THE OXFORD
DICTIONARY
OF
QUOTATIONS

UNIV.
OXONIENSIS

DOM MINA
INUS· TIO·
ILLU MEA

GEOFFREY CUMBERLEGE

OXFORD UNIVERSITY PRESS

LONDON NEW YORK TORONTO

Oxford University Press, Amen House, London E.C.4

GLASGOW NEW YORK TORONTO MELBOURNE WELLINGTON
BOMBAY CALCUTTA MADRAS CAPE TOWN

Geoffrey Cumberlege, Publisher to the University

FIRST EDITION 1941
SECOND IMPRESSION, REVISED 1942
THIRD IMPRESSION, REVISED 1943
FOURTH IMPRESSION 1944
FIFTH IMPRESSION 1948
SIXTH IMPRESSION 1949
SEVENTH IMPRESSION 1950

PRINTED IN GREAT BRITAIN

INTRODUCTION

By BERNARD DARWIN

QUOTATION brings to many people one of the intensest joys of living. If they need any encouragement they have lately received it from the most distinguished quarters. Mr. Roosevelt quoted Longfellow to Mr. Churchill; Mr. Churchill passed on the quotation to us and subsequently quoted Clough on his own account. Thousands of listeners to that broadcast speech must have experienced the same series of emotions. When the Prime Minister said that there were some lines that he deemed appropriate we sat up rigid, waiting in mingled pleasure and apprehension. How agreeable it would be if we were acquainted with them and approved the choice! How flat and disappointing should they be unknown to us! A moment later we heard 'For while the tired waves, vainly breaking' and sank back in a pleasant agony of relief. We whispered the lines affectionately to ourselves, following the speaker, or even kept a word or two ahead of him in order to show our familiarity with the text. We were if possible more sure than ever that Mr. Churchill was the man for our money. He had given his ultimate proofs by flattering our vanity. He had chosen what we knew and what, if we had thought of it, we could have quoted ourselves. This innocent vanity often helps us over the hard places in life; it gives us a warm little glow against the coldness of the world and keeps us snug and happy. It certainly does its full share in the matter of quotations. We are puffed up with pride over those that we know and, a little illogically, we think that everyone else must know them too. As to those which lie outside our line of country we say, with Jowett as pictured by some anonymous genius at Balliol, 'What I don't know isn't knowledge.' Yet here again we are illogical and unreasonable, for we allow ourselves to be annoyed by those who quote from outside our own small preserves. We accuse them in our hearts, as we do other people's children at a party, of 'showing off'. There are some departments of life in which we are ready to strike a bargain of mutual accommodation. The golfer is prepared to listen to his friend's story of missed putts, in which he takes no faintest interest, on the understanding that he may in turn impart his own heart-rending tale, and the bargain is honourably kept by both parties. The same rule does not apply to other people's quotations, which are not merely tedious but wound us in our tenderest spot. And the part played by vanity is perhaps worth pointing out because everybody, when he first plunges adventurously into this great work, ought in justice to the compilers to bear it in mind.

It is safe to say that there is no single reader who will not have a mild grievance or two, both as to what has been put in and what has been left out. In particular he will 'murmur a little sadly' over some favourite that is not there. I, for instance, have a small grievance. William Hepworth Thompson, sometime Master of Trinity, the author of many famous and mordant sayings on which I have been brought up, is represented by but a single one. Can it be, I ask myself, that this is due to the

fact that an Oxford Scholar put several of the Master's sayings into his Greek exercise book but attributed them to one Talirantes? Down, base thought! I only mention this momentary and most unworthy suspicion to show other readers the sort of thing they should avoid as they would the very devil. It is not that of which any one of us is fondest that is entitled as of right to a place. As often as he feels ever so slightly aggrieved, the reader should say to himself, if need be over and over again, that this is not a private anthology, but a collection of the quotations which the public knows best. In this fact, moreover, if properly appreciated, there ought to be much comfort. 'My head', said Charles Lamb, 'has not many mansions nor spacious', and is that not true of most of us? If in this book there are a great many quotations that we do not know, there are also a great many that we do. There is that example of Clough with which I began. We may have to admit under cross-examination that we have only a rather vague acquaintance with Clough's poems, but we do know 'Say not the struggle'; and there on page so-and-so it is. Both we and the dictionary's compilers are thereupon seen to be persons of taste and discrimination.

If I may be allowed to harp a little longer on this string of vanity, it is rather amusing to fancy the varied reception given to the book by those who are quoted in it. They will consist largely of more or less illustrious shades, and we may picture them looking over one another's pale shoulders at the first copy of the dictionary to reach the asphodel. What jealousies there will be as they compare the number of pages respectively allotted to them! What indignation at finding themselves in such mixed company! Alphabetical order makes strange bedfellows. Dickens and Dibdin must get on capitally and convivially together, but what an ill-assorted couple are Mrs. Humphry Ward and the beloved Artemus of the same name! George Borrow may ask, 'Pray, who is this John Collins Bossidy?' Many readers may incidentally echo his question, and yet no man better merits his niche, for Mr. Bossidy wrote the lines ending 'And the Cabots talk only to God', which have told the whole world of the blue blood of Boston. John Hookham Frere, singing of the mailed lobster clapping his broad wings, must feel his frivolity uncomfortably hushed for a moment by his next-door neighbour, Charles Frohman, on the point of going down with the *Lusitania*. And apropos of Frere, there rises before me the portentous figure of my great-great-grandfather, Erasmus Darwin. He was thought a vastly fine poet in his day and there is a family legend that he was paid a guinea a line for his too fluent verses. And yet he is deservedly forgotten, while those who parodied him in the *Anti-Jacobin* attain an equally well-deserved immortality. He was a formidable old gentleman, with something of the Johnson touch, but not without a sense of humour, and I do not think he will be greatly hurt.

The most famous poets must be presumed to be above these petty vanities, though it would be agreeable to think of Horace contemplating his array of columns and saying, 'I told you so—Exegi monumentum'. In any case the number of columns or pages does not constitute the only test. Another is the number of words in each

line by which any particular quotation can be identified, and this gives me a chance of making my compliments to the ingenuity and fullness of the index. The searcher need never despair and should he draw blank under 'swings' he is pretty sure to find what he wants under 'roundabouts'. There is a little game to be played (one of the many fascinating games which the reader can devise for himself) by counting the number of 'key words' in each line and working out the average of fame to which any passage is entitled. Even a short time so spent shows unexpected results, likely to spread envy and malice among the shades. It might be imagined that Shakespeare would be an easy winner. It has been said that every drop of the Thames is liquid history and almost every line of certain passages in Shakespeare is solid quotation. Let us fancy that his pre-eminence is challenged, that a sweepstake is suggested, and that he agrees to be judged by 'To be or not to be'. It seems a sufficiently sound choice and is found to produce fifty-five key words in thirty-three lines. All the other poets are ready to give in at once; they cannot stand against such scoring as that and Shakespeare is about to pocket the money when up sidles Mr. Alexander Pope. What, he asks, about that bitter little thing of his which he sent to Mr. Addison? And he proves to be right, for in those two and twenty lines to Atticus there are fifty-two key words. I have not played this game nearly long enough to pronounce Pope the winner. Very likely Shakespeare or someone else can produce a passage with a still higher average, but here at any rate is enough to show that it is a good game and as full of uncertainties as cricket itself.

Though the great poets may wrangle a little amongst themselves, they do not stand in need of anything that the dictionary can do for them. Very different is the case of the small ones, whose whole fame depends upon a single happy line or even a single absurd one. To them exclusion from these pages may virtually mean annihilation, while inclusion makes them only a little lower than the angels. Their anxiety therefore must be pitiful and their joy when they find themselves safe in the haven proportionately great. Sometimes that joy may be short-lived. Think of Mr. Robert Montgomery, who was highly esteemed till the ruthless Macaulay fell upon him. With trembling hand he turns the pages and finds no less than four extracts from 'The Omnipresence of the Deity'. Alas! under his own letter M the traducer is waiting for him, and by a peculiar refinement of cruelty there are quoted no less than five of Lord Macaulay's criticisms on that very poem. This is a sad case; let us take a more cheerful one and still among the M's. Thomas Osbert Mordaunt has full recognition as the author of 'Sound, sound the clarion, fill the fife', after having for years had to endure the attribution of his lines to Sir Walter Scott, who in pure innocency put them at the head of a chapter. This to be sure was known already, but whoever heard before the name of the author of 'We don't want to fight', the man who gave the word 'Jingo' to the world? We know that the Great McDermott sang it, but even he may not have known who wrote it, just as Miss Fotheringay did not know who wrote 'The Stranger'. Now G. W. Hunt comes into his kingdom and with him another who helped many thousands of

soldiers on their way during the last war. Mr. George H. Powell is fortunately still alive to enjoy the celebrity of 'Pack up your troubles in your old kit bag'. How many thousands, too, have sung 'Wrap me up in my tarpaulin jacket' without realizing that it was by Whyte-Melville? To him, however, recognition is of less account. His place was already secure.

Among the utterers of famous sayings some seem to have been more fortunate than others. Lord Westbury, for instance, has always had the rather brutal credit of telling some wretched little attorney to turn the matter over 'in what you are pleased to call your mind'; but how many of us knew who first spoke of a 'blazing indiscretion' or called the parks 'the lungs of London'? We may rejoice with all these who, having for years been wronged, have come into their rights at last, but there are others with whom we can only sympathize. They must be contented with the fact that their sayings or their verses have been deemed worth recording, even though their names 'shall be lost for evermoe'. The Rugby boy who called his headmaster 'a beast but a just beast' sleeps unknown, while through him Temple lives. He can only enjoy what the dynamiter Zero called 'an anonymous infernal glory'. So do the authors of many admirable limericks, though some of the best are attributed to a living divine of great distinction, who has not disclaimed such juvenile frolics. So again do those who have given us many household words from the advertisement hoardings, the beloved old jingle of 'the Pickwick, the Owl, and the Waverley pen', the alluring alliteration of 'Pink Pills for Pale People'. Let us hope that it is enough for them that they did their duty and sent the sales leaping upward.

So much for the authors without whom this book could never have been. Now for the readers and some of the happy uses to which they will put it. 'Hand me over the Burton's *Anatomy*', said Captain Shandon, 'and leave me to my abominable devices.' It was Greek and Latin quotations that he sought for his article, but fashion has changed and to-day it would rather be English ones. Here is one of the most obvious purposes for which the dictionary will be used. It cannot accomplish impossibilities. It will not prevent many an honest journalist from referring to 'fresh fields and pastures new' nor from describing a cup-tie as an example of 'Greek meeting Greek'. There is a fine old crusted tradition of misquoting not lightly to be broken and it might almost seem pedantry to deck these ancient friends in their true but unfamiliar colours. Misquoting may even be deemed an amiable weakness, since Dickens in one of his letters misquoted Sam Weller; but here at least is a good chance of avoiding it. There is likewise a chance of replenishing a stock grown somewhat threadbare. 'Well, you're a boss word', exclaimed Jim Pinkerton, when he lighted on 'hebdomadary' in a dictionary. 'Before you're very much older I'll have you in type as long as yourself.' So the hard-pressed writer in turning over these pages may find and note many excellent phrases against future contingencies, whether to give a pleasing touch of erudition or to save the trouble of thinking for himself. These, however, are sordid considerations, and the mind loves rather

to dwell on fireside quoting-matches between two friends, each of whom thinks his own visual memory the more accurate. There are certain writers well adapted to this form of contest and among the moderns Conan Doyle must, with all respect to Mr. Wodehouse, be assigned the first place. Sherlock Holmes scholars are both numerous and formidable; they set themselves and demand of others a high standard. It is one very difficult to attain since there often seems no reason why any particular remark should have been made on any particular occasion. This is especially true of Dr. Watson. He was constantly saying that his practice was not very absorbing or that he had an accommodating neighbour, but when did he say which? Even the most learned might by a momentary blunder confuse 'A Case of Identity' with 'The Final Problem'. It would be dry work to plough through all the stories, even though the supreme satisfaction of being right should reward the search. Now a glance at the dictionary will dispose of an argument which would otherwise 'end only with the visit'.

It is incidentally curious and interesting to observe that two authors may each have the same power of inspiring devotion and the competitive spirit, and yet one may be, from the dictionary point of view, infinitely more quotable than the other. Hardly any prose writer, for instance, produces a more fanatical adoration than Miss Austen, and there are doubtless those who can recite pages of her with scarce a slip; but it is perhaps pages rather than sentences that they quote. Mr. Bennet provides an exception, but generally speaking she is not very amenable to the treatment by scissors and paste. George Eliot, if we leave out Mrs. Poyser, a professed wit and coiner of aphorisms, is in much poorer case. Another and a very different writer, Borrow, can rouse us to a frantic pitch of romantic excitement, but it is the whole scene and atmosphere that possess this magic and we cannot take atmosphere to pieces. These are but three examples of writers who do not seem to lend themselves to brief and familiar quotations. They have jewels in plenty, but these form part of a piece of elaborate ornament from which they cannot be detached without irreparable damage. The works of some other writers may by contrast be said to consist of separate stones, each of which needs no setting and can sparkle on its own account. Dickens is an obvious and unique instance. Stevenson, too, has the gift of producing characters such as Prince Florizel and Alan Breck, John Silver and Michael Finsbury, whose words can stand memorable by themselves, apart from context or atmosphere. Those who share my love for Florizel will rejoice to observe that he has had some faithful friend among the compilers. As for Michael I cannot help feeling that he has been rather scurvily used, for 'The Wrong Box' is admirably suited to competition and even learned Judges of the Court of Appeal have been known, all unsuspected by their ignorant auditors, to bandy quotations from it on the Bench. Here, however, I take leave to give any indignant reader a hint. Let him not cry too loudly before he is hurt! It is true that 'nothing like a little judicious levity' is not in the main body of the dictionary, but someone awoke just in time and it is among the addenda.

To return to those friends by the fireside whom I pictured indulging in a heated quoting-match, it may be that they will presently become allies and unite to use the dictionary over a cross-word puzzle. It is hardly too much to say that the setters of these problems should not use a quotation unless it is to be found in the dictionary. A cross-word quotation should not be too simple, but it should be such that that hypothetical personage, the reasonable man, might have heard of it. The solver demands fair play, and the setter who takes a volume of verse at haphazard, finds a word that fits, and substitutes a blank for it, is not playing the game. There are solvers whose standard of sportsmanship is so high that they would as soon allow themselves to cheat at patience as have recourse to a book. We may admire though we cannot emulate this fine austere arrogance. It is the best fun to win unaided, but there is good fun too in ferreting out a quotation. It well repays the ardours of the chase. Moreover a setter of puzzles who oversteps honourable limits should be fought with his own weapons. He has palpably used books and this is an epoch of reprisals. Then let us use books too and hoist him with his own petard.

It is difficult to-day not to deal in warlike metaphors, but perhaps the truest and most perfect use of the dictionary is essentially peaceful. Reviewers are apt to say of a detective story that it is 'impossible to lay it down till the last page is reached'. It is rather for books of reference that such praise should be reserved. No others are comparable with them for the purposes of eternal browsing. They suggest all manner of lovely, lazy things, in particular the watching of a cricket match on a sunshiny day. We have only dropped in for half an hour, but the temptation to see just one more over before we go is irresistible. Evening draws on, the shadows of the fielders lengthen on the grass, nothing much is happening, a draw becomes every minute more inevitable, and still we cannot tear ourselves away. So it is with works of reference, even with the most arid, even with Bradshaw, whose vocabulary, as Sherlock Holmes remarked, is 'nervous and terse but limited'. Over the very next page of Bradshaw there may be hidden a Framlingham Admiral; adventure may always be in wait a little farther down the line. So, but a thousand times more so, is some exciting treasure-trove awaiting us over the next page of this dictionary. What it is we cannot guess, but it is for ever calling in our ears to turn over just one more. We have only taken down the book to look up one special passage, but it is likely enough that we shall never get so far. Long before we have reached the appropriate letter we shall have been waylaid by an earlier one, and shall have clean forgotten our original quest. Nor is this all, for, if our mood changes as we browse, it is so fatally, beautifully easy to change our pasture. We can play a game akin to that 'dabbing' cricket, so popular in private-school days, in which the batsman's destiny depended or was supposed to depend—for we were not always honest—on a pencil delivered with eyes tightly shut. We can close the book and open it again at random, sure of something that shall set us off again on a fresh and enchanting voyage of not too strenuous discovery.

Under this enchantment I have fallen deep. I have pored over the proofs so that

only by a supreme effort of will could I lay them down and embark on the impertinent task of trying to write about them. I now send them back to their home with a sense of privation and loneliness. Here seems to me a great book. Then

Deem it not all a too presumptuous folly,

this humble tribute to Oxford from another establishment over the way.

May 1941   B. D.

THE COMPILERS TO THE READER

'Classical quotation', said Johnson, 'is the *parole* of literary men all over the world.' Although this is no longer strictly true the habit of quoting, both in speech and writing, has steadily increased since his day, and Johnson would undoubtedly be surprised to find here eight and a half pages of his own work that have become part of the *parole* of the reading public. Small dictionaries of quotations have been published for many years—in 1799 D. E. Macdonnel brought out a *Dictionary of Quotations chiefly from Latin and French translated into English*— and during comparatively recent years several large works of American editorship have been produced. In this book the Oxford Press publishes what it is hoped will be a valuable addition to the Oxford Books of Reference already in existence.

The work remained in contemplation for some time before it first began to take shape under the general editorship of Miss Alice Mary Smyth, who worked, for purposes of selection, with a small committee formed of members of the Press itself. The existing dictionaries were taken as a foundation and the entries, pasted on separate cards, considered individually for rejection or inclusion. With these as a basis the most important authors were again dealt with either by the expert, or in committee, or by both. The Press is indebted for a great deal of work to the late Charles Fletcher, who among others made the original selections from Shakespeare, Milton, Pope, Tennyson, and Dryden: among those who dealt with single authors were Lady Charnwood and Mr. Bernard Darwin, who did the Dickens entries, Professor Dewar the Burns, Professor Ernest de Selincourt the Wordsworth: Mr. Colin Ellis did the Surtees, Sterne and Whyte-Melville, Mr. E. Latham contributed the French quotations, and Mr. Harold Child made many valuable suggestions. A great many people, whom it is impossible to name individually, sent in one or more quotations.

During the whole work of selection a great effort was made to restrict the entries to actual current quotations and not to include phrases which the various editors or contributors believed to be quotable or wanted to be quoted: the work is primarily intended to be a dictionary of *familiar* quotations and not an anthology of every author good and bad; popularity and not merit being the password to inclusion. The selections from the Bible and Shakespeare were the most difficult because a great part of both are familiar to most people; but as concordances of both the Bible and Shakespeare are in print the quotations here included are meant to be the most well known where all is well known.

It has been found very difficult to put into precise words the standard of familiarity that has been aimed at or to imagine one man who might be asked whether or not the particular words were known to him. But it is believed that any of the quotations here printed might be found at some time in one or other of the leading articles of the daily and weekly papers with their wide range

of matter—political, literary, descriptive, humorous, &c. So much for the very elastic standard to which the quotations conform. No one person having been imagined to whom everything included in this book would be familiar, the committee have tried to keep in mind that a number of different kinds of readers would be likely to use the book: these are the 'professionals', such as journalists, writers, public speakers, &c.; the crossword devotee, since this form of intellectual amusement appears to have come to stay; the man who has in his mind either a few or many half-completed or unidentified quotations which he would like to complete or verify; and (since, as Emerson wrote—'By necessity, by proclivity—and by delight, we all quote') everyone who has found joy and beauty in the words of the writers and wishes to renew that pleasure by using the words again—he whom perhaps Johnson meant by 'the literary man'. The book is not intended as a substitute for the complete works nor as an excuse to anyone not to drink deep of the Pierian spring. But it *is* hoped that the lover of Dickens, for instance, may find pleasure in reading through his entries and that even his detractors will have to admit how good he is in quotation: that the man who has always regarded Milton as a heavy and dull poet may here come across some lovely line and be inclined to read *Paradise Lost*. If the book serves to start people reading the poets it will have accomplished a great deal besides being a work of reference.

It is interesting to observe that the following are the most quoted writers (arranged in the order in which they appear here): Browning, Byron, Cowper, Dickens, Johnson, Kipling, Milton, Shakespeare, Shelley, Tennyson, Wordsworth, the Bible, and the Book of Common Prayer. On the other hand, certain authors of accepted merit or favour such as Trollope, Henry James, Jane Austen, and P. G. Wodehouse have none of them as much as one page to their credit: it would seem that their charm depends on character and atmosphere and that quotability is no real criterion of either popularity or merit in a writer.

The arrangement of authors is alphabetical and not chronological. The Book of Common Prayer and the Bible come after this alphabetical arrangement, followed immediately by the Anonymous and Miscellaneous entries. After this come the Latin and Greek sections and then the foreign quotations. A short section of Addenda has been added containing a few quotations that have become familiar since the first part was printed off and certain omissions that have been noted in time for inclusion. Under each author the arrangement of the extracts is alphabetical according to the title of the poem or work from which the quotation is taken. When authors have written both poetry and prose the poetry is given first. The text is, wherever possible, the acknowledged authoritative text and the source of the quotation is always given as fully as possible. Some quotations have had to be omitted because every effort to trace their source has failed—e.g. 'Home, James, and don't spare the horses'. Proverbs and phrases are not included, since these have been dealt with fully in the *Oxford Dictionary of English Proverbs*.

It is to be expected that almost every reader will be shocked by what he considers obvious omissions. Should the reader's indignation be strong enough to prompt him to write pointing these out it is to be hoped that he will give the source of all his suggestions. It is not possible to give all the quotations familiar to every reader; almost all households have favourite books and authors from whom they frequently quote: to one family Stevenson is known and quoted by heart, to another the whole of the *Beggar's Opera* is as familiar as the extracts given here. Nor must the user expect to find here every quotation given in crossword puzzles: compilers of these often seek to be obscure rather than familiar.

Latin is no longer a normal part of the language of educated people as it was in the eighteenth century; but from that age certain classical phrases have survived to become part of contemporary speech and writing. It is these 'survivals' that have been included here together with a few of the sayings or writings of the Schoolmen and early theologians. In many places more of the context of the actual familiar phrase has been given than is strictly necessary; but this has been a practice throughout the book, and one which it was thought would add to its value and charm. The translations are usually taken from the works of the better-known translators. Some one or two of the Greek quotations may be known to the general reader in their English versions—e.g. 'The half is better than the whole' or 'Call no man happy till he dies'; but no apology is needed for the inclusion of two pages of matter most of which cannot pretend to be familiar to any but classical scholars.

The foreign quotations are not intended to satisfy the foreigner: they include such things as have become part of the speech and writings of English-speaking people either in their own language, such as 'les enfants terribles', or in an English translation, such as 'We will not go to Canossa'. As hardly any Spanish and no Russian or Swedish quotations are familiar to English readers most of these have been given only in translation.

The index occupies approximately one-third of the total bulk of the book. A separate note will be found at the beginning of the index explaining the arrangement that has been adopted. Of the Latin quotations only those phrases that are familiar to the reader have been indexed; the unfamiliar context has not. In the English translations much the same principle has been followed: where the quotation is known to the reader in its English equivalent it has been indexed; where only the Latin is familiar and a translation is merely supplied to assist the reader it is left unindexed. A great deal of care has been spent on the index and the compilers look at it with some pride, believing that unless the searcher has to say 'Iddy tiddity' for every important word in the quotation he is looking for he will be able to find it; if, like Pig-wig (in Beatrix Potter's *Pigling Bland*), he has only forgotten some of the words, the index is full enough for him to trace it.

CONTENTS

INTRODUCTION iii

THE COMPILERS TO THE READER . . . xi

AUTHORS WRITING IN ENGLISH

Alphabetically arranged 1

Addenda 570

THE BOOK OF COMMON PRAYER . . . 478

HOLY BIBLE 492

ENGLISH LITERATURE

Anonymous 522, 573

Ballads 528

Nursery Rhymes 532

From *Punch* 535

FOREIGN QUOTATIONS

With Translations

Latin 537, 574

Greek 559

French 561, 574

Italian 566

Spanish 567

German 567

In English

Russian, Norwegian, Swedish 567

ADDENDA 570

INDEX 577

DICTIONARY OF QUOTATIONS

CHARLES FOLLEN ADAMS
1842–1918

But ven he vash asleep in ped,
  So quiet as a mouse,
I prays der Lord, 'Dake anyding,
  But leaf dot Yawcob Strauss.' *Yawcob Strauss.*

CHARLES FRANCIS ADAMS
1807–1886

It would be superfluous in me to point out to your lordship that this is war.
  Dispatch to Earl Russell. Sept 5, 1863. C. F. Adams's 'Charles Francis Adams', p. 342.

JOHN QUINCY ADAMS
1767–1848

Think of your forefathers! Think of your posterity!
  Speech, 22 Dec. 1802.

SAMUEL ADAMS
1722–1803

A Nation of shop-keepers are very seldom so disinterested. *Oration said to have been delivered at Philadelphia*, 1776, p. 10. [Phrase 'nation of shop-keepers' also said to have been used by Napoleon and others.]

SARAH FLOWER ADAMS
1805–1848

Nearer, my God, to Thee,
  Nearer to Thee!
E'en though it be a cross
  That raiseth me:
Still all my song shall be
Nearer, my God, to Thee—
  Nearer to Thee! *Nearer, my God, to Thee!*

JOSEPH ADDISON
1672–1719

Pray consider what a figure a man would make in the republic of letters. *Ancient Medals*, 1.

There is nothing more requisite in business than dispatch. *Ib.* 5.

And, pleas'd th' Almighty's Orders to perform,
Rides in the Whirl-wind, and directs the Storm.
  The Campaign, l. 291.

And those who Paint 'em truest Praise 'em most.
  Ib. l. 476.

The dawn is overcast, the morning lowers,
And heavily in clouds brings on the day,
The great, the important day, big with the fate
Of Cato and of Rome. *Cato*, I. i. 1.

'Tis not in mortals to command success,
But we'll do more, Sempronius; we'll deserve it.
  Ib. ii. 43.

Blesses his stars, and thinks it luxury. *Ib.* iv. 70.

'Tis pride, rank pride, and haughtiness of soul;
I think the Romans call it stoicism. *Ib.* 82.

Were you with these, my prince, you'd soon forget
The pale, unripened beauties of the north. *Ib.* 134.

Am I distinguished from you but by toils,
Superior toils, and heavier weight of cares?
Painful pre-eminence! *Ib.* III. v. 23.

The woman that deliberates is lost. *Ib.* IV. i. 31.

Curse on his virtues! they've undone his country.
Such popular humanity is treason. *Ib.* iv. 35.

Content thyself to be obscurely good.
When vice prevails, and impious men bear sway,
The post of honour is a private station. *Ib.* 139.

It must be so—Plato, thou reason'st well!—
Else whence this pleasing hope, this fond desire,
This longing after immortality?
Or whence this secret dread, and inward horror,
Of falling into naught? Why shrinks the soul
Back on herself, and startles at destruction?
'Tis the divinity that stirs within us;
'Tis heaven itself, that points out an hereafter,
And intimates eternity to man.
Eternity! thou pleasing, dreadful thought! *Ib.* v. i. 1.

If there's a power above us,
(And that there is all nature cries aloud
Through all her works) he must delight in virtue.
  Ib. 15.

But thou shalt flourish in immortal youth,
Unhurt amidst the wars of elements,
The wrecks of matter, and the crush of worlds. *Ib.* 28.

From hence, let fierce contending nations know
What dire effects from civil discord flow. *Ib.* iv. 111.

Music, the greatest good that mortals know,
  And all of heaven we have below.
  Song for St. Cecilia's Day, st. 3.

Round-heads and Wooden-shoos are standing Jokes.
  Prologue to the Drummer.

I should think my self a very bad Woman, if I had done what I do, for a Farthing less.
  The Drummer, Act I.

He more had pleas'd us, had he pleas'd us less.
  English Poets (referring to Cowley).

For wheresoe'er I turn my ravished eyes,
Gay gilded scenes and shining prospects rise,
Poetic fields encompass me around,
And still I seem to tread on classic ground.
  Letter from Italy.

A painted meadow, or a purling stream. *Ib.* 1701.

Thus I live in the world rather as a spectator of mankind than as one of the species. *The Spectator*, No. 1.

When I am in a serious humour, I very often walk by myself in Westminster Abbey. *Ib.* No. 26.

A perfect Tragedy is the noblest Production of human Nature. *The Spectator*, No. 39.

In all thy Humours, whether grave or mellow,
Thou'rt such a touchy, testy, pleasant Fellow;
Hast so much Wit, and Mirth, and Spleen about thee,
There is no living with thee, nor without thee.
Ib. No. 68.

There is no place in the town which I so much love to frequent as the Royal Exchange. *Ib.* No. 69.

The infusion of a China plant sweetened with the pith of an Indian cane. *Ib.* No. 69.

Sir Roger . . . will suffer nobody to sleep in it [the church] besides himself; . . . if he sees anybody else nodding, either wakes them himself, or sends his servants to them. *Ib.* No. 112.

Sir Roger told them, with the air of a man who would not give his judgment rashly, that much might be said on both sides. *Ib.* No. 122.

My friends Sir Roger de Coverley and Sir Andrew Freeport are of different principles, the first of them inclined to the *landed* and the other to the *monied* interest. *Ib.* No. 126.

It was a saying of an ancient philosopher, which I find some of our writers have ascribed to Queen Elizabeth, who perhaps might have taken occasion to repeat it, that a good face is a letter of recommendation. *Ib.* No. 221.

I have often thought, says Sir Roger, it happens very well that Christmas should fall out in the Middle of Winter. *Ib.* No. 269.

These Widows, Sir, are the most perverse Creatures in the World. *Ib.* No. 335.

One Englishman could beat three Frenchmen.
Ib. No. 383.

This Mr. Dryden calls 'the fairy way of writing'.
Ib. No. 419.

The Lord my Pasture shall prepare,
And feed me with a Shepherd's Care;
His Presence shall my wants supply,
And guard me with a watchful Eye.
Ib. No. 441.

When all thy Mercies, O my God,
  My rising Soul surveys;
Transported with the View, I'm lost
  In Wonder, Love, and Praise.
Ib. No. 453.

For oh! Eternity's too short
  To utter all thy Praise. *Ib.*

We have in England a particular bashfulness in every thing that regards religion. *Ib.* No. 458.

The spacious firmament on high,
With all the blue ethereal sky.
Ib. No. 465. *Ode.*

And nightly to the listening Earth
Repeats the story of her birth. *Ib.*

Whilst all the stars that round her burn,
And all the planets, in their turn,
Confirm the tidings as they roll,
And spread the truth from pole to pole. *Ib.*

In Reason's ear they all rejoice,
And utter forth a glorious Voice,
For ever singing as they shine,
'The Hand that made us is Divine.' *Ib.*

A woman seldom asks advice before she has bought her wedding clothes. *Ib.* No. 475.

Our Disputants put me in mind of the Skuttle Fish, that when he is unable to extricate himself, blackens all the Water about him, till he becomes invisible.
Ib. No. 476.

I value my garden more for being full of blackbirds than of cherries, and very frankly give them fruit for their songs. *Ib.* No. 477.

If we may believe our logicians, man is distinguished from all other creatures by the faculty of laughter.
Ib. No. 494.

'We are always doing', says he, 'something for Posterity, but I would fain see Posterity do something for us.' *Ib.* No. 583.

I remember when our whole island was shaken with an earthquake some years ago, there was an impudent mountebank who sold pills which (as he told the country people) were very good against an earthquake. *The Tatler*, No. 240.

I have but ninepence in ready money, but I can draw for a thousand pounds. [On his deficiency in conversation.] *Boswell's Life of Johnson*, 7 May, 1773.

See in what peace a christian can die.
Dying words to his stepson Lord Warwick.
Young's *Conjectures on Original Composition*, 1759.

Should the whole frame of nature round him break,
In ruin and confusion hurled,
He, unconcerned, would hear the mighty crack,
And stand secure amidst a falling world.
Translation of Horace, Odes, Bk. III. iii.

THOMAS ADY
c. 1655

Matthew, Mark, Luke, and John,
The Bed be blest that I lie on.
Four angels to my bed,
Four angels round my head,
One to watch, and one to pray,
And two to bear my soul away.
A Cradle in the Dark, p. 58 (1655).

CHARLES HAMILTON AÏDÉ
1830–1906

I sit beside my lonely fire,
  And pray for wisdom yet—
For calmness to remember
  Or courage to forget. *Remember or Forget.*

ARTHUR CAMPBELL AINGER
1841–1919

God is working His purpose out as year succeeds to year,
God is working His purpose out and the time is drawing near;
Nearer and nearer draws the time, the time that shall surely be,
When the earth shall be fill'd with the glory of God as the waters cover the sea.
God is Working His Purpose Out.

MARK AKENSIDE

1721–1770

Such and so various are the tastes of men.
Pleasures of Imagination, bk. iii, l. 567.

HENRY ALDRICH

1648–1710

Hark! the bonny Christchurch Bells,
One, two, three, four, five, six;
   They sound so woundy great,
   So wond'rous sweet,
And they troul so merrily.
Hark the Bonny Christchurch Bells.

If all be true that I do think,
There are five reasons we should drink;
Good wine—a friend—or being dry—
Or lest we should be by and by—
Or any other reason why.   *Reasons for Drinking.*

THOMAS BAILEY ALDRICH

1836–1907

   The fair, frail palaces,
The fading alps and archipelagoes,
And great cloud-continents of sunset-seas.
Sonnet: Miracles.

CECIL FRANCES ALEXANDER

1818–1895

All things bright and beautiful,
  All creatures great and small,
All things wise and wonderful,
  The Lord God made them all.
All Things Bright and Beautiful.

The rich man in his castle,
  The poor man at his gate,
God made them, high or lowly,
  And order'd their estate.   *Ib.*

By Nebo's lonely mountain,
  On this side Jordan's wave,
In a vale in the land of Moab
  There lies a lonely grave.   *The Burial of Moses.*

Do no sinful action,
  Speak no angry word;
Ye belong to Jesus,
  Children of the Lord.   *Do No Sinful Action.*

There's a wicked spirit
  Watching round you still,
And he tries to tempt you
  To all harm and ill.

But ye must not hear him,
  Though 'tis hard for you
To resist the evil,
  And the good to do.   *Ib.*

Every morning the red sun
  Rises warm and bright.
Every Morning the Red Sun.

Jesus calls us; o'er the tumult
  Of our life's wild restless sea.   *Jesus Calls Us.*

Once in royal David's city
  Stood a lowly cattle shed,
Where a Mother laid her Baby
  In a manger for His bed:
Mary was that Mother mild,
Jesus Christ her little Child,
      Once in Royal David's City.

With the poor, and mean, and lowly,
  Lived on earth our Saviour Holy.   *Ib.*

Christian children all must be
  Mild, obedient, good as He.   *Ib.*

For He is our childhood's pattern,
  Day by day like us He grew,
He was little, weak, and helpless,
  Tears and smiles like us He knew;
And He feeleth for our sadness,
And He shareth in our gladness.   *Ib.*

There is a green hill far away,
  Without a city wall,
Where the dear Lord was crucified,
  Who died to save us all.
      There is a Green Hill.

He only could unlock the gate
  Of Heav'n, and let us in.   *Ib.*

The roseate hues of early dawn,
  The brightness of the day,
The crimson of the sunset sky,
  How fast they fade away!
      The Roseate Hues of Early Dawn.

We are but little children weak
  Nor born in any high estate.
      We are but Little Children Weak.

There's not a child so small and weak
  But has his little cross to take,
His little work of love and praise
  That he may do for Jesus' sake.   *Ib.*

SIR WILLIAM ALEXANDER, EARL OF STIRLING

1567?–1640

The weaker sex, to piety more prone.
Doomsday, Hour v, lv.

Yet with great toil all that I can attain
By long experience, and in learned schools,
Is for to know my knowledge is but vain,
And those that think them wise, are greatest fools.
The Tragedy of Crœsus, ii. i.

HENRY ALFORD

1810–1871

Come, ye thankful people, come,
  Raise the song of Harvest-home:
All is safely gathered in,
  Ere the winter storms begin.
      Come, Ye Thankful People, Come.

Ten thousand times ten thousand,
  In sparkling raiment bright.
      Ten Thousand Times Ten Thousand.

RICHARD ALISON

fl. c. 1606

There cherries grow, that none can buy
Till cherry ripe themselves do cry.
An Hour's Recreation in Music.

ELIZABETH AKERS ALLEN

1832–1911

Backward, turn backward, O Time, in your flight,
Make me a child again, just for to-night!
Rock Me To Sleep, Mother.

WILLIAM ALLEN

1803–1879

Fifty-four forty (54° 40′ N.), or fight.
*In the U.S. Senate. On the Oregon Boundary
Question* (1844).

WILLIAM ALLINGHAM

1828–1889

Up the airy mountain,
Down the rushy glen,
We daren't go a-hunting,
For fear of little men.   *The Fairies.*

Four ducks on a pond,
A grass-bank beyond,
A blue sky of spring,
White clouds on the wing:
What a little thing
To remember for years—
To remember with tears!   *A Memory.*

MAXWELL ANDERSON

1888–

What Price Glory.   *Title of Play,* 1924

BISHOP LANCELOT ANDREWES

1555–1626

The nearer the Church the further from God.
Sermon on the Nativity before James I (1622).

ARCHIBALD DOUGLAS, FIFTH EARL OF ANGUS

1449?–1514

I shall bell the cat.
*Attr. by J. Man in Buchanan's Rerum Scoticarum
Historia,* 1762, bk. xii, § 41, *note.*

CHRISTOPHER ANSTEY

1724–1805

If ever I ate a good supper at night,
I dream'd of the devil, and wak'd in a fright.
The New Bath Guide. Letter 4. *A Consultation of the Physicians.*

You may go to Carlisle's, and to Almack's too;
And I'll give you my head if you find such a host,
For coffee, tea, chocolate, butter, and toast:
How he welcomes at once all the world and his wife,
And how civil to folk he ne'er saw in his life.
Ib. (1766), *Letter* 13, *A Public Breakfast.*

Hearken, Lady Betty, hearken,
To the dismal news I tell,
How your friends are all embarking
For the fiery gulf of hell.   *Ib. Letter* 14.

CHARLES JAMES APPERLEY

see

NIMROD

THOMAS APPLETON

1812–1884

A Boston man is the east wind made flesh.   *Attr.*

Good Americans, when they die, go to Paris.
O. W. Holmes, *Autocrat of the Breakfast
Table,* ch. 6.

JOHN ARBUTHNOT

1667–1735

He warns the heads of parties against believing their
own lies.   *The Art of Political Lying,* 1712.

John Bull.   *The History of John Bull,* 1712.

Law is a bottomless pit.   *Ib.*, ch. xxiv.

Hame's hame, be it never so hamely.
Law is a Bottomless Pit.

One of the new terrors of death.
[Of Edmund Curll's biographies.] R. Carruthers' *Life of Pope* (1857), p. 199.

ROBERT ARMIN

fl. 1610

A flea in his ear.   *Foole upon Foole,* 1605, c. 3.

LEWIS ADDISON ARMISTEAD

1817–1863

Give them the cold steel, boys!
Attr. remark during Am. Civil War, 1863.

JOHN ARMSTRONG

1709–1779

Virtuous and wise he was, but not severe;
He still remember'd that he once was young.
Art of Preserving Health, 1744, bk. iv, l. 226.

        Much had he read,
Much more had seen; he studied from the life,
And in th' original perus'd mankind.   *Ib.* l. 231.

'Tis not for mortals always to be blest.   *Ib.* l. 260.

Of right and wrong he taught
Truths as refin'd as ever Athens heard;
And (strange to tell!) he practis'd what he preach'd.
Ib. l. 303.

'Tis not too late to-morrow to be brave.   *Ib.* l. 460.

GEORGE ARNOLD

1834–1865

The living need charity more than the dead.
The Jolly Old Pedagogue.

EDWIN ARNOLD

1832–1904

That what will come, and must come, shall come well.
The Light of Asia, bk. vi.

Veil after veil will lift—but there must be
Veil upon veil behind. *Ib.* bk. viii.

Nor ever once ashamed
So we be named
Press-men; Slaves of the Lamp; Servants of Light.
The Tenth Muse, st. 18.

MATTHEW ARNOLD

1822–1888

And we forget because we must,
And not because we will. *Absence.*

Hath man no second life?—Pitch this one high!

Was Christ a man like us?—Ah! let us try
If we then, too, can be such men as he!
Anti-desperation.

Their ineffectual feuds and feeble hates,
Shadows of hates, but they distress them still.
Balder Dead, iii. 472.

The same heart beats in every human breast.
The Buried Life, l. 23.

A bolt is shot back somewhere in our breast
And a lost pulse of feeling stirs again:

A man becomes aware of his life's flow,
And there arrives a lull in the hot race

And then he thinks he knows
The Hills where his life rose,
And the Sea where it goes. *Ib.* l. 84.

The sea of faith
Was once, too, at the full, and round earth's shore
Lay like the folds of a bright girdle furl'd;
But now I only hear
Its melancholy, long, withdrawing roar,
Retreating to the breath
Of the night-wind down the vast edges drear
And naked shingles of the world.
Dover Beach, l. 21.

And we are here as on a darkling plain
Swept with confused alarms of struggle and flight,
Where ignorant armies clash by night. *Ib.* l. 35.

The Will is free:
Strong is the Soul, and wise, and beautiful:
The seeds of godlike power are in us still:
Gods are we, Bards, Saints, Heroes, if we will!
Written in a copy of Emerson's Essays.

Be neither Saint nor Sophist led, but be a man.
Empedocles on Etna, I. ii. 136.

We do not what we ought;
What we ought not, we do;
And lean upon the thought
That Chance will bring us through;
But our own acts, for good or ill, are mightier powers.
Ib. 237.

Nature, with equal mind,
Sees all her sons at play,
Sees man control the wind,
The wind sweep man away. *Ib.* 257.

Is it so small a thing
To have enjoy'd the sun,
To have liv'd light in the spring,
To have lov'd, to have thought, to have done;
To have advanc'd true friends, and beat down baffling
foes? *Ib.* 396.

Far, far from here,
The Adriatic breaks in a warm bay
Among the green Illyrian hills;

And there, they say, two bright and aged snakes,
Who once were Cadmus and Harmonia,
Bask in the glens or on the warm sea-shore,
In breathless quiet, after all their ills. *Ib.* 427.

Not here, O Apollo!
Are haunts meet for thee.
But, where Helicon breaks down
In cliff to the sea. *Ib.* II. 421.

'Tis Apollo comes leading
His choir, the Nine.
The Leader is fairest,
But all are divine. *Ib.* 445.

The Day in his hotness,
The strife with the palm;
The Night in her silence,
The Stars in their calm. *Ib.* 465.

Eyes too expressive to be blue,
Too lovely to be grey. *Faded Leaves,* 4. *On the Rhine.*

This heart, I know,
To be long lov'd was never fram'd;
For something in its depths doth glow
Too strange, too restless, too untam'd.
A Farewell, st. 5.

I too have long'd for trenchant force
And will like a dividing spear;
Have prais'd the keen, unscrupulous course,
Which knows no doubt, which feels no fear.
Ib. st. 9.

Come, dear children, let us away;
Down and away below. *The Forsaken Merman,* l. 1.

Now the great winds shoreward blow;
Now the salt tides seaward flow;
Now the wild white horses play,
Champ and chafe and toss in the spray. *Ib.* l. 4.

Sand-strewn caverns, cool and deep,
Where the winds are all asleep;
Where the spent lights quiver and gleam;
Where the salt weed sways in the stream;
Where the sea-beasts rang'd all round
Feed in the ooze of their pasture-ground;

Where great whales come sailing by,
Sail and sail, with unshut eye,
Round the world for ever and aye? *Ib.* l. 35.

Children dear, was it yesterday
(Call yet once) that she went away?
                    The Forsaken Merman, l. 48.

Children dear, were we long alone?
The sea grows stormy, the little ones moan.
'Long prayers', I said, 'in the world they say.'
                                        Ib. l. 64.

But, ah, she gave me never a look,
For her eyes were seal'd to the holy book.
Loud prays the priest; shut stands the door.
Come away, children, call no more.
Come away, come down, call no more.   *Ib.* l. 80.

She will start from her slumber
When gusts shake the door;
She will hear the winds howling,
Will hear the waves roar.
We shall see, while above us
The waves roar and whirl,
A ceiling of amber,
A pavement of pearl.
Singing, 'Here came a mortal,
But faithless was she.
And alone dwell for ever
The kings of the sea.'   *Ib.* l. 112.

Who saw life steadily, and saw it whole:
The mellow glory of the Attic stage;
Singer of sweet Colonus, and its child.
          Sonnet to a Friend: 'Who prop, thou ask'st.'

A wanderer is man from his birth.
He was born in a ship
On the breast of the River of Time.
                        The Future, l. 1.

And the width of the waters, the hush
Of the grey expanse where he floats,
Freshening its current and spotted with foam
As it draws to the Ocean, may strike
Peace to the soul of the man on its breast:
As the pale Waste widens around him—
As the banks fade dimmer away—
As the stars come out, and the night-wind
Brings up the stream
Murmurs and scents of the infinite Sea.   *Ib.* l. 78.

Ah! not the nectarous poppy lovers use,
Not daily labour's dull, Lethaean spring,
Oblivion in lost angels can infuse
Of the soil'd glory, and the trailing wing.
            To a Gipsy Child by the Sea-shore.

Not as their friend or child I speak!
But as on some far northern strand,
Thinking of his own Gods, a Greek
In pity and mournful awe might stand
Before some fallen Runic stone—
For both were Faiths, and both are gone.
          The Grande Chartreuse, st. 14, l. 79.

What helps it now, that Byron bore,
With haughty scorn which mock'd the smart,
Through Europe to the Aetolian shore
The pageant of his bleeding heart?
That thousands counted every groan,
And Europe made his woe her own?
                        Ib. st. 23, l. 133.

There may, perhaps, yet dawn an age,
More fortunate, alas! than we,
Which without hardness will be sage,
And gay without frivolity.   *Ib.* st. 27, l. 157.

It is—last stage of all—
When we are frozen up within, and quite
The phantom of ourselves,
To hear the world applaud the hollow ghost
Which blamed the living man.   *Growing Old.*

So thou arraign'st her, her foe;
So we arraign her, her sons
Yes, we arraign her! but she,
The weary Titan! with deaf
Ears, and labour-dimmed eyes,
. . . goes passively by,
Staggering on to her goal;
Bearing on shoulders immense,
Atlanteän, the load . . .
Of the too vast orb of her fate.   *Heine's Grave*, l. 85.

                          Who, Goethe said,
'Had every other gift, but wanted love.'   *Ib.* l. 99.

Only he,
His soul well-knit, and all his battles won,
Mounts, and that hardly, to eternal life.   *Immortality.*

I must not say that thou wert true,
    Yet let me say that thou wert fair;
And they that lovely face who view,
    They will not ask if truth be there.   *Indifference*, 1.

The solemn peaks but to the stars are known,
But to the stars, and the cold lunar beams:
Alone the sun arises, and alone
    Spring the great streams.   *In Utrumque Paratus.*

The unplumb'd, salt, estranging sea.
              Isolation, or To Marguerite (contd.)

Calm soul of all things! make it mine
    To feel, amid the city's jar,
That there abides a peace of thine,
    Man did not make, and cannot mar!
              Lines written in Kensington Gardens.

Calm, calm me more! nor let me die
Before I have begun to live.   *Ib.* st. 11.

Let the long contention cease!
Geese are swans, and swans are geese.
                        The Last Word, l. 5.

Let the victors, when they come,
When the forts of folly fall,
Find thy body by the wall.   *Ib.* l. 13.

This truth—to prove, and make thine own:
'Thou hast been, shalt be, art, alone.'   *To Marguerite.*

When Byron's eyes were shut in death,
We bow'd our head and held our breath.
He taught us little: but our soul
Had felt him like the thunder's roll.

We watch'd the fount of fiery life
Which serv'd for that Titanic strife.
                        Memorial Verses, l. 6.

He spoke, and loos'd our heart in tears.
He laid us as we lay at birth
On the cool flowery lap of earth.   [Wordsworth]
                                        Ib. l. 47.

Time may restore us in his course
Goethe's sage mind and Byron's force:
But where will Europe's latter hour
Again find Wordsworth's healing power?   *Ib.* l. 60.

All this I bear, for, what I seek, I know:
Peace, peace is what I seek, and public calm:
Endless extinction of unhappy hates. *Merope*, l. 100.

With women the heart argues, not the mind.
Merope, l. 341.

He bears the seed of ruin in himself.   *Ib.* l. 862.

For this is the true strength of guilty kings,
When they corrupt the souls of those they rule.
Ib. l. 1451.

We cannot kindle when we will
    The fire that in the heart resides,
The spirit bloweth and is still,
    In mystery our soul abides:
But tasks in hours of insight will'd
Can be through hours of gloom fulfill'd.
Morality, st. 1.

With aching hands and bleeding feet
    We dig and heap, lay stone on stone;
We bear the burden and the heat
    Of the long day, and wish 'twere done.
Not till the hours of light return
All we have built do we discern.   *Ib.* st. 2.

Ere the parting hour go by,
Quick, thy tablets, Memory!   *To My Friends.*

Strew no more red roses, maidens,
Leave the lilies in their dew:
Pluck, pluck cypress, O pale maidens!
Dusk, O dusk the hall with yew!
The New Sirens, l. 269.

But Wordsworth's eyes avert their ken
From half of human fate.
In Memory of the Author of Obermann, l. 53.

What shelter to grow ripe is ours?
What leisure to grow wise?   *Ib.* l. 71.

Too fast we live, too much are tried,
Too harass'd, to attain
Wordsworth's sweet calm, or Goethe's wide
And luminous view to gain.   *Ib.* l. 77.

We, in some unknown Power's employ,
Move on a rigorous line:
Can neither, when we will, enjoy;
Nor, when we will, resign.   *Ib.* l. 133.

On that hard Pagan world disgust
And secret loathing fell.
Deep weariness and sated lust
Made human life a hell.
Obermann Once More, l. 93.

The East bow'd low before the blast,
In patient, deep disdain.
She let the legions thunder past,
And plunged in thought again.   *Ib.* l. 109.

That gracious Child, that thorn-crown'd Man!
He lived while we believed.

Now he is dead. Far hence he lies
In the lorn Syrian town,
And on his grave, with shining eyes,
The Syrian stars look down.   *Ib.* l. 167.

Say, has some wet bird-haunted English lawn
Lent it the music of its trees at dawn?   *Parting.*

Hark! ah, the Nightingale!
The tawny-throated!
Hark! from that moonlit cedar what a burst!
What triumph! hark—what pain!

Listen, Eugenia—
How thick the bursts come crowding through the
    leaves!

Again—thou hearest!
Eternal Passion!
Eternal Pain!   *Philomela*, l. 32.

Cruel, but composed and bland,
Dumb, inscrutable and grand,
So Tiberius might have sat,
Had Tiberius been a cat.   *Poor Matthias.*

Nature's great law, and law of all men's minds?
To its own impulse every creature stirs:
Live by thy light, and Earth will live by hers.
Religious Isolation.

Strew on her roses, roses,
    And never a spray of yew.
In quiet she reposes:
    Ah! would that I did too.

Her cabin'd ample Spirit,
    It flutter'd and fail'd for breath.
To-night it doth inherit
    The vasty Hall of Death.   *Requiescat.*

Coldly, sadly descends
The autumn evening. The Field
Strewn with its dark yellow drifts
Of wither'd leaves, and the elms,
Fade into dimness apace,
Silent.   *Rugby Chapel*, l. 1.

Somewhere, surely, afar,
In the sounding labour-house vast
Of being, is practised that strength,
Zealous, beneficent, firm.   *Ib.* l. 40.

Friends who set forth at our side
Falter, are lost in the storm!
We, we only, are left!   *Ib.* l. 102.

Therefore to thee it was given
Many to save with thyself;
And, at the end of thy day,
O faithful shepherd! to come,
Bringing thy sheep in thy hand.   *Ib.* l. 140.

Then, in such hour of need
Of your fainting, dispirited race,
Ye, like angels, appear,
Radiant with ardour divine.
Beacons of hope, ye appear!
Languor is not in your heart,
Weakness is not in your word,
Weariness not on your brow.   *Ib.* l. 188.

Ye fill up the gaps in our files,
Strengthen the wavering line,
Stablish, continue our march,
On, to the bound of the waste,
On, to the City of God.   *Ib.* l. 204.

But so many books thou readest,
But so many schemes thou breedest,
But so many wishes feedest,
    That thy poor head almost turns.   *The Second Best.*

Others abide our question. Thou art free.
We ask and ask: Thou smilest and art still,
Out-topping knowledge.   *Sonnet, Shakespeare.*

And thou, who didst the stars and sunbeams know,
Self-school'd, self-scann'd, self-honour'd, self-secure,
Didst walk on Earth unguess'd at. Better so!
All pains the immortal spirit must endure,
All weakness that impairs, all griefs that bow,
Find their sole voice in that victorious brow.   *Ib.*

Curl'd minion, dancer, coiner of sweet words!
Sohrab and Rustum, l. 458.

Truth sits upon the lips of dying men.   *Ib.* l. 656.

But the majestic River floated on,
Out of the mist and hum of that low land,
Into the frosty starlight, and there mov'd,
Rejoicing, through the hush'd Chorasmian waste,
Under the solitary moon: he flow'd
Right for the Polar Star, past Orgunjè,
Brimming, and bright, and large: then sands begin
To hem his watery march, and dam his streams,
And split his currents; that for many a league
The shorn and parcell'd Oxus strains along
Through beds of sand and matted rushy isles—
Oxus, forgetting the bright speed he had
In his high mountain cradle in Pamere,
A foil'd circuitous wanderer—till at last
The long'd-for dash of waves is heard, and wide
His luminous home of waters opens, bright
And tranquil, from whose floor the new-bath'd stars
Emerge, and shine upon the Aral Sea.   *Ib.* l. 875.

France, fam'd in all great arts, in none supreme.
To a Republican Friend (contd.)
The high
Uno'erleap'd Mountains of Necessity.   *Ib.*

Not deep the Poet sees, but wide.   *Resignation*, l. 212.

Yet they, believe me, who await
No gifts from Chance, have conquer'd Fate.
Ib. l. 245.

Go, for they call you, Shepherd, from the hill.
The Scholar-Gipsy, st. 1.

All the live murmur of a summer's day.   *Ib.* st. 2.

Tir'd of knocking at Preferment's door.   *Ib.* st. 4.

In hat of antique shape, and cloak of grey,
The same the Gipsies wore.   *Ib.* st. 6.

Crossing the stripling Thames at Bab-lock-hithe,
Trailing in the cool stream thy fingers wet,
As the slow punt swings round.   *Ib.* st. 8.

Rapt, twirling in thy hand a wither'd spray,
And waiting for the spark from Heaven to fall.
Ib. st. 12.

The line of festal light in Christ-Church hall.
Ib. st. 13.

Thou waitest for the spark from Heaven: and we,
Vague half-believers in our casual creeds
       .   .
Who hesitate and falter life away,
And lose to-morrow the ground won to-day—
Ah, do not we, Wanderer, await it too? *Ib.* st. 18.

With close-lipp'd Patience for our only friend,
Sad Patience, too near neighbour to Despair.
Ib. st. 20.

This strange disease of modern life.   *Ib.* st. 21.

Still nursing the unconquerable hope,
Still clutching the inviolable shade.   *Ib.* st. 22.

As some grave Tyrian trader, from the sea,
Descried at sunrise an emerging prow
Lifting the cool-hair'd creepers stealthily,
The fringes of a southward-facing brow
    Among the Aegean isles;
And saw the merry Grecian coaster come,

Freighted with amber grapes, and Chian wine,
Green bursting figs, and tunnies steep'd in brine;
And knew the intruders on his ancient home,

The young light-hearted Masters of the waves;
And snatch'd his rudder, and shook out more sail,
And day and night held on indignantly
Oe'r the blue Midland waters with the gale,
    Betwixt the Syrtes and soft Sicily,
        To where the Atlantic raves
Outside the Western Straits, and unbent sails
    There, where down cloudy cliffs, through sheets
        of foam,
    Shy traffickers, the dark Iberians come;
        And on the beach undid his corded bales.
Ib. st. 24, 25.

Resolve to be thyself: and know, that he
Who finds himself, loses his misery.
Self-Dependence, l. 31.

And see all sights from pole to pole,
    And glance, and nod, and bustle by;
And never once possess our soul
    Before we die.   *A Southern Night*, l. 69.

Mild o'er her grave, ye mountains, shine!
    Gently by his, ye waters, glide!
To that in you which is divine
    They were allied.   *Ib.* l. 237.

Still bent to make some port he knows not where,
Still standing for some false impossible shore.
A Summer Night.

The signal-elm, that looks on Ilsley downs,
    The Vale, the three lone weirs, the youthful Thames.
Thyrsis, st. 2.

And that sweet City with her dreaming spires,
    She needs not June for beauty's heightening. *Ib.*

But Thyrsis of his own will went away.   *Ib.* st. 4.

It irk'd him to be here, he could not rest.
       .   .
He went; his piping took a troubled sound
Of storms that rage outside our happy ground;
He could not wait their passing, he is dead!
Ib. st. 5.

So have I heard the cuckoo's parting cry,
    From the wet field, through the vext garden-trees,
    Come with the volleying rain and tossing breeze:
'The bloom is gone, and with the bloom go I.'
Ib. st. 6.

Too quick despairer, wherefore wilt thou go?
    Soon will the high Midsummer pomps come on,
    Soon will the musk carnations break and swell,
Soon shall we have gold-dusted snapdragon,
    Sweet-William with its homely cottage-smell,
    And stocks in fragrant blow.   *Ib.* st. 7.

For Time, not Corydon, hath conquer'd thee.
Ib. st. 8.

She loved the Dorian pipe, the Dorian strain.
    But ah, of our poor Thames she never heard!
    Her foot the Cumner cowslips never stirr'd!
And we should tease her with our plaint in vain.
Ib. st. 10.

I know what white, what purple fritillaries
    The grassy harvest of the river-fields,
    Above by Ensham, down by Sandford, yields,
And what sedg'd brooks are Thames's tributaries.
Ib. st. 11.

[8]

The foot less prompt to meet the morning dew,
The heart less bounding at emotion new,
And hope, once crushed, less quick to spring again.
Thyrsis, st. 14.

Hear it, O Thyrsis, still our Tree is there!—
Ah, vain! These English fields, this upland dim,
These brambles pale with mist engarlanded,
That lone, sky-pointing tree, are not for him.
To a boon southern country he is fled,
And now in happier air,
Wandering with the great Mother's train divine

. . . . .

Within a folding of the Apennine.   *Ib*. st. 18.

Why faintest thou? I wander'd till I died,
Roam on! the light we sought is shining still.
Dost thou ask proof? Our Tree yet crowns the hill,
Our Scholar travels yet the loved hill-side. *Ib*. st. 24.

Know, man hath all which Nature hath, but more,
And in that *more* lie all his hopes of good.
To an Independent Preacher.

Philip's peerless son,
Who carried the great war from Macedon
Into the Soudan's realm, and thunder'd on
To die at thirty-five in Babylon. *Tristram and Iseult*, iii.

For this and that way swings
The flux of mortal things,
Though moving inly to one far-set goal.
Westminster Abbey.

Nor bring, to see me cease to live,
Some doctor full of phrase and fame,
To shake his sapient head and give
The ill he cannot cure a name.   *A Wish.*

Calm's not life's crown, though calm is well.
'Tis all perhaps which man acquires,
But 'tis not what our youth desires. *Youth and Calm.*

And sigh that only one thing has been lent
To youth and age in common—discontent.
Youth's Agitations.

[Oxford] Beautiful city! so venerable, so lovely, so
unravaged by the fierce intellectual life of our century, so serene! . . . whispering from her towers the
last enchantments of the Middle Age. . . . Home of
lost causes, and forsaken beliefs, and unpopular
names, and impossible loyalties!
Essays in Criticism, First Series, preface.

The magnificent roaring of the young lions of the
Daily Telegraph.   *Ib.*

Wragg is in custody.
Ib. Functions of Criticism at the Present Time.

I am bound by my own definition of criticism: a disinterested endeavour to learn and propagate the
best that is known and thought in the world.   *Ib.*

It always seems to me that the right sphere for
Shelley's genius was the sphere of music, not of
poetry.   *Ib. Maurice de Guérin*, footnote.

Philistine must have originally meant, in the mind of
those who invented the nickname, a strong, dogged,
unenlightened opponent of the chosen people, of
the children of the light.   *Ib. Heinrich Heine.*

Philistinism!—We have not the expression in English.
Perhaps we have not the word because we have so
much of the thing.   *Ib.*

The absence, in this country, of any force of educated
literary and scientific opinion.
Ib. Literary Influence of Academies.

The great apostle of the Philistines, Lord Macaulay.
Ib. Joubert.

His expression may often be called bald . . . but it is
bald as the bare mountain tops are bald, with a
baldness full of grandeur.
Ib., Second Series, preface to *Poems of Wordsworth.*

Nature herself seems, I say, to take the pen out of his
hand, and to write for him with her own bare,
sheer, penetrating power.   *Ib.*

In poetry, no less than in life, he is 'a beautiful and
ineffectual angel, beating in the void his luminous
wings in vain'.
Essays in Criticism, Second Series, Shelley.
[Quoting his own sentence in his essay on
Byron, *Essays on Criticism, Second Series.*]

The difference between genuine poetry and the poetry
of Dryden, Pope, and all their school, is briefly
this: their poetry is conceived and composed in
their wits, genuine poetry is conceived and composed in the soul.   *Ib. Thomas Gray.*

Our society distributes itself into Barbarians, Philistines, and Populace; and America is just ourselves,
with the Barbarians quite left out, and the Populace
nearly.   *Culture and Anarchy*, preface.

The great aim of culture [is] the aim of setting ourselves to ascertain what perfection is and to make
it prevail.   *Ib*. p. 12.

The pursuit of perfection, then, is the pursuit of
sweetness and light . . . He who works for sweetness
and light united, works to make reason and the will
of God prevail.   *Ib*. p. 47.

The men of culture are the true apostles of equality.
Ib. p. 49.

One has often wondered whether upon the whole
earth there is anything so unintelligent, so unapt to
perceive how the world is really going, as an ordinary young Englishman of our upper class.
Ib. pp. 70–1.

For this [Middle] class we have a designation which
now has become pretty well known, and which we
may as well still keep for them, the designation of
Philistines.   *Ib*. p. 97.

But that vast portion, lastly, of the working-class
which . . . is now issuing from its hiding-place to
assert an Englishman's heaven-born privilege of
doing as he likes, and is beginning to perplex us by
marching where it likes, meeting where it likes,
bawling what it likes, breaking what it likes—to this
vast residuum we may with great propriety give the
name of Populace.
Thus we have got three distinct terms, Barbarians,
Philistines, Populace, to denote roughly the three
great classes into which our society is divided.
Ib. pp. 104–5.

Hebraism and Hellenism—between these two points
of influence moves our World. . . . Hebraism and
Hellenism are, neither of them, the law of human
development . . .; they are, each of them, contributions to human development.   *Ib*. pp. 143, 157.

'He knows', says Hebraism, 'his Bible!'—whenever we hear this said, we may, without any elaborate defence of culture, content ourselves with answering simply: 'No man, who knows nothing else, knows even his Bible.' *Culture and Anarchy*, pp. 181–2.

The grand, old, fortifying, classical curriculum.
Friendship's Garland.

The translator of Homer should above all be penetrated by a sense of four qualities of his author:— that he is eminently rapid; that he is eminently plain and direct both in the evolution of his thought and in the expression of it, that is, both in his syntax and in his words; that he is eminently plain and direct in the substance of his thought, that is, in his matter and ideas; and, finally, that he is eminently noble. *On Translating Homer*, i.

Wordsworth says somewhere that wherever Virgil seems to have composed 'with his eye on the object', Dryden fails to render him. Homer invariably composes 'with his eye on the object', whether the object be a moral or a material one: Pope composes with his eye on his style, into which he translates his object, whatever it is. *Ib.*

He [the Translator] will find one English book and one only, where, as in the *Iliad* itself, perfect plainness of speech is allied with perfect nobleness; and that book is the Bible. *Ib.* iii.

Nothing has raised more questioning among my critics than these words—noble, the grand style. ... I think it will be found that the grand style arises in poetry, when a noble nature, poetically gifted, treats with simplicity or with severity a serious subject. *Ib.* Last Words.

Miracles do not happen.
Literature and Dogma, preface to 1883 edition, last words.

Culture, the acquainting ourselves with the best that has been known and said in the world, and thus with the history of the human spirit.
Ib. preface to 1873 edition.

Terms like grace, new birth, justification . . . : terms, in short, which with St. Paul are literary terms, theologians have employed as if they were scientific terms. *Ib.* ch. i, § 1.

When we are asked further, what is conduct?—let us answer: Three-fourths of life. *Ib.* ch. i, § 1.

The true meaning of religion is thus not simply morality, but morality touched by emotion.
Ib. ch. i, § 2.

Conduct is three-fourths of our life and its largest concern. *Ib.* ch. i, § 3.

Let us put into their 'Eternal' and 'God' no more science than they [the Hebrew writers] did:—the enduring power, not ourselves, which makes for righteousness. *Ib.* ch. i, § 5.

For it is what we call the Time-Spirit that is sapping the proof from miracles. . . . The human mind, as its experience widens, is turning away from them. *Ib.* ch. v, § 3.

What is called 'orthodox divinity' is, in fact, an immense literary misapprehension. *Ib.* ch. vi, § 3.

The eternal not ourselves which makes for righteousness. *Ib.* ch. viii, § 1.

But there remains the question: what righteousness really is. The method and secret and sweet reasonableness of Jesus. *Ib.* ch. xii, § 2.

For the total man, therefore, the truer conception of God is as 'the Eternal Power, not ourselves, by which all things fulfil the law of their being'.
Ib. Conclusion, § 2.

So we have the Philistine of genius in religion— Luther; the Philistine of genius in politics— Cromwell; the Philistine of genius in literature— Bunyan. *Mixed Essays, Lord Falkland.*

SAMUEL JAMES ARNOLD
1774–1852

Our ships were British oak,
And hearts of oak our men. *Death of Nelson.*

THOMAS ARNOLD
1795–1842

What we must look for here is, 1st, religious and moral principles: 2ndly, gentlemanly conduct: 3rdly, intellectual ability.
Arnold of Rugby (ed. *J. J. Findlay*), p. 65.

My object will be, if possible, to form Christian men, for Christian boys I can scarcely hope to make.
Letter, in 1828, on appointment to Headmastership of Rugby.

GEORGE ARTHURS

Where there's a girl there's a boy. *Title of song.*

GEORGE ASAF
(GEORGE H. POWELL)
1880–

What's the use of worrying?
It never was worth while,
So, pack up your troubles in your old kit-bag,
And smile, smile, smile.
Pack Up Your Troubles In Your Old Kit-Bag.

THOMAS ASHE
1836–1889

Meet we no angels, Pansie? *At Altenahr*, ii. *Poems.*

HERBERT HENRY ASQUITH,
EARL OF OXFORD
1852–1928

Wait and see.
Phrase used repeatedly in speeches in 1910. Spender and Cyril Asquith's *Life of Lord Oxford and Asquith*, vol. i, p. 275.

We shall never sheathe the sword which we have not lightly drawn until Belgium receives in full measure all and more than all that she has sacrificed, until France is adequately secured against the menace of aggression, until the rights of the smaller nationalities of Europe are placed upon an unassailable foundation, and until the military domination of Prussia is wholly and finally destroyed. *Speech at the Guildhall*, 9 Nov. 1914.

SIR JACOB ASTLEY

1579–1652

O Lord! thou knowest how busy I must be this day:
if I forget thee, do not thou forget me.
Prayer before the Battle of Edgehill (*Sir Philip
Warwick, Memoires*, 1701, p. 229).

HARRIET AUBER

1773–1862

And His that gentle voice we hear,
  Soft as the breath of even,
That checks each fault, that calms each fear,
  And speaks of heaven.
        Our Blest Redeemer, ere He breathed.

JOHN AUBREY

1626–1697

He was so fair that they called him *the lady of
Christ's College.*   *Brief Lives. John Milton.*

When he killed a calf he would do it in a high style,
and make a speech.   *Ib. William Shakespeare.*

He was a handsome, well-shaped man: very good
company, and of a very ready and pleasant smooth
wit.   *Ib.*

ALEXANDER BOSWELL, LORD AUCHINLECK

1706–1782

He gart kings ken they had a *lith* in their neck.
[Of Cromwell.] gart ken = made to know; lith =
joint.   *Boswell*, v. 382, n 2.

JANE AUSTEN

1775–1817

An egg boiled very soft is not unwholesome. (Mr.
Woodhouse.)   *Emma*, ch. 3.

One half of the world cannot understand the pleasures
of the other. (Emma.)   *Ib.* ch. 9.

A basin of nice smooth gruel, thin, but not too thin.
    Ib. ch. 12.

She believed he had been drinking too much of Mr.
Weston's good wine.   *Ib.* ch. 15.

So extremely like Maple Grove. (Mrs. Elton.)
    Ib. ch. 32.

They will have their barouche-landau, of course.
(Mrs. Elton.)   *Ib.*

How shall we ever recollect half the dishes for grandmamma? (Miss Bates.)   *Ib.* ch. 38.

Let other pens dwell on guilt and misery.
    Mansfield Park, ch. 48.

'And what are you reading, Miss —?' 'Oh! it is only
a novel!' replies the young lady: while she lays
down her book with affected indifference, or momentary shame.—'It is only Cecilia, or Camilla,
or Belinda:' or, in short, only some work in which
the most thorough knowledge of human nature,
the happiest delineation of its varieties, the liveliest
effusions of wit and humour are conveyed to the
world in the best chosen language.
    Northanger Abbey, ch. 5.

But are they all horrid, are you sure they are all
horrid? (Catherine.)   *Ib.* ch. 6.

All the privilege I claim for my own sex . . . is that
of loving longest, when existence or when hope is
gone. (Anne.)   *Persuasion*, ch. 23.

It is a truth universally acknowledged, that a single
man in possession of a good fortune, must be in
want of a wife.   *Pride and Prejudice*, ch. 1.

'Kitty has no discretion in her coughs,' said her
father: 'she times them ill.'
'I do not cough for my own amusement,' replied
Kitty fretfully.   *Ib.* ch. 2.

How can you contrive to write so even? (Miss Bingley.)
    Ib. ch. 10.

Mr. Collins had only to change from Jane to Elizabeth
—and it was soon done—done while Mrs. Bennet
was stirring the fire.   *Ib.* ch. 15.

An unhappy alternative is before you, Elizabeth.
From this day you must be a stranger to one of your
parents.—Your mother will never see you again if
you do *not* marry Mr. Collins, and I will never see
you again if you *do*. (Mr. Bennet.)   *Ib.* ch. 20.

Nobody is on my side, nobody takes part with me: I
am cruelly used, nobody feels for my poor nerves.
(Mrs. Bennet.)   *Ib.*

No arguments shall be wanting on my part, that can
alleviate so severe a misfortune: or that may comfort you, under a circumstance that must be of all
others most afflicting to a parent's mind. The
death of your daughter would have been a blessing
in comparison of this. (Mr. Collins.)   *Ib.* ch. 48.

You ought certainly to forgive them as a christian,
but never to admit them in your sight, or allow
their names to be mentioned in your hearing. (Mr.
Collins.)   *Ib.* ch. 57.

For what do we live, but to make sport for our
neighbours, and laugh at them in our turn? (Mr.
Bennet.)   *Ib.*

I have been a selfish being all my life, in practice,
though not in principle. (Mr. Darcy.) *Ib.* ch. 58.

If any young men come for Mary or Kitty, send
them in, for I am quite at leisure. (Mr. Bennet.)
    Ib. ch. 59.

An annuity is a very serious business. (Mrs. Dash-
wood.)   *Sense and Sensibility*, ch. 1.

'I am afraid,' replied Elinor, 'that the pleasantness of
an employment does not always evince its propriety.'   *Ib.* ch. 13.

Lady Middleton . . . exerted herself to ask Mr.
Palmer if there was any news in the paper.
'No, none at all,' he replied, and read on. *Ib.* ch. 19.

ALFRED AUSTIN
1835–1913

An earl by right, by courtesy a man.   *The Season.*

Across the wires the electric message came:
'He is no better, he is much the same.'
> *On the Illness of the Prince of Wales, afterwards
> Edward VII.* Attr. to Austin, but probably
> not his. *See* J. Lewis May in the Dublin
> Review, July 1937.

ROBERT AYTOUN
1570–1638

I loved thee once, I'll love no more,
  Thine be the grief, as is the blame;
Thou art not what thou wast before,
  What reason I should be the same?
> *To an Inconstant Mistress.*

WILLIAM EDMONDSTOUNE AYTOUN
1813–1865

Take away that star and garter—
  Hide them from my aching sight!
Neither king nor prince shall tempt me
From my lonely room this night.
> *Charles Edward at Versailles on the Anniversary
> of Culloden.*

Nowhere beats the heart so kindly
  As beneath the tartan plaid!
> *Ib.* 1. 219.

Sound the fife, and cry the slogan—
  Let the pibroch shake the air.
> *The Burial-march of Dundee,* l. 1.

On the heights of Killiecrankie
  Yester-morn our army lay.
> *Ib.* l. 49.

Like a tempest down the ridges
  Swept the hurricane of steel,
Rose the slogan of Macdonald—
  Flashed the broadsword of Locheill!
> *Ib.* l. 137.

So, amidst the battle's thunder,
  Shot and steel, and scorching flame,
In the glory of his manhood
  Passed the spirit of the Graeme!
> *Ib.* l. 165.

News of battle!—news of battle!
  Hark! 'tis ringing down the street:
And the archways and the pavement
  Bear the clang of hurrying feet.
> *Edinburgh after Flodden,* st. 1.

Warder—warder! open quickly!
  Man—is this a time to wait?
> *Ib.* st. 2.

Do not lift him from the bracken,
  Leave him lying where he fell—
Better bier ye cannot fashion:
  None beseems him half so well
As the bare and broken heather,
  And the hard and trampled sod,

Whence his angry soul ascended
  To the judgement-seat of God!
> *The Widow of Glencoe,* st. 1.

They bore within their breasts the grief
  That fame can never heal—
The deep, unutterable woe
  Which none save exiles feel.
> *The Island of the Scots,* xii.

Fhairshon swore a feud
  Against the clan M'Tavish;
Marched into their land
  To murder and to rafish;
For he did resolve
  To extirpate the vipers,
With four-and-twenty men
  And five-and-thirty pipers.
> *The Massacre of the Macpherson,* i.

Fhairshon had a son,
  Who married Noah's daughter,
And nearly spoiled ta Flood,
  By trinking up ta water:

Which he would have done,
  I at least pelieve it,
Had the mixture peen
  Only half Glenlivet.
> *Ib.* vii, viii.

Come hither, Evan Cameron!
  Come, stand beside my knee.
> *The Execution of Montrose,* i.

And some that came to scoff at him
  Now turned aside and wept.
> *Ib.* vi.

But onwards—always onwards,
  In silence and in gloom,
The dreary pageant laboured,
  Till it reached the house of doom.
> *Ib.* vii.

The master-fiend Argyle!
> *Ib.*

The Marquis gazed a moment,
  And nothing did he say.
> *Ib.* viii.

Then nail my head on yonder tower—
  Give every town a limb—
And God who made shall gather them:
  I go from you to Him!
> *Ib.* xii.

'He is coming! he is coming!'
  Like a bridegroom from his room,
Came the hero from his prison
  To the scaffold and the doom.
> *Ib.* xiv.

The grim Geneva ministers
  With anxious scowl drew near,
As you have seen the ravens flock
  Around the dying deer.
> *Ib.* xvii.

Like a brave old Scottish Cavalier,
  All of the olden time!   *The Old Scottish Cavalier.*

Have you heard of Philip Slingsby,
  Slingsby of the manly chest;
How he slew the Snapping Turtle
  In the regions of the West?
> *The Fight with the Snapping Turtle.*

The earth is all the home I have,
The heavens my wide roof-tree.
> *The Wandering Jew,* l. 49.

FRANCIS BACON

1561–1626

For all knowledge and wonder (which is the seed of knowledge) is an impression of pleasure in itself.
Advancement of Learning, bk. I. i. 3 (ed. 1605).

Time, which is the author of authors.
Ib. iv. 12.

If a man will begin with certainties, he shall end in doubts; but if he will be content to begin with doubts, he shall end in certainties.   *Ib.* v. 8.

[Knowledge is] a rich storehouse for the glory of the Creator and the relief of man's estate.   *Ib.* 11.

Antiquities are history defaced, or some remnants of history which have casually escaped the shipwreck of time.   *Ib.* bk. II. ii. 1.

The knowledge of man is as the waters, some descending from above, and some springing from beneath; the one informed by the light of nature, the other inspired by divine revelation.   *Ib.* v. 1.

There was never miracle wrought by God to convert an atheist, because the light of nature might have led him to confess a God.   *Ib.* vi. 1.

They are ill discoverers that think there is no land, when they can see nothing but sea.   *Ib.* vii. 5.

Words are the tokens current and accepted for conceits, as moneys are for values.   *Ib.* xvi. 3.

But men must know, that in this theatre of man's life it is reserved only for God and angels to be lookers on.   *Ib.* xx. 8.

We are much beholden to Machiavel and others, that write what men do, and not what they ought to do.
Ib. xxi. 9.

Men must pursue things which are just in present, and leave the future to the divine Providence.
Ib. 11.

Did not one of the fathers in great indignation call poesy *vinum dæmonum*?   *Ib.* xxii. 13.

All good moral philosophy is but an handmaid to religion.   *Ib.* 14.

Man seeketh in society comfort, use, and protection.
Ib. xxiii. 2.

A man must make his opportunity, as oft as find it.
Ib. 3.

Cæsar, when he went first into Gaul, made no scruple to profess 'That he had rather be first in a village than second at Rome'.   *Ib.* 36.

Fortunes . . . come tumbling into some men's laps.
Ib. 43.

That other principle of Lysander, 'That children are to be deceived with comfits, and men with oaths.'
Ib. 45.

It is in life as it is in ways, the shortest way is commonly the foulest, and surely the fairer way is not much about.   *Ib.*

There are in nature certain fountains of justice, whence all civil laws are derived but as streams.
Ib. 49.

The inseparable propriety of time, which is ever more and more to disclose truth.   *Ib.* xxiv.

Books must follow sciences, and not sciences books.
Proposition touching Amendment of Laws.

Anger makes dull men witty, but it keeps them poor.
[Related as a remark of Queen Elizabeth.]
Apothegms, 5.

A beautiful face is a silent commendation.   *Ib.* 12.

Wise nature did never put her precious jewels into a garret four stories high: and therefore . . . exceeding tall men had ever very empty heads.
Ib. 17.

Hope is a good breakfast, but it is a bad supper.
Ib. 36.

Like strawberry wives, that laid two or three great strawberries at the mouth of their pot, and all the rest were little ones.
[A saying of Queen Elizabeth.] *Ib.* 54.

Sir Henry Wotton used to say, 'That critics are like brushers of noblemen's clothes.'   *Ib.* 64.

Mr. Savill was asked by my lord of Essex his opinion touching poets; who answered my lord; 'He thought them the best writers, next to those that write prose.'   *Ib.* 66.

Alonso of Arragon was wont to say, in commendation of age, That age appeared to be best in four things: 'Old wood best to burn; old wine to drink; old friends to trust; and old authors to read.'   *Ib.* 97.

Demosthenes when he fled from the battle, and that it was reproached to him, said; 'That he that flies mought fight again.'   *Ib.* 169.

One of the Seven was wont to say; 'That laws were like cobwebs; where the small flies were caught, and the great brake through.'   *Ib.* 181.

Pyrrhus, when his friends congratulated to him his victory over the Romans, under the conduct of Fabricius, but with great slaughter of his own side, said to them again; 'Yes, but if we have such another victory, we are undone.'   *Ib.* 193.

Cosmus duke of Florence was wont to say of perfidious friends; 'That we read that we ought to forgive our enemies; but we do not read that we ought to forgive our friends.'   *Ib.* 206.

One of the fathers saith . . . that old men go to death, and death comes to young men.   *Ib.* 270.

Diogenes said of a young man that danced daintily, and was much commended: 'The better, the worse.'
Ib. 266.

Riches are a good handmaid, but the worst mistress.
De Augmentis Scientiarum, pt. i, bk. vi, ch. 3.
Antitheta, 6 (ed. 1640, trans. by Gilbert Watts).

The voice of the people hath some divineness in it, else how should so many men agree to be of one mind?   *Ib.* 9.

Envy never makes holiday.   *Ib.* 16.

No terms of moderation takes place with the vulgar.
Ib. 30.

Silence is the virtue of fools.   *Ib.* 31.

The worst solitude is to be destitute of sincere friendship. *Ib.* 37.

Omnia mutari, et nil vere interire, ac summam materiae prorsus eandem manere, satis constat.
(That all things are changed, and that nothing really perishes, and that the sum of matter remains exactly the same, is sufficiently certain. Tr. Spedding.) *Cogitationes de Natura Rerum,* v.

I hold every man a debtor to his profession.
The Elements of the Common Law, preface.

My essays . . . come home, to men's business, and bosoms. *Essays. Dedication of 1625 edition.*

What is truth? said jesting Pilate; and would not stay for an answer. *Ib.* 1. *Of Truth.*

A mixture of a lie doth ever add pleasure. *Ib.*

It is not the lie that passeth through the mind, but the lie that sinketh in, and settleth in it, that doth the hurt. *Ib.*

The inquiry of truth, which is the love-making, or wooing of it, the knowledge of truth, which is the presence of it, and the belief of truth, which is the enjoying of it, is the sovereign good of human nature. *Ib.*

Certainly, it is heaven upon earth, to have a man's mind . . . turn upon the poles of truth. *Ib.*

Men fear death as children fear to go in the dark; and as that natural fear in children is increased with tales, so is the other. *Ib.* 2. *Of Death.*

There is no passion in the mind of man so weak, but it mates and masters the fear of death . . . Revenge triumphs over death; love slights it; honour aspireth to it; grief flieth to it. *Ib.*

It is as natural to die as to be born; and to a little infant, perhaps, the one is as painful as the other. *Ib.*

Above all, believe it, the sweetest canticle is *Nunc dimittis,* when a man hath obtained worthy ends and expectations. Death hath this also, that it openeth the gate to good fame, and extinguisheth envy. *Ib.*

All colours will agree in the dark.
Ib. 3. *Of Unity in Religion.*

Revenge is a kind of wild justice, which the more man's nature runs to, the more ought law to weed it out. *Ib.* 4. *Of Revenge.*

Why should I be angry with a man for loving himself better than me? *Ib.*

A man that studieth revenge keeps his own wounds green. *Ib.*

It was a high speech of Seneca (after the manner of the Stoics) that, 'the good things which belong to prosperity are to be wished, but the good things that belong to adversity are to be admired.'
Ib. 5. *Of Adversity.*

It is yet a higher speech of his than the other, . . . 'It is true greatness to have in one the frailty of a man, and the security of a God.' *Ib.*

Prosperity is the blessing of the Old Testament, adversity is the blessing of the New. *Ib.*

The pencil of the Holy Ghost hath laboured more in describing the afflictions of Job than the felicities of Solomon. *Ib.*

Prosperity is not without many fears and distastes; and adversity is not without comforts and hopes. *Ib.*

Prosperity doth best discover vice, but adversity doth best discover virtue. *Ib.*

The joys of parents are secret, and so are their griefs and fears. *Ib.* 7. *Of Parents and Children.*

Children sweeten labours, but they make misfortunes more bitter. *Ib.*

The noblest works and foundations have proceeded from childless men, which have sought to express the images of their minds where those of their bodies have failed. *Ib.*

He that hath wife and children hath given hostages to fortune; for they are impediments to great enterprises, either of virtue or mischief.
Ib. 8. *Of Marriage and Single Life.*

There are some other that account wife and children but as bills of charges. *Ib.*

A single life doth well with churchmen, for charity will hardly water the ground where it must first fill a pool. *Ib.*

Wives are young men's mistresses, companions for middle age, and old men's nurses. *Ib.*

He was reputed one of the wise men that made answer to the question when a man should marry? 'A young man not yet, an elder man not at all.' *Ib.*

The speaking in a perpetual hyperbole is comely in nothing but in love. *Ib.* 10. *Of Love.*

It has been well said that 'the arch-flatterer with whom all the petty flatterers have intelligence is a man's self.' *Ib.*

Men in great place are thrice servants: servants of the sovereign or state, servants of fame, and servants of business. *Ib.* 11. *Of Great Place.*

It is a strange desire to seek power and to lose liberty. *Ib.*

The rising unto place is laborious, and by pains men come to greater pains; and it is sometimes base, and by indignities men come to dignities. The standing is slippery, and the regress is either a downfall, or at least an eclipse. *Ib.*

Set it down to thyself, as well to create good precedents as to follow them. *Ib.*

Severity breedeth fear, but roughness breedeth hate. Even reproofs from authority ought to be grave, and not taunting. *Ib.*

As in nature things move violently to their place and calmly in their place, so virtue in ambition is violent, in authority settled and calm. *Ib.*

All rising to great place is by a winding stair. *Ib.*

There is in human nature generally more of the fool than of the wise. *Ib.* 12. *Boldness.*

He said it that knew it best. *Ib.*

In civil business; what first? boldness; what second and third? boldness: and yet boldness is a child of ignorance and baseness. *Ib.*

Boldness is an ill keeper of promise. *Ib.*

Mahomet made the people believe that he would call a hill to him, and from the top of it offer up his prayers for the observers of his law. The people assembled: Mahomet called the hill to come to him again and again; and when the hill stood still, he was never a whit abashed, but said, 'If the hill will not come to Mahomet, Mahomet will go to the hill.' *Essays.* 12. *Boldness.*

The inclination to goodness is imprinted deeply in the nature of man; insomuch, that if it issue not towards men, it will take unto other living creatures. *Ib.* 13. *Goodness, and Goodness of Nature.*

If a man be gracious and courteous to strangers, it shows he is a citizen of the world. *Ib.*

It is a reverend thing to see an ancient castle or building not in decay. *Ib.* 14. *Of Nobility.*

New nobility is but the act of power, but ancient nobility is the act of time. *Ib.*

Nobility of birth commonly abateth industry. *Ib.*

The four pillars of government . . . (which are religion, justice, counsel, and treasure). *Ib.* 15. *Of Seditions and Troubles.*

The surest way to prevent seditions (if the times do bear it) is to take away the matter of them. *Ib.*

Money is like muck, not good except it be spread. *Ib.*

The remedy is worse than the disease. *Ib.*

I had rather believe all the fables in the legend, and the Talmud, and the Alcoran, than that this universal frame is without a mind. *Ib.* 16. *Atheism.*

God never wrought miracle to convince atheism, because his ordinary works convince it. *Ib.*

A little philosophy inclineth man's mind to atheism, but depth in philosophy bringeth men's minds about to religion. *Ib.*

They that deny a God destroy man's nobility; for certainly man is of kin to the beasts by his body; and, if he be not of kin to God by his spirit, he is a base and ignoble creature. *Ib.*

It were better to have no opinion of God at all than such an opinion as is unworthy of him; for the one is unbelief, the other is contumely. *Ib.* 17. *Of Superstition.*

There is a superstition in avoiding superstition. *Ib.*

Travel, in the younger sort, is a part of education; in the elder, a part of experience. He that travelleth into a country before he hath some entrance into the language, goeth to school, and not to travel. *Ib.* 18. *Of Travel.*

Let diaries, therefore, be brought in use. *Ib.*

It is a miserable state of mind to have few things to desire and many things to fear. *Ib.* 19. *Of Empire.*

Books will speak plain when counsellors blanch. *Ib.* 20. *Of Counsel.*

There be that can pack the cards and yet cannot play well; so there are some that are good in canvasses and factions, that are otherwise weak men. *Ib.* 22. *Of Cunning.*

In things that are tender and unpleasing, it is good to break the ice by some whose words are of less weight, and to reserve the more weighty voice to come in as by chance. *Ib.*

I knew one that when he wrote a letter he would put that which was most material in the postscript, as if it had been a bymatter. *Ib.*

Nothing doth more hurt in a state than that cunning men pass for wise. *Ib.*

Be so true to thyself as thou be not false to others. *Ib.* 23. *Of Wisdom for a Man's Self.*

It is a poor centre of a man's actions, himself. *Ib.*

It is the nature of extreme self-lovers, as they will set a house on fire, and it were but to roast their eggs. *Ib.*

It is the wisdom of the crocodiles, that shed tears when they would devour. *Ib.*

As the births of living creatures at first are ill-shapen, so are all innovations, which are the births of time. *Ib.* 24. *Of Innovations.*

He that will not apply new remedies must expect new evils; for time is the greatest innovator. *Ib.*

I knew a wise man that had it for a by-word, when he saw men hasten to a conclusion, 'Stay a little, that we may make an end the sooner.' *Ib.* 25. *Of Despatch.*

To choose time is to save time. *Ib.*

The French are wiser than they seem, and the Spaniards seem wiser than they are. *Ib.* 26. *Of Seeming Wise.*

It had been hard for him that spake it to have put more truth and untruth together, in a few words, than in that speech: 'Whosoever is delighted in solitude is either a wild beast, or a god.' *Ib.* 27. *Of Friendship.*

A crowd is not company, and faces are but a gallery of pictures, and talk but a tinkling cymbal where there is no love. *Ib.*

It [friendship] redoubleth joys, and cutteth griefs in halves. *Ib.*

Cure the disease and kill the patient. *Ib.*

Riches are for spending. *Ib.* 28. *Of Expense.*

A man ought warily to begin charges which once begun will continue. *Ib.*

Neither is money the sinews of war (as it is trivially said). *Ib.* 29. *Of The True Greatness of Kingdoms.*

Neither will it be, that a people overlaid with taxes should ever become valiant and martial. *Ib.*

Thus much is certain; that he that commands the sea is at great liberty, and may take as much and as little of the war as he will. *Ib.*

Age will not be defied. *Ib.* 30. *Of Regimen of Health.*

Suspicions amongst thoughts are like bats amongst birds, they ever fly by twilight. *Ib.* 31. *Of Suspicion.*

There is nothing makes a man suspect much, more than to know little. *Ib.*

Intermingle . . . jest with earnest. *Ib. 32. Of Discourse.*

If you dissemble sometimes your knowledge of that you are thought to know, you shall be thought, another time, to know that you know not.   *Ib.*

Defer not charities till death; for certainly, if a man weigh it rightly, he that doth so is rather liberal of another man's than of his own.   *Ib. 34. Of Riches.*

[Dreams and predictions] ought to serve but for winter talk by the fireside.   *Ib. 35. Of Prophecies.*

He that plots to be the only figure among ciphers, is the decay of the whole age.   *Ib. 36. Of Ambition.*

Nature is often hidden, sometimes overcome, seldom extinguished.   *Ib. 38. Of Nature in Men.*

Chiefly the mould of a man's fortune is in his own hands.   *Ib. 40. Of Fortune.*

Young men are fitter to invent than to judge, fitter for execution than for counsel, and fitter for new projects than for settled business.
        Ib. 42. Of Youth and Age.

Virtue is like a rich stone, best plain set.
        Ib. 43. Of Beauty.

That is the best part of beauty, which a picture cannot express.   *Ib.*

There is no excellent beauty that hath not some strangeness in the proportion.   *Ib.*

Houses are built to live in and not to look on; therefore let use be preferred before uniformity, except where both may be had.   *Ib. 45. Of Building.*

God Almighty first planted a garden; and, indeed, it is the purest of human pleasures. *Ib. 46. Of Gardens.*

It is generally better to deal by speech than by letter.
        Ib. 47. Of Negotiating.

Lookers-on many times see more than gamesters.
        Ib. 48. Of Followers and Friends.

There is little friendship in the world, and least of all between equals.   *Ib.*

Studies serve for delight, for ornament, and for ability.   *Ib. 50. Of Studies.*

To spend too much time in studies is sloth.   *Ib.*

They perfect nature and are perfected by experience.
        Ib.

Read not to contradict and confute, nor to believe and take for granted, nor to find talk and discourse, but to weigh and consider.   *Ib.*

Some books are to be tasted, others to be swallowed, and some few to be chewed and digested; that is, some books are to be read only in parts; others to be read but not curiously; and some few to be read wholly, and with diligence and attention. Some books also may be read by deputy, and extracts made of them by others.   *Ib.*

Reading maketh a full man; conference a ready man and writing an exact man.   *Ib.*

Histories make men wise; poets, witty; the mathematics, subtile; natural philosophy, deep; moral, grave; logic and rhetoric, able to contend.   *Ib.*

Light gains make heavy purses.
        Ib. 52. Of Ceremonies and Respects.

Small matters win great commendation.   *Ib.*

He that . . . giveth another occasion of satiety, maketh himself cheap.   *Ib.*

A wise man will make more opportunities than he finds.   *Ib.*

Fame is like a river, that beareth up things light and swollen, and drowns things weighty and solid.
        Ib. 53. Of Praise.

It was prettily devised of Aesop, 'The fly sat upon the axletree of the chariot-wheel and said, what a dust do I raise.'   *Ib. 54. Of Vain-Glory.*

The place of justice is a hallowed place.
        Ib. 56. Of Judicature.

In the youth of a state arms do flourish; in the middle age of a state, learning; and then both of them together for a time; in the declining age of a state, mechanical arts and merchandise.
        Ib. 58. Of Vicissitude of Things.

I have often thought upon death, and I find it the least of all evils.   *An Essay on Death, § 1.*

I do not believe that any man fears to be dead, but only the stroke of death.   *Ib. 3.*

Why should man be in love with his fetters, though of gold?   *Ib. 4.*

He is the fountain of honour.   *Essay of a King.*

Lucid intervals and happy pauses.
        History of King Henry VII, par. 3.

Quare videmus araneam aut muscam aut formicam, in electro, monumento plus quam regio, sepultas, aeternizari.
    (Whence we see spiders, flies, or ants, entombed and preserved for ever in amber, a more than royal tomb. Tr. Spedding.)
        Historia Vitae et Mortis, Provisional Rules Concerning the Duration of Life and the Form of Death, rule 1, Explanation.

I have taken all knowledge to be my province.
        Letter to Lord Burleigh, 1592.

Opportunity makes a thief.
        Letter to the Earl of Essex, 1598.

I am too old, and the seas are too long, for me to double the Cape of Good Hope.
        Memorial of Access.

I would live to study, and not study to live.   *Ib.*

God's first Creature, which was Light.   *New Atlantis.*

Quatuor sunt genera Idolorum quae mentes humanas obsident. Iis (docendi gratia) nomina imposuimus; ut primum genus, Idola Tribus; secundum, Idola Specus; tertium, Idola Fori; quartum, Idola Theatri vocentur.
    (There are four classes of Idols which beset men's minds. To these for distinction's sake I have assigned names—calling the first class, Idols of the Tribe; the second, Idols of the Cave; the third, Idols of the Market-place; the fourth, Idols of the Theatre. Tr. Spedding.)
        Novum Organon, Aphor. xxxix.

Quod enim mavult homo verum esse, id potius credit.
    (For what a man had rather were true he more readily believes. Tr. Spedding.)   *Ib. xlix.*

Magna ista scientiarum mater.
(This great mother of the sciences [natural philosophy]. Tr. Spedding.) *Ib.* lxxx.

Naturae enim non imperatur, nisi parendo.
(We cannot command nature except by obeying her. Tr. Spedding.) *Ib.* cxxix.

Nam et ipsa scientia potestas est. (Knowledge itself is power.) *Religious Meditations. Of Heresies.*

De Sapientia Veterum. (The wisdom of the ancients. Tr. Sir Arthur Gorges, 1619.) *Title of Work.*

Praecipue autem lignum, sive virga, versus superiorem partem curva est.
(Every rod or staff of empire is truly crooked at the top.) *Ib.* 6, *Pan, sive Natura.*

Universities incline wits to sophistry and affectation.
Valerius Terminus of the Interpretation of Nature, ch. 26.

I have rather studied books than men.
Advice to Sir Geo. Villiers, Works, ed. 1765, vol. ii, p. 258.

For my name and memory, I leave it to men's charitable speeches, and to foreign nations, and the next ages.
Last Will (Dec. 19, 1625). *Ib.* vol. iii, p. 677.

The world's a bubble; and the life of man
Less then a span. *The World.*

Who then to frail mortality shall trust,
But limns the water, or but writes in dust. *Ib.*

What is it then to have or have no wife,
But single thraldom, or a double strife? *Ib.*

What then remains, but that we still should cry,
Not to be born, or being born, to die. *Ib.*

WALTER BAGEHOT

1826-1877

The mystic reverence, the religious allegiance, which are essential to a true monarchy, are imaginative sentiments that no legislature can manufacture in any people.
The English Constitution. Ch. 1. The Cabinet.

The Crown is, according to the saying, the 'fountain of honour'; but the Treasury is the spring of business. *Ib.*

It has been said that England invented the phrase, 'Her Majesty's Opposition'; that it was the first government which made a criticism of administration as much a part of the polity as administration itself. This critical opposition is the consequence of cabinet government. *Ib.*

The *Times* has made many ministries. *Ib.*

We turned out the Quaker (Lord Aberdeen), and put in the pugilist (Lord Palmerston). (Change of Ministry, 1855). *Ib*

The best reason why Monarchy is a strong government is, that it is an intelligible government. The mass of mankind understand it, and they hardly anywhere in the world understand any other.
Ib. Ch. 2. The Monarchy.

The characteristic of the English Monarchy is that it retains the feelings by which the heroic kings governed their rude age, and has added the feelings by which the constitutions of later Greece ruled in more refined ages. *Ib.*

Women—one half the human race at least—care fifty times more for a marriage than a ministry. *Ib.*

Royalty is a government in which the attention of the nation is concentrated on one person doing interesting actions. A Republic is a government in which that attention is divided between many, who are all doing uninteresting actions. Accordingly, so long as the human heart is strong and the human reason weak, Royalty will be strong because it appeals to diffused feeling, and Republics weak because they appeal to the understanding. *Ib.*

An Englishman whose heart is in a matter is not easily baffled. *Ib.*

Throughout the greater part of his life George III was a kind of 'consecrated obstruction'. *Ib.*

But of all nations in the world the English are perhaps the least a nation of pure philosophers. *Ib.*

The order of nobility is of great use, too, not only in what it creates, but in what it prevents. It prevents the rule of wealth—the religion of gold. This is the obvious and natural idol of the Anglo-Saxon.
Ib. Ch. 4. The House of Lords.

The House of Peers has never been a House where the most important peers were most important. *Ib.*

A severe though not unfriendly critic of our institutions said that 'the *cure* for admiring the House of Lords was to go and look at it.' *Ib.*

Nations touch at their summits. *Ib.*

Years ago Mr. Disraeli called Sir Robert Peel's Ministry—the last Conservative Ministry that had real power—'an organized hypocrisy', so much did the ideas of its 'head' differ from the sensations of its 'tail'. *Ib.*

It has been said, not truly, but with a possible approximation to truth, 'that in 1802 every hereditary monarch was insane'. *Ib.*

Queen Anne was one of the smallest people ever set in a great place.
Ib. Ch. 7. Checks and Balances.

The soldier—that is, the great soldier—of to-day is not a romantic animal, dashing at forlorn hopes, animated by frantic sentiment, full of fancies as to a love-lady or a sovereign; but a quiet, grave man, busied in charts, exact in sums, master of the art of tactics, occupied in trivial detail; thinking, as the Duke of Wellington was said to do, *most* of the shoes of his soldiers; despising all manner of *éclat* and eloquence; perhaps, like Count Moltke, 'silent in seven languages'. *Ib.*

The most melancholy of human reflections, perhaps, is that, on the whole, it is a question whether the benevolence of mankind does most good or harm.
Physics and Politics, No. v.

Wordsworth, Tennyson, and Browning; or, Pure, Ornate, and Grotesque Art in English Poetry.
Title of Essay, National Review, November 1864.

PHILIP JAMES BAILEY

1816–1902

We live in deeds, not years; in thoughts, not breaths;
In feelings, not in figures on a dial.
We should count time by heart-throbs. He most lives
Who thinks most—feels the noblest—acts the best.
Festus, v.

Envy's a coal comes hissing hot from hell.   *Ib.*

America, thou half-brother of the world;
With something good and bad of every land.   *Ib.* x.

And these are joys like beauty, but skin deep.   *Ib.*

A double error sometimes sets us right.   *Ib.* xx.

JOANNA BAILLIE

1762–1851

Uprouse ye, then, my merry men!
It is our op'ning day.   *Orra.* III. i.

HENRY WILLIAMS BAKER

1821–1877

The King of Love my Shepherd is,
Whose goodness faileth never.
*Hymns Ancient and Modern. The King of
Love my Shepherd is.*

There is a blessed home
Beyond this land of woe.
Ib. There is a Blessed Home.

JOHN BALE

1495–1563

Though it be a foul great lie: Set upon it a good face.
King John, l. 1978.

ARTHUR JAMES BALFOUR

1848–1930

Defence of philosophic doubt.   Article in *Mind*, 1878.

The energies of our system will decay, the glory of the
sun will be dimmed, and the earth, tideless and
inert, will no longer tolerate the race which has for
a moment disturbed its solitude. Man will go down
into the pit, and all his thoughts will perish.
The Foundations of Belief, pt. i, ch. 1.

It is unfortunate, considering that enthusiasm moves
the world, that so few enthusiasts can be trusted to
speak the truth.   *Letter to Mrs. Drew*, 1918.

Frank Harris . . . said . . . : 'The fact is, Mr. Balfour,
all the faults of the age come from Christianity and
journalism.' 'Christianity, of course, but why
journalism?'
Autobiography of Margot Asquith, vol. i, ch. 10.

JOHN CODRINGTON BAMPFYLDE

1754–1796

Rugged the breast that beauty cannot tame.
Sonnet in Praise of Delia.

GEORGE BANCROFT

fl. 1548

Where Christ erecteth his church, the devil in the
same churchyard will have his chapel.
Sermon preached at Paul's Cross, 9 Feb. 1588.

GEORGE BANCROFT

1800–1891

It [Calvinism in Switzerland] established a religion
without a prelate, a government without a king.
History of the United States vol. iii, ch. 6.

EDWARD BANGS

fl. 1775

Yankee Doodle, keep it up,
Yankee Doodle dandy;
Mind the music and the step,
And with the girls be handy.
Yankee Doodle: or Father's Return to Camp. See
Nicholas Smith, *Stories of Great National Songs.*

Yankee Doodle came to town
Riding on a pony;
Stuck a feather in his cap
And called it Macaroni.   *Ib.*

GEORGE LINNÆUS BANKS

1821–1881

For the cause that lacks assistance,
For the wrong that needs resistance,
For the future in the distance,
And the good that I can do.
Daisies in the Grass. What I Live For.

ANNA LETITIA BARBAULD

1743–1825

So fades a summer cloud away;
So sinks the gale when storms are o'er;
So gently shuts the eye of day;
So dies a wave along the shore.
The Death of the Virtuous.

The world has little to bestow
Where two fond hearts in equal love are joined.
Delia.

And when midst fallen London, they survey
The stone where Alexander's ashes lay,
Shall own with humbled pride the lesson just
By Time's slow finger written in the dust.
Eighteen Hundred and Eleven.

Of her scorn the maid repented,
And the shepherd—of his love.
Leave Me, Simple Shepherd.

Life! we've been long together,
Through pleasant and through cloudy weather.
Life

Then steal away, give little warning,
  Choose thine own time;
Say not Good-night, but in some brighter clime
  Bid me Good-morning!   *Ib.*

Society than solitude is worse,
And man to man is still the greatest curse.
                    Ovid to His Wife.

JOHN BARBOUR

1316?–1395

Storys to rede ar delitabill,
Suppos that thai be nocht bot fabill.
                    The Bruce, bk. i, l. 1.

A! fredome is a noble thing!
Fredome mays man to haiff liking.   *Ib.* l. 225.

REV. RICHARD HARRIS BARHAM

1788–1845

You intoxified brute!—you insensible block!—
Look at the clock!—Do!—Look at the clock!
  The Ingoldsby Legends. Patty Morgan. Fytte i.

'He won't—won't he? Then bring me my boots!' said
  the Baron.   *Ib. Grey Dolphin.*

There, too, full many an Aldermanic nose
Roll'd its loud diapason after dinner.
                    Ib. The Ghost.

Though I've always considered Sir Christopher Wren,
As an architect, one of the greatest of men;
And, talking of Epitaphs,—much I admire his,
'Circumspice, si Monumentum requiris';
Which an erudite Verger translated to me,
'If you ask for his Monument, Sir-come-spy-see!'
                    Ib. The Cynotaph.

The Jackdaw sat on the Cardinal's chair!
Bishop, and abbot, and prior were there;
  Many a monk, and many a friar,
  Many a knight, and many a squire,
With a great many more of lesser degree,—
In sooth a goodly company;
And they served the Lord Primate on bended knee.
          Never, I ween,
          Was a prouder seen,
Read of in books, or dreamt of in dreams,
Than the Cardinal Lord Archbishop of Rheims!
                    Ib. The Jackdaw of Rheims.

And six little Singing-boys,—dear little souls!
In nice clean faces, and nice white stoles.   *Ib.*

He cursed him in sleeping, that every night
He should dream of the devil, and wake in a fright.
                    Ib.

Never was heard such a terrible curse!
  But what gave rise To no little surprise,
Nobody seem'd one penny the worse!   *Ib.*

Heedless of grammar, they all cried, 'That's him!' *Ib.*

Here's a corpse in the case with a sad swell'd face,
And a Medical Crowner's a queer sort of thing!
                    Ib. A Lay of St. Gengulphus.
    A German,
Who smoked like a chimney. *Ib. Lay of St. Odille.*

So put that in your pipe, my Lord Otto, and smoke
  it!   *Ib.*

And her bosom went in, and her tail came out.
                    Ib. A Lay of St. Nicholas.

She drank Prussic acid without any water,
And died like a Duke-and-a-Duchess's daughter!
                    Ib. The Tragedy.

There was cakes and apples in all the Chapels,
With fine polonies, and rich mellow pears.
          Ib. Barney Maguire's Account of the Coronation.

Tallest of boys, or shortest of men,
He stood in his stockings, just four foot ten.
                    Ib. Hon. Mr. Sucklethumbkin's Story.

Tiger Tim, come tell me true,
What may a Nobleman find to do?   *Ib.*

What *was* to be done?—'twas perfectly plain
That they could not well hang the man over again;
What *was* to be done?—The man was dead!
Nought *could* be done—nought could be said;
So—my Lord Tomnoddy went home to bed!   *Ib.*

She help'd him to lean, and she help'd him to fat,
And it look'd like hare—but it might have been cat.
                    Ib. The Bagman's Dog.

Take a suck at the lemon, and at him again!
                    Ib. The Black Mousquetaire.

Like a blue-bottle fly on a rather large scale,
With a rather large corking-pin stuck through his tail.
                    Ib. The Auto-da-Fé.

A servant's too often a negligent elf;
—If it's business of consequence, *do it yourself!*
                    Ib. The Ingoldsby Penance. Moral.

They were a little less than 'kin', and rather more than
  'kind'.   *Ib. Nell Cook.*

'Twas in Margate last July, I walk'd upon the pier,
I saw a little vulgar Boy—I said, 'What make you
  here?'   *Ib. Misadventures at Margate.*

He had no little handkerchief to wipe his little nose!
                    Ib.

And now I'm here, from this here pier it is my fixed
  intent
To jump, as Mr. Levi did from off the Monu-ment!
                    Ib.

I could not see my little friend—because he was not
  there!   *Ib.*

But when the Crier cried, 'O Yes!' the people cried,
  'O No!'   *Ib.*

It's very odd that Sailor-men should talk so very
  queer—
And then he hitch'd his trousers up, as is, I'm told,
  their use,
It's very odd that Sailor-men should wear those things
  so loose.   *Ib.*

He smiled and said, 'Sir, does your mother know that
  you are out?'   *Ib.*

Be kind to those dear little folks
When our toes are turned up to the daisies!
                    Ib. The Babes in the Wood.

Though his cassock was swarming
With all sorts of vermin,
He'd not take the life of a flea!
Ib. The Lay of St. Aloys.

Ah, ha! my good friend!—Don't you wish you may
get it?   *Ib.*

Though port should have age,
Yet I don't think it sage
To entomb it, as some of your *connoisseurs* do,
Till it's losing its flavour, and body, and hue;
—I question if keeping it does it much good
After ten years in bottle and three in the wood.
Ib. The Wedding-Day. Moral.

The Lady Jane was tall and slim,
The Lady Jane was fair.
Ib. The Knight and the Lady.

He would pore by the hour, O'er a weed or a flower,
Or the slugs that come crawling out after a shower.
Ib.

Or great ugly things, All legs and wings,
With nasty long tails arm'd with nasty long stings.
Ib.

Go—pop Sir Thomas again in the pond—
Poor dear!—he'll catch us some more!!
Ib.

Cob was the strongest, *Mob* was the wrongest,
Chittabob's tail was the finest and longest!
Ib. The Truants.

What Horace says is,
Eheu fugaces
Anni labuntur, Postume, Postume!
Years glide away, and are lost to me, lost to me!
Ib. Epigram: Eheu fugaces.

SABINE BARING-GOULD
1834-1924

Now the day is over,
  Night is drawing nigh,
Shadows of the evening
  Steal across the sky.
*Hymns Ancient and Modern. Now the Day is
Over.*

Birds and beasts and flowers
  Soon will be asleep.   *Ib.*

Guard the sailors tossing
  On the deep blue sea.   *Ib.*

Onward, Christian soldiers,
  Marching as to war,
With the Cross of Jesus
  Going on before. *Ib. Onward, Christian Soldiers.*

Hell's foundations quiver
  At the shout of praise;
Brothers, lift your voices,
  Loud your anthems raise.   *Ib.*

Gates of hell can never
  'Gainst that Church prevail;
We have Christ's own promise,
  And that cannot fail.   *Ib.*

Through the night of doubt and sorrow
Onward goes the pilgrim band,
Singing songs of expectation,
Marching to the Promised Land.
*Ib. Tr. from the Danish of B. S. Ingemann,
1789-1862. Through the Night of Doubt and
Sorrow.*

Brother clasps the hand of brother,
Stepping fearless through the night.   *Ib.*

Soon shall come the great awaking,
Soon the rending of the tomb,
Then, the scattering of all shadows
And the end of toil and gloom.   *Ib.*

LADY ANNE BARNARD
1750-1825

When the sheep are in the fauld, when the cows come
  hame,
When a' the weary world to quiet rest are gane.
Auld Robin Gray.

My mither she fell sick—my Jamie was at sea—
And Auld Robin Gray, oh! he came a-courting me. *Ib.*

My father argued sair—my mother didna speak,
But she look'd in my face till my heart was like to
  break.   *Ib.*

I hadna been his wife, a week but only four,
When mournfu' as I sat on the stane at my door,
I saw my Jamie's ghaist—I cou'dna think it he,
Till he said, 'I'm come hame, my love, to marry thee!'
Ib.

CHARLOTTE ALINGTON BARNARD
1840-1869

I cannot sing the old songs
I sang long years ago.
Fireside Thoughts. I Cannot Sing the Old Songs.

RICHARD BARNFIELD
1574-1627

As it fell upon a day,
In the merry month of May,
Sitting in a pleasant shade,
Which a grove of myrtles made.
Poems: in Divers Humors, An Ode.

Beasts did leap and birds did sing,
Trees did grow and plants did spring,
Everything did banish moan,
Save the nightingale alone.
She, poor bird, as all forlorn,
Lean'd her breast up-till a thorn,
And there sung the dolefullest ditty
That to hear it was great pity.
Fie, fie, fie, now would she cry;
Tereu, Tereu, by and by.   *Ib.*

King Pandion, he is dead,
All thy friends are lapp'd in lead.   *Ib.*

If Music and sweet Poetry agree,
As they must needs (the Sister and the Brother)
Then must the love be great, 'twixt thee and me,
Because thou lov'st the one, and I the other.
Ib. Sonnet 1.

Nothing more certain than incertainties;
Fortune is full of fresh variety:
Constant in nothing but inconstancy.
The Shepherd's Content, xi.

My flocks feed not,
My ewes breed not,
My rams speed not,
    All is amiss.
Love is dying,
Faith 's defying,
Heart 's denying,
    Causer of this.   *A Shepherd's Complaint.*

She [*Pecunia*] is the sovereign queen, of all delights:
For her the lawyer pleads; the soldier fights.
Encomion of Lady Pecunia, xvi.

The waters were his winding sheet, the sea was made
    his tomb;
Yet for his fame the ocean sea, was not sufficient
    room.
Ib. To the Gentlemen Readers [*On the death of
Hawkins.*]

BARNABE BARNES

1569?–1609

Ah, sweet Content! where doth thine harbour hold?
Parthenophil and Parthenophe, Sonnet lxvi.

WILLIAM BARNES

1801–1886

An' there vor me the apple tree
Do leän down low in Linden Lea.
My Orcha'd in Linden Lea.

But still the neäme do bide the seäme—
'Tis Pentridge—Pentridge by the river.
Pentridge by the River.

My love is the maïd ov all maïdens,
Though all mid be comely.
In the Spring.

Since I noo mwore do zee your feäce.
The Wife A-Lost.

MATTHIAS BARR

fl. 1870

Only a baby small,
    Dropt from the skies. *Poems. Only a Baby Small.*

Small, but how dear to us,
    God knoweth best.   *Ib.*

EATON STANNARD BARRETT

1786–1820

She, while Apostles shrank, could dangers brave,
Last at His cross and earliest at His grave.
Woman, pt. i, l. 143.

JAMES MATTHEW BARRIE

1860–1937

His lordship may compel us to be equal upstairs, but
there will never be equality in the servants' hall.
The Admirable Crichton, Act I.

I'm a second eleven sort of chap.   *Ib.* Act III.

Never ascribe to an opponent motives meaner than
    your own.
'*Courage*', *Rectorial Address, St. Andrews, 3 May 1922.*

Courage is the thing. All goes if courage goes.   *Ib.*

I do loathe explanations.
My Lady Nicotine. Ch. 16.

When the first baby laughed for the first time, the
laugh broke into a thousand pieces and they all went
skipping about, and that was the beginning of
fairies.   *Peter Pan,* Act I.

Every time a child says 'I don't believe in fairies'
there is a little fairy somewhere that falls down
dead.   *Ib.*

To die will be an awfully big adventure.   *Ib.* Act III.

Do you believe in fairies? . . . If you believe, clap your
hands!   *Ib.* Act IV.

That is ever the way. 'Tis all jealousy to the bride and
good wishes to the corpse.   *Quality Street,* Act I.

Oh the gladness of her gladness when she 's glad,
And the sadness of her sadness when she 's sad,
But the gladness of her gladness
And the sadness of her sadness
Are as nothing, Charles,
To the badness of her badness when she's bad.
Rosalind.

It is wonderful how much you can conceal between
the touch of the handle and the opening of the door
if your heart is in it.   *Tommy and Grizel.*

The Twelve-Pound Look.   *Title of Play.*

Have you ever noticed, Harry, that many jewels make
women either incredibly fat or incredibly thin?
The Twelve-pound Look.

It's a sort of bloom on a woman. If you have it
[charm], you don't need to have anything else; and if
you don't have it, it doesn't much matter what else
you have.   *What Every Woman Knows,* Act I.

A young Scotsman of your ability let loose upon the
world with £300, what could he not do? It 's almost
appalling to think of; especially if he went among
the English.   *Ib.*

You've forgotten the grandest moral attribute of a
Scotsman, Maggie, that he'll do nothing which
might damage his career.   *Ib.* Act II.

There are few more impressive sights in the world
than a Scotsman on the make.   *Ib.*

Every man who is high up loves to think that he has
done it all himself; and the wife smiles, and lets it
go at that. It's our only joke. Every woman knows
that.   *Ib.* Act IV.

WILLIAM BASSE

d. 1653?

Renowned Spencer, lie a thought more nigh
To learned Chaucer, and rare Beaumont lie,
A little nearer Spenser, to make room
For Shakespeare, in your threefold, fourfold tomb.
Poetical Works. On Shakespeare.

EDGAR BATEMAN

Wiv a ladder and some glasses,
You could see to 'Ackney Marshes,
If it wasn't for the 'ouses in between.
If It Wasn't For The 'Ouses In Between.

KATHERINE LEE BATES

1859–1929

America! America!
  God shed His grace on thee
And crown thy good with brotherhood
  From sea to shining sea!   *America the Beautiful.*

RICHARD BAXTER

1615–1691

I preach'd as never sure to preach again,
And as a dying man to dying men!
Love Breathing Thanks and Praise, pt. ii.

BERNARD BAYLE

fl. 1854

A Storm in a Teacup.   *Title of farce,* 1854.

THOMAS HAYNES BAYLY

1797–1839

I'd be a butterfly born in a bower,
Where roses and lilies and violets meet.
                            I'd be a Butterfly.

I'm saddest when I sing.   *Title of poem.*

Absence makes the heart grow fonder,
  Isle of Beauty, Fare thee well!   *Isle of Beauty.*

It was a dream of perfect bliss,
Too beautiful to last.   *It was a Dream.*

The mistletoe hung in the castle hall,
The holly branch shone on the old oak wall.
                   The Mistletoe Bough.

Oh! no! we never mention her,
  Her name is never heard;
My lips are now forbid to speak
  That once familiar word.
        Oh! No! We Never Mention Her.

Oh, Pilot! 'tis a fearful night,
  There's danger on the deep.   *The Pilot.*

Fear not, but trust in Providence
  Wherever thou may'st be.   *Ib.*

She wore a wreath of roses,
The night that first we met.
            She Wore a Wreath of Roses.

Gaily the Troubadour
Touch'd his guitar.   *Welcome Me Home.*

We met, 'twas in a crowd, And I thought he would
  shun me.   *We Met, 'twas in a Crowd.*

Why don't the men propose, mamma,
Why don't the men propose?
        Why Don't the Men Propose?

JAMES BEATTIE

1735–1803

His harp, the sole companion of his way.
           The Minstrel, bk. i. iii.

In truth, he was a strange and wayward wight,
Fond of each gentle and each dreadful scene.
In darkness and in storm he found delight. *Ib.* xxii.

DAVID BEATTY, EARL BEATTY

1871–1936

There's something wrong with our bloody ships
  to-day, Chatfield.
    *Remark during the Battle of Jutland, 1916: Win-
    ston Churchill, The World Crisis (1927), Pt. i,
    p. 129. The additional words commonly attri-
    buted: 'Steer two points nearer the enemy' are
    denied by Lord Chatfield.*

TOPHAM BEAUCLERK

1739–1780

[On Boswell saying that a certain man had good
  principles.] Then he does not wear them out in
  practice. *Boswell's Life of Johnson, 14 April, 1778.*

FRANCIS BEAUMONT

1584–1616

What things have we seen,
Done at the Mermaid! heard words that have been
So nimble, and so full of subtil flame,
As if that every one from whence they came,
Had meant to put his whole wit in a jest,
And had resolv'd to live a fool, the rest
Of his dull life.   *Letter to Ben Jonson.*

Here are sands, ignoble things,
Dropt from the ruin'd sides of Kings;
Here's a world of pomp and state,
Buried in dust, once dead by fate.
        On the Tombs in Westminster Abbey.

FRANCIS BEAUMONT

1584–1616
and
JOHN FLETCHER

1579–1625

There is no drinking after death.
        The Bloody Brother, ii. ii.

And he that will to bed go sober,
Falls with the leaf still in October.   *Ib.*

Three merry boys, and three merry boys,
  And three merry boys are we,
As ever did sing in a hempen string
    Under the gallows-tree.   *Ib.* III. ii.

Bad 's the best of us.   *Ib.* IV. ii.

You are no better than you should be.
                        The Coxcomb, IV. iii.

I care not two-pence.   *Ib.* V. i.

Death hath so many doors to let out life.
                The Customs of the Country, II. ii.

But what is past my help, is past my care.
                        The Double Marriage, I. i.

            It is always good
When a man has two irons in the fire.
                        The Faithful Friends, I. ii.

Our acts our angels are, or good or ill,
Our fatal shadows that walk by us still.
                Upon an Honest Man's Fortune, V.

Let 's meet, and either do, or die.
                        The Island Princess, II. ii.

Nose, nose, jolly red nose,
and who gave thee this jolly red nose? . . .
Nutmegs and ginger, cinamon and cloves,
And they gave me this jolly red nose.
                Knight of the Burning Pestle, I. iii.

This is a pretty flim-flam.   *Ib.* II. iii.

Go to grass.   *Ib.* IV. vi.

Something given that way.
                        The Lovers' Progress, I. i.

Deeds, not words shall speak me.   *Ib.* III. vi.

Thou wilt scarce be a man before thy mother.
                                Ib. ii.

I find the medicine worse than the malady.   *Ib.*

Faith Sir, he went away with a flea in 's ear. *Ib.* IV. iii.

I'll put on my considering cap.
                        The Loyal Subject, II. i.

I'll put a spoke among your wheels.
                        The Mad Lover, III. vi.

Upon my buried body lay lightly gentle earth.
                        The Maid's Tragedy, II. i.

Fountain heads, and pathless groves,
Places which pale passion loves.
                        The Nice Valour, Song, III. iii.

Nothing's so dainty sweet, as lovely melancholy. *Ib.*

            All your better deeds
Shall be in water writ, but this in marble. *Ib.* V. iii.

'Tis virtue, and not birth that makes us noble:
Great actions speak great minds, and such should
  govern.   *The Prophetess*, II. iii.

I'll have a fling.
                Rule a Wife and have a Wife, III. v.

Kiss till the cow come home.   *Scornful Lady*, II. ii.

There is no other purgatory but a woman.   *Ib.* III. i.

It would talk:
Lord how it talk't!   *Ib.* IV. i.

Daisies smell-less, yet most quaint,
            And sweet thyme true,
Primrose first born child of Ver,
Merry Spring—time's Harbinger.
                        Two Noble Kinsmen, I. i.

God Lyeus ever young,
Ever honour'd, ever sung.   *Valentinian*, V. viii.

Come sing now, sing; for I know ye sing well,
I see ye have a singing face.
                        The Wild Goose Chase, II. ii.

Though I say't, that should not say't.
                        Wit at Several Weapons, II. ii.

Whistle and she'll come to you.
                        Wit Without Money, IV. iv.

Let the world slide.   *Ib.* V. ii.

Have not you maggots in your brains?
                        Women Pleased, III. iv.

PETER BECKFORD

1740–1811

The colour I think of little moment; and am of
  opinion with our friend Foote, respecting his negro
  friend, that a good dog, like a good candidate,
  cannot be of a bad colour.
    Thoughts upon Hare and Fox Hunting, letter 3.

WILLIAM BECKFORD

1759–1844

When he was angry, one of his eyes became so terrible,
  that no person could bear to behold it; and the
  wretch upon whom it was fixed instantly fell backward, and sometimes expired. For fear, however,
  of depopulating his dominions, and making his
  palace desolate, he but rarely gave way to his anger.
                        Vathek (1893), p. 1.

He did not think, with the Caliph Omar Ben Adalaziz,
  that it was necessary to make a hell of this world to
  enjoy paradise in the next.   *Ib.* p. 2.

Your presence I condescend to accept and beg you
  will let me be quiet, for I am not over-fond of resisting temptation.   *Ib.* p. 134.

THOMAS BECON

1512–1567

For when the wine is in, the wit is out.
                        Catechism, 375.

THOMAS LOVELL BEDDOES

1798–1851

If thou wilt ease thine heart
Of love and all its smart,
Then sleep, dear, sleep.
                        Death's Jest Book, II. ii.

But wilt thou cure thine heart
Of love and all its smart,
Then die, dear, die.   *Ib.*

If man could see
The perils and diseases that he elbows,
Each day he walks a mile; which catch at him,
Which fall behind and graze him as he passes;
Then would he know that Life's a single pilgrim,
Fighting unarmed amongst a thousand soldiers.
Ib. iv. i. (MS. III).

I have a bit of FIAT in my soul,
And can myself create my little world.   *Ib.* v. i.

Old Adam, the carrion crow.   *Ib.* v. iv.

King Death hath asses' ears.   *Ib.*

If there were dreams to sell,
  What would you buy?
Some cost a passing bell;
  Some a light sigh,
That shakes from Life's fresh crown
Only a roseleaf down.
If there were dreams to sell,
Merry and sad to tell,
And the crier rung the bell,
  What would you buy?   *Dream-Pedlary.*

            Him
Who was the planet's tyrant, dotard Death.
                  Letter from Göttingen.

How many times do I love thee, dear?
Tell me how many thoughts there be
  In the atmosphere
  Of a new-fal'n year,
Whose white and sable hours appear
The latest flakes of Eternity:
So many times do I love thee, dear.
                  Torrismond. i. iii.

BEDE

673–735

Talis, inquiens, mihi videtur, rex, vita hominum
  praesens in terris, ad conparationem eius, quod
  nobis incertum est, temporis, quale cum te resi-
  dente ad caenam cum ducibus ac ministris tuis
  tempore brumali, ... adveniens unus passerum do
  mum citissime pervolaverit; qui cum per unum
  ostium ingrediens, mox per aliud exierit. Ipso quidem tempore, quo intus est, hiemis tempestate non
  tangitur, sed tamen parvissimo spatio serenitatis ad
  momentum excurso, mox de hieme in hiemem re-
  grediens, tuis oculis elabitur. Ita haec vita hominum ad modicum apparet; quid autem sequatur,
  quidve praecesserit, prorsus ignoramus.

  ['Such,' he said, 'O King, seems to me the present
  life of men on earth, in comparison with that time
  which to us is uncertain, as if when on a winter's
  night you sit feasting with your ealdormen and
  thegns,—a single sparrow should fly swiftly into the
  hall, and coming in at one door, instantly fly out
  through another. In that time in which it is indoors
  it is indeed not touched by the fury of the winter,
  but yet, this smallest space of calmness being passed
  almost in a flash, from winter going into winter
  again, it is lost to your eyes. Somewhat like this
  appears the life of man; but of what follows or what
  went before, we are utterly ignorant.']
          Ecclesiastical History, bk. ii, ch. 13.

Scio, inquiens, quia ubi navem ascenderitis, tempestas vobis et ventus contrarius superveniet: sed
  pestas vobis et ventus contrarius superveniet: sed

tu memento ut hoc oleum quod tibi do, mittas in
  mare; et statim quiescentibus ventis, serenitas maris
  vos læta prosequetur.

  [I know, he said, that when you go on board ship,
  a storm and contrary wind will come upon you: but
  remember to pour this oil that I give you, on the
  water; and immediately with the winds dropping
  happy calm of ocean will ensue.]   *Ib.* bk. iii, ch. 15.

BERNARD ELLIOTT BEE

1823–1861

Let us determine to die here, and we will conquer.
  There is Jackson standing like a stone wall. Rally
  behind the Virginians.
      First Battle of Bull Run, 1861. Poore, *Reminis-
      cences of Metropolis*, ii. 85.

HENRY CHARLES BEECHING

1859–1919

With lifted feet, hands still,
I am poised, and down the hill
Dart, with heedful mind;
The air goes by in a wind.
                  Going Down Hill on a Bicycle.

Alas, that the longest hill
Must end in a vale; but still,
Who climbs with toil, wheresoe'er
Shall find wings waiting there.   *Ib.*

Not when the sense is dim,
  But now from the heart of joy,
I would remember Him:
  Take the thanks of a boy.   *Prayers.*

MAX BEERBOHM

1872–

I belong to the Beardsley period.   *Diminuendo.*

There is always something rather absurd about the
  past.   *1880.*

To give an accurate and exhaustive account of that
  period would need a far less brilliant pen than
  mine.   *Ib.*

She swam to the bell-rope and grasped it for a tinkle.
  [Parody of Meredith.] *Euphemia Clashthought.*

Not that I had any special reason for hating school.
  Strange as it may seem to my readers, I was not
  unpopular there. I was a modest, good-humoured
  boy. It is Oxford that has made me insufferable.
                  Going Back to School.

Mankind is divisible into two great classes: hosts and
  guests.   *Hosts and Guests.*

I maintain that though you would often in the fif-
  teenth century have heard the snobbish Roman say,
  in a would-be off-hand tone, 'I am dining with the
  Borgias to-night,' no Roman ever was able to say,
  'I dined last night with the Borgias.'   *Ib.*

The Nonconformist Conscience makes cowards of
  us all.   *King George the Fourth.*

Fate wrote her [Queen Caroline] a most tremendous
  tragedy, and she played it in tights.   *Ib.*

They so very indubitably *are*, you know! [Parody of Henry James.]   *Mote in the Middle Distance.*

'After all', as a pretty girl once said to me, 'women are a sex by themselves, so to speak.'
The Pervasion of Rouge.

Savonarola love-sick! Ha, ha, ha!
Love-sick? He, love-sick? 'Tis a goodly jest!
The confirm'd misogyn a ladies' man!
Savonarola Brown, Act I.

Had Sav'narola spoken less than thus,
Methinks me, the less Sav'narola he.   *Ib.*

LUC. And what name gave he?
PORTER. Something-arola—
LUC   Savon?—show him up.   *Ib.* Act II.

Enter Michael Angelo. Andrea del Sarto appears for a moment at a window. Pippa passes. *Ib.* Act III.

    O the disgrace of it!—
The scandal, the incredible come-down! *Ib.* Act IV.

A pretty sort of prison I have come to,
In which a self-respecting lady's cell
Is treated as a lounge   *Ib.*

'Your mentality, too, is bully, as we all predicate.'
Zuleika Dobson, ch. 8.

Deeply regret inform your grace last night two black owls came and perched on battlements remained there through night hooting at dawn flew away none knows whither awaiting instructions Jellings.
Ib. ch. 14.

'The Socratic manner is not a game at which two can play.'   *Ib.* ch. 15.

'Ah, say that again,' she murmured. 'Your voice is music.'
  He repeated his question.
  'Music!' she said dreamily; and such is the force of habit that 'I don't', she added, 'know anything about music, really. But I know what I like.'
Ib. ch. 16.

ETHEL LYNN BEERS
1827–1879

All quiet along the Potomac to-night,
  No sound save the rush of the river,
While soft falls the dew on the face of the dead—
  The picket's off duty forever.
All Quiet along the Potomac.

APHRA BEHN
1640–1689

Oh, what a dear ravishing thing is the beginning of an Amour!   *The Emperor of the Moon*, I. I.

Of all that writ, he was the wisest bard, who spoke this mighty truth—
He that knew all that ever learning writ,
Knew only this—that he knew nothing yet. *Ib.* III.

Love ceases to be a pleasure, when it ceases to be a secret.   *The Lover's Watch, Four o'clock.*

Faith, Sir, we are here to-day, and gone to-morrow.
The Lucky Chance, IV.

I owe a duty, where I cannot love.
The Moor's Revenge, III. iii.

Oh, I am arm'd with more than complete steel,
The justice of my quarrel.   *Ib.* IV. 5.

A brave world, Sir, full of religion, knavery, and change: we shall shortly see better days.
The Roundheads, I. i.

Variety is the soul of pleasure.
The Rover, Part II, Act I.

Come away; poverty's catching.   *Ib.*

Money speaks sense in a language all nations understand.   *Ib.* III. i.

Beauty unadorn'd.   *Ib.* IV. ii.

'Sure, I rose the wrong way to-day, I have had such damn'd ill luck every way.'   *The Town Fop*, V. i.

The soft, unhappy sex.   *The Wandering Beauty.*

W. H. BELLAMY

Old Simon the Cellarer keeps a rare store
  Of Malmsey and Malvoisie.
Song: Simon the Cellarer.

HILAIRE BELLOC
1870–

The road went up, the road went down,
  And there the matter ended it.
He broke his heart in Clermont town,
  At Pontgibaud they mended it.   *Auvergnat.*

Child! do not throw this book about;
Refrain from the unholy pleasure
Of cutting all the pictures out!
  Preserve it as your chiefest treasure.
Bad Child's Book of Beasts, dedication.

Your little hands were made to take
The better things and leave the worse ones:
They also may be used to shake
The massive paws of elder persons.   *Ib.*

A manner rude and wild
Is common at your age.   *Ib.* introduction.

Who take their manners from the Ape,
  Their habits from the Bear,
Indulge the loud unseemly jape,
  And never brush their hair.   *Ib.*

The Dromedary is a cheerful bird:
I cannot say the same about the Kurd.
Ib. The Dromedary.

I shoot the Hippopotamus
With bullets made of platinum,
Because if I use leaden ones
His hide is sure to flatten 'em. *Ib. The Hippopotamus.*

Mothers of large families, who claim to common sense,
Will find a Tiger well repay the trouble and expense.
Ib. The Tiger.

Yet may you see his bones and beak
All in the Mu-se-um.   *Ib. The Dodo.*

When people call this beast to mind,
They marvel more and more
At such a little tail behind,
So large a trunk before.   *Ib. The Elephant.*

You have a horn where other brutes have none:
Rhinoceros, you are an ugly beast.
Ib. The Rhinoceros.

The Frog is justly sensitive
To epithets like these. *Ib. The Frog.*

Here is a House that armours a man
With the eyes of a boy and the heart of a ranger.
To the Balliol Men still in Africa.

I have said it before, and I say it again,
There was treason done, and a false word spoken,
And England under the dregs of men,
And bribes about, and a treaty broken. *Ib.*

Balliol made me, Balliol fed me,
Whatever I had she gave me again;
And the best of Balliol loved and led me,
God be with you, Balliol men. *Ib.*

The chief defect of Henry King
Was chewing little bits of string.
Cautionary Tales. Henry King.

Physicians of the utmost fame
Were called at once; but when they came
They answered, as they took their fees,
'There is no cure for this disease.' *Ib.*

'Oh, my friends, be warned by me,
That breakfast, dinner, lunch, and tea
Are all the human frame requires . . .'
With that, the wretched child expires. *Ib.*

'Ponto!' he cried, with angry frown,
'Let go, Sir! Down, Sir! Put it down!' *Ib. Jim.*

The nicest child I ever knew
Was Charles Augustus Fortescue.
Ib. Charles Augustus Fortescue.

Godolphin Horne was nobly born;
He held the human race in scorn.
Ib. Godolphin Horne.

Children in ordinary dress
May always play with sand.
Ib. Franklin Hyde.

Lord Lundy from his earliest years
Was far too freely moved to tears. *Ib. Lord Lundy.*

Towards the age of twenty-six,
They shoved him into politics. *Ib.*

For every time she shouted 'Fire!'
They only answered 'Little liar!' *Ib. Matilda.*

She was not really bad at heart,
But only rather rude and wild;
She was an aggravating child. *Ib. Rebecca.*

Her funeral sermon (which was long
And followed by a sacred song)
Mentioned her virtues, it is true,
But dwelt upon her vices too. *Ib.*

Of Courtesy—it is much less
Than courage of heart or holiness;
Yet in my walks it seems to me
That the Grace of God is in Courtesy. *Courtesy.*

But I will sit beside the fire,
And put my hand before my eyes,
And trace, to fill my heart's desire,
The last of all our Odysseys. *Dedicatory Ode.*

We were? Why then, by God, we *are*—
Order! I call the Club to session! *Ib.*

Remote and ineffectual Don
That dared attack my Chesterton. *Lines to a Don.*

Don different from those regal Dons!
With hearts of gold and lungs of bronze,
Who shout and bang and roar and bawl
The Absolute across the hall,
Or sail in amply billowing gown,
Enormous through the Sacred Town. *Ib.*

The moon on the one hand, the dawn on the other:
The moon is my sister, the dawn is my brother.
The moon on my left and the dawn on my right.
My brother, good morning: my sister, good night.
The Early Morning.

Dear Mr. Noman, does it ever strike you,
The more we see of you, the less we like you?
Epigrams. On Noman, A Guest.

I said to Heart, 'How goes it?' Heart replied·
'Right as a Ribstone Pippin!' But it lied.
Ib. The False Heart.

Of this bad world the loveliest and the best
Has smiled and said 'Good Night,' and gone to rest.
Ib. On a Dead Hostess.

The accursed power which stands on Privilege
(And goes with Women, and Champagne, and Bridge)
Broke—and Democracy resumed her reign:
(Which goes with Bridge, and Women and Champagne). *Ib. On a Great Election.*

The Devil, having nothing else to do,
Went off to tempt my Lady Poltagrue.
My Lady, tempted by a private whim,
To his extreme annoyance, tempted him.
Ib. On Lady Poltagrue, a Public Peril.

When I am dead, I hope it may be said:
'His sins were scarlet, but his books were read.'
Ib. On his Books.

Sally is gone that was so kindly,
Sally is gone from Ha'nacker Hill.
Ha'nacker Mill.

But Catholic men that live upon wine
Are deep in the water, and frank, and fine;
Wherever I travel I find it so,
Benedicamus Domino.
Heretics All.

She died because she never knew
These simple little rules and few;—
The Snake is living yet.
More Beasts for Worse Children. The Python.

With an indolent expression and an undulating throat
Like an unsuccessful literary man. *Ib.*

Birds in their little nests agree
With Chinamen, but not with me.
New Cautionary Tales. On Food.

A smell of burning fills the startled air—
The Electrician is no longer there!
Newdigate Poem.

When I am living in the Midlands
That are sodden and unkind

the great hills of the South Country
Come back into my mind.
The South Country.

A lost thing could I never find,
  Nor a broken thing mend.   *Ib.*

  The faith in their happy eyes
Comes surely from our Sister the Spring
When over the sea she flies;
The violets suddenly bloom at her feet,
She blesses us with surprise.   *Ib.*

I never get between the pines
But I smell the Sussex air.   *Ib.*

If I ever become a rich man,
Or if ever I grow to be old,
I will build a house with deep thatch
To shelter me from the cold,
And there shall the Sussex songs be sung
And the story of Sussex told.   *Ib.*

I will hold my house in the high wood
Within a walk of the sea,
And the men that were boys when I was a boy
Shall sit and drink with me.   *Ib.*

Do you remember an Inn,
Miranda?   *Tarantella.*

We also know the sacred height
  Up on Tugela side,
Where those three hundred fought with Beit
  And fair young Wernher died.
      *Verses to a Lord who said that those who opposed
      the South African adventure confused soldiers
      with money-grubbers.*

Tall Goltman, silent on his horse,
  Superb against the dawn.
The little mound where Eckstein stood
  And gallant Albu fell,
And Oppenheim, half blind with blood
Went fording through the rising flood—
  My Lord, we know them well.   *Ib.*

They sell good beer at Haslemere
  And under Guildford Hill.
At Little Cowfold as I've been told
  A beggar may drink his fill:
There is a good brew in Amberley too,
  And by the bridge also;
But the swipes they take in at Washington Inn
  Is the very best Beer I know.
                    West Sussex Drinking Song.

It is the best of all trades, to make songs, and the
second best to sing them.
                    On Everything. On Song.

From the towns all Inns have been driven: from the
villages most. . . . Change your hearts or you will
lose your Inns and you will deserve to have lost
them. But when you have lost your Inns drown
your empty selves, for you will have lost the last of
England.   *This and That. On Inns.*

ENOCH ARNOLD BENNETT
1867–1931

'Ye can call it influenza if ye like,' said Mrs. Machin.
'There was no influenza in my young days. We
called a cold a cold.'   *The Card*, ch. 8.

Being a husband is a whole-time job.
                    The Title, Act I.

Journalists say a thing that they know isn't true, in
the hope that if they keep on saying it long enough
it *will* be true.   *Ib.* Act II.

HENRY BENNETT
1785–?

Oh, St. Patrick was a gentleman,
  Who came of decent people;
He built a church in Dublin town,
  And on it put a steeple.
      *St. Patrick was a Gentleman (Oxford Song
      Book.)*

JEREMY BENTHAM
1748–1832

All punishment is mischief: all punishment in itself is
evil. *Principles of Morals and Legislation*, ch. 13, § 2.

EDMUND CLERIHEW BENTLEY
1875–

The art of Biography
Is different from Geography.
Geography is about maps,
But Biography is about chaps.
                    Biography for Beginners.

What I like about Clive
Is that he is no longer alive.
There is a great deal to be said
For being dead.   *Ib. Clive.*

Sir Christopher Wren
Said, 'I am going to dine with some men.
If anybody calls
Say I am designing St. Paul's.'
                    Ib. Sir Christopher Wren.

Chapman and Hall
Swore not at all.
Mr. Chapman's yea was yea,
And Mr. Hall's nay was nay.
                    Ib. Mr. Chapman and Mr. Hall.

Edward the Confessor
Slept under the dresser.
When that began to pall
He slept in the hall.   *Ib. Edward the Confessor.*

THOMAS BENTLEY
?1693–1742

No man is demolished but by himself.
                    A Letter to Mr. Pope, 1735.

LORD CHARLES BERESFORD
1846–1919

The idea of a Commercial Alliance with England
based on the integrity of China and the open door
for all nations' trade.
      *The Break-Up of China, a Report to the
      British Associated Chambers of Commerce,
      from Shanghai*, 20 Nov. 1898.

GEORGE BERKELEY
1684–1753

All the choir of heaven and furniture of earth—in a word, all those bodies which compose the mighty frame of the world—have not any subsistence without a mind. *Principles of Human Knowledge.*

Westward the course of empire takes its way;
　The four first acts already past,
A fifth shall close the drama with the day:
　Time's noblest offspring is the last.
　　On the Prospect of Planting Arts and Learning in America.

[Tar water] is of a nature so mild and benign and proportioned to the human constitution, as to warm without heating, to cheer but not inebriate.
　　　　　　　Siris, par. 217.

IRVING BERLIN
1888–

Come on and hear, come on and hear, Alexander's Ragtime Band. *Alexander's Ragtime Band.*

RICHARD BETHELL, BARON WESTBURY
1800–1873

His Lordship says he will turn it over in what he is pleased to call his mind. Nash, *Life of Westbury*, i. 158.

ISAAC BICKERSTAFFE
?1735–?1812

There was a jolly miller once,
　Lived on the river Dee;
He worked and sang from morn till night;
　No lark more blithe than he.
　　　　Love in a Village, i. v.

And this the burthen of his song,
　For ever us'd to be,
I care for nobody, not I,
　If no one cares for me. *Ib.*

We all love a pretty girl—under the rose.
　　　　　　Ib. ii. ii.

Perhaps it was right to dissemble your love,
But—why did you kick me downstairs?
　　　　　An Expostulation.

EDWARD HENRY BICKERSTETH
1825–1906

Peace, perfect peace, in this dark world of sin?
The Blood of Jesus whispers peace within.
　　　Hymnal Companion, Second Edition.

ROGER BIGOD
1245–1306

(Edward I: 'By God, earl, you shall either go or hang!')
'O King, I will neither go nor hang!'
　　　Hemingburgh's Chronicle, ii. 121.

LAURENCE BINYON
1869–

With proud thanksgiving, a mother for her children,
England mourns for her dead across the sea.
　　　　　　Poems For the Fallen.

They shall grow not old, as we that are left grow old:
Age shall not weary them, nor the years condemn.
At the going down of the sun and in the morning
We will remember them. *Ib.*

That many-memoried name. *Tristram's End.*

FREDERICK EDWIN SMITH, EARL OF BIRKENHEAD
1872–1931

The world continues to offer glittering prizes to those who have stout hearts and sharp swords.
Rectorial Address, Glasgow University, 7 Nov. 1923.

AUGUSTINE BIRRELL
1850–1933

That great dust-heap called 'history'.
　　　　Obiter Dicta. Carlyle.

In the name of the Bodleian. *Ib. Dr. Johnson.*

What then did happen at the Reformation?
　　　　　Title of Essay.

WILLIAM BLACKSTONE
1723–1780

Man was formed for society.
　　　　Commentaries, introd. § 2.

Mankind will not be reasoned out of the feelings of humanity. *Ib.* bk. i. 5.

The king never dies. *Ib.* 7.

The royal navy of England hath ever been its greatest defence and ornament; it is its ancient and natural strength; the floating bulwark of the island.
　　　　　　　Ib. 13.

Time whereof the memory of man runneth not to the contrary. *Ib.* 18.

That the king can do no wrong, is a necessary and fundamental principle of the English constitution.
　　　　　Ib. iii. 17.

HELEN SELINA BLACKWOOD, LADY DUFFERIN
1807–1867

I'm sitting on the stile, Mary,
　Where we sat, side by side.
　　　Lament of the Irish Emigrant

The corn was springing fresh and green,
　And the lark sang loud and high,
And the red was on your lip, Mary,
　The love-light in your eye. *Ib.*

a   **b**

I'm very lonely now, Mary,—
  The poor make no new friends:—
But, oh! they love the better still
  The few our Father sends.   *Ib.*

I'm bidding you a long farewell,
  My Mary—kind and true!
But I'll not forget you, darling,
  In the land I'm going to.
They say there's bread and work for all,
  And the sun shines always there:
But I'll not forget old Ireland,
  Were it fifty times as fair.   *Ib.*

ROBERT BLAIR

1699–1747

    The good he scorn'd
Stalk'd off reluctant, like an ill-us'd ghost,
Not to return; or if it did, its visits
Like those of angels, short, and far between.
                 The Grave, l. 586.

CHARLES DUPEE BLAKE

1846–1903

Rock-a-bye-baby on the tree top,
When the wind blows the cradle will rock,
When the bough bends the cradle will fall,
Down comes the baby, cradle and all.   *Attr.*

WILLIAM BLAKE

1757–1827

The errors of a wise man make your rule,
Rather than the perfections of a fool.
             On Art and Artists, viii.

When Sir Joshua Reynolds died
All Nature was degraded:
The King dropped a tear into the Queen's ear,
And all his pictures faded.   *Ib.* xxi.

I understood Christ was a carpenter
And not a brewer's servant, my good Sir.   *Ib.* xxvi.

To see a World in a Grain of Sand,
  And a Heaven in a Wild Flower,
Hold Infinity in the palm of your hand,
  And Eternity in an hour.   *Auguries of Innocence.*

A Robin Redbreast in a Cage
Puts all Heaven in a Rage.   *Ib.*

A dog starv'd at his master's gate
Predicts the ruin of the State,
A horse misus'd upon the road
Calls to Heaven for human blood.
Each outcry of the hunted hare
A fibre from the brain does tear,
A skylark wounded in the wing,
A cherubim does cease to sing.   *Ib.*

The bat that flits at close of eve
Has left the brain that won't believe.   *Ib.*

He who shall hurt the little wren
Shall never be belov'd by men.
He who the ox to wrath has mov'd
Shall never be by woman lov'd.   *Ib.*

The caterpillar on the leaf
Repeats to thee thy mother's grief.
Kill not the moth nor butterfly,
For the Last Judgement draweth nigh.   *Ib.*

A truth that's told with bad intent
Beats all the lies you can invent.
It is right it should be so;
Man was made for Joy and Woe;
And when this we rightly know,
Thro' the World we safely go,
Joy and woe are woven fine,
A clothing for the soul divine.   *Ib.*

Every tear from every eye
Becomes a babe in Eternity.   *Ib.*

The bleat, the bark, bellow, and roar
Are waves that beat on Heaven's shore.   *Ib.*

The strongest poison ever known
Came from Caesar's laurel crown.   *Ib.*

He who doubts from what he sees
Will ne'er believe, do what you please.
If the Sun and Moon should doubt,
They'd immediately go out.
To be in a passion you good may do,
But no good if a passion is in you.
The whore and gambler, by the state
Licensed, build that nation's fate.
The harlot's cry from street to street
Shall weave old England's winding sheet.   *Ib.*

God appears, and God is Light,
To those poor souls who dwell in Night;
But does a Human Form display
To those who dwell in realms of Day.   *Ib.*

Does the Eagle know what is in the pit
Or wilt thou go ask the Mole?
Can Wisdom be put in a silver rod,
Or Love in a golden bowl?
          Book of Thel, Thel's motto.

Everything that lives,
Lives not alone, nor for itself.   *Ib.* II.

My brother John, the evil one.
    To Thomas Butts. 'With Happiness stretch'd
    across the Hills', l. 15.

For double the vision my eyes do see,
And a double vision is always with me.
With my inward eye 'tis an Old Man grey,
With my outward, a Thistle across my way.
               Ib. l. 27.

'What,' it will be questioned, 'when the sun rises, do
  you not see a round disc of fire somewhat like a
  guinea?' 'O no, no, I see an innumerable company
  of the heavenly host crying, "Holy, Holy, Holy is
  the Lord God Almighty!"'
    Descriptive Catalogue, 1810. *The Vision of
    Judgment.*

The Vision of Christ that thou dost see
Is my vision's greatest enemy.
Thine has a great hook nose like thine,
Mine has a snub nose like to mine.
            The Everlasting Gospel. a.

Both read the Bible day and night,
But thou read'st black where I read white.   *Ib.*

This life's five windows of the soul
Distorts the Heavens from pole to pole,
And leads you to believe a lie
When you see with, not thro', the eye.   *Ib. γ.*

Jesus was sitting in Moses' chair.
They brought the trembling woman there.
Moses commands she be ston'd to death.
What was the sound of Jesus' breath?
He laid His hand on Moses' law;
The ancient Heavens, in silent awe,
Writ with curses from pole to pole,
All away began to roll.   *Ib. ξ.*

I am sure this Jesus will not do,
Either for Englishman or Jew.   *Ib. Epilogue.*

[Of Hayley's birth]
    Of H—'s birth this was the happy lot:
    His mother on his father him begot.
          On Friends and Foes, iv.

[On Hayley]
    To forgive enemies H— does pretend,
    Who never in his life forgave a friend,
    And when he could not act upon my wife
    Hired a villain to bereave my life.   *Ib. v.*

To H[ayley]
    Thy friendship oft has made my heart to ache:
    Do be my enemy—for friendship's sake.   *Ib. vi.*

On H[ayle]y's Friendship.
    When H—y finds out what you cannot do,
    That is the very thing he'll set you to;
    If you break not your neck, 'tis not his fault;
    But pecks of poison are not pecks of salt.   *Ib. vii.*

[On Cromek]
    A petty sneaking knave I knew—
    O! Mr. Cr—, how do ye do?   *Ib. xxi.*

Mutual Forgiveness of each vice,
Such are the Gates of Paradise.
          The Gates of Paradise, prologue.

Truly, my Satan, thou art but a dunce,
And dost not know the garment from the man;
Every harlot was a virgin once,
Nor canst thou ever change Kate into Nan.

Tho' thou art worshipp'd by the names divine
Of Jesus and Jehovah, thou art still
The Son of Morn in weary Night's decline,
The lost traveller's dream under the hill.   *Ib.* epilogue.

Great things are done when men and mountains meet;
This is not done by jostling in the street.
          Gnomic Verses, i.

If you have form'd a circle to go into,
Go into it yourself, and see how you would do.
          Ib. ii. *To God.*

Abstinence sows sand all over
The ruddy limbs and flaming hair,
But Desire gratified
Plants fruits of life and beauty there.   *Ib. x.*

The sword sung on the barren heath,
The sickle in the fruitful field:
The sword he sung a song of death,
But could not make the sickle yield.   *Ib. xiv.*

He who bends to himself a Joy
Doth the winged life destroy;
But he who kisses the Joy as it flies
Lives in Eternity's sunrise.   *Ib. xvii.* 1.

What is it men in women do require?
The lineaments of gratified desire.
What is it women do in men require?
The lineaments of gratified desire.   *Ib. xvii.* 4.

Since all the riches of this world
May be gifts from the Devil and earthly kings,
I should suspect that I worshipp'd the Devil
If I thank'd my God for worldly things.   *Ib. xix.*

The Angel that presided o'er my birth
Said 'Little creature, form'd of joy and mirth,
Go, love without the help of anything on earth.'
          Ib. xxi.

I must Create a System, or be enslav'd by another
    Man's;
I will not Reason and Compare: my business is to
    Create.   *Jerusalem*, f. 10, l. 20.

          Near mournful
Ever-weeping Paddington.   *Ib.* f. 12, l. 27.

The fields from Islington to Marybone,
To Primrose Hill and Saint John's Wood,
Were builded over with pillars of gold;
And there Jerusalem's pillars stood.   *Ib.* f. 27.

Pancras and Kentish Town repose
Among her golden pillars high,
Among her golden arches which
Shine upon the starry sky.   *Ib.*

For a tear is an intellectual thing,
And a sigh is the sword of an Angel King,
And the bitter groan of the martyr's woe
Is an arrow from the Almighty's bow.   *Ib.* f. 52.

He who would do good to another must do it in
    Minute Particulars.
General Good is the plea of the scoundrel, hypocrite,
    and flatterer;
For Art and Science cannot exist but in minutely
    organized Particulars.   *Ib.* f. 55, l. 54.

I give you the end of a golden string;
    Only wind it into a ball,
It will lead you in at Heaven's gate,
    Built in Jerusalem's wall.   *Ib.* f. 77.

O ye Religious, discountenance every one among you
    who shall pretend to despise Art and Science!
          Ib.

Let every Christian, as much as in him lies, engage
    himself openly and publicly, before all the World,
    in some mental pursuit for the Building up of
    Jerusalem.   *Ib.*

England! awake! awake! awake!
    Jerusalem thy sister calls!
Why wilt thou sleep the sleep of death,
    And close her from thy ancient walls?   *Ib.*

And now the time returns again:
    Our souls exult, and London's towers
Receive the Lamb of God to dwell
    In England's green and pleasant bowers.   *Ib.*

I care not whether a man is Good or Evil; all that I
    care

Is whether he is a Wise man or a Fool. Go! put off Holiness,
And put on Intellect. *Jerusalem, f. 91.*

Father, O father! what do we here
In this land of unbelief and fear?
The Land of Dreams is better far,
Above the light of the morning star.
The Land of Dreams.

Little Mary Bell had a Fairy in a nut,
Long John Brown had the Devil in his gut.
Long John Brown and Little Mary Bell.

Energy is Eternal Delight.
Marriage of Heaven and Hell: The Voice of the Devil.

The reason Milton wrote in fetters when he wrote of Angels and God, and at liberty when of Devils and Hell, is because he was a true Poet, and of the Devil's party without knowing it. *Ib.* note.

The road of excess leads to the palace of wisdom.
Ib. Proverbs of Hell.

Prudence is a rich, ugly, old maid courted by Incapacity. *Ib.*

He who desires but acts not, breeds pestilence. *Ib.*

A fool sees not the same tree that a wise man sees. *Ib.*

Eternity is in love with the productions of time. *Ib.*

Bring out number, weight, and measure in a year of dearth. *Ib.*

If the fool would persist in his folly he would become wise. *Ib.*

Prisons are built with stones of Law, brothels with bricks of Religion. *Ib.*

The pride of the peacock is the glory of God.
The lust of the goat is the bounty of God.
The wrath of the lion is the wisdom of God.
The nakedness of woman is the work of God. *Ib.*

The tigers of wrath are wiser than the horses of instruction. *Ib.*

Damn braces. Bless relaxes. *Ib.*

Sooner murder an infant in its cradle than nurse unacted desires. *Ib.*

Truth can never be told so as to be understood, and not be believ'd. *Ib.*

Then I asked: 'Does a firm persuasion that a thing is so, make it so?'
He replied: 'All Poets believe that it does, and in ages of imagination this firm persuasion removed mountains; but many are not capable of a firm persuasion of anything.' *Ib. A Memorable Fancy.*

And did those feet in ancient time
Walk upon England's mountains green?
And was the holy Lamb of God
On England's pleasant pastures seen?

And did the Countenance Divine
Shine forth upon our clouded hills?
And was Jerusalem builded here
Among these dark Satanic mills?

Bring me my bow of burning gold!
Bring me my arrows of desire!
Bring me my spear! O clouds, unfold!
Bring me my chariot of fire!

I will not cease from Mental Fight,
Nor shall my Sword sleep in my hand,
Till we have built Jerusalem,
In England's green & pleasant Land.
Milton, preface.

He has observ'd the golden rule,
Till he's become the golden fool.
Miscellaneous Epigrams ii.

Wondrous the gods, more wondrous are the men,
More wondrous, wondrous still, the cock and hen,
More wondrous still the table, stool and chair;
But oh! more wondrous still the charming fair.
Ib. xiii. Imitation of Pope.

To Chloe's breast young Cupid slyly stole,
But he crept in at Myra's pocket-hole. *Ib. xv.*

Mock on, mock on, Voltaire, Rousseau;
Mock on, mock on, 'tis all in vain!
You throw the sand against the wind,
And the wind blows it back again.
Mock on, mock on, Voltaire.

Whether on Ida's shady brow,
Or in the chambers of the East,
The chambers of the sun, that now
From ancient melody have ceas'd;

Whether in Heaven ye wander fair,
Or the green corners of the earth,
Or the blue regions of the air
Where the melodious winds have birth;

Whether on crystal rocks ye rove,
Beneath the bosom of the sea
Wand'ring in many a coral grove,
Fair Nine, forsaking Poetry!

How have you left the ancient love
That bards of old enjoy'd in you!
The languid strings do scarcely move!
The sound is forc'd, the notes are few!
To the Muses.

My Spectre around me night and day
Like a wild beast guards my way;
My Emanation far within
Weeps incessantly for my sin.
My Spectre around Me Night and Day, i.

And throughout all Eternity
I forgive you, you forgive me.
As our dear Redeemer said:
'This the Wine, and this the Bread.' *Ib. xiv.*

Never seek to tell thy love,
Love that never told can be;
For the gentle wind does move
Silently, invisibly. *Never Seek to Tell Thy Love.*

Soon as she was gone from me,
A traveller came by,
Silently, invisibly:
He took her with a sigh. *Ib.*

Hear the voice of the Bard!
Who present, past, and future sees.
Songs of Experience, introduction.

Tiger! Tiger! burning bright
In the forests of the night,
What immortal hand or eye
Could frame thy fearful symmetry?

In what distant deeps or skies
Burnt the fire of thine eyes?
On what wings dare he aspire?
What the hand dare seize the fire?

And what shoulder, and what art,
Could twist the sinews of thy heart?
And when thy heart began to beat,
What dread hand? and what dread feet?

What the hammer? What the chain?
In what furnace was thy brain?
What the anvil? what dread grasp
Dare its deadly terrors clasp?

When the stars threw down their spears,
And water'd heaven with their tears,
Did he smile his work to see?
Did he who made the Lamb make thee?

Tiger! Tiger! burning bright
In the forests of the night,
What immortal hand or eye,
Dare frame thy fearful symmetry?   *Ib. The Tiger*

Love seeketh not itself to please,
Nor for itself hath any care,
But for another gives its ease,
And builds a Heaven in Hell's despair.
                        Ib. The Clod and the Pebble.

Love seeketh only Self to please,
To bind another to its delight,
Joys in another's loss of ease,
And builds a Hell in Heaven's despite.   *Ib.*

Then the Parson might preach, and drink, and sing,
And we'd be as happy as birds in the spring;
And modest Dame Lurch, who is always at church,
Would not have bandy children, nor fasting, nor
birch.   *Ib. The Little Vagabond.*

I was angry with my friend
I told my wrath, my wrath did end.
I was angry with my foe:
I told it not, my wrath did grow.
                        Ib. A Poison Tree.

Youth of delight, come hither,
And see the opening morn,
Image of truth new-born,
                Ib. Voice of the Ancient Bard.

Ah, Sun-flower! weary of time,
Who countest the steps of the Sun;
Seeking after that sweet golden clime,
Where the traveller's journey is done;

Where the Youth pined away with desire,
And the pale Virgin shrouded in snow,
Arise from their graves and aspire
Where my Sun-flower wishes to go.
                        Ib. Ah, Sun-Flower!

My mother groan'd, my father wept,
Into the dangerous world I leapt;
Helpless, naked, piping loud,
Like a fiend hid in a cloud.   *Ib. Infant Sorrow.*

Piping down the valleys wild,
Piping songs of pleasant glee,
On a cloud I saw a child,
And he laughing said to me:

'Pipe a song about a Lamb!
So I piped with merry cheer.
'Piper, pipe that song again;'
So I piped: he wept to hear

'Drop thy pipe, thy happy pipe;
Sing thy songs of happy cheer:'
So I sang the same again,
While he wept with joy to hear.

'Piper, sit thee down and write
In a book, that all may read.'
So he vanish'd from my sight,
And I pluck'd a hollow reed.

And I made a rural pen,
And I stain'd the water clear,
And I wrote my happy songs
Every child may joy to hear.
                Songs of Innocence, introduction.

Little Lamb, who made thee?
Dost thou know who made thee?
Gave thee life, and bid thee feed,
By the stream and o'er the mead;
Gave thee clothing of delight,
Softest clothing, woolly, bright;
Gave thee such a tender voice,
Making all the vales rejoice?
Little Lamb, who made thee?
Dost thou know who made thee?

Little Lamb, I'll tell thee,
Little Lamb, I'll tell thee:
He is callèd by thy name,
For He calls Himself a Lamb,
He is meek, and He is mild;
He became a little child.
I a child, and thou a lamb,
We are callèd by His name.
Little Lamb, God bless thee!
Little Lamb, God bless thee!   *Ib. The Lamb.*

How sweet is the Shepherd's sweet lot!
                        Ib. The Shepherd.

'I have no name:
I am but two days old.'
What shall I call thee?
'I happy am,
Joy is my name.'
Sweet joy befall thee!   *Ib. Infant Joy.*

My mother bore me in the southern wild,
And I am black, but O! my soul is white;
White as an angel is the English child,
But I am black, as if bereav'd of light.
                        Ib. The Little Black Boy.

When the voices of children are heard on the green,
And laughing is heard on the hill.   *Ib. Nurse's Song.*

'Twas on a Holy Thursday, their innocent faces clean,
The children walking two and two, in red and blue
and green.   *Ib. Holy Thursday.*

Then cherish pity, lest you drive an angel from your
door.

When my mother died I was very young,
And my father sold me while yet my tongue
Could scarcely cry, "'weep! 'weep! 'weep! 'weep!'
So your chimneys I sweep, and in soot I sleep.
                        Ib. The Chimney Sweeper.

To Mercy, Pity, Peace, and Love
All pray in their distress.   *Ib. The Divine Image.*

For Mercy has a human heart,
Pity a human face,
And Love, the human form divine,
And Peace, the human dress.   *Ib.*

And there the lion's ruddy eyes
Shall flow with tears of gold,
And pitying the tender cries,
And walking round the fold,
Saying, 'Wrath, by His meekness,
And, by His health, sickness,
Is driven away
From our immortal day.'   *Ib. Night.*

Can I see another's woe,
And not be in sorrow too?
Can I see another's grief,
And not seek for kind relief?   *Ib. On Another's Sorrow.*

Cruelty has a human heart,
And Jealousy a human face;
Terror the human form divine,
And Secrecy the human dress.   *Appendix to Songs of Innocence and of Experience. A Divine Image.*

Good English hospitality, O then it did not fail!   *Songs from an Island in the Moon,* xi.

SUSANNA BLAMIRE
1747–1794
And ye shall walk in silk attire,
And siller ha'e to spare.   *The Siller Crown.*

PHILIPP BLISS
1838–1876
Hold the fort, for I am coming.'
The Charm. Ho, My Comrades, See the Signal!

ROBERT BLOOMFIELD
1766–1823
Strange to the world, he wore a bashful look,
The Fields his study, Nature was his book.   *Farmer's Boy. Spring,* l. 31.

HENRY BLOSSOM
1866–1919
I want what I want when I want it.   *Title of song in Mlle. Modiste.*

EDMUND CHARLES BLUNDEN
1896–
All things they have in common, being so poor.   *The Almswomen.*

WILFRID SCAWEN BLUNT
1840–1922
I would not, if I could, be called a poet.
I have no natural love of the 'chaste muse'.
If aught be worth the doing I would do it;
And others, if they will, may tell the news.   *Love Sonnets,* xcv.

I like the hunting of the hare
Better than that of the fox.   *The Old Squire.*

I like to be as my fathers were,
In the days e'er I was born.   *Ib.*

To-day, all day, I rode upon the Down,
With hounds and horsemen, a brave company.   *St. Valentine's Day.*

Your face my quarry was. For it I rode,
My horse a thing of wings, myself a god.   *Ib.*

J. E. BODE
1816–1874
I see the sights that dazzle.
The tempting sounds I hear.
Hymns from the Gospel for the Day. O Jesus, I Have Promised.

HENRY ST. JOHN, VISCOUNT BOLINGBROKE
1678–1751
The Idea of a Patriot King.   *Title of Book.*

What a world is this, and how does fortune banter us!   *Letter 3 Aug.* 1714.

Pests of society; because their endeavours are directed to loosen the bands of it, and to take at least one curb out of the mouth of that wild beast man.   *Ib.* 12 *Sept.* 1724.

Truth lies within a little and certain compass, but error is immense.   *Reflections upon Exile.*

I have read somewhere or other—in Dionysius of Halicarnassus, I think—that History is Philosophy teaching by examples.   *On the Study of History,* letter 2.

Nations, like men, have their infancy.   *Ib.* letter 4.

They [Thucydides and Xenophon] maintained the dignity of history.   *Ib.* letter 5.

HORATIUS BONAR
1808–1889
A few more years shall roll,
A few more seasons come,
And we shall be with those that rest,
Asleep within the tomb.
Songs for the Wilderness. A Few More Years.

A few more suns shall set
O'er these dark hills of time,
And we shall be where suns are not,
A far serener clime.   *Ib.*

BARTON BOOTH
1681–1733
True as the needle to the pole,
Or as the dial to the sun.   *Song.*

c

GEORGE BORROW

1803–1881

The author of 'Amelia', the most singular genius which their island ever produced, whose works it has long been the fashion to abuse in public and to read in secret.   *The Bible in Spain*, ch. 1.

My favourite, I might say, my only study, is man.
Ib. ch. 5.

The genuine spirit of localism.   *Ib.* ch. 31.

There are no countries in the world less known by the British than these selfsame British Islands.
Lavengro, preface.

'There's night and day, brother, both sweet things; sun, moon, and stars, brother, all sweet things; there's likewise a wind on the heath. Life is very sweet, brother; who would wish to die? *Ib.* ch. 25.

There's the wind on the heath, brother; if I could only feel that, I would gladly live for ever. *Ib.*

A losing trade, I assure you, sir: literature is a drug.
Ib. ch. 30.

Good ale, the true and proper drink of Englishmen. He is not deserving of the name of Englishman who speaketh against ale, that is good ale. *Ib.* ch. 48.

Youth will be served, every dog has his day, and mine has been a fine one.   *Ib.* ch. 92.

Fear God, and take your own part.
The Romany Rye, ch. 16.

Tip them Long Melford.   *Ib.*

JOHN COLLINS BOSSIDY

1860–1928

And this is good old Boston,
   The home of the bean and the cod,
Where the Lowells talk to the Cabots,
   And the Cabots talk only to God.
          On the Aristocracy of Harvard.

GORDON BOTTOMLEY

1874–

When you destroy a blade of grass
You poison England at her roots:
Remember no man's foot can pass
Where evermore no green life shoots.
          To Ironfounders and Others.

FRANCIS WILLIAM BOURDILLON

1852–1921

The night has a thousand eyes,
   And the day but one;
Yet the light of the bright world dies,
   With the dying sun.

The mind has a thousand eyes,
   And the heart but one;
Yet the light of a whole life dies,
   When love is done.   *Light.*

W. ST. HILL BOURNE

1846–1929

The sower went forth sowing,
The seed in secret slept.
          Church Bells. The Sower Went Forth Sowing.

EDWARD ERNEST BOWEN

1836–1901

Forty years on, when afar and asunder
Parted are those who are singing to-day.
          Forty Years On. Harrow School Song.

Follow up! Follow up! Follow up! Follow up!
   Follow up!
Till the field ring again and again,
With the tramp of the twenty-two men,
Follow up!   *Ib.*

CHARLES, BARON BOWEN

1835–1894

The rain it raineth on the just
   And also on the unjust fella:
But chiefly on the just, because
   The unjust steals the just's umbrella.
          Sichel, Sands of Time.

WILLIAM LISLE BOWLES

1762–1850

The cause of Freedom is the cause of God!
          Edmund Burke, l. 78.

JOHN BRADFORD

1510?–1555

'But for the grace of God there goes John Bradford.'
Exclamation on seeing some criminals taken to execution. Dict. of Nat. Biog.

JOHN BRADSHAW

1602–1659

Rebellion to tyrants is obedience to God.
Suppositious epitaph. Randall's Life of Jefferson, vol. iii, appendix No. IV, p. 585.

JOHN BRAHAM

1774?–1856

England, home and beauty.
   The Americans (1811). Song, *The Death of Nelson.*

HARRY BRAISTED

Nineteenth Century

If you want to win her hand,
Let the maiden understand
That she's not the only pebble on the beach.
          You're Not the Only Pebble on the Beach.

ERNEST BRAMAH

contemporary

It is a mark of insincerity of purpose to spend one's time in looking for the sacred Emperor in the low-class tea-shops.
The Wallet of Kai Lung. Transmutation of Ling.

An expression of no-encouragement.
Ib. Confession of Kai Lung.

The whole narrative is permeated with the odour of joss-sticks and honourable high-mindedness.
Ib. Kin Yen.

However entrancing it is to wander unchecked through a garden of bright images, are we not enticing your mind from another subject of almost equal importance?
Kai Lung's Golden Hours. Story of Hien.

REV. JAMES BRAMSTON

1694?–1744

What's not destroy'd by Time's devouring hand?
Where's Troy, and where's the Maypole in the Strand?　　*Art of Politics*, l. 71.

RICHARD BRATHWAITE

1588?–1673

To Banbery came I, O profane one!
Where I saw a Puritane-one
Hanging of his cat on Monday,
For killing of a mouse on Sunday.
Barnabee's Journal, pt. i.

JANE BRERETON

1685–1740

The picture plac'd the busts between,
　Adds to the thought much strength,
Wisdom, and wit are little seen,
　But folly's at full length.
Poems. On Mr. Nash's Picture at full Length between the Busts of Sir Isaac Newton and Mr. Pope. [*attr. also to Lord Chesterfield.*]

NICHOLAS BRETON

1545?–1626?

We rise with the lark and go to bed with the lamb.
The Court and Country, par. 8.

I wish my deadly foe, no worse
Than want of friends, and empty purse.
A Farewell to Town.

A Mad World, My Masters.　*Title of Dialogue*, 1635.

He is as deaf as a door.　*Miseries of Mavillia*, v.

In the merry month of May,
In a morn by break of day,
Forth I walked by the wood side,
Whenas May was in his pride:
There I spied all alone,
Phillida and Coridon.
Much ado there was, God wot,
He would love, and she would not.

She said never man was true,
He said, none was false to you.
He said, he had lov'd her long,
She said, Love should have no wrong.
Coridon would kiss her then,
She said, Maids must kiss no men,
Till they did for good and all.　*Phillida and Coridon.*

Come little babe, come silly soul,
Thy father's shame, thy mother's grief,
Born as I doubt to all our dole,
And to thy self unhappy chief:
　Sing lullaby and lap it warm,
　Poor soul that thinks no creature harm.
A Sweet Lullaby.

ROBERT BRIDGES

1844–1930

All women born are so perverse
No man need boast their love possessing.
All Women Born Are So Perverse.

Angel spirits of sleep,
White-robed, with silver hair,
In your meadows fair,
Where the willows weep,
And the sad moonbeam
On the gliding stream
Writes her scattered dream.　*Angel Spirits of Sleep.*

Wanton with long delay the gay spring leaping cometh;
The blackthorn starreth now his bough on the eve of
　May.　　　*April 1885.*

Awake, my heart, to be loved, awake, awake!
Awake, My Heart, To Be Loved.

Awake, the land is scattered with light, and see,
Uncanopied sleep is flying from field and tree:
And blossoming boughs of April in laughter shake.
Ib.

Clear and gentle stream!
Known and loved so long.　*Clear and Gentle Stream.*

The cliff-top has a carpet
Of lilac, gold and green:
The blue sky bounds the ocean,
The white clouds scud between.　*The Cliff-Top.*

Above my head the heaven,
The sea beneath my feet.　　*Ib.*

Were I a cloud I'd gather
My skirts up in the air,
And fly I well know whither,
And rest I well know where.
　　Ib. The Ocean.

Wherefore tonight so full of care,
My soul, revolving hopeless strife,
Pointing at hindrance, and the bare
Painful escapes of fitful life?　*Dejection.*

O soul, be patient: thou shalt find
A little matter mend all this;
Some strain of music to thy mind,
Some praise for skill not spent amiss.　*Ib.*

I praise my days for all they bring,
Yet are they only not enough.　　**Ib.**

O bold majestic downs, smooth, fair and lonely;
O still solitude, only matched in the skies.
Perilous in steep places,
Soft in the level races.   *The Downs.*

Gay Robin is seen no more:
He is gone with the snow.
                    Gay Robin Is Seen No More.

The whole world now is but the minister
Of thee to me.   *Growth of Love,* 3.

                    That old feud
'Twixt things and me is quash'd in our new truce.
                                    Ib.

The very names of things belov'd are dear,
And sounds will gather beauty from their sense,
As many a face thro' love's long residence
Groweth to fair instead of plain and sere.   *Ib.* 4.

Thus may I think the adopting Muses chose
Their sons by name, knowing none would be heard
Or writ so oft in all the world as those,—
Dan Chaucer, mighty Shakespeare, then for third
The classic Milton, and to us arose
Shelley with liquid music in the word.   *Ib.*

And hither tempt the pilgrim steps of spring. *Ib.* 6.

   Beauty being the best of all we know
Sums up the unsearchable and secret aims
Of nature.   *Ib.* 8.

Winter was not unkind because uncouth;
His prison'd time made me a closer guest,
And gave thy graciousness a warmer zest,
Biting all else with keen and angry tooth. *Ib.* 10.

There's many a would-be poet at this hour,
Rhymes of a love that he hath never woo'd,
And o'er his lamp-lit desk in solitude
Deems that he sitteth in the Muses' bower. *Ib.* 11.

So none of all our company, I boast,
But now would mock my penning, coud they see
How down the right it maps a jagged coast.   *Ib.*

Lo, Shakespeare, since thy time nature is loth
To yield to art her fair supremacy;
In conquering one thou hast so enrichèd both.
What shall I say? for God—whose wise decree
Confirmeth all He did by all He doth—
Doubled His whole creation making thee. *Ib.* 21.

I would be a bird, and straight on wings I arise,
And carry purpose up to the ends of the air. *Ib.* 22.

O my uncared-for songs, what are ye worth,
That in my secret book with so much care
I write you, this one here and that one there,
Marking the time and order of your birth? *Ib.* 51.

The dark and serious angel, who so long
Vex'd his immortal strength in charge of me. *Ib.* 61.

What make ye and what strive for? keep ye thought
Of us, or in new excellence divine
Is old forgot? or do ye count for nought
What the Greek did and what the Florentine? *Ib.* 64.

Ah heavenly joy! But who hath ever heard,
Who hath seen joy, or who shall ever find
Joy's language? There is neither speech nor word;
Nought but itself to teach it to mankind. *Ib.* 65.

Eternal Father, who didst all create,
In whom we live, and to whose bosom move,
To all men be Thy name known, which is Love,
Till its loud praises sound at heaven's high gate.
                                    Ib. 69.

Christ with His lamp of truth
Sitteth upon the hill
Of everlasting youth,
And calls His saints around.   *Hymn of Nature,* v.

Gird on thy sword, O man, thy strength endue,
In fair desire thine earth-born joy renew.
Live thou thy life beneath the making sun
Till Beauty, Truth, and Love in thee are one.
                                    Ib. vii.

And every eve I say,
Noting my step in bliss,
That I have known no day
In all my life like this.   *The Idle Life I Lead.*

I have loved flowers that fade,
Within whose magic tents
Rich hues have marriage made
With sweet unmemoried scents.
                    I Have Loved Flowers That Fade.

I heard a linnet courting
His lady in the spring,
His mates were idly sporting,
Nor stayed to hear him sing
   His song of love.—
I fear my speech distorting
   His tender love.   *I Heard a Linnet Courting.*

I love all beauteous things,
I seek and adore them;
God hath no better praise,
And man in his hasty days
Is honoured for them.

I too will something make
And joy in the making;
Altho' tomorrow it seem
Like the empty words of a dream
   Remembered on waking.
                    I Love All Beauteous Things.

I made another song,
In likeness of my love:
And sang it all day long,
Around, beneath, above:
I told my secret out,
That none might be in doubt.   *I Made Another Song.*

I never shall love the snow again
   Since Maurice died.
                I Never Shall Love the Snow Again.

I will not let thee go.
Ends all our month-long love in this?
Can it be summed up so,
Quit in a single kiss?
I will not let thee go.   *I Will Not Let Thee Go.*

I will not let thee go.
Had not the great sun seen, I might;
Or were he reckoned slow
To bring the false to light,
Then might I let thee go.   *Ib.*

Thou sayest farewell, and lo!
I have thee by the hands,
And will not let thee go.   *Ib.*

When men were all asleep the snow came flying,
In large white flakes falling on the city brown,
Stealthily and perpetually settling and loosely lying.
London Snow.

'O look at the trees!' they cried, 'O look at the trees!'
Ib.

My delight and thy delight
Walking, like two angels white,
In the gardens of the night.
My Delight and Thy Delight.

My eyes for beauty pine,
My soul for Goddës grace.
My Eyes for Beauty Pine.

Beautiful must be the mountains whence ye come,
And bright in the fruitful valleys the streams, where-
from
Ye learn your song:
Where are those starry woods? O might I wander
there,
Among the flowers, which in that heavenly air
Bloom the year long! *Nightingales.*

Nay, barren are those mountains and spent the
streams:
Our song is the voice of desire, that haunts our
dreams,
A throe of the heart. *Ib.*

As night is withdrawn
From these sweet-springing meads and bursting
boughs of May,
Dream, while the innumerable choir of day
Welcome the dawn. *Ib.*

Rejoice ye dead, where'er your spirits dwell,
Rejoice that yet on earth your fame is bright,
And that your names, remembered day and night,
Live on the lips of those who love you well.
Ode to Music.

Perfect little body, without fault or stain on thee,
With promise of strength and manhood full and fair!
On a Dead Child.

He
Must gather his faith together, and his strength make
stronger. *Ib.*

O youth whose hope is high,
Who dost to Truth aspire,
Whether thou live or die,
O look not back nor tire.
O Youth Whose Hope is High.

If thou canst Death defy,
If thy Faith is entire,
Press onward, for thine eye
Shall see thy heart's desire. *Ib.*

Whither, O splendid ship, thy white sails crowding,
Leaning across the bosom of the urgent West,
That fearest nor sea rising, nor sky clouding,
Whither away, fair rover, and what thy quest?
A Passer-By.

Days, that the thought of grief refuse,
Days that are one with human art,
Worthy of the Virgilian muse,
Fit for the gaiety of Mozart.
The Sea Keeps not the Sabbath Day.

Since to be loved endures,
To love is wise:
Earth hath no good but yours,
Brave, joyful eyes:
Earth hath no sin but thine,
Dull eye of scorn:
O'er thee the sun doth pine
And angels mourn. *Since to be Loved Endures.*

So sweet love seemed that April morn,
When first we kissed beside the thorn,
So strangely sweet, it was not strange
We thought that love could never change.

But I can tell—let truth be told—
That love will change in growing old;
Though day by day is nought to see,
So delicate his motions be.
So Sweet Love Seemed.

I wonder, bathed in joy complete,
How love so young could be so sweet. *Ib.*

Back on budding boughs
Come birds, to court and pair,
Whose rival amorous vows
Amaze the scented air. *Spring, ode i.*

And country life I praise,
And lead, because I find
The philosophic mind
Can take no middle ways. *Ib.* 7.

With ecstasies so sweet
As none can even guess,
Who walk not with the feet
Of joy in idleness. *Ib.* 10.

Spring goeth all in white,
Crowned with milk-white may:
In fleecy flocks of light
O'er heaven the white clouds stray.

White butterflies in the air;
White daisies prank the ground:
The cherry and hoary pear
Scatter their snow around.
Spring Goeth All in White.

There is a hill beside the silver Thames,
Shady with birch and beech and odorous pine:
And brilliant underfoot with thousand gems
Steeply the thickets to his floods decline.
There is a Hill.

Nor this the only time
Thou shalt set love to rhyme.
Thou Didst Delight My Eyes.

Fight, to be found fighting: nor far away
Deem, nor strange thy doom.
Like this sorrow 'twill come,
And the day will be today.
Weep Not To-Day.

When Death to either shall come,—
I pray it be first to me,—
Be happy as ever at home,
If so, as I wish, it be.
Possess thy heart, my own;
And sing to the child on thy knee,
Or read to thyself alone
The songs that I made for thee.
When Death to Either Shall Come.

When first we met we did not guess
That Love would prove so hard a master.
When First We Met We Did Not Guess.

When June is come, then all the day
I'll sit with my love in the scented hay:
And watch the sunshot palaces high,
That the white clouds build in the breezy sky.
When June is Come.

That
Sheep-worry of Europe. (Napoleon)
Wintry Delights, l. 121.

JOHN BRIGHT
1811–1889

The knowledge of the ancient languages is mainly a luxury. *Letter in Pall Mall Gaz. 30 Nov. 1886.*

The angel of death has been abroad throughout the land; you may almost hear the beating of his wings. *Speech: House of Commons, 23 Feb. 1855.*

I am for 'Peace, retrenchment, and reform', the watchword of the great Liberal party 30 years ago. *Ib. Birmingham, 28 April 1859.*

England is the mother of Parliaments. *Ib. 18 Jan. 1865.*

The right hon. Gentleman . . . has retired into what may be called his political Cave of Adullam—and he has called about him every one that was in distress and every one that was discontented. *Ib. House of Commons, 13 Mar. 1866.*

This party of two is like the Scotch terrier that was so covered with hair that you could not tell which was the head and which was the tail. *Ib.*

Force is not a remedy. *Ib. Birmingham, 16 Nov. 1880.*

ALEXANDER BROME
1620–1666

Something there is moves me to love, and I
Do know I love, but know not how, nor why.
Love's without Reason, v.

I have been in love, and in debt, and in drink,
This many and many a year. *The Mad Lover, l. 1.*

RICHARD BROME
–1652?

You rose o' the wrong side today.
The Court-Beggar, Act II.

I am a gentleman, though spoiled i' the breeding.
The Buzzards are all gentlemen. We came in with the Conqueror. *English Moor, III. ii.*

J. BROMFIELD
fl. 1840

'Tis a very good world we live in,
To spend, and to lend, and to give in;
But to beg, or to borrow, or ask for our own,
'Tis the very worst world that ever was known.
The Gatherer, The Mirror, 12 Sept. 1840.

ISAAC HILL BROMLEY
1833–1898

Conductor, when you receive a fare,
Punch in the presence of the passenjare!—
Punch, brothers! Punch with care!
Punch in the presence of the passenjare!
Punch, Brother, Punch. N. G. Osborn's 'Isaac H. Bromley'.

John A. Logan is the Head Centre, the Hub, the King Pin, the Main Spring, Mogul, and Mugwump of the final plot. *New York Tribune, 16 Feb. 1877.*

ANNE BRONTË
1820–1849

Oh, I am very weary,
Though tears no longer flow;
My eyes are tired of weeping,
My heart is sick of woe. *Appeal.*

Because the road is rough and long,
Shall we despise the skylark's song? *Views of Life.*

CHARLOTTE BRONTË
1816–1855

Reader, I married him. *Jane Eyre, ch. 38.*

Alfred and I intended to be married in this way almost from the first; we never meant to be spliced in the humdrum way of other people. *Villette, ch. 42.*

EMILY BRONTË
1818–1848

No coward soul is mine,
No trembler in the world's storm-troubled sphere:
I see Heaven's glories shine,
And faith shines equal, arming me from fear.
Last Lines.

O God within my breast,
Almighty! ever-present Deity!
Life—that in me has rest,
As I—undying Life—have power in Thee! *Ib.*

Vain are the thousand creeds
That move men's hearts: unutterably vain;
Worthless as withered weeds,
Or idlest froth amid the boundless main. *Ib.*

So surely anchor'd on
The stedfast rock of immortality. *Ib.*

Though earth and man were gone,
And suns and universes ceased to be,
And Thou wert left alone,
Every existence would exist in Thee. *Ib.*

There is not room for Death,
Nor atom that his might could render void:
Thou—THOU art Being and Breath,
And what THOU art may never be destroy'd. *Ib.*

Oh! dreadful is the check—intense the agony—
When the ear begins to hear, and the eye begins to
    see;
When the pulse begins to throb, the brain to think
    again;
The soul to feel the flesh, and the flesh to feel the
    chain.   *The Prisoner*.

Cold in the earth—and fifteen wild Decembers,
From those brown hills, have melted into spring.
                                Remembrance.

I lingered round them, under that benign sky:
    watched the moths fluttering among the heath and
    hare-bells; listened to the soft wind breathing
    through the grass; and wondered how any one
    could ever imagine unquiet slumbers for the
    sleepers in that quiet earth.
              Wuthering Heights. Last Words.

HENRY BROOKE

1703?–1783

For righteous monarchs,
Justly to judge, with their own eyes should see;
To rule o'er freemen, should themselves be free.
        Earl of Essex, 1 [parodied by Dr. Johnson].

RUPERT BROOKE

1887–1915

The hawthorn hedge puts forth its buds,
And my heart puts forth its pain.
        All Suddenly the Spring Comes Soft.

And I shall find some girl perhaps,
And a better one than you,
With eyes as wise, but kindlier,
And lips as soft, but true.
And I daresay she will do.   *The Chilterns*.

Blow out, you bugles, over the rich Dead!
    There's none of these so lonely and poor of old,
But, dying, has made us rarer gifts than gold.
These laid the world away; poured out the red
Sweet wine of youth; gave up the years to be
    Of work and joy, and that unhoped serene,
    That men call age; and those who would have been,
Their sons, they gave, their immortality.
                    The Dead.

Honour has come back, as a king, to earth,
    And paid his subjects with a royal wage;
And Nobleness walks in our ways again;
    And we have come into our heritage.   *Ib.*

The cool kindliness of sheets, that soon
Smooth away trouble; and the rough male kiss of
    blankets.   *The Great Lover*.

The benison of hot water.   *Ib.*

Fish say, they have their stream and pond;
But is there anything beyond?   *Heaven*.

One may not doubt that, somehow, good
Shall come of water and of mud;
And, sure, the reverent eye must see
A purpose in liquidity.   *Ib.*

But somewhere, beyond space and time,
Is wetter water, slimier slime!   *Ib.*

Immense, of fishy form and mind,
Squamous, omnipotent, and kind;
And under that Almighty Fin,
The littlest fish may enter in.   *Ib.*

Oh! never fly conceals a hook,
Fish say, in the Eternal Brook,
But more than mundane weeds are there,
And mud, celestially fair.   *Ib.*

Unfading moths, immortal flies,
And the worm that never dies.
And in that Heaven of all their wish,
There shall be no more land, say fish.   *Ib.*

Breathless, we flung us on the windy hill,
Laughed in the sun, and kissed the lovely grass.
                           The Hill.

—And then you suddenly cried, and turned away.
                                   Ib.

With snuffle and sniff and handkerchief,
    And dim and decorous mirth,
With ham and sherry, they'll meet to bury
    The lordliest lass of earth.
        Lines Written in the Belief that the Ancient
        Roman Festival of the Dead was called Ambar-
        valia.

Spend in pure converse our eternal day;
Think each in each, immediately wise;
Learn all we lacked before; hear, know, and say
What this tumultuous body now denies;
And feel, who have laid our groping hands away;
And see, no longer blinded by our eyes.
                      Not With Vain Tears.

Oh! Death will find me, long before I tire
Of watching you; and swing me suddenly
Into the shade and loneliness and mire
Of the last land!   *Oh! Death Will Find Me*.

Oh! there the chestnuts, summer through,
Beside the river make for you
A tunnel of green gloom, and sleep
Deeply above.   *The Old Vicarage, Grantchester*.

Here tulips bloom as they are told;
Unkempt about those hedges blows
An English unofficial rose.   *Ib.*

And there the unregulated sun
Slopes down to rest when day is done,
And wakes a vague unpunctual star,
A slippered Hesper.   *Ib.*

Curates, long dust, will come and go
On lissom, clerical, printless toe;
And oft between the boughs is seen
The sly shade of a Rural Dean.   *Ib.*

God! I will pack, and take a train,
And get me to England once again!
For England's the one land, I know,
Where men with splendid hearts may go;
And Cambridgeshire, of all England,
The shire for men who understand;
And of *that* district I prefer
The lovely hamlet Grantchester.   *Ib.*

For Cambridge people rarely smile,
Being urban, squat, and packed with guile. *Ib.*

They love the Good; they worship Truth;
They laugh uproariously in youth;
(And when they get to feeling old,
They up and shoot themselves, I'm told.) *Ib.*

Stands the Church clock at ten to three?
And is there honey still for tea? *Ib.*

Now, God be thanked Who has matched us with His
hour,
And caught our youth, and wakened us from sleeping.
Peace.

Leave the sick hearts that honour could not move,
And half-men, and their dirty songs and dreary,
And all the little emptiness of love. *Ib.*

Naught broken save this body, lost but breath;
Nothing to shake the laughing heart's long peace
there
But only agony, and that has ending;
And the worst friend and enemy is but Death. *Ib.*

Safe shall be my going,
Secretly armed against all death's endeavour;
Safe though all safety's lost; safe where men fall;
And if these poor limbs die, safest of all. *Safety.*

Some white tremendous daybreak. *Second Best.*

If I should die, think only this of me:
That there's some corner of a foreign field
That is for ever England. There shall be
In that rich earth a richer dust concealed;
A dust whom England bore, shaped, made aware,
Gave, once, her flowers to love, her ways to roam,
A body of England's breathing English air,
Washed by the rivers, blest by suns of home.
And think, this heart, all evil shed away,
A pulse in the eternal mind, no less
Gives somewhere back the thoughts by England
given.
Her sights and sounds; dreams happy as her day;
And laughter, learnt of friends; and gentleness,
In hearts at peace, under an English heaven.
The Soldier.

But there's wisdom in women, of more than they
have known,
And thoughts go blowing through them, are wiser
than their own. *There's Wisdom in Women.*

And there's an end, I think, of kissing,
When our mouths are one with Mouth.
Tiare Tahiti.

PHILLIPS BROOKS
1835–1893

O little town of Bethlehem,
How still we see thee lie;
Above thy deep and dreamless sleep
The silent stars go by.
The Church Porch. O Little Town of Bethlehem.

Yet in the dark streets shineth
The everlasting light;
The hopes and fears of all the years
Are met in thee to-night. *Ib.*

THOMAS BROOKS
1608–1680

For (magna est veritas & prævalebit) great is truth,
& shall prevail.
The Crown and Glory of Christianity, 1662, p. 407.

ROBERT BARNABAS BROUGH
1828–1860

My Lord Tomnoddy is thirty-four;
The Earl can last but a few years more.
My Lord in the Peers will take his place:
Her Majesty's councils his words will grace.
Office he'll hold and patronage sway;
Fortunes and lives he will vote away;
And what are his qualifications?—ONE!
He's the Earl of Fitzdotterel's eldest son.
My Lord Tomnoddy.

LORD BROUGHAM
1778–1868

In my mind, he was guilty of no error,—he was
chargeable with no exaggeration,—he was betrayed
by his fancy into no metaphor, who once said, that
all we see about us, Kings, Lords, and Commons,
the whole machinery of the State, all the apparatus
of the system, and its varied workings, end in
simply bringing twelve good men into a box.
*Speech on the Present State of the Law, 7 Feb. 1828,
p. 5.*

Look out, gentlemen, the schoolmaster is abroad!
*Attr. to Speech, London Mechanics' Institute
1825.*

Education makes a people easy to lead, but difficult
to drive; easy to govern, but impossible to enslave.
Attr.

JOHN BROWN
1715–1766

Truth's sacred Fort th' exploded laugh shall win;
And Coxcombs vanquish Berkley by a grin.
Essay on Satire. On the Death of Pope, l. 223.

Altogether upon the high horse.
*Letter to Garrick, 27 Oct. 1765. Correspon-
dence of Garrick (1831), vol. I, p. 205.*

JOHN BROWN
1800–1859

I, John Brown, am now quite certain that the crimes
of this guilty land will never be purged away but
with blood. *Last Statement, 2 Dec. 1859. R. J.
Hinton, John Brown and His Men.*

THOMAS BROWN
1663–1704

In the reign of King Charles the Second, a certain
worthy Divine at Whitehall, thus address'd himself
to the auditory at the conclusion of his sermon:
'In short, if you don't live up to the precepts of the
Gospel, but abandon your selves to your irregular
appetites, you must expect to receive your reward
in a certain place, which 'tis not good manners to
mention here.' *Laconics.*

A little before you made a leap into the dark.
Letters from the Dead.

I do not love you Dr. Fell,
But why I cannot tell;
But this I know full well,
I do not love you, Dr. Fell.
[tr. of *Martial, Epigrams*, i. 32.] *Wks.* 1719,
vol. iv. 113.

THOMAS EDWARD BROWN
1830–1897

O blackbird, what a boy you are!
How you do go it. *The Blackbird.*

Money is honey—my little sonny!
And a rich man's joke is allis funny! *The Doctor.*

A garden is a lovesome thing, God wot!
My Garden.

Not God! in gardens! when the eve is cool?
Nay, but I have a sign;
'Tis very sure God walks in mine. *Ib.*

CHARLES FARRAR BROWNE
see ARTEMUS WARD

SIR THOMAS BROWNE
1605–1682

He who discommendeth others obliquely commendeth himself.
Christian Morals, pt. i, § xxxiv.

That unextinguishable laugh in heaven.
Cyrus' Garden, ch. 2.

Life itself is but the shadow of death, and souls
departed but the shadows of the living. All things
fall under this name. The sun itself is but the dark
simulacrum, and light but the shadow of God.
Ib. ch. 4.

Flat and flexible truths are beat out by every hammer;
but Vulcan and his whole forge sweat to work out
Achilles his armour. *Ib.* ch. 5.

But the quincunx of heaven runs low, and 'tis time
to close the five ports of knowledge. *Ib.*

All things began in order, so shall they end, and so
shall they begin again; according to the ordainer
of order and mystical mathematics of the city of
heaven. *Ib.*

Though Somnus in Homer be sent to rouse up
Agamemnon, I find no such effects in these drowsy
approaches of sleep. To keep our eyes open longer
were but to act our Antipodes. The huntsmen are
up in America, and they are already past their first
sleep in Persia. But who can be drowsy at that
hour which freed us from everlasting sleep? or
have slumbering thoughts at that time, when sleep
itself must end, and, as some conjecture, all shall
awake again? *Ib.*

I dare, without usurpation, assume the honourable
style of a Christian. *Religio Medici*, pt. i, § 1.

C 3

At my devotion I love to use the civility of my knee,
my hat, and hand. *Ib.* § 3.

I could never divide my self from any man upon the
difference of an opinion, or be angry with his
judgment for not agreeing with me in that, from
which perhaps within a few days I should dissent
my self. *Ib.* § 6.

Many . . . have too rashly charged the troops of error,
and remain as trophies unto the enemies of truth.
Ib.

A man may be in as just possession of truth as of a
city, and yet be forced to surrender. *Ib.*

Me thinks there be not impossibilities enough in
Religion for an active faith. *Ib.* § 9.

Who can speak of eternity without a solecism, or
think thereof without an ecstasy? Time we may
comprehend, 'tis but five days elder than ourselves.
Ib. § 11.

I have often admired the mystical way of Pythagoras,
and the secret magic of numbers. *Ib.* § 12.

We carry within us the wonders, we seek without us.
There is all Africa, and her prodigies in us.
Ib. § 15.

All things are artificial, for nature is the art of God.
Ib. § 16.

'Twill be hard to find one that deserves to carry the
buckler unto Samson. *Ib.* § 21.

Obstinacy in a bad cause, is but constancy in a good.
Ib. § 25.

Persecution is a bad and indirect way to plant religion.
Ib.

There are many (questionless) canonized on earth,
that shall never be Saints in Heaven. *Ib.* § 26.

Not pickt from the leaves of any author, but bred
amongst the weeds and tares of mine own brain.
Ib. § 35.

This reasonable moderator and equal piece of justice,
Death. *Ib.* § 37.

I am not so much afraid of death, as ashamed thereof;
'tis the very disgrace and ignominy of our natures.
Ib. § 39.

Certainly there is no happiness within this circle of
flesh, nor is it in the optics of these eyes to behold
felicity; the first day of our Jubilee is death.
Ib. § 43.

I have tried if I could reach that great resolution . . . .
to be honest without a thought of Heaven or Hell.
Ib. § 46.

To believe only possibilities, is not faith, but mere
Philosophy. *Ib.* § 46.

There is no road or ready way to virtue. *Ib.* § 53.

My desires only are, and I shall be happy therein, to
be but the last man, and bring up the rear in
heaven. *Ib.* § 57.

I am of a constitution so general, that it consorts and
sympathiseth with all things. I have no antipathy,
or rather idiosyncrasy, in diet, humour, air, any
thing. *Ib.* pt. ii, § 1.

I feel not in myself those common antipathies that I can discover in others; those national repugnances do not touch me, nor do I behold with prejudice the French, Italian, Spaniard, or Dutch; but where I find their actions in balance with my countrymen's, I honour, love and embrace them in the same degree. *Religio Medici*, pt. ii, § 1.

All places, all airs make unto me one country; I am in England, everywhere, and under any meridian. *Ib.*

It is the common wonder of all men, how among so many millions of faces, there should be none alike. *Ib.* § 2.

No man can justly censure or condemn another, because indeed no man truly knows another. *Ib.* § 4.

Charity begins at home, is the voice of the world. *Ib.*

Sure there is music even in the beauty, and the silent note which Cupid strikes, far sweeter than the sound of an instrument. For there is a music wherever there is a harmony, order or proportion; and thus far we may maintain the music of the spheres; for those well ordered motions, and regular paces, though they give no sound unto the ear, yet to the understanding they strike a note most full of harmony. *Ib.* § 9.

For even that vulgar and tavern music, which makes one man merry, another mad, strikes in me a deep fit of devotion, and a profound contemplation of the first Composer, there is something in it of divinity more than the ear discovers. *Ib.*

We all labour against our own cure, for death is the cure of all diseases. *Ib.*

For the world, I count it not an inn, but an hospital, and a place, not to live, but to die in. *Ib.* § 12.

There is surely a piece of divinity in us, something that was before the elements, and owes no homage unto the sun. *Ib.*

[Sleep is] in fine, so like death, I dare not trust it without my prayers. *Ib.* § 13.

Sleep is a death, O make me try,
By sleeping what it is to die.
And as gently lay my head
On my grave, as now my bed. *Ib.*

Conclude in a moist relentment. *Urn Burial*, ch. 1.

With rich flames, and hired tears, they solemnized their obsequies. *Ib.* ch. 3.

Hercules is not only known by his foot. *Ib.*

Men have lost their reason in nothing so much as their religion, wherein stones and clouts make martyrs. *Ib.* ch. 4.

They carried them out of the world with their feet forward. *Ib.*

Were the happiness of the next world as closely apprehended as the felicities of this, it were a martyrdom to live. *Ib.*

These dead bones have . . . quietly rested under the drums and tramplings of three conquests. *Ib.* ch. 5.

Time, which antiquates antiquities, and hath an art to make dust of all things, hath yet spared these minor monuments. *Ib.*

The long habit of living indisposeth us for dying. *Ib.*

Misery makes Alcmena's nights. *Ib.*

What song the Syrens sang, or what name Achilles assumed when he hid himself among women. *Ib.*

Circles and right lines limit and close all bodies, and the mortal right-lined circle, must conclude and shut up all. *Ib.*

Old families last not three oaks. *Ib.*

To be nameless in worthy deeds exceeds an infamous history. *Ib.*

But the inequity of oblivion blindly scattereth her poppy, and deals with the memory of men without distinction to merit of perpetuity. *Ib.*

Herostratus lives that burnt the Temple of Diana—he is almost lost that built it. *Ib.*

The night of time far surpasseth the day, and who knows when was the equinox? *Ib.*

Mummy is become merchandise, Mizraim cures wounds, and Pharaoh is sold for balsams. *Ib.*

Man is a noble animal, splendid in ashes, and pompous in the grave. *Ib.*

Ready to be any thing, in the ecstasy of being ever, and as content with six foot as the *moles* of Adrianus. *Ib.*

WILLIAM BROWNE
1591–1643

And all the former causes of her moan
Did therewith bury in oblivion.
Britannia's Pastorals, bk. i, Song 2.

Well languag'd Daniel. *Ib.* bk. ii, Song 2.

Underneath this sable hearse
Lies the subject of all verse,
Sidney's sister, Pembroke's mother;
Death! ere thou hast slain another,
Fair and learn'd, and good as she,
Time shall throw a dart at thee.
Epitaph. On the Countess of Pembroke.

May! Be thou never grac'd with birds that sing,
Nor Flora's pride!
In thee all flowers and roses spring,
Mine only died. *In Obitum M.S. x°. Maij.*

SIR WILLIAM BROWNE
1692–1774

The King to Oxford sent a troop of horse,
For Tories own no argument but force:
With equal skill to Cambridge books he sent,
For Whigs admit no force but argument.
Reply to Trapp's epigram 'The King, observing with judicious eyes,' *q.v.*
Nichols' Literary Anecdotes, vol. ii, p. 330.

ELIZABETH BARRETT BROWNING

1806–1861

Here's God down on us! what are you about?
How all those workers start amid their work,
Look round, look up, and feel, a moment's space,
That carpet-dusting, though a pretty trade,
Is not the imperative labour after all,
Aurora Leigh, bk. i.

Near all the birds
Will sing at dawn,—and yet we do not take
The chaffering swallow for the holy lark. *Ib.*

God answers sharp and sudden on some prayers,
And thrusts the thing we have prayed for in our face,
A gauntlet with a gift in 't. *Ib.* bk. ii.

The music soars within the little lark,
And the lark soars. *Ib.* bk. iii.

I think it frets the saints in heaven to see
How many desolate creatures on the earth
Have learnt the simple dues of fellowship
And social comfort, in a hospital. *Ib.*

Now may the good God pardon all good men!
Ib. bk. iv.

Since when was genius found respectable? *Ib.* bk. vi.

The devil's most devilish when respectable.
Ib. bk. vii.

Earth's crammed with heaven,
And every common bush afire with God;
But only he who sees, takes off his shoes,
The rest sit round it and pluck blackberries,
And daub their natural faces unaware
More and more from the first similitude. *Ib.*

'Jasper first,' I said,
'And second sapphire; third chalcedony;
The rest in order,—last an amethyst.' *Ib.* bk. ix.

Speak low to me, my Saviour, low and sweet
From out the hallelujahs, sweet and low,
Lest I should fear and fall, and miss Thee so
Who art not missed by any that entreat. *Comfort.*

O poets, from a maniac's tongue was poured the
deathless singing!
O Christians, at your cross of hope, a hopeless hand
was clinging!
O men, this man in brotherhood your weary paths
beguiling,
Groaned inly while he taught you peace, and died
while ye were smiling. *Cowper's Grave.*

And kings crept out again to feel the sun.
Crowned and Buried.

Do ye hear the children weeping, O my brothers,
Ere the sorrow comes with years?
The Cry of the Children.

But the young, young children, O my brothers,
They are weeping bitterly!
They are weeping in the playtime of the others,
In the country of the free. *Ib.*

And lips say, 'God be pitiful,'
Who ne'er said, 'God be praised.'
Cry of the Human.

Oh, the little birds sang east, and the little birds sang
west, *Toll slowly.*
And I smiled to think God's greatness flowed around
our incompleteness,—
Round our restlessness, His rest.
Rime of the Duchess May, last stanza.

Thou large-brained woman and large-hearted man.
To George Sand. A Desire.

Or from Browning some 'Pomegranate', which, if
cut deep down the middle,
Shows a heart within blood-tinctured, of a veined
humanity. *Lady Geraldine's Courtship*, xli.

By thunders of white silence, overthrown.
Hiram Power's Greek Slave.

'Yes,' I answered you last night;
'No,' this morning, sir, I say.
Colours seen by candle-light
Will not look the same by day. *The Lady's Yes.*

In the pleasant orchard closes,
'God bless all our gains,' say we;
But 'May God bless all our losses,'
Better suits with our degree. *The Lost Bower.*

What was he doing, the great god Pan,
Down in the reeds by the river?
Spreading ruin and scattering ban,
Splashing and paddling with hoofs of a goat,
And breaking the golden lilies afloat
With the dragon-fly on the river.
A Musical Instrument.

Yet half a beast is the great god Pan,
To laugh as he sits by the river,
Making a poet out of a man:
The true gods sigh for the cost and pain,—
For the reed which grows nevermore again
As a reed with the reeds in the river. *Ib.*

And her smile, it seems half holy,
As if drawn from thoughts more far
Than our common jestings are.

And if any poet knew her,
He would sing of her with falls
Used in lovely madrigals. *A Portrait.*

God keeps a niche
In Heaven, to hold our idols: and albeit
He brake them to our faces, and denied
That our close kisses should impair their white,—
I know we shall behold them raised, complete,
The dust swept from their beauty,—glorified,
New Memnons singing in the great God-light.
Sonnets. Futurity.

I tell you, hopeless grief is passionless.
Sonnets. Grief.

Straightway I was 'ware,
So weeping, how a mystic shape did move
Behind me, and drew me backward by the hair,
And a voice said in mastery while I strove, . . .
'Guess now who holds thee?'—'Death', I said, but
there
The silver answer rang, . . . 'Not Death, but Love.'
Sonnets from the Portuguese, 1.

The face of all the world is changed, I think,
Since first I heard the footsteps of thy soul
Move still, oh, still, beside me, as they stole
Betwixt me and the dreadful outer brink
Of obvious death, where I, who thought to sink,
Was caught up into love, and taught the whole
Of a new rhythm. *Ib.* 7.

If thou must love me, let it be for naught
Except for love's sake only.   *Ib.* 14.

When our two souls stand up erect and strong
Face to face, silent, drawing nigh and nigher.
     Ib. 22.

Let us stay
Rather on earth, Beloved—where the unfit
Contrarious moods of men recoil away
And isolate pure spirits, and permit
A place to stand and love in for a day,
With darkness and the death-hour rounding it.   *Ib.*

God's gifts put man's best dreams to shame. *Ib.* 26.

First time he kissed me, he but only kissed
The fingers of this hand wherewith I write;
And, ever since, it grew more clean and white. *Ib.* 38.

And think it soon when others cry, 'Too late'. *Ib.* 40.

How do I love thee? Let me count the ways.
I love thee to the depth and breadth and height
My soul can reach, when feeling out of sight
For the ends of Being and ideal Grace.
I love thee to the level of every day's
Most quiet need, by sun and candle light.
I love thee freely, as men strive for Right;
I love thee purely, as they turn from Praise.
I love thee with the passion put to use
In my old griefs, and with my childhood's faith.
I love thee with a love I seemed to lose
With my lost saints—I love thee with the breath,
Smiles, tears, of all my life!—and, if God choose,
I shall but love thee better after death.   *Ib.* 43.

Of all the thoughts of God that are
Borne inward unto souls afar,
   Along the Psalmist's music deep,
Now tell me if that any is,
For gift or grace, surpassing this—
   'He giveth His beloved, sleep.'   *The Sleep.*

O earth, so full of dreary noises!
O men, with wailing in your voices!
O delvèd gold, the wailers heap!
O strife, O curse, that o'er it fall!
God strikes a silence through you all,
And giveth His belovèd, sleep.   *Ib.*

Let One, most loving of you all,
Say, 'Not a tear must o'er her fall;
He giveth His belovèd, sleep.'   *Ib.*

There, Shakespeare, on whose forehead climb
The crowns o' the world. Oh, eyes sublime,
With tears and laughters for all time!
     A Vision of Poets, verse 100.

Life treads on life, and heart on heart:
We press too close in church and mart
To keep a dream or grave apart.   *Ib.* (conclusion).

Knowledge by suffering entereth;
And Life is perfected by Death.   *Ib.*

And the rolling anapaestic
   Curled like a vapour over shrines!
     Wine of Cyprus, x.

Our Euripides, the human,
With his droppings of warm tears,
And his touches of things common
Till they rose to touch the spheres!   *Ib.* xii.

ROBERT BROWNING
1812–1889

Burrow awhile and build, broad on the roots of things.
     Abt Vogler, ii.

On the earth the broken arcs; in the heaven, a perfect
   round.   *Ib.* ix.

All we have willed or hoped or dreamed of good shall
   exist.   *Ib.* x.

The high that proved too high, the heroic for earth too
   hard,
The passion that left the ground to lose itself in the
   sky,
Are music sent up to God by the lover and the bard;
Enough that he heard it once: we shall hear it by and
   by.   *Ib.*

But God has a few of us whom he whispers in the
   ear;
The rest may reason and welcome; 'tis we musicians
   know.   *Ib.* xi.

The C Major of this life.   *Ib.* xii.

How he lies in his rights of a man!
Death has done all death can.   *After.*

So free we seem, so fettered fast we are!
     Andrea del Sarto.

Ah, but a man's reach should exceed his grasp,
Or what's a heaven for?   *Ib.*

Four great walls in the New Jerusalem.   *Ib.*

It all comes to the same thing at the end.
     Any Wife to Any Husband.

Why need the other women know so much?   *Ib.*

A minute's success pays the failure of years.
     Apollo and the Fates, prologue.

The Doric little Morgue!   *Apparent Failure.*

It's wiser being good than bad;
   It's safer being meek than fierce:
It's fitter being sane than mad.
   My own hope is, a sun will pierce
The thickest cloud earth ever stretched;
   That, after Last, returns the First,
Though a wide compass round be fetched;
   That what began best can't end worst,
   Nor what God blessed once, prove accurst.   *Ib.*

That one Face, far from vanish, rather grows,
Or decomposes but to recompose,
Become my universe that feels and knows.
     Ib. epilogue, third speaker, xii.

But, thanks to wine-lees and democracy,
We've still our stage where truth calls spade a spade!
     Aristophanes' Apology, l. 392.

He lies now in the little valley, laughed
   And moaned about by those mysterious streams.
     Ib. l. 5679.

There up spoke a brisk little somebody,
Critic and whippersnapper, in a rage
To set things right.
     Balaustion's Adventure, pt. i, l. 308.

A man can have but one life and one death,
One heaven, one hell.   *In a Balcony*, l. 13.

I count life just a stuff
To try the soul's strength on. *Ib. 1. 651.*

Truth that peeps
Over the glass's edge when dinner's done,
And body gets its sop and holds its noise
And leaves soul free a little.
Bishop Blougram's Apology.

A piano-forte is a fine resource,
All Balzac's novels occupy one shelf,
The new edition fifty volumes long. *Ib.*

The funny type
They get up well at Leipsic. *Ib.*

Just when we're safest, there's a sunset-touch,
A fancy from a flower-bell, some one's death,
A chorus-ending from Euripides,
And that's enough for fifty hopes and fears,—
The grand Perhaps. *Ib.*

All we have gained then by our unbelief
Is a life of doubt diversified by faith,
For one of faith diversified by doubt:
We called the chess-board white—we call it black. *Ib.*

Demireps
That love and save their souls in new French books. *Ib.*

You, for example, clever to a fault,
The rough and ready man that write apace,
Read somewhat seldomer, think perhaps even less
Ib.

Be a Napoleon and yet disbelieve!
Why, the man's mad, friend, take his light away. *Ib.*

And that's what all the blessed Evil's for. *Ib.*

Set you square with Genesis again. *Ib.*

No, when the fight begins within himself,
A man's worth something. *Ib.*

Gigadibs the literary man. *Ib.*

He said true things, but called them by wrong names.
Ib.

By this time he has tested his first plough,
And studied his last chapter of St. John. *Ib.*

Saint Praxed's ever was the church for peace.
The Bishop orders His Tomb.

Mistresses with great smooth marbly limbs. *Ib.*

See God made and eaten all day long. *Ib.*

Good, strong, thick, stupefying incense-smoke. *Ib.*

Aha, ELUCESCEBAT quoth our friend?
No Tully, said I, Ulpian at the best. *Ib.*

All *lapis*, all sons. *Ib.*

There's a woman like a dew-drop, she's so purer than
the purest. *A Blot in the 'Scutcheon,* 1. iii.

Morning, evening, noon and night,
'Praise God!' sang Theocrite.
The Boy and the Angel.

How well I know what I mean to do
When the long dark autumn-evenings come.
By the Fireside, i.

Not verse now, only prose! *Ib.* ii.

O woman-country, wooed not wed. *Ib.* vi.

That great brow
And the spirit-small hand propping it. *Ib.* xxiii.

We two stood there with never a third. *Ib.* xxxviii.

Oh, the little more, and how much it is!
And the little less, and what worlds away!
Ib. xxxix.

If you join two lives, there is oft a scar.
They are one and one, with a shadowy third;
One near one is too far. *Ib.* xlvi.

One born to love you, sweet! *Ib.* li.

Letting the rank tongue blossom into speech.
Caliban upon Setebos, 1. 23.

Setebos, Setebos, and Setebos!
'Thinketh, He dwelleth i' the cold o' the moon.
'Thinketh He made it, with the sun to match,
But not the stars; the stars came otherwise. *Ib.* 1. 24.

'Let twenty pass, and stone the twenty-first.
Loving not, hating not, just choosing so. *Ib.* 1. 103.

A bitter heart that bides its time and bites. *Ib.* 1. 167.

Kentish Sir Byng stood for his King,
Bidding the crop-headed Parliament swing.
Cavalier Tunes. 1 *Marching Along.*

Marching along, fifty-score strong,
Great-hearted gentlemen, singing this song. *Ib.*

King Charles, and who'll do him right now?
Ib. 2. *Give a Rouse.*

By the old fool's side that begot him. *Ib.*

Noll's damned troopers shot him. *Ib.*

Boot, saddle, to horse, and away!
Ib. 3. *Boot and Saddle.*

'Tis the Last Judgment's fire must cure this place,
Calcine its clods and set my prisoners free.
Childe Roland, xi.

One stiff blind horse, his every bone a-stare.
Ib. xiii.

I never saw a brute I hated so;
He must be wicked to deserve such pain. *Ib.* xiv.

Dauntless the slug-horn to my lips I set,
And blew. '*Childe Roland to the Dark Tower came.*'
Ib. xxxiv.

Out of the little chapel I burst
Into the fresh night-air again. *Christmas Eve,* i.

The preaching man's immense stupidity. *Ib.* iii.

In the natural fog of the good man's mind. *Ib.* iv.

He was there.
He himself with his human air. *Ib.* viii.

Our best is bad, nor bears Thy test;
Still, it should be our very best. *Ib.*

Some thrilling view of the surplice-question.
Ib. xiv.

That sallow, virgin-minded, studious
Martyr to mild enthusiasm. *Ib.*

The exhausted air-bell of the Critic. *Ib.* xvi.

While I watched my foolish heart expand
In the lazy glow of benevolence,
O'er the various modes of man's belief. *Ib.* xx.

The raree-show of Peter's successor. *Ib.* xxii.

For the preacher's merit or demerit,
It were to be wished the flaws were fewer
In the earthen vessel, holding treasure,
Which lies as safe in a golden ewer;
But the main thing is, does it hold good measure?
Heaven soon sets right all other matters !   *Ib.*

       The sprinkled isles,
Lily on lily, that o'erlace the sea.
And laugh their pride when the light wave lisps
'Greece'.   *Cleon*, l. 1.

I have written three books on the soul,
Proving absurd all written hitherto,
And putting us to ignorance again.   *Ib.* l. 57.

What is he buzzing in my ears?
   'Now that I come to die,
Do I view the world as a vale of tears?'
   Ah, reverend sir, not I!   *Confessions.*

To mine, it serves for the old June weather
   Blue above lane and wall;
And that farthest bottle labelled 'Ether'
   Is the house o'ertopping all.   *Ib.*

How sad and bad and mad it was—
   But then, how it was sweet!   *Ib.*

There are flashes struck from midnights,
   There are fire-flames noondays kindle,
Whereby piled-up honours perish,
   Whereby swollen ambitions dwindle,
While just this or that poor impulse,
   Which for once had play unstifled,
Seems the sole work of a life-time
   That away the rest have trifled.   *Cristina*, 4.

Stung by the splendour of a sudden thought.
       A Death in the Desert, l. 59.

Such ever was love's way: to rise, it stoops.   *Ib.* l. 134.

For life, with all it yields of joy and woe,
And hope and fear,—believe the aged friend—
Is just a chance o' the prize of learning love.
       Ib. l. 245.

I say, the acknowledgment of God in Christ
Accepted by thy reason, solves for thee
All questions in the earth and out of it.   *Ib.* l. 474.

For I say, this is death and the sole death,
When a man's loss comes to him from his gain,
Darkness from light, from knowledge ignorance,
And lack of love from love made manifest. *Ib.* l. 482.

Progress, man's distinctive mark alone,
Not God's, and not the beasts': God is, they are,
Man partly is and wholly hopes to be.   *Ib.* l. 586.

'Twas Cerinthus that is lost.   *Ib.* last line.

Your ghost will walk, you lover of trees,
   (If our loves remain)
   In an English lane.   *De Gustibus.*

The bean-flowers' boon.   *Ib.*

A castle, precipice-encurled,
In a gash of the wind-grieved Apennine.   *Ib.*

Italy, my Italy!
Queen Mary's saying serves for me—
   (When fortune's malice
   Lost her—Calais)
Open my heart and you will see
Graved inside of it, 'Italy'.   *Ib.*

Reads verse and thinks she understands.
       Dis aliter visum, iv.

Schumann's our music-maker now.   *Ib.* viii.

Ingres's the modern man who paints.   *Ib.*

Heine for songs; for kisses, how?   *Ib.*

Sure of the Fortieth spare Arm-chair
When gout and glory seat me there.   *Ib.* xii.

With loves and doves, at all events
With money in the Three per Cents.   *Ib.* xiii.

Here comes my husband from his whist.   *Ib.* xxx.

How very hard it is to be
   A Christian!   *Easter Day*, i.

      'Tis well averred,
A scientific faith's absurd.   *Ib.* vi.

'Condemned to earth for ever, shut
From heaven!'
      But Easter-Day breaks! But
Christ rises! Mercy every way
Is infinite—and who can say?   *Ib.* xxxiii.

Karshish, the picker-up of learning's crumbs.
       An Epistle.

Beautiful Evelyn Hope is dead!   *Evelyn Hope.*

Your mouth of your own geranium's red.   *Ib.*

You will wake, and remember, and understand.   *Ib.*

What if this friend happen to be—God?
       Fears and Scruples, xii.

Truth never hurts the teller.
       Fifine at the Fair, xxxii.

'What, and is it really you again?' quoth I:
'I again, what else did you expect?' quoth she.
       Ib. epilogue, i.

When the liquor's out why clink the cannikin?
       The Flight of the Duchess, xvi.
You're my friend—
What a thing friendship is, world without end! *Ib.* xvii.

I must learn Spanish, one of these days,
Only for that slow sweet name's sake.
       The Flower's Name.

Is there no method to tell her in Spanish?   *Ib.*

If you get simple beauty and nought else,
You get about the best thing God invents.
       Fra Lippo Lippi, l. 217.

You should not take a fellow eight years old
And make him swear to never kiss the girls. *Ib.* l. 224.

       This world's no blot for us,
Nor blank; it means intensely, and means good:
To find its meaning is my meat and drink. *Ib.* l. 313.

'Tis the faith that launched point-blank her dart
At the head of a lie—taught Original Sin,
The corruption of Man's Heart. (Christianity)
       Gold Hair.

The moth's kiss, first!
Kiss me as if you made believe
You were not sure, this eve,
How my face, your flower, had pursed
It's petals up. . . .
The bee's kiss, now!
Kiss me as if you entered gay
My heart at some noonday.   *In a Gondola.*

Let us begin and carry up this corpse,
Singing together.   *A Grammarian's Funeral.*

He's for the morning.   *Ib.*

This is our master, famous, calm, and dead,
Borne on our shoulders.   *Ib.*

He said, 'What's time? leave Now for dogs and apes!
Man has Forever.'   *Ib.*

That low man seeks a little thing to do,
Sees it and does it:
This high man, with a great thing to pursue,
Dies ere he knows it.
That low man goes on adding one to one,
His hundred's soon hit:
This high man, aiming at a million,
Misses an unit.
That, has the world here—should he need the next,
Let the world mind him!
This, throws himself on God, and unperplext
Seeking shall find Him.   *Ib.*

He settled *Hoti's* business—let it be!—
Properly based *Oun*—
Gave us the doctrine of the enclitic *De,*
Dead from the waist down.   *Ib.*

Lofty designs must close in like effects.   *Ib.*

O, world, as God has made it! all is beauty.
The Guardian Angel.

This is Ancona, yonder is the sea.   *Ib.*

Infinite mercy, but, I wis,
As infinite a justice too.
The Heretic's Tragedy, i.

(And wanteth there grace of lute or clavicithern, ye
shall say to confirm him who singeth—)
We bring John now to be burned alive.   *Ib.* ii.

Forth John's soul flared into the dark.   *Ib.* x.

God help all poor souls lost in the dark!   *Ib.*

I liken his Grace to an acorned hog.
Holy-Cross Day, iv.

The Lord will have mercy on Jacob yet,
And again in his border see Israel set.   *Ib.* xiii.

Thou! if thou wast He, who at mid-watch came,
By the starlight, naming a dubious name!   *Ib.* xvi.

We gave the Cross, when we owed the Throne.   *Ib.*

We withstood Christ then? Be mindful how
At least we withstand Barabbas now!   *Ib.* xviii.

We march, thy band,
South, East, and on to the Pleasant Land.   *Ib.* xx.

Oh, to be in England
Now that April's there,
And whoever wakes in England
Sees, some morning, unaware,
That the lowest boughs and the brushwood sheaf
Round the elm-tree bole are in tiny leaf,
While the chaffinch sings on the orchard bough
In England—now!   *Home Thoughts from Abroad.*

That's the wise thrush; he sings each song twice over,
Lest you should think he never could recapture
The first fine careless rapture!   *Ib.*

All will be gay when noontide wakes anew
The buttercups, the little children's dower
—Far brighter than this gaudy melon-flower!   *Ib.*

Nobly, nobly Cape St. Vincent to the North-West
died away;
Sunset ran, one glorious blood-red, reeking into
Cadiz Bay.
Home-Thoughts from the Sea.

'Here and here did England help me: how can I help
England?'—say,
Whoso turns as I, this evening, turn to God to praise
and pray,
While Jove's planet rises yonder, silent over Africa.
Ib.

'With this same key
Shakespeare unlocked his heart' once more!
Did Shakespeare? If so, the less Shakespeare he!
House, x.

How it strikes a Contemporary.   *Title.*

He took such cognizance of men and things.
How it Strikes a Contemporary, l. 30.

I sprang to the stirrup, and Joris, and he;
I galloped, Dirck galloped, we galloped all three.
How they brought the Good News from Ghent to Aix.

You know, we French stormed Ratisbon.
Incident of the French Camp.

'You're wounded!' 'Nay,' the soldier's pride
Touched to the quick, he said:
'I'm killed, Sire!' And his chief beside
Smiling the boy fell dead.   *Ib.*

Ignorance is not innocence but sin.
The Inn Album, v.

Just my vengeance complete,
The man sprang to his feet,
Stood erect, caught at God's skirts, and prayed!
—So, *I* was afraid!   *Instans Tyrannus.*

I wager 't is old to you
As the story of Adam and Eve, and possibly quite as
true.   *Iván Ivànovitch,* l. 15.

The swallow has set her six young on the rail,
And looks seaward.   *James Lee,* iii. i.

Oh, good gigantic smile o' the brown old earth.
Ib. vii. i.

I should be dead of joy, James Lee.
Ib. ix. viii.

There's heaven above, and night by night
I look right through its gorgeous roof.
Johannes Agricola in Meditation.

I said—Then, dearest, since 'tis so,
Since now at length my fate I know,
Since nothing all my love avails,
Since all, my life seemed meant for, fails,
Since this was written and needs must be—
My whole heart rises up to bless
Your name in pride and thankfulness!
Take back the hope you gave,—I claim
Only a memory of the same.
The Last Ride Together, i.

Who knows but the world may end tonight?   *Ib.* ii.

Hush! if you saw some western cloud
All billowy-bosomed, over-bowed
By many benedictions—sun's
And moon's and evening-star's at once. *Ib.* iii.

My soul
Smoothed itself out, a long-cramped scroll
Freshening and fluttering in the wind. *Ib.* iv.

Might she have loved me? just as well
She might have hated, who can tell! *Ib.*

The petty done, the undone vast. *Ib.* v.

What hand and brain went ever paired? *Ib.* vi.

They scratch his name on the Abbey-stones.
My riding is better, by their leave. *Ib.*

Sing, riding's a joy! For me, I ride. *Ib.* vii.

Ride, ride together, for ever ride? *Ib.* x.

Escape me?
Never—
Beloved! *Life in a Love.*

To dry one's eyes and laugh at a fall,
And, baffled, get up and begin again. *Ib.*

No sooner the old hope goes to ground
Than a new one, straight to the self-same mark. *Ib.*

So, I gave her eyes my own eyes to take,
 My hand sought hers as in earnest need,
And round she turned for my noble sake,
 And gave me herself indeed. *A Light Woman.*

'Tis an awkward thing to play with souls,
And matter enough to save one's own. *Ib.*

And, Robert Browning, you writer of plays,
Here's a subject made to your hand! *Ib.*

A face to lose youth for, to occupy age
With the dream of, meet death with. *A Likeness.*

Just for a handful of silver he left us,
 Just for a riband to stick in his coat.
 The Lost Leader.

We that had loved him so, followed him, honoured
 him,
 Lived in his mild and magnificent eye,
Learned his great language, caught his clear accents,
 Made him our pattern to live and to die! *Ib.*

Shakespeare was of us, Milton was for us,
Burns, Shelley, were with us—they watch from their
 graves! *Ib.*

We shall march prospering,—not thro' his presence;
 Songs may inspirit us,—not from his lyre;
Deeds will be done,—while he boasts his quiescence,
 Still bidding crouch whom the rest bade aspire. *Ib.*

One more devils'-triumph and sorrow for angels,
One wrong more to man, one more insult to God!
 Ib.

Never glad confident morning again! *Ib.*

All's over, then; does truth sound bitter
As one at first believes? *The Lost Mistress.*

I will hold your hand but as long as all may,
Or so very little longer! *Ib.*

Where the quiet-coloured end of evening smiles.
 Love among the Ruins.

Earth's returns
For whole centuries of folly, noise and sin! *Ib.*

Love is best. *Ib.*

How the March sun feels like May! *A Lovers' Quarrel.*

Oppression makes the wise man mad. *Luria,* IV.

But a bird's weight can break the infant tree
Which after holds an aery in its arms. *Ib.*

The only fault's with time;
All men become good creatures: but so slow! *Ib.* v.

Argument's hot to the close.
 Master Hugues of Saxe-Gotha, xiii.

One dissertates, he is candid;
Two must discept,—has distinguished. *Ib.* xiv.

Do I carry the moon in my pocket? *Ib.* xxix.

As I gain the cove with pushing prow,
And quench its speed i' the slushy sand.
 Meeting at Night.

A mile of warm sea-scented beach. *Ib.*

A tap at the pane, the quick sharp scratch
And blue spurt of a lighted match,
And a voice less loud, thro' its joys and fears,
Than the two hearts beating each to each! *Ib.*

Ah, did you once see Shelley plain,
 And did he stop and speak to you
And did you speak to him again?
 How strange it seems, and new! *Memorabilia.*

A moulted feather, an eagle-feather!
Well, I forget the rest. *Ib.*

Have you found your life distasteful?
 My life did, and does, smack sweet.
Was your youth of pleasure wasteful?
 Mine I saved and hold complete.
Do your joys with age diminish?
 When mine fail me, I'll complain.
Must in death your daylight finish?
 My sun sets to rise again. *At the 'Mermaid'.*

I find earth not grey but rosy,
Heaven not grim but fair of hue.
Do I stoop? I pluck a posy.
Do I stand and stare? All's blue. *Ib.*

'Next Poet'—(Manners, Ben!) *Ib.*

If such as came for wool, sir, went home shorn,
Where is the wrong I did them?
 Mr. Sludge, 'The Medium', l. 630.

Solomon of saloons
And philosophic diner-out. *Ib.* l. 773.

This trade of mine—I don't know, can't be sure
But there was something in it, tricks and all!
Really, I want to light up my own mind. *Ib.* l. 809.

Boston's a hole, the herring-pond is wide,
V-notes are something, liberty still more.
Beside, is he the only fool in the world? *Ib.* last lines.

This is the spray the bird clung to. *Misconceptions.*

This is a heart the Queen leant on. *Ib.*

That's my last Duchess painted on the wall.
 My Last Duchess, I. i.

What matter to me if their star is a world?
Mine has opened its soul to me; therefore I love it.
My Star.

Give me of Nelson only a touch.
Nationality in Drinks.

All I can say is—I saw it!   *Natural Magic.*

Never the time and the place
  And the loved one all together!
Never the Time and the Place.

A lion who dies of an ass's kick,
The wronged great soul of an ancient Master
Old Pictures in Florence, vi.

What's come to perfection perishes.
Things learned on earth, we shall practise in heaven.
Works done least rapidly, Art most cherishes.
Ib. xvii.

There remaineth a rest for the people of God:
And I have had troubles enough, for one.   *Ib.* xxii.

All June I bound the rose in sheaves.
One Way of Love.

Lose who may—I still can say,
Those who win heaven, blest are they!   *Ib.*

There they are, my fifty men and women.
One Word More, i.

Rafael made a century of sonnets,
Made and wrote them in a certain volume
Dinted with the silver-pointed pencil
Else he only used to draw Madonnas.   *Ib.* ii.

Suddenly, as rare things will, it vanished.   *Ib.* iv.

Dante once prepared to paint an angel:
Whom to please? You whisper 'Beatrice'.   *Ib.* v.

Dante, who loved well because he hated,
Hated wickedness that hinders loving.   *Ib.*

Does he paint? he fain would write a poem—
Does he write? he fain would paint a picture.
Ib. viii.

Heaven's gift takes earth's abatement.   *Ib.* ix.

Even he, the minute makes immortal,
Proves, perchance, but mortal in the minute.   *Ib.*

Never dares the man put off the prophet.   *Ib.* x.

Other heights in other lives, God willing:
All the gifts from all the heights, your own, Love!
Ib. xii.

He who blows thro' bronze, may breathe thro' silver.
Ib. xiii.

I am mine and yours—the rest be all men's.   *Ib.* xiv.

Where my heart lies, let my brain lie also.   *Ib.*

Lo, the moon's self!
Here in London, yonder late in Florence,
Still we find her face, the thrice-transfigured.
Curving on a sky imbrued with colour,
Drifted over Fiesole by twilight,
Came she, our new crescent of a hair's-breadth.
Full she flared it, lamping Samminiato,
Rounder 'twixt the cypresses and rounder,
Perfect till the nightingales applauded.   *Ib.* xv.

Blank to Zoroaster on his terrace,
Blind to Galileo on his turret,
Dumb to Homer, dumb to Keats—him, even!
Ib. xvi.

God be thanked, the meanest of his creatures
Boasts two soul-sides, one to face the world with,
One to show a woman when he loves her!   *Ib.* xvii.

Silent silver lights and darks undreamed of,
Where I hush and bless myself with silence.   *Ib.* xviii.

Oh, their Rafael of the dear Madonnas,
Oh, their Dante of the dread Inferno,
Wrote one song—and in my brain I sing it,
Drew one angel—borne, see, on my bosom!   *Ib.* xix.

I see my way as birds their trackless way,
I shall arrive! what time, what circuit first,
I ask not: but unless God send his hail
Or blinding fireballs, sleet or stifling snow,
In some time, his good time, I shall arrive:
He guides me and the bird. In His good time!
Paracelsus, pt. I.

Truth is within ourselves.   *Ib.*

      Are there not, dear Michal,
Two points in the adventure of the diver,
One—when, a beggar, he prepares to plunge,
One—when, a prince, he rises with his pearl?
Festus, I plunge!   *Ib.*

PARACELSUS:
  I am he that aspired to *know*: and thou?
APRILE:
  I would *love* infinitely, and be loved!   *Ib.* pt. II.

      God is the perfect poet,
Who in his person acts his own creations.   *Ib.*

Measure your mind's height by the shade it casts!
Ib. pt. III.

Heap cassia, sandal-buds and stripes
Of labdanum, and aloe-balls.   *Ib.* pt. IV.

As when a queen, long dead, was young.   *Ib.*

Over the sea our galleys went.   *Ib.*

All at once they leave you, and you know them!
Ib. pt. V.

I give the fight up: let there be an end,
A privacy, an obscure nook for me.
I want to be forgotten even by God.   *Ib.*

      Progress is
The law of life, man is not
  Man as yet.   *Ib.*

Thus the Mayne glideth
Where my Love abideth.
Sleep's no softer.   *Ib.*

Like plants in mines which never saw the sun,
But dream of him, and guess where he may be,
And do their best to climb and get to him.   *Ib.*

      If I stoop
Into a dark tremendous sea of cloud,
It is but for a time; I press God's lamp
Close to my breast; its splendour, soon or late,
Will pierce the gloom: I shall emerge one day.   *Ib.*

Round the Cape of a sudden came the sea,
And the sun looked over the mountain's rim;
And straight was a path of gold for him,
And the need of a world of men for me.
Parting at Morning.

It was roses, roses, all the way.   *The Patriot.*

The air broke into a mist with bells.   *Ib.*

Sun-treader, life and light be thine for ever! (Shelley)
     Pauline, l. 148.

Ah, thought which saddens while it soothes!
     Pictor Ignotus.

Hamelin Town's in Brunswick,
   By famous Hanover city;
The river Weser, deep and wide,
   Washes its walls on the southern side.
     The Pied Piper of Hamelin.

   Shrieking and squeaking
In fifty different sharps and flats.   *Ib.*

Anything like the sound of a rat
Makes my heart go pit-a-pat!   *Ib.*

A plate of turtle green and glutinous.   *Ib.*

In did come the strangest figure!   *Ib.*

So munch on, crunch on, take your nuncheon,
Breakfast, supper, dinner, luncheon.   *Ib.*

So, Willy, let me and you be wipers
Of scores out with all men, especially pipers!   *Ib.*

Day! Faster and more fast,
O'er night's brim, day boils at last.
     Pippa Passes, introduction.

The year's at the spring,
And day's at the morn;
Morning's at seven;
The hill-side's dew-pearled;
The lark's on the wing;
The snail's on the thorn:
   God's in his heaven—
All's right with the world!   *Ib.* pt. I.

Some unsuspected isle in the far seas!
Some unsuspected isle in far-off seas!   *Ib.* pt. iii.

In the morning of the world,
When earth was nigher heaven than now.   *Ib.*

No need that sort of king should ever die!   *Ib.*

You'll look at least on love's remains,
   A grave's one violet:
Your look?—that pays a thousand pains.
   What's death? You'll love me yet!   *Ib.*

All service ranks the same with God—
With God, whose puppets, best and worst,
Are we; there is no last nor first.   *Ib.* pt. iv.

Stand still, true poet that you are!
I know you; let me try and draw you.
Some night you'll fail us: when afar
You rise, remember one man saw you,
Knew you, and named a star!   *Popularity.*

   With ardours manifold,
The bee goes singing to her groom,
Drunken and overbold.   *Ib.*

   Who fished the murex up?
What porridge had John Keats?   *Ib.*

The rain set early in tonight.   *Porphyria's Lover.*

   All her hair
In one long yellow string I wound
Three times her little throat around,
And strangled her. No pain felt she;
I am quite sure she felt no pain.   *Ib.*

And all night long we have not stirred,
And yet God has not said a word!   *Ib.*

But flame? The bush is bare. *Prologue.* (*Asolando.*)

Fear death?—to feel the fog in my throat,
   The mist in my face.   *Prospice.*

Where he stands, the Arch Fear in a visible form.
     Ib.

I was ever a fighter, so—one fight more,
   The best and the last!
I would hate that death bandaged my eyes, and forbore,
   And bade me creep past.   *Ib.*

No! let me taste the whole of it, fare like my peers
   The heroes of old,
Bear the brunt, in a minute pay glad life's arrears
   Of pain, darkness and cold.   *Ib.*

O thou soul of my soul! I shall clasp thee again,
   And with God be the rest!   *Ib.*

   Grow old along with me!
   The best is yet to be,
The last of life, for which the first was made:
   Our times are in his hand
   Who saith, 'A whole I planned,
Youth shows but half; trust God: see all, nor be
   afraid!'   *Rabbi ben Ezra,* i.

Irks care the crop-full bird? Frets doubt the maw-
   crammed beast?   *Ib.* iv.

   Then, welcome each rebuff
   That turns earth's smoothness rough,
Each sting that bids nor sit nor stand but go!
   Be our joys three-parts pain!
   Strive, and hold cheap the strain;
Learn, nor account the pang; dare, never grudge the
   throe!   *Ib.* vi.

   For thence,—a paradox
   Which comforts while it mocks,—
Shall life succeed in that it seems to fail:
   What I aspired to be,
   And was not, comforts me.
A brute I might have been, but would not sink i' the
   scale.   *Ib.* vii.

   Let us not always say
   'Spite of this flesh today
I strove, made head, gained ground upon the whole!'
   As the bird wings and sings,
   Let us cry 'All good things
Are ours, nor soul helps flesh more, now, than flesh
   helps soul.'   *Ib.* xii.

Once more on my adventure brave and new. *Ib.* xiv.

   When evening shuts,
   A certain moment cuts
The deed off, calls the glory from the grey. *Ib.* xvi.

   Now, who shall arbitrate?
   Ten men love what I hate,
Shun what I follow, slight what I receive:
   Ten, who in ears and eyes
   Match me: we all surmise,
They, this thing, and I, that: whom shall my soul
   believe?   *Ib.* xxii.

Fancies that broke through language and escaped.
     Ib. xxv.

All that is, at all,
Lasts ever, past recall;
Earth changes, but thy soul and God stand sure.
Rabbi ben Ezra, xxvii.

Time's wheel runs back or stops: potter and clay
    endure.   *Ib.*

He fixed thee mid this dance
Of plastic circumstance.   *Ib.* xxviii.

Look not thou down but up!
To uses of a cup.   *Ib.* xxx.

My times be in Thy hand!
Perfect the cup as planned!
Let age approve of youth, and death complete the
    same!   *Ib.* xxxii.

Do you see this square old yellow Book, I toss
I' the air, and catch again.
         The Ring and the Book, bk. i, l. 33.

The Life, Death, Miracles of Saint Somebody,
Saint Somebody Else, his Miracles, Death and Life.
             Ib. l. 80.

Well, British Public, ye who like me not,
(God love you!)   *Ib.* l. 410.

'Go get you manned by Manning and new-manned
By Newman and, mayhap, wise-manned to boot
By Wiseman.'   *Ib.* l. 444.

     A dusk mis-featured messenger,
No other than the angel of this life,
Whose care is lest men see too much at once.
             Ib. l. 593.

Let this old woe step on the stage again!   *Ib.* l. 824.

         Youth means love,
Vows can't change nature, priests are only men.
             Ib. l. 1056.

O lyric Love, half angel and half bird
And all a wonder and a wild desire.   *Ib.* l. 1391.

Boldest of hearts that ever braved the sun,
Took sanctuary within the holier blue,
And sang a kindred soul out to his face,—
Yet human at the red-ripe of the heart.   *Ib.* l. 1393.

This is the same voice: can thy soul know change?
             Ib. l. 1401.

Never may I commence my song, my due
To God who best taught song by gift of thee,
Except with bent head and beseeching hand.
             Ib. l. 1403.

Their utmost up and on.   *Ib.* l. 1413.

The story always old and always new. *Ib.* bk. ii, l. 214.

But facts are facts and flinch not.   *Ib.* l. 1049.

     Go practise if you please
With men and women: leave a child alone
For Christ's particular love's sake!   *Ib.* bk. iii, l. 88.

In the great right of an excessive wrong.   *Ib.* l. 1055.

Everyone soon or late comes round by Rome.
             Ib. bk. v, l. 296.

'Twas a thief said the last kind word to Christ:
Christ took the kindness and forgave the theft.
             Ib. bk. vi, l. 869.

O great, just, good God! Miserable me!   *Ib.* l. 2105.

The uncomfortableness of it all.   *Ib.* bk. vii, l. 400.

True life is only love, love only bliss.
             Ib. l. 960.

O lover of my life, O soldier-saint.   *Ib.* l. 1786.

       Through such souls alone
God stooping shows sufficient of His light
For us i' the dark to rise by. And I rise.
             Ib. l. 1843.

Faultless to a fault.   *Ib.* bk. ix, l. 1177.

     Of what I call God,
And fools call Nature.   *Ib.* bk. x, l. 1073

Why comes temptation but for man to meet
And master and make crouch beneath his foot,
And so be pedestaled in triumph?   *Ib.* l. 1185.

White shall not neutralize the black, nor good
Compensate bad in man, absolve him so:
Life's business being just the terrible choice.
             Ib. l. 1236.

     There's a new tribunal now,
Higher than God's—the educated man's! *Ib.* l. 1976.

     That sad obscure sequestered state
Where God unmakes but to remake the soul
He else made first in vain; which must not be.
             Ib. l. 2130.

     It is the glory and good of Art,
That Art remains the one way possible
Of speaking truths, to mouths like mine at least.
             Ib. bk. xii, l. 842.

Thy rare gold ring of verse (the poet praised)
Linking our England to his Italy.   *Ib.* l. 873.

Good, to forgive;
    Best, to forget!
Living, we fret;
Dying, we live.   *La Saisiaz*, dedication.

How good is man's life, the mere living! how fit to
    employ
All the heart and the soul and the senses, for ever in
    joy!   *Saul*, ix.

All's love, yet all's law.   *Ib.* xvii.

'Tis not what man does which exalts him, but what
    man would do!   *Ib.* xviii.

          It is by no breath,
Turn of eye, wave of hand, that salvation joins issue
    with death!
As thy Love is discovered almighty, almighty be
    proved
Thy power, that exists with and for it, of being
    beloved!   *Ib.*
            O Saul, it shall be
A Face like my face that receives thee; a Man like to
    me,
Thou shalt love and be loved by, for ever: a Hand like
    this hand
Shall throw open the gates of new life to thee! See
    the Christ stand!'   *Ib.*

     Because a man has shop to mind
In time and place, since flesh must live,
    Needs spirit lack all life behind,
All stray thoughts, fancies fugitive,
All loves except what trade can give?
                 Shop, **xx.**

I want to know a butcher paints,
A baker rhymes for his pursuit,
Candlestick-maker much acquaints
His soul with song, or, haply mute,
Blows out his brains upon the flute.   *Shop*, xxi.

Nay but you, who do not love her,
Is she not pure gold, my mistress?   *Song.*

Who will, may hear Sordello's story told.
                                        Sordello, bk. i

Who would has heard Sordello's story told.
                                        Ib. bk. vi.

Sidney's self, the starry paladin.   *Ib.*

Whence the grieved and obscure waters slope
Into a darkness quieted by hope;
Plucker of amaranths grown beneath God's eye
In gracious twilights where his chosen lie.   *Ib.*

Still more labyrinthine buds the rose.   *Ib.*

                    A touch divine—
And the scaled eyeball owns the mystic rod;
Visibly through his garden walketh God.   *Ib.*

                    Any nose
May ravage with impunity a rose   *Ib.* bk. vi.

You are not going to marry your old friend's love,
    after all?   *A Soul's Tragedy*, Act. ii.

I have known *Four*-and-twenty leaders of revolts.
                                        Ib.

Gr-r-r- there go, my heart's abhorrence!
Water your damned flower-pots, do!
                Soliloquy of the Spanish Cloister.

I the Trinity illustrate,
    Drinking watered orange-pulp—
In three sips the Arian frustrate;
    While he drains his at one gulp.   *Ib.*

There's a great text in Galatians,
    Once you trip on it, entails
Twenty-nine distinct damnations,
    One sure, if another fails.   *Ib.*

My scrofulous French novel
On grey paper with blunt type.   *Ib.*

'St, there's Vespers! Plena gratia
Ave, Virgo! Gr-r-r—you swine!   *Ib.*

The glory dropped from their youth and love,
And both perceived they had dreamed a dream.
                The Statue and the Bust.

The world and its ways have a certain worth.   *Ib.*

The soldier-saints, who row on row,
Burn upward each to his point of bliss.   *Ib.*

The sin I impute to each frustrate ghost
Is—the unlit lamp and the ungirt loin,
Though the end in sight was a vice, I say.   *Ib.*

All the breath and the bloom of the year in the bag of
    one bee.   *Summum Bonum.* (*Asolando.*)

At the midnight in the silence of the sleep-time,
When you set your fancies free.   *Ib.* epilogue.

Greet the unseen with a cheer.   *Ib.*

One who never turned his back but marched breast
    forward,
    Never doubted clouds would break,
Never dreamed, though right were worsted, wrong
    would triumph,
    Held we fall to rise, are baffled to fight better,
    Sleep to wake.   *Ib.*

I've a Friend, over the sea;
I like him, but he loves me.
It all grew out of the books I write;
                    Time's Revenges.

There may be heaven; there must be hell;
Meantime, there is our earth here—well!   *Ib.*

Hark, the dominant's persistence till it must be
    answered to!   *A Toccata of Galuppi's*, viii.

What of soul was left, I wonder, when the kissing had
    to stop?   *Ib.* xiv.

Dear dead women, with such hair, too—what's
    become of all the gold
Used to hang and brush their bosoms? I feel chilly
    and grown old.   *Ib.* xv.

As I ride, as I ride.
            Through the Metidja to Abd-el-kadr.

Grand rough old Martin Luther
    Bloomed fables—flowers on furze,
The better the uncouther:
    Do roses stick like burrs?   *The Twins.*

            Only I discern—
Infinite passion, and the pain
Of finite hearts that yearn.   *Two in the Campagna.*

Sky—what a scowl of cloud
    Till, near and far,
Ray on ray split the shroud
    Splendid, a star!   *The Two Poets of Croisic.*

Bang-whang-whang goes the drum, tootle-te-tootle
    the fife.   *Up at a Villa—Down in the City.*

Wanting is—what?
    Summer redundant,
    Blueness abundant,
    —Where is the blot?   *Wanting—is what?*

What's become of Waring
Since he gave us all the slip?   *Waring*, i. i.

Monst'-inform'-ingens-horrend-ous
Demoniaco-seraphic
Penman's latest piece of graphic.   *Ib.* iv.

Some lost lady of old years.   *Ib.*

In vishnu-land what Avatar?   *Ib.* vi.

'When I last saw Waring . . .'
(How all turned to him who spoke!
You saw Waring? Truth or joke?
In land-travel or sea-faring?)   *Ib.* ii. i.

            Oh, never star
Was lost here but it rose afar!   *Ib.* iii.

But little do or can the best of us:
That little is achieved through Liberty.
        In Andrew Reid's Why I am a Liberal.

Let's contend no more, Love,
    Strive nor weep:
All be as before, Love,
    —Only sleep!   *A Woman's Last Word.*

What so wild as words are?   *Ib.*

Where the apple reddens,
    Never pry—
Lest we lose our Edens,
    Eve and I.   *Ib.*

That shall be tomorrow
  Not tonight:
I must bury sorrow
  Out of sight.   *Ib.*

I knew you once: but in Paradise,
  If we meet, I will pass nor turn my face.
                          The Worst of It, xix.

We have not sighed deep, laughed free,
  Starved, feasted, despaired,—been happy.
                          Youth and Art.

And nobody calls you a dunce,
  And people suppose me clever:
This could but have happened once,
  And we missed it, lost it for ever.   *Ib.*

MICHAEL BRUCE
1746–1767

Sweet bird! thy bower is ever green,
  Thy sky is ever clear:
Thou hast no sorrow in thy song,
  No winter in thy year!
            To the Cuckoo. Also attr. to John Logan.

In ev'ry pang that rends the heart,
The Man of sorrows had a part
                    The Enthroned High Priest.

GEORGE BRYAN BRUMMELL
1778–1840

Who's your fat friend? (Of the Prince of Wales)
        Gronow, *Reminiscences* (1862), p. 63.

ALFRED BRYAN
Nineteenth Century

Who paid the rent for Mrs. Rip Van Winkle
When Rip Van Winkle went away?
    Who Paid the Rent for Mrs. Rip Van Winkle?

WILLIAM JENNINGS BRYAN
1860–1925

The humblest citizen of all the land, when clad in the
  armor of a righteous cause, is stronger than all the
  hosts of error.
      *Speech at the National Democratic Convention,
      Chicago, 1896.*

You shall not press down upon the brow of labour this
  crown of thorns, you shall not crucify mankind
  upon a cross of gold.   *Ib.*

WILLIAM CULLEN BRYANT
1794–1878

So live, that when thy summons comes to join
The innumerable caravan, which moves
To that mysterious realm, where each shall take
His chamber in the silent halls of death,
Thou go not, like the quarry-slave at night,
Scourged to his dungeon, but, sustained and soothed
By an unfaltering trust, approach thy grave

Like one who wraps the drapery of his couch
About him, and lies down to pleasant dreams.
                          Thanatopsis, l. 73.

            They seemed
Like old companions in adversity.
                          A Winter Piece, l. 26.

ROBERT WILLIAMS BUCHANAN
1841–1901

The Fleshly School of Poetry.   *Title.*

          She just wore
Enough for modesty—no more.
                  White Rose and Red, 1, v, l. 60.

The sweet post-prandial cigar.   *De Berny.*

GEORGE VILLIERS, SECOND DUKE OF BUCKINGHAM
1628–1687

The world is made up for the most part of fools and
  knaves. *To Mr. Clifford, on his Humane Reason.*

What the devil does the plot signify, except to bring
  in fine things?   *The Rehearsal*, III. i.

Ay, now the plot thickens very much upon us.
                                        Ib. ii.

HENRY J. BUCKOLL
1803–1871

Lord, behold us with Thy blessing
  Once again assembled here.
      *Psalms and Hymns for the Use of Rugby School
      Chapel. Lord, Behold us with Thy Blessing.*

Lord, dismiss us with Thy blessing,
  Thanks for mercies past receive.
      Ib. Lord, Dismiss us with Thy Blessing.

JOHN BALDWIN BUCKSTONE
1802–1879

On such an occasion as this,
  All time and nonsense scorning,
Nothing shall come amiss,
  And we won't go home till morning.
                          Billy Taylor, 1. ii.

ALFRED BUNN
1796?–1860

Alice, where art thou?   *Title of Song.*

When other lips, and other hearts,
  Their tales of love shall tell.
                  Bohemian Girl, Act III.

I dreamt that I dwelt in marble halls,
With vassals and serfs at my side.
              Song: I Dreamt That I Dwelt.

The light of other days is faded,
And all their glory past.
The Maid of Artois, Act II.

JOHN BUNYAN
1628–1688

Mr. Badman died . . . as they call it, like a Chrisom-child, quietly and without fear.
Life and Death of Mr. Badman.

As I walk'd through the wilderness of this world.
Pilgrim's Progress, pt. i.

The name of the one was Obstinate and the name of the other Pliable.   *Ib.*

The name of the slough was Despond.   *Ib.*

The gentleman's name was Mr. Worldly-Wise-Man.
Ib.

Set down my name, Sir.   *Ib.*

Come in, come in;
Eternal glory thou shalt win.   *Ib.*

And behold there was a very stately palace before him, the name of which was Beautiful.   *Ib.*

The valley of Humiliation.   *Ib.*

A foul Fiend coming over the field to meet him; his name is Apollyon.   *Ib.*

Then Apollyon straddled quite over the whole breadth of the way.   *Ib.*

Set your faces like a flint.   *Ib.*

It beareth the name of Vanity-Fair, because the town where 'tis kept, is lighter than vanity.   *Ib.*

So soon as the man overtook me, he was but a word and a blow.   *Ib.*

Hanging is too good for him, said Mr. Cruelty.   *Ib.*

Yet my great-grandfather was but a water-man, looking one way, and rowing another: and I got most of my estate by the same occupation.
[Mr. By-Ends]

They came at a delicate plain, called Ease, where they went with much content; but that plain was but narrow, so they went quickly over it.   *Ib.*

Remember Lot's Wife.   *Ib.*

A castle, called Doubting-Castle, the owner whereof was Giant Despair.   *Ib.*

Now Giant Despair had a wife, and her name was Diffidence.   *Ib.*

A grievous crab-tree cudgel.   *Ib.*

They came to the Delectable Mountains.   *Ib.*

Sleep is sweet to the labouring man.   *Ib.*

A great horror and darkness fell upon Christian. *Ib.*

Then I saw that there was a way to hell, even from the gates of heaven.   *Ib.*

So I awoke, and behold it was a dream.   *Ib.*

A man that could look no way but downwards, with a muckrake in his hand.   *Ib.* pt. ii.

One leak will sink a ship, and one sin will destroy a sinner.   *Ib.*

One Great-heart.   *Ib.*

He that is down needs fear no fall,
He that is low no pride.
Ib. Shepherd Boy's Song in the Valley of Humiliation.

A man there was, tho' some did count him mad,
The more he cast away, the more he had.   *Ib.*

An ornament to her profession.   *Ib.*

Whose name is Valiant-for-Truth.   *Ib.*

Who would true valour see,
  Let him come hither;
One here will constant be,
  Come wind, come weather.
There's no discouragement
Shall make him once relent
His first avow'd intent
  To be a pilgrim.

[*Popular version of above:*
He who would valiant be
  'Gainst all disaster,
Let him in constancy
  Follow the Master. &c.]   *Ib.*

Who so beset him round
  With dismal stories,
Do but themselves confound—
  His strength the more is.   *Ib.*

Then fancies flee away!
I'll fear not what men say,
I'll labour night and day
  To be a pilgrim.   *Ib.*

Mr. Standfast.   *Ib.*

My sword, I give to him that shall succeed me in my pilgrimage, and my courage and skill to him that can get it.   *Ib.*

So he passed over, and all the trumpets sounded for him on the other side.   *Ib.*

SAMUEL DICKINSON BURCHARD
1812–1891

We are Republicans and don't propose to leave our party and identify ourselves with the party whose antecedents are rum, Romanism, and rebellion.
Speech, New York City, 29 Oct. 1884.

GELETT BURGESS
1866–

Are you a bromide?
Title of Essay in 'Smart Set' (1906).

I never saw a Purple Cow,
  I never hope to see one;
But I can tell you, anyhow,
  I'd rather see than be one!
Burgess Nonsense Book. The Purple Cow.

Ah, yes! I wrote the 'Purple Cow'—
  I'm sorry, now, I wrote it!
But I can tell you anyhow,
  I'll kill you if you quote it!   *Ib.*

JOHN WILLIAM BURGON

1813–1888

A rose-red city—half as old as Time! *Petra*, l. 132.

JOHN BURGOYNE

1722–1792

You have only, when before your glass, to keep pronouncing to yourself nimini-pimini—the lips cannot fail of taking their plie.
The Heiress, III. ii.

EDMUND BURKE

1728–1797

Would twenty shillings have ruined Mr. Hampden's fortune? No! but the payment of half twenty shillings, on the principle it was demanded, would have made him a slave.
Speech on American Taxation, 1774.

It is the nature of all greatness not to be exact. *Ib.*

Falsehood has a perennial spring. *Ib.*

It did so happen that persons had a single office divided between them, who had never spoken to each other in their lives; until they found themselves, they knew not how, pigging together, heads and points, in the same truckle-bed. *Ib.*

For even then, sir, even before this splendid orb was entirely set, and while the western horizon was in a blaze with his descending glory, on the opposite quarter of the heavens arose another luminary, and, for his hour, became lord of the ascendant. *Ib.*

Great men are the guide-posts and landmarks in the state. *Ib.*

Passion for fame; a passion which is the instinct of all great souls. *Ib.*

To tax and to please, no more than to love and to be wise, is not given to men. *Ib.*

The only liberty I mean, is a liberty connected with order; that not only exists along with order and virtue, but which cannot exist at all without them.
Speech at his arrival at Bristol (1774).

Applaud us when we run; console us when we fall; cheer us when we recover: but let us pass on—for God's sake, let us pass on!
Speech at Bristol previous to the Election, 1780.

Bad laws are the worst sort of tyranny. *Ib.*

The worthy gentleman [Mr. Coombe], who has been snatched from us at the moment of the election, and in the middle of the contest, whilst his desires were as warm, and his hopes as eager as ours, has feelingly told us, what shadows we are, and what shadows we pursue.
Speech at Bristol on Declining the Poll, 1780.

The cold neutrality of an impartial judge.
Preface to the Address of M. Brissot.

I have in general no very exalted opinion of the virtue of paper government.
Speech on Conciliation with America, 1775.

The noble lord in the blue riband. *Ib.*

The concessions of the weak are the concessions of fear. *Ib.*

Young man, there is America—which at this day serves for little more than to amuse you with stories of savage men, and uncouth manners; yet shall, before you taste of death, show itself equal to the whole of that commerce which now attracts the envy of the world. *Ib.*

When we speak of the commerce with our colonies, fiction lags after truth; invention is unfruitful, and imagination cold and barren. *Ib.*

A people who are still, as it were, but in the gristle and not yet hardened into the bone of manhood. *Ib.*

Through a wise and salutary neglect [of the colonies], a generous nature has been suffered to take her own way to perfection; when I reflect upon these effects, when I see how profitable they have been to us, I feel all the pride of power sink and all presumption in the wisdom of human contrivances melt and die away within me. My rigour relents. I pardon something to the spirit of liberty. *Ib.*

The use of force alone is but *temporary*. It may subdue for a moment; but it does not remove the necessity of subduing again: and a nation is not governed, which is perpetually to be conquered. *Ib.*

Nothing less will content me, than *whole America*. *Ib.*

Abstract liberty, like other mere abstractions, is not to be found. *Ib.*

All protestantism, even the most cold and passive, is a sort of dissent. But the religion most prevalent in our northern colonies is a refinement on the principle of resistance: it is the dissidence of dissent, and the protestantism of the Protestant religion. *Ib.*

In no country perhaps in the world is the law so general a study. . . . This study renders men acute, inquisitive, dexterous, prompt in attack, ready in defence, full of resources. . . . They augur misgovernment at a distance, and snuff the approach of tyranny in every tainted breeze. *Ib.*

The mysterious virtue of wax and parchment. *Ib.*

I do not know the method of drawing up an indictment against an whole people. *Ib.*

It is not, what a lawyer tells me I *may* do; but what humanity, reason, and justice, tell me I ought to do. *Ib.*

Govern two millions of men, impatient of servitude, on the principles of freedom. *Ib.*

I am not determining a point of law; I am restoring tranquillity. *Ib.*

The march of the human mind is slow. *Ib.*

Freedom and not servitude is the cure of anarchy; as religion, and not atheism, is the true remedy for superstition. *Ib.*

Instead of a standing revenue, you will have therefore a perpetual quarrel. *Ib.*

Slavery they can have anywhere. It is a weed that grows in every soil.
Conciliation with America, 1775.

Deny them this participation of freedom, and you break that sole bond, which originally made, and must still preserve the unity of the empire. *Ib.*

It is the love of the people; it is their attachment to their government, from the sense of the deep stake they have in such a glorious institution, which gives you your army and your navy, and infuses into both that liberal obedience, without which your army would be a base rabble, and your navy nothing but rotten timber. *Ib.*

Magnanimity in politics is not seldom the truest wisdom; and a great empire and little minds go ill together. *Ib.*

By adverting to the dignity of this high calling, our ancestors have turned a savage wilderness into a glorious empire: and have made the most extensive, and the only honourable conquests, not by destroying, but by promoting the wealth, the number, the happiness of the human race. *Ib.*

The people never give up their liberties but under some delusion.
Speech at County Meeting of Bucks, 1784.

Corrupt influence, which is itself the perennial spring of all prodigality, and of all disorder; which loads us more than millions of debt; which takes away vigour from our arms, wisdom from our councils, and every shadow of authority and credit from the most venerable parts of our constitution.
Speech on the Economical Reform, 1780.

Individuals pass like shadows; but the commonwealth is fixed and stable. *Ib.*

The people are the masters. *Ib.*

A rapacious and licentious soldiery.
Speech on Fox's East India Bill, 1783.

He has put to hazard his ease, his security, his interest, his power, even his darling popularity, for the benefit of a people whom he has never seen. *Ib.*

What the greatest inquest of the nation has begun, its highest Tribunal [the British House of Commons] will accomplish.
Impeachment of Warren Hastings, 15 Feb. 1788.

Religious persecution may shield itself under the guise of a mistaken and over-zealous piety.
Ib. 17 Feb. 1788.

An event has happened, upon which it is difficult to speak, and impossible to be silent.
Ib. 5 May 1789.

Resolved to die in the last dyke of prevarication.
Ib. 7 May 1789.

There is but one law for all, namely, that law which governs all law, the law of our Creator, the law of humanity, justice, equity—the law of nature, and of nations. *Ib. 28 May 1794.*

I impeach him in the name of the people of India, whose rights he has trodden under foot, and whose country he has turned into a desert. Lastly, in the name of human nature itself, in the name of both sexes, in the name of every age, in the name of every rank, I impeach the common enemy and oppressor of all!
Impeachment of Warren Hastings, as recorded by Macaulay in his essay on Warren Hastings.

His virtues were his arts.
Inscription on the statue of the Marquis of Rockingham in Wentworth Park.

The greater the power, the more dangerous the abuse.
Speech on the Middlesex Election, 1771.

It is not a predilection to mean, sordid, home-bred cares, that will avert the consequences of a false estimation of our interest, or prevent the shameful dilapidation, into which a great empire must fall, by mean reparations upon mighty ruins.
Speech on the Nabob of Arcot's Debts.

Old religious factions are volcanoes burnt out.
Speech on the Petition of the Unitarians, 1792.

Dangers by being despised grow great. *Ib.*

To complain of the age we live in, to murmur at the present possessors of power, to lament the past, to conceive extravagant hopes of the future, are the common dispositions of the greatest part of mankind.
Thoughts on the Cause of the Present Discontents.

The power of the crown, almost dead and rotten as Prerogative, has grown up anew, with much more strength, and far less odium, under the name of Influence. *Ib.*

The wisdom of our ancestors. *Ib.*

When bad men combine, the good must associate; else they will fall, one by one, an unpitied sacrifice in a contemptible struggle. *Ib.*

Of this stamp is the cant of *Not men, but measures*; a sort of charm by which many people get loose from every honourable engagement. *Ib.*

There is, however, a limit at which forbearance ceases to be a virtue.
Observations on a Publication, 'The present state of the nation'.

Well stored with pious frauds, and, like most discourses of the sort, much better calculated for the private advantage of the preacher than the edification of the hearers. *Ib.*

It is a general popular error to imagine the loudest complainers for the public to be the most anxious for its welfare. *Ib.*

I flatter myself that I love a manly, moral, regulated liberty as well as any gentleman.
Reflections on the Revolution in France.

Whenever our neighbour's house is on fire, it cannot be amiss for the engines to play a little on our own. *Ib.*

Politics and the pulpit are terms that have little agreement. No sound ought to be heard in the church but the healing voice of Christian charity. . . . Surely the church is a place where one day's truce ought to be allowed to the dissensions and animosities of mankind. *Ib.*

A state without the means of some change is without the means of its conservation. *Ib.*

Make the Revolution a parent of settlement, and not a nursery of future revolutions. *Ib.*

The confused jargon of their Babylonian pulpits. *Ib.*

People will not look forward to posterity, who never look backward to their ancestors. *Ib.*

Government is a contrivance of human wisdom to provide for human *wants*. Men have a right that these wants should be provided for by this wisdom. *Ib.*

It is now sixteen or seventeen years since I saw the Queen of France, then the Dauphiness, at Versailles; and surely never lighted on this orb, which she hardly seemed to touch, a more delightful vision. I saw her just above the horizon, decorating and cheering the elevated sphere she just began to move in,—glittering like the morning star, full of life, and splendour, and joy. . . . Little did I dream that I should have lived to see disasters fallen upon her in a nation of gallant men, in a nation of men of honour, and of cavaliers. I thought ten thousand swords must have leaped from their scabbards to avenge even a look that threatened her with insult. But the age of chivalry is gone. That of sophisters, economists, and calculators, has succeeded; and the glory of Europe is extinguished for ever. *Ib.*

The unbought grace of life, the cheap defence of nations, the nurse of manly sentiment and heroic enterprise is gone! *Ib.*

It is gone, that sensibility of principle, that chastity of honour, which felt a stain like a wound. *Ib.*

Vice itself lost half its evil, by losing all its grossness. *Ib.*

The offspring of cold hearts and muddy understandings. *Ib.*

In the groves of *their* academy, at the end of every visto, you see nothing but the gallows. *Ib.*

Kings will be tyrants from policy, when subjects are rebels from principle. *Ib.*

Learning will be cast into the mire, and trodden down under the hoofs of a swinish multitude. *Ib.*

France has always more or less influenced manners in England: and when your fountain is choked up and polluted, the stream will not run long, or will not run clear with us, or perhaps with any nation. *Ib.*

Because half a dozen grasshoppers under a fern make the field ring with their importunate chink, whilst thousands of great cattle, reposed beneath the shadow of the British oak, chew the cud and are silent, pray do not imagine that those who make the noise are the only inhabitants of the field; that of course, they are many in number; or that, after all, they are other than the little, shrivelled, meagre, hopping, though loud and troublesome *insects* of the hour. *Ib.*

Who now reads Bolingbroke? Who ever read him through? Ask the booksellers of London what is become of all these lights of the world. *Ib.*

Man is by his constitution a religious animal. *Ib.*

A perfect democracy is therefore the most shameless thing in the world. *Ib.*

The men of England, the men, I mean, of light and leading in England. *Ib.*

Nobility is a graceful ornament to the civil order. It is the Corinthian capital of polished society. *Ib.*

Superstition is the religion of feeble minds. *Ib.*

He that wrestles with us strengthens our nerves, and sharpens our skill. Our antagonist is our helper. *Ib.*

Our patience will achieve more than our force. *Ib.*

Good order is the foundation of all good things. *Ib.*

The delicate and refined play of the imagination. *On the Sublime and Beautiful*, introduction.

I am convinced that we have a degree of delight, and that no small one, in the real misfortunes and pains of others. *Ib.* pt. i, § xiv.

No passion so effectually robs the mind of all its powers of acting and reasoning as fear. *Ib.* pt. ii, § ii.

Custom reconciles us to everything. *Ib.* pt. iv, § xviii.

Laws, like houses, lean on one another. *Tracts on the Popery Laws*, ch. 3, pt. i.

In all forms of Government the people is the true legislator. *Ib.*

And having looked to government for bread, on the very first scarcity they will turn and bite the hand that fed them. *Thoughts and Details on Scarcity.*

The writers against religion, whilst they oppose every system, are wisely careful never to set up any of their own. *A Vindication of Natural Society*, preface.

The fabric of superstition has in our age and nation received much ruder shocks than it had ever felt before; and through the chinks and breaches of our prison we see such glimmerings of light, and feel such refreshing airs of liberty, as daily raise our ardour for more. *A Vindication of Natural Society.*

A good parson once said, that where mystery begins, religion ends. Cannot I say, as truly at least, of human laws, that where mystery begins, justice ends? *Ib.*

The lucrative business of mystery. *Ib.*

The only infallible criterion of wisdom to vulgar judgments—success. *Letter to a Member of the National Assembly.*

Those who have been once intoxicated with power, and have derived any kind of emolument from it, even though but for one year, can never willingly abandon it. *Ib.*

Cromwell was a man in whom ambition had not wholly suppressed, but only suspended the sentiments of religion. *Ib.*

Tyrants seldom want pretexts. *Ib.*

You can never plan the future by the past. *Ib.*

To innovate is not to reform. *A Letter to a Noble Lord, 1796.*

These gentle historians, on the contrary, dip their pens in nothing but the milk of human kindness.
Ib.

The king, and his faithful subjects, the lords and commons of this realm,—the triple cord, which no man can break. *Ib.*

The coquetry of public opinion, which has her caprices, and must have her way.
Letter to Thos. Burgh, New Year's Day, 1780.

The arrogance of age must submit to be taught by youth. *Letter to Fanny Burney, 29 July 1782.*

People crushed by law have no hopes but from power. If laws are their enemies, they will be enemies to laws; and those, who have much to hope and nothing to lose, will always be dangerous, more or less. *Letter to the Hon. C. J. Fox, 8 Oct. 1777.*

The grand Instructor, Time.
Letter to Sir H. Langrishe, 26 May 1795.

All men that are ruined are ruined on the side of their natural propensities.
Letters on a Regicide Peace, letter 1.

Example is the school of mankind, and they will learn at no other. *Ib.*

Never, no, never, did Nature say one thing and Wisdom say another. *Ib. No. 3.*

Well is it known that ambition can creep as well as soar. *Ib.*

I know many have been taught to think, that moderation, in a case like this, is a sort of treason.
Letter to the Sheriffs of Bristol.

Between craft and credulity, the voice of reason is stifled. *Ib.*

If any ask me what a free government is, I answer, that for any practical purpose, it is what the people think so. *Ib.*

Liberty, too, must be limited in order to be possessed.
Ib.

Nothing in progression can rest on its original plan. We may as well think of rocking a grown man in the cradle of an infant. *Ib.*

Among a people generally corrupt, liberty cannot long exist. *Ib.*

Nothing is so fatal to religion as indifference, which is, at least, half infidelity.
Letter to Wm. Smith, 29 Jan. 1795.

The silent touches of time. *Ib.*

Somebody has said, that a king may make a nobleman, but he cannot make a gentleman. *Ib.*

Not merely a chip of the old 'block', but the old block itself. *On Pitt's First Speech, 1781.*

Mr. Burke observed that Johnson had been very great that night; Mr. Langton . . . could have wished to hear more from another person; (plainly intimating that he meant Mr. Burke). 'O, no (said Mr. Burke), it is enough for me to have rung the bell to him.' *Boswell's Johnson, vol. iv, p. 26.*

'No, no,' said he, 'it is not a good imitation of Johnson; it has all his pomp, without his force; it has all the nodosities of the oak without its strength; it has all the contortions of the Sybil without the inspiration.'
Remark to Boswell who had spoken of Croft's 'Life of Dr. Young' as a good imitation of Johnson's style. Boswell's Life of Johnson, vol. iv, p. 59.

WILLIAM CECIL, LORD BURLEIGH

1520–1598

What! all this for a song?
To Queen Elizabeth (when ordered to give £100 to Spenser for some poems). Birch, Life of Spenser, p. xiii.

SIR FRANCIS COWLEY BURNAND

1836–1917

It's no matter what you do
If your heart be only true,
And his heart *was* true to Poll.   *True to Poll.*

FANNY BURNEY
(Mme D'ARBLAY)

1752–1840

In the bosom of her respectable family resided Camilla. *Camilla, bk. i, ch. 1.*

Travelling is the ruin of all happiness! There's no looking at a building here after seeing Italy. [Mr. Meadows.] *Cecilia, ed. 1904, bk. iv, ch. 2.*

'True, very true, ma'am,' said he [Mr. Meadows], yawning, 'one really lives no where; one does but vegetate, and wish it all at an end.'
Ib. bk. vii, ch. 5.

Indeed, the freedom with which Dr. Johnson condemns whatever he disapproves is astonishing.
Diary, 23 Aug. 1778.

All the delusive seduction of martial music.
Ib. Ce 4 florial, 1802.

'Do you come to the play without knowing what it is?' [Mr. Lovel]. 'O yes, Sir, yes, very frequently: I have no time to read play-bills; one merely comes to meet one's friends, and show that one's alive.'
Evelina, letter 20.

ROBERT BURNS

1759–1796

O thou! whatever title suit thee,
Auld Hornie, Satan, Nick, or Clootie.
Address to the Deil.

But fare you weel, auld Nickie-ben!
O wad ye tak a thought an' men'!
Ye aiblins might—I dinna ken—
        Still hae a stake:
I'm wae to think upo' yon den,
        Ev'n for your sake!   *Ib.*

Ye're aiblins nae temptation.
                    Address To the Unco Guid.

Then gently scan your brother man,
    Still gentler sister woman;
Tho' they may gang a kennin wrang,
    To step aside is human.   *Ib.*

Then at the balance let's be mute,
    We never can adjust it;
What's done we partly may compute,
    But know not what's resisted.   *Ib.*

Ae fond kiss, and then we sever.   *Ae Fond Kiss.*

But to see her was to love her,
Love but her, and love for ever.   *Ib.*

Had we never lov'd sae kindly,
Had we never lov'd sae blindly,
Never met—or never parted,
We had ne'er been broken-hearted.   *Ib.*

Should auld acquaintance be forgot,
    And never brought to mind?   *Auld Lang Syne.*

We twa hae run about the braes,
    And pu'd the gowans fine.   *Ib.*

We'll tak' a right gude-willie waught
    For auld lang syne.   *Ib.*

We'll tak a cup o' kindness yet,
    For auld lang syne.   *Ib.*

And there's a hand, my trusty fiere,
    And gie's a hand o' thine.   *Ib.*

But tell me whisky's name in Greek,
        I'll tell the reason.
        The Author's Earnest Cry and Prayer, xxx.

Freedom and Whisky gang thegither!   *Ib.* xxxi.

Sleep I can get nane
    For thinking on my dearie.   *Ay Waukin O.*

The poor inhabitant below
Was quick to learn and wise to know,
And keenly felt the friendly glow,
        And softer flame;
But thoughtless follies laid him low,
        And stain'd his name!   *A Bard's Epitaph.*

Know prudent cautious self-control
        Is wisdom's root.   *Ib.*

Come, Firm Resolve, take thou the van,
Thou stalk o' carl-hemp in man!
And let us mind, faint heart ne'er wan
A lady fair;
Wha does the utmost that he can,
Will whyles do mair.   *To Dr. Blacklock.*

To make a happy fire-side clime
    To weans and wife,
That's the true pathos and sublime
    Of human life.   *Ib.*

But aye the tear comes in my ee,
To think on him that's far awa.
        The Bonnie Lad that's far awa.

O saw ye bonnie Lesley
    As she gaed o'er the border?
She's gane, like Alexander,
    To spread her conquests farther.
To see her is to love her,
    And love but her for ever,
For Nature made her what she is,
    And ne'er made anither!   *Bonnie Lesley.*

The Deil he could na scaith thee,
    Or aught that wad belang thee;
He'd look into thy bonnie face,
    And say, 'I canna wrang thee'.   *Ib.*

Bonnie wee thing, cannie wee thing,
    Lovely wee thing, wert thou mine,
I wad wear thee in my bosom,
    Lest my jewel it should tine.
                    The Bonnie Wee Thing.

Your poor narrow foot-path of a street,
Where twa wheel-barrows tremble when they meet.
                    The Brigs of Ayr.

Hark! the mavis' evening sang
Sounding Clouden's woods amang;
Then a-faulding let us gang,
    My bonnie dearie.   *Ca' the Yowes.*

She draiglet a' her petticoatie,
    Coming through the rye
        Coming through the Rye (taken from an old
song, *The Bob-tailed Lass.*)

Gin a body meet a body
    Coming through the rye;
Gin a body kiss a body
    Need a body cry?   *Ib.*

Contented wi' little and cantie wi' mair.
                    Contented wi' Little.

Th' expectant wee-things, toddlin', stacher through
    To meet their Dad, wi' flichterin' noise an' glee.
His wee bit ingle, blinkin bonnilie,
    His clean hearth-stane, his thrifty wifie's smile,
The lisping infant prattling on his knee,
    Does a' his weary kiaugh and care beguile,
An' makes him quite forget his labour an' his toil.
                    The Cotter's Saturday Night, iii.

The mother, wi' her needle an' her sheers,
Gars auld claes look amaist as weel's the new. *Ib.* v.

They never sought in vain that sought the Lord
    aright!   *Ib.* vi.

A wretch, a villain, lost to love and truth.   *Ib.*

The halesome parritch, chief of Scotia's food.
                                        Ib. xi.

He wales a portion with judicious care,
And 'Let us worship God!' he says with solemn air.
                                        Ib. xii.

From scenes like these old Scotia's grandeur springs,
    That makes her loved at home, revered abroad:
Princes and lords are but the breath of kings,
    'An honest man's the noblest work of God.' *Ib.* xix.

Ev'n ministers, they hae been kenn'd,
        In holy rapture,
A rousing whid at times to vend,
        And nail't wi' Scripture.
                    Death and Dr. Hornbook, i.

I wasna fou, but just had plenty.   *Ib*. iii.

The auld kirk-hammer strak the bell
Some wee short hour ayont the twal.   *Ib* xxxi.

On ev'ry hand it will allow'd be,
He's just—nae better than he should be.
A Dedication to Gavin Hamilton, l. 25.

The De'il's Awa' Wi' the Exciseman.   *Title of Song.*

But Facts are chiels that winna ding,
    An' downa be disputed.   *A Dream.*

Yet aft a ragged cowt's been known
    To mak a noble aiver.   *Ib.*

Duncan Gray cam here to woo,
    Ha, ha, the wooing o't,
On blithe Yule-nicht when we were fou,
    Ha, ha, the wooing o't.
Maggie coost her head fu' high,
Look'd asklent and unco skeigh,
Gart poor Duncan stand abeigh;
    Ha, ha, the wooing o't.   *Duncan Gray.*

Meg was deaf as Ailsa Craig,
    Ha, ha, the wooing o't,
Duncan sighed baith out and in,
Grat his een baith bleer't and blin',
Spak o' lowpin o'er a linn;
    Ha, ha, the wooing o't.   *Ib.*

How it comes let doctors tell,
    Ha, ha, the wooing o't,
Meg grew sick as he grew haill,
    Ha, ha, the wooing o't.   *Ib.*

A Gentleman who held the patent for his honours
immediately from Almighty God.
Elegy on Capt. Matthew Henderson: from the title.

Perhaps it may turn out a sang,
    Perhaps turn out a sermon.
Epistle to a Young Friend, 1786.

But still keep something to yoursel
Ye scarcely tell to ony.   *Ib.*

I wa[i]ve the quantum o' the sin,
    The hazard of concealing;
But och; it hardens a' within,
    And petrifies the feeling!   *Ib.*

An atheist laugh's a poor exchange
    For Deity offended.   *Ib.*

And may ye better reck the rede
Than ever did th' adviser!   *Ib.*

The heart aye's the part aye
That makes us right or wrang.   *Epistle to Davie.*

What's a' your jargon o' your schools,
Your Latin names for horns and stools;
If honest Nature made you fools,
        What sairs your grammars?
First Epistle to John Lapraik.

Gie me ae spark o' Nature's fire,
That's a' the learning I desire.   *Ib.*

For thus the royal mandate ran,
When first the human race began,
'The social, friendly, honest man,
        Whate'er he be,
'Tis he fulfils great Nature's plan,
        And none but he!'
Second Epistle to Lapraik.

My barmie noddle's working prime.
Epistle to James Smith.

Some rhyme a neebor's name to lash;
Some rhyme (vain thought!) for needfu' cash;
Some rhyme to court the country clash,
        An' raise a din;
For me, an aim I never fash;
        I rhyme for fun.   *Ib.*

Farewell dear, deluding Woman,
The joy of joys!   *Ib.*

Flow gently, sweet Afton, among thy green braes,
Flow gently, I'll sing thee a song in thy praise.
My Mary's asleep by thy murmuring stream,
Flow gently, sweet Afton, disturb not her dream.
Flow gently, sweet Afton.

The rank is but the guinea's stamp;
    The man's the gowd for a' that!
For a' that and a' that.
A man's a man for a' that.   *Ib.*

A prince can mak a belted knight,
    A marquis, duke, and a' that;
But an honest man's aboon his might,
    Guid faith he mauna fa' that!   *Ib.*

    It's coming yet, for a' that,
That man to man the warld o'er
    Shall brothers be for a' that.   *Ib.*

My heart is sair, I daur na tell,
My heart is sair for Somebody.
For the Sake of Somebody.

There's Death in the cup—so beware!
On a Goblet.

Go fetch to me a pint o' wine,
An' fill it in a silver tassie.   *Go Fetch to Me a Pint.*

    Green grow the rashes O,
    Green grow the rashes O;
The sweetest hours that e'er I spend,
    Are spent amang the lasses O!

    There's nought but care on ev'ry han',
    In ev'ry hour that passes O;
What signifies the life o' man,
    An' 'twere na for the lasses O.
Green Grow the Rashes.

But gie me a canny hour at e'en,
    My arms about my dearie O;
An' warly cares, an' warly men,
    May a' gae tapsalteerie O!   *Ib.*

The wisest man the warl' saw,
    He dearly lov'd the lasses O.   *Ib.*

Auld nature swears, the lovely dears
    Her noblest work she classes O;
Her prentice han' she tried on man,
    An' then she made the lasses O.   *Ib.*

That I for poor auld Scotland's sake,
Some usefu' plan or beuk could make,
Or sing a sang at least.
To the Guidwife of Wauchope-House.

Fair fa' your honest sonsie face,
Great chieftain o' the puddin'-race!
Aboon them a' ye tak your place,
        Painch, tripe, or thairm:
Weel are ye wordy o' a grace
        As lang's my arm.   *To a Haggis.*

His spindle shank a guid whip-lash,
His nieve a nit.   *Ib.*

It's guid to be merry and wise,
It's guid to be honest and true,
It's guid to support Caledonia's cause,
And bide by the buff and the blue.
                    Here's a Health to Them that's Awa'.

O, gie me the lass that has acres o' charms,
O, gie me the lass wi' the weel-stockit farms.
                    Hey for a Lass wi' a Tocher.

Then hey, for a lass wi' a tocher—
The nice yellow guineas for me!   *Ib.*

The golden hours on angel wings
Flew o'er me and my dearie;
For dear to me as light and life
Was my sweet Highland Mary.
                    Highland Mary.

But oh! fell death's untimely frost,
That nipt my flower sae early!   *Ib.*

Here some are thinkin' on their sins,
An' some upo' their claes.   *The Holy Fair,* x.

Leeze me on drink! it gi'es us mair
Than either school or college.   *Ib.* xix.

There's some are fou o' love divine,
There's some are fou o' brandy.   *Ib.* xxvii.

I hae a wife o' my ain.   *I Hae a Wife o' My Ain.*

Naebody cares for me,
I care for naebody.   *Ib.*

It was a' for our rightfu' King
We left fair Scotland's strand.
                    It was a' for our Rightfu' King.

Now a' is done that men can do,
And a' is done in vain.   *Ib.*

He turn'd him right and round about
Upon the Irish shore;
And gae his bridle-reins a shake,
With adieu for evermore, My dear,
Adieu for evermore.   *Ib.*

John Anderson my jo, John,
When we were first acquent,
Your locks were like the raven,
Your bonny brow was brent.
                    John Anderson My Jo.

John Anderson my jo, John,
We clamb the hill thegither;
And mony a canty day, John,
We've had wi' ane anither:
Now we maun totter down, John,
And hand in hand we'll go,
And sleep thegither at the foot,
John Anderson, my jo.   *Ib.*

Partly wi' love o'ercome sae sair,
And partly she was drunk.
                    The Jolly Beggars, l. 221.

Their tricks an' craft hae put me daft,
They've ta'en me in, an' a' that,
But clear your decks, an' 'here's the Sex!'
I like the jads for a' that.   *Ib.* l. 266.

A fig for those by law protected!
Liberty's a glorious feast!
Courts for cowards were erected,
Churches built to please the priest.   *Ib.* l. 292.

Life is all a variorum,
We regard not how it goes;
Let them cant about decorum
Who have characters to lose.   *Ib.* l. 308.

As cauld a wind as ever blew,
A caulder kirk, and in't but few;
A caulder preacher never spak;—
Ye'se a' be het ere I come back.
                    The Kirk of Lamington.

I've seen sae mony changefu' years,
On earth I am a stranger grown;
I wander in the ways of men,
Alike unknowing and unknown.
                    Lament for James, Earl of Glencairn.

The mother may forget the child
That smiles sae sweetly on her knee;
But I'll remember thee, Glencairn,
And a' that thou hast done for me.   *Ib.*

O had she been a country maid,
And I the happy country swain.
                    The Lass of Ballochmyle.

When o'er the hill the eastern star
Tells bughtin-time is near, my jo;

I'll meet thee on the lea-rig,
My ain kind dearie O.   *The Lea-Rig.*

True it is, she had one failing,
Had a woman ever less?
                    Lines written under the Picture of Miss Burns

Ha! whare ye gaun, ye crowlin' ferlie!
Your impudence protects you sairly:
I canna say but ye strunt rarely,
Owre gauze and lace;
Tho' faith! I fear ye dine but sparely
On sic a place.   *To a Louse.*

O wad some Pow'r the giftie gie us
To see oursels as others see us!
It wad frae mony a blunder free us,
And foolish notion.   *Ib*

Their sighin', cantin', grace-proud faces,
Their three-mile prayers, and half-mile graces.
                    To the Rev. John M'Math.

May coward shame distain his name,
The wretch that dares not die!
                    Macpherson's Farewell.

Nature's law,
That man was made to mourn.
                    Man was made to Mourn.

Man's inhumanity to man
Makes countless thousands mourn!   *Ib.*

O Death, the poor man's dearest friend,
The kindest and the best!   *Ib.*

Thou lingering star, with lessening ray,
That lov'st to greet the early morn,
Again thou usherest in the day
My Mary from my soul was torn.
                    To Mary in Heaven.

Time but the impression deeper makes,
As streams their channels deeper wear.   *Ib.*

I sigh'd, and said amang them a',
'Ye are na Mary Morison.'   *Mary Morison.*

Wee modest crimson-tippèd flow'r.
> *To a Mountain Daisy.*

Ev'n thou who mourn'st the Daisy's fate,
That fate is thine—no distant date;
Stern Ruin's ploughshare drives elate
    Full on thy bloom,
Till crush'd beneath the furrow's weight
    Shall be thy doom!   *Ib.*

Wee, sleekit, cow'rin, tim'rous beastie,
O what a panic's in thy breastie!
> *To a Mouse.*

I'm truly sorry Man's dominion
Has broken Nature's social union,
An' justifies th' ill opinion
    Which makes thee startle
At me, thy poor, earth-born companion
An' fellow-mortal!   *Ib.*

The best laid schemes o' mice an' men
    Gang aft a-gley.   *Ib.*

My heart's in the Highlands, my heart is not here;
My heart's in the Highlands a-chasing the deer;
Chasing the wild deer, and following the roe,
My heart's in the Highlands, wherever I go.
> *My Heart's in the Highlands.*

O, my Luve's like a red red rose
    That's newly sprung in June:
Oh my Luve's like the melodie
    That's sweetly play'd in tune.
> *My Love is like a Red Red Rose.*

The minister kiss'd the fiddler's wife,
An' could na preach for thinkin' o't.
> *My Love she's but a Lassie yet.*

She is a winsome wee thing,
She is a handsome wee thing,
She is a lo'esome wee thing,
    This sweet wee wife o'mine.
> *My Wife's a Winsome Wee Thing.*

Of a' the airts the wind can blaw,
I dearly like the west.   *Of a' the Airts.*

If there's another world, he lives in bliss;
If there's none, he made the best of this.
> *On a Friend. Epitaph on Wm. Muir.*

He ne'er was gi'en to great misguidin',
Yet coin his pouches wad na bide in.
> *On a Scotch Bard.*

Hear, Land o' Cakes, and brither Scots.
> *On Captain Grose's Peregrinations.*

If there's a hole in a' your coats,
    I rede you tent it:
A chield's amang you taking notes,
    And, faith, he'll prent it.   *Ib.*

He has a fouth o' auld nick-nackets.   *Ib.*

An idiot race to honour lost,
Who know them best, despise them most.
> *On Seeing Stirling Palace in Ruins.*

O, wert thou in the cauld blast,
    On yonder lea, on yonder lea,
My plaidie to the angry airt,
    I'd shelter thee, I'd shelter thee.
> *O, Wert Thou in the Cauld Blast.*

Thy bield should be my bosom,
To share it a', to share it a'.   *Ib.*

Or were I in the wildest waste,
    Sae black and bare, sae black and bare,
The desert were a paradise,
    If thou wert there, if thou wert there.   *Ib.*

The teeth o' Time may gnaw Tantallan,
    But thou's for ever!   *To Pastoral Poetry.*

The mair they talk I'm kent the better.
> *E'en Let Them Clash.*

O Luve will venture in, where it daur na weel be
    seen.   *The Posie.*

And I will pu' the pink, the emblem o' my dear,
For she's the pink o' womankind, and blooms with-
    out a peer.   *Ib.*

It's aye the cheapest lawyer's fee,
    To taste the barrel.   *Scotch Drink.*

Scots, wha hae wi' Wallace bled,
Scots, wham Bruce has aften led,
Welcome to your gory bed,
    Or to victorie.
Now's the day, and now's the hour;
See the front o' battle lour!
See approach proud Edward's power—
    Chains and slaverie!   *Scots, Wha Hae.*

Liberty's in every blow!
    Let us do or die!   *Ib.*

Some hae meat, and canna eat,
    And some wad eat that want it;
But we hae meat and we can eat,
    And sae the Lord be thankit.
> *The Selkirk Grace. As attributed to Burns.*

The Muse, nae poet ever fand her,
Till by himself he learned to wander
Adown some trotting burn's meander,
        An' no think lang;
> *To William Simpson.*

Good Lord, what is man! for as simple he looks,
Do but try to develop his hooks and his crooks,
With his depths and his shallows, his good and his
    evil,
All in all, he's a problem must puzzle the devil.
> *Sketch: inscribed to C. J. Fox.*

Tho' poor in gear, we're rich in love.
> *The Soldier's Return.*

Whare sits our sulky sullen dame,
Gathering her brows like gathering storm,
Nursing her wrath to keep it warm.
> *Tam o'Shanter*, l. 10.

Auld Ayr, wham ne'er a town surpasses
For honest men and bonnie lasses.   *Ib.* l. 15.

Ah, gentle dames! it gars me greet
To think how mony counsels sweet,
How mony lengthen'd sage advices,
The husband frae the wife despises!   *Ib.* l. 33.

His ancient, trusty, drouthy crony;
Tam lo'ed him like a vera brither;
They had been fou for weeks thegither.   *Ib.* l. 43.

Kings may be blest, but Tam was glorious,
O'er a' the ills o' life victorious!   *Ib.* l. 57.

But pleasures are like poppies spread—
You seize the flow'r, its bloom is shed;
Or like the snow falls in the river—
A moment white—then melts for ever.   *Ib.* l. 59.

Nae man can tether time or tide.   *Ib.* l. 67.

That hour, o' night's black arch the key-stane.
        Ib. l. 69.

Inspiring bold John Barleycorn!
What dangers thou canst make us scorn!
Wi' tippenny, we fear nae evil;
Wi' usquebae, we'll face the devil!   *Ib.* l. 105.

The mirth and fun grew fast and furious. *Ib.* l. 143.

But Tam kent what was what fu' brawlie. *Ib.* l. 163.

Ah, Tam! ah, Tam! thou'll get thy fairin'!
In hell they'll roast thee like a herrin'! *Ib.* l. 201.

He'll hae misfortunes great and sma',
But aye a heart aboon them a';   *There was a Lad.*

A man may drink and no be drunk;
   A man may fight and no be slain;
A man may kiss a bonnie lass,
   And aye be welcome back again.
       There was a Lass, they ca'd her Meg.

We labour soon, we labour late,
   To feed the titled knave, man,
And a' the comfort we're to get,
   Is that ayont the grave, man.
      The Tree of Liberty, attributed to Burns.

His lockèd, lettered, braw brass collar,
Shew'd him the gentleman and scholar.
        The Twa Dogs, l. 13.

The fient a pride na pride had he.   *Ib.* l. 16.

And there began a lang digression
About the lords of the creation.   *Ib.* l. 45.

But human bodies are sic fools,
For a' their colleges and schools,
That when nae real ills perplex them,
They mak enow themsels to vex them.   *Ib.* l. 195.

But hear their absent thoughts o' ither,
They're a' run deils an' jads thegither.   *Ib.* l. 221.

Rejoiced they were na men but dogs.   *Ib.* l. 236.

Up in the morning's no' for me,
Up in the morning early.   *Up in the Morning.*

Misled by fancy's meteor ray,
   By passion driven;
But yet the light that led astray
   Was light from Heaven.
       The Vision, Duan ii, xviii.

What can a young lassie, what shall a young lassie,
What can a young lassie do wi' an auld man?
       What can a Young Lassie.

And then his auld brass 'ill buy me a new pan. *Ib.*

O whistle, and I'll come to you, my lad:
O, whistle, and I'll come to you, my lad:
Tho' father and mither and a' should gae mad,
O whistle, and I'll come to you, my lad.
     Whistle, and I'll come to you, my Lad.

Now we're married—speir nae mair—
   Whistle owre the lave o't.
       Whistle owre the lave o't.

We are na that fou, we're nae that fou,
But just a drappie in our ee.
      Willie Brewed a Peck o' Maut.

It is the moon, I ken her horn,
   That's blinkin' in the lift sae hie;
She shines sae bright to wyle us hame,
   But, by my sooth! she'll wait a wee.   *Ib.*

Sic a wife as Willie had,
I wad na gie a button for her!   *Willie's Wife.*

Her nose and chin they threaten ither.   *Ib.*

Her face wad fyle the Logan-water.   *Ib.*

The heart benevolent and kind
   The most resembles God.   *A Winter Night.*

Ye banks and braes o' bonny Doon,
   How can ye bloom sae fresh and fair?
How can ye chant, ye little birds,
   And I sae weary fu' o' care?
      Ye Banks and Braes o' Bonny Doon.

Thou minds me o' departed joys,
Departed never to return.   *Ib.*

And ilka bird sang of its love,
   And fondly sae did I o' mine.   *Ib.*

And my fause lover stole my rose,
But ah! he left the thorn wi' me.   *Ib.*

'Don't let the awkward squad fire over me.'
    *A. Cunningham's Works of Burns; with his
    Life,* 1834, vol. i, p. 344.

JEREMIAH BURROUGHS
1599–1646

We use to say, it's a woman's reason to say, I will do
   such a thing, because I will do it.
       On Hosea, vol. iv, p. 80.

BENJAMIN HAPGOOD BURT

When you're all dressed up and no place to go.
       Title of Song.

HENRY BURTON
fl. 1886

Have you had a kindness shown?
   Pass it on!
'Twas not given for thee alone,
   Pass it on!
Let it travel down the years,
Let it wipe another's tears,
Till in Heaven the deed appears—
   Pass it on!   *Pass It On.*

JOHN BURTON
1773–?

Holy Bible, Book divine,
Precious treasure, thou art mine;
Mine to teach me whence I came,
Mine to teach me what I am.
      Holy Bible, Book Divine.

ROBERT BURTON

1577–1640

All my joys to this are folly,
Naught so sweet as Melancholy.
Anatomy of Melancholy. Author's Abstract of Melancholy.

They lard their lean books with the fat of others' works. *Ib. Democritus to the Reader.*

We can say nothing but what hath been said. . . . Our poets steal from Homer. . . . Divines use Austin's words *verbatim* still, and our story-dressers do as much, he that comes last is commonly best. *Ib.*

I had not time to lick it into form, as she [a bear] doth her young ones. *Ib.*

Like watermen, that row one way and look another. *Ib.*

Him that makes shoes go barefoot himself. *Ib.*

All poets are mad. *Ib.*

A loose, plain, rude writer. *Ib.*

Cookery is become an art, a noble science: cooks are gentlemen. *Ib. pt. i, § 2, memb. 2, subsect. 2.*

No rule is so general, which admits not some exception. *Ib. subsect. 3.*

Die to save charges. *Ib. memb. 3. subsect. 12.*

I may not here omit those two main plagues, and common dotages of human kind, wine and women, which have infatuated and besotted myriads of people. They go commonly together. *Ib. subsect. 13.*

Hinc quam sit calamus sævior ense patet. [From this it is clear how much the pen is worse than the sword.] *Ib. memb. 4, subsect. 4.*

One was never married, and that's his hell; another is, and that's his plague. *Ib. memb. 4, subsect. 7.*

[Fabricius] finds certain spots and clouds in the sun. *Ib. pt. ii, § 2, memb. 3.*

Seneca thinks he takes delight in seeing thee. The gods are well pleased when they see great men contending with adversity. *Ib. § 3, memb. 1, subsect. 1.*

Every thing, saith Epictetus, hath two handles, the one to be held by, the other not. *Ib. memb. 3.*

Who cannot give good counsel? 'tis cheap, it costs them nothing. *Ib.*

What is a ship but a prison? *Ib. memb. 4.*

All places are distant from Heaven alike. *Ib.*

The Commonwealth of Venice in their armoury have this inscription, 'Happy is that city which in time of peace thinks of war.' *Ib. memb. 6.*

Tobacco, divine, rare, superexcellent tobacco, which goes far beyond all their panaceas, potable gold, and philosopher's stones, a sovereign remedy to all diseases. . . . But, as it is commonly abused by most men, which take it as tinkers do ale, 'tis a plague, a mischief, a violent purger of goods, lands, health, hellish, devilish, and damned tobacco, the ruin and overthrow of body and soul. *Ib. § 4, memb. 2, subsect. 1.*

Let me not live, saith Aretine's Antonia, if I had not rather hear thy discourse than see a play! *Ib. pt. iii, § 1, memb. 1, subsect. 1.*

And this is that Homer's golden chain, which reacheth down from Heaven to earth, by which every creature is annexed, and depends on his Creator. *Ib. subsect. 2.*

To enlarge or illustrate this—is to set a candle in the sun. *Ib. § ii, memb. 1, subsect. 2.*

Cornelia kept her in talk till her children came from school, and these, said she, are my jewels. *Ib. memb. 2, subsect. 3.*

To these crocodile's tears, they will add sobs, fiery sighs, and sorrowful countenance. *Ib. subsect. 4.*

Diogenes struck the father when the son swore. *Ib*

England is a paradise for women, and hell for horses: Italy a paradise for horses, hell for women, as the diverb goes. *Ib. § 3, memb. 1, subsect. 2.*

The miller sees not all the water that goes by his mill. *Ib. memb. 4, subsect. 1.*

The fear of some divine and supreme powers, keeps men in obedience. *Ib. § 4, memb. 1, subsect. 2.*

One religion is as true as another. *Ib. memb. 2, subsect. 1.*

JOSEPH BUTLER

1692–1752

Things and actions are what they are, and the consequences of them will be what they will be: why then should we desire to be deceived? *Fifteen Sermons.* No. 7, § 16.

SAMUEL BUTLER

1612–1680

When civil fury first grew high,
And men fell out they knew not why.
Hudibras, pt. i, c. 1, l. 1.

And pulpit, drum ecclesiastic,
Was beat with fist, instead of a stick. *Ib.* l. 11.

Beside, 'tis known he could speak Greek,
As naturally as pigs squeak:
That Latin was no more difficile,
Than to a black-bird 'tis to whistle. *Ib.* l. 51.

He was in logic a great critic,
Profoundly skill'd in analytic.
He could distinguish, and divide
A hair 'twixt south and south-west side.
On either which he would dispute,
Confute, change hands, and still confute. *Ib.* l. 65.

He'd run in debt by disputation,
And pay with ratiocination. *Ib.* l. 77.

For rhetoric he could not ope
His mouth, but out there flew a trope. *Ib.* l. 81.

For all a rhetorician's rules
Teach nothing but to name his tools. *Ib.* l. 89.

A Babylonish dialect
Which learned pedants much affect.   *Ib.* l. 93.

For he, by geometric scale,
Could take the size of pots of ale; . . .
And wisely tell what hour o' th' day
The clock doth strike, by algebra.   *Ib.* l. 121.

Beside, he was a shrewd philosopher,
And had read ev'ry text and gloss over.   *Ib.* l. 127.

What ever sceptic could inquire for;
For every why he had a wherefore.   *Ib.* l. 131.

He knew what's what, and that's as high
As metaphysic wit can fly.   *Ib.* l. 149.

Such as take lodgings in a head
That's to be let unfurnished.   *Ib.* l. 160.

He could raise scruples dark and nice,
And after solve 'em in a trice:
As if Divinity had catch'd
The itch, of purpose to be scratch'd.   *Ib.* l. 163.

'T was Presbyterian true blue.   *Ib.* l. 189.

Such as do build their faith upon
The holy text of pike and gun.   *Ib.* l. 193.

And prove their doctrine orthodox
By apostolic blows and knocks.   *Ib.* l. 197.

And still be doing, never done:
As if Religion were intended
For nothing else but to be mended.   *Ib.* l. 202.

Compound for sins, they are inclin'd to
By damning those they have no mind to.   *Ib.* l. 213.

The trenchant blade, Toledo trusty,
For want of fighting was grown rusty,
And eat into it self, for lack
Of some body to hew and hack.   *Ib.* l. 357.

For rhyme the rudder is of verses,
With which like ships they steer their courses.
   Ib. l. 457.

He ne'er consider'd it, as loth
To look a gift-horse in the mouth.   *Ib.* l. 483.

Quoth Hudibras, I smell a rat;
Ralpho, thou dost prevaricate.   *Ib.* l. 815.

Great actions are not always true sons
Of great and mighty resolutions.   *Ib.* l. 885.

There was an ancient sage philosopher,
That had read Alexander Ross over.   *Ib.* c. 2, l. 1.

Through perils both of wind and limb,
Through thick and thin she follow'd him.   *Ib.*

And bid the devil take the hin'most.   *Ib.* l. 633.

Ay me! what perils do environ
The man that meddles with cold iron!   *Ib.* c. 3, l. 1.

    I'll make the fur
Fly 'bout the ears of the old cur.   *Ib.* l. 277.

These reasons made his mouth to water.   *Ib.* l. 379.

Then while the honour thou hast got
Is spick and span-new, piping hot.   *Ib.* l. 398.

And though th' art of a different church,
I will not leave thee in the lurch.   *Ib.* l. 763.

He that is down can fall no lower.   *Ib.* l. 878.

Cheer'd up himself with ends of verse,
And sayings of philosophers.   *Ib.* l. 1011.

Cleric before, and Lay behind;
A lawless linsy-woolsy brother,
Half of one order, half another.   *Ib.* l. 1226.

Learning that cobweb of the brain,
Profane, erroneous, and vain.   *Ib.* l. 1339.

For nothing goes for sense, or light,
That will not with old rules jump right;
As if rules were not in the schools
Derived from truth, but truth from rules.   *Ib.* l. 1353.

Quoth Hudibras, Friend Ralph, thou hast
Outrun the constable at last.   *Ib.* l. 1367.

Some force whole regions, in despite
O' geography, to change their site:
Make former times shake hands with latter,
And that which was before, come after.
   Ib. pt. ii, c. 1, l. 23.

Not by your individual whiskers,
But by your dialect and discourse.   *Ib.* l. 155.

Some have been beaten till they know
What wood a cudgel's of by th' blow;
Some kick'd, until they can feel whether
A shoe be Spanish or neats-leather.   *Ib.* l. 221.

Such great achievements cannot fail,
To cast salt on a woman's tail.   *Ib.* l. 277.

Quoth she, I've heard old cunning stagers
Say, Fools for arguments use wagers.   *Ib.* l. 297.

She that with poetry is won
Is but a desk to write upon.   *Ib.* l. 591.

Love is a boy, by poets styl'd,
Then spare the rod, and spoil the child.   *Ib.* l. 844.

The sun had long since in the lap
Of Thetis, taken out his nap,
And like a lobster boil'd, the morn
From black to red began to turn.   *Ib.* c. 2, l. 29.

And after many circumstances,
Which vulgar authors in romances
Do use to spend their time and wits on,
To make impertinent description.   *Ib.* l. 41.

Have always been at daggers-drawing,
And one another clapper-clawing.   *Ib.* l. 79.

Oaths are but words, and words but wind.
   Ib. l. 107.

For saints may do the same things by
The Spirit, in sincerity,
Which other men are tempted to.   *Ib.* l. 235.

     As the ancients
Say wisely, Have a care o' th' main chance,
And look before you ere you leap;
For, as you sow, you are like to reap.   *Ib.* l. 501.

Doubtless the pleasure is as great
Of being cheated, as to cheat.
As lookers-on feel most delight,
That least perceive a juggler's sleight,
And still the less they understand,
The more th' admire his sleight of hand.
   Ib. c. 3, l. 1.

He made an instrument to know
If the moon shine at full or no.   *Ib.* l. 261.

And fire a mine in China, here,
With sympathetic gunpowder.
Hudibras, pt. ii, c. 3, l. 295.

To swallow gudgeons ere th'are catch'd,
And count their chickens ere th'are hatch'd.
Ib. l. 923.

T'enforce a desperate amour.
Ib. pt. iii, c. 1, l. 2.

Still amorous, and fond, and billing,
Like Philip and Mary on a shilling.   *Ib.* l. 687.

For in what stupid age or nation
Was marriage ever out of fashion?   *Ib.* l. 817.

Discords make the sweetest airs.   *Ib.* l. 919.

What makes all doctrines plain and clear?
About two hundred pounds a year.
And that which was prov'd true before,
Prove false again? Two hundred more.   *Ib.* l. 1277.

With crosses, relics, crucifixes,
Beads, pictures, rosaries, and pixes,
The tools of working out salvation
By mere mechanic operation.   *Ib.* l. 1495.

The saints engage in fierce contests
About their carnal interests.   *Ib.* c. 2, introd.

Although there's nothing lost nor won,
The public business is undone.   *Ib.* l. 159.

Neither have the hearts to stay,
Nor wit enough to run away.   *Ib.* l. 569.

For if it be but half denied,
'Tis half as good as justified.   *Ib.* l. 803.

For, those that fly, may fight again,
Which he can never do that's slain.   *Ib.* c. 3, l. 243.

He that complies against his will,
Is of his own opinion still.   *Ib.* l. 547.

For Justice, though she's painted blind,
Is to the weaker side inclin'd.   *Ib.* l. 709.

For money has a power above
The stars, and Fate, to manage love;
Whose arrows learned poets hold,
That never miss, are tipp'd with gold.
Ib. l. 1279.

And counted *breaking Priscian's head* a thing
More capital than to behead a king.
Genuine Remains: Satire on the Imperfection of Human Learning, pt. 2, l. 149.

The best of all our actions tend
To the preposterousest end.
Ib. Satire upon the Weakness and Misery of Man, l. 41.

The greatest saints and sinners have been made
The proselytes of one another's trade.
Miscellaneous Thoughts.

All love at first, like generous wine,
Ferments and frets until 'tis fine;
But when 'tis settled on the lee,
And from th' impurer matter free,
Becomes the richer still the older,
And proves the pleasanter the colder.   *Ib.*

The souls of women are so small,
That some believe they've none at all.   *Ib.*

The law can take a purse in open court,
While it condemns a less delinquent for't.   *Ib.*

For trouts are tickled best in muddy water.
On a Hypocritical Nonconformist, iv.

SAMUEL BUTLER

1835–1902

A wound in the solicitor is a very serious thing.
The Humour of Homer. Ramblings in Cheapside.

I keep my books at the British Museum and at Mudie's.   *Ib.*

The most perfect humour and irony is generally quite unconscious.   *Life and Habit*, ch. 2.

Life is one long process of getting tired.
Note Books. Life, vii.

Life is the art of drawing sufficient conclusions from insufficient premises.   *Ib.* ix.

All progress is based upon a universal innate desire on the part of every organism to live beyond its income.   *Ib.* xvi.

When the righteous man turneth away from his righteousness that he hath committed and doeth that which is neither quite lawful nor quite right, he will generally be found to have gained in amiability what he has lost in holiness.
Ib. Elementary Morality. Counsels of Imperfection.

It costs a lot of money to die comfortably.
Ib. A Luxurious Death.

The healthy stomach is nothing if not conservative. Few radicals have good digestions.
Ib. Mind and Matter. Indigestion.

The history of art is the history of revivals.
Ib. Handel and Music. Anachronism.

Though wisdom cannot be gotten for gold, still less can it be gotten without it. Gold, or the value of that is equivalent to gold, lies at the root of wisdom, and enters so largely into the very essence of the Holy Ghost that 'no gold, no Holy Ghost' may pass as an axiom.
Ib. Cash and Credit. Modern Simony.

Genius . . . has been defined as a supreme capacity for taking trouble. . . . It might be more fitly described as a supreme capacity for getting its possessors into trouble of all kinds and keeping them therein so long as the genius remains.
Ib. Genius, i.

The phrase 'unconscious humour' is the one contribution I have made to the current literature of the day.
Ib. The Position of a Homo Unius Libri. Myself and 'Unconscious Humour'.

We were saying what a delightful dispensation of providence it was that prosperous people will write their memoirs. We hoped Tennyson was writing his (1890).
P.S. We think his son has done nearly as well (1898).
Ib. The Enfant Terrible of Literature.

An apology for the Devil: It must be remembered that we have only heard one side of the case. God has written all the books.
Ib. Higgledy-Piggledy. An Apology for the Devil

God is Love, I dare say. But what a mischievous devil Love is.   *Ib. God is Love.*

To live is like love, all reason is against it, and all healthy instinct for it.   *Ib. Life and Love.*

The public buys its opinions as it buys its meat, or takes in its milk, on the principle that it is cheaper to do this than to keep a cow. So it is, but the milk is more likely to be watered.
    Ib. Material for a Projected Sequel to Alps and Sanctuaries. Public Opinion.

I do not mind lying, but I hate inaccuracy.
    Ib. Truth and Convenience. Falsehood, iv.

The world will, in the end, follow only those who have despised as well as served it.
    Ib. Life of the World to Come. The World.

An honest God's the noblest work of man.
    Further Extracts from the Note-Books (1934), p. 26.

Dulce et decorum est desipere in loco.
    Ib. p. 92. [Horace, *Odes*, III. ii. 14, and IV. xii. 28.]

Jesus! with all thy faults I love thee still.   *Ib.* p. 117.

'Tis better to have loved and lost, than never to have lost at all.   *The Way of All Flesh*, ch. 77.

Oh God! Oh Montreal!   *Psalm of Montreal.*

Preferrest thou the gospel of Montreal to the gospel of Hellas,
The gospel of thy connexion with Mr. Spurgeon's haberdasher to the gospel of the Discobolus?
Yet none the less hath he blasphemed beauty saying,
'The Discobolus hath no gospel,
But my brother-in-law is haberdasher to Mr. Spurgeon.'   *Ib.*

Yet meet we shall, and part, and meet again,
Where dead men meet on lips of living men.
    Poems. Life after Death.

I would not be—not quite—so pure as you.
    Ib. A Prayer.

WILLIAM BUTLER
1535–1618

'Doubtless God could have made a better berry [strawberry], but doubtless God never did.'
    Walton, Compleat Angler, pt. i, ch. 5.

JOHN BYROM
1692–1763

Some say, that Signor Bononchini,
Compar'd to Handel's a mere ninny;
Others aver, to him, that Handel
Is scarcely fit to hold a candle.
Strange! that such high dispute shou'd be
'Twixt Tweedledum and Tweedledee.
    Epigram on the Feuds between Handel and Bononcini.

I shall prove it—as clear as a whistle.
    Epistle to Lloyd, I. xii.

    When you find
Bright passages that strike your mind.

And which perhaps you may have reason
To think on at another season,—
—Take them down in black and white.
    Hint to a Young Person.

Christians awake, salute the happy morn,
Whereon the Saviour of the world was born.
    Hymn for Christmas Day.

But now she is gone, and has left me behind,
What a marvellous change on a sudden I find!
When things were as fine as could possibly be,
I thought 'twas the spring; but alas! it was she.
    Pastoral.

God bless the King, I mean the Faith's Defender;
God bless—no harm in blessing—the Pretender;
But who Pretender is, or who is King,
God bless us all—that's quite another thing.
    To an Officer in the Army.

GEORGE GORDON NOEL BYRON, LORD BYRON
1788–1824

The 'good old times'—all times when old are good—
Are gone.   *The Age of Bronze*, i.

For what were all these country patriots born?
To hunt, and vote, and raise the price of corn?
    Ib. xiv.

Year after year they voted cent. per cent.,
Blood, sweat, and tear-wrung millions—why? for rent!   *Ib.*

Woe is me, Alhama!   *Siege and Conquest of Alhama*, i.

And thou art dead, as young and fair
    As aught of mortal birth.
    And Thou Art Dead.

And wilt thou weep when I am low?
    And Wilt Thou Weep?

Just like a coffin clapt in a canoe [gondola].
    Beppo, xix.

In short, he was a perfect cavaliero,
And to his very valet seem'd a hero.   *Ib.* xxxiii.

His heart was one of those which most enamour us,
Wax to receive, and marble to retain.   *Ib.* xxxiv.

Besides, they always smell of bread and butter.
    Ib. xxxix.

One hates an author that's *all author*, fellows
In foolscap uniforms turn'd up with ink.
    Ib. lxxv.

I am ashes where once I was fire.
    To the Countess of Blessington.

Know ye the land where the cypress and myrtle
    Are emblems of deeds that are done in their clime?
Where the rage of the vulture, the love of the turtle,
    Now melt into sorrow, now madden to crime!
    Bride of Abydos, c. I. i.

Where the virgins are soft as the roses they twine,
And all, save the spirit of man, is divine?   *Ib.*

Mark! where his carnage and his conquests cease!
He makes a solitude, and calls it—peace!
    Ib. c. II. xx.

Hark! to the hurried question of Despair:
'Where is my child?'—an echo answers—
      'Where?'   *Ib.* xxvii.

Adieu, adieu! my native shore
    Fades o'er the waters blue.
          Childe Harold, c. I. xiii.

My native land—Good Night!   *Ib.* xiii.

In Biscay's sleepless bay.   *Ib.* xiv.

Here all were noble, save Nobility.   *Ib.* lxxxv.

War, war is still the cry, 'War even to the knife!'
                      Ib. lxxxvi.

A schoolboy's tale, the wonder of an hour! *Ib.* c. II. ii.

The dome of Thought, the palace of the Soul. *Ib.* vi.

Well didst thou speak, Athena's wisest son!
'All that we know is, nothing can be known.' *Ib.* vii.

Ah! happy years! once more who would not be a boy?
                      Ib. xxiii.

None are so desolate but something dear,
    Dearer than self, possesses or possess'd
A thought, and claims the homage of a tear. *Ib.* xxiv.

    The joys and sorrows sailors find,
Coop'd in their winged sea-girt citadel.   *Ib.* xxviii.

Fair Greece! sad relic of departed worth!
Immortal, though no more; though fallen, great!
                      Ib. lxxiii.

Hereditary bondsmen! know ye not
Who would be free themselves must strike the blow?
                      Ib. lxxvi.

Where'er we tread 'tis haunted, holy ground.
                      Ib. lxxxviii.

What is the worst of woes that wait on age?
    What stamps the wrinkle deeper on the brow?
To view each loved one blotted from life's page,
    And be alone on earth, as I am now.   *Ib.* xcviii.

Ada! sole daughter of my house and heart. *Ib.* c. III. i.

Once more upon the waters! yet once more!
And the waves bound beneath me as a steed
That knows his rider.   *Ib.* ii.

        Years steal
Fire from the mind as vigour from the limb;
And life's enchanted cup but sparkles near the brim.
                      Ib. viii.

Stop!—for thy tread is on an Empire's dust!
An earthquake's spoil is sepulchred below! *Ib.* xvii.

And is this all the world has gain'd by thee,
Thou first and last of fields! king-making Victory?
                      Ib.

There was a sound of revelry by night,
    And Belgium's capital had gather'd then
Her beauty and her chivalry, and bright
    The lamps shone o'er fair women and brave men;
A thousand hearts beat happily; and when
    Music arose with its voluptuous swell,
Soft eyes look'd love to eyes which spake again,
    And all went merry as a marriage bell;
But hush! hark! a deep sound strikes like a rising knell!
                      Ib. xxi.

Did ye not hear it?—No; 'twas but the wind,
    Or the car rattling o'er the stony street;
On with the dance! let joy be unconfined;
    No sleep till morn, when Youth and Pleasure meet
To chase the glowing Hours with flying feet.
                      Ib. xxii.

Arm! Arm! it is—it is—the cannon's opening roar!
                      Ib. xxii.

Within a window'd niche of that high hall
Sate Brunswick's fated chieftain.   *Ib.* xxiii.

He rush'd into the field, and foremost fighting, fell.
                      Ib.

And there was mounting in hot haste.   *Ib.* xxv.

    Swiftly forming in the ranks of war;
And the deep thunder peal on peal afar.   *Ib.*

Or whispering, with white lips—'The foe! they come!
they come!'   *Ib.*

Grieving, if aught inanimate e'er grieves,
Over the unreturning brave,—alas!   *Ib.* xxvii.

Burning with high hope shall moulder cold and low.
                      Ib.

Battle's magnificently stern array!   *Ib.* xxviii.

Rider and horse,—friend, foe,—in one red burial
blent!   *Ib.*

Bright names will hallow song.   *Ib.* xxix.

The tree will wither long before it fall.   *Ib.* xxxii.

Like to the apples on the Dead Sea's shore,
All ashes to the taste.   *Ib.* xxxiv.

There sunk the greatest, nor the worst of men,
Whose spirit, antithetically mixt,
One moment of the mightiest, and again
On little objects with like firmness fixt [Napoleon].
                      Ib. xxxvi.

That untaught innate philosophy.   *Ib.* xxxix.

Quiet to quick bosoms is a hell.   *Ib.* xlii.

The castled crag of Drachenfels
Frowns o'er the wide and winding Rhine.   *Ib.* lv.

But these are deeds which should not pass away,
And names that must not wither.   *Ib.* lxvii.

Lake Leman woos me with its crystal face.
                      Ib. lxviii.

To fly from, need not be to hate, mankind. *Ib.* lxix.

I live not in myself, but I become
Portion of that around me; and to me
High mountains are a feeling, but the hum
Of human cities torture.   *Ib.* lxxii.

The self-torturing sophist, wild Rousseau. *Ib.* lxxvii.

        Exhausting thought,
And hiving wisdom with each studious year. *Ib.* cvii.

Sapping a solemn creed with solemn sneer.   *Ib.*

I have not loved the world, nor the world me;
    I have not flatter'd its rank breath, nor bow'd
To its idolatries a patient knee.   *Ib.* cxiii.

        I stood
Among them, but not of them; in a shroud
Of thoughts which were not their thoughts.   *Ib.*

I stood in Venice, on the Bridge of Sighs;
A palace and a prison on each hand.
Childe Harold, c. IV. i.

Where Venice sate in state, throned on her hundred
isles! *Ib.*

The spouseless Adriatic mourns her lord. *Ib.* xi.

Oh for one hour of blind old Dandolo!
Th' octogenarian chief, Byzantium's conquering foe.
Ib. xii.

The moon is up, and yet it is not night;
Sunset divides the sky with her; a sea
Of glory streams along the Alpine height
Of blue Friuli's mountains; Heaven is free
From clouds, but of all colours seems to be,—
Melted to one vast Iris of the West,—
Where the day joins the past Eternity. *Ib.* xxvii.

The Ariosto of the North [Scott]. *Ib.* xl.

Italia! oh Italia! thou who hast
The fatal gift of beauty. *Ib.* xlii.

Let these describe the undescribable. *Ib.* liii.

Love watching Madness with unalterable mien.
Ib. lxxii.

Then farewell, Horace; whom I hated so,
Not for thy faults, but mine. *Ib.* lxxvii.

Oh Rome! my country! city of the soul! *Ib.* lxxviii.

The Niobe of nations! there she stands,
Childless and crownless, in her voiceless woe.
Ib. lxxix.

Yet, Freedom! yet thy banner, torn, but flying,
Streams like the thunder-storm *against* the wind.
Ib. xcviii.

Thou wert a beautiful thought, and softly bodied
forth. *Ib.* cxv.

Alas! our young affections run to waste,
Or water but the desert. *Ib.* cxx.

Of its own beauty is the mind diseased. *Ib.* cxxii.

Time, the avenger! *Ib.* cxxx.

The arena swims around him—he is gone,
Ere ceased the inhuman shout which hail'd the wretch
who won. *Ib.* cxl.

He heard it, but he heeded not—his eyes
Were with his heart, and that was far away;
He reck'd not of the life he lost nor prize,
But where his rude hut by the Danube lay,
There were his young barbarians all at play,
There was their Dacian mother—he, their sire,
Butcher'd to make a Roman holiday. *Ib.* cxli.

A ruin—yet what ruin! from its mass
Walls, palaces, half-cities, have been rear'd.
Ib. cxliii.

While stands the Coliseum, Rome shall stand;
When falls the Coliseum, Rome shall fall;
And when Rome falls—the World. *Ib.* cxlv.

Spared and blest by time;
Looking tranquillity. *Ib.* cxlvi.

The Lord of the unerring bow,
The God of life, and poesy, and light. *Ib.* clxi.

So young, so fair,
Good without effort, great without a foe. *Ib.* clxxii.

Oh! that the desert were my dwelling-place,
With one fair spirit for my minister. *Ib.* clxxvii.

There is a pleasure in the pathless woods,
There is a rapture on the lonely shore,
There is society, where none intrudes,
By the deep sea, and music in its roar:
I love not man the less, but Nature more,
From these our interviews, in which I steal
From all I may be, or have been before,
To mingle with the Universe, and feel
What I can ne'er express, yet cannot all conceal.
Ib. clxxviii.

Roll on, thou deep and dark blue Ocean—roll!
Ten thousand fleets sweep over thee in vain;
Man marks the earth with ruin—his control
Stops with the shore. *Ib.* clxxix.

He sinks into thy depths with bubbling groan,
Without a grave, unknell'd, uncoffin'd, and unknown.
Ib.

Time writes no wrinkle on thine azure brow:
Such as creation's dawn beheld, thou rollest now.
Ib. clxxxii.

Thou glorious mirror, where the Almighty's form
Glasses itself in tempests. *Ib.* clxxxiii.

Dark-heaving—boundless, endless, and sublime,
The image of eternity. *Ib.*

And I have loved thee, Ocean! and my joy
Of youthful sports was on thy breast to be
Borne, like thy bubbles, onward: from a boy
I wanton'd with thy breakers, . . .
And trusted to thy billows far and near,
And laid my hand upon thy mane—as I do here.
Ib. clxxxiv.

Eternal spirit of the chainless mind!
Sonnet on Chillon.

Chillon! thy prison is a holy place,
And thy sad floor an altar—for 'twas trod,
Until his very steps have left a trace
Worn, as if thy cold pavement were a sod,
By Bonnivard! May none those marks efface!
For they appeal from tyranny to God. *Ib.*

My hair is grey, but not with years,
Nor grew it white
In a single night,
As men's have grown from sudden fears.
The Prisoner of Chillon, i.

Regain'd my freedom with a sigh. *Ib.* xiv.

The comet of a season. *Churchill's Grave.*

The glory and the nothing of a name. *Ib.*

We were a gallant company,
Riding o'er land, and sailing o'er sea.
Oh! but we went merrily! *Siege of Corinth*, prologue.

Thus was Corinth lost and won! *Ib.* xxxiii.

The fatal facility of the octo-syllabic verse.
The Corsair, preface.

O'er the glad waters of the dark blue sea,
Our thoughts as boundless, and our souls as free.
Ib. I. i.

Such hath it been—shall be—beneath the sun
The many still must labour for the one. *Ib.* c. I. viii.

There was a laughing devil in his sneer.   *Ib.* ix.

The weak alone repent.   *Ib.* c. II. x.

Oh! too convincing—dangerously dear—
In woman's eye the unanswerable tear!   *Ib.* xv.

> She for him had given
Her all on earth, and more than all in heaven!
   Ib. c. III. xvii.

He left a Corsair's name to other times,
Link'd with one virtue, and a thousand crimes.
   Ib. xxiv.

Slow sinks, more lovely ere his race be run,
Along Morea's hills the setting sun;
Not, as in northern climes, obscurely bright,
But one unclouded blaze of living light.
   Curse of Minerva, I. I, and *The Corsair*, III. i.

I had a dream, which was not all a dream.
   Darkness.

I tell thee, be not rash; a golden bridge
Is for a flying enemy.
   The Deformed Transformed, pt. II, sc. ii.

Through life's road, so dim and dirty,
I have dragg'd to three-and-thirty.
What have these years left to me?
Nothing—except thirty-three.
   Diary, 21 Jan. 1821. In Moore's *Life of Byron*,
   vol. ii, p. 414 (1st ed.).

I wish he would explain his explanation.
   Don Juan, c. 1, dedication ii.

The intellectual eunuch Castlereagh.   *Ib.* xi.

My way is to begin with the beginning.   *Ib.* c. I, vii

In virtues nothing earthly could surpass her,
Save thine 'incomparable oil', Macassar!   *Ib.* xvii

But—Oh! ye lords of ladies intellectual,
Inform us truly, have they not hen-peck'd you all?
   Ib. xxii.

> She
Was married, charming, chaste, and twenty-three.
   Ib. lix.

Her stature tall—I hate a dumpy woman.   *Ib.* lxi.

What men call gallantry, and gods adultery,
Is much more common where the climate's sultry.
   Ib. lxiii.

Christians have burnt each other, quite persuaded
That all the Apostles would have done as they did.
   Ib. lxxxiii.

A little still she strove, and much repented,
And whispering 'I will ne'er consent'—consented.
   Ib. cxvii.

'Tis sweet to hear the watch-dog's honest bark
   Bay deep-mouth'd welcome as we draw near home;
'Tis sweet to know there is an eye will mark
   Our coming, and look brighter when we come.
   Ib. cxxiii.

Sweet is revenge—especially to women.   *Ib.* cxxiv.

Pleasure's a sin, and sometimes sin's a pleasure.
   Ib. cxxxiii.

Man's love is of man's life a thing apart,
'Tis woman's whole existence.   *Ib.* cxciv.

My grandmother's review—the British.   *Ib.* ccix.

So for a good old-gentlemanly vice,
I think I must take up with avarice.   *Ib.* ccxvi.

There's nought, no doubt, so much the spirit calms
   As rum and true religion.   *Ib.* c. II. xxxiv

'Twas twilight, and the sunless day went down
   Over the waste of waters.   *Ib.* xlix.

A solitary shriek, the bubbling cry
Of some strong swimmer in his agony.   *Ib.* liii.

> If this be true, indeed,
Some Christians have a comfortable creed. *Ib.* lxxxvi.

He could, perhaps, have pass'd the Hellespont,
As once (a feat on which ourselves we prided)
Leander, Mr. Ekenhead, and I did.   *Ib.* cv.

Let us have wine and women, mirth and laughter,
Sermons and soda-water the day after.   *Ib.* clxxviii.

Man, being reasonable, must get drunk;
The best of life is but intoxication.   *Ib.* clxxix.

Alas! they were so young, so beautiful,
So lonely, loving, helpless.   *Ib.* cxcii.

> A group that's quite antique,
Half naked, loving, natural, and Greek.   *Ib.* cxciv.

Alas! the love of women! it is known
To be a lovely and a fearful thing!   *Ib.* cxcix.

In her first passion woman loves her lover,
   In all the others all she loves is love. *Ib.* c. III. iii.

Romances paint at full length people's wooings,
   But only give a bust of marriages:
For no one cares for matrimonial cooings,
   There's nothing wrong in a connubial kiss:
Think you, if Laura had been Petrarch's wife,
He would have written sonnets all his life?   *Ib.* viii.

Dreading that climax of all human ills,
The inflammation of his weekly bills.   *Ib.* xxxv.

He was the mildest manner'd man
   That ever scuttled ship or cut a throat,
With such true breeding of a gentleman,
   You never could divine his real thought.
   Ib. xli.

But Shakspeare also says, 'tis very silly
'To gild refined gold, or paint the lily.'   *Ib.* lxxvi.

The isles of Greece, the isles of Greece!
   Where burning Sappho loved and sung,
Where grew the arts of war and peace,
   Where Delos rose, and Phœbus sprung!
Eternal summer gilds them yet,
But all, except their sun, is set.   *Ib.* lxxxvi. 1.

The mountains look on Marathon—
   And Marathon looks on the sea;
And musing there an hour alone,
   I dream'd that Greece might still be free.   *Ib.* 3.

A king sate on the rocky brow
   Which looks o'er sea-born Salamis;
And ships, by thousands, lay below,
   And men in nations;—all were his!
He counted them at break of day—
And when the sun set where were they?   *Ib.* 4.

Earth! render back from out thy breast
A remnant of our Spartan dead!
Of the three hundred grant but three,
To make a new Thermopylæ!   *Ib.* 7.

Fill high the cup with Samian wine!
Don Juan, c. III. lxxxvi. 9.

You have the Pyrrhic dance as yet;
  Where is the Pyrrhic phalanx gone!
Of two such lessons, why forget
  The nobler and the manlier one?
You have the letters Cadmus gave—
Think ye he meant them for a slave?   *Ib.* 10.

Place me on Sunium's marbled steep,
  Where nothing, save the waves and I,
May hear our mutual murmurs sweep;
  There, swan-like, let me sing and die:
A land of slaves shall ne'er be mine—
Dash down yon cup of Samian wine!   *Ib.* 16.

Milton's the prince of poets—so we say;
  A little heavy, but no less divine.   *Ib.* xci.

A drowsy frowzy poem, call'd the 'Excursion',
Writ in a manner which is my aversion.   *Ib.* xciv.

We learn from Horace, 'Homer sometimes sleeps';
We feel without him, Wordsworth sometimes wakes.
                             Ib. xcviii.

Ave Maria! 'tis the hour of prayer!
  Ave Maria! 'tis the hour of love!   *Ib.* ciii.

Imagination droops her pinion.   *Ib.* c. IV. iii.

And if I laugh at any mortal thing,
'Tis that I may not weep.   *Ib.* iv.

'Whom the gods love die young' was said of yore.
                              Ib. xii.

'Arcades ambo', *id est*—blackguards both. *Ib.* xciii.

I've stood upon Achilles' tomb,
And heard Troy doubted; time will doubt of Rome.
                              Ib. ci.

Oh! 'darkly, deeply, beautifully blue',
  As some one somewhere sings about the sky. *Ib.* cx.

When amatory poets sing their loves
  In liquid lines mellifluously bland,
And pair their rhymes as Venus yokes her doves.
                       Ib. c. V. i.

I have a passion for the name of 'Mary',
  For once it was a magic sound to me:
And still it half calls up the realms of fairy,
  Where I beheld what never was to be.   *Ib.* iv.

A lady in the case.   *Ib.* xix.

And put himself upon his good behaviour. *Ib.* xlvii.

That all-softening, overpowering knell,
The tocsin of the soul—the dinner-bell. *Ib.* xlix.

Not to admire is all the art I know.   *Ib.* ci.

Why don't they knead two virtuous souls for life
Into that moral centaur, man and wife? *Ib.* clviii.

There is a tide in the affairs of women,
  Which, taken at the flood, leads—God knows
  where.   *Ib.* c. VI. ii.

A lady of a 'certain age', which means
Certainly aged.   *Ib.* lxix.

A 'strange coincidence', to use a phrase
By which such things are settled now-a-days.
                       Ib. lxxviii.

'Let there be light!' said God, 'and there was light!'
'Let there be blood!' says man, and there's a sea!
                 Ib. c. VII. xli.

'Carnage, (so Wordsworth tells you), is God's
  daughter.'   *Ib.* c. VIII. ix.

Oh, Wellington! (or 'Villainton')—for Fame
Sounds the heroic syllables both ways. *Ib.* c. IX. i.

Call'd 'Saviour of the Nations'—not yet saved,
And 'Europe's Liberator'—still enslaved [Welling-
ton].   *Ib.* v.

Never had mortal man such opportunity,
Except Napoleon, or abused it more.   *Ib.* ix.

That water-land of Dutchmen and of ditches.
                    Ib. c. X. lxiii.

When Bishop Berkeley said 'there was no matter',
  And proved it—'twas no matter what he said.
                   Ib. c. XI. i.

But Tom's no more—and so no more of Tom.
                     Ib. xx.

And, after all, what is a lie? 'Tis but
  The truth in masquerade.   *Ib.* xxxvii.

  I—albeit I'm sure I did not know it,
Nor sought of foolscap subjects to be king.—
Was reckon'd, a considerable time,
The grand Napoleon of the realms of rhyme. *Ib.* lv.

But Juan was my Moscow, and Faliero
My Leipsic, and my Mont Saint Jean seems Cain.
                      Ib. lvi.

John Keats, who was kill'd off by one critique,
Just as he really promised something great,
If not intelligible, without Greek
Contrived to talk about the Gods of late,
Much as they might have been supposed to speak.
Poor fellow! His was an untoward fate;
'Tis strange the mind, that very fiery particle,
Should let itself be snuff'd out by an article. *Ib.* lx.

Nought's permanent among the human race,
Except the Whigs *not* getting into place. *Ib.* lxxxii.

Love rules the camp, the court, the grove—for love
Is heaven, and heaven is love.   *Ib.* c. XII. xiii.

And hold up to the sun my little taper. *Ib.* xxi.

For talk six times with the same single lady,
And you may get the wedding dresses ready. *Ib.* lix.

  Merely innocent flirtation,
Not quite adultery, but adulteration.   *Ib.* lxiii.

A Prince . . .
With fascination in his very bow.   *Ib.* lxxxiv.

A finish'd gentleman from top to toe.   *Ib.*

Beauteous, even where beauties most abound.
                    Ib. c. XIII. ii.

Now hatred is by far the longest pleasure;
Men love in haste, but they detest at leisure. *Ib.* vi.

Cervantes smiled Spain's chivalry away. *Ib.* xi.

I hate to hunt down a tired metaphor. *Ib.* xxxvi.

The English winter—ending in July,
  To recommence in August.   *Ib.* xlii.

Society is now one polish'd horde,
Form'd of two mighty tribes, the *Bores* and *Bored*.
                     Ib. xcv.

I for one venerate a petticoat.   *Ib.* c. XIV. xxvi.

Of all the horrid, hideous notes of woe,
  Sadder than owl-songs or the midnight blast,
Is that portentous phrase, 'I told you so.'
                                    Don Juan, c. XIV. 1.

'Tis strange—but true; for truth is always strange;
Stranger than fiction.   *Ib.* ci.

A lovely being, scarcely form'd or moulded,
A rose with all its sweetest leaves yet folded.
                                    Ib. c. xv. xliii.

The antique Persians taught three useful things,
To draw the bow, to ride, and speak the truth.
                                    Ib. c. XVI. i.

Not so her gracious, graceful, graceless Grace.
                                    Ib. xlix.

The loudest wit I e'er was deafen'd with.   *Ib.* lxxxi.

And both were young, and one was beautiful.
                                    The Dream, ii.

A change came o'er the spirit of my dream.   *Ib.* v.

Still must I hear?—shall hoarse Fitzgerald bawl
His creaking couplets in a tavern hall.
        English Bards and Scotch Reviewers.

        I'll publish, right or wrong:
Fools are my theme, let satire be my song.   *Ib.*

'Tis pleasant, sure, to see one's name in print;
A book's a book, although there's nothing in 't.   *Ib.*

A man must serve his time to every trade
Save censure—critics all are ready made.   *Ib.*

With just enough of learning to misquote.   *Ib.*

        As soon
Seek roses in December—ice in June;
Hope constancy in wind, or corn in chaff;
Believe a woman or an epitaph,
Or any other thing that's false, before
You trust in critics, who themselves are sore.   *Ib.*

Better to err with Pope, than shine with Pye.   *Ib.*

Sense and wit with poesy allied.   *Ib.*

Who both by precept and example, shows
That prose is verse, and verse is merely prose.   *Ib.*

Be warm, but pure: be amorous, but be chaste.   *Ib.*

Perverts the Prophets, and purloins the Psalms.   *Ib.*

Oh, Amos Cottle!—Phoebus! what a name
To fill the speaking trump of future fame!   *Ib.*

The petrifactions of a plodding brain.   *Ib.*

To sanction Vice, and hunt Decorum down.   *Ib.*

To live like Clodius, and like Falkland fall.   *Ib.*

Lords too are bards, such things at times befall,
And 'tis some praise in peers to write at all.   *Ib.*

Forsook the labours of a servile state,
Stemm'd the rude storm, and triumph'd over fate. *Ib.*

'Twas thine own genius gave the final blow,
And help'd to plant the wound that laid thee low:
So the struck eagle, stretch'd upon the plain,
No more through rolling clouds to soar again,
View'd his own feather on the fatal dart,
And wing'd the shaft that quiver'd in his heart;
Keen were his pangs, but keener far to feel
He nursed the pinion which impell'd the steel;

While the same plumage that had warm'd his nest
Drank the last life-drop of his bleeding breast.   *Ib.*

Yet Truth sometimes will lend her noblest fires,
And decorate the verse herself inspires:
This fact in Virtue's name let Crabbe attest;
Though nature's sternest painter, yet the best.   *Ib.*

That mighty master of unmeaning rhyme [Darwin].
                                    Ib.

Let simple Wordsworth chime his childish verse,
And brother Coleridge lull the babe at nurse.   *Ib.*

Glory, like the phoenix 'midst her fires,
Exhales her odours, blazes, and expires.   *Ib.*

I too can hunt a poetaster down.   *Ib.*

The world is a bundle of hay,
  Mankind are the asses who pull;
Each tugs it a different way,
  And the greatest of all is John Bull.   *Epigram.*

My sister! my sweet sister! if a name
Dearer and purer were, it should be thine.
                                    Epistle to Augusta.

And know, whatever thou hast been,
'Tis something better not to be.   *Euthanasia.*

Fare thee well! and if for ever,
  Still for ever, fare thee well.   *Fare Thee Well!*

I only know we loved in vain—
I only feel—Farewell!—Farewell!
                    Farewell! if ever Fondest Prayer.

Nor be, what man should ever be,
  The friend of Beauty in distress?   *To Florence.*

He who hath bent him o'er the dead
Ere the first day of death is fled,
The first dark day of nothingness,
The last of danger and distress,
(Before Decay's effacing fingers
Have swept the lines where beauty lingers).
                                    The Giaour, l. 68.

So fair, so calm, so softly seal'd,
The first, last look by death reveal'd!   *Ib.* l. 88.

Clime of the unforgotten brave!   *Ib.* l. 103.

For Freedom's battle once begun,
Bequeath'd by bleeding Sire to Son,
Though baffled oft is ever won.   *Ib.* l. 123.

Dark tree, still sad when others' grief is fled,
The only constant mourner o'er the dead [cypress]!
                                    Ib. l. 286.

And lovelier things have mercy shown
To every failing but their own,
And every woe a tear can claim
Except an erring sister's shame.   *Ib.* l. 418.

The harp the monarch minstrel swept.   *Title.*

Or lend fresh interest to a twice-told tale.
                        Hints from Horace, l. 184.

Friendship is Love without his wings!
                        Hours of Idleness. L'Amitié.

I have tasted the sweets and the bitters of love.
                        Ib. To Rev. J. T. Becher.

Though women are angels, yet wedlock's the devil.
Ib. To Eliza.

Then receive him as best such an advent becomes,
With a legion of cooks, and an army of slaves!
The Irish Avatar.

More happy, if less wise.   *The Island, c. II. xi.*

Jack was embarrassed—never hero more,
And as he knew not what to say, he swore.
Ib. c. IV. v.

Who killed John Keats?
  'I,' says the Quarterly,
    So savage and Tartarly;
  ''Twas one of my feats.'   *John Keats.*

Weep, daughter of a royal line.
Lines to a Lady Weeping.

Left by his sire, too young such loss to know,
Lord of himself—that heritage of woe.
Lara, c. I. ii.

His madness was not of the head, but heart.
Ib. xviii.

Maid of Athens, ere we part,
Give, oh give me back my heart!
Or, since that has left my breast,
Keep it now, and take the rest!   *Maid of Athens.*

Mont Blanc is the monarch of mountains;
  They crown'd him long ago
On a throne of rocks, in a robe of clouds,
  With a diadem of snow.   *Manfred, I. i.*

When the moon is on the wave,
And the glow-worm in the grass,
And the meteor on the grave,
And the wisp on the morass;
When the falling stars are shooting,
And the answer'd owls are hooting,
And the silent leaves are still
In the shadow of the hill.   *Ib.*

By that most seeming-virtuous eye.   *Ib.*

          The heart ran o'er
With silent worship of the great of old—
The dead but sceptred sovereigns, who still rule
Our spirits from their urns.   *Ib. III. iv.*

Old man! 'tis not so difficult to die.   *Ib.*

          You have deeply ventured;
But all must do so who would greatly win.
Marino Faliero, I. ii.

My boat is on the shore,
  And my bark is on the sea;
But, before I go, Tom Moore,
  Here's a double health to thee! *To Thomas Moore.*

Here's a sigh to those who love me,
  And a smile to those who hate;
And, whatever sky's above me,
  Here's a heart for every fate.   *Ib.*

My Murray.   *To Mr. Murray.*

There be none of Beauty's daughters
  With a magic like thee.
Stanzas for Music. 'There be none of Beauty's daughters.'

There's not a joy the world can give like that it takes
  away.   *Ib. 'There's not a joy the world can give.'*

'Tis done—but yesterday a King!
  And arm'd with Kings to strive—
And now thou art a nameless thing:
  So abject—yet alive! *Ode to Napoleon Bonaparte.*

The Arbiter of others' fate
A Suppliant for his own!   *Ib.*

The Cincinnatus of the West.   *Ib.*

But the poor dog, in life the firmest friend,
The first to welcome, foremost to defend.
Inscription on a Newfoundland Dog.

Oh! snatched away in beauty's bloom,
On thee shall press no ponderous tomb·
But on thy turf shall roses rear
Their leaves, the earliest of the year.
Oh! Snatched Away in Beauty's Bloom.

It is not in the storm nor in the strife
  We feel benumb'd, and wish to be no more,
  But in the after-silence on the shore,
When all is lost, except a little life.
On Hearing Lady Byron was Ill.

The moral Clytemnestra of thy lord.   *Ib.*

My days are in the yellow leaf;
  The flowers and fruits of love are gone;
The worm, the canker, and the grief
  Are mine alone!
On This Day I Complete my Thirty-Sixth Year.

Seek out—less often sought than found—
  A soldier's grave, for thee the best;
Then look around, and choose thy ground,
  And take thy rest.   *Ib.*

It is the hour when from the boughs
  The nightingale's high note is heard;
It is the hour when lovers' vows
  Seem sweet in every whisper'd word.   *Parisina.*

Yet in my lineaments they trace
Some features of my father's face.   *Ib.*

Thy Godlike crime was to be kind,
  To render with thy precepts less
  The sum of human wretchedness.   *Prometheus.*

Oh, talk not to me of a name great in story;
The days of our youth are the days of our glory;
And the myrtle and ivy of sweet two-and-twenty
Are worth all your laurels, though ever so plenty.
Stanzas Written on the Road between Florence and Pisa.

Oh Fame!—if I e'er took delight in thy praises,
'Twas less for the sake of thy high-sounding phrases,
Than to see the bright eyes of the dear one discover,
She thought that I was not unworthy to love her. *Ib.*

I knew it was love, and I felt it was glory.   *Ib.*

By all that's good and glorious take this counsel.
Sardanapalus, I. ii.

I am the very slave of circumstance
And impulse—borne away with every breath!
Ib. IV. i.

The Assyrian came down like the wolf on the fold,
And his cohorts were gleaming in purple and gold;
And the sheen of their spears was like stars on the sea,
When the blue wave rolls nightly on deep Galilee.

Destruction of Sennacherib.

For the Angel of Death spread his wings on the
blast. *Ib.*

And the might of the Gentile, unsmote by the sword,
Hath melted like snow in the glance of the Lord! *Ib.*

She walks in beauty, like the night
Of cloudless climes and starry skies;
And all that's best of dark and bright
Meet in her aspect and her eyes:
Thus mellow'd to that tender light
Which heaven to gaudy day denies.

Hebrew Melodies. She Walks in Beauty.

And on that cheek, and o'er that brow,
So soft, so calm, yet eloquent,
The smiles that win, the tints that glow
But tell of days in goodness spent,
A mind at peace with all below,
A heart whose love is innocent! *Ib.*

Born in the garret, in the kitchen bred,
Promoted thence to deck her mistress' head.

A Sketch.

So, we'll go no more a roving
So late into the night,
Though the heart be still as loving,
And the moon be still as bright.

So, We'll Go No More a Roving.

For the sword outwears its sheath,
And the soul wears out the breast.
And the heart must pause to breathe,
And love itself have rest. *Ib.*

Though the night was made for loving,
And the day returns too soon,
Yet we'll go no more a-roving
By the light of the moon. *Ib.*

Could Love for ever
Run like a river. *Stanzas.*

Part in friendship—and bid good-night. *Ib.*

Though the day of my destiny's over,
And the star of my fate hath declined.

Stanzas to Augusta.

In the desert a fountain is springing,
In the wide waste there still is a tree,
And a bird in the solitude singing,
Which speaks to my spirit of *thee.* *Ib.*

And Freedom hallows with her tread
The silent cities of the dead.

On the Star of 'The Legion of Honour'.

And when we think we lead, we are most led.

The Two Foscari, II. i.

The Mede is at his gate!
The Persian on his throne! *Vision of Belshazzar.*

Saint Peter sat by the celestial gate:
His keys were rusty, and the lock was dull.

Vision of Judgement i.

The angels all were singing out of tune,
And hoarse with having little else to do,
Excepting to wind up the sun and moon,
Or curb a runaway young star or two. *Ib.* ii.

A better farmer ne'er brushed dew from lawn,
A worse king never left a realm undone. *Ib.* viii.

'Midst them an old man
With an old soul, and both extremely blind. *Ib.* xxiii.

Yet still between his Darkness and his Brightness
There pass'd a mutual glance of great politeness.

Ib. xxxv.

The Archangel bow'd, not like a modern beau.

Ib. xxxvi.

Satan met his ancient friend
With more hauteur, as might an old Castilian
Poor noble meet a mushroom rich civilian. *Ib.*

And when the tumult dwindled to a calm,
I left him practising the hundredth psalm. *Ib.* cvi.

Seductive Waltz! *The Waltz.*

Voluptuous Waltz! *Ib.*

When we two parted
In silence and tears,
Half broken-hearted
To sever for years,
Pale grew thy cheek and cold,
Colder thy kiss. *When We Two Parted.*

If I should meet thee
After long years,
How should I greet thee?—
With silence and tears. *Ib.*

The fault was Nature's fault not thine,
Which made thee fickle as thou art.

To a Youthful Friend.

As he [Lord Byron] himself briefly described it in his
Memoranda, 'I awoke one morning and found
myself famous.'—Moore's *Life of Byron, 1830,*
vol. i, p. 347 (referring to the instantaneous success
of *Childe Harold*).

No *Manual,* no letters, no tooth-powder, no *extract*
from Moore's *Italy* concerning Marino Falieri, no
nothing—as a man hallooed out at one of Burdett's
elections, after a long ululatus of No Bastille! No
Governor Aris! No '— God knows what;—but his
ne plus ultra was, 'no nothing!'

Letter to Murray 4 June 1817.

HENRY JAMES BYRON

1834–1884

Life's too short for chess. *Our Boys, Act.* I.

He's up to these grand games, but one of these days
I'll loore him on to skittles—and astonish him.

Ib. Act. II.

JAMES BRANCH CABELL

1879-

I am willing to taste any drink once. *Jurgen*, ch. 1.

A man possesses nothing certainly save a brief loan of his own body: and yet the body of man is capable of much curious pleasure. *Ib.* ch. 20.

The optimist proclaims that we live in the best of all possible worlds; and the pessimist fears this is true. *The Silver Stallion*, bk. iv, ch. 26.

'CAESER'

Swanee, how I love you! how I love you!
My dear old Swanee. *Swanee.*

CHARLES STUART CALVERLEY

1831-1884

The auld wife sat at her ivied door,
  (*Butter and eggs and a pound of cheese*)
A thing she had frequently done before;
  And her spectacles lay on her apron'd knees.
  Ballad.

The farmer's daughter hath soft brown hair;
  (*Butter and eggs and a pound of cheese*)
And I met with a ballad, I can't say where,
  Which wholly consisted of lines like these. *Ib.*

And this song is consider'd a perfect gem,
  And as to the meaning, it's what you please. *Ib.*

O Beer! O Hodgson, Guinness, Allsopp, Bass!
Names that should be on every infant's tongue! *Beer.*

When 'Dulce est desipere in loco'
Was written, real Falernian winged the pen. *Ib.*

'Fate cannot touch me: I have dined to-day.' *Ib.*

I cannot sing the old songs now!
  It is not that I deem them low;
'Tis that I can't remember how
  They go. *Changed.*

Sikes, housebreaker, of Houndsditch,
  Habitually swore;
But so surpassingly profane
  He never was before. *Charades*, vi.

Aspect anything but bland. *Ib.*

You see this pebble-stone? It's a thing I bought
Of a bit of a chit of a boy i' the mid o' the day—
I like to dock the smaller parts-o'-speech,
As we curtail the already curtail'd cur
(You catch the paronomasia, play 'po' words?).
  The Cock and the Bull.

The basis or substratum—what you will—
Of the impending eighty thousand lines. *Ib.*

Donn'd galligaskins, antigropeloes. *Ib.*

Ombrifruge (Lord love you!), case o' rain. *Ib.*

A bare-legg'd beggarly son of a gun. *Ib.*

Fiddlepin's end! Get out, you blazing ass!
Gabble o' the goose. Don't bugaboo-baby *me*! *Ib.*

Pretty i' the Mantuan! *Ib.*

It takes up about eighty thousand lines,
A thing imagination boggles at:
And might, odds-bobs, sir! in judicious hands,
Extend from here to Mesopotamy. *Ib.*

Life is with such all beer and skittles;
They are not difficult to please
About their victuals. *Contentment.*

'Twas ever thus from childhood's hour!
  My fondest hopes would not decay:
I never loved a tree or flower
  Which was the first to fade away! *Disaster.*

For king-like rolls the Rhine,
And the scenery's divine,
And the victuals and the wine
  Rather good. *Dover to Munich.*

Forever! 'Tis a single word!
  Our rude forefathers deemed it two:
Can you imagine so absurd
  A view? *Forever.*

Wherefore bless ye, O beloved ones:—
  Now unto mine inn must I,
Your 'poor moraliɛ', betake me,
  In my 'solitary fly'. *'Hic Vir, Hic Est.'*

For I've read in many a novel that, unless they've souls that grovel,
Folks *prefer* in fact a hovel to your dreary marble halls. *In the Gloaming.*

Grinder, who serenely grindest
  At my door the Hundredth Psalm.
  Lines on Hearing the Organ.

Meaning, however, is no great matter.
  Lovers, and a Reflection.

Thro' the rare red heather we danced together,
  (O love my Willie!) and smelt for flowers:
I must mention again it was gorgeous weather,
  Rhymes are so scarce in this world of ours. *Ib.*

Study first propriety. *Of Propriety.*

How Eugene Aram, though a thief, a liar, and a murderer,
Yet, being intellectual, was amongst the noblest of mankind. *Of Reading.*

Thou, who when fears attack,
Bidst them avaunt, and Black
Care, at the horseman's back
  Perching, unseatest;
Sweet, when the morn is grey;
Sweet, when they've cleared away
Lunch; and at close of day
  Possibly sweetest. *Ode to Tobacco.*

I have a liking old
For thee, though manifold
Stories, I know, are told
  Not to thy credit. *Ib.*

How they who use fusees
All grow by slow degrees
Brainless as chimpanzees,
    Meagre as lizards:
Go mad, and beat their wives;
Plunge (after shocking lives)
Razors and carving knives
    Into their gizzards.   *Ode to Tobacco.*

Jones—(who, I'm glad to say,
Asked leave of Mrs. J.)—
Daily absorbs a clay
    After his labours.   *Ib.*

Cats may have had their goose
Cooked by tobacco-juice;
Still why deny its use
    Thoughtfully taken?
We're not as tabbies are:
Smith, take a fresh cigar!
Jones, the tobacco-jar!
    Here's to thee, Bacon!   *Ib.*

RICHARD OWEN CAMBRIDGE
1717–1802

What is the worth of anything,
But for the happiness 'twill bring?   *Learning*, 1. 23.

WILLIAM CAMDEN
1551–1623

My friend, judge not me,
Thou seest I judge not thee.
Betwixt the stirrup and the ground
Mercy I asked, mercy I found.
    *Remains. Epitaph for a Man Killed by Falling
            from His Horse.*

HERBERT CAMPBELL

Now we sha'n't be long.   *Title of Song.*

JANE MONTGOMERY CAMPBELL
1817–1878

We plough the fields, and scatter
The good seed on the land,
But it is fed and watered
By God's Almighty Hand;
He sends the snow in winter,
The warmth to swell the grain,
The breezes and the sunshine,
And soft refreshing rain.
All good gifts around us
Are sent from Heaven above,
Then thank the Lord, O thank the Lord,
For all His love.
    *We Plough the Fields. Tr. from the German.
            C. S. Bere's Garland of Songs.*

He paints the wayside flower,
He lights the evening star.   *Ib.*

THOMAS CAMPBELL
1777–1844

'Tis Lethe's gloom, but not its quiet,—
    The pain without the peace of death!   *Absence.*

Of Nelson and the North
Sing the glorious day's renown,
When to battle fierce came forth
All the might of Denmark's crown,
And her arms along the deep proudly shone,—
By each gun the lighted brand
In a bold determined hand;
And the Prince of all the land
Led them on.   *Battle of the Baltic.*

There was silence deep as death,
And the boldest held his breath
For a time.   *Ib.*

Again! again! again!
And the havoc did not slack,
Till a feeble cheer the Dane
To our cheering sent us back.   *Ib.*

Out spoke the victor then
As he hailed them o'er the wave,
'Ye are brothers! ye are men!
And we conquer but to save;
So peace instead of death let us bring:
But yield, proud foe, thy fleet
With the crews at England's feet,
And make submission meet
To our King.'   *Ib.*

Let us think of them that sleep,
Full many a fathom deep,
By thy wild and stormy steep,
Elsinore!   *Ib.*

With the gallant good Riou.   *Ib.*

O leave this barren spot to me!
Spare, woodman, spare the beechen tree.
                    The Beech-Tree's Petition.

The lordly, lovely Rhine.   *The Child and the Hind.*

There came to the beach a poor Exile of Erin.
                                  Exile of Erin.

He sang the bold anthem of 'Erin go bragh!'   *Ib.*

Gay lilied fields of France.
                    Gertrude of Wyoming, pt. II, 15.

When Transatlantic Liberty arose.   *Ib.* pt. III, 6.

To-morrow let us do or die!   *Ib.* 37.

To live in hearts we leave behind
    Is not to die.   *Hallowed Ground.*

On the green banks of Shannon, when Sheelah was
    nigh,
No blithe Irish lad was so happy as I;
No harp like my own could so cheerily play,
And wherever I went was my poor dog Tray.
                              The Harper.

On Linden, when the sun was low,
All bloodless lay the untrodden snow,
And dark as winter was the flow
Of Iser, rolling rapidly.   *Hohenlinden.*

Then shook the hills with thunder riven,
Then rushed the steed to battle driven,
And louder than the bolts of heaven
Far flashed the red artillery. *Ib.*

The combat deepens. On, ye brave,
Who rush to glory, or the grave!
Wave, Munich! all thy banners wave,
And charge with all thy chivalry! *Ib.*

Few, few shall part where many meet!
The snow shall be their winding-sheet,
And every turf beneath their feet
Shall be a soldier's sepulchre. *Ib.*

Better be courted and jilted
Than never be courted at all. *The Jilted Nymph.*

All worldly shapes shall melt in gloom,
The sun himself must die,
Before this mortal shall assume
Its immortality. *The Last Man.*

'Tis the sunset of life gives me mystical lore,
And coming events cast their shadows before.
Lochiel's Warning.

A chieftain to the Highlands bound
Cries, 'Boatman, do not tarry!
And I'll give thee a silver pound
To row us o'er the ferry.' *Lord Ullin's Daughter.*

'O, I'm the chief of Ulva's isle,
And this Lord Ullin's daughter.' *Ib.*

Then who will cheer my bonny bride
When they have slain her lover? *Ib.*

I'll meet the raging of the skies,
But not an angry father. *Ib.*

One lovely hand she stretched for aid,
And one was round her lover. *Ib.*

'Come back! come back!' he cried in grief
Across the stormy water:
'And I'll forgive your Highland chief,
My daughter! oh my daughter!' *Ib.*

The waters wild went o'er his child,
And he was left lamenting. *Ib.*

With Freedom's lion-banner
Britannia rules the waves. *Ode to the Germans.*

'Tis distance lends enchantment to the view,
And robes the mountain in its azure hue.
Pleasures of Hope, pt. i, l. 7.

The proud, the cold untroubled heart of stone,
That never mused on sorrow but its own. *Ib.* l. 185.

Hope, for a season, bade the world farewell,
And Freedom shrieked—as Kosciusko fell!
Ib. l. 381.

Who hath not owned, with rapture-smitten frame,
The power of grace, the magic of a name?
Ib. pt. ii, l. 5.

And muse on Nature with a poet's eye. *Ib.* l. 98.

Since first he called her his before the holy man.
Ib. l. 130.

What millions died—that Caesar might be great!
Ib. l. 174.

Who hail thee, Man! the pilgrim of a day,
Spouse of the worm, and brother of the clay.
Ib. l. 305.

Truth, ever lovely,—since the world began
The foe of tyrants, and the friend of man. *Ib.* l. 347.

But, sad as angels for the good man's sin,
Weep to record, and blush to give it in! *Ib.* l. 357.

Cease, every joy, to glimmer on my mind,
But leave, oh! leave the light of Hope behind!
What though my wingèd hours of bliss have been,
Like angel-visits, few and far between? *Ib.* l. 375.

Well can ye mouth fair Freedom's classic line,
And talk of Constitutions o'er your wine.
On Poland, l. 65.

One moment may with bliss repay
Unnumbered hours of pain;
Such was the throb and mutual sob
Of the knight embracing Jane. *The Ritter Bann.*

And the sentinel stars set their watch in the sky.
The Soldier's Dream.

Drink ye to her that each loves best,
And, if you nurse a flame
That's told but to her mutual breast,
We will not ask her name.
Song. Drink Ye To Her.

Bind the sea to slumber stilly,
Bind its odour to the lily,
Bind the aspen ne'er to quiver,
Then bind Love to last for ever!
Song. How Delicious is the Winning.

Can you keep the bee from ranging,
Or the ringdove's neck from changing?
No! nor fettered Love from dying
In the knot there's no untying. *Ib.*

Again to the Battle, Achaians!
Our hearts bid the tyrants defiance;
Our land, the first garden of Liberty's tree—
It has been, and shall yet be, the land of the free!
Song of the Greeks.

Her women fair; her men robust for toil;
Her vigorous souls, high-cultured as her soil:
Her towns, where civic independence flings
The gauntlet down to senates, courts, and kings.
Theodric, l. 160.

It was not strange; for in the human breast
Two master-passions cannot co-exist. *Ib.* l. 488.

'Twas the hour when rites unholy
Called each Paynim voice to prayer.
The Turkish Lady.

Ye Mariners of England
That guard our native seas,
Whose flag has braved, a thousand years,
The battle and the breeze—
Your glorious standard launch again
To match another foe!
And sweep through the deep,
While the stormy winds do blow,—
While the battle rages loud and long,
And the stormy winds do blow.
Ye Mariners of England.

Britannia needs no bulwarks,
No towers along the steep;
Her march is o'er the mountain waves,
Her home is on the deep.   *Ib.*

The meteor flag of England
Shall yet terrific burn,
Till danger's troubled night depart
And the star of peace return.   *Ib.*

An original something, fair maid, you would win me
To write—but how shall I begin?
For I fear I have nothing original in me—
Excepting Original Sin.
            To a Young Lady, Who Asked Me to Write
            Something Original for Her Album.

SIR HENRY CAMPBELL-BANNERMAN
1836–1908

When was a war not a war? When it was carried on
by methods of barbarism.
            Speech at Dinner of National Reform Union,
            14 June, 1901.

THOMAS CAMPION
d. 1619

Rose-cheeked Laura, come;
Sing thou smoothly with thy beauty's
Silent music, either other
    Sweetly gracing.
        Observations in the Art of English Poesie. Laura.

Lovely forms do flow
From conceit divinely framed;
Heaven is music, and thy beauty's
    Birth is heavenly.   *Ib.*

But still moves delight,
Like clear springs renewed by flowing,
Ever perfect, ever in them-
    selves eternal.   *Ib.*

My sweetest Lesbia let us live and love,
And though the sager sort our deeds reprove,
Let us not weigh them: Heav'n's great lamps do dive
Into their west, and straight again revive,
But soon as once set is our little light,
Then must we sleep one ever-during night.
            A Book of Airs. My Sweetest Lesbia.

Follow thy fair sun, unhappy shadow,
    Though thou be black as night,
    And she made all of light,
Yet follow thy fair sun, unhappy shadow.
            Ib. Follow Thy Fair Sun.

When to her lute Corinna sings,
Her voice revives the leaden strings,
And both in highest notes appear,
As any challeng'd echo clear.
But when she doth of mourning speak,
Ev'n with her sighs the strings do break.
            Ib. When to Her Lute Corinna.

Follow your Saint, follow with accents sweet;
Haste you, sad notes, fall at her flying feet.
            Ib. Follow Your Saint.

Hark, all you ladies that do sleep;
The fairy Queen Proserpina
Bids you awake and pity them that weep.
            Ib. Hark, all you Ladies.

When thou must home to shades of under ground,
And there arriv'd, a new admired guest,
The beauteous spirits do ingirt thee round,
White Iope, blithe Helen, and the rest,
To hear the stories of thy finisht love
From that smooth tongue whose music hell can move.
            Ib. When Thou Must Home.

Never weather-beaten sail more willing bent to shore,
Never tired pilgrim's limbs affected slumber more.
        Two Books of Airs. Divine and Moral Songs.
                    Never Weather-Beaten Sail.

Kind are her answers,
But her performance keeps no day;
    Breaks time, as dancers
From their own Music when they stray.
        Book of Airs, III. vii. Kind Are Her Answers.

Lost is our freedom,
When we submit to women so:
    Why do we need them,
When in their best they work our woe?   *Ib.*

There is a garden in her face,
Where roses and white lilies grow;
A heav'nly paradise is that place,
Wherein all pleasant fruits do flow.
There cherries grow, which none may buy
Till 'Cherry ripe' themselves do cry.
        Book of Airs, IV. vii. There is a Garden in her Face.

Those cherries fairly do enclose
Of orient pearl a double row;
Which when her lovely laughter shows,
They look like rosebuds fill'd with snow.
Yet them nor peer nor prince can buy,
Till 'Cherry ripe' themselves do cry.   *Ib.*

GEORGE CANNING
1770–1827

In matters of commerce the fault of the Dutch
Is offering too little and asking too much.
The French are with equal advantage content,
So we clap on Dutch bottoms just twenty per cent.
        Dispatch, in Cipher, to Sir Charles Bagot,
        English Ambassador at The Hague, 31 Jan. 1826.

Needy Knife-grinder! whither are you going?
Rough is the road, your wheel is out of order—
Bleak blows the blast;—your hat has got a hole in't.
    So have your breeches.
        The Friend of Humanity and the Knife-Grinder.

Story! God bless you! I have none to tell, Sir.   *Ib.*

I give thee sixpence! I will see thee damn'd first—
Wretch! whom no sense of wrongs can rouse to
        vengeance;
Sordid, unfeeling, reprobate, degraded,
                    Spiritless outcast!   *Ib.*

So down thy hill, romantic Ashbourne, glides
The Derby dilly, carrying *Three* Insides.
            The Loves of the Triangles, l. 178.

And finds, with keen discriminating sight,
Black's not so black;—nor white so very white.
                    New Morality, l. 199.

Save me, oh, save me from the candid friend.
Ib. l. 210.

Man, only—rash, refined, presumptuous man,
Starts from his rank, and mars creation's plan.
Progress of Man, l. 55.
A sudden thought strikes me, let us swear an eternal
  friendship.   *The Rovers*, i. i.

Whene'er with haggard eyes I view
This Dungeon, that I'm rotting in,
I think of those Companions true
Who studied with me at the U-
    -NIVERSITY of GOTTINGEN,-
    -NIVERSITY of GOTTINGEN.   *Song.*

Sun, moon, and thou vain world, adieu.   *Ib.*

I called the New World into existence, to redress the
  balance of the Old.   *Dec. 12, 1826. Speech.*

CANUTE

994 ?-1035

Merrily sang the monks in Ely
When Cnut, King, rowed thereby;
Row, my knights, near the land,
And hear we these monkes' song.
    Attr. *Song of the Monks of Ely, Historia
    Eliensis* (1066). *Green, Conquest of England*, ix.

RICHARD CAREW

1555-1620

Take the miracle of our age, Sir Philip Sidney.
An Epistle on the Excellency of the English Tongue.

THOMAS CAREW

1595 ?-1639 ?

He that loves a rosy cheek,
  Or a coral lip admires,
Or, from star-like eyes, doth seek
  Fuel to maintain his fires;
As old Time makes these decay,
So his flames must waste away.
         Disdain Returned.

Here lies a King that rul'd, as he thought fit
The universal monarchy of wit;
Here lies two Flamens, and both those the best:
Apollo's first, at last the true God's priest.
       Elegy on the Death of Donne.

The purest soul that e'er was sent
Into a clayey tenement.
       On the Lady Mary Villiers.

Know, Celia (since thou art so proud,)
'Twas I that gave thee thy renown.
Thou had'st in the forgotten crowd
Of common beauties liv'd unknown,
Had not my verse extoll'd thy name,
And with it ympt the wings of fame.
      Ingrateful Beauty Threatened.

Wise poets that wrapt Truth in tales,
Knew her themselves through all her veils.   *Ib.*

An untimely grave.
     Inscription on Tomb of the Duke of Buckingham.

Good to the poor, to kindred dear,
To servants kind, to friendship clear,
To nothing but herself severe.
     Inscription on Tomb of Lady Mary Wentworth.

So though a virgin, yet a bride
To every Grace, she justified
A chaste polygamy, and died.   *Ib.*

Give me more love or more disdain;
The torrid or the frozen zone:
Bring equal ease unto my pain;
The temperate affords me none.
      Mediocrity in Love Rejected.

When thou, poor excommunicate
From all the joys of love, shalt see
The full reward and glorious fate
Which my strong faith shall purchase me,
Then curse thine own inconstancy.
       To My Inconstant Mistress.

Ask me no more where Jove bestows,
When June is past, the fading rose;
For in your beauty's orient deep
These flowers, as in their causes, sleep.   *A Song.*

Ask me no more whither doth haste
The nightingale when May is past;
For in your sweet dividing throat
She winters and keeps warm her note.   *Ib.*

Ask me no more if east or west
The Phoenix builds her spicy nest;
For unto you at last she flies,
And in your fragrant bosom dies.   *Ib.*

HENRY CAREY

1693 ?-1743

Aldiborontiphoscophornio!
Where left you Chrononhotonthologos?
       Chrononhotonthologos, i. i.

His cogitative faculties immers'd
In cogibundity of cogitation.   *Ib.*

To thee, and gentle Rigdum-Funnidos,
Our gratulations flow in streams unbounded. *Ib.* iii.

God save our gracious king!
Long live our noble king!
  God save the king!   *God Save the King.*

Confound their politics,
Frustrate their knavish tricks.   *Ib.*

Of all the girls that are so smart
  There's none like pretty Sally,
She is the darling of my heart,
  And she lives in our alley.   *Sally in our Alley.*

When she is by I leave my work,
  (I love her so sincerely)
My master comes like any Turk,
  And bangs me most severely.   *Ib.*

Of all the days that's in the week
  I dearly love but one day—
And that's the day that comes betwixt
  A Saturday and Monday.   *Ib.*

WILLIAM CARLETON

1794–1869

Things at home are crossways, and Betsey and I are out. *Farm Ballads. Betsey and I Are Out.*

We arg'ed the thing at breakfast, we arg'ed the thing at tea,
And the more we arg'ed the question, the more we didn't agree. *Ib.*

THOMAS CARLYLE

1795–1881

A well-written Life is almost as rare as a well-spent one.
> *Critical and Miscellaneous Essays*, vol. i. *Richter.*

'Providence has given to the French the empire of the land, to the English that of the sea, to the Germans that of—the air!' [quoting a remark of J. P. F. Richter.] *Ib.*

The three great elements of modern civilisation, Gunpowder, Printing, and the Protestant Religion.
> *Ib. State of German Literature.*

The 'golden-calf of Self-love.' *Ib. Burns.*

So here has been dawning
Another blue day. *Ib. To-day.*

> Out of Eternity
This new Day is born;
> Into Eternity
At night, will return. *Ib.*

It is the Age of Machinery, in every outward and inward sense of that word.
> *Ib. vol. ii. Signs of the Times.*

The Bible-Society . . . is found, on inquiry, to be . . . a machine for converting the Heathen. *Ib.*

Thought, he [Dr. Cabanis] is inclined to hold, is still secreted by the brain; but then Poetry and Religion (and it is really worth knowing) are 'a product of the smaller intestines'! *Ib.*

What is all knowledge too but recorded experience, and a product of history; of which, therefore, reasoning and belief, no less than action and passion, are essential materials? *Ib. On History.*

History is the essence of innumerable biographies. *Ib.*

The foul sluggard's comfort: 'It will last my time.'
> *Ib. vol. iii. Count Cagliostro. Flight Last.*

This Mirabeau's work, then, is done. He sleeps with the primeval giants. He has gone over to the majority: *Abiit ad plures*. *Ib. Mirabeau.*

There is no life of a man, faithfully recorded, but is a heroic poem of its sort, rhymed or unrhymed.
> *Ib. vol. iv. Sir Walter Scott.*

Under all speech that is good for anything there lies a silence that is better. Silence is deep as Eternity; speech is shallow as Time. *Ib.*

To the very last, he (Napoleon) had a kind of idea; that, namely, of *La carrière ouverte aux talents*, The tools to him that can handle them. *Ib.*

It can be said of him [Scott], When he departed, he took a man's life along with him. No sounder piece of British manhood was put together in that eighteenth century of Time. *Ib.*

A witty statesman said, you might prove anything by figures. *Ib. Chartism, ch. 2.*

Surely of all 'rights of man', this right of the ignorant man to be guided by the wiser, to be, gently or forcibly, held in the true course by him, is the indisputablest. *Ib. ch. 6.*

In epochs when cash payment has become the sole nexus of man to man. *Ib.*

Thou wretched fraction, wilt thou be the ninth part even of a tailor? *Ib. Francia.*

This idle habit of 'accounting for the moral sense', as they phrase it . . . The moral sense, thank God, is a thing you never will 'account for'. . . . By no greatest happiness principle, greatest nobleness principle, or any principle whatever, will you make that in the least clearer than it already is.
> *Ib. vol. v. Shooting Niagara: and After?*

'Genius' (which means transcendent capacity of taking trouble, first of all).
> *Frederick the Great*, bk. iv, ch. 3.

If they could forget, for a moment, the correggiosity of Correggio, and the learned babble of the sale-room and varnishing auctioneer. *Ib. ch. 6.*

Happy the people whose annals are blank in history-books! *Ib. bk. xvi, ch. 1.*

Indeed it is well said, 'in every object there is inexhaustible meaning; the eye sees in it what the eye brings means of seeing.'
> *Hist. of the French Revolution*, pt. 1, bk. i, ch. 2.

Is not every meanest day 'the conflux of two eternities!' *Ib. bk. iv, ch. 4.*

A whiff of grapeshot. *Ib. bk. v, ch. 3.*

History a distillation of rumour. *Ib. bk. vii, ch. 5.*

The gospel according to Jean Jacques.
> *Ib. pt. 11, bk. i, ch. 6.*

The difference between Orthodoxy or My-doxy and Heterodoxy or Thy-doxy. *Ib. bk. iv, ch. 2.*

The seagreen Incorruptible [Robespierre]. *Ib. ch. 4.*

Aristocracy of the Moneybag. *Ib. bk. vii, ch. 7.*

It is well said, in every sense, that a man's religion is the chief fact with regard to him.
> *Heroes and Hero-Worship*, i. *The Hero as Divinity.*

Worship is transcendent wonder. *Ib.*

No sadder proof can be given by a man of his own littleness than disbelief in great men. *Ib.*

No great man lives in vain. The history of the world is but the biography of great men. *Ib.*

The greatest of faults, I should say, is to be conscious of none. *Ib. ii. The Hero as Prophet.*

The Hero can be Poet, Prophet, King, Priest or what you will, according to the kind of world he finds himself born into. *Ib. iii. The Hero as Poet.*

In books lies the *soul* of the whole Past Time; the articulate audible voice of the Past, when the body and material substance of it has altogether vanished like a dream. *Ib.* v. *The Hero as Man of Letters.*

The true University of these days is a collection of books. *Ib.*

Burke said there were Three Estates in Parliament; but, in the Reporters' Gallery yonder, there sat a *Fourth Estate* more important far than they all. *Ib.*

Adversity is sometimes hard upon a man; but for one man who can stand prosperity, there are a hundred that will stand adversity. *Ib.*

I hope we English will long maintain our *grand talent pour le silence.* *Ib.* vi. *The Hero as King.*

Maid-servants, I hear people complaining, are getting instructed in the 'ologies'.
Inaugural Address at Edinburgh, 1866.

Speech is human, silence is divine, yet also brutish and dead: therefore we must learn both arts.
Journal.

Respectable Professors of the Dismal Science. [Political Economy.]
Latter-Day Pamphlets, No. 1. *The Present Time.*

Little other than a redtape Talking-machine, and unhappy Bag of Parliamentary Eloquence. *Ib.*

A healthy hatred of scoundrels.
Ib. No. 2. *Model Prisons.*

Idlers, game-preservers and mere human clothes-horses. [Exodus from Houndsditch.]
Ib. No. 3. *Downing Street.*

Nature admits no lie. *Ib.* No. 5. *Stump Orator.*

A Parliament speaking through reporters to Buncombe and the twenty-seven millions mostly fools.
Ib. No. 6. *Parliaments.*

'May the Devil fly away with the fine arts!' exclaimed . . . in my hearing, one of our most distinguished public men. *Ib.* No. 8.

Mother of dead dogs.
Letter to John Carlyle, 11 Sept. 1840 (Froude's *Carlyle*, 1884, vol. i, p. 196).

Whatsoever thy hand findeth to do, *do* that with all thy might and leave the issues calmly to God.
Letter to W. Graham, 29 Mar. 1844.

The unspeakable Turk should be immediately struck out of the question.
Letter to G. Howard, 24 Nov. 1876.

Transcendental moonshine.
Life of John Sterling, Pt. 1, ch. 15.

The progress of human society consists . . . in . . . the better and better apportioning of wages to work.
Past and Present, bk. i, ch. 3.

Brothers, I am sorry I have got no Morrison's Pill for curing the maladies of Society. *Ib.* ch. 4.

Thou and I, my friend, can, in the most flunkey world, make, each of us, *one* non-flunkey, one hero, if we like: that will be two heroes to begin with.
Ib. ch. 6.

Cash-payment is not the sole nexus of man with man. *Ib.* bk. iii, ch. 9.

Blessed is he who has found his work; let him ask no other blessedness. *Ib.* ch. 11.

Captains of industry. *Ib.* bk. iv, title of ch. 4.

The sunny plains and deep indigo transparent skies of Italy are all indifferent to the great sick heart of a Sir Walter Scott: on the back of the Apennines, in wild spring weather, the sight of bleak Scotch firs, and snow-spotted heath and desolation, brings tears into his eyes. *Ib.* ch. 5.

Upwards of five-hundred-thousand two-legged animals without feathers lie round us, in horizontal positions; their heads all in nightcaps, and full of the foolishest dreams. *Sartor Resartus*, bk. i, ch. 3.

He who first shortened the labour of copyists by device of *Movable Types* was disbanding hired armies, and cashiering most Kings and Senates, and creating a whole new democratic world: he had invented the art of printing. *Ib.* ch. 5.

Man is a tool-using animal. . . . Without tools he is nothing, with tools he is all. *Ib.*

Language is called the garment of thought: however, it should rather be, language is the flesh-garment, the body, of thought. *Ib.* ch. 11.

Man's unhappiness, as I construe, comes of his greatness; it is because there is an Infinite in him, which with all his cunning he cannot quite bury under the Finite. *Ib.* bk. ii, ch. 9.

'Do the duty which lies nearest thee', which thou knowest to be a duty! Thy second duty will already have become clearer. *Ib.*

What printed thing soever I could meet with I read.
Ib. bk. ii, ch. 3.

The end of man is an action, and not a thought.
Ib. ch. 6.

The everlasting no. *Ib.* ch. 7, title.

The folly of that impossible precept, 'Know thyself'; till it be translated into this partially possible one, 'Know what thou canst work at'. *Ib.*

My spiritual new-birth, or Baphometic Fire-baptism.
Ib.

Great men are the inspired [speaking and acting] texts of that divine Book of Revelations, whereof a chapter is completed from epoch to epoch, and by some named History. *Ib.* ch. 8.

The everlasting yea. *Ib.* ch. 9, title.

Close thy Byron; open thy Goethe. *Ib.*

Be no longer a chaos, but a world, or even worldkin. Produce! Produce! Were it but the pitifullest infinitesimal fraction of a product, produce it in God's name! 'Tis the utmost thou hast in thee: out with it, then. *Ib.*

As the Swiss Inscription says: *Sprechen ist silbern, Schweigen ist golden* (Speech is silvern, Silence is golden); or as I might rather express it: Speech is of Time, Silence is of Eternity. *Ib.* bk. iii, ch. 3.

Two men I honour, and no third. *Ib.* ch. 4.

I don't pretend to understand the Universe—it's a great deal bigger than I am. . . . People ought to be modester.
Remark to Wm. Allingham. D. A. Wilson's and D. Wilson MacArthur's *Carlyle in Old Age.*

If Jesus Christ were to come to-day, people would not even crucify him. They would ask him to dinner, and hear what he had to say, and make fun of it.
> *Remark.* D. A. Wilson's *Carlyle at his Zenith.*

It were better to perish than to continue schoolmastering.
> *Remark.* D. A. Wilson's *Carlyle Till Marriage.*

Macaulay is well for a while, but one wouldn't *live* under Niagara.
> *Remark.* R. M. Milnes' *Notebook, 1838.*

A good book is the purest essence of a human soul.
> *Speech in support of The London Library, 1840.* F. Harrison's *Carlyle and The London Library.*

' "Thou's gey" [pretty, pronounced *gyei*] "ill to deal wi"—Mother's allocution to me once, in some unreasonable moment of mine', is Carlyle's note on this phrase (which, indeed, is an old-fashioned country formula), cited by his wife in a letter to his mother in Dec. 1835. . . . The readers of Mr. Froude's *Life of Carlyle* will remember that he harps upon this phrase, using it as a sort of refrain, but always with the significant change of the word 'deal' to 'live'—'gey ill to *live* wi'.
> C. Eliot Norton, *Letters of Thomas Carlyle* (1888), I, 44.

Who never ate his bread in sorrow,
Who never spent the darksome hours
Weeping and watching for the morrow
He knows ye not, ye heavenly Powers.
> Translation of Goethe's *Wilhelm Meister's Apprenticeship*, Bk. II, ch. 13.

Carlyle and Milnes were talking . . . of the Administration just formed by Sir Robert Peel, and Milnes was evincing some disappointment . . . that he had not been offered a post in it. 'No, no,' said Carlyle, 'Peel knows what he is about; there is only one post fit for you, and that is the office of perpetual president of the Heaven and Hell Amalgamation Society.'
> T. E. Wemyss Reid, *The Life of Lord Houghton* (1890), p. 187.

MARGARET FULLER:
I accept the universe.
CARLYLE:
Gad! she'd better! *Attr.*

JULIA CARNEY

1823–1908

Little drops of water, little grains of sand,
Make the mighty ocean, and the pleasant land.
So the little minutes, humble though they be,
Make the mighty ages of eternity.
> *Little Things.* (Attr. also to E. C. Brewer, D. C. Colesworthy, and F. S. Osgood.)

Little deeds of kindness, little words of love,
Help to make earth happy, like the heaven above.
> (Changed by later compilers to 'make this earth an Eden'.) *Ib.*

JOSEPH EDWARDS CARPENTER

1813–?

What are the wild waves saying
Sister, the whole day long,
That ever amid our playing,
I hear but their low lone song?
> *What Are the Wild Waves Saying?*

Yes! but there's something greater,
That speaks to the heart alone;
The voice of the great Creator,
Dwells in that mighty tone! *Ib.*

LEWIS CARROLL [CHARLES LUTWIDGE DODGSON]

1832–1898

'What is the use of a book', thought Alice, 'without pictures or conversations?'
> *Alice in Wonderland*, ch. 1.

Do cats eat bats? . . . Do bats eat cats? *Ib.*

'Curiouser and curiouser!' cried Alice. *Ib.* ch. 2.

How doth the little crocodile
Improve his shining tail,
And pour the waters of the Nile
On every golden scale! *Ib.*

How cheerfully he seems to grin,
How neatly spreads his claws,
And welcomes little fishes in
With gently smiling jaws! *Ib.*

'I'll be judge, I'll be jury,' said cunning old Fury;
'I'll try the whole cause, and condemn you to death.'
> *Ib.* ch. 3.

'I can't explain *myself*, I'm afraid, sir,' said Alice, 'because I'm not myself, you see.' 'I don't see,' said the Caterpillar. *Ib.* ch. 5.

'You are old, Father William,' the young man said,
'And your hair has become very white;
And yet you incessantly stand on your head—
Do you think, at your age, it is right?'

'In my youth,' Father William replied to his son.
'I feared it might injure the brain;
But now that I'm perfectly sure I have none,
Why, I do it again and again.' *Ib.*

'I have answered three questions, and that is enough,'
Said his father; 'don't give yourself airs!
Do you think I can listen all day to such stuff?
Be off, or I'll kick you downstairs!' *Ib.*

'I shall sit here,' he said, 'on and off, for days and days.' *Ib.* ch. 6.

'If everybody minded their own business,' said the Duchess in a hoarse growl, 'the world would go round a deal faster than it does.' *ib.*

Speak roughly to your little boy,
And beat him when he sneezes;
He only does it to annoy,
Because he knows it teases. *Ib.*

For he can thoroughly enjoy
   The pepper when he pleases!   *Ib.*

'Did you say pig, or fig?' said the Cat.   *Ib.*

This time it vanished quite slowly, beginning with the end of the tail, and ending with the grin, which remained some time after the rest of it had gone. [The Cheshire Cat.]   *Ib.*

'Have some wine,' the March Hare said in an encouraging tone. Alice looked all round the table, but there was nothing on it but tea. 'I don't see any wine,' she remarked. 'There isn't any,' said the March Hare.   *Ib.* ch. 7.

'Then you should say what you mean,' the March Hare went on. 'I do,' Alice hastily replied; 'at least —at least I mean what I say—that's the same thing, you know.'
'Not the same thing a bit!' said the Hatter. 'Why, you might just as well say that "I see what I eat" is the same thing as "I eat what I see!"'   *Ib.*

'It was the *best* butter,' the March Hare meekly replied.   *Ib.*

'Twinkle, twinkle, little bat!
How I wonder what you're at!
Up above the world you fly!
Like a teatray in the sky.'   *Ib.*

'Take some more tea,' the March Hare said to Alice, very earnestly.
'I've had nothing yet,' Alice replied in an offended tone, 'so I can't take more.'
'You mean you can't take *less*,' said the Hatter: 'it's very easy to take *more* than nothing.'   *Ib.*

'Let's all move one place on.'   *Ib.*

'But they were *in* the well,' Alice said to the Dormouse . . . . 'Of course they were,' said the Dormouse,—'well in.'   *Ib.*

'They drew all manner of things—everything that begins with an M——' 'Why with an M?' said Alice. 'Why not?' said the March Hare.   *Ib.*

The Queen was in a furious passion, and went stamping about, and shouting, 'Off with his head!' or 'Off with her head!' about once in a minute.   *Ib.* ch. 8.

'A cat may look at a king,' said Alice.   *Ib.*

'And the moral of that is—"Oh, 'tis love, 'tis love, that makes the world go round!"'   *Ib.* ch. 9.

Take care of the sense, and the sounds will take care of themselves.   *Ib.*

'That's nothing to what I could say if I chose,' the Duchess replied.   *Ib.*

'Just about as much right,' said the Duchess, 'as pigs have to fly.'   *Ib.*

'That's the reason they're called lessons,' the Gryphon remarked: 'because they lessen from day to day.'   *Ib.*

'Will you walk a little faster?' said a whiting to a snail, 'There's a porpoise close behind us, and he's treading on my tail.'   *Ib.* ch. 10.

'Will you, won't you, will you, won't you, will you join the dance?'   *Ib.*

The further off from England the nearer is to France—
Then turn not pale, beloved snail, but come and join the dance.   *Ib.*

'Tis the voice of the lobster; I heard him declare, 'You have baked me too brown, I must sugar my hair.'   *Ib.*

Soup of the evening, beautiful Soup!   *Ib.*

The Queen of Hearts, she made some tarts,
   All on a summer day:
The Knave of Hearts, he stole those tarts,
   And took them quite away!   *Ib.* ch. 11.

'Write that down,' the King said to the jury, and the jury eagerly wrote down all three dates on their slates, and then added them up, and reduced the answer to shillings and pence.   *Ib.*

Here one of the guinea-pigs cheered, and was immediately suppressed by the officers of the court. *Ib.*

'Where shall I begin, please your Majesty?' he asked. 'Begin at the beginning,' the King said, gravely, 'and go on till you come to the end: then stop.'   *Ib.*

'*Un*important, of course, I meant,' the King hastily said, and went on to himself in an undertone, 'important—unimportant—unimportant—important—' as if he were trying which word sounded best.   *Ib.* ch. 12.

'That's not a regular rule: you invented it just now.' 'It's the oldest rule in the book,' said the King. 'Then it ought to be Number One,' said Alice.   *Ib.*

They told me you had been to her,
   And mentioned me to him:
She gave me a good character,
   But said I could not swim.   *Ib.*

The jury all wrote down on their slates, '*She* doesn't believe there's an atom of meaning in it.'   *Ib.*

'Do I look like it?' said the Knave. (Which he certainly did *not*, being made entirely of cardboard.)   *Ib.*

'The horror of that moment,' the King went on, 'I shall never, *never* forget!' 'You will, though,' the Queen said, 'if you don't make a memorandum of it.'   *Through the Looking-Glass*, ch. 1.

'My precious Lily! My imperial kitten!'—
'Imperial fiddlestick!'   *Ib.*

'Twas brillig, and the slithy toves
   Did gyre and gimble in the wabe;
All mimsy were the borogoves,
   And the mome raths outgrabe.

'Beware the Jabberwock, my son!
   The jaws that bite, the claws that catch!
Beware the Jubjub bird, and shun
   The frumious Bandersnatch!'

He took his vorpal sword in hand:
   Long time the manxome foe he sought—
So rested he by the Tumtum tree,
   And stood awhile in thought.

And as in uffish thought he stood,
   The Jabberwock, with eyes of flame,
Came whiffling through the tulgey wood,
   And burbled as it came!

One, two! One, two! And through and through
  The vorpal blade went snicker-snack!
He left it dead, and with its head
  He went galumphing back.
'And hast thou slain the Jabberwock?
  Come to my arms, my beamish boy!
O frabjous day! Callooh! Callay!'
  He chortled in his joy.

Through the Looking-Glass, ch. 1.

Curtsey while you're thinking what to say. It saves
  time.   *Ib.* ch. 2.

Speak in French when you can't think of the English
  for a thing.   *Ib.*

'Now! Now!' cried the Queen. 'Faster! Faster!' *Ib.*

'Now, *here*, you see, it takes all the running *you* can
  do, to keep in the same place. If you want to get
  somewhere else, you must run at least twice as
  fast as that!'   *Ib.*

'Sap and sawdust,' said the Gnat.   *Ib.* ch. 3.

Tweedledum and Tweedledee
  Agreed to have a battle;
For Tweedledum said Tweedledee
  Had spoiled his nice new rattle.

Just then flew down a monstrous crow,
  As black as a tar-barrel;
Which frightened both the heroes so,
  They quite forgot their quarrel.

                        Ib. ch. 4.

'Contrariwise,' continued Tweedledee, 'if it was so,
  it might be; and if it were so, it would be: but as
  it isn't, it ain't. That's logic.'   *Ib.*

The sun was shining on the sea,
  Shining with all his might:
He did his very best to make
  The billows smooth and bright—
And this was odd, because it was
  The middle of the night.

Ib. The Walrus and the Carpenter.

'It's very rude of him,' she said
  'To come and spoil the fun!'   *Ib.*

You could not see a cloud, because
  No cloud was in the sky:
No birds were flying overhead—
  There were no birds to fly.   *Ib.*

The Walrus and the Carpenter
  Were walking close at hand;
They wept like anything to see
  Such quantities of sand:
'If this were only cleared away,'
  They said, 'it would be grand!'

'If seven maids with seven mops
  Swept it for half a year,
Do you suppose,' the Walrus said,
  'That they could get it clear?'
'I doubt it,' said the Carpenter,
  And shed a bitter tear.   *Ib.*

But four young Oysters hurried up,
  All eager for the treat:
Their coats were brushed, their faces washed,
  Their shoes were clean and neat—
And this was odd, because, you know,
  They hadn't any feet.   *Ib.*

And thick and fast they came at last,
  And more, and more, and more.   *Ib.*

The Walrus and the Carpenter
  Walked on a mile or so,
And then they rested on a rock
  Conveniently low:
And all the little Oysters stood
  And waited in a row.

'The time has come,' the Walrus said,
  'To talk of many things:
Of shoes—and ships—and sealing wax—
  Of cabbages—and kings—
And why the sea is boiling hot—
  And whether pigs have wings.'   *Ib.*

'For some of us are out of breath,
  And all of us are fat!'   *Ib.*

'A loaf of bread,' the Walrus said,
  'Is what we chiefly need:
Pepper and vinegar besides
  Are very good indeed—
Now if you're ready, Oysters dear,
  We can begin to feed.'   *Ib.*

'The night is fine,' the Walrus said.
  'Do you admire the view?'   *Ib.*

The Carpenter said nothing but
  'The butter's spread too thick!'   *Ib.*

'I weep for you,' the Walrus said:
  'I deeply sympathize.'
With sobs and tears he sorted out
  Those of the largest size,
Holding his pocket-handkerchief
  Before his streaming eyes.   *Ib.*

But answer came there none—
  And this was scarcely odd because
  They'd eaten every one.   *Ib.*

'Fit to snore his head off!' as Tweedledum remarked.
                        Ib.

'Let's fight till six, and then have dinner,' said
  Tweedledum.   *Ib.*

'You know,' he said very gravely, 'it's one of the most
  serious things that can possibly happen to one in a
  battle—to get one's head cut off.'   *Ib.*

'I'm very brave generally,' he went on in a low voice:
  'only to-day I happen to have a headache.'   *Ib.*

'Twopence a week, and jam every other day.' *Ib.* ch. 5.

The rule is, jam to-morrow and jam yesterday—but
  never jam to-day.   *Ib.*

'It's a poor sort of memory that only works backwards,' the Queen remarked.   *Ib.*

'Consider anything, only don't cry!'   *Ib.*

'I can't believe *that*!' said Alice. 'Can't you?' the
  Queen said in a pitying tone. 'Try again: draw a
  long breath, and shut your eyes.' Alice laughed.
  'There's no use trying,' she said: 'one *can't* believe
  impossible things.' 'I daresay you haven't had
  much practice,' said the Queen. 'When I was your
  age, I always did it for half-an-hour a day. Why,
  sometimes I've believed as many as six impossible
  things before breakfast.'   *Ib.*

'It's very provoking,' Humpty Dumpty said after a
  long silence,—'to be called an egg—*very!' Ib.* ch. 6.

Humpty Dumpty sat on a wall,
  Humpty Dumpty had a great fall;
All the king's horses and all the king's men
Couldn't put Humpty Dumpty together again.   *Ib.*

With a name like yours, you might be any shape,
  almost.   *Ib.*

'They gave it me,—for an un-birthday present.'   *Ib.*

'There's glory for you!' 'I don't know what you mean
by "glory",' Alice said. 'I meant, "there's a nice
knock-down argument for you!"' 'But "glory"
doesn't mean "a nice knock-down argument",'
Alice objected. 'When *I* use a word,' Humpty
Dumpty said in a rather scornful tone, 'it means
just what I choose it to mean,—neither more nor
less.'   *Ib.*

'The question is,' said Humpty Dumpty, 'which is to
be master—that's all.'   *Ib.*

'I can explain all the poems that ever were invented—
and a good many that haven't been invented just
yet.'   *Ib.*

'*I* can repeat poetry as well as other folk if it comes to
that—' 'Oh, it needn't come to that!' Alice hastily
said.   *Ib.*

The little fishes of the sea,
  They sent an answer back to me.

The little fishes' answer was
  'We cannot do it, Sir, because——'   *Ib.*

I took a kettle large and new,
  Fit for the deed I had to do.   *Ib.*

I said it very loud and clear;
  I went and shouted in his ear.

But he was very stiff and proud;
  He said 'You needn't shout so loud!'

And he was very proud and stiff;
  He said 'I'd go and wake them, if——'   *Ib.*

You see it's like a portmanteau—there are two
meanings packed up into one word.   *Ib.*

He's an Anglo-Saxon Messenger—and those are
Anglo-Saxon attitudes.   *Ib.* ch. 7.

The other Messenger's called Hatta. I must have
two you know—to come and go. One to come, and
one to go.   *Ib.*

'There's nothing like eating hay when you're faint.' ...
'I didn't say there was nothing *better*,' the King
replied, 'I said there was nothing *like* it.'   *Ib.*

'I'm sure nobody walks much faster than I do!'
'He can't do that,' said the King, 'or else he'd have
been here first.'   *Ib.*

It's as large as life, and twice as natural!   *Ib.*

'If you'll believe in me, I'll believe in you.'   *Ib.*

The [White] Knight said ... 'It's my own invention.'
  Ib.

'But you've no idea what a difference it makes, mixing
it with other things—such as gunpowder and
sealing-wax.'   *Ib.*

I'll tell thee everything I can:
  There's little to relate.
I saw an aged, aged man,
  A-sitting on a gate.

'Who are you, aged man?' I said.
  'And how is it you live?'
And his answer trickled through my head
  Like water through a sieve.

He said, 'I look for butterflies
  That sleep among the wheat:
I make them into mutton-pies,
  And sell them in the street.'   *Ib.*

I cried, 'Come, tell me how you live!'
  And thumped him on the head.   *Ib.*

He said, 'I hunt for haddocks' eyes
  Among the heather bright,
And work them into waistcoat-buttons
  In the silent night.

And these I do not sell for gold
  Or coin of silvery shine,
But for a copper halfpenny,
  And that will purchase nine.

I sometimes dig for buttered rolls,
  Or set limed twigs for crabs;
I sometimes search the grassy knolls
  For wheels of hansom-cabs.'   *Ib.*

Or madly squeeze a right-hand foot
  Into a left-hand shoe.   *Ib.*

'Speak when you're spoken to!' the Red Queen
sharply interrupted her.   *Ib.* ch. 9.

'No admittance till the week after next!'   *Ib.*

'It isn't etiquette to cut any one you've been introduced to. Remove the joint.'   *Ib.*

'Un-dish-cover the fish, or dishcover the riddle.' *Ib.*

He thought he saw an Elephant,
  That practised on a fife:
He looked again, and found it was
  A letter from his wife.
'At length I realize,' he said,
  'The bitterness of life!'   *Sylvie and Bruno, ch. 5.*

He thought he saw a Buffalo
  Upon the chimney-piece:
He looked again, and found it was
  His sister's husband's niece.
'Unless you leave this house,' he said,
  'I'll send for the Police!'   *Ib.* ch. 6.

He thought he saw a Banker's Clerk
  Descending from the bus:
He looked again, and found it was
  A Hippopotamus:
'If this should stay to dine,' he said,
  'There won't be much for us.'   *Ib.* ch. 7.

He thought he saw an Albatross
  That fluttered round the lamp:
He looked again, and found it was
  A penny-postage-stamp.
'You'd best be getting home,' he said,
  'The nights are very damp.'   *Ib.* ch. 12.

What I tell you three times is true.
      Hunting of the Snark, Fit 1. *The Landing.*

He had forty-two boxes, all carefully packed,
  With his name painted clearly on each:
But, since he omitted to mention the fact,
  They were all left behind on the beach.   *Ib.*

He would answer to 'Hi!' or to any loud cry,
  Such as 'Fry me!' or 'Fritter-my-wig!'   *Ib.*

His intimate friends called him 'Candle-ends',
  And his enemies, 'Toasted-cheese'.   *Ib.*

Then the bowsprit got mixed with the rudder sometimes.   *Ib.*

But the principal failing occurred in the sailing,
  And the Bellman, perplexed and distressed,
Said he *had* hoped, at least, when the wind blew due
  East,
   That the ship would *not* travel due West!
       Ib. Fit 2. *The Bellman's Speech.*

But oh, beamish nephew, beware of the day,
  If your Snark be a Boojum! For then
You will softly and suddenly vanish away,
  And never be met with again!
       Ib. Fit 3. *The Baker's Tale.*

They sought it with thimbles, they sought it with care;
  They pursued it with forks and hope;
They threatened its life with a railway-share;
  They charmed it with smiles and soap.
       Ib. Fit 5. *The Beaver's Lesson.*

Recollecting with tears how, in earlier years,
  It had taken no pains with its sums.   *Ib.*

And in charity-meetings it stands at the door,
  And collects—though it does not subscribe.   *Ib.*

For the Snark *was* a Boojum, you see.
       Ib. Fit 8. *The Vanishing.*

WILLIAM HERBERT CARRUTH

1859–1924

Some call it evolution,
And others call it God.
   Each In His Own Tongue, and Other Poems,
   1908.

PHOEBE CARY

1824–1871

And though hard be the task,
'Keep a stiff upper lip'.   *Keep a Stiff Upper Lip.*

Nearer my Father's house,
  Where the many mansions be,
Nearer the great white throne,
  Nearer the crystal sea.   *Nearer Home.*

HARRY CASTLING

What-Ho! She bumps!   *Title of Song.*
Let's all go down the Strand.   *Title of Song.*

REV. EDWARD CASWALL

1814–1878

Days and moments quickly flying,
  Blend the living with the dead;
Soon will you and I be lying
  Each within our narrow bed.
   *Hymns & Poems. Days and Moments Quickly
   Flying.*

Earth has many a noble city;
Bethlehem, thou dost all excel.
       Ib. Earth Has Many a Noble City.

My God, I love Thee; not because
I hope for heaven thereby.
       Ib. My God, I Love Thee (tr. from Latin).

Come, Thou Holy Spirit, come;
  And from Thy celestial home
   Shed a ray of light Divine;
Come, Thou Father of the poor,
Come, Thou source of all our store,
  Come, within our bosoms shine.
   Ib. Come Thou Holy Spirit, Come (tr. from Latin).

In our labour rest most sweet,
Grateful coolness in the heat,
  Solace in the midst of woe.   *Ib.*

Hark! a thrilling voice is sounding;
'Christ is nigh,' it seems to say
   Ib. Hark! A Thrilling Voice is Sounding.

Jesu, the very thought of Thee
With sweetness fills the breast.
   Ib. Jesu, The Very Thought of Thee (tr. from Latin).

EDITH CAVELL

1865–1915

I realize that patriotism is not enough. I must have
no hatred or bitterness towards any one.
   Last Words, 12 Oct. 1915. The Times, 23 Oct.
   1915.

SUSANNAH CENTLIVRE

1667?–1723

The real Simon Pure.
       Bold Stroke for a Wife, v. i.

And lash the vice and follies of the age.
       The Man's Bewitched, prologue.

He is as melancholy as an unbrac'd drum.
       Wonder, ii. i.

JOHN CHALKHILL

fl. 1600

Oh, the sweet contentment
The countryman doth find.   *Coridon's Song.*

PATRICK REGINALD CHALMERS

1874–

'I find,' said 'e, 'things very much as 'ow I've always
  found,
For mostly they goes up and down or else goes round
  and round.'
   *Green Days and Blue Days: Roundabouts and
   Swings.*

What's lost upon the roundabouts we pulls up on the
  swings!   *Ib.*

JOSEPH CHAMBERLAIN

1836-1914

But the cup is nearly full. The career of high-handed wrong is coming to an end. *Speech, 20 Oct. 1884.*

Provided that the City of London remains as it is at present, the clearing-house of the world.
Ib. Guildhall, London, 19 Jan. 1904.

Learn to think Imperially. *Ib.*

The day of small nations has long passed away. The day of Empires has come.
Ib. Birmingham, 12 May, 1904.

We are not downhearted. The only trouble is, we cannot understand what is happening to our neighbours. *Ib. Smethwick, 18 Jan. 1906.*

ROBERT CHAMBERS

1802-1871

To change the name, and not the letter,
Is a change for the worse, and not for the better.
Book of Days, vol. ii, June, p. 723.

JOHN CHANDLER

1806-1876

Conquering kings their titles take
From the foes they captive make:
Jesu, by a nobler deed,
From the thousands He hath freed.
Hymns Ancient and Modern. Conquering Kings Their Titles Take, tr. from Latin.

ARTHUR CHAPMAN

1873-

Out where the handclasp's a little stronger,
Out where the smile dwells a little longer,
That's where the West begins.
Out Where the West Begins.

GEORGE CHAPMAN

1559?-1634?

I know an Englishman,
Being flatter'd, is a lamb; threaten'd, a lion;
Alphonsus Emperor of Germany, i. ii.

Berenice's ever-burning hair.
Blind Beggar of Alexandria.

Speed his plough. *Bussy D'Ambois, i. i.*

Who to himself is law, no law doth need,
Offends no law, and is a king indeed. *Ib. ii. i.*

Terror of darkness! O, thou king of flames! *Ib. v. i.*

Give me a spirit that on this life's rough sea
Loves t'have his sails fill'd with a lusty wind,
Even till his sail-yards tremble, his masts crack,
And his rapt ship run on her side so low
That she drinks water, and her keel ploughs air.
Byron's Conspiracy, iii. i.

O incredulity! the wit of fools,
That slovenly will spit on all things fair,
The coward's castle, and the sluggard's cradle.
De Guiana, l. 82.

We have watered our horses in Helicon.
May-Day, iii. iii.

For one heat, all know, doth drive out another,
One passion doth expel another still.
Monsieur D'Olive, v. i.

They're only truly great who are truly good.
Revenge for Honour, v. ii.

A poem, whose subject is not truth, but things like truth.
Revenge of Bussy D'Ambois, dedication.

Danger, the spur of all great minds. *Ib. v. i.*

And let a scholar all Earth's volumes carry,
He will be but a walking dictionary.
Tears of Peace, l. 266.

CHARLES I OF ENGLAND

1600-1649

Never make a defence of apology before you be accused.
Letter to Lord Wentworth, 3 Sept. 1636.

Remember.
To Bishop Juxon, on the Scaffold, 30 Jan. 1649. Rushworth's Hist. Collections, 1701, pt. iv.

CHARLES II OF ENGLAND

1630-1685

He [Charles II] said once to myself, he was no atheist, but he could not think God would make a man miserable only for taking a little pleasure out of the way.
Burnet, History of My Own Time, vol. i, bk. ii, ch. i.

He [Lauderdale] told me, the king spoke to him to let that [Presbytery] go, for it was not a religion for gentlemen. *Ib. ch. 2.*

King Charles gave him [Godolphin] a short character when he was page, which he maintained to his life's end, of being never *in* the way, nor *out* of the way.
Ib. vol. ii, bk. iii, ch. ii, n. (The Earl of Dartmouth).

Let not poor Nelly starve. *Ib. ch. 17.*

Better than a play.
(On the Debates in the House of Lords on Lord Ross's Divorce Bill, 1670.) A. Bryant, King Charles II.

Brother, I am too old to go again to my travels.
Hume's History of Great Britain, vol. ii, 1757, ch. 7.

That is very true: for my words are my own, and my actions are my ministers'.
Reply to Lord Rochester's Epitaph on him, [q.v.].

I am sure no man in England will take away my life to make you King. (To his brother James.)
W. King's Political & Lit. Anecdotes.

He had been, he said, an unconscionable time dying; but he hoped that they would excuse it.
Macaulay's Hist. England, 1849, vol. i, ch. 4, p. 437.

SALMON PORTLAND CHASE
1808–1873

No more slave States; no slave Territories.
Platform of the Free Soil National Convention, 1848.

The Constitution, in all its provisions, looks to an indestructible Union composed of indestructible States.
Decision in Texas v. White, 7 Wallace, 725.

The way to resumption is to resume.
Letter to Horace Greeley, 17 May 1866.

EARL OF CHATHAM
see
WILLIAM PITT

THOMAS CHATTERTON
1752–1770

O! synge untoe mie roundelaie,
O! droppe the brynie teare wythe mee,
Daunce ne moe atte hallie daie,
Lycke a reynynge ryver bee;
  Mie love ys dedde,
  Gon to hys death-bedde,
Al under the wyllowe-tree.
Mynstrelles Songe.

GEOFFREY CHAUCER
1340?–1400

Singest with vois memorial in the shade.
Anelida and Arcite, proem.

Whanne that Aprille with his shoures sote
The droghte of Marche hath perced to the rote.
Canterbury Tales. Prologue. l. 1.

And smale fowles maken melodye,
That slepen al the night with open yë,
(So priketh hem nature in hir corages):
Than longen folk to goon on pilgrimages.   *Ib.* l. 9.

    He loved chivalrye,
Trouthe and honour, fredom and curteisye. *Ib.* l. 45.

He was a verray parfit gentil knight.   *Ib.* l. 72.

He was as fresh as is the month of May.   *Ib.* l. 92.

He coude songes make and wel endyte.   *Ib.* l. 95.

Curteys he was, lowly, and servisable,
And carf biforn his fader at the table.   *Ib.* l. 99.

Hir gretteste ooth was but by sëynt Loy. *Ib.* l. 120.

Ful wel she song the service divyne,
Entuned in hir nose ful semely;
And Frensh she spak ful faire and fetisly,
After the scole of Stratford atte Bowe,
For Frensh of Paris was to hir unknowe.   *Ib.* l. 122.

She wolde wepe, if that she sawe a mous
Caught in a trappe, if it were deed or bledde.
Of smale houndes had she, that she fedde
With rosted flesh, or milk and wastel-breed.
But sore weep she if oon of hem were deed.
     Ib. l. 144.

He yaf nat of that text a pulled hen,
That seith, that hunters been nat holy men.
     Ib. l. 177.

A Frere ther was, a wantown and a merye. *Ib.* l. 208.

He knew the tavernes wel in every toun. *Ib.* l. 240.

He was the best beggere in his hous. *Ib.* l. 252.

Somwhat he lipsed, for his wantownesse,
To make his English swete up-on his tonge.
     Ib. l. 264.

A Clerk ther was of Oxenford also.   *Ib.* l. 285.

For him was lever have at his beddes heed
Twenty bokes, clad in blak or reed,
Of Aristotle and his philosophye,
Than robes riche, or fithele, or gay sautrye.
But al be that he was a philosophre,
Yet hadde he but litel gold in cofre.   *Ib.* l. 293.

And gladly wolde he lerne, and gladly teche.
     Ib. l. 308.

No-wher so bisy a man as he ther nas,
And yet he semed bisier than he was.   *Ib.* l. 321.

For he was Epicurus owne sone.   *Ib.* l. 336.

It snewed in his hous of mete and drinke. *Ib.* l. 345.

A Shipman was ther, woning fer by weste:
For aught I woot, he was of Dertemouthe. *Ib.* l. 388.

And, certeinly, he was a good felawe.   *Ib.* l. 395.

Of nyce conscience took he no keep.
If that he faught, and hadde the hyer hond,
By water he sente hem hoom to every lond.
     Ib. l. 398.

His studie was but litel on the bible.   *Ib.* l. 438.

She was a worthy womman al hir lyve,
Housbondes at chirche-dore she hadde fyve,
Withouten other companye in youthe;
But therof redeth nat to speke as nouthe.
And thryes hadde she been at Jerusalem;
She hadde passed many a straunge streem;
At Rome she hadde been, and at Boloigne,
In Galice at seint Jame, and at Coloigne.   *Ib.* l. 459.

A good man was ther of religioun,
And was a povre Persoun of a toun.   *Ib.* l. 477.

This noble ensample to his sheep he yaf,
That first he wroghte, and afterward he taughte.
     Ib. l. 496.

But Cristes lore, and his apostles twelve,
He taughte, but first he folwed it him-selve.
     Ib. l. 527.

That hadde a fyr-reed cherubinnes face. *Ib.* l. 624.

Wel loved he garleek, oynons, and eek lekes,
And for to drinken strong wyn, reed as blood.
Canterbury Tales. Prologue. l. 634.

His walet lay biforn him in his lappe,
Bret-ful of pardoun come from Rome al hoot.
Ib. l. 686.

He hadde a croys of latoun, ful of stones,
And in a glas he hadde pigges bones.
But with thise relikes, whan that he fond
A povre person dwelling up-on lond,
Up-on a day he gat him more moneye
Than that the person gat in monthes tweye.
And thus, with feyned flaterye and japes,
He made the person and the peple his apes.
Ib. l. 690.

Who-so shal telle a tale after a man,
He moot reherce, as ny as ever he can,
Everich a word, if it be in his charge,
Al speke he never so rudeliche and large;
Or elles he moot telle his tale untrewe,
Or feyne thing, or finde wordes newe. *Ib.* l. 731.

And therfore, at the kinges court, my brother,
Ech man for him-self, ther is non other.
Ib. Knightes Tale, l. 323.

And whan a beest is deed, he hath no peyne;
But man after his deeth moot wepe and pleyne.
Ib. l. 461.

The bisy larke, messager of day. *Ib.* l. 633.

For pitee renneth sone in gentil herte. *Ib.* l. 903.

Up roos the sonne, and up roos Emelye. *Ib.* l. 1415.

Yet in our asshen olde is fyr y-reke.
Ib. The Reves Prologue, l. 28.

So was hir joly whistle wel y-wet.
Ib. The Reves Tale, l. 235.

She is mirour of alle curteisye.
Ib. Tale of the Man of Lawe, l. 68.

He wolde sowen som difficultee,
Or springen cokkel in our clene corn.
Ib. The Shipmannes Prologue, l. 20.

He can nat stinte of singing by the weye.
Ib. The Prioresses Tale, l. 105.

'Thou lokest as thou woldest finde an hare,
For ever up-on the ground I see thee stare.'
Ib. Prologue to Sir Thopas, l. 6.

What is bettre than wisdom? Womman. And what
is bettre than a good womman? No-thing.
Ib. The Tale of Melibeus, § 15.

Ful wys is he that can him-selven knowe.
Ib. The Monkes Tale, l. 149.

Redeth the grete poete of Itaille,
That highte Dant, for he can al devyse
Fro point to point, nat o word wol he faille.
Ib. l. 470.

The month in which the world bigan,
That highte March, whan god first maked man.
Ib. The Nonne Preestes Tale, l. 367.

Daun Russel the fox sterte up at ones. *Ib.* l. 514.

And on a Friday fil al this meschaunce. *Ib.* l. 521.

And lightly as it comth, so wol we spende.
Ib. Pardoners Tale, l. 453.

The bacoun was nat fet for hem, I trowe,
That som men han in Essex at Dunmowe.
Ib. The Prologe of the Wyves' Tale of Bathe, l. 217.

And for to see, and eek for to be seye. *Ib.* l. 552.

But yet I hadde alwey a coltes tooth.
Gat-tothed I was, and that bicam me weel.
Ib. l. 602.

This is a long preamble of a tale. *Ib.* l. 831.

As thikke as motes in the sonne-beem.
Ib. Tale of the Wyf of Bathe, l. 12.

'My lige lady, generally,' quod he,
'Wommen desyren to have sovereyntee
As wel over hir housbond as hir love.' *Ib.* l. 181.

He is gentil that doth gentil dedis. *Ib.* l. 314.

The carl spak oo thing, but he thoghte another.
Ib. The Freres Tale, l. 270.

Thus with hir fader, for a certeyn space,
Dwelleth this flour of wyfly pacience,
That neither by hir wordes ne hir face
Biforn the folk, ne eek in hir absence,
Ne shewed she that hir was doon offence.
Ib. The Clerkes Tale, l. 862.

O stormy peple! unsad and ever untrewe. *Ib.* l. 939.

A doghter hadde this worthy king also,
That yongest was, and highte Canacee.
Ib. The Squieres Tale, l. 27.

Trouthe is the hyeste thing that man may kepe.
Ib. The Frankeleyns Tale, l. 751.

Lat take a cat, and fostre him wel with milk,
And tendre flesh, and make his couche of silk,
And lat him seen a mous go by the wal;
Anon he weyveth milk, and flesh, and al,
And every deyntee that is in that hous,
Swich appetyt hath he to ete a mous.
Ib. The Maunciples Tale, l. 71.

Ful craftier to pley she was
Than Athalus, that made the game
First of the ches: so was his name.
The Book of the Duchesse, l. 662.

O litel book, thou art so unconning,
How darst thou put thy-self in prees for drede?
The Flower and the Leaf, l. 591.

Venus clerk, Ovyde,
That hath y-sowen wonder wyde
The grete god of Loves name.
Ib. The Hous of Fame, iii, l. 397.

And as for me, thogh that I can but lyte,
On bokes for to rede, I me delyte,
And to hem yeve I feyth and ful credence,
And in myn herte have hem in reverence
So hertely, that ther is game noon,
That fro my bokes maketh me to goon,
But hit be seldom, on the holyday;
Save, certeynly, whan that the month of May
Is comen, and that I here the foules singe,
And that the floures ginnen for to springe,
Farwel my book and my devocion.
Legend of Good Women, Prologue, l. 29.

That, of alle the floures in the mede,
Than love I most these floures whyte and rede,
Swiche as men callen daysies in our toun.   *Ib.*

Til that myn herte dye.   *Ib.* l. 57.

That wel by reson men hit calle may
The dayesye or elles the ye of day,
The emperice and flour of floures alle.
I pray to god that faire mot she falle,
And alle that loven floures, for hir sake !   *Ib.* l. 183.

For lo, the gentil kind of the lioun!
For whan a flye offendeth him or byteth,
He with his tayl awey the flye smyteth
Al esily; for, of his genterye,
Him deyneth nat to wreke him on a flye,
As doth a curre, or elles another beste.   *Ib.* l. 377.

And she was fair as is the rose in May.
     Ib. Legend of Cleopatra, l. 34.

The lyf so short, the craft so long to lerne,
Thassay so hard, so sharp the conquering.
     The Parlement of Foules, l. 1.

For out of olde feldes, as men seith,
Cometh al this newe corn froe yeer to yere;
And out of olde bokes, in good feith,
Cometh al this newe science that men lere.
     Ib. l. 22.

Thou shalt make castels than in Spayne,
And dreme of joye, al but in vayne.
     Romaunt of the Rose, B. l. 2573.

But the Troyane gestes, as they felle,
In Omer, or in Dares, or in Dyte,
Who-so that can, may rede hem as they wryte.
     Troilus and Criseyde, i, l. 145.

For it is seyd, man maketh ofte a yerde
With which the maker is him-self y-beten. *Ib.* l. 740.

O wind, O wind, the weder ginneth clere.
     Ib. ii, l. 2.

Til crowes feet be growe under your yë.   *Ib.* l. 403.

And we shal speke of thee som-what, I trowe,
Whan thou art goon, to do thyne eres glowe!
     Ib. l. 1021.

It is nought good a sleping hound to wake.
     Ib. iii, l. 764.

For I have seyn, of a ful misty morwe,
Folwen ful ofte a mery someres day.   *Ib.* l. 1060.

Right as an aspes leef she gan to quake.   *Ib.* l. 1200.

And as the newe abaysshed nightingale,
That stinteth first whan she biginneth singe.
     Ib. l. 1233.

For of fortunes sharp adversitee
The worst kinde of infortune is this,
A man to have ben in prosperitee,
And it remembren, whan it passed is.   *Ib.* l. 1625.

Oon ere it herde, at the other out it wente.
     Ib. iv, l. 434.

But manly set the world on Sixe and Sevene;
And, if thou deye a martir, go to hevene.   *Ib.* l. 622.

For tyme y-lost may not recovered be.   *Ib.* l. 1283.

Ye, fare-wel al the snow of ferne yere!   *Ib.* v, l. 1176.

Eek greet effect men wryte in place lyte. [i.e. little space]
Thentente is al, and nought the lettres space.
     Ib. l. 1629.

Go, litel book, go litel myn tragedie.   *Ib.* l. 1786.

O yonge fresshe folkes, he or she.   *Ib.* l. 1835.

O moral Gower, this book I directe
To thee.   *Ib.* l. 1856

ANDREW CHERRY

1762–1812

Loud roar'd the dreadful thunder,
   The rain a deluge show'rd.   *The Bay of Biscay*

Till next day,
There she lay,
In the Bay of Biscay, O!   *Ib.*

PHILIP DORMER STANHOPE, EARL OF CHESTERFIELD

1694–1773

In scandal, as in robbery, the receiver is always thought as bad as the thief.
     Advice to his Son. Rules for Conversation, Scandal.

In my mind, there is nothing so illiberal and so ill-bred, as audible laughter.   *Ib. Graces, Laughter.*

In my opinion, parsons are very like other men, and neither the better nor the worse for wearing a black gown.   *Letter to his Son, 5 Apr. 1746.*

The knowledge of the world is only to be acquired in the world, and not in a closet.   *Ib. 4 Oct. 1746.*

An injury is much sooner forgotten than an insult.
     Ib. 9 Oct. 1746.

Courts and camps are the only places to learn the world in.   *Ib. 2 Oct. 1747.*

There is a Spanish proverb, which says very justly, Tell me whom you live with, and I will tell you who you are.   *Ib. 9 Oct. 1747.*

Take the tone of the company that you are in.   *Ib.*

Do as you would be done by is the surest method that I know of pleasing.   *Ib. 16 Oct. 1747.*

I recommend you to take care of the minutes; for hours will take care of themselves. *Ib. 6 Nov. 1747.*

Advice is seldom welcome; and those who want it the most always like it the least. *Ib. 29 Jan. 1748.*

Speak of the moderns without contempt, and of the ancients without idolatry.   *Ib. 22 Feb. 1748.*

Wear your learning, like your watch, in a private pocket: and do not merely pull it out and strike it; merely to show that you have one.   *Ib.*

Sacrifice to the Graces.   *Ib. 9 Mar. 1748.*

If Shakespeare's genius had been cultivated, those beauties, which we so justly admire in him, would have been undisgraced by those extravagancies, and that nonsense, with which they are so frequently accompanied.   *Ib. 1 Apr. 1748.*

Women, then, are only children of a larger growth: they have an entertaining tattle, and sometimes wit; but for solid, reasoning good-sense, I never knew in my life one that had it, or who reasoned or acted consequentially for four and twenty hours together. *Ib. 5 Sept. 1748.*

A man of sense only trifles with them [women], plays with them, humours and flatters them, as he does with a sprightly and forward child; but he neither consults them about, nor trusts them with, serious matters. *Ib.*

It must be owned, that the Graces do not seem to be natives of Great Britain; and I doubt, the best of us here have more of rough than polished diamond. *Ib. 18 Nov. 1748.*

Idleness is only the refuge of weak minds. *Ib. 20 July, 1749.*

Women are much more like each other than men: they have, in truth, but two passions, vanity and love; these are their universal characteristics. *Ib. 19 Dec. 1749.*

Knowledge may give weight, but accomplishments give lustre, and many more people see than weigh. *Ib. 8 May 1750.*

Is it possible to love such a man? No. The utmost I can do for him is to consider him as a respectable Hottentot. [Lord Lyttelton] *Ib. 28 Feb. 1751.*

It is commonly said, and more particularly by Lord Shaftesbury, that ridicule is the best test of truth. *Ib. 6 Feb. 1752.*

Every woman is infallibly to be gained by every sort of flattery, and every man by one sort or other. *Ib. 16 Mar. 1752.*

In matters of religion and matrimony I never give any advice; because I will not have anybody's torments in this world or the next laid to my charge. *Letter to A. C. Stanhope, 12 Oct. 1765.*

Religion is by no means a proper subject of conversation in a mixed company. *Undated Letter to his Godson, No. 112.*

I assisted at the birth of that most significant word, *flirtation*, which dropped from the most beautiful mouth in the world. *The World, No. 101.*

Tyrawley and I have been dead these two years; but we don't choose to have it known. *Boswell's Johnson, 3 Apr. 1773.*

He once exclaimed to Anstis, Garter King at Arms, 'You foolish man, you do not even know your own foolish business.' *Jesse's Memoirs of the Court of England from 1688 to Geo. II, vol. ii.*

Give Dayrolles a chair. *Last Words. W. H. Craig, Life of Chesterfield.*

The dews of the evening most carefully shun,
Those tears of the sky for the loss of the sun. *Advice to a Lady in Autumn.*

Unlike my subject will I frame my song,
It shall be witty and it sha'n't be long. *Epigram on ['Long'] Sir Thomas Robinson. D.N.B.*

The picture plac'd the busts between,
Adds to the thought much strength;
Wisdom and Wit are little seen,
But Folly's at full length. *Wit and Wisdom of Lord Chesterfield. Epigrams. On the Picture of Richard Nash.. between the Busts of..Newton and..Pope..at Bath. (Attr. also to Mrs. Jane Brereton.)*

GILBERT KEITH CHESTERTON
1874–1936

Are they clinging to their crosses,
F. E. Smith? *Antichrist, or the Reunion of Christendom.*

Talk about the pews and steeples
And the cash that goes therewith!
But the souls of Christian peoples . . .
Chuck it, Smith! *Ib.*

Heaven shall forgive you Bridge at dawn,
The clothes you wear—or do not wear— *Ballade d'une Grande Dame.*

But for the virtuous things you do,
The righteous work, the public care,
It shall not be forgiven you. *Ib.*

They spoke of progress spiring round,
Of Light and Mrs. Humphry Ward—
It is not true to say I frowned,
Or ran about the room and roared;
I might have simply sat and snored—
I rose politely in the club
And said, 'I feel a little bored;
Will some one take me to a pub?' *A Ballade of an Anti-Puritan.*

I'll read 'Jack Redskin on the Quest'
And feed my brain with better things. *A Ballade of a Book Reviewer.*

Prince, Prince-Elective on the modern plan,
Fulfilling such a lot of people's Wills,
You take the Chiltern Hundreds while you can—
A storm is coming on the Chiltern Hills. *A Ballade of the First Rain.*

The gallows in my garden, people say,
Is new and neat and adequately tall. *A Ballade of Suicide.*

The strangest whim has seized me. . . . After all
I think I will not hang myself to-day. *Ib.*

Prince, I can hear the trumpet of Germinal,
The tumbrils toiling up the terrible way;
Even to-day your royal head may fall—
I think I will not hang myself to-day. *Ib.*

Before the gods that made the gods
Had seen their sunrise pass,
The White Horse of the White Horse Vale
Was cut out of the grass. *Ballad of the White Horse, bk. i.*

There was not English armour left,
Nor any English thing,
When Alfred came to Athelney
To be an English king. *Ib.*

I tell you naught for your comfort,
  Yea, naught for your desire,
Save that the sky grows darker yet
  And the sea rises higher.   *Ib.*

Last of a race in ruin—
  He spoke the speech of the Gaels.   *Ib.* bk. ii.

For the great Gaels of Ireland
  Are the men that God made mad,
For all their wars are merry,
  And all their songs are sad.   *Ib.*

The thing on the blind side of the heart,
  On the wrong side of the door,
The green plant groweth, menacing
  Almighty lovers in the spring;
There is always a forgotten thing,
  And love is not secure.   *Ib.* bk. iii.

We have more lust again to lose
  Than you to win again.   *Ib.*

And when the last arrow
    Was fitted and was flown,
When the broken shield was hung on the breast,
And the hopeless lance was laid in rest,
    And the hopeless horn blown,
The King looked up.   *Ib.* bk. vii.

Nelson turned his blindest eye
On Naples and on liberty.
            Blessed are the Peacemakers.

The Christ-child stood at Mary's knee,
  His hair was like a crown,
And all the flowers looked up at Him,
  And all the stars looked down.
                  A Christmas Carol.

When fishes flew and forests walked
  And figs grew upon thorn,
Some moment when the moon was blood
  Then surely I was born.

With monstrous head and sickening cry
  And ears like errant wings,
The devil's walking parody
  Of all four-footed things.   *The Donkey.*

Fools! For I also had my hour;
  One far fierce hour and sweet:
There was a shout about my ears,
  And palms before my feet.   *Ib.*

There is one creed: 'neath no world-terror's wing
Apples forget to grow on apple-trees.
                  Ecclesiastes.

The men that worked for England
  They have their graves at home:
  .   .   .   .
And they that rule in England,
  In stately conclave met,
Alas, alas for England
  They have no graves as yet.
          Elegy in a Country Churchyard.

But since he stood for England
  And knew what England means,
Unless you give him bacon
  You must not give him beans.   *The Englishman.*

Mr. Mandragon, the Millionaire.
                  The Good Rich Man.

When Man is the Turk, and the Atheist,
  Essene, Erastian Whig,
And the Thug and the Druse and the Catholic
  And the crew of the Captain's gig.
                    The Higher Unity

But our best is as far as the fire-drake swings
And our peace is put in impossible things
Where clashed and thundered unthinkable wings
  Round an incredible star.
              The House of Christmas.

Or must Fate act the same grey farce again,
  And wait, till one, amid Time's wrecks and scars,
Speaks to a ruin here, 'What poet-race
  Shot such Cyclopean arches at the stars?'
                  King's Cross Station.

White founts falling in the courts of the sun,
And the Soldan of Byzantium is smiling as they run.
                          Lepanto.

The cold queen of England is looking in the glass;
The shadow of the Valois is yawning at the Mass.
                                Ib.

Strong gongs groaning as the drums beat far.   *Ib.*

Don John of Austria is going to the war.   *Ib.*

It is he that saith not 'Kismet'; it is he that knows
    not fate;
It is Richard, it is Raymond, it is Godfrey in the
    gate!   *Ib.*

Cervantes on his galley sets the sword back in the
    sheath,
(Don John of Austria rides homeward with a wreath.)
                                              Ib.

And he smiles, but not as Sultans smile, and settles
    back the blade. . . .
(But Don John of Austria rides home from the
    Crusade.)   *Ib.*

For I come from Castlepatrick, and me heart is on me
    sleeve,
But a lady stole it from me on St. Gallowglass's Eve.
                          Me Heart.

The folk that live in Liverpool, their heart is in their
    boots;
They go to hell like lambs, they do, because the
    hooter hoots.   *Ib.*

And they think we're burning witches when we're
    only burning weeds.   *Ib.*

You saw the moon from Sussex Downs,
  A Sussex moon, untravelled still,
I saw a moon that was the town's,
  The largest lamp on Campden Hill.
          The Napoleon of Notting Hill, dedication.

This did not end by Nelson's urn
  Where an immortal England sits—
Nor where your tall young men in turn
  Drank death like wine at Austerlitz.   *Ib.*

Yes, Heaven is everywhere at home,
The big blue cap that always fits.   *Ib.*

The legend of an epic hour
  A child I dreamed, and dream it still,
Under the great grey water-tower
  That strikes the stars on Campden Hill.   *Ib.*

John Grubby, who was short and stout
And troubled with religious doubt,
Refused about the age of three
To sit upon the curate's knee.
The New Freethinker.

From all the easy speeches
    That comfort cruel men. *O God of Earth and Altar.*

'What of vile dust?' the preacher said.
    Methought the whole world woke.
The Praise of Dust.

Before the Roman came to Rye or out to Severn strode,
The rolling English drunkard made the rolling English road. *The Rolling English Road.*

That night we went to Birmingham by way of Beachy Head. *Ib.*

My friends we will not go again or ape an ancient rage,
Or stretch the folly of our youth to be the shame of age. *Ib.*

For there is good news yet to hear and fine things to be seen,
Before we go to Paradise by way of Kensal Green. *Ib.*

And a few men talked of freedom, while England talked of ale. *The Secret People.*

But the squire seemed struck in the saddle; he was foolish, as if in pain.
He leaned on a staggering lawyer, he clutched a cringing Jew,
He was stricken; it may be, after all, he was stricken at Waterloo. *Ib.*

We only know the last sad squires ride slowly towards the sea,
And a new people takes the land: and still it is not we. *Ib.*

Smile at us, pay us, pass us; but do not quite forget.
For we are the people of England, that never have spoken yet. *Ib.*

Lord Lilac thought it rather rotten
That Shakespeare should be quite forgotten,
And therefore got on a Committee
With several chaps out of the City.
The Shakespeare Memorial.

The souls most fed with Shakespeare's flame
Still sat unconquered in a ring,
Remembering him like anything. *Ib.*

But not with that grand constancy
Of Clement Shorter, Herbert Tree,
Lord Rosebery and Comyns Carr
And all the other names there are;
Who stuck like limpets to the spot,
Lest they forgot, lest they forgot.

Lord Lilac was of slighter stuff;
Lord Lilac had had quite enough. *Ib.*

God made the wicked Grocer
    For a mystery and a sign,
That men might shun the awful shop
    And go to inns to dine.
Song Against Grocers.

The evil-hearted Grocer
    Would call his mother 'Ma'am,'
And bow at her and bob at her,
    Her aged soul to damn. *Ib.*

He crams with cans of poisoned meat
    The subjects of the King,
And when they die by thousands
    Why, he laughs like anything. *Ib.*

He keeps a lady in a cage
    Most cruelly all day,
And makes her count and calls her 'Miss'
    Until she fades away. *Ib.*

The righteous minds of innkeepers
    Induce them now and then
To crack a bottle with a friend
    Or treat unmoneyed men,

But who hath seen the Grocer
    Treat housemaids to his teas
Or crack a bottle of fish-sauce
    Or stand a man a cheese? *Ib.*

And I dream of the days when work was scrappy,
    And rare in our pockets the mark of the mint,
And we were angry and poor and happy,
    And proud of seeing our names in print.
A Song of Defeat.

And sword in hand upon Afric's passes
    Her last republic cried to God. *Ib.*

And the faith of the poor is faint and partial,
    And the pride of the rich is all for sale,
And the chosen heralds of England's Marshal
    Are the sandwich-men of the *Daily Mail*. *Ib.*

They haven't got no noses,
    The fallen sons of Eve. *The Song of Quoodle.*

And goodness only knowses
    The Noselessness of Man. *Ib.*

But I, I cannot read it
    (Although I run and run)
Of them that do not have the faith,
    And will not have the fun.
The Song of the Strange Ascetic.

Where his aunts, who are not married,
    Demand to be divorced. *Ib.*

Tea, although an Oriental,
Is a gentleman at least;
Cocoa is a cad and coward,
Cocoa is a vulgar beast.
The Song of Right and Wrong.

When old unbroken Pickwick walked
    Among the broken men.
When I Came Back to Fleet Street.

Still he that scorns and struggles
    Sees, frightful and afar,
All that they leave of rebels
    Rot high on Temple Bar. *Ib.*

And Noah he often said to his wife when he sat down to dine,
'I don't care where the water goes if it doesn't get into the wine.' *Wine and Water.*

Step softly, under snow or rain,
    To find the place where men can pray;
The way is all so very plain
    That we may lose the way. *The Wise Men.*

'Call upon the wheels, master, call upon the wheels;
We are taking rest, master, finding how it feels.'
Song of the Wheels.

And that is the meaning of Empire Day.
> *Songs of Education. Geography.*

All slang is metaphor, and all metaphor is poetry.
> *The Defendant. A Defence of Slang.*

There is nothing the matter with Americans except their ideals. The real American is all right; it is the ideal American who is all wrong.
> *New York Times, 1 Feb. 1931.* Reprinted in *Sidelights.*

He [Tennyson] could not think up to the height of his own towering style.
> *Victorian Age in Literature, ch. 3.*

ALBERT CHEVALIER
1861–1923

'Wot's the good of Hanyfink? Why—Nuffink!'
> *Cockney Complaint.*

We've been together now for forty years,
    An' it don't seem a day too much;
There ain't a lady livin' in the land
    As I'd 'swop' for my dear old Dutch! *My Old Dutch.*

Knocked 'em in the Old Kent Road. *Title of Song.*

WILLIAM CHILLINGWORTH
1602–1644

The Bible and the Bible only is the religion of Protestants. *The Religion of Protestants.*

RUFUS CHOATE
1799–1858

Its constitution the glittering and sounding generalities of natural right which make up the Declaration of Independence.
> *Letter to the Maine Whig State Central Committee, 9 Aug. 1856.*

HENRY FOTHERGILL CHORLEY
1808–1872

God the All-terrible! King, Who ordainest
Great winds Thy clarions, the lightnings Thy sword.
> *Hullah's Part Music. God The All-Terrible!*

DAVID CHRISTY
1802–?

Cotton is King. *Title of book, 1855.*

CHARLES CHURCHILL
1731–1764

Greatly his foes he dreads, but more his friends;
He hurts me most who lavishly commends.
> *The Apology, l. 19.*

Though by whim, envy, or resentment led,
They damn those authors whom they never read.
> *The Candidate, l. 57.*

The only difference, after all their rout,
Is, that the one is in, the other out.
> *The Conference, l. 165.*

If all, if all alas! were well at home. *Ib. l. 226.*

Be England what she will,
With all her faults, she is my country still.
> *The Farewell, l. 27.*

It can't be Nature, for it is not sense. *Ib. l. 200.*

England—a happy land we know,
Where follies naturally grow.
> *The Ghost, bk. i, l. 111.*

Fame
Is nothing but an empty name. *Ib. l. 229.*

And adepts in the speaking trade
Keep a cough by them ready made. *Ib. bk. ii, l. 545.*

Who wit with jealous eye surveys,
And sickens at another's praise. *Ib. l. 663.*

Just to the windward of the law. *Ib. bk. iii, l. 56.*

He for subscribers baits his hook,
And takes your cash; but where's the book?
No matter where; wise fear, you know,
Forbids the robbing of a foe;
But what, to serve our private ends,
Forbids the cheating of our friends? *Ib. l. 801.*

A joke's a very serious thing. *Ib. bk. iv, l. 1386.*

Railing at life, and yet afraid of death.
> *Gotham, i, l. 215.*

Thy danger chiefly lies in acting well;
No crime's so great as daring to excel.
> *Epistle to William Hogarth, l. 51.*

Candour, who, with the charity of Paul,
Still thinks the best, whene'er she thinks at all,
With the sweet milk of human kindness bless'd,
The furious ardour of my zeal repress'd. *Ib. l. 55.*

By different methods different men excel;
But where is he who can do all things well?
> *Ib. l. 573.*

Keep up appearances; there lies the test;
The world will give thee credit for the rest.
Outward be fair, however foul within;
Sin if thou wilt, but then in secret sin. *Night, l. 311.*

As one with watching and with study faint,
Reel in a drunkard, and reel out a saint. *Ib. l. 323.*

Who often, but without success, have pray'd
For apt Alliteration's artful aid.
> *The Prophecy of Famine, l. 85.*

A heart to pity, and a hand to bless. *Ib. l. 178.*

He sicken'd at all triumphs but his own.
> *The Rosciad, l. 64.*

Ne'er blush'd unless, in spreading Vice's snares,
She blunder'd on some virtue unawares. *Ib. l. 137.*

Genius is of no country. *Ib. l. 207.*

He mouths a sentence, as curs mouth a bone.
> *Ib. l. 322.*

Fashion!—a word which knaves and fools may use,
Their knavery and folly to excuse. *Ib. l. 455.*

So much they talk'd, so very little said. *Ib. l. 550.*

Not without art, but yet to nature true. *Ib. l. 699.*

But, spite of all the criticizing elves,
Those who would make us feel, must feel themselves.
Ib. l. 961.

The two extremes appear like man and wife,
Coupled together for the sake of strife.
The Rosciad, l. 1005.

Where he falls short, 'tis Nature's fault alone;
Where he succeeds, the merit's all his own.
Ib. l. 1025.

The best things carried to excess are wrong.
Ib. l. 1039.

With the persuasive language of a tear.
The Times, l. 308.

LORD RANDOLPH SPENCER CHURCHILL

1849–1894

The old gang. [Members of the Conservative Government.]
Speech, House of Commons, 7 Mar. 1878.

He told them that he would give them and all other subjects of the Queen much legislation, great prosperity, and universal peace, and he has given them nothing but chips. Chips to the faithful allies in Afghanistan, chips to the trusting native races of South Africa, chips to the Egyptian fellah, chips to the British farmer, chips to the manufacturer and the artisan, chips to the agricultural labourer, chips to the House of Commons itself.
Ib. 24 Jan. 1884.

An old man in a hurry. [Gladstone.]
Ib. To the Electors of South Paddington, June 1886.

Ulster will fight; Ulster will be right.
Letter, 7 May 1886.

All great men make mistakes. Napoleon forgot Blücher, I forgot Goschen.
Leaves from the Notebooks of Lady Dorothy Nevill, p. 21.

The duty of an Opposition is to oppose.
1830. Quoted by Lord Randolph Churchill. W. S. Churchill, *Lord Randolph Churchill,* vol. i, ch. 5.

WINSTON LEONARD SPENCER CHURCHILL

1874–

It cannot in the opinion of His Majesty's Government be classified as slavery in the extreme acceptance of the word without some risk of terminological inexactitude.   *Speech, H. of C., 22 Feb. 1906.*

COLLEY CIBBER

1671–1757

O say! What is that thing called Light,
Which I can ne'er enjoy.   *The Blind Boy.*

Whilst thus I sing, I am a King,
Altho' a poor blind boy.   *Ib.*

Oh! how many torments lie in the small circle of a wedding-ring!   *The Double Gallant,* i. ii.

Dumb 's a sly dog.   *Love Makes a Man,* iv. i.

One had as good be out of the world, as out of the fashion.   *Love's Last Shift,* Act ii.

Off with his head—so much for Buckingham.
Richard III, altered, iv. iii.

A weak invention of the enemy.   *Ib.* v. iii.

Conscience avaunt, *Richard 's* himself again:
Hark! the shrill trumpet sounds, to horse, away,
My soul 's in arms, and eager for the fray.   *Ib.*

Perish the thought!   *Ib.* v.

Losers must have leave to speak.
The Rival Fools, Act i.

Stolen sweets are best.   *Ib.*

This business will never hold water.
She Would and She Would Not, Act iv.

Persuasion tips his tongue whene'er he talks,
And he has chambers in the King's Bench Walks.
Parody of Pope's lines on William Murray, Lord Mansfield, in Satires and Epistles of Horace Imitated, Bk. I, Ep. vi.

EARL OF CLARENDON

see

EDWARD HYDE

HENRY CLAY

1777–1852

I had rather be right than be President.
To Senator Preston of South Carolina, 1839.

The gentleman [Josiah Quincy] can not have forgotten his own sentiments, uttered even on the floor of this House, 'peaceably if we can, forcibly if we must'.
Speech, 8 Jan. 1813; Works, 1904, vol. vi, p. 58.

STEPHEN GROVER CLEVELAND

1837–1908

I have considered the pension list of the republic a roll of honour.
Veto of Dependent Pension Bill, 5 July 1888.

ROBERT CLIVE LORD CLIVE

1725–1774

By God, Mr. Chairman, at this moment I stand astonished at my own moderation!
Reply during Parliamentary cross-examination, 1773.

I feel that I am reserved for some end or other.
　　*Words when his pistol failed to go off twice, in
　　his attempt to commit suicide. G. R. Gleig,
　　Life, ch. 1.*

ARTHUR HUGH CLOUGH

1819–1861

Juxtaposition, in short; and what is juxtaposition?
　　　　　　　　Amours de Voyage, I. xi. 25.

Allah is great, no doubt, and Juxtaposition his prophet.
　　　　　　　　Ib. III. vi. 1.

Mild monastic faces in quiet collegiate cloisters.
　　　　　　　　Ib. III. ix. 1.

Tibur is beautiful, too, and the orchard slopes, and
　　the Anio
Falling, falling yet, to the ancient lyrical cadence.
　　　　　　　　Ib. III. xi. 1.

Whither depart the souls of the brave that die in the
　　battle,
Die in the lost, lost fight, for the cause that perishes
　　with them?　　　　　　*Ib.* V. vi. 6.

Say, 'I am flitting about many years from brain unto
　　brain of
Feeble and restless youths born to inglorious days:
But,' so finish the word, 'I was writ in a Roman
　　chamber,
When from Janiculan heights thundered the cannon
　　of France.'　　　　　　*Ib.* end.

The grave man, nicknamed Adam.
　　　　　The Bothie of Tober-na-Vuolich, i.

　　　　　　　　Over a ledge of granite
Into a granite basin the amber torrent descended. *Ib.*

Petticoats up to the knees, or even, it might be, above
　them.　　　　　　　　　*Ib.* ii.

Hope an Antinoüs mere, Hyperion of calves the
　Piper.　　　　　　　　　*Ib.*

Sesquipedalian blackguard.　　　　*Ib.*

Thicksides and *hairy* Aldrich.　　　*Ib.*

Grace is given of God, but knowledge is bought in the
　market.　　　　　　　　*Ib.* iv.

Bright October was come, the misty-bright October.
　　　　　　　　　　　　Ib. vi.

Dangerous Corryvreckan.　　　　*Ib.* ix.

This Rachel-and-Leah is marriage.　　*Ib.*

They are married and gone to New Zealand.　*Ib.*

'There is no God,' the wicked saith,
　'And truly it's a blessing,
For what He might have done with us
　It's better only guessing.'　　*Dipsychus*, pt. I. v.

But country folks who live beneath
　The shadow of the steeple;
The parson and the parson's wife,
　And mostly married people;

Youths green and happy in first love,
　So thankful for illusion;
And men caught out in what the world
　Calls guilt, in first confusion;

And almost every one when age,
　Disease, or sorrows strike him,
Inclines to think there is a God,
　Or something very like Him.　　　　*Ib.*

　　　　Delicious. Ah!
What else is like the gondola?　　*Ib.* pt. II. ii.

How pleasant it is to have money.　　*Ib.*

Home, Rose, and home, Provence and La Palie.
　　　　Ite Domum Saturae, Venit Hesperus.

Thou shalt have one God only; who
Would be at the expense of two?
　　　　　　The Latest Decalogue.

Do not adultery commit;
Advantage rarely comes of it.　　　　*Ib.*

Thou shalt not kill; but need'st not strive
Officiously to keep alive.　　　　　*Ib.*

Lo, here is God, and there is God,
　Believe it not, O Man.　　*The New Sinai.*

What voice did on my spirit fall,
Peschiera, when thy bridge I crost?
"T is better to have fought and lost,
Than never to have fought at all.'　　*Peschiera.*

As ships, becalmed at eve, that lay
　With canvas drooping, side by side,
Two towers of sail at dawn of day
　Are scarce long leagues apart, descried.
　　　　　　Qua Cursum Ventus.

O bounding breeze, O rushing seas!
　At last, at last, unite them there!　　　*Ib.*

Say not, the struggle naught availeth,
　The labour and the wounds are vain,
The enemy faints not, nor faileth,
　And as things have been they remain.

If hopes were dupes, fears may be liars;
　It may be, in yon smoke concealed,
Your comrades chase e'en now the fliers,
　And, but for you, possess the field.

For while the tired waves, vainly breaking,
　Seem here no painful inch to gain,
Far back, through creeks and inlets making,
　Comes silent, flooding in, the main.

And not by eastern windows only,
　When daylight comes, comes in the light,
In front, the sun climbs slow, how slowly,
　But westward, look, the land is bright.
　　Say Not, the Struggle Naught Availeth.

Green fields of England! whereso'er
　Across this watery waste we fare,
Your image at our hearts we bear
　Green fields of England, everywhere.
　　Songs in Absence. Green Fields of England!

To finger idly some old Gordian knot,
Unskilled to sunder, and too weak to cleave,
And with much toil attain to half-believe.
　　　　Ib. Come back, Come back.

Some future day when what is now is not,
When all old faults and follies are forgot.
　　　　　Ib. Some Future Day.

Where lies the land to which the ship would go?
Far, far ahead, is all her seamen know,
And where the land she travels from? Away.
Far, far behind, is all that they can say.
Ib. Where Lies the Land.

That out of sight is out of mind
Is true of most we leave behind.
Ib. That Out of Sight.

WILLIAM COBBETT
1762–1835

The slavery of the tea and coffee and other slop-kettle. *Advice to Young Men, Letter* i, 31.

Nouns of number, or multitude, such as *Mob*, Parliament, Rabble, House of Commons, Regiment, Court of King's Bench, Den of Thieves, and the like.
English Grammar, Letter xvii, *Syntax as Relating to Pronouns.*

All is vulgar, all clumsy, all dull, all torpid inanity.
Ib. Letter xxiv, *Six Lessons, Lesson* 4.

From a very early age, I had imbibed the opinion, that it was every man's duty to do all that lay in his power to leave his country as good as he had found it. *Political Register, 22 Dec. 1832.*

Give me, Lord, neither poverty nor riches. *Ib.*

But what is to be the fate of the great wen (London) of all? The monster, called . . . 'the metropolis of the empire?' *Rural Rides, 1821.*

RICHARD COBDEN
1804–1865

I believe it has been said that one copy of *The Times* contains more useful information than the whole of the historical works of Thucydides.
Speech, Manchester, 27 Dec. 1850.

CHARLES COBORN
1852–

Two lovely black eyes,
Oh! what a surprise!
Only for telling a man he was wrong,
Two lovely black eyes! *Two Lovely Black Eyes.*

ALISON COCKBURN
1713–1794

I've seen the smiling of Fortune beguiling,
I've felt all its favours and found its decay.
The Flowers of the Forest.

I've seen the forest adorn'd the foremost,
With flowers of the fairest, most pleasant and gay:
Sae bonny was their blooming, their scents the air perfuming,
But now they are wither'd and weeded away. *Ib.*

For the flowers of the forest are withered away. *Ib.*

ASTON COKAYNE
1608–1684

Sydney, whom we yet admire
Lighting our little torches at his fire,
Funeral Elegy on Mr. Michael Drayton.

SIR EDWARD COKE
1552–1634

Magna Charta is such a fellow, that he will have no sovereign.
On the Lords' Amendment to the Petition of Right, 17 May 1628. Rushworth's Hist. Coll., 1659, i.

How long soever it hath continued, if it be against reason, it is of no force in law.
Institutes: Commentary upon Littleton. First Institute, § 80.

Reason is the life of the law, nay the common law itself is nothing else but reason. . . . The law, which is perfection of reason. *Ib.* § 138.

The gladsome light of Jurisprudence. *Ib. epilogus.*

For a man's house is his castle, *et domus sua cuique est tutissimum refugium. Ib. Third Institute,* cap. 73.

The house of every one is to him as his castle and fortress. *Semayne's Case,* 5 Rep. 91*b.*

Six hours in sleep, in law's grave study six,
Four spend in prayer, the rest on Nature fix.
Pandects, lib. II, tit. iv, *De in Jus vocando.*

They [corporations] cannot commit treason, nor be outlawed, nor excommunicate, for they have no souls. *Sutton's Hospital Case,* 10 Rep. 32*b.*

HARTLEY COLERIDGE
1796–1849

But what is Freedom? Rightly understood,
A universal licence to be good. *Liberty.*

She is not fair to outward view
As many maidens be;
Her loveliness I never knew
Until she smiled on me.
Oh! then I saw her eye was bright,
A well of love, a spring of light. *Song. She is not Fair.*

Her very frowns are fairer far,
Than smiles of other maidens are. *Ib.*

Old times unqueen thee, and old loves endear thee.
To a Lofty Beauty, from her Poor Kinsman.

SIR JOHN COLERIDGE,
BARON COLERIDGE
1820–1894

I speak not of this college or of that, but of the University as a whole; and, gentlemen, what a *whole* Oxford is!
G. W. E. Russell's Collections and Recollections, ch. 29.

MARY ELIZABETH COLERIDGE

1861–1907

Mother of God! no lady thou:
Common woman of common earth!   *Our Lady.*

We were young, we were merry, we were very, very
        wise,
And the door stood open at our feast,
When there passed us a woman with the West in her
        eyes,
And a man with his back to the East.   *Unwelcome.*

SAMUEL TAYLOR COLERIDGE

1772–1834

It is an ancient Mariner,
And he stoppeth one of three.
'By thy long grey beard and glittering eye,
Now wherefore stopp'st thou me?'
                The Ancient Mariner, pt. i.

The guests are met, the feast is set:
May'st hear the merry din.   *Ib.*

He holds him with his skinny hand,
'There was a ship,' quoth he.
'Hold off! unhand me, grey-beard loon!'
Eftsoons his hand dropt he.

He holds him with his glittering eye—
The Wedding-Guest stood still,
And listens like a three years' child:
The Mariner hath his will.

The Wedding-Guest sat on a stone:
He cannot choose but hear;
And thus spake on that ancient man,
The bright-eyed Mariner.   *Ib.*

The ship was cheered, the harbour cleared,
Merrily did we drop
Below the kirk, below the hill,
Below the lighthouse top.

The Sun came up upon the left.
Out of the sea came he!
And he shone bright, and on the right
Went down into the sea.   *Ib.*

The Wedding-Guest here beat his breast,
For he heard the loud bassoon.   *Ib.*

The bride hath paced into the hall,
Red as a rose is she.   *Ib.*

As who pursued with yell and blow
Still treads the shadow of his foe,
And forward bends his head.   *Ib.*

And ice, mast-high, came floating by,
As green as emerald.   *Ib.*

The ice was here, the ice was there,
The ice was all around:
It cracked and growled, and roared and howled,
Like noises in a swound!   *Ib.*

It ate the food it ne'er had eat,
And round and round it flew.

The ice did split with a thunder-fit;
The helmsman steered us through!   *Ib.*

And a good south wind sprung up behind;
The Albatross did follow,
And every day, for food or play,
Came to the mariner's hollo!   *Ib.*

'God save thee, ancient Mariner!
From the fiends that plague thee thus!—
Why look'st thou so?'—With my cross-bow
I shot the Albatross.   *Ib.*

Nor dim nor red, like God's own head,
The glorious Sun uprist.   *Ib.* pt. ii.

We were the first that ever burst
Into that silent sea.   *Ib.*

All in a hot and copper sky,
The bloody Sun, at noon,
Right up above the mast did stand,
No bigger than the Moon.   *Ib.*

As idle as a painted ship
Upon a painted ocean.   *Ib.*

Water, water, every where,
And all the boards did shrink;
Water, water, everywhere,
Nor any drop to drink.

The very deep did rot: O Christ!
That ever this should be!
Yea, slimy things did crawl with legs
Upon the slimy sea.

About, about, in reel and rout
The death-fires danced at night;
The water, like a witch's oils,
Burnt green, and blue and white.   *Ib.*

Nine fathom deep he had followed us
        From the land of mist and snow.   *Ib.*

There passed a weary time. Each throat
Was parched, and glazed each eye.
A weary time! a weary time!
How glazed each weary eye.   *Ib.* pt. iii.

I bit my arm, I sucked the blood,
And cried, A sail! a sail!   *Ib.*

Gramercy! they for joy did grin,
And all at once their breath drew in,
As they were drinking all.   *Ib.*

When that strange shape drove suddenly
        Betwixt us and the Sun.   *Ib.*

And straight the Sun was flecked with bars,
(Heaven's Mother send us grace!)
As if through a dungeon-grate he peered
With broad and burning face.   *Ib.*

Her lips were red, *her* looks were free,
Her locks were yellow as gold:
Her skin was white as leprosy,
The Night-mare LIFE-IN-DEATH was she,
Who thicks man's blood with cold.

The naked hulk alongside came,
And the twain were casting dice;
'The game is done! I've won! I've won!'
Quoth she, and whistles thrice.   *Ib.*

The Sun's rim dips; the stars rush out:
At one stride comes the dark;
With far-heard whisper, o'er the sea,
Off shot the spectre-bark. *The Ancient Mariner*, pt. iii.

We listened and looked sideways up!   *Ib.*

The hornèd Moon, with one bright star
Within the nether tip.   *Ib.*

Each turned his face with a ghastly pang,
And cursed me with his eye.   *Ib.*

And every soul, it passed me by,
Like the whizz of my cross-bow!   *Ib.*

'I fear thee, ancient Mariner!
I fear thy skinny hand!
And thou art long, and lank, and brown,
As is the ribbed sea-sand.'   *Ib.* pt. iv.

Alone, alone, all, all alone,
Alone on a wide wide sea!
And never a saint took pity on
My soul in agony.   *Ib.*

And a thousand thousand slimy things
Lived on; and so did I.   *Ib.*

An orphan's curse would drag to hell
A spirit from on high;
But oh! more horrible than that
Is the curse in a dead man's eye.   *Ib.*

The moving Moon went up the sky,
And no where did abide:
Softly she was going up,
And a star or two beside.   *Ib.*

And everywhere the blue sky belongs to them, and
is their appointed rest and their native country
and their own natural homes, which they enter unannounced, as lords that are certainly expected,
and yet there is a silent joy at their arrival [the
stars].   *Ib. gloss.*

But where the ship's huge shadow lay,
The charmed water burned alway
A still and awful red.   *Ib.*

A spring of love gushed from my heart,
And I blessed them unaware.   *Ib.*

Oh Sleep! it is a gentle thing,
Beloved from pole to pole!
To Mary Queen the praise be given!
She sent the gentle sleep from Heaven,
That slid into my soul.   *Ib.* pt. v.

The silly buckets on the deck,
That had so long remained,
I dreamt that they were filled with dew;
And when I awoke, it rained.   *Ib.*

Sure I had drunken in my dreams,
And still my body drank.   *Ib.*

Beneath the lightning and the Moon
The dead men gave a groan.   *Ib.*

It had been strange, even in a dream,
To have seen those dead men rise.   *Ib.*

We were a ghastly crew.   *Ib.*

The body of my brother's son
Stood by me, knee to knee:
The body and I pulled at one rope,
But he said nought to me.   *Ib.*

How they seemed to fill the sea and air
With their sweet jargoning!   *Ib.*

It ceased; yet still the sails made on
A pleasant noise till noon,
A noise like of a hidden brook
In the leafy month of June,
That to the sleeping woods all night
Singeth a quiet tune.   *Ib.*

With a short uneasy motion.   *Ib.*

Quoth he, 'The man hath penance done,
And penance more will do.'   *Ib.*

The air is cut away before,
And closes from behind.   *Ib.* pt. vi.

Like one, that on a lonesome road
Doth walk in fear and dread,
And having once turned round walks on,
And turns no more his head;
Because he knows, a frightful fiend
Doth close behind him tread.   *Ib.*

It raised my hair, it fanned my cheek
Like a meadow-gale of spring.   *Ib.*

Oh! dream of joy! is this indeed
The lighthouse top I see?
Is this the hill? is this the kirk?
Is this mine own countree?   *Ib.*

O let me be awake, my God!
Or let me sleep alway.   *Ib.*

A man all light, a seraph-man,
On every corse there stood.

This seraph-band, each waved his hand:
It was a heavenly sight!
They stood as signals to the land,
Each one a lovely light.   *Ib.*

No voice; but oh! the silence sank
Like music on my heart.   *Ib.*

This Hermit good lives in that wood
Which slopes down to the sea.
How loudly his sweet voice he rears!
He loves to talk with mariners
That come from a far countree.

He kneels at morn, and noon, and eve—
He hath a cushion plump:
It is the moss that wholly hides
The rotted old oak-stump.   *Ib.* pt. vii.

Brown skeletons of leaves that lag
My forest-brook along;
When the ivy-tod is heavy with snow,
And the owlet whoops to the wolf below,
That eats the she-wolf's young.   *Ib.*

Under the water it rumbled on,
  Still louder and more dread:
It reached the ship, it split the bay;
  The ship went down like lead.   *Ib.*

I moved my lips—the Pilot shrieked
And fell down in a fit;
The holy Hermit raised his eyes,
And prayed where he did sit.

I took the oars: the Pilot's boy,
Who now doth crazy go,
Laughed loud and long, and all the while
His eyes went to and fro.
'Ha! ha!' quoth he, 'full well I see,
The Devil knows how to row.'   *Ib.*

I pass, like night, from land to land;
I have strange powers of speech;
That moment that his face I see,
I know the man that must hear me:
To him my tale I teach. *The Ancient Mariner*, pt. vii.

And hark the little vesper-bell,
Which biddeth me to prayer!   *Ib.*

O Wedding-Guest! this soul hath been
Alone on a wide wide sea:
So lonely 'twas, that God himself
Scarce seemed there to be.   *Ib.*

O sweeter than the marriage-feast,
'Tis sweeter far to me,
To walk together to the kirk
With a goodly company.
To walk together to the kirk,
And all together pray,
While each to his great Father bends,
Old men, and babes, and loving friends
And youths and maidens gay!   *Ib.*

He prayeth well, who loveth well
Both man and bird and beast.
He prayeth best, who loveth best
All things both great and small;
For the dear God who loveth us,
He made and loveth all.   *Ib.*

He went like one that hath been stunned,
And is of sense forlorn:
A sadder and a wiser man,
He rose the morrow morn.   *Ib.*

That he sings, and he sings; and for ever sings he—
'I love my Love, and my Love loves me!'
                    Answer to a Child's Question.

And the Spring comes slowly up this way,
                              Christabel, pt. i.

I guess, 'twas frightful there to see
A lady so richly clad as she—
Beautiful exceedingly!   *Ib.*

Carved with figures strange and sweet,
All made out of the carver's brain.   *Ib.*

A sight to dream of, not to tell!   *Ib.*

But this she knows, in joys and woes,
That saints will aid if men will call:
For the blue sky bends over all!   *Ib.*

Each matin bell, the Baron saith,
Knells us back to a world of death.   *Ib.* pt. ii.

Alas! they had been friends in youth;
But whispering tongues can poison truth.   *Ib.*

And constancy lives in realms above;
And life is thorny; and youth is vain;
And to be wroth with one we love
Doth work like madness in the brain.   *Ib.*

They stood aloof, the scars remaining,
Like cliffs which had been rent asunder;
A dreary sea now flows between.   *Ib.*

In Köhln, a town of monks and bones,
And pavements fang'd with murderous stones
And rags, and hags, and hideous wenches;
I counted two and seventy stenches,
All well defined, and several stinks!

Ye Nymphs that reign o'er sewers and sinks,
The river Rhine, it is well known,
Doth wash your city of Cologne;
But tell me, Nymphs, what power divine
Shall henceforth wash the river Rhine?   *Cologne.*

My eyes make pictures, when they are shut.
                              A Day-Dream.

Well! If the Bard was weatherwise, who made
The grand old ballad of Sir Patrick Spence.
                    Dejection: an Ode.

I see them all so excellently fair,
I see, not feel, how beautiful they are!   *Ib.*

O Lady! we receive but what we give,
And in our life alone does Nature live   *Ib*

A light, a glory, a fair luminous cloud
    Enveloping the Earth.   *Ib.*

Joy is the sweet voice, joy the luminous cloud—
    We in ourselves rejoice!
And thence flows all that charms or ear or sight,
    All melodies the echoes of that voice,
All colours a suffusion from that light.   *Ib.*

From his brimstone bed at break of day
    A walking the Devil is gone,
To visit his snug little farm the earth,
    And see how his stock goes on.
                    The Devil's Thoughts.

And backward and forward he switched his long tail
As a gentleman switches his cane.   *Ib.*

His jacket was red and his breeches were blue,
And there was a hole where the tail came through.
                                                 Ib.

He saw a Lawyer killing a viper
    On a dunghill hard by his own stable;
And the Devil smiled, for it put him in mind
    Of Cain and his brother, Abel.   *Ib.*

He saw a cottage with a double coach-house,
    A cottage of gentility;
And the Devil did grin, for his darling sin
    Is pride that apes humility.   *Ib.*

As he went through Cold-Bath Fields he saw
    A solitary cell;
And the Devil was pleased, for it gave him a hint
    For improving his prisons in Hell.   *Ib.*

With Donne, whose muse on dromedary trots,
Wreathe iron pokers into true-love knots.
                        On Donne's Poetry.

What is an Epigram? a dwarfish whole,
Its body brevity, and wit its soul.   *Epigram.*

Swans sing before they die—'twere no bad thing
Did certain persons die before they sing.
                    Epigram on a Volunteer Singer.

Stop, Christian passer-by!—Stop, child of God.
                        Epitaph for Himself.

Ere sin could blight or sorrow fade,
    Death came with friendly care:
The opening bud to Heaven convey'd,
    And bade it blossom *there*.   *Epitaph on an Infant.*

Forth from his dark and lonely hiding-place
(Portentous sight)! the owlet Atheism,
Sailing on obscene wings athwart the noon,
Drops his blue-fringèd lids, and holds them close,
And hooting at the glorious sun in Heaven,
Cries out, 'Where is it?'   *Fears in Solitude.*

Letters four do form his name [Pitt].
Fire, Famine and Slaughter.

With what deep worship I have still adored
The spirit of divinest Liberty.   *France.*

So for the mother's sake the child was dear,
And dearer was the mother for the child.
*Sonnet to a Friend Who Asked How I Felt
When the Nurse First Presented My Infant
to Me.*

The frost performs its secret ministry,
Unhelped by any wind.   *Frost at Midnight.*

Only that film, which fluttered on the grate,
Still flutters there, the sole unquiet thing.   *Ib.*

Therefore all seasons shall be sweet to thee,
Whether the summer clothe the general earth
With greenness, or the redbreast sit and sing
Betwixt the tufts of snow on the bare branch
Of mossy apple-tree, while the nigh thatch
Smokes in the sun-thaw; whether the eave-drops
          fall
Heard only in the trances of the blast,
Or if the secret ministry of frost
Shall hang them up in silent icicles,
Quietly shining to the quiet moon.   *Ib.*

It sounds like stories from the land of spirits
If any man obtain that which he merits
Or any merit that which he obtains.
The Good, Great Man.

'Tis sweet to him who all the week
     Through city-crowds must push his way,
To stroll alone through fields and woods,
     And hallow thus the Sabbath-day.   *Home-Sick.*

Hast thou a charm to stay the morning-star
In his steep course?
Hymn before Sun-rise, in the Vale of Chamouni.

Earth, with her thousand voices, praises God.   *Ib.*

The Knight's bones are dust,
And his good sword rust;—
His soul is with the saints, I trust.
The Knight's Tomb.

In Xanadu did Kubla Khan
A stately pleasure-dome decree:
Where Alph, the sacred river, ran
Through caverns measureless to man
     Down to a sunless sea.
So twice five miles of fertile ground
With walls and towers were girdled round:
And there were gardens bright with sinuous rills,
Where blossomed many an incense-bearing tree;
And here were forests ancient as the hills,
Enfolding sunny spots of greenery.
But oh! that deep romantic chasm which slanted
Down the green hill athwart a cedarn cover!
A savage place! as holy and enchanted
As e'er beneath a waning moon was haunted
By woman wailing for her demon-lover!
And from this chasm, with ceaseless turmoil seething,
As if this earth in fast thick pants were breathing,
A mighty fountain momently was forced.
Kubla Khan.

And 'mid these dancing rocks at once and ever
It flung up momently the sacred river.
Five miles meandering with a mazy motion

Through wood and dale the sacred river ran,
Then reached the caverns measureless to man,
And sank in tumult to a lifeless ocean:
And 'mid this tumult Kubla heard from far
Ancestral voices prophesying war!

The shadow of the dome of pleasure
Floated midway on the waves;
Where was heard the mingled measure
From the fountain and the caves.
It was a miracle of rare device,
A sunny pleasure-dome with caves of ice!

A damsel with a dulcimer
In a vision once I saw:
It was an Abyssinian maid,
And on her dulcimer she played,
Singing of Mount Abora.
Could I revive within me
Her symphony and song,
To such a deep delight 'twould me,
That with music loud and long,
I would build that dome in air,
That sunny dome! those caves of ice!
And all who heard should see them there,
And all should cry, Beware! Beware!
His flashing eyes, his floating hair!
Weave a circle round him thrice,
And close your eyes with holy dread,
For he on honey-dew hath fed,
And drunk the milk of Paradise.   *Ib.*

Image of Lewti! from my mind
Depart, for Lewti is not kind.   *Lewti.*

This Lime-tree Bower my Prison.   *Title.*

A charm
For thee, my gentle-hearted Charles, to whom
No sound is dissonant which tells of Life.   *Ib. l. 74.*

All thoughts, all passions, all delights,
     Whatever stirs this mortal frame,
All are but ministers of Love,
     And feed his sacred flame.   *Love.*

Trochee trips from long to short.   *Metrical Feet.*

Iambics march from short to long;—
With a leap and a bound the swift Anapaests throng.
Ib.

Choose thou whatever suits the line;
Call me Sappho, call me Chloris,
Call me Lalage or Doris,
     Only, only call me thine.   *Names.*

'Most musical, most melancholy' bird!
A melancholy bird? Oh! idle thought!
     In Nature there is nothing melancholy.
The Nightingale.

In the hexameter rises the fountain's silvery column;
In the pentameter aye falling in melody back.
Ovidian Elegiac Metre.

The fair humanities of old religion.
Piccolomini, II. iv.

But still the heart doth need a language, still
Doth the old instinct bring back the old names.   *Ib.*

Something childish, but very natural.   *Title.*

O! I do love thee, meek *Simplicity*!
*Sonnets Attempted in the Manner of Contem-
porary Writers. 2. To Simplicity.*

And this reft house is that the which he built,
Lamented Jack!
Ib. 3. *On a Ruined House in a Romantic Country.*

A mother is a mother still,
The holiest thing alive. *The Three Graves*, pt. III. x.

We ne'er can be
Made happy by compulsion *Ib.* pt. IV. xii.

Never, believe me,
Appear the Immortals,
Never alone.
Visit of the Gods (Imit. from Schiller).

All Nature seems at work. Slugs leave their lair—
The bees are stirring—birds are on the wing—
And Winter slumbering in the open air,
Wears on his smiling face a dream of Spring!
And I the while, the sole unbusy thing,
Nor honey make, nor pair, nor build, nor sing.
Work Without Hope.

Work without hope draws nectar in a sieve,
And hope without an object cannot live. *Ib.*

Poor little Foal of an oppressed race!
I love the languid patience of thy face.
To a Young Ass.

Verse, a breeze mid blossoms straying,
Where Hope clung feeding, like a bee—
Both were mine! Life went a-maying
With Nature, Hope, and Poesy,
When I was young! *Youth and Age.*

Like some poor nigh-related guest,
That may not rudely be dismist;
He hath outstay'd his welcome while,
And tells the jest without the smile. *Ib.*

He who begins by loving Christianity better than
Truth will proceed by loving his own sect of church
better than Christianity, and end by loving himself
better than all.
*Aids to Reflection: Moral and Religious
Aphorisms*, xxv.

Until you understand a writer's ignorance, presume
yourself ignorant of his understanding.
Biographia Literaria, ch. 12.

That willing suspension of disbelief for the moment,
which constitutes poetic faith. *Ib.* ch. 14.

Our *myriad-minded* Shakespeare. Note 'Ἀνὴρ μυριόνους,
a phrase which I have borrowed from a Greek
monk, who applies it to a Patriarch of Constantinople. *Ib.* ch. 15.

No man was ever yet a great poet, without being at the
same time a profound philosopher. *Ib.*

The dwarf sees farther than the giant, when he has the
giant's shoulder to mount on.
The Friend, § i, Essay 8.

Reviewers are usually people who would have been
poets, historians, biographers, &c., if they could;
they have tried their talents at one or at the other,
and have failed; therefore they turn critics.
Lectures on Shakespeare and Milton, i.

Summer has set in with its usual Severity.
Remark quoted in *Lamb's Letter to V. Novello*,
9 May, 1826.

The last speech, [Iago's soliloquy] the motive-
hunting of motiveless malignity—how awful!
Notes on the Tragedies of Shakespeare, Othello.

From whatever place I write you will expect that part
of my 'Travels' will consist of excursions in my own
mind.
Satyrane's Letters, ii. [*The Friend, 7 Dec. 1809*,
No. 16. *Biographia Literaria.*]

Schiller has the material sublime.
Table Talk, 29 Dec. 1822.

You abuse snuff! Perhaps it is the final cause of the
human nose. *Ib. 4 Jan. 1823.*

To see him [Kean] act, is like reading Shakespeare by
flashes of lightning. *Ib. 27 April, 1823.*

I wish our clever young poets would remember my
homely definitions of prose and poetry; that is,
prose = words in their best order;—poetry = the
best words in the best order. *Ib. 12 July, 1827.*

The man's desire is for the woman; but the woman's
desire is rarely other than for the desire of the
man. *Ib. 23 July, 1827.*

My mind is in a state of philosophical doubt as to
animal magnetism. *Ib. 30 April, 1830.*

The misfortune is, that he [Tennyson] has begun to
write verses without very well understanding what
metre is. *Ib. 24 April, 1833.*

That passage is what I call the sublime dashed to
pieces by cutting too close with the fiery four-in-
hand round the corner of nonsense.
Ib. 20 Jan. 1834.

This dark freeze-coated, hoarse, teeth-chattering
Month. *Watchman*, No. 6.

JESSE COLLINGS
1831–1920

Three acres and a cow. [See J. S. Mill.]
*Phrase used in his land-reform propaganda of
1885.*

JOHN CHURTON COLLINS
1848–1908

To ask advice is in nine cases out of ten to tout for
flattery. *Maxims and Reflections*, No. 59.

MORTIMER COLLINS
1827–1876

A man is as old as he's feeling,
A woman as old as she looks.
The Unknown Quantity.

WILLIAM COLLINS
1721–1759

Fair Fidele's grassy tomb. *Dirge in Cymbeline.*

And rifle all the breathing Spring. *Ib.*

Each lonely scene shall thee restore,
For thee the tear be duly shed;
Belov'd till life can charm no more,
And mourn'd, till Pity's self be dead. *Ib.*

If ought of oaten stop, or pastoral song,
May hope, O pensive Eve, to soothe thine ear.
Ode to Evening.

While now the bright-haired sun
Sits in yon western tent, whose cloudy skirts,
With brede ethereal wove,
O'erhang his wavy bed:
Now air is hush'd, save where the weak-ey'd bat,
With short shrill shriek flits by on leathern wing,
Or where the beetle winds
His small but sullen horn,
As oft he rises 'midst the twilight path,
Against the pilgrim borne in heedless hum. *Ib.*

Hamlets brown, and dim-discover'd spires. *Ib.*

Bathe thy breathing tresses, meekest Eve! *Ib.*

Round the moist marge of each cold Hebrid isle.
Ode on the Popular Superstitions of the Highlands.

Tho' taste, tho' genius bless,
To some divine excess,
Faints the cold work till thou inspire the whole.
Ode to Simplicity.

How sleep the brave, who sink to rest,
By all their country's wishes blest!
Ode Written in the Year 1746.

By fairy hands their knell is rung,
By forms unseen their dirge is sung;
There Honour comes, a pilgrim grey,
To bless the turf that wraps their clay,
And Freedom shall awhile repair,
To dwell a weeping hermit there! *Ib.*

When Music, heav'nly maid, was young.
The Passions, an Ode for Music.

With eyes up-rais'd, as one inspir'd,
Pale Melancholy sate retir'd,
And from her wild sequester'd seat,
In notes by distance made more sweet,
Pour'd thro' the mellow horn her pensive soul. *Ib.*

In hollow murmurs died away. *Ib.*

O Music, sphere-descended maid. *Ib.*

Too nicely Jonson knew the critic's part,
Nature in him was almost lost in Art.
Verses to Sir Thomas Hanmer.

GEORGE COLMAN

1762–1836

Like two single gentlemen roll'd into one.
Broad Grins. Lodgings for Single Gentlemen.

Love and a cottage! Eh, Fanny! Ah, give me indifference and a coach and six!
The Clandestine Marriage, i. ii.

When taken, To be well shaken.
Ib. Newcastle Apothecary.

Says he, 'I am a handsome man, but I'm a gay deceiver.'
Broad Grins, &c. Unfortunate Miss Bailey.

Praise the bridge that carried you over.
Heir-at-Law, i. i.

Lord help you! Tell 'em Queen Anne's dead. *Ib.*

Oh, London is a fine town,
A very famous city,
Where all the streets are paved with gold,
And all the maidens pretty. *Ib.* ii.

Oh, Miss Bailey!
Unfortunate Miss Bailey!
Love Laughs at Locksmiths. Act ii, *Song.*

Mynheer Vandunck, though he never was drunk,
Sipped brandy and water gayly.
Mynheer Vandunck.

My father was an eminent button maker—but I had
a soul above buttons—I panted for a liberal profession. *Sylvester Daggerwood,* i. x.

His heart runs away with his head.
Who Wants a Guinea? i. i.

Johnson's style was grand and Gibbon's elegant; the
stateliness of the former was sometimes pedantic,
and the polish of the latter was occasionally finical.
Johnson marched to kettle-drums and trumpets;
Gibbon moved to flutes and hautboys; Johnson
hewed passages through the Alps, while Gibbon
levelled walks through parks and gardens.
Random Records (1830) i. 121.

CHARLES CALEB COLTON

1780?–1832

When you have nothing to say, say nothing.
Lacon, vol. i, No. 183.

Imitation is the sincerest of flattery. *Ib.* No. 217.

Examinations are formidable even to the best prepared, for the greatest fool may ask more than the
wisest man can answer. *Ib.* No. 322.

If you would be known, and not know, vegetate in
a village; if you would know, and not be known,
live in a city. *Ib.* No. 334.

Man is an embodied paradox, a bundle of contradictions. *Ib.* No. 408.

That debt which cancels all others.
Ib. vol. ii, No. 66.

WILLIAM CONGREVE

1670–1729

Is there in the world a climate more uncertain than
our own? And which is a natural consequence,
is there any where a people more unsteady, more
apt to discontent, more *saturnine, dark,* and *melancholic* than our selves? Are we not of all people
the most unfit to be alone, and most unsafe to be
trusted with our selves? . . .'
Amendments of Mr. Collier's False and Imperfect Citations.

Careless she is with artful care,
Affecting to seem unaffected. *Amoret.*

She likes her self, yet others hates
For that which in herself she prizes;
And while she laughs at them, forgets
She is the thing that she despises.   *Ib.*

It is the business of a comic poet to paint the vices
and follies of human kind.
The Double Dealer, Epistle Dedicatory.

Retired to their tea and scandal, according to their
ancient custom.   *Ib.* i. i.

There is nothing more unbecoming a man of quality
than to laugh; Jesu, 'tis such a vulgar expression
of the passion!   *Ib.* iv.

Tho' marriage makes man and wife one flesh, it leaves
'em still two fools.   *Ib.* ii. iii.

She lays it on with a trowel.   *Ib.* iii. x.

When people walk hand in hand there's neither overtaking nor meeting.   *Ib.* iv. ii.

See how love and murder will out.   *Ib.* vi.

No mask like open truth to cover lies,
As to go naked is the best disguise.   *Ib.* v. iv.

I cannot help it, if I am naturally more delighted
with any thing that is amiable, than with any thing
that is wonderful.   *Preface to Dryden.*

What he has done in any one species, or distinct
kind, would have been sufficient to have acquired
him a great name. If he had written nothing but
his Prefaces, or nothing but his Songs, or his
Prologues, each of them would have intituled him
to the preference and distinction of excelling in
his kind [*Dryden*].   *Ib.*

O Sleep! thou flatterer of happy minds.
Elegy to Sleep.
The good receiv'd, the giver is forgot.
Epistle to Lord Halifax, l. 40.

Music alone with sudden charms can bind
The wand'ring sense, and calm the troubled mind.
Hymn to Harmony.

Ah! Madam, . . . you know every thing in the
world but your perfections, and you only know
not those, because 'tis the top of perfection not to
know them.   *Incognita.*

I am always of the opinion with the learned, if they
speak first.   *Ib.*

For 'tis some virtue, virtue to commend.
To Sir Godfrey Kneller.

But soon as e'er the beauteous idiot spoke,
Forth from her coral lips such folly broke,
Like balm the trickling nonsense heal'd my wound,
And what her eyes enthral'd, her tongue unbound.
Lesbia.

I confess freely to you, I could never look long upon
a monkey, without very mortifying reflections.
*Letter to Dennis, concerning Humour in
Comedy,* 1695.

If I can give that Cerberus a sop, I shall be at rest
for one day.   *Love for Love,* i. iv.

I warrant you, if he danced till doomsday, he thought
I was to pay the piper.   *Ib.* ii. v.

Ferdinand Mendez Pinto was but a type of thee, thou
liar of the first magnitude.   *Ib.*

Has he not a rogue's face? . . . a hanging-look
to me . . . has a damn'd Tyburn-face, without the
benefit o' the Clergy. . . .   *Ib.* vii.

I came upstairs into the world; for I was born in a
cellar.   *Ib.*

What, wouldst thou have me turn pelican, and feed
thee out of my own vitals?   *Ib.*

Oh fie Miss, you must not kiss and tell.   *Ib.* x.

He that first cries out stop thief, is often he that has
stoln the treasure.   *Ib.* iii. xiv.

Women are like tricks by slight of hand,
Which, to admire, we should not understand.
Ib. iv. xxi.

A branch of one of your antediluvian families,
fellows that the flood could not wash away.
Ib. v. ii.

To find a young fellow that is neither a wit in his
own eye, nor a fool in the eye of the world, is a
very hard task.   *Ib.*

Musick has charms to sooth a savage breast.
The Mourning Bride, i. i.

How reverend is the face of this tall pile,
Whose ancient pillars rear their marble heads,
To bear aloft its arch'd and pond'rous roof,
By its own weight made stedfast and immoveable,
Looking tranquillity. It strikes an awe
And terror on my aching sight.   *Ib.* ii. iii.

Heav'n has no rage, like love to hatred turn'd,
Nor Hell a fury, like a woman scorn'd.   *Ib.* iii. viii.

Is he then dead?
What, dead at last, quite, quite for ever dead!
Ib. v. xi.

In my conscience I believe the baggage loves me,
for she never speaks well of me her self, nor
suffers any body else to rail at me.
The Old Bachelor, i. i.

One of love's April-fools.   *Ib.*

The Devil watches all opportunities.   *Ib.* vi.

Man was by Nature Woman's cully made:
We never are, but by ourselves betrayed. *Ib.* iii. i.

Bilbo's the word, and slaughter will ensue.
Ib. iii. vii.

Ask all the tyrants of thy sex, if their fools are not
known by this party-coloured livery—I am
melancholy when thou art absent; look like an ass
when thou art present; wake for thee, when I
should sleep, and even dream of thee, when I am
awake; sigh much, drink little, eat less, court
solitude, am grown very entertaining to my self,
and (as I am informed) very troublesome to everybody else. If this be not love, it is madness, and
then it is pardonable—Nay yet a more certain sign
than all this; I give thee my money.   *Ib.* x.

Eternity was in that moment.   *Ib.* iv. vii.

You were about to tell me something, child—but
you left off before you began.   *Ib.* viii.

Now am I slap-dash down in the mouth.   *Ib.* ix.

Well, Sir Joseph, you have such a winning way with
you.   *Ib.* v. vii.

SHARPER.

Thus grief still treads upon the heels of pleasure:
Marry'd in haste, we may repent at leisure.

SETTER.

Some by experience find those words mis-plac'd:
At leisure marry'd, they repent in haste.
     Ib. viii and ix.

I could find it in my heart to marry thee, purely to
be rid of thee.   *Ib.* x.

Courtship to marriage, as a very witty prologue to
a very dull Play.   *Ib.*

O Sleep, why dost thou leave me?
Why thy visionary joys remove?
O Sleep again deceive me,
To my arms restore my wand'ring Love.
     Semele, ii. ii.

Whom she refuses, she treats still
With so much sweet behaviour,
That her refusal, through her skill,
Looks almost like a favour.   *Song: Doris.*

False though she be to me and love,
I'll ne'er pursue revenge;
For still the charmer I approve,
Tho' I deplore her change.
     Song: False Though She Be.

Wou'd I were free from this restraint,
Or else had hopes to win her;
Wou'd she cou'd make of me a saint,
Or I of her a sinner.
     Song: Pious Selinda Goes to Prayers.

Say what you will, 'tis better to be left than never to
have been loved.   *The Way of the World,* ii. vi.

Here she comes i' faith full sail, with her fan spread
and streamers out, and a shoal of fools for tenders.
     Ib. iv.

O ay, letters—I had letters—I am persecuted with
letters—I hate letters—no body knows how to
write letters; and yet one has 'em, one does not
know why—They serve one to pin up one's hair. . . .
     Ib.

WITWOUD.
Pray, Madam, do you pin up your hair with all your
letters; I find I must keep copies.

MILLAMANT.
Only with those in verse, Mr. Witwoud. I never
pin up my hair with prose.   *Ib.*

MILLAMANT.
I believe I gave you some pain.
MIRABEL.
Does that please you?
MILLAMANT.
Infinitely; I love to give pain.
MIRABEL.
You wou'd affect a cruelty which is not in your
nature; your true vanity is in the power of pleasing.
MILLAMANT.
O I ask your pardon for that—one's cruelty is one's
power, and when one parts with one's cruelty,
one parts with one's power; and when one has
parted with that, I fancy one's old and ugly.   *Ib.*

Beauty is the lover's gift.   *Ib.*

E 3

Lord, what is a lover, that it can give? Why one
makes lovers as fast as one pleases, and they live
as long as one pleases, and they die as soon as one
pleases: and then if one pleases one makes more. *Ib.*

Fools never wear out—they are such *drap-de-berry*
things.   *Ib.* iii. x.

Love's but a frailty of the mind
When 'tis not with ambition join'd.   *Ib.* xii.

I nauseate walking; 'tis a country diversion, I loathe
the country.   *Ib.* iv. iv.

O, I hate a lover that can dare to think he draws a
moment's air, independent on the bounty of his
mistress. There is not so impudent a thing in
Nature, as the saucy look of an assured man,
confident of success.   *Ib.* v.

My dear liberty, shall I leave thee? My faithful
solitude, my darling contemplation, must I bid
you then adieu? Ay-h adieu—My morning
thoughts, agreeable wakings, indolent slumbers,
all ye *douceurs,* ye *sommeils du matin,* adieu—I
can't do 't, 'tis more than impossible.   *Ib.*

Don't let us be familiar or fond, nor kiss before
folks, like my Lady Fadler and Sir Francis: Nor
go to Hyde-Park together the first Sunday in a
new chariot, to provoke eyes and whispers, and
then never be seen there together again; as if we
were proud of one another the first week, and
asham'd of one another ever after. . . . Let us be
very strange and well-bred: Let us be as strange
as if we had been married a great while, and as
well-bred as if we were not married at all.   *Ib.*

These articles subscrib'd, if I continue to endure
you a little longer, I may by degrees dwindle into
a wife.   *Ib.*

O horrid provisos!   *Ib.*

I hope you do not think me prone to any iteration
of nuptials.   *Ib.* xii.

Alack he's gone the way of all flesh.
     'Squire Bickerstaff Detected. (Attr. to Con-
greve.)

T. W. CONNOR

She was one of the early birds,
And I was one of the worms.
     She Was One of the Early Birds.

HENRY CONSTABLE

1562–1613

Diaphenia, like the daffadowndilly,
White as the sun, fair as the lily,
Heigh ho, how I do love thee!
I do love thee as my lambs
Are beloved of their dams;
How blest were I if thou wouldst prove me!
     [*Damelus' Song to his*] *Diaphenia.*

ELIZA COOK

1818–1889

I love it, I love it; and who shall dare
To chide me for loving that old arm-chair?
     The Old Armchair.

Better build schoolrooms for 'the boy',
Than cells and gibbets for 'the man'.
A Song for the Ragged Schools.

CALVIN COOLIDGE

1872–1933

I do not choose to run for President in 1928.
Announcement in 1927.

GEORGE COOPER

1840–1927

O Genevieve, sweet Genevieve,
  The days may come, the days may go,
But still the hands of mem'ry weave
  The blissful dreams of long ago.
Sweet Genevieve.

JAMES FENIMORE COOPER

1789–1851

The last of the Mohicans.   *Title of Novel.*

RICHARD CORBET

1582–1635

Farewell rewards and fairies.
The Fairy's Farewell.

  Who of late for cleanliness,
Finds sixpence in her shoe?   *Ib.*

Let others write for glory or reward,
Truth is well paid when she is sung and heard.
Elegy on Lord Howard, Baron of Effingham.

FRANCES CROFTS CORNFORD

1886–

O fat white woman whom nobody loves,
Why do you walk through the fields in gloves,

    .   .   .   .

  Missing so much and so much?
To a Fat Lady Seen from a Train.

BARRY CORNWALL (BRYAN WALLER PROCTER)

1787–1874

The sea! the sea! the open sea!
The blue, the fresh, the ever free!   *The Sea.*

WILLIAM JOHNSON CORY

1823–1892

They told me, Heraclitus, they told me you were
  dead,
They brought me bitter news to hear and bitter tears
  to shed.   *Heraclitus.*

      How often you and I
Had tired the sun with talking and sent him down
  the sky.   *Ib.*

A handful of grey ashes, long long ago at rest.   *Ib.*

You promise heavens free from strife.
Mimnermus in Church.

This warm kind world is all I know.   *Ib.*

But oh, the very reason why
I clasp them, is because they die.   *Ib.*

NATHANIEL COTTON

1705–1788

Yet still we hug the dear deceit.
Visions. iv, *Content.*

THOMAS COVENTRY

1578–1640

The wooden walls are the best walls of this kingdom.
*Speech to the Judges, 17 June 1635, given in
Rushworth's Hist. Coll.* (1680), vol. ii, p. 297.

ABRAHAM COWLEY

1618–1667

Love in her sunny eyes does basking play;
Love walks the pleasant mazes of her hair;
Love does on both her lips for ever stray;
And sows and reaps a thousand kisses there.
In all her outward parts Love's always seen;
  But, oh, he never went within.
The Change.

Nothing is there to come, and nothing past,
But an eternal Now does always last.
Davideis, bk. i, l. 361.

Poet and Saint! to thee alone are given
The two most sacred names of earth and Heaven.
On the Death of Mr. Crashaw.

      Thou
Wert living the same poet which thou'rt now,
Whilst Angels sing to thee their airs divine,
And joy in an applause so great as thine.
Equal society with them to hold,
Thou need'st not make new songs, but say the old.
Ib.

His faith perhaps, in some nice tenents might
Be wrong; his life, I'm sure, was in the right.   *Ib.*

Hail, Bard trumphant! and some care bestow
On us, the Poets Militant below!   *Ib.*

The thirsty earth soaks up the rain,
And drinks, and gapes for drink again.
The plants suck in the earth, and are
With constant drinking fresh and fair.   *Drinking.*

Fill all the glasses there, for why
Should every creature drink but I,
Why, man of morals, tell me why?   *Ib.*

God the first garden made, and the first city Cain.
The Garden.

Ye fields of Cambridge, our dear Cambridge, say,
Have ye not seen us walking every day?
Was there a tree about which did not know
   The love betwixt us two? *On William Harvey.*

The world's a scene of changes, and to be
Constant, in Nature were inconstancy.
Inconstancy.

What shall I do to be for ever known,
And make the age to come my own? *The Motto.*

This only grant me, that my means may lie
Too low for envy, for contempt too high.
Of Myself.

Acquaintance I would have, but when't depends
Not on the number, but the choice of friends. *Ib.*

I would not fear nor wish my fate,
   But boldly say each night,
To-morrow let my sun his beams display,
Or in clouds hide them; I have lived to-day. *Ib.*

Nothing so soon the drooping spirits can raise
As praises from the men, whom all men praise.
Ode upon a Copy of Verses of My Lord Broghill's

Who lets slip Fortune, her shall never find.
Occasion once pass'd by, is bald behind.
Pyramus and Thisbe, xv.

Lukewarmness I account a sin
As great in love as in religion.
The Request.

Life is an incurable disease. *To Dr. Scarborough*, vi.

Let but thy wicked men from out thee go,
And all the fools that crowd thee so,
Even thou, who dost thy millions boast,
A village less than Islington wilt grow,
A solitude almost. *Of Solitude*, xii.

Well then; I now do plainly see
This busy world and I shall ne'er agree;
The very honey of all earthly joy
Does of all meats the soonest cloy,
   And they (methinks) deserve my pity,
Who for it can endure the stings,
The crowd, and buz, and murmurings
   Of this great hive, the city.
The Mistress, or Love Verses.

Ah, yet, e'er I descend to th' grave
May I a small house, and a large garden have!
And a few friends, and many books, both true,
   Both wise, and both delightful too!
And since Love ne'er will from me flee,
A Mistress moderately fair,
And good as guardian angels are,
   Only belov'd, and loving me!
The Wish.

The Dangers of an Honest Man in much Company.
Discourses by Way of Essays, in Verse and Prose, 8, title.

Hence, ye profane; I hate ye all;
Both the great vulgar, and the small.
Trans. of Horace, Bk. III, Ode 1.

HANNAH COWLEY

1743-1809

Five minutes! Zounds! I have been five minutes too
late all my life-time! *The Belle's Stratagem* I. i.

Vanity, like murder, will out. *Ib.* iv.

But what is woman?—only one of Nature's agreeable
   blunders. *Who's the Dupe?* II.

WILLIAM COWPER

1731-1800

Let my obedience then excuse
   My disobedience now. *Beau's Reply.*

When the British warrior queen,
   Bleeding from the Roman rods,
Sought with an indignant mien,
   Counsel of her country's gods,

Sage beneath a spreading oak
   Sat the Druid, hoary chief. *Boadicea.*

Rome shall perish—write that word
   In the blood that she has spilt. *Ib.*

Hark! the Gaul is at her gates! *Ib.*

Regions Caesar never knew
   Thy posterity shall sway,
Where his eagles never flew,
   None invincible as they. *Ib.*

Ruffians, pitiless as proud,
   Heav'n awards the vengeance due;
Empire is on us bestow'd,
   Shame and ruin wait for you. *Ib.*

Obscurest night involv'd the sky,
   Th' Atlantic billows roar'd,
When such a destin'd wretch as I,
   Wash'd headlong from on board,
Of friends, of hope, of all bereft,
His floating home for ever left. *The Castaway.*

But misery still delights to trace
Its semblance in another's case. *Ib.*

   We perish'd, each alone:
But I beneath a rougher sea,
And whelm'd in deeper gulphs than he. *Ib.*

Truth is the golden girdle of the globe. *Charity*, l. 86.

Grief is itself a med'cine. *Ib.* l. 159.

He found it inconvenient to be poor. *Ib.* l. 189.

India's spicy shores. *Ib.* l. 442.

Pelting each other for the public good. *Ib.* l. 623.

Spare the poet for his subject's sake. *Ib.* l. 636.

But strive to be a man before your mother.
Motto to Connoisseur, No. 111

Not more distinct from harmony divine,
The constant creaking of a country sign.
Conversation, l. 9.

Though syllogisms hang not on my tongue,
I am not surely always in the wrong!
'Tis hard if all is false that I advance—
A fool must now and then be right, by chance.
Ib. l. 93.

But still remember, if you mean to please,
To press your point with modesty and ease.
Conversation, l. 103.

A noisy man is always in the right. *Ib.* l. 114.

A moral, sensible, and well-bred man
Will not affront me, and no other can. *Ib.* l. 193.

A tale should be judicious, clear, succinct;
The language plain, and incidents well link'd;
Tell not as new what ev'ry body knows;
And, new or old, still hasten to a close. *Ib.* l. 235.

The pipe, with solemn interposing puff,
Makes half a sentence at a time enough;
The dozing sages drop the drowsy strain,
Then pause, and puff—and speak, and pause again.
Ib. l. 245.

Pernicious weed! whose scent the fair annoys,
Unfriendly to society's chief joys,
Thy worst effect is banishing for hours
The sex whose presence civilizes ours. *Ib.* l. 251.

A fine puss-gentleman that's all perfume. *Ib.* l. 284.

His wit invites you by his looks to come,
But when you knock it never is at home. *Ib.* l. 303.

Our wasted oil unprofitably burns,
Like hidden lamps in old sepulchral urns. *Ib.* l. 357.

Whose only fit companion is his horse. *Ib.* l. 412.

A poet does not work by square or line. *Ib.* l. 789.

What appears
In England's case to move the muse to tears?
Expostulation, l. 1.

Th' embroid'ry of poetic dreams. *Ib.* l. 234.

War lays a burden on the reeling state,
And peace does nothing to relieve the weight.
Ib. l. 306.

The busy trifler. *Ib.* l. 322.

A pick-lock to a place. *Ib.* l. 379.

Thousands . . .
Kiss the book's outside who ne'er look within.
Ib. l. 389.

Religion, if in heav'nly truths attir'd,
Needs only to be seen to be admired. *Ib.* l. 492.

The man that hails you Tom or Jack,
And proves by thumps upon your back
How he esteems your merit,
Is such a friend, that one had need
Be very much his friend indeed
To pardon or to bear it. *Friendship.*

John Gilpin was a citizen
Of credit and renown,
A train-band captain eke was he
Of famous London town.

John Gilpin's spouse said to her dear—
Though wedded we have been
These twice ten tedious years, yet we
No holiday have seen. *John Gilpin.*

To-morrow is our wedding-day,
And we will then repair
Unto the Bell at Edmonton
All in a chaise and pair.

My sister and my sister's child,
Myself and children three,
Will fill the chaise; so you must ride
On horseback after we. *Ib.*

He soon replied—I do admire
Of womankind but one,
And you are she, my dearest dear,
Therefore it shall be done.

I am a linen-draper bold,
As all the world doth know,
And my good friend the calender
Will lend his horse to go. *Ib.*

O'erjoy'd was he to find
That, though on pleasure she was bent,
She had a frugal mind. *Ib.*

And all agog
To dash through thick and thin! *Ib.*

John Gilpin at his horse's side
Seiz'd fast the flowing mane,
And up he got, in haste to ride,
But soon came down again. *Ib.*

So down he came; for loss of time,
Although it griev'd him sore,
Yet loss of pence, full well he knew,
Would trouble him much more. *Ib.*

Good lack! quoth he—yet bring it me,
My leathern belt likewise,
In which I bear my trusty sword
When I do exercise. *Ib.*

So, fair and softly, John he cried,
But John he cried in vain.

So stooping down, as needs he must
Who cannot sit upright,
He grasp'd the mane with both his hands,
And eke with all his might. *Ib.*

His horse, who never in that sort
Had handled been before,
What thing upon his back had got
Did wonder more and more.

Away went Gilpin, neck or nought,
Away went hat and wig! *Ib.*

The dogs did bark, the children scream'd.
Up flew the windows all;
And ev'ry soul cried out—Well done!
As loud as he could bawl.

Away went Gilpin—who but he?
His fame soon spread around—
He carries weight! he rides a race!
'Tis for a thousand pound! *Ib.*

The dinner waits, and we are tired:
Said Gilpin—So am I *Ib.*

Which brings me to
The middle of my song. *Ib.*

My hat and wig will soon be here—
They are upon the road. *Ib.*

The calendar, right glad to find
His friend in merry pin. *Ib.*

My head is twice as big as yours,
  They therefore needs must fit.   *John Gilpin.*

Said John—It is my wedding-day,
  And all the world would stare,
If wife should dine at Edmonton
  And I should dine at Ware   *Ib.*

'Twas for your pleasure you came here,
  You shall go back for mine.   *Ib.*

Nor stopp'd till where he had got up
  He did again get down.   *Ib.*

Now let us sing—Long live the king,
  And Gilpin long live he;
And, when he next doth ride abroad,
  May I be there to see!   *Ib.*

An honest man, close-button'd to the chin,
Broad-cloth without, and a warm heart within
           Epistle to Jos. Hill, 1. 62.

No dancing bear was so genteel,
  Or half so dégagé.   *Of Himself.*

Painful passage o'er a restless flood.   *Hope*, l. 3.

Men deal with life as children with their play,
Who first misuse, then cast their toys away.
                   Ib. l. 127.

Some eastward, and some westward, and all wrong.
                   Ib. l. 281.

Could he with reason murmur at his case,
Himself sole author of his own disgrace? *Ib.* l. 316.

And diff'ring judgements serve but to declare
That truth lies somewhere, if we knew but where.
                   Ib. l. 423.

Seek to delight, that they may mend mankind,
And, while they captivate, inform the mind.
                   Ib. l. 758.

Absence from whom we love is worse than death,
And frustrate hope severer than despair.
           '*Hope, Like the Short-Liv'd Ray.*'

The twentieth year is well-nigh past,
Since first our sky was overcast;
Ah would that this might be the last!
           My Mary!   *To Mary.*

Thy needles, once a shining store,
For my sake restless heretofore,
Now rust disus'd, and shine no more,
           My Mary!   *Ib.*

Partakers of thy sad decline,
Thy hands their little force resign;
Yet, gently prest, press gently mine,
           My Mary!   *Ib.*

Greece, sound thy Homer's, Rome thy Virgil's name,
But England's Milton equals both in fame.
                   To John Milton.

Oh that those lips had language! Life has pass'd
With me but roughly since I heard thee last.
Those lips are thine—thy own sweet smiles I see,
The same that oft in childhood solac'd me.
     On the Receipt of My Mother's Picture, l. 1.

Blest be the art that can immortalize.   *Ib.* l. 8.

Wretch even then, life's journey just begun.
                   Ib. l. 24.

Perhaps thou gav'st me, though unseen, a kiss;
Perhaps a tear, if souls can weep in bliss.   *Ib.* 25.

Disappointed still, was still deceiv'd.   *Ib. l.* 39.

Where once we dwelt our name is heard no more,
Children not thine have trod my nursery floor;
And where the gard'ner Robin, day by day,
Drew me to school along the public way,
Delighted with my bauble coach, and wrapt
In scarlet mantle warm, and velvet capt,
'Tis now become a history little known.   *Ib.* l. 46.

Thy morning bounties ere I left my home,
The biscuit, or confectionary plum.   *Ib. l.* 60.

The fragrant waters on my cheek bestow'd. *Ib. l.* 62.

Not scorn'd in heaven, though little notic'd here.
                   Ib. l. 73.

  I should ill requite thee to constrain
Thy unbound spirit into bonds again.   *Ib. l.* 86.

Me howling winds drive devious, tempest toss'd,
Sails ript, seams op'ning wide, and compass lost.
                   Ib. l. 102.

Some people are more nice than wise.
           Mutual Forbearance, l. 20.

Oh, fond attempt to give a deathless lot
To names ignoble, born to be forgot!
     *On Observing Some Names of Little Note
     Recorded in the Biographia Britannica.*

There goes the parson, oh! illustrious spark,
And there, scarce less illustrious, goes the clerk! *Ib.*

Thought again—but knew not what to think.
           The Needless Alarm, l. 54.

Beware of desp'rate steps. The darkest day
(Live till to-morrow) will have pass'd away.
                   Ib. l. 132.

Hence jarring sectaries may learn
Their real int'rest to discern;
That brother should not war with brother,
And worry and devour each other.
           The Nightingale and Glow-Worm.

Oh! for a closer walk with God,
  A calm and heav'nly frame;
A light to shine upon the road
  That leads me to the Lamb!
           Olney Hymns, 1.

What peaceful hours I once enjoy'd!
  How sweet their mem'ry still!
But they have left an aching void,
  The world can never fill.   *Ib.*

The dearest idol I have known,
  Whate'er that idol be;
Help me to tear it from thy Throne,
  And worship only thee.   *Ib.*

Nor sword nor spear the stripling took,
But chose a pebble from the brook.   *Ib.* 4.

Oh make this heart rejoice, or ache;
  Decide this doubt for me;
And if it be not broken, break,
  And heal it, if it be.   *Ib.* 9.

So unaccustom'd to the yoke,
So backward to comply.   *Olney Hymns*, 12.

There is a fountain fill'd with blood.   *Ib.* 15.

When this poor lisping stammering tongue
Lies silent in the grave.   *Ib.*

Hark, my soul! it is the Lord;
'Tis thy Saviour, hear his word;
Jesus speaks, and speaks to thee;
'Say, poor sinner, lov'st thou me?'   *Ib.* 18.

I deliver'd thee when bound,
And, when bleeding, heal'd thy wound;
Sought thee wand'ring, set thee right,
Turn'd thy darkness into light.   *Ib.*

'Can a woman's tender care
Cease, towards the child she bare?
Yes, she may forgetful be,
Yet will I remember thee.'   *Ib.*

Mine is an unchanging love,
Higher than the heights above;
Deeper than the depths beneath,
Free and faithful, strong as death.   *Ib.*

Lord, it is my chief complaint,
That my love is weak and faint;
Yet I love thee and adore,
Oh for grace to love thee more!   *Ib.*

What various hindrances we meet
In coming to a mercy-seat!   *Ib.* 29.

And Satan trembles, when he sees
The weakest saint upon his knees.   *Ib.*

While Moses stood with arms spread wide,
Success was found on Israel's side;
But when thro' weariness they fail'd,
That moment Amalek prevail'd.   *Ib.*

I seem forsaken and alone,
I hear the lion roar;
And ev'ry door is shut but one,
And that is mercy's door.   *Ib.* 33.

God moves in a mysterious way
His wonders to perform;
He plants his footsteps in the sea,
And rides upon the storm.

Deep in unfathomable mines
Of never failing skill
He treasures up his bright designs,
And works his sovereign Will.

Ye fearful saints fresh courage take,
The clouds ye so much dread
Are big with mercy, and shall break
In blessings on your head.

Judge not the Lord by feeble sense,
But trust him for his grace;
Behind a frowning providence
He hides a smiling face.   *Ib.* 35.

The bud may have a bitter taste,
But sweet will be the flow'r.   *Ib.*

Blind unbelief is sure to err,
And scan his work in vain;
God is his own interpreter,
And he will make it plain.   *Ib.*

Sometimes a light surprises
The Christian while he sings;
It is the Lord who rises
With healing in his wings;
When comforts are declining,
He grants the soul again
A season of clear shining
To cheer it after rain.   *Ib.*

I shall not ask Jean Jacques Rousseau,
If birds confabulate or no.
        Pairing Time Anticipated.

The poplars are fell'd, farewell to the shade
And the whispering sound of the cool colonnade.
        The Poplar-Field.

Unmiss'd but by his dogs and by his groom.
        Progress of Error, l. 95.

Oh, laugh or mourn with me the rueful jest,
A cassock'd huntsman and a fiddling priest!
        Ib. l. 110.

Himself a wand'rer from the narrow way,
His silly sheep, what wonder if they stray?
        Ib. l. 118.

Remorse, the fatal egg by pleasure laid.   *Ib.* l. 239.

Woman, lovely woman, does the same.   *Ib.* l. 274.

Caesar's image is effac'd at last.   *Ib.* l. 280.

As creeping ivy clings to wood or stone,
And hides the ruin that it feeds upon.   *Ib.* l. 285.

How much a dunce that has been sent to roam
Excels a dunce that has been kept at home.
        Ib. l. 415.

Talks of darkness at noon-day.   *Ib.* l. 451.

Thou god of our idolatry, the press.   *Ib.* l. 461.

The nobler tenants of the flood.   *Ib.* l. 482.

Laugh at all you trembled at before.   *Ib.* l. 592.

Pleasure is labour too, and tires as much. *Hope*, l. 20.

He blam'd and protested, but join'd in the plan;
He shar'd in the plunder, but pitied the man.
        Pity for Poor Africans.

Then, shifting his side, (as a lawyer knows how).
        Report of an Adjudged Case.

But vers'd in arts that, while they seem to stay
A falling empire, hasten its decay. *Retirement*, l. 383.

The disencumber'd Atlas of the state.   *Ib.* l. 394.

Prison'd in a parlour snug and small,
Like bottled wasps upon a southern wall. *Ib.* l. 493.

Play the fool, but at a cheaper rate.   *Ib.* l. 562.

He likes the country, but in truth must own,
Most likes it, when he studies it in town. *Ib.* l. 573.

        Philologists who chase
A panting syllable through time and space,
Start it at home, and hunt it in the dark,
To Gaul, to Greece, and into Noah's ark. *Ib.* l. 619.

Absence of occupation is not rest,
A mind quite vacant is a mind distress'd. *Ib.* l. 623.

Built God a church, and laugh'd his word to scorn.
    [Voltaire]   *Ib.* l. 688.

Beggars invention and makes fancy tame. *Ib.* l. 709.

I praise the Frenchman, his remark was shrewd—
How sweet, how passing sweet, is solitude!
But grant me still a friend in my retreat,
Whom I may whisper—solitude is sweet. *Ib.* l. 739.

Fast by the banks of the slow winding Ouse.
Ib. l. 804.

The tear that is wip'd with a little address,
May be follow'd perhaps by a smile. *The Rose.*

Toll for the brave—
　The brave! that are no more:
All sunk beneath the wave,
　Fast by their native shore.
Loss of the Royal George.

A land-breeze shook the shrouds,
　And she was overset;
Down went the Royal George,
　With all her crew complete. *Ib.*

Toll for the brave—
Brave Kempenfelt is gone,
His last sea-fight is fought,
　His work of glory done.

It was not in the battle,
　No tempest gave the shock,
She sprang no fatal leak,
　She ran upon no rock;

His sword was in the sheath,
　His fingers held the pen,
When Kempenfelt went down
　With twice four hundred men. *Ib.*

Weigh the vessel up,
　Once dreaded by our foes. *Ib.*

He and his eight hundred
　Must plough the waves no more. *Ib.*

Oh, happy shades—to me unblest!
Friendly to peace, but not to me! *The Shrubbery.*

Chief monster that has plagued the nations yet.
(Napoleon) *Table Talk*, l. 38.

The lie that flatters I abhor the most. *Ib.* l. 88.

Th' unwashed artificer. *Ib.* l. 152.

As if the world and they were hand and glove.
Ib. l. 173.

Admirals, extoll'd for standing still,
Or doing nothing with a deal of skill. *Ib.* l. 192.

The leathern ears of stock-jobbers and Jews.
Ib. l. 197.

The Frenchman, easy, debonair, and brisk,
Give him his lass, his fiddle, and his frisk,
Is always happy, reign whoever may,
And laughs the sense of mis'ry far away. *Ib.* l. 236.

Freedom has a thousand charms to show,
That slaves, howe'er contented, never know.
Ib. l. 260.

Stamps God's own name upon a lie just made,
To turn a penny in the way of trade. *Ib.* l. 420.

Suspend your mad career. *Ib.* l. 435.

Feels himself spent, and fumbles for his brains.
Ib. l. 537.

Ages elaps'd ere Homer's lamp appear'd,
And ages ere the Mantuan swan was heard:
To carry nature lengths unknown before,
To give a Milton birth, ask'd ages more. *Ib.* l. 556.

By low ambition and the thirst of praise. *Ib.* l. 591.

Made poetry a mere mechanic art;
And ev'ry warbler has his tune by heart. *Ib.* l. 654.

Pity religion has so seldom found
A skilful guide into poetic ground! *Ib.* l. 716.

Hail Sternhold, then; and Hopkins, hail! *Ib.* l. 759.

I sing the Sofa. *The Task*, bk. i, *The Sofa*, l. 1.

The Fair commands the song. *Ib.* l. 7.

So sit two kings of Brentford on one throne.
Ib. l. 78.

Thus first necessity invented stools,
Convenience next suggested elbow-chairs,
And luxury the accomplish'd Sofa last. *Ib.* l. 86.

Nor rural sights alone, but rural sounds,
Exhilarate the spirit, and restore
The tone of languid Nature. *Ib.* l. 181.

Toils much to earn a monumental pile,
That may record the mischiefs he has done.
Ib. l. 276.

God made the country, and man made the town.
Ib. l. 749.

There is a public mischief in your mirth. *Ib.* l. 769.

Oh for a lodge in some vast wilderness,
Some boundless contiguity of shade,
Where rumour of oppression and deceit,
Of unsuccessful or successful war,
Might never reach me more.
Ib. bk. ii, *The Timepiece*, l. 1.

Mountains interpos'd
Make enemies of nations, who had else,
Like kindred drops, been mingled into one. *Ib.* l. 17.

Slaves cannot breathe in England, if their lungs
Receive our air, that moment they are free;
They touch our country, and their shackles fall.
Ib. l. 40.

England, with all thy faults, I love thee still—
My country! *Ib.* l. 206.

I would not yet exchange thy sullen skies,
And fields without a flow'r for warmer France
With all her vines. *Ib.* l. 212.

Presume to lay their hand upon the ark
Of her magnificent and awful cause. *Ib.* l. 231.

Praise enough
To fill th' ambition of a private man,
That Chatham's language was his mother tongue,
And Wolfe's great name compatriot with his own.
Ib. l. 235.

Chatham heart-sick of his country's shame.
Ib. l. 244.

There is a pleasure in poetic pains
Which only poets know. *Ib.* l. 285.

Variety's the very spice of life,
That gives it all its flavour. *Ib.* l. 606.

His head,
Not yet by time completely silver'd o'er,
Bespoke him past the bounds of freakish youth,
But strong for service still, and unimpair'd. *Ib.* l. 702.

Domestic happiness, thou only bliss
Of Paradise that has surviv'd the fall!
Ib. bk. iii, *The Garden*, l. 41.

Guilty splendour. *Ib.* l. 70.

I was a stricken deer, that left the herd
Long since. *Ib.* l. 108.

Charge
His mind with meanings that he never had.
Ib. l. 148.

Great contest follows, and much learned dust
Involves the combatants. *Ib.* l. 161.

From reveries so airy, from the toil
Of dropping buckets into empty wells,
And growing old in drawing nothing up! *Ib.* l. 188.

Exercise all functions of a man. *Ib.* l. 198.

Newton, childlike sage!
Sagacious reader of the works of God. *Ib.* l. 252.

Riches have wings. *Ib.* l. 263.

The only amaranthine flower on earth
Is virtue. *Ib.* l. 268.

Detested sport,
That owes its pleasures to another's pain. *Ib.* l. 326.

Studious of laborious ease. *Ib.* l. 361.

Who loves a garden loves a greenhouse too.
Ib. l. 566.

To combat may be glorious, and success
Perhaps may crown us; but to fly is safe. *Ib.* l. 686.

He comes, the herald of a noisy world,
With spatter'd boots, strapp'd waist, and frozen locks;
News from all nations lumb'ring at his back.
Ib. bk. iv, *The Winter Evening*, l. 5.

Now stir the fire, and close the shutters fast,
Let fall the curtains, wheel the sofa round,
And, while the bubbling and loud-hissing urn
Throws up a steamy column, and the cups,
That cheer but not inebriate, wait on each,
So let us welcome peaceful ev'ning in. *Ib.* l. 34.

Katterfelto, with his hair on end
At his own wonders, wond'ring for his bread.
Ib. l. 85.

'Tis pleasant through the loopholes of retreat
To peep at such a world; to see the stir
Of Babel, and not feel the crowd. *Ib.* l. 88.

O Winter, ruler of th' inverted year. *Ib.* l. 120.

I love thee, all unlovely as thou seem'st
And dreaded as thou art. *Ib.* l. 128.

I crown thee king of intimate delights,
Fire-side enjoyments, home-born happiness.
Ib. l. 139.

A Roman meal;

a radish and an egg. *Ib.* ll. 168–73.

The slope of faces, from the floor to th' roof,
(As if one master-spring controll'd them all),
Relax'd into a universal grin. *Ib.* l. 202.

With spots quadrangular of di'mond form,
Ensanguin'd hearts, clubs typical of strife,
And spades, the emblem of untimely graves.
Ib. l. 217.

In indolent vacuity of thought. *Ib.* l. 297.

It seems the part of wisdom. *Ib.* l. 336.

All learned, and all drunk! *Ib.* l. 478.

Gloriously drunk, obey th' important call! *Ib.* l. 510.

Sidney, warbler of poetic prose. *Ib.* l. 516.

I never fram'd a wish, or form'd a plan,
That flatter'd me with hopes of earthly bliss,
But there I laid the scene. *Ib.* l. 695.

Entangled in the cobwebs of the schools. *Ib.* l. 726.

The fragrant weed,
The Frenchman's darling [mignonette]. *Ib.* l. 764.

Prepost'rous sight! the legs without the man.
Ib. bk. v, *The Winter Morning Walk*, l. 20.

Half lurcher and half cur. *Ib.* l. 46.

Silently as a dream the fabric rose;—
No sound of hammer or of saw was there. *Ib.* l. 144.

Great princes have great playthings. *Ib.* l. 175.

But war's a game, which, were their subjects wise,
Kings would not play at. *Ib.* l. 187.

And the first smith was the first murd'rer's son.
Ib. l. 219.

The beggarly last doit. *Ib.* l. 316.

All constraint,
Except what wisdom lays on evil men,
Is evil. *Ib.* l. 448.

He is the freeman whom the truth makes free.
Ib. l. 733.

Give what thou canst, without thee we are poor;
And with thee rich, take what thou wilt away.
Ib. l. 905.

There is in souls a sympathy with sounds;
And, as the mind is pitch'd the ear is pleas'd
With melting airs, or martial, brisk, or grave:
Some chord in unison with what we hear,
Is touch'd within us, and the heart replies.
Ib. bk. vi, *The Winter Walk at Noon*, l. 1.

Knowledge dwells
In heads replete with thoughts of other men;
Wisdom in minds attentive to their own. *Ib.* l. 89.

Knowledge is proud that he has learn'd so much;
Wisdom is humble that he knows no more. *Ib.* l. 96.

Books are not seldom talismans and spells. *Ib.* l. 98.

Nature is but a name for an effect,
Whose cause is God. *Ib.* l. 223.

A cheap but wholesome salad from the brook.
Ib. l. 304.

Anger insignificantly fierce. *Ib.* l. 320.

I would not enter on my list of friends
(Tho' grac'd with polish'd manners and fine sense,
Yet wanting sensibility) the man
Who needlessly sets foot upon a worm. *Ib.* l. 560.

The crested worm. *Ib.* l. 780.

Stillest streams
Oft water fairest meadows, and the bird
That flutters least is longest on the wing. *Ib.* l. 929.

Public schools 'tis public folly breeds.
Tirocinium, l. 250.

We love the play-place of our early days. *Ib.* l. 297.

The little ones, unbutton'd, glowing hot,
Playing our games, and on the very spot;
As happy as we once, to kneel and draw
The chalky ring, and knuckle down at taw;
To pitch the ball into the grounded hat,
Or drive it devious with a dext'rous pat. *Ib.* l. 304.

The parson knows enough who knows a duke.
Ib. l. 403.

As a priest,
A piece of mere church furniture at best. *Ib.* l. 425.

His fav'rite stand between his father's knees.
Ib. l. 570.

Tenants of life's middle state,
Securely plac'd between the small and great.
Ib. l. 807.

If it chance, as sometimes chance it will,
That, though school-bred, the boy be virtuous still.
Ib. l. 839.

Humility may clothe an English dean. *Truth*, l. 118.

He has no hope who never had a fear. *Ib.* l. 298.

Just knows, and knows no more, her Bible true—
A truth the brilliant Frenchman never knew.
[Voltaire.] *Ib.* l. 327.

Envy, ye great, the dull unletter'd small. *Ib.* l. 375.

One who wears a coronet, and prays. *Ib.* l. 378.

His mind his kingdom, and his will his law.
Ib. l. 406.

Mary! I want a lyre with other strings.
Sonnet to Mrs. Unwin.

Verse, that immortalizes whom it sings! *Ib.*

I am monarch of all I survey,
  My right there is none to dispute;
From the centre all round to the sea
  I am lord of the fowl and the brute.
Oh, solitude! where are the charms
  That sages have seen in thy face?
Better dwell in the midst of alarms,
  Than reign in this horrible place.
*Verses Supposed to be Written by Alexander
Selkirk.*

Never hear the sweet music of speech. *Ib.*

Society, friendship, and love,
  Divinely bestow'd upon man. *Ib.*

But the sound of the church-going bell
  These valleys and rocks never heard,
Ne'er sigh'd at the sound of a knell,
  Or smil'd when a sabbath appear'd. *Ib.*

Our severest winter, commonly called the spring.
Letters. To the Rev. W. Unwin, 8 June, 1783.

He kissed likewise the maid in the kitchen, and
seemed upon the whole a most loving, kissing,
kind-hearted gentleman.
Ib. To the Rev. J. Newton, 29 Mar. 1784.

GEORGE CRABBE

1754–1832

What is a church?—Our honest sexton tells,
'Tis a tall building, with a tower and bells.
The Borough, letter ii, *The Church*, l. 11.

Virtues neglected then, adored become,
And graces slighted blossom on the tomb. *Ib.* l. 133.

Intrigues half-gather'd, conversation-scraps,
Kitchen-cabals, and nursery-mishaps.
Ib. letter iv, *The Vicar*, l. 71.

Habit with him was all the test of truth,
'It must be right: I've done it from my youth.'
Ib. l. 138.

Lo! the poor toper whose untutor'd sense,
Sees bliss in ale, and can with wine dispense;
Whose head proud fancy never taught to steer,
Beyond the muddy ecstasies of beer.
Inebriety, l. 120 (Imitation of Pope).

This, books can do—nor this alone: they give
New views to life, and teach us how to live;
They soothe the grieved, the stubborn they chastise;
Fools they admonish, and confirm the wise.
Their aid they yield to all: they never shun
The man of sorrow, nor the wretch undone;
Unlike the hard, the selfish, and the proud,
They fly not sullen from the suppliant crowd;
Nor tell to various people various things,
But show to subjects, what they show to kings.
The Library, l. 41.

Here come the grieved, a change of thought to find,
The curious here, to feed a craving mind;
Here the devout their peaceful temple choose;
And here the poet meets his favouring muse.
With awe around these silent walks I tread:
These are the lasting mansions of the dead. *Ib.* l. 101.

And mighty folios first, a lordly band,
Then quartos, their well-order'd ranks maintain,
And light octavos fill a spacious plain;
See yonder, ranged in more frequented rows,
A humbler band of duodecimos. *Ib.* l. 128.

Hence, in these times, untouch'd the pages lie,
And slumber out their immortality. *Ib.* l. 157.

Fashion, though Folly's child, and guide of fools,
Rules e'en the wisest, and in learning rules. *Ib.* l. 167.

Against her foes Religion well defends
Her sacred truths, but often fears her friends.
Ib. l. 249.

Coldly profane, and impiously gay. *Ib.* l. 265.

The murmuring poor, who will not fast in peace.
The Newspaper, l. 158.

A master-passion is the love of news. *Ib.* l. 279.

Hold their glimmering tapers to the sun.
The Parish Register, introd. to pt. i, l. 92.

Our farmers round, well pleased with constant gain,
Like other farmers, flourish and complain.
Ib. pt. i, *Baptisms*, l. 273.

I preach for ever; but I preach in vain!
Ib. pt. ii, *Marriages*, l. 130.

When from the cradle to the grave I look,
Mine I conceive a melancholy book.
Ib. pt. iii, *Burials*, l. 21.

Grave Jonas Kindred, Sybil Kindred's sire,
Was six feet high, and look'd six inches higher.
Tales, vi, *The Frank Courtship*, l. 1.

When the coarse cloth she saw, with many a stain,
Soil'd by rude hinds who cut and came again.
Ib. vii, *The Widow's Tale*, l. 25.

Who often reads, will sometimes wish to write.
Ib. xi, *Edward Shore*, l. 109.

The wife was pretty, trifling, childish, weak;
She could not think, but would not cease to speak
Ib. xiv, *Struggles of Conscience*, l. 343

But 'twas a maxim he had often tried,
That right was right, and there he would abide.
Ib. xv, *The Squire and the Priest*, l. 365.

That all was wrong because not all was right.
Ib. xix, *The Convert*, l. 313.

He tried the luxury of doing good.
Tales of the Hall, iii, *Boys at School*, l. 139.

Secrets with girls, like loaded guns with boys,
Are never valued till they make a noise.
Ib. xi, *The Maid's Story*, l. 84.

'The game', he said, 'is never lost till won.'
Ib. xv, *Gretna Green*, l. 334.

The face the index of a feeling mind.
Ib. xvi, *Lady Barbara*, l. 124.

Love warps the mind a little from the right.
Ib. xxi, *Smugglers and Poachers*, l. 216.

Lo! where the heath, with withering brake grown o'er,
Lends the light turf that warms the neighbouring
poor;
From thence a length of burning sand appears,
Where the thin harvest waves its wither'd ears;
Rank weeds, that every art and care defy,
Reign o'er the land, and rob the blighted rye:
There thistles stretch their prickly arms afar,
And to the ragged infant threaten war;
There poppies, nodding, mock the hope of toil;
There the blue bugloss paints the sterile soil;
Hardy and high, above the slender sheaf,
The slimy mallow waves her silky leaf;
O'er the young shoot the charlock throws a shade,
And clasping tares cling round the sickly blade.
The Village, bk. i, l. 63.

I sought the simple life that Nature yields.
Ib. l. 110.

And the cold charities of man to man. *Ib.* l. 245.

A potent quack, long versed in human ills,
Who first insults the victim whom he kills;
Whose murd'rous hand a drowsy Bench protect,
And whose most tender mercy is neglect. *Ib.* l. 282.

The ring so worn, as you behold,
So thin, so pale, is yet of gold:
The passion such it was to prove;
Worn with life's cares, love yet was love.
His Mother's Wedding Ring.

DINAH MARIA CRAIK
1824-1887

Douglas, Douglas, tender and true.
Songs of Our Youth, 'Douglas, Douglas, Tender
and True.'

THOMAS CRANMER
1489-1556

This hand hath offended.
Strype's Memorials of Cranmer, 1694, vol. iii.

RICHARD CRASHAW
1612?-1649

Nympha pudica Deum vidit, et erubuit.
The conscious water saw its God, and blushed.
Epigrammata Sacra. Aquae in Vinum Versae.
(His own translation.)

All those fair and flagrant things.
*The Flaming Heart Upon the Book of Saint
Teresa*, l. 34.

Love's passives are his activ'st part.
The wounded is the wounding heart. *Ib.*

O thou undaunted daughter of desires! *Ib.*

By thy large draughts of intellectual day. *Ib.*

By all the eagle in thee, all the dove. *Ib.* l. 95.

By the full kingdom of that final kiss
That seized thy parting soul, and seal'd thee His;
By all the Heavens thou hast in Him—
Fair sister of the Seraphim!—
By all of Him we have in thee;
Leave nothing of myself in me.
Let me so read thy life, that I
Unto all life of mine may die! *Ib.* l. 101.

I would be married, but I'd have no wife,
I would be married to a single life. *On Marriage.*

I sing the Name which none can say
But touch'd with an interior ray.
To the Name Above Every Name.

Narrow, and low, and infinitely less. *Ib.*

Come; and come strong,
To the conspiracy of our spacious song. *Ib.*

Gloomy night embrac'd the place
Where the noble Infant lay.
The Babe look't up and shew'd his face;
In spite of darkness, it was day.
It was Thy day, sweet! and did rise
Not from the East, but from thine eyes.
Hymn of the Nativity.

Poor World (said I) what wilt thou do
To entertain this starry stranger?
Is this the best thou canst bestow?
A cold, and not too cleanly, manger?
Contend, ye powers of heav'n and earth
To fit a bed for this huge birth. *Ib.*

Proud world, said I; cease your contest
And let the mighty Babe alone.
The phoenix builds the phoenix' nest.
Love's architecture is his own.   *Ib.*

I saw the curl'd drops, soft and slow,
Come hovering o'er the place's head;
Off'ring their whitest sheets of snow
To furnish the fair Infant's bed.
Forbear, said I; be not too bold.
Your fleece is white but 'tis too cold.   *Ib.*

I saw the obsequious Seraphims
Their rosy fleece of fire bestow.
For well they now can spare their wings
Since Heaven itself lies here below.
Well done, said I: but are you sure
Your down so warm, will pass for pure?   *Ib.*

We saw thee in thy balmy nest,
Young dawn of our eternal day!
We saw thine eyes break from their East
And chase the trembling shades away.
We saw thee; and we blest the sight
We saw thee by thine own sweet light.   *Ib.*

Welcome, all wonders in one sight!
Eternity shut in a span.   *Ib.*

Love's great artillery.   *Prayer, l. 15.*

Lo here a little volume, but large book.
         On a Prayer-Book Sent to Mrs. M. R.

Happy soul she shall discover
    What joy, what bliss,
  How many heavens at once it is,
To have a God become her lover.   *Ib.*

Why, 'tis a point of faith. Whate'er it be,
I'm sure it is no point of charity.
              On a Treatise of Charity.

Two walking baths; two weeping motions;
Portable, and compendious oceans.
      Saint Mary Magdalene, or The Weeper, xix.

Love, thou art absolute sole Lord
Of life and death.
  *Hymn to the Name & Honour of the Admirable
  Saint Teresa, l. 1.*

Farewell house, and farewell home!
She's for the Moors, and martyrdom.   *Ib. l. 63*

Two went to pray? O rather say
One went to brag, th'other to pray:

One nearer to God's Altar trod,
The other to the Altar's God.
  *Steps to the Temple, Two Went up into the
  Temple to Pray.*

All is Caesar's; and what odds
So long as Caesar's self is God's?   *Ib. Mark 12.*

And when life's sweet fable ends,
Soul and body part like friends;
No quarrels, murmurs, no delay;
A kiss, a sigh, and so away.   *Temperance.*

Whoe'er she be,
That not impossible she
That shall command my heart and me;

Where'er she lie,
Lock'd up from mortal eye,
In shady leaves of destiny.
      Wishes to His Supposed Mistress.

Meet you her my wishes,
Bespeake her to my blisses,
And be ye call'd my absent kisses.

I wish her beauty,
That owes not all his duty
To gaudy tire, or glist'ring shoe-tie.   *Ib*

Life, that dares send
A challenge to his end,
And when it comes say 'Welcome Friend'.   *Ib.*

Sydnaean showers
Of sweet discourse, whose powers
Can crown old Winter's head with flowers.   *Ib.*

'Tis she, and here
Lo I unclothe and clear,
My wishes' cloudy character.   *Ib.*

Let her full Glory,
My fancies, fly before ye,
Be ye my fictions; but her story.   *Ib.*

JULIA CRAWFORD
fl. 1835

Kathleen Mavourneen! the grey dawn is breaking,
  The horn of the hunter is heard on the hill;
The lark from her light wing the bright dew is shaking;
  Kathleen Mavourneen! what, slumbering still?
Oh! hast thou forgotten how soon we must sever?
  Oh! hast thou forgotten this day we must part?
It may be for years, and it may be for ever,
  Oh! why art thou silent, thou voice of my heart?
    *Kathleen Mavourneen. Metropolitan Magazine,
    London, 1835.*

MANDELL CREIGHTON
1843–1901

No people do so much harm as those who go about
  doing good.   *Life, 1904, vol. ii, p. 503.*

JOHN WILSON CROKER
1780–1857

We now are, as we always have been, decidedly and
  conscientiously attached to what is called the Tory,
  and which might with more propriety be called the
  Conservative, party.
      Article, Quarterly Review, Jan. 1830, p. 276.

A game which a sharper once played with a dupe,
  entitled, 'Heads I win, tails you lose.'
                  Croker Papers, iii. 59.

OLIVER CROMWELL
1599–1658

A few honest men are better than numbers.
          Letter to Sir W. Spring, Sept. 1643.

I beseech you, in the bowels of Christ, think it possible
  you may be mistaken.
      *Letter to the General Assembly of the Church of
      Scotland, 3 Aug. 1650.*

The dimensions of this mercy are above my thoughts.
  It is, for aught I know, a crowning mercy.
      *Letter for the Honourable William Lenthall,
      4 Sept. 1651*

Mr. Lely, I desire you would use all your skill to paint my picture truly like me, and not flatter me at all; but remark all these roughnesses, pimples, warts, and everything as you see me, otherwise I will never pay a farthing for it.
Remark, Walpole's Anecdotes of Painting, ch. 12.

Take away these baubles.
Remark, Sydney Papers (1825), p. 141.

It's a maxim not to be despised, 'Though peace be made, yet it's interest that keeps peace.'
Speech to Parliament, 4 Sept. 1654.

Necessity hath no law. Feigned necessities, imaginary necessities, . . . are the greatest cozenage that men can put upon the Providence of God, and make pretences to break known rules by.
Speech to Parliament, 12 Sept. 1654.

Your poor army, those poor contemptible men, came up hither. *Speech to Parliament, 21 Apr. 1657.*

You have accounted yourselves happy on being environed with a great ditch from all the world beside.
Speech to Parliament, 25 Jan. 1658.

My design is to make what haste I can to be gone.
Last Words. Morley, *Life*, v, ch. 10.

Not what they want but what is good for them.
Attr. remark.

RICHARD ASSHETON, VISCOUNT CROSS
1823–1914
[When the House of Lords laughed at his speech in favour of Spiritual Peers]
I hear a smile.
G. W. E. Russell's *Collections and Recollections*, ch. 29.

JOHN CROWNE
1640?–1703?
River Thames, attended by two nymphs, representing Peace and Plenty.
Calisto, prologue, stage directions.

RICHARD CUMBERLAND
1631–1718
It is better to wear out than to rust out.
G. *Horne, The Duty of Contending for the Faith.*

ALLAN CUNNINGHAM
1784–1842
A wet sheet and a flowing sea,
A wind that follows fast
And fills the white and rustling sail
And bends the gallant mast.
A Wet Sheet and a Flowing Sea.

While the hollow oak our palace is,
Our heritage the sea. *Ib.*

It's hame and it's hame, hame fain wad I be,

O, hame, hame, hame to my ain countree!
It's hame and It's hame. [Hogg includes this poem among his *Jacobite Relics*, i. 135. In his notes, i. 294, he says he took it from Cromek's *Galloway and Nithsdale Relics*, and supposes that it owed much to Allan Cunningham.]

The lark shall sing me hame in my ain countree. *Ib.*

But the sun through the mirk blinks blithe in my e'e,
'I'll shine on ye yet in your ain countree.' *Ib.*

Wha the deil hae we got for a King,
But a wee, wee German lairdie!
The Wee, Wee German Lairdie.

JOHN PHILPOT CURRAN
1750–1817
The condition upon which God hath given liberty to man is eternal vigilance; which condition if he break, servitude is at once the consequence of his crime, and the punishment of his guilt.
Speech on the Right of Election of Lord Mayor of Dublin, 10 July 1790.

GEORGE NATHANIEL CURZON, MARQUESS OF KEDLESTON
1859–1925
I do not exclude the intelligent anticipation of facts even before they occur.
Speech, House of Commons, 29 Mar. 1898.

HENRY CUST
1861–1917
Let Hell afford
The pavement of her Heaven. *Non Nobis, Domine.*

HARRY DACRE
fl. 1892
Daisy, Daisy, give me your answer, do!
I'm half crazy, all for the love of you!
It won't be a stylish marriage,
I can't afford a carriage,
But you'll look sweet on the seat
Of a bicycle made for two! *Daisy Bell.*

CHARLES ANDERSON DANA
1819–1897
When a dog bites a man that is not news, but when a man bites a dog that is news.
What is News? The New York Sun, 1882.

SAMUEL DANIEL
1562–1619
Princes in this case
Do hate the traitor, though they love the treason.
Tragedy of Cleopatra, IV. i.

Unless above himself he can
Erect himself, how poor a thing is man!
      To the Lady Margaret, Countess of Cumberland,
      xii.

Custom that is before all law, Nature that is above
all art.   *A Defence of Rhyme.*

Love is a sickness full of woes,
  All remedies refusing:
A plant that with most cutting grows,
  Most barren with best using.
             Why so?
More we enjoy it, more it dies,
If not enjoy'd, it sighing cries,
             Hey ho.
        Hymen's Triumph, i. v.

This is the thing that I was born to do.
        Musophilus, l. 577.

And who, in time, knows whither we may vent
The treasure of our tongue, to what strange shores
This gain of our best glory shall be sent,
T'enrich unknowing nations with our stores?
What worlds in th'yet unformed Occident
May come refin'd with th'accents that are ours?
        Ib. l. 957.

But years hath done this wrong,
To make me write too much, and live too long.
      Philotas, [Ded.] *To the Prince*, l. 108.

Pity is sworn servant unto love:
And this be sure, wherever it begin
To make the way, it lets your master in.
      The Queen's Arcadia, ii. i.

Care-charmer Sleep, son of the sable Night,
Brother to Death, in silent darkness born:
Relieve my languish, and restore the light,
With dark forgetting of my care return,
And let the day be time enough to mourn
The shipwreck of my ill adventured youth:
Let waking eyes suffice to wail their scorn,
Without the torment of the night's untruth.
      Sonnets to Delia, liv.

Come worthy Greek, Ulysses come
  Possess these shores with me:
The winds and seas are troublesome,
  And here we may be free.
Here may we sit, and view their toil
  That travail on the deep,
And joy the day in mirth the while,
  And spend the night in sleep.
      Ulysses and the Siren.

JOHN JEREMIAH DANIELL

1819–1898

Sing, boys, in joyful chorus
  Your hymn of praise to-day,
And sing, ye gentle maidens,
  Your sweet responsive lay.
      Hymns Ancient & Modern, Come, Sing with
      Holy Gladness.

CHARLES ROBERT DARWIN

1809–1882

We must, however, acknowledge, as it seems to me,
  that man with all his noble qualities, . . . still bears
  in his bodily frame the indelible stamp of his lowly
  origin.
      Descent of Man, vol. ii, pt. iii, ch. 21, last words.

I have called this principle, by which each slight
  variation, if useful, is preserved, by the term of
  Natural Selection.
      The Origin of Species, ch. 3.

We will now discuss in a little more detail the struggle
  for existence.   *Ib.*

The expression often used by Mr. Herbert Spencer
  of the Survival of the Fittest is more accurate, and
  is sometimes equally convenient.   *Ib.*

CHARLES D'AVENANT

1656–1714

Custom, that unwritten law,
By which the people keep even kings in awe.
      Circe, ii. iii.

WILLIAM DAVENANT

1606–1668

I shall sleep like a top.   *The Rivals*, Act iii.

The lark now leaves his wat'ry nest,
And climbing, shakes his dewy wings;
He takes this window for the east;
And to implore your light, he sings,
Awake, awake, the morn will never rise,
Till she can dress her beauty at your eyes.   *Song.*

JOHN DAVIDSON

1857–1909

When the pods went pop on the broom, green broom.
      A Runnable Stag.

A runnable stag, a kingly crop.   *Ib.*

SIR JOHN DAVIES

1569–1626

Skill comes so slow, and life so fast doth fly,
  We learn so little and forget so much.
      Nosce Teipsum, introduction, xix.

Wit to persuade, and beauty to delight.
      Orchestra, v.

Why should your fellowship a trouble be,
Since man's chief pleasure is society?   *Ib.* xxxii.

Judge not the play before the play be done.
      Respice Finem.

SCROPE BERDMORE DAVIES

c. 1783–1852

Babylon in all its desolation is a sight not so awful
as that of the human mind in ruins.
Letter to Thomas Raikes. May 1835. See
Journal T. Raikes, 1831 to 1847, 1856, vol. ii.

WILLIAM HENRY DAVIES

1870–1940

A rainbow and a cuckoo's song
May never come together again;
   May never come
   This side the tomb.   *A Great Time.*

The simple bird that thinks two notes a song.
                   April's Charms.

A flowery, green, bird-singing land.   *In May*

What is this life if, full of care,
We have no time to stand and stare?   *Leisure.*

No time to see, in broad daylight,
Streams full of stars, like skies at night.   *Ib.*

Sweet Stay-at-Home, sweet Well-content
               Sweet Stay-at-Home.

JEFFERSON DAVIS

1808–1889

All we ask is to be let alone.
   *Attr. Remark in Inaugural Address as President
   of the Confederate States of America, 18 Feb.
   1861.*

THOMAS OSBORNE DAVIS

1813–1845

Come in the evening, or come in the morning,
Come when you're looked for, or come without
warning.   *The Welcome.*

STEPHEN DECATUR

1779–1820

Our country! In her intercourse with foreign nations,
may she always be in the right; but our country,
right or wrong.
   A. S. Mackenzie, *Life of Decatur,* ch. xiv.

DANIEL DEFOE

1660?–1731

The best of men cannot suspend their fate:
The good die early, and the bad die late.
   Character of the late Dr. S. Annesley.

We lov'd the doctrine for the teacher's sake.   *Ib.*

Nature has left this tincture in the blood,
That all men would be tyrants if they could.
     The Kentish Petition, addenda, l. 11.

I was born in the year 1632, in the city of York, of a
good family, though not of that county, my father
being a foreigner of Bremen, who settled first at
Hull.
   The Life and Adventures of Robinson Crusoe,
   pt. i.

Robin, Robin, Robin Crusoe, poor Robin Crusoe!
Where are you, Robin Crusoe? Where are you?
Where have you been?   *Ib.*

It happened one day, about noon, going towards
my boat, I was exceedingly surprised with the
print of a man's naked foot on the shore, which
was very plain to be seen in the sand. I stood like
one thunderstruck, or as if I had seen an apparition.
                                    Ib.

I takes my man Friday with me.   *Ib.*

In trouble to be troubl'd
Is to have your trouble doubl'd.
   Robinson Crusoe, The Farther Adventures.

Necessity makes an honest man a knave.
   Serious Reflections of Robinson Crusoe, ch. 2.

Wherever God erects a house of prayer,
The Devil always builds a chapel there;
And 'twill be found, upon examination,
The latter has the largest congregation.
        The True-Born Englishman, pt. i, l. 1.

From this amphibious ill-born mob began
That vain, ill-natur'd thing, an Englishman.
                     Ib. l. 132.

Your Roman–Saxon–Danish–Norman English.
                     Ib. l. 139.

Great families of yesterday we show,
And lords whose parents were the Lord knows who.
                     Ib. l. 374.

In their religion they are so uneven,
That each man goes his own By-way to heaven.
                     Ib. l. 104.

And of all plagues with which mankind are curst,
Ecclesiastic tyranny's the worst.   *Ib.* pt. ii, l. 299.

When kings the sword of justice first lay down,
They are no kings, though they possess the crown.
Titles are shadows, crowns are empty things,
The good of subjects is the end of kings.   *Ib.* l. 313.

THOMAS DEKKER

1570?–1632

The best of men
That ere wore earth about him, was a sufferer,
A soft, meek, patient, humble, tranquil spirit,
The first true gentleman that ever breath'd.
        The Honest Whore, pt. I. i. ii.

That great fishpond (the sea).   *Ib.*

This principle is old, but true as fate,
Kings may love treason, but the traitor hate.
                 Ib. pt. IV. iv.

Art thou poor, yet hast thou golden slumbers:
   Oh sweet content!
Art thou rich, yet is thy mind perplexed?
   Oh, punishment!
Dost thou laugh to see how fools are vexed
To add to golden numbers, golden numbers?
O, sweet content, O sweet, O sweet content!
   Work apace, apace, apace, apace;
Honest labour bears a lovely face;
Then hey nonny, nonny; hey nonny nonny.
               Patient Grissill, Act I.

Canst drink the waters of the crisped spring?
    O sweet content!
Swim'st thou in wealth, yet sink'st in thine own
    tears?
    O punishment!   *Ib.*

Golden slumbers kiss your eyes,
Smiles awake you when you rise:
Sleep, pretty wantons, do not cry,
And I will sing a lullaby:
Rock them, rock them, lullaby.

Care is heavy, therefore sleep you;
You are care, and care must keep you.   *Ib.* iv. ii.

Cold's the wind, and wet's the rain,
    Saint Hugh be our good speed:
Ill is the weather that bringeth no gain,
    Nor helps good hearts in need.

Trowle the bowl, the jolly nut-brown bowl,
    And here kind mate to thee:
Let's sing a dirge for Saint Hugh's soul,
    And down it merrily.
    Shoemaker's Holiday, Second Three-man's Song.

WALTER DE LA MARE

1873–

Oh, no man knows
Through what wild centuries
Roves back the rose.   *All That's Past.*

Very old are we men;
Our dreams are tales
Told in dim Eden
By Eve's nightingales;
We wake and whisper awhile,
But, the day gone by,
Silence and sleep like fields
Of amaranth lie.   *Ib.*

Far are the shades of Arabia,
Where the Princes ride at noon.   *Arabia.*

'He is crazed with the spell of far Arabia,
They have stolen his wits away.'   *Ib.*

What can a tired heart say,
Which the wise of the world have made dumb?
Save to the lonely dreams of a child,
    'Return again, come!'   *Dreams.*

Bright towers of silence [clouds].   *England.*

Here lies a most beautiful lady,
    Light of step and heart was she;
I think she was the most beautiful lady
    That ever was in the West Country.
But beauty vanishes; beauty passes;
    However rare—rare it be;
And when I crumble, who will remember
    This lady of the West Country?   *Epitaph.*

When I lie where shades of darkness
Shall no more assail mine eyes.   *Fare Well.*

Memory fades, must the remembered
Perishing be?   *Ib.*

Look thy last on all things lovely,
Every hour—let no night
Seal thy sense in deathly slumber
Till to delight

Thou hast paid thy utmost blessing;
Since that all things thou wouldst praise
Beauty took from those who loved them
In other days.   *Fare Well*, iii.

'Is there anybody there?' said the traveller,
Knocking on the moonlit door.   *The Listeners.*

'Tell them I came, and no one answered,
That I kept my word,' he said.   *Ib.*

Never the least stir made the listeners.   *Ib.*

Ay, they heard his foot upon the stirrup,
And the sound of iron on stone,
And how the silence surged softly backward,
When the plunging hoofs were gone.   *Ib.*

It's a very odd thing—
As odd as can be—
That whatever Miss T. eats
Turns into Miss T.   *Miss T.*

Never more, Sailor,
Shalt thou be
Tossed on the wind-ridden
Restless sea.   *Never More, Sailor.*

No robin ever
On the deep
Hopped with his song
To haunt thy sleep.   *Ib.*

Three jolly Farmers
Once bet a pound
Each dance the others would
Off the ground.   *Off the Ground.*

And still would remain
    My wit to try—
My worn reeds broken,
    The dark tarn dry,
All words forgotten—
    Thou, Lord, and I.   *The Scribe.*

Slowly, silently, now the moon
Walks the night in her silver shoon.   *Silver.*

Ages and ages have fallen on me—
On the wood and the pool and the elder tree.
    Song of Enchantment.

Of all the trees in England,
Oak, Elder, Elm and Thorn,
The Yew alone burns lamps of peace
For them that lie forlorn.   *Trees.*

JOHN DENHAM

1615–1669

Where, with like haste, though several ways they run;
Some to undo, and some to be undone.
    Cooper's Hill, l. 31.

Oh, could I flow like thee, and make thy stream
My great example, as it is my theme!
Though deep, yet clear; though gentle, yet not dull;
Strong without rage, without o'erflowing full.
    The Thames, l. 189.

Youth, what man's age is like to be doth show;
We may our ends by our beginnings know.
    Of Prudence, l. 225.

THOMAS DENHAM
1779–1854

Trial by jury itself, instead of being a security to persons who are accused, will be a delusion, a mockery, and a snare.
Judgment in O'Connell v. *the Queen, 4 Sept. 1844.*

JOHN DENNIS
1657–1734

A man who could make so vile a pun would not scruple to pick a pocket.
The Gentleman's Magazine, 1781, p. 324 (Edit. note).

Damn them! They will not let my play run, but they steal my thunder!
W. S. Walsh, Handy-book of Literary Curiosities.

THOMAS DE QUINCEY
1785–1859

Set up as a theatrical scarecrow for superstitious terrors.
Confessions of an English Opium Eater. Preface, 1856.

The burden of the incommunicable. *Ib.* pt. i.

Thou hast the keys of Paradise, oh just, subtle, and mighty opium! *Ib.* pt. ii, *The Pleasures of Opium.*

An Iliad of woes. *Ib.* pt. iii, *The Pains of Opium.*

Everlasting farewells! and again, and yet again reverberated—everlasting farewells! *Ib.*

Murder Considered as One of the Fine Arts.
Title of Essay.

There is first the literature of *knowledge,* and secondly, the literature of *power. Essays on the Poets; Pope.*

Books, we are told, propose to *instruct* or to *amuse.* Indeed! . . . The true antithesis to knowledge, in this case, is not *pleasure,* but *power.* All that is literature seeks to communicate power; all that is not literature, to communicate knowledge.
Letters to a Young Man, Letter iii. (De Quincey adds that he is indebted for this distinction to 'many years' conversation with Mr. Wordsworth.')

AUBREY THOMAS DE VERE
1814–1902

Love thy God and love Him only,
And thy breast will ne'er be lonely.
The Waldenses.

Vainly strives the soul to mingle
With a being of our kind;
Vainly hearts with hearts are twined,
For the deepest still is single. *Ib.*

Mortal! Love that Holy One,
Or dwell for aye alone. *Ib.*

EDWARD DE VERE,
EARL OF OXFORD
1550–1604

If women could be fair and yet not fond.
Women's Changeableness.

ROBERT DEVEREUX,
EARL OF ESSEX
1566–1601

Reasons are not like garments, the worse for wearing.
To Lord Willoughby, 4 Jan. 1598–9. [See *Notes and Queries,* Ser. X, vol. ii, p. 23.]

GEORGE DEWEY
1837–1917

You may fire when you are ready, Gridley.
Dewey's *Autobiography.*

CHARLES DIBDIN
1745–1814

Did you ever hear of Captain Wattle?
He was all for love and a little for the bottle.
Captain Wattle and Miss Roe.

For a soldier I listed, to grow great in fame,
And be shot at for sixpence a-day. *Charity.*

In every mess I finds a friend,
In every port a wife. *Jack in his Element.*

And did you not hear of a jolly young waterman,
Who at Blackfriars Bridge used for to ply;
And he feather'd his oars with such skill and dexterity,
Winning each heart, and delighting each eye.
The Jolly Young Waterman.

As he row'd along, thinking of nothing at all. *Ib.*

What argufies sniv'ling and piping your eye?
Poor Jack.

For they say there's a Providence sits up aloft,
To keep watch for the life of poor Jack! *Ib.*

Then farewell, my trim-built wherry!
Oars, and coat, and badge, farewell! *Poor Tom.*

But the standing toast that pleased the most
Was—The wind that blows, the ship that goes,
And the lass that loves a sailor!
The Standing Toast, from the opera, *The Round Robin.*

Spanking Jack was so comely, so pleasant, so jolly,
Though winds blew great guns, still he'd whistle and sing;
Jack lov'd his friend, and was true to his Molly,
And if honour gives greatness, was great as a king.
The Sailor's Consolation.

THOMAS JOHN DIBDIN
1771–1841

Oh! what a snug little Island,
A right little, tight little Island!
The Snug Little Island.

Then a very great war-man call'd Billy the Norman.
Ib.

Here, a sheer hulk, lies poor Tom Bowling,
The darling of our crew.   *Tom Bowling.*

Faithful, below, he did his duty;
But now he's gone aloft.   *Ib.*

CHARLES DICKENS

1812–1870

Rather a tough customer in argeyment, Joe, if
anybody was to try and tackle him. [*Parkes.*]
     Barnaby Rudge, ch. 1.

Something will come of this. I hope it mayn't be
human gore. [*Simon Tappertit.*]   *Ib.* ch. 4.

Polly put the kettle on, we'll all have tea. [*Grip.*]
     Ib. ch. 17.

'There are strings,' said Mr. Tappertit, '. . . in the
human heart that had better not be wibrated.'
     Ib. ch. 22.

Oh gracious, why wasn't I born old and ugly?
[*Miss Miggs.*]   *Ib.* ch. 70.

Jarndyce and Jarndyce still drags its dreary length
before the Court, perennially hopeless.
     Bleak House, ch. 1.

This is a London particular. . . . A fog, miss.
     Ib. ch. 3.

Educating the natives of Borrioboola-Gha, on the
left bank of the Niger. [*Mrs. Jellyby.*]   *Ib.* ch. 4.

The wind's in the east. . . . I am always conscious
of an uncomfortable sensation now and then when
the wind is blowing in the east. [*Mr. Jarndyce.*]
     Ib. ch. 6.

I only ask to be free. The butterflies are free.
Mankind will surely not deny to Harold Skimpole
what it concedes to the butterflies!   *Ib.*

'Not to put too fine a point upon it'—a favourite
apology for plain-speaking with Mr. Snagsby
     Bleak House, ch. 11.

He wos wery good to me, he wos! [*Jo.*]   *Ib.*

He [Mr. Turveydrop] is celebrated, almost everywhere, for his Deportment. [*Caddy.*]   *Ib.* ch. 14.

'It was a maxim of Captain Swosser's', said Mrs.
Badger, 'speaking in his figurative naval manner,
that when you make pitch hot, you cannot make it
too hot; and that if you only have to swab a plank,
you should swab it as if Davy Jones were after
you.'   *Ib.* ch. 17.

The Professor made the same remark, Miss Summer-
son, in his last illness; when (his mind wandering)
he insisted on keeping his little hammer under the
pillow, and chipping at the countenances of the
attendants. The ruling passion! [*Mrs. Badger.*]
     Ib.

'What is peace? Is it war? No. Is it strife? No.'
[*Mr. Chadband.*]   *Ib.* ch. 19.

The Chadband style of oratory is widely received
and much admired.   *Ib.*

You are a human boy, my young friend. A human
boy. O glorious to be a human boy! . . .

O running stream of sparkling joy
To be a soaring human boy! [*Mr. Chadband.*]
     Ib.

Jobling, there *are* chords in the human mind. [*Guppy.*]
     Ib. ch. 20.

'It is', says Chadband, 'the ray of rays, the sun of
suns, the moon of moons, the star of stars. It is the
light of Terewth.'   *Ib.* ch. 25.

'Lo, the city is barren, I have seen but an eel.'   *Ib.*

It's my old girl that advises. She has the head. But
I never own to it before her. Discipline must be
maintained. [*Mr. Bagnet.*]   *Ib.* ch. 27.

It is a melancholy truth that even great men have
their poor relations.   *Ib.* ch. 28.

Never have a mission, my dear child. [*Mr. Jellyby.*]
     Ib. ch. 30.

England has been in a dreadful state for some weeks.
Lord Coodle would go out, and Sir Thomas Doodle
wouldn't come in, and there being nobody in
Great Britain (to speak of) except Coodle and
Doodle, there has been no Government.
     Ib. ch. 40.

She's Colour-Sergeant of the Nonpareil battalion.
[*Mr. Bagnet.*]   *Ib.* ch. 52.

Hasn't a doubt—zample—far better hang wrong fler
than no fler. [*The 'debilitated cousin'.*]   *Ib.* ch. 53.

A smattering of everything, and a knowledge of
nothing. [*Minerva House.*]
     Sketches by Boz. Tales, ch. 3. *Sentiment.*

Grief never mended no broken bones, and as good
people's wery scarce, what I says is, make the
most on 'em.   *Ib. Scenes,* ch. 22, *Gin-Shops.*

O let us love our occupations,
Bless the squire and his relations,
Live upon our daily rations,
And always know our proper stations
     The Chimes, 2nd Quarter.

In came a fiddler—and tuned like fifty stomach-aches.
In came Mrs. Fezziwig, one vast substantial smile.
     A Christmas Carol, stave 2.

'God bless us every one!' said Tiny Tim, the last of
all.   *Ib.* stave 3.

It *was* a turkey! He could never have stood upon
his legs, that bird. He would have snapped 'em
off short in a minute, like sticks of sealing-wax.
     Ib. stave 5.

'Somebody's sharp.' 'Who is?' asked the gentleman, laughing. I looked up quickly; being curious
to know. 'Only Brooks of Sheffield,' said Mr.
Murdstone. I was relieved to that to find it was only
Brooks of Sheffield; for, at first, I really thought
it was I.   *David Copperfield,* ch. 2.

'I am a lone lorn creetur',' were Mrs. Gummidge's
words, . . . 'and everythink goes contrairy with me.'
     Ib. ch. 3.

'I feel it more than other people,' said Mrs. Gummidge.   *Ib.*

I'd better go into the house, and die and be a riddance! [*Mrs. Gummidge.*]   *Ib.*

She's been thinking of the old 'un! [*Mr. Peggotty, of Mrs. Gummidge.*]   *David Copperfield*, ch. 3.

Barkis is willin'.   *Ib.* ch. 5.

'There was a gentleman here yesterday,' he said—'a stout gentleman, by the name of Topsawyer ... he came in here, ... ordered a glass of this ale—*would* order it—I told him not—drank it, and fell dead. It was too old for him. It oughtn't to be drawn; that's the fact.' [*The Waiter.*]   *Ib.*

I live on broken wittles—and I sleep on the coals. [*The Waiter.*]   *Ib.*

'When a man says he's willin',' said Mr. Barkis, ... 'it's as much as to say, that a man's waitin' for a answer.'   *Ib.* ch. 8.

Experientia does it—as papa used to say. [*Mrs. Micawber.*]   *Ib.* ch. 11.

I have known him [Micawber] come home to supper with a flood of tears, and a declaration that nothing was now left but a jail; and go to bed making a calculation of the expense of putting bow-windows to the house, 'in case anything turned up,' which was his favourite expression.   *Ib.*

I never will desert Mr. Micawber. [*Mrs. Micawber.*]   *Ib.* ch. 12.

Annual income twenty pounds, annual expenditure nineteen nineteen six, result happiness. Annual income twenty pounds, annual expenditure twenty pounds ought and six, result misery. [*Mr. Micawber.*]   *Ib.*

Mr. Dick had been for upwards of ten years endeavouring to keep King Charles the First out of the Memorial; but he had been constantly getting into it, and was there now.   *Ib.* ch. 14.

The mistake was made of putting some of the trouble out of King Charles's head into my head.   *Ib.* ch. 17.

We are so very 'umble. [*Uriah Heep.*]   *Ib.*

'Orses and dorgs is some men's fancy. They're wittles and drink to me—lodging, wife, and children—reading, writing and 'rithmetic—snuff, tobacker, and sleep.   *Ib.* ch. 19.

I only ask for information. [*Miss Rosa Dartle.*]   *Ib.* ch. 20.

'It was as true', said Mr. Barkis, '... as taxes is. And nothing's truer than them.'   *Ib.* ch. 21.

What a world of gammon and spinnage it is, though, ain't it! [*Miss Mowcher.*]   *Ib.* ch. 22.

The whole social system ... is a system of Prince's nails. [*Miss Mowcher.*]   *Ib.*

'Oh, surely! surely!' said Mr. Spenlow. ... 'I should be happy, myself, to propose two months, ... but I have a partner. Mr. Jorkins.'   *Ib.* ch. 23.

Other things are all very well in their way, but give me Blood! [*Mr. Waterbrook.*]   *Ib.* ch. 25.

I assure you she's the dearest girl. [*Traddles.*]   *Ib.* ch. 27.

Accidents will occur in the best-regulated families; and in families not regulated by that pervading influence which sanctifies while it enhances the

—a—I would say, in short, by the influence of Woman, in the lofty character of Wife, they may be expected with confidence, and must be borne with philosophy. [*Mr. Micawber.*]   *Ib.* ch. 28.

He told me, only the other day, that it was provided for. That was Mr. Micawber's expression, 'Provided for.' [*Traddles.*]   *Ib.*

'People can't die, along the coast,' said Mr. Peggotty, 'except when the tide's pretty nigh out. They can't be born, unless it's pretty nigh in—not properly born, till flood. He's a going out with the tide.'   *Ib.* ch. 30.

Mrs. Crupp had indignantly assured him that there wasn't room to swing a cat there; but, as Mr. Dick justly observed to me, sitting down on the foot of the bed, nursing his leg, 'You know, Trotwood, I don't want to swing a cat. I never do swing a cat. Therefore, what does that signify to *me!*' *Ib.* ch. 35.

It's only my child-wife. [*Dora.*]   *Ib.* ch. 44.

Circumstances beyond my individual control. [*Mr. Micawber.*]   *Ib.* ch. 49.

I'm Gormed—and I can't say no fairer than that! [*Mr. Peggotty.*]   *Ib.* ch. 63.

He's tough, ma'am, tough, is J. B. Tough, and devilish sly! [*Major Bagstock.*]   *Dombey and Son*, ch. 7.

There was no light nonsense about Miss Blimber. ... She was dry and sandy with working in the graves of deceased languages. None of your live languages for Miss Blimber. They must be dead—stone dead—and then Miss Blimber dug them up like a Ghoul.   *Ib.* ch. 11.

As to Mr. Feeder, B.A., Doctor Blimber's assistant, he was a kind of human barrel-organ, with a little list of tunes at which he was continually working, over and over again, without any variation.   *Ib.*

If I could have known Cicero, and been his friend, and talked with him in his retirement at Tusculum (beautiful Tusculum), I could have died contented. [*Mrs. Blimber.*]   *Ib.*

'Wal'r, my boy,' replied the Captain, 'in the Proverbs of Solomon you will find the following words, "May we never want a friend in need, nor a bottle to give him!" When found, make a note of.' [*Captain Cuttle.*]   *Ib.* ch. 15.

Train up a fig-tree in the way it should go, and when you are old sit under the shade of it. [*Captain Cuttle*].   *Ib.* ch. 19.

Cows are my passion. [*Mrs. Skewton.*]   *Ib.* ch. 21.

Mr. Toots devoted himself to the cultivation of those gentle arts which refine and humanize existence, his chief instructor in which was an interesting character called the Game Chicken, who was always to be heard of at the bar of the Black Badger, wore a shaggy white great-coat in the warmest weather, and knocked Mr. Toots about the head three times a week.   *Ib.* ch. 22.

It's of no consequence. [*Mr. Toots.*]   *Ib.*

The bearings of this observation lays in the application on it. [*Bunsby.*]   *Ib.* ch. 23.

Say, like those wicked Turks, there is no What's-his-name but Thingummy, and What-you-may-call-it is his prophet! [*Mrs. Skewton.*]
Dombey and Son, ch. 27.

I positively adore Miss Dombey;—I—I am perfectly sore with loving her. [*Mr. Toots.*] *Ib.* ch. 30.

England, Home, and Beauty! [*Captain Cuttle.*]
Ib. ch. 48.

If you could see my legs when I take my boots off, you'd form some idea of what unrequited affection is. [*Mr. Toots.*] *Ib.*

Whatever was required to be done, the Circumlocution Office was beforehand with all the public departments in the art of perceiving—HOW NOT TO DO IT. *Little Dorrit*, bk. i, ch. 10.

Look here. Upon my soul you mustn't come into the place saying you want to know, you know. [*Barnacle Junior.*] *Ib.*

One remark . . . I wish to make, one explanation I wish to offer, when your Mama came and made a scene of it with my Papa and when I was called down into the little breakfast-room where they were looking at one another with your Mama's parasol between them seated on two chairs like mad bulls what was I to do? [*Flora Finching.*]
Ib. ch. 13.

The Great Fire of London was not the fire in which your uncle George's workshops was burned down. [*Mr. F.'s Aunt.*] *Ib*

I hate a fool! [*Mr. F.'s Aunt.*] *Ib.*

Take a little time—count five-and-twenty, Tatty-coram. [*Mr. Meagles.*] *Ib.* ch. 16

In company with several other old ladies of both sexes. *Ib.* ch. 17.

There's milestones on the Dover Road! [*Mr. F.'s Aunt.*] *Ib.* ch. 23.

You can't make a head and brains out of a brass knob with nothing in it. You couldn't when your Uncle George was living; much less when he's dead. [*Mr. F.'s Aunt.*] *Ib.*

He [Mr. Finching] proposed seven times once in a hackney-coach once in a boat once in a pew once on a donkey at Tunbridge Wells and the rest on his knees. [*Flora Finching.*] *Ib.* ch. 24.

I revere the memory of Mr. F. as an estimable man and most indulgent husband, only necessary to mention Asparagus and it appeared or to hint at any little delicate thing to drink and it came like magic in a pint bottle it was not ecstasy but it was comfort. [*Flora Finching.*] *Ib.*

E please. Double good! [*Mrs. Plornish.*] *Ib.* ch. 25.

Father is rather vulgar, my dear. The word Papa, besides, gives a pretty form to the lips. Papa, potatoes, poultry, prunes and prism, are all very good words for the lips; especially prunes and prism. [*Mrs. General.*] *Ib.* bk. ii, ch. 5.

Dante—known to that gentleman [Mr. Sparkler] as an eccentric man in the nature of an Old File, who used to put leaves round his head, and sit upon a stool for some unaccountable purpose, outside the cathedral at Florence. *Ib.* ch. 6.

Once a gentleman, and always a gentleman. [*Rigaud.*]
Ib. ch. 28.

Stranger, pause and ask thyself the question, Canst thou do likewise? If not, with a blush retire.
Edwin Drood, ch. 4.

Circumstances alter cases. *Ib.* ch. 9.

'Dear me,' said Mr. Grewgious, peeping in, 'it's like looking down the throat of Old Time.' *Ib.*

'Umps', said Mr. Grewgious. *Ib.* ch. 11.

Your sister is given to government. [*Joe Gargery.*]
Great Expectations, ch. 7.

I had cherished a profound conviction that her bringing me up by hand, gave her no right to bring me up by jerks. *Ib.* ch. 8.

On the Rampage, Pip, and off the Rampage, Pip; such is Life! [*Joe Gargery.*] *Ib.* ch. 15.

Get hold of portable property. [*Wemmick.*]
Ib. ch. 24.

You don't object to an aged parent, I hope? [*Wemmick.*] *Ib.* ch. 25.

'Have you seen anything of London, yet?' [*Herbert.*] 'Why, yes. Sir—but we didn't find that it come up to its likeness in the red bills—it is there drawd too architectooralooral.' [*Joe Gargery.*] *Ib.* ch. 27.

'Halloa! Here's a church! . . . Let's go in! . . . Here's Miss Skiffins! Let's have a wedding.' [*Wemmick.*]
Ib. ch. 55.

Now, what I want is, Facts. . . . Facts alone are wanted in life. [*Mr. Gradgrind.*]
Hard Times, bk. i, ch. 1.

The Lord No Zoo. [*Toby Chuzzlewit.*]
Martin Chuzzlewit, ch. 1.

'The name of those fabulous animals (pagan, I regret to say) who used to sing in the water, has quite escaped me.' Mr. George Chuzzlewit suggested 'Swans.' 'No,' said Mr. Pecksniff. 'Not swans. Very like swans, too. Thank you.' The nephew . . . propounded 'Oysters.' 'No,' said Mr. Pecksniff, . . . 'nor oysters. But by no means unlike oysters; a very excellent idea; thank you, my dear sir, very much. Wait. Sirens! Dear me! sirens, of course.' *Ib.* ch. 4.

Any man may be in good spirits and good temper when he's well dressed. There an't much credit in that. [*Mark Tapley.*] *Ib.* ch. 5.

Some credit in being jolly. [*Mark Tapley.*] *Ib.*

A highly geological home-made cake. *Ib.*

'Let us be merry.' Here he took a captain's biscuit. [*Mr. Pecksniff.*] *Ib.*

With affection beaming in one eye, and calculation shining out of the other. [*Mrs. Todgers.*]
Ib. ch. 8.

Oh, Todger's could do it when it chose! Mind that.
Ib. ch. 9.

Charity and Mercy. Not unholy names, I hope? [*Mr. Pecksniff.*] *Ib.*

'Do not repine, my friends,' said Mr. Pecksniff, tenderly. 'Do not weep for me. It is chronic.'
Ib.

Let us be moral. Let us contemplate existence. [*Mr. Pecksniff.*]   *Martin Chuzzlewit*, ch. 9.

Here's the rule for bargains: 'Do other men, for they would do you.' That's the true business precept. [*Jonas Chuzzlewit.*]   *Ib.* ch. 11.

Mrs. Harris,' I says, 'leave the bottle on the chimley-piece, and don't ask me to take none, but let me put my lips to it when I am so dispoged.' [*Mrs. Gamp.*]   *Ib.* ch. 19.

Some people . . . may be Rooshans, and others may be Prooshans; they are born so, and will please themselves. Them which is of other naturs thinks different. [*Mrs. Gamp.*]   *Ib.*

Therefore I *do* require it, which I makes confession, to be brought reg'lar and draw'd mild. [*Mrs. Gamp.*]   *Ib.* ch. 25.

'She's the sort of woman now,' said Mould, . . . 'one would almost feel disposed to bury for nothing: and do it neatly, too!'   *Ib.*

He'd make a lovely corpse. [*Mrs. Gamp.*]   *Ib.*

All the wickedness of the world is print to him. [*Mrs. Gamp.*]   *Ib.* ch. 26.

'Sairey,' says Mrs. Harris, 'sech is life. Vich likeways is the hend of all things!' [*Mrs. Gamp.*]   *Ib.* ch. 29.

Our backs is easy ris. We must be cracked-up, or they rises, and we snarls. . . . You'd better crack up, you had! [*Chollop.*]   *Ib.* ch. 33.

'Our fellow-countryman is a model of a man, quite fresh from Natur's mould! . . . Rough he may be. So air our Barrs. Wild he may be. So air our Buffalers.' [*Pogram.*]   *Ib.* ch. 34.

'To be presented to a Pogram,' said Miss Codger, 'by a Hominy, indeed, a thrilling moment is it in its impressiveness on what we call our feelings.'   *Ib.*

'Mind and matter,' said the lady in the wig, 'glide swift into the vortex of immensity. Howls the sublime, and softly sleeps the calm Ideal, in the whispering chambers of Imagination.'   *Ib.*

'The Ankworks package,' . . . 'I wish it was in Jonadge's belly, I do,' cried Mrs. Gamp; appearing to confound the prophet with the whale in this miraculous aspiration.   *Ib.* ch. 40.

Oh Sairey, Sairey, little do we know wot lays afore us! [*Mrs. Gamp.*]   *Ib.*

I know'd she wouldn't have a cowcumber! [*Betsey Prig.*]   *Ib.* ch. 49.

'Who deniges of it?' Mrs. Gamp enquired.   *Ib.*

Ever since afore her First, which Mr. Harris who was dreadful timid went and stopped his ears in a empty dog-kennel, and never took his hands away or come out once till he was showed the baby, wen bein' took with fits, the doctor collared him and laid him on his back upon the airy stones, and she was told to ease her mind, his owls was organs. [*Mrs. Gamp.*]   *Ib.*

'Bother Mrs. Harris!' said Betsey Prig. . . . 'I don't believe there's no sich a person!'   *Ib.*

The words she spoke of Mrs. Harris, lambs could not forgive . . . nor worms forget. [*Mrs. Gamp.*] *Ib.*

Which fiddle-strings is weakness to expredge my nerves this night! [*Mrs. Gamp.*]   *Ib.* ch. 51.

Farewell! Be the proud bride of a ducal coronet, and forget me! . . . Unalterably, never yours, Augustus. [*Augustus Moddle.*]   *Ib.* ch. 54.

United Metropolitan Improved Hot Muffin and Crumpet Baking and Punctual Delivery Company.   *Nicholas Nickleby*, ch. 2.

He had but one eye, and the popular prejudice runs in favour of two. [*Mr. Squeers.*]   *Ib.* ch. 4.

Serve it right for being so dear. [*Mr. Squeers.*]   *Ib.* ch. 5.

Subdue your appetites, my dears, and you've conquered human natur. [*Mr. Squeers.*]   *Ib.*

C-l-e-a-n, clean, verb active, to make bright, to scour. W-i-n, win, d-e-r, der, winder, a casement. When the boy knows this out of the book, he goes and does it. [*Mr. Squeers.*]   *Ib.* ch. 8.

As she frequently remarked when she made any such mistake, it would be all the same a hundred years hence. [*Mrs. Squeers.*]   *Ib.* ch. 9.

There are only two styles of portrait painting; the serious and the smirk. [*Miss La Creevy.*]   *Ib.* ch. 10.

Oh! they're too beautiful to live, much too beautiful! [*Mrs. Kenwigs.*]   *Ib.* ch. 14.

Sir, My pa requests me to write to you, the doctors considering it doubtful whether he will ever recuvver the use of his legs which prevents his holding a pen. [*Fanny Squeers.*]   *Ib.* ch. 15.

One mask of brooses both blue and green. [*Fanny Squeers.*]   *Ib.*

I am screaming out loud all the time I write and so is my brother which takes off my attention rather and I hope will excuse mistakes. [*Fanny Squeers.*]   *Ib.*

I pity his ignorance and despise him. [*Fanny Squeers.*]   *Ib.*

This is all very well, Mr. Nickleby, and very proper, so far as it goes—so far as it goes, but it doesn't go far enough. [*Mr. Gregsbury.*]   *Ib.* ch. 16.

We've got a private master comes to teach us at home, but we ain't proud, because ma says it's sinful. [*Mrs. Kenwigs.*]   *Ib.*

'What's the water in French, sir?' 'L'eau,' replied Nicholas. 'Ah!' said Mr. Lillyvick, shaking his head mournfully. 'I thought as much. Lo, eh? I don't think anything of that language—nothing at all.'   *Ib.*

'It's very easy to talk.' said Mrs. Mantalini.
'Not so easy when one is eating a demnition egg,' replied Mr. Mantalini; 'for the yolk runs down the waistcoat, and yolk of egg does not match any waistcoat but a yellow waistcoat, demmit.'   *Ib.* ch. 17.

Language was not powerful enough to describe the infant phenomenon.   *Ib.* ch. 23.

'I hope you have preserved the unities, sir?' said Mr. Curdle. . . .

'The unities, sir, . . . are a completeness—a kind of a universal dovetailedness with regard to place and time.' *Nicholas Nickleby*, ch. 24.

She's the only sylph I ever saw, who could stand upon one leg, and play the tambourine on her other knee, like a sylph. [*Mr. Crummles*]. *Ib.* ch. 25.

The two countesses had no outlines at all, and the dowager's was a demd outline. [*Mr. Mantalini.*] *Ib.* ch. 34.

A demd, damp, moist, unpleasant body. [*Mr. Mantalini.*] *Ib.*

In the absence of the planet Venus, who has gone on business to the Horse Guards. [*The Gentleman in the Small-clothes.*] *Ib.* ch. 41.

Bring in the bottled lightning, a clean tumbler, and a corkscrew. [*The Gentleman in the Small-clothes.*] *Ib.* ch. 49.

All is gas and gaiters. [*The Gentleman in the Small-clothes.*] *Ib.*

My life is one demd horrid grind! [*Mr. Mantalini.*] *Ib.* ch. 64.

He has gone to the demnition bow-wows. [*Mr. Mantalini.*] *Ib.*

Is the old min agreeable? [*Dick Swiveller.*] *The Old Curiosity Shop*, ch. 2.

What is the odds so long as the fire of soul is kindled at the taper of conwiviality, and the wing of friendship never moults a feather! [*Dick Swiveller.*] *Ib.*

Fan the sinking flame of hilarity with the wing of friendship; and pass the rosy wine. [*Dick Swiveller.*] *Ib.* ch. 7.

Codlin's the friend, not Short. [*Codlin.*] *Ib.* ch. 19.

If I know'd a donkey wot wouldn't go
To see Mrs. Jarley's waxwork show,
Do you think I'd acknowledge him,
Oh no no! *Ib.* ch. 27.

I never nursed a dear Gazelle, to glad me with its soft black eye, but when it came to know me well, and love me, it was sure to marry a market-gardener. [*Dick Swiveller.*] *Ib.* ch. 56.

'Did you ever taste beer?' 'I had a sip of it once,' said the small servant. 'Here's a state of things!' cried Mr. Swiveller. . . . 'She *never* tasted it—it can't be tasted in a sip!' *Ib.* ch. 57.

It was a maxim with Foxey—our revered father, gentlemen—'Always suspect everybody.' [*Sampson Brass.*] *Ib.* ch. 66.

Oliver Twist has asked for more! [*Bumble.*] *Oliver Twist*, ch. 2.

Known by the *sobriquet* of 'The artful Dodger.' *Ib.* ch. 8.

'Hard,' replied the Dodger. 'As nails,' added Charley Bates. *Ib.* ch. 9.

There is a passion for hunting something deeply implanted in the human breast. *Ib.* ch. 10.

I'll eat my head. [*Mr. Grimwig.*] *Ib.* ch. 14.

I only know two sorts of boys. Mealy boys, and beef-faced boys. [*Mr. Grimwig.*] *Ib.*

Oh, Mrs. Corney, what a prospect this opens! What a opportunity for a jining of hearts and house-keepings! [*Bumble.*] *Ib.* ch. 27.

'If the law supposes that,' said Mr. Bumble . . . 'the law is a ass—a idiot.' *Ib.* ch. 51.

Why then we should drop into poetry. [*Boffin.*] *Our Mutual Friend*, bk. i, ch. 5.

Decline-and-Fall-Off-The-Rooshan-Empire. [*Mr. Boffin.*] *Ib.*

'Mrs. Boffin, Wegg,' said Boffin, 'is a highflyer at Fashion.' *Ib.*

Meaty jelly, too, especially when a little salt, which is the case when there's ham, is mellering to the organ. [*Silas Wegg.*] *Ib.*

'It is Rooshan; ain't it, Wegg?'
'No, sir. Roman. Roman.'
'What's the difference, Wegg?'
'The difference, sir?—There you place me in a difficulty, Mr. Boffin. Suffice it to observe, that the difference is best postponed to some other occasion when Mrs. Boffin does not honour us with her company.' *Ib.*

I didn't think this morning there was half so many Scarers in Print. [*Boffin.*] *Ib.*

A literary man—*with* a wooden leg. [*Mr. Boffin on Silas Wegg.*] *Ib.* ch. 8.

Professionally he declines and falls, and as a friend he drops into poetry. [*Mr. Boffin on Silas Wegg.*] *Ib.*

Mr. Podsnap settled that whatever he put behind him he put out of existence. . . . Mr. Podsnap had even acquired a peculiar flourish of his right arm in often clearing the world of its most difficult problems, by sweeping them behind him. *Ib.* ch. 11.

The question [with Mr. Podsnap] about everything was, would it bring a blush into the cheek of the young person? *Ib.*

The gay, the gay and festive scene,
The halls, the halls of dazzling light. [*Mrs. Boffin.*] *Ib.* ch. 15.

Oh! *I* know their tricks and their manners. [*Fanny Cleaver.*] *Ib.* bk. ii, ch. 1.

Who comes here?
A Grenadier.
What does he want?
A pot of beer. *Ib.* ch. 2.

I think . . . that it is the best club in London. [*Mr. Twemlow, on the House of Commons.*] *Ib.* ch. 3.

I don't care whether I am a Minx, or a Sphinx. [*Lavvy.*] *Ib.* ch. 8.

A slap-up gal in a bang-up chariot. *Ib.*

Queer street is full of lodgers just at present. [*Fledgeby.*] *Ib.* bk. iii, ch. 1.

O Mrs. Higden, Mrs. Higden, you was a woman and a mother, and a mangler in a million million. [*Sloppy.*] *Ib.* ch. 9.

He'd be sharper than a serpent's tooth, if he wasn't as dull as ditch water. [*Fanny Cleaver.*]
Our Mutual Friend, bk. iii, ch. 10.

T'other governor. [*Mr. Riderhood.*] *Ib.* bk. iv, ch. 1.
The dodgerest of the dodgers. [*Mr. Fledgeby.*]
Ib. ch. 8.

The Golden Dustman. *Ib.* ch. 11.

He had used the word in its Pickwickian sense. . . . He had merely considered him a humbug in a Pickwickian point of view. [*Mr. Blotton.*]
Pickwick Papers, ch. 1.

Heads, heads . . .! . . . five children—mother—tall lady, eating sandwiches—forgot the arch—crash—knock—children look round—mother's head off—sandwich in her hand—no mouth to put it in—head of a family off—shocking, shocking! [*Jingle.*] *Ib.* ch. 2.

Half-a-crown in the bill, if you look at the waiter.—Charge you more if you dine at a friend's than they would if you dined in the coffee-room. [*Jingle.*] *Ib.*

Not presume to dictate, but broiled fowl and mushrooms—capital thing! [*Jingle.*] *Ib.*

Kent, sir—everybody knows Kent—apples, cherries, hops, and women. [*Jingle.*] *Ib.*

'It wasn't the wine,' murmured Mr. Snodgrass, in a broken voice. 'It was the salmon.' *Ib.* ch. 8.

I wants to make your flesh creep. [*The Fat Boy.*] *Ib.*

'It's always best on these occasions to do what the mob do.' 'But suppose there are two mobs?' suggested Mr. Snodgrass. 'Shout with the largest,' replied Mr. Pickwick. *Ib.* ch. 13.

'Can I unmoved see thee dying
On a log,
Expiring frog!' [*Mrs. Leo Hunter.*] *Ib.* ch. 15.

'Sir,' said Mr. Tupman, 'you're a fellow.' 'Sir,' said Mr. Pickwick, 'you're another!' *Ib.*

The word poltics surprises by himself. [*Count Smorltork.*] *Ib.*

Right as a trivet, sir. [*Sam Weller.*] *Ib.* ch. 16.
Tongue; well that's a wery good thing when it an't a woman's. [*Mr. Weller.*] *Ib.* ch. 19.

Mr. Weller's knowledge of London was extensive and peculiar. *Ib.* ch. 20.

The wictim o' connubiality, as Blue Beard's domestic chaplain said, with a tear of pity, ven he buried him. [*Mr. Weller.*] *Ib.*

'It's a wery remarkable circumstance, sir,' said Sam, 'that poverty and oysters always seems to go together.' *Ib.* ch. 22.

It's over, and can't be helped, and that's one consolation, as they always says in Turkey, ven they cuts the wrong man's head off. [*Sam Weller.*]
Ib. ch. 23.

Dumb as a drum vith a hole in it, sir. [*Sam Weller.*]
Ib. ch. 25.

Wery glad to see you, indeed, and hope our acquaintance may be a long 'un, as the gen'l'm'n said to the fi' pun' note. [*Sam Weller.*] *Ib.*

Wen you're a married man, Samivel, you'll understand a good many things as you don't understand now; but vether it's worth while goin' through so much to learn so little, as the charity-boy said ven he got to the end of the alphabet, is a matter o' taste. [*Mr. Weller.*] *Ib.* ch. 27.

Our noble society for providing the infant negroes in the West Indies with flannel waistcoats and moral pocket handkerchiefs. *Ib.* ch. 27.

'Eccentricities of genius, Sam,' said Mr. Pickwick.
Ib. ch. 30.

Keep yourself to yourself. [*Mr. Raddle.*] *Ib.* ch. 32.

Pursuit of knowledge under difficulties, Sammy? [*Mr. Weller.*] *Ib.* ch. 33.

A double glass o' the inwariable. [*Mr. Weller.*] *Ib.*

Poetry's unnat'ral; no man ever talked poetry 'cept a beadle on boxin' day, or Warren's blackin' or Rowland's oil, or some o' them low fellows. [*Mr. Weller.*] *Ib.*

Wot's the good o' callin' a young 'ooman a Wenus or a angel, Sammy? [*Mr. Weller.*] *Ib.*

'That's rather a sudden pull up, ain't it, Sammy?' inquired Mr. Weller.
'Not a bit on it,' said Sam; 'she'll vish there wos more, and that's the great art o' letter writin'.' *Ib.*

If your governor don't prove a alleybi, he'll be what the Italians call reg'larly flummoxed. [*Mr. Weller.*] *Ib.*

She's a swellin' wisibly before my wery eyes. [*Mr. Weller.*] *Ib.*

It's my opinion, sir, that this meeting is drunk, sir! [*Mr. Stiggins.*] *Ib.*

A Being, erect upon two legs, and bearing all the outward semblance of a man, and not of a monster. [*Buzfuz.*] *Ib.* ch. 34.

Chops and Tomata sauce. Yours, Pickwick. *Ib.*

'Do you spell it with a "V" or a "W"?' inquired the judge.
'That depends upon the taste and fancy of the speller, my Lord,' replied Sam. *Ib.*

Put it down a we, my Lord, put it down a we. [*Mr. Weller.*] *Ib.*

'Little to do, and plenty to get, I suppose?' said Sergeant Buzfuz, with jocularity.
'Oh, quite enough to get, sir, as the soldier said ven they ordered him three hundred and fifty lashes,' replied Sam.
'You must not tell us what the soldier, or any other man, said, sir,' interposed the judge; 'it's not evidence.' *Ib.*

'Yes, I have a pair of eyes,' replied Sam, 'and that's just it. If they wos a pair o' patent double million magnifyin' gas microscopes of hextra power, p'raps I might be able to see through a flight o' stairs and a deal door; but bein' only eyes, you see my wision's limited.' *Ib.*

Oh Sammy, Sammy, vy worn't there a alleybi! [*Mr. Weller.*] *Ib.*

A friendly swarry, consisting of a boiled leg of mutton with the usual trimmings. *Pickwick Papers*, ch. 37.

'You disliked the killibeate taste, perhaps?'
'I don't know much about that 'ere,' said Sam. 'I thought they'd a wery strong flavour o' warm flat-irons.'
'That *is* the killibeate, Mr. Weller,' observed Mr. John Smauker, contemptuously. *Ib.*

'That 'ere young lady,' replied Sam. 'She knows wot's wot, she does.' *Ib.*

We know, Mr. Weller—we, who are men of the world —that a good uniform must work its way with the women, sooner or later. *Ib.*

You're a amiably-disposed young man, sir, I don't think. [*Sam Weller.*] *Ib.* ch. 38.

'And a bird-cage, sir,' says Sam. 'Veels vithin veels, a prison in a prison.' *Ib.* ch. 40.

'It would make anyone go to sleep, that bedstead would, whether they wanted to or not.' [*Mr. Roker.*]
'I should think,' said Sam, ... 'poppies was nothing to it.' *Ib.* ch. 41.

They don't mind it; it's a regular holiday to them— all porter and skittles. [*Sam Weller.*] *Ib.*

If he damned hisself in confidence, o' course that was another thing. [*Mr. Weller.*] *Ib.* ch. 43.

The have-his-carcase, next to the perpetual motion, is vun of the blessedest things as wos ever made. [*Sam Weller.*] *Ib.*

Anythin' for a quiet life, as the man said wen he took the sitivation at the lighthouse. [*Sam Weller.*] *Ib.*

Wich puts me in mind o' the man as killed hisself on principle, wich o' course you've heerd on, sir. [*Sam Weller.*] *Ib.* ch. 44.

Which is your partickler wanity? Vich wanity do you like the flavour on best, sir? [*Sam Weller.*]
Ib. ch. 45.

You've got the key of the street, my friend. [*Lowten.*]
Ib. ch. 47.

'Never ... see ... a dead postboy, did you?' inquired Sam. ... 'No,' rejoined Bob, 'I never did.' 'No!' rejoined Sam triumphantly. 'Nor never vill; and there's another thing that no man never see, and that's a dead donkey.' *Ib.* ch. 51.

'Vell, gov'ner, ve must all come to it, one day or another.'
'So we must, Sammy,' said Mr. Weller the elder.
'There's a Providence in it all,' said Sam.
'O' course there is,' replied his father with a nod of grave approval. 'Wot 'ud become of the under-takers vithout it, Sammy?' *Ib.* ch. 52.

''Cos a coachman's a privileged indiwidual,' replied Mr. Weller, looking fixedly at his son. ''Cos a coachman may do vithout suspicion wot other men may not; 'cos a coachman may be on the wery amicablest terms with eighty mile o' females, and yet nobody think that he ever means to marry any vun among them.' *Ib.*

Recalled to life. That's a Blazing strange answer.— Much of that wouldn't do for you, Jerry! I say, Jerry! You'd be in a Blazing bad way, if recalling

to life was to come into fashion, Jerry! [*Jerry Cruncher.*] *A Tale of Two Cities*, bk. i, ch. 2.

I pass my whole life, miss, in turning an immense pecuniary Mangle. [*Mr. Lorry.*] *Ib.* ch. 4.

If you must go flopping yourself down, flop in favour of your husband and child, and not in opposition to 'em. [*Jerry Cruncher.*] *Ib.* bk. ii, ch. 1.

'I tell thee,' said madame—'that although it is a long time on the road, it is on the road and coming. I tell thee it never retreats, and never stops.' [*Mme Defarge.*]
'It is possible—that it may not come, during our lives.... We shall not see the triumph.' [*Defarge.*]
'We shall have helped it,' returned madame.
Ib. ch. 16.

There might be medical doctors ... a cocking their medical eyes. [*Jerry Cruncher.*] *Ib.* bk. iii, ch. 9.

It is a far, far better thing that I do, than I have ever done; it is a far, far better rest that I go to, than I have ever known. [*Sidney Carton.*] *Ib.* ch. 15.

EMILY DICKINSON
1830–1886

I asked no other thing,
No other was denied.
I offered Being for it;
The mighty merchant smiled.

Brazil? He twirled a button,
Without a glance my way:
'But, madam, is there nothing else
That we can show to-day?' *Poems. Life.*

I got so I could hear his name
Without—
Tremendous gain!—
That stop-sensation in my Soul
And thunder in the room. *Ib. I Got so I Could Hear.*

Parting is all we know of heaven,
And all we need of hell. *Ib. Parting.*

JOHN DICKINSON
1732–1808

Our cause is just. Our union is perfect.
Declaration on Taking Up Arms in 1775.

Then join in hand brave Americans all,
By uniting we stand, by dividing we fall.
The Liberty Song. Memoirs of the Historical Soc. of Pennsylvania, vol. xiv.

WENTWORTH DILLON,
EARL OF ROSCOMMON
1633?–1685

But words once spoke can never be recall'd.
Art of Poetry, l. 438.

The last loud trumpet's wondrous sound,
Shall through the rending tombs rebound,
And wake the nations under ground.
On the Day of Judgement.

Choose an author as you choose a friend.
Essay on Translated Verse, l. 96.

Immodest words admit of no defence,
For want of decency is want of sense. *Ib.* l. 113.

The multitude is always in the wrong. *Ib.* l. 183.

BENJAMIN DISRAELI
1804–1881

Though I sit down now, the time will come when you will hear me.
Maiden Speech, 7 Dec. 1837. Meynell, Disraeli, i. 43.

The Continent will not suffer England to be the workshop of the world.
Speech, H. of C., 15 March 1838.

The noble Lord [Lord Stanley] is the Rupert of Parliamentary discussion. *Ib. 24 April 1844.*

The right hon. Gentleman [Sir Robert Peel] caught the Whigs bathing, and walked away with their clothes. *Ib. 28 Feb. 1845.*

Protection is not a principle, but an expedient.
Ib. 17 March 1845.

A Conservative Government is an organized hypocrisy. *Ib.*

He traces the steam-engine always back to the teakettle. *Ib. 11 April 1845.*

A precedent embalms a principle. *Ib. 22 Feb. 1848.*

Justice is truth in action. *Ib. 11 Feb. 1851.*

I read this morning an awful, though monotonous, manifesto in the great organ of public opinion, which always makes me tremble: Olympian bolts; and yet I could not help fancying amid their rumbling terrors I heard the plaintive treble of the Treasury Bench. *Ib. 13 Feb. 1851.*

England does not love coalitions. *Ib. 16 Dec. 1852.*

Finality is not the language of politics.
Ib. 28 Feb. 1859.

This shows how much easier it is to be critical than to be correct. *Ib. 24 Jan. 1860.*

The Church of England is not a mere depositary of doctrine. *Ib. 27 Feb. 1861.*

To put an end to these bloated armaments.
Ib. 8 May 1862.

He seems to think that posterity is a pack-horse, always ready to be loaded. *Ib. 3 June 1862.*

Colonies do not cease to be colonies because they are independent. *Ib. 5 Feb. 1863.*

Never take anything for granted.
Ib. at Salthill, 5 Oct. 1864.

I hold that the characteristic of the present age is craving credulity.
Ib. at Meeting of Society for Increasing Endowments of Small Livings in the Diocese of Oxford, 25 Nov. 1864.

Party is organized opinion. *Ib.*

Is man an ape or an angel? Now I am on the side of the angels. *Ib.*

Assassination has never changed the history of the world. *Ib. H. of C., 1 May 1865.*

Change is inevitable. In a progressive country change is constant. *Ib. Edinburgh, 29 Oct. 1867.*

I had to prepare the mind of the country, and . . . to educate our party. *Ib.*

We have legalized confiscation, consecrated sacrilege, and condoned high treason.
Ib. H. of C., 27 Feb. 1871.

I believe that without party Parliamentary government is impossible.
Ib. Manchester, 3 April 1872.

As I sat opposite the Treasury Bench the ministers reminded me of one of those marine landscapes not very unusual on the coasts of South America. You behold a range of exhausted volcanoes. *Ib.*

Increased means and increased leisure are the two civilizers of man. *Ib.*

A University should be a place of light, of liberty, and of learning. *Ib. H. of C., 11 March 1873.*

All those institutions and all those principles . . . in due time will become great and 'burning' questions.
Ib. 20 March 1873.

An author who speaks about his own books is almost as bad as a mother who talks about her own children.
Ib. at Banquet Given by Glasgow to Ld. Rector, 19 Nov. 1873.

King Louis Philippe once said to me that he attributed the great success of the British nation in political life to their talking politics after dinner. *Ib.*

Upon the education of the people of this country the fate of this country depends.
Ib. H. of C., 15 June 1874.

He is a great master of gibes and flouts and jeers.
[*Referring to his Colleague, the Marquis of Salisbury.*] *Ib. H. of C., 5 Aug. 1874.*

Lord Salisbury and myself have brought you back peace—but a peace I hope with honour.
Ib. 16 July 1878.

A series of congratulatory regrets. [*Lord Harrington's Resolution on the Berlin Treaty.*] *Ib. at Banquet in Riding School, Knightsbridge, 27 July 1878.*

A sophistical rhetorician, inebriated with the exuberance of his own verbosity. [*Gladstone.*] *Ib.*

The hare-brained chatter of irresponsible frivolity.
Ib. Guildhall, London, 9 Nov. 1878.

One of the greatest of Romans, when asked what were his politics, replied, *Imperium et Libertas.* That would not make a bad programme for a British Ministry.
Ib. Mansion House, London, 10 Nov. 1879.

The key of India is in London.
Ib. H. of Lords, 5 March 1881.

Damn your principles! Stick to your party.
Attr. Remark to Bulwer Lytton (Latham, Famous Sayings).

Between ourselves, I could floor them all. This *entre nous*: I was never more confident of anything than that I could carry everything before me in that House. The time will come.
Letters, 7 Feb. 1833.

In the 'Town' yesterday, I am told 'some one asked Disraeli, in offering himself for Marylebone, on what he intended *to stand*. "On my head," was the reply.'
Ib. 8 Apr. 1833.

There can be no economy where there is no efficiency.
Ib. To Constituents, 3 Oct. 1868.

Everyone likes flattery; and when you come to Royalty you should lay it on with a trowel.
Remark to Matthew Arnold. G. W. E. Russell, *Collections and Recollections*, ch. 23.

She is an excellent creature, but she never can remember which came first, the Greeks or the Romans. [Of his wife.] *Ib. ch. 1.*

Your Majesty is the head of the literary profession.
Remark to Queen Victoria. Ib. ch. 23.

There is no reason to doubt the story which represents him as using more than once, in conversation with Her Majesty on literary subjects, the words: 'We authors, Ma'am.'
Buckle's Disraeli (1920), v. 49.

'I am dead: dead, but in the Elysian fields,' was Benjamin's reply to an acquaintance among the peers, who, when welcoming him to the Lords, expressed a fear lest he should miss the excitement of the Commons. *Ib. 522.*

Tadpole and Taper were great friends. Neither of them ever despaired of the Commonwealth.
Coningsby, bk. i, ch. 1.

No Government can be long secure without a formidable Opposition. *Ib. bk. ii, ch. 1.*

Conservatism discards Prescription, shrinks from Principle, disavows Progress; having rejected all respect for antiquity, it offers no redress for the present, and makes no preparation for the future.
Ib. ch. 5.

'A sound Conservative government,' said Taper, musingly. 'I understand: Tory men and Whig measures.' *Ib. ch. 6.*

Adventures are to the adventurous. *Ib. bk. iii, ch. 1.*

The still hissing bacon and the eggs that looked like tufts of primroses. *Ib.*

Almost everything that is great has been done by youth. *Ib.*

Youth is a blunder; Manhood a struggle; Old Age a regret. *Ib.*

It seems to me a barren thing this Conservativism—an unhappy cross-breed, the mule of politics that engenders nothing. *Ib. ch. 5.*

I have been ever of opinion that revolutions are not to be evaded. *Ib. bk. iv, ch. 11.*

The depositary of power is always unpopular. *Ib.*

Where can we find faith in a nation of sectaries?
Ib. ch. 13.

Man is only truly great when he acts from the passions. *Ib.*

I grew intoxicated with my own eloquence.
Contarini Fleming, pt. i, ch. 7.

Read no history: nothing but biography, for that is life without theory. *Ib. ch. 23.*

The practice of politics in the East may be defined by one word—dissimulation. *Ib. pt. v, ch. 10.*

He flits across the stage a transient and embarrassed phantom. *Endymion, bk. i, ch. 3.*

His Christianity was muscular. *Ib. ch. 14.*

The Athanasian Creed is the most splendid ecclesiastical lyric ever poured forth by the genius of man.
Ib. ch. 54.

'As for that,' said Waldershare, 'sensible men are all of the same religion.' 'And pray, what is that?' inquired the prince. 'Sensible men never tell.'
Ib. ch. 81.

The sweet simplicity of the three per cents.
Ib. ch. 91.

I believe they went out, like all good things, with the Stuarts. *Ib. ch. 99.*

What we anticipate seldom occurs; what we least expect generally happens. *Ib. bk. ii, ch. 4.*

Time is the great physician. *Ib. bk. vi, ch. 9.*

They [the Furies] mean well; their feelings are strong, but their hearts are in the right place.
The Infernal Marriage, pt. i, 1.

The blue ribbon of the turf. [The Derby.]
Life of Lord George Bentinck, ch. 26.

Every day when he looked into the glass, and gave the last touch to his consummate toilette, he offered his grateful thanks to Providence that his family was not unworthy of him. *Lothair, ch. 1.*

'I could have brought you some primroses but I do not like to mix violets with anything.'
'They say primroses make a capital salad,' said Lord St. Jerome. *Ib. ch. 13.*

A Protestant, if he wants aid or advice on any matter, can only go to his solicitor. *Ib. ch. 27.*

London; a nation, not a city. *Ib.*

The gondola of London. [A hansom.] *Ib.*

When a man fell into his anecdotage it was a sign for him to retire from the world. *Ib. ch. 28.*

He was not an intellectual Crœsus, but his pockets were full of sixpences. *Ib. ch. 28.*

What I admire in the order to which you belong is that they do live in the air; that they excel in athletic sports; that they can only speak one language; and that they never read. This is not a complete education, but it is the highest education since the Greek. *Ib. ch. 29.*

You know who the critics are? The men who have failed in literature and art. *Ib. ch. 35.*

'My idea of an agreeable person,' said Hugo Bohun, 'is a person who agrees with me.' *Ib. ch. 41.*

St. Aldegonde had a taste for marriages and public executions.   *Ib.* ch. 88.

'I rather like bad wine,' said Mr. Mountchesney; 'one gets so bored with good wine.'
Sybil, bk. i, ch. 1.

The Egremonts had never said anything that was remembered, or done anything that could be recalled.   *Ib.* ch. 3.

To do nothing and get something, formed a boy's ideal of a manly career.   *Ib.* ch. 5.

Little things affect little minds.   *Ib.* bk. iii, ch. 2.

Mr. Kremlin himself was distinguished for ignorance, for he had only one idea,—and that was wrong.
Ib. bk. iv, ch. 5.

I was told that the Privileged and the People formed Two Nations.   *Ib.* ch. 8.

A public man of light and leading in the country.
Ib. bk. v, ch. 1.

The Youth of a Nation are the trustees of Posterity.
Ib. bk. vi, ch. 13.

Guanoed her mind by reading French novels.
Tancred, bk. ii, ch. 9.

That fatal drollery called a representative government.
Ib. ch. 13.

A majority is always the best repartee.   *Ib.* ch. 14.

All is race; there is no other truth.   *Ib.*

The East is a career.   *Ib.*

London is a modern Babylon.   *Ib.* bk. v, ch. 5.

The microcosm of a public school.
Vivian Grey, bk. i, ch. 2.

I hate definitions.   *Ib.* bk. ii, ch. 6.

Information upon points of practical politics.
Ib. ch. 15

Experience is the child of Thought, and Thought is the child of Action. We cannot learn men from books.   *Ib.* bk. v, ch. 1.

There is moderation even in excess.
Ib. bk. vi, ch. 1.

I repeat . . . that all power is a trust—that we are accountable for its exercise—that, from the people, and for the people, all springs, and all must exist.
Ib. ch. 7.

A dark horse, which had never been thought of, and which the careless St. James had never even observed in the list, rushed past the grand stand in sweeping triumph.   *Ib.* bk. ii, ch. 5.

'The age of chivalry is past,' said May Dacre. 'Bores have succeeded to dragons.'
The Young Duke, bk. ii, ch. 5.

A man may speak very well in the House of Commons, and fail very completely in the House of Lords. There are two distinct styles requisite: I intend, in the course of my career, if I have time, to give a specimen of both.   *Ib.* bk. v, ch. 6.

ISAAC DISRAELI

1766–1848

He wreathed the rod of criticism with roses. [Bayle]
Curiosities of Literature, 1834, vol. i, p. 20.

There is an art of reading, as well as an art of thinking, and an art of writing.   *Literary Character*, ch. 11.

SIDNEY THOMPSON DOBELL

1824–1874

'Ho, sailor of the sea!
How's my boy—my boy?'
'What's your boy's name, good wife,
And in what good ship sailed he?'

'My boy John—
He that went to sea—
What care I for the ship, sailor?
My boy's my boy to me.'   *How's My Boy?*

The murmur of the mourning ghost
That keeps the shadowy kine,
'Oh, Keith of Ravelston,
The sorrows of thy line!'   *A Nuptial Eve.*

HENRIETTA OCTAVIA DE LISLE DOBREE

1831–1894

Safely, safely gather'd in,
Far from sorrow, far from sin.
Children's Hymn Book, 1881. *Safely, Safely Gather'd In.*

HENRY AUSTIN DOBSON

1840–1921

This was the Pompadour's Fan!
On a Fan that Belonged to the Marquise de Pompadour.

And I wove the thing to a random rhyme,
For the Rose is Beauty, the Gardener, Time.
A Fancy from Fontenelle.

His Christian name, I think, was John,—
His surname, Leisure.
A Gentleman of the Old School.

It may be that he could not count
The sires and sons to Jesse's fount,—
He liked the 'Sermon on the Mount,'—
And more, he read it.   *Ib.*

All passes. Art alone
Enduring stays to us;
The Bust outlasts the throne,—
The Coin, Tiberius.   *Ars Victrix.*

And where are the galleons of Spain?
Ballad to Queen Elizabeth.

O, Love's but a dance,
    Where Time plays the fiddle!
See the couples advance,—
O, Love's but a dance!
A whisper, a glance,—
    'Shall we twirl down the middle?'
O, Love's but a dance,
    Where Time plays the fiddle!   *Cupid's Alley.*

Ah, would but one might lay his lance in rest,
And charge in earnest . . . were it but a mill!
                              Don Quixote.

Fame is a food that dead men eat,—
I have no stomach for such meat.
          Fame is a Food that Dead Men Eat.

Once at the Angelus
(Ere I was dead),
Angels all glorious
Came to my bed;
Angels in blue and white
Crowned on the head.   *Good-night, Babette.*

    He held his pen in trust
To Art, not serving shame or lust.   *In After Days.*

The ladies of St. James's!
    They're painted to the eyes,
Their white it stays for ever,
    Their red it never dies:
But Phyllida, my Phyllida!
    Her colour comes and goes;
It trembles to a lily,—
    It wavers to a rose.   *The Ladies of St. James's.*

The ladies of St. James's!
    They have their fits and freaks;
They smile on you—for seconds;
    They frown on you—for weeks.   *Ib.*

But Phyllida, my Phyllida!
    She takes her buckled shoon,
When we go out a-courting
    Beneath the harvest moon.   *Ib.*

Time goes, you say? Ah no!
Alas, Time stays, *we* go.   *The Paradox of Time.*

For I respectfully decline
To dignify the Serpentine,
And make *hors-d'œuvres* for fishes.
                    To 'Lydia Languish'.

I intended an Ode,
    And it turned to a Sonnet.
It began *à la mode*,
I intended an Ode;
But Rose crossed the road
    In her latest new bonnet;
I intended an Ode;
    And it turned to a Sonnet.   *Rose-Leaves.*

Rose kissed me to-day.
Will she kiss me to-morrow?
Let it be as it may,
Rose kissed me to-day,
But the pleasure gives way
To a savour of sorrow;—
Rose kissed me to-day,—
Will she kiss me to-morrow?   *Ib.*

PHILIP DODDRIDGE
1702–1751

'Live, while you live,' the epicure would say,
'And seize the pleasures of the present day.'

'Live, while you live,' the sacred preacher cries,
'And give to God each moment as it flies.'
Lord, in my views let both united be;
I live in pleasure, when I live to Thee.
          *Epigram on His Family Arms, 'Dum Vivimus
          Vivamus'.* J. Orton, *Memoirs of Doddridge.*

Hark, the glad sound! The Saviour comes,
The Saviour promised long.
          Hymns (1755). *Hark, The Glad Sound.*

O God of Bethel, by whose hand
    Thy people still are fed.   *Ib. O God of Bethel.*

God of our fathers, be the God
    Of their succeeding race.   *Ib.*

Ye servants of the Lord,
    Each in his office wait,
Observant of His heav'nly Word,
    And watchful at His Gate.
          Ib. Ye Servants of the Lord.

MARY ABIGAIL DODGE
See GAIL HAMILTON.

CHARLES LUTWIDGE DODGSON
See LEWIS CARROLL.

GEORGE BUBB DODINGTON
1691–1762

Love thy country, wish it well,
    Not with too intense a care,
'Tis enough, that when it fell,
    Thou its ruin didst not share.
                    Spence's *Anecdotes.*

CHARLES FLETCHER DOLE
1845–?

Democracy is on trial in the world, on a more colossal
scale than ever before.   *The Spirit of Democracy.*

ALFRED DOMETT
1811–1887

It was the calm and silent night!—
    Seven hundred years and fifty-three
Had Rome been growing up to might,
    And now was Queen of land and sea!
No sound was heard of clashing wars;
    Peace brooded o'er the hushed domain;
Apollo, Pallas, Jove and Mars,
    Held undisturbed their ancient reign,
        In the solemn midnight
            Centuries ago!   *Christmas Hymn.*

JOHN DONNE
1571?–1631

Twice or thrice had I loved thee,
Before I knew thy face or name.
So in a voice, so in a shapeless flame,
Angels affect us oft, and worshipped be.
                    Air and Angels.

Just such disparity
As is 'twixt air and Angels' purity,
'Twixt women's love, and men's will ever be.　　*Ib.*

All other things, to their destruction draw,
Only our love hath no decay;
This, no to-morrow hath, nor yesterday,
Running it never runs from us away,
But truly keeps his first, last, everlasting day.
　　　　　　　　　　　　The Anniversary.

Let us love nobly, and live, and add again
Years and years unto years, till we attain
To write threescore: this is the second of our reign.
　　　　　　　　　　　　　　　　Ib.

Come live with me, and be my love,
And we will some new pleasures prove
Of golden sands, and crystal brooks,
With silken lines, and silver hooks.　　*The Bait.*

A naked thinking heart, that makes no show,
Is to a woman, but a kind of ghost.　　*The Blossom*

The day breaks not, it is my heart.
　　Break of Day (attr. also to John Dowland).

For God sake hold your tongue, and let me love.
　　　　　　　　　　　　The Canonization.

Wilt thou forgive that sin, where I begun,
Which is my sin, though it were done before?
Wilt thou forgive those sins through which I run
And do them still, though still I do deplore?
When thou hast done, thou hast not done,
　　For I have more.

Wilt thou forgive that sin, by which I'have won
Others to sin, and made my sin their door?
Wilt thou forgive that sin which I did shun
A year or two, but wallowed in a score?
When thou hast done, thou hast not done,
　　For I have more.

I have a sin of fear that when I have spun
My last thread, I shall perish on the shore;
Swear by thy self that at my death, thy Sun
Shall shine as it shines now, and heretofore;
And having done that, thou hast done,
　　I have no more.　　　　　　*To Christ.*

Dear love, for nothing less than thee
Would I have broke this happy dream,
　　It was a theme
For reason, much too strong for fantasy,
Therefore thou wak'd'st me wisely; yet
My dream thou brok'st not, but continued'st it.
　　　　　　　　　　　　The Dream.

Love built on beauty, soon as beauty, dies.
　　　　　Elegies, No. 2.　*The Anagram.*

The grim eight-foot-high iron-bound serving-man,
That oft names God in oaths and only then.
　　　　　　Ib. No. 4.　*The Perfume.*

She, and comparisons are odious.
　　　　　　Ib. No. 8.　*The Comparison.*

No Spring, nor Summer beauty hath such grace,
As I have seen in one Autumnal face.
　　　　　　Ib. No. 9.　*The Autumnal.*

So, if I dream I have you, I have you,
For, all our joys are but fantastical.
　　　　　　Ib. No. 10.　*The Dream.*

By our first strange and fatal interview.
　　　　　Ib. No. 16.　*On His Mistress.*

All will spy in thy face
A blushing womanly discovering grace.　　*Ib.*

Whoever loves, if he do not propose
The right true end of love, he's one that goes
To sea for nothing but to make him sick.
　　　　　　Ib. No. 18.　*Love's Progress.*

　　The straight Hellespont between
The Sestos and Abydos of her breasts.　　*Ib.*

Those set our hairs, but these our flesh upright.
　　　　　Ib. No. 19.　*On Going to Bed.*

O my America! my new-found-land.　　*Ib.*

Where harmless fish monastic silence keep.
　　*Epicedes and Obsequies. Elegy on Mrs. Boul-
　　stred,* l. 14.

O strong and long-liv'd death, how cam'st thou in?
　　　　　　　　　　　　Ib. l. 21.

Hail, Bishop Valentine, whose day this is,
　　All the air is thy Diocese.
　　Epithalamions. 1, *On the Lady Elizabeth and
　　Count Palatine being Married on St. Valentine's
　　Day.*

The household bird, with the red stomacher.　　*Ib.*

So, so, break off this last lamenting kiss,
Which sucks two souls, and vapours both away,
Turn thou ghost that way, and let me turn this,
And let our selves benight our happiest day.
　　　　　　　　　　　　The Expiration.

Where, like a pillow on a bed,
A pregnant bank swelled up, to rest
The violets' reclining head,
Sat we two, one another's best.　　*The Extasy.*

So to 'entergraft our hands, as yet
Was all the means to make us one,
And pictures in our eyes to get
Was all our propagation.　　　　　　*Ib.*

And whilst our souls negotiate there,
We like sepulchral statues lay;
All day, the same our postures were,
And we said nothing, all the day.　　*Ib.*

But O alas, so long, so far
Our bodies why do we forbear?
They're ours, though they're not we, we are
The intelligencies, they the sphere.　　*Ib.*

So must pure lovers' souls descend
T' affections, and to faculties,
Which sense may reach and apprehend,
Else a great Prince in prison lies.　　*Ib.*

She, she is dead; she's dead; when thou know'st this,
Thou know'st how dry a cinder this world is.
　　　　　　The First Anniversary, l. 427.

Who ever comes to shroud me, do not harm
Nor question much
That subtle wreath of hair, which crowns my arm;
The mystery, the sign you must not touch,
　　For 'tis my outward soul,
Viceroy to that, which then to heaven being gone,
　　Will leave this to control,
And keep these limbs, her Province, from dissolution.
　　　　　　　　　　　　The Funeral.

What ere she meant by it, bury it with me,
  For since I am
Love's martyr, it might breed idolatry,
If into other's hands these relics came;
  As 'twas humility
To afford to it all that a soul can do,
  So, 'tis some bravery,
That since you would save none of me, I bury some
    of you.   *Ib.*

I wonder by my troth, what thou, and I
Did, till we lov'd? were we not wean'd till then?
But suck'd on country pleasures, childishly?
                        The Good-Morrow.

And now good morrow to our waking souls,
Which watch not one another out of fear.   *Ib.*

Without sharp North, without declining West. *Ib.*

That All, which always is All everywhere.
                Holy Sonnets. Annunciation.

Immensity cloistered in thy dear womb.   *Ib.*

As due by many titles I resign
My self to thee, O God, first I was made
By thee, and for thee, and when I decayed
Thy blood bought that, the which before was thine.
                                         Ib. ii.

I am a little world made cunningly
Of elements, and an angelic sprite.   *Ib.* v.

At the round earth's imagined corners, blow
Your trumpets, Angels, and arise, arise.   *Ib.* vii.

All whom war, dearth, age, agues, tyrannies,
Despair, law, chance, hath slain.   *Ib.* vii.

Death be not proud, though some have called thee
Mighty and dreadful, for, thou art not so,
For, those, whom thou think'st, thou dost overthrow,
Die not, poor death.   *Ib.* x.

One short sleep past, we wake eternally,
And death shall be no more; death, thou shalt die.
                                            Ib.

What if this present were the world's last night?
                                         Ib. xiii.

Batter my heart, three person'd God; for, you
As yet but knock, breathe, shine, and seek to mend.
                                         Ib. xiv.

Take me to you, imprison me, for I
Except you enthrall me, never shall be free,
Nor ever chaste, except you ravish me.   *Ib.*

Show me, dear Christ, thy spouse, so bright and
  clear.   *Ib.* xviii.
                  As thou
Art jealous, Lord, so I am jealous now,
Thou lov'st not, till from loving more, thou free
My soul: whoever gives, takes liberty:
  O, if thou car'st not whom I love
  Alas, thou lov'st not me.
    *Hymn to Christ, at the author's last going into
    Germany.*

Seal then this bill of my Divorce to all.   *Ib.*

To see God only, I go out of sight:
  And to scape stormy days, I choose
    An everlasting night.   *Ib.*

Since I am coming to that holy room,
Where, with thy quire of Saints for evermore,

I shall be made thy Music; as I come
I tune the instrument here at the door,
And what I must do then, think here before.
            Hymn to God in My Sickness.

Will no other vice content you?   *The Indifferent.*

Rob me, but bind me not, and let me go.   *Ib.*

And by Love's sweetest part, Variety, she swore. *Ib.*

And said, alas, some two or three
Poor heretics in love there be,
Which think to stablish dangerous constancy. *Ib.*

Stand still, and I will read to thee
A lecture, Love, in love's philosophy.
            A Lecture upon the Shadow.

When I died last, and, Dear, I die
As often as from thee I go,
Though it be but an hour ago,
And lovers' hours be full eternity.   *The Legacy.*

Love is a growing or full constant light;
And his first minute, after noon, is night.   *Ib.*

If yet I have not all thy love,
Dear, I shall never have it all.   *Lovers' Infiniteness.*

I long to talk with some old lover's ghost,
Who died before the god of love was born.
                        Love's Deity.

Rebel and Atheist too, why murmur I,
As though I felt the worst that love could do? *Ib.*

'Tis the year's midnight, and it is the day's.
            Nocturnal upon S. Lucy's Day.

  The world's whole sap is sunk:
The general balm th' hydroptic earth hath drunk. *Ib.*

I sing the progress of a deathless soul.
            Progress of the Soul, i.

Great Destiny the Commissary of God.   *Ib.* iv.

To my six lustres almost now outwore.   *Ib.* v.

This soul to whom **Luther**, and **Mahomet** were
Prisons of flesh.   *Ib.* vii.

When my grave is broke up again
Some second guest to entertain,
(For graves have learnt that woman-head
To be to more than one a bed).   *The Relic.*

A bracelet of bright hair about the bone.   *Ib.*

As till God's great *Venite* change the song.
            The Second Anniversary, l. 44.

Think then, my soul, that death is but a groom,
Which brings a taper to the outward room. *Ib.* l. 85.

      Her pure and eloquent blood
Spoke in her cheeks, and so distinctly wrought,
That one might almost say, her body thought.
                            Ib. l. 244.

Whose twilights were more clear, than our mid-day.
                            Ib. l. 463.

Sweetest love, I do not go,
  For weariness of thee,
Nor in hope the world can show
A fitter Love for me;
  But since that I
Must die at last, 'tis best,
To use my self in jest
Thus by fain'd deaths to die.   *Song.*

Go, and catch a falling star,
Get with child a mandrake root,
Tell me, where all past years are,
Or who cleft the Devil's foot.
Song, Go and Catch a Falling Star.

And swear
No where
Lives a woman true and fair.   *Ib.*

Though she were true, when you met her,
And last, till you write your letter,
Yet she
Will be
False, ere I come, to two, or three.   *Ib.*

Busy old fool, unruly Sun,
Why dost thou thus,
Through windows, and through curtains call on us?
Must to thy motions lovers' seasons run?
The Sun Rising.

Love, all alike, no season knows, nor clime,
Nor hours, days, months, which are the rags of time.
Ib.

I am two fools, I know,
For loving, and for saying so
In whining Poetry.   *The Triple Fool.*

Who are a little wise, the best fools be.   *Ib.*

I have done one braver thing
Than all the Worthies did,
And yet a braver thence doth spring,
Which is, to keep that hid.
The Undertaking.

So let us melt, and make no noise,
No tear-floods, nor sigh-tempests move,
'Twere profanation of our joys
To tell the laity our love.
A Valediction Forbidding Mourning.

Dull sublunary lovers' love
(Whose soul is sense) cannot admit
Absence, because it doth remove
Those things which elemented it.

But we, by a love so much refined,
That ourselves know not what it is,
Inter-assured of the mind,
Care less, eyes, lips, and hands to miss.

Our two souls therefore, which are one,
Though I must go, endure not yet
A breach, but an expansion,
Like gold to airy thinness beat.

If they be two, they are two so
As stiff twin compasses are two,
Thy soul the fixt foot, makes no show
To move, but doth, if the other do.

And though it in the centre sit,
Yet when the other far doth roam,
It leans, and hearkens after it,
And grows erect, as that comes home.

Such wilt thou be to me, who must
Like th' other foot, obliquely run;
Thy firmness makes my circle just,
And makes me end, where I begun.   *Ib.*

A Day that hath no *pridie*, nor *postridie*, yesterday
doth not usher it in, nor tomorrow shall not drive

it out. Methusalem, with all his hundreds of
years, was but a mushroom of a night's growth,
to this Day, and all the four Monarchies, with all
their thousands of years, and all the powerful
Kings and Queens of this world, were but as a
bed of flowers, some gathered at six, some at
seven, some at eight, all in one morning, in respect
of this Day.
Sermons, i, p. 747, No. lxxiii. *Eternity.*

I throw myself down in my chamber, and I call in,
and invite God, and his Angels thither, and when
they are there, I neglect God and his Angels, for
the noise of a fly, for the rattling of a coach, for the
whining of a door.
Ib. p. 820, No. lxxx. *At the Funeral of Sir
William Cokayne.*

JULIA CAROLINE RIPLEY DORR
1825-1913

O true, brave heart! God bless thee, wheresoe'er
In God's great universe thou art to-day!
*Friar Anselm and other Poems. How Can I
Cease to Pray for Thee?*

CHARLES SACKVILLE, EARL OF DORSET
1638-1706

To all you ladies now at land,
We men, at sea, indite.
But first would have you understand
How hard it is to write:
The Muses now, and Neptune too,
We must implore to write to you—
With a fa, la, la, la, la.
To All You Ladies Now at Land.

Yet if rough Neptune rouse the wind
To wave the azure main,
Our paper, pen, and ink, and we,
Roll up and down our ships at sea.   *Ib.*

SARAH DOUDNEY
1843-1926

But the waiting time, my brothers,
Is the hardest time of all.
Psalms of Life, The Hardest Time of All.

GAVIN DOUGLAS
1474?-1522

Dame naturis menstralis.
Eneados, bk. xii, prol., l. 231.

And all small fowlys singis on the spray:
Welcum the lord of lycht and lamp of day. *Ib.* l. 251.

WILLIAM DOUGLAS

1672–1748

And for bonnie Annie Laurie
I'd lay me doun and dee.   *Annie Laurie.*

LORENZO DOW

1777–1834

Observing the doctrine of Particular Election . . . and those who preached it up to make the Bible clash and contradict itself, by preaching somewhat like this:
You can and you can't—You shall and you shan't—You will and you won't—And you will be damned if you do—
And you will be damned if you don't.
     Reflections on the Love of God, vi (1836), 30.

ERNEST DOWSON

1867–1900

And I was desolate and sick of an old passion.
       Non Sum Qualis Eram.

I have been faithful to thee, Cynara! in my fashion.
       Ib.

Dancing, to put thy pale, lost lilies out of mind.   *Ib.*

They are not long, the weeping and the laughter,
Love and desire and hate;
I think they have no portion in us after
We pass the gate.   *Vitae Summa Brevis.*

SIR ARTHUR CONAN DOYLE

1859–1930

What of the bow?
The bow was made in England:
Of true wood, of yew-wood,
The wood of English bows.   *Song of the Bow.*

To Sherlock Holmes she [Irene Adler] is always *the* woman.
     The Adventures of Sherlock Holmes. Scandal in Bohemia.

It is a capital mistake to theorize before one has data.
       Ib.

It is quite a three-pipe problem.
      Ib. The Red-Headed League.

I have nothing to do to-day. My practice is never very absorbing.   *Ib.*

The husband was a teetotaller, there was no other woman, and the conduct complained of was that he had drifted into the habit of winding up every meal by taking out his false teeth and hurling them at his wife.   *Ib. A Case of Identity.*

It has long been an axiom of mine that the little things are infinitely the most important.   *Ib.*

'It seems . . . to be one of those simple cases which are so extremely difficult.' 'That sounds a little paradoxical.' 'But it is profoundly true. Singu-

larity is almost invariably a clue. The more featureless and commonplace a crime is, the more difficult is it to bring it home.'
     Ib. The Boscombe Valley Mystery.

A little monograph on the ashes of one hundred and forty different varieties of pipe, cigar, and cigarette tobacco.   *Ib.*

A man should keep his little brain attic stocked with all the furniture that he is likely to use, and the rest he can put away in the lumber-room of his library, where he can get it if he wants it.
     Ib. Five Orange Pips.

Circumstantial evidence is occasionally very convincing, as when you find a trout in the milk, to quote Thoreau's example.
      Ib. The Noble Bachelor.

It is my belief, Watson, founded upon my experience, that the lowest and vilest alleys of London do not present a more dreadful record of sin than does the smiling and beautiful countryside.
      Ib. Copper Beeches.

A long shot, Watson; a very long shot!
     The Memoirs of Sherlock Holmes. Silver Blaze.

You know my methods in such cases, Watson.
      Ib. The Musgrave Ritual.

These are much deeper waters than I had thought.
      Ib. Reigate Squires.

You know my methods, Watson.
       Ib. The Crooked Man.

'Excellent!' I [Dr. Watson] cried. 'Elementary,' said he [Holmes].   *Ib.*

My practice could get along very well for a day or two.   *Ib. The Naval Treaty.*

He [Professor Moriarty] is the Napoleon of crime.
      Ib. The Final Problem.

'The practice is quiet,' said I [Dr. Watson], 'and I have an accommodating neighbour.'   *Ib.*

'Arrest you!' said Holmes. 'This is really most grati—most interesting!'
      Ib. The Norwood Builder.

'It is my duty to warn you that it will be used against you,' cried the Inspector, with the magnificent fair play of the British criminal law.
      Ib. Dancing Men.

There is a spirituality about the face, however . . . which the typewriter does not generate. The lady is a musician.
     The Return of Sherlock Holmes. The Solitary Cyclist.

You will ruin no more lives as you ruined mine. You will wring no more hearts as you wrung mine. I will free the world of a poisonous thing. Take that, you hound, and that!—and that!—and that!   *Ib. Charles Augustus Milverton.*

We have not yet met our Waterloo, Watson, but this is our Marengo.   *Ib. Abbey Grange.*

Now, Watson, the fair sex is your department.
      Ib. The Second Stain.

But here, unless I am mistaken, is our client.
His Last Bow. Wisteria Lodge.

There is but one step from the grotesque to the horrible.   *Ib.*

All other men are specialists, but his specialism is omniscience.   *Ib. Bruce-Partington Plans.*

I thought I knew my Watson.   *Ib. The Devil's Foot.*

'I [Sherlock Holmes] followed you—' 'I saw no one.' 'That is what you may expect to see when I follow you.'   *Ib.*

Good old Watson! You are the one fixed point in a changing age.   *Ib. His Last Bow.*

The giant rat of Sumatra, a story for which the world is not yet prepared.
The Case Book. Sussex Vampire.

London, that great cesspool into which all the loungers of the Empire are irresistibly drained.
A Study in Scarlet.

'Wonderful!' I [Dr. Watson] ejaculated. 'Commonplace,' said Holmes.   *Ib.*

'I should have more faith,' he said; 'I ought to know by this time that when a fact appears opposed to a long train of deductions it invariably proves to be capable of bearing some other interpretation.'   *Ib.*

Detection is, or ought to be, an exact science, and should be treated in the same cold and unemotional manner. You have attempted to tinge it with romanticism, which produces much the same effect as if you worked a love-story or an elopement into the fifth proposition of Euclid.
The Sign of Four.

An experience of women which extends over many nations and three separate continents.   *Ib.*

How often have I said to you that when you have eliminated the impossible, whatever remains, *however improbable*, must be the truth?   *Ib.*

You know my methods. Apply them.   *Ib.*

The Baker Street irregulars.   *Ib.*

'I am inclined to think—' said I [Dr. Watson]. 'I should do so,' Sherlock Holmes remarked, impatiently.   *The Valley of Fear.*

The vocabulary of 'Bradshaw' is nervous and terse, but limited.   *Ib.*

Mediocrity knows nothing higher than itself, but talent instantly recognizes genius.   *Ib.*

FRANCIS HASTINGS CHARLES DOYLE

1810–1888

Right on our flank the crimson sun went down,
The deep sea rolled around in dark repose,
When, like a wild shriek from some captured town,
The cry of women rose.
Loss of the Birkenhead.

Last night, among his fellow roughs,
He jested, quaff'd, and swore.
The Private of the Buffs.

To-day, beneath the foeman's frown,
He stands in Elgin's place,
Ambassador from Britain's crown
And type of all her race.   *Ib.*

Poor, reckless, rude, low-born, untaught,
Bewilder'd, and alone,
A heart with English instinct fraught
He yet can call his own.   *Ib.*

Vain, mightiest fleets of iron framed;
Vain, those all-shattering guns;
Unless proud England keep, untamed,
The strong heart of her sons.   *Ib.*

A man of mean estate,
Who died, as firm as Sparta's king,
Because his soul was great.   *Ib.*

His creed no parson ever knew,
'For this was still his simpler plan,'
To have with clergymen to do
As little as a Christian can.
The Unobtrusive Christian.

FRANCIS DRAKE

1540?–1596

I remember Drake, in the vaunting style of a soldier, would call the Enterprise [of Cadiz, 1587] the singeing of the King of Spain's Beard.
Bacon, *Considerations touching a War with Spain* (*Harleian Misc.* 1745, vol. v, p. 85, col. 1).

There is plenty of time to win this game, and to thrash the Spaniards too.   *Attr. in the D.N.B.*
[The tradition goes, that Drake would needs see the game up; but was soon prevail'd on to go and play out the rubber with the Spaniards. W. Oldys' *Life of Raleigh* in Raleigh's *Hist. of the World*, 1736.]

MICHAEL DRAYTON

1563–1631

Ill news hath wings, and with the wind doth go,
Comfort's a cripple and comes ever slow.
The Barrons' Wars, bk. II, xxviii.

He was a man (then boldly dare to say)
In whose rich soul the virtues well did suit,
In whom so mix'd the elements all lay,
That none to one could sovereignty impute,
As all did govern yet all did obey;
He of a temper was so absolute,
As that it seem'd when Nature him began,
She meant to shew all, that might be in man.
Ib. bk. III, xl.

The mind is free, whate'er afflict the man,
A King's a King, do Fortune what she can.
Ib. bk. v, xxxvi.

Thus when we fondly flatter our desires,
Our best conceits do prove the greatest liars.
Ib. bk. VI, xciv.

Fair stood the wind for France
When we our sails advance,
Nor now to prove our chance
    Longer will tarry.
                To the Cambro-Britans. Agincourt.

They now to fight are gone,
Armour on armour shone,
Drum now to drum did groan,
    To hear, was wonder;
That with the cries they make,
The very earth did shake,
Trumpet to trumpet spake,
    Thunder to thunder.   *Ib.*

Suffolk his axe did ply,
Beaumont and Willoughby
Bare them right doughtily,
    Ferrers and Fanhope.

Upon Saint Crispin's Day
Fought was this noble fray,
Which fame did not delay
    To England to carry.
O when shall English men
With such acts fill a pen?
Or England breed again
    Such a King Harry?   *Ib.*

Care draws on care, woe comforts woe again,
Sorrow breeds sorrow, one grief brings forth twain.
    England's Heroical Epistles. Henry Howard,
    Earl of Surrey, to the Lady Geraldine, l. 87.

When Time shall turn those amber locks to grey,
My verse again shall gild and make them gay.
                            Ib. l. 123.

Had in him those brave translunary things,
That the first poets had. [Marlowe.]
    To Henry Reynolds, of Poets and Poesy, l. 106.

For that fine madness still he did retain
Which rightly should possess a poet's brain.
                            Ib. l. 109.

Next these, learn'd Jonson, in this list I bring,
Who had drunk deep of the Pierian spring.
                            Ib. l. 129.

I pray thee leave, love me no more,
    Call home the heart you gave me,
I but in vain the saint adore,
    That can, but will not, save me.
                        To His Coy Love.

These poor half-kisses kill me quite.   *Ib.*

He made him turn and stop, and bound,
To gallop, and to trot the round,
He scarce could stand on any ground,
    He was so full of mettle.
            Nymphidia, The Court of Fairy, lxv.

That shire which we the heart of England well may
    call.   *Poly-olbion,* song xiii, l. 2.

Crave the tuneful nightingale to help you with her lay,
The ousel and the throstlecock, chief music of our May.
        Shepherd's Garland, eclogue iii, 17–18.

How many paltry, foolish, painted things,
That now in coaches trouble ev'ry street,
Shall be forgotten, whom no poet sings,
Ere they be well wrapped in their winding sheet?

F 3

Where I to thee Eternity shall give,
When nothing else remaineth of these days,
And Queens hereafter shall be glad to live
Upon the alms of thy superfluous praise.
                        Sonnets. Idea, vi.

Since there's no help, come let us kiss and part,
Nay, I have done: you get no more of me,
And I am glad, yea glad with all my heart,
That thus so cleanly, I myself can free,
Shake hands for ever, cancel all our vows,
And when we meet at any time again,
Be it not seen in either of our brows,
That we one jot of former love retain;
Now at the last gasp of Love's latest breath,
When his pulse failing, Passion speechless lies,
When Faith is kneeling by his bed of death,
And Innocence is closing up his eyes,
Now if thou wouldst, when all have given him over,
From death to life, thou might'st him yet recover.
                            Ib. lxi.

WILLIAM DRENNAN
1754–1820

The men of the Emerald Isle.   *Erin.*

JOHN DRINKWATER
1882–1937

He comes on chosen evenings,
My blackbird bountiful.   *Blackbird.*

Moon-washed apples of wonder.   *Moonlit Apples.*

For all their courteous words they are not one,
    This Youth and Age, but civil strangers still;
Age with the best of all his seasons done,
    Youth with his face towards the upland hill.
                Olton Pools, Dedication.

Knowledge we ask not—knowledge Thou hast lent,
But, Lord, the will—there lies our bitter need,
Give us to build above the deep intent
    The deed, the deed.   *A Prayer.*

THOMAS DRUMMOND
1797–1840

Property has its duties as well as its rights.
    Letter to the Earl of Donoughmore, 22 May 1838.

WILLIAM DRUMMOND
1585–1649

This fair volume which we World do name.
                The World. Flowers of Sion.

Or if by chance our minds do muse on ought,
It is some picture on the margin wrought.   *Ib.*

The last and greatest herald of Heaven's King.
                Poems. For the Baptist.

Only the echoes which he made relent,
Ring from their marble caves, repent, repent.   *Ib.*

Like the Idalian Queen
Her hair about her eyne,
With neck and breasts ripe apples to be seen.
Ib. Madrigal, iii.

A hyacinth I wisht me in her hand.   *Ib.*

Phœbus, arise,
And paint the sable skies,
With azure, white, and red.   *Ib. Song* (ii).

I long to kiss the image of my death.
Ib. sonnet ix, *Sleep, Silence Child.*

Alexis, here she stay'd among these pines.   *Ib.* xlvi.

     A morn
Of bright carnations did o'erspread her face.   *Ib.*

JOHN DRYDEN

1631–1701

In pious times, ere priestcraft did begin,
Before polygamy was made a sin.
Absalom and Achitophel, pt. i, l. 1.

     And, wide as his command,
Scatter'd his Maker's image through the land.
Ib. l. 9.

Whate'er he did was done with so much ease,
In him alone, 'twas natural to please.   *Ib.* l. 27.

Plots, true or false, are necessary things,
To raise up commonwealths and ruin kings.
Ib. l. 83.

Of these the false Achitophel was first,
A name to all succeeding ages curst.
For close designs and crooked counsels fit,
Sagacious, bold, and turbulent of wit,
Restless, unfixed in principles and place,
In power unpleas'd, impatient of disgrace;
A fiery soul, which working out its way,
Fretted the pigmy body to decay:
And o'er informed the tenement of clay.
A daring pilot in extremity;
Pleased with the danger, when the waves went high
He sought the storms; but for a calm unfit,
Would steer too nigh the sands to boast his wit.
Great wits are sure to madness near alli'd,
And thin partitions do their bounds divide.
Ib. l. 150.

Bankrupt of life, yet prodigal of ease.   *Ib.* l. 168.

And all to leave what with his toil he won
To that unfeather'd two-legg'd thing, a son.
Ib. l. 169.

Resolv'd to ruin or to rule the state.   *Ib.* l. 174.

And Heav'n had wanted one immortal song.
Ib. l. 197.

The people's prayer, the glad diviner's theme,
The young men's vision and the old men's dream!
Ib. l. 238.

All empire is no more than power in trust.
Ib. l. 411.

Better one suffer, than a nation grieve.   *Ib.* l. 416.

Who think too little, and who talk too much.
Ib. l. 534.

A man so various that he seem'd to be
Not one, but all mankind's epitome.
Stiff in opinions, always in the wrong;
Was everything by starts, and nothing long:
But, in the course of one revolving moon,
Was chemist, fiddler, statesman, and buffoon.
Ib. l. 545.

So over violent, or over civil,
That every man, with him, was God or Devil.
Ib. l. 557.

In squandering wealth was his peculiar art:
Nothing went unrewarded, but desert.
Beggar'd by fools, whom still he found too late:
He had his jest, and they had his estate.   *Ib.* l. 559.

During his office treason was no crime,
The sons of Belial had a glorious time.   *Ib.* l. 597.

His tribe were God Almighty's gentlemen.
Ib. l. 645.

Youth, beauty, graceful action seldom fail:
But common interest always will prevail:
And pity never ceases to be shown
To him, who makes the people's wrongs his own.
Ib. l. 723.

For who can be secure of private right,
If sovereign sway may be dissolv'd by might?
Nor is the people's judgement always true:
The most may err as grossly as the few.   *Ib.* l. 779.

Never was patriot yet, but was a fool.   *Ib.* l. 968.

Beware the fury of a patient man.   *Ib.* l. 1005.

Henceforth a series of new time began,
The mighty years in long procession:
Once more the God-like David was restored,
And willing nations knew their lawful lord.
Ib. l. 1028.

Doeg, though without knowing how or why,
Made still a blund'ring kind of melody;
Spurr'd boldly on, and dash'd through thick and thin,
Through sense and nonsense, never out nor in;
Free from all meaning, whether good or bad,
And in one word, heroically mad.
Ib. pt. ii, l. 412.

Rhyme is the rock on which thou art to wreck.
Ib. l. 486.

     The god-like hero sate
     On his imperial throne;
     His valiant peers were plac'd around;
Their brows with roses and with myrtles bound.
     (So should desert in arms be crowned:)
The lovely Thais by his side,
Sate like a blooming Eastern bride
In flow'r of youth and beauty's pride.
     Happy, happy, happy pair!
        None but the brave,
        None but the brave,
     None but the brave deserves the fair.
Alexander's Feast, l. 4

     Assumes the god,
     Affects to nod,
And seems to shake the spheres.   *Ib.* l. 44.

Bacchus ever fair, and ever young.   *Ib.* l. 48.

Sound the trumpets; beat the drums;
  Flush'd with a purple grace
  He shows his honest face:
Now gives the hautboys breath; he comes, he comes.
Ib. l. 50.

Drinking is the soldier's pleasure. *Ib.* l. 57.

  Rich the treasure;
  Sweet the pleasure;
Sweet is pleasure after pain. *Ib.* l. 58.

And thrice he routed all his foes, and thrice he slew
  the slain. *Ib.* l. 68.

Fallen from his high estate,
  And welt'ring in his blood:
Deserted at his utmost need
By those his former bounty fed;
On the bare earth expos'd he lies,
With not a friend to close his eyes. *Ib.* l. 78.

Revolving in his alter'd soul
  The various turns of chance below. *Ib.* l. 85.

Softly sweet, in Lydian measures,
Soon he sooth'd his soul to pleasures.
War, he sung, is toil and trouble;
Honour but an empty bubble.
  Never ending, still beginning,
Fighting still, and still destroying,
  If all the world be worth the winning,
Think, oh think, it worth enjoying.
  Lovely Thais sits beside thee,
  Take the good the gods provide thee. *Ib.* l. 97.

Sigh'd and look'd, and sigh'd again. *Ib.* l. 120.

And, like another Helen, fir'd another Troy.
  Ib. l. 154.

Could swell the soul to rage, or kindle soft desire.
  Ib. l. 160.

Let old Timotheus yield the prize,
  Or both divide the crown:
He rais'd a mortal to the skies;
  She drew an angel down. *Ib.* l. 177.

All For Love, or the World Well Lost.
  Title of Play.

Fool that I was, upon my eagle's wings
I bore this wren, till I was tired with soaring,
And now he mounts above me.
  All For Love, ii. i.

  Give, you gods,
Give to your boy, your Caesar,
The rattle of a globe to play withal,
This gewgaw world, and put him cheaply off:
I'll not be pleased with less than Cleopatra. *Ib.*

The wretched have no friends. *Ib.* iii. i.

Nature has cast me in so soft a mould,
That but to hear a story, feigned for pleasure,
Of some sad lover's death, moistens my eyes,
And robs me of my manhood. *Ib.* iv. i.

Men are but children of a larger growth;
Our appetites as apt to change as theirs,
And full as craving too, and full as vain. *Ib.*

Your Cleopatra; Dolabella's Cleopatra; every man's
  Cleopatra. *Ib.*

Welcome, thou kind deceiver!
Thou best of thieves; who, with an easy key,
Dost open life, and, unperceived by us,
Even steal us from ourselves. *Ib.* v. i.

A knock-down argument; 'tis but a word and a blow.
  Amphitryon, i. i.

I am devilishly afraid, that's certain; but ... I'll sing,
  that I may seem valiant. *Ib.* ii. i.

Whistling to keep myself from being afraid. *Ib.* iii. i.

I never saw any good that came of telling truth. *Ib.*

I am the true Amphitryon. *Ib.* v. i.

As one that neither seeks, nor shuns his foe.
  Annus Mirabilis, xli.

By viewing nature, nature's handmaid art,
  Makes mighty things from small beginnings grow:
Thus fishes first to shipping did impart,
  Their tail the rudder, and their head the prow.
  Ib. clv.

And on the lunar world securely pry. *Ib.* clxiv.

An horrid stillness first invades the ear,
And in that silence we the tempest fear.
  Astræa Redux, l. 7.

He made all countries where he came his own.
  Ib. l. 76.

Death, in itself, is nothing; but we fear,
To be we know not what, we know not where.
  Aureng-Zebe, iv. i.

When I consider life, 'tis all a cheat;
Yet, fool'd with hope, men favour the deceit;
Trust on, and think to-morrow will repay:
To-morrow's falser than the former day;
Lies worse, and, while it says, we shall be blest
With some new joys, cuts off what we possest.
Strange cozenage! None would live past years again,
Yet all hope pleasure in what yet remain;
And, from the dregs of life, think to receive,
What the first sprightly running could not give. *Ib.*

From harmony, from heavenly harmony
  This universal frame began:
  From harmony to harmony
Through all the compass of the notes it ran,
The diapason closing full in Man. *St. Cecilia's Day*, i.

What passion cannot Music raise and quell? *Ib.* ii.

The trumpet's loud clangour
  Excites us to arms. *Ib.* iii.

The soft complaining flute. *Ib.* iv.

The trumpet shall be heard on high,
The dead shall live, the living die,
And Music shall untune the sky. *Ib. Grand Chorus.*

And made almost a sin of abstinence.
  Character of a Good Parson, l. 11.

I am as free as nature first made man,
Ere the base laws of servitude began,
When wild in woods the noble savage ran.
  The Conquest of Granada, pt. i, i. i.

Forgiveness to the injured does belong;
But they ne'er pardon, who have done the wrong.
  Ib. pt. ii, i. ii

Thou strong seducer, opportunity!   *Ib.* IV. iii.

For he was great, ere fortune made him so.
         Death of Oliver Cromwell, vi.

Old as I am, for ladies' love unfit,
The power of beauty I remember yet.
         Cymon and Iphigenia, l. 1.

When beauty fires the blood, how love exalts the
     mind.   *Ib.* l. 41.

He trudg'd along unknowing what he sought,
And whistled as he went, for want of thought.
         Ib. l. 84.

She hugg'd th' offender, and forgave th' offence,
Sex to the last.   *Ib.* l. 367.

Ill fortune seldom comes alone.   *Ib.* l. 392.

Of seeming arms to make a short essay,
Then hasten to be drunk, the business of the day.
         Ib. l. 407.

Theirs was the giant race before the flood.
         Epistles. To Mr. Congreve, l. 5.

Our builders were with want of genius curst;
The second temple was not like the first;
Till you, the best Vitruvius, come at length.
         Ib. l. 13.

For Tom the Second reigns like Tom the First.
         Ib. l. 48.

Heav'n, that but once was prodigal before,
To Shakespeare gave as much; she could not give
     him more.   *Ib.* l. 62.

How blessed is he, who leads a country life,
Unvex'd with anxious cares, and void of strife!
Who studying peace, and shunning civil rage,
Enjoy'd his youth, and now enjoys his age:
All who deserve his love, he makes his own;
And, to be lov'd himself, needs only to be known.
         Ib. To John Driden of Chesterton, l. 1.

Lord of yourself, uncumber'd with a wife.   *Ib.* l. 18.

Better to hunt in fields, for health unbought,
Than fee the doctor for a nauseous draught.
The wise, for cure, on exercise depend;
God never made his work, for man to mend.
         Ib. l. 92.

Ev'n victors are by victories undone.   *Ib.* l. 164.

His colours laid so thick on every place,
As only showed the paint, but hid the face.
         Ib. To Sir R. Howard, l. 75.

Here lies my wife: here let her lie!
Now she's at rest, and so am I.
         Epitaph Intended for Dryden's Wife.

He had brought me to my last legs; I was fighting as
     low as ever was Squire Widdrington.
         An Evening's Love, II. i.

She fear'd no danger, for she knew no sin.
         The Hind and the Panther, pt. i, l. 4.

And doom'd to death, though fated not to die.
         Ib. l. 8.

For truth has such a face and such a mien
As to be lov'd needs only to be seen.   *Ib.* l. 33.

Reason to rule, mercy to forgive:
The first is law, the last prerogative.   *Ib.* l. 261.

For all have not the gift of martyrdom. *Ib.* pt. ii, l. 59.

Either be wholly slaves or wholly free.   *Ib.* l. 285.

Much malice mingled with a little wit. *Ib.* pt. iii, l. 1.

Think you your new French proselytes are come
To starve abroad, because they starv'd at home?
Your benefices twinkl'd from afar,
They found the new Messiah by the star. *Ib.* l. 173.

For present joys are more to flesh and blood
Than a dull prospect of a distant good.   *Ib.* l. 364.

By education most have been misled;
So they believe, because they so were bred.
The priest continues what the nurse began,
And thus the child imposes on the man. *Ib.* l. 389.

The wind was fair, but blew a mack'rel gale.
         Ib. l. 456.

T' abhor the makers, and their laws approve,
Is to hate traitors and the treason love.   *Ib.* l. 706.

For those whom God to ruin has design'd,
He fits for fate, and first destroys their mind.
         Ib. l. 1093.

And love's the noblest frailty of the mind.
         The Indian Emperor, II. ii.

Repentance is the virtue of weak minds. *Ib.* III. i.

For all the happiness mankind can gain
Is not in pleasure, but in rest from pain. *Ib.* IV. i.

Since heav'n's eternal year is thine.
         To the Memory of Mrs. Killigrew, l. 15.

While yet a young probationer,
And candidate of heav'n.   *Ib.* l. 21.

When rattling bones together fly
From the four corners of the sky.   *Ib.* l. 184.

That fairy kind of writing which depends only upon
     the force of imagination.
         King Arthur, Dedication.

All heiresses are beautiful.   *Ib.* I. i.

War is the trade of kings.   *Ib.* II. ii.

Ovid, the soft philosopher of love.
         Love Triumphant, II. i.

Thou tyrant, tyrant Jealousy,
Thou tyrant of the mind!
         Song of Jealousy. Love Triumphant

All human things are subject to decay,
And, when fate summons, monarchs must obey.
         Mac Flecknoe, l. 1.

The rest to some faint meaning make pretence,
But Shadwell never deviates into sense.
Some beams of wit on other souls may fall,
Strike through and make a lucid interval;
But Shadwell's genuine night admits no ray,
His rising fogs prevail upon the day.   *Ib.* l. 19.

And torture one poor word ten thousand ways.
Ib. l. 208.

We burn daylight. *The Maiden Queen*, ii. i.

I am resolved to grow fat and look young till forty,
and then slip out of the world with the first wrinkle
and the reputation of five-and-twenty. *Ib.* iii. i.

I am to be married within these three days; married
past redemption. *Marriage à la Mode*, i. i.

For secrets are edged tools,
And must be kept from children and from fools.
Sir Martin Mar-All, ii. ii.

We loathe our manna, and we long for quails
The Medal, l. 131.

But treason is not own'd when 'tis descried;
Successful crimes alone are justified. *Ib.* l. 207.

Three poets, in three distant ages born,
Greece, Italy and England did adorn.
The first in loftiness of thought surpass'd;
The next in majesty, in both the last:
The force of nature could no farther go;
To make a third she join'd the former two.
Lines Under Portrait of Milton.

Whatever, is, is in its causes just. *Oedipus*, iii. i.

Wit will shine
Through the harsh cadence of a rugged line.
To the Memory of Mr. Oldham.

But love's a malady without a cure.
Palamon and Arcite, bk. ii, l. 110.

Fool, not to know that love endures no tie,
And Jove but laughs at lovers' perjury. *Ib.* l. 148.

And Antony, who lost the world for love. *Ib.* l. 607.

Up rose the Sun, and up rose Emily.
Ib. bk. iii, l. 190.

Unsham'd, though foil'd he does the best he can.
Ib. l. 741.

Repentance is but want of power to sin. *Ib.* l. 813.

Since ev'ry man who lives is born to die,
And none can boast sincere felicity,
With equal mind, what happens, let us bear,
Nor joy nor grieve too much for things beyond our
    care.
Like pilgrims to th' appointed place we tend;
The world's an inn, and death the journey's end.
Ib. l. 883.

A virgin-widow and a *Mourning Bride.* *Ib.* l. 927.

Happy who in his verse can gently steer,
From grave to light; from pleasant to severe.
The Art of Poetry, canto i, l. 75.

Errors, like straws, upon the surface flow;
He who would search for pearls must dive below.
Prologues and Epilogues: Prologue, All For Love.

Bold knaves thrive without one grain of sense,
But good men starve for want of impudence.
Ib. Epilogue, Constantine the Great.

For, Heaven be thank'd we live in such an age,
When no man dies for love, but on the stage.
Ib. Epilogue, Mithridates.

But 'tis the talent of our English nation,
Still to be plotting some new reformation.
Ib. Prologue, Sophonisba, l. 9.

So poetry, which is in Oxford made
An art, in London only is a trade.
Prologue to the University of Oxford.

Oxford to him a dearer name shall be,
Than his own mother University.
Thebes did his green unknowing youth engage,
He chooses Athens in his riper age. *Ib.*

I strongly wish for what I faintly hope:
Like the day-dreams of melancholy men,
I think and think on things impossible,
Yet love to wander in that golden maze.
Rival Ladies, iii. i.

Learn to write well, or not to write at all.
Essay on Satire, l. 281.

This is the porcelain of humankind.
Don Sebastian, i. i.

Brutus and Cato might discharge their souls,
And give them furloughs for another world;
But we, like sentries, are obliged to stand
In starless nights, and wait the 'pointed hour.
Ib. ii. i.

A very merry, dancing, drinking,
Laughing, quaffing, and unthinking time.
Secular Masque, l. 39.

Joy rul'd the day, and Love the night. *Ib.* l. 81.

There is a pleasure sure,
In being mad, which none but madmen know!
The Spanish Friar, ii. i.

Lord of humankind. *Ib.*

And, dying, bless the hand that gave the blow. *Ib.*

They say everything in the world is good for something. *Ib.* iii. ii.

Or break the eternal Sabbath of his rest. *Ib.* v. ii.

'Peace, and the butt.' *The Tempest*, iv. iii.

The clouds dispell'd, the sky resum'd her light,
And Nature stood recover'd of her right.
But fear, the last of ills, remain'd behind,
And horror heavy sat on ev'ry mind.
Theodore and Honoria, l. 336.

And that one hunting which the Devil design'd,
For one fair female, lost him half the kind.
Ib. l. 427.

Mute and magnificent, without a tear.
Threnodia Augustalis, ii.

Men met each other with erected look,
The steps were higher that they took;
Friends to congratulate their friends made haste;
And long inveterate foes saluted as they passed.
Ib. iv.

Freedom which in no other land will thrive,
Freedom an English subject's sole prerogative.
Ib. x.

All delays are dangerous in war. *Tyrannic Love*, i. i.

Pains of love be sweeter far
Than all other pleasures are.   *Ib.* IV. i.

We must beat the iron while it is hot, but we may
polish it at leisure.   *Dedication of the Aeneis.*

I trade both with the living and the dead, for the
enrichment of our native language.   *Ib.*

A thing well said will be wit in all languages.
     Essay of Dramatic Poesy.

He was the man who of all modern, and perhaps
ancient poets, had the largest and most compre-
hensive soul . . . He was naturally learn'd; he
needed not the spectacles of books to read Nature;
he looked inwards, and found her there. . . . He
is many times flat, insipid; his comic wit degenerat-
ing into clenches, his serious swelling into bombast.
But he is always great, when some occasion is presented to him. [Shakespeare]   *Ib.*

The consideration of this made Mr. Hales of Eaton
say, that there was no subject of which any poet
ever writ, but he would produce it much better
done in Shakespeare.   *Ib.*

He invades authors like a monarch; and what would
be theft in other poets, is only victory in him.
[Ben Jonson.]   *Ib.*

If by the people you understand the multitude, the
hoi polloi, 'tis no matter what they think; they
are sometimes in the right, sometimes in the wrong:
their judgement is a mere lottery.   *Ib.*

He [Shakespeare] is the very Janus of poets; he
wears almost everywhere two faces; and you have
scarce begun to admire the one, ere you despise
the other.
     Essay on the Dramatic Poetry of the Last Age.

One of the greatest, most noble, and most sublime
poems which either this age or nation has produced.
[Paradise Lost.]
     Essays, Apology for Heroic Poetry.

What judgment I had increases rather than dimi-
nishes; and thoughts, such as they are, come
crowding in so fast upon me, that my only difficulty is to choose or reject; to run them into verse
or to give them the other harmony of prose.
     Preface to Fables.

'Tis sufficient to say [of Chaucer], according to the
proverb, that here is God's plenty.   *Ib.*

It becomes not me to draw my pen in defence of a
bad cause, when I have so often drawn it for a
good one.   *Ib.*

He [Chaucer] is a perpetual fountain of good sense.
     Ib.

Cousin Swift, you will never be a poet.
     Johnson's *Lives of the Poets: Swift.*

Happy the man, and happy he alone,
He, who can call today his own:
He who, secure within, can say,
Tomorrow do thy worst, for I have lived today.
     Trans. of Horace, bk. iii, Ode xxix.

Not Heav'n itself upon the past has pow'r;
But what has been, has been, and I have had my
hour.   *Ib.*

I can enjoy her while she's kind;
But when she dances in the wind,
And shakes the wings, and will not stay,
I puff the prostitute away. [Fortune]   *Ib.*

Look round the habitable world! how few
Know their own good; or knowing it, pursue.
     Trans. of Juvenal, x.

To see and to be seen, in heaps they run;
Some to undo, and some to be undone.
     Trans. of Ovid, Art of Love, I. 109.

Thus, while the mute creation downward bend
Their sight, and to their earthly mother tend,
Man looks aloft; and with erected eyes
Beholds his own hereditary skies.
     Trans. of Ovid, Metamorphoses, I. 107.

Who, for false quantities, was whipt at school.
     Trans. of Persius, Satires, I. 135.

Swear, fool, or starve; for the dilemma's even;
A tradesman thou! and hope to go to heaven?
     Ib. V. 204.

She knows her man, and when you rant and swear,
Can draw you to her *with a single hair.*   *Ib.* 246.

Arms, and the man I sing, who, forced by fate,
And haughty Juno's unrelenting hate.
     Trans. of Virgil, Æneid, I. i.

SIR HENRY BATE DUDLEY
1745–1824

Wonders will never cease.
     *Letter to Garrick, 13 Sept. 1776. Correspon-
dence of Garrick,* ed. 1832, vol. ii.

GEORGE DUFFIELD
1818–1888

Stand up!—stand up for Jesus!
     The Psalmist. Stand Up, Stand Up for Jesus.

WILLIAM DUNBAR
1465?–1530?

Timor mortis conturbat me.
     Lament for the Makaris.

London, thou art of townes *A per se.*   *London,* l. 1.

Thou lusty Troynovaunt.   *Ib.* l. 9.

London, thou art the flower of cities all!
Gemme of all joy, jasper of jocunditie.   *Ib.* l. 16.

Fair be their wives, right lovesom, white and small.
Ib. l. 46.

Thy famous Maire, by pryncely governaunce,
With sword of justice thee ruleth prudently.
No Lord of Parys, Venyce, or Floraunce
In dignitye or honour goeth to hym nigh.   *Ib.* l. 49.

All love is lost but upon God alone.
The Merle and the Nightingale, ii.

FINLEY PETER DUNNE
1867–1936

'Th' American nation in th' Sixth Ward is a fine
people,' he says. 'They love th' eagle,' he says,
'on th' back iv a dollar.'
> *Mr. Dooley in Peace and War. Oratory on
> Politics.*

THOMAS D'URFEY
1653–1723

Neighbours o'er the Herring Pond.
> *Pills to Purge Melancholy,* 1719, vol. ii, p. 333.
> *Fable of the Lady, the Lurcher, and the Marrow-
> Puddings,* xiv.

EDWARD DYER
c. 1540–1607

My mind to me a kingdom is,
Such perfect joy therein I find,
That it excels all other bliss
That world affords or grows by kind:
Though much I want which most would have,
Yet still my mind forbids to crave.
My Mind to Me a Kingdom Is.

Some have too much, yet still do crave;
   I little have, and seek no more.
They are but poor though much they have,
   And I am rich with little store;
They poor, I rich; they beg, I give;
They lack, I have; they pine, I live.   *Ib.*

And he that will this health deny,
Down among the dead men let him lie.
Toast: Here's a Health to the King.

JOHN DYER
1699–1758

A little rule, a little sway,
A sunbeam in a winter's day,
Is all the proud and mighty have
Between the cradle and the grave.   *Grongar Hill,* l. 89.

While the wanton Zephyr sings,
And in the vale perfumes his wings.   *Ib.* l. 139.

There is a kindly mood of melancholy,
That wings the soul and points her to the skies.
The Ruins of Rome, l. 347.

MARIA EDGEWORTH
1767–1849

Well! some people talk of morality, and some of
religion, but give me a little snug property.
The Absentee, ch. 2.

And all the young ladies . . . said . . . that to be sure
a love match was the only thing for happiness,
where the parties could any way afford it.
Castle Rackrent (Continuation of Memoirs).

I've a great fancy to see my own funeral afore I die.
Ib.

Come when you're called;
And do as you're bid;
Shut the door after you;
And you'll never be chid.   *The Contrast,* ch. 1.

Business was his aversion; pleasure was his business.
Ib. ch. 2.

There is one distinguishing peculiarity of the Irish
bull—its horns are tipped with brass [i.e. with impudence or assurance].   *Essay on Irish Bulls,* ch. 9.

THOMAS ALVA EDISON
1847–1931

Genius is one per cent. inspiration and ninety-nine
per cent. perspiration.
Newspaper Interview. Life (1932), ch. 24.

JAMES EDMESTON
1791–1867

Lead us, Heavenly Father, lead us
O'er the world's tempestuous sea;
Guard us, guide us, keep us, feed us,
For we have no help but Thee.
Sacred Lyrics, Set 2. Lead Us, Heavenly Father.

EDWARD III
1312–1377

Let the boy win his spurs.
Of the Black Prince at Crécy, 1345.

[Also say to them, that they suffre hym this day to
wynne his spurres, for if god be pleased, I woll this
iourney be his, and the honoure therof.
> Lord Berners, *Froissart's Chron.,* 1812, 1. cxxx.
> 158.]

RICHARD EDWARDES
1523?–1566

In going to my naked bed, as one that would have
   slept,
I heard a wife sing to her child, that long before had
   wept.
She sighed sore, and sang full sweet, to bring the
   babe to rest,
That would not cease, but cried still in sucking at her
   breast.
She was full weary of her watch and grieved with her
   child,
She rocked it, and rated it, till that on her it smiled.
Then did she say, 'Now have I found this proverb true
   to prove:
The falling out of faithful friends, renewing is of
   love.'   *Amantium Irae,* ed. 1580.

OLIVER EDWARDS

1711–1791

I have tried too in my time to be a philosopher; but, I don't know how, cheerfulness was always breaking in.   Boswell's *Johnson, 17 Apr. 1778.*

'For my part, now, I consider supper as a turnpike through which one must pass, in order to get to bed.' [Boswell's *Note*: I am not absolutely sure but this was my own suggestion, though it is truly in the character of Edwards.]   *Ib.*

'GEORGE ELIOT'

1819–1880

A prophetess? Yea, I say unto you, and more than a prophetess—a uncommon pretty young woman.   *Adam Bede,* ch. 1.

It's but little good you'll do a-watering the last year's crop.   *Ib.* ch. 18.

It was a pity he couldna be hatched o'er again, an' hatched different.   *Ib.*

Our deeds determine us, as much as we determine our deeds.   *Ib.* ch. 29.

Mrs. Poyser 'has her say out'.   *Ib.* title of ch. 32.

It's them as take advantage that get advantage i' this world.   *Ib.* ch. 32.

A maggot must be born i' the rotten cheese to like it.   *Ib.*

He was like a cock who thought the sun had risen to hear him crow.   *Ib.* ch. 33.

We hand folks over to God's mercy, and show none ourselves.   *Ib.* ch. 42.

I'm not one o' those as can see the cat i' the dairy, an' wonder what she's come after.   *Ib.* ch. 52.

I'm not denyin' the women are foolish: God Almighty made 'em to match the men.   *Ib.* ch. 53.

Men's men: gentle or simple, they're much of a muchness.   *Daniel Deronda,* bk. iv, ch. 31.

Friendships begin with liking or gratitude—roots that can be pulled up.   *Ib.* ch. 32.

Our deeds still travel with us from afar,
And what we have been makes us what we are.   *Middlemarch,* heading to ch. 70.

The law's made to take care o' raskills.   *The Mill on the Floss,* bk. iii, ch. 4.

This is a puzzling world, and Old Harry's got a finger in it.   *Ib.* ch. 9.

The small old-fashioned book, for which you need only pay sixpence at a bookstall, works miracles to this day, turning bitter waters into sweetness. . . . It was written down by a hand that waited for the heart's prompting: it is the chronicle of a solitary hidden anguish, struggle, trust and triumph. [*The Imitation of Christ*]   *Ib.* bk. iv, ch. 3.

I've never any pity for conceited people, because I think they carry their comfort about with them.   *Ib.* bk. v, ch. 4.

The happiest women, like the happiest nations, have no history.   *Ib.* bk. vi, ch. 3.

If you please to take the privilege o' sitting down.   *Ib.* ch. 4.

I should like to know what is the proper function of women, if it is not to make reasons for husbands to stay at home, and still stronger reasons for bachelors to go out.   *Ib.* ch. 6.

In every parting there is an image of death.   *Scenes of Clerical Life, Amos Barton,* ch. 10.

Animals are such agreeable friends—they ask no questions, they pass no criticisms.   *Mr. Gilfil's Love-Story,* ch. 7.

Nothing is so good as it seems beforehand.   *Silas Marner,* ch. 18.

Oh may I join the choir invisible
Of those immortal dead who live again
In minds made better by their presence.   *Poems: Oh May I Join the Choir Invisible.*

So shall I join the choir invisible
Whose music is the gladness of the world.   *Ib.*

'Tis God gives skill,
But not without men's hands: He could not make
Antonio Stradivari's violins
Without Antonio.   *Ib. Stradivarius,* l. 140.

THOMAS STEARNS ELIOT

1888–

April is the cruellest month, breeding
Lilacs out of the dead land, mixing
Memory and desire, stirring
Dull roots with spring rain.   *The Waste Land,* i. *The Burial of the Dead.*

And I will show you something different from either
Your shadow at morning striding behind you,
Or your shadow at evening rising to meet you
I will show you fear in a handful of dust.   *Ib.*

'Jug Jug' to dirty ears.   *Ib.* ii. *A Game of Chess.*

Musing upon the king my brother's wreck
And on the king my father's death before him.   *Ib.* iii. *The Fire Sermon.*

O the moon shines bright on Mrs. Porter
And on her daughter
They wash their feet in soda water.   *Ib.*

When lovely woman stoops to folly and
Paces about her room again, alone,
She smoothes her hair with automatic hand,
And puts a record on the gramophone.   *Ib.*

When the evening is spread out against the sky
Like a patient etherized upon a table.   *Love Song of J. Alfred Prufrock.*

In the room the women come and go
Talking of Michelangelo.   *Ib.*

The yellow fog that rubs its back upon the window-panes.   *Ib.*

I should have been a pair of ragged claws
Scuttling across the floors of silent seas.   *Ib.*

And I have seen the eternal Footman hold my coat
    and snicker,
And in short, I was afraid.   *Ib.*

I grow old . . . I grow old . . .
I shall wear the bottoms of my trousers rolled   *Ib.*

I am aware of the damp souls of housemaids
Sprouting despondently at area gates.
              Morning at the Window.

                    Turning
Wearily, as one would turn to nod good-bye to
    Rochefoucauld,
If the street were time and he at the end of the street.
              The Boston Evening Transcript.

Webster was much possessed by death.
                  Whispers of Immortality.

The sapient sutlers of the Lord.
             Mr. Eliot's Sunday Morning Service.

The nightingales are singing near
The Convent of the Sacred Heart
And sang within the bloody wood
When Agamemnon cried aloud.
           Sweeney Among the Nightingales.

We are the hollow men
We are the stuffed men
Leaning together.   *The Hollow Men.*

This is the way the world ends
Not with a bang but a whimper.   *Ib.*

QUEEN ELIZABETH
1533–1603

God may forgive you, but I never can. [To the
    Countess of Nottingham.]
[The Queen . . . crying to her that God might pardon
    her, but she never could.]
       Hume, *History of England under the House of
       Tudor*, vol. ii, ch. 7.

I know I have the body of a weak and feeble woman,
    but I have the heart and stomach of a king, and
    of a king of England too; and think foul scorn
    that Parma or Spain, or any prince of Europe
    should dare to invade the borders of my realm.
       *Speech to the Troops at Tilbury on the Approach
       of the Armada, 1588.*

As for me, I see no such great cause why I should
    either be fond to live or fear to die. I have had
    good experience of this world, and I know what
    it is to be a subject and what to be a sovereign.
    Good neighbours I have had, and I have met with
    bad: and in trust I have found treason.
       Speech to Parliament, 1586. Camden's *Annals*,
       p. 98.

Good-morning, gentlemen both. [To a delegation of
    eighteen tailors.]
       Chamberlin, *Sayings of Queen Elizabeth*, p. 28.

To your text, Mr. Dean! to your text!
                    Ib. p. 137.

I am your anointed Queen. I will never be by
    violence constrained to do anything. I thank God
    I am endued with such qualities that if I were
    turned out of the Realm in my petticoat I were
    able to live in any place in Christome. *Ib.* p. 138.

I will make you shorter by the head.
       Recueil des Dépôts, trans. by Cooper, vol. ii,
       p. 169, *cit.* Chamberlin, p. 224.

Madam I may not call you; mistress I am ashamed
    to call you; and so I know not what to call you;
    but howsoever, I thank you. [To the wife of the
    Archbishop of Canterbury. The Queen did not
    approve of married clergy.]
       Harington, *Brief View of the State of the
       Church*, 1607.

Though God hath raised me high, yet this I count
    the glory of my crown: that I have reigned with
    your loves.
       The Golden Speech, 1601. D'Ewes' *Journal*,
       p. 659.

Semper eadem.   *Motto.*

'Twas God the word that spake it,
He took the Bread and brake it;
And what the word did make it;
That I believe, and take it.
       *Answer on being asked her opinion of Christ's
       presence in the Sacrament.* S. Clarke's *Marrow
       of Ecclesiastical History*, pt. ii, *Life of Queen
       Elizabeth*, ed. 1675.

If thy heart fails thee, climb not at all.
       *Lines written on a window after Sir Walter
       Raleigh's line* 'Fain would I climb, yet fear I
       to fall.' Fuller, *Worthies of England*, vol. i,
       p. 419.

The daughter of debate, that eke discord doth sow.
    [Mary Queen of Scots.]
       Chamberlin, *Sayings of Queen Elizabeth*, p. 301.

JOHN ELLERTON
1826–1893

Now the labourer's task is o'er;
Now the battle-day is past;
Now upon the farther shore
Lands the voyager at last.
       *Hymns for the Society for Promoting Christian
       Knowledge. Now the Labourer's Task.*

Father, in Thy gracious keeping
Leave we now Thy servant sleeping.   *Ib.*

We stand to bless Thee ere our worship cease;
Then, lowly kneeling, wait Thy word of peace.
       *Hymns Ancient and Modern. Saviour, Again to
       Thy Dear Name We Raise.*

The day Thou gavest, Lord, is ended,
The darkness falls at Thy behest.
       *A Liturgy for Missionary Meetings. The Day
       Thou Gavest.*

JANE ELLIOT
1727–1805

I've heard them lilting, at the ewe milking.
    Lasses a' lilting, before dawn of day;
But now they are moaning, on ilka green loaning;
    The flowers of the forest are a' wede awae.
              The Flowers of the Forest.

CHARLOTTE ELLIOTT

1789–1871

'Christian! seek not yet repose,'
Hear thy guardian angel say;
Thou art in the midst of foes—
    'Watch and pray.'
        Morning and Evening Hymns. Christian! Seek
        Not Yet Repose.

Just as I am, without one plea
But that Thy blood was shed for me,
And that Thou bidd'st me come to Thee,
    O Lamb of God, I come!
        Invalid's Hymn Book. Just As I Am.

EBENEZER ELLIOTT

1781–1849

What is a communist? One who hath yearnings
For equal division of unequal earnings.
        Poetical Works. Epigram.

When wilt thou save the people?
    Oh, God of Mercy! when?
The people, Lord, the people!
    Not thrones and crowns, but men!
        Ib. The People's Anthem.

GEORGE ELLIS

See GREGORY GANDER.

HENRY HAVELOCK ELLIS

1859–1939

Every artist writes his own autobiography.
        The New Spirit. Tolstoi II.

ELSTOW

Elstow smiling said ... 'With thanks to God we know
    the way to heaven, to be as ready by water as by
    land, and therefore we care not which way we go.'
        When threatened with drowning by Henry VIII.
    Stow, *Annales*, 1615, p. 543. ['One Elstow, a
    friar of the order of Observant Friars.']

RALPH WALDO EMERSON

1803–1882

There is no great and no small
    To the Soul that maketh all:
And where it cometh, all things are;
    And it cometh everywhere. *The Absorbing Soul.*

Of Caesar's hand, and Plato's brain,
Of Lord Christ's heart, and Shakespeare's strain. *Ib.*

If the red slayer think he slays,
    Or if the slain think he is slain,
They know not well the subtle ways
    I keep, and pass, and turn again.   *Brahma.*

Far or forgot to me is near.   *Ib.*

I am the doubter and the doubt,
    And I the hymn the Brahmin sings.   *Ib.*

But thou, meek lover of the good!
    Find me, and turn thy back on heaven.   *Ib.*

By the rude bridge that arched the flood,
    Their flag to April's breeze unfurled,
Here once the embattled farmers stood,
    And fired the shot heard round the world.
        Hymn Sung at the Completion of the Concord
        Monument.

Knows he who tills this lonely field,
    To reap its scanty corn,
What mystic fruit his acres yield
    At midnight and at morn? *Dirge. Concord, 1838.*

Ye cannot unlock your heart,
    The key is gone with them;
The silent organ loudest chants
    The master's requiem.   *Dirge.*

Nor knowest thou what argument
Thy life to thy neighbour's creed has lent.
All are needed by each one;
Nothing is fair or good alone.   *Each and All.*

O fair and stately maid, whose eyes
Were kindled in the upper skies
At the same torch that lighted mine.   *To Eva.*

Hast thou named all the birds without a gun?
        Forbearance.

Give all to love:
Obey thy heart;
Friends, kindred, days,
Estate, good fame,
Plans, credit, and the Muse,—
Nothing refuse.   *Give All to Love.*

Cling with life to the maid;
But when the surprise,
First vague shadow of surmise
Flits across her bosom young
Of a joy apart from thee,
Free be she, fancy-free.   *Ib.*

It was not for the mean;
It requireth courage stout.   *Ib.*

Heartily know,
When half-gods go,
The gods arrive.   *Ib.*

Good-bye, proud world! I'm going home:
Thou art not my friend, and I'm not thine. *Good-bye.*

For what are they all in their high conceit,
When man in the bush with God may meet?   *Ib.*

Thou animated torrid-zone.   *To the Humble Bee.*

A subtle chain of countless rings
The next unto the farthest brings,
And, striving to be man, the worm
Mounts through all the spires of form.   *May Day.*

The mountain and the squirrel
Had a quarrel;
And the former called the latter 'Little Prig'.
Bun replied,
'You are doubtless very big;
But all sorts of things and weather
Must be taken in together,
To make up a year
And a sphere.'
        Fable, The Mountain and the Squirrel.

Things are in the saddle,
    And ride mankind.
        Ode, Inscribed to W. H. Channing.

The sinful painter drapes his goddess warm,
Because she still is naked, being dressed:
The godlike sculptor will not so deform
Beauty, which limbs and flesh enough invest.
Painting and Sculpture.

Olympian bards who sung
   Divine ideas below,
Which always find us young,
   And always keep us so.   *The Poet.*

I like a church; I like a cowl;
I love a prophet of the soul;
And on my heart monastic aisles
Fall like sweet strains, or pensive smiles;
Yet not for all his faith can see,
Would I that cowlèd churchman be.   *The Problem.*

Not from a vain or shallow thought
His awful Jove young Phidias brought.   *Ib.*

The hand that rounded Peter's dome,
And groined the aisles of Christian Rome,
Wrought in a sad sincerity;
Himself from God he could not free;
He builded better than he knew;—
The conscious stone to beauty grew.   *Ib.*

Taylor, the Shakespeare of divines.   *Ib.*

Some of your hurts you have cured,
   And the sharpest you still have survived,
But what torments of grief you endured
   From evils which never arrived!
Quatrains. Borrowing (from the French).

Rhodora! if the sages ask thee why
This charm is wasted on the earth and sky,
Tell them, dear, that if eyes were made for seeing,
Then Beauty is its own excuse for being.
The Rhodora.

Though love repine, and reason chafe,
   There came a voice without reply,—
' 'Tis man's perdition to be safe,
   When for the truth he ought to die.'   *Sacrifice.*

The frolic architecture of the snow.   *The Snowstorm.*

Nor sequent centuries could hit
Orbit and sum of Shakespeare's wit.   *Solution.*

Wilt thou seal up the avenues of ill?
Pay every debt, as if God wrote the bill.   *Ib.*

It is time to be old,
To take in sail.   *Terminus.*

House and tenant go to ground,
Lost in God, in Godhead found.   *Threnody.*

So nigh is grandeur to our dust,
   So near is God to man,
When Duty whispers low, *Thou must,*
   The youth replies, *I can.*   *Voluntaries,* iii.

There is no way to success in our art but to take off
   your coat, grind paint, and work like a digger on
   the railroad, all day and every day.
Conduct of Life. Power.

Art is a jealous mistress.   *Ib. Wealth.*

The louder he talked of his honour, the faster we
   counted our spoons.   *Ib. Worship.*

London is the epitome of our times, and the Rome
   of to-day.   *English Traits,* xviii. *Result.*

So ... I feel in regard to this aged England ... pressed
upon by transitions of trade and . . . competing
populations,—I see her not dispirited, not weak,
but well remembering that she has seen dark days
before;—indeed, with a kind of instinct that she
sees a little better in a cloudy day, and that, in
storm of battle and calamity, she has a secret vigour
and a pulse like a cannon.
Ib. ch. 19 (*Speech at Manchester, 1847*).

Every reform was once a private opinion, and when
it shall be a private opinion again it will solve the
problem of the age.   *Essays,* i. *History.*

There is properly no history; only biography.   *Ib.*

To believe your own thought, to believe that what is
true for you in your private heart is true for all
men,—that is genius.   *Ib.* ii. *Self-Reliance.*

To-morrow a stranger will say with masterly good
sense precisely what we have thought and felt all
the time, and we shall be forced to take with shame
our own opinion from another.   *Ib.*

Society everywhere is in conspiracy against the manhood of every one of its members.   *Ib.*

Whoso would be a man must be a nonconformist. *Ib.*

A foolish consistency is the hobgoblin of little minds,
adored by little statesmen and philosophers and
divines. With consistency a great soul has simply
nothing to do. . . . Speak what you think to-day
in words as hard as cannon-balls, and to-morrow
speak what to-morrow thinks in hard words again,
though it contradict every thing you said to-day. *Ib.*

Is it so bad, then, to be misunderstood? Pythagoras
was misunderstood, and Socrates, and Jesus, and
Luther, and Copernicus, and Galileo, and Newton,
and every pure and wise spirit that ever took flesh.
To be great is to be misunderstood.   *Ib.*

Shoves Jesus and Judas equally aside.   *Ib.*

I like the silent church before the service begins,
better than any preaching.   *Ib.*

As men's prayers are a disease of the will so are their
creeds a disease of the intellect.   *Ib.*

Every Stoic was a Stoic; but in Christendom where
is the Christian?   *Ib.*

Men are better than this theology.
Ib. iii. *Compensation.*

There are not in the world at any one time more than
a dozen persons who read and understand Plato:—
never enough to pay for an edition of his works;
yet to every generation these come duly down, for
the sake of those few persons, as if God brought
them written in his hand.   *Ib.* iv. *Spiritual Laws.*

If you would not be known to do anything, never
do it.   *Ib.*

All mankind love a lover.   *Ib.* v. *Love.*

Yet these uneasy pleasures and fine pains are for
curiosity, and not for life.   *Ib.* vi. *Friendship.*

A friend may well be reckoned the masterpiece of
Nature.   *Ib.*

In skating over thin ice, our safety is in our speed.
Ib. vii. *Prudence.*

Tart, cathartic virtue.   *Ib.* viii. *Heroism.*

O friend, never strike sail to a fear! Come into port greatly, or sail with God the seas.   *Ib.*

It was a high counsel that I once heard given to a young person, 'Always do what you are afraid to do.'   *Ib.*

We are wiser than we know.   *Ib.* ix. *The Over-Soul.*

Converse with a mind that is grandly simple, and literature looks like word-catching.   *Ib.*

Beware when the great God lets loose a thinker on this planet.   *Ib.* x. *Circles.*

People wish to be settled: only as far as they are unsettled is there any hope for them.   *Ib.*

Nothing great was ever achieved without enthusiasm.   *Ib.*

God offers to every mind its choice between truth and repose.   *Ib.* xi. *Intellect.*

He in whom the love of truth predominates...submits to the inconvenience of suspense and imperfect opinion; but he is a candidate for truth . . . and respects the highest law of his being.   *Ib.*

Nothing astonishes men so much as common-sense and plain dealing.   *Ib.* xii. *Art.*

Though we travel the world over to find the beautiful we must carry it with us or we find it not.   *Ib.*

Words and deeds are quite indifferent modes of the divine energy. Words are also actions, and actions are a kind of words.   *Ib.* xiii. *The Poet.*

It is not metres, but a metre-making argument, that makes a poem.   *Ib.*

We are symbols, and inhabit symbols.   *Ib.*

Language is fossil poetry.   *Ib.*

The poet knows that he speaks adequately, then, only when he speaks somewhat wildly, or, 'with the flower of the mind.'   *Ib.*

I knew a witty physician who found the creed in the biliary duct, and used to affirm that if there was disease in the liver, the man became a Calvinist, and if that organ was sound, he became a Unitarian.   *Ib.* xiv. *Experience.*

To fill the hour—that is happiness.   *Ib.*

The wise through excess of wisdom is made a fool.   *Ib.*

The years teach much which the days never know.   *Ib.*

Those who listened to Lord Chatham felt that there was something finer in the man, than anything which he said.   *Ib.* xv. *Character.*

Men are conservatives when they are least vigorous, or when they are most luxurious. They are conservatives after dinner.   *Ib. New England Reformers.*

The reward of a thing well done, is to have done it.   *Ib.*

We are always getting ready to live, but never living.   *Journals, 13 Apr. 1834.*

Man does not live by bread alone, but by faith, by admiration, by sympathy.   *Lectures and Biographical Sketches. The Sovereignty of Ethics.*

Great men are they who see that spiritual is stronger than any material force, that thoughts rule the world.   *Letters and Social Aims. Progress of Culture, Phi Beta Kappa Address, 18 July 1876.*

By necessity, by proclivity,—and by delight, we all quote.   *Ib. Quotation and Originality.*

Next to the originator of a good sentence is the first quoter of it.   *Ib.*

When Nature has work to be done, she creates a genius to do it.   *Method of Nature.*

I have heard with admiring submission the experience of the lady who declared that the sense of being well-dressed gives a feeling of inward tranquillity which religion is powerless to bestow. [Miss C. F. Forbes, 1817–1911]   *Ib. Social Aims.*

Every hero becomes a bore at last.   *Representative Men. Uses of Great Men.*

Is not marriage an open question, when it is alleged, from the beginning of the world, that such as are in the institution wish to get out; and such as are out wish to get in.   *Ib. Montaigne.*

Belief consists in accepting the affirmations of the soul; Unbelief, in denying them.   *Ib.*

Hitch your wagon to a star.   *Society and Solitude. Civilization.*

We boil at different degrees.   *Ib. Eloquence.*

One of our statesmen said, 'The curse of this country is eloquent men.'   *Ib.*

Invention breeds invention.   *Ib. Works and Days.*

Never read any book that is not a year old. *Ib. Books.*

'Tis the good reader that makes the good book.   *Ib. Success.*

America is a country of young men.   *Ib. Old Age.*

Glittering generalities! They are blazing ubiquities.   *Attr. remark on Rufus Choate (see p. 94) sneering at the ideas of the Declaration of Independence as 'glittering generalities'.*

If a man write a better book, preach a better sermon, or make a better mouse-trap than his neighbour, tho' he build his house in the woods, the world will make a beaten path to his door.
[Mrs. Sarah S. B. Yule (1856–1916) credits the quotation to Emerson in her *Borrowings* (1889), stating in *The Docket*, Feb. 1912, that she copied this in her handbook from a lecture delivered by Emerson. The 'mouse-trap' quotation was the occasion of a long controversy, owing to Elbert Hubbard's claim to its authorship.]

He who has a thousand friends has not a friend to spare,
And he who has one enemy will meet him everywhere.   *Translations. From Omar Chiam.*

THOMAS DUNN ENGLISH
1819–1902

Oh! don't you remember sweet Alice, Ben Bolt,
Sweet Alice, whose hair was so brown,
Who wept with delight when you gave her a smile,
And trembled with fear at your frown?   *Ben Bolt.*

SIR HENRY ERSKINE

1746–1817

In the garb of old Gaul, wi' the fire of old Rome.
In the Garb of Old Gaul.

GEORGE ETHEREGE

1635?–1691

I must confess I am a fop in my heart; ill customs influence my very senses, and I have been so used to affectation that without the help of the air of the court what is natural cannot touch me.
Letter to Mr. Poley, 2/12 Jan. 1687/8.

Few of our plays can boast of more wit than I have heard him speak at a supper. [Sir Charles Sedley]
Letter to Mr. Will. Richards, undated.

I walk within the purlieus of the Law.
Love in a Tub, I. iii.

Do not vow—Our love is frail as is our life, and full as little in our power; and are you sure you shall out-live this day? *The Man of Mode,* II. i.

When love grows diseas'd, the best thing we can do is to put it to a violent death; I cannot endure the torture of a lingring and consumptive passion.
Ib. ii.

Writing Madam's a mechanic part of wit! A gentle-man should never go beyond a song or a billet.
Ib. IV. i.

What e'er you say, I know all beyond High-Park's a desart to you. *Ib.* v. ii.

ABEL EVANS

1679–1737

Under this stone, Reader, survey
Dead Sir John Vanbrugh's house of clay.
Lie heavy on him, Earth! for he
Laid many heavy loads on thee!
Epitaph on Sir John Vanbrugh, Architect of Blenheim Palace.

When Tadlow walks the streets, the paviours cry,
'God bless you, Sir!' and lay their rammers by.
Epigram. On Dr. Tadlow.

VISCOUNT EVERSLEY
(CHARLES SHAW-LEFEVRE)

1794–1888

What is that fat gentleman in such a passion about?
Remark as a child on hearing Mr. Fox speak in Parliament. G. W. E. Russell, Collections and Recollections, ch. 11.

JOHN EVELYN

1620–1706

This knight was indeed a valiant gentleman; but not a little given to romance, when he spake of him-self. *Diary, 6 Sept. 1651.*

Mulberry Garden, now the only place of refreshment about the town for persons of the best quality to be exceedingly cheated at. *Ib. 10 May 1654.*

That miracle of a youth, Mr. Christopher Wren.
Ib. 11 July 1654.

I saw Hamlet Prince of Denmark played, but now the old plays began to disgust this refined age.
Ib. 26 Nov. 1661.

DAVID EVERETT

1769–1813

You'd scarce expect one of my age
To speak in public on the stage;
And if I chance to fall below
Demosthenes or Cicero,
Don't view me with a critic's eye,
But pass my imperfections by.
Large streams from little fountains flow,
Tall oaks from little acorns grow.
Lines Written for a School Declamation.

JOHN EWEN

1741–1821

O weel may the boatie row,
And better may she speed! *The Boatie Rows.*

WILLIAM NORMAN EWER

b. 1885

I gave my life for freedom—This I know:
For those who bade me fight had told me so.
Five Souls, 1917.

How odd
Of God
To choose
The Jews. *How Odd.*

FREDERICK WILLIAM
FABER

1814–1863

Have mercy on us worms of earth.
Jesus and Mary. Have Mercy on Us, God Most High.

My God, how wonderful Thou art!
Thy majesty how bright,
How beautiful Thy mercy-seat
In depths of burning light!
Ib. My God, How Wonderful Thou Art!

Thine endless wisdom, boundless power,
And awful purity! *Ib.*

Hark! Hark! my soul, angelic songs are swelling
O'er earth's green fields and ocean's wave-beat shore!
How sweet the truth those blessed strains are telling
Of that new life when sin shall be no more!
Oratory Hymns. The Pilgrims of the Night.

The music of the Gospel leads us home.   *Ib.*

Rest comes at length; though life be long and dreary,
   The day must dawn, and darksome night be passed.
                                                    Ib.

O Paradise! O Paradise!
   Who doth not crave for rest?   *Ib. Paradise.*

Faith of our fathers! holy faith!
We will be true to thee till death.
                      Ib. A Pledge of Faithfulness.

Small things are best:
Grief and unrest,
   To rank and wealth are given;
But little things
On little wings
   Bear little souls to Heaven.
            Written in a Little Lady's Little Album.

ROBERT FABYAN
d. 1513

Finally he paid the debt of nature.
                            Chronicles, pt. ii, xli.

GEORGE FARQUHAR
1678–1707

Sir, you shall taste my *Anno Domini*.
                        The Beaux Stratagem, I. i.

I have fed purely upon ale; I have eat my ale, drank
   my ale, and I always sleep upon ale.   *Ib.*

My Lady Bountiful.   *Ib.*

Says little, thinks less, and does—nothing at all, faith.
                                                    Ib.

'Tis still my maxim, that there is no scandal like rags,
   nor any crime so shameful as poverty.   *Ib.* II. ii.

There's some diversion in a talking blockhead; and
   since a woman must wear chains, I would have the
   pleasure of hearing 'em rattle a little.   *Ib.* II. ii.

No woman can be a beauty without a fortune.   *Ib.*

I believe they talked of me, for they laughed consumedly.   *Ib.* III. i.

'Twas for the good of my country that I should be
   abroad.—Anything for the good of one's country—
   I'm a Roman for that.   *Ib.* ii.

Captain is a good travelling name, and so I take it. *Ib.*

AIMWELL:
Then you understand Latin, Mr. Bonniface?
BONNIFACE:
Not I, Sir, as the saying is, but he talks it so very fast
   that I'm sure it must be good.   *Ib.*

There are secrets in all families.   *Ib.* iii.

How a little love and good company improves a
   woman!   *Ib.* IV. i.

It is a maxim that man and wife should never have it
   in their power to hang one another.   *Ib.* ii.

Spare all I have, and take my life.   *Ib.* V. ii.

I hate all that don't love me, and slight all that do.
                        The Constant Couple, I. ii.

Grant me some wild expressions, Heavens, or I shall
   burst— ... Words, words or I shall burst. *Ib.* V. iii.

Charming women can true converts make,
We love the precepts for the teacher's sake.   *Ib.*

Crimes, like virtues, are their own rewards.
                            The Inconstant, IV. ii.

'Tis an old saying, Like master, like man; why not as
   well, Like mistress, like maid?
                            Love and a Bottle, I. i.

Money is the sinews of love, as of war.   *Ib.* II. i.

Poetry's a mere drug, Sir.   *Ib.* III. ii.

He answered the description the page gave to a T,
   Sir.   *Ib.* IV. iii.

And there's a pleasure sure, in being mad,
Which none but mad-men know.
                        The Recruiting Officer, I. iii.

Hanging and marriage, you know, go by Destiny.
                                    Ib. III. ii.

I cou'd be mighty foolish, and fancy my self mighty
   witty; Reason still keeps its throne, but it nods a
   little, that's all.   *Ib.*

A lady, if undrest at Church, looks silly,
One cannot be devout in dishabilly.
                        The Stage Coach, prologue.

I'm privileg'd to be very impertinent, being an
   Oxonian.   *Sir Harry Wildair*, II. i.

The King of Spain is dead.   *Ib.* ii.

FREDERICK WILLIAM FARRAR
1831–1903

Russell . . . acted invariably from the highest principles.   *Eric, or Little by Little*, pt. i, ch. 3.

'Russell, let me always call you Edwin, and call me
   Eric.'   *Ib.* ch. 4.

'By heavens, this is *too* bad!' he exclaimed, stamping
   his foot with anger. 'What have I ever done to you
   young blackguards, that you should treat me thus?'
                            Ib. pt. ii, ch. 1.

JOHN FERRIAR
1761–1815

Now cheaply bought for thrice their weight in gold.
         Illustrations of Sterne. Bibliomania, 1. 65.

WILLIAM PITT FESSENDEN
1806–1869

Repudiate the repudiators.
            Presidential Campaign Slogan, 1868.

EUGENE FIELD
1850–1895

But I, when I undress me
   Each night, upon my knees
Will ask the Lord to bless me
   With apple pie and cheese. *Apple Pie and Cheese.*

When I demanded of my friend what viands he
   preferred,
He quoth: 'A large cold bottle, and a small hot bird!'
                        The Bottle and the Bird.

The little toy dog is covered with dust,
  But sturdy and staunch he stands;
And the little toy soldier is red with rust,
  And his musket moulds in his hands.
Time was when the little toy dog was new,
  And the soldier was passing fair;
And that was the time when our Little Boy Blue
  Kissed them and put them there.
                       Little Boy Blue.

A little peach in an orchard grew,—
A little peach of emerald hue;
Warmed by the sun and wet by the dew,
  It grew.   *The Little Peach.*

Listen to my tale of woe.   *Ib.*

Wynken, Blynken, and Nod one night
  Sailed off in a wooden shoe—
Sailed on a river of crystal light,
  Into a sea of dew.   *Wynken, Blynken, and Nod.*

HENRY FIELDING

1707–1754

'*Tace*, madam,' answered Murphy, 'is Latin for a candle.'   *Amelia*, bk. i, ch. 10.

There are moments in life worth purchasing with worlds.   *Ib.* bk. iii, ch. 2.

It hath been often said, that it is not death, but dying, which is terrible.   *Ib.* ch. 4.

These are called the pious frauds of friendship.
                   Ib. bk. vi, ch. 6.

When widows exclaim loudly against second marriages, I would always lay a wager, that the man, if not the wedding-day, is absolutely fixed on.   *Ib.* ch. 8.

One fool at least in every married couple.
                 Ib. bk. ix, ch. 4.

I am not the least versed in the chrematistic art.
                 Ib. ch. 5.

There is not in the universe a more ridiculous, nor a more contemptible animal, than a proud clergyman.   *Ib.* ch. 10.

One of my illustrious predecessors.
   Covent-Garden Journal, No. 3, 11 Jan. 1752.

I am as sober as a Judge.
        Don Quixote in England, iii. xiv.

Oh! The roast beef of England,
And old England's roast beef.
       The Grub Street Opera, iii. iii.

He in a few minutes ravished this fair creature, or at least would have ravished her, if she had not, by a timely compliance, prevented him.
         Jonathan Wild, bk. iii, ch. 7.

But pray, Mr. Wild, why bitch?   *Ib.* ch. 8.

To whom nothing is given, of him can nothing be required.   *Joseph Andrews*, bk. ii, ch. 8.

I describe not men, but manners; not an individual, but a species.   *Ib.* bk. iii, ch. 1.

They are the affectation of affectation.   *Ib.* ch. 3.

Public schools are the nurseries of all vice and immorality.   *Ib.* ch. 5.

I defy the wisest man in the world to turn a good action into ridicule.   *Ib.* ch. 6.

Some folks rail against other folks, because other folks have what some folks would be glad of.
             Ib. bk. iv, ch. 6.

Love and scandal are the best sweeteners of tea.
     Love in Several Masques, iv. xi.

Yes, I had two strings to my bow; both golden ones, agad! and both cracked.   *Ib.* v. xiii.

We must eat to live, and not live to eat.
            The Miser, iii. iii.

Map me no maps, sir, my head is a map, a map of the whole world.   *Rape upon Rape*, i. v.

Every physician almost hath his favourite disease.
       Tom Jones, bk. ii, ch. 9.

Thwackum was for doing justice, and leaving mercy to heaven.   *Ib.* bk. iii, ch. 10.

A late facetious writer, who told the public that whenever he was dull they might be assured there was a design in it.   *Ib.* bk. v, ch. 1.

O! more than Gothic ignorance.   *Ib.* bk. vii, ch. 3.

'I did not mean to abuse the cloth; I only said your conclusion was a *non sequitur*.'—
'You are another,' cries the sergeant, 'an you come to that, no more a *sequitur* than yourself.'
            Ib. bk. ix, ch. 6.

An amiable weakness.   *Ib.* bk. x, ch. 8.

His designs were strictly honourable, as the phrase is; that is, to rob a lady of her fortune by way of marriage.   *Ib.* bk. xi, ch. 4.

Composed that monstrous animal a husband and wife.
            Ib. bk. xv, ch. 9.

Nay, you may call me coward if you will; but if that little man there upon the stage is not frightened, I never saw any man frightened in my life.
            Ib. bk. xvi, ch. 5.

'He the best player!' cries Partridge, with a contemptuous sneer. 'Why, I could act as well as he myself. I am sure, if I had seen a ghost, I should have looked in the very same manner, and done just as he did. . . . The king for my money! He speaks all his words distinctly, half as loud again as the other. Anybody may see he is an actor.'   *Ib.*

All Nature wears one universal grin.
       Tom Thumb the Great, i. i.

To sun my self in Huncamunca's eyes.   *Ib.* iii.

When I'm not thank'd at all, I'm thank'd enough,
I've done my duty, and I've done no more.   *Ib.*

The dusky night rides down the sky,
  And ushers in the morn;
The hounds all join in glorious cry,
  The huntsman winds his horn:
    And a-hunting we will go.
            A-Hunting We Will Go.

JOHN ARBUTHNOT FISHER, LORD FISHER
1841–1920

You will always be fools! We shall never be gentlemen.

The Times, 26 June 1919. [Quoted by him as 'the apposite words spoken by a German naval officer to his English confrère.... On the whole I think I prefer to be the fool—even as a matter of business.']

Sack the lot!   *Ib. 2 Sept. 1919.*

ALBERT H. FITZ

You are my honey, honey-suckle,
I am the bee.   *The Honey-Suckle and the Bee.*

CHARLES FITZGEFFREY
fl. 1617

And bold and hard adventures t' undertake,
Leaving his country for his country's sake.
          Life and Death of Sir Francis Drake (1596), ccxiii.

EDWARD FITZGERALD
1809–1883

Awake! for Morning in the Bowl of Night
Has flung the Stone that puts the Stars to Flight:
   And Lo! the Hunter of the East has caught
The Sultan's Turret in a Noose of Light.
          Omar Khayyám, ed. 1, i.

Wake! For the Sun, who scatter'd into flight
The Stars before him from the Field of Night,
   Drives Night along with them from Heav'n, and
      strikes
The Sultan's Turret with a Shaft of Light. *Ib.* ed. 4, i.

Dreaming when Dawn's Left Hand was in the Sky
I heard a Voice within the Tavern cry,
   'Awake, my Little ones, and fill the Cup
Before Life's Liquor in its Cup be dry.' *Ib.* ed. 1, ii.

Before the phantom of False morning died,
Methought a Voice within the Tavern cried,
   'When all the Temple is prepared within,
Why nods the drowsy Worshipper outside?'
          Ib. ed. 4, ii.

Now the New Year reviving old Desires,
The thoughtful Soul to Solitude retires.
          Ib. eds. 1 and 4, iv.

Iram indeed is gone with all its Rose,
And Jamshyd's Sev'n-ring'd Cup where no one
      knows;
   But still the Vine her ancient Ruby yields,
And still a Garden by the Water blows. *Ib.* ed. 1, v.

Iram indeed is gone with all his Rose. *Ib.* ed. 4, v.

   But still a Ruby kindles in the Vine,
And many a Garden by the Water blows.   *Ib.*

In divine
High piping Pehlevi, with 'Wine! Wine! Wine!'
'Red Wine!'—the Nightingale cries to the Rose
That yellow Cheek of her's to incarnadine.
          Ib. ed. 1, vi.

That sallow cheek of hers to incarnadine.
          Ib. ed. 4, vi.

Come, fill the Cup, and in the Fire of Spring
The Winter Garment of Repentance fling:
   The Bird of Time has but a little way
To fly—and Lo! the Bird is on the Wing.
          Ib. ed. 1, vii.

Come, fill the Cup, and in the fire of Spring
Your Winter-garment of Repentance fling:
   The Bird of Time has but a little way
To flutter—and the Bird is on the wing.
          Ib. ed. 4, vii.

And look—a thousand Blossoms with the Day
Woke—and a thousand scatter'd into Clay.
          Ib. ed. 1, viii.

Each Morn a thousand Roses brings, you say;
Yes, but where leaves the Rose of Yesterday?
          Ib. ed. 4, ix.

But come with old Khayyám, and leave the Lot
Of Kaikobad and Kaikhosru forgot:
   Let Rustum lay about him as he will,
Or Hatim Tai cry Supper—heed them not.
          Ib. ed. 1, ix.

Well, let it take them! What have we to do
With Kaikobad the Great, or Kaikhosru?
   Let Zal and Rustum bluster as they will,
Or Hatim call to Supper—heed not you.
          Ib. ed. 4, x.

And pity Sultan Mahmud on his Throne.
          Ib. ed. 1, x.

And Peace to Mahmud on his golden Throne.
          Ib. ed. 4, xi.

Here with a Loaf of Bread beneath the bough,
A Flask of Wine, a Book of Verse—and Thou
   Beside me singing in the Wilderness—
And Wilderness is Paradise enow.   *Ib.* ed. 1, xi.

A Book of Verses underneath the Bough,
A Jug of Wine, a Loaf of Bread—and Thou
   Beside me singing in the Wilderness—
Oh, Wilderness were Paradise enow!   *Ib.* ed. 4, xii.

   Ah, take the Cash in hand and waive the Rest;
Oh, the brave Music of a *distant* Drum!
          Ib. ed. 1, xii.

   Ah, take the Cash, and let the Credit go,
Nor heed the rumble of a distant Drum!
          Ib. ed. 4, xiii.

The Worldly Hope men set their Hearts upon
Turns Ashes—or it prospers; and anon,
   Like Snow upon the Desert's dusty Face
Lighting a little Hour or two—is gone.
          Ib. ed. 1, xiv; ed. 4, xvi.

And those who husbanded the Golden grain,
And those who flung it to the winds like Rain,
   Alike to no such aureate Earth are turn'd
As, buried once, Men want dug up again.
          Ib. eds. 1 and 4, xv.

Think, in this batter'd Caravanserai
Whose Doorways are alternate Night and Day,
   How Sultan after Sultan with his Pomp
Abode his Hour or two, and went his way.
          Ib. ed. 1, xvi.

Think, in this batter'd Caravanserai
Whose Portals are alternate Night and Day,
  How Sultan after Sultan with his Pomp
Abode his destin'd Hour, and went his way.
           Omar Khayyám, ed. 4, xvii.

They say the Lion and the Lizard keep
The Courts where Jamshyd gloried and drank deep:
  And Bahram, that great Hunter—the Wild Ass
Stamps o'er his Head, and he lies fast asleep.
           Ib. ed. 1, xvii.

Stamps o'er his Head, but cannot break his Sleep.
           Ib. ed. 4, xviii.

I sometimes think that never blows so red
The Rose as where some buried Caesar bled;
  That every Hyacinth the Garden wears
Dropt in her Lap from some once lovely Head.
           Ib. ed. 1, xviii; ed. 4, xix.

To-morrow!—Why, To-morrow I may be
Myself with Yesterday's Sev'n thousand Years.
           Ib. ed. 1, xx; ed. 4, xxi.

Lo! some we loved, the loveliest and best
That Time and Fate of all their Vintage prest,
  Have drunk their Cup a Round or two before,
And one by one crept silently to Rest.
           Ib. ed. 1, xxi.

For some we loved, the loveliest and the best
That from his Vintage rolling Time hath prest.
           Ib. ed. 4, xxii.

Ah, make the most of what we yet may spend,
Before we too into the Dust descend;
  Dust into Dust, and under Dust, to lie,
Sans Wine, sans Song, sans Singer, and—sans End!
           Ib. ed. 1, xxiii; ed. 4, xxiv.

Oh, come with old Khayyám, and leave the Wise
To talk; one thing is certain, that Life flies;
  One thing is certain, and the Rest is Lies;
The Flower that once hath blown for ever dies.
           Ib. ed. 1, xxvi.

Oh threats of Hell and Hopes of Paradise!
One thing at least is certain—*This* Life flies.
           Ib. ed. 4, lxiii.

Myself when young did eagerly frequent
Doctor and Saint, and heard great argument
  About it and about: but evermore
Came out by the same door as in I went.
           Ib. ed. 1, xxvii.

Came out by the same Door where in I went.
           Ib. ed. 4, xxvii.

I came like Water, and like Wind I go.
           Ib. eds. 1 and 4, xxviii.

Into this Universe, and *Why* not knowing
Nor *Whence*, like Water willy-nilly flowing;
  And out of it, as Wind along the Waste,
I know not *Whither*, willy-nilly blowing.
           Ib. eds. 1 and 4, xxix.

What, without asking, hither hurried *whence*?
And, without asking, *whither* hurried hence!
  Another and another Cup to drown
The Memory of this Impertinence!
           Ib. ed. 1, xxx.

Oh, many a Cup of this forbidden Wine
Must drown the memory of that insolence!
           Ib. ed. 4, xxx.

There was a Door to which I found no Key:
There was a Veil past which I could not see:
  Some little Talk awhile of ME and THEE
There seem'd—and then no more of THEE and ME.
           Ib. ed. 1, xxxii.

There was the Door to which I found no Key;
There was the Veil through which I might not see:
  Some little talk awhile of ME and THEE
There was—and then no more of THEE and ME.
           Ib. ed. 4, xxxii.

  And with its all obliterated Tongue
It murmur'd—'Gently, Brother, gently, pray!'
           Ib. eds. 1 and 4, xxxvi.

Ah, fill the Cup:—what boots it to repeat
How Time is slipping underneath our Feet:
  Unborn TOMORROW, and dead YESTERDAY,
Why fret about them if TODAY be sweet!
           Ib. ed. 1, xxxvii. Not in ed. 4.

One Moment in Annihilation's Waste,
One Moment, of the Well of Life to taste—
  The Stars are Setting and the Caravan
Starts for the Dawn of Nothing—Oh, make haste!
           Ib. ed. 1, xxxviii.

A Moment's Halt—a momentary taste
Of BEING from the Well amid the Waste—
  And lo!—the phantom Caravan has reach'd
The Nothing it set out from—Oh, make haste!
           Ib. ed. 4, xlviii.

Was never deep in anything but—Wine.
           Ib. ed. 1, xli; ed. 4, lvi.

The Grape that can with Logic absolute
The Two-and Seventy jarring Sects confute.
           Ib. ed. 1, xliii; ed. 4, lix.

'Tis all a Chequer-board of Nights and Days
Where Destiny with Men for Pieces plays:
  Hither and thither moves, and mates, and slays,
And one by one back in the Closet lays.
           Ib. ed. 1, xlix.

But helpless Pieces of the Game He plays
Upon this Chequer-board of Nights and Days;
  Hither and thither moves, and checks, and slays,
And one by one back in the Closet lays.
           Ib. ed. 4, lxix.

The Moving Finger writes; and, having writ
Moves on: nor all thy Piety nor Wit
  Shall lure it back to cancel half a Line,
Nor all thy Tears wash out a Word of it. *Ib.* ed. 1, li.

[Ed. 4, lxxi, reads 'your' instead of 'thy'.]

And that inverted Bowl we call The Sky,
Whereunder crawling coop't we live and die,
  Lift not thy hands to *It* for help—for It
Rolls impotently on as Thou or I.   *Ib.* ed. 1, lii.

And that inverted Bowl they call the Sky.
           Ib. ed. 4, lxxii.

As impotently moves as you or I.   *Ib.*

  One glimpse of it within the Tavern caught
Better than in the Temple lost outright. *Ib.* ed. 1, lvi.

One Flash of it within the Tavern caught.
Omar Khayyám, ed. 4, lxxvii.

Oh Thou, who didst with Pitfall and with Gin
Beset the Road I was to wander in,
 Thou wilt not with Predestination round
Enmesh me, and impute my Fall to Sin?
Ib. ed. 1, lvii.

Thou wilt not with Predestined Evil round
Enmesh, and then impute my Fall to Sin!
Ib. ed. 4, lxxx.

Oh, Thou, who Man of baser Earth didst make,
And who with Eden didst devise the Snake;
 For all the Sin wherewith the Face of Man
Is blacken'd, Man's Forgiveness give—and take!
Ib. ed. 1, lviii.

And even with Paradise devise the Snake.
Ib. ed. 4, lxxxi.

'Who *is* the Potter, pray, and who the Pot?'
Ib. ed. 1, lx; ed. 4, lxxxvii.

'He's a Good Fellow, and 'twill all be well.'
Ib. ed. 1, lxiv; ed. 4, lxxxviii.

And much as Wine has play'd the Infidel,
And robb'd me of my Robe of Honour—Well,
 I wonder often what the Vintners buy
One half so precious as the Goods they sell.
Ib. ed. 1, lxxi.

One half so precious as the stuff they sell.
Ib. ed. 4, xcv.

Alas, that Spring should vanish with the Rose!
That Youth's sweet-scented manuscript should close!
 The Nightingale that in the branches sang,
Ah, whence, and whither flown again, who knows!
Ib. ed. 1, lxxii.

Yet Ah, that Spring should vanish with the Rose!
Ib. ed. 4, xcvi.

Ah Love! could thou and I with Fate conspire
To grasp this sorry Scheme of Things entire,
 Would not we shatter it to bits—and then
Re-mould it nearer to the Heart's Desire!
Ib. ed. 1, lxxiii.

Ah Love! could you and I with Him conspire.
Ib. ed. 4, xcix.

Ah, Moon of my Delight who know'st no wane,
The Moon of Heav'n is rising once again:
 How oft hereafter rising shall she look
Through this same Garden after me—in vain!
Ib. ed. 1, lxxiv.

Yon rising Moon that looks for us again.
How oft hereafter will she wax and wane;
 How oft hereafter rising look for us
Through this same Garden—and for *one* in vain!
Ib. ed. 4, c.

And when Thyself with shining Foot shall pass
Among the Guests Star-scattered on the Grass,
 And in thy joyous Errand reach the Spot
Where I made one—turn down an empty Glass!
Ib. ed. 1, lxxv.

And when like her, O Saki, you shall pass.
Ib. ed. 4, ci.

And in your joyous errand reach the spot. *Ib.*

The Wine of Life keeps oozing drop by drop,
The Leaves of Life keep falling one by one.
Ib. ed. 4, viii. Not in ed. 1.

Drink! for you know not whence you came, nor why:
Drink! for you know not why you go, nor where.
Ib. ed. 4, lxxiv. Not in ed. 1.

A Mr Wilkinson, a clergyman.
 Benson's *Life of FitzGerald*, p. 62, and Hallam
 Tennyson's *Tennyson*, i. 153. [An imitation of
 Wordsworth's worst style.]

JAMES ELROY FLECKER
1884–1915

Voiced like a great bell swinging in a dome.
The Bridge of Fire, iv.

For pines are gossip pines the wide world through.
Brumana.

Half to forget the wandering and the pain,
Half to remember days that have gone by,
And dream and dream that I am home again! *Ib.*

The Kings of England lifting up their swords
Shall gather at the gate of Paradise.
The Burial in England.

Noon strikes on England, noon on Oxford town,
Beauty she was statue cold—there's blood upon her
 gown:
Noon of my dreams, O noon!
Proud and godly kings had built her, long ago,
With her towers and tombs and statues all arow,
With her fair and floral air and the love that lingers
 there,
And the streets where the great men go.
The Dying Patriot.

Evening on the olden, the golden sea of Wales,
When the first star shivers and the last wave pales:
O evening dreams! *Ib.*

West of these out to seas colder than the Hebrides
 I must go
Where the fleet of stars is anchored and the young
 star-captains glow. *Ib.*

The dragon-green, the luminous, the dark, the
 serpent-haunted sea.
The Gates of Damascus. West Gate.

When the great markets by the sea shut fast
 All that calm Sunday that goes on and on:
When even lovers find their peace at last,
 And Earth is but a star, that once had shone.
The Golden Journey to Samarkand. Prologue.

And some to Meccah turn to pray, and I toward thy
 bed, Yasmin. *Hassan*, 1. ii.

 For one night or the other night
Will come the Gardener in white, and gathered flowers
 are dead, Yasmin. *Ib.*

For lust of knowing what should not be known,
We take the Golden Road to Samarkand.
Ib. v. ii.

And old Mæonides the blind
Said it three thousand years ago.
To a Poet a Thousand Years Hence.

A ship, an isle, a sickle moon—
  With few but with how splendid stars
The mirrors of the sea are strewn
  Between their silver bars.
         A Ship, an Isle, and a Sickle Moon.

And with great lies about his wooden horse
Set the crew laughing, and forgot his course.
         The Old Ships.

It was so old a ship—who knows, who knows?
And yet so beautiful, I watched in vain
To see the mast burst open with a rose,
  And the whole deck put on its leaves again.   *Ib.*

And walk with you, and talk with you, like any other
  boy.   *Rioupéroux.*

RICHARD FLECKNOE
d. 1678?

Still-born Silence! thou that art
Floodgate of the deeper heart.   *Poems*, 1653.
Was wont to be as still as mouse. *Diarium*, 9 (1656).

MARJORIE FLEMING
1803–1811

A direful death indeed they had
That would put any parent mad
But she was more than usual calm
She did not give a singel dam.   *Journal*, p. 29.

The most devilish thing is 8 times 8 and 7 times 7
  it is what nature itselfe cant endure.   *Ib.* p. 47.

Today I pronounced a word which should never come
  out of a lady's lips it was that I called John a
  Impudent Bitch.   *Ib.* p. 51.

I am going to turn over a new life and am going to be
  a very good girl and be obedient to Isa Keith, here
  there is plenty of gooseberries which makes my
  teeth watter.   *Ib.* p. 76.

I hope I will be religious again but as for regaining
  my character I despare.   *Ib.* p. 80.

An annibabtist is a thing I am not a member of.
         Ib. p. 99.

Sentiment is what I am not acquainted with.   *Ib.*

O lovely O most charming pug
Thy graceful air and heavenly mug. . . .
His noses cast is of the roman
He is a very pretty weomen
I could not get a rhyme for roman
And was oblidged to call it weoman.   *Poems.*

My dear Isa,
  I now sit down on my botom to answer all your
kind and beloved letters which you was so good as to
write to me.   *Letters. I, To Isabella.*

ANDREW FLETCHER
OF SALTOUN
1655–1716

I knew a very wise man so much of Sir Chr—'s sentiment, that he believed if a man were permitted to
  make all the ballads, he need not care who should
  make the laws of a nation.
    Letter to the Marquis of Montrose, and Others.
    Political Works.

PHINEAS FLETCHER
1582–1650

The way to God is by our selves.
         The Purple Island. To the Readers.

Poorly (poor man) he liv'd; poorly (poor man) he
  di'd.   *Ib.* I. xix.

His little son into his bosom creeps,
The lively picture of his father's face.   *Ib.* XII. vi.

Drop, drop, slow tears,
  And bathe those beauteous feet,
Which brought from Heav'n
  The news and Prince of Peace.   *An Hymn.*

In your deep floods
  Drown all my faults and fears;
Not let His eye
  See sin, but through my tears.   *Ib.*

Love is like linen often chang'd, the sweeter.
         Sicelides, III. v.

The coward's weapon, poison.   *Ib.* v. iii.

Love's tongue is in the eyes.
         Piscatory Eclogues, eclog. v, xiii.

SAMUEL FOOTE
1720–1777

Born in a cellar, . . . and living in a garret.
         The Author, II.

So she went into the garden to cut a cabbage-leaf, to
  make an apple-pie; and at the same time a great
  she-bear, coming up the street, pops its head into
  the shop. 'What! no soap?' So he died, and she
  very imprudently married the barber; and there
  were present the Picninnies, and the Joblillies, and
  the Garyalies, and the grand Panjandrum himself,
  with the little round button at top, and they all fell
  to playing the game of catch as catch can, till the
  gun powder ran out at the heels of their boots.
  In Maria Edgeworth, *Harry and Lucy Concluded.*

For as the old saying is,
When house and land are gone and spent
Then learning is most excellent.   *Taste*, I. i.

He is not only dull in himself, but the cause of dullness in others. *Remark.* Boswell's *Life of Johnson*,
  ed. Powell, IV, p. 178. [Parody of Shakespeare,
  Henry IV, pt. ii, IV. i. 2.]

HENRY FORD
1863–

History is bunk.
    In the witness box during his libel suit v. the
    Chicago Tribune, July 1919.

JOHN FORD
1586–1639?

We can drink till all look blue,
         The Lady's Trial, IV. ii.

    Tell us, pray, what devil
This melancholy is, which can transform
Men into monsters.   *Ib.* III. i.

'Tis Pity She's a Whore.   *Title of Play.*

LENA GUILBERT FORD
d. 1916?

Keep the home fires burning, while your hearts are
    yearning,
    Though your lads are far away they dream of home;
There's a silver lining through the dark cloud shining:
    Turn the dark cloud inside out, till the boys come
    home.   *Keep the Home Fires Burning.*

THOMAS FORD
c. 1580–1648

There is a lady sweet and kind,
Was never face so pleased my mind;
I did but see her passing by,
And yet I love her till I die.
    There is a Lady. (*Music of Sundry Kinds*,
    1607, IX. i.)

SAM WALTER FOSS
1858–1911

I say the very things that make the greatest stir,
An' the most interestin' things, are things that didn't
occur.
    Back Country Poems. Things That Didn't
    Occur.

CHARLES FOSTER
1828–1904

Isn't this a billion dollar country?
    At the 51st Congress; retorting to a Democratic
    gibe about a 'million dollar Congress'.

SIR GEORGE EULAS FOSTER
1847–1931

In these somewhat troublesome days when the great
    Mother Empire stands splendidly isolated in
    Europe.
    Speech, Canadian House of Commons, 16 Jan.
    1896.

STEPHEN COLLINS FOSTER
1826–1864

I come down dah wid my hat caved in,
    Doodah! doodah!
I go back home wid a pocket full of tin,
    Oh! doodah day!
Gwine to run all night!
Gwine to run all day!
I'll bet my money on de bob-tail nag,
Somebody bet on de bay.   *Camptown Races.*

De blind hoss stick'n in a big mud hole,
    Doodah! doodah!
Can't touch de bottom wid a ten-foot pole,
    Oh! doodah day!   *Ib.*

Weep no more, my lady,
    Oh! weep no more today!
We will sing one song for the old Kentucky Home,
    For the old Kentucky Home far away.
        My Old Kentucky Home.

'Way down upon de Swanee Ribber,
    Far, far away,
Dere's where my heart is turning ebber:
    Dere's where de old folks stay.
All up and down de whole creation
    Sadly I roam,
Still longing for de old plantation,
    And for de old folks at home.
    Old Folks at Home (*Swanee Ribber*).

I'm coming, I'm coming,
For my head is bending low,
I hear their gentle voices calling
    'Poor old Joe.'   *Poor Old Joe.*

He had no wool on de top of his head,
In de place where de wool ought to grow.   *Uncle Ned.*

Dere's no more hard work for poor old Ned,
He's gone whar de good niggers go.   *Ib.*

CHARLES JAMES FOX
1749–1806

How much the greatest event it is that ever happened
    in the world! and how much the best!
    On the Fall of the Bastille. Letter to Fitzpatrick,
    30 July 1789. Russell's *Life and Times of C. J.*
    Fox, vol. ii, p. 361.

I die happy.
    Last Words. Russell, *ib.* vol. iii, ch. 69.

No man could be so wise as Thurlow looked.
    Campbell's *Lives of the Lord Chancellors*, 1846,
    vol. v, p. 661.

He was uniformly of opinion which, though not a
    popular one, he was ready to aver, that the right of
    governing was not property, but a trust.
    On Pitt's scheme of Parliamentary Reform.
    J. L. Hammond, *C. J. Fox* (1903), p. 75.

HENRY FOX
1705–1774

If Mr. Selwyn calls again, shew him up; if I am alive
    I shall be delighted to see him; and if I am dead he
    would like to see me.
    Last Words. J. H. Jesse, *George Selwyn and his*
    Contemporaries, 1844, vol. iii, p. 50.

BENJAMIN FRANKLIN
1706–1790

Remember, that time is money.
    Advice to Young Tradesman, 1748. Writings,
    vol. ii.

No nation was ever ruined by trade.
    Essays. Thoughts on Commercial Subjects.

Be in general virtuous, and you will be happy.
    Ib. On Early Marriages.

But in this world nothing can be said to be certain,
    except death and taxes.
    Letter to Jean Baptiste Le Roy, 13 Nov. 1789.
    Writings, vol. x.

Here Skugg lies snug,
As a bug in a rug.
    Letter to Miss G. Shipley, 26 Sept. 1772.
    Ib. vol. v.

A little neglect may breed mischief, ... for want of a nail, the shoe was lost; for want of a shoe the horse was lost; and for want of a horse the rider was lost.
> *Maxims ... Prefixed to Poor Richard's Almanac, 1758.*

Three removes is as bad as a fire.   *Ib.*

Fools make feasts, and wise men eat them.
> *Poor Richard's Almanac, May 1733.*

Some are weather-wise, some are otherwise.
> *Ib. Feb. 1735.*

Necessity never made a good bargain. *Ib. Apr. 1735.*

Three may keep a secret, if two of them are dead.
> *Ib. July 1735.*

Early to bed, and early to rise,
Makes a man healthy, wealthy, and wise.
> *Ib. Oct. 1735.*

God helps them that helps themselves. *Ib. June 1736.*

At twenty years of age, the will reigns; at thirty, the wit; and at forty, the judgement.   *Ib. June 1741.*

Experience keeps a dear school, but fools will learn in no other.   *Ib. 1743.*

Dost thou love life? Then do not squander time, for that's the stuff life is made of.   *Ib. June 1746.*

Many have been ruined by buying good pennyworths.
> *Ib. Sept. 1747.*

Little strokes fell great oaks.   *Ib. Aug. 1750.*

If you would know the value of money, go and try to borrow some; for he that goes a borrowing goes a sorrowing.   *Ib. Apr. 1754.*

He that lives upon hope will die fasting.
> *Ib. 1758, preface.*

Poor man, said I, you pay too much for your whistle.
> *The Whistle, 10 Nov. 1779.*

We must indeed all hang together, or, most assuredly, we shall all hang separately.
> *Remark to John Hancock, at Signing of the Declaration of Independence, 4 July 1776.*

Man is a tool-making animal.
> *Boswell's Life of Johnson, 7 Apr. 1778.*

There never was a good war, or a bad peace.
> *Letter to Quincey, 11 Sept. 1783.*

Ça ira.   *Attr.*

THOMAS FREEMAN
b. c. 1591

I love thee Cornwall, and will ever,
  And hope to see thee once again,
For why? thine equal knew I never,
  For honest minds and active men.
> *Encomion Cornubiæ.*

PHILIP MOCIN FRENEAU
1752–1832

What madness is ambition!
What is there in that little breath of men,
Which they call Fame, that should induce the brave
To forfeit ease and that domestic bliss
Which is the lot of happy ignorance?
> *Columbus in Chains, l. 12.*

JOHN HOOKHAM FRERE
1769–1846

The feather'd race with pinions skim the air—
Not so the mackerel, and still less the bear!
> *Progress of Man, l. 34. Poetry of the Anti-Jacobin, 1799.*

Ah! who has seen the mailed lobster rise,
Clap her broad wings, and soaring claim the skies?
> *Ib. l. 44.*

CHARLES FROHMAN
1860–1915

Why fear death? It is the most beautiful adventure in life. *His last words before going down in the* Lusitania, *7 May 1915.*
> I. F. Marcosson and D. Frohman, *Charles Frohman*, ch. 19.

ROBERT FROST
1875–

Something there is that doesn't love a wall.
> *North of Boston. Mending Wall.*

My apple trees will never get across
And eat the cones under his pines, I tell him.
He only says, 'Good fences make good neighbours.'
> *Ib.*

JAMES ANTHONY FROUDE
1818–1894

Wild animals never kill for sport. Man is the only one to whom the torture and death of his fellow-creatures is amusing in itself.   *Oceana, ch. 5.*

Human improvement is from within outwards.
> *Short Studies on Great Subjects. 3rd Ser. Divus Caesar.*

Men are made by nature unequal. It is vain, therefore, to treat them as if they were equal.
> *Ib. Party Politics.*

Experience teaches slowly, and at the cost of mistakes.
> *Ib.*

Fear is the parent of cruelty.   *Ib.*

THOMAS FULLER
1608–1661

Thus this brook hath conveyed his [Wickliff's] ashes into Avon; Avon into Severn; Severn into the narrow seas; they, into the main ocean. And thus the ashes of Wickliff are the emblem of his doctrine, which now, is dispersed all the world over.
> *The Church History (1655), bk. iv, sec. ii, par. 53, p. 171.*

A proverb is much matter decocted into few words.
> *The History of the Worthies of England, ch. 2.*

Know most of the rooms of thy native country before thou goest over the threshold thereof.
> *The Holy and Profane State (1642), bk. ii, ch. 4, p. 159. Of Travelling.*

A little skill in antiquity inclines a man to Popery;
but depth in that study brings him about again to
our religion.
> *Ib.* ch. 6, p. 69. *The True Church Antiquary.*

Light (God's eldest daughter).
> *Ib.* ch. 7, p. 167. *Of Building.*

Learning hath gained most by those books by which
the printers have lost.
> *Ib.* bk. iii, ch. 18, p. 200. *Of Books.*

He was one of a lean body and visage, as if his eager
soul, biting for anger at the clog of his body, desired to fret a passage through it.
> *Ib.* bk. v, ch. 19, p. 441. *Life of the Duke of
> Alva.*

It is always darkest just before the day dawneth.
> *Pisgah Sight,* bk. ii, ch. 11, § 5.

Worldly wealth he cared not for, desiring only to
make both ends meet. [Of Edmund Grindall.]
> *Worthies of England. Worthies of Cumberland.*

It is a silly game where nobody wins.
> *Gnomologia,* No. 2880.

THOMAS GAINSBOROUGH

1727–1788

We are all going to heaven, and Vandyke is of the
company.
> *Last Words.* Boulton, *Thomas Gainsborough,* ch. 9.

THOMAS GAISFORD

1779–1855

The advantages of a classical education are two-fold—
it enables us to look down with contempt on those
who have not shared its advantages, and also fits us
for places of emolument not only in this world, but
in that which is to come.
> *Good Friday Sermon in the Cathedral, Oxford.
> On the authority of Dr. Strong, Bishop of
> Oxford, to whom Canon Liddon told the story.*

RICHARD GALL

1776–1801

Baloo, baloo, my wee wee thing.　　*Poems and Songs.*

SIR GREGORY GANDER
(GEORGE ELLIS)

1745–1815

Snowy, Flowy, Blowy,
Showery, Flowery, Bowery,
Hoppy, Croppy, Droppy,
Breezy, Sneezy, Freezy.　　*The Twelve Months.*

AUGUSTUS P. GARDNER

1865–1918

Wake up America.　　*Speech, 16 Oct. 1916.*

JAMES ABRAM GARFIELD

1831–1881

Fellow-citizens: God reigns, and the Government at
Washington lives!
> *Speech on Assassination of Lincoln, 1865.*

DAVID GARRICK

1717–1779

Prologues precede the piece—in mournful verse;
As undertakers—walk before the hearse.
> *Apprentice,* prologue.

Are these the choice dishes the Doctor has sent us?
Is this the great poet whose works so content us?
This Goldsmith's fine feast, who has written fine
books?
Heaven sends us good meat, but the Devil sends
cooks.
> *On Doctor Goldsmith's Characteristical Cookery.*

Come, cheer up, my lads! 'tis to glory we steer,
To add something more to this wonderful year;
To honour we call you, not press you like slaves,
For who are so free as the sons of the waves?
　Heart of oak are our ships,
　Heart of oak are our men:
　　We always are ready;
　　Steady, boys, steady;
We'll fight and we'll conquer again and again.
> *Heart of Oak.*

We ne'er see our foes but we wish 'em to stay,
They never see us but they wish us away;
If they run, why, we follow, and run 'em ashore,
For if they won't fight us, we cannot do more.　*Ib.*

Here lies Nolly Goldsmith, for shortness call'd Noll,
Who wrote like an angel, but talk'd like poor Poll.
> *Impromptu Epitaph.*

I've that within—for which there are no plaisters.
> *Prologue* to Goldsmith's *She Stoops to Conquer.*

A fellow-feeling makes one wond'rous kind.
> *An Occasional Prologue on Quitting the Theatre,
> 10 June 1776.*

That blessed word Mesopotamia.
> [Garrick tells of the power of George White-
> field's voice, that 'he could make men either
> laugh or cry by pronouncing the word Meso-
> potamia'. Related by Francis Jacox. A story
> goes (Harvey's *Companion to English Literature*)
> that an old woman told her pastor that she
> found great support in that comfortable word
> Mesopotamia.]
> *Notes and Queries,* Ser. xi, i. 458.

WILLIAM LLOYD GARRISON

1805–1879

I am in earnest—I will not equivocate—I will not
excuse—I will not retreat a single inch—and I will
be heard!
> *Salutatory Address of The Liberator, 1 Jan.
> 1831.*

Our country is the world—our countrymen are all mankind. *Prospectus of The Liberator, 15 Dec.1837.*

The compact which exists between the North and the South is 'a covenant with death and an agreement with hell'.
> *Resolution adopted by the Massachusetts Anti-Slavery Society, 27 Jan. 1843.*

SAMUEL GARTH
1661–1719

Hard was their lodging, homely was their food;
For all their luxury was doing good.
> *Claremont, l. 148.*

A barren superfluity of words.
> *The Dispensary, c. 2, l. 95.*

ELIZABETH CLEGHORN GASKELL
1810–1865

Get her a flannel waistcoat and flannel drawers, ma'am, if you wish to keep her alive. But my advice is, kill the poor creature at once. [*Capt. Brown on Miss Betsey Barker's cow.*]
> *Cranford, ch. 1.*

We were none of us musical, though Miss Jenkyns beat time, out of time, by way of appearing to be so.
> *Ib.*

Bombazine would have shown a deeper sense of her loss. *Miss Jenkyns.* *Ib.* ch. 7.

JOHN GAY
1685–1732

I rage, I melt, I burn,
The feeble God has stabb'd me to the heart.
> *Acis and Galatea, ii.*

Bring me an hundred reeds of decent growth,
To make a pipe for my capacious mouth. *Ib.*

O ruddier than the cherry,
O sweeter than the berry. *Ib.*

Wou'd you gain the tender creature?
Softly, gently, kindly treat her,
Suff'ring is the lover's part.
Beauty by constraint, possessing,
You enjoy but half the blessing,
Lifeless charms, without the heart. *Ib.*

Love sounds the alarm, and Fear is a flying. *Ib.*

How, like a moth, the simple maid
Still plays about the flame!
> *The Beggar's Opera, Act I, sc. iv, air iv.*

Our Polly is a sad slut! nor heeds what we have taught her.
I wonder any man alive will ever rear a daughter!
> *Ib.* viii, air vii.

Do you think your mother and I should have liv'd comfortably so long together, if ever we had been married? *Ib.*

There are not many husbands and wives who can bear the charges of plaguing one another in a handsome way. *Ib.*

Can Love be controll'd by advice? *Ib.* air viii.

O Polly, you might have toy'd and kist,
By keeping men off, you keep them on. *Ib.* air ix.

Well, Polly; as far as one woman can forgive another,
I forgive thee. *Ib.*

POLLY.
Then all my sorrows are at an end.
MRS. PEACHUM.
A mighty likely speech, in troth, for a wench who is just married! *Ib.*

Money, wife, is the true fuller's earth for reputations, there is not a spot or a stain but what it can take out.
> *Ib.* ix.

A fox may steal your hens, sir

If lawyer's hand is fee'd, sir
He steals your whole estate. *Ib.* air xi.

The comfortable estate of widowhood, is the only hope that keeps up a wife's spirits. *Ib.* x.

Oh, ponder well! be not severe;
So save a wretched wife:
For on the rope that hangs my dear
Depends poor Polly's life. *Ib.* air xii.

Away, hussy. Hang your husband and be dutiful.
> *Ib.*

Even butchers weep! *Ib.* xii.

Pretty Polly, say,
When I was away,
Did your fancy never stray
To some newer lover? *Ib.* xiii, air xiv.

I sipt each flower,
I chang'd ev'ry hour,
But here ev'ry flower is united. *Ib.* air xv.

If with me you'd fondly stray,
Over the hills and far away. *Ib.* air xvi.

O what pain it is to part! *Ib.* air xvii.

We retrench the superfluities of mankind. *Ib.* II. i.

Fill ev'ry glass, for wine inspires us,
And fires us
With courage, love and joy.
Women and wine should life employ.
Is there ought else on earth desirous? *Ib.* air xix.

If the heart of a man is deprest with cares,
The mist is dispell'd when a woman appears.
> *Ib.* iii, air xxi.

I must have women. There is nothing unbends the mind like them. *Ib.*

Youth's the season made for joys,
Love is then our duty. *Ib.* iv, air xxii.

To cheat a man is nothing; but the woman must have fine parts indeed who cheats a woman! *Ib.*

Man may escape from rope and gun;
Nay, some have outliv'd the doctor's pill:
Who takes a woman must be undone,
That basilisk is sure to kill.
The fly that sips treacle is lost in the sweets,
So he that tastes woman, woman, woman,
He that tastes woman, ruin meets. *Ib.* viii, air xxvi.

MACHEATH.
Have you no bowels, no tenderness, my dear Lucy, to see a husband in these circumstances?
LUCY.
A husband!
MACHEATH.
In ev'ry respect but the form. *Ib.* ix.

I am ready, my dear Lucy, to give you satisfaction—
if you think there is any in marriage?   *Ib.*

In one respect indeed, our employment may be
reckoned dishonest, because, like great Statesmen,
we encourage those who betray their friends. *Ib.* x.

I think you must ev'n do as other widows—buy yourself weeds, and be cheerful.   *Ib.* xi.

How happy could I be with either,
Were t'other dear charmer away!
But while ye thus tease me together,
To neither a word will I say.   *Ib.* xiii, air xxxv.

One wife is too much for one husband to hear,
But two at a time there's no mortal can bear.
This way, and that way, and which way I will,
What would comfort the one, t'other wife would take
ill.   *Ib.* III. xi, air liii.

The charge is prepar'd; the lawyers are met;
The Judges all rang'd (a terrible show!). *Ib.* air lvii.

That that Jemmy Twitcher should peach me, I own
surprised me!   *Ib.* xiv.

She who has never lov'd, has never liv'd.
       The Captives, II. i.

If e'er your heart has felt the tender passion
You will forgive this just, this pious fraud. *Ib.* IV. x.

She who trifles with all
Is less likely to fall
   Than she who but trifles with one.
    The Coquet Mother and the Coquet Daughter.

Then nature rul'd, and love, devoid of art,
Spoke the consenting language of the heart.
       Dione, prologue.

Behold the victim of Parthenia's pride!
He saw, he sigh'd, he lov'd, was scorn'd and died.
       Ib. I. i.

He best can pity who has felt the woe.   *Ib.* II. ii.

Woman's mind
Oft' shifts her passions, like th'inconstant wind;
Sudden she rages, like the troubled main,
Now sinks the storm, and all is calm again.   *Ib.* v.

A woman's friendship ever ends in love.   *Ib.* IV. vi.

Behold the bright original appear.
       Epistle to a Lady, l. 85.

Praising all alike, is praising none.   *Ib.* l. 114.

One always zealous for his country's good. *Ib.* l. 118.

Variety's the source of joy below.
       Epistle to Bernard Lintott, l. 41.

Yet why should learning hope success at Court?
Why should our patriots virtue's cause support?
Why to true merit should they have regard?
They know that virtue is its own reward.
       Epistle to Methuen, l. 39.

Life is a jest; and all things show it.
I thought so once; but now I know it.
       My Own Epitaph.

Whence is thy learning? Hath thy toil
O'er books consum'd the midnight oil?
     Fables. Series I, introduction, l. 15.

Where yet was ever found a mother,
Who'd give her booby for another?
   Ib. The Mother, the Nurse, and the Fairy, iii, l. 33.

Envy's a sharper spur than pay,
No author ever spar'd a brother,
Wits are gamecocks to one another.
     Ib. The Elephant and the Bookseller, l. 74.

An open foe may prove a curse,
But a pretended friend is worse.
   Ib. xvii. *The Shepherd's Dog and the Wolf,* l. 33.

In ev'ry age and clime we see,
Two of a trade can ne'er agree.
     Ib. xxi. *The Rat-Catcher and Cats,* l. 43.

Where there is life, there's hope, he cried,
Then why such haste? so groan'd and died.
     Ib. xxvii. *The Sick Man and the Angel,* l 49.

Those who in quarrels interpose,
Must often wipe a bloody nose.
       Ib. xxxiv. *The Mastiff,* l. 1.

How many saucy airs we meet
From Temple-bar to Aldgate-street.
     Ib. xxxv. *The Barley-Mow and Dunghill,* l. 1.

Fools may our scorn, not envy raise,
For envy is a kind of praise.
     Ib. xliv. *The Hound and the Huntsman,* l. 29.

Friendship, like love, is but a name.
     Ib. l. *The Hare and Many Friends,* l. 1.

And when a lady's in the case,
You know, all other things give place.   *Ib.* l. 41.

Give me, kind heaven, a private station,
A mind serene for contemplation.
     Ib. Series II, ii. *The Vulture, the Sparrow, and
Other Birds,* l. 69.

Studious of elegance and ease.
     Ib. viii. *The Man, the Cat, the Dog, and the
Fly,* l. 127.

'Tis a gross error, held in schools,
That Fortune always favours fools.
     Ib. xii. *Pan and Fortune,* l. 119.

Like a stuck pig I gaping stare.
     A New Song of New Similes.

Soft as silk.   *Ib.*

Sound as a top.   *Ib.*

Lighter than a feather.   *Ib.*

Brown as a berry.   *Ib.*

Sharp as a needle.   *Ib.*

Happy as a king.   *Ib.*

Whoever heard a man of fortune in England talk of
the necessaries of life? . . . Whether we can afford
it or no, we must have superfluities.   *Polly,* I. i.

How little are our customs known on this side of the
herring-pond!   *Ib.*

Why, all our fine ladies, in what they call pin-money,
have no other views.   *Ib.*

No, sir, tho' I was born and bred in England, I can
dare to be poor, which is the only thing now-a-
days men are asham'd of.   *Ib.* xi.

An inconstant woman, tho' she has no chance to be
very happy, can never be very unhappy.   *Ib.* xiv.

Sleep, O Sleep,
With thy rod of incantation
Charm my imagination.

.   .   .   .

What's to sleep?
'Tis a visionary blessing;
A dream that's past expressing;
Our utmost wish possessing
So may I always keep.   *Ib.* II. i.

Where I behold the farmer's early care
In the revolving labours of the year.
                    Rural Sports, c. I, l. 37.

And one slight hair the mighty bulk commands.
                    Ib. l. 244.

All in the Downs the fleet was moor'd,
    The streamers waving in the wind,
When black-ey'd Susan came aboard.
    Sweet William's Farewell to Black-Eyed Susan.

We only part to meet again.
Change, as ye list, ye winds; my heart shall be
The faithful compass that still points to thee.   *Ib.*

They'll tell thee, sailors, when away,
    In ev'ry port a mistress find.   *Ib.*

If to far India's coast we sail,
    Thy eyes are seen in di'monds bright,
Thy breath is Africk's spicy gale,
    Thy skin is ivory, so white.
Thus ev'ry beauteous object that I view,
Wakes in my soul some charm of lovely Sue.   *Ib.*

Adieu, she cries! and wav'd her lily hand.   *Ib.*

A miss for pleasure, and a wife for breed.
                    The Toilette.

With thee conversing, I forget the way.
                    Trivia, bk. ii, l. 480.

Now Cynthia nam'd, fair regent of the Night.
                    Ib. bk. iii, l. 4.

Dispute the reign of some luxurious mire. *Ib.* l. 48.

'Twas when the seas were roaring
    With hollow blasts of wind;
A damsel lay deploring,
    All on a rock reclin'd.
    The What D'ye Call It, II. viii.

GEORGE I OF ENGLAND
1660–1727

I hate all Boets and Bainters.
        Campbell, *Lives of the Chief Justices*, ch. 30,
        Lord Mansfield.

GEORGE II OF ENGLAND
1683–1760

Non, j'aurai des maîtresses.
    *Reply to Queen Caroline when, as she lay dying,
    she urged him to marry again. Her reply to this
    was 'Ah! mon Dieu! cela n'empêche pas.'*
    Hervey, *Memoirs of George the Second*, 1848,
    vol. ii.

Oh! he is mad, is he? Then I wish he would *bite*
some other of my generals.
    *Reply to one who complained that General Wolfe
    was a madman.* F. Thackeray, *History of
    William Pitt*, vol. i, ch. 15, note.

GEORGE V OF ENGLAND
1865–1936

Wake up England.
        *Title of a reprint in 1911 of a speech made by the
        King when Prince of Wales in the Guildhall on
        5 Dec. 1901 on his return from a tour of the
        Empire.*

[I venture to allude to the impression which seemed
    generally to prevail among their brethren across
    the seas, that the old country must wake up if she
    intends to maintain her old position of pre-
    eminence in her colonial trade against foreign
    competitors. *Speech.*]

How is the Empire?
        Last Words. The Times, 21 Jan. 1936.

HENRY GEORGE
1839–1897

So long as all the increased wealth which modern
    progress brings goes but to build up great fortunes,
    to increase luxury and make sharper the contrast
    between the House of Have and the House of Want,
    progress is not real and cannot be permanent.
        Progress and Poverty. Introductory, The Problem.

EDWARD GIBBON
1737–1794

My early and invincible love of reading, which I would
    not exchange for the treasures of India.
        Autobiography (World's Classics ed.), p. 27.

I spent fourteen months at Magdalen College; they
    proved the fourteen months the most idle and
    unprofitable of my whole life.   *Ib.* p. 36.

The monks of Magdalen.   *Ib.* p. 40.

Decent easy men, who supinely enjoyed the gifts of
    the founder.   *Ib.*

Their dull and deep potations excused the brisk in-
    temperance of youth.   *Ib.*

Dr.— well remembered that he had a salary to receive,
    and only forgot that he had a duty to perform.
                    Ib. p. 44.

It was here that I suspended my religious inquiries
    (*aged 17*).   *Ib.* p. 63.

I saw and loved.   *Ib.* p. 83.

I sighed as a lover, I obeyed as a son.   *Ib.*

Crowds without company, and dissipation without
    pleasure. (*Of London.*)   *Ib.* p. 90.

I was never less alone than when by myself. *Ib.* p. 92.

The captain of the Hampshire grenadiers . . . has not
    been useless to the historian of the Roman empire.
                    Ib. p. 106.

It was at Rome, on the 15th of October, 1764, as I
    sat musing amidst the ruins of the Capitol, while
    the barefooted friars were singing vespers in the
    Temple of Jupiter, that the idea of writing the
    decline and fall of the city first started to my mind.
                    Ib. p. 160.

The first of earthly blessings, independence.
Ib. p. 176.

I will not dissemble the first emotions of joy on the recovery of my freedom, and, perhaps, the establishment of my fame. But my pride was soon humbled, and a sober melancholy was spread over my mind, by the idea that I had taken an everlasting leave of an old and agreeable companion, and that whatsoever might be the future date of my History, the life of the historian must be short and precarious. *Ib.* p. 205.

The various modes of worship, which prevailed in the Roman world, were all considered by the people as equally true; by the philosopher, as equally false; and by the magistrate, as equally useful.
Decline and Fall of the Roman Empire, ch. 2.

The principles of a free constitution are irrecoverably lost, when the legislative power is nominated by the executive. *Ib.* ch. 3.

Titus Antoninus Pius.... His reign is marked by the rare advantage of furnishing very few materials for history; which is, indeed, little more than the register of the crimes, follies, and misfortunes of mankind. *Ib.*

If a man were called to fix the period in the history of the world during which the condition of the human race was most happy and prosperous, he would, without hesitation, name that which elapsed from the death of Domitian to the accession of Commodus. *Ib.*

All taxes must, at last, fall upon agriculture. *Ib.* ch. 8.

Corruption, the most infallible symptom of constitutional liberty. *Ib.* ch. 21.

In every deed of mischief he (Commenus) had a heart to resolve, a head to contrive, and a hand to execute. *Ib.* ch. 48.

A victorious line of march had been prolonged above a thousand miles from the rock of Gibraltar to the banks of the Loire; the repetition of an equal space would have carried the Saracens to the confines of Poland and the Highlands of Scotland: the Rhine is not more impassable than the Nile or Euphrates, and the Arabian fleet might have sailed without a naval combat into the mouth of the Thames. Perhaps the interpretation of the Koran would now be taught in the schools of Oxford, and her pulpits might demonstrate to a circumcised people the sanctity and truth of the revelation of Mahomet.
Ib. ch. 52.

Vicissitudes of fortune, which spares neither man nor the proudest of his works, which buries empires and cities in a common grave. *Ib.* ch. 71.

All that is human must retrograde if it does not advance. *Ib.*

WILLIAM HAMILTON GIBSON
1850–1896

Oh, the lovely fickleness of an April day!
Pastoral Days: Spring.

HUMPHREY GIFFORD
1550–1600

I cannot say the crow is white,
But needs must call a spade a spade.
Song, A Woman's Face is Full of Wiles. Ault, *Elizabethan Lyrics.*

Ye curious carpet knights, that spend the time in sport and play,
Abroad, and see new sights, your country's cause calls you away. *For Soldiers. Posie of Gilloflowers.*

WILLIAM GIFFORD
1756–1826

In all the sad variety of woe. *The Baviad*, l. 164.

The insatiate itch of scribbling.
Trans. of Juvenal, vii. 79.

Virtue alone is true nobility. *Ib.* viii. 32.

REV. RICHARD GIFFORD
1725–1807

Verse softens toil, however rude the sound;
She feels no biting pang the while she sings;
Nor, as she turns the giddy wheel around,
Revolves the sad vicissitude of things.
Contemplation.

FRED GILBERT
1850–1903

At Trinity Church I met my doom. *Title of Song.*

Woa, mare! Woa, mare!
You've earned your little bit o' corn!
Down the Road.

As I walk along the Bois Bou-long,
With an independent air,
You can hear the girls declare,
'He must be a millionaire';
You can hear them sigh and wish to die,
You can see them wink the other eye
At the man who broke the Bank at Monte Carlo.
The Man Who Broke the Bank at Monte Carlo.

HUMPHREY GILBERT
1539?–1583

We are as near to heaven by sea as by land!
Hakluyt's Voyages, iii (1600), p. 159.

WILLIAM SCHWENCK GILBERT
1836–1911

It is my duty, and I will.
The 'Bab' Ballads. Captain Reece.

It was their duty, and they did. *Ib.*

The mildest curate going.
Ib. The Rival Curates.

From a highly impossible tree
In a highly impossible scene.   *Ib. Only a Dancing Girl.*

There were captains by the hundred, there were
   baronets by dozens.   *Ib. Ferdinando and Elvira.*

Only find out who it is that writes those lovely cracker
   mottoes!
                                                Ib.

Oh, I am a cook and a captain bold,
   And the mate of the *Nancy* brig,
And a bo'sun tight, and a midshipmite,
   And the crew of the captain's gig.
            Ib. The Yarn of the 'Nancy Bell'.

Among them was a Bishop, who
Had lately been appointed to
The balmy isle of Rum-ti-Foo,
   And Peter was his name.
            Ib. The Bishop of Rum-ti-Foo.

Which is pretty, but I don't know what it means.
            Ib. Story of Prince Agib.

Then they began to sing
That extremely lovely thing,
'Scherzando! ma non troppo ppp.'
                                                Ib.

Roll on, thou ball, roll on!
Through pathless realms of Space
            Roll on!
What though I'm in a sorry case?
What though I cannot meet my bills?
What though I suffer toothache's ills?
What though I swallow countless pills?
            Never *you* mind!
            Roll on!
            Ib. To the Terrestrial Globe.

It's true I've got no shirts to wear;
It's true my butcher's bill is due;
It's true my prospects all look blue—
But don't let that unsettle you!
            Never *you* mind!
            Roll on!   (*It rolls on.*) *Ib.*

The padre said, 'Whatever have you been and gone
   and done?'   *Ib. Gentle Alice Brown.*

A very good girl was Emily Jane,
   Jimmy was good and true,
John was a very good man in the main
   (And I am a good man too.)
            Ib. Emily, John, James, and I.

Down went the owners—greedy men whom hope of
   gain allured:
Oh, dry the starting tear, for they were heavily
   insured.   *Ib. Etiquette.*

He had often eaten oysters, but had never had enough.
                                                Ib.

In all the woes that curse our race
There is a lady in the case.   *Fallen Fairies*, II.

He led his regiment from behind—
   He found it less exciting.   *The Gondoliers*, I.

That celebrated,
Cultivated,
Underrated
            Nobleman,
The Duke of Plaza Toro!   *Ib.*

Of that there is no manner of doubt—
No probable, possible shadow of doubt—
No possible doubt whatever.   *Ib.*

His terrible taste for tippling.   *Ib.*

A taste for drink, combined with gout,
Had doubled him up for ever.   *Ib.*

Oh, 'tis a glorious thing, I ween,
To be a regular Royal Queen!
No half-and-half affair, I mean,
But a right-down regular Royal Queen!   *Ib.*

All shall equal be.   *Ib.*

The Earl, the Marquis, and the Dook,
The Groom, the Butler, and the Cook,
The Aristocrat who banks with Coutts,
The Aristocrat who cleans the boots.   *Ib.*

   But the privilege and pleasure
   That we treasure beyond measure
Is to run on little errands for the Ministers of State.
                                            Ib. II.

With the gratifying feeling that our duty has been
   done!   *Ib.*

Take a pair of sparkling eyes.   *Ib.*

Take my counsel, happy man;
Act upon it, if you can!   *Ib.*

He wished all men as rich as he
(And he was rich as rich could be),
So to the top of every tree
   Promoted everybody.   *Ib.*

Dukes were three a penny.   *Ib.*

When every blessed thing you hold
Is made of silver, or of gold,
   You long for simple pewter.
When you have nothing else to wear
But cloth of gold and satins rare,
For cloth of gold you cease to care—
   Up goes the price of shoddy.   *Ib.*

When everyone is somebodee,
Then no one's anybody!   *Ib.*

I see no objection to stoutness, in moderation.
                                    Iolanthe, I.

For I'm to be married today—today—
Yes, I'm to be married to-day!   *Ib.*

Thou the singer; I the song!   *Ib.*

Bow, bow, ye lower middle classes!
Bow, bow, ye tradesmen, bow, ye masses.   *Ib.*

The Law is the true embodiment
Of everything that's excellent.
It has no kind of fault or flaw,
And I, my Lords, embody the Law.   *Ib.*

Pretty young wards in Chancery.   *Ib.*

A pleasant occupation for
A rather susceptible Chancellor!   *Ib.*

For I'm not so old, and not so plain,
And I'm quite prepared to marry again.   *Ib.*

Spurn not the nobly born with love affected,
Nor treat with virtuous scorn the well-connected. *Ib.*

Hearts just as pure and fair
May beat in Belgrave Square
As in the lowly air
            Of Seven Dials.   *Ib.*

When I went to the Bar as a very young man,
    (Said I to myself, said I).   *Iolanthe*, I.

My son in tears—and on his wedding day!   *Ib.*

He exercises of his brains,
That is, assuming that he's got any.   *Ib.* II.

I am an intellectual chap,
And think of things that would astonish you.
I often think it's comical
    How Nature always does contrive
That every boy and every gal,
    That's born into the world alive,
Is either a little Liberal,
    Or else a little Conservative!   *Ib.*

The House of Peers, throughout the war,
Did nothing in particular,
    And did it very well:
Yet Britain set the world ablaze
In good King George's glorious days!   *Ib.*

    Oh, Captain Shaw!
Type of true love kept under!
    Could thy Brigade
    With cold cascade
Quench my great love, I wonder!   *Ib.*

For you dream you are crossing the Channel, and
    tossing about in a steamer from Harwich—
Which is something between a large bathing machine
    and a very small second class carriage.   *Ib.*

And bound on that journey you find your attorney
    (who started that morning from Devon);
He's a bit undersized, and you don't feel surprised
    when he tells you he's only eleven.   *Ib.*

Faint heart never won fair lady!
Nothing venture, nothing win—
Blood is thick, but water's thin—
In for a penny, in for a pound—
It's Love that makes the world go round!   *Ib.*

A wandering minstrel I—
A thing of shreds and patches,
Of ballads, songs and snatches,
And dreamy lullaby!   *The Mikado*, I.

Are you in sentimental mood?
I'll sigh with you.   *Ib.*

But the happiest hour a sailor sees
    Is when he's down
    At an inland town,
With his Nancy on his knees, yo ho!
And his arm around her waist!   *Ib.*

    And I am right,
    And you are right,
And all is right as right can be!   *Ib.*

It revolts me, but I do it!   *Ib.*

I accept refreshment at any hands, however lowly.
                                                Ib.

And the brass will crash,
    And the trumpets bray,
And they'll cut a dash
    On their wedding day.   *Ib.*

I am happy to think that there will be no difficulty
    in finding plenty of people whose loss will be a
    distinct gain to society at large.   *Ib.*

As some day it may happen that a victim must be
    found,
    I've got a little list—I've got a little list
Of society offenders who might well be under ground
    And who never would be missed—who never
        would be missed!   *Ib.*

The idiot who praises, with enthusiastic tone,
All centuries but this, and every country but his own.
                                                Ib.

Three little maids from school are we,
Pert as a schoolgirl well can be,
Filled to the brim with girlish glee.   *Ib.*

Life is a joke that's just begun.   *Ib.*

Three little maids who, all unwary,
Come from a ladies' seminary.   *Ib.*

Modified rapture!   *Ib.*

Awaiting the sensation of a short, sharp shock,
From a cheap and chippy chopper on a big black
    block.   *Ib.*

For he's going to marry Yum-Yum—
                          Yum-Yum.   *Ib.*

There's not a trace
Upon her face
Of diffidence or shyness.   *Ib.* II.

Ah, pray make no mistake,
    We are not shy;
We're very wide awake,
    The moon and I!   *Ib.*

Brightly dawns our wedding day;
Joyous hour, we give thee greeting!   *Ib.*

Sing a merry madrigal.   *Ib.*

Matrimonial devotion
Doesn't seem to suit her notion.   *Ib.*

Here's a how-de-doo!   *Ib.*

Ha! ha! Family Pride, how do you like *that*, my buck?
                                                Ib.

My object all sublime
I shall achieve in time—
To make the punishment fit the crime—
    The punishment fit the crime.   *Ib.*

A source of innocent merriment!
    Of innocent merriment.   *Ib.*

    Sent to hear sermons
    From mystical Germans
Who preach from ten till four.   *Ib.*

The music-hall singer attends a series
Of masses and fugues and 'ops'
    By Bach, interwoven
    With Spohr and Beethoven,
At classical Monday Pops.   *Ib*

The billiard sharp whom any one catches,
    His doom's extremely hard—
        He's made to dwell—
        In a dungeon cell
On a spot that's always barred.
And there he plays extravagant matches
    In fitless finger-stalls
        On a cloth untrue
        With a twisted cue
And elliptical billiard balls.   *Ib*

The criminal cried, as he dropped him down,
    In a state of wild alarm—
With a frightful, frantic, fearful frown,
    I bared my big right arm.   *Ib*

I drew my snickersnee! *Mikado*, II.

Her terrible tale
You can't assail,
With truth it quite agrees;
Her taste exact
For faultless fact
Amounts to a disease. *Ib.*

Though trunkless, yet
It couldn't forget
The deference due to me! *Ib.*

Something lingering, with boiling oil in it, I fancy. *Ib.*

Merely corroborative detail, intended to give artistic
verisimilitude to an otherwise bald and unconvincing narrative. *Ib.*

She has a left elbow which people come miles to see!
Ib.

The flowers that bloom in the spring, Tra la,
Have nothing to do with the case. *Ib.*

I've got to take under my wing,
tra la,
A most unattractive old thing,
tra la,
With a caricature of a face
And that's what I mean when I say, or I sing,
'Oh bother the flowers that bloom in the spring.' *Ib.*

On a tree by a river a little tom-tit
Sang 'Willow, titwillow, titwillow!'
And I said to him, 'Dicky-bird, why do you sit
Singing 'Willow, titwillow, titwillow?' *Ib.*

'Is it weakness of intellect, birdie?' I cried,
'Or a rather tough worm in your little inside?'
With a shake of his poor little head he replied,
'Oh, willow, titwillow, titwillow!' *Ib.*

He sobbed and he sighed, and a gurgle he gave,
Then he plunged himself into the billowy wave,
And an echo arose from the suicide's grave—
'Oh willow, titwillow, titwillow!' *Ib.*

There's a fascination frantic
In a ruin that's romantic;
Do you think you are sufficiently decayed? *Ib.*

When your Majesty says, 'Let a thing be done,' it's
as good as done—practically, it *is* done—because
your Majesty's will is law. *Ib.*

Twenty love-sick maidens we,
Love-sick all against our will. *Patience*, I.

When I first put this uniform on. *Ib.*

Am I alone,
And unobserved? I am! *Ib.*

If you're anxious for to shine in the high aesthetic line
as a man of culture rare. *Ib.*

You must lie upon the daisies and discourse in novel
phrases of your complicated state of mind,
The meaning doesn't matter if it's only idle chatter of
a transcendental kind.
And everyone will say,
As you walk your mystic way,
'If this young man expresses himself in terms too
deep for *me*,
Why, what a very singularly deep young man this
deep young man must be!' *Ib.*

For Art stopped short in the cultivated court of the
Empress Josephine. *Ib.*

Then a sentimental passion of a vegetable fashion
must excite your languid spleen,
An attachment à la Plato, for a bashful young potato,
or a not too French French bean!
Though the Philistines may jostle, you will rank as an
apostle in the high aesthetic band,
If you walk down Piccadilly with a poppy or a lily in
your medieval hand.
And everyone will say,
As you walk your flowery way,
'If he's content with a vegetable love which would
certainly not suit *me*,
Why, what a most particularly pure young man this
pure young man must be!' *Ib.*

Prithee, pretty maiden—prithee, tell me true. *Ib.*

Nobody I care for comes a-courting me. *Ib.*

Prithee, pretty maiden, will you marry me?
(Hey, but I'm hopeful, willow, willow, waly!)
I may say, at once, I'm a man of propertee—
Hey willow waly O!
Money, I despise it;
Many people prize it,
Hey willow waly O! *Ib.*

The pain that is all but a pleasure will change
For the pleasure that's all but pain. *Ib.*

There will be too much of me
In the coming by and by! *Ib.* II.

While this magnetic,
Peripatetic
Lover, he lived to learn,
By no endeavour
Can magnet ever
Attract a Silver Churn! *Ib.*

Sing 'Hey to you—good day to you'—
Sing 'Bah to you—ha! ha! to you'—
Sing 'Booh to you—pooh, pooh to you'. *Ib.*

He will have to be contented
With our heartfelt sympathy! *Ib.*

'High diddle diddle'
Will rank as an idyll,
If I pronounce it chaste! *Ib.*

Who's fond of his dinner
And doesn't get thinner
On bottled beer and chops. *Ib.*

Francesca di Rimini, miminy, piminy,
Je-ne-sais-quoi young man! *Ib.*

A greenery-yallery, Grosvenor Gallery,
Foot-in-the-grave young man! *Ib.*

A Sewell and Cross young man,
A Howell & James young man,
A pushing young particle—'What's the next article?'
Waterloo House young man! *Ib.*

I'm called Little Buttercup—dear Little Buttercup,
Though I could never tell why.
H.M.S. Pinafore, I.

I am the Captain of the *Pinafore*;
And a right good captain too! *Ib.*

And I'm never, never sick at sea!
     What, never?
     No, never!
     What, *never*?
     Hardly ever!
He's hardly ever sick at sea!
Then give three cheers, and one cheer more,
For the hardy Captain of the *Pinafore*!   *Ib.*

You're exceedingly polite,
And I think it only right
To return the compliment.   *Ib.*

I never use a big, big D.   *Ib.*

And so do his sisters and his cousins and his aunts!
     His sisters and his cousins,
     Whom he reckons up by dozens,
          And his aunts!   *Ib.*

When I was a lad I served a term
As office boy to an Attorney's firm.
I cleaned the windows and I swept the floor,
And I polished up the handle of the big front door.
     I polished up that handle so carefullee
     That now I am the Ruler of the Queen's Navee!
          Ib.

And I copied all the letters in a big round hand. *Ib.*

I always voted at my party's call,
And I never thought of thinking for myself at all. *Ib.*

Stick close to your desks and never go to sea,
And you all may be Rulers of the Queen's Navee! *Ib.*

His energetic fist should be ready to resist
A dictatorial word.   *Ib.*

His bosom should heave and his heart should glow,
And his fist be ever ready for a knock-down blow.
          Ib.

Things are seldom what they seem,
Skim milk masquerades as cream.   *Ib.* II.

The merry maiden and the tar.   *Ib.*

It was the cat!   *Ib.*

He is an Englishman!
     For he himself has said it,
     And it's greatly to his credit,
That he is an Englishman!   *Ib.*

For he might have been a Roosian,
A French, or Turk, or Proosian,
     Or perhaps Ital-ian!
But in spite of all temptations
To belong to other nations,
     He remains an Englishman!   *Ib.*

The other, upper crust,
A regular patrician.   *Ib.*

It is, it is a glorious thing
To be a Pirate King.   *Pirates of Penzance*, I.

The question is, had he not been
     A thing of beauty,
Would she be swayed by quite as keen
     A sense of duty?   *Ib.*

Poor wandering one!
Though thou hast surely strayed,
Take heart of grace,
Thy steps retrace,
Poor wandering one!   *Ib.*

Take heart, fair days will shine;
Take any heart, take mine!   *Ib.*

I am the very model of a modern Major-General.
          Ib.

When the foeman bares his steel,
     Tarantara, tarantara!
We uncomfortable feel,
     Tarantara.   *Ib.* II.

When constabulary duty's to be done,
The policeman's lot is not a happy one.   *Ib.*

When the enterprising burglar's not a-burgling. *Ib.*

When the coster's finished jumping on his mother—
He loves to lie a-basking in the sun.   *Ib.*

No Englishman unmoved that statement hears,
Because, with all our faults, we love our House of
     Peers.   *Ib.*

Politics we bar,
     They are not our bent;
On the whole we are
     Not intelligent.   *Princess Ida*, I.

Yet everybody says I'm such a disagreeable man!
     And I can't think why!   *Ib.* I.

To everybody's prejudice I know a thing or two;
I can tell a woman's age in half a minute—and I do!
          Ib.

Man is Nature's sole mistake!   *Ib.* II.

My natural instinct teaches me
     (And instinct is important, O!)
You're everything you ought to be,
     And nothing that you oughtn't, O!   *Ib.*

Oh, don't the days seem lank and long
When all goes right and nothing goes wrong,
And isn't your life extremely flat
With nothing whatever to grumble at!   *Ib.*

All baronets are bad.   *Ruddigore*, I.

I'll wager in their joy they kissed each other's cheek
     (Which is what them furriners do).   *Ib.*

You must stir it and stump it,
     And blow your own trumpet,
Or trust me, you haven't a chance.   *Ib.*

He combines the manners of a Marquis with the
     morals of a Methodist.   *Ib*

When he's excited he uses language that would make
     your hair curl.   *Ib.*

For duty, duty must be done;
The rule applies to everyone.   *Ib*

If a man can't forge his own will, whose will can he
     forge?   *Ib.*

For you are such a smart little craft—
Such a neat little, sweet little craft,
Such a bright little, tight little,
Slight little, light little,
Trim little, prim little craft!   *Ib.* II.

Desperate deeds of derring do.   *Ib.*

Some word that teems with hidden meaning—like
     Basingstoke.   *Ib.*

This particularly rapid, unintelligible patter
Isn't generally heard, and if it is it doesn't matter.   *Ib.*

Time was when Love and I were well acquainted.
                                        The Sorcerer, 1.

Forsaking even military men.   *Ib.*

I was a pale young curate then.   *Ib.*

Oh! My name is John Wellington Wells,
I'm a dealer in magic and spells.   *Ib.*

If anyone anything lacks,
He'll find it all ready in stacks,
      If he'll only look in
      On the resident Djinn,
Number seventy, Simmery Axe!   *Ib.*

Now for the tea of our host,
Now for the rollicking bun,
Now for the muffin and toast,
      Now for the gay Sally Lunn!   *Ib.*

So I fell in love with a rich attorney's
      Elderly ugly daughter.   *Trial by Jury.*

She may very well pass for forty-three
      In the dusk with a light behind her!   *Ib.*

And many a burglar I've restored
To his friends and his relations.   *Ib.*

For now I am a Judge,
And a good Judge too.   *Ib.*

And a good job too!   *Ib.*

Oh never, never, never, since I joined the human race,
Saw I so exquisitely fair a face.   *Ib.*

Is life a boon?
      If so, it must befall
      That Death, whene'er he call,
Must call too soon.   *The Yeomen of the Guard*, 1.

Perchance, in June!   *Ib.*

I have a song to sing O!
Sing me your song, O!   *Ib.*

It's the song of a merryman, moping mum,
Whose soul was sad, and whose glance was glum,
Who sipped no sup, and who craved no crumb,
      As he sighed for the love of a ladye.   *Ib.*

His pains were o'er, and he sighed no more,
      For he lived in the love of a ladye!   *Ib.*

The prisoner comes to meet his doom.   *Ib.*

'Tis ever thus with simple folk—an accepted wit has
but to say 'Pass the mustard', and they roar their
ribs out!   *Ib.* 11.

THOMAS GILLESPIE
1777–1844

An attitude, not only of defence, but defiance.
      The Mountain Storm. (*Wilson's Tales of the
      Borders*, No. 145.)
      'Defence not defiance' became the motto of
      the Volunteer Movement in 1859.

JAMES GILLRAY
1757–1815

Political Ravishment, or, The Old Lady of Thread-
      needle Street in Danger.   *Title of Caricature*, 1797.

CHARLOTTE PERKINS STETSON GILMAN
1860–

'I do not want to be a fly!
I want to be a worm!'
                  In This Our World. A Conservative.

WILLIAM EWART GLADSTONE
1809–1898

I am come among you unmuzzled.
      *Speech in Free Trade Hall, Manchester, Aug.
      1865.*

[The Turks] one and all, bag and baggage, shall, I
      hope, clear out from the province they have deso-
      lated and profaned.
                  Ib. in H. of C., 7 May 1877.

Out of the range of practical politics.
                  Ib. at Dalkeith, 26 Nov. 1879.

I would tell them of my own intention to keep my own
      counsel . . . and I will venture to recommend them,
      as an old Parliamentary hand, to do the same.
                  Ib. H. of C., 21 Jan. 1886.

All the world over, I will back the masses against the
      classes.   *Ib. Liverpool, 28 June 1886.*

The resources of civilization are not yet exhausted.
            Ib. Leeds, Speech at Banquet, 7 Oct. 1881.

This is the negation of God erected into a system of
      Government.
            *First Letter to the Earl of Aberdeen on the State
            prosecutions of the Neapolitan Government*, § 8,
            1851, p. 9, note.

The impregnable rock of Holy Scripture.
                  Title of Book, 1890.

Throw his mind into the common stock.
            *Phrase. G. W. Russell, Collections and Recollec-
            tions*, ch. 33.

WILLIAM HENRY, DUKE OF GLOUCESTER
1743–1805

Another damned, thick, square book! Always scribble,
      scribble, scribble! Eh! Mr. Gibbon?
            Best's Literary Memorials. (*Boswell's Johnson*,
            vol. ii, p. 2, n.)

ALFRED DENIS GODLEY
1856–1925

Blest spot! where childlike Learning sits
      Remote from worldly cares,
And leaves to skilled financiers its
      Pecuniary affairs.
            *Fifty Poems. Ode on a Distant Prospect of Oriel
            College.*

HANNAH GODWIN

Good sense without vanity, a penetrating judgement
   without a disposition to satire, good nature and
   humility, with about as much religion as my
   William likes, struck me with a wish that she was
   my William's wife.
> *Letter of 29 June 1784 (to her brother William,*
> *recommending Miss Gay).* C. Kegan Paul,
> *William Godwin,* vol. i.

WILLIAM GODWIN

The miner's dream of home.   *Title of Song.*

The log was burning brightly,
'Twas a night that should banish all sin,
For the bells were ringing the Old Year out,
And the New Year in. *The Miner's Dream of Home.*

OLIVER GOLDSMITH

1728–1774

The king himself has follow'd her,—
  When she has walk'd before.
> *Elegy on Mrs. Mary Blaize.*

The doctor found, when she was dead,—
  Her last disorder mortal.   *Ib.*

To the last moment of his breath
  On hope the wretch relies;
And e'en the pang preceding death
  Bids expectation rise.

Hope, like the gleaming taper's light,
  Adorns and cheers our way;
And still, as darker grows the night,
  Emits a brighter ray.   *The Captivity,* ii.

A night-cap decked his brows instead of bay;
A cap by night—a stocking all the day!
> *Description of an Author's Bedchamber.* In
> *Citizen of the World,* letter 30. *The Author's*
> *Club* (1760).

Sweet Auburn! loveliest village of the plain.
> *The Deserted Village,* l. 1.

Dear lovely bowers of innocence and ease.   *Ib.* l. 5.

The bashful virgin's side-long looks of love,
The matron's glance that would those looks reprove.
> *Ib.* l. 29.

Ill fares the land, to hast'ning ills a prey,
Where wealth accumulates, and men decay;
Princes and lords may flourish, or may fade;
A breath can make them, as a breath has made;
But a bold peasantry, their country's pride,
When once destroy'd, can never be supplied.
A time there was, ere England's griefs began,
When every rood of ground maintain'd its man;
For him light labour spread her wholesome store,
Just gave what life requir'd, but gave no more;
His best companions, innocence and health;
And his best riches, ignorance of wealth.   *Ib.* l. 51.

How happy he who crowns in shades like these,
A youth of labour with an age of ease.   *Ib.* l. 99.

Bends to the grave with unperceiv'd decay,
While resignation gently slopes the way;
And, all his prospects bright'ning to the last,
His heaven commences ere the world be pass'd
                      Ib. l. 109.

The watchdog's voice that bay'd the whisp'ring wind,
And the loud laugh that spoke the vacant mind.
                      Ib. l. 121.

A man he was to all the country dear,
And passing rich with forty pounds a year;
Remote from towns he ran his godly race,
Nor e'er had chang'd nor wished to change his place;
Unpractis'd he to fawn, or seek for power,
By doctrines fashion'd to the varying hour;
Far other aims his heart had learned to prize,
More skill'd to raise the wretched than to rise.
                      Ib. l. 141.

He chid their wand'rings, but reliev'd their pain.
                      Ib. l. 150.

Wept o'er his wounds, or tales of sorrow done,
Shoulder'd his crutch, and show'd how fields were
  won.   *Ib.* l. 157.

Careless their merits, or their faults to scan,
His pity gave ere charity began.
Thus to relieve the wretched was his pride,
And e'en his failings lean'd to Virtue's side.
But in his duty prompt at every call,
He watch'd and wept, he pray'd and felt, for all.
And, as a bird each fond endearment tries
To tempt its new-fledg'd offspring to the skies,
He tried each art, reprov'd each dull delay,
Allur'd to brighter worlds, and led the way.
                      Ib. l. 161.

At church, with meek and unaffected grace,
His looks adorn'd the venerable place;
Truth from his lips prevail'd with double sway,
And fools, who came to scoff, remain'd to pray.
                      Ib. l. 177.

Even children follow'd with endearing wile,
And pluck'd his gown, to share the good man's smile.
                      Ib. l. 183.

A man severe he was, and stern to view;
I knew him well, and every truant knew;
Well had the boding tremblers learn'd to trace
The day's disasters in his morning face;
Full well they laugh'd with counterfeited glee,
At all his jokes, for many a joke had he;
Full well the busy whisper, circling round,
Convey'd the dismal tidings when he frown'd;
Yet he was kind; or if severe in aught,
The love he bore to learning was in fault. *Ib.* l. 197.

In arguing too, the parson own'd his skill,
For e'en though vanquish'd, he could argue still;
While words of learned length, and thund'ring sound
Amazed the gazing rustics rang'd around,
And still they gaz'd, and still the wonder grew,
That one small head could carry all he knew.
                      Ib. l. 211.

The white-wash'd wall, the nicely sanded floor,
The varnish'd clock that click'd behind the door;
The chest contriv'd a double debt to pay,
A bed at night, a chest of drawers by day. *Ib.* l. 227.

The twelve good rules, the royal game of goose.
                      Ib. l. 232.

And, e'en while fashion's brightest arts decoy,
The heart distrusting asks, if this be joy. *Ib.* l. 263.

       How wide the limits stand
Between a splendid and a happy land. *Ib.* l. 267.

Her modest looks the cottage might adorn,
Sweet as the primrose peeps beneath the thorn.
Ib. l. 329.

In all the silent manliness of grief.   *Ib.* l. 384.

Thou source of all my bliss, and all my woe,
That found'st me poor at first, and keep'st me so.
Ib. l. 413.

The fat was so white, and the lean was so ruddy.
The Haunch of Venison, l. 4.

Turn, gentle Hermit of the dale,
 And guide my lonely way,
To where yon taper cheers the vale
 With hospitable ray.
Edwin and Angelina, or The Hermit.

Taught by the Power that pities me,
 I learn to pity them.   *Ib.*

Man wants but little here below,
 Nor wants that little long.   *Ib.*

And what is friendship but a name,
 A charm that lulls to sleep:
A shade that follows wealth or fame,
 But leaves the wretch to weep?   *Ib.*

The blossom opening to the day,
 The dews of heav'n refined,
Could nought of purity display,
 To emulate his mind.   *Ib.*

'Turn, Angelina, ever dear.'   *Ib.*

Thus let me hold thee to my heart,
 And ev'ry care resign:
And shall we never, never part,
 My life,—my all that's mine?   *Ib.*

The sigh that rends thy constant heart,
 Shall break thy Edwin's too.   *Ib.*

Brutes never meet in bloody fray,
Nor cut each others' throats, for pay.
Logicians Refuted, l. 39.

Good people all, of every sort,
 Give ear unto my song;
And if you find it wond'rous short,
 It cannot hold you long.
Elegy on the Death of a Mad Dog.

That still a godly race he ran,
 Whene'er he went to pray.   *Ib.*

The naked every day he clad,
 When he put on his clothes.   *Ib.*

And in that town a dog was found,
 As many dogs there be,
Both mongrel, puppy, whelp, and hound,
 And curs of low degree.   *Ib.*

The dog, to gain some private ends,
 Went mad and bit the man.   *Ib.*

And swore the dog had lost his wits,
 To bite so good a man.   *Ib.*

The man recover'd of the bite,
 The dog it was that died.   *Ib.*

Our Garrick's a salad; for in him we see
Oil, vinegar, sugar, and saltness agree.
Retaliation, l. 11.

Who mix'd reason with pleasure, and wisdom with
 mirth:
If he had any faults, he has left us in doubt. [Dr.
 Barnard, Dean of Derry]   *Ib.* l. 24.

Here lies our good Edmund, whose genius was such,
We scarcely can praise it, or blame it too much;
Who, born for the Universe, narrow'd his mind,
And to party gave up what was meant for mankind.
Though fraught with all learning, yet straining his
 throat
To persuade Tommy Townshend to lend him a vote;
Who, too deep for his hearers, still went on refining,
And thought of convincing, while they thought of
 dining;
Though equal to all things, for all things unfit,
Too nice for a statesman, too proud for a wit.
[Edmund Burke]   *Ib.* l. 29.

Too fond of the *right* to pursue the *expedient*.
[Edmund Burke]   *Ib.* l. 46.

His conduct still right, with his argument wrong.
[William Burke]   *Ib.* l. 46.

Here lies David Garrick, describe me, who can,
An abridgment of all that was pleasant in man.
Ib. l. 93.

As a wit, if not first, in the very first line. [Garrick]
Ib. l. 96.

On the stage he was natural, simple, affecting;
'Twas only that when he was off he was acting.
[Garrick]   *Ib.* l. 101.

He cast off his friends as a huntsman his pack,
For he knew when he pleas'd he could whistle them
 back.
Of praise a mere glutton, he swallow'd what came,
And the puff of a dunce he mistook it for fame.
[Garrick]   *Ib.* l. 107.

He was, could he help it?—a special attorney.
[Joseph Hickey]   *Ib.* l. 136.

Here Reynolds is laid, and to tell you my mind,
He has not left a better or wiser behind:
His pencil was striking, resistless, and grand;
His manners were gentle, complying, and bland;
Still born to improve us in every part,
His pencil our faces, his manners our heart. *Ib.* l. 137.

When they talk'd of their Raphaels, Correggios, and
 stuff,
He shifted his trumpet, and only took snuff.
[Reynolds]   *Ib.* l. 145.

Thou best-humour'd man with the worst-humour'd
 muse. [Whitefoord]   *Ib.* l. 174.

Let schoolmasters puzzle their brain,
 With grammar, and nonsense, and learning,
Good liquor, I stoutly maintain,
 Gives genius a better discerning.
She Stoops to Conquer, i. i, song.

Remote, unfriended, melancholy, slow,
Or by the lazy Scheldt, or wandering Po.
The Traveller, l

Where'er I roam, whatever realms to see,
My heart untravell'd fondly turns to thee;
Still to my brother turns with ceaseless pain,
And drags at each remove a lengthening cha

And learn the luxury of doing good. *Ib.* l. 22.

These little things are great to little man. *Ib.* l. 42.

Who can direct, when all pretend to know? *Ib.* l. 64.

Such is the patriot's boast, where'er we roam,
His first, best country ever is, at home. *Ib.* l. 73.

Where wealth and freedom reign, contentment fails,
And honour sinks where commerce long prevails.
Ib. l. 91.

Man seems the only growth that dwindles here.
Ib. l. 126.

But winter ling'ring chills the lap of May. *Ib.* l. 172.

At night returning, every labour sped,
He sits him down the monarch of a shed;
Smiles by his cheerful fire, and round surveys
His children's looks, that brighten at the blaze;
While his lov'd partner, boastful of her hoard,
Displays her cleanly platter on the board. *Ib.* l. 191.

They please, are pleas'd; they give to get esteem,
Till, seeming bless'd, they grow to what they seem.
Ib. l. 265.

To men of other minds my fancy flies,
Embosom'd in the deep where Holland lies.
Methinks her patient sons before me stand,
Where the broad ocean leans against the land.
Ib. l. 282.

Pride in their port, defiance in their eye,
I see the lords of human kind pass by. *Ib.* l. 327.

The land of scholars, and the nurse of arms.
Ib. l. 356.

Laws grind the poor, and rich men rule the law.
Ib. l. 386.

When lovely woman stoops to folly
And finds too late that men betray,
What charm can soothe her melancholy,
What art can wash her guilt away?
The only art her guilt to cover,
To hide her shame from every eye,
To give repentance to her lover,
And wring his bosom—is to die.
Song. From the Vicar of Wakefield, ch. 29.

For he who fights and runs away
May live to fight another day;
But he who is in battle slain
Can never rise and fight again.
Art of Poetry on a New Plan. Written by
Newbery, revised by Goldsmith.

I am resolved to write on, if it were only to spite them.
The Bee, No. 4. 27 Oct. 1759. *Miscellaneous.*

As writers become more numerous, it is natural for
readers to become more indolent.
Ib. No. 175. *Upon Unfortunate Merit.*

The volume of nature is the book of knowledge.
Citizen of the World. Letter 4.

'The Republic of Letters' is a very common expression among the Europeans. *Ib.* Letter 20.

He writes indexes to perfection. *Ib.* Letter 29.

To a philosopher no circumstance, however trifling,
is too minute. *Ib.* Letter 30.

'Did I say so?' replied he coolly; 'to be sure, if I said
so, it was so.' *Ib.* Letter 54.

Had Caesar or Cromwell exchanged countries, the one
might have been a sergeant, and the other an exciseman. *Essays*, i. *Introductory Paper.*

The true use of speech is not so much to express our
wants as to conceal them.
Ib. v. *The Use of Language.*

Bacon, that great and hardy genius.
Ib. xviii. *Travel in Asia.*

Here's to the memory of Shakespeare, Falstaff, and
all the merry men of East-cheap.
Ib. xix. *At The Boar's Head Tavern.*

I hate the French because they are all slaves, and wear
wooden shoes.
Ib. xxiv. *Distresses of a Common Soldier.*

This same philosophy is a good horse in the stable, but
an arrant jade on a journey.
The Good-Natured Man, i.

We must touch his weaknesses with a delicate hand.
There are some faults so nearly allied to excellence,
that we can scarce weed out the fault without
eradicating the virtue. *Ib.*

All his faults are such that one loves him still the
better for them. *Ib.*

I'm now no more than a mere lodger in my own
house. *Ib.*

Life at the greatest and best is but a froward child,
that must be humour'd and coax'd a little till it
falls asleep, and then all the care is over. *Ib.*

Friendship is a disinterested commerce between
equals; love, an abject intercourse between tyrants
and slaves. *Ib.*

Don't let us make imaginary evils, when you know
we have so many real ones to encounter. *Ib.*

LEONTINE:
An only son, sir, might expect more indulgence.
CROAKER:
An only father, Sir, might expect more obedience.
Ib.

I am told he makes a very handsome corpse, and becomes his coffin prodigiously. *Ib.*

Silence is become his mother tongue. *Ib.* ii.

Measures, not men, have always been my mark. *Ib.*

All men have their faults; too much modesty is his. *Ib.*

You, that are going to be married, think things can
never be done too fast; but we, that are old, and
know what we are about, must elope methodically,
madam. *Ib.*

She stoops to conquer. *Title of play.*

In my time, the follies of the town crept slowly
among us, but now they travel faster than a stage-
coach. *She Stoops to Conquer*, i.

I love every thing that's old; old friends, old times,
old manners, old books, old wines. *Ib.*

As for disappointing them I should not so much
mind; but I can't abide to disappoint myself. *Ib.*

Is it one of my well-looking days, child? Am I in
face today? *Ib.*

The very pink of perfection.   *Ib.*

In a concatenation accordingly.   *Ib.*

I'll be with you in the squeezing of a lemon.   *Ib.*

This is Liberty-Hall, gentlemen.   *Ib.* II.

We are the boys
That fears no noise
Where the thundering cannons roar.   *Ib.*

Ask me no questions, and I'll tell you no fibs.
   Ib. III.

Was there ever such a cross-grained brute?   *Ib.*

Women and music should never be dated.   *Ib.*

As for murmurs, mother, we grumble a little now and then, to be sure. But there's no love lost between us.   *Ib.* IV.

A book may be amusing with numerous errors, or it may be very dull without a single absurdity.
   The Vicar of Wakefield, advertisement.

I was ever of opinion, that the honest man who married and brought up a large family, did more service than he who continued single and only talked of population.   *Ib.* ch. 1.

All our adventures were by the fire-side, and all our migrations from the blue bed to the brown.   *Ib.*

A mutilated courtesy.   *Ib.*

The virtue which requires to be ever guarded is scarcely worth the sentinel.   *Ib.* ch. 5.

I find you want me to furnish you with argument and intellects too. No, Sir, there I protest you are too hard for me.   *Ib.* ch. 7.

'Very well,' cried I, 'that's a good girl, I find you are perfectly qualified for making converts, and so go help your mother to make the gooseberry-pie.'   *Ib.*

By the living jingo, she was all of a muck of sweat.
   Ib. ch. 9.

With other fashionable topics, such as pictures, taste, Shakespeare, and the musical glasses.   *Ib.*

Mr. Burchell . . . at the conclusion of every sentence would cry out '*Fudge!*'— an expression which displeased us all.   *Ib.* ch. 11.

Conscience is a coward, and those faults it has not strength enough to prevent it seldom has justice enough to accuse.   *Ib.* ch. 13.

It seemed to me pretty plain, that they had more of love than matrimony in them.   *Ib.* ch. 16.

As ten millions of circles can never make a square, so the united voice of myriads cannot lend the smallest foundation to falsehood.   *Ib.* ch. 27.

There is no arguing with Johnson; for when his pistol misses fire, he knocks you down with the butt end of it.
   Remark. Boswell's *Life of Johnson, 26 Oct. 1769.*

As I take my shoes from the shoemaker, and my coat from the tailor, so I take my religion from the priest.   *Ib. 9 April 1773.*

[To Johnson who was laughing when he said that the little fishes in a proposed fable should talk like little fishes.]
   Why, Dr. Johnson, this is not so easy as you seem to think; for if you were to make little fishes talk, they would talk like whales.
   Ib. 27 April 1773.

[To Boswell, for talking of Johnson as entitled to the honour of unquestionable superiority.]
   Sir, are you for making a monarchy of what should be a republic.   *Ib. 7 May 1773.*

[To Boswell, of Johnson.]
   Is he like Burke, who winds into a subject like a serpent?   *Ib. 10 May 1773.*

ADAM LINDSAY GORDON
1833–1870

Yet if man, of all the Creator plann'd,
   His noblest work is reckoned,
Of the works of His Hand, by sea or by land,
   The horse may at least rank second.
   Hippodromania, pt. 1, iii.

She was iron-sinew'd and satin-skinn'd,
   Ribb'd like a drum and limb'd like a deer,
Fierce as the fire and fleet as the wind—
   There was nothing she couldn't climb or clear.
   The Romance of Britomarte, vi.

I should live the same life over, if I had to live again;
And the chances are I go where most men go.
   The Sick Stockrider.

A little season of love and laughter,
Of light and life, and pleasure and pain,
And a horror of outer darkness after,
And dust returneth to dust again.
Then the lesser life shall be as the greater,
And the lover of life shall join the hater,
And the one thing cometh sooner or later,
And no one knoweth the loss or gain.
   The Swimmer.

The restless throbbings and burnings
   That hope unsatisfied brings,
The weary longings and yearnings
   For the mystical better things.
   Wormwood and Nightshade.

No game was ever yet worth a rap
   For a rational man to play,
Into which no accident, no mishap,
   Could possibly find its way.
   Ye Wearie Wayfarer, Fytte 4.

Yet if once we efface the joys of the chase
From the land, and outroot the Stud,
Goodbye to the Anglo-Saxon race!
   Farewell to the Norman blood.   *Ib. Fytte 7.*

Question not, but live and labour
   Till yon goal be won,
Helping every feeble neighbour,
   Seeking help from none;
Life is mostly froth and bubble,
   Two things stand like stone,
Kindness in another's trouble,
   Courage in your own.   *Ib. Fytte 8.*

EVA GORE-BOOTH

1872–1926

The little waves of Breffny go stumbling through my
  soul.   *Poems. The Little Waves of Breffny.*

GEORGE JOACHIM, FIRST VISCOUNT GOSCHEN

1831–1907

I have the courage of my opinions, but I have not the
temerity to give a political blank cheque to Lord
Salisbury.   *Speech, H. of C., 19 Feb. 1884.*

If so we shall make our wills and do our duty.
                    Speech, 14 Apr. 1886.

We have stood alone in that which is called isolation—
our splendid isolation, as one of our colonial friends
was good enough to call it. [See G. E. Foster.]
                    Speech at Lewes, 26 Feb. 1896.

EDMUND GOSSE

1849–1928

Papa, don't tell me that she's a Paedobaptist?
                    Father and Son, ch. 10.

JOHN GOWER

1325?–1408

It hath and schal ben evermor
That love is maister wher he wile.
              Confessio Amantis, prologue, l. 34.

RICHARD GRAFTON

?–1572?

Thirty days hath November,
April, June, and September,
February hath twenty-eight alone,
And all the rest have thirty-one.
    Abridgement of the Chronicles of England
(1570), introductory matter, sig. 1 ¶ j. b.

CHARLES GRAHAM

Two little girls in blue, lad,
Two little girls in blue,
They were sisters, we were brothers,
And learned to love the two.
                    Two Little Girls In Blue.

HARRY GRAHAM

1874–1936

Aunt Jane observed, the second time
  She tumbled off a bus,
The step is short from the Sublime
  To the Ridiculous.
              Ruthless Rhymes. Equanimity.

Billy, in one of his nice new sashes,
Fell in the fire and was burnt to ashes;
Now, although the room grows chilly,
I haven't the heart to poke poor Billy.
              Ib. Tender-Heartedness.

Auntie, did you feel no pain
  Falling from that apple-tree?
Would you do it, please, again?
  Cos my friend here didn't see.   *Ib. Appreciation.*

O'er the rugged mountain's brow
  Clara threw the twins she nursed,
And remarked, 'I wonder now
  Which will reach the bottom first?'
                    Ib. Calculating Clara.

Philip, foozling with his cleek,
Drove his ball through Helen's cheek;
Sad they bore her corpse away,
Seven up and six to play.   *Ib. Philip.*

'There's been an accident!' they said,
'Your servant's cut in half; he's dead!'
'Indeed!' said Mr. Jones, 'and please
Send me the half that's got my keys.' *Ib. Mr. Jones.*

ROBERT CUNNINGHAME-GRAHAM

1735–1797

If doughty deeds my lady please,
Right soon I'll mount my steed.
    If Doughty Deeds My Lady Please, or *O Tell
    Me How To Woo Thee.*

For you alone I ride the ring.   *Ib.*

JAMES GRAHAME

1765–1811

Hail, Sabbath! thee I hail, the poor man's day.
                    The Sabbath, l. 29.

What strong, mysterious links enchain the heart
To regions where the morn of life was spent!
                    Ib. l. 404.

JAMES GRAINGER

1721?–1766

What is fame? an empty bubble;
Gold? a transient, shining trouble.   *Solitude,* l. 96.

Now, Muse, let's sing of rats.
    The Sugar Cane. MS. quoted in Boswell's *Life
    of Johnson, 21 March 1776. The passage was
    not printed.*

SIR ROBERT GRANT

1779–1838

The Ancient of Days,
Pavilioned in splendour,
And girded with praise.
    *Bickersteth's Church Psalmody. O Worship the
    King.*

Frail children of dust,
And feeble as frail.   *Ib.*

ULYSSES SIMPSON GRANT
1822–1885

I know no method to secure the repeal of bad or obnoxious laws so effective as their stringent execution.   *Inaugural Address, 4 March, 1869.*

I purpose to fight it out on this line, if it takes all summer.
Dispatch to Washington, From Head-Quarters in the Field, 11 May 1864.

Let no guilty man escape, if it can be avoided. . . . No personal considerations should stand in the way of performing a public duty.
Indorsement of a Letter relating to the Whiskey Ring, 29 July 1875.

Let us have peace.
Letter of Acceptance of Nomination, 29 May 1868.

No terms except unconditional and immediate surrender can be accepted. I propose to move immediately upon your works.
Fort Donelson, 16 Feb. 1862.

GEORGE GRANVILLE, BARON LANSDOWNE
1667–1735

I'll be this abject thing no more;
Love, give me back my heart again.
Adieu l'Amour.

Who to a woman trusts his peace of mind,
Trusts a frail bark, with a tempestuous wind.
The British Enchanters, II. i.

Of all the plagues with which the world is curst,
Of every ill, a woman is the worst.   *Ib.*

Marriage the happiest bond of love might be,
If hands were only joined when hearts agree.
Ib. v. i.

Oh Love! thou bane of the most generous souls!
Thou doubtful pleasure, and thou certain pain.
Heroic Love, II. i.

'Tis the talk, and not the intrigue, that's the crime.
The She Gallants, III. i.

Cowards in scarlet pass for men of war.   *Ib. v.*

Whimsey, not reason, is the female guide.
The Vision, l. 81.

ARTHUR PERCEVAL GRAVES
1846–1931

Of priests we can offer a charmin' variety,
Far renowned for larnin' and piety.   *Father O'Flynn.*

Powerfulest preacher and tinderest teacher
And kindliest creature in ould Donegal.   *Ib.*

Checkin' the crazy ones, coaxin' onaisy ones,
Liftin' the lazy ones on wid the stick.   *Ib.*

JOHN WOODCOCK GRAVES
1795–1886

D'ye ken John Peel with his coat so gray?
D'ye ken John Peel at the break of the day?
D'ye ken John Peel when he's far far away
With his hounds and his horn in the morning?

'Twas the sound of his horn called me from my bed,
And the cry of his hounds has me oft-times led;
For Peel's view-hollo would waken the dead,
Or a fox from his lair in the morning.   *John Peel.*

ROBERT GRAVES
1895–

Goodbye to all that.   *Title of Book.*

THOMAS GRAY
1716–1771

Daughter of Jove, relentless power,
Thou tamer of the human breast,
Whose iron scourge and tort'ring hour
The bad affright, afflict the best.
Hymn to Adversity, l. 1.

What sorrow was, thou bad'st her know,
And from her own, she learn'd to melt at others' woe.
Ib. l. 15.

And leave us leisure to be good.   *Ib. l. 20.*

Ruin seize thee, ruthless King!
Confusion on thy banners wait,
Tho' fann'd by Conquest's crimson wing
They mock the air with idle state.   *The Bard, I. i.*

To arms! cried Mortimer, and couch'd his quiv'ring lance.   *Ib.*

To high-born Hoel's harp, or soft Llewellyn's lay.
Ib. I. ii.

Weave the warp, and weave the woof,
The winding-sheet of Edward's race.
Give ample room, and verge enough
The characters of hell to trace.   *Ib. II. i.*

Fair laughs the morn, and soft the zephyr blows,
While proudly riding o'er the azure realm
In gallant trim the gilded vessel goes,
Youth on the prow, and Pleasure at the helm;
Regardless of the sweeping whirlwind's sway,
That, hush'd in grim repose, expects his evening prey.   *Ib. II. ii.*

Ye towers of Julius, London's lasting shame,
With many a foul and midnight murther fed.
Ib. II. iii.

Visions of glory, spare my aching sight,
Ye unborn ages, crowd not on my soul!   *Ib. III. i.*

And Truth severe, by fairy Fiction drest.   *Ib. III. ii.*

What female heart can gold despise?
What cat's averse to fish?
Ode on the Death of a Favourite Cat.

A fav'rite has no friend!   *Ib.*

Not all that tempts your wand'ring eyes
And heedless hearts, is lawful prize;
Nor all, that glisters, gold.   *Ib.*

Now my weary lips I close;
Leave me, leave me to repose!
Descent of Odin, l. 71.

To warm their little loves the birds complain.
Sonnet on the Death of Richard West.

And weep the more because I weep in vain.   *Ib.*

The social smile, the sympathetic tear.
     Alliance of Education and Government, l. 37.

When love could teach a monarch to be wise,
And gospel-light first dawn'd from Bullen's eyes.
         Ib. l. 108.

The curfew tolls the knell of parting day,
   The lowing herd wind slowly o'er the lea,
The ploughman homeward plods his weary way,
   And leaves the world to darkness and to me.

Now fades the glimmering landscape on the sight,
   And all the air a solemn stillness holds.
Save where the beetle wheels his droning flight,
   And drowsy tinklings lull the distant folds.
     Elegy Written in a Country Churchyard, i–ii.

Save that from yonder ivy-mantled tow'r,
   The moping owl does to the moon complain.
         Ib. iii.

Each in his narrow cell for ever laid,
   The rude forefathers of the hamlet sleep.   *Ib.* iv.

The breezy call of incense-breathing Morn,
   The swallow twitt'ring from the straw-built shed,
The cock's shrill clarion, or the echoing horn,
   No more shall rouse them from their lowly bed.

For them no more the blazing hearth shall burn,
   Or busy housewife ply her evening care:
No children run to lisp their sire's return,
   Or climb his knees the envied kiss to share.
         Ib. v–vi.

Let not ambition mock their useful toil,
   Their homely joys, and destiny obscure;
Nor grandeur hear with a disdainful smile,
   The short and simple annals of the poor.

The boast of heraldry, the pomp of pow'r,
   And all that beauty, all that wealth e'er gave,
Awaits alike th' inevitable hour,
   The paths of glory lead but to the grave.
         Ib. viii–ix.

Where thro' the long-drawn aisle and fretted vault
   The pealing anthem swells the note of praise.
         Ib. x.

Can storied urn or animated bust
   Back to its mansion call the fleeting breath?
Can honour's voice provoke the silent dust,
   Or flatt'ry soothe the dull, cold ear of death?
         Ib. xi.

Hands, that the rod of empire might have sway'd,
   Or wak'd to ecstasy the living lyre.   *Ib.* xii.

But knowledge to their eyes her ample page
   Rich with the spoils of time did ne'er unroll;
Chill penury repress'd their noble rage,
   And froze the genial current of the soul.

Full many a gem of purest ray serene,
   The dark unfathom'd caves of ocean bear:
Full many a flower is born to blush unseen,
   And waste its sweetness on the desert air.

Some village-Hampden, that with dauntless breast
   The little tyrant of his fields withstood;
Some mute inglorious Milton here may rest,
   Some Cromwell guiltless of his country's blood.

Th' applause of list'ning senates to command,
   The threats of pain and ruin to despise,
To scatter plenty o'er a smiling land,
   And read their hist'ry in a nation's eyes.
         Ib. xiii–xvi.

Forbad to wade through slaughter to a throne,
   And shut the gates of mercy on mankind.
         Ib. xvii.

Far from the madding crowd's ignoble strife,
   Their sober wishes never learn'd to stray;
Along the cool sequester'd vale of life
   They kept the noiseless tenor of their way.

Yet ev'n these bones from insult to protect
   Some frail memorial still erected nigh,
With uncouth rhymes and shapeless sculpture deck'd,
   Implores the passing tribute of a sigh.
         Ib. xix–xx.

And many a holy text around she strews,
   That teach the rustic moralist to die.   *Ib.* xxi.

For who to dumb Forgetfulness a prey,
   This pleasing anxious being e'er resign'd,
Left the warm precincts of the cheerful day,
   Nor cast one longing, ling'ring look behind?

On some fond breast the parting soul relies,
   Some pious drops the closing eye requires;
Ev'n from the tomb the voice of Nature cries,
   Ev'n in our ashes live their wonted fires.
         Ib. xxii–xxiii.

Mindful of th' unhonour'd dead.   *Ib.* xxiv.

Brushing with hasty steps the dews away
   To meet the sun upon the upland lawn.   *Ib.* xxv.

His listless length at noontide would he stretch,
   And pore upon the brook that babbles by. *Ib.* xxvi.

Here rests his head upon the lap of Earth
   A youth to fortune and to fame unknown.
Fair Science frown'd not on his humble birth,
   And Melancholy mark'd him for her own.

Large was his bounty, and his soul sincere,
   Heav'n did a recompense as largely send:
He gave to Mis'ry all he had, a tear,
   He gain'd from Heav'n ('twas all he wish'd) a
     friend.

No farther seek his merits to disclose,
   Or draw his frailties from their dread abode,
(There they alike in trembling hope repose),
   The bosom of his Father and his God.
         Ib. xxx–xxxii.

Ye distant spires, ye antique towers,
   That crown the wat'ry glade.
     Ode on a Distant Prospect of Eton College, l. 1.

Urge the flying ball.   *Ib.* l. 30.

Still as they run they look behind,
They hear a voice in every wind,
   And snatch a fearful joy.   *Ib.* l. 38.

Alas, regardless of their doom,
   The little victims play!
No sense have they of ills to come,
   Nor care beyond to-day.   *Ib.* l. 51.

Ah, tell them, they are men. *Ib.* l. 60.

Grim-visag'd, comfortless Despair. *Ib.* l. 69.

Slow-consuming Age. *Ib.* l. 90.

To each his suff'rings: all are men,
  Condemn'd alike to groan;
The tender for another's pain,
  Th' unfeeling for his own.

Yet ah! why should they know their fate?
Since sorrow never comes too late,
  And happiness too swiftly flies.
Thought would destroy their paradise.
No more; where ignorance is bliss,
  'Tis folly to be wise. *Ib.* l. 91.

Iron-sleet of arrowy shower
  Hurtles in the darken'd air. *The Fatal Sisters.*

Rich windows that exclude the light,
And passages, that lead to nothing. *A Long Story*, ii.

Full oft within the spacious walls,
  When he had fifty winters o'er him,
My grave Lord-Keeper led the brawls;
  The Seal, and Maces, danc'd before him. *Ib.* iii.

Hence, avaunt, ('tis holy ground)
Comus, and his midnight-crew.
  Ode for Music, or Installation Ode, l. 1.

Servitude that hugs her chain. *Ib.* l. 6.

There sit the sainted sage, the bard divine,
The few, whom genius gave to shine
Thro' every unborn age, and undiscover'd clime.
  Ib. l. 15.

Their tears, their little triumphs o'er,
Their human passions now no more. *Ib.* l. 48.

The meanest flowret of the vale,
The simplest note that swells the gale,
The common sun, the air, and skies,
To him are opening paradise.
  Ode. On the Pleasure Arising from Vicissitude,
  l. 49.

The bloom of young desire and purple light of love.
  The Progress of Poesy, i. 3.

Nature's darling [Shakespeare]. *Ib.* iii. 1.

The dauntless child
Stretched forth his little arms, and smiled
  [Shakespeare]. *Ib.*

Or ope the sacred source of sympathetic tears. *Ib.*

Nor second he, that rode sublime
  Upon the seraph-wings of ecstasy,
  The secrets of th' abyss to spy.
He pass'd the flaming bounds of place and time:
The living throne, the sapphire-blaze,
Where angels tremble, while they gaze,
He saw; but blasted with excess of light,
Closed his eyes in endless night [*Milton*]. *Ib.* iii. 2.

Two coursers of ethereal race,
With necks in thunder clothed, and long-resounding
  pace. *Ib.*

Bright-eyed Fancy, hovering o'er,
Scatters from her pictured urn
Thoughts, that breathe, and words, that burn. *Ib.* 3.

Beyond the limits of a vulgar fate,
Beneath the good how far—but far above the great.
  Ib.

Too poor for a bribe, and too proud to importune,
He had not the method of making a fortune.
  Sketch of his own Character.

The Attic warbler pours her throat,
Responsive to the cuckoo's note.
  Ode on the Spring, l. 5.

How vain the ardour of the crowd,
How low, how little are the proud,
  How indigent the great! *Ib.* l. 18.

Contemplation's sober eye. *Ib.* l. 31.

It has been usual to catch a mouse or two (for form's
  sake) in public once a year [On refusing the
  Laureateship].
  Ib. 259, To Mason, 19 Dec. 1757.

Now as the paradisaical pleasures of the Mahometans
  consist in playing upon the flute and lying with
  Houris, be mine to read eternal new romances of
  Marivaux and Crebillon.
  Letters. 103, To West [8] Apr., [1742].

Any fool may write a most valuable book by chance,
  if he will only tell us what he heard and saw
  with veracity.
  Ib. 475, To Walpole, 25 Feb. 1768.

MATTHEW GREEN

1696–1737

I live by pulling off the hat.
  On Barclay's Apology, l. 84.

They politics like ours profess,
The greater prey upon the less. *The Grotto*, l. 69.

Fling but a stone, the giant dies.
Laugh and be well. *The Spleen*, l. 92.

Or to some coffee-house I stray,
For news, the manna of a day,
And from the hipp'd discourses gather
That politics go by the weather. *Ib.* l. 168.

Experience joined with common sense,
To mortals is a providence. *Ib.* l. 312.

Who their ill-tasted, home-brewed prayer
To the State's mellow forms prefer. *Ib.* l. 336.

By happy alchemy of mind
They turn to pleasure all they find. *Ib.* l. 610.

ALBERT GORTON GREENE

1802–1868

Old Grimes is dead! that good old man
  We never shall see more:
He used to wear a long, black coat
  All buttoned down before. *Old Grimes.*

ROBERT GREENE

1560?–1592

A noble mind disdains to hide his head,
And let his foes triumph in his overthrow.
Alphonso, King of Aragon, i.

Friar Bacon and Friar Bungay.   *Title of play*.

Hangs in the uncertain balance of proud time.
Friar Bacon and Friar Bungay, III. i.

Cupid abroad was lated in the night,
His wings were wet with ranging in the rain.
Sonnet: Cupid Abroad was Lated.

Sweet Adon, darest not glance thine eye
    N'oserez vous, mon bel ami?
Upon thy Venus that must die?
    Je vous en prie, pity me:
N'oserez vous, mon bel, mon bel,
    N'oserez vous, mon bel ami?   *Infida's Song*.

Ah! were she pitiful as she is fair,
Or but as mild as she is seeming so.
Dorastus in Praise of Fawnia. Pandosto, ed. 1694.

O glorious sun, imagine me the west!
Shine in my arms, and set thou in my breast!   *Ib*.

Love in my bosom like a bee
    Doth suck his sweet;
Now with his wings he plays with me,
    Now with his feet.
Within mine eyes he makes his nest,
His bed amid my tender breast;
My kisses are his daily feast,
And yet he robs me of my rest.
    Ah, wanton, will ye?   *Rosalind's Madrigal*.

Like to Diana in her summer weed,
Girt with a crimson robe of brightest dye,
       Goes fair Samela.
Whiter than be the flocks that straggling feed,
When washed by Arethusa's fount they lie,
       Is fair Samela.   *Samela*.

Weep not, my wanton, smile upon my knee;
When thou art old there's grief enough for thee.
    Mother's wag, pretty boy,
    Father's sorrow, father's joy.
When thy father first did see
Such a boy by him and me,
He was glad, I was woe:
Fortune changed made him so,
When he left his pretty boy,
Last his sorrow, first his joy.   *Sephestia's Song*.

The wanton smiled, father wept;
Mother cried, baby lept;
More he crowed, more we cried;
Nature could not sorrow hide.
He must go, he must kiss
Child and mother, baby bliss;
For he left his pretty boy,
Father's sorrow, father's joy.   *Ib*.

The swain did woo, she was nice,
Following fashion nayed him twice.
    The Shepherd's Ode.

Ah! what is love! It is a pretty thing,
As sweet unto a shepherd as a king,
   And sweeter too;

For kings have cares that wait upon a crown,
And cares can make the sweetest love to frown.
   Ah then, ah then,
If country loves such sweet desires do gain,
What lady would not love a shepherd swain?
       The Shepherd's Wife's Song.

For there is an upstart crow, beautified with our
feathers, that with his tiger's heart wrapped in a
player's hide, supposes he is as well able to
bumbast out a blank verse as the best of you;
and being an absolute *Iohannes fac totum*, is in
his own conceit the only Shake-scene in a country.
*The Groatsworth of Wit Bought with a Million
of Repentance*.

STEPHEN GRELLET

1773–1855

I expect to pass through this world but once; any
good thing therefore that I can do, or any kindness
that I can show to any fellow-creature, let me do it
now; let me not defer or neglect it, for I shall not
pass this way again.
*Attr. 'Treasure Trove', collected by John o'
London, 1925. Many other claimants to authorship*.

CHARLES CAVENDISH
FULKE GREVILLE

1794–1865

Knowing, as 'the man in the street' (as we call him
at Newmarket) always does, the greatest secrets of
kings, and being the confidant of their most hidden
thoughts.   *Memoirs, 22 March 1831*.

FULKE GREVILLE,
FIRST BARON BROOKE

1554–1628

More than most fair, full of that heavenly fire,
    Kindled above to show the Maker's glory;
Beauty's first-born, in whom all powers conspire
    To write the Graces' life, and Muses' story:
If in my heart all saints else be defaced,
Honour the shrine, where you alone are placed.
       Cælica, sonnet iii.

Fire and people do in this agree,
They both good servants, both ill masters be.
       Inquisition upon Fame, lxvii.

Do what you can: mine shall subsist by me:
I am the measure of Felicity.
    Mustapha. Chorus Tertius, Eternity.

Oh wearisome condition of humanity!
Born under one law, to another bound.
       Mustapha, v. iv.

Silence augmenteth grief, writing increaseth rage,
Stal'd are my thoughts, which loved and lost, the
    wonder of our age,
Yet quick'ned now with fire, though dead with frost
    ere now,
Enraged I write, I know now what: dead, quick, I
    know not how.
    Elegy on the Death of Sir Philip Sidney.

Fulke Greville, Servant to Queen Elizabeth, Councillor to King James, and Friend to Sir Philip Sidney.
> *Epitaph Written for Himself, on his Monument in Warwick.*

EDWARD, VISCOUNT GREY OF FALLODEN
1862–1933

The British Army should be a projectile to be fired by the British Navy.
> *Lord Fisher, Memories*, ch. 1.

The lamps are going out all over Europe; we shall not see them lit again in our lifetime.
> *3 Aug. 1914. Twenty-Five Years*, vol. ii, ch. 20.

GERALD GRIFFIN
1803–1840

I knew a gentle maid,
Flower of the hazel glade,—
> Eileen Aroon.   *Eileen Aroon.*

Dear were her charms to me,
Dearer her laughter free,
Dearest her constancy,—
> Eileen Aroon!   *Ib.*

NICHOLAS GRIMALD
1519–1562

Of all the heavenly gifts that mortal men commend,
What trusty treasure in the world can countervail a
    friend?   *Of Friendship.*

In working, if travail you sustain,
Into the wind shall lightly pass the pain;
But of the deed the glory shall remain,
And cause your name with worthy wights to reign.
In working wrong, if pleasure you attain,
The pleasure soon shall fade, and void as vain;
But of the deed throughout the life the shame
Endures, defacing you with foul defame.
> *Musonius the Philosopher's Saying.*

GEORGE GROSSMITH
1847–1912
and
WALTER WEEDON GROSSMITH
1854–1919

What's the good of a home if you are never in it?
> *The Diary of a Nobody*, ch. 1.

I . . . recognized her as a woman who used to work years ago for my old aunt at Clapham. It only shows how small the world is.   *Ib.* ch. 2.

'One, two, three; go! Have you an estate in Greenland?'   *Ib.* ch. 10.

'That's right.' (*Mr. Padge*)   *Ib.* ch. 11.

Without an original there can be no imitation.   *Ib.*

I left the room with silent dignity, but caught my foot in the mat.   *Ib.* ch. 12.

Tum, tum; then the band played.   *Ib.* ch. 13.

What's the matter with Gladstone? He's all right.
> *Ib.* ch. 17.

TEXAS GUINAN
1884–1933

Fifty million Frenchmen can't be wrong.
> *Attr. New York World-Telegram 21 Mar. 1931.*

DOROTHY FRANCES GURNEY
1858–1932

The kiss of the sun for pardon,
    The song of the birds for mirth,
One is nearer God's Heart in a garden
    Than anywhere else on earth.   *God's Garden.*

DOUGLAS HAIG, EARL HAIG
1861–1928

Every position must be held to the last man: there must be no retirement. With our backs to the wall, and believing in the justice of our cause, each one of us must fight on to the end.
> *Order to the British Troops, 12 Apr. 1918. The Times, 13 Apr.*

SARAH JOSEPHA HALE
1788–1879

Mary had a little lamb,
    Its fleece was white as snow,
And everywhere that Mary went
    The lamb was sure to go.

'What makes the lamb love Mary so?'
    The eager children cry.
'Oh, Mary loves the lamb, you know,'
    The teacher did reply.
> *Poems for Our Children. Mary's Little Lamb.*

THOMAS CHANDLER HALIBURTON
1796–1865

I want you to see Peel, Stanley, Graham, Shiel, Russell, Macaulay, Old Joe, and so on. These men are all upper crust here.
> *Sam Slick in England*, ch. 24.

GEORGE SAVILE, MARQUIS OF HALIFAX
1633–1695

Love is a passion that hath friends in the garrison.
> *Advice to a Daughter: Behaviour and Conversation.*

This innocent word 'Trimmer' signifies no more than
this, that if men are together in a boat, and one part
of the company would weigh it down on one side,
another would make it lean as much to the contrary.
Character of a Trimmer, preface.

He would rather die, than see a spire of English grass
trampled down by a foreign Trespasser.
Character of a Trimmer.

Men are not hanged for stealing horses, but that
horses may not be stolen.
Political Thoughts and Reflections: Of Punishment.

To the question, What shall we do to be saved in this
World? there is no other answer but this, Look to
your Moat.
A Rough Draft of a New Model at Sea.

CHARLES SPRAGUE HALL

fl. 1860

John Brown's body lies a mould'ring in the grave,
His soul is marching on!
John Brown's Body. Nicholas Smith's *Stories
of Great National Songs.*

JOSEPH HALL

1574–1656

Ah me! how seldom see we sons succeed
Their fathers' praise, in prowess and great deed. *Ib.
Satires*, bk. iv, no. 3.

All his dealings are square, and above the board.
Virtues and Vices (1608), bk. i, p. 15.

FITZ-GREENE HALLECK

1790–1867

Lord Stafford mines for coal and salt,
The Duke of Norfolk deals in malt,
  The Douglas in red herrings.   *Alnwick Castle.*

Forever, float that standard sheet!
Where breathes the foe but falls before us,
With Freedom's soil beneath our feet,
And Freedom's banner streaming o'er us?
The American Flag.
    [Attr. also to Joseph Rodman Drake, 1795–
1820.]

They love their land because it is their own,
  And scorn to give aught other reason why;
Would shake hands with a king upon his throne,
  And think it kindness to his Majesty.
Connecticut.

Green be the turf above thee,
Friend of my better days!
None knew thee but to love thee,
Nor named thee but to praise.
On the Death of J. R. Drake.

Come to the bridal-chamber, Death!
  Come to the mother's, when she feels,
For the first time, her first-born's breath.
Marco Bozzaris.

PHILIP GILBERT HAMERTON

1834–1894

The art of reading is to skip judiciously.
Intellectual Life, pt. iv, letter iv.

ALEXANDER HAMILTON

1757–1804

A national debt, if it is not excessive, will be to us a
national blessing.
Letter to Robert Morris, 30 Apr. 1781.

GAIL HAMILTON

1838–1896

The total depravity of inanimate things.   *Epigram.*

WILLIAM HAMILTON

1704–1754

Busk ye, busk ye, my bonny bonny bride,
Busk ye, busk ye, my winsome marrow.
Poetical Works. The Braes of Yarrow.

SIR WILLIAM HAMILTON

1788–1856

Truth, like a torch, the more it's shook it shines.
Discussions on Philosophy, title-page.

PERCY HAMMOND

1873–

The human knee is a joint and not an entertainment.
Mark Sullivan, *Our Times*, vol. iii, ch. 10.

RICHARD ROLLE DE HAMPOLE

1290?–1349

When Adam dalfe and Eve spane
So spire if thou may spede,
Whare was than the pride of man,
That nowe merres his mede?
Religious Pieces in Prose and Verse, vii. *Early
English Text Society, Original Series*, No. 26.
An altered form was used by John Ball (*d.*
1381) as the text of his revolutionary sermon
on the outbreak of the Peasants' Revolt, 1381:
When Adam delved and Eve span,
Who was then the gentleman?

JOHN HANCOCK

1737–1793

There, I guess King George will be able to read that.
Remark on signing the Declaration of Independence, 4 July 1776.

MINNY MAUD HANFF

fl. 1900

Since then they called him Sunny Jim.
Sunny Jim. [Advertisement for Force, a breakfast food.]

KATHERINE HANKEY

1834–1911

Tell me the old, old story,
Of unseen things above.
The Story Wanted. Tell Me the Old, Old Story.

PHILIP YORKE,
EARL OF HARDWICKE

1690–1764

His doubts are better than most people's certainties.
[Referring to the book *Dirleton's Doubts.*]
Boswell's *Johnson* (1934), iii, p. 205.

THOMAS HARDY

1840–1928

'He was a man who used to notice such things.'
Afterwards.

Some nocturnal blackness, mothy and warm,
When the hedgehog travels furtively over the lawn.
Ib.

As the hope-hour stroked its sum.
A Broken Appointment.

Twin halves of one august event.
Convergence of the Twain.

A dear dark-eyed gentleman.
The Dark-Eyed Gentleman.

And he came and he tied up my garter for me.   *Ib.*

An aged thrush, frail, gaunt, and small,
In blast-beruffled plume.   *The Darkling Thrush.*

So little cause for carolings
   Of such ecstatic sound
Was written on terrestrial things
   Afar or nigh around,
That I could think there trembled through
   His happy good-night air
Some blessed Hope, whereof he knew
   And I was unaware.   *Ib.*

Patriotism, grown Godlike.   *Departure.*

And foreign constellations west
Each night above his mound.   *Drummer Hodge.*

What of the Immanent Will and its designs?—
It works unconsciously as heretofore,
Eternal artistries in Circumstance.
The Dynasts, pt. i. *Fore-Scene.*

            Like a knitter drowsed,
Whose fingers play in skilled unmindfulness,
The Will has woven with an absent heed
Since life first was; and ever so will weave.   *Ib.*

The nether sky opens, and Europe is disclosed as a prone and emaciated figure, the Alps shaping like a backbone, and the branching mountain-chains like ribs, the peninsular plateau of Spain forming a head. Broad and lengthy lowlands stretch from the north of France across Russia like a grey-green garment hemmed by the Ural mountains and the glistening Arctic Ocean.

The point of view then sinks downwards through space, and draws near to the surface of the perturbed countries, where the peoples, distressed by events which they did not cause, are seen writhing, crawling, heaving, and vibrating in their various cities and nationalities.
Ib. Stage Direction.

A local cult called Christianity.   *Ib.* i. vi.

My argument is that War makes rattling good history; but Peace is poor reading.   *Ib.* ii. v.

But O, the intolerable antilogy
Of making figments feel!   *Ib.* iv. vi.

Each captain, petty officer, and man
Is only at his post when under fire.   (*Villeneuve*)
Ib. v. i.

The all-urging Will, raptly magnipotent.   *Ib.* vi. viii.

But—a stirring thrills the air
Like to sounds of joyance there
      That the rages
      Of the ages
Shall be cancelled, and deliverance offered from the
   darts that were,
Consciousness the Will informing, till It fashion all
   things fair!
Ib. pt. iii, last lines.

The selfsame bloody mode.   *Embarcation.*

William Dewy, Tranter Reuben, Farmer Ledlow late
   at plough,
Robert's kin, and John's, and Ned's,
And the Squire, and Lady Susan, lie in Mellstock
   churchyard now!   *Friends Beyond.*

Mothy curfew-tide.   *Ib.*

A lone cave's stillicide.   *Ib.*

If ye break my best blue china, children, I shan't care
or ho.   *Ib.*

And shakes this fragile frame at eve
With throbbings of noontide.   *I Look Into My Glass.*

If way to the Better there be, it exacts a full look at the
worst.   *In Tenebris.*

Only a man harrowing clods
   In a slow silent walk
With an old horse that stumbles and nods
   Half asleep as they stalk.

Only thin smoke without flame
   From the heaps of couch grass;
Yet this will go onward the same
   Though Dynasties pass.

Yonder a maid and her wight
   Come whispering by:
War's annals will cloud into night
   Ere their story die.
In Time of 'The Breaking of Nations'.

That long drip of human tears.
> *On an Invitation to the United States.*

Let me enjoy the earth no less
Because the all-enacting Might
That fashioned forth its loveliness
Had other aims than my delight.
> *Let Me Enjoy the Earth.*

Here's not a modest maiden elf
But dreads the final Trumpet,
Lest half of her should rise herself,
And half some sturdy strumpet!
> *The Levelled Churchyard.*

What of the faith and fire within us
Men who march away
Ere the barn-cocks say
Night is growing gray?
> *Men Who March Away.*

Your face, and the God-curst sun, and a tree,
And a pond edged with grayish leaves.
> *Neutral Tones.*

And both of us, scorning parochial ways,
Had lived like the wives in the patriarchs' days.
> *Over the Coffin.*

Christmas Eve, and twelve of the clock.
'Now they are all on their knees,'
An elder said as we sat in a flock
By the embers in hearthside ease.   *The Oxen.*

So fair a fancy few would weave
In these years!   *Ib.*

I should go with him in the gloom,
Hoping it might be so.   *Ib.*

Read that moderate man Voltaire.
> *The Respectable Burgher.*

I have lived with Shades so long.
> *Retrospect: I Have Lived with Shades.*

Love is lame at fifty years.   *The Revisitation.*

A little ball of feather and bone.   *Shelley's Skylark.*

Patiently adjust, amend, and heal.
> *The Sleep-Worker.*

And the spirits of those who were homing
Passed on, rushingly,
Like the Pentecost Wind.   *Souls of the Slain.*

This is the weather the cuckoo likes,
And so do I.   *Weathers.*

And maids come forth sprig-muslin drest.   *Ib.*

This is the weather the shepherd shuns,
And so do I.   *Ib.*

Rooks in families homeward go.   *Ib.*

When I set out for Lyonnesse,
A hundred miles away.
> *When I Set Out for Lyonnesse.*

When I came back from Lyonnesse
With magic in my eyes.   *Ib.*

Goodbye is not worth while.   *Without Ceremony.*

'Life offers—to deny!'   *Yellham-Wood's Story.*

The kingly brilliance of Sirius pierced the eye with
a steely glitter, the star called Capella was yellow,
Aldebaran and Betelgueux shone with a fiery red.
To persons standing alone on a hill during a clear
midnight such as this, the roll of the world eastward is almost a palpable movement.
> *Far From the Madding Crowd*, ch. 2.

A nice unparticular man.   *Ib.* ch. 8.

We ought to feel deep cheerfulness that a happy
Providence kept it from being any worse.   *Ib*

'Ah! stirring times we live in—stirring times.'
> *Ib.* ch. 15.

Five decades hardly modified the cut of a gaiter,
the embroidery of a smock-frock, by the breadth
of a hair. Ten generations failed to alter the turn
of a single phrase. In these Wessex nooks the
busy outsider's ancient times are only old; his
old times are still new; his present is futurity.
> *Ib.* ch. 22.

'And the people of Bath', continued Cain, 'never
need to light their fires except as a luxury, for
the water springs up out of the earth ready boiled
for use.' ''Tis true as the light', testified Matthew
Moon. 'I've heard other navigators say the same
thing.'   *Ib.* ch. 33.

All that's the matter with me is the affliction called a
multiplying eye.   *Ib.* ch. 42.

Ethelberta breathed a sort of exclamation, not right
out, but stealthily, like a parson's damn.
> *The Hand of Ethelberta.*

'Done because we are too menny.'
> *Jude the Obscure*, pt. vi, ch. 2.

Life's Little Ironies.   *Title.*

'Well, poor soul; she's helpless to hinder that or
anything now', answered Mother Cuxsom. 'And
all her shining keys will be took from her, and
her cupboards opened, and things a' didn't wish
seen, anybody will see; and her little wishes and
ways will all be as nothing.'
> *The Mayor of Casterbridge*, ch. 18.

Dialect words—those terrible marks of the beast to
the truly genteel.   *Ib.* ch. 20.

Michael Henchard's Will.
That Elizabeth-Jane Farfrae be not told of my death,
or made to grieve on account of me.
& that I be not buried in consecrated ground.
& that no sexton be asked to toll the bell.
& that nobody is wished to see my dead body.
& that no murners walk behind me at my funeral.
& that no flours be planted on my grave.
& that no man remember me.
To this I put my name.   *Ib.* ch. 45.

The heaven being spread with this pallid screen and
the earth with the darkest vegetation, their meeting-
line at the horizon was clearly marked. In such
contrast the heath wore the appearance of an
instalment of night which had taken up its place
before its astronomical hour was come: darkness
had to a great extent arrived hereon, while day
stood distinct in the sky.
> *The Return of the Native*, ch. 1.

In fact, precisely at this transitional point of its
nightly roll into darkness the great and particular
glory of the Egdon waste began, and nobody
could be said to understand the heath who had
not been there at such a time.   *Ib.*

The great inviolate place had an ancient permanence which the sea cannot claim. Who can say of a particular sea that it is old? Distilled by the sun, kneaded by the moon, it is renewed in a year, in a day, or in an hour. The sea changed, the fields changed, the rivers, the villages, and the people changed, yet Egdon remained.   *Ib.*

A little one-eyed, blinking sort o' place.
Tess of the D'Urbervilles, ch. 1.

Always washing, and never getting finished.
Ib. ch. 4.

The New Testament was less a Christiad than a Pauliad to his intelligence.   *Ib.* ch. 25.

The President of the Immortals (in Æschylean phrase) had ended his sport with Tess. *Ib.* ch. 59.

The courses of the *Victory* were absorbed into the main, then her topsails went, and then her top-gallants. She was now no more than a dead fly's wing on a sheet of spider's web; and even this fragment diminished. Anne could hardly bear to see the end, and yet she resolved not to flinch. The admiral's flag sank behind the watery line, and in a minute the very truck of the last main-mast stole away. The *Victory* was gone.
The Trumpet Major, ch. 34.

'Good, but not religious-good.'
Under the Greenwood Tree, ch. 2.

'Silent? Ah, he is silent! He can keep silence well. That man's silence is wonderful to listen to.'
Ib. ch. 14.

'You was a good man, and did good things.'
The Woodlanders, ch. 48.

JULIUS CHARLES HARE
1795–1855
and
AUGUSTUS WILLIAM HARE
1792–1834

Man without religion is the creature of circumstances.
Guesses at Truth, Series 1.

The ancients dreaded death: the Christian can only fear dying.   *Ib.*

Half the failures in life arise from pulling in one's horse as he is leaping.   *Ib.*

Purity is the feminine, Truth the masculine, of Honour.   *Ib.*

Every Irishman, the saying goes, has a potato in his head.   *Ib.*

Everybody has his own theatre, in which he is manager, actor, prompter, playwright, sceneshifter, boxkeeper, doorkeeper, all in one, and audience into the bargain.   *Ib.* Series 2.

JOHN HARINGTON
1561–1612

When I make a feast,
I would my guests should praise it, not the cooks.
Epigrams, bk. i, No. 5. *Against Writers that Carp at Other Men's Books.*

Treason doth never prosper: what's the reason?
For if it prosper, none dare call it treason.
Ib. bk. iv, No. 5. *Of Treason.*

WILLIAM WALLACE HARNEY
1831–1912

On the road, the lonely road,
Under the cold, white moon;
Under the rugged trees he strode,
Whistled and shifted his heavy load—
Whistled a foolish tune.   *The Stab.*

ROBERT GOODLOE HARPER
1765–1825

Millions for defence but not a cent for tribute.
Toast at the dinner given by Congress at Phila-delphia, 18 June 1798. (Claypoole's *American Daily Advertiser*, 20 June 1798. A. J. Beveridge's *Life of John Marshall*, vol. ii.)

CHARLES K. HARRIS
1865–1930

After the ball is over.   *After the Ball.*

Somewhere the sun is shining.   *Somewhere.*

CLIFFORD HARRIS

You called me Baby Doll a year ago. *A Broken Doll.*

You left behind a broken doll.   *Ib.*

JOEL CHANDLER HARRIS
1848–1908

'Law, Brer Tarrypin!' sez Brer Fox, sezee, 'you ain't see no trouble yit. Ef you wanter see sho' nuff trouble, you des oughter go 'longer me; I'm de man w'at kin show you trouble,' sezee.
Nights with Uncle Remus, ch. 17.

W'en folks git ole en strucken wid de palsy, dey mus' speck ter be laff'd at.   *Ib.* ch. 23.

Hit look lak sparrer-grass, hit feel like sparrer-grass, hit tas'e lak sparrer-grass, en I bless ef 'taint sparrer-grass.   *Ib.* ch. 27.

All by my own-alone self.   *Ib.* ch. 36.

No 'pollygy aint gwine ter make h'ar come back whar de b'iling water hit.   *Ib.* ch. 45.

We er sorter po'ly, Sis Tempy, I'm 'blige ter you. You know w'at de jay-bird say ter der squinch-owll 'I'm sickly but sassy.'   *Ib.* ch. 50.

A contrapshun what he call a Tar-Baby.
Uncle Remus. Legends of the Old Plantation, ch. 2. *Tar-Baby Story.*

Tar-baby ain't sayin' nuthin', en Brer Fox, he lay low.
Ib.

Bred en bawn in a brier-patch!   *Ib.* ch. 4.

Lounjun 'roun' en suffer'n'.   *Ib.* ch. 12.

Ole man Know-All died las' year.
Ib. ch. 34. *Plantation Proverbs.*

Licker talks mighty loud w'en it git loose fum de jug.
Ib.

Hongry rooster don't cackle w'en he fine a wum. *Ib.*

Youk'n hide de fier, but w'at you gwine do wid de
smoke? *Ib.*

Oh, whar shill we go w'en de great day comes,
Wid de blowin' er de trumpits en de bangin' er de
drums?
How many po' sinners'll be kotched out late
En find no latch ter de golden gate?
Uncle Remus. His Songs, i.

FRANCIS BRETT HART
or BRET HARTE
1836–1902

'Put Watts into 'em—Boys, give 'em Watts!'
Coldwell of Springfield.

You see this yer Dow
Hed the worst kind of luck;
He slipped up somehow
On each thing thet he struck.
Why, ef he'd a straddled that fence-rail, the derned
thing 'ed get up an buck. *Dow's Flat.*

Thar ain't no sense
In gittin' riled! *Jim.*

Never a tear bedims the eye
That time and patience will not dry;
Never a lip is curved with pain
That can't be kissed into smiles again.
The Lost Galleon.

Over the trackless past, somewhere,
 Lie the lost days of our tropic youth,
Only regained by faith and prayer,
Only recalled by prayer and plaint:
Each lost day has its patron saint! *Ib.*

For there be women fair as she,
Whose verbs and nouns do more agree.
Mrs. Judge Jenkins.

If, of all words of tongue and pen,
The saddest are, 'It might have been,'
More sad are these we daily see:
'It is, but hadn't ought to be!' *Ib.*

Which I wish to remark,
And my language is plain,
That for ways that are dark
And for tricks that are vain,
The heathen Chinee is peculiar,
Which the same I would rise to explain.
Plain Language from Truthful James.

But his smile it was pensive and childlike. *Ib.*

But he smiled as he sat by the table,
With the smile that was childlike and bland. *Ib.*

And the same with intent to deceive. *Ib.*

We are ruined by Chinese cheap labour. *Ib.*

And we found on his nails, which were taper,
What is frequent in tapers—that's wax. *Ib.*

He wore, I think, a chasuble, the day when first we
met. *The Ritualist.*

I reside at Table Mountain, and my name is Truthful
James. *The Society upon the Stanislaus.*

And he smiled a kind of sickly smile, and curled up
on the floor,
And the subsequent proceedings interested him no
more. *Ib.*

With unpronounceable awful names.
The Tale of a Pony.

CHRISTOPHER HARVEY
1597–1663
My mind's my kingdom.
Schola Cordis, Ode iv, st. v.

GABRIEL HARVEY
1545?–1630
Now sick, as a dog.
Letters, &c., Works (1884), vol. i, p. 161.

WILLIAM HAUGHTON
fl 1598
As fit as a fiddle. *English-Men for My Money,* iv. i.

STEPHEN HAWES
fl. 1502–1521
When the lytle byrdes swetely dyd syng
Laudes to their maker early in the mornyng.
Passetyme of Pleasure, cap. 33, xxxiii.

For though the day be never so longe,
At last the belles ringeth to evensonge. *Ib.* cap. 42.

ROBERT STEPHEN HAWKER
1803–1875
And have they fixed the where and when?
 And shall Trelawny die?
Here's twenty thousand Cornish men
 Will know the reason why!
Song of the Western Men. The last three lines
have existed since the imprisonment by James
II, 1688, of the seven Bishops, including
Trelawny, Bishop of Bristol.

ANTHONY HOPE HAWKINS
See ANTHONY HOPE.

ALICE HAWTHORNE
Contemp.
What is home without a mother? *Title of Song.*

NATHANIEL HAWTHORNE
1804–1864
Dr. Johnson's morality was as English an article as a
beefsteak. *Our Old Home. Lichfield and Uttoxeter.*

LORD CHARLES HAY

?–1760

Gentlemen of the French Guard, fire first! [Messieurs les gardes françaises, tirez.]
Battle of Fontenoy, 1745. E. Fournier, *L'Esprit dans l'Histoire* (1883), ch. 52, p. 349.

JOHN HAY

1838–1905

He never flunked, and he never lied,—
I reckon he never knowed how.　　*Jim Bludso.*

And I think that saving a little child,
　　And fotching him to his own,
Is a derned sight better business
　　Than loafing around The Throne.
Little Breeches, vii.

WILLIAM HAZLITT

1778–1830

His sayings are generally like women's letters; all the pith is in the postscript. [Chas. Lamb.]
Conversations of Northcote. Boswell Redivivus.

The only specimen of Burke is, *all that he wrote.*
English Literature, ch. ix. *Character of Mr. Burke.*

He writes as fast as they can read, and he does not write himself down. *Ib. ch. xiv. Sir Walter Scott.*

His worst is better than any other person's best. *Ib.*

His works (taken together) are almost like a new edition of human nature. This is indeed to be an author! *Ib.*

The round-faced man in black entered, and dissipated all doubts on the subject, by beginning to talk. He did not cease while he stayed; nor has he since, that I know of. [Coleridge.]
Ib. ch. xvii. My First Acquaintance with Poets.

'For those two hours,' he [Coleridge] afterwards was pleased to say, 'he was conversing with W. H.'s forehead!' *Ib.*

He [Coleridge] lamented that Wordsworth was not prone enough to belief in the traditional superstitions of the place, and that there was a something corporeal, a *matter-of-fact-ness*, a clinging to the palpable, or often to the petty, in his poetry, in consequence. *Ib.*

At Godwin's . . . they [Lamb, Holcroft, and Coleridge] were disputing fiercely which was the best— Man as he was, or man as he is to be. 'Give me,' says Lamb, 'man as he is *not* to be.' This saying was the beginning of a friendship between us, which I believe still continues. *Ib.*

The temple of fame stands upon the grave: the flame that burns upon its altars is kindled from the ashes of great men.
Lectures on the English Poets. Lecture viii, *On the Living Poets.*

He [Coleridge] talked on for ever; and you wished him to talk on for ever. *Ib.*

The dupe of friendship, and the fool of love; have I not reason to hate and to despise myself? Indeed I do; and chiefly for not having hated and despised the world enough.
The Plain Speaker. On the Pleasure of Hating.

The love of liberty is the love of others; the love of power is the love of ourselves.
Political Essays. The Times Newspaper.

Those who make their dress a principal part of themselves, will, in general, become of no more value than their dress.
Ib. On the Clerical Character.

There is nothing good to be had in the country, or, if there is, they will not let you have it.
Ib. 1817. Observations on Mr. Wordsworth's Excursion.

The art of pleasing consists in being pleased.
Round Table, vol. i. *On Manner.*

The greatest offence against virtue is to speak ill of it.
Sketches and Essays. On Cant and Hypocrisy.

The most fluent talkers or most plausible reasoners are not always the justest thinkers.
Ib. On Prejudice.

We never do anything well till we cease to think about the manner of doing it. *Ib.*

There is an unseemly exposure of the mind, as well as of the body. *Ib. On Disagreeable People.*

A nickname is the heaviest stone that the devil can throw at a man. *Ib. Nicknames.*

Rules and models destroy genius and art.
Ib. On Taste.

But of all footmen the lowest class is *literary footmen.*
Ib. Footmen.

His [Leigh Hunt's] light, agreeable, polished style . . . hits off the faded graces of 'an Adonis of fifty'.
The Spirit of the Age: Mr. Leigh Hunt.

Cavanagh's blows were not undecided and ineffectual —lumbering like Mr. Wordsworth's epic poetry, nor wavering like Mr. Coleridge's lyric prose, nor short of the mark like Mr. Brougham's speeches, nor wide of it like Mr. Canning's wit, nor foul like the *Quarterly,* nor *let* balls like the *Edinburgh Review.* Cobbett and Junius together would have made a Cavanagh.
Table Talk, vii. *The Indian Jugglers.*

When I am in the country I wish to vegetate like the country. *Ib. xix. On Going a Journey.*

Give me the clear blue sky over my head, and the green turf beneath my feet, a winding road before me, and a three hours' march to dinner—and then to thinking! It is hard if I cannot start some game on these lone heaths. *Ib.*

The English (it must be owned) are rather a foul-mouthed nation. *Ib. xxii. On Criticism.*

We can scarcely hate any one that we know. *Ib.*

Venerate art as art.   *Ib.* xxx.

So have I loitered my life away, reading books, looking at pictures, going to plays, hearing, thinking, writing on what pleased me best. I have wanted only one thing to make me happy, but wanting that have wanted everything.
Winterslow. My First Acquaintance with Poets.

Well, I've had a happy life.
Last words. W. C. Hazlitt's *Memoirs of William Hazlitt,* 1867.

REGINALD HEBER
1783–1826

Brightest and best of the sons of the morning!
Dawn on our darkness and lend us Thine aid!
Hymns, &c. Brightest and Best.

By cool Siloam's shady rill
How sweet the lily grows!   *Ib. By Cool Siloam's.*

From Greenland's icy mountains,
From India's coral strand,
Where Afric's sunny fountains
Roll down the golden sand.
Ib. From Greenland's Icy Mountains.

What though the spicy breezes
Blow soft o'er Ceylon's isle;
Though every prospect pleases,
And only man is vile:
In vain with lavish kindness
The gifts of God are strown;
The heathen in his blindness
Bows down to wood and stone.
[This is the most familiar version. Bishop Heber originally wrote 'The savage in his blindness'. He altered this, and also altered 'Ceylon's' to 'Java's'.]   *Ib.*

Holy, Holy, Holy! Lord God Almighty!
Early in the morning our song shall rise to Thee:
Holy, Holy, Holy! Merciful and Mighty!
God in Three Persons, Blessed Trinity!

Holy, Holy, Holy! all the Saints adore Thee,
Casting down their golden crowns around the glassy
     sea.   *Ib. Holy, Holy, Holy!*

The Son of God goes forth to war,
A Kingly crown to gain;
His blood-red banner streams afar:—
Who follows in His train?
Ib. The Son of God Goes Forth.

A noble army, men and boys,
The matron and the maid,
Around the Saviour's throne rejoice
In robes of light array'd.   *Ib.*

They climb'd the steep ascent of Heav'n
Through peril, toil and pain;
O God, to us may grace be given
To follow in their train.   *Ib.*

ARTHUR HELPS
1813–1875

Somebody, I suppose, was excusing something on the score of temper, to which the bishop replied, 'Temper is nine-tenths of Christianity.'
Friends in Council, bk. i, ch. 8.

Reading is sometimes an ingenious device for avoiding thought.   *Ib.* bk. ii, ch. 1.

What a blessing this smoking is! perhaps the greatest that we owe to the discovery of America.
Ib. Series II, 1859, vol. i, ch. 1, *Worry.*

There is one statesman of the present day, of whom I always say that he would have escaped making the blunders that he has made if he had only ridden more in omnibuses.
Ib. vol. ii, ch. 9, *On Government.*

FELICIA DOROTHEA HEMANS
1793–1835

I hear thee speak of the better land,
Thou call'st its children a happy band;
Mother! oh, where is that radiant shore?
Shall we not seek it, and weep no more?
The Better Land.

Not there, not there, my child!   *Ib.*

The boy stood on the burning deck
Whence all but he had fled;
The flame that lit the battle's wreck
Shone round him o'er the dead.   *Casabianca.*

There came a burst of thunder sound—
The boy—oh! where was he?   *Ib.*

But the noblest thing which perish'd there
Was that young faithful heart!   *Ib.*

Oh! call my brother back to me!
I cannot play alone;
The summer comes with flower and bee—
Where is my brother gone?
The Child's First Grief.

Calm on the bosom of thy God,
Young spirit! rest thee now!
Even while with us thy footstep trod,
His seal was on thy brow.   *A Dirge.*

Go, stranger! track the deep,
Free, free the white sail spread!
Wave may not foam, nor wild wind sweep,
Where rest not England's dead.
England's Dead.

They grew in beauty, side by side,
They fill'd one home with glee;—
Their graves are sever'd, far and wide,
By mount, and stream, and sea.
The Graves of a Household.

One sleeps where Southern vines are drest
Above the noble slain;
He wrapt his colours round his breast
On a blood-red field of Spain.   *Ib.*

She faded 'midst Italian flowers—
The last of that bright band.   *Ib.*

He Never Smiled Again!   *Title.*

The stately homes of England,
How beautiful they stand!
Amidst their tall ancestral trees,
O'er all the pleasant land.
The Homes of England.

The cottage homes of England!
  By thousands on her plains.   *Ib.*

Leaves have their time to fall,
And flowers to wither at the north wind's breath,
  And stars to set—but all,
Thou hast *all* seasons for thine own, O Death!
                          The Hour of Death.

It is written on the rose,
In its glory's full array—
Read what those buds disclose—
'Passing away.'   *Passing Away.*

Home of the Arts! where glory's faded smile
Sheds lingering light o'er many a mouldering pile.
          Restoration of the Works of Art to Italy.

In the busy haunts of men.
          Tale of the Secret Tribunal, pt. i, l. 203.

WILLIAM ERNEST HENLEY
1849–1903

Out of the night that covers me,
Black as the Pit from pole to pole,
I thank whatever gods may be
For my unconquerable soul.

In the fell clutch of circumstance,
I have not winced nor cried aloud:
Under the bludgeonings of chance
My head is bloody, but unbowed.
      Echoes, iv. *Invictus. In Mem. R. T. H. B.*

It matters not how strait the gate,
How charged with punishments the scroll,
I am the master of my fate:
I am the captain of my soul.   *Ib.*

The friendly and comforting breast
Of the old nurse, Death.   *Ib.* xxix. *To R. L. S.*

A late lark twitters from the quiet skies.
          Ib. xxxv. *Margaritæ Sororis.*

Night with her train of stars
And her great gift of sleep.   *Ib.*

So be my passing!
My task accomplished and the long day done,
My wages taken, and in my heart
Some late lark singing,
Let me be gathered to the quiet west,
The sundown splendid and serene,
Death.   *Ib.*

I was a King in Babylon
And you were a Christian Slave.
                      Ib. xxxvii. *To W. A.*

What have I done for you,
  England, my England?
What is there I would not do,
  England, my own?
          For England's Sake, iii. *Pro Rege Nostro.*

Ever the faith endures,
  England, my England:—
'Take and break us: we are yours,
  England, my own!
Life is good, and joy runs high
Between English earth and sky;
Death is death; but we shall die
  To the Song on your bugles blown, England.' *Ib.*

A poor old tramp explains his poor old ulcers.
Life is (I think) a blunder and a shame.
                    In Hospital, ii. *Waiting.*

    Far in the stillness a cat
Languishes loudly.   *Ib.* vii. *Vigil.*

Much is she worth, and even more is made of her.
              Ib. viii. *Staff-Nurse: Old Style.*

Valiant in velvet, light in ragged luck,
Most vain, most generous, sternly critical,
Buffoon and poet, lover and sensualist:
A deal of Ariel, just a streak of Puck,
Much Antony, Hamlet most of all,
And something of the Shorter-Catechist. [Stevenson]
              Ib. xxv. *Apparition.*

Gulls in an aery morrice.   *Rhymes and Rhythms*, xi.

MATTHEW HENRY
1662–1714

Many a dangerous temptation comes to us in gay,
  fine colours, that are but skin-deep.
              Commentaries, Genesis, III. i.

The better day, the worse deed.   *Ib.* vi.

To their own second and sober thoughts.
                    Ib. Job VI. xxix.

He rolls it under his tongue as a sweet morsel.
                    Ib. Ps. XXXVI, ii.

They that die by famine die by inches.
                    Ib. Ps. LIX, xv.

Men of polite learning and a liberal education.
                    Ib. Acts X. i.

There are shallows in them in which a lamb may wade
  . . . and there are depths in which an elephant may
  swim.
      *Exposition of the Poetical Books of the O.T.,
      Solomon's Song*, Introductory observation.

O. HENRY (WILLIAM SYDNEY PORTER)
1862–1910

Life is made up of sobs, sniffles, and smiles, with
  sniffles predominating.   *Gifts of the Magi.*

Turn up the lights, I don't want to go home in the
  dark.
      Last words, quoting popular song. C. A. Smith's
      O. Henry, ch. 9.

PATRICK HENRY
1736–1799

Cæsar had his Brutus—Charles the First, his Cromwell—and George the Third—('Treason,' cried
  the Speaker) . . . *may profit by their example.* If *this*
  be treason, make the most of it.
      Speech in the Virginia Convention, 1765. W.
      Wirt's *Patrick Henry* (1818), p. 65.

I am not a Virginian, but an American.
                    Ib. Sept. *1774.*

I know not what course others may take; but as for
me, give me liberty, or give me death!
> *Ib. 23 Mar. 1775.* W. Wirt's, *Patrick Henry*
> (1818), p. 123.

PHILIP HENRY
1631–1696

They are not amissi, but præmissi.
[Not lost, but gone before.]
> Matthew Henry, *Life of Philip Henry*, ch. 5,
> ed. 1825, p. 111.

ALAN PATRICK HERBERT
1890–

Don't let's go to the dogs tonight,
For mother will be there.
> *Don't Let's Go to the Dogs.*

Don't tell my mother I'm living in sin,
  Don't let the old folks know:
Don't tell my twin that I breakfast on gin,
  He'd never survive the blow.
> *Don't Tell My Mother.*

It may be life, but ain't it slow?   *It May Be Life.*

I wouldn't be too ladylike in love if I were you.
> *I Wouldn't Be Too Ladylike.*

Let's stop somebody from doing something!
> Everybody does too much. *Let's Stop Somebody.*

Let's find out what everyone is doing,
  And then stop everyone from doing it.   *Ib.*

As my poor father used to say
  In 1863,
Once people start on all this Art
  Good-bye, moralitee!
And what my father used to say
  Is good enough for me.
> *Lines for a Worthy Person.*

This high official, all allow,
Is grossly overpaid.
There wasn't any Board; and now
There isn't any trade.
> *On the President of the Board of Trade.*

  Saturday night!
  Saturday night!
I want to make Hammersmith hum.
> *Saturday Night.*

  Harriet, Hi!
  Light of my eye!
Come to the pictures and have a good cry,
For it's jolly old Saturday,
Mad-as-a-hatter-day,
Nothing-much-matter-day-night!   *Ib.*

Well, fancy giving money to the Government!
  Might as well have put it down the drain.
Fancy giving money to the Government!
  Nobody will see the stuff again.
Well, they've no idea what money's for—
  Ten to one they'll start another war.
I've heard a lot of silly things, but, Lor'!
  Fancy giving money to the Government!
> *Too Much!*

EDWARD HERBERT, BARON
HERBERT OF CHERBURY
1583–1648

Now that the April of your youth adorns
  The garden of your face.
> *Poems. Ditty: Now That the April.*

GEORGE HERBERT
1593–1633

He shoots higher that threatens the moon than he
  that aims at a tree.
> *A Priest to the Temple, To the Reader.*

The book of books, the storehouse and magazine of
  life and comfort, the holy Scriptures.
> *Ib.* ch. 4.

Hearken unto a Verser, who may chance
Rhyme thee to good, and make a bait of pleasure:
A verse may find him who a sermon flies,
And turn delight into a sacrifice.
> *The Temple: The Church Porch,* i.

Drink not the third glass—which thou canst not tame
When once it is within thee.   *Ib.* v.

Dare to be true: nothing can need a lie;
A fault, which needs it most, grows two thereby.
> *Ib.* xiii.

Chase brave employment with a naked sword
Throughout the world.   *Ib.* xv.

O England, full of sin, but most of sloth;
Spit out thy phlegm, and fill thy breast with glory.
> *Ib.* xvi.

Think the king sees thee still; for his King does.
> *Ib.* xxi.

Never was scraper brave man. Get to live;
Then live, and use it.   *Ib.* xxvi.

Wit's an unruly engine, wildly striking
Sometimes a friend, sometimes the engineer.
> *Ib.* xli.

Towards great persons use respective boldness.
> *Ib.* xliii.

But love is lost, the way of friendship's gone,
Though David had his Jonathan, Christ his John.
> *Ib.* xlvi.

Be calm in arguing; for fierceness makes
Error a fault and truth discourtesy.   *Ib.* lii

Calmness is great advantage; he that lets
Another chafe, may warm him at his fire.   *Ib.* liii

     Who aimeth at the sky
Shoots higher much than he that means a tree.
> *Ib.* lvi.

Man is God's image; but a poor man is
Christ's stamp to boot.   *Ib.* lxiv

Kneeling ne'er spoil'd silk stocking; quit thy state;
All equal are within the Church's gate.   *Ib.* lxviii

     O, be drest;
Stay not for th' other pin! Why, thou hast lost
A joy for it worth worlds.   *Ib.* lxix

Judge not the preacher, for He is thy Judge;
If thou mislike him, thou conceiv'st Him not:
God calleth preaching folly: do not grudge
To pick out treasures from an earthen pot:
The worst speaks something good; if all want sense,
God takes a text, and preacheth patience.
Ib. lxxii.

Look not on pleasures as they come, but go.
Ib. lxxvii.

But who does hawk at eagles with a dove?
Ib. The Sacrifice, xxiii.

I got me flowers to strew Thy way,
I got me boughs off many a tree;
But Thou wast up by break of day,
And brought'st Thy sweets along with Thee.
Ib. Easter Song.

Lord, with what care Thou hast begirt us round!
Parents first season us; then schoolmasters
Deliver us to laws; they send us, bound
To rules of reason, holy messengers,

Pulpits and Sundays, sorrow dogging sin,
Afflictions sorted, anguish of all sizes,
Fine nets and stratagems to catch us in,
Bibles laid open, millions of surprises.   *Ib. Sin.*

Yet all these fences and their whole array
One cunning bosom sin blows quite away.   *Ib.*

I read, and sigh, and wish I were a tree—
     For sure then I should grow
To fruit or shade; at least some bird would trust
Her household to me, and I should be just.
Ib. Affliction.

Ah, my dear God, though I am clean forgot,
Let me not love Thee, if I love Thee not.   *Ib.*

Let all the world in ev'ry corner sing
     My God and King.
The heav'ns are not too high,
His praise may thither fly;
The earth is not too low,
His praises there may grow.
Let all the world in ev'ry corner sing
     My God and King.
The Church with psalms must shout,
No door can keep them out:
But above all, the heart
Must bear the longest part.   *Ib. Antiphon.*

Death is still working like a mole,
And digs my grave at each remove.   *Ib. Grace.*

Enrich my heart, mouth, hands in me,
With faith, with hope, with charity,
That I may run, rise, rest with Thee.
Ib. Trinity Sunday.

My God, my verse is not a crown,
No point of honour, or gay suit,
No hawk, no banquet, or renown,
Nor a good sword, nor yet a lute.
Ib. The Quiddity.

The Sundays of man's life,
Threaded together on Time's string,
Make bracelets to adorn the wife
Of the eternal glorious King:
On Sunday heaven's gate stands ope;
Blessings are plentiful and rife,
   More plentiful than hope.   *Ib. Sunday.*

Money, thou bane of bliss and source of woe.
Ib. Avarice.

How well her name an 'Army' doth present,
In whom the 'Lord of Hosts' did pitch His tent!
Ib. Anagram, Mary.

Oh that I were an orange-tree,
     That busy plant!
Then I should ever laden be,
     And never want
Some fruit for Him that dressed me.
Ib. Employment.

Sweet day, so cool, so calm, so bright,
The bridal of the earth and sky,
The dew shall weep thy fall to-night;
     For thou must die.

Sweet rose, whose hue angry and brave
Bids the rash gazer wipe his eye,
Thy root is ever in its grave,
     And thou must die.

Sweet spring, full of sweet days and roses,
A box where sweets compacted lie.   *Ib. Virtue.*

Only a sweet and virtuous soul,
Like season'd timber, never gives;
But though the whole world turn to coal,
     Then chiefly lives.   *Ib.*

     For us the winds do blow,
The earth resteth, heav'n moveth, fountains flow;
   Nothing we see but means our good,
     As our delight or as our treasure;
The whole is either our cupboard of food
     Or cabinet of pleasure.   *Ib. Man.*

Oh mighty love! Man is one world, and hath
   Another to attend him.   *Ib.*

Lord, make me coy and tender to offend:
In friendship, first I think if that agree
     Which I intend
Unto my friend's intent and end;
I would not use a friend as I use Thee.
Ib. Unkindness.

My friend may spit upon my curious floor;
Would he have gold? I lend it instantly;
     But let the poor,
And Thou within them, starve at door:
I cannot use a friend as I use Thee.   *Ib.*

I made a posy while the day ran by;
Here will I smell my remnant out, and tie
   My life within this band;
But Time did beckon to the flow'rs, and they
By noon most cunningly did steal away,
     And wither'd in my hand.   *Ib. Life.*

But Thou shalt answer, Lord, for me. *Ib. The Quip.*

SAVIOUR:
That as I did freely part
With my glory and desert,
Left all joys to feel all smart—
MAN:
Ah, no more: Thou break'st my heart.
Ib. Dialogue.

Grasp not at much, for fear thou losest all.
Ib. The Size.

King of glory, King of peace,
     I will love Thee;
And, that love may never cease,
     I will move Thee.   *Ib. Praise.*

Sev'n whole days, not one in seven,
　　I will praise Thee;
In my heart, though not in heaven,
　　I can raise Thee.　　　　　　　*Ib.*

I struck the board, and cried, 'No more;
　　I will abroad.'
What, shall I ever sigh and pine?
My lines and life are free; free as the road,
Loose as the wind, as large as store.
　　Shall I be still in suit?
Have I no harvest but a thorn
To let me blood, and not restore
What I have lost with cordial fruit?
　　Sure there was wine
Before my sighs did dry it; there was corn
Before my tears did drown it;
Is the year only lost to me?
Have I no bays to crown it?　　*Ib. The Collar.*

　　Away! take heed;
　　I will abroad.
Call in thy death's-head there, tie up thy fears;
　　He that forbears
To suit and serve his need
　　Deserves his load.
But as I rav'd and grew more fierce and wild
　　At every word,
Methought I heard one calling, 'Child';
　　And I replied, 'My Lord.'　　*Ib.*

He would adore my gifts instead of Me,
And rest in Nature, not the God of Nature:
So both should losers be.
　　　　　　　Ib. The Pulley.

　　Yet let him keep the rest,
But keep them with repining restlessness;
Let him be rich and weary, that at least,
If goodness lead him not, yet weariness
　　May toss him to My breast.　　*Ib.*

And now in age I bud again,
After so many deaths I live and write;
I once more smell the dew and rain,
And relish versing: O, my only Light,
　　It cannot be
　　That I am he
On whom Thy tempests fell all night.
　　　　　　　Ib. The Flower.

　　　　Like summer-friends,
Flies of estates and sunshine.　*Ib. The Answer.*

The God of love my Shepherd is,
And He that doth me feed,
While He is mine, and I am His,
What can I want or need?　　*Ib. 23rd Psalm.*

Throw away Thy rod,
Throw away Thy wrath;
　　O my God,
Take the gentle path.　　*Ib. Discipline.*

Love is swift of foot;
Love's a man of war,
　　And can shoot,
And can hit from far.　　*Ib.*

Teach me, my God and King,
In all things Thee to see,
And what I do in any thing
To do it as for Thee.　　*Ib. The Elixir.*

A servant with this clause
Makes drudgery divine;
Who sweeps a room as for Thy laws
Makes that and th' action fine.　　*Ib.*

Love bade me welcome; yet my soul drew back,
　　Guilty of dust and sin.
But quick-ey'd Love, observing me grow slack
　　From my first entrance in,
Drew nearer to me, sweetly questioning
　　If I lack'd any thing.
　　　　　　　Ib. Love.

'You must sit down,' says Love, 'and taste My meat.'
　　So I did sit and eat.　　*Ib.*

OLIVER HERFORD

1863–1935

The bubble winked at me, and said,
'You'll miss me brother, when you're dead.'
　　　　Toast. The Bubble Winked.

ROBERT HERRICK

1591–1674

With thousand such enchanting dreams, that meet
To make sleep not so sound, as sweet.
　　Hesperides. A Country Life: to his Brother,
　　M. Tho. Herrick.

Blest is the bride, on whom the sun doth shine.
　　　　　Ib. A Nuptial Song.

I sing of brooks, of blossoms, birds, and bowers:
Of April, May, of June, and July-flowers.
I sing of May-poles, Hock-carts, wassails, wakes,
Of bride-grooms, brides, and of their bridal-cakes.
　　　　　Ib. Argument of his Book.

A little saint best fits a little shrine,
A little prop best fits a little vine,
As my small cruse best fits my little wine.
　　Ib. A Ternary of Littles, upon a Pipkin of Jelly
　　sent to a Lady.

A little stream best fits a little boat;
A little lead best fits a little float;
As my small pipe best fits my little note.

A little meat best fits a little belly,
As sweetly Lady, give me leave to tell ye,
This little pipkin fits this little jelly.　　*Ib.*

Fair pledges of a fruitful tree,
Why do ye fall so fast?
Your date is not so past;
But you may stay yet here a while,
To blush and gently smile;
And go at last.　　　　*Ib. Blossoms.*

Cherry ripe, ripe, ripe, I cry,
Full and fair ones; come and buy:
If so be, you ask me where
They do grow? I answer, there,
Where my Julia's lips do smile;
There's the land, or cherry-isle.
　　　　　　Ib. Cherry Ripe.

What needs complaints
When she a place
Has with the race
    Of Saints?
In endless mirth,
She thinks not on
What's said or done
    In earth.
    Ib. Comfort to a Youth that had Lost his Love.

Nor do's she mind,
Or think on't now,
That ever thou
    Wast kind.   *Ib.*

Get up, get up for shame, the blooming morn
Upon her wings presents the god unshorn.
    Ib. Corinna's Going a-Maying.

Get up, sweet Slug-a-bed, and see
The dew bespangling herb and tree.   *Ib.*

    'Tis sin,
Nay, profanation to keep in.   *Ib.*

Come, let us go, while we are in our prime;
And take the harmless folly of the time.   *Ib.*

So when or you or I are made
A fable, song, or fleeting shade;
All love, all liking, all delight
Lies drown'd with us in endless night.
Then while time serves, and we are but decaying;
Come, my Corinna, come, let's go a-Maying.   *Ib.*

Fair daffodils, we weep to see
You haste away so soon:
As yet the early-rising sun
    Has not attain'd his noon.
    Stay, stay,
Until the hasting day
    Has run
But to the even-song;
And, having pray'd together, we
Will go with you along.   *Ib. Daffodils.*

We have short time to stay, as you,
We have as short a Spring;
As quick a growth to meet decay,
As you or any thing.   *Ib.*

A sweet disorder in the dress
Kindles in clothes a wantonness:
A lawn about the shoulders thrown
Into a fine distraction:
An erring lace, which here and there
Enthralls the crimson stomacher:
A cuff neglectful, and thereby
Ribbands to flow confusedly:
A winning wave (deserving note)
In the tempestuous petticoat:
A careless shoe-string, in whose tie
I see a wild civility:
Do more bewitch me, than when Art
Is too precise in every part. *Ib. Delight in Disorder.*

Here a solemn Fast we keep,
While all beauty lies asleep
Husht be all things; (no noise here)
But the toning of a tear:
Or a sigh of such as bring
Cowslips for her covering.
    Ib. Epitaph upon a Virgin.

Only a little more
I have to write,
Then I'll give o'er,
And bid the world Good-night.
    Ib. His Poetry his Pillar.

Roses at first were white,
Till they co'd not agree,
Whether my Sappho's breast,
Or they more white sho'd be.
    Ib. How Roses Came Red.

'Twixt kings and tyrants there's this difference
    known;
Kings seek their subjects' good: tyrants their own.
    Ib. Kings and Tyrants.

You say, to me-wards your affection's strong;
Pray love me little, so you love me long.
    Ib. Love me Little, Love me Long.

Love is a circle that doth restless move
In the same sweet eternity of love.
    Ib. Love What It Is.

Night makes no difference 'twixt the Priest and Clerk;
Joan as my Lady is as good i' th' dark.
    Ib. No Difference i' th' Dark.

I do love I know not what;
Sometimes this, and sometimes that.
    Ib. No Luck in Love.

Because thou prizest things that are
Curious, and unfamiliar.   *Ib. Oberon's Feast.*

Made us nobly wild, not mad.
    Ib. Ode for Ben Jonson.

Out-did the meat, out-did the frolic wine.   *Ib.*

Fain would I kiss my Julia's dainty leg,
Which is as white and hairless as an egg.
    Ib. On Julia's Legs.

Men are suspicious; prone to discontent:
Subjects still loathe the present Government.
    Ib. Present Government Grievous

The readiness of doing, doth express
No other, but the doer's willingness. *Ib. Readiness.*

Attempt the end, and never stand to doubt;
Nothing's so hard, but search will find it out.
    Ib. Seek and Find.

And once more yet (ere I am laid out dead)
Knock at a star with my exalted head.
    Ib. The Bad Season Makes the Poet Sad.

It is the end that crowns us, not the fight.
    Ib. The End.

Good morrow to the day so fair;
Good morning Sir to you:
Good morrow to mine own torn hair
Bedabbled with the dew.
    Ib. The Mad Maid's Song.

Her eyes the glow-worm lend thee,
The shooting-stars attend thee;
    And the elves also,
    Whose little eyes glow,
Like the sparks of fire, befriend thee.

No Will-o'-th'-Wisp mislight thee;
Nor snake, or slow-worm bite thee:
    But on, on thy way
    Not making a stay,
Since ghost there's none to affright thee.
    Ib. The Night-Piece, to Julia.

Praise they that will times past, I joy to see
My self now live: this age best pleaseth me.
Ib. The Present Time Best Pleaseth.

Some ask'd how pearls did grow, and where?
Then spoke I to my girl,
To part her lips, and shew'd them there
The quarelets of pearl.
Ib. The Rock of Rubies, and the Quarry of Pearls.

Now is the time, when all the lights wax dim;
And thou (Anthea) must withdraw from him
Who was thy servant.
Ib. To Anthea: Now is the Time.

Give me a kiss, and to that kiss a score;
Then to that twenty, add a hundred more:
A thousand to that hundred: so kiss on,
To make that thousand up a million.
Treble that million, and when that is done,
Let's kiss afresh, as when we first begun.
Ib. To Anthea: Ah, My Anthea!

Bid me to live, and I will live
Thy Protestant to be:
Or bid me love, and I will give
A loving heart to thee.
A heart as soft, a heart as kind,
A heart as sound and free,
As in the whole world thou canst find,
That heart I'll give to thee.
Ib. To Anthea, Who May Command Him Anything.

Bid me to weep, and I will weep,
While I have eyes to see.   *Ib.*

Bid me despair, and I'll despair,
Under that cypress tree:
Or bid me die, and I will dare
E'en Death, to die for thee.   *Ib.*

Thou art my life, my love, my heart,
The very eyes of me:
And hast command of every part,
To live and die for thee.   *Ib.*

No marigolds yet closed are;
No shadows great appear.
Ib. To Daisies, not to Shut so Soon.

Sweet, be not proud of those two eyes,
Which star-like sparkle in their skies.
Ib. To Dianeme.

I dare not ask a kiss;
I dare not beg a smile;
Lest having that, or this,
I might grow proud the while.

No, no, the utmost share
Of my desire, shall be
Only to kiss that air,
That lately kissed thee.   *Ib. To Electra.*

He loves his bonds, who when the first are broke,
Submits his neck unto a second yoke.
Ib. To Love.

Gather ye rosebuds while ye may,
Old Time is still a-flying:
And this same flower that smiles to-day,
To-morrow will be dying.

The glorious lamp of Heaven, the sun,
The higher he's a getting;
The sooner will his race be run,
And nearer he's to setting.

That age is best, which is the first,
When youth and blood are warmer;
But being spent, the worse, and worst
Times, still succeed the former.

Then be not coy, but use your time;
And while ye may, go marry:
For having lost but once your prime,
You may for ever tarry.
Ib. To Virgins, to Make Much of Time.

Welcome maids of honour,
   You do bring
   In the Spring;
And wait upon her.   *Ib. To Violets.*

Her pretty feet
Like snails did creep
A little out, and then,
As if they started at bo-peep,
Did soon draw in agen.   *Ib. Upon her Feet.*

Whenas in silks my Julia goes,
Then, then (methinks) how sweetly flows
That liquefaction of her clothes.

Next, when I cast mine eyes and see
That brave vibration each way free;
O how that glittering taketh me!
Ib. Upon Julia's Clothes.

So smooth, so sweet, so silv'ry is thy voice,
As, could they hear, the damn'd would make no noise,
But listen to thee (walking in thy chamber)
Melting melodious words, to lutes of amber.
Ib. Upon Julia's Voice.

Here a little child I stand,
Heaving up my either hand;
Cold as paddocks though they be,
Here I lift them up to Thee,
For a benison to fall
On our meat, and on us all. Amen.
Noble Numbers: Another Grace for a Child.

Lord, Thou hast given me a cell
     Wherein to dwell,
A little house, whose humble roof
     Is weather-proof;
Under the spars of which I lie
     Both soft, and dry.
Ib. A Thanksgiving to God for his House.

A little buttery, and therein
     A little bin,
Which keeps my little loaf of bread
     Unchipt, unflead:
Some brittle sticks of thorn or briar
     Make me a fire,
Close by whose living coal I sit,
     And glow like it.   *Ib.*

To him, who longs unto his Christ to go,
Celerity even itself is slow.
Ib. Coming to Christ.

When the artless doctor sees
No one hope, but of his fees,
And his skill runs on the lees;
     Sweet Spirit comfort me!

When his potion and his pill,
His, or none, or little skill,
Meet for nothing, but to kill;
   Sweet Spirit comfort me!
    Ib. His Litany to the Holy Spirit.

In prayer the lips ne'er act the winning part,
Without the sweet concurrence of the heart.
    Ib. The Heart.

But, for Man's fault, then was the thorn,
Without the fragrant rose-bud, born;
But ne'er the rose without the thorn. *Ib. The Rose.*

To work a wonder, God would have her shown,
At once, a bud, and yet a rose full-blown.
    Ib. The Virgin Mary.

If any thing delight me for to print
My book, 'tis this; that Thou, my God, art in't.
    Ib. To God.

JAMES HERVEY
1714–1758
E'en crosses from his sov'reign hand
Are blessings in disguise.
  Works. Reflections on a Flower-Garden.

DU BOSE HEYWARD
1885–
Roll dem bones.   *Gamesters All.*

JOHN HEYWOOD
1497?–1580?
All a green willow, willow;
All a green willow is my garland.
    The Green Willow.

EMILY HENRIETTA HICKEY
1845–1924
Beloved, it is morn!
 A redder berry on the thorn,
 A deeper yellow on the corn,
For this good day new-born:
  Pray, Sweet, for me
  That I may be
  Faithful to God and thee.
    Beloved, It Is Morn.

WILLIAM EDWARD HICKSON
1803–1870
'Tis a lesson you should heed,
Try, try again.
If at first you don't succeed,
Try, try again.
    Try and Try Again.

AARON HILL
1685–1750
Tender-handed stroke a nettle,
 And it stings you for your pains;
Grasp it like a man of mettle,
 And it soft as silk remains.
   Verses Written on Window.

'Tis the same with common natures,
 Use 'em kindly, they rebel:
But be rough as nutmeg-graters,
 And the rogues obey you well. *Ib.*

ROWLAND HILL
1744–1833
He did not see any reason why the devil should have all the good tunes.
 E. W. Broome, Rev. Rowland Hill, vii.

ARTHUR CLEMENT HILTON
1851–1877
And we found in his palms which were hollow,
What are frequent in palms,—that is dates.
    The Heathen Pass-ee.

PRINCE HOARE
1755–1834
The saucy Arethusa. *Song: The Arethusa.*

THOMAS HOBBES
1588–1679
Geometry (which is the only science that it hath pleased God hitherto to bestow on mankind).
   Leviathan, pt. i, ch. 4.

They that approve a private opinion, call it opinion; but they that mislike it, heresy: and yet heresy signifies no more than private opinion.
    Ib. ch. 11.

No arts; no letters; no society; and which is worst of all, continual fear and danger of violent death; and the life of man, solitary, poor, nasty, brutish, and short.   *Ib. ch. 13.*

Force, and fraud, are in war the two cardinal virtues.
    Ib.

The Papacy is not other than the Ghost of the deceased Roman Empire, sitting crowned upon the grave thereof. *Ib. pt. iv, ch. 47.*

He was wont to say that if he had read as much as other men, he should have known no more than other men. *Aubrey, Life of Hobbes.*

I am about to take my last voyage, a great leap in the dark.
  Last Words. (Watkins, Anecdotes of Men of Learning.)

EDWARD WALLIS HOCH

1849–1925

There is so much good in the worst of us,
And so much bad in the best of us,
That it hardly becomes any of us
To talk about the rest of us.
    Good and Bad. Attr. to many other authors.

RALPH HODGSON

1871–

Eve, with her basket, was
Deep in the bells and grass,
Wading in bells and grass
Up to her knees,
Plucking a dish of sweet
Berries and plums to eat,
Down in the bells and grass
Under the trees.   *Poems. Eve.*

Picture that orchard sprite,
Eve, with her body white,
Supple and smooth to her
Slim finger tips.   *Ib.*

But oh, the den of wild things in
The darkness of her eyes!   *Ib. The Gipsy Girl.*

Reason has moons, but moons not hers,
     Lie mirror'd on her sea,
Confounding her astronomers,
     But, O! delighting me.
         Ib. Reason Has Moons.

God loves an idle rainbow,
No less than labouring seas.   *Ib.*

'Twould ring the bells of Heaven
The wildest peal for years,
If Parson lost his senses
And people came to theirs,
And he and they together
Knelt down with angry prayers
For tamed and shabby tigers
And dancing dogs and bears,
And wretched, blind, pit ponies,
And little hunted hares.
         Ib. The Bells of Heaven.

See an old unhappy bull,
Sick in soul and body both.   *Ib. The Bull.*

I did not pray him to lay bare
The mystery to me;
Enough the rose was heaven to smell,
And His own face to see.   *Ib. The Mystery.*

I climbed a hill as light fell short,
And rooks came home in scramble sort,
And filled the trees and flapped and fought
And sang themselves to sleep.
         Ib. The Song of Honour.

Hear flocks of shiny pleiades
Among the plums and apple trees
Sing in the summer day.   *Ib.*

When stately ships are twirled and spun
Like whipping tops and help there's none
And mighty ships ten thousand ton
Go down like lumps of lead.   *Ib.*

I stood upon that silent hill
And stared into the sky until
My eyes were blind with stars and still
I stared into the sky.   *Ib.*

Time, you old gypsy man,
     Will you not stay,
Put up your caravan
     Just for one day?
         Ib. Time, You Old Gypsy Man.

HEINRICH HOFFMAN

1809–1874

Anything to me is sweeter
Than to see Shock-headed Peter.
         Struwwelpeter. Shock-Headed Peter.

Here is cruel Frederick, see!
A horrid wicked boy was he.   *Ib. Cruel Frederick.*

The trough was full, and faithful Tray
Came out to drink one sultry day;
He wagged his tail, and wet his lip.   *Ib.*

At this, good Tray grew very red,
And growled, and bit him till he bled.   *Ib.*

But good dog Tray is happy now;
He has no time to say 'Bow-wow!'
He seats himself in Frederick's chair
And laughs to see the good things there:
The soup he swallows, sup by sup—
And eats the pies and puddings up.   *Ib.*

It almost makes me cry to tell
What foolish Harriet befell.
         Ib. Harriet and the Matches.

Now tall Agrippa lived close by—
So tall, he almost touch'd the sky;
He had a mighty inkstand, too,
In which a great goose-feather grew.
         Ib. The Inky Boys.

He finds it hard, without a pair
Of spectacles, to shoot the hare.
The hare sits snug in leaves and grass,
And laughs to see the green man pass.
         Ib. The Man Who Went Out Shooting.

And now she's trying all she can,
To shoot the sleepy, green-coat man.   *Ib.*

'Help! Fire! Help! The Hare! The Hare!'   *Ib.*

The hare's own child, the little hare.   *Ib.*

The door flew open, in he ran,
The great, long, red-legged scissor-man.
         Ib. The Little Suck-a-Thumb.

'Ah!' said Mamma, 'I knew he'd come
To naughty little Suck-a-Thumb.'   *Ib.*

Augustus was a chubby lad;
Fat ruddy cheeks Augustus had:
And everybody saw with joy
The plump and hearty, healthy boy.
He ate and drank as he was told,
And never let his soup get cold.

But one day, one cold winter's day,
He screamed out, 'Take the soup away!
O take the nasty soup away!
I won't have any soup to-day.'   *Ib. Augustus.*

Let me see if Philip can
Be a little gentleman;
Let me see, if he is able
To sit still for once at table.
Ib. Fidgety Philip.

But fidgety Phil,
He won't sit still;
He wriggles
And giggles,
And then, I declare,
Swings backwards and forwards,
And tilts up his chair.   *Ib.*

'Look at little Johnny there,
Little Johnny Head-In-Air!'
Ib. Johnny Head-in-Air.

'Silly little Johnny, look,
You have lost your writing-book!'   *Ib.*

JAMES HOGG
1770-1835

My love she's but a lassie yet.   *Title of Song.*

Bonny Kilmeny gaed up the glen.
The Queen's Wake, ii. Kilmeny. Thirteenth Bard's Song, l. 1.

Late, late in the gloamin' Kilmeny came hame!
Ib. l. 24.

For Kilmeny had been she knew not where,
And Kilmeny had seen what she could not declare.
Ib. l. 38.

And hey, then, up go we.
Jacobite Relics of Scotland, i. 15. Title.

Wha the deil hae we goten for a King
But a wee wee German lairdie?
And when we gade to bring him hame,
He was delving in his kail-yardie.
Ib. 83. The Wee, Wee German Lairdie.

Listen a while, and I'll tell you a tale,
Of a new device of a Protestant Flail.
Ib. 324. The Protestant Flail.

God bless our Lord the king!
God save our lord the king!
God save the king!
Make him victorious,
Happy, and glorious,
Long to reign over us:
God save the king!
Ib. ii. 50. God Save The King.

We'll o'er the water, we'll o'er the sea,
We'll o'er the water to Charlie;
Come weel, come wo, we'll gather and go,
And live or die wi' Charlie.
Ib. 76. O'er the Water to Charlie.

There grows a bonny brier bush in our kail yard.
Ib. 78. An You Be He.

'Twas on a Monday morning,
Right early in the year,
That Charlie came to our town,
The young Chevalier.
And Charlie he's my darling,
My darling, my darling,

And Charlie he's my darling,
The young Chevalier.
Ib. 93. The Young Chevalier.
(Another version by Lady Nairne.)

Hey, Johnnie Cope, are ye wauking yet?
And are your drums a-beatin' yet?
Ib. 113. Johnnie Cope.

Cock up your beaver, and cock it fu' sprush;
We'll over the Border and gi'e them a brush;
There's somebody there we'll teach better behaviour.
Hey, Johnnie lad, cock up your beaver!
Ib. 127. Cock Up Your Beaver.

Will you no come back again?
Better lo'ed you'll never be,
And will you no come back again?
Ib. 195. Will You No Come Back Again?

HENRY RICHARD VASSAL FOX, 3rd BARON HOLLAND
1773-1840

Nephew of Fox, and friend of Grey,—
Enough my meed of fame
If those who deign'd to observe me say
I injur'd neither name.
Memoirs of Rev. Sidney Smith (1855), i. 334.

SIR RICHARD HOLLAND
c. 1450

O Dowglas, O Dowglas,
tendir and trewe!   *Buke of the Howlat, xxxi.*

OLIVER WENDELL HOLMES
1809-1894

Lean, hungry, savage anti-everythings.
Poems: A Modest Request.

Sweet is the scene where genial friendship plays
The pleasing game of interchanging praise.
Ib. An After-Dinner Poem.

Uncursed by doubt, our earliest creed we take;
We love the precepts for the teacher's sake.
Ib. A Rhymed Lesson (Urania).

And, when you stick on conversation's burrs,
Don't strew your pathway with those dreadful *urs*. *Ib.*

Man wants but little drink below,
But wants that little strong.
Ib. A Song of other Days (Parody on Goldsmith).

Day hath put on his jacket, and around
His burning bosom buttoned it with stars.
Ib. Evening.

We greet the monarch-peasant.
Ib. For the Burns Centennial Celebration.

Wisdom has taught us to be calm and meek,
To take one blow, and turn the other cheek;
It is not written what a man shall do
If the rude caitiff smite the other too!
Ib. Non-Resistance.

H

Ay, tear her tattered ensign down!
Long has it waved on high,
And many an eye has danced to see
That banner in the sky;
Beneath it rung the battle shout,
And burst the cannon's roar;—
The meteor of the ocean air
Shall sweep the clouds no more.   *Ib. Old Ironsides.*

Have you heard of the wonderful one-hoss shay,
That was built in such a logical way
It ran a hundred years to a day?
     Ib. The Deacon's Masterpiece.

A general flavor of mild decay.   *Ib.*

When the last reader reads no more.
     Ib. The Last Reader.

Feels the same comfort while his acrid words
Turn the sweet milk of kindness into curds.
     Ib. The Moral Bully.

And silence, like a poultice, comes
To heal the blows of sound.   *Ib. The Music Grinders.*

It cannot be,—it is,—it is,—
A hat is going round!   *Ib.*

Go very quietly and drop
A button in the hat!   *Ib.*

Call him not old, whose visionary brain
Holds o'er the past its undivided reign.
For him in vain the envious seasons roll
Who bears eternal summer in his soul.
     Ib. The Old Player.

To be seventy years young is sometimes far more
cheerful and hopeful than to be forty years old.
   On the Seventieth Birthday of Julia Ward Howe.

I think I said, I can make it plain to Benjamin
Franklin here that there are at least six person-
alities distinctly to be recognized as taking part in
that dialogue between John and Thomas.

Three Johns.
{
1. The real John; known only to his Maker.
2. John's ideal John; never the real one, and often very unlike him.
3. Thomas' ideal John; never the real John, nor John's John, but often very unlike either.
}

Three Thomases.
{
1. The real Thomas.
2. Thomas' ideal Thomas.
3. John's ideal Thomas.
}
   The Autocrat of the Breakfast-Table, ch. 3.

Build thee more stately mansions, O my soul,
     As the swift seasons roll!
     Leave thy low-vaulted past!
Let each new temple, nobler than the last,
     Shut thee from heaven with a dome more vast,
     Till thou at length art free,
Leaving thine outgrown shell by life's unresting sea!
     Ib. ch. 4. The Chambered Nautilus.

Boston State-House is the hub of the solar system.
You couldn't pry that out of a Boston man if you
had the tire of all creation straightened out for a
crowbar.   *Ib.*

The axis of the earth sticks out visibly through the
centre of each and every town or city.   *Ib.*

The world's great men have not commonly been great
scholars, nor its great scholars great men.   *Ib.*

His humid front the cive, anheling, wipes.
And dreams of erring on ventiferous ripes.
     Ib. ch. 11. Aestivation.

Depart,—be off,—excede,—evade,—erump!   *Ib.*

Fate tried to conceal him by naming him Smith
[Samuel Francis Smith].   *The Boys.*

It is the province of knowledge to speak and it is the
privilege of wisdom to listen.
     The Poet at the Breakfast Table, ch. 10.

It is the folly of the world, constantly, which confounds its wisdom.
     The Professor at the Breakfast Table, ch. 1.

A moment's insight is sometimes worth a life's experience.   *Ib. ch. 10.*

JOHN HOME
1722–1808

       In the first days
Of my distracting grief, I found myself—
As women wish to be, who love their lords.
     Douglas, I. 1.

My name is Norval; on the Grampian hills
My father feeds his flocks; a frugal swain,
Whose constant cares were to increase his store.
     Ib. II. 1.

       He seldom errs
Who thinks the worst he can of womankind.
     Ib. III. iii.

Like Douglas conquer, or like Douglas die.   *Ib. v.*

WILLIAM HONE
1780–1842

A good lather is half the shave.
     Every-Day Book, vol. i, 1269.

John Jones may be described as 'one of the *has* beens.'
     Ib. vol. ii, 820.

THOMAS HOOD
1799–1845

When Eve upon the first of Men
     The apple press'd with specious cant,
Oh! what a thousand pities then
     That Adam was not Adamant!   *A Reflection.*

It was not in the winter
     Our loving lot was cast!
It was the time of roses,
     We plucked them as we passed!
     Ballad: It Was Not in the Winter.

O saw ye not fair Inez?   *Fair Inez.*

Ben Battle was a soldier bold,
     And used to war's alarms:
But a cannon-ball took off his legs,
     So he laid down his arms!   *Faithless Nellie Gray.*

For here I leave my second leg,
     And the Forty-second Foot!   *Ib.*

The love that loves a scarlet coat
  Should be more uniform. *Ib.*

His death, which happen'd in his berth,
  At forty-odd befell:
They went and told the sexton, and
  The sexton toll'd the bell. *Faithless Sally Brown.*

I remember, I remember,
The house where I was born,
The little window where the sun
Came peeping in at morn;
He never came a wink too soon,
Nor brought too long a day,
But now, I often wish the night
Had borne my breath away! *I Remember.*

I remember, I remember,
The roses, red and white,
The vi'lets, and the lily-cups,
Those flowers made of light!
The lilacs where the robin built,
And where my brother set
The laburnum on his birthday,—
The tree is living yet! *Ib.*

I remember, I remember,
The fir trees dark and high;
I used to think their slender tops
Were close against the sky:
It was a childish ignorance,
But now 'tis little joy
To know I'm farther off from heav'n
Than when I was a boy. *Ib.*

    That fierce thing
They call a conscience. *Lamia,* sc. vii.

For that old enemy the gout
  Had taken him in toe! *Lieutenant Luff.*

Alas! my everlasting peace
  Is broken into pieces. *Mary's Ghost.*

And then, in the fulness of joy and hope,
Seem'd washing his hands with invisible soap,
  In imperceptible water.
      Miss Kilmansegg. Her Christening.

There's Bardus, a six-foot column of fop,
A lighthouse without any light atop.
      Ib. Her First Step.

For one of the pleasures of having a rout,
Is the pleasure of having it over. *Ib. Her Dream.*

Yet Wedlock's a very awful thing!
'Tis something like that feat in the ring,
  Which requires good nerve to do it—
When one of a 'Grand Equestrian Troop'
Makes a jump at a gilded hoop,
    Not certain at all
    Of what may befall
After his getting through it! *Ib. Her Marriage.*

Home-made dishes that drive one from home.
      Ib. Her Misery.

No sun—no moon!
No morn—no noon!
No dawn—no dusk—no proper time of day. *No!*

No warmth, no cheerfulness, no healthful ease,
No comfortable feel in any member—
No shade, no shine, no butterflies, no bees,
No fruits, no flowers, no leaves, no birds,—
  November! *Ib.*

I saw old Autumn in the misty morn
Stand shadowless like Silence, listening
To silence. *Ode: Autumn.*

Thou'lt find thy Manhood all too fast—
Soon come, soon gone! and Age at last
  A sorry *breaking-up!*
      Ode: Clapham Academy.

And there is ev'n a happiness
That makes the heart afraid! *Ode to Melancholy.*

Not one of those self-constituted saints,
Quacks—not physicians—in the cure of souls.
      Ode to Rae Wilson, l. 13.

Dear bells! how sweet the sounds of village bells
When on the undulating air they swim!
Now loud as welcomes! faint, now, as farewells!
      Ib. l. 159.

She stood breast high amid the corn,
Clasp'd by the golden light of morn,
Like the sweetheart of the sun,
Who many a glowing kiss had won. *Ruth.*

Thus she stood amid the stooks,
Praising God with sweetest looks. *Ib.*

Sure, I said, heav'n did not mean,
Where I reap thou shouldst but glean,
Lay thy sheaf adown and come,
Share my harvest and my home. *Ib.*

There is a silence where hath been no sound,
There is a silence where no sound may be,
In the cold grave—under the deep deep sea,
Or in the wide desert where no life is found.
      Sonnet. Silence.

One more Unfortunate,
Weary of breath,
Rashly importunate,
Gone to her death!

Take her up tenderly,
Lift her with care;
Fashion'd so slenderly,
Young, and so fair!

Look at her garments
Clinging like cerements.
      The Bridge of Sighs.

Loving, not loathing. *Ib.*

All that remains of her
Now is pure womanly. *Ib.*

Past all dishonour,
Death has left on her
Only the beautiful. *Ib.*

Still, for all slips of hers,
One of Eve's family. *Ib.*

Was there a dearer one
Still, and a nearer one
Yet, than all other? *Ib.*

Alas! for the rarity
Of Christian charity
Under the sun!
Oh! it was pitiful!
Near a whole city full,
Home had she none! *Ib.*

Even God's providence
Seeming estranged.   *Ib.*

Mad from life's history,
Glad to death's mystery,
Swift to be hurl'd—
Anywhere, anywhere
Out of the world!   *Ib.*

Picture it—think of it,
Dissolute man!
Lave in it, drink of it,
Then, if you can!   *Ib.*

Owning her weakness,
Her evil behaviour,
And leaving, with meekness,
Her sins to her Saviour!   *Ib*

Our very hopes belied our fears,
    Our fears our hopes belied—
We thought her dying when she slept,
    And sleeping when she died!   *The Death Bed.*

Much study had made him very lean,
    And pale, and leaden-ey'd.
                    The Dream of Eugene Aram.

But Guilt was my grim Chamberlain
    That lighted me to bed.   *Ib.*

Two stern-faced men set out from Lynn,
    Through the cold and heavy mist;
And Eugene Aram walked between,
    With gyves upon his wrist.   *Ib.*

Where folks that ride a bit of blood,
May break a bit of bone.   *The Epping Hunt,* l. 99.

He keeps a parlour boarder of a pig.
                    The Irish Schoolmaster, v

He never spoils the child and spares the rod,
But spoils the rod and never spares the child.
                                          Ib. xii.

But evil is wrought by want of thought,
    As well as want of heart!   *The Lady's Dream.*

On Margate beach, where the sick one roams,
    And the sentimental reads;
Where the maiden flirts, and the widow comes—
    Like the ocean—to cast her weeds.
                        The Mermaid of Margate.

The shrill sweet lark.
            The Plea of the Midsummer Fairies, xxx.

            The bird forlorn,
That singeth with her breast against a thorn.   *Ib.*

We will not woo foul weather all too soon,
Or nurse November on the lap of June.   *Ib.* xcii.

With fingers weary and worn,
With eyelids heavy and red,
A woman sat in unwomanly rags,
Plying her needle and thread—
Stitch! stitch! stitch!
In poverty, hunger, and dirt.
                        The Song of the Shirt.

O! men with sisters dear,
    O! men with mothers and wives!
It is not linen you're wearing out,
    But human creatures' lives!   *Ib.*

Sewing at once, with a double thread,
    A shroud as well as a shirt.   *Ib.*

Oh! God! that bread should be so dear,
    And flesh and blood so cheap!   *Ib.*

No blessed leisure for love or hope,
    But only time for grief!   *Ib.*

My tears must stop, for every drop
    Hinders needle and thread!   *Ib.*

A wife who preaches in her gown,
And lectures in her night-dress!
                    The Surplice Question.

Our hands have met, but not our hearts;
Our hands will never meet again. *To a False Friend.*

There are three things which the public will always
    clamour for, sooner or later: namely, Novelty,
    novelty, novelty.
            Announcement of Comic Annual for 1836.

The sedate, sober, silent, serious, sad-coloured sect
    [Quakers].   *The Doves and the Crows.*

'Extremes meet', as the whiting said with its tail in
    its mouth.   *Ib.*

I don't set up for being a cosmo-polite, which, to
    my mind, signifies being polite to every country
    except your own.
                    Up the Rhine. To Gerard Brooke.

Holland . . . lies so low they're only saved by being
    dammed.   *Ib. To Rebecca Page.*

RICHARD HOOKER
1554?–1600

He that goeth about to persuade a multitude, that
    they are not so well governed as they ought to be,
    shall never want attentive and favourable hearers.
                Ecclesiastical Polity, bk. i, § 1.

Of Law there can be no less acknowledged, than that
    her seat is the bosom of God, her voice the har-
    mony of the world: all things in heaven and earth
    do her homage, the very least as feeling her care,
    and the greatest as not exempted from her power.
                                      Ib. § xvi.

Change is not made without inconvenience, even from
    worse to better.
            *Quoted by Johnson, as from Hooker, in the
            Preface to the 'English Dictionary'.*

ELLEN STURGIS HOOPER
1816–1841

I slept, and dreamed that life was Beauty;
I woke, and found that life was Duty.
                                    Life a Duty.

HERBERT CLARK HOOVER
1874–

Our country has deliberately undertaken a great
    social and economic experiment, noble in motive
    and far-reaching in purpose. [The Eighteenth
    Amendment, enacting Prohibition.]
        Letter to Senator W. H. Borah, 28 Feb. 1928.

ANTHONY HOPE (ANTHONY HOPE HAWKINS)

1863–1933

'You oughtn't to yield to temptation.'
'Well, somebody must, or the thing becomes absurd.'
Dolly Dialogues, No. 14.

'Boys will be boys——'
'And even that . . . wouldn't matter if we could only
   prevent girls from being girls.'   *Ib*. No 16.

'*Bourgeois*,' I observed, 'is an epithet which the riff-
   raff apply to what is respectable, and the aristocracy
   to what is decent.'   *Ib*. No. 17.

He is very fond of making things which he doesn't
   want, and then giving them to people who have no
   use for them.   *Ib.*

'I wish you would read a little poetry sometimes.
   Your ignorance cramps my conversation.'
          Ib. No. 22.

'I may not understand, but I am willing to admire.'
          Ib.

Good families are generally worse than any others.
          Prisoner of Zenda, ch. 1.

LAURENCE HOPE (ADELA FLORENCE NICOLSON)

1865–1904

Pale hands I loved beside the Shalimar,
Where are you now? Who lies beneath your spell?
    Indian Love Lyrics. Pale Hands I Loved.

Pale hands, pink-tipped, like lotus-buds that float
On those cool waters where we used to dwell,
I would have rather felt you round my throat
Crushing out life than waving me farewell.   *Ib.*

Less than the dust beneath thy chariot wheel,
Less than the weed that grows beside thy door,
Less than the rust that never stained thy sword,
Less than the need thou hast in life of me,
   Even less am I.
         Ib. Less than the Dust.

GERARD MANLEY HOPKINS

1844–1889

Not, I'll not, carrion comfort, Despair, not feast on
   thee;
Not untwist—slack they may be—these last strands
   of man
In me or, most weary, cry *I can no more*. I can;
Can something, hope, wish day come, not choose not
   to be.   *Carrion Comfort.*

    That night, that year
Of now done darkness I wretch lay wrestling with
   (my God!) my God.   *Ib.*

Towery city and branchy between towers.
          Duns Scotus' Oxford.

Didst fettle for the great grey drayhorse his bright
   and battering sandal!   *Felix Randal.*

The world is charged with the grandeur of God.
          God's Grandeur.

Because the Holy Ghost over the bent
World broods with warm breast and with ah! bright
   wings.   *Ib.*

I have desired to go
Where springs not fail,
To fields where flies no sharp and sided hail
And a few lilies blow.

And I have asked to be
Where no storms come,
Where the green swell is in the havens dumb,
And out of the swing of the sea.
          Heaven-Haven.

What would the world be, once bereft
Of wet and of wildness? Let them be left,
O let them be left, wildness and wet;
Long live the weeds and the wilderness yet.
          Inversnaid.

          All
Life death does end and each day dies with sleep.
          No Worst, There Is None.

Glory be to God for dappled things.
          Pied Beauty.

All things counter, original, spare, strange;
Whatever is fickle, freckled (who knows how?)
With swift, slow; sweet, sour; adazzle, dim;
He fathers-forth whose beauty is past change:
     Praise him.   *Ib.*

I am all at once what Christ is, since he was what I
   am, and
This Jack, joke, poor potsherd, patch, matchwood,
   immortal diamond,
    Is immortal diamond.
          That Nature is a Heraclitean Fire.

Wild air, world-mothering air,
Nestling me everywhere.
       *The Blessed Virgin Compared to the Air We
       Breathe.*

Some candle clear burns somewhere I came by.
I muse at how its being puts blissful back
With yellowy moisture mild night's blear-all black,
Or to-fro tender trambeams truckle at the eye.
          The Candle Indoors.

Elected Silence, sing to me
And beat upon my whorlèd ear,
Pipe me to pastures still and be
The music that I care to hear.
          The Habit of Perfection.

Palate, the hutch of tasty lust,
Desire not to be rinsed with wine:
The can must be so sweet, the crust
So fresh that come in fasts divine!   *Ib.*

And you unhouse and house the Lord.   *Ib.*

Look at the stars! look, look up at the skies!
O look at all the fire-folk sitting in the air!
The bright boroughs, the circle-citadels there!
          The Starlight Night.

Ah well! it is all a purchase, all is a prize.
Buy then! bid then!—What?—Prayer, patience, alms,
vows.
Look, look: a May-mess, like on orchard boughs!
Look! March-bloom, like on mealed-with-yellow
sallows!
These are indeed the barn; withindoors house
The shocks. This piece-bright paling shuts the
spouse
Christ home, Christ and his mother and all his
hallows. *Ib.*

Thou art indeed just, Lord, if I contend
With thee; but, sir, so what I plead is just.
Why do sinners' ways prosper? and why must
Disappointment all I endeavour end?
Thou Art Indeed Just, Lord.

Birds build—but not I build; no, but strain,
Time's eunuch, and not breed one work that wakes.
Mine, O thou lord of life, send my roots rain. *Ib.*

I caught this morning morning's minion, kingdom of
daylight's dauphin, dapple-dawn-drawn Falcon.
The Windhover.

The achieve of, the mastery of the thing! *Ib.*

JOSEPH HOPKINSON
1770–1842

Hail, Columbia! happy land!
Hail, ye heroes! heaven-born band! *Hail, Columbia!*

RICHARD HENRY HORNE
1803–1884

'Tis always morning somewhere in the world.
Orion, bk. iii, canto ii.

Ye rigid Ploughmen! Bear in mind
Your labour is for future hours.
Advance! Spare not! Nor look behind!
Plough deep and straight with all your powers!
The Plough.

JOHN HOSKINS
1566–1638

Absence, hear thou my protestation
Against thy strength,
Distance and length:
Do what thou canst for alteration,
For hearts of truest mettle
Absence doth join, and time doth settle.
Absence: A Poetical Rhapsody. Attr.

By absence this good means I gain,
That I can catch her,
Where none can watch her,
In some close corner of my brain:
There I embrace and kiss her,
And so I both enjoy and miss her. *Ib.*

RICHARD MONCKTON
MILNES, BARON HOUGHTON
1809–1885

'Lady Moon, Lady Moon, where are you roving?'
'Over the sea.'
'Lady Moon, Lady Moon, whom are you loving?'
'All that love me.' *A Child's Song: Lady Moon.*

A fair little girl sat under a tree,
Sewing as long as her eyes could see;
Then smoothed her work, and folded it right,
And said, 'Dear work! Good Night! Good Night!'
Good Night and Good Morning.

I wander'd by the brookside,
I wander'd by the mill,—
I could not hear the brook flow,
The noisy wheel was still;
There was no burr of grasshopper,
No chirp of any bird;
But the beating of my own heart
Was all the sound I heard. *Song: The Brookside.*

A Second Class in the School of Life.
G. W. E. Russell. Collections and Recollections
ch. 5.

ALFRED EDWARD HOUSMAN
1859–1936

Loveliest of trees, the cherry now
Is hung with bloom along the bough,
And stands about the woodland ride
Wearing white for Eastertide.

Now, of my three score years and ten,
Twenty will not come again,
And take from seventy years a score,
It only leaves me fifty more.

And since to look at things in bloom
Fifty springs are little room,
About the woodlands I will go
To see the cherry hung with snow.
A Shropshire Lad, ii.

And naked to the hangman's noose
The morning clocks will ring
A neck God made for other use
Than strangling in a string. *Ib. ix.*

In farm and field through all the shire
The eye beholds the heart's desire;
Ah, let not only mine be vain
For lovers should be loved again. *Ib. x.*

Lovers lying two and two
Ask not whom they sleep beside,
And the bridegroom all night through
Never turns him to the bride. *Ib. xii.*

When I was one-and-twenty
I heard a wise man say,
'Give crowns and pounds and guineas
But not your heart away.' *Ib. xiii.*

But I was one-and-twenty,
No use to talk to me. *Ib.*

When I was one-and-twenty
I heard him say again,
'The heart out of the bosom
Was never given in vain;
'Tis paid with sighs a plenty
And sold for endless rue.'
And I am two-and-twenty,
And oh, 'tis true, 'tis true. *Ib*

His folly has not fellow
Beneath the blue of day
That gives to man or woman
His heart and soul away. *Ib. xiv*

Oh, when I was in love with you,
　Then I was clean and brave,
And miles around the wonder grew
　How well I did behave.

And now the fancy passes by,
　And nothing will remain,
And miles around they'll say that I
　Am quite myself again.　　*A Shropshire Lad*, xviii.

In summertime on Bredon
　The bells they sound so clear;
Round both the shires they ring them
　In steeples far and near,
　A happy noise to hear.

Here of a Sunday morning
　My love and I would lie,
And see the coloured counties,
　And hear the larks so high
　About us in the sky.

And I would turn and answer
　Among the springing thyme,
'Oh, peal upon our wedding,
　And we will hear the chime,
　And come to church in time.'　　*Ib.* xxi.

They tolled the one bell only,
　Groom there was none to see,
The mourners followed after,
　And so to church went she,
　And would not wait for me.　　*Ib.*

The bells they sound on Bredon,
　And still the steeples hum.
'Come all to church, good people,'—
　Oh, noisy bells, be dumb;
　I hear you, I will come.　　*Ib.*

The lads that will die in their glory and never be old.
　　　　　　　　　　　　　　Ib. xxiii.

Is my team ploughing,
　That I was used to drive?　　*Ib.* xxvii.

Ay, the horses trample,
　The harness jingles now;
No change though you lie under
　The land you used to plough.　　*Ib.*

The goal stands up, the keeper
　Stands up to keep the goal.　　*Ib.*

Yes, lad, I lie easy,
　I lie as lads would choose;
I cheer a dead man's sweetheart,
　Never ask me whose.　　*Ib.*

To-day the Roman and his trouble
　Are ashes under Uricon.　　*Ib.* xxxi.

'Oh, go where you are wanted, for you are not wanted
　here.'
And that was all the farewell when I parted from my
　dear.　　　　*Ib.* xxxiv. *The New Mistress.*

'And the enemies of England they shall see me and
　be sick.'　　　　　　　　　　*Ib.*

White in the moon the long road lies,
　The moon stands blank above;
White in the moon the long road lies
　That leads me from my love.　　*Ib.* xxxvi.

Oh tarnish late on Wenlock Edge,
　Gold that I never see;
Lie long, high snowdrifts in the hedge
　That will not shower on me.　　*Ib.* xxxix.

Into my heart an air that kills
　From yon far country blows.
What are those blue remembered hills,
　What spires, what farms are those?

That is the land of lost content,
　I see it shining plain,
The happy highways where I went
　And cannot come again.　　*Ib.* xl.

But play the man, stand up and end you,
　When your sickness is your soul.　　*Ib.* xlv.

Be still, be still, my soul; it is but for a season;
　Let us endure an hour and see injustice done.
　　　　　　　　　　　　　　Ib. xlviii.

Oh 'tis jesting, dancing, drinking
Spins the heavy world around.
If young hearts were not so clever,
Oh, they would be young for ever:
Think no more; 'tis only thinking
Lays lads underground.　　　　*Ib.* xlix.

Think no more, lad; laugh, be jolly:
Why should men make haste to die?
Empty heads and tongues a-talking
Make the rough road easy walking,
And the feather pate of folly
Bears the falling sky.　　　　*Ib.*

Far in a western brookland
　That bred me long ago
The poplars stand and tremble
　By pools I used to know.　　*Ib.* lii.

There, by the starlit fences,
　The wanderer halts and hears
My soul that lingers sighing
　About the glimmering weirs.　　*Ib.*

Many a rose-lipt maiden
　And many a lightfoot lad.　　*Ib.* liv.

I shall have lived a little while
　Before I die for ever.　　*Ib.* lvii.

In all the endless road you tread
　There's nothing but the night.　　*Ib.* lx.

Say, for what were hop-yards meant,
Or why was Burton built on Trent?　　*Ib.* lxii.

Malt does more than Milton can,
To justify God's ways to man.　　*Ib.*

Mithridates, he died old.　　*Ib.*

We'll to the woods no more,
　The laurels all are cut.　*Last Poems*, introductory.

And lads are in love with the grave.　　*Ib.* iv.

Peace is come and wars are over,
　Welcome you and welcome all.　　*Ib.* viii.

May will be fine next year as like as not:
　Oh ay, but then we shall be twenty-four.　*Ib.* ix.

We for a certainty are not the first
　Have sat in taverns while the tempest hurled
Their hopeful plans to emptiness, and cursed
　Whatever brute and blackguard made the world.
　　　　　　　　　　　　　　Ib.

The troubles of our proud and angry dust
Are from eternity, and shall not fail.
Bear them we can, and if we can we must.
Shoulder the sky, my lad, and drink your ale   *Ib.*

Pass me the can, lad; there's an end of May.   *Ib.*

But men at whiles are sober
And think by fits and starts.
And if they think, they fasten
Their hands upon their hearts.   *Ib.* x.

I, a stranger and afraid
In a world I never made.   *Ib.* xii.

The Wain upon the northern steep
Descends and lifts away.
Oh I will sit me down and weep
For bones in Africa.   *Ib.* xvii. *Astronomy.*

Made of earth and sea
His overcoat for ever,
And wears the turning globe.   *Ib.* xx.

The fairies break their dances
And leave the printed lawn,
And up from India glances
The silver sail of dawn.

The candles burn their sockets,
The blinds let through the day,
The young man feels his pockets
And wonders what's to pay.   *Ib.* xxi.

See, in mid heaven the sun is mounted; hark,
The belfries tingle to the noonday chime.
'Tis silent, and the subterranean dark
Has crossed the nadir, and begins to climb.
                                    Ib. xxxvi.

These, in the day when heaven was falling,
The hour when earth's foundations fled,
Followed their mercenary calling
And took their wages and are dead.

Their shoulders held the sky suspended;
They stood, and earth's foundations stay;
What God abandoned, these defended,
And saved the sum of things for pay.
        Ib. xxxvii. *Epitaph on an Army of Mercenaries.*

RICHARD HOVEY

1864–1900

I do not know beneath what sky
Nor on what seas shall be thy fate;
I only know it shall be high,
I only know it shall be great.
                            Unmanifest Destiny.

WILLIAM WALSHAM HOW

1823–1897

For all the Saints who from their labours rest,
Who Thee by faith before the world confess'd,
Thy Name, O Jesu, be for ever blest,
                            Alleluia!
        *E. Nelson's Hymns For Saints' Days; For All
        the Saints.*

And when the strife is fierce, the warfare long,
Steals on the ear the distant triumph-song,
And hearts are brave again, and arms are strong.
                            Alleluia!   *Ib.*

From earth's wide bounds, from ocean's farthest
coast,
Through gates of pearl streams in the countless host,
Singing to Father, Son, and Holy Ghost,
                            Alleluia!   *Ib.*

O Lord, stretch forth thy mighty hand
And guard and bless our fatherland.
        Church Hymns, 1871. *To Thee, Our God,
        We Fly.*

O Jesu, thou art standing
Outside the fast-closed door.
                    Psalms and Hymns, 1867.

Shame on us, Christian brethren,
His Name and sign who bear.   *Ib.*

SAMUEL HOWARD

1710–1782

Gentle Shepherd, tell me where.   *Song.*

ELLEN CLEMENTINE HOWARTH

1827–1899

'Tis but a little faded flow'r,
But oh, how fondly dear!
'Twill bring me back one golden hour,
Through many a weary year.
            'Tis But a Little Faded Flower.

JULIA WARD HOWE

1819–1910

Mine eyes have seen the glory of the coming of the
Lord:
He is trampling out the vintage where the grapes of
wrath are stored.
            Battle Hymn of the American Republic.

His truth is marching on.   *Ib.*

Oh, be swift, my soul, to answer Him, be jubilant,
my feet!   *Ib.*

In the beauty of the lilies Christ was born, across the
sea,
With a glory in His bosom that transfigures you and
me:
As He died to make men holy, let us die to make men
free.   *Ib.*

JAMES HOWELL

1594?–1666

Some hold translations not unlike to be
The wrong side of a Turkey tapestry.
            Familiar Letters, bk. i, § 6.

One hair of a woman can draw more than a hundred
pair of oxen.   *Ib.* bk. ii, let. 4.

This life at best is but an inn,
And we the passengers.   *Ib.* let. 73.

MARY HOWITT

1799–1888

Old England is our home and Englishmen are we,
Our tongue is known in every clime, our flag on every
    sea.   *Old England Is Our Home.*

'Will you walk into my parlour?' said a spider to a fly:
''Tis the prettiest little parlour that ever you did spy.'
        The Spider and the Fly.

EDMOND HOYLE

1672–1769

When in doubt, win the trick.
   Hoyle's Games. Whist. Twenty-four Short
   Rules for Learners.

ELBERT HUBBARD

1859–1915

Heaven is largely a matter of digestion.
       A Thousand and One Epigrams, p. 34.

Life is just one damned thing after another.
       Ib. p. 137.

THOMAS HUGHES

1822–1896

Life isn't all beer and skittles.
    Tom Brown's Schooldays, pt. i, ch. 2.

He never wants anything but what's right and fair;
only when you come to settle what's right and fair,
it's everything that he wants and nothing that you
want. And that's his idea of a compromise. Give
me the Brown compromise when I'm on his side.
       Ib. pt. ii, ch. 2.

DAVID HUME

1711–1776

Avarice, the spur of industry.
       Essays. Of Civil Liberty.

A miracle may be accurately defined, a transgression
of a law of nature by a particular volition of the
Deity, or by the interposition of some invisible
agent.   *On Miracles,* pt. 1, *note.*

No testimony is sufficient to establish a miracle,
unless the testimony be of such a kind, that its
falsehood would be more miraculous than the fact
which it endeavours to establish: and even in that
case there is a mutual destruction of arguments,
and the superior only gives us an assurance suitable
to that degree of force which remains after de-
ducting the inferior.   *Ib.* pt. 1.

There is not to be found, in all history, any miracle
attested by a sufficient number of men, of such
unquestioned good sense, education, and learning,
as to secure us against all delusion in themselves;
of such undoubted integrity, as to place them
beyond all suspicion of any design to deceive

others; of such credit and reputation in the eyes
of mankind, as to have a great deal to lose in case
of their being detected in any falsehood; and at
the same time attesting facts, performed in such
a public manner, and in so celebrated a part of
the world, as to render the detection unavoidable.
       Ib. pt. 2.

The usual propensity of mankind towards the
marvellous.   *Ib.*

The Christian religion not only was at first attended
with miracles, but even at this day cannot be
believed by any reasonable person without one.
Mere reason is insufficient to convince us of its
veracity: and whoever is moved by faith to assent
to it, is conscious of a continued miracle in his
own person, which subverts all the principles of
his understanding, and gives him a determination
to believe what is most contrary to custom and
experience.   *Ib.*

Custom, then, is the great guide of human life.
   Inquiry Concerning Human Understanding, sec.
   5, pt. 1.

Never literary attempt was more unfortunate than my
Treatise of Human Nature. It fell *dead-born from*
the press.   *My Own Life,* ch. 1.

Opposing one species of superstition to another, set
them a quarrelling; while we ourselves, during
their fury and contention, happily make our escape
into the calm, though obscure, regions of philosophy.   *The Natural History of Religion.*

Though I throw out my speculations to entertain
the learned and metaphysical world, yet in other
things I do not think so differently from the rest
of the world as you imagine.
   Remark. Alexander Carlyle's Autobiography.

G. W. HUNT

fl. 1878

We don't want to fight, but, by jingo if we do,
We've got the ships, we've got the men, we've got the
   money too.
We've fought the Bear before, and while Britons shall
   be true,
The Russians shall not have Constantinople.
   We Don't Want to Fight. Music Hall Song,
   1878.

JAMES HENRY LEIGH HUNT

1784–1859

Abou Ben Adhem (may his tribe increase!)
Awoke one night from a deep dream of peace,
And saw, within the moonlight in his room,
Making it rich, and like a lily in bloom,
An angel writing in a book of gold:—
Exceeding peace had made Ben Adhem bold,
And to the presence in the room he said,
'What writest thou?'—The vision raised its head,
And with a look made of all sweet accord,
Answered, 'The names of those who love the Lord.'
       Abou Ben Adhem and the Angel.

H 3

a

b

'I pray thee then,
Write me as one that loves his fellow-men.'   *Ib.*

And lo! Ben Adhem's name led all the rest.   *Ib.*

'By God!' said Francis, 'rightly done!' and he rose
    from where he sat:
'No love,' quoth he, 'but vanity, sets love a task like
    that.'   *The Glove and the Lions.*

Green little vaulter in the sunny grass.
    To the Grasshopper and the Cricket.

The laughing queen that caught the world's great
    hands.   *The Nile.*

If you become a nun, dear,
A friar I will be.
In any cell you run, dear,
Pray look behind for me.   *The Nun.*

Jenny kissed me when we met,
Jumping from the chair she sat in;
Time, you thief, who love to get
Sweets into your list, put that in:
Say I'm weary, say I'm sad,
Say that health and wealth have missed me,
Say I'm growing old, but add,
Jenny kissed me.   *Rondeau.*

Where the light woods go seaward from the town.
    The Story of Rimini, i, l. 18.

But most he loved a happy human face.
    Ib. iii, l. 110.

The two divinest things this world has got,
A lovely woman in a rural spot!   *Ib.* l. 257.

Places of nestling green, for poets made.   *Ib.* l. 430.

This Adonis in loveliness was a corpulent man of
    fifty. [George IV]
    The Examiner, 22 Mar. 1812.

ANNE HUNTER
1742–1821

My mother bids me bind my hair
    With bands of rosy hue,
Tie up my sleeves with ribbons rare,
    And lace my bodice blue.

'For why,' she cries, 'sit still and weep,
    While others dance and play?'
Alas! I scarce can go or creep
    While Lubin is away.
    My Mother Bids Me Bind My Hair.

FRANCIS HUTCHESON
1694–1746

Wisdom denotes the pursuing of the best ends by the
    best means.
    *Inquiry into the Original of our Ideas of Beauty
    and Virtue,* 1725. Treatise, I, sec. v, § 18.

That action is best, which procures the greatest happi-
    ness for the greatest numbers.
    Ib. Treatise II. *Concerning Moral Good and
    Evil,* sec. 3, § 8.

ALDOUS LEONARD HUXLEY
1894–

But when the wearied Band
Swoons to a waltz, I take her hand,
And there we sit in peaceful calm,
Quietly sweating palm to palm.   *Frascati's.*

Seated upon the convex mound
Of one vast kidney, Jonah prays
And sings his canticles and hymns,
Making the hollow vault resound
God's goodness and mysterious ways,
Till the great fish spouts music as he swims.   *Jonah.*

Bewildered furrows deepen the Thunderer's scowl;
This world so vast, so variously foul—
Who can have made its ugliness? In what
Revolting fancy were the Forms begot
Of all these monsters? What strange deity—
So barbarously not a Greek was he?   *Leda.*

Your maiden modesty would float face down,
And men would weep upon your hinder parts.   *Ib.*

Beauty for some provides escape,
Who gain a happiness in eyeing
The gorgeous buttocks of the ape
Or Autumn sunsets exquisitely dying.
    The Ninth Philosopher's Song.

Then brim the bowl with atrabilious liquor!
We'll pledge our Empire vast across the flood:
For Blood, as all men know, than water's thicker,
But water's wider, thank the Lord, than Blood.   *Ib.*

THOMAS HENRY HUXLEY
1825–1895

The chess-board is the world; the pieces are the
phenomena of the universe; the rules of the game
are what we call the laws of Nature. The player on
the other side is hidden from us. We know that
his play is always fair, just, and patient. But also
we know, to our cost, that he never overlooks a
mistake, or makes the smallest allowance for ignorance.
    Lay Sermons, &c., iii. *A Liberal Education.*

If some great Power would agree to make me always
think what is true and do what is right, on condition of being turned into a sort of clock and
wound up every morning before I got out of bed,
I should instantly close with the offer.
    *On Descartes' Discourse on Method. Method &
    Results* iv.

The great end of life is not knowledge but action.
> *Science & Culture*, iii. *Technical Education.*

Logical consequences are the scarecrows of fools and the beacons of wise men.
> *Ib.* ix. *On the Hypothesis that Animals are Automata.*

Irrationally held truths may be more harmful than reasoned errors.
> *Ib.* xii. *The Coming of Age of the Origin of Species.*

It is the customary fate of new truths to begin as heresies and to end as superstitions.   *Ib.*

I took thought, and invented what I conceived to be the appropriate title of 'agnostic'.
> *Science and Christian Tradition*, ch. 7.

EDWARD HYDE
EARL OF CLARENDON
1609–1674

Without question, when he [Hampden] first drew the sword, he threw away the scabbard.
> *History of the Great Rebellion*, III. vii. 84.

He [Hampden] had a head to contrive, a tongue to persuade, and a hand to execute any mischief.
> *Ib.*

He [Falkland] . . . would, with a shrill and sad accent, ingeminate the word *Peace, Peace.*   *Ib.* 233.

WILLIAM RALPH INGE
1860–

Literature flourishes best when it is half a trade and half an art.
> *The Victorian Age* (1922), p. 49.

A man may build himself a throne of bayonets, but he cannot sit on it.
> Marchant, *Wit and Wisdom of Dean Inge*, No. 108.

The nations which have put mankind and posterity most in their debt have been small states—Israel, Athens, Florence, Elizabethan England.
> *Ib.* No. 181.

JEAN INGELOW
1820–1897

But two are walking apart for ever,
  And wave their hands for a mute farewell.
> *Divided.*

When sparrows build, and the leaves break forth,
My old sorrow wakes and cries.
> *Supper at the Mill.*

Play up 'The Brides of Enderby'.
> *The High Tide on the Coast of Lincolnshire, 1571.*

Come up Whitefoot, come up Lightfoot,
Come up Jetty, rise and follow,
Jetty, to the milking shed.   *Ib.*

A sweeter woman ne'er drew breath
Than my son's wife, Elizabeth.   *Ib.*

And awesome bells they were to me,
That in the dark rang 'Enderby'.   *Ib.*

That flow strewed wrecks about the grass,
That ebb swept out the flocks to sea;
A fatal ebb and flow, alas!
  To many more than mine and me.   *Ib.*

ROBERT GREENE
INGERSOLL
1833–1899

An honest God is the noblest work of man.
> *Gods*, pt. 1, p. 2.

In nature there are neither rewards nor punishments —there are consequences.
> *Lectures & Essays*, 3rd Series. *Some Reasons Why*, viii.

JOHN KELLS INGRAM
1823–1907

Who fears to speak of Ninety-Eight?
> *The Nation*, April 1843.

WASHINGTON IRVING
1783–1859

A tart temper never mellows with age, and a sharp tongue is the only edged tool that grows keener with constant use.   *Rip Van Winkle.*

They who drink beer will think beer.
> *The Sketch Book. Stratford.*

A woman's whole life is a history of the affections.
> *Ib. The Broken Heart.*

Free-livers on a small scale; who are prodigal within the compass of a guinea.   *The Stout Gentleman.*

I am always at a loss to know how much to believe of my own stories.
> *Tales of a Traveller*, To the Reader.

There is a certain relief in change, even though it be from bad to worse; as I have found in travelling in a stage-coach, that it is often a comfort to shift one's position and be bruised in a new place.   *Ib.*

The almighty dollar, that great object of universal devotion throughout our land, seems to have no genuine devotees in these peculiar villages.
> *Wolfert's Roost. The Creole Village.*

ANDREW JACKSON
1767–1845

You are uneasy; you never sailed with *me* before, I see.
> *J. Parton's Life of Jackson*, vol. iii, ch. 35.

Our Federal Union: it must be preserved.
> *Toast given on the Jefferson Birthday Celebration 13 Apr. 1830.* Benton, *Thirty Years' View*, vol. i.

CARRIE JACOBS-BOND

1862–

When you come to the end of a perfect day.
> *Roads of Melody* (1927). *A Perfect Day.*

RICHARD JAGO

1715–1781

With leaden foot time creeps along
While Delia is away.
> *Absence: With Leaden Foot.*

JAMES I OF ENGLAND AND VI OF SCOTLAND

1566–1625

A branch of the sin of drunkenness, which is the root of all sins.
> *A Counterblast to Tobacco* (1604).

A custom loathsome to the eye, hateful to the nose, harmful to the brain, dangerous to the lungs, and in the black, stinking fume thereof, nearest resembling the horrible Stygian smoke of the pit that is bottomless.
> *Ib.*

Herein is not only a great vanity, but a great contempt of God's good gifts, that the sweetness of man's breath, being a good gift of God, should be wilfully corrupted by this stinking smoke.
> *Ib.*

The wisest fool in Christendom. [James.]
> *Ascribed to Henry IV of France in Green's Short History of the English People* (1888), p. 477.

HENRY JAMES

1843–1916

It takes a great deal of history to produce a little literature.
> *Life of Nathaniel Hawthorne.*

[Thoreau] was worse than provincial—he was parochial.
> *Ib. ch. 4.*

Dramatise, dramatise!
> *Prefaces. Altar of the Dead, and elsewhere.*

The note I wanted; that of the strange and sinister embroidered on the very type of the normal and easy.
> *Ib.*

The terrible *fluidity* of self-revelation.
> *Ib. The Ambassadors.*

The deep well of unconscious cerebration.
> *Ib. The American.*

The historian, essentially, wants more documents than he can really use; the dramatist only wants more liberties than he can really take.
> *Ib. The Aspern Papers, &c.*

I have always fondly remembered a remark that I heard fall years ago from the lips of Ivan Turgenieff in regard to his own experience of the usual origin of the fictive picture. It began for him almost always with the vision of some person or persons, who hovered before him, soliciting him, as the active or passive figure, interesting him and appealing to him just as they were and by what they were. He saw them in that fashion, as *disponibles*, saw them subject to the chances, the complications of existence, and saw them vividly, but then had to find for them the right relations, those that would bring them out.
> *Ib. The Portrait of a Lady.*

The fatal futility of Fact.
> *Ib. The Spoils of Poynton, &c.*

The only obligation to which in advance we may hold a novel, without incurring the accusation of being arbitrary, is that it be interesting.
> *The Art of Fiction. Partial Portraits.*

Experience is never limited, and it is never complete; it is an immense sensibility, a kind of huge spider-web of the finest silken threads suspended in the chamber of consciousness, and catching every air-borne particle in its tissue.
> *Ib.*

What is character but the determination of incident? what is incident but the illustration of character?
> *Ib.*

We must grant the artist his subject, his idea, his *donné*: our criticism is applied only to what he makes of it.
> *Ib.*

Vereker's secret, my dear man—the general intention of his books: the string the pearls were strung on, the buried treasure, the figure in the carpet.
> *The Figure in the Carpet, ch. 11.*

Cats and monkeys, monkeys and cats—all human life is there.
> *The Madonna of the Future.*

Tennyson was not Tennysonian.
> *The Middle Years.*

'Print it as it stands—beautifully.'
> *Terminations. The Death of the Lion, x.*

THOMAS JEFFERSON

1743–1826

In the full tide of successful experiment.
> *First Inaugural Address, 4 March 1801.*

Peace, commerce, and honest friendship with all nations—entangling alliances with none.
> *Ib.*

A little rebellion now and then is a good thing.
> *Letter to James Madison, 30 Jan. 1787.*

The tree of liberty must be refreshed from time to time with the blood of patriots and tyrants. It is its natural manure.
> *Ib. To W. S. Smith, 13 Nov. 1787.*

Whenever a man has cast a longing eye on them [offices], a rottenness begins in his conduct.
> *Ib. To Tench Coxe, 1799.*

To seek out the best through the whole Union, we must resort to other information, which, from the best of men, acting disinterestedly and with the purest motives, is sometimes incorrect.
> *Letter to Elias Shipman and others of New Haven, 12 July, 1801.*

If a due participation of office is a matter of right, how are vacancies to be obtained? Those by death are few; by resignation, none.
[Usually quoted, 'Few die and none resign'.]   *Ib.*

Indeed I tremble for my country when I reflect that God is just.
Notes on Virginia, Query xviii. Manners.

When a man assumes a public trust, he should consider himself as public property.
Remark to Baron von Humboldt, 1807. Rayner's Life of Jefferson, p. 356.

No duty the Executive had to perform was so trying as to put the right man in the right place.
J. B. MacMaster, *History of the People of the U.S.*; vol. ii, ch. 13, p. 586.

CHARLES JEFFERYS
1807–1865

I have heard the mavis singing
His love-song to the morn;
I have seen the dew-drop clinging
To the rose just newly born.   *Mary of Argyle.*

The bud is on the bough again,
The leaf is on the tree.
The Meeting of Spring and Summer.

FRANCIS LORD JEFFREY
1773–1850

This will never do.
On Wordsworth's 'Excursion'. Edinburgh Review, Nov. 1814, p. 1.

SOAME JENYNS
1704–1787

A fair where thousands meet, but none can stay;
An inn where travellers bait, then post away.
The Immortality of the Soul, bk. i, l. 399.
Tr. from the Latin of Isaac Hawkins Browne, 1705–60.

JEROME KLAPKA JEROME
1859–1927

It is impossible to enjoy idling thoroughly unless one has plenty of work to do.
Idle Thoughts of an Idle Fellow. On Being Idle.

Love is like the measles; we all have to go through it.
Ib. On Being in Love

I like work: it fascinates me. I can sit and look at it for hours. I love to keep it by me: the idea of getting rid of it nearly breaks my heart.
Three Men in a Boat, ch. 15.

DOUGLAS WILLIAM JERROLD
1803–1857

Honest bread is very well—it's the butter that makes the temptation.   *The Catspaw*, Act III.

Religion's in the heart, not in the knees.
The Devil's Ducat, I. ii.

He is one of those wise philanthropists who, in a time of famine, would vote for nothing but a supply of toothpicks.
Wit and Opinions of Douglas Jerrold (1859), p. 2. *A Philanthropist.*

Love's like the measles—all the worse when it comes late in life.   *Ib.* p. 6.

The best thing I know between France and England is—the sea.
Ib. p. 13. *The Anglo-French Alliance.*

That fellow would vulgarize the day of judgment.
Ib. A Comic Author.

The ugliest of trades have their moments of pleasure. Now, if I were a grave-digger, or even a hangman, there are some people I could work for with a great deal of enjoyment.   *Ib.* p. 14. *Ugly Trades.*

Earth is here [Australia] so kind, that just tickle her with a hoe and she laughs with a harvest.
Ib. A Land of Plenty.

Some people are so fond of ill-luck that they run half-way to meet it.
Ib. Meeting Troubles Half-way.

He was so good he would pour rose-water over a toad.   *Ib.* p. 17. *A Charitable Man.*

Talk to him of Jacob's ladder, and he would ask the number of the steps.
Ib. p. 29. *A Matter-of-fact Man.*

We love peace, as we abhor pusillanimity; but not peace at any price. There is a peace more destructive of the manhood of living man than war is destructive of his material body. Chains are worse than bayonets.   *Ib.* p. 155. *Peace.*

If an earthquake were to engulf England to-morrow, the English would manage to meet and dine somewhere among the rubbish, just to celebrate the event.
Remark. Blanchard Jerrold's Life of D. Jerrold, ch. 14.

The only athletic sport I ever mastered was backgammon.
W. Jerrold, *Douglas Jerrold* (1914), vol. i, ch. 1, p. 22.

JOHN JEWEL
1522–1571

In old time we had treen chalices and golden priests, but now we have treen priests and golden chalices.
Certain Sermons Preached Before the Queen's Majesty, 1609, p. 176.

ANDREW JOHNSON
1808–1875

We are swinging round the circle.
Speech on the Presidential Reconstruction, August 1866.

LIONEL PIGOT JOHNSON

1867–1902

There Shelley dream'd his white Platonic dreams.
Oxford.

In her ears the chime
Of full, sad bells brings back her old springtide. *Ib.*

I know you: solitary griefs,
Desolate passions, aching hours.
The Precept of Silence.

The saddest of all Kings
Crown'd, and again disown'd.
By the Statue of King Charles I at Charing Cross.

Stars in their stations set;
And every wandering star. *Ib.*

The fair and fatal King. *Ib.*

Speak after sentence? Yea:
And to the end of time. *Ib.*

King, tried in fires of woe!
Men hunger for thy grace:
And through the night I go,
Loving thy mournful face. *Ib.*

PHILANDER CHASE JOHNSON

1866–

Cheer up, the worst is yet to come.
Shooting Stars. See Everybody's Magazine,
May, 1920.

SAMUEL JOHNSON

1709–1784

The rod produces an effect which terminates in itself. A child is afraid of being whipped, and gets his task, and there's an end on't; whereas, by exciting emulation and comparisons of superiority, you lay the foundation of lasting mischief; you make brothers and sisters hate each other.
Boswell's Life of Johnson (L. F. Powell's revision of G. B. Hill's edition), vol. i, p. 46.

Johnson. I had no notion that I was wrong or irreverent to my tutor.
Boswell. That, Sir, was great fortitude of mind.
Johnson. No, Sir; stark insensibility.
Ib. p. 60. *5th Nov. 1728.*

Sir, we are a nest of singing birds. *Ib.* p. 75. *1730.*

If you call a dog *Hervey,* I shall love him.
Ib. p. 106. *1737.*

My old friend, Mrs. Carter, could make a pudding, as well as translate Epictetus. *Ib.* p. 123 n. *1738.*

Sleep, undisturb'd, within this peaceful shrine,
Till angels wake thee with a note like thine!
Ib. p. 149. *1741.*

Great George's acts let tuneful Cibber sing;
For Nature form'd the Poet for the King. *Ib.*

Tom Birch is as brisk as a bee in conversation; but no sooner does he take a pen in his hand, than it becomes a torpedo to him, and benumbs all his faculties. *Ib.* p. 159. *1743.*

[When asked how he felt upon the ill success of *Irene*]
Like the Monument. *Ib.* p. 199. *Feb. 1799.*

I'll come no more behind your scenes, David; for the silk stockings and white bosoms of your actresses excite my amorous propensities. *Ib.* p. 201. *1750.*

A man may write at any time, if he will set himself doggedly to it. *Ib.* p. 203. *Mar. 1750.*

[Of F. Lewis]
Sir, he lived in London, and hung loose upon society.
Ib. p. 226. *1750.*

[To Beauclerk]
Thy body is all vice, and thy mind all virtue.
Ib. p. 250. *1752.*

[On being knocked up at 3 a.m. by Beauclerk and Langton]
What, is it you, you dogs! I'll have a frisk with you.
Ib.

Wretched un-idea'd girls. *Ib.* p. 251. *1753.*

I had done all I could; and no man is well pleased to have his all neglected, be it ever so little.
Ib. p. 261. *Letter to Lord Chesterfield, 7 Feb. 1755.*

The shepherd in Virgil grew at last acquainted with Love, and found him a native of the rocks. *Ib.*

Is not a Patron, my Lord, one who looks with unconcern on a man struggling for life in the water, and, when he has reached ground, encumbers him with help? The notice which you have been pleased to take of my labours, had it been early, had been kind; but it has been delayed till I am indifferent, and cannot enjoy it; till I am solitary, and cannot impart it; till I am known, and do not want it. *Ib.*

[Of Lord Chesterfield]
This man I thought had been a Lord among wits; but, I find, he is only a wit among Lords.
Ib. p. 266. *1754.*

[Of Lord Chesterfield's *Letters*]
They teach the morals of a whore, and the manners of a dancing master. *Ib.*

[Of Bolingbroke and his editor, Mallet]
Sir, he was a scoundrel, and a coward: a scoundrel, for charging a blunderbuss against religion and morality; a coward, because he had not resolution to fire it off himself, but left half a crown to a beggarly Scotchman, to draw the trigger after his death! *Ib.* p. 268. *6 Mar. 1754.*

Mr. Millar, bookseller, undertook the publication of Johnson's Dictionary. When the messenger who carried the last sheet to Millar returned, Johnson asked him, 'Well, what did he say?' 'Sir,' answered the messenger, 'he said, thank God I have done with him.'
'I am glad', replied Johnson, with a smile, 'that he thanks God for any thing.' *Ib.* p. 287. *April 1755.*

I respect Millar, Sir; he has raised the price of literature. *Ib.* p. 288. *1755.*

There are two things which I am confident I can do very well: one is an introduction to any literary work, stating what it is to contain, and how it should be executed in the most perfect manner; the other is a conclusion, shewing from various causes why the execution has not been equal to what the author promised to himself and to the public. *Ib.* p. 292. *1755.*

[When asked by a lady why he defined 'pastern' as the 'knee' of a horse, in his Dictionary]
Ignorance, madam, pure ignorance. *Ib.* p. 293. *1755.*

Lexicographer: a writer of dictionaries, a harmless drudge. *Ib.* p. 296. *1755.*

I have protracted my work till most of those whom I wished to please have sunk into the grave; and success and miscarriage are empty sounds.
Ib. p. 297. *1755.*

A man, Sir, should keep his friendship in constant repair. *Ib.* p. 300. *1755.*

The booksellers are generous liberal-minded men.
Ib. p. 304. *1756.*

The worst of Warburton is, that he has a rage for saying something, when there's nothing to be said.
Ib. p. 329. *1758.*

No man will be a sailor who has contrivance enough to get himself into a jail; for being in a ship is being in a jail, with the chance of being drowned. . . . A man in a jail has more room, better food, and commonly better company. *Ib.* p. 348. *16 Mar. 1759.*

'Are you a botanist, Dr. Johnson?'
'No, Sir, I am not a botanist; and (alluding, no doubt, to his near sightedness) should I wish to become a botanist, I must first turn myself into a reptile.'
Ib. p. 377. *20 July 1762.*

Boswell: I do indeed come from Scotland, but I cannot help it. . . .
Johnson: That, Sir, I find, is what a very great many of your countrymen cannot help.
Ib. p. 392. *16 May 1763.*

[On Dr. Blair's asking whether any man of a modern age could have written *Ossian*]
Yes, Sir, many men, many women, and many children. *Ib.* p. 396. *24 May 1763.*

Sir, it was like leading one to talk of a book when the author is concealed behind the door. *Ib.*

He insisted on people praying with him; and I'd as lief pray with Kit Smart as any one else.
Ib. p. 397. *24 May 1763.*

[Of Kit Smart]
He did not love clean linen; and I have no passion for it. *Ib.*

[Of literary criticism]
You may scold a carpenter who has made you a bad table, though you cannot make a table. It is not your trade to make tables. *Ib.* p. 409. *25 June 1763.*

[Of Dr. John Campbell]
I am afraid he has not been in the inside of a church for many years; but he never passes a church without pulling off his hat. This shews that he has good principles. *Ib.* p. 418. *1 July 1763.*

[Of Dr. John Campbell]
He is the richest author that ever grazed the common of literature. *Ib.* n.

Norway, too, has noble wild prospects; and Lapland is remarkable for prodigious noble wild prospects. But, Sir, let me tell you, the noblest prospect which a Scotchman ever sees, is the high road that leads him to England! *Ib.* p. 425. *6 July 1763.*

A man ought to read just as inclination leads him; for what he reads as a task will do him little good.
Ib. p. 428. *14 July 1763.*

But if he does really think that there is no distinction between virtue and vice, why, Sir, when he leaves our houses let us count our spoons.
Ib. p. 432. *14 July 1763.*

Truth, Sir, is a cow, which will yield such people [sceptics] no more milk, and so they are gone to milk the bull. *Ib.* p. 444. *21 July 1763.*

Your levellers wish to level *down* as far as themselves; but they cannot bear levelling *up* to themselves.
Ib. p. 448. *21 July 1763.*

Sir, it is no matter what you teach them [children] first, any more than what leg you shall put into your breeches first. *Ib.* p. 452. *26 July 1763.*

Why, Sir, Sherry [Thomas Sheridan] is dull, naturally dull; but it must have taken him a great deal of pains to become what we now see him. Such an excess of stupidity, Sir, is not in Nature.
Ib. p. 453. *28 July 1763.*

[Of Sheridan's influence on the English language]
Sir, it is burning a farthing candle at Dover, to shew light at Calais. *Ib.* p. 454. *28 July 1763.*

Sir, a woman's preaching is like a dog's walking on his hinder legs. It is not done well; but you are surprised to find it done at all.
Ib. p. 463. *31 July 1763.*

I look upon it, that he who does not mind his belly will hardly mind anything else.
Ib. p. 467. *5 Aug. 1763.*

This was a good dinner enough, to be sure; but it was not a dinner to *ask* a man to.
Ib. p. 470. *5 Aug. 1763.*

Sir, we could not have had a better dinner had there been a *Synod of Cooks.* *Ib.*

[Talking of Bishop Berkeley's theory of the non-existence of matter, Boswell observed that though they were satisfied it was not true, they were unable to refute it. Johnson struck his foot against a large stone, till he rebounded from it, saying]
I refute it *thus.* *Ib.* p. 471. *6 Aug. 1763.*

[Of Sir John Hawkins]
A very unclubable man. *Ib.* p. 480 n. *1764.*

Our tastes greatly alter. The lad does not care for the child's rattle, and the old man does not care for the young man's whore.
Ib. vol. ii, p. 14. *Spring, 1766.*

It was not for me to bandy civilities with my Sovereign. *Ib.* p. 35. *Feb. 1767.*

Johnson: Well, we had a good talk.
Boswell: Yes, Sir; you tossed and gored several persons. *Ib.* p. 66. *1769.*

Let me smile with the wise, and feed with the rich.
Ib. p. 79. *6 Oct. 1769.*

Sir, We *know* our will is free, and *there's* an end on't.
Ib. p. 82. *16 Oct. 1769.*

Inspissated gloom. *Ib.*

I do not know, Sir, that the fellow is an infidel; but if he be an infidel, he is an infidel as a dog is an infidel; that is to say, he has never thought upon the subject. *Ib.* p. 95. *19 Oct. 1769.*

I would not *coddle* the child.
Ib. p. 101. *26 Oct. 1769.*

Boswell: So, Sir, you laugh at schemes of political improvement?

Johnson: Why, Sir, most schemes of political improvement are very laughable things.
> Boswell's *Life of Johnson*, vol. ii, p. 102. *26 Oct. 1769.*

It matters not how a man dies, but how he lives.
> *Ib.* p. 106. *26 Oct. 1769.*

Burton's *Anatomy of Melancholy*, he said, was the only book that ever took him out of bed two hours sooner than he wished to rise.   *Ib.* p. 121. *1770.*

[On Jonas Hanway, who followed his *Travels to Persia* with *An Eight Day's Journey from London to Portsmouth*]
Jonas acquired some reputation by travelling abroad, but lost it all by travelling at home.
> *Ib.* p. 122. *1770.*

That fellow seems to me to possess but one idea, and that is a wrong one.   *Ib.* p. 126. *1770.*

A gentleman who had been very unhappy in marriage, married immediately after his wife died: Johnson said, it was the triumph of hope over experience.
> *Ib.* p. 128. *1770.*

Every man has a lurking wish to appear considerable in his native place.
> *Ib.* p. 141. *Letter to Sir Joshua Reynolds, 17 July 1771.*

Nobody can write the life of a man, but those who have eat and drunk and lived in social intercourse with him.   *Ib.* p. 166. *31 Mar. 1772.*

I would not give half a guinea to live under one form of government rather than another. It is of no moment to the happiness of an individual.
> *Ib.* p. 170. *31 Mar. 1772.*

[To Sir Adam Fergusson]
Sir, I perceive you are a vile Whig.   *Ib.*

There is a remedy in human nature against tyranny, that will keep us safe under every form of government.   *Ib.*

A man who is good enough to go to heaven, is good enough to be a clergyman. *Ib.* p. 171. *5 Apr. 1772.*

Sir, there is more knowledge of the heart in one letter of Richardson's, than in all *Tom Jones*.
> *Ib.* p. 174. *6 Apr. 1772.*

Why, Sir, if you were to read Richardson for the story, your impatience would be so much fretted that you would hang yourself.
> *Ib.* p. 175. *6 Apr. 1772.*

[On Lord Mansfield, who was educated in England]
Much may be made of a Scotchman, if he be *caught* young.   *Ib.* p. 194. *Spring 1772.*

[On Goldsmith's apology in the *London Chronicle* for beating Evans the bookseller]
It is a foolish thing well done.
> *Ib.* p. 210. *3 Apr. 1773.*

Elphinston: What, have you not read it through? . . .
Johnson: No, Sir, do *you* read books *through*?
> *Ib.* p. 226. *19 Apr. 1773.*

[Quoting a college tutor]
Read over your compositions, and where ever you meet with a passage which you think is particularly fine, strike it out.   *Ib.* p. 237. *30 Apr. 1773.*

He [Goldsmith] is now writing a Natural History and will make it as entertaining as a Persian Tale.   *Ib.*

[Of Lady Diana Beauclerk]
The woman's a whore, and there's an end on't.
> *Ib.* p. 247. *7 May 1773.*

I hope I shall never be deterred from detecting what I think a cheat, by the menaces of a ruffian.
> *Ib.* p. 298. *Letter to James Macpherson, 20 Jan. 1775.*

[To Dr. Barnard, Bishop of Killaloe]
The Irish are a fair people;—they never speak well of one another.   *Ib.* p. 307. *1775.*

[To William Strahan]
There are few ways in which a man can be more innocently employed than in getting money.
> *Ib.* p. 323. *27 Mar. 1775.*

He [Thomas Gray] was dull in a new way, and that made many people think him *great*.
> *Ib.* p. 327. *28 Mar. 1775.*

I never think I have hit hard, unless it rebounds.
> *Ib.* p. 335. *2 Apr. 1775.*

I think the full tide of human existence is at Charing-Cross.   *Ib.* p. 337. *2 Apr. 1775.*

Most vices may be committed very genteelly: a man may debauch his friend's wife genteelly: he may cheat at cards genteelly. *Ib.* p. 340. *6 Apr. 1775.*

George the First knew nothing, and desired to know nothing; did nothing, and desired to do nothing; and the only good thing that is told of him is, that he wished to restore the crown to its hereditary successor.   *Ib.* p. 342. *6 Apr. 1775.*

A man will turn over half a library to make one book.
> *Ib.* p. 344. *6 Apr. 1775.*

Patriotism is the last refuge of a scoundrel.
> *Ib.* p. 348. *7 Apr. 1775.*

That is the happiest conversation where there is no competition, no vanity, but a calm quiet interchange of sentiments.   *Ib.* p. 359. *14 Apr. 1775.*

[On the Scotch]
Their learning is like bread in a besieged town: every man gets a little, but no man gets a full meal.
> *Ib.* p. 363. *18 Apr. 1775.*

Knowledge is of two kinds. We know a subject ourselves, or we know where we can find information upon it.   *Ib.* p. 365. *18 Apr. 1775.*

In lapidary inscriptions a man is not upon oath.
> *Ib.* p. 407. *1775.*

There is now less flogging in our great schools than formerly, but then less is learned there; so that what the boys get at one end they lose at the other.   *Ib.*

When men come to like a sea-life, they are not fit to live on land.   *Ib.* p. 438. *18 Mar. 1776.*

Sir, it is a great thing to dine with the Canons of Christ-Church.   *Ib.* p. 445. *20 Mar. 1776.*

There is nothing which has yet been contrived by man, by which so much happiness is produced as by a good tavern or inn.
> *Ib.* p. 452. *21 Mar. 1776.*

Marriages would in general be as happy, and often more so, if they were all made by the Lord Chancellor.
> Boswell's *Life of Johnson*, vol. ii, p. 461. 22 Mar. 1776.

Questioning is not the mode of conversation among gentlemen.   *Ib.* p. 472. *Mar. 1776.*

Fine clothes are good only as they supply the want of other means of procuring respect.
> *Ib.* p. 475. *27 Mar. 1776.*

[Johnson had observed that a man is never happy for the present, but when he is drunk, and Boswell said: 'Will you not add,—or when driving rapidly in a post-chaise?']
No, Sir, you are driving rapidly *from* something, or *to* something.   *Ib.* vol. iii, p. 5. *29 Mar. 1776.*

If a madman were to come into this room with a stick in his hand, no doubt we should pity the state of his mind; but our primary consideration would be to take care of ourselves. We should knock him down first, and pity him afterwards.   *Ib.* p. 11. *3 Apr. 1776.*

Consider, Sir, how should you like, though conscious of your innocence, to be tried before a jury for a capital crime, once a week.   *Ib.*

We would all be idle if we could. *Ib.* p. 13. *3 Apr. 1776.*

No man but a blockhead ever wrote, except for money.   *Ib.* p. 19. *5 Apr. 1776.*

His [Lord Shelburne's] parts, Sir, are pretty well for a Lord; but would not be distinguished in a man who had nothing else but his parts.
> *Ib.* p. 35. *11 Apr. 1776.*

A man who has not been in Italy, is always conscious of an inferiority.   *Ib.* p. 36. *11 Apr. 1776.*

'Does not Gray's poetry tower above the common mark?'
'Yes, Sir, but we must attend to the difference between what men in general cannot do if they would, and what every man may do if he would. Sixteen-string Jack towered above the common mark.'
> *Ib.* p. 38. *12 Apr. 1776.*

'Sir, what is poetry?'
'Why, Sir, it is much easier to say what it is not. We all *know* what light is; but it is not easy to *tell* what it is.'   *Ib.*

[To Mrs. Thrale, who had interrupted him and Boswell by a lively extravagant sally on the expense of clothing children]
Nay, Madam, when you are declaiming, declaim; and when you are calculating, calculate.
> *Ib.* p. 49. *26 Apr. 1776.*

Every man of any education would rather be called a rascal, than accused of deficiency in *the graces*.
> *Ib.* p. 54. *May 1776.*

Sir, you have but two topics, yourself and me. I am sick of both.   *Ib.* p. 57. *May 1776.*

Dine with Jack Wilkes, Sir! I'd as soon dine with Jack Ketch.   *Ib.* p. 66. *15 May 1776.*

Sir, it is not so much to be lamented that Old England is lost, as that the Scotch have found it.
> *Ib.* p. 78. *15 May 1776.*

Olivarii Goldsmith, Poetae, Physici, Historici, Qui nullum fere scribendi genus non tetigit, Nullum quod tetigit non ornavit.
[To Oliver Goldsmith, A Poet, Naturalist, and Historian, who left scarcely any style of writing untouched, and touched nothing that he did not adorn.]
> *Ib.* p. 82. *22 June 1776.* Epitaph on Goldsmith.

That distrust which intrudes so often on your mind is a mode of melancholy, which, if it be the business of a wise man to be happy, it is foolish to indulge; and if it be a duty to preserve our faculties entire for their proper use, it is criminal.
> *Ib.* p. 135. *Letter to Boswell, 11 Sept. 1777.*

If I had no duties, and no reference to futurity, I would spend my life in driving briskly in a post-chaise with a pretty woman.
> *Ib.* p. 162. *19 Sept. 1777.*

Depend upon it, Sir, when a man knows he is to be hanged in a fortnight, it concentrates his mind wonderfully.   *Ib.* p. 167. *19 Sept. 1777.*

No, Sir, when a man is tired of London, he is tired of life; for there is in London all that life can afford.
> *Ib.* p. 178. *20 Sept. 1777.*

He was so generally civil, that nobody thanked him for it.   *Ib.* p. 183. *21 Sept. 1777.*

He who praises everybody praises nobody.
> *Ib.* p. 225 n.

Round numbers are always false.
> *Ib.* p. 226, n. 4. *30 Mar. 1778. Wks. 1787,*

[Of the appearance of the spirit of a person after death]
All argument is against it; but all belief is for it.
> *Ib.* p. 230. *31 Mar. 1776.*

John Wesley's conversation is good, but he is never at leisure. He is always obliged to go at a certain hour. This is very disagreeable to a man who loves to fold his legs and have out his talk, as I do.   *Ib.*

Though we cannot out-vote them we will out-argue them.   *Ib.* p. 234. *3 Apr. 1778.*

[To a clergyman who asked: 'Were not Dodd's sermons addressed to the passions?']
They were nothing, Sir, be they addressed to what they may.   *Ib.* p. 248. *7 Apr. 1778.*

Seeing Scotland, Madam, is only seeing a worse England.   *Ib.*

Goldsmith, however, was a man, who, whatever he wrote, did it better than any other man could do.
> *Ib.* p. 253. *9 Apr. 1778.*

Every man thinks meanly of himself for not having been a soldier, or not having been at sea.
> *Ib.* p. 265. *10 Apr. 1778.*

A mere antiquarian is a rugged being.
> *Ib.* p. 278. *Letter to Boswell, 23 Apr. 1778.*

Johnson had said that he could repeat a complete chapter of 'The Natural History of Iceland', from the Danish of Horrebow, the whole of which was exactly thus:—'CHAP. LXXII. *Concerning snakes.* 'There are no snakes to be met with throughout the whole island.'   *Ib.* p. 279. *13 Apr. 1778.*

A country governed by a despot is an inverted cone. Boswell's *Life of Johnson*, vol. iii, p. 283. *14 Apr. 1778.*

I am willing to love all mankind, *except an American.* *Ib.* p. 290. *15 Apr. 1778.*

As the Spanish proverb says, 'He, who would bring home the wealth of the Indies, must carry the wealth of the Indies with him.' So it is in travelling; a man must carry knowledge with him, if he would bring home knowledge. *Ib.* p. 302. *17 Apr. 1778.*

All censure of a man's self is oblique praise. It is in order to shew how much he can spare. *Ib.* p. 323. *25 Apr. 1778.*

[On Boswell's expressing surprise at finding a Staffordshire Whig] Sir, there are rascals in all countries. *Ib.* p. 326. *28 Apr. 1778.*

I have always said, the first Whig was the Devil. *Ib.*

It is thus that mutual cowardice keeps us in peace. Were one half of mankind brave and one half cowards, the brave would be always beating the cowards. Were all brave, they would lead a very uneasy life; all would be continually fighting; but being all cowards, we go on very well. *Ib.*

The King of Siam sent ambassadors to Louis XIV, but Louis XIV sent none to the King of Siam. *Ib.* p. 336. *29 Apr. 1776.*

Were it not for imagination, Sir, a man would be as happy in the arms of a chambermaid as of a Duchess. *Ib.* p. 341. *9 May 1778.*

Dr. Mead lived more in the broad sunshine of life than almost any man. *Ib.* p. 355. *16 May 1778.*

Claret is the liquor for boys; port for men; but he who aspires to be a hero must drink brandy. *Ib.* p. 381. *7 Apr. 1779.*

A man who exposes himself when he is intoxicated, has not the art of getting drunk. *Ib.* p. 389. *24 Apr. 1779.*

Remember that all tricks are either knavish or childish. *Ib.* p. 396. *Letter to Boswell, 9 Sept. 1779.*

Boswell: Is not the Giant's-Causeway worth seeing? Johnson: Worth seeing? yes; but not worth going to see. *Ib.* p. 410. *12 Oct. 1779.*

If you are idle, be not solitary; if you are solitary, be not idle. *Ib.* p. 415. *Letter to Boswell, 27 Oct. 1779.*

Sir, among the anfractuosities of the human mind, I know not if it may not be one, that there is a superstitious reluctance to sit for a picture. *Ib.* vol. iv, p. 4. *1780.*

[On being asked why Pope had written:
   Let modest Foster, if he will, excel
   Ten metropolitans in preaching well]
Sir, he hoped it would vex somebody. *Ib.* p. 9. *1780.*

A Frenchman must be always talking, whether he knows anything of the matter or not; an Englishman is content to say nothing, when he has nothing to say. *Ib.* p. 15. *1780.*

Greek, Sir, is like lace; every man gets as much of it as he can. *Ib.* p. 23. *1780.*

Are we alive after all this satire! *Ib.* p. 29. *1780.*

[Of Goldsmith] No man was more foolish when he had not a pen in his hand, or more wise when he had. *Ib.* p. 29. *1780.*

Mrs. Montagu has dropt me. Now, Sir, there are people whom one should like very well to drop, but would not wish to be dropped by. *Ib.* p. 73. *Mar. 1781.*

This merriment of parsons is mighty offensive. *Ib.* p. 76. *Mar. 1781.*

[Of Lord North] He fills a chair. *Ib.* p. 81. *1 Apr. 1781.*

[At the sale of Thrale's brewery] We are not here to sell a parcel of boilers and vats, but the potentiality of growing rich, beyond the dreams of avarice. *Ib.* p. 87. *6 Apr. 1781.*

'The woman had a bottom of good sense.'
The word '*bottom*' thus introduced, was so ludicrous, . . . that most of us could not forbear tittering . . .
'Where's the merriment? . . . I say the *woman* was *fundamentally* sensible.' *Ib.* p. 99. *20 Apr. 1781.*

Classical quotation is the *parole* of literary men all over the world. *Ib.* p. 102. *8 May 1781.*

[To Miss Monckton, afterwards Lady Corke, who said that Sterne's writings affected her] Why, that is, because, dearest, you're a dunce. *Ib.* p. 109. *May 1781.*

Sir, I have two very cogent reasons for not printing any list of subscribers;—one, that I have lost all the names,—the other, that I have spent all the money. *Ib.* p. 111. *May 1763.*

My friend [Johnson] was of opinion, that when a man of rank appeared in that character [as an author], he deserved to have his merit handsomely allowed. *Ib.* p. 114. *May 1781.*

A wise Tory and a wise Whig, I believe, will agree. Their principles are the same, though their modes of thinking are different. *Ib.* p. 117. *Written statement given to Boswell, May 1781.*

Officious, innocent, sincere,
Of every friendless name the friend.

Yet still he fills affection's eye,
Obscurely wise, and coarsely kind. *Ib.* p. 127. *20 Jan. 1782.* On the death of Mr. Levett.

In Misery's darkest caverns known,
His ready help was ever nigh. *Ib.*

His virtues walk'd their narrow round,
Nor made a pause, nor left a void;
And sure th' Eternal Master found
His single talent well employ'd. *Ib.*

Then, with no throbs of fiery pain,
No cold gradations of decay,
Death broke at once the vital chain,
And freed his soul the nearest way. *Ib.*

I never have sought the world; the world was not to seek me.
>Boswell's *Life of Johnson*, vol. iv, p. 172. 23 *Mar. 1783.*

Thurlow is a fine fellow; he fairly puts his mind to yours. *Ib.* p. 179. *1783.*

[Of Ossian]
Sir, a man might write such stuff for ever, if he would *abandon* his mind to it. *Ib.* p. 183. *1783.*

[When Dr. Adam Smith was expatiating on the beauty of Glasgow, Johnson had cut him short by saying 'Pray, Sir, have you ever seen Brentford?']
Boswell: My dear Sir, surely that was *shocking*?
Johnson: Why, then, Sir, *you* have never seen Brentford. *Ib.* p. 186. *1783.*

[To Maurice Morgann who asked him whether he reckoned Derrick or Smart the better poet]
Sir, there is no settling the point of precedency between a louse and a flea. *Ib.* p. 192. *1783.*

When I observed he was a fine cat, saying, 'why yes, Sir, but I have had cats whom I liked better than this'; and then as if perceiving Hodge to be out of countenance, adding, 'but he is a very fine cat, a very fine cat indeed.' *Ib.* p. 197. *1783.*

[Johnson had said 'public affairs vex no man', and Boswell had suggested that the growing power of the Whigs vexed Johnson]
Sir, I have never slept an hour less, nor eat an ounce less meat. I would have knocked the factious dogs on the head, to be sure; but I was not *vexed*.
>*Ib.* p. 220. *15 May 1783.*

Clear your *mind* of cant. *Ib.* p. 221. *15 May 1783.*

Sir, he is a cursed Whig, a *bottomless* Whig, as they all are now. *Ib.* p. 223. *26 May 1783.*

As I know more of mankind I expect less of them, and am ready now to call a man *a good man*, upon easier terms than I was formerly.
>*Ib.* p. 239. *Sept. 1783.*

Boswell is a very clubable man.
>*Ib.* p. 254 n. *1783.*

[Of George Psalmanazar, whom he reverenced for his piety]
I should as soon think of contradicting a Bishop.
>*Ib.* p. 274. *15 May 1784.*

[To Bennet Langton who brought him texts on Christian charity when he was ill]
What is your drift, Sir?
>*Ib.* p. 281. *30 May 1784.*

[On the roast mutton he had for dinner at an inn]
It is as bad as bad can be: it is ill-fed, ill-killed, ill-kept, and ill-drest. *Ib.* p. 284. *3 June 1784.*

[To Miss Hannah More, who had expressed a wonder that the poet who had written *Paradise Lost* should write such poor Sonnets]
Milton, Madam, was a genius that could cut a Colossus from a rock; but could not carve heads upon cherry-stones. *Ib.* p. 305. *13 June 1784.*

Don't cant in defence of savages.
>*Ib.* p. 308. *15 June 1784.*

[On hearing the line in Brooke's *Earl of Essex* 'Who rules o'er freemen should himself be free']
It might as well be 'Who drives fat oxen should himself be fat.' *Ib.* p. 313. *June 1784.*

Sir, I have found you an argument; but I am not obliged to find you an understanding. *Ib.*

[On Sir Joshua Reynolds's observing that the real character of a man was found out by his amusements]
Yes, Sir; no man is a hypocrite in his pleasures.
>*Ib.* p. 316. *June 1784.*

Blown about by every wind of criticism.
>*Ib.* p. 319. *June 1784.*

Talking of the Comedy of 'The Rehearsal', he [Johnson] said, 'It has not wit enough to keep it sweet.' This was easy;—he therefore caught himself, and pronounced a more rounded sentence; 'It has not vitality enough to preserve it from putrefaction.' *Ib.* p. 320. *June 1784.*

Who can run the race with Death?
>*Ib.* p. 360. *Letter to Dr. Burney, 2 Aug. 1784.*

Sir, I look upon every day to be lost, in which I do not make a new acquaintance. *Ib.* p. 374. *Nov. 1784.*

I will be conquered; I will not capitulate. *Ib.*

Are you sick or are you sullen?
>*Ib.* p. 380. *Letter to Boswell, 3 Nov. 1784.*

This world where much is to be done and little to be known.
>*Johnsonian Miscellanies* ed. G. B. Hill (1897), vol. i. *Prayers and Meditations. Against inquisitive and perplexing Thoughts*, p. 118.

Trick'd in antique ruff and bonnet,
Ode, and elegy, and sonnet.
>*Ib. Anecdotes of Johnson by Mrs. Piozzi*, p. 190.

Hermit hoar, in solemn cell,
Wearing out life's evening gray;
Strike thy bosom, sage! and tell
What is bliss, and which the way?
Thus I spoke, and speaking sigh'd,
Scarce repress'd the starting tear,
When the hoary Sage reply'd,
'Come, my lad, and drink some beer.' *Ib.* p. 193.

If the man who turnips cries,
Cry not when his father dies,
'Tis a proof that he had rather
Have a turnip than his father
>*Burlesque of Lopez de Vega's lines, 'Se acquien los leones vence,' etc. Ib.*

He [Charles James Fox] talked to me at club one day concerning Catiline's conspiracy—so I withdrew my attention, and thought about Tom Thumb.
>*Ib.* p. 202.

Dear Bathurst (said he to me one day) was a man to my very heart's content: he hated a fool, and he hated a rogue, and he hated a whig; he was a very good hater. *Ib.* p. 204.

[Of a Jamaica gentleman, then lately dead]
He will not, whither he is now gone find much difference, I believe, either in the climate or the company. *Ib.* p. 211.

Goldsmith: Here's such a stir about a fellow that has written one book [Beattie's *Essay on Truth*], and I have written many.
Johnson: Ah, Doctor, there go two-and-forty sixpences you know to one guinea. *Ib.* p. 269.

It is very strange, and very melancholy, that the paucity of human pleasures should persuade us ever to call hunting one of them.   *Ib*. p. 288.

You could not stand five minutes with that man [Edmund Burke] beneath a shed while it rained, but you must be convinced you had been standing with the greatest man you had ever yet seen.
Ib. p. 290.

Johnson observed that 'he did not care to speak ill of any man behind his back, but he believed the gentleman was an *attorney*'.   *Ib*. p. 327, note.

Was there ever yet anything written by mere man that was wished longer by its readers, excepting *Don Quixote*, *Robinson Crusoe*, and the *Pilgrim's Progress*?   *Ib*. p. 332.

[On his Parliamentary reports]
I took care that the *Whig Dogs* should not have the best of it.
Ib. An Essay on Johnson, by Arthur Murphy, p. 379.

Books that you may carry to the fire, and hold readily in your hand, are the most useful after all.
Ib. vol. ii. *Apophthegms from Hawkins's edition of Johnson's works*, p. 2.

A man is in general better pleased when he has a good dinner upon his table, than when his wife talks Greek.   *Ib*. p. 11.

I would rather see the portrait of a dog that I know, than all the allegorical paintings they can shew me in the world.   *Ib*. p. 15.

There is a time of life, Sir, when a man requires the repairs of a table.
Ib. Anecdotes by Joseph Cradock, p. 64.

I have heard him assert, that a tavern chair was the throne of human felicity.
Ib. Extracts from Hawkins' Life of Johnson, p. 91.

I dogmatise and am contradicted, and in this conflict of opinions and sentiments I find delight. *Ib*. p. 92.

Abstinence is as easy to me, as temperance would be difficult.   *Ib. Anecdotes by Hannah More*, p. 197.

Of music Dr. Johnson used to say that it was the only sensual pleasure without vice.
Ib. Anecdotes by William Seward, p. 301.

[Of the performance of a celebrated violinist.]
Difficult do you call it, Sir? I wish it were impossible.
Ib. p. 308.

As with my hat upon my head
  I walk'd along the Strand,
I there did meet another man
  With his hat in his hand.
Ib. Anecdotes by George Steevens, p. 315.

Where you see a Whig you see a rascal.
Ib. Minor Anecdotes of Dr. Johnson, p. 393.

Madam, before you flatter a man so grossly to his face, you should consider whether or not your flattery is worth his having.
Remark to Hannah More. Mme. D'Arblay's *Diary and Letters* (1891), vol. i, ch. ii, p. 55.

Let him go abroad to a distant country; let him go to some place where he is *not* known. Don't let him go to the devil where he is known!
Boswell's *Tour to the Hebrides*, *18 Aug. 1773*.

I wonder, however, that so many people have written who might have let it alone.
Ib. 19 Aug., p. 197.

[To Boswell who would excuse Sir Alexander Gordon's boring of them by saying it was all kindness]
True, Sir; but sensation is sensation.
Ib. 23 Aug., p. 219.

I inherited a vile melancholy from my father, which has made me mad all my life, at least not sober.
Ib. 16 Sept., p. 302.

I am always sorry when any language is lost, because languages are the pedigree of nations.
Ib. 18 Sept., p. 310.

[Johnson, railing against Scotland, said that the wine the Scots had before the Union would not make them drunk. Boswell assured Johnson there was much drunkenness]
No, Sir; there were people who died of dropsies, which they contracted in trying to get drunk.
Ib. 23 Sept., p. 326.

I do not like much to see a Whig in any dress; but I hate to see a Whig in a parson's gown.
Ib. 24 Sept., p. 331.

The known style of a dedication is flattery: it professes to flatter.   *Ib. 4 Oct.*, p. 352.

[Calling for a gill of whisky]
Come, let me know what it is that makes a Scotchman happy!   *Ib. 23 Oct.*, p. 393.

Sir, are you so grossly ignorant of human nature, as not to know that a man may be very sincere in good principles, without having good practice?
Ib. 25 Oct., p. 403.

In all pointed sentences, some degree of accuracy must be sacrificed to conciseness.
On the Bravery of the English Common Soldier. Works (1787), vol. x, p. 286.

I am not yet so lost in lexicography, as to forget that words are the daughters of earth, and that things are the sons of heaven.
Dictionary of the English Language. Preface.

Every quotation contributes something to the stability or enlargement of the language.   *Ib*.

But these were the dreams of a poet doomed at last to wake a lexicographer.   *Ib*.

If the changes that we fear be thus irresistible, what remains but to acquiesce with silence, as in the other insurmountable distresses of humanity? It remains that we retard what we cannot repel, that we palliate what we cannot cure.   *Ib*.

The chief glory of every people arises from its authors.   *Ib*.

To make dictionaries is dull work.
Ib. Dull. 8.

Excise. A hateful tax levied upon commodities.   *Ib*.

Oats. A grain, which in England is generally given to horses, but in Scotland supports the people.
Ib.

Patron. Commonly a wretch who supports with insolence, and is paid with flattery.   *Ib*.

Pension. An allowance made to anyone without an equivalent. In England it is generally understood to mean pay given to a state hireling for treason to his country.   *Ib.*

Whig. The name of a faction.   *Ib.*

Every man is, or hopes to be, an idler.
    The Idler, No. 1.

When two Englishmen meet, their first talk is of the weather.   *Ib.* No. 11.

Promise, large promise, is the soul of an advertisement.   *Ib.* No. 41.

He is no wise man who will quit a certainty for an uncertainty.   *Ib.* No. 57.

Unmov'd tho' witlings sneer and rivals rail;
Studious to please, yet not asham'd to fail.
    Irene, Prologue.

Learn that the present hour alone is man's.
    Ib. III. ii. 33.

At seventy-seven it is time to be in earnest.
    Journey to the Western Islands, Col, p. 110.

Whatever withdraws us from the power of our senses; whatever makes the past, the distant, or the future, predominate over the present, advances us in the dignity of thinking beings.
    Ib. Inch Kenneth, p. 134.

How small, of all that human hearts endure,
That part which laws or kings can cause or cure!
Still to ourselves in every place consigned,
Our own felicity we make or find:
With secret course, which no loud storms annoy,
Glides the smooth current of domestic joy.
    Lines added to Goldsmith's Traveller.

Language is the dress of thought.
    Lives of the English Poets, ed. G. B. Hill (1905),
    vol. i, *Cowley,* § 181, p. 58.

An acrimonious and surly republican.
    Ib. Milton, § 168, p. 156.

The great source of pleasure is variety.
    Ib. Butler, § 35, p. 212.

The father of English criticism [Dryden].
    Ib. Dryden, § 193, p. 410.

But what are the hopes of man! I am disappointed by that stroke of death, which has eclipsed the gaiety of nations and impoverished the public stock of harmless pleasure. (*Garrick's death.*)
    Ib. vol. ii, *Edmund Smith,* § 76, p. 21.

About things on which the public thinks long it commonly attains to think right.
    Ib. Addison, § 136, p. 132.

Whoever wishes to attain an English style, familiar but not coarse, and elegant but not ostentatious, must give his days and nights to the volumes of Addison.   *Ib.* § 168, p. 150.

By the common sense of readers uncorrupted with literary prejudices . . . must be finally decided all claim to poetical honours. *Ib. Gray,* § 51, p. 441.

And, bid him go to Hell, to Hell he goes.
    London, l. 116.

Of all the griefs that harrass the distresst,
Sure the most bitter is a scornful jest;
Fate never wounds more deep the gen'rous heart,
Than when a blockhead's insult points the dart.
    Ib. l. 166.

This mournful truth is ev'rywhere confess'd,
Slow rises worth by poverty depress'd.   *Ib.* l. 176.

Ye who listen with credulity to the whispers of fancy, and pursue with eagerness the phantoms of hope; who expect that age will perform the promises of youth, and that the deficiencies of the present day will be supplied by the morrow; attend to the history of Rasselas, Prince of Abyssinia.
    Rasselas, ch. 1.

The business of a poet, said Imlac, is to examine, not the individual, but the species; . . . he does not number the streaks of the tulip, or describe the different shades in the verdure of the forest.   *Ib.* ch. 10.

Human life is everywhere a state in which much is to be endured, and little to be enjoyed.   *Ib.* ch. 11.

Marriage has many pains, but celibacy has no pleasures.   *Ib.* ch. 26.

Example is always more efficacious than precept.
    Ib. ch. 29.

The endearing elegance of female friendship.
    Ib. ch. 45.

The power of punishment is to silence, not to confute.
    Sermons, No. xxiii.

Notes are often necessary, but they are necessary evils.
    Shakespeare, preface, sig. E4.

When learning's triumph o'er her barb'rous foes
First rear'd the Stage, immortal Shakespeare rose;
Each change of many-colour'd life he drew,
Exhausted worlds, and then imagin'd new:
Existence saw him spurn her bounded reign,
And panting Time toil'd after him in vain.
    Prologue at the Opening of the Theatre in
    Drury Lane, 1747.

Cold approbation gave the ling'ring bays,
For those who durst not censure, scarce could praise.
    Ib.

The wild vicissitudes of taste.   *Ib.*

The stage but echoes back the public voice.
The drama's laws, the drama's patrons give,
For we that live to please, must please to live.   *Ib.*

Let observation with extensive view,
Survey mankind, from China to Peru;
Remark each anxious toil, each eager strife,
And watch the busy scenes of crowded life.
    Vanity of Human Wishes, l. 1.

Our supple tribes repress their patriot throats,
And ask no questions but the price of votes.
    Ib. l. 95.

Deign on the passing world to turn thine eyes,
And pause awhile from letters to be wise;
There mark what ills the scholar's life assail,
Toil, envy, want, the patron, and the jail.
See nations slowly wise, and meanly just,
To buried merit raise the tardy bust.   *Ib.* l. 157.

A frame of adamant, a soul of fire,
No dangers fright him and no labours tire. *Ib.* l. 193.

His fall was destined to a barren strand,
A petty fortress, and a dubious hand;
He left the name, at which the world grew pale,
To point a moral, or adorn a tale.   *Ib.* l. 219.

'Enlarge my life with multitude of days!'
In health, in sickness, thus the suppliant prays:
Hides from himself its state, and shuns to know,
That life protracted is protracted woe.
Time hovers o'er, impatient to destroy,
And shuts up all the passages of joy.   *Ib.* l. 225.

An age that melts with unperceiv'd decay,
And glides in modest innocence away.   *Ib.* l. 293.

Superfluous lags the vet'ran on the stage. *Ib.* l. 308.

In life's last scene what prodigies surprise,
Fears of the brave, and follies of the wise!
From Marlb'rough's eyes the streams of dotage flow,
And Swift expires a driv'ler and a show.   *Ib* l. 315.

What ills from beauty spring.   *Ib.* l. 321.

Still raise for good the supplicating voice,
But leave to Heaven the measure and the choice,
                                             Ib. l. 351.

Secure, whate'er he gives, he gives the best. *Ib.* l. 356.

   Faith, that, panting for a happier seat,
Counts death kind Nature's signal of retreat. *Ib.* l. 363.
With these celestial Wisdom calms the mind,
And makes the happiness she does not find. *Ib.* l. 367.

Grief is a species of idleness.
   Letters of Johnson (ed. *G. B. Hill, 1892*), vol. i,
   p. 212. No. 302, *to Mrs. Thrale, 17 Mar. 1773.*

There is no wisdom in useless and hopeless sorrow.
   Ib. vol. ii, p. 215. No. 722, *to Mrs. Thrale,
   12 Apr. 1781.*

Fly fishing may be a very pleasant amusement; but
   angling or float fishing I can only compare to a stick
   and a string, with a worm at one end and a fool at
   the other.
      Attributed to Johnson by Hawker in *Instruc-
      tions to Young Sportsmen, 1859*, p. 197. Not
      found in his works. See *Notes and Queries,*
      11 Dec. 1915.

[William Gerard Hamilton of Johnson.]
Johnson is dead.—Let us go to the next best:—there
   is nobody; no man can be said to put you in mind
   of Johnson.
      Boswell's *Life of Johnson* (1934), vol. iv, p. 420.

JOHN PAUL JONES
1747–1792

I have not yet begun to fight.
   *Remark on being hailed to know whether he had
   struck his flag, as his ship was sinking, 23 Sept.
   1779.* De Koven's *Life and Letters of
   J. P. Jones,* vol. i.

SIR WILLIAM JONES
1746–1794

On parent knees, a naked new-born child,
Weeping thou sat'st, when all around thee smil'd;
So live, that, sinking in thy last long sleep,
Calm thou may'st smile, while all around thee weep.
   Persian Asiatick Miscellany (1786), vol. ii, p.
   374, *A Moral Tetrastich.*

My opinion is, that power should always be distrusted,
   in whatever hands it is placed.
      Ld. Teignmouth's Life of Sir W. Jones (1835),
      vol. i. *Letter to Ld. Althorpe, 5 Oct. 1782.*

Seven hours to law, to soothing slumber seven,
Ten to the world allot, and *all* to Heaven.
   Ib. vol. ii. *Lines in Substitution for Sir E.
   Coke's lines:* Six hours in sleep, [etc.].

BENJAMIN JONSON
1572–1637

Fortune, that favours fools.   *The Alchemist,* prologue.

I will eat exceedingly, and prophesy.
                         Bartholomew Fair, I. vi.

Neither do thou lust after that tawney weed tobacco.
                                        Ib. II. vi.

When I mock poorness, then heaven make me poor.
                         The Case is Altered, III. i.

PEOPLE:
The Voice of Cato is the voice of Rome.
CATO:
The voice of Rome is the consent of heaven!
                  Catiline his Conspiracy, III. i.

      Where it concerns himself,
Who's angry at a slander makes it true.   *Ib.*

Slow, slow, fresh fount, keep time with my salt tears:
   Yet, slower, yet; O faintly, gentle springs:
List to the heavy part the music bears,
   Woe weeps out her division, when she sings.
                         Cynthia's Revels, I. i.

      So they be ill men,
If they spake worse, 'twere better: for of such
To be dispraised, is the most perfect praise. *Ib.* III. ii.

      True happiness
Consists not in the multitude of friends,
But in the worth and choice.   *Ib.*

Queen and huntress, chaste and fair,
Now the sun is laid to sleep,
Seated in thy silver chair,
State in wonted manner keep:
   Hesperus entreats thy light,
   Goddess, excellently bright.   *Ib.* v. iii.

      If he were
To be made honest by an act of parliament,
I should not alter in my faith of him.
                         The Devil is An Ass, IV. i.

I remember the players have often mentioned it as
   an honour to Shakespeare that in his writing
   (whatsoever he penned) he never blotted out a
   line. My answer hath been 'Would he had
   blotted a thousand'. Which they thought a malevolent speech. I had not told posterity this, but for
   their ignorance, who chose that circumstance to
   commend their friend by wherein he most faulted;
   and to justify mine own candour: for I loved the
   man, and do honour his memory, on this side
   idolatry, as much as any. He was (indeed) honest,
   and of an open and free nature; had an excellent
   phantasy, brave notions, and gentle expressions;
   wherein he flowed with that facility, that sometimes it was necessary he should be stopped:
   sufflaminandus erat, as Augustus said of Haterius.
   His wit was in his own power, would the rule of
   it had been so too. . . . But he redeemed his vices
   with his virtues. There was ever more in him to
   be praised than to be pardoned.
      *Discoveries. De Shakespeare Nostrati.
      Augustus in Haterium.*

His hearers could not cough, or look aside from him,
without loss. . . . The fear of every man that heard
him was, lest he should make an end. (Bacon)
Ib. lxxviii. *Dominus Verulamius.*

In his adversity I ever prayed, that God would give
him strength; for greatness he could not want.
Ib. lxxx. *De Augmentis Scientiarum,—Lord
St. Alban.*

Yet the best pilots have needs of mariners, besides
sails, anchor, and other tackle.
Ib. Illiteratus Princeps.

Talking and eloquence are not the same: to speak,
and to speak well, are two things.
Ib. Praecept. Element.

Alas, all the castles I have, are built with air, thou
know'st. *Eastward Ho,* II. ii. 226.

Still to be neat, still to be drest.
As you were going to a feast;
Still to be powder'd, still perfum'd,
Lady, it is to be presumed,
Though art's hid causes are not found,
All is not sweet, all is not sound.

Give me a look, give me a face,
That makes simplicity a grace;
Robes loosely flowing, hair as free:
Such sweet neglect more taketh me,
Than all the adulteries of art;
They strike mine eyes, but not my heart.
Epicoene, I. i.

HAUGHTY:
Is this the silent woman?
CENTAURE:
Nay, she has found her tongue since she was married.
Ib. III. vi.

But that which most doth take my Muse and me,
Is a pure cup of rich Canary wine,
Which is the Mermaid's now, but shall be mine:
Of which, had Horace or Anacreon tasted,
Their lives, as do their lines, till now had lasted.
Epigrams, ci. *Inviting a Friend to Supper.*

Weep with me, all you that read
  This little story:
And know for whom a tear you shed
  Death's self is sorry.
'Twas a child that so did thrive
  In grace and feature,
As Heaven and Nature seem'd to strive
  Which own'd the creature.
Years he number'd scarce thirteen
  When Fates turn'd cruel,
Yet three fill'd Zodiacs had he been
  The stage's jewel;
And did act, what now we moan,
  Old men so duly,
As sooth the Parcae thought him one,
  He play'd so truly.
So, by error, to his fate
  They all consented;
But viewing him since, alas, too late!
  They have repented:
And have sought (to give new birth)
  In baths to steep him;
But being so much too good for earth,
  Heaven vows to keep him.
Ib. cxx. *An Epitaph on Salathiel Pavy, a
Child of Queen Elizabeth's Chapel.*

Underneath this stone doth lie
As much beauty as could die;
Which in life did harbour give
To more virtue than doth live.
If at all she had a fault,
Leave it buried in this vault.
One name was Elizabeth,
The other let it sleep with death:
Fitter, where it died, to tell,
Than that it lived at all! Farewell!
Ib. cxxiv. *Epitaph on Elizabeth, L. H.*

Helter skelter, hang sorrow, care'll kill a cat, up-tails
all, and a louse for the hangman.
Every Man in His Humour, I. iii.

As sure as death. *Ib.* II. i.

I do honour the very flea of his dog. *Ib.* IV. ii.

I have it here in black and white. *Ib.*

It must be done like lightning. *Ib.* IV. v.

There shall be no love lost.
Every Man out of His Humour, II. i.

Blind Fortune still
Bestows her gifts on such as cannot use them. *Ib.* ii.

How near to good is what is fair!
Love Freed from Ignorance and Folly.

Thou art not to learn the humours and tricks of that
old bald cheater, Time. *The Poetaster,* I. i.

Ramp up my genius, be not retrograde;
But boldly nominate a spade a spade. *Ib.* v. i.

Detraction is but baseness' varlet;
And apes are apes, though clothed in scarlet. *Ib.*

This is Mab, the Mistress-Fairy
That doth nightly rob the dairy. *The Satyr.*

She that pinches country wenches
If they rub not clean their benches. *Ib.*

But if so they chance to feast her,
In a shoe she drops a tester. *Ib.*

Tell proud Jove,
Between his power and thine there is no odds:
'Twas only fear first in the world made gods.
Sejanus, II. ii.

This figure that thou here seest put,
It was for gentle Shakespeare cut,
Wherein the graver had a strife
With Nature, to out-do the life:
O could he but have drawn his wit
As well in brass, as he has hit
His face; the print would then surpass
All that was ever writ in brass:
But since he cannot, reader, look
Not on his picture, but his book.
On the Portrait of Shakespeare, To the Reader.

While I confess thy writings to be such,
As neither man, nor muse, can praise too much.
*To the Memory of My Beloved, the Author,
Mr. William Shakespeare.*

Soul of the Age!
The applause! delight! the wonder of our stage!
My Shakespeare, rise; I will not lodge thee by
Chaucer, or Spenser, or bid Beaumont lie
A little further, to make thee a room:
Thou art a moniment, without a tomb,
And art alive still, while thy book doth live,
And we have wits to read, and praise to give. *Ib.*

Marlowe's mighty line. *Ib.*

And though thou hadst small Latin, and less Greek. *Ib.*

Call forth thundering Aeschylus. *Ib.*

To hear thy buskin tread,
And shake a stage: or, when thy socks were on,
Leave thee alone, for the comparison
Of all, that insolent Greece, or haughty Rome
Sent forth, or since did from their ashes come. *Ib.*

He was not of an age, but for all time! *Ib.*

For a good poet's made, as well as born. *Ib.*

Sweet Swan of Avon! what a sight it were
To see thee in our waters yet appear,
And make those flights upon the banks of Thames,
That so did take Eliza, and our James! *Ib.*

THOMAS:
They write here, one Cornelius-Son
Hath made the Hollanders an invisible eel.
To swim the haven at Dunkirk, and sink all
The shipping there. . . .
CYMBAL:
It is an automa, runs under water,
With a snug nose, and has a nimble tail
Made like an auger, with which tail she wriggles
Betwixt the costs of a ship, and sinks it straight.
The Staple of News, III. i.

Well, they talk we shall have no more Parliaments,
God bless us! *Ib.*

Hark you, John Clay, if you have
Done any such thing, tell troth and shame the devil.
Tale of a Tub, II. i.

Mother, the still sow eats up all the draff.
Ib. III. v.

Calumnies are answered best with silence.
Volpone, II. ii.

Come, my Celia, let us prove,
While we can, the sports of love. *Ib.* III. v.

Suns, that set, may rise again;
But if once we lose this light,
'Tis with us perpetual night. *Ib.*

You have a gift, sir, (thank your education,)
Will never let you want, while there are men,
And malice, to breed causes. [To a lawyer.]
Ib. v. i.

Follow a shadow, it still flies you,
Seem to fly it, it will pursue:
So court a mistress, she denies you;
Let her alone, she will court you.
Say, are not women truly, then,
Styl'd but the shadows of us men?
The Forest, vii. *Song: That Women are but
Men's Shadows.*

Drink to me only with thine eyes,
And I will pledge with mine;
Or leave a kiss but in the cup,
And I'll not look for wine.
The thirst that from the soul doth rise
Doth ask a drink divine;
But might I of Jove's nectar sup,
I would not change for thine.

I sent thee late a rosy wreath,
Not so much honouring thee,
As giving it a hope that there
It could not wither'd be.
But thou thereon didst only breathe,
And sent'st it back to me;
Since when it grows and smells, I swear,
Not of itself, but thee. *Ib.* ix. *To Celia.*

I sing the birth was born to-night,
The author both of life and light.
Underwoods. Poems of Devotion, iii. *Hymn on
the Nativity.*

Have you seen but a bright lily grow,
Before rude hands have touch'd it?
Have you mark'd but the fall o' the snow
Before the soil hath smutch'd it?
.   .   .   .   .
O so white! O so soft! O so sweet is she!
Ib. Celebration of Charis, iv. *Her Triumph.*

She is Venus when she smiles;
But she's Juno when she walks,
And Minerva when she talks. *Ib.* v.

Greek was free from rhyme's infection,
Happy Greek, by this protection,
Was not spoiled:
Whilst the Latin, queen of tongues,
Is not yet free from rhyme's wrongs,
But rests foiled.
Ib. xlviii. *A Fit of Rhyme against Rhyme.*

Vulgar languages that want
Words, and sweetness, and be scant
Of true measure,
Tyrant rhyme hath so abused,
That they long since have refused
Other cesure.
He that first invented thee,
May his joints tormented be,
Cramp'd for ever;
Still may syllabes jar with time,
Still may reason war with rhyme,
Resting never! *Ib.*

England's high Chancellor: the destin'd heir,
In his soft cradle, to his father's chair.
Ib. lxx. *On Lord Bacon's [Sixtieth] Birthday.*

It is not growing like a tree
In bulk, doth make men better be;
Or standing long an oak, three hundred year,
To fall a log at last, dry, bald, and sere:
A lily of a day,
Is fairer far in May,
Although it fall and die that night;
It was the plant and flower of light.
In small proportions we just beauties see;
And in short measures, life may perfect be.
Ib. lxxxviii. *A Pindaric Ode on the Death of
Sir H. Morison.*

What gentle ghost, besprent with April dew,
Hails me so solemnly to yonder yew?
Ib. ci. *Elegy on the Lady Jane Pawlet.*

The voice so sweet, the words so fair,
As some soft chime had stroked the air;
And though the sound were parted thence,
Still left an echo in the sense. *Ib. Eupheme*, iv.

O rare Ben Jonson.
> *Epitaph written on his tombstone in Westminster Abbey, by Jack Young.* See Aubrey's '*Brief Lives*', Ben Jonson.

DOROTHEA JORDAN
1762–1816

'Oh where, and Oh! where is your Highland laddie gone?'
'He's gone to fight the French, for King George upon the throne,
And it's Oh! in my heart, how I wish him safe at home!'   *The Blue Bells of Scotland.*

THOMAS JORDAN
1612?–1685

Our God and soldier we alike adore,
Just at the brink of ruin, not before:
The danger past, both are alike requited;
God is forgotten, and our soldier slighted.
> *Epigram.* J. Nichols's *Select Collection of Poems*, 1781, vol. vii, p. 64.

JAMES JOYCE
1882–1941

Portrait of the artist as a young man.   *Title of Book.*

JUNIUS
fl. 1770

The liberty of the press is the *Palladium* of all the civil, political, and religious rights of an Englishman.   *Letters*, dedication.

The right of election is the very essence of the constitution.   *Ib. Letter 11, 24 Apr. 1769.*

Is this the wisdom of a great minister? or is it the ominous vibration of a pendulum?   *Ib. Letter 12, 30 May 1769.*

There is a holy mistaken zeal in politics as well as in religion. By persuading others, we convince ourselves.   *Ib. Letter 35, 19 Dec. 1769.*

Whether it be the heart to conceive, the understanding to direct, or the hand to execute.   *Ib. Letter 37, 19 Mar. 1770.*

The injustice done to an Individual is sometimes of service to the public.   *Ib. Letter 41, 14 Nov. 1770.*

DENIS KEARNEY
1847–1907

Horny-handed sons of toil.
> *Speech.* San Francisco, *c.* 1878.

JOHN KEATS
1795–1821

The imagination of a boy is healthy, and the mature imagination of a man is healthy; but there is a space of life between, in which the soul is in a ferment, the character undecided, the way of life uncertain, the ambition thick-sighted: thence proceeds mawkishness.   *Endymion*, preface.

A thing of beauty is a joy for ever:
Its loveliness increases; it will never
Pass into nothingness; but still will keep
A bower quiet for us, and a sleep
Full of sweet dreams, and health, and quiet breathing.   *Ib.* bk. 1. i.

The inhuman dearth
Of noble natures.   *Ib.* l. 8.

The grandeur of the dooms
We have imagined for the mighty dead.   *Ib.* l. 20.

They must be always with us, or we die.   *Ib.* l. 33.

The unimaginable lodge
For solitary thinkings; such as dodge
Conception to the very bourne of heaven,
Then leave the naked brain.   *Ib.* l. 293.

Wherein lies happiness? In that which becks
Our ready minds to fellowship divine,
A fellowship with essence.   *Ib.* l. 777.

The crown of these
Is made of love and friendship, and sits high
Upon the forehead of humanity.   *Ib.* l. 800.

Who, of men, can tell
That flowers would bloom, or that green fruit would swell
To melting pulp, that fish would have bright mail,
The earth its dower of river, wood, and vale,
The meadows runnels, runnels pebble-stones,
The seed its harvest, or the lute its tones,
Tones ravishment, or ravishment its sweet
If human souls did never kiss and greet?   *Ib.* l. 835.

Never, I aver,
Since Ariadne was a vintager.   *Ib.* bk. 2, l. 442.

O Sorrow,
Why dost borrow
Heart's lightness from the merriment of May?   *Ib.* bk. 4, l. 164.

To Sorrow,
I bade good-morrow,
And thought to leave her far away behind;
But cheerly, cheerly,
She loves me dearly;
She is so constant to me, and so kind.   *Ib.* l. 173.

'Come hither, lady fair, and joined be
To our wild minstrelsy!'   *Ib.* l. 236.

Great Brahma from his mystic heaven groans,
And all his priesthood moans.   *Ib.* l. 265.

Their smiles,
Wan as primroses gather'd at midnight
By chilly finger'd spring.   *Ib.* l. 969.

Sweet are the pleasures that to verse belong,
And doubly sweet a brotherhood in song.   *Epistle to G. F. Mathew.*

Oh, never will the prize
High reason, and the love of good and ill,
Be my award!   *Epistle to J. H. Reynolds*, l. 74.

Lost in a sort of Purgatory blind.   *Ib.* l. 80.

It is a flaw
In happiness, to see beyond our bourn,—
It forces us in summer skies to mourn,
It spoils the singing of the nightingale.   *Ib.* l. 82.

Dry your eyes—O dry your eyes,
For I was taught in Paradise
To ease my breast of melodies.
　　　　　　　　Fairy Song: Shed No Tear.

Fanatics have their dreams, wherewith they weave
A paradise for a sect.　　*The Fall of Hyperion,* l. 1.

'None can usurp this height', return'd that shade,
'But those to whom the miseries of the world
Are misery, and will not let them rest.'　　*Ib.* l. 147.

　　　　　They are no dreamers weak,
They seek no wonder but the human face;
No music but a happy-noted voice.　　*Ib.* l. 162.

The poet and the dreamer are distinct,
Diverse, sheer opposite, antipodes.
The one pours out a balm upon the world,
The other vexes it.　　　　*Ib.* l. 199.

His flaming robes stream'd out beyond his heels,
And gave a roar, as if of earthly fire,
That scared away the meek ethereal hours,
And made their dove-wings tremble. On he flared.
　　　　　　　　Ib. c. ii, l. 58.

Ever let the fancy roam,
Pleasure never is at home.　　*Fancy,* l. 1.

O sweet Fancy! let her loose;
Summer's joys are spoilt by use.　　*Ib.* l. 9.

Where's the cheek that doth not fade,
Too much gaz'd at? Where's the maid
Whose lip mature is ever new?　　*Ib.* l. 69.

　　　　　Where's the face
One would meet in every place?　　*Ib.* l. 73.

　　　Where—where slept thine ire,
When like a blank idiot I put on thy wreath,
　　　Thy laurel, thy glory,
　　　The light of thy story,
Or was I a worm—too low crawling, for death?
　　O Delphic Apollo!　　*Hymn to Apollo.*

Far from the fiery noon, and eve's one star.
　　　　　　Hyperion, bk. 1, l. 3.

　　　　No stir of air was there,
Not so much life as on a summer's day
Robs not one light seed from the feather'd grass,
But where the dead leaf fell, there did it rest. *Ib.*l. 7.

How beautiful, if sorrow had not made
Sorrow more beautiful than Beauty's self. *Ib.* l. 35.
That large utterance of the early Gods. *Ib.* l. 51.
O aching time! O moments big as years! *Ib.* l. 64.

As when, upon a trancèd summer-night,
Those green-rob'd senators of mighty woods,
Tall oaks, branch-charmèd by the earnest stars,
Dream, and so dream all night without a stir.
　　　　　　　　Ib. l. 72.

And all those acts which Deity supreme
Doth ease its heart of love in.　　*Ib.* l. 111.

He enter'd, but he enter'd full of wrath.　*Ib.*l. 213.

Unseen before by Gods or wondering men.
　　　　　　　　Ib. l. 183.

Instead of sweets, his ample palate took
Savour of poisonous brass and metal sick. *Ib.* l. 188.

For as in theatres of crowded men
Hubbub increases more they call out, 'Hush!'
　　　　　　　　Ib. l. 253.

And still they were the same bright, patient stars.
　　　　　　　　Ib. l. 353.

Who cost her mother Tellus keener pangs,
Though feminine, than any of her sons.
　　　　　　　Ib. bk. 2, l. 54.

Now comes the pain of truth, to whom 'tis pain;
O folly! for to bear all naked truths,
And to envisage circumstance, all calm,
That is the top of sovereignty.　　*Ib.* l. 202.

A solitary sorrow best befits
Thy lips, and antheming a lonely grief.
　　　　　　　Ib. bk. 3, l. 5.

　　　　Point me out the way
To any one particular beauteous star,
And I will flit into it with my lyre,
And make its silvery splendour pant with bliss.
　　　　　　　　Ib. l. 99.

Knowledge enormous makes a God of me. *Ib.*l. 113.

But, for the general award of love,
The little sweet doth kill much bitterness.
　　　　　　　　Isabella, xiii.

Why were they proud? again we ask aloud,
Why in the name of Glory were they proud? *Ib.* xvi.

So the two brothers and their murder'd man
Rode past fair Florence.　　　　*Ib.* xxvii.

And she forgot the stars, the moon, the sun,
　And she forgot the blue above the trees,
And she forgot the dells where waters run,
　And she forgot the chilly autumn breeze;
She had no knowledge when the day was done,
　And the new moon she saw not: but in peace
Hung over her sweet Basil evermore.　*Ib.* liii.

　　　'For cruel 'tis,' said she,
'To steal my Basil-pot away from me.'　*Ib.* lxii.

I stood tip-toe upon a little hill.　　*Title.*

　　　　And then there crept
A little noiseless noise among the leaves,
Born of the very sigh that silence heaves.
　　I Stood Tip-toe upon a Little Hill.

Here are sweet peas, on tiptoe for a flight.　*Ib.*

Oh what can ail thee, Knight at arms
　Alone and palely loitering;
The sedge is wither'd from the lake,
　And no birds sing.　*La Belle Dame Sans Merci.*

I see a lily on thy brow,
　With anguish moist and fever dew;
And on thy cheek a fading rose
　Fast withereth too.　　　　*Ib.*

I met a lady in the meads
　Full beautiful, a faery's child;
Her hair was long, her foot was light,
　And her eyes were wild.

I set her on my pacing steed,
　And nothing else saw all day long;
For sideways would she lean, and sing
　A faery's song.　　　　*Ib.*

She look'd at me as she did love,
　And made sweet moan.　　*Ib.*

And sure in language strange she said,
　'I love thee true!'　　*Ib.*

And there I shut her wild, wild eyes
  With kisses four.   *Ib.* (Ld. Houghton's version.)

      'La belle Dame sans Merci
  Hath thee in thrall!'   *Ib.*

I saw their starv'd lips in the gloam
  With horrid warning gapèd wide,
And I awoke, and found me here
  On the cold hill side.   *Ib.*

She was a gordian shape of dazzling hue,
Vermilion-spotted, golden, green, and blue;
Striped like a zebra, freckled like a pard,
Eyed like a peacock, and all crimson barr'd.
               Lamia, pt. i, l. 47.

Real are the dreams of Gods, and smoothly pass
Their pleasures in a long immortal dream.
               Ib. l. 127.

Love in a hut, with water and a crust,
Is—Love, forgive us!—cinders, ashes, dust;
Love in a palace is perhaps at last
More grievous torment than a hermit's fast.
               Ib. pt. 2, l. 1.

That purple-lined palace of sweet sin.   *Ib.* l. 31.

In pale contented sort of discontent.   *Ib.* l. 135.

         Do not all charms fly
At the mere touch of cold philosophy?
There was an awful rainbow once in heaven:
We know her woof, her texture; she is given
In the dull catalogue of common things.
Philosophy will clip an Angel's wings.   *Ib.* l. 229.

Souls of poets dead and gone,
What Elysium have ye known,
Happy field or mossy cavern,
Choicer than the Mermaid Tavern?
Have ye tippled drink more fine
Than mine host's Canary wine?
          Lines on the Mermaid Tavern.

Pledging with contented smack
The Mermaid in the Zodiac.   *Ib.*

This living hand, now warm and capable
Of earnest grasping, would, if it were cold
And in the icy silence of the tomb,
So haunt thy days and chill thy dreaming nights
That thou would wish thine own heart dry of blood
So in my veins red life might stream again,
And thus be conscience-calm'd—see here it is—
I hold it towards you.
      *Lines Supposed to have been Addressed to
      Fanny Brawne.*

Old Meg was brave as Margaret Queen
And tall as Amazon:
An old red blanket cloak she wore;
A chip hat had she on.   *Meg Merrilies.*

Bards of Passion and of Mirth,
Ye have left your souls on earth!
Have ye souls in heaven too?
  [Written on the blank page before Beaumont
  and Fletcher's *Fair Maid of the Inn*.] *Bards
  of Passion and of Mirth.*

Where the nightingale doth sing
Not a senseless, tranced thing,
But divine melodious truth.   *Ib.*

Let none profane my Holy See of love,
    Or with a rude hand break
    The sacramental cake.   *Ode to Fanny.*

Thou still unravish'd bride of quietness,
Thou foster-child of silence and slow time.
           Ode on a Grecian Urn.

What men or gods are these? What maidens loth?
What mad pursuit? What struggle to escape?
What pipes and timbrels? What wild ecstasy?   *Ib.*

Heard melodies are sweet, but those unheard
Are sweeter; therefore, ye soft pipes, play on;
Not to the sensual ear, but, more endear'd,
Pipe to the spirit ditties of no tone.   *Ib.*

For ever wilt thou love, and she be fair!   *Ib.*

For ever piping songs for ever new.   *Ib.*

All breathing human passion far above.   *Ib.*

Who are these coming to the sacrifice?
To what green altar, O mysterious priest,
Lead'st thou that heifer lowing at the skies,
And all her silken flanks with garlands drest?
What little town by river or sea shore,
Or mountain-built with peaceful citadel,
Is emptied of this folk, this pious morn?   *Ib.*

O Attic shape! Fair attitude!   *Ib.*

Thou, silent form, dost tease us out of thought
As doth eternity: Cold Pastoral!   *Ib.*

'Beauty is truth, truth beauty,'—that is all
Ye know on earth, and all ye need to know.   *Ib.*

For I would not be dieted with praise,
A pet-lamb in a sentimental farce! *Ode on Indolence.*

By bards who died content on pleasant sward,
Leaving great verse unto a little clan. *Ode to Maia.*

Rich in the simple worship of a day.   *Ib.*

No, no, go not to Lethe, neither twist
Wolf's-bane, tight-rooted, for its poisonous wine.
           Ode on Melancholy.

Nor let the beetle, nor the death-moth be
Your mournful Psyche.   *Ib.*

She dwells with Beauty—Beauty that must die;
And Joy, whose hand is ever at his lips
Bidding adieu; and aching Pleasure nigh,
Turning to Poison while the bee-mouth sips:
Ay, in the very temple of delight
Veil'd Melancholy has her sovran shrine.
Though seen of none save him whose strenuous
     tongue
Can burst Joy's grape against his palate fine;
His soul shall taste the sadness of her might,
And be among her cloudy trophies hung.   *Ib.*

My heart aches, and a drowsy numbness pains
My sense.   *Ode to a Nightingale.*

'Tis not through envy of thy happy lot,
But being too happy in thine happiness,—
That thou, light-winged Dryad of the trees,
    In some melodious plot
Of beechen green, and shadows numberless,
Singest of summer in full-throated ease.   *Ib.*

O, for a draught of vintage! that hath been
Cool'd a long age in the deep-delvèd earth,
Tasting of Flora and the country green,
Dance, and Provençal song, and sunburnt mirth!
O for a beaker full of the warm South,
Full of the true, the blushful Hippocrene,
With beaded bubbles winking at the brim,
And purple-stainèd mouth;
That I might drink, and leave the world unseen,
And with thee fade away into the forest dim.   *Ib.*

Fade far away, dissolve, and quite forget
What thou among the leaves hast never known,
The weariness, the fever, and the fret,
Here, where men sit and hear each other groan. *Ib.*

Where youth grows pale, and spectre-thin, and dies.
Ib.

Where but to think is to be full of sorrow
And leaden-eyed despairs. *Ib.*

Where Beauty cannot keep her lustrous eyes,
Or new Love pine at them beyond tomorrow. *Ib.*

Away! away! for I will fly to thee,
Not charioted by Bacchus and his pards,
But on the viewless wings of Poesy,
Though the dull brain perplexes and retards. *Ib.*

But here there is no light,
Save what from heaven is with the breezes blown
Through verdurous glooms and winding mossy ways.
Ib.

I cannot see what flowers are at my feet,
Nor what soft incense hangs upon the boughs. *Ib.*

Fast fading violets cover'd up in leaves;
And mid-May's eldest child,
The coming musk-rose, full of dewy wine,
The murmurous haunt of flies on summer eves. *Ib.*

Darkling I listen; and, for many a time
I have been half in love with easeful Death,
Call'd him soft names in many a mused rhyme,
To take into the air my quiet breath;
Now more than ever seems it rich to die,
To cease upon the midnight with no pain,
While thou art pouring forth thy soul abroad
In such an ecstasy!
Still wouldst thou sing, and I have ears in vain—
To thy high requiem become a sod.

Thou wast not born for death, immortal Bird!
No hungry generations tread thee down;
The voice I hear this passing night was heard
In ancient days by emperor and clown:
Perhaps the self-same song that found a path
Through the sad heart of Ruth, when sick for home,
She stood in tears amid the alien corn;
The same that oft-times hath
Charm'd magic casements, opening on the foam
Of perilous seas, in faery lands forlorn. *Ib.*

Forlorn! the very word is like a bell
To toll me back from thee to my sole self!
Adieu! the fancy cannot cheat so well
As she is fam'd to do, deceiving elf.
Adieu! adieu! thy plaintive anthem fades
Past the near meadows, over the still stream,
Up the hill-side; and now 'tis buried deep
In the next valley-glades:
Was it a vision, or a waking dream?
Fled is that music:—Do I wake or sleep? *Ib.*

'Mid hush'd, cool-rooted flowers, fragrant-eyed,
Blue, silver-white, and budded Tyrian. *Ode to Psyche.*

To make delicious moan
Upon the midnight hours. *Ib.*

Thy voice, thy lute, thy pipe, thy incense sweet
From swinged censer teeming;
Thy shrine, thy grove, thy oracle, thy heat
Of pale-mouth'd prophet dreaming. *Ib.*

Yes, I will be thy priest, and build a fane
In some untrodden region of my mind,
Where branched thoughts, new grown with pleasant
pain,
Instead of pines shall murmur in the wind. *Ib.*

With buds, and bells, and stars without a name,
With all the gardener Fancy e'er could feign,
Who breeding flowers, will never breed the same. *Ib.*

A bright torch, and a casement ope at night,
To let the warm Love in! *Ib.*

Stop and consider! life is but a day;
A fragile dew-drop on its perilous way
From a tree's summit; a poor Indian's sleep
While his boat hastens to the monstrous steep
Of Montmorenci. *Sleep and Poetry*, l. 85.

O for ten years, that I may overwhelm
Myself in poesy; so I may do the deed
That my own soul has to itself decreed. *Ib.* l. 96.

They sway'd about upon a rocking horse,
And thought it Pegasus. *Ib.* l. 186.

The blue
Bared its eternal bosom, and the dew
Of summer nights collected still to make
The morning precious. *Ib.* l. 189.

A drainless shower
Of light is poesy; 'tis the supreme of power;
'Tis might half slumb'ring on its own right arm.
Ib. l. 235.

The great end
Of poesy, that it should be a friend
To soothe the cares, and lift the thoughts of man.
Ib. l. 245.

They shall be accounted poet kings
Who simply tell the most heart-easing things.
Ib. l. 267.

Bright star, would I were stedfast as thou art—
Not in lone splendour hung aloft the night
And watching, with eternal lids apart,
Like nature's patient, sleepless Eremite,
The moving waters at their priestlike task
Of pure ablution round earth's human shores.
Sonnet. 'Bright Star.'

Still, still to hear her tender-taken breath,
And to live ever—or else swoon to death. *Ib.*

Much have I travell'd in the realms of gold,
And many goodly states and kingdoms seen;
Round many western islands have I been
Which bards in fealty to Apollo hold.
Oft of one wide expanse had I been told
That deep-brow'd Homer ruled as his demesne;
Yet did I never breathe its pure serene
Till I heard Chapman speak out loud and bold:
Then I felt like some watcher of the skies
When a new planet swims into his ken;
Or like stout Cortez when with eagle eyes
He star'd at the Pacific—and all his men
Look'd at each other with a wild surmise—
Silent, upon a peak in Darien.
Ib. On First Looking into Chapman's Homer.

O Chatterton! how very sad thy fate!
Ib. To Chatterton.

Mortality
Weighs heavily on me like unwilling sleep.
Ib. On Seeing the Elgin Marbles.

The poetry of earth is never dead:
When all the birds are faint with the hot sun,
And hide in cooling trees, a voice will run
From hedge to hedge about the new-mown mead.
Ib. On the Grasshopper and Cricket.

Happy is England! I could be content
To see no other verdure than its own;
To feel no other breezes than are blown
Through its tall woods with high romances blent.
Ib. 'Happy is England!'

Happy is England, sweet her artless daughters;
Enough their simple loveliness for me.   *Ib.*

Other spirits there are standing apart
Upon the forehead of the age to come.
Ib. To Haydon, ii. *'Great Spirits Now On Earth.'*

There is a budding morrow in midnight.
Ib. To Homer.

Four seasons fill the measure of the year.
Ib. Human Seasons.

Glory and loveliness have pass'd away.
Ib. To Leigh Hunt.

Son of the old moon-mountains African!
Chief of the Pyramid and Crocodile! *Ib. To the Nile.*

It keeps eternal whisperings around
Desolate shores, and with its mighty swell
Gluts twice ten thousand Caverns. *Ib. On the Sea.*

O soft embalmer of the still midnight. *Ib. To Sleep.*

Turn the key deftly in the oiled wards,
And seal the hushed casket of my soul.   *Ib.*

The sweet converse of an innocent mind.
Ib. To Solitude.

The day is gone, and all its sweets are gone!
Sweet voice, sweet lips, soft hand, and softer breast.
Ib. 'The Day Is Gone.'

To one who has been long in city pent;
'Tis very sweet to look into the fair
And open face of heaven.
Ib. 'To One Who Has Been Long.'

A debonair
And gentle tale of love and languishment.   *Ib.*

O fret not after knowledge—I have none,
And yet my song comes native with the warmth.
O fret not after knowledge—I have none,
And yet the Evening listens.
Ib. What the Thrush Said.

When I have fears that I may cease to be
Before my pen has glean'd my teeming train.
Ib. 'When I Have Fears.'

When I behold upon the night's starr'd face,
Huge cloudy symbols of a high romance.   *Ib.*

Then on the shore
Of the wide world I stand alone, and think
Till love and fame to nothingness do sink.   *Ib.*

In a drear-nighted December,
Too happy, happy tree,
Thy branches ne'er remember
Their green felicity.
Stanzas. 'In a Drear-nighted December.'

But were there ever any
Writh'd not at passing joy?
To know the change and feel it,
When there is none to heal it,
Nor numbed sense to steel it,
Was never said in rhyme.   *Ib.*

St. Agnes' Eve—Ah, bitter chill it was!
The owl, for all his feathers, was a-cold;
The hare limp'd trembling through the frozen grass,
And silent was the flock in woolly fold.
The Eve of S. Agnes, i.

The silver, snarling trumpets 'gan to chide. *Ib.* iv.

Upon the honey'd middle of the night.   *Ib.* vi.

The music, yearning like a God in pain.   *Ib.* vii.

A poor, weak, palsy-stricken, churchyard thing.
Ib. xviii.

A casement high and triple-arch'd there was,
All garlanded with carven imag'ries
Of fruits, and flowers, and bunches of knot-grass,
And diamonded with panes of quaint device,
Innumerable of stains and splendid dyes,
As are the tiger-moth's deep-damask'd wings;
And in the midst, 'mong thousand heraldries,
And twilight saints, and dim emblazonings,
A shielded scutcheon blush'd with blood of queens
 and kings.   *Ib.* xxiv.

By degrees
Her rich attire creeps rustling to her knees.
Ib. l. xxvi.

Her soft and chilly nest.   *Ib.* xxvii.

As though a rose should shut, and be a bud again.
Ib. xxvii.

And lucent syrops, tinct with cinnamon;
Manna and dates, in argosy transferr'd
From Fez; and spiced dainties, every one,
From silken Samarcand to cedar'd Lebanon.
Ib. xxx.

He play'd an ancient ditty, long since mute,
In Provence call'd, 'La belle dame sans mercy'.
Ib. xxxiii.

And they are gone: aye, ages long ago
These lovers fled away into the storm.   *Ib.* xlii.

The Beadsman, after thousand aves told,
For aye unsought-for slept among his ashes cold. *Ib.*

Upon a Sabbath-day it fell;
Twice holy was the Sabbath-bell,
That call'd the folk to evening prayer.
The Eve of Saint Mark, l. 1.

Season of mists and mellow fruitfulness,
Close bosom-friend of the maturing sun;
Conspiring with him how to load and bless
With fruit the vines that round the thatch-eves run.
To Autumn.

Who hath not seen thee oft amid thy store?
Sometimes whoever seeks abroad may find
Thee sitting careless on a granary floor,
Thy hair soft-lifted by the winnowing wind;
Or on a half-reap'd furrow sound asleep,
Drows'd with the fume of poppies, while thy hook
Spares the next swath and all its twined flowers. *Ib.*

Then in a wailful choir the small gnats mourn
Among the river sallows, borne aloft
Or sinking as the light wind lives or dies.   *Ib.*

The red-breast whistles from a garden-croft;
And gathering swallows twitter in the skies.   *Ib.*

Woman! when I behold thee flippant, vain,
Inconstant, childish, proud, and full of fancies.
      Woman! When I Behold Thee.

Like a whale's back in the sea of prose.
    Letters (ed. M. B. Forman, 1935), 14. *To
Leigh Hunt, 10 May 1817.*

What a thing to be in the mouth of fame.   *Ib.*

I remember your saying that you had notions of a
good Genius presiding over you. I have of late
had the same thought—for things which [I] do
half at random are afterwards confirmed by my
judgment in a dozen features of propriety. Is it
too daring to fancy Shakespeare this Presider?
    Ib. 15. *To B. R. Haydon, 10–11 May, 1817.*

I am quite disgusted with literary men.
    Ib. 25. *To Benjamin Bailey, 8 Oct. 1817.*

A long poem is a test of invention which I take to
be the Polar star of poetry, as fancy is the sails,
and imagination the rudder.   *Ib.*

A man should have the fine point of his soul taken
off to become fit for this world.
    Ib. 30. *To J. H. Reynolds, 22 Nov. 1817.*

I am certain of nothing but the holiness of the
heart's affection and the truth of imagination—
what the imagination seizes as beauty must be
truth—whether it existed before or not.
    Ib. 31. *To Benjamin Bailey, 22 Nov. 1817.*

I have never yet been able to perceive how anything
can be known for truth by consecutive reasoning—
and yet it must be.   *Ib.*

O for a life of sensations rather than of thoughts! *Ib.*

The excellency of every art is its intensity, capable
of making all disagreeables evaporate, from their
being in close relationship with beauty and truth.
    Ib. 32. *To G. and F. Keats, 21 Dec. 1817.*

Negative Capability, that is, when a man is capable
of being in uncertainties, mysteries, doubts, without any irritable reaching after fact and reason—
Coleridge, for instance, would let go by a fine
isolated verisimilitude caught from the Penetralium of mystery, from being incapable of remaining
content with half-knowledge.   *Ib.*

There is nothing stable in the world; uproar's your
only music.
    Ib. 37. *To G. and T. Keats, 13 Jan. 1818.*

So I do believe . . . that works of genius are the first
things in this world.   *Ib.*

For the sake of a few fine imaginative or domestic
passages, are we to be bullied into a certain
philosophy engendered in the whims of an egotist.
    Ib. 44. *To J. H. Reynolds, 3 Feb. 1818.*

We hate poetry that has a palpable design upon us—
and if we do not agree, seems to put its hand in its
breeches pocket. Poetry should be great and unobtrusive, a thing which enters into one's soul, and
does not startle or amaze it with itself, but with its
subject.   *Ib.*

When man has arrived at a certain ripeness in intellect any one grand and spiritual passage serves
him as a starting-post towards all 'the two-and-
thirty palaces'.
    Ib. 48. *To J. H. Reynolds, 19 Feb. 1818.*

Poetry should surprise by a fine excess, and not by
singularity; it should strike the reader as a wording
of his own highest thoughts, and appear almost a
remembrance. Its touches of beauty should never
be half-way, thereby making the reader breathless,
instead of content. The rise, the progress, the
setting of imagery should, like the sun, come
natural to him.
    Ib. 51. *To John Taylor, 27 Feb. 1818.*

If poetry comes not as naturally as leaves to a tree it
had better not come at all.   *Ib.*

I have good reason to be content, for thank God I
can read and perhaps understand Shakespeare to
his depths.   *Ib.*

Scenery is fine—but human nature is finer.
    Ib. 53. *To Benjamin Bailey, 13 March 1818.*

As if the roots of the earth were rotten, cold, and
drenched.
    Ib. 60. *To J. H. Reynolds, 9 April 1818.*

A country which is continually under hatches.
    Ib. 61. *To J. H. Reynolds, 10 Apr. 1818.*

I have been hovering for some time between the
exquisite sense of the luxurious and a love for
philosophy—were I calculated for the former I
should be glad—but as I am not I shall turn all
my soul to the latter.
    Ib. 62. *To John Taylor, 24 Apr. 1818.*

Axioms in philosophy are not axioms until they are
proved upon our pulses: we read fine things but
never feel them to the full until we have gone the
same steps as the author.
    Ib. 64. *To J. H. Reynolds, 3 May 1818.*

I am in that temper that if I were under water I would
scarcely kick to come to the top.
    Ib. 66. *To Benjamin Bailey, 21 May 1818.*

Were it in my choice I would reject a petrarchal
coronation—on account of my dying day, and
because women have cancers.
    Ib. 69. *To Benjamin Bailey, 10 June 1818.*

I do think better of womankind than to suppose
they care whether Mister John Keats five feet
high likes them or not.
    Ib. 79. *To Benjamin Bailey, 18 July 1818.*

His identity presses upon me.
    Ib. 86. *To C. W. Dilke, 21 Sept. 1818.*

I never was in love—yet the voice and the shape of
a woman has haunted me these two days.
    Ib. 87. *To J. H. Reynolds, 22 Sept. 1818.*

There is an awful warmth about my heart like a load
of immortality.   *Ib.*

In Endymion, I leaped headlong into the sea, and
thereby have become better acquainted with the
soundings, the quicksands, and the rocks, than if
I had stayed upon the green shore, and piped a
silly pipe, and took tea and comfortable advice.
    Ib. 90. *To James Hessery, 9 Oct. 1818.*

I would sooner fail than not be among the greatest.
> *Ib.*

As to the poetical character itself (I mean that sort of which, if I am anything, I am a member; that sort distinguished from the Wordsworthian or egotistical sublime; which is a thing *per se* and stands alone) it is not itself—it has no self. . . . It has as much delight in conceiving an Iago as an Imogen.
> *Ib.* 93. *To Richard Woodhouse, 27 Oct. 1818.*

I think I shall be among the English Poets after my death.
> *Ib.* 94. *To George and Georgiana Keats, 14 Oct. 1818.*

The mighty abstract idea I have of beauty in all things stifles the more divided and minute domestic happiness. The opinion I have of the generality of women—who appear to me as children to whom I would rather give a sugar plum than my time.
> *Ib.*

I never can feel certain of any truth but from a clear perception of its beauty.
> *Ib.* 98. *To George and Georgiana Keats, 16 Dec. 1818–4 Jan. 1819.*

I have come to this resolution—never to write for the sake of writing or making a poem, but from running over with any little knowledge or experience which many years of reflection may perhaps give me; otherwise I shall be dumb.
> *Ib.* 115. *To B. R. Haydon, 8 Mar. 1819.*

It is true that in the height of enthusiasm I have been cheated into some fine passages; but that is not the thing.
> *Ib.*

I should like the window to open onto the Lake of Geneva—and there I'd sit and read all day like the picture of somebody reading.
> *Ib.* 116. *To Fanny Keats, 13 Mar. 1819.*

A man's life of any worth is a continual allegory.
> *Ib.* 123. *To George and Georgiana Keats, 14 Feb.–3 May 1819.*

Shakespeare led a life of allegory: his works are the comments on it.
> *Ib.*

Nothing ever becomes real till it is experienced—even a proverb is no proverb to you till your life has illustrated it.
> *Ib.*

Call the world if you please 'The vale of Soul-making'.
> *Ib.*

I have met with women whom I really think would like to be married to a poem, and to be given away by a novel.
> *Ib.* 136. *To Fanny Brawne, 8 July 1819.*

I have two luxuries to brood over in my walks, your loveliness and the hour of my death. O that I could have possession of them both in the same minute.
> *Ib.* 139. *To Fanny Brawne, 25 July 1809.*

I am convinced more and more day by day that fine writing is next to fine doing.
> *Ib.* 145. *To J. H. Reynolds, 24 Aug. 1819.*

Give me books, fruit, french wine and fine weather and a little music out of doors, played by somebody I do not know.
> *Ib.* 146. *To Fanny Keats, 29 Aug. 1819.*

All clean and comfortable I sit down to write.
> *Ib.* 156. *To George and Georgiana Keats, 17 Sept. 1819.*

I have but lately been on my guard against Milton. Life to him would be death to me. Miltonic verse cannot be written but it [*for* in] the vein of art—I wish to devote myself to another sensation. *Ib.*

The only means of strengthening one's intellect is to make up one's mind about nothing—to let the mind be a thoroughfare for all thoughts. Not a select party. *Ib.*

You have ravished me away by a power I cannot resist; and yet I could resist till I saw you; and even since I have seen you I have endeavoured often 'to reason against the reason of my Love'.
> *Ib.* 160. *To Fanny Brawne, 13 Oct. 1819.*

'If I should die', said I to myself, 'I have left no immortal work behind me—nothing to make my friends proud of my memory—but I have loved the principle of beauty in all things, and if I had had time I would have made myself remembered.'
> *Ib.* 186. *To Fanny Brawne, Feb. 1820?*

I long to believe in immortality. . . . If I am destined to be happy with you here—how short is the longest life. I wish to believe in immortality—I wish to live with you for ever.
> *Ib.* 223. *To Fanny Brawne, July 1820.*

I wish you could invent some means to make me at all happy without you. Every hour I am more and more concentrated in you; every thing else tastes like chaff in my mouth.
> *Ib.* 224. *To Fanny Brawne, Aug. 1820.*

You, I am sure, will forgive me for sincerely remarking that you might curb your magnanimity, and be more of an artist, and load every rift of your subject with ore. *Ib.* 227. *To Shelley, Aug. 1829.*

He already seemed to feel the flowers growing over him.
> *Words reported by Severn.* W. Sharp, *Life and Letters of Severn,* ch. 4.

Here lies one whose name was writ in water.
> *Epitaph.* Lord Houghton, *Life of Keats,* ii. 91.

JOHN KEBLE
1792–1866

Hues of the rich unfolding morn,
That, ere the glorious sun be born,
By some soft touch invisible
Around his path are taught to swell.
> *The Christian Year. Morning.*

Oh! timely happy, timely wise,
Hearts that with rising morn arise! *Ib.*

New every morning is the love
Our wakening and uprising prove. *Ib.*

If on our daily course our mind
Be set to hallow all we find,
New treasures still, of countless price,
God will provide for sacrifice. *Ib.*

We need not bid, for cloister'd cell,
Our neighbour and our work farewell. *Ib.*

Nor strive to wind ourselves too high
For sinful man beneath the sky.   *Ib.*

The trivial round, the common task,
Would furnish all we ought to ask;
Room to deny ourselves; a road
To bring us, daily, nearer God.   *Ib.*

And help us, this and every day,
To live more nearly as we pray.   *Ib.*

Sun of my soul! Thou Saviour dear,
It is not night if Thou be near.   *Ib. Evening*

Abide with me from morn till eve,
For without Thee I cannot live:
Abide with me when night is nigh;
For without Thee I dare not die.   *Ib.*

Like infants' slumbers, pure and light.   *Ib.*

There is a book, who runs may read,
   Which heavenly truth imparts,
And all the lore its scholars need,
   Pure eyes and Christian hearts.
                        Ib. Septuagesima.

Thou, who hast given me eyes to see
   And love this sight so fair,
Give me a heart to find out Thee,
   And read Thee everywhere.   *Ib.*

The many-twinkling smile of ocean.
                Ib. 2nd Sunday after Trinity.

Red o'er the forest peers the setting sun,
   The line of yellow light dies fast away
That crown'd the eastern copse: and chill and dun
   Falls on the moor the brief November day.
                Ib. 23rd Sunday after Trinity.

Bless'd are the pure in heart,
For they shall see our God.   *Ib. The Purification.*

   Still to the lowly soul
   He doth Himself impart,
And for His cradle and His throne
   Chooseth the pure in heart.   *Ib.*

The voice that breathed o'er Eden.
                        Poems. Holy Matrimony.

The English *Virgil* [Spenser].
   Lectures on Poetry, lect. v, 1912, vol. i, p. 82.
As fire is kindled by fire, so is a poet's mind kindled
   by contact with a brother poet.
              Ib. lect. xvi, 1912, vol. i, p. 317.

THOMAS KELLY
1769–1854

The Head that once was crowned with thorns
Is crowned with glory now.
   Hymns on Various Passages of Scripture (1820).
   The Head that Once Was Crowned.

JOHN KEMPTHORNE
1775–1838

Praise the Lord! ye heavens adore Him,
   Praise Him, Angels in the height;
Sun and moon, rejoice before Him,
   Praise Him, all ye stars and light.
   Hymns of Praise. For Foundling Apprentices
   (1796). *Praise the Lord! Ye Heavens Adore*
   Him.

THOMAS KEN
1637–1711

Awake my soul, and with the sun
The daily stage of duty run;
Shake off dull sloth, and joyful rise
To pay thy morning sacrifice.
         Morning Hymn (1709). *Awake My Soul.*

Each present day thy last esteem.   *Ib.*

Teach me to live, that I may dread
The grave as little as my bed.
      Evening Hymn. Glory to Thee My God This
      Night.

Praise God, from whom all blessings flow,
Praise Him, all creatures here below,
Praise Him above, ye heavenly host,
Praise Father, Son, and Holy Ghost.
               Morning and Evening Hymn.

LADY CAROLINE KEPPEL
1735–?

What's this dull town to me?
   Robin's not near.
He whom I wished to see,
   Wished for to hear;
Where's all the joy and mirth
Made life a heaven on earth?
O! they're all fled with thee,
   Robin Adair.   *Robin Adair.*

WILLIAM KETHE
fl. 1560

All people that on earth do dwell,
Sing to the Lord with cheerful voice;
Him serve with fear, His praise forth tell,
Come ye before Him, and rejoice.

The Lord, ye know, is God indeed;
Without our aid He did us make.
      Daye's Psalter (1560). *All People That on*
      Earth.

For it is seemly so to do.   *Ib.*

For why? The Lord our God is good.   *Ib.*

RALPH KETTELL
1563–1693

Here is Hey for Garsington! and Hey for Cuddesdon!
and Hey Hockley! but here's nobody cries, Hey
for God Almighty!
      Sermon at Garsington Revel. Aubrey's *Brief*
      Lives, vol. ii.

FRANCIS SCOTT KEY
1779–1843

'Tis the star-spangled banner; O long may it wave
O'er the land of the free, and the home of the brave!
               The Star-Spangled Banner.

JOYCE KILMER

1888–1918

I think that I shall never see
A poem lovely as a tree.
Poems, Essays, and Letters, 1917, i. *Trees*.

Poems are made by fools like me,
But only God can make a tree.   *Ib.*

BENJAMIN FRANKLIN KING

1857–1894

Nothing to do but work,
Nothing to eat but food,
Nothing to wear but clothes
To keep one from going nude.   *The Pessimist.*

Nothing to breathe but air,
Quick as a flash 'tis gone;
Nowhere to fall but off,
Nowhere to stand but on!   *Ib.*

HARRY KING

Young men taken in and done for.   *Title of Song.*

HENRY KING

1592–1669

We that did nothing study but the way
To love each other, with which thoughts the day
Rose with delight to us, and with them set,
Must learn the hateful art, how to forget.
A Renunciation.

Nature's true-born child, who sums his years
(Like me) with no arithmetic but tears.
The Anniverse. Elegy.

Accept, thou shrine of my dead Saint,
Instead of dirges this complaint;
And for sweet flowers to crown thy hearse,
Receive a strew of weeping verse
From thy griev'd friend, whom thou might'st see
Quite melted into tears for thee.   *The Exequy.*

Sleep on my Love in thy cold bed,
Never to be disquieted!
My last good night! Thou wilt not wake
Till I thy fate shall overtake:
Till age, or grief, or sickness must
Marry my body to that dust
It so much loves; and fill the room
My heart keeps empty in thy tomb.
Stay for me there; I will not fail
To meet thee in that hollow vale.
And think not much of my delay;
I am already on the way,
And follow thee with all the speed
Desire can make, or sorrows breed.   *Ib.*

'Tis true, with shame and grief I yield,
Thou like the van first took'st the field,
And gotten hast the victory
In thus adventuring to die
Before me, whose more years might crave
A just precedence in the grave.

But hark! My pulse like a soft drum
Beats my approach, tells thee I come;
And slow howe'er my marches be,
I shall at last sit down by thee.   *Ib.*

STODDARD KING

1889–1933

There's a long, long trail a-winding
Into the land of my dreams,
Where the nightingales are singing
And a white moon beams:
There's a long, long night of waiting
Until my dreams all come true;
Till the day when I'll be going down
That long long trail with you.
The Long, Long Trail.

WILLIAM KING

1663–1712

Beauty from order springs.   *Art of Cookery*, l. 55.

Cornwall squab-pie, and Devon white-pot brings,
And Leicester beans and bacon, food of kings!
Ib. l. 165.

ALEXANDER WILLIAM KINGLAKE

1809–1891

Soon the men of the column began to see that though
the scarlet line was slender, it was very rigid and
exact.   *Invasion of the Crimea*, vol. ii, p. 455.

CHARLES KINGSLEY

1819–1875

Airly Beacon, Airly Beacon;
Oh the pleasant sight to see
Shires and towns from Airly Beacon,
While my love climb'd up to me!   *Airly Beacon.*

Airly Beacon, Airly Beacon;
Oh the weary haunt for me,
All alone on Airly Beacon,
With his baby on my knee!   *Ib.*

And no one but the baby cried for poor Lorraine,
Lorrèe.   *Ballad: 'Lorraine, Lorraine, Lorrèe.'*

My fairest child, I have no song to give you;
No lark could pipe to skies so dull and grey.
A Farewell. To C. E. G.

Be good, sweet maid, and let who can be clever;
Do noble things, not dream them, all day long;
And so make Life, Death, and that vast For Ever,
One grand sweet song.   *Ib.*

It was Earl Haldan's daughter,
She looked across the sea.
It Was Earl Haldan's Daughter.

The locks of six princesses
Must be my marriage fee,

'So hey bonny boat, and ho bonny boat!
Who comes a-wooing me?'   *Ib.*

Leave to Robert Browning
Beggars, fleas, and vines;
Leave to squeamish Ruskin
Popish Apennines,
Dirty stones of Venice
And his gas-lamps seven;
We've the stones of Snowdon
And the lamps of heaven.
Letter to Thomas Hughes.

What we can we will be,
Honest Englishmen.
Do the work that's nearest,
Though it's dull at whiles,
Helping, when we meet them,
Lame dogs over stiles.   *Ib.*

Welcome, wild North-easter!
Shame it is to see
Odes to every zephyr;
Ne'er a verse to thee.   *Ode to the North East Wind.*

Jovial wind of winter
Turn us out to play!   *Ib.*

Chime, ye dappled darlings,
Down the roaring blast;
You shall see a fox die
Ere an hour be past.   *Ib.*

'Tis the hard grey weather
Breeds hard English men.   *Ib.*

Come; and strong within us
Stir the Vikings' blood;
Bracing brain and sinew;
Blow, thou wind of God!   *Ib.*

I once had a sweet little doll, dears,
The prettiest doll in the world;
Her cheeks were so red and so white, dears,
And her hair was so charmingly curled.
Songs from The Water Babies. My Little Doll.

Yet, for old sakes' sake she is still, dears,
The prettiest doll in the world.   *Ib.*

Undefiled for the undefiled;
Play by me, bathe in me, mother and child.
Ib. The Tide River.

When all the world is young, lad,
And all the trees are green;
And every goose a swan, lad,
And every lass a queen;
Then hey for boot and horse, lad,
And round the world away:
Young blood must have its course, lad,
And every dog his day.

When all the world is old, lad,
And all the trees are brown;
And all the sport is stale, lad,
And all the wheels run down;
Creep home, and take your place there,
The spent and maimed among:
God grant you find one face there,
You loved when all was young. *Ib. Young and Old.*

The merry brown hares came leaping
Over the crest of the hill,
Where the clover and corn lay sleeping
Under the moonlight still.   *The Bad Squire.*

Oh! that we two were maying.
The Saint's Tragedy, II. ix.

With our limbs at rest on the quiet earth's breast,
And our souls at home with God!   *Ib.*

'O Mary, go and call the cattle home,
And call the cattle home,
And call the cattle home,
Across the sands of Dee:'
The western wind was wild and dank with foam,
And all alone went she.   *The Sands of Dee.*

The cruel crawling foam.   *Ib.*

The western tide crept up along the sand,
And o'er and o'er the sand,
And round and round the sand,
As far as eye could see.
The rolling mist came down and hid the land:
And never home came she.   *Ib.*

Three fishers went sailing away to the west,
Away to the west as the sun went down;
Each thought on the woman who loved him the best,
And the children stood watching them out of the
town.   *The Three Fishers.*

And the night-rack came rolling up ragged and
brown.   *Ib.*

For men must work, and women must weep,
And there's little to earn, and many to keep,
Though the harbour bar be moaning.   *Ib.*

For men must work, and women must weep,
And the sooner it's over, the sooner to sleep;
And good-bye to the bar and its moaning.   *Ib.*

To be discontented with the divine discontent, and to
be ashamed with the noble shame, is the very germ
and first upgrowth of all virtue.
Health and Education (1874), p. 20.

Truth, for its own sake, had never been a virtue with
the Roman clergy.
*Review of Froude's History of England, in
Macmillan's Magazine for Jan. 1864.*

He did not know that a keeper is only a poacher
turned outside in, and a poacher a keeper turned
inside out.   *The Water Babies,* ch. 1.

As thorough an Englishman as ever coveted his
neighbour's goods.   *Ib.* ch. 4.

And still the lobster held on.   *Ib.* ch. 5.

Mrs. Bedonebyasyoudid is coming.   *Ib.*

The loveliest fairy in the world; and her name is
Mrs. Doasyouwouldbedoneby.   *Ib.*

All the butterflies and cockyolybirds would fly past
me.   *Ib.* ch. 8.

Till the coming of the Cocqcigrues.   *Ib.*

Don Desperado
Walked on the Prado,
And there he met his enemy.   *Westward Ho,* ch. 12.

More ways of killing a cat than choking her with
cream.   *Ib.* ch. 20.

Eustace is a man no longer; he is become a thing, a
tool, a Jesuit.   *Ib.* ch. 23.

What, then, does Dr. Newman mean?
Title of a pamphlet, 1864.

Some say that the age of chivalry is past, that the
spirit of romance is dead. The age of chivalry is
never past, so long as there is a wrong left unredressed on earth.   *Life* (1879), vol. ii, ch. 28.

RUDYARD KIPLING

1865–1936

When you've shouted 'Rule Britannia', when you've
  sung 'God save the Queen',
When you've finished killing Kruger with your
  mouth.   *The Absent-Minded Beggar.*

He's an absent-minded beggar, and his weaknesses
  are great—
But we and Paul must take him as we find him—
He's out on active service, wiping something off a
  slate—
And he's left a lot of little things behind him!   *Ib.*

Duke's son—cook's son—son of a hundred Kings—
(Fifty thousand horse and foot going to Table Bay!)
                                     Ib.

Pass the hat for your credit's sake, and pay—pay—
  pay!   *Ib.*

If you'd go to Mother Carey
(Walk her down to Mother Carey!),
Oh, we're bound to Mother Carey where she feeds
  her chicks at sea!   *Anchor Song.*

England's on the anvil—hear the hammers ring—
Clanging from the Severn to the Tyne!
Never was a blacksmith like our Norman King—
England's being hammered, hammered, hammered
  into line!   *The Anvil.*

Back to the Army again.   *Title.*

A-layin' on to the Sergeant I don't know a gun from
  a bat.   *Back to the Army Again.*

I 'eard the feet on the gravel—the feet o' the men
  what drill—
An' I sez to my flutterin' 'eart-strings, I sez to 'em,
  'Peace, be still!'   *Ib.*

Rolling down the Ratcliffe Road drunk and raising
  Cain.   *The Ballad of the 'Bolivar'.*

Oh, East is East, and West is West, and never the
  twain shall meet,
Till Earth and Sky stand presently at God's great
  Judgment Seat;
But there is neither East nor West, Border, nor
  Breed, nor Birth,
When two strong men stand face to face, though they
  come from the ends of the earth!
    The Ballad of East and West.

With the mouth of a bell and the heart of Hell and the
  head of the gallows-tree.   *Ib.*

The little silver crucifix
  That keeps a man from harm.
    The Ballad of Fisher's Boarding-House.

And the talk slid north, and the talk slid south,
With the sliding puffs from the hookah-mouth.
Four things greater than all things are,—
Women and Horses and Power and War.
    Ballad of the King's Jest.

It was not part of their blood,
  It came to them very late
With long arrears to make good,
  When the English began to hate.
    The Beginnings.

There's peace in a Larañaga, there's calm in a Henry
  Clay.   *The Betrothed.*

And a woman is only a woman, but a good cigar is a
  Smoke.   *Ib.*

Gentlemen unafraid.
    *Beyond the Path of the Outmost Sun. (Barrack-
    Room Ballads: Dedication.)*

E'en as he trod that day to God so walked he from his
  birth,
In simpleness and gentleness and honour and clean
  mirth.   *Ib.*

'Oh, where are you going to, all you Big Steamers,
With England's own coal, up and down the salt seas?'
'We are going to fetch you your bread and your butter,
Your beef, pork, and mutton, eggs, apples, and
  cheese.'   *Big Steamers.*

'Oh, the Channel's as bright as a ball-room already,
And pilots are thicker than pilchards at Looe.'   *Ib.*

'For the bread that you eat and the biscuits you nibble,
The sweets that you suck and the joints that you
  carve,
They are brought to you daily by all us Big Steam-
  ers—
And if any one hinders our coming you'll starve!' *Ib.*

We're foot—slog—slog—slog—sloggin' over Africa—
Foot—foot—foot—foot—sloggin' over Africa—
(Boots—boots—boots—boots—movin' up an' down
  again!)
There's no discharge in the war!   *Boots.*

Try—try—try—try—to think o' something different—
Oh—my—God—keep—me from goin' lunatic!
(Boots—boots—boots—boots—movin' up an' down
  again!)   *Ib.*

I—'ave—marched—six—weeks in 'Ell an' certify
It—is—not—fire—devils, dark, or anything,
But boots—boots—boots—boots—movin' up an' down
  again.   *Ib.*

O ye who tread the Narrow Way
By Tophet-flare to Judgement Day.
    Buddha at Kamakura.

I've a head like a concertina, I've a tongue like a
  button-stick,
I've a mouth like an old potato, and I'm more than a
  little sick,
But I've had my fun o' the Corp'ral's Guard; I've
  made the cinders fly,
And I'm here in the Clink for a thundering drink and
  blacking the Corporal's eye.   *Cells.*

'Drunk and resisting the Guard!'
Mad drunk and resisting the Guard—
'Strewth, but I socked it them hard!
So it's pack-drill for me and a fortnight's C.B.
For 'drunk and resisting the Guard'.   *Ib.*

Take of English earth as much
As either hand may rightly clutch.
In the taking of it breathe
Prayer for all who lie beneath. . . .
Lay that earth upon thy heart,
And thy sickness shall depart!   *A Charm.*

Land of our birth, we pledge to thee
Our love and toil in the years to be;
When we are grown and take our place,
As men and women with our race.

Father in Heaven who lovest all,
Oh, help Thy children when they call;
That they may build from age to age
An undefilèd heritage.

Teach us to bear the yoke in youth,
With steadfastness and careful truth;
That, in our time, Thy Grace may give
The truth whereby the nations live.
The Children's Song.

That we, with Thee, may walk uncowed
By fear or favour of the crowd.   *Ib.*

That, under Thee, we may possess
Man's strength to comfort man's distress.

Teach us delight in simple things,
And mirth that has no bitter springs;
Forgiveness free of evil done,
And love to all men 'neath the sun!

Land of our birth, our faith, our pride,
For whose dear sake our fathers died;
O Motherland, we pledge to thee
Head, heart, and hand through the years to be!   *Ib.*

High noon behind the tamarisks—the sun is hot
          above us—
As at Home the Christmas Day is breaking wan.
They will drink our healths at dinner—those who
          tell us how they love us,
And forget us till another year be gone!
          Christmas in India.

So Time, that is o'er-kind,
To all that be,
Ordains us e'en as blind,
As bold as she:
That in our very death,
And burial sure,
Shadow to shadow, well persuaded, saith,
'See how our works endure!'
          Cities and Thrones and Powers (*Puck of Pook's
          Hill*).

We must go back with Policeman Day—
          Back from the City of Sleep!   *The City of Sleep.*

The coastwise lights of England watch the ships of
          England go!   *The Coastwise Lights.*

They know the worthy General as 'that most im-
          moral man'.   *A Code of Morals.*

Gold is for the mistress—silver for the maid—
Copper for the craftsman cunning at his trade.
'Good!' said the Baron, sitting in his hall,
'But Iron—Cold Iron—is master of them all.'
          Cold Iron.

We have learned to whittle the Eden Tree to the shape
          of a surplice-peg,
We have learned to bottle our parents twain in the
          yolk of an addled egg,
We know that the tail must wag the dog, for the horse
          is drawn by the cart;
But the Devil whoops, as he whooped of old: 'It's
          clever, but is it Art?'
          The Conundrum of the Workshops.

Our father Adam sat under the Tree and scratched
          with a stick in the mould;
And the first rude sketch that the world had seen was
          joy to his mighty heart,
Till the Devil whispered behind the leaves, 'It's
          pretty, but is it Art?'   *Ib.*

By the favour of God we might know as much—
          as our father Adam knew!   *Ib.*

And that is called paying the Dane-geld;
But we've proved it again and again,
That if once you have paid him the Dane-geld
You never get rid of the Dane.   *Dane-Geld.*

'What are the bugles blowin' for?' said Files-on-
          Parade.
'To turn you out, to turn you out,' the Colour-Ser-
          geant said.   *Danny Deever.*

'For they're hangin' Danny Deever, you can hear the
          Dead March play,
The Regiment's in 'ollow square—they're hangin'
          'im to-day;
They've taken of 'is buttons off an' cut 'is stripes
          away,
An' they're hangin' Danny Deever in the mornin'.'
          Ib.

The 'eathen in 'is blindness bows down to wood an'
          stone;
'E don't obey no orders unless they is 'is own;
'E keeps 'is side-arms awful: 'e leaves 'em all about,
An' then comes up the Regiment an' pokes the 'eathen
          out.   *The 'Eathen.*

All along o' dirtiness, all along o' mess,
All along o' doin' things rather-more-or-less,
All along of abby-nay*, kul*, an' hazar-ho*,
Mind you keep your rifle an' yourself jus' so!   *Ib.*
          * Not now   * tomorrow   * wait a bit.

The 'eathen in 'is blindness must end where 'e began,
But the backbone of the Army is the Non-commis-
          sioned man!   *Ib.*

The first dry rattle of new-drawn steel
Changes the world to-day!   *Edgehill Fight.*

Who are neither children nor Gods, but men in a
          world of men!   *England's Answer to the Cities.*

Winds of the World, give answer! They are whim-
          pering to and fro—
And what should they know of England who only
          England know?   *The English Flag.*

I barred my gates with iron, I shuttered my doors
          with flame,
Because to force my ramparts your nutshell navies
          came.   *Ib.*

Never was isle so little, never was sea so lone,
But over the scud and the palm-trees an English Flag
          was flown.   *Ib.*

I could not look on Death, which being known,
Men led me to him, blindfold and alone.
          Epitaphs of the War. The Coward.

All that pentecostal crew.   *Et Dona Ferentes.*

But it never really mattered till the English grew
          polite.   *Ib.*

The breed that take their pleasures as Saint Lawrence
          took his grid.   *Ib.*

'Something lost behind the Ranges.'   *The Explorer.*

Your 'Never-never country'.   *Ib.*

Anybody might have found it, but—His Whisper
          came to me!   *Ib.*

For the Red Gods call us out and we must go!
          The Feet of the Young Men.

When the Hymalayan peasant meets the he-bear in
          his pride,
He shouts to scare the monster, who will often turn
          aside.

But the she-bear thus accosted rends the peasant
tooth and nail
For the female of the species is more deadly than the
male.   *The Female of the Species.*

Man propounds negotiations, Man accepts the com-
promise.
Very rarely will he squarely push the logic of a fact
To its ultimate conclusion in unmitigated act.   *Ib.*

Buy my English posies!
Kent and Surrey may—
Violets of the Undercliff
Wet with Channel spray;
Cowslips from a Devon combe—
Midland furze afire—
Buy my English posies
And I'll sell your heart's desire!   *The Flowers.*

Weed ye trample underfoot
   Floods his heart abrim—
Bird ye never heeded,
   Oh, she calls his dead to him!   *Ib.*

Take the flower and turn the hour, and kiss your love
again!   *Ib.*

So it's knock out your pipes an' follow me!
An' it's finish up your swipes an' follow me!
Oh, 'ark to the big drum callin',
Follow me—follow me 'ome!   *Follow Me 'Ome.*

For it's 'Three rounds blank' an' follow me,
An' it's 'Thirteen rank' an' follow me;
Oh, passin' the love o' women,
Follow me—follow me 'ome!   *Ib.*

For all we have and are,
For all our children's fate,
Stand up and take the war.
The Hun is at the gate!   *For All We Have and Are.*

There is but one task for all—
One life for each to give.
What stands if Freedom fall?
Who dies if England live?   *Ib.*

Ford, ford, ford o' Kabul river,
Ford o' Kabul river in the dark!
There's the river up an' brimmin', an' there's 'arf a
squadron swimmin'
'Cross the ford o' Kabul river in the dark.
     Ford o' Kabul River.

For to admire an' for to see,
For to be'old this world so wide
It never done no good to me,
But I can't drop it if I tried!   *For to Admire.*

So 'ere's to you, Fuzzy-Wuzzy, at your 'ome in the
Soudan;
You're a pore benighted 'eathen but a first-class
fightin' man;
An' 'ere's to you, Fuzzy-Wuzzy, with your 'ayrick
'ead of 'air—
You big black boundin' beggar—for you broke a
British square!   *Fuzzy-Wuzzy.*

'E's all 'ot sand an' ginger when alive,
An' 'e's generally shammin' when 'e's dead.   *Ib.*

'E's the only thing that doesn't give a damn
For a Regiment o' British Infantree!   *Ib.*

When 'e's 'oppin' in an' out among the bush
With 'is coffin-'eaded shield an' shovel-spear,
An 'appy day with Fuzzy on the rush
Will last an 'ealthy Tommy for a year.   *Ib.*

To the legion of the lost ones, to the cohort of the
damned.   *Gentlemen Rankers.*

Gentlemen-rankers out on the spree,
Damned from here to Eternity.   *Ib.*

We have done with Hope and Honour, we are lost to
Love and Truth,
We are dropping down the ladder rung by rung;
And the measure of our torment is the measure of our
youth.
God help us, for we knew the worst too young! *Ib.*

The wild hawk to the wind-swept sky,
   The deer to the wholesome wold,
And the heart of a man to the heart of a maid,
   As it was in the days of old.   *The Gipsy Trail.*

Our England is a garden that is full of stately views,
Of borders, beds and shrubberies and lawns and
avenues,
With statues on the terraces and peacocks strutting
by;
But the Glory of the Garden lies in more than meets
the eye.   *The Glory of the Garden.*

The Glory of the Garden it abideth not in words. *Ib.*

Our England is a garden, and such gardens are not
made
By singing:—'Oh, how beautiful!' and sitting in the
shade,
While better men than we go out and start their
working lives
At grubbing weeds from gravel paths with broken
dinner-knives.

There's not a pair of legs so thin, there's not a head
so thick,
There's not a hand so weak and white, nor yet a
heart so sick,
But it can find some needful job that's crying to be
done,
For the Glory of the Garden glorifieth every one.

Then seek your job with thankfulness and work till
further orders,
If it's only netting strawberries or killing slugs on
borders;
And when your back stops aching and your hands
begin to harden,
You will find yourself a partner in the Glory of the
Garden.

Oh, Adam was a gardener, and God who made him
sees
That half a proper gardener's work is done upon his
knees,
So when your work is finished, you can wash your
hands and pray
For the Glory of the Garden, that it may not pass
away!
And the Glory of the Garden it shall never pass
away!   *Ib.*

You may talk o' gin an' beer
When you're quartered safe out 'ere,
An' you're sent to penny-fights an' Aldershot it;
But when it comes to slaughter
You will do your work on water,
An' you'll lick the bloomin' boots of 'im that's got it.
     Gunga Din.

The uniform 'e wore
Was nothin' much before,
An' rather less than 'arf o' that be'ind.   *Ib.*

An' for all 'is dirty 'ide
'E was white, clear white, inside
When 'e went to tend the wounded under fire! *Ib.*

So I'll meet 'im later on
At the place where 'e is gone—
Where it's always double drills and no canteen. *Ib.*

'E'll be squattin' on the coals
Givin' drink to poor damned souls,
An' I'll get a swig in Hell from Gunga Din. *Ib.*

Though I've belted you an' flayed you,
By the livin' Gawd that made you,
You're a better man than I am, Gunga Din! *Ib.*

But O, 'tis won'erful good for the Prophet!
Hal o' the Draft. (Puck of Pook's Hill.)

Ere yet we loose the legions—
Ere yet we draw the blade,
Jehovah of the Thunders,
Lord God of Battles, aid! *Hymn Before Action.*

There are nine and sixty ways of constructing tribal
lays,
And—every—single—one—of—them—is—right!
In the Neolithic Age.

If you can keep your head when all about you
Are losing theirs and blaming it on you,
If you can trust yourself when all men doubt you,
But make allowance for their doubting too;
If you can wait and not be tired by waiting,
Or being lied about, don't deal in lies,
Or being hated, don't give way to hating,
And yet don't look too good, nor talk too wise:

If you can dream—and not make dreams your master;
If you can think—and not make thoughts your aim;
If you can meet with Triumph and Disaster
And treat those two impostors just the same. *If—*

If you can make one heap of all your winnings
And risk it on one turn of pitch-and-toss,
And lose, and start again at your beginnings
And never breathe a word about your loss. *Ib.*

If you can talk with crowds and keep your virtue,
Or walk with Kings—nor lose the common touch,
If neither foes nor loving friends can hurt you,
If all men count with you, but none too much;
If you can fill the unforgiving minute
With sixty seconds' worth of distance run,
Yours is the Earth and everything that's in it,
And—which is more—you'll be a Man, my son!
Ib.

I have eaten your bread and salt,
I have drunk your water and wine.
*I Have Eaten Your Bread. (Departmental
Ditties: Prelude.)*

Dear hearts across the seas. *Ib.*

No doubt but ye are the People. *The Islanders.*

Then ye returned to your trinkets; then ye contented
your souls
With the flannelled fools at the wicket or the muddied
oafs at the goals. *Ib.*

Given to strong delusion, wholly believing a lie. *Ib.*

He wrote that monarchs were divine,
And left a son who—proved they weren't! *James I.*

Jane went to Paradise:
That was only fair,
Good Sir Walter met her first,
And led her up the stair.
Henry and Tobias,
And Miguel of Spain,
Stood with Shakespeare at the top
To welcome Jane. *Jane's Marriage.*

Jane lies in Winchester, blessèd be her shade!
Praise the Lord for making her, and her for all she
made.
And, while the stones of Winchester—or Milsom
Street—remain,
Glory, Love, and Honour unto England's Jane! *Ib.*

Cold, commanded lust. *Justice.*

Let them relearn the Law. *Ib.*

I've never sailed the Amazon,
I've never reached Brazil.
Just-So Stories. Beginning of the Armadilloes.

Yes, weekly from Southampton,
Great steamers, white and gold,
Go rolling down to Rio
(Roll down—roll down to Rio!).
And I'd like to roll to Rio
Some day before I'm old! *Ib.*

I've never seen a Jaguar,
Nor yet an Armadill-
o dilloing in his armour,
And I s'pose I never will. *Ib.*

The Camel's hump is an ugly hump
Which well you may see at the Zoo;
But uglier yet is the Hump we get
From having too little to do.
Ib. How the Camel Got His Hump.

We get the Hump—
Cameelious Hump—
The Hump that is black and blue! *Ib.*

The cure for this ill is not to sit still,
Or frowst with a book by the fire;
But to take a large hoe and a shovel also,
And dig till you gently perspire. *Ib.*

Old Man Kangaroo first, Yellow-Dog Dingo behind.
Ib. Sing-Song of Old Man Kangaroo.

'Confound Romance!' . . . And all unseen
Romance brought up the nine-fifteen. *The King.*

For Allah created the English mad—the maddest of
all mankind! *Kitchener's School.*

I've taken my fun where I've found it,
An' now I must pay for my fun,
For the more you 'ave known o' the others
The less will you settle to one;
An' the end of it's sittin' an' thinkin',
An' dreamin' Hell-fires to see.
So be warned by my lot (which I know you will not),
An' learn about women from me! *The Ladies.*

An' I learned about women from 'er! *Ib.*

But the things you will learn from the Yellow an'
Brown,
They'll 'elp you a lot with the White! *Ib.*

For the Colonel's Lady an' Judy O'Grady
Are sisters under their skins! *Ib.*

'Have it jest *as* you've a mind to, but, if I was you, I'd
dreen.' *The Land.*

'Hev it just as you've a mind to, *but*'—and here he
takes command.
For whoever pays the taxes old Mus' Hobden owns
the land. *Ib.*

Thus said the Lord in the vault above the Cherubim,
Calling to the Angels and the Souls in their degree.
The Last Chantey.

Then said the soul of the Angel of the Off-shore
Wind. *Ib.*

'And Ye take mine honour from me if Ye take away
the sea!'   *Ib.*

'Are we babes that we should clamour for a vengeance
on the sea?'   *Ib.*

Then cried the soul of the stout Apostle Paul to God.
       Ib.

'When they learned Thy Grace and Glory under
Malta by the sea!'   *Ib.*

Loud sang the souls of the jolly, jolly mariners,
Plucking at their harps, and they plucked unhandily:
'Our thumbs are rough and tarred,
And the tune is something hard—
May we lift a Deepsea Chantey such as seamen use
at sea?'   *Ib.*

'Heave or sink it, leave or drink it, we were masters
of the sea!'   *Ib.*

Loud sang the souls of the jolly, jolly mariners,
Crying: 'Under Heaven, here is neither lead nor lee!
Must we sing for evermore
On the windless, glassy floor?
Take back your golden fiddles and we'll beat to open
sea!'   *Ib.*

Then stooped the Lord, and He called the good sea
up to Him,
And 'stablishèd its borders unto all eternity,
That such as have no pleasure
For to praise the Lord by measure,
They may enter into galleons and serve Him on the
Sea.   *Ib.*

And the ships shall go abroad
To the Glory of the Lord
Who heard the silly sailor-folk and gave them back
their sea!   *Ib.*

'I ha' harpit ye up to the Throne o' God,
I ha' harpit your midmost soul in three.
I ha' harpit ye down to the Hinges o' Hell,
And—ye—would—make—a Knight o' me!'
       The Last Rhyme of True Thomas.

Now this is the Law of the Jungle—as old and as true
as the sky.   *The Law of the Jungle.*

This is the sorrowful story
Told as the twilight fails
And the monkeys walk together
Holding their neighbours' tails.
       The Legends of Evil.

Thin Noah spoke him fairly, thin talked to him
sevairely,
An' thin he cursed him squarely to the glory av the
Lord:—
'Divil take the ass that bred you, an' the greater ass
that fed you!
Divil go wid you, ye spalpeen!' an' the Donkey wint
aboard.   *Ib.*

Till Noah said:—'There's wan av us that hasn't paid
his fare!'   *Ib.*

We have had an Imperial lesson; it may make us an
Empire yet!   *The Lesson.*

And that's how it all began, my dears,
And that's how it all began!
       The Light that Failed, chapter heading.

The Liner she's a lady, an' she never looks nor
'eeds—
The Man-o'-War's 'er 'usband, an' 'e gives 'er all
she needs;
But, oh, the little cargo-boats, that sail the wet sea
roun',
They're just the same as you an' me a-plyin' up an
down!   *The Liner She's a Lady.*

There's a whisper down the field where the year has
shot her yield,
And the ricks stand grey to the sun,
Singing:—'Over then, come over, for the bee has quit
the clover,
And your English summer's done.' *The Long Trail.*

You have heard the beat of the off-shore wind,
And the thresh of the deep-sea rain;
You have heard the song—how long? how long?
Pull out on the trail again!
Ha' done with the Tents of Shem, dear lass,
We've seen the seasons through,
And it's time to turn on the old trail, our own trail,
the out trail,
Pull out, pull out, on the Long Trail—the trail that
is always new!   *Ib.*

It's North you may run to the rime-ringed sun,
Or South to the blind Horn's hate;
Or East all the way into Mississippi Bay,
Or West to the Golden Gate.   *Ib.*

The Queen was in her chamber, and she was middling
old,
Her petticoat was satin, and her stomacher was gold.
Backwards and forwards and sideways did she pass,
Making up her mind to face the cruel looking-glass.
The cruel looking-glass that will never show a lass
As comely or as kindly or as young as what she was!
       The Looking Glass.

The Queen was in her chamber, her sins were on her
head.
She looked the spirits up and down and statelily she
said:—
'Backwards and forwards and sideways though I've
been,
Yet I am Harry's daughter and I am England's
Queen!'   *Ib.*

There's a Legion that never was 'listed.
       The Lost Legion.

To go and find out and be damned
                (Dear boys!),
To go and get shot and be damned.   *Ib.*

Lord, Thou hast made this world below the shadow
of a dream,
An', taught by time, I tak' it so—exceptin' always
Steam.
From coupler-flange to spindle-guide I see Thy
Hand, O God—
Predestination in the stride o' yon connectin'-rod.
       McAndrew's Hymn.

Alone wi' God an' these
My engines.   *Ib.*

Yon's strain, hard strain, o' head an' hand, for though
Thy Power brings
All skill to naught, Ye'll understand a man must
think o' things.   *Ib.*

Ye thought? Ye are not paid to think.   *Ib.*

Mister McAndrew, don't you think steam spoils
   romance at sea?   *Ib.*

Romance! Those first-class passengers they like it
   very well,
Printed an' bound in little books; but why don't
   poets tell?   *Ib.*

While, out o' touch o' vanity, the sweatin' thrust-
   block says:
'Not unto us the praise, or man—not unto us the
   praise!'   *Ib.*

By the old Moulmein Pagoda, lookin' eastward to the
   sea,
There's a Burma girl a-settin', and I know she thinks
   o' me;
For the wind is in the palm-trees, an' the temple-
   bells they say:
'Come you back, you British soldier; come you back
   to Mandalay!'
Come you back to Mandalay,
Where the old Flotilla lay:
Can't you 'ear their paddles chunkin' from Rangoon
   to Mandalay?
On the road to Mandalay,
Where the flyin'-fishes play,
An' the dawn comes up like thunder outer China
   'crost the Bay!   *Mandalay.*

An' I seed her first a-smokin' of a whackin' white
   cheroot,
An' a-wastin' Christian kisses on an 'eathen idol's
   foot.   *Ib.*

When the mist was on the rice-fields an' the sun was
   droppin' slow,
She'd git 'er little banjo an' she'd sing 'Kulla-lo-lo!'
   Ib.

But that's all shove be'ind me—long ago an' fur away,
An' there ain' no 'buses runnin' from the Bank to
   Mandalay;
An' I'm learnin' 'ere in London wot the ten-year
   soldier tells:
'If you've 'eard the East a-callin', you won't never
   'eed naught else.'   *Ib.*

I am sick o' wastin' leather on these gritty pavin'-
   stones,
An' the blasted English drizzle wakes the fever in my
   bones;
Tho' I walks with fifty 'ousemaids outer Chelsea to
   the Strand,
An' they talks a lot o' lovin', but wot do they under-
   stand?
Beefy face an' grubby 'and—
Law! Wot do they understand?
I've a neater, sweeter maiden in a cleaner, greener
   land!   *Ib.*

Ship me somewheres east of Suez, where the best is
   like the worst,
Where there aren't no Ten Commandments, an' a man
   can raise a thirst:
For the temple-bells are callin', an' it's there that I
   would be—
By the old Moulmein Pagoda, looking lazy at the sea.
   Ib.

Ten thousand men on the pay-roll, and forty
   freighters at sea!   *The 'Mary Gloster'.*

Harrer an' Trinity College! I ought to ha' sent you
   to sea.   *Ib.*

For you muddled with books and pictures, an' china
   an' etchin's an' fans,
And your rooms at college was beastly—more like a
   whore's than a man's.   *Ib.*

I've seen your carriages blocking the half o' the
   Cromwell Road,
But never the doctor's brougham to help the missus
   unload.   *Ib.*

For a man he must go with a woman, which women
   don't understand—
Or the sort that say they can see it, they aren't the
   marrying brand.   *Ib.*

I'm sick of the hired women. I'll kiss my girl on her
   lips!   *Ib.*

Nice while it lasted, an' now it is over—
Tear out your 'eart an' good-bye to your lover!
What's the use o' grievin', when the mother that bore
   you
(Mary, pity women!) knew it all before you?
   Mary, Pity Women.

There runs a road by Merrow Down—
   A grassy track to-day it is—
An hour out of Guildford town,
   Above the river Wey it is.   *Merrow Down.*

But as the faithful years return
   And hearts unwounded sing again,
Comes Taffy dancing through the fern
   To lead the Surrey spring again.   *Ib.*

'Mines reported in the fairway,
Warn all traffic and detain.
'Send up *Unity, Claribel, Assyrian, Stormcock,* and
   Golden Gain.'   *Mine Sweepers.*

'Good rest to all
That keep the Jungle Law.'
   Morning Song in the Jungle.

If I were hanged on the highest hill,
Mother o' mine, O mother o' mine!
I know whose love would follow me still,
Mother o' mine, O mother o' mine!
   Mother O' Mine.

If I were damned of body and soul,
I know whose prayers would make me whole,
Mother o' mine, O mother o' mine!   *Ib.*

'Have you news of my boy Jack?'
   Not this tide.
'When d'you think that he'll come back?'
   Not with this wind blowing, and this tide.
   My Boy Jack.

My new-cut ashlar takes the light
Where crimson-blank the windows flare.
   My New-cut Ashlar.

The depth and dream of my desire,
The bitter paths wherein I stray—
Thou knowest Who hast made the Fire,
Thou knowest Who hast made the Clay.   *Ib*

One stone the more swings into place
In that dread Temple of Thy worth.
It is enough that, through Thy Grace,
I saw nought common on Thy Earth.   *Ib*

Now it is not good for the Christian health to hustle
    the Aryan brown,
For the Christian riles, and the Aryan smiles, and it
    weareth the Christian down;
And the end of the fight is a tombstone white with
    the name of the late deceased,
And the epitaph drear: 'A Fool lies here who tried to
    hustle the East.'   *Naulahka*, heading of ch. 5.

The Saxon is not like us Normans. His manners are
    not so polite.
But he never means anything serious till he talks
    about justice and right,
When he stands like an ox in the furrow with his
    sullen set eyes on your own,
And grumbles, 'This isn't fair dealing,' my son, leave
    the Saxon alone.   *Norman and Saxon.*

The 'orse 'e knows above a bit, the bullock's but a
    fool,
The elephant's a gentleman, the battery-mule's a
    mule;
But the commissariat cam-u-el, when all is said an'
    done,
'E's a devil an' a ostrich an' a orphan-child in one.
                                   Oonts.

Excellent herbs had our fathers of old—
Excellent herbs to ease their pain.
                     'Our Fathers of Old.'

Anything green that grew out of the mould
Was an excellent herb to our fathers of old.   *Ib.*

A Nation spoke to a Nation,
A Throne sent word to a Throne:
Daughter am I in my mother's house,
But mistress in my own.
The gates are mine to open,
As the gates are mine to close,
And I abide by my Mother's House.'
Said our Lady of the Snows.   *Our Lady of the Snows.*

In the Name of the Empress, the Overland Mail!
                     The Overland Mail.

The toad beneath the harrow knows
Exactly where each tooth-point goes;
The butterfly upon the road
Preaches contentment to that toad.   *Pagett M.P.*

Pagett, M.P., was a liar, and a fluent liar therewith.
                                      Ib.

After me cometh a Builder. Tell him, I too have
    known.   *The Palace.*

Can't! Don't! Sha'n't! Won't!
Pass it along the line!
Somebody's pack has slid from his back,
Wish it were only mine!
Somebody's load has tipped off in the road—
Cheer for a halt and a row!
Urrh! Yarrh! Grr! Arrh!
Somebody's catching it now!
     Parade-Song of the Camp-Animals. Commis-
     sariat Camels.

But a man in khaki kit who could handle men a bit,
With his bedding labelled Sergeant Whatsisname.
                     Pharaoh and the Sergeant.

He drank strong waters and his speech was coarse;
He purchased raiment and forbore to pay;
He stuck a trusting junior with a horse,
And won gymkhanas in a doubtful way,
Then, 'twixt a vice and folly, turned aside
To do good deeds—and straight to cloak them, lied.
     Plain Tales from the Hills. Chapter heading
     to 'A Bank Fraud'.

The Three in One, the One in Three? Not so!
To my own Gods I go.
It may be they shall give me greater ease
Than your cold Christ and tangled Trinities.
          Ib. Chapter heading to 'Lispeth'.

Bade farewell to Minnie Boffkin in one last, long
    lingering fit.   *The Post that Fitted.*

Year by year, in pious patience, vengeful Mrs. Boff-
    kin sits
Waiting for the Sleary babies to develop Sleary's fits.
                                      Ib.

There is sorrow enough in the natural way
From men and women to fill our day;
But when we are certain of sorrow in store,
Why do we always arrange for more?
Brothers and Sisters, I bid you beware
Of giving your heart to a dog to tear.
                     The Power of the Dog.

Valour and Innocence
Have latterly gone hence
To certain death by certain shame attended.
                     The Queen's Men.

God of our fathers, known of old,
Lord of our far-flung battle-line,
Beneath whose awful Hand we hold
Dominion over palm and pine—
Lord God of Hosts, be with us yet,
Lest we forget—lest we forget!

The tumult and the shouting dies;
The Captains and the Kings depart:
Still stands Thine ancient sacrifice,
An humble and a contrite heart.
Lord God of Hosts, be with us yet,
Lest we forget—lest we forget!   *Recessional.*

Lo, all our pomp of yesterday
Is one with Nineveh and Tyre!   *Ib.*

If, drunk with sight of power, we loose
Wild tongues that have not Thee in awe,
Such boastings as the Gentiles use,
Or lesser breeds without the Law.   *Ib.*

For heathen heart that puts her trust
In reeking tube and iron shard,
All valiant dust that builds on dust,
And, guarding, calls not Thee to guard,
For frantic boast and foolish word—
Thy mercy on Thy People, Lord!   *Ib.*

If England was what England seems,
    An' not the England of our dreams,
But only putty, brass, an' paint,
    'Ow quick we'd drop 'er! But she ain't!
                     The Return.

English they be and Japanee that hang on the Brown
    Bear's flank,
And some be Scot, but the worst of the lot, and the
    boldest thieves, be Yank!
                   The Rhyme of the Three Sealers.

I 3

And I've lost Britain, and I've lost Gaul,
And I've lost Rome and, worst of all,
I've lost Lalage!   'Rimini.'

I walk my beat before London Town,
Five hours up and seven down,
Up I go till I end my run
At Tide-end-town, which is Teddington.
                    The River's Tale.

Brother, thy tail hangs down behind!
                    Road Song of the Bandar-Log.

Who hath desired the Sea?—the sight of salt water
    unbounded.   The Sea and the Hills.

So and no otherwise—so and no otherwise—hillmen
    desire their Hills!   Ib.

Cheer for the Sergeant's weddin'—
    Give 'em one cheer more!
Grey gun-'orses in the lando,
    An' a rogue is married to a whore.
                    The Sergeant's Weddin'.

Shillin' a day,
Bloomin' good pay—
Lucky to touch it, a shillin' a day!   Shillin' a Day.

Give 'im a letter—
Can't do no better,
Late Troop-Sergeant-Major an'—runs with a letter!
Think what 'e's been,
Think what 'e's seen.
Think of 'is pension an'—
GAWD SAVE THE QUEEN!   Ib.

So it was 'Rounds! What Rounds?' at two of a frosty
    night.
'E's 'oldin' on by the Sergeant's sash, but, sentry,
    shut your eye.   The Shut-Eye Sentry.

But you ought to 'ave 'eard 'em markin' time
To 'ide the things 'e said!   Ib.

There was two-an'-thirty Sergeants,
    There was Corp'rals forty-one,
There was just nine 'undred rank an' file
    To swear to a touch o' sun.   Ib.

We'll 'elp 'im for 'is mother, an' 'e'll 'elp us by-an'-
    by!   Ib.

Them that asks no questions isn't told a lie.
Watch the wall, my darling, while the Gentlemen go
    by!
    Five and twenty ponies
    Trotting through the dark—
    Brandy for the Parson,
    'Baccy for the Clerk;
Laces for a lady, letters for a spy,
Watch the wall, my darling, while the Gentlemen go
    by!   A Smuggler's Song.

Sez 'e, 'I'm a Jolly—'Er Majesty's Jolly—soldier an'
    sailor too!'   Soldier an' Sailor too!

'E's a kind of a giddy harumfrodite—soldier an'
    sailor too!   Ib.

I'm the Prophet of the Utterly Absurd,
Of the Patently Impossible and Vain.
                    The Song of the Banjo.

I am all that ever went with evening dress!   Ib.

Let the organ moan her sorrow to the roof—
I have told the naked stars the Grief of Man!
Let the trumpet snare the foeman to the proof—
I have known Defeat, and mocked it as we ran!   Ib.

With my 'Tinka-tinka-tinka-tinka-tink!'   Ib.

There's never a wave of all her waves
But marks our English dead. The Song of the Dead, ii

If blood be the price of admiralty,
Lord God, we ha' paid in full!   Ib.

For the Lord our God Most High
He hath made the deep as dry,
He hath smote for us a pathway to the ends of all th
    earth!   A Song of the English

Keep ye the Law—be swift in all obedience—
Clear the land of evil, drive the road and bridge th
    ford.
Make ye sure to each his own
That he reap where he hath sown;
By the peace among our peoples let men know w
    serve the Lord!   Ib.

Ere Mor the Peacock flutters, ere the Monkey Peopl
    cry,
Ere Chil the Kite swoops down a furlong sheer,
Through the Jungle very softly flits a shadow and
    sigh—
He is Fear, O Little Hunter, he is Fear!
                    The Song of the Little Hunter

But thy throat is shut and dried, and thy heart agains
    thy side
Hammers: 'Fear, O Little Hunter—this is Fear!'   Ib.

Mithras, God of the Morning, our trumpets wake
    the Wall!
'Rome is above the Nations, but Thou art over all
                    A Song to Mithras

The Sons of Mary seldom bother, for they have in
    herited that good part;
But the Sons of Martha favour their Mother of th
    careful soul and the troubled heart.
And because she lost her temper once, and becaus
    she was rude to the Lord her Guest,
Her Sons must wait upon Mary's Sons, world withou
    end, reprieve, or rest.   The Sons of Marth

They do not preach that their God will rouse them
    little before the nuts work loose.
They do not teach that His Pity allows them to leav
    their job when they damn-well choose.   Ib.

They sit at the Feet—they hear the Word—they se
    how truly the Promise runs.
They have cast their burden upon the Lord, and—
    the Lord He lays it on Martha's Sons!   Ib.

'Let us now praise famous men'—
    Men of little showing—
For their work continueth,
And their work continueth,
Broad and deep continueth,
    Greater than their knowing!
                    Stalky & Co. A School Song

An' it all goes into the laundry,
But it never comes out in the wash,
'Ow we're sugared about by the old men
('Eavy-sterned amateur old men!)
That 'amper an' 'inder an' scold men
For fear o' Stellenbosch!   Stellenbosch

No tender-hearted garden crowns,
  No bosomed woods adorn
Our blunt, bow-headed whale-backed Downs,
  But gnarled and writhen thorn.   *Sussex.*

Half-wild and wholly tame,
The wise turf cloaks the white cliff-edge
  As when the Romans came.   *Ib.*

The barrow and the camp abide,
  The sunlight and the sward.   *Ib.*

And here the sea-fogs lap and cling
  And here, each warning each,
The sheep-bells and the ship-bells ring
  Along the hidden beach.   *Ib.*

Little, lost, Down churches praise
  The Lord who made the hills.   *Ib.*

Huge oaks and old, the which we hold
  No more than Sussex weed.   *Ib.*

God gives all men all earth to love,
  But, since man's heart is small,
Ordains for each one spot shall prove
  Belovèd over all.
Each to his choice, and I rejoice
  The lot has fallen to me
In a fair ground—in a fair ground—
  Yea, Sussex by the sea!   *Ib.*

Till I 'eard a beggar squealin' out for quarter as 'e
  ran,
An' I thought I knew the voice an'—it was me!
    That Day.

'Once on a time there was a Man.'
    Things and the Man.

And, Thomas, here's my best respects to you!
    *To Thomas Atkins. Prelude to Barrack-Room
    Ballads.*

One man in a thousand, Solomon says,
Will stick more close than a brother.
    The Thousandth Man.

But the Thousandth Man will stand by your side
To the gallows-foot—and after!   *Ib.*

With maids of matchless beauty and parentage unguessed,
And a Church of England parson for the Islands of
  the Blest.   *The Three-Decker.*

Till he heard as the roar of a rain-fed ford the roar of
  the Milky Way.   *Tomlinson.*

Stand up, stand up now, Tomlinson, and answer
  loud and high
The good that ye did for the sake of men or ever ye
  came to die.'   *Ib.*

But now ye wait at Heaven's Gate and not in Berkeley Square.'   *Ib.*

Though we called your friend from his bed this night,
  he could not speak to you,
For the race is run by one and one and never by two
  and two.'   *Ib.*

Oh, this I have read in a book,' he said, 'and that
  was told to me,
And this I have thought that another man thought of
  a Prince in Muscovy.'   *Ib.*

'Ye have read, ye have heard, ye have thought,' he
  said, 'and the tale is yet to run:
By the worth of the body that once ye had, give
  answer—what ha' ye done?'   *Ib.*

'Oh, this I have felt, and this I have guessed, and
  this I have heard men say,
And this they wrote that another man wrote of a carl
  in Norroway.'   *Ib.*

'And—the faith that ye share with Berkeley Square
  uphold you, Tomlinson!'   *Ib.*

The Wind that blows between the Worlds, it nipped
  him to the bone,
And he yearned to the flare of Hell-gate there as the
  light of his own hearth-stone.   *Ib.*

'For the sin ye do by two and two ye must pay for one
  by one!'   *Ib.*

'Once I ha' laughed at the power of Love and twice at
  the grip of the Grave,
And thrice I ha' patted my God on the head that men
  might call me brave.'   *Ib.*

'I see no worth in the hobnailed mirth or the jolt-head
  jest ye did
That I should waken my gentlemen that are sleeping
  three on a grid.'   *Ib.*

'Have ye sinned one sin for the pride o' the eye or the
  sinful lust of the flesh?'   *Ib.*

Then Tomlinson he gripped the bars and yammered,
  'Let me in—
For I mind that I borrowed my neighbour's wife to
  sin the deadly sin.'
The Devil he grinned behind the bars, and banked
  the fires high:
'Did ye read of that sin in a book?' said he; and
  Tomlinson said 'Ay!'   *Ib.*

The Devil he blew upon his nails, and the little devils
  ran.   *Ib.*

'Ye have scarce the soul of a louse,' he said, 'but the
  roots of sin are there.'   *Ib.*

'And—the God that you took from a printed book be
  with you, Tomlinson!'   *Ib.*

Oh, it's Tommy this, an' Tommy that, an' 'Tommy,
  go away';
But it's 'Thank you, Mister Atkins,' when the band
  begins to play.   *Tommy.*

It's Tommy this an' Tommy that, an' 'Chuck him
  out, the brute!'
But it's 'Saviour of 'is country' when the guns begin
  to shoot.   *Ib.*

Then it's Tommy this, an' Tommy that, an' 'Tommy,
  'ow's yer soul?'
But it's 'Thin·red line of 'eroes' when the drums
  begin to roll.   *Ib.*

We aren't no thin red 'eroes, nor we aren't no blackguards too.
But single men in barricks, most remarkable like you;
An' if sometimes our conduck isn't all your fancy
  paints,
Why, single men in barricks don't grow into plaster
  saints.   *Ib.*

Of all the trees that grow so fair,
  Old England to adorn,
Greater are none beneath the Sun,
  Than Oak, and Ash, and Thorn.   *A Tree Song.*

England shall bide till Judgement Tide,
  By Oak, and Ash, and Thorn!   *Ib.*

I tell this tale, which is strictly true,
Just by way of convincing you
How very little, since things were made,
Things have altered in the building trade.
                     A Truthful Song.

The young man kindly answered them:
'It might be Lot or Methusalem,
Or it might be Moses (a man I hate),
Whereas it is Pharaoh surnamed the Great.

Your glazing is new and your plumbing's strange,
But otherwise I perceive no change;
And in less than a month, if you do as I bid,
I'd learn you to build me a Pyramid!'   *Ib.*

The old man kindly answered them:
'It might be Japheth, it might be Shem,
Or it might be Ham (though his skin was dark),
Whereas it is Noah, commanding the Ark.

Your wheel is new and your pumps are strange,
But otherwise I perceive no change;
And in less than a week, if she did not ground,
I'd sail this hooker the wide world round!'   *Ib.*

Much I owe to the Lands that grew—
  More to the Lives that fed—
But most to Allah Who gave me two
  Separate sides to my head.   *The Two-Sided Man.*

The dark eleventh hour
Draws on and sees us sold.   *Ulster.*

A fool there was and he made his prayer
  (Even as you and I!)
To a rag and a bone and a hank of hair
(We called her the woman who did not care)
But the fool he called her his lady fair—
  (Even as you and I!)   *The Vampire.*

But a fool must follow his natural bent
  (Even as you and I!)   *Ib.*

Oh, was there ever sailor free to choose,
  That didn't settle somewhere near the sea?
                     The Virginity.

They that have wrought the end unthought
  Be neither saint nor sage,
But only men who did the work
  For which they drew the wage. *The Wage-Slaves.*

They shut the road through the woods
Seventy years ago.   *The Way Through the Woods.*

Steadily cantering through
The misty solitudes,
As though they perfectly knew
The old lost road through the woods—
But there is no road through the woods!   *Ib.*

Father, Mother, and Me,
Sister and Auntie say
All the people like us are We,
And every one else is They.   *We and They.*

When Earth's last picture is painted and the tubes are
  twisted and dried,
When the oldest colours have faded, and the youngest
  critic has died,
We shall rest, and, faith, we shall need it—lie down
  for an æon or two,
Till the Master of All Good Workmen shall put us to
  work anew.   *When Earth's Last Picture.*

And those that were good shall be happy: they shall
  sit in a golden chair;
They shall splash at a ten-league canvas with brushes
  of comets' hair.   *Ib.*

And only The Master shall praise us, and only The
  Master shall blame;
And no one shall work for money, and no one shall
  work for fame,
But each for the joy of the working, and each, in his
  separate star,
Shall draw the Thing as he sees It for the God of
  Things as They are!   *Ib.*

When 'Omer smote 'is bloomin' lyre,
  'E'd 'eard men sing by land an' sea;
An' what 'e thought 'e might require,
  'E went an' took—the same as me!
    When 'Omer Smote. (Barrack-Room Ballads.
    Introduction.)

They knew 'e stole; 'e knew they knowed.
  They didn't tell, nor make a fuss,
But winked at 'Omer down the road,
  An' 'e winked back—the same as us!   *Ib*

Take up the White Man's burden—
  Send forth the best ye breed—
Go, bind your sons to exile
  To serve your captives' need;
To wait in heavy harness
  On fluttered folk and wild—
Your new-caught, sullen peoples,
  Half-devil and half-child.
             The White Man's Burden

By all ye cry or whisper,
  By all ye leave or do,
The silent, sullen peoples
  Shall weigh your Gods and you.   *Ib*

Take up the White Man's burden—
  And reap his old reward:
The blame of those ye better,
  The hate of those ye guard.   *Ib*

'Ave you 'eard o' the Widow at Windsor
  With a hairy gold crown on 'er 'ead?
She 'as ships on the foam—she 'as millions at 'ome,
  An' she pays us poor beggars in red.
             The Widow at Windsor

Take 'old o' the Wings o' the Mornin',
  An' flop round the earth till you're dead;
But you won't get away from the tune that they play
  To the bloomin' old rag over 'ead.   *Ib*

Down to Gehenna or up to the Throne,
He travels the fastest who travels alone.
              The Winners

When the 'arf-made recruity goes out to the East
'E acts like a babe an' 'e drinks like a beast,
An' 'e wonders because 'e is frequent deceased
Ere 'e's fit for to serve as a soldier.
          The Young British Soldier

When you're wounded and left on Afghanistan's plains,
An' the women come out to cut up what remains,
Jest roll to your rifle an' blow out your brains
An' go to your Gawd like a soldier. *Ib.*

How can I crown thee further, O Queen of the Sovereign South? *The Young Queen.*

'Ha! Ha!' said the duck, laughing.
The Day's Work. The Brushwood Boy.

What shall I do when I see you in the light? *Ib.*

Good hunting! *The Jungle Book. Kaa's Hunting.*

'We be of one blood, thou and I.' *Ib.*

'Nice,' said the small 'stute Fish. 'Nice but nubbly.'
Just-So Stories. How the Whale Got His Throat.

You must *not* forget the Suspenders, Best Beloved. *Ib.*

A man of infinite-resource-and-sagacity. *Ib.*

Most 'scruciating idle.
Ib. How the Camel Got His Hump.

Humph yourself!'
And the Camel humphed himself. *Ib.*

There lived a Parsee from whose hat the rays of the sun were reflected in more-than-oriental-splendour. *Ib. How the Rhinoceros Got His Skin.*

An Elephant's Child—who was full of 'satiable curtiosity. *Ib. The Elephant's Child.*

The great grey-green, greasy Limpopo River, all set about with fever-trees. *Ib.*

Led go! You are hurtig be! *Ib.*

This is too butch for be! *Ib.*

He was a Tidy Pachyderm. *Ib.*

The Cat. He walked by himself, and all places were alike to him.
Ib. The Cat That Walked By Himself.

He went back through the Wet Wild Woods, waving his wild tail, and walking by his wild lone. But he never told anybody. *Ib.*

Tho' tay is not my diversion.
Life's Handicap. The Courting of Dinah Shadd.

Glory's no compensation for a belly-ache. *Ib.*

What's the good of argifying? *Ib. On Greenlow Hill.*

hold by the Ould Church, for she's the mother of them all—ay, an' the father, too. I like her bekaze she's most remarkable regimental in her fittings. *Ib.*

Asia is not going to be civilized after the methods of the West. There is too much Asia and she is too old. *Ib. The Man Who Was.*

Man that is born of woman is small potatoes and few in the hill. *Ib. The Head of the District.*

Some were married, which was bad, and some did other things which were worse.
Ib. The Mark of the Beast.

You haf too much Ego in your Cosmos.
Ib. Bertran and Bimi.

He did not rave, as do many bridegrooms, over the strangeness and delight of seeing his own true love sitting down to breakfast with him every morning 'as though it were the most natural thing in the world'. 'He had been there before', as the Americans say. *Ib. Georgie Porgie.*

The Light that Failed. *Title of Novel.*

Every one is more or less mad on one point.
Plain Tales from the Hills. On the Strength of a Likeness.

Open and obvious devotion from any sort of man is always pleasant to any sort of woman. *Ib.*

He gave way to the queer, savage feeling that sometimes takes by the throat a husband twenty years' married, when he sees, across the table, the same face of his wedded wife, and knows that, as he has sat facing it, so must he continue to sit until the day of its death or his own.
Ib. The Bronckhurst Divorce Case.

'Twas like a battle field wid all the glory missin'.
Ib. The Daughter of the Regiment.

On all three counts, as Ortheris says, ''e didn't deserve no consideration'. *Ib. The Three Musketeers.*

Take my word for it, the silliest woman can manage a clever man; but it needs a very clever woman to manage a fool. *Ib. Three and—an Extra.*

But that is another story. *Ib.*

Lalun is a member of the most ancient profession in the world. *Soldiers Three. On the City Wall.*

Being kissed by a man who didn't wax his moustache was—like eating an egg without salt.
Ib. The Gadsbys. Poor Dear Mamma.

Steady the Buffs. *Ib.*

Been trotting out the Gorgonzola! *Ib.*

Almost inevitable Consequences. *Ib. Fatima.*

I gloat! Hear me gloat! *Stalky and Co., ch. i.*

Your Uncle Stalky. *Ib.*

We ain't goin' to have any beastly Erickin'.
Ib. The Moral Reformers.

'This man,' said M'Turk, with conviction, 'is *the* Gadarene Swine.'
Ib. The Flag of Their Country.

It's boy; only boy. *Ib. An Unsavoury Interlude.*

'Tisn't beauty, so to speak, nor good talk necessarily. It's just IT. Some women'll stay in a man's memory if they once walked down a street.
Traffics and Discoveries. Mrs. Bathurst.

The Waddy is an infectious disease herself.
Wee Willie Winkie. A Second-Rate Woman.

Once upon a time there was a Man and his Wife and a Tertium Quid. *Ib. At the Pit's Mouth.*

Gawd knows, an' 'E won't split on a pal.
Ib. Drums of the Fore and Aft.

HORATIO HERBERT KITCHENER
1850–1916

You are ordered abroad as a soldier of the King to help our French comrades against the invasion of a common enemy. You have to perform a task which will need your courage, your energy, your patience. Remember that the honour of the British Army depends on your individual conduct. It will be your duty not only to set an example of discipline and perfect steadiness under fire but also to maintain the most friendly relations with those whom you are helping in this struggle. In this new experience you may find temptations both in wine and women. You must entirely resist both temptations, and, while treating all women with perfect courtesy, you should avoid any intimacy. Do your duty bravely. Fear God. Honour the King.

A message to the soldiers of the British Expeditionary Force, 1914, to be kept by each soldier in his Active Service Pay-Book. Sir G. Arthur's Life of Kitchener, vol. iii, p. 27.

CHARLES KNIGHT

Here we are! here we are!! here we are again!!!
There's Pat and Mac and Tommy and Jack and Joe.
When there's trouble brewing,
When there's something doing,
Are we downhearted?
No! let 'em all come!
Here We Are! Here We Are Again!!

MARY KNOWLES
1733–1807

He [Dr. Johnson] gets at the substance of a book directly; he tears out the heart of it.
Boswell's Johnson (ed. 1934), vol. iii, p. 284. 15 Apr. 1778.

JOHN KNOX
1505–1572

The First Blast of the Trumpet Against the Monstrous Regiment of Women.
Title of Pamphlet, 1558.

RONALD ARBUTHNOT KNOX
1888–

When suave politeness, tempering bigot zeal,
Corrected *I believe* to *One does feel.*
Absolute and Abitofhell.

THOMAS KYD
1557?–1595?

In time the savage bull sustains the yoke,
In time all haggard hawks will stoop to lure,
In time small wedges cleave the hardest oak,
In time the flint is pierced with softest shower.
The Spanish Tragedy, I. vi. 3.

What outcries pluck me from my naked bed?
Ib. II. v. 1.

Oh eyes, no eyes, but fountains fraught with tears;
Oh life, no life, but lively form of death;
Oh world, no world, but mass of public wrongs.
Ib. III. ii. 1

Thus must we toil in other men's extremes,
That know not how to remedy our own.
Ib. III. vi. 1.

My son—and what's a son? A thing begot
Within a pair of minutes, thereabout,
A lump bred up in darkness.
Ib. III. xi. Additions, l. 5

Duly twice a morning
Would I be sprinkling it with fountain water.
At last it grew, and grew, and bore, and bore,
Till at the length
It grew a gallows and did bear our son,
It bore thy fruit and mine: O wicked, wicked plant
Ib. III. xii. Additions, l. 66

HENRY LABOUCHERE
1831–1912

He [Labouchere] did not object, he once said, to Gladstone's always having the ace of trumps up his sleeve, but only to his pretence that God had put it there.
D.N.B., 1912–1921. Cf. Thorold's Life of Labouchere, p. 375.

CHARLES LAMB
1775–1834

I have no ear.   *Essays of Elia. A Chapter on Ears*

I even think that sentimentally I am disposed to harmony. But organically I am incapable of a tune.
Ib

'Presents', I often say, 'endear Absents.'
Ib. A Dissertation upon Roast Pig

It argues an insensibility.   *Ib*

We are not of Alice, nor of thee, nor are we children at all. The children of Alice called Bartrum father. We are nothing; less than nothing, and dreams. We are only what might have been, and must wait upon the tedious shores of Lethe millions of ages before we have existence, and a name.
Ib. Dream Children

Why have we none [i.e. no grace] for books, those spiritual repasts—a grace before Milton—a grace before Shakspeare—a devotional exercise proper to be said before reading the Faerie Queene?
Ib. Grace Before Meat

Coleridge holds that a man cannot have a pure mind who refuses apple-dumplings. I am not certain but he is right.   *Ib*

I am, in plainer words, a bundle of prejudices—made up of likings and dislikings.
Ib. Imperfect Sympathies

I have been trying all my life to like Scotchmen, and am obliged to desist from the experiment in despair.
Ib

A clear fire, a clean hearth, and the rigour of the game.' This was the celebrated wish of old Sarah Battle (now with God), who, next to her devotions, loved a good game at whist.

Ib. Mrs. Battle's Opinions on Whist.

All people have their blind side—their superstitions; and I have heard her declare, under the rose, that Hearts was her favourite suit. *Ib.*

She unbent her mind afterwards—over a book. *Ib.*

Methinks it is better that I should have pined away seven of my goldenest years, when I was thrall to the fair hair, and fairer eyes, of Alice W - -n, than that so passionate a love-adventure should be lost.

Ib. New Year's Eve.

A votary of the desk—a notched and cropt scrivener —one that sucks his substance, as certain sick people are said to do, through a quill.

Ib. Oxford in the Vacation.

In everything that relates to science, I am a whole Encyclopaedia behind the rest of the world.

Ib. The Old and the New Schoolmaster.

He is awkward, and out of place, in the society of his equals. . . . He cannot meet you on the square.

Ib.

The human species, according to the best theory I can form of it, is composed of two distinct races, *the men who borrow*, and *the men who lend*.

Ib. The Two Races of Men.

What a liberal confounding of those pedantic distinctions of *meum* and *tuum*! *Ib.*

I mean your *borrowers of books*—those mutilators of collections, spoilers of the symmetry of shelves, and creators of odd volumes. *Ib.*

To lose a volume to C[oleridge] carries some sense and meaning in it. You are sure that he will make one hearty meal on your viands, if he can give no account of the platter after it. *Ib.*

That princely woman, the thrice noble Margaret Newcastle. *Ib.*

I counsel thee, shut not thy heart, nor thy library, against S. T. C[oleridge]. *Ib.*

I love to lose myself in other men's minds. When I am not walking, I am reading; I cannot sit and think. Books think for me.

Last Essays of Elia. Detached Thoughts on Books and Reading.

I can read any thing which I call a book. There are things in that shape which I cannot allow for such. In this catalogue of books which are no books— biblia a-biblia—I reckon Court Calendars, Directories . . . the works of Hume, Gibbon, Robertson, Beattie, Soame Jenyns, and, generally, all those volumes which 'no gentleman's library should be without'. *Ib.*

Things in books' clothing. *Ib.*

Milton almost requires a solemn service of music to be played before you enter upon him. *Ib.*

A poor relation—is the most irrelevant thing in nature. *Ib. Poor Relations.*

An Oxford scholar, meeting a porter who was carrying a hare through the streets, accosts him with this extraordinary question: 'Prithee, friend, is that thy own hare, or a wig?'

Ib. Popular Fallacies. That the Worst Puns are the Best.

Cultivate simplicity Coleridge.

Letter to Coleridge, 8 Nov. 1796.

I could forgive a man for not enjoying Milton; but I would not call that man my friend who should be offended with 'the divine chit-chat of Cowper'.

Quoting Coleridge's own phrase in Letter to Coleridge, 5 Dec. 1796.

The scene for the most part laid in a Brothel. O tempora, O mores! but as friend Coleridge said when he was talking bawdy to Miss — 'to the pure all things are pure'. *Ib. to Southey, July 1798.*

An old woman clothed in grey,
 Whose daughter was charming and young,
And she was deluded away
 By Roger's false flattering tongue.

Quoted in letter to Southey, 29 Oct. 1798.

I came home . . . hungry as a hunter.

Letter to Coleridge, probably 16 or 17 Apr. 1800.

The man must have a rare recipe for melancholy, who can be dull in Fleet Street.

The Londoner in letter to Thomas Manning, 15 Feb. 1802.

Nursed amid her noise, her crowds, her beloved smoke—what have I been doing all my life, if I have not lent out my heart with usury to such scenes? *Ib.*

It was Lamb who, when Dr. Parr asked him how he managed to emit so much smoke, replied that he had toiled after it as other men after virtue. And Macready relates that he remarked in his presence that he wished to draw his last breath through a pipe and exhale it in a pun.

Ib. to W. and D. Wordsworth, 28 Sept. 1805, note.

A little thin, flowery border round, neat, not gaudy.

Ib. to Wordsworth, June 1806.

To do this it will be necessary to leave off Tobacco. But I had some thoughts of doing that before, for I sometimes think it does not agree with me.

Ib. to W. Wordsworth, 26 June 1806.

I have made a little scale, supposing myself to receive the following various accessions of dignity from the king, who is the fountain of honour— As at first, 1, Mr. C. Lamb; . . . 10th, Emperor Lamb; 11th, Pope Innocent, higher than which is nothing but the Lamb of God.

Ib. to Thomas Manning, 2 Jan. 1810.

I was at Hazlitt's marriage, and had like to have been turned out several times during the ceremony. Anything awful makes me laugh. I misbehaved once at a funeral. *Ib. to Southey, 9 Aug. 1815.*

This very night I am going to leave off tobacco! Surely there must be some other world in which this unconquerable purpose shall be realized. The soul hath not her generous aspirings implanted in her in vain. *Ib. to Thomas Manning, 26 Dec. 1815.*

His face when he repeats his verses hath its ancient
glory, an Archangel a little damaged. [Coleridge.]
Ib. to W. Wordsworth, 26 April 1816.

The rogue gives you Love Powders, and then a strong
horse drench to bring 'em off your stomach that
they mayn't hurt you. [Coleridge.]
Ib. to Wordsworth, 23 Sept. 1816.

Fanny Kelly's divine plain face.
Ib. to Mrs. Wordsworth, 18 Feb. 1818.

How I like to be liked, and what I do to be liked!
Ib. to D. Wordsworth, 8 Jan. 1821.

Who first invented Work—and tied the free
And holy-day rejoicing spirit down
To the ever-haunting importunity
Of business, in the green fields, and the town—
To plough—loom—anvil—spade—and, oh, most sad,
To this dry drudgery of the desk's dead wood?
Ib. to Barton, Sept. 1822.

Those fellows hate us. [Booksellers and authors.]
Ib. to Barton, 9 Jan. 1823.

Old as I am waxing, in his eyes I was still the child
he [Randall Norris] first knew me. To the last he
called me Charley. I have none to call me Charley
now. *Ib. to Robinson, 20 Jan. 1827.*

We should be modest for a modest man—as he is for
himself. *Ib. to Mrs. Montagu [Summer 1827].*

You are knee deep in clover.
Letter to C. C. Clarke, Dec. [1828].

When my sonnet was rejected, I exclaimed, 'Damn
the age; I will write for Antiquity!'
Ib. to B. W. Procter, 22 Jan. 1829.

Books of the true sort, not those things in boards that
moderns mistake for books—what they club for
at book clubs. *Ib. to J. Gillman, 30 Nov. 1829.*

The golden works of the dear, fine, silly old angel.
[Thomas Fuller.] *Ib. to J. Gillman 1830.*

Did G[eorge] D[yer] send his penny tract to me to
convert me to Unitarianism? Dear blundering
soul! why I am as old a one-Goddite as himself.
Ib. to Moxon, 24 Oct. 1831.

Half as sober as a judge.
Ib. to Mr. and Mrs. Moxon, August, 1833.

The greatest pleasure I know, is to do a good action
by stealth, and to have it found out by accident.
*Table Talk by the late Elia. The Athenæum,
4 Jan. 1834.*

'What a lass that were to go a-gipseying through the
world with.'
The Jovial Crew. The Examiner, July 1819.

For thy sake, Tobacco, I
Would do any thing but die.
A Farewell to Tobacco, l. 122.

         Gone before
To that unknown and silent shore. *Hester.*

Riddle of destiny, who can show
What thy short visit meant, or know
What thy errand here below?
On an Infant Dying as soon as Born.

Slow journeying on
To the green plains of pleasant Hertfordshire.
Sonnet: The Lord of Light Shakes Of

I have had playmates, I have had companions,
In my days of childhood, in my joyful school-days,—
All, all are gone, the old familiar faces.
The Old Familiar Face.

Free from self-seeking, envy, low design,
I have not found a whiter soul than thine.
To Martin Charles Burney

I like you, and your book, ingenuous Hone!
To the Editor of the Every-Day Book

Truths, which transcend the searching School-men'
vein,
And half had stagger'd that stout Stagirite.
Written at Cambridg

If ever I marry a wife,
   I'll marry a landlord's daughter,
For then I may sit in the bar,
   And drink cold brandy and water.
Written in a copy of Coelebs in Search of a Wif

Martin, if dirt were trumps, what hands you woul
hold!
Leigh Hunt's Ld. Byron and his Contemporarie
(1828), p. 299.

I do not [know the lady]; but damn her at a venture
E. V. Lucas, Charles Lamb (1905), vol. i, p. 320, r

MARY LAMB
1764–1847

He [Henry Robinson] says he never saw a man s
happy in *three wives* as Mr. Wordsworth is.
Letter to Sarah Hutchinson, Nov. 181

A child's a plaything for an hour.
Parental Recollection

Thou straggler into loving arms,
   Young climber up of knees,
When I forget thy thousand ways,
   Then life and all shall cease.   *I*

LETITIA ELIZABETH
LANDON
1802–1838

Few, save the poor, feel for the poor. *The Poo*

WALTER SAVAGE LANDOR
1775–1864

Around the child bend all the three
   Sweet Graces; Faith, Hope, Charity.
Around the man bend other faces;
   Pride, Envy, Malice, are his Graces.
Around the Chil

Ah, what avails the sceptred race!
Ah, what the form divine!
What every virtue, every grace!
Rose Aylmer, all were thine.

Rose Aylmer, whom these wakeful eyes
May weep, but never see,
A night of memories and of sighs
I consecrate to thee. *Rose Aylmer.*

There is delight in singing, tho' none hear
Beside the singer. *To Robert Browning.*

Shakespeare is not our poet, but the world's,
Therefore on him no speech! *Ib.*

Browning! Since Chaucer was alive and hale,
No man hath walked along our roads with step
So active, so inquiring eye, or tongue
So varied in discourse. But warmer climes
Give brighter plumage, stronger wing: the breeze
Of Alpine heights thou playest with, borne on
Beyond Sorrento and Amalfi, where
The Siren waits thee, singing song for song. *Ib.*

Such stains there are—as when a Grace
Sprinkles another's laughing face
    With nectar, and runs on. *On Catullus.*

Child of a day, thou knowest not
The tears that overflow thy urn. *Child of a Day.*

The witty and the tender Hood.
    Confessions of Jealousy.

Stand close around, ye Stygian set,
    With Dirce in one boat convey'd!
Or Charon, seeing, may forget
    That he is old and she a shade. *Dirce.*

Death stands above me, whispering low
    I know not what into my ear;
Of his strange language all I know
    Is, there is not a word of fear. *Epigrams, c. Death.*

Wearers of rings and chains!
Pray do not take the pains
    To set me right.
In vain my faults ye quote;
I write as others wrote
    On Sunium's height. *Ib. ci.*

I strove with none; for none was worth my strife;
    Nature I loved, and next to Nature, Art;
I warmed both hands before the fire of life;
    It sinks, and I am ready to depart. *Finis.*

I have sinuous shells, of pearly hue.
    Gebir, bk. 1, l. 170.
            Apply
Its polished lips to your attentive ear. *Ib.* l. 174.

And it remembers its august abodes,
And murmurs as the ocean murmurs there. *Ib.* l. 174.

'Is this the mighty ocean? is this all?'
    Ib. bk. v, l. 130.

From you, Ianthe, little troubles pass
Like little ripples down a sunny river.
    Ianthe's Troubles.

In his own image the Creator made,
His own pure sunbeam quickened thee, O man!
Thou breathing dial! since thy day began
The present hour was ever mark'd with shade!
    In His own Image the Creator Made.

I loved him not; and yet now he is gone
    I feel I am alone.
I check'd him while he spoke; yet, could he speak,
    Alas! I would not check. *The Maid's Lament.*

Mother, I cannot mind my wheel. *Title.*

No longer could I doubt him true—
    All other men may use deceit;
He always said my eyes were blue,
    And often swore my lips were sweet.
        Mother, I Cannot Mind My Wheel.

Proud word you never spoke, but you will speak
    Four not exempt from pride some future day.
Resting on one white hand a warm wet cheek
    Over my open volume you will say,
'This man loved *me*!' then rise and trip away.
        Proud Word You Never Spoke.

We are what suns and winds and waters make us;
The mountains are our sponsors, and the rills
Fashion and win their nursling with their smiles.
        Regeneration.

Well I remember how you smiled
    To see me write your name upon
The soft sea-sand—'O! what a child!
    You think you're writing upon stone!'

I have since written what no tide
    Shall ever wash away, what men
Unborn shall read o'er ocean wide
    And find Ianthe's name again.
        Well I Remember How You Smiled.

I know not whether I am proud,
But this I know, I hate the crowd. *With an Album.*

Chatting on deck was Dryden too,
The Bacon of our rhyming crew.
    *To Wordsworth: Those Who Have Laid the
    Harp Aside.*

Tho' never tender nor sublime,
He struggles with and conquers Time. [Dryden.]
            Ib.

Thee gentle Spenser fondly led;
But me he mostly sent to bed. *Ib.*

George the First was always reckoned
Vile, but viler George the Second;
And what mortal ever heard
Any good of George the Third?
When from earth the Fourth descended
God be praised, the Georges ended!
    Epigram in *The Atlas,* 28 Apr. 1855. See
    Notes and Queries, 3 May 1902, pp. 318, 354.

Laodameia died; Helen died; Leda, the beloved of
Jupiter, went before.
    Imaginary Conversations, Æsop and Rhodope, ii.

There are no fields of amaranth on this side of the
grave: there are no voices, O Rhodopè! that are not
soon mute, however tuneful: there is no name, with
whatever emphasis of passionate love repeated, of
which the echo is not faint at last. *Ib.*

Prose on certain occasions can bear a great deal of
poetry: on the other hand, poetry sinks and swoons
under a moderate weight of prose.
    Ib. Archdeacon Hare and Walter Landor.

I shall dine late; but the dining-room will be well
lighted, the guests few and select. *Ib.*

When it was a matter of wonder how Keats, who was
ignorant of Greek, could have written his 'Hyperion', Shelley, whom envy never touched, gave
as a reason, 'Because he *was* a Greek'.
    Ib. Southey and Landor, ii.

Goodness does not more certainly make men happy
　than happiness makes them good.
　　　　　　　　Ib. Lord Brooke and Sir Philip Sidney.

LEONORA:
But tell him, tell Torquato . . . go again; entreat,
　persuade, command him, to forget me.
PANIGAROLA:
Alas! even the command, even the command from
　you and from above, might not avail perhaps.
　You smile, Madonna!
LEONORA:
I die happy.　　*Ib. Leonora di Este and Panigarola.*

States, like men, have their growth, their manhood,
　their decrepitude, their decay.　　　　　*Ib.*

ANDREW LANG
1844–1912

St. Andrews by the Northern Sea,
That is a haunted town to me!　　*Almae Matres.*

The surge and thunder of the Odyssey.
　　　　As One that for a Weary Space has Lain

There's a joy without canker or cark,
　There's a pleasure eternally new,
'T is to gloat on the glaze and the mark
　Of china that's ancient and blue.
　　　　　　　Ballade of Blue China.

Here's a pot with a cot in a park,
　In a park where the peach-blossoms blew,
Where the lovers eloped in the dark,
　Lived, died, and were changed into two
Bright birds that eternally flew
Through the boughs of the may, as they sang
'T is a tale was undoubtedly true
　In the reign of the Emperor Hwang.　　*Ib.*

If the wild bowler thinks he bowls,
　Of if the batsman thinks he's bowled,
They know not, poor misguided souls,
　They too shall perish unconsoled.
I am the batsman and the bat,
　I am the bowler and the ball,
The umpire, the pavilion cat,
　The roller, pitch, and stumps, and all.
　　　　Brahma (in imitation of Emerson).

But he shaved with a shell when he chose,—
'Twas the manner of Primitive Man.
　　　　　Double Ballad of Primitive Man.

FREDERICK LANGBRIDGE
1849–1923

Two men look out through the same bars:
One sees the mud, and one the stars.
　　A Cluster of Quiet Thoughts, 1896 (*Religious
　　Tract Society Publication*).

JOHN LANGHORNE
1735–1779

Cold on Canadian hills, or Minden's plain,
Perhaps that parent mourn'd her soldier slain;
.　.　.　.　.　.
The child of misery, baptiz'd in tears!
　The Country Justice, pt. i. *Apology for Vagrants.*

WILLIAM LANGLAND
1330?–1400?

In a somer seson whan soft was the sonne.
　　*The Vision of William concerning Piers the
　　Plowman* (ed. Skeat), B Text, Prologue, l. 1.

A glotoun of wordes.　　　　*Ib.* l. 139.

Bakers and brewers, bouchers and cokes—
For thees men doth most harme to the mene puple.
　　　　　Ib. C Text, Passus 4, l. 80.

Grammere, that grounde is of alle.
　　　　　　　Ib. Passus 18, l. 107.

'After sharpest shoures,' quath Pees [Peace] 'most
　sheene is the sonne;
Ys no weder warmer than after watery cloudes.'
　　　　　　　Ib. Passus 21, l. 456.

SIDNEY LANIER
1842–1881

Into the woods my Master went,
Clean forspent, forspent.
Into the woods my Master came,
Forspent with love and shame.
　　Poems. A Ballad of Trees and the Master.

HUGH LATIMER
1485?–1555

Be of good comfort Master Ridley, and play the man.
　We shall this day light such a candle by God's
　grace in England, as (I trust) shall never be put out.
　　Foxe, *Actes and Monuments* (1570), p. 1937.

SIR HARRY LAUDER
1870–1950

I love a lassie.　　　　*Title of Song.*

O! it's nice to get up in the mornin'
But it's nicer to lie in bed.
　　　It's Nice To Get Up In The Mornin'.

Roamin' in the Gloamin'.　　*Title of Song.*

ANDREW BONAR LAW
1858–1923

If, therefore, war should ever come between these
　two countries [Great Britain and Germany], which
　Heaven forbid! it will not, I think, be due to
　irresistible natural laws, it will be due to the want
　of human wisdom.
　　Speech, House of Commons, 27 Nov. 1911.

I said [in 1911] that if ever war arose between Great
　Britain and Germany it would not be due to
　inevitable causes, for I did not believe in inevitable
　war. I said it would be due to human folly.
　　Speech, House of Commons, 6 Aug. 1914.

DAVID HERBERT LAWRENCE

1885–1930

The terror, the agony, the nostalgia of the heathen past was a constant torture to her mediumistic soul. *The Lost Girl*, ch. 15.

She is dear to me in the middle of my being. But the gold and flowing serpent is coiling up again, to sleep at the root of my tree.
The Man Who Died, part ii.

Be a good animal, true to your animal instincts.
The White Peacock, pt. ii, ch. 2.

Along the avenue of cypresses,
All in their scarlet cloaks and surplices
Of linen, go the chanting choristers,
The priests in gold and black, the villagers.
Giorno dei Morti.

The silence of the many villagers,
The candle-flame beside the surplices.   *Ib.*

SIR AUSTEN HENRY LAYARD

1817–1894

I have always believed that successes would be the inevitable result if the two services, the army and navy, had fair play, and if we sent the right man to fill the right place.
Speech in Parliament, 15 Jan. 1855.

STEPHEN BUTLER LEACOCK

1869–

Lord Ronald . . . flung himself upon his horse and rode madly off in all directions.
Nonsense Novels. Gertrude the Governess.

EDWARD LEAR

1812–1888

There was an Old Man with a beard,
Who said, 'It is just as I feared!—
  Two Owls and a Hen,
  Four Larks and a Wren,
Have all built their nests in my beard!'
Book of Nonsense.

There was an Old Man in a tree,
Who was horribly bored by a bee;
When they said, 'Does it buzz?'
He replied, 'Yes, it does!
It's a regular brute of a bee!'   *Ib.*

There was an Old Man in a boat,
Who said, 'I'm afloat, I'm afloat!'
When they said, 'No, you ain't!'
He was ready to faint,
That unhappy Old Man in a boat.   *Ib.*

There was an Old Person of Basing,
Whose presence of mind was amazing;
He purchased a steed,
Which he rode at full speed,
And escaped from the people of Basing.   *Ib.*

There was an old man who said, 'Hush!
I perceive a young bird in this bush!'
When they said, 'Is it small?'
He replied, 'Not at all!
It is four times as big as the bush!'   *Ib.*

'How pleasant to know Mr. Lear!'
Who has written such volumes of stuff!
Some think him ill-tempered and queer,
But a few think him pleasant enough.
Nonsense Songs, preface.

Who, or why, or which, or what,
Is the Akond of Swat?   *Ib. The Akond of Swat.*

In the middle of the woods
Lived the Yonghy-Bonghy-Bò.
Two old chairs, and half a candle,—
One old jug without a handle,—
These were all his worldly goods.
Ib. The Courtship of the Yonghy-Bonghy-Bò.

When awful darkness and silence reign
Over the great Gromboolian plain,
Through the long, long wintry nights.
Ib. The Dong with the Luminous Nose.

Far and few, far and few,
Are the lands where the Jumblies live;
Their heads are green, and their hands are blue,
And they went to sea in a Sieve.
Ib. The Jumblies.

In spite of all their friends could say,
On a winter's morn, on a stormy day,
In a Sieve they went to sea!   *Ib.*

The Owl and the Pussy-Cat went to sea
In a beautiful pea-green boat.
Ib. The Owl and The Pussy-Cat.

They sailed away for a year and a day,
To the land where the Bong-tree grows.   *Ib.*

They dined on mince, and slices of quince,
Which they ate with a runcible spoon;
And hand in hand, on the edge of the sand,
They danced by the light of the moon.   *Ib.*

His Aunt Jobiska made him drink
Lavender water tinged with pink,
For she said, 'The world in general knows
There's nothing so good for a Pobble's toes!'
Nonsense Songs. The Pobble Who Has No Toes.

For his Aunt Jobiska said, 'No harm
Can come to his toes if his nose is warm,
And it's perfectly known that a Pobble's toes
Are safe, provided he minds his nose.'   *Ib.*

'It's a fact the whole world knows,
That Pobbles are happier without their toes.'   *Ib.*

MARY ELIZABETH LEASE

1853–1933

Kansas had better stop raising corn and begin raising hell.   *attr.*

WILLIAM EDWARD HARTPOLE LECKY

1838–1903

The stately ship is seen no more,
The fragile skiff attains the shore;
And while the great and wise decay,
And all their trophies pass away,
Some sudden thought, some careless rhyme,
Still floats above the wrecks of Time.
On an Old Song.

GERALD STANLEY LEE

Business to-day consists of persuading crowds.
Crowds, bk. ii, ch. 5.

HENRY LEE

1756–1818

First in war, first in peace, first in the hearts of his
fellow citizens.
*Resolutions in the House of Representatives on
the death of Washington.*

NATHANIEL LEE

1653?–1692

'Tis beauty calls and glory leads the way.
Alexander the Great, II. ii.

When the sun sets, shadows, that showed at noon
But small, appear most long and terrible.
Œdipus, IV. i.

Man, false man, smiling, destructive man.
Theodosius, III. ii.

He speaks the kindest words, and looks such things,
Vows with so much passion, swears with so much
grace.
That 'tis a kind of Heaven to be deluded by him.
The Rival Queens, Act I.

Love itself, that tyrant of the soul.   *Ib.*

See the conquering hero comes,
Sound the trumpets, beat the drums.   *Ib.* Act II.

When Greeks joined Greeks, then was the tug of war!
Ib. IV. ii.

Philip fought men, but Alexander women.   *Ib.*

Terror haunts the guilty mind.   *Ib.* I. i.

RICHARD LE GALLIENNE

1866–

The cry of the Little Peoples goes up to God in vain.
The Cry of the Little Peoples.

Give back the little nation leave to live.
Christmas in War-Time.

Loud mockers in the roaring street
Say Christ is crucified again:
Twice pierced His gospel-bearing feet,
Twice broken His great heart in vain,
The Second Crucifixion.

The quest of the Golden Girl.   *Title of Novel.*

HENRY SAMBROOKE LEIGH

1837–1883

In form and feature, face and limb,
I grew so like my brother
That folks got taking me for him
And each for one another.
Carols of Cockayne, The Twins.

For one of us was born a twin
And not a soul knew which.   *Ib.*

The rapturous, wild, and ineffable pleasure
Of drinking at somebody else's expense.
Ib. Stanzas to an Intoxicated Fly.

I know where little girls are sent
For telling taradiddles.   *Ib. Only Seven.*

CHARLES GODFREY LELAND

1824–1903

Hans Breitmann gife a barty—
Vhere ish dat barty now?
Hans Breitmann's Party.

All goned afay mit de lager-beer—
Afay in de ewigkeit!   *Ib.*

Und efery dime she gife a shoomp
She make der vinders sound.   *Ib.*

They saw a Dream of Loveliness descending from
the train.   *Brand New Ballads. The Masher.*

WILLIAM LENTHALL

1591–1662

I have neither eye to see, nor tongue to speak here,
but as the House is pleased to direct me.
Rushworth's Historical Collections, iv. 238.

ROGER L'ESTRANGE

1616–1704

It is with our passions as it is with fire and water, they
are good servants, but bad masters.
Æsop's Fables, no. 38, *Reflection.*

Though this may be play to you, 'tis death to us.
Ib. no. 398.

GEORGE LEVESON-GOWER, EARL GRANVILLE

1815–1891

Spheres of action.
Letter to Count Münster, 29 April 1885 (Sir
Edward Hertslet, *Map of Africa by Treaty,*
1894, vol. ii, p. 596).

GEORGE HENRY LEWES

1817–1878

Many a genius has been slow of growth. Oaks that
flourish for a thousand years do not spring up into
beauty like a reed.   *Spanish Drama*, ch. 2.

Murder, like talent, seems occasionally to run in families. *The Physiology of Common Life*, ch. 12.

We must never assume that which is incapable of proof.   *Ib.* ch. 13.

GEORGE LILLO
1693–1739

There's sure no passion in the human soul,
But finds its food in music.   *Fatal Curiosity*, 1. ii.

ABRAHAM LINCOLN
1809–1865

I intend no modification of my oft-expressed personal wish that all men everywhere could be free.
     Speeches and Letters (1907), *Letter to H. Greeley, 22 Aug. 1862.*

I claim not to have controlled events, but confess plainly that events have controlled me.
     Ib. Letter to A. G. Hodges, 4 Apr. 1864.

The ballot is stronger than the bullet.
     Ib. Speech, 19 May 1856.

'A house divided against itself cannot stand.' I believe this government cannot endure permanently, half slave and half free. *Ib. Speech, 17 June 1858.*

What is conservatism? Is it not adherence to the old and tried, against the new and untried?
     Ib. Speech, 27 Feb. 1860.

Let us have faith that right makes might; and in that faith let us to the end, dare to do our duty as we understand it.   *Ib.*

I take the official oath to-day with no mental reservations, and with no purpose to construe the Constitution or laws by any hypercritical rules.
     Ib.   *First Inaugural Address, 4 Mar. 1861.*

In giving freedom to the slave, we assure freedom to the free,—honourable alike in what we give and what we preserve.
     Ib. Annual Message to Congress, 1 Dec. 1862.

Fourscore and seven years ago our fathers brought forth upon this continent a new nation, conceived in liberty, and dedicated to the proposition that all men are created equal. Now we are engaged in a great civil war, testing whether that nation, or any nation so conceived and so dedicated, can long endure. We are met on a great battlefield of that war. We have come to dedicate a portion of that field as a final resting-place of those who here gave their lives that that nation might live. It is altogether fitting and proper that we should do this. But in a larger sense we cannot dedicate, we cannot consecrate, we cannot hallow this ground. The brave men, living and dead, who struggled here, have consecrated it far above our power to add or detract. The world will little note, nor long remember, what we say here, but it can never forget what they did here. It is for us, the living, rather to be dedicated here to the unfinished work which they have thus far so nobly advanced. It is rather for us to be here dedicated to the great task remaining before us, that from these honoured dead we take increased devotion to that cause for which they here gave the last full measure of devotion; that we here highly resolve that the dead shall not have died in vain, that this nation, under God, shall have a new birth of freedom; and that government of the people, by the people, and for the people, shall not perish from the earth.
     Ib. Address at Dedication of National Cemetery at Gettysburg, 19 Nov. 1863.

With malice toward none; with charity for all; with firmness in the right, as God gives us to see the right.
     Ib. Second Inaugural Address, 4 Mar. 1865.

You can fool all the people some of the time, and some of the people all the time, but you can not fool all the people all of the time.
     Attr. words in a speech at Clinton, 8 Sept. 1858. N. W. Stephenson, *Autobiography of A. Lincoln* (1927). *Attr. also to Phineas Barnum, 1810–91.*

It is not best to swap horses while crossing the river.
     Reply to National Union League, 9 June 1864. J. E. Nicolay and J. Hay, *Abraham Lincoln.* Bk. ix.

As President, I have no eyes but constitutional eyes; I cannot see you.
     Attr. reply to the South Carolina Commissioners.

People who like this sort of thing will find this the sort of thing they like.
     Judgement on a book. G. W. E. Russell, *Collections and Recollections*, ch. 30.

GEORGE LINLEY
1798–1865

Ever of thee I'm fondly dreaming,
Thy gentle voice my spirit can cheer.
     Poems. Ever of Thee.

Among our ancient mountains,
And from our lovely vales,
Oh, let the prayer re-echo:
'God bless the Prince of Wales!'
     Ib. God Bless the Prince of Wales.

Thou art gone from my gaze like a beautiful dream,
And I seek thee in vain by the meadow and stream.
     Ib. Thou Art Gone.

Tho' lost to sight, to mem'ry dear
Thou ever wilt remain.
     Song. Attr. to Linley. Notes and Queries, Ser. 5, vol. x, p. 417.

SIR THOMAS LITTLETON
1422–1481

[From] time whereof the memory of man runneth not to the contrary.   *Tenures* (? 1481), § 170.

DAVID LLOYD GEORGE
1863–1945

The stern hand of fate has scourged us to an elevation where we can see the great everlasting things

that matter for a nation; the great peaks of honour we had forgotten—duty and patriotism clad in glittering white; the great pinnacle of sacrifice pointing like a rugged finger to Heaven.
Speech, Queen's Hall, London, 19 Sept. 1914.

What is our task? To make Britain a fit country for heroes to live in.
Speech, Wolverhampton, 24 Nov. 1918.

ROBERT LLOYD
1733–1764

Slow and steady wins the race.
Poems. The Hare and the Tortoise.

JOHN LOCKE
1632–1704

New opinions are always suspected, and usually opposed, without any other reason but because they are not already common.
Essay on the Human Understanding, dedicatory epistle.

Nature never makes excellent things for mean or no uses.   *Ib.* bk. ii, ch. 1, sec. 15.

No man's knowledge here can go beyond his experience.   *Ib.* sec. 19.

It is one thing to show a man that he is in an error, and another to put him in possession of truth.
Ib. bk. iv, ch. 7, sec. 11.

All men are liable to error; and most men are, in many points, by passion or interest, under temptation to it.   *Ib.* ch. 20, sec. 17.

FREDERICK LOCKER-LAMPSON
1821–1895

The world's as ugly, ay, as sin,
And almost as delightful.   *The Jester's Plea.*

And many are afraid of God—
And more of Mrs. Grundy.   *Ib.*

Some men are good for righting wrongs,—
And some for writing verses.   *Ib.*

If you lift a guinea-pig up by the tail
His eyes drop out!   *A Garden Lyric.*

FRANCIS LOCKIER
1667–1740

In all my travels I never met with any one Scotchman but what was a man of sense. I believe everybody of that country that has any, leaves it as fast as they can.   *Spence's Anecdotes* (1858), p. 55.

THOMAS LODGE
1558?–1625

Devils are not so black as they are painted.
A Margarite of America.

Love, in my bosom, like a bee,
Doth suck his sweet.   *Love, In My Bosom.*
Heigh ho, would she were mine!
Rosalind's Description.

JOHN LOGAN
1748–1788

Behold congenial Autumn comes,
The sabbath of the year!
Ode on a Visit to the Country in Autumn.

For never on thy banks shall I
Behold my love, the flower of Yarrow.
The Braes of Yarrow.

Sweet bird! thy bow'r is ever green,
Thy sky is ever clear;
Thou hast no sorrow in thy song,
No winter in thy year!
To the Cuckoo. Attr. (See *Notes and Queries,* April 1902, p. 309; 14 June, 1902, p. 469.) Attr. also to Michael Bruce.

HENRY WADSWORTH LONGFELLOW
1807–1882

I shot an arrow into the air,
It fell to earth, I knew not where.
The Arrow and the Song.

And the song, from beginning to end,
I found again in the heart of a friend.   *Ib.*

I know a maiden fair to see,
     Take care!
She can both false and friendly be,
     Beware! Beware!
     Trust her not,
     She is fooling thee! *Beware!* (From the German.)

I stood on the bridge at midnight,
As the clocks were striking the hour.   *The Bridge.*

In the elder days of Art,
     Builders wrought with greatest care
Each minute and unseen part;
     For the Gods see everywhere.   *The Builders.*

'Build me straight, O worthy Master!
Staunch and strong, a goodly vessel,
That shall laugh at all disaster,
And with wave and whirlwind wrestle!'
The Building of the Ship.

Thou too, sail on, O Ship of State!
Sail on, O Union, strong and great!
Humanity with all its fears,
With all the hopes of future years,
Is hanging breathless on thy fate!   *Ib.*

Ye are better than all the ballads
     That ever were sung or said;
For ye are living poems,
     And all the rest are dead.   *Children.*

Between the dark and the daylight,
     When the night is beginning to lower,
Comes a pause in the day's occupations,
     That is known as the Children's Hour.
The Children's Hour.

Singing the Hundredth Psalm, the grand old Puritan anthem.   *The Courtship of Miles Standish,* iii.

Archly the maiden smiled, and, with eyes overrunning with laughter,
Said, in a tremulous voice, 'Why don't you speak for yourself, John?'   *Ib.*

God had sifted three kingdoms to find the wheat for
   this planting.   *Ib. iv.*

The day is done, and the darkness
Falls from the wings of Night,
As a feather is wafted downward
   From an eagle in his flight.   *The Day is Done.*

A feeling of sadness and longing,
   That is not akin to pain,
And resembles sorrow only
   As the mist resembles the rain.   *Ib.*

The bards sublime,
Whose distant footsteps echo
   Through the corridors of Time.   *Ib.*

The cares that infest the day
Shall fold their tents, like the Arabs,
   And as silently steal away.   *Ib.*

If you would hit the mark, you must aim a little above
   it;
Every arrow that flies feels the attraction of earth.
                             Elegiac Verse.

This is the forest primeval.
         Evangeline, introduction, l. 1.

When she had passed, it seemed like the ceasing of
   exquisite music.   *Ib.* pt. 1. i, l. 62.

Talk not of wasted affection, affection never was
   wasted;
If it enrich not the heart of another, its waters, returning
Back to their springs, like the rain, shall fill them full
   of refreshment.   *Ib.* pt. II. i, l. 55.

Sorrow and silence are strong, and patient endurance
   is godlike.   *Ib.* l. 60.

And, as she looked around, she saw how Death, the
   consoler,
Laying his hand upon many a heart, had healed it for
   ever.   *Ib.* v, l. 88.

The shades of night were falling fast,
As through an Alpine village passed
A youth, who bore, 'mid snow and ice,
A banner with the strange device,
       Excelsior!   *Excelsior.*

'Try not the Pass!' the old man said;
'Dark lowers the tempest overhead.'   *Ib.*

'O stay,' the maiden said, 'and rest
Thy weary head upon this breast!'   *Ib.*

'Beware the pine-tree's withered branch!
Beware the awful avalanche!'   *Ib.*

A traveller, by the faithful hound,
Half-buried in the snow was found.   *Ib.*

Spake full well, in language quaint and olden,
One who dwelleth by the castled Rhine,
When he called the flowers, so blue and golden,
   Stars, that in earth's firmament do shine. *Flowers.*

That is best which lieth nearest;
Shape from that thy work of art.   *Gaspar Becerra.*

   Giotto's tower,
The lily of Florence blossoming in stone.
                Giotto's Tower.

I like that ancient Saxon phrase, which calls
   The burial-ground God's-Acre!   *God's-Acre.*

Ah, the souls of those that die
Are but sunbeams lifted higher.
     The Golden Legend, pt. IV. *The Cloisters.*

I heard the trailing garments of the Night
Sweep through her marble halls! *Hymn to the Night.*

Hold the fleet angel fast until he bless thee. *Kavanagh.*

Saint Augustine! well hast thou said,
   That of our vices we can frame
A ladder, if we will but tread
   Beneath our feet each deed of shame!
         The Ladder of Saint Augustine.

The heights by great men reached and kept
   Were not attained by sudden flight,
But they, while their companions slept,
   Were toiling upward in the night.   *Ib.*

Live I, so live I,
To my Lord heartily,
To my Prince faithfully,
To my Neighbour honestly,
Die I, so die I.
   Law of Life. From the Sinngedichte of Fried-
   rich von Logau.

Know how sublime a thing it is
   To suffer and be strong.   *The Light of Stars.*

Standing, with reluctant feet,
Where the brook and river meet,
Womanhood and childhood fleet!   *Maidenhood.*

You would attain to the divine perfection,
And yet not turn your back upon the world.
          Michael Angelo, pt. 1. v.

Would seem angelic in the sight of God,
Yet not too saint-like in the eyes of men;
In short, would lead a holy Christian life
In such a way that even your nearest friend
Would not detect therein one circumstance
To show a change from what it was before.   *Ib.*

The men that women marry,
And why they marry them, will always be
A marvel and a mystery to the world.   *Ib.* vi.

A boy's will is the wind's will,
And the thoughts of youth are long, long thoughts.
               My Lost Youth.

Angels in broad-brimmed hats and russet cloaks,
The colour of the Devil's nutting-bag!
  New England Tragedies. John Endicott, 1. ii.

A solid man of Boston.
A comfortable man, with dividends,
And the first salmon, and the first green peas. *Ib.* IV. i.

Emigravit is the inscription on the tombstone where
   he lies;
Dead he is not, but departed,—for the artist never dies.
               Nuremburg, xiii.

Not in the clamour of the crowded street,
Not in the shouts and plaudits of the throng,
But in ourselves, are triumph and defeat. *The Poets.*

Tell me not, in mournful numbers,
   Life is but an empty dream!
For the soul is dead that slumbers,
   And things are not what they seem.

Life is real! Life is earnest!
   And the grave is not its goal;
Dust thou art, to dust returnest,
   Was not spoken of the soul.   *A Psalm of Life.*

Art is long, and Time is fleeting,
  And our hearts, though stout and brave,
Still, like muffled drums, are beating
  Funeral marches to the grave.   *Ib.*

Trust no Future, howe'er pleasant!
Let the dead Past bury its dead!
Act,—act in the living Present!
  Heart within, and God o'erhead!   *Ib.*

Lives of great men all remind us
  We can make our lives sublime,
And, departing, leave behind us
  Footprints on the sands of time.

Footprints, that perhaps another,
  Sailing o'er life's solemn main,
A forlorn and shipwrecked brother,
  Seeing, shall take heart again.

Let us, then, be up and doing,
  With a heart for any fate;
Still achieving, still pursuing,
  Learn to labour and to wait.   *Ib.*

There is a Reaper whose name is Death,
  And with his sickle keen,
He reaps the bearded grain at a breath,
  And the flowers that grow between.
            The Reaper and the Flowers.

O, not in cruelty, not in wrath,
  The Reaper came that day;
'Twas an angel visited the green earth,
  And took the flowers away.   *Ib.*

There is no flock, however watched and tended,
  But one dead lamb is there!
There is no fireside, howsoe'er defended,
  But has one vacant chair!   *Resignation.*

There is no Death! What seems so is transition;
  This life of mortal breath
Is but a suburb of the life elysian,
  Whose portal we call Death.   *Ib.*

Though the mills of God grind slowly, yet they grind
  exceeding small;
Though with patience he stands waiting, with exactness grinds he all.
       Retribution. From the Sinngedichte of Fried-
       rich von Logau.

A Lady with a Lamp shall stand
In the great history of the land,
  A noble type of good,
  Heroic womanhood.   *Santa Filomena.*

'Wouldst thou'—so the helmsman answered,—
  'Learn the secret of the sea?
Only those who brave its dangers
  Comprehend its mystery!'   *The Secret of the Sea.*

Beside the ungather'd rice he lay,
His sickle in his hand.   *The Slave's Dream.*

He did not feel the driver's whip,
  Nor the burning heat of day;
For Death had illumined the land of Sleep,
  And his lifeless body lay
A worn-out fetter, that the soul
Had broken and thrown away!   *Ib.*

Stay, stay at home, my heart, and rest;
Home-keeping hearts are happiest.
       Song: Stay, Stay at Home.

Should you ask me, whence these stories?
Whence these legends and traditions?
       The Song of Hiawatha, introduction.

I should answer, I should tell you,
'From the forests and the prairies,
From the great lakes of the Northland,
From the land of the Ojibways,
From the land of the Dacotahs,
From the mountains, moors, and fenlands,
Where the heron, the Shuh-shuh-gah,
Feeds among the reeds and rushes.'   *Ib.*

Gitche Manito, the mighty. *Ib.* i. *The Peaceful Pipe.*

By the shores of Gitche Gumee,
By the shining Big-Sea-Water,
Stood the wigwam of Nokomis,
Daughter of the Moon, Nokomis.
Dark behind it rose the forest,
Rose the black and gloomy pine-trees,
Rose the firs with cones upon them;
Bright before it beat the water,
Beat the clear and sunny water,
Beat the shining Big-Sea-Water.
       Ib. iii. *Hiawatha's Childhood.*

'Ewa-yea! my little owlet!
Who is this, that lights the wigwam?
With his great eyes lights the wigwam?'   *Ib.*

Called them 'Hiawatha's Chickens'.   *Ib.*

And his heart was hot within him,
Like a living coal his heart was.
       Ib. iv. *Hiawatha and Mudjekeewis.*

From the waterfall he named her,
Minnehaha, Laughing Water.   *Ib.*

As unto the bow the cord is,
So unto the man is woman;
Though she bends him, she obeys him,
Though she draws him, yet she follows;
Useless each without the other!
       Ib. x. *Hiawatha's Wooing.*

'Onaway! Awake, beloved!'   *Ib.*

'He is dead, the sweet musician!
He the sweetest of all singers!
He has gone from us for ever,
He has moved a little nearer
To the Master of all music,
To the Master of all singing!
O my brother, Chibiabos!'
       Ib. xv. *Hiawatha's Lamentation.*

The secret anniversaries of the heart.
       Sonnets. Holidays.

Stars of the summer night!
  Far in yon azure deeps,
Hide, hide your golden light!
  She sleeps!
  My lady sleeps!
  Sleeps!   *The Spanish Student*, I. iii.

Dreams of the summer night!
  Tell her, her lover keeps
Watch! while in slumbers light
  She sleeps!   *Ib.*

Thinking the deed, and not the creed,
Would help us in our utmost need.
> *Tales of a Wayside Inn*, pt. I, Prelude, l. 221.

At all feasts where ale was strongest
Sat the merry monarch longest,
  First to come and last to go.
> *Ib. The Musician's Tale. The Saga of King Olaf,* ii.

He seemed the incarnate 'Well, I told you so!'
> *Ib. The Poet's Tale. The Birds of Killingworth.*

Our ingress into the world
  Was naked and bare;
Our progress through the world
  Is trouble and care;
Our egress from the world
  Will be nobody knows where;
But if we do well here
  We shall do well there;
And I could tell you no more,
  Should I preach a whole year!
> *Ib.* pt. II. *The Student's Tale. The Cobbler of Hagenau.*

Ships that pass in the night, and speak each other in
    passing;
Only a signal shown and a distant voice in the dark-
    ness;
So on the ocean of life we pass and speak one another,
Only a look and a voice; then darkness again and a
    silence.
> *Ib.* pt. III. *The Theologian's Tale. Elizabeth,* iv.

Under a spreading chestnut-tree
  The village smithy stands;
The smith, a mighty man is he,
  With large and sinewy hands;
And the muscles of his brawny arms
  Are strong as iron bands.
> *The Village Blacksmith.*

He earns whate'er he can,
And looks the whole world in the face,
  For he owes not any man.   *Ib.*

Toiling,—rejoicing,—sorrowing,
  Onward through life he goes;
Each morning sees some task begin,
  Each evening sees it close;
Something attempted, something done,
  Has earned a night's repose.   *Ib.*

It was the schooner Hesperus,
  That sailed the wintry sea;
And the skipper had taken his little daughter,
  To bear him company.
> *The Wreck of the Hesperus.*

But the father answered never a word,
  A frozen corpse was he.   *Ib.*

And fast through the midnight dark and drear,
  Through the whistling sleet and snow,
Like a sheeted ghost, the vessel swept
  Towards the reef of Norman's Woe.   *Ib.*

There was a little girl
Who had a little curl
Right in the middle of her forehead,
When she was good
She was very, very good,
But when she was bad she was horrid.
> B. R. T. Machetta, *Home Life of Longfellow.*

ANITA LOOS
1893–

Gentlemen Prefer Blondes.   *Title of Novel.*

RICHARD LOVELACE
1618–1658

Am not I shot
With the self-same artillery?
> *Amyntor from Beyond the Sea to Alexis.*

Lucasta that bright northern star.   *Ib.*

And when she ceas'd, we sighing saw
The floor lay pav'd with broken hearts.
> *Gratiana Dancing and Singing.*

So did she move; so did she sing
Like the harmonious spheres that bring
Unto their rounds their music's aid;
Which she performed, such a way,
As all th' inamour'd world will say
The Graces danced, and Apollo play'd.   *Ib.*

Forbear thou great good husband, little ant.
> *The Ant.*

Cease large example of wise thrift a while.   *Ib.*

When Love with unconfined wings
  Hovers within my gates;
And my divine Althea brings
  To whisper at the grates:
When I lie tangled in her hair,
  And fettered to her eye,
The Gods, that wanton in the air,
  Know no such liberty.   *To Althea, From Prison.*

When flowing cups run swiftly round
  With no allaying Thames.   *Ib.*

When thirsty grief in wine we steep,
  When healths and draughts go free,
Fishes, that tipple in the deep,
  Know no such liberty.   *Ib.*

When (like committed linnets) I
  With shriller throat shall sing
The sweetness, mercy, majesty,
  And glories of my King;
When I shall voice aloud, how good
  He is, how great should be;
Enlarged winds that curl the flood,
  Know no such liberty.

Stone walls do not a prison make
  Nor iron bars a cage;
Minds innocent and quiet take
  That for an hermitage;
If I have freedom in my love,
  And in my soul am free;
Angels alone, that soar above,
  Enjoy such liberty.   *Ib.*

If to be absent were to be
  Away from thee;
Or that when I am gone,
  You or I were alone;
Then my Lucasta might I crave
Pity from blust'ring wind, or swallowing wave.
> *To Lucasta, Going Beyond the Seas.*

And greet as angels greet.   *Ib.*

Tell me not (Sweet) I am unkind,
  That from the nunnery
Of thy chaste breast, and quiet mind,
  To war and arms I fly.

True; a new mistress now I chase,
  The first foe in the field;
And with a stronger faith embrace
  A sword, a horse, a shield.

Yet this inconstancy is such,
  As you too shall adore;
I could not love thee (Dear) so much,
  Lov'd I not honour more.
       To Lucasta, Going to the Wars.

SAMUEL LOVER

1797–1868

When once the itch of literature comes over a man,
nothing can cure it but the scratching of a pen.
       Handy Andy, ch. 36.

'Now women are mostly troublesome cattle to deal
  with mostly', said Goggins.   *Ib.*

JAMES RUSSELL LOWELL

1819–1891

No man is born into the world, whose work
Is not born with him; there is always work,
And tools to work withal, for those who will:
And blessèd are the horny hands of toil!
       A Glance Behind the Curtain, l. 201.

An' you've gut to git up airly
  Ef you want to take in God.
       The Biglow Papers, First Series, No. 1.

God'll send the bill to you.   *Ib.*

You've a darned long row to hoe.   *Ib.*

This goin' ware glory waits ye haint one agreeable
  feetur.   *Ib.* No. 2.

      But John P.
      Robinson he
Sez theyn't know everythin' down in Judee. *Ib.* No. 3.

A marciful Providence fashioned us holler,
O' purpose thet we might our principles swaller.
       Ib. No. 4.

I du believe in Freedom's cause,
  Ez fur away ez Payris is;
I love to see her stick her claws
  In them infarnal Phayrisees;
It's wal enough agin a king
  To dror resolves an' triggers,—
But libbaty's a kind o' thing
  Thet don't agree with niggers.
       Ib. No. 6. *The Pious Editor's Creed.*

An' in convartin' public trusts
  To very privit uses.   *Ib.*

I *don't* believe in princerple,
  But O, I *du* in interest.   *Ib.*

It ain't by princerples nor men
  My preudunt course is steadied,—
I scent wich pays the best. an' then
  Go into it baldheaded.   *Ib.*

God makes sech nights, all white an' still
  Fur 'z you can look or listen,
Moonshine an' snow on field an' hill,
  All silence an' all glisten.
      Ib. Introduction to the Second Series. The
      Courtin'.

'Twas kin' o' kingdom-come to look
  On sech a blessed cretur.   *Ib.*

He was six foot o' man, A 1,
  Clear grit an' human natur'.   *Ib.*

She thought no v'ice hed sech a swing
  Ez hisn in the choir;
My! when he made Ole Hunderd ring,
  She *knowed* the Lord was nigher.   *Ib.*

His heart kep' goin' pity-pat,
  But hern went pity-zekle.   *Ib.*

I tell ye wut, my jedgement is you're pooty sure to
  fail,
Ez long 'z the head keeps turnin' back for counsel to
  the tail.   *Ib. Second Series*, No. 3, l. 223.

We've a war, an' a debt, an' a flag; an' ef this
Ain't to be inderpendunt, why, wut on airth is?
       Ib. No. 4.

Earth's biggest Country's gut her soul
An' risen up Earth's Greatest Nation!
       Ib. No. 7, last lines

But somehow, when the dogs hed gut asleep,
Their love o' mutton beat their love o' sheep.
       Ib. No. 11, l. 291.

Before Man made us citizens, great Nature made us
  men.   *On the Capture of Fugitive Slaves.*

In life's small things be resolute and great
To keep thy muscle trained: know'st thou when Fate
Thy measure takes, or when she'll say to thee,
'I find thee worthy; do this deed for me'? *Epigram.*

They believed—faith, I'm puzzled—I think I may
  call
Their belief a believing in nothing at all,
Or something of that sort; I know they all went
For a general union of total dissent.
       A Fable for Critics, l. 733.

They are slaves who fear to speak
For the fallen and the weak.   *Stanzas on Freedom.*

They are slaves who dare not be
In the right with two or three.   *Ib.*

The birch, most shy and ladylike of trees.
       An Indian-Summer Reverie.

These pearls of thought in Persian gulfs were bred,
Each softly lucent as a rounded moon;
The diver Omar plucked them from their bed,
FitzGerald strung them on an English thread.
       In a Copy of Omar Khayyám.

Once to every man and nation comes the moment to
  decide,
In the strife of Truth with Falsehood, for the good or
  evil side.   *The Present Crisis.*

Truth forever on the scaffold, Wrong forever on the
  throne.   *Ib.*

         Behind the dim unknown,
Standeth God within the shadow, keeping watch
  above his own.   *Ib.*

Then to side with Truth is noble when we share her
 wretched crust,
Ere her cause bring fame and profit, and 'tis prosperous to be just;
Then it is the brave man chooses, while the coward
 stands aside,
Doubting in his abject spirit, till his Lord is crucified.
             Ib.

New occasions teach new duties: Time makes ancient
 good uncouth;
They must upward still, and onward, who would
 keep abreast of Truth.   *Ib.*

May is a pious fraud of the almanac.
       Under the Willows, l. 21.

And what is so rare as a day in June?
 Then, if ever, come perfect days;
 Then Heaven tries earth if it be in tune,
 And over it softly her warm ear lays.
    Vision of Sir Launfal. Pt. I, prelude.

Who gives himself with his alms feeds three,—
 Himself, his hungering neighbour, and Me.
        Ib. pt. II. viii.

A wise scepticism is the first attribute of a good critic.
   Among My Books. Shakespeare Once More.

Let us be of good cheer, however, remembering that
 the misfortunes hardest to bear are those which
 never come.
    Democracy and Addresses. Democracy.

There is no good in arguing with the inevitable. The
 only argument available with an east wind is to put
 on your overcoat.   *Ib.*

JOHN LYDGATE

1370?–1451?

Dowel, Dobet, et Dobest.
  Piers Plowman. MS. Laud 851, passus viii,
  heading.

Woord is but wynd; leff woord and tak the dede.
    Secrees of old Philisoffres, 1224.

Sithe off oure language he [Chaucer] was the lodesterre.   *The Fall of Princes*, prol. l. 252.

Sithe he off Inglissh in makyng was the beste,
Preie onto God to yiue his soule good reste. *Ib.* l. 356.

Comparisouns doon offte gret greuaunce.
       Ib. bk. iii, l. 2188.

Love is mor than gold or gret richesse.
   The Siege of Thebes. Pt. III, l. 2716.

JOHN LYLY

1554?–1606

CAMPASPE:
Were women never so fair, men would be false.
APELLES:
Were women never so false, men would be fond.
        Campaspe, III. iii.

Cupid and my Campaspe play'd
At cards for kisses, Cupid paid;
He stakes his quiver, bow, and arrows,
His mother's doves, and team of sparrows;

Loses them too; then, down he throws
The coral of his lip, the rose
Growing on 's cheek (but none knows how);
With these, the crystal of his brow,
And then the dimple on his chin:
All these did my Campaspe win.
At last he set her both his eyes;
She won, and Cupid blind did rise.
 O Love! has she done this to thee?
 What shall, alas! become of me? *Ib.* III. v.

What bird so sings, yet so does wail?
O 'tis the ravish'd nightingale.
 Jug, jug, jug, jug, tereu, she cries,
 And still her woes at midnight rise. *Ib.* v. i.

How at heaven's gates she claps her wings,
The morn not waking till she sings.   *Ib.*

Be valiant, but not too venturous. Let thy attire be
 comely, but not costly.
   Euphues, Anatomy of Wit (Arber), p. 39.

Night hath a thousand eyes.
    Maides Metamorphose, III. i.

If all the earth were paper white
 And all the sea were ink
'Twere not enough for me to write
 As my poor heart doth think.
  Poems, Early Autobiographical. Lyly's *Works,*
  ed. Bond (1902), vol. iii, p. 452.

HENRY FRANCIS LYTE

1793–1847

Abide with me; fast falls the eventide;
The darkness deepens; Lord, with me abide;
When other helpers fail, and comforts flee,
Help of the helpless, O, abide with me.

Swift to its close ebbs out life's little day;
Earth's joys grow dim, its glories pass away;
Change and decay in all around I see;
O Thou, who changest not, abide with me.
      Remains. Abide with Me.

I fear no foe with Thee at hand to bless;
Ills have no weight, and tears no bitterness;
Where is death's sting? Where, Grave, thy victory?
I triumph still, if Thou abide with me.

Hold Thou Thy Cross before my closing eyes;
Shine through the gloom, and point me to the skies;
Heaven's morning breaks, and earth's vain shadows
 flee;
In life, in death, O Lord, abide with me. *Ib.*

GEORGE LYTTELTON, BARON LYTTELTON

1709–1773

What is your sex's earliest, latest care,
Your heart's supreme ambition?—To be fair.
      Advice to a Lady, l. 17.

Seek to be good, but aim not to be great;
A woman's noblest station is retreat. *Ib.* l. 51.

Where none admire, 'tis useless to excel;
Where none are beaux, 'tis vain to be a belle.
   Soliloquy of a Beauty in the Country.

Tell me, my heart, if this be love?
      Song. When Delia.

EDWARD GEORGE BULWER-LYTTON, BARON LYTTON

1803–1873

Ah, never can fall from the days that have been
A gleam on the years that shall be! *A Lament.*

Take away the sword—
States can be saved without it!
Richelieu, II. ii.

In the lexicon of youth, which Fate reserves
For a bright manhood, there is no such word
As—*fail!* *Ib.*

Here Stanley meets,—how Stanley scorns, the glance!
The brilliant chief, irregularly great,
Frank, haughty, rash,—the Rupert of Debate.
The New Timon, pt. I. vi.

Out-babying Wordsworth and out-glittering Keats.
Ib.

When stars are in the quiet skies,
Then most I pine for thee;
Bend on me, then, thy tender eyes,
As stars look on the sea!
Ernest Maltravers, bk. iii, ch. i.

Poverty has strange bedfellows.
The Caxtons, pt. iv, ch. 4.

Revolutions are not made with rose-water.
The Parisians, bk. v, ch. 7.

There is no man so friendless but what he can find
a friend sincere enough to tell him disagreeable
truths.
What Will He Do With It?, bk. iii, ch. 15
(heading).

EDWARD ROBERT BULWER-LYTTON, EARL OF LYTTON

see

OWEN MEREDITH

THOMAS BABINGTON MACAULAY, BARON MACAULAY

1800–1859

Attend, all ye who list to hear our noble England's
praise;
I tell of the thrice famous deeds she wrought in
ancient days. *The Armada.*

Many a light fishing-bark put out to pry along the
coast,
And with loose rein and bloody spur rode inland
many a post;
With his white hair unbonneted, the stout old sheriff
comes;
Behind him march the halberdiers; before him sound
the drums. *Ib.*

Night sank upon the dusky beach, and on the purple
sea,
Such night in England ne'er had been, nor e'er again
shall be. *Ib.*

The rugged miners poured to war from Mendip's
sunless caves. *Ib.*

The sentinel on Whitehall gate looked forth into the
night. *Ib.*

At once on all her stately gates arose the answering
fires;
At once the wild alarum clashed from all her reeling
spires. *Ib.*

And broader still became the blaze, and louder still
the din,
As fast from every village round the horse came spurring in;
And eastward straight from wild Blackheath the warlike errand went,
And roused in many an ancient hall the gallant squires
of Kent. *Ib.*

Till Belvoir's lordly terraces the sign to Lincoln sent,
And Lincoln sped the message on o'er the wide vale
of Trent;
Till Skiddaw saw the fire that burned on Gaunt's em-
battled pile,
And the red glare on Skiddaw roused the burghers of
Carlisle. *Ib.*

Obadiah Bind-their-kings-in-chains-and-their-
nobles-with-links-of-iron. *The Battle of Naseby.*

Oh, wherefore come ye forth in triumph from the
north,
With your hands, and your feet, and your raiment
all red?
And wherefore doth your rout send forth a joyous
shout?
And whence be the grapes of the wine-press which
ye tread? *Ib.*

And the Man of Blood was there, with his long
essenced hair,
And Astley, and Sir Marmaduke, and Rupert of the
Rhine. *Ib.*

For God! for the Cause! for the Church! for the
laws!
For Charles King of England, and Rupert of the
Rhine! *Ib.*

The furious German comes, with his clarions and
his drums. *Ib.*

He looked upon his people, and a tear was in his eye;
He looked upon the traitors, and his glance was stern
and high. *Ivry.*

'Press where ye see my white plume shine, amidst the
ranks of war,
And be your oriflamme today the helmet of Navarre.'
Ib.

Their ranks are breaking like thin clouds before a
Biscay gale. *Ib.*

To my true king I offer'd free from stain
Courage and faith; vain faith, and courage vain.
A Jacobite's Epitaph.

And pined by Arno for my lovelier Tees. *Ib.*

By those white cliffs I never more must see,
By that dear language which I spake like thee,
Forget all feuds, and shed one English tear
O'er English dust. A broken heart lies here. *Ib.*

Lars Porsena of Clusium
  By the nine gods he swore
That the great house of Tarquin
  Should suffer wrong no more.
By the Nine Gods he swore it,
  And named a trysting day,
And bade his messengers ride forth,
  East and west and south and north,
    To summon his array.
          Lays of Ancient Rome. Horatius, i.

From lordly Volaterræ,
  Where scowls the far-famed hold
Piled by the hands of giants
  For godlike kings of old.   *Ib.* iv.

The harvests of Arretium,
  This year, old men shall reap.
This year, young boys in Umbro
  Shall plunge the struggling sheep;
And in the vats of Luna,
  This year, the must shall foam
Round the white feet of laughing girls
  Whose sires have marched to Rome.   *Ib.* viii.

A proud man was Lars Porsena
  Upon the trysting day.   *Ib.* xi.

And with a mighty following
  To join the muster came
The Tusculan Mamilius,
  Prince of the Latian name.   *Ib.* xii.

And plainly and more plainly
  Now might the burghers know,
By port and vest, by horse and crest,
  Each warlike Lucumo.   *Ib.* xxiii.

But the Consul's brow was sad,
  And the Consul's speech was low,
And darkly looked he at the wall,
  And darkly at the foe.   *Ib.* xxvi.

Then out spake brave Horatius,
  The Captain of the Gate:
'To every man upon this earth
  Death cometh soon or late.
And how can man die better
  Than facing fearful odds,
For the ashes of his fathers,
  And the temples of his Gods?'   *Ib.* xxvii.

To save them from false Sextus
  That wrought the deed of shame.   *Ib.* xxviii.

'Now who will stand on either hand,
  And keep the bridge with me?'   *Ib.* xxix.

And straight against that great array
  Forth went the dauntless Three.   *Ib.* xxxi.

Then none was for a party;
  Then all were for the state;
Then the great man helped the poor,
  And the poor man loved the great:
Then lands were fairly portioned;
  Then spoils were fairly sold:
The Romans were like brothers
  In the brave days of old.   *Ib.* xxxii.

Was none who would be foremost
  To lead such dire attack;
But those behind cried 'Forward!'
  And those before cried 'Back!'   *Ib.* l.

Thrice looked he at the city;
  Thrice looked he at the dead;
And thrice came on in fury,
  And thrice turned back in dread.   *Ib.* lii.

'Come back, come back, Horatius!'
  Loud cried the Fathers all.
'Back, Lartius! back, Herminius!
  Back, ere the ruin fall!'   *Ib.* liii.

But when they turned their faces,
  And on the farther shore
Saw brave Horatius stand alone,
  They would have crossed once more.   *Ib.* liv.

Round turned he, as not deigning
  Those craven ranks to see;
Nought spake he to Lars Porsena,
  To Sextus nought spoke he;
But he saw on Palatinus
  The white porch of his home!
And he spake to the noble river
  That rolls by the towers of Rome.   *Ib.* lviii.

'Oh, Tiber! father Tiber!
  To whom the Romans pray,
A Roman's life, a Roman's arms,
  Take thou in charge this day!'   *Ib.* lix.

And even the ranks of Tuscany
  Could scarce forbear to cheer.   *Ib.* lx.

Never, I ween, did swimmer,
  In such an evil case,
Struggle through such a raging flood
  Safe to the landing place.   *Ib.* lxii.

'Heaven help him!' quoth Lars Porsena,
  'And bring him safe to shore;
For such a gallant feat of arms
  Was never seen before.'   *Ib.* lxiii.

When the oldest cask is opened,
  And the largest lamp is lit.   *Ib.* lxix.

With weeping and with laughter
  Still is the story told,
How well Horatius kept the bridge
  In the brave days of old.   *Ib.* lxx.

In lordly Lacedaemon,
  The city of two kings.
          The Battle of Lake Regillus, ii.

Those trees in whose dim shadow
  The ghastly priest doth reign,
The priest who slew the slayer,
  And shall himself be slain.   *Ib.* x.

Herminius glared on Sextus.   *Ib.* xv.

Ah! woe is me for the good house
  That loves the people well!   *Ib.* xvii.

For aye Valerius loathed the wrong,
  And aye upheld the right.   *Ib.* xviii.

Away, away went Auster
  Like an arrow from the bow:
Black Auster was the fleetest steed
  From Aufidus to Po.   *Ib.* xxv.

One of us two, Herminius,
  Shall never more go home.
I will lay on for Tusculum
  And lay thou on for Rome!   *Ib.* xxvii.

Herminius smote Mamilius
  Through breast-plate and through breast;
And fast flowed out the purple blood
  Over the purple vest.
Mamilius smote Herminius
  Through headpiece and through head;
And side by side those chiefs of pride
  Together fell down dead.   *Ib.* xxviii.

The pass was steep and rugged,
  The wolves they howled and whined;
But he ran like a whirlwind up the pass,
  And he left the wolves behind.   *Ib.* xxix.

'The furies of thy brother
  With me and mine abide,
If one of your accursed house
  Upon black Auster ride!'   *Ib.* xxx.

So spake he; and was buckling
  Tighter black Auster's band,
When he was aware of a princely pair
  That rode at his right hand.
So like they were, no mortal
  Might one from other know:
White as snow their armour was:
  Their steeds were white as snow.   *Ib.* xxxii.

And all who saw them trembled,
  And pale grew every cheek.   *Ib.* xxxiii.

Let no man stop to plunder,
  But slay, and slay, and slay;
The Gods who live for ever
  Are on our side to-day.   *Ib.* xxxv.

And fliers and pursuers
  Were mingled in a mass;
And far away the battle
  Went roaring through the pass.   *Ib.* xxxvi.

These be the great Twin Brethren
  To whom the Dorians pray.   *Ib.* xl.

      Thou, through all change,
Fix thy firm gaze on virtue and on me.
         Lines Written in August.

Ye diners-out from whom we guard our spoons.
  Political Georgics. See his letter to Hannah
  Macaulay, 29 June 1831.

Knowledge advances by steps, and not by leaps.
    Essays and Biographies. History.

The business of everybody is the business of nobody.
  *Historical Essays Contributed to the 'Edinburgh
  Review'.* Hallam's *Constitutional History*
  (Sept. 1828).

The gallery in which the reporters sit has become a
  fourth estate of the realm.   *Ib.*

He knew that the essence of war is violence, and that
  moderation in war is imbecility. [John Hampden.]
  Ib. Lord Nugent's Memorials of Hampden
  (Dec. 1831).

The reluctant obedience of distant provinces generally costs more than it [the territory] is worth.
  Ib. Lord Mahon's War of the Succession (Jan.
  1833).

The history of England is emphatically the history of
  progress.
  *Ib. Sir J. Mackintosh's History of the Revolu-
  tion* (July 1835).

The rising hope of those stern and unbending Tories.
  Ib. Gladstone on Church and State (April 1839).

Every schoolboy knows who imprisoned Montezuma,
  and who strangled Atahualpa.
    Ib. Lord Clive (Jan. 1840).

They [the Nabobs] raised the price of everything in
  their neighbourhood, from fresh eggs to rotten
  boroughs.   *Ib.*

When some traveller from New Zealand shall, in the
  midst of a vast solitude, take his stand on a broken
  arch of London Bridge to sketch the ruins of St.
  Paul's.   *Ib. Von Ranke* (Oct. 1840).

The Chief Justice was rich, quiet, and infamous.
    Ib. Warren Hastings (Oct. 1841).

The great Proconsul.   *Ib.*

In order that he might rob a neighbour whom he had
  promised to defend, black men fought on the coast
  of Coromandel, and red men scalped each other by
  the Great Lakes of North America.
    Ib. Frederic the Great (April 1842).

We hardly know any instance of the strength and
  weakness of human nature so striking, and so
  grotesque, as the character of this haughty, vigilant,
  resolute, sagacious blue-stocking, half Mithridates
  and half Trissotin, bearing up against a world in
  arms, with an ounce of poison in one pocket and a
  quire of bad verses in the other. [Frederick.] *Ib.*

Lues Boswelliana, or disease of admiration.
    Ib. Earl of Chatham (Jan. 1834).

The dust and silence of the upper shelf.
    *Literary Essays Contributed to the 'Edinburgh
  Review'. Milton* (Aug. 1825).

As civilization advances, poetry almost necessarily declines.   *Ib.*

Perhaps no person can be a poet, or can even enjoy
  poetry, without a certain unsoundness of mind. *Ib.*

Nobles by the right of an earlier creation, and priests
  by the imposition of a mightier hand.   *Ib.*

That propensity which, for want of a better name, we
  will venture to christen Boswellism.   *Ib.*

Out of his surname they have coined an epithet for a
  knave, and out of his Christian name a synonym
  for the Devil.   *Ib. Machiavelli* (March 1827).

Nothing is so useless as a general maxim.   *Ib.*

We have heard it said that five per cent. is the natural
  interest of money.
    Ib. Southey's Colloquies (Jan. 1830).

His writing bears the same relation to poetry which
  a Turkey carpet bears to a picture. There are
  colours in the Turkey carpet out of which a picture
  might be made. There are words in Mr. Montgomery's writing which, when disposed in certain
  orders and combinations, have made, and will
  make again, good poetry. But, as they now stand,
  they seem to be put together on principle in such
  a manner as to give no image of anything 'in the
  heavens above, or in the earth beneath, or in the
  waters under the earth.'
    Ib. Mr. Robert Montgomery's Poems (April
  1830).

The use of a mirror, we submit, is not to be painted
  upon.   *Ib.*

But Mr. Robert Montgomery's readers must take such grammar as they can get, and be thankful.   *Ib.*

We take this to be, on the whole, the worst similitude in the world. In the first place, no stream meanders, or can possibly meander, level with its fount. In the next place, if streams did meander level with their founts, no two motions can be less like each other than that of meandering level and that of mounting upwards.   *Ib.*

His theory is therefore this, that God made the thunder, but that the lightning made itself.   *Ib.*

He had a head which statuaries loved to copy, and a foot the deformity of which the beggars in the street mimicked.
    Ib. Moore's Life of Lord Byron (June 1830).

We know no spectacle so ridiculous as the British public in one of its periodical fits of morality.   *Ib.*

We prefer a gipsy by Reynolds to his Majesty's head on a sign-post.   *Ib.*

The world, we believe, is pretty well agreed in thinking that the shorter a prize poem is, the better.   *Ib.*

From the poetry of Lord Byron they drew a system of ethics, compounded of misanthropy and voluptuousness, a system in which the two great commandments were, to hate your neighbour, and to love your neighbour's wife.   *Ib.*

Very few and very weary are those who are in at the death of the Blatant Beast.
    Ib. Southey's Edition of Pilgrim's Progress (Dec. 1830).

What schoolboy of fourteen is ignorant of this remarkable circumstance?
    Ib. Sir William Temple (Oct. 1838).

There is a vile phrase of which bad historians are exceedingly fond, 'the dignity of history'.   *Ib.*

The conformation of his mind was such that whatever was little seemed to him great, and whatever was great seemed to him little.
    Ib. Horace Walpole (Oct. 1833).

With the dead there is no rivalry. In the dead there is no change. Plato is never sullen. Cervantes is never petulant. Demosthenes never comes unseasonably. Dante never stays too long. No difference of political opinion can alienate Cicero. No heresy can excite the horror of Bossuet.
    Ib. Lord Bacon.

An acre in Middlesex is better than a principality in Utopia.   *Ib.* (July 1837).

The checkered spectacle of so much glory and so much shame.   *Ib.*

The Life of Johnson is assuredly a great, a very great work. Homer is not more decidedly the first of heroic poets, Shakespeare is not more decidedly the first of dramatists, Demosthenes is not more decidedly the first of orators, than Boswell is the first of biographers.
    Ib. Boswell's Life of Johnson (Sept. 1831).

They knew luxury; they knew beggary; but they never knew comfort.   *Ib.*

In the foreground is that strange figure which is as familiar to us as the figures of those among whom we have been brought up, the gigantic body, the huge massy face, seamed with the scars of disease, the brown coat, the black worsted stockings, the grey wig with the scorched foretop, the dirty hands, the nails bitten and pared to the quick.   *Ib.*

Like Sir Condy Rackrent in the tale, she survived her own wake, and overheard the judgment of posterity.   *Ib. Madame D'Arblay* (Jan. 1843).

A sort of broken Johnsonese.   *Ib.*

He was a rake among scholars, and a scholar among rakes. [Richard Steele.]
    Ib. Aikin's Life of Addison (July 1843).

The old philosopher is still among us in the brown coat with the metal buttons and the shirt which ought to be at wash, blinking, puffing, rolling his head, drumming with his fingers, tearing his meat like a tiger, and swallowing his tea in oceans.
    Life of Johnson (ad fin.).

I shall cheerfully bear the reproach of having descended below the dignity of history.
    History of England, vol. i, ch. 1.

Thus our democracy was, from an early period, the most aristocratic, and our aristocracy the most democratic in the world.   *Ib.*

Persecution produced its natural effect on them. It found them a sect; it made them a faction.   *Ib.*

It was a crime in a child to read by the bedside of a sick parent one of those beautiful collects which had soothed the griefs of forty generations of Christians.   *Ib.* ch. 2.

The Puritan hated bear-baiting, not because it gave pain to the bear, but because it gave pleasure to the spectators.   *Ib.*

There were gentlemen and there were seamen in the navy of Charles the Second. But the seamen were not gentlemen; and the gentlemen were not seamen.   *Ib.* ch. 3.

The English Bible, a book which, if everything else in our language should perish, would alone suffice to show the whole extent of its beauty and power.
    Edinburgh Review, Jan. 1828. On John Dryden.

His imagination resembled the wings of an ostrich. It enabled him to run, though not to soar.   *Ib.*

The object of oratory alone is not truth, but persuasion.   *Works* (1898), vol. xi. *Essay on Athenian Orators.*

Dark and terrible beyond any season within my remembrance of political affairs was the day of their flight. Far darker and far more terrible will be the day of their return. [The Tory Government, defeated in Nov. 1830.]   *Speech, 20 Sept. 1831.*

Thank you, madam, the agony is abated. [Reply, aged four.]
    Trevelyan's Life and Letters of Macaulay, ch. 1.

I shall not be satisfied unless I produce something which shall for a few days supersede the last fashionable novel on the tables of young ladies.
    Ib. ch. 13.

JOSEPH McCARTHY

You made me love you,
I didn't want to do it.   *You Made Me Love You.*

JOHN McCRAE

d. 1918

Take up our quarrel with the foe:
To you from falling hands we throw
  The torch; be yours to hold it high.
If ye break faith with us who die
We shall not sleep, though poppies grow
  In Flanders fields.
    In Flanders Fields. (*Punch*, vol. cxlix, *8 Dec. 1915.*)

GEORGE MACDONALD

1824–1905

Where did you come from, baby dear?
Out of the everywhere into here.
    At the Back of the North Wind, xxxiii, *Song.*

Where did you get your eyes so blue?
Out of the sky as I came through.   *Ib.*

Here lie I, Martin Elginbrodde:
Hae mercy o' my soul, Lord God;
As I wad do, were I Lord God,
And ye were Martin Elginbrodde.
    David Elginbrod, bk. i, ch. 13.

Alas, how easily things go wrong!
A sigh too much, or a kiss too long,
And there follows a mist and a weeping rain,
And life is never the same again.
    Phantastes: Down the Lane.

They all were looking for a king
To slay their foes, and lift them high;
Thou cam'st, a little baby thing,
That made a woman cry.   *That Holy Thing.*

CHARLES MACKAY

1814–1889

Cheer! Boys, cheer!   *Title of Song.*

There's a good time coming, boys,
  A good time coming.   *The Good Time Coming.*

Old Tubal Cain was a man of might
In the days when earth was young.   *Tubal Cain.*

SIR JAMES MACKINTOSH

1765–1832

Men are never so good or so bad as their opinions.
    Ethical Philosophy, section 6. *Bentham.*

The frivolous work of polished idleness.
    Ib. Remarks on Thomas Brown.

The Commons, faithful to their system, remained in
  a wise and masterly inactivity.
    Vindiciæ Gallicæ, sec. 1.

MURDOCH McLENNAN

fl. 1715

There's some say that we wan, some say that they wan,
  Some say that nane wan at a', man;
But one thing I'm sure, that at Sheriffmuir
  A battle there was which I saw, man:
And we ran, and they ran, and they ran, and we ran,
  And we ran; and they ran awa', man!
    Sheriffmuir. Roxburghe Ballads (1889), vol. vi.
    In Hogg's *Jacobite Relics*, 1821, vol. ii, the last
    line is: 'But Florence ran fastest of a', man.'
    (Florence was the Marquis of Huntley's horse.)

NORMAN MACLEOD

1812–1872

Courage, brother! do not stumble,
  Though thy path is dark as night;
There's a star to guide the humble:
  'Trust in God, and do the Right.'
    Book of Praise. Courage, Brother.

LEONARD McNALLY

1752–1820

This lass so neat, with smiles so sweet,
Has won my right good-will,
I'd crowns resign to call thee mine,
Sweet lass of Richmond Hill.
    The Lass of Richmond Hill. E. Duncan,
    Minstrelsy of England (1905), i. 254. Attr. also
    to W. Upton in *Oxford Song Book*, and to
    W. Hudson in Baring-Gould, *English Minstrel-
    sie* (1895), iii. 54.

SAMUEL MADDEN

1687–1765

Words are men's daughters, but God's sons are things.
    Boulter's Monument, l. 377.

ALFRED THAYER MAHAN

1840–1914

Those far distant, storm-beaten ships, upon which
  the Grand Army never looked, stood between it
  and the dominion of the world.
    *The Influence of Sea Power upon the French
    Revolution and Empire 1793–1812* (1892),
    ii. 118.

FRANCIS SYLVESTER MAHONY

see FATHER PROUT

SIR HENRY JAMES SUMNER MAINE

1822–1888

Except the blind forces of Nature, nothing moves in
  this world which is not Greek in its origin.
    Rede Lecture, 1875. Village Communities.

DAVID MALLET

1705?–1765

O grant me, Heaven, a middle state,
Neither too humble nor too great;
More than enough for nature's ends,
With something left to treat my friends.

Imitation of Horace, bk. ii, sat. vi.

SIR THOMAS MALORY

fl. 1470

It is notoriously known through the universal world that there be nine worthy and the best that ever were. That is to wit three paynims, three Jews, and three Christian men. As for the paynims they were ... the first Hector of Troy, ... the second Alexander the Great; and the third Julius Caesar. ... As for the three Jews ... the first was Duke Joshua ...; the second David, King of Jerusalem; and the third Judas Maccabaeus.... And sith the said Incarnation ... was first the noble Arthur.... The second was Charlemagne or Charles the Great ...; and the third and last was Godfrey of Bouillon.

> *Le Morte D'Arthur*, vol. I. *Caxton's Original Preface.*

I, according to my copy, have done set it in imprint, to the intent that noble men may see and learn the noble acts of chivalry, the gentle and virtuous deeds that some knights used in those days. *Ib.*

Wherein they shall find many joyous and pleasant histories, and noble and renowned acts of humanity, gentleness, and chivalries. For herein may be seen noble chivalry, courtesy, humanity, friendliness, hardiness, love, friendship, cowardice, murder, hate, virtue, and sin. Do after the good and leave the evil, and it shall bring you to good fame and renown. *Ib.*

Me repenteth, said Merlin; because of the death of that lady thou shalt strike a stroke most dolorous that ever man struck, except the stroke of our Lord, for thou shalt hurt the truest knight and the man of most worship that now liveth, and through that stroke three kingdoms shall be in great poverty, misery and wretchedness twelve years, and the knight shall not be whole of that wound for many years. *Ib.* bk. II, ch. 8.

What, nephew, said the king, is the wind in that door? *Ib.* bk. VII, ch. 34.

The questing beast. *Ib.* bk. IX, ch. 12.

God defend me, said Dinadan, for the joy of love is too short, and the sorrow thereof, and what cometh thereof, dureth over long.

Ib. bk. x, ch. 56.

It is his day, said Dinadan. *Ib.* ch. 70.

Nay, by my knighthood, said Palomides, I never espied that ever she loved me more than all the world, nor never had I pleasure with her, but the last day she gave me the greatest rebuke that ever I had, the which shall never go from my heart.

Ib. ch. 82.

Fair lord, salute me to my lord, Sir Launcelot, my father, and as soon as ye see him, bid him remember of this unstable world. *Ib.* bk. XVII, ch. 22.

Thus endeth the story of the Sangreal, that was briefly drawn out of French into English, the which is a story chronicled for one of the truest and the holiest that is in this world.

Ib. ch. 23, end.

And thus it passed on from Candlemass until after Easter, that the month of May was come, when every lusty heart beginneth to blossom, and to bring forth fruit; for like as herbs and trees bring forth fruit and flourish in May, in likewise every lusty heart that is in any manner a lover, springeth and flourisheth in lusty deeds.

Ib. bk. XVIII, ch. 25.

Therefore all ye that be lovers call unto your remembrance the month of May, like as did Queen Guenevere, for whom I make here a little mention, that while she lived she was a true lover, and therefore she had a good end. *Ib.*

Through this man and me hath all this war been wrought, and the death of the most noblest knights of the world; for through our love that we have loved together is my most noble lord slain. *Ib.* bk. XXI, ch. 9.

Therefore, Sir Launcelot, I require thee and beseech thee heartily, for all the love that ever was betwixt us, that thou never see me more in the visage. *Ib.*

Wherefore, madam, I pray you kiss me and never no more. Nay, said the queen, that shall I never do, but abstain you from such works: and they departed. But there was never so hard an hearted man but he would have wept to see the dolour that they made. *Ib.* ch. 10.

And Sir Launcelot awoke, and went and took his horse, and rode all that day and all night in a forest, weeping. *Ib.*

Then Sir Launcelot saw her visage, but he wept not greatly, but sighed. *Ib.* ch. 11.

Said Sir Ector ... Sir Launcelot ... thou wert never matched of earthly knights' hand; and thou wert the courteoust knight that ever bare shield; and thou wert the truest friend to thy lover that ever bestrad horse; and thou wert the truest lover of a sinful man that ever loved woman; and thou wert the kindest man that ever struck with sword; and thou wert the goodliest person that ever came among press of knights; and thou wert the meekest man and the gentlest that ever ate in hall among ladies; and thou wert the sternest knight to thy mortal foe that ever put spear in the rest.

Ib. ch. 13.

W. R. MANDALE

19th cent.

Up and down the City Road,
In and out the Eagle,
That's the way the money goes—
Pop goes the weasel!

Pop Goes the Weasel.

JAMES CLARENCE MANGAN
1803–1849

There's wine from the royal Pope
  Upon the ocean green;
And Spanish ale shall give you hope,
  My Dark Rosaleen!   *Dark Rosaleen.*

Your holy delicate white hands
  Shall girdle me with steel.   *Ib.*

The fair hills of Eiré, O.   *Title of Poem.*

Roll forth, my song, like the rushing river.
    The Nameless One.

He, too, had tears for all souls in trouble
  Here, and in hell.   *Ib.*

MARY DE LA RIVIERE MANLEY
1663–1724

No time like the present.   *The Lost Lover,* IV. i.

HORACE MANN
1796–1859

The object of punishment is, prevention from evil; it never can be made impulsive to good.
    Lectures and Reports on Education, 1867, lecture vii.

Lost, yesterday, somewhere between Sunrise and Sunset, two golden hours, each set with sixty diamond minutes. No reward is offered, for they are gone forever.   *Lost, Two Golden Hours.*

LORD JOHN MANNERS, DUKE OF RUTLAND
1818–1906

Let wealth and commerce, laws and learning die,
But leave us still our old nobility!
    England's Trust, pt. III, l. 227.

WILLIAM MURRAY, EARL OF MANSFIELD
1705–1793

Consider what you think justice requires, and decide accordingly. But never give your reasons; for your judgement will probably be right, but your reasons will certainly be wrong.
    Advice. Campbell's *Lives of the Chief Justices,* 1874, vol. iv, p. 26.

RICHARD MANT
1776–1848

Bright the vision that delighted
Once the sight of Judah's seer.
    Ancient Hymns. Bright the Vision.

WILLIAM LEARNED MARCY
1786–1857

To the victor belong the spoils of the enemy.
    Parton's *Life of Jackson* (1860), vol. iii, p. 378.

EDWIN MARKHAM
1852–1940

Bowed by the weight of centuries he leans
Upon his hoe and gazes on the ground,
The emptiness of ages in his face,
And on his back the burden of the world.
    The Man with the Hoe.

CHRISTOPHER MARLOWE
1564–1593

My men, like satyrs grazing on the lawns,
Shall with their goat feet dance an antic hay.
    Edward II, I. i. 59.

For when we hear one rack the name of God,
Abjure the Scriptures, and his Saviour Christ,
We fly, in hope to get his glorious soul.
    Faustus, i. 282.

MEPHISTOPHELES:
O by aspiring pride and insolence,
For which God threw him from the face of heaven.
FAUSTUS:
And what are you that live with Lucifer?
MEPHISTOPHELES:
Unhappy spirits that fell with Lucifer,
Conspired against our God with Lucifer,
And are for ever damned with Lucifer.   *Ib.* l. 303.

Why this is hell, nor am I out of it:
Thinkst thou that I who saw the face of God,
And tasted the eternal joys of heaven,
Am not tormented with ten thousand hells
In being deprived of everlasting bliss?   *Ib.* l. 312.

           When all the world dissolves,
And every creature shall be purified,
All places shall be hell that are not heaven.   *Ib.* l. 556.

Was this the face that launch'd a thousand ships,
And burnt the topless towers of Ilium?
Sweet Helen, make me immortal with a kiss!
Her lips suck forth my soul: see, where it flies!
Come Helen, come give me my soul again.
Here will I dwell, for heaven be in these lips,
And all is dross that is not Helena.   *Ib.* l. 1328.

O thou art fairer than the evening air,
Clad in the beauty of a thousand stars,
Brighter art thou than flaming Jupiter,
When he appeared to hapless Semele,
More lovely than the monarch of the sky
In wanton Arethusa's azured arms,
And none but thou shalt be my paramour.   *Ib.* l. 1341.

Now hast thou but one bare hour to live,
And then thou must be damned perpetually;
Stand still you ever-moving spheres of heaven,
That time may cease, and midnight never come.
    Ib. l. 1420.

O lente, lente currite noctis equis:
The stars move still, time runs, the clock will strike,
The devil will come, and Faustus must be damn'd.
O I'll leap up to my God: who pulls me down?
See see where Christ's blood streams in the firmament.
One drop would save my soul, half a drop, ah my Christ.   *Ib.* l. 1428.

Ah Pythagoras metempsychosis.   *Ib.* l. 1461.

Cut is the branch that might have grown full straight,
And burnèd is Apollo's laurel bough,
That sometime grew within this learned man.
Ib. l. 1478.

It lies not in our power to love, or hate,
For will in us is over-rul'd by fate.
When two are stripped, long ere the course begin,
We wish that one should lose, the other win;
And one especially do we affect
Of two gold ingots, like in each respect.
The reason no man knows; let it suffice,
What we behold is censured by our eyes.
Where both deliberate, the love is slight;
Who ever loved that loved not at first sight?
Hero and Leander. First Sestiad, l. 167.

I count religion but a childish toy,
And hold there is no sin but ignorance.
The Jew of Malta, l. 14.

And as their wealth increases, so enclose
Infinite riches in a little room. *Ib.* l. 71.

As for myself, I walke abroad a nights
And kill sick people groaning under walls:
Sometimes I go about and poison wells. *Ib.* l. 939.

Come live with me and be my love;
And we will all the pleasures prove
That hills and valleys, dales and fields,
Woods or steepy mountain yields.
The Passionate Shepherd to his Love.

By shallow rivers to whose falls
Melodious birds sing madrigals. *Ib.*

And I will make thee beds of roses
And a thousand fragrant posies. *Ib.*

Jigging veins of rhyming mother wits.
Conquests of Tamburlaine, prologue.

Zenocrate, lovelier than the Love of Jove,
Brighter than is the silver Rhodope,
Fairer than whitest snow on Scythian hills.
Ib. pt. 1, l. 283.

Our swords shall play the orators for us. *Ib.* l. 328.

With Nature's pride, and richest furniture,
His looks do menace heaven and dare the Gods.
Ib. l. 351.

His deep affections make him passionate. *Ib.* l. 359.

These are the men that all the world admires.
Ib. l. 418.

Accurst be he that first invented war. *Ib.* l. 664.

Is it not passing brave to be a King,
And ride in triumph through Persepolis? *Ib.* l. 758.

Nature that fram'd us of four elements,
Warring within our breasts for regiment,
Doth teach us all to have aspiring minds:
Our souls, whose faculties can comprehend
The wondrous Architecture of the world:
And measure every wand'ring planet's course,
Still climbing after knowledge infinite,
And always moving as the restless Spheres,
Will us to wear ourselves and never rest,
Until we reach the ripest fruit of all,
That perfect bliss and sole felicity,
The sweet fruition of an earthly crown. *Ib.* l. 869.

Virtue is the fount whence honour springs. *Ib.* l. 1769.

Ah fair Zenocrate, divine Zenocrate,
Fair is too foul an epithet for thee. *Ib.* l. 1916.

What is beauty saith my sufferings then?
If all the pens that ever poets held,
Had fed the feeling of their masters' thoughts,
And every sweetness that inspir'd their hearts,
Their minds, and muses on admired themes:
If all the heavenly quintessence they still
From their immortal flowers of Poesy,
Wherein as in a mirror we perceive
The highest reaches of a human wit.
If these had made one poem's period
And all combin'd in beauty's worthiness,
Yet should there hover in their restless heads,
One thought, one grace, one wonder at the least,
Which into words no virtue can digest. *Ib.* l. 1941.

Now walk the angels on the walls of heaven,
As sentinels to warn th' immortal souls,
To entertain divine Zenocrate. *Ib.* pt. II, l. 2983.

Yet let me kiss my Lord before I die,
And let me die with kissing of my Lord. *Ib.* l. 3037.

Helen, whose beauty summoned Greece to arms,
And drew a thousand ships to Tenedos. *Ib.* l. 3055.

More childish valourous than manly wise. *Ib.* l. 3690.

Holla, ye pampered Jades of Asia:
What, can ye draw but twenty miles a day?
Ib. l. 3980.

I'm arm'd with more than complete steel—
The justice of my quarrel.
Lust's Dominion, IV, iii. Play probably not by Marlowe.

SHACKERLEY MARMION
1603–1639
Familiarity begets boldness. *The Antiquary*, Act I.

Great joys, like griefs, are silent.
Holland's Leaguer, v. I.

DONALD ROBERT PERRY MARQUIS
1878–1937
The great open spaces
where cats are cats.
Archy and Mehitabel, xiv. *Mehitabel Has an Adventure*, l. 100.

FREDERICK MARRYAT
1792–1848
There's no getting blood out of a turnip.
Japhet in Search of a Father, ch. 4.

'If you please, ma'am, it was a very little one.' [The nurse excusing her illegitimate baby.]
Midshipman Easy, ch. 3.

All zeal . . . All zeal, Mr. Easy. *Ib.* ch. 9.

As savage as a bear with a sore head.
The King's Own, ch. 26.

I never knows the children. It's just six of one and half-a-dozen of the other. *The Pirate*, ch. 4.

I think it much better that ... every man paddle his
own canoe.   *Settlers in Canada*, ch. 8.

JOHN MARSTON
1575?-1634.

Who winks and shuts his apprehension up.
    Antonio's Revenge, prologue.

ANDREW MARVELL
1620-1678

Thrice happy he who, not mistook,
Hath read in Nature's mystic book.
    Upon Appleton House. To My Lord Fairfax,
lxxiii.

Where the remote Bermudas ride
In th' ocean's bosom unespied.   *Bermudas.*

           Orange bright,
Like golden lamps in a green night.   *Ib.*

And makes the hollow seas, that roar,
Proclaim the ambergris on shore.
He cast (of which we rather boast)
The Gospel's pearls upon our coast.   *Ib.*

Echo beyond the Mexique Bay.   *Ib.*

Had we but world enough, and time,
This coyness Lady were no crime.
We would sit down, and think which way
To walk, and pass our long love's day.
    To His Coy Mistress.

           I would
Love you ten years before the Flood:
And you should if you please refuse
Till the conversion of the Jews.
My vegetable love should grow
Vaster than empires, and more slow.   *Ib.*

But at my back I always hear
Time's wingèd chariot hurrying near.
And yonder all before us lie
Deserts of vast eternity.
Thy beauty shall no more be found;
Nor, in thy marble vault, shall sound
My echoing song: then worms shall try
That long preserved virginity:
And your quaint honour turn to dust;
And into ashes all my lust.
The grave's a fine and private place,
But none I think do there embrace.   *Ib.*

My love is of a birth as rare
As 'tis for object strange and high:
It was begotten by despair
Upon impossibility.

Magnanimous Despair alone
Could show me so divine a thing,
Where feeble Hope could ne'er have flown
But vainly flapt its tinsel wing.   *Definition of Love.*

As lines so loves oblique may well
Themselves in every angle greet
But ours so truly parallel,
Though infinite can never meet.

Therefore the love which us doth bind,
But Fate so enviously debars,
Is the conjunction of the mind,
And opposition of the stars.   *Ib.*

Earth cannot shew so brave a sight
As when a single soul does fence
The batteries of alluring sense,
And Heaven views it with delight.
    *Dialogue between the Resolved Soul and Created
Pleasure.*

All this fair, and soft, and sweet,
Which scatteringly doth shine,
Shall within one Beauty meet,
And she be only thine.   *Ib.*

And want new worlds to buy.   *Ib.*

Not full sails hasting loaden home,
Nor the chaste lady's pregnant womb,
Nor Cynthia teeming shows so fair,
As two eyes swoln with weeping are.   *Eyes and Tears*

Thus let your streams o'erflow your springs,
Till eyes and tears be the same things:
And each the other's difference bears;
These weeping eyes, those seeing tears.   *Ib.*

They neither build the Temple in their days,
Nor matter for succeeding founders raise.
    *The First Anniversary of the Government under
Oliver Cromwell*, l. 33.

Choosing each stone, and poising every weight,
Trying the measures of the breadth and height;
Here pulling down, and there erecting new,
Founding a firm state by proportions true.   *Ib.* l. 245

How vainly men themselves amaze
To win the palm, the oak, or bays;
And their uncessant labours see
Crown'd from some single herb or tree,
Whose short and narrow vergèd shade
Does prudently their toils upbraid;
While all flowers and all trees do close
To weave the garlands of repose.   *The Garden*

Fair quiet, have I found thee here,
And Innocence thy Sister dear!   *Ib.*

Society is all but rude,
To this delicious solitude.   *Ib.*

The Gods, that mortal beauty chase,
Still in a tree did end their race.
Apollo hunted Daphne so,
Only that she might laurel grow.
And Pan did after Syrinx speed,
Not as a nymph, but for a reed.   *Ib.*

What wond'rous life is this I lead!
Ripe apples drop about my head;
The luscious clusters of the vine
Upon my mouth do crush their wine;
The nectarine and curious peach,
Into my hands themselves do reach;
Stumbling on melons, as I pass,
Insnar'd with flow'rs, I fall on grass.   *Ib.*

Meanwhile the mind, from pleasure less,
Withdraws into its happiness.   *Ib.*

Annihilating all that's made
To a green thought in a green shade.   *Ib.*

lere at the fountain's sliding foot,
)r at some fruit-tree's mossy root,
Casting the body's vest aside,
My soul into the boughs does glide:
There like a bird it sits, and sings,
Then whets, and combs its silver wings;
And, till prepar'd for longer flight,
Waves in its plumes the various light.   *Ib.*

uch was that happy garden-state,
While man there walk'd without a mate.   *Ib.*

But 'twas beyond a mortal's share
To wander solitary there:
Two Paradises 'twere in one
To live in Paradise alone.   *Ib.*

Of a tall stature and of sable hue,
Much like the son of Kish that lofty Jew,
Twelve years complete he suffer'd in exile
And kept his father's asses all the while.
    An Historical Poem.

He nothing common did or mean
Upon that memorable scene:
But with his keener eye
The axe's edge did try.
    Horatian Ode upon Cromwell's Return from Ireland, l. 57.

But bowed his comely head,
own as upon a bed.   *Ib.*

And now the Irish are ashamed
To see themselves in one year tamed:
So much one man can do
That does both act and know.   *Ib. l. 75.*

e living lamps, by whose dear light
The nightingale does sit so late,
And studying all the summer night,
Her matchless songs does meditate.
    The Mower to the Glow-worms.

The wanton troopers riding by
ave shot my fawn and it will die.
    Nymph Complaining for the Death of her Fawn.

hy love was far more better than
he love of false and cruel men.   *Ib.*

is a wond'rous thing, how fleet
was on those little silver feet.
ith what a pretty skipping grace,
oft would challenge me the race:
nd when 't had left me far away,
would stay, and run again, and stay.
r it was nimbler much than hinds;
nd trod, as on the four winds.   *Ib.*

have a garden of my own,
ut so with roses overgrown,
nd lilies, that you would it guess
o be a little wilderness.   *Ib.*

ad it liv'd long, it would have been
lies without, roses within.   *Ib.*
    The Picture of little T.C. in a Prospect of Flowers.
    Title of Poem.

ho can foretell for what high cause
nis darling of the Gods was born?
    The Picture of Little T.C.

r though the whole world cannot shew such another,
t we'd better by far have him than his brother.
    Statue in Stocks-Market.

He is Translation's thief that addeth more,
As much as he that taketh from the store
Of the first author.   *To Dr. Witty.*

MARY TUDOR
1516–1558

When I am dead and opened, you shall find 'Calais'
lying in my heart.   *Holinshed, Chron.* iii. 1160.

THEOPHILE JULIUS HENRY MARZIALS
1850–

'Ahoy! and Oho, and it's who's for the ferry?'
  (The briar's in bud and the sun going down:)
'And I'll row ye so quick and I'll row ye so steady,
  And 'tis but a penny to Twickenham Town.'
    Twickenham Ferry.

JOHN MASEFIELD
1878–

Over the grasses of the ancient way
Rutted this morning by the passing guns.
    August 1914.

Coming in solemn beauty like slow old tunes of Spain.
    Beauty.

But the loveliest things of beauty God ever has
  showed to me,
Are her voice, and her hair, and eyes, and the dear red
  curve of her lips.   *Ib.*

Quinquireme of Nineveh from distant Ophir
Rowing home to haven in sunny Palestine,
With a cargo of ivory,
And apes and peacocks,
Sandalwood, cedarwood, and sweet white wine.
    Cargoes.

Dirty British coaster with a salt-caked smoke stack,
Butting through the Channel in the mad March days,
With a cargo of Tyne coal,
Road-rail, pig-lead,
Firewood, iron-ware, and cheap tin trays.   *Ib.*

Oh some are fond of Spanish wine, and some are fond
  of French,
And some'll swallow tay and stuff fit only for a wench.
    Captain Stratton's Fancy.

And fifteen arms went round her waist.
(And then men ask, Are Barmaids chaste?)
    The Everlasting Mercy.

To get the whole world out of bed
And washed, and dressed, and warmed, and fed,
To work, and back to bed again,
Believe me, Saul, costs worlds of pain.   *Ib.*

And he who gives a child a treat
Makes joy-bells ring in Heaven's street,
And he who gives a child a home
Builds palaces in Kingdom come,
And she who gives a baby birth
Brings Saviour Christ again to Earth.   *Ib.*

O Christ, the plough, O Christ, the laughter
Of holy white birds flying after.   *Ib.*

The corn that makes the holy bread
By which the soul of man is fed,
The holy bread, the food unpriced,
Thy everlasting mercy, Christ.   *Ib.*

Death opens unknown doors. It is most grand to die.
    Pompey the Great. i. *The Chief Centurions.*
    '*Man is a sacred city.*'

                    The house is falling,
The beaten men come into their own.
                    The Rider at the Gate.

One road leads to London,
    One road runs to Wales,
My road leads me seawards
    To the white dipping sails.   *Roadways.*

My road calls me, lures me
    West, east, south, and north;
Most roads lead men homewards,
    My road leads me forth.   *Ib.*

I must down to the seas again, to the lonely sea and
    the sky,
And all I ask is a tall ship and a star to steer her by,
And the wheel's kick and the wind's song and the
    white sail's shaking,
And a grey mist on the sea's face and a grey dawn
    breaking.   *Sea Fever.*

I must down to the seas again, for the call of the
    running tide
Is a wild call and a clear call that may not be denied.
                                        Ib.

I must down to the seas again, to the vagrant gypsy
    life,
To the gull's way and the whale's way where the
    wind's like a whetted knife;
And all I ask is a merry yarn from a laughing fellow-
    rover,
And quiet sleep and a sweet dream when the long
    trick's over.   *Ib.*

Friends and loves we have none, nor wealth nor
    blessed abode,
But the hope of the City of God at the other end of
    the road.   *The Seekers.*

It is good to be out on the road, and going one knows
    not where.   *Tewkesbury Road.*

It's a warm wind, the west wind, full of birds' cries;
I never hear the west wind but tears are in my
    eyes.
For it comes from the west lands, the old brown
    hills,
And April's in the west wind, and daffodils.
                                    The West Wind.

JACKSON MASON

1833–1889

'Rise up, My love, My fair one,
    Arise and come away.
For lo, 'tis past, the winter,
    The winter of thy year;
The rain is past and over,
    The flowers on earth appear.

And now the time of singing
    Is come for every bird;
And over all the country
    The turtle dove is heard.'
        Suppl. Hymns to Hymns A. and M., 1889.
        O Voice of the Beloved.

PHILIP MASSINGER

1583–1640

Ambition, in a private man a vice,
Is, in a prince, the virtue.
                    The Bashful Lover, I. ii

He that would govern others, first should be
The master of himself.   *The Bondman,* I. iii

                            Be wise;
Soar not too high to fall; but stoop to rise.
                        Duke of Milan, I. ii

        Greatness, with private men
Esteem'd a blessing, is to me a curse;
And we, whom, for our high births, they conclude
The only freemen, are the only slaves.
Happy the golden mean! *Great Duke of Florence,* I. i

        I am driven
Into a desperate strait and cannot steer
A middle course.   *Ib.* III. i

A New Way to Pay Old Debts.   *Title of Play*

The devil turned precisian!
            A New Way to Pay Old Debts, I. i

I write *nil ultra* to my proudest hopes.   *Ib.* IV. i

Patience, the beggar's virtue.   *Ib.* V. i

Some undone widow sits upon my arm,
And takes away the use of 't; and my sword,
Glued to my scabbard with wrong'd orphans' tears
Will not be drawn.   *Ib*

            View yourselves
In the deceiving mirror of self-love.
                    Parliament of Love, I. v

What pity 'tis, one that can speak so well,
Should in his actions be so ill!   *Ib.* III. iii

        All words,
And no performance!   *Ib.* IV. i

There are a thousand doors to let out life.   *Ib*

        Serves and fears
The fury of the many-headed monster,
The giddy multitude. *The Unnatural Combat,* III. i

CHARLES ROBERT
MATURIN

1782–1824

'Tis well to be merry and wise,
'Tis well to be honest and true;
'Tis well to be off with the old love,
Before you are on with the new.
                        Bertram. Motto

GEORGE LOUIS PALMELLA BUSSON DU MAURIER

1834–1896

Life ain't all beer and skittles, and more's the pity;
but what's the odds, so long as you're happy?
Trilby, pt. I.

The salad, for which, like everybody else I ever met,
he had a special receipt of his own. *Ib.*

A little work, a little play
To keep us going—and so, good-day!

A little warmth, a little light
Of love's bestowing—and so, good-night!

A little fun, to match the sorrow
Of each day's growing—and so, good-morrow!

A little trust that when we die
We reap our sowing! and so—good-bye! *Ib.* (end).

WILLIAM LAMB, VISCOUNT MELBOURNE

1779–1848

I wish I was as cocksure of anything as Tom Macau-
lay is of everything.
*Earl Cowper's Preface to Lord Melbourne's
Papers*, 1889, p. xii.

Things have come to a pretty pass when religion is
allowed to invade the sphere of private life.
*Remark on hearing an Evangelical Sermon.
G. W. E. Russell's Collections and Recollections*,
ch. 6.

THOMAS MELLOR

1880–1926

I wouldn't leave my little wooden hut for you!
I've got one lover and I don't want two.
I Wouldn't Leave My Little Wooden Hut for You.

GEORGE MEREDITH

1828–1909

With patient inattention hear him prate.
Bellerophon, iv.

Sword of Common Sense!
Our surest gift. *To the Comic Spirit.*

He who has looked upon Earth
Deeper than flower and fruit,
Losing some hue of his mirth,
As the tree striking rock at the root.
The Day of the Daughter of Hades, i.

And we go,
And we drop like the fruits of the tree,
Even we,
Even so. *Dirge in Woods.*

Is it accepted of Song? *The Empty Purse.*

Keep the young generations in hail,
And bequeath them no tumbled house! *Ib.*

The Man of England circled by the sands.
Epitaph on Gordon of Khartoum.

Shall man into the mystery of breath
From his quick beating pulse a pathway spy?
Or learn the secret of the shrouded death,
By lifting up the lid of a white eye?
Cleave thou thy way with fathering desire
Of fire to reach to fire. *Hymn to Colour*, v.

Not forfeiting the beast with which they are crossed,
To stature of the gods they will attain.
Ib. xiv.

The song had ceased; my vision with the song.
Ib. xv.

Death met I too,
And saw the dawn glow through. *Ib.*

Bring the army of the faithful through.
To J[ohn] M[orley].

I've studied men from my topsy-turvy
Close, and, I reckon, rather true.
Some are fine fellows: some, right scurvy:
Most, a dash between the two. *Juggling Jerry*, vii.

I'm the bird dead-struck! *Ib.* xiii.

Under yonder beech-tree single on the greensward,
Couched with her arms behind her golden head,
Knees and tresses folded to slip and ripple idly,
Lies my young love sleeping in the shade.
Love in the Valley, i.

She whom I love is hard to catch and conquer,
Hard, but O the glory of the winning were she won!
Ib. ii.

Lovely are the curves of the white owl sweeping
Wavy in the dusk lit by one large star.
Lone on the fir-branch, his rattle-note unvaried,
Brooding o'er the gloom, spins the brown eve-jar.
Darker grows the valley, more and more forgetting:
So were it with me if forgetting could be willed.
Tell the grassy hollow that holds the bubbling well-
spring,
Tell it to forget the source that keeps it filled. *Ib.* v.

Fain would fling the net, and fain have her free. *Ib.* vi.

Pure from the night, and splendid for the day. *Ib.* ix.

In arrowy rain. *Ib.* xii.

Quaintest, richest carol of all the singing throats!
[Blackbird.] *Ib.* xvii.

Straight rains and tiger sky. *Ib* xix.

Gossips count her faults; they scour a narrow
chamber
Where there is no window, read not heaven or her.
Ib. xxii.

Our souls were in our names. *Ib.* xxiii.

Around the ancient track marched, rank on rank,
The army of unalterable law.
Lucifer in Starlight.

Each wishing for the sword that severs all.
Modern Love, i.

Not till the fire is dying in the grate,
Look we for any kinship with the stars. *Ib.* iv.

With hindward feather, and with forward toe
Her much-adored delightful Fairy Prince! *Ib.* x.

And if I drink oblivion of a day,
So shorten I the stature of my soul.   *Ib.* xii.

'I play for Seasons; not Eternities!'
Says Nature.   *Ib.* xiii.

It is in truth a most contagious game:
HIDING THE SKELETON, shall be its name.   *Ib.* xvii.

They have the secret of the bull and lamb.
'Tis true that when we trace its source, 'tis beer.
   Ib. xviii.

      We'll sit contentedly
And eat our pot of honey on the grave.   *Ib.* xxix.

      That rarest gift
To Beauty, Common Sense.   *Ib.* xxxii.

O have a care of natures that are mute!   *Ib.* xxxv.

God, what a dancing spectre seems the moon.
   Ib. xxxix.

      In tragic life, God wot,
No villain need be! Passions spin the plot:
We are betrayed by what is false within.   *Ib.* xliii.

We saw the swallows gathering in the sky.   *Ib.* xlvii.

The pilgrims of the year waxed very loud
In multitudinous chatterings.   *Ib.*

Their sense is with their senses all mixed in,
Destroyed by subtleties these women are!
   Ib. xlviii.

More brain, O Lord, more brain!   *Ib.*

Thus piteously Love closed what he begat.   *Ib.* l.

Ah, what a dusty answer gets the soul
When hot for certainties in this our life!   *Ib.*

God! of whom music
And song and blood are pure,
The day is never darkened
That had thee here obscure.
   Phoebus with Admetus.

You with shelly horns, rams! and, promontory goats,
You whose browsing beards dip in coldest dew!
Bulls, that walk the pastures in kingly-flashing coats!
Laurel, ivy, vine, wreathed for feasts not few!   *Ib.*

Narrows the world to my neighbour's gate.
   Seed Time.

Through the sermon's dull defile.
   The Sage Enamoured, v.

Into the breast that gives the rose,
Shall I with shuddering fall?
   The Spirit of Earth in Autumn.

      Broad as ten thousand beeves
At pasture!   *The Spirit of Shakespeare,* i.

As the birds do, so do we,
Bill our mate, and choose our tree.
   The Three Singers to Young Blood, i.

Lowly, with a broken neck,
The crocus lays her cheek to mire.
   The Thrush in February.

Full lasting is the song, though he,
The singer, passes: lasting too,
For souls not lent in usury,
The rapture of the forward view.
   Ib.

We spend our lives in learning pilotage,
And grow good steersmen when the vessel's crank!
   The Wisdom of Eld.

Sweet as Eden is the air,
And Eden-sweet the ray.   *Woodland Peace.*

Enter those enchanted woods,
      You who dare.
   The Woods of Westermain.

Thoughts of heroes were as good as warming-pans.
   Beauchamp's Career, ch. 4.

'Wilt thou?' said the winged minute.   *Ib.* ch. 22.

They that make of his creed a strait jacket for humanity.   *Ib.* ch. 29.

He had by nature a tarnishing eye that cast discolouration.   *Diana of the Crossways,* ch. 1.

Men may have rounded Seraglio Point: they have not yet doubled Cape Turk.   *Ib.*

Sentimental people, in her phrase, fiddle harmonics on the strings of sensualism.   *Ib.*

Rose pink and dirty drab will alike have passed away.
   Ib.

'Tis Ireland gives England her soldiers, her generals too.   *Ib.* ch. 2.

She did not seduce, she ravished.   *Ib.* ch. 7.

'Hog's my feed,' said Andrew Hedger . . . 'Ah could eat hog a solid hower!'   *Ib.* ch. 8.

She was a lady of incisive features bound in stale parchment.   *Ib.* ch. 14.

Prose can paint evening and moonlight, but poets are needed to sing the dawn.   *Ib.* ch. 16.

'But how divine is utterance!' she said. 'As we to the brutes, poets are to us.'   *Ib.*

Brittle is foredoomed.   *Ib.* ch. 28.

Between the ascetic rocks and the sensual whirlpools.
   Ib. ch. 37.

He had his nest of wishes piping to him all the time.
   Ib. ch. 42.

There is nothing the body suffers the soul may not profit by.   *Ib.* ch. 43.

He has a leg.   *The Egoist,* ch. 2.

A Phoebus Apollo turned fasting friar.   *Ib.*

A dainty rogue in porcelain.   *Ib.* ch. 5.

Cynicism is intellectual dandyism.   *Ib.* ch. 7.

In . . . the book of Egoism, it is written, Possession without obligation to the object possessed approaches felicity.   *Ib.* ch. 14.

I have but a girl to give!   *Ib.* ch. 20.

Are you quite well, Laetitia?   *Ib.* ch. 40.

None of your dam punctilio.
   One of Our Conquerors, ch. 1.

I expect that Woman will be the last thing civilized by Man.   *The Ordeal of Richard Feverel,* ch. 1.

In action Wisdom goes by majorities.   *Ib.*

Who rises from prayer a better man, his prayer is answered.   *Ib.* ch. 12.

A youth educated by a system.   *Ib.* ch. 15.

Kissing don't last: cookery do!   *Ib.* ch. 28.

Speech is the small change of silence.   *Ib.* ch. 34.

Italia, Italia shall be free.   *Vittoria,* ch. 21.

Much benevolence of the passive order may be traced
to a disinclination to inflict pain upon oneself.
Ib. ch. 42.

OWEN MEREDITH
(EDWARD ROBERT BULWER, EARL OF LYTTON)
1831–1891

There's nothing certain in man's life but this:
That he must lose it.   *Clytemnestra,* pt. xx.

He may live without books,—what is knowledge but
grieving?
He may live without hope,—what is hope but
deceiving?
He may live without love,—what is passion but
pining?
But where is the man that can live without dining?
Lucile, pt. 1, c. ii, xxiv.

Genius does what it must, and Talent does what it
can.
Poems. Last Words of a Sensitive Second-Rate Poet.

ALICE MEYNELL
1847–1922

Flocks of the memories of the day draw near
The dovecote doors of sleep.   *At Night.*

With this ambiguous earth
His dealings have been told us. These abide:
The signal to a maid, the human birth,
The lesson, and the young Man crucified.
Christ in the Universe.

I come from nothing; but from where
Come the undying thoughts I bear?
The Modern Poet, or A Song of Derivations.

I must not think of thee; and, tired yet strong,
I shun the thought that lurks in all delight—
The thought of thee—and in the blue heaven's height,
And in the sweetest passage of a song.
Renouncement (ed. 1923).

With the first dream that comes with the first sleep
I run, I run, I am gathered to thy heart.   *Ib.*

She walks—the lady of my delight—
A shepherdess of sheep.   *The Shepherdess.*

She holds her little thoughts in sight,
Though gay they run and leap.
She is so circumspect and right;
She has her soul to keep.   *Ib.*

Sudden as sweet
Come the expected feet.
All joy is young, and new all art,
And He too, Whom we have by heart.
Unto us a Son is Given.

HUGO MEYNELL
1727–1808

The chief advantage of London is, that a man is
always so near his burrow.
Boswell's Johnson (ed. 1934), vol. iii, p. 379,
1 Apr. 1779.

For anything I see, foreigners are fools.
Ib. vol. iv, p. 15, 1780.

WILLIAM JULIUS MICKLE
1734–1788

The dews of summer night did fall,
The moon, sweet regent of the sky,
Silver'd the walls of Cumnor Hall,
And many an oak that grew thereby.
Cumnor Hall.

THOMAS MIDDLETON
1570?–1627

I never heard
Of any true affection, but 'twas nipt
With care.   *Blurt, Master-Constable,* iii. i. 39.

By many a happy accident.
No Wit, No Help, Like a Woman's, iv. i. 66.

Though I be poor, I'm honest.   *The Witch,* iii. ii.

There's no hate lost between us.   *Ib.* iv. iii. 10.

Black spirits and white, red spirits and gray,
Mingle, mingle, mingle, you that mingle may!
Ib. v. ii. 60.

ALBERT MIDLANE
1825–1909

There's a Friend for little children
Above the bright blue sky,
A Friend Who never changes,
Whose love will never die.
Good News for the Little Ones. There's a Friend for Little Children.

JOHN STUART MILL
1806–1873

Ask yourself whether you are happy, and you cease
to be so.   *Autobiography,* ch. 5.

No great improvements in the lot of mankind are
possible, until a great change takes place in the
fundamental constitution of their modes of thought.
Ib. ch. 7.

As often as a study is cultivated by narrow minds,
they will draw from it narrow conclusions.
Auguste Comte and Positivism, 1865, p. 82.

When society requires to be rebuilt, there is no use in
attempting to rebuild it on the old plan.
Dissertations and Discussions, Essays on Coleridge, 1859, vol. i, p. 423.

Unearned increment.   *Ib.* vol. iv, p. 299.

K 3

The sole end for which mankind are warranted, individually or collectively, in interfering with the liberty of action of any of their number, is self-protection.   *Liberty*, introduction.

If all mankind minus one, were of one opinion, and only one person were of the contrary opinion, mankind would be no more justified in silencing that one person, than he, if he had the power, would be justified in silencing mankind.   *Ib*. ch. 2.

We can never be sure that the opinion we are endeavouring to stifle is a false opinion; and if we were sure, stifling it would be an evil still.   *Ib*.

A party of order or stability, and a party of progress or reform, are both necessary elements of a healthy state of political life.   *Ib*.

The liberty of the individual must be thus far limited; he must not make himself a nuisance to other people.   *Ib*. ch. 3.

All good things which exist are the fruits of originality.   *Ib*.

Liberty consists in doing what one desires. *Ib*. ch. 5.

The worth of a State, in the long run, is the worth of the individuals composing it.   *Ib*.

A State which dwarfs its men, in order that they may be more docile instruments in its hands even for beneficial purposes—will find that with small men no great thing can really be accomplished.   *Ib*.

When the land is cultivated entirely by the spade and no horses are kept, a cow is kept for every three acres of land.   *Political Economy. A Treatise on Flemish Husbandry*.

The great majority of those who speak of perfectibility as a dream, do so because they feel that it is one which would afford them no pleasure if it were realized.   *Speech on Perfectibility*, 1828.

EDNA ST. VINCENT MILLAY
1892–

Euclid alone has looked on Beauty bare.
    The Harp-Weaver, pt. IV, sonnet xxii.

MRS. EMILY MILLER
1833–1913

I love to hear the story
Which angel voices tell.
    The Little Corporal. I Love to Hear.

WILLIAM MILLER
1810–1872

Wee Willie Winkie
Rins through the town,
Upstairs and downstairs
In his nicht-gown,
Tirling at the window,
Crying at the lock,
'Are the weans in their bed,
For it's now ten o'clock?'   *Willie Winkie.*

A. J. MILLS

Just like the ivy I'll cling to you.   *Title of Song.*

HENRY HART MILMAN
1791–1868

When our heads are bowed with woe,
When our bitter tears o'erflow.
    Hymns. 'When Our Heads.'

Ride on! ride on in majesty!
In lowly pomp ride on to die.   *Ib. Ride On!*

ALAN ALEXANDER MILNE
1882–

Time for a little something.
    Winnie-the-Pooh, ch. 6.

James James
Morrison Morrison
Weatherby George Dupree
Took great
Care of his Mother
Though he was only three.
    When We Were Very Young. Disobedience.

'You must never go down to the end of the town if you don't go down with me.'   *Ib.*

The King asked
The Queen, and
The Queen asked
The Dairymaid:
'Could we have some butter for
The Royal slice of bread?'
    Ib. The King's Breakfast.

'I do like a little bit of butter to my bread!'   *Ib.*

JOHN MILTON
1608–1674

Such sweet compulsion doth in music lie.
    Arcades, l. 68.

Before the starry threshold of Jove's Court
My mansion is.   *Comus*, l. 1.

Above the smoke and stir of this dim spot,
Which men call Earth.   *Ib*. l. 5.

Yet some there be that by due steps aspire
To lay their just hands on that golden key
That opes the palace of Eternity.   *Ib*. l. 12.

Rich and various gems inlay
The unadorned bosom of the deep.   *Ib*. l. 22.

An old, and haughty nation proud in arms. *Ib*. l. 33.

What never yet was heard in tale or song.
From old or modern bard in hall or bower. *Ib*. l. 44.

And the gilded car of day,
His glowing axle doth allay
In the steep Atlantic stream.   *Ib*. l. 95.

What hath night to do with sleep?   *Ib*. l. 122.

Ere the babbling eastern scout,
The nice Morn on the Indian steep
From her cabin'd loop-hole peep.   *Ib*. l. 138.

Come, knit hands, and beat the ground,
In a light fantastic round.　　　　　*Comus*, l. 143.

　　　　　　When the grey-hooded Even
Like a sad votarist in palmer's weed,
Rose from the hindmost wheels of Phœbus' wain.
　　　　　　　　　　　　Ib. l. 188.

　　　　　　O thievish Night,
Why shouldst thou, but for some felonious end,
In thy dark lantern thus close up the stars,
That nature hung in heaven, and filled their lamps
With everlasting oil, to give due light
To the misled and lonely traveller?　*Ib.* l. 195.

Calling shapes and beckoning shadows dire,
And airy tongues that syllable men's names
On sands, and shores, and desert wildernesses.
These thoughts may startle well, but not astound
The virtuous mind, that ever walks attended
By a strong siding champion, Conscience.
　　　　　　　　　　　　Ib. l. 207.

O welcome pure-ey'd Faith, white-handed Hope,
Thou hovering angel girt with golden wings.
　　　　　　　　　　　　Ib. l. 213.

Was I deceived, or did a sable cloud
Turn forth her silver lining on the night?　*Ib.* l. 221.

Sweet Echo, sweetest nymph, that liv'st unseen
　Within thy airy shell
By slow Meander's margent green,
　And in the violet-embroidered vale.　　*Ib.* l. 230.

Can any mortal mixture of earth's mould
Breathe such divine enchanting ravishment?
　　　　　　　　　　　　Ib. l. 244.

How sweetly did they float upon the wings
Of silence, through the empty-vaulted night,
At every fall smoothing the raven down
Of darkness till it smiled!　　　　*Ib.* l. 249.

Such sober certainty of waking bliss
I never heard till now.　　　　　*Ib.* l. 263.

　　　　　Shepherd, I take thy word,
And trust thy honest offer'd courtesy,
Which oft is sooner found in lowly sheds
With smoky rafters, than in tap'stry halls
And courts of princes.　　　　　*Ib.* l. 321.

With thy long levell'd rule of streaming light.
　　　　　　　　　　　　Ib. l. 340.

What need a man forestall his date of grief,
And run to meet what he would most avoid?
　　　　　　　　　　　　Ib. l. 362.

Virtue could see to do what virtue would
By her own radiant light, though sun and moon
Were in the flat sea sunk. And Wisdom's self
Oft seeks to sweet retired solitude,
Where with her best nurse Contemplation
She plumes her feathers, and lets grow her wings
That in the various bustle of resort
Were all too ruffled, and sometimes impair'd.
He that has light within his own clear breast
May sit i' th' centre and enjoy bright day;
But he that hides a dark soul and foul thoughts
Benighted walks under the midday sun.　*Ib.* l. 373.

　　　　　The unsunned heaps
Of miser's treasure.　　　　　*Ib.* l. 398.

'Tis Chastity, my brother, Chastity:
She that has that, is clad in complete steel.　*Ib.* l. 420.

How charming is divine philosophy!
Not harsh, and crabbed as dull fools suppose,
But musical as is Apollo's lute,
And a perpetual feast of nectared sweets,
Where no crude surfeit reigns.　　*Ib.* l. 476.

What the sage poets taught by the heavenly Muse,
Storied of old in high immortal verse
Of dire chimeras and enchanted isles
And rifted rocks whose entrance leads to Hell,—
For such there be, but unbelief is blind.
　　　　　　　　　　　　Ib. l. 515.

And fill'd the air with barbarous dissonance.
　　　　　　　　　　　　Ib. l. 550.

A steam of rich distill'd perfumes.　*Ib.* l. 556.

　　　　　I was all ear,
And took in strains that might create a soul
Under the ribs of Death.　　　　*Ib.* l. 560.

　　　　　　That power
Which erring men call Chance.　　*Ib.* l. 587.

Virtue may be assailed, but never hurt,
Surprised by unjust force, but not enthralled.
　　　　　　　　　　　　Ib. l. 589.

　　　　　If this fail,
The pillared firmament is rottenness,
And earth's base built on stubble.　*Ib.* l. 597.

　　　　　　The dull swain
Treads on it daily with his clouted shoon.
　　　　　　　　　　　　Ib. l. 634.

Hast thou betrayed my credulous innocence
With vizor'd falsehood, and base forgery?
　　　　　　　　　　　　Ib. l. 697.

　　　　　None
But such as are good men can give good things,
And that which is not good, is not delicious
To a well-govern'd and wise appetite.　*Ib.* l. 702.

Budge doctors of the Stoic fur.　*Ib.* l. 707.

Praising the lean and sallow abstinence.　*Ib.* l. 709.

Beauty is Nature's coin, must not be hoarded,
But must be current, and the good thereof
Consists in mutual and partaken bliss.　*Ib.* l. 739.

Beauty is Nature's brag, and must be shown
In courts, at feasts, and high solemnities,
Where most may wonder at the workmanship;
It is for homely features to keep home,
They had their name thence; coarse complexions
And cheeks of sorry grain will serve to ply
The sampler, and to tease the huswife's wool.
What need a vermeil-tinctur'd lip for that,
Love-darting eyes, or tresses like the morn?
　　　　　　　　　　　　Ib. l. 745.

Obtruding false rules pranked in reason's garb.
　　　　　　　　　　　　Ib. l. 759.

　　Through the porch and inlet of each sense
Dropt in ambrosial oils till she reviv'd.
　　　　　　　　　　　　Ib. l. 839.

Sabrina fair,
　Listen where thou art sitting
Under the glassy, cool, translucent wave,
　In twisted braids of lilies knitting
The loose train of thy amber-dropping hair.
　　　　　　　　　　　Comus, l. 859.

Thus I set my printless feet
O'er the cowslip's velvet head,
That bends not as I tread.　　　*Ib.* l. 897.

Love virtue, she alone is free,
She can teach ye how to climb
Higher than the sphery chime;
Or, if virtue feeble were,
Heaven itself would stoop to her.　*Ib.* l. 1019.

O fairest flower, no sooner blown but blasted,
Soft silken primrose fading timelessly.
　　On the Death of a Fair Infant, Dying of a Cough,
　l. 1.

Hence, vain deluding joys,
The brood of Folly without father bred.
　　　　　　　　　　Il Penseroso, l. 1.

Hail divinest Melancholy.　　　*Ib.* l. 12.

And looks commercing with the skies,
Thy rapt soul sitting in thine eyes:
There held in holy passion still,
Forget thyself to marble.　　　*Ib.* l. 39.

And join with thee calm Peace, and Quiet,
Spare Fast, that oft with gods doth diet.
　　　　　　　　　　　　Ib. l. 45.

And add to these retired Leisure,
That in trim gardens takes his pleasure.　*Ib.* l. 49.

Him that yon soars on golden wing,
Guiding the fiery-wheeled throne,
The Cherub Contemplation.　　　*Ib.* l. 52.

Sweet bird, that shunn'st the noise of folly,
Most musical, most melancholy!　*Ib.* l. 61.

　　　　　　　I walk unseen
On the dry smooth-shaven green,
To behold the wandering moon,
Riding near her highest noon,
Like one that had been led astray
Through the heav'n's wide pathless way;
And oft, as if her head she bow'd,
Stooping through a fleecy cloud.　　*Ib.* l. 65.

Oft, on a plat of rising ground,
I hear the far-off curfew sound
Over some wide-watered shore,
Swinging slow with sullen roar.　*Ib.* l. 73.

Where glowing embers through the room
Teach light to counterfeit a gloom,
Far from all resort of mirth,
Save the cricket on the hearth.　*Ib.* l. 79.

Where I may oft outwatch the Bear,
With thrice great Hermes, or unsphere
The spirit of Plato.　　　　*Ib.* l. 87.

Sometime let gorgeous Tragedy
In sceptred pall come sweeping by,
Presenting Thebes, or Pelops' line,
Or the tale of Troy divine.　　*Ib.* l. 97.

Or bid the soul of Orpheus sing
Such notes as, warbled to the string,
Drew iron tears down Pluto's cheek.　*Ib.* l. 105.

Or call up him that left half told
The story of Cambuscan bold.　*Ib.* l. 109.

Where more is meant than meets the ear.　*Ib.* l. 120.

While the bee with honied thigh,
That at her flowery work doth sing,
And the waters murmuring
With such consort as they keep,
Entice the dewy-feather'd sleep.　*Ib.* l. 142.

But let my due feet never fail
To walk the studious cloister's pale.　*Ib.* l. 155.

With antique pillars massy proof,
And storied windows richly dight,
Casting a dim religious light.
There let the pealing organ blow,
To the full-voiced quire below,
In service high, and anthems clear
As may, with sweetness, through mine ear,
Dissolve me into ecstasies,
And bring all Heaven before mine eyes.　*Ib.* l. 158.

Till old experience do attain
To something like prophetic strain.　*Ib.* l. 173.

Hence, loathed Melancholy,
　Of Cerberus, and blackest Midnight born,
In Stygian cave forlorn,
　'Mongst horrid shapes, and shrieks, and sights un-
　　holy.　　　　　　　*L'Allegro*, l. 1.

So buxom, blithe, and debonair.　*Ib.* l. 24.

Haste thee Nymph, and bring with thee
Jest and youthful jollity,
Quips and cranks, and wanton wiles,
Nods, and becks, and wreathed smiles.　*Ib.* l. 25.

Sport that wrinkled Care derides,
And Laughter holding both his sides.
Come, and trip it as ye go
On the light fantastic toe.　　*Ib.* l. 31.

The mountain nymph, sweet Liberty.　*Ib.* l. 36.

Mirth, admit me of thy crew,
To live with her, and live with thee,
In unreproved pleasures free.
To hear the lark begin his flight,
And singing startle the dull night,
From his watch-tower in the skies,
Till the dappled dawn doth rise;
Then to come in spite of sorrow,
And at my window bid good-morrow.　*Ib.* l. 38.

While the cock with lively din
Scatters the rear of darkness thin,
And to the stack, or the barn door,
Stoutly struts his dames before.　*Ib.* l. 49.

Right against the eastern gate,
Where the great Sun begins his state.　*Ib.* l. 59.

　　　　The ploughman near at hand,
Whistles o'er the furrowed land,
And the milkmaid singeth blithe,
And the mower whets his scythe,
And every shepherd tells his tale
Under the hawthorn in the dale.　*Ib.* l. 63.

Meadows trim with daisies pied,
Shallow brooks and rivers wide.
Towers, and battlements it sees
Bosom'd high in tufted trees,
Where perhaps some beauty lies,
The cynosure of neighbouring eyes. *L'Allegro*, l. 75.

Of herbs, and other country messes,
Which the neat-handed Phyllis dresses.   *Ib.* l. 85.

To many a youth, and many a maid,
Dancing in the chequered shade.
And young and old come forth to play
On a sunshine holiday.   *Ib.* l. 95.

Then to the spicy nut-brown ale.   *Ib.* l. 100.

Towered cities please us then,
And the busy hum of men.   *Ib.* l. 117.

Store of ladies, whose bright eyes
Rain influence.   *Ib.* l. 121.

And pomp, and feast, and revelry,
With masks, and antique pageantry,
Such sights as youthful poets dream,
On summer eves by haunted stream.
Then to the well-trod stage anon,
If Jonson's learnèd sock be on,
Or sweetest Shakespeare, Fancy's child,
Warble his native wood-notes wild
And ever against eating cares,
Lap me in soft Lydian airs,
Married to immortal verse
Such as the meeting soul may pierce
In notes, with many a winding bout
Of linked sweetness long drawn out.   *Ib.* l. 127.

The melting voice through mazes running;
Untwisting all the chains that tie
The hidden soul of harmony.   *Ib.* l. 142.

Such strains as would have won the ear
Of Pluto, to have quite set free
His half regain'd Eurydice.   *Ib.* l. 148.

Yet once more, O ye laurels, and once more
Ye myrtles brown, with ivy never sere,
I come to pluck your berries harsh and crude,
And with forc'd fingers rude,
Shatter your leaves before the mellowing year.
     Lycidas, l. 1.

   He knew
Himself to sing, and build the lofty rhyme.
     Ib. l. 10

Without the meed of some melodious tear.
     Ib. l. 14.

Hence, with denial vain, and coy excuse,
So may some gentle Muse
With lucky words favour my destin'd urn,
And as he passes turn,
And bid fair peace be to my sable shroud.
     Ib. l. 18.

For we were nursed upon the self-same hill.
     Ib. l. 23.

Under the opening eyelids of the morn.   *Ib.* l. 26.

But, O the heavy change, now thou art gone,
Now thou art gone, and never must return!
     Ib. l. 37.

The gadding vine.   *Ib.* l. 40.

As killing as the canker to the rose.   *Ib.* l. 45.

Flowers that their gay wardrobe wear.   *Ib.* l. 47.

Where were ye, Nymphs, when the remorseless deep
Closed o'er the head of your loved Lycidas?
     Ib. l. 50.

Whom universal Nature did lament.   *Ib.* l. 60.

Alas! what boots it with uncessant care
To tend the homely, slighted, shepherd's trade,
And strictly meditate the thankless Muse?
Were it not better done, as others use,
To sport with Amaryllis in the shade,
Or with the tangles of Neæra's hair.
Fame is the spur that the clear spirit doth raise
(That last infirmity of noble mind)
To scorn delights, and live laborious days;
But the fair guerdon when we hope to find,
And think to burst out into sudden blaze,
Comes the blind Fury with th' abhorred shears
And slits the thin-spun life.   *Ib.* l. 64.

Touch'd my trembling ears.   *Ib.* l. 77.

Fame is no plant that grows on mortal soil.
     Ib. l. 78.

As he pronounces lastly on each deed,
Of so much fame in Heaven expect thy meed.
     Ib. l. 83.

That strain I heard was of a higher mood.   *Ib.* l. 87.

It was that fatal and perfidious bark
Built in th' eclipse, and rigged with curses dark,
That sunk so low that sacred head of thine. *Ib.* l. 100.

Last came, and last did go,
The Pilot of the Galilean lake,
Two massy keys he bore of metals twain,
The golden opes, the iron shuts amain.   *Ib.* l. 108.

       Such as for their bellies' sake,
Creep and intrude, and climb into the fold.
Of other care they little reckoning make,
Than how to scramble at the shearers' feast,
And shove away the worthy bidden guest.
     Ib. l. 114.

Blind mouths! that scarce themselves know how to
hold
A sheep-hook, or have learn'd aught else the least
That to the faithful herdman's art belongs!
     Ib. l. 119.

       Their lean and flashy songs
Grate on their scrannel pipes of wretched straw,
The hungry sheep look up, and are not fed,
But, swoln with wind and the rank mist they draw,
Rot inwardly and foul contagion spread;
Besides what the grim wolf with privy paw
Daily devours apace, and nothing said.
But that two-handed engine at the door
Stands ready to smite once, and smite no more.
     Ib. l. 123.

a

Throw hither all your quaint enamell'd eyes
That on the green turf suck the honied showers,
And purple all the ground with vernal flowers,
Bring the rathe primrose that forsaken dies,
The tufted crow-toe, and pale jessamine,
The white pink, and the pansy freakt with jet,
The glowing violet,
The musk-rose, and the well-attir'd woodbine,
With cowslips wan that hang the pensive head,
And every flower that sad embroidery wears.
Bid amaranthus all his beauty shed,
And daffadillies fill their cups with tears,
To strew the laureate hearse where Lycid lies.
Lycidas, l. 139.

So to interpose a little ease. *Ib.* l. 152.

Whether beyond the stormy Hebrides,
Where thou perhaps under the whelming tide
Visit'st the bottom of the monstrous world;
Or whether thou, to our moist vows denied,
Sleep'st by the fable of Bellerus old,
Where the great Vision of the guarded mount
Looks toward Namancos and Bayona's hold.
Look homeward, Angel, now, and melt with ruth.
Ib. l. 156.

For Lycidas your sorrow is not dead,
Sunk though he be beneath the watery floor;
So sinks the day-star in the ocean bed,
And yet anon repairs his drooping head,
And tricks his beams, and with new spangled ore,
Flames in the forehead of the morning sky:
So Lycidas sunk low, but mounted high,
Through the dear might of Him that walked the
waves. *Ib.* l. 166.

In solemn troops, and sweet societies. *Ib.* l. 179.

Thus sang the uncouth swain. *Ib.* l. 186.

He touch'd the tender stops of various quills,
With eager thought warbling his Doric lay. *Ib.* l. 188.

At last he rose, and twitch'd his mantle blue;
To-morrow to fresh woods, and pastures new.
Ib. l. 192.

The bright morning star, day's harbinger.
On May Morning.

This is the month, and this the happy morn,
Wherein the Son of Heaven's eternal King,
Of wedded maid, and virgin mother born,
Our great redemption from above did bring;
For so the holy sages once did sing,
That He our deadly forfeit should release,
And with His Father work us a perpetual peace.
Hymn. On the Morning of Christ's Nativity,
l. 1.

The star-led wizards haste with odours sweet!
Ib. l. 23.

It was the winter wild
While the Heav'n-born child
All meanly wrapt in the rude manger lies. *Ib.* l. 29.

Nor war, nor battle's sound
Was heard the world around,
The idle spear and shield were high uphung.
Ib. l. 53.

Birds of calm sit brooding on the charmèd wave.
Ib. l. 68.

b

Perhaps their loves, or else their sheep,
Was all that did their silly thoughts so busy keep.
Ib. l. 91.

The helmed Cherubim
And sworded Seraphim,
Are seen in glittering ranks with wings display'd.
Ib. l. 112.

Time will run back, and fetch the age of gold.
Ib. l. 135.

And speckled Vanity
Will sicken soon and die. *Ib.* l. 136.

Swinges the scaly horror of his folded tail. *Ib.* l. 172.

The oracles are dumb,
No voice or hideous hum
Runs through the arched roof in words deceiving.
Apollo from his shrine
Can no more divine,
With hollow shriek the steep of Delphos leaving.
No nightly trance or breathèd spell,
Inspires the pale-eyed priest from the prophetic cell.
Ib. l. 173.

From haunted spring and dale
Edg'd with poplar pale
The parting genius is with sighing sent. *Ib.* l. 184.

Peor and Baalim
Forsake their temples dim. *Ib.* l. 197.

So when the sun in bed,
Curtain'd with cloudy red,
Pillows his chin upon an orient wave. *Ib.* l. 229.

But see the Virgin blest,
Hath laid her Babe to rest.
Time is our tedious song should here have ending,
Heav'ns youngest teemed star,
Hath fixt her polisht car,
Her sleeping lord with handmaid lamp attending:
And all about the courtly stable,
Bright-harnest Angels sit in order serviceable.
Ib. l. 237.

Rhyme being no necessary adjunct or true ornament
of poem or good verse, in longer works especially,
but the invention of a barbarous age, to set off
wretched matter and lame metre.
The Verse. Preface to Paradise Lost, 1668 ed.

The troublesome and modern bondage of Rhyming.
Ib.

Of Man's first disobedience, and the fruit
Of that forbidden tree, whose mortal taste
Brought death into the world, and all our woe,
With loss of Eden. *Paradise Lost, bk. i, l. 1.*

Or if Sion hill
Delight thee more, and Siloa's brook that flow'd
Fast by the oracle of God. *Ib.* l. 10.

Things unattempted yet in prose or rhyme. *Ib.* l. 16.

What in me is dark
Illumine, what is low raise and support;
That to the highth of this great argument
I may assert eternal Providence,
And justify the ways of God to Men. *Ib.* l. 22.

For one restraint, lords of the world besides.
Ib. l. 32.

The infernal serpent; he it was, whose guile
Stirr'd up with envy and revenge, deceived
The mother of mankind. *Ib.* l. 34.

JOHN MILTON

Him the Almighty Power
Hurled headlong flaming from th' ethereal sky
With hideous ruin and combustion down
To bottomless perdition, there to dwell
In adamantine chains and penal fire
Who durst defy th' Omnipotent to arms.
Paradise Lost, bk. i, l. 44.

As far as angels' ken. *Ib.* l. 59.

A dungeon horrible, on all sides round
As one great furnace flam'd; yet from those flames
No light, but rather darkness visible
Serv'd only to discover sights of woe,
Regions of sorrow, doleful shades, where peace
And rest can never dwell, hope never comes
That comes to all. *Ib.* l. 60.

As far removed from God and light of heav'n
As from the centre thrice to th' utmost pole.
Ib. l. 73.

But O how fall'n! how changed
From him who, in the happy realms of light,
Clothed with transcendent brightness didst outshine
Myriads though bright. *Ib.* l. 84.

United thoughts and counsels, equal hope,
And hazard in the glorious enterprise. *Ib.* l. 88.

Yet not for those
Nor what the potent victor in his rage
Can else inflict do I repent or change,
Though changed in outward lustre; that fixed mind
And high disdain, from sense of injured merit.
Ib. l. 94.

What though the field be lost?
All is not lost; th' unconquerable will,
And study of revenge, immortal hate,
And courage never to submit or yield:
And what is else not to be overcome? *Ib.* l. 105.

Vaunting aloud, but racked with deep despair.
Ib. l. 126.

Fall'n Cherub, to be weak is miserable
Doing or suffering: but of this be sure,
To do ought good never will be our task,
But ever to do ill our sole delight. *Ib.* l. 157.

And out of good still to find means of evil. *Ib.* l. 165.

The seat of desolation, void of light. *Ib.* l. 181.

What reinforcement we may gain from hope,
If not what resolution from despair. *Ib.* l. 190.

The will
And high permission of all-ruling Heaven
Left him at large to his own dark designs,
That with reiterated crimes he might
Heap on himself damnation. *Ib.* l. 211.

Is this the region, this the soil, the clime,
Said then the lost Archangel, this the seat
That we must change for Heav'n, this mournful gloom
For that celestial light? *Ib.* l. 242.

Farthest from him is best
Whom reason hath equalled, force hath made supreme
Above his equals. Farewell happy fields
Where joy for ever dwells: Hail horrors, hail
Infernal world, and thou profoundest Hell
Receive thy new possessor: one who brings
A mind not to be changed by place or time.
The mind is its own place, and in it self
Can make a Heav'n of Hell, a Hell of Heav'n.
Ib. l. 247.

Here we may reign secure, and in my choice
To reign is worth ambition though in hell:
Better to reign in hell, than serve in heav'n.
Ib. l. 261.

His spear, to equal which the tallest pine
Hewn on Norwegian hills, to be the mast
Of some great ammiral, were but a wand,
He walk'd with to support uneasy steps
Over the burning marle. *Ib.* l. 292.

Thick as autumnal leaves that strow the brooks
In Vallombrosa, where th' Etrurian shades
High over-arch'd imbower. *Ib.* l. 302.

Busiris and his Memphian chivalry. *Ib.* l. 307.

'Awake, arise, or be for ever fall'n!'
They heard, and were abashed, and up they sprung
Upon the wing, as when men wont to watch
On duty, sleeping found by whom they dread,
Rouse and bestir themselves ere well awake.
Ib. l. 330.

First Moloch, horrid king, besmear'd with blood
Of human sacrifice, and parents' tears. *Ib.* l. 392.

For spirits when they please
Can either sex assume, or both; so soft
And uncompounded is their essence pure. *Ib.* l. 423.

Execute their aery purposes. *Ib.* l. 430.

Astarte, Queen of Heav'n, with crescent horns.
Ib. l. 439.

Thammuz came next behind,
Whose annual wound in Lebanon allur'd
The Syrian damsels to lament his fate
In amorous ditties all a summer's day,
While smooth Adonis from his native rock
Ran purple to the sea. *Ib.* l. 446.

A leper once he lost and gain'd a king. *Ib.* l. 471.

Jehovah, who in one night when he passed
From Egypt marching. *Ib.* l. 487.

And when night
Darkens the streets, then wander forth the sons
Of Belial, flown with insolence and wine. *Ib.* l. 500.

Shone like a meteor streaming to the wind. *Ib.* l. 537.

Sonorous metal blowing martial sounds:
At which the universal host up sent
A shout that tore hell's concave, and beyond
Frighted the reign of Chaos and old Night. *Ib.* l. 540.

Anon they move
In perfect phalanx to the Dorian mood
Of flutes and soft recorders. *Ib.* l. 549.

That small infantry
Warred on by cranes. *Ib.* l. 575.

What resounds
In fable or romance of Uther's son
Begirt with British and Armoric knights;
And all who since, baptized or infidel
Jousted in Aspramont or Montalban,
Damasco, or Marocco, or Trebisond,
Or whom Biserta sent from Afric shore
When Charlemain with all his peerage fell
By Fontarabbia. *Ib.* l. 579.

He above the rest
In shape and gesture proudly eminent
Stood like a tower; his form had yet not lost
All her original brightness, nor appeared
Less than archangel ruined, and th' excess
Of glory obscur'd.   *Paradise Lost*, bk. i, l. 589.

The sun . . .
In dim eclipse disastrous twilight sheds
On half the nations, and with fear of change
Perplexes monarchs.   *Ib*. l. 594.

His face
Deep scars of thunder had intrenched, and care
Sat on his faded cheek, but under brows
Of dauntless courage, and considerate pride
Waiting revenge.   *Ib*. l. 600.

Who overcomes
By force, hath overcome but half his foe.   *Ib*. l. 648.

Mammon led them on,
Mammon, the least erected Spirit that fell
From heav'n, for ev'n in heav'n his looks and thoughts
Were always downward bent, admiring more
The riches of heaven's pavement, trodden gold,
Than aught divine or holy else enjoy'd
In vision beatific.   *Ib*. l. 678.

Let none admire
That riches grow in hell; that soil may best
Deserve the precious bane.   *Ib*. l. 690.

Anon out of the earth a fabric huge
Rose like an exhalation.   *Ib*. l. 710.

From morn
To noon he fell, from noon to dewy eve,
A summer's day; and with the setting sun
Dropt from the zenith like a falling star.   *Ib*. l. 742.

Fairy elves,
Whose midnight revels, by a forest side
Or fountain some belated peasant sees,
Or dreams he sees, while overhead the moon
Sits arbitress.   *Ib*. l. 781.

High on a throne of royal state, which far
Outshone the wealth of Ormus and of Ind,
Or where the gorgeous East with richest hand
Showers on her kings barbaric pearl and gold,
Satan exalted sat, by merit raised
To that bad eminence; and from despair
Thus high uplifted beyond hope.   *Ib*. bk. ii, l. 1.

The strongest and the fiercest Spirit
That fought in Heav'n; now fiercer by despair.
His trust was with th' Eternal to be deemed
Equal in strength, and rather than be less
Cared not to be at all.   *Ib*. l. 44.

My sentence is for open war: of wiles
More unexpert, I boast not.   *Ib*. l. 51.

When the scourge
Inexorably, and the torturing hour
Calls us to penance.   *Ib*. l. 90.

Belial, in act more graceful and humane;
A fairer person lost not Heav'n; he seemed
For dignity compos'd and high exploit:
But all was false and hollow; though his tongue
Dropt manna, and could make the worse appear
The better reason.   *Ib*. l. 109.

For who would lose,
Though full of pain, this intellectual being,
Those thoughts that wander through eternity,
To perish rather, swallowed up and lost
In the wide womb of uncreated night,
Devoid of sense and motion?   *Ib*. l. 146.

His red right hand.   *Ib*. l. 174.

Unrespited, unpitied, unreprieved,
Ages of hopeless end.   *Ib*. l. 185.

Thus Belial with words clothed in reason's garb
Counselled ignoble ease, and peaceful sloth,
Not peace.   *Ib*. l. 226.

Our torments also may in length of time
Become our elements.   *Ib*. l. 274.

With grave
Aspect he rose, and in his rising seem'd
A pillar of state; deep on his front engraven
Deliberation sat and public care;
And princely counsel in his face yet shone,
Majestic though in ruin.   *Ib*. l. 300.

To sit in darkness here
Hatching vain empires.   *Ib*. l. 377.

Who shall tempt with wand'ring feet
The dark unbottom'd infinite abyss
And through the palpable obscure find out
His uncouth way.   *Ib*. l. 404.

Long is the way
And hard, that out of hell leads up to light.   *Ib*. l. 432.

O shame to men! devil with devil damn'd
Firm concord holds, men only disagree
Of creatures rational.   *Ib*. l. 496.

In discourse more sweet
(For eloquence the soul, song charms the sense,)
Others apart sat on a hill retir'd,
In thoughts more elevate, and reason'd high
Of providence, foreknowledge, will, and fate,
Fix'd fate, free will, foreknowledge absolute,
And found no end, in wand'ring mazes lost.
     Ib. l. 555.

Vain wisdom all, and false philosophy.   *Ib*. l. 565.

A gulf profound as that Serbonian bog
Betwixt Damiata and Mount Casius old,
Where armies whole have sunk: the parching air
Burns frore, and cold performs th' effect of fire.
     Ib. l. 592.

The bitter change
Of fierce extremes, extremes by change more fierce.
     Ib. l. 598.

O'er many a frozen, many a fiery Alp,
Rocks, caves, lakes, fens, bogs, dens, and shades of
death.   *Ib*. l. 620.

Worse
Than fables yet have feigned, or fear conceived,
Gorgons and Hydras, and Chimæras dire.   *Ib*. l. 626.

The other shape,
If shape it might be call'd that shape had none
Distinguishable in member, joint, or limb,
Or substance might be call'd that shadow seem'd,
For each seem'd either; black it stood as night,
Fierce as ten furies, terrible as hell,
And shook a dreadful dart; what seem'd his head
The likeness of a kingly crown had on.   *Ib*. l. 666.

Whence and what art thou, execrable shape?
Paradise Lost, bk. ii, l. 681.
Incens'd with indignation Satan stood
Unterrifi'd, and like a comet burn'd
That fires the length of Ophiucus huge
In th' arctic sky, and from his horrid hair
Shakes pestilence and war. *Ib.* l. 707.

Their fatal hands
No second stroke intend. *Ib.* l. 712.

I fled, and cry'd out, *Death*;
Hell trembled at the hideous name, and sigh'd
From all her caves, and back resounded, *Death*.
Ib. l. 787.

On a sudden open fly
With impetuous recoil and jarring sound
Th' infernal doors, and on their hinges grate
Harsh thunder. *Ib.* l. 879.
A dark
Illimitable ocean without bound,
Without dimension, where length, breadth, and highth,
And time and place are lost. *Ib.* l. 891.

Chaos umpire sits,
And by decision more embroils the fray
By which he reigns: next him high arbiter
Chance governs all. *Ib.* l. 907.

This wild abyss,
The womb of nature and perhaps her grave. *Ib.* l. 910.

To compare
Great things with small. *Ib.* l. 921.

So eagerly the fiend
O'er bog or steep, through strait, rough, dense, or rare,
With head, hands, wings, or feet pursues his way,
And swims or sinks, or wades, or creeps, or flies.
Ib. l. 947.

Sable-vested Night, eldest of things. *Ib.* l. 962.

With ruin upon ruin, rout on rout,
Confusion worse confounded. *Ib.* l. 995.

So he with difficulty and labour hard
Moved on, with difficulty and labour he. *Ib.* l. 1021.

Hail, holy light, offspring of Heaven first-born,
Or of th' Eternal co-eternal beam,
May I express thee unblamed? Since God is light,
And never but in unapproached light
Dwelt from eternity. *Ib.* bk. iii, l. 1.

So thick a drop serene hath pierced their orbs,
Or dim suffusion veiled. Yet not the more
Cease I to wander where the Muses haunt
Clear spring, or shady grove, or sunny hill. *Ib.* l. 25.

Nor sometimes forget
Those other two equall'd with me in fate,
So were I equall'd with them in renown,
Blind Thamyris and blind Mæonides,
And Tiresias and Phineus, prophets old.
Then feed on thoughts, that voluntary move
Harmonious numbers; as the wakeful bird
Sings darkling, and in shadiest covert hid,
Tunes her nocturnal note. Thus with the year
Seasons return, but not to me returns
Day, or the sweet approach of ev'n or morn,
Or sight of vernal bloom, or summer's rose,

Or flocks, or herds, or human face divine;
But cloud instead, and ever-during dark
Surrounds me, from the cheerful ways of men
Cut off, and for the book of knowledge fair
Presented with a universal blank
Of Nature's works to me expung'd and raz'd,
And wisdom at one entrance quite shut out.
So much the rather thou celestial light
Shine inward. *Ib.* l. 32.

Freely they stood who stood, and fell who fell.
Ib. l. 102.

Dark with excessive bright. *Ib.* l. 380.

Sericana, where Chineses drive
With sails and wind their cany waggons light.
Ib. l. 438.
Embryos and idiots, eremites and friars,
White, black and grey, with all their trumpery.
Ib. l. 474.
Dying put on the weeds of Dominic,
Or in Franciscan think to pass disguised. *Ib.* l. 479.

Then might ye see
Cowls, hoods, and habits, with their wearers, tost
And fluttered into rags, then reliques, beads,
Indulgences, dispenses, pardons, bulls,
The sport of winds. *Ib.* l. 489.

Into a Limbo large and broad, since called
The Paradise of Fools, to few unknown. *Ib.* l. 495.

For neither man nor angel can discern
Hypocrisy, the only evil that walks
Invisible, except to God alone. *Ib.* l. 682.

At whose sight all the stars
Hide their diminished heads. *Ib.* bk. iv, l. 34.

Warring in Heav'n against Heav'n's matchless King.
Ib. l. 41.
And understood not that a grateful mind
By owing owes not, but still pays, at once
Indebted and discharged. *Ib.* l. 55.

Me miserable! which way shall I fly
Infinite wrath, and infinite despair?
Which way I fly is Hell; myself am Hell;
And in the lowest deep a lower deep
Still threatening to devour me opens wide,
To which the Hell I suffer seems a Heaven.
Ib. l. 73.

So farewell hope, and with hope farewell fear,
Farewell remorse: all good to me is lost;
Evil be thou my Good. *Ib.* l. 108.

Off at sea north-east winds blow
Sabæan odours from the spicy shore
Of Araby the blest. *Ib.* l. 161.

Many a league
Cheer'd with the grateful smell old Ocean smiles.
Ib. l. 164.

So clomb this first grand thief into God's fold:
So since into his church lewd hirelings climb.
Thence up he flew, and on the tree of life,
The middle tree and highest there that grew,
Sat like a cormorant. *Ib.* l. 192.

A heaven on earth. *Ib.* l. 208.

Groves whose rich trees wept odorous gums and balm,
Others whose fruit burnished with golden rind
Hung amiable, Hesperian fables true,
If true, here only.   *Paradise Lost*, bk. iv, l. 248.

Flowers of all hue, and without thorn the rose.
                                                Ib. l. 256.

The mantling vine.   *Ib.* l. 258.

Not that fair field
Of Enna, where Proserpin gathering flowers,
Herself a fairer flower by gloomy Dis
Was gathered.   *Ib.* l. 268.

Nor where Abassin kings their issue guard,
Mount Amara, though this by some supposed
True Paradise.   *Ib.* l. 280.

Two of far nobler shape erect and tall,
Godlike erect, with native honour clad
In naked majesty seemed lords of all.   *Ib.* l. 288.

For contemplation he and valour formed;
For softness she and sweet attractive grace,
He for God only, she for God in him:
His fair large front and eye sublime declared
Absolute rule.   *Ib.* l. 297.

Which implied
Subjection, but required with gentle sway
And by her yielded, by him best received;
Yielded with coy submission, modest pride,
And sweet reluctant amorous delay.   *Ib.* l. 307.

Adam, the goodliest man of men since born
His sons; the fairest of her daughters Eve.   *Ib.* l. 323.

The savoury pulp they chew, and in the rind
Still as they thirsted scooped the brimming stream.
                                                Ib. l. 335.

Sporting the lion ramped, and in his paw,
Dandled the kid; bears, tigers, ounces, pards
Gamboll'd before them, th' unwieldly elephant
To make them mirth us'd all his might, and wreathed
His lithe proboscis.   *Ib.* l. 343.

So spake the Fiend, and with necessity,
The tyrant's plea, excus'd his devilish deeds.
                                                Ib. l. 393.

With eyes
Of conjugal attraction unreprov'd.   *Ib.* l. 492.

Imparadised in one another's arms.   *Ib.* l. 506.

Now came still evening on, and twilight gray
Had in her sober livery all things clad;
Silence accompanied, for beast and bird,
They to their grassy couch, these to their nests,
Were slunk, all but the wakeful nightingale;
She all night long her amorous descant sung;
Silence was pleas'd: now glow'd the firmament
With living sapphires: Hesperus that led
The starry host, rode brightest, till the moon,
Rising in clouded majesty, at length
Apparent queen unveil'd her peerless light,
And o'er the dark her silver mantle threw. *Ib.* l. 598.

God is thy law, thou mine: to know no more
Is woman's happiest knowledge and her praise.
                                                Ib. l. 637.

With thee conversing I forget all time.   *Ib.* l. 639.

Sweet is the breath of morn, her rising sweet,
With charm of earliest birds.   *Ib.* l. 641.

Sweet the coming on
Of grateful evening mild, then silent night
With this her solemn bird and this fair moon,
And these the gems of Heav'n, her starry train.
                                                Ib. l. 646.

Millions of spiritual creatures walk the earth
Unseen, both when we wake, and when we sleep.
                                                Ib. l. 677.

Into their inmost bower
Handed they went; and eas'd the putting off
These troublesome disguises which we wear,
Strait side by side were laid, nor turned I ween
Adam from his fair spouse, nor Eve the rites
Mysterious of connubial love refus'd:
Whatever hypocrites austerely talk
Of purity and place and innocence,
Defaming as impure what God declares
Pure, and commands to some, leaves free to all.
                                                Ib. l. 738.

Hail wedded love, mysterious law, true source
Of human offspring, sole propriety,
In Paradise of all things common else.   *Ib.* l. 750.

Sleep on,
Blest pair; and O yet happiest if ye seek
No happier state, and know to know no more.
                                                Ib. l. 773.

Him there they found
Squat like a toad, close at the ear of Eve. *Ib.* l. 799.

Him thus intent Ithuriel with his spear
Touched lightly; for no falsehood can endure
Touch of celestial temper, but returns
Of force to its own likeness; up he starts
Discover'd and surpris'd.   *Ib.* l. 810.

Not to know me argues yourselves unknown.
                                                Ib. l. 830.

Abash'd the Devil stood,
And felt how awful goodness is, and saw
Virtue in her shape how lovely.   *Ib.* l. 846.

Of regal port,
But faded splendour wan.   *Ib.* l. 869.

But wherefore thou alone? Wherefore with thee
Came not all hell broke loose?   *Ib.* l. 917.

Then when I am thy captive talk of chains,
Proud limitary Cherub.   *Ib.* l. 970.

Like Teneriff or Atlas unremov'd.   *Ib.* l. 987.

Fled
Murmuring, and with him fled the shades of night.
                                                Ib. l. 1014.

His sleep
Was aery light, from pure digestion bred.
                                          Ib. bk. v, l. 3.

My fairest, my espoused, my latest found,
Heaven's last best gift, my ever new delight.
                                                Ib. l. 18.

Good, the more
Communicated, more abundant grows.   *Ib.* l. 71.

Best image of myself and dearer half.   *Ib.* l. 95.

These are thy glorious works, Parent of Good,
Almighty, thine this universal frame,
Thus wondrous fair; thyself how wondrous then!
Paradise Lost, bk. v, l. 153.

Him first, him last, him midst, and without end.
Ib. l. 165.

A wilderness of sweets. *Ib.* l. 294.

Another morn
Ris'n on mid-noon. *Ib.* l. 310.

So saying, with despatchful looks in haste
She turns, on hospitable thoughts intent. *Ib.* l. 331.

From many a berry, and from sweet kernels press'd
She tempers dulcet creams. *Ib.* l. 346.

Nor jealousy
Was understood, the injured lover's hell. *Ib.* l. 449.

Son of Heav'n and Earth,
Attend: that thou art happy, owe to God;
That thou continuest such, owe to thyself,
That is, to thy obedience; therein stand. *Ib.* l. 519.

Freely we serve,
Because we freely love, as in our will
To love or not; in this we stand or fall. *Ib.* l. 538.

What if earth
Be but the shadow of Heaven, and things therein
Each to other like, more than on earth is thought?
Ib. l. 574.

Hear all ye Angels, progeny of light,
Thrones, Dominations, Princedoms, Virtues, Powers.
Ib. l. 600.

All seemed well pleased, all seemed but were not all.
Ib. l. 617.

And in their motions harmony divine
So smoothes her charming tones, that God's own ear
Listens delighted. *Ib.* l. 625.

Satan, so call him now, his former name
Is heard no more in heaven. *Ib.* l. 655.

So spake the Seraph Abdiel, faithful found
Among the faithless, faithful only he;
Among innumerable false, unmoved,
Unshaken, unseduced, unterrified
His loyalty he kept, his love, his zeal. *Ib.* l. 893.

All night the dreadless angel unpursued
Through Heaven's wide champain held his way till
morn,
Waked by the circling hours, with rosy hand
Unbarred the gates of light. *Ib.* bk. vi, l. 1.

Servant of God, well done, well hast thou fought
The better fight, who singly hast maintained
Against revolted multitudes the cause
Of truth, in word mightier than they in arms.
Ib. l. 29.

He onward came; far off his coming shone. *Ib.* l. 768.

Headlong themselves they threw
Down from the verge of Heaven, eternal wrath
Burnt after them to the bottomless pit. *Ib.* l. 864.

Standing on earth, not rapt above the Pole,
More safe I sing with mortal voice, unchang'd
To hoarse or mute, though fall'n on evil days,
On evil days though fall'n, and evil tongues.
In darkness, and with dangers compass'd round,

And solitude; yet not alone, while thou
Visit'st my slumbers nightly, or when morn
Purples the east: still govern thou my song,
Urania, and fit audience find, though few:
But drive far off the barb'rous dissonance
Of Bacchus and his revellers. *Ib.* bk. vii, l. 23.

The affable Archangel. *Ib.* l. 41.

Necessity and chance
Approach not me, and what I will is fate. *Ib.* l. 172.

There Leviathan
Hugest of living creatures, on the deep
Stretch'd like a promontory sleeps or swims,
And seems a moving land, and at his gills
Draws in, and at his trunk spouts out a sea.
Ib. l. 412.

Now half appear'd
The tawny lion, pawing to get free
His hinder parts. *Ib.* l. 463.

The Planets in their stations list'ning stood,
While the bright Pomp ascended jubilant.
Open, ye everlasting gates, they sung,
Open, ye heavens, your living doors; let in
The great Creator from his work return'd
Magnificent, his six days' work, a world. *Ib.* l. 563.

The Angel ended, and in Adam's ear
So charming left his voice that he a while
Thought him still speaking, still stood fixed to hear.
Ib. bk. viii, l. 1.

He his fabric of the Heavens
Hath left to their disputes, perhaps to move
His laughter at their quaint opinions wide
Hereafter, when they come to model Heaven
And calculate the stars, how they will wield
The mighty frame, how build, unbuild, contrive
To save appearances, how gird the sphere
With centric and eccentric scribbled o'er,
Cycle and epicycle, orb in orb. *Ib.* l. 76.

Heaven is for thee too high
To know what passes there; be lowly wise:
Think only what concerns thee and thy being.
Ib. l. 172.

Liquid lapse of murmuring streams. *Ib.* l. 263.

And feel that I am happier than I know. *Ib.* l. 282.

In solitude
What happiness? Who can enjoy alone,
Or all enjoying, what contentment find? *Ib.* l. 364.

I waked
To find her, or for ever to deplore
Her loss, and other pleasures all abjure. *Ib.* l. 478.

Grace was in all her steps, heaven in her eye,
In every gesture dignity and love. *Ib.* l. 488.

Her virtue, and the conscience of her worth,
That would be wooed, and not unsought be won.
Ib. l. 502.

The amorous bird of night
Sung spousal, and bid haste the evening star
On his hill top, to light the bridal lamp. *Ib.* l. 518.

The sum of earthly bliss. *Ib.* l. 522.

So absolute she seems
And in herself complete, so well to know
Her own, that what she wills to do or say
Seems wisest, virtuousest, discreetest, best.
Paradise Lost, bk. viii, l. 547.

To whom the Angel with contracted brow.
Accuse not Nature, she hath done her part;
Do thou but thine, and be not diffident
Of wisdom, she deserts thee not, if thou
Dismiss not her.   *Ib.* l. 560.

Oft-times nothing profits more
Than self-esteem, grounded on just and right
Well manag'd.   *Ib.* l. 571.

With a smile that glowed
Celestial rosy red, love's proper hue.   *Ib.* l. 618.

My celestial Patroness, who deigns
Her nightly visitation unimplor'd,
And dictates to me slumb'ring, or inspires
Easy my unpremeditated verse:
Since first this subject for heroic song
Pleas'd me long choosing, and beginning late.
Ib. bk. ix, l. 21.

Unless an age too late, or cold
Climate, or years damp my intended wing.
Ib. l. 44.

The serpent subtlest beast of all the field. *Ib.* l. 86.

For nothing lovelier can be found
In woman, than to study household good,
And good works in her husband to promote.
Ib. l. 232.

For solitude sometimes is best society,
And short retirement urges sweet return. *Ib.* l. 249.

Wouldst thou approve thy constancy, approve
First thy obedience.   *Ib.* l. 367.

As one who long in populous city pent,
Where houses thick and sewers annoy the air,
Forth issuing on a summer's morn to breathe
Among the pleasant villages and farms
Adjoin'd, from each thing met conceives delight.
Ib. l. 445.

She fair, divinely fair, fit love for Gods.   *Ib.* l. 489.

Hope elevates, and joy
Brightens his crest.   *Ib.* l. 633.

God so commanded, and left that command
Sole daughter of his voice; the rest, we live
Law to ourselves, our reason is our law.   *Ib.* l. 652.

Her rash hand in evil hour
Forth reaching to the fruit, she pluck'd, she eat:
Earth felt the wound, and Nature from her seat
Sighing through all her works gave signs of woe
That all was lost.   *Ib.* l. 780.

Adam shall share with me in bliss or woe:
So dear I love him, that with him all deaths
I could endure, without him live no life. *Ib.* l. 831.

O fairest of creation! last and best
Of all God's works! creature in whom excell'd
Whatever can to sight or thought be form'd,
Holy, divine, good, amiable, or sweet!
How art thou lost, how on a sudden lost,
Defac'd, deflower'd, and now to Death devote?
Ib. l. 896.

For with thee
Certain my resolution is to die;
How can I live without thee, how forgo
Thy sweet converse and love so dearly joined,
To live again in these wild woods forlorn?
Should God create another Eve, and I
Another rib afford, yet loss of thee
Would never from my heart; no no, I feel
The link of nature draw me: flesh of flesh,
Bone of my bone thou art, and from thy state
Mine never shall be parted, weal or woe. *Ib.* l. 906.

What thou art is mine;
Our state cannot be sever'd, we are one,
One flesh; to lose thee were to lose myself.
Ib. l. 957.

A pillared shade
High overarched, and echoing walks between.
Ib. l. 1106.

He hears
On all sides, from innumerable tongues,
A dismal universal hiss, the sound
Of public scorn.   *Ib.* bk. x, l. 506.

Complicated monsters, head and tail,
Scorpion and asp, and Amphisbaena dire,
Cerastes horned, Hydrus, and Ellops drear.
Ib. l. 523.

Chew'd bitter ashes, which th' offended taste
With spattering noise rejected.   *Ib.* l. 566.

Oh! why did God,
Creator wise, that peopled highest Heaven
With Spirits masculine, create at last
This novelty on Earth, this fair defect
Of Nature?   *Ib.* l. 888.

Demoniac frenzy, moping melancholy,
And moon-struck madness.   *Ib.* bk. xi, l. 485.

So may'st thou live, till like ripe fruit thou drop
Into thy mother's lap, or be with ease
Gathered, not harshly plucked, for death mature:
This is old age.   *Ib.* l. 535.

Nor love thy life, nor hate; but what thou liv'st
Live well, how long or short permit to Heaven.
Ib. l. 553.

The evening star,
Love's harbinger.   *Ib.* l. 588.

The brazen throat of war had ceased to roar:
All now was turned to jollity and game,
To luxury and riot, feast and dance. *Ib.* l. 713.

For now I see
Peace to corrupt no less than war to waste. *Ib.* l. 779.

Then wilt thou not be loth
To leave this Paradise, but shalt possess
A Paradise within thee, happier far. *Ib.* bk. xii, l. 585.

In me is no delay; with thee to go,
Is to stay here; without thee here to stay,
Is to go hence unwilling; thou to me
Art all things under Heaven, all places thou,
Who for my wilful crime art banished hence.
Ib. l. 615.

They looking back, all th' eastern side beheld
Of Paradise, so late their happy seat,
Wav'd over by that flaming brand, the Gate
With dreadful faces throng'd and fiery arms.
Some natural tears they dropped, but wiped them
     soon;
The world was all before them, where to choose
Their place of rest, and Providence their guide:
They hand in hand with wandering steps and slow
Through Eden took their solitary way.
Paradise Lost, bk. xii, l. 641.

Satan, bowing low
His gray dissimulation, disappeared.
Paradise Regained, bk. i, l. 497.

Skill'd to retire, and in retiring draw
Hearts after them tangled in amorous nets.
Ib. bk. ii, l. 161.

Beauty stands
In the admiration only of weak minds
Led captive.   *Ib.* l. 220.

And now the herald lark
Left his ground-nest, high tow'ring to descry
The morn's approach, and greet her with his song.
Ib. l. 279.

Ladies of th' Hesperides, that seemed
Fairer than feign'd of old, or fabled since
Of faery damsels met in forest wide
By knights of Logres, or of Lyones,
Lancelot or Pelleas, or Pellenore.   *Ib.* l. 357.

Of whom to be dispraised were no small praise.
Ib. bk. iii, l. 56.

But on Occasion's forelock watchful wait. *Ib.* l. 173.

As he who, seeking asses, found a kingdom.
Ib. l. 242.

Elephants endorsed with towers.   *Ib.* l. 329.

Dusk faces with white silken turbans wreath'd.
Ib. bk. iv, l. 76.

The childhood shows the man,
As morning shows the day. Be famous then
By wisdom; as thy empire must extend,
So let extend thy mind o'er all the world. *Ib.* l. 220.

Athens, the eye of Greece, mother of arts
And eloquence, native to famous wits
Or hospitable, in her sweet recess,
City or suburban, studious walks and shades;
See there the olive grove of Academe,
Plato's retirement, where the Attic bird
Trills her thick-warbled notes the summer long.
Ib. l. 240.

The first and wisest of them all professed
To know this only, that he nothing knew. *Ib.* l. 293.

Deep versed in books and shallow in himself.
Ib. l. 327.

In them is plainest taught, and easiest learnt,
What makes a nation happy, and keeps it so.
Ib. l. 361.

Till morning fair
Came forth with pilgrim steps in amice grey.
Ib. l. 426.

Without wing
Of hippogriff.   *Ib.* l. 541.

And, as that Theban monster that proposed
Her riddle, and him who solved it not devoured;
That once found out and solved, for grief and spite
Cast herself headlong from th' Ismenian steep,
So strook with dread and anguish fell the Fiend;
And to his crew, that sat consulting, brought
Joyless triumphals of his hop't success,
Ruin, and desperation, and dismay,
Who durst so proudly tempt the Son of God.
Ib. l. 572.

He unobserved
Home to his mother's house private returned.
Ib. l. 638.

But headlong joy is ever on the wing.
The Passion, l. 5.

A little onward lend thy guiding hand
To these dark steps, a little further on.
Samson Agonistes, l. 1.

Eyeless in Gaza, at the mill with slaves. *Ib.* l. 41.

O dark, dark, dark, amid the blaze of noon,
Irrecoverably dark, total eclipse
Without all hope of day!   *Ib.* l. 80.

The sun to me is dark
And silent as the moon,
When she deserts the night
Hid in her vacant interlunar cave.   *Ib.* l. 86.

To live a life half dead, a living death.   *Ib.* l. 100.

Ran on embattled armies clad in iron,
And, weaponless himself,
Made arms ridiculous.   *Ib.* l. 129.

Wisest men
Have erred, and by bad women been deceived;
And shall again, pretend they ne'er so wise.
Ib. l. 210.

Just are the ways of God,
And justifiable to men;
Unless there be who think not God at all.
Ib. l. 293.

Of such doctrine never was there school,
But the heart of the fool,
And no man therein doctor but himself. *Ib.* l. 297.

What boots it at one gate to make defence,
And at another to let in the foe?   *Ib.* l. 560.

My race of glory run, and race of shame,
And I shall shortly be with them that rest. *Ib.* l. 597.

But who is this, what thing of sea or land?
Female of sex it seems,
That so bedeck'd, ornate, and gay,
Comes this way sailing
Like a stately ship
Of Tarsus, bound for th' isles
Of Javan or Gadier,
With all her bravery on, and tackle trim,
Sails fill'd, and streamers waving,
Courted by all the winds that hold them play,
An amber scent of odorous perfume
Her harbinger.   *Ib.* l. 710.

That grounded maxim
So rife and celebrated in the mouths
Of wisest men; that to the public good
Private respects must yield.   *Ib.* l. 865.

Yet beauty, though injurious, hath strange power,
After offence returning, to regain
Love once possess'd.　　　*Samson Agonistes*, l. 1003.

Love-quarrels oft in pleasing concord end.
　　　　　　　　　　　　　Ib. l. 1008.

Therefore God's universal law
Gave to the man despotic power
Over his female in due awe.　　　*Ib.* l. 1053.

He's gone, and who knows how may he report
Thy words by adding fuel to the flame?　*Ib.* l. 1350.

Lords are lordliest in their wine.　*Ib.* l. 1418.

For evil news rides post, while good news baits.
　　　　　　　　　　　　　Ib. l. 1538.

And as an ev'ning dragon came,
Assailant on the perched roosts
And nests in order rang'd
Of tame villatic fowl.　　　*Ib.* l. 1692.

Like that self-begotten bird
In the Arabian woods embost,
That no second knows nor third,
And lay erewhile a holocaust.　　　*Ib.* l. 1699.

And though her body die, her fame survives,
A secular bird, ages of lives.　　　*Ib.* l. 1706.

　　　　Samson hath quit himself
Like Samson, and heroically hath finish'd
A life heroic.　　　　　　*Ib.* l. 1709.

Nothing is here for tears, nothing to wail
Or knock the breast; no weakness, no contempt,
Dispraise or blame; nothing but well and fair,
And what may quiet us in a death so noble.
　　　　　　　　　　　　　Ib. l. 1721.

All is best, though we oft doubt,
What th' unsearchable dispose
Of highest wisdom brings about,
And ever best found in the close.
Oft he seems to hide his face,
But unexpectedly returns
And to his faithful champion hath in place
Bore witness gloriously; whence Gaza mourns
And all that band them to resist
His uncontrollable intent,
His servants he with new acquist
Of true experience from this great event
With peace and consolation hath dismiss'd,
And calm of mind all passion spent.　*Ib.* l. 1745.

What needs my Shakespeare for his honour'd bones,
The labour of an age in piled stones,
Or that his hallow'd relics should be hid
Under a star-y-pointing pyramid?
Dear son of memory, great heir of fame,
What need'st thou such weak witness of thy name?
　　　　　　　　[Epitaph] on Shakespeare.

Blest pair of Sirens, pledges of Heaven's joy,
Sphere-born harmonious sisters, Voice and Verse.
　　　　　　　　At a Solemn Music, l. 1.

Where the bright Seraphim in burning row
Their loud up-lifted Angel trumpets blow.　*Ib.*

　　　Till disproportion'd sin
Jarr'd against nature's chime.　　　*Ib.*

O nightingale, that on yon bloomy spray
Warblest at eve, when all the woods are still.
　　　　　　　Sonnet i. To the Nightingale.

All is, if I have grace to use it so,
As ever in my great Task-Master's eye.
　　Ib. ii. *On his having arrived at the age of
　　twenty-three.*

Captain or Colonel, or Knight in arms.
　　Ib. viii. *When the assault was intended to the
　　city.*

The great Emathian conqueror bid spare
The house of Pindarus, when temple and tower
Went to the ground.　　　　　　*Ib.*

　　　As that dishonest victory
At Chæronea, fatal to liberty,
Killed with report that old man eloquent.
　　　　　Ib. x. *To the Lady Margaret Ley.*

Those rugged names to our like mouths grow sleek,
That would have made Quintilian stare and gasp.
Thy age, like ours, O soul of Sir John Cheek,
Hated not learning worse than toad or asp,
When thou taught'st Cambridge, and King Edward
　Greek.　　　*Ib.* xi. 'A book was writ of late.'

Licence they mean when they cry Liberty;
For who loves that, must first be wise and good.
　　　Ib. xii. *On the Same.* [The detraction, &c.]

Avenge, O Lord, thy slaughtered saints, whose bones
Lie scattered on the Alpine mountains cold;
Ev'n them who kept thy truth so pure of old,
When all our fathers worshipped stocks and stones,
Forget not.　*Ib.* xv. *On the late Massacre in Piedmont.*

That one talent which is death to hide.
　　　　　　　Ib. xvi. *On his Blindness.*

They also serve who only stand and wait.　*Ib.*

In mirth, that after no repenting draws.
　　　　　　　Ib. xviii. *To Cyriac Skinner.*

To measure life learn thou betimes, and know
Toward solid good what leads the nearest way;
For other things mild Heaven a time ordains,
And disapproves that care, though wise in show,
That with superfluous burden loads the day,
And, when God sends a cheerful hour, refrains.　*Ib.*

Methought I saw my late espousèd Saint
Brought to me like Alcestis from the grave.
　　　　　　　Ib. xix. *On His Deceased Wife.*

Love, sweetness, goodness, in her person shined. *Ib.*

But O as to embrace me she inclined,
I waked, she fled, and day brought back my night. *Ib.*

New Presbyter is but old Priest writ large.
　　*Ib. On the New Forces of Conscience under the
　　Long Parliament.*

For what can war but endless war still breed?
　　　Ib. On the Lord General Fairfax.

　　　Peace hath her victories
No less renowned than war.
　　Ib. [*To the Lord General Cromwell, May* 1652.]

Help us to save free conscience from the paw
Of hireling wolves, whose gospel is their maw.　*Ib.*

Fly, envious Time, till thou run out thy race:
Cail on the lazy leaden-stepping hours. *On Time*, l. 1.

Beldam Nature.
　　　At a Vacation Exercise in the College, l. 46.

He who would not be frustrate of his hope to write well hereafter in laudable things ought himself to be a true poem.
Apology for Smectymnuus, introd. to sec. 1.

His words . . . like so many nimble and airy servitors trip about him at command. *Ib.* sec. 12.

Books are not absolutely dead things, but do contain a potency of life in them to be as active as that soul was whose progeny they are; nay they do preserve as in a vial the purest efficacy and extraction of that living intellect that bred them. *Areopagitica.*

As good almost kill a man as kill a good book: who kills a man kills a reasonable creature, God's image; but he who destroys a good book, kills reason itself, kills the image of God, as it were in the eye. *Ib.*

A good book is the precious life-blood of a master spirit, embalmed and treasured up on purpose to a life beyond life. *Ib.*

I cannot praise a fugitive and cloistered virtue, unexercised and unbreathed, that never sallies out and sees her adversary, but slinks out of the race, where that immortal garland is to be run for, not without dust and heat. *Ib.*

Our sage and serious poet Spenser. *Ib.*

Where there is much desire to learn, there of necessity will be much arguing, much writing, many opinions; for opinion in good men is but knowledge in the making. *Ib.*

Methinks I see in my mind a noble and puissant nation rousing herself like a strong man after sleep, and shaking her invincible locks. Methinks I see her as an eagle mewing her mighty youth, and kindling her undazzled eyes at the full midday beam. *Ib.*

Though all the winds of doctrine were let loose to play upon the earth, so Truth be in the field, we do injuriously by licensing and prohibiting to misdoubt her strength. Let her and Falsehood grapple; who ever knew Truth put to the worse, in a free and open encounter. *Ib.*

But because about the manner and order of this government, whether it ought to be Presbyterial, or Prelatical, such endless question, or rather uproar is arisen in this land, as may be justly termed, what the fever is to the physicians, the eternal reproach of the divines.
Reason of Church Government, preface.

This manner of writing [*i.e.* prose] wherein knowing myself inferior to myself . . . I have the use, as I may account it, but of my left hand.
Ib. bk. ii, introd. to ch. 1.

A poet soaring in the high region of his fancies with his garland and singing robes about him. *Ib.*

By labour and intent study (which I take to be my portion in this life) joined with the strong propensity of nature, I might perhaps leave something so written to after-times, as they should not willingly let it die. *Ib.*

Inquisitorious and tyrannical duncery. *Ib.*

Beholding the bright countenance of truth in the quiet and still air of delightful studies. *Ib.*

Let not England forget her precedence of teaching nations how to live.
The Doctrine and Discipline of Divorce.

I call therefore a complete and generous education that which fits a man to perform justly, skilfully and magnanimously all the offices both private and public of peace and war. *Of Education.*

I will point ye out the right path of a virtuous and noble Education; laborious indeed at the first ascent, but else so smooth, so green, so full of goodly prospect, and melodious sounds on every side, that the harp of Orpheus was not more charming.
Ib.

Brave men, and worthy patriots, dear to God, and famous to all ages. *Ib.*

Ornate rhetorick taught out of the rule of Plato, . . . To which poetry would be made subsequent, or indeed rather precedent, as being less subtle and fine, but more simple, sensuous and passionate.
Ib.

In those vernal seasons of the year, when the air is calm and pleasant, it were an injury and sullenness against Nature not to go out, and see her riches, and partake in her rejoicing with Heaven and Earth. *Ib.*

For such kind of borrowing as this, if it be not bettered by the borrower, among good authors is accounted plagiary. *Iconoclastes*, ch. 23.

None can love freedom heartily, but good men; the rest love not freedom, but licence.
Tenure of Kings and Magistrates.

No man who knows aught, can be so stupid to deny that all men naturally were born free. *Ib.*

JAMES, DUKE OF MONMOUTH
1649–1685

Do not hack me as you did my Lord Russell.
Words to his executioner. Macaulay, Hist. of England, vol. i, ch. 5.

JOHN SAMUEL BEWLEY MONSELL
1811–1875

Fight the good fight with all thy might,
Christ is thy strength, and Christ thy right;
Lay hold on life, and it shall be
Thy joy and crown eternally.

Run the straight race through God's good grace,
Lift up thine eyes, and seek His Face;
Life with its way before us lies,
Christ is the path, and Christ the prize.
Hymns of Love and Praise. Fight of Faith.

Faint not nor fear, His arms are near,
He changeth not, and thou art dear;
Only believe, and thou shalt see
That Christ is all in all to thee. *Ib.*

LADY MARY WORTLEY MONTAGU

1689–1762

This world consists of men, women, and Herveys.
Letters, vol. i, p. 67.

But the fruit that can fall without shaking,
   Indeed is too mellow for me.
      *Letters and Works. Answered, for Lord William
      Hamilton.*

He comes too near that comes to be denied.
      Ib. The Lady's Resolve.

And we meet, with champagne and a chicken, at last.
      Ib. The Lover.

General notions are generally wrong.
      *Ib. Letter to Mr. Wortley Montagu 28 March
      1710.*

JAMES MONTGOMERY

1771–1854

'For ever with the Lord!'
   Amen; so let it be;
Life from the dead is in that word,
   'Tis immortality.   *At Home in Heaven.*

Here in the body pent,
   Absent from Him I roam,
Yet nightly pitch my moving tent
   A day's march nearer home.   *Ib.*

He was—whatever thou hast been;
He is—what thou shalt be.   *The Common Lot.*

Prayer is the soul's sincere desire,
   Uttered or unexpressed,
The motion of a hidden fire
   That trembles in the breast.   *What is Prayer?*

A day in such serene enjoyment spent
Were worth an age of splendid discontent.
      Greenland, Canto II, l. 224.

ROBERT MONTGOMERY

1807–1855

The solitary monk who shook the world.
      Luther. Man's Need and God's Supply, l. 68.

With fearful gaze, still be it mine to see
How all is fill'd and vivified by Thee;
Upon thy mirror, earth's majestic view,
To paint Thy Presence, and to feel it too.
      The Omnipresence of the Deity (ed. 1830),
      pt. I, l. 105.

And thou, vast ocean! on whose awful face
Time's iron feet can print no ruin-trace.
      Ib. l. 141.

Ye quenchless stars! so eloquently bright,
Untroubled sentries of the shadowy night. *Ib.* l. 305.

The soul aspiring pants its source to mount,
As streams meander level with their fount. *Ib.* l. 339.

JAMES GRAHAM, MARQUIS OF MONTROSE

1612–1650

My dear and only love, I pray
   This noble world of thee,
Be govern'd by no other sway
   But purest Monarchy.
For if confusion have a part,
   Which virtuous souls abhor,
And hold a synod in thy heart,
   I'll never love thee more. *My Dear and Only Love.*

He either fears his fate too much,
   Or his deserts are small,
That puts it not unto the touch,
   To win or lose it all.   *Ib.*

But if thou wilt be constant then,
   And faithful of thy word,
I'll make thee glorious by my pen,
   And famous by my sword.   *Ib.*

Let them bestow on every airth a limb;
Then open all my veins, that I may swim
To thee, my Maker! in that crimson lake;
Then place my parboiled head upon a stake—
Scatter my ashes—strew them in the air;—
Lord! since thou know'st where all these atoms are,
I'm hopeful thou'lt recover once my dust,
And confident thou'lt raise me with the just.
      *Lines Written on the Window of his Jail the
      Night before his Execution. Scottish Poetry of
      the Seventeenth Century.*

PERCY MONTROSE

In a cavern, in a canyon,
   Excavating for a mine,
Dwelt a miner, Forty-niner,
   And his daughter, Clementine.
Oh, my darling, oh my darling, oh my darling
   Clementine!
Thou art lost and gone for ever, dreadful sorry,
   Clementine.

Light she was and like a fairy,
   And her shoes were number nine;
Herring boxes without topses,
   Sandals were for Clementine.   *Ib.*

But I kissed her little sister,
   And forgot my Clementine.   *Ib.*

CLEMENT C. MOORE

1779–1863

'T was the night before Christmas, when all through
   the house
Not a creature was stirring, not even a mouse;
The stockings were hung by the chimney with care,
In hopes that St. Nicholas soon would be there.
      The Night before Christmas.

EDWARD MOORE

1712–1757

This is adding insult to injuries. *The Foundling*, v. ii.

I am rich beyond the dreams of avarice.
      The Gamester, II. ii.

GEORGE MOORE

1852–1933

All reformers are bachelors.
The Bending of the Bough, Act 1.

Art must be parochial in the beginning to become
cosmopolitan in the end.
Hail and Farewell! 1925, vol. i, p. 5.

Acting is therefore the lowest of the arts, if it is an art
at all.   *Mummer-Worship.*

THOMAS MOORE

1779–1852

For you know, dear—I may, without vanity, hint—
Though an angel should write, still 'tis *devils* must
print.   *The Fudges in England*, letter iii, l. 64.

Yet, who can help loving the land that has taught us
Six hundred and eighty-five ways to dress eggs?
The Fudge Family in Paris, letter viii. l. 64.

As that Countess of Desmond, of whom I've been
told
That she liv'd to much more than a hundred and ten,
And was kill'd by a fall from a cherry-tree then!
Ib. letter x, l. 23.

Weep on; and, as thy sorrows flow,
I'll taste the luxury of woe.
Juvenile Poems. Anacreontic: Press the Grape.

Where I love I must not marry;
Where I marry, cannot love.
Ib. Love and Marriage.

'Twere more than woman to be wise;
'Twere more than man to wish thee so!
Ib. The Ring (ed. 1882).

To love you was pleasant enough,
And, oh! 'tis delicious to hate you!
Ib. To — When I Lov'd You.

Go where glory waits thee,
But, while fame elates thee,
Oh! still remember me.
Irish Melodies. Go Where Glory.

Erin, the tear and the smile in thine eyes,
Blend like the rainbow that hangs in thy skies!
Ib. Erin, the Tear.

Oh! breathe not his name, let it sleep in the shade,
Where cold and unhonour'd his relics are laid.
Ib. Oh! Breathe not his Name.

The harp that once through Tara's halls
The soul of music shed,
Now hangs as mute on Tara's walls
As if that soul were fled.—
So sleeps the pride of former days,
So glory's thrill is o'er;
And hearts, that once beat high for praise,
Now feel that pulse no more.
Ib. The Harp that Once.

Rich and rare were the gems she wore,
And a bright gold ring on her wand she bore.
Ib. Rich and Rare.

There is not in the wide world a valley so sweet
As that vale in whose bosom the bright waters meet.
Ib. The Meeting of the Waters.

Believe me, if all those endearing young charms,
Which I gaze on so fondly to-day.
Ib. Believe Me, if All.

And around the dear ruin each wish of my heart
Would entwine itself verdantly still.   *Ib.*

No, the heart that has truly lov'd never forgets,
But as truly loves on to the close,
As the sun-flower turns on her god, when he sets,
The same look which she turn'd when he rose. *Ib.*

Oh! blame not the bard.   *Ib. Oh! Blame Not.*

And, when once the young heart of a maiden is stolen,
The maiden herself will steal after it soon.
Ib. Ill Omens.

'Tis sweet to think, that, where'er we rove,
We are sure to find something blissful and dear,
And that, when we're far from the lips we love,
We've but to make love to the lips we are near.
Ib. 'Tis Sweet to Think.

No, there's nothing half so sweet in life
As love's young dream. *Ib. Love's Young Dream.*

Lesbia hath a beaming eye,
But no one knows for whom it beameth.
Ib. Lesbia Hath.

Eyes of most unholy blue!   *Ib. By that Lake.*

She is far from the land where her young hero sleeps,
And lovers are round her, sighing:
But coldly she turns from their gaze, and weeps,
For her heart in his grave is lying. *Ib. She is Far.*

This life is all chequer'd with pleasures and woes.
Ib. This Life is All Chequered.

'Tis the last rose of summer
Left blooming alone;
All her lovely companions
Are faded and gone.   *Ib. 'Tis the Last Rose.*

Then awake! the heavens look bright, my dear;
'Tis never too late for delight, my dear;
And the best of all ways
To lengthen our days
Is to steal a few hours from the night, my dear!
Ib. The Young May Moon.

The Minstrel Boy to the war is gone,
In the ranks of death you'll find him;
His father's sword he has girded on,
And his wild harp slung behind him.
Ib. The Minstrel Boy.

You may break, you may shatter the vase, if you will,
But the scent of the roses will hang round it still.
Ib. Farewell! But Whenever.

Has sorrow thy young days shaded?
Ib. Has Sorrow Thy Young.

Come, child of misfortune, come thither,
I'll weep with thee, tear for tear.   *Ib.*

The light, that lies
In woman's eyes,
Has been my heart's undoing. *Ib. The Time I've Lost.*

My only books
Were woman's looks,
And folly's all they've taught me.   *Ib.*

Come, rest in this bosom, my own stricken deer,
Though the herd have fled from thee, thy home is still
here.   *Ib. Come, Rest In This Bosom.*

I know not, I ask not, if guilt's in that heart,
But I know that I love thee, whatever thou art.   *Ib.*

And doth not a meeting like this make amends,
For all the long years I've been wand'ring away?
                    Ib. And Doth Not a Meeting.

Sing—sing—Music was given,
To brighten the gay, and kindle the loving.
                    Ib. Sing—Sing—Music Was Given.

Who, that surveys this span of earth we press—
This speck of life in time's great wilderness,
This narrow isthmus 'twixt two boundless seas,
The past, the future, two eternities!—
                    Lalla Rookh. The Veiled Prophet, ii, l. 136.

There's a bower of roses by Bendemeer's stream,
And the nightingale sings round it all the day long.
                    Ib. l. 247.

And, when all hope seem'd desp'rate, wildly hurl'd
Himself into the scale, and sav'd a world.
                    Ib. iii, l. 211.

But Faith, fanatic Faith, once wedded fast
To some dear falsehood, hugs it to the last. *Ib.* l. 356.

One Morn a Peri at the gate
Of Eden stood, disconsolate.
                    Ib. Paradise and the Peri, l. 1.

Some flow'rets of Eden ye still inherit,
But the trail of the Serpent is over them all!
                    Ib. l. 206.
Oh! ever thus, from childhood's hour,
I've seen my fondest hopes decay;
I never lov'd a tree or flow'r,
But 't was the first to fade away.
I never nurs'd a dear gazelle,
To glad me with its soft black eye,
But when it came to know me well,
And love me, it was sure to die!
                    Ib. The Fire-Worshippers, i, l. 279.

Like Dead Sea fruits, that tempt the eye,
But turn to ashes on the lips!   *Ib.* l. 484.

'Come, come', said Tom's father, 'at your time of life,
'There's no longer excuse for thus playing the
rake—
'It is time you should think, boy, of taking a wife'—
'Why, so it is, father—whose wife shall I take?'
                    Miscellaneous Poems. A Joke Versified.

Disguise our bondage as we will,
'Tis woman, woman, rules us still.
                    Ib. Sovereign Woman.

Those evening bells! those evening bells!
How many a tale their music tells,
Of youth, and home, and that sweet time
When last I heard their soothing chime.
                    National Airs. Those Evening Bells.

Oft, in the stilly night,
Ere Slumber's chain has bound me,
Fond Memory brings the light
Of other days around me;
The smiles, the tears,
Of boyhood's years,
The words of love then spoken;
The eyes that shone,
Now dimm'd and gone,
The cheerful hearts now broken!
                    Ib. Oft in the Stilly Night.
I feel like one
Who treads alone
Some banquet-hall deserted,
Whose lights are fled,
Whose garlands dead,
And all but he departed!   *Ib.*

If I speak to thee in Friendship's name,
Thou think'st I speak too coldly;
If I mention Love's devoted flame,
Thou say'st I speak too boldly.
                    Ib. How Shall I Woo?

Faintly as tolls the evening chime
Our voices keep tune and our oars keep time.
Soon as the woods on shore look dim,
We'll sing at St. Ann's our parting hymn.
Row, brothers, row, the stream runs fast,
The Rapids are near and the daylight's past.
                    Poems Relating to America. Canadian Boat Song.

This world is all a fleeting show,
For man's illusion given;
The smiles of joy, the tears of woe,
Deceitful shine, deceitful flow—
There's nothing true, but Heaven!
                    Sacred Songs. This World is All.

Sound the loud timbrel o'er Egypt's dark sea!
Jehovah has triumph'd—his people are free.
                    Ib. Miriam's Song. Sound the Loud Timbrel.

There was a little Man, and he had a little Soul,
And he said, 'Little Soul, let us try, try, try'.
                    Satirical and Humorous Poems. Little Man and Little Soul.

And one wild Shakespeare, following Nature's lights,
Is worth whole planets, filled with Stagyrites.
                    The Sceptic.

Now in his palace of the West,
Sinking to slumber, the bright Day,
Like a tir'd monarch fann'd to rest,
'Mid the cool airs of evening lay;
While round his couch's golden rim
The gaudy clouds, like courtiers, crept—
Struggling each other's light to dim,
And catch his last smile e'er he slept.
                    The Summer Fête, l. 232.

Your priests, whate'er their gentle shamming,
Have always had a taste for damning.
                    Twopenny Post-Bag, letter iv.

Good at a fight, but better at a play,
Godlike in giving, but—the devil to pay!
                    *On a Cast of Sheridan's Hand. Memoirs of the
                    Life of R. B. Sheridan,* 1825, p. 712.

THOMAS OSBERT MORDAUNT

1730–1809

Sound, sound the clarion, fill the fife,
   Throughout the sensual world proclaim,
One crowded hour of glorious life
   Is worth an age without a name.
     The Bee, 12 Oct. 1791. Verses Written During
     the War, 1756–1763.

HANNAH MORE

1745–1833

For you'll ne'er mend your fortunes, nor help the just
   cause,
By breaking of windows, or breaking of laws.
     Address to the Meeting in Spa Fields (1817).
     H. Thompson's Life, 1838, p. 398.

   A crown! what is it?
It is to bear the miseries of a people!
To hear their murmurs, feel their discontents,
And sink beneath a load of splendid care!
     Daniel, pt. vi, l. 72.

Small habits, well pursued betimes,
May reach the dignity of crimes.   *Florio*, l. 77.

He lik'd those literary cooks
Who skim the cream of others' books;
And ruin half an author's graces
By plucking bon-mots from their places. *Ib.* l. 123.

   Did not God
Sometimes withhold in mercy what we ask,
We should be ruined at our own request.
     Moses in the Bulrushes, Pt. I, l. 34.

The sober comfort, all the peace which springs
From the large aggregate of little things;
On these small cares of daughter, wife, or friend,
The almost sacred joys of home depend.
     Sensibility, l. 315.

SIR THOMAS MORE

1478–1535

'In good faith, I rejoiced, son,' quoth he, 'that I had
given the devil a foul fall, and that with those Lords
I had gone so far, as without great shame I could
never go back again.'
     Roper, *Life of Sir Thomas More* (1935), p. 69.

'By god body, master More, *Indignatio principis mors
est.*'
'Is that all, my Lord?' quoth he. "Then in good faith
is there no more difference between your grace and
me, but that I shall die today, and you tomorrow.'
     Ib. p. 71.

Son Roper, I thank our Lord the field is won.
     Ib. p. 73.

Is not this house [the Tower of London] as nigh
heaven as my own?   *Ib.* p. 83.

I pray you, master Lieutenant, see me safe up, and
my coming down let me shift for my self. [On
mounting the scaffold.]   *Ib.* p. 103.

Pluck up thy spirits, man, and be not afraid to do
thine office; my neck is very short; take heed therefore thou strike not awry, for saving of thine
honesty.   [*To the Executioner.*] *Ib.* p. 103.

This hath not offended the king. [As he drew his
beard aside on placing his head on the block.]
     Bacon, *Apophthegms*, 22.

Yea, marry, now it is somewhat, for now it is rhyme;
before, it was neither rhyme nor reason. [Advising
an author to put his ill-written work into verse.]
     A. Cayley's *Memoirs of Sir Thos. More* (1808),
     vol. i, p. 247.

They roll and rumble,
They turn and tumble,
   As pigges do in a poke.
     Works, 1557, ¶. ii. 6. *How a Sergeant would*
     learn to Play the Frere.

This is a fair tale of a tub told us of his elects.
     Ib. p. 576. *Confutation of Tyndale's Answers.*

Your sheep, that were wont to be so meek and tame,
and so small eaters, now, as I hear say, be become
so great devourers, and so wild, that they eat up
and swallow down the very men themselves.
     Utopia, bk. 1.

DR. THOMAS MORELL

1703–1784

See, the conquering hero comes!
Sound the trumpets, beat the drums! *Joshua*, pt. iii.

AUGUSTUS DE MORGAN

1806–1871

Great fleas have little fleas upon their backs to bite
   'em,
And little fleas have lesser fleas, and so *ad infinitum.*
     A Budget of Paradoxes (1872), p. 377.

ALBERT EDMUND PARKER, EARL OF MORLEY

1843–1905

I am always very glad when Lord Salisbury makes a
great speech, . . . It is sure to contain at least one
blazing indiscretion which it is a delight to remember.   *Speech, Hull, 25 Nov. 1887.*

JOHN, VISCOUNT MORLEY OF BLACKBURN

1838–1923

No man can climb out beyond the limitations of his
own character.
     Critical Miscellanies (1886), i, *Robespierre*, p.
     93.

[Letter-writing,] that most delightful way of wasting
time.   *Ib.* iii. *Life of Geo. Eliot*, p. 96.

CHARLES MORRIS

1745–1838

If one must have a villa in summer to dwell,
Oh, give me the sweet shady side of Pall Mall!
     The Contrast.

A house is much more to my taste than a tree,
And for groves, oh! a good grove of chimneys for me. *Ib.*

GEORGE POPE MORRIS

1802–1867

Woodman, spare that tree!
  Touch not a single bough!
In youth it sheltered me,
  And I'll protect it now.
Woodman, Spare That Tree.

WILLIAM MORRIS

1834–1896

'One of these cloths is heaven, and one is hell,
Now choose one cloth for ever; which they be,
I will not tell you, you must somehow tell
Of your own strength and mightiness.'
Defence of Guenevere.

And one of these strange choosing cloths was blue,
Wavy and long, and one cut short and red;
No man could tell the better of the two.

After a shivering half-hour you said:
'God help! heaven's colour, the blue;' and he said:
  'hell'.
Perhaps you then would roll upon your bed,

And cry to all good men that loved you well,
'Ah Christ! if only I had known, known, known.' *Ib.*

The idle singer of an empty day.
The Earthly Paradise. An Apology.

Dreamer of dreams, born out of my due time,
  Why should I strive to set the crooked straight?
Let it suffice me that my murmuring rhyme
  Beats with light wing against the ivory gate,
  Telling a tale not too importunate
To those who in the sleepy region stay,
Lulled by the singer of an empty day. *Ib.*

Forget six counties overhung with smoke,
Forget the snorting steam and piston stroke,
Forget the spreading of the hideous town;
Think rather of the pack-horse on the down,
And dream of London, small and white and clean,
The clear Thames bordered by its gardens green.
Ib. Prologue. *The Wanderers*, l. 1.

Death have we hated, knowing not what it meant;
Life we have loved, through green leaf and through
  sere,
Though still the less we knew of its intent.
Ib. L'Envoi, xiii.

Had she come all the way for this,
To part at last without a kiss?
Yea, had she borne the dirt and rain
That her own eyes might see him slain
Beside the haystack in the floods?
The Haystack in the Floods.

I know a little garden close
Set thick with lily and red rose,
Where I would wander if I might
From dewy dawn to dewy night,
And have one with me wandering.
The Life and Death of Jason, l. 577.

Love is enough: though the world be a-waning,
And the woods have no voice but the voice of
  complaining. *Love is Enough*, i.

But lo, the old inn, and the lights, and the fire,
And the fiddler's old tune and the shuffling of feet;
Soon for us shall be quiet and rest and desire,
And tomorrow's uprising to deeds shall be sweet.
The Message of the March Wind.

'You must be very old, Sir Giles.' *Old Love.*

They hammer'd out my basnet point
Into a round salade. *Ib.*

My lady seems of ivory
Forehead, straight nose, and cheeks that be
Hollow'd a little mournfully.
Beata mea Domina! Praise of my Lady.

Across the empty garden-beds,
When the Sword went out to sea.
The Sailing of the Sword.

There were four of us about that bed;
The mass-priest knelt at the side.
Shameful Death.

He did not die in the night,
  He did not die in the day. *Ib.*

It is the longest night in all the year,
Near on the day when the Lord Christ was born;
Six hours ago I came and sat down here,
And ponder'd sadly, wearied and forlorn.
Sir Galahad, A Christmas Mystery, l. 1.

O servant of the high God, Galahad! *Ib.* i. 153.

Speak but one word to me over the corn,
Over the tender, bow'd locks of the corn.
Summer Dawn.

And ever she sung from noon to noon,
'Two red roses across the moon.'
Two Red Roses Across the Moon.

Wind, wind! thou art sad, art thou kind? *The Wind.*

Forsooth, brothers, fellowship is heaven, and lack of
  fellowship is hell: fellowship is life, and lack of
  fellowship is death: and the deeds that ye do upon
  the earth, it is for fellowship's sake that ye do them.
The Dream of John Ball, ch. 4.

RICHARD MORTON

Twiggy voo, my boys, *twiggy voo?*
Twiggy Voo.

THOMAS MORTON

1764?–1838

Approbation from Sir Hubert Stanley is praise indeed.
A Cure for the Heartache, v. ii.

I eat well, and I drink well, and I sleep well—but
  that's all. *A Roland for an Oliver*, I. ii.

Always ding, dinging Dame Grundy into my ears—
  what will Mrs. Grundy zay? What will Mrs.
  Grundy think? *Speed the Plough*, I. i.

THOMAS MOSS

1740–1808

Pity the sorrows of a poor old man,
  Whose trembling limbs have borne him to your
    door,
Whose days are dwindled to the shortest span;
  Oh! give relief, and Heaven will bless your store.
The Beggar's Petition.

JOHN LOTHROP MOTLEY

1814–1877

As long as he lived, he was the guiding-star of a brave
    nation, and when he died the little children cried in
    the streets. [William of Orange]
            Rise of the Dutch Republic, pt. vi, ch. vii.

Give us the luxuries of life, and we will dispense with
    its necessities.
            Remark. O. W. Holmes' *Autocrat of the
            Breakfast-Table*, ch. 6.

PETER ANTHONY MOTTEUX

1660–1718

The devil was sick, the devil a monk wou'd be;
The devil was well, and the devil a monk he'd be.
            Translation of Rabelais. *Gargantua and Panta-
            gruel*, Bk. iv, ch. 24.

HENRY PHIPPS, EARL OF MULGRAVE

1755–1831

And toast before each Martial tune—
'Howe, and the Glorious First of June!'
                        Our Line Was Formed.

DINAH MARIA MULOCK

see

DINAH MARIA CRAIK

ANTHONY MUNDAY

1553–1603

Beauty sat bathing by a spring
    Where fairest shades did hide her;
The winds blew calm, the birds did sing,
    The cool streams ran beside her.
My wanton thoughts enticed mine eye
To see what was forbidden:
But better memory said, fie!
    So vain desire was chidden.
            Hey nonny, nonny.
            England's Helicon. To Colin Clout.

HECTOR HUGH MUNRO

see

SAKI

C. W. MURPHY

We all go the same way home.   *Title of Song.*

Has anybody here seen Kelly?
Kelly from the Isle of Man?
            Has Anybody Here seen Kelly?

Kelly from the Em'rald Isle.   *Ib.*

FRED MURRAY

Carve a little bit off the top for me!
            A Little Bit Off The Top.

Our lodger's such a nice young man.   *Title of Song.*

FREDERICK WILLIAM HENRY MYERS

1843–1901

Moses on the mountain
Died of the kisses of the lips of God.   *S. Paul.*

CAROLINA BARONESS NAIRNE

1766–1845

Will ye no come back again?
Better lo'ed ye canna be,
Will ye no come back again?
            Life and Songs (1869),
            Bonnie Charlie's now awa'.

Wha'll buy my caller herrin'?
    They're bonnie fish and halesome farin';
Wha'll buy my caller herrin',
    New drawn frae the Forth?   *Ib. Caller Herrin'.*

Oh, ye may ca' them vulgar farin',
Wives and mithers maist despairin',
    Ca' them lives o' men.   *Ib.*

Charlie is my darling, my darling, my darling,
Charlie is my darling, the young Chevalier.
            Ib. Charlie is My Darling.

Gude nicht, and joy be wi' you a'.   *Ib. Gude Nicht.*

Wi' a hundred pipers an' a', an' a',
Wi' a hundred pipers an' a', an' a',
We'll up an' gie them a blaw, a blaw,
Wi' a hundred pipers an' a', an' a'.
            Ib. The Hundred Pipers.

A penniless lass wi' a lang pedigree.
            Ib. The Laird of Cockpen.

I'm wearin' awa'
    To the land o' the leal.   *Ib. The Land o' the Leal.*

There's nae sorrow there, John,
There's neither cauld nor care, John,
The day is aye fair
    In the land o' the leal.   *Ib.*

SIR WILLIAM NAPIER

1785–1860

Then was seen with what a strength and majesty the
    British soldier fights.
            History of the War in the Peninsula, bk. xii,
            ch. 6, *Albuera.*

THOMAS NASHE

1567–1601

Brightness falls from the air;
Queens have died young and fair;
Dust hath closed Helen's eye.
                    In Time of Pestilence.

Spring, the sweet spring, is the year's pleasant king;
Then blooms each thing, then maids dance in a ring,
Cold doth not sting, the pretty birds do sing:
  Cuckoo, jug-jug, pu-we, to-witta-woo!
Spring.

JAMES BALL NAYLOR

1860–

King David and King Solomon
Led merry, merry lives,
With many, many lady friends
And many, many wives;
But when old age crept over them,
With many, many qualms,
King Solomon wrote the Proverbs
And King David wrote the Psalms.
David and Solomon.

JOHN MASON NEALE

1818–1866

All glory, laud, and honour
To Thee, Redeemer, King,
To whom the lips of children
Made sweet Hosannas ring.
  All Glory, Laud and Honour, tr. from Latin,
  Gloria, Laus et Honor tibi sit.

Jerusalem the golden,
  With milk and honey blest,
Beneath thy contemplation
  Sink heart and voice opprest.
I know not, oh, I know not,
  What joys await us there,
What radiancy of glory,
  What bliss beyond compare.
  Jerusalem the Golden, tr. from Latin, *Urbs
  Syon Aurea.*

And bright with many an angel
  And all the martyr throng.   *Ib.*

The pastures of the blessèd
  Are deck'd in glorious sheen.   *Ib.*

The shout of them that triumph,
  The song of them that feast.   *Ib.*

O sweet and blessèd country
  That eager hearts expect!   *Ib.*

Around the throne of God a band
Of glorious Angels always stand.
  *Around the Throne of God. Hymns for Children,
  First Series* (1842).

Art thou weary, art thou languid,
  Art thou sore distressed?
      Art Thou Weary, tr. from Greek.

'Angels, Martyrs, Prophets, Virgins,
          Answer, Yes!'   *Ib.*

Brief life is here our portion;
Brief sorrow, short-lived care.
  Brief Life is Here, tr. from Latin, *Hic breve
  Vivitur.*

Christian, dost thou see them
  On the holy ground,
How the troops of Midian
  Prowl and prowl around?

Christian, up and smite them,
  Counting gain but loss;
Smite them by the merit
  Of the holy Cross.
  Christian, Dost Thou See Them, tr. from Greek.

Laud and honour to the Father,
Laud and honour to the Son,
Laud and honour to the Spirit,
Ever Three and ever One;
Consubstantial, co-eternal,
While unending ages run.
  *Come ye Faithful, Raise the Anthem. The
  Christian Remembrancer,* July 1863.

Loosed from Pharaoh's bitter yoke
Jacob's sons and daughters;
Led them with unmoisten'd foot
Through the Red Sea waters.
  Come ye Faithful, Raise the Strain, tr. from
  Greek.

Endless noon-day, glorious noon-day.
  Light's Abode, Celestial Salem, tr. from Latin,
  Hierusalem Luminosa.

For thee, O dear, dear Country,
  Mine eyes their vigils keep.
    For Thee, O Dear, Dear Country, tr. from
    Latin, *O Bona Patria.*

Good Christian men, rejoice
With heart, and soul, and voice.
  Good Christian Men, Helmore and Neale,
  Carols for Christmastide.

Good King Wenceslas look'd out,
  On the Feast of Stephen;
When the snow lay round about,
  Deep and crisp and even.
  Good King Wenceslas. Helmore and Neale,
  Carols for Christmastide.

'Hither, page, and stand by me,
  If thou know'st it, telling,
Yonder peasant, who is he?
  Where and what his dwelling?'   *Ib.*

'Bring me flesh and bring me wine,
  Bring me pine-logs hither.'   *Ib.*

Page and monarch, forth they went,
  Forth they went together.   *Ib.*

'Sire, the night is darker now,
  And the wind blows stronger,
Fails my heart, I know not how;
  I can go no longer.'
'Mark my footsteps, good my page,
  Tread thou in them boldly,
Thou shalt find the winter's rage
  Freeze thy blood less coldly.'   *Ib.*

In his master's steps he trod,
  Where the snow lay dinted;
Heat was in the very sod
  Which the Saint had printed.
Wherefore, Christian men, be sure,
  Wealth or rank possessing,
Ye who now do bless the poor
  Shall yourselves find blessing.   *Ib.*

O come, O come, Emmanuel,
And ransom captive Israel.
  O Come, O Come, Emmanuel, tr. from Latin,
  Veni, Veni, Emmanuel.

O happy band of pilgrims,
  If onward ye will tread.
    *O Happy Band of Pilgrims. Hymns of the
    Eastern Church.*

O happy band of pilgrims,
  Look upward to the skies,
Where such a light affliction
  Shall win you such a prize!   *Ib.*

Oh, what the joy and the glory must be,
Those endless Sabbaths the blessèd ones see.
    Oh, what the Joy, tr. from Latin of Abelard,
    O quanta qualia sunt illa Sabbata.

Raise the 'Trisagion' ever and aye.
    *Stars of the Morning. Hymns of the Eastern
    Church.*

Safe home, safe home in port!
  Rent cordage, shatter'd deck,
Torn sails, provisions short,
  And only not a wreck.
    *Safe Home, Safe Home. Hymns of the Eastern
    Church.*

The prize, the prize secure!
  The athlete nearly fell.   *Ib.*

They whose course on earth is o'er
Think they of their brethren more?
    *They Whose Course on Earth. Hymns for the
    Young* (1844).

HORATIO, VISCOUNT NELSON

1758–1805

It is my turn now; and if I come back, it is yours.
    Southey's *Life of Nelson. Nelson's Memoir of
    His Services.*

Westminster Abbey or victory!
    [Battle of Cape S. Vincent]   *Ib.* ch. 4.

Before this time to-morrow I shall have gained a
  peerage, or Westminster Abbey.
    [Battle of the Nile]   *Ib.* ch. 5.

Victory is not a name strong enough for such a scene.
    [Battle of the Nile]   *Ib.*

It is warm work; and this day may be the last to
  any of us at a moment. But mark you! I would
  not be elsewhere for thousands.
    [Battle of Copenhagen]   *Ib.* ch. 7.

I have only one eye,—I have a right to be blind
  sometimes: . . . I really do not see the signal!
    [Copenhagen]   *Ib.*

Sent Admiral Collingwood the Nelson touch.
    Private Diary, 9 Oct. 1805.

England expects every man will do his duty.
    [Battle of Trafalgar] *Ib.* ch. 9.

This is too warm work, Hardy, to last long.   *Ib.*

Thank God, I have done my duty.   *Ib.*

Kiss me, Hardy.   *Ib.*

EDITH NESBIT

1858–1924

Little brown brother, oh! little brown brother,
  Are you awake in the dark?   *Baby Seed Song.*

SIR HENRY JOHN NEWBOLT

1862–1938

Effingham, Grenville, Raleigh, Drake,
  Here's to the bold and free!
Benbow, Collingwood, Byron, Blake,
  Hail to the kings of the sea!   *Admirals All,* i.

Admirals all, for England's sake,
  Honour be yours, and fame!
And honour, as long as waves shall break,
  To Nelson's peerless name!   *Ib.*

He clapped the glass to his sightless eye,
  And 'I'm damned if I see it', he said.   *Ib.*

To set the Cause above renown,
  To love the game beyond the prize,
To honour, while you strike him down,
  The foe that comes with fearless eyes:
To count the life of battle good,
  And dear the land that gave you birth,
And dearer yet the brotherhood
  That binds the brave of all the earth.
    The Island Race, Clifton Chapel.

'Qui procul hinc', the legend's writ,—
  The frontier-grave is far away—
'Qui ante diem periit:
  Sed miles, sed pro patria.'   *Ib.*

'Take my drum to England, hang et by the shore,
  Strike et when your powder's runnin' low;
If the Dons sight Devon, I'll quit the port o' Heaven,
  An' drum them up the Channel as we drummed them
  long ago.'   *Ib. Drake's Drum.*

Drake he's in his hammock till the great Armadas
  come.
  (Capten, art tha sleepin' there below?)
Slung atween the round shot, listenin' for the drum,
  An' dreamin' arl the time o' Plymouth Hoe.
Call him on the deep sea, call him up the Sound,
  Call him when ye sail to meet the foe;
Where the old trade's plyin' an' the old flag flyin'
  They shall find him ware an' wakin', as they found
  him long ago!   *Ib.*

There's a breathless hush in the Close to-night—
  Ten to make and the match to win—
A bumping pitch and a blinding light,
  An hour to play and the last man in.
And it's not for the sake of a ribboned coat,
  Or the selfish hope of a season's fame,
But his Captain's hand on his shoulder smote—
  'Play up! play up! and play the game!'
    Ib. Vitaï Lampada.

The voice of the schoolboy rallies the ranks:
  'Play up! play up! and play the game!'   *Ib.*

Now the sunset breezes shiver,
  And she's fading down the river,
But in England's song for ever
  She's the Fighting Téméraire.
    The Fighting Téméraire.

'Ye have robb'd', said he, 'ye have slaughter'd and
  made an end,
Take your ill-got plunder, and bury the dead.'
    He Fell Among Thieves.

But cared greatly to serve God and the King,
  And keep the Nelson touch.   *Minora Sidera.*

MARGARET DUCHESS OF NEWCASTLE

1624 ?–1673

Her name was Margarett Lucas, yongest sister to the Lord Lucas of Colchester, a noble familie; for all the Brothers were Valiant, and all the Sisters virtuous. *Epitaph, Westminster Abbey.*

JOHN HENRY, CARDINAL NEWMAN

1801–1890

It is very difficult to get up resentment towards persons whom one has never seen.
Apologia pro Vita Sua (1864). *Mr. Kingsley's Method of Disputation.*

There is such a thing as legitimate warfare: war has its laws; there are things which may fairly be done, and things which may not be done. . . . He has attempted (as I may call it) to *poison the wells*. *Ib.*

I will vanquish, not my Accuser, but my judges.
Ib. True Mode of meeting Mr. Kingsley.

I used to wish the Arabian Tales were true.
Ib. History of My Religious Opinions to the Year 1833.

Two and two only supreme and luminously self-evident beings, myself and my Creator. *Ib.*

Growth [is] the only evidence of life. *Ib.*

The motto [of *Lyra Apostolica*] shows the feeling of both [Hurrell] Froude and myself at the time: we borrowed from M. Bunsen a Homer, and Froude chose the words in which Achilles, on returning to the battle, says, 'You shall know the difference now that I am back again'. *Ib.*

It would be a gain to the country were it vastly more superstitious, more bigoted, more gloomy, more fierce in its religion than at present it shows itself to be.
Ib. History of My Religious Opinions from 1833–9.

From the age of fifteen, dogma has been the fundamental principle of my religion: I know no other religion; I cannot enter into the idea of any other sort of religion; religion, as a mere sentiment, is to me a dream and a mockery. *Ib.*

This is what the Church is said to want, not party men, but sensible, temperate, sober, well-judging persons, to guide it through the channel of no-meaning, between the Scylla and Charybdis of Aye and No.
Ib. History of My Religious Opinions from 1839 to 1841.

I recollect an acquaintance saying to me that 'the Oriel Common Room stank of Logic'.
Ib. History of My Religious Opinions from 1841 to 1845.

Cowards! If I advanced one step, you would run away. *Ib.*

Trinity had never been unkind to me. There used to be much snap-dragon growing on the walls opposite my freshman's rooms there, and I had for years taken it as the emblem of my own perpetual residence even unto death in my University.
On the morning of the 23rd I left the Observatory. I have never seen Oxford since, excepting its spires, as they are seen from the railway. *Ib.*

Ten thousand difficulties do not make one doubt.
Ib. Position of My Mind since 1845.

The all-corroding, all-dissolving scepticism of the intellect in religious enquiries. *Ib.*

Take a mere beggar-woman, lazy, ragged, filthy, and not over-scrupulous of truth,—but if she is chaste, and sober, and cheerful, and goes to her religious duties—she will, in the eyes of the Church, have a prospect of heaven, quite closed and refused to the State's pattern-man, the just, the upright, the generous, the honourable, the conscientious, if he be all this, not from a supernatural power,—but from mere natural virtue.
Lectures on Anglican Difficulties. Lecture VIII.

She [the Catholic Church] holds that it were better for sun and moon to drop from heaven, for the earth to fail, and for all the many millions who are upon it to die of starvation in extremest agony, as far as temporal affliction goes, than that one soul, I will not say, should be lost, but should commit one single venial sin, should tell one wilful untruth, . . . or steal one poor farthing without excuse. *Ib.*

May He support us all the day long, till the shades lengthen, and the evening comes, and the busy world is hushed, and the fever of life is over, and our work is done! Then in His mercy may He give us a safe lodging, and a holy rest, and peace at the last. *Sermon*, 1834. *Wisdom and Innocence.*

Firmly I believe and truly
God is Three, and God is One;
And I next acknowledge duly
Manhood taken by the Son. *Firmly I Believe.*

Lead, kindly Light, amid the encircling gloom,
Lead thou me on;
The night is dark, and I am far from home,
Lead thou me on.
Keep Thou my feet; I do not ask to see
The distant scene; one step enough for me.
The Pillar of Cloud. Lead Kindly Light.

I loved the garish day, and, spite of fears,
Pride ruled my will: remember not past years. *Ib.*

And with the morn those Angel faces smile,
Which I have loved long since, and lost awhile. *Ib.*

Prune thou thy words, the thoughts control
That o'er thee swell and throng;
They will condense within thy soul,
And change to purpose strong.
Flowers Without Fruit. Prune Thou Thy Words.

Praise to the Holiest in the height,
And in the depth be praise;
In all His words most wonderful,
Most sure in all His ways. *Praise to the Holiest.*

A second Adam to the fight
And to the rescue came. *Ib.*

O wisest love! that flesh and blood
  Which did in Adam fail,
Should strive afresh against their foe,
  Should strive and should prevail. *Ib.*

ISAAC NEWTON

1642–1727

I do not know what I may appear to the world, but
to myself I seem to have been only a boy playing
on the sea-shore, and diverting myself in now and
then finding a smoother pebble or a prettier shell
than ordinary, whilst the great ocean of truth lay
all undiscovered before me.
  Brewster's Memoirs of Newton, vol. ii, ch. 27.

O Diamond! Diamond! thou little knowest the mischief done!
  *Remark to a dog who knocked down a candle and
  so set fire to some papers and 'destroyed the almost
  finished labours of some years'.* Thomas Maude,
  Wensley-Dale . . . a Poem, 1780, p. 28, note.

JOHN NEWTON

1725–1807

How sweet the name of Jesus sounds
  In a believer's ear!
It soothes his sorrows, heals his wounds,
  And drives away his fear.
  Olney Hymns (1779), *How Sweet the Name.*

Glorious things of thee are spoken,
  Zion, city of our God.
  Ib. Glorious Things of Thee.

ADELA FLORENCE NICOLSON
See LAURENCE HOPE.

'NIMROD'
[CHARLES JAMES APPERLEY]

1779–1843

'Who is that under his horse in the brook?'—
'Only Dick Christian', answers Lord Forester, 'and
  it's nothing new to him.'
'But he'll be drowned', exclaims Lord Kinnaird.
'I shouldn't wonder', observes Mr. William Coke.
'But the pace is too good to inquire.'
  The Chase.

'Quite the cream of the thing, I suppose', says
  Lord Gardner. *Ib.*

RODEN BERKELEY
WRIOTHESLEY NOEL

1834–1894

After battle sleep is best,
After noise, tranquillity. *The Old.*

Loving, adorable,
  Softly to rest,
Here in my crystalline,
  Here in my breast!
  The Water-Nymph and the Boy.

THOMAS NOEL

1799–1861

'Rattle his bones over the stones;
He's only a pauper, whom nobody owns!'
  Rhymes and Roundelays, The Pauper's Drive.

REV. JOHN NORRIS

1657–1711

Were angels to write, I fancy we should have but few
  Folios. *Collection of Miscellanies* (1678), *Preface.*

How fading are the joys we doat upon!
Like apparitions seen and gone.
But those which soonest take their flight
Are the most exquisite and strong,—
Like angels' visits, short and bright;
Mortality's too weak to bear them long.
  Ib. The Parting.

CHRISTOPHER NORTH
(JOHN WILSON)
1785–1854

Minds like ours, my dear James, must always be
above national prejudices, and in all companies it
gives me true pleasure to declare, that, as a people,
the English are very little indeed inferior to the
Scotch. *Noctes Ambrosianae*, no. 9.

His Majesty's dominions, on which the sun never sets.
  Ib. No. 20 (April 1829).

Laws were made to be broken.
  Ib. No. 24 (May 1830).

Insultin the sun, and quarrellin wi' the equawtor.
(*Ettrick Shepherd*). *Ib.* (May 1830).

Animosities are mortal, but the Humanities live for
ever. *Ib.* No. 35 (Aug. 1834).

I cannot sit still, James, and hear you abuse the
shopocracy. *Ib.* No. 39 (Feb. 1835).

SIR STAFFORD HENRY
NORTHCOTE, EARL OF
IDDESLEIGH

1818–1887

Argue as you please, you are nowhere, that grand old
man, the Prime Minister, insists on the other thing.
  Speech at Liverpool, 12 Apr. 1882.

CAROLINE ELIZABETH SARAH
NORTON

1808–1877

My beautiful, my beautiful! that standest meekly by,
With thy proudly-arched and glossy neck, and dark
  and fiery eye!
Fret not to roam the desert now, with all thy winged
  speed:
I may not mount on thee again!—thou'rt sold, my
  Arab steed! *The Arab's Farewell to His Steed.*

The stranger hath thy bridle-rein, thy master hath his
  gold;—
Fleet-limbed and beautiful, farewell; thou'rt sold, my
  steed, thou'rt sold. *Ib.*

L

And sitting down by the green well, I'll pause and
sadly think—
''Twas here he bowed his glossy neck when last I saw
him drink.' *Ib.*

They tempted me, my beautiful! for hunger's power
is strong—
They tempted me, my beautiful! but I have loved too
long. *Ib.*

'Tis false! 'tis false, my Arab steed! I fling them back
their gold! *Ib.*

A soldier of the Legion lay dying in Algiers—
There was lack of woman's nursing, there was
dearth of woman's tears. *Bingen on the Rhine.*

I do not love thee!—no! I do not love thee!
And yet when thou art absent I am sad.
I Do Not Love Thee.

For death and life, in ceaseless strife,
Beat wild on this world's shore,
And all our calm is in that balm—
Not lost but gone before. *Not Lost but Gone Before.*

ALFRED NOYES
1880–

Go down to Kew in lilac-time, in lilac-time, in lilac-
time;
Go down to Kew in lilac-time (it isn't far from
London!)
And you shall wander hand in hand with love in
summer's wonderland;
Go down to Kew in lilac-time (it isn't far from
London!) *Barrel Organ.*

The wind was a torrent of darkness among the gusty
trees,
The moon was a ghostly galleon tossed upon cloudy
seas,
The road was a ribbon of moonlight over the purple
moor,
And the highwayman came riding—
Riding—riding—
The highwayman came riding, up to the old inn-door.
The Highwayman.

The landlord's black-eyed daughter,
Bess, the landlord's daughter,
Plaiting a dark red love-knot into her long black hair.
Ib.

Look for me by moonlight;
Watch for me by moonlight;
I'll come to thee by moonlight, though hell should
bar the way! *Ib.*

There's a magic in the distance, where the sea-line
meets the sky. *Forty Singing Seamen,* ix.

Calling as he used to call, faint and far away,
In Sherwood, in Sherwood, about the break of day.
Sherwood.

Sherwood in the red dawn, is Robin Hood asleep? *Ib.*

FREDERICK OAKELEY
1802–1880

O come, all ye faithful,
Joyful and triumphant,
O come ye, O come ye to Bethlehem.
O Come, All Ye Faithful, tr. from Latin,
Adeste Fideles.

SEAN O'CASEY
1884–

The whole world is in a state of chassis.
Juno and the Paycock, I. i.

JOHN O'KEEFE
1747–1833

Amo, amas, I love a lass,
As a cedar tall and slender;
Sweet cowslip's grace
Is her nom'native case,
And she's of the feminine gender.
Rorum, corum, sunt Divorum!
Harum, scarum, Divo!
Tag rag, merry derry, periwig and hatband!
Hic hoc horum Genitivo!
Agreeable Surprise, II. ii. *Song: Amo, Amas.*

You should always except the present company.
London Hermit, I. ii.

DENNIS O'KELLY
1720 ?–1787

Eclipse first, the rest nowhere.
Epsom, 3 May 1769. Annals of Sporting,
vol. ii, p. 271.

JOHN OLDHAM
1653–1683

And all your fortune lies beneath your hat.
*A Satire addressed to a Friend about to leave
the University,* l. 25.

Racks, gibbets, halters, were their arguments.
Satires Upon the Jesuits, Sat. 1, *Garnet's
Ghost,* l. 176.

WILLIAM OLDYS
1696–1761

Busy, curious, thirsty fly.
Busy, Curious, Thirsty Fly, l. 1.

JOHN OPIE
1761–1807

[When asked with what he mixed his colours.]
I mix them with my brains, sir.
Samuel Smiles, Self-Help. ch. 4.

BARONESS ORCZY
contemp.

We seek him here, we seek him there,
Those Frenchies seek him everywhere.
Is he in heaven?—Is he in hell?
That demmed, elusive Pimpernel?
The Scarlet Pimpernel, ch. 12.

JOHN BOYLE O'REILLY

1844–1890

The organized charity, scrimped and iced,
In the name of a cautious, statistical Christ.
Life, Poems, and Speeches (1891), *In Bohemia*,
l. 37.

ARTHUR WILLIAM EDGAR O'SHAUGHNESSY

1844–1881

We are the music makers,
  We are the dreamers of dreams,
Wandering by lonely sea-breakers,
  And sitting by desolate streams;—
World-losers and world-forsakers,
  On whom the pale moon gleams:
We are the movers and shakers
  Of the world for ever, it seems.
      Ode: 'We are the Music Makers.'

One man with a dream, at pleasure,
  Shall go forth and conquer a crown;
And three with a new song's measure
  Can trample a kingdom down.   *Ib.*

For each age is a dream that is dying,
  Or one that is coming to birth.   *Ib.*

SIR WILLIAM OSLER

1849–1919

The uselessness of men above sixty years of age,
and the incalculable benefit it would be in commercial, political, and in professional life if, as a
matter of course, men stopped work at this age.
Address, Johns Hopkins Univ. Feb. 1905.
H. Cushing's *Life of Sir W. Osler* (1925),
vol. i, p. 667.

JOHN O'SULLIVAN

1813–1895

Our manifest destiny to overspread the continent
allotted by Providence for the free development
of our yearly multiplying millions.
U.S. Magazine and Democratic Review, vol.
xvii, p. 5.

A torchlight procession marching down your throat.
[Description of some whisky] G. W. E.
Russell's *Collections and Recollections*, ch. 19.

THOMAS OTWAY

1652–1685

These are rogues that pretend to be of a religion
now! Well, all I say is, honest atheism for my
money.   *The Atheist*, Act III, l. 31.

Ere man's corruptions made him wretched, he
Was born most noble that was born most free:
Each of himself was lord; and unconfin'd
Obey'd the dictates of his godlike mind.
      Don Carlos, Act II, l. 3.

Destructive, damnable, deceitful woman!
      The Orphan, Act III, l. 586.

And for an apple damn'd mankind.   *Ib.* l. 594.

You wags that judge by rote, and damn by rule.
      Titus and Berenice, prologue, l. 3.

Oh woman! lovely woman! Nature made thee
To temper man: we had been brutes without you;
Angels are painted fair, to look like you;
There's in you all that we believe of heav'n,
Amazing brightness, purity, and truth,
Eternal joy, and everlasting love.
      Venice Preserved, Act I, l. 337.

No praying, it spoils business.   *Ib.* Act II, l. 87.

SIR THOMAS OVERBURY

1581–1613

In part to blame is she,
Which hath without consent been only tried;
He comes too near, that comes to be denied.
      Miscellaneous Works, A Wife, xxvi.

He disdains all things above his reach, and preferreth
all countries before his own.
      Ib. An Affectate Traveller.

You cannot name any example in any heathen author
but I will better it in Scripture.
  Ib. Crumms Fal'n From King James's Table,
§ 10.

JOHN OWEN

1560?–1622

God and the doctor we alike adore
But only when in danger, not before;
The danger o'er, both are alike requited,
God is forgotten, and the Doctor slighted.
      Epigrams.

EDWARD OXENFORD

1847–1929

I fear no foe in shining armour.   *Song.*

THOMAS PAINE

1737–1809

The sublime and the ridiculous are often so nearly
related, that it is difficult to class them separately.
One step above the sublime, makes the ridiculous;
and one step above the ridiculous, makes the
sublime again. *Age of Reason* (1795), pt. ii, p. 20.

These are the times that try men's souls.
  The American Crisis, No. 1. Writings (1894),
  vol. 1, p. 170.

Government, even in its best state, is but a necessary
evil; in its worst state, an intolerable one.
      Common Sense, ch. 1.

The final event to himself [Mr. Burke] has been,
that as he rose like a rocket, he fell like the stick.
  Letter to the Addressers on the late Proclama-
  tion, 1792, p. 4.

[Burke] is not affected by the vality of distress touch-ing his heart, but by the showy resemblance of it striking his imagination. He pities the plumage, but forgets the dying bird.

Rights of Man, 1791, p. 26.

My country is the world, and my religion is to do good. *Ib. pt. ii, ch. 5.*

WILLIAM PALEY
1743–1805

Who can refute a sneer?
Moral Philosophy, bk. v, ch. 9.

HENRY JOHN TEMPLE, VISCOUNT PALMERSTON
1784–1865

Accidental and fortuitous concurrence of atoms.
Speech, H. of C., 5 March 1857.

What is merit? The opinion one man entertains of another.
(Quoted by Carlyle in *Critical and Miscel-laneous Essays*, viii, 'Shooting Niagara.')

'Die, my dear Doctor, that's the last thing I shall do!' *Attr. last words.*

JOHN PALSGRAVE
d. 1554

In the country of the blind the one-eyed man is king.
(Caecorum in patria luscus rex imperat omnis.)
Fullonius' *Comedye of Acolastus.*

EDWARD HAZEN PARKER

Life's race well run,
Life's work well done,
Life's victory won,
Now cometh rest.
See *Notes and Queries*, 9th Series, vol. iv, p. 167, and vol. vii, p. 406.

MARTIN PARKER
–1656?

Country men of England, who live at home with ease,
And little think what dangers are incident o' th' seas:
Give ear unto the sailor who unto you will show
His case, his case: *How e'er the wind doth blow.*
Sailors for My Money (Roxburghe Ballads, vol. vi, p. 797).

You gentlemen of England
Who live at home at ease,
How little do you think
On the dangers of the seas.
The Valiant Sailors (Early Naval Ballads, Percy Society, 1841, p. 34).

But all's to no end, for the times will not mend
Till the king enjoys his own again.
Upon Defacing of Whitehall (The Loyal Garland, 1671). Later title: When the King Enjoys His Own Again (Ritson's Ancient Songs, 1792, p. 231).

My skill goes beyond the depths of a pond,
Or rivers, in the greatest rain;
Whereby I can tell, all things will be well,
When the King enjoys his own again. *Ib.*

THEODORE PARKER
1810–1860

A democracy, that is, a government of all the people, by all the people, for all the people; of course, a government after the principles of eternal justice, the unchanging law of God; for shortness' sake, I will call it the idea of freedom.
The American Idea. Speech at N. E. Anti-Slavery Convention, Boston, 29 May, 1850. Discourses of Slavery (1863), i.

CHARLES STEWART PARNELL
1846–1891

No man has a right to fix the boundary of the march of a nation; no man has a right to say to his country —thus far shalt thou go and no further.
Speech at Cork, 21 Jan. 1885.

THOMAS PARNELL
1679–1717

When thy beauty appears,
In its graces and airs,
All bright as an angel new dropt from the sky;
At distance I gaze, and am aw'd by my fears,
So strangely you dazzle my eye!
Poems (1894). Song, 'When thy Beauty Appears.'

Still an angel appear to each lover beside,
But still be a woman to you. *Ib*

We call it only pretty Fanny's way.
Ib. An Elegy, to an Old Beauty, l. 34

WALTER HORATIO PATER
1839–1894

A white bird, she told him once, looking at him gravely, a bird he must carry in his bosom across a crowded public place—his own soul was like that.
Marius the Epicurean, pt. i, ch. 2

The presence that thus rose so strangely beside the waters, is expressive of what in the ways of a thousand years men had come to desire. Hers is the head upon which all 'the ends of the world are come', and the eyelids are a little weary. . . . Set it for a moment beside one of those white Greek goddesses or beautiful women of antiquity and how would they be troubled by this beauty, into which the soul with all its maladies has passed? [Mona Lisa.]
The Renaissance. Leonardo da Vinci

She is older than the rocks among which she sits; like the vampire, she has been dead many times, and learned the secrets of the grave; and has been a diver in deep seas, and keeps their fallen day about her; and trafficked for strange webs with Eastern merchants: and, as Leda, was the mother of Helen of Troy, and, as Saint Anne, the mother of Mary; and all this has been to her but as the sound of lyres and flutes, and lives only in the delicacy with which it has moulded the changing lineaments, and tinged the eyelids and the hands.

Ib.

To burn always with this hard, gemlike flame, to maintain this ecstasy, is success in life.

Ib. Conclusion.

COVENTRY KERSEY DIGHTON PATMORE

1823–1896

For dear to maidens are their rivals dead.

Amelia, l. 135.

Grant me the power of saying things
 Too simple and too sweet for words!
 The Angel in the House, ed. 1904, bk. 1, c. 1, Prelude 1, *The Impossibility*, l. 7.

 Love, sole mortal thing
Of worth immortal.

Ib. Prelude 2, *Love's Reality*, l. 9.

The fair sum of six thousand years'
 Traditions of civility.

Ib. The Cathedral Close, v. l. 27.

Ah, wasteful woman, she who may
 On her sweet self set her own price,
Knowing man cannot choose but pay,
 How has she cheapen'd paradise!
How given for nought her priceless gift,
 How spoil'd the bread and spill'd the wine,
Which, spent with due, respective thrift,
 Had made brutes men, and men divine.

Ib. c. iii, Prelude 3, *Unthrift*.

Leave us alone! After a while,
 This pool of private charity
Shall make its continent an isle,
 And roll, a world-embracing sea.

Ib. c. vi, Prelude 2, *Love Justified*, l. 9.

Kind souls, you wonder why, love you,
 When you, you wonder why, love none
We love, Fool, for the good we do,
 Not that which unto us is done!

Ib. Prelude 4, *A Riddle Solved*.

Love wakes men, once a lifetime each;
 They lift their heavy lids, and look;
And, lo, what one sweet page can teach,
 They read with joy, then shut the book.
And some give thanks, and some blaspheme,
 And most forget; but, either way,
That and the Child's unheeded dream
 Is all the light of all their day.

Ib. c. viii, Prelude 2, *The Revelation*, l. 5.

I drew my bride, beneath the moon,
 Across my threshold; happy hour!

But, ah, the walk that afternoon
 We saw the water-flags in flower!

Ib. Prelude 3, *The Spirit's Epochs*, l. 9.

God's grace is the only grace,
And all grace is the grace of God.

Ib. c. x, Prelude 1, *The Joyful Wisdom*.

'I'll hunt for dangers North and South,
 To prove my love, which sloth maligns!'
What seems to say her rosy mouth?
 'I'm not convinced by proofs but signs.'

Ib. c. iv, Prelude 3, *Valour Misdirected*.

'I saw you take his kiss!' ''Tis true.'
 'O, modesty!' ''Twas strictly kept:
He thought me asleep; at least, I knew
 He thought I thought he thought I slept.

Ib. c. viii, Prelude 3, *The Kiss*.

Why, having won her, do I woo?
 Because her spirit's vestal grace
Provokes me always to pursue,
 But, spirit-like, eludes embrace.

Ib. c. xii, Prelude 1, *The Married Lover*, l. 1.

Because, though free of the outer court
 I am, this Temple keeps its shrine
 Sacred to Heaven; because, in short,
She's not and never can be mine.   *Ib.* l. 29.

Some dish more sharply spiced than this
Milk-soup men call domestic bliss.   *Olympus*, l. 15.

Maud burst in, while the Earl was there,
With 'Oh, Mama, do be a bear!'
 The Victories of Love, bk. ii, ii. *From Lady Clitheroe to Mary Churchill*, l. 89.

No magic of her voice or smile
Suddenly raised a fairy isle,
But fondness for her underwent
An unregarded increment,
Like that which lifts, through centuries,
The coral-reef within the seas,
Till, lo! the land where was the wave,
Alas! 'tis everywhere her grave.

Ib. v. *From Mrs. Graham*, l. 57.

Faults had she, child of Adam's stem,
But only Heaven knew of them.

Ib. xii. *From Felix to Honoria*, l. 167.

Well dost thou, Love, thy solemn Feast to hold
In vestal February.
 The Unknown Eros, bk. 1, i. *St. Valentine's Day*, l. 1.

Fair as the rash oath of virginity
Which is first-love's first cry.
O, Baby Spring,
That flutter'st sudden 'neath the breast of Earth
A month before the birth.   *Ib.* l. 9.

Thy heart with dead, wing'd innocencies fill'd,
Ev'n as a nest with birds
After the old ones by the hawk are kill'd.   *Ib.* l. 51.

But, in a while,
The immeasurable smile
Is broke by fresher airs to flashes blent
With darkling discontent.   *Ib.* l. 15.

I, singularly moved
To love the lovely that are not beloved,
Of all the Seasons, most
Love Winter.   *Ib.* iii. *Winter*, l. 1.

It *was* the azalea's breath, and she *was* dead!
      Ib. vii. *The Azalea*, l. 17.

So, till to-morrow eve, my Own, adieu!
Parting's well-paid with soon again to meet,
Soon in your arms to feel so small and sweet,
Sweet to myself that am so sweet to you!   *Ib.* l. 22.

It was not like your great and gracious ways!
Do you, that have nought other to lament,
Never, my Love, repent
Of how, that July afternoon,
You went,
With sudden, unintelligible phrase,
And frighten'd eye,
Upon your journey of so many days,
Without a single kiss, or a good-bye?
      Ib. viii. *Departure*, l. 1.

And the only loveless look the look with which you
pass'd.   *Ib.* l. 31.

My little Son, who look'd from thoughtful eyes
And moved and spoke in quiet grown-up wise,
Having my law the seventh time disobey'd,
I struck him, and dismiss'd
With hard words and unkiss'd,
His Mother, who was patient, being dead.
      Ib. x. *The Toys*, l. 1.

Then, fatherly, not less
Than I whom Thou hast moulded from the clay,
Thou'lt leave Thy wrath, and say,
'I will be sorry for their childishness.'   *Ib.*

For want of me the world's course will not fail:
When all its work is done, the lie shall rot;
The truth is great, and shall prevail,
When none cares whether it prevail or not.
      Ib. xii. *Magna est Veritas*, l. 7.

In the year of the great crime,
When the false English Nobles and their Jew,
By God demented, slew
The Trust they stood twice pledged to keep from
    wrong,
One said, Take up thy Song,
That breathes the mild and almost mythic time
Of England's prime!   *Ib.* xiii, 1867, l. 1.

If I were dead, you'd sometimes say, Poor Child!
      Ib. xiv. *'If I were dead*,' l. 1.

With all my will, but much against my heart,
We two now part.
My Very Dear,
Our solace is, the sad road lies so clear.
It needs no art,
With faint, averted feet
And many a tear,
In our opposed paths to persevere.
      Ib. xvi. *A Farewell*, l. 1.

Haply yon wretch, so famous for his falls,
Got them beneath the Devil-defended walls
Of some high Virtue he had vow'd to win.
      Ib. xx. *'Let Be*,' l. 17.

That shaft of slander shot
Miss'd only the right blot.
I see the shame
They cannot see:
'Tis very just they blame
The thing that's not.   *Ib.* l. 35.

Through delicatest ether feathering soft their solitary
beat.   *Ib.* bk. II. i. *To the Unknown Eros*, l. 8.

What in its ruddy orbit lifts the blood,
Like a perturbed moon of Uranus,
Reaching to some great world in ungauged darkness
hid.   *Ib.* l. 33.

Who is this only happy She,
Whom, by a frantic flight of courtesy,
Born of despair
Of better lodging for his Spirit fair,
He adores as Margaret, Maude, or Cecily?   *Ib.* l. 30.

                The Jebusite,
That, maugre all God's promises could do,
The chosen People never conquer'd quite;
Who therefore lived with them,
And that by formal truce and as of right,
In metropolitan Jerusalem.
      Ib. vii. *To the Body*, l. 32.

Enoch, Elijah, and the Lady, she
Who left the lilies in her body's lieu.   *Ib.* l. 45.

Who has thy birth-time's consecrating dew
For death's sweet chrism retain'd,
Quick, tender, virginal, and unprofaned!   *Ib.* l. 51.

There of pure Virgins none
Is fairer seen,
Save One,
Than Mary Magdalene.   *Ib.*   127.

Shall I, the gnat which dances in thy ray,
Dare to be reverent?
      Ib. xiv. *Psyche's Discontent*, l. 72.

This is to say, my dear Augusta,
We've had another awful buster:
Ten thousand Frenchmen sent below!
Thank God from whom all blessings flow.
      Epigram on King William's dispatch to Queen
      Augusta reported in *The Times*, 8 Aug. 1870.
      B. Champneys, *Coventry Patmore* (1900), i.
      286.

JAMES PAYN

1830–1898

I had never had a piece of toast
Particularly long and wide,
But fell upon the sanded floor,
And always on the buttered side.
      Chambers's Journal, 2 Feb., 1884.

JOHN HOWARD PAYNE

1791–1852

Mid pleasures and palaces though we may roam,
Be it ever so humble, there's no place like home;
A charm from the sky seems to hallow us there,
Which, seek through the world, is ne'er met with
    elsewhere.
Home, home, sweet, sweet home!
There's no place like home! there's no place like
    home!
      Clari, the Maid of Milan. Home, Sweet Home.

THOMAS LOVE PEACOCK

1785–1866

Ancient sculpture is the true school of modesty. But where the Greeks had modesty, we have cant; where they had poetry, we have cant; where they had patriotism, we have cant; where they had anything that exalts, delights, or adorns humanity, we have nothing but cant, cant, cant.

Crotchet Castle, ch. 7.

Modern literature having attained the honourable distinction of sharing with blacking and Macassar oil the space which used to be monopolized by razor-strops and the lottery. *Ib.* ch. 15.

The march of mind—has marched in through my back-parlour shutters, and out again with my silver spoons, in the dead of the night. The policeman, who was sent down to examine, says my house has been broken open on the most scientific principles. *Ib.* ch. 17.

Nothing can be more obvious than that all animals were created solely and exclusively for the use of man. *Headlong Hall*, ch. 2.

'Indeed, the loaves and fishes are typical of a mixed diet; and the practice of the Church in all ages shows—'
'That it never loses sight of the loaves and fishes.'
Ib.

'I distinguish the picturesque and the beautiful, and I add to them, in the laying out of grounds, a third and distinct character, which I call *unexpectedness*.'
'Pray, sir', said Mr. Milestone, 'by what name do you distinguish this character, when a person walks round the grounds for the second time?'
Ib. ch. 4.

Sir, I have quarrelled with my wife; and a man who has quarrelled with his wife is absolved from all duty to his country.
Nightmare Abbey, ch. 11.

Long night succeeds thy little day
  Oh blighted blossom! can it be,
That this gray stone and grassy clay
  Have closed our anxious care of thee?
Epitaph on his Daughter. Works of Peacock, ed. Cole, 1875, Biographical Notice by E. Nicolls.

In his last binn Sir Peter lies,
  Who knew not what it was to frown:
Death took him mellow by surprise,
  And in his cellar stopped him down.
Headlong Hall, ch. 5.

Hail to the Headlong! the Headlong Ap-Headlong!
All hail to the Headlong, the Headlong Ap-Headlong!
  The Headlong Ap-Headlong
  Ap-Breakneck Ap-Headlong
Ap-Cataract Ap-Pistyll Ap-Rhaiader Ap-Headlong!
Ib. ch. 13. *Chorus.*

The mountain sheep are sweeter,
  But the valley sheep are fatter;
We therefore deemed it meeter
  To carry off the latter.
The Misfortunes of Elphin, ch. 11. *The War-Song of Dinas Vawr.*

The bowl goes trim. The moon doth shine,
And our ballast is old wine.
Nightmare Abbey, ch. 11.

In a bowl to sea went wise men three,
  On a brilliant night in June:
They carried a net, and their hearts were set
  On fishing up the moon.
The Wise Men of Gotham. Paper Money Lyrics.

GEORGE PEELE

1558?–1597

Fair and fair, and twice so fair,
  As fair as any may be;
The fairest shepherd on our green,
  A love for any lady.
Works, ed. Bullen, vol. i. *Arraignment of Paris*, i. ii, 55. *Song of Oenone and Paris.*

What thing is love for (well I wot) love is a thing.
It is a prick, it is a sting,
It is a pretty, pretty thing;
It is a fire, it is a coal
Whose flame creeps in at every hole.
Ib. vol. ii. *Miscellaneous Poems. The Hunting of Cupid*, l. 1.

His golden locks time hath to silver turn'd;
  O time too swift, O swiftness never ceasing!
His youth 'gainst time and age hath ever spurn'd
  But spurn'd in vain; youth waneth by increasing:
Beauty, strength, youth, are flowers but fading seen;
Duty, faith, love, are roots, and ever green.
Ib. Polyhymnia, Sonnet ad finem. A Farewell to Arms.

His helmet now shall make a hive for bees,
  And, lovers' sonnets turn'd to holy psalms,
A man-at-arms must now serve on his knees,
  And feed on prayers, which are age his alms:
But though from court to cottage he depart,
His saint is sure of his unspotted heart. *Ib.*

Goddess, allow this aged man his right,
To be your beadsman now that was your knight. *Ib.*

HENRY HERBERT, EARL OF PEMBROKE

1734–1794

My noble friend Lord Pembroke said once to me at Wilton, with a happy pleasantry and some truth, that, 'Dr. Johnson's sayings would not appear so extraordinary, were it not for his *bow-wow way*'.
Boswell's *Life of Johnson*, 27 Mar. 1775, note.

WILLIAM PENN

1644–1718

No Cross, No Crown. *Title of Pamphlet*, 1669.

It is a reproach to religion and government to suffer so much poverty and excess.
Reflexions and Maxims, pt. i, No. 52.

Men are generally more careful of the breed of their horses and dogs than of their children. *Ib.* No. 85.

The country life is to be preferred, for there we see the works of God, but in cities little else but the works of men.　　*Ib. No. 220.*

SAMUEL PEPYS

1633-1703

Strange the difference of men's talk!
　　　　　　Diary, 4 Jan. 1659-60.

And so to bed.　　　　*Ib. 20 April 1660.*

A silk suit, which cost me much money, and I pray God to make me able to pay for it.
　　　　　　Ib. 1 July 1660.

I . . . sent for Mr. Butler, who was now all full of his high discourse in praise of Ireland, . . . but so many lies I never heard in praise of anything as he told of Ireland.　　*Ib. 28 July 1660.*

I went out to Charing Cross, to see Major-general Harrison hanged, drawn, and quartered; which was done there, he looking as cheerful as any man could do in that condition.　　*Ib. 13 Oct. 1660.*

Very merry, and the best fritters that ever I eat in my life.　　*Ib. 26 Feb. 1660-1 (Shrove Tues.).*

A good honest and painful sermon.
　　　　　　Ib. 17 March 1661.

If ever I was foxed it was now.　*Ib. 23 April 1661.*

But methought it lessened my esteem of a king, that he should not be able to command the rain.
　　　　　　Ib. 19 July 1662.

I see it is impossible for the King to have things done as cheap as other men.　　*Ib. 21 July 1662.*

But Lord! to see the absurd nature of Englishmen, that cannot forbear laughing and jeering at everything that looks strange.　　*Ib. 27 Nov. 1662.*

My wife, who, poor wretch, is troubled with her lonely life.　　　*Ib. 19 Dec. 1662.*

Went to hear Mrs. Turner's daughter . . . play on the harpsichon; but, Lord! it was enough to make any man sick to hear her; yet was I forced to commend her highly.　　*Ib. 1 May 1663.*

Most of their discourse was about hunting, in a dialect I understand very little.
　　　　　　Ib. 22 Nov. 1663.

While we were talking came by several poor creatures carried by, by constables, for being at a conventicle. . . . I would to God they would either conform, or be more wise, and not be catched!
　　　　　　Ib. 7 Aug. 1664.

Pretty witty Nell. [Nell Gwynne.]
　　　　　　Ib. 3 April 1665.

But Lord! what a sad time it is to see no boats upon the River; and grass grows all up and down White Hall Court.　　*Ib. 20 Sept. 1665.*

Strange to see how a good dinner and feasting reconciles everybody.　　*Ib. 9 Nov. 1665.*

Strange to say what delight we married people have to see these poor fools decoyed into our condition.
　　　　　　Ib. 25 Dec. 1665.

And mighty proud I am (and ought to be thankful to God Almighty) that I am able to have a spare bed for my friends.　　*Ib. 8 Aug. 1666.*

I bless God I do find that I am worth more than ever I yet was, which is £6,200, for which the Holy Name of God be praised!　*Ib. 31 Oct. 1666.*

But it is pretty to see what money will do.
　　　　　　Ib. 21 March 1667.

JOHN JOSEPH PERSHING

1860-

LaFayette, we are here.
　　Address at the grave of LaFayette, 4 July 1917.
　　G. Morgan's *True LaFayette*, 1919, preface.

EDWARD JOHN PHELPS

1822-1900

The man who makes no mistakes does not usually make anything.
　　Speech at Mansion House, 24 Jan. 1899.

AMBROSE PHILIPS

1675?-1749

The flowers, anew, returning seasons bring!
But beauty faded has no second spring.
　　　　The First Pastoral, Lobbin, l. 55.

Timely blossom, infant fair,
Fondling of a happy pair,
Every morn, and every night,
Their solicitous delight,
Sleeping, waking, still at ease,
Pleasing without skill to please.
Little gossip, blithe and hale,
Tattling many a broken tale.
　　To Mistress Charlotte Pulteney, l. 1.

JOHN PHILIPS

1676-1709

Happy the man, who, void of cares and strife,
In silken or in leathern purse retains
A Splendid Shilling.　　*The Splendid Shilling,* l. 1.

STEPHEN PHILLIPS

1864-1915

I am deaf with praises, and all dazed with flowers.
　　　　　　Herod, I. i.

A man not old, but mellow, like good wine.
　　　　　　Ulysses, III. ii.

WENDELL PHILLIPS

1811-1884

One, on God's side, is a majority.
　　Speeches (1880), *Lecture at Brooklyn, N. Y.*
　　1 Nov. 1859.

Every man meets his Waterloo at last.　　*Ib.*

Revolutions never go backward.
Ib. Address at Boston. 17 Feb. 1861.

We live under a government of men and morning
newspapers. *Address: The Press.*

EDEN PHILLPOTTS
1862–

His father's sister had bats in the belfry and was put
away. *Peacock House. My First Murder.*

SIR ARTHUR WING PINERO
1855–1934

What beautiful fruit! I love fruit when it's expensive.
The Second Mrs. Tanqueray, Act 1.

WILLIAM PITT,
EARL OF CHATHAM
1708–1778

The atrocious crime of being a young man . . . I
shall neither attempt to palliate nor deny.
Speeches. H. of C., 27 Jan. 1741.

I rejoice that America has resisted. Three millions
of people, so dead to all the feelings of liberty, as
voluntarily to submit to be slaves, would have
been fit instruments to make slaves of the rest.
Ib. 14 Jan. 1766.

I cannot give them my confidence; pardon me,
gentlemen, confidence is a plant of slow growth
in an aged bosom: youth is the season of credulity.
Ib.

Unlimited power is apt to corrupt the minds of those
who possess it.
Ib. House of Lords, 9 Jan. 1770.

There is something behind the throne greater than
the King himself. *Ib. 2 March 1770.*

We have a Calvinistic creed, a Popish liturgy, and
an Arminian clergy. *Ib. 19 May 1772.*

If I were an American, as I am an Englishman, while
a foreign troop was landed in my country, I never
would lay down my arms,—never—never—never!
Ib. 18 Nov. 1777.

I invoke the genius of the Constitution! *Ib.*

The poorest man may in his cottage bid defiance to
all the forces of the Crown. It may be frail—its
roof may shake—the wind may blow through it—
the storm may enter—the rain may enter—but the
King of England cannot enter—all his force dares
not cross the threshold of the ruined tenement!
Ib. Date unknown. *Brougham's Statesmen
in the Time of George III, First Series.*

Our watchword is security. *Attr.*

It was a saying of Lord Chatham, that the parks were
the lungs of London.
*William Windham, in a Speech in House of
Commons, 30 June 1808.*

L 3

WILLIAM PITT
1759–1806

Necessity is the plea for every infringement of human
freedom. It is the argument of tyrants; it is the
creed of slaves.
Speeches, H. of C., 18 Nov. 1783.

Roll up that map; it will not be wanted these ten
years. [On a map of Europe, after hearing the
news of the Battle of Austerlitz.]
*Stanhope's Life of the Rt. Hon. William Pitt,
1862, vol. iv, p. 369.*

England has saved herself by her exertions and
Europe by her example.
Ib. At the Guildhall, 1805.

Oh, my country! how I love my country. [*Attr. last
words.*] *Ib. p. 382.*

Oh, my country! how I leave my country! [*Attr. last
words.*] *Ib. 1879, vol. iii, p. 391.*

My country! oh, my country! [*Attr. last words.*]
G. Rose, Diary, 23 Jan. 1806.

I think I could eat one of Bellamy's veal pies.
Alternative attributed last words.

JAMES ROBINSON PLANCHÉ
1796–1880

Ching-a-ring-a-ring-ching! Feast of lanterns!
What a crop of chop-sticks, hongs and gongs!
Hundred thousand Chinese crinkum-crankums,
Hung among the bells and ding-dongs!
The Drama at Home, or An Evening With Puff.

It would have made a cat laugh.
*Extravaganzas (1879), The Queen of the Frogs,
1. iv.*

JOSEPH MARY PLUNKETT
1887–1916

I see His blood upon the rose
And in the stars the glory of His eyes.
Poems (1916), 'I See His Blood.'

EDGAR ALLAN POE
1809–1849

This maiden she lived with no other thought
Than to love and be loved by me. *Annabel Lee.*

I was a child and she was a child,
In this kingdom by the sea;
But we loved with a love which was more than love—
I and my Annabel Lee;
With a love that the wingèd seraphs of heaven
Coveted her and me. *Ib.*

The beautiful Annabel Lee. *Ib.*

In the sepulchre there by the sea,
In her tomb by the sounding sea. *Ib.*

The fever call'd 'Living'
Is conquer'd at last. *For Annie.*

Keeping time, time, time,
  In a sort of Runic rhyme,
To the tintinabulation that so musically wells
From the bells, bells, bells, bells.   *The Bells,* l. 9.

They are neither man nor woman—
They are neither brute nor human,
    They are Ghouls.   *Ib.* l. 86.

Vastness! and Age! and Memories of Eld!
Silence! and Desolation! and dim Night!
                    The Coliseum, l. 10.

While the angels, all pallid and wan,
  Uprising, unveiling, affirm
That the play is the tragedy, 'Man',
  And its hero the Conqueror Worm.
                The Conqueror Worm, l. 39.

All that we see or seem
Is but a dream within a dream.
            A Dream within a Dream, l. 10.

Helen, thy beauty is to me
  Like those Nicean barks of yore,
That gently, o'er a perfumed sea,
  The weary, wayworn wanderer bore
    To his own native shore.

On desperate seas long wont to roam,
  Thy hyacinth hair, thy classic face,
Thy Naiad airs have brought me home
  To the glory that was Greece
And the grandeur that was Rome.   *To Helen,* l. 1.

If I could dwell where Israfel
Hath dwelt, and he where I,—
He might not sing so wildly well
A mortal melody,
While a bolder note than his might swell
From my lyre within the sky.   *Israfel.*

And, Guy de Vere, hast *thou* no tear?—weep now or
  nevermore!   *Lenore,* l. 3.

Peccavimus; but rave not thus! and let a Sabbath song
Go up to God so solemnly the dead may feel no
  wrong.   *Ib.* l. 13.

And all my days are trances,
  And all my nightly dreams
Are where thy grey eye glances,
  And where thy footstep gleams—
In what ethereal dances,
  By what eternal streams. *To One in Paradise,* l. 21.

Once upon a midnight dreary, while I pondered,
  weak and weary,
Over many a quaint and curious volume of forgotten
  lore,
While I nodded, nearly napping, suddenly there came
  a tapping,
As of some one gently rapping.   *The Raven,* i.

      Sorrow for the lost Lenore—
For the rare and radiant maiden whom the angels
  name Lenore—
      Nameless here for evermore.   *Ib.* ii.

Deep into that darkness peering, long I stood there
  wondering, fearing,
Doubting, dreaming dreams no mortal ever dared to
  dream before.   *Ib.* v.

Ghastly grim and ancient raven wandering from the
  Nightly shore—
Tell me what thy lordly name is on the Night's
  Plutonian shore!   *Ib.* viii.

'Prophet!' said I, 'thing of evil—prophet still, if bird
  or devil!
By that heaven that bends above us—by that God
  we both adore.'   *Ib.* xvi.

Take thy beak from out my heart, and take thy form
  from off my door!
Quoth the Raven, 'Nevermore'.   *Ib.* xvii.

The skies they were ashen and sober;
  The leaves they were crisped and sere—
  The leaves they were withering and sere;
It was night in the lonesome October
  Of my most immemorial year.   *Ulalume,* l. 1.

Here once, through an alley Titanic,
  Of cypress, I roamed with my Soul—
  Of cypress, with Psyche, my Soul.   *Ib.* l. 10.

JOHN POMFRET
1667–1703

We live and learn, but not the wiser grow.
                    Reason, l. 112.

JOHN POOLE
1786?–1872

I hope I don't intrude?   *Paul Pry,* 1. ii.

ALEXANDER POPE
1688–1744

To wake the soul by tender strokes of art,
To raise the genius, and to mend the heart;
To make mankind in conscious virtue bold,
Live o'er each scene, and be what they behold:
For this the Tragic Muse first trod the stage.
            Prologue to Addison's Cato, l. 1.

A brave man struggling in the storms of fate,
And greatly falling, with a falling State.
While Cato gives his little senate laws,
What bosom beats not in his country's cause?
                          Ib. l. 21.

Ye gods! annihilate but space and time,
And make two lovers happy.
          The Art of Sinking in Poetry, ch. 11.

And thou Dalhoussy, the great God of War,
Lieutenant-Colonel to the Earl of Mar.   *Ib.*

Poetic Justice, with her lifted scale,
Where, in nice balance, truth with gold she weighs,
And solid pudding against empty praise.
                    The Dunciad, bk. i, l. 52.

Now night descending, the proud scene was o'er,
But liv'd in Settle's numbers one day more. *Ib.* l. 89.

Or where the pictures for the page atone,
And Quarles is sav'd by beauties not his own.
                          Ib. l. 139

And gentle dullness ever loves a joke.   *Ib.* bk. ii, l. 34

Earless on high, stood unabash'd De Foe. *Ib.* l. 147.

Another, yet the same.   *Ib.* bk. iii, l. 40.

Lo, where Maeotis sleeps, and hardly flows
The freezing Tanais thro' a waste of snows. *Ib.* l. 87.

Peel'd, patch'd, and piebald, linsey-wolsey brothers,
Grave mummers! sleeveless some, and shirtless
     others.   *Ib.* l. 115.

All crowd, who foremost shall be damn'd to fame.
             Ib. l. 158.

Some free from rhyme or reason, rule or check,
Break Priscian's head, and Pegasus's neck.
             Ib. l. 161.

So sweetly mawkish, and so smoothly dull.
             Ib. l. 171.

May you, my Cam and Isis, preach it long!
The Right Divine of Kings to govern wrong.
             Ib. bk. iv, l. 187.

Stretch'd on the rack of a too easy chair. *Ib.* l. 341.

She comes! she comes! the sable Throne behold
Of Night primæval, and of Chaos old!
Before her, Fancy's gilded clouds decay,
And all its varying rain-bows die away. *Ib.* l. 629.

See skulking Truth to her old cavern fled,
Mountains of Casuistry heap'd o'er her head!
Philosophy, that lean'd on Heav'n before,
Shrinks to her second cause, and is no more.
Physic of Metaphysic begs defence,
And Metaphysic calls for aid on Sense!
See Mystery to Mathematics fly!
In vain! they gaze, turn giddy, rave, and die.
Religion blushing veils her sacred fires,
And unawares Morality expires.
Nor public flame, nor private, dares to shine;
Nor human spark is left, nor glimpse divine!
Lo! thy dread empire, Chaos! is restor'd;
Light dies before thy uncreating word;
Thy hand, great Anarch! lets the curtain fall,
And universal darkness buries all.   *Ib.* l. 641.

Vital spark of heav'nly flame!
Quit, oh quit this mortal frame:
Trembling, hoping, ling'ring, flying,
Oh the pain, the bliss of dying!
        The Dying Christian to his Soul.

Tell me, my soul, can this be death?   *Ib.*

What beck'ning ghost, along the moon-light shade
Invites my steps, and points to yonder glade?
    Elegy to the Memory of an Unfortunate Lady,
    l. 1.

Is it, in heav'n, a crime to love too well?   *Ib.* l. 6.

Is there no bright reversion in the sky,
For those who greatly think, or bravely die?
             Ib. l. 9.

Ambition first sprung from your bless'd abodes;
The glorious fault of angels and of gods. *Ib.* l. 13.

By foreign hands thy dying eyes were closed,
By foreign hands thy decent limbs composed,
By foreign hands thy humble grave adorned,
By strangers honoured, and by strangers mourned!
             Ib. l. 51.

Yet shall thy grave with rising flow'rs be dressed,
And the green turf lie lightly on thy breast.
             Ib. l. 63.

So peaceful rests, without a stone, a name,
What once had beauty, titles, wealth, and fame.
How loved, how honoured once, avails thee not,
To whom related, or by whom begot;
A heap of dust alone remains of thee;
'Tis all thou art, and all the proud shall be!
             Ib. l. 69.

Line after line my gushing eyes o'erflow,
Led through a sad variety of woe:
Now warm in love, now with'ring in my bloom,
Lost in a convent's solitary gloom!
         Eloisa to Abelard, l. 35.

No, make me mistress to the man I love
If there be yet another name more free
More fond than mistress, make me that to thee!
             Ib. l. 8.

How happy is the blameless vestal's lot!
The world forgetting, by the world forgot.
             Ib. l. 207.

One thought of thee puts all the pomp to flight,
Priests, tapers, temples, swim before my sight.
             Ib. l. 273.

See my lips tremble, and my eye-balls roll,
Suck my last breath, and catch my flying soul!
             Ib. l. 323.

Teach me at once, and learn of me to die.
             Ib. l. 328.

You beat your pate, and fancy wit will come:
Knock as you please, there's nobody at home.
        Epigrams. An Empty House.

Has she no faults then (Envy says), Sir?
   Yes, she has one, I must aver;
When all the world conspires to praise her,
   The woman's deaf, and does not hear.
       Ib. On a Certain Lady at Court.

I am his Highness' dog at Kew;
Pray tell me, sir, whose dog are you?
     Ib. On the Collar of a Dog which I gave to
     his Royal Highness.

Here rests a woman, good without pretence.
       Epitaphs. On Mrs. Corbet.

Heav'n, as its purest gold, by tortures tried;
The saint sustain'd it, but the woman died.   *Ib.*

Whether thou choose Cervantes' serious air,
Or laugh and shake in Rab'lais' easy chair,
Or in the graver gown instruct mankind,
Or, silent, let thy morals tell thy mind.
       Ib. To Swift. 22 Oct. 1727.

In wit a man; simplicity a child.   *Ib. On Gay.*

Form'd to delight at once and lash the age. *Ib.* l. 4.

Nature and Nature's laws lay hid in night:
God said, *Let Newton be!* and all was light.
      Ib. Intended for Sir Isaac Newton.

            Prais'd, wept,
And honour'd by the Muse he lov'd.
       Epitaph on James Craggs in
       Westminster Abbey.

Ten censure wrong for one who writes amiss;
A fool might once himself alone expose,
Now one in verse makes many more in prose.
'Tis with our judgments as our watches, none
Go just alike, yet each believes his own.
           Essay on Criticism, !. 6.

Let such teach others who themselves excel,
And censure freely who have written well.
           Ib. l. 15.

Some are bewildered in the maze of schools,
And some made coxcombs nature meant but fools.
           Ib. l. 26.

A little learning is a dang'rous thing;
Drink deep, or taste not the Pierian spring:
There shallow draughts intoxicate the brain,
And drinking largely sobers us again.   *Ib.* l. 215.

Hills peep o'er hills, and Alps on Alps arise!
           Ib. l. 232.

'Tis not a lip, or eye, we beauty call,
But the joint force and full result of all.   *Ib.* l. 245.

Poets, like painters, thus unskilled to trace
The naked nature, and the living grace,
With gold and jewels cover ev'ry part,
And hide with ornaments their want of art.
           Ib. l. 293.

True wit is nature to advantage dressed,
What oft was thought, but ne'er so well expressed.
           Ib. l. 297.

Such laboured nothings, in so strange a style,
Amaze th' unlearn'd, and make the learned smile.
           Ib. l. 326.

Be not the first by whom the new are tried,
Nor yet the last to lay the old aside.   *Ib.* l. 335.

       As some to church repair,
Not for the doctrine, but the music there.
These equal syllables alone require,
Tho' oft the ear the open vowels tire;
While expletives their feeble aid do join;
And ten low words oft creep in one dull line.
           Ib. l. 342

Where'er you find 'the cooling western breeze',
In the next line, it 'whispers through the trees':
If crystal streams 'with pleasing murmurs creep',
The reader's threatened, not in vain, with 'sleep':
Then, at the last and only couplet fraught
With some unmeaning thing they call a thought,
A needless Alexandrine ends the song,
That, like a wounded snake, drags its slow length
   along.   *Ib.* l. 350.

True ease in writing comes from art, not chance,
As those move easiest who have learned to dance.
'Tis not enough no harshness gives offence,
The sound must seem an echo to the sense.
Soft is the strain when zephyr gently blows,
And the smooth stream in smoother numbers flows;
But when loud surges lash the sounding shore,
The hoarse, rough verse should like the torrent roar:
When Ajax strives some rock's vast weight to throw,
The line too labours, and the words move slow:
Not so, when swift Camilla scours the plain,
Flies o'er th' unbending corn, and skims along the
   main.   *Ib.* l. 362.

Yet let not each gay turn thy rapture move;
For fools admire, but men of sense approve.
           Ib. l. 390.

What woeful stuff this madrigal would be,
In some starved hackney sonneteer, or me!
But let a lord once own the happy lines,
How the wit brightens; how the style refines
           Ib. l. 418.

Some praise at morning what they blame at night;
But always think the last opinion right.   *Ib.* l. 430.
To err is human, to forgive, divine.   *Ib.* l. 525.
The bookful blockhead, ignorantly read,
With loads of learned lumber in his head. *Ib.* l. 612.
For fools rush in where angels fear to tread.
           Ib. l. 625.

Still pleased to teach, and yet not proud to know
           Ib. l. 632.

Awake, my St. John! leave all meaner things
To low ambition, and the pride of kings.
Let us, since life can little more supply
Than just to look about us and to die,
Expatiate free o'er all this scene of man;
A mighty maze! but not without a plan.
      An Essay on Man: Epistle i, l. 1.

Eye Nature's walks, shoot folly as it flies,
And catch the manners living as they rise.
Laugh where we must, be candid where we can;
But vindicate the ways of God to man.
Say first, of God above or man below,
What can we reason but from what we know?
           Ib. l. 13.

Observe how system into system runs,
What other planets circle other suns.   *Ib.* l. 25.
Who sees with equal eye, as God of all,
A hero perish, or a sparrow fall,
Atoms or systems into ruin hurled,
And now a bubble burst, and now a world.
           Ib. l. 87.

Hope springs eternal in the human breast;
Man never is, but always to be blessed.
The soul, uneasy, and confined from home,
Rests and expatiates in a life to come.
Lo, the poor Indian! whose untutored mind
Sees God in clouds, or hears him in the wind;
His soul proud science never taught to stray
Far as the solar walk or milky way;
Yet simple nature to his hope has giv'n,
Behind the cloud-topped hill, an humbler heav'n.
           Ib. l. 95.

But thinks, admitted to that equal sky,
His faithful dog shall bear him company. *Ib.* l. 111.
In pride, in reas'ning pride, our error lies;
All quit their sphere and rush into the skies!
Pride still is aiming at the bless'd abodes,
Men would be angels, angels would be gods.
Aspiring to be gods if angels fell,
Aspiring to be angels men rebel.   *Ib.* l. 123.
       The first Almighty Cause
Acts not by partial, but by gen'ral laws.   *Ib.* l. 145.
Why has not man a microscopic eye?
For this plain reason, man is not a fly.   *Ib.* l. 193.
Die of a rose in aromatic pain?   *Ib.* l. 200.
The spider's touch how exquisitely fine!
Feels at each thread, and lives along the line.
           Ib. l. 217.

All are but parts of one stupendous whole,
Whose body nature is, and God the soul.
An Essay on Man: Epistle i, l. 267.

Warms in the sun, refreshes in the breeze,
Glows in the stars, and blossoms in the trees.
Ib. l. 271.

As the rapt Seraph that adores and burns. *Ib.* l. 278.

All nature is but art unknown to thee,
All chance, direction which thou canst not see;
All discord, harmony not understood;
All partial evil, universal good;
And, spite of pride, in erring reason's spite,
One truth is clear, Whatever is, is right. *Ib.* l. 284.

Know then thyself, presume not God to scan,
The proper study of mankind is man.
Placed on this isthmus of a middle state,
A being darkly wise, and rudely great:
With too much knowledge for the sceptic side,
With too much weakness for the stoic's pride,
He hangs between; in doubt to act or rest;
In doubt to deem himself a god, or beast;
In doubt his mind or body to prefer;
Born but to die, and reas'ning but to err;
Alike in ignorance, his reason such,
Whether he thinks too little or too much;
Chaos of thought and passion, all confused;
Still by himself abused, or disabused;
Created half to rise, and half to fall;
Great lord of all things, yet a prey to all;
Sole judge of truth, in endless error hurled;
The glory, jest, and riddle of the world!
Ib. Ep. ii, l. 1.

Go, teach eternal wisdom how to rule—
Then drop into thyself, and be a fool! *Ib.* l. 29.

Fix'd like a plant on his peculiar spot,
To draw nutrition, propagate, and rot. *Ib.* l. 63.

And hence one master-passion in the breast,
Like Aaron's serpent, swallows up the rest.
Ib. l. 131.

The young disease, that must subdue at length,
Grows with his growth, and strengthens with his
strength. *Ib.* l. 135.

Vice is a monster of so frightful mien,
As to be hated needs but to be seen;
Yet seen too oft, familiar with her face,
We first endure, then pity, then embrace.
But where th' extreme of vice, was ne'er agreed:
Ask where's the North? at York, 'tis on the Tweed;
In Scotland, at the Orcades; and there,
At Greenland, Zembla, or the Lord knows where.
Ib. l. 217.

Till one man's weakness grows the strength of all.
Ib. l. 252.

The learn'd is happy nature to explore,
The fool is happy that he knows no more.
Ib. l. 263.

Behold the child, by nature's kindly law
Pleased with a rattle, tickled with a straw:
Some livelier plaything gives his youth delight,
A little louder, but as empty quite:
Scarfs, garters, gold, amuse his riper stage,
And beads and pray'r-books are the toys of age:
Pleased with this bauble still, as that before;
Till tired he sleeps, and life's poor play is o'er.
Ib. l. 275.

For forms of government let fools contest;
Whate'er is best administered is best:
For modes of faith let graceless zealots fight;
His can't be wrong whose life is in the right:
In faith and hope the world will disagree,
But all mankind's concern is charity. *Ib.* Ep. iii, l. 303.

O Happiness! our being's end and aim,
Good, pleasure, ease, content! whate'er thy name:
That something still which prompts th' eternal sigh,
For which we bear to live, or dare to die.
Ib. Ep. iv, l. 1.

Order is Heav'n's first law. *Ib.* l. 49.

Buries madmen in the heaps they raise. *Ib.* l. 76.

Shall gravitation cease, if you go by?
Or some old temple, nodding to its fall,
For Chartres' head reserve the hanging wall?
Ib. l. 128.

Go, like the Indian, in another life
Expect thy dog, thy bottle, and thy wife. *Ib.* l. 177.

Worth makes the man, and want of it the fellow;
The rest is all but leather or prunella. *Ib.* l. 203.

What can ennoble sots, or slaves, or cowards?
Alas! not all the blood of all the Howards.
Ib. l. 215.

A wit's a feather, and a chief a rod;
An honest man's the noblest work of God.
Ib. l. 247.

And more true joy Marcellus exil'd feels,
Than Caesar with a senate at his heels. *Ib.* l. 257.

Truths would you teach, or save a sinking land?
All fear, none aid you, and few understand.
Ib. l. 265.

If parts allure thee, think how Bacon shined,
The wisest, brightest, meanest of mankind:
Or ravished with the whistling of a name,
See Cromwell, damned to everlasting fame!
Ib. l. 281.

Know then this truth, enough for man to know,
'Virtue alone is happiness below.' *Ib.* l. 309.

Slave to no sect, who takes no private road,
But looks through nature up to nature's God.
Ib. l. 331.

Formed by thy converse, happily to steer
From grave to gay, from lively to severe. *Ib.* l. 379.

Say, shall my little bark attendant sail,
Pursue the triumph, and partake the gale? *Ib.* l. 385.

Thou wert my guide, philosopher, and friend.
Ib. l. 390.

That true self-love and social are the same.
Ib. l. 396.

To observations which ourselves we make,
We grow more partial for th' observer's sake.
Moral Essays, Ep. i, l. 11.

Like following life through creatures you dissect,
You lose it in the moment you detect. *Ib.* l. 29.

Alas! in truth the man but changed his mind,
Perhaps was sick, in love, or had not dined.
Ib. l. 127.

'Tis from high life high characters are drawn;
A saint in crape is twice a saint in lawn. *Ib.* l. 135.

'Odious! in woollen! 'twould a saint provoke!'
(Were the last words that poor Narcissa spoke:)
Moral Essays, Ep. i, l. 246.

'One would not, sure, be frightful when one's dead:
And,—Betty,—give this cheek a little red.'
Ib. l. 250.

And you, brave Cobham! to the latest breath,
Shall feel your ruling passion strong in death.
Ib. l. 262.

Most women have no characters at all.
Ib. Ep. ii. *To Mrs. M. Blount*, l. 2.

Choose a firm cloud, before it fall, and in it
Catch, ere she change, the Cynthia of this minute.
Ib. l. 19.

Chaste to her husband, frank to all beside,
A teeming mistress, but a barren bride. *Ib.* l. 71.

Flavia's a wit, has too much sense to pray;
To toast our wants and wishes is her way;
Nor asks of God, but of her stars, to give
The mighty blessing, 'while we live, to live'.
Ib. l. 87.

Wise wretch! with pleasures too refined to please;
With too much spirit to be e'er at ease;
With too much quickness ever to be taught;
With too much thinking to have common thought.
Ib. l. 95.

'With every pleasing, every prudent part,
Say, what can Chloe want?'—She wants a heart.
Ib. l. 159.

Virtue she finds too painful an endeavour,
Content to dwell in decencies for ever. *Ib.* l. 163.

In men, we various ruling passions find;
In women, two almost divide the kind;
Those, only fixed, they first or last obey,
The love of pleasure, and the love of sway.
Ib. l. 207.

Men, some to business, some to pleasure take;
But every woman is at heart a rake:
Men, some to quiet, some to public strife;
But every lady would be queen for life. *Ib.* l. 215.

See how the world its veterans rewards!
A youth of frolics, an old age of cards. *Ib.* l. 243.

She who ne'er answers till a husband cools,
Or, if she rules him, never shows she rules;
Charms by accepting, by submitting, sways,
Yet has her humour most, when she obeys.
Ib. l. 261.

And mistress of herself, though China fall.
Ib. l. 268.

Woman's at best a contradiction still. *Ib.* l. 270.

Who shall decide, when doctors disagree,
And soundest casuists doubt, like you and me?
Ib. Ep. iii. *To Lord Bathurst.* l. 1.

But thousands die, without or this or that,
Die, and endow a college, or a cat. *Ib.* l. 95.

The ruling passion, be it what it will,
The ruling passion conquers reason still.
Ib. l. 153.

Rise, honest Muse! and sing the Man of Ross!
Ib. l. 250.

In the worst inn's worst room, with mat half-hung,

Great Villiers lies—alas! how changed from him,

Gallant and gay, in Cliveden's proud alcove
The bower of wanton Shrewsbury and love.
Ib. ll. 299–308.

Where London's column, pointing at the skies
Like a tall bully, lifts the head, and lies. *Ib.* l. 339.

Grove nods at grove, each alley has a brother,
And half the platform just reflects the other.
Ib. Ep. iv, l. 117. *To Lord Burlington.*

To rest, the cushion and soft dean invite,
Who never mentions hell to ears polite. *Ib.* l. 149.

Such were the notes, thy once-loved Poet sung,
Till Death untimely stopped his tuneful tongue.
Ib. Ep. v. *To the Earl of Oxford and Earl
Mortimer*, l. 1.

Statesman, yet friend to truth! of soul sincere,
In action faithful, and in honour clear;
Who broke no promise, served no private end,
Who gained no title, and who lost no friend.
Ib. Ep. vii. *To Mr. Addison.* l. 67.

Where'er you walk cool gales shall fan the glade;
Trees, where you sit, shall crowd into a shade;
Where'er you tread, the blushing flow'rs shall rise,
And all things flourish where you turn your eyes.
Pastorals, Summer. l. 73.

What dire offence from am'rous causes springs,
What mighty contests rise from trivial things!
The Rape of the Lock, c. i, l. 1.

Here files of pins extend their shining rows,
Puffs, powders, patches, bibles, billets-doux.
Ib. l. 137.

On her white breast a sparkling cross she wore,
Which Jews might kiss, and infidels adore.
Ib. c. ii, l. 7.

Bright as the sun, her eyes the gazers strike,
And, like the sun, they shine on all alike. *Ib.* l. 13.

If to her share some female errors fall,
Look on her face, and you'll forget 'em all.
Ib. l. 17.

Fair tresses man's imperial race insnare,
And beauty draws us with a single hair. *Ib.* l. 27.

Here thou, great Anna! whom three realms obey,
Dost sometimes counsel take—and sometimes tea.
Ib. c. iii, l. 7.

The hungry judges soon the sentence sign,
And wretches hang that jurymen may dine.
Ib. l. 21.

Let spades be trumps! she said, and trumps they
were. *Ib.* l. 46.

Not louder shrieks to pitying heav'n are cast,
When husbands, or when lap-dogs breathe their last.
Ib. l. 157.

Sir Plume, of amber snuff-box justly vain,
And the nice conduct of a clouded cane.
Ib. c. iv, l. 123.

Shut, shut the door, good John! fatigued I said,
Tie up the knocker; say I'm sick, I'm dead.
*Epistles and Satires of Horace Imitated.
Prologue, Ep. to Dr. Arbuthnot*, l. 1.

Is there a parson, much bemused in beer,
A maudlin poetess, a rhyming peer,
A clerk, foredoomed his father's soul to cross,
Who pens a stanza, when he should engross?
                                        Ib. l. 15.

Fired that the house reject him, ''Sdeath I'll print it,
And shame the fools.'   *Ib.* l. 61.

Destroy his fib or sophistry—in vain!
The creature's at his dirty work again.   *Ib.* l. 91.

As yet a child, nor yet a fool to fame,
I lisped in numbers, for the numbers came.
                                        Ib. l. 127.

This long disease, my life.   *Ib.* l. 132.

Pretty! in amber to observe the forms
Of hairs, or straws, or dirt, or grubs, or worms!
The things we know are neither rich nor rare,
But wonder how the devil they got there.
                                        Ib. l. 169.

And he, whose fustian's so sublimely bad,
It is not poetry, but prose run mad.   *Ib.* l. 187.

Were there one whose fires
True genius kindles, and fair fame inspires;
Blest with each talent, and each art to please,
And born to write, converse, and live with ease:
Should such a man, too fond to rule alone,
Bear, like the Turk, no brother near the throne,
View him with scornful, yet with jealous eyes,
And hate for arts that caused himself to rise;
Damn with faint praise, assent with civil leer,
And, without sneering, teach the rest to sneer;
Willing to wound, and yet afraid to strike,
Just hint a fault, and hesitate dislike.
Alike reserved to blame, or to commend,
A timorous foe, and a suspicious friend;
Dreading e'en fools, by flatterers besieged,
And so obliging, that he ne'er obliged;
Like Cato, give his little senate laws,
And sit attentive to his own applause;
While wits and Templars every sentence raise,
And wonder with a foolish face of praise—
Who but must laugh, if such a man there be?
Who would not weep, if Atticus were he!
[Addison]   *Ib.* l. 193.

Let Sporus tremble.—A. What? that thing of silk,
Sporus, that mere white curd of ass's milk?
Satire or sense, alas! can Sporus feel?
Who breaks a butterfly upon a wheel?   *Ib.* l. 305.

This painted child of dirt, that stinks and stings.
                                        Ib. l. 310.

So well-bred spaniels civilly delight
In mumbling of the game they dare not bite.
Eternal smiles his emptiness betray,
As shallow streams run dimpling all the way.
                                        Ib. l. 313.

Wit that can creep, and pride that licks the dust.
                                        Ib. l. 333.

That not in fancy's maze he wandered long,
But stooped to truth, and moralised his song.
                                        Ib. l. 340.

Unlearned, he knew no schoolman's subtle art,
No language, but the language of the heart.
By nature honest, by experience wise,
Healthy by temperance, and by exercise. *Ib.* l. 398.

There St. John mingles with my friendly bowl
The feast of reason and the flow of soul.
          Ib. I. *Hor.* II, *Sat.* 1. *To Mr. Fortescue*, l. 127.

For I, who hold sage Homer's rule the best,
Welcome the coming, speed the going guest.
          Ib. II. *Hor.* II, *Sat.* 2. *To Mr. Bethel*, l. 159.

In life's cool evening satiate of applause.
          Ib. III. *Hor.* I, *Ep.* 1. *To Lord Bolingbroke*, l. 9.

Not to go back, is somewhat to advance,
And men must walk at least before they dance.
                                        Ib. l. 53.

Get place and wealth—if possible with grace;
If not, by any means, get wealth and place.
                                        Ib. l. 103.

The worst of madmen is a saint run mad.
          Ib. IV. *Hor.* I, *Ep.* 6. *To Mr. Murray*, l. 27.

Shakespeare (whom you and every play-house bill
Style the divine, the matchless, what you will)
For gain, not glory, winged his roving flight,
And grew immortal in his own despite.
          Ib. V. *Hor.* II, *Ep.* 1. *To Augustus*, l. 69.

Who now reads Cowley? if he pleases yet,
His moral pleases, not his pointed wit;
Forgot his epic, nay Pindaric art,
But still I love the language of his heart. *Ib.* l. 75.

The people's voice is odd,
It is, and it is not, the voice of God.   *Ib.* l. 89.

In quibbles, angel and archangel join,
And God the Father turns a school-divine.
          [On *Paradise Lost*]   *Ib.* l. 101.

The mob of gentlemen who wrote with ease.
                                        Ib. l. 108.

Waller was smooth; but Dryden taught to join
The varying verse, the full-resounding line,
The long majestic march and energy divine.
                                        Ib. l. 267.

Ev'n copious Dryden wanted, or forgot,
The last and greatest art, the art to blot. *Ib.* l. 280.

There still remains to mortify a wit,
The many-headed monster of the pit.   *Ib.* l. 304.

Let humble Allen, with an awkward shame,
Do good by stealth, and blush to find it fame.
                          Ib. Epilogue, Dial. i, l. 136.

Argyll, the state's whole thunder born to wield,
And shake alike the senate and the field.
                                  Ib. Dial. ii, l. 86.

Ask you what provocation I have had?
The strong antipathy of good to bad.   *Ib.* l. 197.

Yes, I am proud; I must be proud to see
Men not afraid of God, afraid of me.   *Ib.* l. 208.

Vain was the chief's, the sage's pride!
They had no poet, and they died.
                  Imitations of Horace, Odes, IV. IX. iv.

Bathos, the art of sinking in Poetry.
                              Miscellanies. Title.

Happy the man whose wish and care
   A few paternal acres bound,
Content to breathe his native air,
   In his own ground.   *Ode on Solitude.*

And the touched needle trembles to the pole.
Temple of Fame, l. 431.

Father of all! in ev'ry age,
In ev'ry clime adored,
By saint, by savage, and by sage,
Jehovah, Jove, or Lord!

Thou Great First Cause, least understood!
Who all my sense confined
To know but this, that thou art good,
And that myself am blind.
The Universal Prayer.

What conscience dictates to be done,
Or warns me not to do,
This teach me more than hell to shun,
That, more than heav'n pursue. *Ib.*

Teach me to feel another's woe,
To hide the fault I see;
That mercy I to others show,
That mercy show to me. *Ib.*

Oft, as in airy rings they skim the heath,
The clam'rous lapwings feel the leaden death:
Oft, as the mounting larks their notes prepare,
They fall, and leave their little lives in air.
Windsor Forest, l. 131.

This is the Jew
That Shakspeare drew.
Of Macklin's performance of Shylock, 14 Feb. 1741. Baker, Reed, & Jones, *Biographia Dramatica* (1812), vol. i, pt. ii, p. 469.

Party-spirit, which at best is but the madness of many for the gain of a few.
Letters. To E. Blount, 27 Aug. 1714.

'Blessed is the man who expects nothing, for he shall never be disappointed', was the ninth beatitude which a man of wit (who, like a man of wit, was a long time in gaol) added to the eighth.
Ib. To Fortescue, 23 Sept. 1725.

How often are we to die before we go quite off this stage? In every friend we lose a part of ourselves, and the best part. *Ib. To Swift*, 5 Dec. 1732.

To endeavour to work upon the vulgar with fine sense, is like attempting to hew blocks with a razor. *Thoughts on Various Subjects.*

When men grow virtuous in their old age, they only make a sacrifice to God of the devil's leavings. *Ib.*

Not to admire, is all the art I know
To make men happy, and to keep them so.
Trans. of Horace, Epistles, I. vi.

WALTER POPE

1630–1714

If I live to be old, for I find I go down,
Let this be my fate in a country town;
May I have a warm house with a stone at the gate,
And a cleanly young girl to rub my bald pate.
May I govern my passion with an absolute sway,
And grow wiser and better as my strength wears away,
Without gout or stone, by a gentle decay.
The Old Man's Wish. H. Playford, *Theater of Musick*, 1685, bk. i, p. 50.

RICHARD PORSON

1759–1808

When Dido found Æneas would not come,
She mourn'd in silence, and was Di-do-dum.
Epigram: On Latin Gerunds. J. S. Watson, Life of Porson (1861), p. 418.

'Madoc will be read,—when Homer and Virgil are forgotten.' [To Southey]
Rogers, Table Talk, p. 330.

He sometimes draws out the thread of his verbosity finer than the staple of his argument.
[Of Gibbon's *Decline and Fall*] *Letters to Travis*, 1790, preface, p. xxix.

I went to Frankfort, and got drunk
With that most learn'd professor, Brunck;
I went to Worts, and got more drunken
With that more learn'd professor, Ruhnken.
Facetiæ Cantabrigienses, 1825.

BEILBY PORTEUS

1731–1808

In sober state,
Through the sequester'd vale of rural life,
The venerable Patriarch guileless held
The tenor of his way. *Death*, l. 108.

One murder made a villain,
Millions a hero. *Ib.* l. 155.

War its thousands slays, Peace its ten thousands.
Ib. l. 179.

Teach him how to live,
And, oh! still harder lesson! how to die. *Ib.* l. 319.

WILLIAM SYDNEY PORTER

see O. HENRY

FRANCIS POTT

1832–1909

The strife is o'er, the battle done;
Now is the Victor's triumph won;
O let the song of praise be sung. Alleluia!
The Strife is O'er. Hymns fitted to the Order of Common Prayer (1861), tr. of Latin, *Finita Iam Sunt Proelia.*

HENRY CODMAN POTTER

1835–1908

We have exchanged the Washingtonian dignity for the Jeffersonian simplicity, which in due time came to be only another name for the Jacksonian vulgarity.
Address, Washington Centennial, 30 Apr. 1889.

SIR JOHN POWELL

1645–1713

Let us consider the reason of the case. For nothing is law that is not reason.
Coggs v. Bernard, 2 Lord Raymond, 911.

WINTHROP MACKWORTH PRAED

1802–1839

I think that nought is worth a thought,
And I'm a fool for thinking.
The Chart of the Brazen Head.

My own Araminta, say 'No!'
A Letter of Advice.

A happy boy, at Drury's.
School and Schoolfellows.

Just Eton boys grown heavy. *Ib.*

Of science and logic he chatters,
  As fine and as fast as he can;
Though I am no judge of such matters,
  I'm sure he's a talented man.
The Talented Man.

Whate'er the stranger's caste or creed,
  Pundit or Papist, saint or sinner,
He found a stable for his steed,
  And welcome for himself, and dinner.
The Vicar.

If he departed as he came,
  With no new light on love or liquor,—
Good sooth, the traveller was to blame,
  And not the Vicarage, nor the Vicar. *Ib.*

His talk was like a stream, which runs
  With rapid change from rocks to roses:
It slipped from politics to puns,
  It passed from Mahomet to Moses;
Beginning with the laws which keep
  The planets in their radiant courses,
And ending with some precept deep
  For dressing eels, or shoeing horses. *Ib.*

The Baptist found him far too deep;
  The Deist sighed with saving sorrow;
And the lean Levite went to sleep,
  And dreamed of tasting pork to-morrow. *Ib.*

For all who understood admired,
  And some who did not understand them. *Ib.*

CHARLES PRATT, EARL CAMDEN

1714–1794

The British Parliament has no right to tax the Americans. . . . Taxation and representation are inseparably united. God hath joined them; no British Parliament can put them asunder. To endeavour to do so is to stab our very vitals.
Speech, House of Lords, 1765.

ARCHIBALD PHILIP PRIMROSE, EARL OF ROSEBERY

1847–1929
See ROSEBERY

SIR JAMES PRIOR

1790?–1869

Mr. Cruger . . . at the conclusion of one of Mr. Burke's eloquent harangues, finding nothing to add, or perhaps as he thought to add with effect, exclaimed earnestly, in the language of the counting-house, 'I say ditto to Mr. Burke—I say ditto to Mr. Burke.' *Life of Burke, ch. 5.*

MATTHEW PRIOR

1664–1721

He's half absolv'd who has confess'd.
Alma, c. ii, l. 22.

Dear Cloe, how blubber'd is that pretty face!
A Better Answer [to Cloe Jealous].

Odds life! must one swear to the truth of a song? *Ib.*

I court others in verse: but I love thee in prose:
And they have my whimsies, but thou hast my heart.
Ib.

Serene yet strong, majestic yet sedate,
Swift without violence, without terror great.
Carmen Seculare, l. 282.

The song too daring, and the theme too great!
Ib. l. 308.

She may receive and own my flame,
  For tho' the strictest prudes should know it,
She'll pass for a most virtuous Dame,
  And I for an unhappy poet.
To a Child of Quality Five Years Old.

That I shall be past making love,
  When she begins to comprehend it. *Ib.*

Be to her virtues very kind;
Be to her faults a little blind;
Let all her ways be unconfin'd;
And clap your padlock—on her mind.
An English Padlock, l. 79.

To John I ow'd great obligation;
  But John, unhappily, thought fit
To publish it to all the nation:
  Sure John and I are more than quit. *Epigram.*

Nobles and heralds, by your leave,
  Here lies what once was Matthew Prior;
The son of Adam and of Eve,
  Can Bourbon or Nassau go higher? *Epitaph.*

Without love, hatred, joy, or fear,
They led—a kind of—as it were:
Nor wish'd, nor car'd, nor laugh'd, nor cried:
And so they liv'd, and so they died.
An Epitaph, l. 59.

All jargon of the schools.
On Exod. iii. 14. I am that I am. An Ode,
l. 65.

And oft the pangs of absence to remove
By letters, soft interpreters of love.
Henry and Emma, l. 147.

No longer shall the bodice, aptly lac'd
From thy full bosom to thy slender waist,
That air and harmony of shape express,
Fine by degrees, and beautifully less. *Ib. l. 427.*

From ignorance our comfort flows,
The only wretched are the wise.
> *To the Hon. C. Montague*, l. 35.

For the idiom of words very little she heeded,
Provided the matter she drove at succeeded,
She took and gave languages just as she needed.
> *Jinny the Just.*

Her religion so well with her learning did suit
That in practice sincere, and in controverse mute,
She shewed she knew better to live than dispute. *Ib.*

Venus, take my votive glass;
Since I am not what I was,
What from this day I shall be,
Venus, let me never see.
> *The Lady who Offers her Looking-Glass to Venus.*

My noble, lovely, little Peggy.
> *A Letter to the Honourable Lady Miss Margaret Cavendish-Holles-Harley.*

The merchant, to secure his treasure,
Conveys it in a borrowed name:
Euphelia serves to grace my measure;
But Chloe is my real flame.
> *An Ode, 'The Merchant to Secure his Treasure.'*

They never taste who always drink;
They always talk, who never think.
> *Upon this Passage in the Scaligeriana.*

He rang'd his tropes, and preach'd up patience;
Back'd his opinion with quotations.
> *Paulo Purganti and his Wife*, l. 138.

Entire and sure the monarch's rule must prove,
Who founds her greatness on her subjects' love.
> *Prologue Spoken on Her Majesty's Birthday, 1704*, l. 17.

Cur'd yesterday of my disease,
I died last night of my physician.
> *The Remedy Worse than the Disease.*

Abra was ready ere I call'd her name;
And, though I call'd another, Abra came.
> *Solomon*, bk. ii, l 362.

What is a King?—a man condemn'd to bear
The public burden of the nation's care.
> *Ib.* bk. iii, l. 275.

Now fitted the halter, now travers'd the cart;
And often took leave: but was loth to depart.
> *The Thief and the Cordelier*, v.

I never strove to rule the roast,
She ne'er refus'd to pledge my toast.
> *Turtle and Sparrow*, l. 334.

A Rechabite poor Will must live,
And drink of Adam's ale.
> *The Wandering Pilgrim*, iii.

ADELAIDE ANN PROCTER
1825–1864

I do not ask, Oh Lord, that life may be
A pleasant road.
> *A Chaplet of Verses. Per Pacem ad Lucem.*

Joy is like restless day; but peace divine
Like quiet night:
Lead me, Oh Lord—till perfect Day shall shine,
Through Peace to Light.
> *Ib.*

Seated one day at the organ,
I was weary and ill at ease,
And my fingers wandered idly
Over the noisy keys.
> *Legends and Lyrics. A Lost Chord.*

But I struck one chord of music,
Like the sound of a great Amen.
> *Ib.*

It may be that only in Heaven
I shall hear that grand Amen.
> *Ib.*

Rise! for the day is passing,
And you lie dreaming on;
The others have buckled their armour,
And forth to the fight are gone:
A place in the ranks awaits you,
Each man has some part to play;
The Past and the Future are nothing,
In the face of the stern To-day.
> *Ib. Now.*

BRYAN WALLER PROCTER
See BARRY CORNWALL

FATHER PROUT
(FRANCIS SYLVESTER MAHONY)
1804–1866

With deep affection,
And recollection,
I often think of
Those Shandon bells.   *The Bells of Shandon.*

'Tis the bells of Shandon,
That sound so grand on
The pleasant waters
Of the River Lee.   *Ib.*

WILLIAM JEFFREY PROWSE
1836–1870

Though the latitude's rather uncertain,
And the longitude also is vague,
The persons I pity who know not the city,
The beautiful city of Prague.   *The City of Prague.*

WILLIAM PULTENEY, EARL OF BATH
1684–1764

Since twelve honest men have decided the cause,
And were judges of fact, tho' not judges of laws.
> *The Honest Jury*, iii. In *The Craftsman*, 1731, vol. 5, 337. Refers to Sir Philip Yorke's unsuccessful prosecution of *The Craftsman* (1729).

a

b

ISRAEL PUTNAM

1718-1790

Men, you are all marksmen—don't one of you fire
  until you see the whites of their eyes.
  Bunker Hill, 1775. Frothingham, *History of
  the Siege of Boston* (1873), ch. 5, note.

FRANCIS QUARLES

1592-1644

The heart is a small thing, but desireth great matters.
  It is not sufficient for a kite's dinner, yet the whole
  world is not sufficient for it.
  Emblems, bk. i, No. 12. *Hugo de Anima.*

We spend our midday sweat, our midnight oil;
We tire the night in thought, the day in toil.
  Ib. bk. ii, No. 2, l. 33.

Be wisely worldly, be not worldly wise. *Ib.* l. 46.

Man is Heaven's masterpiece. *Ib.* No. 6, Epig. 6.

The road to resolution lies by doubt:
The next way home's the farthest way about.
  Ib. bk. iv, No. 2, Epig. 2.

My soul, sit thou a patient looker-on;
Judge not the play before the play is done:
Her plot hath many changes; every day
Speaks a new scene; the last act crowns the play.
  Epigram. Respice Finem.

No man is born unto himself alone;
Who lives unto himself, he lives to none.
  Esther, Sect. 1, Medit. 1.

He that had no cross deserves no crown.
  Ib. Sect. 9, Medit. 9.

He teaches to deny that faintly prays.
  A Feast for Worms, Sect. 7, Medit. 7, l. 2.

Man is man's A.B.C. There is none that can
Read God aright, unless he first spell Man.
  Hieroglyphics, i, l. 1.

He that begins to live, begins to die.
  Ib. 1, Epig. 1.

Physicians of all men are most happy; what good
  success soever they have, the world proclaimeth,
  and what faults they commit, the earth covereth.
  Ib. iv. *Nicocles.*

Come then, my brethren, and be glad,
  And eke rejoice with me;
Lawn sleeves and rochets shall go down,
  And hey! then up go we!
  The Shepherd's Oracles. Eglogue xi, *Song of
  Anarchus*, i.

We'll cry both arts and learning down,
  And hey! then up go we! *Ib.* iv.

ARTHUR QUILLER-COUCH

1863-

Know you her secret none can utter?
Hers of the Book, the tripled Crown?
  Poems. Alma Mater.

Once, my dear—but the world was young then. *Ib.*

Yet if at last, not less her lover,
You in your hansom leave the High;
Down from her towers a ray shall hover—
  Touch you, a passer-by! *Ib.*

O pastoral heart of England! like a psalm
Of green days telling with a quiet beat.
  Ib. Ode Upon Eckington Bridge.

Turns in her sleep, and murmurs of the Spring. *Ib.*

JOSIAH QUINCY

1772-1864

As it will be the right of all, so it will be the duty of
  some, definitely to prepare for a separation,
  amicably if they can, violently if they must.
  Abridgment of Debates of Congress, 14 *Jan.
  1811*, vol. iv, p. 327.

THOMAS RAINBOROWE

-1648

The poorest he that is in England hath a life to live
  as the greatest he. Peacock, *Life of Rainborowe.*

SIR WALTER RALEIGH

1552?-1618

Go, Soul, the body's guest,
  Upon a thankless arrant:
Fear not to touch the best;
  The truth shall be thy warrant:
  Go, since I needs must die,
  And give the world the lie. *The Lie*, i.

If all the world and love were young,
And truth in every shepherd's tongue,
These pretty pleasures might me move
To live with thee, and be thy love.
  The Nymph's Reply to the [*Passionate*]
  Shepherd.

Give me my scallop-shell of quiet,
My staff of faith to walk upon,
My scrip of joy, immortal diet,
My bottle of salvation,
My gown of glory, hope's true gage,
And thus I'll take my pilgrimage.
  The Passionate Man's Pilgrimage.

As you came from the holy land
  Of Walsinghame,
Met you not with my true love
  By the way as you came?

How shall I know your true love,
  That have met many a one
As I went to the holy land,
  That have come, that have gone? *Walsinghame.*

Fain would I climb, yet fear I to fall.
  Line Written on a Window-Pane. Queen
  Elizabeth wrote under it 'If thy heart fails
  thee, climb not at all.' Fuller, *Worthies*
  (1840), i, 419.

Even such is time, which takes in trust
Our youth, our joys, and all we have,
And pays us but with age and dust,
Who in the dark and silent grave,

When we have wandered all our ways,
Shuts up the story of our days.
And from which earth, and grave, and dust,
The Lord shall raise me up, I trust.
> *Written the night before his death. Found in his Bible in the Gate-house at Westminster.*

O eloquent, just, and mighty Death! whom none could advise, thou hast persuaded; what none hath dared, thou hast done; and whom all the world hath flattered, thou only hast cast out of the world and despised: thou hast drawn together all the far-stretched greatness, all the pride, cruelty, and ambition of man, and covered it all over with these two narrow words, *Hic jacet*.
> *A History of the World*, bk. v, ch. vi, § 12.

[Feeling the edge of the axe before his execution]
'Tis a sharp remedy, but a sure one for all ills.
> Hume, *History of Great Britain* (1754), vol. i, ch. iv, p. 72.

[When asked which way he preferred to lay his head on the block]
So the heart be right, it is no matter which way the head lies.
> W. Stebbing, *Sir Walter Raleigh*, ch. xxx.

SIR WALTER A. RALEIGH
1861–1922

I wish I loved the Human Race;
I wish I loved its silly face;
I wish I liked the way it walks;
I wish I liked the way it talks;
And when I'm introduced to one
I wish I thought *What Jolly Fun!*
> *Laughter from a Cloud* (1923), p. 228. *Wishes of an Elderly Man.*

JULIAN RALPH
1853–1903

News value.
> *Lecture to Brander Matthews' English Class, Columbia, 1892.* Thomas Beer's *Mauve Decade.*

ALLAN RAMSAY
1686–1758

Farewell to Lochaber, and farewell my Jean.
> *Works* (1851), ii, *Lochaber No More.*

JAMES RYDER RANDALL
1839–1908

The despot's heel is on thy shore,
  Maryland!
His torch is at thy temple door,
  Maryland!
Avenge the patriotic gore
That flecked the streets of Baltimore,
And be the battle-queen of yore,
  Maryland, my Maryland!
> *Maryland! My Maryland*, i.

THOMAS RAVENSCROFT
1592?–1635?

We be three poor mariners
Newly come from the seas.
> *Deuteromelia*, 1609.
> *Oxford Song Book*, vol. ii.

WALTER RAYMOND
1852–1931

Right as rain.   *Love and Quiet Life*, ch. 10.

THOMAS BUCHANAN READ
1822–1872

The terrible grumble, and rumble, and roar,
Telling the battle was on once more,
And Sheridan twenty miles away.
> *Sheridan's Ride*, i.

EBEN REXFORD

Darling, I am growing old,
Silver threads among the gold
Shine upon my brow to-day;
Life is fading fast away.
> *Silver Threads among the Gold.*

FREDERIC REYNOLDS
1765–1841

How goes the enemy? [Said by Mr. Ennui, 'the time-killer'.]   *The Dramatist*, I. i.

SIR JOSHUA REYNOLDS
1723–1792

If you have great talents, industry will improve them: if you have but moderate abilities, industry will supply their deficiency.
> *Discourse to Students of the Royal Academy, 11 Dec. 1769.*

A mere copier of nature can never produce anything great.   *Ib. 14 Dec. 1770.*

He who resolves never to ransack any mind but his own, will be soon reduced, from mere barrenness, to the poorest of all imitations; he will be obliged to imitate himself, and to repeat what he has before often repeated.   *Ib. 10 Dec. 1774.*

I should desire that the last words which I should pronounce in this Academy, and from this place might be the name of—Michael Angelo.
> *Ib. 10 Dec. 1790.*

He [Dr. Johnson] has no formal preparation, no flourishing with his sword; he is through your body in an instant.
> Boswell's *Johnson* (ed. 1934), vol. ii, p. 365. *18 Apr. 1775.*

WALTER REYNOLDS
(DE REYNEL or REGINALD)
d. 1327

Vox Populi, vox Dei.
  The voice of the people, the voice of God.
    Text of Sermon when Edward III ascended the throne, 1 Feb. 1327. Walsingham, Historia Anglicana (ed. 1863), i, 186.

CECIL JOHN RHODES
1853-1902

So little done, so much to do.
  Last words. L. Michell, Life, vol. ii, ch. 39.

WILLIAM BARNES RHODES
1772-1826

'Who dares this pair of boots displace,
Must meet Bombastes face to face.'
Thus do I challenge all the human race.
    Bombastes Furioso, sc. iv.
BOMBASTES:
So have I heard on Afric's burning shore,
A hungry lion give a grievous roar;
The grievous roar echo'd along the shore.
KING:
So have I heard on Afric's burning shore
Another lion give a grievous roar,
And the first lion thought the last a bore.   *Ib.*

GRANTLAND RICE
1880-

For when the One Great Scorer comes
  To write against your name,
He marks—not that you won or lost—
  But how you played the game.
    Alumnus Football.

SIR STEPHEN RICE
1637-1715

Sir Stephen Rice . . . having been often heard to say, before he was a judge, that he will drive a coach and six horses through the Act of Settlement.
    W. King, *State of the Protestants of Ireland,* 1672, ch. 3, § 3, par. 6.

GEORGE RIDDING,
BISHOP OF SOUTHWELL
1828-1904

I feel a feeling which I feel you all feel.
    Sermon in the London Mission of 1885. G. W. E. Russell's *Collections and Recollections,* ch. 29.

JAMES WHITCOMB RILEY
1852-1916

An' the gobble-uns 'll git you
  Ef you don't watch out!
    Poems. Little Orphant Annie.

SIR BOYLE ROCHE
1743-1807

Mr. Speaker, I smell a rat; I see him forming in the air and darkening the sky; but I'll nip him in the bud.   *Attr.*

JOHN WILMOT,
EARL OF ROCHESTER
1647-1680

Since 'tis Nature's law to change,
Constancy alone is strange.
    Works (1926), *A Dialogue between Strephon and Daphne,* l. 31.

The best good man, with the worst-natur'd muse.
    To Lord Buckhurst.

An age in her embraces past,
Would seem a winter's day.   *Ib. The Mistress.*

Nothing! thou elder brother ev'n to shade.
    Ib. Upon Nothing.

A merry monarch, scandalous and poor.
    Ib. A Satire on King Charles II for which he was Banished from the Court, l. 19.

Reason, an *ignis fatuus* of the mind.
    Ib. A Satire Against Mankind, l. 11.

Then Old Age, and Experience, hand in hand,
Lead him to Death, and make him understand,
After a search so painful, and so long,
That all his life he has been in the wrong.
Huddled in dirt the reasoning engine lies,
Who was so proud, so witty and so wise.   *Ib.* l. 25.

For all men would be cowards if they durst.
    Ib. l. 158.

Here lies a great and mighty king
  Whose promise none relies on;
He never said a foolish thing,
  Nor ever did a wise one.
    The King's Epitaph. An alternative version of the first line is: *Here lies our sovereign lord the King.* For Charles II's answer, see p. 87.

E. W. ROGERS

Ev'ry member of the force
Has a watch and chain, of course;
If you want to know the time,
Ask a P'liceman!   *Ask A P'liceman.*

Hi-tiddley-hi-ti.   *Title of song.*

ROBERT CAMERON ROGERS
1862-1912

The hours I spent with thee, dear heart,
  Are as a string of pearls to me;
I count them over, every one apart,
  My rosary.   *The Rosary.*

SAMUEL ROGERS
1763-1855

Think nothing done while aught remains to do.
    Human Life, l. 49.

But there are moments which he calls his own,
Then, never less alone than when alone,
Those whom he loved so long and sees no more,
Loved and still loves—not dead—but gone before,
He gathers round him. *Ib.* l. *755*.

By many a temple half as old as Time.
Italy. A Farewell, ii. 5.

Go—you may call it madness, folly;
    You shall not chase my gloom away.
There's such a charm in melancholy,
    I would not, if I could, be gay. *To —, 1814.*

Mine be a cot beside the hill;
    A bee-hive's hum shall soothe my ear;
A willowy brook, that turns a mill,
    With many a fall shall linger near. *A Wish.*

Sheridan was listened to with such attention that
you might have heard a pin drop. *Table Talk.*

Ward has no heart, they say; but I deny it;—
He has a heart, and gets his speeches by it.
Ib. Epigram upon Lord Dudley.

JAMES ROLMAZ

'Where did you get that hat?
Where did you get that tile?
Isn't it a nobby one, and just the proper style?
I should like to have one just the same as that!'
Where'er I go they shout, 'Hello!
Where did you get that hat?'
Where Did You Get That Hat?

FRANKLIN DELANO ROOSEVELT
1882–1945

I pledge you—I pledge myself—to a new deal for
the American people.
Speech at Convention, Chicago, 2 July 1932.
(*New York Times,* 3 July, sect. 1, p. 8, col. 7.)
E. K. Lindley, *The Roosevelt Revolution,*
ch. 1

THEODORE ROOSEVELT
1858–1919

I wish to preach, not the doctrine of ignoble ease,
but the doctrine of the strenuous life.
Speech, Hamilton Club, Chicago, 10 Apr. 1899.

Speak softly and carry a big stick.
Ib. Minnesota State Fair, 2 Sept. 1901.

The first requisite of a good citizen in this Republic
of ours is that he shall be able and willing to pull
his weight. *Ib. New York, 11 Nov. 1902.*

A man who is good enough to shed his blood for
the country is good enough to be given a square
deal afterwards. More than that no man is entitled
to, and less than that no man shall have.
*Ib. At the Lincoln Monument, Springfield
(Illinois), 4 June 1903.*

The men with the muck-rakes are often indispensable
to the well-being of society; but only if they know
when to stop raking the muck.
*Ib. At the laying of the Corner-stone of the
Office Building of House of Representatives,
14 Apr. 1906.*

There can be no fifty-fifty Americanism in this
country. There is room here for only 100 per cent.
Americanism, only for those who are Americans
and nothing else.
Ib. Republican Convention, Saratoga.

No man is justified in doing evil on the ground of
expediency.
*The Strenuous Life, Essays. Latitude and
Longitude among Reformers.*

We demand that big business give the people a
square deal; in return we must insist that when
any one engaged in big business honestly en-
deavors to do right he shall himself be given a
square deal. *Autobiography,* 1913, p. 615.

Hyphenated Americans.
Metropolitan Magazine, Oct. 1915, p. 7.

ARCHIBALD PHILIP PRIMROSE, EARL OF ROSEBERY
1847–1929

It is beginning to be hinted that we are a nation of
amateurs.
Rectorial Address, Glasgow, 16 Nov. 1900.

I must plough my furrow alone.
*Speech, City of London Liberal Club, 19 July
1901.*

What is the advice I have to offer you? The first is
this—that you have to clean your slate. [To the
Liberal Party] *Speech, Chesterfield, 16 Dec. 1901.*

ALEXANDER ROSS
1699–1784

Marri'd an' woo'd an' a',
Marri'd an' woo'd an' a',
The dandilly toss[1] of the parish,
Is marri'd and woo'd an' a'.
    [1] = toast.
The Fortunate Shepherdess (1768), p. 139.

CHRISTINA GEORGINA ROSSETTI
1830–1894

My heart is like a singing bird
Whose nest is in a watered shoot;
My heart is like an apple-tree
Whose boughs are bent with thickset fruit;
My heart is like a rainbow shell
That paddles in a halcyon sea;
My heart is gladder than all these
Because my love is come to me. *A Birthday.*

Because the birthday of my life
Is come, my love is come to me. *Ib.*

Oh where are you going with your love-locks
  flowing?   *Amor Mundi*, i.

We shall escape the uphill by never turning back. *Ib.*

This downhill path is easy, but there's no turning
  back.   *Ib.* v.

For there is no friend like a sister
In calm or stormy weather;
To cheer one on the tedious way,
To fetch one if one goes astray,
To lift one if one totters down,
To strengthen whilst one stands.
         Goblin Market (end).

In the bleak mid-winter
  Frosty wind made moan,
Earth stood hard as iron,
  Water like a stone;
Snow had fallen, snow on snow,
  Snow on snow,
In the bleak mid-winter,
  Long ago.   *Mid-Winter*.

In the bleak mid-winter
  A stable-place sufficed
The Lord God almighty,
  Jesus Christ.   *Ib.*

A breastful of milk,
  And a mangerful of hay.   *Ib.*

There was no hurry in her hands,
  No hurry in her feet.
         The Prince's Progress, lxxxv.

Remember me when I am gone away,
  Gone far away into the silent land.   *Remember*.

Better by far you should forget and smile
Than that you should remember and be sad.   *Ib.*

O Earth, lie heavily upon her eyes;
Seal her sweet eyes weary of watching, Earth.   *Rest.*

Silence more musical than any song.   *Ib.*

Oh roses for the flush of youth,
  And laurel for the perfect prime;
But pluck an ivy branch for me
  Grown old before my time.
         Song: 'Oh Roses for the Flush.'

When I am dead, my dearest,
  Sing no sad songs for me;
Plant thou no roses at my head,
  Nor shady cypress tree:
Be the green grass above me
  With showers and dewdrops wet;
And if thou wilt, remember,
  And if thou wilt, forget.
         Song: 'When I am Dead.'

And dreaming through the twilight
  That doth not rise nor set,
Haply I may remember,
  And haply may forget.   *Ib.*

Does the road wind up-hill all the way?
  Yes, to the very end.
Will the day's journey take the whole long day?
  From morn to night, my friend.   *Up-Hill.*

They will not keep you standing at that door.   *Ib.*

Will there be beds for me and all who seek?
  Yea, beds for all who come.   *Ib.*

DANTE GABRIEL ROSSETTI
1828–1882

Mother of the Fair Delight,
Thou handmaid perfect in God's sight.   *Ave*, l. 1.

Like the sweet apple which reddens upon the topmost bough,
A-top on the topmost twig,—which the pluckers
  forgot,—
Forgot it not, nay, but got it not, for none could get
  it till now.   *Beauty: A Combination from Sappho.*

The blessed damozel leaned out
  From the gold bar of Heaven;
Her eyes were deeper than the depth
  Of waters stilled at even;
She had three lilies in her hand,
  And the stars in her hair were seven.
         The Blessed Damozel, i.

Her hair that lay along her back
  Was yellow like ripe corn.   *Ib.* ii.

So high, that looking downward thence,
  She scarce could see the sun.   *Ib.* v.

  As low as where this earth
Spins like a fretful midge.   *Ib.* vi.

And the souls mounting up to God
  Went by her like thin flames.   *Ib.* vii.

'We two', she said, 'will seek the groves
  Where the lady Mary is,
With her five handmaidens, whose names
  Are five sweet symphonies,
Cecily, Gertrude, Magdalen,
  Margaret and Rosalys.'   *Ib.* xviii.

         Them
Who are just born, being dead.   *Ib.* xix.

And laid her face between her hands,
  And wept. (I heard her tears.)   *Ib.* xxiv.

Still we say as we go,—
  'Strange to think by the way,
Whatever there is to know,
  That shall we know one day.'
         The Cloud Confines.

Heard through all spheres one song increase,—
'Even I, even I am Beatrice.'   *Dante at Verona*, xii.

Where the lean black craft like flies
  Seem well-nigh stagnated,
  Soon to drop off dead.   *Even So.*

Peace in her chamber, wheresoe'er
It be, a holy place.   *First Love Remembered*, i.

A sonnet is a moment's monument,—
Memorial from the Soul's eternity
To one dead deathless hour.
         The House of Life, pt. 1. Introd.

Love's throne was not with these; but far above
All passionate wind of welcome and farewell
He sat in breathless bowers they dream not of.
         Ib. i. *Love Enthroned.*

When do I see thee most, beloved one?
         Ib. iv. *Lovesight.*

O love, my love! if I no more should see
Thyself, nor on the earth the shadow of thee,
Nor image of thine eyes in any spring,—
How then should sound upon life's darkening slope
The ground-whirl of the perished leaves of Hope,
The wind of Death's imperishable wing? *Ib.*

Lady, I fain would tell how evermore
Thy soul I know not from thy body, nor
Thee from myself, neither our love from God.
Ib. v. *Heart's Hope.*

I was a child beneath her touch,—a man
When breast to breast we clung, even I and she,—
A spirit when her spirit looked through me,—
A god when all our life-breath met to fan
Our life-blood, till love's emulous ardours ran,
Fire within fire, desire in deity. *Ib.* vi. *The Kiss.*

Known for my soul's birth-partner well enough!
Ib. xv. *The Birth-Bond.*
Beauty like hers is genius.
Ib. xviii. *Genius in Beauty.*

'Tis visible silence, still as the hour-glass.
Ib. xix. *Silent Noon.*

Deep in the sun-searched growths the dragon-fly
Hangs like a blue thread loosened from the sky:—
So this wing'd hour is dropt to us from above.
Oh! clasp we to our hearts, for deathless dower,
This close-companioned inarticulate hour
When twofold silence was the song of love. *Ib.*

Shall my sense pierce love,—the last relay
And ultimate outpost of eternity?
Ib. xxxiv. *The Dark Glass.*

Not in thy body is thy life at all,
But in this lady's lips and hands and eyes.
Ib. xxxvi. *Life-in-Love.*

The hour when you too learn that all is vain
And that Hope sows what Love shall never reap.
Ib. xliv. *Cloud and Wind.*

If to grow old in Heaven is to grow young,
(As the Seer saw and said,) then blest were he
With youth for evermore, whose heaven should be
True Woman, she whom these weak notes have sung.
Ib. lviii. *True Woman,* sonnet iii.

The sunrise blooms and withers on the hill
Like any hillflower; and the noblest troth
Dies here to dust. Yet shall Heaven's promise clothe
Even yet those lovers who have cherished still
This test for love:—in every kiss sealed fast
To feel the first kiss and forebode the last. *Ib.*

Upon the sight of lidless eyes in Hell.
Ib. pt. II, lxiii, *Inclusiveness.*

Thenceforth their incommunicable ways
Follow the desultory feet of Death.
Ib. lxv. *Known in Vain.*

And see the gold air and the silver fade
And the last bird fly into the last night.
Ib. lxx. *The Hill Summit.*

Eat thou and drink; to-morrow thou shalt die.
Ib. lxxi. *The Choice,* i.

They die not,—for their life was death,—but cease;
And round their narrow lips the mould falls close. *Ib.*

Think thou and act; to-morrow thou shalt die.
Ib. iii.

Nay, come up hither. From this wave-washed mound
Unto the furthest flood-brim look with me;
Then reach on with thy thought till it be drown'd.
Miles and miles distant though the last line be,
And though thy soul sail leagues and leagues beyond,—
Still, leagues beyond those leagues, there is more sea.
Ib.

Give honour unto Luke Evangelist;
For he it was (the aged legends say)
Who first taught Art to fold her hands and pray.
Ib. lxxiv. *Old and New Art,* i.

This is that Lady Beauty, in whose praise
Thy voice and hand shake still,—long known to thee
By flying hair and fluttering hem,—the beat
Following her daily of thy heart and feet,
How passionately and irretrievably,
In what fond flight, how many ways and days!
Ib. lxxvii. *Soul's Beauty.*

Lo! as that youth's eyes burned at thine, so went
Thy spell through him, and left his straight neck bent
And round his heart one strangling golden hair.
Ib. lxxviii. *Body's Beauty.*

And in regenerate rapture turns my face
Upon the devious coverts of dismay?
Ib. lxxix. *The Monochord.*

The lost days of my life until to-day,
What were they, could I see them on the street
Lie as they fell? *Ib.* lxxxvi. *Lost Days.*

I do not see them here; but after death
God knows I know the faces I shall see,
Each one a murdered self, with low last breath.
'I am thyself,—what hast thou done to me?'
'And I—and I—thyself', (lo! each one saith,)
'And thou thyself to all eternity!' *Ib.*

Even as, heavy-curled,
Stooping against the wind, a charioteer
Is snatched from out his chariot by the hair,
So shall Time be; and as the void car, hurled
Abroad by reinless steeds, even so the world.
Ib. xc. *'Retro me, Sathana!'*

Thou still, upon the broad vine-sheltered path,
Mayst wait the turning of the phials of wrath
For certain years, for certain months and days. *Ib.*

My name is Might-have-been;
I am also called No-more, Too-late, Farewell.
Ib. xcvii. *A Superscription.*

Sleepless with cold commemorative eyes. *Ib.*

When vain desire at last and vain regret
Go hand in hand to death. *Ib.* ci. *The One Hope.*

Teach the unforgetful to forget. *Ib.*

The wan soul in that golden air. *Ib.*

Scriptured petals. *Ib.*

The one Hope's one name be there,—
Not less nor more, but even that word alone. *Ib.*

It makes a goblin of the sun. *Jenny,* l. 205.

Between the hands, between the brows,
Between the lips of Love-Lily. *Love-Lily.*

Whose speech Truth knows not from her thought
Nor Love her body from her soul.   *Ib.*

This is that blessed Mary, pre-elect
God's Virgin.   *Mary's Girlhood.*

Thou fill'st from the winged chalice of the soul
Thy lamp, O Memory, fire-winged to its goal.
     Mnemosyne.

Amid the bitterness of things occult.
     For Our Lady of the Rocks.

And your own footsteps meeting you,
And all things going as they came.
     The Portrait, iii.

Yearned loud the iron-bosomed sea.   *Ib.* x.

Like tombs of pilgrims that have died
About the Holy Sepulchre.   *Ib.* xii.

(O Mother, Mary Mother,
Three days to-day, between Hell and Heaven!)
     Sister Helen.

Unto the man of yearning thought
And aspiration, to do nought
Is in itself almost an act.   *Soothsay,* x.

I have been here before,
     But when or how I cannot tell:
I know the grass beyond the door,
     The sweet keen smell,
The sighing sound, the lights around the shore.
     Sudden Light, i.

Heavenborn Helen, Sparta's queen,
     (O Troy Town!)
Had two breasts of heavenly sheen,
The sun and moon of the heart's desire.
     Troy Town, i.

The sea hath no king but God alone.
     The White Ship, l. 6.

From perfect grief there need not be
Wisdom or even memory:
One thing then learnt remains to me,—
The woodspurge has a cup of three.
     The Woodspurge.

'I saw the Sibyl at Cumæ'
(One said) 'with mine own eye.
She hung in a cage, and read her rune
     To all the passers-by.
Said the boys, 'What wouldst thou, Sibyl?'
     She answered, "I would die".'
     Fragments. The Sibyl.

Was it a friend or foe that spread these lies?
Nay, who but infants question in such wise?
'Twas one of my most intimate enemies.   *Fragment.*

MARTIN JOSEPH ROUTH
1755–1854

You will find it a very good practice always to verify
     your references, sir!
     Burgon, *Memoir of Dr. Routh.*   *Quarterly
Review,* July 1878, vol. cxlvi.

NICHOLAS ROWE
1674–1718

That false Lothario!   *The Fair Penitent,* ii. i.

To be good is to be happy.   *Ib.* iii. i.

The evening of my age.   *Ib.* iv. i.

I feel the pangs of disappointed love.   *Ib.*

Is this that haughty, gallant, gay Lothario?   *Ib.* v. i.

Like Helen, in the night when Troy was sack'd,
Spectatress of the mischief which she made.   *Ib.*

Death is the privilege of human nature,
And life without it were not worth our taking.   *Ib.*

       Had I but early known
Thy wond'rous worth, thou excellent young man,
We had been happier both.   *Ib.*

With rough, majestic force he mov'd the heart,
With strength and nature made amends for art.
     [Shakespeare.]   *Jane Shore,* prologue.

       If I boast of aught,
Be it, to have been Heaven's happy instrument,
The means of good to all my fellow-creatures;
This is a King's best praise.
     Tamerlaine, ii. ii.

       Death is parting,
'Tis the last sad adieu 'twixt soul and body.   *Ib.*

Think on the sacred dictates of thy faith,
And let that arm thy virtue, to perform
What Cato's daughter durst not,—live Aspasia,
And dare to be unhappy.   *Ib.* iv. i.

MATTHEW ROYDON
fl. 1580–1622

A sweet attractive kind of grace,
     A full assurance given by looks,
Continual comfort in a face,
     The lineaments of Gospel books;
I trow that countenance cannot lie,
Whose thoughts are legible in the eye.
     An Elegy, or Friend's Passion, for his Astrophill
     (i.e. Sir Philip Sidney), xviii.

Was never eye, did see that face,
     Was never ear, did hear that tongue,
Was never mind, did mind his grace,
     That ever thought the travel long—
       But eyes, and ears, and ev'ry thought,
       Were with his sweet perfections caught.   *Ib.* xix.

JOHN RUSKIN
1819–1900

You know there are a great many odd styles of
architecture about; you don't want to do anything
ridiculous; you hear of me, among others, as a
respectable architectural man-milliner; and you
send for me, that I may tell you the leading fashion.
     The Crown of Wild Olive, § 53, lecture ii.
     Traffic.

Thackeray settled like a meat-fly on whatever one
had got for dinner, and made one sick of it.
     Fors Clavigera, letter xxxi.

[On Whistler's 'Nocturne in Black and Gold']
I have seen, and heard, much of Cockney impudence
before now; but never expected to hear a coxcomb
ask two hundred guineas for flinging a pot of paint
in the public's face.
     Ib. letter lxxix, 18 June 1877.

No person who is not a great sculptor or painter *can* be an architect. If he is not a sculptor or painter, he can only be a *builder*.
> *Lectures on Architecture and Painting*, § 61, Addenda.

There is nothing in sea-description, detailed, like Dickens' storm at the death of Ham, in 'David Copperfield'.
> *Modern Painters* (1888), vol. i, pt. ii, p. 425, note.

What is poetry? The suggestion, by the imagination, of noble grounds for the noble emotions.
> *Ib.* vol. iii.

Mountains are the beginning and the end of all natural scenery.   *Ib.* vol. iv, pt. v, ch. 20, § 1.

That mysterious forest below London Bridge.
> *Ib.* vol. v, pt. ix, ch. 9, § 7.

Its symmetry be as of thunder answering from two horizons. [A sentence of Johnson.]
> *Praeterita*, I. xii. *Rosslyn Chapel*, § 251.

There was a rocky valley between Buxton and Bakewell, . . . divine as the vale of Tempe; you might have seen the gods there morning and evening,— Apollo and the sweet Muses of the Light. . . . You enterprised a railroad, . . . you blasted its rocks away. . . . And now, every fool in Buxton can be at Bakewell in half-an-hour, and every fool in Bakewell at Buxton.
> *Ib.* III. iv. *Joanna's Cave*, § 84 note.

All books are divisible into two classes: the books of the hour, and the books of all time.
> *Sesame and Lilies*, Lect. i. *Of Kings' Treasuries*, § 8.

But whether thus submissively or not, at least be sure that you go to the author to get at *his* meaning, not to find yours.   *Ib.* § 13.

Which of us . . . is to do the hard and dirty work for the rest—and for what pay? Who is to do the pleasant and clean work, and for what pay?
> *Ib.* § 30, note.

What do we, as a nation, care about books? How much do you think we spend altogether on our libraries, public or private, as compared with what we spend on our horses?   *Ib.* § 32.

How long most people would look at the best book before they would give the price of a large turbot for it!   *Ib.*

We call ourselves a rich nation, and we are filthy and foolish enough to thumb each other's books out of circulating libraries!   *Ib.*

Will you not covet such power as this, and seek such throne as this, and be no more housewives, but queens?   *Ib.* Lect. ii. *Of Queens' Gardens*, § 87.

There is no putting by that crown; queens you must always be; queens to your lovers; queens to your husbands and your sons; queens of higher mystery to the world beyond. . . . But, alas! you are too often idle and careless queens, grasping at majesty in the least things, while you abdicate it in the greatest.   *Ib.* § 90.

I believe the right question to ask, respecting all ornament, is simply this: Was it done with enjoyment— was the carver happy while he was about it?
> *Ib.* ch. 5. *The Lamp of Life*.

Better the rudest work that tells a story or records a fact, than the richest without meaning. There should not be a single ornament put upon great civic buildings, without some intellectual intention.
> *The Seven Lamps of Architecture*, ch. 6. *The Lamp of Memory*, § 7.

When we build, let us think that we build for ever.
> *Ib.* § 10.

Remember that the most beautiful things in the world are the most useless; peacocks and lilies for instance.   *The Stones of Venice*, vol. i, ch. 2, § 17.

The purest and most thoughtful minds are those which love colour the most.
> *Ib.* vol. ii, ch. 5, § 30.

All things are literally better, lovelier, and more beloved for the imperfections which have been divinely appointed, that the law of human life may be Effort, and the law of human judgment, Mercy.   *Ib.* ch. vi, § 25.

Fine art is that in which the hand, the head, and the heart of man go together.
> *The Two Paths*, lecture ii.

Not only is there but one way of *doing* things rightly, but there is only one way of *seeing* them, and that is, seeing the whole of them.   *Ib.*

Nobody cares much at heart about Titian; only there is a strange undercurrent of everlasting murmur about his name, which means the deep consent of all great men that he is greater than they.   *Ib.*

No human being, however great, or powerful, was ever so free as a fish.   *Ib.* lect. v.

Labour without joy is base. Labour without sorrow is base. Sorrow without labour is base. Joy without labour is base.   *Time and Tide*, letter v.

Your honesty is *not* to be based either on religion or policy. Both your religion and policy must be based on *it*. Your honesty must be based, as the sun is, in vacant heaven; poised, as the lights in the firmament, which have rule over the day and over the night.   *Ib.* letter viii.

To make your children *capable of honesty* is the beginning of education.   *Ib.*

I hold it for indisputable, that the first duty of a State is to see that every child born therein shall be well housed, clothed, fed, and educated, till it attain years of discretion. But in order to the effecting this the Government must have an authority over the people of which we now do not so much as dream.   *Ib.* letter xiii.

It ought to be quite as natural and straightforward a matter for a labourer to take his pension from his parish, because he has deserved well of his parish, as for a man in higher rank to take his pension from his country, because he has deserved well of his country.   *Unto this Last*, preface, § 6 (4).

Soldiers of the ploughshare as well as soldiers of the sword.   *Unto this Last*, Essay iii, § 54.

Government and co-operation are in all things the laws of life; anarchy and competition the laws of death. *Ib.*

Whereas it has long been known and declared that the poor have no right to the property of the rich, I wish it also to be known and declared that the rich have no right to the property of the poor. *Ib.*

There is no wealth but life. *Ib.* Essay iv, § 77.

Trust thou thy Love: if she be proud, is she not sweet?
Trust thou thy Love: if she be mute, is she not pure?
Lay thou thy soul full in her hands, low at her feet;—
Fail, Sun and Breath!—yet, for thy peace, she shall endure. *Trust Thou Thy Love.*

LORD JOHN RUSSELL
1792–1878

If peace cannot be maintained with honour, it is no longer peace.
Speech. Greenock, 19 Sept. 1853. The Times, 21 Sept. 1853.

Among the defects of the Bill, which were numerous, one provision was conspicuous by its presence and another by its absence.
Speech to the electors of the City of London, April 1859.

WILLIAM HOWARD RUSSELL
1820–1907

[The Russians] dash on towards that thin red line tipped with steel.
The British Expedition to the Crimea, 1877, p. 156.

CHARLES SACKVILLE
See EARL OF DORSET

JOHN L. ST. JOHN

Archibald—certainly not! *Title of song.*

'SAKI'
(HECTOR HUGH MUNRO)
1870–1916

The cook was a good cook, as cooks go; and as cooks go she went.
Reginald. Reginald on Besetting Sins.

The Western custom of one wife and hardly any mistresses.
Reginald in Russia. A Young Turkish Catastrophe.

But, good gracious, you've got to educate him first. You can't expect a boy to be depraved until he's been to a good school. *Ib. The Baker's Dozen.*

He's simply got the instinct for being unhappy highly developed.
Chronicles of Clovis. The Match-Maker.

Oysters are more beautiful than any religion. . . . There's nothing in Christianity or Buddhism that quite matches the sympathetic unselfishness of an oyster. *Ib.*

'The man is a common murderer.'
'A common murderer, possibly, but a very uncommon cook.'
Beasts and Super-Beasts. The Blind Spot.

When she inveighed eloquently against the evils of capitalism at drawing-room meetings and Fabian conferences she was conscious of a comfortable feeling that the system, with all its inequalities and iniquities, would probably last her time. It is one of the consolations of middle-aged reformers that the good they inculcate must live after them if it is to live at all.
Ib. The Byzantine Omelette.

Waldo is one of those people who would be enormously improved by death.
Ib. The Feast of Nemesis.

Children with Hyacinth's temperament don't know better as they grow older; they merely know more.
The Toys of Peace. Hyacinth.

IRA DAVID SANKEY
1840–1908

God be with you till we meet again!
Sacred Songs, No. 298. God Be With You.

Light in the darkness, sailor, day is at hand!
See o'er the foaming billows fair Heaven's land.
Drear was the voyage, sailor, now almost o'er;
Safe within the lifeboat, sailor, pull for the shore.
Pull for the shore, sailor, pull for the shore!
Heed not the rolling waves, but bend to the oar.
Ib. The Life Boat.

Is there room for Mary there?
Yes, there's room; yes, there's room;
Room in the beautiful heavenly land.
Ib. Room Among the Angels.

Shall we gather at the river? . . .
Yes, we'll gather at the river,
The beautiful, the beautiful river,
Gather with the saints at the river,
That flows by the throne of God.
Ib. No. 1000. Shall We Gather.

In the sweet by-and-by,
We shall meet on that beautiful shore.
Ib. Sweet By-and-By.

That will be glory for me.
Ib. That Will Be Heaven For Me.

EPES SARGENT
1813–1880

A life on the ocean wave,
A home on the rolling deep.
A Life on the Ocean Wave.

SIEGFRIED SASSOON

1886–

Everyone suddenly burst out singing.

Everyone Sang.

The song was wordless;
The singing will never be done. *Ib.*

RICHARD SAVAGE

d. 1743

No tenth transmitter of a foolish face.
The Bastard, l. 8.

Perhaps been poorly rich, and meanly great,
The slave of pomp, a cipher in the state. *Ib.* l. 39.

May see thee now, though late, redeem thy name,
And glorify what else is damn'd to fame.
Character of the Rev. James Foster, l. 45.

HENRY J. SAYERS

Ta-ra-ra-boom-de-ay. *Title of song.*

GEORGE SAVILE,
MARQUIS OF HALIFAX

See HALIFAX

SIR WALTER SCOTT

1771–1832

To the Lords of Convention 'twas Claver'se who
spoke,
'Ere the King's crown shall fall there are crowns to
be broke;
So let each cavalier who loves honour and me,
Come follow the bonnet of Bonny Dundee.
Come fill up my cup, come fill up my can,
Come saddle your horses, and call up your men;
Come open the West Port, and let me gang free,
And it's room for the bonnets of Bonny Dundee!'
Bonny Dundee. (The Doom of Devorgoil, Act
II, sc. ii.)

But answer came there none.
Bridal of Triermain, c. III. x.

The stag at eve had drunk his fill,
Where danced the moon on Monan's rill,
And deep his midnight lair had made
In lone Glenartney's hazel shade.
The Lady of the Lake, c. I. i.

A moment gazed adown the dale,
A moment snuff'd the tainted gale. *Ib.* ii.

Two dogs of black Saint Hubert's breed,
Unmatchd for courage, breath, and speed. *Ib.* vii.

Woe worth the chase, woe worth the day,
That costs thy life, my gallant grey! *Ib.* ix.

In listening mood, she seem'd to stand,
The guardian Naiad of the strand. *Ib.* xvii.

And ne'er did Grecian chisel trace
A Nymph, a Naiad, or a Grace
Of finer form, or lovelier face!
What though the sun, with ardent frown,
Had slightly tinged her cheek with brown. *Ib.* xviii.

The will to do, the soul to dare. *Ib.* xxi.

His ready speech flow'd fair and free,
In phrase of gentlest courtesy;
Yet seem'd that tone, and gesture bland,
Less used to sue than to command. *Ib.*

Soldier, rest! thy warfare o'er,
Sleep the sleep that knows not breaking,
Dream of battled fields no more,
Days of danger, nights of waking. *Ib.* xxxi.

Huntsman, rest! thy chase is done. *Ib.* xxxii.

Hail to the Chief who in triumph advances!
Ib. xix.

Speed, Malise, speed! the dun deer's hide
On fleeter foot was never tied. *Ib.* c. III. xiii.

Like the dew on the mountain,
Like the foam on the river,
Like the bubble on the fountain,
Thou art gone, and for ever! *Ib.* xvi.

Which spills the foremost foeman's life,
That party conquers in the strife! *Ib.* c. IV. vi.

'These are Clan Alpine's warriors true;
And, Saxon,—I am Roderick Dhu!' *Ib.* c. V. ix.

'Come one, come all! this rock shall fly
From its firm base as soon as I.' *Ib.* x.

Respect was mingled with surprise,
And the stern joy which warriors feel
In foemen worthy of their steel. *Ib.*

Where, where was Roderick then?
One blast upon his bugle-horn
Were worth a thousand men! *Ib.* c. VI. xviii.

The way was long, the wind was cold,
The Minstrel was infirm and old;
His wither'd cheek and tresses grey,
Seem'd to have known a better day.
The harp, his sole remaining joy,
Was carried by an orphan boy.
The last of all the Bards was he,
Who sung of Border chivalry;
For, welladay! their date was fled,
His tuneful brethren all were dead;
And he, neglected and oppress'd,
Wish'd to be with them, and at rest.
The Lay of the Last Minstrel, introd. l. 1.

The unpremeditated lay. *Ib.* l. 18.

Old times were changed, old manners gone;
A stranger fill'd the Stuarts' throne;
The bigots of the iron time
Had call'd his harmless art a crime. *Ib.* l. 19.

Nine-and-twenty knights of fame
Hung their shields in Branksome Hall;
Nine-and-twenty squires of name
Brought them their steeds to bower from stall;
Nine-and-twenty yeomen tall
Waited, duteous, on them all:
They were all knights of mettle true,
Kinsmen to the bold Buccleuch. *Ib.* c. I. iii.

They carv'd at the meal
With gloves of steel,
And they drank the red wine through the helmet
barr'd. *Ib.* iv.

Such is the custom of Branksome Hall. *Ib.* vii.

Vengeance, deep-brooding o'er the slain,
  Had lock'd the source of softer woe;
And burning pride and high disdain
  Forbade the rising tear to flow.
          The Lay of the Last Minstrel, c. I. ix.

To her bidding she could bow
  The viewless forms of air.   *Ib.* xii.

What shall be the maiden's fate?
Who shall be the maiden's mate?   *Ib.* xvi.

Steady of heart, and stout of hand.   *Ib.* xxi.

Sir William of Deloraine, good at need.   *Ib.* xxii.

Yet, through good heart, and Oure Ladye's grace,
At length he gain'd the landing-place.   *Ib.* xxix.

If thou would'st view fair Melrose aright,
Go visit it by the pale moonlight;
For the gay beams of lightsome day
Gild, but to flout, the ruins grey.   *Ib.* c. II. i.

Strange sounds along the chancel pass'd,
The banners wav'd without a blast.   *Ib.* xvi.

Yet somewhat was he chill'd with dread,
And his hair did bristle upon his head.   *Ib.*

I cannot tell how the truth may be;
I say the tale as 'twas said to me.   *Ib.* xxii.

In peace, Love tunes the shepherd's reed;
In war, he mounts the warrior's steed;
In halls, in gay attire is seen;
In hamlets, dances on the green.
Love rules the court, the camp, the grove,
And men below, and saints above;
For love is heaven, and heaven is love.   *Ib.* c. III. ii.

And laugh'd, and shouted, 'Lost! lost! lost!'
          Ib. xiii.

Why, when the volleying musket play'd
Against the bloody Highland blade,
Why was not I beside him laid!
Enough, he died the death of fame;
Enough, he died with conquering Graeme.
          Ib. c. IV. ii.

          For ne'er
Was flattery lost on poet's ear:
A simple race! they waste their toil
For the vain tribute of a smile.   *Ib.* conclusion.

Call it not vain; they do not err,
  Who say, that when the Poet dies,
Mute Nature mourns her worshipper,
  And celebrates his obsequies.   *Ib.* c. v. i.

The secret sympathy,
The silver link, the silken tie,
Which heart to heart, and mind to mind,
In body and in soul can bind.   *Ib.* c. v. xiii.

Breathes there the man, with soul so dead,
Who never to himself hath said,
  This is my own, my native land!
Whose heart hath ne'er within him burn'd,
As home his footsteps he hath turn'd
  From wandering on a foreign strand!
If such there breathe, go, mark him well;
For him no Minstrel raptures swell;
High though his titles, proud his name,
Boundless his wealth as wish can claim;
Despite those titles, power, and pelf,
The wretch, concentred all in self,

Living, shall forfeit fair renown,
And, doubly dying, shall go down
To the vile dust, from whence he sprung,
Unwept, unhonour'd, and unsung.

O Caledonia! stern and wild,
Meet nurse for a poetic child!
Land of brown heath and shaggy wood,
Land of the mountain and the flood,
Land of my sires! what mortal hand
Can e'er untie the filial band
That knits me to thy rugged strand!   *Ib.* c. VI. i–ii.

For Love will still be lord of all.   *Ib.* xi.

The elvish page fell to the ground,
And, shuddering, mutter'd, 'Found! found! found!'
          Ib. xxiv.

That day of wrath, that dreadful day,
When heaven and earth shall pass away.   *Ib.* xxxi.

The dew that on the violet lies
Mocks the dark lustre of thine eyes.
          The Lord of the Isles, c. I. iii.

To show the form it seem'd to hide.   *Ib.* v.

Thus, then, my noble foe I greet;
Health and high fortune till we meet,
  And then—what pleases Heaven.   *Ib.* c. III. vi.

Scenes sung by him who sings no more!
His bright and brief career is o'er,
  And mute his tuneful strains.   *Ib.* c. IV. xi.

O! many a shaft, at random sent,
Finds mark the archer little meant!
And many a word, at random spoken,
May soothe or wound a heart that's broken.
          Ib. c. v. xviii.

To that dark inn, the grave!   *Ib.* c. VI. xxvi.

O hush thee, my babie, thy sire was a knight,
Thy mother a lady, both lovely and bright.
          Lullaby of an Infant Chief.

Then hush thee, my darling, take rest while you may,
For strife comes with manhood, and waking with
  day.   *Ib.*

O lovers' eyes are sharp to see,
  And lovers' ears in hearing.
          The Maid of Neidpath.

Till through her wasted hand, at night,
  You saw the taper burning.   *Ib.*

November's sky is chill and drear,
November's leaf is red and sear.
          Marmion, c. I, introd. i.

To him, as to the burning levin,
Short, bright, resistless course was given.   *Ib.* vi.

Had'st thou but liv'd, though stripp'd of power,
A watchman on the lonely tower. [On Pitt]
          Ib. viii.

Now is the stately column broke,
The beacon-light is quench'd in smoke,
The trumpet's silver sound is still,
The warder silent on the hill! [On Pitt]   *Ib.*

Drop upon Fox's grave the tear,
'Twill trickle to his rival's bier;
O'er Pitt's the mournful requiem sound,
And Fox's shall the notes rebound.   *Ib.* xi.

But search the land of living men,
Where wilt thou find their like agen?
Marmion, c. I, introd. xi.

Profan'd the God-given strength, and marr'd the
　lofty line.　　　　　　　　　　　　*Ib.* xvi.

His square-turn'd joints, and strength of limb,
Show'd him no carpet knight so trim,
But in close fight a champion grim,
　In camps a leader sage.　　　　　*Ib.* c. I. v.

Stout heart, and open hand!　　　*Ib.* x.

And come he slow, or come he fast,
It is but Death who comes at last.　*Ib.* c. II. xxx.

When Prussia hurried to the field,
And snatch'd the spear, but left the shield!
Ib. c. III, introd. l. 63.

Where shall the lover rest,
　Whom the fates sever
From his true maiden's breast,
　Parted for ever?
Where, through groves deep and high,
　Sounds the far billow,
Where early violets die,
　Under the willow.　　　　　　*Ib.* c. III. x.

In the lost battle,
　Borne down by the flying,
Where mingles war's rattle
　With groans of the dying.　　　*Ib.* xi.

Still is thy name in high account,
　And still thy verse has charms,
Sir David Lindesay of the Mount,
　Lord Lion King-at-arms!　　　*Ib.* c. IV. vii.

O, young Lochinvar is come out of the west,
Through all the wide Border his steed was the best.
Ib. c. V. xii.

So faithful in love, and so dauntless in war,
There never was knight like the young Lochinvar.
Ib.

For a laggard in love, and a dastard in war,
Was to wed the fair Ellen of brave Lochinvar.　*Ib.*

'O come ye in peace here, or come ye in war,
Or to dance at our bridal, young Lord Lochinvar?'
Ib.

'To lead but one measure, drink one cup of wine.'
Ib.

With a smile on her lips, and a tear in her eye.　*Ib.*

'Now tread we a measure!' said young Lochinvar.
Ib.

'She is won! we are gone, over bank, bush, and
　scaur;
They'll have fleet steeds that follow' quoth young
　Lochinvar.　　　　　　　　　　　　*Ib.*

Heap on more wood!—the wind is chill;
But let it whistle as it will,
We'll keep our Christmas merry still.
Ib. c. VI, introd. i.

England was merry England, when
Old Christmas brought his sports again.
'Twas Christmas broach'd the mightiest ale;
'Twas Christmas told the merriest tale;
A Christmas gambol oft could cheer
The poor man's heart through half the year.　*Ib.* iii.

What skilful limner e'er would choose
To paint the rainbow's varying hues,
Unless to mortal it were given
To dip his brush in dyes of heaven?　　*Ib.* c. VI. v.

My castles are my King's alone,
From turret to foundation-stone—
The hand of Douglas is his own.　　　*Ib.* xiii.

'And dar'st thou then
To beard the lion in his den,
The Douglas in his hall?
And hop'st thou thence unscathed to go?
No, by Saint Bride of Bothwell, no!
Up drawbridge, grooms—what, warder, ho!
Let the portcullis fall.'　　　　　　*Ib.* xiv.

O what a tangled web we weave,
When first we practise to deceive!　　*Ib.* xvii.

Scarce could they hear, or see their foes,
Until at weapon-point they close.
They close, in clouds of smoke and dust,
With sword-sway, and with lance's thrust;
And such a yell was there,
Of sudden and portentous birth,
As if men fought upon the earth,
And fiends in upper air.　　　　　　*Ib.* xxv.

Good-night to Marmion.　　　　　　*Ib.* xxviii.

O Woman! in our hours of ease,
Uncertain, coy, and hard to please,
And variable as the shade
By the light quivering aspen made;
When pain and anguish wring the brow,
A ministering angel thou!　　　　　*Ib.* xxx.

'Charge, Chester, charge! On, Stanley, on!'
Were the last words of Marmion.　　*Ib.* xxxii.

Where's now their victor vaward wing,
Where Huntley, and where Home?—
O, for a blast of that dread horn,
On Fontarabian echoes borne!　　　*Ib.* xxxiii.

The stubborn spear-men still made good
Their dark impenetrable wood,
Each stepping where his comrade stood,
　The instant that he fell.　　　　*Ib.* xxxiv.

Still from the sire the son shall hear
Of the stern strife, and carnage drear,
　Of Flodden's fatal field,
Where shiver'd was fair Scotland's spear,
　And broken was her shield!　　　*Ib.*

To all, to each, a fair good-night,
And pleasing dreams, and slumbers light!
Ib. L'envoy.

But Nora's heart is lost and won,
—She's wedded to the Earlie's son!　*Nora's Vow.*

Pibroch of Donuil Dhu,
　Pibroch of Donuil,
Wake thy wild voice anew,
　Summon Clan-Conuil.
Come away, come away,
　Hark to the summons!
Come in your war array,
　Gentles and commons.　*Pibroch of Donuil Dhu.*

Leave untended the herd,
　The flock without shelter;
Leave the corpse uninterr'd,
　The bride at the altar.　　　　　　*Ib.*

Come as the winds come, when
　　Forests are rended,
Come as the waves come, when
　　Navies are stranded. *Ib.*

Still are the thoughts to memory dear. *Rokeby*, xxxiii.

A mother's pride, a father's joy! *Ib.* c. III. xv.

O, Brignal banks are wild and fair,
　　And Greta woods are green,
And you may gather garlands there
　　Would grace a summer queen. *Ib.* xvi.

A weary lot is thine, fair maid,
　　A weary lot is thine!
To pull the thorn thy brow to braid,
　　And press the rue for wine! *Ib.* xxviii.

He turn'd his charger as he spake,
　　Upon the river shore,
He gave his bridle-reins a shake,
　　Said 'Adieu for evermore,
　　　　　　　　　　　　My love!
And adieu for evermore.' *Ib.*

Tramp! tramp! along the land they rode,
Splash! splash! along the sea. *William and Helen.*

You . . . whirl'd them to the back o' beyont.
The Antiquary, ch. 2.

Praetorian here, Praetorian there, I mind the bigging
o't. *Ib.* ch. 4.

It's no fish ye're buying—it's men's lives. *Ib.* ch. 11.

Widow'd wife, and married maid,
Betrothed, betrayer, and betray'd!
The Betrothed, ch. 15.

Woman's faith, and woman's trust—
Write the characters in dust. *Ib.* ch. 20.

Look not thou on beauty's charming,—
Sit thou still when kings are arming,—
Taste not when the wine-cup glistens,—
Speak not when the people listens,—
Stop thine ear against the singer,—
From the red gold keep thy finger;—
Vacant heart and hand, and eye,—
Easy live and quiet die.
The Bride of Lammermoor, ch. 3.

When the last Laird of Ravenswood to Ravenswood
　　shall ride,
And woo a dead maiden to be his bride,
He shall stable his steed in the Kelpie's flow,
And his name shall be lost for evermoe! *Ib.* ch. 18.

I live by twa trades, sir, . . . fiddle, sir, and spade;
filling the world, and emptying of it. *Ib.* ch. 24.

Her winding-sheet is up as high as her throat
already. *Ib.* ch. 34.

An ower true tale. *Ib.*

Touch not the cat but[1] a glove.
The Fair Maid of Perth, ch. 34.

But no one shall find me rowing against the stream.
I care not who knows it—I write for the general
amusement.
The Fortunes of Nigel, introductory epistle.

It's ill taking the breeks aff a wild Highlandman.
Ib. ch. 5.

[1] = without.

For a con-si-de-ra-tion. *Ib.* ch. 22.

To be plain, if your lordship does not ken when you
have a good servant, I ken when I have a kind
master. *Ib.* ch. 31.

(He) was ever after designated as a 'stickit minister'.
Guy Mannering, ch. 2.

Twist ye, twine[2] ye! even so
Mingle shades of joy and woe,
Hope and fear, and peace and strife,
In the thread of human life. *Ib.* ch. 4.

Ride your ways, Ellangowan. *Ib.* ch. 8.

Mrs. Bertram:
'That sounds like nonsense, my dear.'
Mr. Bertram:
'May be so, my dear; but it may be very good law
for all that.' *Ib.* ch. 9.

Sophia, as you well know, followed me to India. She
was as innocent as gay; but, unfortunately for us
both, as gay as innocent. *Ib.* ch. 12.

'Pro-di-gi-ous!' exclaimed Dominie Sampson.
Ib. ch. 14.

Gin by pailfuls, wine in rivers,
Dash the window-glass to shivers!
For three wild lads were we, brave boys,
And three wild lads were we;
Thou on the land, and I on the sand,
And Jack on the gallows-tree! *Ib.* ch. 34.

The ancient and now forgotten pastime of high jinks.
Ib. ch. 36.

And Bertram's right and Bertram's might
Shall meet on Ellangowan's height. *Ib.* ch. 46.

The hour is come, but not the man.
The Heart of Midlothian, ch. 4, heading.

The passive resistance of the Tolbooth-gate.
Ib. ch. 6.

Jock, when ye hae naething else to do, ye may be ay
sticking in a tree; it will be growing, Jock, when
ye're sleeping. *Ib.* ch. 8.

Proud Maisie is in the wood,
　　Walking so early,
Sweet Robin sits in the bush,
　　Singing so rarely. *Ib.* ch. 40.

Come, trowl the brown bowl to me,
　　Bully boy, bully boy,
Come, trowl the brown bowl to me:
　　Ho! jolly Jenkin, I spy a knave in drinking,
Come, trowl the brown bowl to me. *Ivanhoe*, ch. 20.

'Pax vobiscum' will answer all queries. *Ib.* ch. 26.

When Israel, of the Lord belov'd,
　　Out of the land of bondage came,
Her fathers' God before her mov'd,
　　An awful guide in smoke and flame. *Ib.* ch. 39.

His morning walk was beneath the elms in the
churchyard; 'for death', he said, 'had been his
next-door neighbour for so many years, that he
had no apology for dropping the acquaintance.'
The Legend of Montrose, introduction.

But, my lord, there is a Southern proverb,—fine
words butter no parsnips. *Ib.* ch. 3.

[2] = divide.

March, march, Ettrick and Teviotdale,
Why the deil dinna ye march forward in order?
March, march, Eskdale and Liddesdale,
All the Blue Bonnets are bound for the Border.
The Monastery, ch. 25.

Though his suit was rejected,
He sadly reflected,
  That a lover forsaken
    A new love may get;
But a neck that's once broken
    Can never be set.   *Peveril of the Peak*, ch. 39.

Ah! County Guy, the hour is nigh,
  The sun has left the lea,
The orange flower perfumes the bower,
  The breeze is on the sea.
Quentin Durward, ch. 4.

And it's ill speaking between a fou man and a
  fasting.
    Redgauntlet, Letter 11, *Wandering Willie's
    Tale.*

Better a finger off, as ay wagging.   *Ib.* ch. 2.

The ae half of the warld thinks the tither daft.
Ib. ch. 7.

Over the water, and over the sea,
  And over the water to Charlie;
Come weal, come woe, we'll gather and go,
  And live or die with Charlie.   *Ib.* ch. 11.

But with the morning cool repentance came.
Rob Roy, ch. 12.

Come fill up my cup, come fill up my cann,
Come saddle my horses, and call my man;
Come open your gates, and let me gae free,
I daurna stay langer in bonny Dundee.   *Ib.* ch. 23.

If your honour disna ken when ye hae a gude servant,
  I ken when I hae a gude master, and the deil be in
  my feet gin I leave ye.   *Ib.* ch. 24.

It's a far cry to Lochow.   *Ib.* ch. 29, note.

There's a gude time coming.   *Ib.* ch. 32.

'Speak out, sir, and do not Maister or Campbell me—
  my foot is on my native heath, and my name is
  MacGregor!'   *Ib.* ch. 34.

Fair, fat, and forty.   *St. Ronan's Well*, ch. 7.

The play-bill, which is said to have announced the
  tragedy of Hamlet, the character of the Prince of
  Denmark being left out.
    The Talisman, introduction. For an earlier
    report of this anecdote, see *T.L.S.* 3 June 1939.

Rouse the lion from his lair.   *Ib.* ch. 6.

My heart's in the Highlands, my heart is not here,
My heart's in the Highlands a-chasing the deer;
A-chasing the wild deer, and following the roe,
My heart's in the Highlands wherever I go.
Waverley, ch. 28.

Bring the bowl which you boast,
  Fill it up to the brim;
Here's to him we love most,
  And to all who love him.
Brave gallants, stand up,
  And avaunt ye, base carles!
Were there death in the cup,
  Here's a health to King Charles!
Woodstock, ch. 20.

A man may drink and not be drunk;
A man may fight and not be slain;
A man may kiss a bonnie lass,
  And yet be welcome back again.   *Ib.* ch. 27.

The Big Bow-Wow strain I can do myself like any
  now going; but the exquisite touch, which renders
  ordinary commonplace things and characters
  interesting, from the truth of the description and
  the sentiment, is denied to me. [On Jane Austen.]
    Journal, 14 Mar. 1826.

I would like to be there, were it but to see how the
  cat jumps.   *Ib.* 7 Oct. 1826.

From the lone shieling of the misty island
  Mountains divide us, and the waste of seas—
Yet still the blood is strong, the heart is Highland,
  And we in dreams behold the Hebrides!
Fair these broad meads, these hoary woods are grand;
But we are exiles from our fathers' land.
Canadian Boat Song.
Of disputed authorship. See *Times Literary
Supplement*, 23 Dec. 1904, G. M. Fraser's
article.

WILLIAM SCOTT, LORD STOWELL

1745–1836

The elegant simplicity of the three per cents.
  Campbell's *Chancellors* (1857), vol. x, ch. 212,
  p. 218.

SIR OWEN SEAMAN

1861–1935

New Art would better Nature's best,
But Nature knows a thing or two.
  Battle of the Bays.   Ars Postera, v.

EDMUND HAMILTON SEARS

1810–1876

Calm on the listening ear of night
  Came Heaven's melodious strains,
Where wild Judea stretches far
  Her silver-mantled plains.
    Boston Observer, 1834.   *Christmas Hymn:
    Calm on the Listening Ear.*

It came upon the midnight clear,
  That glorious song of old.
    The Christian Register, 1850.   *That Glorious
    Song of Old.*

SIR CHARLES SEDLEY

1639?–1701

Ah, Chloris! that I now could sit
  As unconcerned as when
Your infant beauty could beget
  No pleasure, nor no pain!   *Child and Maiden*

Love still has something of the sea
  From whence his mother rose.
    Love still has Something.

Phyllis is my only joy,
 Faithless as the winds or seas;
Sometimes coming, sometimes coy,
 Yet she never fails to please.
*   Song. Phyllis is my Only Joy.*
   She deceiving,
   I believing;
What need lovers wish for more?   *Ib.*

Phyllis, without frown or smile,
Sat and knotted all the while.
*   Song [Phyllis Knotting]. Hears not my
   Phyllis.*

Not, Celia, that I juster am
 Or better than the rest,
For I would change each hour like them,
 Were not my heart at rest.
*   Song [To Celia]. Not, Celia, that I juster am.*

Why then should I seek farther store,
 And still make love anew;
When change itself can give no more,
 'Tis easy to be true.   *Ib.*

ALAN SEEGER
1888–1916

I have a rendezvous with Death
At some disputed barricade.
*   I Have a Rendezvous with Death.*

JOHN SELDEN
1584–1654

Scrutamini scripturas. These two words have undone
 the world.
*   Table Talk* (1892), p. 10. *Bible, Scripture.*

Old friends are best. King James used to call for
 his old shoes; they were easiest for his feet.
*   Ib.* p. 71, *Friends.*

'Tis not the drinking that is to be blamed, but the
 excess.   *Ib.* p. 78. *Humility.*

Ignorance of the law excuses no man; not that all
 men know the law, but because 'tis an excuse
 every man will plead, and no man can tell how
 to confute him.   *Ib.* p. 99. *Law.*

Take a straw and throw it up into the air, you shall
 see by that which way the wind is.
*   Ib.* p. 105. *Libels.*

Marriage is nothing but a civil contract.
*   Ib.* p. 109. *Marriage.*

There is not anything in the world so much abused
 as this sentence, *Salus populi suprema lex esto.*
*   Ib.* p. 131. *People.*

Philosophy is nothing but discretion.
*   Ib.* p. 132. *Philosophy.*

Pleasure is nothing else but the intermission of pain.
*   Ib. Pleasure.*

Preachers say, Do as I say, not as I do.
*   Ib.* p. 147. *Preaching.*

WALTER CARRUTHERS SELLAR
contemp.
and
ROBERT JULIAN YEATMAN
contemp.

1066 and all that.   *Title of Book.*

Julius Caesar (the *memorable* Roman Emperor.)
*   1066 And All That*, ch. 1.

The Roman Conquest was, however, a *Good Thing.*
*   Ib.*

THOMAS SEWARD
1708–1790

Seven wealthy towns contend for Homer dead,
Through which the living Homer begg'd his bread.
 Attr. *On Homer,* or *A Cure for Poetry.* H. P.
 Dodd, *The Epigrammatists* (1875), p. 397.

WILLIAM HENRY SEWARD
1801–1872

The Constitution devotes the domain to union, to
 justice, to defence, to welfare, and to liberty. But
 there is a higher law than the Constitution.
*   Speech in U.S. Senate, 11 March 1850.*

I know, and all the world knows, that revolutions
 never go backward.
*   Ib. At Rochester on the Irrepressible Conflict,
 Oct. 1858.*

EDWARD SEXBY
d. 1658

Killing no Murder Briefly Discourst in Three Questions.
*   Title of Pamphlet,* 1657.

RICHARD SHACKLOCK
c. 1565

Proud as peacocks.
*   Hatchet of Heresies* (1565), p. 26b.

THOMAS SHADWELL
1642?–1692

Words may be false and full of art,
Sighs are the natural language of the heart.
*   Psyche,* Act III.

'Tis the way of all flesh. *The Sullen Lovers,* v. ii.

And wit's the noblest frailty of the mind.
*   A True Widow,* II. i.

The haste of a fool is the slowest thing in the world.
*   Ib.* III. i.

I am, out of the ladies' company, like a fish out of
 the water.   *Ib.*

Every man loves what he is good at.   *Ib.* v. i.

Instantly, in the twinkling of a bed-staff.
    Virtuoso, I. i.

ANTHONY ASHLEY COOPER, EARL OF SHAFTESBURY

1621–1683

'People differ in their discourse and profession about these matters, but men of sense are really but of one religion.' . . . 'Pray, my lord, what religion is that which men of sense agree in?' 'Madam,' says the earl immediately, 'men of sense never tell it.'
    Burnet, *History of My Own Time*, vol. I, bk. ii, ch. 1, note by Onslow.

WILLIAM SHAKESPEARE

1564–1616

[In the references the line number is given without brackets where the scene is all verse up to the quotation and the line number is certain. It is given in square brackets where prose makes it variable, and the references are to the Oxford Standard Authors Shakespeare in one volume.]

It were all one
That I should love a bright particular star
And think to wed it, he is so above me.
    All's Well That Ends Well, I. i. [97].

My friends were poor but honest.   *Ib.* iii. [203].

They say miracles are past.   *Ib.* II. iii. [1].

A young man married is a man that's marred. *Ib.* [315].

I know a man that had this trick of melancholy sold a goodly manor for a song.   *Ib.* III. ii. [8].

The web of our life is of a mingled yarn, good and ill together : our virtues would be proud if our faults whipped them not; and our crimes would despair if they were not cherished by our own virtues.
    Ib. IV. iii. [83].

There's place and means for every man alive.
    Ib. [379].

The flowery way that leads to the broad gate and the great fire.   *Ib.* v. [58].

Praising what is lost
Makes the remembrance dear.   *Ib.* v. iii. 19.

The triple pillar of the world transform'd
Into a strumpet's fool. *Antony and Cleopatra*, I. i. 12.

CLEOPATRA :
If it be love indeed, tell me how much.
ANTONY :
There's beggary in the love that can be reckoned.
CLEOPATRA :
I'll set a bourn how far to be belov'd.
ANTONY :
Then must thou needs find out new heaven, new earth.
    Ib. 14.

The scarce-bearded Cæsar.   *Ib.* 21.

Let Rome in Tiber melt, and the wide arch
Of the rang'd empire fall! Here is my space.
Kingdoms are clay; our dungy earth alike
Feeds beast as man; the nobleness of life
Is to do thus; when such a mutual pair
And such a twain can do 't.   *Ib.* 33.

Whom everything becomes, to chide, to laugh,
To weep; whose every passion fully strives
To make itself, in thee, fair and admir'd.   *Ib.* 49.

In Nature's infinite book of secrecy
A little I can read.   *Ib.* ii. [11].

You shall be yet far fairer than you are.   *Ib.* [18].

You shall be more beloving than belov'd.   *Ib.* [24].

O excellent! I love long life better than figs.
    Ib. [34].

Mine, and most of our fortunes, tonight, shall be,—drunk to bed.   *Ib.* [47].

But a worky-day fortune.   *Ib.* [57].

On the sudden
A Roman thought hath struck him.   *Ib.* [90].

The nature of bad news infects the teller. *Ib.* [103].

These strong Egyptian fetters I must break,
Or lose myself in dotage.   *Ib.* [125].

I have seen her die twenty times upon far poorer moment. I do think there is mettle in death which commits some loving act upon her, she hath such a celerity in dying.   *Ib.* [150].

We cannot call her winds and waters sighs and tears; they are greater storms and tempests than almanacs can report.   *Ib.* [157].

O sir! you then had left unseen a wonderful piece of work which not to have been blessed withal would have discredited your travel.   *Ib.* [164].

Indeed the tears live in an onion that should water this sorrow.   *Ib.* [181].

If you find him sad,
Say I am dancing; if in mirth, report
That I am sudden sick.   *Ib.* iii. 3.

CHARMIAN :
In each thing give him way, cross him in nothing.
CLEOPATRA :
Thou teachest like a fool; the way to lose him. *Ib.* 9.

In time we hate that which we often fear.   *Ib.* 12.

It cannot thus be long, the sides of nature
Will not sustain it.   *Ib.* 16.

Eternity was in our lips and eyes,
Bliss in our brows bent.   *Ib.* 35.

Quietness, grown sick of rest, would purge
By any desperate change.   *Ib.* 53.

Though age from folly could not give me freedom,
It does from childishness.   *Ib.* 57.

At the last, best.   *Ib.* 61.

O! my oblivion is a very Antony,
And I am all forgotten.   *Ib.* 90.

'Tis sweating labour
To bear such idleness so near the heart
As Cleopatra this.   *Ib.* 93.

This common body,
Like to a vagabond flag upon the stream,
Goes to and back, lackeying the varying tide,
To rot itself with motion.   *Ib.* iv. 44.

On the Alps
It is reported thou didst eat strange flesh,
Which some did die to look on.   *Ib.* 66.

Give me to drink mandragora. . . .
That I might sleep out this great gap of time
My Antony is away.   *Antony and Cleopatra*, I. v. 4.

The demi-Atlas of this earth, the arm
And burgonet of men.   *Ib.* 23.

Where's my serpent of old Nile?   *Ib.* 25.

Think on me,
That am with Phœbus' amorous pinches black,
And wrinkled deep in time? Broad-fronted Cæsar,
When thou wast here above the ground I was
A morsel for a monarch, and great Pompey
Would stand and make his eyes grow in my brow;
There would he anchor his aspect and die
With looking on his life.   *Ib.* 27.

My salad days,
When I was green in judgment.   *Ib.* 73.

We, ignorant of ourselves,
Beg often our own harms, which the wise powers
Deny us for our good; so find we profit
By losing of our prayers.   *Ib.* II. i. 5.

I do not much dislike the matter, but
The manner of his speech.   *Ib.* ii. 117.

No worse a husband than the best of men.   *Ib.* 135.

The barge she sat in, like a burnish'd throne,
Burn'd on the water; the poop was beaten gold,
Purple the sails, and so perfumed, that
The winds were love-sick with them, the oars were
    silver,
Which to the tune of flutes kept stroke, and made
The water which they beat to follow faster,
As amorous of their strokes. For her own person,
It beggar'd all description; she did lie
In her pavilion,—cloth-of-gold of tissue,—
O'er-picturing that Venus where we see
The fancy outwork nature; on each side her
Stood pretty-dimpled boys, like smiling Cupids,
With divers-colour'd fans, whose wind did seem
To glow the delicate cheeks which they did cool,
And what they undid did.   *Ib.* [199].

Her gentlewomen, like the Nereides,
So many mermaids, tended her i' the eyes,
And made their bends adornings; at the helm
A seeming mermaid steers; the silken tackle
Swell with the touches of those flower-soft hands,
That yarely frame the office. From the barge
A strange invisible perfume hits the sense
Of the adjacent wharfs. The city cast
Her people out upon her, and Antony,
Enthron'd i' the market-place, did sit alone,
Whistling to the air; which, but for vacancy,
Had gone to gaze on Cleopatra too
And made a gap in nature.   *Ib.* [214].

I saw her once
Hop forty paces through the public street;
And having lost her breath, she spoke, and panted
That she did make defect perfection,
And, breathless, power breathe forth.   *Ib.* [236].

Age cannot wither her, nor custom stale
Her infinite variety; other women cloy
The appetites they feed, but she makes hungry
Where most she satisfies; for vilest things
Become themselves in her, that the holy priests
Bless her when she is riggish.   *Ib.* [243].

Read not my blemishes in the world's report;
I have not kept the square, but that to come
Shall all be done by the rule.   *Ib.* iii. 5.

Music, moody food
Of us that trade in love.   *Ib.* v. 1.

I laugh'd him out of patience; and that night
I laugh'd him into patience: and next morn,
Ere the ninth hour, I drunk him to his bed.   *Ib.* 19.

There is gold, and here
My bluest veins to kiss; a hand that kings
Have lipp'd, and trembled kissing.   *Ib.* 28.

Pour out the pack of matter to mine ear,
The good and bad together.   *Ib.* 54.

Though it be honest, it is never good
To bring bad news; give to a gracious message
A host of tongues, but let ill tidings tell
Themselves when they be felt.   *Ib.* 85.

I will praise any man that will praise me.   *Ib.* vi. [88].

LEPIDUS:
What manner o' thing is your crocodile?
ANTONY:
It is shaped, sir, like itself, and it is as broad as it
    hath breadth; it is just so high as it is, and moves
    with its own organs; it lives by that which nourish-
    eth it; and the elements once out of it, it trans-
    migrates.
LEPIDUS:
What colour is it of?
ANTONY:
Of its own colour too.
LEPIDUS:
'Tis a strange serpent.
ANTONY:
'Tis so; and the tears of it are wet.   *Ib.* vii. [47].

Ah! this thou shouldst have done,
And not have spoken on 't. In me 'tis villainy;
In thee 't had been good service.   *Ib.* [80].

Come, thou monarch of the vine,
Plumpy Bacchus with pink eyne!
In thy fats our cares be drown'd,
With thy grapes our hairs be crown'd:
    Cup us, till the world go round,
    Cup us, till the world go round!   *Ib.* [119].

Ambition,
The soldier's virtue.   *Ib.* III. i. 22.

The swan's down-feather,
That stands upon the swell at full of tide,
And neither way inclines.   *Ib.* ii. 48.

The ostentation of our love, which, left unshown,
Is often left unlov'd.   *Ib.* vi. 52.

But let determin'd things to destiny
Hold unbewail'd their way.   *Ib.* 84.

We have kiss'd away
Kingdoms and provinces.   *Ib.* viii. 17.

Fortune knows
We scorn her most when most she offers blows.   *Ib.* ix. 73.

Which had superfluous kings for messengers
Not many moons gone by.   *Ib.* x. 5.

He wears the rose
Of youth upon him.   *Ib.* xi. 20.

Men's judgments are
A parcel of their fortunes, and things outward
Do draw the inward quality after them,
To suffer all alike.   *Antony and Cleopatra*, III. xi. 31.

Against the blown rose may they stop their nose,
That kneel'd unto the buds.   *Ib.* 39.

       Yet he that can endure
To follow with allegiance a fall'n lord,
Does conquer him that did his master conquer,
And earns a place i' the story.   *Ib.* 43.

       Your Cæsar's father oft,
When he hath mus'd of taking kingdoms in,
Bestow'd his lips on that unworthy place,
As it rain'd kisses.   *Ib.* 82.

But when we in our viciousness grow hard,—
O misery on't!—the wise gods seel our eyes;
In our own filth drop our clear judgments; make us
Adore our errors; laugh at's while we strut
To our confusion.   *Ib.* 111.

I found you as a morsel cold upon
Dead Cæsar's trencher.   *Ib.* 116.

My playfellow, your hand; this kingly seal
And plighter of high hearts.   *Ib.* 125.

       Henceforth,
The white hand of a lady fever thee,
Shake thou to look on't.   *Ib.* 137.

Let's have one other gaudy night.   *Ib.* 182.

       Since my lord
Is Antony again, I will be Cleopatra.   *Ib.* 185.

Know that tomorrow the last of many battles
We mean to fight.   *Ib.* IV. i. 11.

To business that we love we rise betime,
And go to't with delight.   *Ib.* iv. 20.

       O! my fortunes have
Corrupted honest men.   *Ib.* v. 16.

I am alone the villain of the earth,
And feel I am so most.   *Ib.* vi. 30.

Ride on the pants triumphing.   *Ib.* viii. 16.

O infinite virtue! com'st thou smiling from
The world's great snare uncaught?   *Ib.* 17.

       My nightingale,
We have beat them to their beds.   *Ib.* 18.

O sovereign mistress of true melancholy. *Ib.* ix. 12.

       Swallows have built
In Cleopatra's sails their nests; the augurers
Say they know not, they cannot tell.   *Ib.* x. 16.

       The hearts
That spaniel'd me at heels, to whom I gave
Their wishes, do discandy, melt their sweets
On blossoming Cæsar.   *Ib.* 33.

The soul and body rive not more in parting
Than greatness going off.   *Ib.* xi. 5.

Sometimes we see a cloud that's dragonish;
A vapour sometime like a bear or lion,
A tower'd citadel, a pendant rock,
A forked mountain, or blue promontory
With trees upon 't, that nod unto the world
And mock our eyes with air: thou hast seen these
signs;
They are black vesper's pageants.   *Ib.* xii. 2.

That which is now a horse, even with a thought
The rack dislimns, and makes it indistinct,
As water is in water.   *Ib.* 9.

Unarm, Eros; the long day's task is done,
And we must sleep.   *Ib.* 35.

I will o'ertake thee, Cleopatra, and
Weep for my pardon. So it must be, for now
All length is torture; since the torch is out,
Lie down, and stray no further. Now all labour
Mars what it does; yea, very force entangles
Itself with strength; seal then, and all is done.
Eros!—I come, my queen.—Eros!—Stay for me:
Where souls do couch on flowers, we'll hand in hand,
And with our sprightly port make the ghosts gaze;
Dido and her Æneas shall want troops,
And all the haunt be ours.   *Ib.* 44.

       Since Cleopatra died,
I have liv'd in such dishonour, that the gods
Detest my baseness.   *Ib.* 55.

       But I will be
A bridegroom in my death, and run into 't
As to a lover's bed.   *Ib.* 99.

All strange and terrible events are welcome,
But comforts we despise.   *Ib.* xiii. 3.

ANTONY:
Not Cæsar's valour hath o'er thrown Antony
But Antony's hath triumphed on itself.
CLEOPATRA:
So it should be, that none but Antony
Should conquer Antony.   *Ib.* 14.

I am dying, Egypt, dying; only
I here importune death awhile, until
Of many thousand kisses the poor last
I lay upon thy lips.   *Ib.* 18.

The miserable change now at my end
Lament nor sorrow at; but please your thoughts
In feeding them with those my former fortunes
Wherein I liv'd, the greatest prince o' the world,
The noblest; and do now not basely die,
Not cowardly put off my helmet to
My countryman; a Roman by a Roman
Valiantly vanquished.   *Ib.* 51.

Hast thou no care of me? shall I abide
In this dull world, which in thy absence is
No better than a sty? O! see my women,
The crown o' the earth doth melt. My lord!
O! wither'd is the garland of the war,
The soldier's pole is fall'n; young boys and girls
Are level now with men; the odds is gone,
And there is nothing left remarkable
Beneath the visiting moon.   *Ib.* 60.

No more, but e'en a woman and commanded
By such poor passion as the maid that milks
And does the meanest chares.   *Ib.* 73.

       What's brave, what's noble,
Let's do it after the high Roman fashion,
And make death proud to take us.   *Ib.* 86.

       A rarer spirit never
Did steer humanity; but you, gods, will give us
Some faults to make us men.   *Ib.* v. i. 31.

My desolation does begin to make
A better life. 'Tis paltry to be Cæsar;
Not being Fortune, he's but Fortune's knave,
A minister of her will; and it is great
To do that thing that ends all other deeds,
Which shackles accidents, and bolts up change,
Which sleeps, and never palates more the dug,
The beggar's nurse and Cæsar's.
Antony and Cleopatra, v. ii. 1.

Nor once be chastis'd with the sober eye
Of dull Octavia. Shall they hoist me up
And show me to the shouting varletry
Of censuring Rome? Rather a ditch in Egypt
Be gentle grave unto me! rather on Nilus' mud
Lay me stark naked, and let the water-flies
Blow me into abhorring!   *Ib.* 54.

His legs bestrid the ocean; his rear'd arm
Crested the world; his voice was propertied
As all the tuned spheres, and that to friends;
But when he meant to quail and shake the orb,
He was as rattling thunder. For his bounty,
There was no winter in't; an autumn was
That grew the more by reaping; his delights
Were dolphin-like, they show'd his back above
The element they liv'd in; in his livery
Walk'd crowns and crownets, realms and islands were
As plates dropp'd from his pocket.   *Ib.* 82.

He words me, girls, he words me, that I should not
Be noble to myself.   *Ib.* 190.

Finish, good lady; the bright day is done,
And we are for the dark.   *Ib.* 192.

         Antony
Shall be brought drunken forth, and I shall see
Some squeaking Cleopatra boy my greatness
I' the posture of a whore.   *Ib.* 217.

       I am again for Cydnus,
To meet Mark Antony.   *Ib.* 227.

His biting is immortal; those that do die of it do
   seldom or never recover.   *Ib.* [246].

A very honest woman, but something given to lie.
                              Ib. [251].

I know that a woman is a dish for the gods if the
   devil dress her not.   *Ib.* [274].

         I have
Immortal longings in me.   *Ib.* [282].

       Husband, I come:
Now to that name my courage prove my title!
I am fire and air; my other elements
I give to baser life.   *Ib.* [289].

If thou and nature can so gently part,
The stroke of death is as a lover's pinch,
Which hurts, and is desir'd.   *Ib.* [296].

If thus thou vanishest, thou tell'st the world
It is not worth leave-taking.   *Ib.* [299].

CLEOPATRA:
If she first meet the curled Antony,
He'll make demand of her, and spend that kiss
Which is my heaven to have. Come, thou mortal
   wretch,
With thy sharp teeth this knot intrinsicate
Of life at once untie; poor venomous fool,
Be angry, and dispatch. O! couldst thou speak,
That I might hear thee call great Cæsar ass
Unpolicied.

CHARMIAN:
         O eastern star!
CLEOPATRA: Peace! peace!
Dost thou not see my baby at my breast,
That sucks the nurse asleep?   *Ib.* [303].

Now boast thee, death, in thy possession lies
A lass unparallel'd.   *Ib.* [317].

It is well done, and fitting for a princess
Descended of so many royal kings.   *Ib.* [328].

As she would catch another Antony
In her strong toil of grace.   *Ib.* [348].

She hath pursu'd conclusions infinite
Of easy ways to die.   *Ib.* [356].

Let us sit and mock the good housewife Fortune
   from her wheel, that her gifts may henceforth be
   bestowed equally.   *As You Like It*, I. ii. [35].

How now, wit! whither wander you?   *Ib.* [60].

Your heart's desires be with you!   *Ib.* [214].

One out of suits with fortune.   *Ib.* [263].

My pride fell with my fortunes.   *Ib.* [269].

Sir, you have wrestled well, and overthrown
More than your enemies.   *Ib.* [271].

Hereafter, in a better world than this,
I shall desire more love and knowledge of you.
                             Ib. [301].

Thus must I from the smoke into the smother;
From tyrant duke unto a tyrant brother.   *Ib.* [304].

O, how full of briars is this working-day world!
                           Ib. iii. [12].

We'll have a swashing and a martial outside,
As many other mannish cowards have
That do outface it with their semblances.   *Ib.* [123].

Hath not old custom made this life more sweet
Than that of painted pomp? Are not these woods
More free from peril than the envious court?
Here feel we but the penalty of Adam,
The seasons' difference; as, the icy fang
And churlish chiding of the winter's wind,
Which, when it bites and blows upon my body,
Even till I shrink with cold, I smile and say,
'This is no flattery.'   *Ib.* II. i. 2.

Sweet are the uses of adversity,
Which like the toad, ugly and venomous,
Wears yet a precious jewel in his head;
And this our life, exempt from public haunt,
Finds tongues in trees, books in the running brooks,
Sermons in stones, and good in everything.   *Ib.* 12.

       The big round tears
Cours'd one another down his innocent nose,
In piteous chase.   *Ib.* 38.

'Poor deer,' quoth he, 'thou mak'st a testament
As worldlings do, giving thy sum of more
To that which had too much.'   *Ib.* 47.

Sweep on, you fat and greasy citizens!   *Ib.* 55.

I love to cope him in these sullen fits,
For then he's full of matter.   *Ib.* 67.

      Though I look old, yet I am strong and lusty;
For in my youth I never did apply
Hot and rebellious liquors in my blood.   *Ib.* iii. 47.

Therefore my age is as a lusty winter,
Frosty, but kindly. *As You Like It*, ii. iii. 52.

O good old man! how well in thee appears
The constant service of the antique world,
When service sweat for duty, not for meed!
Thou art not for the fashion of these times,
Where none will sweat but for promotion,
And having that, do choke their service up
Even with the having. *Ib.* 56.

Ay, now am I in Arden; the more fool I. When I
was at home I was in a better place: but travellers
must be content. *Ib.* iv. [16].

As true a lover
As ever sigh'd upon a midnight pillow. *Ib.* [26].

If thou remember'st not the slightest folly
That ever love did make thee run into,
Thou hast not lov'd. *Ib.* [34].

We that are true lovers run into strange capers.
Ib. [53].

Thou speakest wiser than thou art ware of.
Ib. [57].

I shall ne'er be ware of mine own wit till I break my
shins against it. *Ib.* [59].

My master is of churlish disposition
And little recks to find the way to heaven
By doing deeds of hospitality. *Ib.* [81].

Under the greenwood tree
Who loves to lie with me,
And turn his merry note
Unto the sweet bird's throat,
Come hither, come hither, come hither:
    Here shall he see
    No enemy
But winter and rough weather. *Ib.* v. i.

I can suck melancholy out of a song as a weasel sucks
eggs. *Ib.* [12].

Who doth ambition shun
And loves to live i' the sun,
Seeking the food he eats,
And pleas'd with what he gets. *Ib.* [38].

I'll rail against all the first-born in Egypt. *Ib.* [60].

A fool, a fool! I met a fool i' the forest,
A motley fool. *Ib.* vii. 12.

And rail'd on Lady Fortune in good terms,
In good set terms. *Ib.* 16.

'Call me not fool till heaven hath sent me fortune.'
And then he drew a dial from his poke,
And, looking on it with lack-lustre eye,
Says very wisely, 'It is ten o'clock;
Thus may we see,' quoth he, 'how the world wags.'
Ib. 19.

And so, from hour to hour, we ripe and ripe,
And then from hour to hour, we rot and rot:
And thereby hangs a tale. *Ib.* 26.

My lungs began to crow like chanticleer,
That fools should be so deep-contemplative,
And I did laugh sans intermission
An hour by his dial. O noble fool!
A worthy fool! Motley's the only wear. *Ib.* 30.

And says, if ladies be but young and fair,
They have the gift to know it: and in his brain,—

Which is as dry as the remainder biscuit
After a voyage,—he hath strange places cramm'd
With observation, the which he vents
In mangled forms. *Ib.* 37.

I must have liberty
Withal, as large a charter as the wind,
To blow on whom I please. *Ib.* 47.

The 'why' is plain as way to parish church. *Ib.* 52.

But whate'er you are
That in this desert inaccessible,
Under the shade of melancholy boughs,
Lose and neglect the creeping hours of time;
If ever you have look'd on better days,
If ever been where bells have knoll'd to church,
If ever sat at any good man's feast,
If ever from your eyelids wip'd a tear,
And know what 'tis to pity, and be pitied,
Let gentleness my strong enforcement be. *Ib.* 109.

There is an old poor man,
    .   .   .
Oppress'd with two weak evils, age and hunger.
Ib. 129.

All the world's a stage,
And all the men and women merely players;
They have their exits and their entrances;
And one man in his time plays many parts,
His acts being seven ages. At first the infant,
Mewling and puking in the nurse's arms.
And then the whining schoolboy, with his satchel,
And shining morning face, creeping like snail
Unwillingly to school. And then the lover,
Sighing like furnace, with a woful ballad
Made to his mistress' eyebrow. Then a soldier,
Full of strange oaths, and bearded like the pard,
Jealous in honour, sudden and quick in quarrel,
Seeking the bubble reputation
Even in the cannon's mouth. And then the justice,
In fair round belly with good capon lin'd,
With eyes severe, and beard of formal cut,
Full of wise saws and modern instances;
And so he plays his part. The sixth age shifts
Into the lean and slipper'd pantaloon,
With spectacles on nose and pouch on side,
His youthful hose well sav'd a world too wide
For his shrunk shank; and his big manly voice,
Turning again towards childish treble, pipes
And whistles in his sound. Last scene of all,
That ends this strange eventful history,
Is second childishness, and mere oblivion,
Sans teeth, sans eyes, sans taste, sans everything.
Ib. 139.

Blow, blow, thou winter wind,
Thou art not so unkind
    As man's ingratitude:
Thy tooth is not so keen,
Because thou art not seen,
    Although thy breath be rude.
Heigh-ho! sing, heigh-ho! unto the green holly:
Most friendship is feigning, most loving were folly.
    Then heigh-ho! the holly!
        This life is most jolly.

Freeze, freeze, thou bitter sky,
That dost not bite so nigh
    As benefits forgot:
Though thou the waters warp,
Thy sting is not so sharp
        As friend remember'd not. *Ib.* 174.

Run, run, Orlando: carve on every tree
The fair, the chaste, and unexpressive she.
As You Like It, III. ii. 9.

Hast any philosophy in thee, shepherd? *Ib.* [22].

He that wants money, means, and content is without
three good friends. *Ib.* [25].

Thou art in a parlous state. *Ib.* [46].

I earn that I eat, get that I wear, owe no man hate,
envy no man's happiness, glad of other men's
good, content with my harm. *Ib.* [78].

From the east to western Ind,
No jewel is like Rosalind. *Ib.* [94].

This is the very false gallop of verses. *Ib.* [120].

Let us make an honourable retreat; though not with
bag and baggage, yet with scrip and scrippage.
Ib. [170].

O wonderful, wonderful, and most wonderful wonderful! and yet again wonderful, and after that, out of
all whooping! *Ib.* [202].

It is as easy to count atomies as to resolve the propositions of a lover. *Ib.* [246].

Do you not know I am a woman? what I think, I
must speak. *Ib.* [265].

I do desire we may be better strangers. *Ib.* [276].

You have a nimble wit; I think 'twas made of
Atalanta's heels. *Ib.* [294].

I will chide no breather in the world but myself,
against whom I know most faults. *Ib.* [298].

Time travels in divers paces with divers persons.
I'll tell you who Time ambles withal, who Time
trots withal, who Time gallops withal, and who
he stands still withal. *Ib.* [328].

Every one fault seeming monstrous till his fellow
fault came to match it. *Ib.* [377].

Truly, I would the gods had made thee poetical.
Ib. iii. [16].

I am not a slut, though I thank the gods I am foul.
Ib. [40].

ROSALIND:
His hair is of a good colour.
CELIA:
An excellent colour; your chestnut was ever the only
colour. *Ib.* iv. [10].

Down on your knees,
And thank heaven, fasting, for a good man's love.
Ib. v. 57.

Dead shepherd, now I find thy saw of might:
'Who ever lov'd that lov'd not at first sight?' *Ib.* 81.

It is a melancholy of mine own, compounded of many
simples, extracted from many objects, and indeed
the sundry contemplation of my travels, which,
by often rumination, wraps me in a most humorous
sadness. *Ib.* IV. i. [16].

Farewell, Monsieur Traveller: look you lisp and
wear strange suits, disable all the benefits of your
own country, be out of love with your nativity,
and almost chide God for making you that countenance you are, or I will scarce think you have
swam in a gondola. *Ib.* [35].

Break an hour's promise in love! He that will divide
a minute into a thousand parts, and break but a
part of the thousandth part of a minute in the
affairs of love, it may be said of him that Cupid
hath clapped him o' the shoulder, but I'll warrant
him heart-whole. *Ib.* [46].

For now I am in a holiday humour. *Ib.* [70].

When you were gravelled for lack of matter.
Ib. [76].

Men have died from time to time, and worms have
eaten them, but not for love. *Ib.* [110].

Men are April when they woo, December when they
wed: maids are May when they are maids, but the
sky changes when they are wives. *Ib.* [153].

The horn, the horn, the lusty horn
Is not a thing to laugh to scorn. *Ib.* ii. [17].

Chewing the food of sweet and bitter fancy.
Ib. iii. [103].

Cæsar's thrasonical brag of 'I came, saw, and overcame'. *Ib.* v. ii. [35].

No sooner met, but they looked; no sooner looked
but they loved; no sooner loved but they sighed;
no sooner sighed but they asked one another the
reason; no sooner knew the reason but they sought
the remedy. *Ib.* [37].

Oh! how bitter a thing it is to look into happiness
through another man's eyes. *Ib.* [48].

PHEBE:
Good shepherd, tell this youth what 'tis to love.
SILVIUS:
It is to be all made of sighs and tears;—

It is to be all made of faith and service;—

It is to be all made of fantasy,
All made of passion, and all made of wishes;
All adoration, duty, and observance;
All humbleness, all patience, and all impatience;
All purity, all trial, all obeisance. *Ib.* [90].

'Tis like the howling of Irish wolves against the
moon. *Ib.* [120].

It was a lover and his lass,
With a hey, and a ho, and a hey nonino,
That o'er the green cornfield did pass,
In the spring time, the only pretty ring time,
When birds do sing, hey ding a ding, ding;
Sweet lovers love the spring. *Ib.* iii. [18].

Between the acres of the rye,
With a hey, and a ho, and a hey nonino,
These pretty country folks would lie,
In the spring time, &c. *Ib.* [24].

This carol they began that hour,
With a hey, and a ho, and a hey nonino,
How that life was but a flower,
In the spring time, &c. *Ib.* [28].

And therefore take the present time,
With a hey, and a ho, and a hey nonino;
For love is crowned with the prime
In the spring time, &c. *Ib.* [32].

Here comes a pair of very strange beasts, which in
all tongues are called fools. *Ib.* iv. [36].

An ill-favoured thing, sir, but mine own.
As You Like It, v. iv. [60].

Rich honesty dwells like a miser, sir, in a poor house; as your pearl in your foul oyster. *Ib*. [62].

The retort courteous . . . the quip modest . . . the reply churlish . . . the reproof valiant . . . the countercheck quarrelsome . . . the lie circumstantial . . . the lie direct. *Ib*. [96].

Your 'if' is the only peace-maker; much virtue in 'if'. *Ib*. [108].

He uses his folly like a stalking-horse, and under the presentation of that he shoots his wit. *Ib*. [112].

If it be true that, 'good wine needs no bush', 'tis true that a good play needs no epilogue.
Epilogue [3].

They brought one Pinch, a hungry, lean-fac'd villain,
A mere anatomy, a mountebank,
A threadbare juggler, and a fortune-teller,
A needy, hollow-ey'd, sharp-looking wretch,
A living-dead man. *The Comedy of Errors*, v. i. 238.

He's a very dog to the commonalty.
Coriolanus, i. i. [29].

The kingly crowned head, the vigilant eye,
The counsellor heart, the arm our soldier,
Our steed the leg, the tongue our trumpeter. *Ib*. [121].

What's the matter, you dissentious rogues,
That, rubbing the poor itch of your opinion,
Make yourselves scabs? *Ib*. [170].

They threw their caps
As they would hang them on the horns o' the moon,
Shouting their emulation. *Ib*. [218].

Oh! I warrant, how he mammocked it! *Ib*. iii. [71].

My gracious silence, hail! *Ib*. ii. i. [194].

Such eyes the widows in Corioli wear,
And mothers that lack sons. *Ib*. [197].

Custom calls me to 't:
What custom wills, in all things should we do't,
The dust on antique time would lie unswept,
And mountainous error be too highly heap'd
For truth to o'erpeer. *Ib*. ii. iii. [124].

I thank you for your voices, thank you,
Your most sweet voices. *Ib*. [179].

The mutable, rank-scented many. *Ib*. iii. i. 65.

Hear you this Triton of the minnows? mark you
His absolute 'shall'? *Ib*. 88.

His nature is too noble for the world:
He would not flatter Neptune for his trident,
Or Jove for 's power to thunder. His heart's his mouth:
What his breast forges, that his tongue must vent.
Ib. 254.

You common cry of curs! whose breath I hate
As reek o' the rotten fens, whose loves I prize
As the dead carcases of unburied men
That do corrupt my air,—I banish you. *Ib*. iii. 118.

The beast
With many heads butts me away. *Ib*. iv. i. 1.

Under the canopy . . . I' the city of kites and crows.
Ib. v. [41].

I'll never
Be such a gosling to obey instinct, but stand
As if a man were author of himself
And knew no other kin. *Ib*. v. iii. 34.

Like a dull actor now,
I have forgot my part, and I am out,
Even to a full disgrace. *Ib*. 40.

O! a kiss
Long as my exile, sweet as my revenge!
Now, by the jealous queen of heaven, that kiss
I carried from thee, dear, and my true lip
Hath virgin'd it e'er since. *Ib*. 44.

Chaste as the icicle
That's curdied by the frost from purest snow,
And hangs on Dian's temple. *Ib*. 65.

Thou hast never in thy life
Show'd thy dear mother any courtesy;
When she—poor hen! fond of no second brood—
Has cluck'd thee to the wars, and safely home,
Loaden with honour. *Ib*. 160.

If you have writ your annals true, 'tis there,
That, like an eagle in a dove-cote, I
Flutter'd your Volscians in Corioli:
Alone I did it. *Ib*. v. 114.

On her left breast
A mole cinque-spotted, like the crimson drops
I' the bottom of a cowslip. *Cymbeline*, ii. ii. 37.

Hark! hark! the lark at heaven's gate sings,
And Phœbus 'gins arise,
His steeds to water at those springs
On chaliced flowers that lies;
And winking Mary-buds begin
To ope their golden eyes:
With everything that pretty is,
My lady sweet, arise! *Ib*. iii. [22].

Is there no way for men to be, but women
Must be half-workers? *Ib*. v. 1.

As chaste as unsunn'd snow. *Ib*. 13.

There be many Cæsars
Ere such another Julius. Britain is
A world by itself, and we will nothing pay
For wearing our own noses. *Ib*. III. i. 11.

The natural bravery of your isle, which stands
As Neptune's park, ribbed and paled in
With rocks unscalable, and roaring waters. *Ib*. 18.

O, for a horse with wings! *Ib*. ii. [49].

What should we speak of
When we are as old as you? when we shall hear
The rain and wind beat dark December, how,
In this our pinching cave, shall we discourse
The freezing hours away? *Ib*. iii. 35.

Some jay of Italy,
Whose mother was her painting, hath betray'd him:
Poor I am stale, a garment out of fashion.
Ib. iv. [51].

I have not slept one wink. *Ib*. [103].

Hath Britain all the sun that shines? *Ib*. [139].

To lapse in fulness
Is sorer than to lie for need, and falsehood
Is worse in kings than beggars. *Ib*. vi. 12.

Weariness
Can snore upon the flint when resty sloth
Finds the down pillow hard.   *Cymbeline*, III. vi. 33.

Thou shalt not lack
The flower that's like thy face, pale primrose, nor
The azur'd harebell, like thy veins.   *Ib.* IV. ii. 220.

Great griefs, I see, medicine the less.   *Ib.* 243.

Though mean and mighty rotting
Together, have one dust, yet reverence—
That angel of the world—doth make distinction
Of place 'tween high and low.   *Ib.* 246.

Thersites' body is as good as Ajax'
When neither are alive.   *Ib.* 252.

Fear no more the heat o' the sun,
 Nor the furious winter's rages;
Thou thy worldly task hast done,
 Home art gone and ta'en thy wages:
Golden lads and girls all must,
As chimney-sweepers, come to dust.

Fear no more the frown o' the great,
 Thou art past the tyrant's stroke:
Care no more to clothe and eat;
 To thee the reed is as the oak:
The sceptre, learning, physic, must
All follow this, and come to dust.

Fear no more the lightning flash,
 Nor the all-dreaded thunder-stone;
Fear not slander, censure rash;
 Thou hast finish'd joy and moan:
All lovers young, all lovers must
Consign to thee, and come to dust.

No exorciser harm thee!
 Nor no witchcraft charm thee!
Ghost unlaid forbear thee!
 Nothing ill come near thee!
Quiet consummation have;
And renowned be thy grave!   *Ib.* 258.

Every good servant does not all commands.
   Ib. v. i. 6.

He that sleeps feels not the toothache. *Ib.* iv. [176].

He spake of her as Dian had hot dreams,
And she alone were cold.   *Ib.* v. 181.

IMOGEN:
Why did you throw your wedded lady from you?
Think that you are upon a rock; and now
Throw me again.
POSTHUMUS:
     Hang there like fruit, my soul,
Till the tree die!   *Ib.* 262.

Pardon's the word to all.   *Ib.* 423.

You come most carefully upon your hour.
   Hamlet, I. i. 6.

For this relief much thanks; 'tis bitter cold,
And I am sick at heart.   *Ib.* 8.

O! farewell, honest soldier.   *Ib.* 16.

BERNARDO:
What! is Horatio there?

M 3

HORATIO:
     A piece of him.   *Ib.* 19.
What! has this thing appear'd again tonight?
   Ib. 21.

Look, where it comes again!   *Ib.* 40.

But in the gross and scope of my opinion,
This bodes some strange eruption to our state.
   Ib. 68.

This sweaty haste
Doth make the night joint-labourer with the day.
   Ib. 77.

Of unimproved metal hot and full.   *Ib.* 96.

This post-haste and romage in the land.   *Ib.* 107.

In the most high and palmy state of Rome,
A little ere the mightiest Julius fell,
The graves stood tenantless and the sheeted dead
Did squeak and gibber in the Roman streets.
   Ib. 113.

The moist star
Upon whose influence Neptune's empire stands
Was sick almost to doomsday with eclipse. *Ib.* 118.

I'll cross it, though it blast me.   *Ib.* 127.

We do it wrong, being so majestical,
To offer it the show of violence;
For it is, as the air, invulnerable,
And our vain blows malicious mockery.   *Ib.* 143.

And then it started like a guilty thing
Upon a fearful summons.   *Ib.* 148.

Whether in sea or fire, in earth or air,
The extravagant and erring spirit hies
To his confine.   *Ib.* 153.

It faded on the crowing of the cock.
Some say that ever 'gainst that season comes
Wherein our Saviour's birth is celebrated,
The bird of dawning singeth all night long;
And then, they say, no spirit can walk abroad;
The nights are wholesome; then no planets strike,
No fairy takes, nor witch hath power to charm,
So hallow'd and so gracious is the time.   *Ib.* 157.

But, look, the morn, in russet mantle clad,
Walks o'er the dew of yon high eastward hill.
   Ib. 166.

The memory be green.   *Ib.* ii. 2.

Therefore our sometime sister, now our queen.
   Ib. 8.

With one auspicious and one dropping eye,
With mirth in funeral and with dirge in marriage,
In equal scale weighing delight and dole.   *Ib.* 11.

The head is not more native to the heart.   *Ib.* 47.

A little more than kin, and less than kind.   *Ib.* 65.

Not so, my lord; I am too much i' the sun.   *Ib.* 67.

Good Hamlet, cast thy nighted colour off,
And let thine eye look like a friend on Denmark.
   Ib. 68.

QUEEN:
Thou know'st 'tis common; all that live must die,
Passing through nature to eternity.
HAMLET:
Ay, madam, it is common.   *Ib.* 72.

Seems, madam! Nay, it is; I know not 'seems'.
'Tis not alone my inky cloak, good mother,
Nor customary suits of solemn black,
Nor windy suspiration of forc'd breath,
No, nor the fruitful river in the eye,
Nor the dejected 'haviour of the visage,
Together with all forms, modes, shows of grief,
That can denote me truly; these indeed seem,
For they are actions that a man might play:
But I have that within which passeth show;
These but the trappings and the suits of woe.
Hamlet, I. ii. 76.

But to persever
In obstinate condolement is a course
Of impious stubbornness; 'tis unmanly grief;
It shows a will most incorrect to heaven,
A heart unfortified, a mind impatient.   *Ib.* 92.

HAMLET:
I shall in all my best obey you, madam.
QUEEN:
Why, 'tis a loving and a fair reply.   *Ib.* 120.

O! that this too too solid flesh would melt,
Thaw, and resolve itself into a dew;
Or that the Everlasting had not fix'd
His canon 'gainst self-slaughter! O God! O God!
How weary, stale, flat, and unprofitable
Seem to me all the uses of this world.
Fie on't! O fie! 'tis an unweeded garden,
That grows to seed; things rank and gross in nature
Possess it merely   That it should come to this!
But two months dead: nay, not so much, not two:
So excellent a king; that was, to this,
Hyperion to a satyr: so loving to my mother,
That he might not beteem the winds of heaven
Visit her face too roughly. Heaven and earth!
Must I remember? Why, she would hang on him,
As if increase of appetite had grown
By what it fed on; and yet, within a month,
Let me not think on 't: Frailty, thy name is woman!
A little month; or ere those shoes were old
With which she follow'd my poor father's body,
Like Niobe, all tears; why she, even she,——
O God! a beast, that wants discourse of reason,
Would have mourn'd longer,—married with mine
    uncle,
My father's brother, but no more like my father
Than I to Hercules.   *Ib.* 129.

It is not, nor it cannot come to good;
But break, my heart, for I must hold my tongue!
    Ib. 158.

A truant disposition, good my lord.   *Ib.* 169.

We'll teach you to drink deep ere you depart.
    Ib. 175.

Thrift, thrift, Horatio! the funeral bak'd meats
Did coldly furnish forth the marriage tables.
Would I had met my dearest foe in heaven
Ere I had ever seen that day, Horatio!   *Ib.* 180.

In my mind's eye, Horatio.   *Ib.* 185.

He was a man, take him for all in all,
I shall not look upon his like again.   *Ib.* 187.

Season your admiration for a while.   *Ib.* 192.

In the dead vast and middle of the night.   *Ib.* 198.

Armed at points exactly, cap-a-pe.   *Ib.* 200.

Distill'd
Almost to jelly with the act of fear.   *Ib.* 204.

These hands are not more like.   *Ib.* 212.

But answer made it none.   *Ib.* 215.

A countenance more in sorrow than in anger.
    Ib. 231.

While one with moderate haste might tell a hundred.
    Ib. 237.

HAMLET:
His beard was grizzled, no?
HORATIO:
It was, as I have seen it in his life,
A sable silver'd.   *Ib.* 239.

Give it an understanding, but no tongue.   *Ib.* 249.

Upon the platform, 'twixt eleven and twelve.
    Ib. 251.

All is not well;
I doubt some foul play.   *Ib.* 254.

Foul deeds will rise,
Though all the earth o'erwhelm them, to men's eyes.
    Ib. 256.

A violet in the youth of primy nature,
Forward, not permanent, sweet, not lasting.
The perfume and suppliance of a minute.
    Ib. iii. 7.

His greatness weigh'd, his will is not his own,
For he himself is subject to his birth;
He may not, as unvalu'd persons do,
Carve for himself, for on his choice depends
The safety and the health of the whole state. *Ib.* 17.

And keep you in the rear of your affection.   *Ib.* 34.

Do not, as some ungracious pastors do,
Show me the steep and thorny way to heaven,
Whiles, like a puff'd and reckless libertine,
Himself the primrose path of dalliance treads,
And recks not his own rede.   *Ib.* 47.

A double blessing is a double grace;
Occasion smiles upon a second leave.   *Ib.* 53.

And these few precepts in thy memory
See thou character. Give thy thoughts no tongue,
Nor any unproportion'd thought his act.
Be thou familiar, but by no means vulgar;
The friends thou hast, and their adoption tried,
Grapple them to thy soul with hoops of steel;
But do not dull thy palm with entertainment
Of each new-hatch'd, unfledg'd comrade. Beware
Of entrance to a quarrel; but, being in,
Bear 't that th' opposed may beware of thee.
Give every man thine ear, but few thy voice;
Take each man's censure, but reserve thy judgment.
Costly thy habit as thy purse can buy,
But not express'd in fancy; rich, not gaudy;
For the apparel oft proclaims the man,
And they in France of the best rank and station
Are most select and generous, chief in that.
Neither a borrower, nor a lender be;
For loan oft loses both itself and friend,
And borrowing dulls the edge of husbandry.
This above all: to thine own self be true,
And it must follow, as the night the day,
Thou canst not then be false to any man.
Farewell; my blessing season this in thee!   *Ib.* 58.

You speak like a green girl,
Unsifted in such perilous circumstance.
Hamlet, I. iii. 101.

Ay, springes to catch woodcocks. I do know,
When the blood burns, how prodigal the soul
Lends the tongue vows. *Ib*. 115.

Be somewhat scanter of your maiden presence.
Ib. 121.

I would not, in plain terms, from this time forth,
Have you so slander any moment's leisure. *Ib*. 132.

HAMLET:
The air bites shrewdly; it is very cold.
HORATIO:
It is a nipping and an eager air. *Ib*. iv. 1.

But to my mind,—though I am native here,
And to the manner born,—it is a custom
More honour'd in the breach than the observance.
Ib. 14.

Angels and ministers of grace defend us!
Be thou a spirit of health or goblin damn'd,
Bring with thee airs from heaven or blasts from hell,
Be thy intents wicked or charitable,
Thou com'st in such a questionable shape
That I will speak to thee: I'll call thee Hamlet,
King, father; royal Dane, O! answer me:
Let me not burst in ignorance; but tell
Why thy canoniz'd bones, hearsed in death,
Have burst their cerements; why the sepulchre,
Wherein we saw thee quietly inurn'd,
Hath op'd his ponderous and marble jaws,
To cast thee up again. What may this mean,
That thou, dead corse, again in complete steel
Revisit'st thus the glimpses of the moon,
Making night hideous; and we fools of nature
So horridly to shake our disposition
With thoughts beyond the reaches of our souls?
Ib. 39.

Look, with what courteous action
It waves you to a more removed ground. *Ib*. 60.

I do not set my life at a pin's fee;
And for my soul, what can it do to that,
Being a thing immortal as itself? *Ib*. 65.

My fate cries out,
And makes each petty artery in this body
As hardy as the Nemean lion's nerve. *Ib*. 81.

Unhand me, gentlemen,
By heaven! I'll make a ghost of him that lets me.
Ib. 84.

Something is rotten in the state of Denmark. *Ib*. 90.

Whither wilt thou lead me? speak; I'll go no further.
Ib. v. 1.

Alas! poor ghost. *Ib*. 4.

I am thy father's spirit;
Doom'd for a certain term to walk the night. *Ib*. 9.

But that I am forbid
To tell the secrets of my prison-house,
I could a tale unfold whose lightest word
Would harrow up thy soul, freeze thy young blood,
Make thy two eyes, like stars, start from their spheres,
Thy knotted and combined locks to part,
And each particular hair to stand an end,
Like quills upon the fretful porpentine:
But this eternal blazon must not be
To ears of flesh and blood. List, list, O, list! *Ib*. 13.

Revenge his foul and most unnatural murder. *Ib*. 25.

Murder most foul, as in the best it is;
But this most foul, strange, and unnatural. *Ib*. 27.

And duller shouldst thou be than the fat weed
That rots itself in ease on Lethe wharf. *Ib*. 32.

O my prophetic soul!
My uncle! *Ib*. 40.

That it went hand in hand even with the vow
I made to her in marriage. *Ib*. 49.

But, soft! methinks I scent the morning air. *Ib*. 58.

In the porches of mine ears. *Ib*. 63.

Cut off even in the blossoms of my sin,
Unhousel'd, disappointed, unanel'd,
No reckoning made, but sent to my account
With all my imperfections on my head:
O, horrible! O, horrible! most horrible!
If thou hast nature in thee, bear it not. *Ib*. 76.

Leave her to heaven,
And to those thorns that in her bosom lodge,
To prick and sting her. *Ib*. 86.

The glow-worm shows the matin to be near,
And 'gins to pale his uneffectual fire. *Ib*. 89.

While memory holds a seat
In this distracted globe. Remember thee!
Yea, from the table of my memory
I'll wipe away all trivial fond records,
All saws of books, all forms, all pressures past,
That youth and observation copied there. *Ib*. 96.

O most pernicious woman!
O villain, villain, smiling, damned villain!
My tables,—meet it is I set it down,
That one may smile, and smile, and be a villain;
At least I'm sure it may be so in Denmark. *Ib*. 105.

HAMLET:
There's ne'er a villain dwelling in all Denmark,
But he's an arrant knave.
HORATIO:
There needs no ghost, my lord, come from the grave,
To tell us this. *Ib*. 123.

And, for mine own poor part,
Look you, I'll go pray. *Ib*. 131.

It is an honest ghost, that let me tell you. *Ib*. 138.

Art thou there, true-penny?
Come on,—you hear this fellow in the cellarage.
Ib. 150.

Hic et ubique? then we'll shift our ground. *Ib*. 156.

Well said, old mole! canst work i' the earth so fast?
Ib. 162.

O day and night, but this is wondrous strange!
Ib. 164.

There are more things in heaven and earth, Horatio,
Than are dreamt of in your philosophy. *Ib*. 166.

To put an antic disposition on. *Ib*. 172.

Rest, rest, perturbed spirit! *Ib*. 182.

The time is out of joint; O cursed spite,
That ever I was born to set it right! *Ib*. 188.

Your bait of falsehood takes this carp of truth.
Ib. II. i. 63.

By indirections find directions out. *Hamlet*, II. i. 66.

Lord Hamlet, with his doublet all unbrac'd. *Ib.* 78.

Ungarter'd, and down-gyved to his ankle. *Ib.* 80.

Such thanks
As fits a king's remembrance. *Ib.* ii. 25.

Thou still hast been the father of good news. *Ib.* 42.

Brevity is the soul of wit. *Ib.* 90.

More matter with less art. *Ib.* 95.

That he is mad, 'tis true; 'tis true 'tis pity;
And pity 'tis 'tis true: a foolish figure;
But farewell it, for I will use no art. *Ib.* 97.

That's an ill phrase, a vile phrase; 'beautified' is a
vile phrase. *Ib.* [110].

Doubt thou the stars are fire;
Doubt that the sun doth move;
Doubt truth to be a liar;
But never doubt I love. *Ib.* [115].

Lord Hamlet is a prince, out of thy star. *Ib.* [141].

If circumstances lead me, I will find
Where truth is hid, though it were hid indeed
Within the centre. *Ib.* [157].

Let me be no assistant for a state,
But keep a farm, and carters. *Ib.* [166].

POLONIUS:
Do you know me, my lord?
HAMLET:
Excellent well; you are a fishmonger. *Ib.* [173].

Ay, sir; to be honest, as this world goes, is to be one
man picked out of ten thousand. *Ib.* [179].

Still harping on my daughter. *Ib.* [190].

POLONIUS:
What do you read, my lord?
HAMLET:
Words, words, words. *Ib.* [195].

All which, sir, though I most powerfully and potently
believe, yet I hold it not honesty to have it thus set
down. *Ib.* [206].

Though this be madness, yet there is method in it.
Ib. [211].

Except my life, except my life, except my life.
Ib. [225].

These tedious old fools! *Ib.* [227].

As the indifferent children of the earth. *Ib.* [235].

HAMLET:
Then you live about her waist, or in the middle of
her favours?
GUILDENSTERN:
Faith, her privates we.
HAMLET:
In the secret parts of Fortune? O! most true; she is
a strumpet. What news?
ROSENCRANTZ:
None, my lord, but that the world's grown honest.
HAMLET:
Then is doomsday near. *Ib.* [240].

There is nothing either good or bad, but thinking
makes it so. *Ib.* [259].

O, God! I could be bounded in a nut-shell, and
count myself a king of infinite space, were it not
that I have bad dreams. *Ib.* [263].

GUILDENSTERN:
The very substance of the ambitious is merely the
shadow of a dream.
HAMLET:
A dream itself is but a shadow.
ROSENCRANTZ:
Truly, and I hold ambition of so airy and light a
quality that it is but a shadow's shadow. *Ib.* [268].

Beggar that I am, I am poor even in thanks.
Ib. [286].

It goes so heavily with my disposition that this goodly
frame, the earth, seems to me a sterile promontory;
this most excellent canopy, the air, look you, this
brave o'erhanging firmament, this majestical roof
fretted with golden fire, why, it appears no other
thing to me but a foul and pestilent congregation
of vapours. What a piece of work is a man! How
noble in reason! how infinite in faculty! in form,
in moving, how express and admirable! in action
how like an angel! in apprehension how like a god!
the beauty of the world! the paragon of animals!
And yet, to me, what is this quintessence of dust?
man delights not me; no, nor woman neither, though,
by your smiling, you seem to say so. *Ib.* [316].

There was no such stuff in my thoughts. *Ib.* [332].

What lenten entertainment the players shall receive
from you. *Ib.* [337].

Make those laugh whose lungs are tickle o' the sere.
Ib. [346].

There is something in this more than natural, if
philosophy could find it out. *Ib.* [392].

I am but mad north-north-west; when the wind is
southerly, I know a hawk from a handsaw.[1]
Ib. [405].

That great baby you see there is not yet out of his
swaddling-clouts. *Ib.* [410].

Seneca cannot be too heavy, nor Plautus too light.
Ib. [428].

One fair daughter and no more,
The which he loved passing well. *Ib.* [435].

Come, give us a taste of your quality. *Ib.* [460].

The play, I remember, pleased not the million; 'twa
caviare to the general. *Ib.* [465].

The rugged Pyrrhus, like the Hyrcanian beast.
Ib. [481].

Head to foot
Now is he total gules. *Ib.* [487].

The mobled queen. *Ib.* [533].

Good my lord, will you see the players well be
stowed? Do you hear, let them be well used
for they are the abstracts and brief chronicles o
the time: after your death you were better have
bad epitaph than their ill report while you live.
Ib. [553].

Use every man after his desert, and who shoul
'scape whipping? *Ib.* [561].

O, what a rogue and peasant slave am I! *Ib.* [584].

1 = heron-shaw, or heron.

What's Hecuba to him or he to Hecuba
That he should weep for her?   *Hamlet*, II. ii. [593].

He would drown the stage with tears,
And cleave the general ear with horrid speech,
Make mad the guilty, and appal the free,
Confound the ignorant, and amaze, indeed,
The very faculties of eyes and ears.   *Ib.* [596].

A dull and muddy-mettled rascal.   *Ib.* [602].

But I am pigeon-livered, and lack gall
To make oppression bitter.   *Ib.* [613].

I should have fatted all the region kites
With this slave's offal.   *Ib.* [615].

          I have heard,
That guilty creatures sitting at a play
Have by the very cunning of the scene
Been struck so to the soul that presently
They have proclaim'd their malefactions;
For murder, though it have no tongue, will speak.
With most miraculous organ.   *Ib.* [625].

Abuses me to damn me.   *Ib.* [640].

         The play's the thing
Wherein I'll catch the conscience of the king.
                 Ib. [641].

Nor do we find him forward to be sounded,
But, with a crafty madness, keeps aloof,
When we would bring him on to some confession
Of his true state.   *Ib.* III. i. 7.

'Tis too much prov'd—that with devotion's visage
And pious action, we do sugar o'er
The devil himself.   *Ib.* 47.

To be, or not to be: that is the question:
Whether 'tis nobler in the mind to suffer
The slings and arrows of outrageous fortune,
Or to take arms against a sea of troubles,
And by opposing end them? To die: to sleep;
No more; and, by a sleep to say we end
The heart-ache and the thousand natural shocks
That flesh is heir to, 'tis a consummation
Devoutly to be wish'd. To die, to sleep;
To sleep: perchance to dream: ay, there's the rub;
For in that sleep of death what dreams may come
When we have shuffled off this mortal coil,
Must give us pause. There's the respect
That makes calamity of so long life;
For who would bear the whips and scorns of time,
The oppressor's wrong, the proud man's contumely,
The pangs of dispriz'd love, the law's delay,
The insolence of office, and the spurns
That patient merit of the unworthy takes,
When he himself might his quietus make
With a bare bodkin? Who would fardels bear,
To grunt and sweat under a weary life,
But that the dread of something after death,
The undiscover'd country from whose bourn
No traveller returns, puzzles the will,
And makes us rather bear those ills we have,
Than fly to others that we know not of?
Thus conscience doth make cowards of us all;
And thus the native hue of resolution
Is sicklied o'er with the pale cast of thought,
And enterprises of great pith and moment
With this regard their currents turn awry,
And lose the name of action.   *Ib.* 56.

          Nymph, in thy orisons
Be all my sins remember'd.   *Ib.* 89.

        For, to the noble mind,
Rich gifts wax poor when givers prove unkind.
                 Ib. 100.

Get thee to a nunnery.   *Ib.* [124].

I am myself indifferent honest.   *Ib.* [125].

I am very proud, revengeful, ambitious; with more
offences at my beck, than I have thoughts to put
them in, imagination to give them shape, or time
to act them in. What should such fellows as I do
crawling between heaven and earth?   *Ib.* [128].

Let the doors be shut upon him, that he may play
the fool nowhere but in's own house.   *Ib.* [137].

Be thou as chaste as ice, as pure as snow, thou shalt
not escape calumny.   *Ib.* [142].

I have heard of your paintings too, well enough. God
hath given you one face, and you make yourself
another.   *Ib.* [150].

I say, we will have no more marriages.   *Ib.* [156].

O! what a noble mind is here o'erthrown:
The courtier's, soldier's, scholar's, eye, tongue, sword;
The expectancy and rose of the fair state,
The glass of fashion, and the mould of form,
The observed of all observers, quite, quite, down!
And I, of ladies most deject and wretched,
That suck'd the honey of his music vows,
Now see that noble and most sovereign reason,
Like sweet bells jangled, out of tune and harsh;
That unmatch'd form and figure of blown youth,
Blasted with ecstasy: O! woe is me,
To see what I have seen, see what I see!   *Ib.* [159].

Speak the speech, I pray you, as I pronounced it to
you, trippingly on the tongue; but if you mouth
it, as many of your players do, I had as lief the
town-crier spoke my lines. Nor do not saw the
air too much with your hand, thus; but use all
gently: for in the very torrent, tempest, and—as
I may say—whirlwind of passion, you must
acquire and beget a temperance, that may give it
smoothness. O! it offends me to the soul to hear
a robustious periwig-pated fellow tear a passion to
tatters, to very rags, to split the ears of the groundlings, who for the most part are capable of nothing
but inexplicable dumb-shows and noise: I would
have such a fellow whipped for o'erdoing Termagant; it out-herods Herod: pray you, avoid it.
                 Ib. ii. 1.

Be not too tame neither, but let your own discretion
be your tutor: suit the action to the word, the word
to the action; with this special observance, that
you o'erstep not the modesty of nature.   *Ib.* [19].

The purpose of playing, whose end, both at the first
and now, was and is, to hold, as 'twere, the mirror
up to nature.   *Ib.* [24].

To show . . . the very age and body of the time his
form and pressure.   *Ib.* [26].

Neither having the accent of Christians nor the gait
of Christian, pagan, nor man.   *Ib.* [35].

I have thought some of nature's journeymen had
made men, and not made them well, they imitated
humanity so abominably.   *Ib.* [38].

FIRST PLAYER:
I hope we have reformed that indifferently with
us, sir.
HAMLET:
O, reform it altogether.   *Hamlet*, III. ii. [41].

That's villainous, and shows a most pitiful ambition
in the fool that uses it.   *Ib.* [49].

Horatio, thou art e'en as just a man
As e'er my conversation cop'd withal.   *Ib.* [59].

     Nay, do not think I flatter:
For what advancement may I hope from thee,
That no revenue hast, but thy good spirits? *Ib.* [61].

Since my dear soul was mistress of her choice
And could of men distinguish, her election
Hath seal'd thee for herself.   *Ib.* [68].

A man that fortune's buffets and rewards
Hast ta'en with equal thanks; and bless'd are those
Whose blood and judgment are so well co-mingled
That they are not a pipe for Fortune's finger
To sound what stop she please. Give me that man
That is not passion's slave, and I will wear him
In my heart's core, ay, in my heart of heart,
As I do thee. Something too much of this.
     Ib. [72].

And my imaginations are as foul
As Vulcan's stithy.   *Ib.* [88].

The chameleon's dish: I eat the air, promise-
crammed.   *Ib.* [98].

Here's metal more attractive.   *Ib.* [117].

That's a fair thought to lie between maids' legs.
     Ib. [126].

Die two months ago, and not forgotten yet? Then
there's hope a great man's memory may outlive
his life half a year; but, by'r lady, he must build
churches then.   *Ib.* [140].

For, O! for, O! the hobby-horse is forgot. *Ib.* [145].

Marry, this is miching mallecho.   *Ib.* [148].

OPHELIA:
'Tis brief, my lord.
HAMLET:
As woman's love.   *Ib.* [165].

Where love is great, the littlest doubts are fear;
When little fears grow great, great love grows there.
     Ib. [183].

What to ourselves in passion we propose,
The passion ending, doth the purpose lose.
     Ib. [206].

This world is not for aye, nor 'tis not strange
That even our love should with our fortunes change.
     Ib. [212].

The great man down, you mark his favourite flies;
The poor advanc'd makes friends of enemies.
     Ib. [216].

Our wills and fates do so contrary run
That our devices still are overthrown.   *Ib.* [223].

     Sleep rock thy brain;
And never come mischance between us twain!
     Ib. [239].

The lady doth protest too much, methinks.
     Ib. [242].

We that have free souls, it touches us not: let the
galled jade wince, our withers are unwrung.
     Ib. [255].

The story is extant, and writ in very choice Italian.
     Ib. [277].

What! frighted with false fire?   *Ib.* [282].

So runs the world away.   *Ib.* [289].

Put your discourse into some frame, and start not so
wildly from my affair.   *Ib.* [325].

O wonderful son, that can so astonish a mother!
     Ib. [347].

The proverb is something musty.   *Ib.* [366].

It will discourse most eloquent music.   *Ib.* [375].

You would play upon me; you would seem to know
my stops; you would pluck out the heart of my
mystery; you would sound me from my lowest
note to the top of my compass.   *Ib.* [387].

Do you think I am easier to be played on than a pipe?
Call me what instrument you will, though you can
fret me, you cannot play upon me.   *Ib.* [393].

HAMLET:
Do you see yonder cloud that's almost in shape of
a camel?
POLONIUS:
By the mass, and 'tis like a camel, indeed.
HAMLET:
Methinks it is like a weasel.
POLONIUS:
It is backed like a weasel.
HAMLET:
Or like a whale?
POLONIUS:
Very like a whale.   *Ib.* [400].

They fool me to the top of my bent   *Ib.* [408].

By and by is easily said.   *Ib.* [411].

'Tis now the very witching time of night.   *Ib.* [413].

Let me be cruel, not unnatural;
I will speak daggers to her, but use none.   *Ib.* [420].

O! my offence is rank, it smells to heaven. *Ib.*iii. 36.

My stronger guilt defeats my strong intent;
And, like a man to double business bound,
I stand in pause where I shall first begin,
And both neglect.   *Ib.* 40.

     Whereto serves mercy
But to confront the visage of offence?   *Ib.* 46.

May one be pardon'd and retain the offence? *Ib.* 56.

     'Tis not so above;
There is no shuffling, there the action lies
In his true nature, and we ourselves compell'd,
Even to the teeth and forehead of our faults
To give in evidence.   *Ib.* 60.

Now might I do it pat, now he is praying.   *Ib.* 73.

He took my father grossly, full of bread,
With all his crimes broad blown, as flush as May;
And how his audit stands who knows save heaven?
     Ib. 80.

Tell him his pranks have been too broad to bear
with.   *Ib.* iv. 2.

You go not, till I set you up a glass
Where you may see the inmost part of you.
Hamlet, III. iv. 19.

How now! a rat? Dead, for a ducat, dead! *Ib.* 23.

A bloody deed! almost as bad, good mother,
As kill a king, and marry with his brother. *Ib.* 28.

As false as dicers' oaths. *Ib.* 45.

A rhapsody of words. *Ib.* 48.

Ay me! what act,
That roars so loud, and thunders in the index?
Ib. 51.

Look here, upon this picture, and on this. *Ib.* 53.

Could you on this fair mountain leave to feed
And batten on this moor? *Ib.* 66.

At your age
The hey-day in the blood is tame, it's humble,
And waits upon the judgment. *Ib.* 68.

Speak no more;
Thou turn'st mine eyes into my very soul. *Ib.* 88.

A cut-purse of the empire and the rule,
That from a shelf the precious diadem stole,
And put it in his pocket! *Ib.* 99.

A king of shreds and patches. *Ib.* 102.

Do you not come your tardy son to chide? *Ib.* 106.

Conceit in weakest bodies strongest works. *Ib.* 113.

Bring me to the test,
And I the matter will re-word, which madness
Would gambol from. Mother, for love of grace,
Lay not that flattering unction to your soul. *Ib.* 142.

Confess yourself to heaven;
Repent what's past; avoid what is to come. *Ib.* 149.

For in the fatness of these pursy times,
Virtue itself of vice must pardon beg. *Ib.* 153.

QUEEN:
O Hamlet! thou hast cleft my heart in twain.
HAMLET:
O! throw away the worser part of it,
And live the purer with the other half. *Ib.* 156.

Assume a virtue, if you have it not.
That monster, custom, who all sense doth eat,
Of habits devil, is angel yet in this. *Ib.* 160.

And when you are desirous to be bless'd,
I'll blessing beg of you. *Ib.* 171.

I must be cruel, only to be kind. *Ib.* 178.

For 'tis the sport to have the enginer
Hoist with his own petar: and it shall go hard
But I will delve one yard below their mines,
And blow them to the moon. *Ib.* 206.

He keeps them, like an ape doth nuts, in the corner
of his jaw; first mouthed, to be last swallowed.
Ib. IV. ii. [19].

A knavish speech sleeps in a foolish ear. *Ib.* [25].

Diseases desperate grown,
By desperate appliances are reliev'd,
Or not at all. *Ib.* iii. 9.

A certain convocation of politic worms are e'en at
him. Your worm is your only emperor for diet.
Ib. [21].

A man may fish with the worm that hath eat of a
king, and eat of the fish that hath fed of that worm.
Ib. [29].

We go to gain a little patch of ground,
That hath in it no profit but the name. *Ib.* iv. 18.

How all occasions do inform against me,
And spur my dull revenge! What is a man,
If his chief good and market of his time
Be but to sleep and feed? a beast, no more.
Sure he that made us with such large discourse,
Looking before and after, gave us not
That capability and god-like reason
To fust in us unus'd. *Ib.* 32.

Some craven scruple
Of thinking too precisely on the event. *Ib.* 40.

Rightly to be great
Is not to stir without great argument,
But greatly to find quarrel in a straw
When honour's at the stake. *Ib.* 53.

So full of artless jealousy is guilt,
It spills itself in fearing to be spilt. *Ib.* v. 19.

How should I your true love know
From another one?
By his cockle hat and staff,
And his sandal shoon. *Ib.* [23].

He is dead and gone, lady,
He is dead and gone,
At his head a grass-green turf;
At his heels a stone. *Ib.* [29].

White his shroud as the mountain snow. *Ib.* [36].

Larded with sweet flowers;
Which bewept to the grave did go
With true-love showers. *Ib.* [38].

Then up he rose, and donn'd his clothes. *Ib.* [53].

Come, my coach! Good night, sweet ladies; good
night. *Ib.* [72].

When sorrows come, they come not single spies,
But in battalions. *Ib.* [78].

We have done but greenly
In hugger-mugger to inter him. *Ib.* [83].

There's such divinity doth hedge a king,
That treason can but peep to what it would.
Ib. [123].

To hell, allegiance! vows, to the blackest devil!
Conscience and grace, to the profoundest pit!
I dare damnation. *Ib.* [130].

Nature is fine in love, and where 'tis fine
It sends some precious instance of itself
After the thing it loves. *Ib.* [160].

They bore him barefac'd on the bier;
Hey non nonny, nonny, hey nonny;
And in his grave rain'd many a tear. *Ib.* [163].

There's rosemary, that's for remembrance; pray,
love, remember: and there is pansies, that's for
thoughts. *Ib.* [174].

You must wear your rue with a difference. There's
a daisy; I would give you some violets, but they
withered all when my father died. *Ib.* [181].

They say he made a good end. *Ib.* [184].

For bonny sweet Robin is all my joy.
Hamlet, iv. v. [186].

No, no, he is dead;
Go to thy death-bed,
He never will come again.   *Ib.* [191].

He is gone, he is gone,
And we cast away moan;
God ha' mercy on his soul!   *Ib.* [196].

His means of death, his obscure funeral,
No trophy, sword, nor hatchment o'er his bones,
No noble rite nor formal ostentation.   *Ib.* [213].

And where the offence is let the great axe fall.
Ib. [218].

You must not think
That we are made of stuff so fat and dull
That we can let our beard be shook with danger
And think it pastime.   *Ib.* vii. 30.

It warms the very sickness in my heart,
That I shall live and tell him to his teeth,
'Thus diddest thou.'   *Ib.* 55.

A very riband in the cap of youth.   *Ib.* 77.

He grew into his seat,
And to such wondrous doing brought his horse,
As he had been incorps'd and demi-natur'd
With the brave beast.   *Ib.* 85.

No place, indeed, should murder sanctuarize.
Ib. 127.

There is a willow grows aslant a brook,
That shows his hoar leaves in the glassy stream;
There with fantastic garlands did she come,
Of crow-flowers, nettles, daisies, and long purples,
That liberal shepherds give a grosser name,
But our cold maids do dead men's fingers call them:
There, on the pendent boughs her coronet weeds
Clambering to hang, an envious sliver broke,
When down her weedy trophies and herself
Fell in the weeping brook. Her clothes spread wide,
And, mermaid-like, awhile they bore her up;
Which time she chanted snatches of old tunes,
As one incapable of her own distress.   *Ib.* 167.

Too much of water hast thou, poor Ophelia,
And therefore I forbid my tears; but yet
It is our trick, nature her custom holds,
Let shame say what it will.   *Ib.* 186.

Is she to be buried in Christian burial that wilfully
seeks her own salvation?   *Ib.* v. i. 1.

Ay, marry, is 't; crowner's quest law.   *Ib.* [23].

There is no ancient gentlemen but gardeners, ditchers,
and grave-makers; they hold up Adam's profession.
Ib. [32].

The gallows-maker; for that frame outlives a thousand
tenants.   *Ib.* [47].

Cudgel thy brains no more about it, for your dull ass
will not mend his pace with beating.   *Ib.* [61].

The houses that he makes last till doomsday.
Ib. [64].

Has this fellow no feeling of his business?   *Ib.* [71].

The hand of little employment hath the daintier
sense.   *Ib.* [75].

The pate of a politician, . . . one that could circumvent God.   *Ib.* [84].

How absolute the knave is! we must speak by the
card, or equivocation will undo us.   *Ib.* [147].

The age is grown so picked that the toe of the peasant
comes so near the heel of the courtier, he galls his
kibe.[1]   *Ib.* [150].

FIRST CLOWN:
He that is mad, and sent into England.
HAMLET:
Ay, marry; why was he sent into England?
FIRST CLOWN:
Why, because he was mad: he shall recover his wits
there; or, if he do not, 'tis no great matter there.
HAMLET:
Why.
FIRST CLOWN:
'Twill not be seen in him there; there the men are
as mad as he.   *Ib.* [160].

Alas! poor Yorick. I knew him, Horatio; a fellow of
infinite jest, of most excellent fancy; he hath
borne me on his back a thousand times; and now,
how abhorred in my imagination it is! my gorge
rises at it. Here hung those lips that I have kissed
I know not how oft. Where be your gibes now?
your gambols? your songs? your flashes of merriment, that were wont to set the table on a roar?
Not one now, to mock your own grinning? quite
chap-fallen? Now get you to my lady's chamber,
and tell her, let her paint an inch thick, to this
favour she must come.   *Ib.* [201].

'Twere to consider too curiously to consider so.
Ib. [226].

Imperious Cæsar, dead, and turn'd to clay,
Might stop a hole to keep the wind away.   *Ib.* [235].

We should profane the service of the dead,
To sing a requiem, and such rest to her
As to peace-parted souls.   *Ib.* [258].

Lay her i' the earth;
And from her fair and unpolluted flesh
May violets spring! I tell thee, churlish priest,
A minstering angel shall my sister be,
When thou liest howling.   *Ib.* [260].

Sweets to the sweet: farewell!   *Ib.* [265].

I thought thy bride-bed to have deck'd, sweet maid,
And not have strewed thy grave.   *Ib.* [267].

For, though I am not splenetive and rash
Yet have I in me something dangerous.   *Ib.* [283].

Forty thousand brothers
Could not, with all their quantity of love,
Make up my sum.   *Ib.* [291].

And thus a while the fit will work on him;
Anon, as patient as the female dove,
When that her golden couplets are disclos'd,
His silence will sit drooping.   *Ib.* [307].

This grave shall have a living monument.   *Ib.* [319].

There's a divinity that shapes our ends,
Rough-hew them how we will.   *Ib.* ii. 10.

It did me yeoman's service.   *Ib.* 36.

1 = chap on the heel.

HAMLET:
  Dost know this water-fly?
HORATIO:
                    No, my good lord.
HAMLET:
Thy state is the more gracious; for 'tis a vice to
  know him.   *Hamlet*, v. ii. [84].

What imports the nomination of this gentleman?
                                   Ib. [134].

The phrase would be more german to the matter, if
  we could carry cannon by our sides.   *Ib.* [165].

'Tis the breathing time of day with me.   *Ib.* [181].

But thou wouldst not think how ill all's here about
  my heart.   *Ib.* [222].

Not a whit, we defy augury; there's a special providence in the fall of a sparrow. If it be now, 'tis
  not to come; if it be not to come, it will be now;
  if it be not now, yet it will come: the readiness is
  all.   *Ib.* [232].

I have shot mine arrow o'er the house,
And hurt my brother.   *Ib.* [257].

Now the king drinks to Hamlet!   *Ib.* [292].

A hit, a very palpable hit.   *Ib.* [295].

Why, as a woodcock to mine own springe, Osric;
I am justly kill'd with my own treachery. *Ib.* [320].

O villainy! Ho! let the door be lock'd:
Treachery! seek it out.   *Ib.* [325].

The point envenom'd too!—
Then, venom, to thy work.   *Ib.* [335].

              This fell sergeant, death,
Is strict in his arrest.   *Ib.* [350].

Report me and my cause aright.   *Ib.* [353].

I am more an antique Roman than a Dane.
                                   Ib. [355].

              Horatio, what a wounded name,
Things standing thus unknown, shall live behind me.
If thou didst ever hold me in thy heart,
Absent thee from felicity awhile,
And in this harsh world draw thy breath in pain,
To tell my story.   *Ib.* [358].

The potent poison quite o'ercrows my spirit.
                                   Ib. [367].

The rest is silence.   *Ib.* [372].

Now cracks a noble heart. Good-night, sweet prince,
And flights of angels sing thee to thy rest! *Ib.* [373].

              O proud death!
What feast is toward in thine eternal cell? *Ib.* [378].

              Purposes mistook
Fall'n on the inventors' heads.   *Ib.* [308].

For he was likely, had he been put on,
To have prov'd most royally.   *Ib.* [411].

Hence! home, you idle creatures, get you home:
Is this a holiday?   *Julius Cæsar*, I. i. I.

What trade, thou knave? thou naughty knave, what
  trade?   *Ib.* [15].

FLAVIUS:
  Thou art a cobbler, art thou?
2ND COMMONER:
Truly, sir, all that I live by is with the awl: ... I am
  indeed, sir, a surgeon to old shoes.   *Ib.* [22].

As proper men as ever trod upon neat's-leather.
                                   Ib. [27].

Wherefore rejoice? What conquest brings he home?
                                   Ib. [36].

You blocks, you stones, you worse than senseless
  things!
O you hard hearts, you cruel men of Rome,
Knew you not Pompey?   *Ib.* [39].

Have you not made a universal shout,
That Tiber trembled underneath her banks,
To hear the replication of your sounds
Made in her concave shores?   *Ib.* [48].

Speak; Cæsar is turn'd to hear.   *Ib.* ii. 17.

Beware the Ides of March.   *Ib.* 18.

He is a dreamer; let us leave him: pass.   *Ib.* 24.

I am not gamesome: I do lack some part
Of that quick spirit that is in Antony.   *Ib.* 28.

Brutus, I do observe you now of late:
I have not from your eyes that gentleness
And show of love as I was wont to have:
You bear too stubborn and too strange a hand
Over your friend that loves you.   *Ib.* 32.

              Poor Brutus, with himself at war,
Forgets the shows of love to other men.   *Ib.* 46.

Set honour in one eye and death i' the other,
And I will look on both indifferently.   *Ib.* 86.

Well, honour is the subject of my story.
I cannot tell what you and other men
Think of this life: but, for my single self,
I had as lief not be as live to be
In awe of such a thing as I myself.   *Ib.* 92.

              'Dar'st thou Cassius, now,
Leap in with me into this angry flood,
And swim to yonder point?' Upon the word,
Accoutred as I was, I plunged in,
And bade him follow.   *Ib.* 102.

Stemming it with hearts of controversy.   *Ib.* 109.

His coward lips did from their colour fly,
And that same eye whose bend doth awe the world
Did lose his lustre.   *Ib.* 122.

              Ye gods, it doth amaze me,
A man of such a feeble temper should
So get the start of the majestic world,
And bear the palm alone.   *Ib.* 128.

Why, man, he doth bestride the narrow world
Like a Colossus; and we petty men
Walk under his huge legs, and peep about
To find ourselves dishonourable graves.
Men at some time are masters of their fates:
The fault, dear Brutus, is not in our stars,
But in ourselves, that we are underlings.   *Ib.* 134.

Brutus' will start a spirit as soon as 'Cæsar'.
Now in the names of all the gods at once,
Upon what meat doth this our Cæsar feed,
That he is grown so great?   *Ib.* 146.

Now is it Rome indeed and room enough.
Julius Cæsar, I. ii. 155.

But, look you, Cassius,
The angry spot, doth glow on Cæsar's brow.
Ib. 181.

Let me have men about me that are fat;
Sleek-headed men and such as sleep o' nights;
Yond' Cassius has a lean and hungry look;
He thinks too much: such men are dangerous.
Ib. 191.

Would he were fatter! But I fear him not:
Yet if my name were liable to fear,
I do not know the man I should avoid
So soon as that spare Cassius. He reads much;
He is a great observer, and he looks
Quite through the deeds of men; he loves no plays,
As thou dost, Antony; he hears no music;
Seldom he smiles, and smiles in such a sort
As if he mock'd himself, and scorn'd his spirit,
That could be mov'd to smile at anything.
Such men as he be never at heart's ease,
Whiles they behold a greater than themselves,
And therefore are they very dangerous.
I rather tell thee what is to be fear'd
Than what I fear, for always I am Cæsar. *Ib.* 197.

'Tis very like: he hath the falling sickness.
Ib. [255].

If Cæsar had stabbed their mothers, they would
have done no less.   *Ib.* [277].

For mine own part, it was Greek to me.   *Ib.* [288].

Therefore 'tis meet
That noble minds keep ever with their likes;
For who so firm that cannot be seduc'd? *Ib.* [315].

Besides—I have not since put up my sword,—
Against the Capitol I met a lion,
Who glar'd upon me, and went surly by,
Without annoying me.   *Ib.* iii. 19.

Yesterday the bird of night did sit,
Even at noon-day, upon the market-place,
Hooting and shrieking.   *Ib.* 26.

But men may construe things after their own fashion,
Clean from the purpose of the things themselves.
Ib. 34.

Cassius from bondage will deliver Cassius.   *Ib.* 90.

Nor stony tower, nor walls of beaten brass,
Nor airless dungeon, nor strong links of iron,
Can be retentive to the strength of spirit;
But life, being weary of these worldly bars,
Never lacks power to dismiss itself.   *Ib.* 93.

So every bondman in his own hand bears
The power to cancel his captivity.   *Ib.* 101.

I will set this foot of mine as far
As who goes farthest.   *Ib.* 119.

O! he sits high in all the people's hearts:
And that which would appear offence in us,
His countenance, like richest alchemy,
Will change to virtue and to worthiness.   *Ib.* 157.

It is the bright day that brings forth the adder;
And that craves wary walking.   *Ib.* II. i. 14.

'Tis a common proof,
That lowliness is young ambition's ladder,
Whereto the climber-upward turns his face;

But when he once attains the upmost round,
He then unto the ladder turns his back,
Looks in the clouds, scorning the base degrees
By which he did ascend.   *Ib.* 21.

Therefore think him as a serpent's egg
Which, hatch'd, would, as his kind, grow mischievous,
And kill him in the shell.   *Ib.* 32.

Between the acting of a dreadful thing
And the first motion, all the interim is
Like a phantasma, or a hideous dream:
The genius and the mortal instruments
Are then in council; and the state of man,
Like to a little kingdom, suffers then
The nature of an insurrection.   *Ib.* 63.

O conspiracy!
Sham'st thou to show thy dangerous brow by night,
When evils are most free?   *Ib.* 77.

For if thou path, thy native semblance on,
Not Erebus itself were dim enough
To hide thee from prevention.   *Ib.* 83.

For he will never follow anything
That other men begin.   *Ib.* 151.

Let us be sacrificers, but not butchers, Cassius.
Ib. 166.

Let's carve him as a dish fit for the gods.
Not hew him as a carcase fit for hounds.   *Ib.* 173.

For he is superstitious grown of late,
Quite from the main opinion he held once
Of fantasy, of dreams, and ceremonies.   *Ib.* 195.

But when I tell him he hates flatterers,
He says he does, being then most flattered. *Ib.* 207.

Enjoy the honey-heavy dew of slumber.   *Ib.* 230.

With an angry wafture of your hand,
Gave sign for me to leave you.   *Ib.* 246.

What! is Brutus sick,
And will he steal out of his wholesome bed
To dare the vile contagion of the night?   *Ib.* 263.

That great vow
Which did incorporate and make us one.   *Ib.* 272.

PORTIA:
Dwell I but in the suburbs
Of your good pleasure? If it be no more,
Portia is Brutus' harlot, not his wife.
BRUTUS:
You are my true and honourable wife,
As dear to me as are the ruddy drops
That visit my sad heart.   *Ib.* 285.

I grant I am a woman, but, withal,
A woman that Lord Brutus took to wife;
I grant I am a woman, but, withal,
A woman well-reputed, Cato's daughter.
Think you I am no stronger than my sex,
Being so fathered and so husbanded?   *Ib.* 292.

Enter Cæsar, in his night-gown.
Ib. ii.   *Stage Direction.*

Nor heaven nor earth have been at peace to-night.
Ib. ii. 1.

CALPURNIA:
>>> These things are beyond all use,
And I do fear them.
CÆSAR:
>>> What can be avoided
Whose end is purpos'd by the mighty gods?
Julius Cæsar, II. ii. 25.

CALPURNIA:
When beggars die, there are no comets seen;
The heavens themselves blaze forth the death of
>> princes.
CÆSAR:
Cowards die many times before their deaths
The valiant never taste of death but once.
Of all the wonders that I yet have heard,
It seems to me most strange that men should fear;
Seeing that death, a necessary end,
Will come when it will come. *Ib*. 30.

>> Danger knows full well
That Cæsar is more dangerous than he:
We are two lions litter'd in one day,
And I the elder and more terrible:
And Cæsar shall go forth. *Ib*. 44.

The cause is in my will: I will not come. *Ib*. 71.

See! Antony, that revels long o' nights,
Is notwithstanding up. *Ib*. 116.

My heart laments that virtue cannot live
Out of the teeth of emulation. *Ib*. iii. [13].

O constancy! be strong upon my side;
Set a huge mountain 'tween my heart and tongue;
I have a man's mind, but a woman's might.
How hard it is for women to keep counsel! *Ib*. iv. 6.

CÆSAR:
The ides of March are come.
SOOTHSAYER:
Ay, Cæsar; but not gone. *Ib*. III. i. 1.

>> Sweet words,
Low-crooked curtsies, and base spaniel fawning. *Ib*. 42.

If I could pray to move, prayers would move me;
But I am constant as the northern star,
Of whose true-fix'd and resting quality
There is no fellow in the firmament.
The skies are painted with unnumber'd sparks,
They are all fire and every one doth shine,
But there's but one in all doth hold his place:
So, in the world; 'tis furnish'd well with men,
And men are flesh and blood, and apprehensive;
Yet in the number I do know but one
That unassailable holds on his rank,
Unshak'd of motion: and that I am he,
Let me a little show it, even in this,
That I was constant Cimber should be banish'd,
And constant do remain to keep him so. *Ib*. 59.

Et tu, Brute! *Ib*. 77.

Ambition's debt is paid. *Ib*. 83.

That we shall die, we know; 'tis but the time
And drawing days out, that men stand upon. *Ib*. 99.

He that cuts off twenty years of life
Cuts off so many years of fearing death. *Ib*. 101.

CASSIUS:
>> How many ages hence
Shall this our lofty scene be acted o'er,
In states unborn, and accents yet unknown!
BRUTUS:
How many times shall Cæsar bleed in sport. *Ib*. 111.

O mighty Cæsar! dost thou lie so low?
Are all thy conquests, glories, triumphs, spoils,
Shrunk to this little measure? *Ib*. 148.

>> Your swords, made rich
With the most noble blood of all this world. *Ib*. 155.

>> Live a thousand years,
I shall not find myself so apt to die. *Ib*. 159.

The choice and master spirits of this age. *Ib*. 163.

Let each man render me his bloody hand
First, Marcus Brutus, will I shake with you. *Ib*. 184.

Though last, not least in love. *Ib*. 189.

My credit now stands on such slippery ground,
That one of two bad ways you must conceit me,
Either a coward or a flatterer. *Ib*. 191.

>> Here wast thou bay'd, brave hart;
Here didst thou fall; and here thy hunters stand,
Sign'd in thy spoil, and crimson'd in thy lethe.
O world! thou wast the forest to this hart;
And this, indeed, O world! the heart of thee. *Ib*. 204.

The enemies of Cæsar shall say this;
Then, in a friend, it is cold modesty. *Ib*. 212.

O! pardon me, thou bleeding piece of earth,
That I am meek and gentle with these butchers;
Thou art the ruins of the noblest man
That ever lived in the tide of times. *Ib*. 254.

>> Cæsar's spirit, ranging for revenge,
With Ate by his side, come hot from hell,
Shall in these confines, with a monarch's voice
Cry, 'Havoc!' and let slip the dogs of war. *Ib*. 270.

Passion, I see, is catching. *Ib*. 283.

Not that I loved Cæsar less, but that I loved Rome
more. *Ib*. ii. [22].

As he was valiant I honour him: but, as he was
ambitious, I slew him. *Ib*. [27].

Who is here so base that would be a bondman? If
any, speak; for him have I offended. Who is here
so rude that would not be a Roman? If any,
speak; for him have I offended. Who is here so
vile, that will not love his country? If any, speak;
for him have I offended. I pause for a reply. *Ib*. [31].

Friends, Romans, countrymen, lend me your ears;
I come to bury Cæsar, not to praise him.
The evil that men do lives after them,
The good is oft interred with their bones;
So let it be with Cæsar. The noble Brutus
Hath told you Cæsar was ambitious;
If it were so, it was a grievous fault;
And grievously hath Cæsar answer'd it. *Ib*. [79].

For Brutus is an honourable man;
So are they all, all honourable men. *Ib*. [88].

He was my friend, faithful and just to me:
But Brutus says he was ambitious;
And Brutus is an honourable man.
Julius Cæsar, III. ii. [91].

When that the poor have cried, Cæsar hath wept;
Ambition should be made of sterner stuff. *Ib.* [97].

You all did love him once, not without cause.
Ib. [108].

O judgment! thou art fled to brutish beasts,
And men have lost their reason. *Ib.* [110].

But yesterday the word of Cæsar might
Have stood against the world; now lies he there,
And none so poor to do him reverence. *Ib.* [124].

Let but the commons hear this testament—
Which, pardon me, I do not mean to read—
And they would go and kiss dead Cæsar's wounds
And dip their napkins in his sacred blood,
Yea, beg a hair of him for memory,
And, dying, mention it within their wills,
Bequeathing it as a rich legacy
Unto their issue. *Ib.* [136].

The will, the will! we will hear Cæsar's will.
Ib. [145].

You are not wood, you are not stones, but men.
Ib. [148].

If you have tears, prepare to shed them now.
You all do know this mantle: I remember
The first time ever Cæsar put it on;
'Twas on a summer's evening, in his tent,
That day he overcame the Nervii. *Ib.* [174].

See what a rent the envious Casca made. *Ib.* [180].

For Brutus, as you know, was Cæsar's angel.
Ib. [186].

This was the most unkindest cut of all. *Ib.* [188].

Ingratitude, more strong than traitors' arms,
Quite vanquish'd him: then burst his mighty heart;
And, in his mantle muffling up his face,
Even at the base of Pompey's statua,
Which all the while ran blood, great Cæsar fell.
O! what a fall was there, my countrymen;
Then I, and you, and all of us fell down,
Whilst bloody treason flourish'd over us.
O! now you weep, and I perceive you feel
The dint of pity; these are gracious drops.
Ib. [190].

Good friends, sweet friends, let me not stir you up
To such a sudden flood of mutiny.
They that have done this deed are honourable:
What private griefs they have, alas! I know not,
That made them do it; they are wise and honourable,
And will no doubt with reasons answer you.
I come not, friends, to steal away your hearts:
I am no orator, as Brutus is;
But, as you know me all, a plain, blunt man,
That love my friend. *Ib.* [214].

For I have neither wit, nor words, nor worth,
Action, nor utterance, nor power of speech,
To stir men's blood: I only speak right on;
I tell you that which you yourselves do know.
Ib. [225].

But were I Brutus,
And Brutus Antony, there were an Antony

Would ruffle up your spirits, and put a tongue
In every wound of Cæsar, that should move
The stones of Rome to rise and mutiny.
Ib. [230].

Here was a Cæsar! when comes such another?
Ib. [257].

Now let it work; mischief, thou art afoot,
Take thou what course thou wilt! *Ib.* [265].

Fortune is merry,
And in this mood will give us anything. *Ib.* [271].

Tear him for his bad verses, tear him for his bad
verses. *Ib.* iii. [34].

He shall not live; look, with a spot I damn him.
Ib. IV. i. 6.

This is a slight unmeritable man,
Meet to be sent on errands. *Ib.* 12.

OCTAVIUS:
He's a tried and valiant soldier.
ANTONY:
So is my horse, Octavius; and for that
I do appoint him store of provender. *Ib.* 28.

We are at the stake,
And bay'd about with many enemies;
And some that smile have in their hearts, I fear,
Millions of mischiefs. *Ib.* 48.

Not with such familiar instances,
Nor with such free and friendly conference,
As he hath us'd of old. *Ib.* ii. 16.

When love begins to sicken and decay,
It useth an enforced ceremony.
There are no tricks in plain and simple faith.
Ib. 20.

CASSIUS:
In such a time as this it is not meet
That every nice offence should bear his comment.
BRUTUS:
Let me tell you, Cassius, you yourself
Are much condemn'd to have an itching palm.
Ib. iii. 7.

Remember March, the ides of March remember.
Ib. 18.

Shall we now
Contaminate our fingers with base bribes? *Ib.* 23.

I had rather be a dog, and bay the moon,
Than such a Roman. *Ib.* 27.

Away, slight man! *Ib.* 37.

I'll use you for my mirth, yea, for my laughter,
When you are waspish. *Ib.* 49.

For mine own part,
I shall be glad to learn of noble men. *Ib.* 53.

You wrong me every way; you wrong me, Brutus;
I said an elder soldier, not a better:
Did I say 'better'? *Ib.* 55.

Do not presume too much upon my love;
I may do that I shall be sorry for. *Ib.* 63.

There is no terror, Cassius, in your threats;
For I am arm'd so strong in honesty
That they pass me by as the idle wind,
Which I respect not. *Ib.* 66.

By heaven, I had rather coin my heart,
And drop my blood for drachmas, than to wring
From the hard hands of peasants their vile trash
By any indirection. *Julius Cæsar*, IV. iii. 72.

Should I have answer'd Caius Cassius so?
When Marcus Brutus grows so covetous,
To lock such rascal counters from his friends,
Be ready, gods, with all your thunderbolts;
Dash him to pieces! *Ib.* 78.

A friend should bear his friend's infirmities,
But Brutus makes mine greater than they are.
Ib. 85.

A friendly eye could never see such faults. *Ib.* 89.

All his faults observ'd,
Set in a note-book, learn'd and conn'd by rote,
To cast into my teeth. *Ib.* 96.

O Cassius! you are yoked with a lamb
That carries anger as the flint bears fire;
Who, much enforced, shows a hasty spark,
And straight is cold again. *Ib.* 109.

O Cassius! I am sick of many griefs. *Ib.* 143.

I have as much of this in art as you,
But yet my nature could not bear it so. *Ib.* 193.

Good reasons must, of force, give place to better.
Ib. 202.

There is a tide in the affairs of men,
Which, taken at the flood, leads on to fortune;
Omitted, all the voyage of their life
Is bound in shallows and in miseries.
On such a full sea are we now afloat,
And we must take the current when it serves,
Or lose our ventures. *Ib.* 217.

The deep of night is crept upon our talk,
And nature must obey necessity. *Ib.* 225.

This was an ill beginning of the night:
Never come such division 'tween our souls! *Ib.* 233.

BRUTUS:
Then I shall see thee again?
GHOST:
Ay, at Philippi.
BRUTUS:
Why, I will see thee at Philippi, then. *Ib.* 283.

But for your words, they rob the Hybla bees,
And leave them honeyless. *Ib.* v. i. 34.

You know that I held Epicurus strong,
And his opinion; now I change my mind,
And partly credit things that do presage. *Ib.* 77.

The gods to-day stand friendly, that we may,
Lovers in peace, lead on our days to age! *Ib.* 94.

I know not how,
But I do find it cowardly and vile,
For fear of what might fall, so to prevent
The time of life. *Ib.* 103.

Think not, thou noble Roman,
That ever Brutus will go bound to Rome;
He bears too great a mind: but this same day
Must end that work the ides of March begun;
And whether we shall meet again, I know not.
Therefore our everlasting farewell take:
For ever, and for ever, farewell, Cassius!
If we do meet again, why, we shall smile!
If not, why then, this parting was well made.
Ib. 111.

O! that a man might know
The end of this day's business, ere it come;
But it sufficeth that the day will end,
And then the end is known. *Ib.* 123.

This day I breathed first: time is come round,
And where I did begin, there shall I end;
My life is run his compass. *Ib.* iii. 23.

O hateful error, melancholy's child!
Why dost thou show, to the apt thoughts of men,
The things that are not? *Ib.* 67.

O Julius Cæsar! thou art mighty yet!
Thy spirit walks abroad, and turns our swords
In our own proper entrails. *Ib.* 94.

Are yet two Romans living such as these?
The last of all the Romans, fare thee well!
It is impossible that ever Rome
Should breed thy fellow. Friends, I owe more tears
To this dead man than you shall see me pay.—
I shall find time, Cassius, I shall find time. *Ib.* 98.

When you do find him, or alive or dead,
He will be found like Brutus, like himself.
Ib. iv. 24.

I had rather have
Such men my friends than enemies. *Ib.* 28.

Thou seest the world, Volumnius, how it goes;
Our enemies have beat us to the pit:
It is more worthy to leap in ourselves,
Than tarry till they push us. *Ib.* v. 22.

Thou art a fellow of a good respect;
Thy life hath had some smatch of honour in it.
Ib. 45.

Cæsar, now be still;
I kill'd not thee with half so good a will. *Ib.* 50.

This was the noblest Roman of them all. *Ib.* 68.

He, only, in a general honest thought
And common good to all, made one of them.
His life was gentle, and the elements
So mix'd in him that Nature might stand up
And say to all the world, 'This was a man!' *Ib.* 71.

LEAR:
So young, and so untender?
CORDELIA:
So young, my lord, and true. *King Lear*, I. i. [108].

A still-soliciting eye. *Ib.* [234].

Love is not love
When it is mingled with regards that stand
Aloof from the entire point. *Ib.* [239].

Fairest Cordelia, that art most rich, being poor;
Most choice, forsaken; and most lov'd, despis'd!
Ib. [253].

Who in the lusty stealth of nature take
More composition and fierce quality
Than doth, within a dull, stale, tired bed,
Go to the creating a whole tribe of fops. *Ib.* ii. 11.

These late eclipses in the sun and moon portend no
good to us. *Ib.* [115].

We have seen the best of our time: machinations,
hollowness, treachery, and all ruinous disorders,
follow us disquietly to our graves. *Ib.* [125].

This is the excellent foppery of the world. *Ib.* [132].

We make guilty of our disasters the sun, the moon,
and the stars; as if we were villains by necessity,
fools by heavenly compulsion.
King Lear, i. ii. [134].

An admirable evasion of whoremaster man, to lay
his goatish disposition to the charge of a star!
Ib. [141].

My nativity was under Ursa Major; so that it follows
I am rough and lecherous. *Ib.* [145].

Pat he comes, like the catastrophe of the old comedy;
my cue is villainous melancholy, with a sigh like
Tom o' Bedlam. *Ib.* [150].

KENT:
You have that in your countenance which I would
fain call master.
LEAR:
What's that?
KENT:
Authority. *Ib.* iv. [29].

Not so young, sir, to love a woman for singing, nor
so old to dote on her for any thing. *Ib.* [40].

Lady the brach may stand by the fire and stink.
Ib. [125].

Have more than thou showest,
Speak less than thou knowest,
Lend less than thou owest. *Ib.* [132].

LEAR:
Dost thou call me fool, boy?
FOOL:
All thy other titles thou hast given away; that thou
wast born with. *Ib.* [163].

The hedge-sparrow fed the cuckoo so long,
That it had it head bit off by it young. *Ib.* [238].

Ingratitude, thou marble-hearted fiend,
More hideous, when thou show'st thee in a child,
Than the sea-monster. *Ib.* [283].

Into her womb convey sterility!
Dry up in her the organs of increase. *Ib.* [302].

How sharper than a serpent's tooth it is
To have a thankless child! *Ib.* [312].

How far your eyes may pierce I cannot tell;
Striving to better, oft we mar what's well.
Ib. [370].

A knave; a rascal; an eater of broken meats.
Ib. ii. ii. [15].

Thou whoreson zed! thou unnecessary letter!
Ib. [68].

I'd drive ye cackling home to Camelot. *Ib.* [89].

I have seen better faces in my time
Than stands on any shoulder that I see
Before me at this instant. *Ib.* [99].

Winter's not gone yet, if the wild-geese fly that way.
Ib. iv. [46].

Down, thou climbing sorrow!
Thy element's below. *Ib.* [57].

That sir which serves and seeks for gain,
And follows but for form,
Will pack when it begins to rain,
And leave thee in the storm. *Ib.* [79].

O, sir! you are old;
Nature in you stands on the very verge
Of her confine. *Ib.* [148].

But I'll not chide thee;
Let shame come when it will, I do not call it:
I do not bid the thunder-bearer shoot,
Nor tell tales of thee to high-judging Jove.
Ib. [228].

Our basest beggars
Are in the poorest thing superfluous:
Allow not nature more than nature needs,
Man's life is cheap as beast's. *Ib.* [267].

You see me here, you gods, a poor old man,
As full of grief as age; wretched in both! *Ib.* [275].

I will have such revenges on you both
That all the world shall—I will do such things,—
What they are yet I know not,—but they shall be
The terrors of the earth. *Ib.* [282].

To wilful men,
The injuries that they themselves procure
Must be their schoolmasters. *Ib.* [305].

Contending with the fretful elements;
Bids the wind blow the earth into the sea,
Or swell the curled waters 'bove the main.
Ib. iii. i. 4.

Strives in his little world of man to out-scorn
The to-and-fro conflicting wind and rain.
This night, wherein the cub-drawn bear would couch,
The lion and the belly-pinched wolf
Keep their fur dry. *Ib.* 10.

Blow, winds, and crack your cheeks! rage! blow!
You cataracts and hurricanoes, spout
Till you have drench'd our steeples, drown'd the
cocks!
You sulphurous and thought-executing fires,
Vaunt-couriers to oak-cleaving thunderbolts,
Singe my white head! And thou, all-shaking thunder,
Strike flat the thick rotundity o' the world!
Crack nature's moulds, all germens spill at once
That make ingrateful man! *Ib.* ii. 1.

I tax not you, you elements, with unkindness;
I never gave you kingdom, call'd you children,
You owe me no subscription: then, let fall
Your horrible pleasure; here I stand, your slave,
A poor, infirm, weak, and despis'd old man.
But yet I call you servile ministers,
That have with two pernicious daughters join'd
Your high-engender'd battles 'gainst a head
So old and white as this. *Ib.* [16].

There was never yet fair woman but she made mouths
in a glass. *Ib.* [35].

Things that love night
Love not such nights as these. *Ib.* [42].

Let the great gods,
That keep this dreadful pother o'er our heads,
Find out their enemies now. Tremble, thou wretch,
That hast within thee undivulged crimes,
Unwhipp'd of justice. *Ib.* [49].

Close pent-up guilts,
Rive your concealing continents, and cry
These dreadful summoners grace. I am a man
More sinned against than sinning. *Ib.* [57].

The art of our necessities is strange,
That can make vile things precious.
                              King Lear, III. ii. [70].

When the mind's free,
The body's delicate.   *Ib*. iv. 11.

O! that way madness lies; let me shun that.   *Ib*. 21.

Poor naked wretches, wheresoe'er you are,
That bide the pelting of this pitiless storm,
How shall your houseless heads and unfed sides,
Your looped and window'd raggedness, defend you
From seasons such as these?   *Ib*. 28.

          Take physic, pomp;
Expose thyself to feel what wretches feel.   *Ib*. 33.

Tom's a-cold.   *Ib*. [57].

Pillicock set on Pillicock-hill:
Halloo, halloo, loo, loo!   *Ib*. [75].

Take heed o' the foul fiend!   *Ib*. [79].

A serving-man, proud in heart and mind; that curled
my hair, wore gloves in my cap, served the lust of
my mistress' heart, and did the act of darkness
with her; swore as many oaths as I spake words,
and broke them in the sweet face of heaven; one
that slept in the contriving of lust, and waked to
do it.   *Ib*. [84].

Keep thy foot out of brothels, thy hand out of
plackets, thy pen from lenders' books, and defy
the foul fiend.   *Ib*. [96].

Thou art the thing itself; unaccommodated man is
no more but such a poor, bare, forked animal as
thou art.   *Ib*. [109].

'Tis a naughty night to swim in.   *Ib*. [113].

Drinks the green mantle of the standing pool.
                                         Ib. [136].

But mice and rats and such small deer
Have been Tom's food for seven long year.
                                         Ib. [142].

The prince of darkness is a gentleman.   *Ib*. [148].

I'll talk a word with this same learned Theban.
                                         Ib. [161].

Child Roland to the dark tower came,
His word was still, Fie, foh, and fum,
I smell the blood of a British man.   *Ib*. [185].

Nero is an angler in the lake of darkness. *Ib*. vi. [8].

          The little dogs and all,
Tray, Blanch, and Sweet-heart, see, they bark at me.
                                         Ib. [65].

Mastiff, greyhound, mongrel grim,
Hound or spaniel, brach or lym,
Or bobtail tyke, or trundle-tail.   *Ib*. [71].

You, sir, I entertain for one of my hundred; only I
do not like the fashion of your garments: you will
say, they are Persian attire; but let them be
changed.   *Ib*. [83].

          'Tis most ignobly done
To pluck me by the beard.   *Ib*. vii. [35].

I am tied to the stake, and I must stand the course.
                                         Ib. [54].

The sea, with such a storm as his bare head
In hell-black night endur'd, would have buoy'd up,
And quench'd the stelled fires.   *Ib*. [59].

Out, vile jelly!   *Ib*. [83].

The lowest and most dejected thing of fortune.
                                         Ib. IV. i. 3.

The lamentable change is from the best;
The worst returns to laughter.   *Ib*. 5.

          The worst is not,
So long as we can say, 'This is the worst.' *Ib*. 27.

As flies to wanton boys, are we to the gods;
They kill us for their sport.   *Ib*. 36.

You are not worth the dust which the rude wind
Blows in your face.   *Ib*. ii. 30.

She that herself will sliver and disbranch
From her material sap, perforce must wither
And come to deadly use.   *Ib*. 34.

Wisdom and goodness to the vile seem vile;
Filths savour but themselves.   *Ib*. 38.

Crown'd with rank fumiter and furrow weeds,
With burdocks, hemlock, nettles, cuckoo-flowers,
Darnel, and all the idle weeds that grow
In our sustaining corn.   *Ib*. iv. 3.

How fearful
And dizzy 'tis to cast one's eyes so low!
The crows and choughs that wing the midway air
Show scarce so gross as beetles; half-way down
Hangs one that gathers samphire, dreadful trade!
Methinks he seems no bigger than his head
The fishermen that walk upon the beach
Appear like mice, and yond tall anchoring bark
Diminish'd to her cock, her cock a buoy
Almost too small for sight. The murmuring surge,
That on the unnumber'd idle pebbles chafes,
Cannot be heard so high.   *Ib*. vi. 12.

          The shrill-gorg'd lark so far
Cannot be seen or heard.   *Ib*. 59.

Think that the clearest gods, who make them honours
Of men's impossibilities, have preserv'd thee.
                                         Ib. 74.

They told me I was every thing; 'tis a lie, I am not
ague-proof.   *Ib*. [107].

GLOUCESTER:
Is't not the king?
LEAR:
                    Ay, every inch a king.
                                         Ib. [110].

The wren goes to 't, and the small gilded fly
Does lecher in my sight.   *Ib*. [115].

Give me an ounce of civet, good apothecary, to
sweeten my imagination.   *Ib*. [133].

A man may see how this world goes with no eyes.
Look with thine ears: see how yond justice rails
upon yond simple thief. Hark, in thine ear: change
places; and, handy-dandy, which is the justice,
which is the thief?   *Ib*. [154].

          Get thee glass eyes;
And, like a scurvy politician, seem
To see the things thou dost not.   *Ib*. [175].

When we are born we cry that we are come
To this great stage of fools.   *Ib*. [187].

Mine enemy's dog,
Though he had bit me, should have stood that night
Against my fire.   *King Lear*, IV. vii. 36.

Thou art a soul in bliss; but I am bound
Upon a wheel of fire, that mine own tears
Do scald like molten lead.   *Ib.* 46.

I am a very foolish, fond old man,
Fourscore and upward, not an hour more or less;
And, to deal plainly,
I fear I am not in my perfect mind.   *Ib.* 60.

For, as I am a man, I think this lady
To be my child Cordelia.   *Ib.* 69.

Pray you now, forget and forgive.   *Ib.* [85].

Men must endure
Their going hence, even as their coming hither:
Ripeness is all.   *Ib.* v. ii. 9.

Come, let's away to prison;
We two alone will sing like birds i' the cage:
When thou dost ask me blessing, I'll kneel down,
And ask of thee forgiveness: and we'll live,
And pray, and sing, and tell old tales, and laugh
At gilded butterflies, and hear poor rogues
Talk of court news; and we'll talk with them too,
Who loses, and who wins; who's in, who's out;
And take upon 's the mystery of things,
As if we were God's spies; and we'll wear out,
In a wall'd prison, packs and sets of great ones
That ebb and flow by the moon.   *Ib.* iii. 8.

Upon such sacrifices, my Cordelia,
The gods themselves throw incense.   *Ib.* 20.

The gods are just, and of our pleasant vices
Make instruments to plague us.   *Ib.* [172].

The wheel has come full circle.   *Ib.* [176].

His flaw'd heart,—
Alack! too weak the conflict to support;
'Twixt two extremes of passion, joy and grief,
Burst smilingly.   *Ib.* [198].

Her voice was ever soft,
Gentle, and low, an excellent thing in woman.
                    Ib. [274].

I have seen the day, with my good biting falchion
I would have made them skip.   *Ib.* [278].

And my poor fool is hang'd! No, no, no life!
Why should a dog, a horse, a rat, have life,
And thou no breath at all? Thou'lt come no more,
Never, never, never, never, never!
Pray you, undo this button.   *Ib.* [307].

Vex not his ghost: O! let him pass; he hates him
That would upon the rack of this tough world
Stretch him out longer.   *Ib.* [314].

The oldest hath borne most: we that are young,
Shall never see so much, nor live so long.   *Ib.* [327].

Let fame, that all hunt after in their lives,
Live register'd upon our brazen tombs.
                    Love's Labour's Lost, I. i. 1.

Spite of cormorant devouring Time.   *Ib.* 4.

Why, all delights are vain; but that most vain,
Which, with pain purchas'd, doth inherit pain.
                    Ib. 72.

Study is like the heaven's glorious sun,
That will not be deep-search'd with saucy looks;
Small have continual plodders ever won,
Save base authority from others' books.   *Ib.* 84.

At Christmas I no more desire a rose
Than wish a snow in May's new-fangled mirth;
But like of each thing that in season grows. *Ib.* 105.

So study evermore is overshot.   *Ib.* [141].

If I break faith, this word shall speak for me,—
I am forsworn 'on mere necessity'.   *Ib.* [152].

A child of our grandmother Eve, a female; or, for
thy more sweet understanding, a woman.
                    Ib. [263].

The world was very guilty of such a ballad some three
ages since; but, I think, now 'tis not to be found.
                    Ib. ii. [117].

Devise, wit! write, pen! for I am for whole volumes
in folio!   *Ib.* [194].

Beauty is bought by judgment of the eye,
Not utter'd by base sale of chapmen's tongues.
                    Ib. II. i. 15.

A merrier man,
Within the limit of becoming mirth,
I never spent an hour's talk withal.   *Ib.* 66.

Your wit's too hot, it speeds too fast, 'twill tire.
                    Ib. [119].

Thy own wish wish I thee in every place! *Ib.* [178].

Warble, child; make passionate my sense of hearing.
                    Ib. III. i. 1.

A very beadle to a humorous sigh.   *Ib.* [185].

This wimpled, whining, purblind, wayward boy,
This senior-junior, giant-dwarf, Dan Cupid;
Regent of love rhymes, lord of folded arms,
The anointed sovereign of sighs and groans,
Liege of all loiterers and malcontents.   *Ib.* [189].

With two pitch balls stuck in her face for eyes.
                    Ib. [207].

Some men must love my lady, and some Joan.
                    Ib. [215].

He hath not fed of the dainties that are bred in a
book; he hath not eat paper, as it were; he hath
not drunk ink.   *Ib.* IV. ii. [25].

These are begot in the ventricle of memory, nourished
in the womb of pia mater, and delivered upon the
mellowing of occasion.   *Ib.* [70].

Old Mantuan! old Mantuan! Who understandeth
thee not, loves thee not.   *Ib.* [102].

The elegancy, facility, and golden cadence of poesy.
                    Ib. [126].

By heaven, I do love, and it hath taught me to rhyme,
and to be melancholy.   *Ib.* iii. [13].

The heavenly rhetoric of thine eye.   *Ib.* [60].

Love, whose month is ever May,
Spied a blossom passing fair,
Playing in the wanton air:
Through the velvet leaves the wind,
All unseen, 'gan passage find;
That the lover, sick to death,
Wish'd himself the heaven's breath.   *Ib.* [102].

Thou for whom e'en Jove would swear
Juno but an Ethiop were;
And deny himself for Jove,
Turning mortal for thy love.
Love's Labour's Lost, IV. iii. [119].

Now step I forth to whip hypocrisy.   *Ib.* [151].

From women's eyes this doctrine I derive:
They are the ground, the books, the academes,
From whence doth spring the true Promethean fire.
Ib. [302].

For where is any author in the world
Teaches such beauty as a woman's eye?
Learning is but an adjunct to ourself.   *Ib.* [312].

But love, first learned in a lady's eyes,
Lives not alone immured in the brain,
But, with the motion of all elements,
Courses as swift as thought in every power,
And gives to every power a double power,
Above their functions and their offices.
It adds a precious seeing to the eye;
A lover's eyes will gaze an eagle blind;
A lover's ears will hear the lowest sound,
When the suspicious head of theft is stopp'd:
Love's feeling is more soft and sensible
Than are the tender horns of cockled snails:
Love's tongue proves dainty Bacchus gross in taste.
For valour, is not love a Hercules,
Still climbing trees in the Hesperides?
Subtle as Sphinx; as sweet and musical
As bright Apollo's lute, strung with his hair;
And when Love speaks, the voice of all the gods
Makes heaven drowsy with the harmony.
Never durst poet touch a pen to write
Until his ink were temper'd with Love's sighs
Ib. [327].

From women's eyes this doctrine I derive:
They sparkle still the right Promethean fire;
They are the books, the arts, the academes,
That show, contain, and nourish all the world.
Ib. [350].

He draweth out the thread of his verbosity finer than
the staple of his argument.   *Ib.* v. i. [18].

Priscian a little scratched; 'twill serve.   *Ib.* [31].

MOTH:
They have been at a great feast of languages, and
stolen the scraps.

COSTARD:
O! they have lived long on the alms-basket of words.
I marvel thy master hath not eaten thee for a
word; for thou art not so long by the head as
honorificabilitudinitatibus: thou art easier swallowed than a flap-dragon.   *Ib.* [39].

In the posteriors of this day; which the rude multitude call the afternoon.   *Ib.* [96].

Had she been light, like you,
Of such a merry, nimble, stirring spirit,
She might ha' been a grandam ere she died;
And so may you; for a light heart lives long.
Ib. ii. 15.

Taffeta phrases, silken terms precise,
Three-pil'd hyperboles, spruce affectation,
Figures pedantical.   *Ib.* 407.

In russet yeas and honest kersey noes.   *Ib.* 414.

When in the world I liv'd, I was the world's com-
mander;
By east, west, north, and south, I spread my conquer-
ing might:
My scutcheon plain declares that I am Alisander.
Ib. [563].

Let me take you a button-hole lower.   *Ib.* [705].

A world-without-end bargain.   *Ib:* [797].

A jest's prosperity lies in the ear
Of him that hears it, never in the tongue
Of him that makes it.   *Ib.* [869].

When daisies pied and violets blue
And lady-smocks all silver-white
And cuckoo-buds of yellow hue
Do paint the meadows with delight,
The cuckoo then, on every tree,
Mocks married men; for thus sings he,
Cuckoo;
Cuckoo, cuckoo; O, word of fear,
Unpleasing to a married ear!   *Ib.* [902].

When icicles hang by the wall,
And Dick, the shepherd, blows his nail,
And Tom bears logs into the hall,
And milk comes frozen home in pail,
When blood is nipp'd and ways be foul,
Then nightly sings the staring owl,
Tu-who;
Tu-whit, tu-who—a merry note,
While greasy Joan doth keel the pot.
When all aloud the wind doth blow,
And coughing drowns the parson's saw;
And birds sit brooding in the snow,
And Marion's nose looks red and raw,
When roasted crabs hiss in the bowl,   *Ib.* [920].

The words of Mercury are harsh after the songs of
Apollo.   *Ib.* [938].

FIRST WITCH:
When shall we three meet again
In thunder, lightning, or in rain?
SECOND WITCH:
When the hurly-burly's done,
When the battle's lost and won.
THIRD WITCH:
That will be ere the set of sun.
FIRST WITCH:
Where the place?
SECOND WITCH:
Upon the heath.
THIRD WITCH:
There to meet with Macbeth.
FIRST WITCH:
I come, Graymalkin!
SECOND WITCH:
Paddock calls.
THIRD WITCH:
Anon!
ALL:
Fair is foul, and foul is fair:
Hover through the fog and filthy air.
Macbeth, I. i. 1.
DUNCAN:
What bloody man is that? . . .
MALCOLM:
This is the sergeant.
Ib. ii. 1.

Disdaining fortune, with his brandish'd steel,
Which smok'd with bloody execution,
Like valour's minion carv'd out his passage.
Macbeth, i. ii. 17.

Memorize another Golgotha. *Ib*. 41.

So well thy words become thee as thy wounds;
They smack of honour both. *Ib*. 44.

Banners flout the sky. *Ib*. 50.

Till that Bellona's bridegroom, lapp'd in proof,
Confronted him with self-comparisons,
Point against point, rebellious arm 'gainst arm,
Curbing his lavish spirit. *Ib*. 55.

A sailor's wife had chestnuts in her lap,
And munch'd, and munch'd, and munch'd: 'Give
me,' quoth I:
'Aroint thee, witch!' the rump-fed ronyon cries.
Her husband's to Aleppo gone, master o' the Tiger:
But in a sieve I'll thither sail,
And, like a rat without a tail,
I'll do, I'll do, and I'll do. *Ib*. iii. 4.

Sleep shall neither night nor day
Hang upon his pent-house lid.
He shall live a man forbid.
Weary se'nnights nine times nine
Shall he dwindle, peak, and pine:
Though his bark cannot be lost,
Yet it shall be tempest-tost. *Ib*. 19.

So foul and fair a day I have not seen. *Ib*. 38.

What are these,
So withered, and so wild in their attire,
That look not like th' inhabitants o' the earth,
And yet are on 't? *Ib*. 39.

You should be women,
And yet your beards forbid me to interpret
That you are so. *Ib*. 45.

If you can look into the seeds of time,
And say which grain will grow and which will not.
Ib. 58.

Stay, you imperfect speakers, tell me more. *Ib*. 70.

The Thane of Cawdor lives,
A prosperous gentleman; and to be king
Stands not within the prospect of belief;
No more than to be Cawdor. Say, from whence
You owe this strange intelligence? or why
Upon this blasted heath you stop our way
With such prophetic greeting? *Ib*. 72.

BANQUO:
The earth hath bubbles, as the water has,
And these are of them.
Were such things here as we do speak about?
Or have we eaten on the insane root
That takes the reason prisoner? *Ib*. 83.

Strange images of death. *Ib*. 97.

What! can the devil speak true? *Ib*. 107.

And oftentimes, to win us to our harm,
The instruments of darkness tell us truths;
Win us with honest trifles, to betray 's
In deepest consequence. *Ib*. 123.

Two truths are told,
As happy prologues to the swelling act
Of the imperial theme. *Ib*. 127.

This supernatural soliciting
Cannot be ill, cannot be good; if ill,
Why hath it given me earnest of success,
Commencing in a truth? I am Thane of Cawdor:
If good, why do I yield to that suggestion
Whose horrid image doth unfix my hair
And make my seated heart knock at my ribs,
Against the use of nature? Present fears
Are less than horrible imaginings;
My thought, whose murder yet is but fantastical,
Shakes so my single state of man that function
Is smother'd in surmise, and nothing is
But what is not. *Ib*. 130.

If chance will have me king, why, chance may crown
me. *Ib*. 143.

Come what come may,
Time and the hour runs through the roughest day.
Ib. 146.

MALCOLM:
Nothing in his life
Became him like the leaving it; he died
As one that had been studied in his death
To throw away the dearest thing he owed
As 'twere a careless trifle.
DUNCAN:
There's no art
To find the mind's construction in the face;
He was a gentleman on whom I built
An absolute trust. *Ib*. iv. 7.

Glamis thou art, and Cawdor; and shalt be
What thou art promis'd. Yet do I fear thy nature;
It is too full o' the milk of human kindness
To catch the nearest way; thou wouldst be great,
Art not without ambition; but without
The illness should attend it; what thou wouldst
highly,
That wouldst thou holily; wouldst not play false,
And yet wouldst wrongly win; thou'dst have, great
Glamis,
That which cries, 'Thus thou must do, if thou have
it';
And that which rather thou dost fear to do
Than wishest should be undone. *Ib*. v. [16].

The golden round,
Which fate and metaphysical aid doth seem
To have thee crown'd withal. *Ib*. [29].

The raven himself is hoarse
That croaks the fatal entrance of Duncan
Under my battlements. Come, you spirits
That tend on mortal thoughts! unsex me here,
And fill me from the crown to the toe top full
Of direst cruelty; make thick my blood,
Stop up the access and passage to remorse,
That no compunctious visitings of nature
Shake my fell purpose, nor keep peace between
The effect and it! Come to my woman's breasts,
And take my milk for gall, you murdering ministers,
Wherever in your sightless substances
You wait on nature's mischief! Come, thick night,
And pall thee in the dunnest smoke of hell,
That my keen knife see not the wound it makes,
Nor heaven peep through the blanket of the dark,
To cry 'Hold, hold!' *Ib*. [38].

Greater than both, by the all-hail hereafter! *Ib*. [56].

Your face, my thane, is as a book where men
May read strange matters. To beguile the time,
Look like the time; bear welcome in your eye,
Your hand, your tongue: look like the innocent
flower,
But be the serpent under 't. *Macbeth*, I. v. [63].

DUNCAN:
This castle hath a pleasant seat; the air
Nimbly and sweetly recommends itself
Unto our gentle senses.

BANQUO:
This guest of summer,
The temple-haunting martlet, does approve
By his lov'd mansionry that the heaven's breath
Smells wooingly here: no jutty, frieze,
Buttress, nor coign of vantage, but this bird
Hath made his pendent bed and procreant cradle:
Where they most breed and haunt, I have observ'd,
The air is delicate. *Ib*. vi. 1.

If it were done when 'tis done, then 'twere well
It were done quickly: if the assassination
Could trammel up the consequence, and catch
With his surcease success; that but this blow
Might be the be-all and the end-all here,
But here, upon this bank and shoal of time,
We'd jump the life to come. *Ib*. vii. 1.

This even-handed justice. *Ib*. 10.

Besides, this Duncan
Hath borne his faculties so meek, hath been
So clear in his great office, that his virtues
Will plead like angels trumpet-tongu'd, against
The deep damnation of his taking-off;
And pity, like a naked new-born babe,
Striding the blast, or heaven's cherubim, hors'd
Upon the sightless couriers of the air,
Shall blow the horrid deed in every eye,
That tears shall drown the wind. I have no spur
To prick the sides of my intent, but only
Vaulting ambition, which o'erleaps itself,
And falls on the other. *Ib*. 16.

We will proceed no further in this business:
He hath honour'd me of late; and I have bought
Golden opinions from all sorts of people. *Ib*. 31.

Was the hope drunk,
Wherein you dress'd yourself? hath it slept since,
And wakes it now, to look so green and pale
At what it did so freely? From this time
Such I account thy love. Art thou afeard
To be the same in thine own act and valour
As thou art in desire? Wouldst thou have that
Which thou esteem'st the ornament of life,
And live a coward in thine own esteem,
Letting 'I dare not' wait upon 'I would,'
Like the poor cat i' the adage. *Ib*. 35.

I dare do all that may become a man;
Who dares do more is none. *Ib*. 46.

LADY MACBETH:
I have given suck, and know
How tender 'tis to love the babe that milks me:
I would, while it was smiling in my face,
Have pluck'd my nipple from his boneless gums,
And dash'd the brains out, had I so sworn as you
Have done to this.

MACBETH:
If we should fail,—

LADY MACBETH:
We fail!
But screw your courage to the sticking-place,
And we'll not fail. *Ib*. 54.

That memory, the warder of the brain,
Shall be a fume. *Ib*. 65.

Bring forth men-children only;
For thy undaunted mettle should compose
Nothing but males. *Ib*. 72.

Away, and mock the time with fairest show:
False face must hide what the false heart doth know.
Ib. 81.

There's husbandry in heaven;
Their candles are all out. *Ib*. II. i. 4.

Merciful powers!
Restrain in me the cursed thoughts that nature
Gives way to in repose. *Ib*. 7.

Shut up
In measureless content. *Ib*. 16.

Is this a dagger which I see before me,
The handle toward my hand? Come, let me clutch
thee:
I have thee not, and yet I see thee still.
Art thou not, fatal vision, sensible
To feeling as to sight? or art thou but
A dagger of the mind, a false creation,
Proceeding from the heat-oppressèd brain? *Ib*. 33.

Now o'er the one half-world
Nature seems dead, and wicked dreams abuse
The curtain'd sleep; witchcraft celebrates
Pale Hecate's offerings; and wither'd murder,
Alarum'd by his sentinel, the wolf,
Whose howl's his watch, thus with his stealthy pace,
With Tarquin's ravishing strides, towards his design
Moves like a ghost. Thou sure and firm-set earth,
Hear not my steps, which way they walk, for fear
The very stones prate of my whereabout,
And take the present horror from the time,
Which now suits with it. Whiles I threat he lives:
Words to the heat of deeds too cold breath gives.
I go, and it is done; the bell invites me.
Hear it not, Duncan; for it is a knell
That summons thee to heaven or to hell.
Ib. 49.

That which hath made them drunk hath made me
bold,
What hath quench'd them hath given me fire.
Ib. ii. 1.

It was the owl that shriek'd, the fatal bellman,
Which gives the stern'st good-night. *Ib*. 4.

The attempt and not the deed,
Confounds us. *Ib*. 12.

Had he not resembled
My father as he slept I had done 't. *Ib*. 14.

I have done the deed. Didst thou not hear a noise?
Ib. 16.

As they had seen me with these hangman's hands.
Ib. 29.

Consider it not so deeply. *Ib*. 31.

I had most need of blessing, and 'Amen'
Stuck in my throat. *Ib*. 33.

These deeds must not be thought
After these ways; so, it will make us mad.
Macbeth, II. ii. 34.

Methought I heard a voice cry, 'Sleep no more!
Macbeth does murder sleep,' the innocent sleep,
Sleep that knits up the ravell'd sleave of care,
The death of each day's life, sore labour's bath,
Balm of hurt minds, great nature's second course,
Chief nourisher in life's feast. *Ib*. 36.

Glamis hath murder'd sleep, and therefore Cawdor
Shall sleep no more, Macbeth shall sleep no more!
Ib. 43.

You do unbend your noble strength to think
So brainsickly of things. *Ib*. 46.

MACBETH:
I am afraid to think what I have done;
Look on 't again I dare not.
LADY MACBETH:
　　　　　　　　Infirm of purpose!
Give me the daggers. The sleeping and the dead
Are but as pictures; 'tis the eye of childhood
That fears a painted devil. *Ib*. 52.

Will all great Neptune's ocean wash this blood
Clean from my hand? No, this my hand will rather
The multitudinous seas incarnadine,
Making the green one red. *Ib*. 61.

Here's a farmer that hanged himself on the expectation of plenty. *Ib*. iii. [5].

Faith, here's an equivocator. *Ib*. [9].

The primrose way to the everlasting bonfire.
Ib. [22].

The labour we delight in physics pain. *Ib*. [56].

The night has been unruly: where we lay
Our chimneys were blown down; and, as they say,
Lamentings heard i' the air; strange screams of
death,
And prophesying with accents terrible
Of dire combustion and confus'd events
New-hatch'd to the woeful time. The obscure bird
Clamour'd the live-long night: some say the earth
Was feverous and did shake. *Ib*. [60].

Confusion now hath made his masterpiece!
Most sacrilegious murder hath broke ope
The Lord's anointed temple, and stole thence
The life o' the building! *Ib*. [72].

Shake off this downy sleep, death's counterfeit,
And look on death itself! up, up, and see
The great doom's image! *Ib*. [83].

Had I but died an hour before this chance,
I had liv'd a blessed time; for, from this instant,
There's nothing serious in mortality:
All is but toys; renown, and grace is dead,
The wine of life is drawn, and the mere lees
Is left this vault to brag of. *Ib*. [98].

Who can be wise, amazed, temperate, and furious,
Loyal and neutral, in a moment? No man.
Ib. [115].

In the great hand of God I stand, and thence
Against the undivulg'd pretence I fight
Of treasonous malice. *Ib*. [137].

There's daggers in men's smiles. *Ib*. [147].

A falcon, towering in her pride of place,
Was by a mousing owl hawk'd at and kill'd.
Ib. iv. 12.

Thriftless ambition, that wilt ravin up
Thine own life's means! *Ib*. 28.

Thou hast it now: King, Cawdor, Glamis, all,
As the weird women promis'd; and, I fear,
Thou play'dst most foully for 't; yet it was said
It should not stand in thy posterity,
But that myself should be the root and father
Of many kings. *Ib*. III. i. 1.

I must become a borrower of the night
For a dark hour or twain. *Ib*. 27.

　　　　　　　　　To be thus is nothing;
But to be safely thus. *Ib*. 48.

　　　　　　　　There is none but he
Whose being I do fear; and, under him
My genius is rebuk'd: as, it is said,
Mark Antony's was by Cæsar. *Ib*. 54.

　　　　　　　　Mine eternal jewel
Given to the common enemy of man. *Ib*. 68.

FIRST MURDERER:
　　　　　　　　We are men, my liege.
MACBETH:
Ay, in the catalogue ye go for men. *Ib*. 91.

FIRST MURDERER:
　　　　　　　　　I am one, my liege,
Whom the vile blows and buffets of the world
Have so incens'd, that I am reckless what
I do to spite the world.
SECOND MURDERER:
　　　　　　　　I another,
So weary with disasters, tugg'd with fortune,
That I would set my life on any chance,
To mend it or be rid on 't. *Ib*. 108.

Leave no rubs nor botches in the work. *Ib*. 134.

　　　　　　　　Thy soul's flight,
If it find heaven, must find it out to-night. *Ib*. 141.

　　　　　　Naught's had, all's spent,
Where our desire is got without content:
'Tis safer to be that which we destroy,
Than, by destruction, dwell in doubtful joy.
Ib. ii. 4.

LADY MACBETH:
　　　　　　　　Things without all remedy
Should be without regard: what's done is done.
MACBETH:
We have scotch'd[1] the snake, not killed it:
She'll close and be herself, whilst our poor malice
Remains in danger of her former tooth
But let the frame of things disjoint, both the worlds
suffer,
Ere we will eat our meal in fear, and sleep
In the affliction of these terrible dreams
That shake us nightly. Better be with the dead,
Whom we, to gain our peace, have sent to peace,
Than on the torture of the mind to lie
In restless ecstasy. Duncan is in his grave;
After life's fitful fever he sleeps well;
Treason has done his worst: nor steel, nor poison,
Malice domestic, foreign levy, nothing,
Can touch him further. *Ib*. 11.

---

[1] Theobald's emendation of First Folio 'scorched'.

a

Make our faces vizards to our hearts,
Disguising what they are.   *Macbeth*, III. ii. 34.

But in them nature's copy's not eterne.   *Ib.* 38.

A deed of dreadful note.   *Ib.* 44.

Be innocent of the knowledge, dearest chuck,
Till thou applaud the deed. Come, seeling night,
Scarf up the tender eye of pitiful day,
And with thy bloody and invisible hand,
Cancel and tear to pieces that great bond
Which keeps me pale! Light thickens, and the crow
Makes wing to the rooky wood;
Good things of the day begin to droop and drowse,
Whiles night's black agents to their preys do rouse.
        Ib. 45.

Things bad begun make strong themselves by ill.
        Ib. 55.

Now spurs the lated traveller apace
To gain the timely inn.   *Ib.* iii. 6.

Ourself will mingle with society
And play the humble host.   *Ib.* iv. 3.

But now I am cabin'd, cribb'd, confin'd, bound in
To saucy doubts and fears.   *Ib.* 24.

Now good digestion wait on appetite,
And health on both!   *Ib.* 38.

Which of you have done this?   *Ib.* 49.

Thou canst not say I did it: never shake
Thy gory locks at me.   *Ib.* 50.

The air-drawn dagger.   *Ib.* 62.

        The times have been,
That, when the brains were out, the man would die,
And there an end; but now they rise again,
With twenty mortal murders on their crowns,
And push us from our stools: this is more strange
Than such a murder is.   *Ib.* 78.

I drink to the general joy of the whole table.
        Ib. 89.

Thy bones are marrowless, thy blood is cold;
Thou hast no speculation in those eyes
Which thou dost glare with.   *Ib.* 94.

Take any shape but that, and my firm nerves
Shall never tremble.   *Ib.* 102.

                Hence, horrible shadow!
Unreal mockery, hence!   *Ib.* 106.

LADY MACBETH:
You have displaced the mirth, broke the good
        meeting,
With most admir'd disorder.

MACBETH:
                Can such things be,
And overcome us like a summer's cloud,
Without our special wonder?   *Ib.* 109.

Stand not upon the order of your going,
But go at once.   *Ib.* 119.

MACBETH:
It will have blood, they say; blood will have blood:
Stones have been known to move and trees to speak;
Augurs and understood relations have
By maggot-pies and choughs and rooks brought forth
The secret'st man of blood. What is the night?

b

LADY MACBETH:
Almost at odds with morning, which is which.
        Ib. 122.

        I am in blood
Stepp'd in so far that, should I wade no more,
Returning were as tedious as go o'er.   *Ib.* 136.

You lack the season of all natures, sleep.   *Ib.* 141.

Upon the corner of the moon
There hangs a vaporous drop profound;
I'll catch it ere it come to ground.   *Ib.* v. 23.

And you all know, security
Is mortals' chiefest enemy.   *Ib.* 32.

Round about the cauldron go;
In the poison'd entrails throw.   *Ib.* IV. i. 4.

Double, double toil and trouble;
Fire burn, and cauldron bubble.   *Ib.* 10.

Eye of newt and toe of frog,
Wool of bat and tongue of dog.   *Ib.* 14.

        Slips of yew
Sliver'd in the moon's eclipse.   *Ib.* 27.

Finger of birth-strangled babe,
Ditch-deliver'd by a drab,
Make the gruel thick and slab.   *Ib.* 30.

Black spirits and white,
    Red spirits and grey,
Mingle, mingle, mingle,
    You that mingle may.[1]   *Ib.* 44. *Stage direction.*

By the pricking of my thumbs,
Something wicked this way comes.
        Open, locks,
        Whoever knocks.   *Ib.* 44.

How now, you secret, black, and midnight hags!
        Ib. 48.

A deed without a name.   *Ib.* 49.

Though you untie the winds and let them fight
Against the churches; though the yesty waves
Confound and swallow navigation up.   *Ib.* 52.

Be bloody, bold, and resolute; laugh to scorn
The power of man, for none of woman born
Shall harm Macbeth.   *Ib.* 79.

But yet I'll make assurance double sure,
And take a bond of fate.   *Ib.* 83.

That I may tell pale-hearted fear it lies,
And sleep in spite of thunder.   *Ib.* 85.

        Wears upon his baby brow the round
And top of sovereignty.   *Ib.* 88.

        Take no care
Who chafes, who frets, or where conspirers are:
Macbeth shall never vanquish'd be until
Great Birnam wood to high Dunsinane hill
Shall come against him.   *Ib.* 90.

Show his eyes, and grieve his heart;
Come like shadows, so depart!   *Ib.* 110.

What! will the line stretch out to the crack of doom?
        Ib. 117.

For the blood-bolter'd Banquo smiles upon me.
        Ib. 123.

        [1] Davenant's version of *Macbeth.*

The weird sisters.　　　　　*Macbeth*, IV. i. 136.

The flighty purpose never is o'ertook,
Unless the deed go with it.　　　　　*Ib.* 145.

The very firstlings of my heart shall be
The firstlings of my hand.　　　　　*Ib.* 147.

His flight was madness: when our actions do not,
Our fears do make us traitors.　　　　　*Ib.* ii. 3.

He wants the natural touch; for the poor wren,
The most diminutive of birds, will fight—
Her young ones in her nest—against the owl.
　　　　　Ib. 9.

Angels are bright still, though the brightest fell.
　　　　　Ib. iii. 22.

MACDUFF:
Stands Scotland where it did?
ROSS:
　　　　　　　　　Alas! poor country;
Almost afraid to know itself. It cannot
Be call'd our mother, but our grave.　　*Ib.* 164.

What! man; ne'er pull your hat upon your brows;
Give sorrow words: the grief that does not speak
Whispers the o'erfraught heart, and bids it break.
　　　　　Ib. 208.

　　　　　　All my pretty ones?
Did you say all? O hell-kite! All?
What! all my pretty chickens and their dam,
At one fell swoop?　　　　　*Ib.* 216.

MALCOLM:
Dispute it like a man.
MACDUFF:
　　　　　　　　I shall do so;
But I must also feel it as a man;
I cannot but remember such things were,
That were most precious to me.　　*Ib.* 219.

DOCTOR:
You see her eyes are open.
GENTLEWOMAN:
Ay, but their sense is shut.　　　*Ib.* v. i. [27].

Out, damned spot! out, I say! One; two: why then,
'tis time to do't. Hell is murky! Fie, my lord, fie!
a soldier, and afeard? What need we fear who
knows it, when none can call our power to
account? Yet who would have thought the old
man had so much blood in him?　　*Ib.* [38].

The Thane of Fife had a wife: where is she now?
What! will these hands ne'er be clean?　*Ib.* [46].

She has spoke what she should not, I am sure of
that: Heaven knows what she has known.
　　　　　Ib. [52].

All the perfumes of Arabia will not sweeten this
little hand.　　　　　*Ib.* [56].

I would not have such a heart in my bosom for the
dignity of the whole body.　　　　*Ib.* [60].

Foul whisperings are abroad.　　　*Ib.* [78].

More needs she the divine than the physician.
　　　　　Ib. [81].

Those he commands move only in command,
Nothing in love; now does he feel his title
Hang loose about him, like a giant's robe
Upon a dwarfish thief.　　　　　*Ib.* ii. 19.

All that is within him does condemn
Itself for being there.　　　　　*Ib.* 24.

Bring me no more reports; let them fly all:
Till Birnam wood remove to Dunsinane
I cannot taint with fear.　　　　*Ib.* iii. 1.

　　　　The spirits that know
All mortal consequences have pronounc'd me thus.
　　　　　Ib. 4.

The devil damn thee black, thou cream-faced loon!
Where gott'st thou that goose look?　　*Ib.* 11.

　　　　　This push
Will cheer me ever or dis-seat me now.
I have lived long enough: my way of life
Is fall'n into the sear, the yellow leaf;
And that which should accompany old age,
As honour, love, obedience, troops of friends,
I must not look to have; but in their stead,
Curses, not loud but deep, mouth-honour, breath,
Which the poor heart would fain deny, and dare not.
　　　　　Ib. 20.

DOCTOR:
　　　　　Not so sick, my lord,
As she is troubled with thick-coming fancies,
That keep her from her rest.
MACBETH:
　　　　　Cure her of that:
Canst thou not minister to a mind diseas'd,
Pluck from the memory a rooted sorrow,
Raze out the written troubles of the brain,
And with some sweet oblivious antidote
Cleanse the stuff'd bosom of that perilous stuff
Which weighs upon the heart?
DOCTOR:
　　　　　Therein the patient
Must minister to himself.
MACBETH:
Throw physic to the dogs; I'll none of it.　*Ib.* 37.

　　　If thou couldst, doctor, cast
The water of my land, find her disease,
And purge it to a sound and pristine health,
I would applaud thee to the very echo,
That should applaud again.　　　　*Ib.* 50.

Hang out our banners on the outward walls;
The cry is still, 'They come'; Our castle's strength
Will laugh a siege to scorn.　　　*Ib.* v. 1.

I have almost forgot the taste of fears.
The time has been my senses would have cool'd
To hear a night-shriek, and my fell of hair
Would at a dismal treatise rouse and stir
As life were in 't. I have supp'd full with horrors;
Direness, familiar to my slaughterous thoughts,
Cannot once start me.　　　　　*Ib.* 9.

SEYTON:
The queen, my lord, is dead.
MACBETH
She should have died hereafter;
There would have been a time for such a word.
To-morrow, and to-morrow, and to-morrow,
Creeps in this petty pace from day to day,
To the last syllable of recorded time;
And all our yesterdays have lighted fools
The way to dusty death. Out, out, brief candle!
Life's but a walking shadow, a poor player,
That struts and frets his hour upon the stage,
And then is heard no more; it is a tale
Told by an idiot, full of sound and fury,
Signifying nothing.　　　　　*Ib.* 16.

I pull in resolution, and begin
To doubt the equivocation of the fiend
That lies like truth: 'Fear not, till Birnam wood
Do come to Dunsinane.'   *Macbeth*, V. V. 42.

I 'gin to be aweary of the sun,
And wish the estate o' the world were now undone.
                    Ib. 49.

       Blow, wind! come, wrack!
At least we'll die with harness on our back.   *Ib.* 51.

Those clamorous harbingers of blood and death.
                    Ib. vi. 10.

They have tied me to a stake; I cannot fly.
But bear-like I must fight the course.   *Ib.* vii. 1.

Why should I play the Roman fool, and die
On mine own sword?   *Ib.* 30.

I bear a charmed life.   *Ib.* 41.

And let the angel whom thou still hast served
Tell thee, Macduff was from his mother's womb
Untimely ripp'd.   *Ib.* 43.

And be these juggling fiends no more believ'd,
That palter with us with a double sense;
That keep the word of promise to our ear,
And break it to our hope.   *Ib.* 48.

Live to be the show and gaze o' the time.   *Ib.* 53.

        Lay on, Macduff;
And damn'd be he that first cries, 'Hold, enough!'
                    Ib. 62.

SIWARD:
       Had he his hurts before?
ROSS:
Ay, on the front.
SIWARD:
       Why, then, God's soldier be he!
Had I as many sons as I have hairs,
I would not wish them to a fairer death.   *Ib.* 75.

        For if our virtues
Did not go forth of us, 'twere all alike
As if we had them not. Spirits are not finely touch'd
But to fine issues.   *Measure for Measure*, I. i. 33.

The sanctimonious pirate, that went to sea with the
    Ten Commandments, but scraped one out of the
    table.   *Ib.* ii. [7].

And liberty plucks justice by the nose.   *Ib.* iii. 29.

I hold you as a thing ensky'd and sainted. *Ib.* iv. 34.

       A man whose blood
Is very snow-broth; one who never feels
The wanton stings and motions of the sense.
                    Ib. 57.

       Our doubts are traitors,
And make us lose the good we oft might win,
By fearing to attempt.   *Ib.* 77.

We must not make a scarecrow of the law,
Setting it up to fear the birds of prey,
And let it keep one shape, till custom make it
Their perch and not their terror.   *Ib.* II. i. 1.

'Tis one thing to be tempted, Escalus,
Another thing to fall. I not deny,
The jury, passing on the prisoner's life,
May in the sworn twelve have a thief or two
Guiltier than him they try.   *Ib.* 17.

Some rise by sin, and some by virtue fall.   *Ib.* 38.

This will last out a night in Russia,
When nights are longest there.   *Ib.* [144].

       I am
At war 'twixt will and will not.   *Ib.* ii. 32.

Condemn the fault and not the actor of it? *Ib.* 37.

No ceremony that to great ones 'longs,
Not the king's crown, nor the deputed sword,
The marshal's truncheon, nor the judge's robe,
Become them with one half so good a grace
As mercy does.   *Ib.* 59.

Why, all the souls that were were forfeit once;
And He that might the vantage best have took,
Found out the remedy. How would you be,
If He, which is the top of judgment, should
But judge you as you are?   *Ib.* 73.

        O! it is excellent
To have a giant's strength, but it is tyrannous
To use it like a giant.   *Ib.* 107.

Merciful Heaven!
Thou rather with thy sharp and sulphurous bolt
Split'st the unwedgeable and gnarled oak
Than the soft myrtle; but man, proud man,
Drest in a little brief authority,
Most ignorant of what he's most assur'd,
His glassy essence, like an angry ape,
Plays such fantastic tricks before high heaven,
As make the angels weep.   *Ib.* 114.

Great men may jest with saints; 'tis wit in them,
But, in the less foul profanation.   *Ib.* 127.

That in the captain's but a choleric word,
Which in the soldier is flat blasphemy.   *Ib.* 130.

      I am that way going to temptation,
Where prayers cross.   *Ib.* 158.

Having waste ground enough,
Shall we desire to raze the sanctuary
And pitch our evils there?   *Ib.* 170.

O cunning enemy, that, to catch a saint,
With saints dost bait thy hook! Most dangerous
Is that temptation that doth goad us on
To sin in loving virtue.   *Ib.* 180.

When I would pray and think, I think and pray
To several subjects: Heaven hath my empty words.
                    Ib. iv. 1.

CLAUDIO:
The miserable have no other medicine
But only hope:
I have hope to live, and am prepar'd to die.
DUKE:
Be absolute for death; either death or life
Shall thereby be the sweeter. Reason thus with life:
If I do lose thee, I do lose a thing
That none but fools would keep: a breath thou art
Servile to all the skyey influences.   *Ib.* III. i. 2.

       If thou art rich, thou'rt poor;
For, like an ass whose back with ingots bows,
Thou bear'st thy heavy riches but a journey,
And death unloads thee.   *Ib.* 25.

       Thou hast nor youth nor age;
But, as it were, an after-dinner's sleep,
Dreaming on both.   *Ib.* 32.

Palsied eld.　　　　*Measure for Measure*, III. i. 35.

　　　　　　Dar'st thou die?
The sense of death is most in apprehension,
And the poor beetle, that we tread upon,
In corporal sufferance finds a pang as great
As when a giant dies.　　　　　　*Ib.* 75.

　　　　　　If I must die,
I will encounter darkness as a bride,
And hug it in mine arms.　　　　*Ib.* 81.

The cunning livery of hell.　　　*Ib.* 93.

CLAUDIO:
　　　　　Death is a fearful thing.
ISABELLA:
And shamed life a hateful.
CLAUDIO:
Ay, but to die, and go we know not where;
To lie in cold obstruction and to rot;
This sensible warm motion to become
A kneaded clod; and the delighted spirit
To bathe in fiery floods, or to reside
In thrilling region of thick-ribbèd ice;
To be imprisoned in the viewless winds,
And blown with restless violence round about
The pendent world!　　　　　　*Ib.* 114.

The weariest and most loathèd worldly life
That age, ache, penury, and imprisonment
Can lay on nature, is a paradise
To what we fear of death.　　　　*Ib.* 127.

　　　　　O, fie, fie, fie!
Thy sin's not accidental, but a trade.　　*Ib.* 146.

The hand that made you fair hath made you good.
　　　　　　　　　　　　　Ib. [182].

Virtue is bold, and goodness never fearful.
　　　　　　　　　　　　　Ib. [214].

There, at the moated grange, resides this dejected
　Mariana.　　　　　　　　　*Ib.* [279].

A very superficial, ignorant, unweighing fellow.
　　　　　　　　　　　　Ib. ii. [151].

Take, O take those lips away,
　That so sweetly were forsworn;
And those eyes, the break of day,
　Lights that do mislead the morn:
But my kisses bring again, bring again;
Seals of love, but seal'd in vain, seal'd in vain.
　　　　　　　　　　　　Ib. IV. i. 1.

　Though music oft hath such a charm
To make bad good, and good provoke to harm.
　　　　　　　　　　　　　Ib. 16.

He will discredit our mystery.　　*Ib.* ii. [29].

Every true man's apparel fits your thief.　*Ib.* [46].

Look, here's the warrant, Claudio, for thy death:
'Tis now dead midnight, and by eight to-morrow
Thou must be made immortal.　　*Ib.* [66].

A man that apprehends death no more dreadfully
　but as a drunken sleep.　　　　*Ib.* [148].

Look, the unfolding star calls up the shepherd.
　　　　　　　　　　　　　Ib. [219].

I am a kind of burr; I shall stick.　*Ib.* iii. [193].

A forted residence 'gainst the tooth of time,
And razure of oblivion.　　　　*Ib.* v. i. 12.

　　　　　Let the devil
Be sometime honour'd for his burning throne.
　　　　　　　　　　　　　Ib. [289].

Haste still pays haste, and leisure answers leisure;
Like doth quit like, and Measure still for Measure.
　　　　　　　　　　　　　Ib. [411].

They say best men are moulded out of faults,
And, for the most, become much more the better
For being a little bad.　　　　*Ib.* [440].

In sooth I know not why I am so sad:
It wearies me; you say it wearies you;
But how I caught it, found it, or came by it,
What stuff 'tis made of, whereof it is born,
I am to learn.　　*The Merchant of Venice*, I. i. 1.

There, where your argosies with portly sail,—
Like signiors and rich burghers on the flood,
Or, as it were, the pageants of the sea,—
Do overpeer the petty traffickers.　　*Ib.* 9.

Nature hath fram'd strange fellows in her time:
Some that will evermore peep through their eyes
And laugh like parrots at a bagpiper:
And other of such vinegar aspect
That they'll not show their teeth in way of smile,
Though Nestor swear the jest be laughable.　*Ib.* 51.

I hold the world but as the world, Gratiano;
A stage where every man must play a part,
And mine a sad one.　　　　　*Ib.* 77.

Why should a man, whose blood is warm within,
Sit like his grandsire cut in alabaster?　*Ib.* 83.

There are a sort of men whose visages
Do cream and mantle like a standing pond.　*Ib.* 88.

As who should say, 'I am Sir Oracle,
And when I ope my lips let no dog bark!'
O, my Antonio, I do know of these,
That therefore only are reputed wise,
For saying nothing.　　　　　*Ib.* 93.

　　　Fish not, with this melancholy bait,
For this fool gudgeon, this opinion.　*Ib.* 101.

　　　Silence is only commendable
In a neat's tongue dried and a maid not vendible.
　　　　　　　　　　　　　Ib. 111.

Gratiano speaks an infinite deal of nothing, more
than any man in all Venice. His reasons are as
two grains of wheat, hid in two bushels of chaff:
you shall seek all day ere you find them; and
when you have found them, they are not worth
the search.　　　　　　　　*Ib.* 114.

My purse, my person, my extremest means
Lie all unlock'd to your occasion.　*Ib.* [139].

　　　Sometimes from her eyes
I did receive fair speechless messages.　*Ib.* [164].

By my troth, Nerissa, my little body is aweary of
this great world.　　　　　*Ib.* ii. 1

They are as sick that surfeit with too much, as they
that starve with nothing.　　　*Ib.* [5]

Superfluity comes sooner by white hairs, but compe-
tency lives longer.　　　　　*Ib.* [9]

If to do were as easy as to know what were good to
do, chapels had been churches, and poor men'
cottages princes' palaces.　　　*Ib.* [13]

It is a good divine that follows his own instructions;
I can easier teach twenty what were good to be
done, than be one of the twenty to follow mine
own teaching. *The Merchant of Venice*, i. ii. [15].

He doth nothing but talk of his horse. *Ib.* [43].

God made him, and therefore let him pass for a man.
Ib. [59].

If I should marry him, I should marry twenty
husbands. *Ib.* [66].

I think he bought his doublet in Italy, his round hose
in France, his bonnet in Germany, and his
behaviour everywhere. *Ib.* [78].

I will do anything, Nerissa, ere I will be married to
a sponge. *Ib.* [105].

I dote on his very absence. *Ib.* [118].

Ships are but boards, sailors but men; there be land-
rats and water-rats, land-thieves and water-thieves.
Ib. iii. [22].

I will buy with you, sell with you, talk with you,
walk with you, and so following; but I will not
eat with you, drink with you, nor pray with you.
What news on the Rialto? *Ib.* [36].

How like a fawning publican he looks!
I hate him for he is a Christian;
But more for that in low simplicity
He lends out money gratis, and brings down
The rate of usance here with us in Venice.
If I can catch him once upon the hip,
I will feed fat the ancient grudge I bear him.
He hates our sacred nation, and he rails,
Even there where merchants most do congregate,
On me, my bargains, and my well-won thrift.
Ib. [42].

The devil can cite Scripture for his purpose.
Ib. [99].

A goodly apple rotten at the heart.
O, what a goodly outside falsehood hath! *Ib.* [102].

Signior Antonio, many a time and oft
In the Rialto you have rated me. *Ib.* [107].

For sufferance is the badge of all our tribe.
Ib. [111].

'Hath a dog money? Is it possible
A cur can lend three thousand ducats?' or
Shall I bend low, and in a bondman's key,
With bated breath, and whispering humbleness,
Say this:—
'Fair sir, you spet on me on Wednesday last;
You spurn'd me such a day; another time
You call'd me dog; and for these courtesies
I'll lend you thus much moneys?' *Ib.* [122].

For when did friendship take
A breed for barren metal of his friend? *Ib.* [134].

O father Abram! what these Christians are,
Whose own hard dealing teaches them suspect
The thoughts of others! *Ib.* [161].

I like not fair terms and a villain's mind. *Ib.* [180].

Mislike me not for my complexion,
The shadow'd livery of the burnished sun.
Ib. II. i. 1.

An honest man's son,—or rather an honest woman's
son;—for, indeed, my father did something smack,
something grow to, he had a kind of taste;—
well, my conscience says, 'Launcelot, budge not.'
'Budge,' says the fiend. 'Budge not,' says my
conscience. 'Conscience,' say I, 'you counsel
well;' 'fiend,' say I, 'you counsel well.' *Ib.* ii. [16].

O heavens! this is my true-begotten father. *Ib.* [36].

An honest exceeding poor man. *Ib.* [54].

The very staff of my age, my very prop. *Ib.* [71].

It is a wise father that knows his own child.
Ib. [83].

Truth will come to light; murder cannot be hid long.
Ib. [86].

Lord worshipped might he be! What a beard hast
thou got! *Ib.* [101].

There is some ill a-brewing towards my rest,
For I did dream of money-bags to-night. *Ib.* v. 17.

Then it was not for nothing that my nose fell a-
bleeding on Black Monday. *Ib.* [24].

And the vile squealing of the wry-neck'd fife.
Ib. [30].

But love is blind, and lovers cannot see
The pretty follies that themselves commit.
Ib. vi. 36.

What! must I hold a candle to my shames? *Ib.* 41.

> Men that hazard all
Do it in hope of fair advantages:
A golden mind stoops not to shows of dross.
Ib. vii. 18.

Pause there, Morocco. *Ib.* 24.

Young in limbs, in judgment old. *Ib.* 71.

My daughter! O my ducats! O my daughter!
Fled with a Christian! O my Christian ducats!
Ib. viii. 15.

The fool multitude, that choose by show. *Ib.* ix. 26.

> Like the martlet,
Builds in the weather on the outward wall,
Even in the force and road of casualty.
I will not choose what many men desire,
Because I will not jump with common spirits
And rank me with the barbarous multitude.
Ib. 28.

> Let none presume
To wear an undeserved dignity.
O! that estates, degrees, and offices
Were not deriv'd corruptly, and that clear honour
Were purchased by the merit of the wearer! *Ib.* 39.

The fire seven times tried this:
Seven times tried that judgment is
That did never choose amiss.
Some there be that shadows kiss;
Such have but a shadow's bliss. *Ib.* 63.

Thus hath the candle sing'd the moth.
O, these deliberate fools! *Ib.* 79.

The ancient saying is no heresy:
'Hanging and wiving goes by destiny.' *Ib.* 82.

The Goodwins, I think they call the place; a very dangerous flat, and fatal, where the carcasses of many a tall ship lie buried, as they say, if my gossip Report be an honest woman of her word.
The Merchant of Venice, III. i. [4].

Let him look to his bond.   *Ib.* [51, 52, 54].

Hath not a Jew eyes? hath not a Jew hands, organs, dimensions, senses, affections, passions? fed with the same food, hurt with the same weapons, subject to the same diseases, healed by the same means, warmed and cooled by the same winter and summer, as a Christian is? If you prick us, do we not bleed? if you tickle us, do we not laugh? if you poison us, do we not die? and if you wrong us, shall we not revenge?   *Ib.* [63].

The villany you teach me I will execute, and it shall go hard but I will better the instruction.
Ib. [76].

Thou stick'st a dagger in me.   *Ib.* [118].

TUBAL:
One of them showed me a ring that he had of your daughter for a monkey.
SHYLOCK:
I would not have given it for a wilderness of monkeys.   *Ib.* [126].

He makes a swan-like end
Fading in music.   *Ib.* III. ii. 44.

   Tell me where is fancy bred,
  Or in the heart or in the head?
  How begot, how nourished?
    Reply, reply.

  It is engender'd in the eyes,
  With gazing fed; and fancy dies
  In the cradle where it lies.
   Let us all ring fancy's knell:
   I'll begin it,—Ding, dong, bell.
        Ib. 63.

So may the outward shows be least themselves:
The world is still deceived with ornament.
In law, what plea so tainted and corrupt
But, being season'd with a gracious voice,
Obscures the show of evil? In religion,
What damned error, but some sober brow
Will bless it and approve it with a text,
Hiding the grossness with fair ornament?   *Ib.* 73.

  Ornament is but the guiled shore
To a most dangerous sea; the beauteous scarf
Veiling an Indian beauty; in a word,
The seeming truth which cunning times put on
To entrap the wisest.   *Ib.* 97.

   Thou pale and common drudge
'Tween man and man.   *Ib.* 103.

  Rash-embrac'd despair,
And shuddering fear, and green-ey'd jealousy.
        Ib. 109.

   What demi-god
Hath come so near creation?   *Ib.* 115.

 An unlesson'd girl, unschool'd, unpractis'd;
Happy in this, she is not yet so old
But she may learn; happier than this,
She is not bred so dull but she can learn.   *Ib.* 160.

I wish you all the joy that you can wish.   *Ib.* 191.

My eyes, my lord, can look as swift as yours:
You saw the mistress, I beheld the maid.   *Ib.* 198.

Here are a few of the unpleasant'st words
That ever blotted paper!   *Ib.* 252.

I will have my bond.   *Ib.* iii. 17.

This comes too near the praising of myself.
Ib. iv. 22.

How every fool can play upon the word!
Ib. v. [48].

Wilt thou show the whole wealth of thy wit in an instant? I pray thee, understand a plain man in his plain meaning.   *Ib.* [62].

    I'll not answer that:
But say it is my humour.   *Ib.* IV. i. 42.

A harmless necessary cat.   *Ib.* 55.

I am not bound to please thee with my answer.
Ib. 65.

What judgment shall I dread, doing no wrong?
Ib. 89.

I am a tainted wether of the flock,
Meetest for death: the weakest kind of fruit
Drops earliest to the ground.   *Ib.* 114.

I never knew so young a body with so old a head.
Ib. [163].

PORTIA:
   Then must the Jew be merciful.
SHYLOCK:
On what compulsion must I? tell me that.
PORTIA:
The quality of mercy is not strain'd,
It droppeth as the gentle rain from heaven
Upon the place beneath: it is twice bless'd;
It blesseth him that gives and him that takes:
'Tis mightiest in the mightiest: it becomes
The throned monarch better than his crown;
His sceptre shows the force of temporal power,
The attribute to awe and majesty,
Wherein doth sit the dread and fear of kings;
But mercy is above this sceptred sway,
It is enthroned in the hearts of kings,
It is an attribute to God himself,
And earthly power doth then show likest God's
When mercy seasons justice. Therefore, Jew,
Though justice be thy plea, consider this,
That in the course of justice none of us
Should see salvation: we do pray for mercy,
And that same prayer doth teach us all to render
The deeds of mercy.   *Ib.* [182].

My deeds upon my head! I crave the law.
Ib. [206].

Wrest once the law to your authority:
To do a great right, do a little wrong.   *Ib.* [215].

'Twill be recorded for a precedent,
And many an error by the same example
Will rush into the state.   *Ib.* [220].

A Daniel come to judgment! yea, a Daniel!
O wise young judge, how I do honour thee!
Ib. [223].

An oath, an oath, I have an oath in heaven:
Shall I lay perjury upon my soul?
No, not for Venice.   *Ib.* [228].

I charge you by the law,
Whereof you are a well-deserving pillar,
Proceed to judgment.
                              The Merchant of Venice, IV. i. [238].

Is it so nominated in the bond?   *Ib.* [260].

'T is not in the bond.   *Ib.* [263].

For herein Fortune shows herself more kind
Than is her custom: it is still her use
To let the wretched man outlive his wealth,
To view with hollow eye and wrinkled brow
An age of poverty.   *Ib.* [268].

The court awards it, and the law doth give it.
                                           Ib. [301].

              Thyself shalt see the act;
For, as thou urgest justice, be assur'd
Thou shalt have justice, more than thou desir'st.
                                           Ib. [315].

A second Daniel, a Daniel, Jew!
Now, infidel, I have thee on the hip.   *Ib.* [334].

I thank thee, Jew, for teaching me that word.
                                           Ib. [342].

You take my house when you do take the prop
That doth sustain my house; you take my life
When you do take the means whereby I live. *Ib.* [376].

He is well paid that is well satisfied.   *Ib.* 416.

You taught me first to beg, and now methinks
You teach me how a beggar should be answer'd.
                                           Ib. [440].

LORENZO:
              In such a night
Troilus methinks mounted the Troyan walls,
And sigh'd his soul toward the Grecian tents,
Where Cressid lay that night.
JESSICA:
              In such a night
Did Thisbe fearfully o'ertrip the dew,
And saw the lion's shadow e'er himself,
And ran dismay'd away.
LORENZO:
              In such a night
Stood Dido with a willow in her hand
Upon the wild sea-banks, and waft her love
To come again to Carthage.
JESSICA:
              In such a night
Medea gather'd the enchanted herbs
That did renew old Æson.   *Ib.* v. i. 3.

How sweet the moonlight sleeps upon this bank!
Here we will sit, and let the sounds of music
Creep in our ears: soft stillness and the night
Become the touches of sweet harmony.
Sit, Jessica: look, how the floor of heaven
Is thick inlaid with patines of bright gold:
There's not the smallest orb which thou behold'st
But in his motion like an angel sings,
Still quiring to the young-eyed cherubins;
Such harmony is in immortal souls;
But, whilst this muddy vesture of decay
Doth grossly close it in, we cannot hear it. *Ib.* 54.

I am never merry when I hear sweet music. *Ib.* 69.

              Therefore the poet
Did feign that Orpheus drew trees, stones, and floods;
Since nought so stockish, hard, and full of rage,

But music for the time doth change his nature.
The man that hath no music in himself,
Nor is not mov'd with concord of sweet sounds,
Is fit for treasons, stratagems, and spoils;
The motions of his spirit are dull as night,
And his affections dark as Erebus:
Let no such man be trusted.   *Ib.* 79.

PORTIA:
How far that little candle throws his beams!
So shines a good deed in a naughty world.
NERISSA:
When the moon shone, we did not see the candle.
PORTIA:
So doth the greater glory dim the less:
A substitute shines brightly as a king
Until a king be by, and then his state
Empties itself, as doth an inland brook
Into the main of waters.   *Ib.* 90.

The crow doth sing as sweetly as the lark
When neither is attended, and I think
The nightingale, if she should sing by day,
When every goose is cackling, would be thought
No better a musician than the wren.
How many things by season season'd are
To their right praise and true perfection!
Peace, ho! the moon sleeps with Endymion,
And would not be awak'd!   *Ib.* 102.

This night methinks is but the daylight sick.
                                           Ib. 124.

For a light wife doth make a heavy husband.
                                           Ib. 130.

These blessed candles of the night.   *Ib.* 220.

I will make a Star-Chamber matter of it.
                              The Merry Wives of Windsor, I. i. 1.

She has brown hair, and speaks small like a woman.
                                           Ib. [48].

Drink down all unkindness.   *Ib.* [203].

I had rather than forty shillings I had my Book of
Songs and Sonnets here.   *Ib.* [205].

I will make an end of my dinner; there's pippins and
seese to come.   *Ib.* ii. [12].

'Convey,' the wise it call. 'Steal!' foh! a fico for the
phrase!   *Ib.* iii. [30].

Here will be an old abusing of God's patience, and
the king's English.   *Ib.* iv. [5].

We burn daylight.   *Ib.* II. i. [54].

There's the humour of it.   *Ib.* [139].

Faith, thou hast some crotchets in thy head now.
                                           Ib. [158].

Why, then the world's mine oyster,
Which I with sword will open.   *Ib.* ii. 2.

Marry, this is the short and the long of it. *Ib.* [62].

Like a fair house built upon another man's ground.
                                           Ib. [229].

Ah, sweet Anne Page!   *Ib.* III. i. [40].

I cannot tell what the dickens his name is.
                                           Ib. ii. [20].

He capers, he dances, he has eyes of youth, he writes
verses, he speaks holiday, he smells April and May.
The Merry Wives of Windsor, III. ii. [71].

O, what a world of vile ill-favour'd faults
Looks handsome in three hundred pounds a year!
Ib. iv. [32].

If it be my luck, so; if not, happy man be his dole!
Ib. [67].

If I be served such another trick, I'll have my brains
ta'en out, and buttered, and give them to a dog
for a new year's gift.   *Ib.* v. [7].

I have a kind of alacrity in sinking.   *Ib.* [13].

As good luck would have it.   *Ib.* [86].

A man of my kidney.   *Ib.* [119].

Vengeance of Jenny's case!   *Ib.* IV. i. [65].

So curses all Eve's daughters, of what complexion
soever.   *Ib.* ii. [24].

This is the third time; I hope good luck lies in odd
numbers. . . . There is divinity in odd numbers,
either in nativity, chance or death.   *Ib.* v. i. 2.

Fairies, black, grey, green, and white,
You moonshine revellers, and shades of night.
Ib. v. [43].

To live a barren sister all your life,
Chanting faint hymns to the cold fruitless moon.
A Midsummer Night's Dream, I. ii. 72.

But earthlier happy is the rose distill'd,
Than that which withering on the virgin thorn
Grows, lives, and dies, in single blessedness. *Ib.* 76.

Ay me! for aught that ever I could read,
Could ever hear by tale or history,
The course of true love never did run smooth.
Ib. 132.

O hell! to choose love by another's eye. *Ib.* 140.

If there were a sympathy in choice,
War, death, or sickness did lay siege to it,
Making it momentany as a sound,
Swift as a shadow, short as any dream,
Brief as the lightning in the collied night,
That, in a spleen, unfolds both heaven and earth,
And ere a man hath power to say, 'Behold!'
The jaws of darkness do devour it up:
So quick bright things come to confusion. *Ib.* 141.

        Your tongue's sweet air
More tuneable than lark to shepherd's ear,
When wheat is green, when hawthorn buds appear.
Ib. 183.

Love looks not with the eyes, but with the mind,
And therefore is wing'd Cupid painted blind.
Ib. 234.

The most lamentable comedy, and most cruel death
of Pyramus and Thisby.   *Ib.* ii. [11].

Masters, spread yourselves.   *Ib.* [16].

A part to tear a cat in, to make all split. *Ib.* [32].

This is Ercles' vein.   *Ib.* [43].

I'll speak in a monstrous little voice. *Ib.* [55].

I am slow of study.   *Ib.* [70].

I will roar, that I will do any man's heart good to
hear me.   *Ib.* [73].

I will aggravate my voice so that I will roar you as
gently as any sucking dove; I will roar you as
'twere any nightingale.   *Ib.* [84].

A proper man, as one shall see in a summer's day.
Ib. [89].

Hold, or cut bow-strings.   *Ib.* [115].

Over hill, over dale,
  Thorough bush, thorough brier,
Over park, over pale,
  Thorough flood, thorough fire.   *Ib.* II. i. 2.

The cowslips tall her pensioners be;
In their gold coats spots you see;
Those be rubies, fairy favours,
In those freckles live their savours.   *Ib.* 10.

I must go seek some dew-drops here,
And hang a pearl in every cowslip's ear. *Ib.* 14.

The middle summer's spring.   *Ib.* 82.

Therefore the moon, the governess of floods,
Pale in her anger, washes all the air,
That rheumatic diseases do abound:
And thorough this distemperature we see
The seasons alter: hoary-headed frosts
Fall in the fresh lap of the crimson rose. *Ib.* 103.

Since once I sat upon a promontory,
And heard a mermaid on a dolphin's back
Uttering such dulcet and harmonious breath,
That the rude sea grew civil at her song,
And certain stars shot madly from their spheres,
To hear the sea-maid's music.   *Ib.* 149.

But I might see young Cupid's fiery shaft
Quench'd in the chaste beams of the wat'ry moon,
And the imperial votaress passed on,
In maiden meditation, fancy-free.
Yet mark'd I where the bolt of Cupid fell:
It fell upon a little western flower,
Before milk-white, now purple with love's wound,
And maidens call it, Love-in-idleness. *Ib.* 161.

I'll put a girdle round about the earth
In forty minutes.   *Ib.* 175.

I know a bank whereon the wild thyme blows,
Where oxlips and the nodding violet grows
Quite over-canopied with luscious woodbine,
With sweet musk-roses, and with eglantine:
There sleeps Titania some time of the night,
Lull'd in these flowers with dances and delight;
And there the snake throws her enamell'd skin,
Weed wide enough to wrap a fairy in. *Ib.* 249.

Some to kill cankers in the musk-rose buds,
Some war with rere-mice for their leathern wings,
To make my small elves coats.   *Ib.* ii. 3.

The clamorous owl, that nightly hoots, and wonders
At our quaint spirits.   *Ib.* 6.

  You spotted snakes with double tongue,
  Thorny hedge-hogs, be not seen;
  Newts, and blind-worms, do no wrong;
  Come not near our fairy queen.   *Ib.* 9.

  Weaving spiders come not here;
  Hence, you long-legg'd spinners, hence!
  Beetles black, approach not near;
  Worm nor snail, do no offence.   *Ib.* 20

This green plot shall be our stage, this hawthorn-
brake our tiring-house.
A Midsummer Night's Dream, III. i. [3].

God shield us!—a lion among ladies, is a most
dreadful thing; for there is not a more fearful
wild-fowl than your lion living.   *Ib.* [32].

What hempen home-spuns have we swaggering here,
So near the cradle of the fairy queen?   *Ib.* [82].

Bless thee, Bottom! bless thee! thou art translated.
Ib. [124].

The throstle with his note so true,
The wren with little quill.   *Ib.* [133].

As wild geese that the creeping fowler eye,
Or russet-pated choughs, many in sort,
Rising and cawing at the gun's report,
Sever themselves, and madly sweep the sky.
Ib. ii. 20.

Lord, what fools these mortals be!   *Ib.* 115.

       So we grew together,
Like to a double cherry, seeming parted,
But yet an union in partition;
Two lovely berries moulded on one stem.   *Ib.* 208.

For night's swift dragons cut the clouds full fast,
And yonder shines Aurora's harbinger;
At whose approach, ghosts, wandering here and there,
Troop home to churchyards.   *Ib.* 379.

Cupid is a knavish lad,
Thus to make poor females mad.   *Ib.* 440.

       Jack shall have Jill;
       Nought shall go ill;
The man shall have his mare again,
And all shall be well.   *Ib.* 461.

I must to the barber's, mounsieur, for methinks I
am marvellous hairy about the face. *Ib.* IV. i. [25].

I have a reasonable good ear in music: let us have
the tongs and the bones.   *Ib.* [32].

Methinks I have a great desire to a bottle of hay:
good hay, sweet hay, hath no fellow.   *Ib.* [37].

But, I pray you, let none of your people stir me: I
have an exposition of sleep come upon me.
Ib. [43].

But as the fierce vexation of a dream.   *Ib.* [75].

My Oberon! what visions have I seen!
Methought I was enamour'd of an ass.   *Ib.* [82].

Then, my queen, in silence sad,
Trip we after the night's shade;
We the globe can compass soon,
Swifter than the wandering moon.   *Ib.* [101].

HIPPOLYTA:
I was with Hercules and Cadmus once,
When in a wood of Crete they bay'd the bear
With hounds of Sparta: never did I hear . . .
So musical a discord, such sweet thunder.
THESEUS:
My hounds are bred out of the Spartan kind,
So flew'd, so sanded; and their heads are hung
With ears that sweep away the morning dew;
Crook-knee'd, and dew-lapp'd like Thessalian bulls;
Slow in pursuit, but match'd in mouth like bells.
Ib. [118].

       Saint Valentine is past:
Begin these wood-birds but to couple now?
Ib. [145].

I have had a dream, past the wit of man to say what
dream it was.   *Ib.* [211].

The eye of man hath not heard, the ear of man hath
not seen, man's hand is not able to taste, his tongue
to conceive, nor his heart to report, what my
dream was.   *Ib.* [218].

The lunatic, the lover, and the poet,
Are of imagination all compact:
One sees more devils than vast hell can hold,
That is, the madman; the lover, all as frantic,
Sees Helen's beauty in a brow of Egypt:
The poet's eye, in a fine frenzy rolling,
Doth glance from heaven to earth, from earth to
heaven;
And, as imagination bodies forth
The forms of things unknown, the poet's pen
Turns them to shapes, and gives to airy nothing
A local habitation and a name.
Such tricks hath strong imagination,
That, if it would but apprehend some joy,
It comprehends some bringer of that joy;
Or in the night, imagining some fear,
How easy is a bush suppos'd a bear!   *Ib.* v. i. 7.

What revels are in hand? Is there no play,
To ease the anguish of a torturing hour?   *Ib.* 36.

Very tragical mirth.   *Ib.* [57].

For never anything can be amiss,
When simpleness and duty tender it.   *Ib.* 82.

That is the true beginning of our end.
Consider then we come but in despite.
We do not come as minding to content you,
Our true intent is. All for your delight,
We are not here.   *Ib.* 111.

Whereat, with blade, with bloody blameful blade,
He bravely broach'd his boiling bloody breast.
Ib. [148].

The best in this kind are but shadows, and the worst
are no worse, if imagination amend them.
Ib. [215].

A very gentle beast, and of a good conscience.
Ib. [233].

Well roared, Lion.   *Ib.* [272].

This passion, and the death of a dear friend, would
go near to make a man look sad.   *Ib.* [295].

The iron tongue of midnight hath told twelve;
Lovers, to bed; 'tis almost fairy time.   *Ib.* [372].

Now the hungry lion roars,
And the wolf behowls the moon;
Whilst the heavy ploughman snores,
All with weary task fordone.   *Ib.* ii. 1.

       Not a mouse
Shall disturb this hallow'd house:
I am sent with broom before,
To sweep the dust behind the door.   *Ib.* 17.

A victory is twice itself when the achiever brings
home full numbers.
Much Ado About Nothing, I. i. [8].

He hath indeed better bettered expectation than you must expect of me to tell you how.

Much Ado About Nothing, I. i. [15].

He is a very valiant trencher-man. *Ib.* [52].

I see, lady, the gentleman is not in your books.
Ib. [79].

BEATRICE:
I wonder that you will still be talking, Signior Benedick: nobody marks you.
BENEDICK:
What! my dear Lady Disdain, are you yet living?
Ib. [121].

Shall I never see a bachelor of three-score again?
Ib. [209].

BENEDICK:
I will live a bachelor.
DON PEDRO:
I shall see thee, ere I die, look pale with love.
BENEDICK:
With anger, with sickness, or with hunger, my lord; not with love. *Ib.* [256].

'In time the savage bull doth bear the yoke.' *Ib.* [271].

Benedick the married man. *Ib.* [278].

What need the bridge much broader than the flood?
Ib. [326].

Would it not grieve a woman to be over-mastered with a piece of valiant dust? to make an account of her life to a clod of wayward marl? *Ib.* ii. 1. [64].

Wooing, wedding, and repenting, is as a Scotch jig, a measure, and a cinque-pace. *Ib.* [77].

I have a good eye, uncle: I can see a church by day-light. *Ib.* [86].

Speak low, if you speak love. *Ib.* [104].

Friendship is constant in all other things
Save in the office and affairs of love. *Ib.* [184].

She speaks poniards, and every word stabs: if her breath were as terrible as her terminations, there were no living near her; she would infect to the north star. *Ib.* [257].

Silence is the perfectest herald of joy: I were but little happy, if I could say how much. *Ib.* [319].

Speak, cousin, or, if you cannot, stop his mouth with a kiss. *Ib.* [322].

There was a star danced, and under that was I born.
Ib. [351].

Lie ten nights awake, carving the fashion of a new doublet. *Ib.* iii. [18].

Note this before my notes;
There's not a note of mine that's worth the noting.
Ib. [57].

Is it not strange that sheeps' guts should hale souls out of men's bodies? *Ib.* [62].

Sigh no more, ladies, sigh no more,
    Men were deceivers ever;
One foot in sea, and one on shore,
    To one thing constant never.
        Then sigh not so,
        But let them go,
    And be you blithe and bonny,

Converting all your sounds of woe
Into Hey nonny, nonny.

Sing no more ditties, sing no mo
    Of dumps so dull and heavy;
The fraud of men was ever so,
    Since summer first was leavy. *Ib.* [65].

Sits the wind in that corner? *Ib.* [108].

Doth not the appetite alter? A man loves the meat in his youth that he cannot endure in his age.
Ib. [258].

Paper bullets of the brain. *Ib.* [261].

The world must be peopled. When I said I would die a bachelor, I did not think I should live till I were married. *Ib.* [262].

Disdain and scorn ride sparkling in her eyes.
Ib. III. i. 51.

One doth not know
How much an ill word may empoison liking.
Ib. 85.

Contempt, farewell! and maiden pride, adieu!
No glory lives behind the back of such.
And, Benedick, love on; I will requite thee,
Taming my wild heart to thy loving hand.
Ib. 109.

He hath a heart as sound as a bell, and his tongue is the clapper; for what his heart thinks his tongue speaks. *Ib.* ii. [12].

BENEDICK:
I have the toothache.
                      .   .   .
DON PEDRO:
What! sigh for the toothache? *Ib.* [21].

Well, every one can master a grief but he that has it.
Ib. [28].

A' brushes his hat a mornings; what should that bode? *Ib.* [41].

The barber's man hath been seen with him; and the old ornament of his cheek hath already stuffed tennis-balls. *Ib.* [45].

Are you good men and true? *Ib.* iii. 1.

To be a well-favoured man is the gift of fortune; but to write and read comes by nature. *Ib.* [14].

Well, for your favour, sir, why, give God thanks, and make no boast of it; and for your writing and reading, let that appear when there is no need of such vanity. You are thought here to be the most senseless and fit man for the constable of the watch.
Ib. [19].

You shall comprehend all vagrom men. *Ib.* [25].

SECOND WATCH:
How, if a' will not stand?
DOGBERRY:
Why, then, take no note of him, but let him go; and presently call the rest of the watch together, and thank God you are rid of a knave. *Ib.* [28].

For the watch to babble and to talk is most tolerable and not to be endured. *Ib.* [36].

If they make you not then the better answer, you may say they are not the men you took them for. *Much Ado About Nothing*, III. iii. [49].

The most peaceable way for you, if you do take a thief, is, to let him show himself what he is and steal out of your company. *Ib.* [61].

I know that Deformed. *Ib.* [132].

I thank God, I am as honest as any man living, that is an old man and no honester than I. *Ib.* v. [15].

Comparisons are odorous. *Ib.* [18].

If I were as tedious as a king, I could find it in my heart to bestow it all of your worship. *Ib.* [23].

A good old man, sir; he will be talking: as they say, 'when the age is in, the wit is out.' *Ib.* [36].

Well, God's a good man. *Ib.* [39].

O! what men dare do! what men may do! what men daily do, not knowing what they do! *Ib.* IV. i. [19].

For it so falls out
That what we have we prize not to the worth
Whiles we enjoy it, but being lack'd and lost,
Why, then we rack the value, then we find
The virtue that possession would not show us
Whiles it was ours. *Ib.* [219].

The idea of her life shall sweetly creep
Into his study of imagination,
And every lovely organ of her life
Shall come apparell'd in more precious habit,
More moving-delicate, and full of life
Into the eye and prospect of his soul. *Ib.* [226].

Write down that they hope they serve God: and write God first; for God defend but God should go before such villains! Masters, it is proved already that you are little better than false knaves, and it will go near to be thought so shortly. *Ib.* ii. [21].

Yea, marry, that's the eftest way. *Ib.* [39].

Flat burglary as ever was committed. *Ib.* [54].

O that he were here to write me down an ass! but, masters, remember that I am an ass; though it be not written down, yet forget not that I am an ass. *Ib.* [80].

A fellow that hath had losses; and one that hath two gowns, and everything handsome about him. *Ib.* [90].

Patch grief with proverbs. *Ib.* v. i. 17.

For there was never yet philosopher
That could endure the toothache patiently. *Ib.* 35.

In a false quarrel there is no true valour. *Ib.* [121].

What though care killed a cat, thou hast mettle enough in thee to kill care. *Ib.* [135].

No, I was not born under a riming planet. *Ib.* ii. [40].

The trumpet of his own virtues. *Ib.* [91].

Done to death by slanderous tongues. *Ib.* iii. 3.

The wolves have prey'd; and look, the gentle day,
Before the wheels of Phœbus, round about
Dapples the drowsy east with spots of grey. *Ib.* 25.

Horribly stuff'd with epithets of war.
Othello, I. i. 14.

A fellow almost damn'd in a fair wife. *Ib.* 21.

The bookish theoric. *Ib.* 24.

This counter-caster. *Ib.* 31.

'Tis the curse of the service,
Preferment goes by letter and affection,
Not by the old gradation, where each second
Stood heir to the first. *Ib.* 35.

I follow him to serve my turn upon him;
We cannot all be masters, nor all masters
Cannot be truly follow'd. *Ib.* 42.

Wears out his time, much like his master's ass,
For nought but provender, and when he's old, cashier'd;
Whip me such honest knaves. *Ib.* 47.

In following him, I follow but myself. *Ib.* 58.

But I will wear my heart upon my sleeve
For daws to peck at: I am not what I am. *Ib.* 64.

An old black ram
Is tupping your white ewe. *Ib.* 88.

'Zounds! sir, you are one of those that will not serve God if the devil bid you. *Ib.* 108.

Your daughter and the Moor are now making the beast with two backs. *Ib.* [117].

The gross clasps of a lascivious Moor. *Ib.* [127].

An extravagant and wheeling stranger
Of here and every where. *Ib.* [137].

I do hate him as I hate hell-pains. *Ib.* [155].

I must show out a flag and sign of love,
Which is indeed but sign. *Ib.* [157].

Though in the trade of war I have slain men,
Yet do I hold it very stuff o' the conscience
To do no contriv'd murder: I lack iniquity
Sometimes to do me service. *Ib.* ii. 1.

I fetch my life and being
From men of royal siege. *Ib.* 21.

I would not my unhoused free condition
Put into circumscription and confine
For the sea's worth. *Ib.* 26.

My parts, my title, and my perfect soul
Shall manifest me rightly. *Ib.* 31.

Keep up your bright swords, for the dew will rust them. *Ib.* 59.

The wealthy curled darlings of our nation. *Ib.* 68.

The sooty bosom
Of such a thing as thou. *Ib.* 70.

My particular grief
Is of so flood-gate and o'erbearing nature
That it engluts and swallows other sorrows
And it is still itself. *Ib.* iii. 55.

The bloody book of law
You shall yourself read in the bitter letter
After your own sense. *Ib.* 67.

Most potent, grave, and reverend signiors,
My very noble and approv'd good masters,
That I have ta'en away this old man's daughter,

It is most true; true, I have married her:
The very head and front of my offending
Hath this extent, no more. Rude am I in my speech,
And little bless'd with the soft phrase of peace;
For since these arms of mine had seven years' pith,
Till now some nine moons wasted, they have us'd
Their dearest action in the tented field;
And little of this great world can I speak,
More than pertains to feats of broil and battle;
And therefore little shall I grace my cause
In speaking for myself. Yet, by your gracious
     patience,
I will a round unvarnish'd tale deliver
Of my whole course of love; what drugs, what charms,
What conjuration, and what mighty magic,
For such proceeding I am charg'd withal,
I won his daughter.   *Othello*, I. iii. 76.

         A maiden never bold;
Of spirit so still and quiet, that her motion
Blush'd at herself.   *Ib.* 94.

Her father lov'd me; oft invited me;
Still question'd me the story of my life
From year to year, the battles, sieges, fortunes
That I have pass'd.
I ran it through, even from my boyish days
To the very moment that he bade me tell it;
Wherein I spake of most disastrous chances,
Of moving accidents by flood and field,
Of hair-breadth 'scapes i' the imminent deadly breach,
Of being taken by the insolent foe
And sold to slavery, of my redemption thence
And portance in my travel's history;
Wherein of antres vast and desarts idle,
Rough quarries, rocks and hills whose heads touch
     heaven,
It was my hint to speak, such was the process;
And of the Cannibals that each other eat,
The Anthropophagi, and men whose heads
Do grow beneath their shoulders. This to hear
Would Desdemona seriously incline.   *Ib.* 128.

And often did beguile her of her tears,
When I did speak of some distressful stroke
That my youth suffer'd. My story being done,
She gave me for my pains a world of sighs:
She swore, in faith, 't was strange, 't was passing
     strange;
'T was pitiful, 't was wondrous pitiful:
She wish'd she had not heard it, yet she wish'd
That heaven had made her such a man; she thank'd
     me,
And bade me, if I had a friend that lov'd her,
I should but teach him how to tell my story,
And that would woo her. Upon this hint I spake:
She lov'd me for the dangers I had pass'd,
And I lov'd her that she did pity them.
This only is the witchcraft I have us'd.   *Ib.* 156.

I do perceive here a divided duty.   *Ib.* 181.

To mourn a mischief that is past and gone
Is the next way to draw new mischief on.   *Ib.* 204.

The robb'd that smiles steals something from the
     thief.   *Ib.* 208.

But words are words; I never yet did hear
That the bruis'd heart was pierced through the ear.
                                        Ib. 218.

The tyrant custom, most grave senators,
Hath made the flinty and steel couch of war
My thrice-driven bed of down.   *Ib.* [230].

         My heart's subdu'd
Even to the very quality of my lord.   *Ib.* [252].

I saw Othello's visage in his mind.   *Ib.* [254].

A moth of peace.   *Ib.* [258].

BRABANTIO:
She has deceiv'd her father, and may thee.
OTHELLO:
My life upon her faith!   *Ib.* [295].

I will incontinently drown myself.   *Ib.* [307].

It is silliness to live when to live is torment; and then
     have we a prescription to die when death is our
     physician.   *Ib.* [310].

Virtue! a fig! 'tis in ourselves that we are thus, or thus.
     Our bodies are our gardens, to which our wills are
     gardeners.   *Ib.* [323].

Put money in thy purse.   *Ib.* [345].

The food that to him now is as luscious as locusts,
     shall be to him shortly as bitter as coloquintida.
                                        Ib. [354].

There are many events in the womb of time which
     will be delivered.   *Ib.* [377].

Thus do I ever make my fool my purse.   *Ib.* [389].

         He holds me well;
The better shall my purpose work on him.   *Ib.* [396].

Framed to make women false.   *Ib.* [404].

The Moor is of a free and open nature,
That thinks men honest that but seem to be so.
                                      Ib. [405].

I have 't; it is engender'd; hell and night
Must bring this monstrous birth to the world's light.
                                      Ib. [409].

Our great captain's captain.   *Ib.* II. i. 74.

         You are pictures out of doors,
Bells in your parlours, wild cats in your kitchens,
Saints in your injuries, devils being offended,
Players in your housewifery, and housewives in your
     beds.   *Ib.* 109.

         Do not put me to 't,
For I am nothing if not critical.   *Ib.* 118.

I am not merry, but I do beguile
The thing I am by seeming otherwise.   *Ib.* 122.

IAGO:
She never yet was foolish that was fair,
For even her folly help'd her to an heir.
DESDEMONA:
These are old fond paradoxes to make fools laugh i'
     the alehouse.   *Ib.* 136.

IAGO:
She that was ever fair and never proud,
Had tongue at will and yet was never loud,
Never lack'd gold and yet went never gay,
Fled from her wish and yet said 'Now I may,'
She that being anger'd, her revenge being nigh,
Bade her wrong stay and her displeasure fly;
She that in wisdom never was so frail
To change the cod's head for the salmon's tail,

She that could think and ne'er disclose her mind,
See suitors following and not look behind,
She was a wight, if ever such wight were,—
DESDEMONA:
To do what?
IAGO:
To suckle fools and chronicle small beer.
DESDEMONA:
O most lame and impotent conclusion!
Othello, II. i. 148.

With as little a web as this will I ensnare as great a fly
as Cassio. *Ib.* [169].

OTHELLO:
        If it were now to die,
'Twere now to be most happy, for I fear
My soul hath her content so absolute
That not another comfort like to this
Succeeds in unknown fate.
DESDEMONA:
        The heavens forbid
But that our loves and comforts should increase
Even as our days do grow! *Ib.* [192].

A slipper and subtle knave, a finder-out of occasions.
Ib. [247].

A pestilent complete knave! and the woman hath
found him already. *Ib.* [253].

This poor trash of Venice. *Ib.* [315].

Make the Moor thank me, love me, and reward me
For making him egregiously an ass. *Ib.* [320].

Let's teach ourselves that honourable stop,
Not to outsport discretion. *Ib.* iii. 2.

She is sport for Jove. *Ib.* [17].

I have very poor and unhappy brains for drinking:
I could well wish courtesy would invent some other
custom of entertainment. *Ib.* [34].

My boat sails freely, both with wind and stream.
Ib. [66].

And let me the canakin clink;
  A soldier's a man;
  A life's but a span;
Why then let a soldier drink. *Ib.* [72].

England, where indeed they are most potent in potting. *Ib.* [79].

King Stephen was a worthy peer,
  His breeches cost him but a crown;
He held them sixpence all too dear,
  With that he call'd the tailor lown. *Ib.* [93].

'Tis pride that pulls the country down. *Ib.* [99].

Well, God's above all; and there be souls must be
saved, and there be souls must not be saved.
Ib. [106].

The lieutenant is to be saved before the ancient.
Ib. [115].

He is a soldier fit to stand by Cæsar
And give direction. *Ib.* [128].

Silence that dreadful bell! it frights the isle
From her propriety. *Ib.* [177].

But men are men; the best sometimes forget. *Ib.* [243].

Thy honesty and love doth mince this matter.
Ib. [249].

        Cassio, I love thee;
But never more be officer of mine. *Ib.* [250].

Reputation, reputation, reputation! O! I have lost
my reputation. I have lost the immortal part of
myself, and what remains is bestial. My reputation,
Iago, my reputation! *Ib.* [264].

O thou invisible spirit of wine! if thou hast no name
to be known by, let us call thee devil! *Ib.* [285].

O God! that men should put an enemy in their
mouths to steal away their brains; that we should,
with joy, pleasance, revel, and applause, transform
ourselves into beasts. *Ib.* [293].

CASSIO:
Every inordinate cup is unblessed, and the ingredient
is a devil.
IAGO:
Come, come; good wine is a good familiar creature if
it be well used; exclaim no more against it.
Ib. [315].

How poor are they that have not patience!
What wound did ever heal but by degrees?
Ib. [379].

O! thereby hangs a tail. *Ib.* III. i. [8].

Talk him out of patience. *Ib.* iii. 23.

Excellent wretch! Perdition catch my soul
But I do love thee! and when I love thee not,
Chaos is come again. *Ib.* 90.

By heaven, he echoes me,
As if there were some monster in his thought
Too hideous to be shown. *Ib.* 106.

  Men should be what they seem;
Or those that be not, would they might seem none!
Ib. 126.

Good name in man or woman, dear my lord,
Is the immediate jewel of their souls;
Who steals my purse steals trash; 'tis something,
  nothing;
'Twas mine, 'tis his, and has been slave to thousands;
But he that filches from me my good name
Robs me of that which not enriches him,
And makes me poor indeed. *Ib.* 155.

  O! beware, my lord, of jealousy;
It is the green-ey'd monster which doth mock
The meat it feeds on. *Ib.* 165.

But, O! what damned minutes tells he o'er
Who dotes, yet doubts; suspects, yet soundly loves!
Ib. 169.

Poor and content is rich, and rich enough. *Ib.* 172.

Think'st thou I'd make a life of jealousy,
To follow still the changes of the moon
With fresh suspicions? No; to be once in doubt
Is once to be resolved. *Ib.* 177.

In Venice they do let heaven see the pranks
They dare not show their husbands; their best
  conscience
Is not to leave 't undone, but keep 't unknown.
Ib. 202.

I humbly do beseech you of your pardon
For too much loving you. *Ib.* 212.

This fellow's of exceeding honesty. *Ib.* 258.

If I do prove her haggard,
Though that her jesses were my dear heart-strings,
I'd whistle her off and let her down the wind,
To prey at fortune.   *Othello*, III. iii. 260.

For I am declin'd
Into the vale of years.   *Ib.* 265.

O curse of marriage!
That we can call these delicate creatures ours,
And not their appetites. I had rather be a toad,
And live upon the vapour of a dungeon,
Than keep a corner in the thing I love
For others' uses.   *Ib.* 268.

If she be false, O! then heaven mocks itself.
I'll not believe it.   *Ib.* 278.

Trifles light as air
Are to the jealous confirmations strong
As proofs of holy writ.   *Ib.* 323.

Not poppy, nor mandragora,
Nor all the drowsy syrups of the world,
Shall ever medicine thee to that sweet sleep
Which thou ow'dst yesterday.   *Ib.* 331.

Avaunt! be gone! thou hast set me on the rack;
I swear 'tis better to be much abus'd
Than but to know 't a little.   *Ib.* 336.

He that is robb'd, not wanting what is stol'n,
Let him not know 't and he's not robb'd at all.
                    Ib. 343.

I had been happy, if the general camp,
Pioners and all, had tasted her sweet body,
So I had nothing known. O! now, for ever
Farewell the tranquil mind; farewell content!
Farewell the plumed troop and the big wars
That make ambition virtue! O, farewell!
Farewell the neighing steed and the shrill trump,
The spirit-stirring drum, the ear-piercing fife,
The royal banner, and all quality,
Pride, pomp, and circumstance of glorious war!
And, O you mortal engines, whose rude throats
The immortal Jove's dread clamours counterfeit,
Farewell! Othello's occupation's gone!   *Ib.* 346.

Be sure of it; give me the ocular proof.   *Ib.* 361.

Never pray more; abandon all remorse;
On horror's head horrors accumulate.   *Ib.* 370.

O wretched fool!
That liv'st to make thine honesty a vice.
O monstrous world! Take note, take note, O world!
To be direct and honest is not safe.   *Ib.* 376.

By the world,
I think my wife be honest and think she is not;
I think that thou art just and think thou art not.
                    Ib. 384.

There are a kind of men so loose of soul
That in their sleeps will mutter their affairs.
                    Ib. 417.

But this denoted a foregone conclusion.   *Ib.* 429.

Swell, bosom, with thy fraught,
For 't is of aspics' tongues!   *Ib.* 450.

O! blood, blood, blood!   *Ib.* 452.

Like to the Pontick sea,
Whose icy current and compulsive course

Ne'er feels retiring ebb, but keeps due on
To the Propontic and the Hellespont,
Even so my bloody thoughts, with violent pace,
Shall ne'er look back, ne'er ebb to humble love,
Till that a capable and wide revenge
Swallow them up.   *Ib.* 454.

For here's a young and sweating devil here,
That commonly rebels.   *Ib.* iv. 43.

The hearts of old gave hands,
But our new heraldry is hands not hearts.   *Ib.* 47.

That handkerchief
Did an Egyptian to my mother give.   *Ib.* 56.

'Tis true; there's magic in the web of it;
A sibyl, that had number'd in the world
The sun to course two hundred compasses,
In her prophetic fury sew'd the work;
The worms were hallow'd that did breed the silk,
And it was dy'd in mummy which the skilful
Conserv'd of maiden's hearts.   *Ib.* 70.

But jealous souls will not be answer'd so;
They are not ever jealous for the cause,
But jealous for they are jealous.   *Ib.* 158.

What! keep a week away? seven days and nights?
Eight score eight hours? and lovers' absent hours,
More tedious than the dial eight score times?
O, weary reckoning!   *Ib.* 172.

I do attend here on the general,
And think it no addition nor my wish
To have him see me woman'd.   *Ib.* 192.

O! it comes o'er my memory,
As doth the raven o'er the infected house,
Boding to all.   *Ib.* IV. i. 20.

Many worthy and chaste dames even thus,
All guiltless, meet reproach.   *Ib.* 47.

To beguile many and be beguil'd by one.   *Ib.* 98.

They laugh that win.   *Ib.* [123].

I would have him nine years a-killing.   *Ib.* [186].

My heart is turned to stone; I strike it, and it hurts
my hand.   *Ib.* [190].

O! the world hath not a sweeter creature; she might
lie by an emperor's side and command him tasks.
                    Ib. [192].

O, she will sing the savageness out of a bear.
                    Ib. [198].

But yet the pity of it, Iago! O! Iago, the pity of it,
Iago!   *Ib.* [205].

The justice of it pleases.   *Ib.* [221].

O well-painted passion!   *Ib.* [268].

Goats and monkeys!   *Ib.* [274].

Whose solid virtue
The shot of accident nor dart of chance
Could neither graze nor pierce?   *Ib.* [277].

Your mystery, your mystery; nay, dispatch.
                    Ib. ii. 29.

Had it pleas'd heaven
To try me with affliction, had he rain'd
All kinds of sores, and shames, on my bare head,
Steep'd me in poverty to the very lips,

Given to captivity me and my utmost hopes,
I should have found in some part of my soul
A drop of patience; but, alas! to make me
The fixed figure for the time of scorn
To point his slow and moving finger at;
Yet could I bear that too; well, very well.
But there, where I have garner'd up my heart,
Where either I must live or bear no life,
The fountain from the which my current runs
Or else dries up; to be discarded thence!
Or keep it as a cistern for foul toads
To knot and gender in! Turn thy complexion there,
Patience, thou young and rose-lipp'd cherubin;
Ay, there, look grim as hell!   *Othello*, IV. ii. 46.

O thou weed!
Who art so lovely fair and smell'st so sweet
That the sense aches at thee, would thou hadst ne'er
   been born!   *Ib.* 66.

Heaven stops the nose at it and the moon winks.
       Ib. 76.

I took you for that cunning whore of Venice
That married with Othello. You, mistress,
That have the office opposite to Saint Peter,
And keep the gate of hell!   *Ib.* 88.

I will be hang'd, if some eternal villain,
Some busy and insinuating rogue,
Some cogging cozening slave, to get some office,
Have not devis'd this slander.   *Ib.* 130.

O heaven! that such companions thou'dst unfold,
And put in every honest hand a whip
To lash the rascals naked through the world,
Even from the east to the west!   *Ib.* 141.

Unkindness may do much;
And his unkindness may defeat my life,
But never taint my love.   *Ib.* 159.

Why, now I see there's mettle in thee, and even from
   this instant do build on thee a better opinion than
   ever before.   *Ib.* [207].

EMILIA:
I would you had never seen him.
DESDEMONA:
So would not I; my love doth so approve him.
       Ib. iii. 18.

The poor soul sat sighing by a sycamore tree,
Sing all a green willow;
Her hand on her bosom, her head on her knee,
Sing willow, willow, willow:
The fresh streams ran by her, and murmur'd her
   moans;
Sing willow, willow, willow:
Her salt tears fell from her, and soften'd the stones;—
Sing willow, willow, willow:
Sing all a green willow must be my garland. *Ib.* [41].

DESDEMONA:
     Mine eyes do itch;
Doth that bode weeping?
EMILIA:
'Tis neither here nor there.   *Ib.* [59].

Who would not make her husband a cuckold to make
   him a monarch?   *Ib.* [76].

He hath a daily beauty in his life
That makes me ugly.   *Ib.* v. i. 19.

This is the night
That either makes me or fordoes me quite. *Ib.* 128.

It is the cause, it is the cause, my soul;
Let me not name it to you, you chaste stars!
It is the cause. Yet I'll not shed her blood,
Nor scar that whiter skin of hers than snow,
And smooth as monumental alabaster.
Yet she must die, else she'll betray more men.
Put out the light, and then put out the light:
If I quench thee, thou flaming minister,
I can again thy former light restore,
Should I repent me; but once put out thy light,
Thou cunning'st pattern of excelling nature,
I know not where is that Promethean heat
That can thy light relume. When I have pluck'd the
   rose,
I cannot give it vital growth again,
It needs must wither: I'll smell it on the tree.
O balmy breath, that dost almost persuade
Justice to break her sword! One more, one more.
Be thus when thou art dead, and I will kill thee,
And love thee after. One more, and this the last:
So sweet was ne'er so fatal. I must weep,
But they are cruel tears; this sorrow's heavenly,
It strikes where it doth love.   *Ib.* ii. 1.

If you bethink yourself of any crime
Unreconcil'd as yet to heaven and grace,
Solicit for it straight.   *Ib.* 26.

Alas! why gnaw you so your nether lip?
Some bloody passion shakes your very frame;
These are portents, but yet, I hope, I hope
They do not point on me.   *Ib.* 43.

For to deny each article with oath
Cannot remove nor choke the strong conception
That I do groan withal.   *Ib.* 54.

Had all his hairs been lives, my great revenge
Had stomach for them all.   *Ib.* 74.

It is the very error of the moon;
She comes more near the earth than she was wont,
And makes men mad.   *Ib.* 107.

Not Cassio kill'd! then murder's out of tune,
And sweet revenge grows harsh.   *Ib.* 113.

A guiltless death I die.   *Ib.* 120.

Nobody; I myself; farewell.   *Ib.* 122.

OTHELLO:
She's like a liar gone to burning hell;
'Twas I that kill'd her.

EMILIA:
     O! the more angel she,
And you the blacker devil.   *Ib.* 127.

     Nay, had she been true,
If heaven would make me such another world
Of one entire and perfect chrysolite,
I'd not have sold her for it.   *Ib.* 141.

She was too fond of her most filthy bargain. *Ib.* 155.

Thou hast not half the power to do me harm
As I have to be hurt.   *Ib.* 160.

You told a lie, an odious damned lie;
Upon my soul, a lie, a wicked lie.   *Ib.* 178.

Curse his better angel from his side,
And fall to reprobation.   *Ib.* 206.

With that recognizance and pledge of love.
Othello, v. ii. 212.

Are there no stones in heaven
But what serve for the thunder?   *Ib.* 232.

Every puny whipster gets my sword.   *Ib.* 242.

I will play the swan,
And die in music.   *Ib.* 245.

Who can control his fate?   *Ib.* 264.

Here is my journey's end, here is my butt,
And very sea-mark of my utmost sail,   *Ib.* 266.

O ill-starr'd wench!
Pale as thy smock! when we shall meet at compt,
This look of thine will hurl my soul from heaven,
And fiends will snatch at it. Cold, cold, my girl!
Even like thy chastity.
O! cursed, cursed slave. Whip me, ye devils,
From the possession of this heavenly sight!
Blow me about in winds! roast me in sulphur!
Wash me in steep-down gulfs of liquid fire!
O Desdemona! Desdemona! dead!   *Ib.* 271.

I look down towards his feet; but that's a fable.
If that thou be'st a devil, I cannot kill thee.
          Ib. 285.

An honourable murderer, if you will;
For nought did I in hate, but all in honour. *Ib.* 293.

OTHELLO:
Will you, I pray, demand that demi-devil
Why he hath thus ensnar'd my soul and body?
IAGO:
Demand me nothing: what you know, you know:
From this time forth I never will speak word.
          Ib. 300.

I have done the state some service, and they know 't;
No more of that. I pray you, in your letters,
When you shall these unlucky deeds relate,
Speak of me as I am; nothing extenuate,
Nor set down aught in malice: then, must you speak
Of one that lov'd not wisely but too well;
Of one not easily jealous, but, being wrought,
Perplex'd in the extreme; of one whose hand,
Like the base Indian, threw a pearl away
Richer than all his tribe; of one whose subdu'd eyes
Albeit unused to the melting mood,
Drop tears as fast as the Arabian trees
Their med'cinable gum. Set you down this;
And say besides, that in Aleppo once,
Where a malignant and a turban'd Turk
Beat a Venetian and traduc'd the state,
I took by the throat the circumcised dog,
And smote him thus.   *Ib.* 338.

All that 's spoke is marred.   *Ib.* 356.

I kiss'd thee ere I kill'd thee.   *Ib.* 357.

See, where she comes apparell'd like the spring.
          Pericles, I. i. 12.

Few love to hear the sins they love to act. *Ib.* 92.

O you gods!
Why do you make us love your goodly gifts,
And snatch them straight away?   *Ib.* III. i. 22.

ABRAHAM:
Do you bite your thumb at us, sir?
SAMPSON:
Is the law of our side if I say ay?
GREGORY:
No.
SAMPSON:
No, sir, I do not bite my thumb at you, sir; but I bite
my thumb, sir.   *Romeo and Juliet*, I. i. [50].

Gregory, remember thy swashing blow.   *Ib.* [68].

Saint-seducing gold.   *Ib.* [220].

And 'tis not hard, I think,
For men so old as we to keep the peace.   *Ib.* ii. 2.

PARIS:
Younger than she are happy mothers made.
CAPULET:
And too soon marr'd are those so early made. *Ib.* 12.

And then my husband—God be with his soul!
A' was a merry man—took up the child:
'Yea,' quoth he, 'dost thou fall upon thy face?
Thou wilt fall backward when thou hast more wit;
Wilt thou not, Jule?' and, by my halidom,
The pretty wretch left crying, and said 'Ay.'
          Ib. iii. 39.

Pretty fool, it stinted and said 'Ay.'   *Ib.* 48.

I am proverb'd with a grandsire phrase;
I'll be a candle-holder, and look on.   *Ib.* iv. 37.

Come, we burn daylight, ho!   *Ib.* 43.

O! then, I see, Queen Mab hath been with you. . . .
She is the fairies' midwife, and she comes
In shape no bigger than an agate-stone
On the forefinger of an alderman,
Drawn with a team of little atomies
Athwart men's noses as they lie asleep:
Her waggon-spokes made of long spinners' legs;
The cover, of the wings of grasshoppers;
The traces, of the smallest spider's web;
The collars, of the moonshine's watery beams;
Her whip, of cricket's bone; the lash, of film;
Her waggoner, a small grey-coated gnat,
Not half so big as a round little worm
Prick'd from the lazy finger of a maid;
Her chariot is an empty hazel-nut,
Made by the joiner squirrel or old grub,
Time out o' mind the fairies' coach-makers.
And in this state she gallops night by night
Through lovers' brains, and then they dream of love;
O'er courtiers' knees, that dream on curtsies straight;
O'er lawyers' fingers, who straight dream on fees;
O'er ladies' lips, who straight on kisses dream;
Which oft the angry Mab with blisters plagues,
Because their breaths with sweetmeats tainted are.
Sometimes she gallops o'er a courtier's nose,
And then dreams he of smelling out a suit;
And sometimes comes she with a tithe-pig's tail,
Tickling a parson's nose as a' lies asleep,
Then dreams he of another benefice;
Sometime she driveth o'er a soldier's neck,
And then dreams he of cutting foreign throats,
Of breaches, ambuscadoes, Spanish blades,
Of healths five fathom deep; and then anon
Drums in his ear, at which he starts and wakes;
And, being thus frighted, swears a prayer or two,

And sleeps again. This is that very Mab
That plats the manes of horses in the night;
And bakes the elf-locks in foul sluttish hairs,
Which once untangled much misfortune bodes;
This is the hag, when maids lie on their backs,
That presses them and learns them first to bear,
Making them women of good carriage.

Romeo and Juliet, I. iv. 53.

For you and I are past our dancing days.
Ib. v. [35].

O! she doth teach the torches to burn bright.
It seems she hangs upon the cheek of night
Like a rich jewel in an Ethiop's ear;
Beauty too rich for use, for earth too dear. *Ib.* [48].

We have a trifling foolish banquet towards.
Ib. [126].

My only love sprung from my only hate! *Ib.* [142].

Young Adam Cupid, he that shot so trim
When King Cophetua lov'd the beggar-maid.
Ib. II. i. 13.

He jests at scars, that never felt a wound.
But, soft! what light through yonder window breaks?
It is the east, and Juliet is the sun. *Ib.* ii. 1.

See! how she leans her cheek upon her hand:
O! that I were a glove upon that hand,
That I might touch that cheek. *Ib.* 23.

O Romeo, Romeo! wherefore art thou Romeo?
Ib. 33.

What's in a name? that which we call a rose
By any other name would smell as sweet. *Ib.* 43.

For stony limits cannot hold love out. *Ib.* 67.

Thou know'st the mask of night is on my face,
Else would a maiden blush bepaint my cheek.
Ib. 85.

Fain would I dwell on form, fain, fain deny
What I have spoke: but farewell compliment!
Ib. 88.

At lovers' perjuries,
They say, Jove laughs. O gentle Romeo!
If thou dost love, pronounce it faithfully:
Or if thou think'st I am too quickly won,
I'll frown and be perverse and say thee nay,
So thou wilt woo; but else, not for the world.
In truth, fair Montague, I am too fond. *Ib.* 92.

I'll prove more true
Than those that have more cunning to be strange.
Ib. 100.

ROMEO:
Lady, by yonder blessed moon I swear
That tips with silver all these fruit-tree tops,—
JULIET:
O! swear not by the moon, the inconstant moon,
That monthly changes in her circled orb,
Lest that thy love prove likewise variable. *Ib.* 107.

Do not swear at all;
Or, if thou wilt, swear by thy gracious self,
Which is the god of my idolatry. *Ib.* 112.

It is too rash, too unadvis'd, too sudden;
Too like the lightning, which doth cease to be

Ere one can say it lightens. Sweet, good-night!
This bud of love, by summer's ripening breath,
May prove a beauteous flower when next we meet.
Ib. 118.

Love goes toward love, as schoolboys from their
books;
But love from love, toward school with heavy looks.
Ib. 156.

O! for a falconer's voice,
To lure this tassel-gentle back again.
Bondage is hoarse, and may not speak aloud,
Else would I tear the cave where Echo lies. *Ib.* 158.

It is my soul that calls upon my name:
How silver-sweet sound lovers' tongues by night,
Like softest music to attending ears! *Ib.* 164.

'Tis almost morning; I would have thee gone;
And yet no further than a wanton's bird,
Who lets it hop a little from her hand,
Like a poor prisoner in his twisted gyves,
And with a silk thread plucks it back again,
So loving-jealous of his liberty. *Ib.* 176.

JULIET:
Yet I should kill thee with much cherishing.
Good-night, good-night! parting is such sweet sorrow
That I shall say good-night till it be morrow.
ROMEO:
Sleep dwell upon thine eyes, peace in thy breast!
Would I were sleep and peace, so sweet to rest!
Ib. 183.

Wisely and slow; they stumble that run fast.
Ib. iii. 94.

One, two, and the third in your bosom.
Ib. iv. [24].

O flesh, flesh, how art thou fishified! *Ib.* [41].

I am the very pink of courtesy. *Ib.* [63].

A gentleman, nurse, that loves to hear himself talk,
and will speak more in a minute than he will stand
to in a month. *Ib.* [156].

Two may keep counsel, putting one away. *Ib.* [211].

These violent delights have violent ends,
And in their triumph die. *Ib.* vi. 9.

Therefore love moderately; long love doth so;
Too swift arrives as tardy as too slow. *Ib.* 14.

O! so light a foot
Will ne'er wear out the everlasting flint. *Ib.* 16.

Thy head is as full of quarrels as an egg is full of
meat. *Ib.* III. i. [23].

A word and a blow. *Ib.* [43].

Men's eyes were made to look, and let them gaze;
I will not budge for no man's pleasure, I. *Ib.* [59].

No, 'tis not so deep as a well, nor so wide as a church
door; but 'tis enough, 'twill serve: ask for me to-
morrow, and you shall find me a grave man. I am
peppered, I warrant, for this world. *Ib.* [100].

A plague o' both your houses!
They have made worms' meat of me. *Ib.* [112].

O! I am Fortune's fool. *Romeo and Juliet*, III. i. [142].

Gallop apace, you fiery-footed steeds,
Towards Phœbus' lodging.   *Ib.* ii. 1.

     Come, civil night,
Thou sober-suited matron, all in black.   *Ib.* 10.

For thou wilt lie upon the wings of night,
Whiter than new snow on a raven's back.   *Ib.* 18.

Give me my Romeo: and, when he shall die,
Take him and cut him out in little stars,
And he will make the face of heaven so fine
That all the world will be in love with night,
And pay no worship to the garish sun.   *Ib.* 21.

     He was not born to shame:
Upon his brow shame is ashamed to sit.   *Ib.* 91.

Romeo, come forth; come forth, thou fearful man:
Affliction is enamour'd of thy parts,
And thou art wedded to calamity.   *Ib.* iii. 1.

Thou cutt'st my head off with a golden axe.   *Ib.* 22.

Adversity's sweet milk, philosophy.   *Ib.* 54.

     Hang up philosophy!
Unless philosophy can make a Juliet.   *Ib.* 56.

Wilt thou be gone? it is not yet near day:
It was the nightingale, and not the lark,
That pierc'd the fearful hollow of thine ear;
Nightly she sings on yon pomegranate tree:
Believe me, love, it was the nightingale.
     Ib. III. v. 1.

Night's candles are burnt out, and jocund day
Stands tiptoe on the misty mountain tops.   *Ib.* 9.

Villain and he be many miles asunder.   *Ib.* 82.

Thank me no thankings, nor proud me no prouds.
     Ib. 153.

Is there no pity sitting in the clouds,
That sees into the bottom of my grief?   *Ib.* 198.

Romeo's a dishclout to him.   *Ib.* 221.

'Tis an ill cook that cannot lick his own fingers.
     Ib. IV. ii. [6].

All things that we ordained festival,
Turn from their office to black funeral;
Our instruments to melancholy bells,
Our wedding cheer to a sad burial feast,
Our solemn hymns to sullen dirges change,
Our bridal flowers serve for a buried corse,
And all things change them to the contrary.
     Ib. v. 84.

My bosom's lord sits lightly in his throne.
     Ib. v. i. 3.

I do remember an apothecary,
And hereabouts he dwells.   *Ib.* 37.

Being holiday, the beggar's shop is shut.   *Ib.* 56.

The world is not thy friend, nor the world's law.
     Ib. 72.

APOTHECARY:
My poverty, but not my will, consents.
ROMEO:
I pay thy poverty, and not thy will.   *Ib.* 75.

The time and my intents are savage-wild,
More fierce and more inexorable far
Than empty tigers or the roaring sea.   *Ib.* iii. 37.

Tempt not a desperate man.   *Ib.* 59.

One writ with me in sour misfortune's book.   *Ib.* 82.

How oft when men are at the point of death
Have they been merry! which their keepers call
A lightning before death.   *Ib.* 88.

     Beauty's ensign yet
Is crimson in thy lips and in thy cheeks,
And death's pale flag is not advanced there.   *Ib.* 94.

     Shall I believe
That unsubstantial Death is amorous,
And that the lean abhorred monster keeps
Thee here in dark to be his paramour?
For fear of that I still will stay with thee,
And never from this palace of dim night
Depart again: here, here will I remain
With worms that are thy chambermaids; O! here
Will I set up my everlasting rest,
And shake the yoke of inauspicious stars
From this world-wearied flesh. Eyes, look your last!
Arms, take your last embrace! and, lips, O you
The doors of breath, seal with a righteous kiss
A dateless bargain to engrossing death!   *Ib.* 102.

Look in the chronicles; we came in with Richard
     Conqueror. *The Taming of the Shrew, Induc.* i. [4].

As Stephen Sly, and old John Naps of Greece,
And Peter Turf, and Henry Pimpernell,
And twenty more such names and men as these,
Which never were nor no man ever saw.   *Ib.* ii. [95].

No profit grows where is no pleasure ta'en;
In brief, sir, study what you most affect.
     Ib. I. i. 39.

There's small choice in rotten apples.   *Ib.* [137].

Nothing comes amiss, so money comes withal.
     Ib. ii. [82].

O! this learning, what a thing it is.   *Ib.* [163].

She is your treasure, she must have a husband;
I must dance bare-foot on her wedding day,
And, for your love to her, lead apes in hell.
     Ib. II. i. 32.

Say that she rail; why then I'll tell her plain
She sings as sweetly as a nightingale:
Say that she frown; I'll say she looks as clear
As morning roses newly wash'd with dew:
Say she be mute and will not speak a word;
Then I'll commend her volubility,
And say she uttereth piercing eloquence.   *Ib.* 171.

And thereby hangs a tale.   *Ib.* IV. i [59].

He kills her in her own humour.   *Ib.* [183].

     She shall watch all night:
And if she chance to nod I'll rail and brawl,
And with the clamour keep her still awake.
This is the way to kill a wife with kindness.
     Ib. [208].

What say you to a piece of beef and mustard?
     Ib. iii. [23].

And as the sun breaks through the darkest clouds,
So honour peereth in the meanest habit.   *Ib.* [175].

PETRUCHIO:
It shall be what o'clock I say it is.
HORTENSIO:
Why, so this gallant will command the sun.
     Ib. [197].

     O vile,
Intolerable, not to be endur'd!   *Ib.* v. ii. 93.

A woman mov'd is like a fountain troubled,
Muddy, ill-seeming, thick, bereft of beauty.
      The Taming of the Shrew, v. ii. 143.
Such duty as the subject owes the prince,
Even such a woman oweth to her husband. *Ib.* 156.

I am asham'd that women are so simple
To offer war where they should kneel for peace.
          Ib. 162.

What cares these roarers for the name of king?
      The Tempest, i. i. [18].

He hath no drowning mark upon him; his complexion is perfect gallows.   *Ib.* [33].

Now would I give a thousand furlongs of sea for an
acre of barren ground.   *Ib.* [70].

The wills above be done! but I would fain die a dry
death.   *Ib.* [72].

        O! I have suffer'd
With those that I saw suffer: a brave vessel,
Who had, no doubt, some noble creatures in her,
Dash'd all to pieces. O! the cry did knock
Against my very heart. Poor souls, they perish'd.
          Ib. ii. 5.
        What seest thou else
In the dark backward and abysm of time? *Ib.* 49.

      My library
Was dukedom large enough.   *Ib.* 109.

Knowing I lov'd my books, he furnish'd me,
From mine own library with volumes that
I prize above my dukedom.   *Ib.* 166.

From the still-vexed Bermoothes.   *Ib.* 229.

I will be correspondent to command
And do my spiriting gently.   *Ib.* 297.

You taught me language; and my profit on't
Is, I know how to curse: the red plague rid you,
For learning me your language!   *Ib.* 363.

Fill all thy bones with aches.   *Ib.* 370.

Come unto these yellow sands,
  And then take hands:
Curtsied when you have, and kiss'd,—
  The wild waves whist,—
Foot it featly here and there;
And, sweet sprites, the burden bear.
  Hark, hark!
        Bow, wow,
  The watch-dogs bark:
        Bow, bow,
Hark, hark! I hear
The strain of strutting Chanticleer
      Cock-a-diddle-dow.
          Ib. 375.

This music crept by me upon the waters,
Allaying both their fury, and my passion,
With its sweet air.   *Ib.* 389.

Full fathom five thy father lies;
  Of his bones are coral made:
Those are pearls that were his eyes:
  Nothing of him that doth fade,
But doth suffer a sea-change
Into something rich and strange.
Sea-nymphs hourly ring his knell:
      Ding-dong.
Hark! now I hear them,—ding-dong, bell. *Ib.* 394.

The fringed curtains of thine eye advance,
And say what thou seest yond.   *Ib.* 405.

      At the first sight
They have changed eyes.   *Ib.* 437.

There's nothing ill can dwell in such a temple:
If the ill spirit have so fair a house,
Good things will strive to dwell with 't.   *Ib.* 454.

What's past is prologue.   *Ib.* ii. i. [261].

They'll take suggestion as a cat laps milk. *Ib.* [296].

Open-ey'd conspiracy
His time doth take.   *Ib.* [309].

A very ancient and fish-like smell.   *Ib.* ii. [27].

When they will not give a doit to relieve a lame
  beggar, they will lay out ten to see a dead Indian.
          Ib. [33].

Misery acquaints a man with strange bedfellows.
          Ib. [42].

Well, here's my comfort. [*Drinks.*]   *Ib.* [48].

For she had a tongue with a tang.   *Ib.* [53].

'Ban, 'Ban, Ca-Caliban,
Has a new master—Get a new man.   *Ib.* [197].

       For several virtues
Have I lik'd several women; never any
With so full soul but some defect in her
Did quarrel with the noblest grace she ow'd,
And put it to the foil.   *Ib.* iii. i. 42.

FERDINAND:
Here's my hand.
MIRANDA:
And mine, with my heart in 't.   *Ib.* 89.

Thou deboshed fish thou.   *Ib.* ii. [30].

Flout 'em, and scout 'em; and scout 'em, and flout
  'em;
Thought is free.   *Ib.* [133].

He that dies pays all debts.   *Ib.* [143].

      The isle is full of noises,
Sounds and sweet airs, that give delight, and hurt
  not.   *Ib.* [147].

Spongy April.   *Ib.* iv. i. 65.

You sun-burn'd sicklemen, of August weary.
          Ib. 134.

Our revels now are ended. These our actors,
As I foretold you, were all spirits and
Are melted into air, into thin air:
And, like the baseless fabric of this vision,
The cloud-capp'd towers, the gorgeous palaces,
The solemn temples, the great globe itself,
Yea, all which it inherit, shall dissolve
And, like this insubstantial pageant faded,
Leave not a rack behind. We are such stuff
As dreams are made on, and our little life
Is rounded with a sleep.   *Ib.* 148.

I do begin to have bloody thoughts.   *Ib.* [221].

With foreheads villanous low.   *Ib.* [252].

Now does my project gather to a head. *Ib.* v. i. 1.

       Demi-puppets, that
By moonshine do the green sour ringlets make
Whereof the ewe not bites.   *Ib.* 36.

Deeper than did ever plummet sound,
I'll drown my book.   *The Tempest*, v. i. 56.

Where the bee sucks, there suck I
In a cowslip's bell I lie;
There I couch when owls do cry.
On the bat's back I do fly
After summer merrily:
Merrily, merrily shall I live now
Under the blossom that hangs on the bough.   *Ib.* 88.

    O brave new world,
That has such people in 't.   *Ib.* 183.

    Retire me to my Milan, where
Every third thought shall be my grave.   *Ib.* [310].

'Tis not enough to help the feeble up,
But to support him after.   *Timon of Athens*, I, i. 108.

He that loves to be flattered is worthy o' the flatterer.   *Ib.* [233].

    The strain of man 's bred out
Into baboon and monkey.   *Ib.* [260].

I wonder men dare trust themselves with men.   *Ib.* ii. [45].

Immortal gods, I crave no pelf;
I pray for no man but myself.   *Ib.* [64].

Like madness is the glory of this life.   *Ib.* [141].

Men shut their doors against a setting sun.   *Ib.* [152].

Nothing emboldens sin so much as mercy.   *Ib.* III. v. 3.

Uncover, dogs, and lap.   *Ib.* vi. [96].

You fools of fortune, trencher-friends, time's flies.   *Ib.* [107].

We have seen better days.   *Ib.* IV. ii. 27.

O! the fierce wretchedness that glory brings us.   *Ib.* 30.

He has almost charmed me from my profession, by persuading me to it.   *Ib.* iii. [457].

    My long sickness
Of health and living now begins to mend,
And nothing brings me all things.   *Ib.* v. i. [191].

Life's uncertain voyage.   *Ib.* [207].

Timon hath made his everlasting mansion
Upon the beached verge of the salt flood;
Who once a day with his embossed froth
The turbulent surge shall cover.   *Ib.* [220].

She is a woman, therefore may be woo'd;
She is a woman, therefore may be won;
She is Lavinia, therefore must be lov'd.
What, man! more water glideth by the mill
Than wots the miller of; and easy it is
Of a cut loaf to steal a shive, we know.   *Titus Andronicus*, II. i. 82.

Come, and take choice of all my library,
And so beguile thy sorrow.   *Ib.* IV. i. 34.

The eagle suffers little birds to sing,
And is not careful what they mean thereby.   *Ib.* iv. [82].

If one good deed in all my life I did,
I do repent it from my very soul.   *Ib.* v. iii. [189].

The ravish'd Helen, Menelaus' queen,
With wanton Paris sleeps.   *Troilus and Cressida*, Prologue, 9.

PANDARUS:
He that will have a cake out of the wheat must tarry the grinding.
TROILUS:
Have I not tarried?
PANDARUS:
Ay, the grinding; but you must tarry the bolting.
TROILUS:
Have I not tarried?
PANDARUS:
Ay, the bolting; but you must tarry the leavening.
TROILUS:
Still have I tarried.
PANDARUS:
Ay, to the leavening; but here's yet in the word 'hereafter' the kneading, the making of the cake, the heating of the oven, and the baking; nay, you must stay the cooling too, or you may chance to burn your lips.   *Ib.* I. i. [15].

    O! that her hand,
In whose comparison all whites are ink,
Writing their own reproach; to whose soft seizure
The cygnet's down is harsh, and spirit of sense
Hard as the palm of ploughman.   *Ib.* [57].

I have had my labour for my travail.   *Ib.* [73].

    Women are angels, wooing:
Things won are done; joy's soul lies in the doing:
That she belov'd knows nought that knows not this:
Men prize the thing ungain'd more than it is.   *Ib.* ii. [310].

    The sea being smooth
How many shallow bauble boats dare sail
Upon her patient breast.   *Ib.* iii. 34.

The heavens themselves, the planets, and this centre
Observe degree, priority, and place,
Insisture, course, proportion, season, form,
Office, and custom, in all line of order.   *Ib.* 85.

    O! when degree is shak'd,
Which is the ladder to all high designs,
The enterprise is sick.   *Ib.* 101.

Take but degree away, untune that string,
And, hark! what discord follows; each thing meets
In mere oppugnancy.   *Ib.* 109.

    The general 's disdain'd
By him one step below, he by the next,
That next by him beneath; so every step,
Exampled by the first pace that is sick
Of his superior, grows to an envious fever
Of pale and bloodless emulation.   *Ib.* 129.

    Like a strutting player, whose conceit
Lies in his hamstring, and doth think it rich
To hear the wooden dialogue and sound
'Twixt his stretch'd footing and the scaffoldage.   *Ib.* 153.

    But we are soldiers;
And may that soldier a mere recreant prove,
That means not, hath not, or is not in love!   *Ib.* 286.

And in such indexes, although small pricks
To their subsequent volumes, there is seen
The baby figure of the giant mass
Of things to come at large.   *Ib.* 343.

Mongrel beef-witted lord.   *Ib.* II. i. [14].

Who wears his wit in his belly, and his guts in his
head. *Troilus and Cressida*, II. i. [78].

The wound of peace is surety,
Surety secure. *Ib.* ii. 14.

TROILUS:
What is aught, but as 'tis valued?
HECTOR:
But value dwells not in particular will;
It holds his estimate and dignity
As well wherein 'tis precious of itself
As in the prizer. 'Tis mad idolatry
To make the service greater than the god.
Ib. 52.

Young men, whom Aristotle thought
Unfit to hear moral philosophy. *Ib.* 166.

Thus to persist
In doing wrong extenuates not wrong,
But makes it much more heavy. *Ib.* 186.

I am giddy, expectation whirls me round.
The imaginary relish is so sweet
That it enchants my sense.
Ib. III. ii. [17].

To be wise, and love,
Exceeds man's might. *Ib.* [163].

Time hath, my lord, a wallet at his back,
Wherein he puts alms for oblivion,
A great-siz'd monster of ingratitudes:
Those scraps are good deeds past; which are devour'd
As fast as they are made, forgot as soon
As done. *Ib.* iii. 145.

Perseverance, dear my lord,
Keeps honour bright: to have done, is to hang
Quite out of fashion, like a rusty mail
In monumental mockery. *Ib.* 150.

For honour travels in a strait so narrow
Where one but goes abreast. *Ib.* 154.

Time is like a fashionable host
That slightly shakes his parting guest by the hand,
And with his arms outstretch'd, as he would fly,
Grasps in the comer: welcome ever smiles,
And farewell goes out sighing. *Ib.* 165.

Beauty, wit,
High birth, vigour of bone, desert in service,
Love, friendship, charity, are subjects all
To envious and calumniating time.
One touch of nature makes the whole world kin,
That all with one consent praise new-born gawds.
Ib. 171.

And give to dust that is a little gilt
More laud than gilt o'er-dusted. *Ib.* 178.

A plague of opinion! a man may wear it on both
sides, like a leather jerkin. *Ib.* [267].

How my achievements mock me! *Ib.* IV. ii. [72].

Sometimes we are devils to ourselves
When we will tempt the frailty of our powers,
Presuming on their changeful potency. *Ib.* iv. [95].

Fie, fie upon her!
There's language in her eye, her cheek, her lip,
Nay, her foot speaks; her wanton spirits look out
At every joint and motive of her body. *Ib.* v. 54.

What's past, and what's to come, is strew'd with
husks
And formless ruin of oblivion. *Ib.* 165.

The end crowns all,
And that old common arbitrator, Time,
Will one day end it. *Ib.* 223.

Words, words, mere words, no matter from the heart.
Ib. v. iii. [109].

If music be the food of love, play on;
Give me excess of it, that, surfeiting,
The appetite may sicken, and so die.
That strain again! it had a dying fall:
O! it came o'er my ear like the sweet sound
That breathes upon a bank of violets,
Stealing and giving odour! Enough! no more:
'Tis not so sweet now as it was before.
O spirit of love! how quick and fresh art thou,
That notwithstanding thy capacity
Receiveth as the sea, nought enters there,
Of what validity and pitch soe'er,
But falls into abatement and low price,
Even in a minute: so full of shapes is fancy,
That it alone is high fantastical. *Twelfth Night*, I. i. 1.

O! when mine eyes did see Olivia first,
Methought she purg'd the air of pestilence.
That instant was I turn'd into a hart,
And my desires, like fell and cruel hounds,
E'er since pursue me. *Ib.* 19.

The element itself, till seven years' heat,
Shall not behold her face at ample view;
But, like a cloistress, she will veiled walk,
And water once a day her chamber round
With eye-offending brine. *Ib.* 26.

Away before me to sweet beds of flowers;
Love-thoughts lie rich when canopied with bowers.
Ib. 40.

And what should I do in Illyria?
My brother he is in Elysium. *Ib.* ii. 2.

O my poor brother! *Ib.* 6.

He's as tall a man as any's in Illyria. *Ib.* iii. [21].

Speaks three or four languages word for word without
book. *Ib.* [28].

Methinks sometimes I have no more wit than a
Christian or an ordinary man has; but I am a great
eater of beef, and I believe that does harm to my
wit. *Ib.* [90].

SIR ANDREW:
I would I had bestowed that time in the tongues that
I have in fencing, dancing, and bear-baiting. O!
had I but followed the arts!
SIR TOBY:
Then hadst thou had an excellent head of hair.
Ib. [99].

Wherefore are these things hid? wherefore have
these gifts a curtain before 'em? are they like to
take dust, like Mistress Mall's picture? why dost
thou not go to church in a galliard, and come home
in a coranto? My very walk should be a jig.
Ib. [135].

Is it a world to hide virtues in? *Ib.* [142].

Diana's lip
Is not more smooth and rubious; thy small pipe
Is as the maiden's organ, shrill and sound;
And all is semblative a woman's part.
Twelfth Night, I. iv. 31.

Many a good hanging prevents a bad marriage.
Ib. v. [20].

What says Quinapalus? 'Better a witty fool than a foolish wit.'
Ib. [37].

Virtue that transgresses is but patched with sin; and sin that amends is but patched with virtue.
Ib. [52].

Good my mouse of virtue, answer me.
Ib. [68].

O! you are sick of self-love, Malvolio.
Ib. [96].

A plague o' these pickle herring!
Ib. [127].

Not yet old enough for a man, nor young enough for a boy; as a squash is before 'tis a peascod, or a codling when 'tis almost an apple: 'tis with him in standing water, between boy and man. He is very well-favoured, and he speaks very shrewishly: one would think his mother's milk were scarce out of him.
Ib. [166].

I would be loath to cast away my speech, for besides that it is excellently well penned, I have taken great pains to con it.
Ib. [184].

I can say little more than I have studied, and that question's out of my part.
Ib. [191].

OLIVIA:
'Tis in grain, sir; 'twill endure wind and weather.
VIOLA:
'Tis beauty truly blent, whose red and white
Nature's own sweet and cunning hand laid on:
Lady, you are the cruell'st she alive
If you will lead these graces to the grave
And leave the world no copy.
Ib. [257].

Item, Two lips, indifferent red; Item, Two grey eyes, with lids to them; Item, One neck, one chin, and so forth.
Ib. [268].

Make me a willow cabin at your gate,
And call upon my soul within the house;
Write loyal cantons of contemned love,
And sing them loud even in the dead of night;
Halloo your name to the reverberate hills,
And make the babbling gossip of the air
Cry out, 'Olivia'.
Ib. [289].

Farewell, fair cruelty.
Ib. [309].

'What is your parentage?'
'Above my fortune, yet my state is well:
I am a gentleman.'
Ib. [310].

She is drowned already, sir, with salt water, though I seem to drown her remembrance again with more.
Ib. II. i. [31].

I am yet so near the manners of my mother, that upon the least occasion more mine eyes will tell tales of me.
Ib. [42].

Not to be a-bed after midnight is to be up betimes. ... To be up after midnight and to go to bed then, is early; so that to go to bed after midnight is to go to bed betimes.
Ib. iii. [1 and 7].

O mistress mine! where are you roaming?
O! stay and hear; your true love's coming,
That can sing both high and low.
Trip no further, pretty sweeting;
Journeys end in lovers meeting,
Every wise man's son doth know.

What is love? 'tis not hereafter;
Present mirth hath present laughter;
What's to come is still unsure:
In delay there lies no plenty;
Then come kiss me, sweet and twenty,
Youth's a stuff will not endure.
Ib. [42].

Am not I consanguineous? am I not of her blood?
Tillyvally, lady!
Ib. [85].

He does it with a better grace, but I do it more natural.
Ib. [91].

Is there no respect of place, persons, nor time, in you?
Ib. [100].

SIR TOBY:
Dost thou think, because thou art virtuous, there shall be no more cakes and ale?
CLOWN:
Yes, by Saint Anne, and ginger shall be hot i' the mouth too.
Ib. [124].

MARIA:
Marry, sir, sometimes he is a kind of puritan.
SIR ANDREW:
O, if I thought that, I'd beat him like a dog!
Ib. [153].

I will drop in his way some obscure epistles of love; wherein, by the colour of his beard, the shape of his leg, the manner of his gait, the expressure of his eye, forehead, and complexion, he shall find himself most feelingly personated.
Ib. [171].

My purpose is, indeed, a horse of that colour.
Ib. [184].

Now, good Cesario, but that piece of song,
That old and antique song we heard last night;
Methought it did relieve my passion much,
More than light airs and recollected terms
Of these most brisk and giddy-paced times:
Come, but one verse.
Ib. II. iv. 2.

DUKE:
If ever thou shalt love,
In the sweet pangs of it remember me;
For such as I am all true lovers are:
Unstaid and skittish in all motions else,
Save in the constant image of the creature
That is belov'd. How dost thou like this tune?
VIOLA:
It gives a very echo to the seat
Where love is enthron'd.
Ib. 15.

Let still the woman take
An elder than herself, so wears she to him,
So sways she level in her husband's heart:
For, boy, however we do praise ourselves,
Our fancies are more giddy and unfirm,
More longing, wavering, sooner lost and worn,
Than women's are.
Ib. 29.

Then let thy love be younger than thyself,
Or thy affection cannot hold the bent.
Ib. 36.

Mark it, Cesario; it is old and plain.
The spinsters and the knitters in the sun
And the free maids that weave their thread with bones
Do use to chant it: it is silly sooth,
And dallies with the innocence of love,
Like the old age.   *Twelfth Night*, II. iv. 43.

Come away, come away, death,
　And in sad cypress let me be laid;
Fly away, fly away, breath:
　I am slain by a fair cruel maid.
My shroud of white, stuck all with yew,
　O! prepare it.
My part of death no one so true
　Did share it.

Not a flower, not a flower sweet,
　On my black coffin let there be strown;
Not a friend, not a friend greet
　My poor corse, where my bones shall be thrown.
A thousand thousand sighs to save,
　Lay me, O! where
Sad true lover never find my grave,
　To weep there.   *Ib.* 51.

Now, the melancholy god protect thee, and the tailor
make thy doublet of changeable taffeta, for thy
mind is a very opal.   *Ib.* [74].

Get thee to yond same sovereign cruelty:
Tell her, my love, more noble than the world,
Prizes not quantity of dirty lands.   *Ib.* [82].

　　There is no woman's sides
Can bide the beating of so strong a passion
As love doth give my heart; no woman's heart
So big, to hold so much; they lack retention.
Alas! their love may be call'd appetite,
No motion of the liver, but the palate,
That suffer surfeit, cloyment, and revolt;
But mine is all as hungry as the sea,
And can digest so much.   *Ib.* [95].

DUKE:
And what's her history?
VIOLA:
A blank, my lord. She never told her love,
But let concealment, like a worm i' the bud,
Feed on her damask cheek: she pin'd in thought;
And with a green and yellow melancholy,
She sat like patience on a monument,
Smiling at grief. Was not this love indeed?
We men may say more, swear more; but, indeed,
Our shows are more than will; for still we prove
Much in our vows, but little in our love.   *Ib.* [111].

I am all the daughters of my father's house,
And all the brothers too.   *Ib.* [122].

How now, my metal of India!   *Ib.* v. [17].

Here comes the trout that must be caught with
tickling.   *Ib.* [25].

Contemplation makes a rare turkey-cock of him:
how he jets under his advanced plumes! *Ib.* [35].

In my branched velvet gown.   *Ib.* [54].

Now is the woodcock near the gin.   *Ib.* [93].

I may command where I adore.   *Ib.* [116].

But be not afraid of greatness: some men are born
great, some achieve greatness, and some have greatness thrust upon them.   *Ib.* [158].

Let thy tongue tang arguments of state; put thyself
into the trick of singularity. She thus advises thee
that sighs for thee. Remember who commended
thy yellow stockings, and wished to see thee ever
cross-gartered.   *Ib.* [165].

Jove and my stars be praised! Here is yet a postscript.
　　　　　　　　　　　　　　　　　　　Ib. [189].

He will come to her in yellow stockings, and 'tis a
colour she abhors; and cross-gartered, a fashion
she detests.   *Ib.* [220].

Now Jove, in his next commodity of hair, send thee
a beard.   *Ib.* III. i. [51].

This fellow's wise enough to play the fool,
And to do that well craves a kind of wit. *Ib.* [68].

Taste your legs, sir; put them to motion.   *Ib.* [88].

Most excellent accomplished lady, the heavens rain
odours on you!   *Ib.* [96].

　　　'Twas never merry world
Since lowly feigning was called compliment.
　　　　　　　　　　　　　　　　　　Ib. [110].

O world! how apt the poor are to be proud.
　　　　　　　　　　　　　　　　　　Ib. [141].

O! what a deal of scorn looks beautiful
In the contempt and anger of his lip.   *Ib.* [159].

Love sought is good, but giv'n unsought is better.
　　　　　　　　　　　　　　　　　　Ib. [170].

They have been grand-jurymen since before Noah
was a sailor.   *Ib.* ii. [18].

You should then have accosted her, and with some
excellent jests, fire-new from the mint, you should
have banged the youth into dumbness.   *Ib.* [23].

Where you will hang like an icicle on a Dutchman's
beard.   *Ib.* [30].

I had as lief be a Brownist as a politician.   *Ib.* [35].

Although the sheet were big enough for the bed of
Ware in England.   *Ib.* [52].

Let there be gall enough in thy ink, though thou
write with a goose-pen, no matter.   *Ib.* [54].

If he were opened, and you find so much blood in
his liver as will clog the foot of a flea, I'll eat the
rest of the anatomy.   *Ib.* [68].

Look, where the youngest wren of nine comes.
　　　　　　　　　　　　　　　　　　Ib. [73].

More lines than are in the new map with the augmentation of the Indies.   *Ib.* [87].

In the south suburbs, at the Elephant.   *Ib.* iii. 39.

I think we do know the sweet Roman hand.
　　　　　　　　　　　　　　　　　　Ib. iv. [31].

Why, this is very midsummer madness. *Ib.* iv. [62].

What, man! defy the devil: consider, he's an enemy
to mankind.   *Ib.* [109].

Go, hang yourselves all! you are idle shallow things:
I am not of your element.   *Ib.* [138].

If this were played upon a stage now, I could condemn
it as an improbable fiction.   *Ib.* [142].

More matter for a May morning.
Twelfth Night, III. iv. [158].

Still you keep o' the windy side of the law. *Ib.* [183].

Fare thee well; and God have mercy upon one of our souls! He may have mercy upon mine, but my hope is better; and so look to thyself. *Ib.* [185].

Nay, let me alone for swearing.   *Ib.* [204].

He is knight dubbed with unhatched rapier, and on carpet consideration.   *Ib.* [260].

I am one that had rather go with sir priest than sir knight; I care not who knows so much of my mettle.   *Ib.* [300].

Out of my lean and low ability
I'll lend you something.   *Ib.* [380].

I hate ingratitude more in a man
Than lying, vainness, babbling drunkenness,
Or any taint of vice whose strong corruption
Inhabits our frail blood.   *Ib.* [390].

In nature there's no blemish but the mind;
None can be call'd deform'd but the unkind. *Ib.* [403].

Out, hyperbolical fiend!   *Ib.* IV. ii. [29].

For I am one of those gentle ones that will use the devil himself with courtesy.   *Ib.* [37].

CLOWN:
What is the opinion of Pythagoras concerning wild fowl?
MALVOLIO:
That the soul of our grandam might haply inhabit a bird.
CLOWN:
What thinkest thou of his opinion?
MALVOLIO:
I think nobly of the soul, and no way approve his opinion.   *Ib.* [55].

Leave thy vain bibble-babble.   *Ib.* [106].

We took him for a coward, but he's the very devil incardinate.   *Ib.* v. i. [185].

And made the most notorious geck and gull
That e'er invention play'd.   *Ib.* [355].

And thus the whirligig of time brings in his revenges.
             Ib. [388].

When that I was and a little tiny boy,
    With hey, ho, the wind and the rain;
A foolish thing was but a toy,
    For the rain it raineth every day.

But when I came to man's estate,
    With hey, ho, the wind and the rain;
'Gainst knaves and thieves men shut their gates,
    For the rain it raineth every day.

But when I came, alas! to wive,
    With hey, ho, the wind and the rain;
By swaggering could I never thrive,
    For the rain it raineth every day.

But when I came unto my beds,
    With hey, ho, the wind and the rain;
With toss-pots still had drunken heads,
    For the rain it raineth every day.

A great while ago the world begun,
    With heigh, ho, the wind and the rain;

But that's all one, our play is done,
    And we'll strive to please you every day. *Ib.* [401].

Home-keeping youth have ever homely wits.
    The Two Gentlemen of Verona, I. i. 2.

For he was more than over shoes in love.   *Ib.* 24.

I have no other but a woman's reason:
I think him so, because I think him so.   *Ib.* ii. 23.

Fie, fie! how wayward is this foolish love
That, like a testy babe, will scratch the nurse
And presently all humbled kiss the rod!   *Ib.* 55.

O! how this spring of love resembleth
The uncertain glory of an April day.   *Ib.* iii. 84.

Or as one nail by strength drives out another,
So the remembrance of my former love
Is by a newer object quite forgotten. *Ib.* II. iv. 194.

He makes sweet music with th' enamell'd stones,
Giving a gentle kiss to every sedge
He overtaketh in his pilgrimage;
And so by many winding nooks he strays
With willing sport, to the wild ocean.   *Ib.* vii. 28.

Except I be by Silvia in the night,
There is no music in the nightingale;
Unless I look on Silvia in the day,
There is no day for me to look upon.
             Ib. III. i. 178.

Ay,
Much is the force of heaven-bred poesy.   *Ib.* ii. 71.

A man I am cross'd with adversity.   *Ib.* IV. i. 12.

        You know that love
Will creep in service where it cannot go.   *Ib.* ii. 19.

Who is Silvia? what is she,
    That all our swains commend her?
Holy, fair, and wise is she;
    The heaven such grace did lend her,
That she might admired be.

Is she kind as she is fair?
    For beauty lives with kindness:
Love doth to her eyes repair,
    To help him of his blindness;
And, being help'd, inhabits there.

Then to Silvia let us sing,
    That Silvia is excelling;
She excels each mortal thing
    Upon the dull earth dwelling;
To her let us garlands bring.   *Ib.* 40.

How use doth breed a habit in a man!
             Ib. v. iv. 1.

        O heaven! were man
But constant, he were perfect.   *Ib.* 110.

Two lads that thought there was no more behind
But such a day to-morrow as to-day,
And to be boy eternal. *The Winter's Tale*, I. ii. 63.

We were as twinn'd lambs that did frisk i' the sun,
And bleat the one at the other: what we chang'd
Was innocence for innocence; we knew not
The doctrine of ill-doing, no, nor dream'd
That any did.   *Ib.* 67.

Three crabbed months had sour'd themselves to death,
Ere I could make thee open thy white hand
And clap thyself my love.   *Ib.* 102.

Paddling palms and pinching fingers.
The Winter's Tale, I. ii. 116.

Still virginalling
Upon his palm. *Ib.* 126.

Affection! thy intention stabs the centre:
Thou dost make possible things not so held,
Communicat'st with dreams. *Ib.* 139.

How like, methought, I then was to this kernel,
This squash, this gentleman. *Ib.* 160.

A sad tale's best for winter.
I have one of sprites and goblins. *Ib.* II. i. 24.

It is a heretic that makes the fire,
Not she which burns in 't. *Ib.* iii. 116.

What's gone, and what's past help
Should be past grief. *Ib.* III. ii. [223].

Bohemia. A desert Country near the Sea.
Ib. iii. *Stage Direction.*

Our ship hath touch'd upon
The desarts of Bohemia. *Ib.* iii. 1.

Exit, pursued by a bear. *Ib. Stage Direction.*

When daffodils begin to peer,
  With heigh! the doxy, over the dale,
Why, then comes in the sweet o' the year;
  For the red blood reigns in the winter's pale.

The white sheet bleaching on the hedge,
  With heigh! the sweet birds, O, how they sing!
Doth set my pugging tooth on edge;
  For a quart of ale is a dish for a king.

The lark, that tirra-lirra chants,
  With, heigh! with, heigh! the thrush and the jay,
Are summer songs for me and my aunts,
  While we lie tumbling in the hay. *Ib.* IV. ii. 1.

But shall I go mourn for that, my dear? *Ib.* [15].

A snapper-up of unconsidered trifles. *Ib.* [26].

For the life to come, I sleep out the thought of it.
Ib. [30].

Prig, for my life, prig; he haunts wakes, fairs, and
bear-baitings. *Ib.* [109].

Jog on, jog on the foot-path way,
  And merrily hent the stile-a:
A merry heart goes all the day,
  Your sad tires in a mile-a. *Ib.* [133].

For you there's rosemary and rue; these keep
Seeming and savour all the winter long. *Ib.* iii. 74.

The fairest flowers o' the season
Are our carnations and streak'd gillyvors,
Which some call nature's bastards. *Ib.* 81.

Yet nature is made better by no mean
But nature makes that mean. *Ib.* 89.

Here's flowers for you;
Hot lavender, mints, savory, marjoram;
The marigold, that goes to bed wi' the sun,
And with him rises weeping. *Ib.* 103.

O Proserpina!
For the flowers now that frighted thou let'st fall
From Dis's waggon! daffodils,
That come before the swallow dares, and take
The winds of March with beauty; violets dim,
But sweeter than the lids of Juno's eyes

Or Cytherea's breath; pale prime-roses,
That die unmarried, ere they can behold
Bright Phœbus in his strength,—a malady
Most incident to maids; bold oxlips and
The crown imperial; lilies of all kinds,
The flower-de-luce being one. *Ib.* 116.

PERDITA:
Sure this robe of mine
Doth change my disposition.
FLORIZEL:
What you do
Still betters what is done. When you speak, sweet,
I'd have you do it ever: when you sing,
I'd have you buy and sell so; so give alms;
Pray so; and, for the ordering your affairs,
To sing them too: when you do dance, I wish you
A wave o' the sea, that you might ever do
Nothing but that; move still, still so,
And own no other function: each your doing,
So singular in each particular,
Crowns what you are doing in the present deed,
That all your acts are queens. *Ib.* 134.

Good sooth, she is
The queen of curds and cream. *Ib.* 160.

Lawn as white as driven snow. *Ib.* [220].

I love a ballad in print, a-life, for then we are sure
  they are true. *Ib.* [262].

The self-same sun that shines upon his court
Hides not his visage from our cottage, but
Looks on alike. *Ib.* [457].

Being now awake, I'll queen it no inch further,
But milk my ewes and weep. *Ib.* [462].

Prosperity's the very bond of love,
Whose fresh complexion and whose heart together
Affliction alters. *Ib.* [586].

Ha, ha! what a fool Honesty is! and Trust his sworn
  brother, a very simple gentleman! *Ib.* [608].

Though I am not naturally honest, I am so sometimes by chance. *Ib.* [734].

That rare Italian master, Julio Romano.
Ib. v. ii. [108].

Thou art a tall fellow of thy hands. *Ib.* [185].

'Tis time; descend; be stone no more; approach.
Ib. iii. 99.

O! she's warm.
If this be magic, let it be an art
Lawful as eating. *Ib.* 109.

Lord of thy presence and no land beside.
King John, I. i. 137.

For new-made honour doth forget men's names.
Ib. 186.

Sweet, sweet, sweet poison for the age's tooth.
Ib. 213.

Bearing their birthrights proudly on their backs.
Ib. II. i. 70.

For courage mounteth with occasion. *Ib.* 82.

Saint George, that swinged the dragon, and e'er since
Sits on his horse back at mine hostess' door.
Ib. 288.

Mad world! Mad kings! Mad composition!
King John, II. i. 561.

That smooth-fac'd gentleman, tickling Commodity,
Commodity, the bias of the world.   *Ib.* 573.

Well, whiles I am a beggar, I will rail,
And say there is no sin, but to be rich;
And, being rich, my virtue then shall be,
To say there is no vice, but beggary.   *Ib.* 593.

         Here I and sorrows sit;
Here is my throne, bid kings come bow to it.
           Ib. III. i. 73.

Thou wear a lion's hide! doff it for shame,
And hang a calf's-skin on those recreant limbs!
           Ib. 128.

         No Italian priest
Shall tithe or toll in our dominions.   *Ib.* 153.

Old Time the clock-setter, that bald sexton, Time.
           Ib. 324.

Bell, book and candle shall not drive me back,
When gold and silver becks me to come on.
           Ib. iii. 12.

KING JOHN:
Death.

HUBERT:
     My lord?

KING JOHN:
         A grave.

HUBERT:
             He shall not live.

KING JOHN:
                   Enough.
I could be merry now.   *Ib.* 66.

Look, who comes here! a grave unto a soul;
Holding the eternal spirit, against her will,
In the vile prison of afflicted breath.   *Ib.* iv. 17.

Grief fills the room up of my absent child,
Lies in his bed, walks up and down with me,
Puts on his pretty looks, repeats his words,
Remembers me of all his gracious parts,
Stuffs out his vacant garments with his form.
           Ib. 93.

Life is as tedious as a twice-told tale,
Vexing the dull ear of a drowsy man.   *Ib.* 108.

Heat me these irons hot.   *Ib.* IV. i. 1.

Methinks nobody should be sad but I:
Yet I remember, when I was in France,
Young gentlemen would be as sad as night,
Only for wantonness.   *Ib.* 13.

I knit my handkercher about your brows,—
The best I had, a princess wrought it me.
           Ib. 41.

To gild refined gold, to paint the lily,
To throw a perfume on the violet,
To smooth the ice, or add another hue
Unto the rainbow, or with taper light
To seek the beauteous eye of heaven to garnish,
Is wasteful and ridiculous excess.   *Ib.* ii. 11.

The spirit of the time shall teach me speed.
           Ib. 176.

Another lean unwash'd artificer.   *Ib.* 201.

It is the curse of kings to be attended
By slaves that take their humours for a warrant
To break within the bloody house of life.   *Ib.* 208.

How oft the sight of means to do ill deeds
Makes ill deeds done!   *Ib.* 219.

Whate'er you think, good words, I think, were best.
           Ib. iii. 28.

Unthread the rude eye of rebellion,
And welcome home again discarded faith. *Ib.* v. iv. 11.

I beg cold comfort.   *Ib.* vii. 42.

This England never did, nor never shall,
Lie at the proud foot of a conqueror,
But when it first did help to wound itself.
Now these her princes are come home again,
Come the three corners of the world in arms,
And we shall shock them: nought shall make us rue,
If England to itself do rest but true.   *Ib.* 112.

Old John of Gaunt, time-honour'd Lancaster.
         King Richard II, I. i. 1.

Let's purge this choler without letting blood.
           Ib. 153.

The purest treasure mortal times afford
Is spotless reputation; that away,
Men are but gilded loam or painted clay.
A jewel in a ten-times-barr'd-up chest
Is a bold spirit in a loyal breast.
Mine honour is my life; both grow in one;
Take honour from me, and my life is done. *Ib.* 177.

We were not born to sue, but to command. *Ib.* 196.

Stay, stay, the king hath thrown his warder down.
           Ib. iii. 119.

         This must my comfort be,
That sun that warms you here shall shine on me.
           Ib. 144.

The language I have learn'd these forty years,
My native English, now I must forego;
And now my tongue's use is to me no more
Than an unstringed viol or a harp.   *Ib.* 159.

I am too old to fawn upon a nurse,
Too far in years to be a pupil now.   *Ib.* 170.

How long a time lies in one little word!
Four lagging winters and four wanton springs
End in a word; such is the breath of kings. *Ib.* 213.

Things sweet to taste prove in digestion sour.
           Ib. 236.

         Boast of nothing else
But that I was a journeyman to grief?   *Ib.* 273.

All places that the eye of heaven visits
Are to a wise man ports and happy havens.
Teach thy necessity to reason thus;
There is no virtue like necessity.   *Ib.* 275.

O! who can hold a fire in his hand
By thinking on the frosty Caucasus?
Or cloy the hungry edge of appetite,
By bare imagination of a feast?
Or wallow naked in December snow
By thinking on fantastic summer's heat?
O, no! the apprehension of the good
Gives but the greater feeling to the worse. *Ib.* 294.

Methinks I am a prophet new inspir'd,
And thus expiring do foretell of him:
His rash fierce blaze of riot cannot last,
For violent fires soon burn out themselves;
Small showers last long, but sudden storms are short;
He tires betimes that spurs too fast betimes.
           Ib. II. i. 31.

This royal throne of kings, this scepter'd isle,
This earth of majesty, this seat of Mars,
This other Eden, demi-Paradise,
This fortress built by Nature for herself
Against infection and the hand of war,
This happy breed of men, this little world,
This precious stone set in the silver sea,
Which serves it in the office of a wall,
Or as a moat defensive to a house,
Against the envy of less happier lands,
This blessed plot, this earth, this realm, this England,
This nurse, this teeming womb of royal kings,
Fear'd by their breed and famous by their birth,
Renowned for their deeds as far from home,—
For Christian service and true chivalry,—
As is the sepulchre in stubborn Jewry
Of the world's ransom, blessed Mary's Son:
This land of such dear souls, this dear, dear land.
King Richard II, II. i. 40.

England, bound in with the triumphant sea. *Ib.* 61.

That England, that was wont to conquer others,
Hath made a shameful conquest of itself. *Ib.* 65.

Can sick men play so nicely with their names?
Ib. 84.

    Lay aside life-harming heaviness,
And entertain a cheerful disposition. *Ib.* ii. 3.

    Believe me, noble lord,
I am a stranger here in Gloucestershire:
These high wild hills and rough uneven ways
Draw out our miles and make them wearisome.
Ib. iii. 2.

I count myself in nothing else so happy
As in a soul remembering my good friends. *Ib.* 46.

Bloody with spurring, fiery-red with haste. *Ib.* 58.

Grace me no grace, nor uncle me no uncle. *Ib.* 87.

The caterpillars of the commonwealth. *Ib.* 166.

Things past redress are now with me past care.
Ib. 171.

Eating the bitter bread of banishment.
Ib. III. i. 21.

    I weep for joy
To stand upon my kingdom once again.
Dear earth, I do salute thee with my hand,
Though rebels wound thee with their horses' hoofs.
Ib. ii. 4.

Not all the water in the rough rude sea
Can wash the balm from an anointed king;
The breath of worldly men cannot depose
The deputy elected by the Lord.
For every man that Bolingbroke hath press'd
To lift shrewd steel against our golden crown,
God for his Richard hath in heavenly pay
A glorious angel; then, if angels fight,
Weak men must fall, for heaven still guards the
    right. *Ib.* 59.

O! call back yesterday, bid time return. *Ib.* 69.

Is not the king's name twenty thousand names?
Arm, arm, my name! A puny subject strikes
At thy great glory. *Ib.* 85.

The worst is death, and death will have his day.
Ib. 103.

Sweet love, I see, changing his property,
Turns to the sourest and most deadly hate. *Ib.* 135.

    Of comfort no man speak:
Let's talk of graves, of worms, and epitaphs;
Make dust our paper, and with rainy eyes
Write sorrow on the bosom of the earth.
Let's choose executors, and talk of wills. *Ib.* 144.

For God's sake, let us sit upon the ground
And tell sad stories of the death of kings:
How some have been depos'd, some slain in war,
Some haunted by the ghosts they have depos'd,
Some poison'd by their wives, some sleeping kill'd;
All murder'd: for within the hollow crown
That rounds the mortal temples of a king
Keeps Death his court, and there the antick sits,
Scoffing his state and grinning at his pomp;
Allowing him a breath, a little scene,
To monarchize, be fear'd, and kill with looks,
Infusing him with self and vain conceit
As if this flesh which walls about our life
Were brass impregnable; and humour'd thus
Comes at the last, and with a little pin
Bores through his castle wall, and farewell king!
Ib. 155.

See, see, King Richard doth himself appear,
As doth the blushing discontented sun
From out the fiery portal of the east. *Ib.* iii. 62.

    O! that I were as great
As is my grief, or lesser than my name,
Or that I could forget what I have been,
Or not remember what I must be now. *Ib.* 136.

What must the king do now? Must he submit?
The king shall do it: must he be depos'd?
The king shall be contented: must he lose
The name of king? o' God's name, let it go.
I'll give my jewels for a set of beads,
My gorgeous palace for a hermitage,
My gay apparel for an almsman's gown,
My figur'd goblets for a dish of wood,
My sceptre for a palmer's walking staff,
My subjects for a pair of carved saints,
And my large kingdom for a little grave,
A little little grave, an obscure grave;
Or I'll be buried in the king's highway,
Some way of common trade, where subjects' feet
May hourly trample on their sovereign's head;
For on my heart they tread now whilst I live;
And buried once, why not upon my head? *Ib.* 143.

You make a leg. *Ib.* 175.

Go, bind thou up yon dangling apricocks,
Which, like unruly children, make their sire
Stoop with oppression of their prodigal weight.
Ib. iv. 29.

Old Adam's likeness, set to dress this garden. *Ib.* 73.

Here did she fall a tear; here, in this place,
I'll set a bank of rue, sour herb of grace;
Rue, even for ruth, here shortly shall be seen,
In the remembrance of a weeping queen. *Ib.* 104.

If I dare eat, or drink, or breathe, or live,
I dare meet Surrey in a wilderness,
And spit upon him, whilst I say he lies,
And lies, and lies. *Ib.* IV. i. 73.

    And there at Venice gave
His body to that pleasant country's earth,
And his pure soul unto his captain Christ,
Under whose colours he had fought so long. *Ib.* 97.

Peace shall go sleep with Turks and infidels.
King Richard II, IV. i. 139.

God save the king! Will no man say, amen?
Am I both priest and clerk? Well then, amen.
Ib. 172.

Give me the crown. Here, cousin, seize the crown;
Here cousin,
On this side my hand and on that side thine.
Now is this golden crown like a deep well
That owes two buckets filling one another;
The emptier ever dancing in the air,
The other down, unseen, and full of water:
That bucket down and full of tears am I,
Drinking my griefs, whilst you mount up on high.
Ib. 181.

You may my glories and my state depose,
But not my griefs; still am I king of those. *Ib.* 192.

Now mark me how I will undo myself. *Ib.* 203.

With mine own tears I wash away my balm,
With mine own hands I give away my crown.
Ib. 207.

God pardon all oaths that are broke to me!
God keep all vows unbroke are made to thee!
Ib. 214.

A mockery king of snow. *Ib.* 260.

An if my word be sterling yet in England. *Ib.* 264.

Julius Caesar's ill-erected tower. *Ib.* v. i. 2.

I am sworn brother, sweet,
To grim Necessity, and he and I
Will keep a league till death. *Ib.* 20.

That were some love but little policy. *Ib.* 84.

As in a theatre, the eyes of men,
After a well-grac'd actor leaves the stage,
Are idly bent on him that enters next,
Thinking his prattle to be tedious. *Ib.* ii. 23.

Who are the violets now
That strew the green lap of the new come spring?
Ib. 46.

Give me my boots I say. *Ib.* 77 and 87.

He prays but faintly and would be denied. *Ib.* iii. 103.

I have been studying how I may compare
This prison where I live unto the world. *Ib.* v. i.

How sour sweet music is,
When time is broke, and no proportion kept!
So is it in the music of men's lives. *Ib.* 42.

Mount, mount, my soul! thy seat is up on high,
Whilst my gross flesh sinks downwards, here to die.
Ib. 112.

So shaken as we are, so wan with care.
King Henry IV, Part I, I. i. 1.

In those holy fields
Over whose acres walk'd those blessed feet,
Which fourteen hundred years ago were nail'd
For our advantage, on the bitter cross. *Ib.* 24.

The blessed sun himself a fair hot wench in flame-
colour'd taffeta. *Ib.* ii. [10].

I see no reason why thou shouldst be so superfluous
to demand the time of the day. *Ib.* [11].

Phoebus, he 'that wandering knight so fair'. *Ib.* [16].

Let us be Diana's foresters, gentlemen of the shade,
minions of the moon. *Ib.* [28].

FALSTAFF:
And is not my hostess of the tavern a most sweet
wench?
PRINCE:
As the honey of Hybla, my old lad of the castle.
Ib. 44.

What, in thy quips and thy quiddities? *Ib.* [50].

Shall there be gallows standing in England when
thou art king, and resolution thus fobbed as it is
with the rusty curb of old father antick, the law?
Ib. [66].

Thou hast the most unsavoury similes. *Ib.* [89].

I would to God thou and I knew where a commodity
of good names were to be bought. *Ib.* [92].

O! thou hast damnable iteration, and art, indeed,
able to corrupt a saint. *Ib.* [101].

Now am I, if a man should speak truly, little better
than one of the wicked. *Ib.* [105].

I'll be damned for never a king's son in Christendom.
Ib. [108].

Why, Hal, 'tis my vocation, Hal; 'tis no sin for a
man to labour in his vocation. *Ib.* [116].

How agrees the devil and thee about thy soul, that
thou soldest him on Good Friday last for a cup
of Madeira and a cold capon's leg? *Ib.* [126].

There's neither honesty, manhood, nor good fellowship in thee. *Ib.* [154].

Farewell, thou latter spring! Farewell, All-hallown
summer! *Ib.* [176].

If he fight longer than he sees reason, I'll forswear
arms. *Ib.* [206].

I know you all, and will awhile uphold
The unyok'd humour of your idleness. *Ib.* [217].

If all the year were playing holidays,
To sport would be as tedious as to work;
But when they seldom come, they wish'd for come.
Ib. [226].

A certain lord, neat, and trimly dress'd,
Fresh as a bridegroom; and his chin, new-reap'd,
Show'd like a stubble-land at harvest home:
He was perfumed like a milliner,
And 'twixt his finger and his thumb he held
A pouncet-box, which ever and anon
He gave his nose and took't away again. *Ib.* iii. 33.

And as the soldiers bore dead bodies by,
He call'd them untaught knaves, unmannerly,
To bring a slovenly, unhandsome corpse
Betwixt the wind and his nobility.
With many holiday and lady terms
He question'd me. *Ib.* 42.

So pester'd with a popinjay. *Ib.* 50.

He made me mad
To see him shine so brisk, and smell so sweet
And talk so like a waiting-gentlewoman
Of guns, and drums, and wounds,—God save the
mark!—

And telling me the sovereign'st thing on earth
Was parmaceti for an inward bruise;
And that it was great pity, so it was,
This villainous saltpetre should be digg'd
Out of the bowels of the harmless earth,
Which many a good tall fellow had destroy'd
So cowardly; and but for these vile guns,
He would himself have been a soldier.
King Henry IV, Part 1, 1. iii. 53.

To put down Richard, that sweet lovely rose,
And plant this thorn, this canker, Bolingbroke.
Ib. 175.

WORCESTER:
As to o'er-walk a current roaring loud,
On the unsteadfast footing of a spear.
HOTSPUR:
If he fall in, good-night! or sink or swim:
Send danger from the east unto the west,
So honour cross it from the north to south,
And let them grapple: O! the blood more stirs
To rouse a lion than to start a hare. *Ib.* 192.

By heaven methinks it were an easy leap
To pluck bright honour from the pale-fac'd moon,
Or dive into the bottom of the deep,
Where fathom-line could never touch the ground,
And pluck up drowned honour by the locks;
So he that doth redeem her thence might wear
Without corrival all her dignities:
But out upon this half-fac'd fellowship! *Ib.* 201.

Why, what a candy deal of courtesy
This fawning greyhound then did proffer me! *Ib.* 251.

I know a trick worth two of that. *Ib.* II. i. [40].

'At hand, quoth pick-purse.' *Ib.* [53].

We have the receipt of fern-seed, we walk invisible.
Ib. [95].

I am bewitched with the rogue's company. If the
rascal have not given me medicines to make me
love him, I'll be hanged. *Ib.* ii. [19].

Farewell, and stand fast. *Ib.* [78].

Happy man be his dole. *Ib.* [84].

On, bacons, on! *Ib.* [99].

It would be an argument for a week, laughter for a
month, and a good jest for ever. *Ib.* 104.

Falstaff sweats to death
And lards the lean earth as he walks along.
Ib. [119].

Out of this nettle, danger, we pluck this flower,
safety. *Ib.* iii. [11].

A good plot, good friends, and full of expectation;
an excellent plot, very good friends. *Ib.* [21].

Constant you are,
But yet a woman: and for secrecy,
No lady closer; for I well believe
Thou wilt not utter what thou dost not know.
Ib. [113].

Show it a fair pair of heels. *Ib.* iv. [52].

I am not yet of Percy's mind, the Hotspur of the
North; he that kills me some six or seven dozen
of Scots at a breakfast, washes his hands, and says
to his wife, 'Fie upon this quiet life! I want work.'
Ib. [116].

Didst thou never see Titan kiss a dish of butter—
pitiful-hearted Titan, that melted at the sweet tale
of the sun? *Ib.* [135].

There live not three good men unhanged in England,
and one of them is fat and grows old. *Ib.* [146].

Call you that backing of your friends? A plague
upon such backing! give me them that will face
me. *Ib.* [168].

A plague of all cowards, still say I. *Ib.* [175].

I am a Jew else; an Ebrew Jew. *Ib.* [201].

All! I know not what ye call all. *Ib.* [208].

Nay, that's past praying for: I have peppered two
of them: two I am sure I have paid, two rogues in
buckram suits. I tell thee what, Hal, if I tell thee a
lie, spit in my face, call me horse. Thou knowest
my old ward; here I lay, and thus I bore my point.
Four rogues in buckram let drive at me—
Ib. [214].

O monstrous! eleven buckram men grown out of two.
Ib. [247].

Three misbegotten knaves in Kendal-green.
Ib. [249].

These lies are like the father that begets them; gross
as a mountain, open, palpable. *Ib.* [253].

Give you a reason on compulsion! if reasons were as
plentiful as blackberries I would give no man a
reason upon compulsion, I. *Ib.* [267].

Mark now, how a plain tale shall put you down.
Ib. [285].

What a slave art thou, to hack thy sword as thou hast
done, and then say it was in fight! *Ib.* [292].

Instinct is a great matter, I was a coward on instinct.
Ib. [304].

Ah! No more of that, Hal, an thou lovest me.
Ib. [316].

What doth gravity out of his bed at midnight?
Ib. [328].

A plague of sighing and grief! It blows a man up
like a bladder. *Ib.* [370].

I will do it in King Cambyses' vein. *Ib.* [430].

QUICKLY:
O Jesu! he doth it as like one of these harlotry players
as ever I see!
FALSTAFF:
Peace, good pint-pot! *Ib.* [441].

Shall the blessed sun of heaven prove a micher and
eat blackberries? A question not to be asked.
Ib. [454].

There is a devil haunts thee in the likeness of a fat
old man; a tun of man is thy companion.
Ib. [498].

That roasted Manningtree ox with the pudding in
his belly, that reverend vice, that grey iniquity,
that father ruffian, that vanity in years. *Ib.* [504].

If sack and sugar be a fault, God help the wicked!
Ib. [524].

No, my good lord; banish Peto, banish Bardolph,
banish Poins; but for sweet Jack Falstaff, kind
Jack Falstaff, true Jack Falstaff, valiant Jack
Falstaff, and therefore more valiant, being, as he
is, old Jack Falstaff, banish not him thy Harry's
company: banish not him thy Harry's company:
banish plump Jack and banish all the world.
King Henry IV, Part 1, II. iv. [528].

Play out the play. *Ib.* [539].

O monstrous! but one half-pennyworth of bread to
this intolerable deal of sack! *Ib.* [598].

GLENDOWER:
　　　　　　At my nativity
The front of heaven was full of fiery shapes,
Of burning cressets; and at my birth
The frame and huge foundation of the earth
Shak'd like a coward.
HOTSPUR:
Why, so it would have done at the same season, if
your mother's cat had but kittened.
　　　　　　　　　　　　Ib. III. i. 13.

And all the courses of my life do show
I am not in the roll of common men. *Ib.* [42].

GLENDOWER:
I can call spirits from the vasty deep.
HOTSPUR:
Why, so can I, or so can any man;
But will they come when you do call for them?
　　　　　　　　　　　　Ib. [53].

O! while you live, tell truth, and shame the devil!
　　　　　　　　　　　　Ib. [62].

See how this river comes me cranking in,
And cuts me from the best of all my land
A huge half-moon, a monstrous cantle out. *Ib.* [99].

I had rather be a kitten and cry mew
Than one of these same metre ballad-mongers.
　　　　　　　　　　　　Ib. [128].

Mincing poetry. *Ib.* [133].

And such a deal of skimble-skamble stuff
As puts me from my faith. *Ib.* [153].

　　　　　O! he's as tedious
As a tired horse, a railing wife;
Worse than a smoky house. I had rather live
With cheese and garlic in a windmill, far,
Than feed on cates and have him talk to me
In any summer-house in Christendom. *Ib.* [158].

I understand thy kisses, and thou mine,
And that's a feeling disputation. *Ib.* [204].

Makes Welsh as sweet as ditties highly penn'd,
Sung by a fair queen in a summer's bower,
With ravishing division, to her lute. *Ib.* [208].

Now I perceive the devil understands Welsh.
　　　　　　　　　　　　Ib. 233.

You swear like a comfit-maker's wife. *Ib.* [252].

Swear me, Kate, like a lady as thou art,
A good mouth-filling oath. *Ib.* [257].

The skipping king, he ambled up and down
With shallow jesters and rash bavin wits. *Ib.* ii. 60.

　　　　Being daily swallow'd by men's eyes,
They surfeited with honey and began

To loathe the taste of sweetness, whereof a little
More than a little is by much too much.
So, when we had occasion to be seen,
He was but as the cuckoo is in June,
Heard, not regarded. *Ib.* 70.

My near'st and dearest enemy. *Ib.* 123.

Well, I'll repent, and that suddenly, while I am in
some liking; I shall be out of heart shortly, and
then I shall have no strength to repent.
　　　　　　　　　　　　Ib. iii. [5].

Company, villainous company, hath been the spoil of
me. *Ib.* [10].

Come, sing me a bawdy song; make me merry.
　　　　　　　　　　　　Ib. [15].

Shall I not take mine ease in mine inn? *Ib.* [91].

I have more flesh than another man, and therefore
more frailty. *Ib.* [187].

　　　　　That daff'd the world aside,
And bid it pass. *Ib.* IV. i. 96.

All plum'd like estridges that wing the wind,
Baited like eagles having lately bath'd. *Ib.* 98.

I saw young Harry, with his beaver on,
His cuisses on his thighs, gallantly arm'd,
Rise from the ground like feather'd Mercury,
And vaulted with such ease into his seat,
As if an angel dropp'd down from the clouds,
To turn and wind a fiery Pegasus,
And witch the world with noble horsemanship.
　　　　　　　　　　　　Ib. 104.

Doomsday is near; die all, die merrily. *Ib.* 134.

I have misus'd the king's press damnably.
　　　　　　　　　　　　Ib. ii. [13].

The cankers of a calm world and a long peace.
　　　　　　　　　　　　Ib. [32].

I am as vigilant as a cat to steal cream. *Ib.* [64].

Tut, tut; good enough to toss; food for powder, food
for powder; they'll fill a pit as well as better:
tush, man, mortal men, mortal men. *Ib.* [72].

To the latter end of a fray and the beginning of a
feast
Fits a dull fighter and a keen guest. *Ib.* [86].

Greatness knows itself. *Ib.* iii. 74.

For mine own part, I could be well content
To entertain the lag-end of my life
With quiet hours. *Ib.* v. i. 23.

Rebellion lay in his way, and he found it. *Ib.* 28.

I do not think a braver gentleman,
More active-valiant or more valiant-young,
More daring or more bold, is now alive
To grace this latter age with noble deeds.
For my part, I may speak it to my shame,
I have a truant been to chivalry. *Ib.* 89.

FALSTAFF:
I would it were bed-time, Hal, and all well.
PRINCE:
Why, thou owest God a death. *Ib.* [125].

Honour pricks me on. Yea, but how if honour prick me off when I come on? how then? Can honour set-to a leg? No. Or an arm? No. Or take away the grief of a wound? No. Honour hath no skill in surgery, then? No. What is honour? A word. What is that word, honour? Air. A trim reckoning! Who hath it? He that died o' Wednesday. Doth he feel it? No. Doth he hear it? No. It is insensible then? Yea, to the dead. But will it not live with the living? No. Why? Detraction will not suffer it. Therefore I'll none of it: honour is a mere scutcheon: and so ends my catechism.

King Henry IV, Part 1, v. i. [131].

Suspicion all our lives shall be stuck full of eyes;
For treason is but trusted like the fox,
Who, ne'er so tame, so cherish'd, and lock'd up,
Will have a wild trick of his ancestors.　*Ib.* ii. 8.

O gentlemen! the time of life is short;
To spend that shortness basely were too long,
If life did ride upon a dial's point,
Still ending at the arrival of an hour.
An if we live, we live to tread on kings;
If die, brave death, when princes die with us!
Now, for our consciences, the arms are fair,
When the intent of bearing them is just.　*Ib.* 81.

Now, *Esperance!* Percy! and set on.　*Ib.* 96.

I have led my ragamuffins where they are peppered: there's not three of my hundred and fifty left alive, and they are for the town's end, to beg during life.　*Ib.* iii. [36].

I like not such grinning honour as Sir Walter hath: give me life; which if I can save, so; if not, honour comes unlooked for, and there's an end.　*Ib.* 61.

Two stars keep not their motion in one sphere.
Ib. iv. 65.

But thought's the slave of life, and life time's fool;
And time, that takes survey of all the world,
Must have a stop.　*Ib.* [81].

　　　　Fare thee well, great heart!
Ill-weav'd ambition, how much art thou shrunk!
When that this body did contain a spirit,
A kingdom for it was too small a bound;
But now two paces of the vilest earth
Is room enough: this earth, that bears thee dead,
Bears not alive so stout a gentleman.　*Ib.* [87].

Thy ignominy sleep with thee in the grave,
But not remember'd in thy epitaph!
What! old acquaintance! could not all this flesh
Keep in a little life? Poor Jack, farewell!
I could have better spar'd a better man.　*Ib.* [100].

The better part of valour is discretion.　*Ib.* [120].

　　　　Full bravely hast thou flesh'd
Thy maiden sword.　*Ib.* [132].

Lord, Lord, how this world is given to lying! I grant you I was down and out of breath; and so was he; but we rose both at an instant, and fought a long hour by Shrewsbury clock.　*Ib.* [148].

For my part, if a lie will do thee grace,
I'll gild it with the happiest terms I have.　*Ib.* [161].

I'll purge, and leave sack, and live cleanly, as a nobleman should do.　*Ib.* [168].

I speak of peace, while covert enmity
Under the smile of safety wounds the world.
　　　King Henry IV, Part 2, Induction, 9.

　　　　Rumour is a pipe
Blown by surmises, jealousies, conjectures,
And of so easy and so plain a stop
That the blunt monster with uncounted heads,
The still-discordant wavering multitude,
Can play upon it.　*Ib.* 15.

Even such a man, so faint, so spiritless,
So dull, so dead in look, so woe-begone,
Drew Priam's curtain in the dead of night,
And would have told him, half his Troy was burn'd.
Ib. I. i. 70.

Yet the first bringer of unwelcome news
Hath but a losing office, and his tongue
Sounds ever after as a sullen bell,
Remember'd knolling a departed friend.　*Ib.* 100.

The brain of this foolish-compounded clay, man, is not able to invent anything that tends to laughter, more than I invent or is invented on me: I am not only witty in myself, but the cause that wit is in other men. I do here walk before thee like a sow that hath overwhelmed all her litter but one.
Ib. ii. [7].

A rascally yea-forsooth knave.　*Ib.* [40].

Your lordship, though not clean past your youth, hath yet some smack of age in you, some relish of the saltness of time.　*Ib.* [111].

This apoplexy is, as I take it, a kind of lethargy, an't please your lordship; a kind of sleeping in the blood, a whoreson tingling.　*Ib.* [127].

It is the disease of not listening, the malady of not marking, that I am troubled withal.　*Ib.* [139].

I am as poor as Job, my lord, but not so patient.
Ib. [145].

Well, I am loath to gall a new-healed wound.
Ib. 169.

You that are old consider not the capacities of us that are young; you measure the heat of our livers with the bitterness of your galls; and we that are in the vaward of our youth, I must confess, are wags too.　*Ib.* [198].

Have you not a moist eye, a dry hand, a yellow cheek, a white beard, a decreasing leg, an increasing belly?　*Ib.* [206].

Every part about you blasted with antiquity.
Ib. [210].

My lord, I was born about three of the clock in the afternoon, with a white head, and something of a round belly. For my voice, I have lost it with hollaing, and singing of anthems.　*Ib.* [213].

CHIEF JUSTICE:
God send the prince a better companion!
FALSTAFF:
God send the companion a better prince! I cannot rid my hands of him.　*Ib.* [227].

All you that kiss our lady Peace at home.　*Ib.* [236].

It was always yet the trick of our English nation, if they have a good thing, to make it too common.
Ib. [244].

I would to God my name were not so terrible to the enemy as it is: I were better to be eaten to death with rust than to be scoured to nothing with perpetual motion.   *King Henry IV*, *Part 2*, I. ii. [247].

I can get no remedy against this consumption of the purse: borrowing only lingers and lingers it out, but the disease is incurable.   *Ib.* [268].

O, thoughts of men accurst!
Past and to come seem best; things present, worst.
   Ib. iii. 107.

A poor lone woman.   *Ib.* II. i. [37].

Away, you scullion! you rampallion! you fustilarian!
I'll tickle your catastrophe.   *Ib.* [67].

He hath eaten me out of house and home.   *Ib.* [82].

Thou didst swear to me upon a parcel-gilt goblet, sitting in my Dolphin-chamber, at the round table, by a sea-coal fire, upon Wednesday in Wheeson week.   *Ib.* [97].

Doth it not show vilely in me to desire small beer?
   Ib. ii. [7].

I do now remember the poor creature, small beer.
   Ib. [12].

Let the end try the man.   *Ib.* [52].

Never a man's thought in the world keeps the road way better than thine.   *Ib.* [64].

He was indeed the glass
Wherein the noble youth did dress themselves.
   Ib. iii. 21.

Hollow pamper'd jades of Asia.   *Ib.* [177].

By my troth, captain, these are very bitter words.
   Ib. [183].

Thou whoreson little tidy Bartholomew boar-pig.
   Ib. [249].

Patch up thine old body for heaven.   *Ib.* [251].

O sleep! O gentle sleep!
Nature's soft nurse, how have I frighted thee,
That thou no more wilt weigh mine eyelids down
And steep my senses in forgetfulness?
Why rather, sleep, liest thou in smoky cribs,
Upon uneasy pallets stretching thee,
And hush'd with buzzing night-flies to thy slumber,
Than in the perfum'd chambers of the great,
Under the canopies of costly state,
And lull'd with sound of sweetest melody?
   Ib. III. i. 5.

Wilt thou upon the high and giddy mast
Seel up the ship-boy's eyes, and rock his brains
In cradle of the rude imperious surge,
And in the visitation of the winds,
Who take the ruffian billows by the top,
Curling their monstrous heads, and hanging them
With deaf'ning clamour in the slippery clouds,
That with the hurly death itself awakes?   *Ib.* 18.

With all appliances and means to boot.   *Ib.* 29.

Then, happy low, lie down!
Uneasy lies the head that wears a crown.   *Ib.* 30.

O God! that one might read the book of fate.   *Ib.* 45.

There is a history in all men's lives,
Figuring the nature of the times deceas'd,
The which observ'd, a man may prophesy,
With a near aim, of the main chance of things
As yet not come to life, which in their seeds
And weak beginnings lie intreasured.   *Ib.* 80.

Death, as the Psalmist saith, is certain to all; all shall die. How a good yoke of bullocks at Stamford fair?   *Ib.* ii. [41].

And is old Double dead?   *Ib.* [58].

A soldier is better accommodated than with a wife.
   Ib. [73].

Most forcible Feeble.   *Ib.* [181].

We have heard the chimes at midnight.   *Ib.* [231].

I care not; a man can die but once; we owe God a death.   *Ib.* [253].

He that dies this year is quit for the next.   *Ib.* [257].

Lord, Lord, how subject we old men are to this vice of lying!   *Ib.* [329].

Like a man made after supper of a cheese-paring: when a' was naked, he was, for all the world, like a forked radish, with a head fantastically carved upon it with a knife.   *Ib.* [335].

Talks as familiarly of John a Gaunt as if he had been sworn brother to him.   *Ib.* [348].

Against ill chances men are ever merry,
But heaviness foreruns the good event. *Ib.* IV. ii. 81.

A peace is of the nature of a conquest;
For then both parties nobly are subdu'd,
And neither party loser.   *Ib.* 89.

That I may truly say with the hook-nosed fellow of Rome, 'I came, saw, and overcame.'   *Ib.* iii. [44].

A man cannot make him laugh; but that's no marvel; he drinks no wine.   *Ib.* [95].

A good sherris-sack hath a two-fold operation in it. It ascends me into the brain; dries me there all the foolish and dull and crudy vapours which environ it; makes it apprehensive, quick, forgetive, full of nimble fiery and delectable shapes; which, deliver'd o'er to the voice, the tongue, which is the birth, becomes excellent wit. The second property of your excellent sherris is, the warming of the blood; which, before cold and settled, left the liver white and pale, which is the badge of pusillanimity and cowardice: but the sherris warms it and makes it course from the inwards to the parts extreme. It illumineth the face, which, as a beacon, gives warning to all the rest of this little kingdom, man, to arm; and then the vital commoners and inland petty spirits muster me all to their captain, the heart, who, great and puffed up with this retinue, doth any deed of courage; and this valour comes of sherris. So that skill in the weapon is nothing without sack, for that sets it a-work; and learning, a mere hoard of gold kept by a devil till sack commences it and sets it in act and use. *Ib.* [103].

If I had a thousand sons, the first human principle I would teach them should be, to forswear thin potations.   *Ib.* [133].

Most subject is the fattest soil to weeds. *Ib.* iv. 54.

Thou art a summer bird,
Which ever in the haunch of winter sings
The lifting up of day.
King Henry IV, Part 2, IV. iv. [91].

O polish'd perturbation! golden care!
That keep'st the ports of slumber open wide
To many a watchful night! Sleep with it now!
Yet not so sound, and half so deeply sweet
As he whose brow with homely biggen bound
Snores out the watch of night. *Ib.* v. 22.

This sleep is sound indeed; this is a sleep
That from this golden rigol hath divorc'd
So many English kings. *Ib.* 34.

Thy wish was father, Harry, to that thought. *Ib.* 91.

Commit
The oldest sins the newest kind of ways. *Ib.* 124.

It hath been prophesied to me many years
I should not die but in Jerusalem,
Which vainly I suppos'd the Holy Land.
But bear me to that chamber; there I'll lie:
In that Jerusalem shall Harry die. *Ib.* 235.

Any pretty little tiny kickshaws, tell William cook.
Ib. v. i. [29].

Not Amurath an Amurath succeeds,
But Harry, Harry. *Ib.* 48.

Sorrow so royally in you appears,
That I will deeply put the fashion on. *Ib.* 51.

'Tis merry in hall when beards wag all. *Ib.* iii. [35].

A foutra for the world, and worldlings base!
I speak of Africa and golden joys. *Ib.* [100].

Under which king, Bezonian? speak, or die!
Ib. [116].

Let us take any man's horses; the laws of England
are at my commandment. *Ib.* [139].

I know thee not, old man: fall to thy prayers;
How ill white hairs become a fool and jester!
I have long dream'd of such a kind of man,
So surfeit-swell'd, so old, and so profane. *Ib.* v. [52].

Make less thy body hence, and more thy grace;
Leave gormandizing; know the grave doth gape
For thee thrice wider than for other men. *Ib.* [57].

Presume not that I am the thing I was. *Ib.* [61].

Master Shallow, I owe you a thousand pound.
Ib. [78].

Where, for anything I know, Falstaff shall die of a
sweat, unless already a' be killed with your hard
opinions; for Oldcastle died a martyr, and this is
not the man.
Ib. Epilogue [32].

O! for a Muse of fire, that would ascend
The brightest heaven of invention.
King Henry V, Chorus, 1.
The flat unraised spirits. *Ib.* 9.

Can this cockpit hold
The vasty fields of France? or may we cram
Within this wooden O the very casques
That did affright the air at Agincourt? *Ib.* 11.

Consideration like an angel came,
And whipp'd the offending Adam out of him.
Ib. I. i. 8

Never came reformation in a flood,
With such a heady currance, scouring faults. *Ib.* 33.

When he speaks,
The air, a charter'd libertine, is still. *Ib.* 47.

O noble English! that could entertain
With half their forces the full pride of France,
And let another half stand laughing by,
All out of work, and cold for action. *Ib.* ii. 111.

And make your chronicle as rich with praise
As is the owse and bottom of the sea
With sunken wreck and sumless treasuries. *Ib.* 163.

For so work the honey-bees,
Creatures that by a rule in nature teach
The act of order to a peopled kingdom.
They have a king and officers of sorts,
Where some, like magistrates, correct at home,
Others, like merchants, venture trade abroad,
Others, like soldiers, armed in their stings,
Make boot upon the summer's velvet buds;
Which pillage they with merry march bring home
To the tent-royal of their emperor:
Who, busied in his majesty, surveys
The singing masons building roofs of gold,
The civil citizens kneading up the honey,
The poor mechanic porters crowding in
Their heavy burdens at his narrow gate,
The sad-ey'd justice, with his surly hum,
Delivering o'er to executors pale
The lazy yawning drone. *Ib.* 187.

His present and your pains we thank you for:
When we have match'd our rackets to these balls,
We will in France, by God's grace, play a set
Shall strike his father's crown into the hazard.
Ib. 260.

Now all the youth of England are on fire,
And silken dalliance in the wardrobe lies;
Now thrive the armourers, and honour's thought
Reigns solely in the breast of every man:
They sell the pasture now to buy the horse,
Following the mirror of all Christian kings,
With winged heels, as English Mercuries.
For now sits Expectation in the air
And hides a sword from hilts unto the point
With crowns imperial, crowns and coronets,
Promis'd to Harry and his followers.
Ib. II. Chorus, 1.

O England! model to thy inward greatness,
Like little body with a mighty heart,
What might'st thou do, that honour would thee do,
Were all thy children kind and natural!
But see thy fault! *Ib.* 16.

I dare not fight; but I will wink and hold out mine
iron. *Ib.* i. [7].

That's the humour of it. *Ib.* [63].

Base is the slave that pays. *Ib.* [100].

For, lambkins, we will live. *Ib.* [134].

Would I were with him, wheresome'er he is, either
in heaven or in hell. *Ib.* iii. [7].

He's in Arthur's bosom, if ever man went to Arthur's
bosom. A' made a finer end, and went away an it
had been any christom child; a' parted even just
between twelve and one, even at the turning o' the

tide: for after I saw him fumble with the sheets and play with flowers and smile upon his fingers' ends, I knew there was but one way; for his nose was as sharp as a pen, and a' babbled of green fields. [Theobald's emendation of the Folio's reading: 'A table of green fields'.]
King Henry V, II. iii. [9].

So a' cried out 'God, God, God!' three or four times: now I, to comfort him, bid him a' should not think of God, I hoped there was no need to trouble himself with any such thoughts yet.   *Ib.* [19].

As cold as any stone.   *Ib.* [25].

BOY:
Yes, that a' did; and said they were devils incarnate.

HOSTESS:
A' never could abide carnation; 'twas a colour he never liked.

BOY:
A' said once, the devil would have him about women.
Ib. [33].

Trust none;
For oaths are straw, men's faiths are wafer-cakes,
And hold-fast is the only dog, my duck.   *Ib.* [53].

Once more unto the breach, dear friends, once more;
Or close the wall up with our English dead!
In peace there's nothing so becomes a man
As modest stillness and humility:
But when the blast of war blows in our ears,
Then imitate the action of the tiger;
Stiffen the sinews, summon up the blood,
Disguise fair nature with hard-favour'd rage;
Then lend the eye a terrible aspect.   *Ib.* III. i. 1.

On, on you noblest English!
Whose blood is fet from fathers of war-proof;
Fathers that, like so many Alexanders,
Have in these parts from morn till even fought,
And sheath'd their swords for lack of argument. *Ib.* 17.

And you, good yeomen,
Whose limbs were made in England, show us here
The mettle of your pasture.   *Ib.* 25.

I see you stand like greyhounds in the slips,
Straining upon the start. The game's afoot:
Follow your spirit; and, upon this charge
Cry 'God for Harry! England and Saint George!'
Ib. 31.

I would give all my fame for a pot of ale, and safety.
Ib. ii. [14].

Men of few words are the best men.   *Ib.* [40].

A' never broke any man's head but his own, and that was against a post when he was drunk.   *Ib.* [43].

He will maintain his argument as well as any military man in the world, in the disciplines of the pristine wars of the Romans.   *Ib.* [89].

One Bardolph, if your majesty know the man: his face is all bubukles, and whelks, and knobs, and flames o' fire.   *Ib.* vi. [110].

I thought upon one pair of English legs
Did march three Frenchmen.   *Ib.* [161].

Give them great meals of beef and iron and steel, they will eat like wolves and fight like devils.
Ib. vii. [166].

Now entertain conjecture of a time
When creeping murmur and the poring dark
Fills the wide vessel of the universe.

From camp to camp, through the foul womb of night,
The hum of either army stilly sounds,
That the fix'd sentinels almost receive
The secret whispers of each other's watch.
Fire answers fire, and through their paly flames
Each battle sees the other's umber'd face:
Steed threatens steed, in high and boastful neighs
Piercing the night's dull ear; and from the tents
The armourers, accomplishing the knights,
With busy hammers closing rivets up,
Give dreadful note of preparation.
Ib. IV. Chorus, 1.

The royal captain of this ruin'd band.   *Ib.* 29.

A largess universal, like the sun
His liberal eye doth give to every one,
Thawing cold fear.   *Ib.* 43.

A little touch of Harry in the night.   *Ib.* 47.

O for pity,—we shall much disgrace,
With four or five most vile and ragged foils,
Right ill dispos'd in brawl ridiculous,
The name of Agincourt.   *Ib.* 49.

Gloucester, 'tis true that we are in great danger;
The greater therefore should our courage be.
Ib. IV. i. 1.

There is some soul of goodness in things evil,
Would men observingly distil it out.   *Ib.* 4.

Thus may we gather honey from the weed,
And make a moral of the devil himself.   *Ib.* 11.

Art thou base, common and popular?   *Ib.* 37.

Trail'st thou the puissant pike?   *Ib.* 40.

If you would take the pains but to examine the wars of Pompey the Great, you shall find, I warrant you, that there is no tiddle-taddle nor pibble-pabble in Pompey's camp.   *Ib.* [69].

There is much care and valour in this Welshman.
Ib. [85].

I think the king is but a man, as I am: the violet smells to him as it doth to me.   *Ib.* [106].

I am afeard there are few die well that die in a battle; for how can they charitably dispose of anything when blood is their argument?   *Ib.* [149].

Every subject's duty is the king's; but every subject's soul is his own.   *Ib.* [189].

Upon the king! let us our lives, our souls,
Our debts, our careful wives,
Our children, and our sins lay on the king!
We must bear all. O hard condition!   *Ib.* [250].

What infinite heart's ease
Must kings neglect, that private men enjoy!
And what have kings that privates have not too,
Save ceremony, save general ceremony?   *Ib.* [256].

'Tis not the balm, the sceptre and the ball,
The sword, the mace, the crown imperial,
The intertissued robe of gold and pearl,
The farced title running 'fore the king,
The throne he sits on, nor the tide of pomp
That beats upon the high shore of this world,
No, not all these, thrice-gorgeous ceremony,
Not all these, laid in bed majestical,
Can sleep so soundly as the wretched slave.

Who with a body fill'd and vacant mind
Gets him to rest, cramm'd with distressful bread;
Never sees horrid night, the child of hell,
But, like a lackey, from the rise to set
Sweats in the eye of Phoebus, and all night
Sleeps in Elysium; next day after dawn,
Doth rise and help Hyperion to his horse,
And follows so the ever-running year
With profitable labour to his grave:
And, but for ceremony, such a wretch,
Winding up days with toil and nights with sleep,
Hath the forehand and vantage of a king.
                    King Henry V, IV. i. [280].

O God of battles! steel my soldiers hearts;
Possess them not with fear; take from them now
The sense of reckoning, if the opposed numbers
Pluck their hearts from them.   *Ib.* [309].

        O! that we now had here
But one ten thousand of those men in England
That do no work to-day.   *Ib.* iii. 16.

If we are mark'd to die, we are enow
To do our country loss; and if to live,
The fewer men, the greater share of honour. *Ib.* 20.

        I am not covetous for gold,
            .   .   .
But if it be a sin to covet honour
I am the most offending soul alive.   *Ib.* 24.

He which hath no stomach to this fight,
Let him depart; his passport shall be made,
And crowns for convoy put into his purse:
We would not die in that man's company
That fears his fellowship to die with us.
This day is called the feast of Crispian:
He that outlives this day and comes safe home,
Will stand a tip-toe when this day is nam'd,
And rouse him at the name of Crispian.
He that shall live this day, and see old age,
Will yearly on the vigil feast his neighbours,
And say, 'To-morrow is Saint Crispian:'
Then will he strip his sleeve and show his scars,
And say, 'These wounds I had on Crispin's day.'
Old men forget: yet all shall be forgot,
But he'll remember with advantages
What feats he did that day. Then shall our names,
Familiar in his mouth as household words,
Harry the King, Bedford and Exeter,
Warwick and Talbot, Salisbury and Gloucester,
Be in their flowing cups freshly remember'd.
This story shall the good man teach his son;
And Crispin Crispian shall ne'er go by,
From this day to the ending of the world,
But we in it shall be remembered;
We few, we happy few, we band of brothers;
For he to-day that sheds his blood with me
Shall be my brother; be he ne'er so vile
This day shall gentle his condition:
And gentlemen in England, now a-bed
Shall think themselves accurs'd they were not here,
And hold their manhoods cheap whiles any speaks
That fought with us upon Saint Crispin's day. *Ib.* 35.

Thou damned and luxurious mountain goat.
                        Ib. iv. [20].

I'll fer him, and firk him, and ferret him. *Ib.* [29].

And all my mother came into mine eyes
And gave me up to tears.   *Ib.* vi. 31.

There is a river in Macedon, and there is also moreover a river at Monmouth: . . . and there is salmons
in both.   *Ib.* vii. [28].

            But now behold,
In the quick forge and working-house of thought,
How London doth pour out her citizens.
                    Ib. v. Chorus, 22.

Were now the general of our gracious empress,—
As in good time he may,—from Ireland coming,
Bringing rebellion broached on his sword. *Ib.* 30.

There is occasions and causes why and wherefore in
all things.   *Ib.* v. i. [3].

Not for Cadwallader and all his goats.   *Ib.* [29].

By this leek, I will most horribly revenge. *Ib.* [49].

Why that the naked, poor, and mangled Peace,
Dear nurse of arts, plenties, and joyful births.
                        Ib. ii. 34.

The even mead, that erst brought sweetly forth
The freckled cowslip, burnet, and green clover,
      .   .   .   .   .   *
Conceives by idleness, and nothing teems
But hateful docks, rough thistles, kecksies, burs.
                        Ib. 48.

If not, to say to thee that I shall die, is true; but for
thy love, by the Lord, no; yet I love thee too.
                        Ib. [157].

For these fellows of infinite tongue, that can rhyme
themselves into ladies' favours, they do always
reason themselves out again.   *Ib.* [162].

Shall not thou and I, between Saint Denis and Saint
George, compound a boy, half-French, half-
English, that shall go to Constantinople and take
the Turk by the beard?   *Ib.* [218].

It is not a fashion for the maids in France to kiss
before they are married.   *Ib.* [287].

God, the best maker of all marriages,
Combine your hearts in one.   *Ib.* [387].

Hung be the heavens with black, yield day to night!
            King Henry VI, Part I, I. i. 1.

Expect Saint Martin's summer, halcyon days.
                        Ib. ii. 131.

            Unbidden guests
Are often welcomest when they are gone.
                        Ib. II. ii. 55.

But in these nice sharp quillets of the law,
Good faith, I am no wiser than a daw. *Ib.* iv. 17.

From off this brier pluck a white rose with me.
                        Ib. 30.

Pluck a red rose from off this thorn with me. *Ib.* 33.

PLANTAGENET:
Hath not thy rose a canker, Somerset?
SOMERSET:
Hath not thy rose a thorn, Plantagenet?   *Ib.* 68.

Delays have dangerous ends.   *Ib.* III. ii. 33.

I owe him little duty and less love.   *Ib.* IV. iv. 34.

So doth the swan her downy cygnets save,
Keeping them prisoners underneath her wings.
                        Ib. v. iii. 56.

She's beautiful and therefore to be woo'd;
She is a woman, therefore to be won.
King Henry VI, Part 1, v. iii. 78.

She bears a duke's revenues on her back,
And in her heart she scorns our poverty.
King Henry VI, Part 2, I. iii. [83].

Could I come near your beauty with my nails
I'd set my ten commandments in your face. *Ib.* [144].

What stronger breastplate than a heart untainted!
Thrice is he arm'd that hath his quarrel just,
And he but naked, though lock'd up in steel,
Whose conscience with injustice is corrupted.
Ib. III. ii. 232.

He dies, and makes no sign. *Ib.* iii. 29.

Forbear to judge, for we are sinners all.
Close up his eyes, and draw the curtains close;
And let us all to meditation. *Ib.* 31.

The gaudy, blabbing, and remorseful day
Is crept into the bosom of the sea. *Ib.* IV. i. 1.

True nobility is exempt from fear. *Ib.* 129.

I say it was never merry world in England since
gentlemen came up. *Ib.* ii. [10].

There shall be in England seven halfpenny loaves
sold for a penny; the three-hooped pot shall have
ten hoops; and I will make it felony to drink small
beer. *Ib.* [73].

The first thing we do, let's kill all the lawyers.
Ib. [86].

Is not this a lamentable thing, that of the skin of an
innocent lamb should be made parchment? that
parchment, being scribbled o'er, should undo a
man? *Ib.* [88].

And Adam was a gardener. *Ib.* [146].

Thou hast most traitorously corrupted the youth of
the realm in erecting a grammar school: and
whereas, before, our forefathers had no other
books but the score and the tally, thou hast
caused printing to be used; and, contrary to the
king, his crown and dignity, thou hast built a
paper-mill. *Ib.* vii. [35].

Away with him! away with him! he speaks Latin.
Ib. [62].

Lord, who would live turmoiled in the court,
And may enjoy such quiet walks as these? *Ib.* x. [18].

This battle fares like to the morning's war,
When dying clouds contend with growing light,
What time the shepherd, blowing of his nails,
Can neither call it perfect day nor night.
King Henry VI, Part 3, II. v. 1.

O God! methinks it were a happy life,
To be no better than a homely swain;
To sit upon a hill, as I do now,
To carve out dials, quaintly, point by point,
Thereby to see the minutes how they run,
How many make the hour full complete;
How many hours bring about the day;
How many days will finish up the year;
How many years a mortal man may live. *Ib.* 21.

Gives not the hawthorn bush a sweeter shade
To shepherds, looking on their silly sheep,

Than doth a rich embroider'd canopy
To kings that fear their subjects' treachery? *Ib.* 42.

See, see! what showers arise,
Blown with the windy tempest of my heart. *Ib.* 85.

Warwick, peace;
Proud setter up and puller down of kings. *Ib.* 156.

A little fire is quickly trodden out,
Which, being suffer'd, rivers cannot quench.
Ib. viii. 7.

Live we how we can, yet die we must.
Ib. v. ii. 27.

Suspicion always haunts the guilty mind;
The thief doth fear each bush an officer. *Ib.* vi. 11.

Down, down to hell; and say I sent thee thither.
Ib. 67.

Now is the winter of our discontent
Made glorious summer by this sun of York.
King Richard III, I. i. 1.

Our stern alarums changed to merry meetings;
Our dreadful marches to delightful measures.
Ib. 7.

He capers nimbly in a lady's chamber
To the lascivious pleasing of a lute. *Ib.* 12.

This weak piping time of peace. *Ib.* 24.

And therefore, since I cannot prove a lover, . . .
I am determined to prove a villain. *Ib.* 28.

No beast so fierce but knows some touch of pity.
Ib. ii. 71.

Was ever woman in this humour woo'd?
Was ever woman in this humour won? *Ib.* 229.

Fram'd in the prodigality of Nature. *Ib.* 245.

By silken, sly, insinuating Jacks? *Ib.* iii. 53.

Since every Jack became a gentleman
There's many a gentle person made a Jack. *Ib.* 72.

And thus I clothe my naked villany
With odd old ends stol'n forth of holy writ,
And seem a saint when most I play the devil.
Ib. 336.

O, I have pass'd a miserable night,
So full of ugly sights, of ghastly dreams,
That, as I am a Christian faithful man,
I would not spend another such a night,
Though 'twere to buy a world of happy days,
So full of dismal terror was the time! *Ib.* iv. 2.

Lord, Lord! methought what pain it was to drown:
What dreadful noise of water in mine ears!
What sights of ugly death within mine eyes!
Methought I saw a thousand fearful wracks;
A thousand men that fishes gnaw'd upon;
Wedges of gold, great anchors, heaps of pearl,
Inestimable stones, unvalu'd jewels,
All scatter'd in the bottom of the sea.
Some lay in dead men's skulls; and in those holes
Where eyes did once inhabit, there were crept
As 'twere in scorn of eyes, reflecting gems,
That woo'd the slimy bottom of the deep,
And mock'd the dead bones that lay scatter'd by.
Ib. 21.

The empty, vast, and wandering air. *Ib.* 39.

Clarence is come,—false, fleeting, perjur'd Clarence.
Ib. 55.

As snow in harvest. *King Richard III*, I. iv. [252].

Woe to the land that's govern'd by a child!
Ib. II. iii. 11.

So wise so young, they say, do never live long.
Ib. III. i. 79.

I moralize two meanings in one word. *Ib.* 83.

My Lord of Ely, when I was last in Holborn,
I saw good strawberries in your garden there.
Ib. iv. 31.

Talk'st thou to me of 'ifs'? Thou art a traitor:
Off with his head! *Ib.* 74.

High-reaching Buckingham grows circumspect.
Ib. IV. ii. 31.

I am not in the giving vein to-day. *Ib.* 117.

The sons of Edward sleep in Abraham's bosom.
Ib. iii. 38.

Let not the heavens hear these tell-tale women
Rail on the Lord's anointed. *Ib.* iv. 150.

A grievous burthen was thy birth to me;
Tetchy and wayward was thy infancy. *Ib.* 168.

An honest tale speeds best being plainly told.
Ib. 359.

Harp not on that string. *Ib.* 365.

Relenting fool, and shallow, changing woman!
Ib. 432.

Is the chair empty? is the sword unsway'd?
Is the king dead? the empire unpossess'd?
Ib. 470.

Thus far into the bowels of the land
Have we march'd on without impediment.
Ib. v. ii. 3.

True hope is swift, and flies with swallow's wings;
Kings it makes gods, and meaner creatures kings.
Ib. 23.

The king's name is a tower of strength.
Ib. iii. 12.

Give me another horse! bind up my wounds!
Have mercy, Jesu! Soft! I did but dream.
O coward conscience, how dost thou afflict me!
Ib. 178.

My conscience hath a thousand several tongues,
And every tongue brings in a several tale,
And every tale condemns me for a villain. *Ib.* 194.

I shall despair. There is no creature loves me;
And if I die, no soul shall pity me:
Nay, wherefore should they, since that I myself
Find in myself no pity to myself? *Ib.* 201.

By the apostle Paul, shadows to-night
Have struck more terror to the soul of Richard
Than can the substance of ten thousand soldiers.
Ib. 217.

Jockey of Norfolk, be not too bold,
For Dickon thy master is bought and sold. *Ib.* 305.

A thing devised by the enemy. *Ib.* 307.

Conscience is but a word that cowards use,
Devis'd at first to keep the strong in awe. *Ib.* 310.

A horse! a horse! my kingdom for a horse!
Ib. iv. 7.

Slave! I have set my life upon a cast,
And I will stand the hazard of the die.
I think there be six Richmonds in the field. *Ib.* 9.

They
Made Britain India: every man that stood
Show'd like a mine. *King Henry VIII*, I. i. 20.

Heat not a furnace for your foe so hot
That it do singe yourself. *Ib.* 140.

If I chance to talk a little wild, forgive me;
I had it from my father. *Ib.* iv. 26.

The mirror of all courtesy. *Ib.* II. i. 53.

Go with me, like good angels, to my end;
And, as the long divorce of steel falls on me,
Make of your prayers one sweet sacrifice,
And lift my soul to heaven. *Ib.* 75.

CHAMBERLAIN:
It seems the marriage with his brother's wife
Has crept too near his conscience.
SUFFOLK:
No; his conscience
Has crept too near another lady. *Ib.* ii. [17].

This bold bad man. *Ib.* [44].

Verily,
I swear, 'tis better to be lowly born,
And range with humble livers in content,
Than to be perk'd up, in a glist'ring grief,
And wear a golden sorrow. *Ib.* iii. 18.

I would not be a queen
For all the world. *Ib.* 45.

Orpheus with his lute made trees,
And the mountain-tops that freeze,
  Bow themselves when he did sing:
To his music plants and flowers
Ever sprung; as sun and showers
  There had made a lasting spring.

Everything that heard him play,
Even the billows of the sea,
  Hung their heads, and then lay by.
In sweet music is such art,
Killing care and grief of heart
  Fall asleep, or hearing die. *Ib.* III. i. 3.

Heaven is above all yet; there sits a judge,
That no king can corrupt. *Ib.* 99.

A spleeny Lutheran. *Ib.* ii. 100.

'Tis well said again;
And 'tis a kind of good deed to say well:
And yet words are no deeds. *Ib.* 153.

And then to breakfast, with
What appetite you have. *Ib.* 203.

That in all you writ to Rome, or else
To foreign princes, '*Ego et Rex meus*'
Was still inscrib'd. *Ib.* 314.

Farewell! a long farewell, to all my greatness!
This is the state of man: to-day he puts forth
The tender leaves of hope; to-morrow blossoms,
And bears his blushing honours thick upon him;
The third day comes a frost, a killing frost;
And, when he thinks, good easy man, full surely
His greatness is a-ripening, nips his root,
And then he falls, as I do. I have ventur'd,

Like little wanton boys that swim on bladders,
This many summers in a sea of glory,
But far beyond my depth: my high-blown pride
At length broke under me, and now has left me
Weary and old with service, to the mercy
Of a rude stream that must for ever hide me.
Vain pomp and glory of this world, I hate ye:
I feel my heart new open'd. O how wretched
Is that poor man that hangs on princes' favours!
There is, betwixt that smile we would aspire to,
That sweet aspect of princes, and their ruin,
More pangs and fears than wars or women have;
And when he falls, he falls like Lucifer,
Never to hope again.   *King Henry VIII*, III. ii. 352.

A peace above all earthly dignities,
A still and quiet conscience.   *Ib.* 380.

A load would sink a navy.   *Ib.* 384.

There was the weight that pull'd me down. O
   Cromwell!
The king has gone beyond me: all my glories
In that one woman I have lost for ever.   *Ib.* 408.

Cromwell, I did not think to shed a tear
In all my miseries; but thou hast forc'd me,
Out of thy honest truth, to play the woman.
     Ib. 429.

Let's dry our eyes: and thus far hear me, Cromwell;
And, when I am forgotten, as I shall be,
And sleep in dull cold marble, where no mention
Of me more must be heard of, say, I taught thee,
Say, Wolsey, that once trod the ways of glory,
And sounded all the depths and shoals of honour,
Found thee a way, out of his wrack, to rise in;
A sure and safe one, though thy master miss'd it.
     Ib. 432.

Cromwell, I charge thee, fling away ambition:
By that sin fell the angels.   *Ib.* 441.

Love thyself last: cherish those hearts that hate thee;
Corruption wins not more than honesty.
Still in thy right hand carry gentle peace,
To silence envious tongues: be just, and fear not.
Let all the ends thou aim'st at be thy country's,
Thy God's, and truth's; then if thou fall'st, O Cromwell!
Thou fall'st a blessed martyr.   *Ib.* 444.

Had I but serv'd my God with half the zeal
I serv'd my king, he would not in mine age
Have left me naked to mine enemies.   *Ib.* 456.

She had all the royal makings of a queen.
     Ib. IV. i. 87.

An old man, broken with the storms of state,
Is come to lay his weary bones among ye;
Give him a little earth for charity.   *Ib.* ii. 21.

He gave his honours to the world again,
His blessed part to Heaven, and slept in peace.
     Ib. 29.

So may he rest; his faults lie gently on him! *Ib.* 31.

He was a man
Of an unbounded stomach.   *Ib.* 33.

His promises were, as he then was, mighty;
But his performance, as he is now, nothing. *Ib.* 41.

Men's evil manners live in brass; their virtues
We write in water.   *Ib.* 45.

He was a scholar, and a ripe and good one;
Exceeding wise, fair-spoken, and persuading:
Lofty and sour to them that lov'd him not;
But, to those men that sought him, sweet as summer.
     Ib. 51.

Those twins of learning that he rais'd in you,
Ipswich and Oxford!   *Ib.* 58.

After my death I wish no other herald,
No other speaker of my living actions,
To keep mine honour from corruption,
Than such an honest chronicler as Griffith.   *Ib.* 69.

To dance attendance on their lordships' pleasures.
     Ib. v. ii. 30.

'Tis a cruelty
To load a falling man.   *Ib.* 76.

In her days every man shall eat in safety
Under his own vine what he plants; and sing
The merry songs of peace to all his neighbours.
     Ib. v. 34.

Those about her
From her shall read the perfect ways of honour.
     Ib. 37.

Nor shall this peace sleep with her; but as when
The bird of wonder dies, the maiden phoenix,
Her ashes new-create another heir
As great in admiration as herself.   *Ib.* 40.

Some come to take their ease
And sleep an act or two.   *Ib.* Epilogue, 2.

The first heir of my invention.
     Venus and Adonis, Preface.

Hunting he lov'd, but love he laugh'd to scorn.
     Ib. l. 4.

Bid me discourse, I will enchant thine ear,
Or like a fairy trip upon the green,
Or, like a nymph, with long dishevell'd hair,
Dance on the sands, and yet no footing seen:
Love is a spirit all compact of fire,
Not gross to sink, but light, and will aspire.
     Ib. l. 145.

Round-hoof'd, short-jointed, fetlocks shag and long,
Broad breast, full eye, small head and nostril wide,
High crest, short ears, straight legs and passing strong,
Thin mane, thick tail, broad buttock, tender hide:
Look, what a horse should have he did not lack,
Save a proud rider on so proud a back.   *Ib.* l. 295.

By this, poor Wat, far off upon a hill,
Stands on his hinder legs with listening ear,
To hearken if his foes pursue him still.   *Ib.* l. 697.

What I have done is yours; what I have to do is
   yours; being part in all I have, devoted yours.
     The Rape of Lucrece, Preface.

Beauty itself doth of itself persuade
The eyes of men without an orator.
     Ib. l. 29.

Or sells eternity to get a toy.   *Ib.* l. 214.

Time's glory is to calm contending kings,
To unmask falsehood, and bring truth to light.
     Ib. l. 939.

Cloud-kissing Ilion.   *Ib.* l. 1370.

From fairest creatures we desire increase,
That thereby beauty's rose might never die.
Sonnets, 1.

When forty winters shall besiege thy brow,
And dig deep trenches in thy beauty's field. *Ib.* 2.

Thou art thy mother's glass, and she in thee
Calls back the lovely April of her prime. *Ib.* 3.

Lo! in the orient when the gracious light
Lifts up his burning head, each under eye
Doth homage to his new-appearing sight. *Ib.* 7.

Music to hear, why hear'st thou music sadly?
Sweets with sweets war not, joy delights in joy:
Why lov'st thou that which thou receiv'st not gladly,
Or else receiv'st with pleasure thine annoy? *Ib.* 8.

True concord of well-tuned sounds. *Ib.*

When lofty trees I see barren of leaves,
Which erst from heat did canopy the herd,
And summer's green all girded up in sheaves,
Borne on the bier with white and bristly beard.
Ib. 12.

If I could write the beauty of your eyes
And in fresh numbers number all your graces,
The age to come would say, 'This poet lies;
Such heavenly touches ne'er touch'd earthly faces.'
Ib. 17.

And stretched metre of an antique song. *Ib.*

Shall I compare thee to a summer's day?
Thou art more lovely and more temperate:
Rough winds do shake the darling buds of May,
And summer's lease hath all too short a date:
Sometime too hot the eye of heaven shines,
And often is his gold complexion dimm'd;
And every fair from fair sometime declines,
By chance, or nature's changing course untrimm'd;
But thy eternal summer shall not fade,
Nor lose possession of that fair thou ow'st,
Nor shall death brag thou wander'st in his shade,
When in eternal lines to time thou grow'st;
So long as men can breathe, or eyes can see,
So long lives this, and this gives life to thee. *Ib.* 18.

My glass shall not persuade me I am old,
So long as youth and thou are of one date;
But when in thee time's furrows I behold,
Then look I death my days should expiate. *Ib.* 22.

As an unperfect actor on the stage,
Who with his fear is put beside his part. *Ib.* 23.

O! let my books be then the eloquence
And dumb presagers of my speaking breast. *Ib.*

The painful warrior famoused for fight,
After a thousand victories once foil'd,
Is from the book of honour razed quite,
And all the rest forgot for which he toil'd. *Ib.* 25.

Weary with toil, I haste me to my bed. *Ib.* 27.

When in disgrace with fortune and men's eyes
I all alone beweep my outcast state,
And trouble deaf heaven with my bootless cries,
And look upon myself and curse my fate,
Wishing me like to one more rich in hope,
Featur'd like him, like him with friends possess'd,
Desiring this man's art, and that man's scope,
With what I most enjoy contented least;

Yet in these thoughts myself almost despising,
Haply I think on thee,—and then my state,
Like to the lark at break of day arising
From sullen earth, sings hymns at heaven's gate;
For thy sweet love remember'd such wealth brings
That then I scorn to change my state with kings.
Ib. 29.

When to the sessions of sweet silent thought
I summon up remembrance of things past,
I sigh the lack of many a thing I sought,
And with old woes new wail my dear time's waste:
Then can I drown an eye, unus'd to flow,
For precious friends hid in death's dateless night,
And weep afresh love's long since cancell'd woe,
And moan the expense of many a vanish'd sight:
Then can I grieve at grievances foregone,
And heavily from woe to woe tell o'er
The sad account of fore-bemoaned moan,
Which I new pay as if not paid before.
But if the while I think on thee, dear friend,
All losses are restor'd and sorrows end. *Ib.* 30.

But since he died, and poets better prove,
Theirs for their style I'll read, his for his love.
Ib. 32.

Full many a glorious morning have I seen
Flatter the mountain-tops with sovereign eye,
Kissing with golden face the meadows green,
Gilding pale streams with heavenly alchemy. *Ib.* 33.

But, out! alack! he was but one hour mine,
The region cloud hath mask'd him from me now. *Ib.*

Suns of the world may stain when heaven's sun
staineth. *Ib.*

Why didst thou promise such a beauteous day,
And make me travel forth without my cloak?
Ib. 34.

Roses have thorns, and silver fountains mud;
Clouds and eclipses stain both moon and sun,
And loathsome canker lives in sweetest bud.
All men make faults. *Ib.* 35.

As a decrepit father takes delight
To see his active child do deeds of youth,
So I, made lame by fortune's dearest spite,
Take all my comfort of thy worth and truth. *Ib.* 37.

Against that time when thou shalt strangely pass,
And scarcely greet me with that sun, thine eye,
When love, converted from the thing it was,
Shall reasons find of settled gravity. *Ib.* 49.

Like stones of worth they thinly placed are,
Or captain jewels in the carcanet. *Ib.* 52.

What is your substance, whereof are you made,
That millions of strange shadows on you tend?
Ib. 53.

You in Grecian tires are painted new. *Ib.*

The spring and foison of the year. *Ib.*

O! how much more doth beauty beauteous seem
By that sweet ornament which truth doth give!
Ib. 54.

Not marble, nor the gilded monuments
Of princes, shall outlive this powerful rhyme.
Ib. 55.

Being your slave, what should I do but tend
Upon the hours and times of your desire?
I have no precious time at all to spend,
Nor services to do, till you require.
Nor dare I chide the world-without-end hour
Whilst I, my sovereign, watch the clock for you,
Nor think the bitterness of absence sour
When you have bid your servant once adieu;
Nor dare I question with my jealous thought
Where you may be, or your affairs suppose,
But like a sad slave, stay and think of nought
Save, where you are, how happy you make those.
So true a fool is love that in your will,
Though you do anything, he thinks no ill.
Sonnets, 57.

Like as the waves make towards the pebbled shore,
So do our minutes hasten to their end.   *Ib.* 60.

Time doth transfix the flourish set on youth
And delves the parallels in beauty's brow.   *Ib.*

Sin of self-love possesseth all mine eye.   *Ib.* 62.

When I have seen by Time's fell hand defac'd
The rich-proud cost of outworn buried age.   *Ib.* 64.

When I have seen the hungry ocean gain
Advantage on the kingdom of the shore.   *Ib.*

Since brass, nor stone, nor earth, nor boundless sea,
But sad mortality o'ersways their power,
How with this rage shall beauty hold a plea,
Whose action is no stronger than a flower?   *Ib.* 65.

Tir'd with all these, for restful death I cry,
As to behold desert a beggar born,
And needy nothing trimm'd in jollity,
And purest faith unhappily forsworn,
And gilded honour shamefully misplac'd,
And maiden virtue rudely strumpeted,
And right perfection wrongfully disgrac'd,
And strength by limping sway disabled,
And art made tongue-tied by authority,
And folly—doctor-like—controlling skill,
And simple truth miscall'd simplicity,
And captive good attending captain ill:
Tir'd with all these, from these I would be gone,
Save that, to die, I leave my love alone.   *Ib.* 66.

No longer mourn for me when I am dead
Than you shall hear the surly sullen bell
Give warning to the world that I am fled
From this vile world, with vilest worms to dwell.
   Ib. 71.

That time of year thou mayst in me behold
When yellow leaves, or none, or few, do hang
Upon those boughs which shake against the cold,
Bare ruin'd choirs, where late the sweet birds sang.
In me thou see'st the twilight of such day
As after sunset fadeth in the west;
Which by and by black night doth take away,
Death's second self, that seals up all in rest.   *Ib.* 73.

This thou perceiv'st, which makes thy love more
   strong,
To love that well which thou must leave ere long.
   Ib.

So all my best is dressing old words new.   *Ib.* 76.

Like unletter'd clerk, still cry 'Amen'.   *Ib.* 85.

Was it the proud full sail of his great verse,
Bound for the prize of all too precious you,

That did my ripe thoughts in my brain inhearse,
Making their tomb the womb wherein they grew?
   Ib. 86.

          That affable familiar ghost
Which nightly gulls him with intelligence.   *Ib.*

Farewell! thou art too dear for my possessing,
And like enough thou know'st thy estimate:
The charter of thy worth gives thee releasing;
My bonds in thee are all determinate.
For how do I hold thee but by thy granting?
And for that riches where is my deserving?
The cause of this fair gift in me is wanting,
And so my patent back again is swerving.
Thyself thou gav'st, thine own worth then not
   knowing,
Or me, to whom thou gav'st it, else mistaking;
So thy great gift, upon misprision growing,
Comes home again, on better judgment making.
Thus have I had thee, as a dream doth flatter,
In sleep a king, but, waking, no such matter.   *Ib.* 87.

Ah, do not, when my heart hath 'scap'd this sorrow,
Come in the rearward of a conquer'd woe;
Give not a windy night a rainy morrow,
To linger out a purpos'd overthrow.   *Ib.* 90.

They that have power to hurt and will do none,
That do not do the thing they most do show,
Who, moving others, are themselves as stone,
Unmoved, cold, and to temptation slow.   *Ib.* 94.

They are the lords and owners of their faces,
Others but stewards of their excellence.
The summer's flower is to the summer sweet,
Though to itself it only live and die.   *Ib.*

Lilies that fester smell far worse than weeds.   *Ib.*

How like a winter hath my absence been
From thee, the pleasure of the fleeting year!
What freezings have I felt, what dark days seen!
What old December's bareness every where!   *Ib.* 97.

From you have I been absent in the spring,
When proud-pied April, dress'd in all his trim,
Hath put a spirit of youth in everything.   *Ib.* 98.

To me, fair friend, you never can be old,
For as you were when first your eye I ey'd,
Such seems your beauty still. Three winters cold
Have from the forests shook three summers' pride,
Three beauteous springs to yellow autumn turn'd
In process of the seasons have I seen,
Three April perfumes in three hot Junes burn'd,
Since first I saw you fresh, which yet are green.
Ah! yet doth beauty, like a dial-hand,
Steal from his figure, and no pace perceiv'd;
So your sweet hue, which methinks still doth stand,
Hath motion, and mine eye may be deceiv'd:
For fear of which, hear this, thou age unbred:
Ere you were born was beauty's summer dead.
   Ib. 104.

And beauty, making beautiful old rhyme.   *Ib.* 106.

Not mine own fears, nor the prophetic soul
Of the wide world dreaming on things to come,
Can yet the lease of my true love control,
Suppos'd as forfeit to a confin'd doom.
The mortal moon hath her eclipse endur'd,
And the sad augurs mock their own presage.
   Ib. 107.

And thou in this shalt find thy monument,
When tyrants' crests and tombs of brass are spent.
Sonnets, 107.

O! never say that I was false of heart,
Though absence seem'd my flame to qualify. *Ib.* 109.

Alas! 'tis true I have gone here and there,
And made myself a motley to the view,
Gor'd mine own thoughts, sold cheap what is most
  dear,
Made old offences of affections new;
Most true it is that I have look'd on truth
Askance and strangely; but, by all above,
These blenches gave my heart another youth,
And worse essays prov'd thee my best of love.
Ib. 110.

    My nature is subdu'd
To what it works in, like the dyer's hand;
Pity me, then, and wish I were renew'd. *Ib.* 111.

Let me not to the marriage of true minds
Admit impediments. Love is not love
Which alters when it alteration finds,
Or bends with the remover to remove:
O, no! it is an ever-fixed mark,
That looks on tempests and is never shaken;
It is the star to every wandering bark,
Whose worth's unknown, although his height be
  taken.
Love's not Time's fool, though rosy lips and cheeks
Within his bending sickle's compass come;
Love alters not with his brief hours and weeks,
But bears it out even to the edge of doom.
If this be error, and upon me prov'd,
I never writ, nor no man ever lov'd. *Ib.* 116.

What potions have I drunk of Siren tears,
Distill'd from limbecks foul as hell within. *Ib.* 119.

O benefit of ill! now I find true
That better is by evil still made better. *Ib.*

'Tis better to be vile than vile esteem'd,
When not to be receives reproach of being. *Ib.* 121.

The expense of spirit in a waste of shame
Is lust in action; and till action, lust
Is perjur'd, murderous, bloody, full of blame,
Savage, extreme, rude, cruel, not to trust. *Ib.* 129.

Mad in pursuit, and in possession so;
Had, having, and in quest to have, extreme;
A bliss in proof,—and prov'd, a very woe;
Before, a joy propos'd; behind, a dream.
All this the world well knows; yet none knows well:
To shun the heaven that leads men to this hell. *Ib.*

My mistress' eyes are nothing like the sun;
Coral is far more red than her lips' red:
If snow be white, why then her breasts are dun;
If hairs be wires, black wires grow on her head.
Ib. 130.

And yet, by heaven, I think my love as rare
As any she belied with false compare. *Ib.*

Whoever hath her wish, thou hast thy *Will*,
And *Will* to boot, and *Will* in over-plus. *Ib.* 135.

When my love swears that she is made of truth,
I do believe her, though I know she lies. *Ib.* 138.

Lo, as a careful housewife runs to catch
One of her feather'd creatures broke away. *Ib.* 143

Two loves I have of comfort and despair,
Which like two spirits do suggest me still:
The better angel is a man right fair,
The worser spirit a woman colour'd ill. *Ib.* 144.

Yet this shall I ne'er know, but live in doubt,
Till my bad angel fire my good one out. *Ib.*

Poor soul, the centre of my sinful earth,
[Fool'd by] these rebel powers that thee array,
Why dost thou pine within and suffer dearth,
Painting thy outward walls so costly gay?
Why so large cost, having so short a lease,
Dost thou upon thy fading mansion spend? *Ib.* 146.

So shalt thou feed on Death, that feeds on men,
And Death once dead, there's no more dying then.
Ib.

For I have sworn thee fair, and thought thee bright,
Who art as black as hell, as dark as night. *Ib.* 147.

Love is too young to know what conscience is;
Yet who knows not conscience is born of love?
Ib. 151.

Crabbed age and youth cannot live together:
Youth is full of pleasance, age is full of care.
The Passionate Pilgrim, xii.

Age, I do abhor thee, youth, I do adore thee. *Ib.*

Good friend, for Jesu's sake forbear
To dig the dust enclosed here.
Blest be the man that spares these stones,
And curst be he that moves my bones.
Shakespeare's Epitaph.

DAVID TAYLOR SHAW
1813–1890

O Britannia, the pride of the ocean,
  The home of the brave and the free,
The shrine of the sailor's devotion,
  No land can compare unto thee!
    The Red, White, and Blue. First line changed
    to 'Columbia, the gem of the ocean', when
    sung by Shaw in America. Attr. also to
    Thomas à Becket, 1850.

GEORGE BERNARD SHAW
1856–

All great truths begin as blasphemies.
    Annajanska (1919), p. 262.

You can always tell an old soldier by the inside of his
  holsters and cartridge boxes. The young ones
  carry pistols and cartridges: the old ones, grub.
    Arms and the Man, Act I.

I never apologize.   *Ib.* Act III.

You're not a man, you're a machine.   *Ib.*

When a stupid man is doing something he is ashamed
  of, he always declares that it is his duty.
    Cæsar and Cleopatra, Act III.

He who has never hoped can never despair.
    Ib. Act IV.

A man of great common sense and good taste,—meaning thereby a man without originality or moral
  courage.   *Ib. Notes. Julius Cæsar.*

We have no more right to consume happiness without producing it than to consume wealth without producing it. *Candida*, Act I.

Do you think that the things people make fools of themselves about are any less real and true than the things they behave sensibly about? *Ib.*

It is easy—terribly easy—to shake a man's faith in himself. To take advantage of that to break a man's spirit is devil's work. *Ib.*

I'm only a beer teetotaller, not a champagne teetotaller. *Ib.* Act III.

The worst sin towards our fellow creatures is not to hate them, but to be indifferent to them: that's the essence of inhumanity.
The Devil's Disciple, Act II.

I never expect a soldier to think.
Ib. Act III.

The British soldier can stand up to anything except the British War Office. *Ib.*

With the single exception of Homer, there is no eminent writer, not even Sir Walter Scott, whom I can despise so entirely as I despise Shakespeare when I measure my mind against his. . . . It would positively be a relief to me to dig him up and throw stones at him.
Dramatic Opinions and Essays (1907), vol. II, p. 52.

It's all that the young can do for the old, to shock them and keep them up to date.
Fanny's First Play, Induction.

You don't expect me to know what to say about a play when I don't know who the author is, do you? . . . If it's by a good author, it's a good play, naturally. That stands to reason. *Ib.* Epilogue.

What God hath joined together no man shall ever put asunder: God will take care of that.
Getting Married (1911), p. 216.

When you loved me I gave you the whole sun and stars to play with. I gave you eternity in a single moment, strength of the mountains in one clasp of your arms, and the volume of all the seas in one impulse of your soul. *Ib.* p. 278.

We possessed all the universe together; and you ask me to give you my scanty wages as well. I have given you the greatest of all things; and you ask me to give you little things. I gave you your own soul: you ask me for my body as a plaything. Was it not enough? Was it not enough? *Ib.*

Go anywhere in England, where there are natural, wholesome, contented, and really nice English people; and what do you always find? That the stables are the real centre of the household.
Heartbreak House, Act III.

The captain is in his bunk, drinking bottled ditch-water; and the crew is gambling in the forecastle. She will strike and sink and split. Do you think the laws of God will be suspended in favour of England because you were born in it? *Ib.*

Money is indeed the most important thing in the world; and all sound and successful personal and national morality should have this fact for its basis.
The Irrational Knot, Preface (1905), p. xiv.

Though the Life Force supplies us with its own purpose, it has no other brains to work with than those it has painfully and imperfectly evolved in our heads. *Ib.* p. xxv.

Reminiscences make one feel so deliciously aged and sad. *Ib.* ch. 14.

A man who has no office to go to—I don't care who he is—is a trial of which you can have no conception. *Ib.* ch. 18.

What really flatters a man is that you think him worth flattering. *John Bull's Other Island*, Act IV.

There are only two qualities in the world: efficiency and inefficiency; and only two sorts of people: the efficient and the inefficient. *Ib.*

The greatest of evils and the worst of crimes is poverty. *Major Barbara*, Preface.

Wot prawce Selvytion nah? *Ib.* Act II.

Nothing is ever done in this world until men are prepared to kill one another if it is not done.
Ib. Act III.

Our political experiment of democracy, the last refuge of cheap misgovernment.
Man and Superman (1903), Epistle Dedicatory, p. xxi.

He who has nothing to assert has no style and can have none: he who has something to assert will go as far in power of style as its momentousness and his conviction will carry him. *Ib.* p. xxxv.

A lifetime of happiness: No man alive could bear it: it would be hell on earth. *Ib.* Act I.

The more things a man is ashamed of, the more respectable he is. *Ib.*

Vitality in a woman is a blind fury of creation.
Ib.

The true artist will let his wife starve, his children go barefoot, his mother drudge for his living at seventy, sooner than work at anything but his art.
Ib.

Is the devil to have all the passions as well as all the good tunes? *Ib.*

Never mind her; go on talking. *Ib.*

You think that you are Ann's suitor; that you are the pursuer and she the pursued; that it is your part to woo, to persuade, to prevail, to overcome. Fool: it is you who are the pursued, the marked-down quarry, the destined prey. *Ib.* Act II.

Marry Ann; and at the end of a week you'll find no more inspiration in her than in a plate of muffins. *Ib.*

Hell is full of musical amateurs: music is the brandy of the damned. *Ib.* Act III.

An Englishman thinks he is moral when he is only uncomfortable. *Ib.*

As an old soldier I admit the cowardice: it's as universal as seasickness, and matters just as little. *Ib.*

When the military man approaches, the world locks up its spoons and packs off its womankind. *Ib.*

Those who talk most about the blessings of marriage and the constancy of its vows are the very people who declare that if the chain were broken and the prisoners left free to choose, the whole social fabric would fly asunder. You cannot have the argument both ways. If the prisoner is happy, why lock him in? If he is not, why pretend that he is?
Ib.

There are two tragedies in life. One is not to get your heart's desire. The other is to get it.
Ib. Act IV.

Do not do unto others as you would they should do unto you. Their tastes may not be the same.
Ib., Maxims for Revolutionists, p. 227.

The golden rule is that there are no golden rules. *Ib.*

Democracy substitutes election by the incompetent many for appointment by the corrupt few.
Ib. p. 228.

Liberty means responsibility. That is why most men dread it. *Ib.* p. 229.

Marriage is popular because it combines the maximum of temptation with the maximum of opportunity. *Ib.* p. 231.

If you strike a child, take care that you strike it in anger, even at the risk of maiming it for life. A blow in cold blood neither can nor should be forgiven. *Ib.* p. 234.

The reasonable man adapts himself to the world: the unreasonable one persists in trying to adapt the world to himself. Therefore all progress depends on the unreasonable man. *Ib.* p. 238.

The man who listens to Reason is lost: Reason enslaves all whose minds are not strong enough to master her. *Ib.*

Home is the girl's prison and the woman's workhouse. *Ib.* p. 240.

Every man over forty is a scoundrel. *Ib.* p. 242.

There is nothing so bad or so good that you will not find Englishmen doing it; but you will never find an Englishman in the wrong. He does everything on principle. He fights you on patriotic principles; he robs you on business principles; he enslaves you on imperial principles. *The Man of Destiny.*

An English army led by an Irish general: that might be a match for a French army led by an Italian general. *Ib.*

A great devotee of the Gospel of Getting On.
Mrs. Warren's Profession, Act IV.

The fickleness of the women I love is only equalled by the infernal constancy of the women who love me. *The Philanderer*, Act II.

It is clear that a novel cannot be too bad to be worth publishing. . . . It certainly is possible for a novel to be too good to be worth publishing.
Plays Pleasant and Unpleasant (1898), vol. 1, Preface, p. vi.

There is only one religion, though there are a hundred versions of it. *Ib.* vol. 2, Preface, p. vii.

Not bloody likely. *Pygmalion,* Act II.

Assassination is the extreme form of censorship.
The Rejected Statement, Pt. I.

If ever I utter an oath again may my soul be blasted to eternal damnation! *St. Joan,* Sc. ii.

How can what an Englishman believes be heresy? It is a contradiction in terms. *Ib.* Sc. iv.

Must then a Christ perish in torment in every age to save those that have no imagination?
Ib. Epilogue.

Well, sir, you never can tell. That's a principle in life with me, sir, if you'll excuse my having such a thing. *You Never Can Tell,* Act II.

RICHARD SHEALE

Sixteenth Century

For Witherington needs must I wail,
  As one in doleful dumps;
For when his legs were smitten off,
  He fought upon his stumps.
Ballad of Chevy Chase, Pt. II, x.

MARY WOLLSTONECRAFT SHELLEY

1797–1851

Mrs. Shelley was choosing a school for her son, and asked the advice of this lady, who gave for advice—to use her own words to me—'Just the sort of banality, you know, one does come out with: "Oh, send him somewhere where they will teach him to think for himself!" . . . Mrs. Shelley answered: 'Teach him to think for himself? Oh, my God, teach him rather to think like other people!'
Matthew Arnold, *Essays in Criticism, Second Series; Shelley.*

PERCY BYSSHE SHELLEY

1792–1822

It might make one in love with death, to think that one should be buried in so sweet a place.
Adonais. Preface.

I weep for Adonais—he is dead!
O, weep for Adonais! though our tears
Thaw not the frost which binds so dear a head!
Ib. I.

Most musical of mourners, weep again!
Lament anew, Urania!—He died,
Who was the Sire of an immortal strain,
Blind, old, and lonely, when his country's pride,
The priest, the slave, and the liberticide,
Trampled and mocked with many a loathed rite
Of lust and blood; he went, unterrified,
Into the gulf of death; but his clear Sprite
Yet reigns o'er earth; the third among the sons of light. *Ib.* IV.

But now, thy youngest, dearest one, has perished—
The nursling of thy widowhood. *Ib.* VI.

To that high Capital, where kingly Death
Keeps his pale court in beauty and decay,
He came. *Adonais*, VII.

He will awake no more, oh, never more! *Ib.* VIII.

The quick Dreams,
The passion-winged Ministers of thought. *Ib.* IX.

Lost Angel of a ruin'd Paradise!
She knew not 'twas her own; as with no stain
She faded, like a cloud which had outwept its rain.
Ib. X.

Desires and Adorations,
Winged Persuasions and veiled Destinies,
Splendours, and Glooms, and glimmering Incarna-
tions
Of hopes and fears, and twilight Phantasies;
And Sorrow, with her family of Sighs,
And Pleasure, blind with tears, led by the gleam
Of her own dying smile instead of eyes,
Came in slow pomp. *Ib.* XIII.

Ah, woe is me! Winter is come and gone,
But grief returns with the revolving year. *Ib.* XVIII.

The great morning of the world when first
God dawned on Chaos. *Ib.* XIX.

Alas! that all we loved of him should be,
But for our grief, as if it had not been,
And grief itself be mortal! *Ib.* XXI.

Whence are we, and why are we? Of what scene
The actors or spectators? *Ib.*

As long as skies are blue, and fields are green,
Evening must usher night, night urge the morrow,
Month follow month with woe, and year wake year
to sorrow. *Ib.*

Why didst thou leave the trodden paths of men
Too soon, and with weak hands though mighty heart
Dare the unpastured dragon in his den?
Defenceless as thou wert, oh, where was then
Wisdom the mirrored shield, or scorn the spear?
Ib. XXVII.

The herded wolves, bold only to pursue;
The obscene ravens, clamorous o'er the dead.
Ib. XXVIII.

The Pilgrim of Eternity, whose fame
Over his living head like heaven is bent,
An early but enduring monument,
Came, veiling all the lightnings of his song
In sorrow. *Ib.* XXX.

A pard-like spirit, beautiful and swift—
A Love in desolation masked;—a Power
Girt round with weakness;—it can scarce uplift
The weight of the superincumbent hour;
It is a dying lamp, a falling shower,
A breaking billow;—even whilst we speak
Is it not broken? *Ib.* XXXII.

A herd-abandoned deer struck by the hunter's dart.
Ib. XXXIII.

Our Adonais has drunk poison—oh!
What deaf and viperous murderer could crown
Life's early cup with such a draught of woe?
Ib. XXXVI.

He wakes or sleeps with the enduring dead;
Thou canst not soar where he is sitting now—

Dust to the dust! but the pure spirit shall flow
Back to the burning fountain whence it came,
A portion of the Eternal. *Ib.* XXXVIII.

He hath awakened from the dream of life—
'Tis we, who lost in stormy visions, keep
With phantoms an unprofitable strife,
And in mad trance, strike with our spirit's knife
Invulnerable nothings. *Ib.* XXXIX.

He has out-soared the shadow of our night;
Envy and calumny and hate and pain,
And that unrest which men miscall delight,
Can touch him not and torture not again;
From the contagion of the world's slow stain
He is secure, and now can never mourn
A heart grown cold, a head grown grey in vain.
Ib. XL.

He lives, he wakes,—'tis Death is dead, not he.
Ib. XLI.

He is made one with Nature: there is heard
His voice in all her music, from the moan
Of thunder, to the song of night's sweet bird.
Ib. XLII.

He is a portion of the loveliness
Which once he made more lovely. *Ib.* XLIII.

The inheritors of unfulfilled renown
Rose from their thrones, built beyond mortal thought,
Far in the Unapparent. *Ib.* XLV.

Sublimely mild, a Spirit without spot. (Sidney) *Ib.*

Oblivion as they rose shrank like a thing reproved.
Ib.

What Adonais is, why fear we to become? *Ib.* LI.

The One remains, the many change and pass;
Heaven's light forever shines, Earth's shadows fly;
Life, like a dome of many-coloured glass,
Stains the white radiance of Eternity. *Ib.* LII.

The soul of Adonais, like a star,
Beacons from the abode where the Eternal are.
Ib. LV.

The lone Chorasmian shore. *Alastor*, l. 272.

But thou art fled
Like some frail exhalation. *Ib.* l. 686.

Pale despair and cold tranquillity,
Nature's vast frame, the web of human things,
Birth and the grave, that are not as they were.
Ib. l. 718.

I am the eye with which the Universe
Beholds itself and knows itself divine;
All harmony of instrument or verse,
All prophecy, all medicine is mine,
All light of art or nature;—to my song
Victory and praise in its own right belong.
Hymn of Apollo.

Arethusa arose
From her couch of snows
In the Acroceraunian mountains,—
From cloud and from crag,
With many a jag,
Shepherding her bright fountains. *Arethusa.*

Like friends once parted
Grown single-hearted. *Ib.*

'Do you not hear the Aziola cry?
    Methinks she must be nigh,'
        Said Mary as we sate
In dusk, ere stars were lit, or candles brought;
        And I, who thought
This Aziola was some tedious woman,
Asked, 'Who is Aziola?'   *The Aziola.*

Give yourself no unnecessary pain,
My dear Lord Cardinal. Here, Mother, tie
My girdle for me, and bind up this hair
In any simple knot; ay, that does well.
And yours I see is coming down. How often
Have we done this for one another; now
We shall not do it any more. My Lord,
We are quite ready. Well, 'tis very well.
      The Cenci, v. iv. 158.

A widow bird sate mourning for her love
    Upon a wintry bough;
The frozen wind crept on above,
    The freezing stream below.

There was no leaf upon the forest bare,
    No flower upon the ground,
And little motion in the air
    Except the mill-wheel's sound.
      Charles the First, sc. v, l. 10.

I bring fresh showers for the thirsting flowers,
    From the seas and the streams;
I bear light shade for the leaves when laid
    In their noonday dreams.   *The Cloud.*

I wield the flail of the lashing hail,
    And whiten the green plains under,
And then again I dissolve it in rain,
    And laugh as I pass in thunder.   *Ib.*

I sift the snow on the mountains below,
    And their great pines groan aghast;
And all the night 'tis my pillow white,
    While I sleep in the arms of the blast.
Sublime on the towers of my skiey bowers,
    Lightning my pilot sits;
In a cavern under is fettered the thunder,
    It struggles and howls at fits.   *Ib.*

And I all the while bask in Heaven's blue smile,
    Whilst he is dissolving in rains.   *Ib.*

That orbèd maiden, with white fire laden,
    Whom mortals call the moon,
Glides glimmering o'er my fleece-like floor,
    By the midnight breezes strewn;
And wherever the beat of her unseen feet,
    Which only the angels hear,
May have broken the woof of my tent's thin roof,
    The stars peep behind her and peer;
And I laugh to see them whirl and flee
    Like a swarm of golden bees,
When I widen the rent in my wind-built tent,
    Till the calm rivers, lakes, and seas,
Like strips of the sky fallen through me on high,
    Are each paved with the moon and these.   *Ib.*

I am the daughter of earth and water,
    And the nursling of the sky;
I pass through the pores of the ocean and shores;
    I change, but I cannot die.
For after the rain when with never a stain
    The pavilion of Heaven is bare,

And the winds and sunbeams with their convex
        gleams
Build up the blue dome of air,
I silently laugh at my own cenotaph,
    And out of the caverns of rain,
Like a child from the womb, like a ghost from the
        tomb,
I arise and unbuild it again.   *Ib.*

    How wonderful is Death,
        Death and his brother Sleep!
One pale as yonder wan and horned moon,
        With lips of lurid blue,
The other glowing like the vital morn,
        When throned on ocean's wave
        It breathes over the world:
Yet both so passing strange and wonderful!
      The Daemon of the World, Part 1, l. 1.

My Song, I fear that thou wilt find but few
Who fitly shall conceive thy reasoning,
Of such hard matter dost thou entertain.
      Epipsychidion. Advertisement.

My last delight! tell them that they are dull,
And bid them own that thou art beautiful.   *Ib.*

            Sweet as stops
Of planetary music heard in trance.   *Ib.* l. 85.

The spirit of the worm beneath the sod
In love and worship, blends itself with God.
      Ib. l. 128.

The fields of Immortality.   *Ib.* l. 133.

    Are we not formed, as notes of music are,
For one another, though dissimilar.   *Ib.* l. 142.

I never was attached to that great sect,
Whose doctrine is, that each one should select
Out of the crowd a mistress or a friend,
And all the rest, though fair and wise, commend
To cold oblivion.   *Ib.* l. 149.

Who travel to their home among the dead
By the broad highway of the world, and so
With one chained friend, perhaps a jealous foe,
The dreariest and the longest journey go. *Ib.* l. 156.

True Love in this differs from gold and clay,
That to divide is not to take away.   *Ib.* l. 160.

A ship is floating in the harbour now,
A wind is hovering o'er the mountain's brow;
There is a path on the sea's azure floor,
No keel has ever ploughed that path before.
      Ib. l. 408.

    An isle under Ionian skies,
Beautiful as a wreck of Paradise.   *Ib.* l. 422.

    Day and night, aloof, from the high towers
And terraces, the Earth and Ocean seem
To sleep in one another's arms, and dream
Of waves, flowers, clouds, woods, rocks, and all that we
Read in their smiles, and call reality.   *Ib.* l. 508.

I pant, I sink, I tremble, I expire!   *Ib.* l. 591.

Chameleons feed on light and air:
Poets' food is love and fame.   *An Exhortation.*

And bloody Faith the foulest birth of time.
      Feelings of a Republican.

            Time's printless torrent grew
A scroll of crystal, blazoning the name
Of Adonais!   *Fragment on Keats.*

My head is wild with weeping.
Fragment: My head is wild.

My spirit like a charmed bark doth swim
  Upon the liquid waves of thy sweet singing.
Fragment: To One Singing.

Good-night? ah! no; the hour is ill
  Which severs those it should unite;
Let us remain together still,
  Then it will be *good* night.   *Good Night.*

To hearts which near each other move
  From evening close to morning light,
The night is good; because, my love,
  They never *say* good-night.   *Ib.*

Life may change, but it may fly not;
Hope may vanish, but can die not:
Truth be veiled, but still it burneth;
Love repulsed,—but it returneth!   *Hellas*, l. 34.

Let there be light! said Liberty,
And like sunrise from the sea,
Athens arose!   *Ib.* l. 682.

The world's great age begins anew,
The golden years return,
The earth doth like a snake renew
  Her winter weeds outworn;
Heaven smiles, and faiths and empires gleam,
Like wrecks of a dissolving dream.

A brighter Hellas rears its mountains
From waves serener far;
A new Peneus rolls his fountains
Against the morning star.
Where fairer Tempes bloom, there sleep
Young Cyclads on a sunnier deep.

A loftier Argo cleaves the main,
Fraught with a later prize;
Another Orpheus sings again,
And loves, and weeps, and dies.
A new Ulysses leaves once more
Calypso for his native shore.   *Ib.* l. 1060.

Riddles of death Thebes never knew.   *Ib.* l. 1083.

Another Athens shall arise,
And to remoter time
Bequeath, like sunset to the skies,
The splendour of its prime;
And leave, if nought so bright may live,
All earth can take or Heaven can give.

Saturn and Love their long repose
Shall burst, more bright and good
Than all who fell, than One who rose,
Than many unsubdued:
Not gold, not blood, their altar dowers,
But votive tears and symbol flowers.

Oh cease! must hate and death return?
Cease! must men kill and die?
Cease! drain not to its dregs the urn
Of bitter prophecy.
The world is weary of the past,
Oh, might it die or rest at last!   *Ib.* l. 1090.

I pursued a maiden and clasped a reed.
Gods and men, we are all deluded thus!
It breaks in our bosom and then we bleed.
Hymn of Pan.

The awful shadow of some unseen Power
  Floats though unseen among us,—visiting
  This various world with as inconstant wing
As summer winds that creep from flower to flower.
Hymn to Intellectual Beauty.

Spirit of Beauty, that dost consecrate
  With thine own hues all thou dost shine upon
  Of human thought or form.   *Ib.*

While yet a boy I sought for ghosts, and sped
  Through many a listening chamber, cave and
    ruin,
  And starlight wood, with fearful steps pursuing
Hopes of high talk with the departed dead.
I called on poisonous names with which our youth
  is fed.   *Ib.*

The day becomes more solemn and serene
  When noon is past—there is a harmony
  In autumn, and a lustre in its sky,
Which through the summer is not heard or seen,
As if it could not be, as if it had not been!   *Ib.*

I arise from dreams of thee
In the first sweet sleep of night.
When the winds are breathing low,
And the stars are shining bright:
I arise from dreams of thee,
And a spirit in my feet
Hath led me—who knows how?
To thy chamber window, Sweet!

The wandering airs they faint
On the dark, the silent stream—
The Champak odours fail
Like sweet thoughts in a dream;
The nightingale's complaint,
It dies upon her heart;—
As I must on thine,
Beloved as thou art!

Oh lift me from the grass!
I die! I faint! I fail!
Let thy love in kisses rain
On my lips and eyelids pale.
My cheek is cold and white, alas!
My heart beats loud and fast;—
Oh! press it to thine own again,
Where it will break at last.   *The Indian Serenade.*

Best and brightest, come away!
Fairer far than this fair day.
To Jane: The Invitation.

'I am gone into the fields
To take what this sweet hour yields;—
Reflection, you may come to-morrow,
Sit by the fireside with Sorrow.—
You with the unpaid bill, Despair,—
You, tiresome verse-reciter, Care,—
I will pay you in the grave,—
Death will listen to your stave.   *Ib.*

The daisy-star that never sets,
And wind-flowers, and violets,
Which yet join not scent to hue.   *Ib.*

  Soothed by every azure breath
That under Heaven is blown.
To Jane: The Recollection.

Less oft is peace in Shelley's mind,
Than calm in waters, seen.   *Ib.*

       I love all waste
And solitary places; where we taste
The pleasure of believing what we see
Is boundless, as we wish our souls to be.
         Julian and Maddalo, l. 14.

Thou Paradise of exiles, Italy!   *Ib.* l. 57.

       It is our will
That thus enchains us to permitted ill—
We might be otherwise—we might be all
We dream of happy, high, majestical.   *Ib.* l. 170.

Me—who am as a nerve o'er which do creep
The else unfelt oppressions of this earth. *Ib.* l. 449.

  Most wretched men
Are cradled into poetry by wrong:
They learn in suffering what they teach in song.
         Ib. l. 543.

     A wonder of this earth—
Like one of Shakespeare's women.   *Ib.* l. 590.

O world! O life! O time!
On whose last steps I climb,
Trembling at that where I had stood before;
When will return the glory of your prime?
No more—Oh, never more!
Fresh spring, and summer, and winter hoar,
Move my faint heart with grief, but with delight
No more—Oh, never more!   *A Lament.*

When the lamp is shattered
  The light in the dust lies dead—
When the cloud is scattered
  The rainbow's glory is shed.
When the lute is broken,
  Sweet tones are remembered not;
When the lips have spoken,
  Loved accents are soon forgot.
       Lines: When the Lamp.

When hearts have once mingled
  Love first leaves the well-built nest;
The weak one is singled
  To endure what it once possessed.
O Love! who bewailest
  The frailty of all things here,
Why choose you the frailest
  For your cradle, your home, and your bier?   *Ib.*

Many a green isle needs must be
In the deep wide sea of misery,
Or the mariner, worn and wan,
Never thus could voyage on.
  Lines written amongst the Euganean Hills, l. 1.

Ay, many flowering islands lie
In the waters of wide Agony.   *Ib.* l. 66.

Beneath is spread like a green sea
The waveless plain of Lombardy,
Bounded by the vaporous air,
Islanded by cities fair;
Underneath Day's azure eyes
Ocean's nursling, Venice lies,
A peopled labyrinth of walls,
Amphitrite's destined halls.   *Ib.* l. 90.

Sun-girt city, thou hast been
Ocean's child, and then his queen;
Now is come a darker day,
And thou soon must be his prey.   *Ib.* l. 115.

    My spirit which so long
Darkened this swift stream of song.   *Ib.* l. 311.

Peopling the lone universe.   *Ib.* l. 319.

Other flowering isles must be
In the sea of Life and Agony.   *Ib.* l. 335.

What! alive, and so bold, O earth?
  *Lines written on hearing the News of the Death
  of Napoleon.*

The fountains mingle with the river,
  And the rivers with the ocean;
The winds of heaven mix for ever
  With a sweet emotion;
Nothing in the world is single;
  All things, by a law divine,
In one another's being mingle.
  Why not I with thine?—

See the mountains kiss high Heaven
  And the waves clasp one another;
No sister-flower would be forgiven
  If it disdained its brother;
And the sunlight clasps the earth
  And the moonbeams kiss the sea:
What are all these kissings worth
  If thou kiss not me?   *Love's Philosophy.*

Under the roof of blue Italian weather.
    Letter to Maria Gisborne, l. 147.

    London, that great sea, whose ebb and flow
At once is deaf and loud, and on the shore
Vomits its wrecks, and still howls on for more.
        Ib. l. 193.

You will see Coleridge—he who sits obscure
In the exceeding lustre and the pure
Intense irradiation of a mind,
Which, through its own internal lightning blind,
Flags wearily through darkness and despair—
A cloud-encircled meteor of the air,
A hooded eagle among blinking owls.
You will see Hunt—one of those happy souls
Which are the salt of the earth, and without whom
This world would smell like what it is—a tomb.
        Ib. l. 202.

     Have you not heard
When a man marries, dies, or turns Hindoo,
His best friends hear no more of him?   *Ib.* l. 235.

   The milk-white Snowdonian antelope
Matched with this cameleopard.   *Ib.* l. 239.

     Wit and sense,
Virtue and human knowledge; all that might
Make this dull world a business of delight,
Are all combined in Horace Smith.   *Ib.* l. 247.

I met Murder in the way—
He had a mask like Castlereagh.
    The Mask of Anarchy, II.

Ye are many—they are few.   *Ib.* XXXVIII.

Its horror and its beauty are divine.
    The Medusa of Leonardo da Vinci.

Some say that gleams of a remoter world
Visit the soul in sleep,—that death is slumber,
And that its shapes the busy thoughts outnumber
Of those who wake and live.   *Mont Blanc*, l. 49.

Art thou pale for weariness
Of climbing heaven, and gazing on the earth,
  Wandering companionless
Among the stars that have a different birth,—
And ever changing, like a joyous eye
That finds no object worth its constancy?
                To the Moon.

Nought may endure but Mutability.   *Mutability.*

A glorious people vibrated again
  The lightning of the nations. *Ode to Liberty*, l. 1.

My soul spurned the chains of its dismay,
  And in the rapid plumes of song
  Clothed itself, sublime and strong,
(As a young eagle soars the morning clouds among.)
                Ib. l. 5.

      When o'er the Aegean main
Athens arose: a city such as vision
  Builds from the purple crags and silver towers
Of battlemented cloud, as in derision
  Of kingliest masonry: the ocean-floors
Pave it; the evening sky pavilions it;
    Its portals are inhabited
    By thunder-zoned winds.   *Ib.* l. 60.

Within the surface of Time's fleeting river
  Its wrinkled image lies, as then it lay
Immovably unquiet, and for ever
  It trembles, but it cannot pass away!   *Ib.* l. 76.

I stood within the City disinterred;
And heard the autumnal leaves like light footfalls
Of spirits passing through the streets; and heard
The Mountain's slumbrous voice at intervals
Thrill through those roofless halls.
              Ode to Naples, l. 1.

Long lost, late won, and yet but half-regained.
                Ib. l. 58.

O wild West Wind, thou breath of Autumn's being,
Thou, from whose unseen presence the leaves dead
Are driven, like ghosts from an enchanter fleeing,

Yellow, and black, and pale, and hectic red,
Pestilence-stricken multitudes: O thou,
Who chariotest to their dark wintry bed

The winged seeds, where they lie cold and low,
Each like a corpse within its grave, until
Thine azure sister of the spring shall blow

Her clarion o'er the dreaming earth, and fill
(Driving sweet buds like flocks to feed in air)
With living hues and odours plain and hill:

Wild Spirit, which art moving everywhere;
Destroyer and preserver; hear, oh, hear!
         Ode to the West Wind, l. 1.

Shook from the tangled boughs of Heaven and Ocean,
Angels of rain and lightning.   *Ib.* l. 17.

Like the bright hair uplifted from the head
Of some fierce Maenad.   *Ib.* l. 20.

                Thou dirge
Of the dying year, to which this closing night
Will be the dome of a vast sepulchre.   *Ib.* l. 23.

Thou who didst waken from his summer dreams
  The blue Mediterranean, where he lay,
Lulled by the coil of his crystalline streams

  Beside a pumice isle in Baiae's bay,
And saw in sleep old palaces and towers
  Quivering within the wave's intenser day,

All overgrown with azure moss and flowers
  So sweet, the sense faints picturing them. *Ib.* l. 29.

              Far below
The sea-blooms and the oozy woods which wear
The sapless foliage of the ocean, know
Thy voice, and suddenly grow gray with fear,
And tremble and despoil themselves.   *Ib.* l. 38.

If I were a dead leaf thou mightest bear;
If I were a swift cloud to fly with thee;
A wave to pant beneath thy power, and share

The impulse of thy strength, only less free
Than thou, O uncontrollable! If even
I were as in my boyhood, and could be

The comrade of thy wanderings over Heaven,
As then, when to outstrip thy skiey speed
Scarce seemed a vision; I would ne'er have striven

As thus with thee in prayer in my sore need.
Oh, lift me as a wave, a leaf, a cloud!
I fall upon the thorns of life! I bleed!   *Ib.* l. 43.

Make me thy lyre, even as the forest is:
What if my leaves are falling like its own?
The tumult of thy mighty harmonies

Will take from both a deep, autumnal tone,
Sweet though in sadness. Be thou, Spirit fierce,
My spirit! Be thou me, impetuous one!

Drive my dead thoughts over the universe
Like withered leaves to quicken a new birth!
And, by the incantation of this verse,

Scatter, as from an unextinguished hearth
Ashes and sparks, my words among mankind!
Be through my lips to unawakened earth

The trumpet of a prophecy! O, Wind,
If Winter comes, can Spring be far behind? *Ib.* 57.

Or *anything*, as the learned Boar observed.
         Oedipus Tyrannus, II. i. 105.

I met a traveller from an antique land
Who said: Two vast and trunkless legs of stone
Stand in the desert.   *Ozymandias.*

My name is Ozymandias, king of kings:
Look on my works, ye Mighty, and despair!   *Ib.*

Nothing beside remains. Round the decay
Of that colossal wreck, boundless and bare
The lone and level sands stretch far away.   *Ib.*

Hell is a city much like London—
A populous and smoky city.
      Peter Bell the Third, Part 3. Hell, **i.**

But from the first 'twas Peter's drift
  To be a kind of moral eunuch,
He touched the hem of Nature's shift,
  Felt faint—and never dared uplift
    The closest, all-concealing tunic.
                Ib. Part 4. Sin, xi.

        Ere Babylon was dust,
The Magus Zoroaster, my dead child,
Met his own image walking in the garden,
That apparition, sole of men, he saw.
     Prometheus Unbound, 1, l. 191.

Dreams and the light imaginings of men,
And all that faith creates or love desires,
Terrible, strange, sublime and beauteous shapes.
                      Ib. 200.

Cruel he looks, but calm and strong,
Like one who does, not suffers wrong.   *Ib*. 238.

It doth repent me: words are quick and vain;
Grief for awhile is blind, and so was mine.
I wish no living thing to suffer pain.   *Ib*. 303.

See a disenchanted nation
Springs like day from desolation;
To Truth its state is dedicate,
And Freedom leads it forth, her mate.   *Ib*. 567.

The good want power, but to weep barren tears.
The powerful goodness want: worse need for them.
The wise want love; and those who love want
  wisdom.   *Ib*. 625.

Thy words are like a cloud of winged snakes;
And yet I pity those they torture not.   *Ib*. 632.

         Peace is in the grave.
The grave hides all things beautiful and good:
I am a God and cannot find it there.   *Ib*. 638.

The dust of creeds outworn.   *Ib*. 697.

On a poet's lips I slept
Dreaming like a love-adept
In the sound his breathing kept;
Nor seeks nor finds he mortal blisses,
But feeds on the aërial kisses
Of shapes that haunt thought's wildernesses.
He will watch from dawn to gloom
The lake-reflected sun illume
The yellow bees in the ivy-bloom,
Nor heed, nor see, what things they be;
But from these create he can
Forms more real than living man,
Nurslings of immortality!   *Ib*. 737.

     That sense, which when the winds of Spring
In rarest visitation, or the voice
Of one beloved heard in youth alone,
Fills the faint eyes with falling tears which dim
The radiant looks of unbewailing flowers,
And leaves this peopled earth a solitude
When it returns no more.   *Ib*. ii. iv. 12.

        To be
Omnipotent but friendless is to reign.   *Ib*. 47.

He gave man speech, and speech created thought,
Which is the measure of the universe.   *Ib*. 73.

All spirits are enslaved which serve things evil.
                        Ib. 110.

Fate, Time, Occasion, Chance, and Change? To
  these
All things are subject but eternal Love.   *Ib*. 119.

My coursers are fed with the lightning,
They drink of the whirlwind's stream,
And when the red morning is bright'ning
They bathe in the fresh sunbeam.   *Ib*. 163.

Life of Life! thy lips enkindle
  With their love the breath between them;
And thy smiles before they dwindle
  Make the cold air fire; then screen them
In those looks, where whoso gazes
Faints, entangled in their mazes.

Child of Light! thy limbs are burning
  Through the vest which seems to hide them;
As the radiant lines of morning
  Through the clouds ere they divide them;
And this atmosphere divinest
Shrouds thee wheresoe'er thou shinest.
                      Ib. v. 48.

  My soul is an enchanted boat,
  Which, like a sleeping swan, doth float
Upon the silver waves of thy sweet singing. *Ib*. 72.

Death is the veil which those who live call life:
They sleep, and it is lifted.   *Ib*. iii. iii. 113.

The loathsome mask has fallen, the man remains
Sceptreless, free, uncircumscribed, but man
Equal, unclassed, tribeless, and nationless,
Exempt from awe, worship, degree, the king
Over himself; just, gentle, wise: but man
Passionless?—no, yet free from guilt or pain,
Which were, for his will made or suffered them,
Nor yet exempt, though ruling them like slaves,
From chance, and death, and mutability,
The clogs of that which else might oversoar
The loftiest star of unascended heaven,
Pinnacled dim in the intense inane.   *Ib*. 193.

Familiar acts are beautiful through love. *Ib*. iv. 403.

Language is a perpetual Orphic song,
Which rules with Daedal harmony a throng
Of thoughts and forms, which else senseless and
  shapeless were.   *Ib*. 415.

Elysian, windless, fortunate abodes
Beyond Heaven's constellated wilderness. *Ib*. 531.

A traveller from the cradle to the grave
Through the dim night of this immortal day.
                      Ib. 551.

To suffer woes which Hope thinks infinite;
To forgive wrongs darker than death or night;
  To defy Power, which seems omnipotent;
To love, and bear; to hope till Hope creates
From its own wreck the thing it contemplates;
  Neither to change, nor falter, nor repent;
This, like thy glory, Titan, is to be
Good, great and joyous, beautiful and free;
This is alone Life, Joy, Empire, and Victory.
                    Ib. 570.

How wonderful is Death,
Death and his brother Sleep!
        Queen Mab, Canto 1, l. 1.

That sweet bondage which is freedom's self.
               Ib. Canto 9, l. 76.

I dreamed that, as I wandered by the way,
  Bare Winter suddenly was changed to Spring,
And gentle odours led my steps astray,
  Mixed with a sound of water's murmuring

Along a shelving bank of turf, which lay
  Under a copse, and hardly dared to fling
Its green arms round the bosom of the stream,
  But kissed it and then fled, as thou mightst in
    dream.   *The Question.*

There grew pied wind-flowers and violets,
  Daisies, those pearled Arcturi of the earth,
The constellated flower that never sets.   *Ib.*

And in the warm hedge grew lush eglantine,
  Green cowbind and the moonlight-coloured may,
And cherry-blossoms, and white cups, whose wine
  Was the bright dew, yet drained not by the day;
And wild roses, and ivy serpentine,
  With its dark buds and leaves, wandering astray;
And flowers azure, black, and streaked with gold,
  Fairer than any wakened eyes behold.   *Ib.*

And nearer to the river's trembling edge
  There grew broad flag-flowers, purple, pranked
    with white,
And starry river buds among the sedge,
  And floating water-lilies, broad and bright.   *Ib.*

With hue like that when some great painter dips
His pencil in the gloom of earthquake and eclipse.
       The Revolt of Islam, C. 5. 2, xxiii.

A Sensitive Plant in a garden grew.
       The Sensitive Plant, Part 1, l. 1.

And the rose like a nymph to the bath addressed,
Which unveiled the depth of her glowing breast,
Till, fold after fold, to the fainting air
The soul of her beauty and love lay bare. *Ib.* l. 29.

And the jessamine faint, and the sweet tuberose,
The sweetest flower for scent that blows. *Ib.* l. 37.

It is a modest creed, and yet
Pleasant if one considers it,
To own that death itself must be
Like all the rest, a mockery.   *Ib. Conclusion.*

Hail to thee, blithe spirit!
  Bird thou never wert,
That from Heaven, or near it,
  Pourest thy full heart
In profuse strains of unpremeditated art.
         To a Skylark.

And singing still dost soar, and soaring ever singest.
         Ib.

Like an unbodied joy whose race is just begun. *Ib.*

Thou art unseen, but yet I hear thy shrill delight.
         Ib.

Keen as are the arrows
  Of that silver sphere,
Whose intense lamp narrows
  In the white dawn clear
Until we hardly see,—we feel that it is there. *Ib.*

Like a Poet hidden
  In the light of thought,
Singing hymns unbidden,
  Till the world is wrought
To sympathy with hopes and fears it heeded not:

Like a high-born maiden
  In a palace-tower,
Soothing her love-laden
  Soul in secret hour
With music sweet as love, which overflows her bower.
         Ib.

Chorus Hymeneal,
  Or triumphal chant,
Matched with thine would be all
  But an empty vaunt,
A thing wherein we feel there is some hidden want.
         Ib.

What objects are the fountains
  Of thy happy strain?
What fields, or waves, or mountains?
  What shapes of sky or plain?
What love of thine own kind? what ignorance of
  pain?   *Ib.*

With thy clear keen joyance
  Languor cannot be:
Shadow of annoyance
  Never came near thee:
Thou lovest—but ne'er knew love's sad satiety.

Waking or asleep,
  Thou of death must deem
Things more true and deep
  Than we mortals dream,
Or how could thy notes flow in such a crystal stream?

We look before and after;
  We pine for what is not;
Our sincerest laughter
  With some pain is fraught;
Our sweetest songs are those that tell of saddest
  thought.   *Ib.*

Better than all measures
  Of delightful sound,
Better than all treasures
  That in books are found,
Thy skill to poet were, thou scorner of the ground!

Teach me half the gladness
  That thy brain must know,
Such harmonious madness
  From my lips would flow
The world should listen then—as I am listening now.
         Ib.

Rarely, rarely, comest thou,
Spirit of Delight!
       Song: Rarely, Rarely, Comest Thou.

I love all that thou lovest,
  Spirit of Delight:
The fresh Earth in new leaves dressed,
  And the starry night;
Autumn evening, and the morn
When the golden mists are born.   *Ib.*

    Everything almost
Which is Nature's, and may be
Untainted by man's misery.   *Ib.*

I love tranquil solitude,
  And such society
As is quiet, wise, and good;
  Between thee and me
What difference? but thou dost possess
The things I seek, not love them less.   *Ib.*

I love Love—though he has wings,
  And like light can flee,
But above all other things,
  Spirit, I love thee—
Thou art love and life! Oh, come,
Make once more my heart thy home.   *Ib.*

Men of England, wherefore plough
For the lords who lay you low?
Song to the Men of England.

An old, mad, blind, despised, and dying king.
Sonnet: England in 1819.

Lift not the painted veil which those who live
Call Life.   *Sonnet: Lift not the Painted Veil.*

          He sought,
For his lost heart was tender, things to love,
But found them not, alas! nor was there aught
The world contains, the which he could approve.
Through the unheeding many he did move,
A splendour among shadows, a bright blot
Upon this gloomy scene, a Spirit that strove
For truth, and like the Preacher found it not.   *Ib.*

The City's voice itself is soft like Solitude's.
Stanzas Written in Dejection, near Naples.

I see the waves upon the shore,
Like light dissolved in star-showers, thrown.   *Ib.*

How sweet! did any heart now share in my emotion.
          Ib.

Alas! I have nor hope nor health,
   Nor peace within nor calm around,
Nor that content surpassing wealth
   The sage in meditation found,
   And walked with inward glory crowned.   *Ib.*

I could lie down like a tired child,
   And weep away the life of care
Which I have borne and yet must bear,
   Till death like sleep might steal on me.   *Ib.*

Away! the moor is dark beneath the moon,
Rapid clouds have drank the last pale beam of even:
Away! the gathering winds will call the darkness soon,
And profoundest midnight shroud the serene lights of
   heaven.
Stanzas.—April 1814: Away! the Moor is Dark.

Swiftly walk over the western wave,
   Spirit of Night!
Out of the misty eastern cave,
Where, all the long and lone daylight,
Thou wovest dreams of joy and fear,
Which make thee terrible and dear,—
   Swift be thy flight!   *To Night.*

Wrap thy form in a mantle gray,
   Star-inwrought!
Blind with thine hair the eyes of Day;
Kiss her until she be wearied out,
Then wander o'er city, and sea, and land,
Touching all with thine opiate wand—
   Come, long-sought!   *Ib.*

Thy brother Death came, and cried,
   Wouldst thou me?
Thy sweet child Sleep, the filmy-eyed,
Murmured like a noontide bee,
Shall I nestle by thy side?
   Wouldst thou me?   *Ib.*

Death will come when thou art dead,
   Soon, too soon—
Sleep will come when thou art fled;
Of neither would I ask the boon
I ask of thee, beloved Night—
   Come soon, soon!   *Ib.*

Music, when soft voices die,
Vibrates in the memory—
Odours, when sweet violets sicken,
Live within the sense they quicken.

Rose leaves, when the rose is dead,
Are heaped for the beloved's bed;
And so thy thoughts, when thou art gone,
Love itself shall slumber on.
To—— Music, When Soft Voices.

I fear thy kisses, gentle maiden,
   Thou needest not fear mine;
My spirit is too deeply laden
   Ever to burthen thine.

I fear thy mien, thy tones, thy motion,
   Thou needest not fear mine;
Innocent is the heart's devotion
   With which I worship thine.
To—— I Fear thy Kisses.

One word is too often profaned
   For me to profane it,
One feeling too falsely disdained
   For thee to disdain it.
To—— One Word is too often Profaned.

The desire of the moth for the star,
   Of the night for the morrow,
The devotion to something afar
   From the sphere of our sorrow.   *Ib.*

And like a dying lady, lean and pale,
Who totters forth, wrapped in a gauzy veil.
          The Waning Moon.

A lovely lady, garmented in light
   From her own beauty.   *The Witch of Atlas,* v.

For she was beautiful—her beauty made
The bright world dim, and everything beside
Seemed like the fleeting image of a shade.   *Ib.* xii.

          The rapid, blind
And fleeting generations of mankind.   *Ib.* lxxi.

In honoured poverty thy voice did weave
Songs consecrate to truth and liberty,—
Deserting these, thou leavest me to grieve,
Thus having been, that thou shouldst cease to be.
          To Wordsworth.

Poets are the unacknowledged legislators of the world.
          A Defence of Poetry.

WILLIAM SHENSTONE
1714–1763

Whoe'er has travell'd life's dull round,
   Where'er his stages may have been,
May sigh to think he still has found
   The warmest welcome, at an inn.
          At an Inn at Henley.

My banks they are furnish'd with bees,
   Whose murmur invites one to sleep;
My grottoes are shaded with trees,
   And my hills are white over with sheep.
          A Pastoral Ballad. Pt. II, Hope, i.

I have found out a gift for my fair;
I have found where the wood-pigeons breed;
But let me that plunder forbear,
She will say 'twas a barbarous deed.   *Ib.* **v.**

A little bench of heedless bishops here,
And there a chancellor in embryo,
Or bard sublime, if bard may e'er be so.
The Schoolmistress, xxviii.

Laws are generally found to be nets of such a texture,
as the little creep through, the great break through,
and the middle-sized are alone entangled in.
Essays on Men and Manners. On Politics.

PHILIP HENRY SHERIDAN
1831–1888

The only good Indian is a dead Indian.
Attr., at Fort Cobb, Jan. 1869.

RICHARD BRINSLEY SHERIDAN
1751–1816

Not a translation—only *taken from the French.*
The Critic, i. i.

The newspapers! Sir, they are the most villainous—
licentious—abominable—infernal— Not that I
ever read them—no—I make it a rule never to
look into a newspaper. *Ib.*

If it is abuse—why one is always sure to hear of it
from one damned good-natured friend or other!
Ib.

Egad, I think the interpreter is the hardest to be
understood of the two! *Ib.* ii.

Yes, sir, puffing is of various sorts; the principal are,
the puff direct, the puff preliminary, the puff col-
lateral, the puff collusive, and the puff oblique, or
puff by implication. *Ib.*

No scandal about Queen Elizabeth, I hope? *Ib.* ii. i.

I open with a clock striking, to beget an awful
attention in the audience: it also marks the time,
which is four o'clock in the morning, and saves a
description of the rising sun, and a great deal
about gilding the eastern hemisphere. *Ib.* ii.

Where they do agree on the stage, their unanimity is
wonderful! *Ib.*

Inconsolable to the minuet in Ariadne! *Ib.*

The Spanish fleet thou canst not see because—
It is not yet in sight! *Ib.*

All that can be said is, that two people happened to
hit on the same thought—and Shakespeare made
use of it first, that's all. *Ib.* iii. i.

Burleigh comes forward, shakes his head, and exit.
Ib. Stage direction.

O Lord, sir, when a heroine goes mad she always goes
into white satin. *Ib.*

An oyster may be crossed in love. *Ib.*

I ne'er could any lustre see
In eyes that would not look on me.
The Duenna, i. ii. Air.

I loved him for himself alone. *Ib.* iii.

Had I a heart for falsehood framed,
I ne'er could injure you. *Ib.* v.

'Tis safest in matrimony to begin with a little
aversion. *The Rivals*, i. ii.

You gentlemen's gentlemen are so hasty.
Ib. ii. ii.

He is the very pine-apple of politeness! *Ib.* iii. iii.

An aspersion upon my parts of speech! *Ib.*

If I reprehend any thing in this world, it is the use
of my oracular tongue, and a nice derangement of
epitaphs! *Ib.*

Too civil by half. *Ib.* iv.

Our ancestors are very good kind of folks; but they
are the last people I should choose to have a
visiting acquaintance with. *Ib.* iv. i.

No caparisons, miss, if you please. Caparisons don't
become a young woman. *Ib.* ii.

You are not like Cerberus, three gentlemen at once,
are you? *Ib.*

There's nothing like being used to a thing. *Ib.* v. iii.

My valour is certainly going!—it is sneaking off! I
feel it oozing out as it were at the palms of my
hands! *Ib.*

I own the soft impeachment. *Ib.*

Thro' all the drama—whether damned or not—
Love gilds the scene, and women guide the plot.
Ib. Epilogue.

You shall see them on a beautiful quarto page, where
a neat rivulet of text shall meander through a
meadow of margin. *The School for Scandal*, i. i.

Here is the whole set! a character dead at every word.
Ib. ii. ii.

I'm called away by particular business. But I leave
my character behind me. *Ib.*

Oh! plague of his sentiments! *Ib.* iii.

Here's to the maiden of bashful fifteen;
Here's to the widow of fifty;
Here's to the flaunting, extravagant quean;
And here's to the housewife that's thrifty.
Let the toast pass,—
Drink to the lass,
I'll warrant she'll prove an excuse for a glass.
Ib. iii. iii. Song.

Here's to the charmer whose dimples we prize;
Now to the maid who has none, sir;
Here's to the girl with a pair of blue eyes,
And here's to the nymph with but one, sir. *Ib.*

ROWLEY:
I believe there is no sentiment he has such faith in
as that 'charity begins at home'.

SURFACE:
And his, I presume, is of that domestic sort which
never stirs abroad at all. *Ib.*

Damned disinheriting countenance. *Ib.* iv. i.

It was an amiable weakness. *Ib.* v. i.

There is no trusting to appearances. *Ib.* ii.

The Right Honourable gentleman is indebted to his memory for his jests, and to his imagination for his facts.

Speech in Reply to Mr. Dundas. T. Moore, *Life of Sheridan* (1825), II. 471.

You write with ease, to show your breeding,
But easy writing's vile hard reading.

Clio's Protest. See Moore's *Life of Sheridan*, I. 55.

WILLIAM TECUMSEH SHERMAN
1820–1891

There is many a boy here to-day who looks on war as all glory, but, boys, it is all hell.

Speech, Columbus, Ohio, 11 Aug. 1880. Lewis's *'Sherman, Fighting Prophet'.*

JAMES SHIRLEY
1596–1666

The glories of our blood and state
Are shadows, not substantial things;
There is no armour against fate;
　　Death lays his icy hand on kings:
　　　　Sceptre and crown
　　　　Must tumble down,
And in the dust be equal made
With the poor crooked scythe and spade.

The Contention of Ajax and Ulysses, I. iii.

Only the actions of the just
Smell sweet, and blossom in their dust.　　*Ib.*

I presume you're mortal, and may err.

The Lady of Pleasure, II. ii.

　　　　How little room
Do we take up in death, that, living know
No bounds?　　　　*The Wedding,* IV. iv.

JOSEPH HENRY SHORTHOUSE
1834–1903

'The Church of England', I said, seeing that Mr. Inglesant paused, 'is no doubt a compromise.'

John Inglesant (1880), ch. 40.

In all probability 'Wordsworth's standard of intoxication was miserably low'.

Remark to some Wordsworthians who were deploring W.'s confession that he got drunk at Cambridge. G. W. E. Russell's *Collections and Recollections,* ch. 8.

ALGERNON SIDNEY
1622–1683

Liars ought to have good memories.

Discourses on Government, ch. 2, sect. xv.

Men lived like fishes; the great ones devour'd the small.　　*Ib.* sect. xviii.

'Tis not necessary to light a candle to the sun.

Ib. sect. xxiii.

SIR PHILIP SIDNEY
1554–1586

High erected thoughts seated in the heart of courtesy.

The Arcadia, bk. i, ch. 2.

Shallow brooks murmur most, deep silent slide away.

Ib. First Eclogues, Lalus and Dorus, st. ii.

Who shoots at the mid-day sun, though he be sure he shall never hit the mark; yet as sure he is he shall shoot higher than who aims but at a bush.

Ib. bk. ii, ch. 6.

My true love hath my heart and I have his,
By just exchange one for the other giv'n;
I hold his dear, and mine he cannot miss,
There never was a better bargain driv'n.

Ib. bk. iii, *ad fin.*

Doubt you to whom my Muse these notes intendeth,
　　Which now my breast o'ercharged to music
　　　lendeth?
To you, to you, all song of praise is due;
　　Only in you my song begins and endeth.

Astrophel and Stella, Song I: Doubt You to Whom.

Have I caught my heav'nly jewel.

Ib. Song II: Have I Caught.

Thy fair hair my heart enchained.

Ib. Certain Sonnets, To the tune of a Neapolitan Villanell.

'Fool!' said my Muse to me, 'look in thy heart, and write.'　　*Ib. Sonnet I.*

With how sad steps, O Moon, thou climb'st the skies!
How silently, and with how wan a face!
What! may it be that even in heavenly place
That busy archer his sharp arrows tries?

Ib. Sonnet XXXI.

Do they call virtue there ungratefulness?　　*Ib.*

Come, Sleep! O Sleep, the certain knot of peace,
　　The baiting-place of wit, the balm of woe,
The poor man's wealth, the prisoner's release,
　　Th' indifferent judge between the high and low.

Ib. Sonnet XXXIX.

Take thou of me smooth pillows sweetest bed,
　　A chamber deaf to noise and blind to light,
A rosy garland and a weary head.　　*Ib.*

That sweet enemy, France.　　*Ib. Sonnet XLI.*

They love indeed who quake to say they love.

Ib. Sonnet LIV.

Oh heav'nly fool, thy most kiss-worthy face
Anger invests with such a lovely grace,
That Anger's self I needs must kiss again.

Ib. Sonnet LXXIII.

I never drank of Aganippe well,
　　Nor ever did in shade of Tempe sit,
And Muses scorn with vulgar brains to dwell;
　　Poor layman I, for sacred rites unfit.

Ib. Sonnet LXXIV.

Highway, since you my chief Parnassus be,
  And that my Muse, to some ears not unsweet,
Tempers her words to trampling horses' feet
  More oft than to a chamber melody,
Now blessed you, bear onward blessed me
  To her, where I my heart, safe-left, shall meet.
                              Ib. Sonnet LXXXIV.

Hundreds of years you Stella's feet may kiss.   *Ib.*

Leave me, O Love, which reacheth but to dust;
  And thou, my mind, aspire to higher things;
Grow rich in that which never taketh rust;
  Whatever fades, but fading pleasure brings.
    *Ib. Sonnet CX: Splendidis Longum Valedico
    Nugis.*

Never love was so abused.
          Pansies from Penshurst and Wilton. V. Love.

O fair! O sweet! when I do look on thee,
  In whom all joys so well agree,
Heart and soul do sing in me,
  Just accord all music makes.
    *Ib. VIII. Verses, To the Tune of a Spanish
    Song.*

With a tale forsooth he cometh unto you, with a tale
  which holdeth children from play, and old men
  from the chimney corner.
              The Defence of Poesy (1923), p. 20.

Certainly I must confess mine own barbarousness, I
  never heard the old song of Percy and Douglas,
  that I found not my heart moved more than with
  a trumpet.   *Ib.* p. 24.

Philip of Macedon reckoned a horse-race won at
  Olympus among his three fearful felicities.   *Ib.*

To be rhymed to death as is said to be done in Ireland.
                                              Ib.

Thy necessity is yet greater than mine.
    *On giving his water-bottle to a dying soldier on
    the battle-field of Zutphen, 1586.* Sir Fulke
    Greville's *Life* (1907), ch. 12.

HAROLD SIMPSON

contemp

Down in the forest something stirred,
It was only the note of a bird.
      A Cycle of Life. No. 2. *Down In The Forest.*

OSBERT SITWELL

1892–

The British Bourgeoisie
Is not born,
And does not die,
But, if it is ill,
It has a frightened look in its eyes.
                      At the House of Mrs. Kinfoot.

JOHN SKELTON

1460?–1529

As patient and as still
And as full of goodwill,
As the fair Isyphill,

Coliander,
Sweet pomander,
Good Cassander,
Steadfast of thought,
Well made, well wrought.
Far may be sought
Erst ye can find
So courteous, so kind,
As Merry Margaret, the midsummer flower,
Gentle as falcon or hawk of the tower.
                      To Mistress Margaret Hussey.

With solace and gladness,
Much mirth and no madness,
All good and no badness;
So joyously,
So maidenly,
So womanly,
Her demeaning.   *Ib.*

She is the violet,
The daisy delectable,
The columbine commendable,
The jelofer amiable;
For this most goodly flower,
This blossom of fresh colour,
So Jupiter me succour,
She flourisheth new and new
In beauty and virtue.
          The Commendations of Mistress Jane Scrope.

For the soul of Philip Sparrow,
That was late slain at Carrow
Among the Nunnes Black,
For that sweet soules sake
And for all sparrows' souls
Set in our bead-rolls,
Pater noster qui
With an *Ave Mari.*

                              The Sparrow's Dirge.

JOHN SKINNER

1721–1807

Let Whig and Tory a' agree,
  Whig and Tory, Whig and Tory,
  Whig and Tory a' agree,
    To drop their Whigmigmorum;
Let Whig and Tory a' agree
To spend the night in mirth and glee,
And cheerfu' sing alang wi' me
    The reel o' Tullochgorum.
    Tullochgorum, st. i.   *The Songs of Scotland,*
    ed. G. F. Graham.
    [A version of 1776 gives line 4 as 'To drop
    their whipmegorum'.]

CHRISTOPHER SMART

1722–1771

For Adoration all the ranks
Of angels yield eternal thanks,
  And David in the midst.   *Song to David.*

Glorious—more glorious is the crown
Of Him that brought salvation down
  By meekness, call'd thy Son;
Thou that stupendous truth believ'd,
And now the matchless deed's achiev'd,
  Determined, dared, and done.   *Ib.*

Glorious the northern lights astream;
Glorious the song, when God's the theme;
  Glorious the thunder's roar:
Glorious hosanna from the den;
Glorious the catholic amen;
  Glorious the martyr's gore. *Ib.*

Glorious the sun in mid-career;
Glorious th' assembled fires appear;
  Glorious the comet's train:
Glorious the trumpet and alarm;
Glorious th' almighty stretch'd-out arm;
  Glorious th' enraptur'd main. *Ib.*

He sung of God—the mighty source
Of all things—the stupendous force
  On which all strength depends;
From whose right arm, beneath whose eyes,
All period, pow'r, and enterprize
  Commences, reigns, and ends. *Ib.*

Strong is the horse upon his speed;
Strong in pursuit the rapid glede,
  Which makes at once his game:
Strong the tall ostrich on the ground;
Strong thro' the turbulent profound
  Shoots xiphias to his aim. *Ib.*

Strong is the lion—like a coal
His eye-ball—like a bastion's mole
  His chest against his foes:
Strong, the gier-eagle on his sail,
Strong against tide, th' enormous whale
  Emerges as he goes. *Ib.*

Tell them I am, Jehova said
To Moses; while earth heard in dread,
  And smitten to the heart,
At once above, beneath, around,
All nature, without voice or sound,
  Replied, O Lord, Thou art. *Ib.*

Where ask is have, where seek is find,
  Where knock is open wide. *Ib.*

FRANCIS EDWARD SMEDLEY
1818–1864

You are looking as fresh as paint.
Frank Fairlegh, ch. 41.

SAMUEL SMILES
1812–1904

A place for everything, and everything in its place.
Thrift, ch. 5.

Cecil's despatch of business was extraordinary, his maxim being, 'The shortest way to do many things is to do only one thing at once.' *Self-Help*, ch. 9.

His (Dr. Priestley's) appointment [to act as astronomer to Captain Cook's expedition to the southern seas] has been cancelled, as the Board of Longitude objected to his theology.
Men of Invention and Industry, ch. 3.

ADAM SMITH
1723–1790

To found a great empire for the sole purpose of raising up a people of customers, may at first sight appear a project fit only for a nation of shop-keepers. It is, however, a project altogether unfit for a nation of shopkeepers; but extremely fit for a nation that is governed by shopkeepers.
Wealth of Nations, vol. ii, bk. iv, ch. 7, Pt. iii.

ALEXANDER SMITH
1830–1867

Like a pale martyr in his shirt of fire.
A Life Drama, ii.

In winter, when the dismal rain
  Came down in slanting lines,
And Wind, that grand old harper, smote
  His thunder-harp of pines. *Ib.*

ALFRED EMANUEL SMITH
1873–

Nothing doing. That's just boloney. Everybody knows I can't lay bricks.
Remark at the laying of the corner-stone of the New York State Office Building.

FREDERICK EDWIN SMITH
EARL OF BIRKENHEAD
See BIRKENHEAD

JAMES SMITH
1775–1839
AND
HORACE SMITH
1779–1849

And hast thou walk'd about (how strange a story!)
  In Thebes's streets three thousand years ago,
When the Memnonium was in all its glory.
Address to a Mummy.

Hail, glorious edifice, stupendous work!
God bless the Regent and the Duke of York!
Rejected Addresses. No. 1. *Loyal Effusion*, l. 1.

Who makes the quartern loaf and Luddites rise?
Who fills the butchers' shops with large blue flies?
Ib. l. 48.

I saw them go: one horse was blind,
The tails of both hung down behind,
  Their shoes were on their feet.
Ib. No. 2. *The Baby's Début*, vi. (*Parody of Wordsworth.*)

What stately vision mocks my waking sense?
Hence, dear delusion, sweet enchantment, hence!
Ib. No. 3. *An Address Without a Phoenix.*

I am a blessed Glendoveer:
'Tis mine to speak, and yours to hear.
Ib. No. 7. *The Rebuilding.*

'Why are you in such doleful dumps?
A fireman, and afraid of bumps!—
What are they fear'd on? fools! 'od rot 'em!'
Were the last words of Higginbottom.
Ib. No. 9. *Drury Lane.* (*Parody of Scott.*)

'In the name of the Prophet—figs!'
Ib. No. 10. Johnson's Ghost.

In Craven-street, Strand, ten attorneys find place,
And ten dark coal-barges are moor'd at its base.
Fly, Honesty, fly! seek some safer retreat;
For there's craft in the river, and craft in the street.
Craven Street, Strand.

LANGDON SMITH

1858–1918

When you were a tadpole, and I was a fish,
In the Palaeozoic time,
And side by side in the ebbing tide
We sprawled through the ooze and slime.
A Toast to a Lady. (The Scrap-Book, April, 1906.)

LOGAN PEARSALL SMITH

1865–

There are two things to aim at in life: first, to get what you want; and, after that, to enjoy it. Only the wisest of mankind achieve the second.
Afterthoughts (1931), p. 4.

There are few sorrows, however poignant, in which a good income is of no avail. *Ib. p. 12.*

People say that life is the thing, but I prefer reading.
Ib. p. 71.

SAMUEL FRANCIS SMITH

1808–1895

My country, 'tis of thee,
Sweet land of liberty,
Of thee I sing:
Land where my fathers died,
Land of the pilgrims' pride,
From every mountain-side
Let freedom ring. *America.*

SYDNEY SMITH

1771–1845

It requires a surgical operation to get a joke well into a Scotch understanding. Their only idea of wit . . . is laughing immoderately at stated intervals.
Lady Holland, Memoirs (1st ed. 1855), I. ii. 15.

I heard him speak disrespectfully of the Equator!
Ib. p. 17.

That knuckle-end of England—that land of Calvin, oat-cakes, and sulphur. *Ib.*

Looked as if she had walked straight out of the Ark.
Ib. ch. 7, p. 157.

No furniture so charming as books.
Ib. ch. 9, p. 240.

Madam, I have been looking for a person who disliked gravy all my life; let us swear eternal friendship. *Ib. p. 257.*

How can a bishop marry? How can he flirt? The most he can say is, 'I will see you in the vestry after service.' *Ib. p. 258.*

Not body enough to cover his mind decently with; his intellect is improperly exposed. *Ib.*

I have, alas, only one illusion left, and that is the Archbishop of Canterbury. *Ib. p. 259.*

You find people ready enough to do the Samaritan, without the oil and twopence. *Ib. p. 261.*

As the French say, there are three sexes—men, women, and clergymen. *Ib. p. 262.*

Praise is the best diet for us, after all. *Ib. p. 265.*

Daniel Webster struck me much like a steam-engine in trousers. *Ib. p. 267.*

He [Macaulay] has occasional flashes of silence, that make his conversation perfectly delightful.
Ib. ch. 11, p. 363.

Let onion atoms lurk within the bowl,
And, scarce-suspected, animate the whole.
Recipe for Salad-Dressing, Ib. p. 373.

You remember Thurlow's answer . . . you never expected justice from a company, did you? They have neither a soul to lose, nor a body to kick.
Ib. p. 376.

Deserves to be preached to death by wild curates.
Ib. p. 384.

I never read a book before reviewing it; it prejudices a man so.
H. Pearson, The Smith of Smiths (1934), ch. iii, p. 54.

It is a place with only one post a day. . . . In the country I always fear that creation will expire before tea-time. *Ib. ch. 5, p. 92.*

Minorities . . . are almost always in the right.
Ib. ch. 9, p. 220.

My idea of heaven is, eating *pâtés de foie gras* to the sound of trumpets. *Ib. ch. 10, p. 236.*

What a pity it is that we have no amusements in England but vice and religion! *Ib.*

Death must be distinguished from dying, with which it is often confused. *Ib. ch. 11, p. 271.*

The only way to deal with such a man as O'Connell is to hang him up and erect a statue to him under the gallows. *Ib. p. 272.*

What two ideas are more inseparable than Beer and Britannia? *Ib.*

I am just going to pray for you at St. Paul's, but with no very lively hope of success.
Ib. ch. 13, p. 308.

Poverty is no disgrace to a man, but it is confoundedly inconvenient. *His Wit and Wisdom (1900), p. 89.*

One of the greatest pleasures of life is conversation.
Essays (1877). Female Education, p. 103.

This great spectacle of human happiness.
Ib. Waterton's Wanderings, p. 465.

The moment the very name of Ireland is mentioned, the English seem to bid adieu to common feeling, common prudence, and common sense, and to act with the barbarity of tyrants, and the fatuity of idiots. *Peter Plymley Letters* (1929), p. 9.

A Curate—there is something which excites compassion in the very name of a Curate!!!
Ib. p. 127. *Persecuting Bishops.*

The Atlantic Ocean beat Mrs. Partington. *Ib.* p. 228.

Bishop Berkeley destroyed this world in one volume octavo; and nothing remained, after his time, but mind; which experienced a similar fate from the hand of Mr. Hume in 1739.
Sketches of Moral Philosophy. Introd.

We shall generally find that the triangular person has got into the square hole, the oblong into the triangular, and a square person has squeezed himself into the round hole. The officer and the office, the doer and the thing done, seldom fit so exactly that we can say they were almost made for each other. *Sketches of Moral Philosophy*, Lect. ix.

I never could find any man who could think for two minutes together. *Ib.* Lect. xix.

The motto I proposed for the [*Edinburgh*] *Review* was: *Tenui musam meditamur avena*—'We cultivate literature upon a little oatmeal.'
Works (1859), vol. i, Preface, p. v.

We can inform Jonathan what are the inevitable consequences of being too fond of glory;—Taxes upon every article which enters into the mouth, or covers the back, or is placed under the foot . . . taxes on everything on earth, and the waters under the earth.
Ib., vol. i. *Review of Seybert's Statistical Annals of the United States*, p. 291.

The schoolboy whips his taxed top—the beardless youth manages his taxed horse, with a taxed bridle, on a taxed road;—and the dying Englishman, pouring his medicine, which has paid seven per cent., into a spoon that has paid fifteen per cent.—flings himself back upon his chintz bed, which has paid twenty-two per cent.—and expires in the arms of an apothecary who has paid a licence of a hundred pounds for the privilege of putting him to death. *Ib.*

What bishops like best in their clergy is a dropping-down-deadness of manner.
Ib., vol. ii, *First Letter to Archdeacon Singleton*, p. 271. *Note.*

I like, my dear Lord, the road you are travelling, but I don't like the pace you are driving; too similar to that of the son of Nimshi. I always feel myself inclined to cry out, Gently, John, gently down hill. Put on the drag.
Ib. vol. ii, *Letter to Lord John Russell*, p. 300.

I look upon Switzerland as an inferior sort of Scotland.
Letters. *Lady Holland, Memoirs*, vol. ii. *To Lord Holland, 1815.*

Tory and Whig in turns shall be my host,
I taste no politics in boil'd and roast.
Ib. To John Murray. Nov. 1834.

What would life be without arithmetic, but a scene of horrors? *Ib. To Miss ——, 22 July 1835.*

I am convinced digestion is the great secret of life.
Ib. To Arthur Kinglake, 30 Sept. 1837.

I have no relish for the country; it is a kind of healthy grave. *Ib. To Miss G. Harcourt, 1838.*

I have seen nobody since I saw you, but persons in orders. My only varieties are vicars, rectors, curates, and every now and then (by way of turbot) an archdeacon.
Ib. To Miss Berry, 28 Jan. 1843.

One very hot evening in summer, Lady Holland and a large party of friends were suffering from the stifling atmosphere, and a general dulness had crept over the company. Then Milnes was seen to enter. 'Ah! here comes the cool of the evening,' cried Sydney Smith, and immediately everybody grew brighter. [Milnes resented this and other nicknames, and Sydney Smith wrote to him: 'The names of "Cool of the evening", "London Assurance", and "In-I-go Jones", are, I give you my word, not mine.']
T. Wemyss Reid, *Life of Lord Houghton* (1890), p. 213.

TOBIAS GEORGE SMOLLETT

1721–1771

Mourn, hapless Caledonia, mourn
Thy banish'd peace, thy laurels torn!
The Tears of Scotland.

I think for my part one half of the nation is mad—and the other not very sound.
The Adventures of Sir Launcelot Greaves, ch. 6.

He was formed for the ruin of our sex.
Roderick Random, ch. 22.

That great Cham of literature, Samuel Johnson.
Letter to John Wilkes, 16 Mar. 1759. (*Boswell's Johnson, 1934*, vol. i, p. 348.)

GEORGE HUNT SMYTTAN

1825–1870

AND

FRANCIS POTT

1852–1909

Forty days and forty nights
Thou wast fasting in the wild,
Forty days and forty nights
Tempted, and yet undefiled.
Hymn: Forty Days and Forty Nights. The Penny Post, 1856.

Prowling beasts about Thy way;
Stones Thy pillow, earth Thy bed. *Ib.*

WILLIAM SOMERVILLE

1675–1742

If this pale rose offend your sight,
It in your bosom, wear;
'Twill blush to find itself less white,
And turn Lancastrian there.
Presenting to a Lady a White Rose and a Red on the Tenth of June.

My hoarse-sounding horn
Invites thee to the chase, the sport of kings;
Image of war, without its guilt.

The Chase, bk. i, l. 13.

CHARLES HAMILTON SORLEY

1895–1915

We have the evil spirits too
That shake our soul with battle-din.
But we have an eviller spirit than you,
We have a dumb spirit within:
The exceeding bitter agony
But not the exceeding bitter cry.   *To Poets.*

We swing ungirded hips,
And lightened are our eyes,
The rain is on our lips,
We do not run for prize.

Song of the Ungirt Runners.

We run because we like it
Through the broad bright land.   *Ib.*

REV. ROBERT SOUTH

1634–1716

An Aristotle was but the rubbish of an Adam, and
Athens but the rudiments of Paradise.

Sermons, vol. I. ii.

THOMAS SOUTHERN

1660–1746

And when we're worn,
Hack'd, hewn with constant service, thrown aside
To rust in peace, or rot in hospitals.

Loyal Brother, Act I.

ROBERT SOUTHEY

1774–1843

It was a summer's evening,
Old Kaspar's work was done,
And he before his cottage door
Was sitting in the sun,
And by him sported on the green
His little grandchild Wilhelmine.

The Battle of Blenheim.

He came to ask what he had found,
That was so large, and smooth, and round.   *Ib.*

'Now tell us all about the war,
And what they fought each other for.'   *Ib.*

But what they fought each other for,
  I could not well make out.   *Ib.*

But things like that, you know, must be
  At every famous victory.   *Ib.*

Great praise the Duke of Marlbro' won,
  And our good Prince Eugene.   *Ib.*

'And everybody praised the Duke,
  Who this great fight did win.'
'But what good came of it at last?'
  Quoth little Peterkin.
'Why that I cannot tell,' said he,
'But 'twas a famous victory.'   *Ib.*

My name is Death: the last best friend am I.

*Carmen Nuptiale.   The Lay of the Laureate.
The Dream*, lxxxvii.

'How does the water
Come down at Lodore?'   *The Cataract of Lodore.*

And this way the water comes down at Lodore.   *Ib.*

Curses are like young chickens, they always come
  home to roost.   *The Curse of Kehama.* Motto.

Water shall hear me,
And know thee and fly thee.   *Ib.* II. 14.

And Sleep shall obey me,
  And visit thee never,
And the Curse shall be on thee
  For ever and ever.   *Ib.*

Hark! at the Golden Palaces
The Brahmin strikes the hour.   *Ib.* v. 1.

They sin who tell us love can die.
With life all other passions fly,
  All others are but vanity.   *Ib.* x. 10.

Thou hast been call'd, O Sleep! the friend of Woe,
But 'tis the happy who have called thee so.

Ib. xv. 12.

From his brimstone bed, at break of day
  A walking the Devil is gone,
To look at his little snug farm of the World,
  And see how his stock went on.

The Devil's Walk, i.

His coat was red and his breeches were blue,
And there was a hole where his tail came through.

Ib. iii.

He passed a cottage with a double coach-house,
  A cottage of gentility!
And he owned with a grin
  That his favourite sin
Is pride that apes humility.   *Ib.* viii.

As he passed through Cold Bath fields, he looked
  At a solitary cell;
And he was well-pleased, for it gave him a hint
  For improving the prisons of Hell.   *Ib.* xv.

And all at once to the Bishop they go.

God's Judgment on a Wicked Bishop.

No stir in the air, no stir in the sea,
The ship was still as she could be.

The Inchcape Rock.

And then they knew the perilous rock,
And blest the Abbot of Aberbrothok.   *Ib.*

'O Christ! It is the Inchcape Rock!'   *Ib.*

Sir Ralph the Rover tore his hair;
He curst himself in his despair.   *Ib.*

Day after day, day after day the same—
A weary waste of waters!

Madoc: Pt. I, *Madoc in Wales.*   IV, *The
Voyage*, l. 32.

Blue, darkly, deeply, beautifully blue.

Ib. V, *Lincoya*, l. 102.

We wage no war with women nor with priests.

Ib. XV, *The Excommunication*, l. 65.

What will not woman, gentle woman dare,
When strong affection stirs her spirit up?
Ib. Pt. II, *Madoc in Aztlan.* II, *The Tidings,*
l. 125.

My days among the dead are passed;
  Around me I behold,
Where'er these casual eyes are cast,
  The mighty minds of old;
My never-failing friends are they,
With whom I converse day by day.
My Days Among the Dead.

Yet leaving here a name, I trust,
That will not perish in the dust.   *Ib.*

You are old, Father William, the young man cried,
  The few locks which are left you are grey;
You are hale, Father William, a hearty old man,
  Now tell me the reason, I pray.
*The Old Man's Comforts, and how he Gained
them.*

You are old, Father William, the young man cried,
  And pleasures with youth pass away,
And yet you lament not the days that are gone,
  Now tell me the reason, I pray.   *Ib.*

In the days of my youth I remembered my God!
  And He hath not forgotten my age.   *Ib.*

The Monk my son, and my daughter the Nun.
The Old Woman of Berkeley.

Their wintry garment of unsullied snow
The mountains have put on.
The Poet's Pilgrimage. Pt. I, *The Journey.*
ii, *Flanders,* 23.

He ran against a shooting star,
So fast for fear did he sail,
And he singed the beard of the Bishop
Against a comet's tail;
And he passed between the horns of the moon,
With Antidius on his back;
And there was an eclipse that night,
Which was not in the Almanac.
St. Antidius, the Pope and the Devil.

  How beautiful is night!
A dewy freshness fills the silent air;
No mist obscures, nor cloud, nor speck, nor stain,
  Breaks the serene of heaven.
Thalaba the Destroyer, bk. I, i.

A vague, a dizzy, a tumultuous joy.   *Ib.* bk. III. xix.

'I had a home once—I had once a husband—
I am a widow, poor and broken-hearted!'
Loud blew the wind, unheard was her complaining,
  On drove the chariot.   *The Widow,* v.

The arts babblative and scribblative.
*Colloquies on the Progress and Prospects of
Society. Coll. x.* Pt. ii.

The march of intellect.   *Ib. Coll. xiv.*

Your true lover of literature is never fastidious.
The Doctor, ch. 17.

Show me a man who cares no more for one place
than another, and I will show you in that same
person one who loves nothing but himself. Beware
of those who are homeless by choice.
Ib. ch. 34.

Live as long as you may, the first twenty years are
the longest half of your life.   *Ib.* ch. 130.

The death of Nelson was felt in England as something
more than a public calamity; men started at the
intelligence, and turned pale, as if they had heard
of the loss of a dear friend.
The Life of Nelson, ch. 9.

The Satanic School.
The Vision of Judgment. Preface.

The pander of posterity.   *Ib.*

ROBERT SOUTHWELL
1561?–1595

As I in hoary winter's night stood shivering in the
  snow,
Surprised I was with sudden heat which made my
  heart to glow;
And lifting up a fearful eye to view what fire was near,
A pretty Babe all burning bright did in the air appear.
The Burning Babe.

'The fuel justice layeth on, and mercy blows the
  coals;
The metal in this furnace wrought are men's defiled
  souls:
For which, as now on fire I am to work them to their
  good,
So will I melt into a bath to wash them in my blood.'
With this he vanished out of sight and swiftly shrunk
  away,
And straight I called unto mind that it was Christmas
  Day.   *Ib.*

Come, Raphael, this Babe must eat,
Provide our little Toby meat.
New Heaven, New War.

Behold, a silly tender Babe
  In freezing winter night
In homely manger trembling lies,
  Alas, a piteous sight!   *New Prince, New Pomp.*

With joy approach, O Christian wight,
  Do homage to thy King;
And highly praise his humble pomp,
  Which he from heaven doth bring.   *Ib.*

Times go by turns, and chances change by course,
From foul to fair, from better hap to worse.
Times go by Turns.

HERBERT SPENCER
1820–1903

Science is organized knowledge.   *Education,* ch. 2.

Absolute morality is the regulation of conduct in such
a way that pain shall not be inflicted.
Essays (1891), vol. iii, p. 152. *Prison Ethics.*

The ultimate result of shielding men from the effects
of folly, is to fill the world with fools.
Ib. p. 354. *State Tamperings with Money and
Banks.*

The Republican form of Government is the highest
form of government; but because of this it requires
the highest type of human nature—a type nowhere
at present existing.   *Ib.* p. 478. *The Americans.*

Evolution . . . is—a change from an indefinite, incoherent homogeneity, to a definite coherent heterogeneity.   *First Principles*, ch. 16, § 138.

This survival of the fittest.
      Principles of Biology, pt. iii, ch. 12, *Indirect Equilibration*, § 165.

Progress, therefore, is not an accident, but a necessity. . . . It is a part of nature.
      Social Statics, pt. i, ch. 2, § 4.

Education has for its object the formation of character.   *Ib.* pt. ii, ch. 17, § 4.

Opinion is ultimately determined by the feelings, and not by the intellect.   *Ib.* pt. iv, ch. 30, § 8.

No one can be perfectly free till all are free; no one can be perfectly moral till all are moral; no one can be perfectly happy till all are happy.   *Ib.* § 16.

It was remarked to me by the late Mr. Charles Roupell . . . that to play billiards well was a sign of an ill-spent youth.
      Remark. Duncan, '*Life and Letters of Spencer*' (1908), ch. 20, p. 298.

WILLIAM ROBERT SPENCER

1770–1834

In fancy's ear he oft would hear
Poor Gêlert's dying yell.   *Beth-Gêlert*, xxiii.

EDMUND SPENSER

1552?–1599

The merry cuckoo, messenger of Spring,
His trumpet shrill hath thrice already sounded.
      Amoretti. Sonnet xix.

Most glorious Lord of life, that on this day
Didst make thy triumph over death and sin:
And, having harrow'd hell, didst bring away
Captivity thence captive, us to win.   *Ib.* lxviii.

Fresh spring the herald of love's mighty king,
In whose coat armour richly are display'd
All sorts of flowers the which on earth do spring
In goodly colours gloriously array'd.   *Ib.* lxx.

One day I wrote her name upon the strand,
But came the waves and washed it away:
Again I wrote it with a second hand,
But came the tide, and made my pains his prey.
Vain man, said she, that dost in vain assay,
A mortal thing so to immortalize,
For I myself shall like to this decay,
And eke my name be wiped out likewise.
Not so, quoth I, let baser things devise
To die in dust, but you shall live by fame:
My verse your virtues rare shall eternize,
And in the heavens write your glorious name,
Where when as death shall all the world subdue,
Our love shall live, and later life renew.   *Ib.* lxxv.

Triton blowing loud his wreathed horn.
      Colin Clout's Come Home Again, l. 245.

The Shepherd of the Ocean (quoth he)
Unto that Goddess' grace me first enhanc'd,
And to mine oaten pipe inclin'd her ear.   *Ib.* l. 358.

So love is Lord of all the world by right.   *Ib.* l. 883.

The woods shall to me answer and my echo ring.
      Epithalamion, l. 18.

Behold whiles she before the altar stands
Hearing the holy priest that to her speaks
And blesseth her with his two happy hands.
      Ib. l. 223.

Ah! when will this long weary day have end,
And lend me leave to come unto my love?
      Ib. l. 278.

Song made in lieu of many ornaments,
With which my love should duly have been deck'd.
      Ib. l. 427.

Fierce wars and faithful loves shall moralize my song.
      The Faerie Queene, bk. I, introd. i. 1.

A gentle knight was pricking on the plain.
      Ib. bk. I, c. i. i.

But on his breast a bloody cross he bore,
The dear remembrance of his dying Lord.   *Ib.* ii.

But of his cheer did seem too solemn sad;
Yet nothing did he dread, but ever was ydrad.   *Ib.*

A bold bad man.   *Ib.* xxxvii.

      Her angel's face
As the great eye of heaven shined bright,
And made a sunshine in the shady place;
Did never mortal eye behold such heavenly grace.
      Ib. c. iii. iv.

      A cruel Crocodile,
While in false grief hiding his harmful guile,
Doth weep full sore, and sheddeth tender tears.
      Ib. c. v. xviii.

As when that devilish iron engine, wrought
In deepest hell, and fram'd by furies' skill,
With windy nitre and quick sulphur fraught,
And ramm'd with bullet round, ordain'd to kill,
Conceiveth fire.   *Ib.* c. vii. xiii.

Still as he fled, his eye was backward cast,
As if his fear still followed him behind.
      Ib. c. ix. xxi.

That darksome cave they enter, where they find
That cursed man, low sitting on the ground,
Musing full sadly in his sullen mind.   *Ib.* xxxv.

Sleep after toil, port after stormy seas,
Ease after war, death after life does greatly please.
      Ib. xl.

So double was his pains, so double be his praise.
      Ib. bk. II, c. ii. xxv.

And all for love, and nothing for reward.
      Ib. c. viii. ii.

Let Grill be Grill, and have his hoggish mind.
      Ib. c. xii. lxxvii.

O goodly usage of those antique times,
In which the sword was servant unto right;
When not for malice and contentious crimes,
But all for praise, and proof of manly might,
The martial brood accustomed to fight:
Then honour was the meed of victory,
And yet the vanquished had no despite.
      Ib. bk. III, c. i. xiii.

Divine tobacco. *Ib.* c. v. xxxii.

Hard is to teach an old horse amble true.
Ib. c. VIII. xxvi.

And painful pleasure turns to pleasing pain.
Ib. c. x. lx.

And as she look'd about, she did behold,
How over that same door was likewise writ,
Be bold, be bold, and everywhere Be bold.

.   .   .   .

At last she spied at that room's upper end,
Another iron door, on which was writ
Be not too bold. *Ib.* c. XI. liv.

Dan Chaucer, well of English undefiled,
On Fame's eternal beadroll worthy to be filed.
Ib. bk. IV, c. II. xxxii.

For all that nature by her mother wit
Could frame in earth. *Ib.* c. x. xxi.

O sacred hunger of ambitious minds.
Ib. bk. V, c. XII. i.

A monster, which the Blatant beast men call,
A dreadful fiend of gods and men ydrad.
Ib. xxxvii.

The gentle mind by gentle deeds is known.
For a man by nothing is so well bewray'd,
As by his manners. *Ib.* bk. VI, c. III. i.

What man that sees the ever-whirling wheel
Of Change, the which all mortal things doth sway,
But that thereby doth find, and plainly feel,
How Mutability in them doth play
Her cruel sports, to many men's decay?
Ib. bk. VII, c. VI. i.

That beauty is not, as fond men misdeem,
An outward show of things, that only seem.
An Hymn in Honour of Beauty, l. 90.

For of the soul the body form doth take;
For soul is form, and doth the body make.
Ib. l. 132.

The hearts of men, which fondly here admire
Fair seeming shews, and feed on vain delight,
Transported with celestial desire
Of those fair forms, may lift themselves up higher,
And learn to love with zealous humble duty
Th' eternal fountain of that heavenly beauty.
Hymn of Heavenly Beauty, l. 16.

Of such deep learning little had he need,
Ne yet of Latin, ne of Greek, that breed
Doubts 'mongst Divines, and difference of texts,
From whence arise diversity of sects,
And hateful heresies.
Complaints. Mother Hubbard's Tale, l. 385.

Full little knowest thou that hast not tried,
What hell it is, in suing long to bide:
To lose good days, that might be better spent;
To waste long nights in pensive discontent;
To speed today, to be put back tomorrow;
To feed on hope, to pine with fear and sorrow;
To have thy Prince's grace, yet want her Peers';
To have thy asking, yet wait many years;
To fret thy soul with crosses and with cares;

To eat thy heart through comfortless despairs;
To fawn, to crouch, to wait, to ride, to run,
To spend, to give, to want, to be undone,
Unhappy wight, born to disastrous end,
That doth his life in so long tendance spend.
Ib. l. 895.

What more felicity can fall to creature,
Than to enjoy delight with liberty.
Muiopotmos, l. 209.

I was promis'd on a time,
To have reason for my rhyme;
From that time unto this season,
I received nor rhyme nor reason.
Lines on his Pension. (*Traditional.*)

Sweet Thames, run softly, till I end my song.
Prothalamion, l. 18.

At length they all to merry London came,
To merry London, my most kindly nurse,
That to me gave this life's first native source:
Though from another place I take my name,
A house of ancient fame.
There when they came, whereas those bricky towers,
The which on Thames' broad aged back do ride,
Where now the studious Lawyers have their bowers
There whilom wont the Templar Knights to bide,
Till they decay'd through pride. *Ib.* l. 127.

To be wise and eke to love,
Is granted scarce to God above.
*The Shepherd's Calendar. March. Willy's
Emblem.*

Bring hither the Pink and purple Columbine,
With Gillyflowers:
Bring Coronation, and Sops in wine,
Worn of paramours.
Strew me the ground with Daffadowndillies,
And Cowslips, and Kingcups, and loved Lilies:
The pretty Pawnce,
And the Chevisaunce,
Shall match with the fair flower Delice.
Ib. April, l. 136.

And he that strives to touch the stars,
Oft stumbles at a straw. *Ib. July,* l. 99.

The rugged brow of careful Policy.
Dedicatory Sonnets. To Sir Christopher Hatton.

WILLIAM ARCHIBALD SPOONER

1844–1930

Kinquering Congs their titles take.
*Announcing the hymn in New
College Chapel, 1879.*

ARTHUR CECIL SPRING-RICE

1859–1918

I vow to thee, my country—all earthly things above—
Entire and whole and perfect, the service of my love.
Last Poem.

Her ways are ways of gentleness and all her paths are
peace. *Ib.*

CHARLES HADDON SPURGEON

1834–1892

The Lord gets his best soldiers out of the highlands of affliction.
Gleanings among the Sheaves (1864), p. 132, *Sorrow's Discipline.*

EDWARD STANLEY, EARL OF DERBY

1799–1869

When I first came into Parliament, Mr. Tierney, a great Whig authority, used always to say that the duty of an Opposition was very simple—it was, to oppose everything, and propose nothing.
House of Commons, 4 June 1841. 3rd Ser. lviii. 1188.

SIR HENRY MORTON STANLEY

1841–1904

Dr. Livingstone, I presume?
How I found Livingstone, ch. 11.

FRANK LEBBY STANTON

1857–1927

Sweetest li'l' feller, everybody knows;
Dunno what to call him, but he's mighty lak' a rose;
Lookin' at his mammy wid eyes so shiny blue
Mek' you think that Heav'n is comin' clost ter you.
Mighty Lak' a Rose.

JOHN STARK

1728–1822

We beat them to-day or Molly Stark's a widow.
Battle of Bennington, 16 Aug. 1777. Appleton's *Cycl. of Am. Biography*, vol. v.

RICHARD STEELE

1671–1729

I have often thought that a story-teller is born, as well as a poet. *The Guardian*, No. 42.

Gained universal applause by explaining a passage in the game-act. *The Spectator*, No. 2.

We were in some little time fixed in our seats, and sat with that dislike which people not too good-natured usually conceive of each other at first sight.
Ib. No. 132.

The noblest motive is the public good.
Ib. No. 200. *Motto in Ed. 1744.*

There are so few who can grow old with a good grace.
Ib. No. 263.

Will Honeycomb calls these over-offended ladies the outrageously virtuous. *Ib.* No. 266.

Fashion, the arbiter, and rule of right.
Ib. No. 478. *Motto in Ed. 1744.*

It is to be noted that when any part of this paper appears dull, there is a design in it.
The Tatler, No. 38.

Though her mien carries much more invitation than command, to behold her is an immediate check to loose behaviour; to love her is a liberal education.
Ib. No. 49.

Every man is the maker of his own fortune.
Ib. No. 52.

The insupportable labour of doing nothing.
Ib. No. 54.

Reading is to the mind what exercise is to the body.
Ib. No. 147.

The truth of it is, the first rudiments of education are given very indiscreetly by most parents.
Ib. No. 173.

Let your precept be, Be easy. *Ib.* No. 196.

The pink of courtesy. *Ib.* No. 204.

These ladies of irresistible modesty are those who make virtue unamiable. *Ib.* No. 217.

GEORGE STEEVENS

1736–1800

And when the Pye was open'd
The birds began to sing,
And was not this a dainty dish
To set before the King!
Recorded in Lamb's Letter to Miss Sarah James, ? April, 1829. Attr. to Steevens in the D.N.B.

JAMES KENNETH STEPHEN

1859–1892

Two voices are there: one is of the deep;
.   .   .   .   .   .
And one is of an old half-witted sheep
Which bleats articulate monotony,
.   .   .   .   .   .
And Wordsworth, both are thine.
Lapsus Calami. Sonnet.

Good Lord! I'd rather be
Quite unacquainted with the A.B.C.
Than write such hopeless rubbish as thy worst. *Ib.*

When the Rudyards cease from kipling
And the Haggards ride no more. *Ib. To R. K.*

Ah! Matt.: old age has brought to me
Thy wisdom, less thy certainty:
The world's a jest, and joy's a trinket:
I knew that once: but now—I think it.
Ib. Senex to Matt. Prior.

JAMES STEPHENS

1882–

I hear a sudden cry of pain!
There is a rabbit in a snare. *The Snare.*

Little One! Oh, Little One!
I am searching everywhere! *Ib.*

ISABELLA S. STEPHENSON

1843–1890

Holy Father, in Thy mercy,
  Hear our anxious prayer,
Keep our loved ones, now far absent,
  'Neath Thy care.
    Holy Father, in Thy Mercy. Hymns A. and M.,
    Supplement to Revised Edition, 1889.

When in sorrow, when in danger,
  When in loneliness,
In Thy love look down and comfort
  Their distress.   *Ib.*

LAURENCE STERNE

1713–1768

They order, said I, this matter better in France.
    A Sentimental Journey, l. 1.

I had had an affair with the moon, in which there
was neither sin nor shame. *Ib. The Monk. Calais.*

The Sentimental Traveller (meaning thereby myself)
who have travell'd, and of which I am now sitting
down to give an account—as much out of necessity,
and the *besoin de voyager*, as any one in the class.
    Ib. Preface. In the Desobligeant.

As an English man does not travel to see English
men, I retired to my room.   *Ib.*

Having been in love with one princess or another,
almost all my life, and I hope I shall go on so, till
I die, being firmly persuaded, that if I ever do a
mean action, it must be in some interval betwixt
one passion and another.   *Ib. Montriul.*

Vive l'amour! et vive la bagatelle!   *Ib. The letter.*

Hail ye small sweet courtesies of life.
    Ib. The Pulse. Paris.

There are worse occupations in this world than
feeling a woman's pulse.   *Ib.*

He gave a deep sigh—I saw the iron enter into his
soul!   *Ib. The Captive. Paris.*

I think there is a fatality in it—I seldom go to the
place I set out for.   *Ib. The Address. Versailles.*

Dear sensibility! source inexhausted of all that's
precious in our joys, or costly in our sorrows!
    Ib. The Bourbonnois.

If the supper was to my taste—the grace which
followed it was much more so. *Ib. The Supper.*

I live in a constant endeavour to fence against the
infirmities of ill health, and other evils of life, by
mirth; being firmly persuaded that every time a
man smiles,—but much more so, when he laughs,
that it adds something to this Fragment of Life.
    Tristram Shandy: Dedication.

'Pray, my dear,' quoth my mother, 'have you not
forgot to wind up the clock?'—'Good G——!' cried
my father, making an exclamation, but taking care
to moderate his voice at the same time,—'Did ever
woman, since the creation of the world, interrupt
a man with such a silly question?' *Ib. bk. i, ch. 1.*

As we jog on, either laugh with me, or at me, or in
short do anything,—only keep your temper.
    Ib. ch. 6.

He was within a few hours of giving his enemies the
slip for ever.   *Ib. ch. 12.*

'Tis known by the name of perseverance in a good
cause,—and of obstinacy in a bad one.
    Ib. ch. 17.

Persuasion hung upon his lips.   *Ib. ch. 19.*

What is the character of a family to an hypothesis?
my father would reply.   *Ib. ch. 21.*

My uncle Toby would never offer to answer this by
any other kind of argument, than that of whistling
half a dozen bars of Lillabullero.   *Ib.*

Digressions, incontestably, are the sunshine;—they
are the life, the soul of reading;—take them out of
this book for instance,—you might as well take
the book along with them.   *Ib. ch. 22.*

I should have no objection to this method, but that
I think it must smell too strong of the lamp.
    Ib. ch. 23.

'I'll not hurt thee,' says my uncle Toby, rising from
his chair, and going across the room, with the fly
in his hand,—'I'll not hurt a hair of thy head:—
Go,' says he, lifting up the sash, and opening his
hand as he spoke, to let it escape;—'go, poor devil,
get thee gone, why should I hurt thee?—This
world surely is wide enough to hold both thee and
me.'   *Ib. bk. ii, ch. 12.*

Whenever a man talks loudly against religion,—
always suspect that it is not his reason, but his
passions which have got the better of his creed.
    Ib. ch. 17.

'Sir,' replied Dr. Slop, 'it would astonish you to
know what improvements we have made of late
years in all branches of obstetrical knowledge, but
particularly in that one single point of the safe and
expeditious extraction of the foetus,—which has
received such lights, that, for my part (holding up
his hands) I declare I wonder how the world
has——.'
'I wish', quoth my uncle Toby, 'you had seen what
prodigious armies we had in Flanders.'
    Ib. ch. 18.

'Our armies swore terribly in Flanders,' cried my
uncle Toby,—'but nothing to this.' *Ib. bk. iii, ch. 11.*

The corregiescity of Corregio.   *Ib. ch. 12.*

Of all the cants which are canted in this canting
world,—though the cant of hypocrites may be the
worst,—the cant of criticism is the most tor-
menting!   *Ib. ch. 12.*

Is this a fit time, said my father to himself, to talk of
Pensions and Grenadiers?   *Ib. bk. iv, ch. 5.*

The nonsense of the old women (of both sexes).
    Ib. ch. 16.

There is a North-west passage to the intellectual
world.   *Ib. ch. 42.*

'The poor soul will die:——'
'He shall not die, by G——,' cried my uncle Toby.—
The Accusing Spirit, which flew up to heaven's chancery with the oath, blush'd as he gave it in;—and the Recording Angel, as he wrote it down, dropp'd a tear upon the word, and blotted it out for ever. *Ib.* bk. vi, ch. 8.

An eye full of gentle salutations—and soft responses—. . . whispering soft—like the last low accents of an expiring saint. . . . It did my uncle Toby's business. *Ib.* bk. viii, ch. 25.

That eternal separation which we are shortly to make. *Ib.* bk. ix, ch. 8.

Said my mother, 'what is all this story about?'—'A Cock and a Bull,' said Yorick. *Ib.* ch. 33.

This sad vicissitude of things. *Sermon xvi*

THOMAS STERNHOLD

?–1549

On cherubs and cherubims
 full royally he rode;
And on the wings of mighty winds
 came flying all abroad.
 A Metrical Version of Psalm xviii, verse 10.

ROBERT LOUIS STEVENSON

1850–1894

The harmless art of knucklebones has seen the fall of the Roman empire and the rise of the United States. *Across the Plains.* VII. *The Lantern-Bearers*, i.

All the while, deep down in the privacy of your fool's heart, to know you had a bull's-eye at your belt, and to exult and sing over the knowledge. *Ib.*

The bright face of danger. *Ib.* iv.

Every one lives by selling something.
 Ib. IX. *Beggars*, iii.

Our frailties are invincible, our virtues barren; the battle goes sore against us to the going down of the sun. *Ib.* XI. *Pulvis et Umbra.*

Surely we should find it both touching and inspiriting, that in a field from which success is banished, our race should not cease to labour.
 Ib. ii.

Still obscurely fighting the lost fight of virtue, still clinging, in the brothel or on the scaffold, to some rag of honour, the poor jewel of their souls! *Ib.*

To make our idea of morality centre on forbidden acts is to defile the imagination and to introduce into our judgments of our fellow-men a secret element of gusto. *Ib.* XII. *A Christmas Sermon*, i.

A mortified appetite is never a wise companion. *Ib.*

To be honest, to be kind—to earn a little and to spend a little less, to make upon the whole a family happier for his presence, to renounce when that shall be necessary and not be embittered, to keep a few friends, but these without capitulation—above all, on the same grim condition, to keep friends with himself—here is a task for all that a man has of fortitude and delicacy. *Ib.*

Here lies one who meant well, tried a little, failed much:—surely that may be his epitaph, of which he need not be ashamed. *Ib.* iv.

There goes another Faithful Failure! *Ib.*

Lamplough was genteel, Eno was omnipresent; Lamplough was trite, Eno original and abominably vulgar. . . . Am I, then, to sink with Lamplough, or to soar with Eno?
 The Dynamiter. The Superfluous Mansion.

He who was prepared to help the escaping murderer or to embrace the impenitent thief, found, to the overthrow of all his logic, that he objected to the use of dynamite. *Ib.*

'Or Opulent Rotunda Strike the Sky,' said the shopman to himself, in the tone of one considering a verse. 'I suppose it would be too much to say "orotunda", and yet how noble it were! "Or Opulent Orotunda Strike the Sky." But that is the bitterness of arts; you see a good effect, and some nonsense about sense continually intervenes.'
 Ib. Epilogue of the Cigar Divan.

These are my politics: to change what we can; to better what we can; but still to bear in mind that man is but a devil weakly fettered by some generous beliefs and impositions; and for no word however sounding, and no cause however just and pious, to relax the stricture of these bonds. *Ib.*

Politics is perhaps the only profession for which no preparation is thought necessary.
 Familiar Studies of Men and Books.
 '*Yoshida-Torajiro*'.

'Am I no a bonny fighter?' [Alan Breck.]
 Kidnapped, ch. 10.

I've a grand memory for forgetting, David. [Alan Breck.] *Ib.* ch. 18.

I have thus played the sedulous ape to Hazlitt, to Lamb, to Wordsworth, to Sir Thomas Browne, to Defoe, to Hawthorne, to Montaigne, to Baudelaire and to Obermann.
 Memories and Portraits, ch. 4.

Each has his own tree of ancestors, but at the top of all sits Probably Arboreal. *Ib.* ch. 6, *Pastoral.*

The devil, depend upon it, can sometimes do a very gentlemanly thing.
 New Arabian Nights. The Suicide Club. Story of the Young Man with the Cream Tarts.

Is there anything in life so disenchanting as attainment? *Ib. The Adventure of the Hansom Cab.*

'I regard you with an indifference closely bordering on aversion.'
 Ib. The Rajah's Diamond. Story of the Bandbox.

For my part, I travel not to go anywhere, but to go. I travel for travel's sake. The great affair is to move.
 Travels with a Donkey. Cheylard and Luc.

I own I like definite form in what my eyes are to rest upon; and if landscapes were sold, like the sheets of characters of my boyhood, one penny plain and twopence coloured, I should go the length of twopence every day of my life. *Ib. Father Apollinaris.*

A faddling hedonist. *Ib. The Boarders.*

The true Babel is a divergence upon morals.
Ib. Florac.

Fifteen men on the dead man's chest
  Yo-ho-ho, and a bottle of rum!
Drink and the devil had done for the rest—
  Yo-ho-ho, and a bottle of rum!
Treasure Island, ch. 1.

Tip me the black spot. *Ib.* ch. 3.

'Pieces of eight!' *Ib.* ch. 10.

'Many's the long night I've dreamed of cheese—toasted, mostly.' [Ben Gunn.] *Ib.* ch. 15.

In marriage, a man becomes slack and selfish, and undergoes a fatty degeneration of his moral being.
Virginibus Puerisque, i. i.

Acidulous vestals. *Ib.*

They have never been in love, or in hate. *Ib.*

Even if we take matrimony at its lowest, even if we regard it as no more than a sort of friendship recognised by the police. *Ib.*

A little amateur painting in water-colour shows the innocent and quiet mind. *Ib.*

Lastly (and this is, perhaps, the golden rule), no woman should marry a teetotaller, or a man who does not smoke. *Ib.*

Marriage is a step so grave and decisive that it attracts light-headed, variable men by its very awfulness. *Ib.*

Marriage is like life in this—that it is a field of battle, and not a bed of roses. *Ib.*

Times are changed with him who marries; there are no more by-path meadows, where you may innocently linger, but the road lies long and straight and dusty to the grave. *Ib.* ii.

To marry is to domesticate the Recording Angel. Once you are married, there is nothing left for you, not even suicide, but to be good. *Ib.*

Man is a creature who lives not upon bread alone, but principally by catchwords. *Ib.*

The cruellest lies are often told in silence.
Ib. iv. *Truth of Intercourse.*

Old and young, we are all on our last cruise.
Ib. Crabbed Age and Youth.

Youth is the time to go flashing from one end of the world to the other both in mind and body; to try the manners of different nations; to hear the chimes at midnight; to see sunrise in town and country; to be converted at a revival; to circumnavigate the metaphysics, write halting verses, run a mile to see a fire, and wait all day long in the theatre to applaud 'Hernani'. *Ib.*

The weak brother is the worst of mankind. *Ib.*

It is better to be a fool than to be dead. *Ib.*

To love playthings well as a child, to lead an adventurous and honourable youth, and to settle when the time arrives, into a green and smiling age, is to be a good artist in life and deserve well of yourself and your neighbour. *Ib.*

I still remember that Emphyteusis is not a disease, nor Stillicide a crime.
Ib. iii. *An Apology for Idlers.*

There is no duty we so much underrate as the duty of being happy. *Ib.*

He sows hurry and reaps indigestion. *Ib.*

By the time a man gets well into the seventies his continued existence is a mere miracle.
Ib. v. *Æs Triplex.*

Into what great waters, not to be crossed by any swimmer, God's pale Prætorian throws us over in the end! *Ib.*

Philosophy, in its more rigid sense, has been at the same work for ages; and . . . has the honour of laying before us . . . her contribution towards the subject: that life is a Permanent Possibility of Sensation. *Ib.*

Even if the doctor does not give you a year, even if he hesitates about a month, make one brave push and see what can be accomplished in a week. *Ib.*

To travel hopefully is a better thing than to arrive, and the true success is to labour.
Ib. vi. *El Dorado.*

The great barons of the mind. *Ib.* x. *Walking Tours.*

Though we are mighty fine fellows nowadays, we cannot write like Hazlitt. *Ib.*

You must not fancy I am sick, only over-driven and under the weather. *The Wrecker*, ch. 4.

'The "Athæneum", that was the name! Golly, what a paper!' ' "Athenæum", you mean,' said Morris.
The Wrong Box, ch. 15.

In winter I get up at night
And dress by yellow candle-light.
In summer, quite the other way,—
I have to go to bed by day.

I have to go to bed and see
The birds still hopping on the tree,
Or hear the grown-up people's feet
Still going past me in the street.

And does it not seem hard to you,
When all the sky is clear and blue,
And I should like so much to play,
To have to go to bed by day?
A Child's Garden of Verses. 1. *Bed in Summer.*

It is very nice to think
The world is full of meat and drink,
With little children saying grace
In every Christian kind of place.
Ib. ii. *A Thought.*

A child should always say what's true,
And speak when he is spoken to,
And behave mannerly at table:
At least as far as he is able.
Ib. v. *Whole Duty of Children.*

Fairy land,
Where all the children dine at five,
And all the playthings come alive.
Ib. viii. *Foreign Lands.*

When I am grown to man's estate
I shall be very proud and great,
And tell the other girls and boys
Not to meddle with my toys.
Ib. XII. *Looking Forward.*

The pleasant land of counterpane.
Ib. XVI. *The Land of Counterpane.*

The child that is not clean and neat,
With lots of toys and things to eat,
He is a naughty child, I'm sure—
Or else his dear papa is poor.
Ib. XIX. *System.*

The friendly cow, all red and white,
I love with all my heart:
She gives me cream with all her might,
To eat with apple-tart.
Ib. XXIII. *The Cow.*

The world is so full of a number of things,
I'm sure we should all be as happy as kings.
Ib. XXIV. *Happy Thought.*

Children, you are very little,
And your bones are very brittle;
If you would grow great and stately,
You must try to walk sedately.
Ib. XXVII. *Good and Bad Children.*

But the unkind and the unruly,
And the sort who eat unduly,
They must never hope for glory—
Theirs is quite a different story!

Cruel children, crying babies,
All grow up as geese and gabies,
Hated, as their age increases,
By their nephews and their nieces.
Ib.

Must we to bed indeed? Well then,
Let us arise and go like men,
And face with an undaunted tread
The long black passage up to bed.
Ib. XLI. *North-West Passage.* 1. *Good-Night.*

Give to me the life I love,
Let the lave go by me,
Give the jolly heaven above
And the byway nigh me.
Bed in the bush with stars to see,
Bread I dip in the river—
There's the life for a man like me,
There's the life for ever.
Songs of Travel. 1. *The Vagabond.*

Let the blow fall soon or late,
Let what will be o'er me;
Give the face of earth around
And the road before me.
Wealth I seek not, hope nor love,
Nor a friend to know me;
All I seek, the heaven above
And the road below me.
Ib.

The untented Kosmos my abode,
I pass, a wilful stranger;
My mistress still the open road
And the bright eyes of danger.
Ib. II. *Youth and Love.*

Here, lady, lo! that servant stands
You picked from passing men,
And should you need nor heart nor hands
He bows and goes again.
Ib. VII.

I will make you brooches and toys for your delight
Of bird-song at morning and star-shine at night.

I will make a palace fit for you and me
Of green days in forests and blue days at sea.
I will make my kitchen, and you shall keep your
room,
Where white flows the river and bright blows the
broom,
And you shall wash your linen and keep your body
white
In rainfall at morning and dewfall at night. *Ib.* XI.

Bright is the ring of words
When the right man rings them,
Fair the fall of songs
When the singer sings them.
Still they are carolled and said—
On wings they are carried—
After the singer is dead
And the maker buried.
Ib. XIV.

Low as the singer lies
In the field of heather,
Songs of his fashion bring
The swains together.
And when the west is red
With the sunset embers,
The lover lingers and sings
And the maid remembers.
Ib.

In the highlands, in the country places,
Where the old plain men have rosy faces,
And the young fair maidens
Quiet eyes.
Ib. XV.

Trusty, dusky, vivid, true,
With eyes of gold and bramble-dew,
Steel-true and blade-straight,
The great artificer
Made my mate.
Ib. XXV. *My Wife.*

Sing me a song of a lad that is gone,
Say, could that lad be I?
Merry of soul he sailed on a day
Over the sea to Skye.
Ib. XLII.

Mull was a-stern, Rum on the port,
Eigg on the starboard bow;
Glory of youth glowed in his soul,
Where is that glory now?
Ib.

Blows the wind to-day, and the sun and the rain are
flying,
Blows the wind on the moors to-day and now,
Where about the graves of the martyrs the whaups
are crying,
My heart remembers how!
Ib. xlv. *To S. R. Crockett.*

Be it granted to me to behold you again in dying,
Hills of home! and to hear again the call;
Hear about the graves of the martyrs the peewees
crying,
And hear no more at all.
Ib.

Of all my verse, like not a single line;
But like my title, for it is not mine.
That title from a better man I stole;
Ah, how much better, had I stol'n the whole!
Underwoods. Foreword.

Go, little book, and wish to all
Flowers in the garden, meat in the hall,
A bin of wine, a spice of wit,
A house with lawns enclosing it,
A living river by the door,
A nightingale in the sycamore! *Ib.* bk. i. i. *Envoy.*

The gauger walked with willing foot,
And aye the gauger played the flute;
And what should Master Gauger play
But 'Over the hills and far away'?
Ib. ii. *A Song of the Road.*

There's nothing under Heav'n so blue
That's fairly worth the travelling to.   *Ib.* iv.

Under the wide and starry sky
Dig the grave and let me lie.
Glad did I live and gladly die,
   And I laid me down with a will.
This be the verse you grave for me:
'Here he lies where he longed to be;
Home is the sailor, home from sea,
   And the hunter home from the hill.'
Ib. xxi. *Requiem.*

If I have faltered more or less
In my great task of happiness;
If I have moved among my race
And shown no glorious morning face;
If beams from happy human eyes
Have moved me not; if morning skies,
Books, and my food, and summer rain
Knocked on my sullen heart in vain:—
Lord, thy most pointed pleasure take
And stab my spirit broad awake;
Or, Lord, if too obdurate I,
Choose thou, before that spirit die,
A piercing pain, a killing sin,
And to my dead heart run them in!
Ib. xxii. *The Celestial Surgeon.*

Unfrowning caryatides.
Ib. xxiii. *Our Lady of the Snows.*

I am a kind of farthing dip,
   Unfriendly to the nose and eyes;
A blue-behinded ape, I skip
Upon the trees of Paradise.   *Ib.* xxx. *A Portrait.*

      In the afternoon of time
A strenuous family dusted from its hands
The sand of granite, and beholding far
Along the sounding coast its pyramids
And tall memorials catch the dying sun,
Smiled well content, and to this childish task
Around the fire addressed its evening hours.
Ib. xxxviii. *Say not of me that weakly I
   declined.*

A mile an' a bittock, a mile or twa,
Abüne the burn, ayont the law,
Davie an' Donal' an' Cherlie an' a',
An' the müne was shinin' clearly!
Ib. bk. ii. iv. *A mile an' a bittock,* 1.

WILLIAM STEVENSON.

1530?–1575.

can not eat but little meat,
   My stomach is not good:
ut sure I think, that I can drink
   With him that wears a hood.
hough I go bare, take ye no care,
   I am nothing a cold:
stuff my skin, so full within,
   Of jolly good ale and old.

[415]

Back and side go bare, go bare,
   Both foot and hand go cold:
But belly God send thee good ale enough,
   Whether it be new or old.
Gammer Gurton's Needle, Act II, *Song.*

SAMUEL JOHN STONE

1839–1901

The Church's one foundation
   Is Jesus Christ her Lord;
She is His new creation
   By water and the Word.
Lyra Fidelium (1866). *The Church's One
   Foundation.*

Yet Saints their watch are keeping,
   Their cry goes up, 'How long?'
And soon the night of weeping
   Shall be the morn of song.   *Ib.*

'Mid toil and tribulation,
   And tumult of her war,
She waits the consummation
   Of peace for evermore;
Till with the vision glorious
   Her longing eyes are blest,
And the great Church victorious
   Shall be the Church at rest.   *Ib.*

Weary of earth and laden with my sin.
Ib. Weary of Earth and Laden.

HARRIET BEECHER STOWE

1812–1896

'Who was your mother?' 'Never had none!' said the
   child, with another grin. 'Never had any mother?
   What do you mean? Where were you born?'
   'Never was born!' persisted Topsy.
Uncle Tom's Cabin, ch. 20.

'Do you know who made you?' 'Nobody, as I knows
   on,' said the child, with a short laugh. . . . 'I 'spect
   I grow'd.'
Ib.

''Cause I's wicked—I is. I's mighty wicked, any
   how. I can't help it.'
Ib.

WILLIAM STUBBS

1825–1901

Froude informs the Scottish youth
That parsons do not care for truth.
The Reverend Canon Kingsley cries
History is a pack of lies.
What cause for judgments so malign?
A brief reflection solves the mystery—
Froude believes Kingsley a divine,
And Kingsley goes to Froude for history.
*In Stubbs's Letter to J. R. Green, 17 Dec. 1871.
   Letters of Stubbs* (1904), p. 162.

GEOFFREY ANKETELL
STUDDERT-KENNEDY

1883–1929

When in the darkest depths the miner striving,
Feels in his arms the vigour of the Lord,
Strikes for a Kingdom and his King's arriving,
Holding his pick more splendid than the sword.
Songs of Faith and Doubt (1922), p. 7. *Then
   Will He Come: 'When Through the Whirl.'*

SIR JOHN SUCKLING

1609–1642

Why so pale and wan, fond lover?
  Prithee, why so pale?
Will, when looking well can't move her,
  Looking ill prevail?
Prithee, why so pale?   *Aglaura*, IV. i. *Song.*

Quit, quit, for shame, this will not move:
  This cannot take her.
If of herself she will not love,
  Nothing can make her:
  The devil take her!   *Ib.*

Her feet beneath her petticoat,
Like little mice, stole in and out,
  As if they fear'd the light.
   Ballad. Upon a Wedding, viii.

For streaks of red were mingled there,
Such as are on a Catherine pear
  (The side that's next the sun).

Her lips were red, and one was thin,   *Ib.*
Compar'd to that was next her chin
  (Some bee had stung it newly).   *Ib.* xi.

The Prince of Darkness is a gentleman.
  The Goblins. Act III, *A Catch.*

I prithee send me back my heart,
  Since I cannot have thine:
For if from yours you will not part,
  Why then shouldst thou have mine?
   Song. I Prithee Send me Back.

But love is such a mystery,
  I cannot find it out:
For when I think I'm best resolv'd,
  I then am in most doubt.   *Ib.*

Out upon it, I have loved
  Three whole days together;
And am like to love three more,
  If it prove fair weather.

Time shall moult away his wings,
  Ere he shall discover
In the whole wide world again
  Such a constant lover.   *A Poem with the Answer.*

Had it any been but she,
  And that very face,
There had been at least ere this
  A dozen dozen in her place.   *Ib.*

HENRY HOWARD,
EARL OF SURREY

1517?–1547

My friend, the things that do attain
  The happy life be these, I find:
The riches left, not got with pain;
  The fruitful ground, the quiet mind;

The equal friend; no grudge, no strife;
  No charge of rule, nor governance;
Without disease the healthy life;
  The household of continuance.
   Martial's Quiet Life, st. i, ii.

The faithful wife, without debate;
  Such sleeps as may beguile the night:
Content thyself with thine estate;
  Neither wish death nor fear his might.   *Ib.* st. iv.

The soote season, that bud and bloom forth brings.
   Spring.

ROBERT SMITH SURTEES

1803–1864

More people are flattered into virtue than bullied out
of vice.
  The Analysis of the Hunting Field (1846), ch. 1.

The only infallible rule we know is, that the man who
is always talking about being a gentleman never is
one.   *Ask Mamma* (1858), ch. 1.

Major Yammerton was rather a peculiar man, inasmuch as he was an ass, without being a fool.
   Ib. ch. 25.

'Unting is all that's worth living for—all time is lost
  wot is not spent in 'unting—it is like the hair we
  breathe—if we have it not we die—it's the sport
  of kings, the image of war without its guilt, and
  only five-and-twenty per cent. of its danger.
   Handley Cross (1930), ch. 7.

'Unting fills my thoughts by day, and many a good
  run I have in my sleep. Many a dig in the ribs I
  gives Mrs. J. when I think they're running into
  the warmint (renewed cheers). No man is fit to be
  called a sportsman wot doesn't kick his wife out of
  bed on a haverage once in three weeks! *Ib.* ch. 11.

Tell me a man's a fox-hunter, and I loves him at
  once.   *Ib.*

Come Hup! I say, you hugly beast!   *Ib.* ch. 13.

He will bring his nightcap with him, for where the
  M.F.H. dines he sleeps, and where the M.F.H.
  sleeps he breakfasts.   *Ib.* ch. 15.

I'll fill hup the chinks wi' cheese.   *Ib.*

Well did that great man, I think it was Sir Walter
  Scott, but if it warn't, 'twas little Bartley, the bootmaker, say, that there was no young man that
  would not rather have a himputation on his
  morality than on his 'ossmanship.   *Ib.* ch. 16.

It ar'n't that I loves the fox less, but that I loves the
  'ound more.   *Ib.*

The 'oss loves the 'ound, and I loves both.   *Ib.*

Dinner lost! 'ounds lost, self lost—all lost together!
   Ib. ch. 21.

I can stand a wast of praise.   *Ib.* ch. 24.

From the bonded warehouse of my knowledge.
   Ib. ch. 27.

Bishops' boots Mr. Radcliffe also condemned, an
  spoke highly in favour of tops cleaned with champagne and abricot jam.   *Ib.*

Unless a man has a good many servants, he had
  better have them cleanin' his 'oss than cleanin' his
  breeches.   *Ib.*

Full o' beans and benevolence!   *Ib.*

Paid for catching my 'oss, 6*d.*   *Ib.* ch. 29.

Letting in the Latchfords. *Ib.* ch. 31.

Con-found all presents wot eat! *Ib.* ch. 37.

Hellish dark, and smells of cheese! *Ib.* ch. 50.

I feels all over trembulation and fear, like a maid that thinks she's not a-goin' to be married. *Ib.* ch. 52.

'Hurrah! blister my kidneys!' exclaimed he in delight, 'it is a frost!—the dahlias are dead!'
Ib. ch. 59.

Howsomever, never mind—the country has its charms—cheapness for one.
Hillingdon Hall (1931), ch. 5.

Three things I never lends—my 'oss, my wife, and my name. *Ib.* ch. 33.

Every man shouting in proportion to the amount of his subscription.
Jorrocks's Jaunts and Jollities (1929). No. 1. *Swell and the Surrey.*

Jorrocks, who is not afraid of 'the pace' so long as there is no leaping. *Ib.*

And a nod or a wink for every pretty maid that showed at the windows; for . . . , as he says, 'there is no harm in looking'.
Ib. No. 4. *Surrey Stag-Hounds.*

Champagne certainly gives one werry gentlemanly ideas, but for a continuance, I don't know but I should prefer mild hale.
Ib. No. 9. *Mr. Jorrocks in Paris.*

No one knows how ungentlemanly he can look, until he has seen himself in a shocking bad hat.
Mr. Facey Romford's Hounds (1892), ch. 9.

Bob Short, who had replied to Facey's advertisement for a 'strong persevering man, to clean horses'.
Ib. ch. 19.

Better be killed than frightened to death. *Ib.* ch. 32.

Thinking that life would be very pleasant if it were not for its enjoyments. *Ib.*

These sort of boobies think that people come to balls to do nothing but dance; whereas everyone knows that the real business of a ball is either to look out for a wife, to look after a wife, or to look after somebody else's wife. *Ib.* ch. 56.

The young ladies entered the drawing-room in the full fervour of sisterly animosity.
Mr. Sponge's Sporting Tour (1892), ch. 17.

Women never look so well as when one comes in wet and dirty from hunting. *Ib.* ch. 21.

He was a gentleman who was generally spoken of as having nothing a-year, paid quarterly. *Ib.* ch. 24.

There is no secret so close as that between a rider and his horse. *Ib.* ch. 31.

He had a tremendous determination of words to the mouth. *Ib.* ch. 34.

When at length they rose to go to bed, it struck each man as he followed his neighbour upstairs that the one before him walked very crookedly. *Ib.* ch. 35.

P

JONATHAN SWIFT

1667–1745

I conceive some scattered notions about a superior power to be of singular use for the common people, as furnishing excellent materials to keep children quiet when they grow peevish, and providing topics of amusement in a tedious winter-night.
An Argument Against Abolishing Christianity.

Satire is a sort of glass, wherein beholders do generally discover everybody's face but their own.
The Battle of the Books, preface.

Instead of dirt and poison we have rather chosen to fill our hives with honey and wax; thus furnishing mankind with the two noblest of things, which are sweetness and light. *Ib.*

I have heard of a man who had a mind to sell his house, and therefore carried a piece of brick in his pocket, which he shewed as a pattern to encourage purchasers.
The Drapier's Letters, No. 2 (4 Aug. 1724).

Laws are like cobwebs, which may catch small flies, but let wasps and hornets break through.
A Tritical Essay upon the Faculties of the Mind.

There is nothing in this world constant, but inconstancy. *Ib.*

He [the emperor] is taller by almost the breadth of my nail than any of his court, which alone is enough to strike an awe into the beholders.
Gulliver's Travels. Voyage to Lilliput, ch. 2.

The colonel and his officers were in much pain, especially when they saw me take out my penknife.
Ib.

He put this engine [a watch] to our ears, which made an incessant noise like that of a water-mill; and we conjecture it is either some unknown animal, or the god that he worships; but we are more inclined to the latter opinion. *Ib.*

Flimnap, the Treasurer, is allowed to cut a caper on the straight rope, at least an inch higher than any other lord in the whole empire. I have seen him do the summerset several times together. *Ib.* ch. 3.

It is alleged indeed, that the high heels are most agreeable to our ancient constitution: but however this be, his Majesty hath determined to make use of only low heels in the administration of the government. *Ib.* ch. 4.

He could not forbear taking me up in his right hand, and stroking me gently with the other, after an hearty fit of laughing, asked me whether I were a Whig or a Tory.
Ib. Voyage to Brobdingnag, ch. 3.

I cannot but conclude the bulk of your natives to be the most pernicious race of little odious vermin that nature ever suffered to crawl upon the surface of the earth. *Ib.* ch. 6.

He was amazed how so impotent and grovelling an insect as I (these were his expressions) could entertain such inhuman ideas. *Ib.* ch. 7.

And he gave it for his opinion, that whoever could make two ears of corn or two blades of grass to grow upon a spot of ground where only one grew before, would deserve better of mankind, and do more essential service to his country than the whole race of politicians put together. *Ib.*

He had been eight years upon a project for extracting sun-beams out of cucumbers, which were to be put into vials hermetically sealed, and let out to warm the air in raw inclement summers.
Ib. Voyage to Laputa, etc., ch. 5.

I said the thing which was not.
Ib. A Voyage to the Houyhnhms, ch. 3.

I told him . . . that we ate when we were not hungry, and drank without the provocation of thirst.
Ib. ch. 6.

Plaguy twelvepenny weather.
Journal to Stella, 26 Oct. 1710.

'Tis very warm weather when one's in bed.
Ib. 8 Nov. 1710.

With my own fair hands. *Ib. 4 Jan. 1711.*

We are so fond of one another, because our ailments are the same. *Ib. 1 Feb. 1711.*

Will she pass in a crowd? Will she make a figure in a country church? *Ib. 9 Feb. 1711.*

I love good creditable acquaintance; I love to be the worst of the company. *Ib. 17 May 1711.*

He was a fiddler, and consequently a rogue.
Ib. 25 July 1711.

He showed me his bill of fare to tempt me to dine with him; poh, said I, I value not your bill of fare, give me your bill of company. *Ib. 2 Sept. 1711.*

We were to do more business after dinner; but after dinner is after dinner—an old saying and a true, 'much drinking, little thinking'. *Ib. 26 Feb. 1712.*

Monday is parson's holiday. *Ib. 3 Mar. 1712.*

Not die here in a rage, like a poisoned rat in a hole.
Letter to Bolingbroke, 21 Mar. 1729.

If Heaven had looked upon riches to be a valuable thing, it would not have given them to such a scoundrel.
Letter to Miss Vanhomrigh, 12–13 Aug. 1720.

What they call 'running a man down'.
Letter to a Very Young Lady on her Marriage.

Proper words in proper places, make the true definition of a style.
Letter to a Young Clergyman, 9 Jan. 1720.

Surely man is a broomstick!
A Meditation upon a Broomstick.

I have been assured by a very knowing American of my acquaintance in London, that a young healthy child well nursed is at a year old a most delicious, nourishing, and wholesome food, whether stewed, roasted, baked, or boiled, and I make no doubt that it will equally serve in a fricassee, or a ragout.
A Modest Proposal for Preventing the Children of Ireland from being a Burden to their Parents or Country.

Promises and pie-crust are made to be broken.
Polite Conversation. Dialogue 1.

Bachelor's fare; bread and cheese, and kisses. *Ib.*

Like an owl in an ivy-bush. *Ib.*

I mean, you lie—under a mistake. *Ib.*

Why every one as they like; as the good woman said when she kissed her cow. *Ib.*

Why, madam, Queen Elizabeth's dead. *Ib.*

The sight of you is good for sore eyes. *Ib.*

'Tis as cheap sitting as standing. *Ib.*

Prythee, Tom, sit a little farther: I believe your father was no glazier. *Ib.*

You were half seas over. *Ib.*

I won't quarrel with my bread and butter. *Ib.*

I swear, she's no chicken; she's on the wrong side of thirty, if she be a day. *Ib.*

If it had been a bear, it would have bit you. *Ib.*

She wears her clothes, as if they were thrown on her with a pitchfork. *Ib.*

Faith, that's as well said, as if I had said it myself.
Ib. Dialogue 2.

You must take the will for the deed. *Ib.*

She has more goodness in her little finger, than he has in his whole body. *Ib.*

Lord, I wonder what fool it was that first invented kissing! *Ib.*

I'll give you leave to call me anything, if you don't call me spade. *Ib.*

I always love to begin a journey on Sundays, because I shall have the prayers of the church, to preserve all that travel by land, or by water. *Ib.*

I know Sir John will go, though he was sure it would rain cats and dogs. *Ib.*

'Tis happy for him, that his father was before him.
Ib. Dialogue 3.

There's none so blind as they that won't see. *Ib.*

She watches him, as a cat would watch a mouse. *Ib.*

She pays him in his own coin. *Ib.*

All the world and his wife. *Ib.*

Damn your cards, said he, they are the devil's books. *Ib.*

There's two words to that bargain. *Ib.*

It is a maxim, that those to whom everybody allows the second place, have an undoubted title to the first. *A Tale of a Tub. Dedication.*

I never saw, heard, nor read, that the clergy were beloved in any nation where Christianity was the religion of the country. Nothing can render them popular but some degree of persecution.
Thoughts on Religion.

We have just enough religion to make us hate, but not enough to make us love one another.
Thoughts on Various Subjects.

What they do in heaven we are ignorant of; what they do *not* we are told expressly, that they neither marry, nor are given in marriage. *Ib.*

The reasons why so few marriages are happy, is, because young ladies spend their time in making nets, not in making cages. *Ib.*

Few are qualified to shine in company; but it is in most men's power to be agreeable. *Ib.*

Every man desires to live long; but no man would be old. *Ib.*

A nice man is a man of nasty ideas. *Ib.*

Old men and comets have been reverenced for the same reason; their long beards, and pretences to foretell events. *Ib.*

I never wonder to see men wicked, but I often wonder to see them not ashamed. *Ib.*

A man should never be ashamed to own he has been in the wrong, which is but saying, in other words, that he is wiser today than he was yesterday. *Ib.*

Party is the madness of many, for the gain of a few. *Ib.*

When men grow virtuous in their old age, they only make a sacrifice to God of the devil's leavings. *Ib.*

The most positive men are the most credulous. *Ib.*

Good God! what a genius I had when I wrote that book.
[Of *The Tale of a Tub*] Sir Walter Scott's *Life of Swift. Works of Swift* (1824), vol. i, p. 89.

I shall be like that tree, I shall die at the top.
Sir Walter Scott, *Memoirs of Swift.*

How haughtily he cocks his nose,
To tell what every schoolboy knows.
The Country Life, l. 81.

Lose no time to contradict her,
Nor endeavour to convict her. *Daphne*, l. 29.

Only take this rule along,
Always to advise her wrong;
And reprove her when she's right;
She may then grow wise for spite. *Ib.* l. 35.

In all distresses of our friends,
We first consult our private ends;
While nature, kindly bent to ease us,
Points out some circumstance to please us.
On the Death of Dr. Swift, l. 7.

Poor Pope will grieve a month, and Gay
A week, and Arbuthnot a day.
St. John himself will scarce forbear
To bite his pen, and drop a tear.
The rest will give a shrug, and cry,
'I'm sorry—but we all must die!' *Ib.* l. 207.

Yet malice never was his aim;
He lash'd the vice, but spared the name;
No individual could resent,
Where thousands equally were meant. *Ib.* l. 512.

He gave the little wealth he had
To build a house for fools and mad;
And show'd, by one satiric touch,
No nation wanted it so much. *Ib.* l. 538.

They never would hear,
But turn the deaf ear,
As a matter they had no concern in.
Dingley and Brent, ii.

A coming shower your shooting corns presage.
Description of a City Shower, l. 9.

I often wish'd that I had clear,
For life, six hundred pounds a-year,
A handsome house to lodge a friend,
A river at my garden's end,
A terrace walk, and half a rood
Of land, set out to plant a wood.
Imitation of Horace, bk. II, sat. vi, ll. 1-6.

Removed from kind Arbuthnot's aid,
Who knows his art, but not the trade.
Preferring his regard for me
Before his credit, or his fee. *In Sickness*, l. 9.

Convey a libel in a frown,
And wink a reputation down.
Journal of a Modern Lady, l. 192.

'Libertas et natale solum':
Fine words! I wonder where you stole 'em.
Lines written in 1724 on Chief Justice Whitshed's motto on his coach, after the trial of Drapier.

Hail, fellow, well met,
All dirty and wet:
Find out, if you can,
Who's master, who's man.
My Lady's Lamentation, l. 171.

Th' artillery of words. *Ode to Sancroft*, i.

Philosophy, the lumber of the schools.
Ode to Sir W. Temple, ii.

Walls have tongues, and hedges ears.
Pastoral Dialogue, l. 8.

Say, Britain, could you ever boast,—
Three poets in an age at most?
Our chilling climate hardly bears
A sprig of bays in fifty years. *On Poetry*, l. 5.

Then, rising with Aurora's light,
The Muse invoked, sit down to write;
Blot out, correct, insert, refine,
Enlarge, diminish, interline. *Ib.* l. 85.

As learned commentators view
In Homer more than Homer knew. *Ib.* l. 103.

So geographers, in Afric-maps,
With savage-pictures fill their gaps;
And o'er unhabitable downs
Place elephants for want of towns. *Ib.* l. 177.

Read all the prefaces of Dryden,
For these our critics much confide in,
(Tho' merely writ at first for filling
To raise the volume's price, a shilling.) *Ib.* l. 251.

He gives directions to the town,
To cry it up, or run it down. *Ib.* l. 269.

Hobbes clearly proves, that every creature
Lives in a state of war by nature. *Ib.* l. 319.

So, naturalists observe, a flea
Hath smaller fleas that on him prey;
And these have smaller fleas to bite 'em,
And so proceed *ad infinitum.*
Thus every poet, in his kind,
Is bit by him that comes behind. *Ib.* l. 337.

To guide his steps afford your kindest aid,
And gently pity whom ye can't persuade;
Leave to avenging Heaven his stubborn will,
For, O, remember, he's your brother still.

Swan Tripe Club in Dublin, l. 489.

Humour is odd, grotesque, and wild,
Only by affectation spoil'd;
'Tis never by invention got,
Men have it when they know it not.

To Mr. Delany, 10 Oct. 1718, l. 25.

Hated by fools, and fools to hate,
Be that my motto and my fate.   *Ib.* l. 171.

A beggarly people!
A church and no steeple! [Of St. Ann's Church,
Dublin]
> Attr. to Swift by Malone. See Prior's *Life
> of Malone* (1860), p. 381.

Ubi saeva indignatio ulterius cor lacerare nequit.
> Where fierce indignation can no longer tear the heart.

Swift's Epitaph.

ALGERNON CHARLES SWINBURNE

1837–1909

Superflux of pain.   *Anactoria,* l. 27.

Maiden, and mistress of the months and stars
Now folded in the flowerless fields of heaven.
> *Atalanta in Calydon. Collected Poetical Works*
> (1924), vol. ii, p. 247, l. 1.

When the hounds of spring are on winter's traces,
    The mother of months in meadow or plain
Fills the shadows and windy places
    With lisp of leaves and ripple of rain;
And the brown bright nightingale amorous
Is half assuaged for Itylus,
For the Thracian ships and the foreign faces,
    The tongueless vigil and all the pain.

Come with bows bent and with emptying of quivers,
    Maiden most perfect, lady of light,
With a noise of winds and many rivers,
    With a clamour of waters, and with might;
Bind on thy sandals, O thou most fleet,
Over the splendour and speed of thy feet;
For the faint east quickens, the wan west shivers,
    Round the feet of the day and the feet of the night.

Where shall we find her, how shall we sing to her,
    Fold our hands round her knees, and cling?
O that man's heart were as fire and could spring to
    her,
Fire, or the strength of the streams that spring!
For the stars and the winds are unto her
As raiment, as songs of the harp-player;
For the risen stars and the fallen cling to her,
    And the southwest-wind and west-wind sing.

For winter's rains and ruins are over,
    And all the season of snows and sins;
The days dividing lover and lover,
    The light that loses, the night that wins;
And time remembered is grief forgotten,
And frosts are slain and flowers begotten,

And in green underwood and cover
    Blossom by blossom the spring begins.

Ib. Chorus, p. 249.

And the hoofed heel of a satyr crushes
    The chestnut-husk at the chestnut-root. *Ib.* p. 250.

And Pan by noon and Bacchus by night,
    Fleeter of foot than the fleet-foot kid,
Follows with dancing and fills with delight
    The Maenad and the Bassarid;
And soft as lips that laugh and hide
The laughing leaves of the tree divide,
And screen from seeing and leave in sight
    The god pursuing, the maiden hid.   *Ib.*

The ivy falls with the Bacchanal's hair
    Over her eyebrows hiding her eyes;
The wild vine slipping down leaves bare
    Her bright breast shortening into sighs.   *Ib.*

The wolf that follows, the fawn that flies.   *Ib.*

Before the beginning of years
    There came to the making of man
Time with a gift of tears,
    Grief with a glass that ran.
Pleasure with pain for leaven,
    Summer with flowers that fell,
Remembrance fallen from heaven,
    And Madness risen from hell,
Strength without hands to smite,
    Love that endures for a breath;
Night, the shadow of light,
    And Life, the shadow of death.   *Ib.* p. 258.

For a day and a night and a morrow,
    That his strength might endure for a span
With travail and heavy sorrow,
    The holy spirit of man.   *Ib.* p. 259.

Eyesight and speech they wrought
    For the veil of the soul therein,
A time for labour and thought,
    A time to serve and to sin;
They gave him light in his ways,
    And love, and a space for delight,
And beauty and length of days,
    And night, and sleep in the night.
His speech is a burning fire;
    With his lips he travaileth;
In his heart is a blind desire,
    In his eyes foreknowledge of death;
He weaves, and is clothed with derision;
    Sows, and he shall not reap;
His life is a watch or a vision
    Between a sleep and a sleep.   *Ib.*

We have seen thee, O love, thou art fair; thou art
    goodly, O Love.   *Ib.* p. 273.

For words divide and rend;
But silence is most noble till the end.   *Ib.* p. 299.

Where the narrowing Symplegades whitened the
    straits of Propontis with spray.   *Ib.* p. 327.

Shall I strew on thee rose or rue or laurel,
    Brother, on this that was the veil of thee?
Or quiet sea-flower moulded by the sea,
Or simplest growth of meadow-sweet or sorrel?

Ave atque Vale, i.

Now all strange hours and all strange loves are over,
　Dreams and desires and sombre songs and sweet,
Hast thou found place at the great knees and feet
　Of some pale Titan-woman like a lover,
　　Such as thy vision here solicited,
　Under the shadow of her fair vast head,
The deep division of prodigious breasts,
　The solemn slope of mighty limbs asleep?   *Ib.* vi.

Sleep; and if life was bitter to thee, pardon,
　If sweet, give thanks; thou hast no more to live;
　And to give thanks is good, and to forgive.
　　　　　　　　　　　　　　　　　　Ib. xvii.

For thee, O now a silent soul, my brother,
　Take at my hands this garland and farewell.
　Thin is the leaf, and chill the wintry smell,
And chill the solemn earth, a fatal mother,
　With sadder than the Niobean womb
And in the hollow of her breasts a tomb.   *Ib.* xviii.

　There lies not any troublous thing before,
　Nor sight nor sound to war against thee more,
For whom all winds are quiet as the sun,
　All waters as the shore.   *Ib.*

This is the end of every man's desire.
　　　　　　　A Ballad of Burdens.

Poor splendid wings so frayed and soiled and torn!
Poor kind wild eyes so dashed with light quick tears!
　　　　　　　Ballad of François Villon.

　Villon, our sad bad glad mad brother's name.   *Ib.*

　　Strung with subtle-coloured hair
Of some dead lute-player.   *A Ballad of Life.*

O slain and spent and sacrificed
People, the grey-grown speechless Christ.
　Before a Crucifix. Poetical Works (1924), vol.
　i, p. 744.

No soul that lived, loved, wrought and died,
Is this their carrion crucified.   *Ib.* p. 747.

We shift and bedeck and bedrape us,
　Thou art noble and nude and antique.
　　　　　　　　　　　Dolores, vii.

　　　Change in a trice
The lilies and languors of virtue
　For the raptures and roses of vice.   *Ib.* ix.

O splendid and sterile Dolores,
　Our Lady of Pain.   *Ib.*

Ah beautiful passionate body
That never has ached with a heart !   *Ib.* xi.

But sweet as the rind was the core is;
　We are fain of thee still, we are fain,
O sanguine and subtle Dolores,
　Our Lady of Pain.   *Ib.* xiii.

The delight that consumes the desire,
　The desire that outruns the delight.   *Ib.* xiv.

For the crown of our life as it closes
　Is darkness, the fruit thereof dust;
No thorns go as deep as a rose's,
　And love is more cruel than lust.
Time turns the old days to derision,
　Our loves into corpses or wives;
And marriage and death and division
　Make barren our lives.   *Ib.* xx.

Ringed round with a flame of fair faces,
　And splendid with swords.   *Ib.* xxx.

What ailed us, O gods, to desert you
　For creeds that refuse and restrain?
Come down and redeem us from virtue,
　Our Lady of Pain.   *Ib.* xxxv.

On thy bosom though many a kiss be,
　There are none such as knew it of old.
Was it Alciphron once or Arisbe,
　Male ringlets or feminine gold,
That thy lips met with under the statue,
　Whence a look shot out sharp after thieves
From the eyes of the garden-god at you
　Across the fig-leaves?   *Ib.* xxxviii.

Old poets outsing and outlove us,
　And Catullus makes mouths at our speech. *Ib.* xliii.

Where are they, Cotytto or Venus,
　Astarte or Ashtaroth, where?
Do their hands as we touch come between us?
　Is the breath of them hot in thy hair?
From their lips have thy lips taken fever,
　With the blood of their bodies grown red?
Hast thou left upon earth a believer
　If these men are dead?   *Ib.* lii.

O daughter of Death and Priapus,
　Our Lady of Pain.   *Ib.* liii.

I shall remember while the light lives yet
And in the night time I shall not forget.   *Erotion.*

Bright with names that men remember, loud with
　names that men forget.   *Eton: An Ode.*

What adders came to shed their coats?
　What coiled obscene
Small serpents with soft stretching throats
　Caressed Faustine?   *Faustine.*

Those eyes the greenest of things blue,
　The bluest of things grey.   *Félise.*

In a coign of the cliff between lowland and highland,
At the sea-down's edge between windward and lee,
Walled round with rocks as an inland island,
　The ghost of a garden fronts the sea.
　　　　　　　　　　A Forsaken Garden.

The fields fall southward, abrupt and broken,
To the low last edge of the long lone land.
If a step should sound or a word be spoken,
　Would a ghost not rise at the strange guest's hand?
So long have the grey bare walls lain guestless,
　Through branches and briars if a man make way,
He shall find no life but the sea-wind's, restless
　　　　Night and day.   *Ib.*

Heart handfast in heart as they stood, 'Look thither,'
Did he whisper? 'look forth from the flowers to the
　　sea;
For the foam-flowers endure when the rose-blossoms
　　wither
　And men that love lightly may die—but we?'
And the same wind sang and the same waves
　　whitened,
And or ever the garden's last petals were shed,
In the lips that had whispered, the eyes that had
　　lightened,
　　　　Love was dead.   *Ib.*

Stretched out on the spoils that his own hand spread.
As a god self-slain on his own strange altar,
　　　　Death lies dead.   *Ib.*

Here, where the world is quiet;
  Here, where all trouble seems
Dead winds' and spent waves' riot
  In doubtful dreams of dreams.
              The Garden of Proserpine.

I am tired of tears and laughter,
  And men that laugh and weep;
Of what may come hereafter
  For men that sow and reap:
I am weary of days and hours,
  Blown buds of barren flowers,
Desires and dreams and powers
  And everything but sleep.   *Ib.*

Here life has death for neighbour,
  And far from eye or ear
Wan waves and wet winds labour,
  Weak ships and spirits steer.   *Ib.*

Pale, beyond porch and portal,
  Crowned with calm leaves, she stands
Who gathers all things mortal
  With cold immortal hands.   *Ib.*

Dead dreams of days forsaken,
Blind buds that snows have shaken,
Wild leaves that winds have taken,
  Red strays of ruined springs.   *Ib.*

We are not sure of sorrow,
  And joy was never sure.   *Ib.*

From too much love of living,
  From hope and fear set free,
We thank with brief thanksgiving
  Whatever gods may be
That no man lives forever,
That dead men rise up never;
That even the weariest river
  Winds somewhere safe to sea.   *Ib.*

Then star nor sun shall waken,
  Nor any change of light:
Nor sound of waters shaken,
  Nor any sound or sight:
Nor wintry leaves nor vernal,
Nor days nor things diurnal;
Only the sleep eternal
  In an eternal night.   *Ib.*

Calling a crowned man royal
That was no more than a king. *The Halt before Rome.*

Fiddle, we know, is diddle: and diddle, we take it,
  is dee.
The Heptalogia. The Higher Pantheism in a Nutshell.

  I am that which began;
  Out of me the years roll;
  Out of me God and man;
  I am equal and whole;
God changes, and man, and the form of them bodily;
  I am the soul.   *Hertha.*

  But what thing dost thou now,
  Looking Godward, to cry
  'I am I, thou art thou,
  I am low, thou art high'?
I am thou, whom thou seekest to find him; find thou
  but thyself, thou art I.   *Ib.*

  A creed is a rod,
  And a crown is of night;
  But this thing is God,

  To be man with thy might,
To grow straight in the strength of thy spirit, and live
  out thy life as the light.   *Ib.*

Green leaves of thy labour, white flowers of thy
  thought, and red fruit of thy death.   *Ib.*

Man, equal and one with me, man that is made of me,
  man that is I.   *Ib.*

'Hope thou not much, and fear thou not at all.'
                  Hope and Fear.

  In the fair days when God
  By man as godlike trod,
And each alike was Greek, alike was free.
              To Victor Hugo.

And a bird overhead sang *Follow*,
  And a bird to the right sang *Here*;
And the arch of the leaves was hollow,
  And the meaning of May was clear.
              An Interlude.

I remember the way we parted,
  The day and the way we met;
You hoped we were both broken-hearted,
  And knew we should both forget.   *Ib.*

And the best and the worst of this is
  That neither is most to blame,
If you have forgotten my kisses
  And I have forgotten your name.   *Ib.*

Swallow, my sister, O sister swallow,
  How can thine heart be full of the spring?
A thousand summers are over and dead.
  What hast thou found in the spring to follow?
What hast thou found in thine heart to sing?
  What wilt thou do when the summer is shed?
                Itylus.

Hast thou forgotten ere I forget?   *Ib.*

Sister, my sister, O fleet sweet swallow,
  Thy way is long to the sun and the south;
But I, fulfilled of my heart's desire,
  Shedding my song upon height, upon hollow,
From tawny body and sweet small mouth
  Feed the heart of the night with fire.

I the nightingale all spring through,
  O swallow, sister, O changing swallow,
All spring through till the spring be done,
  Clothed with the light of the night on the dew,
Sing, while the hours and the wild birds follow,
  Take flight and follow and find the sun.   *Ib.*

Till life forget and death remember,
  Till thou remember and I forget.   *Ib.*

Thy lord the summer is good to follow,
  And fair the feet of thy lover the spring:
But what wilt thou say to the spring thy lover? *Ib.*

But mine goes forth among sea-gulfs hollow
  To the place of the slaying of Itylus,
The feast of Daulis, the Thracian sea.   *Ib.*

The small slain body, the flower-like face,
  Can I remember if thou forget?   *Ib.*

Thou hast forgotten, O summer swallow,
But the world shall end when I forget.   *Ib.*

Apples of gold for the king's daughter.
             The King's Daughter.

I came as one whose thoughts half linger,
  Half run before;
The youngest to the oldest singer
  That England bore.
      In Memory of Walter Savage Landor.

O father of all of us, Paian, Apollo,
  Destroyer and healer, hear!   *The Last Oracle.*

God by God goes out, discrowned and disanointed,
But the soul stands fast that gave them shape and
  speech.   *Ib.*

Ah, yet would God this flesh of mine might be
Where air might wash and long leaves cover me;
Where tides of grass break into foam of flowers,
Or where the wind's feet shine along the sea.
      Laus Veneris.

Until God loosen over sea and land
The thunder of the trumpets of the night.   *Ib.*

Let us go hence, my songs; she will not hear.
Let us go hence together without fear.
      A Leave-taking.

But God, if a God there be, is the substance of men
  which is man.   *Hymn of Man.*

Glory to Man in the highest! for Man is the master
  of things.   *Ib.*

If love were what the rose is,
  And I were like the leaf,
Our lives would grow together
  In sad or singing weather.   *A Match.*

If you were thrall to sorrow,
  And I were page to joy.   *Ib.*

If you were April's lady,
  And I were lord in May.   *Ib.*

If you were queen of pleasure,
  And I were king of pain.   *Ib.*

But you would have felt my soul in a kiss,
  And known that once if I loved you well;
And I would have given my soul for this
  To burn for ever in burning hell. *Les Noyades.*

Ask nothing more of me, sweet;
  All I can give you I give.
Heart of my heart, were it more,
  More would be laid at your feet:
Love that should help you to live,
  Song that should spur you to soar. *The Oblation.*

I turn to thee as some green afternoon
Turns toward sunset, and is loth to die;
Ah God, ah God, that day should be so soon!
      In the Orchard.

For a day and a night Love sang to us, played with us,
  Folded us round from the dark and the light;
And our hearts were fulfilled with the music he made
  with us,
Made with our hands and our lips while he stayed
  with us,
  Stayed in mid passage his pinions from flight
    For a day and a night.   *At Parting.*

The world has no such flowers in any land,
And no such pearl in any gulf the sea,
As any babe on any mother's knee. *Pelagius.*

I have lived long enough, having seen one thing, that
  love hath an end;
Goddess and maiden and queen, be near me now and
  befriend.   *Hymn to Proserpine.*

Yea, is not even Apollo, with hair and harpstring of
  gold,
A bitter God to follow, a beautiful God to behold?
I am sick of singing: the bays burn deep and chafe:
  I am fain
To rest a little from praise and grievous pleasure and
  pain.   *Ib.*

Wilt thou yet take all, Galilean? but these thou shalt
  not take,
The laurel, the palms and the paean, the breasts of
  the nymphs in the brake;
Breasts more soft than a dove's, that tremble with
  tenderer breath;
And all the wings of the Loves, and all the joy before
  death.   *Ib.*

For no man under the sky lives twice, outliving his
  day.   *Ib.*

Thou hast conquered, O pale Galilean; the world has
  grown grey from Thy breath;
We have drunken of things Lethean, and fed on the
  fullness of death.
Laurel is green for a season, and love is sweet for a
  day;
But love grows bitter with treason, and laurel outlives
  not May.   *Ib.*

For the old faiths loosen and fall, the new years ruin
  and rend.   *Ib.*

O ghastly glories of saints, dead limbs of gibbeted
  Gods!   *Ib.*

Impelled of invisible tides, and fulfilled of unspeakable things.   *Ib.*

All ye as a wind shall go by, as a fire shall ye pass and
  be past;
Ye are Gods, and behold, ye shall die, and the waves
  be upon you at last.   *Ib.*

Though the feet of thine high priests tread where thy
  lords and our forefathers trod,
Though these that were Gods are dead, and thou
  being dead art a God,
Though before thee the throned Cytherean be fallen,
  and hidden her head,
Yet thy kingdom shall pass, Galilean, thy dead shall
  go down to thee dead.   *Ib.*

As the deep dim soul of a star.   *Ib.*

A little soul for a little bears up this corpse which is
  man.   *Ib.*

Love alone, with yearning
  Heart for astrolabe,
Takes the star's height, burning
  O'er the babe.   *A Rhyme.*

Say, was not this thy Passion, to foreknow
In death's worst hour the works of Christian men?
    On the Russian Persecution of the Jews.

In the heart is the prey for gods,
Who crucify hearts, not hands.
     Satia te Sanguine.

Good hap to the fresh fierce weather,
   The quiver and beat of the sea!
While three men hold together,
   The kingdoms are less by three.
                    A Song in Time of Order 1852.

They have tied the world in a tether,
   They have bought over God with a fee.   *Ib.*

When the devil's riddle is mastered
And the galley-bench creaks with a Pope,
We shall see Buonaparte the bastard
Kick heels with his throat in a rope.   *Ib.*

Had you loved me once, as you have not loved;
Had the chance been with us that has not been.
                    The Triumph of Time.

I have put my days and dreams out of mind,
Days that are over, dreams that are done.   *Ib.*

The strong sea-daisies feast on the sun.   *Ib.*

Who swims in sight of the great third wave
That never a swimmer shall cross or climb.   *Ib.*

A broken blossom, a ruined rhyme.   *Ib.*

I had wrung life dry for your lips to drink,
Broken it up for your daily bread.   *Ib.*

                    Content you;
The gate is strait; I shall not be there.   *Ib.*

I will go back to the great sweet mother,
Mother and lover of men, the sea.
I will go down to her, I and no other,
Close with her, kiss her and mix her with me.   *Ib.*

I shall sleep, and move with the moving ships,
Change as the winds change, veer in the tide.   *Ib.*

There lived a singer in France of old
By the tideless dolorous midland sea.
In a land of sand and ruin and gold
There shone one woman, and none but she.   *Ib.*

                    In heaven,
If I cry to you then, will you hear or know?   *Ib.*

One the last flower of Catholic love, that grows
Amid bare thorns their only thornless rose.
                    Two Leaders.

Sweet red splendid kissing mouth.
                    Translations from Villon.
                    Complaint of the fair Armouress.

There's no good girl's lip out of Paris.
                    Ib. Ballad of the Women of Paris.

JOHN ADDINGTON SYMONDS

1840–1893

These things shall be! A loftier race
Than e'er the world hath known shall rise,
With flame of freedom in their souls,
And light of knowledge in their eyes.   *Hymn.*

JOSEPH TABRAR

19th cent.

In over a year and a half,
I've only sung it once,
And I don't suppose I shall sing it again
For months and months and months.
                    For Months and Months and Months.

ROBERT TANNAHILL

1774–1810

When gloamin' treads the heels o' day,
And birds sit courin' on the spray,
Alang the flow'ry hedge I stray,
To meet mine ain dear somebody.
                    Songs and Poems (1911), Mine ain dear Somebody.

NAHUM TATE

1652–1715

AND

NICHOLAS BRADY

1659–1726

To the hills and the vales,
   To the rocks and the mountains,
To the musical groves
   And the cool shady fountains,
Let the triumphs of Love,
   And of Beauty be shown!
Go revel, ye Cupids,
   The day is your own.
                    Dido and Æneas, Act I (*By Nahum Tate*).

Take a bowsey short leave of your nymphs on the
      shore,
   And silence their mourning
   With vows of returning,
Though never intending to visit them more.
                    Ib. Act III.

As pants the hart for cooling streams
   When heated in the chase.
                    *New Version of the Psalms (1696). As Pants
                    the Hart.*

Through all the changing scenes of life.
                    Ib. Through all the Changing.

Fear Him, ye saints, and you will then
   Have nothing else to fear.   *Ib.*

While shepherds watch'd their flocks by night,
All seated on the ground,
The Angel of the Lord came down,
And glory shone around.

'Fear not,' said he, for mighty dread
Had seized their troubled mind;
'Glad tidings of great joy I bring
To you and all mankind.'
                    *Supplement to the New Version of the Psalms
                    (1700). While Shepherds Watched.*

ANN TAYLOR

1782–1866

AND

JANE TAYLOR

1783–1827

I thank the goodness and the grace
   Which on my birth have smiled,
And made me, in these Christian days,
   A happy English child.
                    Hymns for Infant Minds, 1. *A Child's Hymn
                    of Praise.*

O that it were my chief delight
    To do the things I ought!
Then let me try with all my might
    To mind what I am taught.
           Ib. 18. *For a Very Little Child.*

'Tis a *credit* to any good girl to be neat,
    But quite a *disgrace* to be fine.
        *Hymns for Sunday Schools. The Folly
        of Finery.*

Who ran to help me when I fell,
And would some pretty story tell,
Or kiss the place to make it well?
        My Mother.
    Original Poems. My Mother. (By Ann T.)

How pleasant it is, at the end of the day,
    No follies to have to repent;
But reflect on the past, and be able to say,
    That my time has been properly spent.
        *Rhymes for the Nursery. The Way to be
        Happy. (By Jane T.)*

Twinkle, twinkle, little star,
How I wonder what you are!
Up above the world so high,
Like a diamond in the sky!
        Ib. The Star. (By Jane T.)

BAYARD TAYLOR
1825–1875

Till the sun grows cold,
    And the stars are old,
And the leaves of the Judgment Book unfold.
        Bedouin Song. Refrain.

SIR HENRY TAYLOR
1800–1886

Quoth tongue of neither maid nor wife
    To heart of neither wife nor maid—
Lead we not here a jolly life
    Betwixt the shine and shade?

Quoth heart of neither maid nor wife
    To tongue of neither wife nor maid—
Thou wagg'st, but I am worn with strife,
    And feel like flowers that fade.
        Philip Van Artevelde, Pt. II. v. i. i.

JEREMY TAYLOR
1613–1667

Too quick a sense of a constant infelicity.
        Holy Dying, ch. 1, sect. v.

Every school-boy knows it.
        On the Real Presence, sect. v, par. 1.

The union of hands and hearts.
        Sermons. The Marriage Ring, pt. i.

JOHN TAYLOR
1580–1653

'Tis a mad world, my masters.
        Western Voyage, l. 1.

P 3

SIR WILLIAM TEMPLE
1628–1699

When all is done, human life is, at the greatest and
    the best, but like a froward child, that must be
    play'd with and humoured a little to keep it quiet
    till it falls asleep, and then the care is over.
        Essay on Poetry, ad fin.

ALFRED, LORD TENNYSON
1809–1892

The noblest answer unto such,
    Is kindly silence when they brawl.
        After-Thought, v.

For nothing worthy proving can be proven,
    Nor yet disproven.   *The Ancient Sage*, l. 66.

Cleave ever to the sunnier side of doubt.   *Ib.* l. 68.

The rabbit fondles his own harmless face.
        Aylmer's Field, l. 851.

Her arms across her breast she laid;
    She was more fair than words can say:
Bare-footed came the beggar maid
    Before the king Cophetua.
In robe and crown the king stept down,
    To meet and greet her on her way;
'It is no wonder,' said the lords,
    'She is more beautiful than day.'
        The Beggar Maid.

As shines the moon in clouded skies,
    She in her poor attire was seen:
One praised her ankles, one her eyes,
    One her dark hair and lovesome mien.
So sweet a face, such angel grace,
    In all that land had never been:
Cophetua sware a royal oath:
    'This beggar maid shall be my queen!'   *Ib.*

Break, break, break,
    On thy cold gray stones, O Sea!
And I would that my tongue could utter
    The thoughts that arise in me.

O well for the fisherman's boy,
    That he shouts with his sister at play!
O well for the sailor lad,
    That he sings in his boat on the bay!

And the stately ships go on
    To their haven under the hill;
But O for the touch of a vanish'd hand,
    And the sound of a voice that is still!

Break, break, break,
    At the foot of the crags, O Sea!
But the tender grace of a day that is dead
    Will never come back to me.
        Break, Break, Break.

A happy bridesmaid makes a happy bride.
        The Bridesmaid, l. 4.

For men may come and men may go,
    But I go on for ever.   *The Brook*, l. 33.

Here and there a lusty trout,
    And here and there a grayling.   *Ib.* l. 57.

That petitionary grace
Of Sweet Seventeen.   *Ib.* l. 112.

The Lord let the house of a brute to the soul of a man,
  And the man said, 'Am I your debtor?'
And the Lord—'Not yet: but make it as clean as you can,
  And then I will let you a better.'   *By an Evolutionist.*

He that only rules by terror
  Doeth grievous wrong.   *The Captain*, l. 1.

Slav, Teuton, Kelt, I count them all
  My friends and brother souls,
With all the peoples, great and small,
  That wheel between the poles.
    Epilogue to The Charge of the Heavy Brigade, l. 18.

The song that nerves a nation's heart,
Is in itself a deed.   *Ib.* l. 81.

Half a league, half a league,
Half a league onward.
        The Charge of the Light Brigade.

'Forward, the Light Brigade!'
Was there a man dismay'd?   *Ib.*

Some one had blunder'd.   *Ib.*

Their's not to make reply,
Their's not to reason why,
Their's but to do and die:
Into the valley of Death
Rode the six hundred.   *Ib.*

Cannon to right of them
Cannon to left of them,
Cannon in front of them
  Volley'd and thunder'd.   *Ib.*

Into the jaws of Death,
Into the mouth of Hell.   *Ib.*

When can their glory fade?
O the wild charge they made!
All the world wonder'd.   *Ib.*

        The golden guess
Is morning-star to the full round of truth.
                          Columbus, l. 42.

Come not, when I am dead,
  To drop thy foolish tears upon my grave,
To trample round my fallen head,
  And vex the unhappy dust thou wouldst not save.
        Come Not, When I Am Dead, i.

Sunset and evening star,
  And one clear call for me!
And may there be no moaning of the bar,
  When I put out to sea,

But such a tide as moving seems asleep,
  Too full for sound and foam,
When that which drew from out the boundless deep
  Turns again home.

Twilight and evening bell,
  And after that the dark!
And may there be no sadness of farewell,
  When I embark;

For tho' from out our bourne of Time and Place
  The flood may bear me far,
I hope to see my Pilot face to face
  When I have crost the bar.   *Crossing the Bar.*

O Love what hours were thine and mine,
In lands of palm and southern pine;
  In lands of palm, of orange-blossom,
Of olive, aloe, and maize and vine.   *The Daisy*, i.

A mount of marble, a hundred spires!   *Ib.* xv.

Gray metropolis of the North. [Edinburgh] *Ib.* xxvi.

This proverb flashes thro' his head,
'The many fail: the one succeeds.'
              The Day-dream. The Arrival, ii.

But dallied with his golden chain,
  And, smiling, put the question by.
                        Ib. The Revival.

And on her lover's arm she leant,
  And round her waist she felt it fold,
And far across the hills they went
  In that new world which is the old.
                      Ib. The Departure, i.

And o'er the hills, and far away
  Beyond their utmost purple rim,
Beyond the night, across the day,
  Thro' all the world she follow'd him.   *Ib.* iv.

And is there any moral shut
  Within the bosom of the rose?   *Ib. Moral*, i.

But any man that walks the mead,
  In bud or blade, or bloom, may find,
According as his humours lead,
  A meaning suited to his mind.   *Ib.* ii.

Wearing his wisdom lightly, like the fruit
Which in our winter woodland looks a flower.
                          A Dedication.

And ever upon the topmost roof our banner of England blew.   *The Defence of Lucknow.*

Out of the deep, my child, out of the deep.
                        De Profundis, i, l. 1.

I read, before my eyelids dropt their shade,
  'The Legend of Good Women', long ago
Sung by the morning star of song, who made
  His music heard below.
              A Dream of Fair Women, l. i.

The spacious times of great Elizabeth.   *Ib.* l. 7.

A daughter of the gods, divinely tall,
  And most divinely fair.   *Ib.* l. 87.

A queen, with swarthy cheeks and bold black eyes,
  Brow-bound with burning gold.   *Ib.* l. 127.

He clasps the crag with crooked hands;
Close to the sun in lonely lands,
Ring'd with the azure world, he stands.
The wrinkled sea beneath him crawls;
He watches from his mountain walls,
And like a thunderbolt he falls.   *The Eagle.*

Once more the Heavenly Power
Makes all things new,
And domes the red-plow'd hills
With loving blue;
The blackbirds have their wills,
The throstles too.   *Early Spring*, i.

The curate; he was fatter than his cure.
                          Edwin Morris, l. 15.

God made the woman for the man,
And for the good and increase of the world. *Ib.* l. 50.

  Slight Sir Robert with his watery smile
And educated whisker.   *Ib.* l. 128.

And when they buried him the little port
Had seldom seen a costlier funeral.   *Enoch Arden.*

Barbarous experiment, barbarous hexameters.
> *Experiments. In quantity. On Translation of*
> *Homer.*

O mighty-mouth'd inventor of harmonies,
O skill'd to sing of Time or Eternity,
   God-gifted organ-voice of England,
     Milton, a name to resound for ages.
> *Ib. Milton. Alcaics.*

All that bowery loneliness,
The brooks of Eden mazily murmuring.   *Ib.*

O you chorus of indolent reviewers.
> *Ib. Milton. Hendecasyllabics.*

A tiny poem
All composed in a metre of Catullus,
All in quantity, careful of my motion,
Like the skater on ice that hardly bears him.   *Ib.*

The mellow lin-lan-lone of evening bells.
> *Far-Far-Away.*

O Love, O fire! once he drew
With one long kiss my whole soul thro'
My lips, as sunlight drinketh dew.   *Fatima,* iii.

Read my little fable:
  He that runs may read.
Most can raise the flowers now,
  For all have got the seed.   *The Flower,* v.

Move onward, leading up the golden year.

Flower in the crannied wall,
I pluck you out of the crannies,
I hold you here, root and all, in my hand,
Little flower—but *if* I could understand
What you are, root and all, and all in all,
I should know what God and man is.
> *Flower in the Crannied Wall.*

More black than ashbuds in the front of March.
> *The Gardener's Daughter,* l. 28.

A sight to make an old man young.   *Ib.* l. 140.

Then she rode forth, clothed on with chastity.
> *Godiva,* l. 53.

With twelve great shocks of sound, the shameless
  noon
Was clash'd and hammer'd from a hundred towers.
> *Ib.* l. 74.

Ah! when shall all men's good
Be each man's rule, and universal Peace
Lie like a shaft of light across the land?
> *The Golden Year,* l. 47.

Thro' all the circle of the golden year.   *Ib.* l. 51.

That a lie which is all a lie may be met and fought
  with outright,
But a lie which is part a truth is a harder matter to
  fight.   *The Grandmother,* viii.

That man's the true Conservative
Who lops the moulder'd branch away.
> *Hands All Round,* i.

Pray God our greatness may not fail
Thro' craven fears of being great.   *Ib.* iii.

Gigantic daughter of the West,
We drink to thee across the flood . . .
For art thou not of British blood?
> *Ib.* iv. [In original version, published in *The*
> *Examiner,* 7 Feb. 1852.]

Senlac! Sanguelac,
The lake of Blood!   *Harold,* iii. i.

Sanguelac! Sanguelac! the arrow! the arrow!   *Ib.*

Speak to Him thou for He hears, and Spirit with
  Spirit can meet—
Closer is He than breathing, and nearer than hands
  and feet.   *Higher Pantheism,* vi.

Wearing the white flower of a blameless life,
Before a thousand peering littlenesses,
In that fierce light which beats upon a throne,
And blackens every blot.
> *The Idylls of the King,* Dedication, l. 24

Man's word is God in man.
> *Ib. The Coming of Arthur,* l. 132.

A doubtful throne is ice on summer seas. *Ib.* l. 247.

Clothed in white samite, mystic, wonderful.
> *Ib.* l. 284, and *The Passing of Arthur,* l. 199.
Rain, rain, and sun! a rainbow in the sky!
A young man will be wiser by and by;
An old man's wit may wander ere he die. *Ib.* l. 402.

From the great deep to the great deep he goes.
> *Ib.* l. 410.

Blow trumpet, for the world is white with May.
> *Ib.* l. 481.

Live pure, speak true, right wrong, follow the King—
Else, wherefore born?
> *Ib. Gareth and Lynette,* l. 117.

The city is built
To music, therefore never built at all,
And therefore built for ever.   *Ib.* l. 272.

Lightly was her slender nose
Tip-tilted like the petal of a flower.   *Ib.* l. 576.

Lead, and I follow.   *Ib.* l. 726.

O purblind race of miserable men,
How many among us at this very hour
Do forge a lifelong trouble for ourselves,
By taking true for false, or false for true!
> *Ib. Geraint and Enid,* l. 1.

But o'er her meek eyes came a happy mist
Like that which kept the heart of Eden green.
Before the useful trouble of the rain.   *Ib.* l. 769.

The world will not believe a man repents:
And this wise world of ours is mainly right.
> *Ib.* l. 900.

Too late, too late! ye cannot enter now.
> *Ib. Guinevere,* l. 168.

For manners are not idle, but the fruit
Of loyal nature, and of noble mind.   *Ib.* l. 333.

The children born of thee are sword and fire,
Red ruin, and the breaking up of laws.   *Ib.* l. 422.

To reverence the King, as if he were
Their conscience, and their conscience as their King,
To break the heathen and uphold the Christ,
To ride abroad redressing human wrongs,
To speak no slander, no, nor listen to it,
To honour his own word as if his God's. *Ib.* l. 465.

To love one maiden only, cleave to her,
And worship her by years of noble deeds,
Until they won her; for indeed I knew
Of no more subtle master under heaven
Than is the maiden passion for a maid,
Not only to keep down the base in man,
But teach high thought, and amiable words
And courtliness, and the desire of fame,
And love of truth, and all that makes a man.

> *The Idylls of the King. Guinevere*, l. 472.

Our fair father Christ. *Ib.* l. 559.

Hereafter in that world where all are pure
We two may meet before high God, and thou
Wilt spring to me, and claim me thine, and know
I am thine husband—not a smaller soul,
Nor Lancelot, nor another. *Ib.* l. 560.

> He never mocks,
For mockery is the fume of little hearts. *Ib.* l. 627.

I thought I could not breathe in that fine air
That pure severity of perfect light—
I yearn'd for warmth and colour which I found
In Lancelot. *Ib.* l. 640.

It was my duty to have loved the highest:
It surely was my profit had I known:
It would have been my pleasure had I seen.
We needs must love the highest when we see it,
Not Lancelot, nor another. *Ib.* l. 652.

To where beyond these voices there is peace.
> *Ib.* l. 692.

For good ye are and bad, and like to coins,
Some true, some light, but every one of you
Stamp'd with the image of the King.
> *Ib. The Holy Grail*, l. 25.

The cup, the cup itself, from which our Lord
Drank at the last sad supper with his own. *Ib.* l. 46.

God make thee good as thou art beautiful. *Ib.* l. 136.

For when was Lancelot wanderingly lewd?
> *Ib.* l. 148.

I, maiden, round thee, maiden, bind my belt.
> *Ib.* l. 159.

> Ye follow wandering fires
Lost in the quagmire! *Ib.* l. 319.

This madness has come on us for our sins.
> *Ib.* l. 356.

And lifting up mine eyes, found myself
Alone, and in a land of sand and thorns. *Ib.* l. 374.

I saw the fiery face as of a child
That smote itself into the bread, and went.
> *Ib.* l. 473.

And in the strength of this I rode,
Shattering all evil customs everywhere. *Ib.* l. 483.

I will be deafer than the blue-eyed cat,
And thrice as blind as any noon-tide owl,
To holy virgins in their ecstasies,
Henceforward. *Ib.* l. 865.

So spake the King: I knew not all he meant.
> *Ib.* l. 919.

Elaine the fair, Elaine the loveable,
Elaine, the lily maid of Astolat.
> *Ib. Lancelot and Elaine*, l. 1.

> To me
He is all fault who hath no fault at all:
For who loves me must have a touch of earth.
> *Ib.* l. 131.

> In me there dwells
No greatness, save it be some far-off touch
Of greatness to know well I am not great. *Ib.* l. 447.

I know not if I know what true love is,
But if I know, then, if I love not him,
I know there is none other I can love. *Ib.* l. 672.

The shackles of an old love straiten'd him,
His honour rooted in dishonour stood,
And faith unfaithful kept him falsely true. *Ib.* l. 870.

Sweet is true love tho' given in vain, in vain;
And sweet is death who puts an end to pain.
> *Ib.* l. 1000.

> Never yet
Was noble man but made ignoble talk.
He makes no friend who never made a foe.
> *Ib.* l. 1080.

Our bond is not the bond of man and wife.
> *Ib.* l. 1199.

'Forgive me; mine was jealousy in love.'
He answer'd with his eyes upon the ground,
'That is love's curse; pass on, my Queen, forgiven.'
> *Ib.* l. 1340.

Free love—free field—we love but while we may.
> *Ib. The Last Tournament*, l. 281.

The dirty nurse, Experience, in her kind
Hath foul'd me. *Ib.* l. 317.

The greater man, the greater courtesy. *Ib.* l. 628.

The Ptarmigan that whitens ere his hour
Woos his own end. *Ib.* l. 692.

Our hoard is little, but our hearts are great.
> *Ib. The Marriage of Geraint*, l. 352.

For man is man and master of his fate. *Ib.* l. 355.

Hark, by the bird's song ye may learn the nest.
> *Ib.* l. 359.

They take the rustic murmur of their bourg
For the great wave that echoes round the world.
> *Ib.* l. 419.

Mother, a maiden is a tender thing,
And best by her that bore her understood.
> *Ib.* l. 510.

Brave hearts and clean! and yet—God guide them—
young. *Ib. Merlin and Vivien*, l. 29.

As, on a dull day in an ocean-cave,
The blind wave, feeling round his long sea-hall
In silence. *Ib.* l. 229.

Unfaith in aught is want of faith in all. *Ib.* l. 387.

It is the little rift within the lute,
That by and by will make the music mute,
And ever widening slowly silence all. *Ib.* l. 388.

And trust me not at all or all in all. *Ib.* l. 396.

Lo now, what hearts have men! they never mount
As high as woman in her selfless mood. *Ib.* l. 440.

Man dreams of fame while woman wakes to love.
> *Ib.* l. 458.

With this for motto, 'Rather use than fame'.
The Idylls of the King.
Merlin and Vivien, l. 478.

Where blind and naked Ignorance
Delivers brawling judgments, unashamed,
On all things all day long.   *Ib.* l. 662.

But every page having an ample marge,
And every marge enclosing in the midst
A square of text that looks a little blot.   *Ib.* l. 667.

And none can read the text, not even I;
And none can read the comment but myself.
Ib. l. 679.

Or some black wether of St. Satan's fold.
Ib. l. 748.

O selfless man and stainless gentleman!   *Ib.* l. 790.

Defaming and defacing, till she left
Not even Lancelot brave, nor Galahad clean.
Ib. l. 802.

For men at most differ as Heaven and Earth,
But women, worst and best, as Heaven and Hell.
Ib. l. 812.

Face-flatterer and backbiter are the same.   *Ib.*l. 822.

And the thicket closed
Behind her, and the forest echo'd 'fool'.   *Ib.* l. 971.

O great and sane and simple race of brutes
That own no lust because they have no law!
Ib. Pelleas and Ettarre, l. 471.

I found Him in the shining of the stars,
I mark'd Him in the flowering of His fields,
But in His ways with men I find Him not.
Ib. The Passing of Arthur, l. 9.

Why is all around us here
As if some lesser god had made the world,
But had not force to shape it as he would?   *Ib.* l. 13.

So all day long the noise of battle roll'd
Among the mountains by the winter sea.   *Ib.* l. 170.

On one side lay the Ocean, and on one
Lay a great water, and the moon was full.
Ib. l. 179.

Authority forgets a dying king.   *Ib.* l. 289.

Clothed with his breath, and looking, as he walk'd,
Larger than human on the frozen hills.
He heard the deep behind him, and a cry
Before.   *Ib.* l. 350.

When every morning brought a noble chance,
And every chance brought out a noble knight.
Ib. l. 398.

Among new men, strange faces, other minds.
Ib. l. 406.

And slowly answer'd Arthur from the barge:
'The old order changeth, yielding place to new,
And God fulfils himself in many ways,
Lest one good custom should corrupt the world.'
Ib. l. 407.

If thou shouldst never see my face again,
Pray for my soul. More things are wrought by prayer
Than this world dreams of. Wherefore, let thy voice
Rise like a fountain for me night and day.
Ib. l. 414.

For so the whole round earth is every way
Bound by gold chains about the feet of God.
Ib. l. 422.

I am going a long way
With these thou seest—if indeed I go
(For all my mind is clouded with a doubt)—
To the island-valley of Avilion;
Where falls not hail, or rain, or any snow,
Nor ever wind blows loudly; but it lies
Deep-meadow'd, happy, fair with orchard lawns
And bowery hollows crown'd with summer sea,
Where I will heal me of my grievous wound.
Ib. l. 424.

Like some full-breasted swan
That, fluting a wild carol ere her death,
Ruffles her pure cold plume, and takes the flood
With swarthy webs.   *Ib.* l. 434.

Believing where we cannot prove.
In Memoriam, prologue. [The numbering of
the Cantos follows that of the latest edition,
and includes the additional Canto No.
xxxix, first published in 1869.]

Thou madest man, he knows not why,
He thinks he was not made to die;
And thou hast made him: thou art just.   *Ib.*

Our little systems have their day;
They have their day and cease to be:
They are but broken lights of thee,
And thou, O Lord, art more than they.   *Ib.*

Let knowledge grow from more to more,
But more of reverence in us dwell;
That mind and soul, according well,
May make one music as before.   *Ib.*

I held it truth, with him who sings
To one clear harp in divers tones,
That men may rise on stepping-stones
Of their dead selves to higher things.   *Ib.* i.

Who changest not in any gale,
Nor branding summer suns avail
To touch thy thousand years of gloom.   *Ib.* ii.

For words, like Nature, half reveal
And half conceal the Soul within.   *Ib.* v.

But, for the unquiet heart and brain,
A use in measured language lies;
The sad mechanic exercise,
Like dull narcotics, numbing pain.   *Ib.*

And common is the commonplace,
And vacant chaff well meant for grain.   *Ib.* vi.

Never morning wore
To evening, but some heart did break.   *Ib.*

His heavy-shotted hammock-shroud
Drops in his vast and wandering grave.   *Ib.*

Dark house, by which once more I stand
Here in the long unlovely street,
Doors, where my heart was used to beat
So quickly, waiting for a hand.   *Ib.* vii.

More than my brothers are to me.   *Ib.* ix.

Or where the kneeling hamlet drains
The chalice of the grapes of God.   *Ib.* x.

The last red leaf is whirl'd away,
The rooks are blown about the skies.   *Ib.* xv.

[429]

Thou comest, much wept for: such a breeze
  Compell'd thy canvas.   *In Memoriam*, xvii.

And from his ashes may be made
The violet of his native land.   *Ib.* xviii.

There twice a day the Severn fills;
  The salt sea-water passes by,
  And hushes half the babbling Wye,
And makes a silence in the hills.   *Ib.* xix.

I do but sing because I must,
And pipe but as the linnets sing.   *Ib.* xxi.

The Shadow cloak'd from head to foot,
Who keeps the keys of all the creeds.   *Ib.* xxiii.

And Thought leapt out to wed with Thought
Ere Thought could wed itself with Speech.   *Ib.*

I envy not in any moods
  The captive void of noble rage,
  The linnet born within the cage,
That never knew the summer woods.   *Ib.* xxvii.

'Tis better to have loved and lost
Than never to have loved at all.   *Ib.*

The time draws near the birth of Christ. *Ib.* xxviii.

'Where wert thou, brother, those four days?'
  There lives no record of reply,
  Which telling what it is to die
Had surely added praise to praise.

From every house the neighbours met,
  The streets were fill'd with joyful sound,
  A solemn gladness even crown'd
The purple brows of Olivet.

Behold a man raised up by Christ!
  The rest remaineth unreveal'd;
  He told it not; or something seal'd
The lips of that Evangelist.   *Ib.* xxxi.

Her eyes are homes of silent prayer.   *Ib.* xxxii.

Leave thou thy sister when she prays,
  Her early Heaven, her happy views;
  Nor thou with shadow'd hint confuse
A life that leads melodious days.   *Ib.* xxxiii.

And so the Word had breath, and wrought
  With human hands the creed of creeds
  In loveliness of perfect deeds,
More strong than all poetic thought.   *Ib.* xxxvi.

Short swallow-flights of song, that dip
  Their wings in tears, and skim away.   *Ib.* xlviii.

And Time, a maniac scattering dust,
And Life, a Fury slinging flame.   *Ib.* l.

Do we indeed desire the dead
  Should still be near us at our side?
  Is there no baseness we would hide?
No inner vileness that we dread?   *Ib.* li.

How many a father have I seen,
  A sober man, among his boys,
  Whose youth was full of foolish noise.   *Ib.* liii.

Hold thou the good: define it well:
  For fear divine Philosophy
  Should push beyond her mark, and be
Procuress to the Lords of Hell.   *Ib.*

Oh yet we trust that somehow good
  Will be the final goal of ill.   *Ib.* liv.

That nothing walks with aimless feet;
  That not one life shall be destroy'd,
  Or cast as rubbish to the void,
When God hath made the pile complete;

That not a worm is cloven in vain;
  That not a moth with vain desire
  Is shrivell'd in a fruitless fire,
Or but subserves another's gain.   *Ib.*

      But what am I?
  An infant crying in the night:
  An infant crying for the light:
And with no language but a cry.   *Ib.*

So careful of the type she seems,
So careless of the single life.   *Ib.* lv.

    The great world's altar-stairs
That slope thro' darkness up to God.   *Ib.*

Nature, red in tooth and claw.   *Ib.* lvi.

    Dragons of the prime,
  That tare each other in their slime,
Were mellow music match'd with him.   *Ib.*

Peace; come away: the song of woe
  Is after all an earthly song:
  Peace; come away: we do him wrong
To sing so wildly: let us go.   *Ib.* lvii.

The passing of the sweetest soul
That ever look'd with human eyes.   *Ib.*

O Sorrow, wilt thou live with me
No casual mistress, but a wife.   *Ib.* lix.

As some divinely gifted man,
  Whose life in low estate began
And on a simple village green;

Who breaks his birth's invidious bar,
  And grasps the skirts of happy chance,
  And breasts the blows of circumstance,
And grapples with his evil star.   *Ib.* lxiv.

Yet feels, as in a pensive dream,
  When all his active powers are still,
  A distant dearness in the hill,
A secret sweetness in the stream.   *Ib.*

So many worlds, so much to do,
  So little done, such things to be.   *Ib.* lxxiii.

      Death has made
His darkness beautiful with thee.   *Ib.* lxxiv.

And round thee with the breeze of song
To stir a little dust of praise.   *Ib.* lxxv.

O last regret, regret can die!   *Ib.* lxxviii.

Laburnums, dropping-wells of fire.   *Ib.* lxxxiii.

God's finger touch'd him, and he slept.   *Ib.* lxxxv.

I, the divided half of such
A friendship as had master'd Time.   *Ib.*

Dusty purlieus of the law.   *Ib.* lxxxix.

The hard heir strides about their lands,
And will not yield them for a day.   *Ib.* xc.

When rosy plumelets tuft the larch,
  And rarely pipes the mounted thrush;
  Or underneath the barren bush
Flits by the sea-blue bird of March.   *Ib.* xci.

You tell me, doubt is Devil-born.
In Memoriam, xcvi.

There lives more faith in honest doubt,
Believe me, than in half the creeds.   *Ib.*

Their meetings made December June,
Their every parting was to die.   *Ib.* xcvii.

He seems so near and yet so far.   *Ib.*

Ring out, wild bells, to the wild sky.   *Ib.* cvi.

Ring out the old, ring in the new,
 Ring, happy bells, across the snow:
 The year is going, let him go;
Ring out the false, ring in the true.   *Ib.*

Ring out the feud of rich and poor.   *Ib.*

Ring out a slowly dying cause,
 And ancient forms of party strife;
 Ring in the nobler modes of life,
With sweeter manners, purer laws.

Ring out the want, the care, the sin,
 The faithless coldness of the times;
 Ring out, ring out my mournful rhymes,
But ring the fuller minstrel in.

Ring out false pride in place and blood,
 The civic slander and the spite;
 Ring in the love of truth and right,
Ring in the common love of good.

Ring out old shapes of foul disease;
 Ring out the narrowing lust of gold;
 Ring out the thousand wars of old,
Ring in the thousand years of peace.

Ring in the valiant man and free,
 The larger heart, the kindlier hand;
 Ring out the darkness of the land;
Ring in the Christ that is to be.   *Ib.*

'Tis held that sorrow makes us wise,
Whatever wisdom sleep with thee.   *Ib.* cviii.

Not the schoolboy heat,
The blind hysterics of the Celt.   *Ib.* cix.

And thus he bore without abuse
 The grand old name of gentleman,
 Defamed by every charlatan,
And soil'd with all ignoble use.   *Ib.* cxi.

Now fades the last long streak of snow
 Now burgeons every maze of quick
 About the flowering squares and thick
By ashen roots the violets blow.   *Ib.* cxv.

And drown'd in yonder living blue
The lark becomes a sightless song.   *Ib.* cxv.

But trust that those we call the dead
 Are breathers of an ampler day
 For ever nobler ends.   *Ib.* cxviii.

There, where the long street roars, hath been
The stillness of the central sea.   *Ib.* cxxiii.

And all is well, tho' faith and form
 Be sunder'd in the night of fear.   *Ib.* cxxvii.

The red fool-fury of the Seine.   *Ib.* cxxvii.

Wearing all that weight
Of learning lightly like a flower.
Ib. Conclusion, st. x.

One God, one law, one element,
 And one far-off divine event,
To which the whole creation moves.   *Ib.* st. xxxvi.

All along the valley, stream that flashest white.
In the Valley of Cauteretz.

The voice of the dead was a living voice to me.   *Ib.*

God gives us love. Something to love
 He lends us; but, when love is grown
To ripeness, that on which it throve
 Falls off, and love is left alone.   *To J. S.* iv.

A simple maiden in her flower
 Is worth a hundred coats-of-arms.
Lady Clara Vere de Vere.

Her manners had not that repose
 Which stamps the caste of Vere de Vere.   *Ib.* v.

From yon blue heavens above us bent
The gardener Adam and his wife
 Smile at the claims of long descent.
Howe'er it be, it seems to me,
 'Tis only noble to be good.
Kind hearts are more than coronets,
 And simple faith than Norman blood.   *Ib.* vii.

Oh! teach the orphan-boy to read,
 Or teach the orphan-girl to sew.   *Ib.*

On either side the river lie
Long fields of barley and of rye.
The Lady of Shalott, pt. i.

Willows whiten, aspens quiver,
Little breezes dusk and shiver.   *Ib.*

But who hath seen her wave her hand?
Or at the casement seen her stand?
Or is she known in all the land,
 The Lady of Shalott?   *Ib.*

Only reapers, reaping early
In among the bearded barley,
Hear a song that echoes cheerly
From the river winding clearly
 Down to tower'd Camelot.   *Ib.*

She hath no loyal knight and true,
 The Lady of Shalott.   *Ib.* pt. ii.

Or when the moon was overhead,
Came two young lovers lately wed;
'I am half sick of shadows,' said
 The Lady of Shalott.   *Ib.*

A bow-shot from her bower-eaves,
He rode between the barley-sheaves,
The sun came dazzling thro' the leaves,
And flamed upon the brazen greaves
 Of bold Sir Lancelot.
A red-cross knight for ever kneel'd
To a lady in his shield,
That sparkled on the yellow field,
 Beside remote Shalott.   *Ib.* pt. iii.

All in the blue unclouded weather.   *Ib.*

'Tirra lirra,' by the river
 Sang Sir Lancelot.   *Ib.*

She left the web, she left the loom,
She made three paces thro' the room,
She saw the water-lily bloom,
She saw the helmet and the plume,
 She look'd down to Camelot.
Out flew the web and floated wide;
The mirror crack'd from side to side;
'The curse is come upon me,' cried
 The Lady of Shalott.   *Ib.*

Like some bold seër in a trance,
Seeing all his own mischance—
With a glassy countenance
    Did she look to Camelot.   *Ib.* pt. iv.

Heard a carol, mournful, holy,
Chanted loudly, chanted lowly,
Till her blood was frozen slowly,
And her eyes were darken'd wholly,
    Turn'd to tower'd Camelot.   *Ib.*

Who is this? and what is here?
And in the lighted palace near
Died the sound of royal cheer;
And they cross'd themselves for fear,
    All the knights at Camelot:
But Lancelot mused a little space;
He said, 'She has a lovely face;
God in his mercy lend her grace,
    The Lady of Shalott.'
                           Ib. pt. iv.

Slander, meanest spawn of Hell.   *The Letters.*

Airy, fairy Lilian.   *Lilian.*

Comrades, leave me here a little, while as yet 'tis
    early morn:
Leave me here, and when you want me, sound upon
    your bugle horn.   *Locksley Hall*, l. i.

The fairy tales of science, and the long result of Time.
                           Ib. l. 12.

In the Spring a livelier iris changes on the burnish'd
    dove;
In the Spring a young man's fancy lightly turns to
    thoughts of love.   *Ib.* l. 19.

Love took up the glass of Time, and turn'd it in his
    glowing hands;
Every moment, lightly shaken, ran itself in golden
    sands.

Love took up the harp of Life, and smote on all the
    chords with might;
Smote the chord of Self, that, trembling, pass'd in
    music out of sight.   *Ib.* l. 31.

And our spirits rush'd together at the touching of the
    lips.   *Ib.* l. 38.

As the husband is, the wife is.   *Ib.* l. 47.

He will hold thee, when his passion shall have spent
    its novel force.
Something better than his dog, a little dearer than his
    his horse.   *Ib.* l. 49.

The many-winter'd crow that leads the clanging
    rookery home.   *Ib.* l. 68.

    This is truth the poet sings,
That a sorrow's crown of sorrow is remembering
    happier things.   *Ib.* l. 75.

Like a dog, he hunts in dreams.   *Ib.* l. 79.

With a little hoard of maxims preaching down a
    daughter's heart.   *Ib.* l. 94.

But the jingling of the guinea helps the hurt that
    Honour feels.   *Ib.* l. 105.

Men, my brothers, men the workers, ever reaping
    something new:
That which they have done but earnest of the things
    that they shall do:

For I dipt into the future, far as human eye could see,
Saw the Vision of the world, and all the wonder that
    would be.   *Ib.* l. 117.

Heard the heavens fill with shouting, and there rain'd
    a ghastly dew
From the nations' airy navies grappling in the central
    blue.   *Ib.* l. 123.

In the Parliament of man, the Federation of the
    world.   *Ib.* l. 128.

Science moves, but slowly slowly, creeping on from
    point to point.   *Ib.* l. 134.

Yet I doubt not thro' the ages one increasing purpose
    runs,
And the thoughts of men are widen'd with the process
    of the suns.   *Ib.* l. 137.

Knowledge comes, but wisdom lingers.   *Ib.* l. 143.

I am shamed thro' all my nature to have loved so
    slight a thing.   *Ib.* l. 148.

Woman is the lesser man, and all thy passions,
    match'd with mine,
Are as moonlight unto sunlight, and as water unto
    wine.   *Ib.* l. 151.

I will take some savage woman, she shall rear my
    dusky race.   *Ib.* l. 168.

Not with blinded eyesight poring over miserable
    books.   *Ib.* l. 172.

I the heir of all the ages, in the foremost files of time.
                           Ib. l. 178.

    Forward, forward let us range,
Let the great world spin for ever down the ringing
    grooves of change.   *Ib.* l. 181.

Better fifty years of Europe than a cycle of Cathay.
                           Ib. l. 184.

He is but a landscape-painter,
    And a village maiden she.
                 The Lord of Burleigh, l. 7.

Let us see these handsome houses
    Where the wealthy nobles dwell.   *Ib.* l. 23.

O but she will love him truly!
    He shall have a cheerful home.   *Ib.* l. 37.

Many a gallant gay domestic
    Bows before him at the door.   *Ib.* l. 47.

But he clasp'd her like a lover,
    And he cheer'd her soul with love.
So she strove against her weakness,
    Tho' at times her spirit sank.   *Ib.* l. 67.

And the people loved her much.   *Ib.* l. 76.

But a trouble weigh'd upon her,
    And perplex'd her, night and morn,
With the burthen of an honour
    Unto which she was not born.   *Ib.* l. 77.

             'Oh, that he
Were once more that landscape-painter,
Which did win my heart from me!'   *Ib.* l. 82.

Three fair children first she bore him,
    Then before her time she died.   *Ib.* l. 87.

Weeping, weeping late and early,
    Walking up and pacing down,
Deeply mourn'd the Lord of Burleigh,
    Burleigh-house by Stamford-town.   *Ib.* l. 89.

'Bring the dress and put it on her,
  That she wore when she was wed.' *Ib.* l. 95.

'Courage!' he said, and pointed toward the land.
                                   The Lotos-Eaters.

             A land
In which it seemed always afternoon. *Ib.*

Music that gentlier on the spirit lies,
Than tir'd eyelids upon tir'd eyes.
                          Ib. Choric Song, i.

There is no joy but calm! *Ib.* ii.

          Ah, why
Should life all labour be? *Ib.* iv.

Let us alone. Time driveth onward fast,
  And in a little while our lips are dumb.
Let us alone. What is it that will last?
All things are taken from us, and become
Portions and parcels of the dreadful Past. *Ib.*

The Lotos blooms below the barren peak:
The Lotos blows by every winding creek:
All day the wind breathes low with mellower tone:
Thro' every hollow cave and alley lone,
Round and round the spicy downs the yellow Lotos-
  dust is blown. *Ib.* viii.
          Live and lie reclined
On the hills like Gods together, careless of mankind.
For they lie beside their nectar, and the bolts are
  hurl'd
Far below them in the valleys, and the clouds are
  lightly curl'd
Round their golden houses, girdled with the gleaming
  world. *Ib.*

Surely, surely, slumber is more sweet than toil, the
  shore
Than labour in the deep mid-ocean, wind and wave
  and oar;
Oh rest ye, brother mariners, we will not wander
  more. *Ib.*

Of love that never found his earthly close,
What sequel? Streaming eyes and breaking hearts?
Or all the same as if he had not been?
                          Love and Duty, l. 1.

The long mechanic pacings to and fro,
The set gray life, and apathetic end. *Ib.* l. 17.

Raw Haste, half-sister to Delay.
                          Love thou thy Land, xxiv.

Ruining along the illimitable inane. *Lucretius,* l. 40.

    Nor at all can tell
Whether I mean this day to end myself,
Or lend an ear to Plato where he says,
That men like soldiers may not quit the post
Allotted by the Gods. *Ib.* l. 145.

That stays the rolling Ixionian wheel,
And numbs the Fury's ringlet-snake, and plucks
The mortal soul from out immortal hell. *Ib.* l. 260.

Passionless bride, divine Tranquillity. *Ib.* l. 265.

Without one pleasure and without one pain. *Ib.* l. 268.

The lonely moated grange. *Mariana.*

She only said, 'My life is dreary,
He cometh not,' she said;
She said, 'I am aweary, aweary.
I would that I were dead!' *Ib.*

Her tears fell with the dews at even;
Her tears fell ere the dews were dried. *Ib.*

She wept, 'I am aweary, aweary,
O God, that I were dead!' *Ib.*

I hate the dreadful hollow behind the little wood.
                          Maud, Pt. I. i. i.

The smooth-faced snubnosed rogue. *Ib.* xiii.

Faultily faultless, icily regular, splendidly null. *Ib.* ii.

A monstrous eft was of old the Lord and Master of
  Earth. *Ib.* iv. vi.

The passionate heart of the poet is whirl'd into folly
  and vice. *Ib.* vii.

Maud with her exquisite face,
And wild voice pealing up to the sunny sky,
And feet like sunny gems on an English green.
                                   Ib. v. ii.

That jewell'd mass of millinery,
That oil'd and curl'd Assyrian Bull. *Ib.* vi. vi.

She came to the village church,
And sat by a pillar alone;
An angel watching an urn
Wept over her, carved in stone. *Ib.* viii.

The snowy-banded, dilettante,
Delicate-handed priest intone. *Ib.*

Ah God, for a man with heart, head, hand,
Like some of the simple great ones gone
For ever and ever by,
One still strong man in a blatant land,
Whatever they call him, what care I,
Aristocrat, democrat, autocrat—one
Who can rule and dare not lie.

And ah for a man to arise in me,
That the man I am may cease to be! *Ib.* x. v–vi.

O let the solid ground
  Not fail beneath my feet
Before my life has found
  What some have found so sweet. *Ib.* xi. i.

Birds in the high Hall-garden
When twilight was falling,
Maud, Maud, Maud, Maud,
They were crying and calling. *Ib.* xii. i.

I kiss'd her slender hand,
She took the kiss sedately;
Maud is not seventeen,
But she is tall and stately. *Ib.* iv.

I know the way she went
Home with her maiden posy,
For her feet have touch'd the meadows
And left the daisies rosy. *Ib.* vi.

Gorgonised me from head to foot
With a stony British stare. *Ib.* xiii. ii.

Go not, happy day,
From the shining fields,
Go not, happy day,
Till the maiden yields.
Rosy is the West,
Rosy is the South,
Roses are her cheeks,
And a rose her mouth. *Ib.* xvii.

Blush from West to East,
Blush from East to West,
Till the West is East,
Blush it thro' the West. *Maud*, Pt. I. XVII.

A livelier emerald twinkles in the grass,
A purer sapphire melts into the sea. *Ib.* XVIII. vi.

Come into the garden, Maud,
For the black bat, night, has flown;
Come into the garden, Maud,
I am here at the gate alone;
And the woodbine spices are wafted abroad,
And the musk of the rose is blown.

For a breeze of morning moves,
And the planet of Love is on high,
Beginning to faint in the light that she loves
On a bed of daffodil sky. *Ib.* XXII. i–ii.

All night have the roses heard
The flute, violin, bassoon;
All night has the casement jessamine stirr'd
To the dancers dancing in tune;
Till a silence fell with the waking bird,
And a hush with the setting moon. *Ib.* iii.

Whenever a March-wind sighs
He sets the jewel-print of your feet
In violets blue as your eyes. *Ib.* vii.

The slender acacia would not shake
One long milk-bloom on the tree;
The white lake-blossom fell into the lake
As the pimpernel dozed on the lea;
But the rose was awake all night for your sake,
Knowing your promise to me;
The lilies and roses were all awake,
They sigh'd for the dawn and thee. *Ib.* viii.

Queen rose of the rosebud garden of girls. *Ib.* ix.

There has fallen a splendid tear
From the passion-flower at the gate.
She is coming, my dove, my dear;
She is coming, my life, my fate;
The red rose cries, 'She is near, she is near;'
And the white rose weeps, 'She is late;'
The larkspur listens, 'I hear, I hear;'
And the lily whispers, 'I wait.'

She is coming, my own, my sweet;
Were it ever so airy a tread,
My heart would hear her and beat,
Were it earth in an earthy bed;
My dust would hear her and beat,
Had I lain for a century dead;
Would start and tremble under her feet,
And blossom in purple and red. *Ib.* x–xi.

The Christless code,
That must have life for a blow. *Ib.* Pt. II. I. i.

O that 'twere possible
After long grief and pain
To find the arms of my true love
Round me once again! *Ib.* IV. i.

Ah Christ, that it were possible
For one short hour to see
The souls we loved, that they might tell us
What and where they be. *Ib.* iii.

But the churchmen fain would kill their church,
As the churches have kill'd their Christ. *Ib.* v. ii.

O me, why have they not buried me deep enough?
Is it kind to have made me a grave so rough,
Me, that was never a quiet sleeper? *Ib.* xi.

Bury me, bury me
Deeper, ever so little deeper. *Ib.*

My life has crept so long on a broken wing
Thro' cells of madness, haunts of horror and fear,
That I come to be grateful at last for a little thing. *Ib.* Pt. III. VI. i.

When the face of night is fair on the dewy downs,
And the shining daffodil dies. *Ib.*

The blood-red blossom of war with a heart of fire. *Ib.* iv.

It is better to fight for the good, than to rail at the ill;
I have felt with my native land, I am one with my kind,
I embrace the purpose of God, and the doom assign'd. *Ib.* v.

You must wake and call me early, call me early, mother dear;
To-morrow 'ill be the happiest time of all the glad New-year;
Of all the glad New-year, mother, the maddest merriest day;
For I'm to be Queen o' the May, mother, I'm to be Queen o' the May. *The May Queen.*

It seem'd so hard at first, mother, to leave the blessed sun,
And now it seems as hard to stay, and yet His will be done!
But still I think it can't be long before I find release;
And that good man, the clergyman, has told me words of peace. *Ib. Conclusion.*

All in the wild March-morning I heard the angels call;
It was when the moon was setting, and the dark was over all;
The trees began to whisper, and the wind began to roll,
And in the wild March-morning I heard them call my soul. *Ib.*

Follow the Gleam. *Merlin and the Gleam.*

In after-dinner talk,
Across the walnuts and the wine. *The Miller's Daughter.*

What, it's you,
The padded man—that wears the stays. *The New Timon and the Poets.*

What profits now to understand
The merits of a spotless shirt—
A dapper boot—a little hand—
If half the little soul is dirt? *Ib.*

Dosn't thou' ear my 'erse's legs, as they canters awaäy?
Proputty, proputty, proputty—that's what I 'ears 'em saäy. *Northern Farmer. New Style.*

But I knaw'd a Quaäker feller as often 'as towd me this:
'Doänt thou marry for munny, but goä wheer munny is!' *Ib.*

Taake my word for it, Sammy, the poor in a loomp is bad. *Ib.*

An' I thowt a said whot a owt to 'a said an' I coom'd
  awaäy.   *Northern Farmer. Old Style.*

Do godamoighty knaw what a's doing a-taäkin' o'
  meä?   *Ib.*

Bury the Great Duke
With an empire's lamentation,
Let us bury the Great Duke
To the noise of the mourning of a mighty nation.
    Ode on the Death of the Duke of Wellington, i.

Let the sound of those he wrought for,
And the feet of those he fought for,
Echo round his bones for evermore.   *Ib.* ii.

The last great Englishman is low.   *Ib.* iii.

Foremost captain of his time,
Rich in saving common-sense,
And, as the greatest only are,
In his simplicity sublime.
O good grey head which all men knew!   *Ib.* iv.

O fall'n at length that tower of strength
Which stood four-square to all the winds that blew!
                      Ib.

Under the cross of gold
That shines over city and river.   *Ib.* v.

Mighty Seaman, this is he
Was great by land as thou by sea.   *Ib.* vi.

For this is England's greatest son,
He that gain'd a hundred fights,
Nor ever lost an English gun.   *Ib.*

Clash'd with his fiery few and won.   *Ib.*

In that world-earthquake, Waterloo!   *Ib.*

Thank Him who isled us here, and roughly set
His Briton in blown seas and storming showers.
                     Ib. vii.

That sober freedom out of which there springs
Our loyal passion for our temperate kings.   *Ib.*

Who never sold the truth to serve the hour,
Nor palter'd with Eternal God for power.   *Ib.*

Truth-teller was our England's Alfred named.   *Ib.*

Not once or twice in our rough island-story,
The path of duty was the way to glory.   *Ib.* viii.

He shall find the stubborn thistle bursting
Into glossy purples, which outredden
All voluptuous garden-roses.   *Ib.*

    The shining table-lands
To which our God Himself is moon and sun.   *Ib.*

Speak no more of his renown,
Lay your earthly fancies down,
And in the vast cathedral leave him,
God accept him, Christ receive him.   *Ib.* ix.

There lies a vale in Ida, lovelier
Than all the valleys of Ionian hills.   *Œnone,* l. 1.

O mother Ida, many-fountain'd Ida.   *Ib.* l. 22.

Dear mother Ida, harken ere I die.
It was the deep midnoon: one silvery cloud
Had lost his way between the piney sides
Of this long glen. Then to the bower they came,
Naked they came to that smooth-swarded bower,
And at their feet the crocus brake like fire,
Violet, amaracus, and asphodel,
Lotos and lilies.   *Ib.* l. 89.

Self-reverence, self-knowledge, self-control,
These three alone lead life to sovereign power.
                    Ib. l. 142.

  Because right is right, to follow right
Were wisdom in the scorn of consequence. *Ib.* l. 147.

I built my soul a lordly pleasure-house,
  Wherein at ease for aye to dwell.
                 The Palace of Art, i.

Still as, while Saturn whirls, his stedfast shade
  Sleeps on his luminous ring.   *Ib.* iv.

A haunt of ancient Peace.   *Ib.* xxii.

Plato the wise, and large-brow'd Verulam,
  The first of those who know.   *Ib.* xli.

On corpses three-months-old at noon she came,
  That stood against the wall.   *Ib.* lxi.

Act first, this Earth, a stage so gloom'd with woe
  You all but sicken at the shifting scenes.
And yet be patient. Our Playwright may show
  In some fifth Act what this wild Drama means.
                    The Play.

Dower'd with the hate of hate, the scorn of scorn,
The love of love.   *The Poet.*

And Freedom rear'd in that august sunrise
  Her beautiful bold brow.   *Ib.*

Vex not thou the poet's mind
  With thy shallow wit;
Vex not thou the poet's mind;
  For thou canst not fathom it.
Clear and bright it should be ever,
Flowing like a crystal river;
Bright as light, and clear as wind.   *The Poet's Mind.*

Dark-brow'd sophist, come not anear:
All the place is holy ground.   *Ib.*

And he sat him down in a lonely place,
And chanted a melody loud and sweet,
That made the wild-swan pause in her cloud,
And the lark drop down at his feet.   *The Poet's Song.*

The swallow stopt as he hunted the fly,
The snake slipt under a spray,
The wild hawk stood with the down on his beak,
And stared, with his foot on the prey.   *Ib.*

For some cry 'Quick' and some cry 'Slow',
  But, while the hills remain,
Up hill 'Too-slow' will need the whip,
  Down hill 'Too-quick', the chain.   *Politics.*

The cuckoo of a joyless June
Is calling out of doors.
    Prefatory Poem to my Brother's Sonnets.

The cuckoo of a worse July
Is calling thro' the dark.   *Ib.*

Here, in this roaring moon of daffodil
And crocus.
    Prefatory Sonnet to the 'Nineteenth Century'.

With prudes for proctors, dowagers for deans,
And sweet girl-graduates in their golden hair.
          The Princess, prologue, l. 141.

A rosebud set with little wilful thorns,
And sweet as English air could make her, she.
                    Ib. l. 153.

As thro' the land at eve we went,
  And pluck'd the ripen'd ears,
We fell out, my wife and I,
  O we fell out I know not why,
And kiss'd again with tears.
And blessings on the falling out
  That all the more endears,
When we fall out with those we love
  And kiss again with tears!
                    The Princess, ii. *Introd. Song.*

O hard, when love and duty clash!   *Ib.* ii, l. 273.

And quoted odes, and jewels five-words long,
That on the stretch'd forefinger of all Time
Sparkle for ever.   *Ib.* l. 355.

Sweet and low, sweet and low,
  Wind of the western sea,
Low, low, breathe and blow,
  Wind of the western sea!
Over the rolling waters go,
Come from the dying moon, and blow,
  Blow him again to me;
While my little one, while my pretty one, sleeps.
                    Ib. iii, *Introd. Song.*

A Memnon smitten with the morning Sun.
                    Ib. l. 100.

The splendour falls on castle walls
  And snowy summits old in story:
The long light shakes across the lakes,
  And the wild cataract leaps in glory.
Blow, bugle, blow, set the wild echoes flying,
Blow, bugle; answer, echoes, dying, dying, dying.
                    Ib. iv, *Introd. Song.*

O hark, O hear! how thin and clear,
  And thinner, clearer, farther going!
O sweet and far from cliff and scar
  The horns of Elfland faintly blowing!   *Ib.*

O love, they die in yon rich sky,
  They faint on hill or field or river:
Our echoes roll from soul to soul,
  And grow for ever and for ever.   *Ib.*

Tears, idle tears, I know not what they mean,
Tears from the depth of some divine despair
Rise in the heart, and gather to the eyes,
In looking on the happy Autumn-fields,
And thinking of the days that are no more.
                    Ib. iv, l. 21.

So sad, so fresh, the days that are no more. *Ib.* l. 30.

Ah, sad and strange as in dark summer dawns
The earliest pipe of half-awaken'd birds
To dying ears, when unto dying eyes
The casement slowly grows a glimmering square;
So sad, so strange, the days that are no more.

Dear as remembered kisses after death,
And sweet as those by hopeless fancy feign'd
On lips that are for others: deep as love,
Deep as first love, and wild with all regret;
O Death in Life, the days that are no more.   *Ib.* l. 31.

O Swallow, Swallow, flying, flying South,
Fly to her, and fall upon her gilded eaves,
And tell her, tell her, what I tell to thee.

O tell her, Swallow, thou that knowest each,
That bright and fierce and fickle is the South,
And dark and true and tender is the North.   *Ib.* l. 75.

O tell her, Swallow, that thy brood is flown:
Say to her, I do but wanton in the South,
But in the North long since my nest is made.

O tell her, brief is life but love is long,
And brief the sun of summer in the North,
And brief the moon of beauty in the South.

O Swallow, flying from the golden woods,
Fly to her, and pipe and woo her, and make her mine,
And tell her, tell her, that I follow thee.   *Ib.* l. 90.

Thy voice is heard thro' rolling drums,
  That beat to battle where he stands;
Thy face across his fancy comes,
  And gives the battle to his hands:
A moment, while the trumpets blow,
  He sees his brood about thy knee;
The next, like fire he meets the foe,
  And strikes him dead for thine and thee.
                    Ib. l. 552.

Man is the hunter; woman is his game. *Ib.* v, l. 147.

Man for the field and woman for the hearth:
Man for the sword and for the needle she:
Man with the head and woman with the heart:
Man to command and woman to obey;
All else confusion.   *Ib.* l. 427.

Home they brought her warrior dead.
She nor swoon'd, nor utter'd cry:
All her maidens, watching, said,
'She must weep or she will die.' *Ib.* vi, *Introd. Song.*

Home they brought him slain with spears,
They brought him home at even-fall.
            Version reprinted in Poems (1912), p. 870.

Rose a nurse of ninety years,
  Set his child upon her knee—
Like summer tempest came her tears—
  'Sweet my child, I live for thee.'   *Ib.*

            The woman is so hard
Upon the woman.   *Ib.* vi, l. 205.

Ask me no more: the moon may draw the sea;
The cloud may stoop from heaven and take the shape
With fold to fold, of mountain or of cape;
But O too fond, when have I answer'd thee?
            Ask me no more.

Ask me no more: what answer should I give?
I love not hollow cheek or faded eye:
Yet, O my friend, I will not have thee die!
Ask me no more, lest I should bid thee live;
            Ask me no more.

Ask me no more: thy fate and mine are seal'd:
I strove against the stream and all in vain:
Let the great river take me to the main:
No more, dear love, for at a touch I yield;
            Ask me no more.
                    Ib. vii, *Introd. Song.*

Now sleeps the crimson petal, now the white;
Nor waves the cypress in the palace walk;
Nor winks the gold fin in the porphyry font:
The fire-fly wakens: waken thou with me.

Now droops the milk-white peacock like a ghost,
And like a ghost she glimmers on to me.

Now lies the Earth all Danaë to the stars,
And all thy heart lies open unto me.

Now slides the silent meteor on, and leaves
A shining furrow, as thy thoughts in me.

Now folds the lily all her sweetness up,
And slips into the bosom of the lake:
So fold thyself, my dearest, thou, and slip
Into my bosom and be lost in me.
The Princess, vii, 1. 161.

Come down, O maid, from yonder mountain height:
What pleasure lives in height?   *Ib.* l. 177.

For Love is of the valley, come thou down
And find him; by the happy threshold, he,
Or hand in hand with Plenty in the maize,
Or red with spirted purple of the vats,
Or foxlike in the vine; nor cares to walk
With Death and Morning on the silver horns.
Ib. l. 184.

Sweet is every sound,
Sweeter thy voice, but every sound is sweet;
Myriads of rivulets hurrying thro' the lawn,
The moan of doves in immemorial elms,
And murmuring of innumerable bees.   *Ib.* l. 203.

The woman's cause is man's: they rise or sink
Together.   *Ib.* l. 243.

Like perfect music unto noble words.   *Ib.* l. 270.

Happy he
With such a mother! faith in womankind
Beats with his blood, and trust in all things high
Comes easy to him, and tho' he trip and fall
He shall not blind his soul with clay.   *Ib.* l. 308.

No little lily-handed Baronet he,
A great broad-shoulder'd genial Englishman.
Ib. Conclusion, l. 84.

A pamphleteer on guano and on grain.   *Ib.* l. 89.

This laurel greener from the brows
Of him that utter'd nothing base.
To the Queen, 1851, 'Revered, beloved.'

Her court was pure; her life serene;
God gave her peace; her land reposed;
A thousand claims to reverence closed
In her as Mother, Wife, and Queen;

And statesmen at her council met
Who knew the seasons when to take
Occasion by the hand, and make
The bounds of freedom wider yet.   *Ib.*

Broad-based upon her people's will,
And compass'd by the inviolate sea.   *Ib.*

Our slowly-grown
And crown'd Republic's crowning common-sense.
To the Queen, 'O loyal to the royal in thyself', l. 59.

For it was in the golden prime
Of good Haroun Alraschid.
Recollections of the Arabian Nights, i.

At Flores in the Azores Sir Richard Grenville lay,
And a pinnace, like a fluttered bird, came flying from
far away:
Spanish ships of war at sea! we have sighted fifty-
three!'   *The Revenge*, i.

Then sware Lord Thomas Howard: "Fore God I am
no coward;
But I cannot meet them here, for my ships are out of
gear,

And the half my men are sick. I must fly, but follow
quick.
We are six ships of the line; can we fight with fifty-
three?'   *Ib.*

Then spake Sir Richard Grenville: 'I know you are
no coward;
You fly them for a moment to fight with them again.
But I've ninety men and more that are lying sick
ashore.
I should count myself the coward if I left them, my
Lord Howard,
To these Inquisition dogs and the devildoms of
Spain.'   *Ib.* ii.

So Lord Howard past away with five ships of war
that day,
Till he melted like a cloud in the silent summer
heaven;
But Sir Richard bore in hand all his sick men from
the land
Very carefully and slow,
Men of Bideford in Devon,
And we laid them on the ballast down below;
For we brought them all aboard,
And they blest him in their pain, that they were not
left to Spain,
To the thumbscrew and the stake, for the glory of
the Lord.   *Ib.* iii.

'Shall we fight or shall we fly?
Good Sir Richard, tell us now,
For to fight is but to die!
There'll be little of us left by the time this sun be set.'
And Sir Richard said again: 'We be all good English
men.
Let us bang these dogs of Seville, the children of the
devil,
For I never turn'd my back upon Don or devil yet.'
Ib. iv.

And the sun went down, and the stars came out far
over the summer sea,
But never a moment ceased the fight of the one and
the fifty-three.
Ship after ship, the whole night long, their high-built
galleons came,
Ship after ship, the whole night long, with her battle-
thunder and flame,
Ship after ship, the whole night long, drew back with
her dead and her shame.
For some were sunk and many were shatter'd, and so
could fight us no more—
God of battles, was ever a battle like this in the world
before?   *Ib.* ix.

'Sink me the ship, Master Gunner—sink her, split her
in twain!
Fall into the hands of God, not into the hands of
Spain!'   *Ib.* xi.

And the gunner said 'Ay, ay', but the seamen made
reply:
'We have children, we have wives,
And the Lord hath spared our lives.'   *Ib.* xii.

And they praised him to his face with their courtly
foreign grace;
But he rose upon their decks, and he cried:
'I have fought for Queen and Faith like a valiant man
and true;
I have only done my duty as a man is bound to do:
With a joyful spirit I Sir Richard Grenville die!'
And he fell upon their decks, and he died.   *Ib.* xiii.

And the little Revenge herself went down by the island crags
To be lost evermore in the main. *The Revenge*, xiv.

Form, Form, Riflemen Form! *Riflemen Form!*

Make thou my spirit pure and clear
  As are the frosty skies,
Or the first snowdrop of the year
  That in my bosom lies. *St. Agnes' Eve.*

The sabbaths of Eternity,
One sabbath deep and wide—
A light upon the shining sea—
The Bridegroom with his bride! *Ib.*

Battering the gates of heaven with storms of prayer.
  St. Simeon Stylites, l. 7.

What does little birdie say
In her nest at peep of day? *Sea Dreams*, l. 281.

Birdie, rest a little longer,
Till the little wings are stronger.
So she rests a little longer,
Then she flies away. *Ib.* l. 285.

My strength is as the strength of ten,
  Because my heart is pure. *Sir Galahad.*

So pass I hostel, hall, and grange;
By bridge and ford, by park and pale,
All-arm'd I ride, whate'er betide,
  Until I find the holy Grail. *Ib.*

A man had given all other bliss,
And all his worldly worth for this,
To waste his whole heart in one kiss
  Upon her perfect lips.
    Sir Launcelot and Queen Guinevere.

Alone and warming his five wits,
The white owl in the belfry sits. *Song. The Owl.*

Thou art no sabbath-drawler of old saws,
Distill'd from some worm-canker'd homily.
  Sonnet. To J. M. K.

    Thou from a throne
Mounted in heaven wilt shoot into the dark
Arrows of lightnings. I will stand and mark. *Ib.*

    Oh teach me yet
Somewhat before the heavy clod
Weighs on me, and the busy fret
Of that sharp-headed worm begins
In the gross blackness underneath.
  Supposed Confessions of a Second-Rate Sensitive Mind.

In tea-cup times of hood and hoop,
  Or while the patch was worn.
    The Talking Oak, xvi.

And far below the Roundhead rode,
  And humm'd a surly hymn. *Ib.* lxxv.

We are not cotton-spinners all,
  But some love England and her honour yet.
    The Third of February, 1852, viii.

The woods decay, the woods decay and fall,
The vapours weep their burthen to the ground,
Man comes and tills the field and lies beneath,
And after many a summer dies the swan.
  Tithonus, l. 1.

Here at the quiet limit of the world. *Ib.* l. 7.

Why wilt thou ever scare me with thy tears,
And make me tremble lest a saying learnt,
In days far-off, on that dark earth, be true?
'The gods themselves cannot recall their gifts.'
  Ib. l. 46.

Of happy men that have the power to die,
And grassy barrows of the happier dead. *Ib.* l. 70.

A still small voice spake unto me,
'Thou art so full of misery,
Were it not better not to be?' *The Two Voices*, i.

This truth within thy mind rehearse,
That in a boundless universe
Is boundless better, boundless worse. *Ib.* ix.

'Consider well,' the voice replied,
'His face, that two hours since hath died;
Wilt thou find passion, pain, or pride?' *Ib.* lxxxi.

No life that breathes with human breath
Has ever truly long'd for death. *Ib.* cxxxii.

For, being of that honest few,
Who give the Fiend himself his due,
Should eighty-thousand college-councils
Thunder 'Anathema', friend at you.
  To the Rev. F. D. Maurice, ii.

    A careless-order'd garden
Close to the ridge of a noble down. *Ib.* iv.

You'll have no scandal while you dine,
But honest talk and wholesome wine. *Ib.* v.

It little profits that an idle king,
By this still hearth, among these barren crags,
Match'd with an aged wife, I mete and dole
Unequal laws unto a savage race *Ulysses*, l. 1.

    I will drink
Life to the lees: all times I have enjoy'd
Greatly, have suffer'd greatly, both with those
That loved me, and alone; on shore, and when
Thro' scudding drifts the rainy Hyades
Vext the dim sea: I am become a name;
For always roaming with a hungry heart
Much have I seen and known; cities of men
And manners, climates, councils, governments,
Myself not least, but honour'd of them all;
And drunk delight of battle with my peers,
Far on the ringing plains of windy Troy.
I am a part of all that I have met;
Yet all experience is an arch wherethro'
Gleams that untravell'd world, whose margin fades
For ever and for ever when I move.
How dull it is to pause, to make an end,
To rust unburnish'd, not to shine in use!
As tho' to breathe were life. Life piled on life
Were all too little, and of one to me
Little remains: but every hour is saved
From that eternal silence, something more,
A bringer of new things. *Ib.* l. 6

    This gray spirit yearning in desire
To follow knowledge like a sinking star,
Beyond the utmost bound of human thought.
  Ib. l. 3c

This is my son, mine own Telemachus. *Ib.* l. 33

There lies the port; the vessel puffs her sail:
There gloom the dark broad seas. My mariners,
Souls that have toil'd, and wrought, and thought
    with me—
That ever with a frolic welcome took
The thunder and the sunshine, and opposed
Free hearts, free foreheads—you and I are old;
Old age hath yet his honour and his toil;
Death closes all: but something ere the end,
Some work of noble note, may yet be done,
Not unbecoming men that strove with gods.
The lights begin to twinkle from the rocks:
The long day wanes: the slow moon climbs: the deep
Moans round with many voices. Come, my friends,
'Tis not too late to seek a newer world.
Push off, and sitting well in order smite
The sounding furrows; for my purpose holds
To sail beyond the sunset, and the baths
Of all the western stars, until I die.
It may be that the gulfs will wash us down:
It may be we shall touch the Happy Isles,
And see the great Achilles, whom we knew.
Tho' much is taken, much abides; and tho'
We are not now that strength which in old days
Moved earth and heaven; that which we are, we are;
One equal temper of heroic hearts,
Made weak by time and fate, but strong in will
To strive, to seek, to find, and not to yield. *Ulysses*, l. 44.

What is it all but a trouble of ants in the gleam of a
million million of suns? *Vastness*.

Household happiness, gracious children, debtless
competence, golden mean. *Ib.*

An' I thowt 'twur the will o' the Lord, but Miss Annie
she said it wur draäins. *The Village Wife*, ii.

All the charm of all the Muses often flowering in a
lonely word. *To Virgil*, iii.

I salute thee, Mantovano,
I that loved thee since my day began,
Wielder of the stateliest measure ever moulded by
the lips of man. *Ib.* x.

As 'twere a hundred-throated nightingale.
    The Vision of Sin, II.

God made Himself an awful rose of dawn. *Ib.* III.

Bitter barmaid, waning fast! *Ib.* IV. ii.

Let us have a quiet hour,
Let us hob-and-nob with Death. *Ib.* iii.

Every moment dies a man,
Every moment one is born. *Ib.* ix.

Fill the can, and fill the cup:
All the windy ways of men
Are but dust that rises up,
And is lightly laid again. *Ib.* xviii.

Drink to heavy Ignorance!
Hob-and-nob with brother Death! *Ib.* xxxiii.

We knew the merry world was round,
And we might sail for evermore. *The Voyage*, i.

Give her the wages of going on, and not to die.
    Wages, ii.

Sea-King's daughter from over the sea, Alexandra!
Saxon and Norman and Dane are we,
But all of us Danes in our welcome of thee, Alexandra!
    A Welcome to Alexandra.

Oh well for him whose will is strong!
He suffers, but he will not suffer long;
He suffers, but he cannot suffer wrong. *Will*.

O plump head-waiter at the Cock
To which I most resort.
    Will Waterproof's Lyrical Monologue, i.

Or that eternal want of pence,
  Which vexes public men. *Ib.* vi.

High over roaring Temple-bar,
  And set in Heaven's third story,
I look at all things as they are,
  But thro' a kind of glory. *Ib.* ix.

Right down by smoky Paul's they bore,
  Till, where the street grows straiter,
One fix'd for ever at the door,
  And one became head-waiter. *Ib.* xviii.

A land of settled government,
  A land of just and old renown,
  Where Freedom slowly broadens down
From precedent to precedent. '*You ask me, why*,' iii.

EDWARD TESCHEMACHER
19th cent.

There is a garden that I dream of.
    The Garden of Your Heart.

Where my caravan has rested,
Flowers I leave you on the grass.
    Where My Caravan Has Rested.

WILLIAM MAKEPEACE
THACKERAY
1811–1863

He who meanly admires mean things is a Snob.
    The Book of Snobs, ch. 2.

It is impossible, in our condition of Society, not to be
sometimes a Snob. *Ib.* ch. 3.

'Tis not the dying for a faith that's so hard, Master
Harry—every man of every nation has done that—
'tis the living up to it that is difficult.
    Esmond, bk. i, ch. 6.

'Tis strange what a man may do, and a woman yet
think him an angel. *Ib.* ch. 7.

We love being in love, that's the truth on't.
    Ib. bk. ii, ch. 15.

Why do they always put mud into coffee on board
steamers? Why does the tea generally taste of
boiled boots? *The Kickleburys on the Rhine*.

What woman, however old, has not the bridal-favours
and raiment stowed away, and packed in lavender,
in the inmost cupboards of her heart?
    Lovel the Widower, ch. 28.

When I say that I know women, I mean I know that
I don't know them. Every single woman I ever
knew is a puzzle to me, as, I have no doubt, she is
to herself. *Mr. Brown's Letters*.

A military gent I see—and while his face I scan,
I think you'll all agree with me—He came from
Hindostan. *The Newcomes*, bk. i, ch. 1.

What money is better bestowed than that of a school-boy's tip? *The Newcomes*, ch. 16.

As the last bell struck, a peculiar sweet smile shone over his face, and he lifted up his head a little, and quickly said, 'Adsum!' and fell back. It was the word we used at school, when names were called; and lo, he, whose heart was as that of a little child, had answered to his name, and stood in the presence of The Master. *Ib.* ch. 80.

Rake's progress. *Pendennis, Title of* ch. 19.

Yes, I am a fatal man, Madame Fribsbi. To inspire hopeless passion is my destiny. (*Mirobolant.*) *Ib.* ch. 23.

Remember, it is as easy to marry a rich woman as a poor woman. *Ib.* ch. 28.

For a slashing article, sir, there's nobody like the Capting. *Ib.* ch. 32.

The *Pall Mall Gazette* is written by gentlemen for gentlemen. *Ib.*

Now Valoroso is a man again! (*Valoroso.*) *The Rose and the Ring*, ch. 1.

Business first; pleasure afterwards. (*Queen of Paflagonia.*) *Ib.*

Runs not a river by my palace wall? Have I not sacks to sew up wives withal? (*Valoroso.*) *Ib.* ch. 9.

'No business before breakfast, Glum!' says the King. 'Breakfast first, business next.' (*Valoroso.*) *Ib.* ch. 11.

My bold, my beautiful, my Bulbo! (*Angelica.*) *Ib.*

Illuminated with the Author's own candles. *Vanity Fair. Before the Curtain.*

This I set down as a positive truth. A woman with fair opportunities and without a positive hump, may marry whom she likes. *Ib.* ch. 4.

(Miss Crawley) had been in France—and loved, ever after, French novels, French cookery, and French wines. *Ib.* ch. 10.

Whenever he met a great man he grovelled before him, and my-lorded him as only a free-born Briton can do. *Ib.* ch. 13.

Arms and Hatchments, Resurgam.—Here is an opportunity for moralizing! *Ib.* ch. 14.

Darkness came down on the field and city: and Amelia was praying for George, who was lying on his face, dead, with a bullet through his heart. *Ib.* ch. 32.

Nothing like blood, sir, in hosses, dawgs, and men. [*James Crawley.*] *Ib.* ch. 35.

Ah! *Vanitas Vanitatum!* Which of us is happy in this world? Which of us has his desire? or, having it, is satisfied?—Come, children, let us shut up the box and the puppets, for our play is played out. *Ib.* ch. 67.

'There's no sweeter tobacco comes from Virginia, and no better brand than the Three Castles.' *The Virginians*, ch. 1.

Fashnable fax and polite annygoats. *The Yellowplush Papers*, pt. i, *title.*

My ma wrapped up my buth in a mistry. *Ib.* pt. ii, *Miss Shum's Husband*, ch. 1.

Then sing as Martin Luther sang,
As Doctor Martin Luther sang,
'Who loves not wine, woman and song,
He is a fool his whole life long.' *A Credo.*

Ho, pretty page, with the dimpled chin
That never has known the barber's shear,
All your wish is woman to win,
This is the way that boys begin.
Wait till you come to Forty Year. *The Age of Wisdom.*

Although I enter not,
Yet round about the spot
Ofttimes I hover;
And near the sacred gate,
With longing eyes I wait,
Expectant of her. *At the Church Gate.*

The play is done; the curtain drops,
Slow falling to the prompter's bell:
A moment yet the actor stops,
And looks around, to say farewell.
It is an irksome word and task:
And, when he's laughed and said his say,
He shows, as he removes the mask,
A face that's anything but gay. *The End of the Play.*

Christmas is here:
Winds whistle shrill,
Icy and chill.
Little care we;
Little we fear
Weather without,
Sheltered about
The Mahogany Tree. *The Mahogany Tree.*

There are three sailors of Bristol City
Who took a boat and went to sea.
But first with beef and captain's biscuits
And pickled pork they loaded she.
There was gorging Jack and guzzling Jimmy,
And the youngest he was little Billee.
Now when they got as far as the Equator
They'd nothing left but one split pea. *Little Billee.*

Says gorging Jim to guzzling Jacky,
We have no wittles, so we must eat *we*. *Ib.*

There's little Bill as is young and tender,
We're old and tough—so let's eat *he*. *Ib.*

He scarce had said his Catechism,
When up he jumps: 'There's land I see!
There's Jerusalem and Madagascar,
And North and South Ameri*key.*
There's the British Fleet a-riding at anchor,
With Admiral Napier, K.C.B.' *Ib.*

Werther had a love for Charlotte
Such as words could never utter;
Would you know how first he met her?
She was cutting bread and butter. *Sorrows of Werther.*

Charlotte, having seen his body
Borne before her on a shutter
Like a well-conducted person,
Went on cutting bread and butter. *Ib.*

Oh, Vanity of vanities!
How wayward the decrees of Fate are;
How very weak the very wise,
How very small the very great are! *Vanitas Vanitatum.*

FRANCIS THOMPSON

1859–1907

Pontifical Death, that doth the crevasse bridge
To the steep and trifid God.   *Anthem of Earth.*

Here I shake off
The bur o' the world, man's congregation shun,
And to the antique order of the dead
I take the tongueless vows: my cell is set
Here in thy bosom; my little trouble is ended
In a little peace.   *Ib.*

And thou what needest with thy tribe's black tents
Who hast the red pavilion of my heart?   *Arab Love Song.*

He the Anteros and Eros,
    I the body, He the Cross;
He upbeareth me, *Ischyros,*
    Agios Athanatos!   *Assumpta Maria.*

Lo! He standeth, Spouse and Brother,
    I to Him, and He to me,
Who upraised me where my mother
    Fell beneath the apple-tree.   *Ib.*

Life is a coquetry
Of Death, which wearies me,
     Too sure
    Of the amour.
     To the Dead Cardinal of Westminster.

I have no angels left
    Now, Sweet, to pray to.   *A Carrier Song.*

The hills look over on the South,
    And Southward dreams the sea;
And with the sea-breeze hand in hand,
    Came innocence and she.   *Daisy.*

Where 'mid the gorse the raspberry
    Red for the gatherer springs,
Two children did we stray and talk
    Wise, idle, childish things.   *Ib.*

The fairest things have fleetest end,
    Their scent survives their close:
But the rose's scent is bitterness
    To him that loved the rose.   *Ib.*

She went her unremembering way,
    She went and left in me
The pang of all the partings gone,
    And partings yet to be.

She left me marvelling why my soul
    Was sad that she was glad;
At all the sadness in the sweet,
    The sweetness in the sad.   *Ib.*

Nothing begins and nothing ends
    That is not paid with moan;
For we are born in other's pain,
    And perish in our own.   *Ib.*

Ah, for a heart less native to high Heaven,
A hooded eye, for jesses and restraint,
Or for a will accipitrine to pursue!   *The Dread of Height.*

Go, songs, for ended is our brief sweet play;
    Go, children of swift joy and tardy sorrow:
And some are sung, and that was yesterday,
    And some unsung, and that may be tomorrow.
     Envoy.

Little Jesus, wast Thou shy
Once, and just so small as I?
And what did it feel to be
Out of Heaven and just like me?   *Ex Ore Infantum.*

Did the things
Play 'Can you see me?' through their wings?   *Ib.*

Cast wide the folding doorways of the East,
For now is light increased!
And the wind-besomed chambers of the air,
See they be garnished fair.
     From the Night of Forebeing. Ode to Easter.

Spring is come home with her world-wandering feet.
And all things are made young with young desires.
     Ib.

Let even the slug-abed snail upon the thorn
Put forth a conscious horn!   *Ib.*

Look for me in the nurseries of Heaven.
     To My Godchild.

O nothing, in this corporal earth of man,
That to the imminent heaven of his high soul
Responds with colour and with shadow, can
Lack correlated greatness.   *The Heart,* ii.

And all man's Babylons strive but to impart
The grandeurs of his Babylonian heart.   *Ib.*

I fled Him, down the nights and down the days;
    I fled Him, down the arches of the years;
I fled Him, down the labyrinthine ways
    Of my own mind; and in the mist of tears
I hid from Him, and under running laughter.
     The Hound of Heaven.

But with unhurrying chase,
And unperturb'd pace,
Deliberate speed, majestic instancy,
They beat—and a Voice beat
More instant than the Feet—
'All things betray thee, who betrayest Me.'   *Ib.*

(For, though I knew His love Who followed,
     Yet was I sore adread
Lest, having Him, I must have naught beside.)   *Ib.*

Fear wist not to evade, as Love wist to pursue.   *Ib.*

I said to Dawn: Be sudden—to Eve: Be soon.   *Ib.*

To all swift things for swiftness did I sue;
Clung to the whistling mane of every wind.   *Ib.*

Came on the following Feet,
And a Voice above their beat—
'Naught shelters thee, who wilt not shelter Me.'   *Ib.*

I sought no more that after which I strayed
     In face of man or maid;
But still within the little children's eyes
     Seems something, something that replies,
They at least are for me, surely for me!
I turned me to them very wistfully;
But just as their young eyes grew sudden fair
     With dawning answers there,
Their angel plucked them from me by the hair.   *Ib.*

I was heavy with the even
When she lit her glimmering tapers
Round the day's dead sanctities.   *Ib.*

My harness piece by piece Thou hast hewn from me
And smitten me to my knee.   *Ib.*

Yea, faileth now even dream
The dreamer, and the lute the lutanist;
Even the linked fantasies, in whose blossomy twist
I swung the earth a trinket at my wrist.
The Hound of Heaven.

Ah! must—
    Designer infinite!—
Ah! must Thou char the wood ere Thou canst limn
    with it?   *Ib.*

    Such is; what is to be?
The pulp so bitter, how shall taste the rind?   *Ib.*

Yet ever and anon a trumpet sounds
From the hid battlements of Eternity;
Those shaken mists a space unsettle, then
Round the half-glimpsèd turrets slowly wash again.
                                   Ib.

Whether man's heart or life it be which yields
    Thee harvest, must Thy harvest-fields
    Be dunged with rotten death?   *Ib.*

Now of that long pursuit
    Comes on at hand the bruit;
That Voice is round me like a bursting sea:
    'And is thy earth so marred,
    Shattered in shard on shard?
Lo, all things fly thee, for thou fliest Me!'   *Ib.*

And human love needs human meriting:
    How hast thou merited—
Of all man's clotted clay the dingiest clot?
    Alack, thou knowest not
How little worthy of any love thou art.   *Ib.*

All which I took from thee I did but take,
    Not for thy harms,
But just that thou might'st seek it in My arms.   *Ib.*

Halts by me that footfall:
    Is my gloom, after all,
Shade of His hand, outstretched caressingly?
    'Ah, fondest, blindest, weakest,
    I am He whom thou seekest!
Thou dravest love from thee, who dravest Me.'   *Ib.*

There is no expeditious road
To pack and label men for God,
And save them by the barrel-load.
           Epilogue to 'A Judgment in Heaven'.

O world invisible, we view thee,
O world intangible, we touch thee,
O world unknowable, we know thee,
Inapprehensible, we clutch thee!

Does the fish soar to find the ocean,
The eagle plunge to find the air—
That we ask of the stars in motion
If they have rumour of thee there?

Not where the wheeling systems darken,
And our benumbed conceiving soars!—
The drift of pinions, would we hearken,
Beats at our own clay-shuttered doors.

The angels keep their ancient places;—
Turn but a stone, and start a wing!
'Tis ye, 'tis your estrangèd faces,
That miss the many-splendoured thing.

But (when so sad thou canst not sadder)
Cry;—and upon thy so sore loss
Shall shine the traffic of Jacob's ladder
Pitched betwixt Heaven and Charing Cross.

Yea, in the night, my Soul, my daughter,
Cry,—clinging Heaven by the hems;
And lo, Christ walking on the water
Not of Gennesareth, but Thames!
           The Kingdom of God.

It is little I repair to the matches of the Southron
    folk,
    Though my own red roses there may blow;
It is little I repair to the matches of the Southron
    folk,
    Though the red roses crest the caps, I know.
For the field is full of shades as I near the shadowy
    coast,
And a ghostly batsman plays to the bowling of a
    ghost,
And I look through my tears on a soundless-clapping
    host
    As the run-stealers flicker to and fro,
              To and fro:—
O my Hornby and my Barlow long ago!
                     At Lord's.

Secret was the garden,
Set i' the pathless awe.   *The Mistress of Vision.*

East, ah, east of Himalay,
    Dwell the nations underground.   *Ib.*

Where is the land of Luthany,
And where the region Elenore?
I do faint therefor.

When to the new eyes of thee
All things by immortal power,
Near or far,
Hiddenly
To each other linked are,
That thou canst not stir a flower
Without troubling of a star.   *Ib.*

Lo, in the sanctuaried East,
Day, a dedicated priest
In all his robes pontifical exprest,
Lifteth slowly, lifteth sweetly,
From out its Orient tabernacle drawn,
Yon orbed sacrament confest
Which sprinkles benediction through the dawn.
                         Orient Ode.

Ah! let the sweet birds of the Lord
With earth's waters make accord;
Teach how the crucifix may be
Carven from the laurel-tree,
Fruit of the Hesperides
Burnish take on Eden-trees,
The Muses' sacred grove be wet
With the red dew of Olivet,
And Sappho lay her burning brows
In white Cecilia's lap of snows!
           To a Poet Breaking Silence.

Summer set lip to earth's bosom bare,
And left the flushed print in a poppy there.
                         The Poppy.

The sleep-flower sways in the wheat its head,
Heavy with dreams, as that with bread:
The goodly grain and the sun-flushed sleeper
The reaper reaps, and Time the reaper.

I hang 'mid men my needless head,
And my fruit is dreams, as theirs is bread:
The goodly men and the sun-hazed sleeper
Time shall reap, but after the reaper
The world shall glean of me, me the sleeper.   *Ib.*

I had endured through watches of the dark
The abashless inquisition of each star.
Sister Songs, i.

The innocent moon, which nothing does but shine,
Moves all the labouring surges of the world.   *Ib.*

What heart could have thought you?—
Past our devisal
(O filigree petal!)
Fashioned so purely,
Fragilely, surely,
From what Paradisal
Imagineless metal,
Too costly for cost?   *To a Snowflake.*

His hammer of wind,
And His graver of frost.   *Ib.*

And, while she feels the heavens lie bare,
She only talks about her hair.   *The Way of a Maid.*

WILLIAM HEPWORTH THOMPSON

1810–1886

We are none of us infallible—not even the youngest of us.
Remark referring to G. W. Balfour, then Junior Fellow of Trinity. G. W. E. Russell's Collections and Recollections, ch. 18.

JAMES THOMSON

1700–1748

When Britain first, at heaven's command,
Arose from out the azure main,
This was the charter of the land,
And guardian angels sung this strain:
'Rule, Britannia, rule the waves;
    Britons never will be slaves.'
Alfred: a Masque 1740, Act II, Scene the last.

The world of waters wild.   *Britannia*, l. 27.

A pleasing land of drowsyhead it was.
The Castle of Indolence, c. i. vi.

As when a shepherd of the Hebrid Isles,
Placed far amid the melancholy main.   *Ib.* xxx.

A bard here dwelt, more fat than bard beseems.
Ib. lxviii.

Poured forth his unpremeditated strain.   *Ib.*

A little, round, fat, oily man of God.   *Ib.* lxix.

For ever, Fortune, wilt thou prove
An unrelenting foe to love,
And, when we meet a mutual heart,
Come in between and bid us part?   *To Fortune.*

Come then, expressive Silence, muse His praise.
A Hymn on the Seasons, l. 118.

How the heart listened while he pleading spoke!
While on the enlightened mind, with winning art,
His gentle reason so persuasive stole
That the charmed hearer thought it was his own.
To the Memory of the Lord Talbot, l. 103.

Come, gentle Spring! ethereal mildness, come.
The Seasons, Spring, l. 1.

    The stately-sailing swan
Gives out his snowy plumage to the gale,
And, arching proud his neck, with oary feet
Bears forward fierce, and guards his osier-isle,
Protective of his young.   *Ib.* l. 778.

Delightful task! to rear the tender thought,
To teach the young idea how to shoot.   *Ib.* l. 1152.

An elegant sufficiency, content.   *Ib.* l. 1161.

The sober-suited songstress. [The nightingale.]
Ib. Summer, l. 746.

Ships, dim-discovered, dropping from the clouds.
Ib. l. 946.

And Mecca saddens at the long delay.   *Ib.* l. 979.

Or sighed and looked unutterable things. *Ib.* l. 1188.

While Autumn nodding o'er the yellow plain
Comes jovial on.   *Ib. Autumn*, l. 2.

While listening senates hang upon thy tongue.
Ib. l. 15.

    For loveliness
Needs not the foreign aid of ornament,
But is when unadorned adorned the most. *Ib.* l. 204.

Poor is the triumph o'er the timid hare!   *Ib.* l. 401.

The big round tears run down his dappled face.
Ib. l. 454.

    The Atlantic surge
Pours in among the stormy Hebrides.   *Ib.* l. 864.

Find other lands beneath another sun.   *Ib.* l. 1286.

See, Winter comes to rule the varied year,
Sullen and sad.   *Ib. Winter*, l. 1.

    Welcome, kindred glooms!
Congenial horrors, hail!   *Ib* l. 5.

The redbreast, sacred to the household gods,
Wisely regardful of the embroiling sky,
In joyless fields and thorny thickets leaves
His shivering mates, and pays to trusted man
His annual visit. Half afraid, he first
Against the window beats; then brisk alights
On the warm hearth; then, hopping o'er the floor,
Eyes all the smiling family askance,
And pecks, and starts, and wonders where he is—
Till, more familiar grown, the table-crumbs
Attract his slender feet.   *Ib.* l. 246.
    Studious let me sit,
And hold high converse with the mighty dead.
Ib. l. 431.

Oh! Sophonisba! Sophonisba! oh!
Sophonisba, III. ii.

JAMES THOMSON

1834–1882

The city of dreadful night.   *Title of poem.*

The City is of Night; perchance of Death,
But certainly of Night.   *The City of Dreadful Night.*

As we rush, as we rush in the train,
The trees and the houses go wheeling back,
But the starry heavens above that plain
Come flying on our track. *Sunday at Hampstead*, x.

Give a man a horse he can ride,
Give a man a boat he can sail.
Sunday up the River, xv.

HENRY DAVID THOREAU
1817–1862

The mass of men lead lives of quiet desperation.
Walden. Economy.

It is a characteristic of wisdom not to do desperate
things.   *Ib.*

I have lived some thirty years on this planet, and I
have yet to hear the first syllable of valuable or
even earnest advice from my seniors.   *Ib.*

I long ago lost a hound, a bay horse, and a turtle-
dove, and am still on their trail.   *Ib.*

It is true, I never assisted the sun materially in his
rising, but, doubt not, it was of the last importance
only to be present at it.   *Ib.*

Tall arrowy white pines.   *Ib.*

The owner of the axe, as he released his hold on it,
said that it was the apple of his eye; but I returned
it sharper than I received it.   *Ib.*

For more than five years I maintained myself thus
solely by the labor of my hands, and I found, that
by working about six weeks in a year, I could meet
all the expenses of living.   *Ib.*

As for Doing-good, that is one of the professions
which are full. Moreover, I have tried it fairly,
and, strange as it may seem, am satisfied that it
does not agree with my constitution.   *Ib.*

Simplify, simplify.
Ib. Where I Lived, and What I Lived For.

The three-o'-clock in the morning courage, which
Bonaparte thought was the rarest.   *Ib. Sounds.*

Wherever a man goes, men will pursue him and paw
him with their dirty institutions, and, if they can,
constrain him to belong to their desperate odd-
fellow society.   *Ib. The Village.*

I frequently tramped eight or ten miles through the
deepest snow to keep an appointment with a beech-
tree, or a yellow birch, or an old acquaintance
among the pines.   *Ib. Winter Visitors.*

I once had a sparrow alight upon my shoulder for a
moment while I was hoeing in a village garden,
and I felt that I was more distinguished by that circumstance than I should have been by any epaulet
I could have worn.   *Ib.*

It takes two to speak the truth,—one to speak, and
another to hear.
*A Week on the Concord and Merrimack Rivers,
Wednesday.*

Some circumstantial evidence is very strong, as when
you find a trout in the milk.
*Unpublished MSS. in Miscellanies, Biographi-
cal Sketch* (1918), vol. x, p. 30.

Not that the story need be long, but it will take a
long while to make it short.
Letter to Mr. B., 16 Nov. 1857.

ROSE HARTWICK THORPE
1850–1939

'Curfew must not ring to-night.'   *Title of poem.*

GODFREY THRING
1823–1903

Fierce raged the tempest o'er the deep,
Watch did thine anxious servants keep,
But thou wast wrapp'd in guileless sleep,
                                        Calm and still.
Chope's Hymnal (1862). *Fierce Raged The Tempest.*

EDWARD, FIRST BARON THURLOW
1731–1806

As guardian of his Majesty's conscience.
Speech in the House of Lords, 1779. C. Butler,
Reminiscences, vol. 1, p. 200.

His debt of gratitude also to his Majesty was ample . . . ;
and which, when he forgot, might God forget him!
*Speech in House of Lords, 15 Dec. 1788. Parl.
Hist.* (1814), vol. xxvii, col. 680.

EDWARD, SECOND BARON THURLOW
1781–1829

Nature is always wise in every part.
*Select Poems. Sonnet. To a Bird, that haunted
the Waters of Lacken, in the Winter.*

Did you ever expect a corporation to have a conscience, when it has no soul to be damned, and no
body to be kicked?
Attr. Wilberforce, *Life of Thurlow*, vol. iii,
Appendix.

THOMAS TICKELL
1686–1740

There taught us how to live; and (oh! too high
The price for knowledge) taught us how to die.
Epitaph. On the Death of Mr. Addison, l. 81.
Addison's *Works* (1721), preface, p. xx.

MATTHEW TINDAL
1657–1733

Matters of fact, which as Mr. Budgell somewhere
observes, are very stubborn things.
Will of Matthew Tindal (1733), p. 23.

JOHN TOBIN
1770–1804

The man that lays his hand upon a woman,
Save in the way of kindness, is a wretch
Whom 't were gross flattery to name a coward.
The Honeymoon, II. i.

AUGUSTUS MONTAGUE TOPLADY

1740–1778

Rock of ages, cleft for me,
Let me hide myself in thee.
The Gospel Magazine, Oct. 1775. *Rock of Ages.*

Nothing in my hand I bring,
Simply to thy Cross I cling;
Naked, come to thee for dress;
Helpless, look to thee for grace;
Foul, I to the Fountain fly;
Wash me, Saviour, or I die.   *Ib.*

THOMAS TRAHERNE

1637?–1674

You never enjoy the world aright, till the sea itself
floweth in your veins, till you are clothed with the
heavens, and crowned with the stars: and perceive
yourself to be the sole heir of the whole world, and
more than so, because men are in it who are every
one sole heirs as well as you.   Till you can sing and
rejoice and delight in God, as misers do in gold,
and kings in sceptres, you never enjoy the world.
Centuries of Meditations. Cent. i, § 29.

The corn was orient and immortal wheat, which
never should be reaped, nor was ever sown.
I thought it had stood from everlasting to everlasting.   *Ib.* Cent. iii, § 3.

The Men! O what venerable and reverend creatures
did the aged seem! Immortal Cherubims! And
young men glittering and sparkling Angels, and
maids strange seraphic pieces of life and beauty!
Boys and girls tumbling in the street, and playing,
were moving jewels.   I knew not that they were
born or should die; but all things abided eternally
as they were in their proper places.   *Ib.*

Contentment is a sleepy thing
If it in death alone must die;
A quiet mind is worse than poverty,
Unless it from enjoyment spring!
That's blessedness alone that makes a King!
Of Contentment.

O yonder is the moon
Newly come after me to town,
That shin'd at Lugwardin but yesternight,
Where I enjoy'd the self-same light.
On Leaping over the Moon, viii.

I within did flow
With seas of life, like wine;   *Wonder*, iii.

HENRY DUFF TRAILL

1842–1900

Look in my face.   My name is Used-to-was;
I am also called Played-out and Done-to-death,
And It-will-wash-no-more.
After Dilettante Concetti, viii.

JOSEPH TRAPP

1679–1747

The King, observing with judicious eyes,
The state of both his universities,
To Oxford sent a troop of horse, and why?

That learned body wanted loyalty;
To Cambridge books, as very well discerning,
How much that loyal body wanted learning.
On George I's Donation of Bishop of Ely's
Library to Cambridge University. Nichols's
Literary Anecdotes, vol. iii, p. 330.
For the reply, see Sir William Browne.

Our royal master saw, with heedful eyes,
The wants of his two universities:
Troops he to Oxford sent, as knowing why
That learned body wanted loyalty:
But books to Cambridge gave, as, well discerning,
That that right loyal body wanted learning.
Alternative version recited by Dr. Johnson.
Johnsonian Miscellanies (1897), vol. i, p. 171.

HERBERT TRENCH

1865–1923

But when Night is on the hills, and the great Voices
Roll in from Sea,
By starlight and by candlelight and dreamlight
She comes to me.
She Comes Not When Noon is on the Roses.

Come, let us make love deathless, thou and I.
To Arolilia, No. 2. 'Come, let us make love
deathless.'

O dreamy, gloomy, friendly Trees.   *Title of poem.*

RICHARD CHENEVIX TRENCH

1807–1886

England, we love thee better than we know.
Gibraltar.

I say to thee, do thou repeat
To the first man thou mayest meet
In lane, highway, or open street—

That he and we and all men move
Under a canopy of love,
As broad as the blue sky above.
The Kingdom of God.

This *is* blessing, this *is* life.   *Ib.*

ANTHONY TROLLOPE

1815–1882

He must have known me had he seen me as he was
wont to see me, for he was in the habit of flogging
me constantly. Perhaps he did not recognize me
by my face.   *Autobiography*, ch. 1.

'Unhand it, sir!' said Mrs. Proudie.   From what
scrap of dramatic poetry she had extracted the
word cannot be said; but it must have rested on
her memory, and now seemed opportunely digni-
fied for the occasion.   *Barchester Towers*, ch. 11.

Lilian Dale,—Old Maid.
Last Chronicles of Barset, ch. 35.

It's dogged as does it.   It ain't thinking about it.
Ib. ch. 61.

MARTIN FARQUHAR TUPPER

1810–1889

A good book is the best of friends, the same to-day and for ever.
Proverbial Philosophy, Series 1. *Of Reading.*

WALTER JAMES REDFERN TURNER

1889–

Chimborazo, Cotopaxi,
They had stolen my soul away!   *Romance,* vii.

THOMAS TUSSER

1524?–1580

Make hunger thy sauce, as a medicine for health.
Five Hundred Points of Good Husbandry, ch.
10. *Good Husbandry Lessons.*

At Christmas play and make good cheer,
For Christmas comes but once a year.
Ib. 12. *The Farmer's daily Diet.*

Yet true it is, as cow chaws cud,
And trees at spring do yield forth bud,
Except wind stands as never it stood,
It is an ill wind turns none to good.
Ib. ch. 13. *Description of the Properties of Winds.*

Who goeth a borrowing
Goeth a sorrowing.
Few lend (but fools)
Their working tools.
Ib. ch. 15. *September's Abstract.*

In doing of either, let wit bear a stroke,
For buying or selling of pig in a poke.
Ib. September's Husbandry.

Naught venture, naught have.
Ib. ch. 16. *October's Abstract.*

To dog in the manger some liken I could.
Ib. ch. 28. *Against Fantastical Scrupleness.*

Feb, fill the dyke
With what thou dost like.
Ib. ch. 34: *February's Husbandry.*

March dust to be sold
Worth ransom of gold.
Ib. ch. 36. *March's Husbandry.*

Sweet April showers
Do spring May flowers.
Ib. ch. 38. *April's Husbandry.*

Cold May and windy,
Barn filleth up finely. *Ib.* ch. 40. *May's Husbandry.*

Dry August and warm
Doth harvest no harm.
Ib. ch. 46. *August's Husbandry.*

Look ere thou leap, see ere thou go.
Ib. ch. 56. *Dialogue of Wiving and Thriving.*

Some respite to husbands the weather may send,
But housewives' affairs have never an end.
Ib. Preface to the Book of Housewifery.

The stone that is rolling can gather no moss,
For master and servant, oft changing is loss.
Ib. Housewifely Admonitions.

Dry sun, dry wind;
Safe bind, safe find.   *Ib. Washing.*

LAWRENCE TUTTIETT

1825–1899

Father, let me dedicate
All this year to thee.
Gems of Thought (1864). *Father, Let Me Dedicate.*

MARK TWAIN (SAMUEL LANGHORNE CLEMENS)

1835–1910

There was things which he stretched, but mainly he
told the truth.
The Adventures of Huckleberry Finn, ch. 1.

The statements was interesting, but tough.
Ib. ch. 17.

All kings is mostly rapscallions.   *Ib.* ch. 23.

If there was two birds sitting on a fence, he would bet
you which one would fly first.
The Celebrated Jumping Frog, p. 17.

I don't see no p'ints about that frog that's any
better'n any other frog.   *Ib.* p. 20.

Soap and education are not as sudden as a massacre,
but they are more deadly in the long run.
The Facts concerning the Recent Resignation.
Sketches New & Old, 1900, p. 350.

They spell it Vinci and pronounce it Vinchy;
foreigners always spell better than they pronounce.
Innocents Abroad, ch. 19.

I do not want Michael Angelo for breakfast—for
luncheon—for dinner—for tea—for supper—for
between meals.   *Ib.* ch. 27.

Lump the whole thing! say that the Creator made
Italy from designs by Michael Angelo!   *Ib.*

Guides cannot master the subtleties of the American
joke.   *Ib.*

If you've got a nice *fresh* corpse, fetch him out! *Ib.*

Are you going to hang him *anyhow*—and try him
afterward?   *Innocents at Home,* ch. 5.

You've done yourselves proud.   *Ib.*

When I'm playful I use the meridians of longitude
and parallels of latitude for a seine, and drag the
Atlantic Ocean for whales! I scratch my head with
the lightning and purr myself to sleep with the
thunder!   *Life on the Mississippi,* ch. 3

At bottom he was probably fond of them, but he was
always able to conceal it.
[Thomas Carlyle and Americans.] *My First
Lie.*

There is a sumptuous variety about the New England
weather that compels the stranger's admiration—
and regret. The weather is always doing some-

thing there; always attending strictly to business; always getting up new designs and trying them on the people to see how they will go. But it gets through more business in spring than in any other season. In the spring I have counted one hundred and thirty-six different kinds of weather inside of four-and-twenty hours.

The Weather. Speech at dinner of New England Society, New York, 22 Dec. 1876. Speeches (1910), p. 59.

An experienced, industrious, ambitious, and often quite picturesque liar.

Private History of a Campaign that Failed.

Adam was but human—this explains it all. He did not want the apple for the apple's sake, he wanted it only because it was forbidden.

Pudd'nhead Wilson, Heading of ch. 2.

Whoever has lived long enough to find out what life is, knows how deep a debt of gratitude we owe to Adam, the first great benefactor of our race. He brought death into the world.

Ib. heading of ch. 3.

There's plenty of boys that will come hankering and gruvvelling around when you've got an apple, and beg the core off you; but when *they've* got one, and you beg for the core and remind them how you give them a core one time, they make a mouth at you and say thank you 'most to death, but there ain't-a-going to *be* no core.

Tom Sawyer Abroad, ch. 1.

There ain't no way to find out why a snorer can't hear himself snore.　　*Ib.* ch. 10.

They inwardly resolved that so long as they remained in the business, their piracies should not again be sullied with the crime of stealing.　*Ib.* ch. 13.

The cross of the Legion of Honour has been conferred upon me. However, few escape that distinction.　　*A Tramp Abroad,* ch. 8.

This poor little one-horse town.

The Undertaker's Chat.

HENRY TWELLS

1823–1900

At even ere the sun was set,
The sick, O Lord, around thee lay.

Hymns Ancient and Modern (1868), Appendix. *'At Even Ere the Sun Was Set'.*

W. UPTON

This lass so neat, with smile so sweet,
Has won my right good will,
I'd crowns resign to call thee mine,
Sweet lass of Richmond Hill.

The Lass of Richmond Hill. Oxford Song Book.

SIR JOHN VANBRUGH

1664–1726

The want of a thing is perplexing enough, but the possession of it is intolerable.

The Confederacy, I. ii.

BELINDA:
　Ay, but you know we must return good for evil.
LADY BRUTE:
　That may be a mistake in the translation.　　*Ib.*

Britons, strike home.　　　　　*Ib.* IV. i.

No man worth having is true to his wife, or can be true to his wife, or ever was, or ever will be so.

The Relapse, III. ii.

WILLIAM HENRY VANDERBILT

1821–1885

The public be damned!
[Reply to a question whether the public should be consulted about luxury trains.]
　　A. W. Cole's *Letter, New York Times,* 25 August, 1918.

CHARLES JOHN VAUGHAN

1816–1897

Must you go? Can't you stay?
　[Remark with which he broke up awkward breakfast parties of schoolboys who were too shy to go. Story retold with the words transposed, 'Can't you go? Must you stay?']
　　G. W. E. Russell's *Collections and Recollections,* ch. 24.

HENRY VAUGHAN

1622–1695

Father of lights! what sunny seed,
What glance of day hast Thou confin'd
Into this bird? To all the breed
This busy ray Thou hast assign'd;
　Their magnetism works all night,
　And dreams of Paradise and light.

Silex Scintillans. Cock-Crowing.

I cannot reach it; and my striving eye
Dazzles at it, as at eternity.　*Ib. Childhood.*

Through that pure virgin shrine,
That sacred veil drawn o'er Thy glorious noon,
That men might look and live, as glow-worms shine,
　And face the moon;
Wise Nicodemus saw such light
As made him know his God by night.

Ib. The Night, l. 1.

　Most blest believer he!
Who in that land of darkness and blind eyes
Thy long expected healing wings could see
　When Thou didst rise!
And, what can never more be done,
Did at midnight speak with the Sun!　*Ib.* l. 7.

　Dear Night! this world's defeat;
The stop to busy fools; care's check and curb;
　The day of spirits; my soul's calm retreat
　Which none disturb!
Christ's progress, and His prayer-time;
The hours to which high Heaven doth chime.

Ib. l. 25.

There is in God—some say—
A deep, but dazzling darkness; as men here
Say it is late and dusky, because they
  See not all clear.
O for that Night! where I in Him
Might live invisible and dim!
      Silex Scintillans. The Night, l. 49.

My soul, there is a country
  Far beyond the stars,
Where stands a wingèd sentry
  All skilful in the wars:
There, above noise and danger,
  Sweet Peace is crown'd with smiles,
And One born in a manger
  Commands the beauteous files.   *Ib. Peace.*

If thou canst get but thither,
  There grows the flower of Peace,
The Rose that cannot wither,
  Thy fortress, and thy ease.
Leave then thy foolish ranges;
  For none can thee secure,
But One, who never changes,
  Thy God, thy life, thy cure.   *Ib.*

Happy those early days, when I
Shin'd in my angel-infancy.
Before I understood this place
Appointed for my second race,
Or taught my soul to fancy aught
But a white, celestial thought;
When yet I had not walked above
A mile or two from my first love,
And looking back—at that short space—
Could see a glimpse of His bright face.
       Ib. The Retreat, l. 1.

And in those weaker glories spy
Some shadows of eternity.   *Ib.* l. 13.

But felt through all this fleshly dress
Bright shoots of everlastingness.   *Ib.* l. 19.

O how I long to travel back,
And tread again that ancient track!
That I might once more reach that plain,
Where first I left my glorious train;
From whence th' enlighten'd spirit sees
The shady City of palm-trees.   *Ib.* l. 21.

Some men a forward motion love,
But I by backward steps would move,
And when this dust falls to the urn,
In that state I came, return.   *Ib.* l. 29.

They are all gone into the world of light,
  And I alone sit lingering here;
Their very memory is fair and bright,
  And my sad thoughts doth clear.
       Ib. They Are All Gone.

I see them walking in an air of glory,
  Whose light doth trample on my days:
My days, which are at best but dull and hoary,
  Mere glimmering and decays.   *Ib.*

Dear, beauteous death! the jewel of the just,
  Shining nowhere but in the dark;
What mysteries do lie beyond thy dust,
  Could man outlook that mark!   *Ib.*

He that hath found some fledg'd bird's nest, may
     know
  At first sight, if the bird be flown;
But what fair well or grove he sings in now,
  That is to him unknown.   *Ib.*

And yet, as angels in some brighter dreams
  Call to the soul when man doth sleep,
So some strange thoughts transcend our wonted
     themes,
  And into glory peep.   *Ib.*

I saw Eternity the other night,
Like a great ring of pure and endless light,
  All calm, as it was bright;
And round beneath it, Time in hours, days, years,
  Driv'n by the spheres
Like a vast shadow mov'd; in which the world
  And all her train were hurl'd.   *Ib. The World.*

THOMAS, LORD VAUX
1510–1556

For Age, with stealing steps,
Hath clawed me with his clutch.
      Poems (1872), p. 42. *The Aged Lover Renoun-*
      ceth Love. A Ditty . . . Representing the Image
      of Death.

QUEEN VICTORIA
1819–1901

I will be good.
      Letter from the Baroness Lehzen to Her Majesty,
      2 Dec. 1867. Martin's *The Prince Consort*
      (1875), vol. i, p. 13.

We are not amused.
      Notebooks of a Spinster Lady, 2 Jan. 1900.

He (Mr. Gladstone) speaks to Me as if I was a public
meeting.
      G. W. E. Russell's *Collections and Recollec-*
      tions, ch. 14.

JOSEPH AUGUSTINE WADE
1796?–1845

Meet me by moonlight alone.
      Meet Me by Moonlight.

WILLIAM ROSS WALLACE
? –1881

The hand that rocks the cradle
Is the hand that rules the world.
      John o' London's Treasure Trove.

EDMUND WALLER
1606–1687

So was the huntsman by the bear oppress'd,
Whose hide he sold—before he caught the beast!
      Battle of the Summer Islands, ii, l. 111.

That which her slender waist confin'd.
Shall now my joyful temples bind;
No monarch but would give his crown
His arms might do what this has done.

It was my heaven's extremest sphere,
The pale which held that lovely deer:
My joy, my grief, my hope, my love,
Did all within this circle move.

A narrow compass! and yet there
Dwelt all that's good, and all that's fair:
Give me but what this riband bound,
Take all the rest the sun goes round.
On a Girdle.

Others may use the ocean as their road,
Only the English make it their abode.
Of a War with Spain, l. 25.

The seas are quiet when the winds give o'er;
So, calm are we when passions are no more!
On the Foregoing Divine Poems, l. 7.

The soul's dark cottage, batter'd and decay'd,
Lets in new light through chinks that time has made;
Stronger by weakness, wiser men become,
As they draw near to their eternal home.
Leaving the old, both worlds at once they view,
That stand upon the threshold of the new. *Ib.* l. 18.

Rome, though her eagle through the world had flown,
Could never make this island all her own.
Panegyric to My Lord Protector, xvii.

Illustrious acts high raptures do infuse,
And every conqueror creates a Muse.   *Ib.* xlvi.

    Go, lovely Rose!
Tell her, that wastes her time and me,
    That now she knows,
When I resemble her to thee,
How sweet and fair she seems to be.
Song: 'Go, Lovely Rose!'

Small is the worth
    Of beauty from the light retir'd;
Bid her come forth,
    Suffer herself to be desir'd,
And not blush so to be admir'd.   *Ib.*

Why came I so untimely forth
Into a world which, wanting thee,
Could entertain us with no worth,
Or shadow of felicity?
To My Young Lady Lucy Sidney.

        So all we know
Of what they do above,
Is that they happy are, and that they love.
Upon the Death of My Lady Rich, l. 75.

Under the tropic is our language spoke,
And part of Flanders hath receiv'd our yoke.
Upon the Death of the Lord Protector, l. 21.

HORACE WALPOLE

1717-1797

Alexander at the head of the world never tasted the
    true pleasure that boys of his own age have en-
    joyed at the head of a school.
Letters to Montagu, 6 May, 1736.

Our supreme governors, the mob.
Ib. To Horace Mann, 7 Sept. 1743.

(Strawberry Hill) is a little plaything-house that I got
    out of Mrs. Chenevix's shop, and is the prettiest
    bauble you ever saw. It is set in enamelled
    meadows, with filigree hedges.
To Conway, 8 June, 1747.

But, thank God! the Thames is between me and the
    Duchess of Queensberry.

Every drop of ink in my pen ran cold.
Ib. To Montagu, 3 July, 1752.

It has the true rust of the Barons' Wars.
Ib. To Bentley, Sept. 1753.

At present, nothing is talked of, nothing admired, but
    what I cannot help calling a very insipid and
    tedious performance: it is a kind of novel, called
    The Life and Opinions of Tristram Shandy; the
    great humour of which consists in the whole narra-
    tion always going backwards.
To Dalrymple, 4 Apr. 1760.

One of the greatest geniuses that ever existed,
    Shakespeare, undoubtedly wanted taste.
Ib. To Wren, 9 Aug. 1764.

The works of Richardson . . . which are pictures of
    high life as conceived by a bookseller, and romances
    as they would be spiritualized by a Methodist
    preacher.   *Ib. To Mann, 20 Dec. 1764.*

At Madame du Deffand's, an old blind *débauchée* of
    wit.   *Ib. To Conway, 6 Oct. 1765.*

It is charming to totter into vogue.
Ib. To Selwyn, 2 Dec. 1765.

Yes, like Queen Eleanor in the ballad, I sunk at
    Charing Cross, and have risen in the Faubourg St.
    Germain.   *Ib. To Gray, 25 Jan. 1766.*

The best sun we have is made of Newcastle coal.
Ib. To Montagu, 15 June, 1768.

Everybody talks of the constitution, but all sides
    forget that the constitution is extremely well, and
    would do very well, if they would but let it alone.
Ib. To Sir Horace Mann, 18-19 Jan. 1770.

It was easier to conquer it (the East) than to know
    what to do with it.   *Ib. To Mann, 27 March, 1772.*

The way to ensure summer in England is to have it
    framed and glazed in a comfortable room.
Ib. To Cole, 28 May, 1774.

The next Augustan age will dawn on the other side
    of the Atlantic. There will, perhaps, be a Thucy-
    dides at Boston, a Xenophon at New York, and,
    in time, a Virgil at Mexico, and a Newton at
    Peru. At last, some curious traveller from Lima
    will visit England and give a description of the
    ruins of St. Paul's, like the editions of Balbec and
    Palmyra.   *Ib. To Mann, 24 Nov. 1774.*

By the waters of Babylon we sit down and weep, when
    we think of thee, O America!
Ib. To Mason, 12 June, 1775.

This world is a comedy to those that think, a tragedy
    to those that feel.
*Ib. To the Countess of Upper Ossory, 16 Aug.
1776.*

Prognostics do not always prove prophecies,—at least
    the wisest prophets make sure of the event first.
Ib. To Thos. Walpole, 19 Feb. 1785.

All his [Sir Joshua Reynolds's] own geese are swans,
    as the swans of others are geese.
Ib. To the Countess of Upper Ossory, 1 Dec. 1786.

SIR ROBERT WALPOLE, FIRST EARL OF ORFORD

1676-1745

They now *ring* the bells, but they will soon *wring* their hands.
> Remark on the declaration of war with Spain, 1739. W. Coxe, *Memoirs of Sir Robert Walpole* (1798), vol. i, p. 618.

All those men have their price.   *Ib.* p. 757.

Madam, there are fifty thousand men slain this year in Europe, and not one Englishman.
> Remark to Queen Caroline, 1734. Hervey, *Memoirs* (1848), vol. i, p. 398.

My Lord Bath, you and I are now two as insignificant men as any in England.
> To Pulteney, Earl of Bath, on their promotion to the House of Lords. W. King, *Political & Literary Anecdotes* (1819), p. 43.

The balance of power.
> *Speech in House of Commons, 13 Feb. 1741.*

Sir Robert Walpole's definition of the gratitude of place-expectants, 'That it is a lively sense of *future* favours'.
> W. Hazlitt, *Lectures on the English Comic Writers, Wit and Humour*, p. 27.

WILLIAM WALSH

1663-1708

And sadly reflecting,
That a lover forsaken
  A new love may get,
But a neck when once broken
  Can never be set.   *The Despairing Lover*, l. 17.

Of all the torments, all the cares,
With which our lives are curst;
Of all the plagues a lover bears,
Sure rivals are the worst!
By partners, in each other kind,
Afflictions easier grow;
In love alone we hate to find
Companions of our woe.
> *Song, 'Of All the Torments'.*

I can endure my own despair,
But not another's hope.   *Ib.*

IZAAK WALTON

1593-1683

Angling may be said to be so like the mathematics, that it can never be fully learnt.
> *Compleat Angler. Epistle to the Reader.*

And for winter fly-fishing it is as useful as an almanac out of date.   *Ib.*

As no man is born an artist, so no man is born an angler.   *Ib.*

I shall stay him no longer than to wish him a rainy evening to read this following discourse; and that if he be an honest angler, the east wind may never blow when he goes a-fishing.   *Ib.*

I am, Sir, a Brother of the Angle   *Ib.* pt. I, ch. 1.

It [angling] deserves commendations; . . . it is an art, and an art worthy the knowledge and practice of a wise man.   *Ib.*

Angling is somewhat like poetry, men are to be born so.   *Ib.*

Sir Henry Wotton . . . was also a most dear lover, and a frequent practiser of the art of angling; of which he would say, 'it was an employment for his idle time, which was then not idly spent . . . a rest to his mind, a cheerer of his spirits, a diverter of sadness, a calmer of unquiet thoughts, a moderator of passions, a procurer of contentedness; and that it begat habits of peace and patience in those that professed and practised it.'   *Ib.*

I remember that a wise friend of mine did usually say, 'that which is everybody's business is nobody's business.'   *Ib.* ch. 2.

Good company and good discourse are the very sinews of virtue.   *Ib.*

An excellent angler, and now with God.   *Ib.* ch. 4.

When I was last this way a-fishing.   *Ib.*

I love such mirth as does not make friends ashamed to look upon one another next morning.   *Ib.* ch. 5.

A good, honest, wholesome, hungry breakfast.   *Ib.*

No man can lose what he never had.   *Ib.*

Thus use your frog. . . . Put your hook, I mean the arming-wire, through his mouth, and out at his gills; and then with a fine needle and silk sew the upper part of his leg, with only one stitch, to the arming-wire of your hook; or tie the frog's leg, above the upper joint, to the armed-wire; and, in so doing, use him as though you loved him.   *Ib.* ch. 8.

This dish of meat is too good for any but anglers, or very honest men.   *Ib.*

I love any discourse of rivers, and fish and fishing.   *Ib.* ch. 18.

Look to your health; and if you have it, praise God, and value it next to a good conscience; for health is the second blessing that we mortals are capable of; a blessing that money cannot buy.   *Ib.* ch. 21.

Let the blessing of St. Peter's Master be . . . upon all that are lovers of virtue; and dare trust in His providence; and be quiet; and go a-Angling.   *Ib.*

But God, who is able to prevail, wrestled with him, as the Angel did with Jacob, and marked him; marked him for his own.   *Life of Donne.*

The great Secretary of Nature and all learning, Sir Francis Bacon.   *Life of Herbert.*

Of this best man, let his just praise be given,
Heaven was in him, before he was in heaven.
> *Written in Dr. Richard Sibbes's 'Returning Backslider', now preserved in Salisbury Cathedral Library.*

WILLIAM WARBURTON

1698-1779

Orthodoxy is my doxy; heterodoxy is another man's doxy.
> Remark to Lord Sandwich. Priestley, *Memoirs* (1807), vol. i, p. 372.

ARTEMUS WARD
[CHARLES FARRAR BROWNE]
1834–1867

I now bid you a welcome adoo.
Artemus Ward His Book. The Shakers.

'Mister Ward, don't yur blud bile at the thawt that three million and a half of your culled brethren air a clanking their chains in the South?' Sez I, 'not a bile! Let 'em clank!' *Ib. Oberlin.*

The College has konfired upon me the honery title of T.K., of which I'm suffishuntly prowd. *Ib.*

'I wish thar was winders to my Sole', sed I, 'so that you could see some of my feelins.'
Ib. The Showman's Courtship.

If you mean gettin hitched, I'M IN! *Ib.*

My pollertics, like my religion, bein of a exceedin accommodatin character. *Ib. The Crisis.*

Shall we sell our birthrite for a mess of potash? *Ib.*

N.B. This is rote Sarcasticul.
Ib. A Visit to Brigham Young.

I girdid up my Lions & fled the Seen. *Ib.*

Did you ever hav the measels, and if so how many?
Ib. The Census.

'Fair youth, do you know what I'd do with you if you was my sun?' 'No,' sez he. 'Wall,' sez I, 'I'd appint your funeral tomorrow afternoon & the *korps should be ready!* You're too smart to live on this yearth.' *Ib. Edwin Forrest as Othello.*

Before he retired to his virtuous couch. *Ib.*

The female woman is one of the greatest institooshuns of which this land can boste. *Ib. Woman's Rights.*

Do me eyes deceive me earsight? Is it some dreams?
Ib. Moses, the Sassy.

By a sudden and adroit movement I placed my left eye agin the Secesher's fist.
Ib. Thrilling Scenes in Dixie.

The ground flew up and hit me in the hed. *Ib.*

I presunted myself at Betty's bedside late at nite, with considerbul licker koncealed about my persun.
Ib. Betsy-Jain Re-orgunised.

The happy marrid man dies in good stile at home, surrounded by his weeping wife and children. The old batchelor don't die at all—he sort of rots away, like a polly-wog's tail. *Ib. Draft in Baldinsville.*

It is a pity that Chawcer, who had geneyus, was so unedicated. He's the wuss speller I know of.
Artemus Ward in London, ch. 4. At the Tomb of Shakespeare.

Why these weeps? *Artemus Ward's Lecture.*

One of the principal features of my Entertainment is that it contains so many things that don't have anything to do with it. *Ib.*

I can't sing. As a singist I am not a success. I am saddest when I sing. So are those who hear me. They are sadder even than I am. *Ib.*

He [Brigham Young] is dreadfully married. He's the most married man I ever saw in my life. *Ib.*

Why is this thus? What is the reason of this thusness? *Ib.*

I am happiest when I am idle. I could live for months without performing any kind of labour, and at the expiration of that time I should feel fresh and vigorous enough to go right on in the same way for numerous more months.
Pyrotechny. III. *Pettingill.*

Why care for grammar as long as we are good?
Ib. v.

Let us all be happy, and live within our means, even if we have to borrer the money to do it with.
Science and Natural History.

MRS. HUMPHRY WARD
1851–1920

'Propinquity does it'—as Mrs. Thornburgh is always reminding us. *Robert Elsmere, bk. i, ch. 2.*

REV. NATHANIEL WARD
1578–1652

The world is full of care, much like unto a bubble;
Women and care, and care and women, and women and care and trouble.
Epigram. (Attr. by Ward to a lady at the Court of Queen of Bohemia.) Simple Cobler's Boy (1648), p. 25.

HENRY STEVENSON WASHBURN

We shall meet, but we shall miss him,
There will be one vacant chair:
We shall linger to caress him,
When we breathe our evening prayer.
The Vacant Chair, chorus.

GEORGE WASHINGTON
1732–1799

Father, I cannot tell a lie, I did it with my little hatchet.
Attr. remark. Mark Twain's *Mark Twain as George Washington.* Another version is: I can't tell a lie, Pa; you know I can't tell a lie. I did cut it with my hatchet.
Weems, *Washington, 1800* (ed. 1918), p. 23.

It is our true policy to steer clear of permanent alliance with any portion of the foreign world.
His Farewell Address to the People of the United States, 17 Sept. 1796.

Labour to keep alive in your breast that little spark of celestial fire, called conscience.
Rules of Civility and Decent Behaviour. Sparks's *Life of Washington* (1839), vol. ii, p. 109.

We must consult Brother Jonathan.
> Said to have been a frequent remark of his during the American Revolution, referring to Jonathan Trumbull, 1710–85, Governor of Connecticut. *Norwich Evening Courier*, 12 Nov. 1846, No. 797, p. 2. (*Publications of the Colonial Society of Massachusetts*, 1905, vol. vii, p. 94).

Put none but Americans on guard tonight.
> *Attr. remark, based on his circular letter to regimental commanders, 30 April 1777.*

ROWLAND WATKYNS

fl. 1662

I love him not, but shew no reason can
Wherefore, but this, *I do not love* the man.
> *Flamma sine fumo. Antipathy.*

For every marriage then is best in tune,
When that the wife is May, the husband June.
> *Ib. To the most Courteous and Fair Gentlewoman, Mrs. Elinor Williams.*

SIR WILLIAM WATSON

1858–1936

April, April,
Laugh thy girlish laughter;
Then, the moment after,
Weep thy girlish tears! *April.*

O be less beautiful, or be less brief. *Autumn.*

Slight not the songsmith. *England my Mother.*

Plucked by his hand, the basest weed that grows
Towers to a lily, reddens to a rose. *Epigram.*

How all her care was but to be fair,
  And all her task to be sweet. *The Heart of the Rose.*

When, upon orchard and lane, breaks the white foam
  of the Spring.
> *Hymn to the Sea*, Pt. iii, 12.

Nature! whose lapidary seas
Labour a pebble without cease. *Nature's Way.*

Who never negligently yet
Fashioned an April violet,
Nor would forgive, did June disclose
Unceremoniously the rose. *Ib.*

Time, and the ocean, and some fostering star,
In high cabal have made us what we are.
> *Ode on the Coronation of Edward VII*, l. 8.

Forget not, brother singer, that though Prose
Can never be too truthful or too wise,
Song is not truth, not Wisdom, but the rose
Upon Truth's lips, the light in Wisdom's eyes.
> *Ode to J. C. Collins.*

We are children of splendour and flame,
Of shuddering, also, and tears;
Magnificent out of the dust we came,
And abject from the spheres. *Ode in May.*

The staid, conservative, Came-over-with-the-Conqueror type of mind. *A Study in Contrasts*, i, 1. 42.

The thirst to know and understand,
A large and liberal discontent;
These are the goods in life's rich hand,
The things that are more excellent.
> *Things That Are More Excellent*, viii.

And not without honour my days ran,
  Nor yet without a boast shall end,
For I was Shakespeare's countryman,
  And were not you my friend? *To H. D. Traill.*

Another bruising of the hapless head
Of a wronged people yearning to be free.
> *Ver Tenebrosum. 2. Hasheen.*

In this house with starry dome,
  Floored with gemlike plains and seas,
Shall I never feel at home,
  Never wholly be at ease? *World-Strangeness.*

On from room to room I stray,
  Yet mine Host can ne'er espy,
And I know not to this day
  Whether guest or captive I. *Ib.*

ISAAC WATTS

1674–1748

Whene'er I take my walks abroad,
  How many poor I see!
What shall I render to my God
  For all his gifts to me?
> *Divine Songs for Children*, iv. *Praise for Mercies.*

Lord, I ascribe it to Thy grace,
  And not to chance, as others do,
That I was born of Christian race,
  And not a Heathen, or a Jew.
> *Ib.* vi. *Praise for the Gospel.*

There's no repentance in the grave.
> *Ib.* x. *Solemn Thoughts of God and Death.*

There is a dreadful Hell,
  And everlasting pains;
There sinners must with devils dwell
  In darkness, fire, and chains.
> *Ib.* xi. *Heaven and Hell.*

But liars we can never trust,
  Though they should speak the thing that's true;
And he that does one fault at first,
  And lies to hide it, makes it two.
> *Ib.* xv. *Against Lying.*

Let dogs delight to bark and bite,
  For God hath made them so;
Let bears and lions growl and fight,
  For 'tis their nature too.
> *Ib.* xvi. *Against Quarrelling.*

But, children, you should never let
  Such angry passions rise;
Your little hands were never made
  To tear each other's eyes. *Ib.*

Whatever brawls disturb the street,
  There should be peace at home.
> *Ib.* xvii. *Love between Brothers and Sisters.*

Birds in their little nests agree. *Ib.*

How doth the little busy bee
  Improve each shining hour,
And gather honey all the day
  From every opening flower!
        Ib. xx. *Against Idleness and Mischief.*

In works of labour, or of skill,
  I would be busy too;
For Satan finds some mischief still
  For idle hands to do.   *Ib.*

One sickly sheep infects the flock,
  And poisons all the rest.
        Ib. xxi. *Against Evil Company.*

Let me be dress'd fine as I will,
Flies, worms, and flowers, exceed me still.
        Ib. xxii. *Against Pride in Clothes.*

I have been there, and still would go;
'Tis like a little Heaven below.
        Ib. xxviii. *Lord's Day Evening.*

Hush! my dear, lie still and slumber,
  Holy angels guard thy bed!
Heavenly blessings without number
  Gently falling on thy head.   *Ib. Cradle Hymn.*

Were I so tall to reach the Pole,
  Or grasp the ocean in my span,
I must be measured by my soul;
  The mind 's the standard of the man.
        Ib. False Greatness.

'Tis the voice of the sluggard; I heard him complain,
'You have wak'd me too soon, I must slumber again'.
As the door on its hinges, so he on his bed,
Turns his sides and his shoulders and his heavy head.
        Moral Songs, i. *The Sluggard.*

Abroad in the meadows to see the young lambs
Run sporting about by the side of their dams,
With fleeces so clean and so white.
        Ib. ii. *Innocent Play.*

How rude are the boys that throw pebbles and mire!
        Ib.

I'll not willingly offend,
  Nor be easily offended;
What's amiss I'll strive to mend,
  And endure what can't be mended.
        Ib. vi. *Good Resolution.*

Lord, in the morning thou shalt hear
My voice ascending high.   *Psalms,* v.

O God, our help in ages past,
  Our hope for years to come,
Our shelter from the stormy blast,
  And our eternal home.

Beneath the shadow of Thy Throne
  Thy saints have dwelt secure;
Sufficient is Thine Arm alone,
  And our defence is sure.

Before the hills in order stood,
  Or earth received her frame,
From everlasting Thou art God,
  To endless years the same.

A thousand ages in Thy sight
  Are like an evening gone;
Short as the watch that ends the night
  Before the rising sun.

Time, like an ever-rolling stream,
  Bears all its sons away;
They fly forgotten, as a dream
  Dies at the opening day.   *Ib. Psalm* xc.

How bright these glorious spirits shine!
  Whence all their white array?
How came they to the blissful seats
  Of everlasting day?
        Hymns and Spiritual Songs, bk. i, No. 41,
        How Bright These Glorious Spirits. First
        line altered from Watts's original: *These
        glorious minds how bright they shine.*

Hark! from the tombs a doleful sound.
        Ib. bk. ii, No. 63. *Hark! from the Tombs.*

When I can read my title clear
  To mansions in the skies,
I bid farewell to every fear,
  And wipe my weeping eyes.   *Ib. No.* 65.

There is a land of pure delight,
  Where saints immortal reign;
Infinite day excludes the night,
  And pleasures banish pain.
        Ib. No. 66. *There is a Land of Pure Delight.*

Death, like a narrow sea, divides
  That heavenly land from ours.   *Ib.*

So to the Jews old Canaan stood,
  While Jordan rolled between.   *Ib.*

But timorous mortals start and shrink
  To cross the narrow sea,
And linger shivering on the brink,
  And fear to launch away.   *Ib.*

Could we but climb where Moses stood,
  And view the landscape o'er;
Not Jordan's stream, nor death's cold flood,
  Should fright us from the shore.   *Ib.*

When I survey the wondrous cross.
        Ib. bk. iii, No. 7. *When I Survey the Wondrous
        Cross.*

Were the whole realm of nature mine,
That were an offering far too small;
Love so amazing, so Divine,
Demands my soul, my life, my all.   *Ib.*

WALTER THEODORE
WATTS-DUNTON

1832–1914

Behold, ye builders, demigods who made England's
  Walhalla [Westminster Abbey].
        What the Silent Voices Said, iv. *The Minster
        Spirits.*

FREDERIC EDWARD
WEATHERLY

1848–1929

Where are the boys of the Old Brigade?
        The Old Brigade.

Not in the Abbey proudly laid
  Find they a place or part;
The gallant boys of the old brigade,
  They sleep in old England's heart.   *Ib.*

Why, Jack's the king of all,
For they all love Jack! *They All Love Jack.*

WILLIAM WEBB

fl. 1839

His throat they cut from ear to ear,
His brains they pun*ched* in,
His name was Mr. William Weare,
Wot lived in Lyon's Inn.
> *Ballad.* See Lord William Lennox in *The Sporting Review*, July 1839, vol. ii, p. 42. Also attrib. to Theodore Hook (1788–1841). See C. Hindley's *Life and Times of James Catnach* (1878), p. 145.

DANIEL WEBSTER

1782–1852

The gentleman has not seen how to reply to this, otherwise than by supposing me to have advanced the doctrine that a national debt is a national blessing.
> *Second Speech in the Senate on Foot's Resolution, 20 Jan. 1830.*

He [Alexander Hamilton] smote the rock of the national resources, and abundant streams of revenue gushed forth. He touched the dead corpse of the Public Credit, and it sprung upon its feet.
> *Speech at a Public Dinner at New York, 10 March, 1831.*

On this question of principle, while actual suffering was yet afar off, they [the Colonies] raised their flag against a power, to which, for purposes of foreign conquest and subjugation, Rome, in the height of her glory, is not to be compared; a power which has dotted over the surface of the whole globe with her possessions and military posts, whose morning drum-beat, following the sun, and keeping company with the hours, circles the earth with one continuous and unbroken strain of the martial airs of England.
> *Speech in the Senate on the President's Protest, 7 May, 1834.*

Thank God, I—I also—am an American!
> *Speech on the Completion of Bunker Hill Monument, 17 June 1843.*

The Law: It has honoured us, may we honour it.
> *Ib.*

I was born an American; I will live an American; I shall die an American.
> *Speech in the Senate on 'The Compromise Bill', 17 July, 1850.*

Fearful concatenation of circumstances.
> *Argument on the Murder of Captain Joseph White.*

JOHN WEBSTER

1580?–1625?

She's loose i' th' hilts. *The Duchess of Malfi*, II. v.

Rais'd by that curious engine, your white hand.
> *Ib.* III. ii. 297.

I am acquainted with sad misery
As the tann'd galley-slave is with his oar.
> *Ib.* IV. ii. 25.

I have made a soap-boiler costive. *Ib.* I. 117.

I am Duchess of Malfi still. *Ib.* I. 146.

I know death hath ten thousand several doors
For men to take their exits. *Ib.* I. 222.

So I were out of your whispering. *Ib.* I. 226.

FERDINAND:
Cover her face; mine eyes dazzle: she died young.
BOSOLA:
I think not so; her infelicity
Seem'd to have years too many. *Ib.* I. 267.

We are merely the stars' tennis-balls, struck and bandied
Which way please them. *Ib.* V. iv. 52.

Is not old wine wholesomest, old pippins toothsomest, old wood burn brightest, old linen wash whitest? Old soldiers, sweetheart, are surest, and old lovers are soundest. *Westward Hoe*, II. ii.

I saw him even now going the way of all flesh. *Ib.*

'Tis just like a summer bird-cage in a garden: the birds that are without despair to get in, and the birds that are within despair and are in a consumption for fear they shall never get out.
> *The White Devil*, I. ii.

A mere tale of a tub, my words are idle. *Ib.* II. i.

Call for the robin redbreast and the wren,
Since o'er shady groves they hover,
And with leaves and flowers do cover
The friendless bodies of unburied men. *Ib.* V. iv.

I am i' th' way to study a long silence. *Ib.* vi.

Prosperity doth bewitch men, seeming clear;
But seas do laugh, show white, when rocks are near.
> *Ib.*

I have caught
An everlasting cold. *Ib.*

ARTHUR WELLESLEY
DUKE OF WELLINGTON

1769–1852

All the business of war, and indeed all the business of life, is to endeavour to find out what you don't know by what you do; that's what I called 'guessing what was at the other side of the hill'.
> *Croker Papers* (1885), vol. iii, p. 276.

F.M. the Duke of Wellington presents his compliments to Mr. —— and declines to interfere in circumstances over which he has no control.
> G. A. Sala, *Echoes of the Week* in *London Illustrated News*, 23 Aug. 1884. Vol. lxxxv, p. 171, col. 1.

I never saw so many shocking bad hats in my life.
> *On seeing the first Reformed Parliament.* Sir William Fraser, *Words on Wellington* (1889), p. 12.

The battle of Waterloo was won in the playing fields of Eton. *Ib.* p. 138.

The next greatest misfortune to losing a battle is to gain such a victory as this.
S. Rogers, *Recollections* (1859), p. 215.

'What a glorious thing must be a victory, Sir.' 'The greatest tragedy in the world, Madam, except a defeat.' *Ib.* footnote.

There is no mistake; there has been no mistake; and there shall be no mistake.
Wellingtoniana (1852), p. 78.

Up Guards and at them again!
Attr. to Wellington during the Battle of Waterloo. Capt. Batty's letter, 22 June 1815, in Booth's Battle of Waterloo. J. W. Croker, in a letter to A. Greville, 14 Mar. 1852, wrote 'Perhaps I might also venture to ask his Grace whether he did say "Up Guards and at them". ' *Wellington replied in an undated letter to Croker which is in Croker Correspondence and Diaries, 1884, vol. iii, p. 280:* 'What I must have said and possibly did say was, Stand up Guards! and then gave the commanding officers the order to attack.'

I used to say of him [Napoleon] that his presence on the field made the difference of forty thousand men.
Stanhope's *Life of Wellington*, p. 9.

Ours [our army] is composed of the scum of the earth—the mere scum of the earth. *Ib.* p. 14.

My rule always was to do the business of the day in the day. *Ib.* p. 71.

The Government was contemplating the dispatch of an expedition to Burma, with a view to taking Rangoon, and a question arose as to who would be the fittest general to be sent in command of the expedition. The Cabinet sent for the Duke of Wellington, and asked his advice. He instantly replied, 'Send Lord Combermere.'
'But we have always understood that your Grace thought Lord Combermere a fool.'
'So he is a fool, and a d—d fool; but he can take Rangoon.'
G. W. E. Russell's *Collections and Recollections*, ch. 2.

In refusing the dedication of a song (the Duke of Wellington) informed Mrs. Norton that he had been obliged to make a rule of refusing dedications, 'because, in his situation as Chancellor of the University of Oxford, he had been much exposed to authors.' *Ib.*

I have no small talk and Peel has no manners. *Ib.* ch. 14.

I don't care a twopenny damn what becomes of the ashes of Napoleon Buonaparte.
Attr. Farmer and Henley, *Slang and its Analogues*.

Publish and be damned. *Attr.*

By God, I never saw so many whores
In all my life before.
Hardy, *The Dynasts*, Pt. III. II. iii.
UXBRIDGE:
I have lost my leg, by God!
WELLINGTON:
By God, and have you! *Ib.* VII. viii.

HERBERT GEORGE WELLS
1866–

'I'm a Norfan, both sides,' he would explain, with the air of one who had seen trouble.
Kipps, bk. i, ch. 6, § 1.

'I expect,' he said, 'I was thinking jest what a Rum Go everything is. I expect it was something like that.' *Ib.* bk. iii, ch. 3, § 8.

The shape of things to come. *Title of Book.*

The Time-Machine. *Title of Book.*

The War that will end War. *Title of Book*, 1914.

CHARLES WESLEY
1707–1788

'Christ, the Lord, is risen to-day,'
Sons of men and angels say,
Raise your joys and triumphs high,
Sing, ye heavens, and earth reply.
Hymns and Sacred Poems (1739). *Christ, the Lord, is Risen To-day.*

Jesu, Lover of my soul,
Let me to Thy Bosom fly,
While the nearer waters roll,
While the tempest still is high;
Hide me, O my Saviour, hide,
Till the storm of life is past;
Safe into the haven guide,
O receive my soul at last.
Ib. (1740), *Jesu, Lover of My Soul.*

Other refuge have I none;
Hangs my helpless soul on Thee. *Ib.*

Cover my defenceless head
With the shadow of Thy wing. *Ib.*

Thou of Life the Fountain art;
Freely let me take of Thee;
Spring Thou up within my heart,
Rise to all eternity. *Ib.*

Gentle Jesus, meek and mild,
Look upon a little child;
Pity my simplicity,
Suffer me to come to thee.
Ib. (1742), *Gentle Jesus, Meek and Mild.*

Soldiers of Christ, arise,
And put your armour on.
Ib. (1749), *Soldiers of Christ, Arise.*

Lift up your heart, lift up your voice;
Rejoice, again I say, rejoice.
Hymns for Our Lord's Resurrection (1746): *Rejoice, the Lord is King.*

Hark! the herald-angels sing
Glory to the new-born King;
Peace on earth, and mercy mild,
God and sinners reconciled.
Ib. Christmas Hymn: Hark! the Herald Angels Sing.
First two lines altered by George Whitefield in 1753 from Wesley's original
Hark, how all the welkin rings,
'Glory to the King of kings'.

Lo! He comes with clouds descending.
  Hymns of Intercession for all Mankind (1758)
  Lo! He Comes with Clouds. New version of
  John Cennick's 'Lo! He cometh, countless
  trumpets', in *Collection of Sacred Hymns*,
  1752.

Those who set at naught and sold Him,
Pierced and nail'd Him to the Tree,
    Deeply wailing,
Shall the true Messiah see.   *Ib.*

Let saints on earth in concert sing.
  Funeral Hymns (1759): *Let saints on earth.*
  Altered by F. H. Murray in his *Hymnal for
  Use in the English Church*, 1852, from 'Let all
  the saints terrestrial sing'.

JOHN WESLEY

1703–1791

I look upon all the world as my parish.
              Journal, 11 June 1739.

Though I am always in haste, I am never in a hurry.
  Select Letters (1837). *Letter to a member of the
  Society. 10 Dec. 1777.*

Do all the good you can,
By all the means you can,
In all the ways you can,
In all the places you can,
At all the times you can,
To all the people you can,
As long as ever you can.
            Letters (1915). *Rule of Conduct.*

Let it be observed, that slovenliness is no part of
  religion; that neither this, nor any text of Scripture, condemns neatness of apparel. Certainly this
  is a duty, not a sin. 'Cleanliness is, indeed, next
  to godliness.'   *Sermons*, No. xciii. *On Dress.*

EDWARD NOYES WESTCOTT

1846–1898

'They say a reasonable amount o' fleas is good fer a
  dog—keeps him from broodin' over bein' a dog,
  mebbe.'   *David Harum*, ch. 32.

EDITH WHARTON

1862–1937

Mrs. Ballinger is one of the ladies who pursue Culture in bands, as though it were dangerous to meet
it alone.   *Xingu*, ch. 1.

RICHARD WHATELY
ARCHBISHOP OF DUBLIN

1787–1863

Preach not because you have to say something, but
because you have something to say. *Apophthegms.*

Happiness is no laughing matter.   *Ib.* p. 218.

It is a folly to expect men to do all that they may
reasonably be expected to do.   *Ib.* p. 219.

Honesty is the best policy; but he who is governed
by that maxim is not an honest man.
                                    Ib. p. 219.

WILLIAM WHEWELL

1794–1866

And so no force, however great,
  Can stretch a cord, however fine,
  Into a horizontal line
That shall be absolutely straight.
      Quoted as an example of accidental metre
      and rhyme. Printed in prose in Whewell's
      Elementary Treatise on Mechanics, 1819.

JAMES ABBOTT McNEILL WHISTLER

1834–1903

Listen! There never was an artistic period. There
never was an Art-loving nation.
                        'Ten O'Clock.'

Nature is usually wrong.   *Ib.*

I am not arguing with you—I am telling you.
              Gentle Art of Making Enemies.

'I only know of two painters in the world,' said a
newly introduced feminine enthusiast to Whistler,
'yourself and Velasquez.' 'Why,' answered
Whistler in dulcet tones, 'why drag in Velasquez?'
      D. C. Seitz, *Whistler Stories* (1913), p. 27.

[In answer to a lady who said that a landscape
reminded her of his work]
Yes madam, Nature is creeping up.   *Ib.*

[In answer to the question 'For two days' labour,
you ask two hundred guineas?']
No, I ask it for the knowledge of a lifetime.   *Ib.*

You shouldn't say it is not good. You should say you
do not like it; and then, you know, you're perfectly safe.

[Answering Oscar Wilde's 'I wish I had said that']
You will, Oscar, you will.
              L. C. Ingleby, *Oscar Wilde*, p. 67.

HENRY KIRKE WHITE

1785–1806

Oft in danger, oft in woe,
Onward, Christians, onward go.
      W. J. Hall's *Mitre Hymn Book*, 1836. Adapted
      by Dr. W. B. Collyer from White's original
      'Much in sorrow, oft in woe.'

JOSEPH BLANCO WHITE

1775–1841

Mysterious Night! when our first parent knew
  Thee from report divine, and heard thy name,
  Did he not tremble for this lovely frame,
This glorious canopy of light and blue?
                        To Night, l. 1.

Hesperus with the host of heaven came,
And lo! Creation widened in man's view. *Ib.* l. 8.

If Light can thus deceive, wherefore not Life?
Ib. l. 14.

PAUL WHITEHEAD
1710–1774

Honour's a mistress all mankind pursue;
Yet most mistake the false one for the true:
Lur'd by the trappings, dazzled by the paint,
We worship oft the idol for the saint.
Honour, l. 105.

Why, praise is satire in these sinful days.
Manners, l. 215.

WILLIAM WHITEHEAD
1715–1785

Yes, I'm in love, I feel it now,
And Caelia has undone me;
And yet I'll swear I can't tell how
The pleasing plague stole on me.
The Je ne scay quoi, st. i. Song.

Her voice, her touch, might give th' alarm—
'Twas both perhaps, or neither;
In short, 'twas that provoking charm
Of Caelia altogether. *Ib.*

WILLIAM WHITING
1825–1878

O hear us when we cry to Thee
For those in peril on the sea.
Hymn: Eternal Father Strong to Save.

WALT WHITMAN
? 1819–1892

Silent and amazed even when a little boy,
I remember I heard the preacher every Sunday put
God in his statements,
As contending against some being or influence.
A Child's Amaze.

Give me the splendid silent sun with all his beams
full-dazzling!
Give Me the Splendid Silent Sun.

I dream'd in a dream I saw a city invincible to the
attacks of the whole of the rest of the earth,
I dream'd that was the new city of Friends.
I Dream'd in a Dream.

The institution of the dear love of comrades.
I Hear it was Charged against Me.

Joy, shipmate, joy!
(Pleas'd to my soul at death I cry,)
Our life is closed, our life begins,
The long, long anchorage we leave,
The ship is clear at last, she leaps!
She swiftly courses from the shore,
Joy, shipmate, joy. *Joy, Shipmate, Joy.*

Me imperturbe, standing at ease in Nature.
Me Imperturbe.

O Captain! my Captain! our fearful trip is done,
The ship has weather'd every rack, the prize we
sought is won,

The port is near, the bells I hear, the people all
exulting. *O Captain! My Captain!* i.

The ship is anchor'd safe and sound, its voyage closed
and done.
From fearful trip the victor ship comes in with object
won;
Exult O shores, and ring O bells! But I with mourn-
ful tread
Walk the deck my captain lies, Fallen cold and dead.
Ib. iii.

Out of the cradle endlessly rocking,
Out of the mocking-bird's throat, the musical shuttle,
A reminiscence sing.
Out of the Cradle endlessly Rocking.

O we can wait no longer,
We too take ship O soul,
Joyous we too launch out on trackless seas,
Fearless for unknown shores on waves of ecstasy to
sail,
Amid the wafting winds (thou pressing me to thee,
I thee to me, O soul,)
Caroling free, singing our song of God,
Chanting our chant of pleasant exploration.
Passage to India, 8.

O my brave soul!
O farther, farther, sail!
O daring joy, but safe; are they not all the seas of
God?
O farther, farther, farther sail! *Passage to India,* 9.

Come my tan-faced children,
Follow well in order, get your weapons ready,
Have you your pistols? have you your sharp-edged
axes?
Pioneers! O pioneers!
Pioneers! O Pioneers!

Beautiful that war and all its deeds of carnage must in
time be utterly lost,
That the hands of the sisters Death and Night
incessantly softly wash again, and ever again, this
soil'd world;
For my enemy is dead, a man as divine as myself is
dead,
I look where he lies white-faced and still in the coffin
—I draw near,
Bend down and touch lightly with my lips the white
face in the coffin. *Reconciliation.*

Where the populace rise at once against the never-
ending audacity of elected persons.
Song of the Broad Axe, 5, l. 12.

Where women walk in public processions in the
streets the same as the men,
Where they enter the public assembly and take places
the same as the men;
Where the city of the faithfullest friends stands,
Where the city of the cleanliness of the sexes stands,
Where the city of the healthiest fathers stands,
Where the city of the best-bodied mothers stands,
There the great city stands. *Ib.* l. 20.

I celebrate myself, and sing myself.
Song of Myself, 1.

I loafe and invite my soul. *Ib.*

Urge and urge and urge,
Always the procreant urge of the world. *Ib.* 3.

A child said *What is the grass?* fetching it to one with
full hands;
. . . .
Or I guess it is the handkerchief of the Lord,
A scented gift and remembrancer designedly dropt,
Bearing the owner's name someway in the corners,
that we may see and remark, and say *Whose?*
. . . .
And now it seems to me the beautiful uncut hair of
graves. *Ib.* 6.

The look of the bay mare shames silliness out of me.
Ib. 13.

I also say it is good to fall, battles are lost in the same
spirit in which they are won. *Ib.* 18.

I think I could turn and live with animals, they are so
placid and self-contain'd,
I stand and look at them long and long.
They do not sweat and whine about their condition,
They do not lie awake in the dark and weep for their
sins,
They do not make me sick discussing their duty to
God,
Not one is dissatisfied, not one is demented with the
mania of owning things,
Not one kneels to another, nor to his kind that lived
thousands of years ago,
Not one is respectable or unhappy over the whole
earth. *Ib.* 31.

Behold, I do not give lectures or a little charity,
When I give I give myself. *Ib.* 39.

My rendezvous is appointed, it is certain,
The Lord will be there and wait till I come on perfect
terms,
The great Camerado, the lover true for whom I pine
will be there. *Ib.* 44.

I have said that the soul is not more than the body,
And I have said that the body is not more than the
soul,
And nothing, not God, is greater to one than one's
self is. *Ib.* 47.

In the faces of men and women I see God, and in my
own face in the glass,
I find letters from God dropt in the street, and every
one is sign'd by God's name,
And I leave them where they are, for I know that
wheresoe'er I go,
Others will punctually come for ever and ever.
Ib.

Do I contradict myself?
Very well then I contradict myself,
(I am large, I contain multitudes.) *Ib.* 50.

I sound my barbaric yawp over the roofs of the world.
Ib. 51.

Afoot and light-hearted I take to the open road,
Healthy, free, the world before me,
The long brown path before me leading wherever I
choose. *Song of the Open Road,* 1.

The earth, that is sufficient,
I do not want the constellations any nearer,
I know they are very well where they are,
I know they suffice for those who belong to them.
Ib. l. 8.

I am larger, better than I thought,
I did not know I held so much goodness. *Ib.* 5.

I will put in my poems that with you is heroism upon
land and sea,
And I will report all heroism from an American point
of view. *Starting from Paumanok,* 6.

This dust was once the man,
Gentle, plain, just and resolute, under whose cau-
tious hand,
Against the foulest crime in history known in any
land or age,
Was saved the Union of these States.
This Dust was Once the Man.

When lilacs last in the dooryard bloom'd,
And the great star early droop'd in the western sky in
the night,
I mourn'd, and yet shall mourn with ever-returning
spring.
When Lilacs Last in the Dooryard Bloom'd, 1.

Come lovely and soothing death,
Undulate round the world, serenely arriving, arriving,
In the day, in the night, to all, to each,
Sooner or later, delicate death.
Prais'd be the fathomless universe,
For life and joy, and for objects and knowledge
curious,
And for love, sweet love—but praise! praise! praise!
For the sure-enwinding arms of cool-enfolding death.
Ib. 14.

Camerado, this is no book,
Who touches this touches a man. *Ib. So Long!*

I am he that walks with the tender and growing night,
I call to the earth and sea half-held by the night.
Press close bare-bosom'd night—press close mag-
netic nourishing night!
Night of south winds—night of the large few stars!
Still nodding night—mad naked summer night.
Ib. 21.

Earth of the vitreous pour of the full moon just
tinged with blue! *Ib.*

Far-swooping elbow'd earth—rich apple-blossom'd
earth!
Smile, for your lover comes. *Ib.*

These United States.
A Backward Glance O'er Travell'd Roads.
'These States' is *passim* throughout Whit-
man's verse.

JOHN GREENLEAF
WHITTIER

1807–1892

O brother man! fold to thy heart thy brother.
Worship, l. 49.

I know not where His islands lift
Their fronded palms in air;
I only know I cannot drift
Beyond His love and care.
The Eternal Goodness, xx.

The Indian Summer of the heart! *Memories,* ix.

Up from the meadows rich with corn,
Clear in the cool September morn,
The clustered spires of Frederick stand
Green-walled by the hills of Maryland.
Barbara Frietchie, l. 1.

Bravest of all in Frederick town,
She took up the flag the men hauled down.
Ib. l. 17.

Up the street came the rebel tread,
Stonewall Jackson riding ahead.
Ib. l. 23.

'Shoot, if you must, this old gray head,
But spare your country's flag,' she said.
Ib. l. 35.

'Who touches a hair of yon gray head
Dies like a dog! March on!' he said.
Ib. l. 41.

'Dinna ye hear it?—Dinna ye hear it?
The pipes o' Havelock sound!'
Pipes at Lucknow, iv.

For all sad words of tongue or pen,
The saddest are these: 'It might have been!'
Maud Muller, l. 105.

CORNELIUS WHURR

c. 1845

What lasting joys the man attend
Who has a polished female friend.
The Accomplished Female Friend.

GEORGE JOHN WHYTE-MELVILLE

1821–1878

Then drink, puppy, drink, and let ev'ry puppy drink,
That is old enough to lap and to swallow;
For he'll grow into a hound, so we'll pass the bottle round,
And merrily we'll whoop and we'll holloa.
Drink, Puppy, Drink, chorus.

The swallows are making them ready to fly,
Wheeling out on a windy sky:
Goodbye, Summer, goodbye, goodbye
Goodbye, Summer.

Wrap me up in my tarpaulin jacket,
And say a poor buffer lies low,
And six stalwart lancers shall carry me,
With steps solemn, mournful, and slow.
The Tarpaulin Jacket.

ELLA WHEELER WILCOX

1855–1919

Laugh, and the world laughs with you;
Weep, and you weep alone;
For the sad old earth must borrow its mirth,
But has trouble enough of its own.
Solitude.

So many gods, so many creeds,
So many paths that wind and wind,
While just the art of being kind
Is all the sad world needs.   *The World's Need.*

OSCAR FINGAL O'FLAHERTIE WILLS WILDE

1856–1900

He did not wear his scarlet coat,
For blood and wine are red,
And blood and wine were on his hands
When they found him with the dead.
The Ballad of Reading Gaol, pt. I. i.

I never saw a man who looked
With such a wistful eye
Upon that little tent of blue
Which prisoners call the sky.
Ib. iii.

When a voice behind me whispered low,
'That fellow's got to swing.'
Ib. iv.

Yet each man kills the thing he loves,
By each let this be heard,
Some do it with a bitter look,
Some with a flattering word.
The coward does it with a kiss,
The brave man with a sword!
Ib. vii.

Like two doomed ships that pass in storm
We had crossed each other's way:
But we made no sign, we said no word,
We had no word to say,
Ib. II. xii.

The Governor was strong upon
The Regulations Act:
The Doctor said that Death was but
A scientific fact:
And twice a day the Chaplain called,
And left a little tract.
Ib. III. iii.

And once, or twice, to throw the dice
Is a gentlemanly game,
But he does not win who plays with Sin
In the secret House of Shame.
Ib. xxiii.

Something was dead in each of us,
And what was dead was Hope.
Ib. xxxi.

And the wild regrets, and the bloody sweats,
None knew so well as I:
For he who lives more lives than one
More deaths than one must die.
Ib. xxxvii.

I know not whether Laws be right,
Or whether Laws be wrong;
All that we know who lie in gaol
Is that the wall is strong;
And that each day is like a year,
A year whose days are long.
Ib. v. i.

How else but through a broken heart
May Lord Christ enter in?
Ib. xiv.

Surely there was a time I might have trod
The sunlit heights, and from life's dissonance
Struck one clear chord to reach the ears of God.
Helas! (*Lines prefixed to his Poems, Paris edition, 1903.*)

And yet, and yet,
These Christs that die upon the barricades,
God knows it I am with them, in some ways.
Sonnet to Liberty: Not that I Love Thy Children.

All her bright golden hair
  Tarnished with rust,
She that was young and fair
  Fallen to dust.   *Requiescat.*

O Singer of Persephone!
In the dim meadows desolate
Dost thou remember Sicily?   *Theocritus.*

Art never expresses anything but itself.
    The Decay of Lying (1891), p. 43.

Really, if the lower orders don't set us a good
example, what on earth is the use of them?
    Importance of Being Earnest, Act I.

In married life three is company and two none. *Ib.*

Confirmed and secret Bunburyist.   *Ib.*

I have invented an invaluable permanent invalid
called Bunbury, in order that I may be able to go
down into the country whenever I choose.   *Ib.*

To lose one parent, Mr. Worthing, may be regarded as a
misfortune; to lose both looks like carelessness. *Ib.*

All women become like their mothers. That is their
  tragedy. No man does. That's his.   *Ib.*

The chapter on the Fall of the Rupee you may omit.
It is somewhat too sensational.   *Ib.* Act. II.

On an occasion of this kind it becomes more than a
moral duty to speak one's mind. It becomes a
pleasure.   *Ib.*

Meredith is a prose Browning, and so is Browning.
He used poetry as a medium for writing in prose.
    The Critic as Artist. Part I.
    Intentions.

A little sincerity is a dangerous thing, and a great deal
of it is absolutely fatal.   *Ib.* 2.

Ah! don't say that you agree with me. When people
agree with me I always feel that I must be wrong.
                                 Ib.

As long as war is regarded as wicked, it will always
have its fascination. When it is looked upon as
vulgar, it will cease to be popular.   *Ib.*

There is no sin except stupidity.   *Ib.*

Many a woman has a past, but I am told that she has
at least a dozen, and that they all fit.
    Lady Windermere's Fan. Act. I.

There is nothing in the whole world so unbecoming
to a woman as a Nonconformist conscience.
                         Ib. Act III.

CECIL GRAHAM:
What is a cynic?
LORD DARLINGTON:
A man who knows the price of everything and the
value of nothing.   *Ib.*

DUMBY:
Experience is the name every one gives to their
mistakes.
CECIL GRAHAM:
One shouldn't commit any.
DUMBY:
Life would be very dull without them.   *Ib.*

There is no such thing as a moral or an immoral book.
Books are well written, or badly written.
    Picture of Dorian Gray, preface.

The moral life of man forms part of the subject-
matter of the artist, but the morality of art consists
in the perfect use of an imperfect medium.   *Ib.*

There is only one thing in the world worse than being
talked about, and that is not being talked about.
                           Ib. ch. 1.

A man cannot be too careful in the choice of his
enemies.   *Ib.*

The only way to get rid of a temptation is to yield
to it.   *Ib.* ch. 2.

Children begin by loving their parents; as they grow
older they judge them; sometimes they forgive
them.   *Ib.* ch. 5.

A cigarette is the perfect type of a perfect pleasure.
It is exquisite, and it leaves one unsatisfied. What
more can one want?   *Ib.* ch. 6.

It is better to be beautiful than to be good. But . . .
it is better to be good than to be ugly.
                            Ib. ch. 17.

Anybody can be good in the country.   *Ib.* ch. 19.

As for the virtuous poor, one can pity them, of course,
but one cannot possibly admire them.
    Soul of Man under Socialism.

Democracy means simply the bludgeoning of the
people by the people for the people.   *Ib.*

MRS. ALLONBY:
They say, Lady Hunstanton, that when good Ameri-
cans die they go to Paris.
LADY HUNSTANTON:
Indeed? And when bad Americans die, where do
they go to?
LORD ILLINGWORTH:
Oh, they go to America.
    A Woman of No Importance (1893), Act I.

The youth of America is their oldest tradition. It
has been going on now for three hundred years.
                                   Ib.

One should never trust a woman who tells one her
real age. A woman who would tell one that,
would tell one anything.   *Ib.*

LORD ILLINGWORTH:
The Book of Life begins with a man and a woman in
a garden.
MRS. ALLONBY:
It ends with Revelations.   *Ib.*

GERALD:
I suppose society is wonderfully delightful!
LORD ILLINGWORTH:
To be in it is merely a bore. But to be out of it
simply a tragedy.   *Ib.* Act III.

You should study the Peerage, Gerald. . . . It is the
best thing in fiction the English have ever done.
                                 Ib.

A thing is not necessarily true because a man dies
for it.
    Sebastian Melmoth (1904), p. 12. *Oscariana*
    (1910), p. 8.

(*At the New York Custom House*)
I have nothing to declare except my genius.
    F. Harris, *Oscar Wilde* (1918), p. 75.

(A huge fee [for an operation] was mentioned)
'Ah, well, then,' said Oscar, 'I suppose that I shall
 have to die beyond my means'.
> R. H. Sherard, Life of Oscar Wilde (1906),
> p. 421.

JOHN WILKES
1727–1797

The chapter of accidents is the longest chapter in the
book.
> *Attributed to John Wilkes by Southey in The
> Doctor (1837), vol. iv, p. 166.*

WILLIAM WILKIE
1721–1772

[His] labour for his pains.
> *Fables. The Boy and the Rainbow, ad fin.*

EMMA HART WILLARD
1787–1870

Rocked in the cradle of the deep.　　　　*Song.*

WILLIAM III OF ENGLAND
1650–1702

I will die in the last ditch.
> *Hume, History of Great Britain, vol. ii, 1757,
> p. 226. Charles II, ch. 3.*

Every bullet has its billet.
> *John Wesley, Journal, 6 June, 1765.*

SIR CHARLES HANBURY WILLIAMS
1708–1759

Dear Betty, come, give me sweet kisses,
　For sweeter no girl ever gave:
But why in the midst of our blisses,
　Do you ask me how many I'd have?
I'm not to be stinted in pleasure,
　Then prithee, dear Betty, be kind;
For as I love thee beyond measure,
　To numbers I'll not be confin'd.
> *A Ballad in Imitation of Martial, Lib. 6, Ep. 34.
> Works (1822), vol. i, p. 111.*

HARRY WILLIAMS and JACK JUDGE

It's a long way to Tipperary, it's a long way to go;
It's a long way to Tipperary, to the sweetest girl I
　know!
Good-bye Piccadilly, Farewell Leicester Square;
It's a long, long way to Tipperary, But my heart's
　right there!
> *It's A Long Way to Tipperary.
> Chorus claimed by Alice Smythe B. Jay.
> Written in 1908. See N.Y. Times, 20 Sept.
> 1907.*

In the shade of the old apple tree.　*Title of Song.*

I'm afraid to come home in the dark.
　　　　　　　　　　　　　Title of Song.

ISAAC WILLIAMS
1802–1865

Disposer Supreme,
And Judge of the earth.
> *Hymns translated from the Parisian Breviary
> (1839), p. 271.*

NATHANIEL PARKER WILLIS
1806–1867

At present there is no distinction among the upper
ten thousand of the city.
> *Necessity for a Promenade Drive.*

W. G. WILLS
19th cent.

I'll sing thee songs of Araby,
　And tales of wild Cashmere,
Wild tales to cheat thee of a sigh,
　Or charm thee to a tear.
> *'Lalla Rookh.'*

D. EARDLEY WILMOT
contemp.

It's a corner of heaven itself,
　Though it's only a tumble-down nest,
But with love brooding there, why, no place can
　compare,
With my little grey home in the west.
> *My Little Grey Home.*

JOHN WILSON
1785–1854

See CHRISTOPHER NORTH

JOHN WILSON
d. 1889.

Oh for a book and a shady nook,
　Either in door or out;
With the green leaves whispering overhead,
　Or the street cries all about.
Where I may read all at my ease,
　Both of the new and old;
For a jolly good book whereon to look,
　Is better to me than gold.
> *Lines written as a motto to a second-hand
> books catalogue. Lubbock, Pleasures of Life,
> ed. 1887, p. 48.*

THOMAS WOODROW WILSON

1856–1924

There is such a thing as a man being too proud to fight.   *Address at Philadelphia, 10 May 1915.*

We have stood apart, studiously neutral.
Message to Congress, 7 Dec. 1915.

The world must be made safe for democracy.
Address to Congress, 2 April 1917.

It is indispensable that the governments associated against Germany should know beyond a peradventure with whom they are dealing.
Note to Germany, 14 Oct. 1918.

ARTHUR WIMPERIS

1874–

Gilbert, the Filbert,
The Colonel of the Knuts.
Gilbert, the Filbert.

ROBERT CHARLES WINTHROP

1809–1894

A Star for every State, and a State for every Star.
Speech on Boston Common, 27 Aug. 1862.

GEORGE WITHER

1588–1667

Shall I, wasting in despair,
  Die because a woman's fair?
Or make pale my cheeks with care,
  'Cause another's rosy are?
Be she fairer than the day,
Or the flow'ry meads in May;
  If she be not so to me,
  What care I how fair she be.   *Sonnet.*

I loved a lass, a fair one,
  As fair as e'er was seen;
She was indeed a rare one,
  Another Sheba queen.
I Loved a Lass, a Fair One.

CHARLES WOLFE

1791–1823

Not a drum was heard, not a funeral note,
  As his corse to the rampart we hurried.
The Burial of Sir John Moore at Corunna, i.

We buried him darkly at dead of night,
  The sods with our bayonets turning.   *Ib. ii.*

But he lay like a warrior taking his rest,
  With his martial cloak around him.   *Ib. iii.*

Few and short were the prayers we said,
  And we spoke not a word of sorrow;
But we steadfastly gazed on the face that was dead,
  And we bitterly thought of the morrow.   *Ib. iv.*

We carved not a line, and we raised not a stone—
  But we left him alone with his glory.   *Ib. viii.*

JAMES WOLFE

1727–1759

[*The General . . . repeated nearly the whole of Gray's Elegy . . . adding, as he concluded, that*] he would prefer being the author of that poem to the glory of beating the French to-morrow.
J. Playfair, *Biogr. Acc. of J. Robinson* in *Transactions R. Soc. Edinb. 1814,* vii. 499.

Now, God be praised, I will die in peace.
Dying words. J. Knox, *Historical Journal of Campaigns, 1757–60.* Published 1769. Ed. 1914, vol. ii, p. 114.

THOMAS WOLSEY, CARDINAL

1475?–1530

Father Abbot, I am come to lay my bones amongst you.
Cavendish, *Negotiations of Thomas Woolsey,* 1641, p. 108.

Had I but served God as diligently as I have served the King, he would not have given me over in my gray hairs.   *Ib.* p. 113.

J. T. WOOD

Wait till the clouds roll by, Jenny,
Wait till the clouds roll by;
Jenny, my own true loved one,
Wait till the clouds roll by.
Wait Till the Clouds Roll By.

VIRGINIA WOOLF

1882–1941

A Room of One's Own.   *Title of Book.*

ELIZABETH WORDSWORTH

1840–1932

If all the good people were clever,
  And all clever people were good,
The world would be nicer than ever
  We thought that it possibly could.

But somehow, 'tis seldom or never
  The two hit it off as they should;
The good are so harsh to the clever,
  The clever so rude to the good!
St. Christopher and Other Poems: Good and Clever.

WILLIAM WORDSWORTH

1770–1850

Where art thou, my beloved Son,
Where art thou, worse to me than dead?
The Affliction of Margaret.

To keep
An incommunicable sleep.   *Ib.*

My apprehensions come in crowds;
I dread the rustling of the grass;
The very shadows of the clouds
Have power to shake me as they pass   *Ib.*

Lady of the Mere,
Sole-sitting by the shores of old romance.
A Narrow Girdle of Rough Stones and Crags.

And three times to the child I said,
'Why, Edward, tell me why?'
Anecdote for Fathers.

'At Kilve there was no weather-cock;
And that's the reason why.'   *Ib.*

A Poet!—He hath put his heart to school.
Miscellaneous Sonnets, xxvii. *A Poet!—He
Hath Put.*

A slumber did my spirit seal;
I had no human fears:
She seemed a thing that could not feel
The touch of earthly years.

No motion has she now, no force;
She neither hears nor sees;
Rolled round in earth's diurnal course,
With rocks, and stones, and trees.
A Slumber did My Spirit Seal.

Action is transitory,—a step, a blow,
The motion of a muscle, this way or that—
'Tis done, and in the after-vacancy
We wonder at ourselves like men betrayed:
Suffering is permanent, obscure and dark,
And shares the nature of infinity.
The Borderers, III. 1539.

Love had he found in huts where poor men lie;
His daily teachers had been woods and rills,
The silence that is in the starry sky,
The sleep that is among the lonely hills.
Song at the Feast of Brougham Castle.

But ne'er to a seductive lay
Let faith be given;
Nor deem that 'light which leads astray
Is light from Heaven.'   *To the Sons of Burns.*

The best of what we do and are
Just God, forgive!
Memorials of a Tour in Scotland, 1803. iii.
Thoughts near Burns' Residence.

Sweet childish days, that were as long
As twenty days are now.
To a Butterfly: I've Watched You Now.

I, with many a fear
For my dear country, many heartfelt sighs,
'Mongst men who do not love her, linger here.
Poems Dedicated to National Independence.
pt. I, i. *Near Calais, Aug. 1802: Fair Star of
Evening.*

Jones! as from Calais southward you and I
Went pacing side by side.
Ib. iii. *Composed near Calais, on the Road to
Ardres.*

Isis and Cam, to patient science dear!
Ib. No. 42. *Cathedrals, etc. Open your Gates,
ye Everlasting Piles!*

To be a Prodigal's favourite,—then, worse truth,
A Miser's pensioner,—behold our lot!
O Man, that from thy fair and shining youth
Age might but take the things Youth needed not!
The Small Celandine: There is a Flower.

There's a flower that shall be mine,
'Tis the little celandine.
To the Small Celandine: Pansies, Lilies.

Pleasures newly found are sweet
When they lie about our feet:
February last, my heart
First at sight of thee was glad;
All unheard of as thou art,
Thou must needs, I think have had,
Celandine! and long ago,
Praise of which I nothing know.
To the Same Flower: Pleasures Newly Found.

Small service is true service while it lasts:
Of humblest friends, bright creature! scorn not one:
The daisy, by the shadow that it casts,
Protects the lingering dewdrop from the sun.
To a Child. Written in her Album.

O blithe new-comer! I have heard,
I hear thee and rejoice.
O Cuckoo! Shall I call thee bird,
Or but a wandering voice?
To the Cuckoo: O Blithe New-comer!

Thrice welcome, darling of the Spring!   *Ib.*

'Tis the still hour of thinking, feeling, loving.
On a High Part of the Coast of Cumberland.

Thou unassuming common-place
Of Nature, with that homely face,
And yet with something of a grace
Which love makes for thee.
To the Same Flower [*Daisy*]. *With Little Here
To Do.*

Oft on the dappled turf at ease
I sit, and play with similes,
Loose type of things through all degrees.   *Ib.*

Degenerate Douglas! Oh, the unworthy lord!
Memorials of a Tour in Scotland, 1803. xii.
Sonnet: Degenerate Douglas!

A brotherhood of venerable trees.   *Ib.*

I thought of Thee, my partner and my guide,
As being past away.—Vain sympathies!
For, backward, Duddon! as I cast my eyes,
I see what was, and is, and will abide;
Still glides the Stream, and shall for ever glide;
The Form remains, the Function never dies.
The River Duddon, xxxiv. *After-Thought.*

Enough, if something from our hands have power
To live, and act, and serve the future hour;
And if, as toward the silent tomb we go,
Through love, through hope, and faith's transcen-
dent dower,
We feel that we are greater than we know.   *Ib.*

Stern daughter of the voice of God!
O Duty! if that name thou love
Who art a light to guide, a rod
To check the erring and reprove.   *Ode to Duty.*

But thee I now will serve more strictly, if I may. *Ib.*

Me this unchartered freedom tires;
I feel the weight of chance-desires:
My hopes no more must change their name,
I long for a repose that ever is the same. *Ib.*

Thou dost preserve the stars from wrong;
And the most ancient heavens, through Thee, are fresh
and strong. *Ib.*

Give unto me, made lowly wise,
The spirit of self-sacrifice;
The confidence of reason give;
And in the light of truth thy Bondman let me live! *Ib.*

Thine is the tranquil hour, purpureal Eve!
But long as god-like wish, or hope divine,
Informs my spirit, ne'er can I believe
That this magnificence is wholly thine!
—From worlds not quickened by the sun
A portion of the gift is won;
An intermingling of Heaven's pomp is spread
On ground which British shepherds tread.
*Composed upon an Evening of Extraordinary
Splendour.*

Not in the lucid intervals of life
That come but as a curse to party strife.
*Evening Voluntaries, iv. Not in the Lucid
Intervals.*

By grace divine,
Not otherwise, O Nature, we are thine. *Ib.*

On Man, on Nature, and on Human Life,
Musing in solitude.
The Excursion, preface 1. i.

Joy in widest commonalty spread. *Ib.* 1. 18.

The Mind of Man—
My haunt, and the main region of my song.
Ib. 1. 40.

The discerning intellect of Man,
When wedded to this goodly universe
In love and holy passion, shall find these
A simple produce of the common day. *Ib.* 1. 52.

A metropolitan temple in the hearts
Of mighty Poets. *Ib.* 1. 86.

Oh! many are the Poets that are sown
By Nature; men endowed with highest gifts,
The vision and the faculty divine;
Yet wanting the accomplishment of verse.
Ib. bk. i, 1. 77.

What soul was his, when, from the naked top
Of some bold headland, he beheld the sun
Rise up, and bathe the world in light! *Ib.* 1. 198.

The imperfect offices of prayer and praise.
Ib. 1. 216.

That mighty orb of song
The divine Milton. *Ib.* 1. 249.

The good die first,
And they whose hearts are dry as summer dust
Burn to the socket. *Ib.* 1. 500.

The intellectual power, through words and things,
Went sounding on, a dim and perilous way!
Ib. bk. ii, 1. 700.

Society became my glittering bride,
And airy hopes my children. *Ib.* 1. 735.

'Tis a thing impossible, to frame
Conceptions equal to the soul's desires;
And the most difficult of tasks to *keep*
Heights which the soul is competent to gain.
Ib. bk. iv, 1. 136.

And that unless above himself he can
Erect himself, how poor a thing is man. *Ib.* 1. 330.

As fast as a musician scatters sounds
Out of an instrument. *Ib.* 1. 524.

We live by admiration, hope, and love;
And even as these are well and wisely fixed,
In dignity of being we ascend. *Ib.* 1. 763.

I have seen
A curious child, who dwelt upon a tract
Of inland ground, applying to his ear
The convolutions of a smooth-lipped shell;
To which, in silence hushed, his very soul
Listened intensely; and his countenance soon
Brightened with joy; for from within were heard
Murmurings, whereby the monitor expressed
Mysterious union with its native sea. *Ib.* 1. 1132.

Spires whose 'silent fingers point to heaven.'
Ib. bk. vi, 1. 19. Quoting Coleridge, *The
Friend,* sec. i, No. 14.

The head and mighty paramount of truths,—
Immortal life, in never-fading worlds,
For mortal creatures, conquered and secured.
Ib. bk. vi, 1. 85.

Amid the groves, under the shadowy hills,
The generations are prepared; the pangs,
The internal pangs, are ready; the dread strife
Of poor humanity's afflicted will
Struggling in vain with ruthless destiny. *Ib.* 1. 553.

A man of hope and forward-looking mind.
Ib. bk. vii, 1. 276.

A man he seems of cheerful yesterdays
And confident to-morrows. *Ib.* 1. 557.

'To every Form of being is assigned',
Thus calmly spoke the venerable Sage,
'An *active* Principle.' *Ib.* bk. ix, 1. 1.

Spirit that knows no insulated spot,
No chasm, no solitude; from link to link
It circulates, the Soul of all the worlds. *Ib.* 1. 13.

And hear the mighty stream of tendency
Uttering, for elevation of our thought,
A clear sonorous voice, inaudible
To the vast multitude. *Ib.* 1. 87.

The primal duties shine aloft like stars;
The charities that soothe, and heal, and bless,
Are scattered at the feet of man, like flowers.
Ib. 1. 238.

Nor less I deem that there are Powers
Which of themselves our minds impress;
That we can feed this mind of ours
In a wise passiveness. *Expostulation and Reply.*

Think you mid all this mighty sum
Of things for ever speaking,
That nothing of itself will come,
But we must still be seeking? *Ib.*

How nourished there through that long time
He knows who gave that love sublime. *Fidelity.*

'What is good for a bootless bene?'
With these dark words begins my tale;
And their meaning is, whence can comfort spring
When prayer is of no avail?   *The Force of Prayer.*

My eyes are dim with childish tears,
My heart is idly stirred,
For the same sound is in my ears
Which in those days I heard.   *The Fountain.*

         The wiser mind
Mourns less for what age takes away
Than what it leaves behind.   *Ib.*

And often, glad no more,
We wear a face of joy because
We have been glad of yore.   *Ib.*

A power is passing from the earth
To breathless Nature's dark abyss;
But when the great and good depart,
What is it more than this—

That Man, who is from God sent forth,
Doth yet again to God return?—
Such ebb and flow must ever be,
Then wherefore should we mourn?
       Lines on the Expected Dissolution of Mr. Fox.

Bliss was it in that dawn to be alive,
But to be young was very heaven!
    French Revolution, as it Appeared to Enthusiasts,
    and *The Prelude*, bk. xi, l. 108.

                          Sets . . .
The budding rose above the rose full blown.
       Ib. and *The Prelude*, bk. xi, l. 121.

And homeless near a thousand homes I stood,
And near a thousand tables pined and wanted food.
                   Guilt and Sorrow, xli.

Who is the happy Warrior? Who is he
That every man in arms should wish to be?
It is the generous spirit, who, when brought
Among the tasks of real life, hath wrought
Upon the plan that pleased his childish thought:
Whose high endeavours are an inward light
That makes the path before him always bright:
Who, with a natural instinct to discern
What knowledge can perform, is diligent to learn.
           Character of the Happy Warrior.

Who, doomed to go in company with Pain,
And Fear, and Bloodshed, miserable train!
Turns his necessity to glorious gain;
In face of these doth exercise a power
Which is our human nature's highest dower;
Controls them and subdues, transmutes, bereaves
Of their bad influence, and their good receives.   *Ib.*

More skilful in self-knowledge, even more pure,
As tempted more; more able to endure,
As more exposed to suffering and distress;
Thence also, more alive to tenderness.   *Ib.*

And in himself possess his own desire.   *Ib.*

And therefore does not stoop, nor lie in wait
For wealth, or honours, or for worldly state.   *Ib.*

Whose powers shed round him in the common strife,
Or mild concerns of ordinary life,
A constant influence, a peculiar grace;
But who if he be called upon to face

Some awful moment to which Heaven has joined
Great issues, good or bad for human kind,
Is happy as a lover; and attired
With sudden brightness, like a man inspired;
And, through the heat of conflict, keeps the law
In calmness made, and sees what he foresaw.   *Ib.*

'Tis, finally, the Man, who, lifted high,
Conspicuous object in a Nation's eye,
Or left unthought of in obscurity,—
Who, with a toward or untoward lot,
Prosperous or adverse, to his wish or not—
Plays, in the many games of life, that one
Where what he most doth value must be won:
Whom neither shape of danger can dismay,
Nor thought of tender happiness betray.   *Ib.*

The moving accident is not my trade;
To freeze the blood I have no ready arts:
'Tis my delight, alone in summer shade,
To pipe a simple song for thinking hearts.
                   Hart-leap Well, pt. 2, l. 1.

The Being that is in the clouds and air,
That is in the green leaves among the groves,
Maintains a deep and reverential care
For the unoffending creatures whom he loves.
                          Ib. l. 165.

Never to blend our pleasure or our pride
With sorrow of the meanest thing that feels.
                          Ib. l. 179.

High is our calling, friend! Creative Art
(Whether the instrument of words she use,
Or pencil pregnant with ethereal hues,)
Demands the service of a mind and heart,
Though sensitive, yet, in their weakest part,
Heroically fashioned.
       Miscellaneous Sonnets, iii. *To B. R. Haydon:*
       High is our Calling, Friend!

Sweet Highland Girl, a very shower
Of beauty is thy earthly dower.
       Memorials of a Tour in Scotland, 1803. vi. *To*
       a Highland Girl.

The rapt one, of the godlike forehead,
The heaven-eyed creature sleeps in earth:
And Lamb, the frolic and the gentle,
Has vanished from his lonely hearth.
       Extempore Effusion upon the Death of James Hogg.

How fast has brother followed brother,
From sunshine to the sunless land!   *Ib.*

Him whom you love, your Idiot Boy.
                          The Idiot Boy.

And as her mind grew worse and worse,
Her body—it grew better.   *Ib.*

Wisdom and Spirit of the Universe!
Thou Soul that art the Eternity of thought!
And giv'st to forms and images a breath
And everlasting motion!
       Influence of Natural Objects, and *The Prelude*,
       bk. i, l. 401.

A grandeur in the beatings of the heart.   *Ib.*

         All shod with steel
We hissed along the polished ice, in games
Confederate.   *Ib.* and *The Prelude*, bk. i, l. 414.

With the din
Smitten, the precipices rang aloud;
The leafless trees and every icy crag
Tinkled like iron; while far-distant hills
Into the tumult sent an alien sound
Of melancholy.   *Ib.*

    Leaving the tumultous throng
To cut across the reflex of a star;
Image, that flying still before me, gleamed
Upon the glassy plain.   *Ib.*

    Yet still the solitary cliffs
Wheeled by me—even as if the earth had rolled
With visible motion her diurnal round!
   Ib. and *The Prelude*, bk. i, l. 458.

There was a time when meadow, grove, and stream,
The earth, and every common sight,
   To me did seem
   Apparelled in celestial light,
The glory and the freshness of a dream.
It is not now as it hath been of yore;—
   Turn wheresoe'er I may,
   By night or day,
The things which I have seen I now can see no more.
   Ode. Intimations of Immortality, i.

   The rainbow comes and goes,
   And lovely is the rose,
   The moon doth with delight
Look round her when the heavens are bare,
   Waters on a starry night
   Are beautiful and fair;
   The sunshine is a glorious birth:
   But yet I know, where'er I go,
That there hath passed away a glory from the earth.
      Ib. ii.
And while the young lambs bound
   As to the tabor's sound.   *Ib.* iii.

A timely utterance gave that thought relief,
And I again am strong.   *Ib.*

The winds come to me from the fields of sleep.   *Ib.*

Shout round me, let me hear thy shouts, thou happy
   Shepherd-boy.   *Ib.*

And the babe leaps up on his mother's arm.   *Ib.* iv.

—But there's a tree, of many, one
A single field which I have looked upon,
Both of them speak of something that is gone:
   The pansy at my feet
   Doth the same tale repeat:
Whither is fled the visionary gleam?
Where is it now, the glory and the dream?   *Ib.*

Our birth is but a sleep and a forgetting:
   The Soul that rises with us, our life's Star,
   Hath had elsewhere its setting,
     And cometh from afar:
   Not in entire forgetfulness,
   And not in utter nakedness,
But trailing clouds of glory do we come
   From God, who is our home:
Heaven lies about us in our infancy!
Shades of the prison-house begin to close
   Upon the growing boy,
But he beholds the light, and whence it flows,
   He sees it in his joy;

The youth, who daily farther from the east
   Must travel, still is Nature's priest,
   And by the vision splendid
   Is on his way attended;
At length the man perceives it die away,
And fade into the light of common day.   *Ib.* v.

Behold the child among his new-born blisses,
A six years' darling of a pigmy size!
See, where 'mid work of his own hand he lies,
Fretted by sallies of his mother's kisses,
With light upon him from his father's eyes!   *Ib.* vii.

As if his whole vocation
Were endless imitation.   *Ib.*

Thou, whose exterior semblance doth belie
   Thy soul's immensity.   *Ib.* viii.

   Thou Eye among the blind,
That, deaf and silent, read'st the eternal deep
Haunted for ever by the eternal mind.   *Ib.*

Thou, over whom thy immortality
Broods like the day, a master o'er a slave.   *Ib.*

   Provoke
The years to bring the inevitable yoke.   *Ib.*

And custom lie upon thee with a weight,
Heavy as frost, and deep almost as life!   *Ib.*

   O joy! that in our embers
   Is something that doth live,
   That nature yet remembers
   What was so fugitive!
The thought of our past years in me doth breed
Perpetual benediction.   *Ib.* ix.

Not for these I raise
The song of thanks and praise;
   But for those obstinate questionings
   Of sense and outward things,
   Fallings from us, vanishings;
   Blank misgivings of a creature
Moving about in worlds not realised,
High instincts before which our mortal nature
Did tremble like a guilty thing surprised:
   But for those first affections,
   Those shadowy recollections,
Which, be they what they may,
Are yet the fountain-light of all our day,
Are yet a master-light of all our seeing.   *Ib.*

Our noisy years seem moments in the being
Of the eternal Silence: truths that wake,
   To perish never:
Which neither listlessness, nor mad endeavour,
   Nor Man nor Boy,
Nor all that is at enmity with joy,
Can utterly abolish or destroy!

Hence in a season of calm weather
   Though inland far we be,
Our souls have sight of that immortal sea
   Which brought us hither,
   Can in a moment travel thither,
And see the children sport upon the shore,
And hear the mighty waters rolling evermore.   *Ib.*

Though nothing can bring back the hour
Of splendour in the grass, of glory in the flower;
We will grieve not, rather find
Strength in what remains behind;
   In the primal sympathy
   Which having been must ever be;

In the soothing thoughts that spring
Out of human suffering;
In the faith that looks through death,
In years that bring the philosophic mind.
                    Intimations of Immortality, x.

And O, ye fountains, meadows, hills and groves,
Forbode not any severing of our loves!
Yet in my heart of hearts I feel your might;
I only have relinquished one delight
To live beneath your more habitual sway.   *Ib*. xi.

The innocent brightness of a new-born day
        Is lovely yet;
The clouds that gather round the setting sun
Do take a sober colouring from an eye
That hath kept watch o'er man's mortality;
Another race hath been, and other palms are won.
Thanks to the human heart by which we live,
Thanks to its tenderness, its joys, and fears,
To me the meanest flower that blows can give
Thoughts that do often lie too deep for tears.   *Ib*.

It is a beauteous evening, calm and free,
The holy time is quiet as a nun,
Breathless with adoration; the broad sun
Is sinking down in its tranquillity;
The gentleness of heaven broods o'er the Sea;
Listen! the mighty Being is awake,
And doth with his eternal motion make
A sound like thunder—everlastingly.
Dear Child! dear Girl! that walkest with me here
If thou appear untouched by solemn thought,
Thy nature is not therefore less divine,
Thou liest in Abraham's bosom all the year;
And worshipp'st at the temple's inner shrine,
God being with thee when we know it not.
        Miscellaneous Sonnets, xxx.   *It is a Beauteous*
        Evening.

It is not to be thought of that the Flood
Of British freedom, which, to the open sea
Of the world's praise, from dark antiquity
Hath flowed, 'with pomp of waters, unwithstood.'
        National Independence and Liberty. xvi.   *It is*
        not to be thought of.

        In our halls is hung
Armoury of the invincible Knights of old:
We must be free or die, who speak the tongue
That Shakespeare spake; the faith and morals hold
Which Milton held.—In everything we are sprung
Of Earth's first blood, have titles manifold.   *Ib*.

I travelled among unknown men
        In lands beyond the sea;
Nor, England! did I know till then
        What love I bore to thee.
            I Travelled among Unknown Men.

I wandered lonely as a cloud
That floats on high o'er vales and hills,
When all at once I saw a crowd,
A host, of golden daffodils;
Beside the lake, beneath the trees,
Fluttering and dancing in the breeze.
            I Wandered Lonely as a Cloud.

Continuous as the stars that shine
And twinkle on the milky way.   *Ib*.

A poet could not but be gay,
In such a jocund company:
I gazed—and gazed—but little thought
What wealth to me the show had brought:

For oft, when on my couch I lie
In vacant or in pensive mood,
They flash upon that inward eye
Which is the bliss of solitude;
And then my heart with pleasure fills,
And dances with the daffodils.   *Ib*.

Poetry is the spontaneous overflow of powerful feel-
    ings: it takes its origin from emotion recollected in
    tranquillity.   *Lyrical Ballads: Preface.*

Vanguard of Liberty, ye men of Kent.
        National Independence and Liberty, xxiii. *To the*
        Men of Kent: Vanguard of Liberty.

Give all thou canst; high Heaven rejects the lore
Of nicely-calculated less or more.
        Ecclesiastical Sonnets, xliii.   *King's College*
        Chapel. Tax not the Royal Saint.

Where light and shade repose, where music dwells
Lingering—and wandering on as loth to die;
Like thoughts whose very sweetness yieldeth proof
That they were born for immortality.   *Ib.*

They dreamt not of a perishable home
Who thus could build.
        Ib. xlv. *Continued. They Dreamt not of a Perish-*
        able Home.

        The gods approve
The depth, and not the tumult, of the soul.
        Laodamia, l. 74

Of all that is most beauteous—imaged there
In happier beauty; more pellucid streams,
An ampler ether, a diviner air,
And fields invested with purpureal gleams. *Ib.* l. 103.

Milton! thou shouldst be living at this hour:
England hath need of thee; she is a fen
Of stagnant waters.
        National Independence and Liberty. xiv.
        London. Milton! thou shouldst.

Thy soul was like a star, and dwelt apart;
Thou hadst a voice whose sound was like the sea:
Pure as the naked heavens, majestic, free,
So didst thou travel on life's common way
In cheerful godliness; and yet thy heart
The lowliest duties on herself did lay.   *Ib.*

Plain living and high thinking are no more:
The homely beauty of the good old cause
Is gone; our peace, our fearful innocence,
And pure religion breathing household laws.
        Ib. xiii. *Written in London. O Friend! I Know*
        Not.

I chanced to see at break of day
The solitary child.   *Lucy Gray.*

No mate, no comrade Lucy knew;
She dwelt on a wild moor,
The sweetest thing that ever grew
Beside a human door!   *Ib.*

And sings a solitary song
That whistles in the wind.   *Ib.*

    The cattle are grazing,
    Their heads never raising;
There are forty feeding like one!
                            Written in March.
Like an army defeated
The snow hath retreated.   *Ib.*

Meantime Luke began
To slacken in his duty; and at length,
He in the dissolute city gave himself
To evil courses.   *Michael,* l. 442.

Many and many a day he thither went,
And never lifted up a single stone.   *Ib.* l. 465.

Most sweet it is with unuplifted eyes
To pace the ground, if path there be or none,
While a fair region round the traveller lies,
Which he forbears again to look upon.
                    Most Sweet It Is.

My heart leaps up when I behold
  A rainbow in the sky:
So was it when my life began;
So is it now I am a man;
So be it when I shall grow old,
  Or let me die!
The Child is father of the Man;
And I could wish my days to be
Bound each to each by natural piety.
                    My Heart Leaps Up.

From low to high doth dissolution climb.
  Ecclesiastical Sonnets, xxxiv. *Mutability. From
  Low to High.*

The unimaginable touch of time.   *Ib.*

Soft is the music that would charm for ever;
The flower of sweetest smell is shy and lowly.
  Miscellaneous Sonnets, ix. *Not Love, not War.*

Another year!—another deadly blow!
Another mighty Empire overthrown!
And we are left, or shall be left, alone.
  National Independence and Liberty, xxvii.
  November. Another Year!

We shall exult, if they who rule the land
Be men who hold its many blessings dear,
Wise, upright, valiant; not a servile band,
Who are to judge of danger which they fear,
And honour which they do not understand.   *Ib.*

Nuns fret not at their convent's narrow room;
And hermits are contented with their cells.
  Miscellaneous Sonnets, pt. I, i. *Nuns Fret Not.*

The weight of too much liberty.   *Ib.*

There is a spirit in the woods.   *Nutting.*

But Thy most dreaded instrument
In working out a pure intent,
Is man,—arrayed for mutual slaughter,
Yea, Carnage is Thy daughter.
  Ib. xlv. *Ode* (1815), l. 106. *Imagination Ne'er
  Before Content.*

O dearer far than light and life are dear.
                    To ——: O Dearer Far than Life.

I heard a Stock-dove sing or say
His homely tale, this very day;
His voice was buried among trees,
Yet to be come-at by the breeze:
He did not cease; but cooed—and cooed;
And somewhat pensively he wooed:
He sang of love, with quiet blending,
Slow to begin, and never ending;
Of serious faith, and inward glee;
That was the song,—the song for me!
                    O Nightingale! Thou Surely Art.

Ye sacred Nurseries of blooming Youth!
      Ib. pt. III, ii. *Oxford: Ye Sacred Nurseries.*

A genial hearth, a hospitable board,
And a refined rusticity.
      Ib. pt. iii, No. 18. *Pastoral Character. A
      Genial Hearth.*

The light that never was, on sea or land,
The consecration, and the poet's dream.
      *Elegiac Stanzas Suggested by a Picture of Peele
      Castle in a Storm.*

A deep distress hath humanized my soul.   *Ib.*

Farewell, farewell the heart that lives alone,
Housed in a dream, at distance from the Kind!   *Ib.*

But welcome fortitude, and patient cheer,
And frequent sights of what is to be borne!
Such sights, or worse, as are before me here.—
Not without hope we suffer and we mourn.   *Ib.*

I am not one who oft or much delight
To season my fireside with personal talk.
                    Personal Talk, i.

    Sweetest melodies
Are those that are by distance made more sweet.
                    Ib. ii.

Dreams, books, are each a world; and books, we
    know,
Are a substantial world, both pure and good.
Round these, with tendrils strong as flesh and blood,
Our pastime and our happiness will grow.   *Ib.* iii.

The gentle lady married to the Moor;
And heavenly Una with her milk-white lamb.   *Ib.*

Oh! might my name be numbered among theirs.
                    Ib. iv

There's something in a flying horse,
There's something in a huge balloon.
                    Peter Bell, prologue, l. 1

Full twenty times was Peter feared
For once that Peter was respected.   *Ib.* pt. i, l. 204

A primrose by a river's brim
A yellow primrose was to him,
And it was nothing more.   *Ib.* l. 249

He gave a groan, and then another,
Of that which went before the brother,
And then he gave a third.   *Ib.* l. 443

Is it a party in a parlour?
Cramm'd just as they on earth were cramm'd—
Some sipping punch, some sipping tea,
But, as you by their faces see,
All silent and all damned!   *Ib.* pt. ii, l. 516

The dew was falling fast, the stars began to blink;
I heard a voice; it said, 'Drink, pretty creature
    drink!'   *The Pet Lamb*

Art thou a Man of purple cheer?
A rosy Man, right plump to see?   *A Poet's Epitaph.*

A fingering slave,
One that would peep and botanize
Upon his mother's grave?

A reasoning, self-sufficing thing,
An intellectual All-in-all!   *Ib.*

But who is He, with modest looks,
And clad in homely russet brown?
He murmurs near the running brooks
A music sweeter than their own. *Ib.*

He is retired as noontide dew,
Or fountain in a noon-day grove;
And you must love him, ere to you
He will seem worthy of your love. *Ib.*

Impulses of deeper birth
Have come to him in solitude. *Ib.*

In common things that round us lie
Some random truths he can impart,—
The harvest of a quiet eye,
That broods and sleeps on his own heart.

But he is weak; both Man and Boy,
Hath been an idler in the land;
Contented if he might enjoy
The things which others understand. *Ib.*

Weak as is a breaking wave. *Ib.*

My soul
Once more made trial of her strength, nor lacked
Aeolian visitations. *The Prelude*, bk. i, l. 94.

Feels immediately some hollow thought
Hang like an interdict upon her hopes. *Ib.* l. 259.

Unprofitably travelling towards the grave. *Ib.* l. 267.

Made one long bathing of a summer's day. *Ib.* l. 290.

Fair seed-time had my soul, and I grew up
Fostered alike by beauty and by fear. *Ib.* l. 301.

When the deed was done
I heard among the solitary hills
Low breathings coming after me, and sounds
Of undistinguishable motion, steps
Almost as silent as the turf they trod. *Ib.* l. 321.

Though mean
Our object and inglorious, yet the end
Was not ignoble. *Ib.* l. 328.

With what strange utterance did the loud dry wind
Blow through my ear! the sky seemed not a sky
Of earth—and with what motion moved the clouds!
Ib. l. 337.

Dust as we are, the immortal spirit grows
Like harmony in music; there is a dark
Inscrutable workmanship that reconciles
Discordant elements, makes them cling together
In one society. *Ib.* l. 340.

The grim shape
Towered up between me and the stars, and still,
For so it seemed, with purpose of its own
And measured motion like a living thing,
Strode after me. *Ib.* l. 382.

Unknown modes of being. *Ib.* l. 393.

Huge and mighty forms that do not live
Like living men, moved slowly through the mind
By day, and were a trouble to my dreams.
Ib. l. 398.

Not with the mean and vulgar works of man,
But with high objects, with enduring things.
Ib. l. 408.

Strife too humble to be named in verse.
Ib. l. 513.

The self-sufficing power of Solitude.
Ib. bk. ii, l. 77.

A prop
To our infirmity. *Ib.* l. 214.

Thence did I drink the visionary power;
And deem not profitless those fleeting moods
Of shadowy exultation. *Ib.* l. 311.

The soul,
Remembering how she felt, but what she felt
Remembering not, retains an obscure sense
Of possible sublimity. *Ib.* l. 315.

Where the statue stood
Of Newton, with his prism and silent face,
The marble index of a mind forever
Voyaging through strange seas of thought alone.
Ib. bk. iii, l. 61.

Sweet Spenser, moving through his clouded heaven
With the moon's beauty and the moon's soft pace,
I called him Brother, Englishman, and Friend!
Ib. l. 280.

Here and there
Slight shocks of young love-liking interspersed.
Ib. bk. iv, l. 316.

Bond unknown to me
Was given, that I should be, else sinning greatly,
A dedicated spirit. *Ib.* l. 335.

A day
Spent in a round of strenuous idleness. *Ib.* l. 377.

That uncertain heaven, received
Into the bosom of the steady lake. *Ib.* bk. v, l. 387.

Visionary power
Attends the motions of the viewless winds,
Embodied in the mystery of words. *Ib.* l. 595.

Present themselves as objects recognized,
In flashes, and with glory not their own.
Ib. l. 604.

Whether we be young or old,
Our destiny, our being's heart and home,
Is with infinitude, and only there;
With hope it is, hope that can never die,
Effort, and expectation, and desire,
And something evermore about to be.
Ib. bk. vi, l. 603.

We were brothers all
In honour, as in one community,
Scholars and gentlemen. *Ib.* bk. ix, l. 227.

In the People was my trust,
And in the virtues which mine eyes had seen.
Ib. bk. xi, l. 11.

The dupe of folly, or the slave of crime.
Ib. l. 320.

Not in Utopia—subterranean fields,—
Or some secreted island, Heaven knows where!
But in the very world, which is the world
Of all of us,—the place where, in the end
We find our happiness, or not at all! *Ib.* l. 140.

There is
One great society alone on earth:
The noble living and the noble dead. *Ib.* l. 393.

A sensitive being, a *creative* soul.
The Prelude, bk. xii, l. 207.

Oh! mystery of man, from what a depth
Proceed thy honours. I am lost, but see
In simple childhood something of the base
On which thy greatness stands.   *Ib.* l. 272.

Animate an hour of vacant ease.   *Ib.* l. 335.

Sorrow, that is not sorrow, but delight;
And miserable love, that is not pain
To hear of, for the glory that redounds
Therefrom to human kind, and what we are.
Ib. bk. xiii, l. 246.

Imagination, which, in truth,
Is but another name for absolute power
And clearest insight, amplitude of mind,
And Reason in her most exalted mood.
Ib. bk. xiv, l. 190.

Prophets of Nature, we to them will speak
A lasting inspiration, sanctified
By reason, blest by faith: what we have loved,
Others will love, and we will teach them how;
Instruct them how the mind of man becomes
A thousand times more beautiful than the earth
On which he dwells, above this frame of things
(Which, 'mid all revolution in the hopes
And fears of men, doth still remain unchanged)
In beauty exalted, as it is itself
Of quality and fabric more divine.   *Ib.* l. 444.

Art thou the bird whom man loves best,
The pious bird with the scarlet breast,
    Our little English robin?
The Redbreast Chasing the Butterfly.

Love him, or leave him alone!   *Ib.*

Habit rules the unreflecting herd.
Ecclesiastical Sonnets, xxviii. *Reflections. Grant
that by this Unsparing Hurricane.*

There was a roaring in the wind all night.
Resolution and Independence, i.

As high as we have mounted in delight
In our dejection do we sink as low.   *Ib.* iv.

But how can he expect that others should
Build for him, sow for him, and at his call
Love him, who for himself will take no heed at all?
Ib. vi.

I thought of Chatterton, the marvellous boy,
The sleepless soul, that perished in his pride;
Of him who walked in glory and in joy,
Following his plough, along the mountain side:
By our own spirits are we deified:
We poets in our youth begin in gladness;
But thereof comes in the end despondency and mad-
    ness.   *Ib.* vii.

The oldest man he seemed that ever wore grey hairs.
Ib. viii.

As a huge stone is sometimes seen to lie
Couched on the bald top of an eminence.   *Ib.* ix.

Like a sea-beast crawled forth, that on a shelf
Of rock or sand reposeth, there to sun itself.   *Ib.*

That heareth not the loud winds when they call,
And moveth all together, if it moves at all.   *Ib.* xi.

Choice words, and measured phrase, above the reach
Of ordinary men; a stately speech;
Such as grave livers do in Scotland use.   *Ib.* xiv.

And mighty poets in their misery dead.   *Ib.* xvii.

'How is it that you live, and what is it you do?'   *Ib.*

The good old rule
Sufficeth them, the simple plan,
That they should take, who have the power,
    And they should keep who can.
Memorials of a Tour in Scotland, 1803. xi. *Rob
Roy's Grave.*

Scorn not the Sonnet; Critic, you have frowned,
Mindless of its just honours; with this key
Shakespeare unlocked his heart.
Miscellaneous Sonnets, pt. II, i. *Scorn Not the
Sonnet.*

And when a damp
Fell round the path of Milton, in his hand
The Thing became a trumpet; whence he blew
Soul-animating strains,—alas! too few.   *Ib.*

She dwelt among the untrodden ways
    Beside the springs of Dove,
A maid whom there were none to praise
    And very few to love:

A violet by a mossy stone
    Half hidden from the eye!
Fair as a star, when only one
    Is shining in the sky.

She lived unknown, and few could know
    When Lucy ceased to be;
But she is in her grave, and, oh,
    The difference to me!
She Dwelt Among the Untrodden Ways.

She was a phantom of delight
When first she gleamed upon my sight;
A lovely apparition, sent
To be a moment's ornament;
Her eyes as stars of twilight fair;
Like twilight's, too, her dusky hair;
But all things else about her drawn
From May-time and the cheerful dawn;
A dancing shape, an image gay,
To haunt, to startle, and waylay.
She was a Phantom of Delight.

I saw her upon nearer view,
A spirit, yet a woman too!
Her household motions light and free,
And steps of virgin liberty;
A countenance in which did meet
Sweet records, promises as sweet;
A creature not too bright or good
For human nature's daily food;
For transient sorrows, simple wiles,
Praise, blame, love, kisses, tears, and smiles.   *Ib.*

And now I see with eye serene,
The very pulse of the machine;
A being breathing thoughtful breath,
A traveller betwixt life and death;
The reason firm, the temperate will,
Endurance, foresight, strength, and skill;
A perfect woman, nobly planned,
To warn, to comfort, and command;
And yet a spirit still, and bright
With something of angelic light.   *Ib.*

For still, the more he works, the more
Do his weak ankles swell.   *Simon Lee.*

O reader! had you in your mind
Such stores as silent thought can bring,
O gentle reader! you would find
A tale in every thing.   *Ib.*

I've heard of hearts unkind, kind deeds
With coldness still returning;
Alas! the gratitude of men
Hath oftener left me mourning.   *Ib.*

Characters of the great Apocalypse,
The types and symbols of Eternity,
Of first, and last, and midst, and without end.
    The Simplon Pass: Brook and Road, and *The*
    Prelude, bk. vi, l. 636.

Ethereal minstrel! pilgrim of the sky!
Dost thou despise the earth where cares abound?
Or, while the wings aspire, are heart and eye
Both with thy nest upon the dewy ground?
Thy nest which thou canst drop into at will,
Those quivering wings composed, that music still!
    To a Skylark.

Type of the wise who soar, but never roam;
True to the kindred points of heaven and home!
    Ib.

Behold her, single in the field,
   Yon solitary Highland lass!
    Memorials of a Tour in Scotland, 1803, ix. *The*
    Solitary Reaper.

A voice so thrilling ne'er was heard
In spring-time from the Cuckoo-bird,
Breaking the silence of the seas
Among the farthest Hebrides.   *Ib.*

Will no one tell me what she sings?—
Perhaps the plaintive numbers flow
For old, unhappy, far-off things,
And battles long ago.   *Ib.*

Some natural sorrow, loss, or pain
That has been, and may be again.   *Ib.*

The music in my heart I bore,
Long after it was heard no more.   *Ib.*

Spade! with which Wilkinson hath tilled his lands.
    To the Spade of a Friend.

She gave me eyes, she gave me ears;
And humble cares, and delicate fears;
A heart, the fountain of sweet tears;
   And love, and thought, and joy.
    The Sparrow's Nest.

In that sweet mood when pleasant thoughts
Bring sad thoughts to the mind.
    Lines Written in Early Spring.

And much it grieved my heart to think
What man has made of man.   *Ib.*

And 'tis my faith that every flower
Enjoys the air it breathes.   *Ib.*

Have I not reason to lament
What man has made of man?   *Ib.*

Strange fits of passion I have known.
    Strange Fits of Passion.

What fond and wayward thoughts will slide
Into a Lover's head!

'O mercy!' to myself I cried,
'If Lucy should be dead!'   *Ib.*

Two Voices are there; one is of the sea,
One of the mountains; each a mighty Voice,
In both from age to age thou didst rejoice,
They were thy chosen music, Liberty!
    National Independence and Liberty, xii. *Thought*
    of a Briton on the Subjugation of Switzerland:
    Two Voices are There.

Up! up! my friend, and quit your books;
   Or surely you'll grow double:
Up! up! my friend, and clear your looks;
   Why all this toil and trouble? *The Tables Turned.*

Books! 'tis a dull and endless strife:
   Come, hear the woodland linnet,
How sweet his music! on my life,
   There's more of wisdom in it.

And hark! how blithe the throstle sings!
   He, too, is no mean preacher:
Come forth into the light of things,
   Let Nature be your teacher.   *Ib.*

Spontaneous wisdom breathed by health,
   Truth breathed by cheerfulness.

One impulse from a vernal wood
   May teach you more of man,
Of moral evil and of good,
   Than all the sages can.

Sweet is the lore which Nature brings;
   Our meddling intellect
Misshapes the beauteous forms of things:—
   We murder to dissect.

Enough of science and of art;
   Close up these barren leaves;
Come forth, and bring with you a heart
   That watches and receives.   *Ib.*

Every gift of noble origin
Is breathed upon by Hope's perpetual breath.
    National Independence and Liberty, xx. *These*
    Times Strike Monied Worldlings.

The power of Armies is a visible thing,
Formal, and circumscribed in time and place.
    Ib. pt. ii. xxxii. *The Power of Armies.*

A noticeable man with large grey eyes
And a pale face. (Coleridge.)
    Stanzas written in my pocket copy of Thomson's
    'Castle of Indolence'.

I've measured it from side to side:
'Tis three feet long, and two feet wide.
    The Thorn, iii. [early reading.]

Then nature said, 'A lovelier flower
   On earth was never sown;
This child I to myself will take;
She shall be mine, and I will make
   A lady of my own.'   *Three Years She Grew.*

The stars of midnight shall be dear
To her; and she shall lean her ear
   In many a secret place
Where rivulets dance their wayward round,
And beauty born of murmuring sound
   Shall pass into her face.   *Ib.*

[471]

Sensations sweet,
Felt in the blood, and felt along the heart.
Lines composed a few miles above Tintern Abbey,
l. 27.

That best portion of a good man's life,
His little, nameless, unremembered acts
Of kindness and of love.   *Ib.* l. 33.

That blessed mood,
In which the burthen of the mystery,
In which the heavy and the weary weight
Of all this unintelligible world,
Is lightened:—that serene and blessed mood,
In which the affections gently lead us on,—
Until, the breath of this corporeal frame
And even the motion of our human blood
Almost suspended, we are laid asleep
In body, and become a living soul:
While with an eye made quiet by the power
Of harmony, and the deep power of joy,
We see into the life of things.   *Ib.*

For nature then
(The coarser pleasures of my boyish days,
And their glad animal movements all gone by)
To me was all in all.—I cannot paint
What then I was. The sounding cataract
Haunted me like a passion: the tall rock,
The mountain, and the deep and gloomy wood,
Their colours and their forms, were then to me
An appetite; a feeling and a love,
That had no need of a remoter charm,
By thought supplied, nor any interest
Unborrowed from the eye.   *Ib.* l. 72.

I have learned
To look on nature, not as in the hour
Of thoughtless youth; but hearing often-times
The still, sad music of humanity,
Nor harsh nor grating, though of ample power
To chasten and subdue. And I have felt
A presence that disturbs me with the joy
Of elevated thoughts; a sense sublime
Of something far more deeply interfused,
Whose dwelling is the light of setting suns,
And the round ocean and the living air,
And the blue sky, and in the mind of man.
                                      Ib. l. 88.

All the mighty world
Of eye, and ear,—both what they half create,
And what perceive.   *Ib.* l. 105.

Oh! yet a little while
May I behold in thee what I was once,
My dear, dear Sister! and this prayer I make,
Knowing that Nature never did betray
The heart that loved her; 'tis her privilege,
Through all the years of this our life, to lead
From joy to joy: for she can so inform
The mind that is within us, so impress
With quietness and beauty, and so feed
With lofty thoughts, that neither evil tongues,
Rash judgments, nor the sneers of selfish men,
Nor greetings where no kindness is, nor all
The dreary intercourse of daily life,
Shall e'er prevail against us, or disturb
Our cheerful faith, that all which we behold
Is full of blessings.   *Ib.* l. 121.

Thou hast left behind
Powers that will work for thee; air, earth, and skies;

There's not a breathing of the common wind
That will forget thee; thou hast great allies;
Thy friends are exultations, agonies,
And love, and man's unconquerable mind.
National Independence and Liberty, viii. *To
Toussaint L'Ouverture: Toussaint, the Most
Unhappy.*

Once did she hold the gorgeous East in fee,
And was the safeguard of the West.
Ib. vi. *On the Extinction of the Venetian Repub-
lic: Once Did She Hold.*

Venice, the eldest child of Liberty.
She was a maiden city, bright and free.   *Ib.*

And when she took unto herself a Mate,
She must espouse the everlasting Sea.   *Ib.*

Men are we, and must grieve when even the shade
Of that which once was great is passed away.   *Ib.*

Our tainted nature's solitary boast.
Ecclesiastical Sonnets, pt. ii, No. xxv. *The Virgin Mother! Whose Virgin Bosom.*

A shy spirit in my heart,
That comes and goes—will sometimes leap
From hiding-places ten years deep.
The Waggoner, iv, l. 210.

A simple child, [dear brother Jim]
That lightly draws its breath,
And feels its life in every limb,
What should it know of death?   *We are Seven.*

I take my little porringer
And eat my supper there.   *Ib.*

'But they are dead; those two are dead!
Their spirits are in Heaven!'
'Twas throwing words away; for still
The little Maid would have her will,
And said, 'Nay, we are seven!'   *Ib.*

Earth has not anything to show more fair:
Dull would he be of soul who could pass by
A sight so touching in its majesty:
This City now doth, like a garment, wear
The beauty of the morning; silent, bare,
Ships, towers, domes, theatres, and temples lie
Open unto the fields, and to the sky;
All bright and glittering in the smokeless air.
Never did sun more beautifully steep
In his first splendour, valley, rock, or hill;
Ne'er saw I, never felt, a calm so deep!
The river glideth at his own sweet will:
Dear God! the very houses seem asleep;
And all that mighty heart is lying still!
Miscellaneous Sonnets, xxxvi. *Composed upon
Westminster Bridge.*

What wonder if a Poet now and then,
Among the many movements of his mind,
Felt for thee as a lover or a child! [England]
National Independence and Liberty, xvii. *When
I Have Borne in Memory.*

Where lies the Land to which yon Ship must go?
Miscellaneous Sonnets, xxxi. *Where Lies the
Land.*

With Ships the sea was sprinkled far and nigh.
Ib. xxxii. *With Ships the Sea was Sprinkled.*

The world is too much with us; late and soon,
Getting and spending, we lay waste our powers:
Little we see in Nature that is ours;
We have given our hearts away, a sordid boon!
The Sea that bares her bosom to the moon;
The winds that will be howling at all hours,
And are up-gathered now like sleeping flowers;
For this, for everything, we are out of tune;
It moves us not; Great God! I'd rather be
A Pagan suckled in a creed outworn,
So might I, standing on this pleasant lea,
Have glimpses that would make me less forlorn;
Have sight of Proteus rising from the sea,
Or hear old Triton blow his wreathed horn.
Ib. xxxiii. *The World is Too Much with Us.*

The swan on still St. Mary's Lake
Float double, swan and shadow!
Memorials of a Tour in Scotland, 1803. xiii.
Yarrow Unvisited.

But thou, that didst appear so fair
To fond imagination,
Dost rival in the light of day
Her delicate creation.
*Memorials of a Tour in Scotland, 1814. Yarrow
Visited.*

Like,—but oh how different!
Yes, it was the Mountain Echo.

Fear and trembling Hope,
Silence and Foresight; Death the Skeleton
And Time the Shadow.   *Yew Trees.*

Thou, while thy babes around thee cling,
Shalt show us how divine a thing
A woman may be made.   *To a Young Lady.*

But an old age, serene and bright,
And lovely as a Lapland night,
Shall lead thee to thy grave.   *Ib.*

HENRY CLAY WORK

1832–1884

Bring the good old bugle, boys, we'll sing another
     song;
Sing it with a spirit that will start the world along,
Sing it as we used to sing it—fifty thousand strong,
     As we were marching through Georgia.
Marching Through Georgia.

'Hurrah! hurrah! we bring the Jubilee!
Hurrah! hurrah! the flag that makes you free!'
So we sang the chorus from Atlanta to the sea,
     As we were marching through Georgia. *Ib. Chorus.*

SIR HENRY WOTTON

1568–1639

An ambassador is an honest man sent to lie abroad for
     the good of his country.
*Written in the Album of Christopher Fleck-
more* (1604).

How happy is he born and taught
     That serveth not another's will;
Whose armour is his honest thought,
     And simple truth his utmost skill!
Character of a Happy Life, i.

Who God doth late and early pray
     More of his grace than gifts to lend;
And entertains the harmless day
     With a religious book, or friend.   *Ib.* v.

This man is freed from servile bands,
     Of hope to rise, or fear to fall:—
Lord of himself, though not of lands,
     And having nothing, yet hath all.   *Ib.* vi.

He first deceas'd; she for a little tri'd
To live without him: lik'd it not, and di'd.
Death of Sir Albertus Morton's Wife.

You meaner beauties of the night,
     That poorly satisfy our eyes,
More by your number, than your light;
     You common people of the skies,
What are you when the moon shall rise?
On His Mistress, the Queen of Bohemia.

SIR CHRISTOPHER WREN

1632–1723

Si monumentum requiris, circumspice.
     If you would see his monument look around.
*Inscription over the interior of the North Door
in St. Paul's Cathedral, London. Written by
Wren's son.*

SIR THOMAS WYATT

1503?–1542

Blame not my lute! for he must sound
     Of this and that as liketh me.   *The Lute Obeys,* i.

And wilt thou leave me thus?
Say nay, say nay, for shame!   *An Appeal.*

Forget not yet the tried intent
Of such a truth as I have meant;
My great travail so gladly spent
     Forget not yet!   *Steadfastness.*

They flee from me, that sometime did me seek.
Remembrance.

My lute, awake! perform the last
Labour that thou and I shall waste,
The end that I have now begun;
For when this song is sung and past,
My lute, be still, for I have done.   *To His Lute.*

WILLIAM WYCHERLEY

1640?–1716

Fy! madam, do you think me so ill bred as to love a
     husband?   *Love in a Wood,* III, iv.

Nay, you had both felt his desperate deadly daunting
     dagger:—there are your d's for you!
Gentleman Dancing-Master, Act v.

Go to your business, I say, pleasure, whilst I go to
     my pleasure, business.   *Country Wife,* Act II.

QUAINT:
With sharp invectives—
WIDOW:
Alias, Billingsgate.   *Plain Dealer,* Act. III.

WYNTOUN'S CHRONICLE

Quhen Alysander oure kyng wes dede,
  That Scotland led in luve and le,
Away wes sons of ale and brede,
Of wyne and wax, of gamyn and gle:
Oure gold wes changyd into lede,
  Cryst, borne into virgynyte,
Succour Scotland, and remede,
    That stad is in perplexyte.
    *From Andrew Wyntoun's 'Cronykill', vol. i,
    p. 401, ed. 1795 (the edition used by Scott)
    and in the edition of 1872, vol. ii, p. 266.*

WILLIAM BUTLER YEATS

1865–1939

A line will take us hours may be;
Yet if it does not seem a moment's thought,
Our stitching and unstitching has been naught.
        Adam's Curse.

O heart, be at peace, because
Nor knave nor dolt can break
What's not for their applause,
Being for a woman's sake.
      Against Unworthy Praise.

When I was young,
I had not given a penny for a song
Did not the poet sing it with such airs
That one believed he had a sword upstairs.
      All Things Can Tempt Me.

The phantom, Beauty, in a mist of tears.
      Anashuya and Vijaya.

The old priest Peter Gilligan
Was weary night and day;
For half his flock were in their beds,
Or under green sods lay.
      Ballad of Father Gilligan.

He Who is wrapped in purple robes,
With planets in His care,
Had pity on the least of things
Asleep upon a chair.   *Ib.*

The years like great black oxen tread the world,
And God the herdsman goads them on behind,
And I am broken by their passing feet.
      The Countess Cathleen, Act IV.

    The Light of Lights
Looks always on the motive, not the deed,
The Shadow of Shadows on the deed alone.   *Ib.*

God's laughing in Heaven
To see you so good.   *A Cradle Song.*

Down by the salley gardens my love and I did meet;
She passed the salley gardens with little snow-white
  feet.
She bid me take love easy, as the leaves grow on the
  tree;
But I, being young and foolish, with her would not
  agree.

In a field by the river my love and I did stand,
And on my leaning shoulder she laid her snow-white
  hand.
She bid me take life easy, as the grass grows on the
  weirs;
But I was young and foolish, and now am full of tears.
      Down by the Salley Gardens.

She was more beautiful than thy first love,
This lady by the trees.   *A Dream of Death.*

He found the unpersuadable justice.
      Ego Dominus Tuus.

The coarse-bred son of a livery stable keeper. (Keats.)
      Ib.

We who are old, old and gay
O so old!
Thousands of years, thousands of years,
If all were told.   *A Faery Song.*

But weigh this song with the great and their pride;
I made it out of a mouthful of air,
Their children's children shall say they have lied.
    *He Thinks of Those who have Spoken Evil of
    his Beloved.*

Had I the heavens' embroidered cloths,
Enwrought with golden and silver light,
The blue and the dim and the dark cloths
Of night and light and the half-light,
I would spread the cloths under your feet:
But I, being poor, have only my dreams;
I have spread my dreams under your feet;
Tread softly, because you tread on my dreams.
    He Wishes for the Cloths of Heaven.

I mourn for that most lovely thing; and yet God's
  will be done:
I knew a phoenix in my youth, so let them have their
  day.   *His Phoenix.*

Out-worn heart, in a time out-worn,
Come clear of the nets of wrong and right;
Laugh, heart, again in the grey twilight,
Sigh, heart, again in the dew of the morn.
      Into the Twilight.

And God stands winding His lonely horn,
And time and the world are ever in flight;
And love is less kind than the grey twilight,
And hope is less dear than the dew of the morn. *Ib.*

All the wild witches, those most noble ladies,
For all their broom-sticks and their tears,
Their angry tears, are gone.
      Lines Written in Dejection.

Never give all the heart, for love
Will hardly seem worth thinking of
To passionate women if it seem
Certain, and they never dream
That it fades out from kiss to kiss.
      Never Give All the Heart.

Why, what could she have done, being what she is?
Was there another Troy for her to burn?
      No Second Troy.

To shake their wicked sides at youth
Restraining reckless middle-age?
    *On hearing that the Students of our new Univer-
    sity have joined the Agitation against Immoral
    Literature.*

Was it for this the wild geese spread
The grey wing upon every tide;
For this that all that blood was shed,
For this Edward Fitzgerald died,
And Robert Emmet and Wolfe Tone,
All that delirium of the brave?
Romantic Ireland's dead and gone,
It's with O'Leary in the grave.   *September 1913.*

For the good are always the merry,
Save by an evil chance,
And the merry love the fiddle,
And the merry love to dance.
The Fiddler of Dooney.

When I play on my fiddle in Dooney
Folk dance like a wave of the sea.   *Ib.*

One that is ever kind said yesterday
'Your well-beloved's hair has threads of grey,
And little shadows come about her eyes.'
The Folly of Being Comforted.

Time can but make her beauty over again:
Because of that great nobleness of hers
The fire that stirs about her, when she stirs,
Burns but more clearly. O she had not these ways
When all the wild summer was in her gaze.   *Ib.*

O heart! O heart! if she'd but turn her head,
You'd know the folly of being comforted.   *Ib.*

The little fox murmured,
'O what of the world's bane?'
The sun was laughing sweetly,
The moon plucked at my rein;
But the little red fox murmured,
'O do not pluck at his rein,
He is riding to the townland
That is the world's bane.'   *The Happy Townland.*

The host is riding from Knocknarea
And over the grave of Clooth-na-Bare;
Caoilte tossing his burning hair,
And Niamh calling Away, come away.
The Hosting of the Sidhe.

Who holds the world between His bill and made us
   strong or weak
Is an undying moorfowl, and He lives beyond the
   sky.
The rains are from His dripping wings, the moonbeams from His eye.   *The Indian upon God.*

Who made the world and ruleth it, He hangeth on
   a stalk,
For I am in His image made, and all this tinkling
   tide
Is but a sliding drop of rain between His petals wide.
                           Ib.

     The Stamper of the Skies,
He is a gentle roebuck; for how else, I pray, could He
Conceive a thing so sad and soft, a gentle thing like
   me?   *Ib.*

Who made the grass and made the worms and made
   my feathers gay,
He is a monstrous peacock, and He waveth all the
   night
His languid tail above us, lit with myriad spots of
   light.   *Ib.*

I will arise and go now, and go to Innisfree,
And a small cabin build there, of clay and wattles
   made:
Nine bean-rows will I have there, a hive for the
   honey-bee,
And live alone in the bee-loud glade.

And I shall have some peace there, for peace comes
   dropping slow,
Dropping from the veils of the morning to where
   the cricket sings;

There midnight's all a-glimmer, and noon a purple
   glow,
And evening full of the linnet's wings.

I will arise and go now, for always night and day
I hear lake water lapping with low sounds by the
   shore;
While I stand on the roadway, or on the pavements
   gray
I hear it in the deep heart's core.
             The Lake Isle of Innisfree.

The wind blows out of the gates of the day,
The wind blows over the lonely of heart,
And the lonely of heart is withered away.
            The Land of Heart's Desire.

     The land of faery,
Where nobody gets old and godly and grave,
Where nobody gets old and crafty and wise,
Where nobody gets old and bitter of tongue.
                            Ib.

Of a land where even the old are fair,
And even the wise are merry of tongue.   *Ib.*

     Land of Heart's Desire,
Where beauty has no ebb, decay no flood,
But joy is wisdom, Time an endless song.   *Ib.*

All things uncomely and broken, all things worn out
   and old,
The cry of a child by the roadway, the creak of a
   lumbering cart,
The heavy steps of the ploughman, splashing the
   wintry mould,
Are wronging your image that blossoms a rose in
   the deeps of my heart.
The wrong of unshapely things is a wrong too great to
   be told;
I hunger to build them anew and sit on a green knoll
   apart,
With the earth and the sky and the water, re-made,
   like a casket of gold;
For my dreams of your image that blossoms a rose in
   the deeps of my heart.
       The Lover Tells of the Rose in his Heart.

When I was a boy with never a crack in my heart.
       The Meditation of the Old Fishermen.

I heard the old, old men say,
'All that's beautiful drifts away
Like the waters.'
     The Old Men Admiring Themselves in the Water.

A pity beyond all telling
Is hid in the heart of love.   *The Pity of Love.*

Rose of all Roses, Rose of all the World!
                   The Rose of Battle.

Who dreamed that beauty passes like a dream?
For these red lips, with all their mournful pride,
Mournful that no new wonder may betide,
Troy passed away in one high funeral gleam,
And Usna's children died.

We and the labouring world are passing by:
Amid men's souls, that waver and give place
Like the pale waters in their wintry race,
Under the passing stars, foam of the sky,
Lives on this lonely face.
Bow down, archangels, in your dim abode;

Before you were, or any hearts to beat,
Weary and kind one linger'd by His seat;
He made the world to be a grassy road
Before her wandering feet.   *The Rose of the World.*

Far off, most secret, and inviolate Rose,
Enfold me in my hours of hours.   *The Secret Rose.*

A woman of so shining loveliness
That men threshed corn at midnight by a tress.   *Ib.*

When shall the stars be blown about the sky,
Like the sparks blown out of a smithy, and die?
Surely thine hour has come, thy great wind blows,
Far-off, most sweet, and inviolate Rose?   *Ib.*

It is love that I am seeking for,
But of a beautiful, unheard-of kind
That is not in the world.   *The Shadowy Waters.*

    Do you not know
How great a wrong it is to let one's thought
Wander a moment when one is in love?   *Ib.*

Bend lower, O king, that I may crown you with it.
O flower of the branch, O bird among the leaves,
O silver fish that my two hands have taken
Out of the running stream, O morning star,
Trembling in the blue heavens like a white fawn
Upon the misty border of the wood,
Bend lower, that I may cover you with my hair,
For we will gaze upon this world no longer.   *Ib.*

And pluck till time and times are done
The silver apples of the moon
The golden apples of the sun.
    The Song of Wandering Ængus.

The brawling of a sparrow in the eaves,
  The brilliant moon and all the milky sky,
And all that famous harmony of leaves,
  Had blotted out man's image and his cry.

A girl arose that had red mournful lips
  And seemed the greatness of the world in tears,
Doomed like Odysseus and the labouring ships
  And proud as Priam murdered with his peers;

Arose, and on the instant clamorous eaves,
  A climbing moon upon an empty sky,
And all that lamentation of the leaves,
  Could but compose man's image and his cry.
    The Sorrow of Love.

And the loud chaunting of the unquiet leaves
Are shaken with earth's old and weary cry.
    The Sorrow of Love (1893 version).

Come away, O human child!
To the waters and the wild
With a faery, hand in hand,
For the world's more full of weeping than you can
  understand.   *The Stolen Child.*

Nor know that what disturbs our blood
Is but its longing for the tomb.   *The Wheel.*

I would that we were, my beloved, white birds on the
  foam of the sea!   *The White Birds.*

But was there ever dog that praised his fleas?
  To a Poet, who would have me praise certain
  bad Poets, Imitators of his and mine.

I know what wages beauty gives,
How hard a life her servant lives,
Yet praise the winters gone

There is not a fool can call me friend,
And I may dine at journey's end
With Landor and with Donne.   *To a Young Beauty.*

Know, that I would accounted be
True brother of a company
That sang, to sweeten Ireland's wrong,
Ballad and story, rann and song;
Nor be I any less of them,
Because the red-rose-bordered hem
Of her, whose history began
Before God made the angelic clan,
Trails all about the written page.
    To Ireland in the Coming Times.

For the elemental creatures go
About my table to and fro.   *Ib.*

Ah, faeries, dancing under the moon,
A Druid land, a Druid tune!   *Ib.*

Red Rose, Proud Rose, sad Rose of all my days!
    To the Rose upon the Rood of Time.

Eternal beauty wandering on her way.   *Ib.*

All changed, changed utterly:
A terrible beauty is born.   *Under Saturn.*

Dwell in the house of the Fenians, be they in flames
  or at feast.   *The Wanderings of Oisin,* bk. iii.

When you are old and gray and full of sleep,
And nodding by the fire, take down this book,
And slowly read, and dream of the soft look
Your eyes had once, and of their shadows deep;
How many loved your moments of glad grace,
And loved your beauty with love false or true,
But one man loved the pilgrim soul in you,
And loved the sorrows of your changing face;
And bending down beside the glowing bars,
Murmurs, a little sadly, how Love fled
And paced upon the mountains overhead
And hid his face amid a crowd of stars.
    When you are Old.

ANDREW YOUNG

1807–1889

There is a happy land,
  Far, far away,
Where Saints in glory stand,
  Bright, bright as day.
    Hymn: There is a Happy Land. C. H. Bate-
    man's *Sacred Song Book*, 1843.

EDWARD YOUNG

1683–1765

  Be wise with speed;
A fool at forty is a fool indeed.
    Love of Fame, Sat. ii, l. 281.

For who does nothing with a better grace?
    Ib. Sat. iv, l. 86.

For ever most divinely in the wrong.
    Ib. Sat. vi, l. 106.

For her own breakfast she'll project a scheme,
Nor take her tea without a stratagem.   *Ib.* l. 187.

One to destroy, is murder by the law;
And gibbets keep the lifted hand in awe;
To murder thousands, takes a specious name,
War's glorious art, and gives immortal fame.

Ib. Sat. vii, l. 55.

How commentators each dark passage shun,
And hold their farthing candle to the sun.

Ib. l. 97.

Tir'd Nature's sweet restorer, balmy sleep!
He, like the world, his ready visit pays
Where fortune smiles; the wretched he forsakes.

The Complaint: Night Thoughts, Night i, l. 1.

Night, sable goddess! from her ebon throne
In rayless majesty, now stretches forth
Her leaden sceptre o'er a slumb'ring world.

Ib. l. 18.

Be wise to-day; 'tis madness to defer. *Ib.* l. 390.

Procrastination is the thief of time. *Ib.* l. 393.

Of man's miraculous mistakes, this bears
The palm, 'That all men are about to live'.

Ib. l. 399.

At thirty man suspects himself a fool;
Knows it at forty, and reforms his plan;
At fifty chides his infamous delay,
Pushes his prudent purpose to resolve;
In all the magnanimity of thought
Resolves; and re-resolves; then dies the same.

Ib. l. 417.

All men think all men mortal, but themselves.

Ib. l. 424.

Man wants but little; nor that little, long;

Ib. Night iv, l. 118.

A God all mercy, is a God unjust. *Ib.* l. 233.

To know the world, not love her, is thy point;
She gives but little, nor that little, long.

Ib. Night viii, l. 1276.

Devotion! daughter of astronomy!
An undevout astronomer is mad.

Ib. Night ix, l. 769.

Life is the desert, life the solitude;
Death joins us to the great majority.

The Revenge, Act iv.

Accept a miracle, instead of wit,
See two dull lines, with Stanhope's pencil writ.

Written with Lord Chesterfield's Diamond Pencil.
Spence, Anecdotes, 1820, p. 378.

You are so witty, profligate, and thin,
At once we think thee Milton, Death, and Sin.

Epigram on Voltaire.

ISRAEL ZANGWILL

1864–1926

Scratch the Christian and you find the pagan—
spoiled. *Children of the Ghetto*, bk. ii, ch. 6.

America is God's Crucible, the great Melting-Pot
where all the races of Europe are melting and re-
forming! . . . God is making the American.

The Melting Pot, Act i.

THE BOOK OF COMMON PRAYER

The two extremes, of too much stiffness in refusing, and of too much easiness in admitting any variation. *The Preface.*

There was never any thing by the wit of man so well devised, or so sure established, which in continuance of time hath not been corrupted. *Ib. Concerning the Service of the Church.*

A table of the Moveable Feasts. *Section Heading in Introductory Pages,* p. xxxi.

Dearly beloved brethren, the Scripture moveth us in sundry places to acknowledge and confess our manifold sins and wickedness. *Morning Prayer. Priest's Opening Exhortation.*

We should not dissemble nor cloke them. *Ib.*

When we assemble and meet together. *Ib.*

Those things which are requisite and necessary, as well for the body as the soul. *Ib.*

We have erred, and strayed from thy ways like lost sheep. *Ib. General Confession.*

We have left undone those things which we ought to have done; And we have done those things which we ought not to have done; And there is no health in us. *Ib.*

A godly, righteous, and sober life. *Ib.*

And forgive us our trespasses, As we forgive them that trespass against us. *Ib. The Lord's Prayer.*

As it was in the beginning, is now, and ever shall be: world without end. Amen. *Ib. Gloria.*

Lord God of Sabaoth. *Ib. Te Deum Laudamus.*

An infinite Majesty. *Ib.*

The sharpness of death. *Ib.*

The noble army of martyrs. *Ib.*

O Lord, in thee have I trusted: let me never be confounded. *Ib.*

O all ye Works of the Lord, bless ye the Lord: praise him, and magnify him for ever. *Ib. Benedicite.*

O all ye Green Things upon the Earth, bless ye the Lord: praise him, and magnify him for ever. *Ib.*

O ye Whales, and all that move in the Waters. *Ib.*

O Ananias, Azarias, and Misael, bless ye the Lord: praise him, and magnify him for ever. *Ib.*

Give peace in our time, O Lord.
Because there is none other that fighteth for us, but only thou, O God. *Ib. Versicles.*

The author of peace and lover of concord, in knowledge of whom standeth our eternal life, whose service is perfect freedom. *Ib. Second Collect, for Peace.*

Neither run into any kind of danger. *Ib. Third Collect, for Grace.*

In Quires and Places where they sing. *Ib. Rubric after Third Collect.*

Grant him in health and wealth long to live. *Ib. A Prayer for the King's Majesty.*

The fountain of all goodness. *Ib. Prayer for the Royal Family.*

Almighty and everlasting God, who alone workest great marvels; Send down upon our Bishops, and Curates, and all Congregations committed to their charge, the healthful Spirit of thy grace. *Ib. Prayer for the Clergy and People.*

The continual dew of thy blessing. *Ib.*

With one accord to make our common supplications unto thee. *Ib. Prayer of St. Chrysostom.*

When two or three are gathered together in thy Name thou wilt grant their requests. *Ib.*

From whom all holy desires, all good counsels, and all just works do proceed. *Evening Prayer. Second Collect.*

That peace which the world cannot give. *Ib.*

Lighten our darkness, we beseech thee, O Lord; and by thy great mercy defend us from all perils and dangers of this night. *Ib. Third Collect.*

Whosoever will be saved: before all things it is necessary that he hold the Catholick Faith.
Which Faith except every one do keep whole and undefiled: without doubt he shall perish everlastingly. *Athanasian Creed.*

Neither confounding the Persons: nor dividing the Substance. *Ib.*

As also there are not three incomprehensibles, nor three uncreated: but one uncreated, and one incomprehensible. *Ib.*

Not three Gods: but one God. *Ib.*

Of a reasonable soul and human flesh subsisting. *Ib.*

Not by conversion of the Godhead into flesh: but by taking of the Manhood into God. *Ib.*

Have mercy upon us miserable sinners. *The Litany.*

Neither take thou vengeance of our sins. *Ib.*

The crafts and assaults of the devil. *Ib.*

Envy, hatred, and malice, and all uncharitableness. *Ib.*

Deceits of the world, the flesh, and the devil. *Ib.*

From battle and murder, and from sudden death. *Ib.*

Hardness of heart, and contempt of thy Word and Commandment. *Ib.*

Agony and bloody Sweat. *Ib.*

In the hour of death, and in the day of judgement. *Ib.*

All Bishops, Priests, and Deacons. *Ib.*

Unity, peace, and concord.   *Ib.*

To bring forth the fruits of the Spirit.   *Ib.*

To strengthen such as do stand; and to comfort and help the weak-hearted; and to raise up them that fall; and finally to beat down Satan under our feet. *Ib.*

All that are in danger, necessity, and tribulation. *Ib.*

All that travel by land or by water, all women labouring of child, all sick persons, and young children; and to shew thy pity upon all prisoners and captives. *Ib.*

The fatherless children, and widows.   *Ib.*

Our enemies, persecutors, and slanderers.   *Ib.*

The kindly fruits of the earth, so as in due time we may enjoy them.   *Ib.*

Our sins, negligences, and ignorances.   *Ib.*

The sighing of a contrite heart.   *Ib. First Collect.*

The craft and subtilty of the devil or man.   *Ib.*

We have heard with our ears, and our fathers have declared unto us, the noble works that thou didst in their days, and in the old time before them.

Ib. Sentences after the First Collect.

Turn from us all those evils that we most righteously have deserved.   *Ib. Second Collect.*

Tied and bound with the chain of our sins.
Prayers and Thanksgivings, upon Several Occasions. 'O God, whose nature and property'.

Our Mediator and Advocate.   *Ib.*

Our most religious and gracious King.
Ib. Prayer for the High Court of Parliament.

The safety, honour, and welfare of our Sovereign, and his Dominions.   *Ib.*

All sorts and conditions of men.
Ib. Prayer for All Conditions of Men.

All who profess and call themselves Christians. *Ib.*

Any ways afflicted, or distressed, in mind, body, or estate.   *Ib.*

A happy issue out of all their afflictions.   *Ib.*

Our creation, preservation, and all the blessings of this life.
Ib. Thanksgivings. A General Thanksgiving.

For the means of grace, and for the hope of glory. *Ib.*

The former and the latter rain.   *Ib. For Rain.*

Cast away the works of darkness, and put upon us the armour of light, now in the time of this mortal life.   *Collects. 1st Sunday in Advent.*

Hear them, read, mark, learn, and inwardly digest them.   *Ib. 2nd Sunday in Advent.*

An acceptable people in thy sight.
Ib. 3rd Sunday in Advent.

Sore let and hindered in running the race.
Ib. 4th Sunday in Advent.

Children by adoption and grace. *Ib. Christmas Day.*

The glory that shall be revealed.
Ib. St. Stephen's Day.

That they may both perceive and know what things they ought to do, and also may have grace and power faithfully to fulfil the same.
Ib. 1st Sunday after Epiphany.

Grant us thy peace all the days of our life.
Ib. 2nd Sunday after Epiphany.

By reason of the frailty of our nature we cannot always stand upright.   *Ib. 4th Sunday after Epiphany.*

That most excellent gift of charity.
Ib. Quinquagesima Sunday.

All evil thoughts which may assault and hurt the soul.
Ib. 2nd Sunday in Lent.

Jews, Turks, Infidels, and Hereticks.
Ib. Good Friday. Third Collect.

Thy special grace preventing us.   *Ib. Easter Day.*

The leaven of malice and wickedness.
Ib. 1st Sunday after Easter.

Those things that are contrary to their profession.
Ib. 3rd Sunday after Easter.

The unruly wills and affections of sinful men.
Ib. 4th Sunday after Easter.

The sundry and manifold changes of the world.   *Ib.*

To have a right judgement in all things.
Ib. Whitsun-day.

The weakness of our mortal nature.
Ib. 1st Sunday after Trinity.

We may so pass through things temporal, that we finally lose not the things eternal.
Ib. 4th Sunday after Trinity.

Such good things as pass man's understanding.
Ib. 6th Sunday after Trinity

The author and giver of all good things.
Ib. 7th Sunday after Trinity.

Running the way of thy commandments.
Ib. 11th Sunday after Trinity.

Those things whereof our conscience is afraid.
Ib. 12th Sunday after Trinity.

Increase of faith, hope, and charity.
Ib. 14th Sunday after Trinity.

Because the frailty of man without thee cannot but fall.   *Ib. 15th Sunday after Trinity*

Serve thee with a quiet mind.
Ib. 21st Sunday after Trinity.

Thy household the Church.
Ib. 22nd Sunday after Trinity.

Stir up, we beseech thee, O Lord, the wills of thy faithful people; that they, plenteously bringing forth the fruit of good works, may of thee be plenteously rewarded.
Ib. 25th Sunday after Trinity.

Carried away with every blast of vain doctrine.
Ib. St. Mark's Day.

Whom truly to know is everlasting life.
Ib. St. Philip and St. James's Day.

Constantly speak the truth, boldly rebuke vice, and patiently suffer for the truth's sake.
Ib. St. John the Baptist's Day.

Ordained and constituted the services of Angels and men in a wonderful order.
Ib. St. Michael and All Angels.

Who hast knit together thine elect in one communion and fellowship, in the mystical body of thy Son.   *Ib. All Saints' Day.*

An open and notorious evil liver.
Holy Communion: Introductory Rubric.

Truly repented and amended his former naughty life.
Ib.

A fair white linen cloth.   *Ib.*

Unto whom all hearts be open, all desires known, and from whom no secrets are hid.
Ib. Collect for Purity.

Thou shalt have none other gods but me.
Ib. 1st Commandment.

Incline our hearts to keep this law.
Response to Commandments.

Thou shalt not make to thyself any graven image, nor the likeness of any thing that is in heaven above, or in the earth beneath, or in the water under the earth. Thou shalt not bow down to them, nor worship them: for I the Lord thy God am a jealous God, and visit the sins of the fathers upon the children unto the third and fourth generation.
Ib. 2nd Commandment.

Thou shalt not take the Name of the Lord thy God in vain.   *Ib. 3rd Commandment.*

Remember that thou keep holy the Sabbath-day. Six days shalt thou labour, and do all that thou hast to do; but the seventh day is the Sabbath of the Lord thy God.   *Ib. 4th Commandment.*

The stranger that is within thy gates.   *Ib.*

In six days the Lord made heaven and earth, the sea, and all that in them is, and rested the seventh day.
Ib.

Honour thy father and thy mother; that thy days may be long in the land which the Lord thy God giveth thee.   *Ib. 5th Commandment.*

Thou shalt do no murder.   *Ib. 6th Commandment.*

Thou shalt not commit adultery.
Ib. 7th Commandment.

Thou shalt not steal.   *Ib. 8th Commandment.*

Thou shalt not bear false witness against thy neighbour.   *Ib. 9th Commandment.*

Thou shalt not covet thy neighbour's wife, nor his servant, nor his maid, nor his ox, nor his ass, nor any thing that is his.   *Ib. 10th Commandment.*

All things visible and invisible.   *Nicene Creed.*

The Lord and giver of life.   *Ib.*

Who spake by the Prophets.   *Ib.*

One Catholick and Apostolick Church.   *Ib.*

In a decent bason to be provided by the Parish.
Ib. Rubric before the Prayer for the Church Militant.

The whole state of Christ's Church militant here in earth.   *Ib. Prayer for the Church Militant.*

The spirit of truth, unity, and concord.   *Ib.*

Live in unity and godly love.   *Ib.*

Truly and indifferently minister justice.   *Ib.*

Thy true and lively Word.   *Ib.*

All them, who in this transitory life are in trouble, sorrow, need, sickness, or any other adversity.   *Ib.*

Departed this life in thy faith and fear.   *Ib.*

Discreet and learned Minister of God's Word.
Ib. First Exhortation.

Ghostly counsel and advice.   *Ib.*

We eat and drink our own damnation.
Ib. Third Exhortation.

Ye that do truly and earnestly repent you of your sins, and are in love and charity with your neighbours, and intend to lead a new life.   *Ib. The Invitation.*

Meekly kneeling upon your knees.   *Ib.*

The burden of them is intolerable.
Ib. General Confession.

Hear what comfortable words.
Ib. Comfortable Words.

It is meet and right so to do.   *Ib. Versicles.*

Therefore with Angels and Archangels, and with all the company of heaven.   *Ib. Hymn of Praise.*

Holy, holy, holy, Lord God of hosts, heaven and earth are full of thy glory: Glory be to thee, O Lord most High.   *Ib.*

By the operation of the Holy Ghost.
Ib. Proper Preface for Christmas Day.

A full, perfect, and sufficient sacrifice, oblation, and satisfaction.   *Ib. Prayer of Consecration.*

Who, in the same night that he was betrayed.   *Ib.*

This our bounden duty and service.
Ib. Prayer of Oblation, 1.

Not weighing our merits, but pardoning our offences.
Ib.

The mystical body of thy Son, which is the blessed company of all faithful people.   *Ib. 2.*

Heirs through hope of thy everlasting kingdom.   *Ib.*

The peace of God, which passeth all understanding.
Ib. The Blessing.

Be amongst you and remain with you always.   *Ib.*

All the changes and chances of this mortal life.
Ib. Collects after the Offertory, 1.

Prevent us, O Lord, in all our doings.   *Ib. 4.*

All our works begun, continued, and ended in thee.
Ib.

Those things, which for our unworthiness we dare not, and for our blindness we cannot ask.   *Ib. 5.*

For that were Idolatry, to be abhorred of all faithful Christians.   *Ib. Black Rubric.*

In the vulgar tongue.
Publick Baptism of Infants. Introductory Rubric, 1.

All this I stedfastly believe. *Ib. Vow of Faith.*

Grant that the old Adam in this Child may be so buried, that the new man may be raised up in him. *Ib. Invocation of Blessing on the Child.*

The faith of Christ crucified. *Ib. Reception and Dedication of the Child.*

Dead unto sin, and living unto righteousness. *Ib. Thanksgiving.*

Crucify the old man. *Ib.*

Ministration of Baptism to Such as are of Riper Years. *Title.*

Put on Christ. *Ministration of Baptism to Such as are of Riper Years. Final Exhortation.*

What is your name?
N. or M. *The Catechism.*

A member of Christ, the child of God, and an inheritor of the kingdom of heaven. *Ib.*

What did your Godfathers and Godmothers then for you? *Ib.*

Renounce the devil and all his works, the pomps and vanity of this wicked world, and all the sinful lusts of the flesh. *Ib.*

Believe all the Articles of the Christian Faith. *Ib.*

Yes verily; and by God's help so I will. *Ib.*

Rehearse the Articles of thy Belief. *Ib.*

My duty towards God, and my duty towards my Neighbour. *Ib.*

To love him as myself, and to do to all men, as I would they should do unto me. *Ib.*

Governors, teachers, spiritual pastors and masters. *Ib.*

To keep my hands from picking and stealing, and my tongue from evil speaking, lying and slandering. *Ib.*

To learn and labour truly to get mine own living, and to do my duty in that state of life, unto which it shall please God to call me. *Ib.*

My good child, know this. *Ib.*

Amen, So be it. *Ib.*

Two only, as generally necessary to salvation, that is to say, Baptism, and the Supper of the Lord. *Ib.*

An outward and visible sign of an inward and spiritual grace. *Ib.*

In their Mother Tongue. *Ib. Final Rubric.*

Confirmation, or laying on of hands. *Title.*

Being now come to the years of discretion. *Confirmation.*

Ratify and confirm the same. *Ib.*

Thy manifold gifts of grace. *Ib.*

If any of you know cause, or just impediment, why these two persons should not be joined together in holy Matrimony, ye are to declare it. This is the first time of asking. *Solemnization of Matrimony. The Banns.*

Here in the sight of God, and in the face of this congregation. *Ib. Exhortation.*

Brute beasts that have no understanding. *Ib.*

First, it was ordained for the procreation of children. *Ib.*

A remedy against sin. *Ib.*

Such persons as have not the gift of continency. *Ib.*

Let him now speak, or else hereafter for ever hold his peace. *Ib.*

Wilt thou have this woman to thy wedded wife, to live together after God's ordinance in the holy estate of Matrimony? *Ib. Betrothal.*

Forsaking all other, keep thee only unto her, so long as ye both shall live. *Ib.*

To have and to hold from this day forward, for better for worse, for richer for poorer, in sickness and in health, to love and to cherish, till death us do part, according to God's holy ordinance; and thereto I plight thee my troth. *Ib.*

To love, cherish, and to obey. *Ib.*

With this Ring I thee wed, with my body I thee worship, and with all my worldly goods I thee endow. *Ib. The Wedding.*

This Ring given and received. *Ib. The Prayer.*

Those whom God hath joined together let no man put asunder. *Ib.*

Consented together in holy wedlock. *Ib. Priest's Declaration.*

Peace be to this house. *Visitation of the Sick.*

Unto God's gracious mercy and protection we commit thee. *Ib.*

The inner man. *Ib.*

Against the hour of death. *Ib.*

Laid violent hands upon themselves. *Burial of the Dead. Introductory Rubric.*

Man that is born of a woman hath but a short time to live, and is full of misery. *Ib. First Anthem.*

In the midst of life we are in death. *Ib.*

Suffer us not, at our last hour, for any pains of death, to fall from thee. *Ib.*

We therefore commit his body to the ground; earth to earth, ashes to ashes, dust to dust; in sure and certain hope of the Resurrection to eternal life. *Ib.*

Sat in the seat of the scornful. *Psalms, i. 1.*

He shall be like a tree planted by the water-side. *Ib. 3.*

Why do the heathen so furiously rage together : and why do the people imagine a vain thing? *Ib. ii. 1.*

Let us break their bonds asunder: and cast away their cords from us. *Ib. 3.*

The Lord shall have them in derision. *Ib. 4.*

Thou shalt bruise them with a rod of iron: and break them in pieces like a potter's vessel. *Ib. 9.*

Kiss the Son, lest he be angry. *Ib. 12.*

Stand in awe, and sin not : commune with your own heart, and in your chamber, and be still. *Ib. iv. 4.*

There be many that say : Who will shew us any good?
Psalms iv. 6.

Lord, lift thou up : the light of thy countenance upon us. *Ib.* 7.

The Lord will abhor both the bloodthirsty and deceitful man. *Ib.* v. 6.

Make thy way plain before my face. *Ib.* 8.

Their throat is an open sepulchre : they flatter with their tongue. *Ib.* 10.

Let them perish through their own imaginations. *Ib.* 11.

God is a righteous Judge, strong, and patient : and God is provoked every day. *Ib.* vii. 12.

Out of the mouth of very babes and sucklings hast thou ordained strength, because of thine enemies : that thou mightest still the enemy and the avenger. *Ib.* viii. 2.

For I will consider thy heavens, even the works of thy fingers : the moon and the stars, which thou hast ordained. *Ib.* 3.

What is man, that thou art mindful of him : and the son of man, that thou visitest him?

Thou madest him lower than the angels : to crown him with glory and worship. *Ib.* 4.

The fowls of the air, and the fishes of the sea : and whatsoever walketh through the paths of the seas. *Ib.* 8.

O thou enemy, destructions are come to a perpetual end. *Ib.* ix. 6.

Their memorial is perished with them. *Ib.*

Up, Lord, and let not man have the upper hand. *Ib.* 19.

That the heathen may know themselves to be but men. *Ib.* 20.

In the Lord put I my trust : how say ye then to my soul, that she should flee as a bird unto the hill? *Ib.* xi. 1.

That they may privily shoot at them which are true of heart. *Ib.* 2.

For the foundations will be cast down : and what hath the righteous done? *Ib.* 3.

They do but flatter with their lips, and dissemble in their double heart. *Ib.* xii. 2.

The fool hath said in his heart : there is no God. *Ib.* xiv. 1.

There is none that doeth good, no not one. *Ib.* 2.

They are altogether become abominable. *Ib.* 4.

Lord, who shall dwell in thy tabernacle : or who shall rest upon thy holy hill?

Even he, that leadeth an uncorrupt life : and doeth the thing which is right, and speaketh the truth from his heart.

He that hath used no deceit in his tongue, nor done evil to his neighbour : and hath not slandered his neighbour.

He that setteth not by himself, but is lowly in his own eyes : and maketh much of them that fear the Lord.

He that sweareth unto his neighbour, and dis-

appointeth him not : though it were to his own hindrance.

He that hath not given his money upon usury : nor taken reward against the innocent.

Whoso doeth these things : shall never fall. *Ib.* xv.

Thou shalt maintain my lot.

The lot is fallen unto me in a fair ground : yea, I have a goodly heritage. *Ib.* xvi. 6.

For why? thou shalt not leave my soul in hell : neither shalt thou suffer thy Holy One to see corruption.

Thou shalt shew me the path of life; in thy presence is the fulness of joy : and at thy right hand there is pleasure for evermore. *Ib.* 11.

Keep me as the apple of an eye : hide me under the shadow of thy wings. *Ib.* xvii. 8.

Thou also shalt light my candle : the Lord my God shalt make my darkness to be light. *Ib.* xviii. 28.

With the help of my God I shall leap over the wall. *Ib.* 29.

A people whom I have not known : shall serve me. *Ib.* 44.

The heavens declare the glory of God : and the firmament showeth his handy-work.

One day telleth another : and one night certifieth another.

There is neither speech nor language : but their voices are heard among them.

Their sound is gone out into all lands : and their words into the ends of the world.

In them hath he set a tabernacle for the sun : which cometh forth as a bridegroom out of his chamber, and rejoiceth as a giant to run his course.

It goeth forth from the uttermost part of the heaven, and runneth about unto the end of it again : and there is nothing hid from the heat thereof. *Ib.* xix. 1.

More to be desired are they than gold, yea, than much fine gold : sweeter also than honey, and the honey-comb. *Ib.* 10.

Who can tell how oft he offendeth : O cleanse thou me from my secret faults.

Keep thy servant also from presumptuous sins, lest they get the dominion over me : so shall I be undefiled, and innocent from the great offence.

Let the words of my mouth, and the meditation of my heart : be alway acceptable in thy sight, O Lord : my strength, and my redeemer. *Ib.* 12.

The Lord hear thee in the day of trouble : the name of the God of Jacob defend thee;

Send thee help from the sanctuary : and strengthen thee out of Sion. *Ib.* xx. 1.

Grant thee thy heart's desire : and fulfil all thy mind. *Ib.* 4.

Some put their trust in chariots, and some in horses : but we will remember the name of the Lord our God.

They are brought down, and fallen : but we are risen, and stand upright. *Ib.* 7.

Thou hast given him his heart's desire : and hast not denied him the request of his lips. *Ib.* xxi. 2.

He asked life of thee, and thou gavest him a long life: even for ever and ever.   *Psalms* xxi. 4.

And imagined such a device as they are not able to perform.   *Ib.* 11.

My God, my God, look upon me; why hast thou forsaken me : and art so far from my health, and the voice of my complaint?
Oh my God, I cry in the day-time, but thou hearest not : and in the night-season also I take no rest.
And thou continuest holy : O thou worship of Israel.   *Ib.* xxii. 1.

But as for me, I am a worm, and no man.   *Ib.* 6.

All they that see me laugh me to scorn: they shoot out their lips, and shake their heads, saying,
He trusted in God, that he would deliver him : let him deliver him, if he will have him.   *Ib.* 7.

Many oxen are come about me : fat bulls of Basan close me in on every side.   *Ib.* 12.

For many dogs are come about me.   *Ib.* 16.

They pierced my hands and my feet; I may tell all my bones: they stand staring and looking upon me.
They part my garments among them : and cast lots upon my vesture.   *Ib.* 17.

Deliver my soul from the sword: my darling from the power of the dog.
Save me from the lion's mouth : thou hast heard me also from the horns of the unicorns.   *Ib.* 20.

For he hath not despised, nor abhorred, the low estate of the poor.   *Ib.* 24.

All they that go down into the dust shall kneel before him : and no man hath quickened his own soul.   *Ib.* 30.

The Lord is my shepherd : therefore can I lack nothing.
He shall feed me in a green pasture: and lead me forth beside the waters of comfort.
He shall convert my soul : and bring me forth in the paths of righteousness, for his name's sake.
Yea, though I walk through the valley of the shadow of death, I will fear no evil : for thou art with me; thy rod and thy staff comfort me.
Thou shalt prepare a table before me against them that trouble me : thou hast anointed my head with oil, and my cup shall be full.
But thy loving-kindness and mercy shall follow me all the days of my life: and I will dwell in the house of the Lord for ever.   *Ib.* xxiii.

The earth is the Lord's, and all that therein is : the compass of the world, and they that dwell therein.   *Ib.* xxiv. 1.

Lift up your heads, O ye gates, and be ye lift up, ye everlasting doors: and the King of glory shall come in.   *Ib.* 7.

Who is the King of glory: even the Lord of hosts, he is the King of glory.   *Ib.* 10.

O remember not the sins and offences of my youth.   *Ib.* xxv. 6.

The sorrows of my heart are enlarged.   *Ib.* 16.

Deliver Israel, O God: out of all his troubles. *Ib.* 21.

Examine me, O Lord, and prove me : try out my reins and my heart.   *Ib.* xxvi. 2.

I will wash my hands in innocency, O Lord : and so will I go to thine altar.   *Ib.* 6.

Lord, I have loved the habitation of thy house : and the place where thine honour dwelleth.
O shut not up my soul with the sinners : nor my life with the blood-thirsty.   *Ib.* 8.

The Lord is my light, and my salvation; whom then shall I fear : the Lord is the strength of my life; of whom then shall I be afraid?   *Ib.* xxvii. 1.

When my father and my mother forsake me: the Lord taketh me up.   *Ib.* 12.

I should utterly have fainted: but that I believe verily to see the goodness of the Lord in the land of the living.   *Ib.* 15.

The voice of the Lord maketh the hinds to bring forth young, and discovereth the thick bushes.   *Ib.* xxix. 8.

The Lord sitteth above the water-flood : and the Lord remaineth a King for ever.   *Ib.* 9.

Give thanks unto him for a remembrance of his holiness.
For his wrath endureth but the twinkling of an eye, and in his pleasure is life : heaviness may endure for a night, but joy cometh in the morning.   *Ib.* xxx. 4.

What profit is there in my blood : when I go down to the pit?
Shall the dust give thanks unto thee; or shall it declare thy truth?   *Ib.* 9.

Into thy hands I commend my spirit.   *Ib.* xxxi. 6.

But hast set my feet in a large room.   *Ib.* 9.

I am clean forgotten, as a dead man out of mind.   *Ib.* 14.

Thanks be to the Lord : for he hath shewed me marvellous great kindness in a strong city. *Ib.* 23.

For while I held my tongue : my bones consumed away through my daily complaining. *Ib.* xxxii. 3.

For this shall every one that is godly make his prayer unto thee, in a time when thou mayest be found : but in the great water-floods they shall not come nigh him.   *Ib.* 7.

Thou shalt compass me about with songs of deliverance.   *Ib.* 8.

Be ye not like to horse and mule, which have no understanding : whose mouths must be held with bit and bridle, lest they fall upon thee.   *Ib.* 10.

Rejoice in the Lord, O ye righteous : for it becometh well the just to be thankful.
Praise the Lord with harp : sing praises unto him with the lute, and instrument of ten strings.
Sing unto the Lord a new song : sing praises lustily unto him with a good courage.   *Ib.* xxxiii. 1.

The Lord bringeth the counsel of the heathen to nought : and maketh the devices of the people to be of none effect, and casteth out the counsels of princes.   *Ib.* 10.

There is no king that can be saved by the multitude of an host : neither is any mighty man delivered by much strength.

A horse is counted but a vain thing to save a man : neither shall he deliver any man by his great strength.   *Psalms* xxxiii. 15.

O taste, and see, how gracious the Lord is : blessed is the man that trusteth in him.

O fear the Lord, ye that are his saints : for they that fear him lack nothing.

The lions do lack, and suffer hunger : but they who seek the Lord shall want no manner of thing that is good.   *Ib.* xxxiv. 8.

What man is he that lusteth to live : and would fain see good days?   *Ib.* 12.

Eschew evil, and do good : seek peace, and ensue it.   *Ib.* 14.

Fret not thyself because of the ungodly. *Ib.* xxxvii. 1.

He shall make thy righteousness as clear as the light : and thy just dealing as the noon-day.   *Ib.* 6.

I have been young, and now am old : and yet saw I never the righteous forsaken, nor his seed begging their bread.   *Ib.* 25.

I myself have seen the ungodly in great power : and flourishing like a green bay-tree.

I went by, and lo, he was gone : I sought him, but his place could no where be found.

Keep innocency, and take heed unto the thing that is right : for that shall bring a man peace at the last.   *Ib.* 36.

Lord, thou knowest all my desire : and my groaning is not hid from thee.   *Ib.* xxxviii. 9.

I held my tongue, and spake nothing : I kept silence, yea, even from good words; but it was pain and grief to me.

My heart was hot within me, and while I was thus musing the fire kindled: and at the last I spake with my tongue;

Lord, let me know mine end, and the number of my days : that I may be certified how long I have to live.   *Ib.* xxxix. 3.

Mine age is even as nothing in respect of thee : and verily every man living is altogether vanity.

For man walketh in a vain shadow, and disquieteth himself in vain : he heapeth up riches, and cannot tell who shall gather them.   *Ib.* 6.

Thou makest his beauty to consume away, like as it were a moth fretting a garment : every man therefore is but vanity.   *Ib.* 12.

For I am a stranger with thee : and a sojourner, as all my fathers were.

O spare me a little, that I may recover my strength : before I go hence, and be no more seen.   *Ib.* 14.

I waited patiently for the Lord : and he inclined unto me, and heard my calling.

He brought me also out of the horrible pit, out of the mire and clay : and set my feet upon the rock, and ordered my goings.   *Ib.* xl. 1.

Burnt-offerings, and sacrifice for sin, hast thou not required : then said I, Lo, I come.

In the volume of the book it is written of me, that I should fulfil thy will, O my God.   *Ib.* 9.

Thou art my helper and redeemer : make no long tarrying, O my God.   *Ib.* 21.

Yea, mine own familiar friend . . . hath lifted up his heel against me.   *Ib.* xli. 9 [Bible Version].

Like as the hart desireth the water-brooks : so longeth my soul after thee, O God.   *Ib.* xlii. 1.

Why art thou so full of heaviness, O my soul : and why art thou so disquieted within me?   *Ib.* 6.

The little hill of Hermon.   *Ib.* 8.

One deep calleth another, because of the noise of the water-pipes : all thy waves and storms are gone over me.   *Ib.* 9.

While mine enemies that trouble me cast me in the teeth.   *Ib.* 12.

My heart is inditing of a good matter : I speak of the things which I have made unto the King.

My tongue is the pen: of a ready writer.   *Ib.* xlv. 1.

Gird thee with thy sword upon thy thigh, O thou most Mighty : according to thy worship and renown.

Good luck have thou with thine honour : ride on, because of the word of truth, of meekness, and righteousness; and thy right hand shall teach thee terrible things.   *Ib.* 4.

Kings' daughters were among thy honourable women : upon thy right hand did stand the queen in a vesture of gold, wrought about with divers colours.

Hearken, O daughter, and consider, incline thine ear : forget also thine own people, and thy father's house.

So shall the King have pleasure in thy beauty. *Ib.* 10.

And the daughter of Tyre shall be there with a gift.   *Ib.* 13.

The King's daughter is all glorious within : her clothing is of wrought gold.

She shall be brought unto the King in raiment of needlework : the virgins that be her fellows shall bear her company, and shall be brought unto thee.   *Ib.* 14.

Instead of thy fathers thou shalt have children: whom thou mayest make princes in all lands.   *Ib.* 17.

God is our hope and strength : a very present help in trouble.

Therefore will we not fear, though the earth be moved : and though the hills be carried into the midst of the sea.   *Ib.* xlvi. 1.

God is in the midst of her, therefore shall she not be removed : God shall help her, and that right early.

The heathen make much ado, and the kingdoms are moved : but God hath shewed his voice, and the earth shall melt away.   *Ib.* 5.

He maketh wars to cease in all the world: he breaketh the bow, and knappeth the spear in sunder, and burneth the chariots in the fire.

Be still then, and know that I am God.   *Ib.* 9.

He shall subdue the people under us: and the nations under our feet.   *Ib.* xlvii. 3.

God is gone up with a merry noise: and the Lord with the sound of the trump.   *Ib.* 5.

For God is the King of all the earth : sing ye praises with understanding. *Psalms* xlvii. **7.**

For lo, the kings of the earth : are gathered, and gone by together.
They marvelled to see such things : they were astonished; and suddenly cast down. *Ib.* xlviii. **3.**

Thou shalt break the ships of the sea : through the east-wind. *Ib.* **6.**

Walk about Sion, and go round about her : and tell the towers thereof.
Mark well her bulwarks, set up her houses : that ye may tell them that come after.
For this God is our God for ever and ever : he shall be our guide unto death. *Ib.* **11.**

And yet they think that their houses shall continue for ever : and that their dwelling-places shall endure from one generation to another; and call the lands after their own names. *Ib.* xlix. **11.**

He shall follow the generation of his fathers : and shall never see light.
Man being in honour hath no understanding : but is compared unto the beasts that perish. *Ib.* **19.**

For all the beasts of the forest are mine : and so are the cattle upon a thousand hills. *Ib.* l. **10.**

Thinkest thou that I will eat bulls' flesh : and drink the blood of goats? *Ib.* **13.**

When thou sawest a thief, thou consentedst unto him : and hast been partaker with the adulterers. *Ib.* **18.**

O consider this, ye that forget God. *Ib.* **22.**

For I acknowledge my faults : and my sin is ever before me.
Against thee only have I sinned, and done this evil in thy sight. *Ib.* li. **3.**

Behold, I was shapen in wickedness; and in sin hath my mother conceived me.
But lo, thou requirest truth in the inward parts : and shalt make me to understand wisdom secretly.
Thou shalt purge me with hyssop, and I shall be clean : thou shalt wash me, and I shall be whiter than snow.
Thou shalt make me hear of joy and gladness : that the bones which thou hast broken may rejoice. *Ib.* **5.**

Make me a clean heart, O God : and renew a right spirit within me.
Cast me not away from thy presence : and take not thy holy Spirit from me.
O give me the comfort of thy help again : and stablish me with thy free Spirit.
Then shall I teach thy ways unto the wicked : and sinners shall be converted unto thee.
Deliver me from blood-guiltiness, O God. *Ib.* **10.**

For thou desirest no sacrifice, else would I give it thee : but thou delightest not in burnt-offerings.
The sacrifice of God is a troubled spirit : a broken and contrite heart, O God, shalt thou not despise.
O be favourable and gracious unto Sion : build thou the walls of Jerusalem. *Ib.* **16.**

Then shall they offer young bullocks upon thine altar. *Ib.* **19.**

My guide, and mine own familiar friend.
We took sweet counsel together : and walked in the house of God as friends. *Ib.* lv. **14.**

His words were smoother than oil and yet be they very swords. *Ib.* **22.**

All that they imagine is to do me evil.
They hold all together, and keep themselves close. *Ib.* lvi. **5.**

Thou tellest my flittings; put my tears into thy bottle : are not these things noted in thy book? *Ib.* **8.**

For thou hast delivered my soul from death, and my feet from falling : that I may walk before God in the light of the living. *Ib.* **13.**

Under the shadow of thy wings shall be my refuge, until this tyranny be over-past *Ib.* lvii. **1.**

God shall send forth his mercy and truth : my soul is among lions.
And I lie even among the children of men, that are set on fire : whose teeth are spears and arrows, and their tongue a sharp sword.
Set up thyself, O God, above the heavens : and thy glory above all the earth.
They have laid a net for my feet, and pressed down my soul : they have digged a pit before me and are fallen into the midst of it themselves. *Ib.* **4.**

Awake up, my glory; awake, lute and harp : I myself will awake right early. *Ib.* **9.**

Even like the deaf adder that stoppeth her ears;
Which refuseth to hear the voice of the charmer : charm he never so wisely. *Ib.* lviii. **4.**

Let them consume away like a snail, and be like the untimely fruit of a woman : and let them not see the sun.
Or ever your pots be made hot with thorns : so let indignation vex him, even as a thing that is raw. *Ib.* **7.**

They grin like a dog, and run about through the city. *Ib.* lix. **6.**

God hath spoken in his holiness, I will rejoice, and divide Sichem : and mete out the valley of Succoth.
Gilead is mine, and Manasses is mine; Ephraim also is the strength of my head; Judah is my law-giver.
Moab is my wash-pot; over Edom will I cast out my shoe : Philistia, be thou glad of me.
Who will lead me into the strong city : who will bring me into Edom? *Ib.* lx. **6.**

As for the children of men, they are but vanity : the children of men are deceitful upon the weights, they are altogether lighter than vanity itself.
O trust not in wrong and robbery, give not yourselves unto vanity : if riches increase, set not your heart upon them.
God spake once, and twice I have also heard the same : that power belongeth unto God;
And that thou, Lord, art merciful : for thou rewardest every man according to his work. *Ib.* lxii. **9.**

My soul thirsteth for thee, my flesh also longeth after thee : in a barren and dry land where no water is. *Ib.* lxiii. **2.**

Have I not remembered thee in my bed : and thought upon thee when I was waking? *Ib.* **7.**

Thou that hearest the prayer : unto thee shall all flesh come. *Ib.* lxv. **3.**

Thou that art the hope of all the ends of the earth, and of them that remain in the broad sea.

Who in his strength setteth fast the mountains : and is girded about with power.

Who stilleth the raging of the sea : and the noise of his waves, and the madness of the people.
Psalms, lxv. 5.

Thou that makest the outgoings of the morning and evening to praise thee. *Ib.* 8.

Thou waterest her furrows, thou sendest rain into the little valleys thereof : thou makest it soft with the drops of rain, and blessest the increase of it.

Thou crownest the year with thy goodness : and thy clouds drop fatness.

They shall drop upon the dwellings of the wilderness: and the little hills shall rejoice on every side.

The fold shall be full of sheep : the valleys also shall stand so thick with corn, that they shall laugh and sing. *Ib.* 11.

Who holdeth our soul in life : and suffereth not our feet to slip.

For thou, O God, hast proved us : thou also hast tried us, like as silver is tried. *Ib.* lxvi. 8.

God be merciful unto us, and bless us : and shew us the light of his countenance, and be merciful unto us.

That thy way may be known upon earth : thy saving health among all nations. *Ib.* lxvii. 1.

Then shall the earth bring forth her increase : and God, even our own God, shall give us his blessing. *Ib.* 6.

Let God arise, and let his enemies be scattered : let them also that hate him flee before him.

Like as the smoke vanisheth, so shalt thou drive them away : and like as wax melteth at the fire, so let the ungodly perish at the presence of God. *Ib.* lxviii. 1.

O sing unto God, and sing praises unto his Name : magnify him that rideth upon the heavens, as it were upon an horse; praise him in his Name JAH, and rejoice before him.

He is a Father of the fatherless, and defendeth the cause of the widows : even God in his holy habitation.

He is the God that maketh men to be of one mind in an house, and bringeth the prisoners out of captivity : but letteth the runagates continue in scarceness.

O God, when thou wentest forth before the people : when thou wentest through the wilderness,

The earth shook, and the heavens dropped at the presence of God. *Ib.* 4.

Thou, O God, sentest a gracious rain upon thine inheritance : and refreshedst it when it was weary. *Ib.* 9.

The Lord gave the word : great was the company of the preachers.

Kings with their armies did flee, and were discomfited : and they of the household divided the spoil.

Though ye have lien among the pots, yet shall ye be as the wings of a dove : that is covered with silver wings, and her feathers like gold.

When the Almighty scattered kings for their sake : then were they as white as snow in Salmon.

As the hill of Basan, so is God's hill : even an high hill, as the hill of Basan.

Why hop ye so, ye high hills? this is God's hill, in the which it pleaseth him to dwell. *Ib.* 11.

The chariots of God are twenty thousand, even thousands of angels. *Ib.* 17.

Thou art gone up on high, thou hast led captivity captive, and received gifts for men. *Ib.* 18.

God shall wound the head of his enemies : and the hairy scalp of such a one as goeth on still in his wickedness. *Ib.* 21.

That thy foot may be dipped in the blood of thine enemies : and that the tongue of thy dogs may be red through the same. *Ib.* 23.

The singers go before, the minstrels follow after : in the midst are the damsels playing with the timbrels. *Ib.* 25.

There is little Benjamin their ruler, and the princes of Judah their counsel. *Ib.* 27.

When he hath scattered the people that delight in war. *Ib.* 30.

Lo, he doth send out his voice, yea, and that a mighty voice. *Ib.* 33.

I paid them the things that I never took : God, thou knowest my simpleness. *Ib.* lxix. 5.

The zeal of thine house hath even eaten me. *Ib.* 9.

They that sit in the gate speak against me : and the drunkards make songs upon me. *Ib.* 12.

I looked for some to have pity on me, but there was no man, neither found I any to comfort me.

They gave me gall to eat: and when I was thirsty they gave me vinegar to drink. *Ib.* 21.

Let them for their reward be soon brought to shame: that cry over me, There, there. *Ib.* lxx. 2.

I am become as it were a monster unto many. *Ib.* lxxi. 6.

Give the King thy judgements, O God : and thy righteousness unto the King's son. *Ib.* lxxii. 1.

The mountains also shall bring peace : and the little hills righteousness unto the people. *Ib.* 3.

He shall come down like the rain into a fleece of wool: even as the drops that water the earth. *Ib.* 6.

His enemies shall lick the dust.

The kings of Tharsis and of the isles shall give presents : the kings of Arabia and Saba shall bring gifts.

All kings shall fall down before him : all nations shall do him service. *Ib.* 9.

Therefore fall the people unto them : and thereout suck they no small advantage.

Tush, say they, how should God perceive it : is there knowledge in the Most High? *Ib.* lxxiii. 10.

Then thought I to understand this : but it was too hard for me.

Until I went into the sanctuary of God : then understood I the end of these men. *Ib.* 15.

O deliver not the soul of thy turtle-dove unto the multitude of the enemies. *Ib.* lxxiv. 20.

The earth is weak, and all the inhabiters thereof : I bear up the pillars of it. *Psalms* lxxv. 4.

For promotion cometh neither from the east, nor from the west : nor yet from the south. *Ib.* 7.

For in the hand of the Lord there is a cup, and the wine is red : it is full mixed, and he poureth out of the same. *Ib.* 9.

I have considered the days of old : and the years that are past. *Ib.* lxxvii. 5.

A faithless and stubborn generation. *Ib.* lxxviii. 9.

Who being harnessed, and carrying bows, turned themselves back in the day of battle. *Ib.* 10.

So man did eat angels' food. *Ib.* 26.

Starting aside like a broken bow. *Ib.* 58.

So the Lord awaked as one out of sleep : and like a giant refreshed with wine.
He smote his enemies in the hinder parts : and put them to a perpetual shame. *Ib.* 66.

Thou feedest them with the bread of tears.
Ib. lxxx. 5.

I proved thee also : at the waters of strife. *Ib.* lxxxi. 8.

They will not be learned nor understand, but walk on still in darkness : all the foundations of the earth are out of course. *Ib.* lxxxii. 5.

O how amiable are thy dwellings : thou Lord of hosts!
My soul hath a desire and longing to enter into the courts of the Lord : my heart and my flesh rejoice in the living God.
Yea, the sparrow hath found her an house, and the swallow a nest where she may lay her young : even thy altars, O Lord of hosts, my King and my God.
Ib. lxxxiv. 1.

Who going through the vale of misery use it for a well : and the pools are filled with water.
They will go from strength to strength. *Ib.* 6.

For one day in thy courts : is better than a thousand.
I had rather be a doorkeeper in the house of my God : than to dwell in the tents of ungodliness. *Ib.* 10.

Lord, thou art become gracious unto thy land : thou hast turned away the captivity of Jacob. *Ib.* lxxxv. 1

Mercy and truth are met together : righteousness and peace have kissed each other.
Truth shall flourish out of the earth : and righteousness hath looked down from heaven. *Ib.* 10.

Righteousness shall go before him : and he shall direct his going in the way. *Ib.* 13.

The congregations of naughty men have sought after my soul. *Ib.* lxxxvi. 14.

Show some token upon me for good, that they who hate me may see it, and be ashamed. *Ib.* 17.

Her foundations are upon the holy hills : the Lord loveth the gates of Sion more than all the dwellings of Jacob.
Very excellent things are spoken of thee : thou city of God.
I will think upon Rahab and Babylon : with them that know me. *Ib.* lxxxvii. 1.

The singers also and trumpeters shall he rehearse : all my fresh springs shall be in thee. *Ib.* 7.

Lord, thou hast been our refuge : from one generation to another.
Before the mountains were brought forth, or ever the earth and the world were made : thou art God from everlasting, and world without end.
Thou turnest man to destruction : again thou sayest, Come again, ye children of men.
For a thousand years in thy sight are but as yesterday : seeing that is past as a watch in the night.
As soon as thou scatterest them they are even as a sleep : and fade away suddenly like the grass.
In the morning it is green, and groweth up : but in the evening it is cut down, dried up, and withered.
Ib. xc.

For when thou art angry all our days are gone : we bring our years to an end, as it were a tale that is told.
The days of our age are threescore years and ten; and though men be so strong that they come to fourscore years : yet is their strength then but labour and sorrow; so soon passeth it away, and we are gone. *Ib.* 9.

Prosper thou the work of our hands upon us, O prosper thou our handy-work. *Ib.* 17.

For he shall deliver thee from the snare of the hunter : and from the noisome pestilence.
He shall defend thee under his wings, and thou shalt be safe under his feathers : his faithfulness and truth shall be thy shield and buckler.
Thou shalt not be afraid for any terror by night : nor for the arrow that flieth by day.
For the pestilence that walketh in darkness : nor for the sickness that destroyeth in the noon-day.
A thousand shall fall beside thee, and ten thousand at thy right hand : but it shall not come nigh thee.
Ib. xci. 3.

There shall no evil happen unto thee : neither shall any plague come nigh thy dwelling.
For he shall give his angels charge over thee : to keep thee in all thy ways.
They shall bear thee in their hands : that thou hurt not thy foot against a stone. *Ib.* 10.

An unwise man doth not well consider this : and a fool doth not understand it. *Ib.* xcii. 6.

They also shall bring forth more fruit in their age : and shall be fat and well-liking. *Ib.* 13.

The Lord is King, and hath put on glorious apparel : the Lord hath put on his apparel, and girded himself with strength.
He hath made the round world so sure : that it cannot be moved. *Ib.* xciii. 1.

The floods are risen, O Lord, the floods have lift up their voice : the floods lift up their waves.
The waves of the sea are mighty, and rage horribly : but yet the Lord, who dwelleth on high, is mightier.
Ib. 9.

He that planted the ear, shall he not hear : or he that made the eye, shall he not see? *Ib.* xciv. 9.

Shew ourselves glad in him with psalms. *Ib.* xcv. 2.

In his hand are all the corners of the earth : and the strength of the hills is his also.
The sea is his, and he made it : and his hands prepared the dry land. *Ib.* 4.

The Lord is King, the earth may be glad thereof : yea, the multitude of the isles may be glad thereof.
Psalms xcvii. 1.

With trumpets also, and shawms : O shew yourselves joyful before the Lord the King.   *Ib.* xcviii. 7.

The Lord is King, be the people never so impatient : he sitteth between the cherubims, be the earth never so unquiet.   *Ib.* xcix. 1.

Whoso hath also a proud look and high stomach : I will not suffer him.   *Ib.* ci. 7.

I am become like a pelican in the wilderness : and like an owl that is in the desert.
I have watched, and am even as it were a sparrow : that sitteth alone upon the house-top.   *Ib.* cii. 6.

They shall perish, but thou shalt endure : they shall all wax old as doth a garment;
And as a vesture shalt thou change them, and they shall be changed : but thou art the same, and thy years shall not fail.   *Ib.* 26.

Praise the Lord, O my soul : and forget not all his benefits.   *Ib.* ciii. 2.

Who satisfieth thy mouth with good things : making thee young and lusty as an eagle.   *Ib.* 5.

He will not alway be chiding : neither keepeth he his anger for ever.   *Ib.* 9.

For look how high the heaven is in comparison of the earth : so great is his mercy also toward them that fear him.
Look how wide also the east is from the west : so far hath he set our sins from us.
Yea, like as a father pitieth his own children : even so is the Lord merciful unto them that fear him.
Ib. 11.

The days of man are but as grass : for he flourisheth as a flower of the field.
For as soon as the wind goeth over it, it is gone : and the place thereof shall know it no more.   *Ib.* 15.

Who layeth the beams of his chambers in the waters : and maketh the clouds his chariot, and walketh upon the wings of the wind.
He maketh his angels spirits : and his ministers a flaming fire.
He laid the foundations of the earth : that it never should move at any time.
Thou coveredst it with the deep like as with a garment : the waters stand in the hills.
At thy rebuke they flee : at the voice of thy thunder they are afraid.
They go up as high as the hills, and down to the valleys beneath : even unto the place which thou hast appointed for them.
Thou hast set them their bounds which they shall not pass : neither turn again to cover the earth.
He sendeth the springs into the rivers : which run among the hills.
All beasts of the field drink thereof : and the wild asses quench their thirst.
Beside them shall the fowls of the air have their habitation : and sing among the branches.
Ib. civ. 3.

Wine that maketh glad the heart of man : and oil to make him a cheerful countenance, and bread to strengthen man's heart.

The trees of the Lord also are full of sap : even the cedars of Libanus which he hath planted.   *Ib.* 15.

Wherein the birds make their nests : and the fir-trees are a dwelling for the stork.
The high hills are a refuge for the wild goats : and so are the stony rocks for the conies.
He appointed the moon for certain seasons : and the sun knoweth his going down.
Thou makest darkness that it may be night : wherein all the beasts of the forest do move.
The lions roaring after their prey : do seek their meat from God.
The sun ariseth, and they get them away together : and lay them down in their dens.
Man goeth forth to his work, and to his labour : until the evening.   *Ib.* 17.

So is the great and wide sea also : wherein are things creeping innumerable, both small and great beasts.
There go the ships, and there is that Leviathan : whom thou hast made to take his pastime therein.
These wait all upon thee : that thou mayest give them their meat in due season.   *Ib.* 25.

Whose feet they hurt in the stocks : the iron entered into his soul.   *Ib.* cv. 18.

Wonders in the land of Ham.   *Ib.* 27.

Went a whoring with their own inventions.
Ib. cvi. 38.

Hungry and thirsty : their soul fainted in them.
So they cried unto the Lord in their trouble : and he delivered them from their distress.
He led them forth by the right way : that they might go to the city where they dwelt.
O that men would therefore praise the Lord for his goodness : and declare the wonders that he doeth for the children of men!
For he satisfieth the empty soul : and filleth the hungry soul with goodness.
Such as sit in darkness, and in the shadow of death : being fast bound in misery and iron;
Because they rebelled against the words of the Lord : and lightly regarded the counsel of the most Highest.   *Ib.* cvii. 5.

Their soul abhorred all manner of meat : and they were even hard at death's door.   *Ib.* 18.

They that go down to the sea in ships : and occupy their business in great waters;
These men see the works of the Lord : and his wonders in the deep.   *Ib.* 23.

They reel to and fro, and stagger like a drunken man : and are at their wit's end.
So when they cry unto the Lord in their trouble : he delivereth them out of their distress.   *Ib.* 27.

Then are they glad, because they are at rest : and so he bringeth them unto the haven where they would be.   *Ib.* 30.

Again, he maketh the wilderness a standing water : and water-springs of a dry ground.   *Ib.* 35.

And again, when they are minished, and brought low : through oppression, through any plague, or trouble.
Ib. 39.

Whoso is wise will ponder these things.   *Ib.* 43.

The Lord said unto my Lord : Sit thou on my right hand, until I make thine enemies thy footstool.
Psalms cx. 1.

The Lord sware, and will not repent : Thou art a priest for ever after the order of Melchisedech.
Ib. 4.

The fear of the Lord is the beginning of wisdom : a good understanding have all they that do thereafter; the praise of it endureth for ever. *Ib.* cxi. 10.

A good man is merciful, and lendeth. *Ib.* cxii. 5.

He hath dispersed abroad, and given to the poor.
Ib. 9.

He maketh the barren woman to keep house : and to be a joyful mother of children. *Ib.* cxiii. 8.

They have mouths, and speak not : eyes have they, and see not.
They have ears, and hear not : noses have they, and smell not.
They have hands, and handle not; feet have they, and walk not : neither speak they through their throat.
Ib. cxv. 5.

The snares of death compassed me round about : and the pains of death gat hold upon me. *Ib.* cxvi. 3.

And why? thou hast delivered my soul from death : mine eyes from tears, and my feet from falling.
Ib. 8.

I said in my haste, All men are liars. *Ib.* 10.

The voice of joy and health is in the dwellings of the righteous : the right hand of the Lord bringeth mighty things to pass. *Ib.* cxviii. 15.

The right hand of the Lord hath the pre-eminence.
Ib. 16.

I shall not die, but live : and declare the works of the Lord. *Ib.* 17.

The same stone which the builders refused : is become the head-stone in the corner. *Ib.* 22.

Blessed be he that cometh in the Name of the Lord : we have wished you good luck, ye that are of the house of the Lord. *Ib.* 26.

Wherewithal shall a young man cleanse his way : even by ruling himself after thy word. *Ib.* cxix. 9.

Make me to go in the path of thy commandments : for therein is my desire. *Ib.* 35.

O turn away mine eyes, lest they behold vanity : and quicken thou me in thy law. *Ib.* 37.

In the house of my pilgrimage. *Ib.* 54.

The law of thy mouth is dearer unto me : than thousands of gold and silver. *Ib.* 72.

For I am become like a bottle in the smoke. *Ib.* 83.

I see that all things come to an end : but thy commandment is exceeding broad. *Ib.* 96.

I have more understanding than my teachers : for thy testimonies are my study.
I am wiser than the aged : because I keep thy commandments. *Ib.* 99.

Thy word is a lantern unto my feet : and a light unto my paths.

I have sworn, and am stedfastly purposed : to keep thy righteous judgements. *Ib.* 105.

O stablish me according to thy word. *Ib.* 116.

Princes have persecuted me without a cause. *Ib.* 161.

What reward shall be given or done unto thee, thou false tongue : even mighty and sharp arrows, with hot burning coals.
Woe is me, that I am constrained to dwell with Mesech : and to have my habitation among the tents of Kedar. *Ib.* cxx. 3.

I labour for peace, but when I speak unto them thereof : they make them ready to battle. *Ib.* 6.

I will lift up mine eyes unto the hills : from whence cometh my help. *Ib.* cxxi. 1.

He will not suffer my foot to be moved : and he that keepeth thee will not sleep. *Ib.* 3.

The Lord himself is thy keeper : the Lord is thy defence upon thy right hand;
So that the sun shall not burn thee by day : neither the moon by night. *Ib.* 5.

The Lord shall preserve thy going out, and thy coming in : from this time forth for evermore.
Ib. 8.

I was glad when they said unto me : We will go into the house of the Lord. *Ib.* cxxii. 1.

O pray for the peace of Jerusalem : they shall prosper that love thee.
Peace be within thy walls : and plenteousness within thy palaces.
For my brethren and companions' sakes : I will wish thee prosperity.
Yea, because of the house of the Lord our God : I will seek to do thee good. *Ib.* 6.

Our soul is escaped even as a bird out of the snare of the fowler : the snare is broken, and we are delivered. *Ib.* cxxiv. 6.

The hills stand about Jerusalem : even so standeth the Lord round about his people, from this time forth for evermore.
For the rod of the ungodly cometh not into the lot of the righteous : let the righteous put their hand unto wickedness. *Ib.* cxxv. 2.

Turn our captivity, O Lord : as the rivers in the south.
They that sow in tears : shall reap in joy.
He that now goeth on his way weeping, and beareth forth good seed : shall doubtless come again with joy, and bring his sheaves with him. *Ib.* cxxvi. 5.

Except the Lord build the house : their labour is but lost that build it.
Except the Lord keep the city : the watchman waketh but in vain.
It is but lost labour that ye haste to rise up early, and so late take rest, and eat the bread of carefulness : for so he giveth his beloved sleep.
Lo, children and the fruit of the womb : are an heritage and gift that cometh of the Lord.
Like as the arrows in the hand of the giant : even so are the young children.
Happy is the man that hath his quiver full of them : they shall not be ashamed when they speak with their enemies in the gate. *Ib.* cxxvii. 1.

R 3

Thy wife shall be as the fruitful vine : upon the walls of thine house.
Thy children like the olive-branches : round about thy table. *Psalms* cxxviii. 3.

The plowers plowed upon my back : and made long furrows. *Ib.* cxxix. 3.

Out of the deep have I called unto thee, O Lord : Lord, hear my voice. *Ib.* cxxx. 1.

If thou, Lord, wilt be extreme to mark what is done amiss : O Lord, who may abide it? *Ib.* 3.

My soul fleeth unto the Lord : before the morning watch, I say, before the morning watch. *Ib.* 6.

Lord, I am not high-minded : I have no proud looks.
I do not exercise myself in great matters : which are too high for me.
But I refrain my soul, and keep it low, like as a child that is weaned from his mother : yea, my soul is even as a weaned child. *Ib.* cxxxi. 1.

Lord, remember David : and all his trouble. *Ib.* cxxxii. 1.

Behold, how good and joyful a thing it is : brethren, to dwell together in unity!
It is like the precious ointment upon the head that ran down unto the beard : even unto Aaron's beard, and went down to the skirts of his clothing. *Ib.* cxxxiii. 1.

His mercy endureth for ever. *Ib.* cxxxvi. 1.

By the waters of Babylon we sat down and wept : when we remembered thee, O Sion.
As for our harps, we hanged them up : upon the trees that are therein.
For they that led us away captive required of us then a song, and melody, in our heaviness : Sing us one of the songs of Sion.
How shall we sing the Lord's song : in a strange land?
If I forget thee, O Jerusalem : let my right hand forget her cunning.
If I do not remember thee, let my tongue cleave to the roof of my mouth : yea, if I prefer not Jerusalem in my mirth. *Ib.* cxxxvii. 1.

How they said, Down with it, down with it, even to the ground.
O daughter of Babylon, wasted with misery : yea, happy shall he be that rewardeth thee, as thou hast served us.
Blessed shall he be that taketh thy children : and throweth them against the stones. *Ib.* 7.

O Lord, thou hast searched me out, and known me : thou knowest my down-sitting, and mine uprising; thou understandest my thoughts long before. *Ib.* cxxxix. 1.

Such knowledge is too wonderful and excellent for me : I cannot attain unto it. *Ib.* 5.

If I take the wings of the morning : and remain in the uttermost parts of the sea;
Even there also shall thy hand lead me : and thy right hand shall hold me.
If I say, Peradventure the darkness shall cover me : then shall my night be turned to day.
Yea, the darkness is no darkness with thee, but the night is as clear as the day : the darkness and light to thee are both alike. *Ib.* 8.

I will give thanks unto thee, for I am fearfully and wonderfully made. *Ib.* 13.

And in thy book were all my members written. *Ib.* 15.

Thou hast covered my head in the day of battle. *Ib.* cxl. 7.

Let the lifting up of my hands be an evening sacrifice.
Set a watch, O Lord, before my mouth : and keep the door of my lips. *Ib.* cxli. 2.

Let the righteous rather smite me friendly : and reprove me.
But let not their precious balms break my head. *Ib.* 5.

Let the ungodly fall into their own nets together : and let me ever escape them. *Ib.* 11.

That our sons may grow up as the young plants : and that our daughters may be as the polished corners of the temple. *Ib.* cxliv. 12.

That our oxen may be strong to labour, that there be no decay : no leading into captivity, and no complaining in our streets. *Ib.* 14.

The Lord is gracious, and merciful : long-suffering, and of great goodness. *Ib.* cxlv. 8.

O put not your trust in princes, nor in any child of man : for there is no help in them.
For when the breath of man goeth forth he shall turn again to his earth : and then all his thoughts perish. *Ib.* cxlvi. 2.

The Lord careth for the strangers; he defendeth the fatherless and widow : as for the way of the ungodly, he turneth it upside down. *Ib.* 9.

Yea, a joyful and pleasant thing it is to be thankful.
The Lord doth build up Jerusalem : and gather together the outcasts of Israel.
He healeth those that are broken in heart : and giveth medicine to heal their sickness.
He telleth the number of the stars : and calleth them all by their names. *Ib.* cxlvii. 1.

He hath no pleasure in the strength of an horse : neither delighteth he in any man's legs. *Ib.* 10.

He giveth snow like wool : and scattereth the hoarfrost like ashes. *Ib.* 16.

Praise the Lord upon earth : ye dragons and all deeps;
Fire and hail, snow and vapours : wind and storm, fulfilling his word. *Ib.* cxlviii. 7.

Young men and maidens, old men and children, praise the name of the Lord : for his name only is excellent, and his praise above heaven and earth. *Ib.* 12.

Let the praises of God be in their mouth : and a two-edged sword in their hands. *Ib.* cxlix. 6.

To bind their kings in chains : and their nobles with links of iron. *Ib.* 8.

Praise him upon the well-tuned cymbals : praise him upon the loud cymbals.
Let every thing that hath breath : praise the Lord. *Ib.* cl. 5.

Such as pass on the seas upon their lawful occasions. *Forms of Prayer to be Used at Sea.* 'O Eternal Lord God.'

We therefore commit his body to the deep, to be turned into corruption, looking for the resurrection of the body (when the Sea shall give up her dead).
Ib. At the Burial of their Dead at Sea.

Come, Holy Ghost, our souls inspire,
And lighten with celestial fire.
Thou the anointing Spirit art,
Who dost thy seven-fold gifts impart.
Ordering of Priests. Veni, Creator Spiritus.

Enable with perpetual light
The dulness of our blinded sight.   *Ib.*

Anoint and cheer our soiled face
With the abundance of thy grace,
Keep far our foes, give peace at home:
Where thou art guide, no ill can come.   *Ib.*

Cheerfully for conscience sake.
Accession Service. Almighty God, who rulest over all the kingdoms.

We will see there shall be due Execution upon them.
Articles of Religion. His Majesty's Declaration.

All things necessary to salvation.
Ib. Of the Sufficiency of the Holy Scriptures, vi.

As the Pelagians do vainly talk.
Ib. Of Original Sin, ix.

Of Works of Supererogation.   *Title of Article* xiv.

Man is very far gone from original righteousness. *Ib.*

Fond thing vainly invented. *Ib.* xxii. *Of Purgatory.*

Understanded of the people.
Ib. xxiv. *Of Speaking in the Congregation.*

The corrupt following of the Apostles.
Ib. xxv. *Of the Sacraments.*

Reserved, carried about, lifted up, or worshipped.
Ib. xxviii. *Of the Lord's Supper.*

Blasphemous fables, and dangerous deceits.
Ib. xxxi. *Of the One Oblation.*

The Bishop of *Rome* hath no jurisdiction in this Realm of *England.*
Ib. xxxvii. *Of the Civil Magistrates.*

It is lawful for Christian men, at the commandment of the Magistrate, to wear weapons, and serve in the wars.   *Ib.*

As certain Anabaptists do falsely boast.
Ib. xxxviii. *Of Christian Men's Goods.*

Table of Kindred and Affinity.   *Title.*

A Man may not marry his Grandmother.
Table of Kindred.

THE HOLY BIBLE

THE OLD TESTAMENT

Upon the setting of that bright *Occidental Star*, Queen *Elizabeth* of most happy memory.
Holy Bible, Authorized Translation, Preface.

The appearance of Your Majesty, as of the *Sun* in his strength. *Ib.*

In the beginning God created the heaven and the earth.

And the earth was without form, and void; and darkness was upon the face of the deep. And the Spirit of God moved upon the face of the waters.

And God said, Let there be light: and there was light.
Genesis i. 1.

And the evening and the morning were the first day. *Ib.* 5.

And God saw that it was good. *Ib.* 10.

And God made two great lights; the greater light to rule the day, and the lesser light to rule the night: he made the stars also. *Ib.* 16.

And God said, Let us make man in our image, after our likeness. *Ib.* 26.

Dominion . . . over every creeping thing that creepeth upon the earth. *Ib.*

Male and female created he them. *Ib.* 27.

Be fruitful, and multiply, and replenish the earth, and subdue it: and have dominion over the fish of the sea, and over the fowl of the air, and over every living thing that moveth upon the earth. *Ib.* 28.

But there went up a mist from the earth, and watered the whole face of the ground. *Ib.* ii. 6.

And the Lord God formed man of the dust of the ground and breathed into his nostrils the breath of life; and man became a living soul.

And the Lord God planted a garden eastward in Eden. *Ib.* 7.

The tree of life also in the midst of the garden. *Ib.* 9.

But of the tree of the knowledge of good and evil, thou shalt not eat of it: for in the day that thou eatest thereof thou shalt surely die. *Ib.* 17.

It is not good that the man should be alone. *Ib.* 18.

The Lord God . . . brought them unto Adam to see what he would call them. *Ib.*

And the Lord God caused a deep sleep to fall upon Adam, and he slept: and he took one of his ribs, and closed up the flesh instead thereof;

And the rib, which the Lord God had taken from man, made he a woman. *Ib.* 21.

Bone of my bones, and flesh of my flesh. *Ib.* 23.

Therefore shall a man leave his father and his mother, and shall cleave unto his wife: and they shall be one flesh. *Ib.* 24.

Now the serpent was more subtil than any beast of the field. *Ib.* iii. 1.

Ye shall be as gods, knowing good and evil. *Ib.* 5.

And they sewed fig leaves together, and made themselves aprons.

And they heard the voice of the Lord God walking in the garden in the cool of the day. *Ib.* 7.

The woman whom thou gavest to be with me, she gave me of the tree, and I did eat. *Ib.* 12.

What is this that thou hast done? *Ib.* 13.

The serpent beguiled me, and I did eat. *Ib.*

It shall bruise thy head, and thou shalt bruise his heel. *Ib.* 15.

In sorrow thou shalt bring forth children. *Ib.* 16.

In the sweat of thy face shalt thou eat bread. *Ib.* 19.

For dust thou art, and unto dust shalt thou shalt return. *Ib.*

The mother of all living. *Ib.* 20.

Am I my brother's keeper? *Ib.* iv. 9.

The voice of thy brother's blood crieth unto me from the ground. *Ib.* 10.

My punishment is greater than I can bear. *Ib.* 13.

Dwelt in the land of Nod. *Ib.* 16.

The father of such as dwell in tents. *Ib.* 20.

And Enoch walked with God: and he was not: for God took him. *Ib.* v. 24.

And Noah begat Shem, Ham, and Japheth. *Ib.* 32.

There were giants in the earth in those days. *Ib.* vi. 4.

Mighty men which were of old, men of renown. *Ib.*

But the dove found no rest for the sole of her foot. *Ib.* viii. 9.

For the imagination of man's heart is evil from his youth. *Ib.* 21.

While the earth remaineth, seedtime and harvest, and cold and heat, and summer and winter, and day and night shall not cease. *Ib.* 22.

At the hand of every man's brother will I require the life of man. *Ib.* ix. 5.

Whoso sheddeth man's blood, by man shall his blood be shed. *Ib.* 6.

I do set my bow in the cloud. *Ib.* 13.

Even as Nimrod the mighty hunter before the Lord. *Ib.* x. 9.

Let there be no strife, I pray thee, between thee and me . . . for we be brethren. *Ib.* xiii. 8.

An horror of great darkness fell upon him. *Ib.* xv. 12.

In good old age. *Ib.* 15.

His hand will be against every man, and every man's hand against him. *Ib.* xvi. 12.

Old and well stricken in age. *Genesis* xviii. 11.

And the Lord said unto Abraham, Wherefore did Sarah laugh? *Ib.* 13.

Shall not the Judge of all the earth do right? *Ib.* 25.

But his wife looked back from behind him, and she became a pillar of salt. *Ib.* xix. 26.

Take now thy son, thine only son Isaac, whom thou lovest. *Ib.* xxii. 2.

My son, God will provide himself a lamb. *Ib.* 8.

Behold behind him a ram caught in a thicket by his horns. *Ib.* 13.

Esau was a cunning hunter, a man of the field; and Jacob was a plain man, dwelling in tents. *Ib.* xxv. 27.

And he sold his birthright unto Jacob. *Ib.* 33.

Behold, Esau my brother is a hairy man, and I am a smooth man. *Ib.* xxvii. 11.

The voice is Jacob's voice, but the hands are the hands of Esau. *Ib.* 22.

Thy brother came with subtilty, and hath taken away thy blessing. *Ib.* 35.

And he dreamed, and behold a ladder set up on the earth, and the top of it reached to heaven: and behold the angels of God ascending and descending on it. *Ib.* xxviii. 12.

Surely the Lord is in this place; and I knew it not. *Ib.* 16.

This is none other but the house of God, and this is the gate of heaven. *Ib.* 17.

And Jacob served seven years for Rachel; and they seemed unto him but a few years, for the love he had to her. *Ib.* xxix. 20.

A troop cometh: and she called his name Gad. *Ib.* xxx. 11.

Mizpah; for he said, The Lord watch between me and thee, when we are absent one from another. *Ib.* xxxi. 49.

There wrestled a man with him until the breaking of the day.
And when he saw that he prevailed not against him, he touched the hollow of his thigh; and the hollow of Jacob's thigh was out of joint, as he wrestled with him. *Ib.* xxxii. 24.

I will not let thee go, except thou bless me. *Ib.* 26.

For I have seen God face to face, and my life is preserved. *Ib.* 30.

Now Israel loved Joseph more than all his children, because he was the son of his old age; and he made him a coat of many colours. *Ib.* xxxvii. 3.

Behold, your sheaves stood round about, and made obeisance to my sheaf. *Ib.* 7.

Behold, this dreamer cometh. *Ib.* 19.

Some evil beast hath devoured him. *Ib.* 20.

And she caught him by his garment, saying, Lie with me; and he left his garment in her hand, and fled. *Ib.* xxxix. 12.

And the lean and the ill-favoured kine did eat up the first seven fat kine. *Ib.* xli. 20.

And the thin ears devoured the seven good ears. *Ib.* 24.

Jacob saw that there was corn in Egypt. *Ib.* xlii. 1.

Ye are spies; to see the nakedness of the land ye are come. *Ib.* 9.

Bring down my grey hairs with sorrow to the grave. *Ib.* 38.

Benjamin's mess was five times so much as any of their's. *Ib.* xliii. 34.

Ye shall eat of the fat of the land. *Ib.* xlv. 18.

See that ye fall not out by the way. *Ib.* 24.

Few and evil have the years of my life been. *Ib.* xlvii. 9.

Unstable as water, thou shalt not excel. *Ib.* xlix. 4.

Issachar is a strong ass couching down between two burdens. *Ib.* 14.

Unto the utmost bound of the everlasting hills. *Ib.* 26.

Now there arose up a new king over Egypt, which knew not Joseph. *Exodus* i. 8.

She took for him an ark of bulrushes, and daubed it with slime. *Ib.* ii. 3.

Who made thee a prince and a judge over us? *Ib.* 14.

I have been a stranger in a strange land. *Ib.* 22.

Behold, the bush burned with fire, and the bush was not consumed. *Ib.* iii. 2.

Put off thy shoes from off thy feet, for the place whereon thou standest is holy ground. *Ib.* 5.

And Moses hid his face; for he was afraid to look upon God. *Ib.* 6.

A land flowing with milk and honey; unto the place of the Canaanites, and the Hittites, and the Amorites, and the Perizzites, and the Hivites, and the Jebusites. *Ib.* 8.

I AM THAT I AM. *Ib.* 14.

The Lord God of your fathers, the God of Abraham, the God of Isaac, and the God of Jacob. *Ib.* 15.

But I am slow of speech, and of a slow tongue. *Ib.* iv. 10.

I know not the Lord, neither will I let Israel go. *Ib.* v. 2.

My signs and wonders in the land of Egypt. *Ib.* vii. 3.

Aaron's rod swallowed up their rods.
And he hardened Pharaoh's heart, that he hearkened not. *Ib.* 12.

A boil breaking forth with blains. *Ib.* ix. 10.

Darkness which may be felt. *Ib.* x. 21.

Your lamb shall be without blemish. *Ib.* xii. 5.

Roast with fire, and unleavened bread; and with bitter herbs they shall eat it.
Eat not of it raw, nor sodden at all with water, but roast with fire; his head with his legs, and with the appurtenances thereof. *Ib.* 8.

With your loins girded, your shoes on your feet, and your staff in your hand; and ye shall eat it in haste; it is the Lord's passover.

For I will pass through the land of Egypt this night, and will smite all the firstborn in the land of Egypt, both man and beast.   *Exodus* xii. 11.

And there was a great cry in Egypt.   *Ib.* 30.

And they spoiled the Egyptians.   *Ib.* 36.

And the Lord went before them by day in a pillar of a cloud, to lead them the way; and by night in a pillar of fire, to give them light.   *Ib.* xiii. 21

The Lord is a man of war.   *Ib.* xv. 3.

Would to God we had died by the hand of the Lord in the land of Egypt, when we sat by the fleshpots, and when we did eat bread to the full.   *Ib.* xvi. 3.

But let not God speak with us, lest we die.   *Ib.* xx.

Life for life,
Eye for eye, tooth for tooth, hand for hand, foot for foot,
Burning for burning, wound for wound, stripe for stripe.   *Ib.* xxi. 23.

Thou shalt not suffer a witch to live.   *Ib.* xxii. 18.

Thou shalt not seethe a kid in his mother's milk.   *Ib.* xxiii. 19.

The Urim and the Thummim.   *Ib.* xxviii. 30.

And the people sat down to eat and to drink, and rose up to play.   *Ib.* xxxii. 6.

If not, blot me, I pray thee, out of thy book which thou hast written.   *Ib.* 32.

A stiff-necked people.   *Ib.* xxxiii. 3.

Joshua the son of Nun.   *Ib.* 11.

There shall no man see me, and live.   *Ib.* 20.

Let him go for a scapegoat into the wilderness.   *Leviticus* xvi. 10.

The Lord bless thee, and keep thee:
The Lord make his face shine upon thee, and be gracious unto thee:
The Lord lift up his countenance upon thee, and give thee peace.   *Numbers* vi. 24.

Would God that all the Lord's people were prophets.   *Ib.* xi. 29.

Now the man Moses was very meek, above all the men which were upon the face of the earth.   *Ib.* xii. 3.

Sent to spy out the land.   *Ib.* xiii. 16.

The giants, the sons of Anak.   *Ib.* 33.

Hear now, ye rebels; must we fetch you water out of this rock?   *Ib.* xx. 10.

Smote him with the edge of the sword.   *Ib.* xxi. 24.

He whom thou blessest is blessed, and he whom thou cursest is cursed.   *Ib.* xxii. 6.

Let me die the death of the righteous, and let my last end be like his!   *Ib.* xxiii. 10.

God is not a man, that he should lie.   *Ib.* 19.

I called thee to curse mine enemies, and, behold, thou hast altogether blessed them these three times.   *Ib.* xxiv. 10.

Be sure your sin will find you out.   *Ib.* xxxii. 23.

I call heaven and earth to witness against you this day.   *Deuteronomy* iv. 26.

Man doth not live by bread only, but by every word that proceedeth out of the mouth of the Lord doth man live.   *Ib.* viii. 3.

A dreamer of dreams.   *Ib.* xiii. 1.

The wife of thy bosom.   *Ib.* 6.

Thou shalt not muzzle the ox when he treadeth out the corn.   *Ib.* xxv. 4.

Cursed be he that removeth his neighbour's landmark.   *Ib.* xxvii. 17.

In the morning thou shalt say, Would God it were even! and at even thou shalt say, Would God it were morning!   *Ib.* xxviii. 67.

The secret things belong unto the Lord our God.   *Ib.* xxix. 29.

I have set before you life and death, blessing and cursing; therefore choose life, that both thou and thy seed may live.   *Ib.* xxx. 19.

In the waste howling wilderness.   *Ib.* xxxii. 10.

Jeshurun waxed fat, and kicked.   *Ib.* 15.

As thy days, so shall thy strength be.   *Ib.* xxxiii. 25.

The eternal God is thy refuge, and underneath are the everlasting arms.   *Ib.* 27.

No man knoweth of his sepulchre unto this day.   *Ib.* xxxiv. 6.

As I was with Moses, so I will be with thee: I will not fail thee, nor forsake thee.   *Joshua* i. 5.

Be strong and of a good courage: be not afraid, neither be thou dismayed: for the Lord thy God is with thee, whithersoever thou goest.   *Ib.* 9.

This line of scarlet thread.   *Ib.* ii. 18.

All the Israelites passed over on dry ground.   *Ib.* iii. 17.

When the people heard the sound of the trumpet, and the people shouted with a great shout, that the wall fell down flat, so that the people went up into the city.   *Ib.* vi. 20.

Hewers of wood and drawers of water.   *Ib.* ix. 21.

Sun, stand thou still upon Gibeon; and thou Moon, in the valley of Ajalon.   *Ib.* x. 12.

Is not this written in the book of Jasher?   *Ib.* 13.

I am going the way of all the earth.   *Ib.* xxiii. 14.

He delivered them into the hands of the spoilers.   *Judges* ii. 14.

Then Jael, Heber's wife, took a nail of the tent, and took an hammer in her hand, and went softly unto him, and smote the nail into his temples, and fastened it into the ground: for he was fast asleep and weary.   *Ib.* iv. 21.

I arose a mother in Israel.   *Ib.* v. 7.

The stars in their courses fought against Sisera.   *Ib.* 20.

She brought forth butter in a lordly dish.   *Ib.* 25.

At her feet he bowed, he fell, he lay down.
Judges v. 27.

The mother of Sisera looked out at a window, and cried through the lattice, Why is his chariot so long in coming? why tarry the wheels of his chariot?
Ib. 28.

Have they not divided the prey; to every man a damsel or two? *Ib.* 30.

Is not the gleaning of the grapes of Ephraim better than the vintage of Abi-ezer? *Ib.* viii. 2.

Faint, yet pursuing. *Ib.* 4.

Out of the eater came forth meat, and out of the strong came forth sweetness. *Ib.* xiv. 14.

If ye had not plowed with my heifer, ye had not found out my riddle. *Ib.* 18.

He smote them hip and thigh. *Ib.* xv. 8.

The Philistines be upon thee, Samson. *Ib.* xvi. 9.

He wist not that the Lord was departed from him.
Ib. 20.

He did grind in the prison house. *Ib.* 21.

From Dan even to Beer-sheba. *Ib.* xx. 1.

The people arose as one man. *Ib.* 8.

Intreat me not to leave thee, or to return from following after thee: for whither thou goest, I will go; and where thou lodgest, I will lodge: thy people shall be my people, and thy God my God:
Where thou diest, will I die, and there will I be buried: the Lord do so to me, and more also, if ought but death part thee and me.
Ruth i. 16.

Girded with a linen ephod. *1 Samuel* ii. 18.

The Lord called Samuel: and he answered, Here am I. *Ib.* iii. 4.

Here am I; for thou calledst me. And he said, I called not; lie down again. *Ib.* 5.

Speak, Lord; for thy servant heareth. *Ib.* 9.

The ears of every one that heareth it shall tingle.
Ib. 11.

Quit yourselves like men. *Ib.* iv. 9.

He fell from off the seat backward by the side of the gate, and his neck brake. *Ib.* 18.

Ichabod, saying, The glory is departed from Israel.
Ib. 21.

Is Saul also among the prophets? *Ib.* x. 11.

God save the king. *Ib.* 24.

A man after his own heart. *Ib.* xiii. 14.

I did but taste a little honey with the end of the rod that was in mine hand, and, lo, I must die.
Ib. xiv. 43.

What meaneth then this bleating of the sheep in mine ears, and the lowing of the oxen which I hear?
Ib. xv. 14.

To obey is better than sacrifice, and to hearken than the fat of rams.
For rebellion is as the sin of witchcraft. *Ib.* 22.

Agag came unto him delicately. And Agag said, Surely the bitterness of death is past. *Ib.* 32.

For the Lord seeth not as man seeth: for man looketh on the outward appearance, but the Lord looketh on the heart. *Ib.* xvi. 7.

Now he was ruddy, and withal of a beautiful countenance, and goodly to look to. *Ib.* 12.

I know thy pride, and the naughtiness of thine heart.
Ib. xvii. 28.

Let no man's heart fail because of him [Goliath].
Ib. 32.

Go, and the Lord be with thee. *Ib.* 37.

Five smooth stones out of the brook. *Ib.* 40.

Am I a dog, that thou comest to me with staves?
Ib. 43.

Saul hath slain his thousands, and David his ten thousands. *Ib.* xviii. 7.

And Jonathan gave his artillery unto the lad.
Ib. xx. 40.

As saith the proverb of the Ancients, Wickedness proceedeth from the wicked. *Ib.* xxiv. 13.

I have played the fool. *Ib.* xxvi. 21.

The beauty of Israel is slain upon thy high places: how are the mighty fallen!
Tell it not in Gath, publish it not in the streets of Askelon; lest the daughters of the Philistines rejoice, lest the daughters of the uncircumcised triumph.
Ye mountains of Gilboa, let there be no dew, neither let there be rain, upon you, nor fields of offerings: for there the shield of the mighty is vilely cast away. *2 Samuel* i. 19.

Saul and Jonathan were lovely and pleasant in their lives, and in their death they were not divided: they were swifter than eagles, they were stronger than lions.
Ye daughters of Israel, weep over Saul, who clothed you in scarlet, with other delights, who put on ornaments of gold upon your apparel.
How are the mighty fallen in the midst of the battle!
O Jonathan, thou wast slain in thy high places.
I am distressed for thee, my brother Jonathan: very pleasant hast thou been unto me: thy love to me was wonderful, passing the love of women.
How are the mighty fallen, and the weapons of war perished. *Ib.* 23.

Smote him under the fifth rib. *Ib.* ii. 23.

Set ye Uriah in the forefront of the hottest battle.
Ib. xi. 15.

The poor man had nothing, save one little ewe lamb.
Ib. xii. 3.

Thou art the man. *Ib.* 7.

As water spilt on the ground, which cannot be gathered up again. *Ib.* xiv. 14.

Come out, come out, thou bloody man, thou son of Belial. *Ib.* xvi. 17.

Would God I had died for thee, O Absalom, my son, my son! *Ib.* xviii. 33.

The sweet psalmist of Israel. *2 Samuel* xxiii. 1.

Went in jeopardy of their lives. *Ib.* 17.

I have somewhat to say unto thee. And she said, Say on. *1 Kings* ii. 14.

A proverb and a byword among all people. *Ib.* ix. 7.

And when the queen of Sheba had seen all Solomon's wisdom . . . there was no more spirit in her. *Ib.* x. 4.

Behold, the half was not told me. *Ib.* 7.

Ivory, and apes, and peacocks. *Ib.* 22.

But King Solomon loved many strange women. *Ib.* xi. 1.

My little finger shall be thicker than my father's loins. *Ib.* xii. 10.

My father hath chastised you with whips, but I will chastise you with scorpions. *Ib.* 11.

To your tents, O Israel: now see to thine own house, David. *Ib.* 16.

He slept with his fathers. *Ib.* xiv. 20.

Nevertheless in the time of his old age he was diseased in his feet. *Ib.* xv. 23.

He went and dwelt by the brook Cherith, that is before Jordan.
And the ravens brought him bread and flesh in the morning, and bread and flesh in the evening; and he drank of the brook. *Ib.* xvii. 5.

An handful of meal in a barrel, and a little oil in a cruse. *Ib.* 12.

How long halt ye between two opinions? *Ib.* xviii. 21.

He is talking, or he is pursuing, or he is in a journey, or peradventure he sleepeth, and must be awaked. *Ib.* 27.

There is a sound of abundance of rain. *Ib.* 41.

There ariseth a little cloud out of the sea, like a man's hand. *Ib.* 44.

He girded up his loins, and ran before Ahab. *Ib.* 46.

Sat down under a juniper tree. *Ib.* xix. 4.

But the Lord was not in the wind: and after the wind an earthquake: but the Lord was not in the earthquake: And after the earthquake a fire: but the Lord was not in the fire: and after the fire a still small voice. *Ib.* 11.

And it shall come to pass, that him that escapeth the sword of Hazael shall Jehu slay: and him that escapeth from the sword of Jehu shall Elisha slay. *Ib.* 17.

Elijah passed by him, and cast his mantle upon him. *Ib.* 19.

Let not him that girdeth on his harness boast himself as he that putteth it off. *Ib.* xx. 11.

Hast thou found me, O mine enemy? *Ib.* xxi. 20.

I saw all Israel scattered upon the hills, as sheep that have not a shepherd. *Ib.* xxii. 17.

Feed him with bread of affliction and with water of affliction, until I come in peace.
And Micaiah said, if thou return at all in peace, the Lord hath not spoken by me. *Ib.* 27.

And a certain man drew a bow at a venture, and smote the king of Israel between the joints of his harness. *Ib.* 34.

The chariot of Israel, and the horsemen thereof. *2 Kings* ii. 12.

The spirit of Elijah doth rest upon Elisha. *Ib.* 15.

Go up, thou bald head. *Ib.* 23.

Is it well with the child? And she answered, It is well. *Ib.* iv. 26.

There is death in the pot. *Ib.* 40.

He shall know that there is a prophet in Israel. *Ib.* v. 8.

Are not Abana and Pharpar, rivers of Damascus, better than all the waters of Israel? *Ib.* 12.

I bow myself in the house of Rimmon. *Ib.* 18.

Whence comest thou, Gehazi? *Ib.* 25.

Is thy servant a dog, that he should do this great thing? *Ib.* viii. 13.

Is it peace? And Jehu said, What hast thou to do with peace? turn thou behind me. *Ib.* ix. 18.

The driving is like the driving of Jehu, the son of Nimshi: for he driveth furiously. *Ib.* 20.

She painted her face, and tired her head and looked out at a window. *Ib.* 30.

Had Zimri peace, who slew his master? *Ib.* 31.

Who is on my side? who? *Ib.* 32.

And he said, Throw her down. So they threw her down. *Ib.* 33.

They found no more of her than the skull, and the feet, and the palms of her hands. *Ib.* 35.

Thou trustest upon the staff of this bruised reed, this Egypt, on which if a man lean, it will go into his hand, and pierce it. *Ib.* xviii. 21.

He died in a good old age, full of days, riches, and honour. *1 Chronicles* xxix. 28.

Every one with one of his hands wrought in the work, and with the other hand held a weapon. *Nehemiah* iv. 17.

The man whom the king delighteth to honour. *Esther* vi. 9.

Behold also the gallows fifty cubits high. *Ib.* vii. 9.

The sons of God came to present themselves before the Lord, and Satan came also among them.
And the Lord said unto Satan, Whence comest thou? Then Satan answered the Lord, and said, From going to and fro in the earth, and from walking up and down in it. *Job* i. 6.

Doth Job fear God for naught? *Ib.* 9.

The Lord gave, and the Lord hath taken away; blessed be the name of the Lord. *Ib.* 21.

All that a man hath will he give for his life. *Job* ii. 4.

And he took him a potsherd to scrape himself withal. *Ib.* 8.

Curse God, and die. *Ib.* 9.

Let the day perish wherein I was born, and the night in which it was said, There is a man child conceived. *Ib.* iii. 3.

There the wicked cease from troubling, and there the weary be at rest. *Ib.* 17.

Wherefore is light given to him that is in misery, and life unto the bitter in soul? *Ib.* 20.

Then a spirit passed before my face: the hair of my flesh stood up. *Ib.* iv. 15.

Shall mortal man be more just than God? shall a man be more pure than his maker? *Ib.* 17.

Man is born unto trouble, as the sparks fly upward. *Ib.* v. 7.

He taketh the wise in their own craftiness. *Ib.* 13.

My days are swifter than a weaver's shuttle. *Ib.* vii. 6.

He shall return no more to his house, neither shall his place know him any more. *Ib.* 10.

The land of darkness and the shadow of death. *Ib.* x. 21.

A land ... where the light is as darkness. *Ib.* 22.

Canst thou by searching find out God? *Ib.* xi. 7.

No doubt but ye are the people, and wisdom shall die with you. *Ib.* xii. 2.

With the ancient is wisdom; and in length of days understanding. *Ib.* 12.

Man that is born of a woman is of few days, and full of trouble. *Ib.* xiv. 1.

Miserable comforters are ye all. *Ib.* xvi. 2.

The king of terrors. *Ib.* xviii. 14.

I am escaped with the skin of my teeth. *Ib.* xix. 20.

Oh that my words were now written! oh that they were printed in a book! *Ib.* 23.

I know that my redeemer liveth, and that he shall stand at the latter day upon the earth:
And though after my skin worms destroy this body, yet in my flesh shall I see God. *Ib.* 25.

Seeing the root of the matter is found in me. *Ib.* 28.

The price of wisdom is above rubies. *Ib.* xxviii. 18.

I was eyes to the blind, and feet was I to the lame. *Ib.* xxix. 15.

The house appointed for all living. *Ib.* xxx. 23.

My desire is . . . that mine adversary had written a book. *Ib.* xxxi. 35.

Great men are not always wise. *Ib.* xxxii.

One among a thousand. *Ib.* xxxiii. 23.

Far be it from God, that he should do wickedness. *Ib.* xxxiv. 10.

For I am full of matter, the spirit within me constraineth me. *Ib.* 18.

He multiplieth words without knowledge. *Ib.* xxxv. 16.

Who is this that darkeneth counsel by words without knowledge? *Ib.* xxxviii. 2.

Gird up now thy loins like a man. *Ib.* 3.

Where wast thou when I laid the foundations of the earth? declare, if thou hast understanding. *Ib.* 4.

When the morning stars sang together, and all the sons of God shouted for joy. *Ib.* 7.

Hitherto shalt thou come, but no further: and here shall thy proud waves be stayed. *Ib.* 11.

Hast thou entered into the springs of the sea? or hast thou walked in the search of the depths? *Ib.* 16.

Hath the rain a father? or who hath begotten the drops of dew? *Ib.* 28.

Canst thou bind the sweet influences of Pleiades, or loose the bands of Orion? *Ib.* 31.

Canst thou guide Arcturus with his sons? *Ib.* 32.

He paweth in the valley, and rejoiceth in his strength: he goeth on to meet the armed men. *Ib.* xxxix. 21.

He swalloweth the ground with fierceness and rage: neither believeth he that it is the sound of the trumpet.
He saith among the trumpets, Ha, ha; and he smelleth the battle afar off, the thunder of the captains, and the shouting. *Ib.* 24.

Behold now behemoth, which I made with thee; he eateth grass as an ox. *Ib.* xl. 15.

Canst thou draw out Leviathan with an hook? *Ib.* xli. 1.

Wilt thou play with him as with a bird? or wilt thou bind him for thy maidens? *Ib.* 5.

Hard as a piece of the nether millstone. *Ib.* 24.

He maketh the deep to boil like a pot. *Ib.* 31.

I have heard of thee by the hearing of the ear; but now mine eye seeth thee. *Ib.* xlii. 5.

So the Lord blessed the latter end of Job more than his beginning. *Ib.* 12.

My son, if sinners entice thee, consent thou not. *Proverbs* i. 10.

Surely in vain the net is spread in the sight of any bird. *Ib.* 17.

Wisdom crieth without; she uttereth her voice in the streets. *Ib.* 20.

Length of days is in her right hand; and in her left hand riches and honour. *Ib.* iii. 16.

Her ways are ways of pleasantness, and all her paths are peace. *Ib.* 17.

Wisdom is the principal thing; therefore get wisdom; and with all thy getting get understanding. *Ib.* iv. 7.

The path of the just is as the shining light, that shineth more and more unto the perfect day. *Ib.* 18.

For the lips of a strange woman drop as an honeycomb, and her mouth is smoother than oil:
But her end is bitter as wormwood, sharp as a two-edged sword. *Ib.* v. 3.

Go to the ant, thou sluggard; consider her ways, and be wise.   *Proverbs* vi. 6.

Yet a little sleep, a little slumber, a little folding of the hands to sleep.   *Ib.* 10.

So shall thy poverty come as one that travelleth, and thy want as an armed man.   *Ib.* 11.

Neither let her take thee with her eyelids.   *Ib.* 25.

Can a man take fire in his bosom, and his clothes not be burned?   *Ib.* 27.

Come, let us take our fill of love, until the morning: let us solace ourselves with loves.

For the goodman is not at home, he is gone a long journey.   *Ib.* vii. 18.

As an ox goeth to the slaughter.   *Ib.* 22.

Wisdom is better than rubies.   *Ib.* viii. 11.

Stolen waters are sweet, and bread eaten in secret is pleasant.   *Ib.* ix. 17.

A wise son maketh a glad father: but a foolish son is the heaviness of his mother.   *Ib.* x. 1.

The destruction of the poor is their poverty.   *Ib.* 15.

In the multitude of counsellors there is safety.   *Ib.* xi. 14.

He that is surety for a stranger shall smart for it.   *Ib.* 15.

As a jewel of gold in a swine's snout, so is a fair woman which is without discretion.   *Ib.* 22.

A virtuous woman is a crown to her husband.   *Ib.* xii. 4.

A righteous man regardeth the life of his beast; but the tender mercies of the wicked are cruel.   *Ib.* 10.

Hope deferred maketh the heart sick.   *Ib.* xiii. 12.

The way of transgressors is hard.   *Ib.* 15.

The desire accomplished is sweet to the soul.   *Ib.* 19.

He that spareth his rod hateth his son.   *Ib.* 24.

The heart knoweth his own bitterness; and a stranger doth not intermeddle with his joy.   *Ib.* xiv. 10.

In all labour there is profit.   *Ib.* 23.

Righteousness exalteth a nation.   *Ib.* 34.

A soft answer turneth away wrath.   *Ib.* xv. 1.

A merry heart maketh a cheerful countenance.   *Ib.* 13.

Better is a dinner of herbs where love is, than a stalled ox and hatred therewith.   *Ib.* 17.

A word spoken in due season, how good is it!   *Ib.* 23.

Pride goeth before destruction, and an haughty spirit before a fall.   *Ib.* xvi. 18.

The hoary head is a crown of glory.   *Ib.* 31.

He that is slow to anger is better than the mighty; and he that ruleth his spirit than he that taketh a city.   *Ib.* 32.

He that repeateth a matter separateth very friends.   *Ib.* xvii. 9.

He that begetteth a fool doeth it to his sorrow.   *Ib.* 21.

A merry heart doeth good like a medicine.   *Ib.* 22.

A wounded spirit who can bear?   *Ib.* xviii. 14.

There is a friend that sticketh closer than a brother.   *Ib.* 24.

Wine is a mocker, strong drink is raging.   *Ib.* xx. 1.

Every fool will be meddling.   *Ib.* 3.

Even a child is known by his doings.   *Ib.* 1.

The hearing ear, and the seeing eye.   *Ib.* 12.

It is naught, it is naught, saith the buyer: but when he is gone his way, then he boasteth.   *Ib.* xx. 14.

It is better to dwell in a corner of the housetop than with a brawling woman in a wide house.   *Ib.* xxi. 9.

A good name is rather to be chosen than great riches.   *Ib.* xxii. 1.

Train up a child in the way he should go: and when he is old, he will not depart from it.   *Ib.* 6.

Riches certainly make themselves wings.   *Ib.* xxiii. 5.

Look not thou upon the wine when it is red, when it giveth his colour in the cup; ... at the last it biteth like a serpent, and stingeth like an adder.   *Ib.* 31.

The heart of kings is unsearchable.   *Ib.* xxv. 3.

A word fitly spoken is like apples of gold in pictures of silver.   *Ib.* 11.

Heap coals of fire upon his head.   *Ib.* 22.

As cold waters to a thirsty soul, so is good news from a far country.   *Ib.* 25.

As the bird by wandering, as the swallow by flying, so the curse causeless shall not come.   *Ib.* xxvi. 2.

Answer a fool according to his folly.   *Ib.* 5.

As a dog returneth to his vomit, so a fool returneth to his folly.   *Ib.* 11.

Seest thou a man wise in his own conceit? There is more hope of a fool than of him.   *Ib.* 12.

The slothful man saith, There is a lion in the way: a lion is in the streets.   *Ib.* 13.

The sluggard is wiser in his own conceit than seven men that can render a reason.   *Ib.* 16.

Boast not thyself of to morrow; for thou knowest not what a day may bring forth.   *Ib.* xxvii. 1.

Open rebuke is better than secret love.   *Ib.* 5.

Faithful are the wounds of a friend.   *Ib.* 6.

A continual dropping in a very rainy day and a contentious woman are alike.   *Ib.* 15.

Iron sharpeneth iron: so a man sharpeneth the countenance of his friend.   *Ib.* 17.

Though thou shouldest bray a fool in a mortar among wheat with a pestle, yet will not his foolishness depart from him.   *Ib.* 22.

The wicked flee when no man pursueth; but the righteous are bold as a lion.   *Ib.* xxviii. 1.

He that maketh haste to be rich shall not be innocent.   *Ib.* 20.

A fool uttereth all his mind. *Proverbs* xxix. 11.

Where there is no vision, the people perish. *Ib.* 18.

The horseleech hath two daughters, crying, Give, give. *Ib.* xxx. 15.

There are three things that are never satisfied, yea, four things say not, It is enough:
The grave; and the barren womb; the earth that is not filled with water; and the fire that saith not, It is enough. *Ib.* 15.

The way of an eagle in the air; the way of a serpent upon a rock; the way of a ship in the midst of the sea; and the way of a man with a maid. *Ib.* 19.

Who can find a virtuous woman? for her price is above rubies. *Ib.* xxxi. 10.

Her children arise up, and call her blessed. *Ib.* 28.

All the rivers run into the sea; yet the sea is not full. *Ecclesiastes* i. 7.

Vanity of vanities, saith the Preacher, vanity of vanities; all is vanity.
What profit hath a man of all his labour which he taketh under the sun?

One generation passeth away, and another generation cometh. *Ib.* 2.

All things are full of labour; man cannot utter it: the eye is not satisfied with seeing, nor the ear filled with hearing.
The thing that hath been, it is that which shall be; and that which is done is that which shall be done: and there is no new thing under the sun. *Ib.* 8.

All is vanity and vexation of spirit. *Ib.* 14.

He that increaseth knowledge increaseth sorrow. *Ib.* 18.

Wisdom excelleth folly, as far as light excelleth darkness. *Ib.* ii. 13.

One event happeneth to them all. *Ib.* 14.

To every thing there is a season, and a time to every purpose under the heaven:
A time to be born, and a time to die. *Ib.* iii. 1.

Wherefore I praised the dead which are already dead more than the living which are yet alive. *Ib.* iv. 2.

A threefold cord is not quickly broken. *Ib.* 12.

God is in heaven, and thou upon earth: therefore let thy words be few. *Ib.* v. 2.

Better is it that thou shouldest not vow, than that thou shouldest vow and not pay. *Ib.* 5.

The sleep of a labouring man is sweet. *Ib.* 12.

A good name is better than precious ointment: and the day of death than the day of one's birth.
It is better to go to the house of mourning than to go to the house of feasting. *Ib.* vii. 1.

As the crackling of thorns under a pot, so is the laughter of a fool. *Ib.* 6.

Better is the end of a thing than the beginning thereof. *Ib.* 8.

Say not thou, What is the cause that the former days were better than these? for thou dost not inquire wisely concerning this. *Ib.* 10.

In the day of prosperity be joyful, but in the day of adversity consider. *Ib.* 14.

Be not righteous over much. *Ib.* 16.

One man among a thousand have I found; but a woman among all those have I not found. *Ib.* 28.

God hath made man upright; but they have sought out many inventions. *Ib.* 29.

There is no discharge in that war. *Ib.* viii. 8.

A man hath no better thing under the sun, than to eat, and to drink, and to be merry. *Ib.* 15.

A living dog is better than a dead lion. *Ib.* ix. 4.

Go thy way, eat thy bread with joy, and drink thy wine with a merry heart; for God now accepteth thy works. *Ib.* 7.

Whatsoever thy hand findeth to do, do it with thy might; for there is no work, nor device, nor knowledge, nor wisdom, in the grave, whither thou goest. *Ib.* 10.

The race is not to the swift, nor the battle to the strong. *Ib.* 11.

Dead flies cause the ointment of the apothecary to send forth a stinking savour. *Ib.* x. 1.

He that diggeth a pit shall fall into it. *Ib.* 8.

Wine maketh merry: but money answereth all things. *Ib.* 19.

For a bird of the air shall carry the voice, and that which hath wings shall tell the matter. *Ib.* 20.

Cast thy bread upon the waters: for thou shalt find it after many days. *Ib.* xi. 1.

In the place where the tree falleth, there it shall be. *Ib.* 3.

He that observeth the wind shall not sow; and he that regardeth the clouds shall not reap. *Ib.* 4.

In the morning sow thy seed, and in the evening withhold not thine hand. *Ib.* 6.

Truly the light is sweet, and a pleasant thing it is for the eyes to behold the sun. *Ib.* 7.

Rejoice, O young man, in thy youth; and let thy heart cheer thee in the days of thy youth. *Ib.* 9.

Remember now thy Creator in the days of thy youth, while the evil days come not, nor the years draw nigh, when thou shalt say, I have no pleasure in them;
While the sun, or the light, or the moon, or the stars, be not darkened, nor the clouds return after the rain:
In the day when the keepers of the house shall tremble, and the strong men shall bow themselves, and the grinders cease because they are few, and those that look out of the windows be darkened,
And the doors shall be shut in the streets, when the sound of the grinding is low, and he shall rise up at the voice of the bird, and all the daughters of musick shall be brought low;
Also when they shall be afraid of that which is high, and fears shall be in the way, and the almond tree shall flourish, and the grasshopper shall be a burden, and desire shall fail: because man goeth to

his long home, and the mourners go about the streets:

Or ever the silver cord be loosed, or the golden bowl be broken, or the pitcher be broken at the fountain, or the wheel broken at the cistern.

Then shall the dust return to the earth as it was: and the spirit shall return unto God who gave it.

Ecclesiastes xii. 1.

The words of the wise are as goads.   *Ib.* 11.

Of making many books there is no end; and much study is a weariness of the flesh.   *Ib.* 12.

Fear God, and keep his commandments: for this is the whole duty of man.

For God shall bring every work into judgment, with every secret thing, whether it be good, or whether it be evil.   *Ib.* 13.

The song of songs, which is Solomon's.

Let him kiss me with the kisses of his mouth: for thy love is better than wine.

The Song of Solomon, i. 1.

Thy name is an ointment poured forth, therefore do the virgins love thee.   *Ib.* 3.

I am black, but comely, O ye daughters of Jerusalem, as the tents of Kedar, as the curtains of Solomon.

Ib. 5.

Tell me, O thou whom my soul loveth, where thou feedest, where thou makest thy flock to rest at noon.   *Ib.* 7.

O thou fairest among women.   *Ib.* 8.

A bundle of myrrh is my well beloved unto me; he shall lie all night betwixt my breasts.   *Ib.* 13.

I am the rose of Sharon, and the lily of the valleys.

Ib. ii. 1.

His banner over me was love.   *Ib.* 4.

Stay me with flagons, comfort me with apples: for I am sick of love.

His left hand is under my head, and his right hand doth embrace me.   *Ib.* 5.

Rise up, my love, my fair one, and come away.

For, lo! the winter is past, the rain is over and gone;

The flowers appear on the earth: the time of the singing of birds is come, and the voice of the turtle is heard in our land.   *Ib.* 10.

Take us the foxes, the little foxes, that spoil the vines.

Ib. 15.

My beloved is mine, and I am his: he feedeth among the lilies.

Until the day break, and the shadows flee away.

Ib. 16.

By night on my bed I sought him whom my soul loveth.   *Ib.* iii. 1.

Behold, thou art fair, my love; behold, thou art fair; thou hast doves' eyes within thy locks: thy hair is as a flock of goats, that appear from mount Gilead.

Thy teeth are like a flock of sheep that are even shorn, which came up from the washing; whereof every one bear twins, and none is barren among them.

Thy lips are like a thread of scarlet, and thy speech is comely: thy temples are like a piece of a pomegranate within thy locks.

Thy neck is like the tower of David builded for an armoury, whereon there hang a thousand bucklers, all shields of mighty men.

Thy breasts are like two young roes that are twins, which feed among the lilies.   *Ib.* iv. 1.

Thou art all fair, my love; there is no spot in thee.

Ib. 7.

A garden inclosed is my sister, my spouse; a spring shut up, a fountain sealed.   *Ib.* 12.

Awake, O north wind; and come, thou south; blow upon my garden, that the spices thereof may flow out. Let my beloved come into his garden, and eat his pleasant fruits.   *Ib.* 16.

I sleep, but my heart waketh: it is the voice of my beloved that knocketh, saying, Open to me, my sister, my love, my dove, my undefiled.   *Ib.* v. 2.

My beloved put in his hand by the hole of the door, and my bowels were moved for him.   *Ib.* 4.

I opened to my beloved; but my beloved had withdrawn himself.   *Ib.* 6.

The watchmen that went about the city found me, they smote me, they wounded me; the keepers of the walls took away my veil from me.

I charge you, O daughters of Jerusalem, if ye find my beloved, that ye tell him, that I am sick of love.

What is thy beloved more than another beloved, O thou fairest among women?   *Ib.* 7.

My beloved is white and ruddy, the chiefest among ten thousand.   *Ib.* 10.

His hands are as gold rings set with the beryl: his belly is as bright ivory overlaid with sapphires.

His legs are as pillars of marble, set upon sockets of fine gold: his countenance is as Lebanon, excellent as the cedars.

His mouth is most sweet: yea, he is altogether lovely. This is my beloved, and this is my friend, O daughters of Jerusalem.   *Ib.* 14.

Who is she that looketh forth as the morning, fair as the moon, clear as the sun, and terrible as an army with banners?   *Ib.* vi. 10.

Return, return, O Shulamite; return, return, that we may look upon thee.   *Ib.* 13.

How beautiful are thy feet with shoes, O prince's daughter!   *Ib.* vii. 1.

Thy navel is like a round goblet, which wanteth not liquor: thy belly is like an heap of wheat set about with lilies.   *Ib.* 2.

Thy neck is as a tower of ivory; thine eyes like the fishpools in Heshbon, by the gate of Bath-rabbim: thy nose is as the tower of Lebanon which looketh towards Damascus.   *Ib.* 4.

Like the best wine, for my beloved, that goeth down sweetly, causing the lips of those that are asleep to speak.   *Ib.* 9.

O that thou wert as my brother, that sucked the breasts of my mother! when I should find thee without, I would kiss thee; yea, I should not be despised.

I would lead thee, and bring thee into my mother's house.   *Ib.* viii. 1.

Who is this that cometh up from the wilderness, leaning upon her beloved? I raised thee up under the apple tree: there thy mother brought thee forth: there she brought thee forth that bare thee.

Set me as a seal upon thine heart, as a seal upon thine arm: for love is strong as death; jealousy is cruel as the grave. *The Song of Solomon* viii. 5.

Many waters cannot quench love, neither can the floods drown it: if a man would give all the substance of his house for love, it would be utterly contemned. *Ib.* 7.

We have a little sister, and she hath no breasts. *Ib.* 8.

Make haste, my beloved, and be thou like to a roe or to a young hart upon the mountain of spices. *Ib.* 14.

The ox knoweth his owner, and the ass his master's crib. *Isaiah* i. 3.

The whole head is sick, and the whole heart faint. *Ib.* 5.

As a lodge in a garden of cucumbers. *Ib.* 8.

Bring no more vain oblations; incense is an abomination unto me; the new moons and sabbaths, the calling of assemblies, I cannot away with. *Ib.* 13.

Though your sins be as scarlet, they shall be white as snow. *Ib.* 18.

They shall beat their swords into plowshares, and their spears into pruninghooks; nation shall not lift up sword against nation, neither shall they learn war any more. *Ib.* ii. 4.

Cease ye from man, whose breath is in his nostrils. *Ib.* 22.

The stay and the staff, the whole stay of bread, and the whole stay of water. *Ib.* iii. 1.

Grind the faces of the poor. *Ib.* 15.

Walk with stretched forth necks and wanton eyes, walking and mincing as they go, and making a tinkling with their feet. *Ib.* 16.

In that day seven women shall take hold of one man. *Ib.* iv. 1.

My wellbeloved hath a vineyard in a very fruitful hill. *Ib.* v. 1.

And he looked that it should bring forth grapes, and it brought forth wild grapes. *Ib.* 2.

And he looked for judgment, but behold oppression; for righteousness, but behold a cry. *Ib.* 7.

Woe unto them that join house to house, that lay field to field, till there be no place. *Ib.* 8.

Woe unto them that rise up early in the morning, that they may follow strong drink. *Ib.* 11.

Woe, woe unto them that draw iniquity with cords of vanity, and sin as it were with a cart rope. *Ib.* 18.

Woe unto them that call evil good, and good evil. *Ib.* 20.

For all this his anger is not turned away, but his hand is stretched out still. *Ib.* 25.

In the year that king Uzziah died I saw also the Lord

sitting upon a throne, high and lifted up, and his train filled the temple.

Above it stood the seraphims: each one had six wings; with twain he covered his face, and with twain he covered his feet, and with twain he did fly.

And one cried unto another, and said, Holy, holy, holy, is the Lord of hosts: the whole earth is full of his glory.

And the posts of the door moved at the voice of him that cried, and the house was filled with smoke.

Then said I, Woe is me! for I am undone; because I am a man of unclean lips, and I dwell in the midst of a people of unclean lips. *Ib.* vi. 1.

Whom shall I send, and who will go for us? Then said I, Here am I; send me. *Ib.* 8.

Make the heart of this people fat, and make their ears heavy, and shut their eyes; lest they see with their eyes, and hear with their ears, and understand with their heart, and convert, and be healed. *Ib.* 10.

Then said I, Lord, how long? *Ib.* 11.

Behold, a virgin shall conceive, and bear a son, and shall call his name Immanuel.

Butter and honey shall he eat, that he may know how to refuse the evil, and choose the good. *Ib.* vii. 14.

For a stone of stumbling and for a rock of offence. *Ib.* viii. 14.

The people that walked in darkness have seen a great light: they that dwell in the land of the shadow of death, upon them hath the light shined.

Thou hast multiplied the nation, and not increased the joy: they joy before thee according to the joy in harvest, and as men rejoice when they divide the spoil. *Ib.* ix. 2.

For every battle of the warrior is with confused noise, and garments rolled in blood. *Ib.* 5.

For unto us a child is born, unto us a son is given: and the government shall be upon his shoulder: and his name shall be called Wonderful, Counsellor, The mighty God, The everlasting Father, The Prince of Peace.

Of the increase of his government and peace there shall be no end. *Ib.* 6.

The zeal of the Lord of hosts will perform this. *Ib.* 7.

And there shall come forth a rod out of the stem of Jesse, and a Branch shall grow out of his roots:

And the spirit of the Lord shall rest upon him, the spirit of wisdom and understanding, the spirit of counsel and might, the spirit of knowledge and of the fear of the Lord. *Ib.* xi. 1.

The wolf also shall dwell with the lamb, and the leopard shall lie down with the kid; and the calf and the young lion and the fatling together; and a little child shall lead them. *Ib.* 7.

And the lion shall eat straw like the ox.

And the sucking child shall play on the hole of the asp, and the weaned child shall put his hand on the cockatrice' den.

They shall not hurt nor destroy in all my holy mountain: for the earth shall be full of the knowledge of the Lord, as the waters cover the sea. *Ib.* 7.

Dragons in their pleasant palaces. *Ib.* xiii. 22.

Hell from beneath is moved for thee to meet thee at thy coming. *Isaiah* xiv. 9.

How art thou fallen from heaven, O Lucifer, son of the morning! *Ib.* 12.

I will also make it a possession for the bittern, and pools of water: and I will sweep it with the besom of destruction. *Ib.* 23.

And in mercy shall the throne be established. *Ib.* xvi. 5.

The burden of the desert of the sea. *Ib.* xxi. 1.

Watchman, what of the night? Watchman, what of the night?
The watchman said, The morning cometh, and also the night. *Ib.* 11.

Let us eat and drink; for to morrow we shall die. *Ib.* xxii. 13.

Fasten him as a nail in a sure place. *Ib.* 23.

Whose merchants are princes. *Ib.* xxiii. 8.

Howl, ye ships of Tarshish. *Ib.* 14.

A feast of fat things, a feast of wines on the lees. *Ib.* xxv. 6.

We have as it were brought forth wind. *Ib.* xxvi. 18.

For precept must be upon precept, precept upon precept; line upon line, line upon line; here a little, and there a little. *Ib.* xxviii. 10.

We have made a covenant with death, and with hell are we at an agreement. *Ib.* 15.

They are drunken, but not with wine. *Ib.* xxix. 9.

Their strength is to sit still. *Ib.* xxx. 7.

Now go, write it before them in a table, and note it in a book. *Ib.* 8.

Speak unto us smooth things, prophesy deceits. *Ib.* 10.

In quietness and in confidence shall be your strength. *Ib.* 15.

One thousand shall flee at the rebuke of one. *Ib.* 17.

This is the way, walk ye in it. *Ib.* 21.

And a man shall be as an hiding place from the wind, and a covert from the tempest; as rivers of water in a dry place, as the shadow of a great rock in a weary land. *Ib.* xxxii. 2.

The liberal deviseth liberal things. *Ib.* 8.

An habitation of dragons, and a court for owls. *Ib.* xxxiv. 13.

The wilderness and the solitary place shall be glad for them; and the desert shall rejoice, and blossom as the rose. *Ib.* xxxv. 1.

Strengthen ye the weak hands, and confirm the feeble knees. *Ib.* 3.

Then shall the lame man leap up as an hart, and the tongue of the dumb sing: for in the wilderness shall waters break out, and streams in the desert. *Ib.* 6.

The wayfaring men, though fools, shall not err therein. *Ib.* 8.

Sorrow and sighing shall flee away. *Ib.* 10.

Set thine house in order. *Ib.* xxxviii. 1.

I shall go softly all my years in the bitterness of my soul. *Ib.* 15.

Comfort ye, comfort ye my people, saith your God.
Speak ye comfortably to Jerusalem, and cry unto her, that her warfare is accomplished. *Ib.* xl. 1.

The voice of him that crieth in the wilderness, Prepare ye the way of the Lord, make straight in the desert a highway for our God.
Every valley shall be exalted, and every mountain and hill shall be made low: and the crooked shall be made straight, and the rough places plain:
And the glory of the Lord shall be revealed, and all flesh shall be revealed together: for the mouth of the Lord hath spoken it. *Ib.* 3.

The voice said, Cry. And he said, What shall I cry? All flesh is grass, and all the goodliness thereof is as the flower of the field:
The grass withereth, the flower fadeth: because the spirit of the Lord bloweth upon it: surely the people is grass. *Ib.* 6.

He shall feed his flock like a shepherd: he shall gather the lambs with his arm, and carry them in his bosom, and shall gently lead those that are with young. *Ib.* 11.

The nations are as a drop of a bucket, and are counted as the small dust of the balance: behold, he taketh up the isles as a very little thing. *Ib.* 15.

Have ye not known? hath it not been told you from the beginning? *Ib.* 21.

But they that wait upon the Lord shall renew their strength: they shall mount up with wings as eagles: they shall run, and not be weary: they shall walk, and not faint. *Ib.* 31.

A bruised reed shall he not break, and the smoking flax shall he not quench. *Ib.* xlii. 3.

He warmeth himself, and saith, Aha, I am warm, I have seen the fire. *Ib.* xliv. 16.

Shall the clay say to him that fashioneth it, What makest thou? *Ib.* xlv. 9.

Verily thou art a God that hidest thyself. *Ib.* 15.

I have chosen thee in the furnace of affliction. *Ib.* xlviii. 10.

O that thou hadst hearkened to my commandments! then had thy peace been as a river, and thy righteousness as the waves of the sea. *Ib.* 18.

There is no peace, saith the Lord, unto the wicked. *Ib.* 22.

How beautiful upon the mountains are the feet of him that bringeth good tidings, that publisheth peace; that bringeth good tidings of good, that publisheth salvation; that saith unto Zion, Thy God reigneth! *Ib.* lii. 7.

For they shall see eye to eye, when the Lord shall bring again Zion.
Break forth into joy, sing together, ye waste places of Jerusalem: for the Lord hath comforted his people, he hath redeemed Jerusalem. *Ib.* 9.

Who hath believed our report? and to whom is the arm of the Lord revealed? *Ib.* liii. 1.

He hath no form nor comeliness; and when we shall see him, there is no beauty that we should desire him. He is despised and rejected of men; a man of sorrows, and acquainted with grief: and we hid as it were our faces from him; he was despised, and we esteemed him not.

Surely he hath borne our griefs, and carried our sorrows. *Isaiah* liii. 2.

But he was wounded for our transgressions, he was bruised for our iniquities: the chastisement of our peace was upon him; and with his stripes we are healed.

All we like sheep have gone astray; we have turned every one to his own way; and the Lord hath laid on him the iniquity of us all.

He was oppressed, and he was afflicted, yet he opened not his mouth: he is brought as a lamb to the slaughter, and as a sheep before her shearers is dumb, so he openeth not his mouth. *Ib.* 5.

He was cut off out of the land of the living. *Ib.* 8.

He was numbered with the transgressors; and he bare the sins of many, and made intercession for the transgressors. *Ib.* 12.

Ho, every one that thirsteth, come ye to the waters, and he that hath no money; come ye, buy and eat; yea, come, buy wine and milk without money and without price.
Wherefore do ye spend money for that which is not bread? and your labour for that which satisfieth not? *Ib.* lv. 1.

Seek ye the Lord while he may be found, call ye upon him while he is near. *Ib.* 6.

For my thoughts are not your thoughts, neither are your ways my ways, saith the Lord. *Ib.* 8.

Instead of the thorn shall come up the fir tree, and instead of the brier shall come up the myrtle tree. *Ib.* 13.

I will give them an everlasting name, that shall not be cut off. *Ib.* lvi. 5.

Peace to him that is far off, and to him that is near. *Ib.* lvii. 19.

Is it such a fast that I have chosen? a day for a man to afflict his soul? *Ib.* lviii. 5.

Is not this the fast that I have chosen? to loose the bands of wickedness, to undo the heavy burdens, and to let the oppressed go free, and that ye break every yoke? *Ib.* 6.

Then shall thy light break forth as the morning, and thine health shall spring forth speedily. *Ib.* 8.

They make haste to shed innocent blood. *Ib.* lix. 7.

Arise, shine; for thy light is come, and the glory of the Lord is risen upon thee. *Ib.* lx. 1.

A little one shall become a thousand, and a small one a strong nation. *Ib.* 22.

The spirit of the Lord is upon me. *Ib.* lxi. 1.

To bind up the broken-hearted, to proclaim liberty to the captives, and the opening of the prison to them that are bound;
To proclaim the acceptable year of the Lord, and the day of vengeance of our God; to comfort all that mourn. *Ib.*

To give unto them beauty for ashes, the oil of joy for mourning, the garment of praise for the spirit of heaviness. *Ib.* 3.

Who is this that cometh from Edom, with dyed garments from Bozrah? *Ib.* lxiii. 1.

I have trodden the winepress alone. *Ib.* 3.

In all their affliction he was afflicted. *Ib.* 9.

All our righteousnesses are as filthy rags; and we all do fade as a leaf. *Ib.* lxiv. 6.

For, behold, I create new heavens and a new earth. *Ib.* lxv. 17.

As one whom his mother comforteth, so will I comfort you. *Ib.* lxvi. 13.

They were as fed horses in the morning: every one neighed after his neighbour's wife. *Jeremiah* v. 8.

This people hath a revolting and a rebellious heart. *Ib.* 23.

The prophets prophesy falsely, and the priests bear rule by their means; and my people love to have it so: and what will ye do in the end thereof? *Ib.* 31.

Saying, Peace, peace; when there is no peace. *Ib.* vi. 14.

Do they provoke me to anger? saith the Lord: do they not provoke themselves to the confusion of their own faces? *Ib.* vii. 19.

The harvest is past, the summer is ended, and we are not saved. *Ib.* viii. 20.

Is there no balm in Gilead? *Ib.* 22.

Can the Ethiopian change his skin, or the leopard his spots? *Ib.* xiii. 23.

A man of strife and a man of contention. *Ib.* xv. 10.

The heart is deceitful above all things, and desperately wicked. *Ib.* xvii. 9.

As the partridge sitteth on eggs, and hatcheth them not. *Ib.* 11.

And seekest thou great things for thyself? seek them not. *Ib.* xlv. 5.

Is it nothing to you, all ye that pass by? behold, and see if there be any sorrow like unto my sorrow. *Lamentations* i. 12.

The wormwood and the gall. *Ib.* iii. 19.

It is good for a man that he bear the yoke in his youth. *Ib.* 27.

He giveth his cheek to him that smiteth him. *Ib.* 30.

As if a wheel had been in the midst of a wheel. *Ezekiel* x. 10.

As is the mother, so is her daughter. *Ib.* xvi. 44.

The fathers have eaten sour grapes, and the children's teeth are set on edge. *Ib.* xviii. 2.

When the wicked man turneth away from his wickedness that he hath committed, and doeth that which is lawful and right, he shall save his soul alive. *Ib.* 27.

The king of Babylon stood at the parting of the way.
Ezekiel xxi. 21.

She doted upon the Assyrians her neighbours, captains and rulers clothed most gorgeously, horsemen riding upon horses, all of them desirable young men. *Ib.* xxiii. 12.

The valley which was full of bones. *Ib.* xxxvii. 1.

Can these bones live? *Ib.* 3.

The image that Nebuchadnezzar the king had set up.
Daniel iii. 3.

The sound of the cornet, flute, harp, sackbut, psaltery, dulcimer, and all kinds of musick. *Ib.* 5.

Cast into the midst of a burning fiery furnace. *Ib.* 6.

We are not careful to answer thee in this matter.
Ib. 16.

Commanded that they should heat the furnace one seven times more than it was wont to be heated.
Ib. 19.

Then these men were bound in their coats, their hosen, and their hats, and their other garments, and were cast into the midst of the burning fiery furnace. *Ib.* 21.

Shadrach, Meshach, and Abed-nego, ye servants of the most high God, come forth, and come hither.
Ib. 26.

MENE, MENE, TEKEL, UPHARSIN.
This is the interpretation of the thing: MENE; God hath numbered thy kingdom, and finished it.
TEKEL; Thou art weighed in the balances, and art found wanting.
PERES; Thy kingdom is divided, and given to the Medes and Persians. *Ib.* v. 25.

The Ancient of days. *Ib.* vii. 9.

O Daniel, a man greatly beloved. *Ib.* x. 11.

Many shall run to and fro, and knowledge shall be increased. *Ib.* xii. 4.

They have sown the wind, and they shall reap the whirlwind. *Hosea* viii. 7.

Ye have plowed wickedness, ye have reaped iniquity.
Ib. x. 13.

I drew them . . . with bands of love. *Ib.* xi. 4.

I have multiplied visions, and used similitudes.
Ib. xii. 10.

That which the palmerworm hath left hath the locust eaten. *Joel* i. 4.

I will restore to you the years that the locust hath eaten. *Ib.* ii. 25.

And it shall come to pass afterwards, that I will pour out my spirit upon all flesh; and your sons and your daughters shall prophesy, your old men shall dream dreams, your young men shall see visions.
Ib. 28.

Multitudes in the valley of decision. *Ib.* iii. 14.

Can two walk together, except they be agreed?
Amos iii. 3.

A firebrand plucked from the burning. *Ib.* iv. 11.

Woe to them that are at ease in Zion. *Ib.* vi. 1.

The Lord stood upon a wall made by a plumbline, with a plumbline in his hand.
And the Lord said unto me, Amos, what seest thou? And I said, A plumbline. *Ib.* vii. 7.

Come, and let us cast lots, that we may know for whose cause this evil is upon us. So they cast lots, and the lot fell upon Jonah. *Jonah* i. 7.

Jonah was in the belly of the fish three days and three nights. *Ib.* 17.

They shall sit every man under his vine and under his fig tree. *Micah* iv. 4.

But thou, Beth-lehem Ephratah, though thou be little among the thousands of Judah. *Ib.* v. 2.

Write the vision, and make it plain upon tables, that he may run that readeth it. *Habakkuk* ii. 2.

Your fathers, where are they? And the prophets, do they live for ever? *Zechariah* i. 5.

For who hath despised the day of small things?
Ib. iv. 10.

Turn ye to the stronghold, ye prisoners of hope.
Ib. ix. 12.

I was wounded in the house of my friends.
Ib. xiii. 6.

Have we not all one father? hath not one God created us? *Malachi* ii. 10.

But unto you that fear my name shall the Sun of righteousness arise with healing in his wings.
Ib. iv. 2.

THE NEW TESTAMENT

There came wise men from the east to Jerusalem, Saying, Where is he that is born King of the Jews? for we have seen his star in the east, and are come to worship him. *St. Matthew* ii. 1.

They presented unto him their gifts; gold, and frankincense, and myrrh. *Ib.* 11.

They departed into their own country another way.
Ib. 12.

Rachel weeping for her children, and would not be comforted, because they are not. *Ib.* 18.

Repent ye: for the kingdom of heaven is at hand.
Ib. iii. 2.

The voice of one crying in the wilderness, Prepare ye the way of the Lord, make his paths straight.
Ib. 3.

Raiment of camel's hair, and a leathern girdle about his loins; and his meat was locusts and wild honey.
Ib. 4.

O generation of vipers, who hath warned you to flee from the wrath to come? *Ib.* 7.

And now also the axe is laid unto the root of the trees.
Ib. 10.

Suffer it to be so now: for thus it becometh us to fulfil all righteousness. *Ib.* 15.

This is my beloved Son, in whom I am well pleased.
Ib. 17.

Man shall not live by bread alone, but by every word that proceedeth out of the mouth of God.

St. Matthew iv. 4.

Thou shalt not tempt the Lord thy God. *Ib.* 7.

The devil taketh him up into an exceeding high mountain, and sheweth him all the kingdoms of the world, and the glory of them. *Ib.* 8.

Angels came and ministered unto him. *Ib.* 11.

Fishers of men. *Ib.* 19.

Blessed are the poor in spirit: for their's is the kingdom of heaven.
Blessed are they that mourn: for they shall be comforted.
Blessed are the meek: for they shall inherit the earth.
Blessed are they which do hunger and thirst after righteousness: for they shall be filled.
Blessed are the merciful: for they shall obtain mercy.
Blessed are the pure in heart: for they shall see God.
Blessed are the peacemakers: for they shall be called the children of God. *Ib.* v. 3.

Ye are the salt of the earth: but if the salt have lost his savour, wherewith shall it be salted? *Ib.* 13.

Ye are the light of the world. A city that is set on a hill cannot be hid. *Ib.* 14.

Let your light so shine before men, that they may see your good works. *Ib.* 16.

Think not that I am come to destroy the law, or the prophets: I am come not to destroy, but to fulfil. *Ib.* 17.

Except your righteousness exceed the righteousness of the scribes and Pharisees. *Ib.* 20.

Whosoever shall say, Thou fool, shall be in danger of hell fire. *Ib.* 22.

Agree with thine adversary quickly, whiles thou art in the way with him. *Ib.* 25.

Till thou hast paid the uttermost farthing. *Ib.* 26.

Swear not at all; neither by heaven; for it is God's throne:
Nor by the earth; for it is his footstool. *Ib.* 34.

Let your communication be, Yea, yea; Nay, nay. *Ib.* 37.

Resist not evil: but whosoever shall smite thee on thy right cheek, turn to him the other also. *Ib.* 39.

Whosoever shall compel thee to go a mile, go with him twain. *Ib.* 41.

He maketh his sun to rise on the evil and on the good, and sendeth rain on the just and on the unjust. *Ib.* 45.

Do not even the publicans the same? *Ib.* 46.

Be ye therefore perfect. *Ib.* 48.

When thou doest alms, let not thy left hand know what thy right hand doeth. *Ib.* vi. 3.

Use not vain repetitions, as the heathen do: for they think they shall be heard for their much speaking. *Ib.* 7.

After this manner therefore pray ye: Our Father which art in heaven, Hallowed be thy name.

Thy kingdom come. Thy will be done in earth, as it is in heaven.
Give us this day our daily bread.
And forgive us our debts, as we forgive our debtors.
And lead us not into temptation, but deliver us from evil: For thine is the kingdom, and the power, and the glory, for ever. Amen. *Ib.* 9.

Lay not up for yourselves treasures upon earth, where moth and rust doth corrupt, and where thieves break through and steal. *Ib.* 19.

Lay up for yourselves treasures in heaven. *Ib.* 20.

Where your treasure is, there will your heart be also. *Ib.* 21.

If therefore the light that is in thee be darkness, how great is that darkness! *Ib.* 23.

No man can serve two masters. *Ib.* 24.

Ye cannot serve God and mammon. *Ib.* 24.

Is not the life more than meat, and the body than raiment?
Behold the fowls of the air: for they sow not, neither do they reap, nor gather into barns. *Ib.* 25.

Which of you by taking thought can add one cubit unto his stature? *Ib.* 27.

Consider the lilies of the field, how they grow; they toil not, neither do they spin:
And yet I say unto you, That even Solomon in all his glory was not arrayed like one of these. *Ib.* 28.

Seek ye first the kingdom of God, and his righteousness; and all these things shall be added unto you. *Ib.* 33.

Take therefore no thought for the morrow; for the morrow shall take thought for the things of itself. Sufficient unto the day is the evil thereof. *Ib.* 34.

Judge not, that ye be not judged. *Ib.* vii. 1.

Why beholdest thou the mote that is in thy brother's eye, but considerest not the beam that is in thine own eye? *Ib.* 3.

Neither cast ye your pearls before swine. *Ib.* 6.

Ask, and it shall be given you; seek, and ye shall find; knock, and it shall be opened unto you. *Ib.* 7.

Every one that asketh receiveth; and he that seeketh findeth. *Ib.* 8.

Or what man is there of you, whom if his son ask bread, will he give him a stone? *Ib.* 9.

Therefore all things whatsoever ye would that men should do to you, do ye even so to them: for this is the law and the prophets. *Ib.* 12.

Wide is the gate and broad is the way that leadeth to destruction, and many there be that go in thereat. *Ib.* 13.

Strait is the gate, and narrow is the way which leadeth unto life, and few there be that find it. *Ib.* 14.

Beware of false prophets, which come to you in sheep's clothing, but inwardly they are ravening wolves. *Ib* 15.

Do men gather grapes of thorns, or figs of thistles? *Ib.* 16.

By their fruits ye shall know them.
St. Matthew vii. 20.

And great was the fall of it. *Ib.* 27.

For he taught them as one having authority, and not
as the scribes. *Ib.* 29.

Lord, I am not worthy that thou shouldest come under
my roof. *Ib.* viii. 8.

I am a man under authority, having soldiers under me:
and I say to this man, Go, and he goeth; and to
another, Come, and he cometh; and to my servant,
Do this, and he doeth it. *Ib.* 9.

I have not found so great faith, no, not in Israel.
Ib. 10.

But the children of the kingdom shall be cast out
into outer darkness : there shall be weeping and
gnashing of teeth. *Ib.* 12.

The foxes have holes, and the birds of the air have
nests; but the Son of man hath not where to lay
his head. *Ib.* 20.

Let the dead bury their dead. *Ib.* 22.

The whole herd ran violently down a steep place into
the sea, and perished in the waters. *Ib.* 32.

Sitting at the receipt of custom. *Ib.* ix. 9.

Why eateth your master with publicans and sinners?
Ib. 11.

They that be whole need not a physician, but they
that are sick. *Ib.* 12.

I am not come to call the righteous, but sinners to
repentance. *Ib.* 13.

Can the children of the bridechamber mourn, as long
as the bridegroom is with them? *Ib.* 15.

Neither do men put new wine into old bottles. *Ib.* 17.

The maid is not dead, but sleepeth. *Ib.* 24.

He casteth out devils through the prince of the devils.
Ib. 34.

The harvest truly is plenteous, but the labourers are
few. *Ib.* 37.

Go rather to the lost sheep of the house of Israel.
Ib. x. 6.

Freely ye have received, freely give. *Ib.* 8.

When ye depart out of that house or city, shake off the
dust of your feet. *Ib.* 14.

Be ye therefore wise as serpents, and harmless as
doves. *Ib.* 16.

He that endureth to the end shall be saved. *Ib.* 22.

The disciple is not above his master, nor the servant
above his lord. *Ib.* 24.

Are not two sparrows sold for a farthing? and one of
them shall not fall on the ground without your
Father. *Ib.* 29.

The very hairs of your head are all numbered. *Ib.* 30.

Fear ye not therefore, ye are of more value than many
sparrows. *Ib.* 31.

I came not to send peace, but a sword. *Ib.* 34.

A man's foes shall be they of his own household.
Ib. 36.

He that findeth his life shall lose it : and he that loseth
his life for my sake shall find it. *Ib.* 39.

Whosoever shall give to drink unto one of these little
ones a cup of cold water only. *Ib.* 42.

Art thou he that should come, or do we look for
another? *Ib.* xi. 3.

What went ye out into the wilderness to see? A reed
shaken with the wind?
But what went ye out for to see? A man clothed in
soft raiment? . . .
But what went ye out for to see? A prophet? yea,
I say unto you, and more than a prophet. *Ib.* 7.

The kingdom of heaven suffereth violence, and the
violent take it by force. *Ib.* 12.

We have piped unto you, and ye have not danced.
Ib. 17.

Wisdom is justified of her children. *Ib.* 19.

Come unto me, all ye that labour and are heavy laden,
and I will give you rest.
Take my yoke upon you, and learn of me; for I am
meek and lowly in heart : and ye shall find rest unto
your souls.
For my yoke is easy, and my burden is light. *Ib.* 28.

He that is not with me is against me. *Ib.* xii. 30.

The blasphemy against the Holy Ghost shall not be
forgiven unto men. *Ib.* 31.

The tree is known by his fruit. *Ib.* 33.

Out of the abundance of the heart the mouth speaketh.
Ib. 34.

Every idle word that men shall speak, they shall give
account thereof in the day of judgment. *Ib.* 36.

An evil and adulterous generation seeketh after a sign.
Ib. 39.

Behold, a greater than Solomon is here. *Ib.* 42.

Empty, swept, and garnished. *Ib.* 44.

Then goeth he and taketh with himself seven other
spirits more wicked than himself, and they enter
in and dwell there : and the last state of that man is
worse than the first. *Ib.* 45.

Behold my mother and my brethren! *Ib.* 49.

Some seeds fell by the wayside. *Ib.* xiii. 4.

Because they had no root, they withered away.
Ib. 7.

But other fell into good ground, and brought forth
fruit, some an hundredfold, some sixtyfold, some
thirtyfold. *Ib.* 8.

The care of this world, and the deceitfulness of riches.
Ib. 22.

His enemy came and sowed tares. *Ib.* 25.

An enemy hath done this. *Ib.* 28.

Let both grow together until the harvest. *Ib.* 30.

The kingdom of heaven is like to a grain of mustard
seed. *Ib.* 31.

So that the fowls of the air come and lodge in the branches thereof. *St. Matthew* xiii. 32.

A pearl of great price. *Ib.* 46.

An householder which bringeth forth out of his treasure things new and old. *Ib.* 52.

Is not this the carpenter's son? *Ib.* 55.

A prophet is not without honour, save in his own country and in his own house. *Ib.* 57.

They took up of the fragments that remained twelve baskets full. *Ib.* xiv. 20.

In the fourth watch of the night Jesus went unto them, walking on the sea. *Ib.* 25.

Be of good cheer: it is I; be not afraid. *Ib.* 27.

O thou of little faith, wherefore didst thou doubt? *Ib.* 31.

Not that which goeth into the mouth defileth a man; but that which cometh out of the mouth, this defileth a man. *Ib.* xv. 11.

They be blind leaders of the blind. And if the blind lead the blind, both shall fall into the ditch. *Ib.* 14.

The dogs eat of the crumbs which fall from their masters' table. *Ib.* 27.

When it is evening, ye say it will be fair weather: for the sky is red. *Ib.* xvi. 2.

The signs of the times. *Ib.* 3.

Thou art Peter, and upon this rock I will build my church; and the gates of hell shall not prevail against it. *Ib.* 18.

Get thee behind me, Satan. *Ib.* 23.

What is a man profited, if he shall gain the whole world, and lose his own soul? *Ib.* xvi. 26.

It is good for us to be here. *Ib.* xvii. 4.

If ye have faith as a grain of mustard seed, ye shall say unto this mountain, Remove hence to yonder place; and it shall remove. *Ib.* 20.

Become as little children. *Ib.* xviii. 3.

But whoso shall offend one of these little ones which believe in me, it were better for him that a millstone were hanged about his neck, and that he were drowned in the midst of the sea. *Ib.* 6.

It must needs be that offences come; but woe to that man by whom the offence cometh! *Ib.* 7.

If thine eye offend thee, pluck it out, and cast it from thee: it is better for thee to enter into life with one eye, rather than having two eyes to be cast into hell fire. *Ib.* 9.

For where two or three are gathered together in my name, there am I in the midst of them. *Ib.* 20.

Until seventy times seven. *Ib.* 22.

Lord, have patience with me, and I will pay thee all. *Ib.* 26.

Pay me that thou owest. *Ib.* 28.

What therefore God hath joined together, let not man put asunder. *Ib.* xix. 6.

Thou shalt love thy neighbour as thyself. *Ib.* 19.

If thou wilt be perfect, go and sell that thou hast, and give to the poor, and thou shalt have treasure in heaven. *Ib.* 21.

He went away sorrowful: for he had great possessions. *Ib.* 22.

It is easier for a camel to go through the eye of a needle than for a rich man to enter into the kingdom of God. *Ib.* 24.

With men this is impossible: but with God all things are possible. *Ib.* 26.

But many that are first shall be last; and the last shall be first. *Ib.* 30.

Why stand ye here all the day idle? *Ib.* xx. 6.

Borne the burden and heat of the day. *Ib.* 12.

I will give unto this last, even as unto thee.
Is it not lawful for me to do what I will with mine own? *Ib.* 14.

My house shall be called the house of prayer; but ye have made it a den of thieves. *Ib.* xxi. 13.

For many are called, but few are chosen. *Ib.* xxii. 14.

Whose is this image and superscription? *Ib.* 20.

Render therefore unto Cæsar the things which are Cæsar's. *Ib.* 21.

Last of all the woman died also. *Ib.* 27.

For in the resurrection they neither marry, nor are given in marriage. *Ib.* 30.

They make broad their phylacteries, and enlarge the borders of their garments,
And love the uppermost rooms at feasts, and the chief seats in the synagogues. *Ib.* xxiii. 5.

Whosoever shall exalt himself shall be abased; and he that shall humble himself shall be exalted. *Ib.* 12.

Woe unto you, . . . for ye pay tithe of mint and anise and cummin. *Ib.* 23.

Blind guides, which strain at a gnat, and swallow a camel. *Ib.* 24.

Whited sepulchres, which indeed appear beautiful outward, but are within full of dead men's bones. *Ib.* 27.

O Jerusalem, Jerusalem, thou that killest the prophets and stonest them which are sent unto thee, how often would I have gathered thy children together, even as a hen gathereth her chickens under her wings, and ye would not! *Ib.* 37.

Wars and rumours of wars. *Ib.* xxiv. 6.

But the end is not yet. *Ib.*

For nation shall rise against nation, and kingdom against kingdom. *Ib.* 7.

Abomination of desolation. *Ib.* 15.

Wheresoever the carcase is, there will the eagles be gathered together. *Ib.* 28.

Eating and drinking, marrying and giving in marriage. *Ib.* 38.

One shall be taken, and the other left.
St. Matthew xxiv. 40.

Well done, thou good and faithful servant.
Ib. xxv. 21.

Enter thou into the joy of thy Lord. *Ib.*

Lord, I knew thee that thou art an hard man, reaping where thou hast not sown, and gathering where thou hast not strawed. *Ib.* 24.

Unto every one that hath shall be given, and he shall have abundance; but from him that hath not shall be taken away even that which he hath. *Ib.* 29.

I was a stranger, and ye took me in:
Naked, and ye clothed me: I was sick, and ye visited me: I was in prison, and ye came unto me. *Ib.* 35.

Inasmuch as ye have done it unto the least of these my brethren, ye have done it unto me. *Ib.* 40.

A woman having an alabaster box of very precious ointment. *Ib.* xxvi. 7.

To what purpose is this waste? *Ib.* 8.

What will ye give me, and I will deliver him unto you? And they covenanted with him for thirty pieces of silver. *Ib.* 15.

It had been good for that man if he had not been born. *Ib.* 24.

This night, before the cock crow, thou shalt deny me thrice. *Ib.* 34.

Though I should die with thee, yet will I not deny thee. *Ib.* 35.

If it be possible, let this cup pass from me. *Ib.* 39.

What, could ye not watch with me one hour? *Ib.* 40.

The spirit indeed is willing, but the flesh is weak.
Ib. 41.

Hail, master; and kissed him. *Ib.* 49.

Friend, wherefore art thou come? *Ib.* 50.

All they that take the sword shall perish with the sword. *Ib.* 52.

Thy speech bewrayeth thee.
Then began he to curse and to swear, saying, I know not the man. And immediately the cock crew.
Ib. 73.

Have thou nothing to do with that just man.
Ib. xxvii. 19.

He took water, and washed his hands before the multitude, saying, I am innocent of the blood of this just person: see ye to it. *Ib.* 24.

His blood be on us, and on our children. *Ib.* 25.

He saved others; himself he cannot save. *Ib.* 42.

Eli, Eli, lama sabachthani? ... My God, my God, why hast thou forsaken me? *Ib.* 46.

Simon's wife's mother. *St. Mark* i. 30.

The sabbath was made for man, and not for the sabbath. *Ib.* ii. 27.

If a house be divided against itself, that house cannot stand. *Ib.* iii. 25.

He that hath ears to hear, let him hear. *Ib.* iv. 9.

With what measure ye mete, it shall be measured unto you. *Ib.* 24.

My name is Legion: for we are many. *Ib.* v. 9.

Clothed, and in his right mind. *Ib.* 15.

My little daughter lieth at the point of death. *Ib.* 23.

Had suffered many things of many physicians, and had spent all that she had, and was nothing bettered, but rather grew worse. *Ib.* 26.

Knowing in himself that virtue had gone out of him.
Ib. 30.

I see men as trees, walking. *Ib.* viii. 24.

For what shall it profit a man, if he shall gain the whole world, and lose his own soul? *Ib.* 36.

Where their worm dieth not, and the fire is not quenched. *Ib.* ix. 44.

Suffer the little children to come unto me, and forbid them not: for of such is the kingdom of God.
Ib. x. 14.

Which devour widows' houses, and for a pretence make long prayers. *Ib.* xii. 40.

And there came a certain poor widow, and she threw in two mites. *Ib.* 42.

Go ye into all the world, and preach the gospel to every creature. *Ib.* xvi. 15.

It seemed good to me also ... to write unto thee ... most excellent Theophilus. *St. Luke* i. 3.

To turn the hearts of the disobedient to the wisdom of the just. *Ib.* 17.

Hail, thou that art highly favoured, the Lord is with thee: blessed art thou among women. *Ib.* 28.

My soul doth magnify the Lord,
And my spirit hath rejoiced in God my Saviour.
For he hath regarded the low estate of his handmaiden: for, behold, from henceforth all generations shall call me blessed. *Ib.* 46.

He hath shewed strength with his arm; he hath scattered the proud in the imagination of their hearts.
He hath put down the mighty from their seats, and hath exalted them of low degree.
He hath filled the hungry with good things; and the rich he hath sent empty away. *Ib.* 51.

To give light to them that sit in darkness and in the shadow of death, to guide our feet into the way of peace. *Ib.* 70.

And it came to pass in those days, that there went out a decree from Cæsar Augustus, that all the world should be taxed. *Ib.* ii. 1.

Because there was no room for them in the inn.
Ib. 7.

And, lo, the angel of the Lord came upon them, and the glory of the Lord shone round about them: and they were sore afraid. *Ib.* 9.

Glory to God in the highest, and on earth peace, good will toward men. *Ib.* 14.

Lord, now lettest thou thy servant depart in peace, according to thy word. *Ib.* 29.

Vist ye not that I must be about my Father's business? *St. Luke* ii. 49.

esus increased in wisdom and stature, and in favour with God and man. *Ib.* 52.

Be content with your wages. *Ib.* iii. 14.

Shewed unto him all the kingdoms of the world in a moment of time. *Ib.* iv. 5.

Physician, heal thyself. *Ib.* 23.

Many widows were in Israel in the days of Elias . . . but unto none of them was Elias sent. *Ib.* 25.

Master, we have toiled all the night, and have taken nothing: nevertheless at thy word I will let down the net. *Ib.* v. 5.

Woe unto you, when all men shall speak well of you! *Ib.* vi. 26.

Judge not, and ye shall not be judged. *Ib.* 37.

Give, and it shall be given unto you; good measure, pressed down, and shaken together, and running over, shall men give into your bosom. *Ib.* 38.

The only son of his mother, and she was a widow. *Ib.* vii. 12.

Simon, I have somewhat to say unto thee. And he saith, Master, say on. *Ib.* 40.

Peace be to this house. *Ib.* x. 5.

For the labourer is worthy of his hire. *Ib.* 7.

I beheld Satan as lightning fall from heaven. *Ib.* 18.

I thank thee, O Father, Lord of heaven and earth, that thou hast hid these things from the wise and prudent, and hast revealed them unto babes: even so, Father; for so it seemed good in thy sight. *Ib.* 21.

For I tell you, that many prophets and kings have desired to see those things which you see, and have not seen them; and to hear those things which ye hear, and have not heard them. *Ib.* 24.

Fell among thieves. *Ib.* 30.

He passed by on the other side. *Ib.* 31.

He took out two pence and gave them to the host. *Ib.* 35.

Whatsoever thou spendest more, when I come again I will repay thee. *Ib.* 35.

Go, and do thou likewise. *Ib.* 37.

But Martha was cumbered about much serving. *Ib.* 40.

But one thing is needful; and Mary hath chosen that good part which shall not be taken away from her. *Ib.* 42.

When a strong man armed keepeth his palace, his goods are in peace. *Ib.* xi. 21.

All his armour wherein he trusted. *Ib.* 22.

He that is not with me is against me. *Ib.* 23.

Take heed therefore that the light which is in thee be not darkness. *Ib.* 35.

Woe unto you, lawyers! for ye have taken away the key of knowledge. *Ib.* 52.

Are not five sparrows sold for two farthings, and not one of them is forgotten before God? *Ib.* xii. 6.

Soul, thou hast much goods laid up for many years; take thine ease, eat, drink, and be merry. *Ib.* 19.

Thou fool, this night thy soul shall be required of thee. *Ib.* 20.

Let your loins be girded about, and your lights burning. *Ib.* 35.

But he that knew not, and did commit things worthy of stripes, shall be beaten with few stripes. *Ib.* 48.

Cut it down; why cumbereth it the ground? *Ib.* xiii. 7.

Begin with shame to take the lower room. *Ib.* xiv. 9.

Friend, go up higher. *Ib.* 10.

For whosoever exalteth himself shall be abased; and he that humbleth himself shall be exalted. *Ib.* 11.

They all with one consent began to make excuse. *Ib.* 18.

I pray thee have me excused. *Ib.*

I have married a wife, and therefore I cannot come. *Ib.* 20.

The poor, and the maimed, and the halt, and the blind. *Ib.* 21.

Go out into the highways and hedges, and compel them to come in. *Ib.* 23.

Leave the ninety and nine in the wilderness. *Ib.* xv. 4.

Rejoice with me; for I have found my sheep which was lost. *Ib.* 6.

Joy shall be in heaven over one sinner that repenteth more than over ninety and nine just persons, which need no repentance. *Ib.* 7.

Wasted his substance with riotous living. *Ib.* 13.

He fain would have filled his belly with the husks that the swine did eat: and no man gave unto him.

And when he came to himself, he said, How many hired servants of my father's have bread enough and to spare, and I perish with hunger!
I will arise and go to my father, and will say unto him, Father, I have sinned against heaven, and before thee, And am no more worthy to be called thy son: make me as one of thy hired servants. *Ib.* 16.

Bring hither the fatted calf, and kill it. *Ib.* 23.

This my son was dead, and is alive again; he was lost and is found. *Ib.* 24.

Which hath devoured thy living with harlots. *Ib.* 30.

I cannot dig; to beg I am ashamed. *Ib.* xvi. 3.

Take thy bill, and sit down quickly, and write fifty. *Ib.* 6.

And the lord commended the unjust steward, because he had done wisely; for the children of this world are in their generation wiser than the children of light. *Ib.* 8.

Make to yourselves friends of the mammon of unrighteousness. *Ib.* 9.

He that is faithful in that which is least is faithful also in much. *St. Luke* xvi. 10.

There was a certain rich man, which was clothed in purple and fine linen, and fared sumptuously every day. *Ib.* 19.

The crumbs which fell from the rich man's table. *Ib.* 21.

Carried by the angels into Abraham's bosom. *Ib.* 22.

Between us and you there is a great gulf fixed. *Ib.* 26.

It were better for him that a millstone were hanged about his neck, and he cast into the sea. *Ib.* xvii. 2.

Say, we are unprofitable servants: we have done that which was our duty to do. *Ib.* 10.

Were there not ten cleansed? but where are the nine? *Ib.* 17.

The kingdom of God is within you. *Ib.* 21.

Remember Lot's wife. *Ib.* 32.

Men ought always to pray, and not to faint. *Ib.* xviii. 1.

God, I thank thee, that I am not as other men are. *Ib.* 11.

God be merciful to me a sinner. *Ib.* 13.

How hardly shall they that have riches enter into the kingdom of God. *Ib.* 24.

Have thou authority over ten cities. *Ib.* xix. 17.

Out of thine own mouth will I judge thee. *Ib.* 22.

Thou knewest that I was an austere man. *Ib.* 22.

If these should hold their peace, the stones would immediately cry out. *Ib.* 40.

And when they heard it, they said, God forbid. *Ib.* xx. 16.

In your patience possess ye your souls. *Ib.* xxi. 19.

He shall shew you a large upper room furnished. *Ib.* xxii. 12.

I am among you as he that serveth. *Ib.* 27.

Nevertheless, not my will, but thine, be done. *Ib.* 42.

And the Lord turned, and looked upon Peter. *Ib.* 61.

For if they do these things in a green tree, what shall be done in the dry? *Ib.* xxiii. 31.

Father, forgive them; for they know not what they do. *Ib.* 34.

Lord, remember me when thou comest into thy kingdom. *Ib.* 42.

To day thou shalt be with me in paradise. *Ib.* 43.

Father, into thy hands I commend my spirit. *Ib.* 46.

He was a good man, and a just. *Ib.* 50.

Why seek ye the living with the dead? *Ib.* xxiv. 5.

Their words seemed to them as idle tales. *Ib.* 11.

Did not our hearts burn within us, while he talked with us by the way? *Ib.* 32.

He was known of them in breaking of bread. *Ib.* 35.

A piece of broiled fish, and of an honeycomb. *Ib.* 42.

In the beginning was the Word, and the Word was with God, and the Word was God. *St. John* i. 1

All things were made by him; and without him was not any thing made that was made. *Ib.* 3

And the light shined in darkness; and the darkness comprehended it not. *Ib.* 5

There was a man sent from God, whose name was John. *Ib.* 6

The true light, which lighteth every man that cometh into the world. *Ib.* 9

He came unto his own, and his own received him not. *Ib.* 11

And the Word was made flesh, and dwelt among us, (and we beheld his glory, the glory as of the only begotten of the Father,) full of grace and truth. *Ib.* 14

No man hath seen God at any time. *Ib.* 18

Who coming after me is preferred before me, whose shoe's latchet I am not worthy to unloose. *Ib.* 27

Can there any good thing come out of Nazareth? *Ib.* 46

Behold an Israelite indeed, in whom is no guile. *Ib.* 47

Woman, what have I to do with thee? mine hour is not yet come. *Ib.* ii. 4

When he had made a scourge of small cords, he drove them all out of the temple. *Ib.* 15

The wind bloweth where it listeth, and thou hearest the sound thereof, but canst not tell whence it cometh, and whither it goeth. *Ib.* iii. 8

How can these things be? *Ib.* 9

God so loved the world, that he gave his only begotten Son, that whosoever believeth on him should not perish, but have everlasting life. *Ib.* 16

Men loved darkness rather than light, because their deeds were evil. *Ib.* 19

The friend of the bridegroom . . . rejoiceth greatly because of the bridegroom's voice. *Ib.* 29

He must increase, but I must decrease. *Ib.* 30

God is a Spirit: and they that worship him must worship him in spirit and in truth. *Ib.* iv. 24

They are white already unto harvest. *Ib.* 35

Other men laboured, and ye are entered into their labours. *Ib.* 38

Rise, take up thy bed, and walk. *Ib.* v. 8

Passed from death unto life. *Ib.* 24

He was a burning and a shining light. *Ib.* 35

Search the scriptures. *Ib.* 39

What are they among so many? *Ib.* vi. 9

Gather up the fragments that remain, that nothing be lost. *Ib.* 12

Him that cometh to me I will in no wise cast out. *Ib.* 37

It is the spirit that quickeneth. *St. John* vi. 63.

Never man spake like this man. *Ib.* vii. 46.

Are ye also deceived? *Ib.* 47.

He that is without sin among you, let him first cast a stone at her. *Ib.* viii. 7.

Neither do I condemn thee: go, and sin no more. *Ib.* 11.

The truth shall make you free. *Ib.* 32.

Ye are of your father the devil. *Ib.* 44.

There is no truth in him. *Ib.*

He is a liar, and the father of it. *Ib.*

Which of you convinceth me of sin? *Ib.* 46.

The night cometh when no man can work. *Ib.* ix. 4.

He is of age; he shall speak for himself. *Ib.* 21.

One thing I know, that, whereas I was blind, now I see. *Ib.* 25.

I am the door. *Ib.* x. 9.

The good shepherd giveth his life for his sheep. *Ib.* 11.

The hireling fleeth, because he is an hireling, and careth not for the sheep. *Ib.* 13.

Other sheep I have, which are not of this fold. *Ib.* 16.

I am the resurrection, and the life. *Ib.* xi. 25.

Jesus wept. *Ib.* 35.

It is expedient for us, that one man should die for the people. *Ib.* 50.

Why was not this ointment sold for three hundred pence, and given to the poor? *Ib.* xii. 5.

The poor always ye have with you. *Ib.* 8.

Sir, we would see Jesus. *Ib.* 21.

Walk while ye have the light, lest darkness come upon you. *Ib.* 35.

Lord, dost thou wash my feet? *Ib.* xiii. 6.

Now there was leaning on Jesus' bosom one of his disciples, whom Jesus loved. *Ib.* 23.

That thou doest, do quickly *Ib.* 27.

Let not your heart be troubled: ye believe in God, believe also in me. *Ib.* xiv. 1.

In my father's house are many mansions. *Ib.* 2.

I go to prepare a place for you. *Ib.*

I am the way, the truth, and the life: no man cometh unto the Father, but by me. *Ib.* 6.

Lord, show us the Father, and it sufficeth us. *Ib.* 8.

Have I been so long time with you, and yet hast thou not known me, Philip? *Ib.* 9.

Judas saith unto him, not Iscariot. *Ib.* 22.

Greater love hath no man than this, that a man lay down his life for his friends. *Ib.* xv. 13.

Ye have not chosen me, but I have chosen you. *Ib.* 26.

It is expedient for you that I go away: for if I go not away, the Comforter will not come unto you. *Ib.* xvi. 7.

I have yet many things to say unto you, but ye cannot bear them now. *Ib.* 12.

A little while, and ye shall not see me: and again, a little while, and ye shall see me, because I go to the Father. *Ib.* 16.

Do ye now believe? *Ib.* 31.

In the world ye shall have tribulation: but be of good cheer; I have overcome the world. *Ib.* 33.

The son of perdition. *Ib.* xvii. 12.

Put up thy sword into the sheath. *Ib.* xviii. 11.

Answerest thou the high priest so? *Ib.* 22.

Pilate saith unto him, What is truth? *Ib.* 38.

Now Barabbas was a robber. *Ib.* 40.

Behold the man. *Ib.* xix. 5.

What I have written I have written. *Ib.* 22.

Woman, behold thy son!...
Behold thy mother. *Ib.* 26.

I thirst. *Ib.* 28.

It is finished. *Ib.* 30.

A new sepulchre, wherein was never man yet laid. *Ib.* 41.

The first day of the week cometh Mary Magdalene early, when it was yet dark, unto the sepulchre, and seeth the stone taken away from the sepulchre. *Ib.* xx. 1.

So they ran both together; and the other disciple did outrun Peter, and came first to the sepulchre. *Ib.* 4.

She, supposing him to be the gardener. *Ib.* 15.

She turned herself and saith unto him, Rabboni. *Ib.* 16.

Touch me not. *Ib.* 17.

Except I shall see in his hands the print of the nails, and put my finger into the print of the nails, and thrust my hand into his side, I will not believe. *Ib.* 25.

Be not faithless, but believing. *Ib.* 27.

Thomas, because thou hast seen me, thou hast believed: blessed are they that have not seen, and yet have believed. *Ib.* 29.

Simon Peter saith unto them, I go a fishing. *Ib.* xxi. 3.

Children, have ye any meat? *Ib.* 5.

Simon, son of Jonas, lovest thou me more than these? *Ib.* 15.

Feed my lambs. *Ib.* 15.

Feed my sheep. *Ib.* 16.

Lord, thou knowest all things; thou knowest that I love thee. *Ib.* 17.

When thou wast young, thou girdest thyself, and walkedst whither thou wouldest: but when thou shalt be old, thou shalt stretch forth thy hands, and another shall gird thee, and carry thee whither thou wouldest not. *Ib.* 18.

The disciple whom Jesus loved. *Ib.* 20.

What shall this man do?
Jesus saith unto him, If I will that he tarry till I come,
what is that to thee?   *St. John* xxi. 21.

The former treatise have I made, O Theophilus.
       The Acts of the Apostles i. 1.

Ye men of Galilee, why stand ye gazing up into
heaven?   *Ib.* 11.

His bishoprick let another take.   *Ib.* 20.

A rushing mighty wind.   *Ib.* ii. 2.

Cloven tongues like as of fire.   *Ib.* 3.

Parthians, and Medes, and Elamites, and the dwellers
in Mesopotamia, and in Judæa, and Cappadocia,
in Pontus, and Asia,
Phrygia, and Pamphylia, in Egypt, and in the parts
of Libya about Cyrene, and strangers of Rome,
Jews and proselytes,
Cretes and Arabians, we do hear them speak in our
tongues the wonderful works of God.   *Ib.* 9.

Silver and gold have I none; but such as I have give
I thee.   *Ib.* iii. 6.

I wot that through ignorance ye did it.   *Ib.* 17.

They took knowledge of them that they had been
with Jesus.   *Ib.* iv. 13.

Barnabas, . . . the son of consolation.   *Ib.* 36.

We ought to obey God rather than men. *Ib.* v. 29.

If this counsel or this work be of men, it will come to
nought:
But if it be of God, ye cannot overthrow it; lest
haply ye be found to fight against God.   *Ib.* 38.

It is not reason that we should leave the word of God,
and serve tables.   *Ib.* vi. 2.

The witnesses laid down their clothes at a young
man's feet, whose name was Saul.   *Ib.* vii. 58.

Saul was consenting unto his death.   *Ib.* viii. 1.

Thy money perish with thee.   *Ib.* 20.

Thou hast neither part nor lot in this matter. *Ib.* 21.

In the gall of bitterness, and in the bond of iniquity.
       Ib. 23.

Understandest thou what thou readest? . . .
How can I, except some man should guide me?
       Ib. 30.

Breathing out threatenings and slaughter. *Ib.* ix. 1.

Saul, Saul, why persecutest thou me?   *Ib.* 4.

It is hard for thee to kick against the pricks. *Ib.* 5.

The street which is called Straight.   *Ib.* 11.

Full of good works.   *Ib.* 36.

One Simon a tanner.   *Ib.* 43.

As it had been a great sheet knit at the four corners,
and let down to the earth.   *Ib.* x. 11.

What God hath cleansed, that call not thou common.
       Ib. 15.

God is no respecter of persons.   *Ib.* 34.

It is the voice of a god, and not of a man.
       Ib. xii. 22.

He was eaten of worms, and gave up the ghost.
       Ib. 23.

The gods are come down to us in the likeness of men.
       Ib. xiv. 11.

We also are men of like passions with you. *Ib.* 15.

Come over into Macedonia, and help us.
       Ib. xvi. 9.

Lydia, a seller of purple, of the city of Thyatira.
       Ib. 14.

A certain damsel possessed with a spirit of divination.
       Ib. 16.

Certain lewd fellows of the baser sort. *Ib.* xvii. 5.

These that have turned the world upside down.
       Ib. 6.

What will this babbler say?   *Ib.* 18.

For all the Athenians and strangers which were there
spent their time in nothing else, but either to tell,
or to hear some new thing.   *Ib.* 21.

Ye men of Athens, I perceive that in all things ye are
too superstitious. For as I passed by, and beheld
your devotions, I found an altar with this inscription, TO THE UNKNOWN GOD. Whom therefore ye
ignorantly worship, him declare I unto you.
       Ib. 23.

For in him we live, and move, and have our being.
       Ib. 28.

As certain also of your own poets have said.   *Ib.*

Gallio cared for none of those things. *Ib.* xviii. 17.

Mighty in the scriptures.   *Ib.* 24.

We have not so much as heard whether there be any
Holy Ghost.   *Ib.* xix. 2.

Demetrius, a silversmith.   *Ib.* 24.

Some therefore cried one thing, and some another:
for the assembly was confused; and the more part
knew not wherefore they were come together.
       Ib. 32.

All with one voice about the space of two hours cried
out, Great is Diana of the Ephesians.   *Ib.* 34.

For we are in danger to be called in question for this
day's uproar.   *Ib.* 42.

I go bound in the spirit unto Jerusalem. *Ib.* xx. 22.

It is more blessed to give than to receive.   *Ib.* 35.

A citizen of no mean city.   *Ib.* xxi. 39.

Brought up in this city at the feet of Gamaliel.
       Ib. xxii. 3.

And the chief captain answered, With a great sum
obtained I this freedom. And Paul said, But I was
free born.   *Ib.* 28.

God shall smite thee, thou whited wall. *Ib.* xxiii. 3.

Revilest thou God's high priest?   *Ib.* 4.

I am a Pharisee, the son of a Pharisee.   *Ib.* 6.

A conscience void of offence toward God, and toward
men.   *Ib.* xxiv. 16.

I appeal unto Cæsar.   *Ib.* xxv. 11.

Hast thou appealed unto Caesar? Unto Caesar shalt
thou go.   *The Acts of the Apostles* xxv. 12.

I think myself happy, king Agrippa.   *Ib.* xxvi. 2.

After the most straitest sect of our religion I lived a
Pharisee.   *Ib.* 5.

Paul, thou art beside thyself; much learning doth
make thee mad.   *Ib.* 24.

Words of truth and soberness.   *Ib.* 25.

For this thing was not done in a corner.   *Ib.* 26.

Almost thou persuadest me to be a Christian. *Ib.* 28.

I would to God, that not only thou, but also all that
hear me this day, were both almost, and altogether
such as I am, except these bonds.   *Ib.* 29.

They used helps, undergirding the ship *Ib.* xxvii. 17.

They cast four anchors out of the stern, and wished
for the day.   *Ib.* 29.

Without ceasing I make mention of you always in my
prayers.
        The Epistle of Paul to the Romans, i. 9.

The just shall live by faith.   *Ib.* 17.

Worshipped and served the creature more than the
Creator.   *Ib.* 25.

Patient continuance in well doing.   *Ib.* ii. 7.

For there is no respect of persons with God. *Ib.* 11.

These . . . are a law unto themselves.   *Ib.* 14.

Let God be true, but every man a liar.   *Ib.* iii. 4.

Let us do evil, that good may come.   *Ib.* 8.

For all have sinned, and come short of the glory of
God.   *Ib.* 23.

For where no law is, there is no transgression.
                                          Ib. iv. 15.

Who against hope believed in hope.   *Ib.* 18.

Hope maketh not ashamed.   *Ib.* v. 5.

Where sin abounded, grace did much more abound.
                                          Ib. 20.

Shall we continue in sin, that grace may abound?
                                          Ib. vi. 1.

We also should walk in newness of life.   *Ib.* 4.

Christ being raised from the dead dieth no more;
death hath no more dominion over him.
For in that he died, he died unto sin once: but in that
he liveth, he liveth unto God.   *Ib.* 9.

The wages of sin is death.   *Ib.* 23.

Is the law sin? God forbid. Nay, I had not known
sin, but by the law.   *Ib.* vii. 7.

Now then it is no more I that do it, but sin that
dwelleth in me.   *Ib.* 17.

For the good that I would I do not; but the evil which
I would not, that I do.   *Ib.* 19.

I find then a law, that, when I would do good, evil is
present with me.   *Ib.* 21.

O wretched man that I am! who shall deliver me from
the body of this death?   *Ib.* 24.

They that are after the flesh do mind the things of
the flesh; but they that are after the Spirit the things
of the Spirit.
For to be carnally minded is death.   *Ib.* viii. 5.

For ye have not received the spirit of bondage again
to fear; but ye have received the Spirit of adoption,
whereby we cry, Abba, Father.   *Ib.* 15.

We are the children of God:
And if children, then heirs; heirs of God, and joint-
heirs with Christ.   *Ib.* 16.

For we know that the whole creation groaneth and
travaileth in pain together until now.   *Ib.* 22.

All things work together for good to them that love
God.   *Ib.* 28.

If God be for us, who can be against us?   *Ib.* 31.

For I am persuaded, that neither death, nor life, nor
angels, nor principalities, nor powers, nor things
present, nor things to come,
Nor height, nor depth, nor any other creature, shall
be able to separate us from the love of God, which
is in Jesus Christ our Lord.   *Ib.* 38.

I could wish that myself were accursed from Christ
for my brethren, my kinsmen according to the
flesh.   *Ib.* ix. 3.

Hath not the potter power over the clay, of the same
lump to make one vessel unto honour, and another
unto dishonour?   *Ib.* 21.

A zeal of God, but not according to knowledge.
                                          Ib. x. 2.

I beseech you therefore, brethren, by the mercies of
God, that ye present your bodies a living sacrifice,
holy, acceptable unto God.   *Ib.* xii. 1.

Let love be without dissimulation.   *Ib.* 9.

Be kindly affectioned one to another with brotherly
love: in honour preferring one another;
Not slothful in business; fervent in spirit; serving
the Lord.   *Ib.* 10.

Given to hospitality.   *Ib.* 13

Rejoice with them that do rejoice, and weep with
them that weep.   *Ib.* 15.

Mind not high things, but condescend to men of low
estate. Be not wise in your conceits.   *Ib.* 16.

Vengeance is mine; I will repay, saith the Lord.
                                          Ib. 19.

Be not overcome of evil, but overcome evil with good.
                                          Ib. 21.

Let every soul be subject unto the higher powers.
                                          Ib. xiii. 1.

The powers that be are ordained of God.   *Ib.*

For rulers are not a terror to good works, but to the
evil.   *Ib.* 3.

Render therefore to all their dues: tribute to whom
tribute is due; custom to whom custom; fear to
whom fear; honour to whom honour.
Owe no man anything, but to love one another: for he
that loveth another hath fulfilled the law.   *Ib.* 7.

Love is the fulfilling of the law.   *Ib.* 10.

Now it is high time to awake out of sleep: for now is our salvation nearer than when we believed.

The night is far spent, the day is at hand: let us therefore cast off the works of darkness, and let us put on the armour of light. *Romans* xiii. 11.

Make not provision for the flesh, to fulfil the lusts thereof. *Ib.* 14.

Doubtful disputations. *Ib.* xiv. 1.

Let every man be fully persuaded in his own mind. *Ib.* 5.

We then that are strong ought to bear the infirmities of the weak, and not to please ourselves. *Ib.* xv. 1.

Salute one another with an holy kiss. *Ib.* xvi. 16.

The foolishness of preaching.
First Epistle of Paul to the Corinthians i. 21.

God hath chosen the foolish things of the world to confound the wise; and God hath chosen the weak things of the world to confound the things which are mighty. *Ib.* 27.

I determined not to know any thing among you, save Jesus Christ, and him crucified. *Ib.* ii. 2.

I have planted, Apollos watered; but God gave the increase. *Ib.* iii. 6.

Every man's work shall be made manifest. *Ib.* 13.

Stewards of the mysteries of God. *Ib.* iv. 1.

A spectacle unto the world, and to angels. *Ib.* 9.

Absent in body, but present in spirit. *Ib.* v. 3.

Know ye not that a little leaven leaveneth the whole lump? *Ib.* 6.

Christ our passover is sacrificed for us:
Therefore let us keep the feast, not with the old leaven, neither with the leaven of malice and wickedness; but with the unleavened bread of sincerity and truth. *Ib.* 7.

Your body is the temple of the Holy Ghost. *Ib.* vi. 19.

It is better to marry than to burn. *Ib.* vii. 9.

The unbelieving husband is sanctified by the wife. *Ib.* 14.

The fashion of this world passeth away. *Ib.* 31.

Knowledge puffeth up, but charity edifieth. *Ib.* viii. 1.

Who goeth a warfare any time at his own charges? who planteth a vineyard, and eateth not of the fruit thereof? *Ib.* ix. 7.

I am made all things to all men. *Ib.* 22.

Know ye not that they which run in a race run all, but one receiveth the prize? *Ib.* 24.

Now they do it to obtain a corruptible crown; but we an incorruptible.
I therefore so run, not as uncertainly: so fight I, not as one that beateth the air:
But I keep under my body, and bring it into subjection: lest that by any means, when I have preached to others, I myself should be a castaway. *Ib.* 25.

Let him that thinketh he standeth take heed lest he fall.

There hath no temptation taken you but such as is common to man: but God is faithful, who will not suffer you to be tempted above that ye are able; but will with the temptation also make a way to escape, that ye may be able to bear it *Ib.* x. 12.

All things are lawful for me, but all things are not expedient. *Ib.* 23.

For the earth is the Lord's, and the fulness thereof. *Ib.* 26.

Whether therefore ye eat, or drink, or whatsoever ye do, do all to the glory of God. *Ib.* 31.

If a woman have long hair, it is a glory to her. *Ib.* xi. 15.

Now there are diversities of gifts, but the same Spirit. *Ib.* xii. 4.

Though I speak with the tongues of men and of angels, and have not charity, I am become as sounding brass, or a tinkling cymbal. *Ib.* xiii. 1.

Though I have all faith, so that I could remove mountains, and have not charity, I am nothing.
And though I bestow all my goods to feed the poor, and though I give my body to be burned, and have not charity, it profiteth me nothing.
Charity suffereth long, and is kind; charity envieth not; charity vaunteth not itself, is not puffed up,
Doth not behave itself unseemly, seeketh not her own, is not easily provoked, thinketh no evil;
Rejoiceth not in iniquity, but rejoiceth in the truth;
Beareth all things, believeth all things, hopeth all things, endureth all things.
Charity never faileth: but whether there be prophecies, they shall fail; whether there be tongues, they shall cease; whether there be knowledge, it shall vanish away.
For we know in part, and we prophesy in part. *Ib.* 2.

When I was a child, I spake as a child, I understood as a child, I thought as a child: but when I became a man, I put away childish things.
For now we see through a glass, darkly; but then face to face: now I know in part; but then shall I know even as also I am known.
And now abideth faith, hope, charity, these three; but the greatest of these is charity. *Ib.* 11.

If the trumpet give an uncertain sound, who shall prepare himself to the battle? *Ib.* xiv. 8.

Let your women keep silence in the churches: for it is not permitted unto them to speak. *Ib.* 34.

If they will learn any thing, let them ask their husbands at home: for it is a shame for women to speak in the church. *Ib.* 35.

Let all things be done decently and in order. *Ib.* 40.

Last of all he was seen of me also, as of one born out of due time.
For I am the least of the apostles, that am not meet to be called an apostle, because I persecuted the church of God.
But by the grace of God I am what I am. *Ib.* xv. 8.

I laboured more abundantly than they all: yet not I, but the grace of God which was with me. *Ib.* 10.

We are of all men most miserable. *Ib.* 19.

But now is Christ risen from the dead, and become the firstfruits of them that slept.

For since by man came death, by man came also the resurrection of the dead.

For as in Adam all die, even so in Christ shall all be made alive.   *1 Corinthians* xv. 20.

The last enemy that shall be destroyed is death.
Ib. 26.

If after the manner of men I have fought with beasts at Ephesus.   *Ib.* 32.

Let us eat and drink; for to morrow we die.   *Ib.*

Evil communications corrupt good manners. *Ib.* 33.

One star differeth from another star in glory. *Ib.* 41.

It is sown in corruption; it is raised in incorruption.
Ib. 42.

The first man is of the earth, earthy.   *Ib.* 47.

Behold, I shew you a mystery; We shall not all sleep, but we shall all be changed,

In a moment, in the twinkling of an eye, at the last trump.   *Ib.* 51.

For this corruptible must put on incorruption, and this mortal must put on immortality.   *Ib.* 53.

O death, where is thy sting? O grave, where is thy victory?   *Ib.* 55.

Quit you like men, be strong.   *Ib.* xvi. 13.

Let him be Anathema Maran-atha.   *Ib.* 22.

Fleshy tables of the heart.
Second Epistle of Paul to the Corinthians iii. 3.

Not of the letter, but of the spirit; for the letter killeth, but the spirit giveth life.   *Ib.* 6.

We have this treasure in earthen vessels. *Ib.* iv. 7.

An house not made with hands, eternal in the heavens.
Ib. v. 1.

We walk by faith, not by sight.   *Ib.* 7.

The love of Christ constraineth us.   *Ib.* 14.

Now is the accepted time.   *Ib.* vi. 2.

By honour and dishonour, by evil report and good report.   *Ib.* 8.

As having nothing, and yet possessing all things.
Ib. 10.

Without were fightings, within were fears.
Ib. vii. 5.

God loveth a cheerful giver.   *Ib.* ix. 7.

For ye suffer fools gladly, seeing ye yourselves are wise.   *Ib.* xi. 19.

Are they Hebrews? so am I. Are they Israelites? so am I. Are they the seed of Abraham? so am I. Are they ministers of Christ? (I speak as a fool) I am more.   *Ib.* 22.

Five times received I forty stripes save one. *Ib.* 24.

In perils in the city, in perils in the wilderness, in perils in the sea, in perils among false brethren.
Ib. 26.

Whether in the body, I cannot tell; or whether out of the body, I cannot tell: God knoweth. *Ib.* xii. 2.

There was given to me a thorn in the flesh, the messenger of Satan to buffet me.   *Ib.* 7.

My strength is made perfect in weakness.   *Ib.* 9.

In the mouth of two or three witnesses shall every word be established.   *Ib.* xiii. 1.

The right hands of fellowship.
Epistle of Paul to the Galatians ii. 9.

O foolish Galatians, who hath bewitched you?
Ib. iii. 1.

Weak and beggarly elements.   *Ib.* iv. 9.

Which things are an allegory.   *Ib.* 24.

Ye are fallen from grace.   *Ib.* v. 4.

For the flesh lusteth against the Spirit, and the Spirit against the flesh . . . so that ye cannot do the things that ye would.   *Ib.* 17.

But the fruit of the Spirit is love, joy, peace, long-suffering, gentleness, goodness, faith,

Meekness, temperance.   *Ib.* 22.

Be not deceived; God is not mocked: for whatsoever a man soweth, that shall he also reap.   *Ib.* vi. 7.

Let us not be weary in well doing: for in due season we shall reap, if we faint not.   *Ib.* 9.

Ye see how large a letter I have written unto you with mine own hand.   *Ib.* 11.

You hath he quickened, who were dead in trespasses and sins.   *Epistle of Paul to the Ephesians* ii. 1.

Middle wall of partition.   *Ib.* 14.

Preached peace to you which were afar off, and to them that were nigh.   *Ib.* 17.

The unsearchable riches of Christ.   *Ib.* iii. 8.

To be strengthened with might by his Spirit in the inner man.   *Ib.* 16.

The love of Christ, which passeth knowledge. *Ib.* 19.

Him that is able to do exceeding abundantly above all that we ask or think.   *Ib.* 20.

Worthy of the vocation wherewith ye are called.
Ib. iv. 1.

Carried about with every wind of doctrine.   *Ib.* 14.

We are members one of another.   *Ib.* 25.

Be ye angry, and sin not: let not the sun go down upon your wrath.   *Ib.* 26.

Nor foolish talking, nor jesting, which are not convenient.   *Ib.* v. 4.

Let no man deceive you with vain words: for because of these things cometh the wrath of God upon the children of disobedience.   *Ib.* 6.

Redeeming the time, because the days are evil. *Ib.* 16.

Psalms and hymns and spiritual songs.   *Ib.* 19.

Wives, submit yourselves unto your own husbands, as unto the Lord.   *Ib.* 22.

The first commandment with promise. *Ib.* vi. 2.

Ye fathers, provoke not your children to wrath.
Ib. 4.

Not with eyeservice, as menpleasers. *Ephesians* vi. 6.

Put on the whole armour of God. *Ib.* 11.

For we wrestle not against flesh and blood, but against principalities, against powers, against the rulers of the darkness of this world, against spiritual wickedness in high places.

Wherefore take unto you the whole armour of God, that ye may be able to withstand in the evil day, and having done all, to stand. *Ib.* 12.

Your feet shod with the preparation of the gospel of peace. *Ib.* 15.

The shield of faith, wherewith ye shall be able to quench all the fiery darts of the wicked. *Ib.* 16.

For me to live is Christ, and to die is gain.
Epistle of Paul to the Philippians i. 21.

Having a desire to depart, and to be with Christ; which is far better. *Ib.* 23.

But made himself of no reputation, and took upon him the form of a servant, and was made in the likeness of men. *Ib.* ii. 7.

Given him a name which is above every name:
That at the name of Jesus every knee should bow. *Ib.* 9.

Work out your own salvation with fear and trembling. *Ib.* 12.

An Hebrew of the Hebrews; as touching the law, a Pharisee. *Ib.* iii. 5.

But what things were gain to me, those I counted loss for Christ. *Ib.* 7.

If by any means I might attain unto the resurrection of the dead. *Ib.* 11.

Forgetting those things which are behind, and reaching forth unto those things which are before,
I press toward the mark. *Ib.* 13.

Whose God is their belly, and whose glory is in their shame. *Ib.* 19.

Rejoice in the Lord alway: and again I say, Rejoice. *Ib.* iv. 4.

The peace of God, which passeth all understanding. *Ib.* 7.

Whatsoever things are true, whatsoever things are honest, whatsoever things are just, whatsoever things are pure, whatsoever things are lovely, whatsoever things are of good report; if there be any virtue, and if there be any praise, think on these things. *Ib.* 8.

I can do all things through Christ which strengtheneth me. *Ib.* 13.

Touch not; taste not; handle not.
Epistle of Paul to the Colossians ii. 21.

Set your affection on things above, not on things on the earth. *Ib.* iii. 2.

Where there is neither Greek nor Jew, circumcision nor uncircumcision, Barbarian, Scythian, bond nor free: but Christ is all, and in all. *Ib.* 11.

Husbands, love your wives, and be not bitter against them. *Ib.* 19.

Let your speech be alway with grace, seasoned with salt. *Ib.* iv. 6.

Luke, the beloved physician. *Ib.* 14.

Labour of love.
First Epistle of Paul to the Thessalonians i. 3.

Study to be quiet, and to do your own business. *Ib.* iv. 11.

Pray without ceasing. *Ib.* v. 17.

Prove all things; hold fast that which is good. *Ib.* 21.

If any would not work, neither should he eat.
Second Epistle of Paul to the Thessalonians iii. 10.

Be not weary in well doing. *Ib.* 13.

Fables and endless genealogies.
First Epistle of Paul to Timothy i. 4.

I did it ignorantly in unbelief. *Ib.* 13.

Sinners; of whom I am chief. *Ib.* 15.

If a man desire the office of a bishop, he desireth a good work. *Ib.* iii. 1.

Not greedy of filthy lucre. *Ib.* 3.

For every creature of God is good, and nothing to be refused, if it be received with thanksgiving. *Ib.* iv. 4.

Old wives' fables. *Ib.* 7.

Worse than an infidel. *Ib.* v. 8.

Tattlers also and busybodies, speaking things which they ought not. *Ib.* 13.

Drink no longer water, but use a little wine for thy stomach's sake and thine often infirmities. *Ib.* 23.

For we brought nothing into this world, and it is certain we can carry nothing out. *Ib.* vi. 7.

The love of money is the root of all evil. *Ib.* 10.

Fight the good fight of faith, lay hold on eternal life. *Ib.* 12.

Rich in good works. *Ib.* 18.

Science falsely so called. *Ib.* 20.

For God hath not given us the spirit of fear; but of power, and of love, and of a sound mind.
Second Epistle of Paul to Timothy i. 7.

Hold fast the form of sound words. *Ib.* 13.

From a child thou hast known the holy scriptures. *Ib.* iii. 15.

Be instant in season, out of season. *Ib.* iv. 2.

I have fought a good fight, I have finished my course, I have kept the faith. *Ib.* 7.

For Demas hath forsaken me, having loved this present world. *Ib.* 10.

Only Luke is with me. *Ib.* 11.

Alexander the coppersmith did me much evil: the Lord reward him according to his works. *Ib.* 14.

Unto the pure all things are pure.
Epistle of Paul to Titus i. 15.

Being such an one as Paul the aged, and now also a prisoner of Jesus Christ.
Epistle of Paul to Philemon 9.

At sundry times and in divers manners.
Epistle of Paul to the Hebrews i. 1.

The brightness of his glory, and the express image of his person. *Ib.* 3.

For the word of God is quick, and powerful, and sharper than any twoedged sword, piercing even to the dividing asunder of soul and spirit.
Ib. iv. 12.

They crucify to themselves the Son of God afresh, and put him to an open shame. *Ib.* vi. 6.

Without shedding of blood is no remission.
Ib. ix. 22.

Nor forsaking the assembling of ourselves together, as the manner of some is. *Ib.* x. 25.

It is a fearful thing to fall into the hands of the living God. *Ib.* 31.

Faith is the substance of things hoped for, the evidence of things not seen. *Ib.* xi. 1.

For he looked for a city which hath foundations.
Ib. 10.

These all died in faith. *Ib.* 13.

Esteeming the reproach of Christ greater riches than the treasures in Egypt. *Ib.* 26.

Of whom the world was not worthy. *Ib.* 38.

Wherefore seeing we also are compassed about with so great a cloud of witnesses, let us lay aside every weight, and the sin which doth so easily beset us, and let us run with patience the race that is set before us,
Looking unto Jesus the author and finisher of our faith. *Ib.* xii. 1.

Whom the Lord loveth he chasteneth. *Ib.* 6.

He found no place of repentance, though he sought it carefully with tears. *Ib.* 17.

The spirits of just men made perfect. *Ib.* 23.

Let brotherly love continue.
Be not forgetful to entertain strangers: for thereby some have entertained angels unawares. *Ib.* xiii. 1.

Jesus Christ the same yesterday, and to day, and for ever. *Ib.* 8.

For here have we no continuing city, but we seek one to come. *Ib.* 14.

To do good and to communicate forget not. *Ib.* 16.

Let patience have her perfect work.
General Epistle of James i. 4.

If any of you lack wisdom, let him ask of God, that giveth to all men liberally, and upbraideth not. *Ib.* 5.

Blessed is the man that endureth temptation; for when he is tried, he shall receive the crown of life.
Ib. 12.

Every good gift and every perfect gift is from above, and cometh down from the Father of lights, with whom is no variableness, neither shadow of turning.
Ib. 17.

Be swift to hear, slow to speak, slow to wrath:
For the wrath of man worketh not the righteousness of God. *Ib.* 19.

Superfluity of naughtiness. *Ib.* 21.

Be ye doers of the word, and not hearers only.
Ib. 22.

If any be a hearer of the word, and not a doer, he is like unto a man beholding his natural face in a glass:
For he beholdeth himself, and goeth his way, and straightway forgetteth what manner of man he was.
Ib. 23.

If any man among you seem to be religious, and bridleth not his tongue, but deceiveth his own heart, this man's religion is vain.
Pure religion and undefiled before God and the Father is this, To visit the fatherless and widows in their affliction, and to keep himself unspotted from the world. *Ib.* 26.

Faith without works is dead. *Ib.* ii. 20.

How great a matter a little fire kindleth! *Ib.* iii. 5.

The tongue can no man tame; it is an unruly evil.
Ib. 8.

Doth a fountain send forth at the same place sweet water and bitter? *Ib.* 11.

This wisdom descendeth not from above, but is earthly, sensual, devilish. *Ib.* 15.

Resist the devil, and he will flee from you.
Ib. iv. 7.

For what is your life? It is even a vapour, that appeareth for a little time, and then vanisheth away. *Ib.* 14.

Ye have heard of the patience of Job. *Ib.* v. 11.

Let your yea be yea; and your nay, nay. *Ib.* 12.

Whom having not seen, ye love.
First Epistle General of Peter i. 8.

All flesh is as grass, and all the glory of man is the flower of grass. The grass withereth, and the flower thereof falleth away. *Ib.* 24.

As newborn babes, desire the sincere milk of the word.
Ib. ii. 2.

But ye are a chosen generation, a royal priesthood, an holy nation, a peculiar people. *Ib.* 9.

Abstain from fleshly lusts, which war against the soul.
Ib. 11.

Honour all men. Love the brotherhood. Fear God. Honour the king. *Ib.* 17.

For what glory is it, if, when ye be buffeted for your faults, ye shall take it patiently? but if, when ye do well, and suffer for it, ye take it patiently, this is acceptable with God. *Ib.* 20.

The Shepherd and Bishop of your souls. *Ib.* 25.

Ornament of a meek and quiet spirit. *Ib.* iii. 4.

Giving honour unto the wife, as unto the weaker vessel. *Ib.* 7.

Not rendering evil for evil, or railing for railing: but contrariwise blessing. *Ib.* 9.

The end of all things is at hand. *Ib.* iv. 7.

Charity shall cover the multitude of sins. *Ib.* 8.

Be sober, be vigilant; because your adversary the devil, as a roaring lion, walketh about, seeking whom he may devour. *1 Peter* v. 8.

And the day star arise in your hearts.
Second Epistle General of Peter i. 19.

Not afraid to speak evil of dignities. *Ib.* ii. 10.

The dog is turned to his own vomit again. *Ib.* 22.

If we say that we have no sin, we deceive ourselves, and the truth is not in us.
First Epistle General of John i. 8.

But whoso hath this world's good, and seeth his brother have need, and shutteth up his bowels of compassion from him, how dwelleth the love of God in him? *Ib.* iii. 17.

He that loveth not knoweth not God; for God is love.
Ib. iv. 8.

No man hath seen God at any time. *Ib.* 12.

There is no fear in love; but perfect love casteth out fear. *Ib.* 18.

If a man say, I love God, and hateth his brother, he is a liar: for he that loveth not his brother whom he hath seen, how can he love God whom he hath not seen? *Ib.* 20.

The elder unto the elect lady.
Second Epistle of John 1.

Yet Michael the archangel, when contending with the devil he disputed about the body of Moses, durst not bring against him a railing accusation.
General Epistle of Jude 9.

Spots in your feasts of charity. *Ib.* 12.

Clouds they are without water, carried about of winds.
Ib.

Raging waves of the sea, foaming out their own shame; wandering stars, to whom is reserved the blackness of darkness for ever. *Ib.* 13.

John to the seven churches which are in Asia: Grace be unto you, and peace, from him which is, and which was, and which is to come.
The Revelation of St. John the Divine i. 4.

Behold, he cometh with clouds; and every eye shall see him, and they also which pierced him: and all kindreds of the earth shall wail because of him. Even so, Amen.

I am Alpha and Omega, the beginning and the ending, saith the Lord. *Ib.* 7.

I John, who also am your brother, and companion in tribulation, and in the kingdom and patience of Jesus Christ, was in the isle that is called Patmos, for the word of God, and for the testimony of Jesus Christ.

I was in the spirit on the Lord's day, and heard behind me a great voice, as of a trumpet. *Ib.* 9.

What thou seest, write in a book, and send it unto the seven churches which are in Asia. *Ib.* 11.

Being turned, I saw seven golden candlesticks.
Ib. 12.

Clothed with a garment down to the foot, and girt about the paps with a golden girdle. *Ib.* 13.

His head and his hairs were white like wool, as white as snow; and his eyes were as a flame of fire;

And his feet like unto fine brass, as if they burned in a furnace; and his voice as the sound of many waters.

And he had in his right hand seven stars: and out of his mouth went a sharp twoedged sword: and his countenance was as the sun shineth in his strength.
And when I saw him, I fell at his feet as dead. *Ib.* 14.

I am he that liveth, and was dead; and, behold, I am alive for evermore, Amen; and have the keys of hell and of death. *Ib.* 18.

I have somewhat against thee, because thou hast left thy first love. *Ib.* ii. 4.

Be thou faithful unto death, and I will give thee a crown of life. *Ib.* 10.

I ... will give him a white stone, and in the stone a new name written, which no man knoweth saving he that receiveth it. *Ib.* 17.

I will not blot out his name out of the book of life.
Ib. iii. 5.

I will write upon him my new name. *Ib.* 12.

I know thy works, that thou art neither cold nor hot: I would thou wert cold or hot.
So then because thou art lukewarm, and neither cold nor hot, I will spue thee out of my mouth. *Ib.* 15.

Behold, I stand at the door, and knock. *Ib.* 20.

And he that sat was to look upon like a jasper and a sardine stone: and there was a rainbow round about the throne, in sight like unto an emerald. *Ib.* iv. 3.

And before the throne there was a sea of glass like unto crystal: and in the midst of the throne, and round about the throne, were four beasts full of eyes before and behind. *Ib.* 6.

They were full of eyes within: and they rest not day and night, saying, Holy, holy, holy, Lord God Almighty, which was, and is, and is to come. *Ib.* 8.

Thou hast created all things, and for thy pleasure they are and were created. *Ib.* 11.

Who is worthy to open the book, and to loose the seals thereof? *Ib.* v. 2.

A Lamb as it had been slain, having seven horns and seven eyes. *Ib.* 6.

Golden vials full of odours, which are the prayers of saints. *Ib.* 8.

He went forth conquering, and to conquer. *Ib.* vi. 2.

A measure of wheat for a penny, and three measures of barley for a penny; and see thou hurt not the oil and the wine. *Ib.* 6.

And I looked, and behold a pale horse: and his name that sat on him was Death. *Ib.* 8.

How long, O Lord, holy and true, dost thou not judge and avenge our blood on them that dwell on the earth? *Ib.* 10.

And the stars of heaven fell unto the earth, even as a fig-tree casteth her untimely figs, when she is shaken of a mighty wind. *Ib.* 13.

Said to the mountains and rocks, Fall on us, and hide us from the face of him that sitteth on the throne, and from the wrath of the Lamb. *Revelation* vi. 16.

A great multitude, which no man could number, of all nations, and kindreds, and people, and tongues. *Ib.* vii. 9.

And all the angels stood round about the throne, and about the elders and the four beasts, and fell before the throne on their faces, and worshipped God. *Ib.* 11.

And one of the elders answered, saying unto me, What are these which are arrayed in white robes? and whence came they? *Ib.* 13.

These are they which came out of great tribulation, and have washed their robes, and made them white in the blood of the Lamb. *Ib.* 14.

They shall hunger no more, neither thirst any more; neither shall the sun light on them, nor any heat. *Ib.* 16.

God shall wipe away all tears from their eyes. *Ib.* 17.

There was silence in heaven about the space of half an hour. *Ib.* viii. 1.

And the name of the star is called Wormwood. *Ib.* 11.

Those men which have not the seal of God in their foreheads. *Ib.* ix. 4.

And in those days shall men seek death, and shall not find it; and shall desire to die, and death shall flee from them. *Ib.* 6.

And there were stings in their tails. *Ib.* 10.

It was in my mouth sweet as honey: and as soon as I had eaten it, my belly was bitter. *Ib.* x. 10.

The kingdoms of this world are become the kingdoms of our Lord, and of his Christ. *Ib.* xi. 15.

And there appeared a great wonder in heaven; a woman clothed with the sun, and the moon under her feet, and upon her head a crown of twelve stars. *Ib.* xii. 1.

And there was war in heaven: Michael and his angels fought against the dragon; and the dragon fought and his angels. *Ib.* 7.

The devil is come down unto you, having great wrath, because he knoweth that he hath but a short time. *Ib.* 12.

A time, and times, and half a time. *Ib.* 14.

Who is like unto the beast? who is able to make war with him? *Ib.* xiii. 4.

And that no man might buy or sell, save he that had the mark, or the name of the beast, or the number of his name. *Ib.* 17.

The number of the beast: for it is the number of a man; and his number is Six hundred threescore and six. *Ib.* 18.

They sung as it were a new song . . . and no man could learn that song but the hundred and forty and four thousand, which were redeemed from the earth. *Ib.* xiv. 3.

And in their mouth was found no guile: for they are without fault before the throne of God. *Ib.* 5.

Babylon is fallen, is fallen, that great city. *Ib.* 8.

And the smoke of their torment ascendeth up for ever and ever: and they have no rest day nor night, who worship the beast and his image. *Ib.* 11.

Blessed are the dead which die in the Lord from henceforth: Yea, saith the Spirit, that they may rest from their labours; and their works do follow them. *Ib.* 13.

And I saw as it were a sea of glass mingled with fire. *Ib.* xv. 2.

Behold, I come as a thief. *Ib.* xvi. 15.

And he gathered them together into a place called in the Hebrew tongue Armageddon. *Ib.* 16.

I will shew unto thee the judgment of the great whore that sitteth upon many waters. *Ib.* xvii. 1.

MYSTERY, BABYLON THE GREAT, THE MOTHER OF HARLOTS AND ABOMIN-ATIONS OF THE EARTH.

And I saw the woman drunken with the blood of the saints. *Ib.* 5.

And a mighty angel took up a stone like a great mill-stone, and cast it into the sea, saying, Thus with violence shall that great city Babylon be thrown down, and shall be found no more at all. *Ib.* xviii. 21.

Blessed are they which are called unto the marriage supper of the Lamb. *Ib.* xix. 9.

And I fell at his feet to worship him. And he said unto me, See thou do it not: I am thy fellow-servant. *Ib.* 10.

And I saw heaven opened, and behold a white horse; and he that sat upon him was called Faithful and True. *Ib.* 11.

And he hath on his vesture and on his thigh a name written, KING OF KINGS, AND LORD OF LORDS. *Ib.* 16.

The key of the bottomless pit. *Ib.* xx. 1.

And he laid hold on the dragon, that old serpent, which is the Devil, and Satan, and bound him a thousand years. *Ib.* 2.

On such the second death hath no power. *Ib.* 6.

And I saw a great white throne. *Ib.* 11.

And I saw the dead, small and great, stand before God; and the books were opened. *Ib.* 12.

And the sea gave up the dead which were in it. *Ib.* 13.

And I saw a new heaven and a new earth: for the first heaven and the first earth were passed away; and there was no more sea.

And I John saw the holy city, new Jerusalem, coming down from God out of heaven, prepared as a bride adorned for her husband. *Ib.* xxi. 1.

And God shall wipe away all tears from their eyes; and there shall be no more death, neither sorrow, nor crying, neither shall there be any more pain: for the former things are passed away.

And he that sat upon the throne said, Behold, I make all things new. And he said unto me, Write: for these words are true and faithful. *Ib.* 4.

I will give unto him that is athirst of the fountain of the water of life freely. *Ib.* 6.

The city was pure gold, like unto clear glass.
Revelation xxi. 18.

The first foundation was jasper; the second, sapphire; the third, a chalcedony; the fourth, an emerald;
The fifth, sardonyx; the sixth, sardius; the seventh, chrysolyte; the eighth, beryl; the ninth, a topaz; the tenth, a chrysoprasus; the eleventh, a jacinth; the twelfth, an amethyst. *Ib.* 19.

The twelve gates were twelve pearls. *Ib.* 21.

The street of the city was pure gold. *Ib.*

And I saw no temple therein. *Ib.* 22.

And the city had no need of the sun, neither of the moon, to shine in it: for the glory of God did lighten it, and the Lamb is the light thereof. *Ib.* 23.

And he shewed me a pure river of water of life, clear as crystal, proceeding out of the throne of God and of the Lamb. *Ib.* xxii. 1.

And the leaves of the tree were for the healing of the nations. *Ib.* 2.

He that is unjust, let him be unjust still: and he which is filthy, let him be filthy still: and he that is righteous, let him be righteous still: and he that is holy, let him be holy still.

And, behold, I come quickly. *Ib.* 11.

Whosoever loveth and maketh a lie. *Ib.* 15.

I am the root and the offspring of David, and the bright and morning star.
And the Spirit and the bride say, Come. And let him that heareth say, Come. And let him that is athirst come. And whosoever will, let him take the water of life freely. *Ib.* 16.

If any man shall add unto these things, God shall add unto him the plagues that are written in this book. *Ib.* 18.

God shall take away his part out of the book of life, and out of the holy city, and from the things which are written in this book. *Ib.* 19.

Amen. Even so, come, Lord Jesus. *Ib.* 20.

APOCRYPHA

The first wrote, Wine is the strongest.
The second wrote, The king is strongest.
The third wrote, Women are strongest: but above all things Truth beareth away the victory.
1 Esdras iii. 10.

Great is Truth, and mighty above all things. *Ib.* iv. 41.

I shall light a candle of understanding in thine heart.
2 Esdras xiv. 25.
The holy spirit of discipline.
The Wisdom of Solomon i. 5.

The ear of jealousy heareth all things. *Ib.* 10.

But the souls of the righteous are in the hand of God, and there shall no torment touch them.
In the sight of the unwise they seemed to die: and their departure is taken for misery,
And their going from us to be utter destruction: but they are in peace.
For though they be punished in the sight of men, yet is their hope full of immortality.
And having been a little chastised, they shall be greatly rewarded: for God proved them, and found them worthy for himself. *Ib.* iii. 1.

And in the time of their visitation they shall shine, and run to and fro like sparks among the stubble. *Ib.* 7.

Even so we in like manner, as soon as we were born, began to draw to our end. *Ib.* v. 13.

Passeth away as the remembrance of a guest that tarrieth but a day. *Ib.* 14.

O Lord, thou lover of souls. *Ib.* xi. 26.

For men, serving either calamity or tyranny, did ascribe unto stones and stocks the incommunicable name. *Ib.* xiv. 21.

Be not curious in unnecessary matters: for more things are shewed unto thee than men understand.
Ecclesiasticus iii. 23.

Be not ignorant of any thing in a great matter or a small. *Ib.* v. 15.

A faithful friend is the medicine of life. *Ib.* vi. 16.

Miss not the discourse of the elders. *Ib.* viii. 9.

Open not thine heart to every man. *Ib.* 19.

Give not thy soul unto a woman. *Ib.* ix. 2.

Forsake not an old friend; for the new is not comparable to him: a new friend is as new wine; when it is old, thou shalt drink it with pleasure. *Ib.* 10.

Judge none blessed before his death. *Ib.* xi. 28.

He that toucheth pitch shall be defiled therewith. *Ib.* xiii. 1.

For how agree the kettle and the earthen pot together? *Ib.* 2.

They received the use of the five operations of the Lord, and in the sixth place he imparted them understanding, and in the seventh speech, an interpreter of the cogitations thereof. *Ib.* xvii. 5.

Be not made a beggar by banqueting upon borrowing. *Ib.* xviii. 33.

He that contemneth small things shall fall by little and little. *Ib.* xix. 1.

All wickedness is but little to the wickedness of a woman. *Ib.* xxv. 19.

Neither [give] a wicked woman liberty to gad abroad. *Ib.* 25.
The stroke of the tongue breaketh the bones.
Many have fallen by the edge of the sword: but not so many as have fallen by the tongue. *Ib.* xxviii. 17.

Envy and wrath shorten the life. *Ib.* xxx. 24.

Leave off first for manners' sake. *Ib.* xxxi. 17.

Let thy speech be short, comprehending much in few words. *Ib.* xxxii. 8.

Leave not a stain in thine honour.   *Ib.* xxxiii. 22.

For of the most High cometh healing.   *Ib.* xxxviii. 2.

Let us now praise famous men, and our fathers that begat us.   *Ib.* xliv. 1.

Such as did bear rule in their kingdoms.   *Ib.* 3.

Such as found out musical tunes, and recited verses in writing:
Rich men furnished with ability, living peaceably in their habitations.   *Ib.* 5.

There be of them, that have left a name behind them.   *Ib.* 8.

And some there be, which have no memorial.   *Ib.* 9.

Their bodies are buried in peace; but their name liveth for evermore.   *Ib.* 14.

It is a foolish thing to make a long prologue, and to be short in the story itself.   2 *Maccabees* ii. 32.

When he was at the last gasp.   *Ib.* vii. 9.

It was an holy and good thought.   *Ib.* xii. 45.

ENGLISH LITERATURE

ANONYMOUS

A beast, but a just beast.
> *Of Dr. Temple, Headmaster of Rugby, 1857–69.*

Adam
Had 'em.   *On the Antiquity of Microbes. [Said to be the shortest poem.]*

All present and correct.
> *King's Regulations (Army). Report of the Orderly Sergeant to the Officer of the Day*

All quiet along the Potomac.
> *Originated in the American Civil War. Attr. to General McClellan.*

Always welcome, keep it handy,
Grant's Morella Cherry Brandy.   *Advertisement.*

An old Soldier of the Queen's,
And the Queen's old Soldier.
> *Merry Drollery, 1661–9. An Old Soldier of The Queen's. Oxford Book of 17th Cent. Verse.*

An old song made by an aged old pate,
Of an old worshipful gentleman who had a great estate.   *The Old Courtier.*

A precedent embalms a principle.
> *Attr. to William Scott, Baron Stowell, in an Opinion, while Advocate-General, 1788.*

A rainbow in the morning
Is the Shepherd's warning;
But a rainbow at night
Is the Shepherd's delight.   *Old Weather Rhyme.*

Are we downhearted? No!
> *Expression much used by British soldiers in War of 1914–18, probably based on remark of Joseph Chamberlain, q.v.*

As I sat on a sunny bank,
On Christmas Day in the morning,
I spied three ships come sailing by.
> *Carol: As I Sat on a Sunny Bank. Oxford Book of Carols.*

As Joseph was a-walking,
  He heard an angel sing:
'This night shall be born
  Our heavenly king.'
> *As Joseph was a-walking. Oxford Book of Carols.*

He neither shall be clothed
  In purple nor in pall,
But all in fair linen.
  As were babies all.

He neither shall be rock'd
  In silver nor in gold,
But in a wooden cradle
  That rocks on the mould.   *Ib.*

A swarm of bees in May
Is worth a load of hay;
A swarm of bees in June
Is worth a silver spoon;
A swarm of bees in July
Is not worth a fly.   *Old Rhyme.*

A very gallant gentleman.
> *Epitaph on Capt. Oates (1880–1912), inscribed by A. Cherry-Garrard and Surgeon Atkinson on the cross marking the approximate place of his death. Being almost crippled, he walked to his death in a blizzard to enable his companions to proceed faster on their journey.*

A willing foe and sea room.
> *Naval toast in the time of Nelson. Beckett, A Few Naval Customs, Expressions, Traditions, and Superstitions.*

Begone, dull care! I prithee begone from me!
Begone, dull care, you and I shall never agree.
> *Begone Dull Care.*

Be happy while y'er leevin,
For y'er a lang time deid.
> *Scottish Motto for a house. Notes and Queries, 7 Dec. 1901, p. 469.*

Better is a mess of pottage with love, than a fat ox with evil will.
> *Prov. xv, 17 (Matthew's Bible, 1535).*

Between the stirrup and the ground
I mercy ask'd, I mercy found.
> *Camden's Remains. Epitaph on a wicked man killed by a fall from his horse.*

Born 1820, still going strong.
> *Advertisement for Johnny Walker Whiskey.*

Bovril prevents that sinking feeling.   *Advertisement.*

Christmas is coming, the geese are getting fat,
Please to put a penny in the old man's hat;
If you haven't got a penny, a ha'penny will do,
If you haven't got a ha'penny, God bless you!
> *Beggar's Rhyme.*

Come, landlord, fill the flowing bowl
Until it doth run over. . . .
  For to-night we'll merry be,
  To-morrow we'll be sober.
> *Come, Landlord, Fill the Flowing Bowl. Oxford Song Book.*

Come lasses and lads, get leave of your dads,
And away to the Maypole hie,
For every he has got him a she,
And the fiddler's standing by.
For Willie shall dance with Jane,
And Johnny has got his Joan,
To trip it, trip it, trip it, trip it, trip it up and down.
> *Come Lasses and Lads. Oxford Song Book.*

Cuccu, cuccu, well singes thu, cuccu:
  Ne swike thu never nu;
Sing cuccu, nu, sing cuccu,
  Sing cuccu, sing cuccu, nu!   *Cuckoo Song, c. 1250.*

Dear Sir, Your astonishment's odd:
I am always about in the Quad.
  And that's why the tree
  Will continue to be,
Since observed by Yours faithfully, God.
> *Reply to limerick on Idealism, 'There was once a man who said "God . . .".' q.v.*

Defence, not defiance.
> *Motto of the Volunteers Movement, in 1859.*

Deprive mankind of their hope of eternal damnation.
> *Attr. to Lord Westbury.*

Dollar Diplomacy.
> *Term applied to Secretary Knox's activities in securing opportunities for the investment of American capital abroad, particularly in Latin America and China.* See *Harper's Weekly,* April 23rd, 1910, p. 8.

Dr. Brighton. *Advertisement.*

Dr. Williams' pink pills for pale people.
> *Advertisement.*

Early one morning, just as the sun was rising,
I heard a maid sing in the valley below:
'Oh, don't deceive me; Oh, never leave me!
How could you use a poor maiden so?'
> *Song: Early One Morning.*

Esau selleth his birthright for a mess of potage.
> *Genevan Bible: chapter heading to Genesis ch. 25.*

An intelligent Russian once remarked to us, 'Every country has its own constitution; ours is absolutism moderated by assassination.'
> Georg Herbert, Count Münster, *Political Sketches of the State of Europe, 1814–1867,* ed. 1868, p. 19.

Every minute dies a man,
And one and one-sixteenth is born.
> *Parody by a Statistician of Tennyson's Vision of Sin,* pt. iv, st. 9.

For he must be somebody's son.
> *Title of Music Hall Song.*

God be in my head,
And in my understanding;

God be in my eyes,
And in my looking;

God be in my mouth,
And in my speaking;

God be in my heart,
And in my thinking;

God be at my end,
And at my departing. *Sarum Missal.*

God rest you merry, gentlemen,
Let nothing you dismay.
> *Carol: God Rest You Merry.* Oxford Book of Carols.

O tidings of comfort and joy. *Ib.*

God save great *George* our King.
> *Harmoniana Anglica. The Gentleman's Magazine,* October 1745.

Good-morning! Have you used Pears' Soap?
> *Advertisement.*

Great Chatham with his sabre drawn
Stood waiting for Sir Richard Strachan;
Sir Richard, longing to be at 'em,
Stood waiting for the Earl of Chatham.
> *At Walcheren, 1809.*

Great God, what do I see and hear?
The end of things created.
> *Great God, What do I see.* Collyer's *Hymns: Partly Collected and Partly Original, 1812.*

Greensleeves was all my joy,
  Greensleeves was my delight,
Greensleeves was my heart of gold,
  And who but Lady Greensleeves?
> *A new Courtly Sonnet of the Lady Greensleeves, to the new tune of 'Greensleeves'.* From '*A Handful of Pleasant Delites*' (1584).

Ha-ha-ha, you and me,
Little brown jug, don't I love thee.
> *The Little Brown Jug.* Oxford Song Book.

Here lies Fred,
Who was alive and is dead:
Had it been his father,
I had much rather;
Had it been his brother,
Still better than another;
Had it been his sister,
No one would have missed her;
Had it been the whole generation,
Still better for the nation:
But since 'tis only Fred,
Who was alive and is dead,—
There's no more to be said.
> Horace Walpole, *Memoirs of George II (1882),* vol. i, p. 504.

Here's a health to all those that we love,
Here's a health to all those that love us,
Here's a health to all those that love them that love
  those
That love them that love those that love us.
> *Old Toast.*

Here we come a-wassailing. *Old Song.*

Here we come gathering nuts in May
  Nuts in May,
On a cold and frosty morning. *Children's Song.*

He talked shop like a tenth muse.
> *Of Gladstone's Budget speeches.* G. W. E. Russell's *Collections and Recollections,* ch. 12.

He that fights and runs away
May live to fight another day.
> *Musarum Deliciae, collected by Sir John Mennes and Dr. James Smith, 1656.*

He won't be happy till he gets it.
> *Advertisement for Pears' Soap.*

Hierusalem, my happy home,
  When shall I come to thee?
When shall my sorrows have an end,
  Thy joys when shall I see?
> *Hierusalem.* See *Songs of Praise Discussed.*

Homocea touches the spot. *Advertisement.*

I expect to pass through this world but once. Any good therefore that I can do, or any kindness that I can show to any fellow creature, let me do it now. Let me not defer or neglect it, for I shall not pass this way again.
> *Attr. to many people, probably most reliably to Stephen Grellet. Attributed to Edward Courtenay, Earl of Essex, owing to the resemblance of his epitaph.* See *Literary World,* March 15th, 1905.

I feel no pain dear mother now
But oh, I am so dry!
O take me to a brewery
And leave me there to die.
> C. Fox-Smith's *Book of Shanties,* 1927.

If the Lord Chancellor only knew a little law he
would know something of everything.
Of Lord Brougham. G. W. E. Russell's *Collections and Recollections*, ch. 11.

I know two things about the horse,
And one of them is rather coarse.
The Week-End Book.

In Dublin's fair city, where girls are so pretty,
I first set my eyes on sweet Molly Malone,
As she wheeled her wheelbarrow through streets
    broad and narrow,
Crying, Cockles and mussels! alive, alive, oh!
Cockles and Mussels. Oxford Song Book.

In good King Charles' golden days,
When loyalty no harm meant;
A furious High-Churchman I was,
And so I gain'd preferment.
Unto my flock I daily preach'd,
Kings are by God appointed,
And damned are those who dare resist,
Or touch the Lord's Anointed.
And this is law, I will maintain,
Unto my dying day, Sir,
That whatsoever King shall reign,
I will be the Vicar of Bray, Sir!
The Vicar of Bray. Brit. Musical Miscellany
(1734), i.

The Church of Rome I found would suit
Full well my constitution.   *Ib.*

I turned the cat in pan again,
And swore to him allegiance.   *Ib.*

When George in pudding time came o'er,
And moderate men look'd big, Sir.   *Ib.*

I saw my lady weep,
And Sorrow proud to be exalted so
In those fair eyes where all perfections keep.
Her face was full of woe;
But such a woe, believe me, as wins more hearts,
Than Mirth can do with her enticing parts.
Songs set by John Dowland, iii. *Oxford Book of
16th Cent. Verse.*

I saw three ships a-sailing there,
—A-sailing there, a-sailing there,
Jesu, Mary and Joseph they bare
On Christ's Sunday at morn.

Joseph did whistle and Mary did sing,
—Mary did sing, Mary did sing,
And all the bells on earth did ring
For joy Our Lord was born.

O they sail'd in to Bethlehem!
—To Bethlehem, to Bethlehem;
Saint Michael was the steresman,
Saint John sate in the horn.
I saw three ships. Oxford Book of Carols.

I sing of a maiden
That is makeless;
King of all kings
To her son she ches.
*Carol: I Sing of a Maiden. Oxford Book of
Carols.*

He came all so still
Where His mother was,
As dew in April
That falleth on the grass.   *Ib.*

Mother and maiden
Was never none but she!
Well may such a lady
God's mother be.   *Ib.*

The children of Lord Lytton organized a charade.
The scene displayed a Crusader knight returning
from the wars. At his gate he was welcomed by his
wife to whom he recounted his triumphs and the
number of heathen he had slain. His wife, pointing to a row of dolls of various sizes, replied with
pride, 'And I too, my lord, have not been idle'.
G. W. E. Russell's *Collections and Recollections*,
ch. 31.

It's a long time between drinks.
*The Governor of South Carolina required the
return of a fugitive slave. The Governor of
North Carolina hesitated because of powerful
friends of the fugitive. He gave a banquet to his
official brother. The Governor of South Carolina
in a speech demanded the return of the slave and
ended with 'What do you say?' The Governor
of North Carolina replied as above.*

It is good to be merry and wise,
It is good to be honest and true,
It is best to be off with the old love,
Before you are on with the new.
Songs of England and Scotland. London,
1835, vol. ii, p. 73.

It's love, it's love that makes the world go round.
Chansons Nationales et Populaires de France,
vol. ii, p. 180.

I wish I were single again.   *I Married a Wife.*

Jesus Christ is risen to-day,
Our triumphant holy day;
Who did once upon the cross
Suffer to redeem our loss.
Hallelujah!
*Jesus Christ is Risen To-day. From a Latin Hymn of
the 15th Century. Translator unknown.*

He was a wight of high renown,
And thou's but of low degree.
It's pride that puts this country down:
Man, put thy old cloak about thee!
*The Old Cloak. Oxford Book of 16th Cent.
Verse.*

Like a fine old English gentleman,
All of the olden time.
*The Fine Old English Gentleman. Oxford Song
Book.*

The newly-elected mayor who . . . said that during
his year of office he should lay aside all his political
prepossessions and be, 'like Caesar's wife, all things
to all men'.
G. W. E. Russell's *Collections and Recollections*,
ch. 29.

Love me little, love me long,
Is the burden of my song.
Love me Little, Love me Long (1569–70).

March winds and April showers
Bringeth vo'th May flowers.
> *West Somerset Word-Book*, ed. Frederick Thomas Elworthy (1886). March.

Miss Buss and Miss Beale
Cupid's darts do not feel.
Miss Beale and Miss Buss
They are not like us.
> *Of the Principal and Vice-Principal of the Ladies' College, Cheltenham, Nineteenth Century.*

Monday's child is fair of face,
Tuesday's child is full of grace,
Wednesday's child is full of woe,
Thursday's child has far to go,
Friday's child is loving and giving,
Saturday's child works hard for its living,
And a child that's born on the Sabbath day
Is fair and wise and good and gay.
> Bray, *Traditions of Devon*, ii. 288.

Most Gracious Queen, we thee implore
To go away and sin no more,
But if that effort be too great,
To go away at any rate.
> *Epigram on Queen Caroline, 1820. Quoted in Lord Colchester's Diary, Nov. 15, 1820, sent to him by Francis Burton.*

My Love in her attire doth show her wit,
  It doth so well become her:
For every season she hath dressings fit,
  For winter, spring, and summer.
No beauty she doth miss,
  When all her robes are on;
But beauty's self she is,
  When all her robes are gone.   *Madrigal.*

O God, if there be a God, save my soul, if I have a
soul!   *Quoted in* Newman's *Apologia.*

O God, for as much as without Thee
We are not enabled to doubt Thee,
  Help us all by Thy grace
  To convince the whole race
It knows nothing whatever about Thee.
> *Attr. to R. A. Knox.* Langford Reed, *The Limerick Book.*

Oh, Shenandoah, I long to hear you.
Away, you rolling river,
Oh Shenandoah, I long to hear you.
Away, I'm bound to go
'Cross the wide Missouri.   *Oxford Song Book.*

Oh! the oak, and the ash, and the bonny ivy-tree,
They flourish at home in my own country.
> *O The Oak and The Ash. Oxford Song Book.*

Oh, 'tis my delight on a shining night, in the season
of the year.   *The Poacher. Oxford Song Book.*

Oh, 'twas in the broad Atlantic,
  'Mid the equinoctial gales,
That a young fellow fell overboard
  Among the sharks and whales.
And down he went like a streak of light,
  So quickly down went he,
Until he came to a mer-ma-id
  At the bottom of the deep blue sea.
Singing, Rule Britannia, Britannia, rule the waves!

Britons never, never, never shall be mar-ri-ed to a
  mer-ma-id
At the bottom of the deep blue sea.
> *Oh! 'Twas in the Broad Atlantic. Oxford Song Book.*

Oh! where is my boy to-night?
The boy who was bravest of all.
> *Oh! Where is My Boy To-night?*

Old soldiers never die;
  They only fade away!
> *War Song of the British Soldiers, 1914–18.*

Once a clergyman always a clergyman.
> *Attr. ruling in trial of Horne Tooke.*

One Friday morn when we set sail,
And our ship not far from land,
We there did espy a fair pretty maid,
With a comb and a glass in her hand.
While the raging seas did roar,
And the stormy winds did blow,
And we jolly sailor-boys were all up aloft
And the land-lubbers lying down below.
> *The Mermaid. Oxford Song Book.*

O No John! No John! No John! No!
> *O No, John. Oxford Song Book.*

On Waterloo's ensanguined plain
Full many a gallant man was slain,
But none, by sabre or by shot,
Fell half so flat as Walter Scott.
> *On* Scott's *'Field of Waterloo', 1815.*

O Paddy dear, an' did ye hear the news that's goin'
  round?
The shamrock is by law forbid to grow on Irish
  ground!
No more St. Patrick's Day we'll keep, his colour can't
  be seen,
For there's a cruel law agin the wearin' o' the Green!
I met wid Napper Tandy, and he took me by the
  hand,
And he said, 'How's poor ould Ireland, and how does
  she stand?'
She's the most disthressful country that iver yet was
  seen,
For they're hangin' men an' women there for the
  wearin' o' the Green.
> *The Wearin' o' the Green. (Famous street ballad, later added to by Boucicault.)*

'O where are you going to, my pretty maid?'
> *The Rio Grande. Oxford Song Book.*

'My face is my fortune, kind sir' she said.   *Ib.*

'Nobody asked you, kind sir' she said.   *Ib.*

O ye'll tak' the high road, and I'll tak' the low road,
And I'll be in Scotland afore ye,
But me and my true love will never meet again,
On the bonnie, bonnie banks o' Loch Lomon'.
> *The Bonnie Banks o' Loch Lomon'.*

But the broken heart it kens nae second spring again,
Tho' the waefu' may cease frae their greeting. *Ib.*

Please her the best you may,
She looks another way.
Alas and well a day!
> Phillida flouts me.
> *The Disdainful Shepherdess. Oxford Book of 16th Cent. Verse.*

But she did all disdain,
And threw them back again;
Therefore it's flat and plain
     Phillida flouts me.   *Ib.*

Raise the stone, and there thou shalt find me, cleave the wood and there am I.
     Oxyrhyncus Sayings of Christ. Sayings of Our Lord, Logion 5, l. 23 (1897), p. 12.

Religion is the opium of the people.
     Translation of sentence by Karl Marx in *Kritik der Hegelschen Rechtsphilosophie, Introduction:* 'Die Religion ... ist das Opium des Volkes.'

Remember the Maine!
     Slogan of the Spanish-American War.

She has kilted her coats o' green satin,
   She has kilted them up to the knee,
And she's aff wi' Lord Ronald Macdonald,
   His bride and his darling to be.   *Lizzy Lindsay.*

   Will ye gang wi' me, Lizzy Lindsay,
     Will ye gang to the Highlands wi' me?
   Will ye gang wi' me, Lizzy Lindsay,
     My bride and my darling to be?   *Ib.*

Since first I saw your face, I resolved to honour and renown ye;
If now I be disdained, I wish my heart had never known ye.
What? I that loved and you that liked, shall we begin to wrangle?
No, no, no, my heart is fast, and cannot disentangle.
     Songs set by Thomas Ford, ii. *Oxford Book of 16th Cent. Verse.*

So I wish him joy where'er he dwell,
That first found out the leather bottel.
     The Leather Bottel.

Some talk of Alexander, and some of Hercules;
Of Hector and Lysander, and such great names as these;
But of all the world's brave heroes, there's none that can compare
With a tow, row, row, row, row, row, for the British Grenadier.   *The British Grenadiers.*

Spheres of influence.
     'Spheres of action', found in Earl Granville's letter to Count Münster, April 29, 1885. Hertslet's *Map of Africa by Treaty*, 3rd edn., p. 868.

Sumer is icumen in,
   Lhude sing cuccu!
Groweth sed, and bloweth med,
   And springth the wude nu.
     Cuckoo Song, c. 1250.

That Kruschen feeling.
     Advertisement for Kruschen Salts.

That schoolgirl complexion.
     Advertisement for Palmolive Soap.

That we spent, we had:
That we gave, we have:
That we left, we lost.
     Epitaph of the Earl of Devonshire, quoted by Spenser in The Shepherd's Calendar, May, l. 70.

The animals went in one by one,
There's one more river to cross.
     One More River. Oxford Song Book.

The animals went in four by four,
The big hippopotamus stuck in the door.   *Ib.*

The Campbells are comin', oho, oho.
     The Campbells are Comin'. Oxford Song Book.

The children in Holland take pleasure in making
What the children in England take pleasure in breaking.   *Nursery Rhyme.*

The girl I left behind me.
     Title of song, c. 1759. Oxford Song Book.

The Glorious First of June.
     Page-heading in Sir William Laird Clowes' *The Royal Navy: a History* (1899), vol. iv, p. 225. *Taken from explanatory pamphlet accompanying Cleveley's prints of the action:* 'Two prints ... representing the Glorious and Memorable Action of the First of June 1794.'

The holly and the ivy,
When they are both full grown,
Of all the trees that are in the wood,
The holly bears the crown:
The rising of the sun
And the running of the deer,
The playing of the merry organ,
Sweet singing in the choir.
     The Holly and the Ivy. Oxford Book of Carols.

The King over the Water.
     Jacobite Toast, 18th Cent.

The nature of God is a circle of which the centre is everywhere and the circumference is nowhere.
     Origin unknown; said to have been traced to a lost treatise of Empedocles. Quoted in the Roman de la Rose, and by S. Bonaventura in Itinerarius Mentis in Deum, cap. v. ad fin.

Then he kissed her cold corpus
A thousand times o'er,
He called her his Dinah—
Though she was no more!
He swallowed the pison
Like a true lovier brave,
And Vilikins and his Dinah
Lie a-buried in one grave.
     In Henry Mayhew's *The Wandering Minstrels,* 1834.

The noble Duke of York,
He had ten thousand men,
He marched them up to the top of the hill,
And he marched them down again.
And when they were up, they were up,
And when they were down, they were down,
And when they were only half way up,
   They were neither up nor down.
     The Noble Duke of York.

There is a lady sweet and kind,
Was never face so pleased my mind;
I did but see her passing by,
And yet I love her till I die.
     Attr. to Herrick in the Scottish Students' Song-Book. Found on back of leaf 53 of 'Popish Kingdome or reigne of Antichrist', in Latin verse by Thomas Naogeorgus, and Englished by Barnabe Googe. Printed 1570. See Notes and Queries, S. IX. x. 427.

There is a tavern in the town,
And there my dear love sits him down,
And drinks his wine 'mid laughter free,
And never, never thinks of me.
    Fare thee well, for I must leave thee,
    Do not let this parting grieve thee,
    And remember that the best of friends must part.

Adieu, adieu, kind friends, adieu, adieu, adieu,
I can no longer stay with you.
I'll hang my harp on a weeping willow-tree,
And may the world go well with thee. *There is a Tavern in the Town. Oxford Song Book.*

There's nae luck about the house,
  There's nae luck at a',
There's nae luck about the house
  When our gudeman's awa'.
              The Mariner's Wife.

There was an old Fellow of Trinity,
A Doctor well versed in Divinity;
  But he took to free-thinking,
  And then to deep drinking,
And so had to leave the vicinity.
    A. C. Hilton, in *'The Light Green', No. II,
    1872.*

There was an old man of Boulogne,
Who sang a most topical song.
  It wasn't the words
  Which frightened the birds,
But the horrible double entendre.
    Langford Reed, *The Limerick Book*, p. 51.

There was a young lady named Bright
Who would travel much faster than light.
  She started one day
  In the relative way,
And came back the previous night.
        Relativity. The Week-End Book.

There was a young lady of Kent,
Who said that she knew what it meant
  When men asked her to dine,
  Gave her cocktails and wine,
She knew what it meant—but she went!
    Langford Reed, *The Limerick Book*, p. 49.

There was a young lady of Riga,
Who rode with a smile on a tiger;
  They returned from the ride
  With the lady inside,
And a smile on the face of the tiger.   *Ib.* p. 103.

There was a young man of Devizes,
Whose ears were of different sizes;
  The one that was small
  Was no use at all,
But the other won several prizes.
    Attr. to R. A. Knox. Langford Reed, *The
    Limerick Book*, p. 81.

There was a young man who said, 'Damn!
At last I've found out that I am—
  A creature that moves
  In determinate grooves,
In fact not a bus but a tram.'   *Ib.* p. 43.

There was once a man who said 'God
Must think it exceedingly odd

If he finds that this tree
Continues to be
When there's no one about in the Quad.'
    Attr. to R. A. Knox. Langford Reed, *The Limerick
    Book: Idealism. For the answer, see 'Dear Sir,
    Your astonishment's odd'.*

The Sun himself cannot forget
His fellow traveller.
    *On Sir Francis Drake. Wit's Recreations
    (1640), Epigrams, No. 146.*

They come as a boon and a blessing to men,
The Pickwick, the Owl, and the Waverley pen.
              Advertisement.

'Tis bad enough in man or woman
To steal a goose from off a common;
But surely he's without excuse
Who steals a common from the goose.
    Epigram in Carey's *Commonplace Book of
    Epigrams.*

We don't want to fight; but, by Jingo, if we do,
We won't go to the front ourselves, but we'll send the
  mild Hindoo.
    *1878 parody, on hearing that Indian troops were
    being sent to Malta to help the English.* G. W. E.
    Russell's *Collections and Recollections*, ch. 28.

Weep you no more, sad fountains;
  What need you flow so fast?
    Songs set by John Dowland, viii. *Oxford Book
    of 16th Cent. Verse.*

'Well, what sort of sport has Lord — had?'
'Oh, the young Sahib shot divinely, but God was very
  merciful to the birds.'
    G. W. E. Russell's *Collections and Recollections*,
    ch. 30.

Were I as base as is the lowly plain,
  And you (my Love) as high as Heaven above.
    *Sonnet. Attr. to Joshua Sylvester. Oxford
    Book of 16th Cent. Verse.*

Western wind, when wilt thou blow,
  The small rain down can rain?
Christ, if my love were in my arms
  And I in my bed again!
        Oxford Book of 16th Cent. Verse.

What did you do in the Great War, daddy?
        Recruiting placard, 1914–1918.

What is an epigram? a dwarfish whole,
Its body brevity, and wit its soul.
    Brander Matthews' *American Epigrams. Har-
    per's Mag.*, Nov., 1903.

What shall we do with the drunken sailor?
Early in the morning?
Hoo-ray and up she rises
Early in the morning.
    *What shall we do with the Drunken Sailor?
    Oxford Song Book.*

When Adam delved, and Eve span,
Who was then a gentleman?
    *Text of Ball's revolutionary sermon at Black-
    heath in Wat Tyler's Rebellion 1381.* See
    J. R. Green, *Short Hist.* (1893), ii. 484.

When Johnny Comes Marching Home Again.
    Title of Song. Oxford Song Book.

When Molly smiles beneath her cow,
  I feel my heart—I can't tell how.
                    When Molly smiles, 1732.

Where is the man who has the power and skill
To stem the torrent of a woman's will?
For if she will, she will, you may depend on't;
And if she won't, she won't; so there's an end on't.
          From the Pillar Erected on the Mount in the
          Dane John Field, Canterbury. Examiner, 31
          May 1829.

Where's George? Gone to Lyonch.
          Advertisement for Lyons' lunches.

While ladling butter from alternate tubs
Stubbs butters Freeman, Freeman butters Stubbs.
          (Author revealed as J. E. Thorold Rogers in
          Hutton's Letters of Bishop Stubbs.)

Whilst Adam slept, Eve from his side arose:
Strange his first sleep should be his last repose.
                                    The Consequence.

'Who killed Cock Robin?'
'I', said the Sparrow,
'With my bow and arrow,
I killed Cock Robin.'
All the birds of the air fell a-sighing and a-sobbing,
When they heard of the death of poor Cock Robin.
'Who saw him die?'
'I,' said the Fly,
'With my little eye,
I saw him die.'   *Nursery Rhyme.*

Who passes by this road so late?
  Compagnon de la Majolaine!
Who passes by this road so late?
  Always gay!
Of all the king's knights 'tis the flower,
  Compagnon de la Majolaine,
Of all the king's knights 'tis the flower,
  Always gay!
          Old French Song quoted by Dickens, *Little*
          Dorrit, ch. 1.

Will you hear a Spanish lady
  How she woo'd an Englishman?
Garments gay and rich as may be,
  Decked with jewels had she on.
                    The Spanish Lady's Love.

Within the meaning of the Act.   *The Betting Act.*

Woo'd and married and a',
  Woo'd and married and a'
Was she nae very weel aff,
  Was woo'd and married and a'.
                    Woo'd and Married and a'.

Workers of the world, unite!
          Common form of 'Working men of all countries,
          unite!' *This is the English Translation (1888)*
          by Samuel Moore, revised by Engels, of 'Prole-
          tarien aller Länder, vereinigen Euch!' *which*
          concludes 'The Communist Manifesto' *(1848),*
          by Marx and Engels, and is quoted as the final
          words of the programme of the Communist In-
          ternational (1928). Another common form is
          'Proletarians of the world, unite!'

Worth a guinea a box.
          Advertisement for Beecham's Pills.

You ought to see me on Sunday.
          Advertisement for Knight's Castille Soap.

I am the Dean of Christ Church, Sir:
This is my wife, pray look at her.
She is the Broad, I am the High;
We are the University.
          The Masque of Balliol, a masque composed by
          and current among members of Balliol College
          in the late 1870's.
          The first couplet was unofficially altered to:

I am the Dean, and this is Mrs. Liddell;
She is the first and I the second fiddle.

I am a most superior person,
My name is George Nathaniel Curzon.   *Ib.*

My face is pink, my hair is sleek,
I dine at Blenheim once a week.
                              Ib. (A later addition)

I am rather tall and stately,
And I care not very greatly
What you say, or what you do.
I'm Mackail,—and who are you?   *Ib.*

First come I; my name is Jowett.
There is no knowledge but I know it.
I am Master of this college:
What I don't know isn't knowledge.
          Probably group product of Balliol undergradu-
          ates in the late 1870's.

BALLADS

True Thomas lay on Huntlie bank;
  A ferlie he spied wi' his e'e;
And there he saw a ladye bright
  Come riding down by the Eildon Tree.
    The Oxford Book of Ballads. Thomas the Rhymer.

True Thomas he pu'd aff his cap,
  And louted low down on his knee.   *Ib.*

She's mounted on her milk-white steed,
  She's ta'en true Thomas up behind.   *Ib.*

That is the Road to fair Elfland,
  Where thou and I this night maun gae.   *Ib.*

It was mirk, mirk night, there was nae starlight,
  They waded thro' red blude to the knee;
For a' the blude that's shed on the earth
  Rins through the springs o' that countrie.   *Ib.*

And till seven years were gane and past,
  True Thomas on earth was never seen.   *Ib.*

And she has kilted her green kirtle
  A little abune her knee;
And she has braided her yellow hair
  A little abune her bree.   *Ib. Tam Lin.* v.

About the dead hour of the night
  She heard the bridles ring;
And Janet was as glad at that
  As any earthly thing.   *Ib.* xli.

There were twa sisters sat in a bour;
  Binnorie, O Binnorie!
There came a knight to be their wooer,
  By the bonnie milldams o' Binnorie.   Ib. Binnorie.

Clerk Saunders and may Margaret
  Walk'd owre yon garden green;
And deep and heavy was the love
  That fell thir twa between.

'A bed, a bed,' Clerk Saunders said,
  'A bed for you and me!'
'Fye na, fye na,' said may Margaret,
  'Till anes we married be!'   *Ib. Clerk Saunders.*

There's nae room at my head, Marg'ret,
  There's nae room at my feet;
My bed it is fu' lowly now,
  Among the hungry worms I sleep.   *Ib.*

She hadna sail'd a league, a league,
  A league but barely three,
Till grim, grim grew his countenance
  And gurly grew the sea.

'What hills are yon, yon pleasant hills,
  The sun shines sweetly on?'—
'O yon are the hills o' Heaven,' he said,
  'Where you will never won.'
          Ib. The Daemon Lover.

He strack the top-mast wi' his hand,
  The fore-mast wi' his knee;
And he brake that gallant ship in twain,
  And sank her in the sea.   *Ib.*

It fell about the Martinmass,
  When nights are lang and mirk,
The carline wife's three sons came hame,
  And their hats were o' the birk.

It neither grew in dike nor ditch,
  Nor yet in any sheugh;
But at the gates o' Paradise
  That birk grew fair eneugh.
    Ib. The Wife of Usher's Well.

This ae nighte, this ae nighte,
  —*Every nighte and alle,*
Fire and fleet[1] and candle-lighte,
  And Christe receive thy saule.
          Ib. Lyke-Wake Dirge.

[1] = floor. Other readings are 'sleet' and 'salt'.

From Brig o' Dread when thou may'st pass,
  —*Every nighte and alle,*
To Purgatory fire thou com'st at last;
  And Christe receive thy saule.

If ever thou gavest meat or drink,
  —*Every nighte and alle,*
The fire sall never make thee shrink;
  And Christe receive thy saule.   *Ib.*

The wind doth blow to-day, my love,
  And a few small drops of rain;
I never had but one true love;
  In cold grave she was lain.
    Ib. The Unquiet Grave.

True lovers I can get many an one,
  But a father I can never get mair.
    Ib. The Douglas Tragedy.

O he's gart build a bonny ship,
  To sail on the salt sea;
The mast was o' the beaten gold,
  The sails o' cramoisie.
    Ib. The Lass of Lochroyan.

O well's me o' my gay goss-hawk,
  That he can speak and flee!

He'll carry a letter to my love,
  Bring another back to me.
          Ib. The Gay Gosshawk.

'What gat ye to your dinner, Lord Randal, my Son?
  What gat ye to your dinner, my handsome young
    man?'
'I gat eels boil'd in broo'; mother, make my bed soon,
  For I'm weary wi' hunting, and fain wald lie down.'
          Ib. Lord Randal.

As I was walking all alane,
  I heard twa corbies[1] making a mane:
The tane unto the tither did say,
  'Where sall we gang and dine the day?'

'—In behint yon auld fail[2] dyke
  I wot there lies a new-slain knight;
And naebody kens that he lies there
  But his hawk, his hound, and his lady fair.

'His hound is to the hunting gane,
  His hawk to fetch the wild-fowl hame,
His lady's ta'en anither mate,
  So we may make our dinner sweet.

'Ye'll sit on his white hause-bane,[3]
  And I'll pike out his bonny blue e'en:
Wi' ae lock o' his gowden hair
  We'll theek[4] our nest when it grows bare.'
          Ib. The Twa Corbies.

[1] corbies = ravens.   [2] fail = turf.
[3] hause = neck.   [4] theek = thatch.

There were three ravens sat on a tree,
They were as black as they might be.
The one of them said to his make,
'Where shall we our breakfast take?'
          Ib. The Three Ravens.

Down there comes a fallow doe
As great with young as she might goe.
She lifted up his bloudy head
And kist his wounds that were so red.   *Ib.*

She buried him before the prime,
She was dead herself ere evensong time.
God send every gentleman
Such hounds, such hawks, and such a leman!   *Ib.*

For in my mind, of all mankind
  I love but you alone.
          Ib. The Nut Brown Maid.

For I must to the greenwood go
  Alone, a banished man.   *Ib.*

The king sits in Dunfermline town
  Drinking the blude-red wine.
          Ib. Sir Patrick Spens.

Our king has written a braid letter,
  And seal'd it with his hand,
And sent it to Sir Patrick Spens,
  Was walking on the strand.

'To Noroway, to Noroway,
  To Noroway o'er the faem;
The king's daughter o' Noroway,
  'Tis thou must bring her hame.'

The first word that Sir Patrick read
  So loud, loud laughed he;
The neist word that Sir Patrick read
  The tear blinded his e'e.   *Ib.*

'I saw the new moon late yestreen
   Wi' the auld moon in her arm;
And if we gang to sea, master,
   I fear we'll come to harm.'

Go fetch a web o' the silken claith,
   Another o' the twine,
And wap[1] them into our ship's side,
   And let nae the sea come in.
     [1] wap = wrap.   *Ib. Sir Patrick Spens.*

O laith, laith were our gude Scots lords
   To wat their cork-heel'd shoon;
But lang or a' the play was play'd
   They wat their hats aboon.   *Ib.*

O lang, lang may the ladies sit,
   Wi' their fans into their hand,
Before they see Sir Patrick Spens
   Come sailing to the strand!

And lang, lang may the maidens sit
   Wi' their gowd kames in their hair,
A-waiting for their ain dear loves!
   For them they'll see nae mair.

Half-owre, half-owre to Aberdour,
   'Tis fifty fathoms deep;
And there lies gude Sir Patrick Spens,
   Wi' the Scots lords at his feet!   *Ib.*

Marie Hamilton's to the kirk gane
   Wi' ribbons on her breast;
The King thought mair o' Marie Hamilton
   Than he listen'd to the priest.
          Ib. The Queen's Maries.

Yestreen the Queen had four Maries,
   The night she'll hae but three;
There was Marie Seaton, and Marie Beaton,
   And Marie Carmichael, and me.   *Ib.*

O little did my mother ken,
   The day she cradled me,
The lands I was to travel in
   Or the death I was to die!   *Ib.*

And when we came through Glasgow toun,
   We were a comely sight to see;
My gude lord in the black velvet,
   And I mysel' in cramasie.   *Ib. Jamie Douglas.*

O waly, waly, up the bank,
   And waly, waly, doun the brae,
And waly, waly, yon burn-side,
   Where I and my Love wont to gae!

I lean'd my back unto an aik,
   I thocht it was a trustie tree;
But first it bow'd and syne it brake—
   Sae my true love did lichtlie me.

O waly, waly, gin love be bonnie
   A little time while it is new!
But when 'tis auld it waxeth cauld,
   And fades awa' like morning dew.

O wherefore should I busk my heid,
   Or wherefore should I kame my hair?
For my true Love has me forsook,
   And says he'll never lo'e me mair.
              Ib. Waly, Waly.

But had I wist, before I kist,
   That love had been sae ill to win,
I had lock'd my heart in a case o' gowd,
   And pinn'd it wi' a siller pin.

And O! if my young babe were born,
   And set upon the nurse's knee;
And I mysel' were dead and gane,
   And the green grass growing over me!   *Ib.*

O come ye here to fight, young lord,
   Or come ye here to play?
Or come ye here to drink good wine
   Upon the weddin'-day?
          Ib. Katharine Johnstone.

Ye Highlands and ye Lawlands,
   O where hae ye been?
They hae slain the Earl of Murray,
   And hae laid him on the green.
       Ib. The Bonny Earl of Murray.

He was a braw gallant,
   And he rid at the ring;
And the bonny Earl of Murray,
   O he might hae been a king!   *Ib.*

He was a braw gallant,
   And he play'd at the gluve;
And the bonny Earl of Murray,
   O he was the Queen's luve!

O lang will his Lady
   Look owre the Castle Downe,
Ere she see the Earl of Murray
   Come sounding through the town!   *Ib.*

'Let me have length and breadth enough,
   And under my head a sod;
That they may say when I am dead,
   —*Here lies bold Robin Hood!*'
       Ib. The Death of Robin Hood.

It fell about the Lammas tide
   When husbands win their hay,
The doughty Douglas bound him to ride
   In England to take a prey.
       Ib. The Battle of Otterburn, i.

My wound is deep: I am fayn to sleep,
   Take thou the vaward of me,
And hide me by the bracken bush
   Grows on yonder lilye-lee.   *Ib.* lvii.

The Percy out of Northumberland,
   An avow to God made he
That he would hunt in the mountains
   Of Cheviot within days three,
In the maugre of doughty Douglas,
   And all that e'er with him be.
       Ib. Chevy Chase, I. i.

This began on a Monday at morn,
   In Cheviot the hills so hye;
The child may rue that is unborn,
   It was the more pitye.   *Ib.* iv.

'But I hae dream'd a dreary dream,
   Beyond the Isle of Sky;
I saw a dead man win a fight,
   And I think that man was I.'
   Ib. [xix in the Scottish version, but not included
           in the Oxford Book version.]

For Witherington my heart was woe
   That ever he slain should be:
For when both his legs were hewn in two
   Yet he kneel'd and fought on his knee.   *Ib.* II. i.

'God have mercy on his soul,' said King Harry,
  'Good Lord, if thy will it be!
I've a hundred captains in England,' he said,
  'As good as ever was he:
But Percy, an I brook my life,
  Thy death well quit shall be.'   *Ib.* lviii.

Jesu Christ! our bales[1] bete,[2]
  And to the bliss us bring!
This was the Hunting of the Cheviot:
  God send us all good ending!   *Ib.* lxii.

  [1] bales = woes.   [2] bete = better, relieve.

A ship I have got in the North Country
And she goes by the name of the *Golden Vanity*,
O I fear she will be taken by a Spanish Ga-la-lee,
As she sails by the Low-lands low.
          Ib. The Golden Vanity.

He bored with his augur, he bored once and twice,
And some were playing cards, and some were playing dice,
When the water flowed in it dazzled their eyes,
And she sank by the Lowlands low.

So the Cabin-boy did swim all to the larboard side,
Saying 'Captain! take me in, I am drifting with the tide!'
'I will shoot you! I will kill you!' the cruel Captain cried,
'You may sink by the Low-lands low.'   *Ib.*

Then they laid him on the deck, and he closed his eyes and died,
As they sailed by the Low-lands low.   *Ib.*

O is my basnet a widow's curch?
  Or my lance a wand of the willow-tree?
Or my arm a ladye's lilye hand,
  That an English lord should lightly me!
          Ib. Kinmont Willie, x.

He is either himself a devil frae hell,
  Or else his mother a witch maun be;
I wadna have ridden that wan water
  For a' the gowd in Christentie.   *Ib.* xlvi.

I wish I were where Helen lies,
Night and day on me she cries;
O that I were where Helen lies,
On fair Kirkconnell lea!   *Ib. Helen of Kirkconnell.*

Lady Nancy she died out of pure, pure grief,
Lord Lovel he died out of sorrow. *Ib. Lord Lovel.*

All the trees they are so high,
The leaves they are so green,
The day is past and gone, sweet-heart,
That you and I have seen.
It is cold winter's night,
You and I must bide alone:
Whilst my pretty lad is young
And is growing.   *Ib. The Trees so High.*

In Scarlet town, where I was born,
There was a fair maid dwellin',
Made every youth cry *Well-a-way!*
Her name was Barbara Allen.

All in the merry month of May,
When green buds they were swellin',
Young Jemmy Grove on his death-bed lay,
For love of Barbara Allen.
          Ib. Barbara Allen's Cruelty.

So slowly, slowly rase she up,
And slowly she came nigh him,
And when she drew the curtain by—
'Young man, I think you're dyin'!'.   *Ib.*

'O mother, mother, make my bed,
O make it saft and narrow:
My love has died for me to-day,
I'll die for him to-morrow.'   *Ib.*

'Farewell,' she said, 'ye virgins all,
And shun the fault I fell in:
Henceforth take warning by the fall
Of cruel Barbara Allen.'   *Ib.*

And the Lowlands o' Holland has twin'd my love and
  me.   *Ib. The Lowlands o' Holland.*
'O haud your tongue, my daughter dear, be still and
  be content;
There are mair lads in Galloway, ye neen nae sair
  lament.'
'O there is none in Gallow, there's none at a' for me,
For I never loved a love but one, and he's drown'd in
  the sea.'   *Ib.*

There was a youth, and a well-beloved youth,
  And he was an esquire's son,
He loved the bailiff's daughter dear,
  That lived in Islington.
      Ib. The Bailiff's Daughter of Islington.

But when his friends did understand
  His fond and foolish mind,
They sent him up to fair London,
  An apprentice for to bind.   *Ib.*

She stept to him, as red as any rose,
  And took him by the bridle-ring:
'I pray you, kind sir, give me one penny,
  To ease my weary limb.'

'I prithee, sweetheart, canst thou tell me,
  Where that thou wast born?'
'At Islington, kind sir,' said she,
  'Where I have had many a scorn.'

'I prithee, sweetheart, canst thou tell me
  Whether thou dost know
The bailiff's daughter of Islington?'
  'She's dead, sir, long ago.'

'Then will I sell my goodly steed,
  My saddle and my bow;
I will into some far countrey,
  Where no man doth me know.'

'O stay, O stay, thou goodly youth!
  She's alive, she is not dead;
Here she standeth by thy side,
  And is ready to be thy bride.'   *Ib.*

When captains courageous, whom death could not
  daunt,
Did march to the siege of the city of Gaunt,
They mustered their soldiers by two and by three,
And the foremost in battle was Mary Ambree.
          Mary Ambree.

'Tom Pearse, Tom Pearse, lend me your grey mare,
All along, down along, out along, lee.
For I want for to go to Widdicombe Fair,
Wi' Bill Brewer, Jan Stewer, Peter Gurney, Peter
  Davey, Dan'l Whiddon, Harry Hawk,
    Old Uncle Tom Cobbleigh and all.
    Old Uncle Tom Cobbleigh and all.'
          Ib. Widdicombe Fair.

But ne'er a word wad ane o' them speak,
  For barring of the door.
      Ib. Get Up and Bar the Door.
Goodman, you've spoken the foremost word!
  Get up and bar the door.   *Ib.*

NURSERY RHYMES

Old King Cole
Was a merry old soul,
And a merry old soul was he,
He called for his pipe,
He called for his bowl,
And he called for his fiddlers three.
    Nursery Rhymes Collected by James Orchard
    Halliwell (Phillipps), 1.

I had a little nut-tree, nothing would it bear
But a silver nutmeg and a golden pear;
The king of Spain's daughter came to visit me,
And all because of my little nut tree.   *Ib.* 5.

The King of France went up the hill,
With twenty thousand men;
The King of France came down the hill,
And ne'er went up again.   *Ib.* 8.

Please to remember
The Fifth of November,
  Gunpowder treason and plot;
I know no reason
Why gunpowder treason
  Should ever be forgot.   *Ib.* 13.

A was an apple-pie;
B bit it;
C cut it.   *Ib.* 33.

One, two,
Buckle my shoe;
Three, four,
Shut the door;
Five, six,
Pick up sticks.
Seven, eight,
Lay them straight;
Nine, ten,
A good fat hen.   *Ib.* 35.

Pat-a-cake, pat-a-cake, baker's man!
So I will, master, as fast as I can:
Pat, and prick it, and mark it with T,
Put in the oven for Tony and me.   *Ib.* 36.

Taffy was a Welshman, Taffy was a thief;
Taffy came to my house and stole a piece of beef:
I went to Taffy's house, Taffy was not at home;
Taffy came to my house and stole a marrow-bone.

I went to Taffy's house, Taffy was not in;
Taffy came to my house and stole a silver pin:
I went to Taffy's house, Taffy was in bed,
I took up a poker and flung it at his head.   *Ib.* 42.

Little Jack Horner sat in the corner,
  Eating a Christmas pie:
He put in his thumb, and he took out a plum,
  And said, 'What a good boy am I!'   *Ib.* 43.

There was a crooked man, and he went a crooked mile,
He found a crooked sixpence against a crooked stile:
He bought a crooked cat, which caught a crooked
  mouse,
And they all lived together in a little crooked house.
                                  Ib. 46.

The lion and the unicorn
Were fighting for the crown;
The lion beat the unicorn
All round about the town.

Some gave them white bread,
And some gave them brown;
Some gave them plum-cake,
And sent them out of town.   *Ĭb.* 56.

Three wise men of Gotham
Went to sea in a bowl:
And if the bowl had been stronger,
My song would have been longer.   *Ib.* 59.

Tom, Tom, the piper's son,
Stole a pig, and away he run!
The pig was eat, and Tom was beat,
And Tom went roaring down the street.   *Ib.* 61.

Simple Simon met a pieman
  Going to the fair:
Says Simple Simon to the pieman,
  'Let me taste your ware.'   *Ib.* 63.

The Queen of Hearts
She made some tarts,
  All on a summer's day
The Knave of Hearts
He stole the tarts,
  And took them clean away.   *Ib.* 65.

Solomon Grundy,
Born on a Monday,
Christened on a Tuesday,
Married on a Wednesday,
Took ill on Thursday,
Worse on Friday,
Died on Saturday,
Buried on Sunday:
This is the end
Of Solomon Grundy.   *Ib.* 67.

They that wash on Monday
Have all the week to dry;
They that wash on Tuesday
Are not so much awry;
They that wash on Wednesday
Are not so much to blame;
They that wash on Thursday
Wash for shame;
They that wash on Friday,
Wash in need;
And they that wash on Saturday,
Oh! they're sluts indeed.   *Ib.* 73.

He that would thrive
Must rise at five;
He that hath thriven
May lie till seven.   *Ib.* 76.

See a pin and pick it up,
All the day you'll have good luck;
See a pin and let it lay,
Bad luck you'll have all the day!   *Ib.* 77.

When the wind is in the east,
'Tis neither good for man nor beast;
When the wind is in the north,
The skilful fisher goes not forth;
When the wind is in the south,
It blows the bait in the fishes' mouth;
When the wind is in the west,
Then 'tis at the very best.   *Ib.* 79.

Cross patch,
Draw the latch,
Sit by the fire and spin:
Take a cup,
And drink it up,
Then call your neighbours in. *Ib.* 83.

Cry, baby, cry,
Put your finger in your eye,
And tell your mother it wasn't I. *Ib.* 85.

Mistress Mary, quite contrary,
How does your garden grow?
With cockle shells, and silver bells,
And mussels all a row. *Ib.* 86.

Tell tale, tit!
Your tongue shall be split,
And all the dogs in the town
Shall have a little bit. *Ib.* 88.

Multiplication is vexation,
Division is as bad;
The Rule of Three doth puzzle me,
And Practice drives me mad. *Ib.* 90.

Thirty days hath September,
April, June, and November;
February has twenty-eight alone,
All the rest have thirty-one,
Excepting leap-year, that's the time
When February's days are twenty-nine. *Ib.* 91.

Three blind mice, see how they run!
They all ran after a farmer's wife,
Who cut off their tails with the carving-knife,
Did you ever see such fools in your life?
  Three blind mice. *Ib.* 97.

If I'd as much money as I could spend,
I never would cry old chairs to mend;
Cry chairs to mend, old chairs to mend;
I never would cry old chairs to mend. *Ib.* 100.

The fox jumped up on a moonlight night. *Ib.* 101.

Tom he was a piper's son,
He learned to play when he was young,
But all the tunes that he could play,
Was 'Over the hills and far away.' *Ib.* 106.

London bridge is broken down,
  Dance o'er my lady lee. *Ib.* 110.

The north wind doth blow,
And we shall have snow,
And what will poor robin do then?
                Poor thing!
He'll sit in a barn,
And to keep himself warm,
Will hide his head under his wing.
                Poor thing! *Ib.* 111.

Little Bo-Peep has lost her sheep,
  And can't tell where to find them;
Let them alone, and they'll come home,
  And bring their tails behind them. *Ib.* 120.

Sing a song of sixpence,
  A bag full of rye,
Four and twenty blackbirds,
  Baked in a pie;
When the pie was opened,
  The birds began to sing;
Was not that a dainty dish
  To set before the king?

The king was in his counting-house
  Counting out his money;
The queen was in the parlour
  Eating bread and honey;
The maid was in the garden
  Hanging out the clothes,
There came a little blackbird,
  And snapt off her nose. *Ib.* 122.

As I was going to St. Ives,
I met a man with seven wives,
Every wife had seven sacks,
Every sack had seven cats,
Every cat had seven kits,
Kits, cats, sacks, and wives,
How many were there going to St. Ives? *Ib.* 132.

Humpty Dumpty sate on a wall,
Humpty Dumpty had a great fall;
Three score men and three score more
Cannot place Humpty Dumpty as he was before.
Ib. 135.

Pease-porridge hot, pease-porridge cold,
Pease-porridge in the pot, nine days old. *Ib.* 137.

King Charles walked and talked
Half an hour after his head was cut off. *Ib.* 150.

Peter Piper picked a peck of pickled pepper;
A peck of pickled pepper Peter Piper picked;
If Peter Piper picked a peck of pickled pepper,
Where's the peck of pickled pepper that Peter Piper
  picked? *Ib.* 165.

Lauk a mercy on me, this is none of I! *Ib.* 169.

There was an old woman who lived in a shoe,
She had so many children she didn't know what to do;
She gave them some broth without any bread,
She whipped them all well and put them to bed.
Ib. 171.

Old Mother Hubbard
Went to the cupboard,
To get her poor dog a bone;
But when she came there
The cupboard was bare,
And so the poor dog had none. *Ib.* 184.

Gay go up and gay go down,
To ring the bells of London town. *Ib.* 195.

Oranges and lemons
Say the bells of St. Clement's. *Ib.*

When will you pay me?
Say the bells at Old Bailey.
When I grow rich,
Say the bells at Shoreditch. *Ib.*

Here comes a candle to light you to bed,
And here comes a chopper to chop off your head. *Ib.*

See, saw, Margery Daw,
Sold her bed and lay upon straw;
Was not she a dirty slut,
To sell her bed and lie in the dirt! *Ib.* 198.

Ride a cock-horse to Banbury-cross,
To see an old lady ride upon a white horse,
Rings on her fingers, and bells on her toes,
And so she makes music wherever she goes. *Ib.* 214.

This pig went to market;
This pig stayed at home;
This pig had a bit of meat;
And this pig had none;
This pig said, Wee, wee, wee!
I can't find my way home. *Ib.* 221.

Hickory, Dickory, Dock,
The mouse ran up the clock,
The clock struck one,
The mouse was gone;
O, U, T, spells out!   *Ib.* 226.

How many miles is it to Babylon?—
Threescore miles and ten.
Can I get there by candle-light?—
Yes, and back again!
If you are nimble and light,
You may get there by candle-light.   *Ib.* 230.

The man in the wilderness asked me,
How many strawberries grow in the sea?
I answered him, as I thought good,
As many as red herrings grew in the wood. *Ib.* 259.

Bye, baby bunting,
Daddy's gone a-hunting,
To get a little hare's skin
To wrap a baby bunting in.   *Ib.* 274.

Ding, dong, bell,
Pussy's in the well!
Who put her in?
Little Tommy Lin.   *Ib.* 283.

Cock a doodle doo!
My dame has lost her shoe;
My master's lost his fiddling-stick,
And don't know what to do.   *Ib.* 285.

Hey! diddle-diddle,
The cat and the fiddle,
The cow jumped over the moon;
The little dog laughed
To see such craft,
While the dish ran after the spoon.   *Ib.* 301.

Jack Sprat could eat no fat,
His wife could eat no lean;
And so, between them both, you see,
They licked the platter clean.   *Ib.* 327.

Rowley Poley, pudding and pie,
Kissed the girls and made them cry;
When the girls began to cry,
Rowley Poley ran away.   *Ib.* 347.

Four and twenty tailors went to kill a snail,
The best man among them durst not touch her tail.
She put out her horns like a little Kyloe cow,
Run, tailors, run, or she'll kill you all e'en now.
                                        Ib. 359.

Pussy cat, pussy cat, where have you been?
I've been up to London to look at the queen.
Pussy cat, pussy cat, what did you there?
I frightened a little mouse under the chair. *Ib.* 362.

Hickety, pickety, my black hen,
She lays eggs for gentlemen;
Gentlemen come every day
To see what my black hen doth lay.   *Ib.* 373.

Lady-cow, lady-cow, fly thy way home,
Thy house is on fire, thy children all gone,
All but one that ligs under a stone,
Ply thee home, lady-cow, ere it be gone. *Ib.* 380.

This is the farmer sowing his corn,
That kept the cock that crowed in the morn,
That waked the priest all shaven and shorn,
That married the man all tattered and torn,
That kissed the maiden all forlorn,
That milked the cow with the crumpled horn,

That tossed the dog,
That worried the cat,
That killed the rat,
That ate the malt
That lay in the house that Jack built. *Ib.* 398.

Goosey goosey gander,
Whither shall I wander?
Up stairs, down stairs,
And in my lady's chamber;
There I met an old man
That would not say his prayers;
I took him by the left leg,
And threw him down stairs.   *Ib.* 414.

What are little boys made of, made of?
What are little boys made of?
Snaps and snails, and puppy-dogs' tails;
And that's what little boys are made of, made of.
What are little girls made of, made of, made of?
What are little girls made of?
Sugar and spice, and all that's nice;
And that's what little girls are made of, made of.
                                        Ib. 416.

Who comes here?
A grenadier.
What do you want?
A pot of beer.
Where is your money?
I've forgot.
Get you gone,
You drunken sot!   *Ib.* 420.

Bah, bah, black sheep,
Have you any wool?
Yes, marry, have I,
Three bags full:
One for my master,
And one for my dame,
But none for the little boy
Who cries in the lane.   *Ib.* 440.

Daffy-down-dilly has come up to town,
In a yellow petticoat, and a green gown. *Ib.* 444.

Little Tom Tucker
Sings for his supper;
What shall he eat?
White bread and butter.
How shall he eat it
Without e'er a knife?
How will he be married
Without e'er a wife?   *Ib.* 446.

Come, let's to bed,
Says Sleepy-head;
Tarry a while, says Slow;
Put on the pot,
Says Greedy-gut,
Let's sup before we go.   *Ib.* 447.

When I was a little boy, I had but little wit,
It is some time to go, and I've no more yet;
Nor ever ever shall, until that I die,
For the longer I live, the more fool am I. *Ib.* 455.

Rain, rain, go away,
Come again another day;
Little Arthur wants to play.   *Ib.* 457.

Girls and boys come out to play,
The moon doth shine as bright as day.   *Ib.* 466.

Little boy blue, come blow up your horn,
The sheep's in the meadow, the cow's in the corn;
Where's the little boy that looks after the sheep?
He's under the haycock fast asleep.
Will you wake him? No, not I,
For if I do, he'll be sure to cry.   *Ib.* 468.

Little Polly Flinders
Sate among the cinders,

Warming her pretty little toes
Her mother came and caught her,
And whipped her little daughter
For spoiling her nice new clothes.   *Ib.* 486.

One a penny, two a penny, hot cross-buns;
If your daughters do not like them, give them to your
sons.   *Ib.* 494.

PUNCH

Advice to persons about to marry.—'Don't.'
Punch, vol. viii, p. 1. 1845.

You pays your money and you takes your choice.
Ib. vol. x, p. 16. 1846.

The Half-Way House to Rome, Oxford.
Ib. vol. xvi, p. 36. 1849.

What is better than presence of mind in a railway
accident? Absence of body.
Ib. vol. xvi, p. 231. 1849.

Never do to-day what you can put off till to-morrow.
Ib. vol. xvii, p. 241. 1849.

The cow with the iron tail.
Ib. vol. xxii, p. 13. 1850.

No bread. Then bring me some toast!
Ib. vol. xxii, p. 18. 1852.

A confiseur in the Rue St. Denis at Paris has just
invented a new Cordial for the special use of the
English-French armies in Turkey, to which he has
given the name of 'Entente Cordial'.
Ib. vol. xxvi, p. 76. 1854.

Who's 'im, Bill?
A stranger!
'Eave 'arf a brick at 'im.   *Ib.* vol. xxvi, p. 82. 1854.

What is Matter?—Never mind.
What is Mind?—No matter.
Ib. vol. xxix, p. 19. 1855.

'*Peccavi*—I've Scinde' wrote Lord Ellen so proud.
More briefly Dalhousie wrote—'*Vovi*—I've Oude'.
Ib. vol. xxx, p. 141. 1856.

It ain't the 'unting as 'urts 'un, it's the 'ammer,
'ammer, 'ammer along the 'ard 'igh road.
Ib. vol. xxx, p. 218. 1856.

O 'ill tak zum o' that in a moog.
Ib. vol. xxxvii, p. 156. 1859.

I see it's written by a lady, and I want a book that my
daughters may read. Give me something else.
Ib. vol. liii, p. 252. 1867.

Mun, a had na' been the-erre abune two hours when
—*bang*—went saxpence!!! *Ib.* vol. liv, p. 235. 1868.

Cats is 'dogs' and rabbits is 'dogs' and so's parrots,
but this 'ere 'Tortis' is an insect, and there ain't no
charge for it.   *Ib.* vol. lvi, p. 96. 1869.

Nothink for nothink 'ere, and precious little for sixpence.   *Ib.* vol. lvii, p. 152. 1869.

Sure, the next train has gone ten minutes ago.
Ib. vol. lx, p. 206. 1871.

I may've 'ad too mush, but I 'aven't 'ad enough.
Ib. vol. lxiii, p. 72. 1872.

It appears the Americans have taken umbrage.
The deuce they have! Whereabouts is that?
Ib. vol. lxiii, p. 189. 1872.

Go directly—see what she's doing, and tell her she
mustn't.   *Ib.* vol. lxiii, p. 202. 1872.

There was one poor tiger that hadn't *got* a Christian.
Ib. vol. lxviii, p. 143. 1875.

It's worse than wicked, my dear, it's vulgar.
Ib. Almanac. 1876.

What did you take out of the bag, Mamma? *I* only
got sixpence.   *Ib.* vol. lxx, p. 139. 1876.

'Is Life worth living?' . . . he suspects it is, in a great
measure, a question of the Liver.
Ib. vol. lxxiii, p. 207. 1877.

I never read books—I *write* them.
Ib. vol. lxxiv, p. 210. 1878.

I am not hungry; but thank goodness, I am greedy.
Ib. vol. lxxv, p. 290. 1878.

BISHOP:
Who is it that sees and hears all I do, and before
whom even I am but as a crushed worm?
PAGE:
The Missus, my Lord!

Ib. vol. lxxix, p. 63. 1880.

Ah whiles hae ma doobts aboot the meenister.
Ib. vol. lxxix, p. 275. 1880.

I used your soap two years ago; since then I have used
no other.   *Ib.* vol. lxxxvi, p. 197. 1884.

What sort of a doctor is he?
Oh, well, I don't know very much about his ability;
but he's got a very good bedside manner!
Ib. vol. lxxxvi, p. 121. 1884.

Don't look at me, Sir, with—ah—in that tone of
voice.   *Ib.* vol. lxxxvii, p. 38. 1884.

Oh yes! I'm sure he's not so fond of me as at first.
He's away so much, neglects me dreadfully, and
he's so cross when he comes home. What *shall*
I do?
Feed the brute!   *Ib.* vol. lxxxix, p. 206. 1886.

Hi! James—let loose the Gorgonzola!
Ib. vol. xcvi, p. 82. 1889.

Nearly all our best men are dead! Carlyle, Tennyson, Browning, George Eliot!—I'm not feeling very well myself.   *Ib.* vol. civ, p. 210. 1893.

Botticelli isn't a wine, you Juggins! Botticelli's a *cheese!*   *Ib.* vol. cvi, p. 270. 1894.

I'm afraid you've got a bad egg, Mr. Jones.
Oh no, my Lord, I assure you! Parts of it are excellent!   *Ib.* vol. cix, p. 222. 1895.

Do you know, Carter, that I can actually write my name in the dust on the table?
Faith, Mum, that's more than I can do. Sure there's nothing like education, after all.
Ib. vol. cxxii, p. 142. 1902.

Look here, Steward, if this is coffee, I want tea; but if this is tea, then I wish for coffee.
Ib. vol. cxxiii, p. 44. 1902.

We must gie it up, Alfred.
What, gie up gowff?
Nae, nae, mon. Gie up the meenistry.
Ib. vol. cxxvi, p. 117. 1904.

LATIN QUOTATIONS

PETER ABELARD

1079–1142

O quanta qualia sunt illa sabbata,
Quae semper celebrat superna curia

> O what their joy and their glory must be,
> Those endless sabbaths the blessed ones see!
> *Hymnus Paraclitensis.* Trans. by Neale in
> *Hymnal Noted*, 1858.

THOMAS A KEMPIS

1380–1471

Opto magis sentire compunctionem quam scire eius definitionem.

> I had rather feel compunction, than understand the definition thereof.
> *Imitatio Christi*, ch. 1, § iii. Trans. by Anthony Hoskins.

Sic transit gloria mundi.

> O, how quickly doth the glory of the world pass away! *Ib.* ch. 3, § vi.

Passione interdum movemur et zelum putamus.

> We are sometimes moved with passion, and we think it to be zeal. Quoted in *ib.* ch. 5, § i.

Multo tutius est stare in subiectione quam in praelatura.

> It is much safer to obey, than to govern.
> *Ib.* ch. 9, § i.

Si libenter crucem portas portabit te.

> If thou bear the Cross cheerfully, it will bear thee.
> *Ib.* ch. 12, § v.

Nunquam sis ex toto otiosus, sed aut legens, aut scribens, aut orans, aut meditans, aut aliquid utilitatis pro communi laborans.

> Never be entirely idle: but either be reading, or writing, or praying, or meditating, or endeavouring something for the public good.
> *Ib.* ch. 19, § iv.

Utinam per unam diem essemus bene conversati in hoc mundo.

> O that we had spent but one day in this world thoroughly well! *Ib.* ch. 23, § ii.

ALCUIN

735–804

Vox populi, vox dei.

> The voice of the people is the voice of God.
> *Letter to Charlemagne*, A.D. 800. *Works, Epis.* 127.

ST. AMBROSE

c. 340–397

Si fueris Romae, Romano vivito more;
Si fueris alibi, vivito sicut ibi.

> If you are at Rome live in the Roman style; if you are elsewhere live as they live elsewhere.
> *Quoted by* Jeremy Taylor, *Ductor Dubitantium*, I. i. 5.

ST. AUGUSTINE

354–430

Fecisti nos ad te et inquietum est cor nostrum, donec requiescat in te.

> Thou hast created us for thyself, and our heart cannot be quieted till it may find repose in thee.
> *Confessions*, bk. i, ch. 1. Trans. by Watts.

Et illa erant fercula, in quibus mihi esurienti te inferebatur sol et luna.

> And these were the dishes wherein to me, hunger-starven for thee, they served up the sun and moon. *Ib.* bk. iii, ch. 6.

Fieri non potest, ut filius istarum lacrimarum pereat.

> It is not possible that the son of these tears should be lost. *Ib.* ch. 12.

Da mihi castitatem et continentiam, sed noli modo.

> Give me chastity and continency, but do not give it yet. *Ib.* bk. viii, ch. 7.

Tolle lege, tolle lege.

> Take up and read, take up and read. *Ib.* ch. 12.

Sero te amavi, pulchritudo tam antiqua et tam nova, sero te amavi! et ecce intus eras et ego foris, et ibi te quaerebam.

> Too late came I to love thee, O thou Beauty both so ancient and so fresh, yea too late came I to love thee. And behold, thou wert within me, and I out of myself, where I made search for thee. *Ib.* bk. x, ch. 27.

Da quod iubes et iube quod vis. Imperas nobis continentiam.

> Give what thou commandest, and command what thou wilt.
> Thou imposest continency upon us. *Ib.* ch. 29.

Securus iudicat orbis terrarum.

> The verdict of the world is conclusive.
> *Contra Epist. Parmen.* iii. 24.

Salus extra ecclesiam non est.

> No salvation exists outside the church.
> *De Bapt.* IV, c., xvii. 24, referring back to St. Cyprian's 'Habere non potest Deum patrem qui ecclesiam non habet matrem' (He cannot have God for his Father who has not the church for his mother), *De Cath. Eccl. Unitate.* [vi.

Audi partem alteram.

> Hear the other side. *De Duabus Animabus*, XIV. ii.

Ama et fac quod vis.

Love and do what you will.

Popular version of St. Augustine's 'Dilige et quod vis fac' (Love and do what you will), *In Joann.* vii. 8.

Roma locuta est; causa finita est.

Rome has spoken; the case is concluded.

Sermons, Bk. i.

De vitiis nostris scalam nobis facimus, si vitia ipsa calcamus.

We make a ladder of our vices, if we trample those same vices underfoot.   *Ib.* iii. *De Ascensione.*

AUGUSTUS CAESAR
63 B.C.–A.D. 14

Quintili Vare, legiones redde.

Varus, give me back my legions.

Suetonius, *Divus Augustus,* 23.

Urbem . . . excoluit adeo, ut iure sit gloriatus marmoream se relinquere, quam latericiam accepisset.

He so improved the city that he justly boasted that he found it brick and left it marble.   *Ib.* 28.

JOSHUA BARNES?
1654–1712

Deus quos vult perdere, dementat prius.

Whom God would destroy, He first sends mad.

In his ed. of Euripides, Index Prior, s.v. Deus.

ST. BERNARD
1091–1153

Liberavi animam meam.

I have freed my soul.   *Epistle 371.*

CALIGULA
A.D. 12–41

Utinam populus Romanus unam cervicem haberet!

Would that the Roman people had but one neck!

Suetonius, *Life of Caligula,* 30.

CATO THE ELDER
234–149 B.C.

Delenda est Carthago.

Carthage must be destroyed.

Plutarch, *Life of Cato.*

CATULLUS
87–54? B.C.

Cui dono lepidum novum libellum
Arido modo pumice expolitum?

Here's my small book out, nice and new,
Fresh-bound—whom shall I give it to?

Carmina, i, trans. by Sir W. Marris.

Namque tu solebas
Meas esse aliquid putare nugas.

To you (Cornelius), who of yore
Upon my trifles set some store.   *Ib.*

Plus uno maneat perenne saeclo.

May it outlive an hundred year.   *Ib.*

Lugete, O Veneres Cupidinesque,
Et quantum est hominum venustiorum.
Passer mortuus est meae puellae,
Passer, deliciae meae puellae.

Come, all ye Loves and Cupids, haste
To mourn, and all ye men of taste;
My lady's sparrow, O, he's sped,
The bird my lady loved is dead!   *Ib.* iii.

Qui nunc it per iter tenebricosum
Illuc, unde negant redire quenquam.

And now he treads the gloomy track
Whence no one, so they say, comes back.   *Ib.*

Sed haec prius fuere.

All this is over now.   *Ib.* iv,

Vivamus, mea Lesbia, atque amemus,
Rumoresque senum severiorum
Omnes unius aestimemus assis.
Soles occidere et redire possunt:
Nobis cum semel occidit brevis lux
Nox est perpetua una dormienda.

Lesbia mine, let's live and love!
Give no doit for tattle of
Crabbed old censorious men;
Suns may set and rise again,
But when our short day takes flight
Sleep we must one endless night.   *Ib.* v.

Da mi basia mille.

Kiss me times a thousand o'er.   *Ib.*

Miser Catulle, desinas ineptire.

Forgo your dream, poor fool of love.   *Ib.* viii.

At tu, Catulle, destinatus obdura.

But bide, Catullus, firm and set.   *Ib.*

Nec meum respectet, ut ante, amorem,
Qui illius culpa cecidit velut prati
Ultimi flos, praetereunte postquam
Tactus aratro est.

But ne'er look back again to find my love,
My love, which for her fault has wilted now,
Like meadow flower, upon the marge thereof,
Touched by a passing plough.   *Ib.* xi.

Totum ut te faciant, Fabulle, nasum.

To make you nose and only nose.   *Ib.* xiii.

O quid solutis est beatius curis?
Cum mens onus reponit, ac peregrino
Labore fessi venimus larem ad nostrum,
Desideratoque acquiescimus lecto.
Hoc est quod unum est pro laboribus tantis.
Salve O venusta Sirmio atque hero gaude;
Gaudete vosque O Lydiae lacus undae;
Ridete quidquid est domi cachinnorum.

What joy is like it? to be quit of care
And drop my load, and after weary miles
Come home, and sink upon the bed that so
I used to dream of: this one thing is worth
All that long service. Hail, sweet Sirmio!
Welcome thy lord with laughter, and give back
Your laughter, waters of the Lydian lake:
Laugh, home of mine, with all your maddest mirth.
    Ib. xxxi.

Quidquid est, ubicumque est,
Quodcumque agit, renidet: hunc habet morbum,
Neque elegantem, ut arbitror, neque urbanum.

    Whate'er the case, where'er he be,
Or does, he smiles; with him it is a vice,
And not, I think, a pretty one, nor nice.
                  Carmina, xxxix.

Nam risu inepto res ineptior nulla est.

    Untimely grinning is the silliest sin.   *Ib.*

Iam ver egelidos refert tepores.

    Now Spring restores the balmy days.   *Ib.* xlvi.

Gratias tibi maximas Catullus
Agit pessimus omnium poeta,
Tanto pessimus omnium poeta,
Quanto tu optimus omnium's patronum.

    Catullus gives you warmest thanks,
And he the worst of poets ranks;
As much the worst of bards confessed,
As you of advocates the best.   *Ib.* xlix.

Ille mi par esse deo videtur,
Ille, si fas est, superare divos,
Qui sedens adversus identidem te
    Spectat et audit
Dulce ridentem, misero quod omnis
Eripit sensus mihi.

    Like to a god he seems to me,
    Above the gods, if so may be,
    Who sitting often close to thee
        May see and hear
    Thy lovely laugh: ah, luckless man!   *Ib.* li.

Quid est, Catulle? quid moraris emori?

    How now? why not be quick and die?   *Ib.* lii.

Salaputium disertum!

    He can talk, that little cuss!   *Ib.* liii.

Caeli, Lesbia nostra, Lesbia illa,
Illa Lesbia, quam Catullus unam
Plus quam se atque suos amavit omnes,
Nunc in quadruviis et angiportis
Glubit magnanimis Remi nepotes.

    My Lesbia,—Lesbia, whom once
    Catullus loved of girls alone
    Above himself and all his own—
    Now into lanes and corners runs
    To traffic with proud Remus' sons.   *Ib.* lviii.

Torquatus volo parvulus
Matris e gremio suae
Porrigens teneras manus,
Dulce rideat ad patrem
Semihiante labello.

Sit suo similis patri
Manlio et facile inscieis
Noscitetur ab omnibus,
Et pudicitiam suo
Matris indicet ore.

    I'd a wee Torquatus see
Stretch soft finger-tips
From his mother's lap, and smile
Sweetly at his sire the while
    With half-parted lips;

To his father Manlius so
Very like, in sooth
Even strangers him shall know,
And his face alone shall show
    Forth his mother's truth.   *Ib.* lxi. 209.

Vesper adest, iuvenes, consurgite: Vesper Olympo
Exspectata diu vix tandem lumina tollit.

    Up, lads! 'tis Eve at last: to longing eyes
    Upon Olympus Hesper lifts his ray.   *Ib.* lxii. 1.

Quid datur a divis felici optatius hora?

    What gift hath heaven to match thy happy hour?
                  Ib. 30.

Ut flos in saeptis secretus nascitur hortis,
Ignotus pecori, nullo contusus aratro,
Quem mulcent aurae, firmat sol, educat imber;
Multi illum pueri, multae optavere puellae.

    As grows a flower within a garden close,
    Known to no cattle, by no ploughshare smit,
    Suns give it strength, rain growth, and air repose,
    And many lads and lasses long for it.   *Ib.* 39.

Omnia fanda nefanda malo permixta furore,
Iustificam nobis mentem avertere deorum.

    Then right and wrong confused and all at odds
    Turned from us the just judgment of the gods.
                  Ib. lxiv. 406.

    Sed mulier cupido quod dicit amanti,
In vento et rapida scribere oportet aqua.

    But a woman's sayings to her lover,
    Should be in wind and running water writ. *Ib.* lxx.

Desine de quoquam quicquam bene velle mereri,
Aut aliquem fieri posse putare pium.

    Cease to expect to win men's gratitude,
    To think that human beings can be grateful.
                  Ib. lxxiii.

Siqua recordanti benefacta priora voluptas
Est homini.

    If it be good to mind each kindly act.   *Ib.* lxxvi.

Difficile est longum subito deponere amorem.

    'Tis hard to drop at once old-standing love.   *Ib.*

Si vitam puriter egi.

    If my life be fair.   *Ib.*

O di, reddite mi hoc pro pietate mea.

    Gods, grant me this thing for my piety.   *Ib.*

Chommoda dicebat, si quando commoda vellet
Dicere.

    'Hallowances' said Arrius, (meaning 'allowances').
                  Ib. lxxxiv.

Odi et amo: quare id faciam, fortasse requiris.
Nescio, sed fieri sentio et excrucior.

    I hate, I love—the cause thereof
    Belike you ask of me:
    I do not know, but feel 'tis so,
    And I'm in agony.   *Ib.* lxxxv.

Si quicquam mutis gratum acceptumve sepulcris
Accidere a nostro, Calve, dolore potest.

    If the dumb grave, my Calvus, can receive
    Aught that is dear or grateful from our grief.
                  Ib. xcvi.

Multas per gentes et multa per aequora vectus
Advenio has miseras, frater, ad inferias,
Ut te postremo donarem munere mortis
Et mutam nequiquam alloquerer cinerem.
Quandoquidem fortuna mihi tete abstulit ipsum,
Heu miser indigne frater adempte mihi,

Nunc tamen interea haec prisco quae more parentum
Tradita sunt tristi munere ad inferias,
Accipe fraterno multum manantia fletu,
Atque in perpetuum, frater, ave atque vale.

> By many lands and over many a wave
> I come, my brother, to your piteous grave,
> To bring you the last offering in death
> And o'er dumb dust expend an idle breath;
> For fate has torn your living self from me,
> And snatched you, brother, O, how cruelly!
> Yet take these gifts, brought as our fathers bade
> For sorrow's tribute to the passing shade;
> A brother's tears have wet them o'er and o'er;
> And so, my brother, hail, and farewell evermore!
> *Carmina*, ci.

At non effugies meos iambos.

> You shan't evade
> These rhymes I've made.
> *Fragments*, trans. Sir W. Marris.

THOMAS OF CELANO

c. 1250

Dies irae, dies illa
Solvet saeclum in favilla.

> Day of wrath, on that day the world shall dissolve
> in ashes.   *Analecta Hymnica*, liv, p. 269.

CICERO

106–43 B.C.

Vulgo enim dicitur: Iucundi acti labores.

> For it is commonly said: accomplished labours are
> pleasant.   *De Finibus*, ii. 105.

Id quod est praestantissimum maximeque optabile
omnibus sanis et bonis et beatis, cum dignitate
otium.

> The thing which is the most outstanding and the
> most desirable to all healthy and good and happy
> persons, is comfort with honour.
> *Pro Sestio*, xlv. 98.

Mens cuiusque is est quisque.

> The mind of each man is the man himself.
> *De Republica*, vi. 26.

In Romuli faece.

> Among the dregs of Romulus.
> *Ad Atticum*, ii. i. 8.

Spartam nactus es: hanc (ex)orna.

> Sparta is your inheritance: be worthy of her.
> *Ib*. iv. vi. 2.

Summum bonum.

> The highest good.   *De Officiis*, i. ii. 5.

Cedant arma togae, concedant laurea laudi.

> Let wars yield to peace, laurels to paeans.
> *Ib*. i. xxii. 82.

Nunquam se minus otiosum esse quam cum otiosus,
nec minus solum quam cum solus esset.

> Never less idle than when wholly idle, nor less
> alone than when wholly alone.   *Ib*. iii. i. i.

O fortunatam natam me consule Romam!

> O happy Rome born when I was consul!
> Quoted in *Juvenal*, x. 122.

Omnes artes quae ad humanitatem pertinent habent
quoddam commune vinclum et quasi cognatione
quadam inter se continentur.

> All arts which have anything to do with man have
> a common bond and as it were contain within
> themselves a certain affinity.
> *Pro Archia*, i. ii.

Haec studia adulescentiam acuunt, senectutem oblectant, secundas res ornant, adversis perfugium
ac solacium praebent, delectant domi, non impe-
diunt foris, pernoctant nobiscum, peregrinantur,
rusticantur.

> These studies are an impetus to youth, and a de-
> light to age; they are an adornment to good
> fortune, refuge and relief in trouble; they enrich
> private and do not hamper public life; they are
> with us by night, they are with us on long
> journeys, they are with us in the depths of the
> country.   *Ib*. vii. xvi.

Oderint, dum metuant.

> Let them hate so long as they fear.
> *Philippic*, i. 14 (quoted from the tragedian Accius).

Quod di omen avertant.

> May the gods avert the omen.   *Ib*. iii. xiv. 35.

Silent enim leges inter arma.

> Laws are inoperative in war.   *Pro Milone*, iv. xi.

Cui bono.

> To whose profit.   *Ib*. xii. xxxii.

Ne quid res publica detrimenti caperet.

> Lest any harm should come to the state.
> *Ib*. xxvi. lxx, quoting the senatorial 'ultimate
> decree', beginning 'caveant consules' (let the
> consuls see to it).

Quousque tandem abutere, Catilina, patientia nostra?

> How long will you abuse our patience, Catiline?
> *In Catilinam*, i. i. i.

O tempora, O mores!

> O what times, O what habits!   *Ib*.

Abiit, excessit, evasit, erupit.

> He departed, he withdrew, he went out, he broke
> forth.   *In Catilinam*, ii. i. i.

Salus populi suprema est lex.

> The good of the people is the chief law.
> *De Legibus*, iii. iii. 8.

Civis Romanus sum.

> I am a Roman citizen.   *In Verrem*, v. lvii. 147.

CONSTANTINE

288?–337

In hoc signo vinces.

> In this sign shalt thou conquer.
> *Words of Constantine's vision.* Eusebius, *Life
> of Constantine*, i. 28.

RENÉ DESCARTES

1596–1650

Cogito, ergo sum.

> I think, therefore I am.
> *Le Discours de la Méthode*.

ÆLIUS DONATUS
fl. 4th cent. A.D.

Huic quid simile sententiae et Comicus ait: 'nihil est
dictum, quod non est dictum prius.' (Terent. in
Prolog. Eunuchi.) Unde preceptor meus Donatus,
cum istum versiculum exponeret: Pereant, inquit,
qui ante nos nostra dixerunt.

The same idea is said by the comic poet: 'Nothing
is said which has not been said before.' Whence
my teacher Donatus, when he was speaking of
that verse, said, 'Confound those who have said
our remarks before us.'
St. Jerome, *Commentary on Ecclesiastes*, cap. i.
Migne's Patrologiae Cursus, xxiii. 390.

ENNIUS
239–169 B.C.

Unus homo nobis cunctando restituit rem.

One man by delaying saved the state for us.
Cicero, *De Senectute*, iv. 10.

Moribus antiquis res stat Romana virisque.
The Roman state stands by ancient customs, and
its manhood. *Annals.*

EUCLID
fl. c. 300 B.C.

Quod erat demonstrandum (tr. from the Greek).
Which was to be proved.

VENANTIUS FORTUNATUS
530–609

Vexilla regis prodeunt
Fulget crucis mysterium.

The royal banners forward go
The cross shines forth in mystic glow.
Durham Rituale. Trans. by J. M. Neale.

GAIUS
fl. c. A.D. 110–*c.* 180

Damnosa hereditas.
Ruinous inheritance. *Inst.* ii. 163.

GREGORY I
540–604

Responsum est, quod Angli vocarentur. At ille:
'Bene,' inquit; 'nam et angelicam habent faciem, et
tales angelorum in caelis decet esse coheredes.'

They answered that they were called Angles. 'It
is well,' he said, 'for they have the faces of angels,
and such should be the co-heirs of the angels in
heaven.' Bede, *Historia Ecclesiastica*, II. i.

GREGORY VII
1020–1085

Dilexi iustitiam et odi iniquitatem, propterea morior
in exilio.

I have loved justice and hated iniquity: therefore
I die in exile. Bowden, *Life*, iii, ch. 20.

HADRIAN
A.D. 76–138

Animula vagula blandula,
Hospes comesque corporis,
Quae nunc abibis in loca
Pallidula rigida nudula,
Nec ut soles dabis iocos!

Little soul, wandering, pleasant, guest and companion of the body, into what places wilt thou
now go, pale, stiff, naked, nor wilt thou play any
longer as thou art wont. *To His Soul.*

HORACE
65–8 B.C.

Ut turpiter atrum
Desinat in piscem mulier formosa superne.

Make what at the top was a beautiful woman have
ugly ending in a black fish's tail.
Ars Poetica, 4, trans. by Wickham.

'Pictoribus atque poetis
Quidlibet audendi semper fuit aequa potestas.'
Scimus, et hanc veniam petimusque damusque
vicissim.

'Poets and painters,' you say, 'have always had
an equal licence in daring invention.' We know
it: this liberty we claim for ourselves and give
again to others. *Ib.* 9.

Inceptis gravibus plerumque et magna professis
Purpureus, late qui splendeat, unus et alter
Adsuitur pannus.

Often on a work of grave purpose and high promises
is tacked a purple patch or two to give an effect
of colour. *Ib.* 14.

Amphora coepit
Institui: currente rota cur urceus exit?

It was a wine-jar that was to be moulded: as the
wheel runs round why does it come out a pitcher?
Ib. 21.

Brevis esse laboro,
Obscurus fio.

It is when I am struggling to be brief that I become unintelligible. *Ib.* 25.

Dixeris egregie notum si callida verbum
Reddiderit iunctura novum.

You may gain the finest effects in language by the
skilful setting which makes a well-known word
new. *Ib.* 47.

Multa renascentur quae iam cecidere, cadentque
Quae nunc sunt in honore vocabula, si volet usus,
Quem penes arbitrium est et ius et norma loquendi.

Many a term which has fallen from use shall have
a second birth, and those shall fall that are now
in high honour, if so Usage shall will it, in whose
hands is the arbitrament, the right and rule of
speech. *Ib.* 70.

Grammatici certant et adhuc sub iudice lis est.

Scholars dispute, and the case is still before the
courts. *Ib.* 78.

Proicit ampullas et sesquipedalia verba.

> Throws aside his paint-pots and his words a foot
> and a half long. *Ars Poetica*, 97.

        Si vis me flere, dolendum est
Primum ipsi tibi.

> If you wish to draw tears from me, you must first
> feel pain yourself. *Ib.* 102.

        Servetur ad imum
Qualis ab incepto processerit, et sibi constet.
Difficile est proprie communia dicere.

> See that it [a fresh character in a play] is kept to
> the end such as it starts at the beginning and
> is self-consistent.
> It is a hard task to treat what is common in a way
> of your own. *Ib.* 126.

Parturient montes, nascetur ridiculus mus.

> Mountains will be in labour, the birth will be a
> single laughable little mouse. *Ib.* 139.

Dic mihi, Musa, virum, captae post tempora Troiae
Qui mores hominum multorum vidit et urbis.

> Of him, my Muse, who, when Troy's ramparts fell,
> Saw many cities and men's manners, tell.
> *Ib.* 141.

Non fumum ex fulgore, sed ex fumo dare lucem
Cogitat.

> His thought is not to give flame first and then
> smoke, but from smoke to let light break out.
> *Ib.* 143.

Semper ad eventum festinat et in medias res
Non secus ac notas auditorem rapit.

> He ever hastens to the issue, and hurries his hearers
> into the midst of the story as if they knew it be-
> fore. *Ib.* 148.

Difficilis, querulus, laudator temporis acti
Se puero, castigator, censorque minorum.
Multa ferunt anni venientes commoda secum,
Multa recedentes adimunt.

> Testy, a grumbler, inclined to praise the way the
> world went when he was a boy, to play the critic
> and censor of the new generation. The tide of
> years as it rises brings many conveniences, as it
> ebbs carries many away. *Ib.* 173.

Ne pueros coram populo Medea trucidet.

> You will not let Medea slay her boys before the
> audience. *Ib.* 185.

Quodcumque ostendis mihi sic, incredulus odi.

> Anything that you thus thrust upon my sight, I
> discredit and revolt at. *Ib.* 188.

Nec deus intersit, nisi dignus vindice nodus
Inciderit.

> Neither should a god intervene, unless a knot be-
> falls worthy of his interference. *Ib.* 191.

        Vos exemplaria Graeca
Nocturna versate manu, versate diurna.

> For yourselves, do you thumb well by night and
> day Greek models. *Ib.* 268.

        Fungar vice cotis, acutum
Reddere quae ferrum valet exsors ipsa secandi.

> So I will play the part of a whetstone which can
> make steel sharp, though it has no power itself of
> cutting. *Ib.* 304.

Grais ingenium, Grais dedit ore rotundo
Musa loqui.

> It was the Greeks who had at the Muse's hand
> the native gift, the Greeks who had the utter-
> ance of finished grace. *Ib.* 323.

Omne tulit punctum qui miscuit utile dulci,
Lectorem delectando pariterque monendo.

> He has gained every vote who has mingled profit
> with pleasure by delighting the reader at once
> and instructing him. *Ib.* 343.

Indignor quandoque bonus dormitat Homerus.

> But if Homer, usually good, nods for a moment,
> I think it shame. *Ib.* 359.

Ut pictura poesis.

> As with the painter's work, so with the poet's.
> *Ib.* 361.

        Mediocribus esse poetis
Non homines, non di, non concessere columnae.

> To poets to be second-rate is a privilege which
> neither men, nor gods, nor bookstalls ever al-
> lowed. *Ib.* 372.

Tu nihil invita dices faciesve Minerva.

> You will say nothing, do nothing, unless Minerva
> pleases. *Ib.* 385.

Nonumque prematur in annum.

> Let it be kept quiet till the ninth year. *Ib.* 388.

Solve senescentem mature sanus equum, ne
Peccet ad extremum ridendus et ilia ducat.

> Be wise in time, and turn your horse out to grass
> when he shows signs of age, lest he end in a ludi-
> crous breakdown with straining flanks.
> *Epistles*, 1. i. 8, trans. by Wickham.

Nullius addictus iurare in verba magistri,
Quo me cumque rapit tempestas, deferor hospes.

> I am not bound over to swear allegiance to any
> master: where the wind carries me, I put into
> port and make myself at home. *Ib.* 14.

Virtus est vitium fugere, et sapientia prima
Stultitia caruisse.

> To flee vice is the beginning of virtue, and the be-
> ginning of wisdom is to have got rid of folly.
> *Ib.* 41.

        Hic murus aeneus esto,
Nil conscire sibi, nulla pallescere culpa.

> Be this your wall of brass, to have no guilty secrets,
> no wrong-doing that makes you turn pale. *Ib.* 60.

Si possis recte, si non, quocumque modo rem.

> Money by right means if you can, if not, by any
> means, money. *Ib.* 66.

Olim quod vulpes aegroto cauta leoni
Respondit referam: 'quia me vestigia terrent,
Omnia te adversum spectantia, nulla retrorsum.'

> The wary fox in the fable answered the sick lion:
> 'Because I am frightened at seeing that all the
> footprints point towards your den and none the
> other way.' *Ib.* 73.

Qui quid sit pulchrum, quid turpe, quid utile, quid
non,
Planius ac melius Chrysippo et Crantore dicit.

> Who shows us what is fair, what is foul, what is
> profitable, what not, more plainly and better than
> a Chrysippus or a Crantor. *Epis.*, 1. ii. 3.

Quidquid delirant reges plectuntur Achivi.

> For every folly of their princes the Greeks feel the scourge. *Epistles*, I. ii. 14.

Rursus quid virtus et quid sapientia possit
Utile proposuit nobis exemplar Ulixen.

> Again, of the power of virtue and of wisdom he has given us a profitable example in Ulysses. *Ib.* 17.

Nos numerus sumus et fruges consumere nati.

> We are the ciphers, fit for nothing but to eat our share of earth's fruits. *Ib.* 27.

Dimidium facti qui coepit habet: sapere aude.

> He who has begun his task has half done it. Have the courage to be wise. *Ib.* 40.

Ira furor brevis est.

> Anger is a short madness. *Ib.* 62.

Omnem crede diem tibi diluxisse supremum.
Grata superveniet quae non sperabitur hora.
Me pinguem et nitidum bene curata cute vises
Cum ridere voles Epicuri de grege porcum.

> Hold for yourself the belief that each day that dawns is your last: the hour to which you do not look forward will be a pleasant surprise. If you ask of myself, you will find me, whenever you want something to laugh at, in good case, fat and sleek, a true hog of Epicurus' herd. *Epis.*, I. iv. 13.

Nil admirari prope res est una, Numici,
Solaque quae possit facere et servare beatum.

> Nought to admire is perhaps the one and only thing, Numicius, that can make a man happy and keep him so. *Epis.*, I. vi. 1.

Naturam expellas furca, tamen usque recurret.

> If you drive nature out with a pitchfork, she will soon find a way back. *Epis.*, I. x. 24.

> Tamen illic vivere vellem,
Oblitusque meorum obliviscendus et illis.

> Yet I could find it in my heart to live there, forgetting my friends and forgotten by them. *Epis.*, I. xi. 8.

Caelum non animum mutant qui trans mare currunt,
Strenua nos exercet inertia: navibus atque
Quadrigis petimus bene vivere. Quod petis hic est,
Est Ulubris, animus si te non deficit aequus.

> They change their sky, not their soul, who run across the sea. We work hard at doing nothing: we seek happiness in yachts and four-horse coaches. What you seek is here—is at Ulubrae— if an even soul does not fail you. *Ib.* 27.

Concordia discors.

> Harmony in discord. *Epis.*, I. xii. 19.

Principibus placuisse viris non ultima laus est.
Non cuivis homini contingit adire Corinthum.

> To have found favour with leaders of mankind is not the meanest of glories. It is not every one that can get to Corinth. *Epis.*, I. xvii. 35.

Et semel emissum volat irrevocabile verbum.

> A word once let out of the cage cannot be whistled back again. *Epis.*, I. xviii. 71.

Nam tua res agitur, paries cum proximus ardet.

> It is your own interest that is at stake when your next neighbour's wall is ablaze. *Ib.* 80.

Tu, dum tua navis in alto est,
Hoc age, ne mutata retrorsum te ferat aura.
Oderunt hilarem tristes tristemque iocosi.

> For yourself, my friend, while your bark is on the sea, give all heed lest the breeze shift and turn your course back again. The gloomy hate the cheerful, the mirthful the gloomy. *Ib.* 87.

Fallentis semita vitae.

> The untrodden paths of life. *Ib.* 103.

Sit mihi quod nunc est, etiam minus, et mihi vivam
Quod superest aevi, si quid superesse volunt di;
Sit bona librorum et provisae frugis in annum
Copia, neu fluitem dubiae spe pendulus horae.
Sed satis est orare Iovem qui ponit et aufert,
Det vitam, det opes: aequum mi animum ipse parabo.

> Give me what I have, or even less; and therewith let me live to myself for what remains of life, if the gods will that anything remain. Let me have a generous supply of books and of food stored a year ahead; nor let me hang and tremble on the hope of the uncertain hour. Nay, it is enough to ask Jove, who gives them and takes them away, that he grant life and subsistence; a balanced mind I will find for myself. *Ib.* 107.

Prisco si credis, Maecenas docte, Cratino,
Nulla placere diu nec vivere carmina possunt
Quae scribuntur aquae potoribus.

> You know, Maecenas, as well as I, that, if you trust old Cratinus, no poems can please long, nor live, which are written by water-drinkers. *Epis.*, I. xix. 1.

O imitatores, servum pecus.

> O imitators, you slavish herd. *Ib.* 19.

Graecia capta ferum victorem cepit et artes
Intulit agresti Latio.

> When Greece had been enslaved she made a slave of her rough conqueror, and introduced the arts into Latium, still rude. *Epis.*, II. i. 156.

Si foret in terris, rideret Democritus.

> If he were on earth, Democritus would laugh at the sight. *Ib.* 194.

Atque inter silvas Academi quaerere verum.

> And seek for truth in the garden of Academus. *Epis.*, II. ii. 45.

Singula de nobis anni praedantur euntes.

> Years as they pass plunder us of one thing after another. *Ib.* 55.

Multa fero, ut placem genus irritabile vatum.

> I have to submit to much in order to pacify the sensitive race of poets. *Ib.* 102.

At qui legitimum cupiet fecisse poema,
Cum tabulis animum censoris sumet honesti.

> But the man who shall desire to leave behind him a poem true to the laws of art, when he takes his tables to write will take also the spirit of an honest censor. *Ib.* 109.

Obscurata diu populo bonus eruet atque
Proferet in lucem speciosa vocabula rerum,
Quae priscis memorata Catonibus atque Cethegis
Nunc situs informis premit et deserta vetustas.

> Phrases of beauty that have been lost to popular
> view he will kindly disinter and bring into the
> light, phrases which, though they were on the
> lips of a Cato and a Cethegus of old time, now
> lie uncouth because out of fashion and disused
> because old. *Epistles*, II. ii. 115.

Quid te exempta iuvat spinis de pluribus una?
Vivere si recte nescis, decede peritis.
Lusisti satis, edisti satis atque bibisti
Tempus abire tibi est.

> How does it relieve you to pluck one thorn out of
> many? If you do not know how to live aright,
> make way for those who do. You have played
> enough, have eaten and drunk enough. It is time
> for you to leave the scene. *Ib*. 212.

Beatus ille, qui procul negotiis,
Ut prisca gens mortalium,
Paterna rura bubus exercet suis,
Solutus omni faenore.

> Happy the man who far from schemes of business,
> like the early generations of mankind, ploughs
> and ploughs again his ancestral land with oxen
> of his own breeding, with no yoke of usury on
> his neck! *Epodes*, ii. 1.

Maecenas atavis edite regibus,
O et praesidium et dulce decus meum.

> Maecenas, in lineage the child of kings, but oh! to
> me, my protector, pride, and joy.
> *Odes*, I. i. 1, trans. by Wickham.

Indocilis pauperiem pati.

> To be content without wealth he finds too hard
> a lesson. *Ib*. 18.

Quodsi me lyricis vatibus inseres,
Sublimi feriam sidera vertice.

> But if you give me a place among the bards of
> the lyre, I shall lift my head till it strikes the
> stars. *Ib*. 35.

Audiet pugnas vitio parentum
Rara iuventus.

> How they fought shall be told to a young genera-
> tion scant in number for their parents' crimes.
> *Odes*, I. ii. 23.

Animae dimidium meae.

> The half of my own life. *Odes*, I. iii. 8.

Illi robur et aes triplex
Circa pectus erat, qui fragilem truci
Commisit pelago ratem
Primus.

> His heart was mailed in oak and triple brass who
> was the first to commit a frail bark to the rough
> seas. *Ib*. 9.

Audax omnia perpeti
Gens humana ruit per vetitum nefas.

> In its boldness to bear and to dare all things, the
> race of man rushes headlong into sin, despite of
> law. *Ib*. 25.

Nil mortalibus ardui est.

> No height is too arduous for mortal men. *Ib*. 37

Pallida Mors aequo pulsat pede pauperum tabernas
Regumque turris.

> Pale Death with impartial foot knocks at the doors
> of poor men's hovels and of kings' palaces.
> *Odes*, I. iv. 13.

Vitae summa brevis spem nos vetat incohare longam.

> Life's short span forbids us to enter on far-reaching
> hopes. *Ib*. 15.

Quis multa gracilis te puer in rosa
Perfusus liquidis urget odoribus
Grato, Pyrrha, sub antro?
Cui flavam religas comam,
Simplex munditiis?

> What delicate stripling is it, Pyrrha, that now,
> steeped in liquid perfumes, is wooing thee on
> the heaped rose-leaves in some pleasant grot?
> For whose eyes dost thou braid those flaxen
> locks, so trim, so simple? *Odes*, I. v. 1.

Nil desperandum Teucro duce et auspice Teucro.

> No lot is desperate under Teucer's conduct and
> Teucer's star. *Odes*, I. vii. 27.

Cras ingens iterabimus aequor.

> To-morrow we set out once more upon the bound-
> less sea. *Ib*. 32.

Permitte divis cetera.

> All else leave to the gods. *Odes*, I. ix. 9.

Quid sit futurum cras fuge quaerere et
Quem Fors dierum cumque dabit lucro
Appone.

> What shall be to-morrow, think not of asking.
> Each day that Fortune gives you, be it what it
> may, set down for gain. *Ib*. 13.

Donec virenti canities abest
Morosa.

> So long as youth is green and testy old age is far
> off. *Ib*. 17.

Tu ne quaesieris, scire nefas.

> Pray, ask not,—such knowledge is not for us.
> *Odes*, I. xi. 1.

Dum loquimur, fugerit invida
Aetas: carpe diem, quam minimum credula postero.

> Even while we speak, Time, the churl, will have
> been running. Snatch the sleeve of to-day, and
> trust as little as you may to to-morrow. *Ib*. 7.

Velut inter ignis
Luna minores.

> As shines the moon among the lesser fires.
> *Odes*, I. xii. 47.

Felices ter et amplius
Quos irrupta tenet copula nec malis
Divulsus querimoniis
Suprema citius solvet amor die.

> Thrice happy they, and more than thrice, whom
> an unbroken bond holds fast, and whom love,
> never torn asunder by foolish quarrellings, will
> not loose till life's last day! *Odes*, I. xiii. 17.

O matre pulchra filia pulchrior.

> O fairer daughter of a fair mother. *Odes*, I. xvi. 1.

Mater saeva Cupidinum.

> The imperious mother of Loves. *Odes*, I. xix. 1.

Integer vitae scelerisque purus.

He that is unstained in life and pure from guilt.
Odes, I. xxii. 1.

Dulce ridentem Lalagen amabo,
Dulce loquentem.

Still shall I love Lalage and her sweet laughter,
Lalage and her sweet prattle. *Ib.* 23.

Quis desiderio sit pudor aut modus
Tam cari capitis?

What shame or measure should there be in grief
for one so dear? *Odes*, I. xxiv. 1.

Multis ille bonis flebilis occidit.

Many a good man may weep for his death. *Ib.* 9.

Durum: sed levius fit patientia
Quidquid corrigere est nefas.

'Tis hard. But what may not be altered is made
lighter by patience. *Ib.* 19.

Parcus deorum cultor et infrequens.

A grudging and infrequent worshipper of the gods.
Odes, I. xxxiv. 1.

Nunc est bibendum, nunc pede libero
Pulsanda tellus.

Now we must drink, now beat the earth with free
step. *Odes*, I. xxxvii. 1.

Persicos odi, puer, apparatus.

Persian luxury, boy, I hate. *Odes*, I. xxxviii. 1.

Mitte sectari, rosa quo locorum
Sera moretur.

Cease your efforts to find where the last rose lingers.
Ib. 3.

Incedis per ignis
Suppositos cineri doloso.

You tread over fires hidden under a treacherous
crust of ashes. *Odes*, II. i. 7.

Crescit indulgens sibi dirus hydrops.

The dread dropsy grows by indulging itself.
Odes, II. ii. 13.

Aequam memento rebus in arduis
Servare mentem.

Remember when life's path is steep to keep your
mind even. *Odes*, II. iii. 1.

Omnes eodem cogimur.

We all are driven one road. *Ib.* 25.

Ille terrarum mihi praeter omnis
Angulus ridet.

That nook of earth's surface has a smile for me before all other places. *Odes*, II. vi. 13.

Auream quisquis mediocritatem
Diligit.

Whoso loves well the golden mean. *Odes*, II. x. 5.

Sperat infestis, metuit secundis
Alteram sortem bene praeparatum
Pectus.

The heart that is well forearmed hopes when times
are adverse, and when they are favourable fears,
a change of fortune. *Ib.* 13.

Neque semper arcum
Tendit Apollo.

Nor keeps Apollo his bow for ever strung.
Ib. 19.

Eheu fugaces, Postume, Postume,
Labuntur anni.

Ah me, Postumus, Postumus, the fleeting years
are slipping by. *Odes*, II. xiv. 1.

Domus et placens
Uxor.

House and wife of our choice. *Ib.* 21.

Nihil est ab omni
Parte beatum.

No lot is happy on all sides. *Odes*, II. xvi. 27.

Credite posteri.

Believe it, after-years! *Odes*, II. xix. 2.

Compesce clamorem ac sepulcri
Mitte supervacuos honores.

Check all cries, and let be the meaningless honours
of the tomb. *Odes*, II. xx. 23.

Odi profanum vulgus et arceo;
Favete linguis; carmina non prius
Audita Musarum sacerdos
Virginibus puerisque canto.

I hate the uninitiate crowd and bid them avaunt.
Listen all in silence! Strains unheard before I,
the Muses' hierophant, now chant to maidens
and to boys. *Odes*, III. i. 1.

Omne capax movet urna nomen.

Every name alike is shaken in her roomy urn. *Ib.* 16.

Post equitem sedet atra Cura.

Black Care mounts on the horseman's pillion.
Ib. 40.

Cur valle permutem Sabina
Divitias operosiores?

Why should I exchange my Sabine valley for
wealth which adds to trouble? *Ib.* 47.

Dulce et decorum est pro patria mori.

To die for fatherland is a sweet thing and becoming. *Odes*, III. ii. 13.

Virtus repulsae nescia sordidae
Intaminatis fulget honoribus,
Nec sumit aut ponit securis
Arbitrio popularis aurae.

Virtue, which cannot know the disgrace of rejection,
shines bright with honours that have no stain on
them, nor takes nor resigns the rods at the shifting breath of the people's pleasure. *Ib.* 17.

Raro antecedentem scelestum
Deseruit pede Poena claudo.

Rarely has Punishment, though halt of foot, left
the track of the criminal in the way before her.
Ib. 31.

Iustum et tenacem propositi virum
Non civium ardor prava iubentium,
Non vultus instantis tyranni
Mente quatit solida.

The just man and firm of purpose not the heat
of fellow citizens clamouring for what is wrong,
nor presence of threatening tyrant can shake in
his rocklike soul. *Odes*, III. iii. 1.

Si fractus illabatur orbis,
  Impavidum ferient ruinae.

> If the round sky should crack and fall upon him,
> the wreck will strike him fearless still.
> *Odes*, III. iii. 7.

Aurum irrepertum et sic melius situm.

> The gold unfound, and so the better placed. *Ib.* 49.

Non hoc iocosae conveniet lyrae:
Quo, Musa, tendis?

> This will not suit a mirthful lyre. Whither away,
> my Muse? *Ib.* 69.

Auditis an me ludit amabilis
Insania?

> Do you hear it? Or is it a delightful madness that
> makes sport of me? *Odes*, III. iv. 5.

Non sine dis animosus infans.

> A brave babe, surely, and some god's special care.
> *Ib.* 20.

Fratresque tendentes opaco
Pelion imposuisse Olympo.

> The brothers who strove to leave Pelion set on the
> top of leafy Olympus. *Ib.* 51.

Vis consili expers mole ruit sua.

> Force without mind falls by its own weight.
> *Ib.* 65.

O magna Carthago, probrosis
Altior Italiae ruinis!

> O mighty Carthage, lifted higher for the shameful
> downfall of Italy! *Odes*, III. v. 39.

Delicta maiorum immeritus lues.

> For the sins of your sire, albeit you had no hand
> in them, you must suffer. *Odes*, III. vi. 1.

Aetas parentum peior avis tulit
Nos nequiores, mox daturos
Progeniem vitiosiorem.

> Our sires' age was worse than our grandsires'.
> We their sons are more worthless than they: so
> in our turn we shall give the world a progeny
> yet more corrupt. *Ib.* 46.

Docte sermones utriusque linguae.

> Learned ... in the lore of either tongue.
> *Odes*, III. viii. 5.

Donec gratus eram tibi.

> So long as I found favour in your sight.
> *Odes*, III. ix. 1.

Tecum vivere amem, tecum obeam libens.

> With you I should love to live, with you be ready
> to die. *Ib.* 24.

Splendide mendax et in omne virgo
Nobilis aevum.

> With glorious falsehood ..., a maid famous to
> all time. *Odes*, III. xi. 35.

Miserarum est neque amori dare ludum neque dulci
Mala vino lavere.

> Poor maidens! who may neither let love have his
> way, nor wash away their troubles in sweet wine.
> *Odes*, III. xii. 1.

O fons Bandusiae splendidior vitro.

> O spring of Bandusia, more brilliant than glass.
> *Odes*, III. xiii. 1.

Non ego hoc ferrem calidus iuventa
Consule Planco.

> I should not have borne it in my youth's hot
> blood when Plancus was consul.
> *Odes*, III. xiv. 27.

Magnas inter opes inops.

> A pauper in the midst of wealth. *Odes*, III. xvi. 28.

O nata mecum consule Manlio
... pia testa.

> O born with me when Manlius was consul, ...
> my gentle wine-jar. *Odes*, III. xxi. 1.

      Quid leges sine moribus
Vanae proficiunt?

> What profit laws, which without lives are empty?
> *Odes*, III. xxiv. 35.

Vixi puellis nuper idoneus
Et militavi non sine gloria;
  Nunc arma defunctumque bello
    Barbiton hic paries habebit.

> Though that life is past, I was but now still meet
> for ladies' love, and fought my battles not without
> glory. Now my armour and the lute, whose cam-
> paigns are over, will hang here on yonder wall.
> *Odes*, III. xxvi. 1.

Fumum et opes strepitumque Romae.

> The smoke, and the grandeur and the noise ...
> of Rome. *Odes*, III. xxix. 12.

      Ille potens sui
Laetusque deget, cui licet in diem
  Dixisse 'vixi: cras vel atra
    Nube polum Pater occupato
Vel sole puro'.

> He will through life be master of himself and a
> happy man who from day to day can have said,
> 'I have lived: to-morrow the Sire may fill the
> sky with black clouds or with cloudless sunshine.'
> *Ib.* 41.

Exegi monumentum aere perennius.

> My work is done, the memorial more enduring than
> brass. *Odes*, III. xxx. 1.

Non omnis moriar.

> I shall not all die. *Ib.* 6.

Non sum qualis eram bonae
Sub regno Cinarae. Desine, dulcium
  Mater saeva Cupidinum.

> I am other than I was when poor Cinara was queen.
> Try no more, 'imperious mother of sweet loves'.
> [Cf. Horace, *Odes*, I. xix. 1.] *Odes*, IV. i. 3.

      Numerisque fertur
Lege solutis.

> As he [Pindar] pours along in lawless rhythms.
> *Odes*, IV. ii. 11.

Quod spiro et placeo, si placeo, tuum est.

> Breath of song and power to please, if please I
> may, are alike of thee. *Odes*, IV. iii. 24.

Fortes creantur fortibus et bonis.

> Gallant sons spring from the gallant and good.
> *Odes*, IV. iv. 29.

Duris ut ilex tonsa bipennibus
Nigrae feraci frondis in Algido,
   Per damna, per caedis, ab ipso
     Ducit opes animumque ferro.

   Like the holm-oak shorn by ruthless axes on Al-
     gidus where black leaves grow thick, through
     loss, through havoc, from the very edge of the
     steel draws new strength and heart.
                     Odes, IV. iv. 57.

Merses profundo: pulchrior evenit.

   Plunge it in the depth—it comes forth the fairer.
                             Ib. 65.

       Occidit, occidit
Spes omnis et fortuna nostri
   Nominis Hasdrubale interempto.

   Fallen, fallen is all our hope and the fortune of
     our name in the death of Hasdrubal.   *Ib.* 70.

Diffugere nives, redeunt iam gramina campis
   Arboribusque comae.

   The snows have scattered and fled; already the
     grass comes again in the fields and the leaves on
     the trees.   *Odes*, IV. vii. 1.

Immortalia ne speres, monet annus et almum
   Quae rapit hora diem.   *Ib.* 7.

   That you hope for nothing to last for ever, is the
     lesson of the revolving year and of the flight of time
     which snatches from us the sunny days.   *Ib.* 7.

Damna tamen celeres reparant caelestia lunae:
   Nos ubi decidimus
Quo pater Aeneas, quo Tullus dives et Ancus,
   Pulvis et umbra sumus.

   Yet change and loss in the heavens the swift moons
     make up again. For us, when we have descended
     where is father Aeneas, where are rich old Tullus
     and Ancus, we are but some dust and a shadow.
                             Ib. 13.

Dignum laude virum Musa vetat mori.

   The hero who is worthy of her praise the Muse
     will not let die.   *Odes*, IV. viii. 28.

Vixere fortes ante Agamemnona
Multi; sed omnes illacrimabiles
   Urgentur ignotique longa
     Nocte, carent quia vate sacro.

   Gallant heroes lived before Agamemnon, not a few:
     but on all alike, unwept and unknown, eternal
     night lies heavy because they lack a sacred poet.
                     Odes, IV. ix. 25.

      Quotiens bonus atque fidus
Iudex honestum praetulit utili.

   So often as, on a judgement-seat, generous and leal,
     he has set honour before expediency.   *Ib.* 40.

Non possidentem multa vocaveris
Recte beatum: rectius occupat
   Nomen beati, qui deorum
     Muneribus sapienter uti
Duramque callet pauperiem pati
Peiusque leto flagitium timet.

   It is not the possessor of many things whom you
     will rightly call happy. The name of the happy
     man is claimed more justly by him who has
     learnt the art wisely to use what the gods give,
     and who can endure the hardships of poverty,
     who dreads disgrace as something worse than
     death.   *Ib.* 45.

Misce stultitiam consiliis brevem:
   Dulce est desipere in loco.

   Mix with your sage counsels some brief folly. In
     due place to forget one's wisdom is sweet.
                       Odes, IV. xii. 27.

Qui fit, Maecenas, ut nemo, quam sibi sortem
Seu ratio dederit seu fors obiecerit, illa
Contentus vivat, laudet diversa sequentes?

   How comes it, Maecenas, that, whether it be self-
     chosen or flung to him by chance, every one is
     discontented with his own lot and keeps his
     praises for those who tread some other path?
        Satires, I. i. 1. Trans. by Wickham.

      Quamquam ridentem dicere verum
Quid vetat? Ut pueris olim dant crustula blandi
Doctores, elementa velint ut discere prima.

   And yet, why may one not be telling truth while one
     laughs, as teachers sometimes give little boys
     cakes to coax them into learning their letters?
                            Ib. 24.

       Mutato nomine de te
Fabula narratur.

   Change but the name, and it is of yourself that tale
     is told.   *Ib.* 69.

Est modus in rebus, sunt certi denique fines,
Quos ultra citraque nequit consistere rectum.

   There is measure in everything. There are fixed
     limits beyond which and short of which right
     cannot find resting-place.   *Ib.* 106.

Hoc genus omne.

   All their kith and kin.   *Sat.*, I. ii. 2.

       At ingenium ingens
Inculto latet hoc sub corpore.

   But under that uncouth outside are hidden vast
     gifts of mind.   *Sat.*, I. iii. 33.

Stans pede in uno.

   Without effort.   *Sat.*, I. iv. 10.

Faenum habet in cornu.

   He carries hay on his horns.   *Ib.* 34.

Etiam disiecti membra poetae.

   Even in his dismembered state, the limbs of a poet.
                            Ib. 62.

Hic niger est, hunc tu, Romane, caveto.

   That man is black at heart: mark and avoid him,
     if you are a Roman indeed.   *Ib.* 85.

        Ad unguem
Factus homo.

   The pink of accomplishment.   *Sat.*, I. v. 32.

       Credat Iudaeus Apella,
Non ego.

   Apella the Jew must believe it, not I.   *Ib.* 100.

       Naso suspendis adunco
Ignotos.

   Hang on the crook of your nose those of unknown
     origin.   *Sat.*, I. vi. 5.

Sic me servavit Apollo.

   So Apollo bore me from the fray.   *Sat.*, I. ix. 78.

Solventur risu tabulae, tu missus abibis.

   In a tempest of laughter the Tables will go to
     pieces. You will leave the court without a stain
     on your character.   *Sat.*, II. i. 86.

Nec meus hic sermo est, sed quae praecepit Ofellus
Rusticus, abnormis sapiens crassaque Minerva.

> This is no talk of my own, but the teaching of Ofel-
> lus, the countryman, a philosopher, though not
> from the schools, but of home-spun wit.
> *Sat.*, II. ii. 2.

Par nobile fratrum.

> A noble pair of brothers. *Sat.*, II. iii. 243.

Hoc erat in votis: modus agri non ita magnus,
Hortus ubi et tecto vicinus iugis aquae fons
Et paulum silvae super his foret.

> This used to be among my prayers—a portion of
> land not so very large, but which should contain
> a garden, and near the homestead a spring of
> everflowing water, and a bit of forest to complete
> it. *Sat.*, II. vi. 1.

O rus, quando ego te aspiciam? quandoque licebit
Nunc veterum libris, nunc somno et inertibus horis,
Ducere sollicitae iucunda oblivia vitae?

> O country home, when shall I look on you again!
> when shall I be allowed, between my library of
> classics and sleep and hours of idleness, to drink
> the sweet draughts that make us forget the trou-
> bles of life? *Ib.* 60.

O noctes cenaeque deum!

> O nights and suppers of gods! *Ib.* 65.

Responsare cupidinibus, contemnere honores
Fortis, et in se ipso totus, teres, atque rotundus

> Who has courage to say no again and again to de-
> sires, to despise the objects of ambition, who is a
> whole in himself, smoothed and rounded.
> *Sat.*, II. vii. 85.

JOHN HUSS

1373–1415

O sancta simplicitas!

> O holy simplicity!
> *At the stake, seeing an old peasant bringing a fag-
> got to throw on the pile.* Zincgreff-Weidner,
> *Apophthegmata*, pub. in Amsterdam 1653,
> pt. iii, p. 383. Geo. Büchmann, *Geflügelte
> Worte* (1898), p. 509.

JULIAN

c. 331–363

Vicisti, Galilæe.

> Thou hast conquered, O Galilean.
> *Dying words.* Latin translation of Theodoret,
> *Hist. Eccles.* iii. 20.

JULIUS CAESAR[1]

102?–44 B.C.

Veni, vidi, vici.

> I came, I saw, I conquered.
> Suetonius, *Divus Julius*, xxxvii. 2.
> (*Inscription displayed in Caesar's Pontic triumph,
> or, according to Plutarch, l. 2, written in a letter
> by Caesar, announcing the victory of Zela which
> concluded the Pontic campaign.*)

Iacta alea est.

> The die is cast. *Ib.* xxxii.
> (*Caesar at the crossing of the Rubicon.*)

Et tu, Brute?

> You also, Brutus?
> *Of unknown origin. Quoted by Shakespeare,
> 'Julius Caesar', III. i, perhaps from the (lost)
> Latin play 'Caesar Interfectus', probably from
> 'The True Tragedie of Richard Duke of York.'
> 'Some have written that as M. Brutus came
> running upon him, he said* "καὶ σύ, τέκνον", *"and
> you, my son."'* (Holland's *Suetonius*, p. 33.)

Gallia est omnis divisa in partes tres.

> All Gaul is divided into three parts.
> *De Bello Gallico*, I. i.

Fere libenter homines id quod volunt credunt.

> Men willingly believe what they wish. *Ib.* iii. 18.

JUVENAL

A.D. 60–c. 130

Probitas laudatur et alget.

> Honesty is commended, and starves.
> *Satires*, i. 74. Trans. by Lewis Evans.

Si natura negat, facit indignatio versum.

> If nature denies the power, indignation would give
> birth to verses. *Ib.* 79.

Quidquid agunt homines, votum timor ira voluptas
Gaudia discursus nostri farrago libelli est.

> All that men are engaged in, their wishes, fears,
> anger, pleasures, joys, and varied pursuits, form
> the hotch-potch of my book. *Ib.* 85.

Dat veniam corvis, vexat censura columbas.

> Censure acquits the raven, but falls foul of the
> dove. *Ib.* ii. 63.

Nemo repente fuit turpissimus.

> No one ever reached the climax of vice at one
> step. *Ib.* 83.

Grammaticus rhetor geometres pictor aliptes
Augur schoenobates medicus magus, omnia novit
Graeculus esuriens; in caelum miseris, ibit.

> (*Alternative reading of last line*: in coelum
> iusseris, ibit.)

> Grammarian, rhetorician, geometer, painter, trainer,
> soothsayer, rope-dancer, physician, wizard—he
> knows everything. Bid the hungry Greekling go
> to heaven! He'll go. *Ib.* iii. 76.

Nil habet infelix paupertas durius in se
Quam quod ridiculos homines facit.

> Poverty, bitter though it be, has no sharper pang
> than this, that it makes men ridiculous. *Ib.* 152.

Haud facile emergunt quorum virtutibus opstat
Res angusta domi.

> Difficult indeed is it for those to emerge from ob-
> scurity whose noble qualities are cramped by
> narrow means at home. *Ib.* 164.

1 See also Greek Quotations.

Omnia Romae
Cum pretio.

Everything at Rome is coupled with high price.
Satires, iii. 183.

Credo Pudicitiam Saturno rege moratam
In terris visamque diu.

I believe that while Saturn still was king, chastity
lingered upon earth, and was long seen there.
Ib. vi. 1.

Rara avis in terris nigroque simillima cycno.

A rare bird on the earth and very like a black
swan. *Ib.* 165.

Hoc volo, sic iubeo, sit pro ratione voluntas.

I will it, I insist on it! Let my will stand instead
of reason. *Ib.* 223.

Nunc patimur longae pacis mala, saevior armis
Luxuria incubuit victumque ulciscitur orbem.

Now we are suffering all the evils of long-continued
peace. Luxury more ruthless than war, broods
over Rome, and exacts vengeance for a conquered world. *Ib.* 292.

'Pone seram, prohibe.' Sed quis custodiet ipsos
Custodes? Cauta est et ab illis incipit uxor.

'Put on a lock! keep her in confinement!' But who
is to guard the guards themselves? Your wife
is as cunning as you, and begins with them.
Ib. 347.

Tenet insanabile multos
Scribendi cacoethes et aegro in corde senescit.

An inveterate itch of writing, now incurable, clings
to many, and grows old in their distempered
body. *Ib.* vii. 51.

Occidit miseros crambe repetita magistros.

It is the reproduction of the cabbage that wears
out the master's life. (i.e. cabbage twice cooked.)
Ib. 154.

Summum crede nefas animam praeferre pudori
Et propter vitam vivendi perdere causas.

Deem it to be the summit of impiety to prefer existence to honour, and for the sake of life to
sacrifice life's only end. *Ib.* viii. 83.

Omnibus in terris, quae sunt a Gadibus usque
Auroram et Gangen, pauci dinoscere possunt
Vera bona atque illis multum diversa, remota
Erroris nebula.

In all the regions which extend from Gades even
to the farthest east and Ganges, there are but few
that can discriminate between real blessings and
those that are widely different, all the mist of
error being removed. *Ib.* x. 1.

Nocitura toga, nocitura petuntur
Militia.

Our prayers are put up for what will injure us
in peace, and injure us in war. *Ib.* 8.

Cantabit vacuus coram latrone viator.

The traveller with empty pockets will sing even in
the robber's face. *Ib.* 22.

Verbosa et grandis epistula venit
A Capreis.

A wordy and lengthy epistle came from Capreae.
Ib. 71.

Duas tantum res anxius optat,
Panem et circenses.

Limits its (i.e. the Roman people's) anxious longings to two things only—bread, and the games
of the circus. *Ib.* 80.

I demens et saevas curre per Alpes,
Ut pueris placeas et declamatio fias.

Go then, madman, and hurry over the rugged
Alps, that you may be the delight of boys, and
furnish subjects for declamations. *Ib.* 166.

Mors sola fatetur
Quantula sint hominum corpuscula.

Death alone discloses how very small are the puny
bodies of men. *Ib.* 172.

Da spatium vitae, multos da, Iuppiter, annos.

Grant length of life, great Jove, and many years.
Ib. 188.

Orandum est ut sit mens sana in corpore sano.
Fortem posce animum mortis terrore carentem,
Qui spatium vitae extremum inter munera ponat
Naturae.

Your prayer must be that you may have a sound
mind in a sound body. Pray for a bold spirit,
free from all dread of death; that reckons the
closing scene of life among Nature's kindly
boons. *Ib.* 356.

Nullum numen habes si sit prudentia, nos te,
Nos facimus, Fortuna, deam caeloque locamus.

If we have wise foresight, thou, Fortune, hast
no divinity. It is we that make thee a deity, and
place thy throne in heaven! *Ib.* 365.

Prima est haec ultio quod se
Iudice nemo nocens absolvitur.

This is the punishment that first lights upon him,
that by the verdict of his own breast no guilty
man is acquitted. *Ib.* xiii. 2.

Quippe minuti
Semper et infirmi est animi exiguique voluptas
Ultio. Continuo sic collige, quod vindicta
Nemo magis gaudet quam femina.

Since revenge is ever the pleasure of a paltry spirit,
a weak and abject mind! Draw this conclusion
at once from the fact, that no one delights in revenge more than a woman. *Ib.* 189.

Maxima debetur puero reverentia, siquid
Turpe paras, nec tu pueri contempseris annos.

The greatest reverence is due to a child! If you
are contemplating a disgraceful act, despise not
your child's tender years. *Ib.* xiv. 47.

STEPHEN LANGTON

d. 1228

Veni Sancte Spiritus
Et emitte coelitus
Lucis tuae radium.

Come, thou holy Paraclete,
And from thy celestial seat
Send thy light and brilliancy.
Trans. by J. M. Neale.

LUIS DE LEÓN

c. 1528–1591

Dicebamus hesterna die.

We were saying yesterday.
> On resuming a lecture at Salamanca University after five years' imprisonment. A. F. G. Bell, Luis de León, ch. 8.

LIVY

59 B.C.–A.D. 17

Vae victis.

Woe to the vanquished.   History, v. xlviii. 9.

LUCAN

A.D. 39–65

Victrix causa deis placuit, sed victa Catoni.

The conquering cause was pleasing to the Gods, but the conquered one to Cato.
    i. 128. Trans. by Riley.

Stat magni nominis umbra.

There stood the shadow of a glorious name.
    Ib. 135.

Nil actum credens, dum quid superesset agendum.

Thinking nothing done while anything remains to be done.   Ib. ii. 657.

Clarum et venerabile nomen
Gentibus.

A name illustrious and revered by nations.
    Ib. ix. 203.

Estne Dei sedes nisi terra, et pontus, et aer,
Et coelum, et virtus? Superos quid quaerimus ultra?
Jupiter est quodcumque vides, quocumque moveris.

The abode of God, too, is, wherever is earth and sea and air, and sky, and virtue. Why further do we seek the Gods of heaven? Whatever thou dost behold and whatever thou dost touch, that is Jupiter.   Ib. 578.

LUCRETIUS

99–55 B.C.

Ergo vivida vis animi pervicit, et extra
Processit longe flammantia moenia mundi
Atque omne immensum peragravit, mente animoque.

And so it was that the lively force of his mind won its way, and he passed on far beyond the fiery walls of the world, and in mind and spirit traversed the boundless whole.
    De Rerum Natura, i. 72. Trans. by Bailey.

Tantum religio potuit suadere malorum.

Such evil deeds could religion prompt.   Ib. 101.

Nil posse creari
De nilo.

Nothing can be created out of nothing.   Ib. 155.

Suave, mari magno turbantibus aequora ventis,
E terra magnum alterius spectare laborem;
Non quia vexari quemquamst iucunda voluptas,
Sed quibus ipse malis careas quia cernere suave est.
Suave etiam belli certamina magna tueri
Per campos instructa tua sine parte pericli.
Sed nil dulcius est, bene quam munita tenere
Edita doctrina sapientum templa serena,
Despicere unde queas alios passimque videre
Errare atque viam palantis quaerere vitae,
Certare ingenio, contendere nobilitate,
Noctes atque dies niti praestante labore
Ad summas emergere opes rerumque potiri.

Sweet it is, when on the great sea the winds are buffeting the waters, to gaze from the land on another's great struggles; not because it is pleasure or joy that any one should be distressed, but because it is sweet to perceive from what misfortune you yourself are free. Sweet is it too, to behold great contests of war in full array over the plains, when you have no part in the danger. But nothing is more gladdening than to dwell in the calm high places, firmly embattled on the heights by the teaching of the wise, whence you can look down on others, and see them wandering hither and thither, going astray as they seek the way of life, in strife matching their wits or rival claims of birth, struggling night and day by surpassing effort to rise up to the height of power and gain possession of the world.   Ib. ii. 1.

Sic rerum summa novatur
Semper, et inter se mortales mutua vivunt.
Augescunt aliae gentes, aliae minuuntur,
Inque brevi spatio mutantur saecla animantum
Et quasi cursores vitai lampada tradunt.

Thus the sum of things is ever being replenished, and mortals live one and all by give and take. Some races wax and others wane, and in a short space the tribes of living things are changed, and like runners hand on the torch of life.   Ib. 75.

Medio de fonte leporum
Surgit amari aliquid quod in ipsis floribus angat.

From the heart of this fountain of delights wells up some bitter taste to choke them even amid the flowers.   Ib. iv. 1133.

MARTIN LUTHER

1483–1546

Esto peccator et pecca fortiter, sed fortius fide et gaude in Christo.

Be a sinner and sin strongly, but more strongly have faith and rejoice in Christ.
    Letter to Melanchthon. Epistolæ M. Lutheri (Ienae (1556), i. 345).

MAGNA CARTA

1215

Nisi per legale iudicium parium suorum vel per legem terrae.

Except by the legal judgment of his peers or the law of the land.   Clause 39.

MANILIUS

A.D. 1st cent.

Eripuit caelo fulmen, mox sceptra tyrannis.

He snatched the thunderbolt from heaven, soon the sceptres from tyrants.
i. 104. (*Inscribed on Benjamin Franklin's Statue.*)

MARTIAL

b. A.D. 43

Non est, crede mihi, sapientis dicere 'Vivam':
Sera nimis vita est crastina: vive hodie.

It sorts not, believe me, with wisdom to say 'I shall live'. Too late is to-morrow's life; live thou to-day. *Epigrammata*, i. xv. Trans. by Ker.

Sunt bona, sunt quaedam mediocria, sunt mala plura
Quae legis hic: aliter non fit, Avite, liber.

There are good things, there are some indifferent, there are more things bad that you read here. Not otherwise, Avitus, is a book produced.
Ib. xvi.

Non amo te, Sabidi, nec possum dicere quare:
Hoc tantum possum dicere, non amo te.

I do not love you, Sabidius, and I can't say why. This only I can say, I do not love you. *Ib.* xxxii.

Laudant illa sed ista legunt.

Those they praise, but they read the others.
Ib. IV. xlix.

Bonosque
Soles effugere atque abire sentit,
Qui nobis pereunt et imputantur.

And he feels the good days are flitting and passing away, our days that perish and are scored to our account. *Ib.* V. xx.

Non est vivere, sed valere vita est.

Life is not living, but living in health. *Ib.* VI. lxx.

Rus in urbe.

The country in town. *Ib.* XII. lvii.

TERENTIANUS MAURUS

fl. c. A.D. 200

Pro captu lectoris habent sua fata libelli.

The fate of books depends on the capacity of the reader. *De Literis, Syllabis, &c.*, l. 1286.

MISSAL

O felix culpa, quae talem ac tantum meruit habere Redemptorem.

O happy fault, which has deserved to have such and so mighty a Redeemer.
'Exultet' on Holy Saturday.

NERO

A.D. 37–68

Qualis artifex pereo!

What an artist dies with me!
Suetonius, *Life of Nero*, xlix, 1.

OVID

43 B.C.–A.D. 18?

Et nulli cessura fides, sine crimine mores,
Nudaque simplicitas, purpureusque pudor.

And I have good faith that will yield to none, and ways without reproach, and unadorned simplicity, and blushing modesty.
Amores, I. iii. 13. Trans. by Showerman.

Cetera quis nescit?

The rest who does not know? *Ib.* v. 25.

Procul omen abesto!

Far from us be the omen! *Ib.* xiv. 41.

Vilia miretur vulgus; mihi flavus Apollo
Pocula Castalia plena ministret aqua.

Let what is cheap excite the marvel of the crowd; for me may golden Apollo minister full cups from the Castalian fount. *Ib.* xv. 35.

Procul hinc, procul este, severae!

Away from me, far away, ye austere fair!
Ib. II. i. 3.

Iuppiter ex alto periuria ridet amantum.

Jupiter from on high laughs at the perjury of lovers. *Ars Amatoria*, i. 633.

Forsitan et nostrum nomen miscebitur istis.

Perhaps too my name will be joined to theirs.
Ib. iii. 339.

Nil mihi rescribas, tu tamen ipse veni!

Yet write nothing back to me; yourself come!
Heroides, I. i. 2. Trans. by Showerman.

Iam seges est ubi Troia fuit.

Now are fields of corn where Troy once was.
Ib. 53.

Rudis indigestaque moles.

An unformed and confused mass.
Metamorphoses, i. 7.

Medio tutissimus ibis.

You will go most safely in the middle. *Ib.* ii. 137.

Inopem me copia fecit.

Plenty makes me poor. *Ib.* iii. 466.

Ipse docet quid agam; fas est et ab hoste doceri.

He himself teaches what I should do; it is right to be taught by the enemy. *Ib.* iv. 428.

Video meliora, proboque;
Deteriora sequor.

I see and approve better things, but follow worse.
Ib. vii. 20.

Tempus edax rerum.

Time the devourer of all things. *Ib.* xv. 234.

Iamque opus exegi, quod nec Iovis ira, nec ignes,
Nec poterit ferrum, nec edax abolere vetustas.

And now I have finished the work, which neither the wrath of Jove, nor fire, nor the sword, nor devouring age shall be able to destroy. *Ib.* 871.

Principiis obsta; sero medicina paratur
Cum mala per longas convaluere moras.

Resist beginnings; too late is the medicine prepared when the disease has gained strength by long delays.
Remedia Amoris, 91. Trans. by Showerman.

Qui finem quaeris amoris,
Cedet amor rebus; res age, tutus eris.

You who seek an end of love, love yields to business: be busy, and you will be safe. *Ib.* 144.

Tu quoque.

Thou also. *Tristia*, ii. 39. Trans. by Wheeler.

Teque, rebellatrix, tandem, Germania, magni
Triste caput pedibus supposuisse ducis!

That thou, rebellious Germany, at length hast lowered thy sorrowing head beneath the foot of our leader. *Ib.* III. xii. 47.

Utque solebamus consumere longa loquendo
Tempora, sermonem deficiente die.

As we were wont to pass long hours in converse, till daylight failed our talk. *Ib.* v. xiii. 27.

Nescioqua natale solum dulcedine captos
Ducit et inmemores non sinit esse sui.

By what sweet charm I know not the native land draws all men nor allows them to forget her. *Epistulae Ex Ponto*, I.iii.35. Trans. by Wheeler.

Adde quod ingenuas didicisse fideliter artes
Emollit mores nec sinit esse feros.

Note too that a faithful study of the liberal arts humanizes character and permits it not to be cruel. *Ib.* II. ix. 47.

Gutta cavat lapidem, consumitur annulus usu.

Drops of water hollow out a stone, a ring is worn thin by use. *Ib.* IV. x. 5.

(Gutta cavat lapidem, non vi sed saepe cadendo.

The drop of rain maketh a hole in the stone, not by violence, but by oft falling. Latimer, *7th Sermon before Edw. VI*, 1549.)

PERSIUS
A.D. 34–62

Nec te quaesiveris extra.

Nor ask any opinion but your own. *Satires*, i. 7. Trans. by Conington.

At pulchrum est digito monstrari et dicier 'hic est'.

But it is a fine thing for men to point one out and say 'There he goes'. *Ib.* 28.

Virtutem videant intabescantque relicta.

Let them look upon virtue, and pine that they have lost her for ever. *Ib.* iii. 38.

Venienti occurrite morbo.

Meet the disease at its first stage. *Ib.* 64.

De nihilo nihilum, in nihilum nil posse reverti.

Nothing can come out of nothing, nothing can go back to nothing. *Ib.* 84. Trans. by Conington.

Tecum habita: noris quam sit tibi curta supellex.

Live at home, and learn how slenderly furnished your apartments are. *Ib.* iv. 52.

PETRONIUS
d. c. A.D. 66

Cave canem.

Beware of the dog. *Petronii Arbitri Satyricon*, 29, 1. *Found with picture of a dog on a mosaic floor in Pompeii.*

Horatii curiosa felicitas.

The exact felicity of Horace. *Ib.* 118.

Habes confitentem reum.

You have a confessing prisoner. *Ib.* 130.

PLAUTUS
B.C. 254–184

Miles gloriosus.

The boastful soldier. *Title of Play.*

GRIPUS: Tum tu mendicus es?
LABRAX: Tetigisti acu.

GRIPUS: Then you are a beggar?
LABRAX: You have touched the point with a needle. (You have put your finger on the spot.) *Rudens*, l. 1305.

PLINY
A.D. 23–79

Brutum fulmen.

A harmless thunderbolt. *Historia Naturalis*, II. xliii.

Ex Africa semper aliquid novi.

There is always something new from Africa. *Proverbial from Pliny:* Unde etiam vulgare Graeciae dictum 'semper aliquid novi Africam adferre'.

Whence it is commonly said among the Greeks that 'Africa always offers something new'. *Ib.* viii. 42

In vino veritas.

Truth comes out in wine. *Proverbial from Pliny:* Vulgoque veritas iam attributa vino est.

Now truth is commonly said to be in wine. *Ib.* xiv. 141.

Sal Atticum.

Attic wit. *Ib.* xxxi. 87.

Nulla dies sine linea.

Not a day without a line. *Proverbial from Pliny:* Apelli fuit alioqui perpetua consuetudo numquam tam occupatam diem agendi, ut non lineam ducendo exerceret artem, quod ab eo in proverbium venit.

It was moreover a regular habit of Apelles never to be so occupied in the business of the day that he could not practise his art by drawing a line, and this gave rise to the proverb. *Ib.* xxxv. 36. 12.

Ne supra crepidam sutor iudicaret.

The cobbler should not go beyond his last. *Ib.* 85.

PROPERTIUS
b. c. 51 B.C.

Navita de ventis, de tauris narrat arator,
Enumerat miles vulnera, pastor oves.

The seaman's story is of tempest, the ploughman's of his team of bulls; the soldier tells his wounds, the shepherd his tale of sheep. *Elegies*, ii. i. 43. Trans. by Phillimore.

Quodsi deficiant vires, audacia certe
Laus erit: in magnis et voluisse sat est.

And if my strength fail, at least my boldness will be a title of honour; in great enterprises the very 'I would' is enough. *Ib.* x. 5.

Cedite Romani scriptores, cedite Grai!
Nescio quid maius nascitur Iliade.

> Give place, you Roman writers, give place, you
> Greeks! Here comes to birth something greater
> than the Iliad.   *Ib.* xxxiv. 65.

QUINTILIAN
A.D. 40–*c*. 100

Satura quidem tota nostra est.

> Satire indeed is entirely our own.
>   *De Institutione Oratoria,* x. i. 93.

[Horatius] et insurgit aliquando et plenus est iucunditatis et gratiae et variis figuris et verbis felicissime audax.

> [Horace] soars occasionally, is full of agreeableness
> and grace, and shows a most happy daring in
> certain figures and expressions.   *Ib.* 96.

SALLUST
86–34 B.C.

Sed res docuit id verum esse, quod in carminibus Appius ait, fabrum esse suae quemque fortunae.

> But the case has proved that to be true which
> Appius says in his songs, that each man is the
> maker of his own fate.   *Ad Caesarem,* I. i. 2.

Alieni appetens, sui profusus.

> Coveting the property of others, lavish of his own.
>   *Catiline,* 5.

Idem velle atque idem nolle, ea demum firma amicitia est.

> Friendship is this—to desire, and to dislike, the
> same thing.   *Ib.* 20.

Pro patria, pro liberis, pro aris atque focis suis.

> On behalf of their country, their children, their
> altars, and their hearths.   *Ib.* 59.

Urbem venalem et mature perituram, si emptorem invenerit.

> The venal city soon to perish, if a buyer can be
> found.   *Jugurtha,* 35.

Punica fide.

> With Carthaginian faith [i.e. treachery].   *Ib.* 108, 3.

SENECA
d. A.D. 65

Contra bonum morem.

> Against good custom.   *Dialogues,* VI. i. 2.

Illi mors gravis incubat
Qui notus nimis omnibus
Ignotus moritur sibi.

> On him does death lie heavily who, but too well
> known to all, dies to himself unknown.
>   *Thyestes,* ii, *chorus.* Trans. by Miller.

SUETONIUS
fl. c. A.D. 120

Festina lente. [Σπεῦδε βραδέως.]

> Hasten slowly.   *Divus Augustus,* 25.

Ave, Imperator, morituri te salutant.

> Hail, Emperor, those about to die salute thee.
>   *Life of Claudius,* 21.

PUBLILIUS SYRUS
fl. 1st cent. B.C.

Bis dat qui cito dat.

> He gives twice who gives soon.
>   *Proverbial, attr. to Syrus.*

Beneficium inopi bis dat, qui dat celeriter.

> He doubly benefits the needy who gives quickly.
>   *Sententia,* J. 6.

Iudex damnatur ubi nocens absolvitur.

> The judge is condemned when the criminal is
> acquitted.   *Ib.* 247.

Necessitas dat legem, non ipsa accipit.

> Necessity gives the law and does not itself receive
> it.   *Ib.* 399.

Necessitas non habet legem.

> Necessity has no law.   *Proverbial, attr. to Syrus.*

TACITUS
c. A.D. 55–*c.* 117

Atque omne ignotum pro magnifico est; sed nunc terminus Britanniae patet.

> For wonder grows where knowledge fails. But now
> the very bounds of Britain are laid bare.
>   *Agricola,* 30. Trans. by Fyfe.

Ubi solitudinem faciunt, pacem appellant.

> When they make a wilderness they call it peace.
>   *Ib.*

Proprium humani ingenii est odisse quem laeseris.

> It is human nature to hate the man whom you
> have hurt.   *Ib.* 42.

Felix . . . opportunitate mortis.

> Fortune favoured him . . . in the opportune moment
> of his death.   *Ib.* 45.

Editis annalibus laudatoque M. Bruto C. Cassium Romanorum ultimum dixisset.

> In his history he had praised Brutus and had called
> Cassius the last of the Romans.   *Annals,* iv. 34.

Elegantiae arbiter. (Of Petronius.)

> Judge of taste.   *Ib.* xvi. 18.

Rara temporum felicitate ubi sentire quae velis et quae sentias dicere licet.

> It is the rare fortune of these days that a man may
> think what he likes and say what he thinks.
>   *Histories,* I. i. Trans. by Fyfe.

Maior privato visus dum privatus fuit, et omnium consensu capax imperii nisi imperasset.

> When he was a commoner he seemed too big for
> his station, and had he never been emperor, no
> one would have doubted his ability to reign.
> [*Servius Galba.*]   *Ib.* xlix.

Etiam sapientibus cupido gloriae novissima exuitur.

> For even with philosophers the passion for fame
> is often their last rag of infirmity.   *Ib.* IV. vi.

TERENCE

c. 190–159 B.C.

Id arbitror
Adprime in vita esse utile, ut nequid nimis.
My view is that the most important thing in life
is never to have too much of anything.
Andria, 61.

Davos sum, non Oedipus.
I am Davos, not Oedipus. *Ib.* 194.

Amantium irae amoris integratio est.
The quarrels of lovers are the renewal of love.
Ib. 555.

Homo sum; humani nil a me alienum puto.
I am a man, I count nothing human indifferent to
me. *Heauton Timorumenos*, I. i. 25.

Fortis fortuna adiuvat.
Fortune aids the brave. *Phormio*, 203.

Quot homines tot sententiae; suus cuique mos.
So many men, so many opinions; his own a law to
each. *Ib.* 454.

TERTULLIAN

c. 155–c. 222

Certum est quia impossibile est.
It is certain because it is impossible.
De Carne Christi, ii. 5.

O testimonium animae naturaliter Christianae.
O witness of the soul naturally Christian.
Apol. xvii.

TIBULLUS

54?–18? B.C.

Te spectem, suprema mihi cum venerit hora,
Te teneam moriens deficiente manu.
Let me behold thee when my last hour is come,
thee let me hold with my dying hand.
I. i. 59.

Iupiter pluvius.
Jupiter the rain-bringer. *Ib.* vii. 26.

TITUS VESPASIANUS

A.D. 40 or 41–81

Amici, diem perdidi.
Friends, I have lost a day.
Suetonius, *Titus*, ch. 8, i.

JACOPONI DA TODI

fl. 13th cent. A.D.

Stabat mater dolorosa
Iuxta crucem lacrimosa.
At the cross her station keeping
Stood the mournful mother weeping.
Pachen, *Jacoponi da Todi*. Trans. in English
Hymnal.

VEGETIUS

4th cent. A.D.

Qui desiderat pacem, praeparet bellum.
Let him who desires peace, prepare for war.
De Re Mil. 3, prol.

ST. VINCENT OF LERINS

d. c. A.D. 450

Quod semper, quod ubique, quod ab omnibus credi-
tum est.
What is always, what is everywhere, what is by all
people believed. *Commonitorium*, ii.

VIRGIL

70–19 B.C.

Arma virumque cano, Troiae qui primus ab oris
Italiam fato profugus Lavinaque venit
Litora—multum ille et terris iactatus et alto
Vi superum, saevae memorem Iunonis ob iram.
Arms I sing, and the man, who first from the
shores of Troy came, Fate-exiled, to Italy and her
Lavinian strand—much buffeted he on flood and
field by constraint of Heaven and fell Juno's un-
slumbering ire. *Aeneid*, I. i. Trans. by Jackson.

Quo numine laeso.
Wherein was her godhead affronted. *Ib.* 8.

Tantaene animis caelestibus irae?
Can heavenly spirits cherish resentment so dire?
Ib. 11.

Necdum etiam causae irarum saevique dolores
Exciderant animo; manet alta mente repostum
Iudicium Paridis spretaeque iniuria formae.
Nor yet had the causes of her wrath, nor her hot
resentment, faded from her soul. Deep-written
in her heart the judgement of Paris remained, and
the outrage to her slighted beauty. *Ib.* 25.

Tantae molis erat Romanam condere gentem.
So vast was the struggle to found the Roman
state. *Ib.* 33.

Apparent rari nantes in gurgite vasto.
Here and there in the wastes of ocean a swimmer
was seen. *Ib.* 118.

Furor arma ministrat.
Fury ministers arms. *Ib.* 150.

Fidus quae tela gerebat Achates.
Loyal Achates bore the weapons. *Ib.* 188.

O passi graviora, dabit deus his quoque finem.
Friends, that have endured yet heavier blows,
God will grant an ending even to this. *Ib.* 199.

Forsan et haec olim meminisse iuvabit.
The day may dawn when this plight shall be sweet
to remember. *Ib.* 203.

Durate, et vosmet rebus servate secundis.
Then endure for a while, and live for a happier
day! *Ib.* 207.

Dux femina facti.
A woman the head of their emprize. *Ib.* 364.

Vera incessu patuit dea.

> The goddess indubitable was revealed in her step.
> *Aeneid*, I. 405.

'En Priamus. Sunt hic etiam sua praemia laudi;
Sunt lacrimae rerum et mentem mortalia tangunt.
Solve metus; feret haec aliquam tibi fama salutem.'
Sic ait atque animum pictura pascit inani.

> 'Lo, here is Priam! Even here, virtue hath her
> rewards, and mortality her tears: even here, the
> woes of man touch the heart of man! Dispel
> thy fears; this fame of ours is herald to some
> salvation.' He said, and sated his soul with the
> barren portraiture.   *Ib.* 461.

Impar congressus Achilli.

> Fronted Achilles with unequal arm.   *Ib.* 475.

Mens sibi conscia recti.

> A mind conscious of the right.   *Ib.* 604.

In freta dum fluvii current, dum montibus umbrae
Lustrabunt convexa, polus dum sidera pascet,
Semper honos nomenque tuum laudesque manebunt.

> While the rivers shall run to ocean, while the
> shadows shall move in the mountain valleys,
> while the sky shall feed the stars, always shall thy
> honour, and thy name, and thy glory abide.
>   *Ib.* 607.

Non ignara mali miseris succurrere disco.

> Not unschooled in woe do I learn to succour un-
> happiness!   *Ib.* 630.

Conticuere omnes intentique ora tenebant.

> Every tongue was still, every face turned rapt upon
> him.   *Ib.* ii. 1.

Infandum, regina, iubes renovare dolorem.

> Too deep for words, O queen, lies the sorrow thou
> bidst me renew.   *Ib.* 3.

Quaeque ipse miserrima vidi
Et quorum pars magna fui.

> All the deeds of woe mine eyes have beheld, and
> those whereof I was no small part.   *Ib.* 5.

Et iam nox umida caelo
Praecipitat suadentque cadentia sidera somnos.

> And now dewy Night falls precipitate from heaven,
> and the setting stars counsel sleep!   *Ib.* 8.

Equo ne credite, Teucri.
Quidquid id est, timeo Danaos et dona ferentes.

> Men of Troy, trust not the horse! Be it what it
> may, I fear the Danaans, though their hands
> proffer gifts.   *Ib.* 48.

In utrumque paratus,
Seu versare dolos seu certae occumbere morti.

> Nerved to either event, whether to spin his toils, or
> to fall under death inevitable.   *Ib.* 61.

Crimine ab uno
Disce omnes.

> From a single crime know the nation.   *Ib.* 65.

Horresco referens.

> I shudder at the word.   *Ib.* 204.

Tacitae per amica silentia lunae.

> Through the friendly silence of the mute moon.
>   *Ib.* 255.

Tempus erat quo prima quies mortalibus aegris
Incipit et dono divum gratissima serpit.

> It was the hour when the first sleep of suffering
> mortality begins, and, by the grace of Heaven,
> steals on its sweetest errand of mercy.   *Ib.* 268.

Quantum mutatus ab illo
Hectore qui redit exuvias indutus Achilli.

> How was he changed from that Hector, who wended
> homeward, clad in the spoils of Achilles. *Ib.* 274.

Iam proximus ardet
Ucalegon.

> Already neighbour Ucalegon burns.   *Ib.* 311.

Fuimus Troes, fuit Ilium et ingens
Gloria Teucrorum.

> Trojans we are no more, Ilium is no more, and
> the great glory of the Teucrians is departed!
>   *Ib.* 325.

Una salus victis nullam sperare salutem.

> There is but one safety to the vanquished—to
> hope not safety!   *Ib.* 354.

Dis aliter visum.

> Heaven's thought was otherwise.   *Ib.* 428.

Non tali auxilio nec defensoribus istis
Tempus eget.

> The hour calls not for such succour, nor such
> defenders.   *Ib.* 521.

Sequiturque patrem non passibus aequis.

> Follows his father with unmatched step.   *Ib.* 724.

Quid non mortalia pectora cogis,
Auri sacra fames!

> O cursed lust of gold, to what canst thou not com-
> pel the heart of man!   *Ib.* iii. 56.

Monstrum horrendum, informe, ingens, cui lumen
ademptum.

> A monster fearful and hideous, vast and eyeless.
>   *Ib.* 658.

Agnosco veteris vestigia flammae.

> I feel again a spark of that ancient flame.
>   *Ib.* iv. 23.

Virisque adquirit eundo.

> At every step she gathers strength.   *Ib.* 175.

Sese interea . . .
Temptaturum aditus et quae mollissima fandi
Tempora.

> Himself meanwhile . . . would assay to find access
> and watch what hour might be the smoothest
> for his tale.   *Ib.* 291.

Quis fallere possit amantem?

> Who shall deceive a lover's thought?   *Ib.* 296.

Nec me meminisse pigebit Elissae
Dum memor ipse mei, dum spiritus hos regit artus.

> Nor ever shall the thought of Elissa be bitter to
> me, while yet I have remembrance of myself
> and the breath governs these limbs.   *Ib.* 335.

Varium et mutabile semper
Femina.

> A fickle thing and changeful is woman always!
>   *Ib.* 569.

Exoriare aliquis nostris ex ossibus ultor.

> Arise, thou avenger to come, out of my ashes.
>   *Ib.* 625.

Hos successus alit: possunt, quia posse videntur.

> To those success was good, and the semblance of power gave power indeed. *Aeneid*, v. 231.

Facilis descensus Averno:
Noctes atque dies patet atri ianua Ditis;
Sed revocare gradum superasque evadere ad auras,
Hoc opus, hic labor est.

> Light is the descent to Avernus! Night and day the portals of gloomy Dis stand wide: but to recall thy step and issue to the upper air—there is the toil and there the task! *Ib.* vi. 126.

Primo avulso non deficit alter
Aureus, et simili frondescit virga metallo.

> When the first is rent away a second, golden no less, succeeds, and the bough blossoms with ore as precious. *Ib.* 143.

'Procul, o procul este, profani.'

> Hence, O hence, . . . ye that are uninitiated! *Ib.* 258.

Nunc animis opus, Aenea, nunc pectore firmo.

> Now is the hour, Aeneas, for the dauntless spirit —now for the stout heart. *Ib.* 261.

Vestibulum ante ipsum primis in faucibus Orci
Luctus et ultrices posuere cubilia Curae;
Pallentesque habitant Morbi tristisque Senectus,
Et Metus et malesuada Fames ac turpis Egestas.

> Hard before the portal, in the opening jaws of Hell, Grief and avenging Cares have made their couch; and with them dwell wan Disease and sorrowful Age, and Fear, and Hunger, temptress to Sin, and loathly Want. *Ib.* 273.

Tendebantque manus ripae ulterioris amore.

> Their hands outstretched in yearning for the farther shore. *Ib.* 314.

Inventas aut qui vitam excoluere per artis,
Quique sui memores alios fecere merendo.

> Or who ennobled life by arts discovered; with all whose service to their kind won them remembrance among men. *Ib.* 663.

Spiritus intus alit, totamque infusa per artus
Mens agitat molem et magno se corpore miscet.

> An indwelling spirit sustains, and a mind fused throughout the limbs sways the whole mass and mingles with the giant frame. *Ib.* 726.

Igneus est ollis vigor et caelestis origo
Seminibus.

> To these seeds a flame-like vigour pertains and an origin celestial. *Ib.* 730.

Tu regere imperio populos, Romane, memento
(Hae tibi erunt artes), pacisque imponere morem,
Parcere subiectis et debellare superbos.

> Roman, be this thy care—these thine arts—to bear dominion over the nations and to impose the law of peace, to spare the humbled and to war down the proud! *Ib.* 851.

Sunt geminae Somni portae, quarum altera fertur
Cornea, qua veris facilis datur exitus umbris,
Altera candenti perfecta nitens elephanto,
Sed falsa ad caelum mittunt insomnia manes.

> There are two gates of Sleep:—of horn, fame tells, the one, through which the spirits of truth find an easy passage; the other, wrought smooth-gleaming with sheen of ivory, but false the visions that the nether powers speed therefrom to the heaven above. *Ib.* 893.

Geniumque loci . . .
> precatur.

> Implored the Genius of the place. *Ib.* vii. 136.

Flectere si nequeo superos, Acheronta movebo.

> And if Heaven be inflexible, Hell shall be unleashed! *Ib.* 312.

O mihi praeteritos referat si Iuppiter annos.

> O, would Jupiter restore me the years that are fled! *Ib.* viii. 560.

Quadripedante putrem sonitu quatit ungula campum.

> The sound of galloping hooves shook the crumbling plain. *Ib.* 596.

Me, me, adsum qui feci, in me convertite ferrum.

> On me,—here I stand who did the deed,—on me turn your steel. *Ib.* ix. 427.

Dum domus Aeneae Capitoli immobile saxum
Accolet imperiumque pater Romanus habebit.

> So long as the house of Aeneas shall dwell by the Capitol's unmoved rock and the Father of Rome bear sceptre! *Ib.* 448.

Macte nova virtute, puer, sic itur ad astra.

> Good speed to thy youthful valour, child! So shalt thou scale the stars! *Ib.* 641.

Audentis Fortuna iuvat.

> Fortune is ally to the brave. *Ib.* x. 284.

Experto credite.

> Credit one who has proved. *Ib.* xi. 283.

Audiit et voti Phoebus succedere partem
Mente dedit, partem volucris dispersit in auras.

> Phoebus heard, and in thought vouchsafed that half his vow should prosper: half he scattered to the fleet winds. *Ib.* xi. 794.

Di me terrent et Iuppiter hostis.

> The gods dismay me, and Jove my foe! *Ib.* xii. 895.

Tityre, tu patulae recubans sub tegmine fagi
Silvestrem tenui musam meditaris avena.

> Tityrus, thou liest canopied beneath thy spreading beech and wooing the silvan Muse on thy slender oat. *Eclogues*, i. i. Trans. by Jackson.

Formosam resonare doces Amaryllida silvas.

> Thou teachest the responsive woods to call Amaryllis fair! *Ib.* 5.

O Meliboee, deus nobis haec otia fecit.

> O Meliboeus, it was a god gave us this peace. *Ib.* 6.

Non equidem invideo, miror magis.

> As for me I grudge thee not—rather I marvel! *Ib.* 11.

Verum haec tantum alias inter caput extulit urbes
Quantum lenta solent inter viburna cupressi.

> But, above all other cities, this so far exalts her head as the cypress above the lissom osiers! *Ib.* 24.

Et penitus toto divisos orbe Britannos.

> Or where the Briton dwells utterly estranged from all the world! *Ib.* 66.

Formosum pastor Corydon ardebat Alexim.

> Shepherd Corydon was all aflame for fair Alexis. *Ib.* ii. 1.

O formose puer, nimium ne crede colori!

> Sweet boy, trust not over much to thy hue!
> *Eclogues*, ii. 17.

Quem fugis, a, demens? Habitarunt di quoque silvas.

> Ah, madman, whom dost thou flee? Even gods
> have dwelt in woods. *Ib.* 60.

Trahit sua quemque voluptas.

> Each draws to his best-beloved. *Ib.* 65.

Nunc frondent silvae, nunc formosissimus annus.

> Now the woods are green, and the year is love-
> liest. *Ib.* iii. 57.

Ab Iove principium musae.

> From Jove my lay begins. *Ib.* 60.

Malo me Galatea petit, lasciva puella,
Et fugit ad salices et se cupit ante videri.

> Galatea, wayward girl, pelts me with apples, then
> runs behind the willows—and hopes I saw her
> first! *Ib.* 64.

Latet anguis in herba.

> A snake lurks in the grass! *Ib.* 93.

Non nostrum inter vos tantas componere lites.

> Not ours to decide such high dispute! *Ib.* 108.

Claudite iam rivos, pueri; sat prata biberunt.

> Swains, close now the springs. The meadows have
> drunk enough! *Ib.* 111.

Sicelides Musae, paulo maiora canamus!
Non omnis arbusta iuvant humilisque myrica.
Si canimus silvas, silvae sint consule dignae.
Ultima Cumaei venit iam carminis aetas;
Magnus ab integro saeclorum nascitur ordo.
Iam redit et virgo, redeunt Saturnia regna
Iam nova progenies coelo demittitur alto.

> Sicilian Muses, let us raise a somewhat loftier
> strain. Not all do orchards and the lowly tamarisk
> delight. If the woodland be our theme, let our
> woods be worthy of a consul's ear! The last age,
> heralded in Cumean song, is come, and the great
> march of the centuries begins anew. Now the
> Virgin returns: now Saturn is king again, and a
> new and better race descends from on high.
> *Ib.* iv. 1.

Incipe, parve puer, risu cognoscere matrem.

> Begin, baby boy, to know thy mother with a smile.
> *Ib.* 60.

Incipe, parve puer: qui non risere parenti,
Nec deus hunc mensa, dea nec dignata cubili est.

> Begin, baby boy! Him who had never a smile for
> a parent, no god honours with his board, no god-
> dess with her bed! *Ib.* 62.

Arcades ambo,
Et cantare pares et respondere parati.

> Both Arcadians, both ready to sing in even con-
> test, both ready to make reply! *Ib.* vii. 4.

Saepibus in nostris parvam te roscida mala
(Dux ego vester eram) vidi cum matre legentem.
Alter ab undecimo tum me iam acceperat annus,
Iam fragilis poteram a terra contingere ramos:
Ut vidi, ut perii, ut me malus abstulit error!

> Within our orchard's walls I saw thee—for I was
> there to point the way—a little maid gathering
> dewy apples with my mother! Eleven years I

had numbered, and the twelfth already claimed
me; from the ground already I could reach the
frail boughs. Ah, how I saw! How I fell! How
that fatal blindness swept me away! *Ib.* viii. 37.

Nunc scio quid sit Amor.

> Now do I know what Love is! *Ib.* 43.

Non omnia possumus omnes.

> All power is not to all. *Ib.* 63.

Et me fecere poetam
Pierides, sunt et mihi carmina, me quoque dicunt
Vatem pastores; sed non ego credulus illis.
Nam neque adhuc Vario videor nec dicere Cinna
Digna, sed argutos inter strepere anser olores.

> Me, too, the Pierian sisters have made a singer; I,
> too, have songs: ay, and the shepherds dub me
> *poet*, but I trust them not! For as yet, methinks,
> my strains befit not a Varius nor a Cinna, but,
> gooselike, I cackle amid quiring swans!
> *Ib.* ix. 32.

Omnia vincit Amor: et nos cedamus Amori.

> Love is lord of all: yield we, too, to Love!
> *Ib.* x. 69.

Ite domum saturae, venit Hesperus, ite capellae.

> Get ye home, my full-fed goats, get ye home—the
> Evening-star draws on! *Ib.* 77.

Ultima Thule.

> Farthest Thule. *Georgics*, i. 30. Trans. by Jackson.

Labor omnia vicit
Improbus et duris urgens in rebus egestas.

> Never-flinching labour proved lord of all, and the
> stress of need in a life of struggles! *Ib.* 145.

Imponere Pelio Ossam
Scilicet, atque Ossae frondosum involvere Olympum.

> In sooth . . . to pile Ossa on Pelion and roll leaf-
> crowned Olympus on Ossa. *Ib.* 281.

Miscueruntque herbas et non innoxia verba.

> Mingled herbs and charms of bale. *Ib.* ii. 129.

Salve, magna parens frugum, Saturnia tellus,
Magna virum.

> Hail, Saturn's land, great mother of the harvest,
> great mother of men! *Ib.* 173.

O fortunatos nimium, sua si bona norint,
Agricolas! Quibus ipsa procul discordibus armis
Fundit humo facilem victum iustissima tellus.

> Ah, blest beyond all bliss the husbandmen, did
> they but know their happiness! On whom, far
> from the clash of arms, the most just Earth
> showers from her bosom a toilless sustenance.
> *Ib.* 458.

Felix qui potuit rerum cognoscere causas.

> Happy he, who has availed to read the causes of
> things. *Ib.* 490.

Strepitumque Acherontis avari.

> The roaring of the hungry stream of Death! *Ib.* 492.

Fortunatus et ille deos qui novit agrestis.

> And happy he, who has knowledge of the wood-
> land gods. *Ib.* 493.

Temptanda via est, qua me quoque possim
Tollere humo victorque virum volitare per ora.

> I must assay a path, whereby I may raise me from
> earth and flit conqueror through the mouths of
> men! *Georgics*, iii. 8.

Optima quaeque dies miseris mortalibus aevi
Prima fugit: subeunt morbi tristisque senectus
Et labor, et durae rapit inclementia mortis.

> It is ever the brightest day of life that is first to
> bid adieu to our hapless mortality: disease and
> gloomy eld steal upon us, and anon suffering,
> and the ruthless tyranny of Death, sweep us
> away. *Ib.* 66.

Sed fugit interea, fugit irreparabile tempus.

> Meanwhile, Time is flying—flying, never to re-
> turn. *Ib.* 284.

Hi motus animorum atque haec certamina tanta
Pulveris exigui iactu compressa quiescent.

> Yet all this tumult of soul and all this savagery
> of conflict may be quelled and laid to rest by
> the scattering of a little dust! *Ib.* iv. 86.

Agmine facto
Ignavum fucos pecus a praesepibus arcent.

> They form in array and cast out the drones and their
> idle bands from the homestead. *Ib.* 167.

At genus immortale manet, multosque per annos
Stat fortuna domus, et avi numerantur avorum.

> Yet the race abides immortal, the star of their
> house sets not through many years, and grand-
> sire's grandsire is numbered in the roll. *Ib.* 208.

Victorque volentis
Per populos dat iura viamque adfectat Olympo.

> Assigning, in victorious march, laws to the will-
> ing nations, and assaying on earth the path to
> Heaven! *Ib.* 561.

VULGATE

Fiat lux.

> Let there be light. *Genesis* 1. 3.

Dominus illuminatio mea.

> The Lord is my light. *Psalm* 27.

Quo vadis?

> Whither goest thou? *John* xvi. 5.

Ecce homo.

> Behold the man. *Ib.* xix. 5.

ANONYMOUS

Adeste, fideles,
Laeti triumphantes;
Venite, venite in Bethlehem.

> O come, all ye faithful,
> Joyful and triumphant,
> O come ye, O come ye to Bethlehem.
> *French or German hymn of 18th Cent.* Trans-
> lation by Oakeley in *Murray's Hymnal*, 1852.
> See *Songs of Praise Discussed*.

Ad majorem Dei gloriam.

> To the greater glory of God.
> *Motto of the Society of Jesus.*

Cras amet qui nunquam amavit, quique amavit cras
amet!

> Let those love now, who never lov'd before:
> Let those who always lov'd, now love the more.
> *Pervigilium Veneris*, 1. Trans. by Parnell.

De non apparentibus et de non existentibus eadem est
ratio.

> The reasoning is the same about what does not ap-
> pear to exist and what does not exist.
> *Law Maxim.*

Meum est propositum in taberna mori,
Ubi vina proxima morientis ori:
Tunc cantabunt laetius angelorum chori
'Sit Deus propitius huic potatori.'

> I desire to end my days in a tavern drinking,
> May some Christian hold for me the glass when I
> am shrinking;
> That the Cherubim may cry, when they see me
> sinking,
> 'God be merciful to a soul of this gentleman's
> way of thinking.'
> *The 'Archipoeta'.* Trans. by Leigh Hunt.

Si monumentum requiris, circumspice.

> If you ask where is his monument, look around you.
> *Epitaph of Sir Christopher Wren in St. Paul's
> Cathedral.*

Sic vos non vobis mellificatis apes.
Sic vos non vobis nidificatis aves.
Sic vos non vobis vellera fertis oves.

> So you bees make your honey, not for yourselves.
> So you birds make nests, not for yourselves.
> So you sheep bear fleeces, not for yourselves.
> *Lines attributed to Virgil on Bathyllus' claiming
> the authorship of certain lines by Virgil.*

Surrexit Christus hodie
Humano pro solamine:
Alleluja.

> Jesus Christ is risen to-day,
> Alleluia!
> Our triumphant holy day!
> Alleluia!
> *German Easter Carol of 14th cent.* Transla-
> tion in *Lyra Davidica*, 1708. See *Songs of
> Praise Discussed*.

Te Deum laudamus.

> We praise thee, O God.
> *First words and title of Canticle attr. to S.
> Ambrose.*

GREEK QUOTATIONS

AESCHYLUS
525–456 B.C.
ποντίων τε κυμάτων ἀνήριθμον γέλασμα.

Multitudinous laughter of the waves of ocean.
Prometheus Bound, 88. Trans. by Herbert Weir Smith (Loeb edition).

ALEXANDER
356–323 B.C.
εἰ μὴ ᾽Αλέξανδρος ἤμην, Διογένης ἂν ἤμην.

If I were not Alexander, I would be Diogenes.
Plutarch, Life of Alexander, xiv. 3.

ARCHIMEDES
287–212 B.C.
εὕρηκα.

Eureka! (I have found!)
Vitruvius Pollio, De Architectura, ix. 215.

δός μοι που στῶ καὶ κινῶ τὴν γῆν.

Give me but one firm spot on which to stand, and I will move the earth.
Pappus, Alexandr., Collectio, lib. viii, prop. 10, § xi (ed. Hultsch, Berlin 1878).

ARISTOPHANES
c. 444–c. 380 B.C.
ὁ δ᾽ εὔκολος μὲν ἐνθάδ᾽, εὔκολος δ᾽ ἐκεῖ.

'But he was easy there, is easy here' (Sophocles)
Frogs, 82. Trans. by Rogers.

ARISTOTLE
384–322 B.C.
ἄνθρωπος φύσει πολιτικὸν ζῷον.

Man is by nature a political animal.
Politics, i. 2. 9. 1252 b (ed. Newman).

ἢ θηρίον ἢ θεός.

Either a beast or a god. *Ib.* 14. 1253.

ἔστιν οὖν τραγῳδία μίμησις πράξεως σπουδαίας καὶ τελείας μέγεθος ἐχούσης . . . δι᾽ ἐλέου καὶ φόβου περαίνουσα τὴν τῶν τοιούτων παθημάτων κάθαρσιν.

A tragedy is the imitation of an action that is serious and also, as having magnitude, complete in itself . . . with incidents arousing pity and fear, wherewith to accomplish its purgation of such emotions.
Poetics, 6. 1449 b. Trans. by Bywater.

CALLIMACHUS
fl. 250 B.C.
μέγα βιβλίον μέγα κακόν.

Great book, great evil.
Proverb derived from Callimachus, *Fragments*, 359.

DIOGENES
fl. c. 380 B.C.
"μικρόν", εἶπεν, "ἀπὸ τοῦ ἡλίου μετάστηθι,"

Alexander . . . asked him if he lacked anything. 'Yea,' said he, 'that I do: that you stand out of my sun a little.' Plutarch, *Life of Alexander*, 14 (North's translation).

EURIPIDES
480–406 B.C.
ἡ γλῶσσ᾽ ὀμώμοχ᾽, ἡ δὲ φρὴν ἀνώμοτος.

'Twas but my tongue, 'twas not my soul that swore.
Hippolytus, 612. Trans. by Gilbert Murray.

HERACLEITUS
fl. 513 B.C.
πάντα ῥεῖ, οὐδὲν μένει.

All is flux, nothing is stationary.
Alluded to by Aristotle in De Caelo, 3. 1. 18 (ed. Weise) and elsewhere.

HERODOTUS
484–424? B.C.
οὐ φροντὶς Ἱπποκλείδῃ.

Hippocleides doesn't care. *Histories*, vi. 129.

HESIOD
c. 735 B.C.
πλέον ἥμισυ παντός.

The half is greater than the whole.
Works and Days, 40.

HIPPOCRATES
c. 460–357 B.C.
ὁ βίος βραχύς, ἡ δὲ τέχνη μακρή.

The life so short, the craft so long to learn.
Aphorisms, i. i. Trans. by Chaucer.

HOMER
c. 900 B.C.
μῆνιν ἄειδε, θεά, Πηληϊάδεω ᾽Αχιλῆος
οὐλομένην, ἡ μυρί᾽ ᾽Αχαιοῖς ἄλγε᾽ ἔθηκε.
The wrath of Peleus' son, the direful spring
Of all the Grecian woes, O Goddess, sing!
Iliad, i. 1. Trans. by Pope.

τὸν δ'ἀπαμειβόμενος

To him in answer spake. . .   *Iliad*, i. 84.

δακρυόεν γελάσασα.

Smiling through tears.   *Ib*. vi. 484.

οἵη περ φύλλων γενεή, τοίη δὲ καὶ ἀνδρῶν.

As the generation of leaves, so is that of men.
Ib. vi. 146.

αἰὲν ἀριστεύειν καὶ ὑπείροχον ἔμμεναι ἄλλων.

Always to be best, and distinguished above the
rest.   *Ib*. 208.

εἷς οἰωνὸς ἄριστος, ἀμύνεσθαι περὶ πάτρης.

One omen is best, to fight in defence of one's
country.   *Ib*. xii. 243.

ἄνδρα μοι ἔννεπε, Μοῦσα, πολύτροπον.

Tell me, Muse, of the man of many wiles. (Odysseus.)   *Odyssey*, i. 1.

πολλῶν δ' ἀνθρώπων ἴδεν ἄστεα καὶ νόον ἔγνω.

He saw the cities of many men, and knew their
mind.   *Ib*. 3.

PINDAR
c. 522–442 B.C.

ἄριστον μὲν ὕδωρ.

Water is best. [*Inscription over the Pump Room at
Bath*.]
Olympian Odes, I. i.

φωνᾶντα συνετοῖσιν· ἐς δὲ τὸ πᾶν ἑρμηνέων
χατίζει.

Vocal to the wise; but for the crowd they need
interpreters.   *Ib*. ii. 85.

PROTAGORAS
c. 481–411 B.C.

πάντων χρημάτων ἄνθρωπον μέτρον εἶναι.

Man is the measure of all things.
Quoted by Plato in Theaetetus, 160d.

SIMONIDES
556–468 B.C.

ὦ ξεῖν', ἄγγειλον Λακεδαιμονίοις ὅτι τῇδε
κείμεθα, τοῖς κείνων ῥήμασι πειθόμενοι.

'Go, tell the Spartans, thou who passest by,
That here obedient to their laws we lie.'
Select Epigrams (ed. Mackail), iii. 4.

SOCRATES
469–399 B.C.

ὦ Κρίτων, τῷ Ἀσκληπιῷ ὀφείλομεν ἀλεκτρυόνα· ἀλλὰ
ἀπόδοτε καὶ μὴ ἀμελήσητε.

Crito, we owe a cock to Aesculapius; pay it, therefore, and do not neglect it.
Last words, 399 B.C. *Plato, Phaedo*, 118a.

¹ See also the Latin Quotations.

SOLON
c. 640–*c*. 558 B.C.

γηράσκω δ' ἀεὶ πολλὰ διδασκόμενος.

I grow old ever learning many things.
Poetae Lyrici Graeci (ed. Bergk), Solon, 18.

πρὶν δ' ἂν τελευτήσῃ, ἐπισχεῖν μηδὲ καλέειν κω ὄλβιον,
ἀλλ' εὐτυχέα.

Call no man happy till he dies, he is at best but
fortunate.   Herodotus, *Histories*, i. 32.

SOPHOCLES
495–406 B.C.

πολλὰ τὰ δεινὰ κοὐδὲν ἀνθρώπου δεινότερον πέλει.

Wonders are many, and none is more wonderful
than man.   *Antigone*, 332. Trans. by Jebb.

ὦ παῖ, γένοιο πατρὸς εὐτυχέστερος.

Ah, boy, may'st thou prove happier than thy sire.
Ajax, 550. Trans. by Jebb.

THUCYDIDES
b. c. 471 B.C.

κτῆμα ἐς ἀεί.

A possession for ever.   *Thucydides*, i. 22.

φιλοκαλοῦμέν τε γὰρ μετ' εὐτελείας καὶ φιλοσοφοῦμεν
ἄνευ μαλακίας.

For we are lovers of the beautiful, yet simple in our
tastes, and we cultivate the mind without loss
of manliness.
Ib. ii. 40, § 1. Trans. by Jowett.

ἀνδρῶν γὰρ ἐπιφανῶν πᾶσα γῆ τάφος.

The whole earth is the sepulchre of famous men.
Ib. 43, § 3.

τῆς τε γὰρ ὑπαρχούσης φύσεως μὴ χείροσι γενέσθαι ὑμῖν
μεγάλη ἡ δόξα, καὶ ἧς ἂν ἐπ' ἐλάχιστον ἀρετῆς πέρι ἢ
ψόγου ἐν τοῖς ἄρσεσι κλέος ᾖ.

To a woman not to show more weakness than is
natural to her sex is great glory, and not to be
talked of for good or evil among men.
Ib. 45, § 2.

XENOPHON
b. c. 430 B.C.

θάλαττα θάλαττα.

The sea! the sea!   *Anabasis*, iv. vii. 24.

ANONYMOUS

μηδὲν ἄγαν.

Nothing in excess.
*Written up in the temple at Delphi by Cleobulus,
according to some accounts*. Quoted by *Plato*,
in *Protagoras*, 343 b.

γνῶθι σεαυτόν.

From the gods comes the saying 'Know thyself'.
Juvenal, *Satires*, xi, 27. *The saying was written
up in the temple of Delphi*.

FOREIGN QUOTATIONS

ABBÉ D'ALLAINVAL
1700–1753

L'embarras des richesses.
> The more alternatives, the more difficult the choice.
> *Title of Comedy,* 1726.

COMTE D'ARGENSON
1652–1721

L'ABBÉ GUYOT DESFONTAINES: Il faut que je vive.
D'ARGENSON: Je n'en vois pas la nécessité.
> DESFONTAINES: I must live.
> D'ARGENSON: I do not see the necessity.
> Voltaire, *Alzire, Discours Préliminaire.*

ÉMILE AUGIER
1820–1889

La nostalgie de la boue.
> Homesickness for the gutter.
> *Le Mariage d'Olympe,* i. i.

MARÉCHAL BOSQUET
1810–1861

C'est magnifique, mais ce n'est pas la guerre.
> It is magnificent, but it is not war.
> *Remark on the Charge of the Light Brigade,* 1854.

MME CORNUEL
1605–1694

Il n'y a point de héros pour son valet de chambre.
> No man is a hero to his valet.
> *Lettres de Mlle Aissé,* xii, 13 août 1728.

EMIL COUÉ
1857–1926

Tous les jours, à tous points de vue, je vais de mieux en mieux.
> Every day, in every way, I am getting better and better. *Formula in his clinic at Nancy.*

JACQUES DANTON
1759–1794

De l'audace, et encore de l'audace, et toujours de l'audace!
> Boldness, and again boldness, and always boldness!
> *Speech to the Legislative Committee of General Defence, 2 Sept. 1792. Le Moniteur, 4 Sept. 1792.*

THÉODORE DE BANVILLE
1823–1891

Nous n'irons plus aux bois, les lauriers sont coupés.
> We will go no more to the woods, the laurel-trees are cut. *Les Cariatides, Les Stalactites;*
> (Nursery rhyme, earlier than Banville.)

PIERRE-AUGUSTIN DE BEAUMARCHAIS
1732–1799

Je me presse de rire de tout, de peur d'être obligé d'en pleurer.
> I make myself laugh at everything, for fear of having to weep. *Le Barbier de Séville,* i. ii.

PIERRE-JEAN DE BÉRANGER
1780–1857

Il était un roi d'Yvetot
Peu connu dans l'histoire.
> There was a king of Yvetot
> Little known to history.
> *Œuvres,* i, *Le Roi d'Yvetot.*

GEORGES-LOUIS LECLERC DE BUFFON
1707–1788

Le style est l'homme même.
> Style is the man himself. *Discours sur le Style.*
Le génie n'est qu'une grande aptitude à la patience.
> Genius is only a great aptitude for patience.
> *Attr. to Buffon by Hérault de Séchelles in Voyage à Montbard.*

COMTE DE BUSSY-RABUTIN
1618–1693

L'absence est à l'amour ce qu'est au feu le vent;
il éteint le petit, il allume le grand.
> Absence is to love what wind is to fire; it extinguishes the small, it enkindles the great.
> *Histoire Amoureuse des Gaules, Maximes d'Amours.*

PIERRE-JACQUES, BARON DE CAMBRONNE

1770–1842

La Garde meurt, mais ne se rend pas.

The Guards die but do not surrender.
> *Attr. to Cambronne when called upon to surrender by Col. Halkett. Cambronne denied the saying at a banquet at Nantes, 1835.*

NIVELLE DE LA CHAUSSÉE

1692–1754

Quand tout le monde a tort, tout le monde a raison.

When every one is wrong, every one is right.
> *La Gouvernante*, I. iii.

DUC DE LA ROCHEFOUCAULD

1613–1680

Nous avons tous assez de force pour supporter les maux d'autrui.

We have all enough strength to bear the misfortunes of others.   *Maximes*, 19.

On n'est jamais si heureux ni si malheureux qu'on s'imagine.

One is never so happy or so unhappy as one thinks.
> *Ib.* 49.

L'hypocrisie est un hommage que le vice rend à la vertu.

Hypocrisy is homage paid by vice to virtue. *Ib.* 218.

C'est une grande habileté que de savoir cacher son habileté.

The height of cleverness is to be able to conceal it.
> *Ib.* 245.

Dans l'adversité de nos meilleurs amis, nous trouvons quelque chose qui ne nous déplaît pas.

In the misfortune of our best friends, we find something which is not displeasing to us.
> *Maximes supprimées*, 583.

DUC DE LA ROCHEFOUCAULD-LIANCOURT

1747–1827

LOUIS XVI : C'est une révolte ?
LA ROCHEFOUCAULD-LIANCOURT : Non, Sire, c'est une révolution.

LOUIS XVI : Is it a revolt?
LA R.-LIANCOURT : No, Sire, it is a revolution.
> *When the news arrived at Versailles of the Fall of the Bastille, 1789.*

CHARLES-JOSEPH, PRINCE DE LIGNE

1735–1814

Le congrès ne marche pas, il danse.

The Congress makes no progress; but it dances.
> *Comment on the Congress of Vienna to Comte Auguste de La Garde-Chambonas. La Garde-Chambonas, Souvenirs du Congrès de Vienne, 1814–1815, c. I.*

JOSEPH DE MAISTRE

1753–1821

Toute nation a le gouvernement qu'elle mérite.

Every country has the government it deserves.
> *Lettres et Opuscules Inédits*, i, p. 215, 15 août 1811.

MAURICE DE MAETERLINCK

1862–

Il n'y a pas de morts.

There are no dead.   *L'Oiseau bleu*, IV. ii.

COMTE DE MIRABEAU

1749–1791

La guerre est l'industrie nationale de la Prusse.

War is the national industry of Prussia.
> *Attr. to Mirabeau by Albert Sorel, based on his Introduction to his 'Monarchie Prussienne'.*

ALFRED DE MUSSET

1810–1857

Malgré moi l'infini me tourmente.

I can't help it, the idea of the infinite is a torment to me.   *Premières Poésies, L'Espoir en Dieu*.

MARQUISE DU DEFFAND

1697–1780

La distance n'y fait rien ; il n'y a que le premier pas qui coûte.

The distance is nothing; it is only the first step which counts.
> *Remark on the legend that St. Denis, carrying his head in his hands, walked two leagues. Letter to d'Alembert, 7 July 1763.*

CAMILLE DESMOULINS

1760–1794

My age is that of the *bon Sansculotte Jésus*; an age fatal to Revolutionists.
> *Answer at his trial*. Carlyle, *French Revolution*, bk. vi, ch. 2.

PHILIPPE NÉRICAULT dit DESTOUCHES

1680–1754

Les absents ont toujours tort.

The absent are always in the wrong.
> *L'Obstacle Imprévu*, I. vi.

DENIS DIDEROT

1713–1784

L'esprit de l'escalier.

Staircase wit.
> *An untranslatable phrase, the meaning of which is that one only thinks on one's way downstairs of the smart retort one might have made in the drawing-room. Paradoxe sur le Comédien.*

MARÉCHAL DUMOURIEZ

1739–1823

Les courtisans qui l'entourent n'ont rien oublié et n'ont rien appris.

The courtiers who surround him have forgotten nothing and learnt nothing.
Of Louis XVIII, at the time of the Declaration of Verona, Sept. 1795. Examen. See also Talleyrand.

L'ABBÉ EDGEWORTH DE FIRMONT

1745–1807

Fils de Saint Louis, montez au ciel.

Son of Saint Louis, ascend to heaven.
Attr. words to Louis XVI as he mounted the steps of the guillotine at his execution, 1793. No documentary proof at all.

HENRI ESTIENNE

1532–1598

Si jeunesse savoit; si vieillesse pouvoit.

If youth knew; if age could.
Les Prémices, Épigramme cxci.

MARÉCHAL FOCH

1851–1929

Mon centre cède, ma droite recule, situation excellente. J'attaque!

My centre is giving way, my right is in retreat; situation excellent. I shall attack.
Sir G. Aston, *Biography of Foch* (1929), ch. 13, p. 122.

ANATOLE FRANCE

1844–1924

Le bon critique est celui qui raconte les aventures de son âme au milieu des chefs-d'œuvre.

The good critic is he who relates the adventures of his soul among masterpieces.
La Vie littéraire, preface.

FRANÇOIS Iᴇʀ

1508–1565

Tout est perdu fors l'honneur.

All is lost save honour.
Traditional words in a letter to his mother after his defeat at Pavia, 1525. The actual words were: 'De toutes choses ne m'est demeuré que l'honneur et la vie qui est saulve.' Collection des Documents Inédits sur l'Histoire de France, vol. i, 1847, p. 129.

GAVARNI

1810–1866

Les enfants terribles.   *Title of a series of prints.*
The embarrassing young.

HENRI IV

1553–1610

Pends-toi, brave Crillon; nous avons combattu à Arques et tu n'y étais pas.

Hang yourself, brave Crillon; we fought at Arques and you were not there.
Traditional form given by Voltaire to a letter of Henri to Crillon. Lettres Missives de Henri IV, Collection des Documents Inédits de l'Histoire de France, vol. iv, 1847, p. 848.

Paris vaut bien une messe.

Paris is well worth a mass.
Attr. either to Henry IV or to his minister Sully, in conversation with Henry. Caquets de l'Accouchée, 1622.

The wisest fool in Christendom.
Of James I of England. Remark attr. to Henry IV or Sully. French not known.

ALPHONSE KARR

1808–1890

Plus ça change, plus c'est la même chose.

The more things change, the more they are the same.   *Les Guêpes, Jan. 1849,* vi.

Si l'on veut abolir la peine de mort en ce cas, que MM. les assassins commencent.

If we are to abolish the death penalty, I should like to see the first step taken by our friends the murderers.   *Ib.*

LOUIS XIV

1638–1715

Il n'y a plus de Pyrénées.

The Pyrenees have ceased to exist.
At the accession of his grandson to the throne of Spain, 1700. Attr. by Voltaire in Siècle de Louis XIV, ch. 28.

L'État c'est moi.

I am the State.
Attr. remark before the Parlement de Paris, 13 April 1655. Dulaure, Histoire de Paris.

MARIE-ANTOINETTE

1755–1793

Qu'ils mangent de la brioche.

Let them eat cake.
Attr., but much older. Rousseau refers in his Confessions, 1740, to a similar remark, as a well-known saying.

JEAN MESSELIER

18th cent.

Je voudrais, et ce sera le dernier et le plus ardent de mes souhaits, je voudrais que le dernier des rois fût étranglé avec les boyaux du dernier prêtre.

I should like to see, and this will be the last and the most ardent of my desires, I should like to see the last king strangled with the guts of the last priest.
In his Will, 1733, published by Voltaire.

JEAN-BAPTISTE MOLIÈRE
1622–1673

M. JOURDAIN : Quoi ? quand je dis : 'Nicole, apportez-moi mes pantoufles, et me donnez mon bonnet de nuit', c'est de la prose?

MAÎTRE DE PHILOSOPHIE : Oui, monsieur.

M. JOURDAIN : Par ma foi! il y a plus de quarante ans que je dis de la prose sans que j'en susse rien.

> M. JOURDAIN : What? when I say : 'Nicole, bring me my slippers, and give me my night-cap,' is that prose?
>
> PROFESSOR OF PHILOSOPHY : Yes, Sir.
>
> M. JOURDAIN : Good Heavens! For more than forty years I have been speaking prose without knowing it. *Le Bourgeois Gentilhomme*, II. iv.

Tout ce qui n'est point prose est vers ; et tout ce qui n'est point vers est prose.

> All that is not prose is verse ; and all that is not verse is prose. *Ib.*

Que diable allait-il faire dans cette galère ?

> What the devil is he doing in this galley ?
> *Les Fourberies de Scapin*, II. vii.

Vous l'avez voulu, Georges Dandin, vous l'avez voulu.

> You wanted it, George Dandin, you wanted it.
> *Georges Dandin*, I. ix.

NAPOLEON
1769–1821

A la guerre, les trois quarts sont des affaires morales, la balance des forces réelles n'est que pour un autre quart.

> In war, moral considerations make up three-quarters of the game : the relative balance of manpower accounts only for the remaining quarter. *Correspondance de Napoléon Ier, xvii, no. 14276 (Observations sur les affaires d'Espagne, Saint-Cloud, 27 août 1808).*

Du sublime au ridicule il n'y a qu'un pas.

> There is only one step from the sublime to the ridiculous.
> *To De Pradt, Polish ambassador, after the retreat from Moscow in 1812.* De Pradt, *Histoire de l'Ambassade dans le grand-duché de Varsovie en 1812*, ed. 1815, p. 215.

L'Angleterre est une nation de boutiquiers.

> England is a nation of shopkeepers.
> *Attr. by* B. E. O'Meara, *Napoleon at St. Helena*, vol. ii. The original is probably 'sono mercanti', a phrase of Paoli, quoted by Napoleon ; see Gourgaud, *Journal Inédit de Ste-Hélène*, i. 69.

La carrière ouverte aux talents.

> The career open to talents.
> O'Meara, *Napoleon in Exile* (1822), vol. i, p. 103.

Soldats, songez que, du haut de ces pyramides, quarante siècles vous contemplent.

> Think of it, soldiers ; from the summit of these pyramids, forty centuries look down upon you.
> *Speech to the Army of Egypt on 21 July 1798, before the Battle of the Pyramids.* Gourgaud, *Mémoires, Guerre d'Orient*, i, p. 160.

Tout soldat français porte dans sa giberne la bâton de maréchal de France.

> Every French soldier carries in his cartridge-pouch the baton of a marshal of France.
> E. Blaze, *La Vie Militaire sous l'Empire*, I. v.

Voilà le soleil d'Austerlitz.

> There rises the sun of Austerlitz.
> *To his officers, before Moscow, 7 Sept. 1812.*

Tête d'Armée.   *Last words.*

NICHOLAS I OF RUSSIA
1796–1855

Nous avons sur les bras un homme malade — un homme gravement malade.

> We have on our hands a sick man—a very sick man. (The sick man of Europe, the Turk.)
> *Parliamentary Papers. Accounts and Papers, vol. lxxi, pt. 5. Eastern Papers, p. 2. Sir G. H. Seymour to Lord John Russell, 11 Jan. 1853.*

BLAISE PASCAL
1623–1662

Le nez de Cléopâtre : s'il eût été plus court, toute la face de la terre aurait changé.

> Had Cleopatra's nose been shorter, the whole history of the world would have been different.
> *Pensées*, sect. ii, 162.

Le silence éternel de ces espaces infinis m'effraie.

> The eternal silence of these infinite spaces [the heavens] terrifies me. *Ib.* sect. iii, 206.

Le dernier acte est sanglant, quelque belle que soit la comédie en tout le reste.

> The last act is bloody, however charming the rest of the play may be. *Ib.* 210.

On mourra seul.

> We shall die alone.   *Ib.* 211.

Le cœur a ses raisons que la raison ne connaît point.

> The heart has its reasons which reason knows nothing of. *Ib.* sect. iv, 277.

L'homme n'est qu'un roseau, le plus faible de la nature ; mais c'est un roseau pensant.

> Man is only a reed, the weakest thing in nature ; but he is a thinking reed. *Ib.* sect. vi, 347.

Console-toi, tu ne me chercherais pas si tu ne m'avais trouvé.

> Comfort yourself, you would not seek me if you had not found me. *Ib.* sect. vii, 553.

CHARLES PERRAULT
1628–1703

'Anne, ma sœur Anne, ne vois-tu rien venir ?' Et la sœur Anne lui répondit, 'Je ne vois rien que le soleil qui poudroye, et l'herbe qui verdoye.'

> 'Anne, sister Anne, do you see anybody coming ?'
> And her sister Anne replied, 'I see nothing but

the sun which makes a dust, and the grass looking green.'

Perrault, *Histoires ou Contes du Tems Passé*, 1697. Trans. by R. Samber, 1764.

MARÉCHAL PÉTAIN
1856–

Ils ne passeront pas.

They shall not get past. *Verdun, Feb. 1916.*

MME DE POMPADOUR
1721–1764

Après nous le déluge.

After us the deluge.

Madame de Hausset, *Mémoires*, p. 19.

PIERRE-JOSEPH PROUD'HON
1809–1865

La propriété c'est le vol.

Property is theft. *Qu'est-ce que la Propriété?* ch. 1.

FRANÇOIS RABELAIS
1494?–1553

L'appétit vient en mangeant.

The appetite grows by eating. *Gargantua*, I. v.

Fay ce que vouldras

Do what thou wilt. *Ib.* I. lvii.

Tirez le rideau, la farce est jouée.

Ring down the curtain, the farce is over.
Attr. to Rabelais on his death-bed.

Je m'en vais chercher un grand peut-être.

I go to seek a great perhaps.
Attr. to Rabelais on his death-bed.

Vogue la galère!

A phrase for which it is impossible to find an adequate translation. Literally, the words mean 'loose the galley' or 'hoist sail'.
Works, bk. i, ch. 40.

RACINE
1639–1699

Ce n'est plus une ardeur dans mes veines cachée:
C'est Vénus toute entière à sa proie attachée.

It is no longer a passion hidden in my veins: it is the goddess Venus herself fastened on her prey.
Phèdre, I. iii.

Point d'argent, point de Suisse.

No money, no Swiss (soldiers).
Les Plaideurs, I. i. 15.

MME ROLAND
1754–1793

O liberté! O liberté! que de crimes on commet en ton nom!

O liberty! O liberty! what crimes are committed in thy name!
Lamartine, *Histoire des Girondins*, livre li, ch. 8.

PIERRE RONSARD
1529–1585

Quand vous serez bien vieille, au soir, à la chandelle,
Assise auprès du feu, dévidant et filant,
Direz, chantant mes vers, en vous émerveillant,
Ronsard me célébrait du temps que j'étais belle.

When you are very old, and sit in the candle-light at evening spinning by the fire, you will say, as you murmur my verses, a wonder in your eyes, 'Ronsard sang of me in the days when I was fair.'
Sonnets pour Hélène, ii. 43.

ROUGET DE LISLE
1760–1836

Allons, enfants de la patrie,
Le jour de gloire est arrivé.

Come, children of our country, the day of glory has arrived. *La Marseillaise.*

JEAN-JACQUES ROUSSEAU
1712–1778

L'homme est né libre, et partout il est dans les fers.

Man is born free, and everywhere he is in chains.
Du Contrat Social, ch. 1.

CHARLES-MAURICE DE TALLEYRAND
1754–1838

Ils n'ont rien appris, ni rien oublié.

They have learnt nothing, and forgotten nothing.
Attr. to Talleyrand by the Chevalier de Panat in a letter to Mallet du Pan, Jan. 1796, 'Personne n'est corrigé, personne n'a su ni rien oublier ni rien apprendre.' (*Mémoires et correspondance de Mallet du Pan, 1851*, II. 196.) *See also* Dumouriez.

N'ayez pas de zèle.

Not too much zeal.
Sainte-Beuve, *Critiques et Portraits*, iii. 324.

PIERRE VERGNIAUD
1753–1793

Il a été permis de craindre que la Révolution, comme Saturne, dévorât successivement tous ses enfants.

There was reason to fear that the Revolution, like Saturn, might devour in turn each one of its children.
Lamartine, 'Histoire des Girondins, bk. xxxviii, ch. 20.

FRANÇOIS VILLON
b. 1431

Mais où sont les neiges d'antan?

But where are the snows of yesteryear?
Le Grand Testament, Ballade des Dames du Temps Jadis. Trans. by D. G. Rossetti.

VOLTAIRE

1694–1778

Ce corps qui s'appelait et qui s'appelle encore le saint empire romain n'était en aucune manière ni saint, ni romain, ni empire.

This agglomeration which was called and which still calls itself the Holy Roman Empire is neither holy, nor Roman, nor an empire.
Essai sur les Mœurs et l'Esprit des Nations, lxx.

Dans ce pays-ci il est bon de tuer de temps en temps un amiral pour encourager les autres.

In this country it is thought well to kill an admiral from time to time to encourage the others.
Candide, ch. 23.

Cela est bien dit, répondit Candide, mais il faut cultiver notre jardin.

'That is well said,' replied Candide, 'but we must cultivate our garden.' (We must attend to our own affairs.) *Ib.* 30.

Quoi que vous fassiez, écrasez l'infâme, et aimez qui vous aime.

Whatever you do, trample down abuses, and love those who love you.
Lettres. À M. d'Alembert, 28 Nov. 1762.

On dit que Dieu est toujours pour les gros bataillons.

It is said that God is always for the big battalions.
Ib. A M. le Riche, 6 Feb. 1770.

Si Dieu n'existait pas, il faudrait l'inventer.

If God did not exist, it would be necessary to invent him.
Épîtres, xcvi. A l'Auteur du Livre des Trois Imposteurs.

Ils ne se servent de la pensée que pour autoriser leurs injustices, et n'emploient les paroles que pour déguiser leurs pensées.

Men use thought only to justify their wrongdoings, and speech only to conceal their thoughts.
Dialogue xiv. Le Chapon et la Poularde.

ÉMILE ZOLA

1840–1902

J'accuse.

I accuse.
Title of an open letter to the President of the Republic, in connexion with the Dreyfus case, published in L'Aurore, 13 Jan. 1898.

ANONYMOUS

Ça ira.

Untranslatable phrase, meaning 'That will certainly happen'. *Refrain of French Revolutionary Song.*

Cet animal est très méchant,
Quand on l'attaque il se défend.

This animal is very mischievous; when it is attacked it defends itself.
La Ménagerie, by Théodore P. K., 1868.

Chevalier sans peur et sans reproche.

Knight without fear and without blemish.
Description in contemporary chronicles of Pierre Bayard, 1476–1524.

Il ne faut pas être plus royaliste que le roi.

One must not be more royalist than the king.
Phrase originated under Louis XVI. Chateaubriand, *La Monarchie selon la Charte*, ed. 1876, p. 94.

Liberté! Égalité! Fraternité!

Liberty! Equality! Fraternity!
Phrase of unkown origin dating from before the French Revolution. Aulard, in *Études et Leçons sur la Révolution Française* (6e série), gives the first official use of the phrase in the motion passed by the Club des Cordeliers (30 June 1793): que les propriétaires seront invités, . . . de faire peindre sur la façade de leurs maisons, en gros caractères, ces mots: Unité, indivisibilité de la République, Liberté, Égalité, Fraternité ou la mort.'
(Journal de Paris, No. 182.)

L'ordre règne à Varsovie.

Order reigns in Warsaw.
On 16 Sept. 1831, the Comte Horace Sebastiani, minister of foreign affairs, said that 'La tranquillité règne à Varsovie'. The newspaper Moniteur took it up.

Retournons à nos moutons.

Let us return to our sheep. (Let us get back to the subject.) *Maistre Pierre Pathelin* (line 1191).

Taisez-vous! Méfiez-vous! Les oreilles ennemies vous écoutent.

Be quiet! Be on your guard! Enemy ears are listening to you. *Official Notice in France in 1915.*

DANTE ALIGHIERI

1265–1321

Nel mezzo del cammin di nostra vita.

In the middle of the road of our life.
Divine Comedy. Inferno, I. 1.

Or se' tu quel Virgilio?

Art thou then that Virgil? *Ib.* 79.

Lasciate ogni speranza voi ch'entrate!

All hope abandon, ye who enter here. *Ib.* iii. 9.

Il gran rifiuto.

The great refusal. *Ib.* 60.

Onorate l'altissimo poeta.

Honour to the greatest poet. *Ib.* iv. 80.

Il Maestro di color che sanno.

The Master of them that know. (Aristotle.) *Ib.* 131.

Nessun maggior dolore,
Che ricordarsi del tempo felice
Nella miseria.

There is no greater sorrow than to recall a time of happiness in misery. *Ib.* v. 121.

Galeotto fu il libro e chi lo scrisse:
Quel giorno più non vi leggemmo avante.

Galeotto was the book and writer too: that day we read no more. *Ib.* 137.

E quindi uscimmo a riveder le stelle.

Thence we came forth to rebehold each star.
Ib. xxxiv. 139.

Puro e disposto a salire alle stelle.

Pure and made apt for mounting to the stars.
Ib. Purgatorio, xxxiii. 145.

E la sua volontate è nostra pace.
  In His will is our peace.   *Ib. Paradiso,* iii 85.

Tu proverai sì come sa di sale
Lo pane altrui, e com' è duro calle
Lo scendere e il salir per l'altrui scale.
  You shall find out how salt is the taste of another's
  bread, and how hard a path the going down and
  going up another's stair.   *Ib.* xvii. 58.

L'amor che move il sole e l'altre stelle.
  The love that moves the sun and the other stars.
                              Ib. xxxiii. 145.

GALILEO GALILEI
1564–1642

E pur si muove.
  But it does move.
    Attr. to Galileo after his recantation in 1632.
    The earliest appearance of the phrase is 1761
    (see E. R. Hull, *Galileo*), and it is generally
    conceded to be apocryphal.

CAMILLO BENSO CAVOUR
1810–1861

Noi siamo pronti a proclamare nell' Italia questo gran
principio: Libera Chiesa in libero Stato.
  We are ready to proclaim throughout Italy the great
  principle of a free church in a free state.
    Speech, 27 Mar. 1861. William de la Rive,
    Remin. of Life and Character of Count Cavour
    (1862), ch. 13, p. 276.

LEO TOLSTOY
1828–1910

All happy families resemble each other, each unhappy
family is unhappy in its own way.
  Anna Karenina, pt. i, ch. 1. Trans. by Maude.

Pure and complete sorrow is as impossible as pure
and complete joy.
  War and Peace, bk. xv, ch. 1. Trans. by Maude.

Art is not a handicraft, it is the transmission of
feeling the artist has experienced.
  What is Art? ch. 19. Trans. by Maude.

I sit on a man's back, choking him and making him
carry me, and yet assure myself and others that
I am very sorry for him and wish to ease his lot
by all possible means—except by getting off his
back.
  What Then Must We Do? ch. 16. Trans. by
  Maude.

HENRIK IBSEN
1828–1906

The minority is always right.
        An Enemy of the People, Act IV.

One should never put on one's best trousers to go out
to battle for freedom and truth.   *Ib.* Act v.

Vine-leaves in his hair.   *Hedda Gabler,* Act II.

People don't do such things.   *Ib.* Act IV.

The younger generation will come knocking at my
  door.   *The Master-Builder,* Act I.

MIGUEL DE CERVANTES
1547–1616

El Caballero de la Triste Figura.
  The Knight of the Sorrowful Countenance.
    Don Quixote, pt. I, ch. 19. Trans. by Smollett
    (*see* Lockhart's translation, 1882, vol. i, p. 171).

Dos linages solos hay en el mundo, como decía una
agüela mia, que son el tener y el no tener.
  There are but two families in the world, as my
  grandmother used to say, the Haves and the
  Havenots.   *Ib.* pt. ii, ch. 20. Trans. by Jervas.

COUNT OXENSTIERNA
1583–1654

Dost thou not know, my son, with how little wisdom
the world is governed?   *Letter to his son, 1648.*

ARABIAN NIGHTS

Who will change old lamps for new ones? . . . new
lamps for old ones?   *The History of Aladdin.*

Open Sesame!   *The History of Ali Baba.*

THEOBALD VON BETHMANN HOLLWEG
1856–1921

Just for a word—'neutrality', a word which in war-
time has so often been disregarded, just for a scrap
of paper—Great Britain is going to make war.
    *To Sir Edward Goschen, 4 Aug. 1914. Dispatch
    by Sir Edward Goschen to the British Foreign
    Office.*

OTTO VON BISMARCK
1815–1898

Die Politik ist keine exakte Wissenschaft.
  Politics are not an exact science.
        Speech, Prussian Chamber, 18 Dec. 1863.

Nach Canossa gehen wir nicht.
  We will not go to Canossa.
        Speech, Reichstag, 14 May 1872.

Die gesunden Knochen eines einzigen pommerschen
Musketiers.
  The healthy bones of a single Pomeranian grenadier.
        Speech, Reichstag, 5 Dec. 1876.

Ehrlicher Makler.
  An honest broker.
        Speech, Reichstag, 19 Feb. 1878.

Blut und Eisen.
  Blood and iron.
    Speech, Prussian House of Deputies, 28 Jan. 1886.
  (Legt eine möglichst starke militärische Kraft . . . in
  die Hand des Königs von Preussen, dann wird er
  die Politik machen können, die Ihr wünscht; mit
  Reden und Schützenfesten und Liedern macht sie
  sich nicht, sie macht sich nur durch Blut und
  Eisen.

Place in the hands of the King of Prussia the strong-est possible military power, then he will be able to carry out the policy you wish; this policy cannot succeed through speeches, and festivals, and songs, it can only be carried out through blood and iron.)

I may avail myself of the opportunity of denying once more the truth of the story that Prince Bismarck had ever likened Lord Salisbury to a lath of wood painted to look like iron.
> Sidney Whitman, *Personal Reminiscences of Prince Bismarck* (1902), p. 252.

AUGUST HEINRICH HOFFMANN VON FALLERSLEBEN
1798–1874

Deutschland, Deutschland über alles.

Germany, Germany over all. *Title of Song.*

FREDERICK THE GREAT
1712–1786

Ihr Racker, wollt ihr ewig leben?

Rascals, would you live for ever?
> *When the Guards hesitated, at Köln, 18 June 1757.*

JOHANN WOLFGANG VON GOETHE
1749–1832

Zwei Seelen wohnen, ach! in meiner Brust.

Two souls dwell, alas! in my breast.
> *Faust*, pt. i. *Vor dem Thor.*

Verweile doch! du bist so schön!

Stay then! Thou art so fair! *Ib. Studierzimmer.*

Meine Ruh' ist hin,
Mein Herz ist schwer.

> My peace is gone,
> My heart is heavy.
>> *Ib. Gretchen am Spinnrad.*

Über allen Gipfeln
Ist Ruh'.

Over all the mountain tops is peace.
> *Wanderers Nachtlied.*

Kennst du das Land, wo die Zitronen blühn?
Im dunkeln Laub die Gold-Orangen glühn,
Ein sanfter Wind vom blauen Himmel weht,
Die Myrte still und hoch der Lorbeer steht—
Kennst du es wohl?
> Dahin! Dahin!
Möcht ich mit dir, o mein Geliebter, ziehn!

> Know you the land where the lemon-trees bloom?
> In the dark foliage the gold oranges glow; a soft wind hovers from the sky, the myrtle is still and the laurel stands tall—do you know it well? There, there, I would go, O my beloved, with thee!
>> *Wilhelm Meisters Lehrjahre*, III. i.

Mehr Licht!

More light!
> *Attr. dying words.* (Actually: 'Macht doch den zweiten Fensterladen auch auf, damit mehr Licht hereinkomme': 'Open the second shutter, so that more light can come in.')

Ohne Hast, aber ohne Rast.

Without haste, but without rest. *Motto.*

FRIEDRICH HALM (FRANZ VON MÜNCH-BELLING-HAUSEN)
1806–1871

Mein Herz ich will dich fragen:
Was ist denn Liebe? Sag'!—
'Zwei Seelen und ein Gedanke,
Zwei Herzen und ein Schlag!'
> *Der Sohn der Wildniss*, Act II *ad fin.*

What love is, if thou wouldst be taught,
Thy heart must teach alone,—
Two souls with but a single thought,
Two hearts that beat as one.

> Trans. by Maria Lovell in *Ingomar the Barbarian.*

HEINRICH HEINE
1797–1856

Ich grolle nicht, und wenn das Herz auch bricht.

I do not murmur, even if my heart break.
> *Buch der Lieder. Title of Song.*

Ich weiss nicht, was soll es bedeuten,
Dass ich so traurig bin;
Ein Märchen aus alten Zeiten,
Das kommt mir nicht aus dem Sinn.

> I know not why I am so sad; I cannot get out of my head a fairy-tale of olden times. *Die Lorelei.*

Auf Flügeln des Gesanges.

On the wings of song. *Title of Song.*

IMMANUEL KANT
1724–1804

Zwei Dinge erfüllen das Gemüth mit immer neuer und zunehmender Bewunderung und Ehrfurcht, je öfter und anhaltender sich das Nachdenken damit beschäftigt: der bestirnte Himmel über mir, und das moralische Gesetz in mir.

Two things fill the mind with ever-increasing wonder and awe, the more often and the more intensely the mind of thought is drawn to them: the starry heavens above me and the moral law within me.
> *Critique of Practical Reason*, conclusion.

FRIEDRICH VON KLINGER
1752–1831

Sturm und Drang.

Storm and stress. *Title of Play, 1775.*

MARTIN LUTHER
1483–1546

Ich kann nicht anders.

I can do no otherwise.
Speech at the Diet of Worms, 18 Apr. 1521.
On his monument at Worms.

Wer nicht liebt Wein, Weib und Gesang,
Der bleibt ein Narr sein Leben lang.

Who loves not woman, wine, and song
Remains a fool his whole life long.
Attr. to Luther. Written in the Luther room
in the Wartburg, but no proof exists of its
authorship.

Ein feste Burg ist unser Gott,
Ein gute Wehr und Waffen.

A safe stronghold our God is still,
A trusty shield and weapon.
Klug'sche Gesangbuch, 1529. *Ein Feste Burg.*
Trans. by Carlyle.

Wenn ich gewisst hätte, dass so viel Teufel auf mich
gezielet hätten, als Ziegel auf den Dächern waren
zu Worms, wäre ich dennoch eingeritten.

If I had heard that as many devils would set on me
in Worms as there are tiles on the roofs, still I
would have gone there.
Luthers Sämmtliche Schriften (1745), xvi. 14.

PRINCE METTERNICH
1773–1859

Italien ist ein geographischer Begriff.

Italy is a geographical expression.
Letter, 19 Nov. 1849.

FRIEDRICH WILHELM NIETZSCHE
1844–1900

Jenseits von Gut und Böse.

Beyond good and evil.   *Title of Book.*

Herren-Moral und Sklaven-Moral.

Morality of masters and the morality of slaves.
Jenseits von Gut und Böse.

Blonde Bestie.

Blonde beast.   *Zur Genealogie der Moral.*

NOVALIS
(FRIEDRICH LEOPOLD VON HARDENBERG)
1772–1801

Gott-trunkener Mensch.

A God-intoxicated man.   *Remark about Spinoza*

ERICH MARIA REMARQUE
1898–

Im Westen nichts Neues.

All Quiet on the Western Front.
Title of Novel. Trans. by A. W. Wheen.

FRIEDRICH VON SCHILLER
1759–1805

Mit der Dummheit kämpfen Götter selbst vergebens.

With stupidity the gods themselves struggle in vain.
Jungfrau von Orleans, III. vi.

MAX SCHNECKENBURGER
1819–1849

Die Wacht am Rhein.

The watch on the Rhine.   *Title of Song.*

LOUIS SCHNEIDER

O Tannenbaum, O Tannenbaum,
Wie grün sind deine Blätter!

O pine-tree, O pine-tree,
How green are thy leaves!
Der Kurmärker und die Picarde.

ADDENDA

ALFRED AINGER
1837–1904

No flowers, by request.
At a dinner given to the contributors to the
Dictionary of National Biography, 8 *July* 1897:
his summary of their editor's instructions.

MATTHEW ARNOLD
1822–1888

'Passionate, absorbing, almost blood-thirsty clinging
to life.' *Essays in Criticism, Preface.*

JANE AUSTEN
1775–1817

'The little bit (two inches wide) of ivory on which I
work with so fine a brush as produces little effect
after much labour.' *Letter,* 16 *Dec.* 1816.

CHARLES BRUCE
BAIRNSFATHER
1887–

'Well, if you knows of a better 'ole, go to it.'
Fragments from France, No. 1 (1915).

RICHARD BENTLEY
1662–1742

'He is believed to have liked port, but to have said of
claret that "it would be port if it could".'
R. C. Jebb, *Bentley,* p. 200.

SIR WALTER BESANT
1836–1901

The World went very well then. *Title.*

VALENTINE BLACKER
1778–1823

'Put your trust in God, my boys, and keep your
powder dry.' *Oliver's Advice.*

EDMUND BURKE
1728–1797

My hold of the colonies is in the close affection which
grows from common names, from kindred blood,
from similar privileges, and equal protection.
These are ties which, though light as air, are as
strong as links of iron.
Speech on Conciliation with America, 1775.

GEORGE CANNING
1770–1827

Pitt is to Addington
As London is to Paddington.
The Oracle, c. 1803–4.
(*Pitt:*)
When our perils are past, shall our gratitude sleep?
No,—here's to the pilot that weathered the storm.
Song for the inauguration of the Pitt Club
25 *May* 1802.

GEOFFREY CHAUCER
1328–1400

The smyler with the knyf under the cloke.
Canterbury Tales. Knighte's Tale, l. 1141.

DESMOND F. T. COKE

His blade struck the water a full second before any
other . . . until . . . as the boats began to near the
winning-post, his own was dipping into the water
twice as often as any other.
Sandford of Merton (1903), ch. xii.

Often quoted as 'All rowed fast but none so fast as
stroke', and attrib. to 'Ouida'.

GEORGE COLMAN
1762–1836

Mum's the word. *Battle of Hexham,* II. i.

JOHN CALVIN COOLIDGE
1872–1933

They hired the money, didn't they?
With reference to the war debts incurred by
England and others.

BENJAMIN DISRAELI
EARL OF BEACONSFIELD
1804–1881

'Protection is not only dead, but damned.' (*c.* 1850.
Monypenny and Buckle, *Life of Disraeli,* iii. 241.

ERNEST DOWSON

1867–1900

I have forgot much, Cynara! gone with the wind,
Flung roses, roses, riotously, with the throng
Non Sum Qualis Eram.

EDWARD FITZGERALD

1809–1883

Mrs. Browning's death is rather a relief to me, I must say: no more Aurora Leighs, thank God!
Letter, 15 *July* 1861.

EDWARD AUGUSTUS FREEMAN

1823–1892

A saying which fell from myself in one of the debates in Congregation on the Modern Language Statute has been quoted in several places . . . 'chatter about Shelley' . . . I mentioned that I had lately read a review of a book about Shelley in which the critic . . . praised or blamed the author . . . for his 'treatment of the Harriet problem'.
Contemporary Review, Oct. 1887: 'Literature and Language.'

The two phrases are often telescoped as 'chatter about Harriet'.

GEORGE III

1738–1820

'Was there ever,' cried he, 'such stuff as great part of Shakespeare? Only one must not say so! But what think you?—what?—Is there not sad stuff? what?—what?'
To Fanny Burney (in her *Diary,* 19 Dec. 1785).

EDWARD GIBBON

1737–1794

My English text is chaste, and all licentious passages are left in the decent obscurity of a learned language. *Memoirs of my Life and Writings.*

WILLIAM EWART GLADSTONE

1809–1898

(*The Irish Land League:*) It is perfectly true that these gentlemen wish to march through rapine to disintegration and dismemberment of the Empire, and, I am sorry to say, even to the placing of different parts of the Empire in direct hostility one with the other.
Speech at Knowsley, 27 *Oct.* 1881.

HANNAH GLASSE

fl. 1747

Take your hare when it is cased. . . .
Art of Cookery.

Usually misquoted as 'First catch your hare'.

ALFRED DENIS GODLEY

1856–1925

What asks the Bard? He prays for nought
But what the truly virtuous crave:
That is, the things he plainly ought
To have . . .

His taste in residence is plain:
No palaces his heart rejoice:
A cottage in a lane (Park Lane
For choice)—
Lyra Frivola, 'After Horace'.

KENNETH GRAHAME

1859–1932

'Aunt Maria flung herself on him [the curate]. "O Mr. Hodgitts!" I heard her cry, "you are brave! for my sake do not be rash!" He was not rash.'
The Golden Age, 'The Burglars'.

RICHARD BURDON HALDANE VISCOUNT HALDANE

1856–1928

I had gone to Germany too often, and had read her literature too much, not to give ground to narrow-minded people to say that Germany was my 'spiritual home'. *An Autobiography,* p. 285.

HENRY II

1133–1189

'Who will free me from this turbulent priest?'
History books.

What a parcel of fools and dastards have I nourished in my house, that not one of them will avenge me of this one upstart clerk!
K. Norgate, in *Dictionary of National Biography.*

HENRY VIII

1491–1547

[*Anne of Cleves*]. The King found her so different from her picture . . . that . . . he swore they had brought him a Flanders mare.
Smollett, *Hist. of England* (ed. 3, 1759), vi. 68.

O. HENRY (WILLIAM SYDNEY PORTER)

1862–1910

'Little old New York's good enough for us'—that's what they sing. *A Tempered Wind.*

BENJAMIN JOWETT

1817–1893

The lie in the Soul is a true lie.
From the Introduction to his translation of Plato's *Republic,* bk. ii.

WILLIAM LAMB,
VISCOUNT MELBOURNE
1779–1848

[*Catholic Emancipation*] What all the wise men promised has not happened, and what all the d—d fools said would happen has come to pass.
H. Dunckley, *Lord Melbourne* (1890).

JOHN GEORGE LAMBTON
FIRST EARL OF DURHAM
1792–1840

'... one of his sublimities ... too good to be lost ... he said he considered £40,000 a year a moderate income—such a one as a man *might jog on with.*'
The Creevey Papers (13 Sept. 1821), ii. 32.

WILLIAM LANGLAND
1330?–1400?

Dowel, Dobet, and Dobest.
Piers Plowman. MS. Laud 581, passus viii, heading.

[*This corrects the errors on p. 251a, where the phrase is attributed to Lydgate, and the MS. number given as 851.*]

GEORGE CORNEWALL LEWIS
1806–1863

Life would be tolerable were it not for its amusements.
According to Lord Grey of Fallodon, in his *Twenty-Five Years.*

ROBERT LOWE
VISCOUNT SHERBROOKE
1811–1892

'I believe it will be absolutely necessary that you should prevail on our future masters to learn their letters.'
Speech in House of Commons, 15 July 1867 (on the passing of the Reform Bill).

Popularized as 'We must educate our masters'.

CHARLES BLAIR
MACDONALD

'When ye come to play golf ye maun hae a heid!'
Scotland's Gift—Golf, 1928.

'A caddy at St. Andrews named Lang Willie was teaching one of the professors of the university the noble game. The professor was not a promising pupil.—Willie fairly got out of patience and said to him: "Ye see, Professor, as long as ye are learning thae lads at the College Latin and Greek it is easy work, but when ye come to play golf ye maun hae a heid!" '

JOHN, VISCOUNT MORLEY
OF BLACKBURN
1838–1923

The whole of the golden Gospel of Silence is now effectively compressed in thirty-five volumes.
Critical Miscellanies (1871). *Carlyle.*

ALFRED, LORD MILNER
1854–1925

(*The Peers and the Budget:*) 'If we believe a thing to be bad, and if we have a right to prevent it, it is our duty to try to prevent it and to damn the consequences.' *Speech at Glasgow*, 26 Nov. 1909.

JAMES OGILVY, FIRST
EARL OF SEAFIELD
1664–1730

Now there's ane end of ane old song
(as he signed the engrossed exemplification of the Act of Union, 1706).
Lockhart Papers (1817), i. 223.

WALTER HORATIO PATER
1839–1894

All art constantly aspires towards the condition of music.
The Renaissance. 'The School of Giorgione.'

ARCHIBALD PHILIP PRIMROSE
EARL OF ROSEBERY
1847–1929

Before Irish Home Rule is concluded by the Imperial Parliament, England as the predominant member of the three kingdoms will have to be convinced of its justice and equity.
Speech in the House of Lords, 11 *March* 1894.

'SAKI'
(HECTOR HUGH MUNRO)
1870–1916

Women and elephants never forget an injury.
Reginald. Reginald on Besetting Sins.

JAMES SMITH
1775–1839
AND HORACE SMITH
1779–1849

John Richard William Alexander Dwyer
Was footman to Justinian Stubbs, Esquire.
The Theatre (parodied from Crabbe).

EDMUND SPENSER

1552?–1599

So let us love, deare Love, lyke as we ought,
—Love is the lesson which the Lord us taught.
Amoretti. Sonnet lxviii.

LAURENCE STERNE

1713–1768

God tempers the wind, said Maria, to the shorn lamb.
A Sentimental Journey. Maria.

From a French proverb, but familiar in Sterne's form of words.

ROBERT LOUIS STEVENSON

1850–1894

AND LLOYD OSBOURNE

Nothing like a little judicious levity.
[*Michael Finsbury.*] *The Wrong Box*, chap. 7.

ALFRED, LORD TENNYSON

1809–1892

This way and that dividing the swift mind.
Morte d'Arthur, l. 60.

WILLIAM MAKEPEACE THACKERAY

1811–1863

'Them's my sentiments!' [*Fred Bullock*].
Vanity Fair, chap. 21.

MARK TWAIN (SAMUEL LANGHORNE CLEMENS)

1835–1910

The reports of my death are greatly exaggerated.
Cable from Europe to the Associated Press.

ARTHUR WELLESLEY, DUKE OF WELLINGTON

1769–1852

At Waterloo] Hard pounding this, gentlemen; let's ee who will pound longest.
In Sir W. Scott, *Paul's Letters* (1815).

OSCAR FINGAL O'FLAHERTIE WILLS WILDE

1856–1900

couldn't help it. I can resist everything except temptation.
Lady Windermere's Fan, Act I.

We are all in the gutter, but some of us are looking at the stars. *Ib.*, Act III.

WILLIAM WINDHAM

1750–1810

Those entrusted with arms . . . should be persons of some substance and stake in the country.
In House of Commons, 22 *July* 1807.

PELHAM GRENVILLE WODEHOUSE

1881–

He spoke with a certain what-is-it in his voice, and I could see that, if not actually disgruntled, he was far from being gruntled.
The Code of the Woosters.

Slice him where you like a hellhound is always a hellhound. *Ib.*

Donning the soup-and-fish in preparation for the evening meal. *Jeeves and the Impending Doom.*

Excellent browsing and sluicing.
Jeeves and the Unbidden Guest.

There was another ring at the front door. Jeeves shimmered out and came back with a telegram.
Jeeves takes charge.

SAMUEL WOODFORD

1636–1700

To his very Worthy Friend Mr. Izaak Walton, upon his Writing and Publishing the Life of the Venerable and Judicious Mr. Richard Hooker.
Title of verses prefixed to the Life, 1670.

SIR HENRY WOTTON

1568–1639

At my departure toward Rome . . . I had won confidence enough to beg his advice [Alberto Scipioni's] how I might carry myself securely there without offence of others or of mine own conscience. '*Signor Arrigo mio,*' says he, '*I pensieri stretti ed il viso sciolto* will go safely over the whole world.' ['Sir Henry . . . the thoughts secret and the countenance open.']
Letter to Milton, 13 April 1638, prefixed to *Comus*.

ANONYMOUS

Earned a precarious living by taking in one another's washing.
('It is said that a society was formed (*c.* 1900?) for the purpose of discovering the origin of the phrase, but without result.' *Benham*, 1936.)

Here you are, an able-bodied man, respectably brought-up, instead of which you go about the country stealing ducks.
Said to have been addressed to a prisoner by an Indian judge.

'How different, how very different from the home life of our own dear Queen!'
Irvin S. Cobb, *A Laugh a Day.*

As Cleopatra, Sarah Bernhardt stabbed the slave who bore to her the tidings of Mark Antony's defeat at Actium; she stormed, raved, wrecked some of the scenery in her frenzy and finally, as the curtain fell, dropped in a shuddering, convulsive heap.

As the applause died, a middle-aged British matron was heard to say to her neighbour: 'How different, how very different from the home life of our own dear Queen!' (Victoria).

Know all men by these presents, that I John Griffin make the aforementioned my last will and testament.   Cruise, *Digest*, 1752.

EUCLID

Third century B.C.

A line is length without breadth.

There is no 'royal road' to geometry.
(Said to Ptolemy I. Proclus, *Comment on Euclid*, Prol. G. 20.)

JULIUS CAESAR

102?–44 B.C.

Caesar's wife must be above suspicion.
Traditional, based on Plutarch, *Life of Julius Caesar*, x. 6.

Thou hast Caesar and his fortune with thee.
Plutarch, *Life of Julius Caesar*, xxxviii. 3. Trans. by North.

MARCUS TULLIUS CICERO

106–43 B.C.

'Ipse dixit.' 'Ipse' autem erat Pythagoras.
De Natura Deorum, i.5.10.

'He himself said it', and this 'he himself', it seems, was Pythagoras.

MARCUS AURELIUS ANTONINUS

A.D. 121–180

The poet says, Dear city of Cecrops; and wilt not thou say, Dear City of Zeus?   *tr.* G. Long.

TERTULLIAN

A.D. 192?–220.

Plures efficimur quoties metimur a vobis, semen est sanguis Christianorum.   *Apol.* 50 ad fin.

The more ye mow us down, the more we grow, the seed is the blood of Christians. (Traditionally rendered as 'The blood of the martyrs is the seed of the Church'.)

WILLIAM OF OCCAM

c. 1300–1349

['*Occam's Razor*']: Entia non sunt multiplicanda praeter necessitatem.

Things not known to exist should not, unless it is absolutely necessary, be postulated as existing.
Oxf. Eng. Dict. s.v. 'Razor'.

ANONYMOUS

Et in Arcadia ego.
Inscription on a tomb, frequently reproduced in paintings, e.g. by Guercino, Poussin, and Reynolds.

Usually translated: 'And I too [the occupant of the tomb] was in Arcadia.' But perhaps rather, 'I too [the tomb itself] am in Arcadia': even in Arcadia there am I (Death). (See E. Panofsky in *Philosophy and History*: essays presented to E. Cassirer, 1936.)

Quidquid agas, prudenter agas, et respice finem.
Gesta Romanorum, cap. 103. init.

Whatever you do, do cautiously, and look to the end.

JULIEN BENDA

1868–

La trahison des clercs.

The treason of the educated classes.

NICOLAS BOILEAU

1636–1711

Enfin Malherbe vint, et, le premier en France,
Fit sentir dans les vers une juste cadence.
L'Art Poétique, i. 131–2.

At last comes Malherbe, and, the first to do so in France, makes verse run smoothly.

FRANÇOIS, DUC DE LA ROCHEFOUCAULD

1613–1680

La reconnaissance de la plupart des hommes n'est qu'une secrète envie de recevoir de plus grands bienfaits.   *Maximes*, 298.

In most of mankind gratitude is merely a secret hope of further favours.

A saying ascribed to Sir Robert Walpole by Hazlitt in his 'Wit and Humour': 'The gratitude of place-expectants is a lively sense of future favours' is obviously derived from La Rochefoucauld.

M. E. PATRICE MAURICE DE MACMAHON

1808–1893

J'y suis, j'y reste.

Here I am, and here I stay.
Attr. remark at the taking of the Malakoff, 8 September 1855.

JEAN-BAPTISTE MOLIÈRE

1622–1673

Il m'est permis, disait Molière, de reprendre mon bien où je le trouve.

It is permitted me, said Molière, to take my own where I find it.
Grimarest, *Vie de Molière* (1704), p. 14

Nous avons changé tout cela.
Le Médecin malgré lui, ii. 6.

We have changed all that. (Said by the pretended doctor to justify his mistake as to the relative positions of heart and liver.)

NAPOLEON I

1769–1821

Quant au courage moral, il avait trouvé fort rare, disait-il, celui de deux heures après minuit; c'est-à-dire le courage de l'improviste.
Las Cases, *Mémorial de Ste-Hélène*, Dec. 4–5, 1815.

As to moral courage, I have very rarely met with *the two o'clock in the morning courage*: I mean unprepared courage.

VOLTAIRE

1694–1778

Le mieux est l'ennemi du bien.

The best is the enemy of the good.
Dict. Philosophique, art. Art Dramatique.

ANONYMOUS

An army marches on its stomach.
Attrib. to Napoleon, in, e.g., *Windsor Magazine*, 1904, p. 268.

Probably condensed from a long passage in Las Cases, *Mémorial de Ste-Hélène* (Nov. 1816).

Tout passe, tout casse, tout lasse.
Cahier, *Quelques six mille proverbes*.

Everything passes, everything perishes, everything palls.

Se non è vero, è molto ben trovato.

If it is not true, it is a happy invention.

Apparently a common saying in the sixteenth century. Found in Giordano Bruno (1585) in the above form, and in Antonio Doni (1552) as 'Se non è vero, egli è stato un bel trovato.'

NICHOLAS I

1796–1855

Russia has two generals in whom she can confide—Generals Janvier and Février.
Punch, 10 Mar. 1853. *Speech of the late Emperor of Russia.*

PAUL KRUGER

1825–1904

A bill of indemnity . . . for raid by Dr. Jameson and the British South Africa Company's troops. The amount falls under two heads—first material damage, total of claim, £577,938 3s. 3d.; second, moral or intellectual damage, total of claim, £1,000,000.
Communicated to House of Commons by Joseph Chamberlain, 18 February 1897.

MIGUEL DE CERVANTES

1547–1616

Patience, and shuffle the cards.
Don Quixote, pt. ii, ch. 23.

HERMANN GOERING

1893–

Guns will make us powerful; butter will only make us fat.   *Radio Broadcast, summer of* 1936.

IMMANUEL KANT

1724–1804

There is . . . but one categorical imperative: 'Act only on that maxim whereby thou canst at the same time will that it should become a universal law.'
Tr. A. D. Lindsay, from *Fundamental Principles of . . . Morals*, p. 421.

INDEX

NOTE

The order of the index both in the keywords and in the entries under the keywords is strictly alphabetical. To save space the keyword is replaced by its initial letter in the individual entries, and the following abbreviations have been used with the same intention —shd., wd., cd., yr., yrs., for should, would, could, your, and yours. The general plan has been to allow two words of index for each line of verse—though it has been found impossible to limit the number to two in the most well-known quotations—and to index the principal words in the prose passages. The entries have been made as intelligible as possible in the limited space in order that the index may be used not only to track a known or half-known quota-tion but to supply a quotation on some particular subject.

Irregular spellings (such as occur in Dickens, Artemus Ward, &c.), early English words, dialect words, and Cockneyisms are indexed under their correct or English equivalents, except where the words have no such exact equivalent: thus alleybi, blude, wision, feàce, trouthe, &c., are indexed under alibi, blood, vision, face, and truth respectively, while airts, galumphing, latoun, tapsalteerie, &c., have entries of their own.

Greek, Latin, and other foreign quotations each have a separate index of their own following after the English index.

A was an apple-pie 532a
Aaron: A.'s rod 493b
  even unto A.'s beard 490a
  like A.'s serpent 301a
Abana and Pharpar 496b
Abandon: a. all remorse 362a
  all hope a., ye who enter here 566b
  if he wd. a. his mind to it 211a
Abandoned: what God a., these defended 200a
Abashed: a. the Devil stood 274b
  they heard, and were a. 271b
Abassin: where A. kings their issue guard 274a
Abatement: falls into a. and low price 369b
Abba: we cry, A., Father 513b
Abbey: his name on the A.-stones 48a
  not in the A. proudly laid 453b
Abbot: A. of Aberbrothok 406b
  Father A., I am come 462b
  unacquainted with the 410b
Abdiel: Seraph A. 275a
Abed-nego: Meshach and A. 504a
Abel: Cain and his brother, A. 100b
Aberbrothok: Abbot of A. 406b
Aberdeen: the Quaker (Lord A.) 17a
Aberdour: half-owre to A. 530a
Abhor: age, I do a. thee 389b
Abhorred: he hath not despised, nor a. 483a
  the lean a. monster 366b
  to be a. of all faithful Christians 480b
Abhorring: blow me into a. 325a
Abide: a. with me from morn till eve 224a
  and no where did a. 99a
  O Lord, a. with me 251b
  O Lord, who may a. it 490a
  others a. our question 7b
  what was, and is, and will a. 463b
  with me and mine a. 254a
Abiaed: all things a. eternally 445a
Abides: tho' much is taken, much a. 439a
Abi-ezer: vintage of A. 495a
Ability: men furnished with a. 521a
  out of my lean and low a. 372a
  studies serve for. .a. 16a
  thirdly, intellectual a. 10b
Abject: a. from the spheres 452a
  I'll be this a. thing no more 173a
  so a.—yet alive 73b
Ablaze: yet Britain set the world a. 164a
Able: above that ye are a. 514b
  as far as he is a. 413b
Able-bodied man. .stealing ducks 573b
Ablution: pure a. round earth's human shores 220b
Aboard: we brought them all a. 437b
Abode: archangels, in yr. dim a. 475b
  Kosmos my a. 414a
  nor wealth nor blessed a. 262a
  the English make it their a. 449a

Abodes: aiming at the bless'd a. 300b
  remembers its august a. 241a
  windless, fortunate a. 397b
Abolish: utterly a. or destroy 466b
Abominable: altogether become a. 482a
Abomination: a. of desolation 507b
  incense is an a. 501a
Abominations: mother of harlots and a. 519b
Abora: singing of Mount A. 101b
Abou Ben Adhem 201b
About: a., a., in reel and rout 98b
  heard great argument a. it and a. 153a
  what are you a. 43a
Above: aim a little a. it 247a
  around, beneath, a. 36b
  at once a. beneath, around 403a
  every perfect gift is from a. 517a
  he is so a. me 322a
  some descending from a. 13a
  'tis not so a. 334b
  unless a. himself he can erect 464b
  up a. the world so high 425a
  we know of what they do a. 449a
Abra was ready ere I call'd 306a
Abraham (Abram): A., wherefore did Sarah laugh? 493a
  are they the seed of A. 515a
  carried. .into A.'s bosom 510a
  Edward sleep in A.'s bosom 385a
  O father A...these Christians 353a
  the God of A. 493b
  thou liest in A.'s bosom 467a
Abridgement: an a. of all that was pleasant 169b
Abroad: a., and see new sights 162b
  never stirs a. at all 400b
  no more; I will a. 188a
  pouring forth thy soul a. 220a
  take heed; I will a. 188a
Absalom: O A., my son 495b
Absence: from whom we love 109a
  a., hear thou my protestation 198a
  a. is to love what wind is to fire 561b
  a. makes the heart grow fonder 22a
  a. of body 535a
  a...of. .educated. .opinion 9b
  a. of occupation is not rest 110b
  a. seemed my flame to qualify 389a
  bitterness of a. sour 388a
  by a. this good means 198a
  conspicuous. .by its a. 315a
  eek in hir a. 89b
  hearts of. .mettle a. doth join 198a
  I dote on his very a. 353a
  like a winter hath my a. been 388b
  lovers'. .cannot admit a. 134a
  pangs of a. to remove 305b
  wh. in thy a. is. .a sty 324b

Absent: a. from Him I roam 280a
  a. in body but present in spirit 514a
  a.-minded beggar 227a
  a. one from another 493a
  a. thee from felicity 337a
  call'd my a. kisses 115b
  have I been a. in the spring 388b
  if to be a. were to be away 249b
  our loved ones, now far a. 411a
  the a. are always in the wrong 562b
  thou art a. I am sad 290a
  with an a. heed 179a
Absents: presents. .endear a. 238b
Absolute: be a. for death 351b
  he of a temper was so a. 136b
  how a. the knave is 336b
  Love, thou art a. 115a
  so a. she seems 276a
  the A. across the hall 26b
Absolutism moderated by assassination 523a
Absolved: half a. who has confess'd 305b
Abstain: a. from fleshly lusts 517b
  a. you from such works 257b
Abstinence: a. is as easy to me 212a
  a. sows sand 30a
  made almost a sin of a. 139b
  the lean and sallow a. 267b
Abstract liberty. .not to be found 55b
Abstracts: the a. and brief chronicles 332b
Absurd: or the thing becomes a. 197a
  Prophet of the Utterly A. 234a
  proving a. all written hitherto 46a
  so a. a view 75b
  something. .a. about the past 24b
Abundance: the a. of thy grace 491a
  the a. of the heart 506b
Abundant: good. .more a. grows 274b
Abundantly: to do exceeding a. 515b
Abuse: a. the shopocracy 289b
  if it is a...sure to hear of it 400a
  more dangerous the a. 56b
  to a. in public 34a
Abused: better to be much a. 362a
  except Napoleon, or a. it more 71b
  never love was so a. 402a
  so much a. as this sentence 321a
  still.by himself a. 301a
Abuses me to damn me 333a
Abusing: here will be an old a. 355b
Abydos of her breasts 132b
Abysm of time 367a
Abyss: Nature's dark a. 465a
  secrets of th' a. to spy 175a
  this wild a., the womb of nature 273a
  unbottomed infinite a. 272b
Abyssinian: it was an A. maid 101b
Acacia: the slender a. 434a
Academe: the olive grove of A. 277a
Academes: women's eyes. .the a. 345a

Academy: pronounce in this A. 308b
Accent: the a. of Christians 333b
Accents: a. yet unknown 339b
  caught his clear a. 48a
  follow with a. sweet 78a
  loved a. are soon forgot 395a
  th' a. that are ours 117a
Accept: a., thou shrine 225a
  I a. the Universe 82a
Acceptable: a. year of the Lord 503b
  alway a. in thy sight 482b
  an a. people 479a
Accepted: is it a. of song? 263b
Accident: found out by a. 240a
  many a happy a. 265b
  moving a. is not my trade 465b
  no a., no mishap 171b
  there's been an a. 172b
  the shot of a. 362b
Accidents: a. may be expected 122a
  a. will occur 122a
  chapter of a. is the longest 461a
  moving a. by flood 360a
  which shackles a. 325a
Accipitrine: will a. to pursue 441a
Accommodating: pollertics..exceed-in' a. 451a
Accomplishment of verse 464a
Accomplishments give lustre 91a
Accord: just a. all music makes 402a
  with one a. to make..supplications 478b
Accosted: you shd. then have a. her 371b
Account: but sent to my a. 331b
  shall give a. thereof 506b
Accounted: I wd. a. be true brother 476b
Accounting for the moral sense 80b
Accoutred as I was 337b
Accuracy must be sacrificed 212b
Accursed (accurst): shall think themselves a. 383a
  what God blessed once prove a. 44b
  wish that myself were a. 513b
Accusation: bring against him a railing a. 518a
Accuse: a. not Nature 276a
  I a. 566a
Accused: never make a defence..before..a 87b
Accuser: vanquish, not my A. 288a
Accusing Spirit wh. flew 412a
Ace of trumps up his sleeve 238b
Achaians: to the battle, A. 77b
Achates: loyal A. bore the weapons 554b
Ache: this heart rejoice, or a. 109b
Ached: never has a. with a heart 421a
Aches: fill all thy bones with a. 367a
  the sense a. at thee 363a
Achieve: I shall a. in time 164b
  the a. of, the mastery 198a
Achievements: how my a. mock me 369a
  such great a. cannot fail 65b
Achiever brings home full numbers 357b
Achieving: still a., still pursuing 248a
Achilles: clad in the spoils of A. 555b
  see the great A. 439a
  stood upon A.' tomb 71a
  what name A. assumed 42b
  words in wh. A., on returning 288a
  work out A. his armour 41a
Aching: left an a. void 109b
Achitophel: the false A. 138a
Acidulous vestals 413a
Acknowledge: do you think I'd a. him 125a
  I next a. duly 288b
Acknowledgement of God in Christ 46a
A-cold: owl..was a. 221b
Acorns: oaks from little a. grow 149b
A-courting: comes a. me 165a
  when we go out a. 131a
Acquaintance: a. I wd. have 107a
  an old a. among the pines 444a
  good creditable a. 418a
  have a visiting a. with 400b
  make a new a. 211b
  shd. auld a. be forgot 59a
  what! old a.! 379a
Acquainted (acquent): a. with grief 503a
  a. with sad misery 454b
  Love and I are well a. 167a
  what I am not a. with 155a
  when we were first a. 61a

Acquiesce: but to a. with silence 212b
Acquist: he with new a. 278a
Acre: an a. of barren ground 367a
Acres: every three a. of land 266a
  few paternal a. bound 303b
  lass that has a. o' charms 61a
  mystic fruit his a. yield 146b
  over whose a. walked 376a
  the a. of the rye 327b
  three a. and a cow 102b
Acrimonious and surly republican 213a
Acroceraunian mountains 392b
Act: a. first, this Earth, a stage 435b
  a. in the living Present! 248a
  a. upon it, if you can! 163b
  conclusion in unmitigated a. 229a
  did a. what now we moan 215a
  did the a. of darkness with her 343a
  does both a. and know 261a
  drive a coach..thro' the A. 309a
  I cd. a. as well as he myself 151b
  in some fifth a. 435b
  is in itself almost an a. 313a
  last a. crowns the play 307a
  prologues to the swelling a. 346a
  sleep an a. or two 386b
  some loving a. upon her 322b
  thine own a. and valour 347a
  think thou and a. 312b
  thyself shalt see the a. 355a
  to mind each kindly a. 539b
  unproportioned thought his a. 330b
  what a. that roars so loud 335a
  within the meaning of the A. 528a
Acted: Russell..a. invariably 150b
Acting: a. of a dreadful thing 338b
  a...the lowest of the arts 281a
  danger chiefly lies in a. well 94b
  when he was off he was a. 169b
Action: a. in the tented field 360a
  a. is transitory 463a
  a. lies in his true nature 334b
  a. nor utterance 340a
  cold for a. 381b
  do no sinful a. 3a
  end of life is..a. 203a
  end of man is an a. 81b
  in a. faithful 302b
  in a. how like an angel 332b
  in a. wisdom goes by majorities 264b
  justice is truth in a. 128a
  lose the name of a. 333a
  pious a. 333a
  spheres of a. 244b
  suit the a. to the word 333b
  that and th' a. fine 188b
  thought is the child of a. 130a
  till a., lust is perjur'd 389a
  turn a good a. into ridicule 151b
  whose a. is no stronger 388a
  with what courteous a. it waves 331a
Actions: a. of the just 401a
  a. that a man might play 330a
  best of all our a. tend 66a
  find her a. in balance 42a
  great a. are not always true sons 65a
  great a. speak great minds 23a
  in his a. be so ill 262b
  my a. are my ministers 87b
  speaker of my living a. 386b
  when our a. do not, our fears do 350a
  words are also a. 148a
Active: more a.-valiant 378b
Actor: after a well-graced a. leaves 376a
  a moment yet the a. stops 440b
  anybody may see he is an a. 151b
  as an unperfect a. 387a
  like a dull a. now 328b
  the fault and not the a. of it 351b
Actors: a. or spectators 392a
  these our a. 367b
Actresses: white bosoms of yr. a. 206b
Acts: all those a. wh. Deity 218a
  all yr. a. are queens 373b
  centre on forbidden a. 412a
  feels the noblest-a. the best 18a
  first four a. already past 28a
  illustrious a. high raptures 449a
  nameless, unremembered a. 472a
  our a. our angels are 23a
  our own a...mightier powers 5b

Acts (cont.)
  with such a. fill a pen 137a
Ad infinitum: so proceed a. 419b
Ada! sole daughter 68a
Adage: the poor cat i' the a. 347a
Adam: A. from his fair spouse 274b
  A. had 'em 522a
  A. shall share with me 276a
  A., the goodliest man 274a
  A. was but human 447a
  A. was not Adamant 194b
  a deep sleep to fall upon A. 492a
  and A. was a gardener 384a
  Aristotle..rubbish of an A. 406a
  as in A. all die 515a
  as our Father A. knew 228a
  child of A.'s stem 293b
  drink of A.'s ale 306a
  father A. sat under the tree 228a
  gardener A. and his wife 431b
  God..brought them unto A. 492a
  gratitude we owe to A. 447a
  grave man nicknamed A. 96a
  hold up A.'s profession 336a
  in A.'s ear so charming 275b
  oh, A. was a gardener 229b
  old A. in this child 481a
  old A.'s likeness 375b
  old A., the carrion crow 24a
  old..as the story of A. and Eve 47b
  second A. to the fight 288b
  son of A. and of Eve 305b
  the penalty of A. 325b
  when A. dalfe 178b
  when A. delved 527b
  wh. did in A. fail 289a
  whilst A. slept 528a
  whipped the offending A. 381a
  young A. Cupid 365a
Adamant: Adam was not a. 194b
Adazzle, dim 197b
Add: God shall a. unto him 520b
  if any man shall a. unto 520b
Added: these things shall be a. 505b
Adder: deaf a. that stoppeth her ears 485b
  it stingeth like an a. 498b
  that brings forth the a. 338a
Adders: what a. came to shed 421b
Addington: Pitt is to A. 570b
Addison: days and nights to..A. 213a
Addition: think it no a. 362b
Address: tear..wiped with a little a. 111a
Addressed: a. its evening hours 415a
  be they a. to what they may 209a
Adepts: in the speaking trade 94b
Adieu: a., a., kind friends 527a
  a., a.! my native shore 68a
  a.! a.! thy plaintive anthem 220a
  a. for ever more, my dear 61a
  a. for evermore, my love! 319a
  a., she cries! and waved 161a
  a.! the fancy cannot cheat 220a
  a. 'twixt soul and body 313b
  bid you a welcome a. 451a
  bid yr. servant once a. 388a
  Joy..bidding a. 219b
  thou vain world, a. 79a
  till tomorrow eve, my Own, a. 294a
Adjunct: learning is but an ?. 345a
Adjust: patiently a., amend, and heal 180a
  we never can a. it 59a
Administered: whate'er is best a. is best 301b
Administration: a criticism of 17a
Admiral: kill an a. from time to time 566a
Admirals: A. all 287b
  a., extoll'd for standing still 111a
Admiralty: blood be the price of a. 234b
Admiration: the a. only of weak minds 277a
  disease of a. 254b
  great in a. as herself 386b
  season yr. a. 330a
  we live by a. 464b
Admire: a. his sleight of hand 65b
  do you a. the view 84b
  for fools a. 300b
  for to a. an' for to see 229a
  I am willing to a. 197a
  I do a. of womankind 108b
  let none a. that riches grow 272a
  not to a. is all the art 71a, 304a
  nought to a. is..only thing 543a

Admire (cont.)
one cannot possibly a. them 460b
where none a., 'tis useless to excel 251b
Admired: all who understood a. 305a
in thee, fair and a. 322b
not blush so to be a. 449a
only to be seen to be a. 108a
that she might a. be 372b
Admires: he who meanly a. 439b
the men that all the world a. 259a
Admiring more the riches 272a
Admit: never to a. them in your sight 11b
Admittance: no a. till the week after 85b
Admitted to that equal sky 300b
Ado: much a. there was, God wot 35a
Adon: sweet A., darest not glance 176a
Adonais: blazoning the name of A. 393b
I weep for A. 391b
the soul of A., like a star 392b
what A. is why fear we to become 392b
Adonis: A. from his native rock 271b
an A. of fifty 183b
this A. in loveliness 202a
Adoption: and their a. tried 330b
children by a. and grace 479a
the spirit of a. 513b
Adorable: loving, a., softly to rest 289a
Adoration: all a., duty and observance 327b
breathless with a. 467a
for a. all the ranks of angels 402b
Adorations: desires and a. 392a
Adore: as you too shall a. 250a
I may command where I a. 371a
I seek and a. them 36b
yet I love thee and a. 110a
youth, I do a. thee 389b
Adored: I have still a...Liberty 101a
Adores: he a. as Margaret 294b
Seraph that a. and burns 301a
Adorn: nothing that he did not a. 209b
Adorned: the forest a. the foremost 97a
when unadorned a. the most 443b
Adread: yet was I sore a. 441b
Adrianus: moles of A. 42b
Adriatic: A. breaks in a warm bay 5b
spouseless A. 69a
Adsum: quickly said, 'A.' 440a
Adullam: political Cave of A. 38a
Adulteration: not quite adultery, but a. 71b
Adulterers: partaker with the a. 485a
Adulteries: the a. of art 215a
Adultery: do not a. commit 96b
gods [call] a. 70a
not quite a., but adulteration 71b
thou shalt not commit a. 480a
Advance: a.! spare not! 198a
is somewhat to a. 303b
retrograde if it does not a. 162a
Advanced: cowards! if I a. one step 288a
Advancement: what a. may I hope 334a
nailed for our a. 376a
suck they no small a. 486b
them as take a. that get a. 144a
the private a. of the preacher 56b
with equal a. esteem 78b
Advantages: he'll remember with a. 383a
hope of fair a. 353b
Advent: best such an a. becomes 73a
Adventure: beautiful a. in life 157b
in the a. of a diver 49b
once more on my a. 50b
to die will be an awfully big a. 21b
Adventures: a...to the adventurous 129a
bold and hard a. 152a
our a. were by the fireside 171a
Adventuring: thus a. to die 225a
Adventurous: adventures are to the a. 129a
Adversary: agree with thine a. 505a
mine a. had written a book 497a
yr. a. the devil 518a
Adversity: a. doth best discover virtue 14b
a. is..hard upon a man 81a
a. is not without comforts 14b
a. is the blessing of the New 14a
a.'s sweet milk 366a
hundred that will stand a. 81a
I am crossed with a. 372b
in the day of a. consider 499b

Adversity (cont.)
men contending with a. 64a
of fortunes sharp a. 90a
old companions in a. 53b
or any other a. 480b
sweet are the uses of a. 325b
things that belong to a. 14a
Advertisement: promise..is the soul of an a. 213a
Advice: a. from my seniors 444a
a. is seldom welcome 90b
a. to persons about to marry 535a
can Love be controll'd by a. 159a
never give any a. 91a
tea and comfortable a. 222b
to ask a...flattery 102a
woman seldom asks a. 2b
Advices: mony lengthened sage a. 62b
Advise: always to a. her wrong 419a
Adviser: than ever did th' a. 60a
Advises: it's my old girl that a. 121b
Advocate: our Mediator and A. 479a
Aegean: among the A. Isles 8a
o'er the A. main Athens arose 396a
Æneas: Dido and her A. 324b
Dido found A. wd. not come 304b
Aeon: lie down for an a. or two 236b
Aery: holds an a. in its arms 48b
Aeschylus: thundering A. 216a
Aesculapius: owe a cock to A. 560a
Aeson: herbs that did renew old A. 355a
Æsop: prettily devised of A. 16b
Aesthetic: in the high a. band 165b
in the high a. line 165a
Aetolian: Europe to the A. shore 6a
Afar: a., in the sounding labour-house vast 7b
and cometh from a. 466a
you wh. were a. off 515b
A-faulding let us gang 59b
Afeard: art thou a. to be the same 347a
Affable: the a. Archangel 275b
Affair: had an a. with the moon 411a
no half-and-half a. 163b
Affairs: for the ordering yr. a. 373b
or yr. a. suppose 388a
tide in the a. of men 341a
tide in the a. of women 71a
will mutter their a. 362a
Affect: angels a. us oft 131b
learned pedants much a. 65a
study what you most a. 366b
Affectation: a. of a. 151a
only by a. spoiled 420a
so used to a. 149a
spruce a. 345a
universities incline wits to..a. 17a
Affecting to seem unaffected 103b
Affection: a. beaming in one eye 123b
a. on things above 516a
a.! thy intention stabs 373a
by letter and a. 359b
deep a. and recollection 306b
he fills a.'s eye 210b
rear of yr. a. 330b
strong a. stirs her spirit 407a
talk not of wasted a. 247a
thy a. cannot hold the bent 370b
to me-wards yr. a.'s strong 189b
true a., but 'twas nipt with care 265b
what unrequited a. is 123a
Affectioned: be kindly a. 513b
Affections: a. dark as Erebus 355b
a. gently lead us on 472a
a history of the a. 203b
for those first a. 466b
his deep a. make him passionate 259a
lovers' souls descend t'a. 132b
old offences of a. new 389a
unruly wills and a. 479b
young a. run to waste 69a
Affinity: table of kindred and a. 491b
Affirmations: belief..a. of the soul 148b
Afflict: how dost thou a. me 385a
Afflicted: any ways a., or distressed 479a
he was oppressed and he was a. 503a
in all their affliction he was a. 503b
Affliction: a. is enamoured 366a
feed him with bread of a. 496b
heart together a. alters 373b
in all their a. he was afflicted 503b

Affliction (cont.)
in the furnace of a. 502b
such a light a. 287a
the highlands of a. 410a
try me with a. 362b
Afflictions: a. easier grow 450a
a. sorted 187a
happy issue out of all their a. 479a
Afford: parties cd. any way a. it 143b
Affright: there's none to a. thee 189b
Affront: well-bred man will not a. me 108a
Afghanistan: left on A.'s plains 237a
Afloat: are we now a. 341a
I'm a., I'm a. 243a
Afoot and light-hearted 458a
Afraid: a. of that wh. is high 499b
a. to know itself 350a
a. to look upon God 493b
be not a., neither be..dismayed 494b
do what you are a. to do 148a
half a. he first..beats 443b
happiness that makes the heart a. 195b
I am a. to think 348a
I am devilishly a. 139b
I, a stranger and a. 200a
I'm a. to come home in the dark 461b
in short, I was a. 145a
it is I; be not a. 507a
keep myself from being a. 139b
many are a. of God 246a
men not a. of G., a. of me 303b
not a. to speak evil 518a
not so..a. of death as ashamed 41b
of whom then shall I be a. 483b
so, I was a. 47b
they were sore a. 508b
Afric (Affrick): A.'s sunny fountains 184a
on A.'s burning shore 309a
thy breath is A.'s spicy gale 161a
upon A.'s passes 93b
Africa: I speak of A. 381a
Jove's planet..silent over A. 47b
sloggin' over A. 227b
something new from A. 552b
there is all A. 41b
weep for bones in A. 200a
African: Moon-mountains A. 221a
After: which was before come a. 65b
who coming a. me 510b
Afternoon: in the a. of time 415a
it seemed always a. 433a
some green a. 423a
the walk that a. 293b
wh. the rude multitude call the a. 345a
After-vacancy: in the a. 463a
Afton: flow gently, sweet A. 60b
Agag came unto him delicately 495b
Again: a.! a.! a.! 76b
and at him a. 19b
do it, please, a. 172b
has been, and may be a. 471a
I do it a. and a. 82b
is it really you a. 46b
try, try a. 191a
Against: he that is not with me is a. me 509a
I have somewhat a. thee 518b
who can be a. us 513b
Agamemnon: heroes lived before A. 547a
sent to rouse up A. 41a
when A. cried aloud 145a
Aganippe: I never drank of A. well 401b
Agate: no bigger than an a.-stone 364b
Age: a., ache, penury 352a
a. at last a sorry *breaking-up* 195b
a...best in four things 13b
a. cannot wither her 323a
a. fatal to Revolutionists 562b
a...his seasons done 137b
a., I do abhor thee 383b
a. is as a lusty winter 326a
a. is full of care 389b
A. might but take the things 463b
a. of chivalry is gone 57a
a. of chivalry is past 130a
a. shall not weary them 28b
a. will not be defied 15b
a. will perform the promises 213b
a., with stealing steps 448b
ah! Matt.: old a. 410b

Age (cont.)

a lady of a 'certain a.'	71a
an a. of poverty	355a
an a. that melts with..decay	214a
an a. without a name	283a
an old a., serene and bright	473a
Athens in his riper a.	141b
at your a. the hey-day	335a
build from a. to a.	227b
common at yr. a.	25b
complain of the a. we live in	56b
crabbed a. and youth	389b
damn the a.	240a
days of our a. are threescore	487b
dearth, a., agues	133a
died in a good old a.	496b
each a. is a dream	291a
every one when a...strike him	96b
expect one of my a.	149b
Father of all! in every a.	304a
fixed point in a changing a.	136a
forehead of the a. to come	221a
form'd to..lash the a.	299b
for what a. takes away	465a
green and smiling a.	413a
he cannot endure in his a.	358b
He hath not forgotten my a.	407a
he is of a.; he shall speak	511a
he was not of an a.	216a
he wd. not in mine a.	386a
I can tell a woman's a.	166b
if a. could	563a
in a. I bud again	188a
in a good old a.	492b
in torment in every a.	391b
it is the A. of Machinery	80a
joys with a. diminish	48b
kings governed their rude a.	17b
lead on our days to a.	341a
let a. approve of youth	51a
like the old a.	371a
live this day and see old a.	383a
mine a. is even as nothing	484a
more fruit in their a.	487b
now enjoys his a.	140a
Old A. and Experience	309b
old A. a regret	129a
old a. crept over them	286a
old a. hath yet his honour	439a
outworn buried a.	388a
pays us but with a. and dust	307b
poison for the a.'s tooth	373b
serene, that men call a.	39a
slow-consuming A.	175a
some smack of a. in you	379b
son of his old a.	493a
Soul of the A.!	215b
spirits of this a.	339b
staff of my a.	353a
stopped work at this a.	291a
tells one her real a.	460b
that A. is best	190b
that wh. shd. accompany old a.	350b
the a. is grown so picked	336b
the a. to come my own	107a
the a. to come wd. say	387a
the arrogance of a.	58a
the evening of my a.	313b
there may perhaps yet dawn an a.	6a
the toys of a.	301a
this a. best pleaseth me	190a
this is old a.	276b
this Youth and A.	137b
tho' a. from folly cd. not give	322b
tho' port shd. have a.	20a
thou a. unbred	388b
thou hast nor youth nor a.	351b
thro' every unborn a.	175a
till a., or grief, or sickness	225a
to be the shame of a.	93a
to grace this latter a.	378b
to occupy a. with	48a
towards the a. of twenty-six	26a
to youth and a. in common	9a
two weak evils, a. and hunger	326b
unless an a. too late	276a
Vastness! and A.!	298a
virtuous in their old a.	304a, 419a
well stricken in a.	493a
what stupid a. or nation	66a

Age (cont.)

when the a. is in	359a
wh. are a. his alms	295b
with an a. of ease	168a
woes that wait on a.	68a
world's great a. begins	394a
youth, what man's a. is like to be	119b

Aged: an a. thrush, frail

deliciously a. and sad	390b
I am wiser than the a.	489a
I saw an a. man	85a
object to an a. parent	123b
Paul the a.	516b
venerable..did the a. seem	445a

Agents: night's black a. 349a

Ages: a. and a. have fallen

a. elapsed ere Homer's lamp	111b
a. ere the Mantuan swan	111b
a. of hopeless end	272b
a Milton birth, ask'd a. more	111b
a secular bird, a. of lives	278a
a thousand a. in Thy sight	453a
aye, a. long ago	221b
doubt not thro' the a.	432b
emptiness of a.	258b
how many a. hence	339b
his acts being seven a.	326b
in more refined a.	17b
mighty a. of eternity	82a
our help in a. past	453a
Rock of a.	445a
some three a. since	344b
the rages of the a.	179b
to foreign nations and the next a.	17a
unending a. run	286b

Aggravate: I will a. my voice so 356b

Aggregate of little things 283a

Aggression: against the menace of a. 10b

Agincourt: affright the air at A. 381a
the name of A. 382b

Agios Athanatos 441a

A-gipseying: go a. thro' the world 240a

A-gley: gang aft a. 62a

Agnes: St. A.' Eve 221b

Agnostic: appropriate title of a. 203a

Ago: a great while a. the world 372a

bleak mid-winter long a.	311a
she's dead, sir, long a.	531b

Agog: all a. to dash thro' thick 108b

Agony: a. and bloody sweat 478b

only a., and that has ending	40a
sea of Life and A.	395b
swimmer in his a.	70b
the a. is abated	255b
the exceeding bitter a.	406a
waters of wide a.	395a

Agree: a. with thine adversary 505a

how a. the kettle and the..pot	520b
it does not a. with me	239b
I think if that a.	187b
roses..cd. not a.	189b
sugar, and saltness a.	169a
the more we didn't a.	80a
they do a. on the stage	400a
when people a. with me	460a
with her wd. not a.	474a
you a. with me	460a
you and I shall never a.	522b

Agreeable: idea of an a. person 129b

is the old min a.?	125a
power to be a.	419a

Agreed: a. to have a battle 84a
except they be a. 504a

Agreeing: angry..for not a. with me 41b

Agrees: person who a. with me 129b

Agriculture: all taxes..fall upon a. 162a

Agrippa: tall A. 192b
think myself happy, King A. 513a

Ague-proof: I am not a. 343b

Agues: dearth, age, a. 133a

'Ah!' said Mamma, 'I knew 192b

Aha: a., Elucescebat 45a
a., I am warm 502b

Ahab: ran before A. 496a

A-hunting: a. we will go 151b
daren't go a. 4a

Aid: afford ye kindest a. 420a

a. they yield to all	113b

Alliteration's artful a. 94b
kind Arbuthnot's a. 419b

Aid (cont.)

lend us Thine a.	184a
metaphysical a. doth..have	346b
one lovely hand..for a.	77a
without our a. he did	224b

Aik: my back unto an a. 539a

Ail: Oh what can a. thee 218b

Ailments: our a. are the same 418a

Aim: an a. I never fash 60b

malice never was his a.	419a
shoots xiphias to his a.	403a

Aimless: walks with a. feet 430b

Aims: far other a. his heart had learned 168b

other a. than my delight	180a
unsearchable and secret a.	36a

Ain't: they said 'No, you a.!' 243a

Air: a diviner a. 467b

a. A trim reckoning	379a
all the a. is thy Diocese	132b
all the castles..built with a.	215a
amaze the scented a.	37b
an a. that kills	199b
and fiends in upper a.	318b
as the a., invulnerable	329b
a stirring thrills the a.	179b
behold the fowls of the a.	505b
blue dome of a.	393b
blue regions of the a.	31b
bounded by the vaporous a.	395a
breathe in that fine a.	428a
brightness fall from the a.	285b
chambers of the a.	441b
do corrupt my a.	328a
draws a moment's a.	105b
excellent canopy, the a.	332b
fair and floral a.	154b
fairer than the evening a.	258b
fire-folk sitting in the a.	197b
freshness fills the silent a.	407a
Germans..(empire of)..the a.	80a
glittering in the smokeless a.	472b
gossip of the a.	370a
graceful a. and heavenly mug	155a
happy good-night a.	179a
her keel ploughs a.	87a
he says with solemn a.	59b
hurtles in the darken'd a.	175a
I am fire and a.	325a
I eat the a., promise-crammed	334a
in that heavenly a. bloom	37a
into a., into thin a.	367b
I shot an arrow into the a.	246b
let the pibroch shake the a.	12a
make the cold a. fire	397b
meteor of the ocean's a.	194a
nipping and an eager a.	331a
no stir in the a.	406b
no stir of a. was there	218a
now a. is hush'd	103a
one that beateth the a.	514a
only to kiss that a.	190a
on the undulating a...they swim	195b
out of a mouthful of a.	474b
parching a. burns frore	272b
playing in the wanton a.	344b
plunge to find the a.	442a
purpose up to the ends of the a.	36a
scent the morning a.	331b
she purged the a. of pestilence	369b
sightless couriers of the a.	347a
smell the Sussex a.	27a
still a. of delightful studies	279a
sweet as Eden is the a.	264b
the a., a charter'd libertine	381b
the a. a solemn stillness holds	174a
the a. at Agincourt	381a
the a. bites shrewdly	331a
the a. broke into a mist	50a
the a. goes by in a wind	24b
the a. is calm and pleasant	279b
the a. is cut away before	99b
the a. is delicate	347a
the a. nimbly and sweetly	347a
the fog and filthy a.	345b
the gold a. and the silver	312a
to fill the sea and a.	99b
to take into the a.	220a
to the fainting a...lay bare	398a
'twixt a. and Angels' purity	132a
vast, and wandering a.	384b

Air (*cont.*)

viewless forms of a. 317a
wan soul in that golden a. 312b
where a. might wash 423a
whistling to the a. 323a
wing the midway a. 343b
with an independent a. 162b
with his human a. 45b
with its sweet a. 367a
with pinions skim the a. 157b
world-mothering a. 197b
yr. tongue's sweet a. 356a
Air-bell of the Critic 45b
Airly Beacon 225b
Airs: a. to flashes blent 293b
angels sing..their a. divine 106b
discords make the sweetest a. 66a
don't give yourself a.! 82b
in its graces and a. 292b
martial a. of England 454a
melting a., or martial 112b
more than light a. 370b
saucy a. we meet 160b
sing it with such a. 474a
sounds and sweet a. 367b
the wandering a. they faint 394b
thy Naïad a. 298a
Airth: on every a. a limb 280b
Airts: of a' the a. 62a
Airy: a., fairy Lilian 432a
up the a. mountain 4a
Aisle: the long-drawn a. 174a
Aisles: on my heart monastic a. 147a
Aiver: mak a noble a. 60a
Ajalon: in the valley of A. 494b
Ajax: body is as good as A. 329a
when A. strives..to throw 300a
Akond of Swat 243b
Alabaster: as monumental a. 363b
grandsire cut in a. 352b
Alacrity: kind of a. in sinking 356a
Alan Breck 412b
Alarm (Alarum): at once the wild a. 252b
in a state of wild a. 164b
trumpet and a. 403a
Alarms (alarums): dwell in the midst
of a. 113a
our stern a. changed 384b
swept with confused a. 5a
used to war's a. 194b
Alas: a. and well a day 525b
a., how easily things go wrong 256a
a.! poor ghost 331a
a.! poor Yorick 336b
a., that the longest hill 24b
a.! 'tis true I have gone 389a
Albatross: he saw an a. 85b
I shot the A. 98b
the A. did follow 98b
Albu: gallant A. fell 27a
Alcestis: brought to me like A. 278b
Alchemy: countenance, like richest a. 338a
happy a. of mind 175b
with heavenly a. 387b
Alciphron: A. once or Arisbe 421b
Alcmena: misery makes A.'s nights 42b
Alcoran: *see* Koran
Aldebaran and Betelgueux shone 180b
Alderman: forefinger of an a. 364b
Aldermanic nose 19a
Aldershot: an' A. it 229b
Aldgate-Street: Temple-Bar to A. 160b
Aldiborontiphoscophornio! 79b
Aldrich: *hairy* A. 96a
Ale: a. is a dish for a king 373a
a., that is good a. 34a
always sleep upon a. 150a
Christmas..the mightiest a. 318a
drink of Adam's A. 306a
eat my a., drunk my a. 150a
fame for a pot of a. 382a
feasts where a. was strongest 249a
fed purely upon a. 150a
for a continuance..mild a. 417a
good a., the true and proper 34a
jolly good a. and old 415a
no more cakes and a. 370b
ordered a glass of this a. 122a
sees bliss in a. 113b
send thee good a. enough 415b
sons of a. and brede 474a

Ale (*cont.*)

spicy nut-brown a. 269a
the size of pots of a. 65a
while England talked of a. 93a
Alehouse: fools laugh i' the a. 360b
Aleppo: that in A. once 364a
Alexander (Alisander): A. at the head
of the world 449a
A.'s Ragtime Band 28a
A. the coppersmith 516b
declares that I am A. 345b
fought men, but A. women 244a
if I were not A. 559a
quhen A. owre kyng 474a
read A. Ross over 65a
she's gane, like A. 59b
some talk of A. 526a
the second A. the Great 257a
where A.'s ashes lay 18b
Alexanders: like so many A. 382a
Alexandra: our welcome of thee, A. 439a
Alexandrine: needless A. ends the
song 300a
Alexis: A., here she stay'd 138a
all aflame for fair A. 556b
Alfred: England's A. named 435a
when A. came to Athelney 91b
Algebra: clock doth strike, by a. 65a
Algiers: soldier..lay dying in A. 290a
Alhama: woe is me, A.! 67b
Alibi: if..don't prove a a. 126b
vy worn't there a a. 126b
Alice: A. looked all round 83a
A., where art thou? 53b
fairer eyes, of A. W—n 239a
'in the well', A. said 83a
remember sweet A. 148b
we are not of A. 238b
Alike: a. as if we had them not 351a
a. to no such aureate Earth 152b
faces, there shd. be none a. 42a
Alive: a., a., oh 524a
are we a. after all this satire 210b
art a. still, while thy book 215b
bears not a. so stout a gentleman 379a
born into the world a. 164a
he is no longer a. 27b
I am a. for evermore 518b
If I am a. I shall be delighted 156b
in that dawn to be a. 465a
officiously to keep a. 96b
'ot sand an' ginger when a. 229a
shall all be made a. 515a
she's a., she is not dead 531b
so abject, yet a. 73b
the playthings come a. 413b
was a. and is dead 523b
What! a. and so bold 395b
All: a. along, down along 531b
a. are needed by each one 146b
a. have given him over 137b
a. I can say is—I saw it! 49a
a.! I know not what ye call a. 377b
a. my pretty chickens 350a
a.'s over, then 48a
a. that a man hath 497a
a. that e'er with him be 530b
a. that in them is 480a
a. that is, at a. 51a
a. that therein is 483a
a. things are lawful for me 514b
a. things to a. men 514a, 524b
Christ is a., and in a. 516a
did you say a.? O hell-kite! 350a
for a' that and a' that 60b
her a. on earth 70a
if yet I have not a. thy love 133b
I shall never have it a. 133b
Lord God made them a. 3a
more than a. in heaven 70a
my life, my a. 453b
naught's had, a.'s spent 348b
ripeness is a. 344a
that A., wh. always is A. 133a
woo'd and married and a' 528b
Allah: A. is great, no doubt 96a
most to A. Who gave me two 236a
Allaying: a. both their fury 367a
no a. Thames 249b
Allegiance: follow with a. a fallen
lord 324a

Allegiance (*cont.*)

reverence, the religious a. 17a
swore to him a. 524a
to hell, a.! 335b
Allegorical: all the a. paintings 212a
Allegory: led a life of a. 223a
life..is a continual a. 223a
which things are an a. 515b
Alleluia: song of praise be sung,
A.! 304b
Allen: let humble A...do good 303b
Alley: each a. has a brother 302b
hollow cave and a. lone 433a
she lives in our a. 79b
through an a. Titanic 298b
Alliance: clear of permanent a. 451b
Alliances: entangling a. with none 204b
Allied: to that in you..they were a. 8b
Allies: thou hast great a. 472b
All-in-all: intellectual A. 468b
not at all or a. 428b
to me was a. 472a
Alliteration: apt A.'s artful aid 94b
Allowances: 'a.' said Arrius 539b
Allowed: on every hand it will a. be 60a
Allsopp: Guinness, A., Bass 75a
All-terrible: God the A. 94a
Allured: a. to brighter worlds 168b
Almanac: a. out of date 450a
fraud of the a. 251a
go to Carlisle's, and to A.'s. 4b
which was not in the a. 407a
Almanacs: greater storms..than a.
can report 322b
Almighty: a. be proved thy power 51b
A. scattered kings 486a
A.'s orders to perform 1a
A., thine this universal frame 275a
arrow from the A.'s bow 30b
under that A. Fin 39b
where the A.'s form glasses 69b
Almond: the a. tree shall flourish 499b
Alms: a. for oblivion 369a
a. of thy superfluous praise 137b
his a. feeds three 251a
so give a. 373b
when thou doest a. 505a
Alms-basket of words 345a
Almsman: apparel for an a.'s gown 375b
Aloe: labdanum, and a.-balls 49b
Aloft: lands..of olive, a. 426a
man looks a. 142b
now he's gone a. 121a
Alone: a. on Airly Beacon 225b
all we ask is to be let a. 118a
a., a banished man 529b
a., a., all, all a. 99a
a. and palely loitering 218b
a. and warming his five wits 438a
a. dwell for ever 6a
a. I did it 328b
a. wi' God an' these my engines 231b
a. with his glory 462b
am I a., and unobserved? 165a
as I was walking all a. 529b
be a. on earth 68a
bear the palm a. 337b
but wherefore thou a.? 274b
children dear, were we long a. 6a
dangerous to meet it a. 456a
fastest who travels a. 236b
hast been, shalt be, art, a. 6b
I am here at the gate a. 434a
I cannot play a. 184b
I feel I am a. 241a
ill fortune seldom comes a. 140a
I love but you a. 529b
I seem forsaken and a. 110a
I was never less a. 161b
left blooming a. 281b
let them a. and they'll come home 533a
let us a.. Time driveth 433a
never less a. than when a. 310a
not given for thee a. 63b
not good..that man shd. be a. 302a
nothing is fair or good a. 146b
one who treads a. 282b
or dwell for aye a. 120a
the Immortals, never a. 102a
we perished, each a. 107b
we shall die a. 564b

Alone (cont.)
who can enjoy a. 275b
who might have let it a. 212b
you and I must bide a. 531a
you or I were a. 249b
you weep a. 459a
Along: all a., down a. 531b
we will go with you a. 189a
Alonso of Arragon was wont to say 13b
Aloof: a. from the entire point 341b
a., from the high towers 393b
Alp: many a fiery A. 272b
Alph, the sacred river 101a
Alpha: I am A. and Omega 518a
Alphabet: ven he got. .end of the a. 126b
Alpine: A. mountains cold 278b
streams along the A. height 69a
the breeze of A. heights 241a
thro' an A. village 247a
Alps: A. on A. arise 300a
A. shaping like a backbone 179b
on the A. it is reported 322b
the fading A. 3a
Altar: an a. with this inscription 512b
before the a. stands 408b
bullocks upon thine a. 485a
his own strange a. 421b
nearer to God's A. trod 115a
nearer to. .the A.'s God 115a
so will I go to thine a. 483b
to what green a. 219b
Altars: even thy a., O Lord 487a
their a., and their hearths 553a
Altar-stairs: the great world's a. 430b
Alteration: alters when it a. finds 389a
do what thou canst for a. 198a
Altered in the building trade 236a
Alternative: an unhappy a. is before you 11b
Alternatives: the more a., the more difficult the choice 561a
Alters when it alteration finds 389a
Althea: my divine A. brings 249b
Altogether: charm of Caelia a. 457a
Always: a. gay 528a
I am not. .a. in the wrong 107b
poor a. ye have with you 511a
they must be a. with us 217b
Am: I a. not what I a. 359b
I a. that I a. 493b
I a. what I a. 514b
Amalek: that moment A. prevailed 110a
Amalfi: Sorrento and A. 241a
Amaracus: violet, a., and asphodel 435a
Amaranth: fields of A. lie 119a
no fields of a. on this side 241b
Amaranth's: plucker of a. 52a
Amaranthine flower 112a
Amaranthus: bid amaranthus all his beauty shed 270a
Amaryllis: sport with A. in the shade 269b
Amateurs: a nation of a. 310b
Amaze: a. the scented air 37b
vainly men themselves a. 260b
ye gods, it doth a. me 337b
Amazed: a. the gazing rustics 168b
who can be wise, a. 348a
Amazon and tall as A. 219a
I've never sailed the A. 230b
Ambassador: a. from Britain's Crown 136b
a. is an honest man 473a
Ambassadors: King of Siam sent a. 210a
Amber: a ceiling of a. 6a
preserved forever in a. 16b
pretty! in a. to observe 303a
the a. torrent descended 96a
to lutes of a. 190b
Amber-dropping: thy a. hair 268a
Ambergris: proclaim the a. 260a
Amberley: a good brew in A. 27a
Ambition: a. can creep as well 58a
a. first sprung 299a
a. had not wholly suppressed 57b
a., in a private man a vice 262b
a. of a private man 111b
a. of so airy. .a quality 332b
a.'s debt is paid 339a
a. should be made of sterner stuff 340a
a. the soldier's virtue 323b
a most pitiful a. 334a

Ambition (cont.)
art not without a. 346b
by low a. and. .praise 111b
fling away a. 386a
heart's supreme a. 251b
ill-weaved a. 379a
let not a. mock 174a
meaner things to low a. 300b
not with a. joined 105b
the a. thick-sighted 217a
thriftless a. 348b
to reign is worth a. 271b
vaulting a., wh. o'erleaps itself 347a
virtue in a. is violent 14b
wars that make a. virtue 362a
what madness is a.! 157a
who doth a. shun 326a
young a.'s ladder 338a
Ambitions: swollen a. dwindle 46a
Ambitious: Brutus says he was a. 340a
Caesar was a. 339b
hunger of a. minds 409a
substance of the a. 332b
Amble: teach an old horse a. true 409a
Ambled: he a. up and down 378a
Ambrosial: dropt in a. oils 267b
born of a great A. 421b
Ambuscadoes, Spanish blades 364a
Amelia: A. was praying for George 440a
the author of 'A.' 34a
Amen: A. . . Even so, come, Lord 520b
a., so be it 481a
A.; so let it be 280a
'A.' stuck in my throat 347b
clerk, still cry 'A.' 388a
even so, A. 518a
glorious the catholic a. 403a
hear that grand A. 306b
sound of a great A. 306b
will no man say, a.? 376a
world without end. A. 478a
Amends: meeting like this make a. 282a
America: A.! A.! 22a
A. . . half-brother of the world 18a
A. is a country of young men 148b
A. is God's crucible 477b
A. is just ourselves 9b
huntsmen are up in A. 41a
nothing less. .than *whole A.* 55b
oh, they go to A. 460b
O my A.! My new-found-land 132b
owe to the discovery of A. 184b
rejoice that A. has resisted 297a
smoking. .discovery of A. 184b
wake up A. 158a
when we think of thee, O A. 449b
young man, there's A. 55b
youth of A. is their. .tradition 460b
American: A. nation in th' Sixth Ward 143a
assured by a very knowing A. 418a
God is making the A. 477b
heroism from an A. . .view 458b
I also am an A. 454a
ideal A. who is all wrong 94a
if I were an A. 297a
I was born an A. 454a
love all mankind, *except an A.* 210a
new deal for the A. people 310a
not a Virginian but an A. 185b
subtleties of the A. joke 446b
Americanism: no fifty-fifty A. 310b
only 100 per cent. A. 310b
Americans: A. have taken umbrage 535b
brave A. all 127b
good A., when they die, go to Paris 4b
hyphenated A. 310b
matter with A. except their ideals 94a
put none but A. on guard 452a
when bad A. die 460b
when good A. die 460b
who are A. and nothing else 310b
Amethyst: last an a. 43a
twelfth, an a. 520a
Amiability: gained in a. 66b
Amiable: a. are thy dwellings 487a
an a. weakness 400b
anything that is a. 104a
Amiably-disposed young man 127a
Amicably: separation, a. if they can 307b
Amice: pilgrim steps in a. grey 277a
Amiss: all is a. 21a

Amiss (cont.)
mark what is done a. 490a
never anything can be a. 357b
nothing shall come a. 53b
what 's a. I'll strive to mend 453a
Amissi: not a., but praemissi 186a
Ammiral: mast of some great a. 271b
Amo, amas, I love a lass 290b
Among them, but not of them 68b
Amorites and the Perizzites 493b
Amorous: a. of their strokes 323a
be a., but be chaste 72a
Death is a. 366b
reluctant a. delay 274a
rival a. vows 37b
still a., and fond and billing 66a
Amos, what seest thou? 504b
Amour: beginning of an A. 25a
enforce a desperate a. 66a
too sure of the a. 441a
Amphibious ill-born mob 118b
Amphisboena dire 276b
Amphitrite's destined halls 395a
Amphitryon: I am the true A. 139b
Amurath: not A. an A. succeeds 381a
Amused: we are not a. 448b
Amusement: cough for my own a. 11b
providing topics of a. 417b
write for the general a. 319a
Amusements: *life.* .tolerable were it not for its a. 572a
no a. . .but vice and religion 404b
Amusing with numerous errors 171a
Anabaptists: as certain A. do 491b
Anacreon: Horace or A. tasted 215a
Anak: giants, the sons of A. 494a
Analytic: profoundly skilled in a. 64b
Ananias: O A., Azarias 478a
Anapaestic: rolling a. curled 44a
Anapaests: the swift A. throng 101b
Anarch: thy hand, great A.! 299a
Anarchy: a. .the laws of death 315a
freedom. .the cure of a. 55b
Anathema: thunder 'A.' friend, at you 438b
Anathema Maran-atha: let him be A. 515a
Anatomy: Pinch. .a mere a. 328a
Anatomy of Melancholy. .was the only book 208a
Ancestors: a. are very good kind of folks 400b
his own tree of a. 412b
look backward to their a. 57a
our a. have turned a. .wilderness 56a
wild trick of his a. 379a
wisdom of our a. 56b
Ancestral: a. voices prophesying war 101b
tall a. trees 184b
Anchor: he a. his aspect and die 323a
sails, a. and other tackle 215a
Anchorage: long a. we leave 457a
Anchored on. .immortality 38b
Anchors: they cast four a. out 513a
wedges of gold, great a. 384b
Ancient: a. and fish-like smell 367b
a. castle. .not in decay 15a
a. nobility is the act of time 15a
china that's a. and blue 242a
fear thee, a. Mariner 99a
God save thee, a. Mariner 98b
how have you left the a. love 31b
it is an a. Mariner 98a
lieutenant. .saved before the a. 361a
spake on that a. man 98a
stands Thine a. sacrifice 233b
the A. of days 504a
the A. of Days. .in splendour 172b
with the a. is wisdom 497a
Ancients: a. dreaded death 181a
speak of the a. without idolatry 90b
wisdom of the a. 17a
Ancona: this is A. 47a
Anderson: John A. my jo 61a
Andrea del Sarto appears 25a
Andrew Hedger 264b
Anear: sophist, come not a. 435b
Anecdotage: fell into a. 129b
Anfractuosities of the human mind 210a
Angel: a beautiful and ineffectual a. 9b
a mighty a. took up a stone 519b
an a. visited the green earth 248a

Angel (*cont.*)

a. new dropt from the sky 292b
a. of death has been abroad 38a
A. of Death spread his wings 74a
A. of the Lord came down 424b
a. of the Lord came upon them 508b
A. of the Off-shore Wind 230b
a. of the world 329a
a. of this life 51a
a. spirits of sleep 35b
a. that presided o'er my birth 30b
a.-visits, few and far between 77b
a. watching an urn 433b
a. whom thou still hast served 351a
A. with contracted brow 276a
a. writing in a book of gold 201b
as if an angel dropped down 378b
a Wenus or a a. 126b
a woman yet think him an a. 439b
bright with many an a. 286a
clip an A.'s wings 219a
consideration like an a. 381a
curse his better a. 363b
custom.. is a. yet in this 335a
dark and serious a. 36a
dreadless a. unpursued 275a
drew an a. down 139a
drew one a. 49b
drive an a. from yr. door 32b
fine, silly old a. 240a
heard an a. sing 522a
hear thy guardian a. say 146a
her a.'s face.. shined bright 408b
hold the fleet a. fast 247b
how like an a. 332b
in quibbles, a. and archangel join 303b
is man an ape or an a.? 128b
look homeward, A., now 270a
lost a. of a ruined Paradise 392a
Love, half a. and half bird 51a
ministering a. shall my sister be 336b
ministering a. thou 318b
my bad a. fire my good one 389b
neither man nor a. can discern 273b
pay a glorious a. 375a
prepared to paint an a. 49a
Recording A... dropped a tear 412a
shin'd in my a.-infancy 448a
still an a. appear 292b
sword of an A. King 30b
the A. ended 275b
the better a. is a man 451a
the more a. she 363b
the story wh. a. voices tell 266a
tho' an a. shd. write 281a
those A. faces smile 288b
thou hovering a. 267a
up-lifted A. trumpets blow 278a
who wrote like an a. 158b
Angelic: seem a. in the sight of God 247b
something of a. light 470b
Angelina: turn, A., ever dear 169a
Angels: all the a. stood round 519a
a. affect us oft 131b
a., all pallid and wan 298a
a. all were singing 74b
a. alone, that soar above 249b
a. and ministers of grace 331a
a. are bright still 350a
a. are painted fair 291b
a. came and ministered 505a
a... came to my bed 131a
a. in blue and white 131a
a. in broad-brimmed hats 247b
a. in some brighter dreams 448b
a. into Abraham's bosom 510a
a. keep their ancient places 442a
A., Martyrs, Prophets 286a
a. of God ascending 493a
a. of rain and lightning 396a
A., progeny of light 275a
a. sing to thee their airs 106b
a.' visits, short and bright 289b
a. wd. be gods 300b
a. yield eternal thanks 402b
as far as A. ken 271a
as make the a. weep 351b
aspiring to be a. 300b
blow yr. trumpets, a. 133a
bright-harnest A. 270b

Angels (*cont.*)

by that sin fell the a. 386a
calling to the A. 230b
entertained a. unawares 517a
even thousands of a. 486b
flights of a. sing 337a
four a. round my head 2b
four a. to my bed 2b
give his a. charge over thee 487b
glorious a. always stand 286a
glorious fault of a. 299a
God an a. to be lookers-on 13a
good as guardian a. are 107a
greet as a. greet 250a
guardian a. sung this strain 443a
heard the a. call 434b
he maketh his a. spirits 488a
holy a. guard thy bed 453a
I have no a. left 441a
invite God, and his A. 134b
like a. trumpet-tongued 347a
like good a., to my end 385b
madest him lower than the a. 482a
man did eat a.' food 487a
meet we no a., Pansie 10b
Michael and his a. 519a
nor a., nor principalities 513b
now walk the a. 259b
oblivion in lost a. 6a
o'er thee the.. a. mourn 37b
only the a. hear 393a
on the side of the a. 128b
our acts our a. are 23a
praise Him, a. in the height 224a
services of A. and men 480a
sons of men and a. say 455b
sorrow for a. 48a
sparkling A. 445a
then, if a. fight 375a
therefore with A. and Archangels 480b
they have the faces of a. 541a
till a. wake thee 206a
tongues of men and of a. 514b
'twixt air and A.' purity 132a
unto the world, and to a. 514a
visits like those of a., 29a
walking, like two a. white 37a
were a. to write 289b
where a. fear to tread 300b
where a. tremble 175a
ye like a., appear 7b
Angelus: once at the A. 131a
Anger: a. insignificantly fierce 112b
a. invests with such.. grace 401a
a. is a short madness 543a
a. is not turned away 501a
a. makes dull men witty 13b
a.'s self I needs must kiss 401b
carries a. as the flint 341a
contempt and a. of his lip 371b
do they provoke me to a.? 503b
he that is slow to a. 498a
keepeth.. his a. for ever 488a
more in sorrow than in a. 330b
rarely gave way to his a. 23b
you strike it in a. 391a
Angered: she that being a. 360b
Angle: Brother of the A. 450a
themselves in every a. greet 260a
Angler: excellent a., and now with God 450b
if he be an honest a. 450a
Nero is an a. 343a
no man is born an a. 450a
Anglers, or very honest men 450b
Angles: they were called A. 541a
Angling: a... begat habits of peace 450b
a. deserves commendations 450b
a. is somewhat like poetry 450b
a. or float-fishing 214a
a... rest to his mind 450b
a... so like the mathematics 450a
be quiet; and go a-A. 450a
Wotton.. lover of.. the art of a. 450b
Anglo-Saxon: A. attitudes 85a
gold.. idol of the A. 17b
goodbye to the A. race 171b
he's an A. Messenger 85a
Angry be ye a., and sin not 515b
but not an a. father 77a
I was a. with my foe 32a

Angry (*cont.*)

I was a. with my friend 32a
speak no a. word 3a
when he was a., one of his eyes 23b
when thou art a. all our days 487b
why shd. I be a. with a man 14a
Anguish: a. of all sizes 187a
a. of a torturing hour 357b
solitary hidden a. 144a
when pain and a. wring the brow 318b
with a. moist and fever dew 218b
Animal: a more contemptible a. 151a
be a good a. 243b
man is a noble a. 42b
man is.. a religious a. 57a
man is a tool-making a. 157a
monstrous a. a husband and wife 151b
poor, bare, forked a. 343a
their glad a. movements 472a
this a. is very mischievous 566a
true to yr. a. instincts 243a
Animals: all a... for the use of man 295a
a. are such agreeable friends 144b
a... ask no questions 144b
a. never kill for sport 157b
a... pass no criticisms 144b
500,000 two-legged a. 81b
name of those fabulous a. 123b
the a. went in one by one 526a
the paragon of a. 332b
turn and live with a. 458a
Animate: let onion atoms.. a. the whole 404b
Animated torrid-zone 146b
Animosities are mortal 289b
Animosity: fervour of sisterly a. 417a
Anio: orchard slopes, and the Anio 96a
Anise: mint and a. 507b
Ankle: down-gyved to his a. 332a
Ankles: his weak a. swell 471a
one praised her a. 425b
Ankworks package 124a
Ann Page: sweet A. 355b
Anna: here thou, great A. 302b
Annabel Lee 297b
Annals: a. of the poor 174a
war's a. will cloud into night 179b
writ your a. true 328b
Anne (Annie): A. cd. hardly bear to see the end 181a
for bonnie A. Laurie 135a
Miss A. she said it wur draäins 439a
Sister A., do you see anybody 564a
Annihilate but space and time 298b
Annihilating all that's made 260b
Annihilation: one Moment in A.'s waste 153b
Annibaptist is a thing I am not 155a
Anniversaries: a. of the heart 248b
Anno Domini: taste my A. 150a
Annoy: he only does it to a. 82b
with pleasure thine a. 387a
Annoyance: shadow of a. 398b
Annoying: went surly by, without a. me 338a
Annuity is a very serious business 11b
Annygoats: polite a. 440a
**Anoint.. and cheer our soiled face 491a
Anointed: rail on the Lord's a. 385a
touch the Lord's A. 524a
Anointing: thou the a. spirit art 491a
Another: a groan, and then a. 468b
and each for one a. 244b
a. year! a. deadly blow! 468a
a., yet the same 299a
bind a. to its delight 32a
'cause a.'s rosy are 462a
bring a. back to me 529b
do we look for a. 506b
for a. gives its ease 32a
his bishoprick let a. take 512a
I made a. song 36b
joys in a.'s loss of ease 32a
love by a.'s eyes 356a
members one of a. 515b
Nature.. ne'er made a. 59b
not Lancelot, nor a. 428a
rather liberal of a. man's 16a
see a.'s grief 33a
see a.'s woe 33a
serveth not a.'s will 473a

Another (cont.)
'Sir,' said Mr. Pickwick, 'you're a.' 126a
still better than a. 523b
taste of a.'s bread 567a
that's quite a. thing 67b
true love know from a. one 335b
when comes such a.? 340b
world cannot show such a. 261a
Answer: a. a fool according 498b
a. came there none 84b, 316a
a. made it none 330b
a man's waitin' for a a. 122a
a. trickled thro' my head 85b
be swift, my soul, to a. Him 200b
careful to a. thee 504a
give me yr. a., do! 116b
I a., there 188b
I shd. a., I shd. tell thee 248b
I wd. turn and a. 199a
little fishes' a. was 85a
make you not then the better a. 359a
not bound to please thee with my a. 354b
reduced the a. to shillings 83b
sent an a. back to me 85a
shalt a., Lord, for me 187b
soft a. turneth away wrath 498a
the noblest a. unto such 425b
the silver a. rang 43b
Uncle Toby wd. never offer to a. 411b
what a dusty a. gets the soul 264a
what a. shd. I give 436b
wd. not stay for an a. 14a
Answered: a. Caius Cassius so 341a
a. with his eyes upon the ground 428a
how a beggar shd. be a. 355a
I a. him as I thought good 534a
I came, and no one a. 119b
I have a. three questions 82b
jealous souls will not be a. so 362b
they only a. 'little liar' 26a
when have I a. thee 436b
Answerest thou the high priest 511b
Answers: kind are her a. 78b
ne'er a. till a husband cools 302a
with dawning a. there 441b
Ant: good husband, little a. 249b
go to the a., thou sluggard 498a
Antagonist: our a. is our helper 57b
Antelope: Snowdonian a. 395b
Anteros: he the A. and Eros 441a
Anthea: thou A. must withdraw 190a
Anthem: a. of 'Erin go bragh' 76b
pealing a. swells 174a
thy plaintive a. fades 220a
Antheming a lonely grief 218b
Anthems: hollaing, and singing of a. 379b
loud yr. a. raise 20b
service high, and a. clear 268b
Anthropophagi and men whose heads 360a
Anti: savage a.-everythings 193b
Antic (antick): a. disposition 331b
old father a., the law 376b
there the a. sits 375b
Anticipate: what we a. seldom occurs 129b
Anticipation of facts 116b
Antidius on his back 407a
Antidote: sweet oblivious a. 350b
Antigropeloes: galligaskins, a. 75a
Antilogy: the intolerable a. 179b
Antinoüs: Hope an A. mere 96a
Antipathies: those common a. 42a
Antipathy: a. of good to bad 303b
I have no a...in...anything 41b
Antipodes: sheer opposite, a. 218a
to act our a. 41a
Antiquarian is a rugged beast 209b
Antique: noble and nude and a. 421a
Antiquities: a. are history defaced 13a
time, wh. antiquates a. 42b
Antiquity: a. inclines a man to Popery 158a
blasted with a. 379b
praise, from dark a. 467a
write for A. 240a
Antonia: saith Aretine's A. 64b
Antoninus: Titus A. Pius..His reign 162a
Antonio: make A. Stradivari's violins 144b

Antony: and Brutus A., there were an A. 340a
A. enthroned i' the marketplace 323a
A. shall be brought drunken 325a
A.'s hath triumphed 324b
A., that revels long 339a
A., who lost the world for love 141a
catch another A. 325b
for Cydnus to meet Mark A. 325a
loves no plays, as thou dost, A. 338a
much A. 185b
my A. is away 323a
my lord is A. again 324a
my oblivion is a very A. 322b
none but A. shd. conquer A. 324b
she first meet the curled A. 325a
spirit that is in A. 337b
valour hath o'erthrown A. 324b
Antres vast 360a
Ants: a trouble of a. in the gleam 439a
flies or a...in amber 16b
Anvil: England's on the a. 227a
what the a. 32a
Any: but were there ever a. 221b
Anybody: no one's a.! 163b
Anything: a., as the learned Boar observed 396b
a. that is his 480a
a. to me is sweeter 192b
in case a. turned up 122a
I will do a., Nerissa 353a
never to have too much of a. 554a
not be known to do a. 147b
or in short do a. 411b
thanks God for a. 206b
tho' you do a. 388a
what is the worth of a. 76a
wot's the good of a.? 94a
Anywhere: a.; a., out of the world 196a
A1: six foot o' man, A. 250b
Ap Headlong 295a
Apart: man's love..a thing a. 70a
two are walking a. 203a
Ape: a blue-behinded a., I skip 415a
a. an ancient rage 93a
buttocks of the a. 202b
like an angry a. 351b
like an a. doth nuts 335a
played the sedulous a. 412b
their manners from the A. 25b
Apella the Jew must believe it 547b
Apennine: folding of the A. 9a
wind-grieved A. 46a
Apennines: Popish A. 226a
Apes: a. are a., tho' clothed 215b
cargo of ivory, and a. 261b
ivory, and a., and peacocks 496a
the person and the peple his a. 89a
to her, lead a. in hell 366b
Apocalypse: great A. 471a
Apollo: A. bore me from the fray 547b
A. from his shrine 270b
A. hunted Daphne so 260b
A., Pallas, Jove 131b
A.'s first 79a
A.'s laurel bough 259a
A. turned fasting friar 264b
as bright A.'s lute 345a
bards in fealty to A. hold 220b
Graces danced, and A. play'd 249b
is not even A...a bitter god 423b
musical as is A.'s lute 267b
nor keeps A. his bow 545a
not here, O A.! 5b
O Delphic A.! 218a
Paian, A. 423a
the songs of A. 345b
'tis A. comes leading 5b
Apollos watered 514a
Apollyon: his name is A. 54a
then A. straddled 54a
Apologize: I never a. 389a
Apology: a. before you be accused 87b
no a. ain't gwine ter make h'ar ter 181b
Apoplexy: a. is..a kind of lethargy 379b
Apostle: a. in the high aesthetic band 165b
a. of the Philistines 9b
meet to be called an a. 514b
Apostles: Cristes lore..A. twelve 88b

Apostles (cont.)
following of the A. 491b
she while A. shrank 21a
the A. wd. have done 70a
true a. of equality 9b
Apothecary: I do remember an a. 366a
ointment of the a. 499b
ounce of civet, good a. 343b
Apparel: every true man's a. 352a
gold upon yr. a. 495b
my gay a. for an almsman's gown 375b
put on glorious a. 487b
the a. oft proclaims the man 330b
Apparelled: a. in celestial light 466a
a. in more precious habit 359a
a. like the spring 364a
Apparition: a lovely a. 470b
if I had seen an a. 118b
that a., sole of men 397a
Apparitions: like a. seen and gone 289b
Appeal: I a. unto Caesar 512b
Appealed: hast thou a. unto Caesar 513a
Appear: never..so fair 102a
that didst a. so fair 473a
Appearance: looketh on the outward a. 495b
the a. of Your Majesty 492a
Appearances: contrive to save a. 275b
keep up a. 94b
no trusting to a. 400b
Appeared: thing a. again tonight? 329b
Appeareth for a little time 517b
Appetite: a. grows by eating 565a
as if increase of a. had grown 330a
doth not the a. alter 358b
good digestion wait on a. 349a
govern'd and wise a. 267b
hungry edge of a. 374b
love may be called a. 371a
mortified a. is never..wise 412a
swich a. hath he to ete a mous 89b
the a. may sicken 369b
were then to me an a. 472a
with what a. you have 385b
Appetites: cloy the a. they feed 323a
our a. are apt to change 139a
ours, and not their a. 362a
subdue yr. a., my dears 124b
to yr. irregular a. 40b
Applaud: a. thee to the very echo 350b
a. the hollow ghost 6b
a. us when we run 55a
till thou a. the deed 349a
Applause: a.! delight! the wonder 215b
a. of listening senates 174b
attentive to his own a. 303a
gained universal a. by explaining 410a
joy in an a. so great as thine 106b
satiate of a. 303b
what's not for their a. 474a
Apple: a codling when 'tis almost an a. 370a
an a. damn'd mankind 291b
a. for the a.'s sake 447a
a. pressed with specious cant 194b
cream..to eat with a. tart 414a
goodly a. rotten at the heart 353a
like the sweet a. 311b
pure mind..a. dumplings 238b
the a. of an eye 482b
when you've got an a. 447a
where the a. reddens 52b
Apple pie: A was an a. 532a
cabbage-leaf, to make an a. 155b
with a. and cheese 150b
Apples: a., cherries, hops 126a
a. forget to grow on apple-trees 92a
a. in all the Chapels 19b
a. of gold for the king's 422b
a. on the Dead Sea's shore 68b
breasts ripe a. 138a
comfort me with a. 500a
like a. of gold 498b
moon-washed a. of wonder 137b
ripe a. drop about 260b
silver a. of the moon 476a
small choice in rotten a. 366b
Apple-tree: a. do leän down low 21a
branch of mossy a. 101a
falling from that a. 172b
fell beneath the a. 441a

Apple-tree (*cont.*)
my heart is like an a. 310*b*
raised thee up under the a. 501*a*
shade of the old a. 461*b*
Apple-trees: forget to grow on a. 92*a*
my a. will never get across 157*b*
plums and a. 192*a*
Appliances: all a. and means to boot 380*a*
by desperate a. are relieved 335*a*
Application: lays in the a. on it 122*b*
Apply: know my methods. A. them 136*a*
Appointed: pilgrims to th' a. place 141*a*
wh. thou hast a. for them 488*a*
Appointment with a beech-tree 444*a*
Apprehension: a. of the good 374*b*
death is most in a. 352*a*
in a. how like a god 332*b*
shuts his a. up 260*a*
Apprehensions: my a. come in crowds 463*a*
Apprehensive: men are..a. 339*a*
Apprentice for to bind 531*b*
Approach: descry the morn's a. 277*a*
my pulse..beats my a. 225*b*
the sweet a. of even or morn 273*a*
Approbation: a. from Sir Hubert 284*b*
cold a. gave the lingering bays 213*b*
Approve: a. a private opinion 191*b*
love doth so a. him 363*a*
men of sense a. 300*b*
the wh. he cd. a. 399*a*
wdst. then a. thy constancy 276*a*
Appurtenances thereof 493*b*
Apricocks: dangling a. 375*b*
April: A. is the cruellest month 144*b*
A., June, and September 172*a*
A., June, and November 533*a*
A., laugh thy girlish laughter 452*a*
A. of her prime 387*a*
A. of yr. youth adorns 186*b*
A. showers bringeth..May flowers 525*a*
A.'s in the west wind 262*a*
blossoming boughs of A. 35*b*
dew in A. that falleth 524*b*
fashioned an A. violet 452*a*
fickleness of an A. day 162*a*
flag to A.'s breeze 146*b*
love seemed that A. morn 37*b*
men are A. when they woo 327*b*
now that A.'s there 47*a*
one of love's A. fools 104*b*
proud-pied A. 388*b*
spongy A. 367*b*
sweet A. showers 446*a*
three A. perfumes 388*b*
uncertain glory of an A. day 372*b*
whanne that A. 88*a*
you were A.'s lady 423*a*
Aprons: made themselves a. 492*b*
Apt: a. Alliteration's artful aid 94*b*
find myself so a. to die 339*b*
Arab: sold, my A. steed 289*b*
Arabia: all the perfumes of A. 350*a*
A. and Saba 486*b*
far are the shades of A. 119*a*
spell of far A. 119*a*
Arabian: A. fleet might have sailed 162*a*
A. woods embost 278*a*
fast as the A. trees 364*a*
wish the A. Tales were true 288*a*
Arabians: Cretes and A. 512*a*
Arabs: fold their tents, like the A. 247*a*
Araby: A. the blest 273*b*
songs of A. 461*b*
Aral: shine upon the A. Sea 8*a*
Araminta, say 'No!' 305*a*
Arbiter: A. of others' fate 73*b*
high a. chance 273*a*
Arbitrate: now, who shall a.? 50*b*
Arbitrator: common a., Time 369*b*
Arbitress: moon sits a. 272*a*
Arboreal: sits Probably A. 412*b*
Arbuthnot: A. a day 419*a*
kind A.'s aid 419*b*
'Arcades ambo'..blackguards 71*a*
Arcadians: both A. 557*a*
Arch: A. Fear in a visible form 50*b*
a. of the leaves was hollow 422*b*
experience is an a. 438*b*
forgot the a.—crash 126*a*
hour, o' night's black a. 63*a*

Archangel: affable A. 275*b*
A. a little damaged 240*a*
less than a. ruined 272*a*
the A. bowed 74*b*
the lost A. 271*a*
Archangels: bow down, a. 475*b*
with Angels and A. 480*b*
Archdeacon: by way of turbot, an a. 405*b*
Archer: busy a. his sharp arrows 401*b*
mark the a. little meant 317*b*
Arches: among her golden a. 30*b*
such Cyclopean a. 92*b*
Archibald—certainly not 315*a*
Archipelagoes: alps and a. 3*a*
Architect: a. . . . greatest of men 19*a*
no person..*can* be an a. 314*a*
Architectooralooral 123*b*
Architecture: a. of the snow 147*a*
A. of the world 259*a*
love's a. is his own 115*a*
odd styles of a. about 313*b*
Archways and the pavement 12*a*
Arcs: on the earth the broken a. 44*b*
Arcturi: pearled A. 398*a*
Arcturus: canst thou guide A. 497*b*
Arden: now am I in A. 326*a*
Ardour: a. of the crowd 175*b*
furious a. of my zeal 94*b*
radiant a. divine 7*b*
Ardours: with a. manifold 50*a*
Are: by God, we a. 26*b*
for all we have and a. 229*a*
makes us what we a. 144*a*
that wh. we a., we a. 439*a*
very indubitably a. 25*a*
Area: at a. gates 145*a*
Arena swims around him 69*a*
Arethusa: A. arose from her couch 392*b*
saucy A. 191*b*
wanton A.'s azured arms 258*b*
washed by A.'s fount 176*a*
Argifying: what 's the good of a. 237*a*
Argo: a loftier A. 394*a*
Argosies with portly sail 352*b*
Argue: he cd. a. still 168*b*
Argued: we a...at breakfast 80*a*
Argues: it a. insensibility 238*b*
Argufies: what a. sniv'ling 120*b*
Arguing: be calm in a. 186*b*
I am not a. with you 456*b*
in a. too, the parson 168*b*
no a. with Johnson 171*a*
no good a. with the inevitable 251*a*
there..will be much a. 279*a*
Argument: a knock-down a. 139*b*
all a. is against it 209*b*
an a. for a week 377*a*
a.'s hot to the close 48*b*
a...with an east wind 251*a*
blood is their a. 382*b*
cannot have the a. both ways 391*a*
finer than the staple of his a. 304*b*, 345*a*
heard great a. 153*a*
he will maintain his a. 382*a*
highth of this great a. 270*b*
I have found you an a. 211*b*
knowest thou what a. 146*b*
nice knock-down a. 85*a*
stir without great a. 335*b*
swords for lack of a. 382*a*
with a. and intellects too 171*a*
with his a. wrong 169*b*
Arguments: Fools for a. use wagers 65*b*
halters, were their a. 290*b*
mutual destruction of a. 201*a*
no a. shall be wanting 11*b*
tongue tang with a. 371*b*
Argyll (Argyle): A., the State's..
thunder 303*b*
master-fiend A. 12*b*
Ariadne: since A. was a vintager 217*b*
the minuet in A.! 400*a*
Arian: three sips the A. frustrate 52*a*
Ariel: a deal of A. 185*b*
Ariosto of the North [Scott] 69*a*
Arisbe: Alciphron once or A. 421*b*
Arise: a man to a. in me 433*b*
another Athens shall a. 394*a*
a. and come away 262*a*
a. and go like men 414*a*
a., shine; for thy light is come 503*a*

Arise (*cont.*)
I a. and build it again 393*b*
I a. from dreams of thee 394*b*
I will a. and go now 475*a*
I will a. and go to my father 509*b*
my lady sweet, a.! 328*b*
Aristocracy: A. of the Moneybag 80*b*
a. to what is decent 197*a*
Aristocrat: a., democrat, autocrat 433*b*
A. who banks with Coutts 163*b*
A. who cleans the boots 163*b*
Aristotle: A. and his philosophye 88*b*
[A.] Master of them that know 566*b*
A...the rubbish of an Adam 406*a*
young men whom A. thought unfit 369*a*
Arithmetic: no a. but tears 225*a*
what wd. life be without a. 405*b*
Ark: a. of bulrushes 493*b*
Noah, commanding the A. 236*a*
their hand upon the a. 111*b*
to Greece, and into Noah's a. 110*b*
walked straight out of the a. 404*a*
Arm: a.! a.! it is..the cannon's
opening roar 68*b*
a., a., my name! 375*a*
a. of the Lord revealed 502*b*
bared my big right a. 164*b*
flourish of his right a. 125*b*
from whose right a. 403*a*
his rear'd a. crested the world 325*a*
I bit my a. 98*b*
my a. a ladye's lilye hand 531*a*
rebellious a. 'gainst a. 346*a*
sufficient is Thine A. alone 453*a*
th'almighty stretched-out a. 403*a*
the a. and burgonet of men 323*a*
the a. our soldier 328*a*
the auld moon in her a. 530*a*
wh. crowns my a. 132*b*
widow sits upon my a. 262*b*
Armadas: till the great A. come 287*b*
Armadillo: nor yet an a. 230*b*
Armageddon: in the Hebrew tongue
A. 519*b*
Armaments: these bloated a. 128*a*
Armchair: Fortieth spare A. 46*b*
that old a. 105*b*
Armed: a. against all death 40*a*
a. at points exactly 330*a*
a. with more than compleat steel 25*b*
I'm a. with more than..steel 259*b*
thrice is he a. 384*a*
to meet the a. men 497*b*
when a strong man a. 509*a*
Armies: a. we had in Flanders 411*b*
disbanding hired a. 81*b*
ignorant a. clash 5*a*
kings with their a. 486*a*
our a. swore terribly 411*b*
power of a. is a visible thing 471*b*
ran on embattled a. 277*b*
where a. whole have sunk 272*b*
Armoric: British and A. knights 271*b*
Armour: a. of a righteous cause 53*a*
a. on a. shone 137*a*
as snow their a. was 254*a*
dilloing in his a. 230*b*
his a. wherein he trusted 509*a*
in whose coat a. richly 408*a*
no a. against fate 401*a*
others have buckled their a. 306*b*
put on the a. of light 514*a*
put yr. a. on 455*b*
the a. of light 479*a*
to work out Achilles his a. 41*a*
whole a. of God 516*a*
whose a. is his honest thought 473*a*
Armourers: a., accomplishing the
knights 382*b*
now thrive the a. 381*b*
Armoury: a. of the invincible 467*a*
builded for an a. 500*b*
Arms: and a. are strong 200*a*
Arethusa's azured a. 258*b*
A. and Hatchments 440*a*
a. and the man I sing 142*b*
a. I sing and the man 554*b*
a. of my true love 434*a*
a., take yr last embrace! 366*b*
corners of the world in a. 374*b*
excites us to a. 139*b*

Arms (cont.)
feels in his a. the vigour 415b
fifteen a. went round her 261b
green a. round the bosom 398b
he laid down his a. 194b
her a. across her breast 425b
her a. along the deep 76b
her a. behind her golden head 263b
His a. are near 279b
his a. might do what this has 448b
imparadised in one another's a. 274a
I never wd. lay down my a. 297a
made a. ridiculous 277b
Moses stood with a. spread wide 110a
muscles of his brawny a. 249a
my a. about my dearie 60b
of seeming a. to make 140a
proud in a. 266b
seek it in my a. 442a
since these a. of mine 360a
so shd. desert in a. be crown'd 138b
state a. do flourish 16b
straggler into loving a. 240b
stretched forth his little a. 175a
such a gallant feat of a. 253b
take a. against a sea 333a
takes away vigour from our a. 56a
the a. are fair 379a
the nurse of a. 170a
the sure-enwinding a. 458b
throng'd and fiery a. 277a
'to a.!' cried Mortimer 173b
to war and a. I fly 250a
underneath..the everlasting a. 494b
with his a. outstretched 369a
Army: an a. marches on its stomach 575a
a noble a., men and boys 184a
a. of the faithful 263b
a. of unalterable law 263b
a., those poor contemptible men 116a
a. wd. be a base rabble 56a
backbone of the A. 228b
back to the A. again 227a
British a. shd. be a projectile 177a
English a. led by an Irish general 391a
her name an 'A.' 187b
hum of either a. 382b
like an a. defeated 467b
noble a. of martyrs 478a
our a. is..the scum 455a
terrible as an a. 500b
yestermorn our a. lay 12a
Arno: pined by Arno 252b
Aroint thee, witch 346a
Around: a., beneath, above 36b
why is all a. us here 429a
A-roving: we'll go no more a. 74a
Arragon: Alonso of A. was wont to say 13b
Arraignest: thou a. her, her foe 6b
Arrange: we always a. for more? 233b
Arrant: thankless a. 307b
Array: battle's..stern a. 187b
fences and their whole a. 187a
straight against that great a. 253a
to summon his a. 253a
whence all their white a. 453b
Arrayed like one of these 505b
Arrears: long a. to make good 227a
pay life's glad a. 50b
'Arrest you!' said Holmes 135b
Arretium: harvests of A. 253a
Arrival: silent joy at their a. 99a
Arrive: better thing than to a. 413b
his good time, I shall a. 49b
I shall a.! what time 49b
Arrived: a., a new admired guest 78b
evils wh. never a. 147a
Arriving: serenely a., a. 458b
Arrogance of age must submit 58a
Arrow: a. from the Almighty's bow 30b
a. that flieth by day 487b
every a. that flies 247a
I shot an a. into the air 246b
mine a. o'er the house 337a
Sanguelac! the a.! the a.! 427b
the last a. was fitted 92a
Arrows: archer his sharp a. tries 401b
a. in the hand of the giant 489b
a. of lightning 438a
keen as are the a. 398a
mighty and sharp a. 489b

Arrows (cont.)
my a. of desire 31a
whose a. learned poets hold 66a
Arrowy: a. white pines 444a
in a. rain 263b
iron-sleet of a. shower 175a
Art: adulteries of a. 215a
all a..aspires towards..music 572b
all nature is but a. 301a
all the a. I know 304a
almost lost in A. 103a
an A.-loving nation 456b
an a. of reading 130b
Arbuthnot's aid who knows his a. 419b
a. alone enduring 130b
A. and Science cannot exist 30b
a. is a jealous mistress 147a
a. is long, and Time is fleeting 248a
a. is..transmission of feeling 567a
a. made tongue-tied 388a
a. most cherishes 49a
a. must be parochial 281a
a. never expresses anything 460a
a. of being kind 459a
a. o' letter writin' 126b
a. of our necessities 343a
a. of reading is to skip 178b
a. remains the one way 51b
a. that can immortalize 109a
a. to blot 303b
as much of this in a. as you 341a
but in the vein of a. 223b
chrematistic a. 151a
cookery is become an a. 64a
Creative A...demands the service 465b
desiring this man's a. 387a
each a. to please 303a
elder days of a. 246b
enough of science and of a. 471b
excellency of..a. is its intensity 222a
fine a. is that in wh. 314b
first taught A. to..pray 312b
for A. stopped short 165b
glory and good of a. 51b
half a trade and half an a. 203a
harmless a. a crime 316b
hateful a., how to forget 225a
he tried each a. 168b
hide..their want of a. 300a
his peculiar a. 138b
his pen in trust to A. 131a
invented the a. of printing 81b
it needs no a. 294a
it 's clever, but is it A.? 228a
I will use no a. 332a
let it be an a. lawful as eating 373b
love, devoid of a. 160a
made amends for a. 313b
morality of a. consists 460b
more bewitch me, than when A. 189a
more matter with less a. 332a
music is such a. 385b
nature is loth to yield to a. 36a
nature is the a. of God 41b
nature's handmaid a. 139b
Nature that is above all a. 117a
new A. wd. better Nature's best 320b
next to Nature, A. 241a
not without a., but yet to nature 94b
one with human a. 37a
poetry a mere mechanic a. 111b
poetry..in Oxford made an a. 141b
pretend to despise a. 30b
shape than that they work of a. 247a
start on all this A. 186a
success in our a. 147a
tender strokes of a. 298b
there 's no a. to find 346b
tho' a.'s hid causes 215a
unpremeditated a. 398a
venerate a. as a. 184a
what a. can wash her guilt 170a
what shoulder, and what a. 32a
whole a. of war 454b
work at anything but his a. 390b
writing comes from a., not chance 300a
Artery: each petty a. 331a
Artful: the A. Dodger 125a
Arthur: answered A. from the barge 429a
first the noble A. 257a

Arthur (cont.)
he 's in A.'s bosom 381b
little A. wants to play 534b
Article: for a slashing a. 440a
snuffed out by an a. 71b
to deny each a. with oath 363b
what's the next a. 165b
Articles: a. of the Christian faith 481a
a. of thy belief 481a
Artificer: great a. made my mate 414b
lean unwashed a. 374a
th'unwashed a. 111a
Artificial: all things are a. 4b
Artillery: a. of words 419b
flashed the red a. 77a
Jonathan gave his a. 495b
love's great a. 115a
with the self-same a.? 249b
Artist: a good a. in life 413a
be more of an a. 223b
every a. writes his own 146a
grant the a. his subject 204b
no man is born an a. 450a
Portrait of the A. as a Young Man 217a
subject-matter of the a. 460b
the a. never dies 247b
true a. will let his wife starve 390b
what an a. I perish! 551a
Artistic: never was an a. period 456b
Artistries in Circumstance 179a
Arts: a. that..hasten its decay 110b
away with the fine a. 81a
cry both a. and learning down 307a
dear nurse of a. 383b
France, famed in all great a. 8a
grew the a. of war and peace 70b
his virtues were his a. 56b
home of the A. 185a
I but followed the a.! 369b
I have no ready a. 465b
lowest of the a. 281a
mechanical a. and merchandise 16b
Murder..One of the Fine A. 120a
no a.; no letters 191b
that is the bitterness of a. 412b
women's eyes..the a. 345a
Aryan: A. brown 233a
A. smiles 233a
As it was in the beginning 478a
Ascend: degrees by wh. he did a. 338b
Ascendant: lord of the a. 55a
Ascended: bright Pomp a. jubilant 275b
Ascending: angels..a. and descending 493a
Ash: more black than a.-buds 427a
Oak, and A., and Thorn 236a
oak and the a. and the..ivy-tree 525a
Ashamed: a. that women are so simple 367a
friends a...next morning 450b
hope maketh not a. 513a
nor ever once a. 5a
now the Irish are a. 261a
see it, and be a. 487a
something he is a. of 389b
they shall not be a. 489b
thing now-a-days men are a. of 160b
things a man is a. of 390b
to see them not a. 419a
Ashbourne: thy hill, romantic A. 78b
Ashen: by a. roots the violets 431a
skies they were a. 298b
Ashes (asshen): all a. to the taste 68b
a. of great men 183a
a. of his fathers 253a
a. of Napoleon Bonaparte 455a
a. of Wickliff 157b
a. to a. 481b
a. under Uricon 199a
beauty for a. 503b
but turn to a. on the lips! 282a
chew'd bitter a. 276b
ev'n in our a. live 174b
from his a. may be made 430a
from their a. come 216a
handful of grey a. 106b
her a. new-create another heir 386b
hoar-frost like a. 490b
I am a. where once I was fire 67b
man..splendid in a. 42b

Ashes (*cont.*)
monograph on the a. of ..tobacco 135*b*
slept among his a. cold 221*b*
to a. all my lust 260*a*
Worldly Hope..turns A. 152*b*
yet in our a. olde 89*a*
Ashlar: my new-cut a. 232*b*
Ashtaroth: Astarte or A. 421*b*
Asia: A. is not going to be civilized 237*b*
churches wh. are in A. 518*a*
hollow pampered jades of A. 380*a*
in Pontus and A. 512*a*
there is too much A. 237*a*
ye pampered Jades of A. 259*b*
Ask: all that we a. or think 515*b*
all we ought to a. 224*a*
a., and it shall be given 505*b*
a. for me tomorrow 365*b*
a. me no more 436*b*
a. me no more where Jove 79*b*
a. nothing more of me 423*a*
a. yourself whether you are happy 265*b*
dinner to a. a man to 207*a*
for our blindness we cannot a. 480*b*
he is of age; a. him 511*a*
I do not a. O Lord 306*a*
if his son a. bread 505*b*
if so be, you a. me where 188*b*
never a. me whose 199*a*
shd. I a. me, whence these stories? 248*b*
we a. and a. 7*b*
we will not a. her name 77*b*
where a. is have 403*a*
Askance: truth a. and strangely 389*a*
Asked: a. leave of Mrs. Jones 76*a*
I a. no other thing 127*b*
I have a. to be 197*b*
nobody a. you, kind sir 525*b*
some a. how pearls 190*a*
Askelon: in the streets of A. 495*b*
Asketh: every one that a. receiveth 505*b*
Asking: first time of a. 481*a*
to have thy a. 409*a*
Asklent: look'd a. and unco skeigh 60*a*
Asleep: all beauty lies a. 189*a*
a. upon a chair 474*a*
a. within the tomb 33*b*
as moving seems a. 426*a*
fall a., or hearing die 385*b*
fast a. and weary 494*b*
half a. as they stalk 179*a*
he thought me a. 293*b*
men's noses as they lie a. 364*b*
on a..furrow sound a. 221*b*
quiet till it falls a. 425*b*
soon will be a. 20*a*
sucks the nurse a. 325*b*
under the haycock fast a. 535*a*
vash a. in ped 1*a*
we are laid a. in body 472*a*
when men were all a. 37*a*
Asp: hole of the a. 501*b*
scorpion and a. 276*b*
Asparagus: necessary to mention A. 123*a*
Aspasia: live, A., and dare to be unhappy 313*b*
Aspect: anchor his a. and die 323*a*
a. anything but bland 75*a*
lend the eye a terrible a. 382*a*
meet in her a. 74*a*
of such vinegar a. 352*b*
sweet a. of princes 386*a*
with grave a. he rose 272*b*
Aspen (aspes): bind the a. ne'er to quiver 77*b*
light quivering a. made 318*b*
right as an a. leaf 90*a*
Aspens quiver 431*b*
Aspersion upon my parts of speech 400*b*
Asphodel: amaracus and a. 435*a*
Aspics: 'tis of a.' tongues 362*a*
Aspiration, to do nought 313*a*
Aspire: a. where my sunflower 32*a*
by due steps a. 266*b*
on what wings dare he a.? 32*a*
the rest bade a. 48*a*
Aspired: what I a. to be 50*b*
Aspiring to be gods 300*b*
Aspirings: generous a. implanted 239*b*
Aspramont: jousted in A. 271*b*
Ass: a. that bred you 231*a*

Ass (*cont.*)
a. whose back with ingots bows 351*b*
a., without being a fool 416*b*
Caesar a. unpolicied 325*a*
dies of an a.'s kick 49*a*
dull a. will not mend 336*a*
enamoured of an a. 357*a*
get out, you blazing a.! 75*b*
Issachar is a strong a. 493*b*
making him egregiously an a. 361*a*
much like his master's a. 359*b*
remember that I am an a. 359*a*
the a. his master's crib 501*a*
Wild A. stamps o'er his Head 153*a*
write me down an a. 359*a*
Assail: darkness..no more a. mine eyes 119*a*
tale you can't a. 165*a*
Assailant on the perched roosts 278*a*
Assailed: virtue may be a. 267*b*
Assassination: absolutism moderated by a. 523*a*
a. is the extreme of..censorship 391*b*
a...never changed the history 128*b*
if the a. cd. trammel up 347*a*
Assault and hurt the soul 479*b*
Assaults of the devil 478*b*
Assay: th' a. so hard 90*a*
Assemble and meet together 478*a*
Assembled: once again a. here 53*b*
Assemblies, I cannot away with 501*a*
Assembling: not forsaking the a. 517*a*
Assembly: for the a. was confused 512*b*
they enter the public a. 457*b*
Assert: a. eternal Providence 270*b*
he who has nothing to a. 390*b*
Asses: Death hath a.' ears 24*a*
he who, seeking a. 277*a*
kept his father's a. 261*a*
mankind are the a. who pull 72*b*
wild a. quench their thirst 488*a*
Assistance: cause that lacks a. 18*b*
Assistant: no a. for a state 332*a*
Assuaged: half a. for Itylus 420*a*
Assume: a. a virtue, if you have it not 335*a*
we must never a. that 245*a*
Assumes the God 138*b*
Assuming that he's got any 164*a*
Assurance: a. double sure 349*b*
a. given by looks 313*b*
Assured: of what he's most a. 351*b*
Assyrian: *Claribel, A.* 232*b*
curled A. bull 433*b*
the A. came down 74*a*
Assyrians: she doted upon the A. 504*a*
Astarte: A. or Ashtaroth 421*b*
A., Queen of Heav'n 271*b*
Astley, and Sir Marmaduke 252*b*
Astolat: lily maid of A. 428*a*
Astonish: so a. a mother! 334*b*
things that wd. a. you 164*a*
Astonished: a.; and suddenly cast down 485*a*
a. at my own moderation 95*b*
Astonishes: nothing a. men so much 148*a*
Astonishment: yr. a.'s odd 522*b*
Astray: light that led a. 63*a*
like sheep have gone a. 503*a*
that light wh. leads a. 463*a*
Astrolabe: yearning Heart for a. 423*b*
Astronomer: an undevout a. 477*b*
Astronomers: confounding her a. 192*a*
Astronomy: daughter of a.! 477*b*
Asunder: let no man put a. 481*b*
no man shall ever put a. 390*a*
Atahualpa: who strangled A. 254*b*
Atalanta: made of A.'s heels 327*a*
Ate: A. by his side 339*b*
a. the food it ne'er had eat 98*a*
a. when we were not hungry 418*a*
he a. and drank as he was told 192*b*
Athalus..first of the ches 89*b*
Athanasian Creed is the most splendid..lyric 129*b*
Atheism: honest a. for my money 291*a*
inclineth man's mind to a. 15*a*
miracle to convince a. 15*a*
owlet A. 100*b*
Atheist: an a. laugh's 60*a*
never miracle..to convert an a. 13*a*

Atheist (*cont.*)
rebel and A. too 133*b*
Turk and the A. 92*b*
Athelney: when Alfred came to A. 91*b*
Athena's wisest son! 68*a*
Athenæum!.. golly what a paper 413*b*
Athenians: all the A. and strangers 512*b*
Athens: another A. shall arise 394*a*
as ever A. heard 4*b*
A. arose! 394*a*
A. but the rudiments of Paradise 406*a*
A., the eye of Greece 277*a*
chooses A. in his riper age 141*b*
Israel, A., Florence 203*a*
Maid of A. 73*a*
o'er the Aegean main A. arose 396*a*
ye men of A. 512*b*
Athirst: him that is a. come 520*b*
unto him that is a. 519*b*
Athlete: the a. nearly fell 287*a*
Athletic: only a. sport I ever mastered 205*b*
Atkins: thank you, Mister A. 235*b*
Atlanta: from A. to the sea 473*a*
Atlanteän: shoulders immense, A. 6*b*
Atlantic: A. billows roared 107*b*
A. Ocean beat Mrs. Partington 405*a*
drag the A. for whales 446*b*
steep A. stream 266*b*
the A. surge 443*b*
to where the A. raves 8*b*
'twas in the broad A. 525*a*
Atlas: A. of the state 110*b*
Teneriff or A. 274*b*
the demi-Atlas of this earth 323*a*
Atmosphere: a. divinest shrouds thee 397*b*
a. of a new-fal'n year 24*a*
Atom that his might cd. render void 38*b*
Atomies: team of little a. 364*b*
to count a. 327*a*
Atoms: a. or systems into ruin hurled 300*b*
fortuitous concurrence of a. 292*a*
where all these a. are 280*b*
Attached to that great sect 393*b*
Attachment à la Plato 165*b*
Attack: lead such dire a. 253*a*
Attacked it defends itself 566*a*
Attacks: a city invincible to the a. 457*a*
Attain: a. unto the resurrection 516*a*
I cannot a. unto it 490*a*
with..toil all that I can a. 3*b*
Attained: sun has not a. his noon 189*a*
Attainment: so disenchanting as a. 412*b*
Attains the upmost round 338*b*
Attempt: a. and not the deed confounds 347*b*
a. the end 189*b*
lose..by fearing to a. 351*a*
oh, fond a. to give 109*b*
Attend: another to a. him 187*b*
a., all ye who list 252*a*
I do a. here on the general 362*b*
Attendance: to dance a. on 386*b*
Attendant: bark a. sail 301*b*
Attended: is on his way a. 466*b*
when neither is a. 355*b*
Attention: so I withdrew my a. 211*b*
wh. takes off my a. 124*b*
Attentive to his own applause 303*a*
Attic: A. warbler pours her throat 175*b*
A. wit 552*b*
little brain a. stocked 135*b*
mellow glory of the A. stage 6*a*
O A. shape 219*b*
when the A. bird trills 277*a*
Atticus: if A. were he! 303*a*
Attire: in halls, in gay a. is seen 317*a*
let thy a. be comely 251*b*
my love in her a. 525*a*
rich a. creeps rustling 221*b*
she in her poor a. was seen 425*b*
so wild in their a. 346*a*
ye shall walk in silk a. 33*a*
Attitude: fair a.! 219*b*
Attitudes: Anglo-Saxon a. 85*a*
Attorney: believed..was an a. 212*a*
he was..a special a. 169*b*
office boy to an A.'s firm 166*a*
on that journey you find yr. a. 164*a*
rich a.'s elderly ugly daughter 167*a*

Attorneys: ten a. find place 404a
Attracts light-headed, variable men 413a
Attribute: a. to awe and majesty 354b
  a. to God himself 354b
Auburn: sweet A.! 168a
Auctioneer: varnishing A. 80b
Audacity of elected persons 457b
Audible: ill-bred, as a. laughter 90b
Audience: attention in the a. 400a
  a. into the bargain 181a
  fit a. find, though few 275b
Audit: how his a. stands 334b
Aufidus: from A. to Po 253b
Auger: tail made like an a. 216a
Aught: what is a., but as 'tis valued? 369a
Augur: he bored with his a. 531a
Augurers say they know not 324a
Augurs: a. and understood relations 349a
  sad a. mock 388b
Augury: we defy a. 337a
August: dry A. and warm 446a
  sicklemen, of A. weary 367b
  to recommence in A. 71b
Augusta: say, my dear A. 294b
Augustan: next A. Age 449b
Augustus: A. was a chubby lad 192b
  never yours, A. 124b
Auld: A. Robin Gray 20b
  for a. lang syne 59a
  lassie do wi' an a. man 63a
Aunt (Auntie): A., did you feel no pain 172b
  A. Jane observed 172a
  his A. Jobiska 243b
Aunts: a., who are not married 93b
  cousins and his a.! 166a
  songs for me and my a. 373a
Aurora: A.'s harbinger 357a
  rising with A.'s light 419b
Aurora Leighs: no more A. 571a
Auspicious: one a. and one dropping eye 329b
Auster: black A.'s band 254a
  black A. was the fleetest 253b
  upon black A. ride! 254a
Austere: I was an a. man 510a
Austerlitz: death like wine at A. 92b
  sun of A. 564b
Austin: Divines use A.'s words 64a
Author: an a. that's all a. 67b
  as if a man were a. of himself 328b
  a. and giver of all 479b
  a. both of life and light 216b
  a. concealed behind the door 207a
  A.'s own candles 440a
  a. who speaks..own books 128b
  choose an a. as..friend 128a
  example in any heathen a. 291b
  he is the richest a. 207a
  if it's by a good a. 390a
  Jesus the a. and finisher 517a
  leaves of any a. 41b
  man of rank..[as an a.] 210b
  no a. ever spar'd a brother 160b
  prefer being the a. of that poem 462b
  same steps as the a. 222b
  sole a. of his own disgrace! 109a
  store of the first a. 261b
  the a. of peace 478a
  this is indeed to be an a.! 183a
  time which is the a. of authors 13a
  to the a. to get at his meaning 314a
  where is any a. in the world 345a
Authority: a little brief a. 351b
  as one having a. 506a
  a. forgets a dying king 429a
  a...of wh. we do not..dream 314b
  a. over ten cities 510a
  even reproofs from a. 14b
  man under a. 506a
  save base a. from others! 344b
  shadow of a. and credit 56a
  the law to yr. a. 354b
  tongue-tied by a. 388a
  virtue..in a. settled and calm 14b
  what's that? A. 342a
Authors: damn..a...never read 94a
  glory..arises from its a. 212b
  he invades a. 142a
  much exposed to a. 455a
  old a. to read 13b

Authors (cont.)
  vulgar a. in romances 65b
  we a., Ma'am 129a
Autobiography: writes his own a. 146a
Autocrat: democrat, a. 433b
Automa: it is an a. 216a
Autumn: a. evening, and the morn 398b
  A...grew the more by reaping 325a
  A. nodding o'er the..plain 443b
  a. sunsets exquisitely dying 202b
  breath of A.'s being 396a
  congenial A. comes 246b
  happy A.-fields 436a
  I saw old A. 195b
  she forgot the chilly a. 218b
  there is a harmony in a. 394b
  to yellow a. turned 388b
Autumnal: in one A. face 132a
Availeth: struggle naught a. 96b
Avails: what a. the sceptred race! 240b
Avalanche: beware the awful a. 247a
Avarice: a., the spur of industry 201a
  beyond the dreams of a. 280b
  take up with a. 70b
Avatar: in Vishnu-land what A.? 52b
Avaunt: a.! be gone! 362a
  a. ye, base carles 320a
Avenge, O Lord, thy..saints 278b
Avenger: enemy and the a. 482a
  time, the a. 69a
Avenue of cypresses 243a
Avenues: lawns and a. 229b
  seal up the a. of ill 147a
Avernus: descent to A. 556a
Aversion: begin with a little a. 400b
  closely bordering on a. 412b
  manner which is my a. 71a
Aves: thousand a. told 221b
Avilion: island-valley of A. 429b
Avoid: a. what is to come 335a
  man I shd. a. so soon 338a
  what he wd. most a. 267a
Avoided: what can be a. 339a
Avoiding: in a. superstition 15a
Avon: A. into Severn 157b
  swan of A.! 216a
Avow: an a. to God made he 530b
Await: no gifts from Chance 8a
  do not we, Wanderer, a. it too? 8a
Awake: are you a. in the dark? 287a
  a., arise., or be for ever fall'n! 271b
  a.! for Morning 152a
  a., lute and harp 485b
  a., my heart, to be loved 35b
  a., my little ones 152a
  a., my St. John 300b
  a. my soul 224b
  a. O heart..a., a. 35b
  a.! the heavens look bright 281b
  a., the land is scattered 35b
  a. up, my glory 485b
  being now a. I'll queen it 373b
  bestir themselves ere well a. 271b
  Christians a. 67b
  England! a.! a.! a.! 30b
  he will a. no more 392a
  keep her still a. 366b
  lie ten nights a. 358a
  my lute, awake! perform 473b
  O let me be a. 99b
  Onaway! a. 248b
  the rose was a. 434a
  they do not lie a. 458a
  we're very wide a. 164b
  will a. right early 485b
Awaked (awakened): he hath a. from..life 392b
  moon..wd. not be a. 355b
Awaking: come the great a. 20b
Award: general a. of love 218b
Aware of his life's flow 5a
Away: an I coom'd a. 435a
  a.! a.! for I will fly 220a
  a. before me to sweet beds 360b
  a., I'm bound to go 525a
  a., slight man! 340b
  a.! take heed: I will abroad 188a
  a.! the gathering winds 399a
  a.! the moor is dark 399a
  a. went Gilpin 108b

Away (cont.)
  a. went hat and wig 108b
  a. with him! he speaks Latin 384a
  a., you rolling river 525a
  but they wish us a. 158b
  come a., come down 6a
  dear children, let us a. 5b
  Niamh calling A., come a. 475a
  to be a. from thee 249b
  won't get a. from the tune 236b
Awe: a. into the beholders 417b
  a. of such a thing as I 337b
  female in due a. 278a
  pity and mournful a. 6a
  set i' the pathless a. 442b
  stand in a., and sin not 481b
  to keep the strong in a. 385a
  with a. around these..walks 113b
Aweary: a. of the sun 351a
  she said, 'I am a.' 433a
Awful: anything a. makes me laugh 239b
Awkward: a. thing to play with souls 48a
  don't let the a. squad fire 63b
  he is a., and out of place 239a
Awl: all..I live by is with the a. 337b
Awoke: I a...found myself famous 74b
  so I a. and behold 54a
Axe: a. is laid unto the root 504b
  a.'s edge did try 261a
  head off with a golden a. 366a
  let the great a. fall 336a
  owner of the a. 444a
  Suffolk his a. did ply 137a
Axes: yr. sharp-edged a. 457b
Axiom: long been an a. of mine 135a
Axioms: a. in philosophy..not a. 222b
Axis of the earth sticks out 194a
Axle: fly sat upon the a. tree 16b
  glowing a. 266b
Ay (aye): Charybdis of A. and No 288a
  left crying and said 'A.' 364b
Ayr, wham ne'er a town surpasses 62b
Azalea: it was the a.'s breath 294a
Azarias: Ananias, A. 478a
Aziola: hear the A. cry 393a
Azores: Flores in the A. 437a
Azure: a., white, and red 138a
  by every a. breath 394b
  mountain in its a. hue 77a

B

B bit it 532a
Baalim: Peor and B. 270b
Babblative: and scribblative 407a
Babble: for the watch to b. and talk 358b
  learned to b. of the sale-room 80b
Babbled of green fields 381b
Babbler: what will this b. say? 512b
Babe (baby): a little b. thing 256a
  a Mother laid her B. 3b
  as any b. on any mother's knee 423a
  B. all burning bright 407b
  b. leaps up on his mother's arm 466a
  b. that milks me 347a
  becomes a b. in Eternity 29b
  birth-strangled b. 349b
  bring the b. to rest 143b
  burning o'er the b. 423b
  bye, b. bunting 534a
  come little b., come silly soul 35b
  cry, b., cry 533a
  down comes the b. 29a
  'e acts like a b. 236b
  first b. laughed 21b
  his b. on my knee 225b
  laid her B. to rest 270b
  let the mighty B. alone 115a
  like a testy b. 372b
  little b. thing 256a
  mother cried, b. lept 176a
  my young b. were born 530b
  only a b. small 21a
  rock-a-bye-b. 29a
  see my b. at my breast 325b
  she who gives a b. birth 261b
  silly tender B. 407b
  that great b. you see 332b
  the B. look't up 114b
  this B. must eat 407b

Babe (cont.)
wears upon his b.-brow 349b
where did you come from, b. dear? 256a
Babel: see the stir of B. 112a
true B. is a divergence 413a
Babes (babies): as newborn b., desire
the..milk 517b
as were b. all 522a
cruel children, crying b. 414a
mouth of very b. and sucklings 482a
old men, and b. 100a
revealed them unto b. 509a
while thy b. around thee cling 473a
Bab-lock-hithe: Thames at B. 8a
Baboon: bred out into b. 368a
Baby, see Babe
Babylon: B. be thrown down 519b
B. in all its desolation 118a
B. is fallen 519b
B., wasted with misery 490a
by the waters of B. 449b, 490a
die at thirty-five in B. 449b
ere B. was dust 397a
how many miles is it to B.? 534a
I was a King in B. 185a
king of B. stood 504a
London is a modern B. 130a
Mystery, B. the Great 519b
think upon Rahab and B. 487a
Babylonian: B. pulpits 57a
his B. heart 441b
Babylonish: a B. dialect 65a
Babylons: all man's B. strive 441b
Bacchanal: ivy falls with the B.'s
hair 420b
Bacchus: B. by night 420b
B. ever fair 138b
dissonance of B. 275b
not charioted by B. 220a
Plumpy B. with pink eyne! 323b
proves dainty B. gross 345a
'**Baccy** for the Clerk 234a
Bach: 'Ops' by B. interwoven 164b
Bachelor: b. of three score 358a
b.'s fare; bread and cheese 418b
I wd. die a b. 358b
the old b. don't die at all 451a
Bachelors: all reformers are b. 281a
reasons for b. to go out 144b
Back: at my b. I always hear 260a
b. and side go bare 415b
b., Lartius! b., Herminius! 253b
b. o' beyont 319a
b. to the Army again 227a
borne me on his b. 336b
by getting off his b. 567a
duke's revenues on her b. 384a
fog that rubs its b. 144b
hair that lay along her b. 311b
harness on our b. 351a
I cd. never go b. again 283a
if I come b., it is yrs. 287a
I sit on a man's b. 567a
my b. unto an aik 530a
never come b. to me 425b
never turned his b. 52a
not to go b. is..to advance 303b
now that I am b. again 288a
on the bat's b. 368a
plowers plowed upon my b. 490a
rider on so proud a b. 386b
they show'd his b. above 325a
think that he'll come b. 232b
thoughts..shall ne'er look b. 362b
turn yr. b. upon the world 247b
unto the ladder turns his b. 338b
will ye no come b. again? 285b
will you no come b. again? 193b
yr. b. stops aching 229b
Backbiter: face-flatterer and b. 429a
Backbone of the Army 228b
Backgammon: only sport..mastered
was b. 205a
Backing: call you that b. 377b
Backs: beast with two b. 359b
birthrights proudly on their b. 373b
our b. is easy ris 124a
with our b. to the wall 177b
Backward: b., turn b., O Time 4a
I by backward steps 448a
in the dark b. 367a

Backward (cont.)
look b. to their ancestors 57a
revolutions never go b. 321b
so b. to comply 110a
thou wilt fall b. 364b
Backwards: memory..only works b. 84b
narration always going b. 449b
Bacon: b., food of kings! 225b
B., that great and hardy genius 170b
b. was nat fet 89b
Friar B. and Friar Bungay 176a
here's to thee, B.! 76a
Secretary of Nature..B. 450b
still hissing b. 129a
the B. of our rhyming crew 241b
think how B. shined 301b
unless you give him b. 92a
Bacons: on, b., on 377a
Bad: all baronets are b. 166b
as b. as b. can be 211a
b. affright, afflict the blest 173b
b.'s the best of us 23a
better for being a little b. 352b
charm to make b. good 352a
defence of a b. cause 142a
good and b. together 323b
good compensate b. in man 51b
good ye are and b. 428a
heavens, this is too b. 150b
nothing so b. or so good 391a
not really b. at heart 26a
novel cannot be too b. 391a
our best is b. 45b
sad and b. and mad 46a
some were married, wh. was b. 237a
so much b. in the best of us 192a
the b. die late 118a
think myself a very b. Woman 1b
'tis b. enough in man 527b
when b. men combine 56b
when she was b. she was horrid 249a
wiser being good than b. 44b
Badger: Mrs. B. 121a
Badman: Mr. B. died 54a
Badness: all good and no b. 402b
b. of her b. 21b
Baffled: b., get up and begin again 48a
b. oft is ever won 72b
b. to fight better 52a
Englishman..not easily b. 17b
Bag: b. and baggage 327a
B. of Parliamentary Eloquence 81a
Turks..b. and baggage 167b
what did you take out of the b.? 535b
Bagatelle: vive la b. 411a
Baggage: the b. loves me 104b
Bagpiper: laugh like parrots at a b. 352b
Bags: three b. full 534b
Bah: b., b., black sheep 534b
sing 'B. to you' 165b
Bahram that great Hunter 153a
Baiae's bay 396b
Bailey: unfortunate Miss B. 103b
Bailiff: loved the b.'s daughter 531b
Bait: it blows the b. in 532b
with this melancholy b. 352a
yr. b. of falsehood 331b
Baited like eagles 378b
Baiting: dancing and bear-b. 369b
Baked: you have b. me too brown 83b
Baker: b. rhymes for his pursuit 52a
pat-a-cake, b.'s man 532a
Bakers and brewers 242b
Baker Street irregulars 136a
Bakewell: valley between Buxton
and B. 314a
Balance: at the b. let's be mute 59a
b. of power 450a
b. of proud time 176a
dust of the b. 502b
redress the b. of the Old 79a
Balances: art weighed in the b. 504a
Balbec: editions of B. and Palmyra 449b
Bald: b. and unconvincing narrative 165a
b. as the bare mountain tops 9b
expression may..be called b. 9b
go up, thou b. head 496b
Baldheaded: go into it b. 250a
Baldness: b. full of grandeur 9b
Bales: our b. bete 531a
undid his corded b. 8b

Ball: after the b. is over 181b
bowler and the b. 242a
his b. thro' Helen's cheek 172b
little b. of feather 180a
real business of a b. 417a
to pitch the b. into the..hat 113a
urge the flying b. 174b
wind it into a b. 30b
Ballad: b. and story 476b
b. of Sir Patrick Spence 100b
guilty of such a b. 344b
I love a b. in print 373b
I met with a b. 75a
metre b.-mongers 378a
with a woful b. 326b
Ballads: b., songs and snatches 164a
permitted to make all the b. 155a
ye are better than all the b. 246b
Ballast: on the b. down below 437b
our b. is old wine 295b
Balliol: B. made me, B. fed me 26a
best of B. loved and fed me 26a
Balloon: something in a huge b. 468b
Ballot is stronger than the bullet 245a
Balls: elliptical billiard b. 164b
match'd our rackets to these b. 381b
people come to b. to do nothing 417a
Balm: b. in Gilead 503b
b. of hurt minds 348a
b. upon the world 218a
calm is in that b. 290a
can wash the b. from..king 375a
general b. th' hydroptic earth 133b
mine own tears..wash away my b. 375a
'tis not the b., the sceptre 382b
Balms: their precious b. break my
head 490b
Baloo, baloo, my wee wee thing 158a
Balsams: Pharaoh is sold for b. 42b
Baltimore: flecked the streets of B. 308a
Balzac's novels occupy one shelf 45a
Ban: 'B., 'B., Ca-Caliban 367b
scattering b. 43b
Banbury: cock-horse to B.-cross 533b
to B. came I 35a
Band: Alexander's Ragtime B. 28a
all that b. them to resist 278a
around the throne of God a b. 286a
call'st its children a happy b. 184b
happy b. of pilgrims 287a
last of that bright b. 184b
my life within this b. 187b
not a servile b. 468a
the b. begins to play 235b
then the b. played 177b
this ruined b. 382b
we march, they b. 47a
when the wearied B. swoons 202b
Bandersnatch: frumious B.! 83b
Bands: of rosy hue 202a
drew them..with b. of love 504a
loose the b. of wickedness 503a
strong as iron b. 249a
Bane: deserve the precious b. 272a
money, thou b. of bliss 187b
Oh Love! thou b. 173a
what of the world's b. 475a
Bang: b.—went saxpence!!! 535a
not with a b. but a whimper 145a
Banged the youth into dumbness 371b
Bangs me most severely 79b
Banish: b. Peto, b. Bardolph 378a
b. plump Jack 378a
I b. you 328a
Banished: alone, a b. man 529b
Cimber should be b. 339a
for my..crime art b. hence 276b
Banishment: bread of b. 375a
Banjo: git 'er little b. 232a
Bank: a pregnant b. 132b
a shelving b. of turf 398a
as I sat on a sunny b. 522a
B. to Mandalay 232a
broke the B. at Monte Carlo 162b
I know a b. 356b
moonlight sleeps upon this b.! 355a
waly, up the b. 530a
Banker: he saw a B.'s Clerk 85b
Bankrupt of life 138a
Banks: b. of the slow winding Ouse 111a
b. o' Loch Lomond 525b

Banks (*cont.*)
green b. of Shannon — 76b
my b. they are furnished — 399b
never on thy b. shall I behold — 246b
O, Brignal b. — 319a
the b. fade dimmer away — 6a
ye b. and braes — 63b
Banner: b. with the strange device — 247a
blood-red b. streams afar — 184a
Freedom's b. streaming o'er us — 178a
Freedom's lion-b. — 77a
Freedom! yet thy b., torn — 69a
his b. over me was love — 500a
star-spangled b. — 224b
that b. in the sky — 194a
the royal b., and all quality — 362a
Banners: an army with b. — 500b
b. flout the sky — 346a
b. waved without a blast — 317a
confusion on thy b. — 173b
hang out our b. — 350b
Munich! all thy b. wave — 77a
royal b. forward go — 541a
Banquet: trifling foolish b. — 365a
Banquet-hall deserted — 282b
Banqueting upon borrowing — 520b
Banquo: blood-boltered B. — 349b
Banter: how does fortune b. us! — 33b
Baphometic Fire-baptism — 81b
Baptism: B. and the Supper — 481a
B. to Such as are of Riper Years — 481a
Ministration of B. — 481a
Baptist found him far too deep — 305a
Bar: birth's invidious b. — 430b
gold b. of Heaven — 311b
harbour b. be moaning — 226b
I have crost the b. — 426a
may sit in the b. — 240b
no moaning of the b. — 426a
when I went to the B. — 164a
Barabbas: B. was a robber — 511b
we withstand B. now! — 47a
Barbara Allen — 531a
Barbarian, Scythian — 516a
Barbarians: B. quite left out — 9b
young b. all at play — 69a
Barbaric yawp — 458a
Barbarism: methods of b. — 78a
Barbarous: b. dissonance — 275b
b. experiment — 427a
'twas a b. deed — 399a
Barbarously: so b. not a Greek — 202b
Barbarousness: confess mine own b. — 402a
Barber: b.'s man hath been seen with him — 358b
imprudently married the b. — 155b
I must to the b.'s — 357a
Bard: a b. here dwelt — 443a
b. sublime, if b. may e'er be so — 400a
blame not the b. — 281b
hail, B. triumphant! — 106b
hear the voice of the B.! — 31b
if the B. was weatherwise — 100b
old or modern b. — 266b
the lover and the b. — 44b
the sainted sage, the b. divine — 175a
Bardolph: one B. if yr. majesty know — 382a
Bards: b. in fealty to Apollo — 220b
b. of old enjoy'd in you — 31b
B. of Passion — 219a
b. sublime whose..footsteps — 247a
b. who died content — 219b
Gods are we, B., Saints — 5a
last of all the B. — 316b
lords too are b. — 72a
Olympian b. who sung — 147a
Bare: back and side go b. — 415b
b., sheer, penetrating power — 9b
b. them right doughtily — 137a
brought thee forth that b. thee — 501a
sae black and b. — 62b
tho' I go b., take ye no care — 415a
towards the child she b. — 110a
Bared my big right arm — 164b
Barefaced: bore him b. on the bier — 335b
Barefoot: makes shoes go b. himself — 64a
Bare-legged, beggarly son — 75a
Bareness: old December's b. — 388b
Bargain: better b. driven — 401b
dateless b. to engrossing death — 366b
her most filthy b. — 363b

Bargain (*cont.*)
necessity never made a good b. — 157a
two words to that b. — 418b
world-without-end b. — 345b
Bargains: b., and my well-won thrift — 353a
here's the rule for b. — 124a
Barge: answered Arthur from the b. — 429a
from the b. a strange..perfume — 323a
the b. she sat in — 323a
Bark: bleat, the b., bellow — 29b
charmed b. doth swim — 394a
fatal and perfidious b. — 269b
his b. cannot be lost — 346a
my b. is on the sea — 73a
my little b. attendant — 301b
star to every wandering b. — 389a
trusts a frail b. — 173a
watch-dog's honest b. — 70a
yond tall anchoring b. — 343b
Barkis is willin' — 122a
Barks: Nicean b. of yore — 298a
Barley: among the bearded b. — 431b
rode between the b. sheaves — 431b
three measures of b. for a penny — 518b
Barleycorn: bold John B.! — 63a
Barlow: my Hornby and my B. — 442b
Barmaid: bitter b., waning fast — 439a
Barmaids: are B. chaste? — 261b
Barmie: my b. noddle's working — 60b
Barn: b. filleth up finely — 446a
he'll sit in a b. — 533a
these are indeed the b. — 198a
to the stack, or the b. door — 268b
Barnabas..the son of consolation — 512a
Barn-cocks: ere the b. say — 180a
Barns: nor gather into b. — 505b
Baron: 'boots,' said the B. — 19a
'good!' said the B. — 228a
Baronet: no lily-handed B. — 437a
Baronets: all b. are bad — 166b
b. by dozens — 163a
Barons: b. of the mind — 413b
rust of the B.' Wars — 449b
Barouche: their b.-landau — 11a
Barracks: single men in b. — 235b
Barred: a spot that's always b. — 164b
Barrel: handful of meal in a b. — 496a
to taste the b. — 62b
Barrel-load: save them by the b. — 442a
Barrel-organ: human b. — 122b
Barren: b. are those mountains — 37a
b. woman to keep house — 489a
love..b. with best using — 117a
make b. our lives — 421a
none is b. among them — 500a
Barricade: some disputed b. — 321a
Barricades: Christs..die upon the b. — 459b
Barring: for b. of the door — 531b
Barrow and the camp abide — 235a
Barrows of the happier dead — 438b
Barrs: so air our B. — 124a
Bars: beside the glowing b. — 476b
look out thro' the same b. — 242a
nor iron b. a cage — 249b
Sun was flecked with b. — 98b
Tomlinson he gripped the b. — 235b
weary of these worldly b. — 338a
Bartholomew boar-pig — 380a
Bartley, the bootmaker — 416a
Bartrum: called B. father — 238b
Basan: as the hill of B. — 486b
fat bulls of B. close me in — 483a
Base: b., common and popular — 382b
fly from its firm b. — 316b
him that uttered nothing b. — 437a
keep down the b. in man — 428a
see..something of the b. — 470a
were I as b. as is the..plain — 527b
who is here so b. — 339b
Baseness: boldness—child of..b. — 14b
detraction is but b. — 215b
gods detest my b. — 324b
no b. we wd. hide — 430a
Baser: let b. things devise — 408a
Bashful: he wore a b. look — 33a
Bashfulness: England..b. in..religion — 2a
Basil: hung over her sweet B. — 218b
steal my B.-pot — 218b
Basilisk: that B. is sure to kill — 159b
Basin (bason): in a decent b. — 480a
into a granite b. — 96a

Basing: an old person of B. — 243a
Basingstoke: some word..like B. — 166b
Basis: the b. or substratum — 75a
Basket: Eve, with her b. — 192a
Baskets: twelve b. full — 507a
Basking: he loves to lie a-b. — 166b
Basnet: is my b. a widow's curch? — 531a
Basnet point: hammered out my b. — 284b
Bass: Guinness, Allsopp, B.! — 75a
Bassaria! Maenad and the B. — 420b
Bassoon: flute, violin, b. — 434a
heard the loud b. — 98a
Bastard: Buonaparte the b. — 424a
Bastards: gillyvors..nature's b. — 373a
Bat: batsman and the b. — 242a
b. that flits at close of eve — 29a
black b., night, has flown — 434a
on the b.'s back I do fly — 368a
twinkle, little b. — 83a
where the weak-ey'd b. — 103a
wool of b. — 349b
Bates: 'as nails,' added Charlie B. — 125a
Bath: I melt into a b. — 407b
my Lord B., you and I — 450a
'people of B.,' continued Cain — 180b
sore labour's b. — 348a
Bathe: b. those beauteous feet — 155b
play by me, b. in me — 226a
Bathing: Beauty sat b. — 285a
caught the Whigs b. — 128a
made one long b. — 469a
Bathos..the art of sinking in Poetry — 303b
Baths: b. of all the western stars — 439a
in b. to steep him — 215a
two walking b. — 115a
Bathurst, said he to me — 211b
Baton of a marshal of France — 564b
Bats: in the belfry — 297a
do cats eat b.? — 82b
like b. amongst birds — 15b
Batsman: a ghostly b. plays — 442b
I am the b. and the bat — 242a
if the b. thinks he's bowled — 242a
Battalions: God..for the big b. — 566a
not single spies, but in b. — 335b
Batten on this moor — 335a
Batter my heart — 133a
Batteries of alluring sense — 260b
Battering the gates of heaven — 438a
Battle: a b. there was which I saw — 256b
after b. sleep is best — 289a
again to the b., Achaians! — 77b
agreed to have a b. — 84a
amidst the b.'s thunder — 12a
back in the day of b. — 487a
b. and murder — 478b
b., and not a bed of roses — 413a
b. goes sore against us — 412a
b. rages loud and long — 77b
b.'s magnificently stern array! — 68b
beat to b. where he stands — 436b
Ben B. — 194b
beneath it rung the b. shout — 194a
count the life of b. good — 287b
drunk delight of b. — 438b
each b. sees the other's — 382b
every b. of the warrior — 501b
far away the b. went roaring — 254a
feats of broil and b. — 360a
flame that lit the b.'s wreck — 184b
forefront of the hottest b. — 495b
Freedom's b. once begun — 72b
in the lost b. — 318a
it was not in the b. — 111a
make them ready to b. — 489b
my head in the day of b. — 490b
news of b.! — 12a
next..misfortune to losing a b. — 455a
nor the b. to the strong — 499b
nor war, nor b.'s sound — 270a
prepare himself for the b. — 514b
Sarah B. — 239a
see the front o' b. lour — 62b
serious things..in a b. — 84b
smelleth the b. afar off — 497b
souls..that die in the b. — 96a
the b. and the breeze — 77b
the b. to his hands — 436b
the noise of b. roll'd — 429a
the steed to b. driven — 77a
the strife is o'er, the b. done — 304b

Battle (*cont.*)
this b. fares like..the morning's 384*a*
to b. fierce came forth 76*b*
was ever a b. like this 437*b*
when the b.'s lost and won 345*b*
Battle-day is past 145*b*
Battlefield: b. wid all the glory 237*b*
missin'
we are met on a great b. 245*a*
Battle-line: far-flung b. 233*b*
Battlements: owls came..perched on
b. 25*a*
towers and b. it sees 269*a*
under my b. 346*b*
Battle-queen of yore 308*a*
Battles: all his b. won 6*b*
b. are lost in the same spirit 458*a*
b. long ago 471*a*
b., sieges, fortunes 360*a*
God of B., aid! 230*a*
high-engendered b. 342*b*
last of many b. 324*a*
Battle-thunder and flame 437*b*
Bauble: my b. coach 109*b*
pleased with this b. 301*a*
shallow b. boats 368*b*
Baubles: take away these b. 116*a*
Baudelaire: sedulous ape to..B. 412*b*
Bawdy: sing me a b. song 378*b*
talking to Miss — 239*b*
Bawl: as loud as he cd. b. 108*b*
Bawling what it likes 9*b*
Bay: a night-cap..instead of b. 168*a*
beyond the Mexique B. 260*a*
Biscay's sleepless b. 68*a*
China crost the B.! 232*a*
in the B. of Biscay, O! 90*b*
it split the b. 99*b*
somebody bet on de b. 156*a*
Bayed: here wast thou b. 339*b*
Bayona's hold 270*a*
Bayonets: chains are worse than b. 205*b*
the sods with our b. turning 462*a*
throne of b. 203*a*
Bays: approbation gave the..b. 213*b*
no b. to crown it 188*a*
palm, the oak, or b. 260*b*
sprig of b. in fifty years 419*b*
the b. burn deep 423*b*
Bay-tree: flourishing like a green b. 484*a*
Be: amen, so b. it 481*a*
as if it cd. not b. 394*b*
b. amongst you and remain 480*b*
b. of good cheer 507*a*
b. they what they may 466*b*
b. thou me, impetuous one! 396*b*
better not to b. 438*b*
b. warm, but pure 72*a*
b. what they behold 298*b*
b. ye therefore perfect 505*a*
cared not to b. at all 272*a*
choose not to b. 197*a*
evermore about to b. 469*b*
hadn't ought to b.! 182*a*
hame fain wad I b. 116*a*
haven where they wd. b. 488*b*
having been must ever b. 466*b*
it cannot b.,—it is 194*a*
it is that wh. shall b. 499*a*
let Einstein b.! 26*b*
lief not b. as live to b. in awe 337*b*
man..wholly hopes to b. 46*a*
or those that b. not 361*b*
rather see than b. one! 54*b*
such things to b. 430*b*
their day and cease to b. 429*b*
thou shouldst cease to b. 399*b*
'tis something better not to b. 72*b*
to b., or not to b. 333*a*
tree will continue to b. 522*b*
what and where they b. 434*a*
wish to b. no more 73*b*
Beach: left behind on the b. 85*b*
night sank upon the dusky b. 252*a*
only pebble on the b. 34*b*
on the b. undid his corded bales 8*b*
warm sea-scented b. 48*b*
Beachy Head: Birmingham by way
of B. 93*a*
Beacon: Airly B. 225*b*
face, wh., as a b., gives warning 380*b*

Beacon-light is quenched 317*b*
Beacons: b. from the abode 392*b*
b. of hope, ye appear 7*b*
Beadle: a b. on boxin' day 126*b*
b. to a humorous sigh 344*b*
Beadroll: fame's eternal b. 409*a*
Beadrolls: souls set in our b. 402*b*
Beads: b. and prayer-books 301*a*
b., pictures, rosaries 66*a*
my jewels for a set of b. 375*b*
reliques, b., indulgences 273*b*
Beadsman: be yr. b. now 295*b*
the B., after thousand aves 221*b*
Beak: take thy b. from out my heart 298*b*
Beaker: O for a b. full 219*b*
Beale: Miss B. and Miss Buss 525*a*
Be-all and the end-all 347*a*
Beam: at the full midday b. 279*a*
b. that is in thine own eye 505*b*
th'eternal co-eternal b. 273*a*
Beameth: for whom it b. 281*b*
Beamish: my b. boy! 84*a*
Beams: cold lunar b. 6*b*
daystar..tricks his b. 270*a*
his b. full-dazzling! 457*a*
if b. from happy human eyes 415*a*
little candle throws his b.! 355*b*
quenched in the chaste b. 356*b*
some b. of wit 140*b*
the b. of his chambers 488*a*
Bean: home of the b. and the cod 34*a*
nine b.-rows will I have 475*a*
the b.-flowers' boon 46*a*
too French French b.! 165*a*
Beans: full o' b. and benevolence 416*b*
you must not give him b. 92*a*
Bear: all this I b. 6*b*
as a b. doth her young 64*a*
b.-like I must fight 351*a*
b. thee in their hands 487*b*
b. them we can 200*a*
b. with a sore head 259*b*
Brown B.'s flank 233*b*
bush supposed a b.! 357*b*
by the b. oppressed 448*b*
cub-drawn b. wd. couch 342*b*
exit, pursued by a b. 373*a*
gave pain to the b. 255*b*
he-b. in his pride 228*b*
if it had been a b. 418*b*
learns them first to b. 365*a*
my nature cd. not b. it so 341*a*
no dancing b. 109*a*
nothing wd. it b. 532*a*
Oh, Mama, do be a b.! 293*b*
outwatch the B. 268*a*
she-b. thus accosted 228*b*
still less the b.! 157*b*
their habits from the B. 25*b*
they bayed the b. 357*a*
to pardon or to b. it 108*a*
vapour sometime like a b. 324*a*
we must b. all 382*b*
we've fought the B. 201*b*
ye cannot b. them now 511*b*
ye may be able to b. it 514*b*
yet cd. I b. that too 363*a*
Bear-baiting: Puritan hated b. 255*b*
Bear-baitings: wakes, fairs and b. 373*a*
Beard: b. of formal cut 326*b*
b. the lion in his den 318*b*
by the colour of his b. 370*b*
by thy long grey b. 98*a*
his b. was grizzled 330*b*
Jove..send thee a b. 371*b*
King of Spain's B. 136*b*
let our b. be shook 336*a*
nests in my b. 243*a*
Old Man with a b. 243*a*
ran down unto the b. 490*a*
to pluck me by the b. 343*a*
what a b. hast thou got 353*b*
white and bristly b. 387*a*
yellow cheek, a white b. 379*b*
Bearded: b. like the pard 326*b*
scarce-b. Caesar 322*a*
Beards: long b., and pretences 419*a*
when b. wag all 381*a*
yr. b. forbid me 346*a*
you whose browsing b. 264*a*
Beardsley period 24*b*

Beareth: charity..b. all things 514*b*
Bearing: intent of b. them is just 379*a*
Bearings of this observation 122*b*
Bears: b. and lions growl 452*b*
b. not alive..a gentleman 379*a*
but b. it out even to..doom 389*a*
dancing dogs and b. 192*a*
Beast (beastie): a b., but a just b. 522*a*
a b., no more 335*b*
a b., that wants discourse 330*a*
a very gentle b. 357*b*
before he caught the b.! 448*b*
Blatant B. 255*a*, 409*a*
blonde b. 569*a*
Cocoa is a vulgar b. 93*b*
cow'rin', tim'rous b. 62*a*
curre, or elles another b. 90*a*
deem himself a god, or b. 301*a*
demi-natur'd with the brave b. 336*a*
dialect words..marks of the b. 180*b*
drinks like a b. 236*b*
either a b., or a god 559*a*
either a wild b. or a god 15*b*
evil b. hath devoured him 493*a*
good for man nor b. 532*b*
half a b. is the great god Pan 43*b*
life of his b. 498*a*
like a wild b. guards my way 31*b*
man and bird and b. 100*a*
man's life is as cheap as b.'s 342*b*
no beast so fierce but knows..pity 384*a*
not forfeiting the b. 263*b*
number of the b. 519*a*
people call this b. to mind 25*b*
that wild b. man 33*b*
the b. with two backs 359*b*
the b. with many heads 328*a*
the name of the b. 519*a*
the questing b. 257*a*
whan a b. is deed 89*a*
who is like unto the b. 519*a*
who worship the b. 519*b*
you are an ugly b. 26*a*
you hugly b.! 416*b*
Beastly: any b. Erickin' 237*b*
Beasts: all b. of the field drink 488*a*
b. did leap 20*b*
b. of the forest are mine 485*a*
b. that have no understanding 481*b*
birds and b. and flowers 20*a*
compared unto the b. that perish 485*a*
elders and the four b. 519*a*
fled to brutish b. 340*a*
fought with b. at Ephesus 515*a*
four b. full of eyes 518*b*
man..kin to the b. by..body 15*a*
pair of very strange b. 327*b*
prowling b. about Thy way 405*b*
sea-b. ranged all round 5*b*
small and great b. 488*a*
the b. of the forest do move 488*b*
transform ourselves into b. 361*b*
Beat: b. him when he sneezes 82*b*
b. of her unseen feet 393*a*
b. of the off-shore wind 231*b*
b. wild on this world's shore 290*a*
I'd b. him like a dog! 370*b*
I walk my b. 234*a*
knit hands, and b. the ground 267*a*
soft their solitary b. 294*b*
telling with a quiet b. 307*b*
the b. following her daily 312*b*
they b., and a Voice b. 441*b*
when thy heart began to b. 32*a*
Beata mea Domina 284*b*
Beaten: b. men come into their own 262*a*
some have been b. 65*b*
Beatific: enjoy'd in vision b. 272*a*
Beating: b. of my own heart 198*b*
b. of so strong a passion 571*a*
hear the b. of his wings 38*a*
mend his pace with b. 336*a*
Beatitude: ninth b. 304*a*
Beaton: Marie Seaton and Marie B. 530*a*
Beatrice: even I am B. 311*b*
you whisper 'B.' 49*a*
Beau: not like a modern b. 74*b*
Beaux: where none are b. 251*b*
Beaumont: B. and Willoughby 137*a*
bid B. lie 215*b*
nigh to..rare B. lie 22*a*

Beauteous: all that is most b. 467b
b., even where beauties..abound 71b
I love all b. things 36b
Beauties: b., wh. we so justly admire 90b
crowd of common b. 79a
pale, unripened b. of the north 1b
saved by b. not his own 298b
we just b. see 216b
where b. most abound 71b
you meaner b. of the night 473b
'Beautified' is a vile phrase 332a
Beautiful: a deal of scorn looks b. 371b
all heiresses are b. 140b
all that 's b. drifts 475b
all things bright and b. 3a
and one was b. 72a
b. and therefore to be woo'd 384a
b. as a wreck of Paradise 393b
b. exceedingly! 100a
b. must be the mountains 37a
better to be b. than to be good 460b
for she was b. 399b
full b., a faery's child 218b
good as thou art b. 428a
his darkness b. 430b
how b., if sorrow had not made 218a
how b. they are! 100b
how b. they stand! 184b
how b. Thy mercy-seat 149b
how b. upon the mountains 502b
left on her only the b. 195b
love..of a b., unheard-of kind 476a
lovers of the b. 560b
more b. than day 425b
more b. than the earth 470a
more b. than thy first love 474b
most b. things..useless 314b
my b., my b.! 289b
O be less b. 452a
own that thou art b. 393b
palace..name of which was B. 54a
singing: 'Oh, how b.!' 229b
the b., the b. river 315b
the most b. lady 119a
they're too b. to live 124b
they tempted me, my b.! 290a
they were so young; so b. 70b
Tibur is b., too 96a
too b. to last 22a
travel..to find the b. 148a
Beautifully: as it stands—b. 204b
Beauty: a daily b. in his life 363a
ah! yet doth b., like a dial hand 388b
all b. lies asleep 189a
all is b. 47a
Amaranthus all his b. shed 270a
and b. to delight 117b
as much of b. as cd. die 215b
a thing of b. is a joy 217b
b. and length of days 420b
b. being the best 36a
b. born of murmuring 471b
B. cannot keep her..eyes 220a
b. draws us with a single hair 302b
b. faded has no second spring 296b
b. for some provides escape 202b
b. from order springs 225b
b. from the light retir'd 449a
b. is bought by judgment 344b
B. is its own excuse 147a
B. is Nature's brag 267b
B. is Nature's coin 267b
b. is not..an outward show 409a
b. is the lover's gift 105a
b. is the mind diseased 69a
b. is thy earthly dower 465b
b. is truth 219b
b. itself doth of itself persuade 386b
b. like hers is genius 312a
b. lives with kindness 372b
b. making beautiful old rhyme 388b
b. of a thousand stars 258b
b. of Israel is slain 495b
b. of the morning 472b
b. passes like a dream 475b
B. sat bathing 285a
b.'s birth is heavenly 78a
b.'s ensign yet is crimson 366b
B.'s first-born 176b
b. shd. never be half-way 222b

Beauty (cont.)
b. stands in th' admiration 277a
b., strength, youth, are flowers 295b
b. that hath not..strangeness 16a
b., tho' injurious 278a
b. took from those 119b
b. too rich for use 365a
B. unadorned 25b
b. vanishes; b. passes 119a
b., wit, high birth 369a
been a thing of b. 166a
breast that b. cannot tame 18a
but b.'s self she is 525a
coming in solemn b. 261b
court in b. and decay 392a
doth b. beauteous seem 387b
dreamed that life was B. 196b
dress her b. at yr. eyes 117b
dust swept from their b. 43b
England, Home, and B. 34b, 123a
eternal b. wandering 476b
Euclid alone has looked on B. 266a
fatal gift of b. 69a
for b.'s heightening 8b
fostered alike by b. 469a
friend of B. in distress 72b
fruits of life and b. 30a
gather b. from their sense 36a
give unto them b. for ashes 503b
Gods, that mortal b. chase 260b
Helen, thy b. is to me 298a
her b. and her chivalry 68a
her b. made the bright world dim 399b
his b. to consume away 484a
homely b. of the good 467b
idea I have of b. 223a
if you get simple b. 46b
ills from b. spring 214a
in b. exalted 470a
in b.'s worthiness 259b
in happier b. 467b
in the b. of the lilies 200b
in thy b.'s field 387a
in yr. b.'s orient deep 79b
Isle of B. 22a
it is b. truly blent 370a
its horror and its b. 395b
I wish her b. 115b
joys like b., but skin-deep 18a
King have pleasure in thy b. 484b
light from her own b. 399b
lines where b. lingers 72b
lip or eye, we b. call 300a
look not thou on b.'s charming 319a
love built on b. 132a
loved yr. b. with love false 476b
loveliest things of b. 261b
make her b. over again 475a
more beautiful than B.'s 218a
music even in b. 42a
my eyes for b. pine 37a
new in b. and virtue 402b
no b. she doth miss 525a
no b. that we shd. desire him 503a
no..b. without a fortune 150a
none of B.'s daughters 73a
nor Summer b. hath such grace 132a
of Love, and of B. be shown 424b
of that heavenly b. 409a
parallels in b.'s brow 388a
perception of its b. 223a
perhaps some b. lies 269a
phantom., B., in a mist 474a
power of b. I remember 140a
quietness and b. 472a
rarest gift to B. 264a
relationship with b. and truth 222a
shall b. hold a plea 388a
she dwells with B. 219b
she walks in b. 74a
snatched away in b.'s bloom 73b
soul of her b. 398a
Spirit of B., that dost consecrate 394b
such seems yr. b. still 388b
teaches such b. as a woman's eye 345a
terrible b. is born 476b
the b. of the world! 332b
the best part of b. 16a
the principle of b. in all 223b
thereby b.'s rose 387a
the Rose is B. 130b

Beauty (cont.)
they grew in b. 184b
thick, bereft of b. 367a
this is that Lady B. 312b
thy b. shall no more be found 260a
thy b.'s silent music 78a
till B., Truth and Love 36b
'tis b. calls and glory 244a
'tisn't b., so to speak 237b
troubled by this b. 292b
veiling an Indian b. 354a
wages b. gives 476a
was b.'s summer dead 388b
what is b. saith my sufferings 259b
what once had b. 299b
what the imagination seizes as b. 222a
when b. fires the blood 140a
when thy b. appears 292b
where b. has no ebb 475b
whose b. is past change 197b
will not so deform B. 147a
winds of March with b. 373a
within one B. meet 260b
write the b. of yr. eyes 387a
your b. with my nails 384a
yr. infant b. cd. beget 320b
youth, b., graceful action 138b
Beaver: cock up yr. b. 193b
with his b. on 378b
Because: we cannot do it, Sir, b.— 85a
Become: altogether b. abominable 482a
doth so well b. her 525a
what's b. of Waring 52b
what shall, alas! b. of me 251b
Becomes: hardly b. any of us 192a
nothing so b. a man 382a
whom everything b. 322b
Becometh: it b. us to fulfil 504b
Bed: a b., a b. 529a
a b. at night 168b
a b. for you and me 529a
and so to b. 296a
as little as my b. 224b
as to a lover's b. 324b
b. amid my tender breast 176a
B. be blest that I lie on 2b
b. for this huge birth 114b
b. in the bush 414a
b. majestical 382b
b. of Ware 371b
blue b. to the brown 171a
book..took him out of b. 208a
candle to light you to b. 533b
come, let's to b. 534b
dark wintry b. 396a
down as upon a b. 261a
dull, stale, tired b. 341b
each within our narrow b. 86a
earth in an earthy b. 434a
earth Thy b. 405b
England now a-b. 383a
for the beloved's b. 399b
fortunes..drunk to b. 322b
four angels to my b. 2b
four of us about that b. 284b
from his brimstone b. 100b
from my naked b. 238b
from their lowly b. 174a
go to b. by day 413b
gravity out of his b. 377b
grief..lies in his b. 374a
Guilt..lighted me to b. 196a
hath made his pendent b. 347a
have at his b.'s heed 88b
have to go to b. and see 413b
his brimstone b. 406b
his wholesome b. 338b
I drunk him to his b. 323b
I haste me to my b. 387a
I in my b. again! 527b
in going to my naked b. 143b
in thy cold b. 225a
like a pillow on a b. 132b
Lord Tomnoddy went home to b.! 19b
manger for His b. 3b
me he mostly sent to b. 241b
mother, make my b. 531b
mother, make my b. soon 529b
must we to b. indeed? 414a
my b. it is fu' lowly 529a
nicer to lie in b. 242b

Bed (cont.)
o'erhang his wavy b. 103a
on my grave, as now my b. 42a
passage up to b. 414a
remembered thee in my b. 485b
roll upon yr. b. 284a
smooth pillows sweetest b. 401b
so he on his b. 453a
sold her b. and lay upon straw 533b
spare b. for my friends 296b
take up thy b. 510b
the fair Infant's b. 115a
thrice-driven b. of down 360b
to b. go sober 23a
to go to b. after midnight 370a
to more than one a b. 133b
vash asleep in p. 1a
warm weather when one's in b. 418a
welcome to yr. gory b. 62b
whipped them . . put them to b. 533b
whole world out of b. 261b
work, and back to b. again 261b
Bedeck'd: so b., ornate 277b
Bedfellows: misery . . with strange b. 383a
Bedford and Exeter 383a
Bedonebyasyoudid: Mrs. B. 226b
Beds: beat them to their b. 324a
b. for all who come 311a
b. for me and all 311a
came unto my b. 372a
flock were in their b. 474a
make thee b. of roses 259a
Bedside: good b. manner 535b
Bed-staff: twinkling of a b. 322a
Bedstead: make anyone go to sleep,
that b. 127a
Bed-time: I wd. it were b. 378b
Bee: bag of one b. 52a
b. goes singing 50a
b. has quit the clover 231b
b.-loud glade 475a
b. with honied thigh 268b
bored by a b. 243a
bosom, like a b. 240a
brute of a b.! 243a
hive for the honey-b. 475a
I am the b. 152a
in my bosom like a b. 176a
keep the b. from ranging 77b
like a noontide b. 399a
little busy b. 453a
some b. had stung it 416a
the b.'s kiss, now! 46b
where the b. sucks 368a
Beech (beechen): appointment with
a b.-tree 444a
spare the b. tree 76b
under yonder b.-tree 263b
Beef: b. and iron and steel 382a
b., pork, and mutton 227b
but first with b. 440b
great eater of b. 369b
piece of b. and mustard 366b
roast b. of England 151a
Beehive: a b.'s hum shall soothe 310a
Bee-mouth: while the b. sips 219b
Been: as if he had not b. 433a
as if it had not b. 392a, 394b
b. and gone and done it 163a
think what 'e's b. 234a
what has b. has b. 142b
wh. having b. must ever be 466b
Beer: all b. and skittles 75b, 201a, 263a
and drink some b. 211b
a pot of b. 125b, 534b
B. and Britannia 404b
b. at Haslemere 27a
b. teetotaller 390a
best B. I know 27a
bottled b. and chops 165b
chronicle small b. 361a
did you ever taste b.? 125a
felony to drink small b. 384a
its source, 'tis b. 264a
muddy ecstasies of b. 113b
O B.! O Hodgson 75a
parson, much bemused in b. 303a
poor creature, small b. 380a
talk o' gin and b. 229b
they who drink b. will think b. 203b
to desire small b. 380a

Bees: b. are stirring 102a
b. in the ivy bloom 397a
furnished with b. 399b
innumerable b. 437a
make a hive for b. 295b
rob the Hybla b. 341a
so work the honey-b. 381b
so you b. make yr. honey 558b
swarm of b. in May 522a
swarm of golden b. 393a
Beer-sheba: Dan even to B. 495a
Beetle: nor let the b. 219b
save where the b. wheels 174a
the poor b. 352a
where the b. winds 103a
Beetles: b. black, approach not
here 356b
scarce so gross as b. 343b
Beeves at pasture! 264a
Before: air is cut away b. 99b
all be as b., Love 52b
b., a joy proposed 389a
b. me at this instant 342a
b. you were, or any hearts 476a
but gone b. 290a
events cast their shadows b. 77a
had he his hurts b.? 351a
he had been there b. 237b
I have been here b. 313a
I have said it b. 26a
look b. and after 398b
looking b. and after 335b
nothin' much b. 229b
she has walked b. 168a
that which was b., come after 65b
things wh. are b. 516a
those b. cried 'Back!' 253a
what thou wast b. 12a
who . . is preferred b. me 510b
Beforehand: good as it seems b. 144b
Befriend: be near me now and b. 423b
Beg: taught me first to b. 355a
they b., I give 143a
to b. during life 379a
to b. I am ashamed 509b
to b. . . . 'tis the very worst world 38a
Began: how it all b., my dears 231a
I am that wh. b. 422a
left off before you b. 104b
Beggar: a b., he prepares to plunge 49b
bare-footed came the b. maid 425b
b. by banqueting 520b
b. may drink his fill 27a
b. shd. be answered 355a
b. that I am 332b
beste in his hous 88b
big black boundin' b. 229a
Cophetua loved the b.-maid 365a
desert a b. born 388a
'eard a b. squealin' 235a
patience, the b.'s virtue 262b
relieve a lame b. 367b
the b.'s shop is shut 366a
whiles I am a b. 374a
Beggared all description 323a
Beggarly last doit 112b
Beggars: b., fleas and crimes 226a
b. in the street mimicked 255a
b. invention 111a
our basest b. 342b
poor b. in red 236b
when b. die 339a
Beggary: b. in the love 322a
no vice, but b. 374a
they knew b. 255a
Begin: b. at the beginning 83b
b. . . to take the lower room 509b
b. with the beginning 70a
follow . . that other men b. 338b
get up and b. again 48a
I'll b. it—ding, dong 354a
let us b. and carry up this corpse 47a
slow to b. 468a
where I did b., there shall I end 341b
where I shall first b. 334b
where shall I b.? 83b
Beginning: as it was in the b. 478a
begin at the b. 83b
begin with the b. 70a
b. of an amour 25a
b. of fairies 21b

Beginning (cont.)
better . . than the b. thereof 499b
ill b. of the night 341a
in the b. God created 492a
in the b. was the Word 510b
long choosing, and b. late 276a
Omega, the b. and the ending 518a
the b. of wisdom 489a
told you from the b. 502b
true b. of our end 357b
Beginnings: mighty things from
small b. 139b
our ends by our b. know 119b
resist b. 551b
seeds and weak b. 380b
start again at yr. b. 230a
Begins: nothing b. and nothing ends 441a
Begirt: Thou hast b. us round 187a
Begone, dull care 522a
Begot: b. in the ventricle of memory 344b
fool's side that b. him 45b
how b., how nourished? 354a
Begotten by despair 260a
Beguile: b. many and be beguiled 362b
b. the thing I am 360b
Beguiled: be b. by one 362b
serpent b. me 492b
Beguiling: smiling of Fortune b. 97a
Begun: end, where I b. 134a
our works b., continued 480b
that sin, where I b. 132a
things bad I b. 349a
Behave: b. mannerly at table 413b
how well I did b. 199a
Behaviour: her evil b. 196a
his b. everywhere 353a
put himself upon his good b. 71a
we'll teach better b. 193b
with so much sweet b. 105a
Behead: more capital than to b. a king 66a
Beheld what never was to be 71a
Behemoth: behold now B. 497b
Behind: air . . closes from b. 99b
and has left me b. 67b
'arf o' that b. 229b
get thee b. me, Satan 507a
girl I left b. me 526b
leave her far away b. 217b
led his regiment from b. 163a
ling'ring look b. 174b
little things b. him! 227a
something b. the throne 297a
there was no more b. 372b
things wh. are b. 516a
those b. cried 'Forward!' 253a
thou hast left b. powers 472a
veil upon veil b. 5a
Behold: b. an Israelite indeed 510b
b., a silly tender babe 407b
b., he cometh with clouds 518a
b. her, single in the field 471a
b., how good and joyful 490a
b., I come as a thief 519b
b., I come quickly 520b
b., I make all things new 519b
b., I show you a mystery 515a
b., I stand at the door 518b
b., I was shapen in wickedness 485a
b. now Behemoth 497b
b. the man 511b, 558a
b. this dreamer cometh 493a
b., thou art fair 500a
b. us with thy blessing 53b
for, b., from henceforth 508b
may I b. in them what I was once 472a
power to say, 'B.!' 356a
what we b. is censured 259a
woman! when I b. thee 222a
Beholden: much b. to Machiavel 13a
Beholdeth: he b. himself and goeth 517b
Beholds: Universe b. itself 392b
Being: b. breathing thoughtful 470b
a b. darkly wise 301a
a B., erect upon two legs 126b
a b. of our kind 120a
a momentary taste of B. 153b
a sensitive b. 470a
Beauty is its own excuse for b. 147a
b. what she is 474b
for the ends of B. 44a
in dignity of b. 464b

Being (cont.)

in one another's b. mingle	395b
I offered B. for it	127b
its b. puts blissful back	197b
lovely b., scarcely formed	72a
mighty B. is awake	467a
our b.'s end and aim	301b
our b.'s heart	469b
pleasing anxious b.	174b
receives reproach of b.	389a
selfish b. all my life	11b
sounding labour-house vast of b.	465b
the B. that is in the clouds	272b
this intellectual b.	272b
Thou art B. and Breath	38b
to every Form of b.	464b
unknown modes of b.	469a
we move, and have our b.	512b
whose b. I do fear	348b

Beings: luminously self-evident b. 288a

Beit: fought with B.	27a
Belang: aught that wad b. thee	59b
Beldam Nature	278b
Belfries: in the b. tingle	200a
Belfry: bats in the b.	297a
white owl in the b.	438a
Belgium: B.'s capital had gathered	68a
until B. receives in full measure	10b
Belgrave Square: beat in B.	163b
Belial: B. in act more graceful	272a
sons of B., flown with insolence	271b
sons of B. had a glorious time	138b
thou son of B.	495b
thus B. with words clothed	272b

Belief: all b. is for it 209b

b. a believing in nothing	250b
b. consists in accepting	148b
modes of man's b.	45b
reasoning and b.	80a
within the prospect of b.	346a

Beliefs: home of . . forsaken b. 9a

Believe: b. all the articles 481a

b. also in me	511a
b. it not, O Man	96b
b. me, if all those . . charms	281b
b. of my own stories	203b
b. the aged friend	46a
b. they've none at all	66a
brain that won't b.	29a
can't b. impossible things	84b
corrected 'I b.'	238a
do ye now b.	511b
do you b. in fairies?	21b
firmly I b.	288b
I at least b. it	12b
I b. verily to see	483b
I can't b. that	84b
I do b. her, tho' . . she lies	389a
I don't b. in fairies	21b
I du b. in Freedom's cause	250a
I'll not b. it	362a
I will not b.	511b
ne'er b., do what you please	29b
only b., and thou shalt see	279b
powerfully and potently b.	332a
read not . . to b.	16a
that I b., and take it	145b
they b., because they so were bred	140b
this I stedfastly b.	481a
you'll b. in me, I'll b. in you	85a

Believed: against hope b. in hope 513a

be b. by any reasonable person	201b
b.—faith, I'm puzzled	250b
b. . . . six impossible things	84b
fiends no more b.	351a
nearer than when we b.	514a
seen, and yet have b.	511b
understood and not . . b.	31a
who hath b. our report?	502b

Believer: in a b.'s ear! 289a

left upon earth a b.	421b
most blest b. he!	447b

Believes: as one at first b. 48a

each b. his own	300a
he more readily b.	16b

Believeth: charity . . b. all things 514b

neither b. he that it is the sound	497b
whosoever b. on him	510b

Believing: b. where we cannot prove 429b

not faithless, but b.	511b
pleasure of b. what we see	395b

Believing (cont.)

she deceiving, I b.	321a
Bell: as the last b. struck	440a
b., book and candle	374a
b. to toll me back	220a
church-going b.	113a
crier rung the b.	24a
enough . . rung the b. to him	58a
falling to the prompter's b.	440b
hear them, ding-dong, b.	367a
in a cowslip's b. I lie	368a
I shall b. the cat	4a
kirk-hammer struck the b.	60a
Little Mary B.	31a
matin b., the Baron saith	100a
merry as a marriage b.	68a
sexton tolled the b.	195a
silence that dreadful b.!	361a
some coast a passing b.	24a
sounds ever after as a sullen b.	379b
surly sullen b.	388a
the B. at Edmonton	108a
the b. invites me	347b
tolled the one b. only	199a
twilight and evening b.	426a
voiced like a great b.	154b

Belle: vain to be a b. 251b

Bellerus: fable of B.	270a
Bellies: for their b.' sake	269b
Bellman: B., perplexed	86a
fatal b.	347b
Bellona's bridegroom	346a
Bellow: bleat, the bark, b.	29b
Bell-rope: she swam to the b.	24b

Bells: a mist with b. 50a

at last the b. ringeth	182b
awesome b. they were	203b
b. at Old Bailey	533b
b. at Shoreditch	533b
b. have knoll'd to church	326b
b. in yr. parlours	360b
b. of London town	533b
b. of S. Clement's	533b
b. of Shandon	306b
b. on her toes	533b
b. they sound on Bredon	199a
b. they sound so clear	199a
b. were ringing the Old Year	168a
bonny Christchurch B.	3a
dear b.! how sweet	195b
from the b., b., b.	298a
full, sad b.	206a
how sweet . . . village b.	195b
hung among the b.	297a
instruments to melancholy b.	366a
lan-lone of evening b.	427a
oh, noisy b., be dumb	199a
ring O b.!	457b
ring, happy b.	431a
ring out wild b.	431a
ring the b. now	450a
ring the b. of Heaven	192a
shells, and silver b.	533a
sweet b. jangled	333b
the b. I hear	457b
those evening b.!	282a

Belly: an increasing b. 379b

b. God send thee	415b
b. is as bright ivory	500b
b. is like an heap	500b
b. of the fish	504b
b. with the husks	509b
best fits a little b.	188b
does not mind his b.	207b
fair round b.	326b
God is their b.	516a
Jonadge's b.	124a
my b. was bitter	519a
something of a round b.	379b

Beloved: a man greatly b. 504a

b. as thou art!	394b
b. come into his garden	500b
b. from pole to pole!	99a
b., it is morn	191a
b. of their dams	105b
b. till life can charm no more	103a
best wine for my b.	500b
creature that is b.	370b
for the b.'s bed	399b
he giveth His b. sleep	44a, 489b
how far to be b.	322a

Beloved (cont.)

if ye find my b.	500b
leaning upon her b.	501a
Luke, the b. physician	516b
make haste, my b.	501a
more beloving than b.	322b
my b. had withdrawn	500b
my b. is mine, and I am his	500a
my b. is white and ruddy	500b
my b. put in his hand	500b
names of things b.	36a
one b. heard in youth	397a
only b., and loving me	107a
power . . of being b.!	51b
prove b. over all	235a
Suspenders, Best B.	237a
this is my b.	500b
what is thy b. more	500b
yr. well-b.'s hair	475a

Beloving: more b. than beloved 322b

Below: all of heaven we have b. 1b

down and away b.	5b
little Heaven b.	453a

Belt: my leathern b. likewise 108b

Belted you an' flayed you	230a
Belvoir's lordly terraces	252b
Ben Adhem's name	202a
Benbow, Collingwood	287b
Bench: a drowsy B. protect	114a
b. of heedless bishops	400a
Benches: rub not clean their b.	215b
Bend: around the child b. all	240b
b. lower, O King	476a
b. on me, then, thy tender eyes	252a
Bendemeer's stream	282a
Bends: b. not as I tread	268a
b. with the remover to remove	389a
blue sky b. over all	100a
made their b. adornings	323a
Bene: bootless b.	465a
Beneath: around, b., above	36b
some springing from b.	13a
Benedick: B., love on	358b
B. the married man	358a
Benediction: perpetual b.	466b
sprinkles b. thro' the dawn	442b
Benedictions: over-bowed by many b.	48a
Benefactor: Adam . . first great b.	447a
Benefice: dreams he of another b.	364b
Benefices: yr. b. twinkled from afar	140b
Beneficent: zealous, b., firm	7b
Benefit: O b. of ill!	389a
without the b. o' the Clergy	104b
Benefits: as b. forgot	326b
forget not all his b.	488a
Benevolence: b. of the passive order	265a
full o' beans and b.!	416b
lazy glow of b.	45b
whether the b. of mankind	17b
Ben Gunn	413a
Benight our happiest day	132b
Benighted . . under the mid-day sun	267a
Benison: b. of hot water	39a
for a b. to fall on our meat	190b
Benjamin: B.'s mess	493b
little B. their ruler	486b
Benjamin Franklin: plain to B.	194a
Ben Jonson: O rare B.	217a
Bennet: Mrs. B. was stirring the fire	11b
Bent: affection cannot hold the b.	370b
b. him o'er the dead	72b
still b. to make some port	8b
they are not our b.	166b
to the top of my b.	334b
Benumbed: we feel b., and wish	73b
Benumbs: pen . . b. all his faculties	206a
Bequeath them no tumbled house!	263a
Berenice's ever-burning hair	87a
Berkeley (Berkley): Bishop B. destroyed this world	405a
coxcombs vanquish B.	40b
when Bishop B. said . . no matter	71b
Berkeley Square: not in B.	235a
ye share with B.	235b
Bermoothes: still-vext B.	367a
Bermudas: the remote B.	260a
Berries: b. and plums to eat	192a
b. harsh and crude	269a
two lovely b.	357a
Berry: a redder b. on the thorn	191a
brown as a b.	160b

Berry (cont.)
from many a b. 275a
God cd. have made a better b. 67a
sweeter than the b. 159a
Berth: his death..happened in his b. 195a
Bertram: B.'s right and B.'s might 319b
Beryl: eighth, b. 520a
rings set with the b. 500b
Beseems: none b. him half so well 12a
Beset: who so b. him round 54b
Beside: thou art b. thyself 513a
Besmeared: Moloch..b. with blood 271b
Besoin de voyager 411a
Besom: b. of destruction 502a
Bess, the landlord's daughter 290a
Best: afflict the b. 173b
all is b., tho' we oft doubt 278a
all my b. is dressing old words 388a
any other person's b. 183a
at the last, b. 322b
bad in the b. of us 192a
bad 's the b. of us 23a
beauty being the b. 36a
b. administered is b. 301b
b. and brightest, come away! 394b
b. and the worst of this is 422b
b. ends by the b. means 202b
b. found in the close 278a
b. in this kind are but shadows 357b
b. is like the worst 232a
b. is yet to be 50b
b. men are moulded 352b
b. of life is but intoxication 70b
b. of men..a sufferer 118b
b. of what we do and are 463a
b. that has been known and said 10a
b. things carried to excess 95a
b. thou canst bestow 114b
b., to forget! 51b
b. wh. lieth nearest 247a
change is from the b. 343b
he made the b. of this 62a
how much the b.! 156b
information..from the b. of men 204b
it shd. be our very b. 45b
it was the b. butter 83a
little do or can the b. of us 52b
my handkercher..the b. I had 374a
next b.:—there is nobody 214a
our b. is as far 92b
our b. is bad 45b
please her the b. you may 525b
propagate the b. 9a
said it that knew it b. 14b
sat we two, one another's b. 132b
seen the b. of our time 341b
the b. and the last! 50b
the b. ye breed 236b
'tis at the very b. 532b
what began b. can't end worst 44b
Best-beloved: the Suspenders, B. 237a
Bestial: what remains is b. 361b
Bestir: rouse and b. themselves 271b
Bestow it all of yr. worship 359a
Bestowed: divinely b upon man 113a
Bet: b. you wh. one wd. fly first 446b
Farmers once b. a pound 119b
somebody b. on de bay 156a
Bete: our bales b. 531a
Betelgueux: Aldebaran and B. shone 180b
Bethel: O God of B. 131b
Bethlehem: B. Ephratah 504b
B., thou dost all excel 86b
little town of B. 40a
O come ye to B. 290a, 558a
sailed in to B.! 524a
Betimes: is to be up b. 370a
Betray: all things b. thee 441b
Nature never did b. 472a
she'll b. more men 363b
those who b. their friends 160a
too late that men b. 170a
Betrayed: b. my credulous innocence 267b
but by ourselves b. 104b
night that he was b. 480b
we are b. by what is false 264a
wonder at ourselves like men b. 463a
Betrayer and betrayed 319a
Betrothed, betrayer 319a
Better: become much more the b. 352b
b. by evil still made b. 389a

Better (cont.)
b., had I stol'n the whole! 414b
b. man than I am 230a
b. not to be 438b
b. one than you 39a
be with Christ; wh. is far b. 516a
blame of those ye b. 236b
boundless b. 438b
by God! she'd b. 82a
can't do me b. 234a
did I say 'b.' 340b
didn't say there was nothing b. 85a
far, far b. thing 127b
feed my brain with b. things 91b
for b. for worse 481b
former days were b. than these 499a
friend of my b. days! 178a
good reasons..give place to b. 341a
he is no b. 12a
I am getting b. and b. 561a
if way to the B. there be 179b
I will b. the instruction 354a
little b. than one of the wicked 376b
make men b. be 216b
my riding is b. 48a
mystical b. things 171b
nae b. than he shd. be 60a
no b. than you shd. be 23a
no b. thing under the sun 499b
no man cd. tell the b. 284a
not left a b. nor wiser behind 169b
one day..is b. than a thousand 487a
or b. than the rest 321a
rises from prayer a b. man 264b
see and approve b. things 551b
striving to b., oft we mar 342a
the b. the uncourser 52b
the b., the worse 13b
thy love was far more b. 261a
'tis something b. not to be 72b
to take the b. things and leave 25b
we have seen b. days 368a
what is b. than a good womman? 89a
what is b. than wisdom? 89a
Bettered: better b. expectation 358a
Betters: still b. what is done 373b
Betty (Betsey): B. and I are out 80a
dear B., be kind 461a
dear B., come, give me 461a
Between: angels, short, and far b. 29a
angel-visits, few and far b. 77b
as we touch come b. us 421b
fell thir twa b. 529a
the 'ouses in b. 22a
Beuk: usefu' plan or b. 60b
Beware: b., my lord, of jealousy 361b
b. of desperate steps 199b
b. of false prophets 505b
b. of those who are homeless 407a
b. the awful avalanche 247a
b. the Ides of March 337b
b. the Jabberwock 83b
b. the pine-tree's..branch 247a
cry, B.! B.! 101b
I bid you b. 233b
Beweep my outcast state 387a
Bewildered, and alone 136b
Bewitch: do more b. me 189a
prosperity doth b. men 454b
Bewitched: b. with the rogue's company 377a
who hath b. you? 515b
Bewrayeth: thy speech b. thee 508a
Beyond: back o' b. 319a
know b. a peradventure 462a
Bezonian: under wh. king, B.? 381a
Bias: commodity, the b. of the world 374a
Bibble-babble: leave thy vain b. 372a
Bible: but litel on the B. 88b
Holy B., book divine 63b
knows....her B. true 113a
no man..knows even his B. 10a
read the B. day and night 29b
that book is the B. 10a
the B. clash and contradict itself 135a
the B. only is the religion 94a
the English B...a Book 255b
Bibles: b., billets-doux 302b
B. laid open 187a
Bible-Society machine..heathen 80a
Biblia-a-biblia 239a

Bicycle made for two! 116b
Bid: b. for cloistered cell 223b
b. her come forth 449a
b. me discourse 386b
b. me to live 190a
buy then! b. then! 198a
do as you're b. 143b
or b. me love 190a
Biddest: Thou b. me come to Thee 146a
Bidding: to her b. she cd. bow 317a
Bide: you and I must b. alone 531a
Bideford: men of B. 437b
Bield: thy b. shd. be my bosom 62b
Bier: barefac'd on the b. 335b
better b. ye cannot fashion 12a
sheaves, borne on the b. 387a
trickle to his rival's b. 317b
yr. home, and yr. b. 395a
Big: clouds..are b. with mercy 110a
twice as b. as yours 109a
you are doubtless very b. 146b
Bigger: homely b. 381a
Bigger: no b. than his head 343b
no b. than the Moon 98b
Bigging: I mind the b. o't 319a
bigoted: more b., more gloomy 288a
bigots of the iron time 316b
Big-Sea-Water 248b
Bilbo's the word 104b
Bill: b. our mate, and choose our tree 264a
God 'll send the b. 250a
God wrote the b. 147a
not yr. b. of fare 418a
take thy b... and write fifty 509b
the world between His b. 475a
unpaid b., Despair 394b
Billet: every bullet has its b. 461a
Billets-doux: bibles, b. 302b
Billiard: elliptical b. balls 164b
the b. sharp 164b
Billiards: to play b. well 408a
Billing: still amorous..fond, and b. 66a
Billingsgate: alias, B. 473b
Billow: a breaking b. 392a
where..sounds the far b. 318a
Billows: b. smooth and bright 84a
even the b. of the sea 385b
foaming b. fair Heaven's hand 315b
ruffian b. 380a
trusted to thy b. 69b
Billowy-bosomed: cloud all b. 48a
Bills: children but as b. 14b
I cannot meet my b. 163a
inflammation of his weekly b. 70b
Billy (Billee): B., in one of his..new sashes 172b
B. the Norman 120b
little B. 440b
poke poor B. 172b
Bin (binn): in his last b. Sir Peter lies 295a
therein a little b. 190b
Bind: an apprentice fer to b. 531b
b. him for thy maidens 497b
b. its odour to the lily 77b
b. on thy sandals 420a
b. the aspen ne'er to quiver 77b
b. the sea to slumber 77b
b. up the broken hearted 503a
b...yon dangling apricocks 375b
love wh. us doth b. 260b
rob me, but b. me not 133b
safe b. safe find 446b
then b. Love to last 77b
Binnorie, O Binnorie 528b
Biographies: history is the essence of ..b. 80a
Biography: art of B. 27b
B. is about chaps 27b
no history; only b. 147b
nothing but b. 129b
Birch: appointment with..a b. 444a
b., most shy..of trees 250b
Tom B. 206a
Bird (birdie): a melancholy b. 101b
amorous b. of night 275b
a rare b. on the earth 549a
as a b. each..endearment tries 168b
as a b. unto the hill 482a
as the b. by wandering 498b
as the wakeful b. sings 273a
at least some b. wd. trust 187a

Bird (Birdie) (cont.)
a widow b. sate mourning 393a
beware the Jubjub b. 83b
b. in the solitude singing 74a
B. is on the Wing 152b
b. of dawning singeth 329b
b. of night did sit 338a
b. of the air shall carry 499b
b. of wonder dies 386b
b. overhead sang *Follow* 422b
b., rest a little longer 438a
b.'s weight can break the..tree 48b
b. that flutters least 113a
b. thou never wert 398a
b. whom man loves best 470a
b. wings and sings 50b
b. ye never heeded 229a
confined into this b. 447b
crop-full b. 50b
Dromedary is a cheerful b. 25b
escaped even as a b. 489b
forgets the dying b. 292a
further than a wanton's b. 365b
haply inhabit a b. 372a
hark, by the b.'s song 428b
he guides me and the b. 49b
if b. or devil! 298b
if the b. be flown 448a
ilka b. sang of its love 63b
I'm the b. dead-struck 263b
in the sight of any b. 497b
I wd. be a b. 36a
last b. fly into the last night 312a
Love, half angel and half b. 51a
man and b. and beast 100a
my heart is like a singing b. 310b
no chirp of any b. 198b
not born for death, immortal B.! 220a
O b. among the leaves 476a
only the note of a b. 402a
pious b. with..scarlet breast 470a
play with him as with a b. 497b
poor b., as all forlorn 20b
rise up at the voice of a b. 499b
sea-blue b. of March 430b
secular b., ages of lives 278a
self-begotten b. 278a
shall I call thee b. 463b
silence fell with the waking b. 434a
small hot b.! 150b
some fledged b.'s nest 448a
spray the dying b. 48b
sweet b. that shunn'st the noise 268a
sweet b.! thy bower is..green 53a, 246b
the b. forlorn 196a
the B. of Time 152b
the household b. 132b
the obscure b. 348a
there like a b. it sits 261a
the simple b. that thinks 118a
this b. hath made his..bed 347a
this her solemn b. 274b
thou art a summer b. 381a
time..is come for every b. 262b
unto the sweet b.'s throat 326a
wet b.-haunted English lawn 7a
what b. so sings 251b
what does little b. say 438a
white b...in his bosom 292b
young b. in this bush! 243b
Bird-cage: and a b., sir 127a
summer b. in a garden 454b
Birds: all the b. without a gun 146b
as the b. do, so do we 254a
B...agree with Chinamen 26b
b. and beasts and flowers 20a
b. are faint with the hot sun 221a
b. began to sing 533a
b. build—but not I 198a
b. in the high Hall-garden 433b
b. in their little nests 452b
b. of calm sit brooding 270a
b. of the air fell a-sighing 528a
b. of the air have nests 506a
b. sing madrigals 259a
b. sit brooding in the snow 345b
b. sit cowrin' on the spray 424b
b. still hopping on the tree 413b
b. that are without despair 454b
b., to court and pair 37b
charm of earliest b. 274b

Birds (cont.)
eagle suffers little b. 368a
fear the b. of prey 351a
full of b.' cries 262a
God was very merciful to the b. 527b
heigh! the sweet b. 373a
holy white b. 261b
hours and the wild b. follow 422b
how can ye chant, ye little b. 63b
if b. confabulate 110b
if there was two b. 446b
late the sweet b. sang 388a
like bats amongst b. 15b
little b. sang east 43b
May! be thou never grac'd with b. 42b
most diminutive of b. 350a
near all the b. will sing 43a
nest of singing b. 206a
no b. sing 218b
no b. were flying overhead 84a
one of the early b. 105b
pipe of half-awakened b. 436a
pretty b. do sing 286a
sing like b. i' the cage 344a
song of the b. for mirth 177b
sweet b. of the Lord 442b
two bright b. that..flew 242a
were no b. to fly 84a
when b. do sing 327b
when the lytle b. swetely 182b
wherein the b. make their nests 488b
wh. frightened the b. 527a
white b. on the foam 476a
Bird-singing land 118a
Bird-song at morning 414a
Birk: hats were o' the b. 529a
that b. grew fair enough 529a
Birmingham by way of Beachy Head 93a
Birnam: B. wood to high Dunsinane 349b
till B. wood remove 350b
Birth: a month before the b. 293b
Angel that presided o'er my b. 30b
as we lay at b. 6b
at my b. the frame..of the earth 378a
beauty's b. is heavenly 78a
bed for this huge b. 114b
b. and the grave 392b
b. of that..word flirtation 91a
b.'s invidious bar 430b
bring this monstrous b. 360b
burthen was thy b. to me 385a
death than the day of one's b. 499a
famous by their b. 375a
have sought to give new b. 215a
he himself is subject to his b. 330b
high b., vigour of bone 369a
impulses of deeper b. 469a
I sing the b. was born 216b
land of our b. 227b
my love is of a b. as rare 260a
nobility of b...abateth industry 15a
of H[ayley's] b. 30a
one that is coming to b. 291a
on my b. have smiled 424b
our b. is but a sleep 466a
quicken a new b.! 396b
repeats the story of her b. 2a
signal to a maid, the human b. 265a
sudden and portentous b. 318b
sunshine is a glorious b. 466a
time and order of yr. b. 36a
'tis virtue, and not b. 23a
walked he from his b. 227b
wanderer is man from his b. 6a
Birthday: b. of my life 310b
laburnum on his b. 195a
Birth-partner: soul's b. 312a
Birthright: b. for a mess of potash 451a
Esau selleth his b. 523a
he sold his b. unto Jacob 493a
Birthrights proudly on their backs 373b
Births: b. of living creatures 15b
plenties, and joyful b. 383b
whom, for our high b. 262b
Birth-time's consecrating dew 294b
Biscay: B.'s sleepless bay 68a
clouds before a B. gale 252b
in the Bay of B., O! 90b
Biscuit: b., or confectionary plum 109b
dry as the remainder b. 326b
took a captain's b. 123b

Biscuits: beef and captain's b. 440b
the b. you nibble 227b
Biserta: whom B. sent 271b
Bishop: among them was a B. 163a
B...Abbot..Prior were there 19a
B. of *Rome* hath no jurisdiction 491b
B. of yr. souls 517b
contradicting a B. 211a
desire the office of a B. 516b
hail, B. Valentine 132b
how can a b. marry? 404b
singed the beard of the B. 407a
to the B. they go 406b
Bishoprick: his b. let another take 512a
Bishops: bench of heedless b. 400a
B., Priests and Deacons 478b
upon our B. and Curates 478b
what b. like best 405a
Bit: b. by him that comes behind 419b
b. him till he bled 192b
dogs..shall have a little b. 533a
dog, tho' he had b. me, 344a
held with b. and bridle 483b
I b. my arm 98b
it wd. have b. you 418b
little b. off the top 285b
went mad and b. the man 169a
Bitch: a Impudent B. 155a
why b.? 151a
Bite: b. some..of my generals 161a
b. yr. thumb at us 364b
game they dare not b. 303a
man recovered of the b. 169a
to bark and b. 452b
to b. so good a man 169a
Bites: bides its time and b. 45b
Biting: his b. is immortal 325a
Bitter: be not b. against them 516a
my belly was b. 519a
old and b. of tongue 475b
shed a b. tear 84a
unto the b. in soul 497a
wells up some b. taste 550b
Bittern: possession for the b. 502a
Bitterness: b. of absence sour 388a
b. of death is past 495b
b. of things occult 313a
doth kill much b. 218b
I must have no..b. 86b
in the b. of my soul 502b
in the gall of b. 512a
knoweth his own b. 498a
the b. of life! 85b
Bitters: sweets and the b. of love 72b
Bittock: mile an' a b. 415a
Blabbing: b., and remorseful day 384a
ere the b. eastern scout 266b
Black: as b. as they might be 529b
b. as a tar-barrel 84a
b. as the Pit from pole 185a
b. it stood as night 272b
b. men fought on the coast 254b
b.'s not so b. 78b
b. spirits and white 265b, 349b
but thou read'st b. 29b
down in b. and white 67b
from b. to red began to turn 65b
have it here in b. and white 215b
I am b., as if bereaved 32b
I am b., but comely 500a
I am b., but O! 32b
man is b. at heart 547b
matron, all in b. 366a
more b. than ash-buds 427a
night's blear-all b. 197b
round-faced man in b. 183a
sae b. and bare 62b
silver and b. on flank 202b
suits of solemn b. 330a
take them down in b. 67a
tho' thou be b. as night 78a
white shall not neutralize the b. 51b
who art as b. as hell 389b
Blackberries: micher and eat b. 377b
reasons..plentiful as b. 377b
sit round it and pluck b. 43a
Blackbird: my b. bountiful 137b
O b., what a boy you are! 41a
than to a b. 'tis to whistle 64b
there came a little b. 533b
Blackbirds: b. have their wills 426b

Blackbirds (*cont.*)
four-and-twenty b. 533*a*
full of b. than of cherries 2*b*
Blackens: Skuttlefish..b. all the Water 2*b*
Black-eyed Susan 161*a*
Blackfriars: waterman..B. Bridge 120*b*
Blackguard: sesquipedalian b. 96*a*
whatever brute and b. 199*b*
Blackguards: 'arcades ambo'..b. 71*a*
done to you young b. 150*b*
we aren't no b. too 235*b*
Blackheath: straight from wild B. 252*b*
Blackness: in the gross b. underneath 438*a*
some nocturnal b. 179*a*
to whom is reserved the b. 518*a*
Blacksmith like our Norman King 227*a*
Blackthorn starreth now his bough 35*b*
Bladder: blows a man up like a b. 377*b*
Bladders: boys that swim on b. 386*a*
Blade: against..bloody Highland b. 317*a*
bud or b., or bloom 426*b*
cling round the sickly b. 114*a*
destroy a b. of grass 34*a*
the vorpal b. went snicker-snack! 84*a*
trenchant b., Toledo trusty 65*a*
we draw the b. 230*a*
with bloody, blameful b. 357*b*
Blade-straight: steel-true and b. 414*b*
Blains: breaking forth with b. 493*b*
Blake: Collingwood, Byron, B. 287*b*
Blame: alike reserved to b. 303*a*
b. not my lute! 473*b*
in part to b. is she 291*b*
murderous, bloody, full of b. 389*a*
oh! b. not the bard 281*b*
praise it, or b. it too much 169*b*
that neither is most to b. 422*b*
the b. of those ye better 236*b*
thine be the grief, as the b. 12*a*
'tis very just they b. 294*a*
what they b. at night 300*b*
Blamed: he b. and protested 110*b*
world..b. the living man 6*b*
Blanc: Mont B. is the monarch 73*a*
Blanch: Troy, B. and Sweetheart 343*a*
Bland: aspect anything but b. 75*a*
cruel, but composed and b. 7*b*
his manners..complying, and b. 169*b*
lines mellifluously b. 71*a*
Blank: a b., my Lord 371*a*
b. to Zoroaster 49*b*
presented with a universal b. 273*b*
this world's no blot..nor b. 46*b*
Blanket: peep thro' the b. of the dark 346*b*
red b. cloak she wore 219*a*
Blankets: rough male kiss of b. 39*a*
Blaspheme: some give thanks, and some b. 293*a*
Blasphemies: truths begin as b. 389*b*
Blasphemy: b. against..Holy Ghost 506*b*
in the soldier is flat b. 351*b*
Blast: b. of vain doctrine 479*b*
bleak blows the b. 78*b*
down the roaring b. 226*a*
East bowed low before the b. 7*a*
heard..in the trances of the b. 101*a*
I'll cross it, tho' it b. me 329*b*
pity..striding the b. 347*a*
shelter from the stormy b. 453*a*
sleep in the arms of the b. 393*a*
the banners waved without a b. 317*a*
wert thou in the cauld b. 62*a*
Blast-beruffled plume 179*a*
Blasted: b. with antiquity 379*b*
b. with excess of light 175*a*
no sooner blown but b. 268*a*
Blasts: hollow b. of wind 161*a*
Blatant Beast: death of the B. 255*a*
wh. the B. men call 409*a*
Blaze: b. of living light 70*a*
broader still became the b. 252*b*
burst out into sudden b. 260*b*
his rash fierce b. 374*b*
Blazing: in a B. bad way 127*a*
one b. indiscretion 283*b*
that's a B. strange answer 127*a*
they are b. ubiquities 148*b*
Blazon: this eternal b. 331*a*
Bleat: b., the bark, bellow 29*b*
b. the one at the other 372*b*

Bleating: what meaneth then this b. 495*a*
Bledde: if it were deed or b. 88*b*
Bleed: and then we b. 394*a*
the thorns of life! I b.! 396*b*
Bleeding: thou b. piece of earth 339*b*
Blemish: lamb shall be without b. 493*b*
Blemishes: read not my b. 323*b*
Blenches: these b. gave my heart 389*a*
Blending: love, with quiet b. 468*a*
Blenheim: I dine at B. 528*b*
Bless: angel fast until he b. thee 247*b*
ask the Lord to b. me 150*b*
b. myself with silence 49*b*
b. thee, Bottom! b. thee! 357*a*
b. the hand that gave the blow 141*b*
b. ye the Lord 478*a*
b. ye the man that spares 389*b*
God b. us every one! 121*b*
go, except thou b. me 493*a*
we stand to b. Thee 145*b*
wherefore b. ye, O beloved ones 75*b*
with Thee at hand to b. 251*b*
Blessed: b. are the dead wh. die 519*b*
b. are the poor in spirit 505*a*
b. are the pure in heart 224*a*
b. are they that have not seen 511*b*
b. are they wh. are called 519*b*
b. art thou among women 508*b*
b. be he that cometh 489*a*
b. be the name of the Lord 496*b*
b. is he who has found his work 81*b*
b. is the man..endureth temptation 517*a*
b. is the man that trusteth 484*a*
b. shall be he that taketh 490*a*
b. them these three times 494*a*
b. . . . who expects nothing 304*a*
desirous to be b. 335*a*
generations shall call me b. 508*b*
his b. part to Heaven 386*a*
I b. them unaware 99*a*
none b. before his death 520*b*
now b. you, bear onward b. me 402*a*
pastures of the b. 286*a*
rise up and call her b. 499*a*
Sabbaths the b. ones see 287*a*
the b. damozel leaned out 311*b*
till, seeming b., they grow 170*a*
what God b. once 44*b*
whom thou blessest is b. 494*a*
Blessedness: ask no other b. 81*b*
in single b. 356*a*
Blesses: b. his stars..luxury 1*b*
b. us with surprise 27*a*
Blesseth: b. her with his two..hands 408*b*
it b. him that gives 354*b*
Blessing: b. in comparison of this 11*b*
a b. that money cannot buy 450*b*
a boon and a b. 527*a*
a double b. 330*b*
but contrariwise b. 517*b*
death, b. and cursing 494*b*
dew of thy b. 478*b*
God, shall give us his b. 486*a*
greatness..esteemed a b. 262*b*
I had most need of b. 347*b*
I'll b. beg of you 335*a*
Lord, behold us with Thy b. 53*b*
Lord, dismiss us with Thy b. 53*b*
mighty b. 'while we live, to live' 302*a*
my b. season this in thee 330*b*
national debt..national b. 178*b*, 454*a*
no harm in B. 67*b*
paid thy utmost b. 119*b*
shall yourselves find b. 286*b*
taken away thy b. 493*a*
this *is* b., this is life 445*a*
thou dost ask me b. 344*a*
'tis a visionary b. 161*a*
truly it's a b. 96*a*
you enjoy but half the b. 159*a*
Blessings: all wh. we behold is full of b. 472*a*
b. are plentiful and rife 187*a*
b. in disguise 191*a*
b. of this life 479*a*
b. on the falling out 436*a*
break in b. on yr. head 110*a*
first of earthly b., independence 162*a*
from whom all b. flow 224*b*
heavenly b. without number 453*a*
its many b. dear 468*a*

Blest: bed be b. that I lie on 2*b*
b. him in their pain 437*b*
b. pair of Sirens 278*a*
but always to be b. 300*b*
it is twice b. 354*b*
not for mortals always to be b. 4*b*
while it says we shall be b. 139*b*
Blimber: Dr. B. 122*b*
Miss B. 122*b*
Blind: altho' a poor B. Boy 95*b*
b. as any noon-tide owl 428*a*
b. leaders of the b. 507*a*
b. mouths! 269*b*
b., old, and lonely 391*b*
b. side of the heart 92*a*
b. to Galileo 49*b*
b. unbelief is sure to err 110*a*
I myself am b. 304*a*
in the country of the b. 292*a*
Justice, tho' she's painted b. 66*a*
none so b. as they that won't see 418*b*
old Mæonides the b. 154*b*
ordains us e'en as b. 228*a*
people have their b. side 239*a*
right to be b. sometimes 287*a*
thou Eye among the b. 466*b*
unbelief is b. 267*b*
whereas I was b., now I see 511*a*
winged Cupid painted b. 356*a*
Blinded: no longer b. by our eyes 39*b*
Blindest: fondest, b., weakest 442*a*
Nelson turned his b. eye 92*a*
Blindfold and alone 228*b*
Blindly: never lov'd sae b. 59*a*
Blindness: for our b. we cannot ask 480*b*
help him of his b. 372*b*
the heathen in his b. 184*a*
Blinds let through the day 200*a*
Blind-worms: newts and b. 356*b*
Bliss: a b. in proof 389*a*
a man had given all other b. 438*a*
b. and sole felicity 259*a*
b. beyond compare 286*a*
b. in our brows 322*b*
b. was it in that dawn 465*a*
certainty of waking b. 267*a*
deprived of everlasting b. 258*b*
dream of perfect b. 22*a*
each to his point of b. 52*a*
excels all other b. 143*a*
have but a shadow's b. 353*b*
he lives in b. 62*a*
moment may with b. repay 77*b*
mutual and partaken b. 267*b*
my step in b. 36*b*
my wing'd hours of b. have been 77*b*
sees in ale 113*b*
splendour pant with b. 218*b*
sum of earthly b. 275*b*
the pain, the b. of dying! 299*a*
thou art a soul in b. 344*a*
to the b. us bring 531*a*
what is b., and which the way? 211*b*
where ignorance is b. 175*a*
Blisses: among his new-born b. 466*b*
bespeake her to my b. 115*b*
in the midst of our b. 461*a*
seeks nor finds he mortal b. 397*a*
Blissful: something b. and dear 281*b*
Blisters: angry Mab with b. plagues 364*b*
Blithe: be you b. and bonny 358*a*
buxom, b., and debonair 268*b*
no lark more b. 28*a*
Block: chopper on a big black b. 164*b*
the old b. itself 58*a*
you insensible b.! 19*a*
Blockhead: a talking b. 150*a*
no man but a b. ever wrote 209*a*
the bookful b. 300*b*
when a b.'s insult points the dart 213*a*
Blocks: hew b. with a razor 304*a*
you b., you stones 337*b*
Blondes: Gentlemen Prefer B. 249*b*
Blood: a blow in cold b. 391*a*
all that b. was shed 474*b*
all the while ran b. 340*a*
a man, whose b. is warm within 352*b*
am I not of her b.? 370*b*
a' the b. that 's shed 528*a*
a thorn to let me b. 188*a*
b. and iron 567*b*

Blood (cont.)
b. and judgement are..co-mingled 334a
b. and wine are red 459b
b.-boltered Banquo 349b
b. is their argument 382b
b. is thick, but water's thin 164a
b. more stirs to rouse a lion 377a
b. of all the Howards 301b
B. of Jesus whispers peace 28a
b. of patriots and tyrants 204b
b. of their bodies grown red 421b
b. of the martyrs..seed of the Church 574a
b. of this just person 508a
b. out of a turnip 259b
b. that she has spilt 107b
b. was frozen slowly 432a
b. will have b. 349a
blushed with b. of queens 221b
but give me B.! 122a
but that Thy b. was shed 146a
calls to Heaven for human b. 29a
crimes..purged away but with b. 40b
don't yur b. bile 451a
drink the b. of goats 485a
drunken with the b. of the saints 519b
faith..beats with his b. 437a
felt in the b. 472a
find so much b. in his liver 371b
flowed out the purple b. 254a
folks that ride a bit of b. 196a
foot..in the b. of thine enemies 486b
for B., as all men know 202b
fountain filled with b. 110a
freeze thy b. less coldly 286b
freeze thy young b. 331a
garments rolled in b. 501b
glories of our b. and state 401a
guiltless of his country's b. 174a
harbingers of b. and death 351a
haste to shed innocent b. 503a
hey-day in the b. is tame 335a
his b. be on us 508a
His b. upon the rose 297b
I am in b. stepped 349b
if b. be the price 234b
I'll not shed her b. 363b
inhabits our frail b. 372a
in its ruddy orbit lifts the b. 294b
I smell the b. 343a
I sucked the b. 98b
it was not part of their b. 227a
judge and avenge our b. 518b
let there be b.! 71a
make thick my b. 346b
Man of B. was there 252b
motion of our human b. 472a
my b. for drachmas 341a
napkins in his sacred b. 340a
Neptune's ocean wash this b. 348a
not gold, not b. 394a
nothing like b., sir 440a
O! b., b., b.! 362a
pure and eloquent b. 133b
purge this choler without..b. 374b
red b. reigns in the winter's 373a
rich with the most noble b. 339b
sheds his b. with me 383a
so much b. in him 350a
song and b. are pure 264a
speech to stir men's b. 340a
still the b. is strong 320b
stir the Vikings' b. 226a
summon up the b. 382a
the lake of B.! 427b
the secret'st man of b. 349a
the warming of the b. 380b
they waded thru' red b. 528a
thicks man's b. with cold 98b
thy b. bought that 133a
Thy b. is cold 349a
to freeze the b. 465b
to wash them in my b. 407b
voice of thy brother's b. 492b
water's wider..than B. 202b
we be of one b. 237a
weltering in his b. 139a
what disturbs our b. 476a
what profit is there in my b. 483b
when b. is nipp'd 345b
when the b. burns 331a

Blood (cont.)
when the moon was b. 92a
white in the b. of the Lamb 519a
whose b. is fet from fathers 382a
whose b. is very snow-broth 351a
whoso sheddeth man's b. 492b
wish thine own heart dry of b. 219a
without..b. is no remission 517a
young b. must have its course 226a
youth and b. are warmer 190b
Blood-guiltiness: deliver me from b. 485a
Bloodless lay the untrodden snow 76b
Blood-red banner streams afar 184a
Bloodshed: Fear, and B., miserable train! 465a
Bloodthirsty: b. and deceitful man 482a
b. clinging to life 570a
my life with the b. 483b
Bloody: b., bold, and resolute 349b
b. with spurring 375a
come out, thou b. man 495b
not b. likely 391b
the b. Sun, at noon 98b
the selfsame b. mode 179b
to have b. thoughts 367b
what b. man is that? 345b
wipe a b. nose 160b
Bloom: b. along the bough 198b
b. sae fresh and fair 63b
drives elate full on thy b. 62a
its b. is shed 63a
long milk-b. on the tree 434a
look at things in b. 198b
sort of b. on a woman 21b
withering in my b. 299b
with the b. go I 8b
Blooming: left b. alone 281b
sae bonny their b. 97a
Blooms: then b. each thing 286a
Blossom: a broken b. 424a
bade it b. *there* 100b
blood-red b. of war 434b
b. by b. the spring begins 420b
b. in purple and red 434a
b. of fresh colour 402b
b. opening to the day 169a
desert..b. as the rose 502a
oh blighted b.! can it be 295a
spied a b. passing fair 344b
timely b., infant fair 296b
under the b. that hangs 368a
Blossoms: a thousand B. with the Day 152b
b. in the trees 301a
sing of brooks, of b. 188b
Blot: art to b. 303b
blackens every b. 427b
b. me, I pray thee 494a
b. out, correct 419b
bright b. upon this..scene 399a
only the right b. 294a
text that looks a little b. 429a
this world's no b. 46b
where is the b.? 52b
Blotted: b. it out for ever 412a
had b. a thousand 214b
never b. out a line 214b
Blow: another deadly b.! 468a
bless the hand that gave the b. 141b
b., bugle, b. 436a
b. fall soon or late 414a
b. him again to me 436a
b. in cold blood 391a
b. me about in winds! 364a
b. out, you bugles 39a
b., winds, and crack your cheeks! 342b
for a knock-down b. 166a
genius gave the final b. 72a
gie them a b. 285b
he'd never survive the b. 186a
liberty's in every b.! 62b
must have life for a b. 434a
stormy winds do b. 77b
this b. might be the be-all 347a
'tis but a word and a b. 139b
to take one b., and turn 193b
was but a word and a b. 54a
what wood..by the b. 65b
word and a b. 54a, 365b
Blown: b. with restless violence 352a
rooks are b. about 429b
Blows: apostolic b. and knocks 65a

Blows (cont.)
b. the wind to-day 414b
heal the b. of sound 194a
our vain b. malicious 329b
vile b. and buffets 348b
when most she offers b. 323b
Bludgeoning: democracy means..b. 460b
Bludgeonings of chance 185a
Blue: and she forgot the b. 218b
beneath the b. of day 198b
b. above lane and wall 46a
b. bared its eternal bosom 220b
b., darkly, deeply, beautifully b. 406b
b., the fresh, the ever free! 106a
burnt green, and b. 98b
canopy of light and b. 456b
choosing cloths was b. 284a
do I stand and stare? all's b. 48b
domes the..hills with loving b. 426b
drink till all look b. 155b
flowers..b., silver-white 220a
grappling in the central b. 432b
heaven's colour, the b. 284a
little boy blue 535a
little tent of b. 459b
of most unholy b.! 281b
our Little Boy B. 151a
Presbyterian true b. 65a
said my eyes were b. 241b
the b. and the dim 474b
to bide by the buff and the b 61a
too expressive to be b. 5b
two little girls in b. 172a
within the holier b. 51a
yonder living b. 431a
you get yr. eyes so b.? 256a
Blue Beard's domestic chaplain 126a
Bluebottle: like a b. fly 19b
Blueness abundant 52b
Blue-stocking: sagacious b. 254b
Bluest of things grey 421b
Blunder: frae mony a b. free us 61b
life is I think a b. 185b
Blunderbuss against religion 206b
Blundered; someone had b. 426a
Blundering kind of melody 138b
Blunders: escaped..b. ridden more in omnibuses 184b
Woman?—only one of Nature's..b. 107b
Blush: b. and gently smile 188b
b. from West to East 434a
b. to find itself less white 405b
b. to give it in! 77b
born to b. unseen 174a
else wd. a maiden b. 365a
not b. so to be admired 449a
with a b. retire 123b
wd. it bring a b. into the cheek 125b
Blushed: her motion b. at herself 360a
ne'er b. unless..she blundered 94b
saw its god, and b. 114b
Blushful Hippocrene 219b
Blushing: a b. womanly..grace 132b
his b. honours 385b
Blynken: Wynken, B. and Nod 151a
Boar: as the learned B. observed 396b
Board: a hospitable b. 468b
cleanly platter on the b. 170a
I struck the b. 188a
square, and above the b. 178a
there wasn't any B. 186a
Boards: all the b. did shrink 98b
books..not those things in b. 240a
Boar-pig: Bartholomew b. 380a
Boast: Anabaptists do falsely b. 491b
b. himself as he that putteth it off 496a
b. not thyself of tomorrow 498b
b. of heraldry 174a
b. of nothing else but..grief 374b
b. sincere felicity 141a
b. their love possessing 35b
for frantic b. and foolish word 233b
if I b. of aught 313b
make no b. of it 358b
nature's solitary b. 472b
nor yet without a b. shall end 452b
now b. thee, death 325b
of wh. we rather b. 260a
such is the patriot's b. 170a
Boasteth: gone his way, then he b. 498b
Boastings as the Gentiles use 233b

ENGLISH INDEX

Boat (boatie): a b. he can sail   444a
best fits a little b.   188b
his b. hastens to the..steep   220b
if men are together in a b.   178a
in a beautiful pea-green b.   243b
my b. is on the shore   73a
my b. sails freely   361a
my soul is an enchanted b.   397b
Old Man in a b.   243a
sings in his b. on the bay!   425b
so hey bonny b.   225b
weel may the b. row   149a
who took a b. and went to sea   440b
with Dirce in one b. conveyed!   241a
Boatman, do not tarry!   77a
Boats: shallow bauble b. dare sail   368b
to see no b. upon the River   296a
Bob: B. Short   417a
bow at her and b. at her   93a
Bode: what shd. that b.?   358b
Bodice: b., aptly laced   305b
lace my b. blue   202a
Bodied: softly b. forth   69a
Bodies: blood of their b.   421b
b. of unburied men   454a
circles..close all b.   42b
conceit in weakest b.   335a
our b. are our gardens   360b
our b. why de we forbear?   132b
soldiers bore dead b. by   376b
their b. are buried in peace   521b
yr. b. a living sacrifice   513b
Boding: doth the raven..b. to all   362b
Bodkin: with a bare b.   333a
Bodleian: in the name of the B.   28b
Body: absence of b.   535a
absent in b...present in spirit   514a
as well for the b. as the soul   478a
beautiful passionate b.   421a
blows upon my b.   325b
b. and I pulled at one rope   99a
b. form doth take   409a
b. gets its sop   45a
b. is not more than the soul   458a
b. of a weak and feeble woman   145a
b. of man is capable of..pleasure   75a
b. of my brother's son   99a
b. of this death   513a
b. that once ye had   235b
casting the b.'s vest aside   261a
Charlotte, having seen his b.   440b
clog of his b.   158a
commit this b. to the ground   481b
demd, damp, moist, unpleasant b.   125a
dignity of the whole b.   350a
Eve, with her b. white   192a
find thy b. by the wall   6b
flavour, and b., and hue   20a
fretted the pigmy b.   138a
from tawny b.   422b
gigantic b., the huge massy face   255b
gin a b. kiss a b.   59b
gin a b. meet a b.   59b
he is through your b.   308b
her b. it grew better   465a
her b. thought   133b
here in the b. pent   280a
his b. to that pleasant..earth   375b
his b. to the deep   491a
his lifeless b. lay   248a
his mind or b. to prefer   301a
I keep under my b.   514a
in b. and in soul can bind   317a
I the b.   441a
its b. brevity, and wit its soul   527b
keep yr. b. white   414b
language is..the b., of thought   81b
loan of his own b.   75a
like little b. with a..heart   381b
lilies in her b.'s lieu   294b
little b. is aweary of this..world   352b
make less thy b. hence   381a
man..kin to the beasts by his b.   15a
marry my b. to that dust   225a
motive of her b.   369a
my b. as a plaything   390a
my b. to be burned   514b
mystical b. of thy Son   480b
my Thames-blown b.   202b
need a b. cry?   59b
no b. to be kicked   444b

Body (cont.)
nor a b. to kick   404b
nor Love her b. from her soul   313a
not b. enough to cover his mind   404b
nothing the b. suffers   264b
not in thy b. is thy life   312a
nought broken save this b.   40a
out of the b.   515a
patch up thine old b.   380a
perfect little b.   37a
small slain b.   422b
soul and b. part like friends   115a
soul and b. rive not   324a
soul I know not from thy b.   312a
Soul, the b.'s guest   307b
sound mind in a sound b.   549b
still my b. drank   99a
tasted her sweet b.   362a
than he has in his whole b.   418b
the b.'s delicate   343a
the b. than raiment   505b
Thersites' b. is as good as Ajax   329a
this b. did contain a spirit   379a
this common b.   322b
this tumultuous b.   39b
tho' her b. die   278a
thy b. is all vice   206b
upon my buried b.   23a
whether in the b., I cannot tell   515a
whose b. nature is   301a
who with a b. filled   383a
with my b. I thee worship   481b
yr. b. is the temple   514a
Boffin: Mrs. B. does not honour us   125b
Mrs. B., Wegg..is a highflyer   125b
Boffkin: Minnie B.   233b
Mrs. B. sits   233b
Bog: o'er b. or steep   273a
Boggles: thing imagination b. at   75b
Bogs: fens, b., dens   272b
Bohemia: B. A desert Country
desarts of B.   373a
373a
Boil: b. breaking forth with blains   493b
we b. at different degrees   148b
Bois Bou-long   162b
Bold: as b. as she   228a
be b., and everywhere be b.   409a
be not too b.   409a
bloody, b., and resolute   349b
b. bad man   385b, 408b
b. majestic downs   36a
more daring or more b.   378b
my b., my beautiful, my Bulbo!   440a
that..hath made me b.   347b
Boldest: b. held his breath   76b
b. of hearts   51a
Boldness: b. and again b.   561a
b. is a child of ignorance   14b
b. is an ill keeper of promise   14b
familiarity begets b.   259b
use respective b.   186b
what first? b.   14b
Bole: round the elm-tree b.   47a
Bolingbroke: every man that B. hath pressed   375a
this canker, B.   377a
who now reads B.?   57a
Boloigne: at Rome..and at B.   88b
Boloney: that 's just b.   403b
Bolt: Ben B.   148b
b. is shot back somewhere   5a
b. of Cupid fell   356b
sulphurous b.   351b
Bolting: tarry the b.   368b
Bolts: louder than the b. of heaven   77a
the b. are hurled   433a
Bombastes: meet B. face to face   309a
Bombazine..shown a deeper sense   159a
Bond: b. nor free: but Christ is all   516a
b. nomine to me   469b
I will have my b.   354b
look to his b.   354a
nominated in the b.   355a
our b. is not the b. of man   428b
take a b. of fate   349b
that great b. wh. keeps me pale!   349a
'tis not in the b.   355a
Bondage: b. is hoarse   365b
b. of Rhyming   270b
Cassius from b. will deliver   338a

Bondage (cont.)
disguise our b. as we will   282a
out of the land of b. came   319b
received the spirit of b.   513b
that sweet b.   397b
Bondman: every b. in his own hand bears   338a
here so base that would be a b.   339b
in a b.'s key   353a
thy B. let me live!   464a
Bonds: break their b. asunder   481b
he loves his b.   190a
my b. in thee are all determinate   388b
spirit into b. again   109b
stricture of these b.   412b
such as I am, except these b.   513a
Bondsmen: hereditary b.!   68a
Bone: b. of my bones   492a
b. of my b. thou art   276b
bracelet of..hair about the b.   133b
break a bit of b.   196a
every b. a-stare   45b
into the b. of manhood   55b
to a rag and a b.   236a
to get her poor dog a b.   533b
vigour of b.   369a
Bones: b. of a single Pomeranian   567b
b. wh. thou hast broken   485a
can these b. live?   504a
come to lay my b. amongst you   462b
echo round his b.   435a
fill all thy b. with aches   367a
for his honoured b.   278a
full of dead men's b.   507b
he that moves my b.   389b
I may tell all my b.   483a
in a glas he hadde pigges b.   89a
interréd with their b.   339b
Knight's b. are dust   101a
mocked the dead b.   384b
my b. consumed away   483b
of his b. are coral made   367a
rattle his b.   289b
rattling b. together fly   140b
roll dem b.   191a
saints, whose b. lie scattered   278b
these b. from insult to protect   174b
these dead b. have..rested   42a
the tongs and the b.   357a
the tongue breaketh the b.   520b
to lay his weary b.   386a
thy b. are marrowless   349a
thy canoniz'd b.   331a
valley wh. was full of b.   504a
weave their thread with b.   371a
where my b. shall be thrown   371a
you may see his b. and beak   25b
yr. b. are very brittle   414a
Bonfire: way to the everlasting b.   348a
Bong-tree grows   243b
Bon-mots: plucking b. from their places   283a
Bonnet: antique ruff and b.   211b
in her latest new b.   131a
Bonnets of Bonnie Dundee   316a
Bonnie (bonny): be you blithe and b.   358a
b. wee thing   59b
Bonnivard: by B.!   69b
Bononchini: that Signor B.   67a
Booby: give her b. for another   160b
Booh: sing 'B. to you'   165b
Boojum: the Snark was a B.   86a
if yr. Snark be a B.   86a
Book: a b. may be amusing   171a
a b.'s a b.   72a
a good b. is the..life-blood   279a
a melancholy b.   114a
anything wh. I call a b.   239a
a religious b., or friend   473b
bloody b. of law   359b
blot me..out of thy b.   494a
b...essence of a human soul   82a
b. of books   186b
b. of knowledge fair   273b
b. of Jasher   494b
B. of Life begins   460b
B. of Verses underneath the Bough   152b
b. that my daughters may read   535a
b... without pictures   82b
but where's the b.?   94b
Camerado, this is no b.   458b

Book (cont.)

dainties that are bred in a b.	344*b*
eyes were sealed to the holy b.	6*a*
farewell my b. and my devocion	89*b*
find one English b.	10*a*
for a jolly good b.	461*b*
from the b. of honour razed quite	387*a*
frowst with a b.	230*b*
Galeotto was the b.	566*b*
gets at the substance of a b.	238*a*
God . . from a printed b.	235*b*
go, litil b.	90*b*
go, little b., and wish to all	414*b*
good b. is the best of friends	446*a*
great b., great evil	559*b*
half a library to make one b.	208*b*
Hers of the B.	307*a*
if a man write a better b.	148*b*
I had my B. of Songs	355*b*
I'll drown my b.	368*a*
in a b., that all may read	32*b*
in my secret b.	36*a*
in thy b. were all my members	490*b*
kill a good b.	279*a*
kiss the b.'s outside	108*a*
leading one to talk of a b.	207*a*
little volume, but large b.	115*a*
mine adversary had written a b.	497*a*
my b., 'tis this	191*a*
name out of the b. of life	518*b*
Nature's infinite b. of secrecy	322*b*
Nature's mystic b.	260*a*
Nature was his b.	33*a*
never read any b.	148*b*
no . . moral or an immoral b.	460*a*
note in a b.	502*a*
not on his picture, but his b.	215*b*
Oh for a b.	51*a*
old yellow B.	89*b*
O litel b.	89*b*
out of the b. of life	520*b*
people wd. look at the best b.	314*a*
plagues . . written in this b.	520*b*
read a b. before reviewing	404*b*
reader that makes the good b.	148*b*
read of that sin in a b.?	235*b*
read the b. of fate	385*a*
small old-fashioned b.	144*a*
sour misfortune's b.	366*b*
take down this b.	476*b*
take them out of this b.	411*b*
then shut the b.	293*a*
there is a b., who runs may read	224*a*
they club for at b. clubs	240*a*
they were printed in a b.!	497*a*
thick, square b.!	167*b*
things noted in thy b.	485*b*
things . . written in this b.	520*b*
throw this b. about	25*b*
unbent her mind . . over a b.	239*a*
valuable b. by chance	175*b*
volume of the b. it is written	484*a*
when I wrote that b.	419*a*
while thy b. doth live	215*b*
word for word without b.	369*b*
worthy to open the b.	518*b*
writing in a b. of gold	201*b*
yr. face . . a b. where men may read	347*a*

Bookish: the b. theoric 359*b*

Books: authority from others' b. 344*b*

author who speaks . . own b.	128*b*
b., and my food	415*a*
b. are not absolutely dead things	279*a*
b. are not seldom talismans	112*b*
b. are well written	460*a*
b. . . a substantial world	468*b*
b. by wh. the printers have lost	158*a*
b. . . contain a potency of life	279*a*
b., fruit, French wine	223*a*
b. in the running brooks	325*b*
b. . . may carry to the fire	212*a*
b. must follow sciences	13*b*
b. of the hour	314*a*
b. of the true sort	240*a*
b. . . propose to *instruct*	120*a*
b.! 'tis a dull . . strife	471*b*
b. . . to be read only in parts	16*a*
b. to Cambridge gave	445*b*
b., wh. are no b.	230*a*
b. will speak plain	15*a*
bound in little b.	232*a*

Books (cont.)

but his b. were read	26*b*
cream of others' b.	283*a*
deep versed in b.	277*a*
dreams, b., are each a world	468*b*
fate of b. depends on . . reader	551*a*
forefathers had no b.	384*a*
friends, and many B., both true	107*a*
from my b. maketh me to goon	89*b*
gentleman is not in yr. b.	358*a*
God has written all the b.	66*b*
grew out of the b. I wrote	52*b*
he may live without b.	265*a*
I keep my b. at the . . Museum	66*b*
in b. . . *soul* of . . Past Time	81*a*
I never read b.	535*b*
knowing I loved my b.	367*a*
lard their lean b.	64*a*
let my b. be then the eloquence	387*a*
many b. thou readest	7*b*
moderns mistake for b.	240*a*
my only b. were woman's looks	282*a*
no furniture so charming as b.	404*a*
no grace for b.	238*b*
of making many b. there is no end	500*a*
on b. for to rede	89*b*
out of olde b. . . newe science	90*a*
poring over miserable b.	432*b*
quit yr. b.	471*b*
rather studied b. than men	17*a*
some b. are to be tasted	16*a*
some b. . . may be read by deputy	16*a*
souls in new French b.	45*a*
the b. were opened	519*b*
the spectacles of b.	142*a*
things in b. clothing	239*a*
this, b. can do	113*b*
three b. on the soul	46*a*
thumb each other's b.	314*a*
to Cambridge b.	445*b*
to Cambridge b. he sent	42*b*
treasures that in b. are found	398*b*
true University . . of B.	81*a*
twenty b., clad in blak	88*b*
what do we . . care about b.	314*a*
women's eyes . . the b.	345*a*
yr. borrowers of b.	239*a*

Bookseller: conceived by a b. 449*b*

Booksellers: ask the b. of London 57*a*

b. are generous 207*a*

Boon: a sordid b. 473*a*

bean flowers' b.	46*a*
b. and a blessing to men	527*b*
is life a b.?	167*a*
of neither wd. I ask the b.	399*a*

Boot: a dapper b. 434*b*

b., saddle, to horse	45*b*
hey for b. and horse, lad	226*a*
my legs when I take my b. off	269*b*

Boots: alas! what b. it 163*b*

Aristocrat who cleans the b.	
bishop's b. Mr. Radcliffe also condemned	416*b*
bloomin' b. of 'im	229*b*
b.-b.-b.—movin' up an' down	227*b*
bring me my b.!	19*a*
give me my b. I say	376*a*
taste of boiled b.	439*b*
this pair of b. displace	309*a*
with spattered b.	112*a*

Bo-peep: B. has lost her sheep 533*a*

they started at b. 190*b*

Border: Blue Bonnets . . for the B. 320*a*

B., nor Breed, nor Birth	227*a*
gaed o'er the b.	59*b*
in his b. see Israel set	47*a*
misty of the wood	476*b*
sung of B. chivalry	316*b*
thin flowery b.	239*b*
thro' all the wide B.	318*a*
we'll over the B.	193*b*

Borders: b., beds and shrubberies 229*b*

b. of their garments	507*b*
'stablishèd its b.	231*a*

Bore: awhile they b. her up 336*a*

b., mid snow and ice, a banner	257*a*
by her that b. her understood	428*b*
every hero becomes a b.	148*b*
grew, and b., and b.	238*b*
singer that England b.	423*a*

Bore (cont.)

thus he b. without abuse	431*a*
to be in it is merely a b.	460*b*

Bored: b. by a bee 243*a*

he b. with his augur	531*a*
I feel a little b.	91*b*
two . . tribes the bores and b.	71*b*

Bores: b. have succeeded to dragons 130*a*

b. thro' his castle wall	375*b*
two . . tribes, the b. and bored	71*b*

Borgias: dining with the B. tonight 24*b*

Born: as of one b. out of due time 514*b*

as soon as we were b.	520*a*
better to be lowly b.	385*b*
b. but to die	301*a*
b. 1820	522*b*
b. in a cellar	155*b*
b. in other's pain	441*a*
b. in the garret	74*a*
b. into the world alive	164*a*
b. of Christian race	452*b*
b. out of my due time	284*a*
b. to love you, sweet!	45*b*
b. to set it right!	331*b*
b. under one law	176*b*
Bourgeoisie is not b.	402*a*
but I was free b.	512*b*
day perish wherein I was b.	497*a*
else, wherefore b.?	427*b*
every moment one is b.	439*a*
he was b. most noble	291*a*
Horne was nobly b.	26*a*
house where I was b.	195*a*
how happy is he b. and taught	473*a*
if he had not been b.	508*a*
I knew not that they were b.	445*a*
in silent darkness b.	117*a*
I was b. about three	379*a*
I was b. an American	454*a*
I was b. in a cellar	104*b*
I was b. in the year 1632	118*a*
maggot must be b. i' . . cheese	144*a*
men are to be b. so	450*b*
men naturally were b. free	279*b*
my young babe were b.	530*b*
natural to die as to be b.	14*a*
'never was b.,' persisted Topsy	415*b*
no man is b. an angler	450*a*
one and one-sixteenth is b.	523*a*
people . . b. when the tide's . . in	122*b*
poet's made, as well as b.	216*a*
that thou wast b. with	342*a*
then surely I was b.	92*a*
thing that I was b. to do	117*a*
this night shall be b.	522*b*
time to be b.	499*a*
to the manner b.	331*a*
under that was I b.	358*a*
unto wh. she was not b.	432*b*
we cry, not to be b.	17*a*
when we are b. we cry	343*b*
whereof it is b.	352*b*
where that thou wast b.	531*b*
who are just b., being dead	311*b*
world he finds himself b. into	80*b*

Borne: b. on our shoulders 47*a*

b., see on my bosom	49*b*
sights of what is to be b.!	468*b*
wh. I have b. and yet must bear	399*a*

Borogoves: all mimsy were the b. 83*b*

Boroughs: eggs to rotten b. 254*b*

the bright b. 197*b*

Borrioboola-Gha 121*a*

Borrow: if we have to b. the money 451*b*

Sorrow, why dost b.	217*b*
the men who b.	239*a*
to b. . . 'tis the very worst world	38*a*
try to b. some	157*a*

Borrower: bettered by the b. 279*b*

b. of the night	348*b*
neither a b., nor a lender be	330*b*

Borrowers: yr. b. of books 239*a*

Borrowing: banqueting upon b. 520*b*

b. dulls the edge of husbandry	330*b*
b. only lingers . . it out	380*a*
he that goes a b.	157*a*
kind of b. as this	279*b*
who goeth a b.	446*a*

Bosom: angels into Abraham's b. 510*a*

beneath the b. of the sea	31*b*
bield shd. be my b.	62 . .

Bosom (*cont.*)

blue bared its eternal b. 220*b*
borne, see, on my b.! 49*b*
b. of her respectable family 58*b*
b. of his Father and his God 174*b*
b. of the lake 437*a*
b. of the urgent West 37*a*
cleanse the stuff'd b. 350*b*
flits across her b. young 146*b*
her b. went in 19*b*
his b. shd. heave 166*a*
his burning b. buttoned 193*b*
in Arthur's b. 381*b*
in yr. fragrant b. dies 79*b*
it in yr. b., wear 405*a*
lac'd from thy full b. 305*b*
my cell is set here in thy b. 441*a*
on thy b. tho' many a kiss 421*b*
shall men give into yr. b. 509*a*
slip into my b. 437*a*
son into his b. creeps 155*b*
sooty b. of such a thing 359*b*
such a heart in my b. 350*a*
swell, b., with thy fraught 362*a*
take fire in his b. 498*a*
that in my b. lies 438*a*
the heart out of the b. 198*b*
thorns that in her b. lodge 331*b*
to Thy B. fly 455*b*
to whose b. move 36*b*
unadorned b. of the deep 266*b*
wear thee in my b. 59*b*
what b. beats not 298*b*
white bird. .in his b. 292*b*
wife of thy B. 494*b*
Bosomed high in tufted trees 269*a*
Bosom-friend of the maturing sun 221*b*
Bosoms: come, within our b. shine 86*b*
   men's business and b. 14*a*
   quiet to quick bosoms is a hell 68*b*
   silk stockings and white b. 206*b*
   to hang and brush their b. 52*b*
Bossuet: excite the horror of B. 255*a*
Boston: B. man is the east wind 4*b*
   B.'s a hole 48*b*
   B. state-house is the hub 194*a*
   good old B. 34*a*
   pry that out of a B. man 194*a*
   solid man of B. 247*b*
   Thucydides at B. 449*b*
Bos'un: and a b. tight 163*a*
Boswell: B. is a very clubbable man 211*a*
   B. is the first of biographers 255*a*
Boswellism: christen B. 254*b*
Botanist: no, Sir, I am not a b. 207*a*
Botanize: peep and b. 468*b*
Botches in the work 348*b*
Both: b. perhaps or neither 457*a*
   so, between them b. 534*a*
   such revenges on you b. 342*b*
Botticelli isn't a wine 536*a*
Bottle: a b. of hay 357*a*
   a little for the b. 120*b*
   b. on the chimley-piece 124*a*
   crack it b. of fish-sauce 93*b*
   crack a b. with a friend 93*b*
   farthest b. labelled 'Ether' 46*a*
   large cold b. 150*b*
   like a b. in the smoke 489*a*
   like magic in a pint b. 123*a*
   nor a b. to give him 122*b*
   tears into thy b. 485*b*
   ten years in b. 20*a*
   the leather b. 526*a*
   thy dog, thy b. 301*b*
   we'll pass the b. round 459*a*
Bottled: b. lightning 125*a*
   b. wasps 110*b*
Bottles: new wine into old b. 506*a*
Bottom: bless thee, B.! 357*a*
   b. of my grief 366*a*
   b. of the monstrous world 270*a*
   can't touch de b. 156*a*
   reach the b. first 172*b*
   sit down on my b. 155*a*
   woman has a b. of good sense 210*b*
   wooed the slimy b. 384*b*
Bottoms: b. of my trousers 145*a*
   Dutch b. 78*b*
Bottomless: a b. Whig 211*a*
Bough: Loaf of Bread beneath the b. 152*b*

Bough (*cont.*)

reddens upon the topmost b. 311*b*
starreth now his b. 35*b*
that hangs on the b. 368*a*
touch not a single b.! 284*a*
when the b. bends 29*a*
Boughs: back on budding b. 37*b*
   blossoming b. of April 35*b*
   b. off many a tree 187*a*
   b. of Heaven and Ocean 396*a*
   bursting b. of May 37*a*
   hour when from the b. 73*b*
   incense hangs upon the b. 220*a*
   lowest b. and the brushwood 47*a*
   my soul into the b. does glide 261*a*
   oft between the b. is seen 39*b*
   on the pendent b. 336*a*
   shade of melancholy b. 326*b*
   those b. wh. shake 388*a*
   whose b. are bent 310*b*
Bought: b. golden opinions 347*a*
   knowledge is b. in the market 96*a*
Boulogne: old man of B. 527*a*
Bound: b. each to each 468*a*
   b. him a thousand years 519*b*
   b. in the spirit 512*b*
   b. of human thought 438*b*
   b. of the everlasting hills 493*b*
   Brutus will go b. to Rome 341*a*
   it was too small a b. 379*a*
   men were b. in their coats 504*a*
   prison to them that are b. 503*a*
   the b. of the waste 7*b*
   to another b. 176*b*
   young lambs b. 466*a*
Boundary of the march of a nation 292*b*
Bounding: the heart less b. 9*a*
Boundless: dark-heaving, b. 69*b*
   what we see is b. 395*a*
Bounds: b. of freakish youth 112*a*
   he passed the flaming b. 175*a*
   partitions do their b. divide 138*a*
   thou hast set them their b. 488*a*
Bounties: thy morning b. 109*b*
Bountiful: my blackbird b. 137*b*
   my Lady B. 150*a*
Bounty: for his b., there was no
   winter in it 325*a*
   goat is the b. of God 31*a*
   his former b. fed 139*a*
Bourbon: can B. or Nassau go higher? 305*b*
Bourg: murmur of their b. 428*b*
Bourgeois: . .is an epithet 197*a*
Bourgeoisie: British B. is not born 402*a*
Bourn (Bourne): b. of Time and Place 426*a*
   country from whose b. 333*a*
   I'll set a b. 322*a*
   to see beyond our b. 217*b*
   very b. of heaven 217*b*
Bout: many a winding b. 269*a*
Bovril prevents that sinking 522*b*
Bow: arrow from the Almighty's b. 30*b*
   as unto the b. the cord 30*b*
   b., b., ye lower middle classes! 163*b*
   b. themselves when he did sing 385*b*
   b. was made in England 135*a*
   drew b. at a venture 496*b*
   fascination in his very b. 71*b*
   he breaketh the b. 484*b*
   I b. myself in the house. .Rimmon 496*b*
   I had two strings to my b. 151*b*
   Lord of the unerring b. 69*a*
   my b. of burning gold 31*a*
   my saddle and my b. 531*a*
   set my b. in the cloud 492*b*
   shalt not b. down to them 480*a*
   starting aside like a broken b. 487*a*
   taught. .to draw the b. 72*a*
   what of the b.? 135*a*
   with my b. and arrow 528*a*
   wd. b. at her and bob 93*a*
Bowed: but first it b. 530*a*
   he b., he fell 495*a*
Bowels: b. of the harmless earth 377*a*
   b. of the land 385*a*
   have you no b., no tenderness 159*b*
   his b. of compassion 518*a*
   my b. were moved for him 500*b*
Bower: a b. quiet for us 217*b*
   bard in hall or b. 266*b*
   born in a b. 22*a*

Bower (*cont.*)

b. of wanton Shrewsbury 302*b*
flower perfumes the b. 320*a*
he sitteth in the Muses' b. 36*a*
into their inmost b. 274*b*
overflows her b. 398*a*
queen in a summer's b. 378*a*
smooth-swarded b. 435*a*
there's a b. of roses 282*a*
this Lime-tree B. 101*b*
thy b. is ever green 53*a*, 246*b*
to the b. they came 435*a*
twa sisters sat in a b. 528*b*
Bower-eaves: bow-shot from her b. 431*b*
Bowers: dear lovely b. 168*a*
   green and pleasant b. 30*b*
   he sat in breathless b. 311*b*
   my skiey b. 393*a*
   when canopied with b. 369*b*
Bowery: all that b. loneliness 427*a*
Bowl: atoms lurk within the b. 404*b*
   B. we call the Sky 153*b*
   bring the b. wh. you boast 320*a*
   crabs hiss in the b. 345*b*
   fill the flowing b. 522*b*
   golden b. be broken 500*a*
   he called for his b. 532*a*
   in a b. to sea went wise men 295*b*
   Love in a golden b. 29*b*
   the b. goes trim 295*b*
   trowle the b., the. .nut-brown b. 119*a*
   trowl the brown b. 319*b*
   went to sea in a b. 532*b*
Bowler: I am the b. 242*a*
   if the wild b. 242*b*
Bowling: b. of a ghost 442*b*
   poor Tom B. 121*a*
Bowls: bowler thinks he b. 242*a*
Bows: b. before him at the door 432*b*
   b. down to wood and stone 184*a*
   come with b. bent 420*a*
   harnessed and carrying b. 487*a*
   he b. and goes again 414*a*
   wood of English b. 135*a*
Bowsey: take a b. short leave 424*b*
Bow-shot from her bower 431*b*
Bowsprit got mixed with the rudder 86*a*
Bow-strings: hold, or cut b. 356*b*
Bow-windows: expense of putting b. 122*a*
Bow-wow: hark! b.! 367*a*
   his b. way 295*b*
   no time to say 'b.!' 192*b*
   the Big B. strain 320*b*
Bow-wows: demnition b. 125*a*
Box: alabaster b. of. .ointment 508*a*
   b. where sweets compacted lie 187*b*
   shut up the b. 440*a*
   twelve good men in a b. 40*b*
   worth a guinea a b. 528*b*
Boxes: he had forty-two b. 85*b*
Boy: a b. by him and me 176*a*
   a b. playing on the seashore 289*a*
   a b.'s will 247*b*
   altho' a poor blind b. 95*b*
   amazed even when a little b. 457*a*
   bit of a chit of a b. 75*a*
   blackbird, what a b. you are! 41*a*
   b. my greatness 325*a*
   b. stood on the burning deck 184*b*
   b. who was bravest 525*b*
   build schoolrooms for 'the b.' 106*a*
   carried by an orphan b. 316*b*
   Chatterton, the marvellous b. 470*a*
   close upon the growing b. 466*a*
   compound a b. half-French 383*b*
   every b. and every gal 164*a*
   give to yr. b., yr. Caesar 139*a*
   happy b., at Drury's 305*a*
   hearty, healthy b. 192*b*
   he is weak; both Man and B. 469*a*
   he left his pretty b. 176*a*
   horrid, wicked b. was he 192*b*
   how's my b.—my b. 130*b*
   imagination of a b. is healthy 217*a*
   it's b.; only b. 237*b*
   let the b. win his spurs 143*b*
   like any other b. 155*a*
   little b. blue 535*a*
   little tiny b. 372*a*
   little vulgar B 19*b*
   Love is a b. 65*b*

Boy (*cont.*)
my beamish b.! — 84a
my b. John, he that went to sea — 130b
my b.'s my b. to me — 130b
news of my b. Jack? — 232b
none for the little b. — 534b
nor Man nor B...can..abolish — 466b
office b. to an Attorney's firm — 166a
our Little B. Blue — 151a
purblind, wayward b. — 344b
smiling the b. fell dead — 47b
soaring human b.! — 121b
speak roughly to yr. little b. — 82b
than when I was a b. — 195a
the b. be virtuous still — 113a
the b.—oh! where was he? — 184b
the Minstrel B. — 281b
there's a girl there's a b. — 10b
the thanks of a b. — 24b
to be b. eternal — 372b
what a good b. am I! — 532a
what's yr. b.'s name — 130b
when I was a b. — 475b
when I was a little b. — 534b
when the b. knows this — 124b
where is my b. tonight? — 525b
where's the little b. — 535b
who wd. not be a b.? — 68a
yet a b. I sought for ghosts — 394b
you are a human b. — 121a
Boyhood: if even I were as in my b. — 396b
tears, of b.'s years — 282b
Boyish: pleasures of my b. days — 472a
Boys: as flies to wanton b. — 343b
a sober man, among his b. — 430a
b. and girls are level — 324b
b., in joyful chorus — 117a
b. of the Old Brigade — 453b
b...were moving jewels — 445a
Christian b. I can scarcely..make — 10b
claret is the liquor for b. — 210a
girls and b. come out to play — 534b
how rude are the b. — 453a
like little wanton b. — 386a
mealy b., and beef-faced b. — 125b
men that were b. when I was a boy — 27a
only know two sorts of b. — 125b
pretty, dimpled b. — 323a
the way that b. begin — 440b
three merry b. are we — 23a
till the b. come home — 156a
we are the b. — 171a
what are little b. made of — 534b
what the b. get at one end — 208b
young b. in Umbro — 253a
Bozrah: garments from B. — 503b
Bracelet of bright hair — 133b
Bracelets: make b. to adorn the wife — 187a
Braces: Damn b. Bless relaxes — 31a
Brach: b. or lym — 343a
the b. may stand by the fire — 342a
Bracken: hide me by the b. bush — 530b
lift him from the b. — 12a
Bradford: there goes John B. — 34b
Bradshaw: vocabulary of 'B.' — 136a
Brae: waly, doun the b. — 530a
Braes: run about the b. — 59a
ye banks and b. — 63b
Brag: beauty is nature's b. — 267b
left this vault to b. of — 348a
one went to b., th'other to pray — 115a
Brahma: Great B. from his..heaven — 217b
Brahmin: hymn the B. sings — 146a
B. strikes the hour — 406a
Braids: twisted b. of lilies — 268a
Brain: bracing b. and sinew — 226a
b. of this foolish..clay — 379b
bullets of the b. — 358b
close corner of my b. — 198a
draughts intoxicate the b. — 300a
feed my b. with better things — 91b
fibre from the b. does tear — 29a
from b. unto b. of..youths — 96a
gladness that thy b. must know — 398b
gleaned my teeming b. — 221a
his b., wh. is as dry as..biscuit — 326a
I feared it might injure the b. — 82b
in my b. I sing it — 49b
in what furnace was thy b. — 32a
learning, that cobweb of the b. — 65b
left the b. that won't believe — 29a

Brain (*cont.*)
let my b. lie also — 49a
little b. attic stocked — 135b
more b., O Lord — 264a
not alone immured in the b. — 345a
not old, whose visionary b. — 194a
out of the carver's b. — 100a
petrifactions of a plodding b. — 72a
rightly shd. possess a poet's b. — 137a
sherris..ascends me into the b. — 380b
the b. to think again — 39a
the heat-oppressèd b. — 347b
then leave the naked b. — 217b
though the dull b. perplexes — 220a
thought..secreted by the b. — 80a
[tobacco] harmful to the b. — 204a
troubles of the b. — 350b
unquiet heart and b. — 429b
warder of the b. — 347b
weeds and tares of mine own b. — 41b
what hand and b. went..paired? — 48a
work like madness in the b. — 100a
Brainless as chimpanzees — 76a
Brains: blow out yr b. — 237a
blows out his b. upon the flute — 52a
b. taken out and buttered — 356a
b. they punched in — 454a
cudgel thy b. no more — 336a
dashed the b. out — 347a
exercises of his b. — 164a
fumbles for his b. — 111a
I mix them with my b. — 290b
maggots in yr. b. — 23b
no other b. to work with — 390b
to steal away their b. — 361b
unhappy b. for drinking — 361a
when the b. were out — 349a
Brainsickly: think so b. of things — 348a
Brake: he b. that gallant ship — 529a
He took the Bread and b. it — 145b
syne it b. — 530a
withering b. grown o'er — 114a
Brambles pale with mist — 9a
Branch: B. shall grow out of his roots — 501b
cut is the b. — 259a
lops the mouldered b. — 427a
snow on the bare b. — 101a
Branched: in my b. velvet gown — 371a
Branches: fowls..lodge in the b. — 507a
fowls..sing among the b. — 488a
Nightingale that in the b. sang — 154a
thro' b. and briars — 421b
thy b. ne'er remember — 221b
Branchy between towers — 197a
Brand: by each gun the lighted b. — 76b
wav'd over by that flaming b. — 277a
Brandy: b. for the Parson — 234a
cold b. and water — 240b
Grant's Morella Cherry B. — 522a
hero must drink b. — 210a
sipped b. and water gayly — 103b
some are fou o' b. — 61a
Bransome Hall — 316b
Brass: all that was ever writ in b. — 215b
auld b. will buy me a new pan — 63a
evil manners live in b. — 386a
feet like unto fine b. — 518b
I am become as sounding b. — 514b
its horns are tipped with b. — 143b
more enduring than b. — 546b
nor walls of beaten b. — 338a
putty, b., an' paint — 233b
savours of poisonous b. — 218a
since b., nor stone — 388a
the b. will crash — 164a
this flesh..were b. impregnable — 375b
wit as well in b. — 215b
Brave: a b. man struggling — 298b
binds the b. of all the earth — 287b
b. days of old — 253a
b. Kempenfelt is gone — 111a
b. man with a sword! — 459a
b. to be a King — 259a
b. to forfeit ease — 157a
b. translunary things — 137a
clime of the unforgotten b.! — 72b
delirium of the b. — 474b
how sleep the b. — 103a
I'm very b. generally — 84b
I was clean and b. — 199a
men might call me b. — 235b

Brave (*cont.*)
none but the b. deserves — 138b
not too late tomorrow to be b. — 4b
O b. new world — 368a
old Meg was b. — 219a
on, ye b., who rush to glory — 77a
over the unreturning b. — 68b
that b. vibration — 190b
the b.! that are no more — 111a
the home of the b.! — 224b
then it is the b. man chooses — 251a
toll for the b. — 111a
what's b., what's noble — 324b
Braved: whose flag has b. — 77b
Braver: I have done one b. thing — 134a
yet a b. thence doth spring — 134a
Bravery: all her b. on — 277b
natural b. of yr. isle — 328b
Bravest: boy who was b. of all — 525b
b. of all in Frederick town — 459a
Brawl: ill disposed in b. ridiculous — 382b
kindly silence when they b. — 425b
Brawling of a sparrow in the eaves — 476a
Brawls: b. disturb the street — 452b
Lord-Keeper led the b. — 175a
Bray: b. a fool — 498b
Vicar of B., sir! — 524a
Brazil: B.? He twirled a button — 127b
I've never reached B. — 230b
Breach: imminent deadly b. — 360a
more honoured in the b. — 331a
not yet a b., but an expansion — 134a
once more unto the b. — 382a
Breaches: of b., ambuscadoes — 364b
Bread: 'a loaf of b.,' the Walrus said — 84b
bit of butter to my b.! — 266b
bitter b. of banishment — 375a
b., and the..circus — 549b
b. and work for all — 29a
b. eaten in secret — 498a
b. enough and to spare — 509b
b. I dip in the river — 414a
b. of tears — 487a
b. to strengthen man's heart — 488a
broken it up for yr. daily b. — 424a
broth without any b. — 533b
cast thy b. upon the waters — 499b
corn that makes the holy b. — 262a
crammed with distressful b. — 383a
cutting b. and butter — 440b
eat b. to the full — 494a
eat thy b. with joy — 499b
feed him with b. of affliction — 496b
fire, and unleavened b. — 493b
going to fetch you yr. b. — 227b
grossly, full of b. — 334b
half-pennyworth of b. — 378a
heavy..as that with b. — 442b
he took the B. and brake it — 145b
his seed begging their b. — 484a
honest b. is very well — 293a
how spoil'd the b. — 293a
if his son ask b. — 505b
I have eaten yr. b. and salt — 230a
in the sweat..shalt thou eat b. — 492b
known of them in breaking of b. — 510a
Loaf of B. beneath the bough — 152b
looked to government for b. — 57b
man doth not live by b. only — 494b
man shall not live by b. alone — 505a
money for that wh. is not b. — 503a
my little loaf of b. — 190b
never ate his b. in sorrow — 82a
no b., then bring me some toast — 535a
quarrel with my b. and butter — 418b
ravens brought him b. — 496a
Royal slice of b. — 266b
smell of b. and butter — 67b
smote itself into the b. — 428a
some gave them white b. — 532b
taste of another's b. — 567a
that b. shd. be so dear — 196b
the b. that you eat — 227b
their learning is like b. — 208b
the whole stay of b. — 501a
this day our daily b. — 505b
this the B. — 31b
unleavened b. of sincerity — 514a
Breadth: length and b. enough — 530b
Break: be not broken, b. — 109b
b., b., b., on thy cold grey stones — 425b

Break (cont.)
b. forth into joy   502b
b. it to our hope   351a
b. off this last lamenting kiss   132b
b. their bonds asunder   481b
but b., my heart   330a
grief..bids it b.   350a
take and b. us   185a
thou shalt b. the ships   485a
where it will b. at last   394b
Breakers: wantoned with thy b.   69b
Breakest: thou b. my heart   187b
Breakfast: arg'ed the thing at b.   80a
b., dinner, lunch, and tea   26a
b. first, business next   440a
b. with what appetite you have   385b
for her own b. she'll project   476b
hope is a good b.   13b
impossible things before b.   84b
kills..Scots at a b.   377a
Michael Angelo for b.   446b
shall we our b. take?   529b
wholesome, hungry b.   450b
Breaking: by b. of windows   283a
sleep that knows not b.   316b
take pleasure in b.   526b
working-class..b. what it likes   9b
Breaking-up: a sorry b.   195b
red ruin, and the b. of laws   427b
Breaks: it b. in our bosom   394a
Breast: beats in every human b.   5a
bird with the scarlet b.   470a
boiling bloody b.   357b
bold spirit in a loyal b.   374b
bolt..shot back..in our b.   5a
b. that beauty cannot tame   18a
b. that gives the rose   264a
b. will ne'er be lonely   120a
bright b., shortening into sighs   420b
broad b., full eye   386b
depth of her glowing b.   398a
ease my b. of melodies   218a
friendly and comforting b.   185a
head upon this b.!   247a
heart..has left my b.   73a
here beat his b.   98a
his bed amid my tender b.   176a
his own clear b.   267a
Holy Ghost..with warm b.   197b
hope..eternal in the human b.   300b
leaned her b. against a thorn   20b
lie lightly on thy b.   299b
life-drop of his bleeding b.   72b
may toss him to My b.   188a
'neath the b. of Earth   293b
nunnery of thy chaste b.   250a
on her white b. a sparkling cross   302b
on her left b. a mole   328b
on his b. a bloody cross   408b
on some fond b.   174b
or knock the b.   278a
panic's in thy b.   62a
presagers of my speaking b.   387a
sail upon her patient b.   368b
see my baby at my b.   325b
sooth a savage B.   104b
soul wears out the b.   74a
the man on its b.   6a
thou tamer of the human b.   173b
through breastplate and thro' b.   254a
told but to her mutual b.   77b
to rest..here in my b.!   289a
trembles in the B.   280a
what his b. forges   328a
when b. to b. we clung   312a
whether my Sappho's b.   189b
with her b. against a thorn   196a
wi' ribbons on her b.   530a
with sweetness fills the b.   86b
Breastful of milk   311a
Breast-high amid the corn   195b
Breastplate: thro' b. and thro'
breast   254a
what stronger b.   384a
Breasts: Abydos of her b.   132b
all night betwixt my b.   500a
b. more soft than a dove's   423b
b. of the nymphs in the brake   423b
come to her woman's b.   346b
her b. are dun   389a
hollow of her b. a tomb   421a

Breasts (cont.)
prodigious b.   421a
she hath no b.   501a
thy b. are like two young roes   500b
two b. of heavenly sheen   313a
Breath: a b. can make them   168a
a b. thou art   351b
allowing him a b.   375b
although thy b. be rude   326b
boldest held his b.   76b
borne away with every b.!   73b
borne my b. away!   195a
breathes with human b.   438b
breathing thoughtful b.   470b
b. is in his nostrils   501a
b. of man goeth forth   490b
b. of them hot in thy hair   421b
b. of this corporal frame   472a
b. of worldly men   375a
b., smiles, tears, of all my life   44a
by every azure b.   394b
clothed with his b.   429a
Cobham! to the latest b.   302a
down and out of b.   379a
draw his last b. thro' a pipe   239b
draw thy b. in pain   337a
dulcet and harmonious b.   356b
everything that hath b.   490b
fly away, b.   371a
gives the hautboys b.   139a
giv'st to forms and images a b.   465b
grey from Thy b.   423b
having lost her b.   323a
heaven's b. smells wooingly   347a
her tender-taken b.   220b
himself the heaven's b.   344b
Hope's perpetual b.   471b
if her b. were as terrible   358a
it fluttered and failed for b.   7b
it is by no b...that salvation   51b
last gasp of Love's latest b.   137b
lightly draws its b.   472b
little b. of men   157a
love that endures for a b.   420b
love the b. between them   397b
mystery of b.   263b
nought..lost but b.   40a
O balmy b.   363b
once their b. drew in   98b
princes..but the b. of kings   59b
prison of afflicted b.   374a
soft as the b. of even   11a
some of us are out of b.   84b
so the Word had b.   430a
such is the b. of kings   374b
suck my last b.   299b
suspiration of forced b.   330a
sweetness of man's b.   204a
take into the air my quiet b.   220a
Thou art Being and B.   38b
thou to b. at all   344a
thy b. is Africk's spicy gale   161a
tremble with tenderer b.   423b
with bated b.   353a
with low last b.   312b
Breathe: as tho' to b. were life   438b
b. a word about yr. loss   230a
b. its pure serene   220b
b. not his name   281a
b., shine, and seek to mend   133a
b. thro' silver   49a
if such there b.   317a
in the taking of it b.   227b
nothing to b. but air   225a
summer's morn to b.   276a
thought I cd. not b.   428a
thou thereon didst only b.   216b
Breathed in his nostrils   492a
Breather: chide no b. in the world   327a
Breathers of an ampler day   431a
Breathes: b. there the man, with
soul   317a
b. upon a bank of violets   369b
enjoys the air it b.   471a
Breathing: b. of the common wind   472b
b. out threatenings   512a
b. time of day   337a
health, and quiet b.   217b
in the sound his b. kept   397a
Breathings: low b. coming after me   469a
Breathless: b. we flung us   39b

Breathless (cont.)
b. with adoration   467a
Breaths with sweetmeats tainted   364b
Bred: because they so were b.   140b
b. en bawn in a brier-patch!   181b
b. me long ago   199b
she is not b. so dull   354a
where is fancy b.   354a
Brede: with b. ethereal wove   103a
Bredon: bells they sound in B.   199a
summertime on B.   199a
Bree: a little abune her b.   528b
Breeches: a hole in't. So have yr.
b.   78b
his b. cost him but a crown   361a
his b. were blue   100b, 406b
his 'oss then cleanin' his b.   416b
what leg..into your b. first   207b
Breed: b. of barren metal   353a
b. of their horses and dogs   295b
b. that take their pleasures   228b
fear'd by their b.   375a
happy b. of men   375a
war but endless war still b.   278b
where they most b. and haunt   347a
will never b. the same   220b
Breeding: true b. of a gentleman   70b
write..to show yr. b.   401a
Breeds: lesser b. without the Law   233b
Breeks aff a wild Highlandman   319a
Breeze: a b. of morning moves   434a
chilly autumn b.   218b
cooling western b.   300a
dancing in the b.   467a
O bounding b.   96b
the battle and the b.   77b
the b. is on the sea   320a
the b. of song   430b
to be come-at by the b.   468a
tyranny in every tainted b.   55b
verse, a b. mid blossoms   102a
volleying rain and tossing b.   8b
Breezes: b. and the sunshine   76a
by the midnight b. strewn   393a
feel no other b.   221a
heaven is with the b. blown   220a
little b. dusk and shiver   431b
spicy b. blow..o'er Ceylon's isle   184a
sunset b. shiver   287b
Breezy, Sneezy   158a
Breffny: waves of B.   172a
Bremen: a foreigner of B.   118a
Brent: yr. bonny brow was b.   61a
Brentford: have you ever seen B.?   211a
two kings of B.   111b
Brer Fox   181b
Brer Tarrypin   181b
Bret-ful of pardoun   89a
Brethren: accursed from Christ for
my b.   513b
b., to dwell together in unity!   490a
dearly beloved b.   478a
for my b. and companions' sakes   489b
for we be b.   492b
great Twin B.   254a
his tuneful b. all were dead   316b
least of these my b.   508a
my mother and my b.!   506b
perils among false b.   515a
think they of their b. more?   287a
Brevity: b. is the soul of wit   332a
its body b.   100b, 527b
Brewer: Bill B., Jan Stewer   531b
not a b.'s servant   29a
Brewers: bakers and b.   242b
Brewery: take me to a b.   523b
Briar (brier): from off this b. pluck a
..rose   383b
grows a bonny b. bush   193a
instead of the b...myrtle tree   503a
the b.'s in bud   261b
thorough bush, thorough b.   356b
Briars: how full of b. is this..world   325b
Bribes: and b. about   26a
contaminate our fingers with..b.   340b
Brick: b. in his pocket   417b
'eave 'arf a b. at him   535a
found it b. and left it marble   538a
Bridal: b.-favours..stowed away   439b
b. of the earth and sky   187b
come to the b.-chamber, Death   178a

Bridal (*cont.*)
light the b. lamp — 275*b*

Bride: as a b. adorned for her husband — 519*b*
a *mourning* b. — 141*a*
blooming Eastern b. — 138*b*
bridegroom with his b. — 438*b*
b. hath paced into the hall — 98*a*
b. of a ducal coronet — 124*b*
b. of quietness — 219*b*
b., on whom the sun doth shine — 188*b*
bridesmaid makes a happy b. — 425*b*
busk ye, my bonny bonny b. — 178*b*
but a barren b. — 302*a*
dead maiden to be his b. — 319*a*
encounter darkness as a b. — 352*a*
his b. and his darling — 526*a*
I drew my b., beneath the moon — 293*a*
jealousy to the b. — 21*b*
my b. and my darling — 526*a*
my glittering b. — 464*a*
passionless b. — 433*a*
ready to be thy b. — 531*b*
Spirit and the b. say, Come — 520*b*
the b. at the altar — 318*b*
turns him to the b. — 198*b*
virgin, yet a b. — 79*b*
who will cheer my bonny b. — 77*a*

Bride-bed: thy b. to have deck'd — 336*b*
Bridechamber: children of the b. — 506*a*
Bridegroom: a b. in my death — 324*b*
as the b. is with them — 506*a*
because of the b.'s voice — 510*b*
Bellona's b. — 346*a*
b. all night through — 198*a*
b. with his bride — 438*b*
cometh forth as a b. — 482*b*
fresh as a b. — 376*b*
like a b. from his room — 12*b*

Bridegrooms: I sing of..b. — 188*b*
rave, as do many b. — 237*b*
Brides: 'B. of Enderby' — 203*a*
I sing of..b. — 188*b*
Bridesmaid: happy b. makes a happy bride — 425*b*

Bridge: b. at midnight — 246*b*
by b. and ford — 438*a*
by the rude b. — 146*b*
forgive you B. at dawn — 91*b*
golden b. is for a flying enemy — 70*a*
Horatius kept the b. — 253*b*
keep the b. with me — 253*a*
London B. is broken down — 533*a*
on the B. of Sighs — 69*a*
Peschiera, when thy b. I crost — 96*b*
praise the b. that carried you — 103*b*
what need the b. much broader — 358*a*
Women and Champagne and B. — 26*b*
Bridle: gave his b.-reins a shake — 61*a*, 319*a*
held with bit and b. — 483*b*
stranger hath thy b.-rein — 289*b*
took him by the b.-ring — 531*b*
Bridles: heard the b. ring — 528*b*
Bridleth not his tongue — 517*b*
Brief: b. life is here our portion — 286*a*
b. sorrow, short-lived care — 286*a*
I am struggling to be b. — 541*b*
or be less b. — 452*a*
'tis b., my lord — 334*a*
Brier-patch: bawn in a b. — 181*b*
Brig o' Dread — 529*a*
Brigade: boys of the old B. — 453*b*
cd. thy B. with cold cascade — 164*a*
forward the Light B. — 426*a*
Bright: all b. and glittering — 472*b*
all calm, as it was b. — 448*b*
all things b. and beautiful — 3*a*
behold the b. original appear — 160*a*
best of dark and b. — 74*a*
b. and fierce and fickle — 436*a*
b., b. as day — 476*b*
b. in fruitful valleys — 37*a*
b. is the ring of words — 414*b*
b. October was come — 96*a*
b. the vision that delighted — 258*a*
b. with many an angel — 286*a*
Channel's as b. as a ball-room — 227*b*
creature not too b. or good — 470*b*
dark with excessive b. — 273*b*
how b. these glorious spirits — 453*b*
lady named B. — 527*a*

Bright (*cont.*)
look, the land is b. — 96*b*
more b. and good — 394*a*
myriads though b. — 271*a*
nought so b. may live — 394*a*
rises warm and b. — 3*a*
so quick b. things — 356*a*
stars! so eloquently b. — 280*a*
the path before him always b. — 465*a*
Brighten at the blaze — 170*a*
Brightening: prospects b. to the last — 168*a*
Brighter: b...than flaming Jupiter — 258*b*
b. than is the silver Rhodope — 259*a*
look b. when we come — 394*b*
Brightest: best and b., come away! — 394*b*
b. and best of the sons — 184*a*
tho' the b. fell — 350*a*
Bright-eyed: b. Fancy — 175*a*
the b. Mariner — 98*a*
Brightly dawns our wedding day — 164*b*
Brightness: all her original b. — 272*a*
amazing b., purity — 291*b*
attired with sudden b. — 465*b*
between his Darkness and his B. — 74*b*
b. falls from the air — 285*b*
b. of his glory — 517*a*
b. of the day — 3*b*
innocent b. — 467*a*
with transcendent b. — 271*a*
Brighton: Dr. B. — 523*a*
Brignall banks are wild and fair — 319*a*
Brilliant..with thousand gems — 37*b*
Brillig: 'twas b. — 83*b*
Brim: sparkles near the b. — 68*a*
winking at the b. — 219*b*
Brimstone: from his b. bed .. the Devil is gone — 100*b*, 406*a*
Brine: eye-offending b. — 369*b*
tunnies steeped in b. — 8*b*
Bring: b. another back to me — 529*b*
b. me flesh and b. me wine — 286*b*
b. me up by jerks — 123*b*
b. the good old bugle, boys — 473*b*
my kisses b. again — 352*a*
nothing in my hand I b. — 445*a*
the happiness 'twill b. — 76*a*
to her let us garlands b. — 372*b*
Bringer: b. of new things — 438*b*
some b. of that joy — 357*b*
yet the first b. of..news — 379*b*
Brings: eye sees in it what the eye b. — 80*b*
Brink: at the b. of ruin — 217*a*
dreadful outer b. — 43*b*
shivering on the b. — 453*b*
Bristle: his hair did b. upon his head — 317*a*
Bristol: sailors of B. city — 440*b*
Britain: ambassador from B.'s crown — 136*b*
B. a fit country for heroes — 246*a*
B., cd. you ever boast three poets — 419*b*
B. first, at Heaven's Command — 443*a*
B. is a world by itself — 328*b*
B. set the world ablaze — 164*a*
Graces..not..natives of Great B. — 91*a*
hath B. all the sun — 328*b*
I've lost B. — 234*a*
they made B. India — 385*b*
Britannia: B. needs no bulwark — 78*a*
B. rules the waves — 77*a*
Oh B., the pride of the ocean — 389*b*
rule, B. — 443*a*
singing Rule, B. — 525*a*
two ideas..Beer and B. — 404*b*
British: art thou not of B. blood? — 427*a*
B. and Armoric Knights — 271*b*
B. Bourgeoisie is not born — 402*a*
B. Fleet a-riding — 440*b*
B. public in one of its..fits — 255*a*
B. Public, ye who like me not — 51*a*
B. soldier can stand..anything — 390*a*
B. warrior queen — 107*a*
broke a B. square — 229*a*
dirty B. coaster — 261*b*
fair play of the B. criminal — 135*b*
Flood of B. freedom — 467*a*
for the B. Grenadiers — 526*a*
grandmother's review—the B. — 70*b*
ground wh. B. shepherds tread — 464*a*
no countries less known by..B. — 34*a*
our ships were B. oak — 10*b*
piece of B. manhood — 80*b*
Regiment o' B. Infantree — 229*a*

British (*cont.*)
selfsame B. Islands — 34*a*
smell the blood of a B. man — 343*a*
stony B. stare — 433*b*
British Museum: I keep my **books** at the B. — 66*b*
Briton: as only a free-born B. — 440*a*
roughly set his B. — 435*a*
where the B. dwells..estranged — 556*b*
Britons: B. never..shall be married — 525*b*
B. never will be slaves — 443*a*
B., strike home — 447*b*
while B. shall be true — 201*b*
Brittle: b. is foredoomed — 264*b*
yr. bones are very b. — 414*a*
Broached: he bravely b. his..breast — 357*b*
Broad: b. as it hath breadth — 323*b*
b. as ten thousand beeves — 264*a*
b.-based upon her people's will — 437*a*
his pranks have been too b. — 334*b*
make b. their phylacteries — 507*b*
she is the B., I am the High — 528*b*
Broadcloth without — 109*a*
Broad-shouldered..Englishman — 437*a*
Broadsword of Locheill! — 12*a*
Broil: feats of b. and battle — 360*a*
Broke: pardon all oaths..b. to me — 376*a*
pride at length b. under me — 386*a*
Broken (broke): be not b., break — 109*b*
I am b. by their passing feet — 474*a*
laws were made to be b. — 289*b*
neck that's once b. — 320*a*
nor a b. thing mend — 27*a*
Pickwick walked among..b. men — 93*b*
soul had b. and thrown away! — 248*a*
the golden bowl b. — 500*a*
when my grave is b. up again — 133*b*
whilst we speak is it not b. — 392*a*
Broken-hearted: bind up the b. — 503*a*
half b. — 74*b*
we had ne'er been b. — 59*a*
we were both b. — 422*b*
Broker: an honest b. — 567*b*
Bromide: are you a b.? — 54*b*
Bronze: he who blows thro' b. — 49*a*
Broo': eels boiled in b. — 529*b*
Brooches: I will make you b. — 414*a*
Brood: fond of no second b. — 328*b*
his b. about thy knee — 436*b*
thy b. is flown — 436*b*
Brooding o'er the gloom — 263*b*
Brook: as doth an inland b. — 355*b*
a willow grows aslant a b. — 336*a*
a willowy b., that turns a mill — 310*a*
b. Cherith — 496*a*
chose a pebble from the b. — 109*b*
fell in the weeping b. — 336*a*
fish say, in the Eternal B. — 39*b*
he drank of the b. — 496*a*
I cd. not hear the b. flow — 198*b*
noise like of a hidden b. — 99*b*
pore upon the b. that babbles by — 174*b*
salad from the b. — 112*b*
stones out of the b. — 495*b*
where the b. and river meet — 247*b*
Brookland: far in a western b. — 199*b*
Brooks: books in the running b. — 325*b*
b. of Eden mazily murmuring — 427*a*
B. of Sheffield — 121*b*
golden sands and crystal b. — 132*a*
I sing of b. — 188*b*
murmurs near the running b. — 469*a*
shallow b. and rivers wide — 269*a*
shallow b. murmur most — 401*b*
what sedged b. — 8*b*
Brookside: I wander'd by the b. — 198*b*
Broom: bright blows the b. — 414*b*
I am sent with b. before — 357*b*
pods went pop on the b. — 117*b*
Broomstick: surely man is a b.! — 418*a*
Broomsticks: their b. and their tears — 474*b*
Broth: she gave them some b. — 533*b*
Brothel: in the b. or on the scaffold — 412*a*
scene..laid in a b. — 239*b*
Brothels: b. with bricks of Religion — 31*a*
keep thy foot out of B. — 343*a*
Brother: been sworn b. to him — 380*b*
better..have him than his b. — 261*a*
b. clasps the hand of b. — 261*b*
B., Englishman and Friend! — 469*b*
b. John, the evil one — 29*b*

Brother (cont.)

B. of the Angle | 450a
b. of the clay | 77b
b., on this that was the veil | 420b
b. should not war with b. | 109b
b., thy tail hangs down | 234a
b. whom he hath seen | 518a
dawn is my b. | 26b
elder b. ev'n to shade | 309b
fast has b. followed b. | 465b
fold to thy heart thy b. | 458b
forlorn and shipwrecked b. | 248a
furies of my b. | 254a
'gently, B., gently, pray' | 153b
grew so like my b. | 244b
had it been his b. | 523b
hand of every man's b. | 492b
He standeth, spouse and b. | 441a
he's yr. b. still | 420a
I am sworn b., sweet | 376a
it disdained its b. | 395b
kill a king..marry with his b. | 335a
life is very sweet, b. | 34a
little brown b. | 287a
marriage with his b.'s wife | 385b
more close than a b. | 235a
my b., good morning | 26b
my b., hail, and farewell | 540a
my b. he is in Elysium | 369b
my b. Jonathan | 495b
my b.'s keeper | 492b
my father's b., but no more like | 330a
no author ever spar'd a b. | 160b
no b. near the throne | 303a
O b. man! | 458b
Oh! call my b. back | 184b
O my poor b. | 369b
seeth his b. have need | 518a
sheds his blood..shall be my b. | 383a
shot mine arrow..and hurt my b. | 337a
silent soul, my b. | 421a
sticketh closer than a b. | 498b
still to my b. turns | 169b
sun, moon, and stars, b. | 34a
Tam lo'ed him like a vera b. | 62b
that thou wert as my b. | 500b
that wh. went before the b. | 468b
the king my b.'s wreck | 144b
there's night and day, b. | 34a
thy b. came with subtilty | 493a
true b. of a company | 476b
unto a tyrant b. | 325b
voice of thy b.'s blood | 492b
weak b. is the worst of mankind | 413a
where is my b. gone? | 184b
where my b. set the laburnum | 195a
where wert thou, b., those..days? | 430a
who also am yr. b. | 518a
wind on the heath, b. | 34a
Brotherhood: a b. in song | 217b
b. of venerable trees | 463b
crown thy good with b. | 22a
dearer yet the b. | 287b
love the b. Fear God | 517b
Brotherly: let b. love continue | 517a
Brothers: all the b. too | 371a
all the B. were Valiant | 288a
b. be for a' that | 60b
b., lift yr. voices | 20a
forty thousand b. | 236b
more than my b. are to me | 429b
Romans were like b. | 253a
two b. and their murdered man | 218b
we band of b. | 383a
we were b. all | 469b
ye are b.! ye are men! | 76b
Brougham: Mr. B.'s speeches | 183b
Brought: b. to you daily by .. Steamers | 227b
sea wh. b. us hither | 466b
they are b. down and fallen | 482b
we b. nothing into this world | 516b
Brought'st Thy sweets along | 187a
Brow: beautiful bold b. | 435b
b.-bound with burning gold | 426b
b. with homely biggen bound | 381a
but some sober b. will bless it | 354a
Consul's b. was sad | 253a
crystal of his b. | 251b
dangerous b. by night | 338b
his seal was on thy b. | 184b

Brow (cont.)

hollow eye and wrinkled b. | 355a
in that victorious b. | 7b
on that cheek, and o'er that b. | 74a
on thine azure b. | 69b
rugged b. of careful Policy | 409b
shine upon my b. to-day | 308b
southward-facing b. | 8a
that great b. | 45a
the wrinkle deeper on the b. | 68a
weariness not on yr. b. | 7b
whether on Ida's shady b. | 31b
winters shall besiege thy b. | 387a
yr. bonny b. was brent | 61a
Brown: all the trees are b. | 226a
Aryan b. | 233a
b. as a berry | 160b
in homely russet b. | 469a
learn from the Yellow and B. | 230b
little b. brother | 287a
Long John B. | 31a
tinged her cheek with b. | 316a
you have baked me too b. | 83b
Browne: ape to..Sir Thomas B. | 412b
Browning: B.! Since Chaucer was alive | 241a
from B. some 'Pomegranate' | 43b
leave to Robert B. beggars | 226a
Meredith is a prose B. | 460a
Robert B., you writer of plays | 48a
Wordsworth, Tennyson, and B. | 17b
Brownist as a politician | 371b
Brows: bliss in our b. | 322b
b. of dauntless courage | 272a
gathering her b. like..storm | 62b
handkerchief about yr. b. | 374a
lay her burning b. | 442b
purple brows of Olivet | 430a
seen in either of our b. | 137b
their b. with roses..bound | 138b
yr. b. upon yr. b. | 350a
Browsing and sluicing | 573b
Bruce has aften led | 62b
Bruise: it shall b. thy head | 492b
parmaceti for an inward b. | 377a
Bruises: one mask of b. both blue | 124b
Bruised: be b. in a new place | 203b
b. for our iniquities | 503a
b. reed shall he not break | 502b
Bruising of the hapless head | 452b
Bruit: comes on at hand the b. | 442a
Brunck: professor, B. | 304b
Brunswick: B.'s fated chieftain | 68b
Hamelin Town's in B. | 50a
Brush: dip his b. in dyes of heaven | 318b
gi'e them a b. | 193b
Brushers: critics are like b. | 13b
Brushes: a' b. his hat a mornings | 358b
b. of comets' hair | 236b
Brushing with hasty steps the dews | 174b
Brute: Et tu, B.! | 339a, 548b
Brute: b. I might have been | 50b
cross-grained b. | 171a
feed the b.! | 535b
I never saw a b. I hated so | 45b
lord of the fowl and the b. | 113a
the Lord let the house of a b. | 426a
they are neither b. nor human | 298a
whatever b. and blackguard | 199b
you intoxified b.! | 199b
Brutes: as we to the b., poets..to us | 264b
b. never meet in bloody fray | 169a
had made b. men, and men divine | 293a
horn where other b. have none | 26a
simple race of b. | 429a
we had been b. without you | 291b
Brutish: life of man..b., and short | 191b
Brutus: B. and Cato might discharge | 141b
B., I do observe you now | 337b
B. is an honourable man | 339b, 340a
B. makes mine greater | 341a
B. says he was ambitious | 340a
B...was Caesar's angel | 340a
B. will go bound to Rome | 341a
'B.' will start a spirit | 337b
B. with himself at war | 337b
but were I B., and B. Antony | 340a
fault, dear B., is not in our stars | 337b
he will be found like B. | 341b
I am no orator as B. is | 340a

Brutus (cont.)

the noble B. hath told you | 339b
what! is B. sick | 338b
when..B. grows so covetous | 341a
you wrong me, B. | 340b
Bubble: b. reputation | 326b
b. winked at me, and said | 188b
fame? an empty b. | 172b
honour but an empty b. | 139a
life is mostly froth and bubble | 171b
like the b. on the fountain | 316b
much like unto a b. | 451b
now a b. burst, and now a world | 300b
the world's a b. | 17a
Bubbles: borne, like thy b. | 69b
the earth hath b. | 346a
with beaded b...at the brim | 219b
Bubukles: face is all b. | 382a
Buccleuch: kinsmen to the bold B. | 316b
Buck: derned thing 'ed get up and b. | 182a
Bucket: that b. down | 376a
Buckets: b. into empty wells | 112a
owes two b. filling | 376a
silly b. on the deck | 99a
Buckingham: high-reaching B. | 385a
so much for B. | 95b
Buckled: take her buckled shoon | 131a
Buckler: carry the b. unto Sampson | 41b
Bucklers: there hang a thousand b. | 500b
Buckling..black Auster's band | 254a
Buckram: eleven b. men..out of two | 377b
rogues in b. suits | 377b
Bud: at once, a b., and yet a rose | 191a
b. is on the bough again | 205a
b. may have a bitter taste | 110a
canker lives in sweetest b. | 387b
in age I b. again | 188a
in b. or blade | 426b
opening b. to Heaven | 100b
rose shd. shut, and be a b. again | 221b
this b. of love | 365b
trees..do yield forth b. | 446a
Budge: 'B.' says the fiend | 353b
I will not b. for no man's | 365b
Buds: blown b. of barren flowers | 422a
b. that snows have shaken | 422a
b. they were swellin' | 531a
darling b. of May | 387a
driving sweet b. like flocks | 396a
hawthorn hedge puts forth its b. | 39a
kneeled unto the b. | 324a
starry river b. | 398a
summer's velvet b. | 381b
what those b. disclose | 185a
with b. and bells | 220b
Buff: to bide by the b. and the blue | 61a
Buffalo: he thought he saw a B. | 85b
Buffaloes: so air our B. | 124a
Buffer: poor b. lies low | 459a
Buffet: Satan to me | 515b
Buffets: b. of the world..so incens'd | 334a
fortune's b. and rewards | 334a
Buffoon: b. and poet | 185b
statesman, and b. | 138b
Buffs: steady the B. | 237b
Bug: snug, as a b. in a rug | 156b
Bugaboo: don't b. baby me! | 75b
Bughtin'-time is near | 61b
Bugle: blow, b., blow | 436a
bring the good old b., boys | 473a
one blast upon his b.-horn | 316b
Bugles: blow out, you b. | 39a
Song on yr. b. blown | 185a
what are the b. blowin' for? | 228b
Bugloss: there the blue b. paints | 114a
Build: birds b. but not I | 198a
b. from age to age | 227b
b. me a Pyramid! | 236a
b. me straight, O worthy Master! | 246b
b. on thee a better opinion | 363a
b. thee more stately mansions | 194a
b., unbuild, contrive | 275b
burrow awhile and b. | 44b
I arise and b. it again | 393b
I hunger to b. them | 475b
labour is but lost that b. it | 489b
others shd. b. for him | 470a
they neither b. the Temple | 260b
when we b...b. for ever | 314b
who thus cd. b. | 467b
Builded better than he knew | 147a

Builder: after me cometh a B. 233a
he can only be a b. 314a
Builders: behold, ye b., demigods 453b
b. wrought with greatest care 246b
our b. . . with want of genius 140a
stone wh. the b. refused 489a
Building: altered in the b. trade 236a
ancient . . b. not in decay 15a
church . . 'tis a tall b. 113b
for the B. up of Jerusalem 30b
no looking at a b. here 58b
stole . . the life o' the b. 348a
Built: all we have b. do we discern 7a
b. in such a logical way 194a
b. in th' eclipse 269b
therefore b. for ever 427b
therefore never b. at all 427b
Bulbo: my B.! 440a
Bulk: the mighty b. commands 161a
Bull: a Cock and a B. 412a
curled Assyrian B. 433b
gone to milk the b. 207b
greatest of all is John B. 72b
in time the savage b. doth bear 358a
in time the savage b. sustains 238a
old unhappy b. 192a
peculiarity of the Irish b. 143b
secret of the b. and lamb 264a
Bullen's eyes 174a
Bullet: ballot stronger than a b. 245a
b. thro' his heart 440a
by b. or by shot 525b
every b. has its billet 461a
ramm'd with b. round 408b
Bullets: b. made of platinum 25b
paper b. of the brain 358b
Bullied into a certain philosophy 222a
Bullock's but a fool 233a
Bullocks: good yoke of b. 380b
offer young b. upon thine altar 485a
Bulls: b., that walk the pastures 264a
b., the sport of winds 273b
dew-lapp'd like Thessalian b. 357a
fat b. of Basan close me in 483a
I will eat b.' flesh 485a
seated on two chairs like mad b. 123a
Bull's eye at yr. belt 412a
Bully: b. boy, b. boy 319b
like a tall b. 302b
yr. mentality, too, is b. 25a
Bulrushes: ark of b. 493b
Bulwark: Britannia needs no b. 78a
Bulwarks: floating b. of the island 28b
mark well her b. 485a
Bumble: Mr. B. 125b
Bumps: a fireman, and afraid of b.! 403b
what ho! she b.! 86a
Bun: B. replied 146b
now for the rollicking b. 167a
Bunbury: invalid called B. 460a
Bunburyist: secret B. 460a
Buncombe: Parliament speaking . . to 81a
Bundle of prejudices 238b
Bungay: Friar Bacon and Friar B. 176a
Bunk: history is b. 155b
Buns: hot cross-b. 535b
Bunyan: Philistine of . . literature, B. 10b
Buonaparte the bastard 424a
Buoy: cock a b. . . too small for sight 343b
Bur o' the world 441a
Burbled as it came! 83b
Burchell . . wd. . cry out 'Fudge' 171a
Burden (see also burthen): b. and heat of the day 507b
b. and the heat of the long day 7a
b. of the desert of the sea 502a
b. of the incommunicable 120a
b. of them is intolerable 480b
my b. is light 506b
on his back the b. of the world 258b
public b. of the nation's care 306a
sprites, the b. bear 367a
take up the White Man's b. 236b
they have cast their b. 234b
with superfluous b. loads 278b
Burdens: couching . . between two b. 493b
heavy b. at his narrow gate 381b
undo the heavy b. 503a
Burdocks, hemlock, nettles 343b

Burghers: now might the b. know 253a
rich b. of the flood 352b
Burglar: many a b. I've restored 167a
when the enterprising b. 166b
Burglary: flat b. as ever was committed 359a
Burgling: burglar's not a-b. 166b
Burgonet of men 323a
Burial: and b. sure 228a
buried in Christian b. 336a
in one red b. blent! 68b
to a sad b. feast 366a
Burial-ground God's Acre 247b
Buried: as b. once, Men want dug up 152b
b. him before the prime 529b
b. in so sweet a place 391b
b. in the king's highway 375b
b. once, why not upon my head? 375b
lie a-b. in one grave 526b
not b. me deep enough 434b
there will I be b. 495a
they b. him . . costlier funeral 426b
'tis b. deep in the next valley 220a
we b. him darkly 462a
Buries madmen in the heaps 301b
Burke: B. is not affected by . . distress 292a
B. said there were 'Three Estates' 81a
B., who winds into a subject 171b
I say ditto to Mr. B. 305b
only specimen of B. 183a
Burleigh: B. comes forward 400a
B.-house by Stamford 432b
the Lord of B. 432b
Burma girl a-settin' 232a
Burn: abúne the b., ayont the law 415a
another Troy for her to b. 474b
better to marry than to b. 514a
b. for ever in burning hell 423a
b. to the socket 464a
b. upward each to . . bliss 52a
chance to b. yr. lips 368b
flag . . shall yet terrific b. 78a
stars that round her b. 2a
sun shall not b. thee 489b
trotting b.'s meander 62b
we b. daylight 141a, 355b, 364b
Burned: bush b. with fire 493b
half his Troy was b. 379b
heart hath ne'er within him b. 317a
John now to be b. alive 47a
Burnet: freckled cowslip, b. 383b
Burneth the chariots in the fire 484b
Burning: a b. fiery furnace 504a
Babe all b. bright 407b
b. and a shining light 510b
b. for b. 494a
b. questions 128b
b. Sappho loved 70b
b. with high hope 68b
firebrand plucked from the b. 504a
on the b. deck 184b
smell of b. fills the startled air 26b
tiger! tiger! b. bright 31b
Burnings: restless throbbings and b. 171b
Burnish take on Eden-trees 442b
Burns: b. but more clearly 475a
B., Shelley were with us 48a
not she wh. b. in 't 373a
oil unprofitably b. 108a
Burn-side: waly, yon b. 530a
Burnt: Christians have b. each other 70a
Burnt-offerings: b. and sacrifice 484a
delightest not in b. 485a
Burr: I am a kind of b. 352a
Burrow: b. awhile and build 44b
London . . so near his b. 265b
Burrs: conversation's b. 193b
roses stick like b. 52b
Burs: kecksies, b. 383b
Burst: b. of thunder sound 184b
his flawed heart . . b. smilingly 344a
the first that ever b. 98b
words, words, or I shall b. 150a
Bursts: thick the b. come crowding 7a
Burthen (see also burden): b. of an honour 432b
b. of the mystery 472a
b. was thy birth to me 385a
this the b. of his song 28a
too . . laden ever to b. thine 399b
vapours weep their b. 438a

Burton: why was B. built 199b
Bury: b. it with me 133a
b. me, b. me deeper 434b
b. the Great Duke 435a
ham and sherry . . meet to b. 39b
I b. some of you 133a
I come to b. Cæsar 339b
let the dead b. their dead 506a
sort of woman . . to b. for nothing 124a
Bus: descending from a b. 85b
not a b. but a tram 527a
she tumbled off a b. 172a
Buses: no b. runnin' 232a
Bush: b. burned with fire 493b
b. supposed a bear 357b
but flame? the b. is bare 50b
every common b. afire with God 43a
fear each b. an officer 384b
four times as big as the b.! 243b
'oppin in an' out among the b. 229a
thorough b. thorough brier 356b
underneath the barren b. 430b
who aims but at a b. 401b
young bird in this b. 243b
Bushes: discovereth the thick b. 483b
Busier: semed b. than he was 88b
Business: about my Father's b. 509a
a b. of delight 395b
annuity is a very serious b. 11b
be quiet, and to do yr. own b. 516b
big. b. give . . a square deal 310b
breakfast first, b. next 440a
b. first; pleasure afterwards 440a
b. of everybody . . b. of nobody 254a
b. of the day in the day 455a
b. that we love 324a
b. to-day . . persuading crowds 244a
b. was his aversion 143b
b. will never hold water 95b
called away by particular b. 400b
derned sight better b. 183a
do other men . . true b. precept 124a
end of this day's b. 341b
everybody's b. is nobody's b. 450b
go to yr. b., I say, pleasure 473b
Hoti's b. 47a
if everybody minded their own b. 82b
importunity of b. 240a
in civil b., what first? 14b
man to double b. bound 334b
men's b. and bosoms 14a
men, some to b., some to pleasure 302a
more b. after dinner 418a
no feeling of his b. 336a
no praying, it spoils b. 291b
not slothful in b. 513b
public b. is undone 66a
requisite in b. than dispatch 1a
servants of b. 14b
than for settled b. 16a
their b. in great waters 488b
the Treasury is the spring of b. 17a
yr. own foolish b. 91a
Busiris and his Memphian chivalry 271b
Busk: b. ye, b. ye 178b
wherefore shd. I b. my heid 530a
Buskin: hear thy b. tread 216a
Buss: Miss B. 525a
Bust: B. outlasts the throne 130b
give a b. of marriages 70b
raise the tardy b. 213b
storied urn or animated b. 174a
Buster: another awful b. 294b
Bustle: glance, and nod, and b. by 8b
Busts: picture plac'd . . b. between 35a, 91b
Busy: b. old fool, unruly Sun 134a
I wd. be b. too 453a
Lord! thou knowest how b. 11a
no-wher so b. a man 88b
silly thoughts so b. keep 270b
the b. trifler 108a
Busybodies: tattlers also and b. 516b
Butcher: my b.'s bill is due 163a
to know a b. paints 52a
Butchered to make a Roman holiday 69a
Butchers: b. and cokes 242b
even b. weep! 150b
gentle with these b. 339b
sacrificers, but not b. 338b
who fills the b.' shops 403b
Butler: Mr. B. . . in praise of Ireland 296a

Butt: my journey's end, here is my b. 364a
 peace, and the b. 141b
Butter: bit of b. to my bread 266b
 b. and eggs and a pound of cheese 75a
 b. and honey shall he eat 501b
 b. in a lordly dish 494b
 b.'s spread too thick! 84b
 b. that makes the temptation 205a
 b. will only make us fat 575b
 chocolate, b., and toast 4b
 fetch you yr. bread and yr. b. 227b
 it was the best b. 83a
 kiss a dish of b. 377b
 smell of bread and b. 67b
 while ladling b. from . . tubs 528:1
Buttercup: dear little B. 165b
Buttercups . . little children's dower 47b
Buttered: dig for b. rolls 85b
 fell . . always on the b. side 294b
Butterflies: b. and the cockyolybirds 226b
 deny . . what it concedes to b.! 121a
 I look for b. 85b
 laugh at gilded b. 344a
 white b. in the air 37b
Butterfly: b. upon a wheel 303a
 b. upon the road 233a
 I'd be a b. 22a
 kill not the moth nor b. 29b
Buttery: a little b. 190b
Buttocks of the ape 202b
Button: b. in the hat! 194a
 gie a b. for her! 63b
 he twirled a b. 127b
 little round b. on top 155b
 pray you, undo this b. 344a
Buttoned: all b. down before 175b
 b. it with stars 193b
Button-hole: take you a b. lower 345b
Buttons: I had a soul above b. 103b
 taken of 'is b. off 228b
Buttress nor coign of vantage 347a
Buxton: valley between B. and Bakewell 314a
Buy: b. my English posies! 229a
 b. then! bid then! 198a
 b. wine and milk without money 503a
 cherries grow, that none can b. 4a
 cherries grow, wh. none may b. 78b
 come ye, b. and eat 503a
 dreams to sell, what wd. you b.? 24a
 fair ones, come and b. 188b
 I'd have you b. and sell so 373b
 I will b. with you 353a
 new worlds to b. 260b
 no man might b. or sell 519a
 nor peer nor prince can b. 78b
 what the vintners b. 154a
Buyer: it is naught, saith the b. 498b
Buying: of pig in a poke 446a
Buzfuz: Sergeant B. 126b
Buzz: the stings, the crowd and b. 107a
 they said, 'does it b.?' 243a
Buzzards: the B. are all gentlemen 38a
Buzzing: what is he b. in my ears? 46a
By: and then lay b. 385b
By-and-by: b. is easily said 334b
 in the coming b.! 165b
 sweet b. 315b
Bye, baby bunting 534a
Bymatter: as if it had been a b. 15b
Byng: Kentish Sir B. 45b
Byron: B.'s force 6b
 close thy B. 81b
 Collingwood, B., Blake 287b
 from the poetry of Lord B. 255a
 what helps it now, that B. bore 6a
 when B.'s eyes . . shut in death 6b
Byteth: flye offendeth him or b. 90a
By-way: and the b. nigh me 414a
 his own B. to heaven 118b
Byword: proverb and a b. 496a
Byzantium: B.'s conquering foe 69a
 Soldan of B. is smiling 92b

                  C

C: C. cut it 532a
 C. Major of this life 44b
Ça ira 157a
Cabal: in high c. have made us 452a

Cabbage twice cooked 549a
Cabbage-leaf, to make an apple-pie 155b
Cabbages: of c. and kings 84b
Cabin: small c. build there 475a
 willow c. at yr. gate 370a
Cabin-boy: so the C. did swim 531a
Cabined: c., cribbed, confined 349a
 from her c. loop-hole peep 266b
 her c. ample Spirit 7b
Cabinet: c. of pleasure 187b
 consequence of c. government 17a
Cabots talk only to God 34a
Cackle: hungry rooster don't c. 182a
Cackling home to Camelot 342a
Cad: cocoa a c. 93b
Cadence: c. of a rugged line 141a
 golden c. of poesy 344b
 to the ancient lyrical c. 96a
Cadiz: reeking into C. Bay 47b
Cadmus: I was with Hercules and C. 357a
 snakes . . C. and Harmonia 5b
 the letters C. gave 71a
Cadwallader and all his goats 383b
Caesar: all is C.'s, and what odds 115a
 Ay, C., but not gone 338a
 beggar's nurse and C.'s 325a
 broad-fronted C. 323a
 Brutus . . was C.'s angel 340a
 C. and his fortune 574a
 C. bleed in sport 339b
 C . . . first in a village than second
 at Rome 13b
 C. had his Brutus 185b
 C. hath wept 340a
 C. is more dangerous than he 339a
 C. is turn'd to hear 337b
 C., now be still 341b
 C. shall go forth 339a
 C.'s image is effaced 110b
 C.'s spirit, ranging for revenge 339b
 C.'s thrasonical brag 327b
 C.'s wife . . above suspicion 574a
 C.'s wife, all things to all men 524b
 C. was ambitious 339b
 C. with a senate at his heels 301b
 call great C. ass unpolicied 325a
 cold upon dead C.'s trencher 324a
 doth this our C. feed 337b
 enemies of C. shall say this 339b
 enter C. in his night-gown 338b
 first time ever C. put it on 340a
 for always I am C. 338a
 glow on C.'s brow 338a
 great C. fell 340a
 grievously hath C. answer'd it 339b
 had C. or Cromwell exchanged 170b
 here was a C.! 340b
 I appeal unto C. 512b
 I come to bury C. 339b
 if C. had stabbed their mothers 338a
 imperious C. dead 336b
 in every wound of C. 340a
 kiss dead C.'s wounds 340a
 Mark Antony's was by C. 348b
 not C.'s valour hath o'erthrown 324b
 not that I loved C. less 339b
 of C.'s hand, and Plato's brain 146a
 O Julius C.! thou art mighty yet 341b
 O mighty C.! dost thou lie so low? 339b
 paltry to be C. 325a
 poison . . came from C.'s . . crown 29b
 regions C. never knew 107b
 render therefore unto C. 507b
 scarce-bearded C. 322a
 soldier fit to stand by C. 361a
 so let it be with C. 339b
 so long as C.'s self is God's 115a
 some buried C. bled 153a
 start a spirit as soon as 'Caesar' 337b
 that C. might be great! 77a
 their sweets on blossoming C. 324a
 unto C. shalt thou go 513a
 we will hear C.'s will 340a
 word of C. might have stood 340a
 yr. boy, yr. C. 139a
 yr. C.'s father oft 324a
Caesar Augustus: decree from C. 508b
Caesars: many C. ere such another
 Julius 328b
Cage: born within the c. 430a
 keeps a lady in a c. 93b

Cage (cont.)
 nor iron bars a c. 249b
 Redbreast in a c. 29a
 she hung in a c. 313a
Cages: making nets, not in making c. 419a
Cain: C. and his brother, Abel 100b
 'people of Bath,' continued C. 180b
 the first city C. 107a
Caitiff: if the rude c. smite the other 193b
Cake: gave them plum-c. 532b
 geological home-made c. 123b
 he that will take a c. 368b
 let them eat c. 563b
 the sacramental c. 219a
Cakes: c. and apples in . . chapels 19b
 hear, Land o' C. 62a
 no more c. and ale 370b
Calais: find 'C.' lying in my heart 261b
 fortune's malice lost her C. 46a
 Jones! as from C. southward 403a
 to show light at C. 207b
Calamity: art wedded to c. 366a
 c. of so long life 333a
 more than a public c. 407b
 serving either c. or tyranny 520a
Calcine its clods 45b
Calculate: c. the stars 275b
 when you are calculating, c. 209a
Calculated: were I c. for the former 222b
Calculation shining out of the other 123b
Calculators: sophisters, . . and c. 57a
Caledonia: guid to support C.'s
 cause 61a
 mourn, hapless C. 405b
 O C.! stern and wild 317b
Calendar: c. right glad to find 108b
Calender: good friend the c. 108b
Calf: bring hither the fatted c. 509b
 c. and the young lion 501b
 golden-c. of Self-love 80a
 when he killed a c. 11a
Calf's-skin: hang a c. on those . . limbs 374a
Caliban: 'Ban, 'Ban, Ca-C. 367b
Caliph Omar Ben Abdalaziz 23b
Call: breezy c. of incense 174a
 c. for the robin redbreast 454b
 c. him on the deep sea 287b
 c. him when ye sail 287b
 c. home the heart you gave me 137a
 c. me early, mother dear 434b
 c. me Sappho, call me Chloris 101b
 c. themselves Christians 479a
 c. these delicate creatures ours 362a
 c. up him that left half told 268b
 c. yet once 6a
 c. ye upon them while he is near 503a
 c. you that backing 377b
 children, c. no more 6a
 Death . . must c. too soon 167a
 help Thy children when they c. 227b
 I do not c. it 342b
 know not what to c. you 145b
 leave to c. me anything 418b
 men hit c. may the dayesye 90a
 none dare c. it treason 181b
 obey th'important c. 112b
 Oh! c. my brother back to me! 184b
 one clear c. for me 426a
 only c. me thine 101b
 pleased to c. yr. mind 28a
 prompt at every c. 168b
 Red Gods c. us out 228b
 to hear again the c. 414b
 to see what he wd. c. them 492a
 voted at my party's c. 166a
 whatever they c. him 433b
 wild c. and a clear c. 262a
 will they come when you do c. 378a
Callay: Callooh! C.! 84a
Called: c. him Sunny Jim 179a
 come when you're c. 143b
 he c. for his pipe 532a
 I c. not; lie down again 495a
 science falsely so c. 516b
 since first he c. her his 77a
 tho' I c. another, Abra came 306a
 vocation wherewith ye are c. 515b
 you c. me dog 353a
Caller herrin' 285b
Calling: c. as he used to call 290a
 c. out of doors 435b

Calling (cont.)
  c. thro' the dark 435b
  followed their mercenary c. 200a
  high is our c., friend! 465b
  inclined unto me, and heard my c. 484a
  Maud, they were crying and c. 433b
  one c.. 'Child' 188a
Callooh! Callay! 84a
Calls: c. his dead to him 229a
  it is my soul that c. 365b
Calm: a c. and heavenly frame 109b
  all c., as it was bright 448b
  all is c. again 160a
  be c. in arguing 186b
  c. and still 444b
  c. in waters, seen 395a
  c. is in that balm 290a
  c. me more! nor let me die! 6b
  c. of mind, all passion spent 278a
  c. on the bosom of thy God 184b
  c.'s not life's crown 9a
  for a c. unfit 138a
  never felt, a c. so deep 472b
  no joy but c. 433a
  nor peace within nor c. around 399a
  peace..I seek, and public c. 6b
  she was more than usual c. 155a
  so, c. are we when passions 449a
  tumult dwindled to a c. 74b
  virtue..in authority..c. 14b
  Wordsworth's sweet c. 7a
Calmly: move..c. in their place 14b
Calmness: c. is great advantage 186b
  for c. to remember 2b
  keeps the law in c. made 465b
Calumnies..answered..with silence 216a
Calumny: envy and c. and hate 392b
  thou shalt not escape c. 333b
Calvin: land of C., oat-cakes 404a
Calvinist: disease in the liver..C. 148a
Calvus: if the dumb grave, my C. 539b
Calypso for his native shore 394a
Cam: C., to patient science dear! 463a
  may you, my C...preach it long 299a
Cambridge: books to C. gave 445b
  C. people rarely smile 39b
  fields of C., our dear C. 107a
  to C. books, as..discerning 445b
  to C. books he sent 42b
  when thou taught'st C. 278b
Cambuscan bold 268b
Came: all things going as they c. 313a
  c. they to the blissful seats 453b
  he c. all so still 524b
  I c., I saw, I overcame 548a
  never c. a wink too soon 195a
  tell them I c. 119b
  whence you c., nor why 154b
  when he c. to himself 509b
  who cut and c. again 114a
Cameelious Hump 230b
Camel: C. humphed himself 237a
  C.'s hump is an ugly hump 230b
  c...through the eye of a needle 507b
  cloud..in shape of a c. 334b
  Commissariat c. 233a
  raiment of c.'s hair 504b
  swallow a c. 507b
Cameleopard: matched with this c. 395b
Camelot: all the knights at C. 432a
  cackling home to C. 342a
  did she look to C. 432a
  she looked down to C. 431b
  turned to towered C. 432a
Came-over-with-the-Conqueror 452a
Camerado: C., this is no book 458b
  great C., the lover true 458a
Cameron: come hither, Evan C.! 12b
Camilla: bosom of her..family re-
    sided C. 58b
  swift C. scours the plain 300a
Camp: barrow and the c. abide 235a
  court, the c., the grove 317a
  from c. to c. thro' the..night 382b
  if the general c. 362a
  love rules the c. 71b
  pibble-pabble in Pompey's c. 382b
Campaspe: Cupid and my C. 251a
  did my C. win 251b
Campbell: do not Maister or C. me 320a
Campbells are comin' 526b

Campden Hill: largest lamp on C. 92b
  stars on C. 92b
Camps: Courts and c... learn the
    world 90b
  in c. a leader sage 318a
Can: c. something, hope 197a
  come fill up my c. 316a, 320a
  cry I c. no more 197a
  do all the good you c. 456a
  fill the c., and fill the cup 439a
  if we c. we must 200a
  in all the ways you c. 456a
  pass me the c., lad 200a
  the c. must be so sweet 197b
  they shd. keep who c. 470b
  youth replies, I c. 147a
Canaan: to the Jews old C. stood 453b
Canaanites, and the Hittites 493b
Canacee: highte C. 89b
Canadian: cold on C. hills 242a
Canary: mine host's C. wine 219a
  pure cup of rich C. wine 215a
Cancel: c. all our vows 137b
  c. and tear to pieces that..bond 349a
  to c. half a Line 153b
Cancers: because women have c. 222b
Candid: be c. where we can 300b
  one dissertates, he is c. 48b
Candidate: c. of heav'n 140b
  good c. cannot be..bad colour 23b
Candle: a farthing c. at Dover 207b
  c.-flame beside..surplices 243a
  c. of understanding 520a
  c. singed the moth 353b
  c. throws his beams 355b
  friends called him 'c.-ends' 86a
  Handel..fit to hold a c. 67a
  here comes a c. to light you 533b
  hold a c. to my shames 353b
  hold their farthing c. 477a
  light a c. to the sun 401a
  out, out, brief c.! 350b
  set a c. in the sun 64b
  some c. clear burns 197b
  tace..Latin for a c. 151a
  this day light such a c. 242b
  thou also shalt light my c. 482b
  two old chairs, and half a c. 243b
  we did not see the c. 355b
Candle-holder: a c., and look on 364b
Candle-light: c. and dreamlight 445b
  can I get there by c.? 534a
  colours seen by c. 43b
  dress by yellow c. 413b
  fire and fleet and c. 529a
Candlemass until after Easter 257b
Candles: Author's own c. 440a
  blessed c. of the night 355b
  night's c. are burnt out 366a
  the c. burn their sockets 200a
  their c. are all out 347b
Candlestick-maker..acquaints his soul 52a
Candlesticks: saw seven golden c. 518a
Candour..with the charity of Paul 94b
Candy deal of courtesy 377a
Cane: as a gentleman switches his c. 100b
  conduct of a clouded c. 302b
  pith of an Indian c. 2a
Canker: as killing as the c. 269b
  c. lives in sweetest bud 387b
  joy without c. or cark 242a
Cankers: c. of a calm world 378b
  some to kill c. 356b
Cannibals that each other eat 360a
Cannikin: let me the c. clink 361a
  why clink the c.? 46b
Canning: like Mr. C.'s wit 183b
Cannon: burst the c.'s roar 194a
  c. to left of them 426a
  England..a pulse like a c. 147b
  even in the c.'s mouth 326b
  if we cd. carry c. 337a
  it is the c.'s opening roar 68b
  thundered the c. of France 96a
Cannon-ball took off his legs 194b
Cannons: thundering c. roar 171a
Canny: a c. hour at e'en 60b
Canoe: coffin clapt in a c. 67b
  paddle his own c. 260a
Canon 'gainst self-slaughter 330a
Canonized: many..c. on earth 41b

Canopies of costly state 380a
Canopy: from heat did c. the herd 387a
  rich embroidered c. 384b
  this glorious c. of light 456b
  under the c.—I' the city of kites 328a
Canossa: we will not go to C. 567b
Cans of poisoned meat 93b
Canst thou do likewise 123b
Can't! Don't! Shan't 255a
Cant: apple pressed with specious c. 194b
  c. about decorum 61b
  c. of criticism is..tormenting 411b
  c. of 'Not men but measures' 56b
  clear yr. mind of c. 211a
  don't c. in defence of savages 211a
  we have nothing but c., c., c. 295a
Canteen: drills and no c. 230a
Canterbury: one illusion..Arch-
    bishop of C. 404b
Cantering: steadily c. through 236a
Canticle: the sweetest c. is Nunc
    Dimittis 14a
Canticles: sings his c. and hymn 202b
Cantie (canty): c. wi' mair 59b
  mony a c. day, John 61a
Cantle: a monstrous c. out 378a
Cantons: write loyal c. 370a
Cants: of all the c. wh. are canted 411b
Canvas: a breeze compelled thy c. 430a
  c. drooping, side by side 96b
  splash at a ten-league c. 236b
Canvasses: good in c. and factions 15a
Cany waggons 273b
Caoilte tossing his burning hair 475a
Cap: a c. by night 168a
  big blue c. that always fits 92b
  put on my considering c. 23a
  riband in the c. of youth 336a
  stuck a feather in his c. 18b
  Thomas he pu'd aff his c. 528a
Capability: c. and god-like reason 335b
  Negative C. 222a
Capable: a c. and wide revenge 362b
Capacity: genius..c. of taking
    trouble 80b
  notwithstanding thy c. 369b
Cap-a-pe: armed..c. 330a
Caparisons: no c. miss 400b
Cape: doubled C. Turk 264b
  round the C. of a sudden 49b
Cape of Good Hope: to double the C. 16b
Cape St. Vincent: nobly, nobly C. 47b
Capella: star called C. was yellow 180a
Caper on the straight rope 417b
Capers: c. nimbly in 384b
  lovers run into strange c. 326a
Capital: Belgium's c. had gathered 68a
  C. where kingly Death keeps..court 392a
  Corinthian c. of..society 57b
Capitalism at drawing-room meetings 315b
Capitol: against the C. I met a lion 338a
  amidst the ruins of the C. 161b
Capitulate: I will not c. 211b
Capon: cold c.'s leg 376b
  with good c. lin'd 326b
Cappadocia: in Judea, and in C. 512a
Caprices: public opinion wh. has..c. 58a
Caps: roses crest the c. 442b
  they wither their c. 328a
Captain: a cook and a c. bold 163a
  a train-band c. eke was he 108a
  C. is a good travelling name 150a
  c. jewels in the carcanet 387b
  c. of my soul 185a
  C. of the Gate 253a
  c. of the Hampshire grenadiers 253a
  c. of the Pinafore 165b, 166a
  c. of this ruined band 382b
  C. or Colonel, or Knight in arms 278b
  C.'s hand on his shoulder 287b
  C.! take me in 531a
  crew of the c.'s gig 163a
  each c., petty officer, and man 179b
  foremost c. of his time 435a
  in the c.'s but a choleric word 351b
  O C.! my C. 457a
  our great c.'s c. 360b
  right good c. too 165b
  the c. is in his bunk 390a
  the cruel C. cried 531a
  there's nobody like the C. 440a

Captain (*cont.*)
took a c.'s biscuit — 123b
walk the deck my C. lies — 457b
Captains: c. and rulers clothed — 504a
C. and the Kings depart — 233b
c. by the hundred — 163a
c. of industry — 81b
hundred c. in England — 531a
thunder of the c. — 497b
when c. courageous — 531b
Captain Wattle — 120b
Captivate: they c., inform the mind — 109a
Captive: c. void of noble rage — 430a
from the foes they c. make — 87a
they that led us away c. — 490a
weak minds led c. — 277a
when I am thy c. talk of chains — 274b
whether guest or c. I — 452b
Captives: all prisoners and c. — 479a
proclaim liberty to the c. — 503a
serve yr. c.' need — 236b
Captivity: c. thence captive — 408a
given to c. me and my..hopes — 363a
led c. captive — 486b
no leading into c. — 490b
power to cancel his c. — 338a
turned away the c. of Jacob — 487a
turn our c., O Lord — 489b
Car: as the void c., hurled abroad — 312b
c. rattling o'er the stony street — 68b
fixt her polisht c. — 270b
gilded c. of day — 266b
Caravan: C. starts for the Dawn — 153b
join the innumerable c. — 53a
phantom C. has reached the Nothing — 153b
put up yr. c. — 192b
where my c. has rested — 439b
Caravanserai: this battered C. — 152b
Carcanet: jewels in the c. — 387b
Carcase: not hew him as a c. — 338b
wheresoever the c. is — 507b
Carcases: c. of many a tall ship — 354a
c. of unburied men — 328a
Cardboard: being made entirely of c. — 83b
Cardinal: C...Archbishop of Rheims — 19a
force and fraud..c. virtues — 191b
Jackdaw sat on the C.'s chair — 19a
my dear Lord C. — 393a
Cards: an old age of c. — 302a
c...are the devil's books — 418b
played at c. for kisses — 251a
some..that can pack the c. — 15a
some were playing c. — 531a
Care: a deep and reverential c. — 465b
age is full of c. — 389b
and I c. not very greatly — 528b
begone dull c. — 522b
beyond His love and c. — 458b
black C. mounts on the..pillion — 545b
builders wrought with greatest c. — 246b
burden of the nation's c. — 306a
can a woman's tender c. — 110a
c., at the horseman's back — 75b
c. draws on c. — 137a
c. is heavy, therefore sleep — 119a
c. is lest men see too much — 51a
careless she is with artful c. — 103b
c.'ll kill a cat — 215b
c. o' the main chance — 65b
c. sat on his faded cheek — 272a
c.'s check and curb — 447b
c. was but to be fair — 452a
closed our anxious c. of thee — 295a
death came with friendly c. — 100b
deliberation sat and public c. — 272b
disapproves that c. — 278b
ev'ry c. resign — 169a
forgetting of my c. return — 117a
hast thou no c. of me? — 324b
hours will take c. of themselves — 90b
I c. for nobody — 28a
irks c. the crop-full bird? — 50b
I shan't c. or ho — 179b
killing and grief — 385b
little c. we — 440b
load of splendid c. — 283a
Lord, with what c. — 187a
mettle enough in thee to kill c. — 359a
neither cauld nor c. — 285b

Care (*cont.*)
nor c. beyond to-day — 174b
nor for itself hath any c. — 32a
nought but c. on every han' — 60b
now with me past c. — 375a
our loved ones.. 'neath thy C. — 411a
past my help, is past my c. — 23a
polished perturbation! golden c.! — 381a
sae weary fu' o' c. — 63b
so wan with c. — 376a
take c. of the minutes — 90b
take c. of the sense — 83a
the c. of this world — 506b
the ravelled sleave of c. — 348a
then all the c. is over — 170b
then the c. is over — 425b
they sought it with c. — 86a
tiresome, verse-reciter, C. — 394b
tonight so full of c. — 35b
to take c. of ourselves — 209a
'twas nipt with c. — 265b
wales..with judicious c. — 59b
what c. I how fair she be — 462a
what is this life, if full of c. — 118a
what tho' c. killed a cat — 359a
with incessant c. — 269b
with so much c. I write — 36a
with too intense a c. — 131b
women and c. and trouble — 451b
work, the public c. — 91b
wrinkled C. derides — 268b
you are c., and c. must keep you — 119a
your sex's earliest, latest c. — 251b
Cared: c. greatly to serve — 287b
Gallio c. for none — 512b
nor wished, nor c. — 305b
Career: boy's ideal of a manly c. — 130a
bright and brief c. — 317b
c. open to talents — 564a
nothing wh. might damage his c. — 21b
suspend your mad c. — 111a
the East is a c. — 130a
Careful: a man cannot be too c. — 460b
is not c. what they mean — 368a
more c. of the breed — 295b
not c. to answer thee — 504a
so c. of the type — 430b
Carefully: very c. and slow — 437b
Carefulness: bread of c. — 489b
Careless: c. of the single life — 430b
c. she is with artful care — 103b
c. their merits..to scan — 168b
first fine c. rapture — 47a
Carelessness: lose both looks like c. — 460a
Cares: c. can make the sweetest love — 176b
c. that infest the day — 247a
ever against eating c. — 269a
heavier weight of c. — 1b
home-bred c. — 56b
humble c., and delicate fears — 471a
if no one c. for me — 28a
in thy fats our c. be drown'd — 323b
kings have c. that wait — 176b
man is deprest with c. — 159b
none c. whether it prevail — 294a
of all the torments, all the c. — 450a
remote from worldly c. — 167b
small c. of daughter — 283a
swain, whose constant c. — 194b
thou, who when c. attack — 75b
unvexed with anxious c. — 140a
with crosses and with c. — 409a
worn with life's c. — 114a
Caress: linger to c. him — 451b
Carest: if thou c. not whom I love — 133a
Cargo: c. of ivory — 261b
c. of Tyne coal — 251b
Cargo-boats: Oh, the little c. — 231b
Caricature of a face — 165a
Carl spak oo thing — 89b
Carl-hemp: stalk o' c. in man! — 59a
Carline's wife's three sons came — 529a
Carlisle: burghers of C. — 252b
go to C.'s, and to Almanac's — 4b
Carlyle — 572b
Carmichael: Marie C., and me — 530a
Carnage: all its deeds of c. — 457b
c...is God's daughter — 71b
C. is Thy daughter — 468a
his c. and his conquests cease — 67b
stern strife and c. drear — 318b

Carnal: their c. interests — 66a
Carnally minded is death — 513b
Carnation: never cd. abide c. — 382a
Carnations: morn of bright c. — 138a
our c. and streaked gillyvors — 373a
soon will the musk c. break — 8b
Carol: fluting a wild c. — 429b
heard a c., mournful — 432a
quaintest, richest c. — 263b
this c. they began — 327b
Caroline: [Queen C.]..in tights — 24b
Carolings: cause for c. — 179a
Carolled: still they c. and said — 414b
Carpenter: is not this the c.'s son? — 507a
I understood Christ was a c. — 29a
the Walrus and the C. — 84a
you may scold a c. — 207a
Carpet: cliff-top has a c. — 35b
knight..on c. consideration — 372a
the figure in the c. — 204b
Turkey c. bears to a picture — 254b
Carpet-dusting..not..imperative — 43a
Carpet-knight: showed him no c. — 318a
Carpet-knights: ye curious c. — 162b
Carr: Comyns C. — 93a
Carriage: can't afford a c. — 116b
small second class c. — 164a
women of good c. — 365a
Carriages: I've seen yr. c. blocking — 232b
Carried: c. about with every wind — 515b
c. away with every blast — 479b
c. them out of the world — 42a
on wings they are c. — 414b
Carrion: c. comfort — 197a
is this their c. crucified — 421a
Carrow: Sparrow..late slain at C. — 402b
Carry: c. all he knew — 168b
c. everything before me — 129a
c. thee whither thou wdest. not — 511b
c. them in his bosom — 502b
delay to England to c. — 137a
to c. off the latter — 295a
we can c. nothing out — 516b
we must c. it with us — 148a
Cart: creak of a lumbering c. — 475b
now traversed the c. — 306a
Carter: old friend, Mrs. C. — 206a
Carters: keep a farm, and c. — 332a
Carthage: C. must be destroyed — 538a
to come again to C. — 355a
Carthaginian faith — 553a
Carve: c. beforn his vader — 88a
c. him as a dish — 338b
c. on every tree the fair — 327a
c. out dials — 384a
he may not..c. for himself — 330b
Carved: c. with figures strange — 100a
they c. at the meal — 316b
wept over her c. in stone — 433b
Carver: made out of the c.'s brain — 100a
was the c. happy — 314b
Caryatides: unfrowning c. — 415a
Casca: the envious C. — 340a
Cascade: with cold c. — 164a
Case: a corpse in the c. — 19a
heart in a c. o' gowd — 530a
his c., his c. — 292a
I'm in a sorry c. — 163a
in such an evil c. — 253b
its semblance in another c. — 107b
lady in the c. — 71a, 163a
nothing to do with the c. — 165a
Casement: a c. high and triple arch'd — 221b
at the c. seen her stand — 431b
c. ope at night — 220b
the c. slowly grows — 436a
Casements: charm'd magic c. — 220a
Cases: circumstances alter c. — 123b
know my methods in such c. — 135b
simple c. wh. are so..difficult — 135a
Cash: c. that goes therewith! — 91b
take the C., and let the Credit go — 152b
take the c. in hand — 152b
takes yr. c.; but where's the book — 94b
Cashiered: when he's old, c. — 359b
Cashiering most Kings and Senates — 81b
Cashmere: tales of wild C. — 461b
Cash-payment..not the sole nexus — 81a
Casius: Mount C. old — 272b
Cask: oldest c. is opened — 253b
Casket of my soul — 221a

x

Casques: this wooden O the very c. 381a
Cassander: good C. 402b
Cassia: heap c., sandal-buds 49b
Cassio: as great a fly as C. 361a
  C., I love thee 361b
  not C. killed! 363b
Cassius: answered Caius C. so 341a
  as that spare C. 338a
  C. from bondage will deliver C. 338a
  C. has a lean and hungry look 338a
  dar'st thou C., now leap in 337b
  for ever, farewell, C.l 341a
  let me tell you, C. 340b
Cassock was swarming with..vermin 20a
Cassocked: a c. huntsman 110b
Cast: and suddenly c. down 485a
  c. away the works of darkness 479a
  c. me not away from thy presence 485a
  c. the water of my land 350b
  c. wide the folding doorways 441b
  I will in no wise c. out 510b
  more he c. away, the more he had 54b
  pale c. of thought 333a
  to c. thee up again 331a
  when I e. mine eyes and see 190b
Castaway: I myself shd. be a c. 514a
Caste of Vere de Vere 431b
Castilian: as might an old C. 74b
Casting down their golden crowns 184a
Castle: a man's house is his c. 97b
  ancient c...not in decay 15a
  bores thro' his c. wall 375b
  c. called Doubting-Castle 54a
  c., precipice-encurled 46a
  house of every one..his c. 97b
  mistletoe hung in the c. hall 22a
  old lad of the c. 376b
  our c.'s strength will laugh 350b
  owre the C. Downe 530b
  rich man in his c. 3a
  splendour falls on c. walls 436a
  this c. hath a pleasant seat 347a
Castlepatrick: I come from C. 92b
Castlereagh: eunuch C. 70a
  mask like C. 395b
Castles: alas, all the c...air 215a
  make c. than in Spayne 90a
  my c. are my King's alone 318b
  no better brand than..Three C. 440a
Casualty: force and road of c. 353b
Casuistry: Mountains of C. 299a
Casuists, like you and me 302a
Cat: a c. languishes loudly 185b
  a c. may look at a king 83a
  a harmless necessary c. 354b
  as a c. laps milk 367b
  bought a crooked c. 532a
  c. and the fiddle 534a
  c. had but kittened 378a
  C...He walked by himself 237a
  c. i' the adage 347a
  c. wd. watch a mouse 418b
  deafer than the blue-eyed c. 428a
  dog, that worried the c. 534b
  endow a college, or a c. 302a
  had Tiberius been a c. 7b
  hanging of his c. on Monday 35a
  I am as vigilant as a c. 378b
  I don't want to swing a c. 122b
  I shall bell the c. 4a
  it might have been c. 19b
  I turned the c. in pan again 524a
  it was the c.l 166a
  it wd. have made a c. laugh 297b
  lat take a c. 89b
  more ways of killing a c. 226b
  part to tear a c. in 356a
  pussy c., where have you been? 534a
  see how the c. jumps 320b
  see the c. i' the dairy 144a
  the pavilion c. 242a
  touch not the c. but a glove 319a
  very fine c. indeed 211a
  what c.'s averse to fish? 173b
Catalogue: dull c. of common things 219a
  in the c. ye go for men 348b
Cataract: c. leaps in glory 436a
  the sounding c. haunted me 472a
Cataracts and hurricanes 342b
Catastrophe: c. of the old comedy 342a
  I'll tickle yr. c. 380a

Catch: c. another Antony 325b
  c., ere she change, the Cynthia 302a
  c. him once upon the hip 353a
  first c. yr. hare 571a
  he'll c. us some more 20a
  I'll c. it ere it come to ground 349b
  that I can c. her 198a
  toss i' air and c. again 51a
Catched: be more wise, and not be c. 296a
Catching: for c. my 'oss, 6d. 416b
  passion, I see, is c. 339b
  Poverty's c. 25b
Catchwords: man..lives..by c. 413a
Catechism: scarce had said his C. 440b
  so ends my c. 379a
Categorical imperative 575b
Caterpillar: c. on the leaf 29b
  'I don't see,' said the C. 82b
Caterpillars of the commonwealth 375a
Cates: that feed on c. 378a
Cathartic virtue 148a
Cathay: cycle of C. 432b
Cathedral: in the vast c. leave him 435a
  outside the c. at Florence 123a
Catherine: such as are on a C. pear 416a
Catholic: C. and Apostolick Church 480a
  C. men that live upon wine 26b
  flower of C. love 424a
  glorious the c. amen 403a
  he hold the C. faith 478b
  the Druse and the C. 92b
Catholic Church holds that it were better 288b
Catiline: concerning C. conspiracy 211b
Cato: Brutus and C. might discharge 141b
  C. gives his little senate laws 298b
  C.'s daughter 338b
  fate of C. and of Rome 1a
  like C., give his little senate 303a
  the Voice of C. 214b
  what C.'s daughter durst not 313b
Cats: c. and monkeys..all human life 204b
  c. is 'dogs' 535a
  c. may have had their goose 76a
  c. whom I liked better 211a
  do c. eat bats? 82b
  open spaces where c. are c. 259b
  rain c. and dogs 418b
Cattle: c. upon a thousand hills 485a
  great c...shadow of the..oak 57a
  Mary, go and call the c. home 226b
  mostly troublesome c. 250a
  the c. are grazing 467b
Catullus: C. makes mouths 421b
  metre of C. 427a
Caucasus: frosty C. 374b
Caught: c. my heavenly jewel 401b
  how I c. it 352b
  if he be c. young 208a
Cauldron: c. bubble 349b
  round about the c. go 349b
Cause: armor of a righteous c. 53a
  beauty of the good old c. 467b
  C. above renown 287b
  c. for carolings 179a
  c. is in my will 339a
  c. of this fair gift 388b
  c., or just impediment 481a
  c. that lacks assistance 18b
  c. that perishes with them 96a
  c. that the former days 499a
  ere her c. bring fame 251a
  final c. of the human nose 102b
  first Almighty c. 300b
  foretell for what high c. 261a
  I'll try the whole c. 82b
  it is the c., my soul 363b
  jealous for the c. 362b
  little shall I grace my c. 360a
  love him once, not without c. 340a
  magnificent and awful c. 111b
  no c. however just and pious 412b
  nor help the just c. 283a
  our c. is just 127b
  perseverance in a good c. 411b
  report me and my c. 337a
  ring out a slowly dying c. 431a
  shrinks to her second c. 299a
  Thou Great First C. 304a
  twelve..men have decided the c. 306b
  whose c. is God 112b

Causes: former c. of her moan 42b
  from amorous c. springs 302b
  Home of lost c. 9a
  men, and malice, to breed c. 216a
  there is occasions and c. 383b
Cavalier: brave old Scottish C. 12b
  each c. who loves honour 316a
Cavaliero: he was a perfect c. 67b
Cavanagh's blows 183b
Cave: c.'s stillicide 179b
  c. where Echo lies 365b
  darksome c. they enter 408b
  dull day in an ocean-c. 428b
  Idols of the C. 16b
  in this our pinching c. 328b
  misty eastern c. 399a
  political C. of Adullam 38a
  Stygian c. forlorn 268b
  thro' every hollow c. 433a
  vacant interlunar c. 277b
Cavern: happy field or mossy c. 219a
  in a c. 280b
  to her old c. fled 299a
Caverns: measureless to man 101a
  gluts twice ten thousand C. 221a
  Misery's darkest c. 210b
  sand strewn c., cool 5b
Caves: dark unfathom'd c. 174a
  dome with c. of ice 101b
  from the fountain and the c. 101b
  ring from their marble c. 137b
  sigh'd from all her c. 273a
Caviare to the general 332b
Cawdor: C. shall sleep no more 348a
  Glamis thou art, and C. 346b
  I am Thane of C. 346b
  King, C., Glamis 348b
  no more than to be C. 346a
  the Thane of C. lives 346a
C.B.: a fortnight's C. 227b
Cease: c., every joy, to glimmer 77b
  c. large example of wise thrift 249b
  c., towards the child she bare 110a
  c. ye from man 501a
  fears that I may c. to be 221a
  he did not c.; but cooed 468a
  man I am may c. to be 433b
  oh c.! I must hate and death return 394a
  that love may never c. 187b
  wonders will never c. 142b
Ceased: when she c., we sighing saw 249b
Ceasing: pray without c. 516b
Cecil's despatch of business 403a
Cecilia: C.'s lap of snows 442b
  it is only C., or Camilla 11b
Cecily: C., Gertrude, Magdalen 311b
  Margaret, Maude, or C. 294a
Cecrops: dear city of C. 574a
Cedar: as a c. tall and slender 290b
  from that moonlit c. 7a
Cedarn: athwart a c. cover 101a
Cedars: even the c. of Libanus 488b
  excellent as the c. 500b
Ceiling: of amber 6a
Celandine: C.! and long ago 463b
  'tis the little c. 463b
Celebrate: I c. myself 457b
Celebrated: c., cultivated..nobleman 163a
  c...for his Deportment 121a
Celerity even itself is slow 190b
Celestially: mud, c. fair 39b
Celia (Caelia): C. has undone me 457a
  charm of C. altogether 457a
  come, my C., let us prove 216a
  know, C., since thou art so proud 79a
  not, C., that I juster am 321a
Celibacy has no pleasures 213b
Cell: bid, for cloister'd c. 223b
  each in his narrow c. 174a
  hermit hoar, in solemn c. 211b
  he saw a solitary c. 100b
  in thine eternal c. 337a
  looked at a solitary c. 406b
  my c. is set 441a
  priest from the prophetic c. 270b
  self-respecting lady's c. 25a
  Thou hast given me a c. 190b
Cellar: born in a c. 155b
  in his c. stopped him down 295a
  I was born in a c. 104b
Cellarage: this fellow in the c. 331b

Cellarer: Simon the C. 25b
Cells: contented with their c. 468a
  thro' c. of madness 434b
Celt: hysterics of the C. 431a
Cenotaph: laugh at my own c. 393b
Censer: swinged c. teeming 220a
Censorship: extreme form of c. 391b
Censure: all c. of a man's self 210a
  c. freely who have written well 300a
  every trade save c. 72a
  no man can justly c...another 42a
  slander, c. rash 329a
  take each man's c. 330b
  ten c. wrong 300a
  those who durst not c. 213b
Cent: not a c. for tribute 181b
  they voted c. per c. 67b
Centaur: moral c., man and wife 71a
Centre: and tho' it in the c. sit 134a
  as from the c. thrice 271a
  c. of each and every town 194a
  c. of my sinful earth 389b
  God..c. is everywhere 526b
  hid indeed within the c. 332a
  intention stabs the c. 373a
  may sit i' th' c. 267a
  my c. is giving way 563a
  poor c. of a man's action 15b
  stables are the real c. 390a
Centric and eccentric 275b
Cents: money in the Three per C. 46b
  simplicity of the three per c. 129b, 320b
Centuries: bowed by the weight of c. 258b
  forty c. look down 564b
  nor sequent c. cd. hit 147a
  praises..all c. but this 164b
  solemn midnight c. ago! 131b
  thro' what wild c. 119a
Century: Rafael made a c. of sonnets 49a
Cerastes horned 276b
Cerberus: C., and blackest Midnight 268b
  give that C. a sop 104a
  you are not like C. 400b
Cerebration: unconscious c. 204a
Cerements: burst their c. 331a
  clinging like c. 195b
Ceremonies: superstitious..of dreams
    and c. 338b
Ceremony: an enforced c. 340b
  but for c...hath the forehand 383a
  no c. that to great ones 'longs 351b
  save c., save general c. 382b
  thrice-gorgeous c. 382b
Cerinthus that is lost 46a
Certain: for c. years, for c. months 312b
  I am c. of nothing 222a
  if it seem c. and they never dream 474b
  more c. than incertainties 21a
  not c. at all of what may befall 195a
  nothing c. in man's life 265a
  of a 'c. age' 71a
  one thing at least is c. 153a
Certainties: hot for c. 264a
  if a man will begin with c. 13a
  most people's c. 179a
Certainty: c. for an uncertainty 213a
  such sober c. 267a
  wisdom, less thy c. 410b
Cervantes: C. is never petulant 255a
  C. on his galley 92b
  C.' serious air 299b
  C. smiled Spain's chivalry away 71b
Cesario: mark it, C.; it is old 371a
  now, good C. 370b
Cesspool: London, that great c. 136a
Cesure: refused other c. 216b
Ceylon: blow soft o'er C.'s isle 184a
Chadband style of oratory: 121a
Chæronea: dishonest victory at C. 278b
Chafe: he that lets another c. 186b
Chafes: take no care who c. 349b
Chaff: like c. in my mouth 223b
  two bushels of c. 352b
  vacant c. well meant 429b
Chaffinch sings on the..bough 47a
Chain: a watch and c., of course 309b
  broke at once the vital c. 210b
  c. of countless rings 146b
  c. of our sins 479a
  dallied with his golden c. 426b
  ere Slumber's c. has bound me 282b

Chain (cont.)
  flesh to feel the c. 39a
  Homer's golden c. 64b
  if the c. were broken 391a
  remove a lengthening c. 169b
  servitude that hugs her c. 175a
  what the hammer? what the c.? 32a
Chains: a clanking their c. 451a
  adamantine c. 271a
  bound by gold c. 429b
  c. and slaverie! 62b
  c. are worse than bayonets 205a
  darkness, fire, and c. 452b
  their kings in c. 490b
  untwisting all the c. 269a
  when I am thy captive talk of c. 274b
  woman must wear c. 150a
Chair: asleep upon a c. 474a
  give Dayrolles a c. 91a
  has one vacant c. 248a
  he fills a c. 210b
  is the c. empty? 385a
  mouse under the c. 534a
  rack of a too easy c. 299a
  seated in thy silver c. 214b
  seats himself in Frederick's c. 192b
  sit in a golden c. 236b
  table, stool and c. 31b
  there will be one vacant c. 451b
  tilts up his c. 193a
Chairs: old c. to mend 533a
  seated on two c. like mad bulls 123a
  two old c., and half a candle 243b
Chaise: all in a c. and pair 108a
  children three will fill the c. 108b
Chalcedony: the third, a c. 520a
  third c.; the rest in order 43a
Chalice: c. of the grapes of God 429b
  winged c. of the soul 313a
Chalices: treen c. and golden priests 205b
Challenge: c. all the human race 309a
  oft wd. c. me the race 261a
  send a c. to his end 115b
Cham of literature 405b
Chamber: a c. deaf to noise 401b
  bridegroom out of his c. 482b
  capers nimbly in a lady's c. 384b
  c. in the silent halls of death 53a
  commune..in yr. c., and be still 481b
  in my lady's c. 534b
  many a listening c. 394b
  once a day her c. round 369b
  peace in her c. 311b
Chamberlain: Guilt was my grim C. 196a
Chambermaid: happy in the arms
    of a c. 210a
Chambermaids: worms..are thy c. 366b
Chambers: c. in the King's Bench 95b
  c. of the East 31b
  c. of the sun 31b
  perfumed c. of the great 380a
  wind-besomed c. 441b
Chameleon's dish: I eat the air 334a
Chameleons feed on light 393b
Champagne: c. and abricot jam 416b
  c. certainly gives one..ideas 417a
  c. teetotaller 390a
  we meet, with c. and a chicken 280a
Women, and C., and Bridge 26b
Champain: Heaven's wide c. 275a
Champak odours fail 394b
Champion: in close fight a c. grim 318a
  strong siding c. 267a
  to his faithful c...bore witness 278a
Chance: accident nor dart of c. 362b
  all c., direction 301a
  await no gifts from C. 8a
  be right, by c. 107b
  bludgeonings of c. 185a
  by c., or nature's..course 387a
  care o' th' main c. 65b
  c., and death, and mutability 397b
  c. brought out a noble knight 429a
  c. o' the prize of learning love 46a
  C. will bring us through 5b
  despair, law, c. 133a
  died an hour before this c. 348a
  erring men call C. 267b
  from art, not c. 300a
  had the c. been with us 424a
  high arbiter c. 273a

Chance (cont.)
  I am so sometimes by c. 373b
  if c. will have me king 346b
  main c. of things 380b
  morning brought a noble c. 429a
  necessity and c. approach not 275b
  nor now to prove our c. 137a
  not to c., as others do 452b
  Occasion, C., and Change 397a
  set my life on any c. 348b
  skirts of happy c. 430b
  turns of c. below 139a
Chance-desires: weight of c. 464a
Chancel: strange sounds along the c. 317a
Chancellor: c. in embryo 400a
  England's high C. 216b
  if the Lord C. only knew 524a
  marriages..by the Lord C. 209a
  susceptible C.! 163b
Chancery: young wards in C. 163b
Chances: against ill c. men are..
  merry 380b
  c. change by course 407b
  changes and c. of this..life 480b
  spake of most disastrous c. 360a
Change: a certain relief in c. 203b
  a marvellous c. on a sudden 67b
  appetites as apt to c. as theirs 139a
  as a vesture shalt thou c. them 488a
  bitter c. of fierce extremes 272b
  bolts up c. 325a
  c. and decay in all around 251b
  c. as the winds c. 424a
  c., as ye list, ye winds 161a
  c. came o'er the spirit 72a
  c. for the worst 87a
  c. is constant 128b
  c. is inevitable 128b
  c...not..without inconvenience 196b
  c. of many-coloured life 213b
  fear of c. perplexes monarchs 272a
  I c., but I cannot die 393a
  I deplore her c. 105a
  I perceive no c. 236a
  I wd. c. each hour like them 321a
  lamentable c. is from the best 343b
  life may c. 394a
  love cd. never c. 37b
  love will c. in growing old 37b
  miserable c. now at my end 534b
  more things c...more..the same 563b
  Nature's law to c. 309b
  neither to c., nor falter 397b
  no c. tho' you lie under 199a
  Occasion, Chance and C. 397a
  O the heavy c., now thou art gone 269b
  purge by any desperate c. 322b
  religion, knavery and c. 25b
  ringing grooves of c. 432b
  thou, fix thy..gaze thro' all c. 254a
  to c. what we can 412b
  to know the c. and feel it 221b
  to show a c. from what it was 247b
  when c. itself can give no more 321a
  whirling wheel of C. 409a
  whose beauty is past c. 197b
  without the means of some c. 56b
  wd. not c. for thine 216a
Changed: all c., c. utterly 476b
  all things are c. 14a
  c. in outward lustre 271a
  face of all the world is c. 43b
  how fall'n, how c. from him 271a
  let them be c. 343a
  nor e'er had c. 168b
  sea c., the fields to 181a
  we shall all be c. 515a
Changeful: sae mony c. years 61b
Changes: c. and chances of..life 480b
  c. the world to-day 228b
  follow still the c. of the moon 361b
  Friend Who never c. 265b
  God.., and man 422a
  her plot hath many c. 307a
  if the c. that we fear 212b
  monthly c. in her circled orb 365a
  One, who never c. 448a
  sundry and manifold c. 479b
  world's a scene of c. 107a
Changest: O Thou, who c. not 251b
Changeth: He c. not..thou art dear 279b

Changing: oft c. is loss 446b
the ring dove's neck from c. 77b
Channel: butting thro' the C. 261b
channel of no-meaning 288a
C.'s as bright as a ball room 227b
drum them up the C. 287b
wet with C. spray 229a
Channels: streams their c. deeper wear 61b
Chant: of pleasant exploration 457b
do use to c. it 371a
how can ye c., ye little birds 63b
or triumphal c. 398b
Chanted loudly, chanted lowly 432a
Chantey: lift a Deepsea C. 231a
Chanticleer: crow like c. 326a
strain of strutting C. 367a
Chaos: be no longer a c. 81b
c. is come again 361b
c. umpire sits 273a
God dawned on C. 392a
Night primeval, and of C. old 299a
reign of C. and old Night 271b
state of c. 290b
thy dread empire, C.! 299a
Chapel: Devil always builds a c. there 118b
devil..will have his c. 18b
out of the little c. I burst 45b
Chapels: apples in all the c. 19b
c. had been churches 352b
Chap-fallen: quite c.? 336b
Chaplain: Blue Beard's domestic c. 126a
twice a day the C. called 459b
Chapman: C. and Hall 27b
Mr. C.'s yea 27b
till I heard C. speak 220b
Chapmen: sale of c.'s tongues 344b
Chaps: Biography is about c. 27b
c. out of the City 93a
Chapter: c. is completed from epoch 81b
c. of accidents is the longest 461a
c. on the Fall of the Rupee 460a
repeat a complete c. 209b
studied his last c. of St. John 45a
Char: must Thou c. the wood 442a
Character: c. dead at every word 400b
education..formation of c. 408a
leave my c. behind me 400b
limitations of his own c. 283b
my c. I despare 155a
my wishes' cloudy c. 115b
see thou c. 330b
she gave me a good c. 83b
the poetical c. itself 223a
what is c. but..incident 204b
what is the c. of a family 411b
Characters: c. of hell to trace 173b
c. of the great Apocalypse 471a
high c. are drawn 301b
most women have no c. 302a
who have c. to lose 61b
write the c. in dust 319a
Chares: does the meanest c. 324b
Charge: and c. in earnest 131a
c., Chester, c.! 318b
c. with all thy chivalry! 77a
c. you more if you dine 126a
give his angels c. over thee 487b
I c. you, O daughters 500b
O the wild c. they made! 426a
take thou in c. this day 253b
the c. is prepar'd 160a
vex'd his..strength in c. of me 36a
Charger: he turned his c. as he spake 319a
Charges: a man ought warily to begin c. 15b
children but as bills of c. 14b
die to save c. 64a
goeth a warfare..at his own c. 514a
Charing Cross: heaven and C. 442a
human existence is at C. 208b
I sunk at C. 449b
Chariot: bang-up c. 125b
beneath thy c. wheel 197a
c. of Israel, and the horsemen 496b
her c. is an empty hazel-nut 364b
maketh the clouds his c. 488a
my c. of fire! 31a
on drove the c. 407a
snatched from out his c. 312b
Time's wingèd c. 260a
why tarry the wheels of his c. 495b

Charioted: not c. by Bacchus 220a
Charioteer: against the wind, a c. 312b
Chariotest to their dark wintry bed 396a
Chariots: burneth the c. in the fire 484b
c. of God are twenty thousand 486b
some put their trust in c. 482b
Charitable: to men's c. speeches 17a
Charities: c. of man to man 114a
defer not c. till death 16a
the c. that soothe, and heal 464b
Charity: all mankind's concern is c. 301b
C. and Mercy. Not unholy names 123b
c. begins at home 42a
c...cover the multitude of sins 517b
c. edifieth 514a
c. envieth not 514b
c. never faileth 514b
c. suffereth long 514b
c. vaunteth not itself 514b
c. will hardly water the ground 14b
excellent gift of c. 479b
faith, hope, c. 479b, 514b
give him a little earth for c. 386a
give lectures or a little c. 458a
greatest of these is c. 514b
healing voice of Christian c. 56b
in c.-meetings it stands 86a
it is no point of c. 115a
organized c., scrimped and iced 291a
pity gave ere c. began 168b
pool of private c. 293a
rarity of Christian c. 195b
remove mountains and have not c. 514b
sentiment..'c. begins at home' 400b
speak..and have not c. 514b
spots in yr. feasts of c. 518a
the living need c. 5a
with c. for all 245b
with the c. of Paul 94b
Charity-boy: as the c. said 126b
Charlatan: defamed by every c. 431a
Charlemagne: second was C. 257a
when C. with all his peerage 271b
Charles: C. the First, his Cromwell 185b
for C. King of England 252b
gentle-hearted C. 101b
health to King C. 320a
in good King C.' golden days 524a
keep King C. the first out 122a
King C.'s head..[Mr. Dick] 122a
King C. walked and talked 533b
seamen in the navy of C. II 255b
Charlie (Charley): call me C. now 240a
C. came to our town 193a
C. he's my darling 193a
C. is my darling 285b
Donal' an' C. an' a' 415a
live or die with C. 193a, 320a
o'er the water to C. 193a
over the water to C. 320a
Charlock throws a shade 114a
Charlotte: C., having seen his body 440b
Werther had a love for C. 440b
Charm: ask..why this c. is wasted 147a
c. by wh. many people..get loose 56b
c. from the sky 294b
c. he never so wisely 485b
c. of all the Muses 439a
c. of lovely Sue 161a
c. that lulls to sleep 169a
c. thee to a tear 461b
if you have it [c.] 21b
music oft hath such a c. 352a
music that wd. c. for ever 468a
no need of a remote c. 472a
'twas that provoking c. 457a
what c. can soothe 170a
Charmed: bear a c. life 351a
c. me from my profession 368a
c. water burned alway 99a
Charmer: c. whose dimples we prize 400b
the c. I approve 105a
t'other dear c. away 160a
voice of the c. 485b
Charming: so c. left his voice 275b
Charms: c. by accepting 302a
c., cheapness for one 417a
c. or ear or sight 100b
do not all c. fly 219a
endearing young c. 281b
Freedom has a thousand c. 111a

Charms (cont.)
lass that has acres o' c. 61a
lifeless c., without the heart 159a
music alone with sudden c. 104a
musick has c. 104b
solitude! where are the c. 113a
Charon, seeing, may forget 241a
Charter: as large a c. as the wind 326b
c. of the land 443a
the c. of thy worth 388b
Chartres: for C.' head reserve 301b
Charybdis: Scylla and C...Aye..No 288a
Chase: c., the sport of kings 406a
efface the joys of the c. 171b
heated in the c. 424b
in piteous c. 325b
rest! thy c. is done 316b
with unhurrying c. 441b
woe worth the c. 316a
Chasm: deep romantic c. 101a
no c., no solitude 464b
Chaste: are Barmaids c.? 261b
be amorous, but be c. 72a
be thou as c. as ice 333b
c. as the icicle 328b
c. as unsunned snow 328b
c. to her husband 302a
if I pronounce it c.! 165b
married, charming, c. 70a
nor ever c., except you ravish me 133a
Chasten: power to c. and subdue 472a
Chasteneth: the Lord loveth he c. 517a
Chastised: c. with the sober eye 325a
having been a little c. 520a
my father hath c. you 496a
Chastisement of our peace..upon him 503a
Chastity: c...but..not..yet 537b
clothed on with c. 427a
cold, my girl! even like thy c. 364a
give me c. and continency 537b
that c. of honour 57a
'tis C., my brother, C. 267b
Chasuble: wore, I think, a c. 182b
Chatham: C. heart-sick 111b
C.'s language 111b
great C. with sabre drawn 523a
listened to Lord C. 148a
waiting for the Earl of C. 523a
Chatter: c. about Harriet 571a
c. of a transcendental kind 165a
hare-brained c. 128b
Chatterings: multitudinous c. 264a
Chatterton: C., the marvellous boy 470a
O C.! how very sad thy fate! 220b
Chatting on deck was Dryden 241b
Chaucer: by C., or Spenser 215b
[C.] is a perpetual fountain 142a
C...was so unedicated 451a
Dan C., mighty Shakespeare 36a
Dan C., well of English 409a
nigh to learned C. 22a
since C. was alive and hale 241a
sufficient to say [of C.] 142a
Chaunting of the unquiet leaves 476a
Cheap: c. sitting as standing 418b
counsel 'tis c. 64a
flesh and blood so c. 196b
King to have things done as c. 296a
maketh himself c. 16b
Cheapened paradise 293a
Cheaper: c...this than to keep a cow 67a
fool, but at a c. rate 110b
Cheapness: charms, c. for one 417a
Cheat: c. a man is nothing 159b
detecting what I think a c. 208b
life, 'tis all a c. 139b
of being cheated, as to c. 65b
Cheated: c. into some fine passages 223a
of being c., as to cheat 65b
to be exceedingly c. at 149b
Cheater: bald c., Time 215b
Cheating of our friends 94b
Cheats: who c. a woman! 159b
Check: alas, I wd. not c. 241a
Oh! dreadful is the c. 39a
Checked: I c. him while he spoke 241a
Cheek: a warm wet c. 241b
blush bepaint my c. 365a
care sat on his jaded c. 272a
c. a little red 302a
c. of the young person 125b

Cheek (cont.)

crocus lays her c. to mire	264a
dry hand, a yellow c.	379b
feed on her damask c.	371a
hangs upon the c. of night	365a
he giveth his c. to him	503b
he that loves a rosy c.	79a
I love not hollow c.	436b
I might touch that c.	365a
it fanned my c.	99b
kissed each other's c.	166b
leans her c. upon her hand	365a
my c. is cold	394b
old ornament of his c.	358b
on that c., and o'er that brow	74a
on thy c. a fading rose	218b
pale grew every c.	254a
pale grew thy c.	74b
rose growing on 's c.	251b
sallow c. of hers to incarnadine	152b
smite thee on the right c.	505a
soul of Sir John C.	278b
the c. that does not fade	218a
tinged her c. with brown	316a
waters on my c. bestowed	109b
withered c. and tresses grey	316b
yellow C. of her's to incarnadine	152a

Cheeks: blood spoke in her c. | 133b
c. of sorry grain	267b
c. that be hollow'd	284b
crack yr. c.!	342b
fat ruddy c. Augustus had	192b
her c. were so red	226a
pale my c. with care	462a
queen, with swarthy c.	426b
roses are her c.	433b
to glow the delicate c.	323a

Cheer: a feeble c. the Dane sent | 76b
c.! boys, c.!	256a
c. for a halt and a row	233a
c. my bonny bride	77a
c. one on the tedious way	311a
c. up, the worst is yet to come	206a
c. us when we recover	55a
come, c. up, my lads	158b
cups, that c. but not inebriate	112a
give 'em one c. more!	234a
greet the unseen with a c.	52a
of his c. did seem too..sad	408b
piped with merry c.	32b
play and make good c.	446a
sound of royal c.	432a
this push will c. me ever	350b
to c. but not inebriate	28a
to c. it after rain	110b

Cheered: c. her soul with love | 432b
| c. up himself with ends of verse | 65b |
| the guinea-pigs c. | 83b |

Cheerful: buy yrself weeds, and be c. | 160a
| he looking as c. as any man cd. | 296a |

Cheerfully: c. for conscience sake | 491a
| c. he seems to grin | 82b |

Cheerfulness: c...always breaking in | 144a
| no warmth, no c. | 195a |
| truth breathed by c. | 471b |

Cheering: to our c. sent us back | 76b

Cheerly she loves me | 217b

Cheers: three c...one cheer more | 166a

Cheese: born i' the rotten c. | 144a
Botticelli 's a c.!	536a
c. and garlic in a windmill	378a
dark, and smells of c.!	417a
eggs and a pound of c.	75a
eggs, apples, and c.	227b
fill hup the chinks wi' c.	416b
his enemies, 'Toasted-c.'	86a
I've dreamed of c.	413a
stand a man a c.	93b
with apple-pie and c.	150b

Cheese-paring: man made..of a c. | 380b

Chemist, fiddler, statesman | 138b

Chenevix's shop | 449a

Cheque: political blank c. | 172a

Chequer-board of Nights and Days | 153b

Chequered: this life is all c. | 281b

Cherish: c. those hearts that hate thee | 386a
| to love and to c. | 481b |

Cherishes: Art most c. | 49a

Cherishing: kill thee with much c. | 365b

Cherith: brook C. | 496a

Cheroot: whackin' white c. | 232a

Cherries: c. fairly do enclose | 78b
full of blackbirds than of c.	2b
there c. grow	4a
there c. grow wh. none may buy	78b

Cherry: c. and hoary pear | 37b
c.-blossoms, and white cups	398a
c. now is hung with bloom	198b
c. ripe	188b
like to a double c.	357a
ruddier than the c.	159a
there 's the land, or c. isle	188b
to see the c. hung with snow	198b

Cherry-ripe themselves do cry | 4a, 78b

Cherry-stones: heads upon c. | 211a

Cherry-tree: fall from a c. then | 281a

Cherub: C. Contemplation | 268a
| fall'n c., to be weak | 271a |
| proud limitary c. | 274b |

Cherubim: c. does cease to sing | 29a
fyr-reed c. face	88b
heaven's c., horsed upon the..air	347a
rose-lipped c.	363a
the helmed C.	270b
the vault above the C.	230b

Cherubims: Immortal C. | 445a
on cherubs and c.	412a
sitteth between the c.	488a
young-eyed c.	355a

Cherubs and cherubims | 412a

Cheshire Cat | 83a

Chess: Athralus..first of the c. | 89b
| life 's too short for c. | 74b |

Chess-board: the c. is the world | 202b
| we called the c. white | 45a |

Chest: c. contriv'd a double debt | 168b
c. of drawers by day	168b
his c. against his foes	403a
in a ten-times-barred-up c.	374b
on the dead man's c.	413a
Slingsby of the manly c.	12b

Chester: charge, C., charge! | 18b

Chesterton: dared attack my C. | 26b

Chestnut: c.-husk at the c.-root | 420b
| yr. c. was ever the only colour | 327a |

Chestnuts: sailor's wife had c. | 346a
| there the c., summer through | 39b |

Chestnut-tree: the spreading c. | 249a

Chevalier: the young C. | 193a, 285b

Cheviot: C. within days three | 530b
| Hunting of the C. | 531a |
| in C. the hills so hye | 530b |

Chevisaunce: Pawnce and the C. | 409b

Chewing little bits of string | 26a

Chian: freighted with C. wine | 8a

Chibiabos: Brother, C.! | 248b

Chicken: champagne and a c. | 280a
| I swear, she 's no c. | 418b |

Chickens: all my pretty c. | 350a
| count..c. ere they're hatch'd | 66a |
| hen gathereth her c. | 507b |

Hiawatha's c. | 248b

Chicks: feeds her c. at sea | 227a

Chid: you'll never be c. | 143b

Chidden: vain desire was c. | 285a

Chide: I'll not c. thee | 342b
| to c., to laugh, to weep | 322b |
| your tardy son to c. | 335a |

Chiding: he will not alway be c. | 488a
| icy fang and churlish c. | 325b |

Chief: brilliant c., irregularly great | 252a
c. of Ulva's isle	77a
forgive yon Highland c.	77a
Hail to the C. who..advances	316b
Lord, it is my c. complaint	110a
sinners; of whom I am c.	516b
the Druid, hoary c.	107b
th' octogenarian c.	69a
wit 's a feather and a c. a rod	301b

Chiefest among ten thousand | 500b

Chief Justice was rich | 254b

Chiefs: those c. of pride | 254a

Chieftain: Brunswick's fated c. | 68b
| c. o' the pudding race | 60b |
| c. to the Highlands bound | 77a |

Chiels: Facts are c. | 60a

Child: a c. shd. always say what's | |
true	413b
a c. that so did thrive	215a
a happy English c.	424b
an aggravating c.	26a
an it had been any christom c.	381b

Child (cont.)

around the c. bend all the three	240b
as a lover or a c.	472b
a simple c.	472b
a wife sing to her c.	143b
behold the c.	301a
behold the c. among his..blisses	466b
c. and mother, baby bliss	176a
c.! do not throw this book about	25b
c. imposes on the man	140b
C. is afraid of being whipped	206a
C. is father of the Man	468a
C. may rue that is unborn	530b
c. of a day	241a
c. of our grandmother Eve	344b
C. of Light	397b
c. said What is the Grass	458a
c. 's amang you taking notes	62a
c. 's a plaything	240b
c. shall lead them	501b
c. so small and weak	3b
c...stewed, roasted, baked	418a
C.'s unheeded dream	293a
c. that is not clean	414a
Christ her little C.	3b
come away, O human c.!	476a
cry of a c. by the roadway	475b
dauntless c. stretched forth	175a
dear C.! dear Girl	467a
dearer was the mother for the c.	101a
Elephant's C.	237a
even a c. is known by his doings	498b
every c. born therein	314b
every c. may joy to hear	32b
every time a c. says	21b
father that knows his own c.	353b
fiery face as of a c.	428a
from a c. thou hast known	516b
get with c. a mandrake root	134a
gracious C., that thorn-crowned	7a
half-devil and half-c.	236b
hare's own c.	192b
healthy c. well nursed	418a
He became a little c.	32b
he is a naughty c., I'm sure	414a
here a little c. I stand	190b
I a c., and thou a Lamb	32b
if you strike a c.	391a
I have seen a curious c.	464b
is it well with the c.?	496b
I spake as a c.	514b
it was a crime in a c.	255b
I was a c. beneath her touch	312a
I was a c. and she was a c.	297b
I wd. not coddle the c.	207b
land that 's governed by a c.!	385a
leave a c. alone	51a
life..is but a froward c.	170b
life is..but like a froward c.	425b
like a three years' c.	98a
like a tired c.	399a
lonely dreams of a c.	119a
look upon a little c.	455b
make me a c. again	4a
Monday's c. is fair of face	525a
more hideous..in a c.	342a
mother may forget the c.	61b
mother's sake the c. was dear	101a
my fairest c.	225b
my good c., know this	481a
my husband..took up the c.	364b
my soul is even like a weaned c.	490a
naked new-born c.	214a
never spares the c.	196a
nicest c. I ever knew	26a
nor in any c. of man	490b
not as their friend or c.	6a
not there, my c.!	184b
nurse for a poetic c.	317b
old Adam in this C.	481a
on a cloud I saw a c.	32a
one calling, 'C.'	188a
out of the deep, my c.	426b
O! what a c.!	241b
painted c. of dirt	303a
saving a little c.	163a
say, Poor C.!	294a
see his active c. do deeds	387b
set his c. upon her knee	436b
sing to the c. on thy knee	37b
spare the rod, and spoil the c.	65b

Child (*cont.*)
sprightly and forward c. 91*a*
still the c. he first knew me 240*a*
sucking c. shall play 501*b*
sweet, my c., I live for thee 436*b*
the c. of misery 242*a*
there is a man c. conceived 497*a*
the room up of my absent c. 374*a*
the solitary c. 467*b*
this c. I to myself will take 471*b*
three times to the c. I said 463*a*
to be my c. Cordelia 344*a*
to have a thankless c. 342*a*
to love playthings well as a c. 413*a*
train up a c. 498*b*
unto us a c. is born 501*b*
waters wild went o'er his c. 77*a*
weaned c. shall put his hand 501*b*
when I was a c., I spake 514*b*
where is my c.? 68*a*
while the heaven-born c. 270*a*
who gives a c. a home 261*b*
who gives a c. a treat 261*b*
wretched c. expires 26*a*
Zoroaster, my dead c. 397*a*
Childe Roland to the Dark Tower
came 45*b*, 343*a*
Childhood: c. shows the man 277*a*
ever thus, from c.'s hour 282*a*
eye of c. that fears 348*a*
in my days of c. 240*b*
our c.'s pattern 3*b*
same that oft in c. solaced me 109*a*
see in simple c. 470*a*
'twas ever thus from c.'s hour! 75*b*
with my c.'s faith 44*a*
womanhood and c. fleet 247*b*
Childish: all tricks . . knavish or c. 210*a*
put away c. things 514*b*
something c., but very natural 101*b*
wise, idle, c. things 441*a*
Childishness: it does from c. 322*b*
I will be sorry for their c. 294*a*
second c. 326*b*
Childless: c. and crownless 69*a*
proceeded from c. men 14*b*
Childlike: c. Learning sits remote 167*b*
smile it was pensive and c. 182*a*
Children: all our c.'s fate 229*a*
airy hopes my c. 464*a*
as c. with their play 109*a*
become as little c. 507*a*
blessed . . be that taketh thy c. 490*a*
buttercups, the little c.'s dower 47*b*
called the c. of God 505*a*
called you c. 342*b*
careful of . . dogs than of their c. 295*b*
c. begin by loving their parents 460*b*
c. born of thee are sword 427*b*
c. but as bills 14*b*
c. by adoption 479*a*
c. *capable of honesty* 314*b*
c. cried in the streets 285*a*
c. dear, was it yesterday? 6*a*
c. dear, were we long alone? 6*a*
c. . . . deceived with comfits 13*a*
c. dine at five 413*b*
c., have ye any meat? 511*b*
c. . . . hostages to fortune 14*b*
c. in England take pleasure 526*b*
c. in Holland take pleasure 526*b*
c. in ordinary dress 26*b*
c. like the olive-branches 490*a*
c. not thine have trod 109*b*
c. of Alice called Bartrum 238*b*
c. of disobedience 515*b*
c. of men, they are but vanity 485*b*
c. of the bridechamber 506*a*
c. of the kingdom be cast out 506*a*
c. of the light 9*a*
c. of the Lord 3*a*
c. of this world 509*b*
c. . . . said she, are my jewels 64*b*
c.'s c. shall say they have lied 474*b*
c.'s looks, that brighten 170*a*
c.'s teeth are set on edge 503*b*
c. stood watching them 226*b*
c. sweeten labours 14*b*
c. walking two and two 32*b*
c., you are very little 414*a*
c., you shd. never let 452*b*

Children (*cont.*)
Christian c. all must be 3*b*
come away, c., call no more 6*a*
come again, ye c. of men 487*b*
come, dear c., let us away 5*b*
cruel c., crying babies 414*a*
Dame Lurch . . not have bandy c. 32*a*
do ye hear the c. weeping 43*a*
even c. followed 168*b*
fatherless c., and widows 479*a*
father pitieth his own c. 488*a*
frail c. of dust 172*b*
Friend for little c. 265*b*
go, c. of swift joy 441*a*
gracious c. 439*a*
he doeth for the c. of men 488*b*
her c. arise up 499*a*
holdeth c. from play 402*a*
if c., then heirs 513*b*
I have gathered thy c. 507*b*
I lie even among the c. of men 485*b*
indifferent c. of the earth 332*a*
I never knows the c. 259*b*
instead of fathers . . shalt have c. 484*b*
its c. a happy band 184*b*
joyful mother of c. 489*a*
little c. saying grace 413*b*
little c.'s eyes 441*b*
lo, C. and the fruit of the womb 489*b*
many women, and many c. 207*a*
materials to keep c. quiet 417*b*
men . . c. of a larger growth 139*a*
men fear death as c. 14*a*
mother who talks about . . own c. 128*b*
myself and c. three 108*b*
my tan-faced c. 457*b*
neither c. nor Gods 228*b*
no c. run to lisp 174*a*
Oh, help Thy c. 227*b*
old men and c. 490*b*
opponent of . . c. of the light 9*a*
procreation of c. 481*b*
provoke not yr. c. 515*b*
Rachel weeping for her c. 504*b*
secrets . . must be kept from c. 141*a*
see the c. sport 466*b*
shalt bring forth c. 492*b*
she had so many c. 533*b*
sick persons, and young c. 479*a*
sins of the fathers upon the c. 480*a*
so are the young c. 489*b*
suffer the little c. 508*b*
the C.'s Hour 246*b*
the young, young c. 43*a*
three fair c. first 432*b*
thy c. all gone 534*a*
to whom the lips of c. 286*a*
two c. did we stray 441*a*
Usna's c. died 475*b*
voices of c. . . on the green 32*b*
we are but little c. weak 3*b*
we are c. of splendour 452*a*
we are the c. of God 513*b*
we have c., we have wives 437*b*
were all thy c. kind 381*b*
wisdom is justified of her c. 506*b*
wiser than the c. of light 509*b*
women, then, are only c. 91*a*
Child-wife: only my c. 122*b*
Chill: Ah, bitter c. it was! 221*b*
c. thy dreaming nights 219*a*
Chillon! thy prison! 69*b*
Chilly: altho' the room grows c. 172*b*
I feel c. and grown old 52*b*
Chiltern: storm . . on the C. Hills 91*b*
take the C. Hundreds 91*b*
Chimborazo 446*a*
Chime: C. of full, sad bells 206*a*
c., ye dappled darlings 226*a*
faintly as tolls the evening c. 282*b*
higher than the sphery c. 268*a*
jarr'd against nature's c. 278*a*
last I heard their soothing c. 282*a*
some soft c. had stroked the air 216*b*
we will hear the c. 199*a*
Chimeras: Hydras, and C. dire 272*b*
poets taught . . of dire c. 267*b*
Chimes: heard the c. at midnight 380*b*
Chimney: hung by the c. with
care 280*b*
old men from the c. 402*a*

Chimney (*cont.*)
smoked like a c. 19*a*
Chimney-piece: Buffalo upon the c. 85*b*
Chimneys: c. were blown down 348*a*
good grove of c. 283*b*
so yr. c. I sweep 32*b*
Chimney-sweepers come to dust 329*a*
Chimpanzees: brainless as c. 76*a*
Chin: c. upon an orient wave 270*b*
compared to that was next her c. 416*a*
dimple on his c. 251*b*
her nose and c. they threaten 63*b*
his c., new-reaped 376*b*
page, with the dimpled c. 440*b*
China: break my best blue c. 179*b*
C. 'crost the Bay! 232*a*
c. that's ancient and blue 242*a*
fire a mine in China 66*a*
infusion of c. plant 2*a*
mistress of herself, tho' C. fall 302*a*
Chinamen: with C., but not with
me 26*b*
Chinee: heathen C. is peculiar 182*a*
Chinese: C. cheap labour 182*a*
C. crinkum-crankums 297*b*
Chineses: Sericana, where C. drive 273*b*
Ching-a-ring-a-ring-ching 297*b*
Chink: their importunate c. 57*a*
Chinks: c. that time has made 449*a*
fill hup the c. wi' cheese 416*b*
Chip hat had she on 219*a*
Chipping at the countenances 121*a*
Chips to the faithful allies 95*a*
Chit-chat of Cowper 239*b*
Chittabob's tail 20*a*
Chivalries: gentleness, and c. 257*a*
Chivalry: age of c. is gone 57*a*
age of c. is never past 226*b*
age of c. is past 130*a*
charge with all thy c. 77*a*
Christian service and true c. 375*a*
he loved c. 88*a*
her beauty and her c. 68*a*
his Memphian c. 271*b*
I have a truant been to c. 378*b*
noble acts of c. 257*a*
smiled Spain's c. away 71*b*
sung of Border c. 316*b*
Chloe (Cloe): C. is my real flame 306*a*
dear C., how blubbered 305*b*
to C.'s breast . . Cupid . . stole 31*b*
what can C. want? 302*a*
Chloris: ah, C.! that I now cd. sit 320*b*
call me C. 101*b*
Chocolate: coffee, tea, c. 4*b*
Choice: but the c. of friends 107*a*
c. in rotten apples 366*b*
c. of all my library 368*a*
each to his c. 235*a*
for on his c. depends the safety 330*b*
if there were a sympathy in c. 356*a*
in the worth and c. 214*b*
just the terrible c. 51*b*
most c., forsaken 341*b*
to Heaven the measure and the c. 214*a*
you takes yr. c. 535*a*
Choir: c. invisible 144*b*
ez hisn in the c. 250*b*
in a wailful c. 221*b*
innumerable c. of day 37*a*
leading his c., the Nine 5*b*
sweet singing in the c. 526*b*
Choirs (quires): bare ruin'd c. 388*a*
c. and places where they sing 478*b*
Choler: let's purge this c. 374*b*
Choose: c. thy ground 73*b*
c. to run for President 106*a*
c. . . . whatever suits the line 101*b*
c. what many men desire 353*b*
don't c. to have it known 91*a*
I lie as lads wd. c. 199*a*
leading wherever I c. 458*a*
not c. not to be 197*a*
sailor free to c. 236*a*
that did never c. amiss 353*b*
therefore c. life 494*b*
to c. time is to save time 15*b*
where to c. their place of rest 277*a*
Choosing: c. each stone 260*b*
hating not, just c. so 45*b*
pleased me long c. 276*a*

Chopper: here comes a c. 533b
Choppy: chippy c. 164b
Chops: bottled beer and c. 165b
  C. and Tomato sauce 126b
Chop-sticks: crop of c. 297b
Chorasmian: lone C. shore 392b
  hushed C. waste 8a
Chord: one clear c. to reach 459b
  smote the c. of Self 432a
  some c. in unison 112b
  struck one c. of music 306b
Chords: Jobling, there are c. 121b
  smote on all the c. with might 432a
Choristers: go the chanting c. 243a
Chortled in his joy 84a
Chorus: c. from Atlanta to the sea 473a
  c. Hymeneal 398b
  c. of indolent reviewers 427a
Chorus-ending from Euripides 45a
Chose: to her son she c. 524a
Chosen: twilights where his c. lie 32a
  ye have not chosen me 511a
Choughs: crows and c. 343b
  maggot pies and c. 349a
  russet-pated c. 357a
Chrematistic art 151a
Chrism: death's sweet c. 294b
Chrisom: been any c. child 381b
Christ: acknowledgment of God in C. 46a
  ah, C., that it were possible 434a
  a member of C. 481a
  and uphold the C. 427b
  are they ministers of C.? 515a
  brings Saviour C. again to earth 261b
  but C. rises! 46b
  but C. lore..he taughte 88b
  C. being raised from the dead 513a
  C., borne into virgynyte 474a
  C.-child stood at Mary's knee 92a
  C. his John 186b
  C., if my love were in my arms 527b
  C. is all, and in all 516a
  C. is all in all 279b
  C. is crucified again 244a
  'C. is nigh,' it seems to say 86b
  C. is the path 279b
  C. is thy strength 279b
  C. our passover 514a
  C. receive him 435a
  C. receive thy saule 529a
  C.'s particular love's sake 51a
  C.'s progress 447b
  C.'s stamp to boot 186b
  C.'s Sunday at morn 524a
  C., the Lord, is risen to-day 455b
  C. took the kindness 51a
  C. was born, across the Sea 200b
  C. with His lamp of truth 36b
  churches have killed their C. 434a
  counted loss for C. 516a
  fair father C. 428a
  faith of C. crucified 481a
  his captain C. 375b
  I am all at once what C. is 197b
  in C. shall all be made alive 515a
  joint heirs with C. 513b
  kingdoms of our Lord, and..C. 519a
  lady of C.'s College 11a
  last kind word to C. 51a
  lo, C. walking on the water 442b
  longs unto his C. to go 190b
  love of C. constraineth us 515a
  love of C. wh. passeth 515b
  man raised up by C. 430a
  may Lord C. enter in? 459b
  must then a C. perish 391b
  myself were accursed from C. 513b
  near the birth of C. 430a
  now is C. risen 515a
  of Lord C.'s heart 146a
  put on C. 481a
  reproach of C. greater riches 517a
  ring in the C. 431a
  see the C. stand 51b
  see where C.'s blood 258b
  show me, dear C., thy spouse 133a
  shuts the spouse C. home 198a
  soldiers of C., arise 455b
  statistical C. 291a
  the grey-grown speechless C. 421a

Christ (cont.)
  through C. wh. strengtheneth me 516a
  to live is C. 516a
  understood C. was a carpenter 29a
  unsearchable riches of C. 515b
  Vision of C. that thou dost see 29b
  was C. a man like us? 5a
  we have C.'s own promise 20a
  we withstood C. then 47a
  when the Lord C. was born 284b
  with C.; wh. is far better 516a
  yr. cold C. 233b
Christ Church: dine with the Canons of C. 208b
  festal light in C. hall 8a
  hark! the bonny C. bells 3a
  I am the Dean of C., Sir 528b
Christendom: summer-house in C. 378a
  wisest fool in C. 563b
Christentie: gowd in C. 531a
Christiad than a Pauliad 181b
Christian: approach, O C. wight 407b
  articles of the C. faith 481b
  as little as a C. 136b
  born of C. race 452b
  buried in C. burial 336a
  C. boys I can scarcely..make 10b
  C. can only fear dying 181a
  C. children all must be 3b
  C., dost thou see them 286a
  C. religion not only was 201b
  C.! seek not yet repose 146a
  C., up and smite them 286b
  coined..out of his C. name 254b
  cooled..as a C. is 354a
  darkness fell upon C. 54a
  every C...engage himself openly 30b
  every C. kind of place 413b
  fled with a c. 353b
  forgive them as a c. 11b
  for he is a C. 353a
  for the C. riles 233a
  good C. men, rejoice 286b
  hard it is to be a C.! 46b
  his C. name, I think, was John 130b
  honourable style of C. 41a
  I am a C. faithful man 384b
  in Christendom where is the C.? 147b
  in these C. days 424b
  in what peace a c. can die 2b
  it weareth the C. down 233a
  lawful for C. men 491b
  lead a holy C. life 247b
  mirror of all C. kings 381b
  no more wit than a C. 369b
  not good for the C. health 233a
  only Dick C. 289a
  rarity of C. charity 195b
  scratch the C. 477b
  shame on us, C. brethren 200b
  soul naturally C. 554a
  souls of C. peoples 91b
  stop, C. passer-by! 100b
  the C. while he sings 110b
  the gait of C. 333b
  thou persuadest me to be a C. 513a
  three C. men 257a
  tiger that hadn't got a C. 535b
  to form C. men 10b
  wherefore, C. men, be sure 286b
  works of C. men 423b
  you were a C. slave 185a
Christianity: beloved..where C. was the religion 418b
  C. better than Truth 102a
  C., of course, but why journalism? 18a
  church better than C. 102a
  his C. was muscular 129b
  local cult called C. 179b
  temper is nine-tenths of C. 184a
Christians: abhorred of all faithful C. 480b
  call themselves C. 479a
  C. awake 67b
  C. have burnt each other 70a
  O C., at yr. cross 43a
  onward, C., onward go 456b
  some C. have a comfortable creed 70b
  what these C. are 353a
Christless code 434a
Christmas: at C. I no more desire a rose 344b

Christmas (cont.)
  at C. play and make good cheer 446a
  C. comes but once a year 446a
  C. is coming 522b
  C. is here 440b
  C. shd. fall..in..Winter 2a
  eating a C. pie 532a
  keep our C. merry still 318a
  night before C. 280b
  old C. brought his sports 318a
  'twas C. broached..ale 318a
  'twas C. told..tale 318a
Christmas Day: C. in the morning 522b
  C. is breaking wan 228a
  that it was C. 407b
Christmas Eve..twelve of the clock 180a
Christome: live in any place in C. 145a
  died..like a C.-child 54a
Christs that die upon the barricades 459b
Chronic: do not weep for me. It is c. 123b
Chronicle: c. of a solitary..anguish 144a
  c. small beer 361a
  make yr. c. as rich with praise 381b
Chronicler: honest c. as Griffith 386b
Chronicles: brief c. of the time 332b
  look in the c. 366b
Chrononhontonthologos 79b
Chrysolite: perfect c. 363b
  seventh, a c. 520a
Chrysoprasus: tenth, a c. 520a
Chubby: Augustus was a c. lad 192b
Chuck: c. him out, the brute 235b
  c. it, Smith! 91b
Church: a c. and no steeple 420a
  at c., with meek..grace 168b
  bells have knoll'd to c. 326b
  be the C. at rest 415b
  blood of the martyrs..seed of the C. 574a
  built a c. in Dublin town 27b
  built God a c. 110b
  Catholick and Apostolick C. 480a
  c. better than Christianity 102a
  churchmen..kill their c. 434a
  C. militant 480b
  C. of Rome I found wd. suit 524a
  C.'s one foundation 415b
  C. with psalms must shout 187a
  come all to c. 99a
  come to c. in time 199a
  Dame Lurch, who is always at c. 32a
  figure in a country c. 418a
  free c. in a free State 567a
  'gainst that C. prevail 20a
  go to c. in a galliard 369b
  great C. victorious 415b
  he never passes a c. 207a
  here's a c.!..Let's go in! 123b
  if undrest at c., looks silly 150b
  I hold by the Ould C. 237a
  I like a c. 147a
  I like the silent c. 147b
  into his c. lewd hirelings climb 273b
  I persecuted the c. 514b
  I will build my c. 507a
  mere c. furniture 113a
  nearer the C., the further from God 4a
  no salvation..outside the church 537b
  of a different c. 65a
  press too close in c. and mart 44a
  see a c. by daylight 358a
  she came to the village c. 433b
  Sir Roger..sleep in..c. 2a
  some to c. repair 300a
  so to c. went she 199a
  stands the C. clock 40a
  the c. for peace 45a
  thy household the C. 479b
  what is a c.? 113b
  where Christ erecteth his c. 18b
  women to speak in the c. 514b
Church-door: housbondes at c. 88b
  so wide a c. 365b
Churches: as the c. have killed.. Christ 434a
  chapels had been c. 352b
  c. built to please the priest 61a
  fight against the c. 349b
  he must build c. then 334a
  John to the seven c. 518a
  keep silence in the c. 514b

Churches (cont.)
  lost, Down c. 235a
  send it to the seven c. 518a
Church-going bell 113a
Churchman: wd. I that cowlèd c. be 147a
Churchmen: c. fain wd. kill their
  church 434a
  single life doth well with c. 14b
Church of England: C. . . a com-
  promise 401a
  C. . .depository of doctrine 128a
Churchyard: a poor, weak. .c. thing 221b
  his morning walk. .in the c. 319b
Churchyards: troop home to c. 357a
Churn: magnet ever attract. .Silver C. 165b
Cibber: tuneful C. sing 206a
Cicero: fall below Demosthenes or C. 149b
  no. .opinion can alienate C. 255a
  if I cd. have known C. 122b
Cigar: good c. is a Smoke 227b
  Smith, take a fresh c. 76a
  sweet post-prandial c. 53b
Cigarette is the perfect type 460b
Cimber should be banish'd 339a
Cincinnatus of the West 73b
Cinder: how dry a c. this world is 132b
Cinders: made the c. fly 227b
  sate among the c. 535a
Cinnamon: c. and cloves 23a
  tinct with c. 221b
Cinque-pace: measure, and a c. 358a
Cipher: a c. in the state 316a
Ciphers: the only figure among c. 16a
Circle: all within this c. move 448b
  c. of a wedding-ring 95b
  c. of the golden year 427a
  form'd a c. to go into 30a
  God is a c. 526b
  love is a c. 189b
  swinging round the c. 205b
  the mortal right-lined c. 42b
  thy firmness makes my c. just 134a
  weave a c. round him thrice 101b
  wheel has come full c. 344a
Circles: c. and right lines limit 42b
  millions of c. can never make 171a
Circuitous: foiled c. wanderer 8a
Circumcision nor uncircumcision 516a
Circumlocution Office 123a
Circumscribed in time and place 471b
Circumscription and confine 359b
Circumspect: Buckingham grows c. 385a
  she is so c. and right 265a
Circumstance: artistries in C. 179a
  breasts the blows of c. 430b
  clutch of c. 185a
  dance of plastic c. 51a
  detect therein one c. 247b
  I am the very slave of c. 73b
  in such perilous c. 331a
  pride, pomp, and c. of. .war 362a
  some c. to please us 419a
  to a philosopher no c. 170a
  to envisage c. 218b
Circumstances: and after many c. 65b
  c. alter cases 123b
  c. beyond my. .control 122b
  c. over wh. he has no control 454b
  concatenation of c. 454a
  if c. lead me 332a
  man. .the creature of c. 181a
Circumstantial: c. evidence is. .con-
  vincing 135b
  some c. evidence is very strong 444a
Circus: bread, and the. .c. 549b
Cistern for foul toads 363a
Citadel: a tower'd c. 324a
  winged sea-girt c. 68a
  with peaceful c. 219b
Citadels: circle-c. there 197b
Cities: authority over ten c. 510a
  c. of men 438b
  c. of the dead 74a
  flower of c. all 143a
  hum of human c. torture 68b
  in c. little else but. .works of men 296a
  islanded by c. fair 395a
  towered c. please us 269a
  walls, palaces, half-c. 69a
Citizen: c. of no mean city 512b
  Gilpin was a c. 108a

Citizen (cont.)
  humblest c. of all the land 53a
  I am a Roman c. 540b
  requisite of a good c. 310a
  shows he is a c. of the world 15a
Citizens: before Man made us c. 250b
  civil c. kneading up the honey 381b
  fat and greasy c. 325b
  hearts of his fellow c. 244a
  London doth pour out her c. 383b
City: amid the c.'s jar 6b
  a rose-red c. 55a
  a very famous c. 103b
  beautiful c. of Prague 306b
  chaps out of the C. 93a
  citizen of no mean c. 512b
  c. had no need of the sun 520a
  c. is built to music 427b
  c. of dreadful night 443b
  c. of kites and crows 328a
  C. of palm-trees 448a
  C. of Sleep 228a
  c. of the best-bodied mothers 457b
  c. of the cleanliness 457b
  c. of the faithfullest 457b
  c. of the healthiest fathers 457b
  c. of the soul 69a
  c. of two kings 253b
  c. or suburban 277a
  c. such as vision builds 396a
  C.'s voice itself 399a
  c. that is set on a hill 505a
  c. was pure gold 520a
  c. wh. hath foundations 517a
  C. with her dreaming spires 8b
  dear c. of Cecrops 574a
  dissolute c. 468a
  earth has many a noble c. 86b
  except the Lord keep the c. 489b
  falling on the c. brown 37a
  go to the c. where they dwelt 488b
  happy is that c. 64a
  hell is a c. much like London 396b
  he that taketh a c. 498a
  holy c., new Jerusalem 519b
  hope of the C. of God 262a
  if you wd. know,. .live in a c. 103b
  in Dublin's fair c. 524a
  in populous c. pent 276a
  I saw a c. invincible 457a
  kindness in a strong c. 483b
  lead me into the strong c. 485b
  London; a nation, not a c 129b
  long in c. pent 221a
  looked he at the c. 253b
  lo, the c. is barren 121b
  near a whole c. full 195b
  new c. of Friends 457a
  no continuing c. 517a
  once in royal David's c. 3b
  on, to the C. of God 7b
  out of the holy c. 520b
  perils in the c. 515a
  populous and smoky c. 396b
  possession of truth as of a c. 41b
  run about thro' the c. 485b
  she was a maiden c. 472b
  shines over c. and river 435a
  street of the c. was pure gold 520a
  sun-girt c. 395b
  the c. cast her people out 323a
  the C. is of Night 443b
  the first c. Cain 107a
  there the great c. stands 457b
  this c. now doth. .wear 472b
  this great hive, the c. 107a
  thou c. of God 487a
  through c.-crowds must push 101a
  towery c. 197a
  up and down the C. Road 257b
  within the C. disinterred 396a
  Zion, c. of our God 289a
Cive anheling 194b
Civet: give me an ounce of c. 343a
Civic: where c. independence flings 77b
Civil: c. fury first grew high 64b
  he was so generally c. 209b
  in c. business; what first? 14b
  over violent, or over c. 138b
  too c. by half 400b
  whence all c. laws 13a

Civilian: mushroom rich c. 74b
Civilities with my Sovereign 207b
Civility: c. of my knee, my hat 41b
  I see a wild c. 189a
  traditions of c. 293a
Civilization: as c. advances poetry. .
  declines 254b
  resources of c. 167b
  three great elements of modern c. 80a
Civilized: Asia is not going to be c. 237a
  Woman will be the last thing c. 264b
Civilizes: sex whose presence c. ours 108a
Clad: a lady so richly c. 100a
  c. in complete steel 267b
  c. in homely russet 469a
Claim: spring to me, and c. me thine 428a
Clamour: c. in the slippery clouds 380a
  c. of the crowded street 247b
  with a c. of waters 420a
  with the c. keep her still awake 366b
Clamours: drea dc. counterfeit 362a
Claims of long descent 431b
Clan: before God made the angelic c. 476b
  leaving. .verse unto a little c. 219b
Clan Alpine's warriors 316b
Clan Coniul 318b
Clang of hurrying feet 12a
Clangour: trumpet's loud c. 139b
Clank: not a bile! Let 'em c.! 451a
Clap: c. thyself my love 372b
  if you believe, c. yr. hands! 21b
Clapham: my old aunt at C. 177a
Clapper: one another c.-clawing 65b
Clara threw the twins she nursed 172b
Clarence: perjured C. 384b
Claret: c. is the liquor for boys 210a
  c. wd. be port 570a
Claribel: send up Unity, C. 232b
Clarion: c. o'er the dreaming earth 396a
  sound, the c. 283a
Clarions: great winds Thy c. 94a
Clash: e'en let them c. 62b
Clashed: c. and hammered 427a
  c. with his fiery few 435a
Clasp: I shall c. thee again 50b
  oh! c. we to our hearts 312a
  reason why I c. them 106b
Clasped: c. by the golden light 195b
  c. her like a lover 432b
Clasps of a lascivious Moor 359b
Classes: c. against the masses 167b
  her noblest work she c. 60b
  masses against the c. 167b
  ye lower middle c.! 163b
Classic: for third the c. Milton 36a
Classical: advantages of a c. education 158a
  c. quotation is the parole 210b
  fortifying, c. curriculum 10a
Clause: servant with this c. 188b
Claverhouse: 'twas C. who spoke 316a
Clavicithern: lute or c. 47a
Clawed me with his clutch 448b
Claws: c. that catch 83b
  neatly spreads his c. 82b
  pair of ragged c. 145a
  see her stick her c. 250a
Clay: a thousand scattered into C. 152b
  blinds his soul with c. 437a
  brother of the c. 77b
  daily absorbs a c. 76a
  gilded loam or painted c. 374a
  gray stone and grassy c. 295a
  knowest Who hast made the C. 232b
  of c. and wattles made 475a
  power over the c. 513b
  shall the c. say to him 502b
  turf that wraps their c. 103a
Clayey: into a c. tenement 79a
Clean: all c. and comfortable 223b
  as c. as you can 426a
  child that is not c. 414a
  c., verb active 124b
  grew more c. and white 44a
  have to c. your slate 310b
  I was c. and brave 199a
  will these hands ne'er be c.? 350a
Cleaned: tops c. with champagne 416b
Cleaning: better have them c. his 'oss 416b
Cleanliness: c. is. .next to godliness 456a
  who of late for c. 106a

Cleanly: thus so c. I myself can free 137b
Cleanse thou me from my..faults 482b
Cleansed: what God hath c. 512a
Clear: all doctrines plain and c. 66a
  c. and gentle stream 35b
  c. as a whistle 67a
  nothing we cdn't. climb or c. 171b
  said it very loud and c. 85a
  that they cd. get it c. 84a
  they see not all c. 448a
  thy sky is ever c. 53a, 246b
Cleared: if this were only c. away 84a
Clearer: thinner, c., farther 436a
Clearing-house of the world 87a
Cleave: c. the wood 526a
  c. thou thy way 263b
  too weak to c. 96b
Cleft: who c. the Devil's foot 134a
Clementine: and his daughter, C. 280b
  oh my darling C.! 280b
Cleopatra: C.'s nose been shorter 564b
  gone to gaze on C. too 323a
  in C.'s sails their nests 324a
  I will be C. 324a
  I will o'ertake thee, C. 324b
  pleased with less than C. 139a
  since C. died 324b
  some squeaking C. 325a
  so near the heart as C. this 322b
  yr. C...every man's C. 139a
Clergy: an Arminian c. 297a
  bishops like best in their c. 405a
  c. were beloved in any nation 418b
  without the benefit o' the C. 104b
Clergyman: a proud c. 151a
  good enough to be a c. 208a
  Mr. Wilkinson, a c. 154b
  once a c. always a c. 525b
  that good man, the c. 434b
Clergymen: men, women and c. 404b
  to have with c. to do 136b
Cleric before, and Lay behind 65b
Clerical: lissom, c., printless toe 39b
Clerk: a C. ther was 88b
  am I both priest and c.? 376a
  'Baccy for the C. 234a
  c., foredoomed his father's soul 303a
  C. Saunders 529a
  illustrious, goes the c. 109b
  saw a Banker's C. 85b
  unlettered c., still cry 'Amen' 388a
  Venus c., Ovyde 89b
Clermont: broke his heart in C. town 25b
Clever: all the good people were c. 462b
  c. so rude to the good! 462b
  c. to a fault 45a
  good are so harsh to the c. 462b
  if young hearts were not so c. 199b
  it's c., but is it Art? 228a
  let who will be c. 225b
  manage a c. man 237b
  needs a very c. woman 237b
  people suppose me c. 53a
Client: here.. is our c. 136a
Cliff: c.-top has a carpet 35b
  in a coign of the c. 421b
Cliff-edge: cloaks the white c. 235a
Cliffs: c. wh. had been rent 100a
  still the solitary c. wheeled 466a
  where down cloudy c. 8b
  white c. I never more must see 252b
Climate: c. more uncertain than our 103b
  c. or the company 211b
  cold c., or years damp my..wing 276a
  our chilling c. hardly bears 410b
  where the c.'s sultry 70a
Climates: manners, c., councils 438b
Climax of all human ills 70b
Climb: a swimmer shall cross or c. 424a
  heart fails thee, c. not at all 145b, 307b
  do their best to c. 49b
  fain wd. I c. 307b
  last steps I c. 395b
  nothing she cdn't. c. or clear 171b
  teach ye how to c. 268a
Climbed the steep ascent 184a
Climber: c. up of knees 240b
  c.-upward turns his face 338a
Climbing: still c. after knowledge 259a
Clime: a far serener c. 33b
  c. of the unforgotten brave 72b

Clime (cont.)
  deeds that are done in their c. 67b
  in every c. adored 304a
  in some brighter c. 19a
  that sweet golden c. 32a
  this the soil, the c. 271a
  undiscovered c. 175a
Climes: night of cloudless c. 74a
  warmer c. give brighter plumage 241a
Cling: c. with life to the maid 146b
  hands round her knees, and c. 420a
  like the ivy I'll c. to you 266b
  makes them c. together 469a
  to thy Cross I c. 445a
Clings: as creeping ivy c. 110b
Clink: I'm here in the C. 227b
  let me the canakin c. 361a
Clive: what I like about C. 27b
Cliveden's proud alcove 302b
Cloak: dissemble nor c. them 478a
  his martial c. around him 462a
  in..c. of grey 8a
  old c. about thee 524b
  red blanket c. 219a
  'tis not alone my inky c. 330a
  travel forth without my c. 387b
Cloaked: Shadow c. from head to foot 430a
Cloaks: scarlet c. and surplices 243a
Clock: by Shrewsbury c. 379a
  c. doth strike, by algebra 65a
  c. struck one 534a
  forgot to wind up the c. 411a
  I open with a c. striking 400a
  look at the c. 19a
  mouse ran up the c. 534a
  stands the church C. 40a
  turned into a sort of c. 202b
  varnish'd c. that click'd 168b
  watch the c. for you 388a
Clocks: morning c. will ring 198b
Clod: a c. of wayward marl 358a
  a kneaded c. 352a
  before the heavy c. weighs on me 438a
Clodius: live like C. 72a
Clog of his body 158a
Clogs of that wh. else..oversoar 397b
Cloistered: fugitive and c. virtue 279a
Cloisters: quiet collegiate c. 96a
  studious c. pale 268b
Cloistress, she will veiled walk 369b
Clot: clotted clay the dingiest c. 442a
Clooth-na-Bare: grave of C. 475a
Clootie: Nick, or C. 58b
Close: c., and, I reckon, rather true 263b
  close behind him tread 99b
  c. with her, kiss her 424a
  ever best found in the c. 278a
  gates are mine to c. 233a
  grossly c. it in 355a
  hush in the C. to-night 287b
  never found his earthly c. 433a
  she'll c. and be herself 348b
  still hasten to a c. 108a
  they c., in clouds of smoke 318b
Closed: no marigolds yet c. 190a
Closer is He than breathing 427b
Closet: in the world, and not in a c. 90b
  one by one back in the C. lays 153b
Cloth: choose one c. for ever 284a
  did not mean to abuse the c. 151b
  on a c. untrue 164b
  web o' the silken c. 530a
  when the coarse c. she saw 114a
  white linen c. 480a
Clothe: care no more to c. 329a
  c. my naked villainy 384b
Clothed: c., and in his right mind 508b
  c. in purple and fine linen 510a
  c. in white samite 427b
  c. itself, sublime and strong 396a
  c. with a garment..to the foot 518a
  c. with his breath 429a
  c. with the light of the night 422b
  c. with transcendent brightness 271a
  he neither shall be c. 522a
Clothes: and donn'd his c. 335b
  away with their c. 128a
  bought her wedding c. 2b
  brushers of noblemen's c. 13b
  c. you wear or do not wear 91b
  fine c. are good 209a

Clothes (cont.)
  gars auld c. look..weel 59b
  hanging out the c. 533b
  her c. spread wide 336a
  her nice new c. 535b
  his c. not be burned 498a
  kindles in c. a wantonness 189a
  liquefaction of her c. 190b
  nothing to wear but c. 225a
  she wears her c...with a pitchfork 418b
  some upo' their c. 61a
  when he put on his c. 169a
  witnesses laid down their c. 512a
Clothes-horses: mere human c. 81a
Clothing: c. for the soul divine 29b
  c. is of wrought gold 484b
  gave thee c. of delight 32b
  softest c., woolly, bright 32b
  things in books' c. 239a
Cloth-of-gold: c. of tissue 323a
  for c. you cease to care 163b
Cloths: heaven's embroidered c. 474b
  I wd. spread the c. 474b
  one of these c. is heaven 284a
  the dark c. 474b
  these strange choosing c. 284a
Cloud: a fair luminous c. 100b
  but c. instead 273b
  choose a firm c. 302a
  c. of witnesses 517a
  c. that 's dragonish 324a
  c. wh. had outwept its rain 392a
  did a sable c. turn forth 267a
  do you see yonder c. 334b
  fades a summer c. away 18b
  fiend hid in a c. 32a
  from c. and from crag 392b
  I do set my bow in the c. 492b
  if I were a swift c. 396b
  in a pillar of a c. 494a
  lonely as a c. 467a
  no c. was in the sky 84a
  on a c. I saw a child 32a
  one silvery c. had lost his way 435a
  overcome us like a summer's c. 349a
  saw some western c. 48a
  stooping thro' a fleecy c. 268a
  the c. may stoop from heaven 436b
  there ariseth a little c. 496a
  the region c. hath mask'd him 387b
  the wild-swan pause in her c. 435b
  thickest c. earth ever stretched 44b
  thro' the dark c. shining 156a
  towers of battlemented c. 396a
  tremendous sea of c. 49b
  turn the dark c. inside out 156a
  were I a c. I'd gather 35b
  what a scowl of c. 52b
  when the c. is scattered 395a
  you cd. not see a c. 84a
Cloud-continents 3a
Clouded: shine forth upon our c. hills 31a
Clouden's woods amang 59b
Cloud-kissing Ilion 386b
Clouds: angel dropt..from the c. 378b
  Being that is in the c. 465b
  clamour in the slippery c. 380a
  c. and eclipses stain 387b
  c. are lightly curled 433a
  c. drop fatness 486a
  c. return after the rain 499b
  c. that gather round the..sun 467a
  c. they are without water 518a
  c. ye so much dread 110a
  comes with c. descending 456a
  gaudy c., like courtiers 282b
  heavily in c. brings on the day 1a
  he cometh with c. 518a
  he that regardeth the c. 499b
  looks in the c. 338b
  maketh the c. his chariot 488a
  never doubted c. wd. break 52a
  O c., unfold! 31a
  or in c. hide them 107a
  pity sitting in the c. 366a
  rapid c. have drank the last 399a
  sees God in c. 300b
  shadows of the c. 463a
  ships..dropping from the c. 443b
  soars the morning c. among 396a
  sun breaks thro' the darkest c. 366b

Clouds (cont.)
sweep the c. no more 194a
the c. dispell'd 141b
the white c. build in the..sky 38a
the white c. stray 37b
thro' rolling c. to soar 72a
thro' the c. ere they divide them 397b
trailing c. of glory 466a
wait till the c. roll by 462b
when dying c. contend 384a
white c. on the wing 4a
white c. scud between 35b
with what motion moved the c. 469a
Cloudy: among her c. trophies hung 219b
sees a little better in a c. day 147b
Cloven: not a worm is c. in vain 430b
Clover: burnet, and green c. 383b
c. and corn lay sleeping 226a
knee deep in c. 240a
Cloves: cinamon and c. 23a
Clown: heard..by emperor and c. 220a
Cloy: of all meats the soonest c. 107a
Cloyment and revolt 371a
Club: best c. in London 125b
call the C. to session 26a
rose politely in the c. 91b
Clubable man 211a
Clubs typical of strife 112b
Clucked thee to the wars 328b
Clusium: Lars Porsena of C. 253a
Clutch: clawed me with his c. 448b
c. of circumstance 185a
come, let me c. thee 347b
either hand may rightly c. 227b
Clutching the inviolable shade 8a
Clytemnestra: moral C. 73b
Cnut: when C., King, rowed thereby 79a
Coach: c. and six..thro' the Act 309a
come, my c.! 335b
Coaches trouble ev'ry street 137a
Coach-house: cottage with a double
c. 100b, 406b
Coach-makers: the fairies' c. 364b
Coachman's a privileged indiwidual 127a
Coal: best sun we have...c. 449b
by whose living c. I sit 190b
with hot burning c. 489b
cargo of Tyne c. 261b
envy's a c. comes hissing 18a
it is a fire, it is a c. 295b
like a c. his eye-ball 403a
the whole world turn to c. 187b
Coal-barges: ten dark c. 404a
Coalitions: England does not love c. 128a
Coals: 'e'll be squattin' on the c. 230a
heap c. of fire 498b
I sleep on the c. 122a
Coarse: one of them is rather c. 524a
Coast: I near the shadowy c. 442b
maps a jagged c. 36a
sounding c. its pyramids 415a
to pry along the c. 252a
Coaster: dirty British c. 261b
merry Grecian c. 8a
Coat: brown c., the black..stockings 255b
c. of many colours 493a
he did not wear his scarlet c. 459b
his c. was red 406b
in whose c. armour richly 408a
I take..my c. from the tailor 171a
oars, and c., and badge 120b
riband to stick in his c. 48a
the eternal Footman hold my c. 145a
the love that loves a scarlet c. 195a
the sake of a ribboned c. 287b
wear a long, black c. 175b
with his c. so gray 173a
Coats: a hole in a' yr. c. 62a
bound in their c., their hosen 504a
c. o' green satin 526a
in kingly-flashing c. 264a
in their gold c. spots you see 356b
their c. were brushed 84a
to make my small elves c. 356b
to shed their c. 421b
Coats-of-arms: worth a hundred c. 431b
Cob was the strongest 20a
Cobbett and Junius 183b
Cobbleigh: Uncle Tom C. 531b
Cobbler: c...go beyond his last 552b
thou art a c., art thou? 337b

Cobham: you, brave C.! 302a
Cobweb: learning c...of the brain 65b
Cobwebs: c. of the schools 112b
laws are like c. 417b
laws were like c. 13b
Cock: bark diminished to her c. 343b
c. a doodle doo! 534a
'C. and a bull,' said Yorick 412a
c.'s shrill clarion 174a
c. up yr. beaver 193b
c. with lively din 268b
Crito, we owe a c. to Aesculapius 560b
faded on the crowing of the c. 329b
head-waiter at the C. 439b
he was like a c. 144a
immediately the c. crew 508a
kept the c. that crowed 534a
this night, before the c. crow 508a
wondrous still, the c. and hen 31b
Cock-a-diddle-dow 367a
Cockatrice' dam 501b
Cockle hat and staff 335b
Cockles and mussels 524a
Cockpit: can this c. hold the..fields 381a
Cock Robin: who killed C.? 528a
Cocks: drowned the c. 342b
Cocksure..as Tom Macaulay 263a
Cocktails: gave her c. and wine 527a
Cockyolybirds: butterflies and the c. 226b
Cocoa is a cad 93b
Cocqcigrues: coming of the C. 226b
Cod: change the c.'s head 360b
home of the bean and the c. 34a
Coddle: I wd. not c. the child 207b
Code: Christless c. 434a
Codlin the friend 125a
Codling: when 'tis almost an apple 370a
Co-eternal: consubstantial, c. 286b
Co-exist: two master passions cannot
co-exist 77b
Coffee: c. on board steamers 439b
c., tea, chocolate 4b
if this is c., I want tea 536b
Coffee-house: to some c. I stray 175b
Coffer: but litil gold in c. 88b
Coffin: becomes his c. prodigiously 170b
c. clapt in a canoe 67b
on my black c. 371a
white-faced..in the c. 457b
Cogibundity of cogitation 79b
Cogitations: interpreter of the c. 520b
Cogitative: his c. faculties 79b
Cognizance: took such c. of men 47b
Cohort of the damned 229a
Cohorts: his c. were gleaming 74a
Coign: buttress, nor c. of vantage 347a
Coil: c. of his crystalline streams 396b
shuffled off this mortal c. 333a
Coin: beauty is Nature's c. 267b
c. his pouches wad na bide in 62a
c. of silvery shine 85b
I had rather c. my heart 341a
pays him in his own c. 418b
the C., Tiberius 130b
Coincidence: a 'strange c.' 71a
Coiner of sweet words 8a
Coins, some true, some light 428a
Coke: Mr. William C. 289a
Cokkel: or springen c. 89a
Cold: art neither c. not hot 518b
as c. as any stone 382a
boughs wh. shake against the c. 388a
caught an everlasting c. 454b
c. and heat, and summer 492b
c. as paddocks tho' they be 190b
c., c., my girl! 364a
c., commanded lust 230b
c. doth not sting 286a
c. performs th' effect of fire 272b
even till I shrink with c. 325b
fleece is white but 'tis too c. 115a
foot and hand go c. 415b
give them the c. steel, boys 4b
I am nothing a c. 415a
ink in my pen ran c. 449b
i' the c. o' the moon 45b
let his soup get c. 192b
life's arrears of pain..and c. 50b
living hand..wd., if it were c. 219a
neither c. nor care 285b
she alone were c. 329a

Cold (cont.)
shelter me from the c. 27a
straight is c. again 341a
thick man's blood with c. 98b
Tom's a-c. 343a
we called a c. a c. 27a
wert thou in the c. blast 62a
when its auld wrack c. 530a
Cold Bath Field 100b, 406b
Colder: a c. kirk, and in't but few 61b
a c. preacher never spak 61b
the pleasanter the c. 66a
Coldly: c.,..descends the..evening 7b
c. she turns from their gaze 281b
I speak too c. 282b
Coldness: faithless c. of the times 431a
with c. still returning 471a
Cole: old King C. 532a
Coleridge: as friend C. said 239b
brother C. lull the babe 72b
C., for instance, wd. let go by 222a
[C.] talked on for ever 183b
cultivate simplicity, C. 239b
Lamb, Holcroft and C. 183a
lose a volume to C. 239a
Mr. C.'s lyric prose 183b
thy library against S. T. C. 239a
you will see C. 395b
Coliander 402b
Coliseum: when falls the C. 69a
while stands the C. 69a
Collar: braw brass c. 63a
Collars of the moonshine's..beams 364b
Collects: c.—tho' it does not sub-
scribe 86a
c. wh. had soothed..Christians 255b
College: eighty-thousand c.-councils 438b
endow a c., or a cat 302a
Master of this c. 528b
Colleges: for a' their c. and schools 63a
Collingwood: Benbow, C., Byron 287b
Collins: if you do not marry Mr. C. 11b
Mr. C. had only to change 11b
Cologne: at St. Jame and at C. 88b
wash yr. city of C. 100b
Colonel: Captain or C. or Knight 278b
c. and his officers were in..pain 417b
Colonies: c. do not cease to be c. 128a
C. raised their flag against a power 454a
my hold of the c. 570a
the commerce with our c. 55b
Colonnade: sound of the cool c. 110b
Colonus: singer of sweet C. 6a
Coloquintida: bitter as c. 360b
Colossus: bestride..world like a C. 337b
cut a C. from a rock 211a
Colour: chestnut was ever the only c. 327a
giveth his c. in the cup 498b
good dog..cannot be of a bad c. 23b
heaven's c., the blue 284a
her c. comes and goes 131a
his c. can't be seen 525b
his..lips did from their c. fly 337b
I yearned for warmth and c. 428a
responds with c. and with shadow 441b
sky imbrued with c. 49a
the c. I think of little moment 23b
those wh. love c. the most 314b
'tis a c. she abhors 371b
'twas a c. he never liked 382a
what c. is it of? 323b
Coloured: see the c. counties 199a
Colouring: take a sober c. 467a
Colours: all c. a suffusion 100b
all c. will agree in the dark 14a
coat of many c. 493a
c. in the Turkey carpet 254b
c. seen by candlelight 43b
c., that are but skin-deep 185b
his c. laid so thick 140a
in goodly c. gloriously array'd 408a
their c. and their forms 472a
under whose c. he had fought 375b
when the oldest c. have faded 236b
wrapt his c. round his breast 184b
wrought about with divers c. 484b
Colour-Sergeant: C. said 228b
she's c. of the Nonpareil 121b
Colt: hadde alway a c.'s tooth 89b
Columbia: Hail, C.! 198a
Columbine: c. commendable 402b

Columbine (cont.)
Pink and purple C. 409b
Column: is the stately c. broke 317b
six-foot c. of fop 195a
throws up a streamy c. 112a
where London's c...lifts the head 302b
Comb: c. and a glass in her hand 525b
shd. I c. my hair 530a
Combat: the c. deepens 77a
to c. may be glorious 112a
Combermere: yr. grace thought Lord
C. a fool 455a
Combine: when bad men c. 56b
Combs: gowd c. in their hair 530a
Combustion: accents terrible of..c. 348a
hideous ruin and c. 271a
Come: art thou he that shd. c. 506b
behold, I c. quickly 520b
chaos is c. again 361b
c. again another day 534b
c. again, ye children of men 487b
c.; and c. strong 114b
c. and he cometh 506a
c.; and strong within us 226a
c., and trip it 268b
c. as the waves c. 319a
c. as the winds c. 319a
c. away, c. away 318b
c. away, death 371a
c. back! c. back! 77a
c. back, Horatius! 253b
'c., c,' said Tom's father 282a
c. down, O maid 437a
c., fill the Cup 152b
c. forth, and bring with you 471b
c. forth into the light 471b
c. hither, Evan Cameron! 12b
c. Helen, c. give me my soul 258b
c. hither, lady fair 217b
c., Holy Ghost 491a
c. in, c. in 54a
c. in the evening 118a
c. into the garden, Maud 434a
c. in yr. war-array 318b
c., knit hands 267a
c., landlord, fill the..bowl 522b
c. lasses and lads 522b
c. like shadows, so depart 349b
c., long-sought! 399a
c., my coach! 335b
c., my Corinna 189a
c. my tan-faced children 457b
c. not, when I am dead 426a
c. one, c. all! 316b
c. out, thou bloody man 495b
c. over into Macedonia 512b
c. then, my brethren 307a
c., thou holy Paraclete 549b
c., Thou Holy Spirit, c. 86b
c., thou mortal wretch 325a
c. unto me, all ye that labour 506b
c. unto these yellow sands 367a
c. up Whitefoot 203a
c. weal, c. woe, we'll gather 320a
c. what c. may 346b
c. when you're called 143b
c. with bows bent 420a
c. with old Khayyám 152b
c. without warning 118a
c. worthy Greek, Ulysses c. 117a
c. ye before Him, and rejoice 224b
c. ye here to fight 530b
c. ye here to play 530b
c. ye thankful people, c. 3b
cry is still, 'They c.' 350b
even so, c., Lord Jesus 520b
had she c. all the way for this 284a
he never will c. again 336a
I c. from nothing 265a
if it be now, 'tis not to c. 337a
I hear you, I will c. 199a
it needn't c. to that 85a
let him that heareth, say c. 520b
let him that is athirst c. 520b
look not on pleasures as they c. 187a
may never c. together again 118a
men may c., and men may go 425b
nay, c. up hither 312b
O c., all ye faithful 290a, 558b
O c., Emmanuel 286b
O Lamb of God, I c.! 146a

Come (cont.)
one to c., and one to go 85a
seldom c., they wished-for c. 376b
some c. to take their ease 386b
Spirit and the bride say, C. 520b
tarry till I c. 512a
tells thee I c. 225b
that it shd. c. to this! 330a
the foe! they c.! they c.! 68b
then said I, Lo, I c. 484a
therefore I cannot c. 509b
things present, nor things to c. 513b
thou'lt c. no more, never, never 344a
ve must all c. to it 127a
went and cannot c. again 199b
what's to c. is still unsure 370b
what will c., and must c. 5a
when I c. again I will repay 509a
when shall I c. to thee? 523b
where did you c. from, baby dear? 256a
wherefore art thou c.? 508a
wh. was, and wh. is to c. 518a
whistle, and I'll c. to you 63a
whistle and she'll c. 23b
will c. when it will c. 339a
will they c. when you do call 378a
will ye no c. back again? 285b
will you no c. back again? 193b
you c. most carefully 329a
Come-down: incredible c.! 25a
Comedy: c. to those that think 449b
most lamentable c. 356a
Comeliness: he hath no form nor c. 503a
Comely: all mid be c. 21a
I am black, but c. 500a
let thy attire be c. 251b
show a lass as c. or as kindly 231b
Spanking Jack was so c. 120b
Comer: grasps in the c. 369a
Comes: he c. too near 291b
hope never comes that c. to all 271a
if it c. to that 85a
she c.! she c.! the sable throne 299a
she c. to me 445b
something wicked this way c. 349b
Comest: thou c., much wept for 430a
Comet: against a c.'s tail 407a
c. of a season 69b
glorious the c.'s train 403a
Satan stood..like a c. burn'd 273a
Cometh: canst not tell whence it c. 510b
c. up from the wilderness 501a
he c. not, she said 433a
it c. everywhere 146a
one thing c. sooner 171b
where it c., all things are 146a
Comets: old men and c. 419a
there are no c. seen 339a
Comfit-maker's wife 378a
Comfits: children..deceived with c. 13a
Comfort: another c. like to this 361a
a' the c. we're to get 63a
beside the waters of c. 483a
carrion c., Despair 197a
carry their c. about with them 144b
c. and help the weak-hearted 479a
c. of thy help again 485a
c.'s a cripple 136b
c. ye my people 502b
continual c. in a face 313b
feels the same c. 194a
from ignorance our c. flows 306a
I beg cold c. 374b
naught for yr. c. 92a
neither found I any to c. me 486b
of c. no man speak 375b
O tidings of c. 523a
social c., in hospital 43a
speeches that c. cruel men 93a
sweet Spirit c. me 191a
take all my c. of thy worth 387b
the sober c., all the peace 283a
they never knew c. 255a
this must my c. be 374b
two loves..of c. and despair 389b
was not ecstasy but it was c. 123a
well, here's my c. 367b
what wd. c. the one 160a
whence can c. spring 465a
Comfortable: c. words 480b
some Christians have a c. creed 70b

Comfortably: a lot of money to die c. 66b
Comforted: folly of being c. 475a
for they shall be c. 505a
Rachel..wd. not be c. 504b
Comforter will not come 511a
Comforters: miserable c. 497a
Comforteth: one whom his mother c. 503b
Comfortless Despair 175a
Comforts: c. we despise 324b
c. while it mocks 50b
helpers fail, and c. flee 251b
our loves and c. shd. increase 361a
to be, and was not, c. me 50b
when c. are declining 110b
Comic: business of a c. poet 104a
Comical: I often think it's c. 164a
Coming: an eye will mark our c. 70a
Campbells are c. 526b
c. events cast their shadows 77a
c. of the Cocqcigrues 226b
c. through the rye 59b
c. to that holy room 133a
even as their c. hither 344a
far off his c. shone 275a
going out and thy c. in 489b
he is c.! like a bridegroom 12b
hold the fort, for I am c. 33a
I'm c., I'm c. 156b
it's c. yet, for a' that 60b
meet thee at thy c. 502a
she is c., my dove 434a
she is c., my own, my sweet 434a
the c. by and by 165b
there's a good time c. 256a
welcome the c., speed the going 303b
Command: born to sue, but to c. 374b
c. my heart and me 115a
c. Nature except by obeying her 17a
even the c. from you 242a
hast c. of every part 190a
I may c. where I adore 371a
I will be correspondent to c. 367a
left that c. sole daughter 276a
less used to sue than to c. 316b
move only in c. 350a
not in mortals to c. success 1b
to comfort, and c. 470b
Commander: I was the world's c. 345b
Commandment: first c. with promise 515b
laws..are at my c. 381a
thy c. is exceeding broad 489a
thy Word and C. 478b
Commandments: because I keep thy
c. 489a
fear God, and keep his c. 500a
go in the path of thy c. 489a
hadst hearkened to my c. 502b
I'd set my ten c. in yr. face 384a
running the way of thy c. 479b
Commands: he that c. the sea 15b
servant does not all c. 329a
those he c. move 350a
Commemorative: cold c. eyes 312b
Commences, reigns, and ends 403a
Commend: all our swains c. her 372b
forced to c. her highly 296a
reserved to blame or to c. 303a
Commendable: silence is only c. 352b
Commendation: beautiful face..a..c. 13b
small matters win great c. 16b
Commendations: angling deserves c. 450b
Commendeth: obliquely c. himself 41a
Commends: hurts..who lavishly c. 94a
Comment: none can read the c. 92a
offence shd. bear his c. 340b
Commentators: as learned c. view 419b
how c. each dark passage shun 477a
Commenus had a heart to resolve 162a
Commerce: equal to the whole of..c. 55b
honour sinks where c...prevails 170a
in matters of c...the Dutch 78b
speak of..c. of..colonies 55b
Commissary: Destiny the C. 133b
Commit: do not adultery c. 96b
God's..protection we c. thee 481b
pretty follies they themselves c. 353b
Committee: therefore got on a C. 93a
Commodity: c. of good names 376b
tickling c., c. the bias 374a
Commodus: the accession of C. 162a
Common: all things they have in c. 33a

Common (cont.)

ay, madam, it is c.	329b
because they are not already c.	246a
c. is the commonplace	429b
c, woman of c. earth	98a
hard task to treat what is c.	542a
he nothing c. did	261a
in c. things that round us lie	469a
I saw naught c. on Thy Earth	232b
manner rude..c. at yr. age	25b
nor lose the C. touch	230a
steals a c. from the goose	527b
such as is c. to man	514b
that call not thou c.	512a
the same with c. natures	191b
thou know'st 'tis c.	329b
to make it too c.	379b
touches of things c.	44a
Commonalty: dog to the c.	328a
joy in widest c.	464a
Commoners: vital c.	380b
Commonplace: common is the c.	429b
'c.', said Holmes	136a
c. things and characters	320b
unassuming c.	463b
Commons: C., faithful to..system	256a
highest tribunal..C.	56a
let but the c. hear this	340a
speak..well in the House of C.	130a
Common Sense: c. and plain dealing	148a
experiences joined with c.	175b
gift to Beauty, C.	264a
Republic's crowning c.	437a
rich in saving c.	435a
sword of C.!	263a
Commonwealth: caterpillars of the c.	375a
neither..despaired of the C.	129a
the c. is fixed and stable	56a
Commonwealths: plots..raise up c.	138a
Commune with yr. own heart	481b
Communicate: to do good and to c.	517a
Communicated: good, the more c.	274b
Communication: let yr. c., be Yea	505a
Communications: evil c. corrupt	515a
Communion: one c. and fellowship	480a
Communist: what is a c.?	146a
Community: honour, as in one c.	469b
Compact..between the North.. South	159a
Companion: appetite..never a wise c.	412a
fit c. is his horse	108a
God send the prince a better c.	379b
his harp, the sole c.	22b
leave of an old and agreeable c.	162a
thy poor, earth-born c.	62a
Companions: all her lovely c.	281b
best c., innocence and health	168a
brethren and c.' sakes	489b
c. for middle age	14b
c. of our woe	450a
I have had c.	240b
I think of those C. true	79a
old c. in adversity	53b
that such c. thou'dst unfold	363a
while their c. slept	247b
Company: a crowd is not c.	15b
a little love and good c.	150a
an Honest Man in much C.	107a
climate or the c.	211b
c. of all faithful people	480b
c., villainous c.	378b
die in that man's c.	383a
except the present c.	290b
expected justice from a c.	404b
gay, in such a jocund c.	467a
give me yr. bill of c.	418a
good c. and good discourse	450b
horsemen, a brave c.	33b
none of all our c., I boast	36a
other c. in youthe	88b
Punctual Delivery C.	124b
qualified to shine in c.	419a
religion..in a mixed c.	91a
[Shakespeare]..very good c.	11a
three is c.	460a
take the tone of the c.	90b
to the kirk with a goodly c.	100a
true brother of a c.	476b
we were a gallant c.	69b
Compare: belied with false c.	389a
how I may c. this prison	376a

Compare (cont.)

I will not Reason and C.	30b
shall I c. thee	387a
Comparison: alone, for the c. of all	216a
in whose c. all whites are ink	368b
Comparisons: c. are odorous	359a
c. doon offte gret greuaunce	251a
confronted him with self-c.	346a
she, and c. are odious	132a
Compass: a narrow c.	449a
and c. lost	109b
c. of the world	483a
my heart..the faithful c.	161a
my life is run his c.	341b
thou shalt c. me about	483b
thro' all the c. of the notes	139b
to the top of my c.	334b
we the globe can c. soon	357a
wide c. round be fetched	44b
within his bending sickle's c.	389a
Compassed: c. by the inviolate sea	437a
we also are c. about	517a
Compasses: as stiff twin c. are two	134a
Compassion: c. in the very name of a Curate	405a
his bowels of c.	518a
Compel: c. thee to go a mile	505a
c. them to come in	509b
Compensation: glory 's no c.	237a
Competence: debtless c.	439a
Competency lives longer	352b
Competition: anarchy and c. the laws	315a
where there is no c., no vanity	208b
Complain: farmers, flourish and c.	113b
I heard him c.	453a
to c. of the age we live in	56b
Complainers for the public	56b
Complaining: but the voice of c.	284a
no c. in our streets	490b
thro' my daily c.	483b
unheard was her c.	407a
Complaint: instead of dirges this c.	225a
Lord, it is my chief c.	110a
the voice of my c.	483a
Complaints: what needs c.	189a
Complete: and in herself c.	276a
just my vengeance c.	47b
mine I saved and hold c.	48b
Complexion: c. is perfect gallows	367a
gold c. dimmed	387a
mislike me not for my c.	353a
of what c. soever	356a
schoolgirl c.	526a
turn thy c. there, patience	363a
whose fresh c. and whose heart	373b
Complexions: coarse c. and cheeks	267b
Compliance: timely c. prevented him	151a
Complies: he that c. against his will	66a
Compliment: but farewell c.	365a
feigning was called c.	371b
to return the c.	166a
Comply: so backward to c.	110a
Composer: contemplation of..first C.	42a
Composition: mad c.!	374a
take more c. and fierce quality	341b
Compositions: read over yr. c.	208a
Compound for sins	65a
Comprehend: c. all vagrom men	358b
when she begins to c.	305b
Compromise: Church of England.. a c.	401a
give me the Brown c.	201a
Compulsion: c. doth in music lie	266b
fools by heavenly c.	342a
give you a reason on c.	377b
happy by c.	102a
on what c. must I?	354b
Compute: what 's done we..may c.	59a
Comrade: c. of thy wanderings	396b
new-hatch'd, unfledged c.	330a
no c. Lucy knew	467b
stepping where his c. stood	318b
Comrades: c., leave me here	432a
dear love of c.	457a
yr. c. chase e'en now the fliers	96b
Comus and his midnight crew	175a
Con: taken great pains to c. it	370a
Concatenation: c. of circumstances	454a
in a c. accordingly	171a
Conceal: half c. the Soul within	429b
he was always able to c. it	446b

Conceal (cont.)

how much you can c.	21b
ne'er express, yet cannot all c.	69b
tried to c. him by naming him	194b
use of speech..to c. them	170b
Concealing: hazard of c.	60a
Concealment: but let c., like a worm	371a
Conceit: all in their high c.	146b
a man wise in his own c.	498b
c. divinely framed	78a
c. in weakest bodies	335a
sluggard is wiser in his own c.	498b
strutting player, whose c. lies	368b
with self and vain c.	375b
you must c. me	339b
Conceited: never..pity..c. people	144b
Conceits: best c. do prove..liars	136b
wise in yr. own c.	513b
words..tokens..for c.	13a
Conceives by idleness	383b
Conceivest: thou c. Him not	187a
Conceiving: our benumbed c. soars	442a
Concentrated: more and more c. in you	223b
Concentrates: it c. his mind	209b
Conception: choke the strong c.	363b
such as dodge c.	217b
truer c. of God	10b
Conceptions equal to the soul's	464b
Concern: a matter they had no c. in	419a
conduct its largest c.	10a
Concerns: think only what c. thee	275b
where it c. himself	214b
Concessions of the weak..of fear	55b
Conciseness: accuracy..sacrificed to c.	212b
Conclave: in stately c. met	92a
Conclusion: c. in unmitigated act	229a
denoted a foregone c.	362a
lame and impotent c.	361a
men hasten to a c.	15b
the other is a c.	206b
Conclusions: life is..drawing..c.	66b
narrow minds..narrow c.	265b
pursued c. infinite	325b
Concord: c. of sweet sounds	355b
c. of well-tuned sounds	387a
damn'd firm c. holds	272b
lover of c.	478a
quarrels oft in pleasing c. end	278a
unity, peace, and c.	479a
Concurrence: fortuitous c. of atoms	292a
sweet c. of the heart	191a
Condemn: cause, and c. you to death	82b
c. itself for being here	350b
neither do I c. thee	511a
Condemned to earth for ever	46b
Condemns: Johnson c. whatever he disapproves	58b
Condense within thy soul	288b
Condescend to men of low estate	513b
Condition: cheerful as any man..in that c.	296a
gentle his c.	383a
my unhoused free c.	359b
O hard c.!	382b
wearisome c. of humanity	176b
whine about their c.	458a
Condolement: persevere in..c.	330a
Conduct: c. is three-fourths of..life	10a
c. of a clouded cane	302b
his c. still right	169b
morality is the regulation of c.	407b
our c. isn't all yr. fancy paints	235b
secondly, gentlemanly c.	10b
what is c.?	10b
Conductor, when you receive a fare	38b
Cone: country..is an inverted c.	210a
Cones: eat the c. under his pines	157b
Confabulate: if birds c.	110b
Conference: c. a ready man	16a
free and friendly c.	340b
Confess yourself to heaven	335a
Confessed: faith before the world c.	200a
half absolved who has c.	305b
Confession of his true state	333a
Confide: these our critics much c. in	419b
Confidence: c. is..of slow growth	297a
damned hisself in c.	127a
the c. of reason give	464a
Confident: never more c. of anything	129a

Confine: erring spirit hies to his c. 329b
the very verge of her c. 342b
Confined: cabined, cribbed, c. 349a
to numbers I'll not be c. 461a
Confines: in these c...cry 'Havoc!' 339b
Confirm: c. him who singeth 47a
c. the feeble knees 502a
c...tidings as they roll 2a
ratify and c. the same 481a
Confirmation, or laying on of hands 481a
Confirmations: jealous c. strong 362a
Confiscation: we have legalized c. 128b
Conflict: in this c. of opinions 212a
the heat of c., keeps the law 465b
too weak the c. to support 344a
Conflux of two Eternities 80b
Conform, or be more wise 296a
Conformation of his mind was such 255a
Confound: c. their politics 79b
c. the things wh. are mighty 514a
do but themselves c. 54b
Confounded: let me never be c. 478a
Confounds: not the deed c. us 347b
Confusion: all else c. 436b
bright things come to c. 356a
c. now hath made his masterpiece 348a
c. of their own faces 503b
c. on thy banners 173b
c. worse confounded 273a
if c. have a part 280b
ruin and c. hurled 2b
strut to our c. 324a
world calls guilt, in first c. 96a
Confute: c., change hands, and still c. 64b
no man can tell how to c. him 321a
read not to . . c. 16a
Congratulate: friends to c. 141b
Congratulatory regrets 128b
Congregate: merchants most do c. 353a
Congregation: in the face of this c. 481b
latter has the largest c. 118b
Congregations: C. committed to their
charge 478b
c. of naughty men 487a
Congress makes no progress 562a
Congs: Kinquering C. 409b
Conies: stony rocks for the c. 488b
Conjecture: now entertain c. 382a
Conjugal attraction unreproved 274a
Conjunction of the mind 260b
Conjuration and what . . magic 360a
Connecting-rod: stride o' yon c. 231b
Connoisseurs: as some of yr. c. do 20a
Connubial: nothing wrong in a c. kiss 70b
rites . . of c. love refused 274a
Connubiality: wictim o' c. 126a
Conquer: Antony shd. c. Antony 324b
c. him that did his master c. 324a
easier to c. it (the East) 449b
like Douglas c. 194b
she stoops to c. 170b
that was wont to c. others 375a
we c. but to save 76b
we'll c. again and again 158b
went forth conquering and to c. 518b
Conquered: c., O pale Galilean 423b
I came, I saw, I c. 548a
I will be c. 211b
'living' is c. at last 297b
mortal creatures, c. and secured 464b
People never c. quite 294b
perpetually to be c. 55b
thou hast c., O Galilean 548a
Conquering: c. kings their titles take 87a
he went forth c. 518b
in c. one thou hast so enriched 36a
see the c. hero comes 244a
so sharp the c. 90a
Conqueror: came in with Richard C. 366b
came in with the C. 38a
c. creates a Muse 449a
Emathian c. 278b
its hero the C. Worm 208a
proud foot of a c. 374b
Conquest: fann'd by c.'s crimson 173b
peace is of the nature of a c. 380b
shameful c. of itself 375a
Conquests: are all thy c...shrunk 339b
drums and tramplings of three c. 42a
his carnage and his c. cease 67b
the only honourable c. 56a

Conquests (cont.)
to spread her c. further 59b
what c. brings he home? 337b
Consanguineous: am not I c.? 370b
Conscience: a Nonconformist c. 460a
a still and quiet c. 386a
'budge not,' says my c. 353b
celestial fire, called c. 451b
cheerfully for c. sake 491a
c. and grace, to the . . pit 335b
c. as their King 427b
c. avaunt 95b
c. doth make cowards of us all 333a
c. is a coward 171a
c. is born of love 389b
c. is but a word 385a
c. of the king 333a
c. void of offence 512b
c. with injustice is corrupted 384a
corporation to have a c. 444b
crept too near his c. 385b
gentle beast, and of a good c. 357b
guardian of his Majesty's c. 444b
health. . next to a good c. 450b
his c. has crept too near 385b
hold it very stuff o' the c. 359b
my c. hath a thousand . . tongues 385a
Non-conformist C. makes cowards 24b
O coward c. 385a
of nyce c. took he no keep 88b
save free c. from the paw 278b
siding champion, C. 267a
the c. of her worth 275b
their best c. is not to leave 't 361b
things whereof our c. is afraid 479b
thing they call a c. 195a
thus be c.-calmed 219a
too young to know what c. is 389b
what c. dictates to be done 304a
Consciences: for . . c. the arms are fair 379a
Conscious: the c. stone to beauty 147a
to be c. of none 80b
Consciousness: chamber of c. 204b
c. the Will informing 179b
Consecrate: Beauty, that dost c. 394b
I c. to thee 241a
Consecrated: c... above our power 245a
I be not buried in c. ground 180b
Consecration and the poet's dream 468b
Consent: all with one c. began 509b
c. of all great men 314b
I will ne'er c.—consented 70a
with one c. praise . . gawds 369a
without c. been only tried 291b
Consented: c. together in . . wedlock 481b
I will ne'er consent—c. 70a
to his fate they all c. 215a
Consentedst: thou c. unto him 485a
Consequence: business of c. 19b
it's of no c. 122b
trammel up the c. 347a
wisdom in the scorn of c. 435b
Consequences: almost inevitable C. 237b
betray 's in deepest c. 346a
c. of them will be 64b
damn the c. 572b
know all mortal c. 350a
logical c. are the scarecrows 203a
nor punishments—there are c. 203b
Conservation: state without . . means
of its c. 56b
Conservatism: barren thing this C. 129a
C. discards Prescription 129a
c. offers no redress 129a
what is c.? 245a
Conservative: called the C. party 115b
C. Government . . hypocrisy 128a
healthy stomach is . . c. 66b
last C. Ministry . . hypocrisy 17b
man's the true C. 247a
or else a little C. 164a
sound C. government 129a
staid, c... type of mind 452a
Conservatives: men . . c. after dinner 148a
men are c. when . . least vigorous 148a
Consider: c. anything, only don't cry 84b
c. her ways, and be wise 498a
c. it not so deeply 347b
c. the lilies of the field 505b
'c. well,' the voice replied 438b
in the day of adversity c. 499b

Consider (cont.)
I will c. thy heavens 482a
man doth not well c. 487b
O c. this, ye that forget God 485a
O daughter, and c. 484b
read . . to weigh and c. 16a
to c. too curiously to c. so 336b
Considerable in his native place 208a
Consideration: c. like an angel 381a
deserve no c. 237b
for a c. 319b
our primary c. wd. be 209a
Considered: I have c. the days of old 487a
Considering: put on my c. cap 23a
Consign to thee, and come to dust 329a
Consigned: in every place c. 213a
Consistency: a foolish c. 147b
with c... great soul has nothing 147b
Consolation: Barnabas, the son of c. 512a
that's one c. 126a
with peace and c...dismiss'd 278a
Console us when we fall 55a
Consort: with such c. as they keep 268b
Conspicuous: c... by its absence 315a
c. object in a Nation's eye 465b
Conspiracy: c. of our spacious song 114b
O c.! sham'st thou to show 338b
open-eyed c. 367b
Conspire: you and I with Him c. 154a
Conspirers: where c. are 349b
Conspiring with him how to load 221b
Constable: fit man for the c. of the
watch 358b
outrun the c. 65b
Constabulary duty 's to be done 166b
Constancy: but c. in a good 41b
c. alone is strange 309b
c. lives in realms above 100a
finds no object worth its c. 396a
hope c. in wind 72a
infernal c. of the woman 391a
let him in c. follow 54b
not with that grand c. 93a
O c.! be strong 339a
think to stablish dangerous c. 133b
wdst. thou approve thy c. 276a
Constant: c. as the northern star 339a
c. creaking of a country sign 107b
c. do remain to keep him so 339a
c., in Nature were inconstancy 107a
c. you are, but yet a woman 377a
friendship is c. in all 358a
if thou wilt be c. then 280b
nothing . . c., save inconstancy 417b
one here will c. be 54b
she is so c. to me 217b
to one thing c. never 358a
were man but c. 372b
Constantinople: go to C. and take the
Turk 383b
Russians shall not have C. 201b
Constellated flower that never sets 398a
Constellations: foreign c. west 179a
I do not want the c. any nearer 458a
Constitution: C. devotes the domain 321b
c. is extremely well 449b
C...looks to an . . Union 88a
does not agree with my c. 444a
essence of the c. 217a
everybody talks of the c. 449b
genius of the C. 297a
higher law than the C. 321b
I am of a c. so general 41b
principle of the English c. 28b
suit full well my c. 524a
venerable parts of our c. 56a
Constitutions o'er yr. wine 77b
Constraineth: love of Christ c. us 515a
spirit within me c. me 497a
Constraint: all c... is evil 112b
beauty by c., possessing 159a
Construe: men may c. things 338a
Consubstantial, co-eternal 286b
Consul's brow was sad 253a
Consult: c. Brother Jonathan 452a
c. our private ends 419a
Consults . . about . . serious matters 91a
Consume: c. away like a snail 485b
no more right to c. happiness 390a
Consummation: quiet c. have 329a
she waits the c. 415b

Consummation (cont.)
'tis a c. devoutly to be wish'd   333a
Consumption of the purse   380a
Contact with a brother poet   224a
Contagion: c. of the night   338b
  c. of the world's slow stain   392b
  foul c. spread   269b
Contaminate our fingers with..bribes   340b
Contemned: it wd. be utterly c.   501a
Contemneth: he that c. small things   520b
Contemplates: wreck the thing it c.   397b
Contemplation: beneath thy c.   286a
  best nurse C.   267a
  c. makes a rare turkey-cock   371a
  c.'s sober eye   175b
  for c. he and valour formed   274a
  mind serene for c.   160b
  my darling c.   105b
  the Cherub C.   268a
Contemporary: How it strikes a C.   47b
Contempt: c. of thy Word   478b
  for c. too high   107a
Contemptible: those poor c. men   116a
Contend: c., ye powers of heav'n   114b
  let's c. no more, Love   52b
  Lord, if I c. with thee   198a
Contending: c. with the..elements   342b
  let fierce c. nations know   1b
  put God..as c. against   457a
Content: as c. with six foot   42b
  c. thyself with thine estate   416b
  c. to breathe his native air   303b
  C.! where doth thine harbour hold   21a
  c. with yr. wages   509a
  c. you; the gate is strait   424a
  farewell c.!   362a
  good reason to be c.   222b
  I cd. be well c...with quiet   378b
  land of lost c.   199b
  money, means, and c.   327a
  my soul hath her c.   361a
  nor that c. surpassing wealth   399a
  Oh sweet c.!   118b
  our desire is got without c.   348b
  poor and c. is rich   361b
  range with humble livers in c.   385b
  shut up in measureless c.   347b
  will no other vice c. you?   133b
Contented: c. if he might enjoy   469a
  c. wi' little   59b
  slaves, howe'er c.   111a
  with what I most enjoy c. least   387a
Contention: a man of c.   503b
  let the long c. cease   6b
Contentment: all enjoying, what c.   275b
  c. is a sleepy thing   445a
  oh, the sweet c.   86b
  preaches c. to that toad   233a
  where..freedom reign, c. fails   170a
Contest: great c. follows   112a
  proud world..cease yr. c.   115a
Contests: Saints assuage fierce c.   66a
  what mighty c. rise   302b
Contiguity: boundless c. of shade   111b
Continency: have not the gift of c.   481b
Continent: make its c. an isle   293a
  upon this c. a new nation   245a
Continents: over..three separate c.   136a
  rive yr. concealing c.   342b
Continuance: c...prefer mild hale   417a
  in c. of time   478a
  patient c. in well-doing   513a
  the household of c.   416a
Continue: charges wh. once begun
    will c.   15b
  tree will c. to be   522b
Continuest: that thou c. such, owe   275a
Continueth: for their work c.   234b
Continuous as the stars   467a
Contortions of..sybil..inspiration   58b
Contracted: Angel with c. brow   276a
Contradict: do I c. myself?   458a
  lose no time to c. her   419a
  read not to c.   16a
  tho' it c. everything you said   147b
Contradicting a Bishop   211a
Contradiction: it is a c. in terms   391b
  woman's at best a c.   302a
Contradictions: man..a bundle of c.   103b
Contrairy: everythink goes c.   121b
Contraption..he call a Tar-Baby   181b

'Contrariwise' continued Tweedledee   84a
Contrarious: unfit c. moods   44a
Contrary: change them to the c.   366a
  c. to their profession   479b
  Mistress Mary, quite c.   533a
  time..runneth not to the c.   28b, 245b
Contributions to..development   9b
Contrivance: government is a c...
    wisdom   57a
Contrivances: presumption in..c.   55b
Contrive: c. to write so even   11b
  Nature always does c.   164a
Control: beyond my individual c.   122b
  his c. stops with the shore   69b
  over wh. he has no c.   454b
  who can c. his fate?   364a
  will leave this to c...   132b
Controlled: I claim not to have c.
    events   245a
Controls them and subdues   465a
Controverse: in c. mute   306a
Controversy: with hearts of c.   337b
Contumely: proud man's c.   333a
  the other is c.   15a
Convenience next suggested elbow
    chairs   111b
Convenient: jesting, wh. are not c.   515b
Convent: C. of the Sacred Heart   145a
  c.'s narrow room   468a
  c.'s solitary gloom   299b
Conventicle: for being at a c.   296a
Convention: lords of C. 'twas
    Claver'se   316a
Conversation: as e'er my c. coped   334a
  brisk as a bee in c.   206a
  c. among gentlemen   209a
  c.'s burrs   193b
  c.-scraps, kitchen-cabals   113b
  ignorance cramps my c.   197a
  pleasures of life is c.   404b
  religion..no..subject of c.   91a
  silence that make his c...delightful   404b
  that is the happiest c.   208b
  Wesley's c. is good   209b
Conversations: book..without c.   82b
Converse: born to write, c.   303a
  c. of an innocent mind   221a
  c. with the mighty dead   443b
  forgo thy sweet c.   276b
  formed by thy c.   301b
  I c. day by day   407a
  spend in pure c.   39b
Conversing: c. with W. H.'s forehead   183a
  with thee c. I forget all time   274a
  with thee c. I forget the way   161a
Conversion of the Jews   260a
Convert: c., and be healed   501b
  he shall c. my soul   483a
Converted: sinners shall be c.   485a
  to be c. at a revival   413a
Converting: c. all yr. sounds of woe   358b
  machine for c. the Heathen   80a
Converts: qualified for making c.   171a
  women can true c. make   150b
'Convey' the wise it call   355b
Convict: endeavour to c. her   419a
Convince: by persuading others we
    c.   217a
Convinced: not c. by proofs   293b
Convinceth: wh. of you c. me of sin   511a
Convincing: just by way of c. you   236a
  Oh! too c.—dangerously dear   70a
  thought of c.   169b
Conviviality: taper of c.   125a
Convocation of politic worms   335a
Convoy: crowns for c. put   383a
Coodle: Lord C. wd. go out   121b
Cooed: but c., and c.   468a
Cooings: matrimonial c.   70b
Cook: astronomer to Capt. C.   403a
  Groom, the Butler, and the C.   163b
  I am a c. and a captain bold   163a
  ill c. that cannot lick..finger   366a
  tell William c.   381a
  very uncommon c.   315b
Cookery: c. is become an art   64a
  kissing don't last: c. do!   265a
Cooks: bouchers and c.   242b
  c. are gentlemen   64a
  good cook as c. go   315a
  guests shd. praise it, not the c.   181a

Cooks (cont.)
he lik'd those literary c.   283a
Synod of C.   207b
the Devil sends c.   158b
with a legion of c.   73a
Cool: cheeks wh. they did c.   323a
  garden in the c. of the day   492b
  here comes the c. of the evening   405b
  sweet day, so c.   187b
Cooled a long age in the..earth   219b
Cool-haired: lifting the c. creepers   8a
Cooling: you must stay the c. too   368b
Coolness: grateful c. in the heat   86b
Coombe: [Mr. C.]..snatched from
    us   55a
Co-operation..the laws of life   315a
Coop't: whereunder crawling c.   153b
Cophetua: beggar maid before
    ..C.   425b
  C. sware a royal oath   425b
  when King C. loved   365a
Copier: mere c. of Nature   308b
Copious Dryden   303b
Copper: for a c. halfpenny   85b
  c. for the craftsman   228a
  hot and c. sky   98b
Coppersmith: Alexander the c.   516b
Copse: that crowned the eastern c.   224a
  turf, wh. lay under a c.   398a
Copy: I, according to my c.   257a
  leave the world no c.   370a
  nature's c.'s not eterne   349a
Copyists: shortened the labour of c.   81b
Coquetry: c. of public opinion   58a
  life is a c. of death   441a
Corages: nature in hir c.   88a
Coral: c. is far more red   389a
  c. of his lip   251b
  of his bones are c. made   367a
  or a c. lip admires   79a
  wand'ring in many a c. grove   31b
Coral-reef within the seas   293b
Coranto: home in a c.   369b
Corbies: I heard twa c.   529b
Cord: as unto the bow the c.   248b
  ever the silver c. be loosed   500a
  stretch a c., however fine   456b
  threefold c. is not..broken   499a
  triple c., wh. no man can break   58a
Cordage: rent c., shatter'd deck   287a
Cordelia: to be my child C.   344a
Cordial: lost with c. fruit   188a
  name of 'Entente C.'   535a
Cords: cast away their c.   481b
  scourge of small c.   510b
Core: ain't-a-going to be no c.   447a
  as the rind was the c. is   421a
Corinna: come, my C.   189a
  when to her lute C. sings   78a
Corinth: C. lost and won   69b
  not everyone that can get to C.   543a
Corinthian capital of..society   57b
Corioli: eyes the widows in C. wear   328a
  fluttered yr. Volscians in C.   328b
Corking-pin: a rather large c.   19b
Cormorant: c. devouring Time   344a
  sat like a c.   273b
Corn: bow'd locks of the c.   284b
  breast-high amid the c.   195b
  clover and c. lay sleeping   226a
  cokkel in our clene c.   89a
  cometh al this newe c.   90a
  c. before my tears did drown it   188a
  c. in Egypt   493b
  c. that makes the holy bread   262a
  c. was springing..green   28b
  cow's in the c.   535a
  earn'd yr. little bit o' c.   162b
  flies o'er th' unbending c.   300a
  he treadeth out the c.   494b
  hope..c. in chaff   72a
  in tears amid the alien c.   220a
  make two ears of c...to grow   418a
  meadows rich with c.   458b
  raise the price of c.   67b
  the c. was orient..wheat   445a
  the farmer sowing his c.   534a
  threshed at midnight   476a
  to reap its scanty c.   146b
  valleys..stand so thick with c.   486a
  weeds..in our sustaining c.   343b

Cornelia kept her in talk 64b
Cornelius-Son hath made the Hollanders 216a
Corner: close c. of my brain 198a
head-stone in the c. 489a
keep a c. in the thing I love 362a
not done in a c. 513a
sits the Wind in that c.? 358b
some c. of a foreign field 40a
the world in every c. sing 187a
Corners: come the three c. 374b
in his hand are all the c. 487b
knit at the four c. 512a
polished c. of the temple 490b
round earth's imagined c., blow 133a
Cornet: sound of the c., flute, harp 504a
Corney: Mrs. C., what a prospect 125b
Cornfield: o'er the green c. did pass 327b
Cornish: twenty thousand C. men 182b
Corns: yr. shooting c. presage 419b
Cornwall: C. squab-pie 225b
I love thee C. 157a
Coromandel: fought on the..C. 254b
Coronation: C. and Sops in wine 409b
reject a petrarchal c. 222b
Coroner: c.'s quest law 336a
Medical c.'s a queer..thing 19a
Coronet: wears a c., and prays 113a
Coronets: hearts are more than c. 431b
Corporal: blacking the C.'s eye 227b
fun o' the C.'s guard 227b
Corporals forty-one 234a
Corporation to have a conscience 444b
Corporations cannot commit treason 97b
Corporeal, a matter-of-fact-ness 183a
Corpse (corse): as his c. to the rampart 462a
a slovenly, unhandsome c. 376b
carry up this c. 47a
c. of Public Credit 454a
each like a c. within 396a
flowers serve for a buried c. 366a
frozen c. was he 249a
good wishes to the c. 21b
he'd make a lovely c. 124a
he makes a very handsome c. 170b
here's a c. in the case 19a
kissed her cold c. 526b
leave the c. uninterred 318b
not a friend greet my poor c. 371a
seraph-man on every c. 99b
the c. shd. be ready 451a
they bore her c. away 172b
this c. wh. is man 423b
thou, dead ... revisit'st thus 331a
you've got a nice fresh c. 446b
Corpses: c. three-months-old 435b
loves into c. or wives 421a
Correct: all present and c. 522a
c., insert, refine 419b
like magistrates, c. at home 381b
to be critical than to be c. 128a
Correggio: correggiosity of C. 80b
correggiescity of C. 80b, 411b
Correggios: Raphaels, C. 169b
Correspondent to command 367a
Corridors of Time 247a
Corrival: without c. all her dignities 377a
Corrupt: a judge that no king can c. 385b
a people generally c. 58a
c. influence..prodigality 56a
c. the souls of those they rule 7a
good custom shd. c. the world 429a
power is apt to c. 297a
Corrupted: hath not been c. 478a
my fortunes have c. honest men 324a
Corruptible: obtain a c. crown 514a
this c. must put on incorruption 515a
Corruption: c. of Man's Heart 46b
c., the most infallible symptom 162a
c. wins not more than honesty 386a
it is sown in c. 515a
keep mine honour from c. 386b
thy Holy One to see c. 482b
to be turned into c. 491a
vice whose strong c. inhabits 372a
Corruptions made him wretched 219a
Corryvreckan: dangerous C. 96a
Corsair: left a C.'s name 70a
Cortez: stout C. 220b
Corydon: C. wd. kiss her then 35b

Corydon (cont.)
Phillida and C. 35a
shepherd C. was all aflame 556b
Time, not C. hath conquer'd thee 8b
Cosmopolitan in the end 281a
Cosmopolite: I don't set up for..a c. 196b
Cosmos: too much Ego in yr. C. 237a
Cosmus, Duke of Florence 13b
Cost: gods sigh for the c. and pain 43b
rich-proud c. of outworn..age 388a
too costly for c. 443a
why so large c. 389b
Coster's finished jumping 166b
Costive: soap-boiler c. 454b
Costly thy habit 330b
Cot: here's a pot with a c. 242a
mine be a c. beside the hill 310a
Cotopaxi 446a
Cottage: c. homes of England 185a
c. in a lane, Park Lane for choice 571b
c. of gentility 100b, 406b
c. with a double coach-house 100b, 406b
from court to c. he depart 295b
he before his c. door 406a
her..looks the c. might adorn 169a
hides not his visage from our c. 373b
in his c. bid defiance 297a
love and a c.! 103a
soul's dark c. 449a
Cottages: poor men's c...palaces 352b
Cottle: Amos C. 72a
Cotton is King 94a
Cotton-spinners: we are not c. all 438a
Cotytto or Venus 421b
Couch: make his c. of silk 89b
on my c. I lie 467b
retired to his virtuous c. 451a
round his C.'s golden rim 282b
steel c. of war 360b
there I c. when owls do cry 368a
they to their grassy c. 274a
wraps the drapery of his c. 53b
Couch grass: heaps of c. 179b
Cough: c. for my own amusement 11b
his hearers cd. not c. 215a
keep a c. by them ready 94b
Coughs: no discretion in her c. 11b
Coughing drowns the parson's saw 345b
Council: instruments are then in c. 338b
Councils: climates, c., governments 438b
Her Majesty's c. his words..grace 40b
takes..wisdom from our c. 56a
thousand college-c. 438b
Counsel: c. of her country's gods 107b
c. of the heathen to nought 483b
dost sometimes c. take 302b
'fiend,' say I, you c. well 353b
fitter for execution than for c. 16a
ghostly c. and advice 480b
hard it is for women to keep c. 339a
if this c...be of men 512a
Judah their c. 486b
justice, c., and treasure 15a
lightly regarded the c. 488b
princely c. in his face 272b
spirit of c. and might 501b
take my c., happy man 163b
that darkeneth c. by words 497b
to keep my own c. 167b
took sweet c. together 485a
two may keep c. 365b
who cannot give good c.? 64a
Counsellor: Wonderful, C. 501b
Counsellors: in the multitude of c. 498a
when c. blanch 15a
Counsels: all good c...do proceed 478b
casteth out the c. of princes 483b
designs and crooked c. fit 138a
how mony c. sweet 62b
Count: all men c. with you 230a
c. five-and-twenty 123a
I c. myself in nothing 375a
I c. them all my friends 426a
I c. them over, every one 309a
let me c. the ways 44a
makes her c. and calls her 'Miss' 93b
Counted: he c. them at break of day 70b
Countenance: c. in wh. did meet 470b
c. is as Lebanon 500b
c. like richest alchemy 338a
c. more in sorrow 330b

Countenance (cont.)
damned disinheriting c. 400b
did the C. Divine 31a
grim, grim grew his c. 529a
his c. soon brightened 464b
his c. was as the sun 518b
Knight of the Sorrowful C. 567b
light of thy c. upon us 482a
Lord lift up his c. 494a
maketh a cheerful c. 498a
oil to make him a cheerful c. 488a
perceiving Hodge..out of c. 211a
shew us the light of his c. 486a
sobs..and sorrowful c. 64b
trow that c. cannot lie 313b
with a glassy c. 432a
withal of a beautiful c. 495b
you have that in yr. c. 342a
Counter: all things c., original 197b
Counter-caster: this c. 359b
Countercheck quarrelsome 328a
Counterfeit: sleep, death's c. 348a
Counterpane: land of c. 414a
Countesses had no outlines at all 125a
Counties: see the coloured c. 199a
six c. overhung with smoke 284a
Counting out his money 533b
Counting-house: king was in his c. 533b
Countries: he made all c...his own 139b
preferreth all c. before his own 291b
rascals in all c. 210a
Country: absolved from all duty to his c. 295a
all these c. patriots 67b
anybody can be good in the c. 460b
beats not in his c.'s cause 298b
benefits of yr. own c. 327a
billion dollar c. 156a
but c. folks who live beneath 96a
c...continually under hatches 222b
c. for heroes to live in 246a
c. governed by a despot 210a
c. has its charms 417a
c...kind of healthy grave 405b
c. life I praise 37b
c. life is to be preferred 296a
c. men of England 292a
c.'s cause calls you away 162b
C.'s gut her soul 250b
departed into their own c. 504b
ends thou aim'st at be thy c.'s 386a
every c. has its own constitution 523a
fear for my dear c. 463a
Flora and the c. green 219b
for thee, O dear, dear C. 286b
from yon far c. blows 199b
genius is of no c. 94b
God made the c. 111b
good news from a far c. 498b
had she been a c. maid 61b
he likes the c., but..in town 110b
his first, best c. 170a
how I leave my c.! 297b
how I love my c. 297b
if c. loves such sweet desires 176b
I loathe the c. 105b
in the c. I always fear 404b
in the c. of the free 43a
in the c. places..rosy faces 414b
into the c. whenever I choose 460a
in yr. ain c. 116b
is this mine own c.? 99b
I the happy c. swain 61b
I tremble for my c. 205a
I vow to thee, my c. 409b
I will into some far c. 531b
know..the rooms of thy native c. 157b
leave his c. as good 97a
leaving his c. for his c.'s sake 152a
lie..for the good of his c. 473a
love thy c., wish it well 131b
make unto me one c. 42a
mariners..from a far c. 99b
most disthressful c. 525b
my c. is the world 292a
my c.! oh, my c.! 297b
my c., 'tis of thee 404a
my soul, there is a c. 448a
never-never c. 228b
nothing good..in the c. 183b
Oh Rome! my c.! 69a

Country (*cont.*)

our c. is the world	159a
our c., right or wrong	118a
over all the c. the turtle dove	262b
polite to every c.	196b
praises..every c. but his own	164b
pretty c. folks wd. lie	327b
pride that pulls..c. down	361a, 524b
save in his own c.	507a
she is my c. still	94b
sky..their native c.	99a
springs o' that c.	528a
stake in the c.	573b
sucked on c. pleasures	133a
sweet and blessed c.	286a
the c. in town	551a
the good of one's c.	150a
their c.'s wishes blest	103a
the undiscovered c.	333a
they touch our c.	111b
they've undone his c.	1b
'tis a c. diversion	105b
to a boon southern c.	9a
to do our c. loss	383a
to my ain c.	116b
to vegetate like the c.	183b
vile, that will not love his c.	339b
when his c.'s pride	391b
who leads a c. life	140a
whose c...turned into a desert	56a
zealous for his c.'s good	160a

Countryman: contentment the c.

doth find	86b
I was Shakespeare's c.	452b

Countrymen: friends, Romans, c.

in balance with my c.'s	42a
our c. are all mankind	159a
what a fall was there, my c.!	340a

Countryside: smiling..beautiful c. | 135b

Couple: begin..wood-birds but to c. | 357b

Coupler-flange to spindle-guide | 231b

Couples: see the c. advance | 131a

Couplet fraught with..unmeaning | 300a

Couplets: creaking c. | 72a

golden c. are disclosed	336b

Courage: all goes if c. goes

and of a good c.	494b
brows of dauntless c.	272a
c., breath and speed	316a
c., brother! do not stumble	256b
'c.!' he said and pointed	433a
c. in yr. own	171b
c. is the thing	21b
c. mounteth with occasion	373b
c. never to submit	271a
c. of heart or holiness	26a
doth any deed of c.	380b
fires us with c., love and joy	159b
for c. to forget	2b
greater therefore shd. our c. be	382b
it requireth c. stout	146b
my c. prove my title!	325a
my c...to him that can get it	54b
screw yr. c.	347b
sing praises..with a good c.	483b
three o'clock in the morning c.	444a
two o'clock in the morning c.	575a
vain faith, and c. vain	252b
without originality or moral c.	389b

Courageous: when captains c. | 531b

Couriers of the air | 347a

Course: as a giant to run his c. | 482b

c. of true love	356a
crew laughing, and forgot his c.	155a
current and compulsive c.	362a
earth's diurnal c.	463a
foundations..are out of c.	487a
I have finished my c.	516b
I must fight the c.	351a
I must stand the c.	343a
in our daily c. our mind be set	223b
insisture, c., proportion	368b
keen, unscrupulous c.	5b
long ere the c. begin	259a
morning-star in his steep c.	101a
my preudunt c. is steadied	250a
short, bright, resistless c.	317b
steer a middle c.	262b
take thou what c. thou wilt	340b
they whose c. on earth is o'er	287a
with secret c.	213a

Course (*cont.*)

world's c. will not fail	294b

Coursers: c...fed with the lightning | 397b

two c. of ethereal race	175a

Courses: c. of my life do show | 378a

gave himself to evil c.	468a
planets in their radiant c.	305a
stars in their c.	494b

Court: c. awards it | 355a

C. Calendars, Directories	239a
Death keeps his pale c.	392a
free of the outer c.	293b
from c. to cottage he depart	295b
help of the air of the c.	149a
her c. was pure	437a
keeps Death his c.	375b
learning hope success at C.	160a
let her alone, she will c. you	216a
love rules the c.	317a
peril than the envious c.	325b
sun that shines upon his c.	373b
turmoiled in the c.	384a

Courted: better be c. and jilted | 77a

c. by all the winds	277b
than never be courted at all	77a

Courteous: c. he was, lowly | 88a

if a man be..c. to strangers	15a
so c., so kind, as Merry Margaret	402b

Courtesies: for these c. I'll lend you | 353a

hail ye small sweet c.	411a

Courtesy: a mutilated c. | 171a

by a frantic flight of c.	294b
candy deal of c.	377a
Grace of God is in C.	26a
greater man, the greater c.	428b
he loved..fredom and c.	88a
mirour of alle c.	89a
mirror of all c.	385b
of C. it is much less	26b
phrase of gentlest c.	316b
seated in the heart of c.	401b
show'd thy dear mother any c.	328b
the pink of c.	410b
the very pink of c.	365b
trust thy honest offer'd c.	267a
use the devil himself with c.	372a
wish c. wd. invent some	361a

Courtier: c.'s, soldier's, scholar's | 333b

gallops o'er a c.'s nose	364b
heel of the c.	336b
o'er c.'s knees	364b

Courting: I heard a linnet c. | 36b

Courtliness, and the desire of fame | 428a

Courts: c. for cowards were erected | 61a

c. of the sun	92b
c...to learn the world in	90b
C. where Jamshýd gloried	153a
gauntlet down to..c., and kings	77b
halls and c. of princes	267a
into the c. of the Lord	487b
one day in thy c.	487a
shown in c., at feasts	267b

Courtship to Marriage as a..pro-

logue	105a

Cousin: here, c., seize the crown | 376a

Cousins: his sisters and his c. | 166a

Coutts: Aristocrat who banks with C. | 163b

Cove: gain the c. with pushing prow | 48b

Covenant with death | 502a

Cover: athwart a cedarn c. | 101a

c. her face	454b
c. my defenceless head	455b
c., of the wings of grasshoppers	364b
green underwood and c.	420b
jewels c. every part	300a
leaves and flowers do c.	454b
the turbulent surge shall c.	368a

Coverings: cowslips for her c. | 189a

Covert: c. from the tempest | 502a

in shadiest c. hid	273a

Coverts of dismay | 312b

Covet thy neighbour's wife | 480a

Coveted: an Englishman as ever c. | 226b

Coveting the property of others | 553a

Covetous: Brutus grows so c. | 341a

Cow: a little Kyloe c. | 534a

as c. chaws cud	446a
cheaper..than to keep a c.	67a
c. is kept for every three acres	266a
c. jumped over the moon	534a
c.'s in the corn	535a

Cow (*cont.*)

c. with the crumpled horn	534a
c. with the iron tail	535a
friendly c., all red	414a
I never saw a Purple C.	54b
kiss till the c. come home	23a
Molly smiles beneath her c.	528a
three acres and a c.	102b
when she kissed her c.	418b

Coward: call me c. if you will | 151b

count myself the c.	437b
c. does it with a kiss	459b
c. in thine own esteem	347a
c.'s castle	87b
c.'s weapon, poison	155b
either a c. or a flatterer	339b
flattery to name a c.	444b
'Fore God I am no c.	437a
he was a scoundrel, and a c.	206b
I know you are no c.	437b
I was a c. on instinct	377b
no c. soul is mine	38b
O c. conscience	385a
shaked like a c.	378a
the c. stands aside	251a
we took him for a c.	372a

Cowards: all men wd. be c. | 309b

being all c., we go on very well	210a
conscience doth make c.	333a
courts for c. were erected	61a
c. die many times	339a
C.! if I advanced one step	288a
c. in scarlet	173a
other mannish c. have	325b
plague of all c.	377b
what can ennoble..sots or c.?	301b
word that c. use	385a

Cowardice: c. keeps us in peace | 210a

I admit the c.	390b
pusillanimity and c.	380b

Cowardly: c. put off my helmet | 324b

I do find it c. and vile	341a

Cowbind: green c. | 398a

Cowl: I like a c. | 147a

Cowled: wd. I that c. churchman

be	147a

Cowley: who now reads C.? | 303b

Cowls, hoods, and habits | 273b

Cowper: chit-chat of C. | 239b

Cows: c. are my passion | 122b

when the c. come hame	20b

Cowslip: a pearl in every c.'s ear | 356b

c.'s velvet head	268a
freckled c., burnet	383b
in a c.'s bell I lie	368a
i' the bottom of a c.	328b
sweet c.'s grace	290b

Cowslips: C. and Kingcups | 404b

c. for her covering	189a
c. from a Devon combe	229a
c. tall her pensioners	356b
her foot the Cumnor c.	8b
with c. wan	270a

Cowt: a ragged c.'s been known | 60a

Coxcomb ask two hundred guineas | 313b

Coxcombs: C. vanquish Berkley | 40b

some made c.	300a

Coy: lord, make me c. | 187b

sometimes coming, sometimes c.	321a
then be not c.	190b
uncertain, c., and hard to please	318b

Coyness: this c., Lady..no crime | 260a

Cozenage: strange c.! | 139b

Crabbe: Virtue's name let C. attest | 72b

Crabbed: c. age and youth | 389b

not harsh, and c.	267b

Crabs: roasted c. hiss in the bowl | 345b

set limed twigs for c.	85b

Crab-tree cudgel | 54a

Crack: he..wd. hear the mighty c. | 2b

you'd better c. us up	124a

Cracked: it c. and growled | 98a

two strings..and both c.	151b

Cracked-up: we must be c. | 124a

Cracker: lovely c. mottoes! | 163a

Crackling of thorns under a pot | 499a

Cracks a noble heart | 337a

Cradle: baby, c. and all | 29a

bed and procreant c.	347a
between the c. and the grave	143a
but in a wooden c.	522a

Cradle (*cont.*)
c. endlessly rocking 457b
c. of our fairy queen 357a
c. of the deep 461a
fancy dies in the c. 354a
for His c. and His throne 224a
from the c. to the grave I look 114a
grown man in the c. of an infant 58a
hand that rocks the c. 448b
heir, in his soft c. 216b
mountain c. in Pamere 8a
murder an infant in its c. 31a
the c. will fall 29a
the c. will rock 29a
yr. c., yr. home, and yr. bier 395a
Cradled: c. into poetry 395a
the day she c. me 530a
Craft: between c. and credulity 58a
c. and subtilty of the devil 479a
c. so long to lerne 90a, 559b
dog laughed to see such c. 534a
lean black c. 311b
prim little c. 166b
such a smart little c. 166b
sweet little c. 166b
their tricks and c. 61a
there 's c. in the river 404a
Craftier: ful c. to pley she was 89b
Craftiness: wise in their own c. 497a
Crafts and assaults of the devil 478b
Crafty: old and c. and wise 475b
Crag: castled c. of Drachenfels 68b
from cloud and from c. 392b
he clasps the c. 426b
leafless trees and every icy c. 466a
Crags: among these barren c. 438b
at the foot of thy c., O Sea! 425b
builds from the purple c. 396a
Cramasie: I mysel' in c. 530a
sails o' c. 529a
Crammed: c. just as they on earth 468b
c. with distressful bread 383a
Cramped for ever 216b
Cranes: warred on by c. 271b
Cranking: river comes me c. in 378a
Crannies: pluck you out of the c. 427a
Crave: have too much, yet still do c. 143a
I c. no pelf 368a
my mind forbids to c. 143a
Craven: in C. street, Strand 404a
Craving: and full as c. too 139a
c. credulity 128a
Crawl: slimy things did c. 98b
Crawley: Miss C. had been in France 440a
Crawling: c. between heaven 333b
whereunder c. coop't 153b
Crawls: sea beneath him c. 426b
Crazed: he is c. with..far Arabia 119a
Crazy: checkin' the c. ones 173a
I'm half c. 116b
who now doth c. go 99b
Creaking: constant c. of a..sign 107b
Cream: choking her with c. 226b
c. of others' books 283a
gives me c. with all her might 414a
milk masquerades as c. 166a
quite the c. of the thing 289a
visages do c. and mantle 352a
Creams: tempers dulcet c. 275a
Create: as well to c. good precedents 14b
both what they half c. 472a
can myself c. my little world 24a
Father who didst all c. 36b
from these c. he can 397a
I must C. a System 30b
my business is to C. 30b
Created: end of things c. 523a
God c. the heaven 492a
they are and were c. 518b
thou hast c. all things 518b
Creation: about the lords of the c. 63a
a false c. proceeding 347b
blind fury of c. 390b
c...expire before teatime 404b
doubled His whole c. 36a
lo! C. widened in man's view 457a
mars c.'s plan 79a
O fairest of c.! 276a
our c., preservation 479a
right of an earlier c. 254b
rival..her delicate c. 473a

Creation (*cont.*)
she is His new c. 415b
such as c.'s dawn beheld 69b
the whole c. groaneth 513b
to wh. the whole c. moves 431a
up and down de whole c. 156a
what demi-god..come so near c. 354a
while the mute c. downward bend 142b
Creations: God..acts his own c. 49b
Creator: C. made Italy from designs 446b
creature more than the C. 513a
great C. from his work return'd 275b
in his own image the C. made 241a
knowledge..for the glory of the C. 13a
myself and my C. 513a
O C. Spirit, come 549b
remember now thy C. 499b
voice of the great C. 82b
Creature: blank misgivings of a c. 466b
c., form'd of joy and mirth 30b
c. in whom excelled 276a
c. more than the Creator 513a
c. not too bright or good 470b
c.'s at his dirty work 303a
c. that moves in..grooves 527a
every c. of God is good 516b
every c. shall be purified 258b
God's first c. 16b
heaven-eyed c. sleeps 465b
Heaven..wh. owned the c. 215a
he is a base and ignoble c. 15a
I am a lone lorn c. 121b
image of the c. 370b
kindliest c. in ould Donegal 173a
nor any other c. 513b
not a c. was stirring 280b
of humblest friends, bright c.! 463b
own impulse every c. stirs 7b
some noble c. in her 367a
there is no c. loves me 385a
to look on sech a blessed c. 250b
wine is a good familiar c. 361b
world hath not a sweeter c. 362b
wd. you gain the tender c.? 159a
Creatures: all c. great and small 3a
all c. here below 224b
call these delicate c. ours 362a
c. that by a rule in nature 381b
disagree of c. rational 272b
elemental c. go about my table 476b
feathered c. broke away 389a
for mortal c., conquered 464b
from fairest c. we desire 387a
guilty c. sitting at a play 333a
home, you idle c. 337a
how many desolate c. 43a
meanest of his c. 49b
men become good c. 48b
millons of spiritual c. 274b
take unto other living c. 15a
unoffending c. whom he loves 465b
Widows..most perverse C. 2a
Crebillon: Marivaux and C. 175b
Credence: feyth and ful c. 89b
Credit: an't much c. in that 123b
before his c., or his fee 419b
citizen of c. and renown 108a
corpse of Public C. 454a
give thee c. for the rest 94b
it 's greatly to his c. 166a
let the C. go 152b
my c. now stands on..ground 339b
some c. in being jolly 123b
stories..not to thy c. 75b
'tis a c...to be neat 425a
Credulity: between craft and c. 58a
craving c. 128a
youth is the season of c. 297a
Credulous: positive men..most c. 419a
Creed: a c. is a rod 422a
Christians have a comfortable c. 70b
deed, and not the c. 249a
got the better of his c. 411b
his c. a strait jacket 264b
his c. no parson ever knew 136b
it is a modest c. 398a
our earliest c. we take 193b
sapping a solemn c. 68b
stranger's caste or c. 305a
suckl'd in a c. outworn 473a
the c. in the biliary duct 148a

Creed (*cont.*)
there is one c. 92a
to thy neighbour's c. has lent 146b
we have a Calvinistic c. 297a
Creeds: c. that refuse and restrain 421b
dust of c. out-worn 397a
half-believers in our casual c. 8a
keys of all the c. 430a
more faith..than in half the c. 431a
so many c. 459a
their c. a disease of the intellect 147b
vain are the thousand c. 38b
wrought..the creed of c. 430a
Creek: every winding c. 433a
Creeks: thro' c. and inlets making 96b
Creep: ambition can c. 58a
c. and intrude 269b
c. home, and take yr. place 226a
death..bade me c. past 50b
I wants to make yr. flesh c. 126a
love will c. in service 372b
Creepers: lifting the cool-haired c. 8a
Creeping: c. on from point to point 432b
dominion over every c. thing 492a
Nature is c. up 456b
things c. innumerable 488b
Creeps: c. in this petty pace 350b
wades, or c., or flies 273a
Crept: c. a little noiseless noise 218b
c. silently to Rest 153a
Crescent of a hair's-breadth 49a
Cressets: shapes, of burning c. 378a
Cressid: where C. lay that night 355a
Crest: high c., short ears 386b
joy brightens his c. 276a
Crested: his rear'd arm c. the world 325a
Crete: in a wood of C. 357a
Cretes..and Arabians 512a
Crevasse: Death..doth the c. bridge 441a
Crew: admit me of thy c. 268b
all that pentecostal c. 228b
Comus, and his midnight-c. 175a
c. is gambling in the forecastle 390a
c. of the captain's gig 163a
darling of our c. 121a
set the c. laughing 155a
to his c., that sat consulting 277b
we were a ghastly c. 99a
with all her c. complete 111a
Crib: the ass his master's c. 501a
Cribbed: cabined, c., confined 349a
Cribs: liest thou in smoky c. 380a
Cricket: her whip, of c.'s bone 364b
save the c. on the hearth 268a
where the c. sings 475a
Cried: and c., 'No more' 188a
c. still in sucking 143b
some therefore c. one thing 512b
winced nor c. aloud 185a
you suddenly c. 39b
Crier: C. cried, 'O Yes' 19b
c. rung the bell 24a
Cries: boy who c. in the lane 534b
check all c., and let be 545b
c. out, 'Where is it?' 100b
night and day on me she c. 531a
pitying the tender c. 33a
the street c. all about 461b
trouble..with my bootless c. 387a
who turnips c. 211b
with the c. they make 137a
Crillon: hang yourself, brave C. 563b
Crime: any c. so shameful as poverty 150a
bethink yourself of any c. 363b
call'd his harmless art a c. 316b
capital c., once a week 209a
c. of being a young man 297a
c. to love too well 299a
for my wilful c. art banished 276b
it was c. in a child 255b
Napoleon of c. 135b
no c.'s so great as..to excel 94b
now madden to c. 67b
piracies..c. of stealing 447a
the foulest c. in history 458b
the more..commonplace a c. is 135b
the punishment fit the c. 164b
the slave of c. 469b
this coyness, Lady, were no c. 260a
thy Godlike c. 73b
year of the great c. 294a

Crimes: all his c. broad blown 334b
  c. like virtues..own rewards 150b
  c. of this guilty land 40b
  dignity of c. 283a
  hast within thee undivulged c. 342b
  one virtue, and a thousand c. 70a
  our c. would despair 322a
  successful c. alone are justified 141a
  with reiterated c. 271a
  worst of c. is poverty 390b
Criminal: play of the British c. law 135b
  the c. cried, as he dropped 164b
Crimson: all c. barr'd 219a
  beauty's ensign..c. in thy lips 366b
  c. of the sunset sky 3b
  c.-tipped flow'r 62a
  girt with a c. robe 176a
Crimson-blank: where c. 232b
Cripple: comfort 's a c. 136b
Crispin (Crispian): C. shall ne'er go by 383a
  feast of C. 383a
  tomorrow is Saint C. 383a
  upon St. C.'s Day 137a
Criterion of wisdom to vulgar 57b
Critic: air-bell of the C. 45b
  attribute of a good c. 251a
  c. and whippersnapper 44b
  C., you have frowned 470b
  good c. is he who relates 563a
  he was in logic a great c. 64b
  Jonson knew the c.'s part 103a
  view me with a c.'s eye 149b
  youngest c. has died 236b
Critical: easier..to be c. than correct 128a
  nothing if not c. 360b
Criticism: cant of c...tormenting 411b
  c. of administration 17a
  definition of c. 9a
  every wind of c. 211b
  father of English c. 213a
  our c. is applied only 204b
  rod of c. with roses 130b
Criticizing: spite of all the c. elves 95a
Critics: before you trust in c. 72a
  c. all are ready made 72a
  c. are like brushers 13b
  c...men who have failed 129b
  therefore they turn c. 102a
  these our c. much confide in 419b
Crito, we owe a cock to Aesculapius 560b
Croaks: raven..the fatal entrance 346b
Crocodile: a cruel C. 408b
  how doth the little c. 82b
  Pyramid and C.! 221a
  to these c.'s tears..add sobs 64b
  what manner..is yr. c.? 323b
Crocodiles: wisdom of the c. 15b
Crocus: brake like fire 435a
  C. lays her cheek 264a
  moon of daffodil and c. 435b
Crœsus: an intellectual C. 129b
Cromek: O! Mr C., how do ye do? 30a
Cromwell: Caesar or C. exchanged 170b
  C., I charge thee 386a
  C., I did not think to shed 386a
  C. was a man in whom ambition 57b
  half o' the C. Road 232a
  hear me, C. 386a
  if thou fall'st, O C.! 386a
  Philistine..in politics, C. 10b
  pulled me down, O C.! 386a
  see C., damned 301b
  some C. guiltless 174a
Crony: ancient, trusty, drouthy c. 62b
Crooked: c. shall be made straight 502b
  empire is truly c. at the top 17a
  set the c. straight 284a
  there was a c. man 532a
Crookedly: one before him walked very c. 417a
Crooks: develop his hooks and his c. 62b
Crop: watering the last year's c. 144a
Croppy: Hoppy, C. 158a
Cross: advantage on the bitter c. 376a
  at the c. her station 554a
  c. him in nothing 322b
  c. patch 533a
  c. of latoun 89a
  crucify mankind upon a c. of gold 53a
  e'en though it be a c. 1a

Cross (cont.)
  his little c. to take 3b
  hold Thou Thy C. 251b
  I'll c. it tho' it blast me 329b
  I survey the wondrous c. 453b
  I the body, He the C. 441a
  last at His c. 21a
  merit of the Holy C. 286b
  no c. deserves no crown 307a
  No C., No Crown 295b
  one more river to c. 526a
  on his breast a bloody c. 408b
  sparkling c. she wore 302b
  to thy C. I cling 445a
  under the c. of gold 435a
  we gave the C. 47a
  who did once upon the c. 524b
  with the C. of Jesus 20a
Cross-bow: whizz of my c.! 99a
  with my c. I shot the Albatross 98b
Cross-breed: an unhappy c. 129a
Crossed: beast with wh. they are c. 263b
  c. each other's way 459b
  c. themselves for fear 432a
  c. with adversity 372b
  they wd. have c. once more 253b
Crosses: clinging to their c., F. E. Smith 91b
  c. from his sov'reign hand 191a
  c., relics, crucifixes 66a
Cross-gartered: c., a fashion she detests 371b
  wished to see thee ever c. 371b
Cross-grained brute 171a
Crotchets in thy head 355b
Crouch: make c. beneath his foot 51b
  still bidding c. 48a
Crow: Adam, the carrion c. 24a
  c. doth sing as sweetly 355b
  c. makes wing to the rooky wood 349a
  flew down a monstrous c. 84a
  many-wintered c. 432a
  say the c. is white 162b
  sun had risen to hear him c. 144a
  there is an upstart c. 176b
Crowbar: straightened out for a c. 194a
Crowd: all c...foremost..damned 299a
  ardour of the c. 175b
  at once I saw a c. 467a
  c. is not company 15b
  endure the stings, the c., and buzz 107a
  far from the madding c.'s 174b
  favour of the c. 228a
  fly not..from the suppliant c. 113b
  forgotten c. of common beauties 79a
  I hate the c. 241b
  not feel the c. 112a
  out of the c. a mistress 393b
  she pass in a c. 418a
  we met, 'twas in a c. 22b
Crowded: theatres of c. men 218a
Crowds: business..persuading c. 244a
  c. without company 161b
  if you can talk with c. 230a
  my apprehensions come in c. 463a
Crowed: more he c., more we cried 176a
Crow-flowers, nettles, daisies 336a
Crowling: ye c. ferlie! 61b
Crown: a c. is of night 422a
  a c.! what is it? 283a
  both divide the c. 139a
  breeches cost him but a c. 361a
  calm's not life's c. 9a
  chance may c. me 346b
  corruptible c. 514a
  cousin, seize the c. 376a
  c. him with glory 482a
  c. like a deep well 376a
  c. of our life as it closes 421a
  c. of these is made of love 217b
  c. of twelve stars 519a
  c. o' the earth doth melt 324b
  c. the wat'ry glade 174b
  defiance to the forces of the C. 297a
  ere the King's c. shall fall 316a
  fighting for the c. 532a
  fill me from the c. to the toe 346b
  from Life's fresh c. 24a
  fruition of an earthly c. 259a
  George I..wished to restore the c. 208b
  give me the c. 376a

Crown (cont.)
  give thee a c. of life 518b
  glory of my c. 145b
  go forth and conquer a c. 291a
  hairy gold c. 236b
  head that wears a c. 380a
  his father's c. into the hazard 381b
  his hair was like a c. 92a
  hoary head is a c. of glory 498b
  joy and c. eternally 279b
  likeness of a kingly c. 272b
  mine own hands..give away my c. 376b
  monarch better than his c. 354b
  more glorious is the c. 402b
  my verse is not a c. 187a
  no bays to c. it? 188a
  no cross deserves no c. 307a
  No Cross, no C. 295b
  no putting by that c. 314a
  not the King's c. 351b
  oxlips and the c. imperial 373b
  poison..from Caesar's laurel c. 29b
  power of the c., almost dead 56b
  receive the c. of life 517a
  sceptre and c. must tumble 401a
  steel against our golden c. 375a
  the Book, the tripled C. 307a
  the C. is,..fountain of honour 17a
  the holly bears the c. 526b
  the mace, the c. imperial 382b
  tho' they possess the c. 118b
  within the hollow c...keeps Death 375b
Crowned: calling a c. man royal 422a
  c., and again discrowned 206a
  c. from some single herb 260b
  c. him long ago 73a
  c. upon the grave 191b
  c. with calm leaves 422a
  c. with glory now 224a
  to have thee c. withal 346b
Crowning: a c. mercy 115b
Crownless: childless and c. 69a
Crowns: climb the c. o' the world 44a
  c. are empty things 118b
  c. around the glassy sea 184a
  c. for convoy 383a
  c. in shades like these 168a
  give c. and pounds 198b
  I'd c. resign to call thee mine 256b
  in his livery walked c. 325a
  it is the end that c. us 189b
  mortal murders on their c. 349a
  there are c. to be broke 316a
  with c. imperial, c. and coronets 381b
Crows: c. and choughs 343b
  c. feet be growe under yr. yë 90a
Crow-toe: tufted c. 270a
Crucible: America is God's C. 477b
Crucified: carrion c. 421a
  Jesus Christ, and him c. 514a
  the dear Lord was c. 3b
  young Man c. 265a
Crucifix: how the c. may be carven 442b
  the little silver c. 227a
Crucifixes: crosses, relics, c. 66a
Crucify: c. mankind upon..gold 53a
  c. the old man 481a
  they c...the Son of God afresh 517a
  wd. not even c. him 82a
Cruel: comfort c. men 93a
  c., but composed 7b
  c. he looks, but calm 397a
  c., only to be kind 335a
  'for c. 'tis,' said she 218b
  let me be c., not unnatural 334b
Cruelly: I am c. used 11b
  in a cage most c. all day 93b
Cruelty: c. has a human heart 33a
  c. to load a falling man 386b
  farewell, fair c. 370a
  fear is the parent of c. 157a
  full of direst c. 346b
  one's c. is one's power 105a
  O, not in c...the Reaper came 248a
  said Mr. C. 54a
  yond same sovereign c. 371a
Cruger: Mr. C. 305b
Cruise: all on our last c. 413a
Crumb: who craved no c. 167a
Crumble, who will remember 119a
Crumbs: c...from the rich man's 510a

Crumbs (cont.)
dogs eat of the c. — 507a
Crupp: Mrs. C. — 122b
Crusade: rides home from the C. — 92b
Cruse: a little oil in a c. — 496a
as my small c. best fits — 188b
Crush of worlds — 1b
Crushing out life than..farewell — 197a
Crusoe: Robin C. — 118b
Crust: share her wretched c. — 251a
the c. so fresh — 197b
the other, upper c. — 166a
these men are all upper c. here — 177b
Crutch: shoulder'd his c. — 168b
Cry: a great c. in Egypt — 494a
answer to 'Hi!' or to any loud c. — 86a
bubbling c. of some..swimmer — 70b
but behold a c. — 501a
by all ye c. or whisper — 236b
cherry-ripe themselves do c. — 4a
consider anything, only don't c.! — 84b
c...and upon thy so sore loss — 442a
c., baby, c. — 533a
c., Beware! Beware! — 101b
c.—clinging heaven by the hems — 442b
c. goes up, 'How long?' — 415b
c. is still 'They come' — 350b
c. not when his father dies — 211b
cuckoo's parting c. — 8b
deep behind him, and a c. before — 429a
earth's old and weary c. — 476a
far c. to Lochow — 320a
have a good c. — 186a
he'll be sure to c. — 535a
he said, what shall I c.? — 502b
I c. in the day-time — 483a
in heaven, if I c. to you then — 424a
it almost makes me c. to tell — 192b
man's image and his c. — 476a
monstrous head and sickening c. — 92a
no language but a c. — 430b
not the exceeding bitter c. — 406a
she nor swooned, nor uttered c. — 436b
so when they c. unto the Lord — 488b
sudden c. of pain — 410b
that c. over me, There, there — 486b
the c. did knock..my very heart — 367a
the c. of women rose — 136a
the girls and made them c. — 534a
the voice said, C. — 502b
to c. it up, or run it down — 419b
we still shd. c., not to be born — 17a
when we are born we c. — 334b
Crying: Maud, they were c. — 433b
neither sorrow nor c. — 519b
one c. in the wilderness — 504b
Crystal: c. of his brow — 251b
glass like unto c. — 518b
on c. rocks ye rove — 31b
Crystalline: here in my c. — 289a
Cubit unto his stature — 505b
Cuckold to make him a monarch — 363a
Cuckoo: as the c. is in June — 378b
C., c., well singes thu — 522b
C., jug-jug, pu-we — 286a
c. of a joyless June — 435b
c. of a worse July — 435b
c.; O, word of fear — 345b
c.'s parting cry — 8b
c. then, on every tree mocks — 345b
hedge-sparrow fed the c. — 342a
lhude sing c. — 526a
merry c., messenger — 408a
O C.! shall I call thee bird — 463b
rainbow and a c.'s song — 118a
responsive to the c.'s note — 175b
spring-time from the C.-bird — 471a
the weather the c. likes — 180a
Cuckoo-buds of yellow hue — 345b
Cuckoo-flowers: hemlock, nettles, c. — 343b
Cucumber: she wdn't have a c. — 124a
Cucumbers: a lodge in a garden of c. — 501a
sunbeams out of c. — 418a
Cud: as cow chaws c. — 446a
chew the c. and are silent — 57a
Cuddesdon: Hey for C.! — 11a
Cudgel: crab-tree c. — 54a
what wood a c.'s of — 65b
Cue: with a twisted c. — 164b
Cuisses on his thighs — 378b
Cully: man..by Nature woman's c. — 104b

Cultivated: Shakespeare's genius..c. — 90b
Culture: c.,..acquainting ourselves
with the best — 10a
great aim of c. — 9b
man of c. rare — 165a
men of c...apostles of equality — 9b
pursue C. in bands — 456a
Cumæ: Sibyl at C. — 313a
Cumbered: Martha was c. — 509a
Cumbereth it the ground? — 509b
Cummin: anise and c. — 507b
Cumnor: C. Hall — 265b
her foot the C. cowslips — 8b
Cunning: by the very c. of the scene — 333a
c. men pass for wise — 15b
hand forget her c. — 490a
more c. to be strange — 365a
Cup: ah, fill the C. — 153b
another and another C. — 153a
come fill up my c. — 316a, 320a
c. of this forbidden Wine — 153b
c. us, till the world go round — 323b
drunk their C. a Round or two — 153a
every inordinate c. — 361b
fill the can, and fill the c. — 439a
Jamshyd's Sev'n-ring'd C. — 152a
kiss but in the c. — 216a
let this c. pass from me — 508a
life's enchanted c. — 68a
Liquor in its C. be dry — 152a
Lord there is a c. — 487a
my c. shall be full — 483a
perfect the c. as planned — 51a
tak' a c. o' kindness — 59a
take a c., and drink it up — 533a
the c. is nearly full — 87a
the c., the c. itself — 428a
there's Death in the c. — 60b
to uses of a c. — 51a
Cups: be in their flowing c. — 383a
c., that cheer but not inebriate — 112a
c., whose wine was the bright dew — 398a
when flowing c. run swiftly — 249b
Cupboard: our c. of food — 187b
the c. was bare — 533b
Cupboards: her c. opened — 180b
Cupid: bolt of C. fell — 356b
C. abroad was lated — 176a
C. and my Campaspe — 251a
C. blind did rise — 251b
C. hath clapped him — 327b
C. is a knavish lad — 357a
C. paid — 251a
C.'s darts do not feel — 525a
C.'s fiery shaft — 356b
giant dwarf, Dan C. — 344b
note wh. C. strikes — 42a
to Chloe's breast C...stole — 31b
wing'd C. painted blind — 356a
young Adam C. — 365a
Cupids: boys, like smiling C. — 323a
go revel, ye C. — 424b
Cur: as doth a c. — 90a
c. can lend..ducats — 353a
fly 'bout the ears of that old c. — 65a
half lurcher and half c. — 112b
the already curtailed c. — 75a
Curs: common cry of c. — 328a
c. mouth a bone — 94b
c. of low degree — 169a
Curate: compassion in the..name
of a C.!! — 405a
c.; he was fatter than his cure — 426b
mildest c. going — 162b
pale young c. then — 167a
sit upon the c.'s knee — 93a
Curates: c., long dust, will come — 39b
preached to death by wild c. — 404b
upon our Bishops and C. — 478b
Curch: basnet a widow's c. — 531a
Curd of ass's milk — 303a
Curdied by the frost — 328b
Curds: milk of kindness into c. — 194a
queen of c. and cream — 373b
Cure: c. for admiring the..Lords — 17b
c. her of that — 350b
death is the c. of all diseases — 42a
fire must c. this place — 45b
labour against our own c. — 42a
love's a malady without a c. — 141a
no c, for this disease — 26a

Cure (cont.)
thy life, thy c. — 448a
Cured: c. yesterday of my disease — 306a
hurts you have c. — 147a
Curfew: c. must not ring — 444b
c. tolls the knell — 174a
far-off c. sound — 268a
mothy c.-tide — 179b
Curious: be not c. in unnecessary — 520a
the c. here to feed a..mind — 113b
things..c., and unfamiliar — 189b
Curiouser and curiouser! — 82b
Curiosity: pains are for c. — 147b
'satiable c. — 237a
Curl: girl who had a little c. — 249a
Curled: c. darlings of our nation — 359b
I saw the c. drops — 115a
Curling their monstrous heads — 380a
Currance: heady c. — 381b
Current: Beauty..must be c. — 267b
c. literature of the day — 66b
c. of domestic joy — 213a
fountain from the wh. my c. runs — 363a
freshening its c. — 6a
genial c. of the soul — 174a
o'er-walk a c. roaring — 377a
Pontick sea, whose icy c. — 362a
we must take the c. — 341a
Currents: sands..split his c. — 8a
their c. turn awry — 333a
Curriculum: fortifying, classical c. — 10a
Curse: an orphan's c. — 99a
c. causeless shall not come — 498b
c. God, and die — 497a
c. his better angel — 363b
c. in a dead man's eye — 99a
c. is come upon me — 431b
c. of kings to be attended — 374a
c. of this country — 148b
C. shall be on thee for ever — 406b
c. thine own inconstancy — 79b
c. to party strife — 464a
greatness..is to me a c. — 262b
heard such a terrible c. — 19a
I called thee to c. — 494a
I know how to c. — 367a
man to man is still..greatest c. — 19a
O c. of marriage! — 362a
O strife, O c. — 44a
then began he to c. — 508a
Curses: c. all Eve's daughters — 356a
c. are like young chickens — 406b
c., not loud but deep — 350b
writ with c. from pole to pole — 30a
Cursed: c. him in sleeping — 19a
c. me with his eye — 99a
he c. him squarely — 231a
O! c., c. slave — 364a
whom thou curest is c. — 494a
Curst: c. be he that moves my bones — 389b
c. himself in his despair — 406b
name to all succeeding ages c. — 138a
Curtail the already curtailed — 75a
Curtain: draw the c. by — 531a
drew Priam's c. — 379b
ring down the c. — 565a
the c. drops — 440b
these gifts a c. before 'em — 369b
Curtained with cloudy red — 270b
Curtains: draw the c. close — 384a
fringed c. of thine eye — 367b
let fall the c. — 112a
Curtsey while you're thinking — 84a
Curtsied when you have, and kiss'd — 367a
Curtsies: sweet words, low-crooked
c. — 339a
that dream on c. straight — 364b
Curves: lovely are the c. of the..owl — 263b
Curzon: George Nathaniel C. — 528b
Cushion: c. and soft Dean invite — 302b
he hath a c. plump — 99b
Custody: Wragg is in c. — 9a
Custom: at the receipt of c. — 506a
c. calls me to't — 328a
c. lie upon thee — 466b
c. loathsome to the eye — 204a
c. make it their perch — 351a
c. more honoured in the breach — 331a
c. of Branksome Hall — 316b
c. reconciles us to everything — 57b
c. that is before all law — 117a

Custom (*cont.*)

c., that unwritten law 117b
c., then, is the great guide 201b
c. to whom c. 513b
hath not old c. made this life 325b
lest one good c. shd. corrupt 429a
more kind than is her c. 355a
nature her c. holds 336a
nor c. stale her infinite variety 323a
that monster, c. 335a
the tyrant c. 360b
what c. wills..shd. we do't 328a
Customer: rather a tough c. 121a
Customs: ill c. influence..senses 149a
little are our c. known 160b
shattering all evil c. 428a
Cut: c. deep down the middle 43b
c. him out in little stars 366a
c. is the branch 259a
c. it down; why cumbereth it 509b
c. up what remains 237a
he was c. off out of the land 503a
Horse..was c. out of the grass 91b
in the evening it is c. down 487b
most unkindest c. of all 340a
name, that shall not be c. off 503a
who c. and came again 114a
Cutpurse of the empire 335a
Cuts the wrong man's head off 126a
Cutting: c. all the pictures out 25b
love..that with most c. grows 117a
Cuxsom: Mother C. 180b
Cyclads: young C. on a sunnier deep 394a
Cycle and epicycle 275b
Cyclopean arches 92b
Cydnus: I am again for C. 325a
Cygnet's down is harsh 368b
Cygnets: the swan her downy c. save 383b
Cymbal: become as..a tinkling c. 514b
talk but a tinkling c. 15b
Cymbals: well-tuned c. 490b
Cynara: faithful to thee, C.! 135a
Cynic: ..a man who knows the price 460a
Cynicism is intellectual dandyism 264b
Cynosure of neighbouring eyes 269a
Cynthia: C. nam'd, fair regent 161a
nor C. teeming shows so fair 260b
the C. of this minute 302a
Cypress: [c.] dark tree, still sad 72b
despair, under that c. tree 190a
in sad c. let me be laid 371a
land where the c. and myrtle 67b
nor waves the c. 436b
no shady c. tree 311a
pluck C., O pale maidens 7a
thro' an alley Titanic, of c. 298b
Cypresses: avenue of c. 243a
Cyrene: parts of Libya about C. 512a
Cytherea's breath 373b
Cytherean: throned C. 423b

D

D: a big, big, D. 166a
there are yr. d.'s for you 473b
Dacian: their D. mother 69a
Dacotahs: land of the D. 248b
Daddy: D.'s gone a-hunting 534a
do in the Great War, d.? 527b
Dads: get leave of yr. d. 522b
Daedal harmony 397b
Daffadillies fill their cups 270a
Daffa-down-dilly: D. has come up to
town 534b
Diaphenia, like the d. 105b
Daffadowndillies 409b
Daffed the world aside 378b
Daffodil: moon of d. and crocus 435b
on a bed of d. sky 434a
the shining d. dies 434b
Daffodils: d. begin to peer 373a
d., that come before the swallow 373a
dances with the d. 467b
fair d., we weep to see 189a
host of golden d. 467a
west wind, and d. 262a
Daft: thinks the tither d. 320a
Dagger: a d. of the mind 347b
deadly daunting me 473b
is this a d. wh. I see before me 347b

Dagger (*cont.*)

the air-drawn d. 349a
thou stickst a d. in me 354a
Daggers: been at d.-drawing 65b
give me the d. 348a
speak d. to her, but use none 334b
there's d. in man's smiles 348a
Dahlias: hurrah. .the d. are dead 417a
Daily Mail: Sandwich men of the D. 93b
Dainties: d. that are bred in a book 344b
spiced d., every one 221b
Dainty: every d. that is in that hous 89b
Dairy: Mab. .doth nightly rob the d. 215b
see the cat i' the d. 144a
Dairymaid: Queen asked the d. 266b
Daisies: crowflowers, nettles, d. 336a
d. smell-less 23b
d., those pearled Arcturi 398a
left the d. rosy 433b
meadows trim with d. pied 269a
men callen d. in our toun 90a
strong sea-d. feast on the sun 424a
toes turned up to the d. 19b
when d. pied and violets blue 345b
white d. prank the ground 37b
you must lie upon the d. 165a
Daisy: d., by the shadow that it casts 463b
D., D., give me yr. answer 116b
d.-star that never sets 394b
men hit calle may the d. 90a
mourn'st the D.'s fate 62a
the d. delectable 402b
there's a d. 335b
Dale: a moment gazed adown the d. 316a
doxy, over the d. 373a
haunted spring and d. 270b
Hermit of the d. 169a
over hill, over d. 356b
Dalhousie (Dalhousy): D. wrote—
'Vovi—I've Oude' 535a
thou D. the great God of War 298b
Dalliance: primrose path of d. 330b
silken d. in the wardrobe lies 381b
Dallied with his golden chain 426b
Dallies with the innocence of love 371a
Damage: moral or intellectual d. 575b
nothing wh. might d. his career 21b
Damaged: an Archangel a little d. 240a
Damasco or Marocco 271b
Damascus: Abana and Pharpar of..D. 496b
tower. .wh. looketh toward D. 500b
Dame: Belle D. Sans Merci 219a, 221b
my d. has lost her shoe 534a
one for my d. 534b
our sulky sullen d. 62b
pass for a most virtuous D. 305b
Dames: chaste and worthy d. 362b
gentle d.! it gars me 62b
stoutly struts his d. before 268b
Damian: betwixt D. and. .Casius 272b
Damn: abuses me to d. me 333a
d. by rule 291b
d. her at a venture 240b
d. the consequences 572b
d. those authors. .never read 94a
d. with faint praise 303a
her aged soul to d. 93a
I don't care a twopenny d. 455a
man who said, 'D.!' 527a
she did not give a singel d. 155a
stealthily, like a parson's d. 180b
thing that doesn't give a d. 229a
with a spot I d. him 340b
Damnation: d. of his taking off 347a
drink our own d. 480b
heap on himself d. 271a
hope of eternal d. 523a
I dare d. 335b
Damnations: twenty-nine distinct d. 52a
Damned: all silent and all d.! 468b
be d. (dear boys!) 231b
be d. if you do. .be d. if ye don't 135a
d. are those who dare resist 524a
d. be him that first cries 'Hold' 351a
d. for never a king's son 376b
d. from here to Eternity 229b
d. hisself in confidence 127a
d. if I see it 287b
d. in a fair wife 359b
if I were d. of body and soul 232a
music is the brandy of the d. 390b

Damned (*cont.*)

one d. thing after another 201a
protection is. .damned 570b
publish and be d. 455a
saved by being d. 196b
see thee d. first 78b
the d. wd. make no noise 190b
the public be d. 447b
thou must be d. perpetually 258b
what all the d. fools said 572a
what else is d. to fame 316a
Damning: always had a taste for d. 282b
d. those they have no mind to 65a
Damozel: blessed d. leaned out 311b
Damp: d. fell round . . Milton 470b
the nights are very d. 85b
Dams: run. .by the side of their d. 453a
Damsel: a certain d. possessed 512b
a d. lay deploring 161a
d. with a dulcimer 101b
to every man a d. 495a
Damsels: d. playing on the timbrels 486b
of faery d. met in forest wide 277a
Syrian d. to lament his fate 271b
Dan even to Beersheba 495a
Danaë: Earth all D. to the stars 436b
Dance: come and join the d. 83b
d., and Provençal song 219b
d. attendance on their lordships' 386b
d. ne moe atte hallie daie 88a
d. o'er my lady lee 533a
d. of plastic circumstance 51a
d. on the sands, and yet no footing 386b
each d. the others wd. 119b
easiest who have learned to d. 300a
folk d. like a wave 475a
I must d. barefoot 366b
O, Love's but a d. 131a
on with the d.! 68b
the merry love to d. 475a
to d. at our bridal 318a
to do nothing but d. 417a
walk at least before they d. 303b
when you do d., I wish you 373b
you have the Pyrrhic d. as yet 71a
Danced: d. by. .light of the moon 243b
if he d. till doomsday 104a
many an eye has d. to see 194a
piped. .and ye have not d. 506b
young man that d. daintily 13b
Dancer: curled minion, d. 8a
Dancers: breaks time, as d. 78b
d. dancing in tune 434a
Dances: Congress. .d. 502a
d. with the daffodils 467b
fairies break their d. 200a
in what ethereal d. 298a
lull'd. .with d. and delight 356b
she d. in the wind 142b
Dancing: comes Taffy d. 232b
dancers in tune 434a
d., and bear-baiting 369b
d. in the chequered shade 269a
d., to put thy pale, lost lilies 135a
emptier ever d. in the air 376a
follows with d. 420b
merry d., drinking,. .time 141b
mid these d. rocks 101a
no d. bear was so genteel 109a
past our d. days 365a
say I am d. 322b
Dancing master: manners of a him 206b
Dandolo: blind old D. 69a
Dandyism: cynicism. .intellectual d. 264b
Dane: get rid of the D. 228b
more an antique Roman than a D. 337a
Norman and D. are we 439a
Dane-geld: called paying the D. 228b
paid him the D. 228b
Danes: all of us D. in our welcome 439a
Danger: above noise and d. 448a
all that are in d., necessity 479a
beard be shook with d. 336a
bright eyes of d. 414a
bright face of d. 412a
d. knows full well that Caesar 339a
d. o'er, both are alike requited 291b
d. past, both are alike requited 217a
d., the spur of all great minds 87b
in d. to be called in question 512b

Danger (cont.)
last of d. and distress — 72b
neither shape of d. can dismay — 465b
oft in d., oft in woe — 456b
only when in d., not before — 291b
out of this nettle, the d. — 377a
pleased with the d. — 138a
run into any kind of d. — 478a
send d. from the east — 377a
she fear'd no d. — 140a
there 's in the deep — 22a
thy d. chiefly lies in acting — 94b
till d.'s troubled night depart — 78a
we are in great d. — 382b
when in sorrow, when in d. — 411a
who are to judge of d. — 468a
Dangerous: Caesar is more d. — 339a
D. Corryvreckan — 96a
delays have d. ends — 383b
little learning is a d. thing — 300a
most d. is that temptation — 351b
sincerity is a d. thing — 460a
such men are it — 338a
therefore are they very d. — 338a
think to stablish d. constancy — 133b
yet have I in me something d. — 336b
Dangers: d...despised grow great — 56b
D. of an Honest Man — 107a
d. thou canst make us scorn — 63a
little think what d. are incident — 292a
loved me for the d. I had passed — 360a
no d. fright him — 213b
the d. of the seas — 292a
those who brave its d. — 248a
with d. compassed round — 275a
Daniel: a D. come to judgment! — 354b
a second D. — 355a
O D., a man greatly beloved — 504a
well-languag'd D. — 42b
Dank: Field strewn with its d..drifts — 7b
Danny Deever — 228b
Dante: D...nature of an Old File — 123a
D. never stays too long — 255a
D. of the dread Inferno — 49b
D. once prepared to paint — 49a
D., who loved well — 49a
poete of Itaille, that highte D. — 89a
Danube: rude hut by the D. — 69a
Daphne: Apollo hunted D. so — 260b
Dappled: glory be to God for d. — 197b
Dapples the drowsy east — 359a
Dare: d. its deadly terrors clasp — 32a
d. to be true — 186b
d. to be unhappy — 313b
enter..you who d. — 264b
I d. do all that may become — 347a
I d. meet Surrey — 375b
I d. not ask a kiss — 190a
I d. not beg a smile — 190a
if I d. eat, or drink — 375b
I will d. e'en Death — 190a
letting 'I d. not' wait — 347a
O, what men d. do! — 359a
slaves who d. not be..right — 250b
Dared: determined, d., and done — 402b
Dares: in Omer or in D. — 90a
who d. do more is none — 347a
Daresay: I d. she will do — 39a
Darest: d. thou, Cassius, now leap in — 337b
d. thou then to beard the lion — 318b
how d. thou put thyself — 89b
Darien: a peak in D. — 220b
Daring: more d. or more bold — 378b
Dark: afraid to come home in the d. — 185b
after that the d. — 426a
all colours will agree in the d. — 14a
all that 's best of d. and bright — 74a
are you awake in the d.? — 287a
as children fear..the d. — 14a
between the d. and the daylight — 246b
blanket of the d. — 346b
d. and terrible beyond any season — 255b
d. and true and tender — 436a
d. behind it rose the forest — 248b
d. freeze-coated..Month — 102b
d. horse..rushed past — 130a
d. was over all — 434b
d. with excessive bright — 273b
don't want to go home in the d. — 185b
ever-during d. surrounds me — 273b
for us i' the dark to rise by — 51b

Dark (cont.)
great leap in the d. — 191b
hellish d., and smells of cheese — 417a
Joan..is as good i' th' d. — 189b
keeps thee here in d. — 366b
made a leap into the d. — 41a
nowhere but in the d. — 448a
O d., d., d. — 277b
o'er the d. her silver mantle — 274a
one stride comes the d. — 99a
permanent, obscure and d. — 463a
poring d. fills the wide vessel — 382a
souls lost in the d. — 47a
sun to me is d. — 277b
the subterranean d. — 200a
we are for the d. — 325a
what in me is d. — 270b
when it was yet d. — 511b
Darkened: day is never d. — 264a
stars, be not d. — 499b
Darkeneth: this that d. counsel — 497b
Darkest: always d. just before the day — 158a
Dark-heaving, boundless — 69b
Darkling: as on a d. plain — 5a
d. I listen — 220a
Darkly: d., deeply, beautifully blue — 406b
d. looked he at the wall — 253a
thro' a glass d. — 514b
Darkness: a deep, but dazzling d. — 448a
a great..d. fell upon Christian — 54a
angler in the lake of d. — 343a
arrears of pain, d., and cold — 50b
between his D. and his Brightness — 74b
blackness of d. for ever — 518a
but rather d. visible — 271a
cast away the works of d. — 479a
cast off the works of d. — 514a
cast out into outer d. — 506a
d. again and a silence — 249a
d. and the death-hour — 44a
d. and the light to thee..alike — 490a
d. came down on the field — 440a
d. comprehended it not — 510b
d. falls at Thy behest — 145b
d., fire, and chains — 452b
d. from light — 46a
d. had to a great extent arrived — 180b
d. is no d. with thee — 490a
d. quieted by hope — 52a
d., the fruit thereof dust — 421a
d. was upon the face of the deep — 492a
d. wh. may be felt — 493b
day is done and the d. falls — 247a
Death hath made his d. beautiful — 430b
deep into that d. peering — 298a
did the act of d. with her — 343a
encounter d. as a bride — 352a
horror of great d. fell upon him — 492b
how great is that d.! — 505b
I lie where shades of d. — 119a
in d., and in storm..delight — 22b
in d., and with dangers compass'd — 275a
instruments of d. tell us truths — 346a
in the d. of her eyes! — 192a
in ungauged d. hid — 294b
its nightly roll into d. — 180b
jaws of d. do devour it up — 356a
land of d. and blind eyes — 447b
leaves the world to d. and to me — 174a
lest d. come upon you — 511a
lighten our d. — 478b
light in the d., sailor — 315b
light that is in thee be d. — 505b
light wh. is in thee be not d. — 509a
make my d. to be light — 482b
makest d. that it may be night — 488b
men loved d. rather than light — 510b
people that walked in d. — 501b
peradventure the d. shall cover — 490a
pestilence that walketh in d. — 487b
prince of d. is a gentleman — 343a
rear of d. thin — 268b
ring out the d. — 431a
rulers of the d. of this world — 516a
smoothing the raven down of d. — 267a
spite of d., it was day — 114b
such as sit in d. — 488b
talks of d. at noon-day — 110b
that year of now done d. — 197a
the d. deepens — 251b
them that sit in d. — 508b

Darkness (cont.)
turned thy d. into light — 110a
universal d. buries all — 299a
walk on still in d. — 487a
Darks undreamed of — 49b
Darling: Charlie he 's my d. — 193a
Charlie is my d. — 285b
d. of our crew — 121a
d. of the Gods — 261a
d. of the spring — 463b
his bride and his d. to be — 526a
my bride and my d. to be — 526a
my d. from the power of the dog — 483a
Nature's d. [Shakespeare] — 175a
oh my d. Clementine! — 280b
put to hazard..his d. popularity — 56a
she is the d. of my heart — 79b
six years' d. of a pigmy size — 466b
the Frenchman's d. [Mignonette] — 112b
Darlings: d. of our nation — 359b
ye dappled d. — 226a
Darnel, and all the idle weeds — 343b
Dart: his own feather on the fatal d. — 72a
insult points the d. — 213a
launched point-blank her d. — 46b
shook a dreadful d. — 272b
Time shall throw a d. — 42b
Dartle: Miss Rosa D. — 122a
Dartmouth: he was of D. — 88b
Darts: Cupid's d. do not feel — 525a
deliverance..from the d. that were — 179b
fiery d. of the wicked — 516a
Dash: d. him to pieces! — 341a
d. thro' thick and thin — 108b
most, a d. between the two — 263b
they'll cut a d. — 164a
Dastard: a d. in war — 318a
Data: theorize before one has d. — 135a
Date: yr. d. is not so past — 188b
youth and thou are of one d. — 387a
Dates: all three d. on their slates — 83b
manna and d. — 221b
palms—that is d. — 191b
Daughter: Ada! sole d. of my house — 68a
a d. hadde this worthy king — 89b
any man..will ever rear a d. — 159a
apples..for the King's d. — 422b
as is the mother, so is her d. — 503b
attorney's elderly ugly d. — 167a
beautiful..thy feet..prince's d. — 500b
Carnage is Thy d. — 468a
Cato's d. — 338b
d. am I in my mother's house — 233a
d. of Death and Priapus — 421b
d. of debate — 145b
d. of Jove, relentless power — 173b
d. of the gods, divinely tall — 426b
d. of Tyre shall be there — 484b
d. was charming and young — 239b
death of yr. d...a blessing — 11b
died..Duke-and-a-Duchess' d. — 19b
Earl Haldan's d. — 225b
farmer's d. hath soft..hair — 75a
gigantic d. of the West — 427a
hearken, O d., and consider — 484b
he loved the bailiff's d. — 531b
his d., Clementine — 280b
I am the d. of earth — 393a
I won his d. — 360a
king of Spain's d. — 532a
king's d. is all glorious — 484b
king's d. o' Noroway — 529b
landlord's black-eyed d. — 290a
Light (Child's eldest d.) — 158a
Lord Ullin's d. — 77a
married Noah's d. — 12b
marry a landlord's d. — 240b
my d.! oh my d.! — 77a
my d.! O, my ducats! — 353b
my little d. lieth..death — 508b
O d. of Babylon — 490a
O fairer d. of a fair mother — 544b
O haud yr. tongue, my d. — 531b
one fair d. and no more — 332b
on Mrs. Porter and on her d. — 144b
preaching down a d.'s heart — 432a
skipper had taken his little d. — 249a
sole d. of his voice — 276a
stern d. of the voice of God — 463b
still harping on my d. — 332a
ta'en away this old man's d. — 359b

Daughter (cont.)
undaunted d. of desires — 114a
weep, d. of a royal line — 73a
whipped her little d. — 535b
yr. d. and the Moor — 359b
Daughters: book..my d. may read — 535a
d...as the polished corners — 490b
d. of musick shall be brought low — 499b
d. of the Philistines — 495b
fairest of her d. Eve — 274a
horseleech hath two d. — 499a
I am all the d. — 371a
if yr. d. do not like them — 535b
kings' d. were among thy..women — 484b
none of Beauty's d. — 73a
sweet her artless d. — 221a
with two pernicious d. joined — 342b
words are the d. of earth — 212b
words are men's d. — 256b
ye d. of Israel, weep — 495b
yr. d. shall prophesy — 504a
Daulis: feast of D. — 422b
Daun Russel the fox — 89a
Dauntless the slug-horn to my lips — 45b
Dauphin: kingdom of daylight's d. — 198a
Dauphiness: the D. at Versailles — 57a
David: D. had his Jonathan — 186b
D. his ten thousands — 495b
D. in the midst — 402b
D., King of Jerusalem — 257a
D. wrote the Psalms — 286a
God-like D. was restored — 138b
Lord, remember D. — 490a
once in royal D.'s city — 3b
see to thine own house, D. — 496a
the root and the offspring of D. — 520b
'David Copperfield': storm..in 'D.' — 314a
Davie (Davey): D. an' Donal' — 415a
Peter D. — 531b
Daw: I am no wiser than a d. — 383b
Dawn: a grey d. breaking — 262a
all the birds will sing at d. — 43a
awful rose of d. — 439a
benediction thro' the d. — 442b
choir of day welcome the d. — 37a
dappled d. doth rise — 268b
d. comes up like thunder — 232a
d. is my brother — 26b
d. on my right hand — 26b
d. on our darkness — 184a
D.'s Left Hand was on the sky — 152a
dewy d. to dewy night — 284a
grey d. is breaking — 115a
in the white d. clear — 398a
I said to D.: Be sudden — 441a
May-time and the cheerful d. — 470b
music of its trees at d. — 7a
next day after d., doth rise — 383a
no d.—no dusk — 195a
poets are needed to sing the d. — 264b
roseate hues of early d. — 3b
saw the d. glow through — 263b
sigh'd for the d. and thee — 434a
silver sail of d. — 200a
starts for the D. of Nothing — 153b
superb against the d. — 27a
the d. is overcast — 1a
young of our eternal day — 115a
Dawneth: darkest just before..day d. — 158a
Dawning: bird of d. singeth — 329b
so here has been d. — 80a
Dawns: dark summer d. — 436a
Daws: heart..for d. to peck at — 359b
Day: all d. and every day — 147a
alternate Night and D. — 153a
an 'appy d. with Fuzzy — 229a
and it is the d.'s — 133b
another blue d. — 80a
arrow that flieth by d. — 487b
as it fell upon a d. — 20b
beams of lightsome d. — 317a
beneath the blue of d. — 198b
benight our happiest d. — 132b
beyond the night, across the d. — 426b
blabbing, and remorseful d. — 384a
blind with..hair the eyes of D. — 399a
breathers of an ampler d. — 431a
breathing time of d. — 337a
bright, bright as d. — 476b
bright d. is done — 325a
brightness of a new-born D. — 467a

Day (cont.)
brought too long a d. — 195a
business of the d. in the d. — 455a
caravan just for one d. — 192b
cares that infest the d. — 247a
child of a d. — 241a
clouds brings on the d. — 1a
come again another d. — 534b
counted them at break of d. — 70b
darkest d...will have passed — 109b
d., a dedicated priest — 442b
d. after d. the same — 406b
d. and a night and a morrow — 420b
d. and night, aloof — 393b
d. and night shall not cease — 492b
d. becomes more solemn — 394b
d. be time enough to mourn — 117a
d. boils at last — 50a
d. brought back my night — 278b
d. by d. is nought to see — 37b
d. by d. like us He grew — 3b
d. dies with sleep — 197b
d. excludes the night — 453b
d., faster and more fast — 50a
d. for a man to afflict his soul — 503a
d. hath put on his jacket — 193b
D. in his hotness — 5b
d. in such serene enjoyment — 280a
d. is at hand — 514a
d. is done, and the darkness falls — 247a
d. is never darkened — 264a
d. is past and gone — 531a
d. of Empires has come — 87a
d. of my destiny's over — 74a
d. of small nations — 87a
d. of wrath — 317b, 540a
d. returns too soon — 74a
d.'s at the morn — 50a
D.'s azure eyes — 395a
d.'s dead sanctities — 441b
d.'s march nearer home — 280a
d. spent in a round of..idleness — 469b
d. star arise in yr. hearts — 518a
d. stood distinct in the sky — 180b
d. that brings forth the adder — 338a
d. that comes betwixt a Saturday — 79b
d. that hath no *pridie* — 134a
d. that is dead — 425b
d. Thou gavest, Lord is ended — 145b
d. when I'll be going — 225b
dearly love but one d. — 79b
death of each d.'s life — 348a
dies at the opening d. — 453b
dost rival in the light of d. — 473a
draughts of intellectual d. — 114b
driven away from our immortal d. — 33a
dwell in realms of D. — 29b
each d. is like a year — 459b
each d. that dawns is yr. last — 543a
each lost d...has its patron saint — 182a
each present d. thy last — 224b
eclipse without all hope of d. — 277b
elles the ye of d. — 90a
end of a perfect d. — 204a
enjoy bright d. — 267a
entertains the harmless d. — 473b
ere I had ever seen that d. — 330a
every d.'s most quiet need — 44a
every d. to be lost — 211b
every dog his d. — 226a
every meanest D. the conflux — 80b
eye of pitiful d. — 349a
fairer far than this fair d. — 394b
first d. of death is fled — 72b
first dark d. of nothingness — 72b
fogs prevail upon the d. — 140b
for a d. and a night — 423a
garden in the cool of the d. — 492b
gates of the d. — 475b
gently shuts the eye of d. — 18b
gilded car of d. — 266b
gloamin' treads the heels o' d. — 424b
go not, happy d. — 433b
good-morrow to the d. so fair — 189b
good things of the d. — 349a
go to bed by d. — 413b
guest that tarrieth but a d. — 520a
gwine to run all d. — 156a
heat of the long d. — 7a
heaven to gaudy d. denies — 74a
he that outlives this d. — 383a

Day (cont.)
his first, last, everlasting d. — 132a
how many hours bring about the d. — 384a
idle singer of an empty d. — 284a
I have known no d. — 36b
I loved the garish d. — 288b
immortality broods like the d. — 466b
in her nest at peep of d. — 438a
innumerable choir of d. — 37a
in pure converse our eternal d. — 39b
it don't seem a d. too much — 94a
it is his d., said Dinadan — 257a
it is not yet near d. — 366a
it is our opening d. — 18a
it raineth every d. — 372a
it was Thy d., sweet — 114b
jocund d. stands tiptoe — 366a
journey take the whole long d. — 311a
joy of the d. in mirth the while — 117a
keeps their fallen d. about her — 293a
knell of parting d. — 174a
larke, messenger of d. — 89a
latter d. upon the earth — 497a
let the d. perish..I was born — 497a
let them have their d. — 474b
life's little d. — 251b
lifting up of d. — 381a
light of all our d. — 466b
light of all their d. — 293a
light of common d. — 466b
light to rule the d. — 492a
little systems have their d. — 429b
long d. wanes — 439a
look on Silvia in the d. — 372b
look the same by d. — 43b
loved thee since my d. began — 439a
maddest merriest d. — 434b
many and many a d. — 468a
merry heart goes all the d. — 373a
mery someres d. — 90a
moon doth shine as bright as d. — 534b
more and more unto the perfect d. — 497b
morning star, d.'s harbinger — 270a
morning were the first d. — 492a
murmur of a summer's d. — 8a
named a trysting d. — 253a
nephew, beware of the d. — 86a
night in thought, the d. in toil — 307a
night of this immortal d. — 397b
night succeeds thy little d. — 295a
no d. for me to look upon — 372b
nothing else saw all d. long — 218b
not to me returns d. — 273a
now is come a darker d. — 395b
now's the d. — 62b
now the d. is over — 20a
O d. and night, but this is..strange — 331b
O frabjous d.! — 84a
on a dull d. in an ocean cave — 428b
one d. in thy courts — 487a
one d. telleth another — 482b
on the d. when..Christ was born — 284b
our triumphant holy d. — 524b, 558b
outliving his d. — 423b
out of Eternity this new D. — 80a
perfect d. nor night — 384a
performance keeps no d. — 78b
Policeman D. — 228a
precincts of the cheerful d. — 174b
produce of the common d. — 464a
promise such a beauteous d. — 387b
rare as a d. in June — 251a
rise! for the d. is passing — 306b
round the feet of the d. — 420a
runs thro' the roughest d. — 346b
sailor, d. is at hand — 315b
sang it all d. long — 36b
seats of everlasting d. — 453b
seem'd to have known a better d. — 316b
see'st the twilight of such d. — 388a
since thy d. began — 241a
sinking to slumber, the bright D. — 282b
sister, the whole d. long — 82b
so foul and fair a d. — 346a
spite of darkness, it was d. — 114b
splendid for the d. — 236b
springs like d. from desolation — 397a
stay, until the hasting d. — 189a
sufficeth that the d. will end — 341b
sufficient unto the d. — 505b
sunless d. went down — 70b

Day (cont.)

superfluous burden loads the d.	278b
sweet d., so cool, so calm	187b
that d. shd. be so soon	423a
the better d., the worse deed	185b
the brightness of the d.	3b
the d. and the way we met	422b
the d. be never so longe	182b
the d. breaks not	132a
the d. but one	34a
the d. gone by	119a
the d. is aye fair	285b
the d. is gone	221a
the d. must dawn	150a
the d. of spirits	447b
the d. will be to-day	37b
the gentle d. . . dapples the. .east	359a
the great, the important d.	1a
the long d. done	185a
there 's night and d., brother	34a
this and every d.	224a
this d. I breathed first	341b
this d. is called. .Crispian	383a
the d. is yr. own	424b
this d. may be the last	287a
this d. shall gentle his condition	383a
this good d. new-born	191a
this long weary d. have end	408b
this petty pace from d. to d.	350b
those eyes, the break of d.	352a
tho' the d. be never so long	182b
thousand Blossoms with the D.	152b
till next d., there she lay	90b
to hold from this d. forward	481b
until the breaking of the d.	493a
until the d. break	500a
unto my dying d., sir	524a
welcum the d. . .lamp of d.	134b
w'en de great d. comes	182a
what a d. may bring forth	498b
what glance of d.	447b
when this d. is named	383a
while the d. ran by	187b
wished for the d.	513a
withstand in the evil d.	516a
woe worth the d.	316a
yield d. to night	383b
young dawn of our eternal d.!	115a
Daybreak: white tremendous d.	40a
Day-dreams of melancholy men	141b
Daylight: and the d.'s past	282b
between the dark and d.	246b
d. comes, comes in the light	96b
in death yr. d. finish	48b
long and lone d.	399a
night. .is but the d. sick	355b
see a church by d.	358a
we burn d.	141a, 355b, 364b
Days: all our d. are gone	487b
all the d. that 's in the week	79b
Ancient of D.	172b, 504b
as thy d., so shall thy strength	494b
beauty and length of d.	420b
because the d. are evil	515b
born to inglorious d.	96a
brave d. of old	253a
childish d., that were as long	463a
considered the d. of old	487a
d. and moments quickly flying	86a
d. dividing lover and lover	420a
d. in goodness spent	74a
d. may come, the d. may go	106a
d. of danger, nights of waking	316b
d. of man are but as grass	488a
d. of our tropic youth	182a
d. seem lank and long	166b
d. that are no more	436a
d. that are one with human art	37a
d. that are over	424a
d. . .thought of grief refuse	37a
dreams of d. forsaken	422a
even as our d. do grow	361a
even from my boyish d.	360a
evil d. come not	499b
fain see good d.	484a
fall'n on evil d.	275a
fall from the d. that have been	252a
find it after many d.	499b
forty d. and forty nights	405b
full of d., riches, and honour	496b
green d. in forests	414b

Days (cont.)

how many d. will finish. .year	384a
I am but two d. old	32b
I am weary of d. and hours	422a
I have put my d. . .out of mind	424a
in her d. every man shall eat	386b
in six d. the lord made heaven	480a
in the d. e'er I was born	33b
King Charles' golden d.	524a
lead on our d. to age	341a
leads melodious d.	430a
length of d. is in her	497b
light of other d. around me	282b
light of other d. is faded	54a
live laborious d.	269b
long as twenty d. are now	463a
look'd on better d.	326b
lost d. of my life	312b
man in his hasty d. is honoured	36b
man. .is of few d.	497a
my d. among the dead are passed	407a
my d. are in the yellow leaf	73b
my d. are swifter than. .shuttle	497a
my d. are trances	298a
my d. wh. are at best but dull	448a
my salad d.	323a
nor d. nor things diurnal	422a
not without honour my d. ran	452b
one of my well-looking d.	170b
past our dancing d.	365a
praise my d. for all they bring	35b
psalm of green d.	307b
remember d. that have gone by	154b
Rose of all my d.	476b
seven d. and nights	362b
seven whole d.	188a
she has seen dark d. before	147b
sit here. .on and off, for d. and d.	82b
six d. shalt thou labour	480a
sound. .wh. in those d. I heard	465a
spring, full of sweet d.	187b
then, if ever, come perfect d.	251a
three whole d. together	416a
thy d. may be long in the land	480a
thy young d. shaded	281b
time and drawing d. out	339a
to lengthen our d.	281b
to lose good d.	409a
to scape stormy d.	133a
we have seen better d.	368a
we shall shortly see better d.	25b
what dark d. seen	388b
wh. the d. never know	148a
whose d. are dwindled	284b
wish my d. to be	468a
with multitude of d.	214a
world of happy d.	384b
wrought in ancient d.	252a
you lament not the d.	407a
Day-star: so sinks the d.	270a
Day-time: I cry in the d.	483a
Dayrolles a chair	91a
Dazed: all d. with flowers	296b
Dazzle: mine eyes d.	454b
see the sights that d.	33b
you d. my eye	292b
Dazzled by the paint	457a
Dazzles at it, as at eternity	447b
De: enclitic D.	47a
Deacons: Bishops, Priests and D.	478b
Dead: all our best men are d.	536a
all the rest are d.	246b
and art thou d., as young	67b
and bury the d.	287b
antique order of the d.	441a
apples on the D. Sea's shore	68b
back with her d. and her shame	437b
barrows of the happier d.	438b
beautiful Evelyn Hope is d.	46b
bent him o'er the d.	72b
be thus when thou art d.	363b
better be a fool than to be d.	413a
better be with the d.	348b
blend the living with the d.	86a
blessed are the d.	519b
brother, when you're d.	188b
but marks our English d.	234b
but they are d.: those two are d.	472b
Caesar, d., and turned to clay	336b
calls his d. to him	229a

Dead (cont.)

captain lies, fallen cold and d.	457b
Christ risen from the d.	515a
cities of the d.	74a
come not, when I am d.	426a
contend for Homer d.	321b
converse with the mighty d.	443b
d., but in the Elysian fields	129a
d. dieth no more	513a
d. from the waist down	47a
d. herself ere evensong	529b
d. may feel no wrong	298a
d. men gave a groan	99a
d. men rise up never	422a
d. Past bury its d.	248a
d., quick, I know not how	176b
d. . .sceptred sovereigns	73a
d. shall go down to them d.	423b
d. shall not have died in vain	245b
d. unto sin, and living	481a
d. wh. are already d.	499b
d. who live again	144b
d. with frost ere now	176b
death lies d.	421b
dew on the face of the d.	25a
dooms. .imagined for the. .d.	217b
do we indeed desire the d.	430a
down among the dead men	143a
ere I am laid out d.	189b
fairy. .falls down d.	21b
fame is a food that d. men eat	131a
fell d.–born from the press	201b
found him with the d.	459b
found, when she was d.	168a
frightful when one 's d.	302a
Grimes is d.	175b
had I lain for a century d.	434a
he cd. not wait. .he is d.	8b
he is d. and gone, lady	335b
I cheer a d. man's sweetheart	199a
he is d., the sweet musician	248b
I fell at his feet as d.	518b
if I am d. he wd. like to see me	156b
if I were d., you'd. .say	294a
if it were d. or bledde	88b
if Lucy shd. be d.	471b
if oon of hem were d.	88b
if these men are d.	421b
I have been d. these two years	91a
I mysel' were d. and gone	530b
I saw a d. man win a fight	530b
I saw the d., small and great	519b
is old Double d.?	380b
Johnson is d.	214a
King of Spain is d.	150b
lasting mansions of the d.	113b
let the d. bury their d.	506a
life from the d. is in that word	280a
living need charity more than. .d.	5a
love was d.	421b
man fears to be d.	16b
mie love ys d.	88a
mourn for me when I am d.	388a
much less when he 's d.	123a
my days among the d. are passed	407a
noble living and the noble d.	469b
no, no, he is d.	336a
not d., but gone before	310a
not d., but sleepeth	506a
O God, that I were d.	433b
over the rich D.	39a
profane the service of the d.	336b
queen, my lord, is d.	350b
quite, quite for ever d.	104b
ravens, clamorous o'er the d.	392a
rejoice ye d., where'er yr. spirits	37a
rest not England's d.	184b
round the earth till you're d.	236b
sea gave up the d.	519b
Sea shall give up her d.	491a
seek ye the living with the d.?	510a
seen those d. men rise	99a
shammin' when he 's d.	229a
sheeted d. did squeak	329b
she has been d. many times	293a
she 's alive, she is not d.	531b
she 's d., sir, long ago	531b
she, she is d., she 's d.	132b
she was d.!	294a
shone round him o'er the d.	184b
smiling the boy fell d.	47b

Dead (*cont.*)

something was d. in each	459*b*
soon to drop off d.	311*b*
strikes him d. for thine	436*b*
talk with the departed d.	394*b*
the d. shall live	139*b*
their home among the d.	393*b*
the man was d.	19*b*
there are no d.	562*b*
th' unhonour'd d.	174*b*
the wall up with our English d.	382*a*
they may say when I am d.	530*b*
they told me you were d.	106*a*
this my son was d.	509*b*
those we call the d.	431*a*
thou being d. art a God	423*b*
thrice looked he at the d.	253*b*
to be said for being d.	27*b*
together fell down d.	254*a*
took their wages and are d.	200*a*
trade..with the living and the d.	142*a*
view-hollo wd. waken the d.	173*a*
voice of the d...a living voice	431*b*
was alive and is d.	523*b*
was patient, being d.	294*a*
weep for Adonais..he is d.	391*b*
whan a beest is d.	89*a*
what was d. was Hope	459*b*
when I am d. and opened	261*b*
when I am d., I hope..be said	26*b*
when I am d., my dearest	311*a*
where d. men meet	67*a*
who are just born, being d.	311*b*
who were d. in trespasses	515*b*
with the d. there is no rivalry	255*b*
with the enduring d.	392*a*
worse to me than a d.	462*b*
wd. that I were d.!	433*a*
y'er a lang time d.	522*b*

Deadly in the long run | 446*b*
Dead March: hear the D. play | 228*b*
Dead-struck: I'm the bird d.! | 263*b*
Deaf: as d. as a door | 35*a*

at once is d. and loud	395*b*
d. and silent, read'st th'..deep	466*b*
I am d. with praises	296*b*
Meg was d. as Ailsa Craig	60*a*
the woman's d., and does not hear	299*b*

Deafer than the blue-eyed cat | 428*a*
Deal: big business give..a square d. | 310*b*

gey ill to d. wi'	82*a*
new d. for the American people	310*a*
to be given a square d.	310*a*
to d. plainly, I fear I am not	344*a*

Dealing: common-sense and plain d. | 148*a*

this isn't fair d.	233*a*
thy just d. as the noonday	484*a*

Dealings: his d. have been told | 265*a*

whose own hard d. teach them	353*a*

Dean: D. of Christ Church, sir | 528*b*

humility..clothe an English d.	113*a*
I am the D.	528*b*
sly shade of a Rural D.	39*b*
the cushion and soft d. invite	302*b*
to your text, Mr. D.!	145*a*

Deans: dowagers for d. | 435*b*
Dear: and thou art d. | 279*b*

but oh, how fondly d.	200*b*
d. as remembered kisses	436*a*
D. Sir, yr. astonishment's odd	522*b*
d. to maidens are their rivals	293*a*
d. to me as are the ruddy drops	338*b*
d. to me as light and life	61*a*
d. to me in the middle of my being	243*a*
d. were her charms to me	177*b*
desolate but something d.	68*a*
I hold his d.	401*b*
man..to all the country d.	168*b*
mother's sake the child was d.	101*a*
my dove, my d.	434*a*
names of things beloved are d.	36*a*
serve it right for being so d.	124*b*
small, but how d. to us	21*a*
something blissful and d.	281*b*
that bread shd. be so d.	196*b*
this d..d. land	375*a*
too convincing—dangerously d.	70*a*
too d. for my possessing	388*b*
we two now part. My Very D.	294*a*

Dearer: d. her laughter free | 177*a*

d. was the mother	101*a*

Dearer (*cont.*)

d. yet the brotherhood	287*b*
O d. far than light	468*a*
was there a d. one	195*b*

Dearest: assure you she's the d. girl | 122*a*

d. her constancy	177*a*
d. idol I have known	109*b*
then, d. 'since 'tis so	47*b*

Dearie: for thinking on my d. | 59*a*

my ain kind d. O	61*b*
my arms about my d. O	60*b*
flew o'er me and my d.	61*a*
my bonnie d.	59*b*

Dearness: a distant d. in the hill | 430*b*
Dears: nature swears, the lovely d. | 60*b*
Dearth: all whom war, d., age, agues | 133*a*

inhuman d. of noble natures	217*b*
measure in a year of d.	31*a*
pine within and suffer d.	389*b*

Death: absence..worse than d. | 109*a*

a covenant with d.	159*a*
Adam..brought d. into the world	447*a*
after my d. I wish no..herald	386*b*
against the hour of d.	481*b*
a lightning before d.	366*b*
all seasons for thine own, O D.	185*a*
all the joy before d.	423*b*
a man that apprehends d.	352*a*
anarchy..the laws of d.	315*a*
ancients dreaded d.	181*a*
and back resounded, D.	273*a*
and the shadow of d.	497*a*
angel of d. has been abroad	38*a*
Angel of D. spread his wings	74*a*
armed against all d.'s endeavour	40*a*
arms of cool-enfolding d.	458*b*
at my d., thy Sun shall shine	132*a*
back to a world of d.	100*a*
be absolute for d.	351*b*
be dunged with rotten d.	442*a*
be thou faithful unto d.	518*b*
bitterness of d. is past	495*b*
body of this d.	513*a*
breast of the old nurse, D.	185*a*
brought d. into the world	270*b*
but man after his d. moot wepe	89*a*
Byron's eyes were shut in d.	6*b*
call in thy d.'s-head there	188*a*
can this be d.	299*a*
certain d. by..shame attended	233*b*
certain, except d. and taxes	156*b*
chamber in the silent halls of d.	53*a*
come away, d.	371*a*
come to the bridal-chamber, D.	178*a*
commands she be stoned to d.	30*a*
counts d. kind Nature's signal	214*a*
dare e'en D. to die for thee	190*a*
daughter..at the point of d.	508*b*
daughter of D. and Priapus	421*b*
day of d. than the day of..birth	499*a*
dear, beauteous d.	448*a*
d. after life does greatly please	408*b*
d...amusing in itself	157*b*
D. and his brother Sleep	393*b*, 397*b*
D., and that vast For Ever	225*b*
d., a necessary end	339*a*
d., as the Psalmist saith, is certain	380*b*
d. bandaged my eyes	50*b*
d...been his next-door neighbour	319*b*
d., be not proud	133*a*
d. broke at once the vital chain	210*b*
d. by slanderous tongues	359*a*
d. came with friendly care	100*b*
d. closes all	439*a*
d. comes to young men	13*b*
d. cometh soon or late	253*a*
d. complete the same	51*a*
d...distinguished from dying	404*b*
D.! ere thou hast slain another	42*b*
d...extinguisheth envy	14*a*
d. has done all d. can	44*b*
d. has left on her only	195*b*
d. has made his darkness	430*b*
d. hath no more dominion	513*a*
d. hath so many doors	23*a*
d. hath ten thousand..doors	454*b*
d. have we hated	284*a*
d., in itself, is nothing	139*b*
D. in the cup	60*b*
d. in the pot	496*b*
d. is a fearful thing	352*a*

Death (*cont.*)

d. is but a groom	133*b*
d. is d.; but we shall die	185*a*
d. is our physician	360*b*
d. is parting	313*b*
d. is still working	187*a*
d. is the cure of all diseases	42*a*
d. is the privilege of..nature	313*b*
d. is the veil	397*b*
d. joins us to the majority	477*b*
d. lays his icy hand on kings	401*a*
d. lies dead	421*b*
d., like a narrow sea, divides	453*b*
d. met I too, and saw the dawn	263*b*
d...must be like all the rest	398*a*
d. my days shd. expiate	387*a*
D...My lord? A grave	374*a*
d. of a dear friend	357*b*
d. of each day's life	348*a*
d. of Nelson was felt in England	407*b*
d. of poor Cock Robin	528*a*
d. of the Blatant Beast	255*a*
d. of yr. daughter..a blessing	11*b*
D. once dead	389*b*
d. opens unknown doors	262*a*
D...,.poor man's dearest friend	61*b*
d.'s dateless night	387*b*
d. shall flee from them	519*a*
D.'s imperishable wing	312*a*
d.'s pale flag is not advanced	366*b*
d.'s second self	388*a*
d.'s self is sorry	215*a*
d. stands above me	241*a*
d.'s untimely frost	61*a*
D., the consoler	247*a*
d. the journey's end	141*a*
D.; the last best friend	406*b*
D., the Skeleton	473*a*
d. thou shalt die	133*a*
d. took him mellow	295*a*
d. unloads thee	351*b*
D., when'er he call..too soon	167*a*
d. will come when thou art dead	399*a*
d. will find me..before I tire	39*b*
d. will have his day	375*a*
D. will listen to your stave	394*b*
delivered my soul from d.	485*b*
dens, and shades of d.	272*b*
desultory feet of D.	312*a*
die a dry d.	367*a*
die not, poor d.	133*a*
die the d. of the righteous	494*b*
direful d. indeed they had	155*a*
disappointed by that stroke of d.	213*a*
Doctor said that D. was but a..fact	459*b*
doom'd to d., tho' fated	140*a*
dotard D.	24*a*
drank d. like wine at Austerlitz	92*b*
dread of something after d.	333*a*
dreadful..brink of obvious d.	43*b*
eaten to d. with rust	380*a*
eloquent, just, and mighty D.	308*a*
face to..meet d. with	48*a*
faith that looks thro' d.	467*a*
fear and danger of violent d.	191*b*
fear d.? to feel the fog	50*b*
fears..only the stroke of d.	16*b*
fed on the fullness of d.	423*b*
first day of d. is fled	72*b*
fluting a wild carol ere her d.	420*b*
for any pains of d., to fall	481*b*
for D. had illumined the land	248*a*
for d.'s sweet chrism retain'd	294*b*
for restful d. I cry	388*a*
foreknow in d.'s worst hour	423*b*
friend and enemy is but D.	40*a*
from sudden d.	478*b*
give me liberty or give me d.	186*a*
glad to d.'s mystery	196*a*
go hand in hand to d.	312*b*
gone to her d.!	195*b*
guiltless d. I die	363*b*
half dead, a living d.	277*b*
harbingers of blood and d.	351*a*
here importune d. awhile	324*b*
here life has d. for neighbour	422*a*
he shall be our guide unto d.	485*a*
his d., wh. happened in his berth	195*a*
his means of d.	336*a*
his name that sat on him was D.	518*a*
hob-and-nob with brother D.	439*a*

Death (*cont.*)

honour in one eye..d. i' the other	337b
how wonderful is D.	393b, 397b
hungry stream of D.	557b
I cd. not look on D.	228b
if die, brave d.	379a
if it in d. alone must die	445a
I fled, and cry'd out, D.	273a
if thou canst D. defy	37a
I have often thought upon d.	16b
in d. they were not divided	495b
in d. yr. daylight finish	48b
inherit the vasty Hall of D.	7b
in his eyes foreknowledge of d.	420b
in life, in d., O Lord, abide	251b
in love with easeful D.	220a
in our very d. and burial	228a
in the hour of d.	478b
in those days shall men seek d.	519a
into the gulf of D.	391b
into the jaws of D.	426a
into the valley of Death	426a
it is but D. who comes	318a
I will be a bridegroom in my d.	324b
joins issues with d.	51b
keep a league till d.	376a
keeps D. his court	375b
keys of hell and d.	518b
King D. hath asses' ears	24a
kiss the image of my d.	138a
kneeling by his bed of d.	137b
lapwings feel the leaden d.	304a
last enemy.. is d.	515a
last look by d. revealed	72b
lead him to D.	309b
life d. does end	197b
life is a coquetry of D.	441a
Life is perfected by D.	44a
Life, the shadow of d.	420b
life to him wd. be d. to me	223b
little room do we take up in d.	401a
look on d. itself	348a
love is strong as d.	501a
lovely and soothing d.	458b
love thee better after d.	44a
made a covenant with d.	502a
make d. proud to take us	324b
make one in love with d.	391b
marriage and d. and division	421a
masters the fear of d.	14a
meetest for d.	354b
men fear d. as children	14a
midst of life we are in d.	481b
most cruel d. of Pyramus	356a
must hate and d. return?	394a
my part of d. no one so true	371a
nativity, chance or d.	356a
neither d., nor life, nor angels	513b
neither wish d. nor fear	416b
no drinking after d.	22b
no life, but lively form of d.	238b
none blessed before his d.	520b
nor d.'s cold flood	453b
nor shall d. brag thou wander'st	387a
not born for d., immortal Bird	220a
not d., but, dying, wh. is terrible	151a
not D., but Love	43b
not..plucked, for d. mature	276b
not so much afraid of d.	41a
now boast thee, d.	325b
now to D. devote	276a
O D. in Life	436a
O d., where is thy sting?	515a
of Night; perchance of D.	443b
old men go to d.	13b
one life and one d.	44b
one of the new terrors of d.	4b
on such the second d... no power	519b
O proud d.! what feast is toward	337a
or else swoon to d.	220b
ought but d. part thee and me	495a
our Jubilee is d.	41b
pains of d. gat hold upon me	489a
pain without the peace of d.	76b
parting.. image of d.	144b
passed from d. unto life	510b
play to you, 'tis d. to us	244b
pontifical D.	441a
quiet us in a d. so noble	278a
ranks of d. you'll find him	281b
Reaper whose name is D.	248a

Death (*cont.*)

red fruit of thy d.	422b
rendezvous with D.	321a
revenge triumph over d.	14a
ruling passion strong in d.	302a
Saul was consenting unto his d.	512a
secret of the shrouded d.	263b
sense of d. is.. in apprehension	352a
shalt thou feed on D.	389b
sights of ugly d. within mine eyes	384b
silence deep as d.	76b
since by man came d.	515a
sisters D. and Night	457b
sit.. in the shadow of d.	508b
Sleep,.. brother to D.	117a
sleep, death's counterfeit	348a
sleep is a d.	42a
[sleep is] in fine, so like d.	42a
sleep the sleep of d.	30b
snares of d. compassed me	489a
some mettle in d.	322b
some sad lover's d.	139a
sooner or later, delicate d.	458b
soothe the dull, cold ear of d.	174a
so peace instead of d.	76b
strange images of d.	346a
stroke of d. is as a lover's pinch	325a
strong and long-lived d.	132b
studied in his d.	346b
sundown splendid.. D.	185a
sweet is d. who puts an end	428b
sword he sung a song of d.	30a
taste of d. but once	339a
that d. is slumber	396a
that sleep of d.	333a
the d.-fires danced	98b
the d. I was to die	530a
their life was d.	312a
the pang preceding d.	168a
there is no D.!	248a
there is not room for D.	38b
there shall be no more d.	519b
the sharpness of d.	478a
the warrant, Claudio, for thy d.	352a
the way to dusty d.	350b
they were even hard at d.'s door	488b
this fell sergeant, d.	337a
this is d. and the sole d.	46a
this reasonable moderator.. Death	41b
thou of d. must dream	398b
thou owest God a d.	378b
thy.. bones hearsed in d.	331a
thy brother D. came	399a
thy d. well quit shall be	531a
till d. like sleep.. steal on me	399a
till D... stopped his.. tongue	302b
till d. us do part	481b
till life forget and d. remember	422b
'tis D. is dead, not he	392b
to be carnally minded is d.	513b
to my soul at d. I cry	457a
too low crawling, for d.	18a
true to thee till d.	150a
truly longed for d.	438b
under the ribs of D.	267b
unsubstantial d. is amorous	366b
valley of the shadow of death	483a
wages of sin is d.	513a
Waldo.. improved by d.	315b
war, d., or sickness	356a
Webster was much possessed by d.	145a
we owe God a d.	380b
were there d. in the cup	320a
what's d.? you'll love me yet	50a
what shd. it know of d.?	472b
what we fear of d.	352a
when as d. shall all.. subdue	408a
when D. to either shall come	37b
when men are at the point of d.	366b
where is d.'s sting?	251b
where kingly D. keeps.. court	392a
who can run the race with D.?	211b
whom d. cd. not daunt	531b
whose portal we call D.	248a
why fear d.? It is.. adventure	157b
wish them to a fairer d.	351a
with D. and Morning	437a
with the burly d. itself awakes	380a
worst is d. and d... have his day	375a
years of fearing d.	339a
yet afraid of d.	94b

Death (*cont.*)

yr. loveliness and.. hour of my d.	223a
Death-bed: gon to hys d.	88a
go to thy d.	336a
Jemmy Grove on his d.	531a
Death-fires danced	98b
Death-hour: darkness and the d.	44a
Deathless: make love d.	445b
Death-moth: beetle nor the d.	219b
Deaths: after so many d. I live	188a
by fain'd d. to die	133b
die many times before their d.	339a
more d. than one	459b
with him all d. I cd. endure	276a
Debate: daughter of d.	145b
Rupert of D.	252a
Débauchée of wit	449b
Debonair: blithe, and d.	268b
Frenchman, easy, d.	111a
Deboshed fish thou	367b
Debt: ambition's d. is paid	339a
d. wh. cancels all	103b
double d. to pay	168b
in d. by disputation	64b
in love, and in d.	38a
national d.. a national blessing	178b, 454a
paid the d. of nature	150a
war, an' a d., an' a flag	250b
Debtor: am I yr. d.?	426a
d. to his profession	14a
Debtors: as we forgive our d.	505b
Debts: forgive us our d. as we forgive	505b
he that dies pays all d.	367b
New Way to Pay Old D.	262b
our d., our careful wives	382b
Decades: five d. hardly modified	180b
Decay: all human things.. d.	140b
ancient castle.. not in d.	15a
and found its d.	97a
as quick a growth to meet d.	189a
before D.'s effacing fingers	72b
change and d. in all around	251b
cold gradations of d.	210b
d. no flood	475b
d. of that colossal wreck	396b
d. of the whole age	16a
falling empire, hasten its d.	110b
flavour of mild d.	194a
fondest hopes wd. not d.	75b
her cruel sports, to many men's d.	409a
melts with unperceiv'd d.	214a
myself shall like to this d.	408a
old Time makes these d.	79a
our love hath no d.	132a
seen my fondest hopes d.	282a
that there be no d.	490b
this muddy vesture of d.	355a
to the grave with unperceiv'd d.	168a
woods d. and fall	438a
Decayed: you are sufficiently d.	165a
Decays: glimmering and d.	448a
Deceased: 'e is frequent d.	236b
he first d.	473b
name of the late d.	233a
the d. Roman Empire	191b
Deceit: hug the dear d.	106b
men favour the d.	139b
no d. in his tongue	482a
other men may use d.	241b
Deceitful: bloodthirsty and d. man	482a
d. shine, d. flow	282b
heart is d. above all things	503b
men are d. upon the weights	485b
Deceits: d. of the world	478b
fables, and dangerous d.	491b
prophecy d.	502a
Deceive: d. you with vain words	515b
first we practise to d.	318b
Light can thus d.	457a
Oh, don't d. me	523a
Sleep again d. me	105a
the same with intent to d.	182a
we have no sin, we d. ourselves	518a
Deceived: are ye also d.?	511a
be not d.; God is not mocked	515b
by bad women been d.	277b
children are to be d. with comfits	13a
disappointed still, was still d.	109b
men (d.) with oaths	13a
she has d. her father	360b
shd. we desire to be d.?	64b

Deceived (cont.)
was I d., or did a sable cloud 267a
Deceiver: I'm a gay d. 103a
welcome, thou kind d. 139b
Deceivers: men were d. ever 358a
Deceiving: she d., I believing 321a
what is hope but d.? 265a
December: when they wed 327b
in a drear-nighted D. 221a
old D.'s bareness 388b
seek roses in D. 72a
their meetings made D. June 431a
wind beat dark D. 328b
Decembers: fifteen wild D. 39a
Decencies: dwell in d. for ever 302a
Decency: want of d. is want of sense 128a
Decent: d. easy men 161b
who came of d. people 27b
Decently: let all things be done d. 514b
Decide: comes the moment to d. 250b
d., but never give yr. reasons 258a
d. this doubt for me 109b
who shall d., when doctors disagree 302a
Decision: by d. more embroils 273a
in the valley of d. 504a
Deck: boy stood on the burning d. 184b
d. put on its leaves 155a
promoted..to d. her mistress' head 74a
shatter'd d. 287a
silly buckets on the d. 99a
they laid him on the d. 531a
walk the d. my captain lies 457b
Decks: but he rose upon their d. 437b
he fell upon their d. 437b
Decked: d. with jewels had she on 528a
my love shd. duly have been d. 408b
Declaim: you are declaiming, d. 209a
Declaration of Independence 94a
Declare: d., if thou hast understanding 497b
d. the wonders that he doeth 488b
him d. I unto you 512b
I heard him d. 83b
nothing to d. except my genius 460b
ye are to d. it 481a
Decline: D.-and-fall-off of 125b
partakers of thy sad d. 109a
writing the d. and fall of the city 161b
Declined into the vale of years 362a
Declines: fair from fair sometime d. 387a
he d. and falls 125b
Decomposes but to recompose 44b
Decorum: hunt D. down 72a
let them cant about d. 61b
Decoyed into our condition 296a
Decrease: but I must d. 510b
Decree: d. confirmeth all He did 36a
d. from Cæsar Augustus 508b
Decrees: how wayward the d. of Fate 440b
Decreed: soul has to itself d. 220b
Dedicate: d. a portion of that field 245a
Father let me d. 446b
Dedicated: a d. spirit 469b
Dedication is flattery 212b
Dedications: rule of refusing d. 455a
Deductions: long train of d. 136a
Dee: on the River D. 28a
sands of D. 226b
Deed: a bloody d.! 335a
a..moment cuts the d. off
attempt and not the d., confounds 347b
better day the worse d. 185b
blow the horrid d. in every eye 347a
build..the d., the d. 137b
d. of dreadful note 349a
d...thro' life the shame endures 177a
d. without a name 349b
do this d. for me 250b
each d. of shame 247b
fit for the d. I had 85a
if one good d. in all my life 368a
I have done the d. 347b
kind of good d. to say well 385b
leff woord and tak the d. 251a
of the d. the glory shall remain 177a
pronounces lastly on each d. 260b
Shadows on the d. alone 474a
so I may do the d. 220b
song..is in itself a d. 426a
so shines a good d. 355b
take the will for the d. 418b
the matchless d.'s achieved 402b

Deed (cont.)
they that have done this d. 340a
thinking the d., and not the creed 249a
till in Heaven the d. appears 63b
till thou applaud the d. 349a
unless the d. go with it 350a
when the d. was done I heard 469a
wrought the d. of shame 253a
Deeds: all your better d...in water writ
d., not words shall speak me 23a
d. of derring do 166b
d. wh. should not pass away 68b
d. will be done 48a
excus'd his devilish d. 274a
foul d. will rise 330b
gentil that doth gentil d. 89b
gentle and virtuous d. 257a
grace this..age with noble d. 378b
heart..flourisheth in lusty d. 257b
if doughty d. my lady please 172b
kind d. with coldness..returning 471a
little d. of kindness 82a
looks quite thro' the d. of men 338a
loveliness of perfect d. 430a
means to do ill d. makes ill d. done 374b
my d. upon my head! 354b
our d. determine us 144a
our d. still travel with us 144a
renown'd for their d. 375a
sager sort our d. reprove 78a
these unlucky d. relate 364a
thing that ends all other d. 325a
those scraps are good d. past 369a
thrice famous d. she wrought 252a
turned aside to do good d. 233b
we live in d., not years 18a
words and d...indifferent modes 148a
words are no deeds 385b
words to the heat of d. 347b
years of noble d. 428a
Deep: a home on the rolling d. 315b
call spirits from the vasty d. 378a
Catholic men..d. in the water 26b
commit his body to the d. 491a
Cyclads on a sunnier d. 394a
darkness upon the face of the d. 492a
d. and crisp and even 436a
d. as first love 436a
d. in anything but Wine 153b
d. in unfathomable mines 110a
d. silent slide away 401b
dive into the bottom of the d. 377a
eternal d. haunted for ever 466b
Eve..d. in the bells and grass 192a
from hiding-places ten years d. 472b
from out the boundless d. 426a
full many a fathom d. 76b
he hath made the d. as dry 234b
he heard the d. behind him 429a
her home is on the d. 78a
his wonders in the d. 488b
in terms too d. for me 165a
in the lowest d. a lower d. 273b
maketh the d. to boil like a pot 497b
no robin ever on the d. 119b
not buried me d. enough 434b
not the d. the Poet sees, but wide 8a
not so deep as a well 365b
one d. calleth another 484b
one is of the d. 410b
out of the d. have I called 490a
out of the d., my child 426b
rocked in the cradle of the d. 461a
singularly d. young man 165a
sweep through the d. 77b
that travail on the d. 117a
the d. moans round 439a
there's danger on the d. 22a
tho' d., yet clear 119b
thou coveredst it with the d. 488a
'tis fifty fathoms d. 530a
too d. for his hearers 169b
to the great d. he goes 427b
unadorned bosom of the d. 266b
very d. did rot 98b
when the remorseless d. closed 269b
woo'd the slimy bottom of the d. 384b
you are knee d. in clover 240a
Deep-contemplative: fools..so d. 326a
Deeper: d., ever so little d. 434b

Deeper (cont.)
d. than did ever plummet 368a
d. than the depths beneath 110a
much d. waters than I thought 135b
Deepest: the d. still is single 120a
Deep-meadowed, happy, fair 429b
Deeps: dragons and all d. 490b
far in yon azure d. 248b
in what distant d. or skies 32a
Deer: a-chasing the d. 62a, 320a
a herd-abandoned d. 392a
d. to the wholesome wold 229b
dun d.'s hide on fleeter foot 316b
I was a stricken d. 112a
my own stricken d. 282a
pale wh. held that lovely d. 448b
'Poor d.', quoth he 325b
rats and such small d. 343a
ravens flock around the dying d. 12b
the running of the d. 526b
Defaced: all saints else be d. 176b
antiquities are history d. 13a
d., deflower'd 276a
Defacing: d. you with foul defame 177a
defaming and d. 429a
Defame: defacing you with foul d. 177a
Defaming: d. and defacing 429a
d. as impure what God declares 274a
Defeat: Dear Night!, this world's d. 447b
greatest tragedy..except a d. 455a
known D., and mocked it 234b
Defect: chief d. of Henry King 26a
fair d. of Nature 276b
make d. perfection 323a
some d. in her did quarrel 367a
Defects: among the d. of the Bill 315a
Defence: at one gate to make d. 277b
cheap d. of nations 57a
d., not defiance 167a, 523a
millions for d. 181b
navy of England—its greatest d. 28b
never make a d. of apology 87b
not only of d., but defiance 167a
our d. is sure 453a
thy d. upon thy right hand 489b
Defenceless as thou wert 392a
Defend: d. us from all perils 478b
foremost to d. 73b
Defender: I mean the Faith's D. 67b
Defends: when it is attacked it d. 566a
Defer: d. not charities till death 16a
let me not d. or neglect it 176b, 523b
'tis madness to d. 477a
Deference: forget the d. due to me 165a
Defiance: defence, not d. 167a, 523a
d. in their eye 170a
our hearts bid the tyrants d. 77b
not only of defence, but d. 167a
Defied: age will not be d. 15b
Defile: thro' the sermon's dull d. 264a
Defiled: he that toucheth pitch..be d. 520b
Defileth: not..into the mouth d. 507a
Define: hold thou the good: d. it well 430a
Definitions: d. of prose and poetry 102b
I hate d. 130a
Deflowered: defaced, d. 276a
Defoe: the Sedulous ape to..D. 412b
stood unabashed D. 299a
Deformed: I know that D. 359a
none..d. but the unkind 372a
Defy: d. th' Omnipotent 271a
if thou canst Death d. 37a
Dégagé: no dancing bear..half so d. 109a
Degenerate Douglas! 469b
Degeneration of his moral being 413a
Degree: better suits with our d. 43b
embrace them in the same d. 42a
exalted them of low d. 508b
observe d., priority 368b
O! when d. is shak'd 368b
take but d. away 368b
thou'st but of low d. 524b
Degrees: scorning the base d. 338b
type of things thro' all d. 463b
Deified: by our own spirits are we d. 470a
Deigning: round turned he, as not d. 253b
Deist sighed with saving sorrow 305a
Deity: acts wh. D...doth ease 218a
particular volition of the D. 201a
poor exchange for D. offended 60a
Dejection: in our d. do we sink as low 470a

Delay: chides his infamous d. 477a
Haste, half-sister to D. 433a
in d. there lies no plenty 370b
in me is no d. 276b
Mecca saddens at the long d. 443b
reluctant amorous d. 274a
reprov'd each dull d. 168b
think not much of my d. 225a
wanton with long d. 35b
Delayed till I am indifferent 206b
Delaying: by d. saved the state 541a
Delays: d. are dangerous in war 141b
d. have dangerous ends 383b
Delectable Mountains 54a
Delia: time creeps..while D. is away 204a
Deliberate: both d...love is slight 259a
Deliberates: woman that d. is lost 1b
Deliberation sat and public care 272b
Delicacy: a task..of fortitude and d. 412a
Delicate: so d. his motions be 37b
Delicately: Agag came unto him d. 495b
Delicious: d. Ah!..the gondola 96a
this d. solitude 260b
Delight: Alice..who wept with d. 148b
all d. lies drown'd with us 189a
all for yr. d., we are not here 357b
applause! d.! the wonder 215b
as our d. or as our treasure 187b
bind another to its d. 32a
but still moves d. 78a
conflict of..sentiments I find d. 212a
d. in simple things 228a
d...misfortunes..of others 57b
d. to season my fireside 468b
desire that outruns the d. 421a
drunk of battle 438b
dull world a business of d. 395b
each thing met conceives d. 276a
Energy is Eternal D. 31a
enjoy'd d. with liberty 409b
feed on vain d. 409a
form'd to d. at once and lash 299b
gave thee clothing of d. 32b
give d., and hurt not 367b
go to't with d. 324a
Greensleeves was my d. 523b
had other aims than my d. 180a
Heaven views it with d. 260b
he must d. in virtue 1b
high as we have mounted in d. 470a
if Sion hill d. thee more 270b
I only have relinquished one d. 467a
is the Shepherd's d. 522a
land of pure d. 453b
let dogs d. to bark 452b
love and a space for d. 420b
Moon of my D. 154a
Mother of the Fair D. 311b
my d. and thy d. walking 37a
my d. on a shining night 525a
my ever new d. 274b
my last d.! 393b
never too late for d. 281b
O that it were my chief d. 425a
paint the meadows with d. 345b
rarely, comest thou, Spirit of D. 398b
seek to d., that they may mend 109a
she was a phantom of d. 470b
studies serve for d. 16a
the day rose with d. to us 225a
their solicitous d. 296b
there is d. in singing 241a
thought that lurks in all d. 265a
till to d. thou hast paid 110a
'tis my d., alone in summer shade 465b
to such a deep d. 'twould win me 101b
toys for yr. d. 414a
turn d. into a sacrifice 186b
unrest wh. men miscall d. 392b
very temple of d. 219b
weighing d. and dole 329b
with grief, but with d. no more 395a
yet I hear thy shrill d. 398a
youth of d., come hither 32a
Delighted with anything..amiable 104a
Delightful: ugly..as sin..almost as d. 246a
Delighting: but, O! d. me 192a
Delights: d. were dolphin-like 325a
in scarlet, with other d. 495b
king of intimate d. 112a

Delights (cont.)
[Pecunia]..Queen of all d. 21a
scorn d., and live laborious days 269b
violent d. have violent ends 365b
why, all d. are vain 344a
Delineation: happiest d. of its varieties 11b
Delinquent: condemns a less d. for 't 66b
Delirium of the brave 474b
Deliver: d. any man by his..strength 484a
d. Israel, O God 483a
d. me from blood-guiltiness 485a
d. my soul from the sword 483a
d. thee from the snare 487b
I will d. him unto you 508a
let him d. him 483a
trusted in God, that he wd. d. him 483a
Deliverance: d...from the darts 179b
with songs of d. 483b
Delivered: d. upon the mellowing 344b
I d. thee when bound 110a
Delivereth them from their distress 488b
Dells: she forgot the d. 218b
Deloraine, good at need 317a
Delos: where D. rose 70b
Delphic: O D. Apollo! 218a
Delphos: the steep of D. leaving 270b
Deluded: Heaven to be d. by him 244a
she was d. away by Roger's 239b
we are all d. thus 394a
Deluge: after us the d. 565a
the rain a d. show'rs 90b
Delusion: but under some d. 56a
given to strong d. 230a
hence dear d., sweet enchantment 403b
Delved: when Adam d. 178b
Demand: d. me nothing 364a
d. that demi-devil 364a
he'll make d. of her 325a
Demas hath forsaken me 516b
Demd: d., damp, moist,..body 125a
life is one d. horrid grind 125a
Demeaning: so womanly, her d. 402b
Demesne: Homer ruled as his d. 220b
Demetrius, a silversmith 512b
Demi-devil: demand that d. 364a
Demi-god: what d...come so near 354a
Demi-natured: incorps'd and d. 336a
Demi-puppets, that by moonshine 367b
Demireps that love..French books 45a
Demnition bow-wows 125a
Democracy: a d.,..a government 292b
d...bludgeoning of the people 460b
d. is on trial 131b
d. substitutes election 391a
our d...the most aristocratic 255b
perfect d...most shameless 57a
political experiment of d. 390b
thanks to wine-lees and d. 44b
world must be made safe for d. 462a
Democrat: aristocrat, d., autocrat 433b
Democratic: creating a..new d. world 81b
our aristocracy the most d. 255b
Demolished but by himself 27b
Demoniaco-seraphic 52b
Demon-lover: wailing for her d. 101a
Demosthenes: D. is not more decidedly the first 255a
D. never comes unseasonably 255a
D. when he fled from the battle 13b
fall below D. or Cicero 149b
Den: d. of wild things in..her eyes 192a
glorious hosanna from the d. 403a
wae to think upo' yon d. 59a
Dens: lay them down in their d. 488b
Denial: with d. vain, and coy excuse 269a
Denied: call that may not be d. 262a
d. him the request of his lips 482b
if it be but half d. 66a
no other was d. 127b
prays but faintly and wd. be d. 376a
too near that comes to be d. 280a, 291b
Denies: court a mistress, she d. you 216a
Deniges: who d. of it? 124a
Denmark: a villain dwelling in all D. 331b
Hamlet..Prince of D...left out 320a
it may be so in D. 331b
look like a friend on D. 329b
might of D.'s crown 76b
rotten in the state of D. 331a
Denote: that can d. me truly 330a

Denoted a foregone conclusion 362a
Deny: he that will this health d. 143a
life offers—to d. 180a
poor heart wd. fain d. 350b
room to d. ourselves, a road 224a
teaches to d. that faintly prays 307a
thou shalt d. me thrice 508a
to d. each article with oath 363b
yet will I not d. thee 508a
Depart: d. again, here, here 366b
d., —be off, — excede 194b
having a desire to d. 516a
he will not d. from it 498b
I am ready to d. 241a
thy sickness shall d. 227b
took leave: but was loath to d. 306a
Departed: and all but he d. 282b
d. this life in thy faith 480b
if he d. as he came 305a
Lord was d. from him 495a
minds me o' d. joys 63b
Departing: God be at..my d. 523a
Departure is taken for misery 520a
Deplore: do them still..still I do d. 132a
find her, or ever to d. her loss 275b
Deportment: celebrated..for his D. 121a
Deposed: how some have been d. 375b
must he be d.? 375b
Depositary: mere d. of doctrine 128a
Depraved: expect a boy to be d. 315a
Depravity of inanimate things 178b
Deprive mankind of their hope 523a
Deprived of everlasting bliss 258b
Depth: but far beyond my d. 386a
d. and dream of my desire 232b
d., and not the tumult, of the soul 467b
d. in that study brings him 158a
in the d. be praise 288b
nor height, nor d...separate us 513b
Depths: darkest d. the miner striving 415b
deeper than the d. beneath 110a
d. in wh. an elephant may swim 185b
he sinks into thy d. 69b
in d. of burning light 149b
in its d. doth glow 5b
walked in search of the d. 497b
with his d. and his shallows 62b
Deputy: books also may be read by d. 16a
d. elected by the Lord 375a
Derby: glides the D. dilly 78b
Derision: clothed with d. 420b
Lord shall have them in d. 481b
time turns the old days to d. 421a
Derived: offices were not d. corruptly 353b
Derned sight better business 183a
Derring: deeds of d. do 166b
Descant: her amorous d. sung 274a
Descend: be stone no more 373b
Descent: d. to Avernus 556a
smile at the claims of long d. 431b
Describe the undescribable 69a
Descried: long leagues apart, d. 96b
Description: beggared all d. 323a
make impertinent d. 65b
Descry the moth's approach 277a
Desdemona: O D.! D.! dead! 364a
to her wd. D. seriously incline 360a
Desert: as to behold a d. a beggar born 388a
beyond High-Park's a d. 149a
d. were a paradise 62b
d. where no life is found 195b
fret not to roam the d. 289b
I never will d. Mr. Micawber 122a
in the d. a fountain 74a
in this d. inaccessible 326b
life is the d. 477b
nothing went unrewarded, but d. 138b
oh! that the d. were my dwelling 69b
part with my glory and d. 187b
snow upon the D.'s dusty Face 152b
so shd. d. in arms be crowned 138b
streams in the d. 502a
the d. shall reioice 502a
two..legs of stone..in the d. 396b
use every man after his d. 332b
waste its sweetness on the d. air 174a
waste, or water but the d. 69a
what ailed us, o gods, to d. you 421b
Deserted at his utmost need 139a
Deserting these, thou leavest me 399b
Deserts (desarts): antres vast..d. idle 360a

Deserts (cont.)
d. of Bohemia 373a
d. of vast eternity 260a
his d. are small 280b
the moon, when she d. the night 277b
wisdom, she d. thee not 276a
Deserve: all who d. his love 140a
d. well of yourself 413a
Sempronius; we'll d. it 1b
Deserved: d. well of his parish 314b
we most righteously have d. 479a
Deserving: where is my d. 388b
Design: dull..there was a d. in it 151b
free from..envy, low d. 240b
paper..dull, there is a d. in it 410b
poetry..a palpable d. upon us 222a
towards his d. moves like a ghost 347b
Designer infinite 442a
Designs: at large to his own dark d. 271a
for close d. and..counsels 138a
ladder to all high d. 368b
lofty d. must close 47a
treasures up his bright d. 110a
Desire: all a wonder and a wild d. 51a
bloom of young d. 175a
bring me my arrows of d. 31a
but D. gratified plants fruits 30a
choose what many men d. 353b
cleave..thy way with fathering d. 263b
delight that consumes the d. 421a
depth and dream of my d. 232a
d. accomplished is sweet 498a
d. in deity 312a
d...mine adversary had written a book 497a
d. not to be rinsed with wine 197b
d. of the moth for the star 399b
d. shall fail 499b
d. that outruns the delight 421a
d. the office of a bishop 516b
d...to enter into the courts 487a
effort, and expectation, and d. 469b
for therein is my d. 489a
his heart is a blind d. 420b
I d. to end my days 558b
I, fulfilled of my heart's d. 422b
in fair d. thine..joy renew 36b
in himself possess his own d. 465a
it is a strange d. to seek power 14b
lineaments of gratified d. 30b
Lord, thou knowest all my d. 484a
love and d. and hate 135a
man's d. is for the woman 102b
miserable..to have few things to d. 15a
mixing memory and d. 144b
moon of the heart's d. 313a
naught for yr. d. 92a
nearer to the Heart's D. 154a
no beauty that we shd. d. him 503a
one is not to get yr. heart's d. 391a
or kindle soft d. 139a
our song is the voice of d. 37a
quiet and rest and d. 284b
same..as thou art in d. 347a
shall see thy heart's d. 347a
shd. we d. to be deceived 64b
so vain d. was chidden 285a
the end of every man's d. 421a
the eye beholds the heart's d. 198b
the hours and times of yr. d. 388a
the Youth pined away with d. 32a
this gray spirit yearning in d. 438b
transported with celestial d. 409a
utmost share of my d. 190a
vain d. at last and vain regret 312b
what..men had come to d. 292b
whence..this fond d. 1b
where our d. is got without content 348b
wh. of us has his d.? 440a
with all the speed d. can make 225a
woman's d...for the d. of the man 102b
Desirable: all of them d. young men 504a
Desired: I have d. to go 197b
lover's pinch, wh. hurts and is d. 325a
more to be d. are they than gold 482b
suffer herself to be d. 449a
Desires: all holy d...do proceed 478b
D. and Adorations 392a
d. and dreams and powers 422a
d. but acts not, breeds pestilence 31a

Desires (cont.)
d., like fell and cruel hounds 369b
liberty..doing what one d. 266a
such sweet d. do gain 176b
than nurse unacted d. 31a
the New Year reviving old D. 152a
'tis not what our youth d. 9a
undaunted daughter of d. 114b
unto whom..all d. known 480a
we fondly flatter our d. 136b
young with young d. 441b
your heart's d. be with you 325b
Desirest: justice more than thou d. 355a
Desireth: heart..d. great matters 307a
Desirous: d. to be blessed 335a
ought else on earth d. 159b
Desk: a votary of the d. 239a
but a desk to write upon 65b
drudgery of the d.'s dead wood 240a
o'er his lamplit d. in solitude 36a
Desmond: that Countess of D. 281a
Desolate: d. and sick of an old passion 135a
how many d. creatures on the earth 43a
none..so d. but something dear 68a
Desolation: abomination of d. 507b
my d. does begin 325a
springs like day from d. 397a
the seat of d. 271a
Despair: begotten by d. 260c
bid me d., and I'll d. 190a
builds a Heaven in Hell's d. 32a
carrion comfort, D. 197a
curst himself in his d. 406b
depth of some divine d. 436a
for regaining my character I d. 155a
from d. thus high uplifted 272a
frustrate hope severer than d. 109a
Giant D. had a wife 54a
grim visag'd, comfortless D. 175a
he who has hoped can never d. 389b
I can endure my own d. 450a
I shall d...no creature loves me 385a
loves..of comfort and d. 389b
magnanimous D. 260a
near neighbour to D. 8a
now fiercer by d. 272a
pale d. and cold tranquillity 392b
racked with deep d. 271a
rash-embraced d. 354a
shall I, wasting in d. 462a
the hurried question of D. 68a
the owner whereof was Giant D. 54a
the unpaid bill, D. 394b
what resolution from d. 271a
whom...d., law, chance, hath slain 133a
wrath, and infinite d. 273b
ye Mighty, and d. 396b
Despairer: too quick d. 8b
Despairing: mithers maist d. 285b
Despairs: leaden-eyed d. 220a
eat thy heart thro' comfortless d. 409b
Despatchful looks in haste 275a
Desperate: beware of d. steps 109b
diseases d. grown 335a
enforce a d. amour 66a
on d. seas long wont to roam 298a
tempt not a d. man 366b
wisdom not to do d. things 444a
Desperation: lives of quiet d. 444a
Despise: contrite heart..thou not d. 485a
d. the skylark's song 38b
dost thou d. the earth 471a
know them best, d. them most 62a
money, I d. it 165b
Despised: dangers by being d. 56b
d. and rejected of men 503a
d., and we esteemed him not 503a
d. as well as served 67a
d. old man 342b
d. the day of small things 504b
hath not d. nor abhorred..the poor 483a
I shd. not be d. 500b
Despises: she is the thing that she d. 104a
Despising: myself almost d. 387b
Despite: builds a Hell in Heaven's d. 32a
immortal in his own d. 303b
the vanquished had no d. 408b
Despond: name of the slough was D. 54a
Despondency and madness 470a
Despot's heel is on thy shore 308a

Destined wretch as I 107a
Destinies: veiled D. 392a
Destiny: day of my d.'s over 74a
D. the Commissary 133b
D. with Men for Pieces 153b
hanging and marriage..go by D. 174a
homely joys, and d. obscure 174a
hopeless passion is my d. 440a
let determined things to d. hold 323b
our d., our being's heart 469b
our manifest d. 291a
riddle of d. 240a
shady leaves of d. 115a
struggling..with ruthless d. 464b
Destroy: I am not come to d. 505a
impatient to d. 214a
not..come to d. the law 505a
safer to be that wh. we d. 348b
they shall not hurt nor d. 501b
utterly abolish or d. 466b
when you d. a blade of grass 34a
Destroyed: bold peasantry..once d. 168a
nor one life shall be d. 430b
tall fellow had d. so cowardly 377a
what Thou art may never be d. 38b
Destroyer: D. and healer, hear 423a
d. and preserver, hear 396a
Destroying: fighting still and still d. 139a
Destruction: besom of d. 502a
by d., dwell in doubtful joy 348b
d. of the poor is their poverty 498a
going from us to be utter d. 520a
other things, to their d. draw 132a
pride goeth before d. 498a
startles at d. 1b
thou turnest man to d. 487b
way that leadeth to d. 505b
Destructions: O thou enemy, d. 482a
Desyren to have sovereyntee 89b
Detail: merely corroborative d. 165a
Detect: lose it in the moment you d. 301b
wd. not d...one circumstance 247b
Detection is..an exact science 136a
Determinate: d. grooves 527a
my bonds in thee are all d. 388b
Determination of words to the mouth 417a
Determine: our deeds d. us 144a
Determined, dared, and done 402b
Detest: but they d. at leisure 71b
Detraction: d. is but baseness 215b
d. will not suffer it 379a
Development: contributions to..d. 9b
De Vere, hast *thou* no tear? 298a
Device: banner with the strange d. 247a
imagined such a d. 483a
miracle of rare d. 101b
there is no work nor d. 499b
Devices: d. of the people..of none effect 483b
d. still are overthrown 334a
Devil: abash'd the D. stood 274b
a laughing d. in his sneer 70a
a moral of the d. himself 382b
an apology for the D. 66b
and you the blacker d. 363b
a problem must puzzle the d. 62b
a saint when most I play the d. 384b
a-walking the D. is gone 100b, 406b
can the d. speak true? 346a
cards..are the d.'s books 418b
childhood..fears a painted d. 348a
children of the d. 437b
craft and subtilty of the d. 479a
crafts and assaults of the d. 478b
D. always builds a chapel 118b
d. a monk wd. be 285a
d. be sometimes honoured 352b
d. can cite Scripture 353a
d. damn thee black 350b
D.-defended walls 294a
d...do a very gentlemanly thing 412b
D. fly away with the fine arts 81a
D. go wid you 231a
d...have all the good tunes 191b
D., having nothing else to do 26b
D. he blew upon his nails 235b
d. he couldna scaith her 59b
D. he grinned behind the bars 235b
D. howling 'Ho!' 26b
d. is come down unto you 519a
D. knows how to row 99b

Devil (*cont.*)

d.'s most devilish when respectable — 43a
D.'s nutting-bag — 247b
d.'s riddle is mastered — 424a
d.'s walking parody — 92a
d. take her! — 416a
D. take the ass — 231a
d. take the hindmost — 65a
d. taketh him up into..mountain — 505a
d. turned precisian — 74b, 262b
d. understands Welsh — 378a
d. was sick — 285a
D. watches all opportunities — 104b
d...will have his chapel — 18b
d. with d. damn'd — 272b
d. wd. have him about women — 382a
doubt is D.-born — 431a
dreamed of the d. — 4a
drink and the d. had done — 413a
'e's a d. an' a ostrich — 233a
everyman..was God or D. — 138b
first Whig was the D. — 210a
gifts from the D. and earthly kings — 30b
given the d. a foul fall — 283a
go to the d. where he is known — 212a
half-d. and half-child — 236b
he shd. dream of the d. — 19a
he's the very d. incarnadine — 372a
himself a d. frae hell — 531a
how agrees the d. and thee — 376b
how the d. they got there — 303a
hunting wh. the D. design'd — 141b
if the d. dress her not — 325a
if that thou be'st a d. — 364a
is the d. to have all the passions — 390b
I worshipped the D. — 30b
John Brown had the D. in his gut — 31a
let us call thee d. — 361b
man is but a d. weakly fettered — 412b
Milton..of the D.'s party — 31a
one more d.'s triumph — 48a
renounce the d. and all his works — 481a
resist the d., and he will flee — 517b
sacrifice..of the d.'s leavings — 419a
serpent, wh. is the D. — 519b
serve God if the d. bid — 359b
shame the d. — 216a
sugar o'er the d. himself — 333a
synonym for the D. — 254b
tell truth, and shame the d. — 378a
that..is d.'s work — 390a
the D. did grin — 100b
the D.'s Awa' Wi' the Exciseman — 60a
the D. sends cooks — 158b
the D. smiled — 100b
the D. was pleased — 100b
the d. will come — 258b
the ingredient is a d. — 361b
there is a d. haunts thee — 377b
till the D. whispered — 228a
turn'd my back upon Don or d. — 437b
use the d. himself with courtesy — 372a
what a mischievous d. Love is — 67a
what d. this melancholy is — 155b
what, man! defy the d. — 371b
when contending with the d. — 518a
who caleth the D.'s foot — 134a
wi' usquebae, we'll face the d. — 63a
world, the flesh, and the d. — 478b
young and sweating d. here — 362b
yr. adversary the d. — 518a
yr. father the d. — 511a
Devilish: earthly, sensual, d. — 517b
most d. thing is 8 times 8 — 155a
Devils: as many d...as..tiles — 569a
d. are not so black as..painted — 246a
d. being offended — 360b
he casteth out d. — 506a
it-is-not-fire-d., dark — 227b
one sees more d. than vast hell — 357b
said they were d. incarnate — 382a
sinners must with d. dwell — 452b
the little d. ran — 235b
they're a' run d. — 63a
'tis d. must print — 281a
we are d. to ourselves — 369a
whip me, ye d. — 364a
Devisal: past our d. — 443a
Devise: for he can al d. — 89a
Devizes: young man of D. — 527a

Devoid of sense and motion — 272b
Devon: Bideford in D. — 437b
Cowslips from a D. combe — 229a
D. white-pot brings — 225b
if the Dons sight D. — 287b
started that morning from D. — 164a
Devotion: a deep fit of d. — 42a
at my d. I love to use the civility — 41b
d.! daughter of astronomy — 477b
farwel my book and.my d. — 89b
last full measure of d. — 245b
matrimonial d. — 164b
open and obvious d. — 237b
shrine of the sailor's d. — 389b
the d. to something afar — 399b
with d.'s visage..sugar o'er — 333a
Devour: seeking whom he may d. — 518a
shed tears when they wd. d. — 15b
threatening to d. me opens wide — 273b
worry and d. each other — 109b
Devoured: d. as fast as they are made — 369a
great ones d. the small — 401a
him who solved it not d. — 277b
some evil beast hath d. him — 493a
Devours: the grim wolf..daily d. — 269b
Devout: d. in dishabilly — 150b
here the d. their..temple choose — 113b
Dew: as d. in April that falleth — 524b
bedabbled with the d. — 189b
besprent with April d. — 216b
birth-time's consecrating d. — 294b
continual d. of thy blessing — 478b
d. bespangling herb — 189a
d. of summer nights — 220b
d. on the face of the dead — 25a
d. shall weep thy fall tonight — 187b
d. that on the violet lies — 317b
dreamt..they were filled with d. — 99a
fades awa' like morning d. — 530a
fearfully o'ertrip the d. — 355a
honey-heavy d. of slumber — 338b
into a sea of d. — 151a
leave the lilies in their d. — 7a
like the d. on the mountain — 316b
my lips, as sunlight drinketh d. — 427a
red d. of Olivet — 442b
resolve itself into a d. — 330a
roses newly washed with d. — 366b
the bright d. is shaking — 115b
the d. was falling fast — 468b
the d. will rust them — 359b
there rain'd a ghastly d. — 432b
walks o'er the d. of yon..hill — 329b
who hath begotten the drops of d. — 497b
whose..beards dip in coldest d. — 264a
whose wine was the bright d. — 398a
Dewdrop: fragile d. on its..way — 220b
I have seen the d. clinging — 205a
protects the lingering d. — 463b
there's a woman like a d. — 45a
Dewdrops: go seek some d. here — 356b
showers and d. wet — 311a
Dewfall at night — 414b
Dew-lapped like Thessalian bulls — 357a
Dews: brushing with..steps the d. — 174b
her tears fell with the d. — 433b
the d. of heaven refined — 169a
the d. of summer night did fall — 265b
the d. of the evening..shun — 91a
Dewy: d. dawn to d. night — 284a
William D. — 179b
Diadem: the precious d. stole — 335a
with a d. of snow — 73a
Dial: a d. from his poke — 326a
an hour by his d. — 326a
as the d. to the sun — 33b
ride upon a d.'s point — 379a
thou breathing d. — 241a
Dialect: a Babylonish d. — 65a
a d. I understand very little — 296a
d. and discourse — 65b
d. words..marks of the beast — 180b
Dial-hand: beauty, like a d. — 388b
Dialogue: the wooden d. and sound — 368b
Dials: carve out d. — 384a
Diamond: Britain..rough..d. — 91a
d., is immortal d. — 197b
like a d. in the sky — 425a
O D.! D.! thou little knowest — 289a
spots of d. form — 112b
Diamonds: thy eyes are seen in d. — 161a

Dian: D. had hot dreams — 329a
hangs on D.'s temple — 328b
Diana: burnt the temple of D. — 42b
D. in her summer weed — 176a
D. of the Ephesians — 512b
D.'s lip is not more smooth — 370a
let us be D.'s foresters — 376b
Diapason: d. after dinner — 19b
d. closing full — 139b
Diaphenia..daffadowndilly — 105b
Diaries: let d...be brought in use — 15a
Dice: some were playing d. — 531a
twain were casting d. — 98b
twice, to throw the d. — 459b
Dicers: false as d.' oaths — 335a
Dick: Mr. D. — 122a
Dickens: what the d. his name is — 355b
Dickon thy master — 385a
Dicky-bird why do you sit — 165a
Dictate: not presume to d. — 126a
Dictates: d. of his godlike mind — 291a
d. of thy faith — 313b
d. to me slumbering — 276a
Dictatorial: a d. word — 166a
Dictionaries: a writer of d. — 207a
to make d. is dull work — 212b
Dictionary: a walking d. — 87b
Did: it was their duty, and they d. — 162b
nor ever d. a wise one — 309b
thou canst not say I d. it — 349a
thro' ignorance ye d. it — 512a
whate'er he d. was done — 138a
Diddest: thus d. thou — 336a
Diddle, we take it, is dee — 422a
Dido: D. and her Æneas — 324b
when D. found Æneas — 304b
Di-do-dum — 304b
Die: all life of mine may d. — 114b
all that live must d. — 329b
and am prepared to d. — 351b
and a time to d. — 499a
and wring his bosom is to d. — 170a
as loth to d. — 467b
as much beauty as cd. d. — 215b
as natural to d. — 14a
ay, but to d. — 352a
Beauty that must d. — 219b
before I d. for ever — 199b
begins to live, begins to d. — 307a
behold, ye shall d. — 423b
but I cannot d. — 393a
but we all must d. — 419a
by fain'd death to d. — 133b
cowards d. many times — 339a
curse God, and d. — 497a
dar'st thou d.? — 352a
dead wh..d. in the Lord — 519b
death, thou shalt d. — 133a
death, to d. for thee — 190a
d. all, d. merrily — 378b
d. and be a riddance — 121b
d., and endow a college — 302a
d. at the top — 419a
d. before they sing — 100b
d. beyond my means — 461a
d. by famine d. by inches — 185b
d. in music — 364a
d. in that man's company — 383a
d. in the last ditch — 461a
d. in the lost, lost fight — 96a
d. in yon rich sky — 436a
d. I, so d. I — 247b
d., my dear doctor — 292a
d. not, poor death — 133a
d. on mine own sword — 351a
d. or rest at last — 394a
d. to look on — 322b
d. to make men free — 200b
d. to save charges — 64a
d. two months ago — 334a
d. with harness on — 351a
d. with kissing of my Lord — 259b
d. with looking on his life — 323a
do anything but d. — 240a
do now not basely d. — 324b
easy live and quiet d. — 319a
easy ways to d. — 325b
either do, or d. — 23a
ere their story d. — 179b
ever ye came to d. — 235a
every man..is born to d. — 141a

Die (*cont.*)

faith with us who d.	256a
fall asleep, or hearing d.	385b
fated not to d.	140a
fellowship to d. with us	383a
few d. and none resign	205a
few d. well that d. in a battle	382b
fight is but to d.	437b
for the truth he ought to d.	147a
for thou must d.	187b
for tomorrow we shall d.	502a
going on, and not to d.	439a
good d. early	118a
good d. first	464a
harder lesson! how to d.	304b
hazard of the d.	385b
he shall not d., by G——	412a
he was not made to d.	429b
how can man d. better	253a
how often are we to d.	304a
I d. happy	156b, 242a
I d.! I faint	394b
I'd lay me doun and d.	135a
if I d., no soul shall pity me	385a
If I must d.	352a
'if I shd. d.', said I	223b
if I shd. d., think only this	40a
if it were now to d.	361a
if thou deye a martir	90a
if we are marked to d.	383a
I'll d. for him tomorrow	531b
I love her till I d.	156a, 526b
I must d. at last	133b
in Adam all d.	515a
in death alone must d.	445a
in..Jerusalem shall Harry d.	381a
is because they d.	106b
I shall d. to-day, and you	283a
I shall not d., but live	489a
is loth to d.	423a
is not born, and does not d.	402a
is not to d.	76b
it is most grand to d.	262a
it was sure to d.	282a
I will d. in peace	462b
I will not have thee d.	436b
king shd. ever d.	50a
learn of me to d.	299b
leave me there to d.	523b
let us do or d.	62b, 76b
live and gladly d.	415a
lo, I must d.	495a
look about us and to d.	300b
man can d. but once	380b
men make haste to d.	199b
men..shall desire to d.	519a
men that love lightly may d.	421b
more deaths than one must d.	459b
my Lord before I d.	259b
myn herte d.	90a
my resolution is to d.	276b
nor let me d. before	6b
not d. here in a rage	418a
not d. in the night	284b
not so difficult to d.	73a
not to live, but to d. in	42a
not willingly let it d.	279a
now that I come to d.	46a
old soldiers never d.	525b
or being born, to d.	17a
or bid me d.	190a
or let me d.	468a
parting was to d.	431a
people..tide's..out	122b
perceives it d. away	466b
poor soul will d.	412a
possess..soul before we d.	8b
power to d.	438b
regret can d.	430b
resolved to d...last dyke	56a
ride on to d.	266b
Romeo..when he shall d.	366a
seems it rich to d.	220a
seen her d. twenty times	322b
shall see a fox d.	226a
shall Trelawny d.?	182b
she answered, 'I wd. d.'	313a
shot my faun and it will d.	261a
shd. d. for the people	511a
sicken soon and d.	270b
since I needs must d.	307b

Die (*cont.*)

sinks downward, here to d.	376a
sing before they d.	100b
so apt to d.	339b
stars, until I d.	439a
taught us how to d.	444b
that we shall d., we know	339a
the death I was to d.	530a
the d. is cast	548b
their's but to do and die	426a
the man wd. d.	349a
then d., dear, I	23b
they d. by thousands	93b
they d. not..but cease	312a
they must be..with us or we d.	217b
they seemed to d.	520a
think, or bravely d.	299a
tho' I shd. d. with thee	508a
those about to d. salute thee	553b
those that do d. of it	325a
thou shalt surely d.	492a
thus adventuring to d.	225a
to d...big adventure	21b
to d. for fatherland	545b
to d., I leave my love	388a
to d. is gain	516a
to d.: to sleep	333a
to live and d. for thee	190a
to live, or dare to d.	301b
to live or fear to d.	145a
tomorrow thou shalt d.	312a
to say that I shall d.	383b
turn giddy, rave, and d.	299a
until that I d.	534b
wash me, Saviour, or I d.	445a
weep or she will d.	436b
we shall d. alone	564b
we shall d. to the Song	185a
what it is to d.	430a
what peace a christian can d.	2b
when we d. we reap our sowing	263a
whether thou live or d.	37a
whom the gods love d. young	71a
who saw him d.?	528a
who wd. wish to d.?	34a
wisdom shall d. with you	497a
without Thee I dare not d.	224a
wretch that dares not d.	61b
yet d. we must	384b
yet she must d.	363b

Died: and so they d. | 305a

as He d. to make men holy	200b
bards who d. content	219b
before her time she d.	432b
closed his eyes and d.	531a
d., as firm as Sparta's king	136b
d. before the god of love	133b
d. in a good old age	496b
d...kisses of the lips of God	285b
d...like a Chrisom child	54a
d. like Duke..Duchess's daughter	19b
d...of my physician	306a
d. unto sin once	513a
d. while ye were smiling	43a
d. with conquering Graeme	317a
dog it was that d.	169a
fell upon their decks, and he d.	437b
God I had d. for thee	495b
had I but d. an hour	348a
I cd. have d. contented	122b
Know-all d. las' year	182a
liked it not, and d.	473b
my love has d. for me	531b
queens have d. young	285b
she d. because she never knew	26b
she shd. have d. hereafter	350b
since he d., and poets	387b
since Maurice d.	36b
sleeping when she d.	196a
so groan'd and d.	160b
these all d. in faith	517a
they had no poet, and they d.	303b
two hours since hath d.	438b
wandered till I d.	9a
was scorn'd and d.	160a
when I d. last	133b
where it d., to tell	215b
where thou diest, I will d.	495a
who d. to save us all	3b
would to God we had d.	494a

Dies: artist never d. | 247b

Dies (*cont.*)

because a man d. for it	460b
d. ere he knows it	47a
d. in good stile at home	451a
d. like a dog	459a
every moment d. a man	439a
happy till he d.	559b
he d., and makes no sign	384a
he that d. pays all	367b
he that d. this year	380b
it d. upon her heart	394b
king never d.	28b
loves, and weeps, and d.	394a
matters not how a man d.	208a
more it (love) d.	117a
no man d. for love	141a
once hath blown for ever d.	153a
then d. the same	477a
troth d. here to dust	312a

Diest: where thou d. will I die	495a
Diet: idiosyncrasy, in d.	41b
praise is the best d.	404b
worm..emperor for d.	335a
Dieted with praise	219b
Differ: men at most d.	429a
Difference: between thee and me	
what d.?	398b
d. of 40,000 men	455a
d. of men's talk	296a
know the d. now that I am back	288a
night makes no d.	189b
oh, the d. to me	470b
the only d., after all	94b
the other's d. bears	260b
yr. rue with a d.	335b
Different: an' hatched d.	144a
d. methods d. men	94b
how d. from the home life	573b
like,—but oh how d.!	473a
other naturs thinks d.	124a
something d. from either	144b
think o' something d.	227b
we boil at d. degrees	148b
Difficult: d. do you call it	212a
d. of tasks to keep	464a
d. to please about their victuals	75b
not so d. to die	73a
upon wh. it is d. to speak	56a
Difficulties: d. do not make..doubt	288b
knowledge under d.	126b
Difficulty: sowen som d.	89a
with d. and labour	273a
Diffidence: d. or shyness	164b
wife, and her name was D.	54a
Diffident: be not d. of wisdom	276a
Dig: d. the grave and let me die	415a
d. till you gently perspire	230b
I cannot d.; to beg I am ashamed	509b
to d. the dust enclosed	389b
Digest: and can d. so much	371a
inwardly d. them	479a
Digestion: d. is the great secret	405b
from pure d. bred	274b
heaven..matter of d.	201a
may good d. wait on appetite	349a
prove in d. sour	374b
Digestions: few radicals have good d.	66b
Digged: saltpetre shd. be d.	377a
Digger on the railroad	147a
Dignify: to d. the Serpentine	131a
Dignities: above all earthly d.	386a
men come to d.	14b
speak evil of d.	518a
wear without corrival all her d.	377a
Dignity: an undeserved d.	353b
below the d. of history	255b
d. of crimes	283a
d. of history	33b
d. of the whole body	350a
for d. composed	272a
his estimate and d.	369a
I left the room with silent d.	177a
in d. of being	464b
in d. or honour goeth	143a
in every gesture d.	275b
Digression: there began a long d.	63a
Digressions .. the soul of reading	411b
Dike: grew in d. nor ditch	529a
Dilettante: snowy-banded d.	433b
Dilloing in his armour	230b
Dilly: glides the Derby d.	78b

Dim: nor d. nor red   98b
Dim-discovered: ships d.   443b
Dimension: without d., where length   273a
Dimensions: the d. of this mercy   115b
Diminish: d., interline   419b
   joys with age d.   48b
Diminished: hide their d. heads   273b
Diminutive: wren..most d. of birds   350a
Dimmed: glory of..sun will be d.   18a
Dimness: elms, fade into d. apace   7b
Dimple on his chin   251b
Dimples: whose d. we prize   400b
Dimpling all the way   303a
Din: louder still the d.   252b
   may'st hear the merry d.   98a
   the cock with lively d.   268b
   with the d. smitten   466a
Dinadan: God defend me, said D.   257a
   it is his day, said D.   257a
Dinah: Vilikins and his D.   526b
Dine: children d. at five   413b
   d...among the rubbish   205b
   d. at journey's end   476b
   d. with Jack Ketch   209a
   d. with the Canons   208b
   gang and d. the day   529b
   going to d. with some men   27b
   go to inns to d.   93a
   I d. at Blenheim   528b
   I fear ye d. but sparely   61b
   if this shd. stay to d.   85b
   if you d. at a friend's   126a
   I shall d. late   241b
   I shd. d. at Ware   109a
   men asked her to d.   527a
   scandal while you d.   438b
Dined: I have d. to-day   75a
   in love, or had not d.   301b
Diner-out: philosophic d.   48b
Diners-out from whom we guard   254a
Dines: where the M.F.H. d. he sleeps   416b
Dining: can live without d.   265a
   they thought of d.   169b
Dining-room will be well lighted   241b
Ding: d., dong, bell   534a
   hear them, d. dong bell   367a
   hey d. a d., d.   327b
   I'll begin it—d., dong   354a
Dinner: after d. is after d.   418a
   after-d.'s sleep   351b
   and then have d.   84b
   better is a dish of herbs   498a
   diapason after d.   19a
   d. lost! 'ounds lost   416b
   d., lunch and tea   26a
   d. waits, and we are tired   108a
   glass's edge when d.'s done   45a
   good d. enough, to be sure   207b
   good d...reconciles everybody   296a
   good d. upon his table   212a
   hours' march to d.   183b
   make our d. sweet   529b
   not a d. to *ask* a man to   207b
   talking politics after d.   128b
   they wd. ask him to d.   82a
   welcome for himself, and d.   305a
   what gat ye to yr. d.   529b
   who's fond of his d.   165b
Dinner-bell: tocsin of..soul, the d.   71a
Dint: the d. of pity   340a
Diocese: all the air is thy D.   132b
Diogenes: D. said of a young man   13b
   D. struck the father   64b
   I wd. be D.   559a
Dip: kind of farthing d.   415a
Diplomacy: dollar d.   523a
Dirce: with D. in one boat   241a
Dirck galloped   47b
Direct: who can d., when all pretend   170a
Direction: all chance, d.   301a
Directions: find d. out   332a
   gives d. to the town   419b
   rode madly off in all d.   243a
Direness, familiar to my..thoughts   350b
Dirge: d. for St. Hugh's soul   119a
   d. of the dying year   396b
   their d. is sung   103a
Dirges: instead of d. this complaint   225a
   to sullen d. change   366a
Dirt: borne the d. and rain   284a
   half the little soul is d.   434b

Dirt (cont.)
   if d. was trumps   240b
   instead of d. and poison   417b
   painted child of d.   303a
   poverty, hunger, and d.   196a
Dirtiness: all along o' d.   228b
Dirty: all d. and wet   419b
   life's road, so dim and d.   70a
Dis: by gloomy D.   274a
   thou let'st fall from D.'s waggon   373a
Disable all the benefits   327a
Disagree: men only d. of creatures   272b
Disagreeable: I'm such a d. man   166b
Disagreeables: all d. evaporate   222a
Disappoint: can't abide to d. myself   170b
Disappointed: d. still..still deceived   109b
   d., unaneled   331b
   never be d.   304a
   pangs of d. love   313b
Disappointeth: sweareth..and d. him not   482a
Disappointing: as for d. them   170b
Disappointment all I endeavour end   198a
Disapproves: condemns what..he d.   58b
Disaster: 'gainst all d.   54b
   laugh at all d.   246b
   with Triumph and D.   230a
Disasters: d. fallen upon her   57a
   d. in his morning face   168b
   make guilty of our d.   342a
   so weary with d.   348b
Disastrous twilight sheds   272a
Disbelief: d. in great men   80b
   suspension of d.   102a
Disbelieve: be a Napoleon and..d.   45a
Disbranch: will sliver and d.   343b
Discandy: do d., melt their sweets   324a
Discarded: to be d. thence   363a
Discept: two must d.   48b
Discern: all we have built..d.   7a
   natural instinct to d.   465a
   real interest to d.   109b
Discerning: genius a better d.   169b
Discharge: no d. in that war   499b
   there's no d. in the war   227b
Discharged: indebted and d.   273b
Disciple: d. is not above his master   506a
   d. whom Jesus loved   511b
Disciples: one of..d...Jesus loved   511a
Discipline: d. must be maintained   121b
   holy spirit of d.   520a
   d...steadiness under fire   238a
Disciplines of the pristine wars   382a
Disclose: more and more to d. truth   13b
Discobolus hath no gospel   67a
Discommendeth: he who d. others   41a
Disconsolate: gate of Eden stood d.   282a
Discontent: age of splendid d.   280a
   contented sort of d.   219a
   divine d.   226b
   in pensive d.   409a
   large and liberal d.   452b
   to youth and age in common—d.   9a
   winter of our d.   384b
   with darkling d.   293b
Discontented: everyone that was d.   38a
Discord: d., harmony not understood   301a
   eke d. doth sow   145b
   hark! what d. follows   368b
   harmony in d.   543a
   so musical a d.   357a
Discords: dire effects from civil d.   1b
   d. make the sweetest airs   66a
Discountenance: O ye Religious, d.   30b
Discouragement: there's no d.   54b
Discourse: any d. of rivers   450b
   bid me d.   386b
   company and good d.   450b
   dialect and d.   65b
   d. into some frame   334b
   d. most eloquent music   334b
   d. of the elders   520b
   in d. more sweet   272b
   rather hear thy d.   64b
   showers of sweet d.   115b
   with such large d.   335b
Discourses: the hipp'd d.   175b
Discover: happy soul she shall d.   115a
Discovered and surprised   274b
Discoverers: they are ill d.   13a
Discredit our mystery   352a

Discredited your travel   322b
Discreet and learned minister   480b
Discretion: let your own d. be your tutor   333b
   not to outsport d.   361a
   philosophy is..d.   321a
   valour is d.   379a
   woman wh. is without d.   498a
   years of d.   481a
Disdain: burning pride and high d.   317a
   d. and scorn ride   358b
   for thee to d. it   399b
   more love or more d.   79b
   patient, deep d.   7a
   she did all d.   526a
   that fixed mind and high d.   271a
Disdained: if now I be d.   526a
   one feeling too falsely d.   399b
Disdains: d. to hide his head   176a
   he d. all things above   291b
Disease: cure..d...kill..patient   15b
   d. is incurable   380a
   d. of not listening   379b
   d., or sorrows strike him   96b
   Emphyteusis is not a d.   413b
   find her d., and purge it   350b
   her taste..amounts to a d.   165a
   life is an incurable d.   107a
   no cure for this d.   26a
   physician..hath his favourite d.   151b
   remedy..worse than the d.   15a
   shapes of foul d.   431a
   strange d. of modern life   8a
   this long d., my life   303a
   Waddy is an infectious d.   237b
   without d. the healthy life   416a
   yesterday of my d.   306a
   young d.   301a
Diseased: d. in his feet   496a
   minister to a mind d.   350b
   when love grows d.   149a
Diseases: d., desperate grown   335a
   perils and d. that he elbows   24a
   rheumatic d. do abound   356b
Disenchanting: so d. as attainment   412b
Disentangle: heart..cannot d.   526a
Disgrace: a d. to be fine   425a
   author of his own d.   109a
   even to a full d.   328b
   impatient of d.   138a
   O the d. of it   25a
   we shall much d.   382b
   when in d. with fortune   387a
Disgruntled: if not actually d.   573b
Disguise: blessings in d.   191a
   d. our bondage as we will   282a
Disguised: think to pass d.   273b
Disguises: troublesome d...we wear   274b
Disgust: d. and.. loathing fell   7a
   old plays began to d.   149b
Disgusted with literary men   222a
Dish: carve him as a d.   338b
   for a d. of wood   375b
   lordly d.   494b
   plucking a d. of sweet .. plums   192a
   some d. more sharply spiced   293b
   the d. ran after the spoon   534a
   was not that (this) a dainty d.   410b, 533a
   woman is a d. for the gods   325a
Dishabilly: devout in d.   150b
Dishclout: Romeo's a d. to him   366a
Dishcover the riddle   85b
Dishes: are these the choice d.   158b
   home-made d.   195a
   shall we..recollect half the d.   11a
Dishonest: employment may be reckoned d.   160a
Dishonour: honour rooted in d.   428b
   I have lived in such d.   324b
   past all d.   195b
Disinheriting countenance   400b
Disintegration..of the Empire   571a
Dislike: and hesitate d.   303a
   that d. wh. people   410a
Dislimns: with a thought the rack d.   324b
Dismal: the D. Science   81a
Dismay: chains of its d.   396a
   coverts of d.   312b
   let nothing you d.   523a
   ruin..desperation..d.   277b
Dismayed: neither be thou d.   494b

Dismayed (cont.)
was there a man d.'   426a
Dismiss: if thou d. not her   276a
  Lord, d. us with Thy blessing   53b
  power to d. itself   338a
Dismist: may not rudely be d.   102a
Disobedience: children of d.   515b
  excuse my d. now   107b
  Man's first d.   270b
Disobedient: hearts of the d.   508b
Disorder: a sweet d.   189a
  last d. mortal   168a
  most admired d.   349a
Disorders: all ruinous d., follow 341b
Disparity.. 'twixt air and Angel's 132a
Dispatch: be angry, and d.   325a
  requisite in business than d. 1a
Dispenses, pardons, bulls   273b
Dispersed: he hath d. abroad   489a
Dispirited: fainting, d. race   7b
  I see her not d.   147b
Displeasure: bade..her d. fly   360b
Dispoged: when I am so d.   124a
Disponibles: saw them..as d.   204b
Dispose: how can they charitably d. 382b
  unsearchable d.   278a
Disposed: feel d. to bury for nothing 124a
Disposer Supreme   461b
Disposition: antic d.   331b
  entertain a cheerful d.   375a
  goes so heavily with my d.   332b
  lay his goatish d.   342a
  of churlish d.   326a
  this robe..doth change my d.   373b
  to shake our d.   331a
  truant d.   330a
Dispositions of..mankind   56b
Dispraised: of such to be d.   214a
  of whom to be d.   277a
Disproven: proven nor yet d.   425b
Disputants ..mind of ..skuttlefish 2b
Disputation: run in debt by d.   64b
  that's a feeling d.   378a
Disputations: doubtful d.   514a
Dispute: better to live than d.   306a
  either which he wd. d.   64b
  my right there is none to d.   113a
  such high d. shd. be   67a
Disputed: Facts..downa be d.   60a
Disquieted: never to be d.   225a
  so d. within me   484b
Disquieteth himself in vain   484b
Disraeli: D. called..Peel's Ministry 17b
  someone asked D.   129a
Dissatisfied: not one is d.   458a
Dis-seat: or d. me now   350b
Dissect: thro' creatures you d.   301b
  we murder to d.   471b
Dissemble: d. in their double heart 482a
  d. sometimes yr. knowledge   16a
  not d. nor cloke them   478a
Dissent: all Protestantism..is..d. 55b
  dissidence of d.   55b
  I shd. d. myself   41b
  union of total d.   250b
Dissertates: one d., he is candid 48b
Dissidence: the d. of dissent   55b
Dissimilar: for one another, tho' d. 393b
Dissimulation: by one word—d.   129b
  his gray d.   277a
  let love be without d.   513b
Dissipation without pleasure   161b
Dissolute man!   196a
Dissolution: from low..doth d. climb 468a
  these limbs..from d.   132b
Dissolve: all which it inherit, shall d. 367b
  d., and quite forget   220a
  d. me into ecstasies   268b
Dissonance: barb'rous d.   267b, 275b
Distance: at d. I gaze   292b
  by d. made more sweet   468b
  d. lends enchantment   77a
  for the future in the d.   18b
  magic in the d.   290a
  notes by d. made more sweet   103a
  seconds' worth of d. run   230a
  strength, d. and length   198a
Distasteful: you found your life d. 48b
Distemperature: thorough this d. 356b
Distil: observingly d. it out   382b
Distilled: d. almost to jelly   330b

Distilled (cont.)
  d. from limbecks foul   389a
  d. from..worm-cankered homily 438a
Distinct from harmony divine   107b
Distinction: few escape that d.   447a
  reverence..doth make d.   329a
Distinguish: and cd. of men d.   334a
  he cd. d., and divide   64b
Distinguishable in member, joint 272b
Distinguished: am I d. from you   1b
  two must discept—has d.   48b
Distorting: fear my speech d.   36b
Distraction: into a fine d.   189a
Distress: all pray in their d.   32b
  comfort man's d.   228a
  comfort their d.   411a
  deep d. hath humanized   468b
  delivered them from their d.   488b
  everyone that was in d.   38a
  friend of Beauty in d.   72b
  incapable of her own d.   336a
  last of danger and d.   72b
Distressed: art thou sore d.?   286a
  harrass the d.   213a
  I am d. for thee   495b
Distresses: d. of humanity   212b
  d. of our friends   419a
Distressful: most d. country   525b
Distrust: that d. wh. intrudes   209b
Distrusted: power shd...be d.   214a
Disturb this hallowed house   357b
Disturbs me with the joy   472a
Ditch: both shall fall into the d. 507a
  die in the last d.   461a
  d.-delivered by a drab   349b
  environed with a great d.   116a
  grew in dike nor d.   529a
  rather a d. in Egypt   325a
Ditchers and grave-makers   336a
Ditches: land of Dutchmen and of d. 71b
Ditchwater: drinking bottled d.   390a
Ditto to Mr. Burke   305b
Ditties: as d. highly penned   378a
  d. of no tone   219b
  in amorous d. all..day   271b
  sing no more d.   358b
Ditty: played an ancient d.   221b
  sung the dolefullest d.   20b
Dive: or d. into the bottom   377a
  search..pearls must d. below   141a
Diver: adventure of the d.   49b
  d. in deep seas   293a
Diverse, sheer opposite   218a
Diversion: tay is not my d.   237a
Diversities of gifts   514b
Divide: cd. distinguish, and d.   64b
  or both d. the crown   139a
  to d. is not to take   393b
  two almost d. the kind   302a
  words d. and rend   420b
Divided: I do perceive here a d. duty 360a
  if a house be d.   508a
Dividends: comfortable man, with d. 247b
Dividing: by d. we fall   127b
  d. the swift mind   573a
  yr. sweet d. throat   79b
Divination: with a spirit of d.   512b
Divine: ah, what the form d.   240b
  all save..man..is d.   67b
  aught d. or holy   272a
  but all are d.   276a
  charming is d. philosophy   267b
  did the Countenance D.   31a
  d. discontent   226b
  d. high piping Pehlevi   152a
  doth ask a drink d.   216a
  entertain d. Zenocrate   259b
  good d. that follows..precept 353a
  Hand that made us is D.   2a
  heavy, but no less d.   71a
  holy, d., good   276a
  how d. a thing   473a
  inspired by d. revelation   13a
  knows itself d.   392b
  love so amazing, so D.   453b
  made..men d.   293a
  more needs she the d.   350a
  ray of light D.   86b
  style the d., the matchless   303b
  Terror the human form d.   33a
  that monarchs were d.   230a

Divine (cont.)
  to that in you wh. is d.   8b
  to the d. perfection   247b
Divinely in the wrong   476b
Divineness: people hath some d.   13b
Diviner: glad d.'s theme   138a
Divines: doubts 'mongst D.   409a
  reproach of the d.   279d
Divinest: two d. things   202a
Divinity: as if D. had catch'd the itch 65a
  d. in odd numbers   356a
  d. more than the ear discovers 42a
  d. that stirs within us   1b
  piece of d. in us   42a
  such d. doth hedge   335b
  there's a d. that shapes   336b
  well versed in D.   527a
  what is called 'orthodox d.'   10a
Division: d. is as bad   533a
  d. of prodigious breasts   421a
  equal d. of unequal earnings   146a
  never come such d.   341a
  ravishing d.   378a
  woe weeps out her d.   214b
Divorce: d. of steel   385b
  this bill of my D. to all   133a
Divorced: demand to be d.   93b
  d. so many English kings   381a
Dizzy: how..d. 'tis to cast one's eyes 343b
Djinn: resident D.   167a
Do: as I wd. they shd. d. unto me 481a
  aught remains to d.   309b
  be damned if you d.   135a
  but what man wd. d.   51b
  by all ye leave or d.   236b
  d. after the good   257a
  d. all that thou hast to d.   480a
  d. as I say, not as I d.   321a
  d. as you're bid   143b
  d. as you wd. be done by   90b
  d. exceeding abundantly   515b
  d. in the Great War, Daddy?   527b
  d. it with thy might   499b
  d. noble things, not dream them 225b
  d. not d. unto others   391a
  d. nothing and get something   130a
  d. not put me to 't   360b
  d. other men, for they wd. d. you 124a
  d. only one thing at once   403a
  d. this, and he doeth it   506a
  d. thou but thine   276a
  d. what you are afraid to d.   148a
  d. what you can   176b
  d. what you please   29b
  d. ye even so to them   505b
  don't know what to d.   534a
  either d., or die   23a
  go, and d. thou likewise   509a
  how not to d. it   123a
  I can d. all things   516a
  I'd have you d. it ever   373b
  if to d. were as easy to know 352b
  I'll d., I'll d.   346a
  I may d. that I shall be sorry for 340b
  it is seemly so to d.   224b
  it revolts me, but I d. it   164a
  let me d. it now   523b
  let us d. or die   62b, 76b
  meet and right so to d.   480b
  never d. anything well   183b
  say, or what you d.   528b
  see thou d. it not   519b
  so much to d.   309a
  that d. not d. the thing   388b
  things..men shd. d. to you   505b
  this..I was born to d.   117a
  this will never d.   205a
  thus thou must d.   346b
  thy hand findeth to d., d. that 81a
  Todger's cd. d. it   123b
  wh. I wd. not, that I d.   513a
  what I d. in any thing   188a
  what I mean to d.   45a
  what I must d. then   133b
  what is it you d?   470b
  what men daily d.   359a
  what mightst thou d.   381b
  what were good to d.   352b
  what will ye d. in the end   503b
  what you d. still betters   373b
  write what men d.   13a

Do (cont.)

ye cannot d. the things ye would 515b
Doasyouwouldbedoneby: Mrs. D. 226b
Dobest: Dowel, Dobet, and D. 572a
Dobet: Dowel, D., and Dobest 572a
Dock: Hickory, Dickory, D. 534a
  I like to d. the smaller parts 75a
Docks: hateful d. 383b
Doctor: and folly—d.-like 388a
  and the D. slighted 291b
  but never the d.'s brougham 232b
  dishes the D. has sent 158b
  D. Brighton 523a
  d. found, when she was dead 168a
  D. said that Death was..fact 459b
  D. Slop 411b
  D. well versed in Divinity 527a
  even if the d. does not 413b
  fee the d. for a..draught 140a
  frequent D. and Saint 153a
  God and the d. 291b
  no man d...but himself 277b
  outliv'd the d.'s pill 159b
  some d. full of phrase 9a
  the artless d. sees 190b
Doctors: budge d. of the Stoic fur 267b
  d. considering it doubtful 124b
  how it comes let d. tell 60a
  medical d. a cocking their..eyes 127b
  who..decide, when d. disagree 302a
Doctrine: blast of vain d. 479b
  d. for the teacher's sake 118a
  d. of ill-doing 372b
  d. of the enclitic De 47a
  every wind of d. 515b
  mere depository of d. 128a
  not for the d., but the music 300a
  prove their d. orthodox 65a
  such d. never was there school 277b
  this d. I derive 345a
  tho' all the winds of d. 279a
Doctrines: all d. plain and clear 66a
  by d. fashion'd to the..hour 168b
Documents: historian..wants more d. 204a
Dodd's: were not D.'s sermons 209b
Dodger: the artful D. 125a
Dodgerest of the dodgers 126a
Dodgers: dodgerest of the d. 126a
Doe: comes a fallow d. 529b
Doeg, though without knowing 138b
Doer's willingness 189b
Doers of the word 517b
Does: and d.—nothing at all 150a
  dogged as d. it 445b
Doeth: no more I that d. it 513a
Doff it for shame 374a
Dog: a d. starved..master's gate 29a
  a living d. is better 499b
  am I a d., that thou comest 495b
  a very d. to the commonalty 328a
  beware of the d. 552a
  broodin' over bein' a d. 456a
  but the poor d. 73b
  by the throat the circumcised d. 364a
  call a d. *Hervey* 206a
  d. for a new year's gift 356a
  d. is turned to his own vomit 518a
  d. returneth to his vomit 498b
  d.'s walking on his hinder legs 207b
  Dumb's a sly d. 95b
  ever d. that praised his fleas? 476a
  every d. has his day 34a
  every d. his day 226a
  expect thy d., thy bottle 301b
  fleas is good fer a d. 456a
  from the power of the d. 483a
  good d...bad colour 23b
  grin like a d. 485b
  hath a d. money? 353a
  his faithful d. shall bear 300b
  His Highness' d. at Kew 299b
  hold-fast is the only d. 382a
  I had rather be a d. 340b
  in that town a d. was found 169a
  is thy servant a d. 496b
  let no d. bark 352b
  like a d., he hunts 432a
  little d. laughed 534a
  little toy d. 151a
  mine enemy's d. 344a
  my poor d. Tray 76b

Dog (cont.)

portrait of a d. that I know 212a
sick as a d. 182b
something better than his d. 432a
that tossed the d. 534b
the d. had lost his wits 169a
the d. it was that died 169a
the d., to gain some private ends 169a
the poor d. had none 533b
to d. in the manger 446a
to get her poor d. a bone 533b
tongue of d. 349b
very flea of his d. 215b
when a man bites a d. 116b
whose d. are you? 299b
why shd. a d...have life 344a
your heart to a d. to tear 233b
Dogged as does it 445b
Dog-kennel: in an empty d. 124a
Dogma has been the..principle 288a
Dogmatize: I d. and am contradicted 212a
Dogs: all the d. in the town 533a
  as many d. there be 169a
  blood..in hosses, dawgs 440a
  cats is 'd.' 535a
  dancing d. and bears 192a
  d. eat of the crumbs 507a
  d., wd. you live forever? 568a
  go to the d. tonight 186a
  is it you, you d.? 206b
  knocked the factious d. 211a
  lame d. over stiles 226a
  let d. delight 452b
  many d. are come about me 483a
  mother of dead d. 81a
  'orses and d. 122a
  the d. did bark 108b
  the d. of war 339b
  the little d. and all 343a
  they were na men but d. 63a
  throw physic to the d. 350b
  tongue of the d. may be red 486b
  two d. of black St. Hubert's 316a
  uncover, d. 368a
  unmissed but by his d. 110b
  when the d. hed gut asleep 250b
  Whig d. shd. not have the best 212a
Doing: aught be worth the d. 33a
  be not weary in well d. 516b
  be up and d. 248a
  doctrine of ill-d. 372b
  d. nothing..deal of skill 111a
  each yr. d. 373b
  joy's soul lies in the d. 368b
  manner of d. it 183b
  see what she's d. and tell her 535b
  still be d. never done 65a
  the readiness of d. 189b
  to such..d. brought his horse 336a
  weary in well d. 515b
  writing is next to fine d. 223a
Doings: child is known by his d. 498b
  prevent us, O Lord, in all our d. 480b
Doit: the beggarly last d. 112b
  they will not give a d. 367b
Dole: born..to all our d. 35b
  happy man be his d. 356a, 377a
  I mete and d. unequal laws 438b
Doll: prettiest d. in the world 226a
  sweet little d., dears 226a
  you called me Baby D. 181b
  you left behind a broken d. 181b
Dollar: billion d. country 156a
  D. Diplomacy 523a
  eagle..on the back iv a d. 143a
  the almighty d. 203b
Dolores: sanguine and subtle D. 421a
  splendid and sterile D. 421a
Dolorous: stroke most d. 257a
Dolour that they made 257b
Dolphin: a mermaid on a d.'s back 356a
  delights were d.-like 325a
  in my D.-chamber 380a
Dolt: nor knave nor d. can break 474a
Dombey: I..adore Miss D. 123b
Dome: blue d. of air 393b
  build that d. in air 101b
  d. of pleasure 101b
  house with starry d. 452b
  rounded Peter's d. 147a
  that sunny d. 101b

Dome (cont.)

with a d. more vast 194a
Domes the red-plow'd hills 426b
Domestic: d. bliss wh. is the lot 157a
  d. happiness, thou only bliss 112a
  d. sort wh. never stirs 400b
  gallant gay d. 432b
  milk-soup men call d. bliss 293b
Domina: beata mea D. 284b
Dominant's persistence 52b
Dominations: Thrones, D., Prince-
  doms 275a
Dominic: put on the weeds of D. 273b
Dominion: death hath no more d. 513a
  d...over every creeping thing 492a
  d. over palm and pine 233b
  d. over the fish 492a
  get the d. over me 482b
  I'm truly sorry Man's d. 62a
Dominions: His Majesty's d. 289b
  our Sovereign, and his D. 479a
Domitian..to Commodus 162a
Don: d. different 26b
  ineffectual D. 26b
  turned my back upon D. or devil 437b
Donal' an' Charlie 415a
Don Desperado 226b
Done: a' is d. in vain 61a
  a' is d. that men can do 61a
  been and gone and d. 163a
  crying to be d. 229b
  determined, dared, and d. 402b
  d. anything that cd. be recalled 130a
  d. because we are too menny 180b
  d. one braver thing 134a
  d. while Mrs. Bennet was stirring 11b
  have we d. this for one another 393a
  He might have d. with us 96a
  if it were d. when 'tis d. 347a
  I had d. all I cd. 206b
  I have d. the deed 347b
  it is well d., and fitting 325b
  nay, I have d. 137b
  nothing is ever d. in this world 390b
  reward of a thing well d. 148a
  so little d. 309a
  son has d. nearly as well 66b
  the petty d. 48a
  therefore it shall be d. 108b
  things wh. may fairly be d. 288a
  things wh. may not be d. 288a
  this that thou hast d. 492b
  this thou shdst. have d. 323b
  'tis most ignobly d. 343a
  to have d., is to hang 369a
  to have loved..thought..d. 5b
  'twere well it were d. quickly 347a
  we have d. those things 478a
  we have d. with Hope 229b
  what can never more be d. 447b
  what cd. she have d. 474a
  what have I d. for you 185a
  what have I ever d. to you 150b
  what ha' ye d? 235b
  what I have d. is yours 386b
  what's d. is d. 348b
  what's d. we partly..compute 59a
  what were good to be d. 353a
  when thou hast d. 132a
  where much is to be d. 211b
  wh. of you have d. this? 349a
  wh. unto us is d. 293a
  wh. we ought to have d. 478a
Donegal: kindliest creature in..D. 173a
Done-to-death 445a
Donkey: D. wint aboard 231a
  d. wot wdn't go 125a
  never see..a dead d. 127a
  on a d. at Tunbridge Wells 123a
Donne: with D., whose muse 100b
  with Landor and with D. 476b
Donné: his idea, his *d.* 204b
Don Quixote: excepting D. 212a
Dons: if the D. sight Devon 287b
  those regal D.! 26b
Don't: about to marry, D. 535a
  be damned if you d. 135a
  d. let 's go to the dogs 186a
Donuil Dhu 318b
Doodah! doodah! 156a
Doodle: Sir Thomas D. 121b

Doom: at Trinity Church I met my
d. 162b
comes to meet his d. 167a
even to the edge of d. 389a
God, and the d. assigned 434
great d.'s image 348a
his d.'s extremely hard 164b
nor strange thy d. 37b
reached the house of d. 12b
regardless of their d. 174b
shall be thy d. 62a
stretch out to the crack of d. 349b
to a confined d. 388b
to the scaffold and the d. 12b
Doomed: d. for a certain term 331a
d. like Odysseus 476a
d. to go in company with Pain 465a
Dooms: the grandeur of the d. 217b
Doomsday: d. is near; die all 378b
houses..last till d. 336a
then is d. near 332a
Doon: braes o' bonny D. 63b
Dooney: fiddle in D. 475a
Door: another iron d. 409a
as deaf as a d. 35a
as the d. on its hinges 453a
at her ivied d. 75a
beside a human d. 467b
borne him to yr. d. 284b
by the same D. as in I went 153a
click'd behind the d. 168b
d. of my lips 490b
d. stood open at our feast 98a
D. to wh. I found no Key 153b
dust behind the d. 357b
either in d. or out 461b
engine at the d. 269b
every d. is shut but one 110a
fixed for ever at the d. 439b
for barring of the d. 531b
get up and bar the d. 531b
handle and the opening of the d. 21b
handle of the big front d. 166a
he before his cottage d. 406a
Ho! let the d. be lock'd 337a
I am the d. 511a
I stand at the d. 518b
is the wind in that d.? 257a
it stands at the d. 86a
knocking at my d. 567a
knocking on the moonlit d. 119b
know the grass beyond the d. 313a
my sin their d. 132a
no d. can keep them 187a
outside the fast-closed d. 200b
over that same d...writ 409a
posts of the d. moved 501b
riding, up to the old inn-d. 290a
shut stands the d. 6a
shut the d. after you 143b
standing at that d. 311a
stuck in the d. 526b
that is mercy's d. 110a
the d. flew open, in he ran 192b
the open d. for all nations 27b
three, four, shut the d. 532a
when gusts shake the d. 6a
wrong side of the d. 92a
Doorkeeper: I had rather be a d. 487a
Doors: and the d. shall be shut 499b
clay-shuttered d. 442a
death hath so many d. 23a
death opens unknown d. 262a
d. to let out life 262b
d., where my heart was 429b
I shuttered my d. 228b
let the d. be shut upon him 333b
men shut their d. 368a
ten thousand several d. 454b
th'infernal d. 273a
ye everlasting d. 483a
ye heavens, yr. living d. 275b
Doorways: d. are .. Night and Day 152a
d. of the East 441b
Dorian: the D. pipe, the D. strain 8b
to the D. mood of flutes 271b
Dorians: to whom the D. pray 254a
Doric: the D. little Morgue 44b
warbling his D. lay 270a
Doris: call me Lalage or D. 101b
Dormouse: said the D. 'well in' 83a

Dotage: lose myself in d. 322b
streams of d. flow 214a
Dotages: two main plagues, and..d. 64a
Dote: I d. on his very absence 353a
nor so old to d. on her 342a
Doted: she d. upon the Assyrians 504a
Dotes: who d., yet doubts 361b
Double: a d. strife 17a
and is old D. dead? 380b
d., d., toil and trouble 349b
d. error sometimes sets us right 18a
d. the vision my eyes do see 29b
E please. D. good! 123a
for me to d...Cape..Good Hope 16b
so d. was his pains 408b
you'll grow d. 471b
Doubled: d. him up for ever 163b
d. His whole creation 36a
Double entendre: horrible d. 527a
Doublet: fashion of a new d. 358a
his d. all unbraced 332a
Doubt: all is best, tho' we oft d. 278a
clouded with a d. 429b
decide this d. for me 109b
defence of philosophic d. 18a
d. diversified by faith 45a
d. is Devil-born 431a
d. thou the stars 332a
enabled to d. Thee 525a
frets d. the maw-crammed beast? 50b
'I d. it,' said the Carpenter 84a
if the Sun and Moon shd. d. 29b
I then am in most d. 416a
more faith in honest d. 431a
never d. I love 332a
never stand to d. 189b
no d. but ye are the People 230a
no possible d. whatever 163a
no, to be once in d. 361b
resolution lies by d. 307a
state of philosophical d. 102b
sunnier side of d. 425b
that none might be in d. 36b
the doubter and the d. 146a
the night of d. and sorrow 20b
thousand difficulties..not..one d. 288b
time will d. of Rome 71a
troubled with religious d. 93a
uncursed by d. 193b
when all men d. you 230a
when in d., win the trick 201a
wherefore didst thou d.? 507a
wh. knows no d. 5b
without d. he shall perish 478b
Doubted: and heard Troy d. 71a
Doubter: I am the d. 146a
Doubtful: d. disputations 514a
in a d. way 233b
Doubting: a castle, called D.-Castle 54a
d. in his abject spirit 251a
make allowance for their d. 230a
Doubts: breed d. 'mongst Divines 409a
content to begin with d. 13a
d. aboot the meenister 535b
he who d. from what he sees 29b
his d. are better 179a
our d. are traitors 351a
saucy d. and fears 349a
the littlest d. are fear 334a
who dotes, yet d. 361b
Douceurs: all ye d. 105b
Doughty: if d. deeds my lady please 172b
Douglas: Degenerate D.! 463b
D. bound him to ride 530b
D., D., tender and true 114b
hand of D. is his own 318b
like D. conquer 194b
maugre of doughty D. 530b
O D., tendir and trewe 193b
old song of Percy and D. 402a
the D. in his hall 318b
the D. in red herrings 178a
Dove: all the eagle..all the d. 114b
as the wings of a d. 486a
changes on the burnished d. 432a
hawk at eagles with a d. 187a
patient as the female d. 336b
roar..as any sucking d. 356b
the d. found no rest 492b
the springs of D. 470b
Dovecote doors of sleep 265a

Doves: be ye..harmless as d. 506a
his mother's d. 251a
the moan of d. 437a
thou hast d.' eyes 500a
with loves and d. 46b
Dovetailedness: universal..d. 125a
Dover: a farthing candle at D. 207b
Dover Road: milestones on the D. 123a
Dove-wings: made their d. tremble 218a
Dow: this yer D. hed the worst..
luck 182a
Dowager: the d.'s was a demd
outline 125a
Dowagers for deans 435b
Dowel, Dobet, Dobest 572a
Dower: beauty is thy earthly d. 465b
for deathless d. 312a
human nature's highest d. 465a
Down: d. among the dead men 143a
d. can fall no lower 65a
D. churches praise the Lord 235a
d., d. to hell 384b
d. he went like a streak 525a
d. in the mouth 105a
D., Sir! put it d.! 26a
d., thou climbing sorrow 342a
d. went the Royal George 111a
d. with it, d. with it 490a
for I find I go d. 304a
he did again get d. 109a
he that is d. 54b
I will go d. to her 424a
level d. as far as themselves 207b
look not thou d. but up 51a
my coming d. let me shift 283a
neither up nor d. 526b
or run it d. 419b
road by Merrow D. 232b
smoothing the raven d. 267a
soon came d. again 108b
the cygnet's d. is harsh 368b
the d. on his beak 435b
the ridge of a noble d. 438b
thrice-driven bed of d. 360b
throw her d. 496b
when they were d., they were d. 526a
yr. d. so warm 115a
Downe: look owre the Castle D. 530b
Down-gyved to his ankle 332a
Downhearted: are we d.? No! 238a, 522a
we are not d. 87a
Downhill: this d. path is easy 311a
Downs: all in the D. the fleet 161a
bold majestic d. 36a
o'er unhabitable d. 419b
on the dewy d. 434b
round the spicy d. 433a
whale-backed D. 235a
Down-sitting: thou knowest my d. 490a
Downstairs: I'll kick you d.! 82b
you kick me 28a
Downward: his looks..d. bent 272a
mute creation bend 142b
that looking d. thence 311b
Downwards: cd. look no way but d. 54a
Doxy: d. over the dale 373a
orthodoxy is her d. 450b
Dozen in her place 416a
Drab: ditch-delivered by a d. 349b
rose pink and dirty d. 264b
Drachenfels: castled crag of D. 68b
Drachmas: my blood for d. 341a
Draff: sow eats up all the d. 216a
Drag: put on the d. 405a
why d. in Velasquez? 456b
Dragged to three-and-thirty 70a
Dragon: an ev'ning d. came 278a
dare the unpastured d. 392a
Michael..fought against the d. 519a
St. George, that swinged the d. 373b
the d. fought and his angels 519a
the d.-green, the luminous 154b
the d., that old serpent 519b
Dragon-fly: the d. hangs 312a
with the d. on the river 43b
Dragonish: a cloud that's d. 324a
Dragons: bores have succeeded to d. 130a
d. in their pleasant palaces 501b
d. of the prime 430b
habitation of d. 502a
night's swift d. 357a

Dragons (*cont.*)
ye d. and all deeps — 490*b*
Drain: d. not to its dregs the urn — 394*a*
put it down the d. — 186*a*
Drains: d. his at one gulp — 52*a*
she said it wur d. — 439*a*
Drake: D. he's in his hammock — 287*b*
Grenville, Raleigh, D. — 287*b*
Drama: a fifth shall close the d. — 28*a*
the d.'s laws, the d.'s patrons — 213*b*
thro' all the d.—whether damned — 400*b*
what this wild D. means — 435*b*
Dramatist..wants more liberties — 204*a*
Dramatize, dramatize! — 204*a*
Drank: and still my body d. — 99*a*
d. it, and fell dead — 122*a*
d. strong waters — 233*b*
d. without..thirst — 418*a*
I never d. of Aganippe — 401*b*
Drap-de-berry: such d. things — 105*b*
Drapery: wraps the d. of his couch — 53*b*
Drappie: just a d. in our ee — 63*b*
Draught: fee the doctor for a..d. — 219*a*
for a d. of vintage — 219*b*
Draughts: d. of intellectual day — 114*b*
healths and d. go free — 249*b*
shallow d. intoxicate the brain — 300*a*
Dravest: thou d. love from thee — 442*a*
Draw: began to d. to our end — 520*a*
can ye d. but twenty miles — 259*b*
did soon d. in agen — 190*b*
d. the Thing as he sees It — 236*b*
d. you to her *with a single hair* — 142*b*
let me try and d. you — 50*a*
Drawbridge: up d., grooms — 318*b*
Drawers: d. of water — 494*b*
flannel waistcoat and flannel d. — 159*a*
Drawing: in d. nothing up — 112*a*
Drawn: d. his wit as well in brass — 215*b*
it oughtn't to be d. — 122*a*
new d. frae the Forth — 285*b*
sweetness long d. out — 269*a*
Draws: d. on and sees us sold — 236*a*
tho' she d. him — 248*b*
Drayhorse: the great grey d. — 197*a*
Dread: Brig o' D — 529*a*
close your eyes with holy d. — 101*b*
clouds ye so much d. — 110*a*
for mighty d. had seized — 424*a*
I d. the rustling of the grass — 463*a*
live, that I may d. the grave — 224*b*
somewhat was he chilled with d. — 317*a*
still louder and more d. — 99*b*
the d. and fear of kings — 354*b*
the d. of something after death — 333*a*
thrice turned back in d. — 253*b*
walk in fear and d. — 99*b*
what d. hand? and what d. feet? — 32*a*
whence this secret d. — 1*b*
yet nothing did he d. — 408*b*
Dreaded: and d. as thou art — 112*a*
once d. by our foes — 111*a*
Dreadful: called thee mighty and d. — 133*a*
each gentle and each d. scene — 22*b*
Dreads: greatly his foes he d. — 94*a*
Dream: a deep d. of peace — 201*b*
a d. itself is but a shadow — 332*b*
a d. of perfect bliss — 22*a*
a long immortal d. — 219*a*
and then they d. of love — 364*b*
a phantasma, or a hideous d. — 338*b*
as a d. doth flatter — 388*b*
a sight to d. of — 100*a*
a vision, or a waking dream — 220*a*
before, a joy..behind, a d. — 389*a*
behold it was a d. — 54*a*
broke this happy d. — 132*a*
but a d. within a d. — 298*a*
d., and so d. all night — 218*a*
d. of battled fields no more — 316*b*
d. of joye, al but in vayne — 90*a*
d. that I am home again — 154*b*
d. that's past expressing — 161*a*
each age is a d. — 291*a*
ever dared to d. before — 298*a*
feels, as in a pensive d. — 430*b*
garden that I d. of — 439*b*
gone..like a beautiful d. — 245*b*
had a d., which was not all a d. — 70*a*
he shd. d. of the devil — 19*a*
housed in a d. — 468*b*

Dream (*cont.*)
if I d. I have you — 132*a*
if you can d. — 230*a*
I hae dream'd a dreary d. — 530*b*
I have had a d. — 357*b*
life is but an empty d. — 247*b*
like the empty words of a d. — 36*b*
love's young d. — 281*b*
my d. thou brok'st not — 132*a*
not d. them, all day long — 225*b*
occupy age with the d. of — 48*a*
oh! d. of joy! — 99*b*
one man with a d. — 291*a*
soft! I did but d. — 385*a*
the Child's unheeded d. — 293*a*
the fierce vexation of a d. — 357*a*
the freshness of a d. — 466*a*
the glory and the d. — 466*a*
the lost traveller's d. — 30*a*
the miner's d. of home — 168*a*
the old men's d. — 138*a*
the spirit of my d. — 72*a*
they fly forgotten, as a d. — 453*b*
they had dreamed a d. — 52*a*
they never d. that it fades — 474*b*
they saw a D. of Loveliness — 244*b*
this world..shadow of a d. — 231*b*
to keep a d. or grave apart — 44*a*
to say what d. it was — 357*b*
to sleep: perchance to d. — 333*a*
what my d. was — 357*b*
with the first d. that comes — 265*a*
wrecks of a dissolving d. — 394*a*
writes her scattered d. — 35*b*
you d. you are crossing — 164*a*
yr. old men shall d. — 504*a*
Dreamed: a child I d., and dream — 92*b*
he d., and behold a ladder — 493*a*
I d. in a dream — 457*a*
I d. that, as I wandered — 397*b*
I have long d. of such a..man — 381*a*
who d. that beauty passes — 475*b*
Dreamer: a d. of dreams — 494*b*
behold, this d. cometh — 493*a*
d. of dreams, born out of..time — 284*b*
even dream the d. — 442*a*
he is a d.; let us leave him — 337*b*
the poet and the d. — 218*a*
Dreamers: they are no d. weak — 218*a*
we are the d. of dreams — 291*a*
Dreaming: City with her d. spires — 8*b*
d. arl the time — 287*b*
d. Hell-fires to see — 230*b*
d. on things to come — 388*b*
of thee I'm fondly d. — 245*b*
sleep, d. on both — 351*b*
Dreamlight: by candlelight and d. — 445*b*
Dreams: affliction of these terrible d. — 348*b*
all my nightly d. — 298*a*
and d. of erring on..ripes — 196*b*
and my fruit is d. — 442*b*
as angels in some brighter d. — 448*b*
a sleep full of sweet d. — 217*b*
a trouble to my d. — 469*a*
blissful d. of long ago — 106*a*
dead d. of days forsaken — 422*a*
desires and d. and powers — 422*a*
desire, that haunts our d. — 37*a*
Dian had hot d. — 329*a*
dreamer of d. — 494*b*
d. and desires and sombre songs — 421*a*
d. and the light imaginings — 397*a*
d., books, are each a world — 468*b*
d. happy as her day — 40*a*
d. he of cutting foreign throats — 364*b*
d. no mortal ever dared to dream — 298*a*
d. of joy and fear — 399*a*
d. of Paradise and light — 447*b*
d. of the summer night — 248*b*
d. out of mind — 424*a*
d. that are done — 424*a*
embroidery of poetic d. — 108*a*
England of our d. — 233*b*
fanatics have their d. — 218*a*
full of the foolishest d. — 81*b*
heavy with d. — 442*b*
he hunts in d. — 432*a*
his summer d. — 396*b*
I arise from d. of thee — 394*b*
if there were d. to sell — 24*a*
I had drunken in my d. — 99*a*

Dreams (*cont.*)
I have bad d. — 332*b*
I..have only my d. — 474*b*
in doubtful d. of d. — 422*a*
in their noonday d. — 393*a*
is it some d.? — 451*a*
Land of D. is better far — 31*a*
less than nothing, and d. — 238*b*
lies down to pleasant d. — 53*b*
not make d. yr. master — 230*a*
O evening d.! — 154*b*
opinion he held once..of d. — 338*b*
our d. are tales — 119*a*
pleasing d., and slumbers — 318*b*
put man's best d. to shame — 44*a*
real are the d. of Gods — 219*a*
rich, beyond the d. — 210*b*
so full of..ghastly d. — 384*b*
spread my d. under yr. feet — 474*b*
stuff as d. are made on — 367*a*
the land of my d. — 225*b*
the lonely d. of a child — 119*a*
the quick D., the passion-winged — 392*a*
thou..communicat'st with d. — 373*a*
thousand such enchanting d. — 188*b*
until my d. all come true — 225*b*
we are the dreamers of d. — 291*a*
we in d. behold the Hebrides — 320*b*
what d. may come — 333*a*
white Platonic d. — 206*a*
wicked d. abuse..sleep — 347*b*
you tread on my d. — 474*b*
Dreamt: I d. that I dwelt — 53*b*
than are d. of in yr. philosophy — 331*b*
Drear-nighted: in a d. December — 221*a*
Dregs: from the d. of life — 139*b*
Drenched: rotten, cold, and d. — 222*b*
Dress: all this fleshly d. — 448*a*
bring the d. and put it on her — 433*a*
children in ordinary d. — 26*a*
come to thee for d. — 445*a*
d. by yellow candle light — 413*b*
eighty-five ways to d. eggs — 281*a*
noble youth did d. themselves — 380*a*
no more value than their d. — 183*b*
Peace, the human d. — 33*a*
Secrecy the human d. — 33*a*
sweet disorder in the d. — 189*a*
that ever went with evening d. — 234*a*
their d. a principal part — 183*b*
Dressed: for him that d. me — 187*b*
hope drunk wherein you d. — 347*a*
let me be d. fine as I will — 453*a*
neat, and trimly d. — 376*b*
still is naked, being d. — 147*a*
the sense of being well-d. — 148*b*
when he's well d. — 123*b*
you're all d. up — 63*b*
Dresser: slept under the d. — 27*b*
Dressing: my best d. is old words — 388*a*
Dressings: she hath d. fit — 525*a*
Drest: O, be d., stay not — 186*b*
still to be d. — 215*a*
Drew: d. me backward by the hair — 43*b*
d. nearer to me, sweetly — 188*b*
for wh. they d. the wage — 236*a*
they d. all manner of things — 83*a*
Dries: current runs or else d. up — 363*a*
what is yr. d., sir? — 211*a*
Drift: I only know I cannot d. — 458*b*
Drifting: I am d. with the tide — 531*a*
Drifts: its dank yellow d. of..leaves — 7*b*
thro' scudding d. — 438*b*
Drill: the feet o' the men what d. — 227*a*
Drills: it's always double d. — 230*a*
Drink: all beasts..d. thereof — 488*a*
a man may d. — 63*a*, 320*b*
any..delicate thing to drink — 123*a*
a taste for d. — 163*b*
came out to d. one sultry day — 192*b*
doth ask a d. divine — 216*a*
d. and the devil had done for — 413*a*
d. cold brandy and water — 240*b*
d. deep, or taste not — 300*a*
d. down all unkindness — 355*b*
d.! for you know not whence — 154*b*
d. no longer water — 516*b*
d. not the third glass — 186*b*
d. of it, then, if you can — 196*a*
d., pretty creature, d. — 468*b*
d., puppy, d. — 459*a*

Drink (*cont.*)
d. the visionary powers 469b
d. till all look blue 155b
d. to heavy Ignorance 439a
d. to me only with thine eyes 216a
d. to poor damned souls 230a
d. unto one of these little ones 506b
d. ye to her that each loves 77b
every creature. but I 106b
five reasons we shd. d. 3a
follow strong d. 501a
if ever thou gavest meat or d. 529a
in debt, and in d. 38a
I think, that I cd. d. 415a
leeze me on d. 61a
let a soldier d. 361a
let us eat and d., for tomorrow 515a
man wants but little d. 193b
never taste who always d. 306a
sit and d. with me 27a
snewed. mete and d. 88b
strong d. is raging 498b
teach you to d. deep 330a
that I might d. 219b
they will d. our healths 228a
tippled d. more fine 219a
to eat, and to d., and to be merry 499b
we d. to thee across. flood 427a
when it is old, thou shalt d. it 520b
when last I saw him d. 290a
whether therefore ye eat or d. 514b
who d. beer will think beer 203b
willing to taste any d. once 75a
Drinking: and then to deep d. 527a
as they were d. all 98b
d. at somebody else's expense 244b
d. is the soldier's pleasure 139a
d. largely sobers us again 300a
d. the blude-red wine 529b
end my days in a tavern d. 558b
much d., little thinking 418a
no d. after death 22b
not the d. that is to be blamed 321a
oh 'tis jesting, dancing, d. 199b
unhappy brains for d. 361a
with constant d. fresh and fair 106b
Drinks: d., and gapes for drink again 106b
long time between d. 524b
now the king d. 337a
Drip: long d. of human tears 180a
Drive: he will d. a coach and six 309a
one heat, all know, doth d. out
another 87b
or d. it devious 113a
people. difficult to d. 40b
that I was used to d. 199a
Driveller: Swift expires a d. 214a
Driven into a desperate strait 262b
Driver: feel the d.'s whip 248a
Driveth: d. o'er a soldier's neck 364b
for he d. furiously 496b
Driving: d. rapidly *from* something 209a
spend my life in d. briskly 209b
the d. of Jehu 496b
Drizzle: the blasted English d. 232a
Drollery: that fatal d. 130a
Dromedary: D. is a cheerful bird 25b
whose muse on d. trots 100b
Drone: lazy yawning d. 381b
Drop: a d. of patience 363a
as a d. of a bucket 502b
a vaporous d. profound 349b
can't d. it if I tried 229a
d., d., slow tears 155b
d. into thy mother's lap 276b
d. into thyself, and be a fool 301a
for every d. hinders 196b
nor any d. to drink 98b
one d. wd. save my soul 258b
'ow quick we'd d. 'er 233b
people. one. like. to d. 210b
so thick a d. serene 273a
thou canst d. into at will 471a
we d. like the fruits 263a
we shd. d. into poetry 125b
Dropped: as he d. him down 164b
not wish to be d. by 210b
Dropping: continual d. in a..
rainy day 498b
d.-down-deadness of manner 405a
we are d. down the ladder 229b

Droppings: his d. of warm tears 44a
Drops: dear to me as are the ruddy d. 338b
d. that water the earth 486b
I saw the curl'd d. 115a
like kindred d., been mingled 111b
some pious d. 174b
these are gracious d. 340a
Dropsies. trying to get drunk 212b
Dropsy: the dread d. grows 545a
Dropt: sun d. from the zenith 272a
Dross: all is d. that is not Helena 258b
to shows of d. 353b
Drought: the d. of Marche 88a
Drove: that. shape d. suddenly 98b
Drown: can I d. an eye 387b
corn before my tears did d. it 188a
d. all my faults 155b
I'll d. my book 368a
I seem to d. her remembrance 370a
I will incontinently d. myself 360b
what pain it was to d. 384b
Drowned: delight lies d. with us 189a
d. in yonder living blue 431a
he's d. in the sea 531b
she is d. already, sir 370a
that he were d. in the midst 507a
the chance of being d. 207a
thy thought till it be d. 312b
Drowning: he hath no d. mark 367a
Drowsyhead: land of d. 443a
Drudge: lexicographer. harmless d. 207a
pale and common d. 354a
Drudgery: d. of the desk's 240a
makes d. divine 188b
Drug: literature is a d. 34a
poetry's a mere d. 150b
Drugs: what d., what charms 360a
Druid: a D. land, a D. tune 476b
sat the D., hoary chief 107b
Drum: and pulpit, d. ecclesiastic 64b
'ark to the big d. 229a
d.-beat, following the sun 454a
d. 'em up the Channel 287b
d. now to d. did groan 137a
dumb as a d. 126a
listenin' for the d. 287b
melancholy as an unbraced d. 86b
Music of a *distant* D. 152b
my pulse like a soft d. 225b
not a d. was heard 462a
take my d. to England 287b
the rumble of a distant D.! 152b
the spirit-stirring d. 362a
whang goes the d. 52b
Drums: bangin' er de d. 182a
before him sound the d. 252a
d. and tramplings of. conquests 42a
guns, and d., and wounds 376b
his clarions and his d 252b
like muffled d., are beating 248a
sound the trumpets, beat the
d. 139a, 244a, 283b
the d. beat far 92b
the d. begin to roll 235b
then anon d. in his ear 364b
voice is heard thro' rolling d. 436b
Drunk: against a post when he was d. 382a
all learned, and all d.! 112b
art of getting d. 210a
died of dropsies. trying to get d. 212b
drink and not be d. 320b
d. and raising Cain 227a
d. and resisting the Guard! 227b
d. the milk of Paradise 101b
d. with sight of power 233b
gloriously d., obey the. call 112b
he never was d. 103b
I d. him to his bed 323b
man. must get d. 70b
may drink and no be d. 63a
our fortunes. d. to bed 322b
partly she was d. 61a
that wh. hath made them d. 347b
then hasten to be d. 140a
the stag at eve had d. 316a
this meeting is d., sir! 126b
was the hope d. wherein 347a
went to Frankfort, and got d. 304b
Drunkard: the rolling English d. 93a
Drunkards make songs upon me 486b
Drunken: Antony. be brought d. 325a

Drunken (*cont.*)
do with the d. sailor 527b
d. and overbold 50a
d., but not with wine 502a
d. in my dreams 99a
d. of things Lethean 423b
stagger like a d. man 488b
to Worts, and got more d. 304b
you d. sot 534b
Drunkenness: babbling d. 372a
d., which is the root of all sins 204a
Drury: a happy boy, at D.'s 305a
Druse: the Thug and the D. 92b
Dry: die a d. death 367a
d. sun, d. wind 446b
good wine. or being d. 3a
he hath made the deep as d. 234b
O d. yr. eyes 218a
oh, I am so d.! 523b
water in a d. place 502a
what shall be done in the d.? 510a
wine before my sighs did d. it 188a
Dryad: thou light-winged D. of the
trees 219b
Dryden: all the prefaces of D. 419b
chatting on deck was D. too 241b
D. taught to join the. verse 303b
even copious D. wanted 303b
what [D.] has done 104a
Dublin: built a church in D. town 27b
in D.'s fair city 524a
Ducat: dead, for a d., dead! 335a
Ducats: O, my d.! O my daughter! 353b
Duchess: arms of chambermaid as of
a D. 210a
'as much right', said the D. 83a
I am D. of Malfi still 454b
my last D. 48b
Duck: 'Ha! Ha!' said the d., laughing 237a
Ducks: able-bodied man. stealing d. 573b
four d. on a pond 4a
Duddon: for, backward, D.! 463b
du Deffand: at Madame D. D.'s 449b
Due: as d. by many titles 133a
give the Fiend himself his d. 438b
Dues: render. to all their d. 513b
simple d. of fellowship 43a
Dug: Men want d. up again 152b
never palates more the d. 325a
Duke: a marquis, d., and a' that 60b
bury the Great D. 435a
D.'s son—cook's son 227a
Earl, the Marquis, and the D. 163b
everybody praised the D. 406a
knows enough who knows a d. 113a
Regent and the D. of York 403b
Dukedom: I prize above my d. 367a
my library was d. 367a
Dukes were three a penny 163b
Dulce: when 'd...' was written 75a
Dulcimer: damsel with a d. 101b
d., and all kinds of music 504a
Dull: as d. as ditch water 126a
d. in a new way 208b
d. without a single absurdity 171a
d. wd. he be of soul 472b
he is not only d. himself 155b
Sherry is d. 207b
so d., so dead, in look 379b
so smoothly d. 299a
tell them that they are d. 393b
this paper appears d. 410b
tho' it's d. at whiles 226a
what's this d. town to me? 224b
wherever he was d. a design 151b
Dullness: cause of d. in others 155b
d. ever loves a joke 298b
the d. of our blinded sight 491a
Dumb: d. as a drum 126a
D.'s a sly dog 95b
d. to Homer, d. to Keats 49b
oh, noisy bells, be d. 199a
otherwise I shall be d. 223a
the tongue of the d. sing 502a
the world have made d. 119a
Dumbness: banged the youth into d. 371b
Dumb-shows: inexplicable d. 333b
Dumps: of d. so dull and heavy 358b
such doleful d. 403b
Dumpy: I hate a d. woman 70a
Duncan: D. Gray cam here to woo 60a

Duncan (*cont.*)
  D. hath borne his faculties — 347*a*
  D. is in his grave — 348*b*
  D. sighed baith out and in — 60*a*
  gart poor D. stand — 60*a*
  hear it not, D. — 347*b*
  the fatal entrance of D. — 346*b*
Dunce: dearest, you're a d. — 210*b*
  d...been kept at home — 110*b*
  d. that has been sent to roam — 110*b*
  nobody calls you a d. — 53*a*
  Satan, thou art a d. — 30*a*
  the puff of a d. — 169*b*
Duncery: tyrannical d. — 279*a*
Dundee: stay langer in bonnie D. — 320*a*
  the bonnet of Bonnie D. — 316*a*
Dunfermline: king sits in D. — 529*b*
Dunged with rotten death — 442*a*
Dungeon: a d. horrible — 271*a*
  D., that I'm rotting in — 79*a*
  nor airless d. — 338*a*
  scourged to his d. — 53*a*
  vapour of a d. — 362*a*
Dungeon-grate: thro' a d. he peered — 98*b*
Dunghill hard by his own stable — 100*b*
Dunkirk: swim the haven at D. — 216*a*
Dunmowe: in Essex at D. — 89*b*
Dunsinane: Birnam wood remove to
  D. — 350*b*, 351*a*
  to high D. hill — 349*b*
Duodecimos: a humbler band of d. — 113*b*
Dupree: Weatherby George D. — 266*b*
Dusk: d., O d. the hall with yew — 7*a*
  no dawn—no d. — 195*a*
  the d. with a light behind her — 167*a*
Dusky: d., vivid, true — 414*b*
  it is late and d. — 448*a*
Dust: a d. whom England bore — 40*a*
  a heap of d. alone — 299*b*
  an art to make d. of all — 42*b*
  a piece of valiant d. — 358
  are they like to take d. — 369*b*
  a richer d. concealed — 40*a*
  as chimney-sweepers, come to d. — 329*a*
  blossom in their d. — 401*a*
  buried in d. — 22*b*
  cinders, ashes, d. — 219*a*
  curates, long d., will come — 39*b*
  devise to die in d. — 408*a*
  dig the d. enclosed here — 389*b*
  dry as summer d. — 464*a*
  d. as we are — 469*a*
  d. falls to the urn — 448*a*
  d. hath closed Helen's eyes — 285*b*
  D. into D. and under D. — 153*a*
  d. of creeds outworn — 397*a*
  d. of the balance — 502*b*
  d. returneth to d. again — 171*b*
  d. return to the earth — 500*a*
  d. that builds on d. — 233*b*
  d. that is a little gilt — 369*a*
  d. that rises up — 439*a*
  d. thou art, and unto d. — 492*b*
  d. thou art, to d. returnest — 247*b*
  d. to d. — 481*b*
  d. to the d.! but the..spirit — 392*b*
  earth, and grave, and d. — 308*a*
  fallen to d. — 460*a*
  fear in a handful of d. — 144*b*
  formed man of the d. — 492*a*
  frail children of d. — 172*b*
  have one d., yet reverence — 329*a*
  his enemies shall lick the d. — 486*b*
  less than the d. — 197*a*
  lie beyond thy d. — 448*a*
  little d. of praise — 430*b*
  Love, which reacheth but to d. — 402*a*
  magnificent out of the d. — 452*a*
  make d. our paper — 375*b*
  March d. to be sold — 446*a*
  much learned d. — 112*a*
  my d. wd. hear her — 434*a*
  nigh is grandeur to our d. — 147*a*
  not without d. and heat — 279*a*
  or but writes in d. — 17*a*
  pays us but with age and d. — 307*b*
  proud and angry d. — 200*a*
  provoke the silent d. — 174*a*
  quintessence of d. — 332*b*
  recover once my d. — 280*b*
  scattering of a little d. — 558*a*

Dust (*cont.*)
  shake off the d. of your feet — 506*a*
  shall the d. give thanks — 483*b*
  shed one..tear o'er English d. — 252*b*
  sweep the d. behind the door — 357*b*
  that d. it so much loves — 225*a*
  the d. on antique time — 328*a*
  the d. swept from their beauty — 43*b*
  the fruit thereof d. — 421*a*
  they that go down into the d. — 483*a*
  this d. was once the man — 458*b*
  toy dog is covered with d. — 151*a*
  vex the unhappy d. — 426*a*
  vile d. from whence he sprung — 317*b*
  we too into the D. descend — 153*a*
  what a d. do I raise — 16*b*
  what of vile d.? — 93*a*
  will not perish in the d. — 407*a*
  write my name in the d. — 536*b*
  write the characters in d. — 319*a*
  written in the d. — 18*b*
  you are not worth the d. — 343*b*
Dust-heap called 'history' — 28*b*
Dustman: the Golden D. — 126*a*
Dusty: what a d. answer — 264*a*
Dutch: French, Italian, Spaniard
  or D. — 42*a*
  my dear old D.! — 94*a*
  the fault of the D. — 78*b*
  we clap on D. bottoms — 78*b*
Dutchman: icicle on a D.'s beard — 371*b*
Dutchmen: that water-land of D. — 71*b*
Duties: lowliest d. on herself did
  lay — 467*a*
  new occasions teach new d. — 251*a*
  property has its d. — 137*b*
  the primal d. shine — 464*b*
Duty: absolved..d. to his country — 295*a*
  a divided d. — 389*b*
  as keen a sense of d. — 166*a*
  began to slacken in his d. — 468*a*
  daily stage of d. — 224*b*
  declares that it is his d. — 390*a*
  do yr. d. bravely — 238*a*
  d. and patriotism clad — 246*a*
  d. as we understand it — 245*a*
  d., faith, love, are roots — 295*b*
  d. of an Opposition to oppose — 95*a*, 410*a*
  d. of being happy — 413*b*
  d. to preserve our faculties — 209*b*
  d. we so much underrate — 413*b*
  d. wh. lies nearest thee — 81*b*
  England expects..his d. — 287*a*
  every man's d. to do all — 97*a*
  faithful, below, he did his d. — 121*a*
  for d., d. must be done — 166*b*
  he had a d. to perform — 161*b*
  I have done my d. — 287*a*
  I have only done my d. — 437*b*
  in his d. prompt — 168*b*
  I owe a d. — 25*a*
  I owe him little d. — 383*b*
  it is my d., and I will — 162*b*
  it was their d., and they did — 162*b*
  I've done my d...no more — 151*b*
  love is then our d. — 159*b*
  make me sick discussing their d. — 458*a*
  moral d. to speak one's mind — 460*a*
  my d. in that state of life — 481*a*
  my d. to have loved the highest — 428*a*
  my d. towards God — 481*a*
  O d.! if that name thou love — 463*b*
  off d. for ever — 25*a*
  our d. has been done — 163*b*
  performing a public d. — 173*a*
  simpleness and d. tender — 357*b*
  subject's d. is the king's — 382*b*
  such d. as the subject owes — 367*a*
  that wh. was our d. to do — 510*a*
  the path of d. was the way — 435*a*
  the whole d. of man — 500*a*
  this our bounden d. — 480*b*
  thou knowest to be a d. — 81*b*
  thy second d...clearer — 81*b*
  when constabulary d.'s — 166*b*
  when D. whispers low — 147*a*
  when love and d. clash — 436*a*
  when service sweat for d. — 326*a*
  with zealous humble d. — 409*a*
  woke, and found..life was D. — 196*b*
Dwarf sees farther than the giant — 102*a*

Dwarfish: an Epigram? a d. whole — 100*b*, 527*b*
Dwell: at ease for aye to d. — 435*b*
  better to d. in a corner — 498*b*
  d. in the house of the Fenians — 476*b*
  I cd. d. where Israel — 298*a*
  joy where'er he d. — 526*a*
  or d. for aye alone — 120*a*
  they that d. therein — 483*a*
Dwelleth: d. by the castled Rhine — 247*a*
  He d. i' the cold — 45*b*
Dwelling: a fair maid d. — 531*a*
  where and what his d.? — 286*b*
  whose d. is the light — 472*a*
Dwelling-place: desert were my d. — 69*b*
Dwelling-places: their d. shall endure — 485*a*
Dwellings: how amiable are thy d. — 487*a*
  they shall drop upon the d. — 486*a*
Dwelt: d. among..untrodden ways — 470*b*
  where once we d. — 109*b*
Dwindle: d. into a wife — 105*b*
  d., peak and pine — 346*a*
Dwindles: the only growth that d. — 170*a*
Dwyer: John Richard William..D. — 572*b*
Dyer: like the d.'s hand — 389*a*
Dyes: stains and splendid d. — 221*b*
Dying: a celerity in — 322*b*
  around the d. deer — 12*b*
  as a d. man to d. men — 22*a*
  behold you again in d. — 414*b*
  Christian can only fear d. — 181*a*
  death..distinguished from d. — 404*b*
  doubly d., shall go down — 317*b*
  d., has made us rarer gifts — 39*a*
  d., put on the weeds of Dominic — 273*b*
  d., we live — 51*b*
  echoes d., d., d. — 436*a*
  I am d., Egypt — 324*b*
  living indisposeth us for d. — 42*b*
  not death, but d. — 151*a*
  on account of my d. day — 222*b*
  the d. for a faith — 439*b*
  the pain, the bliss of d. — 299*a*
  there's no more d. then — 389*b*
  till the fire is d. — 263*b*
  tomorrow will be d. — 190*a*
  truth..the lips of d. men — 8*a*
  unconscionable time d. — 88*a*
  unmoved see thee d. — 126*a*
  unto my d. day, sir — 524*a*
  we thought her d. — 196*a*
  with groans of the d. — 318*a*
  young man, I think you're d. — 531*a*
Dyke: Feb., fill the d. — 446*a*
  the last d. of prevarication — 56*a*
  yon auld fail d. — 529*b*
Dynamite: objected to the use of d. — 412*b*
Dynasties: the same tho' D. pass — 179*b*
Dyte: Omer..Dares, or in D. — 90*a*

E

E please. Double good! — 123*a*
Each: e. for one another — 244*b*
  e. to his great Father bends — 100*a*
  think e. in e., immediately wise — 39*b*
Eager for the fray — 95*b*
Eagle: all the e. in thee — 114*b*
  as an e. mewing her mighty youth — 279*a*
  as a young e. soars — 396*a*
  E. know what is in the pit — 29*b*
  e...on th' back iv a dollar — 143*a*
  e. plunge to find the air — 442*a*
  e. suffers little birds to sing — 368*a*
  from an e. in his flight — 247*a*
  hooded e. among blinking owls — 395*b*
  in and out the E. — 257*b*
  like an e. in a dove-cote — 328*b*
  Rome, tho' her e...had flown — 449*a*
  so the struck e. — 72*a*
  strong, the gier-e. on his sail — 403*a*
  upon my e.'s wings..this wren — 139*a*
  way of an e. in the air — 499*a*
  young and lusty as an e. — 488*a*
Eagles: baited like e...lately bath'd — 378*b*
  hawk at e. with a dove — 187*a*
  mount up with wings as e. — 502*b*
  there will the e. be gathered — 507*b*
  they were swifter than e. — 495*b*
  where his e. never flew — 107*b*

ENGLISH INDEX

Ear: a flea in his e. 4b
applying to his e. 467b
apply its..lips to yr. attentive e. 241a
beat upon my whorled e. 197b
by the hearing of the e. 497b
cleave the general e. with..speech 333a
e. of him that hears it 345b
e. of jealousy heareth all things 520a
e. of man hath not seen 357b
give e. unto my song 169a
give every man thine e. 330b
God's own e. listens 275a
he that planted the e. 487b
I have no e. 238b
in Reason's e. they all rejoice 2a
I was all e. 267b
I went and shouted in his e. 85a
I will enchant thine e. 386b
more is meant than meets the e. 268b
more than the e. discovers 42a
never e., did hear that tongue 313b
nor the e. filled with hearing 499a
not to the sensual e. 219b
oaten stop..to soothe thine e. 103a
O! it came o'er my e. 369b
on his..legs with listening e. 386b
on the listening e. of night 320b
oon e. it herde, at the other out 90a
over it softly her warm e. lays 251a
pierc'd the..hollow of thine e. 366a
pierced thro' the e. 360a
reasonable good e. in music 357a
she shall lean her e. 471b
sounds in a believer's e. 289a
speech sleeps in a foolish e. 335a
stillness first invades the e. 139b
stop thine e. against the singer 319a
the e. is pleased 112b
the hearing 498b
the word of promise to our e. 351a
turn the deaf e. 419a
unpleasing to a married e. 345b
vexing the dull e. 374a
went away with a flea in 's e. 23a
when the e. begins to hear 39a
wind blow through my e. 469a
world of eye, and e. 472a
Earl: an e. by right 12a
bonny E. of Murray 530b
E. can last but a few years 40b
E., the Marquis, and the Dook 163b
while the E. was there 293b
Earlie: wedded to the E.'s son 318b
Early: call me e., mother dear 434b
e. in the morning 184a
e. one morning, just as the sun 523a
e. to bed, and e. to rise 157a
happy those e. days 448a
help her, and that right e. 484b
nipt my flower sae e. 61a
play-place of our e. days 113a
right e. in the year 193a
the e.-rising sun 189a
up in the morning e. 63a
up she rises, e. in the morning 527b
you've gut to git up e. 250a
Earn: e. a little and to spend a little 412a
I e. that I eat 327a
there's little to e. 226b
Earned: you've e. yr. little bit 162b
Earnest: charge in e...but a mill 131a
e. of the things..they shall do 432a
given me e. of success 346b
intermingle..jest with e. 16a
time to be in e. 213a
Earnings: division of unequal e. 146a
Earns whate'er he can 249a
Ears: countrymen, lend me your e. 339b
deaf adder that stoppeth her e. 485b
e. like errant wings 92a
e. of every one that heareth 495a
e. of flesh and blood 331a
e. that sweep away the..dew 357a
e. were of different sizes 527a
eyes, and..e., and every thought 313b
faculties of eyes and e. 333a
fur fly 'bout the e. 65a
harvest waves its wither'd e. 114a
he that hath e. to hear 508a
high crest, short e. 386b
I have e. in vain 220a

Ears (cont.)
in the porches of mine e. 331b
'jug jug' to dirty e. 144b
lest they..hear with their e. 501b
look with thine e. 343b
lover's e. will hear the..sound 345a
make their e. heavy 501b
never mentions hell to e. polite 302b
noise of water in mine e. 384b
O lovers' e. in hearing 317b
pipe of..birds to dying e. 436b
plucked the ripened e. 436a
she gave me e. 471a
softest music to attending e. 365a
the leathern e. of stock-jobbers 111a
there was a shout about my e. 92a
they have e., and hear not 489a
thin e. devoured the seven good e. 493b
to do thyne e. glowe 90a
touched my trembling e. 269b
we have heard with our e. 479a
what is he buzzing in my e.? 46a
who in e. and eyes match me 50b
Earsight: do me eyes deceive me e.? 451a
Earth: act first, this E., a stage 435b
a glory from the e. 466a
a heaven on e. 273b
alive, and so bold, O e.? 395b
all e. can take 394a
all people that on e. do dwell 224b
all questions in the e. 46a
all the..furniture of e. 28a
all ye know on e. 219b
as if..roots of the e. were rotten 222b
as if the e. had rolled 466a
as low as where this e. spins 311b
a touch of e. 428b
axis of the e. sticks out 194a
balm th' hydroptic e. hath drunk 133b
be alone on e., as I am now 68a
be the e. never so unquiet 488a
binds the brave of all the e. 287b
bleeding piece of e. 339b
blow the e. into the sea 342b
bowels of the harmless e. 377a
bridal of the e. and sky 187b
call heaven and e. to witness 494b
centre of my sinful e. 389b
chill the solemn e. 421a
cloud enveloping the e. 100b
condemned to e. for ever 46b
corporal e. of man 441b
creatures walk the e. unseen 274b
crown o' the e. doth melt 324b
dear e., I do salute thee 375a
demi-Atlas of the e. 323a
E. all Danaë to the stars 436b
e., and every common sight 466a
e. and man were gone 38b
E. and Ocean seem to sleep 393b
e. cannot show so brave a sight 260b
e. changes, but thy soul and God 51a
e. doth like a snake renew 394a
e. felt the wound 276a
e. hath bubbles 346a
e. has many a noble city 86b
e. has not anything..more fair 472b
e. hath no good but yrs. 37b
e. hath no sin but thine 37b
e. in an earthy bed 434a
e. in fast thick pants 101a
e. is all the home I have 12b
E. is but a star that once..shone 154b
e. is here so kind 205b
e. not grey but rosy 48b
e. of the vitreous pour 458b
e.! render back 70b
e. resteth, heaven moveth 187b
e.'s base built on stubble 267b
e.'s crammed with heaven 43a
e.'s diurnal course 463a
E.'s first blood 467a
e.'s foundations fled 200a
e.'s foundations stay 200a
e. shall be filled with the glory 2b
e. shall be full of the knowledge 501b
e. shook, and the heavens dropped 486a
e.'s joys grow dim 251b
E.'s last picture is painted 236b
e.'s majestic view 280a
e., so full of dreary noises 44a

Earth (cont.)
e.'s old and weary cry 476a
e.'s returns for whole centuries 48b
E.'s shadows fly 392b
e. stood hard as iron 311a
e.'s vain shadows flee 251b
e., that bears thee dead 379a
e. that is not filled 499a
e., tideless and inert 18a
e. to e., ashes to ashes 481b
e. was feverous and did shake 348a
e. was without form 492a
e. where cares abound 471a
E. will live by hers 7b
e., with her thousand voices 101a
ever e. and the world were made 487b
every man upon this e. 253a
faith..round e.'s shores lay 5a
Falstaff..lards the lean e. 377a
far-swooping elbowed e. 458b
faults they commit..e. covereth 307a
feels the attraction of e. 247a
first e. were passed away 519b
flop round the e. 236b
flowery lap of e. 6b
for e. too dear 365a
foundations of the e. 487a
fresh E. in new leaves 398b
from e.'s wide bounds 200b
from going to and fro in the e. 496b
from wh. e., and grave, and dust 308a
gazing on the e. 396a
girdle round about the e. 356b
give him a little e. 386a
gives all men all e. to love 235a
give the face of e. around 414a
glance from heaven to e. 357b
God..in heaven and thou upon e. 499a
green corners of the e. 31b
have mercy on us worms of e. 149b
heaven nor e. have been at peace 338b
Heaven tries e. if it be in tune 251a
help to make e. happy 82a
her all on e. 70a
her clarion o'er the dreaming e. 396a
he who has looked upon E. 263a
high..in comparison of the e. 488a
his head upon the lap of E. 174b
honour..back, as a king to e. 39a
hope of all the ends of the e. 486a
huge foundation of the e. 378a
I create new heavens and a new e. 503b
if all the e. were paper 251b
indifferent children of the e. 332a
in e.'s firmament do shine 247a
in that rich e. 40a
I saw a new heaven and a new e. 519b
I saw nought common on Thy E. 232b
is thy e. so marred 442a
I swing the e. a trinket 442a
I will move the e. 559a
kindly fruits of the e. 479a
laid the foundations of the e. 488a
lay her i' the e. 336b
lay lightly gentle e. 23a
lay that e. upon thy heart 227b
let me enjoy the e. 180a
let us stay rather on e. 44a
lie heavy on him, E.! 149a
long age in the deep-delved e. 219b
Lord and Master of E. 433b
man marks the e. with ruin 69b
meantime, there is our e. here 52b
meek..shall inherit the e. 505a
more beautiful than the e. 470a
more than on e. is thought 275a
mortal mixture of e.'s mould 267a
'neath the breast of E. 293b
needs find out new heaven, new e. 322a
not on things on the e. 516a
O E., lie heavily upon her eyes 311a
o'er e.'s green fields 149b
of the e., earthy 515a
on e. I am a stranger 61b
on e. was never sown 471b
on the bare e. exposed he lies 139a
on the e. the broken arcs 44b
or e. received her frame 453a
or in the e. beneath 480a
our dungy e. alike feeds beast 322a
plants suck in the e. 106b

[646]

Earth (cont.)

poetry of e. is never dead	221a
replenish the e.	492a
rich apple-blossomed e.	458b
risen up E.'s Greatest Nation	250b
round e.'s imagined corners	133a
sad old e. must borrow its mirth	459a
saying learnt. . on that dark e.	438b
set lip to e.'s bosom bare	442b
she comes more near the e.	363b
sheet. . let down to the e.	512a
since brass, nor stone, nor e.	388a
sing, ye heavens, and earth reply	455b
sleepers in that quiet e.	39a
smile o' the brown old e.	47b
snug little farm the e.	100b
so the whole round e. is. .bound	429b
standing on e., not rapt above	275a
summer clothe the general e.	101a
take of English e. as much	227b
takes e.'s abatement	49a
that ere wore e. about him	118b
the e.: for it is his footstool	505a
the e. is not too low	187a
the e. is the Lord's	483a
the e. is the Lord's, and the fulness	514b
the e. its dower of river	217b
the e. may be glad thereof	488a
the e. shall melt away	484b
the e., that is sufficient	458a
th' inhabitants o' the e.	346a
the lark. . arising from sullen e.	387b
the latter day upon the e.	497a
then shall the e. bring forth	486a
there were giants in the e.	492b
they whose course on e. is o'er	287a
things learned on e.	49a
thing that creepeth upon the e.	492a
thirsty e. soaks up the rain	106b
this ambiguous e.	265a
this dim spot, wh. men call E.	266b
this e. of majesty	375a
this e., this realm, this England	375a
this goodly frame, the e.	332b
this peopled. a solitude	397a
this span of e. we press	282a
tho' all the e. o'erwhelm them	330b
tho' the e. be moved	484b
thou sure and firm-set e.	347b
thro' my lips to unawakened e.	396b
thy will be done in e.	505b
till E. and Sky stand presently	227a
to no such aureate E. are turn'd	152b
too good for e.	215a
to that pleasant country's e.	375b
to the listening e. repeats	2a
turn again to cover the e.	488a
two paces of the vilest e.	379a
upon the dull e. dwelling	372b
very e. did shake	137a
villain of the e.	324a
water under the e.	480a
way of all the e.	494b
what if e. be but the shadow	275a
what's said or done in e.	189a
when e. was nigher heaven	50a
when e. was young	256a
wh. in old days moved e.	439a
while e. heard in dread	403a
while the e. remaineth	492b
whole e. is full of his glory	501b
who Man of baser E. didst make	154a
with e.'s waters make accord	442b
ye are the salt of the e.	505a
ye have left yr. souls on e.	219a
yrs. is the e.	230a
Earth-born: poor, e. companion	62a
thine e. joy renew	36b
Earthen: treasures from an e. pot	187a
Earthly: as glad at that as any e. thing	528b
e., sensual, devilish	517b
nothing e. cd. surpass her	70a
to their e. mother tend	142b
Earthquake: after the wind an e.	496a
an e.'s spoil. .sepulchred below	68a
if an e. were to engulf England	205b
in that world-wi., Waterloo	435a
sold pills. .against an e.	2b
the Lord was not in the e.	496a
Ease: a delicate plain, called E.	54a
animate an hour of vacant e.	470a

Ease (cont.)

at e. in Zion	504a
Belial. .counselled ignoble e.	272b
bring equal e. unto my pain	79b
Deity. .doth e. its heart of love	218a
done with so much e.	138a
e. after war	408b
for another gives its e.	32a
give me greater e. than. .Christ	233b
induce the brave to forfeit e.	157a
infinite heart's e.	382b
interpose a little e.	270a
joys in another's loss of e.	32a
live at home at e.	292a
nature, kindly bent to e. us	419a
never wholly be at e.	452b
not the doctrine of ignoble e.	310a
on the dappled turf at e.	463b
prodigal of e.	138a
put to hazard his e.	56a
singest. .in full-throated e.	219b
some come to take their e.	386b
studious of elegance and e.	160b
studious of laborious e.	112a
such men. .be never at heart's e.	338a
take mine e. in mine inn	378b
take thine e., eat, drink	509b
thy fortress, and thy e.	448a
too much spirit to be e'er at e.	302a
true in writing comes from art	300a
Eased the putting off these. .disguises	274b
Easier: I am e. to be played on	334b
Easiness in admitting any variation	478a
East: a man with his back to the E.	98a
ask me no more if e. or west	79b
daily farther from the E.	466b
did rise not from the E.	114b
easier to conquer it (the E.)	449b
e., ah, e. of Himalaya	442b
E. all the way into Mississippi	231b
E. is E.	227a
e. of Suez	232a
e. wind may never blow	450a
fiery portals of the e.	375b
gorgeous E. with richest hand	272a
hold the gorgeous E. in fee	472b
if you've 'eard the E. a-callin'	232a
lo, in the sanctuaried E.	442b
look how wide also the e. is	488a
Lo! the Hunter of the E.	152a
or in the chambers of the E.	31b
Phoebus. .dapples the drowsy e.	359a
politics in the E. . .dissimulation	129b
promotion. .neither from the e.	487a
recruity goes out to the E.	236b
send danger from the e.	377a
takes this window for the e.	117b
the E. bowed low	7a
the E. is a career	130a
the faint e. quickens	420a
the folding doorways of the E.	441b
the little birds sang e.	43b
there came wise men from the e.	504b
there is neither E. nor West	227a
thine eyes break from their E.	115a
tried to hustle the E.	233a
we have seen his star in the e.	504b
wind blew due E.	86a
wind's in the e.	121a
East-cheap: merry men of E.	170b
Easter: but E.-Day breaks!	46b
Eastern: e. side beheld of Paradise	277a
ere the blabbing e. scout	266b
like a blooming E. bride	138b
not by e. windows only	96b
right against the e. gate	268b
Eastertide: wearing white for E.	198b
Eastward: some e. . .some westward	109a
Easy: all zeal, Mr. E.	259b
but he was e. there, is e. here	559a
conclusions. .of e. ways to die	325b
let yr. precept be, 'Be e.'	410b
'tis e. to be true	321a
trust. .comes e. to him	437a
yes, lad, I lie e.	199a
Eat: care no more to clothe and e.	329a
con-found all presents wot e.	417a
e. and drink our own damnation	480b
e. an ounce less meat	211a
e., drink, and be merry	509b
e. exceedingly, and prophesy	214b

Eat (cont.)

e. into itself, for lack	65a
e. like wolves and fight like devils	382a
e. not of it raw	493b
e. the rest of the anatomy	371b
e. thou and drink	312a
e. . .to the glory of God	514b
gave me of the tree, and I did e.	492b
how shall he e. it	534b
I cannot e. but little meat	415a
I cd. e. one of Bellamy's. .pies	297b
I e. well, and I drink well	284b
I e. what I see	83a
if I dare e. . .I dare meet Surrey	375b
I'll e. my head	125a
I will not e. with you	353a
let us e. and drink; for. .we die	502a,515a
lots of toys and things to e.	414a
not work, neither shd. he e.	516b
so I did sit and e.	188b
some hae meat, and canna e.	62b
some wad e. that want it	62b
so we must e. we	440b
the people sat down to e.	494a
the sort who e. unduly	414a
this Babe must e.	407b
thou didst e. strange flesh	322b
thou shalt not e. of it	492a
to e., and to drink, and to be merry	499b
we did e. bread to the full	494a
we hae meat and we can e.	62b
we must e. to live	151b
ye shall e. it in haste	494a
Eaten: e. me out of house and home	380a
have we e. on the insane root	346a
he was e. of worms	512b
they'd e. every one	84b
Eater: e. of broken meats	342a
great e. of beef	369b
out of the e. came forth meat	495a
Eaters: sheep. .tame and so small e.	283b
Eateth yr. master with publicans	506a
Eating: against e. cares lap me	269a
e. and drinking, marrying	507b
Eats: whatever Miss T. e.	119b
Eave-drops: whether the e. fall	101a
Eaves: fall upon her gilded e.	436a
on the instant clamorous e.	476a
Ebb: a fatal e. and flow	203b
e. and flow must ever be	465a
great ones that e. and flow	344a
ne'er e. to humble love	362b
ne'er feels retiring e.	362b
that e. swept out the flocks	203b
Ebrew: I am a Jew else; an E. Jew	377b
Eccentric: centric and e.	275b
Eccentricities of genius	126b
Ecclesiastic tyranny's the worst	118b
Ecclesiastical: Athanasian. .e. lyric	129b
Echo: any challenged e. clear	78a
applaud thee to the very e.	350b
E. answers: Du!	202b
e. is not faint at last	241b
e. round his bones for evermore	435a
it gives a very e. to the seat	370b
left an e. in the sense	216b
sweet E., sweetest nymph	267a
the cave where E. lies	365b
woods. .answer and my e. rings	408b
Echoes: all melodies the e.	100b
answer, e., dying, dying	436a
by heaven, he e. me	361b
our e. roll from soul to soul	436a
set the wild e. flying	436a
the e. wh. he made relent	137b
Echoing walks between	276b
Eckstein: mound where E. stood	27a
Eclipse: E. first, the rest nowhere	290b
gloom of earthquake and e.	398a
irrecoverably dark, total e.	277b
moon hath her e. endured	388b
sick almost to doomsday with e.	329b
sliver'd in the moon's e.	349b
there was an e. that night	407a
Eclipses: clouds and e. stain. .moon	387b
these late in the sun	341b
Economists: sophisters, e.	57a
Economy: no e. where. .no efficiency	129a
Ecstasies: dissolve me into e.	268b
holy virgins in their e.	428a
muddy e. of beer	113b

Ecstasies (*cont.*)
with e. so sweet — 37*b*
Ecstasy: blasted with e. — 333*b*
eternity..without an e. — 41*b*
in the e. of being ever — 42*b*
it was not e. but it was comfort — 123*a*
lie in restless e. — 348*b*
on waves of e. to sail — 457*b*
thy soul abroad in such an e. — 220*a*
upon the seraph-wings of e. — 175*a*
wak'd to e. the living lyre — 174*a*
what wild e.? — 219*b*
Ecstatic: carolings of such e. sound — 179*a*
Ector: said Sir E. — 257*b*
Eden: a Peri at the gate of E. stood — 282*a*
brooks of E. mazily murmuring — 427*a*
burnish take on E.-trees — 442*b*
E.-sweet the ray — 264*b*
kept the heart of E. green — 427*b*
learned to whittle the E. Tree — 228*a*
Lord God planted a garden..in E. — 492*a*
make this earth an E. — 82*a*
some flow'rets of E. — 282*a*
sweet as E. is the air — 264*b*
tales told in dim E. — 119*a*
this other E., demi-Paradise — 375*a*
thro' E. took their solitary way — 277*a*
voice that breath'd o'er E. — 224*a*
with E. didst devise the Snake — 154*a*
with loss of E. — 270*b*
Edens: lest we lose our E., Eve and I — 52*b*
Edge: at the sea-down's e. — 421*b*
hungry e. of appetite — 374*b*
low last e. of the..lone land — 421*b*
the axe's e. did try — 261*a*
Edification: than the e. of the hearers — 56*b*
Edifice: hail, glorious e. — 403*b*
Edinburgh Review: let balls like the E. — 183*b*
Edition: new e. fifty volumes long — 45*a*
new e. of human nature — 183*a*
pay for an e. of (Plato's) works — 147*b*
Edmonton: unto the Bell at E. — 108*a*
wife should dine at E. — 109*a*
Edmund: here lies our good E. — 169*b*
Edom: over E...cast out my shoe — 485*b*
who is this that cometh from E.? — 503*b*
who will bring me into E.? — 485*b*
Educate: got to e. him first — 315*a*
to e. our party — 128*b*
we must e. our masters — 572*a*
Educated: absence..of..e...opinion — 9*b*
a youth e. by a system — 265*a*
new tribunal..the e. man's — 51*b*
Education: by e. most..misled — 140*b*
e. has for its object..character — 408*a*
e. make a people easy to lead — 40*b*
e. that wh. fits a man — 279*b*
first rudiments of e. are given — 410*b*
highest e. since the Greek — 129*b*
honesty is the beginning of e. — 314*b*
learning and a liberal e. — 185*a*
soap and e...more deadly — 446*b*
thank yr. e. — 216*a*
there's nothing like e. — 536*b*
to love her was a liberal e. — 410*b*
travel..is a part of e. — 15*a*
upon the e. of the people — 128*b*
virtuous and noble E. — 279*b*
Edward: approach proud E.'s power — 62*b*
E. the Confessor slept — 27*b*
sons of E. sleep in Abraham's — 385*a*
why, E., tell me why? — 463*a*
winding-sheet of E.'s race — 173*b*
Edwin: break thy E.'s too — 169*a*
E. and Angelina — 169*a*
let me always call you E. — 150*b*
Eel: an invisible e. — 216*a*
I have seen but an e. — 121*b*
Eels: e. boiled in broo' — 529*b*
some precept..for dressing e. — 305*a*
Effaced: Caesar's image is e. — 110*b*
Effect: greet e. men wryte — 90*a*
Nature is but a name for an e. — 112*b*
peace between the e. and it — 346*a*
the rod produces an e. — 206*a*
thy worst e. is banishing — 108*a*
Effects: close in like e. — 47*a*
dire e. from civil discords — 1*b*
when I reflect upon these e. — 55*b*
Efficiency: e. and inefficiency — 390*b*
no economy where there is no e. — 129*a*

Efficient and the inefficient — 390*b*
Effingham, Grenville, Raleigh — 287*b*
Effort: e., and expectation, and desire — 469*b*
if that e. be too great — 525*a*
law of human life may be E. — 314*b*
Effusions: liveliest e. of wit — 11*b*
Eft: a monstrous e. was of old — 433*b*
Eftest: yes, marry, that's the e. way — 359*a*
Eftsoons his hand dropt he — 98*a*
Egdon: glory of the E. waste — 180*b*
yet E. remained — 181*a*
Egg: a radish and an e. — 112*a*
as an e. is full of meat — 365*b*
eating a demnition e. — 124*b*
e. boiled very soft — 11*a*
in the yolk of an addled e. — 228*a*
like eating an e. without salt — 237*b*
provoking..to be called an e. — 84*b*
remorse..e. by Pleasure laid — 110*b*
think him as a serpent's e. — 338*b*
white and hairless as an e. — 189*b*
you've got a bad e., Mr. Jones — 536*a*
Eggs: as a weasel sucks e. — 326*a*
e. and a pound of cheese — 75*a*
e. that looked like..primroses — 129*a*
eighty-five ways to dress e. — 281*a*
fire..but to roast their e. — 15*b*
fresh e. to rotten boroughs — 254*b*
partridge sitteth on e. — 503*b*
she lays e. for gentlemen — 534*a*
Eglantine: in the..hedge grew lush e. — 398*a*
over-canopied..with e. — 356*b*
Ego: too much E. in your Cosmos — 237*a*
Egoism: in the book of E. — 264*b*
Egotist: whims of an e. — 222*a*
Egotistical: Wordsworthian or e. — 223*a*
Egregiously an ass — 361*a*
Egress: our e. from the world — 249*a*
Egypt: arose up a new king over E. — 493*b*
greater..than the treasures in E. — 517*a*
Helen's beauty in a brow of E. — 357*b*
I am dying, E. — 324*b*
Jehovah..passed from E. — 271*b*
o'er E.'s dark sea — 282*b*
Pamphylia, in E. — 512*a*
pass thro' the land of E. — 494*a*
rather a ditch in E. — 325*a*
the first-born in E. — 326*a*
there was a great cry in E. — 494*a*
there was corn in E. — 493*b*
this bruised reed, this E. — 496*b*
Egyptian: handkerchief did an E...
give — 362*b*
strong E. fetters — 322*b*
Egyptians: spoiled the E. — 494*a*
Eigg on the starboard bow — 414*b*
Eight: a fellow e. years old — 46*b*
most devilish thing is 8 times 8 — 155*a*
'pieces of e.!' — 413*a*
seven, e., lay them straight — 532*a*
Eighteen hundred and two: in 1802
every..monarch was insane — 17*b*
Eighteen twenty: born 1820 — 522*b*
Eildon: riding down by the E. Tree — 528*a*
Eileen Aroon — 177*a*
Einstein: Let E. be! — 26*b*
Eiré: fair hills of E. — 258*a*
Either: how happy cd. I be with e. — 160*a*
when Death to e. shall come — 37*b*
Ekenhead: Leander, Mr. E., and I — 70*b*
Elaine: E. the fair — 428*a*
the lily maid — 428*a*
Elamites: Medes, and E. — 512*a*
Elates: while fame e. thee — 281*a*
Elbow wh. people come miles to see — 165*a*
Elbow-chairs: next suggested e. — 111*b*
Eld: Memories of E. — 298*a*
palsied e. — 352*a*
Elder: an e. man not at all — 14*b*
an e. said as we sat in a flock — 180*a*
in the e. days of Art — 246*b*
I said an e. soldier, not a better — 340*b*
I the e. and more terrible — 339*a*
the e. unto the elect lady — 518*a*
travel..in the e...experience — 15*a*
woman take an e. than herself — 370*b*
Elders: discourse of the e. — 520*b*
e. and the four beasts — 519*a*
one of the e. answered — 519*a*
Elder-tree: wood..and the e. — 119*b*
Eldest: Night, e. of things — 273*a*

Elect: knit together thine e. — 480*a*
Elected: audacity of e. persons — 457*b*
Election: doctrine of Particular E. — 135*a*
e. by the incompetent many — 391*a*
e. is the..constitution — 217*a*
her e. hath sealed thee — 334*a*
snatched..at the moment of the e. — 55*a*
Electrician is no longer there — 26*b*
Elegance: studious of e. and ease — 160*b*
Elegancy, facility..of poesy — 344*b*
Elegant: e. but not ostentatious — 213*a*
e. sufficiency, content — 443*b*
Element: above the e. they liv'd in — 325*a*
e. itself, till seven years' heat — 369*b*
I am not of yr. e. — 371*b*
thy e.'s below — 342*a*
'Elementary,' said Holmes — 135*b*
Elemented: those things wh. e. it — 134*a*
Elements: amidst the wars of e. — 1*b*
contending with the fretful e. — 342*b*
e. once out of it, it transmigrates — 323*b*
I tax not you, you e. — 342*b*
my other e. I give to..life — 325*a*
Nature that framed us of four e. — 259*a*
our torments..become our e. — 272*b*
reconciles discordant e. — 469*a*
something that was before the e. — 42*a*
so mix'd the e. all lay — 136*b*
the e. so mixed in him — 341*b*
weak and beggarly e. — 515*b*
with the motion of all e. — 345*a*
Elenore: where the region E.? — 442*b*
Elephant: an E.'s child — 237*a*
depths in wh. an e. may swim — 185*b*
he thought he saw an E. — 85*b*
in the south suburbs, at the E. — 371*b*
the e.'s a gentleman — 233*a*
the unwieldy e. — 274*a*
Elephants: e. endorsed with towers — 277*a*
place e. for want of towns — 419*b*
women and e. never forget — 572*b*
Elevation: scourged us to an e. — 245*b*
uttering, for e. of our thought — 464*b*
Eleven: e. buckram men grown — 377*b*
second e. sort of chap — 21*b*
tells you he's only e. — 164*a*
Eleventh: dark e. hour — 236*a*
Elf: a servant's..a negligent e. — 19*b*
deceiving e. — 220*a*
here's not a modest maiden e. — 180*a*
Elfland: horns of E. faintly blowing — 436*a*
the Road to fair E. — 528*a*
Elf-locks: Mab..bakes the e. — 365*a*
Elgin: he stands in E.'s place — 136*b*
Eli, Eli, lama sabachthani? — 508*a*
Elias: unto none of them was E. sent — 509*a*
Elijah: E...cast his mantle upon him — 496*a*
Enoch, E., and the Lady — 294*b*
spirit of E. doth rest upon Elisha — 496*b*
Elinor: 'I am afraid,' replied E. — 11*b*
Elisha: shall E. slay — 496*a*
spirit of Elijah doth rest upon E. — 496*b*
Eliza: that so did take E. and..James — 216*a*
Elizabeth: change from Jane to E. — 11*b*
my son's wife, E. — 203*b*
no scandal about Queen E. — 400*a*
one name was E. — 215*b*
Queen E.'s dead — 418*b*
saying..ascribed to Queen E. — 2*a*
spacious times of great E. — 426*b*
that E.-Jane Farfrae be not told — 180*b*
Ellangowan: meet on E.'s height — 319*b*
Ellen: E. of brave Lochinvar — 318*a*
Peccavi..wrote Lord E. so proud — 535*a*
Ellops: Hydrus, and E. drear — 276*b*
Elm: the signal-e. — 8*b*
Elms: doves in immemorial e. — 437*a*
e., fade into dimness — 7*b*
Elm-tree: round the e. bole — 47*a*
Elope: we..must e. methodically — 170*b*
Eloped: lovers e. in the dark — 242*a*
Eloquence: Bag of Parliamentary E. — 81*a*
for e. the soul — 272*b*
intoxicated with my own e. — 129*b*
let my books be then the e. — 387*a*
mother of arts and e. — 277*a*
she uttereth piercing e. — 366*b*
talking and e. are not the same — 215*a*
Eloquent: curse..is e. men — 148*b*
e., just and mighty Death — 308*a*
Elsewhere: I wd. not be e. — 287*a*

Elsinore: stormy steep, E. 76b
Elucescebat quoth our friend 45a
Elves: fairy e., whose midnight revels 272a
spite of all the criticizing e. 95a
stars attend thee; and the e. also 189b
small e. coats 356b
Ely: merrily sang the monks in E. 79a
my lord of E. 385a
Elysian: dead, but in the E. fields 129a
E., windless, fortunate abodes 397b
Elysium: all night sleeps in E. 383a
brother he is in E. 369b
what E. have ye known 219a
Emanation: my E. far within 31b
Emathian conqueror 278b
Embalmer: O soft e. 221a
Embark: no sadness..when I e. 426a
Embarking: yr. friends are all e. 4b
Embarrassed: Jack was e. 73a
Embarrassing young 563a
Embattled farmers 146b
Embers: by the e. in hearthside ease 180a
O joy! that in our e...doth live 466b
where glowing is. thro' the room 268a
Emblem: the pink, the e. o' my dear 62b
Emblems of deeds that are done 67b
Embodiment: the Law is the true e. 163b
Embody: I, my Lords, e. the Law 163b
Embosom'd in the deep 170a
Embrace: as to e. me she inclined 278b
none I think do there e. 260a
spirit-like, eludes e. 293b
then I e. and kiss 198a
then pity, then e. 301a
Embraces: age in her e. past 309b
Embroidered: sinister e. on the ..
normal 204a
Embroidery: e. of poetic dreams 108a
every flower that sad e. wears 270a
Embroils: by decision more e. the
fray 273a
Embryo: chancellor in e. 400a
Embryos and idiots 273b
Emerald: a livelier e. 434a
fourth, an e. 520a
men of the E. Isle 137b
peach of e. hue 151a
sight like unto an e. 518b
Emerge: I shall e. one day 49b
Emigravit is the inscription 247b
Emily: a very good girl was E. Jane 163a
up roos the sonne, and up roos E. 89a
up rose the Sun, and up rose E. 141a
Eminence: bald top of an e. 470a
raised to that bad e. 272a
Eminent: in..gesture proudly e. 272a
Emmanuel: O come, E. 286b
Emolument: fits us for places of e. 158a
Emotion: any heart..share in my e. 399a
bounding at e. new 9a
e. recollected in tranquillity 467b
mix for ever with a sweet e. 395b
morality touched by e. 10a
Emotions: noble grounds for..e. 314a
Emperor: [e.] is taller by..my nail 417b
had he never been e. 553b
heard..by e. and clown 220a
lie by an e.'s side 362b
looking for the sacred E. 35a
reign of the E. Hwang 242a
tent-royal of their e. 381b
yr. worm is yr. only e. 335a
Emphyteusis..is not a disease 413b
Empire: another..E. overthrown 468a
as thy e. must extend 277a
cutpurse of the e. 335a
disintegration..of the E. 571a
e. is no more than power 138a
E. is on us bestowed 107b
E. stands splendidly isolated 156a
every..staff of e. is..crooked 17a
fall-off-the-Rooshan-E. 125b
freedom and..the unity of the e. 56a
great e. and little minds 56a
how is the E.? 161b
it may make us an E. yet 231a
loungers of the E. 136a
nor Roman, nor an e. 566a
rod of e. might have sway'd 174a
stay a falling e. 110b
the deceased Roman E. 191b

Empire (cont.)
the e. unpossessed 385a
thy tread is on an E.'s dust 68a
to found a great e. 403a
we'll pledge our E. vast 202b
westward the course of e. 28a
wide arch of the ranged e. fall 322a
wilderness into a glorious e. 56a
with an e.'s lamentation 435a
Empire Day: the meaning of E. 94a
Empires: day of E. has come 87a
hatching vain e. 272b
vaster than e., and more slow 260a
Employment: chase brave e. 186b
the hand of little e. 336a
pleasantness of an e. 11b
Empress: e. and flour of floures 90a
general of our gracious e. 383b
Emptier ever dancing in the air 376a
Emptiness: e. of ages in his face 258b
eternal smiles his e. betray 303a
little e. of love 40a
Empty: a little louder, but as e. quite 301a
e., vast, and wandering 384b
like the e. words of a dream 36b
rich he hath sent e. away 508b
Emulate: to e. his mind 169a
Emulation: bloodless e. 368b
by exciting e. 206a
out of the teeth of e. 339a
shouting their e. 328a
Enable: with perpetual light 491a
Enamelled: quaint e. eyes 270a
snake throws her e. skin 356b
Enamour: one of those wh. most e. 67b
Enamoured: affliction is e. 366a
methought I was e. of an ass 357a
Enchanted: as holy and e. 101a
enter those e. woods, you who dare 264b
Enchanter: ghosts from an e. fleeing 396a
Enchanting: divine e. ravishment 267a
Enchantment: hence .. sweet e.,
hence! 403b
'tis distance lends e. 77a
Enchantments of the Middle Ages 9a
Encounter: in a free and open e. 279a
Encourage: kill an admiral..to e. 566a
Encouragement: expression of no-e. 35a
Encumbers him with help 206b
Encyclopaedia behind the rest 239a
End: ages of hopeless e. 272b
all things come to an e. 489a
a' made a finer e. 381b
be-all and the e.-all 347a
began to draw to our e. 520a
better is the e. of a thing 499a
born to disastrous e. 409b
but the e. is not yet 507b
death, a necessary e., will come 339a
e. of a perfect day 204a
e. of all things is at hand 517b
e. of every man's desire 421a
e. of it's sittin' an' thinkin' 230b
e. of this day's business 341b
e. of toil and gloom 20b
fairest things have fleetest e. 441a
for some felonious e. 267a
God be at my e. 523a
go on till you come to the e. 83b
her e. is bitter as wormwood 497b
he made a good e. 335b
here is my journey's e. 364a
housewives'..have never an e. 446a
it is the e. that crowns us 189b
last, and midst, and without e. 471a
lest he shd. make an e. 215a
let my last e. be like his 494a
let the e. try the man 380a
let there be an e. 49b
like good angels, to my e. 385b
long weary day have e. 408b
Lord, let me know mine e. 484a
make an e. the sooner 15b
makes a swan-like e. 354a
makes me e., where I begun 134a
making many books there is no e. 500a
mean this day to e. myself 433a
miserable change now at my e. 324b
my friend's intent and e. 187b
my sorrows have an e. 523b
our minutes hasten to their e. 388a

End (cont.)
quiet-coloured e. of evening 48a
reserved for some e. or other 96a
right true e. of love 132b
sans Singer, and—sans E. 153a
set gray life, and apathetic e. 433a
silence..noble till the e. 420b
something ere the e. 439a
so there's an e. on't 528a
stand up and e. you 199b
sufficeth that the day will e. 341b
the e. crowns all 369b
the e. in sight was a vice 52a
the e. of all things 124a
the e. of things created 523a
the e. that I have now begun 473b
the man wd. die, and there an e. 349a
then the e. is known 341b
therefore she had a good e. 257b
there's an e. 379a
there's an e., I think, of kissing 40a
there's an e. on't 207b
there shall I e. 341b
the same thing at the e. 44b
the true beginning of our e. 357b
Time, will one day e. it 369b
to pause, to make an e. 438b
understood I the e. of these men 486b
what the boys get at one e. 208b
whose e. is purposed by the..gods 339a
wish it all at an e. 58b
woos his own e. 428b
world may e. tonight 47b
wrought the e. unthought 236a
yet the e. was not ignoble 469a
Endearment: a bird each fond e. tries 168b
Endears: falling out..all the more e. 436a
Endeavour: a disinterested e. to learn 9a
against all death's e. 40a
disappointment all I e. end 198a
listlessness, nor mad e. 466b
nor e. to convict her 419a
Endeavours are an inward light 465a
Ended: our revels now are e. 367b
Enderby: Brides of E. 203a
dark rang 'E.' 203b
Ending: God send us all good e. 531a
slow to begin and never e. 468a
song shd. here have e. 270b
still e. at the arrival 379a
Endless: in all the e. road you tread 199b
Endowed: men e. with highest gifts 464a
Ends: best e. by the best means 202b
delights have violent e. 365b
divinity that shapes our e. 336b
e. all our month-long love 36b
e. of the world are come 292b
for ever nobler e. 431a
let all the e...be thy country's 386a
make both e. meet 158a
odd old e. stol'n forth 384b
our e. by our beginnings know 119b
tend to the preposterousest e. 66a
worthy e. and expectations 14a
Endurance: e., foresight, strength 470b
patient e. is godlike 247a
Endure: all deaths I cd. e. 276a
as tempted more; more able to e. 465a
but thou shalt e. 488a
e. not yet a breach 134a
e. what can't be mended 453a
for thy peace, she shall e. 315a
let us e. an hour 199b
nought may e. but Mutability 396a
see how our works e. 228a
we first e., then pity 301a
youth's a stuff will not e. 370b
Endured: I had e. thro' watches 443a
intolerable, not to be e. 366b
much is to be e. 213b
tolerable and not to be e. 358b
Endures: ever the faith e. 185a
since to be loved e. 37b
Endureth: charity..e. all things 514b
he that e. to the end 506a
his mercy e. for ever 490a
Enduring power, not ourselves 10a
Endymion: in E., I leaped headlong 222b
moon sleeps with E. 355b
Enemies: bay'd about with many e. 340b
careful in the choice of his e. 460b

Enemies (cont.)

e. of Caesar shall say this	339b
e. of England..be sick	199a
e., persecutors, and slanderers	479a
e. shall lick the dust	486b
find out their e. now	342b
giving his e. the slip for ever	411b
his e., 'Toasted-cheese'	86a
I called thee to curse mine e.	494a
if laws are their e.	58a
left me naked to mine e.	386a
let his e. be scattered	486a
make e. of nations	111b
mine e. that trouble me	484b
my most intimate e.	313a
our e. have beat us to the pit	341b
overthrown more than yr. e.	325b
smote his e. in the hinder parts	487a
speak with their e. in the gate	489b
such men my friends than e.	341b
they will be e. to laws	58a
to forgive e. H— does pretend	30a
trophies unto the e. of truth	41b
we read..forgive our e.	13b
wound the head of his e.	486b

Enemy: an e. hath done this

a weak invention of the e.	506b
common e. of man	95a
do be my e.	348b
e. ears are listening	30a
e. faints not, nor faileth	566b
golden bridge is for a flying e.	96b
hast thou found me, O mine e.?	70a
here shall he see no e.	496a
he's an e. to mankind	326a
he who has one e.	371b
his e. came and sowed tares	148b
how goes the e.?	506b
I impeach the common e.	308b
last e. that shall be destroyed	56b
mine e.'s dog, tho' he had bit me	515a
my e. is dead	344a
my vision's greatest e.	457b
name..so terrible to the	29b
near'st and dearest e.	380a
O cunning e.	778b
old the gout	351b
O thou e., destructions are come	195a
put an e. in their mouths	482a
right to be taught by the e.	361b
security is mortals' chiefest e.	551b
still the e. and the avenger	349b
that sweet e., France	482a
there he met his e.	401b
thing devised by man	226b
to the victim..the spoils of the e.	385a
worst friend and e. is but Death	258a
Energies of our system will decay	40a
Energy: e. divine	18a
E. is Eternal Delight	303b
Enforce a desperate amour	31a
Enforced, shows a hasty spark	66a
Enforcement: my strong e. be	341a
Engagement: loose from every..e.	326b
Engendered: I have 't; it is e.	56b
Engine: devilish iron e.	360b
he put this e...to our ears	408b
in dirt the reasoning e. lies	417b
that curious e., yr. white hand	309b
two-handed e. at the door	454a
wit's an unruly e.	269b
Engineer: e. hoist with his..petar	186b
wit..striking..sometimes the e.	335a
Engines: alone wi' God an'..my e.	186b
e. to play a little on our own	231b
O you mortal e.	56b
England: a body of E.'s	362a
admirals all, for E.'s sake	40a
a dust whom E. bore	287b
alas, alas, for E.	40a
as a lover or a child [England]	92a
be E. what she will	472b
between France and E...the sea	94b
born and bred in E.	205b
Cambridgeshire, of all E.	160b
chaffinch sings..in E.—now!	39b
children in E. take pleasure	47a
coastwise lights of E.	526b
cold queen of E.	228a
cottage homes of E.	92b
	185a

England (cont.)

country men of E.	292a
did not delay to E. to carry	137a
earthquake were to engulf E.	205b
E.—a happy land we know	94b
E. and Saint George!	382a
E.! awake! awake!	30b
E...bashfulness in..religion	2a
E., bound in with the..sea	375a
E. does not love coalitions	128a
E. expects every man	287a
E. has been in a dreadful state	121b
E. has saved herself	297b
E. hath need of thee	467b
E., Home, and Beauty	34b, 123a
E. invented the phrase	17a
E. is a garden	229b
E. is a nation of shopkeepers	564a
E. is a paradise for women	64b
E. is the mother of Parliaments	38a
E. mourns for her dead	28b
E., my E.	185a
E., my own	185a
E.'s Alfred named	435a
E.'s being hammered	227a
E.'s green and pleasant bowers	30b
E.'s green and pleasant land	31b
E. shall bide till Judgement	236a
E.'s high Chancellor	216b
E.'s Milton equals both in fame	109a
E.'s on the wall	227a
E.'s the one land, I know	39b
E.'s Walhalla	453b
E.'s winding sheet	29b
E., that was wont to conquer	375a
E. to be the workshop of..world	128a
E. under the dregs of men	26a
E. was merry E.	318a
E., we love thee better	445b
E., where..they are most potent	361a
ere E.'s griefs began	168a
Florence, Elizabethan E.	203a
foreign field that is forever E.	40a
France..influenced manners in E.	57a
further off from E.	83b
gentlemen in E., now a-bed	383a
get me to E. once again	39b
go anywhere in E.	390a
God-gifted organ-voice of E.	427a
Greece, Italy, and E.	141a
green fields of E.	96b
happy is E.	221a
heralds of E.'s marshal	93b
here did E. help me	47b
he that is mad, and sent into E.	336b
high road that leads him to E.	207a
history of E. is..of progress	254a
Honour unto E.'s Jane	230b
how can I help E.?	47b
I am E.'s queen	231b
I am in E., everywhere	42a
if E. to itself do rest but true	374b
if E. was what E. seems	233b
in E. seven halfpenny loaves sold	384a
in E.'s song for ever	287b
in regard to this aged E.	147b
insignificant men as any in E.	450a
Ireland gives E. her soldiers	264b
it was never merry world in E.	384a
I've a hundred captains in E.	531a
knew what E. means	92a
know of E. who only E. know?	228b
knuckle-end of E.	404a
light such a candle..in E.	242b
let not E. forget her precedence	279b
linking our E. to his Italy	51b
lost the last of E.	27a
martial airs of E.	454a
men of E., wherefore plough	399a
men..of light and leading in E.	57b
men that worked for E.	92a
mythic time of E.'s prime	294a
no amusements in E. but vice	404b
noon strikes on E.	154b
nor, E.! did I know till then	467a
not the E. of our dreams	233b
oats..in E...given to horses	212b
O E., full of sin	186b
O E.! model to thy..greatness	381b
of a king of E. too	145a
of all the trees in E.	119b

England (cont.)

oh, to be in E.	47a
old E. is lost	209a
old E. is our home	201a
old E. to adorn	236a
oldest singer that E. bore	423a
on E.'s pleasant pastures	31a
or E. breed again such a king	137a
our banner of England flew	426b
our noble E.'s praise	252a
pastoral heart of E.	307b
proud E. keep, untamed	136b
roast beef of E.	151a
Rome..in this realm of E.	491b
seeing a worse E.	209b
shire..the heart of E...call	137a
since he stood for E.	92a
slaves cannot breathe in E.	111b
sleep in Old E.'s heart	453b
some love E. and her honour yet	438a
stately homes of E.	184b
such night in E. ne'er had been	252a
suspended in favour of E.	390a
take my drum to E.	287b
ten thousand of those men in E.	383a
the Man of E. circled	263a
the meteor flag of E.	78a
the royal navy of E.	28b
they that rule in E.	92a
this E. never did, nor never shall	374b
this is E.'s greatest son	435a
this realm, this E.	375a
thoughts by E. given	40a
three good men unhanged in E.	377b
to ensure summer in E.	449b
to ride in E. to take a prey	530b
wake up E.	161b
walk upon E.'s mountains	31a
we are the people of E.	93a
what appears in E.'s case	108a
where an immortal E. sits	92b
where rest not E.'s dead	184b
while E. talked of ale	93a
who dies if E. live	229a
whoever wakes in E.	47a
whose limbs were made in E.	382a
with E.'s own coal	227b
with the crews at E.'s feet	76b
ye Mariners of E.	77b
you gentlemen of E.	292a
you poison E. at her roots	34a
youth of E. are on fire	381b
English: a body..breathing E. air	40a
a boy, half French, half E.	383b
a happy E. child	424b
Alfred came..to be an E. king	91b
Allah created the E. mad	230b
among the E. poets after my death	223a
an E. Flag was flown	228b
an E. unofficial rose	39b
as E. an article as a beefsteak	182b
best thing in fiction..E...done	460b
between E. earth and sky	185a
breeds hard E. men	226a
buy my E. posies	229a
characteristic of the E. monarchy	17b
E...a foul-mouthed nation	183b
E. army led by an Irish general	391a
E...bid adieu to common feeling	405a
E...least..pure philosophers	17b
E...little inferior to the Scotch	289b
E. man..not travel to see E. men	411a
E. summer's done	231b
E...talent pour le silence	81a
E. they be and Japanese	233b
E. winter—ending in July	71b
false E. Nobles and their Jew	294a
find one E. book..as in the Iliad	10a
fine old E. gentleman	524b
freedom an E. subject's	141b
ghost will walk..in an E. lane	46a
God's patience, and the king's E.	355b
good E. hospitality	33a
heart with E. instinct fraught	136b
he off E.-making was the beste	251a
if he went among the E.	21b
marks our E. dead	234b
my native E., now I must forego	374b
nor any E. thing	91b
only the E. make it their abode	449a
O noble E.!	381b

English (cont.)

on, on, you noblest E.! 382a
O when shall E. men 137a
principle of the E. constitution 28b
really nice E. people 390a
rolling E. drunkard 93a
rolling E. road 93a
shed one E. tear o'er E. dust 252b
strung them on an E. thread 250b
sunny gems on an E. green 433b
sweet as E. air cd. make her 435b
take of E. earth as much 227b
talent of our E. nation 141b
that an E. lord shd. lightly me! 531a
there was not E. armour left 91b
till the E. grew polite 228b
to attain an E. style 213a
to make his E. swete 88b
to the E. . . (empire) of the sea 80a
trick of our E. nation 379b
under an E. heaven 40a
upon one pair of E. legs 382a
up with our E. dead 382a
we be all good E. men 437b
well of E. undefyled 409a
wet bird-haunted E. lawn 7a
when the E. began to hate 227a
when you can't think of the E. 84a
white . . is the E. child 32b
winged heels, as E. Mercuries 381b
yr. . . Saxon-Danish-Norman E. 118b
Englishman: an E. thinks he is moral
as I am an E. 390b
broad-shouldered, genial E. 297a
Brother, E., and Friend 437b
E., being flattered, is a lamb 469b
E. is content to say nothing 87a
E.'s heaven-born privilege 210a
E. whose heart is in a matter 9b
E. who speaketh against ale 17b
he is an E.! 34a
he remains an E. 166a
never find an E. in the wrong 166a
no E. unmoved 391a
not one E. 166b
one E. cd. beat three Frenchmen 450a
ordinary young E. 2a
she woo'd an E. 9b
the last great E. is low 528a
thorough an E. as ever coveted 435a
vain, ill-natured thing, an E. 226b
what an E. believes be heresy? 118b
Englishmen: absurd nature of E. 391b
and E. are we 296a
proper drink of E. 201a
we will be, honest E. 34a
when two E. meet 226a
you will not find E. doing it 213a
Engross: pens a stanza, when he shd. 391a
e. 303a
Enjoy: after that, to e. it [life] 404a
can neither, when we will, e. 7a
e. . . things wh. others understand 469a
he can thoroughly e. the pepper 83a
let me e. the earth no less 180a
Light, wh. I can ne'er e. 95a
more we e. it, more it dies 117a
so as in due time we may e. them 479a
so I both e. and miss her 198a
we prize not . . whiles we e. it 359a
who can e. alone 275b
with what I most e. contented least 387a
you never e. the world aright 445a
Enjoyed: all times I have e. greatly 438b
e. in vision beatific 272a
human life is . . little to be e. 213b
if not e., it sighing cries 117a
supinely e. the gifts of the founder 161b
to have e. the sun 5b
Enjoying: all . . e., what contentment 275b
belief of truth, wh. is the e. of it 14a
think, oh think, it worth e. 139a
Enjoyment: a day in such serene e. 280a
question . . was it done with e.? 314b
unless it from e. spring 445a
Enjoyments: pleasant if it were not
for its e. 417a
Enjoys: e. the air it breathes 471a
the King is his own again 292b
Enlarge: e., diminish, interline 419b
e. my life with multitude of days 214a

Enmesh me, and impute my Fall 154a
Enmity: e. under the smile of safety 379b
nor all that is at e. with joy 466b
Enna: that fair field of E. 274a
Eno: soar with E. 412b
Enoch walked with God 492b
Enormous thro' the Sacred Town 26b
Enough: eaten oysters . . never had e. 163a
e. for nature's ends 257a
e., he died the death of fame 317a
e., if something from our hands 463b
e. of science and of art 471b
first cries, 'hold, e.' 351a
I 'aven't 'ad e. 535b
it is e. that, thro' Thy Grace 232b
patriotism is not e. 86b
saith not, it is e. 499a
'tis e., 'twill serve 365b
was it not e.? 390a
yet are they only not e. 35b
Enquire: e. wisely concerning this 499a
the pace is too good to e. 289a
Enraged I write, I know not what 176b
Enrich: e. my heart, mouth, hands 187a
e. unknowing Nations 117a
Enriched: thou hast e. both 36a
Enriches: robs me of that wh. not e. 361b
Enrichment of our native language 142a
Ensample: noble e. to his sheep 88b
Ensham: above by E. 8b
Ensign: beauty's e. yet is crimson 366b
tear her tattered e. down 194a
Enskyed and sainted 351a
Enslave: education . . impossible to e. 40b
Ensnared: hath thus e. my soul 364a
Entente: name of 'E. Cordial' 535a
Enter: all hope abandon, ye who e. 566b
although I e. not 440b
e. thou into the joy of thy Lord 508a
too late! ye cannot e. now 427b
wh. . . [stars] e. unannounced 99a
Entered: he e., but he e. full of wrath 218a
Entergraft: so to e. our hands 132b
Enterprise: e. is sick 368b
hazard in the glorious e. 271a
nurse of . . heroic e. is gone 57a
period, power and e. 403a
Enterprises: e. of great pith 333a
impediments to great e. 14b
Enters: bent on him that e. next 376a
Entertain: e. a cheerful disposition 375a
e. divine Zenocrate 259b
e. us with no worth 449a
forgetful to e. strangers 517a
some second guest to e. 133b
speculations to be learned 201b
you, sir, I e. for one of my hundred 343a
Entertaining: very e. to myself 104b
Entertainment: dull thy palm with e. 330b
human knee is . . not an e. 178b
invent some other custom of e. 361a
principal features of my E. 451a
what lenten e. 332b
Enthrall: except you e. me 133a
Enthralled: virtue may be assailed . .
but not e. 267b
Enthusiasm: e. moves the world 18a
nothing great . . achieved without e. 148a
studious martyr to mild e. 45b
Enthusiasts: few e. . . speak the truth 18a
Entire: e. and perfect chrysolite 363b
e. and whole and perfect 409b
if thy Faith is e., press onward 37a
Entrails: in the poisoned e. throw 349b
swords in our own proper e. 341b
Entrance: beware of e. to a quarrel 330b
croaks the fatal e. of Duncan 346b
grow slack from my first e. in 188b
Entrances: their exits and their e. 326b
Entrancing it is to wander 35a
Entrap: times put on to e. 354a
Entreat: e. me not to leave thee 495a
not missed by any that e. 43a
Entuned in hir nose ful semely 88b
Entwine itself verdantly still 281b
Environ: what perils do e. the man 65a
Environed with a great ditch 116a
Envy: America . . the e. of the world 55b
death . . extinguisheth e. 14a
e. and calumny and hate and pain 392b

Envy (cont.)

e. and wrath shorten the life 520b
e., hatred, and malice 478b
e. is a kind of praise 160b
e. never makes holiday 13b
e. of less happier lands 375a
e. of thy happy lot 219b
e.'s a coal comes hissing hot 18a
e.'s a sharper spur than pay 160b
e., ye great, the dull unlettered 113a
has she no faults then (E. says) 299b
I e. not in any moods the captive 430a
my means may lie too low for e. 107a
whose guile, stirr'd up with e. 270b
Epaulet I cd. have worn 444a
Ephesians: Diana of the E. 512b
Ephesus: beasts at E. 515a
Ephod: linen e. 495a
Ephraim: E. also is the strength 485b
grapes of E. 495a
Epic: forgot his e., nay Pindaric wit 303b
the legend of an e. hour 92b
Epictetus: everything, saith E., hath
two handles 64a
Mrs. Carter cd. . . translate E. 206a
Epicurus: a true hog of E.' herd 543a
he was E. owne sone 88b
I held E. strong 341a
Epicycle: cycle and e. 275b
Epigram: what is an E.? 100b, 527b
Epilogue: good play needs no e. 328a
Epistle: wordy and lengthy e. 549a
Epistles: obscure e. of love 370b
Epitaph: believe a woman or an e. 72a
better have a bad e. 332b
not remembered in thy e. 379a
surely that may be his e. 412b
the e. drear: 'a Fool lies here' 233a
Epitaphs: a nice derangement of e. 400b
let's talk . . of worms, and e. 375b
talking of E. 19a
Epithet: fair is too foul an e. for thee 259b
Epithets: e. of war 359b
sensitive to e. like these 26a
Epitome: all mankind's e. 138b
London is the e. of our times 147a
Equal: all e. are within the Church's 186b
all men are created e. 245a
all shall e. be 163b
compel us to be e. upstairs 21b
deemed e. in strength 272a
e. division of unequal earnings 146a
I am e. and whole 422a
thine e. knew I never 157a
tho' equal to all things 169b
vain . . treat them as if they were e. 157b
Equality: E.! Fraternity! 566a
never be e. in the servants' hall 21b
true apostles of e. 9b
Equalled with me in fate 273a
Equals: awkward . . society of his e. 239a
friendship . . commerce between e. 170b
least of all between e. 16a
Equator: quarrellin' wi' the e. 289b
speak disrespectfully of the E. 404a
when they got as far as the E. 446b
Equestrian: Grand E. Troop 195a
Equinoctial gales 525a
Equinox: when was the e.? 42b
Equivocate: I will not e. 158b
Equivocator: faith, here's an e. 348a
Equivocation: e. of the fiend 351a
e. will undo us 336b
Ercles: this is E.' vein 356a
Erebus: affections dark as E. 355b
not E. itself were dim enough 338b
Erect: godlike e., with native honour 274a
grows e., as that comes home 134a
of far nobler shape e. and tall 274b
stood e., caught at God's skirts 47b
unless above himself he can e. 464b
Erecting: there e. new 260b
Eremite: nature's patient . . E. 220b
Eremites and friars 273b
Eric: call me E. 150b
Ericking: any beastly E. 237b
Erin: anthem of 'E. go bragh' 76b
a poor Exile of E. 76b
E., the tear and the smile 281a
Eros: Anteros and E. 441a
E.!—I come, my queen 324b

Eros (*cont.*)
unarm, E. 324*b*
Err: better to e. with Pope 72*a*
not e., who say..when the Poet dies 317*a*
the most may e. as grossly 138*b*
to e. is human 300*b*
you're mortal and may e. 401*a*
Errand: joyous E. reach the spot 154*a*
the warlike e. went 252*b*
what thy e. here below? 240*a*
Errands: e. for the Ministers of State 163*b*
meet to be sent on e. 340*b*
Erred, and strayed from thy ways 478*a*
Erring: a rod to check the e. 463*b*
Error: a gross e., held in schools 160*b*
all men are liable to e. 246*a*
double e. sometimes sets us right 18*a*
e. a fault and truth discourtesy 186*b*
e. is immense 33*b*
if this be e., and upon me proved 389*a*
in endless e. hurled 301*a*
in religion, what damned e. 354*a*
it is the very e. of the moon 363*b*
many an e. by the same example 354*b*
mountainous e. 328*a*
O hateful e. 341*b*
rashly charged the troops of e. 41*b*
show a man that he is in an e. 246*a*
stronger than all the hosts of e. 53*a*
Errors: e., like straws 141*a*
e. of a wise man make yr. rule 29*a*
make us adore our e. 324*a*
more harmful than reasoned e. 203*a*
to her share some female e. fall 302*b*
Erump: excede, evade, e. 194*b*
Eruption: strange e. to our state 329*b*
Esau: E...is a hairy man 493*a*
E. selleth his birthright 523*a*
E. was a cunning hunter 493*a*
the hands are the hands of E. 493*a*
Escalus: one thing to be tempted, E. 351*a*
Escape: also make a way to e. 514*b*
beauty for some provides e. 202*b*
e. me? never 48*a*
few e. that distinction 447*a*
let me ever e. them 490*b*
let no guilty man e. 173*a*
man may e. from rope 159*b*
Escapes: hair-breadth 'scapes 360*a*
painful e. of fitful life 35*b*
Escapeth the sword of Hazael 469*a*
Eschew evil 484*a*
Eskdale: march, E. and Liddesdale 320*a*
Esperance! Percy! and set on 379*a*
Espouse the everlasting Sea 472*b*
Espoused: my fairest, my e. 274*b*
Espy a fair pretty maid 525*b*
Esquire: he was an e.'s son 531*b*
Essays: worse e. proved thee my best 389*a*
Essence: a fellowship with e. 217*b*
his glassy e., like an angry ape 351*b*
uncompounded is their e. pure 271*b*
Essene Erastian Whig 92*b*
Essex: in E. at Dunmowe 89*b*
Savill was asked by my Lord of E. 13*b*
Estate: condescend to men of low e. 513*b*
e., good fame 146*b*
e. o' the world were now undone 351*a*
fallen from his high e. 139*a*
gentleman who had a great e. 522*a*
have you an e. in Greenland? 177*a*
he had his jest, and they had his e. 138*b*
he steals yr. whole e. 159*b*
high or lowly, and ordered their e. 3*a*
holy e. of Matrimony 481*b*
mind, body, or e. 479*a*
nor born in any high e. 3*b*
not despised..low e. of the poor 483*a*
sat a Fourth E. more important 81*a*
the low e. of his handmaiden 508*b*
the relief of man's e. 13*a*
when I am grown to man's e. 414*a*
when I came to man's e. 372*a*
whose life in low e. began 430*b*
Estates: Burke said there were Three E. 81*a*
e., degrees, and offices 353*b*
flies of e. and sunshine 188*a*
Esteem: coward in thine own e. 347*a*
they give to get e. 170*a*
Esteemed: better..be vile than vile e. 389*a*
Esteemed (*cont.*)
we e. him not 503*a*
Estimate: it holds his e. and dignity 369*a*
like enough thou know'st thy e. 388*b*
Estranged: God's providence..e. 196*a*
Estranging: unplumbed, salt, e. sea 6*b*
Estridges: all plumed like e. 378*b*
Et tu, Brute! 339*a*
Eternal: abode where the E. are 392*b*
a portion of the E. 392*b*
but an e. now does always last 106*b*
deaf and silent, read'st the e. deep 466*b*
energy is E. Delight 31*a*
e. glory thou shalt win 54*a*
e. Passion! e. Pain 7*a*
e. summer gilds them yet 70*b*
ever in themselves e. 78*a*
fish say, in the E. Brook 39*b*
his trust was with th' E. 272*a*
it keeps e. whisperings 221*a*
let us put into their 'E.' 10*a*
of th' E. co-eternal beam 273*a*
only the sleep e. in an e. night 422*a*
the E. Power, not ourselves 10*b*
Eternities: conflux of two E. 80*b*
I play for Seasons; not E. 264*a*
the past, the future, two e. 282*a*
Eternity: becomes a babe in E. 29*b*
damned from here to E. 229*b*
dazzles at it, as at e. 447*b*
deserts of vast e. 260*a*
E. in an hour 29*a*
E. is in love with..time 31*a*
E. shut in a span 115*a*
E.'s too short to utter 2*a*
e.! thou pleasing, dreadful thought 1*b*
e. was in our lips 322*b*
e. was in that moment 104*b*
from the hid battlements of E. 442*a*
I gave you e. 390*a*
intimates e. to man 1*b*
into E., at night will return 80*a*
I saw E. the other night 448*b*
lives in E.'s sunrise 30*b*
make the mighty ages of e. 82*a*
memorial from the Soul's e. 311*b*
opes the palace of E. 266*b*
out of E. this new Day 80*a*
passing thro' nature to e. 329*b*
Pilgrim of E. 392*a*
rise to all e. 455*b*
sells e. to get a toy 386*b*
silence is deep as E. 80*a*
Silence is of E. 81*b*
skill'd to sing of Time or E. 427*a*
Soul that art the e. of thought 465*b*
speak of e. without a solecism 41*b*
spy some shadows of e. 448*a*
'stablished its borders unto all e. 231*a*
stains the white radiance of E. 392*b*
sweet e. of love 189*b*
tease us out of thought as doth e. 219*b*
the image of e. 69*b*
the latest flakes of E. 24*a*
the sabbaths of E. 438*a*
thoughts that wander thro' e. 272*b*
throughout all E., I forgive you 31*b*
troubles..are from e. 200*a*
types and symbols of E. 471*a*
ultimate outpost of e. 312*a*
where I to thee E. shall give 137*b*
where the day joins the past E. 69*a*
Ethelberta breathed a sort of exclamation 180*b*
Ether: an ampler e. 467*b*
bottle labelled 'E.' 46*a*
thro' delicatest e. feathering 294*b*
Etherized: like a patient e. 144*b*
Ethiop: jewel in an E.'s ear 365*a*
swear Juno but an E. were 345*a*
Ethiopian change his skin 503*b*
Etiquette: isn't e. to cut anyone 85*b*
Eton: E. boys grown heavy 305*a*
playing-fields of E. 454*b*
Etrurian: th' E. shades 271*b*
Ettrick: march, E. and Teviotdale 320*a*
Euclid: E. alone has looked on Beauty 266*a*
worked a love-story..into..E. 136*a*
Eugene: our good Prince E. 406*a*
Eugene Aram: E., tho' a thief 75*b*
E. walked between 196*a*
Eunuch: e. Castlereagh 70*a*
kind of moral e. 397*a*
Time's e. 198*a*
Euphelia serves to grace 306*a*
Eureka! (I have found!) 559*a*
Euripides: chorus-ending from E. 45*a*
our E., the human 44*a*
Europe: better fifty years of E. 432*b*
England has saved..E. by her example 297*b*
E. is disclosed as a prone..figure 179*b*
E. made his woe her own 6*a*
E.'s Liberator—still enslaved 71*b*
glory of E. is extinguished 57*a*
lamps are going out all over E. 177*a*
slain this year in E. 450*a*
Spain, or any prince of E. 145*a*
that sheep-worry of E. 38*a*
the sick man of E., the Turk 564*b*
through E. to the Aetolian shore 6*a*
where will E.'s latter hour 6*b*
Eurydice: half-regained E. 269*a*
Eustace is a man no longer 226*b*
Evaded: revolutions are not to be e. 129*a*
Evangelist: honour unto Luke E. 312*b*
seal'd the lips of that E. 430*a*
Eve: a child of our grandmother E. 344*b*
as thro' the land at e. we went 436*a*
bat that flits at close of e. 29*a*
E. from his side arose 528*a*
E., with her basket 192*a*
E., with her body white 192*a*
every e. I say 36*b*
fairest of her daughters E. 274*a*
from noon to dewy e. 272*a*
in dim Eden by E.'s nightingales 119*a*
like a toad, close at the ear of E. 274*b*
nor E. the rites mysterious 274*b*
old..as the story of Adam and E. 47*b*
one of E.'s family 195*b*
O pensive E. 103*a*
shd. God create another E. 276*b*
so curses all E.'s daughters 356*a*
the fallen sons of E. 93*b*
the son of Adam and of E. 305*b*
the tranquil hour, purpureal E. 464*a*
thy breathing tresses, meekest E. 103*a*
to E.: Be soon 441*b*
we lose our Edens, E. and I 52*b*
when Adam delved and E. span 178*b*, 527*b*
when E. upon the first of Men 194*b*
Evejar: spins the brown e. 263*b*
Evelyn Hope is dead 46*b*
Even: at e. ere the sun 447*a*
at e. thou shalt say 494*b*
deep and crisp and e. 286*b*
depth of waters stilled at e. 311*b*
gie me a canny hour at e. 60*b*
grey-hooded E. like a sad votarist 267*a*
I was heavy with the e. 441*b*
the last pale beam of e. 399*a*
would God it were e. 494*b*
Even-fall: brought him home at e. 436*b*
Evening: addressed its e. hours 415*a*
all that ever went with e. dress 234*a*
and yet the E. listens 221*a*
but in the e. it is cut down 487*b*
come in the e., or..in the morning 118*a*
dews of the e. most carefully shun 91*a*
each e. sees it close 249*a*
e. and the morning..the first day 492*a*
e. full of linnets' wings 475*b*
e. is spread out against the sky 144*b*
e. must usher night 392*a*
e. on the olden..Sea of Wales 154*b*
here comes the cool of..e. 405*b*
in the e. withhold not thine hand 499*b*
it is a beauteous e. 467*a*
it was a summer's e. 406*a*
like an e. gone 453*a*
mid the cool airs of e. lay 282*b*
never morning wore to e. 429*b*
now came still e. on 274*a*
quiet-coloured end of e. smiles 48*a*
sadly descends the autumn e. 7*b*
Soup of the e., beautiful Soup 83*a*
sweet the coming on of grateful e. 274*b*
the e. of my age 313*b*
those e. bells! those e. bells! 282*a*
to his labour: until the e. 488*b*

Evening (*cont.*)
  wearing out life's e. gray 211*b*
  welcome peaceful e. in 112*a*
  when e. shuts 50*b*
  when it is e., ye say..fair weather 507*a*
  wish him a rainy e. to read this 450*a*
  yr. shadow at e. rising to meet you 144*b*
Evenings: he comes on chosen e. 137*b*
  long dark autumn-e. come 45*a*
Evening-star: moon's and e.'s at once 48*a*
Evensong: belles ringeth to e. 182*b*
  day has run but to the e. 189*a*
  dead herself ere e. 529*b*
Event: an e. has happened 56*a*
  heaviness foreruns the good e. 380*b*
  one e. happeneth to them all 499*a*
  one far-off divine e. 431*a*
Eventide: fast falls the e. 251*b*
Events: coming e. cast their shadows 77*a*
  I claim not to have controlled e. 245*a*
  many e. in the womb of time 360*b*
  terrible e. are welcome 324*b*
Ever: e. of thee I'm fondly dreaming 245*b*
  for e., and for e., farewell, Cassius 341*a*
  for e. with the Lord 280*a*
  gone for e. and e. by 433*b*
  grow for e. and for e. 436*a*
  long life: even for e. and e. 483*a*
  now, and e. shall be 478*a*
  what *never*? hardly e.! 166*a*
Everlasting: corn..stood from e. to e. 445*a*
  e. things that matter 245*b*
  I choose an e. night 133*a*
  I have caught an e. cold 454*b*
  shineth the e. light 40*a*
  the E. had not fix'd his canon 330*a*
  thy e. mercy, Christ 262*a*
Everlastingness: shoots of e. 448*a*
Everybody: always suspect e. 125*a*
  business of e. is..of nobody 254*a*
  e. does too much 186*a*
  e. has his own theatre 181*a*
  e. saw with joy 192*b*
  e.'s business is nobody's business 450*b*
Everyone: e. is more or less mad 237*b*
  e. suddenly burst out singing 316*a*
  e. will say, as you walk yr...way 165*a*
  God bless us e. 121*b*
  stop e. from doing it 186*a*
  let's find out what e. is doing 186*a*
  when e. is somebodee 163*b*
Everything: a place for e., and e. in
      its place 403*a*
  e. almost wh. is Nature's 398*b*
  e. by starts, and nothing long 138*b*
  e. did banish moan 20*b*
  e. goes contrary 121*b*
  e...is good for something 141*b*
  e. that heard him play 385*b*
  e. that lives, lives not alone 29*b*
  he wd. know something of e. 524*a*
  let e. that hath breath 490*b*
  sans e. 326*b*
  to e. there is a season 499*a*
  with e. that pretty is 328*a*
Everywhere: e. that Mary went 177*b*
  Heaven is e. at home 92*b*
  out of the into here 256*a*
  what is e...believed 554*b*
Eves: summer e. by haunted stream 269*a*
Evidence: circumstantial e. is..con-
      vincing 135*b*
  compell'd..to give in e. 334*b*
  faith..the e. of things not seen 517*a*
  it's not e. 126*b*
  some circumstantial e. is..strong 444*a*
Evil: all constraint..is e. 112*b*
  all partial e., universal good 301*a*
  all..they imagine is to do me e. 485*b*
  because their deeds were e. 510*b*
  be not overcome of e. 513*b*
  better is by e. still made better 389*a*
  by e. report and good report 515*a*
  care not..a man is Good or E. 30*b*
  charity..thinketh no e. 514*b*
  clear the land of e. 234*b*
  coppersmith did me much e. 516*b*
  deliver us from e. 505*b*
  do e., that good may come 513*a*
  done this e. in thy sight 485*a*
  eschew e., and do good 484*a*

Evil (*cont.*)
  E. be thou my Good 273*b*
  e. is present with me 513*a*
  e. is wrought by want of thought 196*a*
  e. wh. I wd. not, that I do 513*a*
  forgiveness free of e. done 228*a*
  government..is but a necessary e. 291*b*
  his good and his e. 62*b*
  hypocrisy, the only e. 273*b*
  I will fear no e. 483*a*
  know how to refuse the e. 501*b*
  knowledge of good and e. 492*a*
  love of money is the root of all e. 516*b*
  maketh his sun to rise on the e. 505*a*
  man's heart is e. from his youth 492*b*
  no man is justified in doing e. 310*b*
  not rendering e. for e. 517*b*
  obscures the show of e. 354*a*
  of moral e. and of good 471*b*
  punishment..prevention from e. 258*a*
  resist not e. 505*a*
  some soul of goodness in things e. 382*b*
  spirits..wh. serve things e. 397*a*
  still to find means of e. 271*a*
  sufficient unto the day is the e. 505*b*
  the e. that men do lives after 339*b*
  them that call e. good 501*a*
  there shall no e. happen unto thee 487*b*
  this heart, all e. shed away 40*a*
  thing of e.—prophet still 298*b*
  tho' fall'n on e. days 275*a*
  tongue..is an unruly e. 517*b*
  to resist the e. and the good to do 3*a*
  Vice itself lost half its e. 57*a*
  what all the blessed E.'s for 57*a*
  with Predestined E. round enmesh 154*a*
  wi' tippenny, we fear nae e. 63*a*
Evils: death..the least of all e. 16*b*
  don't let us make imaginary e. 170*b*
  must expect new e. 15*b*
  notes are..necessary e. 213*b*
  pitch our e. there 351*b*
  torments..from e...never arrived 147*a*
  two weak e., age and hunger 326*b*
  turn from us all those e. 479*a*
  when e. are most free 338*b*
Evolution: e. is a change for..homo-
      geneity 408*a*
  some call it e. 86*a*
Evolved: imperfectly e. in our heads 390*b*
Ewa-yea my little owlet 248*b*
Ewe: black ram is tupping yr...e. 359*b*
  whereof the e. not bites 367*a*
Ewer: as safe in a golden e. 46*a*
Ewes: my e. breed not 21*a*
Ewigheit: afay in de e. 244*b*
Exact: greatness not to be e. 55*a*
Exactness: with e. grinds he all 248*a*
Exaggerated: reports of my death..
      e. 573*a*
Exalt: whosoever shall e. himself 507*b*
Exalted: e. them of low degree 508*b*
  humble himself shall be e. 507*b*
  knock at a star with my e. head 189*b*
Exalteth: whosoever e. himself 509*b*
Exalts: what man does wh. e. him 51*b*
Examinations are formidable 103*b*
Examine me, O Lord 483*b*
Example: e. is..more efficacious 213*b*
  e. is the school of mankind 58*a*
  George III..profit by their e. 185*b*
  lower orders..set us a good e. 460*a*
  many an error, by the same e. 354*b*
  my great e., as it is my theme 119*b*
Exampled by the first Pace 368*b*
Excavating for a mine 280*b*
Excel: Bethlehem thou dost all e. 86*b*
  by different methods..men e. 94*b*
  crime's so great as daring to e. 94*b*
  teach others who themselves e. 300*a*
  where none admire, 'tis useless to e. 251*b*
Excellence: faults..nearly allied to e. 170*b*
  in new e. divine is old forgot? 36*a*
  stewards of their e. 388*b*
Excellency of art..is its intensity 222*a*
Excellent: embodiment of everything
      that's e. 163*b*
  e. herbs had our fathers 233*a*
  'E.!' I cried. 'Elementary' 135*b*
  e. thing in woman 344*a*
  e. wretch!..but I do love thee 361*b*

Excellent (*cont.*)
  learning is most e. 155*b*
  nature never makes e. things 246*a*
  the things that are more e. 452*b*
Excelling: distinction of e. in his
      kind 104*a*
  Silvia is e. 372*b*
Excels: she e. each mortal thing 372*b*
Excelsior: strange device, E.! 247*a*
Except: e. my life 332*a*
  e. the Lord build the house 489*b*
  e. the present company 290*b*
Exception: admits not some e. 64*a*
Excess: best things carried to e. 95*a*
  e. leads to the palace of wisdom 31*a*
  e. of glory obscur'd 272*a*
  give me e. of it 369*b*
  nothing in e. 560*b*
  not the drinking..but the e. 321*a*
  so much poverty and e. 295*b*
  surprise by a fine e. 222*b*
  there is moderation even in e. 130*a*
  to some divine e. 103*a*
  wasteful and ridiculous e. 374*a*
  wise thro' e. of wisdom 148*a*
Exchange: by just e. one for the other 401*b*
  I wd. not e. thy sullen skies 111*b*
Excise: a hateful tax 212*b*
Exciseman: other an e. 170*b*
  The De'il's Awa' Wi' the E. 60*a*
Exciting: he found it less e. 163*a*
Exclaim no more against it 361*b*
Excommunicate from all the joys 79*b*
Excursion: frowzy poem..the 'E.' 71*a*
Excuse: an e. for the glass 400*b*
  began to make e. 509*b*
  denial vain, and coy e. 269*a*
  surely he's without e. 527*b*
  'tis an e. every man will plead 321*a*
Excused: I pray thee have me e. 509*b*
Execution: fitter for e. than counsel 16*a*
  their stringent e. 173*a*
  there shall be due E. upon them 491*a*
  wh. smok'd with bloody e. 346*a*
Executions: marriage and public e. 130*a*
Executive: legislative..nominated by
      the e. 162*a*
Executors: delivering o'er to e. pale 381*b*
  let's choose e., and talk of wills 375*b*
Exercise: bear my..sword when I do e. 108*b*
  I do not e. myself in great matters 490*a*
  sad mechanic e. 429*a*
  the wise, for cure, on e. depend 140*a*
  what e. is to the body 410*b*
Exeter: Bedford and E. 383*a*
Exhalation: fabric huge rose like an e. 272*a*
  fled like some frail e. 392*b*
Exhausted: e. worlds..imagin'd new 213*b*
  range of e. volcanoes 128*b*
Exhausting thought..hiving wisdom 68*b*
Exile: a kiss long as my e. 328*b*
  a poor E. of Erin 76*b*
  bind yr. sons to e. 236*b*
  therefore I die in e. 541*a*
  twelve years..he suffered in e. 261*a*
Exiles: e. from our fathers' land 320*b*
  Paradise of e., Italy 395*a*
  woe wh. none save e. feel 12*b*
Existence: before we have e. 238*b*
  discuss..the struggle for e. 117*b*
  every e. wd. exist in Thee 38*b*
  e. is a mere miracle 413*b*
  e. saw him spurn her..reign 213*b*
  let us contemplate e. 124*a*
  when e. or when hope is gone 11*b*
  woman's whole e. 70*a*
Exit: e., pursued by a bear 373*a*
  shakes his head, and e. 400*a*
Exits: doors for men to take their e. 454*b*
  they have their e. 326*b*
Exorciser: no e. harm thee 329*a*
Expanse: grey e. where he floats 6*a*
  oft of one wide e. had I been told 220*b*
Expansion: not..a breach, but an e. 134*a*
Expatiates in a life to come 300*b*
Expect: country that eager hearts e. 286*a*
  folly to e. men to do all 456*a*
  how can he e. that others shd. 470*a*
  what else did you e.? 46*b*
  what we least e. 129*b*
  you'd scarce e. one of my age 149*b*

ENGLISH INDEX

Expectancy and rose of the fair state 333b
Expectant. e. of her 440b
  e. wee thing 59b
Expectation: a good plot..full of e. 377a
  bids e. rise 168a
  e., and desire 469b
  e. whirls me round 369a
  he hath..better bettered e. 358a
  now sits E. in the air 381b
  singing songs of e. 20b
Expectations: worthy ends and e. 14a
Expected: reasonably be e. to do 456a
Expects: blessed..who e. nothing 304a
  England e. every man 287a
Expediency: evil on the ground of e. 310b
Expedient: all things are not e. 514b
  e. for you that I go 511a
  it is e. for us..one man shd. die 511a
  to pursue the e. 169b
Expel: one passion..doth e. another 87b
Expenditure nineteen nineteen six 122a
Expense: drinking at somebody else's
  e. 244b
  moan the e. of..a vanish'd sight 387b
  repay the trouble and e. 25b
  who wd. be at the e. of two? 96b
Expenses of living 444a
Expensive: I love fruit when it's e. 297a
Experience: by e. wise 303a
  by long e., and in learned schools 3b
  can go beyond his e. 246a
  dirty nurse, E. 428b
  e. is an arch wherethro' gleams 438b
  e. is never limited 204b
  e. is the child of Thought 130a
  e. is the name..to their mistakes 460a
  e. joined with common sense 175b
  e. keeps a dear school 157b
  e. of woman..over many nations 136a
  e. teaches slowly 157b
  great e. of this world 145a
  insight..worth a life's e. 194b
  knowledge..recorded e. 80a
  Old Age and E. 309b
  perfected by e. 16a
  till old e. do attain 268b
  travel..is..a part of e. 15a
  triumph of hope over e. 208a
  true e. from this great event 278a
Experienced: nothing..real till..e. 223a
Experientia does it 122a
Experiment: a great social..e. 196b
  desist from the e. in despair 238b
  full tide of successful e. 204b
  political e. of democracy 390b
Expiate: death my days shd. e. 387a
Expire: I tremble, I e. 393b
Expires: blazes, and e. 72b
  the wretched child e. 26a
Expiring: thus e. do foretell of him 374b
Explain: e. his explanation 70a
  I can e. all the poems 85a
  I can't e. *myself* 82b
Explanation: explain his e. 70a
Explanations: I do loathe e. 21b
Expletives their feeble aid do join 300a
Exploit: for dignity..and high e. 272a
Exploration: chant of pleasant e. 457b
Exposed: more e. to suffering 465a
  much e. to authors 455a
  on the bare earth e. he lies 139a
Exposes himself when..intoxicated 210a
Exposition of sleep 357a
Exposure: unseemly e. of the mind 183b
Express: beauty..picture cannot e. 16a
  may I e. thee unblamed 273a
  speech..not..to e. our wants 170b
Expressed: but ne'er so well e. 300a
Expresses: art never e. anything 460a
  e. himself in terms too deep 165a
Expression: e. of no-encouragement 35a
  e. wh. displeased us 171a
  his e. may often be called bald 9b
  with an indolent e. 26b
Expressions: notions, and gentle e. 214b
Expressive: eyes too e. to be blue 5b
Expunged: Nature's works to me e. 273b
Exquisite: a cigarette..is e. 460b
  most e. and strong 289b
Extend from here to Mesopotamy 75b
Extensive and peculiar 126a

Extent: e. of its beauty and power 255b
  hath this e., no more 360a
Extenuate: speak of me as I am; nothing e. 364a
Extinction of unhappy hates 6b
Extinguished: Nature is..seldom e. 16a
Extirpate: to the e. vipers 12b
Extolled: admirals, e. for standing still 111a
Extravagancies: undisgraced by..e. 90b
Extravagant and erring spirit 329a
Extreme: if thou, Lord, wilt be e. 490a
  in quest to have, e. 389a
Extremes: e. by change more fierce 272b
  'e. meet', as the whiting said 196b
  must we toil in other men's e. 238b
  two e. of passion, joy and grief 344a
  two e., of too much stiffness 478a
Extremity: a daring pilot in e. 138a
Exuberance of his own verbosity 128b
Exult: we shall e., if they who rule 468a
Exultation: moods of shadowy e. 469b
Exultations: thy friends are e. 472b
Exulting: the people all e. 457b
Eye: adds..seeing to the e. 345a
  a drappie in our e. 63b
  a hooded e. 441a
  a microscopic e. 300b
  an e. will mark our coming 70a
  as the great e. of heaven shined 408b
  a still-soliciting e. 341b
  a wit in his own e. 104b
  aye the tear comes in my e. 59a
  beam that is in thine own e. 505b
  beauteous e. of heaven to garnish 374a
  beauty is bought by..the e. 344b
  bids the rash gazer wipe his e. 187b
  blow the horrid deed in every e. 347a
  crowned head, the vigilant e. 328a
  cursed me with his e. 99a
  curse in a dead man's e. 99a
  custom loathsome to the e. 204a
  dark and fiery e. 289b
  Dead Sea fruits, that tempt the e. 282a
  dull e. of scorn 37b
  each under e. doth homage 387a
  elles the e. of day 90a
  enter into life with one e. 507a
  ever changing, like a joyous e. 396a
  every e. shall see him 518a
  e. beholds the heart's desire 198b
  e. for e., tooth for tooth 494a
  e. full of gentle salutations 412a
  e. is not satisfied with seeing 499a
  e. made quiet by the power 472a
  e. of man hath not heard 357b
  e. sees in it what the e. brings 80b
  e. with wh. the Universe beholds 392b
  fair large front and e. sublime 274a
  far as human e. cd. see 432b
  far from e. or ear 422a
  fettered to her e. 249b
  flash upon that inward e. 467b
  fool in the e. of the world 104b
  friendly e. cd. never see..faults 341a
  fringed curtains of thine e. 367b
  full e., small head 386b
  gently shuts the e. of day 18b
  glad me with its soft black e. 282a
  glass to his sightless e. 287b
  glazed each weary e. 98b
  guard me with a watchful E. 2a
  harvest of a quiet e. 469a
  have you not a moist e. 379b
  heavenly rhetoric of thine e. 344b
  he had but one e. 124b
  he had by nature a tarnishing e. 264b
  he that made the e. 487b
  his e. was backward cast 408b
  his liberal e. doth give 382b
  Homer..with his e. on the object 10a
  if thine e. offend thee 507a
  I have a good e., uncle 358a
  I have neither e. to see 244b
  I have only one e. 287a
  in my great Task-Master's e. 278b
  in my mind's e., Horatio 330a
  interest unborrowed from the e. 472a
  in the twinkling of an e. 515a

Eye (cont.)
  into the e. and prospect of his soul 359a
  lend the e. a terrible aspect 382a
  Lesbia hath a beaming e. 281b
  let thine e. look like a friend 329b
  lifting up the lid of a white e. 263b
  long grey beard and glittering e. 98a
  looked with such a wistful e. 459b
  looking on it with lack-lustre e. 326a
  love-light in yr. e. 28b
  many an e. has danced to see 194a
  mild and magnificent e. 48a
  mine e. may be deceived 388b
  mountain-tops with sovereign e. 387b
  mote that is in thy brother's e. 505b
  my left e. agin the Secesher's fist 451a
  my striving e. dazzles at it 447b
  never a tear bedims the e. 182a
  never e., did see that face 313b
  nor let His e. see sin 155b
  now I see with e. serene 470b
  now mine e. seeth thee 497b
  one auspicious..one dropping e. 329b
  pious drops the closing e. requires 174b
  piping yr. e. 120b
  places that the e. of heaven visits 374a
  press onward, for thine e. shall see 37a
  reverent e. must see a purpose 39a
  rude e. of rebellion 374b
  said the Fly, with my little e. 528a
  sail and sail, with unshut e. 5b
  since first yr. e. I eyed 388b
  so enquiring e. 241a
  sun..blinks blithe in my e. 116b
  take a sober colouring from an e. 467a
  tender e. of pitiful day 349a
  that most seeming-virtuous e. 73a
  that same e. whose bend doth awe 337b
  that sun, thine e. 387b
  the e. begins to see 39a
  the fruitful river in the e. 330a
  then can I drown an e. 387b
  then saw her e. was bright 97b
  there's language in her e. 369a
  the seeing e. 498b
  the sober e. of dull Octavia 325a
  the tear blinded his e. 529b
  they shall see e. to e. 502b
  thou E. among the blind 466b
  thoughts are legible in the e. 313b
  'tis the e. of childhood that fears 348a
  too hot the e. of heaven shines 387a
  trambeams truckle at the e. 197b
  view with hollow e. 355a
  what immortal hand or e. 31b
  where thy grey e. glances 298a
  who sees with equal e., as God 300b
  wink the other e. 162b
  with his glittering e. 98a
  with his keener e. 261a
  with, not thro', the e. 30a
  world of e. and ear 472a
  yr. finger in yr. e. 533a
  you went with..frightened e. 294a
  you dazzle my e. 292b
Eyeball: like a coal his e. 403a
  the scaled e. 52a
Eyeballs: my e. roll 299b
Eyebrow: ballad..to his mistress' e. 326b
Eyebrows: over her e. hiding her eyes 420b
Eyeing: a happiness in e. 202b
Eyeless in Gaza 277b
Eyelids: e. are a little weary 292b
  I read, before my e. dropt 426b
  my lips and e. pale 394b
  take thee with her e. 498a
  the opening e. of the morn 269a
  tinged the e. and the hands 293a
  tired e. upon tired eyes 433a
  wilt weigh mine e. down 380a
  with e. heavy and red 196a
Eyes: as in a theatre, the e. of men 376a
  as long as her e. cd. see 198b
  as 'twere in scorn of e. 384b
  Bacchus with pink e. 323b
  beams from happy human e. 415a
  before my closing e. 251b
  before his streaming e. 84b
  bein' only e...my wision's limited 126b
  bend on me, then, thy tender e. 252a
  brave, joyful e. 37b

Eyes (*cont.*)

bright e. of danger	414a
bright e. of the dear one	73b
bring all Heaven before mine e.	268b
burnt the fire of thine e.	32a
cannot keep her lustrous e.	220a
censured by our e.	259a
closed his e. in endless night	175a
close up his e.	384a
close yr. e. with holy dread	101b
cocking their medical e.	127b
cynosure of neighbouring e.	269a
daily swallowed by men's e.	378a
darkness..no more assail mine e.	119a
death bandaged my e.	50b
do me e. deceive me earsight?	451a
dress her beauty at yr. e.	117b
drink to me only with thine e.	216a
dry yr. e.—O dry yr. e.	218a
elves also,—whose little e. glow	189b
e. all the smiling family	443b
e., and eares, and ev'ry thought	313b
e., and tears, be the same things	260b
e. have they, and see not	489a
e. like the fishpools in Heshbon	500b
e., lips, and hands to miss	134a
e., look yr. last!	366b
e. of conjugal attraction	274a
e. of gold and bramble-dew	414b
e. of most unholy blue!	281b
e. of the garden-god	421b
e. overrunning with laughter	246b
e. swol'n with weeping	260b
e. that wd. not look on me	400a
e. the greenest of things blue	421b
e. too expressive to be blue	5b
e. were blind with stars	192b
e. were darkened wholly	432a
e. were made for seeing	147a
e. were sealed to the holy book	6a
e. where all perfections keep	524a
faculties of e. and ears	333a
fair maidens quiet e.	414b
faith in their happy e.	27a
fills the faint e. with falling tears	397a
foe that comes with fearless e.	287b
four beasts full of e.	518b
frightened look in its e.	402a
from her e. I did receive..messages	352b
from star-like e., doth seek fuel	79a
from women's e. this doctrine	345a
full of e. within	518b
gather to the e.	436a
get thee glass e.	343b
girl with a pair of blue e.	400b
God be in my e.	523a
good for sore e.	418b
grat his e. baith bleer't	60a
happiness thro' another man's e.	327b
hast no speculation in those e.	349a
hath not a Jew e.?	354a
he always said my e. were blue	241b
her eyebrows hiding her e.	426b
her e. are homes of..prayer	430a
her e. as stars of twilight	470b
her e. the gazers strike	302b
her e. the glow-worm lend thee	189b
her e. were deeper than the depth	311b
her e. were wild	218b
her longing e. are blest	415b
her own dying smile instead of e.	392a
her own e. might see him slain	284a
he set her booth his e.	251b
his e. drop out	246a
his e. grow in my brow	323a
his e. went to and fro	99b
his e. were as a flame	518b
his e. were with his heart	69a
his flashing e., his floating hair	101b
his great e. lights the wigwam	248b
his sullen e. set on yr. own	233a
how far yr. e. may pierce	342a
hunt for haddocks' e.	85b
I cast mine e. and see that..vibration	190b
I gave her e. my own e.	48a
I have no e. but constitutional	245b
I'll pike out his bonny blue e.	529b
in the optics of these e.	41b
in the stars the glory of His e.	297b

Eyes (*cont.*)

I shut her wild, wild e.	219a
it dazzled their e.	531a
item, two grey e.	370a
it is engendered in the e.	354a
I was e. to the blind	497a
kindling her undazzled e.	279a
labour-dimmed e.	6b
ladies, whose bright e.	269a
land of darkness and blind e.	447b
let's dry our e.	386a
let waking e. suffice to wail	117a
lids of Juno's e.	373a
lie heavily upon her e.	311a
lift up mine e. unto the hills	489b
lift up thine e.	279b
lightened are our e.	406a
light of knowledge in their e.	424a
light, that lies in woman's e.	281b
lion's ruddy e. shall flow	33a
little shadows come about her e.	475a
Lo! as that youth's e. burned	312b
look'd from thoughtful e.	294a
looked with human e.	430b
love-darting e.	267b
love doth to her e. repair	372b
love, first learned in a lady's e.	345a
love looks not with the e.	356a
lover's e. will gaze an eagle	345a
love's tongue is in the e.	155b
make thy two e...start	331a
man with large grey e.	471b
Mary-buds..ope their golden e.	328b
meet in her aspect and her e.	74a
men's e. were made to look	365b
mind has a thousand e.	34a
mine e. dazzle	454a
mine e. do itch	363a
mine e. from tears	489a
mine e. have seen the glory	200b
mine e. their vigils keep	286b
mine e. will tell tales	370a
mock our e. with air	324a
mocks the dark lustre of thine e.	317b
my e. are dim with childish tears	465a
my e. are tired of weeping	38b
my e. for beauty pine	37a
my e. make pictures	100b
my e., my lord, can look as swift	354a
my gushing e. o'erflow	299b
my hand before my e.	26a
my mistress' e. are nothing	389a
my mother came into mine e.	383a
night hath a thousand e.	34a, 251b
no longer blinded by our e.	39b
not a friend to close his e.	139a
not..the East, but from thine e.	114b
o'er her meek e. came a..mist	427b
oh e., no e., but fountains	238b
Oh, e. sublime, with tears	44a
O lovers' e. are sharp	317b
one of his e. became so terrible	23b
one praised her ankles, one her e.	425b
one whose subdued e...drop tears	364a
on his grave, with shining e.	7a
O turn away mine e.	489a
O! when mine e. did see Olivia	369b
pearls that were his e.	367a
peep thro' their e. and laugh	352b
persuade the e. of men	386b
pictures in our e. to get	132b
poor kind wild e.	421a
proud of those two e.	190a
pure e. and Christian hearts	224a
rapt soul sitting in thine e.	268a
royal master saw, with heedful e.	445b
scornful, yet with jealous e.	303a
see the whites of their e.	307a
seel up the ship-boy's e.	380a
seven horns and seven e.	518b
she gave me e., she gave me ears	471a
show his e., and grieve his heart	349b
sights of..death within mine e.	384b
sight of lidless e. in Hell	312a
slepen al the night with open e.	88a
soft e. looked love	68a
soft look yr. e. had once	476b
stately maid, whose e. were kindled	146b
streaming e. and breaking hearts	433a
strike mine e., but not my heart	215a
stuck full of e.	379a

Eyes (*cont.*)

such e. the widows in Corioli wear	328a
swellin' wisibly before my wery e.	126b
take a pair of sparkling e.	163b
tempts yr. wandering e.	173b
that poorly satisfy our e.	473b
the e. that had lightened	421b
the e. that shone	282b
the e. to behold the sun	499b
the Jabberwock, with e. of flame	84a
the justice..with e. severe	326b
the King..with judicious e.	445a
these e. to behold felicity	41b
these weeping e., those seeing tears	260b
the very e. of me	190a
they have changed e.	367b
they're painted to the e.	131a
they see with their e.	501b
thine e. break from their East	115a
this world goes with no e.	343b
those e., the break of day	352a
thou hast doves' e.	500a
thy dying e. were closed	299a
thy e. are seen in di'monds	161a
tired eyelids upon tired e.	433a
to cast one's e. so low	343b
to dry one's e. and laugh	48a
to tear each other's e.	452b
turn't mine e. into my very soul	335a
two pitch balls..for eyes	344b
two lovely black e.	97a
unfriendly to the nose and e.	415a
violets blue as yr. e.	434a
walk with..wanton e.	501a
what her e. enthrall'd	104a
where'er with haggard e. I view	79a
when I cast mine e. and see	190b
when to the new e. of thee	442b
when unto dying e.	436a
when with eagle e. he star'd	220b
where did you get yr. so blue?	256a
where'er these casual e. are cast	407a
where e. did once inhabit	384b
whereso'er I turn my ravished e.	1b
where you turn yr. e.	302b
while I have e. to see	190a
who hast given me e. to see	224a
whom these wakeful e. may weep	241a
wid e. so shiny blue	410a
wipe away all tears from their e.	519b
wipe my weeping e.	453b
with cold commemorative e.	312b
with erected e. beholds his..skies	142b
with e. as wise, but kindlier	39a
with e. up-rais'd, as one inspir'd	103a
within mine e. he makes his nest	176a
with longing e. I wait	440b
with magic in my e.	180a
with rainy e. write sorrow	375b
with their own e. shd. see	39a
with unuplifted e. to pace	468a
Wordsworth's e. avert their ken	7a
write the beauty of yr. e.	387a
yes, I have a pair of e.	126b
you see her e. are open	350a
young e. grew sudden fair	441b
yr. quaint enamell'd e.	270a
Eyne: Bacchus with pink e.	323b
Eyeservice: not with e.	516a
Eyesight: e. and speech	420b
with blinded e. poring	432b

F

F.: revere the memory of Mr. F.	123a
Fable: but that's a f.	364a
f. of Bellerus	270a
f., song, or fleeting shade	189a
nocht bot f.	19a
read my little f.	427a
what resounds in f. or romance	271b
when life's sweet f. ends	115a
Fables: blasphemous f.	491b
f. and endless genealogies	516b
Hesperian f. true	274a
I had rather believe all the f.	15a
Martin Luther bloomed f.	52b
old wives' f.	516b
worse than f. yet have feigned	272b

Fabric: a f. huge rose 272a
baseless f. of this vision 367b
his f. of the Heavens hath left 275b
of quality and f. more divine 470a
silently as a dream the f. rose 112b
the f. of superstition 57b
whole social f. wd. fly asunder 391a
Fabricius: F. finds certain spots 64a
Romans under . . F. 13b
Face: all will spy in thy f. 132b
am I in f. to-day? 170b
anoint and cheer our soiled f. 491a
a spirit passed before my f. 497a
Babe look't up and shew'd his f. 114b
beautiful f. is a commendation 13b
beauty . . shall pass into her f. 471b
beefy an' grubby 'and 232a
before I knew thy f. or name 131b
behold her f. at ample view 369b
beholding his natural f. 517b
bright f. of danger 412a
but then f. to f. 514b
by hir wordes be hir f. 89b
called upon to f. some . . moment 465a
caricature of a f. 165a
corpse . . with a sad swelled f. 19a
disasters in his morning f. 168b
dost thou fall upon thy f.? 364b
drift f. upwards on the oily tide 202b
dust wh. the . . wind blows in yr. f. 343b
each turned his f. 99a
everybody's f. but their own 417a
f. of all the world changed 43b
f. of him that sitteth on the throne 519a
F. of Man is blacken'd 154a
f. that launched a thousand ships 258b
f. that's anything but gay 440b
f. thro' love's long residence 36a
f. to f., silent, drawing nigh 44a
f. to lose youth for 48a
f. with an undaunted tread 414a
fair and open f. of heaven 221a
false f. must hide 347b
Fanny Kelly's divine plain f. 240a
feel . . the mist in my f. 50b
fiery f. as of a child 428a
fondles his own harmless f. 425b
foolish f. of praise 303a
fyr-reed cherubinnes f. 88b
gazed on the f. that was dead 462b
give me a look, give me a f. 215a
give me them that will f. me 377b
give the f. of earth around 414a
God hath given you one f. 333b
good f. is a letter 2a
grey eyes and a pale f. 471b
has a damned Tyburn-f. 104b
has he not a Rogue's f.? 104b
he'd look into thy bonnie f. 59b
he hides a smiling f. 110a
her angel's f. . . shined bright 408b
her f. wad fyle 63b
her f. was full of woe 524a
he shows his honest f. 139a
hid his f. amid a crowd of stars 476b
his f. deep scars of thunder 272a
his f. is all bubukles 382a
his f., that two hours since 438b
His own f. to see 192a
honest sonsie f. 60b
how blubber'd is that pretty f. 305b
huge massy f. 255b
human f. divine 273b
if thou. . never see my f. again 429a
I have seen God f. to f. 493a
I have seen in one Autumnal f. 132a
illumineth the f., wh., as a beacon 380b
in f. of man or maid 441b
in my own f. in the glass 458a
it shall be a F. like my f. 51b
I will pass never turn my f. 53a
I wish I loved its silly f. 308a
Jealousy a human f. 33a
kissing with golden f. the meadows 387b
laid her f. between her hands 311b
languid patience of thy f. 102a
lives on this lonely f. 475b
look on her f., and you'll forget 302b
looks the whole world in the f. 249a
Lord make his f. shine 494a
loved a happy human f. 202a

Face (cont.)
loving thy mournful f. 206a
make the f. of heaven so fine 366a
marvellous hairy about the f. 357a
Maud with her exquisite f. 433b
mind's construction in the f. 346b
modesty wd. float f. down 202b
Monday's child is fair of f. 525a
my f. is my fortune 525b
my f. is pink, my hair is sleek 528b
my f., yr. flower 46b
Nature, with that homely f. 463b
night's starr'd f. 221a
not a trace upon her f. 164b
no. . transmitter of a foolish f. 316a
of finer form or lovelier f. 316a
oft he seems to hide his f. 278a
peered with broad and burning f. 98b
Pity a human f. 33a
recognize me by my f. 445b
sages have seen in thy f. 113a
same f. of his wedded wife 237b
sang a kindred soul out to his f. 51a
see a glimpse of His bright f. 448a
seek His F. 279b
seek no wonder but the human f. 218a
see my Pilot f. to f. 426a
sees the other's umber'd f. 382b
set my ten commandments in yr. f. 384a
set upon it a good f. 18a
she has a lovely f. 432a
she looked in my f. 20b
she painted her f. 496b
shining morning f. 326b
showed the paint, but hid the f. 140a
shown no glorious morning f. 415a
since first I saw yr. f. 526a
since I no mwore do zee yr. f. 21a
smiling f. a-dream of Spring 102a
so exquisitely fair a f. 167a
so sweet a f., such angel grace 425b
sorrow of yr. changing f. 476b
sprinkles another's laughing f. 241a
still we find her f. 49a
tears run down his dappled f. 443b
that moment that his f. I see 100a
that one F., far from vanish 44b
that very f. 416a
the f. of this tall pile 104b
the f. the index of a . . mind 114a
the flower-like f. 422b
the garden of yr. f. 186b
there is a garden in her f. 78b
they that lovely f. who view 6b
thrusts the thing . . in our f. 43a
thy f. across his fancy comes 436a
thy hyacinth hair, thy classic f. 298a
thy most kiss-worthy f. 401b
two strong men stand f. to f. 227a
upon the f. of the waters 492a
visit her f. too roughly 330a
was never eye, did see that f. 313b
was never f. so pleased 156a, 526b
with his prism and silent f. 469b
with twain he covered his f. 501b
where's the f. one wd. meet 218a
white f. in the coffin 457b
with how wan a f.! 401a
woos me with its crystal f. 68b
ye have a singing f. 23b
you find one f. there 226a
yr. f., and the God-curst sun 180a
yr. f. my quarry was 33b
yr. f., my thane, is as a book 347a
Faces: among so many million of f. 42a
around the man bend other f. 240b
brake them to our f. 43b
cantin', grace-proud f. 61b
daub their natural f. 43a
dusk-f. with white . . turbans 277a
f. are but a gallery of pictures 15b
flame of fair f. 421a
hid as it were our f. 503a
I have seen better f. 342a
I know the f. I shall see 312b
in nice clean f. 19a
in the f. of men and women 458a
lords and owners of their f. 388b
make our f. vizards to our hearts 349a
men have rosy f. 414b
mild monastic f. 96a

Faces (cont.)
ne'er touched earthly f. 387a
new men, strange f. 429a
set yr. f. like a flint 54a
the foreign f. 420a
their f. washed 84a
the old familiar f. 240b
the slope of f. 112a
their innocent f. clean 32b
to the confusion of their own f. 503b
wears almost everywhere two f. 142a
when they turned their f. 253b
with dreadful f. throng'd 277a
you by their f. see 468b
yr. estranged f. 442a
Facey's advertisement 417a
Facility: f. of the octo-syllabic verse 69b
he flowed with that f. 214b
Fact: Death was but a scientific f. 459b
fatal futility of F. 204b
he omitted to mention the f. 85b
judges of f., tho' not. . of laws 306b
man's religion is the chief f. 80b
matters of f. . . very stubborn 444b
push the logic of a f. 229a
when a f. appears opposed 136a
Faction: it made them a f. 255b
Whig. The name of a f. 213a
Factions: good in canvasses and f. 15a
religious f. are volcanoes 56b
Facts: f. alone are wanted in life 123b
F. are chiels 60a
f. are f. and flinch not 51a
fashnable f. and polite annygoats 440a
intelligent anticipation of f. 116b
to his imagination for his f. 401a
what I want is F. 123b
Faculties: descend t'affections, and to f. 132b
his cogitative f. 79b
his f. so meek 347a
souls, whose f. can comprehend 259a
very f. of eyes and ears 333a
Faculty: how infinite in f. 332b
the vision and the f. divine 464a
Faddling hedonist 412b
Fade: elms f. into dimness 7b
f. away suddenly like the grass 487b
f. far away, dissolve 220a
how fast they f. away 3b
I have loved flowers that f. 36b
nothing of him that doth f. 367a
they only f. away 525b
't was the first to f. away 282a
we all do f., as a leaf 503b
when can their glory f.? 426a
where's the cheek that does not f. 218a
wh. was the first to f. away 75b
with thee f. away into the forest 219b
Faded: but a little f. flower 200b
companions are f. and gone 281b
f. on the crowing of the cock 329b
f. splendour wan 274b
she f. like a cloud 392a
she f. 'midst Italian flowers 184b
Fades: f. awa' like morning dew 530a
it f. out from kiss to kiss 494b
now f. the glimmering landscape 174a
until she f. away 93b
whatever f., but fading pleasure 402a
Fading: f. in music 354a
how f. are the joys we doat upon! 289b
she's f. down the river 287b
Fadler: my lady F. 105b
Faeries, dancing under the moon 476b
Faerie Queen: before reading the F. 238b
Faery: full beautiful, a f.'s child 218b
sing a f.'s song 218b
the land of f. 475b
with a f. hand in hand 476a
Fail: and that cannot f. 20a
f. . . completely in the House of Lords 130a
f., Sun and Breath 315a
ground not f. beneath my feet 433b
I faint! I f. 394b
if we shd. f.,—we f.! 347a, 347b
I will not f. thee 494b
I will not f. to meet thee 225a
let no man's heart f. 495b
nat o word wol he f. 89a

Fail (cont.)

not asham'd to f.	213a
sooner f. than not..the greatest	223a
succeed in that it seems to f.	50b
the many f.: the one succeeds	426b
there is no such word as—f.!	252a
when mine f. me, I'll complain	48b
yon auld f. dyke	529b
you're pooty sure to f.	250b

Failed: The Light that F. | 237b
| tried a little, f. much | 412b |
| when thro' weariness they f. | 110a |

Faileth: charity never f. | 514b
| f. now even dream the dreamer | 442a |
| whose goodness f. never | 18a |

Failing: mercy..to every f. but their | |
own	72b
principal f. occurred	86a
she had one f.	61b

Failings: e'en his f. lean'd to Virtue's | 168b

Fails: she never f. to please | 321a

Failure: another Faithful F. | 412b
| pays the f. of years | 44b |

Failures: half the f. in life | 181a

Fain: we are f. of thee | 421a
| would f. see good days | 484a |

Faint: always to pray, and not to f. | 510a
a man, so f., so spiritless	379b
eating hay when you're f.	85a
f. and far away	290a
f. heart never won fair lady	164a
f. not nor fear	279b
f., now, as farewells!	195b
f., yet pursuing	495a
felt f.—and never dared uplift	397a
he was ready to f.	243a
I do f. therefor	442b
the wandering airs they f.	394b
they f. on hill or field	436a
they shall walk, and not f.	502b
we shall reap, if we f. not	515b
with watching and with study f.	94b

Fainted: I shd. utterly have f. | 483b

Faintest: why f. thou? | 9a

Faints: f., entangled in their mazes | 397b
| f. the cold work | 103a |
| the enemy f. not, nor faileth | 96b |

Fair: a f. where thousands meet | 205a
a Mistress moderately f.	107a
all her care was but to be f.	452a
all so excellently f.	100b
all this f., and soft, and sweet	260b
all those f. and flagrant things	114b
anything but what's right and f.	201a
as f. as e'er was seen	462a
Bacchus ever f., and ever young	138b
be f. and yet not fond	120b
behold, thou art f., my love	500a
every f. from f. sometimes declines	387a
f. and f., and twice so f.	295b
f. and softly, John, he cried	108b
f. and wise and good	525a
f. as is the rose in May	90a
f. be their wives, right lovesom	143a
f. daffodils, we weep to see	189a
f., fat, and forty	320a
f. is foul, and foul is f.	345b
f. is too foul an epithet	259b
f. mot she falle	90a
f. stood the wind for France	137a
f. white linen cloth	480a
f. with orchard lawns	429b
groweth to f. instead of plain	36a
heaven not grim but f. of hue	48b
holy, f. and wise is she	372b
how near to good is what is f.	215b
I have found not a gift for my f.	399b
I have sworn thee f.	389b
Irish are a f. people	208b
is she kind as she is f.?	372b
Lady Jane was f.	20a
let me say that thou wert f.	20a
lives a woman true and f.	134a
lose possession of that f.	387a
more than most f.	176b
most faithful f.	426b
never yet was foolish that was f.	360b
not anything to show more f.	472b
O f.! O sweet!	402a
outward be f., however foul within	94b
she f., divinely f., fit love	276a

Fair (cont.)

she is not f. to outward view	97b
she that was ever f.	360b
she that was young and f.	460a
she was more f. than words	425b
so f. a fancy few wd. weave	180a
so f., so calm, so softly seal'd	72b
so young, so f.	69a
sweet and f. she seems	449a
that was only f.	230a
the brave deserves the f.	138b
the day is aye f.	285b
the F. commands the song	111b
the hand that made you f.	352a
thou art all f., my love	500b
thou art dead, as young and f.	67b
thou love, and she be f.	219b
thou, that didst appear so f.	473a
thou weed! who art so lovely f.	363a
thus wondrous f.	275a
to make itself, in thee, f.	322b
were it fifty times as f.	29a
were she pitiful as she is f.	176a
what care I how f. she be	462a
wondrous still the charming f.	31b
yr. heart's..ambition? to be f.	251b

Fairer: be she f. than the day | 462a
f. far than this fair day	394b
f. person lost not Heav'n	272a
f. than any wakened eyes behold	398a
f. than feigned of old	277a
f. than the evening air	258b
her very frowns are f. far	97b
lily of a day is f. far in May	216b
the f. way is not much about	13a
you shall be yet far f.	322b

Fairest: f. among women | 500a
f. things have fleetest end	441a
O f. of creation!	276a
the leader is f.	5b

Fairies: do you believe in f.? | 21b
f., black, grey, green	356a
f. break their dances	200a
farewell, rewards and f.	106a
I don't believe in f.	21b
she is the f.' midwife	364b
that was the beginning of f.	21b
the f.' coach-makers	364b

Fairing: thou'll get thy f. | 63a

Fairs: he haunts wakes, f. | 373a

Fair-spoken, and persuading | 386b

Fairway: mines reported in the f. | 232b

Fairy: by f. hands their knell is rung | 103a
calls up the realms of f.	71a
f. elves, whose midnight revels	272a
f. land where all the children	413b
light she was and like a f.	280b
like a f. trip upon the green	386b
little f..falls down dead	21b
loveliest f. in the world	226b
Mary Bell had a F. in a nut	31a
no f. takes, nor witch hath power	329b
that f. kind of writing	140b
the f. way of writing	2a
'tis almost f. time	357b
wide enough to wrap a f. in	356b

Fairy Prince: much-adored..F. | 263b

Fairy queen: come not near our f. | 356b
| near the cradle of our f. | 357a |

Fairy-tale of olden times | 568b

Faith: all that f. creates | 397a
a scientific f.'s absurd	46b
a stronger f. embrace a sword	250a
author and finisher of our f.	517a
bloody F. the foulest birth	393b
build their f. upon..pike and gun	65a
but F., fanatic F., once wedded	282a
disturb our cheerful f.	472a
doubt diversified by f.	45a
ever the f. endures	185a
f. and ful credence	89b
f. and morals hold wh. Milton held	467a
f. as a grain of mustard seed	507a
f. in a nation of sectaries	129a
f. in their happy eyes	27a
f., meekness, temperance	515b
f. of Christ crucified	481a
f. of our fathers! holy f.!	150a
f. of the poor is faint	93b
f...panting for a happier seat	214a
f.'s defying	21a

Faith (cont.)

f. shines equal, arming me	38b
f.'s transcendent dower	463b
f...substance of things hoped for	517a
f. that looks thro' death	467b
f. that right makes might	245a
f. unfaithful kept him	428b
f. without works is dead	517b
fight the good fight of f.	516b
for modes of f. let..zealots fight	301b
he must gather his f. together	37a
his f.,..in some nice tenets	106b
if I break f., this word shall speak	344b
if thy F. is entire	37a
if ye break f. with us who die	256a
I have kept the f.	516b
I have not found so great f.	506a
I mean the F.'s Defender	67b
impossibilities..for an active f.	41b
increase of f., hope, and charity	479b
in f. and hope the world..disagree	301b
in thy f. and fear	480b
'I shd. have more f.', he said	136a
I shd. not alter in my f. of him	214b
let f. be given	463a
live..but by f., by admiration	148a
made of f. and service	327b
more f. in honest doubt	431a
my f. that every flower enjoys	471a
my life upon her f.!	360b
my staff of f. to walk upon	307b
my strong f. shall purchase me	79b
not f., but mere Philosophy	41b
not for all his f. can see	147a
no tricks in plain and simple f.	340b
not the dying for a f.	439b
now abideth f., hope, charity	514b
of serious f., and inward glee	468a
our f., our pride	228a
O thou of little f.	507a
O welcome pure-ey'd F.	267a
puts me from my f.	378a
sacred dictates of thy f.	313b
sanctified by reason, blest by f.	470a
sea of f. was once..at the full	5a
shake a man's f. in himself	390a
simple f. than Norman blood	431b
that he hold the Catholick F.	478b
the f. that launched..her dart	46b
the f. that ye share	235b
the just shall live by f.	513a
them that do not have the f.	93b
these all died in f.	517a
the shield of f.	516a
tho' f. and form be sunder'd	431a
tho' I have all f.	514b
'tis a point of f.	115a
vain f., and courage vain	252b
want of f. in all	428b
welcome home again discarded f.	374b
we walk by f.	515a
what of the f. and fire within us	180a
when F. is kneeling by his bed	137b
which constitutes poetic f.	102a
wh. f. except every one do keep	478b
with my childhood's f.	44a

Faithful: Abdiel, f. found | 275a
army of the f.	263b
as I am a Christian f. man	384b
be thou f. unto death	518b
called F. and True	519b
f. in that wh. is least	510a
f. of thy word	280b
f. only he	275a
f. to God and thee	191a
he was my friend, f. and just	340a
I have been f. to thee, Cynara	135a
O come, all ye f.	290a, 558a
O f. shepherd! to come	7b
to the f. herdman's art belongs	269b

Faithfulness: his f. and truth | 487b

Faithless: be not f., but believing | 511b
| f. as the winds or seas | 321a |
| mortal, but f. was she | 6a |

Faiths: both were F., and both are gone | 6a
f. and empires gleam	394a
f. are wafer-cakes	382a
the old f. loosen and fall	423b

Falchion: my good biting f. | 344b

Falcon: dapple-dawn-drawn F. | 198a

Falcon (cont.)
f., towering in her pride 348b
gentle as f. or hawk 402b
Falconer: O! for a f.'s voice 365b
Falernian winged the pen 75a
Falkland: F. wd. with a . . sad accent 203a
like F. fall 72a
Fall: aisles f. like sweet strains 147a
altho' it f. and die that night 216b
another thing to f. 351a
created . . half to f. 301a
dew shall weep thy f. 187b
diggeth a pit shall f. into it 499b
doeth these things . . never f. 482b
dost thou f. upon thy face? 364b
fair the f. of songs 414b
f. into the hands of God 437b
f. not out by the way 493b
f. on us, and hide us 519a
flowers, . . thou let'st f. from Dis's 373a
for fear of what might f. 341a
fruit that can f. without shaking 280a
great was the f. of it 506a
haughty spirit before a f. 498a
held we f. to rise 52a
here didst thou f. 339b
he that is down can f. no lower 65a
he that is down needs fear no f. 54b
his f. was destined to a . . strand 213b
hope to rise, or fear to f. 473b
Humpty Dumpty had a great f. 85a, 533b
I had given the devil a foul f. 283a
if he f. in, good night! 377a
impute my F. to Sin 154a
in this we stand or f. 275a
it had a dying f. 369b
it is good to f. 458a
kill'd by a f. from a cherry-tree 281a
laugh at a f. 48a
lest they f. upon thee 483b
man without thee cannot but f. 479b
nowhere to f. but off 225a
only bliss . . that has survived the f. 112a
she who trifles . . less likely to f. 160a
soar not too high to f. 262b
some old temple, nodding to its f. 301b
sparrows . . not f. on the ground 506a
suffer us not . . to f. from thee 481b
take heed lest he f. 514b
take warning by the f. 531b
therefore f. the people unto them 486b
tho' he trip and f. 437a
thou wilt f. backward 364b
what a f. was there 340a
when we f. out with those we love 436a
why do ye f. so fast? 188b
with many a f. shall linger near 310a
yet fear I to f. 307b
Fallen: arise, or be for ever f. 271b
Babylon is f. 519b
Cytherean be f. 423b
f. Cherub, to be weak is miserable 271a
f. from his high estate 139a
f. into the midst of it themselves 485b
how are the mighty f. 495b
how art thou f. from heaven 502a
many . . have f. by the tongue 520b
O f. at length that tower 435a
O how f.! how changed 271a
the f. cling to her 420a
though f. on evil days 275a
ye are f. from grace 515b
Fallest: thou f. a blessed martyr 386a
Falleth: that f. on the grass 524b
Falling: blessings on the f. out 436a
cruelty to load a f. man 386b
f., f., yet, to the ancient . . cadence 96a
f. from that apple-tree 172b
f., with a f. State 298b
folly bears the f. sky 199b
he hath the f. sickness 338a
the f. out of faithful friends 143b
Fallings from us, vanishings 466b
Falls: by shallow rivers to whose f. 259a
famous for his f. 294a
he f. like Lucifer 386a
he wd. sing of her with f. 43b
like a thunderbolt he f. 426b
o'erleaps . . and f. on the other 347a
then he f., as I do 385b
where he f. short 95a

False: all was f. and hollow 272a
among innumerable f., unmoved 275a
any other thing that's f. 72a
as thou be not f. to others 15b
betrayed by what is f. within 264a
by the philosopher, as equally f. 162a
canst not then be f. to any man 330b
f. as dicers' oaths 335a
f. Sextus 253a
f. tho' she be to me 105a
framed to make women f. 360b
if all is f. that I advance 107b
if she be f., O! then heaven mocks 362a
I was f. of heart 389a
ring out the f. 431a
round numbers are always f. 209b
she can both f. and friendly be 246b
she will be f., ere I come 134a
taking true for f. 427b
'tis f.! 'tis f.! my Arab steed! 290a
to bring the f. to light 36b
true before, prove f. again 66a
wouldst not play f. 346b
Falsehood: f. has a perennial spring 55a
f. is worse in kings 328b
f. wd. be more miraculous 201a
goodly outside f. hath 353a
heart for f. framed 400a
let her and F. grapple 279a
no f. can endure . . celestial temper 274a
smallest foundation to f. 171a
strife of Truth with F. 250b
to unmask f. 386b
wedded fast to some dear f. 282a
with glorious f. 546a
with vizor'd f. 267b
yr. bait of f. takes this carp 331b
Falser: tomorrow's f. than the former 139b
Falstaff: but for sweet Jack F. 378a
F. shall die of a sweat 381a
F. sweats to death 377a
to the memory of Shakespeare, F. 170b
Falter: f., are lost in the storm 7b
hesitate and f. life away 8a
Faltered: if I have f. more or less 415a
Fame: blush to find it f. 303b
bring you to good f. and renown 257a
courtliness, and the desire of f. 428a
Cromwell, damned to everlasting f. 301b
death . . openeth the gate to . . f. 14a
died the death of f. 317a
enough my meed of f. 193b
estate, good f., plans 146b
fair f. inspires 303a
f.? an empty bubble 172b
f. for a pot of ale 382a
f. is a food that dead men eat 131a
f. is like a river 16b
f. is no plant 269b
f. is nothing but an empty name 94b
f. is the spur 269b
F.'s eternal bead roll 409a
foremost shall be damned to f. 299a
for his f. the ocean sea 21a
full of phrase and f. 9a
gives immortal f. 477a
great heir of f. 278a
grief that f. can never heal 12b
he mistook it for f. 169b
her f. survives 278a
his f. soon spread around 108b
honour be yrs., and f. 287b
hope of a season's f. 287b
let f., that all hunt after 344a
little breath . . wh. they call F. 157a
no one shall work for f. 236b
nor yet a fool to f. 303a
of so much f. in Heaven 269b
Oh F.! if I e'er took delight 73b
on earth yr. f. is bright 37a
passion for f. 55a
physicians of the utmost f. 26a
poets' food is love and f. 393b
rather use than f. 429a
servants of f. 14b
temple of f. . . upon the grave 183a
till love and f. to nothingness 221a
to be in the mouth of f. 222a
to grow great in f. 120b
trump of future f. 72a
what else is damned to f. 316a

Fame (cont.)
wh. f. did not delay 137a
while f. elates thee 281a
ympt the wings of f. 79a
you shall live by f. 408a
Famed: cheat so well as she is f. to do 220a
Familiar: be thou f. 330b
don't let us be f. or fond 105b
f. acts are beautiful 397b
f. but not coarse 213a
f. with her face 301a
our names, f. in his mouth 383a
the old f. faces 240b
till, more f. grown 443b
Familiarity begets boldness 259b
Families: all happy f. resemble each 567a
best-regulated f. 122a
f. not regulated by that . . influence 122a
good f. are generally worse 197a
great f. of yesterday 118b
mothers of large f. 25b
murder . . seems . . to run in f. 245a
old f. last not three oaks 42b
one of yr. antedeluvian f. 104b
rooks in f. homeward go 180a
secrets in all f. 150a
Family: a f. happier for his presence 412a
bosom of her respectable f. 58b
brought up a large f. 171a
character of a f. to an hypothesis 411b
eyes all the smiling f. askance 443b
Ha! ha! F. Bible 164b
his f. was not unworthy of him 129b
one of Eve's f. 195b
strenuous f. dusted from its hands 415a
Famine: die by f. die by inches 185b
f. . . supply of toothpicks 205b
Famous: be f. then by wisdom 277a
f. by my sword 280b
f. to all ages 279b
I awoke . . and found myself f. 74b
Famoused for fight 387a
Fan: f. spread and streamers out 105a
the Pompadour's F. 130b
Fanatics have their dreams 218a
Fancies: f. that broke thro' language 50b
high region of his f. 279a
lay yr. earthly f. down 435a
my f., fly before ye 115b
our f. are more giddy 370b
proud, and full of f. 222a
stray thoughts, f. fugitive 51b
then f. flee away! 54b
troubled with thick-coming f. 350b
you set yr. f. free 52a
Fancy: all the gardener F. 220b
bright-eyed F. 175a
by hopeless f. feigned 436a
conduck isn't all yr. f. paints 235b
did yr. f. never stray 159b
dorgs is some men's f. 122a
ever let the f. roam 218a
f. cannot cheat so well 220a
f. dies in the cradle 354a
f. from a flower-bell 45a
f. is the sails 222a
f. outwork nature 323a
F.'s gilded clouds 299a
f.'s meteor ray 63a
fellow . . of most excellent f. 336b
food of sweet and bitter f. 327b
full of shapes is f. 360b
let us all ring f.'s knell 354a
listen . . to the whispers of f. 213b
makes f. tame 111a
not expressed in f. 330b
not in f.'s maze he wandered 303a
now the f. passes by 199a
O sweet F.! let her loose 218a
revolting f. were the forms begot 202b
Shakespeare, F.'s child 269a
tell me where is f. bred 354a
thy face across his f. comes 436b
young man's f. lightly turns 432a
Fancy-free: maiden meditation f. 356b
Fang: icy f. and churlish chiding 325b
Fanhope: Ferrers and F. 137a
Fanned by Conquest's crimson wing 173b
Fanny: pretty F.'s way 292b
Fans: Cupids, with divers-coloured f. 323a

Fans (*cont.*)
etchin's an' f. — 232b
wi' their f. into their hand — 530a
Fantastic: light f. toe — 268b
Fantastical: it alone is high f. — 369b
joys are but f. — 132a
murder yet is but f. — 346b
Fantasies: even the linked f. — 442a
Fantasy: all made of f. — 327b
opinion he held once of f. — 338b
too strong for f. — 132a
Far: drawn from thoughts more f. — 43b
f. and few, are the lands — 243b
f., f., ahead, is all her seamen — 97a
f., f. behind is all..they can say — 97a
f., f. better rest that I go to — 127b
f., f. better thing I do — 127b
f. from eye or ear — 422a
f. from here, the Adriatic breaks — 5b
f. from sorrow, f. from sin — 130b
f. from the lips we love — 281b
f. from the madding crowd's — 174b
f. or forgot to me is near — 146a
nor f. away deem..thy doom — 37b
peace to him that is f. — 503a
set this foot of mine as f. — 338a
she is f. from the land — 281b
so near and yet so f. — 431a
think on him that's f. awa — 59a
Farce: lamb in a sentimental f. — 219b
same grey f. again — 92b
the f. is over — 565a
Fardels: who would f. bear — 333a
Fare: thee well! and if for ever — 72b
f. thee well, for I must leave — 527a
f. thee well, great heart — 379a
not yr. bill of f. — 418a
that hasn't paid his f. — 231a
when you receive a f. — 38b
Fared sumptuously every day — 510a
Farewell: bidding you a long f. — 29a
f. all-hallown summer — 376b
f., a long f., to all my greatness — 385b
f. al the snow — 90a
f., and stand fast — 377a
f.! be the proud bride — 124b
f. compliment! — 365a
f. dear, deluding Woman — 60b
f., fair cruelty — 370a
f. goes out sighing — 369a
f., happy fields — 271a
f. house, and f. home — 115a
f. king! — 375b
f.; my blessing season this — 330b
f. my book and my devocion — 89b
f., my trim-built wherry — 120b
f. remorse — 273b
'f.' she said, 'ye virgins all' — 531b
f. the heart that lives alone — 468b
f. the tranquil mind — 362a
f.! thou art too dear — 388b
f. to Lochaber — 308a
for ever, f., Cassius — 341a
hail, and f. evermore! — 540a
hope..bade the world f. — 77a
I bid f. to every fear — 453b
I only feel—F.!—F.! — 72b
looks around, to say f. — 440b
No-more, Too-late, F. — 312b
no sadness of f. — 426a
our everlasting f. take — 341a
our neighbour and our work f. — 223b
so f. hope, and with hope f. fear — 273b
sweets to the sweet: f. — 336b
take..this garland and f. — 421a
that was all the f. — 199a
than waving me f. — 197a
thou sayest f., and lo! — 36b
wave their hands for a mute f. — 203a
wind of welcome and f. — 311b
Farewells: everlasting f.! — 120a
Fairin': ca' them vulgar f. — 285b
halesome f. — 285b
Farm: in f. and field — 198b
keep a f., and carters — 332a
snug f. of the World — 406b
snug little f. the earth — 100b
Farmer: a better f. ne'er brushed — 74b
f.'s daughter hath soft..hair — 75a
f. that hanged himself — 348a

Farmer (*cont.*)
ran after a f.'s wife — 533a
the f.'s early care — 161a
this is the f. sowing his ccrn — 534a
Farmers: our f. round — 113b
the embattled f. stood — 146b
three jolly F. once bet — 119b
Farms: lass wi'the weel-stockit f. — 61a
pleasant villages and f. — 276a
what f. are those? — 199b
Farther: I'm f. off from Heaven — 195a
O f., f. sail! — 457a
Farthest: as far as who goes f. — 338a
f. from him is best — 271a
Farthing: kind of f. dip — 415a
never pay a f. for it — 116a
paid the uttermost f. — 505a
sparrows sold for two f. — 509b
two sparrows sold for a f. — 506a
what I do, for a F. less — 1b
Fascination: a f. frantic — 165a
f. in his very bow — 71b
Fashion: after the high Roman f. — 324b
as out of the f. — 95b
construe..after their own f. — 338a
cross-gartered, a f. she detests — 371b
deeply put the f. on — 381a
faithful to thee, Cynara! in my f. — 135a
f. all things fair — 179b
f.! a word wh. knaves..may use — 94b
f. of a new doublet — 358a
f. of this world passeth — 514a
f.'s brightest arts — 168b
f., the arbiter — 410b
F., tho' Folly's child — 113b
f. to abuse in public — 34a
following f. nayed him twice — 176a
hang quite out of f. — 369a
highflyer at F. — 125b
not for the f. of these times — 326a
was marriage ever out of f.? — 66a
Fashioned: f. so purely — 443a
f. so slenderly — 195b
Fashioneth: clay say to him that f. it — 502b
Fast: come he slow, or come he f. — 318a
f. by their native shore — 111a
f. from every village round — 252b
find thy Manhood all too f. — 195b
fine and as f. as he can — 305a
fun grew f. and furious — 63a
here a solemn F. we keep — 189a
he talks it so very f. — 150a
how f. they fade away — 3b
is not this the f. — 503a
so f. for fear did he sail — 407a
spare F., that oft with gods — 268a
such a f. that I have chosen — 503a
thick and f. they came — 84b
too f. we live — 7a
what need you flow so f. — 527b
why do ye fall so f.? — 188b
poor, who will not f. in peace — 113b
Fasten him as a nail — 502a
Faster: cried the Queen, 'F.! F.!' — 84a
walk a little f. — 83a
world wd. go round a deal f. — 82b
Fastest: he travels the f. — 236b
Fastidious: literature is never f. — 407a
Fasting: a foul man and a f. — 320a
f. in the wild — 405b
hope will die f. — 157a
thank heaven, f., for a good man's — 327a
Fasts: come in f. divine — 197b
Fat: a feast of f. things — 502a
all of us are f. — 84b
drives f. oxen shd. himself be f. — 211a
fair, f., and forty — 320a
f. and look young till forty — 141a
f. and well liking — 487b
f. gentleman in such a passion — 140a
f. of others' works — 64a
f. of the land — 493b
f. was so white — 169a
f. white woman — 106a
Jack Sprat cd. eat no f. — 534a
Jeshurun waxed f. — 494b
jewels make women..f. — 21b
men about me that are f. — 338a
more f. than bard beseems — 443a
one of them is f. — 377b
she helped him to f. — 19b

Fatal: I am a f. man — 440a
fair and f. King — 206a
f. gift of beauty — 69a
great deal of it is absolutely f. — 460a
so sweet was ne'er so f. — 363b
strange and f. interview — 132b
their f. hands no second stroke — 273a
Fatality: there is a f. in it — 411a
Fate: Arbiter of others' f. — 73b
armour against f. — 401a
at length my f. I know — 47b
best of men cannot suspend..f. — 118a
big with the f. of Cato — 1a
build that nation's f. — 29b
cd. thou and I with F. conspire — 154a
equalled with me in f. — 273a
F. cannot touch me — 75a
f. never wounds more deep — 213a
F. so enviously debars — 260b
F. thy measure takes — 250b
F., Time, Occasion — 397a
f. tried to conceal him — 194b
F. wrote her a..tragedy — 24b
fears his f. too much — 280b
for all our children's f. — 229a
foreknowledge, will, and f. — 272b
full reward and glorious f. — 79b
hand of f. has scourged us — 245b
hanging breathless on thy f. — 246b
he fits for f. — 140b
here's a heart for every f. — 73a
he that knows not F. — 92b
his was an untoward f. — 71b
how very sad thy f. — 220b
how wayward the decrees of F. — 440b
I wd. not fear nor wish my f. — 107a
let this be my f. — 304a
limits of a vulgar f. — 175b
look upon myself and curse my f. — 387a
master of my f. — 185a
must F. act the same grey farce — 92b
my f. cries out — 331a
my motto and my f. — 420a
no gifts from Chance..conquered F. — 8a
once dead by f. — 22b
on what seas shall be thy f. — 200a
read the book of f. — 380a
she is coming, my life, my f. — 434a
struggling in the storms of f. — 298b
succeeds in unknown f. — 361a
take a bond of f. — 349b
that f. is thine—no distant date — 62a
the f. of this country depends — 128b
the man I sing, who, forced by f. — 142b
their ken from half of human f. — 7a
thou who mourn'st the Daisy's f. — 62a
thy f. and mine are seal'd — 436b
till I thy f. shall overtake — 225a
Time and F. of all their Vintage — 153a
too vast orb of her f. — 6b
what I will is f. — 275b
what shall be the maiden's f.? — 317a
when f. summons, monarchs..obey — 140b
which f. and metaphysical aid — 346b
who can control his f.? — 364a
why shd. they know their f.? — 175a
will in us is over-ruled by f. — 259a
with a heart for any f. — 248a
youth, wh. f. reserves — 252a
Fates: masters of their f. — 337b
our wills and f...contrary run — 334a
when F. turn'd cruel — 215a
whom the F. sever — 318a
Father: about my F.'s business — 509a
a f. I can never get mair — 529a
a mother's pride, a f.'s joy — 319a
an only f., sir — 170b
arise and go to my f. — 509b
as a decrepit f. takes delight — 387b
be the root and f. of many kings — 348b
but not an angry f. — 77a
carf biforn his f. — 88a
come silly soul, thy f.'s shame — 35b
come, Thou F. of the poor — 86b
cometh unto the F., but by me — 511a
cry not when his f. dies — 211b
Diogenes struck the f. — 64b
down from the F. of lights — 517a
even so, F.; for so it seemed good — 509a
f. answered never a word — 249a

Father (*cont.*)

F., forgive them; for they know not	510a
F., I cannot tell a lie	451b
F., I have sinned against thee	509b
F. in Heaven who lovest all	227b
F., in Thy gracious keeping	145b
F., into thy hands I commend	510a
f. is rather vulgar, my dear	123a
F., let me dedicate	446b
F., Mother and Me	23b
f. of all! in ev'ry age	304a
f., O f.! what do we here	31a
F. of lights! what sunny seed	447b
f. of such as dwell in tents	492b
f. of the fatherless	486a
f.'s sorrow, f.'s joy	176a
F. who didst all create	236a
features of my f.'s face	73b
foredoomed his f.'s soul to cross	303a
full fathom five thy f. lies	367a
had it been his f.	523b
hath the rain a f.?	497b
have a turnip than his f.	211b
have we not all one f.?	504b
her f. loved me	360a
he took my f. grossly	334b
his f.'s sword he has girded on	281b
his f. was before him	418b
his mother on his f. him begot	30a
Holy F., in Thy mercy	411a
honour thy f. and thy mother	480a
how many a f. have I seen	430a
I am thy f.'s spirit	331a
I go to the f.	511b
I had it from my f.	385b
I thank thee, O F.	509a
it is a wise f.	353b
kept his f.'s asses	261a
King, f.; royal Dane	331a
lead us, Heavenly F.	143b
liar, and the f. of it	511a
light upon him from his f.'s eyes	466b
like as a f. pitieth his . . children	488a
Lord, shew us the F.	511a
man leave his f. and his mother	492a
mighty God, The everlasting F.	501b
my f. and my mother forsake me	483b
my f . . . argued sair	20b
my f. did something smack	353b
my f. feeds his flocks	194b
my f.'s brother . . no more . . my f.	330a
my f. sold me	32b
my f. was an . . button maker	103b
my f. wept	32a
my poor f. used to say	186a
O f. of all of us	423a
only begotten of the F.	510b
on the king my f.'s death	144b
our fair F. Christ	428a
our F. wh. art in heaven	505a
picture of his f.'s face	155b
resembled my f. as he slept	347b
she follow'd my poor f.'s body	330a
she has deceived her f.	360b
the Child is f. of the Man	468a
the f. of good news	332a
the wanton smiled, f. wept	176a
thicker than my f.'s loins	496a
this is my true-begotten f.	353b
tho' f. and mither . . gae mad	63a
thus with hir f . . . dwelleth	89b
thy wish was f . . . to that thought	381a
to his great F. bends	100a
we cry, Abba, F.	513b
what my f. used to say	186a
when thy f. first did see	176a
wise son maketh a glad f.	498a
with His F. work us a . . peace	270a
without f. bred	268a
ye are of yr. f. the devil	511a
you are old, F. William	407a
your f. was no glazier	418b
Fathered: being so f.	338b
Fatherland: guard and bless our f.	200b
Fatherless: he defendeth the f.	490b
Fatherly: then, f., not less than I	294a
Fathers: ashes of his f.	253a
a sojourner, as all my f. were	484a
blood is fet from f. of war-proof	382a
city of the healthiest f.	457b

Fathers (*cont.*)

excellent herbs had our f. of old	233a
exiles from our f.' land	320b
faith of our f.! holy faith!	150a
f., provoke not your children	515b
f. that, like so many Alexanders	382a
follow the generation of his f.	485a
for whose sake our . . f. died	228a
God of our f., be the God	131b
God of our f., known of old	233b
I like to be as my f. were	33b
instead of thy f . . . have children	484b
Lord God of yr. f.	493b
loud cried the F. all	253b
our f. have declared unto us	479a
our f. that begat us	521a
our f. worshipped stocks	278b
sins of the f. upon the children	480a
slept with his f.	496a
the f. have eaten sour grapes	503b
we sons succeed their f.' praise	178a
your f., where are they?	504b
Fathers-forth: he f. whose beauty	197b
Fathom: full f. five thy father lies	367a
full many a f. deep	76b
nine f. deep he had followed us	98b
thou canst not f. it	435b
where f.-line cd. never touch	377a
Fathoms: 'tis fifty f. deep	530a
Fatigued I said, tie up the knocker	302b
Fatling: lion and the f. together	501b
Fatness: f. of these pursy times	335a
thy clouds drop f.	486a
Fats: in thy f. our cares be drowned	323b
Fatter: he was f. than his cure	426b
the valley sheep are f.	295a
would he were f.!	338a
Faubourg St. Germain	449b
Fault: a f., wh. needs it most	186b
break yr. neck, 'tis not his f.	30a
but see thy f.!	381b
condemn the f. and not the actor	351b
every one f. seeming monstrous	327a
faultless to a f.	51b
fierceness makes error a f.	186b
for they are without f.	519a
he that does one f. at first	452b
if at all she had a f.	215b
it has no kind of f. or flaw	163b
it was a grievous f.	339b
just hint a f.	303a
scarce weed out the f.	170b
shun the f. I fell in	531b
that checks each f.	11a
the f., dear Brutus	337b
the f. is Nature's, f. not thine	74b
the glorious f. of angels	299a
to hide the f. I see	304a
to me he is all f.	428b
without f. or stain on thee	37a
Faulted: wherein he most f.	214b
Faultless: faultily f.	433b
f. to a fault	51b
taste exact for f. fact	165a
Faults: a heady currance, scouring f.	381b
all his f. are such	170b
all his f. observed	341a
all men have their f.	170b
all men make f.	387b
all old f. and follies are forgot	96b
best men are moulded out of f.	352b
be to her f. a little blind	305b
cleanse thou me from my secret f.	482b
drown'd all my f.	155b
England, with all thy f.	111b
f. had she, child of Adam's stem	293b
f. so nearly allied to excellence	170b
f. they commit, the earth covereth	307a
for I acknowledge my f.	485a
friendly eye cd. never see such f.	341a
gossips count her f.	263b
has she no f.	299b
his f. lie gently on him!	386a
if he had any f.	169b
if our f. whipped them not	322a
I know most f.	327a
Jesus! with all thy f. I love thee	67a
my f. ye quote	241a
not for thy f., but mine	69a
some f. to make us men	324b
teeth and forehead of our f.	334b

Faults (*cont.*)

the greatest of f.	80b
vile ill-favoured f.	356a
with all her f., she is my country	94b
ye be buffeted for yr. f.	517b
Faustine: caressed F.	421b
Faustus must be damned	258b
Favour: f. with God and man	509a
for yr. f . . . give God thanks	358b
looks almost like a f.	105a
to this f. she must come	336b
Favourable: O be f. and gracious	485a
Favoured: that art highly f.	508b
Favourite: a f. has no friend!	173b
a Prodigal's f.	463b
you mark his f. flies	334a
Favours: gratitude . . sense of future f.	574b
hangs on princes' f.	386a
in the middle of her f.	332a
I've felt all its f.	97a
lively sense of *future* f.	450a
those be rubies, fairy f.	356b
Fawn: blue heavens like a white f.	476a
the f. that flies	420b
to f., to crouch, to wait	409b
troopers . . have shot my f.	261a
unpractis'd he to f.	168b
Fawning: base spaniel f.	339a
Fear: all f., none aid you	301b
almost to jelly with the act of f.	330b
Arch F. in a visible form	50b
but I f. him not	338a
continual f. and danger of . . death	191b
crossed themselves for f.	432a
cuckoo, O, word of f.	345b
drives away his f.	289a
ere we will eat our meal in f.	348b
faith shines . . arming me from f.	38b
F., and Bloodshed, miserable train!	465a
F. and trembling Hope	473a
f. God . . keep his commandments	500a
f. God, and take yr. own part	34a
f. God. Honour the king	517b
f. Him, ye saints	424b
f. in a handful of dust	144b
F. is a flying	159a
f. is the parent of cruelty	157b
f. no more the frown o' the great	329a
f. no more the heat o' the sun	329a
f. not, but trust in Providence	22a
'f. not,' said he	424b
f. of change perplexes	272a
f. of the Lord is the beginning	489a
F., O little Hunter	234b
f. or favour of the crowd	228a
f. o' Stellenbosch	234b
f., the last of ills	141b
f. thou not at all	422b
f. to launch away	453b
f. to whom f.	513b
f . . . was, lest he shd. make an end	215a
f. wist not to evade	441b
f. ye not therefore	506a
feels all over trembulation and f.	417a
for f. of little men	4a
for f. of wh., hear this, thou age	388b
fostered . . by beauty and by f.	469a
grow gray with f.	396b
hate that wh. we often f.	322b
have nothing else to f.	424b
his f. still followed him	408b
hope and f. set free	422a
I bid farewell to every f.	453b
I cannot taint with f.	350b
I do f. them	339a
I f. no foe in shining armour	291b
I f. thy kisses, gentle maiden	399b
if my name were liable to f.	338a
I have a sin of f.	132a
I'll f. not what men say	54b
in the night, imagining some f.	357b
I, with many a f. for my . . country	463a
I wd. not f. nor wish my fate	107a
judge of danger wh. they f.	468a
land of unbelief and f.	31a
lest I shd. f. and fall	43a
little we f. weather without	440b
many things to f.	15a
most strange that men shd. f.	339a

Fear (cont.)
never strike sail to a f. — 148a
nobility is exempt from f. — 384a
no hope who never had a f. — 113a
no passion so..robs..as f. — 57b
not given us the spirit of f. — 516b
O f. the Lord, ye..his saints — 484a
perfect love casteth out f. — 518a
possess them not with f. — 383a
severity breedeth f. — 14b
shuddering f. — 354a
spirit of bondage again to f. — 513b
sunder'd in the night of f. — 431a
tell pale-hearted f. it lies — 349b
that calms each f. — 11a
that natural f. in children — 14a
thawing cold f. — 382b
the concessions of f. — 55b
therefore will we not f. — 484b
there is no f. in love — 518a
there is not a word of f. — 241a
the spirit of knowledge and..f. — 501b
they that f. him lack nothing — 484a
thou needest not f. mine — 399b
to be feared than what I f. — 338a
tragedy..arousing pity and f. — 559a
trembled with f. at yr. frown — 148b
'twas only f. first..made gods — 215b
watch not one another out of f. — 133a
we f. to be we know not what — 139b
what need we f. who knows it — 350a
which feels no f. — 5b
which rather thou dost f. to do — 346b
whom then shall I f. — 483b
whose being I do f. — 348b
why f. we to become — 392b
wise f., you know, forbids — 94b
with his f. is put beside his part — 387a
with hope farewell f. — 273b
without f. and without blemish — 566a
work out yr. own salvation with f. — 516a
Feared: it is just as I f. — 243a
tell thee what is to be f. — 338a
twenty times was Peter f. — 468b
what are they f. on? — 403b
Fearful: come forth, thou f. man — 366a
f. thing to fall into the hands — 517a
frame thy f. symmetry — 31b
ye f. saints — 110a
Fearfully and wonderfully made — 490b
Fearless: for unknown shores — 457b
stepping f. thro' night — 20b
Fears: craven f. of being great — 427a
either f. his fate too much — 280b
f. are less than..imaginings — 346b
f. may be liars — 96b
f. of the brave — 214a
f. shall be in the way — 499b
fifty hopes and f. — 45a
forgot the taste of f. — 350b
hopes and f. of all the years — 40a
humble cares, and delicate f. — 471a
I had no human f. — 463a
its tenderness, its joys, and f. — 467a
little f. grow great — 334a
man f. to be dead — 16b
men's have grown from sudden f. — 69b
not mine own f. — 388b
our f. do make us traitors — 350a
our f. our hopes belied — 196a
our very hopes belied our f. — 196a
tie up thy f. — 188a
when I have f. that I may cease — 221a
who f. to speak of Ninety-Eight — 203b
within were f. — 515a
Feast: a f. of fat things — 502a
as you were going to a f. — 215a
by bare imagination of a f. — 374b
door stood open at our f. — 98a
f. of reason and the flow of soul — 303b
Goldsmith's fine f. — 158b
great f. of languages — 345a
if so they chance to f. her — 215b
let us keep f. — 514a
liberty's a glorious f. — 61a
Love, thy solemn F. to hold — 293b
perpetual f. of nectared sweets — 267b
riot, f. and dance — 276b
sat at any good man's f. — 326b
scramble at the shearers' f. — 269b
song of them that f. — 286a

Feast (cont.)
the beginning of a f. — 378b
the f. is set — 98a
what f. is toward in thine..cell — 337a
when I make a f. — 181a
Feasting: go to the house of f. — 499a
Feasts: at all f. when ale was strongest — 249a
fools make f. — 157a
spots in yr. f. of charity — 518a
table of the Moveable F. — 478a
uppermost rooms at f. — 507b
wreathed for f. not few — 264a
Feat: f. on which..we prided — 70b
like that f. in the ring — 195a
such a gallant f. of arms — 253b
Feather: a moulted f., an eagle-f. — 48b
f. is wafted downward — 247a
friendship never moults a f. — 125a
lighter than a f. — 160b
little ball of f. and bone — 180a
stuck a f. in his cap — 18b
viewed his own f. on the..dart — 72a
with hindward f. — 263b
Feathered: f. creatures broke away — 389a
f. race with pinions skim the air — 157b
Feathers: animals without f. — 81b
her f. like gold — 486a
made my f. gay — 475a
safe under his f. — 487b
she plumes her f. — 267a
Feats: f. he did that day — 383a
'twas one of my f. — 73a
Featly: foot it f. — 367a
Feature: haint one agreeable f. — 250a
thrive in grace and f. — 215a
Featured like him — 387a
Features: f. of my Entertainment — 451a
homely f. to keep home — 267b
lady of incisive f. — 264b
some f. of my father's face — 73b
February: F., fill the dyke — 446a
F. has twenty-eight alone — 533a
F. hath twenty-eight alone — 172a
F. last, my heart..was glad — 463b
in vestal F. — 293b
Fed: appetite..grown by what it f. — 330a
but it is f. and watered — 76a
f. with the same food — 354a
sheep look up, and are not f. — 269b
Federal: our F. Union — 203b
Federation of the world — 432b
Fee: aye the cheapest lawyer's f. — 62b
before his credit, or his f. — 419b
bought over God with a f. — 424a
set my life at a pin's f. — 331a
Feeble: f. as frail — 172b
help the f. up — 368a
most forcible F. — 380b
Feed: f. fat the ancient grudge — 353a
f. me in a green pasture — 483a
f. my lambs — 511b
f. my sheep — 511b
f. the brute! — 535b
f. with the rich — 207b
gave thee life, and bid thee f. — 32b
He that doth me f. — 188a
to f. and batten on this moor — 335a
we can begin to f. — 84b
Feeder: Mr. F., B.A. — 122b
Feedest: tell me..where thou f. — 500a
Feedeth: he f. among the lilies — 500a
Feeding: there are forty f. like one — 467b
Feeds: Death, that f. on men — 389b
earth alike f. beast as man — 322a
Feel: antilogy of making figments f. — 179b
f. I am so most — 324a
f. what I can ne'er express — 69b
f. what wretches I — 343a
he already seemed to f. the flowers — 223b
I believe to 'One does f.' — 238a
If f. a feeling wh. If. you all f. — 309a
If it more than other people — 121b
If. like one who treads alone — 282b
I must also f. it as a man — 350a
in yr. arms f. so small — 294a
know the change and f. it — 221b
no comfortable f. in any member — 195a
tragedy to those that f. — 440b
we f. that it there — 398a
what did it f. to be out of Heaven — 441a
wd. make us f., must f. themselves — 95b

Feeleth: He f. for our sadness — 3b
Feeling: a f. and a love — 472a
a fellow-f. makes one..kind — 158b
f. of sadness and longing — 247a
greater f. to the worse — 374b
had fed the f. of their masters' — 259b
I feel a f. — 309a
lost pulse of f. stirs — 5a
love's f. is more soft — 345a
one f. too falsely disdained — 399b
petrifies the f. — 60a
prevents that sinking f. — 522b
sensible to f. as to sight — 347b
that Kruschen f. — 526a
to me high mountains are a f. — 68b
with the gratifying f. — 163b
Feelings: f. by wh...kings governed — 17b
f. by wh...later Greece ruled — 17b
opinion..determined by the f. — 408a
their f. are strong — 129b
we live..in f., not in figures — 18a
Feels: become my universe that f. — 44b
finding how it f. — 93b
Fees: as they took their f. — 26a
no one hope, but of his f. — 190b
straight dream on f. — 364b
Feet: aching hands and bleeding f. — 7a
and did those f. in ancient times — 31a
and my f. from falling — 485b
and what dread f. — 32a
at her f. he bowed — 495a
at the f. of Gamaliel — 512b
at their f. the crocus brake — 435a
bathe those beauteous f. — 155b
beat down Satan under our f. — 479a
beat more instant than the F. — 441b
beat of her unseen f. — 393a
beautiful are thy f. with shoes — 500b
before her wandering f. — 476a
be jubilant, my f.! — 200b
broken by their passing f. — 474a
came on the following F. — 441b
chase the..Hours with flying f. — 68b
clang of hurrying f. — 12a
come the expected f. — 265a
crowes f. be growe under yr. yë — 90a
desultory f. of Death — 312a
diseased in his f. — 496a
fall at her flying f. — 78a
f. have they, and walk not — 489a
f. like sunny gems — 433b
f. like unto fine brass — 518b
f. of joy in idleness — 37b
f. of thine high priests — 423b
f. of those he fought for — 435a
f. o' the men what drill — 227a
f. was I to the lame — 497a
guide our f. into the way — 508b
hear the grown-up people's f. — 413b
her f. beneath her petticoat — 416a
her f. have touched the meadows — 433b
I look down towards his f. — 364a
jewel-print of yr. f. — 434a
keep Thou my f. — 288b
laid a net for my f. — 485b
lark drop down at his f. — 435b
let my due f. never fail — 268a
little snow-white f. — 474a
Lord, dost thou wash my f.? — 511a
making a tinkling with their f. — 501a
my dreams under yr. f. — 474b
my f. from falling — 489a
my f. upon the rock — 484a
nae room at my f. — 529a
now with his f. — 176a
palms before my f. — 92a
pierced His gospel-bearing f. — 244a
place at the great knees and f. — 421a
pretty f. like snails — 190b
put off thy shoes from off thy f. — 493b
round her f. of the day — 420a
scattered at the f. of man — 464b
set my f. in a large room — 483b
shake off the dust of yr. f. — 506a
splendour and speed of thy f. — 420a
spread the cloths under yr. f. — 474b
standing, with reluctant f. — 247b
start and tremble under her f. — 434a
suffereth not our f. to slip — 486a
table-crumbs attract his slender f. — 443b
tempt with wand'ring f. — 272b

Feet (cont.)

the man sprang to his f.	47b
the sea beneath my f.	35b
the shuffling of f.	284b
they hadn't any f.	84a
they lie about our f.	463b
they sit at the F.	234b
those little silver f.	261a
thus I set my printless f.	268a
'tis three f. long, and two f. wide	471b
violets suddenly bloom at her f.	27a
walked those blessed f.	376a
wash their f. in soda water	144b
what flowers are at my f.	220a
white f. of laughing girls	253a
whose f. they hurt in the stocks	488b
with faint, averted f.	294a
with her world-wandering f.	441b
with lifted f., hands still	24b
with oary f. bears forward	443b
with their f. forward	42a
with twain he covered his f.	501b
you Stella's f. may kiss	402a
yr. f. shod with the preparation	516a

Feign thing, or finde wordes newe 89a

Feigned: fairer than f. of old 277a
| thus by f. deaths to die | 133b |

Feigning was called compliment 371b

Felicity: absent thee from f. awhile 337a
exact f. of Horace	552b
I am the measure of f.	176b
ne'er remember their green f.	221a
none can boast sincere f.	141a
optics of these eyes to behold f.	41b
or shadow of f.	449a
our own f. we make or find	213a
perfect bliss and sole f.	259a
possession without obligation..f.	264b
tavern-chair..throne of human f.	212a
what more f. can fall to creature	409b

Felicities: three fearful f. 402a

Fell: at one f. swoop 350a
f. among thieves	509a
foremost fighting, f.	68b
from morn to noon he f.	272a
he bowed, he f.	495a
I do not love you Dr. F.	41a
I f. at his feet as dead	518b
it f. to earth, I know not where	246b
more..good than all who f.	394a
my f. of hair wd...rouse and stir	350b
ran to help me when I f.	425a
stood who stood, and f. who f.	273b
the athlete nearly f.	287a
the instant that he f.	318b
'tis enough, that when it f.	131b
we f. out I know not why	436a
we f. out, my wife and I	436a

Felled: the poplars are f. 110b

Fellow: a f. that hath had losses 359a
a tall f. of thy hands	373b
f. eight years old	46b
forget his f. traveller	527b
has this f. no feeling	336a
hay, hath no f.	357a
he's a good F.	154a
he was a good f.	88b
his folly has not f.	198b
impossible..Rome..breed thy f.	341b
many a good tall f. had destroyed	377a
old F. of Trinity	527a
'sir', said Mr. Tupman, 'you're a f.'	126a
sweetest li'l' f.	410a
testy, pleasant F.	2a
that f.'s got to swing	459b
there is no f. in the firmament	339a
this f.'s of exceeding honesty	361b
this f.'s wise enough	371b
thou art a f. of a good respect	341b
to find a young f.	104b
unweighing f.	352a
you hear this f. in the cellarage	331b
young f. fell overboard	525a

Fellow-countryman is a model 124a
Fellow-creatures: good to all my f. 313b
Fellow-mortal: companion and f. 62a
Fellow-rover: laughing f. 262a
Fellows: certain lewd f. 512b
mighty fine f. nowadays	413b
strange f. in her time	352b
virgins that be her f.	484b

Fellows (cont.)

what shd. such f. as I do?	333b
Fellow-servant: I am thy f. 519b
Fellowship: a f. with essence 217b
fears his f. to die	383a
f. is heaven	284b
f. is life	284b
half-faced f.	377a
it is for f.'s sake	284b
manhood, nor good f. in thee	376b
one communion and F.	480a
ready minds to f. divine	217b
simple dues of f.	43a
the right hands of f.	515b
why shd. yr. f. a trouble be	117b

Felt: darkness wh. may be f. 493b
| how she f., but what she f. | 466b |
| Oh, this I have f. | 235b |

Female: child of..Eve, a f. 344b
elegance of f. friendship	213b
f. of sex it seems	277b
f. of the species is more deadly	229a
for one fair f.	141b
male and f. created he them	492a
over his f. in due awe	278a
polished f. friend	459a
some f. errors fall	302b
the f. woman	451a
what f. heart can gold despise	173b
whimsey..is the f. guide	173a

Females: eighty mile o' f. 127a
| make poor f. mad | 357a |

Feminine: keener pangs, tho' f. 218b
Fen of stagnant waters 467b
Fence-rail: straddled that f. 182a
Fences: good f...good neighbours 157b
| there, by the starlit f. | 199b |
| yet all these f. | 187a |

Fencing: that time..that I have in f. 369b
Fenians: house of the F. 476b
Fer: I'll f. him, and firk him 383a
Ferlie: f. he spied wi' his e'e 528a
| ye crowlin' f. | 61b |

Ferments and frets 66a
Fern: grasshoppers under a f. 57a
Ferne: al the snowe of f. yere 90a
Fern-seed: we have the receipt of f. 377a
Ferrers and Fanhope 137a
Ferret: firk him, and f. him 383a
Ferry: row us o'er the f. 77a
| who's for the f.? | 261b |

Festival: things that we ordained f. 366a
Festus, I plunge! 49b
Fetch: I f. my life and being 359b
| to f. one if one goes astray | 311a |

Fetishly: full faire and f. 88b
Fetlocks shag and long 386b
Fetter: his..body lay a worn-out f. 248a
Fettered: f. Love from dying 77b
| so f. fast we are | 44b |

Fetters: in love with his f. 16b
| strong Egyptian f. | 322b |

Feud: f. of rich and poor 431a
| Fhairshon swore a f. | 12b |
| old f. twixt things and me | 36a |

Feuds: forget all f. and shed one.. tear 252b
| their ineffectual f. | 5a |

Fever-trees: all set about with f. 237a
Fever: after life's fitful f. 348b
anguish moist and f. dew	218b
English drizzle wakes the f.	232a
f. of life is over	288b
grows to an envious f.	368b
hand of a lady f. thee	324a
the f. called 'Living'	297b
thy lips taken f.	421b
what the f. is to the physicians	279a

Février: Generals Janvier and F. 575b
Few: angel-visits, f. and far between 77b
appointment by the corrupt f.	391a
being of that honest f.	438b
but f. are chosen	507b
clash'd with his fiery f.	435a
err as grossly as the f.	138b
far and f.	243b
fear that thou will find but f.	393b
f. and evil have the years..been	493b
f. and short were the prayers	462b
f. die and none resign	205a
f., f. shall part where many meet	77a

Few (cont.)

f. know their own good	142b
f. there be that find it	505b
f. things to desire	15a
f., whom genius gave to shine	175a
fit audience..tho' f.	275b
party..the gain of a f.	419a
strains—alas! too f.	470b
the f. our Father sends	29a
the notes are f.	31b
we f., we happy f.	383a
ye are many—they are f.	395b

Fez: in argosy transferred from F. 221b
Fezziwig: in came Mrs. F. 121b
Fhairshon: F. had a son 12b
| F. swore a feud | 12b |

Fiat: I have a bit of F. in my soul 24a
Fib: destroy his f. of sophistry 303a
Fibre from the brain does tear 29a
Fibs: I'll tell you no f. 171a
Fickle: made thee f. as thou art 74b
| whatever is f., freckled | 197b |

Fickleness: f. of the women I love 391a
| Oh, the lovely f. | 162a |

Fiction: by fairy F. drest 173b
condemn it as an improbable f.	371b
f. lags after truth	55b
Peerage..the best thing in f.	460b
truth..stranger than f.	72a

Fictions: my f., but her story 115b
Fictive: origin of the f. picture 204a
Fiddle: as fit as a f. 182b
f. or gay sautrye	88b
f., sir, and spade	319a
f., we know, is diddle	422a
his lass, his f., and his frisk	111a
I the second f.	528b
my f. in Dooney	475a
the cat and the f.	534a
the merry love the f.	475a
Time plays the f.	131a

Fiddlepin's end! Get out 75b
Fiddler: chemist, f., statesman 138b
he was a f., and..a rogue	418a
in came a f.	121b
the f.'s old tune	284b
the f.'s standing by	522b

Fiddlers: called for his f. three 532a
Fiddles: take back yr. golden f. 231a
Fiddlestick: imperial f.! 83b
Fiddle-strings is weakness to expredge 124b
Fiddling: a f. priest 110b
Fiddling-stick: master's lost his f. 534a
Fidele: Fair F.'s grassy tomb 102b
Fidgety Phil 193a
Fie: f., f. upon her! 369a
F., foh and fum	343a
f. now wd. she cry	20b
O, f., f., f.! thy sin's..but a trade	352a

Field: action in the tented f. 360a
a man of the f.	493a
behold her, single in the f.	471a
but for you, possess the f.	96b
by flood and f.	360a
consider the lilies of the f.	505b
cuckoo's..cry from the wet f.	8b
happy f. or mossy cavern	219a
he rush'd into the f.	68b
I thank our Lord the f. is won	283a
in a f. by the river	474a
like the van first took'st the f.	225a
only inhabitants of the f.	57a
shake alike the senate and the f.	303b
single f. wh. I have looked upon	466a
six Richmonds in the f.	385b
sleep is flying from f. and tree	35b
some corner of a foreign f.	40a
sparkled on the yellow f.	431b
that lay f. to f.	501a
the F. strewn with its dank..drifts	7b
there's a whisper down the f.	231b
the sickle in the fruitful f.	30a
tills the f. and lies beneath	438a
till the f. ring again	34b
when Prussia hurried to the f.	318a
who tills this lonely f.	146b

Fields: a' babbled of green f. 382a
ah, vain! These English f.	9a
as long as..f. are green	392a
better to hunt in f.	140a

Fields (*cont.*)
dream of battled f. 316b
farewell happy f. 271a
f. invested with purpureal gleams 467b
f. without a flower 111b
first and last of f. 68a
flowerless f. of heaven 420a
from the f. of sleep 466a
go not . . from the shining f. 433b
green f. of England 96b
happy Autumn-f. 436a
I am gone into the f. 394b
in joyless f. 443b
in the flowering of His f. 429a
in those holy f. over whose acres 376a
lilied f. of France 76b
long f. of barley and of rye 431b
no f. of amaranth 241b
nor f. of offerings 495b
out of olde . . . newe corn 90a
plough the f., and scatter 76a
poetic f. encompass me 1b
show'd how f. were won 168b
stroll alone through f. and woods 101a
subterranean f. 469b
the f. fall southward 421b
the f. his study 33a
the f. of Immortality 393b
to f. where flies no . . sided hail 197b
tyrant of his f. 174a
vasty f. of France 381a
what f., or waves, or mountains? 398b
ye f. of Cambridge 107a
Fiend: a foul F . . . Apollyon 54a
'budge,' says the f. 353b
doubt the equivocation of the f. 351a
f. hid in a cloud 32a
f. of gods and men ydrad 409a
give the F. himself his due 438b
he knows, a frightful f. 99b
out, hyperbolical f. 372a
so eagerly the f. o'er bog 273a
so spake the F. 274a
so strook . . fell the F. 277b
take heed o' the foul f. 343a
thou marble-hearted f. 342a
Fiends: f. in upper air 318b
f. that plague thee thus 98b
f. will snatch at it 364a
these juggling f. 351a
f. a pride na pride had he 63a
Fierce: anger insignificantly f. 112b
f. as ten furies 272b
f. as the fire 171b
f. raged the tempest o'er the deep 444b
grew more f. and wild 188a
more f. and more inexorable 366a
safer being meek than f. 44b
that f. thing . . conscience 195a
with oary feet bears forward f. 443b
Fierceness makes error a fault 186b
Fiere: there's a hand, my trusty f. 59a
Fiesole: drifted over F. by twilight 49a
Fife: Elephant that practised on a f. 85b
farewell . . the ear-piercing f. 362a
sound the clarion, fill the f. 283a
sound the f., and cry the slogan 12a
the Thane of F. had a wife 350a
the wry-necked f. 353b
tootle-te-tootle the f. 52b
Fifteen: f. men on the dead man's chest 413a
fifteen wild Decembers 39a
maiden of bashful f. 400b
Fifth: f. shall close the drama 28a
the F. of November 532a
Fifty: Adonis of f. 183b
at f. chides his infamous delay 477a
corpulent man of f. 202a
fifty springs are little room 198b
fifty million Frenchmen 177b
here's to the widow of f. 400b
it only leaves me f. more 198b
Fifty-four, forty or fight 4a
Fifty-three: the one and the f. 437b
we fight with f. 437b
Fig: did you say pig, or f.? 83a
Fight: a harder matter to f. 427a
a man may f. and not be slain 63a
a man may f., and not be slain 320b
are baffled to f. better 52a

Fight (*cont.*)
a second Adam to the f. 288b
come ye here to f. 530b
dead man win a f. 530b
die in the lost, lost f. 96a
eat like wolves and f. like devils 382a
end of the f. is a tombstone 233a
famoused for f. 387a
fifty-four forty or f. 4a
f. begins within himself 45a
f. it out on this line 173a
f. of the one and the fifty-three 437b
f. on to the end 177b
f. the good f. 279b
f. the good f. of faith 516b
f., to be found fighting 37b
for if they won't f. us 158b
forth to the f. are gone 306b
fought the better f. 275a
good at a f. 282b
hath no stomach to this f. 383a
he's gone to f. the French 217a
he that flies mought f. again 13b
I dare not f. 381b
if he f. longer than he sees reason 376b
I give the f. up 49b
I have fought a good f. 516b
I have not yet begun to f. 214a
it is better to f. for the good 434b
I will not cease from Mental F. 31b
let's f. till six 84b
live to f. another day 170a, 523b
martial brood accustomed to f. 408b
never rise to f. again 170a
shall we f. or shall we fly? 437b
so cd. f. us no more 437b
so f. I 514a
so, one f. more, the best 50b
then say it was in f. 377b
they now to f. are gone 137a
those that fly, may f. again 66a
those who bade me f. had told me 149b
to f. is but to die 437b
to f. with them again 437b
too proud to f. 462a
Ulster will f. 95a
we don't want to f. 201b, 527b
we'll f. and we'll conquer 158b
who this great f. did win 406a
Fighter: a bonny f. 412b
fits a dull f. 378b
I was ever a f. 50b
Fighteth: none other that f. for us 478a
Fighting: f. still, and still destroying 139a
f. unarmed amongst . . soldiers 24a
fight, to be found f. 37b
foremost f., fell 68b
I was f. as low as . . Widdrington 140a
want of f. was grown rusty 65a
Fighting Téméraire: she's the F. 287b
Fightings: without were f. 515a
Fights: gained a hundred f. 435a
he that f. and runs away 523b
he who f. and runs away 170a
with . . majesty the British soldier f. 285b
Fig-leaves: across the f. 421b
they sewed f. together 492b
Figs: f. grew upon thorn 92a
fig-tree casteth her untimely f. 518b
gather . . f. of thistles 505b
green bursting f. 8b
I love long life better than f. 322b
in the name of the Prophet—f. 404a
Fig-tree: every man . . under his f. 504b
f. casteth her untimely figs 518b
train up a f. 122b
Figure: as the active or passive f. 204b
baby of the giant 368b
f. in a country church 418a
f. in the carpet 204b
in did come the strangest f.! 50a
only f. among ciphers 16a
this f. that thou here seest 215b
to make me the fixed f. 363a
Figures: carved with f. strange 100a
f. pedantical 345a
prove anything by f. 80b
Filbert: Gilbert, the F. 462a
File: in the nature of an Old F. 123a
Files: commands the beauteous f. 448a
here f. of pins extend 302b

Files (*cont.*)
ye fill up the gaps in our f. 7b
Files-on-Parade 228b
Filial: untie the f. band 317b
Fill: a beggar may drink his f. 27a
f. it up to the brim 320a
f. me from the crown to the toe top 346b
f. the unforgiving minute 230a
take our f. of love 498a
Filled: dreamt . . they f. with dew 99a
f. and vivified by Thee 280a
f. to the brim with girlish glee 164b
Filling: merely writ at first for f. 419b
Film: only that f., wh. fluttered 101a
the lash, of f. 364b
Filth: in our own f. drop our . . judgments 324a
Filths savour but themselves 343b
Filthy: greedy of f. lucre 516b
he wh. is f., let him be f. still 520b
Fin: now winks the gold f. 436b
under that Almighty F. 39b
Finality . . not . . language of politics 128a
Financiers: leaves to skilled f. 167b
Find: always f. us young 147a
be sure yr. sin will f. you out 494b
can't tell where to f. them 533a
f. him ware an' wakin' 287b
f. it after many days 499b
f. me, and turn thy back 146a
f. out, if you can, whose master 419b
f. thou but thyself, thou art I 422a
I cannot f. it out 416a
I waked to f. her 275b
lost thing cd. I never f. 27a
must f. it out tonight 348b
seek, and ye shall f. 505b
such perfect joy therein I f. 143a
there thou shalt f. me 526a
until I f. the holy Grail 438a
when you do f. him 341b
where shall we f. her 420a
with men I f. Him not 429a
Finder-out of occasions 361a
Findeth: he that f. his life 506b
he that seeketh 505b
Finds: f. too late that men betray 170a
make more opportunities than he f. 16b
Fine: f. by degrees 305b
frank, and f. 26b
makes that and th' action f. 188b
May will be f. next year 199b
not to put too f. a point 121a
quite a *disgrace* to be f. 425a
some are f. fellows 263b
spider's touch how exquisitely f. 300b
stretch a cord, however f. 456b
Finely: spirits are not f. touched 351a
Finer: something f. in the man 148a
Finger: better a f. off 320a
f. of birth-strangled babe 349b
from the red gold keep thy f. 319a
God's f. touched him 430b
lazy f. of a maid 364b
more goodness in her little f. 418b
my little f. shall be thicker 496a
point his slow and unmoving f. at 363a
put my f. into the print 511b
put yr. f. in yr. eye 533a
smooth to her slim f. tips 192a
the Moving F. writes 153b
'twixt his f. and his thumb 376b
Fingers: before Decay's effacing f. 72b
cannot lick his own f. 366a
do dead men's f. call them 336a
even the works of thy f. 482a
he . . kissed the f. of this hand 44a
his f. held the pen 111a
my f. wandered idly 306b
pinching f. 373a
smile upon his f.' ends 382a
spires whose 'silent f.' 464b
trailing in the . . streams thy f. 8a
with f. weary and worn 196a
with forc'd f. rude 269a
Finger-stalls: in fitless f. 164b
Finish, good lady 325a
Finished: it is f. 511b
Finisher of our faith 517a
Finite: cannot . . bury under the F. 81b
Fir-branch: lone on the f. 263b

Fire: adamantine chains and penal f. 271a
a little f. kindleth 517b
all compact of f. 386b
around the f. addressed its evening 415a
as a f. shall ye pass 423b
as f. is kindled by f. 224a
ashes where once I was f. 67b
as now on f. I am 407a
as the flint bears f. 341a
before the f. of life 241a
be in danger of hell f. 505a
books that you may carry to the f. 212a
bring me my chariot of f. 31a
burnt the f. of thine eyes 32a
by a sea-coal f., upon Wednesday 380a
by night in a pillar of f. 494a
can a man take f. in his bosom 498a
darkness, f., and chains 452b
desire of f. to reach to f. 263b
don't..f...you can see..their eyes 307a
every time she shouted 'F.'! 26a
faith and f. within us 180a
feed the heart of..night with f. 422b
fell in the f. and was burnt to ashes 172b
f. and fleet and candle-light 529a
f. and hail, snow and vapours 490b
f. and people do in this agree 176b
f. answers f. 382b
f. burn, and cauldron bubble 349b
F.! Help! The Hare! 192b
f. my good one out 389b
F. of London was not the f. 123a
f., or the strength of the streams 420a
f. sall never make thee shrink 529a
f. that in the heart resides 7a
f. that saith not, it is enough 499a
f. that stirs about her 475a
f. when you are ready, Gridley 120b
f. within f., desire in deity 312a
French Guard, f. first 183a
fretted with golden f. 332b
frighted with false f. 334b
full of that heavenly f. 176b
gave a roar, as if of earthly f. 218a
heap coals of f. 498b
his eyes were as a flame of f. 518b
his ministers a flaming f. 488a
his speech is a burning f. 420b
hold a f. in his hand 374b
I am f. and air 325a
I am warm, I have seen the f. 502b
in our asshen olde is f. y-reke 89a
in the F. of Spring 152b
I sit beside my lonely f. 2b
it is a f., it is a coal 295b
it is a heretic that makes the f. 373a
it—is—not—f.—devils, dark 227b
I was thus musing the f. kindled 484a
I will sit beside the f. 26b
laburnums, dropping-wells of f. 430b
leads to..the great f. 322a
lighten with celestial f. 491a
lighting our..torches at his f. 97b
like f. he meets the foe 436b
little f. is quickly trodden out 384b
make the cold air f. 397b
martyr in his shirt of f. 403b
men, that are set on f. 485b
motion of a hidden f. 280a
neighbour's house is on f. 56b
nodding by the f. 476b
now stir the f. 112a
O! for a Muse of f. 381a
O love! O f. 427a
only at his post when under f. 179b
ordain'd to kill, conceiveth f. 408b
O that man's heart were as f. 420a
pale his ineffectual f. 331b
quench'd them hath given me f. 347b
run a mile to see a f. 413a
sea of glass mingled with f. 519b
shrivelled in a fruitless f. 430b
smiles by his cheerful f. 170a
spark o' Nature's f. 60a
spring the true Promethean f. 345a
Sticks of..briar make me a f. 190b
stood that night against my f. 344a
the f. is not quenched 508b
the f. seven times tried this 353b
their rosy fleece of f. bestow 115a
the Lord was not in the f. 496a

Fire (cont.)
they are all f. 339a
thorough flood, thorough f. 356b
Thou knowest Who hast made the
F. 232b
three removes is as bad as a f. 157a
till the f. is dying in the grate 263b
tongues like as of f. 512a
to Purgatory f. thou com'st 529a
to view what f. was near 407b
two irons in the f. 23a
upon a wheel of f. 344a
wash me in..gulfs of liquid f. 364a
went to tend the wounded under f. 229b
what the hand dare seize the f.? 32a
whether in sea or f. 329b
with white f. laden 393a
youk'n hide de f. 182a
Fireballs: blinding f., sleet 49b
Fire-baptism: Baphometic F. 81b
Firebrand plucked from the burning 504a
Fire-drake: as far as the f. swings 92b
Fire-flames noondays kindle 46a
Fire-fly wakens 436b
Fire-folk sitting in the air! 197b
Fireman, and afraid of bumps! 403b
Fire-red: hadde a f. cherubinnes face 88b
Fires: arose the answering f. 252b
banked the f. high 235b
fuel to maintain his f. 79a
glorious th' assembled f. 403a
in our ashes live their wonted f. 174b
keep the home f. burning 156a
never need to light their f. 180b
one whose f. true genius kindles 303a
quenched the stelled f. 343a
that f. the length of Ophiucus 273a
thought-executing f. 342b
treading over f. hidden 545a
Truth..will lend her noblest f. 72b
violent f. soon burn out 374b
ye follow wandering f. 428a
Fire-side: adventures were by the f. 171a
f. enjoyments 112a
happy f. clime 59a
season my f. with..talk 468b
there is no f. 248a
winter talk by the f. 16a
Firewood, iron ware 261b
Firk: I'll fer him, and f. him 383a
Firm: who so f...cannot be seduc'd 338a
zealous, beneficent, f. 7b
Firmament: brave o'erhanging f. 332b
Christ's blood streams in the f. 258b
f. showeth his handiwork 482b
now glow'd the f. with..sapphires 274a
the pillared f. is rottenness 267b
there is no fellow in the f. 339a
the spacious f. on high 2a
Firmly I believe and truly 288b
Firmness: thy f. makes my circle just 134a
with f. in the right 245b
First: after Last, returns the F. 44b
an undoubted title to the f. 418b
as a wit, if not f., in the..f. line 169b
be not the f. by whom the new 300a
each second stood heir to the f. 359b
Eclipse f., the rest nowhere 290b
else he'd have been here f. 85a
f., and last, and midst 471a
f. and wisest of them all 277a
f. come I; my name is Jowett 528b
f. fine careless rapture 47a
f. in war, f. in peace 244a
f. love's f. cry 293b
f. put this uniform on 165a
f. shall be last 507b
f. that ever burst 98b
f. to come and last to go 249a
f. to fade away 282a
for wh. the f. was made 50b
Glorious F. of June 285a, 526b
him f., him last 275a
in her f. passion woman loves 70b
last state..is worse than the f. 506b
pray it be to me 37b
rather be f. in a village 13a
she is the f. and I the second 528b
the f., last look 72b
there is no last nor f. 50a

First (cont.)
to feel the f. kiss 312a
we for a certainty are not the f. 199b
when f. we met we did not guess 38a
wh. was the f. to fade away 75b
works of genius are the f. things 222a
First-born: her f.'s breath 178a
smite all the f. 494a
Firstfruits: become the f. 515a
Firstlings of my heart 350a
Fir-tree: shall come up the f. 503a
Fir-trees: f...a dwelling for the stork 488b
f. dark and high 195a
Fish: ever so free as a f. 314b
f. not, with this melancholy bait 352b
f. out of the water 321b
f. say, they have their stream 39a
f. would have bright mail 217b
great f. spouts music as he swims 202b
harmless f. monastic silence 132b
it's no f. ye're buying 319a
Jonah was in the belly of the f. 504b
littlest f. may enter in 39b
man may f. with the worm 335b
no more land, say f. 39b
O silver f. that my two hands 476a
piece of broiled f. 510b
the f. soar to find the ocean 442a
they're bonnie f. and halesome 285b
thou deboshed f. thou 367b
un-dish-cover the f. 85b
what cat's arnese to f.? 173b
you were a tadpole, and I was a f. 404a
Fished: who f. the murex up? 50a
Fisher: skilful f. goes not forth 532b
Fisherman: O well for the f.'s boy 425b
Fishermen that walk upon the beach 343b
Fishers: f. of men 505a
three f. went sailing 226b
Fishes: blows..bait in the f.' mouth 532b
f. first to shipping did impart 139b
f., that tipple in the deep 249b
hors d'œuvres for f. 131a
if you were to make little f. talk 171b
little f.' answer was 85a
little f. of the sea 85a
loses sight of the loaves and f. 295a
men lived like f. 401a
the f. of the sea 482a
thousand men that f. gnawed upon 384b
welcomes little f. in 82b
when f. flew and forests walked 92a
Fishified: how art thou f.! 365b
Fishing: and for winter fly-f. 450a
discourse of..fish and f. 450b
I go a f. 511b
on f. up the moon 295b
when I was last this way a-f. 450b
when he goes a-f. 450a
Fishing-bark: many a light f. 252a
Fish-like: ancient and f. smell 367b
Fishmonger: you are a f. 332a
Fishpond: that great f. (the sea) 118b
Fishpools in Heshbon 500b
Fish-sauce: crack a bottle of f. 93b
Fishy: immense, of f. form and mind 39b
Fist: beat with f., instead of a stick 64b
his energetic f. shd. be ready 166a
his f. be ever ready 166a
my left eye agin the Seceesher's f. 451a
Fit: as f. as a fiddle 182b
a while the f. will work 336b
f. audience find, tho' few 275b
f. for the deed I had to do 85a
f. for to serve as a soldier 236b
one last, long lingering f. 233b
Pilot..fell down in a f. 99b
they therefore needs must f. 109a
Fits: bein' took with f. 124a
blue cap that always f. 92b
cope him in these sullen f. 325b
Sleary's f. 233b
strange f. of passion 471a
they have their f. and freaks 131a
Fitter being sane than mad 44b
Fittest: survival of the f. 117b, 408a
Fitzdotterel: Earl of F.'s eldest 40b
Fitzgerald: F. strung them 250b
for this Edward F. died 474b
shall hoarse F. bawl 72a

Five: f. minutes too late 107b
  f. times received I forty stripes 515a
  housbondes..she hadde f. 88b
  must rise at f. 532b
Fixed: f. like a plant 301a
  f. the where and when 182b
  he f. thee mid this dance
  well and wisely f. 464b
Flag: an English f. was flown 228b
  death's pale f. 366b
  f. and sign of love 359b
  f. that makes you free 473a
  f. to April's breeze unfurled 146b
  like to a vagabond f. 322b
  our f. on every sea 201a
  she took up the f. 459a
  spare yr. country's f. 459a
  the meteor f. of England 78a
  the old f.'s flyin' 287b
  war, an' a debt, an' a f. 250b
  whose f. has braved 77b
Flag-flowers: there grew broad f. 398a
Flagons: stay me with f. 500a
Flags wearily thro' darkness 395b
Flail: f. of the lashing hail 393a
  new device of a Protestant F. 193a
Flakes: in large white f. falling 37a
Flame: absence seem'd my f. to
  qualify 389a
  adding fuel to the f. 278a
  burn..with this hard, gemlike f. 293a
  but f.? the bush is bare 50b
  Chloe is my real f. 306a
  feed his sacred f. 101b
  f. that burns upon its altars 183a
  f. that lit the battle's wreck 184b
  friendly glow, and softer f. 59a
  if you nurse a f. 77b
  love's devoted f. 282b
  moth..still plays about the f. 159a
  nor public f., nor private 299a
  she may receive and own my f. 305b
  so in a shapeless f. 131b
  spark of heavenly f. 299a
  whose f. creeps in at every hole 295b
  words..so full of subtil f. 22b
Flamed upon the brazen greaves 431b
Flamens: here lies two F. 79a
Flames: f. in the forehead 270a
  from those f. no light 271a
  his f. must waste away 79a
  knobs, and f. o' fire 382a
  thou king of f. 87a
  thro' their paly f. 382b
  went by her like thin f. 311b
Flaming: hurled headlong f. 271a
Flanders: F. mare 571b
  our armies swore terribly in F. 411b
  part of F. hath receiv'd our yoke 449a
  poppies grow in F. Fields 256a
  prodigious armies we had in F. 411b
Flank: on our f. the crimson sun 136a
Flanks: her silken f. with garlands 219b
Flannel: get her a f. waistcoat 159a
Flannelled fools at the wicket 230a
Flap-dragon: easier swallowed than
  a f. 345a
Flapped and fought 192a
Flash: one F. of it within the Tavern 154a
Flashes: f. struck from midnights 46a
  fresher airs to f. blent 293b
  in f., and with glory not their own 469b
  this proverb f. thro' his head 426b
Flashing: youth is the time to go f. 413a
Flashy: their lean and f. songs 269b
Flat: a very dangerous f., and fatal 354a
  fell half so f. as Walter Scott 525b
  f. burglary as ever was 359a
  isn't yr. life extremely f. 166b
  stale, f., and unprofitable 330a
  therefore it's f. and plain 526a
Flat-irons: flavour o' warm f. 127a
Flats: fifty different sharps and f. 50a
Flatten: hide is sure to f. 'em 25b
Flatter: before you f. a man 212a
  fondly f. our desires 136b
  nay, do not think I f. 334a
  paint my picture..and not f. me 116a
  they do but f. with their lips 482a
  they f. with their tongue 482a
Flattered: being then most f. 338b

Flattered (cont.)
  Englishman, being f., is a lamb 87a
  f. into virtue 416b
  f. me with hopes of earthly bliss 112b
  he that loves to be f. 368a
  I have not f. its rank breath 68b
Flatterer: either a coward or a f. 339b
  face-f. and back-biter 429a
  General Good is the plea of..f. 30b
  O Sleep! thou f. 104a
  the arch-f...man's self 14b
  worthy of the f. 368a
Flatterers: by f. besieged 303a
  tell him he hates f. 338b
Flattering: think him worth f. 390b
  what really f. a man 390b
Flatters: the lie that f. 111a
Flattery: feyned f. and japes 89a
  f. soothe the dull, cold ear 174a
  f...with a trowel 129a
  gross f. to name a coward 444b
  imitation is the sincerest of f. 103b
  ne'er was f. lost on poet's ear 317a
  style of a dedication is f. 212b
  This is no f. 325b
  to ask advice..to tout for f. 102b
  whether..yr. f. is worth his having 212a
  woman..gained by every sort of f. 91a
Flavia's a wit 302a
Flavour: f. of mild decay 194a
  till it's losing its f. 20a
  variety..gives it all its f. 111b
  vich wanity do you like the f. on 127a
Flaw: it has no kind of fault or f. 163b
  it is a f. in happiness 217b
Flaws: wished the f. were fewer 46a
Flax: smoking f. shall he not quench 502b
Flayed: belted you an' f. you 230a
Flea: clog the foot of a f. 371b
  f. in his ear 4b
  f. in's ear 23a
  precedency between a louse and a
  f. 211a
  take the life of a f. 20a
  very f. of his dog 215b
Fleas: a flea hath smaller f. 419b
  beggars, f., and vines 226a
  dog that praised his f. 476a
  f. is good fer a dog 456a
  great f. have little f. 283b
Fled: all but he had f. 184b
  but thou art f. 392b
  f. murmuring 274b
  I f. Him, down the nights 441b
  I waked, she f. 278b
  kissed it and then f. 398a
  still as he f. 408b
  they're all f. with thee 224b
Flee: f. from the wrath to come 504b
  he can speak and f. 529a
  that hate him f. before him 486a
  they f. from me, that..did me seek 473b
Fleece: f. was white as snow 177b
  like the rain into a f. 486b
  their rosy f. of fire bestow 115a
  yr. f. is white but 'tis too cold 115a
Fleeces so clean and white 453a
Fleet: all in the Downs the f. 161a
  British F. a-riding at anchor 440b
  fire and f. and candle-light 529a
  f.-limbed and beautiful 289b
  how f. 'twas on those little..feet 261a
  O thou most f. 420a
  Spanish f. thou canst not see 400a
  where the f. of stars is anchored 154b
  yield, proud foe, thy f. 76b
Fleet Street: dull in F. 239b
Fleeter of foot than the..kid 420b
Fleets: ten thousand f. sweep over 69b
  vain, mightiest f. of iron 136b
Flesh: all f. is as grass 517b
  all f. is grass 502b
  all f. shall be revealed 502b
  Boston man..east wind made f. 4b
  bring me f. and bring me wine 286b
  but the f. is weak 508a
  cd. not all this f. keep in..life? 379a
  closed up the f. instead 492a
  conversion of..Godhead into f. 478b
  fedde with rosted f. 88b
  f. and blood so cheap 196b

Flesh (cont.)
  f. and blood wh. did in Adam fail 289a
  f. helps soul 50b
  f., how art thou fishified! 365b
  f. lusteth against the Spirit 515b
  f. of f., bone of my bone 276b
  f. of my f. 492a
  given to me a thorn in the f. 515b
  going the way of all f. 454b
  gone the way of all f. 105b
  gross f. sinks downwards 376a
  hair of my f. stood up 497a
  her fair and unpolluted f. 336b
  I have more f. than another man 378b
  I wants to make yr. f. creep 126a
  I will eat bulls' f. 485a
  kinsmen according to the f. 513b
  make not provision for the f. 514a
  men are f. and blood 339a
  milk and tender f. 89b
  mind the things of the f. 513b
  my f. also longeth after thee 485b
  nor soul helps f. 50b
  of..human f. subsisting 478b
  one f...leaves 'em still two fools 104a
  shocks that f. is heir to 333a
  since f. must live 51b
  sinful lusts of the f. 481a
  soul to feel the f. 39a
  spite of this f. to-day 50b
  study is a weariness of the f. 500a
  these our f. upright 132b
  the world, the f., and the devil 478b
  they shall be one f. 492a
  they that are after the f. 513b
  this f. of mine might be 423a
  this f. wh. walls about 375b
  this soul..prisons of f. 133b
  this world-wearied f. 366b
  thou didst eat strange f. 322b
  'tis the way of all f. 321b
  too too solid f. wd..melt 330a
  unto thee shall all f. come 485b
  we are one, one f. 276b
  weyveth milk, and f. 89b
  wh. limbs and f. enough invest 147a
  within this circle of f. 41b
  Word was made f. 510b
  wrestle not against f. 516a
  yet in my f. shall I see God 497a
Fleshed thy maiden sword 379a
Fleshly School of Poetry 53b
Fleshpots: when we sat by the f. 494a
Fleshy tables of the heart 515a
Flew: round and round it f. 98a
Flewed: so f., so sanded 357a
Fliers: chase e'en now the f. 96b
  f. and pursuers mingled 254a
Flies: as f. to wanton boys, are we 343b
  butchers' shops with large blue f. 403b
  cobwebs, where small f. were
  caught 13b
  dead f. cause the ointment 499b
  f. of estate and sunshine 188a
  f. on summer eves 220a
  f., or ants, entombed..in amber 16b
  f., worms, and flowers 453a
  he that has..mought fight again 13b
  lean black craft like f. 311b
  shoot folly as it f. 300b
  then she f. away 438a
  unfading moths, immortal f. 39b
  unto you at last she f. 79b
Flight: alarms of struggle and f. 5a
  by a frantic f. of courtesy 294b
  dark..was the day of their f. 255b
  from an eagle in his f. 247a
  hear the lark begin his f. 268b
  his f. was madness 350a
  in what fond f. 312b
  not attained by sudden f. 247b
  on tiptoe for a f. 218b
  prepared for longer f. 261a
  swift be thy f. 399a
  the beetle wheels his droning f. 174a
Flights upon the banks of Thames 216a
Flighty purpose never is o'ertook 350a
Flim-flam: a pretty f. 23a
Flimnap, the Treasurer 417b
Flinch: facts are facts and f. not 51a
Flinders: little Polly F. 535a

Fling: I'll have a f. — 23a
Flint: as the f. bears fire — 341a
  in time the f. is pierced — 238a
  ne'er wear out the everlasting f. — 365b
  set your faces like a f. — 54a
  weariness can snore upon the f. — 329a
Flirt: how can he [a bishop] f.? — 404b
Flirtation: birth of that..word f. — 91a
  merely innocent f. — 71b
Flit: I will f. into it with my lyre — 218b
Flitting: I am f. about many years — 96a
Flittings: thou tellest my f. — 485b
Float: f. double, swan and shadow — 473a
  f. upon the wings of silence — 267a
  little lead best fits a little f. — 188b
Floated: out flew the web and f. wide — 431b
Float-fishing: angling or f. — 214a
Floating: his f. home for ever left — 107b
Floats: f. tho' unseen among us — 394b
  that f. on high o'er vales — 467a
Flock: feed his f. like a shepherd — 502b
  half his f. were in their beds — 474a
  leave..the f. without shelter — 318b
  makest thy f. to rest at noon — 500a
  one sickly sheep infects the f. — 453a
  silent was the f. in woolly fold — 221b
  tainted wether of the f. — 354b
  there is no f., however watched — 248a
  unto my f. I daily preached — 524a
Flocks: f. of shiny pleiades — 192a
  f. of the memories of the day — 265a
  in fleecy f. of light — 37b
  my f. feed not — 21a
  sweet buds like f. to feed in air — 396a
  watch'd their f. by night — 424a
  whiter than be the f. — 176a
Flodden's fatal field — 318b
Flogging: he was in the habit of f. me — 445b
  less f. in our great schools — 208b
Flood: beached verge of the salt f. — 368a
  bridge much broader than the f. — 358a
  bridge that arched the f. — 146b
  by f. and field — 360a
  drink to thee across the f. — 427a
  Empire vast across the f. — 202b
  fellows..f. cd. not wash away — 104b
  fording thro' their rising f. — 27a
  leap..with me into this angry f. — 337b
  love you ten years before the F. — 260a
  nearly spoiled ta F. — 12b
  never came reformation in a f. — 381b
  nobler tenants of the f. — 110b
  not to be thought of that the F. — 467a
  passage o'er a restless f. — 109a
  struggle thro' such a raging f. — 253b
  taken at the f. — 341a
  the f. may bear me far — 426a
  the giant race before the f. — 140a
  thorough f., thorough fire — 356b
  to such a sudden f. of mutiny — 340a
  winds that curl the f. — 249b
Flood-brim: unto the furthest f. — 312b
Flood-gate: f. and o'er-bearing
  nature — 359b
  f. of the deeper heart — 55a
Flooding: silent, f. in, the main — 96b
Floods: bathe in fiery f. — 352a
  beside the haystack in the f. — 284a
  in yr. deep f. drown — 155b
  neither can the f. drown it — 501a
  the f. are risen, O Lord — 487b
  the f. have lift up their voice — 487b
  the f. lift up their waves — 487b
  the thickets to his f. decline — 37b
Floor: beneath the watery f. — 270a
  f. lay pav'd with broken hearts — 249b
  glimmering o'er my fleece-like f. — 393a
  how the f. of heaven is thick inlaid — 355a
  I cd. f. them all — 129a
  I swept the f. — 166a
  the nicely sanded f. — 168b
  thy sad f. an altar — 69b
  windless, glassy f. — 231a
Floored with gemlike plains — 452b
Floors of silent seas — 145a
Flop in favour of yr. husband — 127b
Flopping: must go f. yourself down — 127b
Flora: nor F.'s pride — 42b
  tasting of F. — 210b
Florence: Cosmus Duke of F. — 13b
  F., Elizabethan England — 203a

Florence (cont.)
  lily of F. blossoming in stone — 247a
  outside the cathedral at F. — 123a
  Parys, Venyce or F. — 143a
  rode past fair F. — 218b
  yonder late in F. — 49a
Florentine: and what the F.? — 36a
Flores in the Azores — 437a
Flotilla: where the old F. lay — 232a
Flourish: all things f. where you turn — 302b
  farmers..f. and complain — 113b
  f. of his right arm — 125b
  they f. at home — 525a
  thou shalt f. in immortal youth — 1b
  truth shall f. out — 487a
Flourisheth: she f. new and new — 402b
Flourishing like a green bay-tree — 484a
Flout: banners f. the sky — 346a
  f. 'em, and scout 'em — 367b
  gild, but to f., the ruins grey — 317a
Flouts: master of gibes and f. — 128b
  Phillida f. me — 525b
Flow: a fatal ebb and f. — 203b
  aware of his life's f. — 5a
  ebb and f. must ever be — 465a
  feast of reason and the f. of soul — 303b
  f. gently, sweet Afton — 60b
  I within did f. with seas — 445a
  Oh, cd. I f. like thee — 119b
  that f. strewed wrecks — 203b
  tho' tears no longer f. — 38b
  what need you f. so fast? — 527b
Flower: action is no stronger than a f. — 388a
  a lovelier f...was never sown — 471b
  as the f. of grass — 517b
  bud of love..prove a beauteous f. — 365b
  constellated f. that never sets — 398a
  creep from f. to f. — 394b
  crimson-tippèd f. — 62a
  deeper than f. and fruit — 263a
  emperice and f. of floures alle — 90a
  every f. enjoys the air — 471a
  every f. that sad embroidery — 270a
  fell upon a little western f. — 356b
  f. in the crannied wall — 427a
  f. of a blameless life — 427b
  f. of a hazel glade — 177a
  f. of Catholic love — 424a
  f. of sweetest smell — 468a
  f. of wyfly pacience — 89b
  F. that once has blown — 153a
  f. that's like thy face — 329a
  f. that smiles today — 190a
  f. thereof falleth away — 517b
  Heaven in a Wild F. — 29a
  he flourisheth as a f. — 488a
  here ev'ry f. is united — 159b
  herself a fairer f. — 274a
  honey..from every opening f. — 453a
  I never loved a tree or f. — 75b
  I sipt each f. — 159b
  life was but a f. — 327b
  little f...but if I cd. understand — 427a
  look like the innocent f. — 347a
  many a f. is born to blush — 174a
  Margaret, the midsummer f. — 402b
  my face, yr. f. — 46b
  nipt my f. sae early — 61a
  no f. upon the ground — 393a
  no sister-f. wd. be forgiven — 395b
  not a f., not a f. sweet — 371a
  O fairest f., no sooner blown — 268a
  O f. of the branch — 476a
  only amaranthine f. — 112a
  orange f. perfumes the bower — 320a
  paints the wayside f. — 76a
  pluck this f., safety — 377a
  pore..o'er a weed or a f. — 20a
  summer comes with f. and bee — 184b
  summer's f. is to the summer — 388b
  sweet will be the f. — 110a
  take the f. and turn the hour — 229a
  the fair f. Delice — 409b
  the grass withereth, the f. fadeth — 502b
  the king's knights 'tis the f. — 528a
  the meanest f. that blows — 467a
  there's a f. that shall be mine — 463b
  this most goodly f. — 402b
  thou canst not stir a f. — 442b
  'tis but a little faded f. — 200b
  wearing..learning..like a f. — 431a

Flower (cont.)
  we saw the waterflags in f. — 293b
  winter woodland looks a f. — 426b
  with the f. of the mind — 148a
  you seize the f. — 63a
Flower-bell: fancy from a f. — 45a
Flower-de-luce being one — 373b
Floweret: meanest f. of the vale — 175a
Flowerets of Eden ye still inherit — 282a
Flowering: mark'd Him in the f. of
  His fields — 429a
  other f. isles must be — 395b
Flower-pots: water yr. damned f. — 52a
Flowers: all dazed with f. — 296b
  alle that loven f. — 90a
  all its twined f. — 221b
  all the f. looked up at Him — 92a
  all the ground with vernal f. — 270a
  are f. but fading seen — 295b
  blown buds of barren f. — 422a
  blushing f. shall rise — 302b
  break into foam of f. — 423a
  bringeth vo'th May f. — 525a
  but as a bed of f. — 134b
  cool-rooted f. — 220a
  fairest f. o' the season — 373a
  Fancy..who breeding f. — 220b
  feel like f. that fade — 425a
  feel the f. growing over him — 223b
  feet of man, like f. — 464b
  flies, worms, and f. — 453a
  f. and fruits of love — 73b
  f., anew, returning seasons bring! — 296b
  f. azure, black — 398a
  f. ginnen for to spring — 89b
  f. I leave you on the grass — 439b
  f. in the garden — 414b
  f. of all hue — 274a
  f. of the forest — 97a, 145b
  f. on earth appear — 262a
  f. on furze — 52b
  f., so blue and golden — 247a
  f. that bloom in the spring, Tra la — 165a
  f. that grow between — 248a
  f. that their gay wardrobe wear — 269b
  f. the wh. on earth do spring — 408a
  f. to crown thy hearse — 225a
  f. to strew Thy way — 187a
  f. to wither at the north wind's — 185a
  f. whyte and rede — 90a
  frosts are slain and f. begotten — 420a
  gathered f. are dead, Yasmin — 154b
  gave once, her f. to love — 40a
  here's f. for you — 373a
  I cannot see what f. — 220a
  I have loved f. that fade — 36b
  immortal f. of Poesy — 259b
  in (May) all f. and roses spring — 42b
  insnared with f., I fall on grass — 260b
  larded with sweet f. — 335b
  Little T.C. in a Prospect of F. — 261a
  might I wander there, among the f. — 37a
  most can raise the f. now — 427a
  no f. be planted on my grave — 180b
  no f., by request — 570a
  no fruits, no f. — 195a
  of alle the f. in the mede — 90a
  oh bother the f. that bloom — 165a
  on chaliced f. that lies — 328b
  O Proserpina! for the f. now — 373a
  our bridal f. serve for a..corse — 366a
  play with and smile — 382a
  radiant looks of unbewailing f. — 397a
  showers for the thirsting f. — 393a
  smelt for f. — 75b
  souls do couch on f. — 324b
  summer with f. that fell — 420b
  sweet beds of f. — 369b
  tell that f. wd. bloom — 217b
  the f. appear on the earth — 500a
  these f., as in their causes, sleep — 79b
  those f. made of light — 195a
  Time did beckon to the f. — 187b
  to his music plants and f. — 385b
  took the f. away — 248a
  up-gathered now like sleeping f. — 473a
  votive tears and symbol f., — 394a
  with f. of the fairest — 97a
  with rising f. be dressed — 299b
  world has no such f. — 423a
Flowery: at her f. work doth sing — 268b

Flowery (cont.)
f. way that leads to the broad gate 322a
Showery, F. 158a
walk yr. f. way 165b
Flowing: clear springs renewed by f. 78a
f. with milk and honey 493b
when f. cups run swiftly 249b
Flown with insolence and wine 271b
Flows: beholds the light and whence
it f. 466a
dreary sea now f. between 100a
f. all that charms or ear 100b
methinks how sweetly f. 190b
Flowy: Snowy, F. 158a
Fluidity of self-revelation 204a
Flummoxed: Italians call reg'larly f. 126b
Flung: who f. it to the winds 152b
Flunked: never f...he never lied 183a
Flunkey: one non-f., one hero 81a
Flushed with a purple grace 139a
Flute: blows out his brains upon the
f., harp, sackbut 52a
f., violin, bassoon 504a
soft complaining f. 434a
the gauger played the f. 139b
Flutes: f. and soft recorders 415a
Gibbon moved to f. and hautboys 271b
to the tune of f. kept stroke 103b
Fluttered: f. and fail'd for breath 323a
f. round the lamp 7b
Fluttering in the wind 85b
Flux: all is f. 48a
f. of mortal things 559b
Fly: all things f. thee 9a
as pigs have to f. 442a
away the f. smyteth 83a
but to f. is safe 90a
curious, thirsty f. 112a
dead f.'s wing on a sheet of spider's 290b
ensnare as great a f. as Cassio 181a
f. away, breath 361a
f., Honesty, f.! 371a
f. infinite wrath 404a
f. I well know whither 273b
f. sat upon the axletree 35b
f. that sips treacle 16b
f. to her, and fall upon her..eaves 159b
f. to her and pipe and woo 436a
I cannot f. 436b
I do not want to be a f. 351a
'I', said the F. 167b
I will f. to thee 528a
in my 'solitary f.' 220a
is not worth a f. 75b
know thee and f. thee 522a
let them f. all 406b
making them ready to f. 350b
man is not a f., 459a
never f. conceals a hook 300b
said a spider to a f. 39b
seem to f. it, it will pursue 201a
shall we fight or shall we f.? 216a
small gilded f. does lecher 437b
swallow stopt as he hunted the f. 343b
they ever f. by twilight 435b
those that f., may fight 15b
to f. from, need not be to hate 66a
to wreke him on a 68b
Uncle Toby..the f. in his hand 90a
whan a f. offendeth 411b
wh. one wd. f. first 90a
wh. way I f. is Hell 446b
with twain he did f. 273b
you f. them for a moment 501b
'ly-fishing..very pleasant amuse-ment 437b
214a
'lying: borne down by the f. 318a
came f. all abroad 412a
come f. on our track 443b
f. from far away 437a
f. still before me 466a
sleep is f. from field and tree 35b
Swallow, f., f. South 436a
Time is still a-f. 190a
'lying-fishes play 232a
'oam: poor little F. 102a
'oam: breaks the..f. of the Spring 452a
cruel crawling f. 226b
f. of perilous seas..forlorn 220a
like the f. on the river 316b

Foam (cont.)
this year, the must shall f. 253a
through sheets of f. 8b
too full for sound and f. 426a
Foam-flowers endure 421b
Foaming out their own shame 518a
Foe: at another to let in the f. 277b
a timorous f. 303a
a willing f. and sea room 522b
darkly at the f. 253a
first f. in the field 250a
f. that comes with fearless eyes 287b
forbids the robbing of a f. 94b
I fear no f. in shining armour 291b
I fear no f. with Thee at hand 251b
I was angry with my f. 32a
like fire he meets the f. 436b
my dearest f. in heaven 330a
my noble f. I greet 317b
neither seeks, nor shuns his f. 139b
open f. may prove a curse 160b
perhaps a jealous f. 393b
rider and horse—friend, f. 68b
take up our quarrel with the f. 256a
taken by the insolent f. 360a
the f.! they come! they come! 68b
the manxome f. he sought 83b
thou arraign'st her, her f. 6b
to match another f. 77b
treads the shadow of his f. 98a
truth..the f. of tyrants 77b
unrelenting f. to love 443a
where breathes the f. but falls 178a
who never made a f. 428b
wish my deadly f., no worse 35a
yield, proud f., thy fleet 76b
Foeman: f. bares his steel 166b
let the trumpet snare the f. 234b
spills the foremost f.'s life 316a
to-day, beneath the f.'s frown 136b
Foemen worthy of their steel 316b
Foes: against her f. Religion 113b
beat down baffling f. 5b
f. saluted as they passed 141b
from the f. they captive make 87a
greatly his f. he dreads 94a
keep far our f. 491a
let his f. triumph in his overthrow 176a
man's f...of his own household 506b
neither f. nor loving friends 230a
once dreaded by our f. 111a
scarce..hear, or see their f. 318b
slay their f., and lift them high 256a
thou art in the midst of f. 146a
thrice he routed all his f. 139a
to hearken if his f. pursue him 386b
we ne'er see our f. 158b
Foetus: extraction of the f. 411b
Fog: a London particular..a f., miss 121a
feel the f. in my throat 50b
f. of the good man's mind 45b
thro' the f. and filthy air 345b
yellow f. that rubs its back 144b
Fogs: his rising f. prevail 140b
Foil: put it to the f. 367b
Foiled: Latin..rests f. 216b
unsham'd, tho' f. 141a
Foils: five most vile and ragged f. 382b
Foison: spring and f. of the year 387b
Fold: climb into the f. 266b
clomb this..thief into God's f. 273b
f. to f., of mountain or of cape 436b
loves to f. his legs 209b
sheep..wh. are not of this f. 511a
silent was the flock in woolly f. 221b
the f. shall be full of sheep 486a
walking round the f. 33a
Folded: f. us round from the dark 423a
smooth'd her work, and f. it right 198b
Folding: f. of the Apennine 9a
little f. of the hands 498a
Folds: f. of a bright girdle 5a
lull the distant f. 174a
Foliage of the ocean 396b
Folio: I am for whole volumes in f.! 344b
Folios: mighty f. first, a lordly band 113b
we shd. have but few F. 289b
Folk: civil to f. he ne'er saw 4b
emptied of this f., this pious morn 219b
fluttered f. and wild 236b
longen f. to goon on pilgrimages 88a

Folks: but country f. who live beneath 96a
be kind to those dear little f. 19b
don't let the old f. know 186a
hand f. over to God's mercy 144a
old f. at home 156b
other f. have what some f...glad of 151b
O yonge fresshe f., he or she 90b
some f. rail against other f. 151b
these pretty country f. wd. lie 327b
where de old f. stay 156a
Follies: all old faults and f. 96b
England..where f. naturally grow 94b
f. of the town crept..among us 170b
f. of the wise 214a
lash the vice and f. of the age 86b
no f. to have to repent 425a
pretty f. that themselves commit 353b
thoughtless f. laid him low 59a
Follow: a bird overhead sang F. 422b
create..precedents, as to f. them 14b
expect to see when I f. you 136a
f. and find the sun 422b
f. a shadow, it still flies you 216a
f. ful ofte a mery someres day 90a
f. me—f. me 'ome 229a
f. thee with all the speed 225a
f. the Gleam 434b
f. thy fair sun 78a
f. up! f. up! 34b
f. well in order 457b
f. yr. Saint, f. with accents 78a
found in the spring to f. 422b
he will never f. anything 338b
I f. him to serve my turn 359b
if they run, why, we f. 158b
I must fly, but f. quick 437b
in following him, I f. but myself 359b
lead, and I f. 427b
love wd. f. me still 232b
must f., as the night the day 330b
plunged in, and bade him f. 337b
tell her, that I f. thee 436b
Followed: all masters cannot be..f. 359b
f. by a sacred song 26a
f. him, honoured him 48a
f. perhaps by a smile 111a
he f. it himselve 88b
his fear still f. him 408b
'I f. you'—'I saw no one' 136a
nine fathom deep he had f. us 98b
thro' all the world she f. him 426b
Following: corrupt f. of the Apostles 491b
in f. him, I follow but myself 359b
with a mighty f. 253a
Follows: f. but for form 342a
f. with dancing 420b
she draws him, yet she f. 248b
who f. in His train? 184a
Folly: all my joys to this are f. 64a
brood of F. without father bred 268a
call it madness, f. 310a
Fashion, tho' F.'s child 113b
feather pate of f. 199b
f.—doctor-like—controlling skill 388a
f. helped her to an heir 360b
f. like a stalking-horse 328a
f...love did make thee run into 326a
f. of being comforted 475a
f. of the world..wh. confounds 194b
f.'s all they've taught me 194b
f.'s at full length 35a, 91b
fool returneth to his f. 498b
from her coral lips such f. broke 104a
harmless f. of the time 189a
his f. has not fellow 198b
knavery and f. to excuse 94b
lovely woman stoops to f. 144b, 170a
public schools 'tis public f. 113a
shielding men from..f. 407b
shoot f. as it flies 300b
shunn'st the noise of f. 268a
the dupe of f. 469b
tho' age from f. cd. not give me 322b
'tis f. to be wise 175a
'twixt a vice and f. 233b
when the forts of f. fall 6b
whirled into f. 433b
whole centuries of f. 48b
wisdom excelleth f. 499a
Fond: be familiar or f. 105b
fair and yet not f. 120b

Fond (*cont.*)

f. and foolish mind	531*b*
he was probably f. of [Americans]	446*b*
Montague, I am too f.	365*a*
O too f., when have I answer'd	436*b*
too f. of her most filthy bargain	363*b*
too f. to rule alone	303*a*
we are so f. of one another	418*a*
Fonder: makes the heart grow f.	22*a*
Fondest, blindest, weakest	442*a*
Fondling of a happy pair	296*b*
Fondly sae did I o' mine	63*b*
Fondness for her underwent..increment	293*b*
Font: gold fin in the porphyry f.	436*b*
Fontarabbia: fell by F.	271*b*
Fontarabian echoes borne	318*b*
Food: books, and my f.	415*a*
chewing the f. of..fancy	327*b*
child..is..wholesome f.	418*a*
every day for f. or play	98*b*
fame is a f. that dead men eat	131*a*
finds its f. in music	245*a*
f. for powder	378*b*
f. that to him now is as luscious	360*b*
have been Tom's f. for seven.. years	343*a*
homely was their f.	159*a*
it ate the f. it ne'er had eat	98*a*
music, moody f. of us..in love	323*b*
nothing to eat but f.	225*a*
our cupboard of f.	187*b*
seeking the f. he eats	326*a*
the f. unpriced	262*a*
Fool: a f., a f.! I met a f.	326*a*
a f. at the other [end]	214*a*
a f. his whole life long	569*a*
a F. lies here	233*a*
a f. there was..made his prayer	236*a*
ambition in the f. that uses it	334*a*
an ass, without being a f.	416*b*
answer a f. according to his folly	498*b*
any f. may write a..valuable book	175*b*
better a witty f.	370*a*
better to be a f. than to be dead	413*a*
bray a f. in a mortar	498*b*
call me f., boy	342*a*
call me not f.	326*a*
clever woman to manage a f.	237*b*
drop into thyself, and be a f.!	301*a*
enough to play the f.	371*b*
every f. can play upon the word	354*b*
every f. in Buxton	314*a*
every f. will be meddling	498*b*
f. all the people all of the time	245*b*
f. at forty is a f. indeed	476*b*
f. doth not understand it	487*b*
f. hath said in his heart	482*a*
f. in the eye of the world	104*b*
f. is happy that he knows no more	301*a*
f.; it is you who are the pursued	390*b*
f. might once himself..expose	300*a*
f. must follow his natural bent	236*a*
f. must now and then be right	107*b*
f. returneth to his folly	498*b*
f.! said my Muse	401*b*
f. sees not the same tree	31*a*
f. uttereth all his mind	499*a*
greatest f. may ask more	103*b*
haste of a f. is the slowest	321*b*
he is a f. and a damned f.	455*a*
he's become the golden f.	31*b*
he that begetteth a f.	408*a*
how ill white hairs become a f.	381*a*
I am fortune's f.	366*a*
if the f. wd. persist in his folly	31*a*
I hate a f.!	123*a*
I have played the f.	495*b*
I'm a f. for thinking	305*a*
is he the only f. in the world?	48*b*
I speak as a f.	515*a*
life time's f.	379*a*
make my f. my purse	360*b*
man suspects himself a f.	477*a*
more hope of a f. than of him	498*b*
more of the f. than of the wise	14*b*
never was patriot..but was a f.	138*b*
nor yet a f. to fame	303*a*
not a f. I can call me friend	476*b*
oh heavenly f.	401*b*
old f.'s side that begot him	45*b*

Fool (*cont.*)

one f. at least in every..couple	151*a*
O noble f.! A worthy f.!	326*a*
O wretched f.!	362*a*
perfections of a f.	29*a*
play the f., but at a cheaper rate	110*b*
play the f...but in 's own house	333*b*
play the Roman f.	351*a*
poor venomous f.	325*a*
privacy of yr. f.'s heart	412*a*
relenting f., and shallow..woman	385*a*
resolved to live a f.	22*b*
so is the laughter of a f.	499*a*
so true a f. is love	388*a*
the f. of love	183*b*
the forest echoed 'f.'	429*a*
the more f. am I	534*b*
the more f. I	326*a*
the wisest f. in Christendom 204*a*,	563*a*
they f. me to the top of my bent	334*b*
thou f., this night thy soul	509*b*
thou teachest like a f.	322*b*
transform'd into a strumpet's f.	322*a*
what a f. Honesty is	373*b*
whether he is a Wise man or a F.	31*a*
whosoever shall say, thou f.	505*a*
wise thro' excess..is made a f.	148*a*
Fooled by these rebel powers	389*b*
Fool-fury of the Seine	431*a*
Fooling: beware..she is f. thee	246*b*
Foolish: a f. consistency	147*b*
f., fond old man	344*a*
f. thing was but a toy	372*a*
f. when he had not a pen	210*b*
God hath chosen the f. things	514*a*
he was f., as if in pain	93*a*
I being young and f.	474*a*
I cou'd be mighty f.	150*b*
it is a f. thing well done	208*a*
never said a f. thing	309*b*
not denyin' the women are f.	144*a*
she never yet was f.	360*b*
you f. man..yr. own f. business	91*a*
Foolishness: f. of preaching	514*a*
yet will not his f. depart	498*b*
Fools: all the f. that crowd thee so	107*a*
beggared by f.	138*b*
build a house for f. and mad	419*a*
coxcombs nature meant but f.	300*a*
dreading e'en f.	303*a*
Fashion..knaves and f. may use	94*b*
flannelled f. at the wicket	230*a*
f. are my theme	72*a*
f. by heavenly compulsion	342*a*
F. for argument use wagers	65*b*
f.! for I also had my hour	92*a*
f. make feasts	157*a*
f. may our scorn, not envy raise	160*b*
f. never wear out	105*b*
f.! 'od rot em	403*b*
f. rush in where angels fear	300*b*
f. they admonish	113*b*
f., who came to scoff	168*b*
f. will learn in no other	157*a*
foreigners are f.	265*b*
fortune always favours f.	160*b*
fortune, that favours f.	214*b*
hated by f.	420*a*
have lighted f. the way to..death	350*b*
human bodies are sic f.	63*a*
I am two f.	134*a*
I call God, and f. call Nature	51*b*
Incredulity! the wit of f.	87*b*
little wise, the best f. be	134*a*
make f. laugh i' the alehouse	360*b*
Nature made you f.	60*a*
none but f. wd. keep	351*b*
one flesh..still two f.	104*a*
O, these deliberate f.	353*b*
poor f. decoyed into our condition	296*a*
print it, and shame the f.	303*a*
secrets..must be kept from..f.	141*a*
see how f. are vexed	118*b*
see such f. in yr. life	533*a*
shoal of f. for tenders	105*a*
silence is the virtue of f.	13*b*
the Paradise of F.	273*b*
the scarecrows of f.	203*a*
these tedious old f.!	332*a*
the wayfaring men, tho' f.	502*a*

Fools (*cont.*)

things people make f. of	390*a*
think them wise, are greatest f.	3*b*
this great stage of f.	343*b*
to fill the world with f.	407*b*
to suckle f.	361*a*
twenty-seven millions mostly f.	81*a*
we f. of nature	331*a*
what all the d—d f. said	572*a*
what f. these mortals be!	357*a*
wh. in all tongues are called f.	327*b*
whosoever shall say, Thou f.	505*a*
world..most part of f. and knaves	53*b*
ye suffer f. gladly	515*a*
you f. of fortune	368*a*
you will always be f.	152*a*
Foolscap: fellows in f. uniforms	67*b*
f. subjects	71*b*
Foot: at the fountain's sliding f.	261*a*
caught my f. in the mat	177*a*
f. and hand go cold	415*b*
f.—f.—f.—sloggin'	227*b*
f. for f.	494*a*
f. is on my native heath	320*a*
f. it featly	367*a*
f. less prompt to meet the..dew	9*a*
f. the deformity of wh.	255*a*
Hercules..known by his f.	42*a*
her f. was light	218*b*
hurt not thy f. against a stone	487*b*
keep thy f. out of brothels	343*a*
led them with unmoisten'd f.	286*b*
like th' other f., obliquely run	134*a*
nay, her f. speaks	369*a*
no man's f. can pass	34*a*
one f. in sea, and one on shore	358*a*
on fleeter f. was never tied	316*b*
print of a man's naked f.	118*b*
set this f. of mine as far	338*a*
so light a f. will ne'er wear out	365*b*
squeeze a right-hand f.	85*b*
suffer thy f. to be moved	489*b*
the Forty-Second F.	194*b*
they heard his f. upon the stirrup	119*b*
thy f. may be dipped in the blood	486*b*
Thyself with shining F. shall pass	154*a*
thy soul the fixed f.	134*a*
Foote: with our friend F.	23*b*
Footfall: halts by me that f.	442*a*
Footfalls: leaves like light f.	396*a*
Footing: 'twixt his stretched f.	368*b*
unsteadfast f. of a spear	377*a*
yet no f. seen	386*b*
Foot-in-the-grave young man	165*b*
Footman: seen the eternal F.	145*a*
Footmen: lowest class is *literary* f.	183*b*
Footpath: jog on the f. way	373*a*
narrow f. of a street	59*b*
Footprints: f. on the sands of time	248*a*
f. point towards yr. den	542*b*
f., that perhaps another	248*a*
Footstep: where thy f. gleams	298*a*
with us thy f. trod	184*b*
Footsteps: f. of thy soul	43*b*
home his f. he hath turn'd	317*a*
mark my f.	286*b*
plants his f. in the sea	110*a*
whose distant f. echo	247*a*
yr. own f. meeting you	313*a*
Footstool: by the earth; for it is his f.	505*a*
thine enemies thy f.	489*a*
Foozling: Philip, f. with his cleek	172*b*
Fop: I am a f.	149*a*
Foppery: excellent f. of the world	341*b*
Fops: whole tribe of f.	341*b*
Forbear: f., said I; be not too bold	115*a*
for Jesus sake f.	389*b*
our bodies why do we f.	132*b*
St. John himself will scarce f.	419*a*
Forbearance ceases to be a virtue	56*b*
Forbears: he that f. to suit..his need	188*a*
wh. he f. again to look upon	468*a*
Forbid: they said, God f.	510*a*
Forbidden: fruit of that f. tree	270*a*
to see what was f.	285*a*
wanted it only because it was f.	447*a*
Force: all his pomp, without his f.	58*b*
ev'ry member of the f. has a watch	309*b*
f. and fraud..in war..virtues	191*b*
f. hath made supreme	271*a*
f. is not a remedy	38*a*

Force (*cont.*)
f. of heaven-bred poesy 372b
f. on wh. all strength depends 403a
had not f. to shape it 429a
it is of no f. in law 97b
longed for trenchant f. 5b
no argument but f. 42b
no f. but argument 42b
no f.,..can stretch a cord 456b
no motion has she now, no f. 463a
passion..spent its novel f. 432a
patience will achieve more than..f. 57b
some f. whole regions 65b
thy hands their little f. resign 109a
use of f. alone is but *temporary* 55b
violent take it by f. 506b
who overcomes by f. 272a
with rough, majestic f. 313b
yea, very f. entangles itself 324b
Forced: f. me..to play the woman 386a
the sound is f. 31b
Forces: entertain with half their f. 381b
Forcible: most f. Feeble 380b
Forcibly if we must 95b
Ford o' Kabul river 229a
Fording thro' the rising flood 27a
Forebode not any severing 467a
Fordoes: makes me or f. me quite 363b
Fordone: with weary task f. 357b
Foredoomed: brittle is f. 264b
Forefathers: our rude f. deemed it two 75b
rude f. of the hamlet 174a
think of yr. f. 1a
Forefinger: f. of all Time 436a
f. of an alderman 364b
Forego: English, now I must f. 374b
Foreground: in the f. is that strange figure 255b
Forehead: conversing with W. H.'s f. 183a
curl..in the middle of her f. 249a
f. of the age to come 221a
high upon the f. of humanity 217b
ivory f., straight nose 284b
one, of the godlike f. 465b
Shakespeare, on whose f. climb 44a
teeth and f. of our faults 334b
Foreheads: f. villainous low 367b
free hearts, free f. 439a
seal of God in their f. 519a
Foreign: by f. hands thy dying eyes 299a
f. constellations west each night 179a
some corner of a f. field 40a
to f. nations, and the next ages 17a
trampled down by a f. Trespasser 178a
wandering on a f. strand 317a
Foreigners: f. always spell better 446b
f. are fools 265b
wh. is what them f. do 166b
Foreknowledge of death 420b
providence, f., will 272b
Forelock: on Occasion's f...wait 277a
Foremast wi' his knee 529a
Foremost: f., fighting fell 68b
f. in battle was Mary 531b
none who wd. be f. 253a
Forest: a fool i' the f. 326a
dark behind it rose the f. 248b
down in the f. something stirr'd 402a
even as the f. is 396b
fade away into the f. dim 219b
faery damsels met in f. wide 277a
flowers of the f. 97a, 145b
f. below London Bridge 314a
I've seen the f. adorn'd 97a
midnight revels, by a f. side 272a
the f. echoed 'fool' 429a
this is the f. primeval 247a
thou wast the f. to this hart 339b
Forests: fishes flew and f. walked 92a
f. ancient as the hills 101a
from the f...and the prairies 248b
green days in f. 414b
in the f. of the night 31b
when f. are rended 319a
Forestall his date of grief 267a
Forest-brook: lag my f. along 99b
Forester: 'Dick Christian', answers Lord F. 289a
Foresters: be Diana's f. 376b
Foretell: pretences to f. events 419a
thus expiring do f. of him 374b

Foretell (*cont.*)
who can f. for what high cause 261a
Foretop: grey wig..scorched f. 255b
Forever: and it may be f. 115b
f., float that standard 178a
F.! tis a single word! 75b
Man has F. 47a
that vast F. 225b
Forfeit: all the souls that were f. 351b
f. to a confined doom 388b
He our deadly f. shd. release 270a
Forgave: never in his life f. a friend 30a
Forge: f. a lifelong trouble 427b
in the quick f. and working-house 383b
Vulcan and his whole f. 41a
Forgery: base f. 267b
Forget: and f. so much 117b
best, to f. 51b
but do not quite f. 93a
can I remember if thou f.? 422b
Charon, seeing, may f. 241a
command him, to f. me 242a
f. also thine own people 484b
f. and forgive 344a
f. not all his benefits 488a
f. not, brother singer 452a
f. not yet the tried intent 473b
f. the pale, unripened beauties 1b
f. thyself to marble 268a
f. thy thousand ways 240b
f. us till another year 228a
forgotten ere I f. 422b
haply may f. 311a
hateful art, how to f. 225a
if I f. thee, do not thou f. me 11a
if I f. thee, O Jerusalem 490a
if thou wilt, f. 311a
I'll not f. old Ireland 29a
I'll not f. you, darling 29a
I shall never, *never* f. 83b
knew we shd. both f. 422b
lest we f. 233b
names that men f. 421b
night time I shall not f. 421b
not a..wind that will f. thee 472b
old men f., yet all shall be forgot 383a
or courage to f. 2b
some blaspheme, and most f. 293a
teach the unforgetful to f. 312b
that I cd. f. what I have been 375b
the best sometimes f. 361a
thou remember and I f. 422b
we f. because we must 5a
well, I f. the rest 48b
world shall end when I f. 422b
you'll f. them all 302b
you shd. f. and smile 311a
Forgetful: yes, she may be 110a
Forgetfulness: not in entire f. 466a
steep my senses in f. 380a
to dumb F. a prey 174b
Forgetive: quick, f. 380b
Forgetteth what manner of man 517b
Forgetting: a sleep and a f. 466a
if f. cd. be willed 263b
I've a grand memory for f. 412b
more and more f. 263b
world f., by the world forgot 299b
Forgive: as far as one woman can f. 159b
Father, f. them 510a
forget and f. 344a
f. me; mine was jealousy 428b
f. them as a christian 11b
f. us our debts, as we f. our debtors 505b
f. us our trespasses, as we f. them 478a
f. you Bridge at dawn 91b
give thanks is good, and to f. 421a
God may f. you 145a
good, to f. 51b
I f. you, you f. me 31b
just God, f.! 463a
nor wd. f., did June disclose 452a
sometimes they f. them 460b
to f., divine 300b
wilt thou f. that sin 132a
Forgiven: it shall not be f. you 91b
pass on, my Queen, f. 428b
Forgiveness: ask of thee f. 344a
f. free of evil done 228a
f. to the injured does belong 139b
Man's F. give—and take 154a

Forgiveness (*cont.*)
mutual F. of each vice 30a
Forgot: all the rest f. 387a
and she f. the stars 218b
born to be f. 109b
f. as soon as done 369a
f. it not, nay, but got it not 311b
f. the taste of fears 350b
I f. Goschen 95a
lest they f. 93a
loved accents are soon f. 395a
quite f. their quarrel 84a
shd. auld acquaintance be f. 59a
tho' I am clean f. 187a
when he f., might God forget him 444b
where is yr. money? I've f. 534a
yet all shall be f. 383a
Forgotten: f. nothing and learnt nothing 563a
hast thou f. ere I forget 422b
I am all f. 322b
I am clean f. 483b
I have f. yr. name 422b
injury is much sooner f. 90b
in the f. crowd of..beauties 79a
newer object quite f. 372b
not one of them is f. before God 509b
oh! hast thou f. how soon 115b
Shakespeare shd. be quite f. 93a
there is always a f. thing 92a
they fly f. as a dream 453b
thou hast f., O summer 422b
to be f. even by God 49b
when I am f., as I shall be 386a
you have f. my kisses 422b
Forked: poor, bare, f. animal 343a
Forks: pursued it with f. and hope 86a
Forlorn: faery lands f. 220a
f.! the very word is like a bell 220a
for them that lie f. 119b
in these wild woods f. 276b
Form: ah, what the f. divine 240b
does a Human F. display 29b
earth was without f. 492a
fain wd. I dwell on f. 365a
fishy f. and mind 39b
follows but for f. 342a
F., F., Riflemen F.! 438a
his f. and pressure 333b
his f. had yet not lost All her ..brightness 272a
hold fast the f. of sound words 516b
in f. and feature 244b
in f., in moving, how express 332b
I own I like definite f. 412b
mouse or two for f.'s sake 175b
no f. nor comeliness 503a
of finer f., or lovelier face 316a
of the soul the body f. doth take 409a
soul is f. 409a
the f. of a servant 516a
the F. remains 463b
the mould of f. 333b
thro' all the spires of f. 146b
to every F. of being is assigned 464b
to lick it into f. 64a
to show the f. it seem'd to hide 317b
unmatch'd f. and figure 333b
Formal, and circumscribed 471b
Formed..for one another 393b
Former: f. days were better 499a
make f. times shake hands 65b
the f. and the latter rain 479a
Forms: all f., all pressures past 331b
bodies forth the f. of things 357b
by f. unseen their dirge is sung 103a
desire of those fair f. 409a
for f. of government let fools 301b
f., modes, shows of grief 330a
f. more real than living man 397a
giv'st to f. and images a breath 465b
he vents in mangled f. 326b
huge and mighty f. 469a
in what..fancy were the F. begot 202b
lovely f. do flow from conceit 78a
the beauteous f. of things 471b
their colours and their f. 472a
viewless f. of air 317a
Forsake: f. not an old friend 520b
f. their temples dim 270b
I will not fail thee, nor f. thee 494b

Forsake (cont.)
my father and my mother f. me	483b
Forsaken: Demas hath f. me	516b
home of . . f. beliefs	9a
I seem f. and alone	110a
most choice, f.	341b
why hast thou f. me	483a, 508a
Forsaking: f. all other, keep thee only	481b
not f. the assembling of ourselves	517a
Forsook: my true Love has me f.	530b
Forspent: clean f.,	242b
Forsworn: faith unhappily f.	388a
I am f. on 'mere necessity'	344b
that so sweetly were f.	352a
Fort: hold the f., for I am coming	33a
Fortescue: Charles Augustus F.	26a
Forth: f. they went together	286b
new drawn frae the F.	285b
virtues did not go f. of us	351a
Fortieth spare Arm-chair	46b
Fortifying, classical curriculum	10a
Fortitude: but welcome f.	468b
great f. of mind	206a
task for all that a man has of f.	412a
Fortress: a petty f . . . a dubious hand	213b
this f. built by Nature	375a
thy f., and thy ease	448a
Forts: when the f. of folly fall	6b
Fortunate: more f. alas! than we	6a
Fortune: above my f.	370a
arrows of outrageous f.	333a
blind F. still bestows her gifts	215b
but a worky-day f.	322b
Caesar and his f. with thee	574a
children . . hostages to f.	14b
disdaining f., with his . . steel	346a
do F. what she can	136b
every man . . maker of his own f.	410b
forever, F., wilt thou prove	443a
f. aids the brave	554a
F. always favours fools	160b
f. changed made him so	176a
F. is ally to the brave	556b
f. is full of fresh variety	21a
f. is merry	340b
F. knows we scorn her most	323b
f.'s buffets and rewards	334a
F. shows herself more kind	355a
f.'s malice lost her Calais	46a
F., that favours fools	214b
great, ere f. made him so	140a
health and high f. till we meet	317b
heaven hath sent me f.	326a
how does f. banter us	33b
I am f.'s fool	366a
I can enjoy her [F.]	142b
ill f. seldom comes alone	140a
I, made lame by f.'s . . spite	387b
in disgrace with f. and men's eyes	387a
in the secret parts of f.?	332a
I puff the prostitute [F.] away	142b
man in possession of a good f.	11b
mock the good housewife f.	325b
most dejected thing of f.	343b
mould of a man's f . . . own hands	16a
my face is my f.	525b
no . . beauty without a f.	150a
not being F., he's but F.'s knave	325a
not the method of making a f.	175b
of f.'s sharp adversitee	90a
one out of suits with f.	325b
pipe for F.'s finger to sound	334a
ready visit pays where f. smiles	477a
smiling of F. beguiling	97a
taken at the flood, leads on to f.	341a
to prey at f.	362a
tugged with f.	348b
vicissitudes of f.	162a
well-favoured man is the gift of f.	358b
who lets slip F.	107a
your f. lies beneath yr. hat	290b
Fortunes: battles, sieges, f.	360a
f. and lives he will vote away	40b
f. . . tumbling into some . . laps	13a
judgments . . a parcel of their f.	324a
mine, and most of our f., tonight	322b
my pride fell with my f.	325b
O! my f. . . corrupted honest men	324a
our love shd. with our f. change	334a
those my former f.	324b
you'll ne'er mend yr. f.	283a

Fortune-teller: juggler and a f.	328a
Forty: at f., the judgement (reigns)	157a
fair, fat and f.	320a
every man over f. is a scoundrel	391a
fool at f. is a fool indeed	476b
f. days and f. nights	405b
f. stripes save one	515a
f. years on	34b
grow fat and look young till f.	141a
his death . . at f.-odd befell	195a
knows it at f.	477a
together now for f. years	94a
wait till you come to F. Year	440b
Forty-niner: dwelt a miner, F.	280b
Forty-three: very well pass for f.	167a
Forward: find him f. to be sounded	333a
f. bends his head	98a
f. let us range	432b
f., not permanent	330b
f., the light Brigade	426a
look f. to posterity	57a
marched breast f.	52a
some men a f. motion love	448a
those behind cried 'F.'	253a
Fotching him to his own	183a
Fou: had been f. for weeks thegither	62b
wasna' f., but just had plenty	60a
we're nae that f.	63b
Fought: a lie . . met and f. with	427a
better to have f. and lost	96b
feet of those he f. for	435a
f. a long hour by Shrewsbury	379a
f. was this noble fray	137a
f. with us upon St. Crispin's	383a
from morn till even f.	382a
if that he f. and had the hyer	88b
I have f. a good fight	516b
I have f. for Queen and Faith	437b
I have f. with beasts at Ephesus	515a
kneel'd and f. on his knee	530b
never to have f. at all	96b
under whose colours he had f.	375b
what they f. each other for	406a
Foul: fair is f.	345b
f., I to the Fountain fly	445a
murder most f.	331b
outward be fair . . f. within	94b
so f. and fair a day	346a
so variously f.	202b
thank the gods I am f.	327a
Foulest: shortest way is . . the f.	13a
Foul-mouthed: English . . f. nation	183b
Found: anybody might have f. it	228b
as 'ow I've always f.	86b
as they f. him long ago	287b
at last I've f. out that I am	527a
awoke, and f. me here	219a
awoke . . and f. myself famous	74b
be f. no more at all	519b
came to ask what he had f.	406a
f. it, or came by it	352b
half-buried in the snow was f.	247a
hast thou f. me, O mine enemy?	496a
have it f. out by accident	240a
he will be f. like Brutus	341b
I f. Him in the . . stars	429a
I mercy ask'd, I mercy f.	522b
in a time when thou mayest be f.	483b
I think, now 'tis not to be f.	344b
less often sought than f.	73b
muttered 'F.! f.! f.!'	317b
my espoused, my latest f.	274b
not seek me if you had not f. me	564b
once f. out and solved	277b
quiet, have I f. thee here	260b
still has f. the warmest welcome	399b
taken my fun where I've f. it	230b
they f. no more of her	496b
'twill be f., upon examination	118b
what some have f. so sweet	433b
when f., make a note of	122b
Foundation: Church's one f.	415b
f. of lasting mischief	206a
good order is the f. of all	57b
huge f. of the earth shak'd	378a
the first f. was jasper	520a
Foundations: all the f. of the earth	487a
earth's f. stay	200a
hell's f. quiver	20a
her f. are upon the holy hills	487a
looked for a city wh. hath f.	517a

Foundations (cont.)
the f. will be cast down	482b
when earth's f. fled	200a
when I laid the f. of the earth	497b
Founder: enjoyed the gifts of the f.	161b
Founders: matter for succeeding f.	260b
Foundest me poor at first	169a
Fount: meander level with . . f.	255a, 280a
slow, slow, fresh f.	214b
watch'd the f. of fiery life	6b
Fountain: a f. filled with blood	110a
a f. sealed	500b
at the f.'s sliding foot	261a
back to the burning f.	392b
by a forest side or f.	272a
[Chaucer] is a . . f. of good sense	142a
doth a f. send forth	517b
eternal f. of that heavenly beauty	409a
foul, I to the F. fly	445a
f. from the wh. my current runs	363a
f. heads, and pathless groves	23a
f. in a noon-day grove	469a
f. of all goodness	478b
f. of the water of life	519b
f.'s silvery column	101b
from the f. and the caves	101b
he is the f. of honour	16b
in the desert a f. is springing	74a
mighty f. momently was forced	101a
the f.-light of all our day	466b
Thou of Life the F. art	455b
voice rise like a f. for me	429a
when yr. f. is choked up	57a
woman mov'd is like a f. troubled	367a
Fountains: a new Peneus rolls his f.	394a
f. mingle with the river	395b
heaven moveth, f. flow	187b
in nature certain f. of justice	13a
O, ye f., meadows, hills	467a
shepherding her bright f.	392b
silver f. mud	387b
streams from little f. flow	149b
the cool shady f.	424b
Weep you no more, sad f.	527b
what objects are the f.	398b
Founts: meander level with their f.	255a
white f. falling	92b
Four: f. spend in prayer	97b
there were f. of us about	284b
three, f., shut the door	532a
Four-footed: parody of all f. things	92a
Four-in-hand round the corner	102b
Fourscore: f. and seven years ago	245a
f. and upward	344a
Four-square to all the winds	435a
Fourteen months at Magdalen College	161b
Fourth estate of the realm	254a
Fouth o' auld nick-nackets	62a
Foutra for the world	381a
Fowl: broiled f. and mushrooms	126a
dominion . . over the f. of the air	492a
Pythagoras concerning wild f.	372a
tame villatic f.	278a
Fowler: bird out of the snare of the f.	489b
geese that the creeping f. eye	357a
Fowls: behold the f. of the air	505b
f. of the air, and the fishes	482a
f. of the air come and lodge	507a
f. of the air have their habitation	488a
I here the f. singe	8b
smale f. maken melodye	88a
small f. singis on the spray	134b
Fox: ar'n't that I loves the f. less	416b
better than that of the f.	33b
[Charles James F.] talked to me	211b
Daun Russell the f.	89a
drop upon F.'s grave the tear	317b
f. from his lair in the morning	173b
f. jumped up on a moonlight night	533a
f. may steal yr. hens	159b
F.'s shall the notes rebound	317b
nephew of F., and friend of Grey	193b
the little red f. murmured	475a
treason . . trusted like the f.	379a
you shall see a f. die	226a
Foxed: if ever I was f. it was now	296a
Foxes: f. have holes	506a
f., that spoil the vines	500a
Foxey: it was a maxim with F.	125a

Foxhunter: tell me a man's a f. 416b
Foxlike in the vine 437a
Frabjous: oh f. day 84a
Fraction: thou wretched f. 80b
Fragilely, surely 443a
Fragments: gather up the f. 510b
took up of the f. 507a
Fragrant: in yr. f. bosom dies 79b
Fragrant-eyed: cool-rooted flowers f. 220a
Frail: feeble as f. 172b
our love is f. 149a
wisdom never was so f. 360b
Frailest: choose you the f. 395a
Frailties: his f. from their . . abode 174b
our f. are invincible 412a
Frailty: by . . the f. of our nature 479b
F., thy name is woman! 330a
love's but a f. of the mind 105b
love's the noblest f. of the mind 140b
tempt the f. of our powers 369a
the f. of all things here 395a
the f. of a man 14a
the f. of man without thee 479b
therefore more f. 378b
Frame: above this f. of things 470a
a calm and heavenly f. 109b
a f. of adamant, a soul of fire 213b
all the human f. requires 26a
bloody passion shakes yr. very f. 363b
breath of this corporeal f. 472a
f. and huge foundation of the earth 378a
f. outlives a thousand tenants 336a
f. thy fearful symmetry 31b
how they will wield the mighty f. 275b
let the f. of things disjoint 348b
man . . still bears in his bodily f. 117b
put yr. discourse into some f. 334a
quit, oh quit this mortal f. 299a
shakes this fragile f. at eve 179b
'tis a thing impossible to f. 464a
tremble for this lovely f. 456b
universal f. is without a mind 15a
whatever stirs this mortal f. 101b
whole f. of Nature . . break 2b
with rapture-smitten f. 77a
Framed: conceit divinely f. 78a
France: best thing . . between F. and
England 205b
bought . . his round hose in F. 353a
entertain . . the full pride of F. 381b
fair stood the wind for F. 137a
fashion for the maids in F. 383b
F., fram'd in all great arts 8a
F. . . influenced manners in England 57a
gay lilied fields of F. 76b
I remember, when I was in F. 374a
I saw the Queen of F. 57a
King of F. went up the hill 532a
lived a singer in F. of old 424a
(Miss Crawley) had been in F. 440a
nearer is to F. 83b
order . . this matter better in F. 411a
that sweet enemy, F. 401b
they in F. of the best rank 330b
thundered the cannon of F. 96a
until F. is adequately secured 10b
vasty fields of F. 381a
warmer F. with all her vines 111b
Francesca di Rimini, miminy piminy 165b
Francis: 'By God!' said F. 202a
Lady Fadler and Sir F. 105b
Franciscan: or in F. think to pass 273b
Frank to all beside 302a
Frankfort: went to F. . . got drunk 304b
Frankincense: gold, and f., and myrrh 504b
Fraud: force, and f. . . virtues 191b
f. of men was ever so 358b
this just, this pious f. 160a
Frauds: f. of friendship 151a
stored with pious f. 56b
Fray: brutes never meet in bloody f. 169a
by decision more embroils the f. 273a
eager for the f. 95b
fought was this noble f. 137a
latter end of a f. 378b
Freaks: their fits and f. 131a
Freckled: whatever is fickle, f. 197b
Freckles: in those f. live their savours 356b
Fred: here lies F. 523b
since 'tis only F. 523b
Frederick: bravest of all in F. town 459a

Frederick (cont.)
clustered spires of F. stand 458b
here is cruel F., see! 192b
seats himself in F.'s chair 192b
Free: a heart as sound and f. 190a
all men everywhere cd. be f. 245a
all men naturally were born f. 279b
appal the f. 333a
ask me what a f. government is 58a
beauteous evening, calm and f. 467a
bond nor f.: but Christ is all 516a
but I was f. born 512b
each alike was Greek, alike was f. 422b
fain have her f. 263b
f. and faithful, strong as death 110a
f. as nature first made man 139b
f. as the road 188a
f. be she, fancy-f. 146b
f. church in a f. state 567a
f., f. the white sail spread! 184b
f. from all meaning . . good or bad 138b
f. love—f. field 428b
f. of the outer court I am 293b
f. the world of a poisonous thing 135b
from loving more, thou f. my soul 133a
great and joyous, beautiful and f. 397b
here's to the bold and f. 287b
here we may be f. 117a
himself from God he cd. not f. 147a
in my soul am f. 249b
in the country of the f. 43a
in unreproved pleasures f. 268b
I only ask to be f. 121a
Italia shall be f. 265a
leaves f. to all 274b
let us die to make men f. 200b
love virtue, she alone is f. 268a
man is born f. 565b
most noble that was born most f. 291a
my lines and life are f. 188a
no one can be . . f. till all are f. 408a
o'er the land of the f. 224b
others abide . . thou art f. 7b
people yearning to be f. 452b
shall yet be, the land of the f. 77b
shd. themselves be f. 39a
so f. we seem, so fettered fast 44b
that Greece might still be f. 70b
that moment they are f. 111b
the butterflies are f. 121a
the fresh, the ever f. 106a
thou at length art f. 194a
thought is f. 367b
thus so cleanly, I myself can f. 137b
to have quite set f. . . Eurydice 269a
truth shall make you f. 511a
we must be f. or die 467a
when evils are most f. 338b
who wd. be f. themselves 68a
wholly slaves or wholly f. 140b
you enthrall me, never shall be f. 133a
Freed: from the thousands He hath f. 87a
Freedom: a new birth of f. 245b
assure f. to the free 245a
battle for f. and truth 567a
bounds of f. wider yet 437a
but what is F.? 97b
cause of F. is the cause of God 34b
deny them this participation of f. 146b
emotions . . on the recovery of my f. 162a
few men talked of f. 93a
flame of f. in their souls 424a
Flood of British f. 467a
f. and curteisye 88a
F. and Whiskey gang thegither 59a
f. an English subject's 141b
F. hallows with her tread 74a
F. has a thousand charms 111a
f. is a noble thing 19a
f. . . is the cure of anarchy 55b
F. leads it forth, her mate 397a
f. mays man to haiff liking 19a
F. reared in that august sunrise 435b
F.'s banner streaming o'er us 178a
F.'s battle once begun 72b
f. shall awhile repair 103a
F. shrieked as Kosciusko fell 77a
F. slowly broadens down 439b
f. . . sole . . unity of the empire 56a
F.'s soil beneath our feet 178a
f. wh. in no other land will thrive 141b

Freedom (cont.)
govern . . on the principles of f. 55b
great sum obtained I this f. 512b
I du believe in F.'s cause 250a
if I have f. in my love 249b
I gave my life for f. 149b
infringement of human f. 297b
in giving f. to the slave 245a
let f. ring 404a
lost is our f. . . to women 78b
me this unchartered f. tries 464a
mouth fair F.'s classic line 77b
none can love f. . . but good men 279b
regain'd my f. with a sigh 69b
rest love not f., but licence 279b
sweet bondage wh. is f.'s self 397b
that sober f. out of wh. . . springs 435a
the idea of f. 292b
what stands if F. fall? 229a
whose service is perfect f. 478a
with F.'s lion-banner 77a
yet, F.! yet thy banner, torn 69a
Free-livers on a small scale 203b
Freely: f. let me take of Thee 455b
f. they stood who stood 273b
f. we serve, because we f. love 275a
f. ye have received 506a
I did f. part with my glory 187b
I love thee f. 44a
take the water of life f. 520b
Freeman: F. butters Stubbs 528a
f. whom the truth makes free 112b
Freemen: only f. . . the only slaves 262b
to rule o'er f. shd. . . be free 39a
Freeport: Sir Andrew F. 2a
Free-thinking: he took to f. 527a
Freeze: f., f., thou bitter sky, 326b
f. thy blood less coldly 286b
Freezings: what f. have I felt 388b
Freighters: forty f. at sea 232a
French: a boy, half F., half English 383b
behold with prejudice the F. 42a
by reading F. novels 130a
F. are wiser than they seem 15b
F. are with equal advantage 78b
F. army led by an Italian 391a
F. Guard, fire first 183a
F. of Paris was to hir unknowe 88b
F., or Turk, or Proosian 166a
F. she spak ful faire 88b
he's gone to fight the F. 217a
I hate the F. 170b
loved . . F. novels, F. cookery 440a
my scrofulous F. novel 52a
not too F. F. bean 165b
only taken from the F. 400a
some are fond of F. (wine) 261b
speak in F. 84a
to help our F. comrades 238a
to the F. the empire of the land 80a
to the glory of beating the F. 462b
we F. stormed Ratisbon 47b
what's the water in F.? 124b
your new F. proselytes 140b
Frenchies seek him everywhere 290b
Frenchman: F. . . always talking 210a
I praise the F. 111a
the F., easy, debonair, and brisk 111a
the F.'s darling [Mignonette] 112b
truth the brilliant F. never knew 113a
Frenchmen: did march three F. 382a
fifty million F. can't be wrong 177b
one Englishman cd. beat three F. 2a
ten thousand F. sent below! 294b
Frenzy: demoniac f. 276b
poet's eye, in a fine f. rolling 357b
Frequent: f. as the Royal Exchange 2a
when young did eagerly f. 153a
Fresh: as f. as paint 403a
f. as is the month of May 88a
since first I saw you f. 388b
yonge f. folkes 90b
Freshening and fluttering in the wind 48a
Freshness: dewy f. fills the silent air 113a
f. of a dream 466a
Fret: fever, and the f. 220a
f. not . . because of the ungodly 484a
f. not to roam the desert now 289b
f. of that sharp-headed worm 438a
living, we f. 51b
tho' you can f. me 334b

Frets: ferments and f.	66a
Fretted: f. by sallies	466b
f. the pigmy body to decay	138a
f. with golden fire	332b
Friar: a f. I will be	202a
a F. ther was	88b
turned fasting f.	264b
Friars: barefooted f. were singing	161b
eremites and f.	273b
Friday: F.'s child is loving	525a
my man F.	118b
on a F. fil al this meschaunce	89a
one F. morn when we set sail	525b
they that wash on F.	532b
worse on F.	532b
Friend: a f. in my retreat	111a
ah, ha! my good f.	20a
a mistress or a f.	393b
and mine own familiar f.	485a
a pretended f. is worse	160b
as a f. he drops into poetry	125b
as f. remembered not	326b
be very much his F. indeed	108a
blunt man, that love my f.	340a
breed of barren metal of his f.	353a
choose an author as..a f.	128a
close-lipped Patience..our only f.	8a
Codlin 's the f.	125a
'cos my f. here didn't see	172b
countervail a f.	177a
crack a bottle with a f.	93b
damned good-natured f. or other	400a
death of a dear f.	357b
Death; the last best f.	406b
Death, the poor man's dearest f.	61b
faithful are the wounds of a f.	498b
fav'rite has no f.	173b
find a f. sincere enough	252a
f., go up higher	509b
f. is the medicine of life	520b
f. of my better days	178a
f. of the bridegroom	510b
f...or foe that spread these lies?	313a
f. shd. bear his f.'s infirmities	341a
f. that sticketh closer..brother	498b
f...the masterpiece of Nature	147b
F. to Sir Philip Sidney	177a
F., wherefore art thou come?	508a
F. Who never changes	265b
forsake not an old f.	520b
gained no title..lost no f.	302b
good f., for Jesu's sake forbear	389b
good wine, a f., or being dry	3a
guide, philosopher, and f.	301b
heard of the loss of a dear f.	407b
he gain'd from Heav'n..a f.	174b
he makes no f...never made a foe	428b
he was my f., faithful and just	340a
his f. in merry pin	108b
I cannot use a f. as I use Thee	187b
I cd. not see my little f.	19b
if I had a f. that loved her	360a
if this f. happen to be—God	46b
in a f., it is cold modesty	339b
in every f. we lose..ourselves	304a
in every mess I finds a f.	120b
in the heart of a f.	246b
I've a F., over the sea	52b
I was angry with my f.	32a
I wd. not use a f. as I use Thee	187b
knolling a departed f.	379b
loses both itself and f.	330b
more if you dine at a f.'s	126a
my f., judge not me	76a
my f. may spit upon my..floor	187b
my f. what viands he preferred	150b
my good f. the calendar	108b
nephew of Fox, and f. of Gray	193b
never in his life forgave a f.	30a
never want a f. in need	122b
new f. is as new wine	520b
no f. like a sister	311a
nor a f. to know me	414a
not a f., not a f. greet	371a
not a f. to close his eyes	139a
not a f. to spare	148b
not as their f. or child	6a
of every friendless name the f.	210b
over yr. f. that loves you	337b
poor dog, in life the firmest f.	73b
rider and horse, f., foe	68b

Friend (cont.)	
save me from the candid f.	79a
Sleep! the f. of Woe	406b
that it shd. be a f. to soothe	220b
the equal f.	416a
the while I think on thee, dear f.	387b
there's a F. for little children	265b
this is my f., O daughters	500b
thou art not my f.	146b
tho' we called yr. f. from his bed	235a
timorous foe, and a suspicious f.	303a
to me, fair f.	388b
truest f. to thy lover	257b
truth..the f. of man	77b
unto my f.'s intent and end	187b
verse from thy grieved f.	225a
were not you my f.?	452b
when it comes say 'Welcome F.'	115b
who has a polished female f.	459a
who's yr. fat f.?	53a
with a religious book or f.	473b
with one chained f.	393b
world is not thy f.	366a
worst f. and enemy is but Death	40a
yea, mine own familiar f.	484b
Yet, O my f...not have thee die	436b
you're my f.	46b
Friendless: omnipotent but f.	397a
there is no man so f.	252a
Friendly: both false and f. be	246b
f. to peace, but not to me!	111a
Friends: a few f., and many books	107a
a good plot, good f.	377a
animals are such agreeable f.	144a
babes, and loving f.	100a
best f. hear no more of him	395b
best of f. must part	527a
call you that backing of yr. f.?	377b
city of the faithfullest f.	457b
distresses of our f.	419a
dreads, but more his f.	94a
falling out of faithful f.	143b
foes nor loving f. can hurt	230a
forbids the cheating of our f.	94b
f. and brother souls	426a
f. and loves we have none	262a
f. are lapped in lead	20b
f. called him 'Candle ends'	86a
f. in the garrison	177b
f., kindred, days, estate	146b
f. of..mammon of unrighteousness	509b
f., Romans, countrymen	339b
f. to congratulate their f.	141b
f. who set forth at our side	7b
good book is the best of f.	446a
good f., sweet f., let me not stir	340a
he cast off his f.	160b
in spite of all their f. cd. say	243b
laughter, learnt of f.	40a
lay down his life for his f.	511a
like f. once parted	392b
like him with f. possessed	387a
make f. ashamed to look upon one	450b
make my f. proud of my memory	223b
makes f. of enemies	334a
many, many lady f.	286a
merely comes to meet one's f.	58b
my never-failing f. are they	407a
not in the multitude of f.	214b
number, but the choice of f.	107a
of f., of hope, of all bereft	107b
of humblest f., bright creature	463b
old f. are best	321a
old f. to trust	13b
ought to forgive our f.	13b
precious f. hid in death's	387b
Religion..often fears her f.	113b
remembering my good f.	375a
separateth very f.	498a
something left to treat my f.	257a
soul and body part like f.	115a
such men my f. than enemies	341b
the f. thou hast	330b
the new city of F.	457a
the poor make no new f.	29a
they had been f. in youth	100a
those who betray their f.	160a
thy f. are exultations	472b
to have advanced true f.	5b
to his f. and his relations	167a

Friends (cont.)	
to keep a few f.	412a
to keep f. with himself	412a
trencher-f., time's flies	368a
troops of f.	350b
tuned spheres, and that to f.	325a
unto the breach, dear f.	382a
walked in the house of God as f.	485a
want of f., and empty purse	35a
when his f. did understand	531b
who has a thousand f.	148b
wd. not enter on my list of f.	112b
wounded in the house of my f.	504b
wretched have no f.	139a
yr. f. are all embarking for..hell	4b
Friendship: be my enemy for f.'s sake	30a
destitute of sincere f.	14a
elegance of female f.	213b
f. is a disinterested commerce	170b
f. is constant in all..save..love	358a
f. is Love without his wings	72b
f., like love, is but a name	160b
f. recognized by the police	413a
honest f. with all nations	204b
in f. first, I think if that agree	187b
keep his f. in constant repair	207a
love, f., charity	369a
made of love and f.	217b
most f. is feigning	326b
part in f.	74a
pious frauds of f.	151a
society, f. and love	113a
speak to thee in F.'s name	282b
such a f. as had mastered Time	430b
swear an eternal f.	79a
swear eternal f.	404a
the dupe of f.	183b
there is little f. in the world	16a
the way of f.'s gone	186b
thy f. oft has made my heart	30a
to f. clear	79b
what a thing f. is	46b
what is f. but a name	169a
when did f. take a breed	353a
where genial f. plays the..game	193b
wing of f. never moults	125a
woman's f. ever ends in love	160a
Friendships begin with liking	144a
Fright: dreamed..Devil..waked in a f.	4a
f. us from the shore	453b
wake in a f.	19a
Frighted: being thus f., swears	364b
f. with false fire	334b
how have I f. thee	380a
Frightened: f. both the heroes so	84a
I never saw any man f. in my life	151b
it has a f. look in its eyes	402a
killed than f. to death	417a
Frightful: be f. when one's dead	302a
he knows, a f. fiend	99b
sees, f. and afar	93b
'twas f. there to see	100a
Fringed curtains of thine eye	367b
Fringes of a southward-facing brow	8a
Frisk: I'll have a f. with you	206b
lambs that did f. i' the sun	372b
Fritillaries: what purple f.	8b
Fritter-my-wig!	86a
Fritters: best f. that ever I eat	296a
Friuli: blue F.'s mountains	69a
Frivolity: chatter of irresponsible f.	128b
gay without f.	6a
Frog: eye of newt and toe of f.	349b
no p'ints about that f.	446b
on a log, expiring f.	126a
the F. is justly sensitive	26a
thus use yr. f.	450b
Frolic: Lamb, the f. and the gentle	465b
Frolics: a youth of f.	302a
Front: ay, on the f.	351a
deep on his f. engraven	272b
his fair large f.	274a
his humid f. the cive..wipes	194b
see the f. o' battle lour	62b
won't go to the f. ourselves	527b
Frontier-grave is far away	287b
Frost: comes a f., a killing f.	385b
death's untimely f.	61a
f. performs its secret ministry	101a

Frost (*cont.*)
f. wh. binds so dear a head! 391*b*
heavy as f. 466*b*
His graver of f. 443*a*
it is a f.! the dahlias are dead 417*a*
Frosts: f. are slain and flowers 420*a*
hoary headed f. fall in the..lap 356*b*
Frosty, but kindly 326*a*
Froth: f. amid the boundless main 38*b*
with his embossed f. 368*a*
Froude: F. believes Kingsley a divine 415*b*
F. informs the Scottish youth 415*b*
the feeling of both F. and myself 288*a*
Froust with a book 230*b*
Frown: convey a libel in a f. 419*b*
frantic, fearful f. 164*b*
I'll f. and be perverse 365*a*
knew not what it was to f. 295*a*
say that she f. 366*b*
they f. on you—for weeks 131*a*
Frowned: dismal tidings when he f. 168*b*
it is not true to say I f. 91*b*
Frowning: behind a f. providence 110*a*
Frowns: her very f. are fairer far 97*b*
Froze the genial current of the soul 174*a*
Frozen: o'er many a f...Alp 272*b*
the torrid or the f. zone 79*b*
when we are f. up within 6*b*
Frugal: she had a f. mind 108*a*
Fruit: bent with thick set f. 310*b*
bring forth more f. in their age 487*b*
deeper than flower and f. 263*a*
eateth not of the f. thereof 514*a*
forth reaching to the f. 276*a*
f. burnished with golden rind 274*a*
f. of the Spirit is love, joy 515*b*
f., some an hundredfold 506*b*
f. that can fall without shaking 280*a*
green f. wd. swell to melting pulp 217*b*
hang there like f., my soul 329*a*
I love f. when it's expensive 297*a*
I shd. grow to f. or shade 187*a*
it bore the f. and mine 238*b*
lo, children and the f. of the womb 489*b*
man's..disobedience, and the f. 270*b*
mystic f. his acres yield 146*b*
never want some f. for Him 187*b*
reach the ripest f. of all 259*a*
the f. thereof dust 421*a*
tree is known by his f. 506*b*
untimely f. of a woman 485*b*
weakest kind of f. drops earliest 354*b*
what I have lost with cordial f. 188*a*
Fruitful: be f., and multiply 492*a*
Fruitfulness: mists and mellow f. 221*b*
Fruition of an earthly crown 259*a*
Fruits: all pleasant f. do flow 78*b*
bring forth the f. of the Spirit 479*a*
by their f. ye shall know them 506*a*
drop like the f. of the tree 263*a*
eat his pleasant f. 500*b*
f. of life and beauty 30*a*
kindly f. of the earth 479*a*
like Dead Sea f. 282*a*
no f., no flowers..November! 195*a*
Fruit-tree: silver all these f. tops 365*a*
some f.'s mossy foot 261*a*
Frumious Bandersnatch 83*b*
Frustrate their knavish tricks 79*b*
Fry: such as 'F. me' 86*a*
Fudge: Mr. Burchell..cry out 'F.' 171*a*
Fuel: adding f. to the flame 278*a*
f. to maintain his fires 79*a*
Fugitive: f. and cloistered virtue 279*a*
remembers what was so f. 466*b*
Fugues: masses and f. and 'ops' 164*b*
Fulfil: faithfully to f. the same 479*b*
not to destroy, but to f. 505*a*
Fulfilled of my heart's desire 422*b*
Full: f. and fair ones 188*b*
f. fathom five thy father lies 367*a*
f. man and a fasting 320*a*
if the moon shine at f. or no 65*b*
reading maketh a f. man 16*a*
some are f. o' brandy 61*a*
some are f. o' love divine 61*a*
too f. for sound 426*a*
wasna f., but just had plenty 60*a*
we're no that f. 63*b*
without o'erflowing, f. 119*b*
Full-blown: a rose f. 191*a*

Fuller: money..is the true f.'s earth 159*b*
Fulness: and the f. thereof 514*b*
f. of joy and hope 195*a*
Fum: fie, foh, and f. 343*a*
Fumble with the sheets 382*a*
Fume: black, stinking f. thereof 204*a*
memory..shall be a f. 347*b*
mockery is the f. of little hearts 428*a*
Fumiter: crown'd with rank f. 343*b*
Fun: a little f., to match the sorrow 263*a*
f. grew fast and furious 63*a*
I've taken my f. 230*b*
make f. of it 82*a*
must pay for my f. 230*b*
to come and spoil the f. 84*a*
will not have the f. 93*b*
wish I thought *What Jolly F.* 308*a*
Function: f. is smother'd in surmise 346*b*
own no other f. 373*b*
the F. never dies 463*b*
Functions: above their f. and..offices 345*a*
exercise all f. of a man 112*a*
Funeral: from their office to black f. 366*a*
f. bak'd meats 330*a*
f. marches to the grave 248*a*
her f. sermon, wh. was long 26*b*
his obscure f., no trophy 336*a*
I'd appint yr. f. tomorrow 451*a*
I misbehave myself once at a f. 239*b*
not a f. note 462*a*
see my own f. afore I die 143*b*
seldom seen a costlier f. 426*b*
with mirth in f. 329*b*
Fur: keep their f. dry 342*b*
make the f. fly 'bout the ears 65*a*
Furies: framed by f.' skill 408*b*
the f. of my brother 254*a*
Furious: a f. High-Churchman I was 524*a*
fun grew fast and f. 63*a*
Furloughs for another world 141*b*
Furnace: as if they burned in a f. 518*b*
as one great f. flamed 271*a*
burning, fiery f. 504*a*
f. for yr. foe so hot 385*a*
heat the f. one seven times more 504*a*
in what f. of thy brain 32*a*
the f. of affliction 502*b*
the lover, sighing like f. 326*b*
Furnish: coldly f. forth the marriage 330*a*
f. all we ought to ask 224*a*
Furniture: mere church f. 113*a*
Nature's pride, and richest f. 259*a*
no f. so charming as books 404*a*
Furrow: crush'd beneath the f.'s 62*a*
I must plough my f. alone 310*b*
leaves a smiling f. 437*a*
on a half-reap'd f...asleep 221*b*
Furrows: bewildered f. deepen 202*b*
plowers..made long f. 490*a*
smite the sounding f. 439*a*
thou waterest her f. 486*a*
when in thee time's f. I behold 387*a*
Further: shalt thou come, but no f. 497*b*
Fury: beware the f. of a patient man 138*b*
civil fury first grew high 64*b*
comes the blind F. 269*b*
full of sound and f. 350*b*
in her prophetic f. sew'd 362*b*
Life, a F. slinging flame 430*a*
nor Hell a F., like a woman scorn'd 104*b*
numbs the F.'s ringlet-snake 433*a*
said cunning old F. 82*b*
their f., and my passion 367*a*
thrice came on in f. 253*b*
Furze: Midland f. afire 229*a*
Fusees: they who use f. 76*a*
Fust in us unus'd 335*b*
Fustian: whose f.'s so sublimely bad 303*a*
Fustilarian: you f. 380*a*
Futility: fatal f. of Fact 204*b*
Future: all the hopes of f. years 246*b*
extravagant hopes of the f. 56*b*
for the f. in the distance 18*b*
I dipt into the f. 432*b*
leave the F. to..Providence 13*a*
makes no preparation for the f. 129*a*
never plan the f. by the past 57*b*
Past and the F. are nothing 306*b*
some f. day..what is now is not 96*b*
the Bard! who..past, and f. sees 31*b*
trust no F., how'er pleasant 248*a*

Future (*cont.*)
yr. labour is for f. hours 198*a*
Fuzzy-Wuzzy 229*a*
Fye: f. na, f. na, said May Margaret 529*a*

G

Gabble o' the goose 75*b*
Gabies: geese and g. 414*a*
Gad: liberty to g. abroad 520*b*
she called his name G. 493*a*
Gadarene: this man..is the G. Swine 237*b*
Gadding: the g. vine 269*b*
Gadier: isles of Javan or G. 277*b*
Gaels: spoke the speech of the G. 92*a*
the great G. of Ireland 92*a*
Gaiety: eclipsed the g. of nations 213*a*
fit for the g. of Mozart 37*a*
Gain: counting g. but loss 286*a*
for g., not glory 303*b*
g. of our best glory 117*a*
g. to society at large 164*a*
go to g. a little patch of ground 335*b*
loss comes to him from his g. 46*a*
madness of many..g. of a few 304*a*
no one knoweth the loss or g. 171*b*
pleased with constant g. 113*b*
sir wh. serves and seeks for g. 342*a*
subserves another's g. 430*b*
the soul is competent to g. 464*b*
turns his necessity to glorious g. 465*a*
what things were g. to me 516*a*
whom hope of g. allured 163*a*
would you g. the tender creatures 159*a*
Gained: g. then by our unbelief 45*a*
he that g. a hundred fights 435*a*
Gains: God bless all our g. 43*b*
light g. make heavy purses 16*a*
Gaiter: modified the cut of a g. 180*b*
Gaiters: all is gas and g. 125*a*
Galahad: Lancelot brave, nor G. 429*a*
servant of the high God, G. 284*b*
Ga-la-lee: Spanish G. 531*a*
Galatea, wayward girl 557*a*
Galatians: great text in G. 52*a*
O foolish G. 515*b*
Gale: blew a mackerel g. 140*b*
his snowy plumage to the g. 443*b*
partake the g. 301*b*
snuffed the tainted g. 316*a*
so sinks the g. 18*b*
who changest not in any g. 429*b*
Galeotto was the book and writer 566*b*
Gales: cool g. shall fan the glade 302*b*
'mid the equinoctial g. 525*a*
Galice at Seint Jame 88*b*
Galilean: Pilot of the G. lake 269*b*
thou hast conquered, O G. 548*a*
thou hast conquered, O pale G. 423*b*
thy kingdom shall pass, G. 423*b*
wilt thou yet take all, G.? 423*b*
Galilee: rolls nightly on deep G. 74*a*
ye men of G., why stand ye 512*a*
Galileo on his turret 49*b*
Gall: g. a new-healed wound 379*b*
g. enough in thy ink 371*b*
gave me g. to eat 486*b*
lack g. to make oppression 333*a*
take my milk for g. 346*b*
the wormwood and the g. 503*b*
Gallant: g. gentleman 522*a*
he was a braw g. 530*b*
many a g. gay domestic 432*b*
this g. will command the sun 366*b*
with this g. good Riou 76*b*
Gallantry: what men call g. 70*a*
Gallants: brave g., stand up 320*a*
Galleon: moon was a ghostly g. 290*a*
Galleons: high-built g. came 437*b*
they may enter into g. 231*a*
where are the g. of Spain 130*b*
Galley: Cervantes on his g. 92*b*
g.-bench creaks with a Pope 424*a*
what..is he doing in this g.? 564*a*
Galleys: over the sea our g. went 49*b*
Galley-slave is with his oar 454*b*
Galliard: go to church in a g. 369*b*
Galligaskins, antigropeloes 75*a*
Gallio cared for none of these 512*b*
Gallop: g. apace, you fiery-footed 366*a*

Gallop (*cont.*)
the very false g. of verses 327a
to g., and to trot the round 137a
trot became a g. soon 108b
Galloped: I g., Dirk g., we g. 47b
Gallops: in this state she g. 364b
Gallow: O there is none in G. 531b
Galloway: there are mair lads in G. 531b
Gallows: g. fifty cubits high 496b
his complexion is perfect g. 367a
it grew a g. and did bear 238b
Jack on the g.-tree 319b
shall there be g. standing 376b
sing..under the g.-tree 23a
the g. in my garden 91b
to the g.-foot—and after 235a
you see nothing but the g. 57a
Gallows-maker; for that frame outlives 336a
Galls: with the bitterness of yr. g. 379b
Galumphing: went g. back 84a
Gamaliel: at the feet of G. 512b
Gambler: whore and g...licensed 29b
Game: a most contagious g. 264a
but how you played the g. 309a
but war's a g. 112b
dice is a gentlemanly g. 459b
g. of interchanging praise 193b
helpless Pieces of the G. 153b
love the g. beyond the prize 287b
makes at once his g. 403a
mumbling of the g...dare not bite 303a
no g. was ever yet worth a rap 171b
passage in the g.-act 410a
play up! and play the g.! 287b
plenty of time to win this g. 136b
silly g. where nobody wins 158a
start some g. on these..heaths 183b
the g. is done! I've won! 98b
the g...is never lost till won 114a
the g.'s afoot 382a
the rigour of the g. 239a
ther is g. noon 89b
turned to jollity and g. 276b
Game Chicken 122b
Game cocks: wits are g. to one
another 160b
Game-preservers: idlers, g. 81a
in g. confederate 74b
playing our g. 113a
plays, in the many g. of life 465b
Gamesome: I am not g. 337b
Gamesters: see more than g. 16a
Gammon: world of g. and spinnach 122a
Gamp: Mrs. G. 474a
Gamyn and gle 534b
Gander: goosey goosey g. 534b
Gang: the old g. 95a
will ye g. wi' me 526a
Gaol: all that we know who lie in g. 459b
sleep out this great g. of time 323a
Gaped: horrid warning g. wide 219a
Gaps: with..pictures fill their g. 419b
ye fill up the g. in our files 7b
Garb: in the g. of old Gaul 149a
Garden: a careless-ordered g. 438b
a g. is a lovesome thing 41a
a large g. have 107a
a river at my g.'s end 419b
birds in the high Hall-g. 433b
blow upon my g. 500b
come into the g., Maud 434a
England is a g. 229b
every Hyacinth the G. wears 153a
g. inclosed in my beloved 500b
g.'s last petals were shed 421b
ghost of a g. fronts the sea 421b
Glory of the G. 229b
God Almighty first planted a g. 16a
God planted a g. 492a
God the first g. made 106b
God walking in the g. 492b
good strawberries in yr. g. there 385a
how does yr. g. grow 533a
I have a g. of my own 261a
I know a little g. close 284a
I value my g. more for..black-
birds 2b
let my beloved come into his g. 500b

Garden (*cont.*)
look thro' this same G. after me 154a
man and woman in a g. 460b
many a G. by the Water blows 152a
nearer God's Heart in a g. 177b
no tender-hearted g. crowns 235a
secret was the g. 442b
set to dress this g. 375b
such was that happy g.-state 261a
the first g. of Liberty's tree 77b
the gallows in my g. 91b
the g. of yr. face 186b
there is a g. in her face 78b
there is a g. that I dream of 439b
thro' a g. of bright images 35a
'tis an unweeded g. 330a
visibly thro' his g. walketh God 52a
walk'd owre yon g. green 529a
we must cultivate our g. 566a
who loves a g. loves a greenhouse 112a
Garden-beds: across the empty g. 284b
Garden-croft: whistles from a g. 222a
Gardener: all the g. Fancy 220b
and Adam was a g. 384a
g. Adam and his wife 431b
half a proper g.'s work 229b
Oh, Adam was a g. 229b
supposing him to be the g. 511b
where the g. Robin 109b
will come the G. in white 154b
Gardeners: no..gentlemen but g. 336a
Garden-god: the eyes of the g. 421b
Gardens: down by the salley g. 474a
g. bright with sinuous rills 101a
in the g. of the night 37a
not God! in g.! 41a
our bodies are our g. 360b
such g. are not made by singing 229b
Thames bordered by its g. green 284a
that in trim g. 268a
Garland: g. and singing robes 279a
green willow is my g. 191a
green willow must..be my g. 363a
immortal g. is to be run for 279a
rosy g. and a weary head 401b
take this..g. and farewell 421a
wither'd is the g. of the war 324b
Garlanded with carven imag'ries 221b
Garlands: let us g. bring 372b
silken flanks with g. drest 219b
weave the g. of repose 260b
whose g. dead 282b
with fantastic g. did she come 336a
you may gather g. there 319a
Garlic: cheese and g. in a windmill 378a
wel loved he g. 89a
Garment: a g. out of fashion 328b
a moth fretting a g. 484a
his g. in her hand 493a
language is the flesh-g. 81b
like a g., wear the beauty 472b
not know the g. from the man 30a
the deep like as with a g. 488a
wax old as doth a g. 488a
wintry g. of unsullied snow 407a
with a g. down to the foot 518a
Garments: do not like the fashion
of yr. g. 343a
dyed g. from Bosrah 503b
enlarge the borders of their g. 507b
g. gay and rich 528a
g. rolled in blood 501b
his vacant g. with his form 374a
look at her g. 195b
reasons are not like a g. 120b
they part my g. among them 483a
trailing g. of the Night 247b
Garnered up my heart 363a
Garnish: eye of heaven to g. 374a
Garnished: empty, swept, and g. 506b
see they be g. fair 441b
Garret: and living in a g. 155b
g. four stories high 13b
Garrick: G.'s a salad 169a
here lies David G. 169b
Garsington: here is Hey for G. 11a
Garter: take away that star and g. 12a
tied up my g. for me 179a
Garyalies 155b
Gas: all is g. and gaiters 125a
Gash of the wind-grieved Apennine 46a

Gas-lamps seven 226a
Gasp: at his last g. 521b
at the last g. of love's 137b
Gate: after we pass the g. 135a
against the eastern g. 268b
against the ivory g. 284a
aged man, a-sitting on a g. 85a
at one g. to make defence 277b
a willow cabin at yr. g. 370a
Captain of the G. 253a
death..openeth the g. to..fame 14a
dog starved at his master's g. 29a
find no latch ter de golden g. 182a
from the passion-flower at the g. 434a
'gainst..thieves men shut their g. 372a
gather at the g. of Paradise 154b
Heaven's g. built in Jerusalem's 30b
heavy burdens at his narrow g. 381b
he only cd. unlock the g. 3b
I am here at the g. alone 434a
keep the g. of hell 303a
matters not how strait the g. 185a
near the sacred g. 440b
Peri at the g. 282a
poor man at his g. 3a
seat..by the side of the g. 495a
sound at heaven's high g. 36b
St. Peter sat by the celestial g. 74b
strait is the g. 505b
the g. is strait 424a
the G. with dreadful faces 277a
the Hun is at the g. 229a
the Mede is at his g. 74a
they that sit in the g. 486b
this is the g. of heaven 493a
watchful at His G. 131b
way that leads to the broad g. 322a
wide is the g. 505b
Gates: g. are mine to open 233a
g. of hell can never 20a
Gaul is at her g. 107b
I barred my g. with iron 228b
lift up yr. heads, O ye g. 483a
Lord loveth the g. of Sion 487a
Love..hovers within my g. 249b
on all her stately g. arose 252a
open the g. of new life to thee 51b
stranger that is within thy g. 480a
such are the G. of Paradise 30a
through g. of pearl 200b
twelve g. were twelve pearls 520a
Gath: tell it not in G. 495b
Gather: cannot tell who shall g. 484a
g. up the fragments 510b
g. ye rosebuds 190a
God who made shall g. 12b
shall we g. at the river? 315a
were I a cloud I'd g. 35b
Gathered: all is safely g. in 276b
be with ease g. 274a
by gloomy Dis was g. 274a
cannot be g. up again 495b
g. and gone by together 485a
g. them..into..Armageddon 510b
g. together in my name 507a
g. together in thy Name 478b
g. to the quiet west 185a
I am g. to thy heart 265a
safely, safely g. in 130b
some g. at six, some at seven 134b
Gatherer: red for the g. springs 441a
Gathering where thou hast not
strawed 508a
Gathers all things mortal 422a
Gat-tothed I was 89b
Gaudy: g., blabbing, and remorseful day 384a
neat, not g. 239b
one other g. night 324a
this g. melon-flower 47b
Gauger: g. walked with willing foot 415a
what shd. Master G. play 415a
Gaul: G. is at her gates 107b
G. is divided into three parts 548b
G., to Greece..into Noah's 110b
in the garb of old G. 149a
I've lost G. 234a
Gaunt: G.'s embattled pile 252b
siege of the city of G. 531b
Gauntlet: a g. with a gift in't 43a
flings the g. down to senates 77b

Gauze: strunt rarely owre gauze 61b
Gave: me herself indeed 48a
  Lord g., and the Lord hath taken 496b
  no man g. unto him 509b
  that we g., we have 526a
Gavest me, tho' unseen, a kiss 109b
Gawds: praise new-born g. 369a
Gay: all will be g. 47b
  always g. 528a
  a poet cd. not but be g. 467a
  as g. as innocent 319b
  face that's anything but g. 440b
  gallant, g. Lothario 313b
  G. grieve a week 419a
  g. go up and g. go down 533b
  g. without frivolity 6a
  I'm a g. deceiver 103a
  impiously g. 113b
  most pleasant and g. 97a
  Music was given, to brighten the g. 282a
  my g. goss-hawk 529a
  so bedeck'd, ornate and g. 277b
  tho' g. they run and leap 265a
  thy outward walls so costly g. 389b
  wise and good and g. 525a
  wd. not, if I cd., be g. 310a
  yet went never g. 360b
Gaza: eyeless is G. 277b
  whence G. mourns 278a
Gaze: fix thy firm g. on virtue 254a
  summer was in her g. 475a
  the show and g. o' the time 351a
  wh. I g. on so fondly 281b
  will g. upon this world 476a
  with fearful g. 280a
Gazed: and still they g. 168b
  but we steadfastly g. on the face 462b
  fade, too much g. at 218a
  I g. and g.—but little thought 467a
Gazelle: never nursed a dear G. 125a, 282a
Gazer: bids the rash g. wipe his eye 187b
Gazers: her eyes the g. strike 302b
Gazes on the ground 258b
Gazing: why stand ye g. up 512a
  with g. fed 354a
Geck: notorious g. and gull 372a
Geese: all grow up as g. and gabies 414a
  g. are getting fat 124a
  g. are swans, and swans are g. 6b
  his own g. are swans 449b
  if the wild-g. fly that way 342a
  this the wild g. spread 474b
  wild g...the creeping fowler eye 357a
Gehazi: whence comest thou, G.? 496b
Gehenna: down to G. 236b
Gêlert's dying yell 408a
Gem: considered a perfect g. 75a
  full many a g. of purest ray 174a
  g. of all joy 143a
Gemlike: burn..with this g...flame 293a
Gems: brilliant underfoot with..g. 37b
  crept..reflecting g. 34b
  feet like sunny g. 433b
  rich and rare were the g. she wore 281a
  rich and various g. inlay 266b
  these the g. of Heaven 274b
Gender: she's of the feminine g. 290b
Genealogies: fables and endless g. 516b
General: caviare to the g. 332b
  G. as 'that most immoral man' 228a
  G. Good..plea of the scoundrel 30b
  g. notions are generally wrong 280a
  g. of our gracious empress 383b
  g.'s disdained by him one step 368b
  I do attend here on the g. 362a
  of a constitution so g. 41b
Generalities: glittering..g. 94a, 148b
  sounding g. 94a
Generals: bite some other of my g. 161a
  g. Janvier and Février 575b
Generation: evil and adulterous g. 506b
  faithless and stubborn g. 487a
  had it been the whole g. 523b
  he shall follow the g. 485a
  O g. of vipers 504b
  one g. passeth away 499a
  unto the third and fourth g. 480a
  ye are a chosen g. 517b
  yet to every g. these come..down 147b
  younger g. will come knocking 567a
Generations: all g...call me blessed 508b

Generations (cont.)
  fleeting g. of mankind 399b
  keep the young g. in hail 263a
  no hungry g. tread thee down 220a
  the g. are prepared 464b
Genesis: square with G. again 45a
Geneva: grim G. ministers 12b
  open on to the Lake of G. 223a
Genevieve: O G., sweet G. 106a
Genius: Bacon, that..hardy g. 170b
  beauty like hers is g. 312a
  builders—with want of g. curst 140a
  Chawcer..had g...unedicated 451a
  creates a g. to do it 148b
  eccentricities of g. 126b
  Edmund, whose g. was such 169b
  g. and the mortal instruments 338b
  g...capacity of taking trouble 80b
  G. does what it must 265a
  g...getting its possessors into trouble 66b
  g. has been slow of growth 244b
  g. is of no country 94b
  g. is one per cent. inspiration 143b
  g. is only a great..patience 561b
  gives g. a better discerning 169b
  good g. presiding over you 222a
  implored the g. of the place 556b
  invoke the g. of the Constitution 297a
  models destroy g. and art 183b
  most singular g. 34a
  my g. is rebuked 348b
  nothing to declare except my g. 460b
  parting g. is with sighing sent 270b
  ramp up my g. 215b
  talent instantly recognizes g. 136a
  that is g. 147b
  tho' taste, tho' g. bless 103a
  to raise the g. 298b
  'twas thine own g. 72a
  what a g. I had 419a
  when was g. found respectable? 43a
  whose fires true g. kindles 303a
  works of g. are the first things 222a
Geniuses: greatest g...wanted taste 449b
Gennesareth: not of G. but Thames 442b
Gent: a military g. 439b
  no dancing bear was g. 109a
Genteel: dialect words..to the..g. 180b
Genteelly: debauch..friend's wife g. 208b
  vices may be committed g. 208b
Genterye: for of his g. him deyneth 90a
Gentile: the might of the G. 74a
Gentiles: boastings as the G. use 233b
Gentility: cottage of g. 100b
Gentle: fond of each g...scene 22b
  g. kind of the lioun 90a
  g. mind by g. deeds is known 409a
  g., plain, just 458b
  he is g. that doth g. dedis 89b
  many a g. person made a Jack 384b
  one of those g. ones 372a
  Sleep! it is a g. thing 99a
  take the g. path 188a
  that g. voice we hear 11a
  these g. historians 58a
  tho' g., yet not dull 119b
  verray parfit g. knight 88a
Gentle-hearted: my g. Charles 101b
Gentleman: a dear dark-eyed g. 179a
  always talking about being a g. 416b
  an old worshipful g. 522a
  a prosperous g. 346a
  as a g. switches his cane 100b
  a very gallant g. 522a
  a very simple g. 373b
  bears not alive so stout a g. 379a
  collar, shewed him the g. and scholar 63a
  every Jack became a g. 384b
  fat g. in such a passion 149a
  fine old English g. 524b
  finished g. from top to toe 71b
  g., nurse, that loves to hear himself 365b
  g. on whom I built..trust 346b
  g. said to the fi' pun' note 126a
  g. shd. never go beyond a song 149a
  g.'s way of thinking 558b
  g., tho' spoiled i' the breeding 38a
  God send every g. 529b
  grand old name of g. 431a

Gentleman (cont.)
  I do not think a braver g. 378b
  king..cannot make a g. 58a
  kissing, kind-hearted g. 113a
  my state is well: I am a g. 370a
  no g.'s library shd. be without 239a
  once a g, and always a g. 123b
  prince of darkness is a g. 343a, 416a
  see if Philip can be a little g. 193a
  stainless g. 429a
  St. Patrick was a g. 27b
  tea..is a g. at least 93b
  that smooth-faced g. 374a
  the first true g. 118b
  the nomination of this g. 337a
  this squash, this g. 373a
  true breeding of a g. 70b
  who was then a g.? 527b
Gentlemanly: devil..do a very g. thing 412b
  secondly, g. conduct 10b
Gentlemen: ancient g. but gardeners 336a
  Buzzards are all g. 38a
  conversation among g. 209a
  cooks are g. 64a
  g. come every day 534a
  g. in England now a-bed 383a
  g. of the shade 376b
  G. Prefer Blondes 249b
  G.-rankers out on the spree 229b
  g. unafraid 227b
  g. wd. be as sad as night 374a
  God Almighty's g. 138b
  God rest you merry, g. 523a
  good-morning g. both 145a
  great-hearted g. 45b
  I shd. waken my g. 235b
  never merry..since g. came up 384a
  (Presbytery)..not a religion for g. 87b
  scholars and g. 469b
  seamen were not g. 255b
  she lays eggs for g. 534a
  two single g. roll'd into one 103a
  we shall never be g. 152a
  while the G. go by 234a
  written by g. for g. 440a
  you g. of England 292a
  you g.'s g. are so hasty 400b
Gentleness: g., goodness, faith 515b
  g., in hearts at peace 40a
  have not from yr. eyes that g. 337b
  her ways are ways of g. 409b
  in simpleness and g. 227b
  let g. my strong enforcement 326b
Gentles and commons 318b
Gentlewomen, like the Nereides 323a
Gently, John, gently down hill 405a
Geographers, in Afric maps 419b
Geographical: Italy is a g. expression 569a
Geography: Biography is different from G. 27b
  G. is about maps 27b
  in despite o' g. 65b
Geological home-made cake 123b
Geometric: he, by g. scale 65a
Geometry..the only science 191b
George: Amelia was praying for G. 440a
  any good of G. the Third 241b
  between St. Denis and St. G. 383b
  G. in pudding time came o'er 524a
  G. the First knew nothing 208b
  G. the First was always reckoned 241b
  G. III..profit by their example 185b
  G. III was a..consecrated obstruction 17b
  God save great G. our king 523a
  Great G.'s acts let..Cibber sing 206a
  King G.'s glorious days 164a
  King G. will be able to read that 178b
  viler G. the Second 241b
  where's G.? Gone to Lyonch 528a
Georges: God be praised, the G. ended 241b
Georgia: marching thro' G 473a
German: a wee, wee G. lairdie 116b, 193a
  G., who smoked like a chimney 19a
  more g. to the matter 337a
  the furious G. comes 252b
Germans: G...(empire) of the air 80a
  sermons from mystical G. 164b
Germany: G. over all 568c

Germany (cont.)
G. was my spiritual home 571b
governments associated against G. 462a
his bonnet in G. 353a
war . . between Great Britain and G. 242b
Germens: all G. spill at once 342b
Germinal: trumpet of G. 91b
Gertrude: Cicely, G., Magdalen 311b
Gestes: the Troyane g. 90a
Gesture: in every g. dignity 275b
in shape and g. proudly eminent 272a
Get: don't you wish you may g. it 20a
earn that I eat, g. that I wear 327a
g. thee to a nunnery 333b
g. to live; then live 186b
g. up and bar the door 531b
g. up, g. up for shame 189a
g. up, sweet Slug-a-bed 189a
g. you gone, you drunken sot 534b
if thou canst g. but thither 448a
none cd. g. it till now 311b
quite enough to g., sir 126b
to do nothing and g. something 130a
to g. what you want 404a
Gets: won't be happy till he g. it 523b
Getting: g. and spending we lay
   waste 473a
Gospel of G. On 391a
with all thy g. get understanding 497b
Gewgaw: this g. world 139a
Gey ill to live wi' 82a
Ghastly: the g. priest doth reign 253b
we were a g. crew 99a
Ghent: see Gaunt
Ghost: alas! poor g. 331a
applaud the hollow g. 6b
blasphemy against the Holy G. 506b
g. of a garden fronts the sea 421b
G. of the deceased Roman Empire 191b
g. unlaid forbear thee! 329a
if I had seen a g. 151b
impute to each frustrate g. 52a
it is an honest g. 331b
like a g. from the tomb 393b
like a g. she glimmers on to me 436b
like a sheeted g., the vessel swept 249a
make a g. of him that lets me 331a
murmur of the morning g. 130b
since g. there's none 189b
some old lover's g. 133b
stalk'd off . . like an ill us'd g. 29a
that affable familiar g. 388b
there needs no g. . . to tell us this 331b
to a woman, but a kind of g. 132a
to the bowling of a g. 442b
towards his design moves like a g. 347b
turn thou g. that way 132b
vex not his g. 344a
wd. a g. not rise 421b
what beckoning g. . . invites 299a
what gentle g. . . hails me 216b
yr. g. will walk . . in an English lane 46a
Ghostly counsel and advice 480b
Ghosts: G. all the country over 567b
g. from an enchanter fleeing 396a
g., wandering here and there 357a
haunted by . . g. they have deposed 375b
make the g. gaze 324b
see G. gliding between the lines 567a
yet a boy I sought for g. 394b
Ghoul: dug them up like a G. 122b
Ghouls: they are G. 298a
Giant: arrows in the hand of the 489b
as when a g. dies 352a
dwarf sees farther than the g. 102a
excellent to have a g.'s strength 351b
fling but a stone, the g. dies 175b
g. refreshed with wine 487a
like a g.'s robe upon a dwarfish 350a
owner whereof was G. Despair 54a
rejoiceth as a g. to run his course 482b
tyrannous to use it like a g. 351b
Giant-dwarf, Dan Cupid 344a
Giants: g., the sons of Anak 494a
piled by the hands of g. 253a
there were g. in the earth 492b
Giant's Causeway worth seeing? 210a
Gibbets: cells and g. for 'the man' 106a
g. keep the lifted hand in awe 477a
Gibbon: G. levelled walks 103b
G. moved to flutes 103b

Gibeon: stand thou still upon G. 494b
Gibes: where be your g. now? 336b
Giddy: g. harumfrodite 234a
I am g., expectation whirls me 369a
Giddy-paced . . times 370b
Gift: all have not . . g. of martyrdom 140b
a portion of the g. is won 464a
cause of this fair g. 388b
Common Sense! our surest g. 263a
every g. of noble origin 471b
every other g., but wanted love 6b
every perfect g. is from above 517a
excellent g. of charity 479b
fatal g. of beauty 69a
for g. or grace, surpassing this 44a
for nought her priceless g. 293a
found out a g. for my fair 399b
gauntlet with a g. in 't 43a
have not the g. of continency 481b
Heaven's last best g. 274b
her great g. of sleep 185a
scented g. and remembrancer 458a
so thy great g. . . comes home 388b
they have the g. to know it 326a
to a dog for a new year's g. 356a
wad some Power the g. gie us 61b
you have a g., sir 216a
Gift-horse: look a g. in the mouth 65a
Gifts: all good g. around us 76a
all the g. from all the heights 49a
blind Fortune still bestows . . g. 215b
endowed with highest g. 464a
for all his g. to me 438b
gods . . cannot recall their g. 438b
God's g. put man's . . to shame 44a
her g. may henceforth be bestowed 325b
he wd. adore my g. instead of Me 188a
make us love yr. goodly g. 364a
manifold g. of grace 481a
no g. from Chance, have conquer'd 8a
of all the heavenly g. 177a
rarer g. than gold 39a
rich g. wax poor 333b
receivedst g. for men 486b
seven-fold g. impart 491a
the g. of G are strown 184a
there are diversities of g. 514b
these g. a curtain before 'em 369b
Gigadibs the literary man 45a
Giggles: he wriggles and g. 193a
Gilbert, the Filbert 462a
Gilboa: ye mountains of G. 495b
Gild: g., but to flout, the ruins grey 317a
g. refined gold 374a
I'll g. it with the happiest terms 379a
my verse again shall g. 137a
Gilead: appear from mount G. 500a
balm in G. 503b
G. is mine 485b
Giles: you must be very old, Sir G. 284b
Gills: at his g. draws in 275b
Gilly flowers (gillyvors): Columbine
   with G. 409b
streaked g. 373a
Gilpin: away went G. 108a
G. at his horse's side 108b
G. long live he 109a
G.'s spouse said to her dear 108a
G. was a citizen 108a
said G.—so am I 108b
Gilt: dust that is a little g. 369a
more laud than g. o'er-dusted 369a
Gimble: gyre and g. in the wabe 83b
Gin: g. by pailfuls 319b
I breakfast on g. 186a
now is the woodcock near the g. 371a
talk o' p. an' beer 229b
with Pitfall and with g. beset 154a
Ginger: g. shall be hot i' the mouth 370b
Nutmegs and G. 23a
'ot sand and g. when alive 229a
Giotto's tower 247a
Gipsies: the same the G. wore 8a
Gird: another shall g. thee 511b
g. on thy sword, O man 36b
g. thee with thy sword 484b
g. up now thy loins 497b
how g. the sphere 275b
Girded with praise 172b
Girdle: about the paps with a golden 518a

Girdle (cont.)
folds of a bright g. 5a
I'll put a g. round . . the earth 356b
leathern g. about his loins 504b
Mother, tie my g. for me 393a
truth . . golden g. of the globe 107b
Girdled: with . . towers were g. round 101a
Girl: a fair little g. sat 198b
a g. arose that had red . . lips 476a
an unlessoned g., unschool'd 354a
cleanly young g. to rub my . . pate 304a
dear Child! dear G.! 467a
every boy and every g. 164a
g. I left behind me 526b
g. with a pair of blue eyes 400b
going to be a very good g. 155a
good g. was Emily Jane 163a
home is the g.'s prison 391a
I have but a g. to give 264b
I shall find some g. perhaps 39a
it's my old g. that advises 121b
no good g.'s lip out of Paris 424a
quest of the Golden G. 244a
she's the dearest g. 122a
slap-up g. in a bang-up chariot 125b
spoke I to my g. 190a
sweeter no g. ever gave 461a
there was a little g. 249a
to the sweetest g. I know 461a
we all love a pretty g. 28a
where there's a g. there's a boy 10b
you speak like a green g. 331a
Girl-graduates: sweet g. 435b
Girlish: laugh thy g. laughter 452a
Girls: boys and g. are level now 324b
g. and boys come out to play 534b
he words me, g. 325a
I know where little g. are sent 244b
of all the g. that are so smart 79b
prevent g. from being g. 197a
rose of the rosebud garden of g. 434a
secrets with g. 114a
swear to never kiss the g. 46b
two little g. in blue 172a
what are little g. made of 534b
where g. are so pretty 524a
white feet of laughing g. 253a
with the g. be handy 18b
wretched un-idea'd g. 206b
Gitchee Gumee 248b
Gitche Manito 248b
Give: all I can g. you I g. 423a
g. all thou canst 467b
g. all to love 146b
g. a man a horse he can ride 444a
g., and it shall be given unto you 509a
g. me but what this riband bound 449a
g. me, . . heaven, a private station 160b
g. me more love 79b
g. me my boots I say 376a
g. me the crown. Here, cousin 376a
g. peace in our time 478a
g. the jolly heaven above 414a
g. to me the life I love 414a
g. unto me, made lowly wise 464a
g. what thou canst 112b
in this mood will g. us anything 340b
it is more blessed to g. 512b
I will g. unto this last 507b
such as I have g. I thee 512a
they beg, I g. 143a
two daughters, crying, G., g. 499a
we receive but what we g. 100b
when I g. I g. myself 458a
Given: ask, and it shall be g. 505b
g. for nought her priceless gift 293a
g. to hospitality 513b
never g. in vain 198b
something g. that way 23a
that hath shall be g. 508a
to whom nothing is g. 151a
Giver: God loveth a cheerful g. 515a
good received, the g. is forgot 104a
Givers: when g. prove unkind 333b
Gives: blesseth him that g. 354b
he g. twice who g. soon 553b
she g. but little 477b
what e'er he g., he g. the best 214a
who g. himself with his alms 251a
Giving: godlike in g. 282b
not in the g. vein to-day 385a

Gizzards: knives into their g.   76a
Glad: at sight of thee was g.   463b
   come then, my brethren, and be g.   307a
   earth may be g. thereof   488a
   g. did I live and gladly die   415a
   g. me with its soft black eye   282a
   g. to death's mystery   196a
   g. to learn of noble men   340b
   g. waters of the dark blue sea   69b
   g., yea g. with all my heart   137b
   he was g., I was woe   176a
   I was g. when they said   489b
   Janet was as g. at that   528b
   often, g. no more   465a
   Queens hereafter..be g. to live   137a
   sad that she was g.   441a
   then are they g., because..at rest   488b
   we have been g. of yore   465a
   wery g. to see you indeed   126a
Gladder: my heart is g. than all   310b
Glade: bee-loud g.   475a
   crown the wat'ry g.   174b
   flower of the hazel g.   177a
   points to yonder g.   299a
Gladly wolde he lerne   88b
Gladness: g. of her g.   21b
   make me hear of joy and g.   485a
   music is the g. of the world   144b
   shareth in our g.   3b
   solemn g. even crowned   430a
   teach me half the g.   398b
   with solace and g.   402b
   youth begin in g.   470a
Gladstone: G...ace..up his sleeve   238b
   Mr. G. speaks to Me   448b
   what's the matter with G.?   177b
Glamis: G. hath murdered sleep   348a
   G. thou art, and Cawdor   346b
   King, Cawdor, G.   348b
Glance: g., and nod, and bustle by   8b
   g. from heaven to earth   357b
   g. of great politeness   74b
   his g. was stern and high   252b
   whose g. was glum   167a
   without a g. my way   127b
Glances: where thy grey eye g.   298a
Glare: eyes wh. thou dost g. with   349a
Glared: lion who g. upon me   338a
Glasgow: when we came thro' G.   530a
Glass: a comb and a g. in her hand   525b
   an excuse for a g.   400b
   dome of many-coloured g.   392b
   double g. o' the inwariable   126b
   drink not the third g.   186b
   fill ev'ry g.   159b
   g. to his sightless eye   287b
   gold like unto clear g.   520a
   grief with a g. that ran   420b
   he was indeed the g.   380a
   his natural face in a g.   517b
   in a g. he hadde pigges bones   89a
   made mouths in a g.   342b
   my g. shall not persuade me   387a
   satire is a sort of g.   417b
   sea of g. like unto crystal   518b
   sea of g. mingled with fire   519b
   the g. of fashion   333b
   thou art thy mother's g.   387a
   thro' a g. darkly   514b
   till I set you up a g.   335a
   truth..peeps over the g.'s edge   45a
   turn down an empty G.   154a
   Venus, take my votive g.   306a
Glasses: fill all the g. there   106b
   g. itself in tempests   69b
   Shakespeare, and the musical g.   171a
   wiv a ladder and some g.   22a
Glassy: windless, g. floor   231a
Glaze: gloat on the g. and the mark   242a
Glazed each weary eye   98b
Glazier: father was no g.   418b
Glazing: yr. g. is new   236a
Gleam: fled the visionary g.   466a
   follow the G.   434b
   g. on the years that shall be   252a
   one high funeral g.   475b
Gleams: g. of a remoter world   396a
   invested with purpureal g.   467b
   sunbeams with their convex g.   393b
Glean: the world shall g. of me   442b
   thou shdst. but g.   195b

Gleaning of the grapes of Ephraim   495a
Glede: the rapid g.   403a
Glee: laugh'd with counterfeited g.   168b
   piping songs of pleasant g.   32a
   serious faith and inward g.   468a
   they filled one home with g.   184b
   to the brim with girlish g.   164b
Glen: down the rushy g.   4a
   piney sides of this long g.   435a
Glenartney's hazel shade   316a
Glencairn: I'll remember thee, G.   61b
Glendoveer: I am a blessed G.   403b
Glenlivet: only half G.   12b
Glens: bask in the g.   5b
Glide: gently by his, ye waters, g.!   8b
   shall for ever g.   463b
Glides glimmering o'er my fleece-like
   floor   393a
Glideth: thus the Mayne g.   49b
Gliding: moonbeam on the g. stream   35b
Glimmer: cease, every joy, to g.   77b
Glimmering: mere g. and decays   448a
Glimmers: she g. on to me   436b
Glimpse: g. of His bright face   448a
   nor g. divine!   299a
   one g. of it within the Tavern   153b
Glimpses: g. of the moon   331a
   g. that wd. make me less forlorn   473a
Glisten: all silence an' all g.   250b
Glittering: g. generalities!   94a, 148b
   holds him with his g. eye   98a
   O how that g. taketh me   190b
Gloaming: roamin' in the G.   242b
   when g. treads the heels o' day   424b
Gloat: g. on the glaze and the mark   242a
   I g.! Hear me g.!   237b
Globe: a seat in this distracted g.   331b
   rattle of a g. to play withal   139a
   the great g. itself   367b
   wears the turning g.   200a
   we the g. can compass   357a
Gloom: end of toil and g.   20b
   go with him in the g.   180a
   in silence and in g.   12b
   inspissated g.   207b
   is my g., after all, shade   442a
   its splendour..will pierce the g.   49b
   light to counterfeit a g.   268a
   shall not chase my g. away   310a
   this mournful g.   271a
   thro' hours of g. fulfill'd   7a
   thy thousand years of g.   429b
   tunnel of green g.   39b
Glooms: blown thro' verdurous g.   220a
   welcome, kindred g.!   443b
Gloomy: more bigoted, more g.   288a
Glories: all my g. in that one woman   386a
   g. of our blood and state   401a
   in those weaker g. spy   448a
   its g. pass away   251b
   you may my g...depose   376a
Glorious: but Tam was g.   62b
   by all that's good and g.   73b
   g. First of June   526b
   g.—more g. is the crown   402b
   g. the northern lights   403a
   g. things of thee are spoken   289a
   King's daughter is all g. within   484b
   make thee g. by my pen   280b
   Sons of Belial had a g. time   138b
Glory: a g., a fair luminous cloud   100b
   all g., laud and honour   286a
   all their g. past   54a
   awake up, my g.   485b
   being too fond of g.   405a
   blaze with his descending g.   55a
   but 'g.' doesn't mean..argument   85a
   but thro' a kind of g.   439b
   calls the g. from the grey   50b
   cataract leaps in g.   436a
   chief g. of every people   212b
   crowned with g. now   224a
   crown him with g. and worship   482a
   day of g. has arrived   565b
   do all to the g. of God   514b
   don't know what you mean by 'g.'   85a
   duty was the way to g.   435a
   earth are full of thy g.   480b
   earth is full of his g.   501b
   eternal g. thou shalt win   54a
   fill thy breast with g.   186b

Glory (cont.)
   for gain, not g.   303b
   for the hope of g.   479a
   for what g. is it   517b
   from another star in g.   515a
   gain of our best g.   117a
   g. above all the earth   485b
   g. and loveliness have pass'd away   221a
   g. and the freshness of a dream   466a
   g. and the nothing of a name   69b
   g. be to thee, O Lord most High   480b
   g. dropped from their youth   52a
   g. is in their shame   516a
   g., jest, and riddle of the world   301a
   g. leads the way   244a
   g., like the phoenix   72b
   g. of Europe is extinguished   57a
   g. of God did lighten it   520a
   g. of man as the flower of grass   517b
   g. of the coming of the Lord   200b
   G. of the Garden   229b
   g. of the Lord is risen   503a
   g. of the Lord shall be revealed   502b
   g. of the Lord shone round   508b
   g. of the world pass away   537a
   g. of this world, I hate ye   386a
   g. of youth glowed   414b
   g. shone around   424b
   g.'s no compensation   237a
   g.'s thrill is o'er   281a
   g. that redounds therefrom   470a
   g. that shall be revealed   479b
   g. that was Greece   298a
   g. to God in the highest   508b
   g. to the King of kings   455b
   g. to the newborn King   455b
   go where g. waits   281a
   him who walked in g.   470a
   his work of g. done   111a
   Ichabod..the g. is departed   495a
   I felt it was g.   73b
   in a sea of g.   386a
   in its g.'s full array   185a
   into g. peep   448b
   it is a g. to her   514b
   joy and their g. must be   537a
   kingdoms of the world, and the g.   505a
   King of g., King of peace   187b
   King of G. shall come in   483a
   left him alone with his g.   462b
   let her full G., my fancies   115b
   let others write for g.   106a
   like madness is the g. of this life   368a
   like thy g., Titan, is to be   397b
   mellow g. of the Attic stage   6a
   Memnonium was in all its g.   403b
   my gown of g.   307a
   never hope for g.   414a
   of the deed the g. shall remain   177a
   passed away a g. from the earth   466a
   paths of g. lead but to the grave   174a
   pride of the peacock..g. of God   31a
   return the g. of yr. prime?   395a
   so doth the greater g.   355b
   Solomon in all his g.   505b
   so much g. and so much shame   255a
   storehouse for the g. of the Creator   13a
   that will be g. for me   315b
   the brightness of his g.   517a
   the g. and the dream   466a
   the joy and the g. must be   287a
   the power, and the g.   505b
   there's g. for you   85a
   the soiled g.   6a
   this goin' ware g. waits ye   250a
   this I count the g. of my crown   145b
   thy laurel, thy g.   218a
   'tis to g. we steer   158b
   to the greater g. of God   558b
   trailing clouds of g. do we come   466a
   trod the ways of g.   386a
   uncertain g. of an April day   372b
   visions of g., spare my..sight   173b
   walking in an air of g.   448a
   we beheld his g.   510b
   What Price G.   4a
   when can their g. fade ?   420a
   when gout and g. seat me   46b
   where is that g. now?   414b
   who rush to g., or the grave   77a
   why in the name of G.   218b

Glory (cont.)

wid all the g. missin'	237b
with a g. in His bosom	200b
with g. not their own	469b
with inward g. crowned	399a
with my g. and desert	187b
wretchedness that g. brings	368a
youth are the days of our g.	73b

Gloss: read ev'ry text and g. over 65a

Gloucester: G...we are in..danger 382b

Salisbury and G. 383a

Gloucestershire: I am a stranger here in G. 375a

Glove: he played at the g. 530b

that I were a g. upon that hand	365a
they were hand and g.	111a
touch not the cat but a g.	319a

Gloves: walk thro' the fields in g. 106a

with g. of steel	316b
wore g. in my cap	343a

Glow: and g. like it 190b

keenly felt the friendly g.	59a
lazy g. of benevolence	45b
lo do thyne eres g.	90a

Glowing: his g. axle doth allay 266b

the other g. like the vital morn 393b

Glow-worm: g. shows the matin 331b

her eyes the g. lend thee	189b
the g. in the grass	73a

Glow-worms: live, as g. shine 447b

Glutton: g. of wordes 242b

of praise a mere g. 169b

Gnarled: g. and writhen thorn 235a

Gnat: grey-coated g. 364b

'Sap and Sawdust', said the g.	84a
strain at a g.	507b
the g. wh. dances in thy ray	294b

Gnats: the small g. mourn 221b

Gnaw you so yr. nether lip? 363b

Go: and as cooks g. she went 315a

and g. at last	188b
as often as from thee I g.	133b
away, I'm bound to g.	525a
before I g. hence	484a
bids nor sit nor stand but g.	50b
but g. at once	349a
expedient for you that I g. away	511a
g., and catch a falling star	134a
g., and do thou likewise	509a
g., and he goeth	506a
g., and the Lord be with thee	495b
g. away and sin no more	525a
g. fetch a web	530a
g., for they call you, Shepherd	8a
g., hang yourselves all!	371b
g., little book, and wish to all	414b
g., lovely Rose!	449a
g. not, happy day	433b
g., songs, for ended is our..play	441a
g., stranger! track the deep	184b
g. thy way, eat thy bread	499b
g. to the ant, thou sluggard	498a
g. up, thou bald head	496b
g. very quietly and drop a button	194a
g. we know not where	352a
g. where glory waits thee	281a
g. where you are wanted	199a
g. with him in the gloom	180a
g. with him twain	505a
g. with me, like good angels	385b
g. ye into all the world	508b
g...you may call it madness	310a
how you do g. it!	41a
I and my Love wont to g.	530a
I can g. no longer	286b
I g. from you to Him	12b
I g. on for ever	425b
I g. where most men g.	171b
in service where it cannot g.	372b
I saw them g., one horse was blind	403b
is to g. hence unwilling	276b
it doesn't g. far enough	124b
I this night maun g.	528a
I will neither g. nor hang!	28a
I will not let thee g.	36b
let g., sir! Down, Sir!	26a
let 's sup before we g.	534b
let us g. hence, my songs	423a
men may come and men may g.	425b
must you g.?	447b
neither will I let Israel g.	493b

Go (cont.)

no, no, g. not to Lethe	219b
no note of him, but let him g.	358b
not..g. except thou bless me	493a
not to g. anywhere, but to g.	412b
now g., write it before them	502a
O' God's name, let it g.	375b
one to come, and one to g.	85a
over the rolling waters g.	436a
sigh not so, but let them g.	358a
still we say as we g.	311b
sweetest love, I do not g.	133b
then might I let thee g.	36b
though I must g.	134a
Thursday's child has far to g.	525a
to g. and find out and be damned	231b
to g. and get shot and be damned	231b
to the Bishop they g.	406b
unto Caesar shalt thou g.	513a
we g., and we drop like the fruits	263a
we will g. into the house	489b
what a Rum G. everything is	455b
who will g. for us?	501b
why you g., nor where	154b
will g. with you along	189a
with thee to g., is to stay here	276b
wrong to sing so loudly: let us g.	430b
you g. not, till I set you up	335a
you shall g. back for mine	109a

Goads: words of the wise are as g. 500a

Goal: one far-set g. 9a

the g. stands up	199a
the grave is not its g.	247b
till yon g. be won	171b

Goat: g. feet dance an antic hay 258b

lust of the g. is the bounty	31a
luxurious mountain g.	383a
with hoofs of a g.	43b

Goats: Cadwallader and all his g. 383b

drink the blood of g.	485a
g. and monkeys!	362b
hair is as a flock of g.	500a
promontory g.	264a
refuge for the wild g.	488b

Goblet: navel is like a round g. 500b

upon a parcel-gilt g. 380a

Goblets: my figured g. for a dish 375b

Goblin: it makes a g. of the sun 312b

spirit of health or g. damned 331a

Goblins: an' the g.'ll git you 309a

one of sprites and g. 373a

God: a beautiful G. to behold 423b

a bitter G. to follow	423b
about the best thing G. invents	46b
about the feet of G.	429b
abusing of G.'s patience	355b
acknowledgement of G. in Christ	46a
a' cried out 'G., G., G.!'	382a
afraid to look upon G.	493b
after G.'s holy ordinance	481b
a G. all mercy, is a G. unjust	477b
a g. when all our life-breath met	312a
a highway for our G.	502b
Ah, my dear G.	187a
all love is lost but upon G.	143a
all the seas of G.?	457a
almost chide G. for making you	327a
alone wi' G. an' these my engines	231b
amaranths grow beneath G.'s eye	52a
America is G.'s crucible	477b
an avow to G. made he	530b
and was the holy lamb of G.	31a
an honest G. is the noblest work	203b
animal, or the g. that he worships	417b
appeal from tyranny to G.	69b
as far removed from G.	271a
a' shd. not think of G.	382a
as if G. brought them	147b
as if some lesser g. had made	429a
assumes the g., affects to nod	138b
a thing of wings, myself a g.	33b
batter my heart, three personed G.	133a
before G. made the angelic clan	476b
being dead art a G.	423b
best of all G.'s works	276a
better to have no opinion of G.	15a
blends itself with G.	393b
blow, thou wind of G.	226a
body nature is, and G. the soul	301a
bought over G. with a fee	424a
broken and contrite heart, O G.	485a

God (cont.

built G. a church, and laugh'd	110b
but for the grace of G.	34b
but G., if a G. there be	423a
but G. is faithful	514b
but if it be of G.	512a
by G.'s Almighty hand	76a
by G.'s help so I will	481a
by searching find out G.	497a
by that G. we both adore	298b
by the grace of G. I am what I am	514b
by the livin' G. that made you	230a
Cabots talk only to G.	34a
called the children of G.	505a
calm on the bosom of thy G.	184b
carnage..is G.'s daughter	71b
caught at G.'s skirts	47b
chalice of the grapes of G.	429b
charged with the grandeur of G.	197b
chariots of G. are twenty thousand	486b
cometh the wrath of G.	515b
consider this, ye that forget G.	485a
Counsellor, the mighty G.	501b
crucify..the Son of G. afresh	517a
cry 'G. for Harry!'	382a
curse G., and die	497a
daughter of the voice of G.	463b
day of vengeance of our G.	503a
dear G.! the very houses	472b
declare the glory of G.	482b
delight in God, as misers..in gold	445a
died of the kisses of..G.	285b
dim nor red, like G.'s own head	98b
do all to the glory of G.	514b
doth Job fear G.	496b
doth then show likest G.'s	354b
doubtless G. cd. have made	67a
durst..tempt the Son of G.	277b
dwelleth the love of G. in him?	518a
ef you want to take in G.	250a
either a beast or a g.	559a
either a wild beast, or a g.	15b
Enoch walked with G.	492b
even G. in his holy habitation	486a
even G.'s providence..estranged	196a
every common bush afire with G.	43a
every creature of G. is good	516b
every man..was G. or Devil	118b
excellent angler, and now with G.	450b
faithful to G. and thee	191a
fall into the hands of G.	437b
far be it from G.	497a
fast by the oracle of G.	270b
fear G., and take yr. own part	34a
fear G. Honour the King 238a, 517b
fear G...keep his commandments	500a
fellow-citizens: G. reigns	158b
fool hath said..there is no G.	482a
for G.! for the Cause	252b
for good to them that love G.	513b
forgotten even by G.	49b
for wh. G. threw him from.. heaven	258b
Freedom the cause of G.	34b
from everlasting Thou art G.	453a
from G., who is our home	466a
fulfil thy will, O my G.	484a
Geometry..pleased G. to bestow	191b
gifts of G. are strown	184a
give to G. each moment	131b
glory be to G. for dappled things	197b
glory of G. did lighten it	520a
glory to G. in the highest	508b
goat is the bounty of G.	31a
go up to G. so solemnly	298a
G. accept him, Christ receive	435a
G. Almighty first planted a garden	16a
G. Almighty's gentlemen	138b
G. and angels to be lookers on	13a
G. and sinners reconciled	455b
G. and soldier we alike adore	217a
G. and the doctor we alike adore	291b
G. answers sharp..some prayers	43a
G. appears, and G. is light	29b
G. be at my eyed	523a
G. be in my eyes..head..heart	523a
G. be merciful to me	510a
G. be merciful unto us	486a
G. being with thee	467a
G. be with you till we meet again!	315b
G. bless all our losses	43b

God (*cont.*)

G. bless our Lord the King	193a
G. bless the Prince of Wales	245b
G. bless us every one	121b
G. by G. goes out	423a
G. calleth preaching folly	187a
G. changes, and man	422a
G. dawned on chaos	392a
G...doubled His whole creation	36a
G., even our own G.	486a
G. for his Richard hath in..pay	375a
G. fulfils Himself in many ways	429a
G. gave the increase	514a
G. gives all men all earth	235a
G. gives us love	431b
G. has a few of us	44b
G. has not said a word	50b
G. has written all the books	66b
G. hath chosen the foolish	514a
G. hath chosen the weak things	514a
G. hath given you one face	333b
G. hath made man upright	499b
G. hath made them so	452b
G. hath made the pile complete	430b
G. hath not given us..fear	516b
G. hath raised me high	145b
G. hath shewed his voice	484b
G. hath spoken in his holiness	485b
G. helps them that helps	157a
G. Himself is moon and sun	435a
G. in his mercy lend her grace	432a
G-intoxicated man	569b
G. is a circle	526b
G. is always for the big battalions	566a
G. is a righteous Judge	482a
G. is a Spirit	510b
G. is forgotten..Doctor slighted	291b
G. is forgotten..soldier slighted	217a
G. is gone up with a merry noise	484b
G. is his own interpreter	110a
G. is in heaven..thou upon earth	499a
G. is in the midst of her	484b
G. is love	518a
G. is Love. I dare say	67a
G. is making the American	477b
G. is no respecter of persons	512a
G. is not a man, that he shd. lie	494a
G. is not mocked	515b
G. is our G. for ever	485a
G. is our hope and strength	484b
G. is provoked every day	482a
G. is the King of all	485a
G. is the perfect poet	49b
G. is, they are	46a
G. is Three, and God is One	288b
G. is thy law, thou mine	274a
G. is working His purpose out	2b
G., I thank thee, that I am not	510a
G. keeps a notice in Heaven	43b
G. knows, an' 'E won't split	237b
G. knows it I am with them	459b
G. lets loose a thinker	148a
G.'ll send the bill	250a
G. loves an idle rainbow	192a
G. loveth a cheerful giver	515a
G. made him, and therefore	353a
G. made Himself an awful rose	439a
G. made the country	111b
G. made them, high or lowly	3a
G. made the thunder, but	255a
G. made the wicked Grocer	93a
G. made the woman for the man	426b
G. made two great lights	492a
G. makes sech nights	250b
G...marked him for his own	450b
G. may forgive you, but I never	145a
G. moves in a mysterious way	110a
G. never made his work	140a
G. never wrought miracles	15a
G. now accepteth thy works	499b
G. of Abraham	493b
G. of battles, was ever a battle	437b
G. offers to every mind its choice	148a
G. of Hosts, be with us yet	233b
G. of Jacob defend thee	482b
G. of life, and poesy, and light	69a
g. of my idolatry	365a
G. of our fathers, be the G.	131b
G. of our fathers, known of old	233b
G. of Things as They are	236b
G.! of whom music and song	264a

God (*cont.*)

G. pardon all good men	43a
G. planted a garden	492a
G. proved them, and found them	520a
g. pursuing, the maiden hid	420b
G. rest you merry, gentlemen	523a
G.'s a good man	359a
G. said, let there be light	492a
G. save great George	523a
G. save our gracious king	79b
G. save the king 79b, 193a, 376a,	495a
G. saw that it was good	492a
G...scarce seemed there to be	100a
G. self-slain on his own..altar	421b
G. send every gentleman	529b
G. send us all good ending	531a
G.'s finger touched him	430b
G.'s first Creature, wh. was Light	16b
G.'s gifts put man's..to shame	44a
G.'s grace is the only grace	293b
G.'s greatness flowed around	43b
G.'s great *Venite*	133b
G. shall add unto him	520b
G. shall bring every work	500a
G. shall help her	484b
G. shall send forth his mercy	485b
G. shall smite thee	512b
G. shall take away his part	520b
G. shall wipe away all tears	519a, b
G. shall wound the head	486b
G. shalt make my darkness	482b
G.'s Heart in a garden	177b
G. shed His grace	22a
G.'s in his heaven	50a
G.'s laughing in heaven	474a
G. so commanded	276a
G. so loved the world	510b
G.'s own ear listens delighted	275a
G.'s own name upon a lie	111a
G. spake once, and twice	485b
G.'s pale Praetorian	413b
G.'s soldier be he	351a
G. stooping shows sufficient	51b
G. strikes a silence thro' you all	44a
G.'s universal law	278a
G. takes a text	187a
G., that giveth to all men liberally	517a
G. that hidest thyself	502b
G. that maketh men to be..one	486a
G. the All-terrible	94a
G., the best maker of..marriages	383b
G. the Father turns a..divine	303b
G. the first garden made	107a
G. the herdsman goads them	474a
G. thou knowest my simpleness	486b
G. unmakes but to remake	51b
G. walking in the garden	492b
G. was very merciful to the birds	527b
G. who best taught song	51a
G. who made shall gather	12b
G. whose puppets..are we	50a
G. will provide for sacrifice	223b
G. will provide himself a lamb	493a
G. will take care of that	390a
G. within the shadow	250b
G. wd. have her shown	191a
G. wd. make a man miserable	87b
G. wrote the bill	147a
granted scarce to G. above	409b
Great G.! I'd rather be a Pagan	473a
great G., what do I see and hear	523a
great, just, good G.	51a
grete g. of Loves name	89b
had I but served G.	462b
had I but served my G.	386a
hand folks over to G.'s mercy	144a
handmaid perfect in G.'s sight	311b
harpit ye up to the Throne o' G.	231a
hath not one G. created us?	504b
have a G. become her lover	115a
have G. for his father	537b
have not the seal of G.	519a
hear one rack the name of G.	258b
heart within, and G. o'erhead	248a
heaven; for it is G.'s throne	505a
he for G. only	274a
heirs of G., and joint-heirs with Christ	513b
here in the sight of G.	481b
here is G.'s plenty	142a
here's G. down on us	43a

God (*cont.*)

her fathers' G. before her	319b
her last republic cried to G.	93b
he sung of G.	403a
he trusted in G.,..deliver him	483a
he was not: for G. took him	492b
Hey for G. Almighty 11a,	224b
himself from G. he cd. not free	147a
his Father and his G.	174b
his own word as if his G.'s	427b
holy, acceptable unto G.	513b
honest G.'s the noblest work of man	67a
how odd of G. to choose the Jews	149b
how shd. G. perceive it	486b
I am a G. and cannot find it	397a
I bless G...I am worth more	296b
I cannot tell: G. knoweth	515a
if G. be for us	513b
if G. did not exist	566a
if he be not of kin to G.	15a
if this friend happen to be—G.	46b
if we were G.'s spies	344a
in apprehension how like a g.	332b
inclines to think there is a G.	96b
in favour with G. and man	500a
in G.'s great universe	134b
in my flesh shall I see G.	497a
in that he liveth, he liveth unto G.	513a
in the beginning G. created	492a
in the bush with G. may meet	146b
in the faces of men..see G.	458a
in the great hand of G. I stand	348a
into the hands of the living G.	517a
into the sanctuary of G.	486b
invisible, except to G. alone	273b
invite G., and his angels thither	134b
I press G.'s lamp close	49b
I remembered my G.	407a
is, and it is not, the voice of G.	303b
I saw the dead..stand before G.	519b
I the Lord thy G. am a jealous G.	480a
it is an attribute to G. himself	354b
it is the voice of a g.	512a
I who saw the face of G.	258b
Jerusalem, coming down from G.	519b
Jew, by G. demented	294a
just are the ways of G.	277b
just G., forgive!	463a
justify G.'s ways to man	199b
justify the ways of G. to men	270b
Kings are by G. appointed	524a
know his G. by night	447b
knowledge..makes a G. of me	218b
know that I am G.	484b
label men for G.	442a
Lamb of G. to dwell in England's	30b
land wh. the Lord thy G. giveth	480a
leap up to my G.	258b
leave the issues calmly to G.	81a
led him to confess a G.	13a
let G. arise	486a
let G. be true	513a
let not G. speak with us	494a
letters from G. dropt	458a
'Let us worship G.'	59b
Light, G.'s eldest daughter	158a
like a G. in pain	221b
lion is the wisdom of G.	31a
Lo, here is G., and there is G.	96b
longeth my soul after thee, O G.	484b
Lord G. Almighty, wh. was, and is	518b
Lord G. formed man of the dust	492a
Lord G. made them all	3a
Lord G. of Battles, aid!	230a
Lord thy G. is with thee	494b
Lord, ye know, is G. indeed	224b
lost in G., in Godhead found	147a
love G. whom he hath not seen?	518a
love thy G. and love Him only	120a
make me a clean heart, O G.	485a
make no long tarrying, O my G.	484b
man be more just than G.?	497a
man sent from G.	510b
many are afraid of G.	246a
men not afraid of G., afraid of me	303b
might G. forget him	444b
Milton..in fetters..wrote of G.	31a
Mother of G.! no lady	98a
my duty towards G.	481a

God (cont.)

my G., how wonderful Thou art 149b
my G., I love Thee 86b
my G., my G., look upon me 483a
my G., why hast thou forsaken me? 508a
my soul for G.'s grace 37a
nakedness of woman..of G. 31a
Name of the Lord thy G. in vain 480a
nearer, my G., to Thee 1a
nearer to G.'s..further from G. 4a
nearer to G.'s Altar trod 115a
neck G. made for other use 198b
neither our love from G. 312a
neither shd. a g. intervene 542a
no man hath seen G. 510b, 518a
none other but the house of G. 493a
nor asks of G., but of her stars 302a
no respect of persons with G. 513a
not G.! in gardens 41a
not G.'s, and not the beasts 46a
not G. sometimes withhold in
  mercy 283a
nothing, not G., is greater to one 458a
not I, but the grace of G. 514b
not one..is forgotten before G 509b
not three Gods: but one G. 478b
now, G. be thanked who has
  matched 40a
of all the thoughts of G. 44a
oft names G. in oaths 132a
of what I call G. 51b
O G., for as much as without Thee 525a
O G., if there be a G. 525a
O G. of battles! steel my soldiers 383a
O G. of Bethel 131b
O G., our help in ages past 453a
O G., when thou wentest forth 486a
O G. within my breast 38b
Oh! for a closer walk with G. 109b
Oh G.! Oh Montreal! 67a
Oh my G., I cry in the day-time 483a
oily man of G. 443a
once a man who said 'G.' 527a
one G., one law, one element 431a
one more insult to G. 48a
one, on G.'s side, is a majority 296b
one that cd. circumvent G. 336a
on their faces, and worshipped G. 519a
on, to the City of G. 7b
others call it G. 86a
out of me G. and man 422a
out of the mouth of G. 505a
paltered with Eternal..G. for
  power 435a
patent for..honours..from..G. 60a
patriots, dear to G. 279b
patted my G. on the head 235b
peace of G. wh. passeth 480b, 516a
peacock is the glory of G. 31a
perish at the presence of G. 486a
power belongeth unto G. 485b
powers that be are ordained of G. 513b
'Praise G.!' sang Theocrite 45a
praising G. with sweetest looks 195b
pre-elect G.'s Virgin 313a
presents the g. unshorn 189a
presume not G. to scan 301a
put G. in his statements 457a
put into their..'G.' no more 10a
put on the whole armour of G. 516a
put yr. trust in G., my boys 570a
reach the ears of G. 459b
reader of the works of G. 112a
read G. aright, unless he..spell 307a
reason and the will of G. prevail 9b
reflect that G. is just 205a
rejoice in the living G. 487a
rejoiced in G. my Saviour 508b
revilest thou G.'s high priest? 512b
righteous are in the hand of G. 520a
Sabbath of the Lord thy G. 480a
sacrifice to G...devil's leavings 419a
safe stronghold our G. is still 569a
said, 'G. be praised' 43a
sail with G. the seas 148a
saith unto Zion, Thy G. reigneth 502b
say first, of G. above or man
  below 300b
say, 'G. be pitiful' 43a
security of a G. 14a

God (cont.)

see G. made and eaten all day 45a
seek their meat from G. 488b
seek ye first the kingdom of G. 505b
seen G. face to face 493a
sees G. in clouds 300b
separate us from the love of G. 513b
servant of G., well done 275a
serve G. and Mammon 505b
serve G. if the devil bid you 359b
service greater than the g. 369a
service ranks the same with G. 50a
set up thyself, O G. 485b
shalt not tempt the Lord thy G. 505a
she for G. in him 274a
short of the glory of G. 513a
shd. G. create another Eve 276b
signed by G.'s name 458a
since G. is light 273a
singing our song of G. 457b
sing my G. and King 187a
slope thro' darkness up to G. 430b
so is G.'s hill 486b
so long as Caesar's self is G.'s 115a
so near is G. to man 147a
sons of G. came to present 496b
sons of G. shouted for joy 497b
souls at home with G. 226b
souls mounting up to G. 311b
steep and trifid G. 441a
stewards of the mysteries of G. 514a
such a lady G.'s mother be 524b
sung 'G. save the Queen' 227a
taking of the Manhood into G. 478b
teach me, my G. and King 188a
thanks G. for anything 206b
that thou art happy, owe to G. 275a
the child of G. 481a
the eternal G. is thy refuge 494b
the feeble G. has stabb'd me 159a
the G. that you took from a..book 235b
the great g. Pan 43b
their G. will rouse them 234b
the melancholy g. protect thee 371a
the most resembles G. 63b
the negation of G. 167b
the noblest work of G. 301b
the other to the Altar's G. 115a
the people, the voice of G. 309a
there is in G.—some say—a deep 448a
'there is no G.', the wicked saith 96a
the true G.'s priest 79a
the Word of G. is quick 517a
the Word was G. 510b
they said, G. forbid 510a
they shall see G. 505a
they shall see our G. 224a
they that deny a G. destroy 15a
this is acceptable with G. 517b
this thing is G. 422a
this, throws himself on G. 47a
those whom G. hath joined 481b
tho' the mills of G. grind slowly 248a
thou art G. from everlasting 487b
thou city of G. 487a
thou g. of our idolatry, the press 110b
Thou, my G. art in't 191a
thou, O G., hast proved us 486a
thou, O G., sentest a gracious rain 486a
thou owest G. a death 378b
thousand voices praises G. 101a
thou shalt have one G. only 96b
thro' his garden walketh G. 52a
thro' nature up to nature's G. 301b
thy G. my G. 495a
thy G.'s, and truth's 386a
thy G., thy life, thy cure 448a
thy soul and G. stand sure 51a
'tis G. gives skill 144b
to bring us, daily, nearer G. 224a
to deem himself a g., or beast 301a
to G. of the devil's leavings 304a
to see G. only 133a
to the judgement seat of G.! 12b
to the unknown G. 512b
tribunal now, higher than G.'s 51b
trod that day to G. 227b
truer conception of G. 10b
turns on her g., when he sets 281b
'twas G. the word that spake it 145b
unknown animal, or the g. 417b

God (cont.)

unless G. send his hail 49b
until G. loosen over sea and land 423a
unto G.'s gracious mercy 481b
very sure G. walks in mine 41a
vindicate the ways of G. to man 300b
void of offence towards G. 512b
walk before G. in the light 485b
water saw its G., and blushed 114b
way to God is by our selves 155b
we are the children of G. 513b
well, G.'s above all 361a
we ought to obey G. 512a
we owe G. a death 380b
were I Lord G. 256a
we see the works of G. 296a
we shd. leave the word of G. 512a
we two may meet before high G. 428a
what G. abandoned 200a
what G. and man is 427a
what G. hath cleansed 512a
what G. hath joined together 390a
what shall I render to my G. 452b
what therefore G. hath joined 507a
when G. by man as godlike trod 422b
when g. first maked man 89a
when G.'s the theme 403a
wherever G. erects a house 118b
wh. it shall please G. to call me 481a
who G. doth late and early pray 473b
whom G. to ruin has design'd 140b
whom G. wd. destroy 538a
whose cause is G. 12b
whose G. is their belly 516a
who think not G. at all 277b
why did G., Creator wise 276b
with equal eye, as G. of all 300b
with G. all things are possible 507b
with G. be the rest 50b
with (my G.!) my G. 197a
wonderful works of G. 512a
worketh not..righteousness of G. 517a
write G. first 359a
ye be found to fight against G. 512a
ye believe in G. 511a
yet again to G. return 465a
yr. G. like a soldier 237a
Yours faithfully, G. 522b
zeal of G., but not..knowledge 513b
Godamoighty knaw what a's doing 435a
Goddess: drapes his g. warm 147a
  g., allow this aged man 295b
  g. and maiden 423b
  g., excellently bright 214b
  g. indubitable was revealed 555a
  night, sable g.! 477a
  unto that G.' grace 408a
Goddesses: one of these..Greek g. 292b
Godfathers and Godmothers then 481a
Godfrey: G. in the gate 92b
  last was G. of Bouillon 257a
Godhead: conversion of the G. 478b
  lost in God, in G. found 147a
God-light: singing in the great G. 43b
God-like: God by man as g. trod 422b
  G. David was restored 138b
  g. hero sate 138b
  patriotism, grown G. 179a
  thy G. crime was to be kind 73b
Godliness: cleanliness..is next to g. 456a
  in cheerful g. 467b
Godly: every one that is g. 483b
  g., righteous and sober life 478a
  nobody gets old and g. and grave 475b
  still a g. race he ran 169a
Godolphin: (G.)..never in the way 87b
  King Charles gave (G.)..character 87b
Gods: angels wd. be g. 300b
  as flies..are we to the g. 343b
  aspiring to be g. if angels fell 300b
  before the g. that made the g. 91b
  be ready, g. with..thunderbolts 341a
  by the Nine G. he swore 253a
  counsel of her country's g. 107b
  darling of the G. 261a
  daughter of the g. 426b
  dead limbs of gibbeted G. 423b
  Fast, that oft with g. doth diet 268a
  fear first in the world made g. 215b
  g. and men, we are all deluded 394a
  G. are we, Bards, Saints 5a

Gods (cont.)

g...cannot recall their gifts	438b
G., that mortal beauty chase	260b
G., that wanton in the air	249b
g. themselves throw incense	344a
G. who live for ever	254a
heart is the prey for g.	423b
in the names of all the g. at once	337b
kings it makes g.	385a
let the great g., that keep	342b
live..on the hills like G.	433a
men that strove with g.	439a
neither children nor G.	228b
none other g. but me	480a
O..g.! why do you make us love	364a
post allotted by the G.	433a
real are the dreams of G.	219a
red-breast..household g.	443b
Red G. call us not	228b
so many g., so many creeds	459a
take the good the g. provide	139a
talk about the G. of late	71b
temples of his G.	253a
thank whatever g. may be	185a
the g. are come down to us	512b
the g. are just	344a
the g. arrive	146b
the g. detest my baseness	324b
the g. to-day stand friendly	341a
these that were G. are dead	423b
thinking of his own G., a Greek	6a
think that the clearest g.	343b
to my own G. I go	233b
to stature of the g. they..attain	263b
true g. sigh for the cost and pain	43b
unseen..by G. or wondering men	218a
utterance of the early G.	218a
voice of all the g. makes heaven	345a
weigh yr. G. and you	236b
what ailed us, O g.	421b
whatever g. may be	422a
whom the g. love die young	71a
wise g. seel our eyes	324a
with stupidity the g.	569b
wondrous the g.	31b
ye are G., and behold ye shall die	423b
ye shall be as g.	492a
God's acre: burial-ground G.	247b
Godward: looking G.	422a
Goes: all g. if courage g.	21b
he bows and g. again	414a
so far as it g., but it doesn't go	124b
they g. up and down	86b
Goest: whither thou g., I will go	495a
Goeth: cometh, and whither it g.	510b
wine..that g. down sweetly	500b
Goethe: G.'s sage mind	6b
G.'s wide and luminous view	7a
open thy G.	81b
Going: all things g. as they came	313a
endure their g. hence	344a
give her the wages of g. on	439a
g. from us to be utter destruction	520a
g. on before	20a
g. one knows not where	262a
g. to and fro in the earth	496b
g. with yr. love-locks flowing?	311a
he shall direct his g.	487a
I am g. a long way	429b
Lord shall preserve thy g. out	489b
not worth g. to see	210a
safe shall be my g.	40a
the order of yr. g.	349a
to keep us g.	263a
Goings: ordered my g.	484a
Gold: a path of g. for him	49b
arrows..are tipped with g.	66a
barbaric pearl and g.	272a
book..better to me than g.	461b
brow bound with burning g.	426b
builded over with pillars of g.	30b
but litel g. in cofre	88b
crucify mankind upon a cross of g.	53a
cursed lust of g.	555b
delvèd g., the wailers heap!	44a
fetch the age of g.	270b
fetters, though of g.	16b
fling them back their g.	290a
flow with tears of g.	33a
for a' the g. in Christentie	531a
from the red g. keep thy finger	319a

Gold (cont.)

gild refined g.	374a
gleaming in purple and g.	74a
g. air and the silver fade	312a
g., and frankincense, and myrrh	504b
g. and silver becks me	374a
g.? a transient, shining trouble	172b
g...idol of the Anglo-Saxon	17b
g. is for the mistress	228b
g...lies at the root of wisdom	66b
g. that I never see	199b
g. to airy thinness beat	134a
Greensleeves was my heart of g.	523b
hair and harpstring of g.	423b
her feathers like g.	486a
I am not covetous for g.	383a
is she not pure g., my mistress?	52a
like a casket of g.	475b
Love..differs from g. and clay	393b
man's the g. for a' that	60b
masons building roofs of g.	381b
mast was o' the beaten g.	529a
my bow of burning g.	31a
never lack'd g. and..never gay	360b
nobility..prevents..religion of g.	17b
no g., no Holy Ghost	66b
nor all, that glisters, g.	173b
not g., not blood, their altar	394a
O cursed lust of g.	555b
ornaments of g. upon yr. apparel	495b
oure g. wes changyd	474a
patines of bright g.	355a
ringlets or feminine g.	421b
rocked in silver nor in g.	522a
saint-seducing g.	364b
silver and g. have I none	512a
silver threads among the g.	308b
so thin, so pale, is yet of g.	114a
street of the city was pure g.	520a
streets are paved with g.	103b
than g., yea, than much fine g.	482b
that sweet g. clime	32a
the narrowing lust of g.	431a
the poop was beaten g.	323a
the queen in a vesture of g.	484b
there is g., and here my..veins	323b
these I do not sell for g.	85b
thousands of g. and silver	489a
thrice their weight in g.	150b
travell'd in the realms of g.	220b
truth with g. she weighs	298b
under the cross of g.	435a
what female heart can g. despise	173b
what's become of all the g.	52b
wd. he have g.? I lend it	187b
Golden: add to g. numbers, g. numbers	118b
among her g. arches	30b
bought g. opinions	347a
end of a g. string	30b
g. lads and girls all must	329a
g. rule is..there are no g. rules	391a
g. slumbers kiss yr. eyes	119a
g. works of the dear..old angel	240a
hast thou g. slumbers	118b
her g. pillars high	30b
he 's become the g. fool	31b
Jerusalem the g.	286a
loves well the g. mean	545a
observed the g. rule	31b
on every g. scale	82b
the g. opes, the iron shuts	269b
two strings..both g. ones	151b
wear a g. sorrow	385b
Golden Gain: Stormcock and G.	232b
Golden Gate: West to the G.	231b
Golden Vanity: the G.	531a
Goldsmith: G...did it better	209b
here lies Nolly G.	158b
Oliver G., a Poet	209b
this G.'s fine feast	158b
Golf: to play g. ye maun hae a heid	572a
what, gie up g.?	536b
Golgotha: memorize another G.	346a
Goliath: fail because of him [G.]	495b
Goltman: tall G., silent on his horse	27a
Gondola: G. of London	129b
swam in a g.	327a
what else is like the g.?	96b
Gone: all, all are g.	240b
all g. afay mit de lager-beer	244b

Gone (cont.)

and they are g.	221b
but now she is g.	67b
companions are faded and g.	281b
g. before to that unknown	240a
g. far away into the silent land	311a
g. whar de good niggers go	156b
g. with the wind	571a
he is g., he is g.	336a
here to-day, and g. tomorrow	25a
he 's g., and who knows how	278a
I am g. into the fields	394b
I have g. here and there	389a
I went by, and lo, he was g.	484a
I wd. have thee g.	365b
man is very far g.	491b
now thou art g.	269b
or that when I am g.	249b
she is won! we are g.	318a
soon as she was g. from me	31b
speak of something that is g.	466a
they are all g. into the world	448a
thou art g., and for ever!	316b
thou art g. from my gaze	245b
what 's g., and what 's past help	373a
what haste I can to be g.	116a
when thou art g.	90a
wilt thou be g.?	366a
yet, now he is g...I am alone	241a
Gongs: hongs and g.!	297b
strong g. groaning	92b
Good: a G. Thing	321b
a g. time coming	256a
all g. and no badness	402b
all g. things wh. exist	266a
all g. to me is lost	273b
all his hopes of g.	9a
all partial evil, universal g.	301a
all their luxury was doing g.	159a
all things work together for g.	513b
all we..dreamed of g. shall exist	44b
a man who is g. enough	310a
and the g. to do	3a
antipathy of g. to bad	303b
anybody can be g. in the country	460b
any g. therefore that I can do	523b
any g. thing..that I can do	176b
apprehension of g.	374b
are you g. men and true?	358b
as for Doing-g...I have tried it	444a
as g. as ever was he	531a
as g. as he had found it	97a
a very g. man in the main	163a
be as gods, knowing g. and evil	492a
be g., sweet maid	225b
beneath the g. how far	175b
benevolence..does most g. or harm	17b
better to fight for the g.	434b
beyond g. and evil	569a
but what is g. for them	116a
by a g. author, it 's a g. play	390a
by all that 's g. and glorious	73b
cannot be ill, cannot be g.	346b
captive g. attending captain ill	388a
care not..man is G. or Evil	30b
crown thy g. with brotherhood	22a
do after the g.	257a
do all the g. you can	456a
do any man's heart g. to hear me	356b
do evil, that g. may come	513a
do g. by stealth, and blush	303b
dull prospect of a distant g.	140b
earth hath no g. but yrs.	37b
English..if they have a g. thing	379b
eschew evil, and do g.	484a
everything..is g. for something	141b
evil be thou my G.	273b
few know their own g.	142b
first be wise and g.	278b
for the g. of my country	150a
Freedom?..licence to be g.	97b
gallant g. Riou	76b
General G. is the plea	30b
glad of other men's g.	327a
G. saw that it was g.	492a
God 's laughing..to see you so g.	474a
g., amiable, or sweet	276a
g. and bad together	323b
g. are always the merry	475a
g. are so harsh to the clever	462b
g. as thou art beautiful	428a

Good (*cont.*)

g., but not religious-g.	181a
g. compensate bad in man	51b
g. die early, and the bad die late	118a
g. enough to go to heaven	208a
g. for man nor beast	532b
g. for that man if he had not been	508a
g. for us to be here	507a
g. God pardon all g. men	43a
g., great and joyous	397b
g. man, and did g. things	181a
g. men can give g. things	267b
g. of subjects. . end of kings	118b
g. people all, of every sort	169a
g. people 's wery scarce	121b
g., pleasure, ease	301b
g. plot, g. friends	377a
g. provoke to harm	352a
g. received, the giver is forgot	104a
g. shall come of water and of mud	39a
g. that came of telling truth	139b
g. that I wd. I do not	513a
g. that ye did for the sake of men	235a
g., the more communicated	274b
g. they inculcate must live	315b
g. things of the day	349a
g. things will strive to dwell	367b
g. to be honest and true	61a
g. to be merry and wise	61a, 524b
g. to be out on the road	262a
g., to forgive; best, to forget	51b
g. to support Caledonia's cause	61a
g. to the poor, to kindred dear	79b
g. we oft might win	351a
g. without effort	69a
g. without pretence	299b
g. ye are, and bad	428a
hath this world's g.	518a
he, only, in. . common g. to all	341b
he was a g. man, and a just	510a
he wos wery g. to me	121a
his chief g. and market	335b
his g. and his evil	62b
hold fast that wh. is g.	516b
hold thou the g.	430a
how near to the g. is what is fair	215b
I am a g. man too	163a
if all the g. people were clever	462b
ill wind turns none to g.	446a
in a passion you g. may do	29b
is g. enough for me	186a
it never done no g. to me	229a
it seemed g. to me also	508b
I will be g.	448b
I will seek to do thee g.	489b
Jimmy was g. and true	163a
know but this, that thou art g.	304a
knowledge of g. and evil	492a
learn the luxury of doing g.	170a
leave us leisure to be g.	173b
love of g. and life, be my award	217b
made you fair hath made you g.	352a
man loves what he is g. at	322a
manner of thing that is g.	484a
means of g. to all my. . creatures	313b
meek lover of the g.	146a
music, the greatest g.	1b
no g. if a passion is in you	29b
none that doeth g.	482a
nor it cannot come to g.	330a
nothing. . g. or bad, but thinking	332a
nothing g. to be had in the country	183b
nothing is so g. as it seems	144b
nothing left for you. . but to be g.	413a
nothing we see but means our g.	187b
not too bright or g.	470b
of moral evil and of g.	471b
often drawn it for a g. one	142a
only truly great who are truly g.	87b
out of the g. still to find. . evil	271a
overcome evil with g.	513b
Parent of G.	275a
pelting each. . for the public g.	107a
portend no g. to us	341b
possible for a novel to be too g.	391a
punishment. . never. . impulsive to g.	258a
refuse the evil, and choose the g.	501b
rhyme thee to g.	186b
ring in the common love of g.	431a
say it is not g.	456b

Good (*cont.*)

secret thing, whether it be g.	500a
seek to be g.	251b
she was very, very g.	249a
show some token upon me for g.	487a
so it seemed g. in thy sight	509a
so much g. in the worst of us	192a
so much too g. for earth	215a
sovereign g. of human nature	14a
still raise for g. the. . voice	214a
take the g. the gods provide	139a
talks. . so very fast. . it must be g.	150a
that to the public g. . . must yield	277b
that wh. is not g., is not delicious	267b
the clever so rude to the g.	462b
the g. die first	464a
the g. he scorned	29a
the g. is oft interred	339b
the g. must associate	56b
the g. that I can do	18b
the g. want power	397a
them that call evil g.	501a
there dwelt all that 's g.	449a
the wine rather g.	75b
the worst speaks something g.	187a
they love the G.	39b
those that were g. shall be happy	236b
those who go about doing g.	115b
Time makes ancient g. uncouth	251a
'tis only noble to be g.	431b
to be beautiful than to be g.	460b
to be g. is to be happy	313a
to be obscurely g.	1b
to do g. and to communicate	517a
to do ought g. never will	271a
toward solid g. what leads	278b
tried the luxury of doing g.	114a
trust that somehow g.	430a
voice aloud, how g. he is	249b
we love, Fool, for the g. we do	293a
we must return g. for evil	447b
what g. came of it at last?	406a
when I wd. do g., evil is present	513a
when shall all men's g. be. . Peace	427a
when the great and g. depart	465a
who will show us any g.?	482a
wiser being g. than bad	44b
work them to their g.	407b
yet don't look too g.	230a
zealous for his country's g.	160a
Good-bye: and so—g.!	263a
g. is not worth while	180a
g., moralitee!	186a
g., proud world	146b
g., Summer	459a
g. to all that	173b
g. to Rochefoucauld	145a
g. to the bar	226b
g. to the Anglo-Saxon race	171b
without a single kiss, or a g.	294a
Good-day: and so g.!	263a
Good Friday: soldest him on G. last	376b
Goodliness thereof is as the flower	502b
Goodly to look to	495b
Goodman: g. is not at home	498a
g., you've spoken the foremost	531b
Good-morning: bid me G.!	19a
g. gentlemen both	145a
G.! Have you used Pears'	523a
Good-morrow: and so g.!	263a
at my window bid g.	268b
G. to mine own torn hair	189b
G. to the day so fair	189b
to Sorrow, I bade g.	217b
Good-natured: dislike wh. people not too g.	410a
Goodness: crownest the year with thy g.	486a
days in g. spent	74a
fountain of all g.	478b
g. does not more certainly	242a
g., faith, meekness	515b
g. never fearful	352a
g. only knowses	93b
how awful g. is	274b
inclination to g. is imprinted	15a
I thank the g. and the grace	424b
know I held so much g.	458a
long-suffering, and of great g.	490b
love, sweetness, g.	278b
more g. in her little finger	418b

Goodness (*cont.*)

praise the Lord for his g.	488b
see the g. of the Lord	483b
some soul of g. in things evil	382b
the powerful g. want	397a
whose g. faileth never	18a
wisdom and g. to the vile	343b
Good-night: and bid the world G.	189b
and so g.!	263a
'Dear work! G.'	198b
gives the stern'st g.	347b
g.? ah! no; the hour is ill	394a
g., and joy be wi' you	285b
g.! parting is such sweet sorrow	365b
g., sweet prince	337a
g. to Marmion	318b
happy g. air	179a
has smiled and said 'G.'	26b
if he fall in, g.	377a
I shall say g. till it be morrow	365b
my last g.	225a
my native land, G.!	68a
part in friendship, and bid g.	74a
say not G.	19a
they never say g.	394a
to each a fair g.	318b
Goods: all my worldly g. . . endow	481b
his g. are in peace	509a
precious as the G. they sell	154a
soul, thou hast much g.	509b
tho' I bestow all my g.	514b
Goodwins, I think they call the place	354a
Goose: every g. a swan, lad	226a
every g. is cackling	355b
gott'st thou that g. look	350b
royal game of g.	168b
steals a common from the g.	527b
Goose-feather: a great g. grew	192b
Goose-pen: write with a g.	371b
Goosey, goosey, gander	534b
Gordian: she was a g. shape	219a
some old G. knot	96b
Gore: avenge the patriotic g.	308a
mayn't be human g.	121a
Gored: tossed and g. several persons	207b
Gorgeous Tragedy in sceptred pall	268a
Gorgonized me	433b
Gorgons and Hydras	272b
Gorgonzola: let loose the G.!	536a
trotting out the G.!	237b
Gormandizing: leave g.	381a
Gormed: I'm G.!	122b
Gorse: 'mid the g. the raspberry red	441a
Gooseberries. . makes my teeth watter	155a
Gory: never shake thy g. locks at me	349a
Goschen: I forgot G.	95a
Gosling to obey instinct	288b
Gospel: g. according to Jean Jacques	80b
Discobolus hath no g.	67a
G. of Getting On	391a
G. of Montreal	67a
G. of Silence	572b
g. of the Discobolus	67a
G.'s pearls upon our coast	260a
music of the G.	150a
preach the g. to every creature	508b
the lineaments of G. books	313b
whose g. is their maw	278b
Gospel-light first dawned	174a
Goss-hawk: my gay g.	529a
Gossip: g. of the air	370a
g. pines	154b
little g., blithe and hale	296b
Gossips count her faults	263b
Gotham: wise men of G.	532b
Gothic: more than G. ignorance	151b
Gottingen: University of G.	79a
Gout: drink, combined with g.	163b
that old enemy the g.	195a
when g. and glory seat me there	46b
without g. or stone	304a
Govern: as all did g. yet all did obey	136b
education makes. . easy to g.	40b
great minds. . such should g.	23a
he that wd. g. others	262b
Governance: by prynceley g.	143a
charge of rule now g.	416a
Governed: a nation is not g.	55b
not so well g. as they ought to be	196b
Governess of floods	356b
Governing was not property	156b

Government: Conservative G. is.
  hypocrisy 128a
every country has the g. it deserves 562b
fancy giving money to the G.! 186a
for forms of g. let fools contest 301b
four pillars of 15a
g. after the principles of..justice 292b
g...contrivance of human wisdom 57a
g...is..a necessary evil 291b
G. must have an authority 314b
g. of all the people 292b
g. of men and morning newspapers 297a
g...the laws of life 315a
g. of the people 245b
g. shall be upon his shoulder 501b
g. without a king 18b
I believe this g. cannot endure 245a
increase of his g. and peace 501b
in..G. the people..legislator 57b
land of settled g. 439b
live under one form of G. 208a
looked to the g. 57b
Monarchy is..an intelligible g. 17a
negation of God..G. 167b
no G. can be long secure 129a
Republican form of G. 407b
still loathe the present G. 189b
there has been no G. 121b
virtue of paper g. 55a
what a free g. is 58a
yr. sister is given to g. 123b
Governments: councils, g. 438b
Governor: t'other g. 126a
  G. was strong upon the..Act 459b
Governors: g., teachers,..pastors 481a
  our supreme g., the mob 449a
Gowans fine 59a
Gower: O moral G. 90b
Gown: amply billowing g. 26b
  branched velvet g. 371a
  graver g. instruct mankind 299b
  petticoat, and a green g. 534b
Gowns: one that hath two g. 359a
Gr-r-r: G.—there go, my heart's 52a
  g.—you swine! 52a
Grace: abundance of thy g. 491a
  all g. is the g. of G. 293b
  a peculiar g. 465a
  ascribe it to Thy g. 452b
  as when a G. sprinkles 241a
  behold such heavenly g. 408b
  by g. divine not otherwise 464a
  by the g. of G. I am what I am 514b
  conscience and g., to the..pit 335b
  courtly foreign g. 437b
  cry these dreadful summoners g. 342b
  double blessing is a double g. 330b
  ends of Being and ideal G. 44a
  every virtue, every g. 240b
  flushed with a purple g. 139a
  for gift or g., surpassing this 44a
  for the means of g. 479a
  full of g. and truth 510b
  God in his mercy lend her g. 432a
  God's g. is the only g. 293b
  God shed His g. on thee 22a
  g. and power faithfully to fulfil 479b
  g. as lang's my arm 60b
  g. before Milton..Shakespeare 238b
  g. did much more abound 513a
  graceful, graceless G. 72a
  G. is given of God 96a
  g. me no g. 375a
  g. of a day that is dead 425b
  g. to love thee more 110a
  g. was in all her steps 275b
  g. wh. followed it was much more 411a
  grow old with a good g. 410a
  have g. to use it so 278b
  healthful Spirit of thy g. 478b
  heaven such g. did lend her 372b
  he does it with a better g. 370b
  her spirit's vestal g. 293b
  if a lie will do thee g. 379a
  in our time, Thy G. may give 228a
  inward and spiritual g. 481a
  let yr. speech be alway with g. 516a
  liken his g. to an acorned hog 47a
  little children saying g. 413b
  look to thee for g. 445a
  make less thy body..more thy g. 381a

Grace (cont.)
  makes simplicity a g. 215a
  manifold gifts of g. 481a
  meek and unaffected g. 168b
  men hunger for thy g. 206a
  moments of glad g. 476b
  my soul for Goddës g. 37a
  naked nature, and the living g. 300a
  not I, but the g. of God 514b
  Nymph, a Naiad, or a G. 316a
  one thought, one g., one wonder 259b
  petitionary g. of Sweet Seventeen 425b
  quarrel with the noblest g. 367b
  renown, and g. is dead 348a
  so sweet a face, such angel g. 425b
  sweet attractive g. 274a
  sweet attractive kind of g. 313b
  sweet cowslip's g. 290b
  take heart of g. 166a
  that g. may abound 513a
  thrive in g. and feature 215a
  Thy special g. preventing us 479b
  to us may g. be given 184a
  trust him for his g. 110a
  Tuesday's child is full of g. 525a
  unbought g. of life 57a
  was never mind, did mind his g. 313b
  who does nothing with a better g.? 476b
  with one half so good a g. 351b
  with such a lovely g. 401b
  with what a pretty skipping g. 261a
  womanly discovering g. 132b
  ye are fallen from g. 515b
  yet a bride to every G. 79b
  yet with something of a g. 463b
Graceful: Belial, in act more g. 272a
  g., graceless Grace 72a
  youth, beauty, g. action 138b
Graceless: graceful, g. Grace 72a
Graces: accused of deficiency in..g. 209a
  G...not..natives of Gt. Britain 91a
  g. slighted blossom on the tomb 113b
  half-mile g. 61b
  its g. and airs 292b
  lead these g. to the grave 370a
  number all yr. g. 387a
  Pride, Envy, Malice, are his G. 240b
  ruin half an author's g. 283a
  sacrifice to the G. 90b
  the G. danced, and Apollo play'd 249b
  write the G.' life 176b
Gracing: either other sweetly g. 78a
Gracious: Lord, thou art become g. 487a
  yr. great and g. ways 294a
Graciousness: gave thy g. a..zest 36a
Gradation: not by the old g. 359b
Gradations: cold g. of decay 210b
Graeme: died with conquering G. 317a
  passed the spirit of the g. 12a
Grail: until I find the holy G. 438a
Grain: cheeks of sorry g. 267b
  husbanded the Golden g. 152b
  pamphleteer on guano and on g. 437a
  reaps the bearded g. at a breath 248a
  say wh. g. will grow 346a
  see a World in a G. of Sand 29a
  the goodly g. 442b
  'tis in g., sir 370a
  vacant chaff well meant for g. 429b
  warmth to swell the g. 76a
Grains: two g. of wheat, hid 352b
Gramophone: puts a record on the g. 144b
Gramercy! they for joy did grin 98b
Grammar: erecting a g. school 384a
  g., that grounde is of alle 242b
  heedless of g. 19a
  such g. as they can get 255a
  why care for g. 451b
  with g., and nonsense 169b
Grampian: on the G. hills 194b
Granary: careless on a g. floor 221b
Grand: g...fortifying,..curriculum 10a
  g. old man, the Prime Minister 280b
  g. style arises in poetry 10a
  inscrutable g. 7b
  sound so g. on the pleasant waters 306b
  they said, 'it would be g.' 84a
  upon wh...G. Army never looked 256b
Grandam: she might ha' been a g. 345a
  soul of our g. 372a
Grandchild Wilhelmine 406a

Grandeur: g. in the beatings 465b
  g. of the dooms 217b
  g. that was Rome 298a
  nor g. hear with a..smile 174a
  old Scotia's g. springs 59b
  so nigh is g. to our dust 147a
Grand-jurymen: they have been g. 371b
Grandmamma: dishes for g. 11a
Grandmother: Man..not marry his g. 491b
  my g.'s review—the British 70b
Grandsire cut in alabaster 352b
Grange: at the moated g...Mariana 352a
  the lonely moated g. 433a
Granite: into a g. basin 96a
  the sand of g. 415a
Grant: G.'s Morella Cherry Brandy 522a
  g. thee thy heart's desire 482b
  g. us thy peace 479b
Grantchester: lovely hamlet G. 4b
Granted: be it g. to me to behold you 414b
  never take anything for g. 128a
  read not to..take for g. 16a
Granting: but by thy g. 388b
Grape that can with Logic absolute 153b
Grapes: brought forth wild g. 501a
  Chalice of the g. of God 429b
  freighted with amber g. 8b
  gather g. of thorns 505b
  looked that it shd. bring forth g. 501a
  g. of wrath 200b
  the fathers have eaten sour g. 503b
  whence be the g. of the wine-press 252b
  with thy g. our hairs be crown'd 323b
Grapeshot: whiff of g. 80b
Graphic: Penman's latest piece of g. 52b
Grapple: g. them to thy soul 330b
  let them g. 377a
Grapples with his evil star 430b
Grasp: g. it like a man 191b
  g. not at much 187b
  g. this sorry Scheme of Things 154a
  man's reach shd. exceed his g. 44b
  or g. the ocean in my span 453a
  what dread g. dare 32a
Grasping: capable of earnest g. 219a
Grass: a child said What is the g.? 458a
  all flesh is as g. 517b
  as the g. grows on the weirs 474a
  be the green g. above me 311a
  days of man are but as g. 488a
  deep in the bells and g. 192a
  dread the rustling of the g. 463a
  fade away suddenly like the g. 487b
  glory of man as the flower of g. 517b
  go to g. 23a
  g. grows all up..White Hall Court 296a
  g. withereth, the flower fadeth 502b
  green g. growing over me 530b
  he eateth g. as an ox 497b
  I fall on g. 260b
  I know the g. beyond the door 313a
  kissed the lovely g. 39b
  lift me from the g. 394b
  little vaulter in the sunny g. 202a
  make..two blades of g. to grow 418a
  seed from the feathered g. 218a
  spire of English g. trampled 178a
  splendour in the g. 466b
  surely the people is g. 502b
  that falleth on the g. 524b
  trembling thro' the frozen g. 221b
  twinkles in the g. 434a
  was cut out of the g. 91b
  when you destroy a blade of g. 34a
  where tides of g. break into foam 423a
  who made the g. and..the worms 475a
Grass-bank: a g. beyond 4a
Grasses of the ancient way 261b
Grasshopper: g. shall be a burden 499b
  there was no burr of g. 8a
Grasshoppers: dozen g. under a fern 57a
  the cover, of the wings of g. 364b
Grassy: search the g. knolls 85b
Grate: film, wh. fluttered on the g. 101a
Grateful: g. mind by owing owes not 273b
  I come to be g. at last 434b
Grates: to whisper at the g. 249b
Gratiano speaks an infinite deal 352a
Gratifying: most g...interesting 135b
Gratitude: alas! the g. of men 471a
  friendships begin with..g. 144a

Gratitude (cont.)

g. also to his Majesty was ample 444b
g. of place-expectants 450a
g...sense of future favours 574b
Gratulations: our g. flow in streams 79b
Grave: a-buried in one g. 526b
a g...He shall not live 374a
a g.'s one violet 50a
a g. unto a soul 374a
a just precedence in the g. 225a
a little, little g., an obscure g. 375b
a mould'ring in the g. 178a
an untimely g. 79a
approach thy g. like one who wraps
a soldier's g., for thee the best 53a
be gentle grave unto me 73b
bends to the g. with..decay 325a
between the cradle and the g. 168a
bewept to the g. did go 143a
birth and the g. 335b
botanize upon his mother's g. 392b
but she is in her g. 468b
call'd our mother, but our g. 470b
come from the g., to tell us 350a
country..a kind of healthy g. 331b
crowned upon the g. thereof 405a
digs my g...at each remove 191b
dig the g. and let me die 187a
dread the g. as little as my bed 415a
Duncan is in his g. 224b
earliest at His g. 348b
eat our pot of honey on the g. 21a
echo arose from the suicide's g. 264a
empires and cities in a common g. 165a
fame stands upon the g. 162a
from the cradle to the g. I look 183a
funeral marches to the g. 114a
gently steer from g. to light 248a
g. hides all things beautiful 141a
g. is not its goal 397a
g. of Clooth-na-Bare 247b
g.'s a fine and private place 475a
g. shall have a living monument 260a
g. with rising flowers be dressed 336b
have sunk into the g. 299b
her heart in his g. 207a
his vast and wandering g. 281b
Humours, whether g. or mellow 429b
ignominy sleep with thee in..g. 2a
in cold g. she was lain 379a
in his g. rain'd many a tear 529a
in the cold g., under the..deep sea 335b
in the dark and silent g. 195b
is that ayont the g., man 307b
I will pay you in the g. 63a
jealousy is cruel as the g. 394b
keep a dream or g. apart 501a
know the g. doth gape for thee 44a
lads are in love with the g. 381a
laugh'd..at the grip of the G. 199b
lead but to the g. 235b
lead these graces to the g. 174a
like Alcestis from the g. 370a
made me a g. so rough 278b
man..pompous in the g. 434b
mild o'er her g., ye mountains 42b
my large kingdom for a little g. 8b
nor wisdom, in the g. 375b
not have strewed thy g. 499b
O g., where is thy victory? 336b
O'Leary in the g. 515a
on his g., with shining eyes 474b
on my g., as now my bed 7a
peace is in the g. 42a
renowned by thy g.! 397a
reproofs..ought to be g. 329a
road lies..dusty to the g. 14b
rush to glory or the g. 413a
shall lead thee to thy g. 77a
soldier's g., for thee the best 473a
the g.; and the barren womb 73b
there lies a lonely g. 499a
there's no repentance in the g. 3a
this side of the g. 452b
thought shall be my g. 241b
thy foolish tears upon my g. 368a
thy humble g. adorned 426a
thy root is ever in its g. 299a
'tis everywhere her g. 187b
to steer from g. to gay 293b
to that dark inn, the g.! 301b
317b

Grave (cont.)

travelling towards the g. 469a
true lover never find my g. 371a
when my g. is broke 133b
where, G., thy victory? 251b
without a g., unknelled 69b
with profitable labour to his g. 383a
womb of Nature..perhaps her g. 273a
you shall find me a g. man 365b
Grave-digger..work..with enjoyment 205b
Gravelled for lack of matter 327b
Grave-makers: ditchers, and g. 336a
Graver: His g. of frost 443a
wherein the g. had a strife 215b
Graves: arise from their g. and aspire 32a
beautiful uncut hair of g. 458a
find ourselves dishonourable g. 337b
follow us disquietly to our g. 341b
g. have learnt that woman-head 133b
g. stood tenantless 329b
have their g. at home 92a
let's talk of g. 375b
their g. are severed 184b
they have no g. as yet 92a
Gravitation: shall g. cease 301b
Gravy: person who disliked g. 404a
Gravity: reasons find of settled g. 387b
what doth g. out of his bed 377b
Gray: Duncan G. cam here to woo 60a
[G]. was dull in a new way 208b
prefer being..author of G.s' Elegy 462b
Grayish: pond edged with g. leaves 180a
Grayling: here and there a g. 425b
Graymalkin: I come, G. 345b
Graze: chance cd. neither g. 362b
g. him as he passes 24a
Great: a g., a very g. work 255a
aim not to be g. 251b
as g. with young as she might goe 529b
because his soul was g. 136b
both the g. vulgar, and the small 107a
brilliant chief, irregularly g. 252a
but far above the g. 175b
ceremony that to g. ones 'longs 351b
craven fears of being g. 427a
died—that Caesar might be g. 77a
disbelief in g. men 80b
everything..g...done by youth 129a
frown o' the g. 329a
g., ere fortune made him so 140a
G. is Diana of the Ephesians 512b
g. is Truth, and mighty 520a
g. is Truth, and shall prevail 40a
g. men are the guide-posts 55a
g. men are the inspired texts 81b
g. men are not always wise 497a
g. men are they who see 148b
g. men contending with adversity 64a
g. men have their poor relations 121b
g. men may jest with saints 351b
g. to do that thing that ends all 325a
g. without a foe 69a
heights by g. men reached 247b
he met a g. man he grovelled 440a
how good he is, how g. shd. be 249b
how indigent the g. 175b
how very small the very g. 440b
I only know it shall be g. 200a
I shall be very proud and g. 414a
just as he..promised something g. 71b
know well I am not g. 428b
little seemed to him g. 255a
lives of g. men all remind us 248a
made many people think him g. 208b
man is only truly g. 129b
neither too humble nor too g. 257a
no force, however g. 456b
no g. and no small to the Soul 146a
no g. man lives in vain 80b
nor its g. scholars g. men 194b
nothing g. was ever achieved 148a
only great g. who are truly good 87b
packs and sets of g. ones 344a
perfumed chambers of the g. 380a
Pharaoh surnamed the G. 236a
poorly rich, and meanly g. 316a
poor man loved the g. 253a
rightly to be g. is not to stir 335b
simple g. ones gone for ever 433b
some men are born g. 371a
that he is grown so g. 337b

Great (cont.)

that wh. once was g. is passed 472b
the g. break through 400a
the g. man down 334a
the g. man helped the poor 253a
though fallen, g.! 68a
thou wouldst be g. 346b
to compare g. things with small 273a
towards g. persons use..boldness 186b
was g. by land as thou by sea 435a
when the g. and good depart 465a
while the g. and wise decay 244a
with the g. and their pride 474b
Great Britain: war arose between G.
and Germany 242b
Greater: behold a g. than themselves 338a
Brutus makes mine g. 341a
feel that we are g. than we know 463b
g. are none beneath the Sun 236a
four things g. than all 227a
g. prey upon the less 175b
g. than both, by the all-hail 346b
g. than Solomon is here 506b
g. than their knowing! 234b
that he (Titian) is g. than they 314b
the g. man, the g. courtesy 428b
there's something g. 82b
Greatest: fail than not be..the g. 223a
g. happiness for the g. numbers 202b
how much the g. event 156b
there sunk the g., nor the worst 68b
Great-Heart: one G. 54b
Greatly his foes he dreads 94a
Greatness: base on wh. thy g. stands 470a
be not afraid of g. 371a
correlated g. 441b
farewell, to all my g.! 385b
for g. he cd. not want 215a
God's g. flowed around 43b
g. knows itself 378b
g. of the world in tears 476a
g., with private men..a blessing 262b
her g. on her subjects' love 306a
his g. weigh'd 330b
if honour gives g. 120b
in me there dwells no g. 428b
model to thy inward g. 381b
nature of all g. not to be exact 55a
Pray God our g. may not fail 427a
some achieve g. 371a
some far-off touch of g. 428b
some have g. thrust upon them 371a
surely his g. is a-ripening 385b
than g. going off 324a
true g. to have in one the frailty 14a
Greaves: flamed upon the brazen g. 431b
Grecian: his soul toward the G. tents 355a
merry G. coaster 8a
ne'er did G. chisel trace 316a
you in G. tires are painted 387b
Greece: Athens, the eye of G. 277a
fair G.! sad relic 68a
glory that was G. 298a
G., Italy, and England 141a
G. might still be free 70b
G. ruled in more refined ages 17b
G., sound thy Homer's..name 109a
summoned G. to arms 259b
that insolent G...sent forth 216a
the constitutions of later G. 17b
the isles of G., the isle of G.! 70b
to Gaul, to G. and into Noah's ark 110b
when the light wave lisps 'G.' 70b
Greedy: g. men whom hope of gain 163a
put on the pot says G.-gut 534b
thank goodness, I am g. 535b
Greek: barbarously not a G. was he? 202b
because he was a G. 241b
each alike was G., alike was free 422b
G. in its origin 256b
G., Sir, is like lace 210b
G. was free from rhyme's 216b
happy G., by this protection 216b
it was G. to me 338a
loving, natural, and G. 70b
neither G. nor Jew 516a
ne yet of Latin, ne of G. 409a
small Latin, and less G. 216a
taught'st..King Edward G. 278b
tell me whiskey's name in G. 59a
thinking of his own gods, a G. 6a

Greek (*cont.*)
'tis known he cd. speak G. 64*b*
what the G. did 36*a*
when his wife talks G. 212*a*
white G. goddesses 292*b*
without G. contrived to talk 71*b*
Greekling: bid the hungry G. go 548*b*
Greeks: when G. joined G. 244*a*
where the G. had modesty 295*a*
wh. came first, the G. 129*a*
Green: all the trees are g. 226*a*
anything g. that grew 233*a*
burnt g., and blue and white 98*b*
by him sported on the g. 406*a*
do these things in a g. tree 510*a*
evermore no g. life shoots 34*a*
fairest shepherd on our g. 295*b*
g. be the turf above thee 178*a*
g. fields of England 96*b*
g. grow the rashes O 60*b*
g. plant groweth, menacing 92*a*
g. thought in a g. shade 260*b*
how g. are thy leaves 569*b*
ice..as g. as emerald 98*a*
in red and blue and g. 32*b*
I saw you fresh, wh. yet are g. 388*b*
it is g., and groweth up 487*b*
I was g. in judgment 323*a*
keeps his own wounds g. 14*a*
knaves in Kendal-g. 377*b*
laid him on the g. 530*b*
laughs to see the g. man pass 192*b*
leaves they are so g. 531*a*
like a fairy trip upon the g. 386*b*
lilac, gold and g. 35*b*
making the g. one red 348*a*
many a g. isle needs must be 395*a*
O all ye G. Things 478*a*
on a simple village g. 430*b*
plot of beechen g. 219*b*
the dry smooth-shaven g. 268*a*
there is a g. hill far away 3*b*
to look so g. and pale 347*a*
voices of children..heard on the
g. 32*b*
wearin' o' the G. 525*b*
youths g. and happy in first love 96*a*
Green-coat: sleepy, g. man 192*b*
Greenery: sunny spots of g. 101*a*
Greenery-yallery 165*b*
Greenest of things blue 421*b*
Greenland: at G., Zembla 301*a*
from G.'s icy mountains 184*a*
have you an estate in G.? 177*a*
Greenly: we have done but g. 335*b*
Greensleeves: G. was all my joy 523*b*
who but Lady G.? 523*b*
Greensward: single on the g. 263*b*
Greenwood: I must to the g. go 529*b*
Greet: g. as angels go 250*a*
how shd. I g. thee? 74*b*
if..souls did never kiss and g. 217*b*
Greeting: joyous day, we give thee
g. 164*b*
may cease frae their g. 525*b*
with such prophetic g. 346*a*
Greetings, where no kindness is 472*a*
Gregory, remember thy swashing
blow 364*b*
Grenadier: for the British G. 526*a*
who comes here? A G. 125*b*, 534*b*
Grenadiers: talk of Pensions and G. 411*b*
Grenville: G., Raleigh, Drake 287*b*
I, Sir Richard G., die 437*b*
Sir Richard G. lay 437*a*
then spake Sir Richard G. 437*b*
Greta woods are green 319*a*
Greville, Servant to Queen Elizabeth 177*a*
Grew: at last it g., and g. 238*b*
it neither g. in dike nor ditch 529*a*
so we g. together 357*a*
that sometime g. within 259*a*
they, g. in beauty, side by side 184*b*
wet by the dew it g. 151*a*
Grewgious: Mr. G. 123*b*
Grey: an old woman clothed in g. 239*b*
bluest of things g. 421*b*
calls the glory from the g. 50*b*
costs thy life, my gallant g. 316*a*
earth not g. but rosy 48*b*

Grey (*cont.*)
eyes..too lovely to be g. 5*b*
has threads of g. 475*a*
my hair is g., but not with years 69*b*
nephew of Fox, and friend of G. 193*b*
Grey-green, greasy Limpopo 237*a*
Greyhound: this fawning g 377*a*
Greyhounds in the slips 382*a*
Gridley: fire when you are ready, G. 120*b*
Grief: acquainted with g. 503*a*
after long g. and pain 434*a*
antheming a lonely g. 218*b*
as great as is my g. 375*a*
can I see another's g.? 33*a*
care and g. of heart 385*b*
everyone can master a g. 358*a*
first days of my distracting g. 194*b*
forestall his date of g. 267*a*
for our g., as if it had not been 392*a*
from perfect g. there need not be 313*a*
full of g. as rage 342*b*
g. and unrest, to rank..given 150*a*
g. fills the room up 374*a*
g. flieth to it (death) 14*a*
g. for awhile is blind 397*a*
g. is a species of idleness 214*a*
g. is itself a medicine 107*b*
g. itself be mortal 392*a*
g. never mended no..bones 121*b*
g. returns with the revolving year 392*a*
g. that fame can never heal 12*b*
g...upon the heels of pleasure 105*a*
g. with a glass that ran 420*b*
hopeless g. is passionless 43*b*
I was a journeyman to g. 374*b*
in false g. hiding his..guile 408*b*
modes, shows of g. 330*a*
move my faint heart with g. 395*a*
my particular g. 359*b*
old, there's g. enough for thee 176*a*
one g. brings forth twain 137*a*
only time for g.l 196*b*
pain and g. to me 484*a*
past help shd. be past g. 373*a*
patch g. with proverbs 359*a*
perk'd up, in a glist'ring g. 385*b*
repeats to thee thy mother's g. 29*b*
sad when others' g. is fled 72*b*
sees into the bottom of my g.? 366*a*
she died out of pure, pure g. 531*a*
silent manliness of g. 169*a*
smiling at g. 371*a*
that the thought of g. refuse 37*a*
the naked stars the G. of Man 234*b*
thine be the g. 12*a*
thy mother's g. 35*b*
till age, or g., or sickness must 225*a*
time remembered is g. forgotten 420*a*
'tis unmanly g. 330*a*
what torments of g. you endured 147*a*
when thirsty g. in wine we steep 249*b*
worm, the canker, and the g. 73*b*
Griefs: all g. that bow 7*b*
cutteth g. in halves 15*b*
drinking my g. 376*a*
great g., I see, medicine the less 329*a*
he hath borne our g. 503*a*
I am sick of many g. 341*a*
my state depose, but not my g. 376*a*
of all the g. that harass 213*a*
passion put to use in my old g. 44*a*
solitary g., desolate passions 206*a*
what private g. they have, alas, 340*a*
Grievances foregone 387*b*
Grieve: do not let this parting g. thee 527*a*
g. when even the shade 472*b*
I g. at grievances 387*b*
nor joy nor g. too much 141*a*
Pope will g. a month 419*a*
we will g. not 466*b*
Grieved: g. with her child 143*b*
here come the g. 113*b*
much it g. my heart to think 471*a*
they soothe the g. 113*b*
Grieving: g., if aught inanimate e'er 68*b*
what 's the use o' g'. 232*b*
Griffith: an honest chronicler as G. 386*b*
Grill: let G. be G. 408*b*
Grim: g. grew his countenance 529*a*
heaven not g. but fair 48*b*
Grimes: Old G. is dead 175*b*

Grin: cheerfully he seems to g. 82*b*
ending with the g. 83*a*
g. like a dog 485*b*
he owned with a g. 406*b*
Nature wears one universal g. 151*b*
relaxed into a universal g. 112*a*
they for joy did g. 98*b*
vanquish Berkley by a g. 40*b*
Grind: g. the faces of the poor 501*a*
he did g. in the prison-house 495*a*
life is one demd horrid g. 125*a*
they g. exceedingly small 248*a*
Grinder, who serenely grindest 75*b*
Grinders cease because they are few 499*b*
Grinding: must needs tarry the g. 368*b*
sound of the g. is low 499*b*
Grinning: mock your own g. 336*b*
Gristle: people who are still..in the g. 55*b*
Grit an' human natur' 250*b*
Groan: bitter g. of the martyr's woe 30*b*
condemned alike to g. 175*a*
dead men gave a g. 99*a*
hear each other g. 220*a*
he gave a g., and then another 468*b*
that I do g. withal 363*b*
thousands counted every g. 6*a*
with bubbling g. 69*b*
Groaned inly while he taught 43*a*
Groaning: my g. is not hid from thee 484*a*
Grocer: evil-hearted G. 93*a*
God made the wicked G. 93*a*
who hath seen the G. 93*b*
Groined the aisles of..Rome 147*a*
Gromboolian: great G. plain 243*b*
Groom: bee goes singing to her g. 50*a*
death is but a g. 133*b*
G., the Butler, and the Cook 163*b*
g. there was none to see 199*a*
Grooves: in determinate g. 527*a*
Groping: laid our g. hands away 39*b*
Gross: g. and scope of my opinion 329*b*
g. as a mountain, open 377*b*
not g. to sink, but light 386*b*
Grossness: hiding the g. with fair 354*a*
Vice..by losing all its g. 57*a*
Grosvenor Gallery..young man 165*b*
Grotesque: g. to the horrible 136*a*
Pure, Ornate and G. 17*b*
Grottoes: my g. are shaded 399*b*
Ground: all seated on the g. 424*b*
as water spilt on the g. 495*b*
between the stirrup and the g. 76*a*, 522*b*
built up on another man's g. 355*b*
catch it ere it come to g. 349*b*
commit his body to the g. 481*b*
drops earliest to the g. 354*b*
down with it, even to the g. 490*a*
dwelt upon a tract of inland g. 464*b*
each dance the others wd. off the g. 119*b*
fathom-line cd. never touch the g. 377*a*
for an acre of barren g. 367*a*
fruitful g., the quiet mind 416*a*
gained g. upon the whole 50*b*
g. flew up and hit me 451*a*
g. maintained its man 168*a*
having waste g. enough 351*b*
he swalloweth the g. 497*b*
in a fair g.—in a fair g. 235*a*
in his own g. 303*b*
let us sit upon the g. 375*b*
look around, and choose thy g. 73*b*
man, low sitting on the g. 408*b*
most sweet..to pace the g. 468*a*
old hope goes to g. 48*a*
O let the solid g. not fail 433*b*
on a plat of rising g. 268*a*
on the g. I see thee stare 89*a*
on the holy g. 286*a*
other fell into good g. 506*b*
passed over on dry g. 494*b*
place..thou standest is holy g. 493*b*
scarce cd. stand on any g. 137*a*
seem to tread on classic g. 1*b*
skilful guide into poetic g. 111*b*
stands on such slippery g. 339*b*
storms..outside our happy g. 8*b*
the elvish page fell to the g. 317*b*
the passion that left the g. 44*b*
'tis haunted, holy g. 68*a*
to a more removed g. 331*a*
to gain a little patch of g. 335*b*

Ground (cont.)
twice five miles of fertile g.　101a
wake the nations under g.　127b
who might well be under g.　164b
with thy nest upon the dewy g.　471a
women's eyes..they are the g.　345a
Groundlings: ears of the g.　333b
Ground-nest: herald lark left his g.　277a
Grounds: in the laying out of g.　295a
walks..the g. for the second time　295a
Ground-whirl of the perished leaves　312a
Group that's quite antique　70b
Grove: clear spring, or shady g.　273a
good g. of chimneys　283b
g. nods at g.　302b
the olive g. of Academe　277a
wand'ring in many a coral g.　31b
wh. a g. of myrtles made　20b
Grovel: they've souls that g.　75b
Grovelled: he g. before him　440a
Groves: amid the g., under the
　shadowy hills　464b
fountain heads, and pathless g.　23a
g. where the lady Mary is　311b
g. where rich trees wept　274a
in the green leaves among the g.　465b
in the g. of *their* academy　57a
meadows, hills and g.　467a
o'er shady g. they hover　454b
thro' g. deep and high　318a
to the musical g.　424b
Grow: ask me where they do g.　188b
for sure then I shd. g.　187a
g. for ever and for ever　436a
g. old along with me　50b
g. up with the country　175b
if you wd. g. great and stately　414a
let both g. together　506b
say wh. grain will g.　346a
they g. to what they seem　170a
Growed: I 'spect I g.　415b
Groweth sed, and bloweth med　526a
Growing: feel the flowers g. over him　223b
it is not g. like a tree　216b
it will be g., Jock　319b
lad is young and is g.　531a
sorrow of each day's g.　263a
Growled: g., and bit him till he bled　192b
it cracked and g.　98a
Grown: when they are both full g.　526b
when we are g. and take our place　227b
Grown-up: hear the g. people's feet　413b
spoke in quiet g. wise　294a
Grows: g. with his growth　301a
it g. and smells I swear　216b
Growth: cannot give it vital g. again　363b
g. [is] the only evidence of life　288a
States..have their g.　242a
Grub: by the joiner squirrel or old g.　364b
young ones..pistols..old ones, g.　389b
Grubby: John G., who was short　93a
Grudge: ancient g. I bear him　353a
no g., no strife　416a
Gruel: basin of nice smooth g.　11a
make the g. thick and slab　349b
Grumble: nothing whatever to g. at　166b
Grundy: ding, dinging Dame G.　284b
more of Mrs. G.　246a
Solomon G.　532b
what will Mrs. G. zay　284b
Grunt and sweat under..weary life　333a
Gruntled: far from being g.　573b
Gryphon: the G. remarked　83a
Guano: pamphleteer on g.　437a
Guanoed her mind　130a
Guard: drunk and resisting the G.!　227b
guarding, calls not Thee to g.　233b
g. the sailors tossing　20a
g. us, guide us　143b
hate of those ye g.　236b
none but Americans on g. tonight　452a
that g. our native seas　77b
who is to g. the guards?　549a
Guardian of His Majesty's conscience　444b
Guarding, calls not Thee to guard　233b
Guards: G. die but do not surrender　562a
up G. and at them again　455a
Gudeman: when our g. 's awa'　527a
Gudgeon: fool g.　352b
Gudgeons: swallow g. ere..catch'd　66a
Guenevere: like as did Queen G.　257b

Guerdon: fair g...we hope to find　269b
Guess: as none can even g.　37b
golden g. is morning-star　426a
g. now who holds thee　43b
g. that Love wd. prove　38a
g. where he may be　49b
I g. King George..read that　178b
Guessed: this I have g.　235b
Guessing: it 's better only g.　96a
Guest: a new admired g.　78b
dull fighter and a keen g.　378b
g. that tarrieth but a day　520a
made me a closer g.　36a
rise at the strange g.'s hand　421b
shakes his parting g. by the hand　369a
some poor nigh-related g.　102a
some second g. to entertain　133b
speed the going g.　303b
the worthy bidden g.　269b
this g. of summer　347a
whether g. or captive I　452b
Guestless: bare walls lain g.　421b
Guests: among the G. Star-scatter'd　154a
mankind..hosts and g.　24b
my g. shd. praise it, not the cooks　181a
the g. are met, the feast is set　98a
the g. few and select　241b
unbidden g. are often welcomest　383b
Guide: an awful g. in smoke　319b
custom..great g. of human life　201b
except some man shd. g. me　512a
guard us, g. us　143b
g. my lonely way　169a
g., philosopher, and friend　301b
he shall be our g. unto death　485a
my g., and mine own..friend　485a
of Thee, my partner and my g.　463b
safe into the haven g.　455b
skilful g. into poetic ground　111b
to g. his steps afford yr...aid　420a
where thou art g., no ill can come　491a
Guide-posts: great men are the g.　55a
Guides: blind g., wh. strain at a gnat　507b
g. cannot master..American joke　446b
Guiding-star of a brave nation　285a
Guildford: an hour out of G.　232b
under G. Hill　27a
Guile: he it was, whose g...deceived　270b
hiding his harmful g.　408b
in their mouth was found no g.　519a
in whom is no g.　510b
squat, and packed with g.　39b
Guilt: full of artless jealousy is g.　335b
G. was my prime Chamberlain　196a
if g.'s in that heart　282a
image of war, without its g.　406a, 416b
my stronger g. defeats my..intent　334b
only art her g. to cover　170a
other pens dwell on g. and misery　11a
what art can wash her g. away?　170a
what the world calls g.　26a
Guiltier than him they try　351a
Guiltless: all g., meet reproach　362b
g. death I die　363b
Guilts: close pent-up g.　342b
Guilty: g. of dust and sin　188b
g. of such a ballad　344b
g. splendour　112a
it started like a g. thing　329b
like a g. thing surprised　466b
make g. of our disasters the sun　342a
make mad the g.　333a
suspicion..haunts the g. mind　384b
terror haunts the g. mind　244a
Guinea: disc of fire..like a g.　29b
42 sixpences..to one g.　211b
jingling of the g.　432a
rank is but the g.'s stamp　60b
within the compass of a g.　203b
worth a g. a box　528b
Guinea-pig: lift a g. up by the tail　246a
Guinea-pigs: one of the g. cheered　83b
Guineas: nice yellow g. for me　61a
you ask two hundred g.　456b
Guinness, Allsopp, Bass　75a
Guitar: the Troubadour touch'd his
　g.　22b
Gules: now is he total g.　332b
Gulf: g. profound as that Serbonian　272b
there is a great g. fixed　510a
Gulfs: the g. will wash us down　439a

Gulfs (cont.)
whelmed in deeper g. than he　107b
Gull: g.'s way and the whale's way　262a
notorious geck and g.　372a
Gulls: g. him with intelligence　388b
g. in an aery morrice　185b
Gulp: drains his at one g.　52a
Gum: their med'cinable g.　364a
Gummidge: Mrs. G.　121b
Gums: from his boneless g.　347a
trees wept odorous g.　274a
Gun: by each g. the lighted brand　76b
cawing at the g.'s report　357a
don't know a g. from a bat　227a
holy text of pike and g.　65a
named all the birds without a g.　146b
nor ever lost an English g.　435a
Gunga Din　230a
Gunner said 'Ay, ay'　437b
Gunpowder: fire a mine..with sym-
　pathetic g.　66a
g. and sealing-wax　85a
G., Printing, and..Religion　80a
g. treason and plot　532a
Guns: but for these vile g.　377a
g., and drums, and wounds　376b
g. will make us powerful　575b
rutted..by the passing g.　261b
vain, those all-shattering g.　136b
when the g. begin to shoot　235b
Gurgle: a g. he gave　165a
Gurly grew the sea　529a
Gurney: Peter G.　531b
Gusto: secret element of g.　412a
Gusts: when g. shake the door　6a
Gut: had the Devil in his g.　31a
Guts: sheeps' g. shd. hale souls　358a
wears..his g. in his head　369a
Gutter: we are all in the g.　573a
Guy: ah, County G.　320a
Gymkhanas: won g. in a doubtful
　way　233b
Gypsy: Time, you old g. man　192b
Gyre and gimble in the wabe　83b
Gyves: g. upon his wrist　196a
prisoner in his twisted g.　365b

H

Ha: h.-h.-h., you and me　523a
'H.! H.!' said the duck　237a
saith among the trumpets H., h.　497b
Haberdasher to Mr. Spurgeon　67a
Habit: apparell'd in more precious h.　359a
costly thy h. as thy purse can buy　330b
h. rules the unreflecting herd　470a
h. with him was all the test　113b
honour peereth in the meanest h.　366b
such is the force of h.　25a
the long h. of living　42b
use doth breed a h. in a man　372b
Habitable: look round the h. world　142b
Habitation: a local h. and a name　357b
h. among the tents of Kedar　489b
I have loved the h. of thy house　483b
Habitations: peaceably in their h.　521a
Habits: of h. devil, is angel yet in this　335a
small h., well pursued betimes　283a
their h. from the Bear　25b
Hack: do not h. me as you did..
　Russell　279b
somebody to hew and h.　65a
Hacked, hewn with constant Service　406a
Hackney: 'A. Marches　22a
Had, having, and in quest to have　389a
Haddocks: hunt for h.' eyes　85b
Hag: this is the h.　365a
Haggard: if I do prove her h.　362a
Haggards ride no more　410b
Hags: rags, and h.　100a
secret, black, and midnight h.　349b
Hail: congenial horrors, h.!　443b
h., Bard triumphant!　106b
h., fellow, well met　419b
h., glorious edifice,　403b
h. horrors, h. infernal world　271a
h., master; and kissed him　508a
h., thou that art highly favoured　508b
h. to thee, blithe spirit　398a
h. ye small sweet courtesies,　411a

ENGLISH INDEX

Hail (cont.)

my brother, h., and farewell	540a
no sharp and sided h.	197b
where falls not h., or rain	429b
wield the flail of the lashing h.	393a
Hailed them o'er the wave	76b
Hails: the man that h. you Tom	108a
Hair: a bracelet of bright h.	133b
ae lock o' his gowden h.	529b
a h. twixt south and south-west	64b
all her bright golden h.	460a
all her h. in one long yellow string	50a
an excellent head of h.	369b
Apollo's lute, strung with his h.	345a
a rag and a bone and a hank of h.	236a
beautiful uncut h. of graves	458a
beauty draws us with a single h.	302b
beg a h. of him for memory	340a
Berenice's ever-burning h.	87a
bind up this h. in any simple knot	393a
blind with thine h. the eyes of Day	399a
by flying h. and fluttering hem	312b
Caoilte tossing his burning h.	475a
dead women, with such h., too	52b
draw you to her *with a single h.*	142b
drew me backward by the h.	43b
each particular h. to stand on end	331a
from his..h. shakes pestilence	273a
from out his chariot by the h.	312b
good morrow to mine own torn h.	189b
gowd kames in their h.	530a
h. as free	215a
h. of my flesh stood up	497a
hath soft brown h.	75a
her dark h. and lovesome mien	425b
her h. about her eyne	138a
her h. that lay along her back	311b
her h. was so charmingly curled	226a
her h. was long, her foot was light	218b
his flashing eyes, his floating h.	101b
his h. did bristle upon his head	317a
his h. is of a good colour	327a
his h. was like a crown	92a
horrid image doth unfix my h.	346b
if a woman have long h.	514b
I lie tangled in her h.	249b
I must sugar my h.	83b
I never pin up my h. with prose	371b
it raised my h., it fanned my cheek	99b
Jove, in his commodity of h.	376b
language that wd. make yr. h. curl	166b
like the bright h. uplifted	396a
like twilight's, too, her dusty h.	470b
love-knot into her long black h.	290a
my face is pink, my h. is sleek	528b
my fell of h. wd...rouse and stir	350b
my h. is grey, but not with years	69b
my mother bids me bind my h.	202a
never brush their h.	25b
nymph, with long dishevelled h.	386b
one h. of a woman can draw more	200b
one slight h...bulk commands	161a
one strangling golden h.	312b
our new crescent of a h.'s breadth	49a
plucked them from me by the h.	441b
ruddy limbs and flaming h.	30a
she has braided her yellow h.	528b
she has brown h.	355b
she only talks about her h.	443a
she smoothes her h.	144b
Sir Ralph the Rover tore his h.	406b
strung with subtle-coloured h.	421a
sweet Alice, whose h. was so brown	148b
terrier..so covered with h.	38a
that curled her h.	343a
that I may cover you with my h.	476a
that subtle wreath of h.	132b
the breath of them hot in thy h.	421b
the pleasant mazes of her h.	106b
the tangles of Neæra's h.	269b
thy amber-dropping h.	268a
thy fair h. my heart enchained	401b
thy h. is as a flock of goats	500a
thy h. soft-lifted by the..wind	221b
thy hyacinth h., thy classic face	298a
vine-leaves in his h.	567a
wherefore shd. I kame my h.?	530a
white-robed, with silver h.	35b
who touches a h. of yon grey head	459a
with his long essenced h.	252b
with his white h. unbonneted	252a

Hair (cont.)

with yr. 'ayrick 'ead of 'air	229a
yr. h. has become very white	82b
yr. well-beloved's h. has threads	475a
Hairless as an egg	189b
Hairs: bring down my grey h.	493b
elf-locks in foul sluttish h.	305a
forms of h., or straws, or dirt	303a
given me over in my gray h.	462b
had all his h. been lives	363b
had I as many sons as I have h.	351a
h. of yr. head are all numbered	506a
his head and his h. were white	518b
how ill white h. become a fool	381a
if h. be wires	389a
oldest man..ever wore grey h.	470a
those set our h...upright	132b
with thy grapes our h. be crown'd	323b
Hairy: Esau my brother is a h. man	493a
marvellous is about the face	357a
thicksides and h. Aldrich	96a
Hal: why, H., 'tis my vocation, H.	376b
Halberdiers: behind him..the h.	252a
Halcyon: St. Martin's summer, h. days	383b
Haldan: Earl H.'s daughter	225b
Hale: Meg grew sick as he grew h.	60a
you are h., Father William	407a
Hales: Mr. H. of Eaton	142a
Half: ae h. of the warld thinks	320a
another h. stand laughing by	381b
h. a league, h. a league onward	426a
h. of one order, h. another	65b
h. slave and h. free	245a
h. that 's got my keys	172b
h. to forget the wandering	154b
h. to remember days..gone by	154b
image of myself and dearer h.	274a
lest h. of her shd. rise herself	180a
one h...world cannot understand	11a
overcome but h. his foe	272a
poor h.-kisses kill me quite	137a
the divided h. of such a friend-ship	430b
the h. is greater than the whole	559b
the h. was not told me	496a
Half-a-crown in the bill	126a
Half-a-dozen of the other	259b
Half-believe: attain to h.	96b
Half-believers in our casual creeds	8a
Half-brother: America thou h.	18a
Half-faced: this h. fellowship	377a
Half-gods go, the gods arrive	146b
Half-hour: after a shivering h.	284b
Half-knowledge: content with h.	222a
Half-owre to Aberdour	530a
Halfpenny: a h. will do	522b
for a copper h.	85b
if you haven't got a h.	522b
Half-workers: women must be h.	328b
Half-world: now o'er the one h.	347b
Hall: Absolute across the h.	26b
bride hath paced into the h.	98a
Chapman and H. swore not at all	27b
he slept in the h.	27b
Mr. H.'s nay was nay	27b
O dusk the h. with yew	7a
roused in many an ancient h.	252b
the Douglas in his h.	318b
this is Liberty-H.	171a
Tom bears logs into the h.	345b
Hall-garden: birds in the high H.	433b
Hallelujah: to redeem our loss, H.	524b
Hallelujahs, sweet and low	43a
Halloo yr. name to the..hills	370a
Hallow: be set to h. all we find	223b
h. thus the Sabbath day	101a
seems to h. us there	294b
Hallowed: place of justice is..h.	16b
so h. and so gracious is the time	329b
Hallows: his mother and all his h.	198a
Halls: a hovel to yr...marble h.	75b
Amphitrite's destined h.	395a
chamber in the silent h. of death	53a
dreamt that I dwelt in marble h.	53a
in h., in gay attire is seen	317a
in our h. is hung armoury	467a
tap'stry h. and courts of princes	267a
the h., the h. of dazzling light	125b
thrill thro' those roofless h.	396a
thro' her marble h.	247b

Halt: cheer for a h. and a row — 233a

how long h. ye	496a
the h., and the blind	509b
Halter: now fitted the h.	306a
Halts by me that footfall	442a
Halves of one august event	179a
Ham: it might be H.	236a
Shem, H., and Japheth	492b
wh. is the case when there's h.	125b
with h. and sherry..meet to bury	39b
wonders in the land of H.	488b
Hamelin Town's in Brunswick	50a
Hamilton: Alexander H. smote the rock	454a
Marie H.'s to the kirk gane	530a
Hamlet: good H., cast thy..colour off	329b
H...Prince of Denmark left out	320a
H. with his doublet all unbrac'd	332a
I'll call thee H.	331a
I saw H. Prince of Denmark played	149b
Lord H. is a prince	332a
much Antony, H. most of all	185b
rude forefathers of the h.	174a
the kneeling h. drains the chalice	429b
the lovely h. Grantchester	39b
Hamlets: h. brown	103a
in h., dances on the green	317a
Hammer: his H. of wind	443a
it's the 'a, 'a., 'a.	535a
keeping his..h. under the pillow	121a
no sound of h. or of saw	112b
what the h.? what the chain?	32a
Hammered: England's being h.	227a
Hammers: busy h. closing rivets up	382b
Hammersmith: make H. hum	186a
Hammock: Drake he's in his h.	287b
his heavy-shotted h.-shroud	429b
Hampden: [H.] had a head to contrive	203a
some village-H.	174a
when [H.] first drew the sword	203a
wd. twenty shillings have ruined Mr. H.?	55a
Hampshire: captain..H. grenadiers	161b
Hamstring: conceit lies in his h.	368b
Hand: a dapper boot—a little h.	434b
adieu..and wav'd her lily h.	161a
admire his sleight of h.	65b
a h. that kings have lipp'd	323b
a h. to bless	94b
a hopeless h. was clinging	43a
a lily in yr. medieval h.	165b
a moist eye, a dry h.	379b
an angry wafture of yr. h.	338b
and h. in h. will go	61a
a petty fortress and a dubious h.	213b
art..in wh. the h...head..heart	314b
as an old Parliamentary h.	167b
at h., quoth pick-purse	377a
at the h. of every man's brother	492b
bear welcome in yr. eye, yr. h.	347a
beat so quickly, waiting for a h.	429b
beefy face and grubby 'a.	232a
beneath whose awful H.	233b
bent head and beseeching h.	51a
bite the h. that fed them	57b
bringing me up by the h.	123b
bringing thy sheep in thy h.	7b
by God's Almighty H.	76a
civility of my knee, my hat, and h.	41b
cloud..like a man's h.	496a
(Commenus) had a..h. to execute	162a
Dawn's Left H. was in the Sky	152a
e'en crosses from his sovereign h.	191a
eftsoons his h. dropt he	98a
either h. may rightly clutch	227b
for the touch of a vanish'd h.	425b
gie 's a h. o' thine	59a
go into his h., and pierce it	496b
gold ring on her h. she bore	281a
hadde the hyer h.	88b
h. for h., foot for foot	494a
h. in h., on the edge of the sand	243b
h. in its breeches pocket	222a
H. like this h. shall throw open	51b
h. of little employment	336a
h. of the Lord hath..pre-eminence	489a
H. that made us is Divine	2b
h. that rocks the cradle	448b
h. to mouth	4b

Hand (cont.)

heaving up my either h. 190b
here's my h. 367b
her h. in whose compassion 368b
her h. on her bosom 363a
her rash h. in evil hour 276a
his h. is stretched out still 501a
his h. will be against every man 492b
his left h. is under my head 500a
his red right h. 272b
holds him with his skinny h. 98a
I cd. make thee open thy white h. 372b
I do salute thee with my h. 375a
I fear thy skinny h. 99a
if you want to win her h. 34b
I have the use..but of my left h. 279a
I kissed her slender h. 433b
imposition of a..mightier h. 254b
in a big round h. 166a
in a bold determined h. 76b
Infinity in the palm of yr. h. 29a
in her left h. riches and honour 497b
in his h. are all the corners 487b
in the h. of the Lord..is a cup 487a
I will hold yr. h. 48a
I wrote it with a second h. 408a
Joy, whose h. is ever at his lips 219b
keep the lifted h. in awe 477a
keep..thy h. out of plackets 343a
laying his h. upon many a heart 247a
length of days is in her right h. 497b
let not thy left h. know 505a
letter..with mine own h. 515b
like the dyer's h. 389a
man's h. is not able to taste 357b
my beloved put in his h. 500b
my h. before my eyes 26a
my h. sought hers 48a
my h. upon thy mane 69b
my playfellow, yr. h. 324a
my right h. forget her cunning 490a
my Sword sleep in my h. 31b
not a h. so weak and white 229b
one lovely h. she stretched for aid 77a
on this side my h. 376a
onward lend thy guiding h. 277b
or with a rude h. break the..cake 219a
our times are in his h. 50b
render me his bloody h. 339b
resting on one white h. 241b
sealed it with his h. 529b
shade of His h. 442a
she laid her snow-white h. 474a
she leans her cheek upon her h. 365a
spirit-small h. propping it 45a
stout heart, and open h. 318a
stretch forth thy mighty h. 200b
sweet and cunning h. laid on 370a
sweeten this little h. 350a
taking me up in his right h. 417b
that curious engine, yr. white h. 454a
that I were a glove upon that h. 365a
the firstlings of my h. 350a
the h. that rounded Peter's 147a
the h. to execute 217a
the larger heart, the kindlier h. 431a
there also shall thy h. lead me 490a
there's a h. my trusty fiere 59a
the sweet Roman h. 371b
they h. in h. with wandering steps 277a
they were h. and glove 111a
this h. hath offended 114b
this living h., now warm 219a
this my h. will rather 348a
three lilies in her h. 311b
thro' her wasted h., at night 317b
thrust my h. into his side 511b
thy defence upon thy right h. 489b
thy right h. shall hold me 490a
thy right h. shall teach thee 484b
too stubborn and too strange a h. 337b
under whose cautious h. 458b
voice and h. shake still 312b
wash this blood clean from my h. 348a
what dread h.? and what dread feet 32a
what h. and brain went ever paired 48a
what immortal h. or eye 32a
whatsoever thy h. findeth to do 81a, 499b
what the h. dare seize the fire? 32a
when people walk h. in h. 104a
white h. of a lady fever thee 324a

Hand (cont.)

who can hold a fire in his h. 374b
who hath seen her wave her h. 431b
whose h., like the base Indian 364a
whose murd'rous h. 114a
who will stand on either h. 253a
with automatic h. 144b
wi' their fans into their h. 530a
withered in my h. 187b
withhold not thine h. 499b
with rosy h. unbarred 275a
with thy bloody and invisible h. 349a
Handclasp: where the h's..stronger 87a
Handed: into their..bower h. they
    went 274b
Handel: compared to H.'s a mere
    memory 67a
    H. is scarcely fit to hold 67a
Handful: h. of grey ashes 106b
    just for a h. of silver 48a
Handiwork: firmament showeth his
    h. 482b
Handkercher about yr. brows 374a
Handkerchief: it is the h. of the
    Lord 458a
    no little h. to wipe his..nose 19b
    snuffle and sniff and h. 39b
    that h. did an Egyptian..give 362b
Handle: between the touch of the
    h. 21b
    h. of the big front door 166a
    I polished up that h. 166a
    old jug without a h. 243b
    taste not; h. not 516a
    the h. toward my hand 347b
    tools to him that can h. them 80a
Handled: horse..never..h...before 108b
Handles: everything..hath two h. 64a
Handmaid: h. perfect in God's sight 311b
    philosophy is but an h. to religion 13a
    riches are a good h. 13b
Handmaiden: the low estate of his h. 508b
Handmaidens whose names..sym-
    phonies 311b
Hands: aching h. and bleeding feet 7a
    at the palms of my h. 400b
    bear thee in their h. 487b
    before rude h. have touch'd it 216b
    between the h., between the brows 312b
    blesseth her with his two happy h. 408b
    blood and wine were on his h. 459b
    but not without men's h. 144b
    clasps the crag with crooked h. 426b
    dirty h., the nails bitten 255b
    do their h. as we touch 421b
    eyes, lips, and h. to miss 134a
    fall into the h. of the living God 517a
    Father, into thy h. I commend 510a
    fish that my two h. have taken 476a
    folding of the h. to sleep 498a
    fold our h. round her knees 420a
    grasp'd the mane with both his h. 108b
    h. are the h. of Esau 493a
    h. outstretched in yearning 556a
    h., that the rod of empire..swayed 174a
    his h. are as gold 500b
    his h. prepared the dry land 487b
    house not made with h. 515a
    if h...joined where hearts agree 173a
    I have thee by the h. 36b
    into the h. of the spoilers 494b
    into thy h. I commend my spirit 483b
    laid our groping h. away 39b
    laid violent h. upon themselves 481b
    laying on of h. 481a
    large and sinewy h. 249a
    lay their..h. on that golden key 266b
    made with our h. and our lips 423a
    man's fortune is in his own h. 16a
    mine own h. I give away my crown 376a
    mischief still fresh for idle h. to do 453a
    my h. from picking and stealing 481a
    no hurry in her h. 311a
    one of his h. wrought in the work 496b
    our h. have met, but not our hearts 196b
    our h. will never meet again 196b
    our new heraldry is h. not hearts 362b
    pale h. I loved 197a
    pale h., pink-tipped 197a
    right h. of fellowship 515b

Hands (cont.)

seen me with these hangman's h. 347b
shake h. with a king 178a
so to entergraft our h. 132b
still the h. of memory weave 106a
strengthen ye the weak h. 502a
strength without h. to smite 420b
the horny h. of toil 250a
their fatal h. no second stroke 273a
their h. are blue 243b
their h. upon their hearts 200a
the lifting up of my h. 490b
then take h. 367a
the palms of her h. 496b
these h. are not more like 330b
they have h., and handle not 489a
they pierced my h. 483a
they will soon *wring* their h. 450a
thou art a tall fellow of thy h. 373b
thy h. their little force resign 109a
tinged the eyelids and the h. 293a
touches of those flower-soft h. 323a
to you from failing h. we throw 256a
turn'd it in his glowing h. 432a
two-edged sword in their h. 490b
union of h. and hearts 425a
washed his h. before the multitude 508a
wave their h. for a mute farewell 203a
weak h. tho' mighty heart 392a
what h. you wd. hold! 240b
who crucify hearts, not h. 423b
will these h. ne'er be clean? 350a
with lifted feet, h. still 24b
with my own fair h. 418a
yr. h. begin to harden 229b
yr. holy delicate white h. 258a
yr. little h. were made to take 25b
yr. little h. were never made 452b
Handsaw: hawk from a h. 332b
Handsome: everything h. about him 359a
    I am a h. man 103a
Handy: always welcome, keep it h. 522a
    more h. to leave this Normandy 120b
    with the girls be h. 18b
Handy-work: prosper thou our h. 487b
Hang: are you going to h. him *any-
    how* 446b
    better h. wrong fler than no fler 121b
    feel his title h. loose about him 350a
    h. him up and erect a statue 404b
    h. out our banners 350b
    h. the man over again 19b
    h. yr. husband and be dutiful 159b
    h. yourself, brave Crillon 563b
    I will neither go nor h. 28a
    I will not h. myself to-day 91b
    man and wife..never..power to
    h. 150a
    she wd. h. on him 330a
    syllogisms h. not on my tongue 107b
    we must all h. together 157a
    we shall all h. separately 157a
    wretches h. that jurymen may dine 302b
    you wd. h. yourself 208a
Hanged: h. for stealing horses 178a
    here's a farmer that h. himself 348a
    if I were h. on the highest hill 232b
    our harps, we h. them up 490a
    see..Harrison h., drawn 296a
    to be h. in a fortnight 209b
Hanging: h. and marriage..go by
    Destiny 150b
    h. and wiving goes by destiny 353b
    h. is too good for him 54a
    many a good h. prevents 370a
    they're h. Danny Deever 228b
    they're h. him to-day 228b
    they're h. men an' women there 525b
Hangman: a louse for the h. 215b
    seen me with these h.'s hands 347b
Hangs: h. my helpless soul on Thee 455b
    he h. between; in doubt 301a
    thereby h. a tale 366b
Ha'nacker Mill 26b
Hanover: by famous H. city 50a
Hans Breitman 244b
Hansom: [h.] the gondola of London 129b
    you in yr. h. leave the High 307b
Hansom-cabs: for wheels of h. 85b
Hanyfink: wot's the good of H. 94a
Hap: from better h. to worse 407b

Hap (cont.)
good h. to the fresh..weather 424a
Happen at the Reformation? 28b
Happened: this cd. but have h. once 53a
Happier: a Paradise within thee, h. 276b
feel that I am h. than I know 275b
h. than this, she is not bred so dull 354a
prove h. than thy sire 560b
we had been h. both 313b
Happiest: h. hour a sailor sees 164a
I am h. when I am idle 451b
O yet h. if ye seek 274b
the h. women..have no history 144b
Happiness: a lifetime of h. 390b
all the h. mankind can gain 140b
but for the h. 'twill bring 76a
by wh. so much h. is produced 208b
domestic h., thou only bliss 112a
envy no man's h. 327a
gain a h. in eyeing 202b
greatest h. for the greatest number 202b
great spectacle of human h. 404b
h. consists not in the multitude 214b
h. is no laughing matter 456a
h. makes them good 242a
h. too swiftly flies 175a
happy in thine h. 219b
home-born h. 112a
in solitude what h.? 275b
it is a flaw in h., to see beyond 217b
look into h. thro' another..eyes 327b
love match..the only thing for h. 143b
makes the h. she does not find 214a
minute domestic h. 223a
my great task of h. 415a
no h. within this circle of flesh 41b
no more right to consume h. 390a
of no moment to the h. 208a
O H.! our being's end 301b
recall a time of h. in misery 566b
round these..our h. will grow 468b
the mind..withdraws into its h. 260b
there is ev'n a h...makes..afraid 195b
thought of tender h. betray 465b
to fill the hour, that is h. 148a
travelling is the ruin of all h. 58b
virtue alone is h. 301b
we find our h., or not at all 469b
were the h., of the next world 42a
wherein lies h.? 217b
Happy: a h. noise to hear 199a
all be as h. as kings 414a
all the art I know to make men h. 304a
all we know..is that they h. are 449a
angry and poor and h. 93b
as h. as we once, to kneel 113a
ask yourself whether you are h. 265b
be h. as ever at home 37b
be h. while y'er leevin 522b
be..virtuous, and you will be h. 156b
business of a wise man to be h. 209b
by many a h. accident 265b
call no man h. till he dies 559b
destined to be h. with you here 223b
dream of h., high, majestical 395a
duty of being h. 413b
earthlier h. is the rose distilled 356a
envy of thy h. lot 219b
h. families resemble each other 567a
feasted, despaired,—been h. 53a
fool is h. that he knows no more 301a
Frenchman..is always h. 111a
h., and glorious 193a
h. as a king 160b
h. for him that, his father 418b
h. he with such a mother 437a
h. in this, she is not yet so old 354a
h. is England! 221a
h. is the man that hath his quiver 489b
h. man be his dole 356a, 377a
h. men that have the power to die 438b
h...people whose annals are blank 80b
h. the man, and h. he alone 142a
h. the man whose wish and care 303b
h. the man, who, void of cares 296b
h. those early days 448a
he won't be h. till he gets it 523b
how h. cd. I be with either 160a
how h. he who crowns 168a
how h. is he born 473a
how h. you make those 388a

Happy (cont.)
I die h. 156b
I had been h., if the general camp 362a
I h. am, Joy is my name 32b
in nothing else so h. 375a
I think myself h., King Agrippa 513a
I've had a h. life 184a
I were but little h. 358a
make me at all h. without you 223b
makes a nation h., and keeps it so 277a
makes a Scotchman h. [whisky] 212b
methinks it were a h. life 384a
more h., if less wise 73a
ne'er be made h. by compulsion 102a
no..Irish lad was so h. as I 76b
no one can be..h. till all are h. 408a
one is never so h...as one thinks 562a
only one thing to make me h. 184a
period..human race was most h. 162a
physicians of all men are most h. 307a
so long as you're h. 263a
that thou art h., owe to God 275a
the h. who have called thee so 406b
then, h. low, lie down 380a
there is a h. land 476b
things that do attain the h. life 416a
thrice h. he who, not mistook 260a
to be good is to be h. 313a
to die, 'twere now to be most h. 361a
too h., h. tree 221a
too h. in thine happiness 219b
Tray is h. now 192b
was the carver h. 314b
wh. of us is h. in this world? 440a
who is the h. Warrior? 465a
Harassed: too h., to attain..calm 7a
Harbinger: odorous perfume her h. 277b
the evening star, love's h. 276b
yonder shines Aurora's h. 357a
Harbingers: clamorous h. of blood 351a
Harbour: where doth thine h. hold 21a
the h. cleared 98a
tho' the h. bar be moaning 226b
Hard: does it not seem h. to you 413b
h. as a piece of..millstone 497b
h., but O the glory of the winning 263b
h. grey weather 226a
'h.,' replied the Dodger 125a
h. to catch and conquer 263b
he finds it h., without..spectacles 192b
how very h. it is to be a Christian 46b
it seem'd so h. at first 434b
it was too h. for me 486b
nothing's so h., but search will find 189b
now it seems as h. to stay 434b
thou art an h. man 508a
though 'tis h. for you 3a
'tis not h...to keep the peace 364b
unlike the h., the selfish 113b
weather breeds h. English men 226a
woman is so h. upon the woman 436b
Hardens: it h. a' within 60a
Hardest: misfortunes h. to bear 251a
Hardly shall they that have riches 510a
Hardness: without h. will be sage 6a
Hardy: kiss me, H. 287a
Hare: each outcry of the hunted h. 29a
first catch yr h. 571a
get a little h.'s skin 534a
h.'s own child, the little h. 192b
Help! the H.! the H.! 192b
I like the hunting of the h. 33b
is that thy own h., or a wig? 239b
it looked like h. 19b
rouse a lion than to start a h. 377a
spectacles, to shoot the h. 192b
the h. limp'd trembling 221b
the h. sits snug in leaves 192b
thou woldest finde an h. 89a
triumph o'er the timid h. 443b
Harebell, like thy veins 329a
Hares: little hunted h. 192a
merry brown h. 226a
Hark: h.! a thrilling voice is sounding 86b
h.! at the Golden Palaces 406b
h., by the bird's song ye may learn 428b
h.! from the tombs a doleful sound 453b
h.! h.! bow, wow 367a
h.! h.! I hear..Chanticleer 367a
h.! h.! my soul, angelic songs 149b
h.! h.! the lark at heaven's gate 328b

Hark (cont.)
h., how all the welkin rings 455b
h.! how blithe the throstle sings 471b
h., my soul! it is the Lord 110a
h.! now I hear them 367a
h. the glad sound! 131b
h. the herald angels sing 455b
h. the little vesper-bell 100a
h.! the mavis' evening sang 59b
O h., O hear! how thin and clear 436a
Harken: mother Ida, h. ere I die 435a
Harlot: every h. was a virgin once 30a
Portia is Brutus' h. 338b
the h.'s cry from street to street 29b
Harlotry: like one of these h. players 377b
Harlots: devoured living with h. 509b
mother of h. 519b
Harm: benevolence..does..good or h. 17b
content with my h. 327a
crucifix that keeps a man from h. 227a
do not h. nor question much 132b
half the power to do me h. 363b
I fear we'll come to h. 530a
no h. in looking 417a
no people do so much h. 115b
tempt you to all h. and ill 3a
thees men doth most h. 242b
to win us to our h. 346a
when loyalty no h. meant 524a
Harmless: stock of h. pleasure 213a
Harmonia: Cadmus and H. 5b
Harmonics: fiddle h. 264b
Harmonies: inventor of h...Milton 427a
tumult of thy mighty h. 396b
Harmony: all discord, h. not understood 301a
all h. of instrument or verse 392b
distinct from h. divine 107b
from h., from heavenly h. 139b
give them the other h. of prose 142a
h. in discord 543a
heaven drowsy with the h. 345a
her voice the h. of the world 196b
I am disposed to h. 238b
music wherever there is h. 42a
rules with Daedal's. 397b
spirit grows like h. in music 469a
strike a note most full of h. 42a
such h. is in immortal souls 355a
their motions h. divine so smoothes 275a
there is a h. in autumn 394b
the touches of sweet h. 355a
tie the hidden soul of h. 269a
Harms: not for thy h. 442a
we beg often our own h. 323a
Harness: between the joints of his h. 496b
die with h. on our back 351a
him that girdeth on his h. 496a
my h. piece by piece 441b
the h. jingles now 199a
to wait in heavy h. 236b
Harnessed, and carrying bows 487a
Haroun Alraschid: good H. 437a
Harp: an unstringed viol or a h. 374b
h. not on that string 385a
h., sackbut, psaltery 504a
his h., the sole companion 22b
his wild h. slung behind him 281b
I'll hang my h. on a..willow tree 527a
Love took up the h. of Life 432a
no h. like my own 76b
praise the Lord with h. 483b
smote his thunder h. of pines 403b
the h., his sole remaining joy 316b
the h. that once thro' Tara's halls 281a
the h. the monarch minstrel swept 72b
who sings to one clear h. 429b
Harper: Wind, that grand old h. 403b
Harping: still h. on my daughter 332a
Harpit: I ha' h. ye up 231a
Harp-player: songs of the h. 420a
Harps: as for our h. 490a
plucking at their h. 231b
Harpsichon: Mrs. Turner's daughter
play on the h. 296a
Harriet: chatter about H. 571a
H., Hi! light of my eye 186a
what foolish H. befel 192b
Harris: bother Mrs. H. 124a
Mr. H. who was dreadful timid 124a
Harrison: see..H. hanged 296a

Harrow: Harrer an' Trinity College 232b
  toad beneath the h. 233a
Harrowing: only a man h. 179b
Harry: but H., H. 381a
  Cry 'God for H.!' 382a
  H. the king, Bedford and Exeter 383a
  I am H.'s daughter 231b
  in that Jerusalem shall H. lie 381a
  I saw young H. 378b
  little touch of H. in the night 382b
  Old H.'s got a finger in it 144a
  promised to H. and his followers 381b
  such a King H. 137a
Harsh: nor h. nor grating 472a
  not h., and crabbed 267b
Harshness: no h. gives offence 300a
Hart: as pants the h. 424b
  here wast thou bay'd, brave h. 339b
  I turned into a h. 369b
  lame man leap up as an h. 502a
  like as the h. desireth 484b
  thou wast the forest to this h. 339b
Harum, scarum, Divo 290b
Harvest: according to the joy in h. 501b
  as snow in h. 385a
  both grow together until the h. 506b
  doth h. no harm 446a
  grassy h. of the river-fields 8b
  h. of a quiet eye 469a
  h. truly is plenteous 506a
  like a stubble-land at h. home 376b
  must Thy h.-fields be dunged 442a
  no h. but a thorn 188a
  share my h. and my home 195b
  she laughs with a h. 205b
  song of H.-home 3b
  the h. is past 503b
  where the thin h. waves 114a
  white already unto h. 510b
Harvests of Arretium 253a
Harwich: in a steamer from H. 164a
Has-beens: one of the h. 194b
Haslemere: sell good beer at H. 27a
Haste: fiery-red with h. 375a
  h. of a fool is the slowest 321b
  h. still pays h. 352b
  h. thee Nymph 268b
  h. to shed innocent blood 503a
  h. you, sad notes 78a
  he that maketh h. to be rich 498b
  I said in my h. 489a
  make h., my beloved 501a
  raw H., half-sister to Delay 433a
  then why such h. 160b
  there was mounting in hot h. 68b
  this sweaty h. 329b
  tho' I am always in h. 456a
  what h. I can to be gone 16a
  where, with like h...they run 19b
  while one with moderate h. 330b
  whither doth h. the nightingale 79b
  without h., but without rest 568b
  you h. away so soon 189a
Hasten: h. slowly 553a
  h. to be drunk 140a
  men h. to a conclusion 15b
  new or old, still h. to a close 108a
Hasting: not full sails h. loaden home 260b
  until the h. day has run 189a
Hasty: man in his h. days 36b
Hat: a' brushes his h. a mornings 358b
  a chip h. had she on 219a
  a h. is going round 194a
  a penny in the old man's h. 522b
  as with my h. upon my head 212a
  by his cockle h. and staff 335b
  civility of my knee, my h., and hand 41b
  come down dah wid my h. caved in 156a
  drop a button in the h. 194a
  his h. in his hand 212a
  I live by pulling off the h. 175b
  in h. of antique shape 8a
  my h. and wig will soon be here 108b
  ne'er pull yr. h. upon yr. brows 350a
  Parsee from whose h. the rays 237a
  pitch the ball into the grounded h. 113a
  seen himself in a shocking bad h. 417a
  where did you get that h.? 310a
  without pulling off his h. 207a
  yr. fortune lies beneath yr. h. 290b
  yr. h. has got a hole in 't 78b

Hatched: couldna be h. o'er again 144a
  count their chickens ere th'are h. 66a
  wh. h., wd.,..grow mischievous 338b
Hatches: country wh. is..under h. 222b
Hatchet: with my little h. 451b
Hatcheth: sitteth on eggs, and h.
  them not 503b
Hatching vain empires 272b
Hatchment: nor h. o'er his bones 336a
Hatchments: Arms and H. 440a
Hate: dower'd with the h. of h. 435b
  enough religion to make us h. 418b
  h. for arts that caused himself 303a
  h. him as I h. hell-pains 359b
  hence, ye profane; I h. ye all 107a
  I h. a fool 123a
  I h. all Boets and Bainters 161a
  I h. all that don't love me 150a
  I h. him for he is a Christian 353a
  I h., I love—the cause thereof 539b
  I h. the crowd 241b
  in time we h. that wh. we..fear 322b
  let them h. so long as they fear 540b
  love and desire and h. 135a
  love sprung from my only h. 365a
  make brothers and sisters h. 200a
  Moses (a man I h.) 236a
  must h. and death return? 394a
  never been in love, or in h. 413a
  no h. lost between us 265b
  nor love thy life, nor h. 276b
  nought did I in h. 364a
  roughness breedeth h. 14b
  scarcely h. anyone that we know 183b
  reason to h. and to despise myself 183b
  study of revenge, immortal h. 271a
  sweet love..turns to..deadly h. 375a
  ten men love what I h. 5b
  the h. of those ye guard 236b
  them..that h. him flee before him 486a
  they who h. me may see it 487a
  those fellows h. us 240a
  'tis delicious to h. you 281a
  when the English began to h. 227a
  worst sin..is not to h. them 390a
Hated: brute I h. so 45b
  Dante..loved well because he h. 49a
  farewell, Horace; whom I h. so 69a
  h., as their age increases 414a
  h. by fools 420a
  he h. a fool, and he h. a rogue 211b
  or being h., don't give way 230a
  she might have h. 48a
  to be h. needs but to be seen 301a
Hater: he was a very good h. 211b
Hates: extinction of unhappy h. 6b
  ineffectual feuds and feeble h. 5a
  likes herself yet others h. 104a
  shadows of h. 5a
Hath: from him that h. not 508a
  taken away even that wh. he h. 508a
  unto every one that h. 508a
Hatim call to Supper 152b
Hatim Tai cry Supper 152b
Hating: don't give way to h. 230a
Hatred: envy, h., and malice 478b
  healthy h. of scoundrels 81a
  I must have no h. 86b
  no rage, like love to h. turned 104b
  now h., is by far the longest 71b
  stalled ox and h. therewith 498a
  without love, h., joy, or fun 305b
Hats: angels in broad-brimmed h. 247b
  bound in their..hosen, and their h. 504a
  never saw so many shocking bad h. 454a
  their h. were o' the birk 529a
  they wat their h. aboon 530a
Hatta: other Messenger's called H. 85a
Hatter: 'you can't take less', said the
  H. 83a
Haughtily: how h. he cocks his nose 419a
Haughtiness of soul 1b
Haunch: in the h. of winter sings 381a
Haunt: a h. of ancient Peace 435b
  exempt from public h. 325b
  oh the weary h. for me 225b
  so h. thy days..chill thy..nights 219a
  the Mind of Man—my h. 464a
  to h., to startle, and waylay 470b
  where they most breed and h. 347a
Haunted: beneath a..moon was h. 101a

Haunted (cont.)
  h. me like a passion 472a
  some h. by the ghosts 375b
  that is a h. town to me 242a
  'tis h. holy ground 68a
Haunts: h. of horror and fear 434b
  in the busy h. of men 185a
  not here..Apollo..h. meet for thee 5b
Hause-bane: his white h. 529b
Hautboys: gives the h. breath 139a
Have: deliver him, if he will h. him 483a
  for all we h. and are 229a
  h. I no bays to crown it 188a
  h. it jest as you've a mind to 230b
  h. more than thou showest 342a
  h. thou nothing to do 508a
  if I dream h. you 132a
  I h. thee not, and yet I see thee 347b
  I must not look to h. 350b
  men h. it when they know it not 420a
  other folk h. what some..be glad 151b
  the House of H. 161b
  to h. and to hold 481b
  what we h. we prize not 359a
Have-his-carcase 127a
Havelock: pipes o' H. 459a
Haven: into the h. where they wd. be 488b
  to their h. under the hill 425b
Havenots: the Haves and the H. 567b
Havens: in the h. dumb 197b
  ports and happy h. 374a
Having: lest, to Him, I..have naught 441b
  lest h. that, or this 190a
Havoc: cry, 'H.!' 339b
  the h. did not slack 76b
Hawk: Harry H. 531b
  h. at eagles with a dove 187a
  h. of the tower 402b
  his h., his hound, and his lady 529b
  his h. to fetch the wild-fowl 529b
  I know a h. from a handsaw 332b
  no h., no banquet, or renown 187a
  old ones by the h. are kill'd 293b
  wild h. stood with the down 435b
  wild h. to the wind-swept sky 229b
Hawks: all haggard h. will stoop 238a
  such h., such hounds 529b
Hawthorn(e): h. hedge puts forth its
  buds 39a
  sedulous ape to..H. 412b
  the h. bush a sweeter shade 384a
  this h. brake our tiring house 357a
  under the h. in the dale 268b
  when h. buds appear 356a
Hay: a mangerful of h. 311a
  dance an antic h. 258b
  good h., sweet h. 357a
  great desire to a bottle of h. 357a
  nothing like eating h. when..faint 85a
  sit with my love in the scented h. 38a
  the world is a bundle of h. 72b
  we lie tumbling in the h. 373a
  when husbands win their h. 530b
  worth a load of h. 522a
Haycock: under the h. fast asleep 535a
Hayley: Of H.'s birth this was the..
  lot 30a
  to forgive enemies H. does pretend 30a
  when H. finds out 30a
Haystack: beside the h. in the floods 284a
Hazael: escapeth the sword of H. 496a
Hazard: equal hope, and h. 271a
  father's crown into the h. 381b
  he has put to h. his ease 56a
  I will stand the h. 385b
  men that h. all do it in hope 353b
  the h. of concealing 60a
Hazel-nut: chariot is an empty h. 364b
Hazlitt: I was at H.'s marriage 239b
  played the sedulous ape to H. 412b
  we cannot write like H. 413b
He: art thou h. that shd. come 506b
  every h. has got him a she 522b
  h. and we and all men 445b
  h. for God only 274a
  h. on whom Thy tempests fell 188a
  H. too, Whom we have by heart 265a
  h.'s for the morning 47a
  I to Him, and H. to me 441a
  poorest h. that is in England 307b
  who is H., with modest looks 469a

Head: above my h. the heaven 35b
after his h. was cut off 533b
a h. fantastically carved upon it 380b
a' never broke any man's h. 382a
a rosy garland and a weary h. 401b
as gently lay my h. on my grave 42a
as if her h. she bow'd 268a
at his h. a grass-green turf 335b
bare h. in hell-black night 343a
binds so dear a h. 391b
bowed his comely h., down 261a
breaking Priscian's h. 66a
bruising of the hapless h. 452b
can't make a h. and brains 123a
change the cod's h. 360b
chopper to chop off yr. h. 533b
cover my defenceless h. 455b
cowslips..that hang the pensive h. 270a
cuts the wrong man's h. off 126a
fit to snore his h. off 84b
forward bends his h. 98a
four angels round my h. 2b
from some once lovely H. 153a
'gainst a h. so old and white 342a
gently falling on thy h. 453a
God be in my h. 523a
gold crown on 'er 'e. 236b
go up, thou bald h. 496b
ground flew up..hit me in the h. 451a
had it h. bit off by it young 342a
hang 'mid men my needless h. 442b
have at his beddes h. twenty bokes 88b
h. grown grey in vain 392b
h., hands, wings, or feet 273a
h., heart, and hand 228a
h. is not more native to the heart 329b
h. keeps turnin' back..to the tail 250b
h. like a concertina 227b
h. of a family off—shocking 126a
H. that once was crowned with
    thorns 224a
h. wh. statuaries loved to copy 255a
he (Commenus)..h. to contrive 162a
here rests his h. upon the lap 174b
her fair vast h. 421a
her h. on her knee 363a
hers is the h. 292b
he seems no bigger than his h. 343b
his answer trickled thro' my h. 85b
his h. and his hairs were white 518b
his h...completely silvered o'er 112a
his h. under his wing 533a
his h. with his legs 493b
his heart runs away with his h. 103b
his madness was not of the h. 73a
his shoulders and his heavy h. 453a
hoary h. is a crown of glory 498a
ideas of its 'h.' differ from the..
    'tail' 17b
if she'd but turn her h. 475a
if you can keep yr. h. 230a
I'll eat my h. 125a
in the heart or in the h. 354a
it shall bruise thy h. 492b
I was born..with a white h. 379b
I will make you shorter by the h. 145b
knock at a star with my exalted
    h. 189b
lifts up his burning h. 387a
like the..ointment upon the h. 490a
my hat upon my h. 212a
my h. is bending low 156b
my h. is bloody, but unbowed 185a
my h. is twice as big as yours 109a
my h. is wild with weeping 394b
my parboiled h. upon a stake 280b
nae room at my h. 529a
nail my h. on yonder tower 12b
not where to lay his h. 506a
now does my project gather to a h. 367b
no wool on top of his h. 156b
o'er the cowslip's velvet h. 268a
o'er the h. of yr. loved Lycidas 269b
off with his h. 83a
off with his h...Buckingham 95b
O good grey h. 129a
'on my h.', was the reply 129a
out of King Charles' h. into my h. 122a
over his living h. like heaven 392a
painted her face, and tired her h. 496b
put leaves round his h. 123a

Head (cont.)
rest thy weary h. upon this breast 247a
ripe apples drop about my h. 260b
savage as a bear with a sore h. 259b
serious..to get one's h. cut off 84b
shake his sapient h. 9a
she lifted up his bloudy h. 529b
she has the h. 121b
singe my white h.! 342b
such as take lodgings in a h. 65a
that one small h. cd. carry all 168b
that sacred h. of thine 269b
the h. of the gallows-tree 227a
their h. the prow 139b
their precious balms break my h. 490b
the kingly crowned h. 328a
there's not a h. so thick 229b
the suspicious h. of theft 345a
the whole h. is sick 501a
the Wild Ass stamps o'er his H. 153a
this old grey h. 459a
thou cutt'st my h. off 366a
thou hast anointed my h. with oil 483a
thou hast covered my h. 490b
thro' headpiece and thro' h. 254a
thumped him on the h. 85b
thy h. is as full of quarrels 365b
thy poor h. almost turns 7b
to deck her mistress' h. 74a
touches a hair of yon grey h. 459a
traitor; off with his h. 385a
trample round my fallen h. 426a
two separate sides to my h. 236a
under my h. a sod 530b
uneasy lies the h. 380a
very h. and front of my offending 360a
what seem'd his h. 272b
wherefore shd. I busk my h. 530a
wh. was the h...wh...the tail 38a
wh. way the h. lies 308a
whose h. proud fancy never taught 113b
why not upon my h.? 375b
with a shake of his poor little h. 165a
with bent h. and beseeching hand 51a
with monstrous h. and sickening
    cry 92a
yet anon repairs his drooping h. 270a
you incessantly stand on yr. h. 82b
yr. royal h. may fall 91b
Headache: I happen to have a h. 84b
Head-in-air: Johnny H. 193a
Headland: top of some bold h. 464a
Headlong: H. Ap-Headlong. 295a
h. themselves they threw down 275a
wash'd h. from on board 107b
Headpiece: thro' h. and thro' head 254a
Heads: beast with many h. 328a
blunt monster with uncounted h. 379b
curling their monstrous h. 380a
empty h. and tongues 199b
fall'n on the inventors' h. 337a
h., h.! five children—mother 126a
h. I win 115b
hide their diminished h. 273b
hills whose h. touch heaven 360a
hover in their restless h. 259b
houseless h. and unfed sides 343a
hung their h., and then lay by 385b
knowledge dwells in h. replete 112b
pillars rear their marble h. 104b
shake their h., saying 483a
tall men had ever very empty h. 13b
their h. all in nightcaps 81b
their h. are green 243b
their h. are hung with ears 357a
their h. never raising 467b
this dreadful pother o'er our h. 342b
toss-pots still had drunken h. 372a
when our h. are bowed with woe 266b
whose h. do grow beneath 360a
Head-stone in the corner 489a
Heal: break, and h. it if it be 109b
grief that fame can never h. 12b
I will h. me of my..wound 429b
physician, h. thyself 509a
there is none to h. it 221b
what wound did ever h. 361b
Healed: convert and be h. 501b
had h. it for ever 247a
with his stripes we are h. 503a
Healer: destroyer and h., hear 423a

Healeth: he h. those that are broken 490b
Healing: arise with h. in his wings 504b
for the h. of the nations 520a
long expected h. wings 447b
rises with h. in his wings 110b
the most High cometh h. 521a
Health: art so far from my h. 483a
a sound and pristine h. 350b
h. and high fortune 317b
h. is the second blessing 450b
h. on both 349a
here's a double h. to thee 73a
here's a h. to all 523b
he that will this h. deny 143a
hunt in fields, for h. unbought 140a
I have nor hope nor h. 399a
in h. and wealth long to live 478b
look to yr. h. 450b
my long sickness of h. 368a
not good for the Christian h. 233a
there is no h. in us 478a
thine h. shall spring forth 503a
thy saving h. among all nations 486a
voice of joy and h. 489a
wisdom breathed by h. 471b
Healths: of h. five-fathom deep 364b
when h. and draughts go free 249b
Healthy: h. by temperance 303a
h., free, the world before me 458a
h., wealthy and wise 157a
imagination of a boy is h. 217a
Heap: one h. of all yr. winnings 230a
Heaps: unsunned h. of miser's 267b
Hear: all that h. me this day 513a
and yrs. to h. 403b
be swift to h., slow to speak 517a
cd. ever h. by tale or history 356a
did ye not h. it? 68b
dinna ye h. it? 459a
do any man's heart good to h. me 356b
few love to h. the sins they..act 364a
h. about the graves of the martyrs 414b
h. a song that echoes cheerly 431b
h. it not, Duncan 347b
h. no more at all 414a
h. the Aziola cry 393a
h. them, read, mark, learn 479a
h. the other side 537b
h. those things wh. ye h. 509a
he cannot choose but h. 98a
he that hath ears to h. 508a
I h. a smile 116a
I h. thee and rejoice 463b
I h. the foules singe 89b
I h. you, I will come 199a
I love to h. the story 266a
in heaven..will you h. or know 424a
men sit and h. each other groan 220a
my heart wd. h. her and beat 434a
O h. us when we cry to Thee 457a
planted the ear, shall he not h. 487b
scarce cd. they h...their foes 318b
she will not h. 423a
still must I h.? 72a
still, still to h. her..breath 220b
still stood fixed to h. 275b
the larkspur listens, 'I h., I h.' 434a
they never wd. h. 419a
time will come when you will h. 128a
to h. some new thing 512b
to h., was wonder 137a
we cannot h. it 355a
we shall h. it by and by 44b
ye must not h. him 3a
Heard: all the sound I h. 198b
ay, they h. his foot 119b
enough that he h. it once 44b
h. for their much speaking 505a
h. melodies are sweet 219b
h., not regarded 378b
h. whether..be any Holy Ghost 512b
he h. it, but he heeded not 69a
her name is never h. 22a
his..name is h. no more in heaven 275a
I have also h. the same 485b
I have h. of these by the..ear 497b
I never h. till now 267a
I've h. old cunning stagers say 65b
I will be h. 158b
lark so far cannot be seen or h. 343b
long after it was h. no more 471a

Heard (cont.)

none wd. be h. or writ so oft	36a
oon ere it h.	90a
she wished she had not h. it	360a
since I h. thee last	109a
then is h. no more	350b
they h., and were abashed	271b
this . . patter isn't generally h.	167a
was h. the world around	270a
what never yet was h. in tale	266b
wh. in those days I h.	465a
ye have read, ye have h.	235b
Hearer: any be a h. of the word	517b
the charmed h.	443a
Hearers: attentive and favourable h.	196b
edification of the h.	196b
his h. cd. not cough	215a
not h. only	517b
Heareth not the loud winds	470a
Hearing: fall asleep, or h. die	385b
h. oftentimes the still, sad music	472a
make passionate my sense of h.	344b
Hearken: h., Lady Betty	4b
h., O daughter, and consider	484b
to h. than the fat of rams	495a
Hearkened to my commandments	502b
Hearkens: it leans, and h. after it	134a
Hears: he h. on all sides	276b
she neither h. nor sees	463a
Hearse: flowers to crown thy h.	225a
h. where Lycid lies	270a
underneath this sable h.	42b
walk before the h.	158b
Heart: a broken and contrite h.	485a
a broken h. lies here	252b
absence makes the h. grow fonder	22a
a h. as soft, a h. as kind	190a
a h. grown cold	392b
a h. to pity, and a hand to bless	94b
a h. unfortified	330a
a h. within blood-tinctured	43b
all 's here about my h.	337a
all that mighty h. is . . still	472b
all thy h. lies open unto me	436b
a loving h. to thee	190a
a man after his own h.	495a
a naked thinking h.	132a
and mine, with my h. in it	367b
and the h. replies	112b
as a seal upon thine h.	501a
a shy spirit in my h.	472b
as my poor h. doth think	251b
as well as want of h.	196a
at the red-ripe of the h.	51a
a throe of the h.	37a
awake, my h., to be loved	35b
a warm h. within	109a
awful warmth about my h.	222b
aye a h. aboon them a'	63a
beating of my own h.	198b
because my h. is pure	438a
bitter h. that bides its time	45b
blessed are the pure in h.	505a
blind side of the h.	92a
blows over the lonely of h.	475b
bread to strengthen man's h.	488a
bring with you a h.	471b
broke his h. in Clermont town	25b
broken h. . . kens nae second spring	525b
broods and sleeps on his own h.	469a
but deceiveth his own h.	517b
but some h. did break	429b
but thou hast my h.	305b
call home the h. you gave me	137a
chooseth the pure in h.	224a
consenting language of the h.	160a
Convent of the Sacred H.	145a
cruelty has a human h.	33a
cry did knock against my very h.	367a
daughter of my house and h.	68a
day breaks not, it is my h.	132a
dissemble in their double h.	482a
drink thy wine with a merry h.	499b
each wish of my h.	281b
enrich my h., mouth, hands	187a
entered . . my h. at some noonday	46b
ever hold me in thy h.	337a
every lusty h. beginneth	257b
ev'ry pang that rends the h.	53a
fails my h. I know not how	286b
faint h. ne'er wan a lady fair	59a

Heart (cont.)

farewell the h. that lives alone	468b
far other aims his h. had learned	168b
feed the h. of the night	422b
felt along the h.	472a
fire that in the h. resides	7a
firstlings of my h.	350a
fit to employ all the h.	51b
fleshy tables of the h.	515a
floodgate of the deeper h.	155a
floods his h. abrim	229a
following her daily of thy h.	312b
fool hath said in his h.	482a
for a man with h., head, hand	433b
for Witherington my h. was woe	530b
found in thine h. to sing	422b
found not my h. moved	402a
friendship . . made my h. to ache	30a
gave my h. another youth	389a
give . . but not yr. h. away	198b
give me a h. to find out Thee	224a
give me back my h.	73a
give me back my h. again	173a
given him his h.'s desire	482b
giving yr. h. to a dog to tear	233b
God be in my h.	523a
grandeur in the beatings of the h.	465b
grandeurs of his Babylonian h.	441b
grant thee thy h.'s desire	482b
Greensleeves was my h. of gold	523b
grieve his h.	349b
happiness that makes the h. afraid	195b
hardness of h.	478b
hast cleft my h. in twain	335a
head, h., and hand	228a
healeth those that are broken in h.	496b
hear it in the deep h.'s core	475b
h. against thy side hammers	234b
h. and soul do sing in me	402a
h. and voice opprest	286a
h. as sound as a bell	358b
h. aye's the part aye	60a
h. benevolent and kind	63b
h. distrusting asks, if this be joy	168b
h. doth need a language	101b
h. for falsehood framed	400a
h. handfast in h. as they stood	421b
h. has its reasons	564b
h. hath ne'er within him burn'd	317a
h. is deceitful above all things	503b
h. is in their boots	92b
h. is sick of woe	38b
h. is turned to stone	362b
h. knoweth his own bitterness	498a
h. less native to high Heaven	441a
h. must pause to breathe	74a
h. of a man to the h. of a maid	229b
h. of a ranger	26a
h. of kings is unsearchable	498b
h. of my h., were it more	423a
h. of oak are our ships	158b
h. puts forth its pain	39a
h. runs away with his head	103b
h.'s denying	21a
h.'s lightness from . . May	217b
h., the fountain of sweet tears	471a
h. to h., and mind to mind	317a
h. [treads] on h.	44a
h. *was* true to Poll	58b
h. whose love is innocent	74a
h. with English instinct	136b
h. within, and God o'erhead	248a
heathen h. that puts her trust	233b
he (Commenus) had a h. to resolve	162a
he hardened Pharaoh's h.	493b
he has a h., and gets his speeches	310a
here's a h. for every fate	73a
her h. in his grave	281b
he tears out the h. of it	238a
his flawed h. . . burst smilingly	344a
his h. and soul away	198b
his h. shd. glow	166a
his h. to report	357b
his h. was hot within	248b
his h. was one of those	67b
his lost h. was tender	399a
his madness was . . of . . h.	73a
hold thee to my h.	169a
holiness of the h.'s affection	222a
hope deferred maketh the h. sick	498a
hours I spent with thee, dear h.	309b

Heart (cont.)

how can thine h. be full	422b
how else but thro' a broken h.	459b
how sweet! did any h. now share	399a
how the h. listened	443a
humble and a contrite h.	233b
I feel my h.—I can't tell how	528a
I feel my h. new opened	386a
if guilt 's in that h.	282a
if it enrich not the h. of another	247a
if the h. of a man is deprest	159b
if thou wilt ease thine h.	23b
if thy h. fails thee	145b
if thy h. fail thee	307b
if yr. h. be only true	58b
if yr. h. is in it	21b
I had locked my h. in a case	530a
I had rather coin my h.	341a
I love the language of his h.	303b
Indian Summer of the h.	458b
infinite h.'s ease . . kings neglect	382b
in his h. is a blind desire	420b
inmost cupboards of her h.	439b
in my h., tho' not in heaven	188a
innocent is the h.'s devotion	399b
in the h. is the prey for gods	423b
in the h. of a friend	246b
into my h. an air that kills	199b
I said to H., 'How goes it?'	26b
I shall be out of h. shortly	378b
I was false of h.	389a
I wish my h. had never known ye	526a
I'll sell yr. h.'s desire	229a
I'll warrant him h.-whole	327b
it 's oh! in my h.	217a
joy to his mighty h.	228a
knocked on my sullen h. in vain	415a
knowledge of . . h. in . . Richardson	208a
Land of H.'s Desire	475b
laugh, h., again	474b
laying his hand upon many a h.	247a
lay that earth upon thy h.	227b
lent out my h. with usury	239b
let no man's h. fail	495b
let not yr. h. be troubled	511a
let thy h. cheer thee	499b
lifeless charms, without the h.	159a
lift up yr. h.	455b
light h. lives long	345a
like a living coal his h. was	248b
little body with a mighty h.	381b
look in thy h., and write	401b
loosed out my h. in tears	6b
made my h. to glow	407b
make me a clean h.	485a
make my seated h. knock	346b
make the h. of this people fat	501b
make this h. rejoice	109b
maketh glad the h. of man	488a
man's h. is small	235a
me h. is on me sleeve	92b
Mercy has a human h.	33a
merry h. doeth good	498b
merry h. goes all the day	373a
merry h. maketh . . cheerful	498a
moon of the h.'s desire	313a
more native to the h.	329b
mountain 'tween my h. and tongue	339a
much against my h.	294a
music in my h. I bore	471a
my foolish h. expand	45b
my h. aches	219b
my h. and my flesh rejoice	487a
my h. beats loud	394b
my h. go pit-a-pat!	50a
my h. hath 'scap'd this sorrow	388b
my h. is gladder than all these	310b
my h. is heavy	568a
my h. is idly stirred	465a
my h. is inditing of a good matter	484b
my h. is like an apple tree	310b
my h. is like a rainbow shell	310b
my h. is like a singing bird	310b
my h. is not here	62a
my h. is sair for Somebody	60b
my h. leaps up when I behold	468a
my h. remembers how!	414b
my h., safe left, shall meet	402a
my h. shall be the faithful compass	161a
my h. 's in the Highlands	62a, 320a
my h. 's right there	461a

Heart (cont.)

alights on the warm h. 443b
my h.'s subdued even to..my lord 360b
my h.'s undoing 281b
my h. thy home 398b
my h. untravell'd fondly turns 169b
my h. upon my sleeve 359b
my h. was hot within me 484a
my h. was like to break 20b
my h. was used to beat 429b
my h. with pleasure fills 467b
my h. wd. hear her and beat 434a
my life, my love, my h. 190a
myn h. dye 90a
my reins and my h. 483b
my true love hath my h. 401b
my whole h. rises up 47b
mysterious links enchain the h. 172b
nearer to the H.'s Desire 154a
never a crack in my h. 475b
never give all the h. 474b
never has ached with a h. 421a
no longer tear the h. 420a
no matter from the h. 369b
no, no, my h. is fast 526a
Nora's h. is lost 318b
nor yet a h. so sick 229b
no, the h. that has truly lov'd 281b
not really bad at h. 26a
now cracks a noble h. 337a
nowhere beats the h. so kindly 12a
no woman's h. so big 371a
obey thy h. 146b
O h. be at peace 474a
O h.! if she'd but turn her head 475a
on my h. they tread now 375b
open my h. and you will see..Italy 46a
open not thine h. to every man 520b
or in the h. or in the head 354a
O that man's h. were as fire 420a
O true, brave h.! 134b
our being's h. and home 469b
out of the abundance of the h. 506b
out-worn h., in a time out-worn 474b
pageant of his bleeding h. 6a
passionate h. of the poet 433b
pavilion of my h. 441a
pitee renneth sone in gentil h. 89a
poor man's h. thro' half the year 318a
possess thy h., my own 37b
pourest thy full h. 398a
privacy of yr. fool's h. 412a
put his h. to school 463a
religion's in the h. 205b
revolting and rebellious h. 503b
rise in the h. 436a
roaming with a hungry h. 438b
room my h. keeps empty 225a
round his h. one..golden hair 312b
ruddy drops that visit my sad h. 338b
same h. beats in every..breast 5a
secret anniversaries of the h. 248b
seeing, shall take h. again 248a
send me back my h. 416a
set not yr. h. upon them 485b
Shakespeare unlocked his h. 47b, 470b
shall see thy h.'s desire 37a
she is the darling of my h. 79b
she wants a h. 302a
shd. you need nor h. nor hands 414a
sigh, h., again in the dew 474b
sighing of a contrite h. 479a
sighs are the..language of the h. 321b
sigh that rends thy constant h. 169a
sleep in old England's h. 453b
so long as the human h. is strong 17b
sorrows of my h. are enlarged 483a
so the h. be right 308a
speaks to the h. alone 82b
spring Thou up within my h. 455b
stabb'd me to the h. 159a
stay at home, my h. 248b
steady of h., and stout of hand 317a
stout h., and open hand 318a
strings..in the human h. 121a
stuff wh. weighs upon the h. 350b
such a h. in my bosom 350a
sure of his unspotted h. 295b
sweet concurrence of the h. 191a
take any h., take mine 166a
take h., fair days will shine 166b

Heart (cont.)

take h. of grace 166a
take thy beak from out my h. 298b
taming my wild h. to thy..hand 358b
tear out yr. h. 232b
tell the most h.-easing things 220b
thanks to the human h. 467a
that h. I'll give to thee 190a
that quivered in his h. 72a
that shire..the h. of England 137a
that young faithful h. 184b
the bruised h. was pierced 360a
the counsellor h. 328a
the h. but one 34a
the h. is a small thing 307a
the h. must bear the longest part 187a
the h. of Hell 227a
the h. out of the bosom 198b
the h. ran o'er with..worship 73a
the h. that loved her 472a
the language of the h. 303a
the larger h., the kindlier hand 431a
the laughing h.'s long peace 40a
them wh. are true of h. 482a
then burst his mighty h. 340a
there will yr. h. be also 505b
the service of a mind and h. 465b
the strong h. of her sons 136b
the wh. shall never go from my h. 257a
the whole h. faint 501a
think, this h., all evil shed 40a
this h., I know, to be long lov'd 5b
this, indeed, O world! the h. of thee 339b
this is a h. the Queen leant on 48b
tho' the h. be still as loving 74a
thou break'st my h. 187b
thou voice of my h. 115b
thro' the sad h. of Ruth 220a
thy fair hair my h. enchained 401b
thy h. the lowliest duties..did lay 467b
thy h. with dead..innocencies fill'd 293b
to eat thy h. thro'..despairs 409b
to get yr. h.'s desire 391a
to mend the h. 298b
to my dead h. run them in 415a
to their captain, the h. 380b
twice broken His great h. 244a
twist the sinews of thy h. 32a
understand with their h. 501b
unquiet h. and brain 429b
untroubled h. of stone 77a
vacant h. and hand 319a
waited for the h.'s prompting 144a
Ward has no h., they say 310a
waste his whole h. in one kiss 438a
weak hands tho' mighty h. 392a
wear him in my h.'s core, ay, 334a
were not my h. at rest 321a
what can a tired h. say 119a
what h. cd. have thought you 443a
what h. he thinks his tongue speaks 358b
what the false h. doth know 347b
when once the young h...is stolen 281b
when thy h. began to beat 32a
when we meet a mutual h. 443a
where I have garnered up my h. 363a
where my h. is turning ebber 156a
where my h. lies 49a
whether it be the h. to conceive 217a
wh. the poor h. wd. fain deny 350b
whispers the o'erfraught h. 350a
whose..complexion and whose h. 373b
wilt thou cure thine h. of love 23b
windy tempest of my h. 384b
win my h. from me 432b
winning each h. 120b
wish thine own h. dry 219a
with a h. for any fate 248a
with h., and soul, and voice 286b
with women the h. argues 7a
wound a h. that's broken 317b
wounded is the wounding h. 114b
ye cannot unlock yr. h. 146b
yet thro' good h., and Our Ladye's 317a
your h.'s desires be with you 325b
Heartache: we end the h. 333a
Heartfelt: with our h. sympathy 165b
Hearth: a genial h. 468b

Hearth (cont.)

as from an unextinguished h. 396b
blazing h. shall burn 174a
by this still h. 438b
Hearths: their altars and their h. 553a
Hearthside: embers in h. ease 180a
Hearthstone: his clean h. 59b
light of his own h. 235b
Heartily know 146b
Hearts: a jining of h...housekeepings 125b
boldest of h. that ever braved 51a
brave h. and clean! 428b
but our h. are great 428b
change yr. h. or..lose yr. Inns 27a
cherish those h. that hate thee 386a
combine yr. h. in one 383b
conserved of maidens' h. 362b
country that eager h. expect 286a
creeds that move men's h. 38b
dear h. across the seas 230a
did not our h. burn 510a
draw h. after them tangled 277a
ensanguin'd h. 112b
floor lay pav'd with broken h. 249b
free h., free foreheads 439a
gentleness, in h. at peace 40a
hands upon their h. 200a
h. are brave again 200a
h. are dry as summer dust 464a
h. just as pure and fair 163b
h. of men, wh. fondly here admire 409a
h. of oak our men 10b
h. of truest metal 198a
h. that honour cd. not move 46a
h., that once beat high 281a
h. that spaniel'd me at heels 324a
h. that with rising morn arise 223b
H. was her favourite suit 239a
helps good h. in need 119a
home-keeping h. are happiest 248b
if hands..joined where h. agree 173a
if young h. were not so clever 199b
incline our h. to keep this law 480a
in the h. of his fellow citizens 244a
I've heard of h. unkind 471a
kind h. are more than coronets 431b
Knave of H., he stole those tarts 83b, 532b
men with splendid h. 39b
neither have the h. to stay 66a
new heraldry is hands not h. 362b
of all that human h. endure 213a
offspring of cold h. 57a
one equal temper of heroic h. 439a
or any h. to beat 476a
other lips, and other h. 53b
our faces vizards to our h. 349a
our h., though stout and brave 248a
our h. were fulfilled 423a
O you hard h., you cruel men 337b
pain of finite h. that yearn 52b
pluck their h. from them 383a
pure eyes and Christian h. 224a
Queen of H...made some tarts 83b, 532b
simple song for thinking h. 465b
some that smile have in their h. 340b
stout h. and sharp swords 28b
streaming eyes and breaking h. 433a
such a woe..as wins more h. 524a
the cheerful h. now broken 282b
the day star arise in yr. h. 518a
the h. of old gave hands 362b
their h. are in the right place 129b
thousand h. beat happily 68a
to h. wh. near each other move 394a
to live in h. we leave behind 76b
to steal away yr. h. 340a
to whom all h. be open 480a
turn the h. of the disobedient 508b
two fond h. in equal love 18b
two h. beating each to each 48b
two h. that beat as one 568b
union of hands and h. 425a
vainly h. with h. are twined 120a
we have given our h. away 473a
what h. have men 428b
when h. have once mingled 395a
while yr. h. are yearning 156a
who crucify h., not hands 423b
with h. of controversy 337b
yr. image at our h. 96b

Heart-sick: Chatham h. 111b
Heart-strings: jesses were my..h. 362a
my flutterin' h. 227a
Heart-throbs: count time by h. 18a
Heat: burden and h. of the day 507b
erst from h. did canopy the head 387a
grateful coolness in the h. 86b
h. me these irons hot 374a
h. not a furnace for yr. foe so hot 385b
h. the furnace one seven times 504a
h. was in the very sod 286b
nothing hid from the h. thereof 482b
not the schoolboy h. 431a
not without dust and h. 279a
one h...doth drive out another 87b
sun light on them, nor any h. 519a
surprised I was with sudden h. 407b
the h. of the long day 7a
thy h. of pale-mouth'd prophet 220a
where is that Promethean h. 363b
Heated in the chase 424b
Heating: to warm without h. 28a
Heath: a wind on the h. 34a
h. wore the appearance of..night 180b
land of brown h. 317b
lo! where the h. 114a
my foot is on my native h. 320a
nobody cd...understand the h. 180b
sword sung on the barren h. 30a
where the place? Upon the h. 345b
why upon this blasted h. 346a
wind on the h., brother 34a
Heathen: any example in any h. 291b
break the h. and uphold the Christ 427b
counsel of the h. to nought 483b
h...bows down to wood and stone 184a
h. Chinee is peculiar 182a
h. heart that puts her trust 233b
h. in 'is blindness 228b
h. so furiously rage together 481b
machine for converting the H. 80a
nostalgia of the h. past 243a
not a H., or a Jew 452b
pokes the h. out 228b
that the h. may know themselves 482a
the h. make much ado 484b
you're a pore benighted h. 229a
Heather: among the h. bright 85b
singer lies in the field of h. 414b
the bare and broken h. 12a
thro' the rare red h. 75b
Heaths: some game on these lone h. 183b
Heaven: above my head the h. 35b
a H. in a Wild Flower 29a
a h. on earth 273b
all H. in a Rage 29a
all I seek, the h. above 414a
all of h. we have below 1b
all places..distant from H. alike 64a
all places..hell that are not h. 258b
all that we believe of h. 291b
all the company of h. 480b
and all to h. 214b
and then—what pleases H. 317b
angels on the walls of h. 259b
an humbler h. 300b
anything that is in h. above 480a
appeared a great wonder in h. 519a
are there no stones in h. 364a
as near to h. by sea 162b
Astarte, Queen of H. 271b
at h.'s gates she claps her wings 251b
a will most incorrect to h. 330a
bask in h.'s blue smile 393a
betwixt H. and Charing Cross 442a
beyond H.'s...wilderness 397b
Brahma from his mystic h. groans 217b
breaks the serene of h. 407a
bring all H. before mine eyes 268b
bring up the rear in h. 41b
bring with thee airs from h. 331a
Britain first, at H.'s command 443a
builds a h. in Hell's despair 32a
by that h. that bends above us 298b
calls to H. for human blood 29a
candidate of h. 140a
choir of h. and furniture of earth 28a
clinging H. by the hems 442b
dip his brush in dyes of h. 318b
drives Night..with them from H. 152a

Heaven (cont.)
earth be but the shadow of H. 275a
earth can take or H. can give 394a
earth resteth, h. moveth 187b
earth's crammed with h. 43a
eternal joys of h. 258b
even from the gates of h. 54a
ev'n in h. his looks..downward bent 272a
fairer person lost not H. 272a
fiercest Spirit that fought in H. 272a
find the way to h. 326a
first h. and..earth were passed 519b
flew up to h.'s chancery 412a
flowerless fields of h. 420a
from a throne mounted in h. 438a
from the gold bar of H. 311b
from the verge of H. 275a
gems of H., her starry train 274a
gentleness of h. broods 467a
give the jolly h. above 414a
glance from h. to earth 357b
God created the h. 492a
God's in his h. 50a
goes his own By-way to h. 118b
good gifts..are sent from H. above 76a
greatest herald of H.'s King 137b
H. and Hell Amalgamation Society 82a
H. and Nature seem'd to strive 215a
H., as its purest gold 299b
h. awards the vengeance due 107b
h. being spread with this..screen 180b
h. be in these lips 258b
H. did a recompense..send 174b
h. has no rage, like love to hatred 104b
H. hath my empty words 351b
H. hath sent me fortune 326a
'H. help him!' quoth Lars Porsena 253b
h. in her eye 275b
h. is above all yet 385b
h. is..a matter of digestion 201a
H. is everywhere at home 92b
H. is for thee too high 275b
H. is free from clouds 69a
h. is like to a grain of mustard 506b
h. is music 78a
H. itself lies here 115a
h. itself wd. stoop to her 268a
H. lies about us in our infancy 466a
h. nor earth have been at peace 338b
h. not grim but fair of hue 48b
H. rejects the lore 467b
h.'s colour, the blue 284a
h. sends us good meat 158b
h.'s eternal year is thine 140b
H.'s gate, built in Jerusalem's wall 30b
h.'s gift takes earth's abatement 49a
H.'s great lamps do dive 78a
H.'s happy instrument 313b
H.'s last best gift 274b
H.'s light forever shines 392b
H.'s melodious strains 320b
h. smiles, and faiths..gleam 394a
h.'s morning breaks 251b
H. soon sets right 46a
H.'s pomp is spread on ground 464a
H. stops the nose 363a
h. such grace did lend her 372b
h. suffereth violence 506b
h.'s wide pathless way 268a
H., that but once was prodigal 140a
H. to gaudy day denies 74a
H. tries earth if it be in tune 251a
H. views it with delight 260b
h. vows to keep him 215a
h. was in him, before he was in h. 450b
he gain'd from H...a friend 174b
Hell afford the pavement of her H. 116b
her early H., her happy views 430a
himself the h.'s breath 344b
his blessed part to H. 386a
his h. commences 168a
his looks do menace h. 259a
his..name is heard no more in h. 275a
hours to wh. high H. doth chime 447b
how the floor of h. is thick inlaid 355a
I call h. and earth to witness 494b
if H. had looked upon riches 418a
if h. wd. make me such another 363b
I have an oath in h. 354b

Heaven (cont.)
I hope for h. thereby 86b
I'm farther off from h. 195a
imminent h. of his high soul 441b
in h., if I cry to you then 424a
inheritor of the kingdom of h. 481a
in my heart, tho' not in h. 188a
in that H. of all their wish 39b
in the day when h. was falling 200a
in the h., a perfect round 44b
in the silent summer h. 437b
I saw a new h. and a new earth 519b
I saw h. opened 519b
is he in h.? is he in hell? 290b
is not this house as nigh h. 283a
it may be that only in H. 306b
it's a corner of h. itself 461b
joy-bells ring in H.'s street 261b
kingdom of h. is at hand 504b
knell that summons thee to h. 347b
lay up..treasures in h. 505b
leave to avenging H. his..will 420a
leave to H. the measure 214a
lift my soul to h. 385b
loftiest star of unascended h. 397b
look for me in the nurseries of H. 441b
look how high the h. is 488a
louder than the bolts of h. 77a
love is h., and h. is love 71b, 317a
make a H. of Hell 271a
makes h. drowsy with the harmony 345a
make the face of h. so fine 366a
man is H.'s masterpiece 307a
mek' you think that H. is comin' 410a
met my dearest foe in h. 330a
mild H. a time ordains 278b
more than all in H. 70a
more than h. pursue 304a
more things in h. and earth 331b
moving thro' his clouded h. 469b
my h.'s extremest sphere 448b
my idea of h. is..pâtés de foie gras 404b
native to high H. 441a
needs find out new h., new earth 322a
not H...upon the past has power 142b
nothing true but H. 282b
nothing under H. so blue 415a
not scorned in h. 109b
now ye wait at H.'s Gate 235a
of so much fame in H. 269b
one h., one hell 44b
one of these cloths is h. 284a
only H. knew of them 293b
on Sunday h.'s gate stands ope 187a
order is H.'s first law 301b
or what's a h. for 44b
our Father wh. art in h. 505a
out of H. and just like me 441b
over his..head like h. is bent 392a
parting is all we know of h. 127b
pavilion of h. 393a
peopled...H. with Spirits masculine 276b
permission of all-ruling H. 271a
Philosophy, that leaned on H. 299a
plays such..tricks before high h. 276b
pomp, wh. he from h. doth bring 407b
quit the port o' H. 287b
read not h. or her 263b
reign in hell, than serve in h. 271b
remembrance fallen from h. 420b
riches of h.'s pavements 272a
ring the bells of H. 192a
see H.'s glories shine 38b
set in third story 439b
shall H.'s promise clothe..lovers 312a
short permit to H. 276b
shun the h. that leads men to..hell 389a
shut from h. 46b
shut thee from h. with a dome 194a
sings hymns at h.'s gate 387b
speaks of h. 11a
steep ascent of H. 184a
sure, I said, h. did not mean 195b
swear not..by h...God's throne 505a
tangled boughs of H. and Ocean 396a
that from H., or near it 398a
that kiss wh. is my h. to have 325a
that uncertain h. 469b
the brightest h. of invention 381a
the fair and open face of h. 221a

Heaven (*cont.*)

theirs is the kingdom of h.   505*a*
their spirits are in H.   472*b*
the lark, at h.'s gate sings   328*b*
then h. mocks itself   362*a*
th'opening bud to H. conveyed   100*b*
there may be h.   52*b*
there's h. above   47*b*
there's husbandry in h.   347*b*
there was silence in h.   519*a*
there was war in h.   519*a*
the seat..we must change for H.   271*a*
this is the gate of h.   493*a*
thorny way to h.   330*b*
those who win h., blest are they   49*a*
threw him from the face of heaven   258*b*
thro' H.'s wide champain   275*a*
thy soul's flight, if it find h.   348*b*
till in H. the deed appears   63*b*
'tis h…points out an hereafter   1*b*
'tis like a little H. below   453*a*
to be young was very h.   465*a*
to-day, between Hell and H.   313*a*
to grow old in H. is to grow young   312*a*
top of it reached to h.   493*a*
to the very bourne of h.   217*b*
to wh. H. has joined great issues   142*b*
to wh. the Hell I suffer seems a H.   273*b*
tradesman..hope to go to h.   387*a*
trouble deaf h. with my..cries   387*a*
turn thy back on h.   146*a*
under an English h.   40*a*
unlock the gate of H…let us in   3*b*
unreconciled as yet to h.   363*b*
uttermost part of the h.   482*b*
voice of Rome is the consent of h.   214*b*
waiting for the spark from H.   8*a*
warring in H. against H.'s..King   273*b*
was light from H.   63*a*
watered h. with their tears   32*a*
waves that beat on H.'s shore   29*b*
we are all going to h.   158*a*
weariness of climbing h.   396*a*
we know the way to h…by water   146*a*
we shall practise in h.   49*a*
what they do in h. we are ignorant   418*b*
when earth was nigher h.   50*a*
when they come to model H.   275*b*
whether in H. ye wander fair   31*b*
wh. in old days moved earth and h.   439*a*
who knows save h.   334*b*
whose h. shd. be true Woman   312*a*
why stand ye gazing up into h.?   512*a*
wish'd..H…made her such a man   360*a*
with him..either in h. or in hell   381*b*
without a thought of H. or Hell   41*b*
women [differ]..as H. and Hell   429*a*
yon are the hills o' H.   529*a*

Heavenly: even in h. place that busy archer   401*b*
h. paradise is that place   78*b*
once more the H. Power   426*b*
thy beauty's birth is h.   78*a*

Heavens: all the H. thou hast in Him   114*b*
ancient H., in silent awe   30*a*
awake! the h. look bright   281*b*
blue h. above us bent   431*b*
distorts the H. from pole to pole   30*a*
eternal in the h.   515*a*
feels the h. lie bare   443*a*
had I the h.' embroidered cloths   474*b*
h. declare the glory of God   482*b*
h. dropped at the presence of God   486*a*
h. fill with shouting   432*b*
his fabric of the H. hath left   275*b*
how many h. at once   115*a*
hung the h. with black   383*b*
I create new h.   503*b*
in the h. like a white fawn   476*a*
I will consider the h.   482*a*
most ancient h., thro' Thee, are fresh   464*a*
pure as the naked h.   467*b*
the h. are not too high   187*a*
the h. my wide roof-tree   12*b*
the h. themselves blaze forth   339*a*
the h. themselves, the planets   368*b*
the starry h. above me   568*b*
the starry h. above that plain   443*b*
till you are clothed with the h.   445*a*
when the h. are bare   466*a*

Heavens (*cont.*)

ye h. adore Him   224*a*
you promise h. free from strife   106*b*
Heaviness: h. foreruns the good event   380*b*
h. may endure for a night   483*b*
lay aside life-harming h.   375*a*
melody, in our h.   490*a*
praise for the spirit of h.   503*b*
so full of h., O my soul   484*b*
Heaving up my either hand   190*b*
Heavy: h., but no less divine   71*a*
light gains make h. purses   16*a*
makes it much more h.   369*a*
spins the h. world around   199*b*
with a weight, h. as frost   466*b*
Heavy-curled: even as, h…a charioteer   312*b*
Heavy-shotted hammock-shroud   429*b*
Hebraism: H. and Hellenism   9*b*
'he knows', says H., 'His Bible'   10*a*
Hebrew: an H. of the Hebrews   516*a*
Hebrews: are they H.? So am I   515*a*
Hebrid: each cold H. isle   103*a*
shepherd of the H. isles   443*a*
Hebrides: among the farthest H.   471*a*
among the stormy H.   443*b*
beyond the stormy H.   270*a*
seas colder than the H.   154*b*
we in dreams behold the H.   320*b*
Hecate: pale H.'s offerings   347*b*
Hector: H. and Lysander   526*a*
how was he changed from that H.   555*b*
the first H. of Troy   257*a*
Hecuba: what's H. to him   333*a*
Hedge: along the flowery h. I stray   424*b*
from h. to h. about the..mead   221*a*
high snowdrifts in the h.   199*b*
in the warm h. grew..eglantine   398*a*
sheets bleaching on the h.   373*a*
Hedgehog travels furtively   179*a*
Hedgehogs: thorny h.   356*b*
Hedges: meadows, with filigree h.   449*a*
unkempt about those h.   39*b*
walls have tongues, and h. ears   419*b*
Hedonist: a faddling h.   412*b*
Heed: h. naught else   232*a*
himself, will take no h. at all   470*a*
take h. o' the foul fiend   343*a*
take h. unto the thing   484*a*
Heeded: he heard it, but he h. not   69*a*
Heel: hoofed h. of a satyr   420*b*
lifted up his h. against me   484*b*
thou shalt bruise his h.   492*b*
Heels: at his h. a stone   335*b*
high h. are most agreeable   417*b*
kick h. with his throat in a rope   424*a*
only low h. in the administration   417*b*
show it a fair pair of h.   377*a*
stream'd out beyond his h.   218*a*
Heifer: plowed with my h.   495*a*
that h. lowing at the skies   219*b*
Heigh: h.-ho! sing h.-ho!   326*b*
h.! the sweet birds   373*a*
Height: altho' his h. be taken   389*a*
h. my soul can reach   44*a*
h. of this great argument   270*b*
in the blue heaven's h.   265*a*
measure yr. mind's h.   49*b*
none can usurp this h.   218*a*
nor h., nor depth   513*b*
on Sunium's h.   241*a*
takes the star's h.   423*b*
to the Holiest in the h.   288
we also know the sacred h.   27*a*
what pleasure lives in h.   437*a*
yonder mountain h.   437*a*
Heights: all the gifts from all the h.   49*a*
h. by great men reached   247*b*
h…soul is competent to gain   464*b*
higher than the h. above   110*a*
on the h. of Killiecrankie   12*a*
other h. in other lives   49*a*
trod the sunlit h.   459*b*
Heine for songs   46*b*
Heir: each second stood h. to the first   359*b*
first h. of my invention   386*b*
great h. of fame   278*a*
h. of all the ages   432*b*
h. of the whole world   445*a*
helped her to an h.   360*b*
her ashes new-create another h.   386*b*

Heir (*cont.*)

the destined h., in his soft cradle   216*b*
the hard h. strides about   430*b*
Heiresses: all h. are beautiful   140*b*
Heirs: h. thro' hope of thy..kingdom   480*b*
if children, then h.   513*b*
sole h. as well as you   445*a*
Helen: come H…give me my soul   258*b*
drove his ball thro' H.'s cheek   172*b*
dust hath closed H.'s eyes   285*b*
Heaven-born H.   313*a*
H. make me immortal with a kiss   258*b*
H.'s beauty in a brow of Egypt   357*b*
H., thy beauty is to me   298*a*
H., whose beauty summoned Greece   259*b*
I wish I were where H. lies   531*a*
Laodameia died; H. died   241*b*
Leda, was the mother of H.   293*a*
like another H., fir'd another Troy   139*a*
like H…when Troy was sacked   313*b*
the ravish'd H., Menelaus' queen   368*b*
white Iope, blithe H.   78*b*
Helena: all is dross that is not H.   258*b*
Helicon: where H. breaks down   5*b*
watered our horses in H.   87*b*
Hell: airs from heaven, or blasts from h.   331*a*
a liar gone to burning h.   363*b*
all h. broke loose   274*b*
all places shall be h.   258*b*
an agreement with h.   159*a*
and that's his h.   64*a*
an orphan's curse wd. drag to h.   99*a*
a swig in H. from Gunga Din   230*a*
Ay, there, look grim as h.   363*a*
better to reign in h.   271*b*
bid him go to H., to H. he goes   213*a*
builds a Heaven in H.'s despair   32*a*
builds a H. in Heaven's despite   32*a*
burn for ever in burning h.   423*a*
characters of h. to trace   173*b*
come hot from h.   339*b*
down, down to h.   384*b*
down to the Hinges o' H.   231*a*
England is a..h. for horses   64*b*
envy's a coal..hot from h.   18*a*
for the fiery gulf of h.   4*b*
for yr. love to her, lead apes in h.   366*b*
gates of h. can never   20*a*
gates of h. shall not prevail   507*a*
go to h. like lambs   92*b*
have the keys of h. and death   518*b*
having harrow'd h.   408*a*
having two eyes to be cast into h.   507*a*
heaven that leads men to this h.   389*a*
H. a fury, like a woman scorn'd   104*b*
Heaven and H. Amalgamation Society   82*a*
h. and night bring this..birth   360*b*
h. from beneath is moved for thee   502*a*
h. is a city much like London   396*b*
h. is full of musical amateurs   390*b*
h. is murky   350*a*
h.'s foundations quiver   20*a*
he said: 'h.'   284*a*
himself a devil frae h.   531*a*
improving..prisons in H.   100*b*, 406*b*
in danger of h. fire   505*a*
in h. they'll roast thee   63*a*
in the dunnest smoke of h.   346*b*
into the mouth of H.   426*a*
Italy a..h. for women   64*b*
it wd. be h. on earth   390*b*
jealousy..the injured lover's h.   275*a*
keep the gate of h.   363*a*
let H. afford the pavement   116*b*
made human life a h.   7*a*
Madness risen from h.   420*b*
make a Heaven of H.   271*a*
make a h. of this world   23*b*
marched—six—weeks in H.   227*b*
Milton wrote..at liberty..of H.   31*a*
more devils than vast h. can hold   357*b*
more than h. to shun   304*a*
myself am H.   273*b*
never mentions h. to ears polite   302*b*
night, the child of h.   383*a*
none admire that riches grow in h.   272*a*
oh threats of H.   153*a*
one heaven, one h.   44*b*

Hell (cont.)
parting..all we need of h. 127b
procuress to the Lords of H. 430a
rocks whose entrance leads to H. 267b
shalt not leave my soul in h. 482b
shout that tore h.'s concave 271b
sight of lidless eyes in H. 312a
slander, meanest spawn of H. 432a
soul from out immortal h. 433a
summons thee to heaven or to h. 347b
tears for all souls..here, and in h. 258a
that out of h. leads up to light 272b
the cunning livery of h. 352a
there is a dreadful H. 452b
there must be h. 52b
there was a way to h. 54a
tho' h. shd. bar the way 290a
thou profoundest H. 271a
to-day, between H. and Heaven 313a
to wh. the H. I suffer 273b
war..is all h. 401a
what h. it is, in suing long 409a
wh. way I fly is H. 273b
who art as black as h. 389b
whose music h. can move 78b
why this is h. 258b
with h. are we at an agreement 502a
without a thought of Heaven or H. 41b
worth ambition tho' in h. 271b
Hellas: a brighter H. 394a
to the gospel of H. 67a
Hellenism: Hebraism and H. 9b
Hellespont: cd..have passed the H. 70b
Propontic and the H. 362b
straight H. between..her breasts 132b
Hell-fires: an' dreamin' h. to see 230b
Hell-gate: flare of H. there 235b
Hellhound: h. always a h. 573b
Hellish dark, and smells of cheese 417a
Hell-kite: O h.! All? 350a
Hell-pains: as I hate h. 359b
Hells: tormented with..thousand h. 258b
Helmet: drank the red wine thro' the h. 316b
his h. now shall make a hive 295b
put off my h. to my countryman 324b
she saw the h. and the plume 431b
Helmsman: h. steered us through 98b
so the h. answered 248a
Help: comfort of thy h. again 485a
'e'll h. us by-an'-by 234a
first did h. to wound itself 374b
from whence cometh my h. 489b
H.! Fire! H.! the hare! 192b
h. from the sanctuary 482b
h. of the helpless 251b
h. us all by Thy grace 525a
h. us, this and every day 224a
here did England h. me 47b
his ready h. was ever nigh 210b
how can I h. England? 47b
I can't h. it 415b
lift not thy hands to It for h. 153b
love without the h. of anything 30b
not enough to h. the feeble up 368a
O God, our h. in ages past 453a
seeking h. from none 171b
since there's no h. 137b
there is no h. in them 490b
very present h. in trouble 484b
we have no h. but Thee 143b
we'll h. 'im for 'is mother 234a
what is past my h. 23a
yr. countrymen cannot h. 207a
Helped: being h., inhabits there 372b
we shall have h. it 127b
Helper: my h. and redeemer 484b
our antagonist is our h. 57b
Helpers: when other h. fail 251b
Helping: h. every feeble neighbour 171b
h., when we meet them, lame dogs 226a
Helpless: h., look to Thee for grace 445a
h.., naked, piping loud 32a
little, weak, and h. 3b
she's h. to hinder that or anything 180b
Helps: God h. them..h. themselves 157a
they used h., undergirding the ship 513a
Helter skelter, hang sorrow 215b
Hem: flying hair and fluttering h. 312b
red-rose-bordered h. 476b
Hemisphere: gilding the eastern h. 400a
Hemlock: burdocks, h., nettles 343b

Hen: h. gathereth her chickens 507b
he yaf nat of that text a pulled h. 88b
hickety, pickety, my black h. 534a
nine, ten, a good fat h. 532a
poor h.! fond of no second brood 328b
two Owls and a H, 243a
wondrous still, the cock and h. 31b
Hence: h., avaunt ('tis holy ground) 175a
h., dear delusion 403b
h., horrible shadow! 349a
h., loathed Melancholy 268b
h., with denial vain,..excuse 269a
h., ye profane; I hate ye all 107a
h., you long-legged spinners 356b
whither hurried h.! 153a
Henpecked: have they not h. you all 70a
Henry and Tobias 230a
Henry Clay: there's calm in a H. 227a
Henry King: chief defect of H. 26a
Henry Pimpernell 366b
Her: h. for all she made 230b
I learned about women from h. 230b
keeps their fallen day about h. 293a
never mind h.; go on talking 390b
Heraclitus: they told me, H. 106a
Herald: hark the h.-angels sing 455b
h. of a noisy world 112a
I wish no other h. 386b
last and greatest h. of Heaven's 137b
spring the h. of love's..king 408a
Heraldries: 'mong thousand h. 221b
Heraldry: boast of h. 174a
our new h. is hands not hearts 362b
Heralds of England's marshal 93b
Herb: sour h. of grace 375b
Herbert Tree 93a
Herbs: bitter h. they shall eat 493b
dinner of h. where love is 498a
excellent h. had our fathers 233a
h., and other country messes 269a
Medea gather'd the enchanted h. 355a
Hercules: H. and Cadmus once 357a
H. is not only known by his foot 42a
is not love a H. 345a
some of H. 526a
than I to H. 330a
Herd: habit rules the unreflecting h. 470a
h. ran violently down a steep place 506a
leave untended the h. 318b
left the h. long since 112a
lowing h. winds slowly 174a
tho' the h. have fled 282a
Herdman: faithful h.'s art 269b
Herdsman: God the h. 474a
Here: a bird to the right sang H. 422b
h. a little, and there a little 502a
h. am I; send me 501b
h. are a few..words 354b
h. did she fall a tear 375b
h. I and sorrows sit 374a
h. in my crystalline, h. in my
breast 289a
h. lies bold Robin Hood 530b
h. lies one who meant well 412b
h.'s a health to all 523b
h.'s to the charmer whose dimple's 400b
h.'s to the maiden of..fifteen 400b
h. to-day, and gone tomorrow 25a
h., unless I am mistaken, is our
client 136a
h. we are again! 238a
h. we come a-wassailing 523b
h. we come gathering nuts in May 523b
h., where the world is quiet 422a
h. will I remain 166b
I have been h. before 313a
it is good for us to be h. 507a
La Fayette, we are h. 296b
no noise h. 189a
of h. and everywhere 359b
Samuel..answered, H. am I 495a
'tis neither h. nor there 363a
Hereabouts he dwells 366a
Hereafter: by the all-hail h.! 346b
heaven..points out an h. 1b
here's yet in the word 'h.' 368b
she shd. have died h. 350b
what is love? 'tis not h. 370b
what may come h. 422a
Hereditary: beholds his own h. skies 142b
h. bondsmen 68a

Heresies: hateful h. 409a
new truths..begin as h. 203a
Heresy: h. signifies no more than..
opinion 191b
what an Englishman believes be h. 391b
Heretic: it is a h. that makes the fire 373a
Heretics: Infidels, and H. 479b
poor h. in love 133b
Heritage: an undefiled h. 227b
h. and gift that cometh 489b
I have a goodly h. 482b
our h. the sea 116a
that h. of woe 73a
we have come into our h. 39a
Hermaphrodite: giddy h. 234a
Hermes: thrice great H. 268a
Herminius: back, H. 253b
H. glared on Sextus 253b
H. smote Mamilus 254a
one of us two, H. 253b
Hermit: dwell a weeping h. there 103a
h. hoar, in solemn cell 211b
H. of the dale 169a
the holy H. raised his eyes 99b
this H. good lives in that wood 99b
Hermitage: minds..take that for an h. 249b
my gorgeous palace for a h. 375b
Hermits..contented with their cells 468a
Hermon: little hill of H. 484b
'Hernani': wait all day..to applaud
'H.' 413a
Hero: a h. must drink brandy 210a
a h. perish, or a sparrow fall 300b
came the h. from his prison 12b
every h. becomes a bore at last 148b
H. can be Poet..or what you will 80b
no man is a h. to his valet 561a
one non-flunky, one h. 81a
see the conquering h. comes 244a
the god-like h. sat 138b
to his very valet seemed a h. 67b
where her young h. sleeps 281b
Herod: it out-herods H. 333b
Heroes: all the world's brave h. 526a
country for h. to live in 246a
frightened both the h. so 84a
hail, ye h.! 198a
h. were good as warming pans 264b
like my peers the h. of old 50b
no thin red h. 235b
Saints, H., if we will 5a
thin red line of h. 235b
two h. to begin with 81a
Heroic: Samson..finished a life h. 278a
the h. for earth too hard 44b
Heroically: h. fashioned 465b
in one word, h. mad 138b
Heroine: when a h. goes mad 400a
Heroism: I will report all h. 458b
with you is h. upon land 458b
Heron, the Shuh-Shuh-gah 248b
Herostratus lives..burnt the Temple 42b
Herring: buy my caller h.' 285b
h. boxes without topses 280b
plague o' these pickle h. 370a
roast thee like a h.' 63a
Herring Pond: neighbours o'er the
H. 143a
the h. is wide 48b
this side of the h. 160b
Herrings: h. grew in the wood 534a
the Douglas in red h. 178a
Herself: gave me h. indeed 48a
Hertfordshire: plains of pleasant H. 240b
Hervey: call a dog H. 206a
men, women, and H.'s 280a
Hesper: a slippered H. 39b
Hesperian fables true 274a
Hesperides: fruit of the H. 442b
ladies of th' H. 277a
still climbing trees in the H. 345a
Hesperus: H. entreats thy light 214b
H. that led the starry host 274a
H. with the host of heaven came 457a
it was the schooner H. 249a
Heterodoxy: h. is another man's doxy 450b
H. or Thy-doxy 80b
Heterogeneity: definite coherent h. 408a
Hew: not h. him as a carcase 338b
somebody to h. and hack 65a
Hewers of wood 494b

Hexameter: in the h. rises the fountain's..column | 101b
Hexameters: barbarous h. | 427a
Hey: h.! diddle-diddle | 534a
H. for Garsington | 11a
H. for God Almighty | 11a, 224b
h., ho, the wind and the rain | 372a
h. nonino | 327b
h., then, up go we | 193a, 307a
into H. nonny, nonny | 358b
sing 'H. to you' | 165b
Hey-day in the blood is tame | 335a
Hi: he wd. answer to 'H.!' | 86a
h.-tiddley-hi-ti | 309b
Hiawatha's Chickens | 248b
Hic et ubique? then we'll shift | 331b
Hic jacet: narrow words H. | 308a
Hickety, pickety, my black hen | 534a
Hickory, Dickory, Dock | 534a
Hid: I will find where truth is h. | 332a
thou hast h. these things | 509a
wherefore are these things h. | 369b
wh. is, to keep that h. | 134a
Hidden: half h. from the eye | 470b
nature is often h. | 16a
Hide: for all 'is dirty h. | 229b
h., h., yr. golden light | 248b
h. me by the bracken | 530b
h. me, O my Saviour | 455b
h. me under the shadow | 482b
is there no baseness we wd. h.? | 430a
let me h. myself in thee | 445a
my h. is sure to flatten 'em | 25b
stream that must for ever h. me | 386a
that one talent wh. is death to h. | 278b
to h. the things 'e said | 234a
whose h. he sold | 448b
Hideous: ingratitude..more h...in a child | 342a
too h. to be shown | 361b
Hides: h. from itself its state | 214a
h. the ruin that it feeds upon | 110b
Hidest: thou art a God that h. thyself | 502b
Hiding the Skeleton | 264a
Hiding-place: as a h. from the wind | 502a
his dark and lonely h. | 100b
Hiding-places ten years deep | 472b
Higden: Mrs. H., you was a woman | 125b
Higginbottom: the last words of H. | 403b
High: afraid of that wh. is h. | 499b
all the trees they are so h. | 531a
as h. as Heaven above | 527b
as h. as we have mounted | 470a
be yrs. to hold it h. | 256a
for of the most H. cometh healing | 521a
from h. life h. characters are drawn | 301b
heaven is for thee too h. | 275b
heavens are not too h. | 187a
I am low, thou art h. | 422a
I only know it shall be h. | 200a
is there knowledge in the Most H. | 486b
it is just so h. as it is | 323b
look how h. the heaven is | 488a
pitch this one h. | 5a
she is the Broad, I am the H. | 528b
slain in thy h. places | 495b
so h., that looking downward | 311b
strive to wind ourselves too h. | 224a
surge..cannot be heard so h. | 343b
the h. that proved too h. | 44b
this h. man, aiming at a million | 47a
this h. man, with a great thing | 47a
thou art gone up on h. | 486b
up above the world so h. | 425a
ye'll tak' the h. road | 525b
you in yr. hansom leave the H. | 307b
High-Churchman: a furious H. I was | 524a
High-cultured: souls, h. as her soil | 77b
High diddle diddle..rank as an idyll | 165b
Higher: friend, go up h. | 509b
h. than the heights above | 110a
look'd six inches h. | 114a
the h. he 's a getting | 190b
the steps were h. that they took | 141b
Highest: counsel of the most H. | 488b
glory to God in the h. | 508b
my duty to have loved the h. | 428a
needs must love the h. | 428a
trouthe is the h. thing | 89b
Highflyer: Mrs. Boffin..a h. | 125b
High-handed: career of h. wrong | 87a

High jinks: forgotten pastime of h. | 319b
Highland: between lowland and h. | 421b
I'll forgive yon H. chief | 77a
my sweet H. Mary | 61a
Oh! where is yr. H. laddie gone? | 217a
sweet H. Girl | 465b
the bloody H. blade | 317a
the heart is H. | 320b
yon solitary H. lass | 471a
Highlandman: breeks aff a wild H. | 319a
Highlands: Chieftain to the H. | 77a
in the h. | 414b
my heart's in the H. | 62a, 320a
will ye gang to the H. wi' me | 526a
ye H. and ye Lowlands | 530b
Highly: what thou wouldst h. | 346b
High-minded: Lord, I am not h. | 490a
High-mindedness: joss-sticks and.. | 35a
High-Park: beyond H.'s a desart | 149a
Highway: a h. for our God | 502b
by the broad h. of the world | 393b
h...you my chief Parnassus be | 402a
I'll be buried in the king's h. | 375b
in lane, h., or open street | 445b
Highwayman came riding | 290a
Highways: go out into the h. and hedges | 509a
happy h. where I went | 199b
Hilarity: sinking flame of h. | 125a
Hill: a distant clearness in the h. | 430b
alas, that the longest h. must end | 24b
as the h. of Basan | 486b
at the other side of the h. | 454b
behind the cloud-topped h. | 300b
below the kirk, below the h. | 98a
city that is set on a h. | 505a
down the h. dart | 24b
flee as a bird unto the h. | 482a
hanged on the highest h. | 232b
h. athwart a cedarn cover | 101a
h. beside the silver Thames | 37b
h. of everlasting youth | 36b
hunter home from the h. | 415a
I climbed a h. as light fell | 192a
if the h. will not come to Mahomet | 15a
is this the h.? is this the kirk? | 99b
I stood tip-toe upon a little h. | 218b
I stood upon that silent h. | 192b
King of France went up the h. | 532a
laughing is heard on the h. | 32b
little h. of Hermon | 484b
nursed upon the self-same h. | 269a
on a h. during a clear midnight | 180b
others apart sat on a h. retir'd | 272b
over h., over dale | 356b
poor Wat, far off upon a h. | 386b
so is God's h. | 486b
the dew of yon high eastward h. | 329b
there is a green h. far away | 3b
the warder silent on the h. [Pitt] | 317b
to sit upon a h., as I do | 384a
to their haven under the h. | 425b
traveller's dream under the h. | 30a
up h. 'Too-slow' will need the whip | 435b
up to the top of the h. | 526b
we clamb the h. thegither | 61a
we flung us on the windy h. | 39b
who shall rest upon thy holy h.? | 482a
youth..face towards the upland h. | 137b
Hillflower: sunrise..like any h. | 312a
Hillmen desire their Hills | 234a
Hills: across the h. they went | 426b
a silence in the h. | 430a
before the h. in order stood | 453a
behold you again..h. of home! | 414b
bound of the everlasting h. | 493b
but, while the h. remain | 435b
by the h. of Maryland | 458b
domes the red-plow'd h. | 426b
fair h. of Éire! | 258a
floats on high o'er vales and h. | 467a
forests ancient as the h. | 101a
foundations are upon the holy h. | 487a
go up as high as the h. | 488a
great h. of the South Country | 26b
hillmen desire their H. | 234a
h. look over on the South | 441a
h. peep o'er h. | 300a
h. stand about Jerusalem | 489b
I heard among the solitary h. | 469a

Hills (cont.)
in Cheviot the h. so hye | 530b
larger than human on..frozen h. | 429a
lift up mine eyes unto the h. | 489b
little h. [bring] righteousness | 486b
little h. shall rejoice | 486a
my h. are white over with sheep | 399b
o'er the h. and far away | 426b
o'er these dark h. of time | 33b
over the h. and far away | 415a, 533a
praise the Lord who made the h. | 235a
rivers: wh. run among the h. | 488a
shine forth upon our clouded h. | 31a
sleep that is among the lonely h. | 463a
stray over the h. and far away | 159b
strength of the h. is his also | 487b
the cattle upon a thousand h. | 485a
the high h. are a refuge | 488b
the h. where his life rose | 5a
then shook the h. with thunder | 77a
these high wild h. | 375a
the waters stand in the h. | 488a
those blue remembered h. | 199b
tho' the h. be carried into the..sea | 484b
to the h. and the vales | 424b
under the shadowy h. | 464b
what h. are yon, yon pleasant h. | 529a
why hop ye so, ye high h. | 486b
yon are the h. o' Heaven | 529a
yr. name to the reverberate h. | 370a
Hill-side: fades..up the h. | 220a
on the cold h. | 219a
the h.'s dew-pearled | 50a
travels yet the loved h. | 9a
Hilts: hides a sword from h. | 381b
she's loose i' the h. | 454a
Him: all of H. we have in thee | 114b
h. first, h. last | 275a
h. that cometh to me | 510b
h. they found squat like a toad | 274b
they all cried 'That 's h.' | 19a
Himalay: east of H. | 442b
Himself: born unto h. alone | 307a
centre of a man's actions, h. | 15b
ech man for h. | 89a
He doth H. impart | 224a
he has done it all h. | 21b
h. he cannot save | 508a
h., his..neighbour, and Me | 251a
h. sole author of his own disgrace | 109a
hurl'd h. into the scale | 282a
in h. possess his own desire | 465a
lord of h., tho' not of lands | 473b
loved him for h. alone | 400a
no man is demolished but by h. | 27b
that can h. knowe | 89a
unless above h. he can erect h. | 117a
when he spake of h. | 149b
when the fight begins within h. | 45a
who finds h., loses his misery | 8b
who to h. is law | 87a
word politics surprises by h. | 126a
Hinder: pawing to get free his h. | 275b
smote his enemies in the h. parts | 487a
Hindered: sore let and h. | 479a
Hinders: if anyone h. our coming | 227b
Hindmost: devil take the h. | 65a
we'll send the mild H. | 527b
Hindoo: marries, dies, or turns H. | 395b
Hindostan: he came from H. | 439b
Hindrance: pointing at h. | 35b
tho' it were to his own h. | 482b
Hindrances: what various h. we meet | 110a
Hinds: h. to bring forth young | 483b
nimbler much than h. | 261a
Hinges grate harsh thunder | 273a
Hint: I may, without vanity, h. | 281a
it gave him a h. | 100b
it was my h. to speak | 360a
upon this h. I spake | 360a
with shadowed h. confuse a life | 430a
Hip: catch him once upon the h. | 353a
I have you on the h. | 355a
smote them h. and thigh | 495a
Hipped discourses | 175b
Hippocleides: H. doesn't care | 559b
Hippocrene: the blushful H. | 219b
Hippogriff: without wing of h. | 277a
Hippopotamus: big h. stuck in the door | 526b

Hippopotamus (*cont.*)
found it was a H. 85b
I shoot the H. 25b
Hips: we swing ungirded h. 406a
Hire: the labourer is worthy of his h. 509a
Hired: they h. the money 570b
Hireling: pay given to a state h. 213a
the h. fleeth, because he is a h. 511a
Hirelings: into his church lewd h. 273b
His: He is mine, and I am H. 188a
Hiss: dismal universal h. 276b
Historian: h. wants more documents 204a
life of the h. must be short 162a
useless to the h. of the Roman Empire 161b
Historians: phrase of wh. bad h. are ..fond 255a
these gentle h. 58a
Histories: h. make men wise 16a
joyous and pleasant h. 257a
History: all knowledge..a product of h. 80a
annals are blank in h.-books! 80b
antiquities are h. defaced 13a
antiquities..some remnants of h. 13a
assassination..never changed..h. 128b
below the dignity of h. 255b
by some named H. 81b
culture..h. of the human spirit 10a
dust-heap called 'h.' 28b
ends this strange eventful h. 326b
exceeds an infamous h. 42b
future date of my H. 162a
happiest women..have no h. 144b
her whose h. began before God 476b
h. a distillation of rumour 80b
h...biography of great men 80b
h. is a pack of lies 415b
h. is bunk 155b
h. is the essence of..biographies 80a
H. is Philosophy..by examples 33b
h. of art is the h. of revivals 66b
h. of England..h. of progress 254a
it takes a great deal of h. 204a
maintained the dignity of h. 33b
no h.; only biography 147b
now become a h. little known 109b
read no h. 129b
read their h. in a nation's eyes 174b
there is a h. in all men's lives 380b
very few materials for h. 162a
vile phrase..'the dignity of h.' 255a
War makes rattling good h. 179b
what 's her h.? 371a
Hit: a h., a very palpable h. 337a
if you wd. h. the mark 247a
I never think I have h. hard 208b
Hitched: you mean gettin' h. 451a
Hither: come h., come h. 326a
h. hurried *whence*? 153a
h., page, and stand by me 286b
Hitherto shalt thou come 497b
Hittites, and the Amorites 493b
Hive: h. for the honey-bee 475a
this great h., the city 107a
Hives: fill our h. with honey 417b
Hiving wisdom with each..year 68b
Hivites, and the Jebusites 493b
Ho, every one that thirsteth 503a
Hoard: boastful of her h. 170a
learning, a mere h. of gold 380b
our h. is little 428b
Hoar-frost: scattereth the h. 490b
Hoarse: h. with..little else to do 74b
the raven himself is h. 346b
Hob-and-nob with..Death 439a
Hobbes clearly proves 419b
Hobby-horse: the h. is forgot 334a
Hobden owns the land 230b
Hobgoblin of little minds 147b
Hockley: Hey H. 11a
Hodge to be out of countenance 211a
Hodgson: O Beer! O H., Guinness 75a
Hoe: darned long row to h. 250a
he leans upon his h. 258b
take a large h. and a shovel also 230b
tickle her with a h. 205b
Hoel's harp 173b
Hog: Ah could eat h. a solid hower 264b
h. 's my feed 264b
liken his Grace to an acorned h. 47a

Hoi polloi no matter what they think 142a
Hoist: h. with his own petar 335a
shall they h. me up and show me 325a
Holborn: when I was last in H. 385a
Holcroft: Lamb, H. and Coleridge 183a
Hold: h. both thee and me 411b
H., enough 351a
h. fast that wh. is good 516b
h. fast the form of sound words 516b
h., or cut bow-strings 356b
h. thee to my heart 169a
how do I h. thee 388b
I h. it towards you 219a
they h. all together 485b
to cry 'H., h.!' 346b
where scowls the far-famed h. 253a
Hold-fast is the only dog 382a
Holds: he h. him with his..eye 98a
he h. me well 360b
h. him with his skinny hand 98a
she h. her little thoughts 265a
Hole: by the h. of the door 500b
creeps in at every h. 295b
h. where..tail came through 100b, 406b
if you knows of a better h. 570a
into the square h. 405a
stick'n in a big mud h. 156a
there's a h. in a' yr. coats 62a
yr. hat has got a h. in't 78b
Holes where eyes..inhabit 384b
Holiday: butcher'd..make Roman h. 69a
but hit be seldom, on the h. 89b
envy never makes h. 13b
get you home: is this a h. 337a
he speaks *holiday* 356a
h., the beggar's shop is shut 366a
in a h. humour 327b
ne moe atte h. 88a
to play on a sunshine h. 269a
we no h. have seen 108a
with many h. and lady terms 376b
Holidays: all the year..playing h. 376b
Holiest: mother..the h. thing alive 102a
Holily: that wouldst thou h. 346b
Holiness: courage of heart or h. 26a
for a remembrance of his h. 483b
go! put off H. 30b
h. of the heart's affection 222a
what he..lost in h. 66b
Hollaing, and singing of anthems 379b
Holland: children in H. take 526b
H...lies so low 196b
in the deep where H. lies 170a
Lowlands o' H. has twin'd my love 531b
Hollanders: the H. an invisible eel 216a
Hollo: came to the mariner's h.! 98b
Holloa: we'll whoop and we'll h. 459a
Hollow: arch of the leaves was h. 422b
h. murmurs died away 103a
h. of Jacob's thigh 493a
I hate the dreadful h. 433b
I plucked a h. reed 32b
makes the h. seas, that roar 260a
Providence fashioned us h. 250a
tell the grassy h. 263b
the fearful h. of thine ear 366a
we are the h. men 145a
Hollowed a little mournfully 284b
Hollowness, treachery, and all.. disorders 341b
Hollows: bowery h. crowned 429b
Holly: heigh-ho! the h. 326b
h. and the ivy 526b
h. bears the crown 526b
the h. branch shone on the old oak 22a
Holmes: 'commonplace', said H. 136a
H. remarked impatiently 136a
to..H... [Irene]..*the* woman 135a
Holocaust: lay erewhile a h. 278a
Holsters and cartridge boxes 390a
Holy: all the place is h. ground 435b
called her his before the h. man 77a
He died to make men h. 200b
hence, avaunt ('tis h. ground) 175a
her smile, it seems half h. 43b
he that is h. let him be h. still 520b
h., divine, good 276a
h., fair, and wise 372b
H., H., H.! Lord God Almighty! 184a
H., h., h., Lord God of hosts 480b

Holy (*cont.*)
h. was the Sabbath bell 221b
hunters been nat h. men 88b
it was an h. and good thought 521b
neither h., nor Roman 566a
said h., h., h., is the Lord 501b
saying H., h., h., Lord God 518b
thou continuest h. 483a
thy H. One to see corruption 482b
whereso'er it be, a h. place 311b
Holy Ghost: by the operation of the H. 480b
come, H., our souls inspire 491a
H. over the bent world broods 197b
no gold, no H. 566a
pencil of the H. hath laboured 14a
whether there be any H. 512b
yr. body is the temple of the H. 514a
Holy Land: wh..I supposed the H. 381a
Homage: claims the h. of a tear 68a
do h. to thy King 407b
each under eye doth h. 387a
owes no h. unto the sun 42a
Home (Hame): a day's march nearer h. 280a
almost sacred joys of h. 283a
as we draw near h. 70a
be happy as ever at h. 37b
behold ye again..hills of h.! 414b
best country ever is, at h. 170a
brought him h. at even-fall 436b
by water he sente hem h. 88b
charity begins at h. 42a
comes safe h. 383a
don't want to go h. in the dark 185b
dream that I am h. again 154b
dreamt not of a perishable h. 467b
dunce that has been kept at h. 110b
earth is all the h. I have 12b
eaten me out of house and h. 380a
England, h. and beauty 34b, 123a
from Thy celestial h. 86b
gade to bring him h. 193a
grows erect, as that comes h. 134a
her h. is on the deep 78a
he shall have a cheerful h. 432b
Hierusalem, my happy h. 523b
his floating h. for ever left 107b
his luminous h. of waters opens 8a
h. art gone and ta'en thy wages 329a
h. had she none 195b
his footsteps he hath turn'd 317a
h. is the girl's prison 391a
h. is the sailor, h. from the sea 415a
h.-keeping youth 372b
h. life of our own dear Queen 573b
H. of lost causes 9a
h. of the Arts 185a
h. on the rolling deep 315b
h., Rose, and h., Provence 96a
h.'s h. be it never so hamely 4b
h., sweet, sweet h. 294b
h. they bought her warrior dead 436b
h. they brought him slain 436b
h., you idle creatures 337a
I am far from h. 288b
if all alas! were well at h. 94b
I had a h. once 407a
I'm come h., my love 20b
intruders on his ancient h. 2b
it's h. and it's h...fain wad I be 116a
lady-cow, fly thy way h. 534a
little grey h. in the west 461b
man goeth to his long h. 500a
near to their eternal h. 449a
never h. came she 226b
of youth and h. 282a
old folks at h. 156a
our eternal h. 453a
pleasure never is at h. 218a
points of heaven and h. 471a
safe h., safe h. in port 287a
shall I never feel at h. 452b
shall never more go h. 253b
sick for h. 220a
the lark shall sing me h. 116b
the next way h. 's the farthest 307a
there is a blessed h. 18a
there shd. be peace at h. 452b
there's no place like h. 294b
they dream of h. 156a

Home (cont.)
they filled one h. with glee — 184b
thou must bring her h. — 529b
thy great gift. .comes h. again — 388b
thy h. is still here — 282a
to their h. among the dead — 393b
turns again h. — 426a
uneasy and confined from h. — 300b
we all go the same way h. — 285a
we won't go h. till morning — 53b
what is h. without a mother? — 182b
what 's the good of a h. — 177a
when I was at h. — 326a
when thou must h. to shades — 78b
where Huntley, and where H.? — 318b
white porch of his h. — 253b
who gives a child a h. — 261b
you'd best be getting h. — 85b
Home-brewed prayer. .prefer — 175b
Home-keeping hearts — 248b
Homeless: h. near a thousand homes — 465a
those who are h. by choice — 407a
Homely: it is for h. features to keep — 267b
Home-made dishes — 195a
Homer: contend for H. dead — 321b
deep-browed H. — 220b
dumb to H., dumb to Keats — 49b
ere H.'s lamp appeared — 111b
Greece, sound thy H.'s. .name — 109a
H. and Virgil are forgotten — 304b
H...'his eye on the object' — 10a
H. is not more decidedly the first — 255a
H.'s golden chain — 64b
H. sometimes sleeps — 71a
H.'s rule the best — 303b
H. usually good, nods — 542b
in H. more than H. knew — 419b
in H. or in Dares — 90a
living H. begg'd his bread — 321b
our poets steal from H. — 64a
the translator of H. — 10a
when H. smote his blooming lyre — 236b
winked at H. down the road — 236b
with the single exception of H. — 390a
Homes: cottage h. of England — 185a
near a thousand h. I stood — 465a
sky. .their own natural h. — 99a
stately h. of England — 184b
Homesickness for the gutter — 561a
Home-spuns: hempen h. — 357a
Homewards: most roads lead men h. — 262a
Homily: worm-cankered h. — 438a
Homing: spirits of those who were h. — 180a
Hominy: to be presented. .by a H. — 124a
Homocea touches the spot — 523b
Homogeneity: incoherent h. — 408a
Hone: ingenuous H. — 240b
Honest: a few h. men. .better than numbers — 115b
anglers, or very h. men — 450b
an h. exceeding poor man — 353b
an h. man's aboon his might — 60b
an h. man's son — 353b
by nature h., by experience wise — 303a
friends were poor but h. — 322a
good to be h. and true — 524b
h. as any man living — 359a
h. by an act of parliament — 214b
h. God's the noblest work of man — 67a
h. man, close-button'd to the chin — 109a
h. man's the noblest work of God — 59b, 301b
h. tale speeds best — 385a
h. without a thought of Heaven — 41b
I am myself indifferent h. — 333b
I am not naturally h. — 373b
I be poor, I'm h. — 265b
is not an h. man — 456b
I think my wife is h. — 362a
necessity makes an h. man a knave — 118b
the world's grown h. — 332a
thinks when h. that but seem. .so — 360b
tho' it be h., it is never good — 323b
to be direct and h. is not safe — 362a
to be h., as this world goes — 332a
to be h., to be kind — 412a
whatsoever things are h. — 516a
Honester: old man and no h. than I — 359a
Honesty: children capable of h. — 314b
corruption wins not more than h. — 386b

Honesty (cont.)
fellow's of exceeding h. — 361b
fly, H., fly! — 404a
for saving of thine h. — 283a
h...based. .in vacant heaven — 314b
H. is the best policy — 456a
h., manhood, nor good fellowship — 376b
I am arm'd so strong in h. — 340b
I hold it not h. to have it thus — 332a
liv'st to make thine h. a vice — 362a
rich h. dwells like a miser — 328a
thy h. and love doth mince — 361a
what a fool H. is — 373b
Honey: as the h. of Hybla — 376b
but taste a little h. — 495a
butter and h. shall he eat — 501b
civil citizens kneading up the h. — 381b
eating bread and h. — 533b
eat our pot of h. on the grave — 264a
fill our hives with h. and wax — 417b
gather h. all the day — 453a
his meat was locusts and wild h. — 504b
h. of all earthly joy — 107a
is there h. still for tea? — 40a
it was in my mouth sweet as h. — 519a
money is h.—my little sonny — 41a
nor h. make, nor pair — 102a
suck'd the h. of his music vows — 333b
sweeter also than h. — 482b
they surfeited with h. — 378a
we gather h. from the weed — 382b
with milk and h. blest — 286a
Honeycomb: broiled fish and. .h. — 510b
Honey-dew: he on h. hath fed — 101b
Honeyed middle of the night — 221b
Honeyless: leave them h. — 341a
Honey-suckle: you are my honey, h. — 152a
Honorificabilitudinitatibus — 345a
Honour: all is lost save h. — 563a
as he was valiant I h. him — 339b
brothers all in h. — 469b
by h. and dishonour — 515a
can h. set-to a leg — 379a
can h.'s voice provoke the. .dust — 174a
clear h. were purchased — 353b
curses. .mouth-h., breath — 350b
days, riches and h. — 496b
depths and shoals of h. — 386a
fear God. H. the king — 517b
fount whence h. springs — 259a
from the book of h. razed — 387a
giving h. unto the wife — 517b
good luck have thou with thine h. — 484b
great peaks of h. — 246a
hearts that h. cd. not move — 40a
he is the fountain of h. — 16b
helps the hurt that H. feels — 432a
his h. and his toil — 439a
h. all men. Love the brotherhood — 517b
h. and clean mirth — 227b
h., as long as waves shall break — 287b
h. aspireth to death — 14a
h. be yours, and fame! — 287b
h. but an empty bubble — 139a
h. comes unlooked for — 379a
h. has come back — 39a
h. hath no skill in surgery — 379a
h. is a mere scutcheon — 379a
h. is the subject of my story — 337b
h., love, obedience — 350b
h. of the British Army — 238a
h. pricks me on — 379a
h. rooted in dishonour — 428b
h.'s a mistress all. .pursue — 457a
h. shamefully misplaced — 388a
h. sinks where commerce — 170a
h.'s thought reigns solely — 381b
h. the shrine where you alone — 176b
h. thy father and thy mother — 480a
h. to whom h. — 513b
h. travels in a strait — 369a
h. was the meed of victorie — 408b
h. wh. they do not understand — 468a
h., while you strike him down — 287b
how I do h. thee! — 354b
idiot race to h. lost — 62a
if h. gives greatness, was great — 120b
if it be a sin to covet h. — 383a
I h., love and embrace them — 42a
I like not such grinning h. — 379a
in action faithful, and in h. clear — 302b

Honour (cont.)
in dignitye or h. goeth to hym — 143a
in h. preferring one another — 513b
jealous in h. — 326b
keep mine h. from corruption — 386b
laud and h. to the Father — 286b
leave not a stain in thine h. — 521a
loaden with h. — 328b
louder he talked of his h. — 147a
loved I not h. more — 250a
loved chivalrye, trouthe and h. — 88a
make one vessel unto h. — 513b
man being in h. — 485a
mine h. is my life — 374b
new-made h. doth forget. .names — 373b
no point of h., or gay suit — 187a
not without h. my days ran — 452b
nought. .in hate, but all in h. — 364a
peace. .maintained with h. — 315a
peace, I hope, with h. — 128b
pension list. .a roll of h. — 95b
perfect ways of h. — 386b
perseverance. .keeps h. bright — 369a
pluck bright h. from the. .moon — 377a
pluck up drowned h. by the locks — 377a
post of h. is a private station — 1b
prophet is not without h. — 507a
robb'd me of my Robe of H. — 154a
set h. in one eye — 337b
so h. cross it from the north — 377a
so h. peereth in. .meanest habit — 366b
some love England and her h. yet — 438a
some snatch of h. — 341b
still clinging. .to some rag of h. — 412a
take h. from me — 374b
that chastity of h. — 57a
that h. wd. thee do — 381b
the greater share of h. — 383a
there H. comes, a pilgrim grey — 103a
they smack of h. both — 346a
to h. we call you — 158b
Truth the masculine of H. — 181a
two men I h., and no third — 81b
welcome maids of h. — 190b
what is h.? a word — 379a
when h.'s at the stake — 335b
where thine h. dwelleth — 483b
while the h. thou hast got — 65a
whom the king delighteth to h. — 496b
with native h. clad — 274a
with the burthen of an h. — 432b
Ye take mine h. from me — 231a
yr. quaint h. turn to dust — 260a
Honourable: Brutus is an h. man — 339b, 340a
h. alike in what we give — 245a
that have done this deed are h. — 340a
Honoured: followed him, h. him — 48a
h. by the Muse he lov'd — 299b
h. for his burning throne — 352b
how loved, how h. once — 299b
Lyeus. .ever h., ever sung — 23b
man. .is h. for them — 36b
more h. in the breach — 331a
not least, but h. of them all — 438b
the Law: It has h. us — 454a
Honouring: not so much h. thee — 216b
Honours: claim to poetical h. — 213a
from what a depth proceed thy h. — 470a
gods, who make them h. — 343b
he gave his h. to the world — 386a
his blushing h. thick upon him — 385b
mindless of its just h. — 470b
patent for his h. .from. .God — 60a
whereby piled-up h. perish — 46a
Hood: him that wears an h. — 415a
tea-cup times of h. and hoop — 438a
the witty and the tender H. — 241a
Hoods: cowls, h., and habits — 273b
Hoofs: h. of a swinish multitude — 57a
when the plunging h. were gone — 119b
Hook: draw out Leviathan with an h. — 497b
he for subscribers baits his h. — 94b
never fly conceals a h. — 39b
while thy h. spares the next — 221b
with saints doth bait thy h. — 351b
Hookah-mouth: puffs from the h. — 227a
Hooker: I'd sail this h. — 236a
Judicious. .H. — 573b
Hook-nosed fellow of Rome — 380b
Hooks: develop his h. and his crooks — 62b

Hooks (*cont.*)

silken lines, and silver h.	132a

Hoop: jump at a gilded h. — 195a
Hoo-ray and up she rises — 527b
Hooter: because the h. hoots — 92b
Hooting: bird of night. . h. — 338a
  h. at the glorious sun — 100b
  remained there thro' night h. — 25a
Hoots: clamorous owl, that nightly h. — 356b
Hop: h. forty paces thro' the public
  street — 323a
  who lets it h. a little — 365b
  why h. ye so, ye high hills? — 486b
Hope: admiration, h. and love — 464b
  against h. believed in h. — 513a
  all h. abandon, ye who enter — 566b
  all h. pleasure in what. . remain — 139b
  a man of h. and forward-looking — 464b
  beacons of h., ye appear! — 7b
  break it to our h. — 351a
  burning with high h. — 68b
  but my h. is better — 372a
  but not another's h. — 450a
  darkness quieted by h. — 52a
  equal h., and hazard — 271a
  faith, h., charity — 514b
  fear and trembling H. — 473a
  frustrate h. severer than despair — 109a
  giving it a h. that there — 216b
  god-like wish, or h. divine — 464a
  heirs thro' h. of thy. . kingdom — 480b
  he may live without h. — 265a
  he that lives upon h. — 157a
  high up lifted beyond h. — 272a
  H. an Antinoüs mere — 96a
  h. and fear, and peace and strife — 319b
  h. and fear set free — 422a
  H. clung feeding, like a bee — 102a
  h. deferred maketh the heart sick — 498a
  h. elevates, and joy brightens — 276a
  h., for a season, bade. . farewell — 77a
  h. is a good breakfast — 13b
  h. is less dear than the dew — 474b
  h. maketh not ashamed — 513a
  h. may vanish, but can die not — 394a
  h. never comes that comes to all — 271a
  h. of all the ends of the earth — 486a
  h. of a season's fame — 287b
  h. of eternal damnation — 523a
  h. of fair advantages — 353a
  h. of the City of God — 262a
  h. once crushed, less quick — 9a
  H. sows what Love. . never reap — 312a
  H.'s perpetual breath — 471b
  h. springs eternal in the. . breast — 300b
  h.'s true gage — 307b
  h. that can never die — 469b
  h. . . the gleaming taper's light — 168a
  h. thou not much — 422b
  h. to write well hereafter — 279a
  h. without an object cannot live — 102a
  I have nor h. nor health — 399a
  I h. for heaven thereby — 86b
  in faith and h. the world — 301b
  in trembling h. repose — 174b
  leave the light of H. behind — 77b
  like Lucifer, never to h. again — 386a
  like to one more rich in h. — 387a
  loving longest. . when h. is gone — 11b
  more h. of a fool than of him — 498b
  much to h. and nothing to lose — 58a
  my own h. is — 44b
  Nature, H., and Poesy — 102a
  never h. for glory — 414a
  no h. who never had a fear — 113a
  no one h., but of his fees — 190b
  no other medicine but only h. — 351b
  not without h. we suffer — 468b
  nursing the unconquerable h. — 8a
  of friends, of h., of all bereft — 107b
  old h. goes to ground — 48a
  one H.'s one name be there — 312b
  on h. the wretch relies — 168a
  our h. for years to come — 453a
  perished leaves of H. — 312a
  pursued it with forks and h. — 86a
  reinforcement we may gain from h. — 271a
  so farewell h., and with h. . . fear — 273b
  some blessed h., whereof he knew — 179a
  sure and certain h. — 481b
  take back the h. you gave — 47b

Hope (*cont.*)

  tender leaves of h. — 385b
  that h. unsatisfied brings — 171b
  their h. full of immortality — 520a
  the phantoms of h. — 213b
  they h. they serve God — 359a
  to feed on h., to pine with fear — 409a
  to h. till H. creates — 397b
  triumph of h. over experience — 208a
  true h. is swift — 385a
  was the h. drunk — 347a
  what is h. but deceiving? — 265a
  what was dead was H. — 459b
  when all h. seem'd desp'rate — 282a
  whence this pleasing h. — 1b
  where. . h. cd. ne'er have flown — 260a
  where there is life, there's h. — 160b
  white-handed H., thou. . angel — 267a
  widowhood, is the only h. — 159b
  wish for what I faintly h. — 141b
  without all h. of day — 277b
  woes wh. H. thinks infinite — 397b
  work without h. draws nectar — 102a
  Worldly H. men set their Hearts — 152b
  yet fooled with h. — 139b
  youth whose h. is high — 37a
Hoped: he who has never h. — 389a
  h. we were both broken-hearted — 422b
  said he *had* h., at least — 86a
Hopeful: hey, but I'm h. — 165b
Hope-hour: as the h. stroked — 179a
Hopeless: h. grief is passionless — 43b
  the h. horn blown — 92a
  the h. lance was laid in rest — 92a
Hopes: airy h. my children — 464a
  all his h. of good — 9a
  all revolution in the h. . . of men — 470a
  all the h. of future years — 246b
  extravagant h. of the future — 56b
  fifty h. and fears — 45a
  had h. to win her — 105a
  h. and fears it heeded not — 398a
  h. and fears of all the years — 40a
  h. of earthly bliss — 112b
  if h. were dupes — 96b
  interdict upon her h. — 469a
  me and my utmost h. — 363a
  my h. no more must change — 464a
  nil ultra to my proudest h. — 262b
  our very h. belied our fears — 196a
  seen my fondest h. decay — 282a
  what are the h. of man — 213a
Hopeth: charity. . h. all things — 514b
Hoping it might be so — 180a
Hopkins, hail! — 111b
Hopped with his song — 119b
Hopping o'er the floor — 443b
Hoppy, Croppy — 158a
Hops: Kent, sir. . h., and women — 126a
Hop-yards: for what were h. meant — 199b
Horace: farewell H.; whom I hated — 69a
  had H. or Anacreon tasted — 215a
  we learn from H. — 71a
  what H. says is, *Eheu Fugaces* — 20a
Horatio: H., thou art e'en as just — 334a
  H., what a wounded name — 337a
  things in heaven and earth, H. — 331b
  what! is H. there? — 329a
Horatius: come back, come back, H. — 253b
  how well H. kept the bridge — 253b
  saw brave H. stand alone — 253b
  then out spake brave H. — 253a
Horde: society is now one polished h. — 71b
Horizon: h. . . a blaze with his. . glory — 55a
  I saw her just above the h. — 57a
Horizontal: into a h. line — 456b
Horn: come blow up yr. h. — 535a
  cow with the crumpled h. — 534a
  for a blast of that dreadful h. — 318b
  her small but sullen h. — 103a
  hoarse-sounding h. invites thee — 406a
  h. of the hunter is heard — 115b
  huntsman winds his h. — 151b
  it is the moon, I ken her h. — 63b
  pour'd thro' the mellow h. — 103a
  put forth a conscious h. — 441b
  St. John sate in the h. — 524a
  shrill clarion, or the echoing h. — 174a
  sound of his h. brought me — 173b
  sound upon yr. bugle h. — 432a
  the hopeless h. blown — 92a

Horn (*cont.*)

  the h., the h., the lusty h. — 327b
  to the blind H.'s hate — 231b
  Triton blow his wreathed h. — 473a
  Triton blowing loud his. . h. — 408a
  winding His loud h. — 474b
  with his hounds and his h. — 173a
  you have a h. where other brutes — 26a
Hornby: O my H. and my Barlow — 442b
Horne: Godolphin H. — 26a
Horned Moon, with one bright star — 99a
Horner: little Jack H. — 532a
Hornie, Satan, Nick, or Clootie — 58b
Horns: from the h. of the unicorns — 483a
  h. are tipped with brass — 143b
  h. of Elfland faintly blowing — 436a
  Morning on the silver h. — 437a
  on the h. o' the moon — 328a
  ram caught in a thicket by his h. — 493a
  seven h. and seven eyes — 518b
  she put out her h. — 534a
  tender h. of cockled snails — 345a
Horny-handed sons of toil — 217a
Horrible: grotesque to the h. — 136a
  O, h.! O, h.! most h.! — 331b
  oh! more h. than that — 99a
Horrid: but are they all h.? — 11b
  when she was bad she was h. — 249a
Horror: a h. of outer darkness — 171b
  h. and darkness fell — 54a
  h. heavy sat on ev'ry mind — 141b
  h. of great darkness fell — 492b
  its h. and its beauty are divine — 395b
  on h.'s head horrors accumulate — 362a
  swinges the scaly h. — 270b
  take the present h. from the time — 347b
  the h. of that moment — 83b
  whence this. . inward h. — 1b
Horrors: congenial h., hail — 443b
  hail h., hail infernal world — 271a
  I have supped full with h. — 350b
  life. . but a scene of h. — 405b
Hors d'œuvres for fishes — 131a
Horse: a dark h. . . rushed past — 130a
  a h.! a h.! my kingdom for a h. — 385a
  a h. of that colour — 370b
  altogether upon the high h. — 40b
  an old h. that stumbles and nods — 179b
  as it were upon an h. — 486a
  a sword, a h., a shield — 250a
  better have them cleanin' his h. — 416b
  between a rider and his h. — 417a
  be ye not like to h. and mule — 483b
  blind h. stick'n in a big mud hole — 156a
  by h. and crest — 253a
  dosn't thou 'ear my h.'s legs — 434b
  e'er since sits on his h. back — 373b
  fit companion is his h. — 108a
  for want of a h. — 157a
  Gilpin at his h.'s side — 108b
  give a man a h. he can ride — 444a
  give me another h. — 385a
  good h. in the stable — 170b
  heaven opened, and behold a. . h. — 519b
  help Hyperion to his h. — 383a
  hey for boot and h., lad — 226a
  his h., who never in that sort — 108b
  h. is counted but a vain thing — 484a
  h. is drawn by the cart — 228a
  h. may at least rank second — 171b
  h. misused upon the road — 29a
  h., my wife, and my name — 417a
  I know two things about the h. — 524a
  I long ago lost a. . bay h. — 444a
  I looked, and behold a pale h. — 518b
  lies about his wooden h. — 155a
  little dearer than his h. — 432a
  my h. a thing of wings — 33b
  nothing but talk of his h. — 353a
  O, for a h. with wings — 328b
  one h. was blind — 403b
  one stiff blind h. — 45b
  paid for catching my h., 6d. — 416b
  pleasure in the strength of an h. — 490b
  pulling in one's h. as he is
    leaping — 181a
  ride a cock h. — 533b
  ride upon a white h. — 533b
  sell the pasture now to buy the h. — 381b
  so is my h., Octavius — 340b
  something in a flying h. — 468b

Horse (cont.)
spit in my face, call me h.   377b
strong is the h. upon his speed   403a
stuck a. .junior with a h.   233b
teach an old h. amble true   409a
tedious as a tired h.   378a
that wh. is now a h.   324b
the h. came spurring in   252b
the h. he knows above a bit   233a
the h. loves the 'ound   416b
the King. .sent a troop of h.   42b
to. .wondrous doing brought his h.   336a
under his h. in the brook   289a
what a h. shd. have   386b
Horseback: ride on h. after we   108b
Horse drench: then a strong h.   240a
Horse Guards: on business to the H.   125a
Horseleech hath two daughters   499a
Horsemanship: on his morality than on his h.   416b
witch the world with noble h.   378b
Horsemen: and the h. thereof   496b
h. riding upon horses   504a
Horse-race won at Olympus   402a
Horses: all the king's h.   85a
ay, the h. trample   199a
come saddle yr. h.   316a, 320a
dressing eels, or shoeing h.   305a
England is. .a hell for h.   64b
grey gun-h. in the lando   234a
hanged for stealing h.   178a
her words to trampling h.' feet   402a
h. and dorgs is some men's fancy   122a
Italy is a paradise for h.   64b
nothing like blood, sir, in h.   440a
not to swap h. . .crossing the river   245b
put their trust. .in h.   482b
strong. .man to clean h.   417a
take any man's h.   381a
the h. of instruction   31a
they were as fed h.   503b
watered our h. in Helicon   87b
we spend on our h.   314a
wild white h. play   5b
Women and H. and Power   227a
Hosanna: h. from the den   403a
made sweet H. ring   286a
Hose(n): bound in their. .h.   504a
his youthful h. well sav'd   326b
Hospitable: h., in her sweet recess with h. ray   277a, 169a
Hospital: learnt. .social comfort, in a h.   43a
the world. .but an h.   42a
Hospitality: doing deeds of h.   326a
given to h.   513b
good English h.   33a
Hospitals: rust in peace, or rot in h.   406a
Host: h. is riding from Knocknarea   475a
if you find such a h.   4b
like a fashionable h.   369a
now for the tea of our h.   167a
on a soundless-clapping h.   442b
play the humble h.   349a
praise Him above, ye heavenly h.   224b
saved by the multitude of an h.   484a
streams in the countless h.   200b
two pence and gave them to the h.   509a
universal h. up sent a shout   271b
yet mine H. can ne'er espy   452b
Hostages: children. .h. to fortune   14b
Hostel: pass 1 h., hall, and grange   438a
Hostess: back at mine h.' door   373b
my h. of the tavern   376b
Hosts: God of H., be with us yet   233b
holy, lord G. of h.   480b
'Lord of H.' did pitch His tent!   187b
mankind. .h. and guests   24b
stronger than all the h. of error   53a
Hot: argument's h. to the close   48b
beat the iron while it is h.   142a
come from Rome al h.   89a
his heart was h. within him   248b
h. cross-buns   535b
sometime too h. the eye of heaven   387a
spick and span new, piping h.   65a
thou art. .neither cold nor h.   518b
when h. for certainties   264a
when you make pitch h.   121a
why the sea is boiling h.   84b

Hot (cont.)
ye'se a' be h. ere I come back   61b
Hoti's business   47a
Hotspur of the North   377a
Hottentot: a respectable H.   91a
Hound: a traveller, by the faithful h.   247a
he'll grow into a h.   459a
his h., and his lady fair   529b
his h. is to the hunting gane   529b
h. or spaniel, brach or lym   343a
I long ago lost a h.   444a
I loves the h. more   416b
nought good a sleping h. to wake   90a
'oss loves the h.   416b
puppy, whelp, and h.   169a
take that, you h.   135b
Hounds: cry of his h.   173b
desires, like fell and cruel h.   369b
dinner lost, h. lost   416b
his h. and his horn   173a
h. all join in glorious cry   151b
my h. are bred out of the Spartan   357a
of smale h. had she   88b
when the h. of spring   420a
with h. and horsemen   33b
with h. of Sparta   357a
Houndsditch: housebreaker, of H.   75a
Hour: abode his destined H.   152b
abode his H. or two   153a
against the h. of death   481b
ah! no; the h. is ill   394a
anguish of a torturing h.   357b
animate an h. of vacant ease   470a
Ave Maria! 'tis the h.   71a
awaits alike th' inevitable h.   174a
books of the h.   314a
break an h.'s promise in love   327b
bring me back one golden h.   200b
but every h. is saved   438b
close-companioned inarticulate h.   312a
come most carefully upon yr. h.   329a
dark eleventh hour draws on   236a
dead h. of the night   528b
ere the parting h. go by   7a
ending at the arrival of an h.   379a
Eternity in an h.   29a
for a dark h. or twain   348b
from h. to h., we ripe   326a
he was but one h. mine   387b
h. calls us to penance   272a
h. is come, but not the man   319b
h. when from the boughs   73b
h. when lovers' vows seem sweet   73b
h. when you too learn. .all is vain   312a
I also had my h.   92a
I chang'd ev'ry h.   159b
I have had my h.   142b
improve each shining h.   453a
in ev'ry h. that passes, O   60b
in my h. of hours   476a
in such h. of need   7b
iron scourge and torturing h.   173b
let us have a quiet h.   439a
make the h. full complete   384a
mine h. is not yet come   510b
not an h. more or less   344a
nothing can bring back the h.   466b
now's the day, and now's the h.   62b
one bare h. to live   258b
one crowded h. of glorious life   283a
one far fierce h. and sweet   92a
present h. . .mark'd with shade   241a
serve the future h.   463b
silence. .the space of half an h.   519a
sold the truth to serve the h.   435a
still h. of thinking   463b
suffer us not, at our last h.   481b
surely thine h. has come   476a
that h., o' night's black arch   63a
the Children's H.   246b
the present h. alone is man's   213a
this wing'd h. is dropt to us   312a
tho' it be but an h. ago   133b
time and the h. runs thro'   346b
to fill the h.—that is happiness   148a
to one dead deathless h.   311b
troublesome insects of the h.   57a
turn the h.   229a
wait the 'pointed h.   141b
watch with me one h.   508a
wee short h. ayont the twal   60a

Hour (cont.)
weight of the superincumbent h.   392a
when God sends a cheerful h.   278b
Who has matched us with His h.   40a
wisely tell what h. o' th' day   65a
wonder of an h.   68a
world-without-end h.   388a
Hour-glass: still as the h.   321a
Hours: about the space of two h.   512b
a line will take us h. may be   474a
chase the glowing H.   68b
desolate passions, aching h.   206a
discourse the freezing h. away   328b
eight score eight h.   362b
five h. up and seven down   234a
golden h. on angel wings   61a
h. and the wild birds follow   422b
h. and times of yr. desire   388a
h. bring about the day   384a
h. I spent with thee, dear heart   309a
h. to wh. high Heaven doth chime   447b
h. will take care of themselves   90b
keeping company with the h.   454a
lag-end of my life with quiet h.   378a
lovers' h. be full eternity   133b
now all strange h. . .are over   421a
O Love what h. were thine   426a
on the lazy leaden-stepping h.   278b
scared away the meek ethereal h.   218a
six h. ago I came   284b
six h. in sleep   97b
steal a few h. from the night   281b
thro' h. of gloom fulfill'd   7a
two golden h. . .set with. .minutes   258a
two h. sooner than he wished   208a
unnumbered h. of pain   77b
upon the midnight h.   220a
waked by the circling h.   275a
what peaceful h. I once enjoy'd   109b
white and sable h. appear   24a
who never spent the darksome h.   82a
Woman! in our h. of ease   318b
House: abide by my Mother's H.   233a
a man's h. is his castle   97b
a moat defensive to a h.   375a
bequeath them no tumbled h.   263a
beste beggar in his h.   88b
bloody h. of life   374a
brawling woman in a wide h.   498b
build a h. for fools and mad   419a
build a h. with deep thatch   27a
but as the H. is pleased to direct   244b
call upon my soul within the h.   370a
called the h. of prayer   507b
daughter am I in my mother's h.   233a
daughter of my h. and heart   68a
dark h., by wh. once more I stand   429b
disturb this hallowed h.   357b
eaten me out of h. and home   380a
everything before me in that H.   129a
except the Lord build the h.   489b
fool nowhere but in's own h.   333b
from every h. the neighbours met   430a
God erects a h. of prayer   118b
go into the h. of the Lord   489b
go to the h. of mourning   499a
here is a H. that armours a man   26a
h. and tenant go to ground   147a
h. appointed for all living   497a
h. divided against itself   245a
h. is much more to my taste   283b
h. not made with hands   515b
h. of ancient fame   409b
h. of every one. .his castle   97b
h. of my pilgrimage   489a
h. on fire. .to roast their eggs   15b
h. that Jack built   534b
h. to lodge a friend   419b
h. was filled with smoke   501b
h. where I was born   195a
h. with lawns enclosing   414b
h. with starry dome   452b
if a h. be divided   508a
ill spirit have so fair a h.   367b
in a little crooked h.   532a
in my father's h. are. .mansions   511a
is not this h. as nigh heaven   283a
it snewed in his h.   88b
I will dwell in the h. of the Lord   483a
keepers of the h. shall tremble   499b
let the h. of a brute   426a

House (*cont.*)
like a fair h. built 355*b*
little h., whose humble roof 190*b*
man who had a mind to sell his h. 417*b*
may I a small h...have 107*a*
may I have a warm h. 304*a*
men to be of one mind in an h. 486*a*
mere lodger in my own h. 170*b*
my h. has been broken open 295*a*
my h. in the high wood 27*a*
nearer my Father's h. 86*a*
one of yr. accursed h. 254*a*
peace be to this h. 481*b*
prop that doth sustain the h. 355*a*
prophet..in his own h. 507*a*
raven o'er the infected h. 362*b*
return no more to his h. 497*a*
see to thine own h. 496*a*
set thine h. in order 502*b*
shot mine arrow o'er the h. 337*a*
sparrow hath found her an h. 487*a*
the h. is falling 262*a*
the h. o'ertopping all 46*a*
there's nae luck about the h. 527*a*
the substance of his h. for Love 501*a*
this reft h. 102*a*
thy h. is on fire 534*a*
unless you leave this h. 85*b*
Vanburgh's h. of clay 149*a*
walked in the h. of God 485*a*
when h. and land are gone 155*b*
woe is me for the good h. 253*b*
woe unto them that join h. to h. 501*a*
worse than a smoky h. 378*a*
yea, because of the h. of the Lord 489*b*
you take my h. 355*a*
you unhouse and h. the Lord 197*b*
zeal of thine h. hath..eaten me 486*b*
House-breaker of Houndsditch 75*a*
Household: breathing h. laws 467*b*
familiar in his mouth as h. words 383*a*
her h. motions light and free 470*b*
h. bird, with the red stomacher 132*b*
h. divided the spoil 486*a*
h. happiness 439*a*
the h. of continuance 416*a*
they of his own h. 506*b*
thy h. the Church 479*b*
to study h. good 276*a*
trust her h. to me 187*a*
Householder wh. bringeth forth 507*a*
Housekeepings: hearts and h. 125*b*
Housemaids: damp souls of h. 145*a*
treat h. to his teas 93*b*
walks with fifty h. 232*a*
House of Lords: *cure* for admiring the H. 17*b*
House of Peers has never been a House 17*b*
Houses: devour widows' h. 508*b*
h. are built to live in 16*a*
h...last till doomsday 336*a*
h. thick and sewers annoy 276*a*
if it wasn't for the h. in between 22*a*
let us see these handsome h. 432*b*
plague o' both yr. h. 365*b*
round their golden h. 433*a*
set up her h. 485*a*
the h. go wheeling back 443*b*
their h. shall continue 485*a*
the very h. seem asleep 472*b*
House-top: dwell in a corner of the h. 498*b*
sitteth alone upon the h. 488*a*
Housewife: busy h. ply her evening 174*a*
here's to the h. that's thrifty 400*b*
lo, as a careful h. runs 389*a*
mock the good h. Fortune 325*b*
Housewives: h.' affairs..never an end 446*a*
h. in your beds 360*b*
no more h., but queens 314*a*
Hovel: folks *prefer* in fact a h. 75*b*
Hover: h. in their restless heads 259*b*
round the spot ofttimes I h. 440*b*
Hovering o'er the place's head 115*a*
How: h. are the mighty fallen 495*b*
h. can these things be? 510*b*
h. you do go it 41*a*
Howard: if I left them, my Lord H. 437*b*
Lord H. past away 437*b*
then sware Lord Thomas H. 437*a*
Howards: blood of all the H. 301*b*
How-de-doo: here's a h. 164*b*
Howe, and the glorious First 285*a*
Howell and James young man 165*b*
Howl: h., ye ships of Tarshish 502*a*
whose h.'s his watch 347*b*
Howling: h. of Irish wolves 327*b*
in the waste h. wilderness 494*b*
when thou liest h. 336*b*
winds..h. at all hours 473*a*
Howls on for more 395*b*
Hub, the King Pin 38*b*
Hubbard: old Mother H. 533*b*
Hubbub increases more 218*a*
Hudibras: Quoth H., Friend Ralph 65*b*
Quoth H., I smell a rat 65*a*
Hue: another h. unto the rainbow 374*a*
flavour, and body, and h. 20*a*
gordian shape of dazzling h. 219*a*
join not scent to h. 394*b*
losing some h. of his mirth 263*a*
shells, of pearly h. 241*a*
so yr. sweet h...hath motion 388*b*
sweet rose, whose h. angry 187*b*
the native h. of resolution 333*a*
with h. like that..some..painter 398*a*
Hues: consecrate with thine own h. 394*b*
h. of the rich unfolding morn 223*b*
living h. and odours 396*a*
rich h. have marriage made 36*b*
Hug: h. it in mine arms 352*a*
h. the dear deceit 106*b*
Huge oaks and old 235*a*
Hugest of living creatures 275*b*
Hugger-mugger: thus h. to inter him 335*b*
Hugh: dirge for St. H.'s soul 119*a*
St. H. be our goodspeed 119*a*
Hugs it to the last 282*a*
Hulk: here, a sheer h. 121*a*
the naked h. alongside came 98*b*
Hull: my father..settled first at H. 118*a*
Hum: h. of either army stilly sounds 382*b*
h. of human cities torture 68*b*
make Hammersmith h. 186*a*
mist and h. of that low land 8*a*
no voice or hideous h. 270*b*
sad-ey'd justice, with his surly h. 381*b*
the busy h. of men 269*a*
Human: all h...are subject to decay 140*b*
all the h. frame requires 26*a*
breathing h. passion 219*b*
but h. creatures' lives 196*a*
come away, O h. child 476*a*
cruelty has a h. heart 33*a*
does a H. Form display 29*b*
ever looked with h. eyes 430*b*
from half of h. fate 7*a*
glory that redounds..to h. kind 470*a*
he himself with his h. air 45*b*
h. at the red-ripe of the heart 51*a*
h. bodies are sic fools 63*a*
h. face divine 273*b*
h. knee is a joint 178*b*
h. love needs h. meriting 442*a*
in the h. breast two..passions 77*b*
I wish I loved the H. Race 308*a*
Jealousy a h. face 33*a*
Love, the h. form divine 33*a*
Mercy has a h. heart 33*a*
nothing h. indifferent to me 554*a*
our Euripides, the h. 44*a*
Peace, the h. dress 33*a*
permanent among the h. race 71*b*
Pity a h. face 33*a*
Secrecy the h. dress 33*a*
Terror the h. form divine 33*a*
the h. mind in ruins 118*a*
they are neither brute nor h. 298*a*
to step aside is h. 59*a*
when first the h. race began 60*a*
wrought with h. hands the creed 430*a*
you are a h. boy 121*a*
Human being: no h...free as a fish 314*b*
Humanities: H. live for ever 289*b*
h. of old religion 101*b*
Humanity: acts of h., gentleness 257*a*
a heart..of a veined h. 43*b*
high upon the forehead of h. 217*b*
h.'s afflicted will 464*b*
h. with all its fears 246*b*
imitated h. so abominably 333*b*
insurmountable distresses of h. 212*b*
Humanity (*cont.*)
rarer spirit never did steer h. 324*b*
reasoned out of the feelings of h. 28*b*
sad music of h. 472*a*
such popular h. is treason 1*b*
wearisome condition of h. 176*b*
what h., reason..tell me I ought 55*b*
Humankind: lord of h. 141*b*
paint the vices and follies of h. 104*a*
porcelain clay of h. 141*b*
see the lords of h. pass 170*a*
Human nature: h. is finer 222*b*
h.'s daily food 470*b*
h.'s highest dower 465*a*
sovereign good of h. 14*a*
there is in h...more of the fool 14*b*
Tragedy..noblest production of h. 2*a*
you've conquered h. 124*b*
Humble: be it ever so h. 294*b*
he that shall h. himself 507*b*
h. and a contrite heart 233*b*
h. livers in content 385*b*
minutes, h. though they be 82*a*
neither too h. nor too great 257*a*
star to guide the h. 256*b*
we are so very h. 122*a*
wisdom is h. 112*b*
Humbled: all h. kiss the rod 372*b*
Humbleness: all h., all patience 327*b*
whispering h. 353*a*
Humbleth: he that h. himself 509*b*
Humbug in a Pickwickian sense 126*a*
Hume: H., Gibbon, Robertson 239*a*
similar fate from..Mr. H. 405*a*
Humiliation: valley of H. 54*a*
Humility: h...clothe an English dean 113*a*
pride that apes h. 100*b*, 406*b*
stillness and h. 382*a*
Humour: has her h. most, when she obeys 302*a*
h...consists in..going backwards 449*b*
h. is odd, grotesque 420*a*
kills her in her own h. 366*b*
perfect h. and irony..unconscious 66*b*
say it is my h. 354*b*
that's the h. of it 381*b*
the phrase 'unconscious h.' 66*b*
there's the h. of it 355*b*
unyoked h. of yr. idleness 376*b*
was ever woman in this h. won 384*b*
when I am in a serious h. 1*b*
Humoured thus comes at the last 375*b*
Humours: according as his h. lead 426*b*
in all thy H. 2*a*
take their h. for a warrant 374*a*
Hump: Cameelious H. 230*b*
Camel's h. is an ugly h. 230*b*
without a positive h. 440*a*
Humph yourself! 237*a*
Humpty Dumpty: H. sat on a wall 85*a*, 533*b*
'the question is', said H. 85*a*
Hun is at the gate 229*a*
Huncamunca: in H.'s eyes 151*b*
Hundred: about two h. pounds a year 66*a*
give me a kiss..add a h. more 190*a*
he and his eight h. 111*a*
his h.'s soon hit 47*a*
I entertain for one of my h. 343*a*
of the three h. grant but three 70*b*
two h. more 66*a*
when he made Ole H. ring 250*b*
wi' a h. pipers an' a' 285*b*
with..haste might tell a h. 330*b*
Hundredfold: brought forth..an h. 506*b*
Hundredth: singing the H. Psalm 246*b*
Hung be the heavens with black 383*b*
Hunger: age and h. 326*b*
for h.'s power is strong 290*a*
h. and thirst after righteousness 505*a*
I perish with h. 509*b*
make h. thy sauce 446*a*
O sacred h. of ambitious mind 409*a*
poverty, h., and dirt 196*a*
they shall h. no more 519*a*
Hungry: but she makes h. 323*a*
he hath filled the h. with good 508*b*
h. and thirsty: their soul fainted 488*b*
I am not h., but..I am greedy 535*b*
I came home h. as a hunter 239*b*
mine is all as h. as the sea 371*a*

Hunt: fame, that all h. after 344a
he wd. h. in the mountains 530b
h. down a tired metaphor 71b
h. it in the dark 110b
H., one of those happy souls 395b
to h., and vote 67b
Hunter: Bahram, that great H. 153a
Fear, O little H., he is Fear 234b
from the snare of the h. 487b
hungry as a h. 239b
h. home from the hill 415a
h. is heard on the hill 115b
man is the h. 436b
Nimrod the mighty h. 492b
struck by the h.'s dart 392a
the H. of the East 152a
Hunters: here thy h. stand 339b
h. been nat holy men 88b
Hunting: call h. one of them [pleasures] 212a
good h.! 237a
hound is to the h. gane 529b
h. fills my thoughts by day 416b
h. he loved, but love he laugh'd 386b
h. is all that's worth living for 416b
h...is like the hair we breathe 416b
h...is the sport of kings 416b
H. of the Cheviot 531a
I like the h. of the hare 33b
it ain't the h. as 'urts 535a
passion for h...deeply implanted 125a
that one h. wh. the Devil design'd 141b
their discourse was about h. 296a
wet and dirty from h. 417a
wot is not spent in h. 416b
Huntley: where H., and where Home 318b
Huntlie: lay on H. bank 528a
Huntress: queen and h. 214b
Huntsman: a cassocked h. 110b
as a h. his pack 169b
h. by the bear oppressed 448b
h., rest! thy chase is done 316b
h. winds his horn 151b
Huntsmen are up in America 41a
Hurled headlong flaming 271a
Hurly: with the h. death itself awakes 380a
Hurly burley: when the h.'s done 345b
Hurrah! we bring the Jubilee 473a
Hurricane: swept the h. of steel 12a
Hurricanoes: cataracts and h. 342b
Hurry: an old man in a h. 95a
he sows h. and reaps indigestion 413b
I am never in a h. 456a
no h. in her hands 311a
Hurt: as I have to be h. 363b
he who shall h. the little wren 29a
'I'll not h. thee' 411b
nothing doth more h. in a state 15b
they shall not h. nor destroy 501b
they that have power to h. 388b
Hurtig: you are h. 237a
Hurtles in the darkened air 175a
Hurts: had he his h. before 351a
he h. me most who..commends 94a
I strike it, and it h. my hand 362b
some of yr. h. you have cured 147a
which h., and is desired 325a
Husband: and then my h.—God be 364b
as the h. is, the wife is 432a
as wel over hir h. 89b
being a h. is a whole-time job 27a
bride adorned for her h. 519b
duty..a woman oweth to her h. 367a
good h., little ant 249b
good works in her h. to promote 276a
hang yr. h. and be dutiful 159b
here comes my h. 46b
her h.'s to Aleppo gone 346a
h. frae the wife despises 62b
h., I come 325a
h.! in ev'ry respect but form 159b
h. twenty years married 237b
I am thine h. 428a
I had once a h. 407a
level in her h.'s heart 370b
light wife doth make a heavy h. 355b
make her h. a cuckold 363a
Mr. F...most indulgent h. 123a
monstrous animal a h. and wife 151b
ne'er answers till a h. cools 302a

Husband (cont.)
no worse a h. than the best 323a
see a h. in these circumstances 159b
she must have a h. 366b
so ill bred as to love a h. 473b
the h. was a teetotaller 135a
the Man-o'-War's 'er h. 231b
too much for one h. to bear 160a
unbelieving h. is sanctified 514a
wife is May, the h. june 452a
woman is a crown to her h. 498a
Husbanded: h. the Golden grain 152b
so fathered and so h. 338b
Husbandry: dulls the edge of h. 330b
there's h. in heaven 347b
Husbands: h. at chirch-dore 88b
h. love yr. wives 516a
h., or when lap-dogs breathe 302b
I shd. marry twenty h. 353a
let them ask their h. at home 514b
pranks they dare not show their h. 361b
reasons for h. to stay at home 144b
respite to h. 514b
submit yourselves unto yr. own h. 515b
when h. win their hay 530b
Hush: a h. with the setting moon 434a
h.! if you saw some western cloud 48a
h.! my dear, lie still 453a
increases more they call out, 'H.!' 218a
O h. thee, my babie 317b
old man who said 'H.!' 243b
there's a breathless h. in the Close 287b
Hushes half the babbling Wye 430a
Husht be all things 189a
Husks: h. that the swine did eat 509b
what's to come, is strewed with h. 369b
Hustle: tried to h. the East 233a
Hut: love in a h. 219a
my little wooden h. 263a
rude h. by the Danube 69a
Hutch: palate, the h. of tasty lust 197b
Huts where poor men lie 463a
Hwang: reign of the Emperor H. 242a
Hyacinth: a h. I wisht me 138a
children with H.'s temperament 315b
every H. the Garden wears 153a
Hyades: the rainy H. 438b
Hybla: as the honey of H. 376b
they rob the H. bees 341a
Hyde Park: beyond H.'s a desart 149a
nor go to H. together 105b
Hydras: Gorgons and H. 272b
Hydrus and Ellops drear 276b
Hymeneal: chorus H. 398b
Hymn: humm'd a surly h. 438a
I the h. the Brahmin sings 146a
St. Ann's our parting h. 282b
your h. of praise to-day 117a
Hymns: chanting faint h. 356a
h. and spiritual songs 515b
singing h. unbidden 398a
sings his canticles and h. 202b
sings h. at heaven's gate 387b
solemn h. to sullen dirges change 366a
Hyperbole: perpetual h. 14b
Hyperboles: three-pil'd h. 345a
Hyperion: help H. to his horse 383a
H. of calves the Piper 96a
H. to a satyr 330a
Hyphenated Americans 310b
Hypocrisy: Conservative Government..h. 128a
h. is homage paid by vice 562a
man nor angel can discern h. 273b
now step I forth to whip h. 345a
Hypocrite: a h. in his pleasures 211b
Good is the plea of the..h. 30b
Hypocrites: cant of h...the worst 411b
h. austerely talk of purity 274b
Hypothesis: character of a family to an h. 411b
Hyrcanian: like the H. beast 332b
Hyssop: purge me with h. 485a
Hysterics: blind h. of the Celt 431a

I

I: Ah, reverend sir, not I! 46a
cleave the wood and there am I 526a
first come I; my name is Jowett 528b

I (cont.)
I again, what else did you expect? 46b
I am a good man too 163a
I am always about in the Quad 522b
I am among you as he 510a
I am he that liveth, and was dead 518b
I am I, thou art thou 422a
I am rather tall and stately 528b
I am that I am 493b
I am the door 511a
I am the High 528b
I, and you, and all of us 340a
I, I also am an American 454a
I in my bed again 527b
I John saw the holy city 519b
I'm Mackail, and who are you 528b
I mysel' were dead and gane 530b
'I', said the Fly 528a
'I', said the Sparrow 528a
I, singularly moved to love 293b
I the elder and more terrible 339a
I the Lord thy God 480a
I the Trinity illustrate 52a
I think that man was I 530b
it is I; be not afraid 507a
I to Him, and He to me 441a
I too, my Lord, have not been idle 524b
I, with many a fear 463a
no more I that doeth it 513a
say, cd. that lad be I? 414b
that I am he, let me a little show 339a
there am I in the midst of them 507a
this is none of I 533b
thou art I 422a
Thou, Lord, and I 119b
what am I? an infant crying 430b
yet not I, but the grace of God 514b
Iago: but yet the pity of it, I.! 362b
conceiving an I. as an Imogen 223a
Iambics march from short to long 101b
Ianthe: find I.'s name again 241b
from you, I., little troubles pass 241a
Iberians: the dark I. come 8b
Ice: as soon seek..i. in June 72a
hissed along the polished i. 465b
i. did split with a thunder-fit 98b
i., mast high, came floating by 98a
i. on summer seas 427b
i. was here, the i. was there 98a
it is good to break the i. 15b
like the skater on i. 427a
pleasure-dome with caves of i. 101b
region of thick-ribbèd i. 352a
skating over thin i. 147b
to smooth the i. 374a
Ichabod..the glory is departed 495a
Icicle: chaste as the i. 328b
i. on a Dutchman's beard 371b
Icicles: hang them up in silent i. 101a
when i. hang by the wall 345b
Icumen: sumer is i. in 526a
Ida: dear mother I., hearken 435a
O mother I., many-fountain'd I. 435a
there lies a vale in I. 435a
whether on I.'s shady brow 31b
Idalian Queen 138a
Idea: he had only one i. 130a
i. of her life shall..creep 359a
one i., and that is a wrong one 208a
teach the young i. 443b
the mighty abstract i. I have 223a
Ideal: i. of a manly career 130a
softly sleeps the calm I. 124a
the i. American who is all wrong 94a
Ideas: all sorts of dead i. 567a
champagne..gives..gentlemanly i. 417a
entertain such inhuman i. 417b
man of nasty i. 419a
sung divine i. below 147a
Identity: his i. presses upon me 222b
Ides: beware the I. of March 337b
that work the I. of March begun 341a
the I. of March are come 339a
Idiom: for the i. of words very little 306a
Idiot: an i. race to honour lost 62a
as e'er the beauteous i. spoke 104a
a tale told by an i. 350b
him whom you love, yr. I. Boy 465b
i. who praises..all centuries 164b
like a blank i. 218a
Idle: every i. word..man shall speak 506b

Idle (cont.)

for i. hands to do	453a
happiest when I am i.	451b
i. as a painted ship	98b
if you are i., be not solitary	210a
I too, my Lord, have not been i.	524b
most 'scruciating i.	237a
stand ye here all the day i.?	507b
we wd. all be i. if we cd.	209a
wise, i., childish things	441a

Idleness: bear such i. so near 322b
conceives by i.	383b
feet of joy in i.	37b
frivolous work of polished i.	256a
grief is a species of i.	214a
i…the refuge of weak minds	91a
round of strenuous i.	469b
unyok'd humour of yr. i.	376b

Idler: every man. .hopes to be, an i. 213a
| hath been an i. in the land | 469a |

Idlers, game-preservers 81a
Idling: to enjoy i. thoroughly 205a
Idly bent on him that enters 376a
Idol: dearest i. I have known 109b
kisses on an 'eathen i.'s foot	232a
whate'er that i. be	109b
worship oft the i. for the saint	457a

Idolatries: bow'd to its i. a patient knee 68b
Idolatry: for that were I. 480b
god of my i.	365a
it might breed i.	133a
on this side i.	214b
'tis mad i. to make the service	369a

Idols: four classes of I. 16b
| God keeps a niche. .hold our i. | 43b |

Idyll: high diddle diddle. .i. 165b
If: I'd go and wake them, i. 85a
i. at first you don't succeed	191a
'i.' is the only peacemaker	328a
i. you can keep yr. reason	230a
much virtue in 'i.'	328a

Ifs: talk'st thou to me of 'i.'? 385a
Ignis fatuus: reason an I. of the mind 309b
Ignoble: base and i. creature 15a
| yet the end was not i. | 469a |

Ignominy: i. of our natures 41b
| thy i. sleep with thee | 379a |

Ignorance: alike in i., his reason such 301a
blind and naked I. delivers	429a
bliss wh. is the lot of happy i.	157a
boldness is a child of i.	14b
distinguished for i.	130a
drink to heavy I.!	439a
from i. our comfort flows	306a
from knowledge i.	46a
I. is not innocence	47b
i., madam, pure i.	207a
i. of the law excuses no man	321a
I pity his i. and despise him	124b
it was a childish i.	195a
let me not burst in i.	331a
more than Gothic i.	151b
no sin but i.	259a
putting us to i. again	46a
the smallest allowance for i.	202b
thro' i. ye did it	512a
understand a writer's i.	102a
what i. of pain?	398b
where i. is bliss	175a
yr. i. cramps my conversation	197a

Ignorances: negligences and i. 479a
Ignorant: be not i. of any thing 520b
confound the i.	333a
i. of his understanding	102a
most i. of what he's most assur'd	351b
right of the i. man	80b
we, i. of ourselves	323a

Ignorantly: I did it ignorantly 516b
Iliad: an I. of woes 120a
Ilion: cloud-kissing I. 386b
Ilium: burnt the topless towers of I. 258b
| I. is no more | 555b |

Ill: attending captain i. 388a
cannot be i., cannot be good	346b
cure for this i. is not to sit still	230b
did not care to speak i. of any	212a
enchains us to permitted i.	395a
gey i. to live wi'	82a
give the i. he cannot cure a name	9a

Ill (cont.)

good. .the final goal of i.	430a
he thinks no i.	388a
how i. all's here about my heart	337a
if it is i…has a frightened look	402a
looking i. prevail	416a
make strong themselves by i.	349a
no i. can come	491a
nothing i. come near thee	329a
nought shall go i.	357a
O benefit of i.!	389a
of every i., a woman is the worst	173a
seal up the avenues of i.	147a
tempt you to all harm and i.	3a
than to rail at the i.	434b
there is some i. a-brewing	353b
there's nothing i. can dwell	367b
to do i. our sole delight	271a
to speak i. of it	183b

Ill-bred: illiberal and so i. 90b
Ill-drest: ill-kept and i. 211a
Ill-favoured thing, sir, but mine own 328a
Ill-fed, ill-killed 211a
Illiberal: so i. and so ill-bred 90b
Ill-luck: so fond of i. 205b
Illness: without the i. shd. attend it 346b
Ills: climax of all human i. 70b
fear, the last of i.	141b
i. have no weight	251b
long versed in human i.	114a
no sense have they of i. to come	174b
o'er a' the i. o' life victorious	62b
quiet, after all their i.	5b
rather bear those i. we have	333a
to hastening i. a prey	168a
what i. from beauty spring	214a
when nae real i. perplex them	63a

Ill-tempered: think him i. and queer 243b
Illumine: what in me is dark i. 270b
Illusion: for man's i. given 282b
| only one i. left | 404b |
| so thankful for i. | 96a |

Illustrious: i. predecessors 151a
| scarce less i. goes the clerk | 109b |

Illyria: tall a man as any 's in I. 369b
| What shd. I do in I.? | 369b |

Illyrian: green I. hills 5b
Ilsley: looks on I. downs 8b
Image: an i. gay, to haunt 470b
best i. of myself	274b
Cæsar's i. is effaced	110b
constant i. of the creature	370b
express i. of his person	517a
I am in His i. made	475a
i. of Lewti!	101b
i. of my death	138a
i. that, flying still before me	466a
i. that Nebuchadnezzar. .set up	504a
in his own i. the Creator made	241a
its wrinkled i. lies	396a
kills the i. of God. .in the eye	279a
let us make man in our i.	492a
man's i. and his cry	476a
nor i. of thine eyes	312a
scatter'd his Maker's i.	138a
see the great doom's i.	348a
shalt not make. .any graven i.	480a
stamp'd with the i. of the King	428a
the fleeting i. of a shade	399b
the i. of eternity	69b
whose horrid i. doth unfix my hair	346b
whose is this i.	507b
worship the beast and his i.	519b
yr. i. at our hearts we bear	96b
yr. i. that blossoms a rose	475b
Zoroaster. .met his own i.	397a

Imageries: garlanded with carven i. 221b
Imagery shd…come natural 222b
Images: express the i. of their minds 14b
| strange i. of death | 346a |
| thro' a garden of bright i. | 35a |

Imagination: appear so fair to fond i. 473a
are of i. all compact	357b
as i. bodies forth the forms	357b
a thing i. boggles at	75b
by bare i. of a feast	374b
civet. .to sweeten my i.	343b
creep into my study of i.	359a
fairy. .writing wh. depends on. .i.	140b
his i…wings of an ostrich	255b
how abhorred in my i. it is!	336b

Imagination (cont.)

if i. amend them	357b
i. cold and barren	55b
i. droops her pinion	71a
i. of a boy is healthy	217a
i. of man's heart is evil	492b
i. the rudder	222a
i. to give them shape	333b
i., wh…is but another name	470a
in ages of i.	31a
in the i. of their hearts	508b
is to defile the i.	412a
O Sleep. .charm my i.	161a
refined play of the i.	57b
such tricks hath strong i.	357b
the truth of i.	222a
to his i. for his facts	401a
to save those that have no i.	391b
were it not for i., Sir	210a
what the i. seizes as beauty	222a
whispering chambers of I.	124a

Imaginations: my i. are as foul as Vulcan's 334a
| perish thro' their own i. | 482a |

Imaginative or domestic passages 222a
Imagine: all that they i. is to do me evil 485b
| the people i. a vain thing? | 481b |

Imagined: exhausted worlds, and then i. new 213b
| i. such a device | 483a |

Imaginings: dreams and the light i. 397a
| less than horrible i. | 346b |

Imbower: high over-arch'd i. 271b
Imitate: i. the action of the tiger 382a
| obliged to i. himself | 308b |

Imitation: i…the sincerest. .of flattery 103b
not a good i. of Johnson	58b
there can be no i.	177a
vocation were endless i.	466b

Imitations: poorest of all i. 308b
Imitators, you slavish herd 543b
Imlac: business of a poet, said I. 213b
Immanuel: call his name I. 501b
Immense, of fishy form 39b
Immensity: belie thy soul's i. 466b
| i. cloistered in thy. .womb | 133a |

Immodest words admit of no defence 128a
Immoral: as that most i. man 228a
Immortal: being a thing i. as itself 331a
driven away from our i. day	33a
Heav'n had wanted one i. song	138a
Helen, make me i. with a kiss	258b
his biting is i.	325a
I have i. longings in me	325a
I have lost the i. part	361b
i. diamond, is i. diamond	197a
i. in his own despite	303b
i., though no more	68a
sole thing of worth i.	293a
the minute makes i.	49a
thou must be made i.	352a
what i. hand or eye	31b

Immortality: born for i. 467b
I long to believe in i.	223b
like a load of i.	222b
nurslings of i.!	397a
over whom thy i. broods	466b
slumber out their i.	113b
the fields of I.	393b
the stedfast rock of i.	38b
they gave, their i.	39a
this longing after i.	1b
this mortal must put on i.	515a
this mortal shall assume its i.	77a
'tis i.	280a
yet is their hope full of i.	520a

Immortalize: art that can i. 109a
| mortal thing so to i. | 408a |

Immortalizes: verse, that i. 113a
Immortals: never. .appear the I. 102a
| President of the I. | 181a |

Immoveable, looking tranquillity 104b
Imogen: conceiving an Iago as an I. 223a
Imparadised in one another's arms 274a
Impart: doth Himself i. 224a
Impatience wd. be so much fretted 208a
Impatient of servitude 55b
Impeach: I i. him in the name of. . India 56a

Impeach (cont.)
I i. the common enemy 56a
Impeachment: own the soft i. 400b
Impediment: cause, or just i. 481a
marched on without i. 385a
Impediments: i. to great enterprises 14b
true minds admit i. 389a
Imperative: categorical i. 575b
not the i. labour after all 43a
Imperfections: i. wh. have been
divinely appointed 314b
pass my i. by 149b
with all my i. on my head 331b
Imperial: i. fiddlestick! 83b
my i. kitten! 83b
the i. votaress passed on 356b
Imperially: learn to think I. 87a
Impertinence: Memory of this I. 153a
Impertinent: i, being an Oxonian 150b
to make i. description 65b
Imperturbe: me i. 457a
Impious: when. .i. men bear sway 150a
Important: infinitely the most i. 135a
unimportant—i. 83b
where the most i. peers. . most i. 17b
Importunate: rashly i. 195b
telling a tale not too i. 284a
Importunity of business 240a
Impossibilities: honours of men's i. 343b
not i. enough in Religion 41b
Impossibility: by despair upon i. 260a
Impossible: can't believe i. things 84b
eliminated the i. 136a
highly i. scene 163a
highly i. tree 163a
i. to be silent 56a
it is certain because it is i. 554a
I wish it were i. 212a
Patently I. and Vain 234a
peace is put in i. things 92b
six i. things before breakfast 84b
some false i. shore 8b
that not i. she 115a
think on things i. 141b
'tis a thing i. to frame 464b
with men this is i. 507b
Impostors: treat those two i. just the
same 230a
Impotently: as i. moves as you or I 153b
rolls i. on as Thou or I 153b
Impression: Time but the i. deeper 61b
Imprint: done set it in i. 257a
Imprison: take me to you, i. me 133a
Imprisoned in the viewless winds 352a
Imprisonment: ache, penury, and i. 352a
Improbable: remains, however i. 136a
Improve: i. his shining tail 82b
still born to i. us in every part 169b
Improvement: i. is from within 157b
schemes of political i. 208a
Improvements in the lot of mankind 265b
Impudence: starve for want of i. 141a
yr. i. protects you sairly 61b
Impulse: i. from a vernal wood 471b
own i. every creature stirs 7b
slave of circumstance and i. 73b
this or that poor i. 46a
Impulses of deeper birth 469a
Impure: defaming as i. what God
declares 274b
Impurer: from th' i. matter free 66a
Impute: i. my Fall to Sin 154a
none to one cd. sovereignty i. 136b
In: birds, without. .despair to get i. 454b
i. for a penny, i. for a pound 164a
such as are i. . .wish to get out 148b
such as are out wish to get i. 148b
the one is i., the other out 94b
who's i., who's out 344a
yammered, 'Let me i.' 235b
Inaccuracy: I hate i. 67a
Inactivity: masterly i. 256a
Inane: along the illimitable i. 433a
in the intense i. 397b
Inanimate: depravity of i. things 178b
if aught i. e'er grieves 68b
Inanity: all torpid i. 97a
Inapprehensible, we clutch thee! 442a
Inarticulate hour 312a
Inattention: with patient i. hear him 263a
Inaudible to the vast multitude 464b

Incantation: i. of this verse 396b
thy rod of i. 161a
Incapable: I am i. of a tune 238b
i. of her own distress 336a
Incapacity: courted by I. 31a
Incarnadine: Cheek of her's to i. 152a
the multitudinous seas i. 348a
Incarnations: glimmering I. 392a
Incense: i.-bearing tree 101a
i. is an abomination 501a
nor what soft i. hangs 220a
stupefying i.—smoke 45a
the gods themselves throw i. 344a
thy pipe, thy i. sweet 220a
Incensed: buffets of the world. .so i. 348b
i. with indignation Satan stood 273a
Incertainties: more certain than i. 21a
Inch: no painful i. to gain 96b
Inchcape Rock 406b
Inches: die by famine die by i. 185b
Incident: what is i. but. .character 204b
Incidents well linked 108a
Inclination: read just. .as i. leads him 207a
Incline our hearts to keep this law 480a
Inclined: as to embrace me she i. 278b
he i. unto me 484a
Inclines: neither way i. 323b
Income: annual i. twenty pounds 122a
in wh. a good i. is of no avail 404a
organism. .live beyond its i. 66b
Incommunicable: burden of the i. 120a
i. sleep 463b
Incompleteness: flowed around our i. 43b
Incomprehensibles: not three i. 478b
Inconsolable to the minuet 400a
Inconstancy: Constant, in Nature
were i. 107a
constant in nothing but i. 21a
curse thine own i. 79b
nothing. .constant, save i. 417b
yet this i. is such 250a
Inconstant: i. woman. .never be very
unhappy 160a
woman. .vain, i., childish 222a
Inconvenience: change is not made
without i. 196b
Inconvenient: i. to be poor 107b
poverty. .is confoundedly i. 404b
Incorpsed: as he had been i. 336a
Incorruptible: but we are i. 514a
sea-green I. [Robespierre] 80b
Incorruption: put on i. 515a
raised in i. 515a
Increase: as if i. of appetite 330a
blessest the i. of it 486a
dry up in her the organs of i. 342a
fairest creatures we desire i. 387a
God gave the i. 514a
good and i. of the world 426b
he must i., but I must decrease 510b
i. of faith, hope, and charity 479b
Incredible: round an i. star 92b
Incredulity! the wit of fools 87b
Increment: an unregarded i. 293b
unearned i. 265b
Ind: from the east to western I. 327a
wealth of Ormus and of I. 272a
Indebted and discharged 273b
Independence: first of. .blessings, i. 162a
make up the Declaration of I. 94a
towns, where civic i. flings 77b
Independent: ef this ain't to be i. 250b
Indestructible: Union. .of i. States 88a
Index: thunders in the i. 335a
Indexes: such i. . .small pricks 368b
writes i. to perfection 170a
India: for the treasures of I. 161b
how now, my metal of I.! 371a
if to far I.'s coast we sail 161a
I.'s coral strand 184a
I.'s spicy shores 107b
in the name of the people of I. 56a
key of I. is in London 128b
they made Britain I. 385b
up from I. glances 200a
Indian: a poor I.'s sleep 220b
go, like the I., in another life 301b
I. Summer of the heart 458b
lay out ten to see a dead I. 367b
like the base I. 364a
lo, the poor I. 300b

Indian (cont.)
only good I. is a dead I. 400a
pith of an I. cane 2a
the nice Morn on the I. steep 266b
Indictment against an whole people 55b
Indies: augmentation of the I. 371b
bring home the wealth of the I. 210a
Indifference: fatal to religion as i. 58a
i. closely bordering on aversion 412b
Indifferent: but to be i. to them. .in-
humanity 390a
i., and cannot enjoy it 206b
Indifferently: i. minister justice 480b
I will look on both i. 337b
Indigent: how i. the great! 175b
Indigestion: sows hurry and reaps i. 413b
Indignantly: day and night held on i. 8b
Indignation: i. wd. give birth 548b
let i. vex him 485b
where fierce i. can no longer tear 420a
Indirection: wring. .vile trash by. .i. 341a
Indirections: by i. find directions 332a
Indiscretion: blazing i. 283b
Indite: songes make and wel i. 88a
Inditing of a good matter 484b
Individual: injustice done to an I. 217a
liberty of the i. 266a
no i. cd. resent 419a
not an i., but a species 151a
not by yr. i. whiskers 65b
Individuals: i. pass like shadows 56a
worth of the i. composing it 266a
Indubitably: they so very i. are 25a
Indulge the loud unseemly jape 25b
Indulgences, dispenses, pardons 273b
Industry: avarice, the spur of i. 201a
captains of i. 81b
i. will improve them 308b
nobility. .abateth i. 15a
Inebriate: cups that cheer but
not i. 112a
to cheer but not i. 28a
Inebriated with. .his own verbosity 128b
Ineffectual: beautiful and i. angel 9b
remote and i. Don 26b
Inert: the earth, tideless and i. 18a
Inevitable: arguing with the i. 251a
I did not believe in i. war 242b
Inexactitude: terminological i. 95a
Inexorable: more fierce and more i. 366a
Inez: saw you not fair I.? 194b
Infallible: none of us i. 443a
Infamous: exceeds an i. history 42b
rich, quiet, and i. 254b
Infancy: lies about us in our i. 466a
nations. .have their i. 33b
wayward was thy i. 385a
Infant: at first the i. 326b
furnish the fair I.'s bed 115a
i. crying in the night 430b
lisping i. prattling on his knee 59b
man in the cradle of an i. 58a
sooner murder an i. 31a
the i. phenomenon 124b
timely blossom, i. fair 296b
to a little i. perhaps. .as painful 14a
to the ragged i. threaten war 114a
where the noble I. lay 114b
yr. i. beauty cd. beget no pleasure 320b
Infantry: Regiment o' British I. 229a
that small i. warred on 271b
Infants: like i.' slumbers 224a
who but i. question in such wise 313a
Infect to the north star 358a
Infection: against i. and. .war 375a
Infelicity: score of constant i. 425a
Inferior: knowing myself i. to myself 279a
Inferiority: conscious of an i. 209a
Infernal: hail i. world 271a
Infidel: as a dog is an i. 207b
now, i., I have you on the hip 355a
the fellow is an i. 207b
Wine has play'd the I. 154a
worse than an i. 516b
Infidelity: indifference. .half i. 58a
Infidels: I., and Hereticks 479b
Jews might kiss, and i. adore 302b
Infinite: an i. Majesty 478a
as i. a justice too 47a
i. is a torment to me 562b
mercy every way is i. 46b

Infinite (cont.)
there is an I. in him 81b
tho' i. can never meet 260a
Infinitude: being's heart..is with i. 469b
Infinity: I. in the palm of yr. hand 29a
shares the nature of i. 463a
Infirm of purpose! give me the dagger 348a
Infirmities: bear his friend's i. 341a
thine often i. 516b
Infirmity: prop to our i. 469b
that last i. of noble mind 269b
Inflammation of his weekly bills 70b
Inflict: can else i. do I repent 271a
Influence: a constant i., a peculiar grace 465a
bereaves of their bad i. 465a
corrupt i. wh. is..prodigality 56a
spheres of i. 526a
under the name of I. 56b
upon whose i. Neptune's empire 329b
whose bright eyes rain i. 269a
Influences: skyey i. 351b
sweet i. of Pleiades 497b
Influenza: call it i. if you like 27a
no i. in my young days 27a
Inform: occasions do i. against me 335a
she can so i. the mind 472a
Information: i...is sometimes incorrect 204b
I only ask for i. 122a
Times contains more useful i. 97a
where we can find i. upon it 208b
Informed the tenement of clay 138a
Infortune: worst kinde i. is this 90a
Ingeminate the word Peace 203a
Ingirt: spirits do i. thee round 78b
Ingle: his wee bit i. 59b
Inglorious: mean our object and i. 469a
Ingots: of two gold i. 259a
whose back with i. bows 351b
Ingratitude: I hate i. more in a man 372a
i., more strong than traitors' 340a
i., thou marble-hearted fiend 342a
unkind as man's i. 326b
Ingratitudes: great-siz'd monster of i. 369a
Ingredient is a devil 361b
Ingres's the modern man 46b
Ingress: our i. into the world 249a
Inhabitant: the poor i. below 59a
Inhabitants: like the i. o' the earth 346a
the only i. of the field 57a
Inhabiters: all the i. thereof 487a
Inhabits: being help'd, i. there 372b
Inhearse: thoughts in my brain i. 388b
Inherit: all who. it i., shall dissolve 367b
meek..shall i. the earth 505a
Inheritance: rain upon thine i. 486a
ruinous i. 541a
Inheritor of..kingdom of heaven 481a
Inheritors of unfulfilled renown 392b
Inhuman: ere ceased the i. shout 69a
Inhumanity: man's i. to man 61b
that's the essence of i. 390a
In-i-go Jones 405b
Iniquities: bruised for our i. 503a
Iniquity: draw i. with cords 501a
I lack i. sometimes 359b
in the bond of i. 512a
laid on him the i. of us all 503a
rejoiceth not in i. 514b
that grey i. 377b
ye have reaped i. 504a
Injure: I ne'er cd. i. you 400a
Injured: forgiveness to the i. 139b
Injuries: adding insult to i. 280b
i. that they themselves procure 342b
Injury..sooner forgotten..insult 90b
Injustice: conscience with i. is corrupted 384a
endure an hour and i. done 199b
i. done to the Individual 217a
Ink: all the sea were i. 251b
gall enough in thy i. 371b
he hath not drunk i. 344b
i. in my pen ran cold 449b
uniforms turned up with i. 67b
until his i. were temper'd 345a
Inkstand: mighty i. too 192b
Inland: he's down at an i. town 164a
i. far we be 466b

Inlets: thro' creeks and i. making 96b
Inmost: see the i. part of you 335a
Inn: an i. where travellers bait 205a
in the worst i.'s worst room 302b
life at best is but an i. 200b
no room for them in the i. 508b
not an i., but an hospital 42a
now unto mine i. must I 75b
old i., and the lights, and the fire 284b
remember an I., Miranda? 27a
take mine ease in mine i. 378b
that dark i., the grave! 317b
to gain the timely i. 349a
warmest welcome, at an i. 399b
wot lived in Lyons' I. 454a
Inner: by his Spirit in the i. man 515b
the i. man 481b
Innisfree: go to I. 475a
Innkeepers: righteous minds of i. 93b
Innocence: betrayed my credulous i. 267b
bowers of i. and ease 168a
came i. and she 441a
companions, i., and health 168a
dallies with the i. of love 371a
glides in modest i. away 214a
ignorance is not i. 47b
I. is closing up his eyes 137b
I., thy Sister dear 260b
our peace, our fearful i. 467b
purity and place and i. 274b
Valour and I. have latterly 233b
was i. for i. 372b
Innocencies: dead, wing'd I. 293b
Innocency: keep i., and take heed 484a
wash my hands in i. 483b
Innocent: be i. of the knowledge 349a
I am i. of the blood 508a
i. from the great offence 482b
i. is the heart's devotion 399b
rich shall not be i. 498b
she was as i. as gay 319b
source of i. merriment 164a
taken reward against the i. 482b
Innocently: be more i. employed 208b
Innovate: to i. is not to reform 57b
Innovator: time is the greater i. 15b
Inns: all I. have been driven 27a
go to i. to dine 93a
you have lost your I. 27a
Innumerable: join the i. caravan 53a
Inquest: greatest i. of the nation 56a
Inquire: ever sceptic could i. for 65a
Inquisition: abashless i. of each star 443a
I. dogs 437b
Inquisitorious..duncery 279a
Insane: every hereditary monarch was i. 17b
Inscriptions: in lapidary i. 208b
Inscrutable: dumb, i., and grand 7b
Insect: so..grovelling an i. as I 417b
this 'ere 'Tortis' is an i. 535a
Insects: troublesome i. of the hour 57a
Insensibility: it argues an i. 238b
stark i. 206a
Inside: worm in yr. little i. 165a
Insides: carrying Three I. 78b
Insight: i., amplitude of mind 470a
moment's i. is sometimes worth 194b
tasks in hours of i. will'd 7a
Insignificant: two as i. men as any 450a
Insincerity: mark of i. of purpose 35a
Insisture, course, proportion 368b
Insolence: aspiring pride and i. 258b
drown the memory of that i. 153b
flown with i. and wine 271b
supports with i. 212b
Inspiration: a lasting i. 470a
contortions..without the i. 58b
find no more i. in her 390b
genius is one per cent. i. 143b
Inspire: till thou i. the whole 103a
Inspired: every sweetness that i. 259b
Inspirit: songs may i. us 48a
Inspissated gloom 207b
Instance: some precious i. of itself 335b
Instances: not with such familiar i. 340b
wise saws and modern i. 326b
Instancy: majestic i. 441b
Instant: be i. in season 516b
Instead: fist i. of a stick 64b
Instinct: a gosling to obey i. 328b

Instinct (cont.)
heart with English i. 136b
i. bring back the old names 101b
i. for being unhappy 315a
i. is a great matter 377b
i. is important, O! 166b
i. of all great souls 55a
I was a coward on i. 377b
my natural i. teaches me 166b
with a natural i. to discern 465a
Instincts: high i. before wh. 466b
Institution: i. of the dear love 457a
such as are in the i. 148b
Institutions: paw him with..dirty i. 444a
woman is one of the greatest i. 451a
Instruct: books..propose to i. 120a
in the graver gown i. mankind 299b
Instruction: I will better the i. 354a
the horses of i. 31a
Instructions: follows his own i. 353a
Instructor: grand I., Time 58a
Instrument: all harmony of i. 392b
i. of ten strings 483b
call me what i. you will 334b
Heaven's happy i. 313b
I tune the i. here 133b
made an i. to know if the moon 65b
scatter sounds out of an i. 464b
sweeter than the sound of an i. 42a
Thy most dreaded i. 468a
Instruments: docile i. in its hands 266a
genius and the mortal i. 338b
i. of darkness tell us truths 346a
make i. to plague us 344a
our i. to melancholy bells 366a
Insufferable: Oxford..made me i. 24b
Insulated: knows no i. spot 464b
Insult: adding i. to injuries 280b
blockhead's i. points the dart 213a
bones from i. to protect 174b
injury sooner forgotten than..i. 90b
look that threatened her with i. 57a
Insults: first i. the victim 114a
Insured: they were heavily i. 163a
Insurrection: nature of an i. 338b
Intangible: O world i. 442a
Intellect: certain ripeness in i. 222b
creeds a disease of the i. 147b
discerning i. of Man 464a
his i. is improperly exposed 404b
is it weakness of i., birdie 165a
living i. that bred them 279a
opinion..determined..not by..i. 408a
our meddling i. misshapes 471b
put on I. 31a
scepticism of the i. 288b
the march of I. 407a
Intellects: furnish you with argument and i. 171a
Intellectual: a tear is an i. thing 30b
he was not an i. Croesus 129b
I am an i. chap 164a
i. All-in-all 468b
lords of ladies i. 70a
lose..this i. being 272b
moral or i. damage 575a
passage to the i. world 411b
the i. power, thro' words 464a
thirdly, i. ability 10b
yet being i...amongst the noblest 75b
Intelligence: gulls him with i. 388b
whence you owe this strange i. 346a
Intelligences: we are the i. 132b
Intelligent: on the whole we are not i. 166b
Intemperance: brisk i. of youth 161b
Intense: not with too i. a care 131b
Intensity: excellence of..art is its i. 222a
Intent: build above the deep i. 137b
forget not yet the tried i. 473b
guilt defeats my strong i. 334b
his first avowed i. 54b
i. of bearing them is just 379a
it is my fixed i. 19b
our true i. is 357b
prick the sides of my i. 347a
resist his uncontrollable i. 278a
same with i. to deceive 182a
th' i. is al 90b
the less we knew of its i. 284a
truth that's told with bad i. 29b
working out a pure i. 468a

ttention: affection! thy i. stabs | 373a
without some intellectual i. | 314b
i. are savage-wild | 366a
ter: in hugger-mugger to i. him | 335b
ter-assured of the mind | 134a
tercession for the transgressors | 503a
terchange: quiet i. of sentiments | 208b
tercourse: dreary i. of daily life | 472a
terdict upon her hopes | 469a
terest: but O, I du in i. | 250a
common i. always will prevail | 138b
5 per cent. is the natural i. | 254b
it's i. that keeps peace | 116a
landed and . . monied i. | 2a
learn their real i. to discern | 109b
lend fresh i. to a . . tale | 72b
nor any i. unborrowed | 472a
teresting: most grati—most i. | 135b
obligation . . that it be i. | 204b
terests: contests about their carnal i. | 66a
terfused: far more deeply i. | 472a
terim: all the i. is . . a phantasma | 338b
terlunar cave | 277b
termission: I did laugh sans i. | 326a
terpretation: bearing some other i. | 136a
i. of the thing | 504a
terpreter: God is his own i. | 110a
i. of the cogitations thereof | 520b
i.'s the hardest to be understood | 400a
terrupt: did ever woman . . i. a man | 411a
terval: make a lucid i. | 140b
tervals: lucid i. and happy pauses | 16b
lucid i. of life | 464a
terview: strange and fatal i. | 132b
testines: Poetry . . of the smaller i. | 80a
tolerable: O vile, i. | 366b
this i. deal of sack | 378a
toxicated: exposes himself when
  he is i. | 210a
i. with my own eloquence | 129b
toxication: best of life is but i. | 70b
Wordsworth's standard of i. | 401a
treasured: weak beginnings lie i. | 380b
trigue, that 's the crime | 173a
rigues half-gather'd | 113b
troduced: cut any one you've been
  i. to | 85b
when I'm i. to one | 308a
troduction to any literary work | 206b
rude: I hope I don't i. | 298b
ruders on his ancient home | 8b
urned: we saw thee quietly i. | 331a
vades: he i. authors | 142a
variable: glass o' the i. | 126b
vasion of a common enemy | 238a
ent: beats all the lies you can i. | 29b
nore than I i. or is invented | 379b
necessary to i. him (God) | 566a
oung men are fitter to i. | 16a
ented: accurst be . . first i. war | 259a
ll the poems that ever were i. | 85a
ond thing vainly i. | 491b
e first i. thee | 216b
nany that haven't been i. | 85a
ho first i. Work | 240a
ou i. it just now | 83b
ention: a long poem is a test of i. | 222a
weak i. of the enemy | 95b
eggars i. | 111a
rightest heaven of i. | 381a
rst heir of my i. | 386b
breeds i. | 148b
is unfruitful | 55b
's my own i. | 85a
at e'er i. played | 372a
is never by i. got | 420a
entions: a-whoring with their . . i. | 488b
ught out many i. | 499b
entor: O mighty-mouthed i. | 427a
entors: fall'n on the i.' heads | 337a
ents: about the best thing God i. | 46b
ncible: none as i. as they | 107b
sible: blackens . . water . . till he
  becomes i. | 2b
ypocrisy . . evil that walks i. | 273b
ve i. and dim | 448a
world i., we view thee | 442a
ceipt of fern-seed, we walk i. | 377a
all I join the choir i. | 144b
sibly: wind does move . . i. | 31b

Invitation: more i. than command | 410b
Invited: oft i. me | 360a
Invites: his wit i. you | 108a
Invulnerable: it is, as the air, i. | 329b
Inward: celestial light shine i. | 273b
  with my i. eye 'tis an Old Man | 29b
Ionian: isle under I. skies | 393b
  valleys of I. hills | 435a
Iope: white I., blithe Helen | 78b
Ipswich and Oxford | 386b
Iram indeed is gone | 152a
Ire: where slept thine i. | 218a
Ireland: discourse in praise of I. | 296a
  general . . from I. coming | 383b
  great Gaels of I. | 92a
  how 's poor ould I? | 525b
  I'll not forget old I. | 29a
  I. gives England her soldiers | 264b
  moment . . name of I. is mentioned | 405a
  romantic I. 's dead | 474b
  said to be done in I. | 402a
  sang, to sweeten I.'s wrong | 476b
Irene: ill-success of I. | 206b
  [I. Adler] is always the woman | 135a
Iris: in the Spring a livelier i. | 432a
  one vast I. of the West | 69a
Irish: forbid to grow on I. ground | 525b
  howling of I. wolves | 327b
  I. are a fair people | 208b
  led by an I. general | 391a
  no blithe I. lad | 76b
  now the I. are ashamed | 261a
  peculiarity of the I. bull | 143b
  upon the I. shore | 61a
Irishman . . potato in his head | 181a
Irked: it i. him to be here | 8b
Iron: armies clad in i. | 277b
  beat the i. while it is hot | 142a
  blood and i. | 567b
  bound in misery and i. | 488b
  bruise them with a rod of i. | 481b
  dungeon, nor strong links of i. | 338a
  every icy crag tinkled like i. | 466a
  I.—Cold I.—is master of them | 228a
  i. entered into his soul | 488b
  i. sharpeneth i. | 498b
  I saw the i. enter into his soul | 411a
  man that meddles with cold i.! | 65a
  the i. shuts amain | 269b
  the sound of i. on stone | 119b
  wink and hold out mine i. | 381b
  wood painted to look like i. | 568a
Iron-bosomed sea | 313a
Ironies: Life's Little I. | 180b
Irons: heat me these i. hot | 374a
  two i. in the fire | 23a
Iron-sleet of arrowy shower | 175a
Irony: humour and i. . . unconscious | 66b
Irradiation of a mind | 395b
Irrationally held truths | 203a
Irregulars: Baker Street i. | 136a
Irrelevant thing in nature | 239a
Is: he i.—what thou shalt be | 280a
  it i., but hadn't ought to be | 182a
  such i.; what i. to be? | 442a
  whatever i., i. in its causes just | 141a
  wh. i., and wh. . . i. to come | 518a
Isa: obedient to I. Keith | 155a
Isaac: God of I. | 493b
  thine only son I. | 493a
Iscariot: Judas . . not I. | 511a
Ischyros: He upbeareth me, I. | 441a
Iser: of I., rolling rapidly | 76b
Isis: in Cam, to patient science | 463a
  may Cam and I., preach it long | 299a
Island: as an inland i. | 412b
  floating bulwark of the i. | 28b
  i. was shaken with an earthquake | 2b
  live on yon beautiful i. | 120b
  right little, tight little I. | 120b
  shieling of the misty i. | 320b
  some secreted i. | 469b
  this i. all her own | 449a
  what a snug little I. | 120b
Islanded by cities fair | 395a
Islands: know not where His i. lift | 458b
  many flowering i. lie | 395a
  parson for the I. of the Blest | 235a
  round many western i. | 220b
Island-story: rough i. | 435a
Island-valley of Avilion | 429b

Isle: a ship, an i., and a sickle moon | 155a
  blow soft o'er Ceylon's i. | 184a
  guards his osier-i. | 443b
  I. of Beauty, Fare thee well! | 22a
  i. of Rum-ti-Foo | 163a
  i. under Ionian skies | 393b
  it frights the i. | 361a
  make its continent an i. | 293a
  many a green i. needs must be | 395a
  men of the Emerald I. | 137b
  natural bravery of yr. i. | 328b
  never was i. so little | 228b
  pumice i. in Baiae's bay | 396b
  some unsuspected i. | 50a
  suddenly raised a fairy i. | 293b
  the i. is full of noises | 367b
  this scepter'd i. | 375a
Isled: thank Him who i. us here | 435a
Isles: among the Ægean I. | 8a
  i. and rifted rocks | 267b
  kings of Tharsis and of the i. | 486b
  other flowering i. must lie | 395b
  sprinkled i., lily on lily | 46a
  taketh up the i. as a very little | 502b
  the i. may be glad thereof | 488a
  the i. of Greece | 70b
  throned on her . . hundred i.! | 69a
  touch the Happy I. | 439a
Islington: bailiff's daughter . . in I. | 531b
  from I. to Marybone | 30b
  village less than I. wilt grow | 107a
Ismenian steep | 277b
Isn't: as it i., it ain't | 84a
Isolate pure spirits | 44a
Isolated: stands splendidly i. | 156a
Isolation: our splendid i. | 172a
Israel: all the waters of I. | 496b
  beauty of I. is slain | 495b
  deliver I., O God | 483a
  gather together the outcasts of I. | 490b
  I arose a mother in I. | 494b
  in his border see I. set | 47a
  I saw all I. scattered | 496a
  I., Athens, Florence | 203a
  I. loved Joseph more than all | 493a
  I., of the Lord beloved | 319b
  lost sheep of the house of I. | 506a
  many widows were in I. | 509a
  neither will I let I. go | 493b
  O thou worship of I. | 483a
  ransom captive I. | 286b
  so great faith, no, not in I. | 506a
  success . . was found on I.'s side | 110a
  sweet psalmist of I. | 496a
  there is a prophet in I. | 496b
  to yr. tents, O I. | 496a
Israelite: behold an I. indeed | 510b
Israelites: Are they I.? so am I | 515a
  I. passed over on dry land | 494b
Israfel: dwell where I. hath dwelt | 298a
Issachar is a strong ass | 493b
Issue: happy i. out of . . affliction | 479a
  kings their i. guard | 274a
  rich legacy unto their i. | 340a
Issues: but to fine i. | 351a
  joined great i., good or bad | 465b
  leave the i. calmly to God | 81a
Issuing on a summer's morn | 276a
Isthmus: i. of a middle state | 301a
  this narrow I. 'twixt two . . seas | 282a
Isyphill: fair I. | 402a
It: it's just I. | 237b
Italia: I., I. shall be free | 265a
  I.! oh I.! | 69a
Italian: French, I., Spaniard | 42a
  led by an I. general | 391a
  no I. priest shall tithe | 374a
  or perhaps I.! | 166a
  rare I. master, Julio Romano | 373b
  roof of blue I. weather | 395b
  she faded 'midst I. flowers | 184b
  writ in very choice I. | 334b
Italians call reg'larly flummoxed | 126b
Italy: after seeing I. | 58b
  a man who has not been in I. | 209a
  Creator made I. from designs | 446b
  graved inside of it, 'I.' | 46a
  Greece, I., and England | 141a
  grete poete of I. | 89a
  his doublet in I. | 353a
  I. a paradise for horses | 64b

ENGLISH INDEX

Italy (cont.)
I...indifferent to..Walter Scott 81b
I. is a geographical expression 569a
I., my I.! 46a
linking our England to his I. 51b
some jay of I. 328b
thou Paradise of exiles, I.! 395a
Itch: Divinity had catch'd the i. 65a
insatiate i. of scribbling 162b
i. of literature comes over a man 250a
i. of writing 549a
mine eyes do i. 363a
poor i. of your opinion 328a
Itching: to have an i. palm 340b
Item, two lips 370a
Iteration: prone to any i. of nuptials 105b
thou hast damnable i. 376b
Ithuriel with his spear 274b
Itself: it is still i. 359b
nor for i. hath any care 32a
nothing of i. will come 464b
nought but i. to teach 36a
seeketh not i. to please 32a
to i. it only live and die 388b
It-will-wash-no-more 445a
Itylus: half assuaged for I. 420a
slaying of I. 422b
Ivory: cargo of i. 261b
i., and apes, and peacocks 496a
i. on which I work 570a
i. overlaid with sapphires 500b
my lady seems of i. forehead 284b
thy neck is as a tower of i. 500b
thy skin is i., so white 161a
Ivy: and the bonny i.-tree 525a
as creeping i. clings to wood 110b
bees in the i.-bloom 397a
i. falls with the Bacchanal's 420b
i. serpentine 398a
just like the i. I'll cling to you 266b
like an owl in an i.-bush 418b
pluck an i. branch for me 311a
the holly and the i. 526b
with i. never sere 269a
Ivy-tod is heavy with snow 99b
Ixionian wheel 433a

J

J: dig in the ribs I gives Mrs. J. 416b
Jabberwock: beware the J. 83b
Jacinth: eleventh, a . 520a
Jack: as soon dine with J. Ketch 209a
banish plump J. 378a
dine with J. Wilkes 209a
gorging J. and guzzling Jimmy 440b
have you news of my boy J.? 232b
house that J. built 534b
J. lov'd his friend 120b
J. on the gallows-tree 319b
J. shall have Jill 357a
J. Sprat cd. eat no fat 534a
J.'s the king of all 454a
J. was embarrassed 73a
lamented J.! 102a
little J. Horner 532a
many a gentle person made a J. 384b
poor J., farewell! 379a
since every J. became a gentleman 384b
sixteen-string J. 209a
Spanking J. was so comely 120b
they all love J. 454a
this J., joke, poor potsherd 197b
watch for the life of poor J. 120b
Jackdaw sat on the Cardinal's chair 19a
Jacket: day hath put on his j. 193b
his j. was red 100b
Jacks: shy, insinuating J. 384b
Jackson standing like a stone wall 24b
Jacksonian vulgarity 304b
Jacob: all the dwellings of J. 487a
God of J. 493b
hollow of J.'s thigh 493a
J. served seven years 493a
J.'s sons and daughters 286b
J. was a plain man 493a
Lord will have mercy on J. yet 47a
sold his birthright unto J. 493a
take away the captivity of J. 487a
talk to him of J.'s ladder 205b

Jacob (cont.)
the voice is J.'s voice 493a
traffic of J.'s ladder 442a
Jade: let the galled j. wince 334b
Jades: holla, ye pampered J. of Asia 259b
hollow pamper'd j. of Asia 380a
Jads: deils an' j. thegether 63a
I like the j. for a' that 61a
Jael Heber's wife 494b
Jagged: maps a j. coast 36a
Jaguar: I've never seen a J. 230b
Jah: praise him in his Name J. 486a
Jail: being in a ship is being in a j. 207a
nothing was now left but a j. 122a
Jam: cleaned with champagne and apricot j. 416b
j. every other day 84b
j. tomorrow and j. yesterday 84b
Jamaica: of a J. gentleman..lately dead 211b
James (Jamie): dead of Joy, J. Lee 47b
Eliza, and our J. 216a
I saw my J.'s ghaist 20b
J. J. Morrison Morrison 266b
King J...call for his old shoes 321a
my J. was at sea 20b
Jamshyd: Courts where J. gloried 153a
J.'s Sev'n-ring'd Cup 152a
Jane: from J. to Elizabeth 11b
Honour unto England's J. 230b
J. lies in Winchester 230b
J. went to Paradise 230a
of the knight embracing J. 77b
Willie shall dance with J. 522b
Janet was as glad at that 528b
Janiculan: when from J. heights 96a
Janus of poets 142a
Janvier: Generals J. and Février 575b
Japanee that hang on 233b
Jape: loud unseemly j. 25b
Japes: feyned flaterye and j. 89a
Japheth: it might be J. 236a
Shem, Ham, and J. 492b
Jar: amid the city's j. 6b
Jargon: j. of the schools 305b
j. o' your schools 60a
Jargoning: their sweet j. 99b
Jarley: Mrs. J.'s waxwork 125a
Jarndyce and Jarndyce 121a
Jarring sectaries may learn 100b
Jasher: book of J. 494b
Jasper: first foundation was j. 520a
'J. first', I said 43a
j. of jocundite 143a
to look upon like a j. 518b
Javan or Gadier 277b
Jaws: gently smiling j. 82b
j. of darkness do devour it 356a
ponderous and marble j. 331a
the j. that bite 83b
Jay: heigh! the thrush and the j. 373a
some j. of Italy 328b
Jay-bird: what de j. say 181b
Jealous: as thou art j., Lord 133a
I the Lord thy God am a j. God 480a
j. for they are j. 362b
j. souls will not be answer'd so 362b
not ever j. for the cause 362b
one not easily j. 364a
to the j. confirmations strong 362a
who wit with j. eye surveys 94b
Jealousies: pipe blown by surmises, j. 379b
Jealousy: all j. to the bride 21b
beware, my lord, of j. 361b
full of artless j. 335b
I'd make a life of j. 361b
J. a human face 33a
j. heareth all things 520a
j. is cruel as the grave 501a
mine was j. in love 428b
nor j. was understood 275a
fear, and green-eyed j. 354a
thou tyrant, tyrant J. 140b
Jean Jacques: gospel according to J. 80b
Jebusite..maugre all God's promises 294b
Jebusites: Hivites and the J. 493b
Jefferson simplicity 304b
Jehovah: J. has triumph'd 282b
J., Jove or Lord! 304a
J. of the Thunders 230a
J., who in one night..pass'd 271b

Jehovah (cont.)
names divine of Jesus and J. 3
tell them I am, J. said 40
Jehu: J. said, what hast thou to do 49
J. the son of Nimshi 49
the sword of J. shall Elisha slay 49
Jelly: distill'd almost to j. with..fear 33
little pipkin fits this little j. 18
meaty j., too..is mellering 12
out, vile j.! 34
Jelofer amiable 40
Jemmy Grove: Young J. 53
Jenkin: ho! jolly J. 31
Jenkyns: Miss J. beat time 15
Jenny: J. kissed me 20
vengeance of J.'s case! 35
wait till the clouds roll by, J. 46
Jeopardy of their lives 49
Jerkin: like a leather j. 36
Jerks: bring me up by J. 12
Jerry: wouldn't do for you, J. 12
Jerusalem: as the curtains of J. 50
build thou the walls of J. 48
Building up of J. 3
built in J.'s wall 3
four great walls in the New J. 4
he hath redeemed J. 5
if I forget thee, O J. 49
if I prefer not J. in my mirth 49
I go bound in the spirit unto J. 51
I John saw the holy city, new J. 51
in metropolitan J. 2
in that J. shall Harry lie 38
I shd. not die but in J. 38
J., my happy home 52
J. the golden 28
J., thy sister calls 3
O J., J., thou that killest 5
O pray for the peace of J. 4
speak ye comfortably to J. 5
the hills stand about J. 4
the Lord doth build up J. 4
there J.'s pillars stood 4
there's J. and Madagascar 8
thryes hadde she been at J. 8
till we have built J. 5
was J. builded here 5
wise men from the east to J. 5
ye waste places of J. 5
Jeshurun waxed fat 4
Jessamine: pale j. 2
the casement j. stirr'd 4
the j. faint 3
Jesse: out of the stem of J. 5
sires and sons to J.'s fount 1
Jesses: for j. and restraints 3
her j. were my dear heart-strings 3
Jessica: look, how the floor of heaven 3
Jest: a fellow of infinite j. 3
a good j. for ever 3
glory, j. and riddle of the world 3
he had his j. 1
intermingle..j. with earnest 2
j. and youthful jollity 2
j.'s prosperity lies in the ear 2
most bitter is a scornful j. 3
Nestor swear the j. be laughable 3
put his whole wit in a j. 3
tells the j. without the smile 1
the jolt-head: ye did 1
to use my self in j. 1
Jested, quaffed, and swore 1
Jesters: shallow j. 1
Jesting: nor foolish talking, nor j.
oh, 'tis j., dancing, drinking
What is truth? said j. Pilate
Jestings: than our common j. are
Jests: with some excellent j.
Jesu: J., by a nobler deed
J., Lover of my soul 4
J., Mary and Joseph they bare
J., the very thought of Thee
O J. thou art standing
Thy Name, O J., be for ever blest
Jesuit: a tool, a J.
Jesus: Blood of J. whispers peace
disciple(s) whom J. loved 511a,
even so, come, Lord J.
gentle J., meek and mild
J. calls us; o'er the tumult
J. increased in wisdom and stature

sus (*cont.*)
J. speaks, and speaks to thee | 110a
J. the author and finisher | 517a
J…walking on the sea | 507a
J. was sitting in Moses' chair | 30a
J. wept | 511a
J.! with all thy faults I love thee | 67a
leaning on J.' bosom | 511a
little J., wast Thou shy | 441b
name of J. every knee shall bow | 516a
names divine of J. and Jehovah | 30a
J.'s and Judas equally aside | 147b
Sir, we wd. see J. | 511a
stand up for J. | 142b
sweet reasonableness of J. | 10b
sweet the name of J. sounds | 289a
that he may do for J.'s sake | 3b
that they had been with J. | 512a
this J. will not do | 30a
what was the sound of J.'s breath | 30a
with the cross of J. | 20a
ye belong to J. | 3a
sus Christ: also a prisoner of J. | 516b
if J. were to come to-day | 82a
is J. her lord | 415b
J., and him crucified | 514a
J. her little Child | 3b
J. is risen to-day | 524b, 558b
J.! our bales bate | 531a
J. the same yesterday | 517a
kingdom and patience of J. | 518a
s: how he j. under his..plumes | 371a
tty: come up J., rise and follow | 203a
v: clutched a cringing J. | 93a
false English Nobles and their J. | 294a
hath not a J. eyes | 354a
I am a Jew else; an Ebrew J. | 377a
neither Greek nor J. | 516a
not a Heathen, or a J. | 452b
son of Kish that lofty J. | 261a
the J. that Shakespeare drew | 304a
then must the J. be merciful | 354b
wel: a precious j. in his head | 325b
have I caught my heavenly j. | 401b
j. in a ten-times-barr'd-up chest | 374b
. of gold in a swine's snout | 498a
lest my j. it shd. tine | 59b
mine eternal j. given | 348b
no j. is like Rosalind | 327a
rich j. in an Ethiop's ear | 365a
sets the j.-print of yr. feet | 434a
the immediate j. of their souls | 361b
the j. of the just | 448a
the poor j. of their souls! | 412a
vels: boys and girls..were..j. | 445a
captain j. in the carcanet | 387b
decked with j. had she on | 528a
I'll give my j. for..beads | 375b
j. five-words long | 436a
j. make women..fat or..thin | 21b
put precious j. into a garret | 13b
these, said she, are my j. | 64b
invalued j. | 384b
wry: sepulchre in stubborn J. | 375a
ws: he that is born King of the
  J. | 504b
J. might kiss, and infidels adore | 302b
., Turks, Infidels | 479b
odd of God to choose the J. | 140b
of Rome, J. and proselytes | 512a
so to the J. old Canaan stood | 453b
stock-jobbers and j. | 111a
three paynims, three J. | 257a
ill the conversion of the J. | 260a
: my very walk shd. be a j. | 360b
wooing..is as a Scotch j. | 358a
ging veins of rhyming..wits | 259a
: Jack shall have J. | 357a
ted: better be courted and j. | 77a
n: they called him Sunny J. | 179a
imy: guzzling J. | 440b
J. was good and true | 163a
go: by j. if we do | 201b
g: the living j. | 171a
n: J. as my lady is as good | 189b
Johnny has got his J. | 522b
ome men must love..Joan | 344b
while greasy J. doth keel the pot | 345b
o: and a good j. too | 167a
blessed the latter end of J. | 497b
describing the afflictions of J. | 14a

Job (*cont.*)
doth J. fear God | 496b
find some needful j. | 229b
heard of the patience of J. | 517b
husband is a whole-time j. | 27a
leave their j. when they..choose | 234b
poor as J…but not so patient | 379b
seek yr. j. with thankfulness | 229b
Jobiska: Aunt J. | 243b
Joblillies and the Garyalies | 155b
Jobling, there *are* chords | 121b
Jockey of Norfolk | 385a
Joe: poor old J. | 156b
Jog: j. on with (£40,000 a year) | 572a
j. on the foot-path | 373a
John: Don J. of Austria | 92b
I J. saw the holy city | 519b
I J., who also am yr. brother | 518a
J. Anderson my Jo, J. | 61a
J. Brown's body | 178a
J. he cried in vain | 108b
J.'s ideal j. | 194a
J. now to be burned alive | 47a
J.'s soul flared into the dark | 47a
J. to the seven churches | 518a
J., unhappily, thought fit | 305b
J. was a very good man | 163a
Long J. Brown | 31a
man..whose name was J. | 510b
Matthew, Mark, Luke, and J. | 2b
maun totter down, J. | 61a
mony a canty day, J. | 61a
my brother J., the evil one | 29b
oh No J.! No J.! | 525b
Sure J. and I are more than quit | 305a
the real J. | 194a
Thomas' ideal J. | 194a
to J. I ow'd great obligation | 305b
John Bull | 4b
John Clay: hark you, J. | 216a
John Naps: old J. of Greece | 366b
Johnnie (Johnny): J. Comes March-
  ing Home Again | 527b
J. has got his Joan | 522b
J. lad, cock up yr. beaver | 193b
little J. Head-in-air | 193a
silly little J., look | 193a
J. Cope, are ye wauking | 193b
John of Gaunt: Old J. | 374b
talks as familiarly of J. | 380b
John Peel | 173a
Johnson: Burke observed that J. | 58a
Cham of literature, J. | 405b
Dr. J. condemns what..he dis-
  approves | 58b
[Dr. J.] gets at the substance | 238a
[Dr. J.] has no formal preparation | 308b
Dr. J.'s morality was as English | 182b
Dr. J.'s sayings wd. not appear | 295b
J…cd. repeat a complete chapter | 209b
J. hewed passages thro' the Alps | 103b
J. is dead | 214a
J. marched to kettle drums | 103b
J.'s style was grand | 103b
Life of J. is assuredly..great | 255a
no arguing with J. | 171a
no man..to put you in mind of J. | 214a
not a good imitation of J. | 58b
Johnsonese: broken J. | 255b
Join: come and j. the dance | 83b
Joined: j. together in..Matrimony | 481a
she j. the former two | 141a
what therefore God hath j. | 507a
whom God hath j. together | 481b
Joint: at every j. and motive of her
  body | 369a
j. heirs with Christ | 513b
human knee is a j. | 178b
remove the j. | 85b
the time is out of j. | 331b
Joint-labourer: with the day | 329b
Joints: between the j. of his harness | 496b
his square-turned j. | 318a
may his j. tormented be | 216b
the j. that you carve | 227b
Joke: J. a's a very serious thing | 94b
dullness ever loves a j. | 298b
it 's our only j. | 21b
j. well into a Scotch understanding | 404a
life is a j. that 's just begun | 164b
many a j. had he | 168b

Joke (*cont.*)
rich man's j. is allis funny | 41a
subtleties of the American j. | 446b
this Jack, j., poor potsherd | 197b
you saw Waring? truth or j.? | 52b
Jokes: laugh'd..at all his j. | 168b
Wooden shoes are standing J. | 1b
Jollity: jest and youthful j. | 268b
nothing trimmed in j. | 388a
turned to j. and game | 276b
Jolly: I'm a J.—'Er Majesty's J. | 234a
some credit in being j. | 123b
so was her j. whistle wel y-wet | 89a
Jonadge's belly | 124a
Jonah: J. was in the belly of the fish | 504b
lot fell upon J. | 504b
of one vast kidney, J. prays | 202b
Jonas acquired some reputation | 208a
Jonas Kindred: grave J. | 114a
Jonathan: distressed for thee, my
  brother J. | 495b
J. gave his artillery | 495b
O J., thou wast slain | 495b
Saul and J. were lovely | 495b
we must consult brother J. | 452a
Jones: 'indeed!' said Mr. J. | 172b
J.! as from Calais southward | 463a
J., the tobacco jar! | 76a
J…daily absorbs a clay | 76a
Jonson: [J.] invades authors | 142a
J.'s learned book be on | 269a
next these, learn'd J. | 137a
too nicely J. knew | 103a
Jordan: Cherith, that is before J. | 496a
not J.'s stream, nor death's | 453b
on this side J.'s wave | 3a
while J. rolled between | 453b
Joris, and he | 47b
Jorkins: I have a partner, Mr. J. | 122a
Jorrocks..not afraid of 'the pace' | 417a
Joseph: as J. was a-walking | 522a
Israel loved J. more | 493a
Jesu, Mary and J. they bare | 524a
J. did whistle and Mary did sing | 524a
new king..wh. knew not J. | 493b
Josephine: court of the Empress J. | 165b
Joshua: Duke J. | 257a
J. the son of Nun | 494a
Joss-sticks and..high-mindedness | 35a
Jostling: by j. in the street | 30a
Jot: one j. of former love retain | 137b
Journalism: Christianity..but why j. | 18a
Journalists say a thing | 27b
Journey: arrant jade on a j. | 170b
death the j.'s end | 141a
he is gone a long j. | 498a
here is my j.'s end | 364a
life's j. just begun | 109b
love to begin a j. on Sundays | 418b
on that j. you find yr. attorney | 164a
or he is in a j. | 496a
the longest j. go | 393b
thy heavy riches but a j. | 351b
will the day's j. take the..day | 311a
yr. j. of so many days | 294b
Journeying on to..Hertfordshire | 240b
Journeyman to grief | 374b
Journeymen: some of nature's j. | 333b
Journeys end in lovers meeting | 370b
Jove: Apollo, Pallas, J. | 131b
ask me no more where J. bestows | 79b
awful J. young Phidias brought | 147a
daughter of J., relentless power | 173b
deny himself for J. | 345a
Jehovah, J. or Lord | 304a
J. and my stars be praised | 371b
J. but laughs at lovers' perjury | 141a
J. for 's power to thunder | 328a
J.'s dread clamours counterfeit | 362a
lovelier than the Love of J. | 259a
might I of J.'s nectar sup | 216a
she is sport for J. | 361a
starry threshold of J.'s court | 266b
tales of thee to high-judging J. | 342b
tell proud J., between his power | 215b
they say, J. laughs | 365a
thou for whom e'en J. wd. swear | 345a
while J.'s planet rises | 47b
Jovial: Autumn..comes j. on | 443b
Jowett: my name is J. | 528b
Joy: a dizzy, a tumultous j. | 407a

Joy (cont.)

ah heavenly j.!	36a
a j. apart from thee	146b
all j. is young	265a
all that is at enmity with j.	466b
all the j. before death	423b
bathed in j. complete	37b
before, a j. proposed	389a
bends to himself a J.	30b
break forth into j.	502b
burst J.'s grape	219b
cease, every j., to glimmer	77b
children of swift j.	441a
come again with j.	489b
creature, form'd of j. and mirth	30b
dead of j., James Lee	47b
doth not intermeddle with his j.	408a
dreme of j., al but in vain	90a
dwell in doubtful j.	348b
each for the j. of the working	236b
enter..into the j. of thy Lord	508a
eternal j., and everlasting love	291b
every child may j. to hear	32b
extremes of passion, j. and grief	344a
fields where j. for ever dwells	271a
fruit of the Spirit is love, j.	515b
general j. of the whole table	349a
Greensleeves was all my j.	523b
headlong j. is ever on the wing	277b
heart..asks, if this be j.	168b
he chortled in his j.	84a
he sees it in his j.	466a
is the fulness of j.	482b
it wd. but apprehend some j.	357b
I were page to j.	423a
I wish him j. where'er he dwell	526a
I wish you all the j.	354b
j. and woe are woven fine	29b
j. be wi' you a'	285b
j. brightens his crest	276a
j. cometh in the morning	483b
j. delights in j.	387a
j. in the making	36b
j. in widest commonalty spread	464a
j. is like restless day	306b
J. is my name	32b
j. is the sweet voice	100b
j. is wisdom	475b
j. of elevated thoughts	472a
j. of love is too short	257a
j., pleasance, revel	361b
j. rul'd the day	141b
j. runs high	185a
j.'s a trinket	410b
j. shall be in heaven	509b
j., shipmate, j.!	457a
j.'s soul lies in the doing	368b
j.! that in our embers..doth live	466b
j. the luminous cloud	100b
j. was never sure	422a
J., whose hand is ever at his lips	219b
j. without canker or cark	242a
kisses the J. as it flies	30b
labour without j. is base	314b
last his sorrow, first his j.	176a
lead from j. to j.	472a
let j. be unconfined	68b
like an unbodied j.	398a
lost a j. for it worth worlds	186b
love, and thought, and j.	471a
make me hear of j. and gladness	485a
man was made for J. and Woe	29b
more true j. Marcellus exil'd	301b
my j., my grief, my hope	448b
my j. of youthful sports	69b
my scrip of j., immortal diet	307b
nor j. nor grieve too much	141a
not a j. the world can give	73b
not increased the j.	501b
now from the heart of j.	24b
now 'tis little j.	195a
O daring j., but safe	457a
oh! dream of j.!	99b
oh, what the j. and the glory	287a
oil of j. for mourning	503b
O tidings of comfort and j.	523a
O what their j. and their glory	537a
Phyllis is my only j.	321a
pledges of Heaven's j.	278a
pure and complete j.	567a
Robin is all my j.	336a

Joy (cont.)

running stream of sparkling j.	121b
shuts up all the passages of j.	214a
silence..perfectest herald of j.	358a
silent j. at their arrival	99a
sing, riding 's a j.	48a
smooth current of domestic j.	213a
snatch a fearful j.	174b
some bringer of that j.	357b
soon brightened with j.	464b
stern j. wh. warriors feel	316b
such perfect j. therein I find	143a
sweet j. befall thee	32b
the deep power of j.	472a
the harp, his sole remaining j.	316b
there is no j. but calm	433a
the senses, for ever in j.	51b
the smiles of j., the tears of woe	282b
the very honey of all earthly j.	107a
they j. before thee	501b
thine earth-born j. renew	36b
thing of beauty is a j. for ever	217b
thou hast finished j. and moan	329a
thy j. and crown eternally	279b
tidings of great j. I bring	424b
variety's the source of j. below	160a
we wear a face of j. because	465a
where's all the j. and mirth	224b
who hath seen j.	36a
who shall ever find J.'s language	36a
with courage, love and j.	159b
with feet of j. in idleness	37b
with j. approach, O Christian Woman, the j. of joys	60b
writh'd not at passing j.	221b
years to be of work and j.	39a
Joyance: like to sounds of j. there	179b
with thy clear keen j.	398b
Joy-bells ring in Heaven's street	261b
Joyful: j. and triumphant	290a
j. before the Lord the King	488a
Joyous: j. hour, we give thee greeting!	164b
j. we too launch out	457b
Joyously: so j., so maidenly	402b
Joys: Africa and golden j.	381a
all my j. to this are folly	64a
all that 's precious in our j.	411a
great j., like griefs, are silent	259b
hence, vain deluding j.	268a
how fading are the j.	289b
in whom all j. so well agree	402a
it [friendship] redoubleth j.	15b
j. are but fantastical	132a
j. like beauty, but skin deep	18a
j. of parents are secret	14b
j. with age diminish	48b
left all j. to feel all smart	187b
minds me o' departed j.	63b
our j. three parts pain	50b
our youth, our j., and all we have	307b
present j. are more	140b
raise yr. j. and triumphs high	455b
sacred j. of home depend	283a
season made for j.	159b
their homely j.	174a
thy j. when shall I see?	523b
'twere profanation of our j.	134a
what j. await us there	286a
what lasting j. the man attend	459a
why thy visionary j. remove?	105a
Jubilant: be j., my feet	200b
Jubilee: our J. is death	41b
we bring the J.	473a
Jubjub: beware the J. bird	83b
Judæa: in J. and in Cappadocia	512a
Judah: among the thousands of J.	504b
J. is my law-giver	485b
J. their counsel	486b
the sight of J.'s seer	258a
Judas: J...not Iscariot	511a
shoves J. and Jesus equally aside	147b
Judas Maccabaeus: the third J.	257a
Judea stretches far	320b
Judee: know everythin' down in J.	250a
Judge: and a good J. too	167a
and J. of the earth	461b
as sober as a j.	151a
as they grow older they j. them	460b
fitter to invent than to j.	16a
God is a righteous J.	482a
forbear to j., for we are sinners	384a

Judge (cont.)

for now I am a J.	167
half as sober as a j.	240
I am no j. of such matters	305
I'll be j., I'll be jury	82
indifferent j. between	401
j. and avenge our blood	518
j. is condemned when	553
j. none blessed before his death	520
j. not, and ye shall not be judged	509
j. not, that ye be not judged	505
j. not the Lord	110
j. not the play before the play be done	117b, 307
j. not the preacher	187
J. of all the earth do right?	493
made thee a prince and a j. over us!	493
monarchs, justly to j.	39
my friend, j. me	76
neutrality of an impartial j.	55
O wise young j.	354
shd. but j. you as you are	351
there sits a j.	385
thine own mouth will I j. thee	510
thou seest I j. not thee	76
you wags that j. by rote	291
Judged: that ye be not j.	505
Judges: hungry j...sentence sign	505
J. all rang'd (a terrible show!)	160
j. of fact, tho' not j. of law	306
vanquish, not my Accuser, but my j.	288
Judgment: angry with his j.	41
bide till J. Tide	236
blood..waits upon the j.	335
bring every work into j.	500
but reserve thy j.	330
by the legal j. of his peers	550
by Tophet-flare to J. Day	227
Daniel come to j.	354
God's great J. Seat	227
he looked for j.	501
He, wh. is the top of j.	351
in the day of j.	478
I was green in j.	323
Last J. draweth nigh	29
law of human j., Mercy	29
leaves of the J. Book unfold	425
my j. is you're pooty sure to fail	250
O j.! thou art fled	340
on better j. making	388
proceed to j.	355
right j. in all things	479
seven times tried that j. is	353
their j. is a mere lottery	142
the j. of the great whore	510
the people's j. always true	138
vulgarize the day of j.	205
what j. I had increases	142
what j. shall I dread	354
young in limbs, in j. old	35
yr. j. will probably be right	25b
Judgments: cause for j. so malign	41
criterion of wisdom to vulgar j.	5
delivers brawling j.	10
differing j. serve but to declare	100
drop our clear j.	324
give the King thy j.	480
men's j. are a parcel	324
rash j., nor the sneers	472
to keep thy righteous j.	480
with our j. as our watches	300
Judicious: j. clear, succinct	108
j. levity	573
J. Mr. Richard Hooker	573
Judy O'Grady	230
Jug: little brown j.	521
one old j. without a handle	24
w'en it git loose fum de j.	182
Juggler: east perceive a j.'s sleight thread-bare j.	6
Jug jug: cuckoo, j.-j.	28
j. j. to dirty ears	14
j., j., j., tereu	25
Jule: wilt thou not, J.?	36
Julia: J.'s dainty leg	18
whenas in silks my J. goes	19
where my J.'s lips do smile	18
Juliet: J. is the sun	36
unless philosophy can make a J.	36
Julio: rare Italian master, J. Romano	37

Julius: ere such another J. 328b
ere the mightiest J. fell 329b
J. Cæsar's ill-erected tower 376a
the third J. Cæsar 257a
ye towers of J. 173b
July: cuckoo of a worse J. 435b
English winter—ending in J. 71b
how, that J. afternoon, you went 294a
swarm of bees in J. 522a
Jumblies live 243b
Jump: I will not j. with common
spirits 353b
j., as Mr. Levi did 19b
j. at a gilded hoop 195a
Jumping from the chair 202a
Jumps: see how the cat j. 320b
June: all J. I bound the rose 49a
April, J., and November 172a, 533a
as the cuckoo is in J. 378b
cuckoo of a joyless J. 435b
Glorious First of J. 285a, 526b
leafy month of J. 99b
newly sprung in J. 62a
nor wd. forgive, did J. disclose 452a
November on the lap of J. 196a
on a brilliant night in J. 295b
perchance, in J.! 167a
rare as a day in J. 251a
serves for the old J. weather 46a
she needs not J. for beauty's 8b
swarm of bees in J. 522a
when J. is come, then all the day 38a
when J. is past, the fading rose 79b
Junes: in three hot J. burned 388b
Jungle: that keep the J. law 232b
this is the Law of the J. 231a
thro' the J. very softly 234b
Junior: struck a trusting j. 233b
Juniper: sat down under a j. tree 496a
Junius: Cobbett and J. 183b
Juno: J. but an Ethiop were 345a
J.'s unrelenting hate 142b
she's J. when she walks 216b
than the lids of J.'s eyes 373a
Jupiter: brighter art thou than..J. 258b
J. the rain-bringer 554a
Leda, the beloved of J. 241b
so J. me succour 402b
Vespers in the Temple of J. 161b
Jurisdiction: Rome hath no j. 491b
Jurisprudence: gladsome light of J. 97b
Jury: I'll be j. 82b
j. all wrote down on their slates 83b
j. eagerly wrote down 83b
j. passing on the prisoner's life 351a
trial by j...will be a delusion 120a
tried before a jury. .once a week 209a
Jury-men: that j. may dine 302b
Just: a beast, but a j. beast 522a
actions of the j. smell sweet 401a
becometh well the j. 483b
be j., and fear not 386a
chiefly on the j., because 34b
I think that thou art j. 362a
j. are the ways of G. 277b
j. as I am, without one plea 146a
ninety and nine j. persons 509b
path of the j. is as the..light 497b
pursue things wh. are j. in present 13a
rain it raineth on the j. 34b
raise me with the j. 280b
reflect that God is j. 205a
sendeth rain on the j. 505a
slowly wise, and meanly j. 213b
the j. shall live by faith 513a
thou art indeed j., Lord 198a
thou hast made him; thou art j. 429b
unjust steals the j.'s umbrella 34b
whatever is, is in its causes j. 141a
what I plead is j. 198a
whatsoever things are j. 516a
Juster: not, Celia, that I j. am 321a
Justice: as infinite a j. too 47a
as thou urgest j., be assur'd 355a
conscience. . j. enough to accuse 171a
crimes, unwhipp'd of j. 342b
he found the unpersuadable j. 474b
I have loved j. and hated iniquity 541a
indifferently minister j. 480b
in nature. .certain fountains of j. 13a
in the course of j. 354b

Justice (cont.)
j., in fair round belly 326b
j. is truth in action 128a
j., more than thou desir'st 355a
J., though she's painted blind 66a
kings the sword of j. . .lay down 118b
liberty plucks j. by the nose 351a
never expected j. from a company 404b
persuade J. to break her sword 363b
place of j. is a hallowed place 16b
poetic J., with her lifted scale 298b
religion, j., counsel 15a
revenge is a kind of wild j. 14a
sad-eyed j., with his surly hum 381b
see how yond j. rails 343b
the fuel j. layeth on 407b
the j. of it pleases 362b
the j. of my quarrel 25b, 259b
this even-handed j. 347a
tho' j. be thy plea 354b
Thwackum was for doing j. 151b
till he talks about j. and right 233a
what you think j. requires 258a
when mercy seasons j. 354b
where mystery begins, j. ends 57b
wh. is the j., wh. is the thief 343b
with sword of j. thee ruleth 143a
Justifiable to men 277b
Justified: 'tis half as good as j. 66a
Justify the ways of God to Men 270b
Jutty: no j., frieze, buttress 347a
Juxtaposition: J. his prophet 96a
j., in short 96a

K

Kabul: ford o' K. river 229a
Kaikobad and Kaikhosru 152b
K. the great 152b
Kail: brier bush in our k. yard 193a
delving in his k.-yardie 193a
Kangaroo: old Man K. first 230b
Kansas had better stop raising corn 243b
Karshish, the picker-up 46b
Kaspar: old K.'s work was done 406a
Kate: change K. into Nan 30a
Kathleen Mavourneen 115b
Katterfelto with his hair on end 112a
Kean: to see him [K.] act 102b
Keats: John K. five feet high 222b
John K., who was killed off 71b
K., who was ignorant of Greek 241b
out-glittering K. 252a
what porridge had John K.? 50a
who killed John K.? 73a
Kecksies, burs 383b
Kedar: among the tents of K. 489b
as the tents of K. 500a
Keel: her k. ploughs air 87a
no k. has ever ploughed that path 393b
Keen: k. were his pangs 72a
swayed by quite as k. a sense 166a
thy tooth is not so k. 326b
Keener with constant use 203b
Keep: always k. us so 147a
and many to k. 226b
care must k. you 119a
faith. .every one do k. whole 478b
heaven vows to k. him 215a
hyeste thing that man may k. 89b
if you can k. yr. head 230a
I k., and pass, and turn again 146a
k. holy the Sabbath day 480a
k. innocency, and take heed 484a
k. it now, and take the rest! 73a
k. me as the apple of an eye 482b
k. something to yoursel 60a
k. thee only unto her 481b
k. the home fires burning 156a
k. themselves close 485b
k. thy servant also from. .sins 482b
k. up appearances 94b
k. ye the Law 234b
k. yourself to yourself 126b
most difficult of tasks to k. 464b
of nyce conscience took he no k. 88b
she has her soul to k. 265a
so may I always k. 161a
they shd. k. who can 470b
to k. thee in all thy ways 487b
to k. them so 304a

Keeper: a k. is only a poacher 226b
am I my brother's k.? 492b
k. stands up to keep the goal 199a
Lord himself is thy k. 489b
Keepers: k. of the house. .tremble 499b
k. of the wall took away my veil 500b
wh. their k. call a lightning 366b
Keepest: poor at first, and k. me so 169a
Keepeth thee will not sleep 489b
Keeping: Father, in Thy gracious k. 145b
if k. it does it much good 20a
Keith of Ravelston 130b
Kelly: Fanny K.'s divine plain face 240a
has anybody here seen K. 285a
K. from the Emerald Isle 285a
K. from the Isle of Man 285a
Kelpie's flow 319a
Kelt: Slav, Teuton, K. 426a
Kempenfelt: brave K. is gone 111a
K. went down 111a
Kendal-green 377b
Kensal Green: Paradise by way
of K. 93a
Kent: I'm k. the better 62b
K. and Surrey may 229a
K., sir—everybody knows K. 126a
knocked him in the Old K. Road 94a
there was a young lady of K. 527a
Vanguard of Liberty, ye men of K. 467b
Kentish: K. Sir Byng 45b
Pancras and K. Town repose 30b
Kentucky: the old K. Home 156a
Kept: that I k. my word, he said 119b
Kernel: like. .I then was to this k. 373a
Kernels: from sweet k. prest 275a
Kettle: how agree the k. and the. .
pot 520b
I took a k. large and new 85a
Polly put the k. on 121a
Kettle-drums: Johnson marched to k. 103b
Kew: go down to K. in lilac-time 290a
I am his Highness' dog at K. 299b
Key: a Door to wh. I found no K. 153b
in a bondman's k. 353a
k. of the bottomless pit 519b
lay. .hands on that golden k. 266b
taken away the k. of knowledge 509a
the k. is gone with them 146b
turn the k. deftly 221a
with an easy k., dost open life 139b
with this k. Shakespeare unlocked 470b
with this same k. Shakespeare 470b
you've got the k. of the street 127a
Keys: have the k. of hell and death 518b
his k. were rusty 74b
keeps the k. of all the creeds 430a
over the noisy k. 306b
send me the half that's got my k. 172b
shining k. will be took from her 180b
two massy k. he bore 269b
Keystone: o' night's black arch the k. 63a
Khayyám: come with old K. 152b, 153a
Kiaugh: a' his weary k...beguile 59b
Kibe: he galls his k. 336b
Kick: I'll k. you downstairs 82b
I wd. scarcely k. to come 222b
k. against the pricks 512a
k. his wife out of bed 416b
you k. me downstairs 28a
Kicked: Jeshurun waxed fat, and k. 494b
some k., until they can feel 65b
Kickshaws: little tiny k. 381a
Kid: in his paw, and killed 274a
leopard. .lie down with the k. 501b
seethe a k. in his mother's milk 494a
the fleet-foot k. 420b
Kidney: man of my k. 356a
mound of one vast k. 202b
Kidneys: blister my k. 417a
Kill: be'st a devil, I cannot k. thee 364a
cease! must men k. and die 394a
I'll k. you if you quote it 54b
I will k. thee, and love thee after 363b
I will shoot you! I will k. you! 531a
k. a man as k. a good book 279a
k. him in the shell 338b
k. sick people groaning 259a
k. thee with much cherishing 365b
k. the poor creature at once 159a
meet for nothing, but to k. 191a
prepared to k. one another 390a

Kill (cont.)

shalt not k.; but need'st not strive	96b
they k. us for their sport	343b
Killed: better be k. than frightened	417a
by a..owl hawked at and k.	348b
I am justly k.	337a
I k. Cock Robin	528a
I k. not thee with half so good	341b
I kissed thee, ere I k. thee	364a
I'm k., Sire!	47b
Keats..k. off by one critique	71b
k. with report that old man	278b
man as k. hisself on principle	127a
scotch'd the snake, not k. it	348b
some sleeping k.	375b
'twas I that k. her	363b
Killibeate taste	127a
Killiecrankie: on the heights of K.	12a
Killing: as k. as the canker	269b
I wd. have him nine years a-k.	362b
k. Kruger with yr. mouth	227a
K. no Murder Briefly Discourst	321b
Kills: each man k. the thing he loves	459b
he k. her in her own humour	366b
he that k. me some six..Scots	377a
k. a man k. a reasonable creature	279a
k. reason itself	279a
k. the image of God	279a
Kilmeny: bonny K. gaed up the glen	193a
K. had been she knew not where	193a
late in the gloamin' K. came home	193a
Kilted: k. her coats o' green satin	526a
k. her green kirtle	528b
k. them up to the knee	526a
Kilve: at K. there was no weather-cock	463a
Kin: a little less than 'k.'	19b
a little more than k.	329b
knew no other k.	328b
makes the whole world k.	369a
Kind: a being of our k.	120a
at distance from the K.	468b
by partners, in each other k.	450a
children k. and natural	381b
cruel, only to be k.	335a
enjoy her while she's k.	142b
Fortune shows herself more k.	355a
Godlike crime was to be k.	73b
I am one with my k.	434b
is she k. as she is fair?	372b
just the art of being k.	459a
k. are her answers	78b
Lewti is not k.	101b
lost him half the k.	141b
makes one wondrous k.	158b
more than kin, and less than k.	329b
obscurely wise, and coarsely k.	210b
of a beautiful, unheard of k.	476a
one that is never k.	475a
rather more than 'k.'	19b
so constant to me, and so k.	217b
squamous, omnipotent, and k.	39b
that ever thou wast k.	189a
Time, that is to o'er k.	228a
to be honest, to be k.	412a
world affords or grows by k.	143a
yet he was k.	168b
Kindest: thou wert the k. man	257b
Kindle: k. the loving	282a
we cannot k. when we will	7a
Kindled: k. above to show the Maker's	176b
k. in the upper skies	146b
Kindliness: cool k. of sheets	39a
Kindly: a k. mood of melancholy	143a
a lass as comely or as k.	231b
beats the heart so k.	12a
had we never lov'd sae k.	59a
Sally is gone that was so k.	26b
use 'em k., they rebel	191b
Kindness: acts of k. and of love	472a
any k. that I can show	523b
beauty lives with k.	372b
Christ took the k.	51a
full o' the milk of human k.	346b
greetings where no k. is	472a
have you had a k. shown?	63b
in vain with lavish k.	184a
kill a wife with k.	366b
k. in another's trouble	171b
little deeds of k.	82a

Kindness (cont.)

milk of human k. blessed	94b
pens in..the milk of human k.	58a
save in the way of k.	444b
showed me marvellous great k.	483b
tak' a cup o' k. yet	59a
think it k. to his Majesty	178a
Kindred: friends, k., days	146b
good to the poor, to k. dear	79b
like k. drops, been mingled	111b
Table of K.	491b
Kindreds: k. of the earth shall wail	518a
nations, and k., and people	519a
Kine: seven fat k.	493b
that keeps the shadowy k.	130b
King: a' for our rightfu' K.	61a
a k. and officers of sorts	381b
a k. may make a nobleman	58a
a K.'s a K., do Fortune	136b
a k. sate on the rocky brow	70b
ale is a dish for a k.	373a
all the k.'s horses	85a
a mockery k. of snow	376a
a name written, K. of Kings	519b
arose up a new k. over Egypt	493b
as I have served the K.	462b
at the k.'s court, my brother	89a
authority forgets a dying k.	429a
a worse k. never left a realm	74b
ay, every inch a k.	343b
bend lower, O k.	476a
blessedness alone that makes a K.	445a
but yesterday a K.!	73b
Byng stood for his K.	45b
castles are my K.'s alone	318b
cat may look at a k.	83a
Cotton is K.	94a
damned for never a k.'s son	376b
despised, and dying k.	399a
died, as firm as Sparta's k.	136b
diel hae we goten for a K.	193a
diel hae we got for a K.	116b
divinity doth hedge a k.	335b
do homage to thy K.	407b
farewell k.!	375b
fear God. Honour the K. 238a, 517b
forehand and vantage of a k.	383a
form'd the Poet for the K.	206a
gallows..in England..thou art k.	376b
give the K. thy judgments	486b
glories of my K.	249b
glory to the K. of Kings	455b
glory to the new born K.	455b
God bless the K.	67b
God is the K. of all the earth	485a
God save great George our k.	523a
God save our gracious k.	79b
God save our lord the k.	193a
God save the K. 79b, 193a, 495a
God save the k.! will no man say, Amen	376a
government without a k.	18b
greater than the K. himself	297a
half the zeal I served my k.	386a
happy as a k.	160b
Harry the K., Bedford and Exeter	383a
heart and stomach of a k.	145a
Heaven's matchless K.	273b
he might hae been a k.	530b
here lies a great and mighty K.	309b
here lies a K. that rul'd	79a
Hero can be..K..or what you will	80b
I am a K., altho' a poor blind boy	95b
Idea of a Patriot K.	33b
if chance will have me k.	346b
if I were as tedious as a k.	359a
I have made unto the K.	484b
I'll catch the conscience of the k.	333a
is a k. indeed	87a
is not the k.'s name	375a
is the k. dead?	385a
it little profits that an idle k.	438b
I was a K. in Babylon	85a
I were k. of pain	423a
judge, that no k. can corrupt	385b
kill a k.,..marry his brother	335a
k., and his faithful subjects	58a
k. can do no wrong	28b
K., Cawdor, Glamis	348b
K. dropped a tear	29a

King (cont.)

K., father, royal Dane	331b
k. hath thrown his warder down	374b
K. have pleasure in thy beauty	484b
K. himself has followed her	168a
k.-making Victory	68a
K., observing with judicious eyes	445a
k. of all kings to her son	524a
K. of England cannot enter	297a
K. of France went up the hill	532a
K. of glory, K. of peace	187b
K. of Glory shall come in	483a
k. of intimate delights	112a
k. of shreds and patches	335a
K. Pandion, he is dead	20b
K. said to the jury	83b
k.'s daughter is all glorious within	484b
k.'s daughter o' Noroway	529b
k. sits in Dunfermline town	529b
k.'s name is a tower of strength	385a
K. thought mair o' Marie	530a
K. to have things done as cheap	296a
K. to Oxford sent a troop	42b
k., tried in fires of woe!	206a
k. was in his counting house	533b
K., Who ordainest great winds	94a
leper once he lost and gain'd a k.	271b
lessened my esteem of a k.	296a
let us sing—long live the K.	109a
long live our noble k.	79b
Lord remaineth a K. for ever	483b
'mercy on his soul,' said K. Harry	531a
Moloch, horrid k.	271b
more capital than to behead a k.	66a
mortal temples of a k.	375b
must he lose the name of k.	375b
myself a k. of infinite space	332b
no k. that can be saved	484a
now the k. drinks to Hamlet	337a
old K. Cole	532a
or who is K.	67b
our k. has written a braid letter	529b
our sins lay on the k.!	382b
passing brave to be a K.	259a
patience and the K.'s English	355b
quhen Alysander oure k.	474a
religious and gracious K.	479a
righteousness unto the K.'s son	486b
roarers for the name of k.	367a
ruin seize thee, ruthless K.!	173b
sea hath no k. but God alone	313a
shake hands with a k.	178a
shall be born our heavenly k.	522a
shines brightly as a k.	355b
sing my God and K.	187a
skipping k., he ambled up	378a
so excellent a k.	330a
so spake the K.; I knew not all	428a
stamp'd with the image of the K.	428a
still am I k. of those	376a
strives for..his K.'s arriving	415b
subject's duty is the k.'s	382b
submission meet to our K.	76b
sword of an Angel K.	30b
take away my life to make you K.	88a
thanks as fits a k.'s remembrance	332a
that sort of k. shd. ever die	50a
that was no more than a k.	422a
the fair and fatal K.	206a
their conscience as their K.	427b
the K. asked the Queen	266b
the k. has gone beyond me	386a
the k. is but a man, as I am	382b
the k. is the strongest	520a
the K. looked up	92a
the k. my brother's wreck	144b
the k. my father's death	144b
the k. never dies	28b
the k. of terrors	497a
the K. over the Water	526b
the k. shall be contented	375b
the k. shall do it	375b
the k. stept down	425b
they all were looking for a k.	256a
the year's pleasant k.	286a
think myself happy, k. Agrippa	513a
think the k. sees thee still	186b
this hath not offended the k.	283b
this is a K.'s best praise	313b
till the K. enjoys his own again	292b
title running 'fore the k.	382b

King (cont.)

to be an English k. 91b
to be a Pirate K. 166a
to be k. stands not within 346a
to my true K. I offered free 252b
to reverence the K., as if he were 427b
to set before the K.! 410b, 533a
to Thee, Redeemer, K. 286a
to the K. in a raiment of needlework 484b
under wh. k., Bezonian? 381a
until a k. be by 355b
upon the k.! 382b
wal enough agin a k. 250a
wash the balm from an anointed k. 375a
what is a K.? a man condemn'd 306a
what must the k. do now 375b
whatsoever K. shall reign 524a
who is the K. of Glory 483a
whom the k. delighteth to honour 496b
wife of the..glorious K. 187a
worm that hath eat of a k. 335b
King-at-arms: Lord Lion K. 318a
King Cambyses' vein 377b
King Charles: K. and who'll do him
right 45b
K. gave him a short character 87b
K.'s head 122a
K. walked and talked 533b
Kingcups: Cowslips and K. 409b
Kingdom: act of order to a peopled k. 381b
advantage on the k. of the shore 388a
a k. for it was too small 379a
builds palaces in K. come 261b
can trample a k. down 291a
full k. of that final kiss 114b
God hath numbered the k. 504a
hardly..riches enter into the k. 510a
I never gave you k. 342b
in this k. by the sea 297b
k. against k. 507b
k. and patience of Jesus Christ 518a
k. of God is within you 510a
k. of heaven..grain of mustard 506b
k. of heaven is at hand 504b
k. of heaven suffereth violence 506b
kin' o' k.-come to look on 250b
like to a little k. 338b
my k. for a horse 385a
my large k. for a little grave 375b
my mind's my k. 182b
my mind to me a k. is 143a
of such is the kingdom of God 508b
rich man to enter into the k. 507b
seeking asses, found a k. 277a
seek ye first the k. of God 505b
stand upon his feet once again 375a
strikes for a K. and his King's 415b
theirs is the k. of heaven 505b
thine is the k.; and the power 505b
this little k., man, to arm 380b
Thy k. come 505b
thy k. is divided 504a
thy k. shall pass, Galilean 423b
when thou comest into thy k. 510a
Kingdoms: bear rule in their k. 521a
devil..sheweth him all the k. 505a
goodly states and k. seen 220b
k. are clay 322a
k. of our lord 519a
k. of this world are become 519a
mus'd of taking k. in 324a
the k. are less by three 424a
the k. are moved 484b
we have kissed away k. 323b
King George: for K. upon the throne 217a
K. will be able to read that 178b
Kingly crown to gain 184a
Kings: accounted poet k. 220b
all be as happy as k. 414a
all k. shall fall down before him 486b
all the powerful K. and Queens 134b
Almighty scattered k. 486a
alone dwell..the k. of the sea 6a
ambition, and the pride of k. 300b
arm'd with K. to strive 73b
as..k. in sceptres 445a
bid k. come bow to it 374a
Captains and the K. depart 233b
change my state with k. 387b
city of two k. 253b

Kings (cont.)

conquering k. their titles take 87a
curse of k. to be attended 374a
death lays his icy hand on k. 401a
descended of so many royal k. 325b
divorc'd so many English k. 381a
enthroned in the hearts of k. 354b
for godlike k. of old 253a
from the ruined sides of K. 22b
gauntlet down to..courts and k. 77b
gifts from the devil and..k. 30b
hand that k. have lipped 323b
heart of k. is unsearchable 498b
heart's ease must k. neglect 382b
he gart k. ken 11a
hunting is..the sport of k. 416b
K. are by God appointed 524a
k. crept out again 43a
k.' daughters..thy..women 484b
k. have cares that wait 176b
k. have desired to see those things 509a
k. is mostly rapscallious 446b
k. it makes gods 385a
K. may be blest 62b
K. may love treason 118b
K. of England lifting up..swords 154b
k. of Tharsis and of the isles 486b
k. that fear their subjects! 384b
K. will be tyrants from policy 57a
k. with their armies did flee 486a
last of the k. strangled 563b
lo, the k. of the earth 485a
meaner creatures k. 385a
mirror of all Christian k. 381b
Obadiah Bind-their-k.-in-chains 252b
of cabbages and k. 84b
or walk with K. 230a
part wh. laws or k. can cause 213a
passion for our temperate k. 435a
people keep even k. in awe 117b
proud and godly k. had built her 154b
raise..commonwealths and ruin k. 138a
root and father of many k. 348b
saddest of all K. 206a
setter up and puller-down of k. 384b
showers on her k. barbaric pearl 272a
sit thou still when k. are arming 319a
stories of the death of k. 375b
such is the breath of k. 374b
superfluous k. for messengers 323b
teeming womb of royal k. 375a
the chase, the sport of k. 406a
the dread and fear of k. 354b
they are no k. 118b
this royal throne of k. 375a
to bind their k. in chains 490b
to calm contending k. 386b
to subjects, what they show to k. 113b
true strength of guilty k. 7a
twixt k. and tyrants 189b
two k. of Brentwood 111b
war is the trade of k. 140b
war's a game..k. wd. not play 112b
we live to tread on k. 379a
what have k. that privates have not 382b
when k. the sword of justice 118b
King's Bench: K. Den of Thieves 97a
K. Walks 95b
Kingsley: Froude believes K. a
divine 415b
King Stephen was a worthy peer 361a
Kinnaird: exclaims Lord K. 289a
Kinquering congs 409b
Kinship with the stars 263b
Kinsmen according to the flesh 513b
Kipling: Rudyards cease from k. 410b
Kirk: a caulder k. 61b
below the k., below the hill 98a
is this the k.? 99b
Marie Hamilton's to the k. gane 530a
walk together to the k. 100a
Kirkconnell: fair K. lea 531a
Kirk-hammer strak the bell 60a
Kirtle: kilted her green k. 528b
Kish: son of K. that lofty Jew 261a
Kismet: he that saith not 'K.' 92b
Kiss: ae fond k. 59a
a gentle k. to every sedge 372b
a k. long as my exile 328b
all humbled k. the rod 372a
a man may k. a bonnie lass 63a, 320b

Kiss (cont.)

break off this last lamenting k. 132b
colder thy k. 74b
come, let us k. and part 137b
Coridon wd. k. her 35b
coward does it with a k. 459b
fades out from k. to k. 474b
felt my soul in a k. 423a
find thee without, I wd. k. thee 500b
full kingdom of that final k. 114b
gav'st me, tho' unseen, a k. 109b
give me a k. 190a
his whole heart in one k. 438a
I dare not ask a k. 190a
if thou k. not me 395b
I needs must k. again 401b
in every k. sealed fast 312a
I saw you take his k. 293b
k. again with tears 436a
k., a sigh and so away 115a
k. before they are married 383b
k. her and mix her with me 424a
k. her till she be wearied 399a
k. me as if you entered gay 46b
k. me as if you made believe 46b
k. me, Hardy 287a
k. my girl on the lips 232b
k. our lady Peace at home 379b
k. the book's outside 108a
k. the place to make it well 425a
k. the Son, lest he be angry 481b
k. till the cow come home 23a
let him k. me with..his mouth 500a
let's k. afresh 190a
madam, I pray you k. me 257b
maids must k. no men 35b
many a glowing k. had won 195b
moth's k. first 46b
never k. and greet 217b
nor k. before folks 105b
nothing wrong in a connubial k. 70b
only to k. that air 190a
on thy bosom tho' many a k. be 421b
or a k. too long 256a
part at last without a k.? 284a
quit in a single k. 36b
rough male k. of blankets 39a
seal with a righteous k. 366b
so k. on 190a
some there be that shadows k. 353b
spend that k. wh. is my heaven 325a
stop his mouth with a k. 358a
swear to never k. the girls 46b
that k. I carried from thee 328b
the bee's k., now! 46b
the envied k. to share 174a
then come k. me, sweet-and-
twenty 370b
to feel the first k. 312a
took the k. sedately 433b
will she k. me to-morrow? 131a
with an holy k. 514a
with one long k. my whole soul 427a
without a single k., or a good-bye? 294a
yet let me k. my Lord 259b
you must not k. and tell 104b
Kissed: curtsied when you have,
and k. 367a
first time he k. me 44a
hail, master; and k. him 508a
he k. likewise the maid 113a
I k. her slender hand 433b
I k. thee ere I killed thee 364a
Jenny k. me 202a
k. again with tears 436a
k. beside the thorn 37b
k. her cold corpus 526b
k. her little sister 280b
k. into smiles again 182a
k. it and then fled 398a
k...man who didn't wax..
moustache 237b
k. the girls and made them cry 534a
only k. the fingers of the hand 44a
Rose k. me to-day 131a
that air, that lately k. thee 190a
they k. each other's cheek 166b
we have k. away kingdoms 323b
Kisses: as it rained k. 324a
bread and cheese, and k. 418b
call'd my absent k. 115b

Kisses (cont.)

come, give me sweet k.	461a
dear as remembered k. after death	436a
died of the k. of the lips of God	285b
feeds on the aërial k.	397a
Heine for songs; for k., how?	46b
I fear thy k., gentle maiden	399b
I understand thy k., and thou mine	378a
k. shd. impair their white	43b
k. the Joy as it flies	30b
my k. are his daily feast	176a
my k. bring again	352a
of many thousand k. the poor last	324b
play'd at cards for k.	251a
poor half-k. kill me quite	137a
sallies of his mother's k.	466b
sows and reaps a thousand K.	106b
straight on k. dream	364b
the k. of his mouth	500a
thy love in k. rain	394b
wastin' Christian k.	232a
with k. four	219a
you have forgotten my k.	422b

Kissing: fool. .that first invented k.

	418b
k. don't last: cookery do	265a
k., kind-hearted gentleman	113a
lipped, and trembled k.	323b
splendid k. mouth	424a
there's an end, I think, of k.	40a
when the k. had to stop	52b

Kissings: all these k. worth? 395b

Kist: had I wist, before I k.

	530a
k. his wounds that were so red	529b

Kit-bag: troubles in yr. old k. 10b

Kitchen: in the k. bred

	74a
I will make my k.	414b

Kitchen-cabals 113b

Kite: Chil the K.

	234b
not sufficient for a k.'s dinner	307a

Kites: fatted all the region k. 333a

Kit Smart: pray with K. 207a

Kitten: I had rather be a k.

	378a
my imperial k.!	83b

Kitty: K. has no discretion in her coughs

	11b
young men come for Mary or K.	11b

Knappeth the spear in sunder 484b

Knave: a k.; a rascal

	342a
a pestilent complete k.!	361a
a rascally yea-forsooth k.	379b
a slipper and subtle k.	361a
but he's an arrant k.	331b
coined an epithet for a k.	254b
'do I look like it?' said the k.	83b
he's but Fortune's k.	325a
I spy a k. in drinking	319b
K. of Hearts, he stole those tarts	83b
necessity makes an honest man a k.	118b
nor k. nor dolt can break	474a
petty sneaking k. I knew	30a
thank God you are rid of a k.	358b
the K. of Hearts	532b
thou naughty k., what trade!	337a
to feed the titled k.	63a

Knavery: k. and folly to excuse religion, k., and change

	94b
	25b

Knavish: frustrate their k. tricks

	79b
k. speech. .in a foolish ear	335a
tricks are either k. or childish	210a

Knaves: bold k. thrive

	141a
called them untaught k.	376b
'gainst k. and thieves men shut	372a
misbegotten k. in Kendal green	377b
whip me such honest k.	359b
word wh. k. and fools may use	94b
world is made up. .of fools and k.	53b

Knead two virtuous souls for life 71a

Knee: civility of my k., my hat

	41b
come, stand beside my k.	12b
human k. is a joint	178b
infant prattling on his k.	59b
kilted them up to her k.	526a
little abune her k.	528b
louted low down on his k.	528a
name of Jesus every k. shd. bow	516a
'pastern' as the 'k.' of a horse	207a
set upon the nurse's k.	530b
sing to the child on thy k.	37b
sit upon the curate's k.	93a
stood by me, k. to k.	99a
the fore-mast wi' his k.	529a

Knee (cont.)

thro' red blude to the k.	528a
to its idolatries a. .patient k.	68b

Kneed: crook-k., and dew-lapped 357a

Kneel: dust shall k. before him 483a

Kneeled: red-cross knight for ever k.

	431b
yet he k. and fought	530b

Kneeling: k. ne'er spoiled silk

	186b
meekly k. upon yr. knees	480b
then, lowly k., wait Thy word	145b

Kneels: k. at morn, and noon, and eve 99b

not one k. to another	458a

Knees: at the great k. and feet

	421a
attire creeps rustling to her k.	221b
between his father's k.	113a
climber up of k.	240b
confirm the feeble k.	502a
down on your k.	327a
each night, upon my k.	150b
grass up to her k.	192a
his Nancy on his k.	164a
meekly kneeling upon yr. k.	480b
now serve on his k.	295b
on parent k., a. .new-born child	214a
petticoats up to the k.	96a
the rest on his k.	123a
they are all on their k.	180a
work is done upon his k.	229b

Knell: all ring fancy's k.

	354a
by fairy hands their k. is rung	103a
k. that summons thee to heaven	347b
sea-nymphs hourly ring his k.	367a
strikes like a rising k.	68a
that. .overpowering k.	71a

Knells us back to a world 100a

Knew: as tho' they perfectly k.

	236a
before I k. thy face	131b
blessed Hope, whereof he k.	179a
builded better than he k.	147a
died because she never k.	26b
'e k. they knowed	236b
he k. himself to sing	269a
he that it it k. it best	14b
he that k. all that learning	25a
he that k. not, and did commit	509a
I k. him well, and every truant k.	168b
I k. my Watson	136a
I k. that once	410b
I k. you once; but in Paradise	53a
k. it all before you	232b
k. only this, that he k. nothing	25a
k. we shd. both forget	422b
men fell out they k. not why	64b
more than Homer k.	419b
nicest child I ever k.	26a
none k. so well as I	459b
none k. thee but to love thee	178a
she k. what it meant	527a
such as k. it of old	421b

Knife: eat it without e'er a k.

	534b
my keen k. see not the wound	346b
smyler with the k.	570b
war even to the k.	68a

Knife-grinder: needy K.! 78b

Knight: a verray parfit gentil k.

	88a
beadsman now that was yr. k.	295b
came a k. to be their wooer	528b
chance brought out a noble k.	429a
courteousest k. that ever bare shield	257b
go with sir priest than sir k.	372a
k. like the young Lochinvar	318a
K. of the Sorrowful Countenance	567b
k. .on carpet consideration	372a
k. was indeed a valiant gentleman	149b
k. was pricking on the plain	408b
k. without fear and. .blemish	566a
prince can mak' a belted k.	60b
red cross k. for ever kneel'd	431b
she hath no loyal k. and true	431b
sternest k. to thy mortal foe	257b
that wandering k. so fair	376b
the K.'s bones are dust	101a
the k. embracing Jane	77b
there lies a new-slain k.	529b
the [White] K. said	85a
what can ail thee, K. at arms	218b
ye wd. make a K. o' me	231a

Knights: all k. of mettle true

	316b
all the king's k. 'tis the flower	528a
all the k. at Camelot	432a
armourers, accomplishing the k.	382b

Knights (cont.)

came among the press of k.	257b
most noblest k. of the world	257b
never matched of earthly k.' hand	257b
nine-and-twenty k. of fame	316b
the invincible K. of old	467a

Knit together thine elect 480a

Knits me to thy rugged strand 317b

Knitter: like a k. drowsed 179a

Knitters in the sun 371a

Knives: broken dinner-k. 229b

Knob: brains out of a brass k. 123a

Knock: I stand at the door, and k.

	518b
k., and it shall be opened	505b
k. as you please	299b
k. at a star with my exalted head	189b
k. him down first	209a
when you k. it never is at home	108a
where k. is open wide	403a
you as pert but k., breathe	133a

Knock-down: a k. argument 139b

a nice k. argument	85a

Knocked him in the Old Kent Road 94a

Knocker: tie up the k. 302b

Knocketh: my beloved that k. 500b

Knocking: k. at Preferment's door 8a

k. on the moonlit door	119b

Knocknarea: riding from K. 475a

Knocks: apostolic blows and k. 65a

open, locks, whoever k.	349b

Knoll: sit on a green k. apart 475b

Knolling a departed friend 379b

Knolls: search the grassy k. 85b

Knot: in the k. there 's no untying 77b

k. .worthy of his interference	542a
some old Gordian k.	96b
this hair in any simple k.	393a
this k. intrinsicate of life. .untie	325a
toads to k. and gender in	363a

Knot grass: bunches of k. 221b

Knots: iron pokers into true-love k. 100b

Knotted all the while 321a

Know: all that we k. is, nothing 68a

all that we k. who lie in gaol	459b
almost afraid to k. itself	350a
as you k. me all, a plain. .man	340a
being with thee when we k. it not	467a
but this I k. full well	41a
but yet I k., where'er I go	466a
by their fruits ye shall k. them	506a
does both act and k.	261a
don't k. better. .merely k. more	315b
do you k. me, my lord	332a
enough for man to k.	301b
every wise man's son doth k.	370b
feel that I am happier than I k.	275b
first of those who k.	435b
for we k. in part	514b
ful wys. .that can him-selven k.	89a
how well I k. what I mean to do	45a
I am he that aspired to k.	49b
I do k. I love	38a
I do k. of these. .reputed wise	352b
I do love I k. not what	189b
I do not k. beneath what sky	200a
if you wd. k., and not be known	103b
I k. a maiden fair to see	246b
I k. not if I k. what true love is	428b
I k. not, oh, I k. not	286a
I k. not the man	508a
I k. not to this day	452b
I k. not where His islands lift	458b
I k. not why I am so sad	352b
I k. that I don't k. them	439b
I k. that I love thee	282a
I k. thee not, old man	381a
I k. two things about the horse	524a
I k. you; let me try and draw you	50a
I k. you all, and will awhile	376b
impossible precept, 'k. thyself'	81b
I only k. I cannot drift	458b
I only k. it shall be great	200a
I only k. it shall be high	200a
I only k. we loved in vain	72b
k. but this, that thou art good	304a
k., that I wd. accounted be	476b
k. thee and fly thee	406b
k. then thyself, presume not God	301a
k. thyself	560b
k. to k. no more	274b
k. what thou canst work at	81b

Know (cont.)

k. what to do with it 449b
let him not k. 't. .he's not robb'd 362a
Master of them that k. 566b
men have it when they k. it not 420a
might one from other k. 254a
more than to k. little 15b
music..by somebody I do not k. 223a
my good child, k. this 481a
not to k. anything among you 514a
not to k. me argues yourselves 274b
not utter what thou dost not k. 377a
now I k. in part 514b
O! that a man might k. the end 341b
other women k. so much 44b
pleasant to k. Mr. Lear 243b
professed to k. this only 277a
quick to learn and wise to k. 59a
reason but from what we k. 300b
saying you want to k., you k. 123a
scarcely hate any one that we k. 183b
shall I k. even as I . .am known 514b
than but to k. 't a little 362a
that is all ye k. on earth 219b
that shall we k. one day 311b
there is no knowledge but I k. it 528b
they k. not what they do 510a
they leave you, and you k. them 49b
theyn't k. everythin' down in Judee 250a
this shall I ne'er k. 389b
this warm kind world is all I k. 106b
thought so once; but now I k. it 160a
thought. .to k. that you k. not 16a
to k. the world, not love her 477b
we are greater than we k. 463b
we are wiser than we k. 148a
we k. a subject ourselves 208b
we might k. as much as. .Adam 228a
whatever there is to k. 311b
what I don't know. isn't knowledge 528b
what you k., you k. 364a
when all pretend to k. 170a
when it came to k. me well 282a
where no man doth me k. 531b
whom truly to k. is. .life 479b
who only England k. 228b
with them that k. me 487a
yet not proud to k. 300b
you yourselves do k. 340a
Know-all: ole man K. 182a
Knowed: reckon he never k. how 183a
Knowest: k. that I love thee 511b
lord, thou k. all things 511b
speak less than thou k. 342a
thou that k. each 436a
Knoweth: name written, wh. no
man k. 518b
no man k. of his sepulchre 494b
Knowing: for lust of k. 154b
greater than their k.! 234b
not k. what they do 359a
Knowledge: a k. of nothing 121b
all k. too but recorded experience 80a
any little k. or experience 223a
be innocent of the k. 349a
bonded warehouse of my k. 416b
but not according to k. 513b
by words without k. 497b
climbing after k. infinite 259a
close the five ports of k. 41a
desire more love and k. of you 325b
dissemble sometimes yr. k. 16a
exult and sing over the k. 412a
follow k. like a sinking star 438b
for all k. and wonder. .pleasure 13a
for the book of k. fair 273b
fret not after k. 221a
full of the k. of the Lord 501b
had no k. when the day was done 218b
he multiplieth words without k. 497b
he that increaseth k. 499a
I ask it for the k. of a lifetime 456b
in k. of whom standeth our. .life 478a
is there k. in the Most High? 486b
it is the province of k. to speak 194b
k. advances by steps 254a
k. by suffering entereth 44a
k. comes, but wisdom lingers 432b
k. dwells in heads replete 112b
k. enormous makes a God of me 218b
k. in the making 279a

Knowledge (cont.)

[k.] is a rich storehouse 13a
k. is bought in the market 96a
k. is of two kinds 208b
k. is proud that he has learn'd 112b
k. itself is power 17a
k. may give weight 91a
k. of man is as the waters 13a
k. of the ancient languages 38a
k. of the world 90b
k. puffeth up 514a
k. shall be increased 504a
k. to their eyes her ample page 174a
k. under difficulties 126b
k. we ask not, k. Thou hast lent 137b
let k. grow from more to more 429b
light of k. in their eyes 424a
love of Christ wh. passeth k. 515b
man must carry k. with him 210a
my k. is but vain 3b
no man's k. here can go beyond 246a
nor device, nor k. . .in the grave 499b
objects and k. curious 458b
out-topping k. 7b
science is organized k. 407b
spirit of k. and of the fear 501b
such k. is too wonderful 490a
taken all k. to be my province 16b
taken away the key of k. 509a
the literature of k. 120a
there be k., it shall vanish away 514b
there is no k. but I know it 528b
they took k. of them 512a
too high the price for k. 444b
too much k. for the sceptic side 301a
tree of the k. of good and evil 492a
true antithesis to k. 120a
volume of nature. .book of k. 170a
what I don't know isn't k. 528b
what is k. but grieving? 265a
what k. can perform 465a
woman's happiest k. 274a
wonder, wh. is the seed of k. 13a
Known: among the leaves hast
never k. 220a
best that has been k. and said 10a
best that is k. and thought 9a
even as also I am k. 514b
go to the devil where he is k. 212a
had I but early k. thy. .worth 313b
have ye not k.? 502b
Heaven knows what she has k. 350a
if only I had k., k., k., 284a
I have k. no day. .like this 36b
I wish my heart had never k. ye 526a
knowing what shd. not be k. 154b
k. and loved so long 35b
k. no more than other men 191b
k. of them in breaking of bread 510a
k. that once if I loved you well 423a
more you 'ave k. o' the others 230b
much have I seen and k. 438b
much. .to be done. .little to be k. 211b
not be k. to do anything 147b
people whom I have not k. 482b
place where he is not k. 212a
so I had nothing k. 362a
tell him, I too have k. 233a
till I am k., and do not want it 206b
to be lov'd. .needs only to be k. 140a
what shall I do to be for ever k. 107a
yet hast thou not k. me, Philip 511a
you wd. be k., and not know 103b
Knows: he k. who gave that love 464b
just k., and k. no more, her Bible 113a
k. nothing whatever about Thee 525a
no man k. thro' what. .centuries 119a
no man truly k. another 42a
now she k., when I resemble her 449a
she beloved k. nought that k. not 368b
she k. her man 142b
she k. wot 's wot, she does 127a
this she k., in joys and woes 100a
this the world well k. 389a
what every schoolboy k. 419a
Knuckle down at taw 113a
Knucklebones: art of k. 412a
Knuckle-end of England 404a
Knuts: Colonel of the K. 462a
Köhln, a town of monks 100a
Koran: believe all the fables in the K. 15a

Koran (cont.)

K. wd. now be taught in. .Oxford 162a
Kosciusko: Freedom shrieked as K.
fell 77a
Kosmos: untented K. 414a
Kruger: finished killing K. 227a
Kruschen feeling 526a
Kubla: in Xanadu did K. Khan 101a
K. heard from far 101b
Kurd: the same about the K. 25b
Kyloe: a little K. cow 534a

L

Labdanum: stripes of l. 49b
Laborious indeed at the first ascent 279b
Labour: all l. mars what it does 324b
all things are full of l. 499a
a time for l. and thought 420b
carpet-dusting. .not. .imperative l. 43a
come unto me all ye that l. 506b
every l. sped 170a
forget his l. an' his toil 59b
for him light l. spread 168a
green leaves of thy l. 422b
had my l. for my travail 368b
[his] l. for his pains 461a
I'll l. night and day 54b
in all l. there is profit 498a
in our l. rest most sweet 86b
insupportable l. of doing nothing 410b
in works of l., or of skill 453a
it is but lost l. that ye haste 489b
l. and the wounds are vain 96b
l. a pebble without cease 452a
l. bears a lovely face 118b
l. in the deep mid-ocean 433a
l. of an age in piled stones 278a
l. of love 516b
l.'s dull, Lethaean spring 6a
l. that thou and I shall waste 473b
l. to keep alive. .conscience 451b
l. truly to get mine own living 481a
l. we delight in physics pain 348a
l. without joy is base 314b
l. without sorrow is base 314b
learn to l. and to wait 248a
many still must l. 69b
our race shd. not cease to l. 412a
pleasure is l. too 110b
press down upon the brow of l. 53a
profit. .of all his l. wh. he taketh 499a
ruined by Chinese cheap l. 182a
six days shalt thou l. 480a
sore l.'s bath 348a
strength then but l. and sorrow 487b
their l. is but lost 489b
the true success is to l. 413b
'tis sweating l. to bear 322b
we l. soon, we l. late 63a
why shd. life all l. be? 433a
with difficulty and l. hard 273a
with profitable l. to his grave 383a
yr. l. for that wh. satisfieth not 503a
yr. l. is for future hours 198a
Laboured: I l. more abundantly 514b
other men l. 510b
Labourer: for a l. to take his pension 314b
l. is worthy of his hire 509a
now the l.'s task is o'er 145b
Labourers: but the l. are few 506a
Labour-house: sounding l. vast 7b
Labouring: sleep is sweet to the l.
man 54a
sleep of a l. man is sweet 499a
Labours: absorbs a clay after his l. 76a
children sweeten l. 14b
forsook the l. of a servile state 72a
no l. tire 213b
notice. .pleased to take of my l. 206b
revolving l. of the year 161a
Saints who from their l. rest 200a
their uncessant l. see crown'd 260b
they may rest from their l. 519b
ye are entered into their l. 510b
Laburnum: my brother set the l. 195a
Laburnums, dropping-wells of fire 430b
Labyrinth: a peopled l. of walls 395a
Labyrinthine: down the l. ways 441b
l. buds the rose 52a

Lace: an erring l. 189a
  Greek, sir, is like l. 210b
  strunt rarely, owre gauze and l. 61b
Laces for a lady 234a
Lack: I sigh the l. of many a thing 387b
  lions do l., and suffer hunger 484a
  that fear him l. nothing 484a
  therefore can I l. nothing 483a
  they l., I have 143a
Lacked: being l. and lost 359a
  questioning if I l. anything 188b
Lackey: like a l., from the rise to set 383a
Lackeying the varying tide 322b
Lacks: if anyone anything l. 167a
Lacedæmon: in lordly L. 253b
Lad: many a lightfoot l. 199b
  my pretty l. is young 531a
  say, cd. that l. be I? 414b
  when I was a l. I served a term 166a
Ladder: [Jacob] dreamed, and behold a l. 493a
  lowliness is young ambition's l. 338a
  of our vices we can frame a l. 247b
  talk to him of Jacob's l. 205b
  the l. to all high designs 368b
  unto the l. turns his back 338b
  we are dropping down the l. 229b
  wiv a l. and some glasses 22a
Laden: then I shd. l. be 187b
  ye that labour and are heavy l. 506b
Ladies: a lion among l. 357a
  all you l. that do sleep 78b
  come from a l.' seminary 164b
  good night, sweet l. 335b
  if l. be but young 326a
  I, of l. most deject 333b
  l. entered the drawing-room 417a
  l. of irresistible modesty 410b
  l. of St. James's 131a
  l. of th' Hesperides 277a
  l., whose bright eyes 269a
  lang may the l. sit 530a
  novel on the tables of young l. 255b
  o'er l.' lips, who..on kisses dream 364b
  old as I am, for l.' love unfit 140a
  old l. of both sexes 123a
  out of the l.'s company 321b
  rhyme themselves into l.' favours 383b
  these over-offended l...virtuous 410a
  to all you l. now at land 134b
  wild witches, those most noble l. 474b
Lads: come, cheer up, my l. 158b
  golden l. and girls all must 329a
  l. are in love with the grave 199b
  l. that will die in their glory 199a
  there are mair l. in Galloway 531b
  thinking lays l. underground 199b
  tho' yr. l. are far away 156a
  three wild l. were we 319b
  two l. that thought..no more 372b
Lady: ain't a l. livin' i the land 94a
  a l., if undrest at Church 150b
  a l. in the case 71a, 163a
  a love for any l. 295b
  a self-respecting l.'s cell 25a
  Colonel's l. an' Judy O'Grady 230b
  come hither, l. fair, and joined be 217b
  crept too near another l. 385b
  every l. wd. be queen 302a
  faint heart never won fair l. 164a
  for secrecy, no l. closer 377a
  gentle l. married to the Moor 468b
  good heart, and Our L.'s grace 317a
  heard a linnet courting his l. 36b
  he is dead and gone, l. 335b
  he keeps a l. in a cage 93b
  here, l., lo! that servant stands 414a
  he saw a l. bright 528a
  his hound, and his l. fair 529b
  his l.'s ta'en anither mate 529b
  I met a l. in the meads 218b
  in my l.'s chamber 534b
  in this l.'s lips and hands 312a
  I saw my l. weep 524a
  I see it's written by a l. 535a
  I think this l. to be my child 344a
  I will make a l. of my own 471b
  kneeled to a l. in his shield 431b
  l.-cow, fly thy way home 534a
  l., I fain wd. tell how evermore 312a
  l., it is to be presumed 215a

Lady (cont.)
  l. of light 420a
  L. of the Mere 463a
  L. of the Snows 233a
  L., she who left the lilies 294b
  l. so richly clad 100a
  l. sweet and kind 156a, 526b
  L. the brach may stand by the fire 342a
  L. with a Lamp 248a
  lang will his L. look owre 530b
  learned in a l.'s eyes 345a
  like a dying l., lean and pale 399a
  like a l. as thou art 378a
  lovely l., garmented in light 399b
  many holiday and l. terms 376b
  most excellent accomplished l. 371b
  Mother of God! no l. thou 98a
  my arm a l.'s lilye hand 531a
  my l. seems of ivory 284b
  my l. sweet, arise 328b
  Old L. of Threadneedle Street 167a
  Our L. of Pain 421a
  she was the most beautiful l. 119a
  shd. never come out of a l.'s lips 155a
  sighed for the love of a l. 167a
  some lost l. of old years 52b
  some men must love my l. 344b
  talk..with the same single l. 71b
  the chaste l.'s pregnant womb 260b
  the elder unto the elect l. 518a
  the l. doth protest too much 334a
  the l. of Christ's College 11a
  the l. of my delight 265a
  the Liner she 's a l. 231b
  this l. by the trees 474b
  this l. of the West Country 119a
  thy mother a l., both lovely 317b
  to see an old l. ride 533b
  well may such a l. 524b
  what l. wd. not love a shepherd? 176b
  when a l. 's in the case 160b
  white hand of a l. fever thee 324a
  why did you throw yr. wedded l. 329a
  will you hear a Spanish l. 528a
  with the l. inside 527a
  you were April's l. 423a
Lady Betty: hearken L. 4b
Lady Disdain 358a
Lady Jane was tall 20a
Ladylike: I wouldn't be too l. in love 186a
Lady-smocks all silver-white 345b
Laetitia: are you quite well, L.? 264b
Lafayette, we are here 296b
Lag-end of my life 378b
Lager-beer: afay mit der l. 244b
Laggard: for a l. in love 318a
Laid: ere I am l. out dead 189b
  hae l. him on the green 530b
  I l. me down with a will 415a
  in sad cypress let me be l. 371a
  lightly l. again 439a
  wherein was never man yet l. 511b
  why was not I not beside him l. 317a
Lain: in cold grave she was l. 529a
Lair: deep his midnight l. had made 316a
  rouse the lion from his l. 320a
Laird: last L. of Ravenswood 319a
Lairdie: wee German l. 116b, 193a
Laith were our gude Scots 530a
Laity: tell the l. our love 134a
Lake: beside the l., beneath the trees 467a
  blossom fell into the l. 434a
  into the bosom of the steady l. 469b
  Sanguelac, the l. of Blood! 427b
  sedge is wither'd from the l. 218b
  slips into the bosom of the l. 437a
  swan on still St. Mary's L. 473a
Lake-blossom: white l. falls 434a
Lakes: long light shakes across the l. 436a
  scalped each other by the Great L. 254b
Lalage: call me L. or Doris 101b
  I've lost L! 234a
  L. and her sweet laughter 545a
Lamb: a L. as it had been slain 518b
  as a l. to the slaughter 503a
  but one dead l. is there! 248a
  Cassius, you are yoked with a l. 341a
  did he who made the L. make thee 32a
  God will provide himself a l. 493a
  go to bed with the l. 35a
  He calls Himself a L. 32b

Lamb (cont.)
  hide us..from the wrath of the l. 519a
  I a child, and thou a l. 32b
  [L., Holcroft, and Coleridge] 183a
  L., the frolic and the gentle 465b
  leads me to the L. 109b
  Little L. God bless thee 32b
  little L., I'll tell thee 32b
  little L. who made thee? 32b
  Mary had a little l. 177b
  of the skin of an innocent l. 384a
  O L. of God, I come 146a
  pet-l. in a sentimental farce 219b
  pipe a song about a L. 32b
  receive the L. of God to dwell 30b
  save one little ewe l. 495b
  sedulous ape to..L. 412b
  shallows..in wh. a l. may wade 185b
  tempers the wind..to the shorn l. 573a
  10th, Emperor L. 239b
  the L. is the light thereof 520a
  the l. was sure to go 177b
  the marriage supper of the L. 519b
  Una with her milk-white l. 468b
  was the Holy L. of God 31a
  what makes the l. love Mary 177b
  white in the blood of the L. 519a
  wolf..shall dwell with the l. 501b
  yr. l. shall be without blemish 493b
Lambkins, we will live 381b
Lambs: feed my l. 511b
  gather the l. with his arm 502b
  I do love thee as my l. 105b
  l. cd. not forgive,..worms forget 124b
  meadows to see the young l. 453a
  we were as twinned l. 372b
  young l. bound as to the tabor's 466a
Lame: helping..l. dogs over stiles 226a
  I, made l. by fortune's..spite 387b
  l. and impotent conclusion 361a
  l. man leap up as an hart 502a
Lament: have I not reason to l. 471a
  have nought other to l. 294a
  l. anew, Urania 391b
  l. nor sorrow at 324b
  whom universal Nature did l. 269b
  ye need nae sair l. 531b
  you l. not the days that are gone 407a
Lamented Jack 102a
Lamenting: he was left l. 77a
Lamentings heard i' the air 348a
Lammas: fell about the L. tide 530b
Lamp: Christ with His l. of truth 36b
  glorious L. of Heaven, the sun 190b
  it is a dying l. 392a
  Lady with a L. 248a
  largest l. is lit 253b
  largest l. on Campden Hill 92b
  light the bridal l. 275b
  press God's l. close 49b
  Press-men; Slaves of the L. 5c
  smell too strong of the l. 411b
  that fluttered round the l. 85b
  thou fill'st..thy l., O Memory 313c
  unlit l. and the ungirt loin 52b
  welcum the..l. of day 134a
  when the l. is shattered 395a
  whose intense l. narrows 398a
  with handmaid l. attending 270a
Lamping Samminiato 49a
Lamplough was genteel, L. was trite 412a
Lamps: and the l. of heaven 226a
  filled their l. with everlasting oil 267a
  Heav'n's great l. do dive 78a
  l. are going out all over Europe 177a
  l. shone o'er fair women 68a
  like golden l. in a green night 260a
  like hidden l. in old..urns 108a
  new l. for old 567a
  ye living l., by whose dear light 261a
  Yew alone burns l. of peace 119a
Lancaster: time honoured L. 374a
Lancastrian: turn L. there 405a
Lance: hopeless l. was laid in rest 92a
  my l. a wand of the willow tree 531a
  sword-sway, and with l.'s thrust 318a
Lancelot: by the river sang Sir L. 428a
  colour wh. I found in L. 428a
  L., budge not 277a
  L., or Pelleas, or Pellenore 277a
  L. mused a little space 432a

Lancelot (cont.)
nor. L., nor another 428a
of bold Sir L. 431b
till she left not even L. brave 429a
when was L. wanderingly lewd? 428a
(See also Launcelot)
Lancers: six stalwart l. 459a
Land: a happy l. we know 94b
along the l. they rode 319a
a new people takes the l. 93a
angel of death..abroad thro' the l. 38a
as thro' the l. at eve we went 436a
beyond this l. of woe 18a
cast the water of my l. 350b
dear the l. that gave you birth 287b
divides that heavenly l. from ours 453b
eat of the fat of the l. 493b
edge of the long lone l. 421b
England's green and pleasant L. 31b
far into the bowels of the l. 385a
flowery, green, bird-singing l. 118a
French the empire of the l. 80a
from sunshine to the sunless l. 465b
from the best of all my l. 378a
from the holy l. of Walsinghame 307b
from the l. of mist and snow 98b
good and bad of every l. 18a
good seed on the l. 76a
half a rood of l., set out 419b
has been..the l. of the free 77b
her l. reposed 437a
his hands prepared the dry l. 487b
Hobden owns the l. 230b
I have felt with my native l. 434b
ill fares the l., to hastening ills 168a
in a barren and dry l. 485b
in a cleaner, greener l. 232a
in all that l. had never been 425b
I never liked my l. 120b
in l.-travel or sea-faring? 52b
in the l. I'm going to 29a
in the l. of the living 483b
I went to the holy l. 307b
is she known in all the l.? 431b
know you the l.? 568a
l. flowing with milk and honey 493b
l. is scattered with light 35b
L. of darkness 497a
L. of Dreams is better far 31a
L. of faery 475b
L. of Heart's Desire 475b
l. of just and old renown 439b
l. of lost content 199b
l. of my sires 317b
l. of our birth 227b
l. of pure delight 453b
l. of sand and ruin 424a
l. of sand and thorns 428a
l. of settled government 439b
l. of the shadow of death 501b
l. of slaves shall ne'er be mine 71a
l. of the pilgrims' pride 404a
l. o' the leal 285b
l. that has taught us 281a
l. that's governed by a child 385a
l.-thieves and water-thieves 353a
L. to wh. yon Ship must go 97a. 472b
l. where even the old are fair 475b
l. where my fathers died 404a
l. where the Bong-tree grows 243b
l. where the cypress and myrtle 67b
l...where the light is as darkness 497a
l. wh. the Lord thy God giveth 480a
lilacs out of the dead l. 144b
Lord's song: in a strange l. 490a
lo! the l. where was the wave 293b
love..l. because it is their own 178a
marching to the Promised L. 20b
men sing by l. an' sea 236b
mighty ocean, and the pleasant l. 82a
mire of the last l.! 39b
mist and hum of that low l. 8a
my native l., Good Night! 68a
my new-found-l. 132b
my own, my native l. 317a
no l. beside 373b
no l. can compare unto thee 389b
ocean leans against the l. 170a
o'er all the pleasant l. 184b
on to the Pleasant L. 47a
our ship not far from l. 525b

Land (cont.)
pass, like night, from l. to l. 100a
person dwelling up-on l. 89a
pleasant l. of counterpane 414a
pleasing l. of drowsy-head 443a
plenty o'er a smiling l. 174b
pointed toward the l. 433a
Prince of all the l. 76b
ready by water as by l. 146a
row, my knights, near the l. 79a
save a sinking l. 301b
search the l. of living men 318a
seems a moving l. 275b
sente hem hoom to every l. 88b
shaft of light across the l. 427a
she is far from the l. 281b
speak of the better l. 184b
splendid and a happy l. 168b
stood as signals to the l. 99b
stranger in a strange l. 493b
strong man in a blatant l. 433b
sweet l. of liberty 404a
the l. you used to plough 199a
there is a happy l. 476b
there shall be no more l. 39b
there's l. I see! 440b
there's the l., or cherry isle 188b
they are not fit to live on l. 208b
they who rule the l. be men 468a
think there is no l. 13a
this dear, dear l. 375a
this was the charter of the l. 443a
thou on the l., and I on the sand 319b
thro' the broad bright l. 406a
to all you ladies now at l. 134b
to see the nakedness of the l. 493b
to spy out the l. 494a
violet of his native l. 430a
was great by l. as thou by sea 435a
when house and l. are gone 155b
when the l. is cultivated 266a
where is the l. of Luthany 442b
where the l. she travels from 97a
whistles o'er the furrowed l. 268b
Landeau: they will have their
barouche-l. 11a
grey gun-'orses in the l. 234a
Land-breeze shook the shrouds 111a
Landed: inclined to the l...interest 2a
Landing-place: he gained the l. 317a
safe to the l. 253b
Landlord: l., fill the flowing bowl 522b
l.'s black-eyed daughter 290a
Land-lubbers lying down below 525b
Landmark: removeth his neighbour's l. 494b
Landmarks: great men..l. in..state 55a
Landor and with Donne 476b
Lands: call the l. after their own
names 485a
close to the sun in lonely l. 426b
envy of less happier l. 375a
faery l. forlorn 220a
hard heir strides about their l. 430b
in l. of palm and southern pine 426a
l. beyond the sea 467a
l. I was to travel in 530a
l. the voyager at last 145b
much I owe to the L. that grew 236a
other l. beneath another sun 443b
princes in all l. 484b
prizes not quantity of dirty l. 371a
sound is gone out into all l. 482b
then l. were fairly portioned 253a
Landscape: fades the glimmering l. 174a
he is but a l. painter 432b
once more that l. painter 432b
view the l. o'er 453b
Landscapes ..sold.. one penny plain 412b
Lane: blue above l. and wall 46a
ghost..in an English l. 46a
l., highway, or open street 445b
little boy who cries in the l. 534b
Language: a use in measured l. lies 429b
Chatham's l...his mother tongue 111b
consenting l. of the heart 160a
dear l. wh. I spake like thee 252b
don't think anything of that l. 124b
effusions..in the best chosen l. 11b
enlargement of the l. 212b
enrichment of our native l. 142a

Language (cont.)
everything..in our l. shd. perish 255b
fancies that broke thro' l. 50b
I love the l. of his heart 303b
l. I have learned..forty years 374b
l. is fossil poetry 148a
l. is a perpetual Orphic song 397b
l. is the dress of thought 213a
l. is..the garment of thought 81b
l. quaint and olden 247a
l. that wd. make yr. hair curl 166b
l. was not powerful enough 124b
learned his great l. 48a
learning me yr. l. 367a
my l. is plain 182a
no l. but a cry 430b
no l., but the l. of the heart 303a
off oure l...the lodesterre 251a
of his strange l. all I know 241a
O that those lips had l. 109a
persuasive l. of a tear 95a
some entrance into the l. 15a
still the heart doth need a l. 101b
sure in l. strange she said 218b
the l. plain 108a
there is neither speech nor l. 482b
there's l. in her eye 369a
they can only speak one l. 129b
under the tropic is our l. spoke 449a
you taught me l. 367a
Languaged: well l. Daniel 42b
Languages: at a great feast of l. 345a
gave l. just as she needed 306a
in the graves of deceased l. 122b
knowledge of the ancient l. 38a
l. are the pedigree of nations 212b
none of yr. live l. for..Blimber 122b
speaks three or four l. 369b
vulgar l. that want words 216b
Languid: art thou weary, art thou l. 286a
l. strings do scarcely move! 31b
Languish: relieve my l. 117a
Languishes: a cat l. loudly 185b
Languishment: tale of love and l. 221a
Languor: l. cannot be 398b
l. is not in yr. heart 7b
Languors: lilies and l. of virtue 421a
Lantern: in thy dark l. thus close up 267a
thy word is a l. unto my feet 489a
Lanterns: feast of l.! 297b
Laodameia died 241b
Lap: biforn him in his l. 89a
dropt in her L. from some..Head 153a
l. me in soft Lydian airs 269a
l. of the crimson rose 356b
old enough to l. and to swallow 459a
on the cool flowery l. of earth 6b
strew the green l. of the..spring 376a
sun..in the l. of Thetis 65b
La Palie: Provence and L. 96b
Lap-dogs: when l. breathe their last 302b
Lapis: all l., all sons 45a
Lapland: L...noble wild prospects 207a
lovely as a L. night 473a
Laps: fortunes..tumbling into ..l. 13a
Lapse of murmuring streams 275b
to l. in fulness is sorer 328b
Lapwings feel the..leaden death 304a
Larañaga: peace in a L. 227a
Larboard: all to the l. side 531a
Larch: rosy plumelets tuft the l. 430b
Lard their lean books 64a
Larded with sweet flowers 335b
Lards the lean earth as he walks 377a
Large: as l. as store 188a
I am l., I contain multitudes 458a
l., and smooth, and round 406a
l. as life, and twice as natural 85a
l.-hearted man 43b
l. was his bounty 174b
so rudeliche and l. 89a
thou l.-brained woman 43b
Larger: I am l., better than I thought 458a
l. than human on the frozen hills 429a
Largess universal, like the sun 382b
Largest: shout with the l. 126a
those of the l. size 84b
Lark: and the l. soars 43a
Hark! hark! the l. 328b
hear the l. begin his flight 268b
herald l. left his ground-nest 277a

Lark (*cont.*)
l. becomes a sightless song — 431*a*
l. drop down at his feet — 435*b*
l. from her light wing — 115*b*
l., messenger of day — 89*a*
l. now leaves his wat'ry nest — 117*b*
l. sang loud and high — 28*b*
l. shall sing me hame — 116*b*
l., that tirra-lirra chants — 373*a*
late l. twitters from the..skies — 185*a*
like to the l. at break of day — 387*b*
music soars within the little l. — 43*a*
no l. cd. pipe to skies so dull — 225*b*
no l. more blithe than he — 28*a*
sing as sweetly as the l. — 355*b*
some late l. singing — 185*a*
swallow for the holy l. — 43*a*
than l. to shepherd's ear — 356*a*
the lark's on the wing — 50*a*
the nightingale, and not the l. — 366*a*
the shrill-gorged l. — 343*b*
the shrill sweet l. — 196*a*
we rise with the l. — 35*a*
Larks: four l. and a Wren — 243*a*
hear the l. so high — 199*a*
mounting l. their notes prepare — 304*a*
Larkspur listens, 'I hear' — 434*a*
Lars Porsena — 253*a, b*
Lartius: back, L. — 253*b*
Lascivious pleasing of a lute — 384*b*
Lash: the vice and follies — 86*b*
the l., of film — 364*b*
whip to l. the rascals naked — 363*a*
Lashes: three hundred and fifty l. — 126*b*
Lass: a l. unparalleled — 325*b*
drink to the l. — 400*b*
every l. a queen — 226*a*
give him his l., his fiddle — 111*a*
hey, for a l. wi' a tocher — 61*a*
I loved a l., a fair one — 462*a*
it was a lover and his l. — 327*b*
l. that has acres o' charms — 61*a*
l. wi' the weel-stockit farms — 61*a*
lordliest l. of earth — 39*b*
man may kiss a bonnie l. — 63*a*
penniless l. wi' a lang pedigree — 285*b*
sweet l. of Richmond Hill — 256*b, 447*a*
the l. that loves a sailor! — 120*b*
this l. so neat — 256*b, 447*a*
what a l. that were — 240*a*
will never show a l. as comely — 231*b*
yon solitary Highland l. — 471*a*
Lasses: come l. and lads — 522*b*
he dearly lov'd the l. O — 60*b*
honest men and bonnie l. — 62*b*
l. a' lilting — 145*b*
spent among the l. O! — 60*b*
then she made the l. O — 60*b*
'twere na for the l. O — 60*b*
Lassie: I love a l. — 242*b*
my love she's but a l. — 193*a*
what can a young l. do — 63*a*
Last: after L., returns the First — 44*b*
ah wd. that this might be the l. — 109*a*
at l. the belles ringeth — 182*b*
at the l., best — 322*b*
cobbler shd. not go beyond his l. — 552*b*
comes at the l. — 375*b*
each day thy l. esteem — 224*b*
first kiss and forebode the l. — 312*a*
first to come and l. to go — 249*a*
he had brought me to my l. legs — 140*a*
he that comes l. is commonly best — 64*a*
it did not l. — 26*b*
it will l. my time — 80*a*
I will give unto this l. — 507*b*
l. an 'ealthy Tommy for a year — 229*a*
l. at His cross — 21*a*
l. came, and l. did go — 269*b*
l. night, among his fellow roughs — 136*b*
l., not least in love — 339*b*
l. of all he was seen of me also — 514*b*
l. of all our Odysseys — 26*b*
l. of all the Bards was he — 316*b*
l. of all the Romans — 341*b*
l. of all the woman died also — 507*b*
l. of life for wh...first was made — 50*b*
l. of that bright band — 184*b*
l. of the Mohicans — 106*a*
l. state of that man is worse — 506*b*

Last (*cont.*)
l., till you write yr. letter — 134*a*
l. to lay the old aside — 300*a*
many that are first shall be l. — 507*b*
next in majesty, in both the l. — 141*a*
noblest offspring is the l. — 28*a*
of many..kisses the poor l. — 324*b*
one more, and this the l. — 363*b*
system..wd. probably l. her time — 315*b*
that's the l. thing I shall do! — 292*a*
the best and the l.! — 50*b*
the l. shall be first — 507*b*
there is no l. nor first — 50*a*
this day may be the l. — 287*a*
what is it that will l. — 433*a*
Lasted: nice while it l. — 232*b*
Lasting: full l. is the song — 264*a*
l. too, for souls not lent — 264*a*
Last Judgement: 'tis the L.'s fire — 45*b*
Lasts ever, past recall — 51*a*
Latch: crosspatch, draw the l. — 533*a*
find no l. ter de golden gate? — 182*a*
Latchet: whose shoe's l. I am not worthy — 510*b*
Latchfords: letting in the L. — 417*a*
Late: all the worse when it comes l. — 205*b*
five minutes too l. — 107*b*
it came to them very l. — 227*a*
l., l. in the gloamin' — 193*a*
never too l. for delight, my dear — 281*b*
not too l. to seek a newer world — 439*a*
some l. lark singing — 185*a*
sorrow never comes too l. — 175*a*
too l., too l.! ye cannot enter now — 427*b*
when others cry, 'Too l.' — 44*a*
white rose weeps, 'she is l.' — 434*a*
who passes by this road so l.? — 528*a*
Lated in the night — 176*a*
Lately that air, that l. kissed thee — 190*a*
Lath of wood painted..like iron — 568*a*
Lather: good l. is half the shave — 194*b*
Latian: Prince of the L. name — 253*a*
Latin: away with him! he speaks L. — 384*a*
L. names for horns and stools — 60*a*
L., queen of tongues — 216*b*
L. was no more difficile — 64*b*
ne yet of L., ne of Greek — 409*a*
small L., and less Greek — 216*a*
you understand L., Mr. Bonniface? — 150*a*
Latitude: parallels of l. for a seine — 446*b*
the l.'s rather uncertain — 306*b*
Latoun: croys of l., ful of stones — 89*a*
Latter: blessed the l. end of Job — 497*b*
former times shake hands with the l. — 65*b*
l. has the largest congregation — 118*b*
to carry off the l. — 295*a*
Laud: all glory, l. and honour — 286*a*
l. and honour to the Father — 286*b*
Laudable: write well..in l. things — 279*a*
Laudes to their Maker — 182*b*
Laugh: an atheist l.'s a poor exchange — 60*a*
anything awful makes me l. — 239*b*
exploded l. shall win — 40*b*
I did l. sans intermission — 326*a*
if I l. at any mortal thing — 71*a*
I make myself l. at everything — 561*b*
it wd. have made a cat l. — 297*b*
l...again in the grey twilight — 474*b*
l. and be well — 175*b*
l., and the world laughs with you — 459*a*
l. as I pass in thunder — 393*a*
l. at all you trembled at before — 110*b*
l. at my own cenotaph — 393*b*
l. at's while we strut — 324*a*
l. at them in our turn — 11*b*
l., be jolly — 199*b*
l. broke into a thousand pieces — 21*b*
l., home of mine — 538*b*
l. to scorn the power of man — 349*b*
l. where we must — 300*b*
l. with me or at me — 411*b*
loud l. that spoke the vacant mind — 168*b*
make those l. whose lungs are tickle — 332*b*
man cannot make him l. — 380*b*
men that l. and weep — 422*a*
that shall l. at all disaster — 246*b*
they l. that win — 362*b*
they l. uproariously in youth — 39*b*
they that see me l. me to scorn — 483*a*

Laugh (*cont.*)
to l...such a vulgar expression — 104*a*
unextinguishable l. in heaven — 41*a*
valleys also..shall l. and sing — 486*a*
wherefore did Sarah l.? — 493*a*
who but must l. — 303*a*
Laughable: schemes..very l. things — 208*a*
Laughed: dey mus' speck ter be l. at — 181*b*
for they l. consumedly — 150*a*
full well they l. — 168*b*
I l. him out of patience — 323*b*
l. and moaned about by..streams — 44*b*
l. in the sun — 39*b*
Pilots boy..l. loud and long — 99*b*
so loud, loud l. he — 529*b*
we have not sighed deep, l. free — 53*a*
when he's l. and said his say — 440*b*
when the first baby l. — 21*b*
Laughing: forbear l. and jeering — 296*a*
happiness is no l. matter — 456*a*
l. immoderately at..intervals — 404*a*
l. is heard on the hill — 32*b*
Laughs: l. the sense of mis'ry far — 111*a*
l. to see the good things there — 192*b*
l. to see the green man pass — 192*b*
when he l., it adds something — 411*a*
while she l. at them, forgets — 104*a*
why, he l. like anything — 93*b*
Laughter: April, laugh thy girlish l. — 452*a*
boughs of April in l. shake — 35*b*
by the faculty of l. — 208*a*
drinks his wine 'mid l. free — 527*a*
invent anything that tends to l. — 379*b*
l. for a month — 377*a*
L. holding both his sides — 268*b*
l., learnt of friends — 40*a*
let us have..mirth and l. — 70*b*
multitudinous l. of the waves — 559*a*
O Christ, the l. — 261*b*
our sincerest l. with some pain — 398*b*
perhaps to move his l. — 275*b*
present mirth hath present l. — 370*b*
so ill-bred, as audible l. — 90*b*
so is the l. of a fool — 499*a*
the weeping and the l. — 135*a*
the worst returns to l. — 343*b*
tired of tears and l. — 422*a*
under running l. — 441*b*
use you..for my l. — 340*b*
when her lovely l. shows — 78*b*
with weeping and with l. — 253*b*
Laughters: tears and l. for all time! — 44*a*
Lauk a mercy on me — 533*b*
Launcelot: salute me to my lord, Sir L. — 257*b*
Sir L. awoke and went — 257*b*
Sir L. I require thee — 257*b*
Sir L. saw her visage — 257*b*
Sir L. thou wert never matched — 257*b*
(*See also* Lancelot)
Launch: fear to l. away — 453*b*
yr. glorious standard l. again — 77*b*
Laundry: it all goes into the l. — 234*b*
Laura: if L. had been Petrarch's wife — 70*b*
rose-cheeked L., come — 78*a*
Laurel: burned is Apollo's l. bough — 259*a*
carven from the l.-tree — 442*b*
l. for the perfect prime — 311*a*
l. greener from the brows — 437*a*
l. is green for a season — 423*b*
l. outlives not May — 423*b*
l., the palms, and the paean — 423*b*
only that she might l. grow — 260*b*
rose or rue or l. — 420*b*
the l.-trees are cut — 561*b*
thy l., thy glory — 218*a*
Laurels: once more, O ye l. — 269*a*
the l. all are cut — 199*b*
thy l. torn! — 405*b*
worth all your l. — 73*b*
Lave: l. in it, drink of it — 196*a*
let the l. go by me — 414*a*
whistle owre the l. o't — 63*a*
Lavender: hot l., mints, savory — 373*a*
l. water tinged with pink — 243*b*
Lavinia: she is L. — 368*a*
Lavish: in vain with l. kindness — 184*a*
Lavishly: who l. commends — 94*a*
Law: a fig for those by l. protected — 61*a*
all's love, yet all's l. — 51*b*
because they have no l. — 429*a*

Law (*cont.*)

Chancellor only knew a little l. 524a
common l... is nothing .. but reason 97b
crowner's quest l. 336a
custom that is before all l. 117a
custom, that unwritten l. 117b
despair, l., chance 133a
dusty purlieus of the l. 430b
fulfil the l. of their being 10b
God is thy l., thou mine 274a
God's universal l. gave to the man 278a
had not known sin, but by the l. 513a
heat of conflict, keeps the l. 465b
higher l. than the Constitution 321b
highest l. of his being 148a
I charge you by the l. 355a
I crave the l. 354b
I find then a l. 513a
ignorance of the l. excuses no man 321a
I, my Lords, embody the L. 163b
incline our hearts to keep this l. 480a
in l.'s grave study six 97b
in l., what plea so tainted 354a
is the l. of our side if I say ay? 364b
is the l. sin? 513a
it is of no force in l. 97b
keep the Jungle L. 232b
laid His hand on Moses' l. 30a
l. can take a purse in open court 66b
l. is a bottomless pit 4b
L. is the true embodiment 163b
l. of nature, and of nations 56a
l. of thy mouth is dearer 489a
l...renders men acute, inquisitive 55b
L...seat is the bosom of God 196b
l.'s made to take care o' raskills 144a
L...the harmony of the world 196b
l. to ourselves..reason is our l. 276a
lesser breeds without the L. 233b
let them relearn the L. 230b
love is the fulfilling of the l. 513b
my l. the seventh time disobey'd 294a
Nature's l...to mourn 61b
necessity has no l. 553b
not determining a point of l. 55b
nothing is l. that is not reason 304b
not make a scarecrow of the l. 351a
old father antick, the l. 376b
people crushed by l...no hopes 58a
prisons.. built with stones of L. 31a
quicken thou me in thy l. 489a
reason is the life of the l. 97b
rich men rule the l. 170a
seven hours to l. 214b
sharp quillets of the l. 383b
that I am come to destroy the l. 505a
that l. wh. governs all l. 56a
that loveth..hath fulfilled the l. 513b
the army of unalterable l. 263b
the bloody book of l. 359b
the first is l. 140b
the l. doth give it 355a
the l. is an ass 125b
the L.: it has honoured us 454a
the l. of humanity, justice 56a
the l. of our Creator 56a
the l.'s delay 333a
the l. so general a study 55b
the more ought l. to weed it out 14a
there is but one l. for all 56a
these are a l. unto themselves 513a
this is l., I will maintain 524a
this is the l. and the prophets 505b
this is the L. of the Jungle 231a
to the windward of the l. 94b
touching the l., a Pharisee 516a
very good l. for all that 319b
where no l. is..no transgression 513a
who to himself is L. 87a
windy side o' the l. 372a
within the purlieus of the L. 149a
wrest once the l. to yr. authority 354b
your Majesty's will is l. 165a
Lawful: all things are l. for me 514b
an art l. as eating 373b
is it not l. for me to do 507b
neither quite l. nor quite right 66b
that wh. is l. and right 503b
upon their l. occasions 490b
Lawn: a l. about the shoulders 189a

Lawn (*cont.*)

bird-haunted English l. 7a
l. as white as driven snow 373b
leave the printed l. 200a
rivulets hurrying thro' the l. 437a
sun upon the upland l. 174b
twice a saint in l. 301b
Laws: and their l. approve 140b
bad l...worst sort of tyranny 55a
ballads..l. of a nation 155a
beginning with the l. 305a
breaking up of l. 427b
if l. are their enemies 58a
I know not whether L. be right 459b
l. and learning die 258a
l...are at my commandment 381a
l. are generally found to be nets 400a
l. are inoperative in war 540b
l. are like cobwebs 417b
l. grind the poor 170a
l...lean on one another 57b
l. of God will be suspended 390a
l. were like cobwebs 13b
l. were made to be broken 289b
not by partial, but by general l. 300b
part wh. l. or kings can cause 213a
repeal of bad or obnoxious l. 173a
schoolmasters deliver us to l. 187a
sweeter manners, purer l. 431a
they will be enemies to l. 58a
unequal l. unto a savage race 438b
whence all civil l. are derived 13a
Lawyer: as a l. knows how 110b
aye the cheapest l.'s fee 62b
for her the l. pleads 21a
he saw a L. killing a viper 100b
if l.'s hand is fee'd 159b
leaned on a staggering l. 93a
not what a l. tells me I *may* do 55b
Lawyers: L. have their bowers 409b
let's kill all the l. 384a
o'er l.' fingers 364b
the l. are met 160a
woe unto you, l. 509a
Lay: Brer Fox, he l. low 181b
Cleric before, and L. behind 65b
he l. like a warrior 462a
l. me, O! where sad true lover 371a
l. not up for yourselves treasures 505b
l. on, Macduff 351a
l. them down in their dens 488b
ne'er to a seductive l. 463a
the unpremeditated l. 316b
your sweet responsive l. 117a
Layman: poor l. I 401b
Lays: constructing tribal l. 230a
little do we know wot l. afore us 124a
she l. it on with a trowel 104a
Lazy: l. leaden-stepping hours 278b
liftin' the l. ones on 173a
Lea: fair Kirkconnell l. 531a
on yonder l. 62a
standing on this pleasant l. 473a
Lead: country life I praise, and l. 37b
friends are lapped in l. 20b
go down like lumps of l. 192a
here is neither l. nor lee 231a
I wd. l. thee, and bring thee 500b
l., and I follow 427b
l., kindly Light 288b
l. those that are with young 502b
l. thou me on 288b
l. us, Heavenly Father, l. us 143b
makes a people easy to l. 40b
ship went down like l. 99b
tears do scald like molten l. 344a
when we think we l...most led 74a
whither wilt thou l. me? 331a
Leaden: if I use l. ones 25b
Leaden-eyed: pale, and l. 196a
Leader: in camps l. sage 318a
the L. is fairest 5b
Leaders: blind l. of the blind 507a
four-and-twenty l. of revolts 52a
Leading: man of light and l. 130a
Leads: l.—God knows where 71a
l. me from my love 199a
Leaf: caterpillar on the l. 29b
elm-tree bole are in tiny l. 47a
fall'n into the sear, the yellow l. 350b
falls with the l. still 23a

Leaf (*cont.*)

if I were a dead l. 396b
I were like the l. 423a
last red l. is whirled away 429b
my days are in the yellow l. 73b
no l. upon the forest bare 393a
November's l. is red 317b
right as an aspen l. 90a
the l. is on the tree 205a
thin is the l. 421a
we all do fade as a l. 503b
where the dead l. fell..did rest 218a
League: a l. but barely three 529a
half a l. onward 426a
keep a l. till death 376a
she hadna sailed a l. 529a
Leagues: still l. beyond those l. 312b
tho' thy soul sail l. 312b
Leak: one l. will sink a ship 54b
sprang no fatal l. 111a
Leal: land o' the l. 285b
Lean: bruised reed..on wh. if a man l. 496b
laws..l. on one another 57b
l. and sallow abstinence 267b
l., hungry, savage anti-everythings 193b
one of a l. body and visage 158a
she helped him to l. 19b
sideways wd. she l., and sing 218b
study had made him very l. 196a
the l. was so ruddy 169a
wife cd. eat no l. 534a
Leander, Mr. Ekenhead, and I 70b
Leaning: stuffed men l. together 145a
Leans: it l., and hearkens after it 134a
Leap: a great l. in the dark 191b
I shall l. over the wall 482b
it were an easy l. 377a
l. in with me into this..flood 337b
look before you ere you l. 65b
made a l. into the dark 41a
more worthy to l. in ourselves 341b
Leaping: pulling..one's horse as he is l. 181a
so long as there is no l. 417a
Leaps: babe l. up on his mother's arm 466a
by steps, and not by l. 254a
Leapt: into the dangerous world I l. 32a
Leap-year, that's the time 533a
Lear: pleasant to know Mr. L. 243b
Lea-rig: meet thee on the l. 61b
Learn: diligent to l. 465a
gladly wolde he l. 88b
if they will l. any thing 514b
l. about women from me 230b
l. all we lacked before 39b
l. and labour truly 481a
l., nor account the pang 50b
not bred so dull but she can l. 354a
not yet so old but she may l. 354a
places to l. the world in 90b
quick to l., and wise to know 59a
we l. so little...forget so much 117b
we live and l. 298b
when there is much desire to l. 279a
whereof it is born, I am to l. 352b
Learned: all l., and all drunk 112b
grew within this l. man 259a
I have l. to look on nature 472a
l. about women from 'er 230b
l. and conned by rote 341a
l. lumber in his head 300b
make the l. smile 300a
obscurity of a l. language 571a
of the opinion with the l. 104a
the l. is happy nature 301a
they will not be l. 487a
things l. on earth 49a
Learning: all that ever l. writ 25a
a' the l. I desire 60a
cry both arts and l. down 307a
enough of l. to misquote 72a
fraught with all l. 169b
hated not l. worse than toad 278b
laws and l. die 258a
l., a mere hoard of gold 380b
l. hath gained most 158a
l. is but an adjunct 345a
l. is most excellent 155b
l., that cobweb of the brain 65b
l. will be cast into the mire 57a

Learning (cont.)
little l. is a dangerous thing 300a
love he bore to l. was in fault 168b
loyal body wanted l. 445b
men of polite l. 185b
middle age of a state, l. 16b
much l. doth make thee mad 513a
of light, of liberty, and of l. 128b
O! this l., what a thing it is 366b
picker-up of l.'s crumbs 46b
religion..with her l. did suit 306a
renowned for l. and piety 173a
sceptre, l., physic, must 329a
such deep l. little had he need 409a
their l. is like bread 208b
those twins of l. 386b
wearing..l. lightly like a flower 431a
wear yr. l., like yr. watch 90b
whence is thy l.? 160a
when l.'s triumph o'er 213b
where childlike L. sits 167b
why shd. l. hope success at Court 160a
Learnt: angling..never be fully l. 450a
plainest taught, and easiest l. 277a
they have l. nothing 565b
Lease: having so short a l. 389b
l. of my true love 388b
summer's l. hath all too short 387a
Least: done it unto the l. of these 508a
faithful in that wh. is l. 510a
l. of all the apostles 514b
Leather: all but l. or prunella 301b
as ever trod upon neat's l. 337b
first found out the l. bottel 526a
I am sick o' wastin' l. 232a
Leathern: my l. belt likewise 108b
L'eau, replied Nicholas 124b
Leave: at once they l. you 49b
by all ye l. or do 236b
Comrades, l. me here a little 432a
fare thee well, for I must l. thee 527a
gave sign for me to l. you 338b
he is a dreamer; let us l. him 337b
how I l. my country 297b
I l. them where they are 458a
intreat me not to l. thee 495a
I pray thee l., love me no more 137a
l. behind us footprints 248a
l. her to heaven 331b
l. me here, and when you want me 432a
l. me, l. me to repose! 173b
l. my little wooden hut for you! 263a
l. nothing of myself in me 114b
l. off first for manners' sake 520b
l. thee alone, for the comparison 216a
l. thee in the lurch 65a
l. then thy foolish ranges 448a
l. the trodden paths of men 392a
l. to Robert Browning beggars 226a
l. us alone! 293a
l. we now Thy servant sleeping 145b
lend me l. to come unto my love 408b
live in hearts we l. behind 76b
love him, or l. him alone! 470a
occasion smiles upon a second l. 330b
often took l...loth to depart 306a
Oh, never l. me 523a
O Sleep, why dost thou l. me 105a
taken an everlasting l. 162a
true of most we l. behind 97a
wh. thou must l. ere long 388a
wilt thou l. me thus? 473b
Leaven: l. of malice and wickedness 479b, 514a
little l. leaveneth the whole 514a
not with the old l. of malice 514a
Leavening: you must tarry the l. 368b
Leaves: all its sweetest l. yet folded 72a
all that famous harmony of l. 476a
all that lamentation of the l. 476a
and the l. break forth 203a
as naturally as l. to a tree 222b
as the generation of l. 560a
as the l. grow on the tree 474a
autumnal l. like light footfalls 396a
bear light shade for the l. 393a
brown skeletons of l. that lag 99b
buds and l., wandering astray 398a
bursts come crowding thro' the l. 7a
chauntings of the unquiet l. 476a
close up these barren l. 471b

Leaves (cont.)
crowned with calm l. 422a
fresh Earth in new l. dressed 398b
from whose..presence the l. dead 396a
green l. among the groves 465b
green l. whispering overhead 461b
laughing l. of the tree 420b
l. have their time to fall 185a
l. it as fast as they can 246a
L. of Life keep falling 154b
l. of the Judgment Book unfold 425a
l. of the tree were for the healing 520a
l. they are so green 531a
l. they were crisped and sere 298b
l. to quicken a new birth 396b
lisp of l. and ripple of rain 420a
lofty trees I see barren of l. 387a
long l. cover me 423a
nor wintry l. nor vernal 422a
pickt from the l. of any author 41b
put l. round his head 123a
roses rear their l. 73b
shady l. of destiny 115a
shatter yr. l. before the..year 269a
shows his hoar l. in the..stream 336a
sun came dazzling thro' the l. 431b
the silent l. are still 73a
thick as autumnal l. 271b
thou amongst the l. 220a
thro' the velvet l. the wind 344b
violets cover'd up in l. 220a
what if my l. are falling 396b
what it l. behind 465a
when yellow l., or none, or few 388a
whole deck put on its l. again 155a
wild l. that winds have taken 422a
yellow drifts of withered l. 7b
Leave-taking: it is not worth l. 325a
Leaving: became him like the l. it 346b
l., with meekness, her sins 196a
Leavy: since summer first was l. 358b
Lebanon: annual wound in L. 271b
his countenance is as L. 500b
nose is as the tower of L. 500b
Samarcand to cedared L. 221b
Lecher: fly does l. in my sight 343b
Lecherous: I am rough and l. 342a
Lecture, Love, in love's philosophy 133b
Lectures: I do not give l. 458a
l. in her night-dress! 196b
Led: by whim, envy, or resentment l. 94a
hath l. me, who knows how? 394b
he l. them forth by the right way 488b
men l. me to him, blindfold 228b
Prince..l. them on 76b
they l...a kind of..as it were 305b
think we lead, we are most l. 74a
Leda: as L., was the mother of Helen 293a
L., the beloved of Jupiter 241b
Ledge: over a l. of granite 96a
Ledlow: Farmer L. late at plough 179b
Lee: between windward and l. 421b
here is neither lead nor l.! 231a
waters of the River L. 306b
Leek: by this l., I will..revenge 383b
Leeks: oynons, and eke l. 89a
Leer: assent with civil l. 303a
Lees: drink life to the l. 438b
the mere l. is left this vault 348a
Left: all l. behind on the beach 85b
cannon to l. of them 426a
have the use..but of my l. hand 279a
he was l. lamenting 77a
his l. hand is under my head 500a
l. a lot of little things 227a
l. a name behind them 521b
Sun came up upon the l. 98a
that we l., we lost 526a
there'll be little of us l. 437b
thou hast l. thy first love 518b
'tis better to be l. 105a
we are l., or shall be l., alone 468a
we, we only, are l.! 7b
when 't l. me far away 261a
you l. off before you began 104b
Leg: a decreasing l. 379b
he has a l. 264b
here I leave my second l. 194b
I have lost my l., by God 455a
kiss my Julia's dainty l. 189b
literary man..with a wooden l. 125b

Leg (cont.)
only sylph who could stand upon
 one l. 125a
our steed the l. 328a
took him by the left l. 534b
what l...into yr. breeches first 207b
you make a l. 375b
Legacy: bequeathing it as a rich l. 340a
Legend: l. of an epic hour 92b
L. of Good Women 426b
the l.'s writ 287b
Legends: whence these l. 248b
Legion: l. of the lost ones 229a
L. that never was 'listed 231b
my name is L. 508b
Legion of Honour has been conferred 447a
Legions: ere yet we loose the l. 230a
give me back my l. 538a
let the l. thunder past 7a
Legislative nominated by..executive 162a
Legislator: people is the true l. 57b
Legislators: poets are the unacknowledged l. 399b
Legislature: no l. can manufacture 17a
Legs: brought me to my last l. 140a
cannon-ball took off his l. 194b
delighteth he in any man's l. 490b
ever recuvver the use of his l. 124b
his l. are as pillars of marble 500b
his l. bestrid the ocean 325a
his l. were hewn in two 530b
if you cd. see my l. 123a
not a pair of l. so thin 229b
stands on his hinder l. 386b
stood upon his l., that bird 121b
taste yr. l., sir 371b
the l. without the man 112b
to lie between maids' l. 334a
trunkless l. of stone 396b
upon one pair of English l. 382a
walk under his huge l. 337b
when his l. were smitten off 391b
Leicester beans and bacon 225b
Leicester Square: farewell L. 461a
Leigh Hunt's light agreeable..style 183b
Leipsic: Faliero my L. 71b
get up well at L. 45a
Leisure: add to these retired L. 268a
at l. marry'd 105a
his surname, L. 130b
I am quite at l. 11b
leave us l. to be good 173b
l. answers l. 352b
no blessed l. for love 196b
polish it at l. 142a
repent at l. 105a
slander any moment's l. 331a
what l. to grow wise 7a
Leman: Lake L. woos me 68b
such hounds, and such a l. 529b
Lemon: in the squeezing of a l. 171a
land where the l.-trees bloom 568a
take a suck at the l. 19b
Lemons: oranges and l. 533b
Lend: cur can l...ducats 353a
few l. (but fools) 446a
good world..to l...in 38a
I l. it instantly 187b
I'll l. you something 372a
I'll l. you this much 353a
l. less than thou owest 342a
the men who l. 239a
Lender: nor a l. be 330b
Lenders: thy pen from l.' books 343a
Lendeth: merciful, and l. 489a
Lends: three things I never l. 417a
Length: all l. is torture 324b
drags its slow l. along 300a
Folly's at full l. 91b
his listless l. at noontide 174b
l. and breadth enough 530b
Lengths: carry nature l. unknown 111b
Lenore: sorrow for the lost L. 298a
Lent out my heart with usury 239b
Lenten entertainment 332b
Leopard: l. shall lie down 501b
the l. (change) his spots 503b
Leper once he lost 271b
Leprosy: skin was white as l. 98b
Lesbia: L. hath a beaming eye 281b
L. mine, let 's live and love! 538b

Lesbia (*cont.*)
L., whom once Catullus loved 539a
my sweetest L. let us live 78a
Lesley: saw ye bonnie L. 59b
Less: and beautifully l. 305b
for nothing l. than thee 132a
greater glory dim the l. 355b
had he pleased us l. 1b
l. than that no man shall have 310a
l. than the dust 197a
low, and infinitely l. 114b
nicely-calculated l. or more 467b
pleased with l. than Cleopatra 139a
rather-more-or-l. 228b
rather than be l. 272a
the l. we like you 26b
the little l., what worlds away 45b
they wd. have done no l. 338a
you mean you can't take l. 83a
Lessen: they l. from day to day 83a
Lesser life shall be as the greater 171b
Lesson: l., and the young Man crucified 265a
Love is the lesson 573a
own with..pride the l. just 18b
'tis a l. you shd. heed 191a
we've had an Imperial l. 231a
Lessons: of two such l., why forget 71a
reason they're called l. 83a
Let: a thorn to l. me blood 188a
I will l. you a better 426a
I will not l. thee go 36b
l. go! You are hurtig be! 237a
l. what will be o'er me 414a
sore l. and hindered in running 479a
then might I l. thee go 36b
to be l. unfurnished 65a
Lethæan: labour's dull L. spring 6a
Lethargy: a kind of l. 379b
Lethe: crimson'd in thy l. 339b
go not to L. 219b
on L. wharf 331b
tedious shores of L. 238b
'tis L.'s gloom, but not its quiet 76b
Lethean: drunken of things L. 423b
Lets: ghost of him that l. me 331a
Letter: a l. from his wife 85b
carry a l. to my love 529b
change the name, and not the l. 87a
deal by speech than by l. 16a
for the l. killeth 515a
give 'im a l. 234a
good face..l. of recommendation 2a
how large a l. I have written 515b
king has written a braid l. 529b
one that when he wrote a l. 15b
preferment goes by l. 359b
read in the bitter l. 359b
runs with a l.! 234a
zed! thou unnecessary l. 342a
Letters: I am persecuted with l. 105a
I copied all the l. 166a
I find l. from God 458a
I hate l. 105a
in the republic of l. 1a
l. for a spy 234a
l. four do form his name [Pitt] 101a
l., soft interpreters of love 305b
l...to pin up one's hair 105a
no arts; no l.; no society 191b
nobody knows how to write l. 105a
nought the l. space 90b
O ay l.—I had l. 105a
pause awhile from l. 213b
the l. Cadmus gave 71a
the Republic of L. 170a
yr. kind and beloved l. 155a
Letter-writing: great art o' l. 126b
[l.] that most delightful way 283b
Levellers: yr. l. wish to level down 207b
Lever: for him was l. have 88b
Levi: jump as Mr. L. did 19b
Leviathan: draw out L. with an hook 497b
there is that l. 488b
there L. hugest of..creatures 275b
Levin: as to the burning l. 317b
Levite: the lean L. went to sleep 305a
Levity: a little judicious l. 573a
Levy: foreign l., nothing, can touch him 348b
Lewd: certain l. fellows 512b

Lewd (*cont.*)
when was Lancelot wanderingly l. 428a
Lewti: image of L. 101b
Lexicographer: l.: a writer of dictionaries 207a
to wake a l. 212b
Lexicography: so lost in l. 212b
Lhude sing cuccu 526a
Liar: a l., and the father of it 511a
but every man a l. 513a
hateth his brother, he is a l. 518a
l. of the first magnitude 104b
often quite picturesque l. 447a
Pagett, M.P., was a l. 233a
she's like a l. gone to..hell 363b
they only answered 'little l.' 26a
Liars: all men are l. 489a
conceits do prove the greatest l. 136b
I ought to have good memories 401a
l. we can never trust 452b
Libanus: even the cedars of L. 488b
Libel in a frown 419b
Liberal: either a little L. 164a
rather l. of another man's 16a
the l. deviseth l. things 502a
watchword of the L. Party 38a
Liberator: Europe's L. [Wellington] 71b
Liberticide: the slave and the l. 391b
Liberties: dramatist..wants more l. 204a
people never give up their l. 56a
Libertine: puffed and reckless l. 330b
the air, a chartered l. 381b
Liberty: abstract l...not to be found 55b
a manly, moral, regulated l. 56b
a new nation, conceived in l. 245a
angels alone..enjoy such l. 249b
consecrate to truth and l. 399b
dead to all the feelings of l. 297a
dishonest victory..fatal to l. 278b
eldest child of L. 472b
enjoy delight with l. 409b
first garden of L.'s tree 77b
fishes..know no such l. 249b
give me l., or give me death 186a
he that commands..sea is at..l. 15b
I must have l. 326b
interfering with the l. of action 266a
let there be light! said L. 394a
l. cannot long exist 58a
l. connected with order 55a
l...doing what one desires 266a
L.! Equality! Fraternity! 566b
l...is eternal vigilance 116b
l. means responsibility 391a
l. of the individual..limited 266a
l. of the press 217a
l. plucks justice by the nose 351a
l.'s a glorious feast 61a
l.'s a kind o' thing 250a
l.'s in every blow 62b
l. still more 48b
l., too, must be limited 58a
Licence..mean when they cry L. 278b
love of l. is the love of others 183b
mountain nymph, sweet L. 268b
my dear l., shall I leave thee? 105b
O l.! what crimes are committed on Naples and on l. 92a
pardon..to the spirit of l. 55b
refreshing airs of l. 57b
seek power and to lose l. 14b
so loving-jealous of his l. 365b
spirit of divinest L. 101a
steps of virgin l. 470b
sweet land of l. 404a
symptom of constitutional l. 162a
that little is achieved thro' L. 52b
the tree of l. must be refreshed 204b
this is L.-Hall 171a
thy chosen music, L. 471b
to proclaim l. to the captives 503a
University..place of light, of l. 128b
vanguard of L., ye men of Kent 467b
weight of too much l. 468a
when Transatlantic L. arose 76b
whoever gives, takes l. 133a
wicked woman l. to gad abroad 520a
Libraries: books out of circulating l. 314a
what do..we spend..on our l. 314a
Library: he furnish'd me from mine own l. 367a

Library (*cont.*)
in the lumber-room of his l. 135b
my l. was dukedom..enough 367a
no gentleman's l. shd. be without 239a
shut not..thy l. against S. T. C. 239a
take choice of all my l. 368a
turn over half a l. 208b
Libya: parts of L. about Cyrene 512a
Licence: L. they mean when they cry Liberty 278b
love not freedom, but l. 279b
universal l. to be good 97b
Licensed: whore and gambler..l. 29b
Licensing: by l. and prohibiting 279a
Licentious soldiery 56a
Lichtlie: love did l. me 530a
Lick: l. the bloomin' boots of 'im 229b
to l. it into form 64a
Licked the platter clean 534a
Lid: hang upon his pent-house l. 346a
lifting up the l. of a white eye 263b
Liddell: this is Mrs. L. 528b
Liddesdale: march, Eskdale and L. 320a
Lids: drops his blue-fringèd l. 100b
they lift their heavy l. 293a
with eternal l. apart 220b
Lie: after all, what is a l.? 71b
a l., a wicked l. 363b
an odious, damned l. 363b
asks no questions isn't told a l. 234a
at the head of a l. 46b
does not stoop, nor l. in wait 465a
dost thou l. so low? 339b
Father, I cannot tell a l. 451b
give the world the l. 307b
here l. I, Martin Elginbrodde 256a
I called not, l. down again 495a
I cd. l. down like a tired child 399a
I fain wald l. down 529b
if a l. will do thee grace 379a
I l. as lads wd. choose 199a
leads you to believe a l. 30a
l. all night betwixt my breasts 500a
l. as they fell 312b
l. at the..foot of a conqueror 374b
l. down, and stray no further 324b
l...for the good of his country 473a
l. heavy on him, Earth 149a
l. in cold obstruction and to rot 352a
l. that passeth thro' the mind 14a
l. wh. is all a l. 427a
l. wh. is part a truth 427a
loveth and maketh a l. 520b
mixture of a l. doth..add pleasure 14a
Nature admits no l. 81a
no change tho' you l. under 199a
not a man, that he shd. l. 494a
nothing can need a l. 186b
prayer for all who l. beneath 227b
renowned Spenser, l...more nigh 22a
rule and dare not l. 433b
saying, L. with me 493a
something given to l. 325a
sorer than to l. for need 328b
stamps God's own name upon a l. 111a
stone is sometimes seen to l. 470a
the l. circumstantial, the l. direct 328a
the l. in the Soul 571b
the l. shall rot 294a
the l. that flatters 111a
tho' it be a foul great l. 18a
under the spars of wh. I l. 190b
where'er she l., lock'd up 115a
wholly believing a l. 230a
who loves to l. with me 326a
yes, lad, I l. easy 199a
you l. dreaming on 306b
you l.—under a mistake 418b
Lied: children shall say they have l. 474b
never flunked, and he never l. 183a
or being l. about 230a
straight to cloak them, l. 233b
Liege of all loiterers 344b
Lies: and the Rest is L. 153a
beats all the l. you can invent 29b
believe her, tho' I know she l. 389a
believing their own l. 4b
cruellest l...told in silence 413a
don't deal in l. 230a
fiend that l. like truth 351a
friend..that spread these l. 313a

Lies (cont.)

great l. about his..horse	155a
history is a pack of l.	415b
I say he l., and l.	375b
I wish I were where Helen l.	531a
l. gude Sir Patrick Spens	530a
l...he told of Ireland	296a
l. to hide it, makes it two	452b
l. where he longed to be	415a
lifts the head and l.	302b
naebody kens that he l. there	529b
now l. he there	340a
tell pale-hearted fear it l.	349b
these l. are like the father	377b
tomorrow's falser..l. worse	139b
Lieutenant is to be saved	361a

Life: after l.'s fitful fever 348b

a godly, righteous and sober l.	478a
all his l...been in the wrong	309b
all is lost, except a little l.	73b
all my l. seemed meant for	47b
all the blessings of this l.	479a
all the changing scenes of l.	424b
all the years of this our l.	472a
all..will he give for his l.	497a
amended his former naughty l.	480a
among the tasks of real l.	465a
and on the tree of l...sat	273b
anythin' for a quiet l.	127a
a Roman's l., a Roman's aims	253b
as I, undying L. have	38b
as tho' to breathe were l.	438b
as yet not come to l.	380b
attain the happy l.	416a
author both of l. and light	216b
awakened from the dream of l.	392b
aware of his l.'s flow	5a
away the l. of care	399a
bankrupt of l.	138a
before L.'s Liquor in its Cup	152a
before my l. has found	433b
begin to make a better l.	325a
bid me take l. easy	474a
birthday of my l. is come	310b
bloodthirsty clinging to l.	570a
blotted from l.'s page	68a
Book of L. begins with a..garden	460b
books..give new views to l.	113b
both hands before the fire of l.	241a
brief l. is here our portion	286a
busy scenes of crowded l.	213b
but have everlasting l.	510b
by l.'s unresting sea	194a
calamity of so long l.	333a
calm's not l.'s crown	9a
certain in man's l. but this	265a
chances of this mortal l.	480b
chief nourisher in l.'s feast	348a
C Major of this l.	44b
conduct is three-fourths of our l.	10a
consider! l. is but a day	220b
cool sequestered vale of l.	174b
costs my l., my gallant grey	316a
country l. I praise	37b
count the l. of battle good	287b
courses of man's l. do show	378a
crown of our l. as it closes	421a
custom..great guide of human l.	201b
cuts off twenty years of l.	339a
death and l., in ceaseless strife	290a
deep almost as l.	466b
delicate, and full of l.	359a
demands my soul, my l., my all	453b
depends poor Polly's l.	159b
desert where no l. is found	195b
die with looking on his l.	323a
digestion is the great secret of l.	405b
doctrine of the strenuous l.	310a
dost thou love l.?	157a
doth the winged l. destroy	30b
dreamed that l. was Beauty	196b
dreary intercourse of daily l.	472a
drink l. to the lees	438b
duty in that state of l.	481a
easy key dost open l.	139b
ebbs out l.'s little day	251b
either death or l...be the sweeter	351b
enter into l. with one eye	507a
entertain the lag-end of my l.	378b
every lovely organ of her l.	359a
except my l., except my l.	332a

Life (cont.)

Facts alone are wanted in l.	123b
feels its l. in every limb	472b
few and evil..the years of my l.	493b
fie upon this quiet l.	377a
flesh wh. walls about our l.	375b
flower of a blameless l.	427b
folk he ne'er saw in his l.	4b
for l., six hundred pounds a year	419b
for the l. to come, I sleep	373a
for what is yr. l.?	517b
friend is the medicine of l.	520b
from l.'s dissonance struck	459b
from L.'s fresh crown	24a
from the dregs of l., think to receive	139b
fruits of l. and beauty	30a
gave my l. for freedom	149b
gavest him a long l.	483a
gave thee l., and bid thee feed	32b
gave what l. required	168a
give me l.	379a
giveth his l. for his sheep	511a
give to me the l. I love	414a
God of l., and poesy, and light	69a
government..the laws of l.	315a
great end of l. is..action	203a
growth is the only evidence of l.	288a
hath man no second l.?	5a
have you found yr. l. distasteful	48b
healthy state of political l.	266a
he asked l. of thee	483a
he hath a daily beauty in his l.	363a
here l. has death for neighbour	422a
her l. serene	437a
hesitate and falter l. away	8a
he studied from the l.	4b
he that findeth his l.	506b
he, that leadeth an uncorrupt l.	482a
high l...conceived by a bookseller	449b
hired a villain to bereave my l.	30a
his l., I'm sure, was in the right	106b
his l. is a watch or a vision	420b
his l. was gentle	341b
his name out of the book of l.	518b
his part out of the the book of l.	520b
his unkindness may defeat my l.	363a
holdeth our soul in l.	486a
how good is man's l.	51b
how hard a l. her servant lives	476a
I am the resurrection, and the l.	511a
I bear a charmed l.	351a
I count l. just a stuff	45a
idea of her l. shall..creep	359a
I fall upon the thorns of l.!	396b
I fetch my l. and being	359b
if l. did ride upon a..point	379a
if l. was bitter to thee	421a
if recalling to l.	127b
I had wrung l. dry	424a
I have set before you l.	494b
I have set my l. upon a cast	385b
I love long l. better than figs	322b
immortal l., in never-fading worlds	464b
I must live or bear no l.	363a
in all my l. like this	36b
in his pleasure is l.	483b
in l., in death..abide with me	251b
in l.'s cool evening	303b
in l.'s last scene what prodigies	214a
in l.'s small things be resolute	250b
in our l. alone does Nature live	100b
intend to lead a new l.	480b
in the thread of human l.	319b
in the time of this mortal l.	479a
in tragic l., God wot	264a
into his nostrils the breath of l.	492a
is l. a boon?	167a
is L. worth living?	535b
I shd. live the same l.	171b
isn't yr. l. extremely flat?	166b
it may be l., but ain't it slow	186a
I've had a happy l.	184a
I will give thee a crown of l.	518b
knot intrinsicate of l...untie	325a
large as l., and twice as natural	85a
last of l., of wh. the first	50b
later l. renew	408a
law of human l. may be Effort	314b
lay down his l. for his friends	511a
lay hold on eternal l.	516b

Life (cont.)

lay hold on l.	279b
lead a holy Christian l.	247b
lead l. to sovereign power	435b
lead we not here a jolly l.	425a
Leaves of L. keep falling	154b
lesser l. shall be as the greater	171b
let me so read thy l.	114b
L., a Fury slinging flame	430a
l. ain't all beer	262a
l. and all shall cease	240b
l. and light be thine	50a
L...art of drawing..conclusions	66b
l. at best is but an inn	200b
l., being weary of these..bars	338a
l. can little more supply	300b
L., Death, and that vast For Ever	225b
l. death does end	197b
l., death, miracles of St. Somebody	51a
l. did harbour see	215b
L., exempt from public haunt	325b
L. Force supplies us	390b
l. for l., eye for eye	494a
l. from the dead is in that word	280a
l. has passed with me but roughly	109a
l. have we loved	284a
l. in low estate began	430b
L. is a coquetry	441a
l. is a jest	160a
l. is a joke that's just begun	164b
l. is all a variorum	61b
l. is all chequered	281b
l. is an incurable disease	107a
l. is a Permanent Possibility	413b
l. is..a state..to be endured	213b
l...is but a froward child	170b
l. is but an empty dream!	247b
l...is but the shadow of death	41a
l. is fading fast away	308b
l. is good, and joy runs high	185a
l. is (I think) a blunder	185b
l...is just a chance o' the prize	46a
l. is just one damned thing	201a
l. is..like a froward child	425b
l. is made up of sobs, sniffles	185b
l. is mostly froth and bubble	171b
l. is never the same again	256a
l. isn't all beer and skittles	201a
l. is one demd horrid grind	125a
L. is perfected by Death	44a
l. is..process of getting tired	66b
L. is real! L. is earnest!	247b
l. is the desert	477b
l. is thorny	100a
l. is very sweet, brother	34a
l. is with such all beer	75b
L., Joy, Empire	397b
l., like a dome of..coloured glass	392b
l. may change, but it may fly not	394a
l. may perfect be	216b
l. more than meat	505b
l. of a man..a heroic poem	80a
I offers, to deny?	180a
L. of L.! thy lips enkindle	397b
l. of..man less than..span	17a
l. on the ocean wave	315b
l. piled on l. were all too little	438b
l. protracted is protracted woe	214a
L.'s a single pilgrim	24a
l.'s business being..the..choice	51b
l.'s but a span	361a
l.'s but a walking shadow	350b
l.'s early cup with such a draught	392a
l.'s enchanted cup but sparkles	68a
l.'s first native source	409b
L.'s five windows of the soul	30a
L.'s Little Ironies	180b
l. so fast doth fly	117b
l.'s poor play is o'er	301a
l.'s race well run	292a
l.'s road, so dim and dirty	70a
l.'s short span forbids us	544b
L.'s too short for chess	74b
l.'s uncertain voyage	368a
l.'s wild restless sea	3b
l...tedious as a twice-told tale	374a
L., that dares send a challenge	115b
L. that in me has rest	38b
l. that leads melodious days	430a
L., the shadow of death	420b
l. time's fool	379a

Life (cont.)

l., 'tis all a cheat 139b
l. to him wd. be death to me 223b
l...tolerable [but] for its amuse-
　ments 572a
l. treads on l. 44a
l. unto the bitter in soul 497a
l. was but a flower 327b
L. went a-maying 102a
l.l we've been long together 18b
l. with its way before us lies 279b
l. without it. .not worth. .taking 313b
l. without theory 129b
l. wd. be very dull without them 460a
l. wd. be very pleasant 417a
light of a whole l. dies 34a
like following l. thro' creatures 301b
lived. .to find out what l. is 447a
live out thy l. as the light 422b
live thou thy l. 36b
longest half of yr. l. 407b
Lord and giver of l. 480a
lost days of my l. 312b
lover of l. shall join the hater 171b
Love took up the harp of L. 432a
lucid intervals of l. 464a
made human l. a hell 7a
made l. a heaven 224b
made this l. more sweet 325b
mad from l.'s history 196a
madness is the glory of this l. 368a
make a l. of jealousy 361b
man can have but one l. 44b
man's l. is cheap as beast's 342b
man's l. of any worth is. .allegory 223a
many-coloured l. he drew 213b
marriage is like l. in this 413a
men deal with l. as children 109a
methinks it were a happy l. 384a
middle of the road of our l. 566b
midst of l. we are in death 481b
mild concerns of ordinary l. 465a
mine honour is my l. 374b
most beautiful adventure in l. 157b
most glorious Lord of l. 408a
most loathèd worldly l. 352a
mounts. .hardly. .to eternal l. 6b
must have l. for a blow 434a
my l. at a pin's fee 331a
my l. did, and does smack sweet 48b
my l. has crept so long 434b
my l. is done 374b
my l. is dreary 433a
my l. is preserved 493a
my l. is run his compass 341b
my l.,—my all that 's mine? 169a
my l. upon her faith! 360b
my l. within this band 187b
my lines and l. are free 188a
narrow. .way wh. leadeth unto l. 505b
needs spirit lack all l. behind 51b
neither death, nor l., nor angels 513b
Nightmare L.-in-Death was she 98b
nobleness of l. is to do thus 322a
no green l. shoots 34a
no l., but lively form of death 238b
no l. but the sea-wind's 421b
no l. that breathes 438b
nor love thy l., nor hate 276b
nor my l. with the bloodthirsty 483b
no sound. .dissonant wh. tells of L. 101b
nothing half so sweet in l. 281b
nothing in his l. became him 346b
not in thy body is thy l. at all 312a
not one l. shall be destroy'd 430b
not so much l. as on a summer's 218a
no wealth but l. 315a
O dearer far than light and l. 468a
O Death in L. 436a
o'er l.'s solemn main 248a
O for a l. of sensations 222a
of the Well of L. to taste 153b
of whom standeth our eternal l. 478a
one crowded hour of glorious l. 283a
one good deed in all my l. I did 368a
one l. for each to give 229a
one thing. .certain. .that L. flies 153a
on Human L., musing in solitude 464a
on the Rampage. .such is L. 123b
on this l.'s rough sea 87a
onward thro' l. he goes 249a

Life (cont.)

other elements I give to baser l. 325a
other men think of this l. 337b
our l. is closed, our l. begins 457a
our l. is of a mingled yarn 322a
our. .l. is rounded with a sleep 367b
our love is frail as is our l. 149a
O world! O l.! O time! 395a
painful escapes of fitful l. 35b
passed from death unto l. 510b
pay l.'s glad arrears 50b
people say that l. is the thing 404a
pieces of l. and beauty 445a
plays, in the many games of l. 465b
portion of a good man's l. 472a
present l. of men on earth 24a
progress is the law of l. 49b
pure river of water of l. 520a
questioned me the story of my l. 360a
railing at l...afraid of death 94b
ravin up thine own l.'s means 348b
reason thus with l. 351b
recalled to l. 127a
receive the crown of l. 517a
reck'd not of the l. he lost 69a
ring in the nobler modes of l. 431a
'Sairey,'. .'sech is l.' 124a
sake of l. to sacrifice l.'s. .end 549a
saw l. steadily 6a
seas of l. like wine 445a
Second class in the School of L. 198b
set grey l., and apathetic end 433a
set my l. on any chance 348b
shall l. succeed in that 50b
shamed l. a hateful (thing) 352a
shew me the path of l. 482b
short is the longest l. 223b
since l. first was 179a
slits the thin-spun l. 269b
smiles, tears, of all my l.! 44a
so have I loitered my l. away 184a
so in my veins red l. 219a
so many doors to let out l. 23a
so to prevent the time of l. 341a
so was it when my l. began 468a
spare all. .and take my l. 150a
stir as l. were in't 350b
stole. .the l. o' the building 348a
storm of l. is past 455b
strange disease of modern l. 8a
suburb of the l. elysian 248a
sweat under a weary l. 333a
tell her, brief is l. 436b
that l. may be a pleasant road 306a
that 's the stuff l. is made of 157a
the angel of this l. 51a
theatre of man's l. 13a
the bitterness of l. 85b
the goods in l.'s rich hand 452b
the Hills where his l. rose 5a
their l. was death 312a
the l. for a man like me 414a
the l. so short 90a, 559b
the ornament of l. 347a
therefore choose l. 494b
there's the l. for ever 414a
the rest of his dull l. 22b
the Resurrection to eternal l. 481b
the time of l. is short 379a
the tree of l. also 492a
the unbought grace of l. 57a
the way, the truth, and the l. 511a
the wine of l. is drawn 348a
things to aim at in l. 404a
this flesh keep in a little l. 379a
this Fragment of L. 411a
this gives l. to thee 387a
this *is* blessing, this *is* l. 445b
this L. flies 153a
this l. is most jolly 326b
this l. of mortal breath 248a
this long disease, my l. 303a
this speck of l. 282a
this transitory l. 480b
tho' l. be long and dreary 150a
thousand doors to let out l. 262b
thou art love and l. 398b
thou art my l. 190a
Thou l. the Fountain art 455b
thy l. hath had some. .honour 341b
till l. can charm no more 103a

Life (cont.)

till l. forget 422b
tired of London, he is tired of l. 209b
'tis the sunset of l. 77a
to a l. beyond l. 279a
to be a good artist in l. 413a
to live a l. half-dead 277b
to measure l. learn thou betimes 278b
to the vagrant gypsy l. 262a
travell'd l.'s dull round 399b
traveller betwixt l. and death 470b
travel on l.'s common way 467b
true l. is only love 51b
true pathos. .of human l. 59a
turn over a new l. 155a
unto all l. of mine may die 114b
upon l.'s darkening slope 312a
variety 's the very spice of l. 111b
veil, wh. those who live call l. 397b, 399a
walk in newness of l. 513a
watch'd the fount of fiery l. 6b
watch for the l. of poor Jack 120b
water of l. freely 519b
way of l. is fallen into the sear 350b
wearing out l.'s evening gray 211b
well-written L. is almost as rare 80a
we see into the l. of things 472a
what argument thy l...has lent 146b
what is this l. if full of care 118a
what signifies the l. o' man 60b
what wond'rous l. is this 260b
what wd. l. be without arithmetic 405b
when l.'s sweet fable ends 115a
wherefore not L.? 457a
where the morn of l. was spent 172b
where there is l., there's hope 160b
who leads a country l. 140a
whom. .to know is everlasting l. 479b
whose l. is in the right 301b
why shd. . .a horse, a rat, have l. 344a
why shd. l. all labour be 433a
will I require the l. of man 492b
Wine of L. keeps oozing 154b
within the bloody house of l. 374a
with l. all other passions fly 406b
with Nature, to out-do the l. 215b
without disease the healthy l. 416a
without him live no l. 276a
woke, and found that l. was Duty 196b
worn with l.'s cares 114a
worthy womman al hir l. 88b
write the l. of a man 208a
you take my l. 355a
Life blood: good book is the. .l. 279a
met to fan our l. 312a
Lifeboat: safe within the l. 315b
Life-breath: all our l. met to fan 312a
Life-drop: drank the last l. 72b
Lifeless: in tumult to a l. ocean 101b
Lifetime: a l. of happiness 390b
knowledge of a l. 456b
love wakes men, once a l. each 293a
not see them lit again in our l. 177a
sole work of a l. 46a
Lift: blinkin' in the l. sae hie 63b
do not l. him from the bracken 12a
I l. them up to Thee 190b
l. her with care 195b
l. me as a wave 396b
l. me from the grass 394b
l. not the painted veil 399a
l. not thy hands to *It* for help 153b
l. themselves up higher 409a
l. up yr. heads, O ye gates 483a
l. up yr. heart, l. up yr. voice 455b
to l. one if one totters down 311a
veil after veil will l. 5a
Lifted up a single stone 468a
Lifteth slowly, lifteth sweetly 442b
Lifts: that wh. l., thro' centuries 293b
Light: a blinding l. 287b
above the l. of the morning star 31a
a l., a glory, a fair. .cloud 100b
a little warmth, a little l. 263a
all know what l. is 209a
all l. of art or nature 392b
and restore the l. 117a
Angels, progeny of l. 275a
apparelled in celestial l. 466a
as far as l. excelleth darkness 499a
as far. .from God and l. of heav'n 271a

Light (cont.)

as if they feared the l.	416a
as l. fell short	192a
a well of love, a spring of l.	97b
bathe the world in l.	464a
beauty from the l. retired	449a
blasted with excess of l.	175a
bright as l., and clear as wind	435b
burning and a shining l.	510b
but he beholds the l.	466a
but in unapproached l. dwelt	273a
but soft! what l. breaks thro'	365a
by the l. of the moon	74a
by thine own sweet l.	115a
can again thy former l. restore	363b
can thy l. relume	363b
celestial l. shine inward	273b
child of L.! thy limbs are burning	397b
come forth into the l. of things	471b
contend with growing l.	384a
darkness and the l. to thee..alike	490a
daylight comes, comes in the l.	96b
depth of burning l.	149b
dim religious l.	268b
each one a lovely l.	99b
each others' l. to dim	282b
enable with perpetual l.	491a
enjoyed the selfsame l.	445a
fade into the l. of common day	466b
faint in the l. that she loves	434a
fame..beareth up things l.	16b
fierce l. wh. beats upon a throne	427b
fleecy flocks of l.	37b
flowers made of l.	195a
fond Memory brings the l.	282b
for thy l. is come	503a
forward, the L. Brigade	426a
gave him l. in his ways	420b
gladsome l. of Jurisprudence	97b
gloom for that celestial l.	271a
God appears, and God is L.	29b
God of life, and poesy, and l.	69a
God said, let there be l.	492a
God's first Creature, wh. was L.	16b
golden and silver l.	474b
gone into a world of l.	448a
greater l. to rule the day	492a
had she been l., like you	345a
hail holy l.	273a
halls of dazzling l.	125b
Harriet, Hi! l. of my eye!	186a
have seen a great l.	501b
here there is no l.	220a
her non-radiant l.	267a
he that has l. within	267a
hide, with yr. golden l.!	248b
high endeavours are an inward l.	465a
if L. can thus deceive	457a
if once we lose this l.	216a
if you are nimble and l.	534a
in a Noose of L.	152a
informed by the l. of nature	13a
in its plumes the various l.	261a
in robes of l. array'd	184a
in the dusk with a l. behind her	167a
in the l. of the living	485b
it is the l. of Terewth	121b
Lamb is the l. thereof	520a
land is scattered with l.	35b
lead, kindly L.	288b
leave the l. of Hope behind!	77b
Let Newton be! and all was l.	299b
lets in new l.	449a
let there be l.	492a, 558a
let there be l.! said Liberty	394a
let yr. l. so shine before men	505a
lie like a shaft of l.	427a
l. and leading in England	57b
L. and Mrs. Humphry Ward	91b
l. and the half-l.	474b
l., and will aspire	386b
l. but the shadow of God	41a
l. dies before thy uncreating word	299a
l. gains made heavy purses	16a
L. (God's eldest daughter)	158a
l. in the darkness, sailor	315b
l. in the dust lies dead	395a
l. of all their day	293b
l. of a whole life dies	34a
l. of nature..led him to confess	13a
l. of other days is faded	54a

Light (cont.)

l. of the bright world dies	34a
l. of thy countenance upon us	482a
l. of thy story	218a
l. she was and like a fairy	280b
l. shined in darkness	510b
l. that is in thee be darkness	505b
l., that lies in woman's eyes	281b
l. that never was, on sea or land	468b
l. thickens..the crow makes wing	349a
l. to shine upon the road	109b
l. up my own mind	48b
l. upon him from his father's	466b
l. upon the shining sea	438a
l. we sought is shining still	9a
l. wh. is in thee be not darkness	509a
l. wh. leads astray is..from Heaven	463a
like l. dissolved in star-showers	399a
line of festal l. in Christ-Church	8a
line of yellow l. dies fast	224a
live by thy l.	7b
live out thy life as the l.	422b
living lamps, by whose dear l.	261a
long l. shakes across the lakes	436a
Lord is my l., and my salvation	483b
loved darkness rather than l.	510b
love is a..full constant l.	133b
love..like l. can flee	398b
lovely lady, garmented in l.	399b
love who art a l. to guide	463b
make my darkness to be l.	482b
man of l. and leading	130a
mellowed to that tender l.	74a
more by yr. number, than yr. l.	473b
more l.!	568b
my new-cut ashlar takes the l.	232b
myriad spots of l.	475a
Nicodemus saw such l.	447b
night, the shadow of l.	420b
no l., but rather darkness	271a
nor any change of l.	422a
nothing goes for sense, or l.	65b
now is l. increased	441b
O, my only L.	188a
once put out thy l.	363b
once set is our little l.	78a
opponent of the one..children of the l.	9a
or with taper l. to seek	374a
out of hell leads up to l.	272b
plant and flower of l.	216b
Press-men..Servants of L.	5a
pure severity of perfect l.	428a
pursuit of sweetness and l.	9b
put on the armour of l.	514a
put out the l.	363b
put upon us the armour of l.	479a
righteousness as clear as the l.	484a
ring of pure and endless l.	448b
rule of streaming l.	267a
sailed on a river of crystal l.	151a
seat of desolation, void of l.	271a
shall never see l.	485a
shed a ray of l. Divine	86b
sheds lingering l.	185a
she made all of l.	78a
shineth the everlasting l.	40a
shower of l. is poesy	220b
shows sufficient of His l.	51b
something of angelic l.	470b
sometimes a l. surprises	110b
such a l. affliction	287a
sun, or the l...be not darkened	499b
take his l. away	45a
teach l. to counterfeit	268a
the just is as the shining l.	497b
the L. of Lights looks always	474a
the L. that Failed	237b
the l. that loses	420a
then shall thy l. break forth	503a
the orient when the gracious l.	387a
third among the sons of l.	391b
thro' Peace to L.	306b
thy word..a l. unto my paths	489a
till the hours of l. return	7a
to bring the false to l.	36b
to give l. to them..in darkness	508b
travel much faster than l.	527a
trifles l. as air	362a
true l., wh. lighteth every man	510b
truly the l. is sweet	499b
turn'd thy darkness into l.	110a

Light (cont.)

two noblest..sweetness and l.	417b
unbarred the gates of l.	275a
University shd. be a place of l.	128b
unveil'd her peerless l.	274a
upon them hath the l. shined	501b
walk while ye have the l.	511a
was l. from Heaven	63a
went like a streak of l.	525a
what is that thing called L.	95a
when I see you in the l.	237a
wherefore is l. given to him	497a
where l. and shade repose	467b
where the l. is as darkness	497a
while the l. lives yet	421b
whose l. doth trample on my days	448a
windows that exclude the l.	175a
wiser than the children of l.	509b
with a Shaft of L.	152a
without any l. atop	195a
ye are the l. of the world	505a
yet the l. that led astray	63a
Lighten: l. our darkness	478b
l. with celestial fire	491a
Lightens: ere one can say it l.	365b
Lighter: l. than a feather	160b
l. than vanity itself	485b
Lightfoot: come up L.	203a
Lighthouse: below the l. top	98a
l. without any light	195a
the l. top I see	99b
the sitivation at the l.	127a
Lighting a little Hour or two	152b
Lightly: English lord shd. l. me	531a
lay l. gentle earth	23a
l. as it comth, so wol we spende	89b
Lightning: a l. before death	366b
angels of rain and l.	396a
beheld Satan as l.	509a
beneath the l. and the Moon	99a
bring in the bottled l.	125a
fear no more the l. flash	329a
fed with the l.	397b
it must be done like l.	215b
its own internal l. blind	395b
l. in the collied night	356a
l. my pilot sits	393a
scratch my head with the l.	446b
Shakespeare by flashes of l.	102b
the l. made itself	255a
the l. of the nations	396a
thunder, l., or in rain	345b
too like the l.	365a
Lightnings: arrows of l.	438a
the l. Thy sword	94a
veiling all the l. of his song	392a
Lights: all the l. wax dim	190a
all these l. of the world	57a
are but broken l. of Thee	429b
coastwise l. of England	228a
cometh down from the Father of l.	517a
Father of l.! what sunny seed	447b
glorious the northern l.	403a
l. that do mislead the morn	352a
l. the evening star	76a
old inn, and the l.	284b
serene l. of heaven	399a
silent silver l. and darks	49b
spent l. quiver and gleam	5b
that l. the wigwam	248b
the l. around the shore	313a
the l. begin to twinkle	439a
turn up the l.	185b
whose l. are fled	282b
your l. burning	509b
Like: always l. it the least	90b
each to other l.	275a
every one as they l.	418b
how l...to this kernel	373a
I know what I l.	25a
I l. him, but he loves me	52b
I l. to be liked	240a
I l. you, and your book	240b
I said there was nothing l. it	85a
I shd. l. to have one	310a
l.—but oh how different	473a
l. doth quit l.	352b
people who l. this sort of thing	245b
say you do not l. it	456b
shall not look upon his l. again	330a
so extremely l. Maple Grove	11a

Like (cont.)
so l. they were, no mortal 254a
these hands are not more l. 330b
we run because we l. it 406a
what else is l. the gondola? 96b
what I l. about Clive 27b
wilt thou find their l. agen? 318a
you who l. me not 51a
Liked: I that loved and you that l. 526a
Likely: l. . .have prov'd most royally 337a
not bloody l. 391b
Likeness: in l. of my love 36b
its l. in the red bills 123b
l. of a kingly crown 272b
l. of anything. .in heaven above 480a
made in the l. of men 516a
returns of force to its own l. 274b
Likes: he l. the country 110b
minds keep ever with their l. 338a
she l. herself, yet others hates 104a
Liketh: of this and that as l. me 473b
Liking: all love, all l. 189a
fredome mays man to haiff l. 19a
friendships begin with l. 144a
I have a l. 75b
ill word may empoison l. 358b
shall be fat and well l. 487b
while I am in some l. 378b
Lilac: l., gold and green 35b
Lord L. had had quite enough 93a
Lilacs: l. out of the dead land 144b
l. where the robin built 195a
l. last in the dooryard bloomed 458b
Lilac-time: down to Kew in l. 290a
Lilian: airy, fairy L. 432a
L. Dale,—Old Maid 445b
Lilied fields of France 76b
Lilies: a few l. blow 197b
consider the l. of the field 505b
heap of wheat set about with l. 500b
he feedeth among the l. 500a
in the beauty of the l. 200b
Kingcups and loved L. 409b
leave the l. in their dew 7a
l. and languors of virtue 421a
l. and roses were all awake 434a
l. and violets meet 22a
l. in her body's lieu 294b
l. of all kinds 373b
l. that fester smell far worse 388b
l. without, roses within 261a
lotos and l. 435a
peacocks and l. for instance 314b
put thy pale, lost l. out of mind 135a
roses overgrown, and l. 261a
the golden l. afloat 43b
three l. in her hand 311b
twisted braids of l. knitting 268a
where roses and white l. grow 78b
wh. feed among the l. 500b
Lillabullero: dozen bars of l. 411b
Lilting: I've heard them l. 145b
Lily: a l. of a day 216b
basest weed. .towers to a l. 452a
bind its odour to the l. 77b
Elaine, the l. maid of Astolat 428a
how sweet the l. grows 184a
I see a l. on thy brow 218b
it trembles to a l. 131a
like a l. in bloom 201b
l.-handed baronet 437a
l. of Florence. .in stone 247a
my precious L.! 83b
now folds the l. all her sweetness 437a
seen but a bright l. grow 216b
set thick with l. and red rose 284a
sprinkled isles, l. on 46a
the l. of the valleys 500a
the l. whispers, 'I wait' 434a
to paint the l. 374a
with a poppy or a l. in yr. . .hand 165b
Lily-cups: the violets, and the l. 195a
Lily-lee: on yonder l. 530b
Lima: curious traveller from L. 449b
Limb: feels its life in every l. 472b
give every town a l. 12b
on every airth a l. 280b
perils both of wind and l. 65a
to ease my weary l. 531b
Limb'd like a deer 171b
Limbecks foul as hell 389a

Limbo large and broad 273b
Limbs: calf-skin on those recreant l. 374a
if these poor l. die 40a
keep these l., her Province 132b
marbly l. 45a
mighty l. asleep 421a
never tired pilgrim's l. 78b
ruddy l. and flaming hair 30a
thy decent l. composed 299a
thy l. are burning 397b
trembling l. have borne him 284b
wh. l. and flesh enough invest 147a
whose l. were made in England 382a
with our l. at rest 226b
young in l., in judgment old 353b
Lime-tree Bower my Prison 101b
Limit: quiet l. of the world 438b
within the l. of becoming mirth 344b
Limitary Cherub 274b
Limitations of his own character 283b
Limited: liberty, too, must be l. 58a
Limits: l. of a vulgar fate 175b
stony l. cannot hold love out 365a
Limn: ere Thou canst l. with it 442a
Limner: skilful l. ere wd. choose 318b
Limnes: but l. the water 17a
Limpets: stuck like l. to the spot 93a
Limpopo River 237a
Lin: little Tommy L. 534a
Lincoln: L. sped the message 252b
the sign to L. sent 252b
Linden when the sun was low 76b
Linden Lea 21a
Lindesay of the Mount 318a
Line: a l. will take us hours 474a
cadence of a rugged l. 141a
creep in one dull l. 300a
fight it out on this l. 173a
into a horizontal l. 456b
like not a single l. 414b
l. is length without breadth 574a
lives along the l. 300b
Marlowe's mighty l. 216a
marr'd the lofty l. 318a
precept upon precept, l. upon l. 502a
Shakespeare. .never blotted. .a l. 214b
strengthen the wavering l. 7b
the full resounding l. 303b
the l. too labours 300a
the scarlet l. was slender 225b
thin red l. tipped with steel 315a
to cancel half a L. 153b
we carved not a l. 462b
will the l. stretch out 349b
Lineaments: in my l. they trace 73b
l. of Gospell bookes 313b
l. of gratified desire 30b
Linen: but all in fair l. 522a
girded with a l. ephod 495a
he did not love clean l. 207a
love is like l. 155b
not l. you're wearing out 196a
old l. wash whitest 454b
you shall wash yr. l. 414b
Linen-draper: I am a l. bold 108b
Liner: the L. she's a lady 231b
Lines: as l. so loves oblique 260a
came down in slanting l. 403b
circles and right l. limit 42b
consisted of l. like these 75a
impending eighty thousand l. 75a
l. where beauty lingers 72b
liquid l. mellifluously bland 71a
more l. than are in the new map 371b
my l. and life are free 188a
once own the happy l. 300a
see two dull l. 477b
takes up about eighty thousand l. 75b
their lives, as do their l. 215a
the radiant l. of morning 397b
when in eternal l. to time 387a
with silken l., and silver hooks 132a
Linger: l. out a purpos'd overthrow 388b
l. shivering on the brink 453b
one whose thoughts half l. 423a
who do not love her, l. here 463a
Lingered: one l. by His seat 476a
Lingering: I alone sit l. here 448a
something l., with boiling oil 165a
Lining: there's a silver l. 156a
turn forth her silver l. 267a

Link: from l. to l. it circulates 464b
I feel the l. of nature draw me 276b
the silver l., the silken tie 317a
Linked: to each other l. are 442b
Links: mysterious l. enchain 172b
their nobles with l. of iron 490b
Lin-lan-lone of evening bells 427a
Linn: lowpin o'er a l. 60a
Linnet: come, hear the woodland l. 471b
full of the l.'s wings 475b
I heard a l. courting 36b
l. born within the cage 430a
Linnets: like committed l. 249b
pipe but as the l. sing 430a
Linsy-woolsy: a lawless l. brother 65b
piebald, l. brothers 299a
Lion: against the Capitol I met a l. 338a
a l. among ladies 357a
a l. is in the streets 498b
another l. give a grievous roar 309a
beard the l. in his den 318b
blood more stirs to rouse a l. 377a
calf and the young l. . .together 501b
devil, as a roaring l., walketh 518a
first l. thought the last a bore 309a
gentil kind of the l. 90a
half appear'd the tawny l. 275b
hardy as the Nemean l.'s nerves 331a
I hear the l. roar 110a
l. and the belly-pinched wolf 342b
L. and the Lizard keep 153a
l. and the unicorn 532a
l. shall eat straw like the ox 501b
l. who dies of an ass's kick 49a
living dog. .better than a dead l. 499b
more fearful wild-fowl than yr. l. 357a
now the hungry l. roars 357b
righteous are bold as a l. 498b
rouse the l. from his lair 320a
save me from the l.'s mouth 483a
saw the l.'s shadow e'er himself 355a
sporting the l. ramped 274a
strong is the l. 403a
there is a l. in the way 498b
there the L.'s ruddy eyes 33a
thou wear a l.'s hide! 374a
well roared, L. 357b
wrath of the l. . .wisdom of God 31a
Lions: bears and l. growl 452b
I girdid up my L. 451a
l. do lack, and suffer hunger 484a
l. of the Daily Telegraph 9a
l. roaring after their prey 488b
my soul is among l. 485b
they were stronger than l. 495b
two l. litter'd in one day 339a
Lip: contempt and anger of his l. 371b
keep a stiff upper l. 86a
my true l. hath virgin'd it 328b
never a l. is curved with pain 182a
no good girl's l. out of Paris 424a
not a l., or eye, we beauty call 300a
or a coral l. admires 79a
the red was on yr. l., Mary 28b
throws the coral of his l. 251b
wagged his tail, and wet his l. 192b
what need a vermeil-tinctur'd l. 267b
whose l. mature is ever new 218a
why gnaw you so yr. nether l. ? 363b
Lipped, and trembled kissing 323b
Lips: a little while our l. are dumb 433a
at the touching of the l. 432a
beauty's. .crimson in thy l. 366b
bestow'd his l. on that. .place 324a
be thro' my l. to unawakened earth 396b
between the l. of Love-Lily 312b
causing the l. of those. .to speak 500b
dear red curve of her l. 261b
eternity was in our l. 322b
eyes, l., and hands to miss 134a
far from the l. we love 281b
far more red than her l.' red 389a
for these red l. 475b
from her coral l. such folly 104a
girl. .that had red mournful l. 476a
here hung those l. 336b
her l. suck forth my soul 258b
her l. were red 98b
her l. were red and one was thin 416a
his coward l. . .from their colour 337b
I am a man of unclean l. 501b

Lips (cont.)

I moved my l., the Pilot shrieked 99b
in one kiss upon her perfect l. 438a
in prayer the l. ne'er act 191a
in the l. that had whispered 421b
in this lady's l. and hands 312a
I saw their starved l. 219a
item, two l. 370a
keep the door of my l. 490b
Life of Life! thy l. enkindle 397b
l. as soft, but true 39a
l. cannot fail of taking 55a
l. of lurid blue 393b
l., O you the doors of breath 366b
l. that are for others 436a
live on the l. of those who love 37a
make love to the l. we are near 281b
my l. and eyelids pale 394b
my l. are now forbid 22a
my weary l. I close 173b
my whole soul thro' my l. 427a
often swore my l. were sweet 241b
oh that those l. had language 109a
on a poet's l. I slept 397a
polished l. to yr. attentive ear 241a
round their narrow l. the mould 312a
seal'd the l. of that Evangelist 430a
see my l. tremble 299b
soft as l. that laugh 420b
take, O take those l. away 352a
the l. of a strange woman drop 497b
their l. have thy l. taken fever 421b
the poor last I lay upon thy l. 324b
they shoot out their l. 483a
those l. are thine 109a
though rosy l. and cheeks 389a
thy l. are like a thread 500a
thy l. met with under the statue 421b
to part her l., and shewed them 190a
to whom the l. of children 286a
turn to ashes on the l. 282a
when I ope my l. let no dog bark 352b
when other l., and other hearts 53b
when the l. have spoken 395a
where my Julia's l. do smile 188b
whispering with white l. 68b
with his l. he travaileth 420b
wrung life dry for yr. l. to drink 424a
Liquefaction of her clothes 190b
Liquid: Shelley with l. music 36a
Liquidity: a purpose in l. 39a
Liquor: atrabilious l. 202b
before Life's L...be dry 152a
good l., I stoutly maintain 169b
l. talks mighty loud 182a
no new light on love or l. 305a
round goblet, wh. wanteth not l. 500b
when the l. 's out 46b
with considerbul l. koncealed 451a
Liquors: hot and rebellious l. 325b
Lisp: look you l. 327a
Lisped: I l. in numbers 303a
somewhat he l. 88b
List: I've got a little l. 164b
l., l., O, l. 331a
love to get sweets into yr. l. 202a
not printing . .l. of subscribers 210b
pension l. of the republic 95b
'Listed: Legion never was 'l. 231b
Listen: darkling l. 220a
l. all day to such stuff 82b
l. to my tale of woe 151a
l. with credulity to..fancy 213b
Sabrina fair, l. 268a
speak no slander, no, nor l. to it 427b
the world shd. l. then 398b
Listened: l. and looked sideways 99a
than he l. to the priest 530a
Listeners: least stir made the l. 316b
Listening: disease of not l. 379b
Listens: l. like a three-years' child 98a
yet the Evening l. 221a
Listeth: wind bloweth where it l. 510b
Listlessness nor mad endeavour 466b
Lit again in our lifetime 177a
Literary: absence..of..l. opinion 9b
disgusted with l. men 222a
Gigadibs the l. man 45a
head of the l. profession 129a
he lik'd those l. cooks 283a
immense l. misapprehension 10a

Literary (cont.)

like an unsuccessful l. man 26b
l. man..with a wooden leg 125b
lowest class is l. footmen 183b
terms wh...with St. Paul are l. 10a
Literature: all that is l. seeks..power 120a
current l. of the day 66b
first the l. of knowledge 120a
grazed the common of l. 207a
great Cham of l. 405b
he has raised the price of l. 206b
history to produce a little l. 204a
l. flourishes best 203a
l. is a drug 34a
l. looks like word-catching 148a
l. upon a little oatmeal 405a
lover of l. is never fastidious 407a
modern l. having attained 295a
once the itch of l. comes..a man 250a
Philistine of genius in l., Bunyan 10b
Lith: Kings..had a l. in their necks 11a
Litter: all her l. but one 379b
Little: a l. more than a l...too much 378b
a l. while,..ye shall not see me 511b
as l. as a Christian can 136b
but l. do or can the best of us 52b
children, you are very l. 414a
cry of the L. Peoples 244a
from having too l. to do 230b
full l. knowest thou 409a
goin' thro' so much to learn so l. 126b
grateful at last for a l. thing 434b
here a l., and there a l. 502a
how l. are the proud 175b
I l. have, and seek 143a
it was a very l. one 259b
life were all too l. 438b
l. among the thousands of Judah 504b
l. deeds of kindness 82a
l. drink..but wants that l. strong 193b
l. drops of water 82a
l. old New York 571b
L. One! Oh, L. One 410b
l. ones a cup of cold water 506b
l. one shall become a thousand 503a
l. saint best fits a l. shrine 188b
l. things affect l. minds 130a
l. things are great to l. men 170a
l. things are..most important 135a
l. things on l. wings 150a
l., weak, and helpless 3b
love me l., love me long 524b
love me l., so you love me long 189b
man wants but l. here below 169a
man wants but l.; nor that l., long 477b
nor wants that l. long 169a
offend one of these l. ones 507a
offering too l...asking too much 78b
of one to me l. remains 438b
Oh, the l. more, and how much 45b
precious l. for sixpence 535b
shall fall by l. and l. 520b
she gives but l., nor that l., long 477b
so l. done, such things to do 430b
that l. is achieved thro' Liberty 52b
the isles as a very l. thing 502a
the l. creep through 400a
the l. less, and what worlds away 45b
the l. nation leave to live 244a
trim l., prim l. craft 166b
whatever was l. seemed..great 255a
you ask me to give you l. things 390a
Little Cowfold 27a
Littleness: proof..of his own l. 80b
Littlenesses: a thousand peering l. 427b
Liturgy: Calvinistic creed, a Popish l. 297a
Live: age and youth cannot l.
together 389b
a grave. He shall not l. 374a
all that l. must die 329b
always getting ready to l. 148a
and how is it you l. 85b
be fond to l. or fear to die 145a
bid me to l., and I will l. 190a
certified how long I have to l. 484a
come l. with me and be my love 259a
die before I have begun to l. 6b
dogs, will you l. forever? 568a
dying, we l. 51b
easy l. and quiet die 319a
either I must l. or bear no life 363a

Live (cont.)

every man desires to l. long 419a
for me to l. is Christ 516a
for what do we l. 11b
get to l...Then l., and use it 186b
glad did I l. and gladly die 415a
he shall not l. 340b
he that begins to l. 307a
he that shall l. this day 383a
how can I l. without thee 276b
how is it that you l. 470b
if it is to l. at all 315b
I have hope to l. 351b
I l. by pulling off the hat 175b
I l. not in myself 68b
in health and wealth long to l. 478b
in him we l., and move 512b
I shall not die, but l. 489a
I shd. l. the same life 171b
I shd. l. till I were married 358b
it were a martyrdom to l. 42a
I wish to l. with you for ever 223b
I would gladly l. for ever 34a
knew better to l. than dispute 306a
lambkins, we will l. 381b
Lesbia, let us l. and love 78a
lest I shd. bid thee l. 436b
let us love nobly, and l. 132a
l. and lie reclined on the hills 433a
l. as long as you may 407b
l. beneath yr. more habitual sway 467a
l. in pleasure, when I l. to Thee 131b
l. invisible and dim! 448a
l. I, so l. I 247b
l. more nearly as we pray 224a
l. o'er each scene 298b
l. pure, speak true 427b
l. till tomorrow 109b
l. together after God's ordinance 481b
l. to study, and not study to l. 16b
l. to tread with kings 379a
l. under one form of government 208a
l. upon our daily rations 121b
l. we how we can, yet die we must 384b
l., while you l. 131a, b
loves to l. i' the sun 326a
love that shd. help you to l. 423a
make me..l. too long 117a
man doth not l. by bread only 494b
man..hath but a short time to l. 481b
may l. to fight another day 523b
merrily, merrily shall I l. now 368a
none wd. l. past years again 139b
nought so bright may l. 394a
one bare hour to l. 258b
power to l., and act 463b
question not, but l. and labour 171b
see so much, nor l. so long 344a
so l., that, sinking in thy..sleep 214a
so l., that when thy summons
comes 53a
so long as ye both shall l. 481b
so may'st thou l. 276b
something..for wh. we bear to l. 301b
something that doth l. 466b
so we'll l. and pray 344a
so wise, so young..never l. long 385a
sweet my child, I l. for thee 436b
take the means whereby I l. 355a
taught us how to l. 444b
teach him how to l. 304b
teaching nations how to l. 279b
tell me how you l. 85b
tell me whom you l. with 90b
that all men are about to l. 477a
there shall no man see me, and l. 494a
they're too beautiful to l. 124b
tho' to itself it only l. and die 388b
thou hast no more to l. 421a
to l. and die for thee 190a
to l. ever..else swoon to death 220b
to l. in hearts we leave behind 76b
to l. is like love 67a
to l. when to l. is torment 360b
to l. with thee, and be thy love 307b
to see me cease to l. 9a
tried to l. without him 473b
we l. and learn 298b
we l. by admiration, hope 464b
we must eat to l. 151b
we that l. to please 213b

Live (cont.)
what man is he that lusteth to l. 484a
what thou liv'st, l. well 276b
whether thou l. or die 37a
while we l., to l. 302a
without Thee I cannot l. 224a
Lived: had it l. long 261a
hadst thou but l. 317b
I had l. a blessed time 348a
I have l. in such dishonour 324b
I have l. long enough 350b, 423b
I have l. today 107a
I have l. with Shades so long 180a
I shall have l. a little while 199b
l. comfortably so long together 159a
l. on; and so did I 99a
no soul that l., loved 421a
poorly (poor man) he l. 155b
she l. to much more 281a
she l. unknown, and few cd. know 470b
so they l., and so they died 305b
than that it l. at all 215b
who has never lov'd, has never l. 160a
Lively: thy true and l. Word 480b
Liver: a question of the L. 535b
disease in the l...a Calvinist 148a
find so much blood in his l. 371b
left the l. white and pale 380b
no motion of the l., but the palate 371a
open and notorious evil l. 480a
Liverpool: folk that live in L. 92b
Livers: grave l. do in Scotland 470b
measure the heat of our l. 379b
Livery: cunning l. of hell 352a
in her sober l. all things clad 274a
in his l. walk'd crowns 325a
shadowed l. of the burnish'd sun 353a
this party-coloured l. 104b
Lives: a history in all men's l. 380b
cares, with wh. our l. are curst 450a
ca' them l. o' men 285b
everyone l. by selling something 412a
fortunes and l. he will vote away 40b
had all his hairs been l. 363b
he l., he wakes, 'tis Death is dead 392b
human creatures' l. 196a
if you join two l...oft a scar 45b
it's no fish..it's men's l. 319a
leave their little l. in air 304a
led merry, merry l. 286a
let us our l...lay on the king 382b
l. more l. than one 459b
l. not alone, nor for itself 29b
l. of great men all remind us 248a
Lord hath spared our l. 437b
make barren our l. 421a
more to the L. that fed 236a
music of men's l. 376a
no man l. forever 422a
no man under the sky l. twice 423b
not how a man dies, but how he l. 208a
one really l. nowhere 58b
other heights in other l. 49a
our l. wd. grow together 423a
pleasant in their l. 495b
so long l. this 387a
start their working l. 229b
their l., as do their lines 215a
virtuous soul..then chiefly l. 187b
went in jeopardy of their l. 496a
who l. unto himself, he l. to none 307a
Liveth: he l. unto God 513a
I am he that l., and was dead 518b
their name l. for evermore 521b
Living: are yet two Romans l. 341b
before God in the light of the l. 485b
be happy while y'er l. 522b
blend the l. with the dead 86a
dead shall live, the l. die 139b
devoured thy l. with harlots 509b
fever called 'L.' is conquer'd 297b
from too much love of l. 422a
good is man's life, the mere l.! 51b
his substance with riotous l. 509b
house appointed for all l. 497a
in the land of the l. 483b
is Life worth l.? 535b
Lady Disdain, are you yet l.? 358a
l. need charity more than..dead 5a
l. now begins to mend 368a
l., shall forfeit fair renown 317b

Living (cont.)
l. the same poet wh. thou'rt now 106b
l., we fret 51b
long habit of l. indisposeth us 42b
meet all the expenses of l. 444a
meet on lips of l. men 67a
Milton! thou shouldst be l. 467b
more than the l. wh. are yet alive 499a
mother of all l. 492b
noble l. and the noble dead 469b
no l. with thee, nor without thee 2a
out of the land of the l. 503a
plain l. and high thinking 467b
search the land of l. men 318a
that, l. know no bounds 401a
the l. up to it that's difficult 439b
there were no l. near her 358a
the Snake is l. yet 26b
trade..with the l. and the dead 142a
truly to get mine own l. 481a
which blamed the l. man 6b
why seek ye the l. 510a
ye are l. poems 246b
Living-dead: a l. man 328a
Livingstone: Dr. L., I presume 410a
Lizard: Lion and the L. keep 153a
Lizards: meagre as l. 76a
Lizzy Lindsay 526a
Llewellyn's lay 173b
Lo: l., all things fly thee 442a
L., eh? I don't think anything 124b
l.! He comes with clouds 456a
l., he doth send out his voice 486b
L.! He standeth, Spouse 441a
l.! in the orient 387a
l., the angel of the Lord came 508b
L., the kings of the earth 485a
l., the moon's self 49a
l., the poor Indian 300b
l., where Maeotis sleeps 299a
then said I, L., I come 484a
Load: a l. wd. sink a navy 386a
beneath a l. of splendid care 283a
cruelty to l. a falling man 386b
deserves his l. 188a
how to l. and bless 221b
shifted his heavy l. 181b
somebody's l. has tipped off 233a
Loaded: pickled pork they l. she 440b
Loads: laid many heavy l. on thee 149a
Loaf: 'l. of bread', the walrus said 84b
of a cut l. to steal a shive 368a
quartern l. and Luddites rise 403b
Loafe: I l. and invite my soul 457b
Loafing around the Throne 183a
Loam: men are but gilded l. 374b
Loan oft loses both itself 330b
Loaning: ilka green l. 145b
Loathe the taste of sweetness 378b
Loathed: most l. worldly life 352a
Loathing: disgust and secret l. fell 7a
loving, not l. 195b
Loaves: loses sight of the l. and fishes 295a
seven halfpenny l. sold for a penny 384a
Lobster: like a l. boiled 65b
seen the mailed l. rise 157b
still the l. held on 226b
'tis the voice of the l. 83b
Local cult called Christianity 179b
Localism: genuine spirit of l. 34a
Lochaber: farewell to L. 308a
Locheill: the broadsword of L. 12a
Lochinvar: young L. 318a
Lochow: a far cry to L. 320a
Lock: ae l. o' his gowden hair 529b
crying at the l. 266a
the l. was dull 74b
Lock'd up from mortal eye 115a
Locks: bow'd l. of the corn 284b
few l. wh. are left you 407a
his golden l. time hath to silver 295b
her l. were yellow 98b
knotted and combined l. to part 331a
l. of six princesses 225b
never shake thy gory l. at me 349a
open, l., whoever knocks 349b
pluck up..honour by the l. 377a
shaking her invincible l. 279a
strapped waist, and frozen l. 112a
Time shall turn those amber l. 137a

Locks (cont.)
yr. l. were like the raven 61a
Locust: hath the l. eaten 504a
years that the l. hath eaten 504a
Locusts: as luscious as l. 360b
l. and wild honey 504b
Lodestar: he [Chaucer] was the l. 251a
Lodge: l. in a garden of cucumbers 501a
oh for a l. 111b
unimaginable l. 217b
Lodger: mere l. in my own house 170b
our l.'s such a nice young man 285b
Lodgest: where thou l. I will lodge 495a
Lodging: born of despair of better l. 294b
hard was their l. 159a
may He give us a safe l. 288b
Lodgings: such as take l. in a head 65a
Lodore: water come down at L. 406b
Loftiness: first in l. of thought 141a
Lofty and sour to them 386b
Log: on a l., expiring frog 126a
the l. was burning brightly 168a
to fall a l. at last 216b
Logan is the Head Centre, the Hub 38b
Logan-water: fyle the L. 63b
Logic: as it isn't, it ain't. That's l. 84a
Common Room stank of L. 288a
Grape that can with L. absolute 153b
he was in l. a great critic 64b
l. and rhetoric, able to contend 16a
push the l. of a fact 229a
science and l. he chatters 305a
Logical: built in such a l. way 194a
l. consequences are..scarecrows 203a
Logres: knights of C. 277a
Logs: Tom bears l. into the hall 345b
Loin: unlit lamp and the ungirt l. 52a
Loins: he girded up his l. 496a
I girdid up my l. 451a
let yr. l. be girded 509b
with yr. l. girded 494a
Loitered my life away 184a
Loiterers: liege of all l. 344b
Loitering: alone and palely l. 218b
Lombardy: waveless plain of L. 395a
Lomond: banks o' Loch L. 525b
London: a L. particular..a fog, Miss 121a
chief advantage of L. is 265b
dream of L., small and white 284a
fate of the great Wen, L. 97a
he lived in L., and hung loose 206b
hell is a city much like L. 396b
here in L., yonder..in Florence 49a
I'm learnin' 'ere in L. 232a
in L. all that life can afford 209b
it isn't far from L. 290a
I've been up to L. 534a
I walk my beat before L. Town 234a
Key of India is in L. 128b
L.; a nation, not a city 129b
L. doth pour out her citizens 383b
L. is a fine town 103b
L. is a modern Babylon 130a
L. is..the Rome of to-day 147a
L., my most kindly nurse 409b
L.'s lasting shame 173b
L.'s towers receive the Lamb 30b
L., that great cesspool 136a
L., that great sea 395b
L...the clearing house..world 87a
L., thou art of townes a per se 142b
L., thou art the flower of cities 143a
lowest and vilest alleys of L. 135b
man is tired of L...tired of life 209b
Mr. Weller's knowledge of L. 126a
names of..'L. Assurance' 405b
of famous L. town 108a
one road leads to L. 262a
parks were the lungs of L. 297a
poetry..in L. only a trade 141b
ring the bells of L. town 533b
seen anything of L., yet? 123b
sent him up to fair L. 531b
the gondola of L. [hansom] 129b
they all to merry L. came 409b
when midst fallen L., they survey 18b
where L.'s column..lifts the head 302b
London Bridge: broken arch of L. 254b
forest below L. 314a
L. is broken down 533a
Lone: walking by his wild l. 237a

Loneliness: all that bowery l. 427a
shade and l. and mire 39b
when in danger, when in l. 411a
Lonely: blows over the l. of heart 475b
I'm very l. now, Mary 29a
none of these so l. 39a
so l. 'twas, that God himself 100a
there lies a l. grave 3a
thy breast will ne'er be l. 120a
Lonesome: one, that on a l. road 99b
Long: but as l. as I have 48a
can't be l. before I find release 434b
days seem lank and l. 166b
every man desires to live l. 419a
foolish..to make a l. prologue 521b
gives but little, nor that little, l. 477b
how I l. to travel back 448a
how l. soever it hath continued 97b
it cannot hold you l. 169a
it sha' n't be l. 91a
l., and lank, and brown 99a
l. folk to goon on pilgrimages 88a
l. is the way and hard 272b
l., l. may the ladies sit 530a
l., l. may the maidens sit 530a
l., l. trail a-winding 225b
l. or a' the play was play'd 530a
love me little, so you love me l. 189b
nor brought too l. a day 195a
not that the story need be l. 444a
now we sha'n't be l. 76a
O l. will his lady look 530b
Shenandoah, I l. to hear you 525a
short and l. of it 355b
so l. as men can breathe 387a
so l. lives this 387a
the cry goes up 'How l.?' 415b
then said I, Lord, how l.? 501b
the seas are too l. 16b
they are not l., the weeping 135a
those whom he loved so l. 310a
tho' the day be never so l. 182b
Longed: he lies where he l. to be 415a
truly l. for death 438b
Longer: l. I live, the more fool am I 534b
or so very little l. 48a
wished l. by its readers 212a
Longest: flutters least is l. on the wing 113a
l. half of yr. life 407b
the heart must bear the l. part 187a
when nights are l. there 351b
Longing: its l. for the tomb 476a
more l., wavering, sooner lost 370b
this l. after immortality 1b
Longings: I have immortal l. in me 325a
weary l. and yearnings 171b
Longitude: Board of L. objected 403a
meridians of l...for a seine 446b
the l. also is vague 306b
Long Melford: tip them L. 34a
Longs unto his Christ to go 190b
Long-suffering: l. and of great goodness 490b
l., gentleness, goodness 515b
Look: also a proud l. 488a
and not l. behind 361a
as they run they l. behind 174b
ay, there, l. grim as hell 363a
Cassius has a lean and hungry l. 338a
don't l. at me, Sir, with..that tone 535b
dream of the soft l. yr. eyes had 476b
exacts a full l. at the worst 179b
eyes were made to l. 365b
first, last l. by death reveal'd 72b
fur 'z you can l. or listen 250b
give me a l., give me a face 215a
go and l. at it 17b
hanging-l. to me 104b
hereafter rising shall she l. 154a
hit l. lak sparrer-grass 181b
I cd. not l. on Death 228b
I'll be a candle-holder, and l. on 364b
I l. at all things as they are 439b
I will l. on both indifferently 337a
just to l. about us and to die 300b
let him l. to his bond 354a
l. around, and choose thy ground 73b
l. before you ere you leap 65b
l. ere thou leap 446a
l. forth from the flowers 421b

Look (cont.)
l. here, upon this picture 335a
l. homeward, Angel, now 270a
l. made of all sweet accord 201b
l. not back nor tire 37a
l. not thou down 51a
l. not thou on beauty's charming 319a
l. not thou upon the wine 498b
l. on't again I dare not 348a
l. round her when the heavens 466a
l. thy last on all things lovely 119a
l. to your Moat 178a
l. upon myself and curse 387a
l. upward to the skies 287a
l., what a horse shd. have 386b
l., where it comes again 329b
met each other with erected l. 141b
my eyes..can l. as swift as yrs. 354a
my God, l. upon me 483a
O l. at the trees 37a
one longing, ling'ring l. 174b
only a l. and a voice 249a
only loveless l. the l...you passed 294a
O sweet! when I do l. on thee 402a
row one way and l. another 64a
same l. wh. she turn'd when he rose 281b
shall not l. upon his like again 330a
she gave me never a l. 6a
so l. to thyself 372a
some did die to l. on 322b
some do it with a bitter l. 459b
that men might l. and live 447b
The Twelve-Pound Look 2b
this is my wife, pray l. at her 528b
this l. of thine will hurl 364a
to l. at things in bloom 198b
we l. before and after 398b
whence a l. shot out sharp 421b
where gott'st thou that goose l.? 350b
wh. he forbears again to l. upon 468a
yr. l.? that pays a thousand 50a
Looked: as she l. about, she did behold 409a
he l. again, and found it was 85b
he who has l. upon Earth 263a
I l. for some to have pity 486b
l. unutterable things 443b
no sooner l. but they loved 327b
she l. at me as she did love 218b
sigh'd and l., and sigh'd again 139a
single field wh. I have l. upon 466a
so wise as Thurlow l. 156b
thrice l. he at the city 253b
thrice l. he at the dead 253b
Looker-on: sit thou a patient l. 307a
Lookers-on: as l. feel most delight 65b
God and angels to l. 13a
l...see more than gamesters 16a
Lookest: l. as thou woldest finde an hare 89a
why l. thou so? 98b
Looking: God be..in my l. 523a
l. before and after 335b
l. one way, and rowing another 54a
no harm in l. 417a
staring and l. upon me 483a
they all were l. for a king 256a
they l. back, all th' eastern side 277a
when l. well can't move her 416a
Looking-glass: face the cruel l. 231b
Looks: a woman as old as she l. 102b
be feared, and kill with l. 375b
clear yr. l. 471b
deep-searched with saucy l. 344b
glance that wd. those l. reprove 168a
he..l. such things 244a
he l. quite through the deeds 338a
her l. were free 98b
his l. do menace heaven 259a
his modest l. the cottage..adorn 169a
I have no proud l. 490a
I'll say she l. as clear 366b
in those l., where whoso gazes 397b
l. adorned the venerable place 168b
l. commercing with the skies 268a
l. handsome in three hundred 356a
l. the whole world in the face 249a
Moon hath l. for us again 154a
my only books were woman's l. 282a
praising God with sweetest l. 195b

Looks (cont.)
puts on his pretty l. 374a
she l. another way 525b
sun..l. on alike 373b
who is He, with modest l. 469a
with despatchful l. in haste 275a
Loom: she left the l. 431b
Loon: thou cream-faced l.! 350b
unhand me, grey-beard l. 98a
Loopholes of retreat 112a
Loose: ere yet we l. the legions 230a
let l. the Gorgonzola 536a
l. as the wind 188a
O sweet Fancy! let her l. 218a
she's l. i' the hilts 454a
wear those things so l. 19b
Lops the mouldered branch 427a
Lord: a certain l., neat, and trimly 376b
a L. among wits 206b
Angel of the L. came down 424b
ask the L. to bless me 150b
bless ye the L. 478a
children of the L. 3a
cometh in the Name of the L. 489a
cry unto the L. in their trouble 488b
cup..from wh. our L. drank 428a
day thou gavest, L., is ended 145b
dead wh. die in the L. 519b
declare the works of the L. 489a
deputy elected by the L. 375a
dwell in the house of the L. 483a
each of himself was l. 291a
English l. shd. lightly me 531a
enter thou into the joy of thy L. 508a
except the L. build the house 489b
except the L. keep the city 489b
five operations of the L. 520b
follow with allegiance a fallen l. 324a
for ever with the L. 280a
for joy Our L. was born 524a
for the glory of the L. 437b
glory of the coming of the L. 200b
glory of the L. is risen 503a
glory of the L. shone round 508b
go, and the L. be with thee 495b
go into the house of the L. 489b
great l. of all things 301a
gude l. in the black velvet 530a
hand of the L. bringeth..to pass 489a
hark, my soul! it is the L. 110a
her sleeping L. 270b
how gracious the L. is 484a
how long, O L., holy and true 518b
how shall we sing the L.'s song 490a
I know not the L. 493b
in the L. put I my trust 482a
in the spirit on the L.'s day 518a
I saw also the L. 501a
is Jesus Christ her L. 415b
is the arm of the L. revealed? 502b
I thowt 'twur the will o' the L. 439a
it is the handkerchief of the L. 458a
it is the L.'s passover 494a
it is the L. who rises 110b
I were l. in May 423a
joyful before the L. the King 488a
kingdoms of our L. 519a
King of Kings and L. of Lords 519b
let a l. once own the happy lines 300b
let me kiss my L. 259b
let men know we serve the L. 234b
L. and giver of life 480a
L. awaked as one out of sleep 487a
L. blessed the latter end of Job 497b
L. careth for the strangers 490b
I commended the unjust steward 509b
L. do so to me, and more also 495a
L. doth build up Jerusalem 490b
L. gave, and the L. hath taken 496b
L. God of Sabaoth 478a
L. hath comforted his people 502b
L. hath laid on him the iniquity 503a
L. hath put on his apparel 487b
L., hear my voice 490a
L. hear thee in..day of trouble 482b
L. himself is thy keeper 489b
L., I am not high-minded 490a
L., I ascribe it to Thy grace 452b
L., I have loved the habitation 483b
L., in the morning thou shalt hear 453a
L. is gracious and merciful 490b

Lord (cont.)
L. is King be the people..impatient
L. is king, the earth may be glad 488a
L., let me know mine end 484a
L., lift thou up 482a
L. lift up his countenance 494a
L. loveth the gates of Sion 487a
L. Lundy from his earliest years 26a
L. make his face to shine 494a
L., now lettest thou thy servant 508b
l. of folded arms 344b
l. of himself..heritage of woe 73a
l. of himself, tho' not of lands 473b
L. of Hosts did pitch His tent! 187b
L. of hosts..is the King of Glory 483a
l. of human kind 141b
L. of our far-flung battle-line 233b
l. of the fowl and the brute 113a
l. of the unerring bow 69a
l. of thy presence and no land 373b
l. of yourself, uncumber'd 140a
L., remember David 490a
L. reward him according 516b
L. round about his people 489b
L. said unto my L. 489a
L. seeth not as man seeth 495b
L. shall have them in derision 481b
L. shall preserve thy going out 489b
L. stood upon a wall 504b
L. sware, and will not repent 489a
L., thou art become gracious 487a
L. thou hast been our refuge 487b
L., thou hast searched me out 490a
L., thou knowest all my desire 484a
L. turned, and looked upon Peter 510a
L. was departed from him 495a
L. watch between me and thee 493a
L. went before them by day 494a
L., who shall dwell 482a
L. will abhor both the bloodthirsty 482a
L. with the sound of the trump 484b
love is L. of all 408b
men see the works of the L. 488b
mongrel beef-witted l. 368b
most glorious L. of life 408a
much of them that fear the L. 482a
my bosom's l. sits lightly 366a
my most noble l. slain 257b
my soul doth magnify the L. 508b
my soul fleeth unto the l. 490a
names of those who love the L. 201b
nations knew their lawful l. 138b
noble l. in the blue riband 55b
O L., in thee have I trusted 478a
O L. of hosts, my King 487a
O L., thou lover of souls 520a
praise the L. upon earth 490b
praise the L. who made the hills 235a
praise the L. with harp 483b
prepare ye the way of the L. 502b
pretty well for a L. 209a
rejoice in the L. alway 516a
rejoice in the L., O ye righteous 483b
remembrance of his dying L. 408b
replied, O L., Thou never 403a
rude to the L. her guest 234b
sae the L. be thankit 62b
said the L. in the vault 230b
sapient sutlers of the L. 145a
seek ye the L. while he may 503a
serving the L. 513b
she knowed the L. was nigher 250b
sing unto the L. a new song 483b
so is the L. merciful 488a
sole L. of life and death 115a
spirit of the L. is upon me 503a
still be L. of all 317b
Supper of the L. 481a
surely the L. is in this place 493a
sweet birds of the L. 442b
the earth is the L.'s 483a
the L. bless thee, and keep thee 494a
the L. called Samuel 495a
the L. gave the word 486a
the L. gets his best soldiers 410a
the L. hath spared our lives 437b
the L. is a man of war 494a
the L. is my light 483b, 558a
the L. is my shepherd 483a
the L. is the strength of my life 483b

Lord (cont.)
the L. let the house of a brute 426a
the L. looketh on the heart 495b
the L. made heaven and earth 480a
the L. my Pasture shall prepare 2a
the L. No Zoo 123b
the L. remaineth a King for ever 483b
the L. sitteth above the water-flood 483b
the L. taketh me up 483b
the L. was not in the wind 496a
the L. will be there 458a
the L., ye know, is God 224b
then said I, L., how long? 501b
then stooped the L. 231a
then thank the L. 76a
they that wait upon the L. 502b
thou, L., art merciful 485b
thou, L., wilt be extreme to mark 490a
thou, O L., art more than they 429a
thou shalt answer, L., for me 187b
thy l. the summer is good 422b
till his L. is crucified 251a
to my L. heartily 247b
to the very quality of my l. 360b
touch the L.'s Anointed 524a
voice of the L. maketh the hinds 483b
waited patiently for the L. 484a
where the dear L. was crucified 3b
whom the L. loveth he chasteneth 517a
ye servants of the L. 131b
ye that are of the house of the L. 489a
you unhouse and house the L. 197b
Lord-Keeper led the brawls 175a
Lords: about the l. of the creation 63a
as l. they are certainly expected 99a
fail..in the House of L. 130a
for the l. who lay you low 399a
laith were our gude Scots l. 530a
l. and owners of their faces 388b
l. are lordliest in their wine 278a
l. of human kind pass by 170a
l. of ladies intellectual 70a
l. of the world besides 270b
L. too are bards 72a
l. where parents were 118b
naked majesty seemed l. of all 274a
'no wonder', said the l. 425b
princes and l. may flourish 168a
Scots l. at his head 530a
with those L. I had gone so far 283a
women..who love their l. 194b
Lore: all the l. its scholars heed 224a
Cristes l., and his apostles 88b
gives me mystical l. 77a
sweet is the l. wh. Nature brings 471b
volume of forgotten l. 298a
Lorraine: poor L. Lorrèe 225b
Lose: if I do l. thee, I l. a thing 351b
I love to l. myself 239a
l. and neglect the creeping hours 326b
l., and start again 230a
l. no time to contradict her 419a
l. who may, I still can say 49a
much to hope and nothing to l. 58a
no man can l. what he never had 450b
our doubts..make us l. the good 351a
seemed to l. with my lost saints 44a
that he must l. it 265a
that one shd. l., the other win 259a
the way to l. him 322b
to l. one parent..a misfortune 460a
to l. thee were to l. myself 276b
to win or l. it all 280b
we have more lust again to l. 92a
who wd. l...this intellectual being 272b
you l. it in the moment 301b
Loser: neither party l. 380b
Losers: l. must have leave to speak 95b
so both shd. l. be 188a
Loses: who l., and who wins 344a
Losest: for fear thou l. all 187b
Loseth: he that l. his life for my sake 506b
Loss: breathe a word about yr. l. 230a
down he came; for l. of time 108b
enow to do our country l. 383a
for ever to deplore her l. 275b
l. of pence, full well he knew 108b
l. of thee wd. never from my heart 276b
man's l. comes to him 46a
no one knoweth the l. or gain 171b

Loss (cont.)
people whose l. will be a..gain 164a
shown a deeper sense of her l. 159a
suffer to redeem our l. 524b
those I counted l. for Christ 516a
too young such l. to know 73a
Losses: a fellow that hath had l. 359a
all l. are restored 387b
God bless all our l. 43b
Lost: all is l., except a little life 73b
all is not l. 271a
a l. thing cd. I never find 27a
better to have fought and l. 96b
better to have loved and l. 430a
dinner l., 'ounds l., self l. 416b
found my sheep wh. was l. 509b
game..is never l. till won 114a
having l. but once yr. prime 190b
he is almost l. that built it 42b
he was l. and is found 509b
his bark cannot be l. 346a
how on a sudden l. 276a
I am l., but see in..childhood 470a
I long ago l. a hound 444a
in time be utterly l. 457b
into my bosom and be l. in me 437a
is the year only l. to me? 188a
laugh'd and shouted, 'L.! l.! l.'! 317a
long l., late won 396a
l. and gone for ever 280b
l. behind the Ranges 228b
l. days of my life 312b
l. in a sort of Purgatory 217b
l. is our freedom 78b
l. to me, l. to me! 20a
l., yesterday, somewhere 258a
loved long since, and l. awhile 288b
marks, not that you won or l. 309a
never star was l. here 52b
never to have l. at all 67a
nor ever l. an English gun 435a
not l. but gone before 290a
one woman I have l. for ever 386a
praising what is l. 322a
sooner l. and won, than women's 370b
that nothing be l. 510b
their labour is but l. 489b
there shall be no love l. 215b
there's no hate l. between us 265b
there's nothing l. nor won 66a
tho' l. to sight, to mem'ry dear 245b
to be l. evermore in the main 438a
'twas Cerinthus that is l. 46a
we are l. to Love 229b
we have missed it, l. it for ever 53a
what I have l. with cordial fruit 188a
what tho' the field be l. 271a
you have l. yr. writing-book 193a
Lot: attempt to give a deathless l. 109b
a weary l. is thine, fair maid 319a
l. is fallen unto me 482b
might be L. or Methusalem 236a
our loving l. was cast 194b
policeman's l...not a happy one 166b
rejoice the l. has fallen to me 235a
remember L.'s Wife 54a, 510a
so be warned by my l. 230b
the l. fell upon Jonah 504b
thou shalt maintain my l. 482b
with a toward or untoward l. 465b
Loth: l. to leave this Paradise 276b
l. to look a gift-horse 65a
Lothario: gallant, gay L. 313b
that false L.! 313a
Lots: cast l. upon my vesture 483a
come, and let us cast l. 504b
Lottery: razor-strops and the l. 295a
their judgement is a mere l. 142a
Lotus: like l.-buds that float 197a
l. and lilies 435a
the L. blooms below 433b
yellow L.-dust is blown 433a
Loud: at once is deaf and l. 395b
curses, not l. but deep 350b
licker talks mighty l. 182a
l. roared the dreadful thunder 90b
now l. as welcome 195b
said it very l. and clear 85a
so l., l. laughed he 529b
yet was never l. 360b
you needn't shout so l. 85a

Louder: a little l. but as empty 301a
  still l. and more dread 99b
Loudly: a cat languishes l. 185b
Louis: son of Saint L. 563a
Louis XIV: Siam sent ambassadors
  to L. 210a
Loungers of the Empire are..drained 136a
Lounjun: 'roun' en suffer'n' 181b
Louse: between a l. and a flea 211a
Louted low down on his knee 528a
Love: a feeling and a l. 472a
  absence is to l. 561b
  absence from whom we l. 109a
  acts of kindness and of L. 472a
  against the reason of my L. 223b
  a grace wh. l. makes for thee 463b
  alas! let l. of women! 70b
  a lecture, L., in l.'s philosophy 133b
  all be as before, L. 52b
  alle that l. floures 90a
  All For L. 139a
  all for l...nothing for reward 408b
  all for the l. of you 116b
  all l., all liking, all delight 189a
  all l. at first, like generous wine 66a
  all l. is lost but upon God 143a
  all mankind l. a lover 147b
  all she loves is l. 70b
  all's l., yet all's law 51b
  all that l. me 198a
  all the little emptiness of l. 40a
  all the world and l. were young 307b
  all things..subject but eternal L. 397a
  all who deserve his l. 140a
  a l. for any lady 295b
  am like to l. three more 416a
  amo, amas, I l. a lass 290b
  and the shepherd of his l. 18b
  an hour's promise in l. 327b
  an oyster may be crossed in l. 400a
  Antony, who lost the world for l. 141a
  are but ministers of l. 101b
  as great in l. as in religion 107a
  a sigh to those who l. me 73a
  as in our will to l. or not 275a
  as l. doth give my heart 371a
  as l.'s young dream 281b
  as L. wist to pursue 441b
  as thy L. is discovered almighty 51b
  at his call l. him 470a
  Ave Maria! 'tis the hour of l.! 71a
  a well of l. 97b
  Beauty, Truth, and L. 36b
  because my l. is come 310b
  before the god of l. was born 133b
  beggary in the l. 322a
  best to be off with the old l. 524b
  be Thy name known, wh. is L. 36b
  beyond His l. and care 458b
  bind L. to last for ever! 77b
  bird sate mourning for her l. 393a
  blunt man, that l. my friend 340a
  boast their l. possessing 35b
  both deliberate, the l. is slight 259a
  brown jug, don't I l. thee? 523b
  but for thy L., by the Lord, no 383b
  but I do l. thee 361b
  but little in our l. 371a
  but l. from l., toward school 365b
  but l. he laughed to scorn 386b
  but l. is long 436b
  but l. is lost 186b
  but never taint my l. 363a
  but quick-eyed L., observing me 188b
  but to l. one another 513b
  by a l. so much refined 134a
  by heaven, I do l. 344b
  can L. be controll'd by advice 159a
  Cassio, I l. thee 361b
  caught up into l. 43b
  cheered her soul with l. 432b
  cherished still this test for l. 312a
  choose l. by another's eyes 356a
  Christ's particular l.'s sake 51a
  clap thyself my l. 372b
  comely in nothing but l. 14b
  conscience is born of l. 389b
  constancy of the women who l. me 391a
  content with a vegetable l. 165b
  converse and l. so dearly joined 276b
  cd. L. for ever run like a river 74a

Love (*cont.*)
  course of true l. never..smooth 356a
  cymbal where there is no l. 15b
  dallies with the innocence of l. 371a
  dearly l. but one day 79b
  deep and heavy was the l. 529a
  deep as first l. 436a
  Deity..doth ease its heart of l. 218a
  dinner of herbs where l. is 498a
  disparity..twixt women's l. 132a
  dost thou l. life? 157a
  dropped from their youth and l. 52a
  dull sublunary lovers' l. 134a
  emphasis of passionate l. repeated 241b
  ends all our month-long l. 36b
  England..I l. thee still 111b
  England we l. thee 445b
  eternal joy, and everlasting l. 291b
  evening star, l.'s harbinger 276b
  ever wilt thou l., and she be fair 219b
  every other gift, but wanted l. 6b
  except for l.'s sake only 44a
  faith creates or l. desires 397a
  falling out..renewing is of l. 143b
  fall out with those we l. 436a
  familiar acts..beautiful thro' l. 397b
  fickleness of the women I l. 391a
  find the arms of my true l. 434a
  fires us with courage, l. and joy 159b
  fit l. for Gods 276a
  flag and sign of l. 359b
  flowers and fruits of l. are gone 73b
  food of us that trade in l. 323b
  for a laggard in l. 318a
  for ladies' l. unfit 140a
  for l., sweet l.—but praise! 458b
  for l. will hardly seem worth 474b
  for a good man's l. 327a
  forspent with l. and shame 242b
  for the l. he had to her 493a
  free l.—free field 428b
  Friendship is L. 72b
  from too much l. of living 422a
  general award of l. 218a
  give all to l.: obey thy heart 146b
  give me more l. or more disdain 79b
  God gives us l. 431b
  God is l. 518a
  God is L., I dare say 67a
  God of l. my Shepherd is 188a
  greater l. hath no man 511a
  green and happy in first l. 96a
  grete god of L.'s name 89b
  hail wedded l., mysterious law 274b
  half in l. with easeful Death 220a
  hard, when l. and duty clash 436a
  has twin'd my l. and me 531b
  hath not, or is not in l. 368b
  have you left the ancient l.? 31b
  health to all those that l. us 523b
  health to all those that we l. 523b
  hear him sing his song of l. 36b
  heart whose l. is innocent 74a
  heigh-ho, how I do l. thee! 105b
  he kept, his l., his zeal 275a
  he'll carry a letter to my l. 529b
  he'll never l. me mair 530a
  he may live without l. 265a
  herald of l.'s mighty king 408a
  here's to him we l. most 320a
  he sang of l. 468a
  he sought..things to l. 399a
  he was all for l. 120b
  he was the Queen's l. 530b
  he will seem worthy of yr. l. 469a
  he wd. l. and she wd. not 35a
  hid in the heart of l. 475b
  him whom you l, yr. Idiot Boy 465b
  his banner over me was l. 500a
  his for his l. 387b
  his tender l. 36b
  hold yr. tongue, and let me l. 132a
  honour, l., obedience 350b
  how a little l...improves..woman 150a
  how do I l. thee? 44a
  how..dwelleth the l. of God 518a
  how I l. my country 297b
  how l. exalts the mind 140a
  how l. so young cd. be so sweet 37b
  how shall I know yr. true l. 307b
  how shd. I yr. true l. know 335b

Love (*cont.*)
  how this spring of l. resembleth 372b
  how wayward is this foolish l. 372b
  human l. needs human meriting 442a
  I am sick of l. 500a
  I and my L. wont to gae 530a
  I cd. not l. thee (Dear) so much 250a
  I do know I l. 38a
  I do l. I know not what 189b
  I do l. thee as my lambs 105b
  I do l. thee, meek *Simplicity* 101b
  I do not l. thee!—no! 290a
  I do not l. you Dr. Fell 41a
  I do not l. you Sabidius 551a
  I drew them with bands of l. 504a
  I felt the worst that l. cd. do 133b
  if ever thou shalt l. 370b
  if I have freedom in my l. 249b
  if I know what true l. is 428b
  if I l. not him 428b
  if I l. Thee not 187a
  if it be l. indeed 322a
  if l. were what the rose is 423a
  if music be the food of l. 369b
  if my l. were in my arms 527b
  if of herself she will not l. 416a
  if this be not l., it is madness 104b
  if thou car'st not whom I l. 133a
  if thou must l. me 44a
  if yet I have not all thy l. 133b
  I hate, I l.—the cause thereof 539b
  I have been in l., and in debt 38a
  I knew it was l. 73b
  I know that I l. thee 282a
  I know whose l. wd. follow me 232b
  I leave my l. alone 388a
  ilka bird sang of its l. 63b
  I'll l. no more 12a
  I'll never l. thee more 280b
  I l. a lassie 242b
  I l. all beauteous things 36b
  I. l. all thou lovest 398b
  I l. but you alone 529b
  I l. everything that's old 170b
  I l. God, and hateth his brother 518a
  I l. her so sincerely 79b
  I l. him not, but shew no reason 452a
  I l. it, I l. it 105b
  I l. L. tho' he hath wings 398b
  I l. my L., and my L. loves me 100a
  I l. not hollow cheek 436b
  I l. thee, all unlovely 112a
  I l. thee and adore 110a
  I l. thee beyond measure 461a
  I l. thee Cornwall 157a
  I l. thee freely 44a
  I l. thee purely 44a
  I l. thee to the depth 44a
  I l. thee to the level 44a
  I l. thee with a l. 44a
  I l. thee with the breath 44a
  I l. thee with the passion 44a
  I never had but one true l. 529a
  I never loved a l. but one 531b
  I never shall l. the snow again 36b
  I never was in l.—yet the voice 222b
  ink..temper'd with L.'s sighs 345a
  in likeness of my l. 370b
  in l. alone we hate..companions 450a
  in l. and holy passion 464a
  in l. with his fetters 16b
  in l. with one princess 411a
  in peace, L. tunes the shepherd's 317a
  in the office and affairs of l. 358a
  in Thy l. look down and comfort 411a
  in Wonder, L. and Praise 2a
  I seek, not l. them less 398b
  I shall be past making l. 305b
  I shall desire more l. 325b
  I shd. l. a..particular star 322a
  is it..a crime to l. too well? 299a
  is it possible to l. such a man? 91a
  is not l. a Hercules 345a
  I think my l. as rare 389a
  it is l. that I am seeking for 476a
  it strikes where it doth l. 363b
  I was in l. with you 199a
  I wd. l. infinitely 49b
  joy of l. is too short 257a
  keep a corner in the thing I l. 362a
  kill thee, and l. thee after 363b

Love (cont.)

King of L. my Shepherd is   18a
kiss yr. l. again   229a
know the l. betwixt us two   107a
labour of l.   516b
lack of l. from l. made manifest   46a
last gasp of L.'s latest breath   137b
laughed at the power of L.   235b
leads me from my l.   199a
lease of my true l. control   388b
leave me, O L.   402a
leave to come unto my l.   408b
Lesbia let us live and l.   78a
Lesbia mine, let's live and l.   538b
lest that thy l. prove . . variable   365a
let brotherly l. continue   517a
let l. be without dissimulation   513b
let me not l. thee   187a
let's contend no more, L.   52b
letters, soft interpreters of l.   305b
let the triumphs of L. . . be shown   424b
let the warm L. in   220b
let thy l. be younger than thyself   370b
let thy l. in kisses rain   394b
let us l. nobly   132a
let us l. our occupation   121b
let us make l. deathless   445b
let us take our fill of l.   498a
lies my young l. sleeping   263b
lightly turns to thoughts of l.   432a
little duty and less l.   383b
little light of l.'s bestowing   263a
little season of l. and laughter   171b
little words of l.   82a
little worthy of any l. thou art   442a
live in unity and godly l.   480b
live with me and be my l.   132a, 259a
live with thee, and be thy l.   307b
look at least on l.'s remains   50a
look'd at me as she did l.   218b
lost to l. and truth   59b
l., all alike, no season knows   134a
l. alone, with yearning heart   423b
l. alters not with his brief hours   389a
l., an abject intercourse   170b
l. and a cottage!   103a
l. and all its smart   23b
l., and a space for delight   420b
l. and charity with yr. neighbours   480b
l. and desire and hate   135a
l. and do what you will   538a
l. and murder will out   104a
l. and scandal . . best sweeteners   151b
l., and thought, and joy   471a
l. and toil in the years to be   227b
l. bade me welcome   188b
L. built on beauty . . dies   132a
l. but her, and l. for ever   59a
l. but her for ever   59b
l. ceases to be a pleasure   25a
L. closed what he begat   264a
l., converted from the thing it was   387b
l. cd. teach a monarch to be wise   174a
L.! cd. thou and I . . conspire   154a
l., devoid of art   160a
L. did make thee run   326a
L. does on both her lips   106b
l. doth to her eyes repair   372b
l. endures no tie   141a
l., first learned in a lady's eyes   345a
l. first leaves the well-built nest   395a
L., forgive us!—cinders, ashes   219a
l., friendship, charity   369a
l. gilds the scene   400b
l., give me back my heart   173a
l. goes toward l., as school-boys   365b
l. grows bitter with treason   423b
l. had been sae ill to win   530a
l. had he found in huts   463b
l. hath an end   423b
l. . . hath friends in the garrison   177b
l. him, or leave him alone!   470a
L. in a golden bowl?   29b
l. in a hut, with water   219a
l. in a palace is perhaps at last   219a
L. in desolation masked   392a
L. in her sunny eyes   106b
l., in my bosom, like a bee   176a, 246a
L. is a boy, by poet's styl'd   65b
l. is a circle   189b
l. is a growing or full . . light   133b

Love (cont.)

l. is a sickness full of woes   117a
l. is a spirit all compact   386b
L. is best   48b
l. is blind, and lovers cannot see   353b
l., is but a name   160b
l. is crowned with the prime   327b
l. is dying   21a
l., I see, changing his property   375a
l. is enough   284a
l. is heaven, and heaven is l.   71b, 317a
l. is lame at fifty   180a
l. is left alone   431b
l. is less kind than . . twilight   474b
l. is like linen often chang'd   155b
l. is like the measles   205a
l. is lord of all   408b, 557b
l. is maister wher he wile   172a
l. is more cruel than lust   421a
l. is more than gold   251a
l. is not l. when it is mingled   341b
l. is not l. wh. alters   389a
l. is not secure   92a
L. is of the valley   437a
l. is strong as death   501a
l. is such a mystery   416a
l. is sweet for a day   423b
l. is swift of foot   188a
l. is the fulfiling of the law   513b
L. is the lesson   573a
l. is then our duty   159b
l. is too young to know   389b
l. itself have rest   74a
l. itself shall slumber on   399b
l. itself, that tyrant of the soul   244a
l., joy, peace   515b
l. looks not with the eyes   356a
l. me, it was sure to die!   282a
l. me little, l. me long   524b
l. me little, so you l. me long   189b
l. moderately; long l. doth so   365b
l. of Christ constraineth us   515a
l. of Christ wh. passeth knowledge   515b
l. of false and cruel men   261a
l. of liberty is the l. of others   183b
l. of money is the root of all evil   516b
l. of pleasure, and . . l. of sway   302a
l. of power is the l. of ourselves   183b
l. only bliss   51b
l. repulsed, but it returneth   394a
lover forsaken a new l. may get,   320a, 450a
L. (ruled) the night   141b
l. rules the camp   71b
l. rules the court   317a
l.'s a malady without a cure   141a
l.'s a man of war   188a
L. sang to us   423a
l.'s architecture is his own   115a
l.'s but a frailty of the mind   105b
L. seeketh not itself to please   32a
L. seeketh only Self to please   32a
l.'s emulous ardours   312a
l.'s feeling is more soft   345a
l.'s great artillery   115a
l. shd. have no wrong   35b
l. shd. with our fortunes change   334a
l. slights it (death)   14a
l.'s long since cancelled woe   387b
l.'s not Time's fool   389a
l. so amazing, so Divine   453b
l., sole mortal thing of worth   293a
l. sought is good   371b
L. sounds the alarm   159a
l.'s passives are his activ'st   114b
L.'s sweetest part, Variety   133b
L.'s the noblest frailty   140b
L.'s throne was not with these   311b
L. still has something of the sea   320b
l.'s tongue is in the eyes   155b
l.'s tongue proves dainty   345a
l., sweetness, goodness   278b
l. that endures for a breath   420b
l. that ever was betwixt us   257b
l. that makes the world go round   164a, 524b
l. that never found his . . close   433a
l. that never told can be   31b
l. that shd. help you   423a
l. that the winged seraphs   297b
l. that was more than l.   297b

Love (cont.)

l. that well wh. thou must leave   388a
l. the babe that milks me   347a
l. the brotherhood   517b
l. thee better after death   44a
L., the human form divine   33a
l. their land because . . their own   178a
l. those who l. you   566a
L., thou art absolute sole Lord   115a
l. thy God and l. Him only   120a
l. thyself last   386a
l. to all men 'neath the sun!   228a
l. to hatred turned   104b
l. took up the glass   432a
l. took up the harp   432a
l. wakes men, once a lifetime   293a
L. walks the pleasant mazes   106b
l. warps the mind   114a
l. was dead   421b
l. watching Madness   69a
l., whose month is ever May   344b
l. will change in growing old   37b
l. will creep in service   372b
L. will still be lord of all   317b
l. without the help of anything   30b
L. wd. prove so hard a master   38a
l. yet was l.   114a
loyal cantons of contemned l.   370a
made of l. and friendship   217b
make l. to the lips we are near   281b
makes thy l. more strong   388a
make the sweetest l. to frown   176b
make us l. yr. goodly gifts   364a
man's l. is of man's life   70a
many waters cannot quench l.   501a
marriage the happiest bond of l.   173a
marry yr. old friend's l.   52a
me and my true l.   525b
medicines to make me l. him   377a
men have died . . but not for l.   327b
men l. in haste . . detest at leisure   71b
men l. what I hate   50b
men that l. lightly may die   421b
mention L.'s devoted flame   282b
met you not with my true l.   307b
mie l. ys dedde   88a
mile or two from my first l.   448a
mine is an unchanging l.   110a
mine was jealousy in l.   428b
miserable l., that is not pain   470a
money has a power . . to manage l.   66a
money is the sinews of l.   150b
'mongst men who do not l. her   463a
moral of that is 'Oh, 'tis l., 'tis l.'   83a
more beautiful than thy first l.   474b
more of l. than matrimony   171a
more than over shoes in l.   372b
mortal! L. that Holy One   120a
murmurs . . how L. fled   476b
my dear and only l.   280b
my God, I l. Thee   86b
my grief, my hope, my l.   448b
my life, my l., my heart   190a
my l. and I did meet   474a
my l. and I did stand   474a
my l. and I met was l.   199a
my l. climb'd up to me   225b
my l. doth so approve him   363a
my l. has died for me today   531b
my L. in her attire doth show   525a
my l. is come to me   310b
my l. is of a birth as rare   260a
my l. is the maïd ov all maïdens   21a
my l., more noble than the world   371a
my l. she's but a lassie   193a
my l. shd. duly have been deck'd   408b
my L.'s like a red, red rose   62a
my L.'s like the melodie   62a
my l., the flower of Yarrow   246b
my true l. did lichtlie me   530a
my true L. has me forsook   530a
my true l. hath my heart   401b
my vegetable l. shd. grow   260a
my whole course of l.   360a
names of those who l. the Lord   201b
nature is fine in l.   335b
needs must l. the highest   428a
ne'er ebb to humble l.   362b
ne'er knew l.'s sad satiety   398b
neither our l. from God   312a
never been in l., or in hate   413a

ENGLISH INDEX

Love (cont.)

never doubt I l. — 332a
never l. was so abused — 402a
never, my l., repent of how — 294a
never seek to tell thy l. — 31b
new every morning is the l. — 223b
new L. pine at them — 220a
no blessed leisure for l. — 196b
no l. lost between us — 171a
'no l,' quoth he, 'but vanity' — 202a
no man dies for l. — 141a
no more, dear l. — 436b
no natural l. of the 'chaste muse' — 33a
none knew thee but to l. thee — 178a
none other I can l. — 428b
none profane my Holy See of l. — 219a
none to praise and very few to l. — 470b
no new light on l. or liquor — 305a
nor fettered L. from dying — 77b
nor L. her body from her soul — 313a
nor l. thy life, nor hate — 276b
not Death, but L. — 43b
not enough to make us l. — 418b
nothing all my l. avails — 47b
not in our power to l. or hate — 259a
not l. her, is thy point — 477b
not unworthy to l. her — 73b
now warm in l. — 299b
oh for grace to l. thee more! — 110a
Oh L.! thou bane — 173a
oh l.! who bewailest the frailty — 395a
O L.! has she done this to thee — 251b
O l., my l.! if I no more shd. see — 312a
O l., O fire! once he drew — 427a
O, L.'s but a dance — 131a
O l. what hours were thine — 426a
O L. will venture in — 62b
O lyric L., half angel — 51a
O mightie l.! Man is one world — 187b
one born to l. you, sweet — 45b
one jot of former l. retain — 137b
one of l.'s April-fools — 104b
one to another with brotherly l. — 513b
only in command, nothing in l. — 350a
only l. sprung from my only hate — 365a
or bid me l., and I will give — 190a
O spirit of l.! how quick — 369b
ostentation of our l. — 323b
our l. hath no decay — 132a
our l. is frail as is our life — 149a
our l. shall live — 408a
outward parts L.'s always seen — 106b
over hir housbond as hir l. — 89b
Ovid, the sweet philosopher of l. — 140b
owe a duty, where I cannot l. — 25a
O wisest l.! that flesh and blood — 289a
pains of l. be sweeter far — 142a
pangs of disappointed l. — 313b
pangs of dispriz'd l. — 333a
partly wi' l. o'ercome — 61a
passing the l. of women — 495b
passin' the l. o' women — 229a
pass our long l.'s day — 260a
perfect l. casteth out fear — 518a
perhaps was sick, in l. — 301b
pity is sworn servant unto l. — 117a
place to stand and l. in — 44a
planet of L. is on high — 434a
poets' food is l. — 393b
poor excommunicate from..l. — 79b
poor heretics in l. — 133b
pray, l., remember — 335b
pray thee leave, l. me no more — 137a
presume too much upon my l. — 340b
prosperity's the very bond of l. — 373b
prove an unrelenting foe to l. — 443a
prov'd thee my best of l. — 389a
prove my l, wh. sloth maligns — 293b
purple light of l. — 175a
purple with l.'s wound — 356b
quarrels of lovers..renewal of l. — 554a
quench my great l. — 164a
reason, and the l. of good and ill — 217b
rebuke is better than secret l. — 498b
recognizance and pledge of l. — 364a
regain l. once possessed — 278a
remembrance of my former l. — 372b
restore my wandering l. — 105a
rhymes of a l....never woo'd — 36a
right to dissemble yr. l. — 28a
rise up, My l., My fair one — 262a, 500a

Love (cont.)

rites..of connubial l. refused — 274b
Romeo! if thou dost l. — 365a
rosy red, l.'s proper hue — 276a
same sweet eternity of l. — 189b
Saturn and L. their long repose — 394a
Scotland led in l. and le — 474a
seals of l., but seal'd in vain — 352a
see thee..look pale with love — 358a
separate us from the l. of God — 513b
sets l. a task like that — 202a
shackles of an old l. — 428b
shall my sense pierce l. — 312a
shalt set l. to rhyme — 37b
she bid me take l. easy — 474a
she never told her l. — 371a
shepherd..grew acquainted with L. — 206b
she said, 'I l. thee true!' — 218b
she whom I l. is hard to catch — 263b
she will l. him truly — 432b
shocks of young l.-liking — 469b
show a fitter L. for me — 133b
show of l. as I was wont to have — 337b
shows of l. to other men — 337b
side-long looks of l. — 168a
sighed for the l. of a ladye — 167a
silence was the song of l. — 312a
since I am l.'s martyr — 133a
singularly moved to l. the lovely — 293b
sit with my l. in the hay — 38a
society, friendship, and l. — 113a
so dear l. him — 276a
so faithful in l. — 318a
soft eyes looked l. — 68a
so ill-bred as to l. a husband — 473b
so many times do I l. thee — 24a
some are fou o' l. divine — 61a
some l. but little policy — 376a
some obscure epistles of l. — 370b
something to he lends — 431b
so sweet l. seemed — 37b
so true a fool is l. — 388a
sows what L. shall never reap — 312a
speak low, if you speak l. — 358a
spirit..of power and of l. — 516b
spring of l. gushed from my heart — 99a
still make l. anew — 321a
stony limits cannot hold l. out — 365a
stories of thy finisht l. — 78b
study..the way to l. each other — 225a
substance of his house for l. — 501a
such ever was l.'s way — 46a
such I account thy l. — 347a
sweetest l., I do not go — 133b
sweet is true l. — 428b
sweets and the bitters of l. — 72b
tale of l. and languishment — 221a
tell him, that I am sick of l. — 500b
tell me, my heart, if this be l. — 251b
tell the laity our l. — 134a
tell this youth what 'tis to l. — 327b
tell us how they l. us — 228a
thank the Lord, for all His L. — 76a
that is l.'s curse; pass on — 428b
that l. may never cease — 187b
that my love is weak and faint — 110a
the fool of l. — 183b
their l. may be called appetite — 371a
their tales of l. shall tell — 53b
the last flower of Catholic l. — 424a
the l. he bore to learning — 168b
the l. of l. — 435b
the l. of the turtle — 67b
the l. that lingers there — 154b
the l. that loves a scarlet coat — 195a
the l. that moves the sun — 567a
the l. wh. doth us bind — 260b
then must the L. be great — 21a
then they dream of l. — 364b
the prize of learning l. — 46a
therefore I l. it — 49a
there is no fear in l. — 518a
there my dear l. sits him down — 527a
there shall be no l. lost — 215b
the right true end of l. — 132b
the service of my l. — 409b
the wise want l. — 397a
they all l. Jack — 454a
they happy are, and that they l. — 449a
they l. indeed who quake to say — 401b
they l. the better still — 29a

Love (cont.)

they shall prosper that l. thee — 489b
they sin who tell us l. can die — 406b
this bud of l. — 365b
tho' I knew His l. Who followed — 441b
tho' last, not least in l. — 339b
tho' l. repine, and reason chafe — 147a
those that l. them that l. those — 523b
those who l. want wisdom — 397a
those who l. you well — 37a
thou art goodly, O l. — 420b
thou art l. and life! — 398b
thou dravest l. from thee — 442a
thought that l. cd. never change — 37b
thou hast left thy first l. — 518b
thou knowest that I l. thee — 511b
thou shalt l. and be loved by — 51b
thou shalt l. thy neighbour — 507b
thro' l.'s long residence — 36a
thro' l., thro' hope — 463b
thro' our l. that we have loved — 257b
thy l. is better than wine — 500a
thy l. to me was wonderful — 495b
thy l. was far more better — 261a
thy sweet l. remembered — 387b
till l. and fame to nothingness — 221a
Time was when L. and I — 167a
'tis brief, my lord. As woman's l. — 334a
to all who l. him — 320a
to be wise and eke to l. — 409b
to be wise, and l. — 369a
to be wroth with one we l. — 100a
to live is like l. — 67a
to l., and bear — 397b
to l. and be loved by me — 297b
to l. and to cherish — 481b
to l., cherish and to obey — 481b
to l. her is a liberal education — 410b
to l. him as myself — 481a
to l. is wise — 37b
to l. one maiden only — 428a
to l. with zealous humble duty — 409a
to l. you was pleasant — 281a
to Mercy, Pity, Peace, and L. — 32b
to see her is to l. her — 59b
to see her was to l. her — 59a
to the seat where l. is throned — 370b
true life is only l. — 51b
true L. in this differs from gold — 393b
true l. sitting down to breakfast — 237b
trust thou thy L. — 315a
turning mortal for thy l. — 345a
two fond hearts in equal l. — 18b
type of true l. kept under — 164a
under a canopy of l. — 445b
virginity..first l.'s first cry — 293b
waft her l. to come again — 355a
waly, waly gin l. be bonnie — 530a
wander hand in hand with l. — 290a
was not this l. indeed? — 371a
we all l. a pretty girl — 28a
we have seen thee, O l. — 420b
well dost thou, L. — 293b
we l. being in l. — 439b
we l. but while we may — 428b
we l., Fool, for the good we do — 293a
we l. our House of Peers — 166b
we're far from the lips we l. — 281b
Werther had a l. for Charlotte — 440b
we serve, because we freely l. — 275a
what a mischievous devil L. is — 67a
what is l.? It is a pretty thing — 176a
what is l.? 'tis not hereafter — 370b
what lady wd. not l. a shepherd — 176b
what l. I bore to thee — 467a
what l. is, if thou wdst. be taught — 568b
what l. of thine own kind? — 398b
what thing is l. — 295b
what we have loved, others will l. — 470a
when I l. thee not, chaos is come — 361b
when l. begins to sicken — 340b
when l. grows diseased — 149a
when l. is done — 34a
when l. is grown to ripeness — 431b
when L. speaks — 345a
when L. with unconfined wings — 249b
when my l. swears — 389a
when one is in l. — 476a
where I l. I must not marry — 281a
where I marry, cannot l. — 281a

[732]

Love (*cont.*)

where l. is great	334a
where my L. abideth	49b
while we can, the sports of l.	216a
who gave that l. sublime	464b
whom having not seen, ye l.	517b
whom the gods l. die young	71a
Whose l. will never die	265b
willing to l. all mankind	210a
with a l. I seemed to lose	44a
with all their quantity of l.	336b
with all thy faults I l. thee still	67a
with l. brooding there	461b
with music sweet as l.	398a
without l., hatred, joy, or fear	305b
with their l. the breath between	397b
woman's friendship..ends in l.	160a
women..passions..vanity and l.	91a
words of l. then spoken	282b
wouldn't be too ladylike in l.	186a
yes, I'm in l., I feel it now	457a
yet I l. her till I die	156a, 526b
yet I l. thee too	383b
you all did l. him	340a
you'll l. me yet!	50a
you made me l. you	256a
you must l. him, ere to you	469a
'you must sit down', says L.	188b
you (my L.) as high as Heaven	527b
yr. true l.'s coming	370b
youth means l.	51a
you who do not l. her	52a
you wonder why, l. you	293a
you, you wonder why, l. none	293a
Love-adept: dreaming like a l.	397a
Love-adventure shd. be lost	239a
Loved: all we l. of him shd. be	392a
better l. ye canna be	285b
better l. you'll never be	193b
better to have l. and lost	430a
but I have l. too long	290a
Dante, who l. well	49a
daughter..wh. he l. passing well	332b
ever l. that l. not at first sight	259a, 327a
for some we l., the loveliest	153a
God so l. the world	510b
had we never l. sae blindly	59a
had we never l. sae kindly	59a
had you l. me once	424a
having l. this present world	516b
heart that has truly l.	281b
he had l. her long	35b
how I l. how honoured once	299b
if I l. you well	423a
I have l. long since	288b
I have l. thee, Ocean	69b
I have not l. the world	68b
I l. a lass, a fair one	462a
I l. her that she did pity	360a
I l. him for himself	400a
I l. him not	241a
I l. thee once	12a
I l. the man..on this side idolatry	214b
I never l. a love but one	531b
I never l. a tree or flower	75b, 282a
I only know we l. in vain	72b
I saw and l.	161b
I that l. and you that liked	526a
I that l. thee since my day	439a
I wd. *love* infinitely, and be l.	49b
keep our l. ones, now far absent	411a
known and l. so long	35b
Lavinia, therefore must be l.	368a
life have we l.	284a
Lo! some we l., the loveliest	153a
l. and still loves	310a
l. at home, revered abroad	59b
l. not wisely but too well	364a
lovers shd. be l. again	198b
l. the sorrows of your..face	476b
l. when all was young	226a
l. yr. beauty with love false	476b
many l. yr. moments of..grace	476b
men that I l. you well	284a
might she have l. me?	48a
most he l. a happy human face	202a
most l., despised	341b
never the time..and the l. one	49a
never to have been l.	105a
never to have l. at all	430a
nor no man ever l.	389a

Loved (*cont.*)

no sooner l. but they sighed	327b
one man l. the pilgrim soul	476b
one of his disciples, whom Jesus l.	511a
out upon it, I have l.	416a
people l. her much	432b
see the souls we l.	434a
she l. me for the dangers	360a
since to be l. endures	37b
the disciple whom Jesus l.	511b
this man l. *me*	241b
thrice had I l. thee	131b
to be long l. was never fram'd	5b
to be l...needs only to be known	140a
to be l. needs only to be seen	140b
to have l. so slight a thing	432b
to have l. the highest	428a
to have l...thought..done	5b
took from those who l. them	119b
use him as tho' you l. him	450b
view each l. one blotted	68a
we that had l. him so	48a
what thou, and I, did till we l.	133a
what we have l., others will love	470a
when you l. me I gave you	390a
who has never l., has never liv'd	160a
with those that l. me, and alone	438b
woman who l. him the best	226b
Love-in-idleness	356b
Love-knot: dark red l.	290a
Lovel: Lord L. he died..of sorrow	531a
Loveless: the only l. look	294a
Lovelier: l. things have mercy shown	72b
nothing l. can be found	276a
Loveliest: l. of trees, the cherry	198b
l. things of beauty	261b
the l. and the best	26b
Love-light in yr. eye	28b
Love-Lily: between the lips of L.	312b
Loveliness: enough their simple l.	221a
fashioned forth its l.	180a
glory and l. have pass'd	221a
her l. I never knew	97b
its l. increases	217b
l. needs not the foreign aid	443b
l. of perfect deeds	430a
portion of the l.	392b
saw a Dream of L. descending	244b
woman of so shining l.	476a
yr. l. and the hour of my death	223a
Love-locks: with your l. flowing	311a
Lovely: look thy last on all things l.	119a
l. as a Lapland night	473a
l. forms do flow	78a
more l. and more temperate	387a
singularly moved to love the l.	293b
wh. once he made more l.	392b
yea, he is altogether l.	500b
Love match was the only thing	143b
Love Powders: rogue gives you L.	240a
Love-quarrels oft in pleasing..end	278a
Lover: all mankind love a l.	147b
a l. forsaken a new love may get	320a
angel appear to each l. beside	292b
as true a l. as ever sigh'd	326a
beauty is the l.'s gift	105a
by the l. and the bard	44b
clasped her like a l.	432b
days dividing l. and l.	420a
feet of thy l. the spring	422b
felt for thee as a l.	472a
give repentance to her l.	170a
God become her l.	115a
good-bye to yr. l.	232b
got one l. and I don't want two	263a
great Camerado, the l. true	458a
happy as a l.	465b
heart that is in any manner a l.	257b
I cannot prove a l.	384b
if at last, not less her l.	307b
I sighed as a l.	161b
it was a l. and his lass	327b
jealousy..the injured l.'s hell	275a
like a true l. brave	526b
Lord, what is a l.	105b
l. and sensualist	185b
l. forsaken a new love may get	450a
l. of life shall join the hater	171b
l. of literature..never fastidious	407a
l.'s ears will hear the lowest	345a

Lover (*cont.*)

l.'s eyes will gaze an eagle	345a
magnetic, peripatetic l.	105b
meek l. of the good	146a
my fause l. stole my rose	63b
of all the plagues a l. bears	450a
O I hate a l. that can dare	105b
O Lord, thou l. of souls	520a
O l. of my life	51b
one was round her l.	77a
on her l.'s arm she leant	426b
pale Titan-woman like a l.	421a
resolve the propositions of a l.	327a
run into 't as to a l.'s bed	324b
sad true l. never find my grave	371a
she was a true l.	257b
slide into a L.'s head	471a
smile, for yr. l. comes	458b
some sad l.'s death	139a
stray to some newer l.	159b
such a constant l.	416a
suff'ring in the l.'s part	159a
talk with some old l.'s ghost	133b
tell her, her l. keeps watch	248b
the l., all as frantic	357b
the l. lingers and sings	414b
the l., sick to death	344b
the l. sighing like a furnace	326b
the lunatic, the l., and the poet	357b
truest l. of a sinful man	257b
when they have slain her l.	77a
where shall the l. rest	318a
why so pale and wan, fond l.?	416a
woman loves her l.	70b
Lovers: all l. young, all l. must	329a
all ye that be l. call	257b
almighty l. in the spring	92a
as I am all true l. are	370b
at l.' perjuries..Jove laughs	365a
even l. find their peace at last	154b
hour when l. vows seem sweet	73b
journeys end in l. meeting	370b
Jove but laughs at l.'s perjury	141a
l.' absent hours, more tedious	362b
l. are round her, sighing	281b
l. cannot see the pretty follies	353b
l.' hours be full eternity	133b
l. in peace, lead on our days	341a
l. lying two and two	198b
l. shd. be loved again	198b
l., to bed	357b
l. who have cherished still	312a
make two l. happy	298b
must pure l.' souls descend	132b
night by night thro' l.' brains	364b
not the nectarous poppy l. use	6a
old l. are soundest	454b
O l.' eyes are sharp	317b
one makes l...as one pleases	105b
quarrels of l. are the renewal	554a
sound l.' tongues by night	365b
sweet l. love the spring	327b
these l. fled away	221b
to thy motions l.' seasons run?	134a
true l. I can get many	529a
we that are true l.	326a
what need l. wish for more?	321a
where the l. eloped in the dark	242a
young l. lately wed	431b
Loves: all l. except what trades can give	51b
all she l. is love	70b
all strange l. are over	421a
all the wings of the L.	423b
amatory poets sing their l.	71a
any severing of our l.	467a
ar'n't that I l. the fox less	416b
as lines so l. oblique	260a
as truly l. on to the close	281b
a-waiting for their ain dear l.	530a
each man kills the thing he l.	459b
every man l. what he is good at	322a
faithful l. shall moralize my song	408b
foxhunter, and I l. him at once	416b
friends and l. we have none	262a
he l. his bonds	190a
her that each l. best	77b
if country l. such sweet desires	176b
if our l. remain	46a
I have reigned with yr. l.	145b
I like him, but he l. me	52b

Loves (cont.)
let us solace ourselves with l. 498a
l., and weeps, and dies 394a
l. nothing but himself 407a
old l. endear thee 97b
one l. him still the better 170b
one that l. his fellowmen 202a
'oss l. the hound and I l. both 416b
our l. and comforts shd. increase 361a
our l. into corpses or wives 421a
perhaps their l., or..their sheep 270b
she l. me dearly 217b
show a woman when he l. her 49b
to warm their little l. 173b
two l. I have 389b
whoever l., if he do not propose 132b
who l. a garden l. a greenhouse 112a
who l. me must have 428b
who l. to lie with me 326a
with l. and doves 46b
woman l. her lover 70b
Love-sick: l. all against our will 165a
Savonarola l.! Ha, ha! 25a
twenty l. maidens we 165a
Lovesome: garden is a l. thing 41a
Love-song: singing his l. to the morn 205a
Lovest: alas, thou l. not me 133a
Father in Heaven who l. all 227b
Hal, an thou l. me 377b
l. thou me more than these 511b
say, poor sinner, l. thou me? 110a
thou l. not, till from loving more 133a
thou l. the one, and I the other 21a
why l. thou that 387a
Love-story: a l...into..Euclid 136a
Loveth: He made and l. all 100a
he that l. another hath fulfilled 513b
he that l. not knoweth not God 518a
prayeth best, who l. best 100a
prayeth well, who l. well 100a
the dear God who l. us 100a
thou whom my soul l. 500a
whom the Lord l. he chasteneth 517a
Love-thoughts lie rich 369b
Loving: begin by l. their parents 460b
for l., and for saying so 134a
Friday's child is l. and giving 525a
I will give a l. heart to thee 190a
Lady Moon, whom are you l.? 198a
l., adorable, softly to rest 289a
l. Christianity better than Truth 102a
l. himself better than me 14a
l. not, hating not 45b
l., not loathing 195b
l. thy mournful face 206a
most l. were folly 326b
my own sex..that of l. longest 11b
night was made for l. 74a
One, most l. of you all 44a
pardon for too much l. you 361b
they talks a lot o' l. 232a
till from l. more 133a
wickedness that hinders l. 49a
Loving-jealous of his liberty 365b
Loving-kindness: thy l. and mercy
shall follow me 483a
Low: from l. to high doth dissolution 468a
he that is l. no pride 54b
hear but the l. lone song? 82b
I am l., thou art high 422a
I deem them l. 75a
I'll tak' the l. road 525b
in..dejection do we sink as l. 470a
last great Englishman is l. 435a
l., l., breathe and blow 436a
on a rock conveniently l. 84b
sweet and l. 436a
that l. man goes on adding 47a
that l. man seeks a little thing 47a
the earth is not too l. 187a
then, happy l., lie down 380a
they are minished, and brought l. 488b
to cast one's eyes so l. 343b
what is l. raise and support 270b
wilt thou weep when I am l.? 67b
Lowells talk to the Cabots 34a
Lower: he that is down can fall no l. 65a
madest him l. than the angels 482a
take you a button-hole l. 345b
Lowing of the oxen wh. I hear? 495a
Lowlands: by the L. low 531a

Lowlands (cont.)
L. o' Holland has twin'd my love 531b
ye Highlands and ye L. 530b
Lowliness is young ambition's ladder 338a
Lowly: any hands, however l. 164a
made them, high or l. 3a
my bed it is fu' l. 529a
l. in his own eyes 482a
poor, and mean, and l. 3b
still to the l. soul 224a
'tis better to be l. born 385b
Lown: he called the tailor l. 361a
Lowpin' o'er a linn 60a
Loyal and neutral, in a moment 348a
Loyalties: home of..impossible l. 9a
Loyalty: that learned body wanted l. 445b
unterrified his l. he kept 275a
when l. no harm meant 524a
Lucas: her name was Margaret L. 288a
Lucasta: L. that bright northern star 249b
my L. might I crave 249b
Lucent: each softly l. 250b
Lucifer: are you that live with L.? 258b
for ever damned with L. 258b
he falls like L. 386a
O L., son of the morning 502a
spirits that fell with L. 258b
Luck: all the day you'll have good l. 532b
as good l. wd. have it 356a
damn'd ill l. every way 25b
good l. have thou 484b
if it be my l., so 356a
light in ragged l. 185b
nae l. about the house 527a
we have wished you good l. 489a
Lucrative business of mystery 57b
Lucre: not greedy of filthy l. 516b
Lucumo: each warlike L. 253a
Lucy: few cd. know when L. ceased 470b
if L. shd. be dead 471b
no comrade L. knew 467b
Luddites: quartern loaf and L. rise 403b
Lues Bostwelliana 254b
Lugwardin: shined at L. 445a
Luke: honour unto L. Evangelist 312b
L. began to slacken in his duty 468a
L., the beloved physician 516b
Matthew, Mark, L., and John 2b
only L. is with me 516b
Lukewarm: because thou art l. 518b
Lukewarmness I account a sin 107a
Lull: arrives a l. in the hot race 5a
Lullaby: and dreamy l. 164a
I will sing a l. 119a
rock them, rock them, l. 119a
sing l. and lap it warm 35b
Lulled in these flowers with dances 356b
Lumber: learned l. in his head 300b
philosophy, the l. of the schools 419b
Lumber-room of his library 135b
Luminary: arose another l. 55a
Luminous: Goethe's wide and l. view 7a
Lump: leaveneth the whole l. 514a
l. bred up in darkness 238b
l. the whole thing! 446b
of the same l. to make one vessel 513b
Lumps: go down like l. of lead 192a
Luna: in the vats of L. 253a
Lunar: on the l. world securely pry 139b
Lunatic: keep me from goin' l. 227b
l., the lover, and the poet 357b
Lunch: dinner, l. and tea 26a
Luncheon: supper, dinner, l. 50a
Lundy: Lord L. from his earliest
years 26a
Lungs: dons..with..l. of bronze 26b
if their l. receive our air 111b
my l. began to crow 326a
parks were the l. of London 297a
[smoking] dangerous to the l. 204a
whose l. are tickle o' the sere 332b
Lurch: Dame L...always at church 32a
Lurcher: half l. and half cur 112b
Lured by the trappings 457a
Lust: cold, commanded l. 230b
for l. of knowing what 154a
into ashes all my l. 260a
is l. in action 389a
love is more cruel than l. 421a
l. of the goat is the bounty 31a
no l. because they have no laws 429a

Lust (cont.)
not serving shame or l. 131a
served the l. of my mistress' heart 343a
slept in the contriving of l. 343a
weariness and sated l. 7a
Lusteth: he that l. to live 484a
Lustre: a l. in its sky 394b
dark l. of thine eyes 317b
I ne'er cd. any l. see 400a
obscure in the exceeding l. 395b
same eye..did lose his l. 337b
Lustres: to my six l. 133b
Lusts: abstain from fleshly l. 517b
fulfil the l. thereof 514a
sinful l. of the flesh 481a
Lusty as an eagle 488a
Lutanist: the lute the l. 442a
Lute: blame not my l. 473b
grace of l. or clavicithern 47a
lascivious pleasing of a l. 384b
musical as is Apollo's l. 267b
my l., awake! perform the last 473b
my l., be still, for I have done 473b
not a good sword, nor yet a l. 187a
Orpheus with his l. 385b
or the l. its tones 217b
ravishing division, to her l. 378a
rift within the l. 428b
sing praises unto him with the l. 483b
when the l. is broken 395a
when to her l. Corinna sings 78a
Lute-player: some dead l. 421a
Lutes: to l. of amber 190b
Luthany: where is the land of L. 442b
Luther: Philistine of..religion, L. 10b
rough old Martin L. 52b
sing as Martin L. sang 440b
this soul to whom L. 133b
Lutheran: a spleeny L. 385b
Luxuries: give us the l. of life 285a
I have two l. to brood over 223a
Luxurious: exquisite sense of the l. 222b
l. mountain goat 383a
Luxury: all their l. was doing good 159a
ancient languages is mainly a l. 38a
and thinks it l. 1b
l. of doing good 114a, 170a
l. the accomplished Sofa last 111b
taste the l. of woe 281a
they knew l.; they knew beggary 255a
to l. and riot 276b
Lycid: hearse where L. lies 270a
Lycidas: head of yr. loved L. 269b
L. yr. sorrow is not dead 270a
so L. sunk low 270a
Lydia, a seller of purple 512b
Lydian: lap me in soft L. airs 269a
softly sweet, in L. measures 139a
Lyeus ever young 23b
Lying: evil-speaking, l., and slandering 481a
hate ingratitude more..than l. 372a
I do not mind l. 67a
land-lubbers l. down below 525b
leave him l. where he fell 12a
settling and loosely l. 37a
soon will you and I be l. 86a
this vice of l. 380b
world is given to l. 379a
Lynn: men set out from L. 196a
Lyon: wot lived in L.'s Inn 454a
Lyonch: gone to L. 528a
Lyones: knights of Logres, or of L. 277a
Lyonesse: when I came back from L. 180a
when I set out for L. 180a
Lyra Apostolica: motto of L. 288a
Lyre: flit into it with my l. 218b
make me thy l. 396b
Mary! I want a l. 113a
my l. within the sky 298a
'Omer smote 'is bloomin' l. 236b
songs..not from his l. 48a
wak'd to ecstasy the living l. 174a
Lyres: sound of l. and flutes 293a
Lyric: most splendid ecclesiastical l. 129b
O l. Love, half angel 51a
Lysander: of Hector and L. 526a
that other principle of L. 13a
Lyte: greet effect..in place l. 90b
men wryte in place l. 90b
tho' that I can but l. (little) 89b

M

M: everything that begins with an M 83a
Ma'am: wd. call his mother 'M.' 93a
Mab: angry M. with blisters plagued 364b
　M., the Mistress-Fairy 215b
　Queen M. hath been with you 364b
　this is that very M. 365a
McAndrew: Mister M. 232a
Macaroni: called it M. 18b
Macassar: blacking and M. oil 295a
　thine 'incomparable oil', M. 70a
Macaulay: apostle of the Philistines..M. 9b
　cocksure..as..M. is of everything 263a
　[M.] has..flashes of silence 404b
　M. is well for a while 82a
Macbeth: M. does murder sleep 348a
　M. shall never vanquish'd be 349b
　M. shall sleep no more 348a
　none of woman born shall harm M. 349b
　there to meet with M. 345b
Macdonald: aff wi' lord Ronald M. 526a
　rose the slogan of M. 12a
Macduff: lay on, M. 351a
　M. was from his mother's womb 351a
Mace: the sword, the m. 382b
Macedon: there is a river in M. 383b
　the great war from M. 9a
Macedonia: come over into M. 512b
Maces: Seal and M. danced 175a
MacGregor: my name is M. 320a
Machiavel: much beholden to M. 13a
Machinations, hollowness, treachery 341b
Machine: a large bathing m. 164a
　m. for converting the Heathen 80a
　the very pulse of the m. 470b
　you're not a man, you're a m. 390a
Machinery: it is the Age of M. 80a
　the whole m. of the State 40b
Mackail: I'm M., and who are you? 528b
Mackerel: blew a m. gale 140b
　not so the m. 157b
M'Tavish: against the clan M. 12b
M'Turk 237b
Mad: Allah created the English m. 230b
　all poets are m. 64a
　a pleasure sure, in being m. 141b, 150b
　build a house for fools and m. 419a
　everyone is..m. on one point 237b
　fitter being sane than m. 44b
　God wd. destroy..first sends m. 538a
　go m., and beat their wives 76a
　he made me m. to see him 376b
　how sad and bad and m. it was 46a
　I am but m. north-north-west 332b
　in one word, heroically m. 138b
　m., and sent into England 336b
　m.-as-a-hatter-day 186a
　made us nobly wild, not m. 189b
　m. from life's history 196a
　m. in pursuit, and in possession 389a
　m. world! m. kings! m. composition! 374a
　makes men m. 363b
　melancholy..made me m. 212b
　men that God made m. 92a
　much learning doth make thee m. 513a
　oh! he is m., is he? 161a
　one half of the nation is m. 405b
　some did count him m. 54b
　that he is m. 'tis true 332a
　tho' father and mither..gae m. 63a
　thus to make poor females m. 357a
　'tis a m. world, my masters 425a
　undevout astronomer is m. 477b
　went m. and bit the man 169a
　when a heroine goes m. 400a
　why, the man's m., friend 45a
Madagascar: Jerusalem and M. 440b
Madam I may not call you 145b
Madden: now m. to crime 67b
Made: dost thou know who m. thee? 32b
　even more is m. of her 185b
　good poet 's m., as well as born 216a
　he was not m. to die 429b
　he who m. the Lamb 32a
　I am fearfully and wonderfully m. 490b
　I know not, that m. them do it 340a

Made (cont.)
　in a world I never m. 200a
　little Lamb, who m. thee? 32b
　m. and wrote them 49a
　see God m. and eaten all day 45a
　soul He else m. first in vain 51b
　thou hast m. him: thou art just 429b
　well m., well wrought 402b
　whereof are you m. 387b
　without him was not anything m. 510b
　you m. me love you 256a
Madeira: for a cup of M. 376b
Madman: if a m. were to come 209a
　that is, the m. 357b
Madmen: buries m. in the heaps 301b
　none but m. know 141b, 150b
　worst of m. is a saint run mad 303b
Madness: for that fine m...he did retain 137a
　despondency and m. 470a
　great wits..to m. near allied 138a
　his m. was not of the head 73a
　if this be not love, it is m. 104b
　like m. is the glory of this life 368a
　Love watching M. 69a
　m. of many for the gain of a few 304a
　M. risen from hell 420b
　m., yet there is method in it 332a
　moon-struck m. 276b
　much mirth and no m. 402b
　such harmonious m. 398b
　that way m. lies 343a
　this is very midsummer m. 371b
　this m. has come on us 428a
　thro' cells of m. 434b
　what m. is ambition! 157a
　wh. m. wd. gambol from 335a
　with a crafty m., keeps aloof 333a
　work like m. in the brain 100a
　you may call it m., folly 310a
Madoc will be read 304b
Madonnas: he only used to draw M. 49a
　Rafael of the dear M. 49b
Madrigal: sing a merry m. 164b
　woeful stuff this m. wd. be 300b
Madrigals: birds sing m. 259a
　falls used in lovely m. 43b
Mænad: head of some fierce M. 396a
　M. and the Bassarid 420b
Mæonides: blind M. 273a
　old M. the blind 154b
Maeotis: lo, where M. sleeps 299a
Magazine of life and comfort 186b
Magdalen: Cicely, Gertrude, M. 311b
　fourteen months at M. College 161b
　the monks of M. 161b
Maggie coost her head fu' high 60a
Maggot must be born i' the..cheese 144a
Maggot-pies and choughs and rooks 349a
Maggots in yr. brains 23b
Magic: a dealer in m. and spells 167a
　if this be m., let it be an art 373b
　no m. of her voice 293b
　once it was a m. sound to me 71a
　secret m. of numbers 41b
　the m. of a name 77a
　there's m. in the web of it 362b
　what conjuration..what mighty m. 360a
　with a m. like thee 73a
　with m. in my eyes 180a
Magistrate: commandment of the M. 491b
Magistrates: some, like m., correct 381b
Magna Charta is such a fellow 97b
Magnanimity: curb yr. m. 223b
　in all the m. of thought 477a
　m. in politics..wisdom 56a
Magnanimous Despair alone cd. show 260a
Magnet..attract a Silver Churn 165b
Magnetic peripatetic lover 165b
Magnetism works all night 447b
Magnificence: this m. is wholly thine 464a
Magnificent: in his mild and m. eye 48a
　it is m., but it is not war 561a
　m. out of the dust we came 452a
　mute and m., without a tear 141b
Magnify: m. him for ever 478a
　m. him that rideth..the heavens 486a
　my soul doth m. the Lord 508a
Magnipotent: raptly m. 179b
Magnitude: liar of the first m. 104b

Mahmud: M. on his golden throne 152b
　pity Sultan M. 152b
Mahogany Tree 440b
Mahomet: hill will not come to M. 15a
　passed from M. to Moses 305a
　soul to whom Luther, and M. 133b
Mahometans: paradisaical pleasures of the M. 175b
Maid: a m. not vendible 352b
　as the m. that milks 324b
　a wink for every pretty m. 417a
　bare-footed came the beggar m. 425b
　cling with life to the m. 146b
　come down, O m. 437a
　espy a fair pretty m. 525b
　from the lazy finger of a m. 364b
　going to, my pretty m.? 525b
　had she been a country m. 61b
　heart of neither m. nor wife 425a
　I beheld the m. 354b
　I heard m. sing in the valley 523a
　I knew a gentle m. 177a
　it was an Abyssinian m. 101b
　like mistress, like m. 150b
　like a moth, the simple m. 159a
　Lily Dale,—Old M. 445b
　little M. wd. have her will 472b
　M. of Athens, ere we part 73a
　m. whom there were none to praise 470b
　m. whose lip mature is ever new 218a
　many a youth, and many a m. 269a
　my love is the m. ov all maidens 21a
　now to the m. who has none, sir 400b
　O fair and stately m. 146b
　of wedded m., and virgin mother 270a
　slain by a fair cruel m. 371a
　the maiden passion for a m. 428a
　the m. remembers 414b
　the m. was in the garden 533b
　the matron and the m. 184a
　there was a fair m. dwellin' 531a
　the signal to a m. 265a
　the way of a man with a m. 499a
　to the heart of a m. 229b
　widow'd wife, and wedded m. 319a
　yonder a m. and her wight 179b
Maiden: a m. never bold 360a
　archly the m. smiled 246b
　a village m. she 432b
　from his true m.'s breast 318a
　God pursuing, the m. hid 420b
　how cd. you use a poor m. so 523a
　I know a m. fair to see 246b
　I, m., round thee, m., bind my belt 428a
　I pursued a m. 394a
　I sing of a m. 524a
　I've a neater, sweeter m. 232a
　kissed the m. all forlorn 534a
　let the m. understand 34b
　like a high-born m. 398a
　m., and mistress of the months 420a
　m. herself will steal after it 281b
　m. meditation, fancy-free 356b
　m. most perfect, lady of light 420a
　many a rose-lipt m. 199b
　mother, a m. is a tender thing 428b
　mother and m. 524b
　prithee, pretty m. 165b
　rare and radiant m. 298a
　she was a m. city 472b
　simple m. in her flower 431b
　that orbèd m., with white fire 393a
　the merry m. and the tar 166a
　this m. she lived 297b
　thy..pipe is as the m.'s organ 370a
　till the m. yields 433b
　to love one m. only 428a
　to the m. of bashful fifteen 400b
　what shall be the m.'s fate 317a
　where the m. flirts 196a
　woo a dead m. to be his bride 319a
Maidens: all her m., watching 436b
　all the m. pretty 103b
　bind him for thy m. 497b
　conserved of m.' hearts 362b
　lang may the m. sit 530a
　not fair..as many m. be 97b
　sing, ye gentle m. 117b
　than smiles of other m. are 97b
　twenty love-sick m. we 165a
　what m. loth? 219b

Maidens (cont.)
young fair m. quiet eyes 414b
young men and m. 490a
youths and m. gay! 100a
Maids: but our cold m. 336a
fashion for the m. in France 383b
free m. that weave their thread 371a
if seven m. with seven mops 84a
m. are May when they are m. 327b
m. come forth sprig-muslin drest 180a
m. dance in a ring 286a
m. lie on their backs 365a
m. must kiss no men 35b
m. of matchless beauty 235a
m. strange seraphic pieces 445a
malady most incident to m. 373b
three little m. from school 164b
to lie between m.' legs 334a
welcome m. of honour 190b
Maid-servants: getting instructed 81a
Mail: out of fashion, like a rusty m. 369a
the Overland M. 233a
Mailed: seen the m. lobster rise 157b
Maimed: the spent and m. among 226a
Main: arose from out the azure m. 443a
comes silent, flooding in, the m. 96b
curled waters 'bove the m. 342b
far amid the melancholy m. 443a
glorious th' enraptured m. 403a
great river take me to the m. 436b
idlest froth amid the boundless m. 38b
like the troubled m. 160a
skims along the m. 300a
Maine: remember the M.! 526a
Maintain: this is law, I will m. 524a
Maire: thy famous M. 143a
Maisie: proud M. is in the wood 319b
Maize: lands of..m. and vine 426a
with Plenty in the m. 437a
Majestic: m. tho' in ruin 272b
m. yet sedate 305b
Majestical: happy, high, m. 395a
we do it wrong, being so m. 329b
Majesty: an infinite M. 478a
attribute to awe and m. 354b
her ebon throne in rayless m. 477a
in naked m. seemed lords of all 274a
ride on! ride on in m.! 266b
sight so touching in its m. 472b
sweetness, mercy, m. 249b
the appearance of Your M. 492a
the next in m. 141a
think it kindness to his M. 178a
this earth of m. 375a
Thy m. how bright 149b
who, busied in his m. 381b
yr. M.'s will is law 165a
Major-General: a modern M. 166b
Majority: death joins us to the..m. 477b
gone over to the m. 80a
m. is always the best repartee 130a
one, on God's side, is a m. 296b
Make: a Scotsman on the m. 21b
does not usually m. anything 296b
he did us m. 224b
I cd. not well m. out 406a
I too will something m. 36b
m. it soft and narrow 531b
m. more opportunities than he
    finds 16b
nothing can m. her 416a
one of them said to his m. 529b
ten to m. and the match to win 287b
what m. ye and what strive for? 36a
Makeless: maiden that is m. 524a
Maker: m. is himself y-beten 90a
more pure than his m. 497a
scatter'd his M.'s image 138a
show the M.'s glory 176b
syng laudes to their m. 182b
the m. buried 414b
Makers: t' abhor the m. 140b
Makes: m. the happiness..does
    not find 214a
night that..m. me or fordoes me 363b
tongue of him that m. it 345b
Makest: what m. thou? 502b
Making: joy in the m. 36b
praise the Lord for m. her 230b
take pleasure in m. 526b
Makings of a queen 386a

Maladies: Pill for..the m. of Society 81a
soul with all its m. 292b
Malady: m. most incident to maids 373b
medicine worse than the m. 23a
Male: m. and female created he them 492a
more deadly than the m. 229a
rough m. kiss of blankets 39a
Malefactions: proclaimed their m. 333a
Males: compose nothing but m. 347b
Malfi: Duchess of M. still 454b
Malice: envy, hatred, and m. 478b
Envy, M., are his Graces 240b
I fight of treasonous m. 348a
leaven of m. and wickedness 479b
m. and contentious crimes 408b
m. domestic, foreign levy 348b
m. never was his aim 419a
men, and m. to breed 216a
much m. mingled with..wit 140b
nor set down aught in m. 364a
not with the old leaven..of m. 514a
whilst our poor m. remains 348b
with m. toward none 245b
Malignity: motiveless m. 102b
Mallow: the slimy m. 114a
Malmsey and Malvoisie 25b
Malt: Duke of Norfolk deals in m. 178a
m. does more than Milton can 199b
rat that ate the m. 534b
Malta: under M. by the sea 231a
Malvoisie: Malmsey and M. 25b
Malvolio: sick of self love, M. 370a
Mamilius: Herminius smote M. 254a
the Tusculan M. 253a
Mammocked: how he m. it! 328a
Mammon: M. led them on 272a
M., the least erected Spirit 272a
the m. of unrighteousness 509b
ye cannot serve God and m. 505b
Mammy: lookin' at his m. 410a
Man: Adam, the goodliest m. of men 274a
a good old man, sir 359a
ah, for a m. to arise in me 433b
ah, God for a m. with heart 433b
a House that armours a m. 26a
all, save the spirit of m. 67b
all that makes a m. 428a
all that was pleasant in m. 169b
alone, a banished m. 529b
a m. all light, a seraph-m. 99b
a m. can have but one life 44b
a m...divine as myself is dead 457b
a m. he must go with a woman 232b
a m. in khaki kit 233a
a M. like to me 51b
a m. may drink 63a, 320b
a m. may fight and no be slain
    63a, 320b
a m. may kiss a bonnie lass 63a, 320b
a m. of an unbounded stomach 386a
a m. of hope and forward-looking 464b
a m. of infinite..resource 237a
a m. of mean estate 136b
a m. of my kidney 356a
a m. of such a feeble temper 337b
a m.'s a m. for a' that 60b
a m. sent from God 510b
a m. severe he was 168b
a m. so various that he seem'd 138b
a m.'s worth something 45a
a m. when breast to breast 312a
a m. who has no office to go to 390b
a m. who is good enough to shed 310a
a m. with his back to the East 98a
a merrier m., within the limit 344b
and the last m. in 287b
an honest exceeding poor m. 353b
an honest m., close-buttoned 109a
an old m., broken with the storms 386a
any m. may be in good spirits 123b
any m. obtain that wh. he merits 101a
any m. that walks the mead 426b
a plain, blunt m. 340a
apparel oft proclaims the m. 330b
appear like m. and wife 95a
a proper m., as one shall see 356b
arms, and the m. I sing 142b
around the m. bend other faces 240b
art thou a M. of purple cheer? 468b
as a dead m. out of mind 483b
as if a m. were author of himself 328b

Man (cont.)
as nature first made m. 139b
a soldier's a m. 361a
at thirty m. suspects himself 477a
a very foolish, fond old m. 344a
a very unclubbable m. 207b
a' was a merry m. 364b
away, slight m.! 340b
bears up this corpse wh. is m. 423b
because a m. has shop to mind 51b
before M. made us citizens 250b
behold a m. raised up by Christ 430a
behold the m. 511b
believe it not, O M. 96b
better angel is a m. right fair 389b
better spar'd a better m. 379a
bird whom m. loves 470a
bite so good a m. 169a
bold bad m. 385b, 408b
breathes there the m. 317a
breath of m. goeth forth 490b
brute to the soul of a m. 426a
but every m. a liar 513a
but m. after his death moot wepe 89a
but m. passionless? 397b
but pitied the m. 110b
by his Spirit in the inner m. 515b
by m. came death 515a
called her his before the holy m. 77a
cash..sole nexus of m. to m. 80b
cease ye from m. 501a
cells and gibbets for 'the m.' 106a
childhood shows the m. 277a
Christian, pagan, nor m. 333b
cold charities of m. to m. 114a
corruption of M.'s Heart 46b
cd. m. outlook that mark! 448a
crucifix..keeps a m. from harm 227a
crucify the old m. 481a
dare do all that may become a m. 347a
dares the m. put off the prophet 49a
deny a god destroy m.'s nobility 15a
devotion from any sort of m. 237b
diapason closing full in M. 139b
discerning intellect of M. 464a
dream'd of such a kind of m. 381a
dull ear of a drowsy m. 374a
each m. render me his bloody
    hand 339b
earl by right, by courtesy a m. 12a
earth and m. were gone 38b
ech m. for him-self 89a
end of m. is an action 81b
ere m.'s corruptions made him 291a
evasion of whoremaster m. 342a
even such a m., so faint 379b
every m. (gained) by (flattery) 91a
every m. in arms shd. wish to be 465a
every m. is..an idler 213a
every m. living is..vanity 484a
every m.'s hand against him 492b
every m...Bolingbroke..press'd 375a
every m. therefore is but vanity 484a
every m. who is high up 21b
every m. who lives is born to die 141a
every m...was God or Devil 138b
every minute dies a m. 523a
exercise all functions of a m. 112a
eye of m. hath not heard 357b
find that cursed m., low sitting 408b
first-class fightin' m. 229a
first m. is of the earth, earthy 515a
first m. thou mayest meet 445b
foot-in-the-grave young m. 165b
for a rational m. to play 171b
for it is the number of a m. 519a
for M.'s fault, then was the thorn 191a
for m. to meet and master 51b
for m.'s illusion given 282b
frailty of m. without thee 479b
gave to the m. despotic power 278a
gently scan yr. brother m. 59a
get a new m. 367b
gird on thy sword, O m. 36b
gird up now thy loins like a m. 497b
give a m. a horse 444a
given to the common enemy of m. 348b
gives to m. or woman his heart 198b
glory of m. as the flower of grass 517b
God above or m. below 300b
God by m. as godlike trod 422b

Man (*cont.*)

God hath made m. upright	499b
God is not a m.	494a
God made the woman for the m.	426b
God's a good m.	359a
good compensate bad in m.	51b
good Lord, what is m.!	62b
good m. was ther of religioun	88b
good name in m. or woman	361b
goodness is imprinted..in..m.	15a
greatest m. you had ever yet seen	212a
grown to m.'s estate	414a
handsome, well-shaped m.	11a
hang the m. over again	19b
happy the m., and happy he alone	142a
has not m. a microscopic eye?	300b
hath m. no second life	5a
heart of a m. to..a maid	229b
Heaven had made her such a m.	360a
he shall live a m. forbid	346a
he was a good m., and a just	510a
he was a m., take him for all	330a
he was six foot o' m., A 1	250b
his little world of m.	342b
horse..a vain thing to save a m.	484a
hour is come, but not the m.	319b
how can m. die better	253a
how he lies in his rights of a m.	44b
how poor a thing is m.	117a, 464b
I am a m., I count nothing human	554a
I am a m. of authority	506a
I am a worm, and no m.	483a
if a m. say, I love God	518a
if m., of all the Creator plann'd	171b
if such a m. there be	303a
I have a m.'s mind	339a
I know not the m.	508a
I know the m. that must hear me	100a
I'm a m. of propertee	165b
I'm truly sorry m.'s dominion	62a
I must also feel it as a m.	350a
infirm, weak, and despised old m.	342b
in one the frailty of m.	14a
in the likeness of a fat old m.	377b
in the mind of m.	472a
in the Parliament of m.	432b
in this corporal earth of m.	441b
in wit a m., simplicity a child	299b
I saw an aged, aged m.	85a
is m. an ape or an angel?	128b
I think that m. was I	530b
I was an austere m.	510a
je-ne-sais-quoi young m.!	165b
justify God's ways to m.	199b
keep down the base in m.	428a
killed..that old m. eloquent	278b
king is but a m., as I am	382b
know what God and m. is	427a
lasting joys the m. attend	459a
legs without the m.	112b
let him pass for a m.	353a
let no m. put asunder	481b
let not m. put asunder	507a
let the end try the m.	380a
'let there be blood!' says m.	71a
let us make m. in our image	492a
life of a m...a heroic poem	80a
life of m. less than a span	17a
like a m. inspired	465b
like a m. made after supper	380b
like a strong m. after sleep	279a
like master, like m.	150b
Lord God formed m. of the dust	492a
made his work, for m. to mend	140a
make me mistress to the m. I love	299b
making a poet out of a m.	43b
M. accepts the compromise	229a
m. after his own heart	495a
m. all tattered and torn	534a
m. and a woman in a garden	460b
m. and bird and beast	100a
m. and wife..never..power to hang one another	150a
m.,—arrayed for mutual slaughter	468a
m. as he is *not* to be	183a
m...aware of his life's flow	5a
m. became a living soul	492a
m. being in honour	485a
m. be more pure than his maker?	497a
m. by nothing is so well bewray'd	409a
m. cannot choose but pay	293a

Man (*cont.*)

m. clothed in soft raiment	506b
m. comes and tills the field	438a
m. delights me not	332b
m. did eat angels' food	487a
m. did not make, and cannot mar	6b
m. does not live by bread alone	148a
m. doth not live by bread only	494b
m. dreams of fame	428b
m., equal and one with me	422b
m. equal, unclassed, tribeless	397b
m., false m.	244a
m...far gone from..righteousness	491b
m. fell into his anecdotage	129b
m. for the field	436b
m. for the sword	436b
m. goeth forth to his work	488b
m. goeth to his long home	499b
M. has Forever	47a
m. hath all wh. Nature hath	9a
m. have the upper hand	482a
m. he was to all the country dear	168b
m. in his hasty days	36b
m. in the bush with God may meet	146b
m. in the wilderness asked me	534a
m...in whose rich soul	136b
m. is..a bundle of contradictions	103b
m. is an embodied paradox	103b
M. is a noble animal	42b
m. is..a political animal	559a
m. is a religious animal	57a
m. is as old as he's feeling	102b
m. is a tool-making animal	157a
m. is a tool-using animal	81b
m. is born free	565b
m. is born unto trouble	497a
m. is but a devil weakly fettered	412b
m. is distinguished..by laughter	2b
m. is God's image	186b
M. is Heaven's masterpiece	307a
m. I shd. avoid so soon	338a
m. is m. and master of his fate	428b
m. is m.'s ABC	307a
m. is Nature's sole mistake!	166b
m. is not a fly	300b
m. is not m. as yet	49b
m. is of kin to beasts	15a
m. is one world	187b
m. is only a reed	564b
m. is only truly great	129b
m...is small potatoes	237a
m. is the hunter	436b
m. is the maker of his..fortune	410b
M. is the Master of things	423a
m. is the measure of all things	560a
m...lays his hand upon a woman	444b
m...lives..by catchwords	413a
m. looketh on the outward	495b
m. looks aloft	142b
m. made the town	111b
m. maketh ofte a yerde	90a
m. marks the earth with ruin	69b
m. may escape from rope	159b
m. more sinned against	342b
m...must get drunk	70b
m. must play a part	352b
m. must serve his time	72a
m. never is, but always to be	300b
M. of baser Earth didst make	154a
m. of sense only trifles with them	91a
M. of sorrows had a part	53a
m...only one..torture..amusing	157b
m. partly is and..hopes to be	46a
M. propounds negotiations	229a
m., proud m.	351b
m., put thy old cloak about thee!	524b
m. remains sceptreless	397b
m.'s Babylons strive..to impart	441b
m.'s chief pleasure is society?	117b
m.'s congregation shun	441a
m.'s desire is for the woman	102b
m.'s distinctive mark	46a
m. seeketh in society comfort	13a
m. seems the only growth	170a
M.'s Forgiveness give—and take!	154a
m. shall have his mare	357a
m. shall not live by bread alone	505a
m.'s heart is evil from his youth	492a
m.'s heart is small	235a
m.'s image and his cry	476a
m.'s inhumanity to m.	61b

Man (*cont.*)

m.'s life is cheap as beasts	342b
m.'s love is of m.'s life..apart	70a
m...some did count him mad	54b
m.'s the gowd for a' that	60b
m...still bears..stamp of..origin	117b
m.'s strength to comfort	228a
m. struggling..in the water	206b
m.'s unconquerable mind	472b
m.'s unhappiness, as I construe	81b
m.'s word is God in m.	427b
m. that is born of a woman	481b, 497a
m. that is I	422b
m. that is made of me	422b
m. that is not passion's slave	334a
m. that meddles with cold iron!	65a
M.! the pilgrim of a day	77b
m. to command..woman to obey	436b
m. to double business bound	334b
m. to m...the greatest curse	19a
m. to m. the warld o'er	60b
m. walketh in a vain shadow	484a
m. wants but little	169a, 477b
m. was formed for society	28b
m. was made for Joy and Woe	29b
m. was made to mourn	61b
m. who cd. make so vile a pun	120a
m. who has the power and skill	528a
M., who is from God sent	465a
m. who needlessly sets foot	112b
m., whose blood is warm	352b
m. who used to notice such things	179a
m...with a muck-rake in his hand	54a
m. without religion	181a
m. with the head	436b
m. will go down to the pit	18a
m...woman's cully made	104b
many years a mortal m. may live	384a
Master Ridley..play the m.	242b
means for every m. alive	322a
mind of m...more beautiful	470a
mind 's the standard of the m.	453a
moral centaur, m. and wife	71a
more like a whore's than a m.'s	232b
more than m. to wish thee so	281a
moulded by the lips of m.	439a
my handsome young m.	529b
my m. Friday with me	118b
my only study..is m.	34a
Nature made thee to temper m.	291b
neither is any mighty m. delivered	484a
neither m. nor angel can discern	273b
neither m., nor muse, can praise	215b
never had..m. such opportunity	71b
never m. spake like this m.	511a
never yet was noble m.	428b
new m. may be raised up in him	481a
noblest work of m.	67a, 203b
noisy m. is always in the right	108a
no m. does. That is his	460a
no m. hath seen God	510b, 518a
no m. is born into the world	250a
no m. is born unto himself	307a
no m. need boast their love	35b
no m...true to his wife, or can be	447b
nor M. nor Boy	466b
nothing to do with that just m.	508a
not good that the m. shd. be alone	492a
not know the garment from the m.	30a
not the bond of m. and wife	428b
not yet old enough for a m.	370a
nowher so bisy a m. as he	88b
O brother m.!	458b
o'er all this scene of m.	300b
of...m.'s clotted clay the dingiest	442a
of M.'s first disobedience	270b
of m.'s miraculous mistakes	477a
O good old m.!	326a
oh! mystery of m.	470a
old m. with an old soul	74b
O M. that from thy fair..youth	463b
O men, this m. in brotherhood	43a
once on a time there was a M.	235a
one m. among a thousand	499b
one m. picked out of ten thousand	321a
one m. with a dream	291a
one still strong m.	433b
only a m. harrowing clods	179b
only m. is vile	184a
on M., on Nature..musing	464a
open not thine heart to every m.	520b

Man (cont.)

O selfless m. and..gentleman 429a
out of me God and m. 422a
outward semblance of a m. 126b
owe more tears to this dead m. 341b
O wretched m. that I am 513a
pass m.'s understanding 479b
pays to trusted m...annual visit 443b
poor m. that hangs on princes' 386a
preaching m.'s immense stupidity 45b
prentice han' she tried on m. 60b
present hour alone is m.'s 213a
proper study of mankind is m. 301a
put m.'s best dreams to shame 44a
rash, refined, presumptuous m. 79a
ready now to call a m. *a good m.* 211a
right m. in the right place 205a
right m. to fill the right place 243a
rocking a grown m. in the cradle 58a
rood of ground maintained its m. 168a
rough and ready m. that write 45a
round, fat, oily m. of God 443a
running a m. down 418a
Sabbath was made for m. 508a
sadder and a wiser m. 100a
Saint nor Sophist led, but be a m. 5a
saucy look of an assured m. 105b
scarce be a m. before thy mother 23a
sees m. control the wind 5b
sensible, and well-bred m. 108a
seven women..take hold of one m. 501a
shake a m.'s faith in himself 390a
shall a young m. cleanse his way 489a
shall..m. be more just than God 497a
shall m. into the mystery..spy 263b
she knows her m. 142b
shew all, that might be in m. 136b
sinful m. beneath the sky 224a
single m. in possession of..fortune 11b
sober m. among his boys 430a
so can I, or so can any m. 378a
social, friendly, honest m. 60a
so is it now I am a m. 468a
some divinely gifted m. 430b
so much one m. can do 261a
so near is God to m. 147a
Son of M. in weary Night's 30a
son of m., that thou visitest him? 482a
soul of the m. on its breast 6a
so unto the m. is woman 248b
strain of m.'s bred out 368a
strange what a m. may do 439b
strive to be a m. before yr. mother 107b
striving to be m., the worm mounts 146b
strong..m., to clean horses 417a
surely m. is a broomstick! 418a
teach you more of m. 471b
tell me a m.'s a foxhunter 416b
that low m. goes on adding 47a
that low m. seeks a little thing 47a
that make ingrateful m. 342b
that parchment..shd. undo a m. 384a
that thorn-crowned M.! 7a
that wild beast m. 33b
the best good m. 399b
the Child is father of the M. 468a
the grave m., nicknamed Adam 96a
the holy spirit of m. 420b
the inner m. 481b
the m. hath penance done 99b
the m. I am may cease to be! 433b
the m. in the street 176b
the m...is absolutely fixed on 151a
the M. of England circled 263a
the m. perceives it die away 466b
the m. recovered of the bite 169a
the m. sprang to his feet 47b
the m. that hails you Tom or Jack 108a
the M., who, lifted high 465b
the mildest mannered m. 70b
the most senseless and fit m. 358b
the old m. kindly answered 236a
the people arose as one m. 495a
the play is the tragedy, 'M.' 298a
there came to the making of m. 420b
there is a m. child conceived 497a
there is an old poor m. 326b
the relief of m.'s estate 13a
there was an Old M. in a boat 243a
there was an Old M. in a tree 243a
there was an old m. of Boulogne 527a

Man (cont.)

there was an old m. who said, 'Hush!' 243b
there was an Old M. with a beard 243a
the ruins of the noblest m. 339b
the secret'st m. of blood 349a
these last strands of m. 197a
the state of m...a little kingdom 338b
the substance of men wh. is m. 423a
the White M.'s burden 236b
they are neither m. nor woman 298a
think of it, dissolute m.! 196a
this dust was once the m. 458b
this foolish-compounded clay, m. 379b
this high m., aiming at a million 47a
this high m., with a great thing 47a
this is a slight unmeritable m. 340b
this is not the m. 381a
this is the state of m. 385b
this little kingdom, m., to arm 380b
this is loved *me* 241b
this pure young m. 165b
this was a m.! 341a
thou art e'en as just a m. 334a
thou art the m. 495b
thou best-humoured m. 169b
thou excellent young m. 313b
thou..large-hearted m. 43b
thou madest m., he knows not why 429b
thousandth M. will stand by 235a
thou stalk o' carl-hemp in m. 59a
thou turnest m. to destruction 487b
thro' this m. and me hath..war 257b
thus the child imposes on the m. 140b
'tis an Old M. grey 29b
'tis m.'s perdition to be safe 147a
'tis not what m. does wh. exalts 51b
to be a well-favoured m. 358b
to be m. with thy might 422b
to cheat a m. is nothing 159b
to every m. a damsel 495a
to every m. upon this earth 253a
told the..stars the Grief of M. 234b
took a m.'s life along with him 80b
tresses m.'s imperial race insnare 302b
truth..the friend of m. 77b
tun of m. is thy companion 377b
unaccommodated m. is no more 343a
unless he first spell M. 307a
untainted by m.'s misery 398b
unto the m. of yearning thought 313a
unwise m. doth not well consider 487b
Valoroso is a m. again 440a
voice of a god, and not of a m. 512a
vulgar works of m. 469a
wanderer is m. from his birth 6a
Waterloo House young m. 165b
way of a m. with a maid 499a
were m. but constant 372b
what a piece of work is a m.! 332b
what bloody m. is that 345b
whate'er afflict the m. 136b
what every m. may do 209a
what is a m. if..but to sleep 335b
what is m., that thou art mindful 482a
what m. has made of m. 471a
what m. shd. ever be 72b
what signifies the life o' m. 60b
when a m. bites a dog 116b
when a m. shd. marry 14b
when a strong m. armed 509a
when god first maked m. 89a
when he thinks, good easy m. 385b
when I became a m. 514b
when I came to m.'s estate 372a
when M. is the Turk 92b
wherever a m. goes 444a
whether m.'s heart or life it be 442a
while m. there walked 261a
who kills a m. kills..God's image 279a
who's master, who's m. 419b
whoso sheddeth m.'s blood 492b
whoso wd. be a m. 147b
who touches this touches a m. 458b
why, m. of morals, tell me why? 106b
wisest m. the warl'saw 60b
woman the lesser m. 432b
woman's cause is m.'s 437a
worth makes the m. 301b
wrath of m. worketh not 517a
wrestled a m. with him 493a

Man (cont.)

wretched m. outlive his wealth 355a
writing (maketh) an exact m. 16a
you gods, a poor old m. 342b
you'll be a M., my Son! 230a
young lassie do wi' an auld m. 63a
young m. feels his pockets 200a
young m. kindly answered 236a
you're not a m., you're a machine 389b
Manager, actor, prompter 181a
Manasses is mine 485b
Man-at-arms must now serve 295b
Mandalay: come you back to M. 232a
from Rangoon to M. 232a
on the road to M. 232a
Mandate: thus the royal m. ran 60a
Mandragon: Mr. M., the millionaire 92a
Mandragora: give me to drink m. 323a
not poppy, nor m. 362a
Mandrake: get with child a m. root 134a
Mane: grasped the m. with both.. hands 108b
my hand upon thy m. 69b
seized fast the flowing m. 108b
thin m., thick tail 386b
Manes: plats the m. of horses 365a
Manger: cold, and not too cleanly, m. 114b
in a m, for His bed 3b
in homely m. trembling 407b
in the rude m. lies 270a
One born in a m. 448a
to dog in the m. some liken I cd. 446a
Mangerful of hay
Mangle: immense pecuniary M. 127b
Mangler in a million 125b
Manhood: by taking of the M. into God 478b
Fate reserves for a bright m. 252a
find thy M. all too fast 195b
hardened into the bone of the m. 55b
in conspiracy against the m. 147b
in the glory of his m. 12a
M. a struggle 129a
m. full and fair 37a
m. taken by the Son 288b
neither..m., nor good fellowship 376b
no sounder piece of British m. 80b
robs me of my m. 139a
Manhoods: hold their m. cheap 383a
Mania of owning things 458a
Maniac: poets, from a m.'s tongue 43a
Time, a m. scattering dust 430a
Manifest: man's work..made m. 514a
my..soul shall m. me rightly 359b
our m. destiny to overspread 291a
Manifold stories, I know 75b
Mankind: all the happiness m. can gain 140b
all m.'s epitome 138b
as a spectator of m. 1b
as I know more of m. 211a
but itself to teach it to m. 36a
common dispositions of..m. 56b
crucify m. upon a cross of gold 53a
deceived the mother of m. 270b
example is the school of m. 58a
fleeting generations of m. 399b
fly from, need not be to hate, m. 68b
for an apple damn'd m. 291b
Gods together, careless of m. 433a
he's an enemy to m. 371b
if all m. minus one 266a
in my mind, of all m. 529b
in th' original perused m. 266a
justified in silencing m. 266a
make m., in conscious virtue bold 298a
m. are the asses who pull 72b
m... hosts and guests 24b
m.'s concern is charity 301b
m. will not be reasoned 28b
mistress all m. pursue 457a
retrench the superfluities of m. 159b
shut the gates of mercy on m. 174b
survey m., from China to Peru 213b
things..in the saddle, and ride m. 146b
to party..what was meant for m. 169b
to you and all m. 424b
Manlier: nobler and the m. one 71a
Manliness: silent m. of grief 169a
Manly: I love a m....moral liberty 56b
Man-milliner: architectural m. 313b

Manna: his tongue dropt m. 272a
m. and dates, in argosy 221b
news, the m. of a day 175b
we loath'd our m. 141a
Manned by Manning 51a
Manner: a m. rude and wild 25b
as the manner of some is 517a
a very good bedside m. 535b
forgetteth what m. of man 517b
Socratic m. is not a game 25a
the m. of his speech 323a
think about the m. of doing it 183b
to the m. born 331a
Manners: catch the m. living 300b
combines the m. of a Marquis 166b
corrupt good m. 515a
first for m.' sake 520b
France..influenced m. in England 57a
her m. had not that repose 431b
his m. are not so polite 233a
his m. our heart 169b
his m. were gentle 169b
I describe not men, but m. 151a
I know their tricks and their m. 125b
m. are not idle 427b
m., climates, councils 438b
'Next Poet'—(M., Ben!) 48b
not good m. to mention here 40b
Peel has no m. 455a
polish'd m. and fine sense 112b
so near the m. of my mother 370a
so well bewrayed, as by his m. 409a
sundry times and in divers m. 517a
take their m. from the ape 25b
teach..m. of a dancing master 206b
with sweeter m., purer laws 431a
Manning: manned by M. 51a
Manningtree ox 377b
Manor: sold a goodly m. for a song 322a
Man-o'-War's 'er 'usband 231b
Mansion: back to its m. call 174a
Jove's Court my m. is 266b
made his everlasting m. 368a
upon thy fading m. spend 389b
Mansionary: his loved m. 347a
Mansions: build thee more stately m. 194a
in my father's house are many m. 511a
lasting m. of the dead 113b
to m. in the skies 453b
where the many m. be 86a
Mantalini: Mr. M. 124a, b, 125a
Mrs. M. 124b
Mantle: Elijah..cast his m. upon
him 496a
green m. of the standing pool 343a
in his m. muffling up his face 340a
m. like a standing pond 352b
morn, in russet m. clad 329b
o'er..dark her silver m. threw 274a
twitched his m. blue 270a
wrapt in scarlet m. warm 109b
wrapt thy form in a m. grey 399a
you all do know this m. 340a
Mantovano: I salute thee, M. 439a
Mantuan: M. swan was heard 111b
Old M.! old M.! 344b
pretty i' the M.! 75b
Manual: no M., no letters 74b
Manure: it is its natural m. 204b
Manuscript: Youth's sweet-
scented M. 154a
Manxome foe he sought 83b
Many: as it were a monster unto m. 486b
do you ask me how m. I'd have? 461a
election by the incompetent m. 391a
few shall part where m. meet 77a
how m. among us at this very hour 427b
if so, how m.? (measles) 451a
madness of m...gain of a few 304a
m. are called, but few are chosen 507b
m. have fallen by the..sword 520b
m. shall run to and fro 504a
m. still must labour for the one 69b
m. there be that go in thereat 505b
m. things to fear 15a
my name is Legion, for we are m. 508b
party is the madness of the m. 419a
the m. change and pass 392b
the m. fail: the one succeeds 426b
the mutable, rank-scented m. 328a
there's a tree, of m., one 466a

Many (cont.)
the unheeding m. he did move 399a
what are they among so m. 510b
ye are m., they are few 395b
yes, sir, m. men, m. women 207a
Many-headed monster..multitude 262b
Map: m. me no maps 151b
m. with the augmentation 371b
my head is a m. 151b
roll up that m. 297b
Maple: extremely like M. Grove 11a
Maps: geographers, in Africa m. 419b
Geography is about m. 27b
Mar: Colonel to the Earl of M. 298b
man did not make, and cannot m. 6b
oft we m. what's well 342a
Marathon: M. looks on the sea 70b
mountains look on M. 70b
Marble: dreamt that I dwelt in m.
halls 53b
forget thyself to m. 268a
found it brick and left it m. 538a
in water writ, but this in m. 23a
m. index of a mind 469b
nor, in thy m. vault, shall sound 260a
not m., nor the gilded monuments 387b
sleep in dull cold m. 386a
wax to receive and m. to retain 67b
Marbled: Sunium's m. steep 71a
Marcellus exiled feels 301b
March: ashbuds in the front of M. 427a
beware the Ides of M. 337b
boundary of the m. of a nation 292b
day's m. nearer home 280a
deil dinna ye m. forward 320a
droghte of M. hath perced 88a
hem his watery m. 8a
iambics m. from short to long 101b
in the mad M. days 261b
in the wild M.-morning 434b
long majestic m, 303b
M. dust to be sold 445a
m. is o'er the mountain waves 78a
m., m., Eskdale and Liddesdale 320a
m., m., Ettrick and Teviotdale 320a
m. of the human mind is slow 55b
'm. on!' he said 459a
M. sun feels like May 48b
M. winds and April showers 525a
remember M., the ides of M. 340b
sea-blue bird of M. 430b
stablish, continue our m. 7b
take the winds of M. with beauty 373a
the ides of M. are come 339a
the m. of intellect 407a
the m. of mind 295a
the month..that highte M. 89a
we shall m. prospering 48a
whenever a M.-wind sighs 434a
with merry m. bring home 381b
March-bloom, like on..sallows 198a
Marched..'ave..m.—six—weeks in
'Ell 227b
he marched them down again 526b
he m. them up to the top 526b
m. into their land 12b
Marches: our delightful m. to..
measures 384b
slow howe'er my m. be 225b
March Hare: 'Why not?' said the M. 83a
Marching: his truth is m. on 200b
Johnny Comes M. Home Again 527b
m. along, fifty score strong 45b
m. as to war 20a
m. thro' Georgia 473a
m. where it likes 9b
passed from Egypt m. 271b
Marcus: first, M. Brutus 339b
Mare: bay m. shames silliness 458a
Flanders m. 571b
lend me yr. grey m. 531b
man shall have his m. again 357a
woa, m.! woa, m.! 162b
Marengo: this is our M. 135b
Margaret: Clerk Saunders and
Mary M. 529a
M. and Rosalys 311b
M., Maude, or Cecily 294b
Merry M., the midsummer flower 402b
noble M. Newcastle 239a
Margate: in M. last July 19b

Margate (cont.)
on M. beach 196a
Marge: every m. enclosing 429a
having an ample m. 429a
m. of each cold Hebrid isle 103a
Margent: Meander's m. green 267a
Margery Daw 533b
Margin: picture on the m. wrought 137b
thro' a meadow of m. 400b
world, whose m. fades for ever 438b
Maria: Ave M.! 'tis the hour 71a
Mariana: resides this dejected M. 352a
Marie: M. Carmichael, and me 530a
M. Hamilton's to the kirk gane 530a
M. Seaton and M. Beaton 530a
Maries: the Queen had four M. 530a
Marigold, that goes to bed 373a
Marigolds: no m. yet closed are 190a
Mariner: came to the m.'s hollo! 98b
God save thee, ancient M.! 98b
I fear thee, ancient M. 99a
it is an ancient M. 98a
or the m., worn and wan 395a
the bright-eyed M. 98a
the M. hath his will 98a
Mariners: best pilots..need of m. 215a
loves to talk with m. 99b
my m., souls that have toil'd 439a
rest ye, brother m. 433a
we be three poor m. 308b
ye M. of England 77b
Marivaux and Crebillon 175b
Marjoram: mints, savory, m. 373a
Mark: cd. man outlook that m. 448a
finds m. the archer little meant 317b
go, m. him well 317a
Gray's poetry..above..common
m. 209a
I press toward the m. 516a
it is an ever-fixed m. 389a
I will stand and m. 438a
Matthew, M., Luke and John 2b
m. my footsteps, good my page 286b
m., or the name of the beast 519a
read, m., learn 479a
straight to the self-same m. 48a
sure he shall never hit the m. 401b
Mark Antony's was by Cæsar 348b
Marked: God..marked him for his
own 450b
if we are m. to die 383a
Market: chief good and m. of his
time 335b
Market-gardener: marry a m. 125a
Market-place: Antony, enthroned i'
the m. 323a
Idols of the M. 16b
noonday, upon the m. 338a
Markets: great m. by the sea 154b
Marking: the malady of not m. 379b
Marks: nobody m. you 358a
Marl: clod of wayward m. 358a
over the burning m. 271b
Marlborough: from M.'s eyes..
dotage flew 214a
praise the Duke of M. won 406a
Marlowe's mighty line 216a
Marmaduke: Astley, and Sir M. 252b
Marmion: good-night to M. 318b
the last words of M. 318b
Marocco: Damasco or M. 271b
Marquis: manners of a M. 166b
m., duke and a' that 60b
the M. gazed a moment 12b
Married: all that's spoke is m. 364a
a young man married is..m. 322a
is thy earth so m. 442a
soon m. are those too early made 364b
Marriage: coldly furnish..the m.
tables 330a
courtship to m...witty prologue 105a
every m. then is best in tune 452a
gentleman..'very unhappy in m. 208a
good hanging prevents a bad m. 370a
hanging and m...go by Destiny 150b
in m., a man becomes slack 413a
is not m. an open question 148b
it won't be a stylish m. 116b
m. and death and division 421a
m. has many pains 213b
m. is..a civil contract 321a

Marriage (cont.)

m. is a step so grave 413a
m. is like life in this 413a
m. is popular because it combines 391a
m. supper of the lamb 519b
m. the happiest bond of love 173a
marrying and giving in m. 507b
merry as a m. bell 68a
more for a m. than a ministry 17b
must be my m. fee 225b
neither marry, nor are given in m. 507b
O curse of m.! 362a
rich hues have m. made 36b
rob a lady . . by way of m. 151b
satisfaction, if . . any in m. 160a
talk . . about the blessings of m. 391a
the m. with his brother's wife 385b
this Rachel-and-Leah is m. 96a
tho' m. makes . . one flesh 104a
to the m. of true minds 389a
was m. ever out of fashion? 66a
with dirge in m. 329a
with the vow I made to her in m. 331b
Marriage-feast: sweeter than the m. 100a
Marriages: best maker of all m. 383b
m. and public executions 130a
m. . . made by the Lord Chancellor 209a
only give a bust of m. 70b
reasons why so few m. are happy 419a
we will have no more m. 333b
widows exclaim . . against second m.151a
Married: Alfred and I intended to
be m. 38b
at leisure m., . . repent in haste 105a
aunts, who are not m. 93b
Benedick the m. man 358a
cuckoo . . mocks m. men 345b
delight we m. people have 296a
ere I will be m. to a sponge 353a
he is dreadfully m. 451b
honest man who m. . . more service 171a
how will he be m. 534b
if ever we had been m. 159a
I'm to be m. to-day 163b
in m. life three is company 460a
I wd. be m. to a single life 114b
like to be m. to a poem 223a
maids . . to kiss before they are m. 383b
m. and gone to New Zealand 96a
m. and woo'd and a' 310b
m., charming, chaste 70a
m. in haste . . repent at leisure 105a
m. man dies in good stile 451a
m. past redemption 141a
m. to a mer-ma-id 525b
m. to immortal verse 269a
mostly m. people 96a
most m. man I ever saw 451b
now we're m. spier nae mair 63a
once you are m. . . nothing left 413a
one fool . . in every m. couple 151a
one was never m. . . his hell 64a
Reader, I m. him 38a
rogue is m. to a whore 234a
some were m., wh. was bad 237a
think I shd. live till I were m. 358b
thinks she's not a-goin' to be m. 417a
till anes we m. be 529a
true, I have m. her 360a
wen you're a m. man, Samivel 126b
wench who is just m. 159b
woo'd and m. and a' 528b
word . . unpleasing to a m. ear 345b
you, that are going to be m. 170b
young man m. is a man . . marred 322a
Marries: m., dies, or turns Hindoo 395b
times . . changed with him who m. 413a
Marrow: busk ye, my winsome m. 178b
Marry: advice to persons about to m. 535a
and why they m. them 247b
as easy to m. a rich woman 440a
better to m. than to burn 514a
come hame, my love, to m. thee 20b
doânt thou m. for monny 434b
he ever means to m. any vun 127a
he's going to m. Yum-Yum 164b
how can a bishop m.? 404b
if I shd. m. him 353a
if you do not m. Mr. Collins 11b
I shd. m. twenty husbands 353a
Man may not m. his grandmother 491b

Marry (cont.)

m. Ann . . no more inspiration 390b
m. thee, purely to be rid of thee 105a
m. yr. old friend's love 52a
neither m., nor . . given in marriage 507b
no woman shd. m. a teetotaller 413a
pretty maiden, will you m. me? 165b
question when a man shd. m. 14b
quite prepared to m. again 163b
sure to m. a market-gardener 125a
to m. is to domesticate 413a
we are told . . that they neither m. 418b
where I love I must not m. 281a
where I m., cannot love 281a
while ye may, go m. 190b
woman . . may m. whom she likes 440a
Marrying: m. and giving in marriage 507b
they aren't the m. brand 232b
Mars: Pallas, Jove and M. 131b
this seat of M. 375a
Marshes: see to 'Ackney M. 22a
Mart: too close in church and m. 44a
Martha: M. was cumbered 509a
Sons of M. 234b
Martial: melting airs, or m. 112b
m. brood accustomed to fight 408b
Martin Elginbrodde 256a
Martinmas: it fell about the M. 529a
Martlet: m. builds in the weather 353b
temple-haunting m. 347a
Martyr: all the m. throng 286a
glorious the m.'s gore 403a
groan of the m.'s woe 30b
I am love's m. 133a
if thou deye a m. 90a
m. to mild enthusiasm 45b
Oldcastle died a m. 381a
pale m. in his shirt of fire 403b
thou fall'st a blessed m. 386a
Martyrdom: all have not the gift
of m. 140b
it were a m. to live 42a
she's for the Moors, and M. 115a
Martyrs: about the graves of the m. 414b
blood of the m. . . seed of the
Church 574a
noble army of m. 478a
stones and clouts make m. 42a
Marvel: but that's no m. 380b
Marvelled to see such things 485a
Marvelling: she left me m. 441a
Marvellous: m. change on a sudden 67b
usual propensity . . towards the m. 201b
Marvels: who alone workest great m. 478b
Mary: Christ-child stood at M.'s
knee 92a
cometh M. Magdalene early 511b
everywhere that M. went 177b
groves where the lady M. is 311b
if any young men come for M. 11b
I'm sitting on the stile, M. 28b
I'm very lonely now, M. 29a
in battle was M. Ambree 531b
is there room for M. there? 315b
Jesu, M. and Joseph they bare 524a
Little M. Bell had a Fairy 31a
M. did sing 524a
M. had a little lamb 177b
M. hath chosen that good part 509a
M.! I want a fairy 113a
M. loves the lamb, you know 177b
M., pity women! 232b
M. was that Mother mild 3b
Mistress M., quite contrary 533a
my M. from my soul was torn 61b
my M.—kind and true! 29a
my M.! 109a
my M.'s asleep by thy . . stream 60b
my sweet Highland M. 61a
O M., go and call the cattle home 226b
O Mother, M. Mother 313a
passion for the name of 'M.' 71a
Philip and M. on a shilling 66a
Queen M.'s saying serves for me 46a
red was on yr. lip, M. 28b
said M. as we sate in dusk 393a
Saint Anne, the mother of M. 293a
save One, than M. Magdalene 294b
Sons o. M. seldom bother 234b
this is that blessed M. 313a
to M. Queen the praise be given! 99a

Mary (cont.)

ye are na M. Morison 61b
Marybone: from Islington to M. 30b
Mary-buds: winking M. begin 328b
Maryland: by the hills of M. 458b
M., my M.! 308a
Mask: he had a m. like Castlereagh 395b
m. of night is on my face 365a
no m. like open truth 104a
one m. of brooses 124b
shows, as he removes the m. 440b
the loathsome m. has fallen 397b
Masks, and antique pageantry 269a
Masonry: kingliest m. 396a
Masons: singing m. building roofs 381b
Masquerade: the truth in m. 71b
Mass: baby figure of the giant m. 368b
jewelled m. of millinery 433b
mingled in a m. 254a
m. of mankind understand it 17a
yawning at the M. 92b
Massacre: not as sudden as a m. 446b
Masses: back the m. against the
classes 167b
bow, ye m.! 163b
m. and fugues and 'ops' 164b
Mass-priest knelt at the side 284b
Massy: antique pillars m. proof 268b
Mast: bends the gallant m. 116a
m. burst open with a rose 155a
m. of some great ammiral 271b
m. was o' the beaten gold 529a
right up above the m. 98b
upon the high and giddy m. 380a
Master: a m. o'er a slave 466b
build me straight, O worthy M. 246b
Caliban, has a new m. 367b
chants the m.'s requiem 146b
Cold Iron—is m. of them all 228a
Dickon thy m. is bought 385a
everyone can m. a grief 358b
he saith, M., say on 509a
I am M. of this College 528b
I am the m. of my fate 185a
I hae a gude m. 320a
in constancy follow the M. 54b
in his m.'s steps he trod 286b
into the woods my M. went 242b
ken when I have a kind m. 319b
like m., like man. 150b
love is m. wher he wile 172a
love wd. prove so hard a m. 38a
man is man and m. of his fate 428b
Man is the m. of things 423a
m. and servant, oft changing 446b
M. of All Good Workmen 236b
m. of gibes and flouts 128b
M. of them that know 566b
m. o' the Tiger 346a
m.'s lost his fiddling-stick 534a
m. of unmeaning rhyme 72b
m., we have toiled all the night 509a
my m. comes like any Turk 79b
my m. is of churlish disposition 326a
no more subtle m. under heaven 428a
one for my m. 534b
one m.-passion in the breast 301a
only The M. shall praise us 236b
our m., famous, calm, and dead 47a
our royal m. saw 445b
pity . . lets yr. m. in 117a
shd. be the m. of himself 262b
soul of an ancient M. 49a
stood in the presence of The M. 440a
that did his m. conquer 324a
th' Eternal M. found his . . talent 210b
tho' thy m. miss'd it 386a
thy m. hath his gold 289b
to the M. of all music 248b
to the M. of all singing 248b
we've got a private m. 124b
wh. I wd. fain call m. 342a
wh. is to be m., that's all 85a
who's m., who's man 419b
Master-fiend Argyle 12b
Master-light of all our seeing 466b
Masterly inactivity 256a
M.F.H.: where the M.F.H. dines 416b
Master-passion is the love of news 113b
Master-passions: two m. cannot co-
exist 77b

Masterpiece: confusion..hath made his m. 348a
Masterpieces: his soul among m. 563a
Masters: all m. cannot be truly follow'd 359b
a Mad World, my M. 35a
both ill m. be 176b
good servants, but bad m. 244b
light-hearted M. of the waves 8b
men..are m. of their fates 337b
noble and approved good m. 359b
no man can serve two m. 505b
spiritual pastors and m. 481a
the people are the m. 56a
we cannot all be m. 359b
we must educate our m. 572a
we were m. of the sea! 231a
Mastery: the m. of the thing 198a
Mast-high: the ice, m. 98a
Mastiff, greyhound, mongrel 343a
Masts: his m. crack 87a
Match: and the m. to win 287b
spurt of a lighted m. 48b
to m. another foe 77b
who in ears and eyes m. me 50b
Matches: m. of the Southron folk 442b
plays extravagant m. 164b
Matchless: the m., what you will 303b
Mate: Freedom leads it forth, her m. 397a
great artificer made my m. 414b
his lady's ta'en anither m. 529b
man there walked without a m. 261a
m. of the *Nancy* brig 163a
she took unto herself a M. 472b
who shall be the maiden's m. 317a
Material: most m. in the postscript 15b
Schiller has the m. sublime 102b
Mates: his m. were idly sporting 36b
his shivering m. 443b
Mathematics: angling..so like the m. 450a
m. (make men) subtile 16a
mystical m. of the city of heaven 41a
see Mystery to M. fly! 299a
Matin: each m. bell, the Baron saith 100a
shows the m. to be near 331b
Matrimonial: m. devotion 164b
no one cares for m. cooings 70b
Matrimony: if we take m. at its lowest 413a
in m. begin with..aversion 400b
in matters of religion and m. 91a
in the holy estate of M. 481b
joined together in holy M. 481a
more of love than m. 171a
Matron: m. and the maid 184a
the m.'s glance 168a
thou sober-suited m. 366a
Matt, old age has brought 410b
Matter: a little m. mend all this 35b
a m. they had no concern in 419a
Berkeley said 'there was no m. 71b
gravelled for lack of m. 327b
great a m. a little fire kindleth 517b
I am full of m. 497a
I do not much dislike the m. 323a
if it is it doesn't m. 167a
in a great m. or a small 520b
I the m. will re-word 335a
m. enough to save one's own 48a
m. for succeeding founders 260b
m. she drove at succeeded 306a
meaning, however, is no great m. 75b
mind and m...glide swift 124a
more m. for a May morning 372a
more m. with less art 332a
neither part nor lot in this m. 512a
order..this m. better in France 411a
pour out the pack of m. 323b
root of the m. is found in me 497a
Star-Chamber m. of it 355b
such hard m. dost thou entertain 393b
sum of m. remains..the same 14a
take away the m. of them 15a
then he's full of m. 325b
the wrecks of m. 1b
to set off wretched m. 270b
'twas no m. what he said 71b
what is M.? never mind 535a
what is Mind?—No m. 535a
wings shall tell the m. 499b
Matter-of-fact-ness..in his poetry 183a

Matters: be not curious in unnecessary m. 520a
not exercise myself in great m. 490a
sets right all other m. 46a
Matthew: M., Mark, Luke, and John 2b
testified M. Moon 180b
Mature: for death m. 276b
whose lip m. is ever new 218a
Maud: come into the garden, M. 434a
M. burst in..the Earl was there 293b
M. is not seventeen 433b
M., M., M., they were crying 433b
M. with her exquisite face 433b
Maugre of doughty Douglas 530b
Maurice: since M. died 36b
Mavis: Hark! the m.' evening sang 59b
I have heard the m. singing 205a
Mavourneen: Kathleen M. 115a
Mawkish: so sweetly m. 299a
Mawkishness: thence proceeds m. 217a
Maxim: a m. he had often tried 114a
he who is governed by that m. 456b
so useless as a general m. 254b
that grounded m. so rife 277b
Maxims: a little hoard of m. 432a
Maximum of temptation 391a
May: all in the merry month of M. 531a
as flush as M. 334b
boughs of the m., as they sang 242a
bringeth vo'th M. flowers 525a
bursting boughs of M. 37a
chills the lap of M. 170a
cold M. and windy 446a
crowned with milk-white m. 37b
do spring M. flowers 446a
fair as is the rose in M. 90a
fresh as is the month of M. 88a
from the merriment of M. 217b
gathering nuts in M. 523b
he smells April and M. 356a
his bough on the eve of M. 35b
I'm to be Queen o' the M., Mother 434b
in the merrie month of M. 20b, 35a
I were lord in M. 423a
love, whose month is ever M. 344b
March sun feels like M. 48b
M.! be..never grac'd with birds 42b
M. is a pious fraud 251a
M. will be fine next year 199b
M.'s new-fangled mirth 344b
meaning of M. was clear 422b
mid-M.'s eldest child 220a
month of M. was come 257b
more matter for a M. morning 372a
remembrance the month of M. 257b
shake the darling buds of M. 387a
swarm of bees in M. 522a
the moonlight coloured m. 398a
there's an end of M. 200a
whan..month of M. is comen 89b
when M. is past 79b
whenas M. was in his pride 35a
world is white with M. 427b
yet said, 'Now I m.' 360b
Maying: let's go a-M. 189a
that we two were M. 226a
May-mess, like on orchard 198a
Mayne glideth 49b
Maypole: away to the M. hie 522b
where's the M. in the strand 35a
Maypoles: I sing of M. 188b
May-time and the cheerful dawn 470b
Maze: a mighty m.! 300b
burgeons every m. of quick 431a
not in fancy's m. he wandered 303a
wander in that golden m. 141b
Mazes: entangled in their m. 397b
in wand'ring m. lost 272b
voice thro' m. running 269a
Mazy: meandering with a m. motion 101a
Me: adore my gifts instead of M. 188a
cometh unto the Father, but by m. 511a
eyes that wd. not look on m. 400a
if you don't go down with m. 266b
I knew the voice an' it was m. 235a
just, good God! miserable m.! 51a
m., that was never a quiet sleeper 434b
m., to whom thou gav'st it 388b
m., who am as a nerve 395a
none other gods but m. 480a
talk awhile of M. and THEE 153b

Me (cont.)
tell them, they are m.! 175a
this is too much for M.! 237a
two topics, yourself and m. 209a
wouldest thou m.? 399a
ye have done it unto m. 508a
Mead: about the new-mown m. 221a
any man that walks the m. 426b
by the stream and o'er the m. 32b
Dr. M...in the..sunshine of life 210a
the even m. 383b
Meadow: a time when m., grove 466a
painted m., or a purling stream 1b
Meadow-gale of spring 99b
Meadow-sweet or sorrel 420b
Meadows: abroad in the m. 453a
her feet have touched the m. 433b
in the dim m. desolate 460a
in your m. fair 35b
m. trim with daisies 269a
Mr. M. 58b
oft water fairest m. 113a
O, ye fountains, m., hills 467a
past the near m. 220a
paint the m. with delight 345b
set in enamelled m. 449a
the m. runnels 217b
there are no more by-path m. 413a
up from the m. rich with corn 458b
with golden face the m. green 387b
Meads: fair these broad m. 320b
flowery m. in May 462a
I met a lady in the m. 218b
these sweet-springing m. 37a
Meagre as lizards 76a
Meal: a Roman m. 112a
eat our m. in fear 348b
handful of m. in a barrel 496a
no man gets a full m. 208b
one hearty m. on yr. viands 239a
Meals: great m. of beef and iron 382a
Mean: careful what they m. thereby 368a
debtless competence, golden m. 439a
for m. or no uses 246a
happy the golden m. 262b
if I ever do a m. action 411a
I know not what they m. 436a
I m. this day to end myself 433a
I m. what I say 83a
it was not for the m. 146b
loves well the golden m. 545a
m. and mighty rotting together 329a
meanly admires m. things 439b
means just what I choose it to m. 85a
nature is made better by no m. 373a
nature makes that m. 373a
nothing common did or m. 261a
poor, and m., and lowly 3b
tho' m. our object 469a
you shd. say what you m. 83a
Meander: by slow M.'s margent 267a
Meandering with a mazy motion 101a
Meanders: no stream m...level 255a
Meanest: m. of his creatures 49b
m. thing that feels 465b
wisest, brightest, m. 301b
Meaneth: what m. then this bleating 495a
Meaning: a m. suited to his mind 426b
an atom of m. in it 83b
as to the m., it 's what you please 75a
free from all m. 138b
m., however, is no great matter 75b
rest to some faint m...pretence 140b
that is the m. of Empire Day 94a
the m. doesn't matter 165a
the m. of May was clear 422b
to find its m. is my meat 46b
to the author to get at his m. 314a
within the m. of the Act 528a
Meanings: two m. in one word 385a
two m. packed up into one word 85a
with m. that he never had 112a
Means: all appliances and m. 380a
by absence this good m. I gain 198a
by any m. I might attain 516a
die beyond my m. 461a
I don't know what it m. 163a
live within our m. 451b
m. intensely, and m. good 46b
m. to do ill deeds 374b
my person, my extremest m. 352b

Means (*cont.*)

priests bear rule by their m.   503*b*
take the m. whereby I live   355*a*
that my m. may lie too low   107*a*
that wants money, m., and content   327*a*

Meant: here lies one who m. well   412*b*
I knew not all he m.   428*a*
knowing not what it m.   284*a*
she knew what it m.   527*a*
what ere she m. by it   133*a*
where thousands equally were m.   419*a*

Measles: did you ever hav the m.   451*a*
love's like the m.   205*b*

Measure: a m. of wheat for a penny   518*b*
as a Scotch jig, a m.   358*a*
be scant of true m.   216*b*
does it hold good m.?   46*a*
Fate thy m. takes   250*b*
good m., pressed down   509*a*
I love thee beyond m.   461*a*
man is the m. of all things   560*a*
M. still for M.   352*b*
now tread we a m.   318*a*
number, weight, and m.   31*a*
praise the Lord by m.   231*a*
shrunk to this little m.   339*b*
stateliest m. ever moulded   439*a*
there is m. in everything   547*b*
to lead but one m.   318*a*
to m. life learn thou betimes   278*b*
was heard the mingled m.   101*b*
wh. is the m. of the universe   397*a*
with a new song's m.   291*a*
with what m. ye meet   508*b*

Measured: I must be m. by my soul   453*a*
I've m. it from side to side   471*b*

Measureless: caverns m. to man   101*a*

Measures: better than all m.   398*b*
cant of '*Not men but m.*'   56*b*
in short m., life may perfect be   216*b*
marches to delightful m.   384*b*
m., not men . . my mark   170*b*
softly sweet, in Lydian m.   139*a*
trying the m. of the breadth   260*b*

Meat: as an egg is full of m.   365*b*
children, have ye any m.?   511*b*
dish of m. is too good   450*b*
I cannot eat but little m.   415*a*
if ever thou gavest m.   529*a*
is not the life more than m.   505*b*
little m. best fits   188*b*
loves the m. in his youth   358*b*
m. in the hall   414*b*
mock the m. it feeds on   361*b*
on our m., and on us all   190*b*
out of the eater came forth m.   495*a*
snewed in his house of m.   88*b*
some hae m., and canna eat   62*b*
soul abhorred all manner of m.   488*b*
taste My m.   188*b*
tearing his m. like a tiger   255*b*
their m. in due season   488*b*
upon what m. doth . . Cæsar feed   337*b*
we hae m. and we can eat   62*b*
world is full of m. and drink   413*b*

Meat-fly: Thackeray settled like a m.   313*b*

Meats: an eater of broken m.   342*a*
of all m. the soonest cloy   107*a*

Meaty jelly, too, . . is mellering   125*b*

Mecca: M. saddens at the long delay   443*b*
some to M. turn   154*a*

Mechanic: mere m. operation   66*a*
writing Madam 's a m. part of wit   149*a*

Meddle with my toys   414*a*

Meddling: every fool will be m.   498*b*

Medea gather'd the enchanted herbs   355*a*

Mede is at his gate   74*a*

Medes: given to the M. and Persians   504*a*
M., and Elamites   512*a*

Mediator: our M. and Advocate   479*a*

Medical doctors a cocking their m. eyes   127*a*

Medicinable: their m. gum   364*a*

Medicine: all m. is mine   392*b*
as a m. for health   446*a*
faithful friend is the m. of life   520*b*
giveth m. to heal their sickness   490*b*
great griefs, I see, m. the less   329*a*
grief is itself a m.   107*b*
m. thee to that sweet sleep   362*a*
m. worse than the malady   23*a*

Medicine (*cont.*)

merry heart doeth good like m.   498*b*
miserable have no other m.   351*b*

Medicines to make me love him   377*a*

Mediocrity knows nothing higher   136*a*

Meditate: her . . songs does m.   261*a*
m. the thankless Muse   269*b*

Meditation: in maiden m., fancy free   356*b*
let us all to m.   384*a*
the m. of my heart   482*b*

Mediterranean, where he lay, lulled   396*b*

Medium: use of an imperfect m.   460*b*

Mede: alle the floures in the m.   90*a*
bloweth m.   526*a*
m. of some melodious tear   269*a*

Meek: blessed are the m.   505*a*
I am m. and gentle   339*b*
I am m. and lowly in heart   506*b*
safer being m. than fierce   44*b*
taught us to be calm and m.   193*b*
the man Moses was very m.   494*a*

Meekest: Launcelot . . thou wert the m. man   257*b*

Meekness: by m., call'd thy Son   402*b*
faith, m., temperance   515*b*
leaving, with m., her sins   196*a*
of m., and righteousness   484*b*

Meet: assemble and m. together   478*a*
face one wd. m. in every place?   218*a*
God be with you till we m. again   315*b*
I cannot m. them here   437*a*
if I shd. m. thee after long years   74*b*
if we do m. again . . we shall smile   341*a*
I'll m. the raging of the skies   77*a*
it is m. and right so to do   480*b*
make both ends m.   158*a*
m. me by moonlight   448*b*
m. thee at that hollow vale   225*a*
m., with champagne and a chicken   280*a*
my heart, safe left, shall m.   402*a*
never the twain shall m.   227*a*
only part to m. again   161*a*
run to m. what he wd. most avoid   267*a*
run half way to m. it   205*b*
she first m. the curled Antony   325*a*
so I'll m. 'im later on   230*a*
soon again to m.   294*a*
there did m. another man   212*a*
tho' infinite can never m.   260*a*
we shall m., but we shall miss him   451*b*
we two may m. before high God   428*a*
when shall we three m. again   345*b*
when we m. at any time again   137*b*
when we shall m. at compt   364*a*
where dead men m.   67*a*
where the brook and river m.   247*b*
whether we shall m. again   341*a*
will never m. again   525*b*
yet m. we shall   67*a*

Meeter: we therefore deemed it m.   295*a*

Meeting: as if I was a public m.   448*b*
broke the good m.   349*a*
doth not a m. like this   282*a*
journeys end in lovers m.   370*b*
neither overtaking nor m.   104*a*
this m. is drunk, sir!   126*b*
working-class . . m. when it likes   9*b*

Meetings: alarums changed to . . m.   384*b*
their m. made December June   431*a*

Meg: M. grew sick as he grew haill   60*a*
M. was deaf   60*a*
Old M. was brave   219*a*

Melancholy: alien sound of m.   466*a*
day-dream of m. men   141*b*
distrust . . is a mode of m.   209*b*
green and yellow m.   371*a*
had this trick of m.   322*a*
hail divinest M.   268*a*
hateful error, m.'s child!   341*b*
hence, loathed M.   268*b*
I can suck m. out of a song   326*a*
I inherited a vile m.   212*b*
in Nature there is nothing m.   101*b*
it is a m. of mine own   327*a*
kindly mood of m.   143*a*
m. as an unbraced drum   86*b*
M. mark'd him for her own   174*b*
mistress of true m.   324*a*
moping m.   276*b*
most m. of human reflections   17*b*
most musical, most m.   268*a*

Melancholy (*cont.*)

most musical, most m. bird!   101*b*
my cue is villainous m.   342*a*
naught so sweet as M.   64*a*
pale M. sate retir'd   103*a*
rare recipe for m.   239*b*
so dainty sweet, as lovely ni.   23*a*
such a charm in m.   310*a*
taught me to rhyme, and to be m.   344*b*
the m. god protect thee   371*a*
veil'd M. has her sovran shrine   219*b*
what charm can soothe her m.   170*a*
what devil this m. is   155*b*

Melchisedech: after the order of M.   489*a*

Mellering to the organ   125*b*

Mellow: death took him m.   295*a*
Humours, whether grave or m.   2*a*
indeed is too m. for me   280*a*
man not old, but m.   296*b*
to the State's m. forms prefer   175*b*

Mellowed to that tender light   74*a*

Mellstock: lie in M. Churchyard now   179*b*

Melodies: all m. the echoes of that voice   100*b*
ease my breast of m.   218*a*
heard m. are sweet   219*b*
sweetest m. are those . . by distance   468*b*

Melody: a mortal m.   298*a*
blundering kind of m.   138*b*
chanted a m. loud and sweet   435*b*
falling in m. back   101*b*
from ancient m. have ceased   31*b*
Luve's like the m.   62*a*
smale fowles maken m.   88*a*
sound of sweetest m.   380*a*
than to a chamber m.   402*a*

Melon: this gaudy m.-flower   47*b*

Melons: stumbling on m., as I pass   260*b*

Melrose: view fair M. aright   317*a*

Melt: I rage, I m.   159*a*
m. at other's woe   173*b*
now m. into sorrow   63*a*
so let us m., and make no noise   134*a*
this too too solid flesh wd. m.   330*a*

Melted: m. into air, into thin air   367*b*
till he m. like a cloud   437*b*

Melting-pot: America . . the great M.   477*b*

Melts: then m. for ever   63*a*

Member: ev'ry m. of the force   309*b*
predominant m. of the three king-doms   572*b*
thing I am not a m. of   155*a*

Members: in thy book were all my m.   490*b*
m. one of another   515*b*

Memnon smitten with the . . Sun   436*a*

Memnonium was in all its glory   403*b*

Memnons: new M. singing   43*b*

Memoirs: people will write their m.   66*b*

Memorable: m. Roman Emperor   321*b*
upon that m. scene   261*a*

Memorandum: if you don't make a m.   83*b*

Memorial: keep King Charles . . out of the M.   122*a*
m. more enduring than brass   546*b*
some frail m. still erected   174*b*
their m. is perished with them   482*a*
wh. have no m.   521*b*

Memorials: tall m. catch the . . sun   415*a*

Memoried: many-m. name   28*b*

Memories: flocks of the m. of the day   265*a*
liars ought to have good m.   401*a*
a night of m. and sighs   241*a*

Memory: a grand m. for forgetting   412*b*
a great man's m. may outlive   334*a*
beg a hair of him for m.   340*a*
begot in the ventricle of m.   344*b*
better m. said, fie   285*a*
dear son of m.   278*a*
drown the M. of this Impertinence   153*a*
drown the m. of that insolence   153*b*
fond M. brings the light   282*b*
for my name and m.   17*a*
from the table of my m. I'll wipe   331*b*
indebted to his m. for his jests   401*a*
it's a poor sort of m.   84*b*
m. and desire, stirring dull roots   144*b*
m. fades, must the remembered   119*a*
m., the warder of the brain   347*b*
need not be wisdom or even m.   313*a*
O! it comes o'er my m.   362*b*

Memory (*cont.*)

only a m. of the same	47b
pluck from the m. a rooted sorrow	350b
quick, thy tablets, M.	7a
still the hands of m. weave	106a
sweet their m. still	109b
the m. be green	329b
their very m. is fair	448a
these few precepts in thy m.	330b
tho' lost to sight, to m. dear	245b
thoughts to m. dear	319a
thy lamp, O M., fire-winged	313a
time whereof the m. of man	28b, 245b
vibrates in the m.	399b
while m. holds a seat	331b
Memphian chivalry	271b
Men: all are m., condemned alike	175a
all his m. looked at each other	220b
all m. are about to live	477a
all m. are liable to error	246a
all m. are liars	489a
all m. become good creatures	48b
all m. everywhere cd. be free	245a
all m. have their faults	170b
all m. make faults	387b
all m. think all m. mortal	477a
all m. wd. be cowards	309b
all m. wd. be tyrants	118a
all other m. may use deceit	241b
all sorts and conditions of m.	479a
all the king's m.	85a
all the m. and women. . players	326b
all the windy ways of m.	439a
all things to all m.	514a
all those m. have their price	450a
among new m., strange faces	429a
among the broken m.	93b
are you good m. and true?	358b
as if m. fought upon the earth	318b
as m.'s have grown from. . fears	69b
as proper m. as ever trod	337b
a State wh. dwarfs its m.	266a
best of m. . .was a sufferer	118b
better m. than we go out	229b
booksellers are generous. . m.	207a
brave m., and worthy patriots	279b
busy hum of m.	269a
but good m. starve	141a
but m. are m.; the best. . forget	361a
by keeping m. off. . keep them on	159a
cheerful ways of m. cut off	273b
deals with the memory of m.	42b
Death, that feeds on m.	389b
disgrace with fortune and m.'s eyes	387a
do not live like living m.	469a
doth make m. better be	216b
do to all m. as I wd. they shd. do	481a
Duke of York. .had ten thousand m.	526b
England under the dregs of m.	26a
Eve upon the first of M.	194b
fair women and brave m.	68a
fewer m., the greater. . honour	383a
fishers of m.	505a
for fear of little m.	4a
for m. must work	226b
forsaking even military m.	167a
fraud of m. was ever so	358b
girls are level now with m.	324b
gods. . in the likeness of m.	512b
going to dine with some m.	27b
good m. that loved you well	284a
good will toward m.	508b
great m. contending with adversity	64a
half-m., and their dirty songs	40a
hearts of oak our m.	10b
her m. robust for toil	77b
honest m. and bonnie lasses	62b
honest minds and active m.	157a
honours of m.'s impossibilities	343b
hosses, dawgs, and m.	440a
husband than the best of m.	323a
if after the manner of m.	515a
if it issue not towards m.	15a
if m. are together in a boat	178a
if these m. are dead	421b
if this counsel. . be of m.	512a
I love not m. the less	69b
in His ways with m.	429a
in m., we various ruling passions	302a
in the busy haunts of m.	185a

Men (*cont.*)

in the catalogue ye go for m.	348b
I see m. as trees, walking	508b
is there no way for m. to be	328b
it ain't by princerples nor m.	250a
I travelled among unknown m.	467a
I've ninety m. and more	437b
justify the ways of God to M.	270b
know themselves to be but m.	482a
learn m. from books	130a
let us arise and go like m.	414a
let us now praise famous m.	521a
life of m. . . a single sparrow	24a
little else but the works of m.	296a
little things. . great to little m.	170a
love of false and cruel m.	261a
love to all m. 'neath the sun!	228a
made brutes m., and m. divine	293a
made 'em to match the m.	144a
made in the likeness of m.	516a
measures, not m. . . been my mark	170b
melancholy. . wh. can transform m.	155b
m. about me that are fat	338a
m. and malice, to breed causes	216a
m. and the sun-hazed sleeper	442b
m. and women with one race	227b
m. are April when they woo	327b
m. are better than this theology	147b
m. are but gilded loam	374b
m. are conservatives. . after dinner	148a
m. are made by nature unequal	157b
m. are never so good or so bad	256a
m. are suspicious	189b
m. are we, and must grieve	472b
m. at most differ as Heaven	429a
m. at some time are masters	337b
m. below, and saints above	317a
m. caught out in. . guilt	96a
m. . . children of a larger growth	139a
m. dare trust themselves with m.	368a
m. deal with life as children	109a
m. (deceived) with oaths	13a
m. fear death as children	14a
m. fell out they knew not why	64b
m. have died from time to time	327b
m. have lost their reason	340a
m. hunger for thy grace	206a
m. in a world of m.	228b
m. in great place are. . servants	14b
m. in nations; all were his	70b
m. in women do require	30b
m. lead lives of. . desperation	444a
m. like soldiers may not quit	433a
m. lived like fishes	401a
m. make haste to die	199b
m. may come and m. may go	425b
m. may rise on stepping-stones	429b
m. met each other	141b
m. must endure their going hence	344a
m. must pursue things. . just	13a
m., my brothers, m. the workers	432a
m. of England, wherefore plough	399a
m. of few words are the best m.	382a
m. . . of light and leading	57b
m. of like passions with you	512b
m. of little showing	234b
m. only disagree of creatures	272b
m. on the pay-roll	232a
m. ought always to pray	510a
m., serving either calamity	520a
m.'s evil manners live in brass	386a
m. shd. be what they seem	361b
m. slain this year in Europe	450a
m.'s m.: gentle or simple	144a
m. so loose of soul	362a
m., some to business	302a
m., some to quiet	302a
m. that all the world admires	259a
m. that God made mad	92a
m. that sow and reap	422a
m. that strove with gods	439a
m. that were boys. . I was a boy	27a
m. that women marry, and why	247b
m. to take their exit	454b
m. were deceivers ever	358a
m. with sisters dear	196a
m. who hold its. . blessings dear	468a
m., with wailing in yr. voices	44a
m. wh. have not the seal	519a
m. who march away	180a
m. whose visages do cream	352b

Men (*cont.*)

m. with splendid hearts	39b
m., women, and clergymen	404b
m. wd. be angels	300b
m. wd. be false	251a
m. wd. be fond	251a
moderate m. look'd big, Sir	524a
more wondrous are the m.	31b
my fifty m. and women	49a
never be beloved by m.	29a
not as other m. are	510a
not in the roll of common m.	378a
not m., but manners	151a
not m., but measures	56b
not the m. you took them for	359a
not thrones and crowns, but m.	146a
not without m.'s hands	144b
obey God rather than m.	512a
of all m. most miserable	514b
old m. so duly	215a
old plain m. have rosy faces	414b
O m., this man in brotherhood	43a
O! m. with mothers	196a
one that loves his fellow-m.	202a
only m. who did the work	236a
O shame to m.!	272b
O that m. wd. therefore praise	488b
pack and label m. for God	442a
picked from passing m.	414a
port for m.	210a
practice. . with m. and women	51a
priests are only m.	51a
quit you like m., be strong	515a
quit yourselves like m.	495a
rather have such m. my friends	341b
rather studied books than m.	17a
safe where m. fall	40a
saint-like in the eyes of m.	247b
saints will aid if m. will call	100a
services of Angels and m.	480a
shall m. seek death	519a
she'll betray more m.	363b
shire for m. who understand	39b
single m. in barracks	235b
sleek-headed m.	338a
so long as m. can breathe	387a
so many m., so many opinions	554a
so they be ill m.	214b
some faults to make us m.	324b
souls out of m.'s bodies	358a
spirits of just m. made perfect	517a
such cognisance of m. and things	47b
such m. as he be never at. . ease	338a
such m. are dangerous	338a
such names and m. as these	366b
swallow down. . m. themselves	283b
tell them they are m.	175a
that m. stand upon	339a
the flag the m. hauled down	459a
the M.! O what venerable	445a
the same as the m.	457b
these m. are all upper-crust	177b
these m. see the works of the Lord	488b
the shadows of us m.	216a
this happy breed of m.	375a
tho' m. be so strong	487b
thousand m. that fishes gnaw'd	384b
three good m. unhanged	377b
tide in the affairs of m.	341a
'tis furnish'd well with m.	339a
to m. of other minds	170a
tramp of the twenty-two m.	34b
twelve good m. into a box	40b
'twixt women's love, and m.'s	132a
two m. look out	242a
two stern-faced m. set out	196a
two strong m. stand face to face	227a
very old are we m.	119a
vexes public m.	439b
wander in the ways of m.	61b
weak m. must fall	375a
wealth accumulates, and m. decay	168a
we m., at sea, indite	134b
we m. may say more, swear more	371a
we petty m. walk under	337b
were na m. but dogs	63a
we then, too, can be such m. as he	5a
we've got the m.	201b
what hearts have m.	428b
what m. dare do, what m. may do	359a
what m. in general cannot do	209a

Men (cont.)
what m. or gods are these? 219b
what you and other m. think 337b
when m. and mountains meet 30a
when m. are at the point of death 366b
where the great m. go 154b
while three m. hold together 424a
who cd. handle m. a bit 233a
why don't the m. propose, mamma 22b
wisest m. have erred 277b
with four-and-twenty m. 12b
with M. for Pieces plays 153b
with small m. no great thing 266a
women in m. do require 30b
world of m. for me 49b
ye are brothers! ye are m. 76b
you are not stones, but m. 340a
young m. and maidens 490b
young m. come for Mary 11b
young m. taken in and done for 225a
yr. tall young m. in turn 92b
Men-children: bring forth m. only 347b
Mend: nor a broken thing m. 27a
old chairs to m. 533a
that they may m. mankind 109a
to m. it or be rid on't 348b
what's amiss I'll strive to m. 453a
Mended: nothing else but to be m. 65a
what can't be m. 453a
Mendip's sunless caves 252a
Mene, mene, tekel 504a
Menelaus: Helen, M.' queen 368b
Menny: done because we are too m. 180b
Menpleasers: eye service as M. 516a
Mental: not cease from M. Fight 31b
Mentality: yr. m., too, is bully 25c
Mention: I make m. of you always 513a
no m. of me more..be heard 386a
oh! no! we never m. her 22a
Mentioned: m. her virtues, it is true 26a
m. me to him 83b
Mercenary: followed their m. calling 200a
Merchandise: arts and m. 16b
Merchant: m. to secure his treasure 306a
the mighty m. smiled 127b
Merchants: others, like m. 381b
where m. most do congregate 353a
whose m. are princes 502a
Merci: Belle Dame sans M. 219a, 221b
Mercies: tender m. of the wicked 498a
thanks for m. past receive 53b
when all thy M., O my God 2a
Merciful: blessed are the m. 505a
God be m. unto us 486a
God was very m. to the birds 527b
good man is m., and lendeth 489a
m. and mighty 184a
so is the Lord m. 488a
then must the Jew be m. 354b
thou, Lord, art m. 485b
Mercuries: as English M. 381b
Mercury: like feathered M. 378b
words of M. are harsh 345b
Mercy: a crowning m. 115b
a God all m., is a God unjust 477b
Charity and M...Not unholy names 123b
clouds..are big with m. 110a
emboldens sin so much as m. 368a
God ha' m. on his soul 336a
God have m. upon one of our souls 372a
God shall send forth his m. 485b
God sometimes withhold in m. 283a
half so good a grace as m. does 351b
have m. on Jacob yet 47a
have m. upon us miserable sinners 478b
his m. endureth for ever 490a
Holy Father, in Thy m. 411a
I m. ask'd, I m. found 522b
infinite m., but, I wis 47a
in m...the throne be established 502a
law of human judgment, M 314b
leaving m. to Heaven 151b
lovelier things have m. shown 72b
m. and truth are met together 487a
m. blows the coals 407b
m. every way is infinite 46b
M. has a human heart 33a
m. I asked, m. I found 76a
m. is above this sceptred sway 354b
m. I to others show 304a

Mercy (cont.)
Oh, God of M.! when? 146a
'O m.!' to myself I cried 471b
peace on earth, and m. mild 455b
quality of m. is not strained 354b
reason to rule, m. to forgive 140b
render the deeds of m. 354b
shut the gates of m. on mankind 174b
so great is his m. also 488a
sweetness, m., majesty 249b
that is m.'s door 110a
that m. show to me 304a
they shall obtain m. 505a
thy everlasting m., Christ 262a
thy loving-kindness and m. 483a
Thy m. on Thy People, Lord 233b
to M., Pity, Peace and Love 32b
unto God's gracious m. 481b
we do pray for m. 354b
when m. seasons justice 354b
whereto serves m. 334b
whose most tender m. is neglect 114a
Mercy-seat: how beautiful Thy m. 149b
in coming to thy m. 110a
Mere: Lady of the M. 463a
Meredith is a prose Browning 460a
Meridian: in England..under any m. 42a
Merit: from sense of injured m. 271a
his m. handsomely allowed 210b
how he esteems yr. m. 108a
or any m. that wh. he obtains 101a
patient m. of the unworthy 333a
Satan exalted sat, by m. raised 272a
smite them by the m. 286b
the m.'s all his own 95a
to buried m. raise the tardy bust 213b
to true m. shd. they have regard? 160a
what is m.? 292a
Meriting: love needs human m. 442a
Merits: careless their m...to scan 168b
not weighing our m. 480b
obtain that wh. he m. 101a
seek his m. to disclose 174b
Merlin: me repenteth, said M. 257a
Mermaid: a seeming m. steers 323a
choicer than the M. Tavern 219a
mar-ri-ed to a m. 525b
m.-like awhile they bore her 336a
m. on a dolphin's back 356b
the M. in the Zodiac 219a
until he came to a m. 525a
what things..done at the M.! 22b
wine, wh. is the M.'s now 215a
Mermaids: so many m., tended her 323a
Merrily: m. did we drop 98a
m., m., shall I live now 368a
oh! but we went m.! 69b
Merriment: source of innocent m. 164b
this m. of parsons..offensive 210b
your flashes of m. 336b
Merrow: road by M. Down 232b
Merry: against ill chances men are.. 380b
a wantown and a m. 88b
eat, drink, and be m. 509b
for to-night we'll m. be 522b
God rest you, m., gentlemen 523a
good to be m. and wise 524b
I am never m...sweet music 355a
I am not m., but I do beguile 360b
I cd. be m. now 374a
it was never m. world in England 384a
let us be m. 123b
makes one man m., another mad 42a
m. as a marriage bell 68a
m., dancing, drinking..time 141b
m. of soul he sailed on a day 414b
point of death have they been m. 366b
such a m., nimble spirit 345a
the good are always the m. 475a
their wars are m. 92a
the m. love the fiddle 475a
the m. love to dance 475a
three m. boys are we 23a
'tis m. in hall when beards wag 381a
to eat, and to drink, and to be m. 499b
uprouse ye then, my m. men 18a
very m., and the best fritters 296a
Merryman: song of a m. 167a
Mesech: to dwell with M. 489b
Meshach, and Abed-nego 504a

Mesopotamia: blessed word M. 158b
dwellers in M. 512a
Mesopotamy: from here to M. 75b
Mess: all along o' m. 228b
Benjamin's m. was five times 493b
birthright for a m. of pottage 523a
in every m. I finds a friend 120b
Message: give to a gracious m. a host 323b
the electric m. came 12a
Messages: fair speechless m. 352b
Messenger: a dusk misfeatured m. 51a
he's an Anglo-Saxon M. 85a
larke, m. of day 89a
M. said in a sullen tone 85a
the m. of Satan 515b
the other M.'s called Hatta 85a
Messengers: his m. ride forth 253a
superfluous kings for m. 323b
Messes: herbs, and other country m. 269a
Messiah: shall the true M. see 456a
they found the new M. 140b
Met: are m. in thee to-night 40a
each thing m. conceives delight 276a
how first he m. her 440b
ne'er m. with elsewhere 294b
never be m. with again 86a
no sooner m., but they looked 327b
part of all that I have m. 438b
she were true, when you m. her 134a
that have m. many a one 307b
the day and the way we m. 422b
we m., 'twas in a crowd 22b
Metal: breed for barren m. 353a
here's m. more attractive 334a
m. in this furnace wrought 407b
my m. of India! 371a
Paradisal imagineless m. 443a
poisonous brass and m. sick 218a
sonorous m. blowing 271b
unimproved m. hot and full 329b
Metals: keys he bore of m. twain 269b
Metaphor: all m. is poetry 94a
hunt down a tired m. 71b
Metaphysic: high as m. wit can fly 65a
M. calls for aid on Sense 299a
Physic of M. begs 299a
Metaphysics: circumnavigate the m. 413a
Mete: with what measure ye m. 508b
Metempsychosis: ah, Pythagoras m. 258b
Meteor: and the m. on the grave 73a
cloud-encircled m. of the air 395b
m. of the ocean air 194a
misled by fancy's m. ray 63a
shone like a m. streaming 271b
slides the silent m. on 437a
the m. flag of England 78a
Method: madness, yet there is m. in it 332a
m. and..reasonableness of Jesus 10b
m. of making a fortune 175b
Methodist: morals of a M. 166b
spiritualized by a M. 449b
Methods: by m. of barbarism 78a
my m. in such cases 135b
you know my m. Apply them 136a
you know my m., Watson 135b
Methusalem: M., with all his..years 134b
might be Lot or M. 236a
Metre: a m.-making argument 148a
in a m. of Catullus 427a
m. of an antique song 387a
[Tennyson] .. write .. without understanding..m. 102b
wretched matter and lame m. 270b
Metres: it is not m...makes a poem 148a
Metropolis: gray m. of the North 426b
the m. of the empire 97a
Metropolitan: in m. Jerusalem 294b
Mettle: he was so full of m. 137a
I see there's m. in thee 363a
like a man of m. 191b
m. enough in thee to kill care 359a
the m. of yr. pasture 382a
there is m. in death 322b
thy undaunted m. shd. compose 347b
who knows so much of my m. 372a
Meum: distinctions of *m.* and *tuum* 239a
Mew: rather be a kitten and cry m. 378a
Mewling: infant, m. and puking 326b
Mexico: a Vergil at M. 449b
Mexique: beyond the M. Bay 260a

Micaiah said, if thou return 496b
Micawber: I never will desert Mr. M. 122a
Mr. M.'s expression 'Provided for' 122b
Mice: fisherman. .appear like m. 343b
her feet. .like little m. stole 416a
m., and rats and such small deer 343a
schemes o' m. an' men 62a
three blind m. 533a
Michael: M. and his angels fought 519a
yet M. the archangel 518a
Michael Angelo: enter M. 25a
made Italy from designs by M. 446b
M. for breakfast 446b
talking of M. 144b
the name of M. 308b
Michael Henchard's Will 180b
Michal: are there not, dear M. 49b
Micher: sun. .prove a m. 377b
Miching mallecho: this is m. 334a
Microcosm of a public school 130a
Microscopes: magnifyin' gas m. 126b
Microscopic: has not man a m. eye 300b
Mid-day: more clear, than our m. 133b
Middle: can take no m. ways 37b
go most safely in the m. 551b
grant me, Heaven, a m. state 257a
in the m. of my being 243a
it was the m. of the night 84a
last enchantments of the M. Age 9a
[M.] class. .of Philistines 9b
m. of the road of our life 566b
m.-sized are alone entangled 400a
shall we twirl down the m. 131a
tenants of life's m. state 113a
to the m. of my song 108b
Middle-age: restraining reckless m.? 474b
Middlesex: an acre in M. 255a
Middleton: Lady M. exerted herself 11b
Midge: spins like a fretful m. 311b
Midian: the troops of M. 286a
Midland: M. furze afire 229a
o'er the blue M. waters 8b
Midlands: when I am living in the M. 26b
Midnight: a budding morrow in m. 221a
at m. and at morn 146b
at the m. in the silence 52a
blackest M. born 268b
came upon the m. clear 320b
consum'd the m. oil 160a
did at m. speak with the Sun 447b
foul and m. murther 173b
heard the chimes at m. 380b
in the solemn m. 131b
m. never come 258b
m.'s all a-glimmer 475b
not to be a-bed after m. 370a
once upon a m. dreary 298a
primroses gather'd at m. 217b
profoundest m. shroud the. .lights 399a
sadder than. .m. blast 72a
soft embalmer of the still m. 221a
stars of the m. shall be dear 471b
still her woes at m. rise 251b
stood on the bridge at m. 246b
the iron tongue of m. 357b
thro' the m. dark and drear 249a
'tis now dead m. 352a
tis the year's m. 133b
to cease upon the m. 220a
you secret, black, and m. hags 349b
Midnights: flashes struck from m. 46a
Mid-noon: another morn ris'n on m. 275a
it was the deep m. 435a
Midshipmite: and a m. 163a
Midsummer: high M. pomps come on 8b
this is very m. madness 371b
Mid-watch: He, who at m. same 47a
Midwife: she is the fairies' m. 364b
Mien: dark hair and lovesome m. 425b
I fear thy m. 399b
sought with an indignant m. 107b
truth has such. .a m. 140b
Might: dear m. of Him that walked 270a
eke with all his m. 108b
heart of hearts I feel yr. m. 467a
I spread my conquering m. 345b
it m. have been 182a, 459a
love, exceeds man's m. 369a
m. of Denmark's crown 76b

Might (cont.)
m. she have loved me? 48a
proof of manly m. 408b
Rome been growing up to m. 131b
sovereign sway. .dissolved by m. 138b
spirit of counsel and m. 501b
the all-enacting M. 180a
'tis m. half slumbering 220b
to be man with thy m. 422b
Tubal Cain was a man of m. 256a
wish death nor fear his m. 416b
Might-have-been: my name is M. 312b
Mightiest: one moment of the m. 68b
'tis m. in the m. 354b
Mighty: all the proud and m. have 143a
called thee m. and dreadful 133a
confound the things wh. are m. 514a
how are the m. fallen 495b
let the m. Babe alone 115a
look on my works, ye M. 396b
mean and m. rotting together 329a
m. in the scriptures 512b
m. men wh. were of old 492b
m. things from small beginnings 139b
promises were, as he then was, m. 386a
put down the m. from their seats 508b
shield of the m. is. .cast away 495b
slow to anger. .better than. .m. 498a
thou art m. yet! 341b
[Mignonette] the fragrant weed 112b
Migrations from the blue bed 171a
Miguel of Spain 230a
Milan: retire me to my M. 368a
Mild: brought reg'lar and draw'd m. 124a
m. as she is seeming 176a
m. monastic faces 96a
m., obedient, good as He 3b
sublimely m.,. .without spot 392b
Mildest: m. curate going 162b
the m. mannered man 70b
Mildness: ethereal m., come 443b
Mile: compel thee to go a m. 505a
each day he walks a m. 24a
eighty m. o' females 127a
he went a crooked m. 532a
m. an' a bittock 415a
m. of warm sea-scented beach 48b
walked on a m. or so 84b
yr. sad tires in a m.-a 373a
Miles: draw out our m. 375a
he be many m. asunder 366a
how many m. is it to Babylon 534a
m. and m. distant tho'. .last line be 312b
m. around they'll say 199a
Sheridan twenty m. away 308b
three-score m. and ten 534a
twice five m. of fertile ground 101a
Milestones on the Dover Road 123a
Militant: Church m. here in earth 480b
the Poets M. below 106b
Military: a m. gent 439b
as well as any m. man 382a
forsaking even m. men 167a
when the m. man approaches 390b
Milk: a breastful of m. 311a
anon he weyveth m. 89b
drunk the m. of Paradise 101b
find a trout in the m. 135b, 444a
flowing with m. and honey 493b
fostre him wel with m. 89b
full o' the m. of human kindness 346b
m. and wastel-breed 88b
m. comes frozen home in pail 345b
m. is more likely to be watered 67a
m. my ewes and weep 373b
m. of kindness into curds 194a
pens in. .m. .of human kindness 58a
seethe a kid in his mother's m. 494a
sincere m. of the word 517b
skim. m. masquerades as cream 166a
sweet m. of human kindness 94b
take my m. for gall 346b
with m. and honey blest 286a
Milking: at the ewe m. 145b
Milkmaid singeth blithe 268b
Milks: love the babe that m. me 347a
Milk-soup men call domestic bliss 293b
Milk-white: before m., now purple 356b
Milky Way: roar of the M. 235a
solar walk or m. 300b
twinkle on the m. 467a

Mill: all the water that goes by his m. 64b
brook, that turns a m. 310a
charge. .were it but a m. 131a
in Gaza, at the m. with slaves 277b
I wandered by the m. 198b
more water glideth by the m. 368a
Millar: I respect M., sir 206b
Milldams o' Binnorie 528b
Miller: m. sees not all the water 64b
more water. .than wots the m. of 368a
there was a jolly m. once 28a
Milliner: perfumed like a m. 376b
Millinery: jewell'd mass of m. 433b
Million: a mangler in a m. m. 125b
high man, aiming at a m. 47a
make that thousand up a m. 190a
Millionaire: he must be a m. 162b
Mr. Mandragon, the M. 92a
Millions: m. a hero 304b
m. died, that Cæsar. .be great 77a
m. for defence 181b
m. of mischiefs 340b
m. of strange shadows 387b
she 'as m. at 'ome 236b
tear-wrung m. 67b
twenty-seven m. mostly fools 81a
Mills: dark Satanic m. 31a
tho' the m. of God grind slowly 248a
Millstone: a stone like a great m. 519b
better for him that a m. 507a, 510a
hard as a piece of the nether m. 497b
Mill-wheel: except the m.'s sound 393a
Milsom Street remain 230b
Milton: a grace before M. 238b
been on my guard against M. 223b
damp fell round the path of M. 470b
England's M. equals both 109a
forgive a man for not enjoying M. 239b
for third the classic M. 36a
malt does more than M. can 199b
M., a name to resound for ages 427a
M. almost requires a. .service 239a
M., Death and Sin 477b
M., Madam, was a genius 211a
M.'s the prince of poets 71a
M.! thou shouldst be living 467b
M. was for us 48a
M. wrote in fetters 31a
morals hold wh. M. held 467a
some mute inglorious M. 174a
the divine M. 464a
to give a M. birth, ask'd ages 111b
Miltonic verse cannot be written 223b
Mimsy: all m. were the borogoves 83b
Min: is the old m. agreeable? 125a
Mince: love doth m. this matter 361a
they dined on m. 243b
Mincing as they go 501a
Mind: a fool uttereth all his m. 499a
agree to be of one m. 13b
all my m. is clouded 429b
a m. impatient 330a
a m. not to changed 271a
a m. quite vacant. .m. distress'd 110b
any substance without a m. 28a
as a dead man out of m. 483b
as her m. grew worse 465b
as the m. is pitched 112b
body filled and vacant m. 383a
bring the philosophic m. 467a
but not astound the virtuous m. 267a
calm the troubled m. 104a
charge his m. with meanings 112a
clap yr. padlock on her m. 305b
clearest insight, amplitude of m. 470a
clear yr. m. of cant 211a
clothed, and in his right m. 508b
converse of an innocent m. 221a
cover his m. decently 404b
dart, with heedful m. 24b
dictates of his godlike m. 291a
dividing the swift m. 573a
down the. .ways of my own m. 441b
ever by the eternal m. 466b
excursions in my own m. 102b
extend thy m. o'er all the world 277a
fair terms and a villain's m. 353a
farewell the tranquil m. 362a
feed this m. of ours 464b
first destroys their m. 140b
fixed m. and high disdain 271a

Mind (cont.)

fog of the good man's m. 45b
forward-looking m. 464b
fruitful ground, the quiet m. 416a
fulfil all thy m. 482b
gentle m. by gentle deeds 409a
God offers to every m. its choice 148a
golden m. stoops not to . . dross 353b
grateful m. by owing owes not 273b
had you in yr. m. such stores 471a
happy alchemy of the m. 175b
have his hoggish m. 408b
heart argues, not the m. 7a
heart to heart, and m. to m. 317a
he bears too great a m. 341a
hev it jest as you've a m. to 230b
he who does not m. his belly 207b
hills . . come back into my m. 26b
his fond and foolish m. 531b
his m. his kingdom 113a
his m. into the common stock 167b
how the m. of man becomes 470a
human m. . . away from (miracles) 10a
if he wd. abandon his m. to it 211a
index of a failing m. 114a
inform the m. that is within us 472a
in my m., of all mankind 529b
in my m.'s eye, Horatio 330a
intense irradiation of a m. 395b
inter-assured of the m. 134a
in the m. of man 472a
I saw Othello's visage in his m. 360b
its own beauty is the m. diseased 69a
last infirmity of noble m. 269b
laugh that spoke the vacant m. 168b
let the m. be a thoroughfare 223b
light up my own m. 48b
love warps the m. 114a
make up one's m. about nothing 223b
man's unconquerable m. 472b
many movements of his m. 472b
marble index of a m. 469b
march of the human m. is slow 55b
march of m. . . has marched in 295a
meaning suited to his m. 426b
measure my m. against his 390a
measure yr. m.'s height 49b
men to be of one m. in an house 486a
m. and matter . . glide swift 124a
m. and soul, according well 429b
m. at peace with all below 74a
m., body, or estate 479a
m., from pleasures less, withdraws 260b
m. not high things 513b
m. or body to prefer 301a
m. serene for contemplation 160b
m. that is grandly simple 148a
m. . . turn upon the poles of truth 14a
m. what I am taught 425a
minister to a m. diseased 350b
moral duty to speak one's m. 460a
moved slowly thro' the m. 469a
musing . . in his sullen m. 408b
my m. forbids to crave 143a
my m.'s my kingdom 182b
my m. to me a kingdom is 143a
narrowed his m. 169b
ne'er disclose her m. 361a
never be brought to m. 59a
never face so pleased my m. 156a, 526b
never to ransack any m. 308b
noblest frailty of the m. 140b, 321b
no passion in the m. of man 14a
nor do's she m. 189a
nothing remained . . but m. 405a
nothing unbends the m. like
(women) 159b
not in my perfect m. 344a
not with the eyes, but with the m. 356a
now I change my m. 341a
of love, and of a sound m. 516b
of loyal nature, and of noble m. 427b
on our daily course our m. 223b
on the enlightened m. 443a
on the torture of the m. to lie 348b
out of sight is out of m. 97a
pale, lost lilies out of m. 135a
passages that strike yr. m. 67a
persuaded in his own m. 514a
philosophic m. can take no middle 37b
poet . . certain unsoundness of m. 254b

Mind (cont.)

poor Indian! whose untutored m. 300b
presence of m. in a railway 535a
presence of m. was amazing 243a
pulse in the eternal m. 40a
puts his m. to yours 211a
quiet m. is worse than poverty 445a
seized their troubled m. 424b
serve thee with a quiet m. 479b
service of a m. and heart 465b
she had a frugal m. 108b
she unbent her m. afterwards 239a
shows the innocent and quiet m. 413a
some strain of music to thy m. 35b
some untrodden region of my m. 220b
sound m. in a sound body 549b
spirit of the chainless m. 69b
that of the human m. in ruins 118a
the conjunction of the m. 260b
the great barons of the m. 413b
the man but changed his m. 301b
the m. has a thousand eyes 34a
the m. is free 136b
the m. is its own place 271a
the m. of man, my haunt 464a
the m.'s construction in the face 346b
the m.'s the standard of the man 453a
the m., that fiery particle 71b
there are chords in the human m. 121b
there's no blemish but the m. 372a
they captivate, inform the m. 109a
this truth within thy m. rehearse 438b
thou, my m., aspire . . higher things 402a
thou tyrant of the m. 140b
thy chaste breast, and quiet m. 250a
thy m. all virtue 206b
thy m. is a very opal 371a
to emulate his m. 169a
to feed a craving m. 113b
to the noble m., rich gifts 333b
two things fill the m. with . . awe 568b
universal frame is without a m. 15a
unseemly exposure of the m. 183b
vex not thou the poet's m. 435b
was never m., did m. his grace 313b
we are not enticing yr. m. 35a
we cultivate the m. 560b
what a noble m. . . here o'erthrown 333b
what is m.? no matter 535a
when the m.'s free 343a
whether 'tis nobler in the m. 333a
wiser m. mourns less 405a
with equal m., what happens 141a
with-the-Conqueror type of m. 452a
with the flower of the m. 148a
years steal fire from the m. 68a
yet is thy m. perplexed 118b
you are pleased to call yr. m. 28a
yr. complicated state of m. 165a
Minden's plain 242a
Mindful: m. of the unhonour'd dead 174b
that thou art m. of him 482a
Minds: balm of hurt m. 348a
express the images of their m. 14b
great actions speak great m. 23a
great empire and little m. 56a
honest m. and active men 157a
idleness . . refuge of weak m. 91a
law of all men's m. 7b
live again in m. made better 144b
lose myself in other men's m. 239a
m. innocent and quiet 249b
m. like ours, my dear James 289b
narrow m. . . draw . . narrow conclusions 265b
noble m. keep ever . . their likes 338a
our m. do muse on ought 137b
purest and most thoughtful m. 314b
ready m. to fellowship divine 217b
religion of feeble m. 57b
repentance . . virtue of weak m. 140b
righteous m. of innkeepers 93b
strange faces, other m. 429a
the mighty m. of old 407a
to have aspiring m. 259a
to the marriage of true m. 259a
wh. of themselves our m. impress 464b
wisdom in m. attentive 112b
Mine: beasts of the forests are m. 485a
every man . . show'd like a m. 385b
excavating for a m. 280b

Mine (cont.)

fire a m. in China 66a
heigh ho, wd. she were m.! 246a
I am m. and yours 49a
Mermaid's now, but shall be m. 215a
m. has been a fine one 34a
m. is an unchanging love 110a
m. to teach me what I am 63b
my all that's m.? 169a
my beloved is m. 500a
she shall be m. 471b
she's not and never can be m. 293b
then shouldst thou have m. 416a
what thou art is m. 276b
while He is m., and I am His 188a
wish it were only m. 233a
Miner: dwelt a m. 280b
in the . . depths the m. striving 415b
m.'s dream of home 168a
Miners: rugged m. poured to war 252a
Minerva when she talks 216b
Mines: deep in unfathomable m. 110a
delve one yard below their m. 335a
like plants in 49b
Lord Stafford m. for coal 178a
m. reported in the fairway 232b
Mingle: in another's being m. 395b
m., m., m., you that m. may 265b, 349b
vainly strives the soul to m. 120a
Mingled: heard the m. measure 101b
when it is m. with regards 341b
Minion: curled m., dancer 8a
morning's m. 198a
Minished, and brought low 488b
Minister: a m. of her will 325a
a 'stickit m.' 319b
discreet and learned M. 480b
hae ma doobts aboot the m. 535b
m. kiss'd the fiddler's wife 62a
m. to a mind diseased 350b
patient must m. to himself 350b
quench thee, thou flaming m. 363b
whole world now is but the m. 36a
wisdom of a great m. 217a
Ministered: angels came and m. 505a
Ministers: all are but m. of love 101b
angels and m. of grace 331a
are they m. of Christ? 515a
errands for the M. of State 163b
ev'n m., they hae been kenned 59b
grim Geneva m. 12b
his m. a flaming fire 488a
I call you servile m. 342b
m. . . exhausted volcanoes 128b
my actions are my m.' 87b
passion-winged M. of thought 392a
you murdering m. 346b
Ministries: Times has made . . m. 17a
Ministry: frost performs its secret m. 101a
more for a marriage than a m. 17b
nae, mon. Gie up the m. 536b
the secret m. of frost 101a
Minnehaha, Laughing Water 248b
Minnows: Triton of the m. 328a
Minorities . . always in the right 404b
Minority is always right 567a
Minstrel: a wandering m. I 164a
ethereal m.! 471a
him no M. raptures swell 317a
M. was infirm and old 316b
ring the fuller m. in 431a
the M. Boy 281b
the harp the monarch m. swept 72b
Minstrels: dame nature's m. 134a
m. follow after 486b
Minstrelsy: our wild m. 217b
Mint: fire-new from the m. 371b
m. and anise 507b
our pockets the mark of the m. 93b
Mints: lavender, m., savory 373a
Minuet in Ariadne 400a
Minute: do it in M. Particulars 30b
fill the unforgiving m. 230a
first m., after noon, is night 133b
he that will divide a m. 327b
he, the m. makes immortal 49a
in a m. pay life's glad arrears 50b
perfume and suppliance of a m. 330b
'wilt thou?' said the winged m. 264b
Minutes: about the earth in forty
m. 356b

Minutes (cont.)
damned m. tells he o'er — 361b
five m. too late — 107b
sixty diamond m. — 258a
so do our m. hasten to their end — 388a
so the little m. — 82a
take care of the m. — 90b
to see the m. how they run — 384a
Minx, or a Sphinx — 125b
Mirabeau's work, then, is done — 80a
Miracle: accept a m., instead of wit — 477b
any m. attested by..men — 201a
continued m. in his own person — 201b
existence is a mere m. — 413b
m. may be accurately defined — 201a
m. of a youth..Christopher Wren — 149b
m. of our age, Sir Philip Sidney — 79a
m. of rare device — 101b
never m...to convert an atheist — 13a
never..m. to convince atheism — 15a
sufficient to establish a m. — 201a
Miracles: God never wrought m. — 15a
m. do not happen — 10a
religion..first attended with m. — 201b
sapping the proof from m. — 10a
they say m. are past — 322a
Miranda: an Inn, M.? — 27a
Mire: learning will be cast into the m. — 57a
out of the m. and clay — 484a
reign of some luxurious m. — 161a
shade and loneliness and m. — 39b
Mirror: deceiving m. of self-love — 262b
hold..the m. up to nature — 333b
m. cracked from side to side — 431b
m. of all Christian kings — 381b
m. of all courtesy — 385b
m. of alle curteisye — 89a
thou glorious m. — 69b
thy m., earth's majestic view — 280a
use of a m...not to be painted — 254b
Mirrors of the sea are strewn — 155a
Mirth: bards of Passion and of M. — 219a
creature, form'd of joy and m. — 30b
dim and decorous m. — 39b
elephant to make them m. — 274a
far from all resort of m. — 268a
fence..evils of life, by m. — 411a
honour and clean m. — 227b
if in m., report that I am..sick — 322b
I'll use you for my m. — 340b
I love such m. as does not make friends — 450b
in endless m. — 189a
joy the day in m. the while — 117a
let us have..m. and laughter — 70b
limit of becoming m. — 344b
losing some hue of his m. — 263a
M., admit me of thy crew — 268b
m. and no madness — 402b
m., that after no repenting draws — 278b
m. that has no bitter springs — 228a
no worth in the hobnailed m. — 235b
old earth must borrow its m. — 459a
prefer not Jerusalem in my m. — 490a
present m. hath present laughter — 370b
public mischief in your m. — 111b
so much..M. and Spleen — 2a
song of the birds for m. — 177b
sunburnt m. — 219b
than M. can do with her..parts — 524a
very tragical m. — 357b
where's all the joy and m. — 224b
you have displaced the m. — 349a
Misael: Azarias, and M. — 478a
Misanthropy and voluptuousness — 255a
Misapprehension: immense literary m. — 10a
Misbehaved: I m. once at a funeral — 239b
Miscarriage: success and m. are empty — 207a
Mischance: never come m. between us — 334a
on a Friday fil al this m. — 89a
seeing all his own m. — 432a
Mischief: a public m. in your mirth — 111b
hand to execute any m. — 203a
in every deed of m. — 162a
m. thou art afoot — 340b
neglect may breed m. — 157a
Satan finds some m. still — 453a
spectators of the m. wh. she made — 313b

Mischief (cont.)
to draw new m. on — 360a
to mourn a m. that is past — 360a
you wait on nature's m. — 346b
Mischiefs: millions of m. — 340b
record the m. he has done — 111b
Mischievous: wd., as his kind, grow m. — 338b
Miser: a M.'s pensioner — 463b
heaps of m.'s treasures — 267b
Miserable: it is a m. state of mind — 15a
me m.! — 273b
mercy upon us m. sinners — 478b
m. comforters are ye all — 497a
of all men most m. — 514b
purblind race of m. men — 427b
the m. have no other medicine — 351b
to be weak is m. — 271a
Miseries: bear the m. of a people — 283a
bound in shallows and in m. — 341a
shed a tear in all my m. — 386a
those to whom the m...are misery — 218a
Misers: as m. do in gold — 445a
Misery: acquainted with sad m. — 454b
and is full of m. — 481b
bound in m. and iron — 488b
child of m., baptiz'd in tears — 242a
dwell on guilt and m. — 11a
gave to M. all he had — 174b
in M.'s darkest cavern — 210b
in the deep wide sea of m. — 395a
laughs the sense of m. far away — 111a
light given to him that is in m. — 497a
mighty poets in their m. dead — 470b
m. acquaints..strange bedfellows — 367b
m., and will not let them rest — 218a
m. makes Alcmena's nights — 42b
m. still delights to trace — 107b
result, m. — 122a
their departure is taken for m. — 520a
thou art so full of m. — 438b
thro' the vale of m. use it — 487a
untainted by man's m. — 398b
who finds himself, loses his m. — 8b
Misfortune: alleviate so severe a m. — 11b
come, child of m. — 281b
in sour m.'s book — 366b
m. of our best friends — 562a
next..m. to losing a battle — 455a
once untangled much m. bodes — 365a
Misfortunes: children..make m. more bitter — 14b
he'll hae m. great — 63a
delight..in the real m...of others — 57b
m. hardest..wh. never come — 251a
Misgivings: blank m. of a creature — 466b
Misgovernment: augur m. at a distance — 55b
refuge of cheap m. — 390b
Misguiding: gi'en to great m. — 62a
Mishap: into wh. no accident, no m. — 171b
Misled: by education most..m. — 140b
Mislike: if thou m. him — 187a
m. me not for my complexion — 353a
they that m. it, heresy — 191b
Misogyn: the confirmed m. — 25a
Misprision: upon m. growing — 388b
Misquote: enough of learning to m. — 72a
Miss: a m. for pleasure — 161a
calls her 'M.' — 93b
mine he cannot m. — 401b
M. Blimber — 122b
M. Codger — 124a
m. not the discourse — 520b
so I both enjoy and m. her — 198a
we shall m. him — 451b
whatever M. T. eats — 119b
you'll m. me, brother — 188b
Missed: health and wealth have m. me — 202a
no one wd. have m. her — 523b
we m. it, lost it forever — 53a
who never wd. be m. — 164b
Missing so much and so much — 106a
Mission: never have a m. — 121b
Mississippi: the way into M. Bay — 231b
Missouri: 'cross the wide M. — 525a
Missus: the M., my Lord! — 535b
to help the m. unload — 232b
Mist: brambles pale with m. — 9a
came a happy m. — 427b

Mist (cont.)
feel..the m. in my face — 50b
follows a m. and a weeping rain — 256a
grey m. on the sea's face — 262a
m...dispell'd..woman appears — 159b
m. resembles the rain — 247a
m. was on the rice-fields — 232a
no m. obscures, nor cloud — 407a
rolling m. came down — 226b
the rank m. they draw — 269b
thro' the cold and heavy m. — 196a
went up a m. from the earth — 492a
Mistake: ah, pray make no m. — 164b
a m. in the translation — 447b
he never overlooks a m. — 202b
man is Nature's sole m.! — 166b
m. the false one for the true — 457a
there is no m. — 455a
you lie—under a m. — 418b
Mistaken: possible you may be m. — 115b
Mistakes: all great men make m. — 95a
experience is a name..m. — 460a
I hope will excuse m. — 124b
man who makes no m. — 296b
of man's miraculous m. — 477a
teaches..at the cost of m. — 157b
Mistaking: gav'st it else m. — 388b
Mistletoe hung in the castle hall — 22a
Mistress: a M. moderately fair — 107a
art is a jealous m. — 147a
a teeming m. — 302a
but m. in my own — 233a
in every port a m. — 161a
is she not pure gold, my m.? — 52a
like m., like maid — 150b
like M. Mall's picture — 369b
m. I am ashamed to call you — 145b
m. of herself, tho' China fall — 302a
m. of the months — 420a
m. of the true melancholy — 324a
m. to the man I love — 299b
more fond than m. — 299b
my m.' eyes are nothing like — 389a
my m. still the open road — 414a
no casual m., but a wife — 430b
O m. mine! — 370b
on the bounty of his m. — 105b
riches..the worst m. — 13b
select out of the crowd a m. — 393b
so court a m., she denies you — 216a
true; a new m. now I chase — 250a
was m. of her choice — 334a
you saw the m., I beheld the maid — 354b
Mistresses: m. with great smooth — 45a
one wife and hardly any m. — 315a
wives are young men's m. — 14b
Mistress-Fairy: Mab, the M. — 215b
Mists: Season of m. — 221b
shaken m. a space unsettle — 442a
when the golden m. are born — 398b
Misty: of a ful m. morwe — 90a
Misunderstood: is it so bad..to be m. — 147b
to be great is to be m. — 147b
Misuse: first m., then cast..away — 109a
Misused the king's press — 378b
Mites: she threw in two m. — 508b
Mithras, God of the Morning — 234b
Mithridates: half M. — 254b
M., he died old — 199b
Mix: I m. them with my brains — 290b
kiss her and m. her with me — 424a
Mixed: it is full m. — 487a
Mixing it with other things — 85a
Mixture: had the m. peen — 12b
m. of a lie doth..add pleasure — 14a
mortal m. of earth's mould — 267a
Mizpah..the Lord watch between — 493a
Mizraim cures wounds — 42b
Moab: a vale in the land of M. — 3a
M. is my wash-pot — 485b
Moan: account of fore-bemoaned m. — 387b
former causes of her m. — 42b
made sweet m. — 218b
make delicious m. — 220a
that is not paid with m. — 441a
the little ones m. — 6a
twa corbies making a m. — 529b
we cast away m. — 336a
Moaned: laughed and m. about — 44b
Moaning: bar and its m. — 226b

Moaning (cont.)
may there be no m. of the bar   426a
now they are m.   145b
Moans: deep m. round with many
   voices   439a
murmured her m.   363a
Moat: as a m. defensive to a house   375a
look to your M.   178a
Moated: the lonely m. grange   433a
Mob: amphibious ill-born m.   118b
do what the m. do   126a
m. of gentlemen who wrote   303b
M. was the wrongest   20a
nouns..as M., Parliament, Rabble   97a
our supreme governors, the m.   449a
Mobled queen   332b
Mobs: suppose there are two m.?   126a
Mock: how my achievements m. me   369a
m. on, m. on, Voltaire, Rousseau   31b
m. the air with idle state   173b
m. the good housewife Fortune   325b
m. the meat it feeds on   361b
Mocked: as if he m. himself   338a
God is not m.   515b
m. it as we ran!   234b
Mockers: loud m. in the..street   244a
Mockery: all the rest, a m.   398a
in monumental m.   369a
m. is the fume of little hearts   428a
our vain blows malicious m.   329b
unreal m., hence!   349a
Mocking-bird's throat   457b
Mocks: comforts while it m.   50b
he never m.   428a
Mode: selfsame bloody m.   179b
Model: England! m. to thy inward
   greatness   381b
m. of a modern Major-General   166b
Models destroy genius and art   183b
Moderate men looked big, Sir   524a
Moderation: astonished at my
   own m.   95b
m. even in excess   130a
m. in war is imbecility   254a
m...is a sort of treason   58a
no terms of m...with the vulgar   13b
Moderator: reasonable m...Death   41b
Modern: Prince-Elective on the m.
   plan   91b
Moderns: speak of..m. without contempt   90b
Modes: unknown m. of being   469a
various m. of man's belief   45b
Modest for a modest man   240a
Modester: people ought to be m.   81b
Modesty: in a friend, it is cold m.   339b
ladies of irresistible m.   410b
'O m.! 'Twas strictly kept'   293b
press yr. point with m.   108a
too much m. is his   170b
where the Greeks had m.   295a
wore enough for m.   53b
Mogul, and Mugwump   38b
Mohicans: last of the M.   106a
Moist: conclude in a m. relentment   42a
Mole: a m. cinque-spotted   328b
death is still working like a m.   187a
go ask the M.   29b
like a bastion's m. his chest   403a
well said, old m.!   331b
Moles of Adrianus   42b
Molly: M. Malone   524a
was true to his M.   120b
when M. smiles beneath her cow   120b
Moloch: first M., horrid king   271b
Moltke, 'silent in seven languages'   17b
Moment: a m. gazed adown the dale   316a
a M.'s Halt   153b
certain m. cuts the deed off   50b
does not seem a m.'s thought   474a
eternity was in that m.   104b
every m., dies a man   439a
every m., lightly shaken   432a
horror of that m...never forget   83b
in a m., in the twinkling of an eye   515a
one M. in Annihilation's Waste   153b
one m. may with bliss repay   77b
some awful m.   465b
sonnet is a m.'s monument   311b
the kingdoms of the world in a
   m. of time   509a

Moment (cont.)
the Marquis gazed a m.   12b
very m. that he bade me tell it   360a
Momentany as a sound   356a
Momentousness: its m. and his conviction   390b
Moments: are m. in life worth..
   worlds   151a
days and m. quickly flying   86a
m. big as years   218a
m. in the being   466b
m. wh. he calls his own   310a
Monan's rill   316a
Monarch: a merry m., scandalous   309b
come, thou m. of the vine   323b
cuckold to make him a m.?   363a
every hereditary m. was insane   17b
like a tired m. fann'd to rest   282b
love cd. teach a m. to be wise   174a
m. better than his crown   354b
m. of all I survey   113a
more lovely than..m. of the sky   258b
no m. but wd. give his crown   448b
page and m., forth they went   286b
sat the merry m. longest   249a
sure the m.'s rule must prove   306a
the m. of a shed   170a
we greet the m.-peasant   193b
with a m.'s voice cry, 'Havoc!'   339b
Monarchies: all the four M.   134b
Monarchize: to m., be feared   375b
Monarchs: fate summons, m. must
   obey   140b
fear of change perplexes m.   272a
righteous m., justly to judge   39a
wrote that m. were divine   230a
Monarchy: are you for making a m.   171b
characteristic of the English M.   17b
mass of mankind understand (M.)   17a
M. is..an intelligible government   17a
mystic reverence..to a true m.   17a
no other sway but purest M.   280b
universal m. of wit   79a
wh. are essential to a true m.   17a
Monastic: mild m. faces   96a
on my heart m. aisles   147a
Monday: began on a M. at morn   530b
betwixt a Saturday and M.   79b
classical M. Pops   164b
fell a-bleeding on Black M.   353b
hanging of his cat on M.   35a
M. is parson's holiday   418a
M.'s child is fair of face   525a
Solomon Grundy, born on a M.   532b
they that wash on M.   532b
'twas on a M. morning   193a
Money: blockhead ever wrote, except
   for m.   209a
borrer the m. to do it   451b
buy wine and milk without m.   503a
counting out his m.   533b
fancy giving m. to the government!   186a
goä wheer m. is   434b
hath a dog m.?   353a
he gat him more m.   89a
he that hath no m.; come ye   503a
he that wants m., means,..content   327a
how pleasant it is to have m.   96b
if I'd as much m. as I cd. spend   533a
if not, by any means, m.   542b
if you wd. know the value of m.   157a
I give thee my m.   104b
I have spent all the m.   210a
lends out m. gratis   353a
lot of m. to die comfortably   66b
love of m. is the root of all evil   516b
m. answereth all things   499b
m. has a power above the stars   66a
m., I despise it   165b
m. in the Three per Cents   46b
m. is honey, my little sonny!   41a
m. is indeed the most important   390a
m. is like muck   15a
m. is the sinews of love   150b
m...is the true fuller's earth   150b
m...language all..understand   25b
m. on de bob-tail nag   156a
[M.]..queen of all delights   21a
m. speaks sense   25b
m., thou bane of bliss   187b

Money (cont.)
more innocently..than in getting m.   208b
natural interest of m.   254b
neither is m. the sinews of war   15b
ninepence in ready m.   2b
no m., no Swiss [soldiers]   565a
no one shall work for m.   236b
not given his m. upon usury   482b
put m. in thy purse   360b
see what m. will do   296b
so m. comes withal   366b
suit wh. cost me much m.   296a
that's the way the m. goes   257b
they hired the m., didn't they?   570b
they've no idea what m.'s for   186a
thy m. perish with thee   512a
time is m.   156b
we've got the m. too   201b
what m. is better bestowed   440a
wherefore do ye spend m.   503a
where is yr. m.?   534b
you pays yr. m...takes yr. choice   535a
Money-bag: aristocracy of the M.   80b
Money-bags: dream of m.   353b
Moneys: as m. for values   13a
lend you thus much m?   353a
Mongrel: greyhound, m. grim   343a
m. beef-witted lord   368b
m., puppy, whelp   169a
Monied interest   2a
Moniment, without a tomb   215b
Monitor: murmurings, whereby the
   m. expressed   464b
Monk: m. who shook the world   280a
the devil a m. wd. be   285a
the M. my son   407a
Monkey: bred out into baboon
   and m.   368a
ere the M. People cry   234b
had of yr. daughter for a m.   354a
never look long upon a m.   104a
Monkeys: for a wilderness of m.   354a
goats and m.!   362b
m. and cats, all human life   204b
the m. walk together   231a
Monks: merrily sang the m. in Ely   79a
the m. of Magdalen   161b
Monmouth: also..a river at M.   383b
Monograph on the ashes of..tobacco   135b
Monotony: bleats articulate m.   410b
Monsr'-inform'-ingens   52b
Monster: a m. fearful and hideous   555b
as it were a m. unto many   486b
blunt m. with uncounted heads   379b
chief m...plagued the natives   111a
great-siz'd m. of ingratitudes   369a
it is the green-ey'd m.   361b
lean abhorred m.   366b
many-headed m. of the pit   303b
many-headed m., the..multitude   262b
m., wh. the Blatant Beast men call   409a
shouts to scare the m.   228b
some m. in his thought   361b
that Theban m.   277b
Monsters: begot of all these m.   202b
complicated m., head and tail   276b
Monstrous: bottom of the m. world   356a
speak in a m. little voice   356a
Montagu: Mrs. M. has dropt me   210b
Montague: in truth, fair M.   365a
Montaigne: sedulous ape to..M.   412b
Montalban: Aspramont or M.   271b
Monte Carlo: broke the bank at M.   162b
Montezuma: who imprisoned M.   254b
Montgomery: Mr. M.'s readers   255a
Mr. M.'s writing   254b
Month: a little m.   330a
April is the cruellest m.   144b
ends all our m.-long love   36b
hoarse, teeth-chattering M.   102b
love, whose m. is ever May   344b
m. follow m. with woe   392a
m. in which the world bigan   89a
this is the M., ..the happy morn   270a
yet, within a m.   330a
Months: but two m. dead   330a
for m. and m. and m.   424a
gat in th. tweye   89a
I cd. live for m. without..labour   451b
three crabbed m. had soured   372b

Montmorenci: monstrous steep of M. 220b
Montreal: Oh God! Oh M. 67a
  the gospel of M. 67a
Mont Saint Jean seems Cain 71b
Monument: an early but enduring m. 392a
  ask where is his m. 558b
  from off the M.! 19b
  grave shall have a living m. 336b
  if you wd. see his m. 473b
  in this shalt find thy m. 389a
  like the M. 206b
  patience on a m. 371a
  thou art a m., without a tomb 216a
  you ask for his m. 19a
Monuments: gilded m. of princes 387b
Mood: albeit unused to the melting m. 364a
  her most exalted m. 470a
  in that sweet m. 471a
  in this m. will give us anything 340b
  in vacant or in pensive m. 467b
  listening m., she seem'd to stand 316a
  that blessed m. 472a
  that strain. .was of a higher m. 269b
  woman in her selfless m. 428b
Moods: m. of shadowy exultation 469b
  unfit contrarious m. 44a
Moon: a climbing m. . .an empty sky 476a
  a huge half m. 378a
  a hush with the setting m. 434a
  a m. that was the town's 92b
  and a white m. beams 225b
  and face the m. 447b
  and the m. be still as bright 74a
  and the m. was full 429a
  an isle, and a sickle m. 155a
  a Sussex m., untravelled still 92b
  auld m. in her arm 530a
  bares her bosom to the m. 473a
  be a dog, and bay the m. 340b
  beams of the watery m. 356b
  behold the wandering m. 268a
  beneath a waning m. was haunted 101a
  beneath the harvest m. 131a
  beneath the lightning and the M. 99a
  beneath the visiting m. 324b
  between the horns of the moon 407a
  blow them to the m. 335a
  bowl goes trim. The m. doth shine 295b
  brief the m. of beauty 436b
  brilliant m. and all the milky sky 476a
  by the light of the m. 74a
  by yonder blessed m. I swear 365a
  city had no need. .of the m. 520a
  come from the dying m. 436a
  course of one revolving m. 138b
  danced by the light of the m. 243b
  danced the m. on Monan's rill 316a
  dancing spectre seems the m. 264a
  do I carry the m. in my pocket? 48b
  drew my bride, beneath the m. 293a
  dwelleth i' the cold o' the m. 45b
  each paved with the m. 393a
  fair as the m. 500b
  follow still the changes of the m. 361b
  God Himself is m. and sun 435a
  hang them on the horns o' the m. 328a
  her solemn bird and this fair m. 274b
  honour from the pale faced M. 377a
  horned M., with one bright star 99a
  hymns to the cold fruitless m. 356a
  if the m. shine at full or no 65b
  if the Sun and M. shd. doubt 29b
  I had had an affair with the m. 411a
  I saw the new m. late 530a
  it is the m., I ken her horn 63b
  it is the very error of the m. 363b
  it was when the m. was setting 434b
  Lady M., Lady M. 198a
  lo, the m.'s self 49a
  lucent as a rounded m. 250b
  minions of the m. 376b
  m. and. .stars. .thou hast ordained 482a
  m. doth shine as bright as day 534b
  m. doth with delight 466a
  m. for certain seasons 488b
  M., in the valley of Ajalon 494b
  m. is my sister 26b
  m. is on the wave 73a
  m. may draw the sea 436b
  M. of Heaven is rising 154a

Moon (cont.)
  M. of my Delight 154a
  m. on my left 26b
  m., or the stars, be not darkened 499b
  m. plucked at my rein 475a
  m., rising in clouded majesty 274a
  m. shines bright on Mrs. Porter 144b
  m. shone, we did not see the candle 355b
  m. sits arbitress 272a
  m. sleeps with Endymion 355b
  m. stands blank above 199a
  m., sweet regent of the sky 265b
  m. under her feet 519a
  m. was a ghostly galleon 290a
  m. was shinin' clearly! 415a
  mortal. hath her eclipse 388b
  neither the m. by night 480b
  new m. she saw not 218b
  no bigger than the M. 98b
  no sun—no m.! 195a
  now the m. walks the night 119b
  on whom the pale m. gleams 291a
  owl does to the m. complain 174a
  O yonder is the m. 445a
  perturbed m. of Uranus 294b
  roaring m. of daffodil and crocus 435b
  saw the m. from Sussex downs 92b
  set on fishing up the m. 295b
  shines the m. in clouded skies 425b
  shining to the quiet m. 101a
  shoots higher. .threatens the m. 186b
  silent as the m. 277b
  silver apples of the m. 476a
  slivered in the m.'s eclipse 349b
  stain both m. and sun 387b
  sun and m., rejoice before Him 224a
  sun, m., and stars, brother 34a
  swear not by the m. 365a
  swifter than the wandering m. 357a
  the cow jumped over the m. 534a
  the glimpses of the m. 331a
  the innocent m. 443a
  the m. is up 69a
  the m.'s beauty. .m.'s soft pace 469b
  the m., the governess of floods 356b
  the m. winks 363a
  the moving M. went up the sky 99a
  the slow m. climbs 439a
  two red roses across the m. 284b
  under the cold, white m. 181b
  under the solitary m. 8a
  upon the corner of the m. 349b
  very wide awake the m. and I 164b
  vitreous pour of the full m. 458b
  when the m. shall rise 473b
  when the m. was blood 92a
  when the m. was overhead 431b
  whom mortals call the m. 393a
  wind up the sun and m. 74b
  with how sad steps, O M. 401b
  wolf behowls the m. 357b
  yonder wan and horned m. 393b
  yon rising M. that looks for us 154a
Moonbeam: the sad m. 35b
Moonbeams: m. from His eye 475a
  the m. kiss the sea 395b
Moonlight: as m. unto sunlight 432b
  fox jumped up on a m. night 533a
  how sweet the m. sleeps 355a
  look for me by m. 290a
  meet me by m. alone 462a
  m. in his room 201b
  under the m. still 226a
  visit it by the pale m. 317a
Moonlit: hark! hnot from that cedar 7a
Moons: new m. and sabbaths 501a
  not many m. gone by 323b
  reason has m., but m. not hers 192a
Moonshine: by m. do the. .ringlets make 367b
  collars of the m.'s watery beams 364b
  m. an' snow on field 250b
  transcendental m. 81a
Moon-struck madness 276b
Moon-washed apples 137b
Moor: away! the m. is dark 399a
  clasps of a lascivious M. 359b
  falls on the m. the brief. .day 224a
  feed and batten on this m. 335a
  gentle lady married to the M. 468b
  make the M. thank me, love me 361a

Moor (cont.)
  over the purple m. 290a
  she dwelt on a wide m. 467b
  the M. is of a free. .nature 360b
  yr. daughter and the M. 359b
Moore: before I go, Tom M. 73a
Moorfowl: an undying m. 475a
Moors: blows the wind on the m. 414b
  she's for the M., and martyrdom 115a
Mops: seven maids with seven m. 84a
Mor the Peacock 234b
Moral: and the m. of that is 83a
  degeneration of his m. being 413a
  Englishman thinks he is m. 390b
  his m. pleases, not his. .wit 303b
  is there any m. shut 426b
  let us be m. 124a
  make a m. of the devil 382b
  m. Clytemnestra 73b
  m. considerations. .three quarters 564a
  m. life of a man forms part 460b
  m. or intellectual damage 575b
  m. sense. .never. .account for 80b
  m., sensible, and well bred 108a
  no one m. . .till all are m. 408a
  no such thing as a m. or an immoral book 460a
  O m. Gower 90a
  the m. law within me 568b
  to point a m., or adorn a tale 213b
Moralist: rustic m. to die 174b
  yr. 'poor m.', betake me 75b
Morality: Dr. Johnson's m. . .English 182b
  good-bye, m.! 186a
  make our idea of m. centre 412a
  m. is the regulation of conduct 407b
  m. of art consists 460b
  m. of masters. .m. of slaves 569a
  m. touched by emotion 10a
  on his m. than on his 'ossmanship 416b
  periodical fits of m. 255a
  personal and national m. 390a
  some people talk of m. 143b
  unawares M. expires 299a
Moralize: I m. two meanings 385a
  loves shall m. my song 408b
Moralized his song 303a
Moral philosophy: m. . .handmaid to religion 13a
  m. (make men) grave 16a
Morals: Babel is a divergence upon m. 413a
  let thy m. tell thy mind 299b
  m. of a Methodist 166b
  teach the m. of a whore 206b
  why, man of m., tell me why? 106b
More: and m., and m., and m. 84b
  by god body, master M. 283a
  easy to take m. than nothing 83a
  for I have m. 132a
  he m. had pleased us 1b
  he will awake no m. 392a
  in that m. lie all his hopes 9a
  (I speak as a fool) I am m. 515a
  I've no m. yet 534b
  knowledge grow from m. to m. 429b
  m. he cast away, the m. he had 54b
  m. than my brothers are to me 429b
  m. than that no man is entitled 310a
  m. we see of you 26b
  m. wd. be laid at yr. feet 423a
  m. you 'ave known o' the others 230b
  no m., but e'en a woman 324b
  no m. of that 364a
  no m. of that, Hal 377b
  no m., oh, never m.! 395a
  oh, the little m., and how much 45b
  Oliver Twist has asked for m. 125a
  once m., O ye laurels 269a
  once m. unto the breach. .once m. 382a
  one m., and this the last 363b
  only a little m. I have to write 189b
  rather-m.-or-less 228b
  she cd. not give him m. 140a
  so I can't take m. 83a
  they merely know m. 315b
  thou, O Lord, art m. than they 429b
  we shall not do it any m. 393a
  where m. is meant than meets 268b
  who dares do m. is none 347a

More (*cont.*)
will whyles do m.	59a
Morea: along M.'s hills	70a
Morgue: the Doric little M.	44b
Moriarty: Professor M.	135b
Morn: a m. of bright carnations	138a
another m. ris'n on mid-noon	275a
as yet 'tis early m.	432a
at midnight and at m.	146b
autumn evening, and the m.	398b
awake, the m. will never rise	117b
beloved, it is m.!	191a
clasped by the. .light of m.	195b
clear in the cool September m.	458b
cock that crowed in the m.	534a
fair laughs the m.	173b
from m. to night, my friend	311a
glowing like the vital m.	393b
hearts that with rising m. arise	223b
hues of the rich unfolding m.	223b
in a m. by break of day	35a
incense-breathing M.	174a
less dear than the dew of the m.	474a
lights that do mislead the m.	352a
lov'st to greet the early m.	61b
M. a thousand Roses brings	152b
m. from black to red began to turn	65b
m., in russet mantle clad	329b
one Friday m. when we set sail	525b
opening eyelids of the m.	269a
salute the happy m.	67b
see the opening m.	32a
shall be the m. of song	415b
sun came peeping in at m.	195a
sweet is the breath of m.	274b
the blooming m. upon her wings	189a
the m. not waking till she sing	251b
the nice M. on the Indian steep	266b
this pious m.	219b
this the happy m.	270a
to descry the m.'s approach	277a
ushers in the m.	151b
when m. purples the east	275b
where the m. of life was spent	172b
with the m. those Angel faces	288b
Morning: a breeze of m. moves	434a
almost at odds with m.	349b
as the radiant lines of m.	397b
before the m. watch	490a
bird-song at m.	414a
break forth as the m.	503a
caught this m. m.'s minion	198a
cold and frosty m.	523b
duly twice a m.	238b
early in the m.	527b
evening and the m. . .first day	492a
every m. brought a noble chance	429a
every m. the red sun rises	3a
full many a glorious m.	387b
glad confident m. again	48a
God of the M.	234b
here of a Sunday m.	199a
he's for the m.	47a
if m. skies, books, and my food	415a
in the m. it is green	487b
in the m. of the world	50a
in rainfall at m.	414b
in the m. sow thy seed	499b
in the m. thou shalt say	494b
it's nice to get up in the m.	242b
joy cometh in the m.	483b
like to the m.'s war	384a
looketh forth as the m.	500b
Lord, in the m. thou shalt hear	453a
Lucifer, son of the m.!	502a
make the m. precious	220b
methinks I scent the m. air	331b
m., evening, noon, and night	45a
M. in the Bowl of Night	152a
m.'s at seven	50a
never m. wore to evening	429b
'No', this m., sir, I say	43b
outgoings of the m. and evening	486a
phantom of False m. died	152a
rainbow in the m.	522a
sees some m., unaware	47a
shown no glorious m. face	415a
take the wings of the m.	490a
the great m. of the world	392a
the m. lowers	1a
the m. stars sang together	497b

Morning (*cont.*)
thy m. bounties	109b
till m. fair came forth	277a
'tis almost m.	365b
'tis always m. somewhere	198a
up in the m. early	63a
veils of the M.	475a
walk with Death and M.	437a
watchman said, The m. cometh	502a
wear the beauty of the m.	472b
when the red m. is brightening	397b
Wings o' the M.	236b
with. .m. cool repentance came	320a
won't go home till m.	53b
would God it were m.	494b
Morning-star: a charm to stay the m.	101a
golden guess is m.	426a
Morocco: pause there, M	353b
Morrice: gulls in an aëry m.	185b
Morrison: M. M. Weatherby George	266b
M.'s Pill for curing. .Society	81a
Morrow: bitterly thought of the m.	462b
budding m. is midnight	221a
day and a night and a m.	420b
good m. to our waking souls	133a
m. shall take thought. .itself	505b
of a ful misty m.	90a
take no thought for the m.	505b
watching for the m.	82a
windy night a rainy m.	388b
Morsel: I found you as a m. col	324a
m. for a monarch	323a
Mortal: all men m., but themselves	477a
a m. thing so to immortalize	408a
beyond a m.'s share	261a
but m. in the minute	49a
change. .all m. things doth sway	409a
fair as aught of m. birth	67b
gathers all things m.	422a
grief itself be m.	392a
he rais'd a m. to the skies	139a
her last disorder m.	168a
I presume you're m.	401a
know all m. consequences	350b
love, sole m. thing	293a
m.! Love that Holy One	120a
no m. might one from other know	254a
purest treasure m. times afford	374b
singing, here comes a m.	6a
swings the flux of m. things	9a
this m. must put on immortality	515a
this m. shall assume its immortality	77a
turning m. for thy love	345a
tush, man, m. men, m. men	378b
unless m. it were given	318b
whatever stirs this m. frame	101b
Mortality: kept watch o'er man's m.	467a
m.'s too weak to bear them	289b
m. weighs heavily on me	221a
sad m. o'ersways their power	388a
there's nothing serious in m.	348a
who then to frail m. shall trust	17a
Mortals: experience. .to m. is a providence	175b
not for m. always to be blest	4b
security is m.'s chiefest enemy	349b
than we m. dream	398b
timorous m. start and shrink	453b
what fools these m. be!	357a
whom m. call the moon	393a
Mortar: bray a fool in a m.	498b
Mortify a wit	303b
Mortimer: 'to arms!' cried M.	173b
Moscow: Juan was my M.	71b
Moses: as I was with M.	494b
climb where M. stood	453b
disputed about the body of M.	518a
His hand on M.' law	30a
I am, Jehova said to M.	403a
it might be M. (a man I hate)	236a
Jesus was sitting in M.' chair	30a
M. commands she be ston'd	30a
M. . .died of the kisses of. .God	285b
M. hid his face	493b
M. stood with arms spread	110a
passed from Mahomet to M.	305a
the man M. was very meek	494a
Moss: azure m. and flowers	396b
m. that wholly hides. .oak-stump	99b
stone. .rolling can gather no m.	446b

Most: make the m. on 'em
Most: make the m. on 'em	121b
the m. may err as grossly	138b
thinks m., feels the noblest	18a
Mote that is in thy brother's eye	505b
Motes: as thikke as m.	89b
Moth: a m. of peace	360b
how, like a m., the simple maid	159a
kill not the m. nor butterfly	29b
m. fretting a garment	484a
not a m. with vain desire	430b
the candle singed the m.	353b
the moth's kiss, first!	46b
where m. and rust doth corrupt	505b
Mother: abide by my M.'s house	233a
all my m. came into mine eyes	383a
all so still where His m. was	524a
a m. for her children	28b
a m. is a m. still	102a
an Egyptian to my m. give	362b
any babe on any m.'s knee	423a
as is the m., so is her daughter	503b
back to the great sweet m.	424a
bathe in me, m. and child	226a
behold my m. and my brethren	506b
behold thy m.	511b
bring thee into my m.'s house	500b
call his m. 'Ma'am'	93a
call me early, m. dear	434b
come to the m.'s, when she feels	178a
coster's. .jumping on his m.	166b
daughter am I in my m.'s house	233a
dearer was the m. for the child	101a
deceived the m. of mankind	270b
does yr. m. know. .you are out?	19b
don't tell my m. I'm living in sin	186a
drop into thy m.'s lap	276b
else his m. a witch maun be	531a
fairer daughter of a fair m.	544b
foolish son. .heaviness of his m.	498a
for m. will be there	186a
from whence his m. rose	320b
great M.'s train divine	9a
happy he with such a m.	437a
Heaven's M. send us grace	98b
here, M., tie my girdle	393a
His m. on his father him begot	30a
his M., who was patient, being dead	294a
home to his m.'s house	277b
I arose a m. in Israel	494b
I feel no pain dear m. now	523b
in sin hath my m. conceived me	485a
it cannot be called our m.	350a
joyful m. of children	489a
little did my m. ken	530a
Mary was that M. mild	3b
m., a maiden is a tender thing	428b
m., and lover of men	424a
m. and maiden	524b
m. bids me bind my hair	202a
m. came and caught her	535b
m. cried, baby lept	176a
m., for love of grace, lay not	335a
m., make my bed soon	529b
m. may forget the child	61b
m. of all living	492b
m. of dead dogs	81a
M. of God! no lady thou	98a
m. of harlots and abominations	519b
m. of months in meadow	420a
m. of Parliaments	38a
m. of Sisera looked out	495a
m. of the Fair Delight	311b
M.! oh, where is that radiant shore	184b
m. o' mine	232b
m.'s milk were scarce out of him	370a
m.'s pride, a father's joy	319a
m.'s sake the child was dear	101a
m.'s wag, pretty boy	176a
m. that bore you. .knew it all	232b
m. . .the holiest thing alive	102a
m. who talks. .her own children	128b
M., Wife and Queen	437a
m., wi' her needle an' her sheers	59b
my m. bore me in the. .wild	32b
my m. didna speak	20b
my m. groaned, my father wept	32a
my m. she fell sick	20b
near the manners of my m.	370a
never had any m.	415b
old M. Hubbard	533b

Mother (cont.)
O M., Mary M. — 313a
O m., make my bed soon — 531b
one whom his m. comforteth — 503b
repeats to thee thy m.'s grief — 29b
rhyming m. wits — 259a
scarce be a man before thy m. — 23a
show'd thy dear m. any courtesy — 328b
Simon's wife's m. — 508a
solemn earth, a fatal m. — 421a
so loving to my m. — 330a
Sons of Martha favour their M. — 234b
stood the mournful m. weeping — 554a
strive to be a man before yr. m. — 107b
such a lady God's m. be — 524b
sucked the breasts of my m. — 500b
tell yr. m. it wasn't I — 533a
there thy m. brought thee forth — 501a
there was their Dacian m. — 69a
this great m. of the sciences — 17a
thou art thy m.'s glass — 387a
thy m. a lady, both lovely — 317b
thy m.'s grief — 35b
took great care of his m. — 266b
upraised me where my m. fell — 441a
virgin m. born — 270a
what is home without a m.? — 182b
when my m. died — 32b
where a M. laid her Baby — 3b
where yet was ever found a m. — 160b
who ran to help me..my M. — 425a
whose m. was her painting — 328b
who was yr. m.? — 415b
yr. m. will never see you again — 11b
Mother Carey: bound to M. — 227a
Motherland, we pledge to thee — 228a
Mothers: all women become like their m. — 460a
city of the best-bodied m. — 457b
if Cæsar had stabbed their m. — 338a
m. of large families — 25b
m. that lack sons — 328a
younger..are happy m. made — 364b
Mother tongue: Chatham's language was his m. — 111b
Mother-wit: Nature by her m. cd. frame — 409a
Moths: unfading m. — 39b
Mothy curfew-tide — 179b
Motion: a breath and everlasting m. — 465b
careful of my m. — 427a
her m. blushed at herself — 360a
in his m. like an angel sings — 355a
little m. in the air — 393a
meandering with a mazy m. — 101a
measured m. like a living thing — 469a
m. of our human blood — 472a
next to the perpetual m. — 127a
no m. has she now, no force — 463a
sounds of undistinguishable m. — 469a
the acting..and the first m. — 338b
the m. of a hidden fire — 280a
this sensible warm m. — 352a
to nothing with perpetual m. — 380a
to rot itself with m. — 322b
unshak'd of m. — 339a
with a short uneasy m. — 99b
with his eternal m. make — 467a
with the m. of all elements — 345a
with visible m. her diurnal round — 466a
with what m. moved the clouds! — 469a
yr. sweet hue..hath m. — 388b
Motions: her household m. light — 470b
m. of his spirit are dull — 355b
m. of the viewless winds — 469b
must to thy m. lovers' seasons — 134a
skittish in all motions — 370b
so delicate his m. be — 37b
those well-ordered m. — 42a
two weeping m. — 115a
Motive: looks always on the m. — 474a
noblest m. is the public good — 410a
Motive-hunting of motiveless malignity — 102b
Motives meaner than your own — 21b
Motley: a m. fool — 326a
made myself a m. — 389a
M.'s the only wear — 326a
Motto: be that my m. and my fate — 420a
m. I proposed for the [Edinburgh] — 405a
Mottoes: lovely cracker m. — 163a

Mould: anything that grew out of the m. — 233a
m. of a man's fortune — 16a
rocks on the m. — 522a
round their..lips the m. falls — 312a
splashing the wintry m. — 475b
the m. of form — 333b
'the sort of woman now,' said M. — 124a
Moulded: scarcely formed or m. — 72a
Moulds: crack nature's m. — 342b
Moulmein Pagoda — 232a
Moult: time shall m. away — 416a
Mound: each night above his m. — 179a
seated upon the convex m. — 202b
this wave-washed m. — 312b
Mount: by m., and stream, and sea — 184b
great Vision of the guarded m. — 270a
I may not m. on thee again — 289b
liked the 'Sermon on the M.' — 130b
M. Amara — 274a
m., m., my soul — 376a
m. of marble, a hundred spires — 426b
whilst you m. up on high — 376a
Mountain: a forked m., or blue promontory — 324a
devil..exceeding high m. — 505a
every m. and hill..made low — 502b
fold to fold, of m. or of cape — 436b
gross as a m. — 377b
heard the M.'s slumbrous voice — 396a
his plough, along the m.-side — 470a
in all my holy m. — 501b
I reside at Table M. — 182b
land of the m. and the flood — 317b
Nebo's lonely m. — 3a
o'er the rugged m.'s brow — 172b
robes the m. in its azure hue — 77a
say unto this m., Remove hence — 507a
set a huge m. 'tween my heart — 339a
sun looked over the m.'s rim — 49b
the m. and the squirrel — 146b
the m. sheep are sweeter — 295a
this fair m. leave to feed — 335a
tiptoe on the misty m. tops — 366a
up the airy m. — 4a
woods or steepy m. yields — 259a
young hart upon the m. of spices — 501a
Mountain-built with peaceful citadel — 219b
Mountains: Acroceraunian m. — 392b
among our ancient m. — 245a
among the m. by the winter sea — 429a
barren are those m. — 37a
beautiful must be the m. — 37a
before the m. were brought forth — 487b
brighter Hellas rears its m. — 394a
came to the Delectable M. — 54a
faith, so that I cd. remove m. — 514b
fields, or waves, or m. — 398b
from Greenland's icy m. — 184a
he wd. hunt in the m. — 530b
his strength setteth fast the m. — 486a
how beautiful upon the m. — 502b
Mont Blanc is the monarch of m. — 73a
m. also shall bring peace — 486b
m. and rocks, Fall on us — 519a
m. are the beginning..of..scenery — 314a
m. divide us, and the waste — 320b
m. interpos'd make enemies — 111b
m., moors, and fenlands — 248b
m. will be in labour — 542a
o'er her grave ye m. shine — 8b
paced upon the m. overhead — 476b
see the m. kiss high Heaven — 395b
snow on the m. below — 393a
snow the m. have put on — 407a
the m. are our sponsors — 241b
the m. look on Marathon — 70b
to me high m. are a feeling — 68b
to the rocks and the m. — 424b
two Voices..one of the m. — 471b
uno'erleap'd M. of Necessity — 8a
upon England's m. green — 31a
when men and m. meet — 30a
ye m. of Gilboa — 495b
Mountain-tops: flatter the m. — 387b
over all the m. is peace — 568a
the m. that freeze — 385b
Mountebank: a mere anatomy, a m. — 328a
m. who sold pills — 2b
Mounted: Lycidas sunk low, but m. — 270a
m. on her milk-white steed — 528a

Mounting: there was m. in hot haste — 68l
Mounts: m., and that hardly — 6b
now he m. above me — 139a
Mourn: blessed are they that m. — 505a
I m. for that most lovely thing — 474b
in summer skies to m. — 217b
makes countless thousands m. — 61b
man was made to m. — 61b
m., hapless Caledonia, m. — 405b
m. with ever-returning spring — 458b
no longer m. for me — 388a
now can never m. a heart — 392b
o'er thee the angels m. — 37b
shall I go m. for that, my dear? — 373a
time enough to m. — 117a
to comfort all that m. — 503a
wherefore shd. we m.? — 465a
Mourned: a beast..wd. have m. longer — 330a
m., till Pity's self be dead — 103a
Mourner: constant m. o'er the dead — 72b
Mourners: most musical of m. — 391b
m. go about the streets — 500a
no m. walk behind me — 180b
the m. followed after — 199a
Mournful: m. that no new wonder — 475b
when m. as I sat — 20b
Mourning: and silence their m. — 424b
better to go to the house of m. — 499a
hath oftener left me m. — 471a
m. of a mighty nation — 435a
oil of joy for m. — 503b
she doth of m. speak — 78a
Mouse: as still as m. — 155a
caught a crooked m. — 532a
good my m. of virtue — 370a
hath he to ete a m. — 89b
I frightened a little m. — 534a
if that she sawe a m. — 88b
killing of a m. on Sunday — 35a
lat him seen a m. — 89b
not a m. shall disturb this..house — 357b
not even a m. — 280b
single laughable little m. — 542a
so quiet as a m. — 1a
the m. ran up the clock — 534a
the m. was gone — 534a
usual to catch a m. or two — 175b
Mouse-trap: make a better m. — 148b
Moustache: kissed by a man who didn't wax his m. — 237b
Mouth: a pipe for my capacious m. — 159a
a rose her m. — 433b
determination of words to the m. — 417a
down in the m. — 105a
God be in my m. — 523a
God be in their m. — 490b
he opened not his m. — 503a
her m. is smoother than oil — 497b
his m. is most sweet — 500b
if you m. it — 333b
in their m. was found no guile — 519a
in the m. of fame — 222a
it was in my m. sweet as honey — 519a
matched in m. like bells — 357a
m. fair Freedom's classic line — 77b
m. like an old potato — 227b
m. of the Lord hath spoken it — 502b
m. of yr. own geranium's red — 46b
not..wh. goeth into the m. defileth — 507a
ope his m., out there flew a trope — 64b
out of his m. went a..sword — 518b
out of the..heart the m. speaketh — 506b
out of the m. of very babes — 482a
out of thine own m. will I judge — 510a
purple-stained m. — 219b
reasons made his m. to water — 65a
sandwich..no m. to put it in — 126a
satisfieth thy m. with good things — 488a
set a watch, O Lord, before my m. — 490b
spue thee out of my m. — 518b
stop his m. with a kiss — 358a
sweet red splendid kissing m. — 424a
sweet small m. — 422b
to look a gift-horse in the m. — 65a
what seems to say her rosy m.? — 293b
with the m. of a bell — 227a
Mouthed: first m. last swallowed — 335a
Mouthful: out of a m. of air — 474b
Mouths: blind m.! — 269b
enemy in their m. — 361b

Mouths (*cont.*)
fair woman..made m. in a glass 342*b*
have m., and speak not 489*a*
he m. a sentence 94*b*
our m. are one with Mouth 40*a*
to m. like mine at least 51*b*
whose m. must be held with bit 483*b*
Move: anon they m. in..phalanx 271*b*
but it does m. 567*a*
for ever and for ever when I m. 438*b*
for in him we live, and m. 512*b*
for shame, this will not m. 416*a*
if I cd. pray to m. 339*a*
it never shd. m. at any time 488*a*
I will m. Thee 187*b*
let's all m. one place on 83*a*
makes no show to m. 134*a*
m. onward, leading up 427*a*
m. still, still so 373*b*
so did she m.; so did she sing 249*b*
the great affair is to m. 412*b*
Moveable Feasts 478*a*
Moved: eyes have m. me not 415*a*
he has m. a little nearer 248*b*
hell from beneath is m. for thee 502*a*
I, singularly m. 293*b*
not suffer thy foot to be m. 489*b*
that it cannot be m. 487*b*
Movement: a sudden and adroit m. 451*a*
Movements: many m. of his mind 472*b*
their glad animal m. 472*a*
Movers and shakers of the world 291*a*
Moves: as impotently m. as you or I 153*b*
having writ m. on 153*b*
it m. us not 473*a*
m., and mates, and slays 153*b*
Moveth all together, if..at all 470*a*
Moving: in m., how express 332*b*
m. about in worlds not realised 466*b*
m. others, are themselves as stone 388*b*
the m. Moon went up 99*a*
tho' m. inly to one far-set goal 9*a*
Moving-delicate, and full of life 359*a*
Mower whets his scythe 268*b*
Mozart: fit for the gaiety of M. 37*a*
Much: and asking too m. 78*b*
but poor tho' m. they have 143*a*
goin' thro' so m...learn so little 126*b*
I have as m. of this in art 341*a*
I may've 'ad too m. 535*b*
is by m. too m. 378*b*
maketh m. of them that fear 482*a*
more to that wh. had too m. 325*b*
m. of a muchness 144*a*
so many worlds, so m. to do 430*b*
something too m. of this 334*a*
there will be too m. of me 165*b*
there won't be m. for us 85*b*
this is too m. for be 237*a*
Muchness: much of a m. 144*a*
Muck: money is like m. 15*a*
stop raking the m. 310*b*
Muck-rake: man..with a m. 54*a*
Muck-rakes..indispensable 310*b*
Mud: m. celestially fair 39*b*
of water and of m. 39*a*
one sees the m. 242*a*
put m. into toffee 439*b*
Muddied oafs at the goals 230*a*
Muddy: m. ecstasies of beer 113*b*
m., ill-seeming, thick 367*a*
trouts..tickled best in m. water 66*b*
Muddy-mettled rascal 333*a*
Mudie's: keep my books at..M. 66*b*
Muffin: now for the m. and toast 167*a*
Muffins: in a plate of m. 390*b*
Mug: graceful air and heavenly m. 155*a*
zum o' that in a m. 535*a*
Mugwump of the final plot 38*b*
Mulberry Garden 149*b*
Mule: be ye not like to horse and m. 483*b*
cross breed, the m. of politics 129*a*
the battery-m.'s a m. 233*a*
Mull was a-stern 414*b*
Multiplication is vexation 533*a*
Multiply: be fruitful, and m. 492*a*
Multiplying eye 180*b*
Multitude: cover the m. of sins 517*b*
fool m., that choose by show 353*b*
goeth about to persuade a m. 196*b*
great m., wh. no man cd. number 519*a*

Multitude (*cont.*)
hoofs of a swinish m. 57*a*
inaudible to the vast m. 464*b*
not in the m. of friends 214*b*
rank me with the barbarous m. 353*b*
saved by the m. of an host 484*a*
still discordant, wavering m. 379*b*
the giddy m. 262*b*
the m. is always in the wrong 128*a*
the rude m. call the afternoon 345*a*
Multitudes: against revolted m. 275*a*
I contain m. 458*a*
m. in the valley of decision 504*a*
pestilence-stricken m. 396*a*
Mum 's the word 570*b*
Mummers: grave m.! 299*a*
Mummy: it was dyed in m. 362*b*
M. is become merchandise 42*b*
Munch on, crunch on 50*a*
Munched, and munched 346*a*
Mundane: more than m. weeds 39*b*
Munich: wave, M.! all thy banners 77*a*
Murder: foul and midnight m. 173*b*
from battle and m. 478*b*
I met M. in the way 395*b*
Killing no M. Briefly Discourst 321*b*
love and m. will out 104*a*
more strange than such a m. is 349*a*
most sacrilegious m. 348*a*
most unnatural m. 331*b*
m. by the law 477*a*
m. cannot be hid long 353*b*
m. most foul 331*b*
M...One of the Fine Arts 120*a*
m...run in families 245*a*
m., tho' it have no tongue 333*a*
m. yet is but fantastical 346*b*
no place..shd. m. sanctuarize 336*a*
one m. made a villain 304*b*
then m.'s out of tune 363*b*
thou shalt do no m. 480*a*
to do no contrived m. 359*b*
to m. and to rafish 12*b*
we m. to dissect 471*b*
withered m., alarum'd 347*a*
Murdered: some sleeping kill'd;
all m. 375*b*
two brothers and their m. man 218*b*
Murderer: an honourable m. 364*a*
deaf and viperous m. 392*a*
Eugene Aram..a liar, and a m. 75*b*
first smith was the first m.'s son 112*b*
help the escaping m. 412*b*
the man is a common m. 315*b*
Murders: twenty mortal m. 349*a*
Murdstone: Mr. M. 121*b*
Murex: who fished the m. up? 50*a*
Murmur: Atheist too, why m. I 133*b*
creeping m. and the pouring dark 382*a*
I do not m. 568*b*
live m. of a summer's day 8*a*
take the rustic m. of their bourg 428*b*
whose m. invites one to sleep 399*b*
with reason m. at his case 109*a*
Murmuring of innumerable bees 437*a*
Murmurings: m. of..the city 107*a*
m., whereby the monitor expressed 464*b*
Murmurs: as for m., mother 171*a*
hear our mutual m. sweep 71*a*
hollow m. died away 103*a*
m. as the ocean m. 241*a*
no quarrels, m., no delay 115*a*
Murphy: 'tace, madam', answered M. 151*a*
Murray: bonny Earl of M. 530*b*
my M. 73*a*
Muscle: keep thy m. trained 250*b*
the motion of a m. 463*a*
Muscovy: of a Prince in M. 235*a*
Muscular: his Christianity was m. 129*b*
Muse: every conqueror creates a M. 449*a*
for this the Tragic M. first trod 298*b*
honour'd by the M. he loved 299*b*
meditate the thankless M. 269*b*
M. invoked, sit down to write 419*b*
my M. these notes intendeth 401*b*
my M., to some ears not unsweet 402*a*
natural love of the 'chaste m.' 33*a*
neither man, nor M., can praise 215*a*
now, M., let's sing of rats 172*b*
O! for a M. of fire 381*a*
plans, credit, and the M. 146*b*

Muse (*cont.*)
poet meets his favouring m. 113*b*
so may some gentle M. 269*a*
talked shop like a tenth m. 523*b*
taught by the heavenly M. 267*b*
the M., nae poet ever fand her 62*b*
wh. most doth take my M. and me 215*a*
with the worst-humour'd m. 169*b*
with the worst natured M. 309*b*
worthy of the Virgilian m. 37*a*
Muses: adopting M. chose their sons 36*a*
charm of all the M. 439*a*
m. on admired themes 259*b*
M.' sacred grove be wet 442*b*
M. scorn with vulgar brains 401*b*
sitteth in the M.' bower 36*a*
wander where the M. haunt 273*a*
write the..M.' story 176*b*
Museum: bones and beak all in the
M. 25*b*
Mushrooms: broiled fowl and m. 126*a*
Music(k): a little m. out of doors 223*a*
all art..aspires towards..m. 572*b*
all kinds of m. 504*a*
along the Psalmist's m. deep 44*a*
but the m. there 300*a*
ceasing of exquisite m. 247*a*
chief m. of our May 137*a*
city is built to m. 427*b*
compulsion doth in m. lie 266*b*
daughters of m...be brought low 499*b*
die in m. 364*a*
discourse most eloquent m. 334*b*
fading in m. 354*a*
finds its food in m. 245*a*
fled is that m. 220*a*
from their own M. when they stray 78*b*
God! of whom m. and song 264*a*
great fish spouts m. 202*b*
hath no m. in himself 355*b*
heard his voice in all her m. 392*b*
hear'st thou m. sadly 387*a*
hear the sweet m. of speech 113*a*
heaven is m. 78*a*
heavy part the m. bears 214*b*
he hears no m. 338*a*
how sour sweet m. is 376*a*
how sweet his m.! 471*b*
I don't..know anything about m. 25*a*
if m. be the food of love 369*b*
in sweet m. is such art 385*a*
I shall be made thy M. 133*b*
just accord all m. makes 402*a*
let the sounds of m. creep 355*a*
like harmony in m. 469*a*
made his m. heard below 426*b*
maintain the m. of the spheres 42*a*
makes m. wherever she goes 533*b*
make the m. mute 428*b*
many a tale their m. tells 282*a*
Master of all m. 248*b*
may make one m. as before 429*b*
mellow m. match'd with him 430*b*
Milton..a solemn service of m. 239*a*
mind the m. and the step 18*b*
m. alone with sudden charms 104*a*
M. and sweet Poetry 21*a*
m. arose..voluptuous swell 68*a*
m. for the time doth change 355*b*
m. has charms to sooth 104*b*
M., heavenly Maid, was young 103*a*
m. in its roar 69*b*
m. in my heart I bore 471*a*
m. is the brandy of the damned 390*b*
m. is the gladness of the world 144*b*
m., moody food of us 323*b*
M. of a *distant* Drum 152*b*
m. of its trees at dawn 7*a*
m. of men's lives 376*a*
m. oft hath such a charm 352*a*
m. of the Gospel leads us home 150*a*
m...sensual pleasure without vice 212*a*
m. sent up to God by the lover 44*b*
M. shall untune the sky 139*b*
m. soars within the little lark 43*a*
M., sphere-descended maid 103*a*
m. sweeter than their own 469*a*
m. that gentlier on the spirit 433*a*
m. that I care to hear 197*b*
m., the greatest good..mortals
know 1*b*

Music(k) (cont.)

m. to hear	387a
m., when soft voices die	399b
m. wherever there is a harmony	42a
m. with th' enamelled stones	372b
m., yearning like a God in pain	221b
never merry when I hear sweet m.	355a
no m. in the nightingale	372b
not formed, as notes of m. are	393b
o'ercharged to m. lendeth	401b
pass'd in m. out of sight	432a
perfect m. unto noble words	437a
reasonable good ear in m.	357a
sank like m. on my heart	99b
seduction of martial m.	58b
Shelley's genius..m. not poetry	9a
Shelley with liquid m.	36a
sing—M. was given, to brighten	282a
softest m. to attending ears	365b
soft is the m. that wd. charm	468a
still, sad m. of humanity	472a
strain of m. to thy mind	35b
struck one chord of m.	306b
sweet as stops of planetary m.	393b
that m. still!	471a
that vulgar and tavern m.	42a
their rounds their m.'s aid	249b
the m. he made with us	423a
there is m. even in beauty	42a
the soul of m. shed	281a
this m. crept by me	367a
thy beauty's silent m.	78a
thy chosen m., Liberty!	471b
to hear the sea-maid's m.	356b
to his m. plants and flowers	385b
uproar's yr. only m.	222a
what passion cannot M. raise	130b
where m. dwells lingering	467b
whose m. hell can move	78b
with m. loud and long	101b
with m. sweet as love	398a
women and m. shd. never be dated	171a
yr. voice is m.	25a

Musical: found out m. tunes

found out m. tunes	521a
most m., most melancholy	268a
Shakespeare, and the m. glasses	171a
silence more m. than any song	311a
we were none of us m.	159a

Musician: as a m. scatters sound

as a m. scatters sound	464b
better a m. than the wren	355b
he is dead, the sweet m.	248b
the lady is a m.	135b

Musicians: 'tis we m. know

'tis we m. know	44b
Music-maker: Schumann's our m.	46b
Music-makers: we are the m.	291a

Musing: m. full sadly in his..mind

m. full sadly in his..mind	408b
m. there an hour alone	70b
thus m. the fire kindled	484a

Musk of the rose is blown

of the rose is blown	434a
Musket: his m. moulds in his hands	151a
when the volleying m. played	317a
Musk-rose: cankers in the m. buds	356b
m., and the well-attir'd woodbine	270a
the coming m.	356b

Mussels: cockles and m., alive, alive

cockles and m., alive, alive	524a
m. all in a row	533a

Must: Duty whispers low *Thou m.*

Duty whispers low *Thou m.*	147a
I do but sing because I m.	430a
this year, the m. shall foam	253a
we forget because we m.	5a

Mustard: but to say 'Pass the m.'

but to say 'Pass the m.'	167a
faith as a grain of m.	507a
like to a grain of m. seed	506b
piece of beef and m.	366b

Muster: to join the m. came 253a

Mustn't: tell her she m. 535b

Musty: proverb is something m. 334b

Mutability: M. in them doth play

M. in them doth play	409a
nought may endure but M.	396a
Mutable, rank-scented many	328a

Mute: at the balance let's be m.

at the balance let's be m.	59a
care of natures that are m.!	264a
ditty, long since m.	221b
if she be m., is she not pure?	315a
make the music m.	428b
m. and magnificent, without a tear	141b
m. on Tara's walls	281a
say she be m.	366b
some m. inglorious Milton	174a
Mutilators of collections	239a

Mutiny: a sudden flood of m. 340a

Mutiny (cont.)

stones of Rome to rise and m.	340b
Mutton: boiled leg of m.	127a
their love o' m.	250b
Mutton-pies: make them into m.	85b
Mutual: m. cowardice keeps us in peace	210a
m. Forgiveness of each vice	30a
told but to her m. breast	77b
Muzzle: not m. the ox	494b
My! when he made Ole Hunderd	250b
My-doxy: Orthodoxy or M.	80b
My-lorded him	440a
Mynheer Vandunck	103b
Myra's pocket-hole	31b
Myriad-minded Shakespeare	102a
Myriads though bright	271a

Myrrh: bundle of m. is my well-beloved

bundle of m. is my well-beloved	500a
frankincense, and m.	504b

Myrtle: land where the cypress and m.

land where the cypress and m.	67b
shall come up the m. tree	503a
than the soft m.	351b
Myrtles: once more ye m. brown	269a
wh. a grove of m. made	20b

Myself: am quite m. again

am quite m. again	199a
because I'm not m.	82b
find in m. no pity to m.	385a
I can't explain m.	82b
I celebrate m.	457b
I follow but m.	359b
I live not in m.	68b
I'm not feeling very well m.	536a
I pray for no man but m.	368a
leave nothing of m. in me	114b
m. and my Creator	288a
m. not least, but honoured of them	438b
m. when young did eagerly	153a
never less alone than when by m.	161b
nobody; I m.; farewell	363b
thinking for m. at all	166a
too near the praising of m.	354b
when I give I give m.	458a

Mysteries: stewards of the m.

stewards of the m.	514a
what m. do lie beyond thy dust	448a

Mystery: burthen of the m.

burthen of the m.	472a
comprehend its m.	248a
embodied in the m. of words	469b
he will discredit our m.	352a
in m. our soul abides	7a
I show you a m.	515a
lay bare the m. to me	192a
love is such a m.	416a
lucrative business of m.	57b
marvel and a m. to the world	247b
M., Babylon the Great	519b
oh! m. of man	470a
Penetralium of m.	222a
pluck out the heart of my m.	334b
reflection solves the m.	415b
see M. to Mathematics fly	299a
take upon 's the m. of things	344a
the m., the sign	132b
where m. begins, justice ends	57b
where m. begins, religion ends	57b
wrapped up my buth in a m.	440b
yr. m., yr. m.; nay, despatch	362b
Mysterious: God moves in a m. way	110a
Mystic: as ye walk yr. m. way	165a
Nature's m. book	260a
Mystical: m. body of thy Son	480b
m. mathematics of the city of heaven	41a

N

N or M	481a
Na: fye n., fye n.	529a
Nabobs raised the price of everything	254b
Nadir: dark has crossed the n.	200a
Nag: money on de bob-tail n.	156a
Naiad: a Nymph, a N. or a Grace	316a
guardian N. of the strand	316a

Nail: Dick, the Shepherd, blows his n.

Dick, the Shepherd, blows his n.	345b
fasten him as a n.	502a
for want of a n., the shoe was lost	157a
one n. by strength drives out	372b
smote the n. into his temples	494b
Nailed: hundred years ago were n.	376a
n. Him to the Tree	456a

Nails: blowing of his n.

blowing of his n.	384a
into the print of the n.	511b
n. bitten and pared to the quick	255b
near yr. beauty with my n.	384a
on his n., which were taper	182a
whole social system..Prince's n.	122a
Nail't wi' Scripture	59b

Naked: a n. thinking heart

a n. thinking heart	132a
he but n., tho' locked up	384a
helpless, n., piping	32a
in going to my n. bed	143b
left me n. to mine enemies	386a
n., and ye clothed me	508a
n., come to thee for dress	445a
n. shingles of the world	5a
n. they came to that..bower	435a
n. to the hangman's noose	198b
on Nilus' mud lay me stark n.	325a
our ingress into the world was n.	249a
still is n., being dressed	147a
the n. every day he clad	169a
the n. hulk alongside came	98b
to go n. is the best disguise	104a
Nakedness: n. of the land	493b
n. of woman..work of God	31a
not in utter n.	466a
Namancos: looks toward N.	270a

Name: a dearer n. shall be

a dearer n. shall be	141b
a deed without a n.	349b
a local habitation and a n.	357b
and stain'd his n.	59a
another place I take my n.	409b
a passion for the n. of Mary	71a
arm, arm, my n.	375a
before we have existence, and a n.	238b
Ben Adhem's n. led all the rest	202a
breathe not his n.	281a
Christian n., I think, was John	130b
conveys it in a borrowed n.	306a
coward shame distain his n.	61b
[Dryden], acquired him a great n.	104a
ease, content! whate'er thy n.	301b
eke my n. be wiped out	408a
fame is nothing but an empty n.	94b
filches from me my good n.	361b
find Ianthe's n. again	241b
for my n. and memory	17a
for that slow sweet n.'s sake	46b
friendship, like love, is but a n.	160b
give the ill he cannot cure a n.	9a
glory and the nothing of a n.	69b
good n. in man or woman	361b
good n. is better than..ointment	499a
good n. is rather to be chosen	498b
grand old n. of gentlemen	431a
grete god of Loves n.	89b
hallowed be thy n.	505a
He is called by thy n.	32b
Hell trembled at the hideous n.	273a
her n. an 'army' doth present	187b
her n. is never heard	22a
her n. was Barbara Allen	531a
high tho' his titles, proud his n.	317a
his former n. is heard no more	275a
His N. and sign who bear	200b
his n. only is excellent	490b
his n. painted clearly on each	85b
his n. shall be lost for evermore	319a
Horatio, what a wounded n.	337a
I am become a n.	438b
if a n. dearer and purer were	72b
if my n. were liable to fear	338a
I got so I cd. hear his n.	127b
I have forgotten yr. n.	422b
I have no n.	32b
I injured neither n.	193b
in the stone a new n. written	518b
I sing the N. wh. none can say	114b
is not the king's n...thousand	375a
I will give them an everlasting n.	503a
I will not blot out his n.	518b
I wrote her n. upon the strand	408a
Joy is my n.	32b
lash'd the vice, but spared the n.	419a
leaving her a n., I trust	407a
left a n. behind them	521b
lesser than my n.	375b
let me not n. it to you	363b
letters four do form his n. [Pitt]	101a
mark, or the n. of the beast	519a
Milton, a n. to resound for ages	427a

Name (*cont.*)

Muses chose their sons by n. 36a
must he lose the n. of king? 375b
my n. is George Nathaniel Curzon 528b
my n. is Jowett 528b
my n. is Legion 508b
my n. is Might-have-been 312b
my n. is Ozymandias 396b
my n. is Used-to-was 445a
my n. were not so terrible 380a
my 'oss, my wife, and my n. 417a
my verse extolled thy n. 79a
n. great in story 73b
n. of the God of Jacob defend thee 482b
N. of the Lord thy God in vain 480a
n. to all succeeding ages curst 138a
n. wh. is above every n. 516a
naming a dubious n.! 47a
no more must change their n. 464a
no profit but the n. 335b
nothing but to n. his tools 64b
O Duty! if that n. thou love 463b
Oh! might my n. be numbered 468b
one Hope's one n. be there 312b
on his thigh a n. 519b
or the number of his n. 519a
our n. is heard no more 109b
owner's n. someway in the corners 458a
Phœbus! what a n. to fill 72a
rose by any other n. 365a
see one's n. in print 72a
set down my n., Sir 54a
still is thy n. in high account 318a
still the n. do bide the seäme 21a
such weak witness of thy n. 278a
takes a specious n. 477a
that many-memoried n. 28b
the incommunicable n. 520a
their n. liveth for evermore 521b
the magic of a n. 77a
the n., at wh. the world grew pale 213b
there is no n...of wh. the echo 241b
the whistling of a n. 301b
they had their n. thence 267b
thy n. is an ointment 500a
Thy N., O Jesus, be for ever blest 200a
to all men be Thy n. known 36b
to bless yr. n. in pride 47b
to change the n...not the letter 87a
Villon, our..glad mad brother's n. 421a
we will not ask her n. 77b
what is friendship but a n.? 169a
what is yr. n.? 481a
what n. Achilles assumed 42b
what n. gave he? 25a
what's in a n.? 365a
what the dickens his n. is 355b
what thy lordly n. is 298b
whose n. was writ in water 223b
with a n. like yrs...any shape 85a
Wolfe's great n. compatriot 111b
worth an age without a n. 283a
write against yr. n. 309a
write upon him my new n. 518b
write yr. n. upon the..sand 241b
yet another n. more free 299b
yr. n. with worthy wights to reign 177a
Named thee but to praise 178a
Nameless: n. here for evermore 298a
thou art a n. thing 73b
to be n. in worthy deeds 42b
Names: a commodity of good n. 376b
bright n. will hallow song 68b
bright with n. that men remember 421b
called him soft n. 220a
called them by the wrong n. 45a
calleth them all by their n. 490b
call the lands after their own n. 485a
deathless lot to n. ignoble 109b
home of..unpopular n. 9a
honour doth forget men's n. 373b
I called on poisonous n. 394b
I have lost all the n. 210b
n. of things belov'd are dear 36a
n. of those who love the Lord 201b
n. that must not wither 68b
not unholy n., I hope 123b
oft n. God in oaths 132a
or allow their n. to be mentioned 11b
our n., familiar in his mouth 383a
our souls were in our n. 263b

Names (*cont.*)

play so nicely with their n. 375a
seeing our n. in print 93b
such great n. as these 526a
syllable men's n. 267a
those rugged n...grow sleek 278b
twenty more such n. and men 366b
two most sacred n. 106b
unpronounceable awful n. 182b
worshipped by the n. divine 30a
yr. n., remembered day and night 37a
Nan: change Kate into N. 30a
Nancy: Lady N. she died 531a
mate of the N. brig 163a
with his N. on his knees 164a
Nap: sun had..taken out his n. 65b
Napier: Admiral N., K.C.B. 440b
Napkins: dip their n. in his..blood 340a
Naples and on liberty 92a
Napoleon: ashes of N. Bonaparte 455a
be a N. and yet disbelieve 45a
chief monster (N.) 111a
except N., or abused it more 71b
N. forgot Blücher 95a
[N.] had a kind of idea 80a
N. of crime 135b
N. of the realms of rhyme 71b
(N.) sheep-worry of Europe 38a
[N.'s] presence on the field 455a
Napper Tandy 525b
Narcissa: last words poor N. spoke 302a
Narcotics, numbing pain 429b
Narrow: each within our n. bed 86a
make it soft and n. 531b
n., and low, and infinitely less 114b
n. minds..n. conclusions 265b
Narrows..world to my neighbour's gate 264a
Nassau: can Bourbon or N. 305b
Nasty: man of n. ideas 419a
n., brutish and short 191b
Nation: a n. is not governed 55b
a N. spoke to a N. 233a
an old, and haughty n. 266b
a small one a strong n. 503a
boundary of the march of a n. 292b
build that n.'s fate 29b
greatest inquest of the n...began 56a
guiding-star of a brave n. 285a
half of the n. is mad 405b
he hates our sacred n. 353a
in what stupid age or n. 66a
London: a n. not a city 129b
mourning of a mighty n. 435a
n. of men of honour..cavaliers 57a
N. of shopkeepers 1a
n. shall not lift up sword 501a
n. shall rise against n. 507b
nerves a n.'s heart 426a
never was an Art-loving n. 456b
noble and puissant n. 279a
no n. wanted it so much 419a
no n. was ever ruined by trade 156b
object in a N.'s eye 465b
once to every man and n. 250b
one suffer, than a n. grieve 138a
publish it to all the n. 305b
righteousness exalteth a n. 498a
risen up Earth's Greatest N. 250b
see a disenchanted n. 397a
still better for the n. 523b
that n., or any n. so conceived 245a
their history in a n.'s eyes 174b
thou hast multiplied the n. 501b
upon this continent a new n. 245a
we are a n. of amateurs 310b
what makes a n. happy 277a
who shd. make the laws of a n. 155a
ye are..an holy n. 517b
National: be above n. prejudices 289b
n. debt..a n. blessing 178b, 454a
Nations: all n. shall do him service 486b
called 'Saviour of the N.' 71b
cheap defence of n. 57a
day of small n...passed away 87a
dwell the n. underground 442b
enrich unknowing n. 117a
for the healing of the n. 520a
languages the pedigree of n. 212b
let fierce contending n. know 1b
n. are as a drop of a bucket 502b

Nations (*cont.*)

n...have their infancy 33b
n. touch at their summits 17b
news from all n. 112a
of all n. and kindreds 519a
saving health among all n. 486a
see n. slowly wise 213b
subdue..the n. under our feet 166a
temptations to belong to other n. 166a
the lightning of the n. 396a
truth whereby the n. live 228a
try the manners of different n. 413a
wake the n. under ground 127b
willing N. knew their..lord 138b
Native: considerable in his n. place 208a
content to breathe his n. air 303b
found him a n. of the rocks 206b
my n. land—Good Night 68a
song comes n. with the warmth 221a
tho' I am n. here 331a
Natives: bulk of yr. n. to be..vermin 417b
n. of Borrioboola-gha 121a
Nativity: at my n. the port of heaven 378a
my n. was under Ursa 342a
n., chance or death 356a
out of love with yr. n. 327a
Natural: as n. to die as to be born 14a
daub their n. faces unaware 43a
follow his n. bent 236a
he wants the n. touch 350a
I do it more n. 370b
loving, n., and Greek 70b
most n. thing in the world 237b
on the stage he was n. 169b
ruined on..their n. propensities 58a
something childish, but very n. 101b
something in this more than n. 332b
'twas n. to please 138a
twice as n. 85a
what is n. cannot touch me 149a
Natural History: now writing a N. 208b
Natural Philosophy (make men) deep 16a
Natural Selection: the term of N. 117b
Naturalists: so, n. observe, a flea 419b
Naturally: poetry..as n. as leaves to a tree 222b
where follies n. grow 94b
Nature: accuse not N. 276a
action lies in his true n. 334b
a friend..the masterpiece of N. 147b
against the use of n. 346b
all N. cries aloud 1b
all n. is but art 301a
all N. seems at work 102a
all N. was degraded 29a
all n., without voice or sound 403a
allow not n. more than n. needs 342b
a mere copier of n. 308b
auld n. swears, the lovely dears 60b
beauty is N.'s brag 267b
beauty is N.'s coin 267b
before wh. our mortal n...tremble 466b
Beldam N. 278b
blind forces of N. 256b
breathless N.'s dark abyss 465a
broken N.'s social union 62a
built by N. for herself 375a
by n.'s kindly law pleased 301a
can't be N., for it is not sense 94b
command n. except by obeying 17a
commonplace of N. 463b
counts death kind N.'s signal 214a
crack n.'s moulds 342b
creatures that by a rule in n. 381b
Dame n.'s menstralis 134b
disguise fair n. with..rage 382a
everything almost wh. is N.'s 398b
eye N.'s walks 300b
feel the link of n. draw me 276b
flood-gate and o'erbearing n. 359b
following N.'s lights 282b
fram'd in the prodigality of N. 384b
free as n. first made man 139b
fresh from N.'s mould 124a
fulfils great N.'s plan 60a
generous n. has been suffered 55b
gillyvors..n.'s bastards 373a
great N. made us men 250b
great N.'s second course 348a
happy n. to explore 301a
Heaven and N. seem'd to strive 215a

Nature (cont.)
he is made one with N. 392b
his n. is too noble 328a
hold..the mirror up to n. 333b
I call God and fools call N. 51b
if thou and n. can so gently part 325a
if thou hast n. in thee 331b
if you drive n. out 543a
I have learned to look on n. 472a
I love..but N. more 69b
informed by the light of n. 13a
in n...fountains of justice 13a
in N.'s infinite book of secrecy 322b
in n. there are neither rewards 203b
in n. there's no blemish 372a
in n. things move violently 14b
in our life alone does N. live 100b
in the lusty stealth of n. 341b
in the youth of primy n. 330b
jarr'd against n.'s chime 278a
law of n., and of nations 56a
let N. be yr. teacher 471b
little we see in N. 473a
lives in a state of war by n. 419b
man hath all wh. N. hath 9a
man is N.'s sole mistake! 166b
manners..the fruit of loyal n. 427b
more than enough for n.'s ends 257a
most irrelevant thing in n. 239a
muse on N. with a poet's eye 77a
music..doth change his n. 355b
mute N. mourns her worshipper 317a
my n. cd. not bear it so 341a
my n. is subdued 389a
naked n., and the living grace 300a
N. admits no lie 81a
N. always does contrive 164a
N. and N.'s laws lay hid in night 299b
n. cd. no farther go 141a
n. cd. not sorrow hide 176a
N. from her seat sighing 276a
n. gives way to in repose 347b
N. has cast me in so soft a mould 139a
N. has left this tincture 118a
n. hath fram'd strange fellows 352b
n. her custom holds 336a
N. herself seems..to write for him 9b
N., Hope, and Poesy 102a
N. I loved, and next to N., Art 241a
N. in him was almost lost in Art 103a
N. in you stands on the very verge 342b
n. is always wise 444b
N. is but a name for an effect 112b
N. is creeping up 456b
n. is fine in love 335b
n. is loth to yield her art 36a
n. is made better by no mean 373a
n. is often hidden 16a
n. is the art of God 41b
N. is usually wrong 456b
n., kindly bent to ease us 419a
N. knows a thing or two 320b
N...led him to confess a god 13a
N. made her what she is 59b
N. made you fools 60a
n. makes that mean 373a
N. might stand up and say 341b
n. must obey necessity 341a
N. never did betray the heart 472a
n. never makes excellent things 246a
N...never put..jewels into garret 13b
n., red in tooth and claw 430b
n. said, 'A lovelier flower' 471b
n.'s changing course untrimm'd 387a
n.'s copy's not eterne 349a
N.'s darling [Shakespeare] 175a
n. seems dead 347b
N.'s great law 7b
n.'s handmaid, art 139b
N.'s law..man was made to mourn 61b
n.'s own sweet and cunning hand 370a
n.'s patient, sleepless Eremite 220b
N.'s soft nurse 380a
N.'s sweet restorer 477a
N. stood recover'd of her sight 141b
N.'s true-born child 225a
N.'s vast frame 392b
N. that framed us of..elements 259a
N. that is above all art 117a

Nature (cont.)
n. then..to me was all in all 472a
N. was his book 33a
N. wears one universal grin 151b
n.! whose lapidary seas 452a
N., with equal mind 5b
n. yet remembers 466b
needed not..books to read N. 142a
never did N. say one thing 58a
new edition of human n. 183a
noble n...poetically gifted 10a
no compunctious visitings of n. 346b
not Eternities! says N. 264a
not without art..yet to n. true 94b
of an open and free n. 214b
one touch of n. makes..world kin 369a
O N., we are thine 464a
on N...musing in solitude 464a
our tainted n.'s solitary boast 472a
paid the debt of n. 150a
pattern of excelling n. 363b
Poets that are sown by N. 464a
progress..is a part of n. 408a
prophets of N. 470a
read in N.'s mystic book 260a
reason of the frailty of our n. 479b
rest in N., not the God of N. 188a
restore the tone of languid N. 111b
secret aims of n. 36a
Secretary of N...Francis Bacon 450b
Shakespeare..found [N.] 142a
shares the n. of infinity 463a
sides of n. will not sustain it 322b
simple life that N. yields 114a
simple n. to his hope has giv'n 300b
some of n.'s journeymen 333b
so priketh hem in 88a
spark o' N.'s fire 60a
standing at ease in N. 457b
stars, that n. hung in heaven 267a
still is N.'s priest 466a
strength and n. made amends 313b
strife with N., to out-do the life 215b
strong propensity of n. 279a
sullenness against N. not to go 279b
sweet is the lore wh. N. brings 471b
that age..can lay on n. 352a
the fault was N.'s 74b
the modesty of n. 333b
the n. of an insurrection 338b
the n. of the times deceased 380b
the rest on N. fix 97b
they perfect n. and are perfected 16a
things rank and gross in n. 330a
this fair defect of N. 276b
tho' n.'s sternest painter 72b
thorough knowledge of human n. 11b
thro' n. up to n.'s God 301b
thy n. is not therefore less divine 467a
'tis N.'s fault alone 95a
'tis N.'s law to change 309b
'tis their n. too 452b
to carry n. lengths unknown 111b
touched the hem of N.'s shrift 397a
true wit is n. to advantage 300a
universal blank of N.'s works 273b
vermin..n. ever suffered to crawl 417b
voice of N. cries 174b
volume of n...book of knowledge 170a
vows can't change n. 51a
we fools of n. 331a
we see the fancy outwork n. 323a
weakness of our mortal n. 479b
what n. itselfe can't endure 155a
when N. has work to be done 148b
when N. him began 136b
whole frame of n...break 2b
whole realm of n. mine 453b
whom universal N. did lament 269b
whose body n. is 301a
with N.'s pride 259a
woman! N. made thee to temper 291b
woman..N.'s agreeable blunders 107b
womb of n. and perhaps her grave 273a
words, like N., half reveal 429b
write and read comes by n. 358b
yet do I fear thy n. 346b
Natures: care of n. that are mute 264a
dearth of noble n. 217b
ignominy of our n. 41b
other n. thinks different 124a

Natures (cont.)
'tis the same with common n. 191b
Naught: horror, of falling into n. 1b
I must have n. beside 441b
I tell you n. for yr. comfort 92a
it is n., saith the buyer 498b
n. for yr. desire 92a
n.'s had, all 's spent 348b
n. venture, n. have 446a
Naughtiness: n. of thine heart 495b
superfluity of n. 517b
Naughty: amended his former n. life 480a
congregations of n. men 487a
n. little Suck-a-thumb 192b
Navarre: helmet of N. 252b
Navel: thy n. is like a round goblet 500b
Navies: airy n. grappling 432b
when n. are stranded 319a
yr. nutshell n. came 228b
Navigation: swallow n. up 349b
Navigators: I've heard other n. say 180b
Navy: a load wd. sink a n. 386a
Army..fired by the British N. 177a
royal n. of England..defence 28b
Rulers of the Queen's N. 166a
yr. n. nothing but rotten timber 56a
Nay: Communication be..N., n. 505a
Hall's n. was n. 27b
yea be yea; and yr. n., n. 517b
Nayed him twice 176a
Nazareth: good..come out of N.? 510b
N.B.: This is rote Sarcasticul 451a
Neæra's hair 269b
Near: as n. to heaven by sea 162b
be n. us at our side 430a
call ye upon him while he is n. 503a
far or forgot to me is n. 146a
he comes too n...to be denied 280a
he seems so n. and yet so far 431a
make love to the lips we are n. 281b
not night if Thou be n. 224a
she is n., she is n. 434a
Nearer: dearer one still, and a n. one 195b
n. and n. draws the time 2b
n. my Father's house 86a
n., my God, to Thee 1a
n. than hands and feet 427b
n. the crystal sea 86a
n. the great white throne 86a
Nearest: do the work that 's n. 226a
that is best wh. lieth n. 247a
Neat: credit to any good girl to be n. 425a
in a n.'s tongue dried 352b
n., not gaudy 239b
Spanish or n.'s-leather 65b
still to be n., still to be drest 215a
trod upon n.'s-leather 337b
Neat-handed Phyllis 269a
Nebo's lonely mountain 3a
Nebuchadnezzar the king 504a
Necessaries: talk of the n. of life 160b
Necessary: a harmless n. cat 354b
generally n. to salvation 481a
government..is but a n. evil 291b
n...he hold the Catholic Faith 478b
n. to leave off Tobacco 239b
plots, true or false, are n. things 138a
Necessities: art of our n. is strange 343a
dispense with its n. 285a
feigned n., imaginary n. 161a
Necessity: as if we were villains by n. 342a
by n...we all quote 148b
I am forsworn 'on mere n.' 344b
I do not see the n. 561a
nature must obey n. 341a
n. and chance approach not me 275b
n. gives the law 553b
n. has no law 553b
n. hath no law 116a
n. invented stools 111b
n. makes an honest man a knave 118b
n. never made a good bargain 157a
n...plea for every infringement 297b
n., the tyrant's plea 274a
no virtue like n. 374b
sworn brother..to grim N. 376a
teach thy n. to reason thus 374b
thy n. is yet greater 402a
turns his n. to glorious gain 465a
uno'erleaped Mountains of N. 8a

Neck: a n. God made for other use 198b
arching proud his n. 443b
he bowed his glossy n. 290a
his n. brake 495a
if you break not yr. n. 30a
item, one n., one chin 370a
kings..had a lith in their n. 11a
left his straight n. bent 312b
lowly, with a broken n. 264a
millstone were hanged about his n.
    507a, 510a
my n. is very short 283a
n. and breasts ripe apples 138a
n. that's once broken 320a
n. when once broken 450a
proudly arched and glossy n. 289b
Roman people had but one n.! 538a
thy n. is as a tower of ivory 500b
thy n. is like the tower of David 500b
Necks: n. in thunder clothed 175a
walk with stretched forth n. 501a
Nectar: of Jove's n. sup 216a
sprinkles..with n., and runs on 241a
they lie beside their n. 433a
Nectarine and curious peach 260b
Ned: work for poor old N. 156b
Need: day's most quiet n. 44a
Deloraine, good at n. 317a
deserted at his utmost n. 139a
helps good hearts in n. 119a
help us in our utmost n. 249a
in such hour of n. of yr...race 7b
is what we chiefly n. 84b
less than the n. thou hast in me 197a
shd. you n. nor heart nor hands 414a
sorer than to lie for n. 328b
sought hers as in earnest n. 48a
suit and serve his n. 188a
there lies our bitter n. 137b
thus with thee in my sore n. 396b
what can I want or n.? 188a
why do we n. them (women) 78b
Needed: all are n. by each 146b
Needle: camel..thro' the eye of a n. 507b
for the n. she 436b
hinders n. and thread 196b
plying her n. and thread 196a
sharp as a n. 160b
the touched n. trembles 304a
true as the n. to the pole 33b
wi' her n. an' her sheers 59b
Needles: thy n., once a shining store 109a
Needlework: raiment of n. 484b
Needy: n., hollow-eyed..wretch 328a
n. Knife-grinder! 78b
Negation of God 167b
Negative Capability 222a
Neglect: defer it or n. it 176b, 523b
first begin, and both n. 334b
most tender mercy is n. 114a
n. may breed mischief 157a
such sweet n. more taketh me 215a
wise and salutary n. 55b
Neglected: he, n. and oppressed 316b
to have his all n. 206b
Negligences, and ignorances 479a
Negligently: who never n. yet 452a
Negociate: our souls n. there 132b
Negroes: providing the infant n. 126b
Neighbour: as he followed his n.
    upstairs 417a
bear false witness against thy n. 480a
borrowed my n.'s wife 235b
death..had been his..n. 319b
duty towards my N. 481a
hath not slandered his n. 482a
helping every feeble n. 171b
he that sweareth unto his n. 482a
his hungering n., and Me 251a
I have an accommodating n. 135b
life to thy n.'s creed has lent 146b
narrows the world to my n.'s gate 264a
near n. to Despair 8a
n.'s house is on fire 56b
neighed after his n.'s wife 503b
nor done evil to his n. 482a
our n. and our work farewell 223b
removeth his n.'s landmark 494b
that he might rob a n. 254b
thou shalt love thy n. 507b
to hate yr. n. 255a

Neighbour (cont.)
to love yr. n.'s wife 255a
to my N. honestly 247b
Neighbours: call yr. n. in 533a
from every house the n. met 430a
good fences make good n. 157b
good n. I have had 145a
holding their n.' tails 231a
love and charity with yr. n. 480b
make sport for our n. 11b
on the vigil feast his n. 383a
what is happening to our n. 87a
Neighed after his neighbour's wife 503b
Neighs: high and boastful n. 382b
Neither: to n. a word will I say 160a
Nell: pretty witty N. 296a
Nelly: let not poor N. starve 87b
Nelson: death of N...felt in England 407b
did not end by N.'s urn 92b
the N. touch 287a, b
N.'s peerless name 287b
N. turned his blindest eye 92a
of N. and the North 76b
of N. only a touch 49a
Nemean lion's nerve 331a
Nephew: beamish n. 86a
Nephews: their n. and their nieces 414a
Neptune: all great N.'s ocean 348a
flatter N. for his trident 328a
N.'s empire stands 329b
stands as N.'s park 328b
Nero is an angler 343a
Nereides: gentlewomen, like the N. 323a
Nerve: me—who am as a n. 395a
Nemean lion's n. 331a
requires n. to do it 195a
Nerves: my firm n...never tremble 349a
nobody feels for my poor n. 11b
strengthens our n. 57b
weakness to expredge my n. 124b
Nervii: he overcame the N. 340a
Nest: ev'n as a n. with birds 293b
found some fledged bird's n. 448a
her soft and chilly n. 221b
her young ones in her n. 350a
his n. of wishes piping to him 264b
in her n. at peep of day 438a
lark now leaves his wat'ry n. 117b
long since my n. is made 436b
n. is in a watered shoot 310b
n. of singing birds 206a
n. wh. thou canst drop into 471a
only a tumble-down n. 461b
Phoenix builds her spicy n. 79b
phoenix builds the phoenix' n. 115a
plumage that had warmed his n. 72b
saw thee in thy balmy n. 115a
swallow a n...lay her young 487a
thy n. upon the dewy ground 471a
we'll theek our n. 529b
within mine eyes he makes his n. 176a
Nestle: I n. by thy side 399a
Nestling me everywhere 197b
Nestor swear the jest be laughable 352b
Nests: birds in their little n. agree 452b
birds of the air have n. 506a
built their n. in my beard 243a
in Cleopatra's sails their n. 324a
n. in order rang'd of tame..fowl 278a
these to their n. 274a
Net: fain wd. fling the n. 263b
in vain the n. is spread 497b
I will let down the n. 509a
laid a n. for my feet 485b
they carried a n. 295b
Nets: come clear of the n. of wrong 474b
ladies spend..time in making n. 419a
laws are generally found to be n. 400a
n. and stratagems to catch us 187a
tangled in amorous n. 277a
ungodly fall into their own n. 490b
Nettle: out of this n., danger 377a
stroke a n., and it stings you 191b
Nettles, daisies, and long purples 336a
Neutral: loyal and n., in a moment 348a
stood apart, studiously n. 462a
Neutrality: just for a word—n. 567b
n. of an impartial judge 55a
Never: escape me? n.—beloved! 48a
I n...form'd a plan 112b
I shall n. have it all 133b

Never (cont.)
n...appear the Immortals, n. alone 102a
n. glad confident morning 48a
n., I ween, did swimmer 253b
n. more, Sailor 119b
n., n., n., n. n. 344a
n., n. thinks of me 527a
n. you mind! roll on! 163a
Oh n., n., n., since I joined 167a
what, n.? no, n.! 166a
wh. n. were nor no man..saw 366b
Never-failing: mines of n. skill 110a
Nevermore: quoth the Raven, 'N.!' 298b
Never-never: yr. 'n. country' 228b
New: a bringer of n. things 438b
against the n. and untried 245a
a little time while it is n.! 530a
al this n. corn 90a
al this n. science 90a
amaist as weel's the n. 59b
before you are on with the n.
    262b, 524b
behold, I make all things n. 519b
both of the n. and old 461b
ever piping songs for ever n. 219b
first by whom the n. are tried 300a
fitter for n. projects 16a
Heavenly Power makes all things n. 426b
how strange it seems, and n.! 48b
in n. excellence divine 36a
n. and neat and adequately tall 91b
n. every morning is the love 223b
n. friend is as n. wine 520b
n. is not comparable to him 520b
n. nobility..the act of power 15a
no n. thing under the sun 499a
story always old and always n. 51a
tell not as n. 108a
things n. and old 507a
to hear some n. thing 512b
upon the threshold of the n. 449a
yielding place to n. 429a
New-caught, sullen peoples 236b
New-comer: blithe n.! 463b
New England weather 446b
New-hatch'd to the woeful time 348b
Newman: new-manned by N. 51a
what, then, does Dr. N. mean? 226a
New-manned by Newman 51a
News: a man bites a dog that is n. 116b
any n. in the paper 11b
bad n. infects the teller 322b
brought from Heaven the n. 155b
brought me bitter n. to hear 106a
evil n. rides post 278a
first bringer of unwelcome n. 379b
for n., the manna of a day 175b
good n. baits 278a
ill n. hath wings 136b
master-passion is the love of n. 113b
never good to bring bad n. 323b
n. from all nations 112a
n. of battle, n. of battle 12a
n. value 308a
others..may tell the n. 33a
poor rogues talk of court n. 344a
so is good n. from a far country 498b
the father of good n. 332a
the n. that's goin' round 525b
there is good n. yet to hear 93a
to the dismal n. I tell 4b
what n.? None, my lord 332a
what n. on the Rialto? 353a
Newspaper: rule never to look into
    a n. 400a
Newspapers: men and morning n. 297a
n.! Sir, they are most villainous 400a
Newt: eye of n. 349b
New Testament: adversity..blessing
    of the N. 14a
N. was less a Christiad 181a
Newton: a N. at Peru 449b
God said, Let N. be! 299b
N., childlike sage! 112a
where the statue stood of N. 469b
Newts, and blind-worms 356b
New World: I called the N. into
    existence 79a
that n. wh. is the old 426b
New Year: N. reviving old desires 152a
of all the glad N. 434b

New York: a Xenophon at N. 449b
  little old N. 571b
New Zealand: married..gone to N. 96a
  some traveller from N. 254b
Next: n., when I cast mine eyes 190b
  that n. by him beneath 368b
Nexus: cash payment is not..sole n. 81a
  cash payment..the sole of man 80b
Niagara: wouldn't *live* under N. 82a
Niamh calling Away 475a
Nice: it's n. to get up in the morning 242b
  more n. than wise 109a
  n. but nubbly 237a
  n. man is a man of nasty ideas 419a
  n. while it lasted 232b
  spice, and all that's n. 534b
  such a n. young man 285b
  swain did woo, she was n. 176a
Nicean barks of yore 298a
Nicer to lie in bed 242b
Niche: God keeps a n. in Heaven 43b
  window'd n. of that high hall 68b
Nick, or Clootie 58b
Nickie-ben: auld N.! 59a
Nickleby: this is all very well, Mr. N. 124b
Nick-nackets: fouth o' auld n. 62a
Nickname is the heaviest stone 183b
Nicodemus saw such light 447b
Niece: his sister's husband's n. 85b
Nieces: their nephews and their n. 414a
Niger: left bank of the N. 121a
Niggers: that don't agree with n. 250a
  whar de good n. go 156b
Nigh: as n. as ever he can 89a
  Christ is n. 86b
  drawing n. and nigher 44a
  it shall not come n. thee 487b
  slowly she came n. him 531a
  to them that were n. 515b
Night: about the dead hour of the n. 528b
  a crown is of n. 422a
  afraid for any terror by n. 487b
  all n. has the casement..stirr'd 434a
  all n. have the roses heard 434a
  all n. long we have not stirred 50b
  alternate N. and Day 153a
  amorous bird of n. 275b
  and so dream all n. 218a
  a n. of memories and of sighs 241a
  appearance of an instalment of n. 180b
  a rainbow at n. 522a
  as a watch in the n. 487b
  as n. is withdrawn 37a
  ate a good supper at n. 4a
  become a borrower of the n. 348b
  beyond the n., across the day 426a
  bird of n. did sit 338a
  black bat, n., has flown 434a
  black n. doth take away 388a
  blessed candles of the n. 355b
  boldly say each n. 107a
  boon I ask of thee, beloved N. 399a
  by n. on my bed I sought him 500a
  call it perfect day nor n. 384a
  came back the previous n. 527a
  certain term to walk the n. 331a
  choose an everlasting n. 133a
  clamoured the live-long n. 348a
  closed his eyes in endless n. 175a
  come, civil n...all in black 366a
  come, seeling n., scarf up 349a
  come, thick n., and pall thee 346b
  danger's troubled n. depart 78a
  darkness that it may be n. 488b
  darksome n. be passed 150a
  dead vast and middle of the n. 330a
  dear N.! this world's defeat 447b
  deep of n. is crept upon our talk 341a
  Desolation! and dim N.! 298a
  dewy n. falls precipitate 555a
  dreams of the summer n. 248b
  drives N. along with them 152a
  dying year, to wh. this closing n. 396b
  each n., upon my knees 150b
  every n. and alle 529a
  falls from the wings of N. 247a
  first minute, after noon, is n. 133b
  first sweet sleep of n. 394b
  fled the shades of n. 274b
  for a day and a n. 423a
  fourth watch of the n. 507a

Night (*cont.*)
  from my lonely room this n. 12a
  from the Field of N. 152a
  give not a windy n. a rainy morrow 388b
  golden lamps in a green n. 260a
  gwine to run all n. 156a
  half-held by the n. 458b
  hangs upon the cheek of n. 365a
  he did not die in the n. 284b
  hell and n. must bring this..birth 360b
  He waveth all the n. 475a
  honey'd middle of the n. 221b
  how beautiful is n. 407a
  hung aloft the n. 220b
  I be by Silvia in the n. 372b
  ignorant armies clash by n. 5a
  I have pass'd a miserable n. 384b
  ill beginning of the n. 341a
  in an eternal n. 422a
  infinite day excludes the n. 453b
  in freezing winter n. 407b
  in hell-black n. endur'd 343a
  in such a n. did Thisbe 355a
  in such a n. Medea 355a
  in such a n. stood Dido 355a
  in such a n. Troilus 355a
  in the Bowl of N. 152a
  in the forests of the n. 31b
  in the gardens of the n. 37a
  in the n., imagining some fear 357b
  in the n., my Soul, my daughter 442b
  in weary N.'s decline 30a
  in winter I get up at n. 413b
  it is cold winter's n. 531a
  it is not n. if Thou be near 224a
  it was mirk, mirk n. 528a
  it was the calm and silent n. 131b
  it was the middle of the n. 84a
  it will be good n. 394b
  know his God by n. 447b
  last bird fly into the last n. 312a
  last out a n. in Russia 351b
  let no n. seal thy sense 119a
  lie upon the wings of n. 366a
  lightning in the collied n. 356a
  light of the n. on the dew 422b
  longest n. in all the year 284b
  long, long n. of waiting 225b
  long n. succeeds thy little day 295a
  lovely as a Lapland n. 473a
  mad naked summer n. 458b
  magnetic, nourishing n. 458b
  making n. hideous 331a
  many a watchful n. 381a
  mask of n. is on my face 365a
  morning cometh, and also the n. 502a
  my delight on a shining n. 525a
  my n. be turned to day 490a
  mysterious N.! 456b
  Nature's laws lay hid in n. 299b
  neither the moon by n. 489b
  never sees horrid n. 383a
  n. and day on me she cries 531a
  n. and light and the half-light 474b
  n., and sleep in the n. 420b
  n. by n. I look right thro' 47b
  n. cometh when no man can work 511a
  n. darkens the streets 271b
  n. embrac'd the place 114b
  n. has a thousand eyes 34a
  n. hath a thousand eyes 251b
  n. in the lonesome October 298b
  n. is as clear as the day 490a
  n. is beginning to lower 246b
  n. is drawing nigh 20a
  n. is growing grey 180a
  n. joint-labourer with the day 329b
  n. makes no difference 189b
  n. of south winds 458b
  n. of the few large stars 458b
  n. of this immortal day 397b
  n. of time..surpasseth the day 42b
  n.! sable goddess 477a
  n. sank upon the dusky beach 252a
  n.'s black agents to their preys 349a
  n.'s blear-all black 197b
  n.'s candles are burnt out 366a
  N.'s Plutonian shore 298b
  n.-season also I take no rest 483a
  n.'s starr'd face 221a
  n.'s swift dragons 357a

Night (*cont.*)
  n. that either makes me 363b
  n. that he was betrayed 480b
  n. that shd. banish all sin 168a
  n., the shadow of light 420b
  n. time I shall not forget 421b
  n. urge the morrow 392a
  n. was made for loving 74a
  n., wherein the cub-drawn bear 342b
  n.-wind brings up the stream 6a
  n. with her train of stars 185a
  nor grew it white in a single n. 69b
  nothing but the n. 199b
  obscurest n. involv'd the sky 107b
  o'er n.'s brim, day boils 50a
  O for that N.! 448a
  of the n. for the morrow 399b
  oft, in the stilly n. 282b
  oh, Pilot! 'tis a fearful n. 22a
  one ever-during n. 78a
  one n. certifieth another 482b
  one n. or the other n. 154b
  one other gaudy n. 324a
  O n.'s black arch the key-stane 63a
  O thievish N. 267a
  out and all is n. 299a
  out of the n. that covers me 185a
  out-soared the shadow of our n. 392b
  palace of dim n. 366b
  perils and dangers of this n. 478b
  piercing the n.'s dull ear 382b
  press close, bare-bosomed n. 458b
  pure from the n. 263b
  reign of Chaos and old N. 271b
  retreating..breath of the n.-wind 5a
  revellers, and shades of n. 356a
  sable-vested N. 273a
  sentries of the shadowy n. 280a
  shades of n. were falling fast 247a
  Shadwell's genuine n. 140b
  ship after ship, the whole n. long 437b
  show thy dangerous brow by n. 338b
  silent n. with this her..bird 274b
  sing..even in the dead of n. 370a
  singing startle the dull n. 268b
  Sire, the n. is darker now 286b
  sleep one ever-during n. 78a
  sleeps as may beguile the n. 416b
  sleep we must one endless n. 538b
  slepen al the n. with open yë 88a
  snores out the watch of n. 381a
  soft stillness and the n. 355a
  so late into the n. 74a
  some n. you'll fail us 50a
  some time of the n. 356b
  song of n.'s sweet bird 392b
  song we heard last n. 376b
  son of the sable N. 117a
  soon the n. of weeping 415b
  souls who dwell in N. 29b
  sound of revelry by n. 68a
  spend the n. in sleep 117a
  spend the n. wi' mirth and glee 402b
  Spirit of N.! 399a
  stars of the summer n. 248b
  steal a few hours from the n. 281b
  stepping fearless thro' the n. 20b
  still, as darker grows the n. 168a
  still-nodding n. 458b
  stood that n. against my fire 344a
  studying all the summer n. 261a
  such n. in England ne'er had
    been 252a
  tender and growing n. 458b
  the City is in N. 443b
  the city of dreadful n. 443b
  the dusky n. rides down 151b
  the feet of the n. 420a
  the n. has been unruly 348a
  the N. in its silence 5b
  the n. is dark 288b
  the n. is far spent 514a
  'the n. is fine', the Walrus said 84b
  the n. is good 394a
  the n. that first we met 22b
  the n. that wins 420a
  there's n. and day, brother 34a
  the sisters Death and N. 457b
  the trumpets of the n. 423a
  the world's last n. 133a
  things that love n. 342b

Night (cont.)

this ae n.	529a
this n...is but the daylight	355b
this n. shall be born	522b
this n. thy soul shall be required	509b
this passing n. was heard	220a
tho' thou be black as n.	78a
thou and I this n. maun gae	528a
Throne behold of N. primaeval	299a
thro' the empty-vaulted n.	267a
thro' the foul womb of n.	382b
thro' the n. of doubt and sorrow	20b
Thy tempests fell all n.	188a
tire the n. in thought	307a
'tis a naughty n. to swim in	343a
toiling upward in the n.	247b
touch of Harry in the n.	382b
trailing garments of the N.	247b
trip we after the n.'s shade	357a
'twas the n. before Christmas	280b
vile contagion of the n.	338b
walks in beauty, like the n.	74a
war's annals will cloud into n.	179b
watchman, what of the n.?	502a
watch that ends the n.	453a
waters on a starry n.	466a
we have toiled all the n.	509a
what hath n. to do with sleep?	266b
what is the n.?	349a
when n. is nigh	224a
when N. is on the hills	445b
when she deserts the n.	277b
when the face of n. is fair	434b
witching time of n.	334b
with us perpetual n.	216a
womb of uncreated n.	272b
world will be in love with n.	366a
wd. not spend another such a n.	384b
'Yes,' I answered you last n.	43b
yet it is not n.	69a
you meaner beauties of the n.	473b

Night-air: into the fresh n. again 45b
Nightcap: a n. decked his brows 168a
bring his n. with him 416b
Nightcaps: heads all in n. 81b
Night-dress: lectures in her n. 196b
Nighted: cast thy n. colour off 329b
Night-flies: hush'd with buzzing n. 380a
Nightgown: downstairs in his n. 266a
enter Cæsar in his n. 338b
Nightingale: all but the wakeful n. 274a
bright n. amorous 420a
crave the tuneful N. 137a
Hark! ah, the N. 7a
hundred-throated n. 439a
I the n. all spring thro' 422b
it was the n. 366a
my n., we have beat them 324a
newe abaysshed n. 90a
N. cries to the Rose 152a
n. does sit so late 261a
n., if she shd. sing by day 355b
n. in the sycamore 414b
n.'s high note is heard 73b
n. sings round it 282a
N. that in the branches sang 154a
no music in the n. 372b
O n., that on yon bloomy spray 278a
O 'tis the ravish'd n. 251b
roar you as 'twere any n. 356b
save the n. alone 20b
sings as sweetly as a n. 366b
spoils the singing of the n. 217b
the n.'s complaint 394b
where the n. doth sing 219a
whither doth haste the n. 79b
Nightingales: n. are singing near 145a
till the n. applauded 49a
told..by Eve's n. 119a
where the n. are singing 225b
Nightly to the listening Earth 2a
Night-mare Life-in-Death 98b
Night-rack came rolling up 226b
Nights: Chequer-board of N. and Days 153a
chill thy dreaming n. 219a
fled Him, down the n. 441b
God makes sech n. 250b
love not such n. as these 342b
misery makes Alcmena's 42b
n. are lang and mirk 529a

Nights (cont.)

n. of waking	316b
summer n. collected still	220b
the n. are very damp	85b
the n. are wholesome	329b
thro' the long, long wintry n.	243b
to waste long n. in..discontent	409a
when n. are longest	351b
Nile: pour the waters of the N.	82b
serpent of old N.	323a
Nil ultra to my proudest hopes	262b
Nilus: on N.' mud lay me	325a
Nimble: if you are n. and light	534a
words that have been so n.	22b
Nimbler much than hinds	261a
Nimini-pimini: pronouncing...n.	55a
Nimrod the mighty hunter	492b
Nimshi: too similar to..the son of N.	405a
Nine: but where are the n.?	510a
fair N., forsaking Poetry	31b
leading his choir, the N.	5b
leave the ninety and n.	509b
n., ten, a good fat hen	532a
that will purchase n.	85b
there be n. worthy and the best	257a
Nine-fifteen: romance brought up the n.	230b
Ninepence: but n. in ready money	2b
Ninety-eight: fears to speak of N.?	203b
Nineveh: one with N. and Tyre	233b
Quinquireme of N.	261b
Ninny: compar'd to Handel's a...n.	67a
Ninth: quiet till the n. year	542b
Niobe: like N., all tears	330a
N. of Nations	69a
Niobean womb	421a
Nip him in the bud	309b
Nipping and an eager air	331a
Nipple: have plucked my n.	347a
Nipt: affection, but 'twas n.	265b
Nitre: windy n. and quick sulphur	408b
No: Araminta, say 'N.!'	305a
are we downhearted? N.!	522a
Charybdis of Aye and N.	288a
n. arts, n. letters, n. society	191b
n.! it is an ever-fixed mark	389a
n.! let 'em all come!	238a
'n., none at all', he replied	11b
n., n., n. my heart is fast	526a
n. sun—n. moon!	195a
'N.,' this morning, sir, I say	43b
Oh n. John! John!	525b
oh! n.! we never mention her	22a
the everlasting n.	81b
the people cried, 'O N.!'	19b
Noah: before N. was a sailor	371b
married N.'s daughter	12b
N. begat Shem, Ham	492b
N. he often said to his wife	93b
N. said: 'There's wan' av us	231a
N. spoke him fairly	231a
to Greece, and into N.'s ark	110b
whereas it is N.	236a
Nobby: isn't it a n. one	310a
Nobility: all were noble save n.	68a
ancient n. is the act of time	15a
betwixt the wind and his n.	376b
deny a god destroy man's n.	15a
leave us still our old n.!	258a
new n...the act of power	15a
n. is a graceful ornament	57b
n. of birth..abateth industry	15a
n...prevents the rule of wealth	17b
true n. is exempt from fear	384a
virtue alone is true n.	162b
Noble: all were n. save nobility	68a
a n. army, men and boys	184a
an old Castilian poor n.	74b
ashamed with the n. shame	226b
Homer..is eminently n.	10a
never yet was n. man	428b
n. and nude	421a
n. grounds for the n. emotions	314a
n. living and the n. dead	469b
n. mind disdain to hide his head	176a
n. nature, poetically gifted	10a
only n. to be good	431b
quiet us in a death so n.	278a
shd. not be n. to myself	325a
some work of n. note	439b
to learn of n. men	340a

Noble (cont.)

virtue..not birth..makes us n.	23a
what's brave, what's n.	324b
where the n. infant lay	114b
Nobleman: as a n. shd. do	379a
celebrated, cultivated...n.	163a
king may make a n.	58a
what may a N. find to do	19b
Noblemen: critics..brushers of n.'s clothes	13b
Nobleness: allied with perfect n.	10a
n. of life is to do thus	322a
N. walks in our ways	39a
that great n. of hers	475a
Nobler and the manlier one	71a
Nobles: n. and heralds, by yr. leave	305b
n. by the right of..creation	254b
their n. with links of iron	490b
where the wealthy n. dwell	432b
Noblest: amongst the n. of mankind	75b
an honest man's the n. work	59b
her n. work she classes	60b
his n. work is reckoned	171b
n. Roman of them all	341b
n. thing wh. perished there	184b
Tragedy is the n. Production	2a
Nobly: let us love n.	132a
spurn not the n. born	163b
Nobody: business of n.	254a
everybody's business is n.'s	450b
I care for n.	61a
I care for n., not I	28a
n. asked you, kind sir	525b
n. calls you a dunce	53a
n. cares for me	61a
n. feels for my poor nerves	11b
n. I care for comes a-courting me	165b
n.; I myself; farewell	363b
n. is on my side	11b
n. shd. be sad but I	374a
n. takes part with me	11b
n. walks much faster than I do	85a
pauper, whom n. owns	289b
there's n. at home	299b
where n. gets old	475b
Nocturnal: some n. blackness	179a
Nod: affects to n.	138b
dwelt in the land of N.	492b
if she chance to n. I'll rail	366b
n. and a wink for every..maid	417a
Wynken, Blynken, and N.	151a
Nodded, nearly napping	298a
Nodding: if he sees anybody else n.	2a
Noddle: my barmie n.	60b
Nodosities of the oak	58b
Nods: Homer...n.	542b
n., and becks, and smiles	268b
Reason...n. a little	150b
why n. the drowsy Worshipper	152a
Noes: honest kersey n.	345a
Noise: above n. and danger	448a
a chamber deaf to n.	401b
after n. tranquillity	289a
a little noiseless n.	218b
a pleasant n. till noon	99b
battle..is with confused n.	501b
body..holds its n.	45a
boys that fears no n.	171a
didst thou not hear a n.?	347b
full of foolish n.	430a
God is gone up with a merry n.	484b
happy n. to hear	199a
inexplicable dumb-shows and n.	333b
melt, and make no n.	134a
n. and sin!	48b
n. like of a hidden brook	99b
n. of the water-pipes	484b
nursed amid her n., her crowds	239b
the n. of battle roll'd	429a
valued till they make a n.	114a
wi' flichterin' n. an' glee	59b
with a n. of winds	420a
with spattering n. rejected	276b
Noises: earth, so full of dreary n.	44a
like n. in a swound	98a
the isle is full of n.	367b
Noiseless tenor of their way	174b
Noisy man is always in the right	108a
Nokomis: Daughter of the Moon, N.	248b
the wigwam of N	248b
Noll: for shortness call'd N.	158b

Noll (cont.)
N.'s damned troopers 45b
Noman: dear Mr. N. 26b
No-meaning: channel of n. 288a
Nominated in the bond 355a
Nomination: what imports the n. 337a
Nominative: grace is her n. case 290b
No-more: I am also called N. 312b
Non-commissioned man 228b
Non-conformist: N. Conscience
　makes cowards 24b
　whoso wd. be a man must be an. 147b
None: by resignation, n. 205a
　few die and n. resign 205a
　I'll n. of it 350b
　perfectly sure I have n. 82b
　there's n. at a' for me 531b
Nonino: hey n. 327b
Nonpareil battalion 121b
Nonsense: grammar, and n. 169b
　n. healed my wound 104a
　round the corner of n. 102b
　that sounds like n. 319b
　thro' sense and n. 138b
　time and n. scorning 53b
Non sequitur: yr. conclusion is a n. 151b
Nook: a book and a shady n. 461b
　an obscure n. for me 49b
Nooks: by many winding n. he strays 372b
Noon: by n. most cunningly did steal 187b
　dark, amid the blaze of n. 277b
　drawn o'er Thy glorious n. 447b
　far from the fiery n. 218a
　from n. to dewy eve 272a
　near her highest n. 268a
　n. a purple glow 475b
　n. behind the tamarisks 228a
　n. of my dream, O n. 154b
　N. strikes on England 154b
　on obscene wings athwart the n. 100b
　Princes ride at n. 119a
　shameless n. 427a
　she sung from n. to n. 284b
　sun has not attained his n. 189a
　when n. is past 394b
Noonday: at n., upon the market-
　place 338a
　fire-flames n. kindled 46a
　my heart at some n. 46b
　sickness. .destroyeth in the n. 487b
　thy just dealing as the n. 484a
　tingle to the n. chime 200a
Noondays: endless n., glorious n. 286b
Noontide: at n. wd. he stretch 174b
　retired as n. dew 469a
　throbbings of n. 179b
　when n. wakes anew 47b
Noose: next to the hangman's n. 198b
Nora's heart is lost 318b
Norfan: I'm a N., both sides 455b
Norfolk: Duke of N. deals in malt 178a
　jockey of N., be not too bold 385a
Normal: very type of the n. 204a
Norman: a blacksmith like our N. 227a
　Billy the N. 120b
　farewell to the N. blood! 171b
　N. and Dane are we 439a
　simple faith than N. blood 431b
　the reef of N.'s Woe 249a
Normandy: handy to leave this N. 120b
Normans: Saxon is not like us N. 233a
North: Ariosto of the N. 69a
　a ship. .in the N. Country 531a
　ask where's the N.? 301a
　at the n. wind's breath 185a
　awake, O n. wind 500b
　compact. .between. .N. and the
　　South 159a
　gray metropolis of the N. 426b
　honour cross it from. .n. to south 377a
　Hotspur of the N. 377a
　hunt for dangers N. and South 293b
　in the N. long since 436b
　in triumph from the n. 252b
　it's N. you may run 231b
　[Lord N.] fills a chair 210b
　of Nelson and the N. 76b
　sum of summer in the N. 436b
　tender is the N. 436a
　the n. wind doth blow 533a
　unripened beauties of the n. 1b

North (cont.)
　without sharp N. 133a
North America: scalped each other
　by. .N. 254b
North-easter: welcome, wild N. 226a
Northern: glorious the n. lights 403a
　Lucasta that bright n. star 249b
　not, as in n. climes 70a
　St. Andrews by the N. Sea 242a
　Wain upon the n. steep 200a
North-north-west: mad N. 332b
Northumberland: Percy out of N. 530b
North-West: N. Passage to the in-
　tellectual 411b
　to the N. died away 47b
Norval: my name is N. 194b
Norway: a carl in N. 235b
　N. o'er the faem 529b
　N., too, has noble wild prospects 207a
Norwegian: hewn on N. hills 271b
Nose: a great hook n. like thine 29b
　any n. may ravage. .a rose 52a
　Cleopatra's n. 564b
　custom. .hateful to the n. 204a
　down his innocent n. 325b
　entuned in hir n. 88b
　ever and anon he gave his n. 376b
　final cause of the human n. 102b
　forehead, straight n. 284b
　gallops o'er a courtier's n. 364b
　he cocks his n. 419a
　her n. and chin they threaten 63b
　his n.'s cast is of the roman 155a
　if his n. is warm 243b
　lightly was her slender n. 427b
　many an Aldermanic n. 19a
　Marion's n. looks red 345b
　may they stop their n. 324a
　my n. fell a-bleeding 353b
　n., n., jolly red n. 23a
　n. was as sharp as a pen 382a
　snapt off her n. 533b
　snub n. like to mine 29b
　thy n. is as the tower of Lebanon 500b
　wipe a bloody n. 160b
　wipe his little n. 19b
　with a snug n. 216a
Noselessness of Man 93b
Noses: athwart men's n. as they lie 364b
　n. have they, and smell not 489a
　they haven't got no n. 93b
　wearing our own n. 328b
Nostalgia of the heathen past 243a
Not: Archibald—certainly n.! 315a
Note: a bolder n. than his 298a
　best fits my little n. 188b
　deed of dreadful n. 349a
　dreadful n. of preparation 382b
　gen'l'm'n said to the fi' pun' n. 126a
　keeps warm her n. 79b
　nightingale's high n. is heard 73b
　not a n. of mine. .worth the noting 358a
　n. most full of harmony 42a
　n. this before my notes 358a
　only the n. of a bird 402b
　simplest n. that swells the gale 175a
　sound me from my lowest n. 334a
　the n. I wanted 204a
　tunes her nocturnal n. 273a
　turn his merry n. 326a
　tu-who, a merry n. 345b
　when found, make a n. of 122b
　with a n. like thine 206a
　with his n. so true 357a
Note-book: set in a n., learn'd 341a
Notes: all the compass of the n. 139b
　both in highest n. appear 78a
　child's amang you taking n. 62a
　cd. thy n. flow in 398b
　formed, as n. of music are 393b
　Fox's shall the n. rebound 317b
　haste you, sad n. 78a
　her thick-warbled n. 277a
　my Muse these n. intendeth 401b
　n. are often necessary 213b
　n. by distance made more sweet 103a
　n., with many a winding bout 269a
　such n. as, warbled to the string 268b
　such were the n. 302b
　the n. are few 31b
　thinks two n. a song 118a

Nothing: and it was n. more 468b
　an infinite deal of n. 352b
　as having n. 515a
　as he is now, n. 386a
　did n. in particular 164a
　does n. with a better grace 476b
　doing n. with a deal of skill 111a
　even as n. in respect of thee 484a
　everything by starts, and n. long 138b
　George the First knew n. 208b
　gives to airy n. a. .habitation 357b
　glory and the n. of a name 69b
　have not charity, I am n. 514b
　having n., yet hath all 473b
　I am n. if not critical 360b
　I come from n. 265a
　I have n. to do to-day 135a
　insupportable labour of doing n. 410b
　is it n. to you 503b
　it profiteth me n. 514b
　knew. .he knew n. yet 25a
　knows n. whatever about Thee 525a
　know. .that he n. knew 277a
　let n. you dismay 523a
　madam, is there n. else 127b
　needy n. trimmed in jollity 388a
　no n. 74b
　n. a-year, paid quarterly 417a
　n. begins and n. ends 441a
　n. beside remains 396b
　n. brings me all things 368a
　n. but the night 199b
　n. but well and fair 278a
　n. can be created out of n. 550a
　n. can be known 68a
　n. can return to n. 552a
　n., can touch him further 348b
　n. comes amiss, so money comes 366b
　n. did he say 12b
　n. for n., 'ere 535b
　n. great was ever achieved 148a
　n. hid from the heat thereof 482b
　n. in his life became him 346b
　n. in my hand I bring 445a
　n., in this corporal earth 441b
　n. is but what is not 346b
　n. is fair or good alone 146b
　n. is here for tears 278a
　n. is there to come 106b
　n. less will content me 55b
　n.-much-matter-day 186a
　n. of him that doth fade 367a
　n. of itself will come 464b
　n. refuse 146b
　n.! thou elder brother. .to shade 309b
　n. to be refused 516b
　n. to do but work 225a
　n. to do with the case 165a
　n. to eat but food 225a
　n. to wear but clothes 225a
　n. to what I cd. say 83a
　n. under Heaven so blue 415a
　n. venture, n. win 164a
　n. we see but means our good 187b
　n. will remain 199a
　passages, that lead to n. 175a
　phantom Caravan has reached the
　　N. 153b
　praise of wh. I n. know 463b
　reputed wise, for saying n. 352b
　signifying n. 350b
　starts for the Dawn of N. 153b
　there is n. either good or bad 332a
　they that starve with n. 352b
　they were n., Sir 209b
　think n. done while aught remains 309b
　to be thus is n. 348b
　to n. but herself severe 79b
　to whom n. is given 151a
　we are n.; less than n. 238b
　we brought n. into this world 516b
　we can carry n. out 516b
　we. .have taken n. 509a
　we that did n. study 225a
　when you have n. to say, say n. 103b
　why—N.! 94a
Nothingness: first dark day of n. 72b
　never pass into n. 217b
Nothings: invulnerable n. 392b
　such laboured n. 300a
Notice: a man who used to n. 179a

Notice (*cont.*)
n...you have been pleased to take 206b
Noticeable: a n. man 471b
Noting: not a note..worth the n. 358a
Notion: and foolish n. 61b
Notions about a superior power 417b
Notorious evil liver 480a
Nought: n. is worth a thought 305a
n. spake he to Lars Porsena 253b
n...so much the spirit calms 70b
Nouns: n. of number, or multitude 97a
verbs and n. do more agree 182a
Nourish: eyes..in all the world 345a
Nourished: how begot, how n. 354a
how n. there 464b
n. in the womb of pia mater 344b
Nourisher: chief n. in life's feast 348a
Nourisheth: lives by that wh. n. it 323b
Novel: a n. cannot be too bad 391a
given away by a n. 223a
n. called..*Tristram Shandy* 449b
obligation to wh...we may hold a n. 204b
oh! it is only a n. 11b
scrofulous French n. 52a
supersede the last fashionable n. 255b
Novels: Balzac's n. occupy one shelf 45a
loved, ever after, French n. 450a
Novelty: create at last this n. Earth 276b
n., n., n. 196b
November: April, June, and N 533a
no leaves, no birds—N.! 195a
N.'s leaf is red 317b
N.'s sky is chill 317b
nurse N. on the lap of June 196a
on the moor the brief N. day 224a
the Fifth of N. 532a
thirty days hath N. 172a
Now: an eternal N. does always last 106b
as it was in the beginning, is n. 478a
if it be n., 'tis not to come 337a
it is not n. as it hath been 466a
leave N. for dogs and apes 47a
let me do it n. 523b
n. is the accepted time 515a
n. sleeps the crimson petal 436b
n. we sha'n't be long 76a
Nowher so bisy a man 88b
Nubbly: nice but n. 237a
Nude: keep one from going n. 225a
noble and n. 421a
Nuisance to other people 266a
Null: spendidly n. 433b
Number: in the n. I do not know but one 339a
more by yr. n., than yr. light 473b
multitude, wh. no man cd. n. 519a
not on the n., but the choice 107a
n. is Six hundred three score 519a
n., weight and measure 31a
telleth the n. of the stars 490b
the n. of his name 519a
the n. of my days 484a
the n. of the beast 519a
Numbered: name be n. among theirs 468b
n. with the transgressors 503a
Numbers: add to golden n. 118b
brings home full n. 357b
divinity in odd n. 356a
honest men are better than n. 115b
I lisped in n. 303a
in fresh n. number all yr. graces 387a
liv'd in Settle's n. 298b
opposed n. pluck their hearts 383a
round n. are always false 209b
secret magic of n. 41b
tell me not, in mournful n. 247b
the plaintive n. flow 471a
to n. I'll not be confin'd 461a
voluntary move harmonious n. 273a
Numbness pains my sense 219b
Nun: if you become a n., dear 202a
Joshua the son of N. 494a
my daughter the N. 407a
quiet as a n. 467a
Nunc dimittis: sweetest canticle is N. 14a
Nuncheon: take yr. n. 50a
Nunnery: from the n. of thy chaste breast 250a
get thee to a n. 333b
Nuns: among the N.' Black 402b
n. fret not 468a

Nuptials: iteration of n. 105b
Nurse: beggar's n. and Cæsar's continues what the n. began 325a, 140b
dirty n., Experience 428b
fawn upon a n. 374b
if you n. a flame 77b
London, my most kindly n. 409b
nature's soft n. 380a
n. for a poetic child 317b
n. of manly sentiment 57a
rose a n. of ninety years 436b
set upon the n.'s knee 530b
sucks the n. asleep 325b
testy babe, will scratch the n. 372b
Nursed: I never n. a dear gazelle 282a
n. upon the self-same hill 269a
Nurseries: in the n. of Heaven 441b
N. of blooming Youth 468a
public schools..n. of all vice 151b
Nursery: n.-mishaps 113b
trod my n. floor 109b
Nurses: wives are..old men's n. 14b
Nursing: lack of woman's n. 290a
n. the unconquerable hope 8a
Nursling of the sky 393a
n. of thy widowhood 391b
win their n. with their smiles 241b
Nurslings: n. of immortality 397a
Nut: a Fairy in a n. 31a
Nut-brown: spicy n. ale 269a
Nutmeg: but a silver n. 532a
Nutmeg-graters: rough as n. 191b
Nutmegs and ginger 23a
Nutrition: draw n., propagate 301a
Nuts: before the n. work loose 234b
gathering n. in May 523b
like an ape does n. 335a
Nutshell: bounded in a n. 332b
Nutting-bag: Devil's n. 247b
Nut tree: I had a little n. 532a
Nymph: a N., a Naiad, or a Grace 316a
Echo, sweetest n. 267a
haste thee, N. 268b
like a n., with long..hair 386b
mountain n., sweet Liberty 268b
not as a n., but for a reed 260b
n., in thy orisons be all my sins 333b
rose like a n. to the bath 398a
to the n. with but one, sir 400b
Nymphs: breasts of the n. 423b
leave of yr. n. on the shore 424b
N. that reign o'er sewers 100b
where were ye, N. 269b

O

O: O all ye Green Things 478a
O all ye works of the Lord 478a
O Ananias, Azarias 478a
O little did my mother ken 530a
O Paddy dear, an' did ye hear 525b
O stablish me according 489b
O! that we now had here 383a
O, U, T, spells out 534a
O ye Whales, and all that move 478a
within this wooden O 381a
Oafs: muddied o. at the goals 230a
Oak: cattle..shadow of the British o. 57a
heart of o. are our ships 158b
hearts of o. our men 10b
hollow o. our palace is 116a
I lean'd my back unto an (aik) o. 530a
many an o. that grew thereby 265b
nodosities of the o. 58b
O., and Ash, and Thorn 236a
o., and the ash, and the bonny ivy 525a
O., Elder, Elm 119b
our ships were British o. 10b
sage beneath the spreading o. 107b
standing long an o. 216b
to thee the reed is as the o. 329a
unwedgeable and gnarled o. 351b
win the palm, the o. or bays 260b
Oaks: huge o. and old 235a
little strokes fell great o. 157a
o., branch-charméd by the..stars 218a
o. that flourish for a thousand years 244b
old families last not three o. 42b
tall o. from little acorns grow 140b
Oak-stump: hides the rotted old o. 99b

Oar: but bend to the o. 315b
tann'd galley-slave is with his o. 454b
Oars: he feathered his o. 120b
I took the o. 99b
o., and coat, and badge 120b
our o. keep time 282b
the o. were silver 323a
Oat-cakes: Calvin, o., and sulphur 404a
Oaten: if ought of o. stop 103a
Oatmeal: literature upon a little o. 405a
Oats. A grain given to horses 212b
Oath: a good mouth-filling o. 378a
a man is not upon o. 208b
an o., an o., I have an o. 354b
Cophetua sware a royal o. 425b
fair as the rash o. of virginity 293b
hir gretteste o...sëynt Loy 88a
if ever I utter an o. again 391b
I take the official o. to-day 245a
Oaths: full of strange o. 326b
God pardon all o. 376a
men (deceived) with o. 13a
o. are but words 65b
o. are straw 382a
oft names God in o. 132a
swore as many o. as I spake 343a
Obadiah Bind-their-kings 252b
Obdurate: if too o. I, choose thou 415a
Obedience: approve first thy o. 276a
fear..keeps men in o. 64b
let my o. then excuse 107b
rebellion..is o. to God 34b
reluctant of distant provinces 254a
that is, to thy o. 275a
Obedient: mild, o., good as He 3b
o. to their laws we lie 560a
Obeisance: made o. to my sheaf 493a
Obermann: sedulous ape to...O. 412b
Oberon! what visions have I seen 357a
Obey: all did govern yet all did o. 136b
'E don't o. no orders 228b
in all my best o. you, madam 330a
o. thy heart 146b
Sleep shall o. me 406b
the rogues o. you well 191b
to love, cherish, and to o. 481b
to o. is better than sacrifice 495a
Obeying: command Nature except by o. her 17a
Obeys: has her humour..when she o. 302a
Object: ev'ry beauteous o. that I view 161a
Homer..with his eye on the o. 10a
my o. all sublime 164b
newer o. quite forgotten 372b
ship come in with o. won 457b
tho' mean our o. and inglorious 469a
'tis for o. strange and high 260a
Objects: but with high o. 469a
on little o. with like firmness 68b
themselves as o. recognized 469b
what o. are the fountains 398b
Oblations: bring no more vain o. 501a
Obligation: only o. to wh...we may hold a novel 204b
possession without o. 264b
to John I owed great o. 305b
Obliged: so obliging that he ne'er o. 303a
Obliquely: like th' other foot, o. run 134a
Oblivion: childishness, and mere o. 326b
commend to cold o. 393b
drink o. of a day 264a
formless ruin of o. 369b
my o. is a very Antony 322b
o. as they rose shrank 392b
o. in lost angels can infuse 6a
puts alms for o. 369a
razure of o. 352a
the inequity of o. 42b
therewith bury in o. 42b
Obscure: Coleridge—he who sits o. 395b
that had thee here o. 264a
thro' the palpable o. 272b
Obscured: excess of glory o. 272a
Obscurely: to be o. good 1b
Obscurity: decent o. of a learned language 571a
left unthought of in o. 465b
Obsequies: celebrates his o. 317a
they solemnized their o. 42a
Obsequious: saw the o. Seraphims 115a
Observance: in the breach than the o. 331a

Observance (cont.)
with this special o. 333b
Observant of His heavenly Word 131b
Observation: bearings of this o. 122b
cramm'd with o. 326b
let o. with extensive view 213b
youth and o. copied there 331b
Observations wh. ourselves we make 301b
Observatory: I left the O. 288b
Observe: Brutus, I do o. you now 337b
Observed: o. of all observers 333b
since o. by Yours faithfully, God 522b
Observer: he is a great o. 338a
partial for th' o.'s sake 301b
Obstinacy: o. in a bad cause 41b
o. in a bad one 411b
Obstinate: name of the one was O. 54a
Obstruction: George III..con-
secrated 17b
lie in cold o. and to rot 352a
Obtain that wh. he merits 101a
Obtains: merits that wh. he o. 101a
Occasion: courage mounteth with o. 373b
lie all unlocked to yr. o. 352b
o...is bald behind 107a
o. smiles upon a second leave 330b
on O.'s forelock..wait 277a
on such an o. as this 53b
take o. by the hand 437a
upon the mellowing of o. 344b
when we had o. to be seen 378b
Occasions: all o. do inform against 335b
new o. teach new duties 251a
there is o. and causes 383b
upon their lawful o. 490b
Occident: in th' yet unformed O. 117a
Occult: bitterness of things o. 313a
Occupation: absence of o. is not rest 110b
my estate by the same o. 54a
Occupations: let us love our o. 121b
pause in the day's o. 246b
there are worse o. in this world 411a
Occur: things that didn't o. 156a
Ocean: a dark illimitable o. 273a
as it draws to the O. 6a
blue sky bounds the o. 35b
Britannia, the pride of the o. 389b
broad o. leans against the land 170a
dark unfathom'd caves of o. bear 174a
deep and dark blue O. 69b
Earth and O. seem to sleep 393b
from o.'s farthest coast 200b
grasp the o. in my span 453a
grateful smell old O. smiles 273b
great Neptune's o. wash..blood 348a
great o. of truth..undiscovered 289a
his legs bestrid the o. 325a
I have loved thee, O.! 69b
in tumult to a lifeless o. 101b
I pass thro' the pores of the o. 393a
is this the mighty o.? 241a
life on the o. wave 315b
make the mighty o. 82a
many-twinkling smile of o. 224a
murmurs as the o. murmurs there 241a
o.'s child, and then his queen 395b
O.'s nursling, Venice lies 395a
o.'s wave-beat shore 149b
on one side lay the O. 429a
on the o.'s bosom, unespy'd 260a
seen the hungry o. gain advantage 388a
shall read o'er o. wide 241b
Shepherd of the O. 408a
so on the o. of life we pass 249a
the day-star in the o. bed 270a
the fish soar to find the o. 442a
the o.-floors pave it 396a
the rivers with the o. 395b
the sapless foliage of the o. 396b
time, and the o. 452a
upon the o. green 258a
use the o. as their road 449a
vast o.! on whose awful face 280a
with willing sport, to the wild o. 372b
Oceans: compendious o. 115a
O'clock: shall be what o. I say it is 366b
O'Connell: to deal with..O.'C. 404b
Octavia: eye of dull O.
Octavos: light o. fill a spacious plain 113b
October: bright O. was come 96a
night in the lonesome O. 298b

October (cont.)
with the leaf still in O. 23a
Octosyllabic: facility of the o. verse 69b
Ocular: give me the o. proof 362a
Odd: and this was o., because, you
know 84a
creators of o. volumes 239a
how o. of God to choose the Jews 149b
humour is o., grotesque 420a
it's a very o. thing 119b
luck lies in o. numbers 356a
must think it exceedingly o. 527a
scarcely o. because they'd eaten 84b
Odd-fellow: desperate o. society 444a
Odds: facing fearful o. 253a
the o. is gone 324b
what's the o., so long as 263a
Ode: I intended an O. 131a
o., and elegy, and sonnet 211b
Odes: o. to every zephyr 226a
quoted o., and jewels 436a
Odious! in woollen! 302a
Odorous: beech and o. pine 37b
comparisons are o. 359a
Odour: stealing and giving o. 369b
Odours: Champak o. fail 394b
gentle o. led my steps 397b
glory..exhales her o. 72b
golden vials full of o. 518b
heavens rein o. on you 371b
living hues and o. 396a
o., when sweet violets sicken 399b
Odysseus: doomed like O. 476a
Odyssey: thunder of the O. 242a
Odysseys: last of all our O. 26a
O'er: then I'll give o. 189b
O'er-dusted: more laud than gilt o. 369a
O'erjoyed was he to find 108b
O'ertake: I will o. thee, Cleopatra 324b
O'erthrown: noble mind is here o. 333b
O'erwhelm: all the earth o. them 330b
Off: be o., or I'll kick you 82b
nowhere to fall but o. 225a
o. with his head! 83a
o. with the old love 262b, 524b
sit here..on and o. for days 82b
when he was o. he was acting 169b
Offal: this slave's o. 333a
Offence: a conscience void of o. 512b
beauty..after o. returning 278a
confront the visage of o. 334b
every nice o...bear his comment 340b
forgave the o. 140a
greatest o. against virtue 183b
his was doon o. 89b
innocent from the great o. 482b
my o. is rank 334b
pardon'd and retain the o. 334b
that wh. wd. appear o. in us 338a
what dire o. from am'rous causes 302b
where the o. is let the..axe fall 336a
Offences: but pardoning our o. 480b
it must needs be that o. come 507a
made old o. of affections new 389a
more o. at my beck 333b
sins and o. of my youth 483a
Offend: coy and tender to o. 187b
not willingly o. 453a
o. one of these little ones 507a
Offended: for him have I o. 330b
nor be easily o. 453a
this hand hath o. 114b
this hath not o. the king 283b
Offender: she hugged the o. 140a
Offenders: a little list of social o. 164b
Offendeth: who can tell how oft he o. 482b
Offending: head and front of my o. 360a
whipped the o. Adam 381a
Offer: instantly close with the o. 202b
Offering: an o. far too small 453b
Office: been so clear in his great o. 347a
be not afraid to do thine o. 283a
Circumlocution O. 123a
during his o. treason..no crime 138b
each in his o. wait 131b
from their o. to black funeral 366a
hands, that yarely frame the o. 323a
hath but a losing o. 379b
insolence of o. 333a
man who has no o. to go to 390b
o. and affairs of love 358a

Office (cont.)
o., and custom, in all line 368b
o. he'll hold and patronage sway 40b
serves it in the o. of a wall 375a
single o. divided between them 55a
the o. opposite to St. Peter 363a
Officer: never more be o. of mine 361b
o. and the office..seldom fit 405a
Officers: a king and o. of sorts 381b
his o. were in much pain 417b
Offices: above their functions and..o. 345a
cast a longing eye on [o.] 204b
estates, degrees, and on 353b
imperfect o. of prayer 464a
o. both private and public 279b
Official: this high o., all allow 186a
Officious, innocent, sincere 210b
Offspring: new-fledg'd o. to the skies 168b
o. of Heaven first born 273a
Time's noblest o. 28a
true source of human o. 274b
Oft: how o. hereafter will she wax 154a
o. in danger, o. in woe 456b
o., in the stilly night 282b
Often: how o. have we done this 393a
how o. wd. I have gathered 507b
Oh: o. don't deceive me 523a
O.! Sophonisba! Sophonisba! O.! 443b
Oil: a little o. in a cruse 496a
anointed my head with o. 483a
consum'd the midnight o. 160a
her mouth is smoother than o. 497b
hurt not the o. and the wine 518b
'incomparable o.,' Macassar 70a
lingering, with boiling o. in it 165a
o. to make him a cheerful 488a
o., vinegar, sugar 169a
our midday sweat, our midnight o. 307a
our wasted o. unprofitably burns 108a
pour this o...on the water 24a
their lamps with everlasting o. 267a
without the o. and twopence 404b
Oils: dropt in ambrosial o. 267b
the water, like a witch's o. 98b
Oily: fat, o. man of God 443a
Ointment: alabaster box of..o. 508a
like the precious o. upon the head 490a
name is better than precious o. 499a
the o. of the apothecary 499b
thy name is an o. poured forth 500a
why was not this o. sold 511a
Ojibways: land of the O. 248b
O'Leary: it's with O. in the grave 474b
Old: adherence to the o. and tried 245a
all..the young can do for the o. 390a
all times when o. are good 67b
a man not o. but mellow 296b
an o. man in a hurry 95a
both of the new and o. 461b
call him not o., whose..brain 194a
crucify the o. man 481a
darling, I am growing o. 308b
die in their glory and never be o. 199a
'eavy-sterned amateur o. men 234b
for o. sakes' sake 226a
growing o. in drawing nothing up 112a
grown o. before my time 311a
grow o. along with me 50b
grow o. with a good grace 410a
half as o. as Time 55a
he is o. and she a shade 241a
holdeth o. men from the chimney 402a
hopeful than to be forty years o. 194a
I am too o...the seas..too long 168a
I am too o. to fawn upon a nurse 374b
I fancy one's o. and ugly 105a
if ever I grow to be o. 27a
if I live to be o. 304a
if to grow o. in Heaven 312a
I grow o...I grow o. 145a
I have been young, and now am o. 484a
I heard the o., o. men say 475b
I love everything that's o. 170b
I'm not so o., and not so plain 163b
is not o. wine wholesomest 454b
it is o. and plain 371a
it was so o. a ship—who knows 155a
it was too o. for him 122a
man is as o. as he's feeling 102b
men as o. as we to keep the peace 364b
Mithridates, he died o. 199b

Old (cont.)
no man wd. be o. 419a
nor so o. to dote on her 342a
not persuade me I am o. 387a
not yet o. enough for a man 370a
off with the o. love 262b
o. Adam in this child 481a
o. and well stricken in age 493a
o. and young..on our last cruise 413a
o. as I am, for ladies' love unfit 140a
o. as I am waxing 240a
o. friends, o times 170b
o. loves endear thee 97b
o., mad, blind..dying king 399a
o. man!..not so difficult to die 73a
o. man's wit may wander 427b
o. men, and babes 100a
o. men and comets..reverenced 419a
o. men go to death 13b
o. there's grief enough for thee 176a
o. times are still new 180b
o. times unqueen thee 97b
o. to you as the story of Adam 47b
one of them is fat and grows o. 377b
O, sir! you are o. 342b
out of o. bokes..newe science 90a
out of o. feldes..newe corn 90a
redress the balance of the O. 79a
ring out the o. 431a
say I'm growing o. 202a
she is not yet so o. 354a
she was middling o. 231b
snowy summits o. in story 436a
so o., and so profane 381a
some day before I'm o.! 230b
sugared about by the o. men 234b
tell me the o., o. story 179a
that new world wh. is the o. 426b
the 'good o. times' 67b
the last to lay the o. aside 300a
the o. man had so much blood 350a
the o. ones, grub 389b
there I met an o. man 534b
they shall not grow o. 28b
thinking of the o. 'un 122a
this year, o. men shall reap 253a
till..the stars are o. 425a
time to be o., to take in sail 147a
to me..you never can be o. 388b
too o. to go again to my travels 87b
very o. are we men 119a
wax o. as doth a garment 488a
w'en folks get o. en strucken 181b
we're o. and tough 440b
we that are left grow o. 28b
we who are o., o. and gay 474b
when all the world is o., lad 226a
when I shall grow o. 468a
when it is o., thou shalt drink it 520b
when they get to feeling o. 39b
when thou shalt be o. 511b
when 'tis o. it waxeth cauld 530a
when we are as o. as you 328b
when you are o. and grey 476b
when you are o. sit under..shade 122b
when you are very o. 565b
where even the o. are fair 475b
where nobody gets o. 475b
whether it be new or o. 415b
whether we be young or o. 469b
why wasn't I born o. and ugly? 121a
woman as o. as she looks 102b
you and I are o. 439a
you are o. Father William 82b, 407a
you must be very o., Sir Giles 284b
you that are o, consider not 379b
young a body with so o. a head 354b
young and o. came forth to play 269a
yr. o. men shall dream dreams 504a
Old Bailey: say the bells at O. 533b
Old Kent Road 94a
Old Testament: prosperity blessing
    of the O. 14a
Oldcastle died a martyr 381a
Olden: all of the o. time 12b, 524b
Older: becomes the richer still the o. 66a
    she is o. than the rocks 293a
Oldest: o. man he seemed 470a
    the o. hath borne most 344a
Old-gentlemanly: a good o. vice 7cb
Olive: lands..of o., aloe, and maize 426a

Olive-branches: children like the o. 490a
Oliver Twist has asked for more 125a
Olivet: purple brows of O. 430a
    wet with the red dew of O. 442b
Olivia: air cry out, 'O.!' 370a
    mine eyes did see O. first 369b
Ologies: instructed in the 'o.' 81a
Olympian: O. bards who sung 147a
    O. bolts 128a
Omar: the diver O. plucked then 250b
Ombrifruge (Lord love you) 75a
Omega: Alpha and O. 518a
Omen: from us be the o. 551b
    may the gods avert the o. 540b
Omitted, all the voyage of their life 341a
Omnibuses: only ridden more in o. 184b
Omnipotent: durst defy th' O. 271a
    o. but friendless 397a
    squamous, o.., and kind 39b
Omniscience: his specialism is o. 136a
On: before you are o. with the new 262b, 524b
    but o., o. thy way 189b
    nowhere to stand but o. 225a
    o., bacons, o.! 377a
    o., o. you noblest English! 382a
    sit here..o. and off, for days 82b
    their utmost up and o. 51a
Onaway! Awake, beloved! 248b
Once: Christmas comes but o. a year 446a
    did you o. see Shelley plain 48b
    not o. or twice 435a
    o. a clergyman 525b
    o...but the world was young then 307a
    o. did she hold the gorgeous East 472b
    o. to every man and nation 250b
    pass thro' this world but o. 176b, 523b
    taste any drink o. 75a
One: all but o. that ligs under 534a
    all their..words they are not o. 137b
    all the means to make us o. 132b
    and for o. in vain 154a
    animals went in two, by o. 526a
    but that's all o. 372b
    incorporate and make us o. 338b
    in the number I do know but o. 339a
    it ought to be Number O. 83b
    it were all o. that I shd. love 322a
    made o. of them 341b
    made o. with Nature 392b
    many..must labour for the o. 69b
    none but doeth good, no, not o. 482a
    o. among a thousand 497a
    o. especially do we affect 259a
    o. fixed for ever at the door 439b
    o. for my master..o. for my dame 534b
    o. God, o. law, o. element 431a
    o. man in a thousand 235a
    O., most loving of you all 44a
    o. near o. is too far 45b
    o. of us two, Herminius 253b
    o. shall be taken 508a
    o. thing is certain,..Life flies 153a
    o. to destroy, is murder 477a
    o. to watch, and o. to pray 2b
    o., two; and the third in yr. bosom 365b
    o.; two: why then, 'tis time 350a
    o. was round her lover 77a
    O., who never changes 448a
    only o. thing at once 403a
    our two souls..wh. are o. 134a
    race is run by o. and o. 235a
    than O. who rose 394a
    the day but o. 34a
    the heart but o. 34a
    the less will you settle to o. 230b
    the many fail: the o. succeeds 426b
    the O. remains, the many change
        and pass 392b
    there's but o. in all doth hold 339a
    the Three in O., the O. in Three 233b
    they are o. and o. 45b
    to o. thing constant never 358a
    to the nymph with but o., sir 400b
    we are o. flesh 276b
    where o. but goes abreast 369a
One-and-twenty: when I was o. 198b
One-eyed: o., blinking sort of place 181a
    o. man is king 292a
One-Goddite: a o. 240a
One-horse: poor little o. town 447a

One-horse (cont.)
    wonderful o. shay 194a
Ones: little o., unbuttoned, glowing 113a
One-sixteenth: one and o. is born 523a
Onion: let o. atoms lurk within 404b
    tears live in an o. 322b
Onions, and eke lekes 89a
Only: nor this the o. time 37b
    o. a little more..to write 189b
    o. a man harrowing clods 179b
    o. Luke is with me 516b
    o. man is vile 184a
    o. thin smoke without flame 179b
Onward: a little o. lend thy guiding
    hand 277b
    half a league o. 426a
    he o. came 275a
    o., Christian Soldiers 20a
    o., Christians, o. go 456b
    o. ye will tread 287a
    press o., for thine eye shall see 37a
Onwards—always onwards 12b
Ooze of their pasture ground 5b
Oozing: I feel it o. out 400b
    feed..o...pasture ground 5b
Opal: thy mind is a very o. 371a
Open: gates are mine to o. 233a
    I o. with a clock striking 400a
    lie o. unto the fields 472b
    on a sudden o. fly 273a
    o. not thine heart to every man 520b
    o. Sesame! 567b
    o. to me, my sister 500b
    o., ye heavens, yr. living doors 275b
    the o. door for all nations 27b
    warder, warder! o. quickly 12a
Opened: I o. to my beloved 500b
    knock, and it shall be o. 505b
    when the Pye was o. 410b
Opening: it is our o. day 18a
    to him are o. paradise 175a
Operation: by mere mechanic o. 66a
    hath a two-fold o. in it 380b
    o. of the Holy Ghost 480b
    surgical o. to get a joke 404a
Operations: five o. of the Lord 520b
Ophelia: water hast thou, poor O. 336a
Ophir: from distant O. 261b
Ophiucus huge in th' arctic sky 273a
Opinion: a better o. than ever before 363a
    absence..of..educated..o. 9b
    a plague of o. 369a
    approve a private o., call it o. 191b
    better to have no o. of God 15a
    coquetry of public o. 58a
    from the main o. he held once 338b
    great organ of public o. 128a
    gross and scope of my o. 329b
    held Epicurus strong, and his o. 341a
    is of his own o. still 66a
    justifies th' ill o. 62a
    of the o. with the learned 104a
    one person..of the contrary o. 266a
    o...determined by the feelings 408a
    o. in good men is but knowledge 279a
    o. one man entertains 292a
    o. we are endeavouring to stifle 266a
    party is organized o. 128b
    reform was once a private o. 147b
    suspense and imperfect o. 148a
    take..our own o. from another 147b
    the poor itch of your o. 328a
    thinks the last o. right 300b
    this fool gudgeon, this o. 352b
    upon the difference of an o. 41b
Opinions: halt ye between two o. 496a
    I have bought golden o. 347a
    killed with yr. hard o. 381a
    never..so bad as their o. 256a
    new o. are always suspected 246a
    so many men, so many o. 554a
    stiff in o. 138b
    their quaint o. wide 275b
    the public buys its o. 67a
Opium: religion..o. of the people 526a
    subtle, and mighty o. 120a
Oppenheim, half-blind with blood 27a
Opponent: ascribe to an o. motives 21b
    o. of the chosen people 9a
Opportune moment of his death 553b
Opportunities: Devil watches all o. 104b

Opportunities (cont.)
make more o. than he finds — 16b
Opportunity: man must make his o. — 13a
marriage..maximum of o. — 391a
never had mortal man such o. — 71b
o. makes a thief — 16b
thou strong seducer, o.! — 140a
Oppose: duty of an Opposition..
to o. — 95a, 410a
Opposed: th' o. may beware of thee — 330b
Opposition: duty of an O..to oppose — 95a, 410a
Her Majesty's O. — 17a
o. of the stars — 260b
without a formidable O. — 129a
Oppressed: he was o., and he was afflicted — 503a
let the o. go free — 503a
Oppression: but behold o. — 501a
lack gall to make o. bitter — 333a
o. makes the wise man mad — 48b
thro' o., thro' any plague — 488b
Oppressions: unfelt o. of this earth — 395a
Oppressor: the o.'s wrong — 333a
Opprest: heart and voice o. — 286a
Oppugnancy: meets in mere o. — 368b
Ops: fugues and 'o.' — 164b
Optimist: in the best of all..worlds — 75a
Opulent Rotunda Strike the Sky — 412b
Oracle: fast by the o. of God — 270b
I am Sir O. — 352b
Oracles: the o. are dumb — 270b
Orange: drinking watered o.-pulp — 52a
lands of palm, of o.-blossom — 426a
o. bright, like golden lamps — 260a
that I were an o.-tree — 187b
Oranges and lemons — 533b
Orator: eyes of men without an o. — 386b
I am no o. — 340a
Orators: swords shall play the o. — 259a
Oratory: Chadband style of o. — 121a
object of o. alone is not truth — 255b
Orb: before this splendid o. was..set — 55a
mighty o. of song..Milton — 464a
quail and shake the o. — 325a
the moon..in her circled o. — 365a
there's not the smallest o. — 355a
too vast o. of her fate — 6b
Orbit: in its ruddy o. lifts the blood — 294b
Orbs: hath pierced their o. — 273a
Orcades: in Scotland, at the O. — 301a
Orchard: chaffinch sings on the o. bough — 47a
in the pleasant o. closes — 43b
little peach in an o. grew — 151a
picture that o. sprite — 192a
when, upon o. and lane — 452a
Ordained: stars, wh. thou hast o. — 482a
Ordains: o. for each one spot — 235a
o. us e'en as blind — 228a
Order: all things began in o. — 41a
Angels sit in o. serviceable — 270b
beauty from o. springs — 225b
best words in the best o. — 102b
good o. is the foundation of all — 57b
in all line of o. — 368b
liberty connected with o. — 55a
men in a wonderful o. — 480a
nobility..ornament to the civil o. — 57b
o. is Heaven's first law — 301b
stand not upon the o. of yr. going — 349a
teach the act of o. — 381b
the old o. changeth — 429a
time and o. of yr. birth — 36a
Ordered their estate — 3a
Orders: Almighty's O. to perform e' don't obey no o. — 1a
e' don't obey no o. — 228b
lower o. don't set us..example — 460a
Ordinance: according to God's holy o. — 481b
live together after God's o. — 481b
Ordinary: a Christian or an o. man — 369b
o. young Englishman — 9b
Ore: load yr. subject with o. — 223b
with new spangled o. — 270a
Organ: every lovely o. of her life — 359a
great o. of public opinion — 128a
let the o. moan her sorrow — 234b
let the pealing o. blow — 268b
mellering to the o. — 125b
o.-voice of England, Milton — 427a

Organ (cont.)
pipe is as the maiden's o. — 370a
playing of the merry o. — 526b
seated one day at the o. — 306b
silent o. loudest chants — 146b
speak with most miraculous o. — 333a
Organism to live beyond its income — 66b
Organs: dry up in her the o. of increase — 342a
his owls was o. — 124a
moves with its own o. — 323b
Orgunjè: flow'd..past O. — 8a
Oriel Common Room — 288a
Orient: from out its O. tabernacle — 442b
in yr. beauty's o. deep — 79b
lo! in the o. — 387a
o. and immortal wheat — 445a
Oriental: tea, an O. is a gentleman — 93b
Oriflamme: be your o. to-day — 252b
Origin: every gift of noble o. — 471b
stamp of his lowly o. — 117b
wh. is not Greek in its o. — 256b
Original: all things counter, o. — 197b
an o. something, fair maid — 78a
behold the bright o. appear — 160a
in the o. perused mankind — 4b
nothing o. in me, excepting O. sin — 78a
without an o...no imitation — 177a
Originality: fruits of o. — 266a
without o. or moral courage — 389b
Originator of a good sentence — 148b
Orion: loose the bands of O. — 497b
Orisons: in thy o. be all my sins — 333b
Orlando: run, run O. — 327a
Ormus and of Ind — 272a
Ornament: an o. to her profession — 54b
hiding the grossness with fair o. — 354a
navy..defence and o. — 28b
needs not the foreign aid of o. — 443b
o. is but the guiled shore — 354a
o. of a meek and quiet spirit — 517b
o. put upon..civic buildings — 314b
sent to be a moment's o. — 470b
still deceived with o. — 354a
studies serve for..o. — 16a
sweet o. wh. truth doth give! — 387b
the old o. of his cheek — 358b
wh. thou esteem'st the o. of life — 347a
Ornaments: hide with o. their want — 300a
made in lieu of many o. — 408b
Ornate: Pure, O., and Grotesque Art — 17b
Orphan: an o.'s curse — 99a
I'm an O., both sides — 455b
o.-child in one — 233a
teach the o.-boy to read — 431b
teach the o.-girl to sew — 431b
Orphans: wrong'd o.' tears — 262b
Orpheus: another O. sings — 394a
bid the soul of O. sing — 268b
O. was not more charming — 279b
O. with his lute — 385b
that O. drew trees, stones — 355a
Orphic: language is a perpetual O. song — 397b
Ortheris: as O. says — 237b
Orthodox: prove their doctrine o. — 65a
what is called 'o. divinity' — 10a
Orthodoxy: o. is my doxy — 450b
O. or My-doxy — 8ob
Oscar: you will, O., you will — 456b
Ossa: to pile O. on Pelion — 557b
Ostentation: o. of our love — 323a
rite nor formal o. — 336a
Ostrich: 'e's a devil an' a o. — 233a
his imagination..wings of an o. — 255b
strong the tall o. on the ground — 403a
Othello: O.'s occupation's gone — 362a
O.'s visage in his mind — 360b
whore of Venice..married with O. — 363a
Other: follow anything that o. men begin — 338b
I and no o. — 424a
no o. was denied — 127b
since then I have used no o. — 535b
the o. down, unseen — 376a
ther is non o. — 89a
when the o. far doth roam — 134a
Others: delight..in..pains of o. — 57b
do not do unto o. as you wd. — 391a
fly to o. that we know not — 333a
he that wd. govern o. — 262b

Others (cont.)
learn'd to melt at o.' woe — 173b
o. apart sat on a hill — 272b
o...may tell the news — 33a
o. will punctually come for ever — 458a
Otherwise: I can do no o. — 569a
so and no o. — 234a
some are o. — 157a
we might be o. — 395a
Oude: vovi—I've O. — 535a
Ought: it is, but hadn't o. to be — 182a
not what they o. to do — 13a
to do the things I o.! — 425a
we do not what we o. — 5b
you're everything you o. to be — 166b
Oughtn't: nothing that you o., O! — 166b
Oun: properly based O. — 47a
Ours: all the haunt be o. — 324b
little..in Nature that is o. — 473a
whiles it was o. — 359a
Ourself will mingle with society — 349a
Ourselves: even steal us from o. — 139b
in o., are triumph and defeat — 247b
not in our stars, but in o. — 337b
not to please o. — 514a
still to o. in every place — 213a
the enduring power, not o. — 10a
the eternal, not o. — 10a
the Eternal Power, not o. — 10b
the way to God is by o. — 155b
'tis in o. that we are thus — 360b
Ouse: slow winding O. — 111a
Ousel and the throstlecock — 137a
Out: at the other o. it wente — 90a
Betsey and I are o. — 80a
fear they shall never get o. — 454b
one is in, the other o. — 94b
o., damned spot! O. I say! — 350a
o., vile jelly! — 343b
o. with it, then — 81b
such as are in..wish to get o. — 148b
such as are o. wish to get in — 148b
they'd immediately go o. — 29b
this is hell, nor am I o. of it — 258b
vanity, like murder, will o. — 107b
yr. mother know that you are o.? — 19b
Out-argue: we will o. them — 209b
Outcast: degraded, spiritless o.! — 78b
Outcasts: the o. of Israel — 490b
Outcries: what o. pluck me — 238b
Outcry: each o. of the hunted hare — 29a
Outdid the meat, o. the frolic wine — 180b
Outface it with their semblances — 325b
Outgoings of the morning — 486a
Outgrabe: mome raths o. — 83b
Outlines: two countesses had no o. — 125a
Outlive: o. his life half a year — 334a
o. this powerful rhyme — 387b
sure you shall o. this day? — 149a
Outpost: ultimate o. of eternity — 312a
Outrun: disciple did o. Peter — 511b
o. the constable at last — 65b
Outside: goodly o. falsehood hath — 353a
swashing and a martial o. — 325b
Outsider: busy o.'s ancient times — 180b
Outsing and outlove — 421b
Out-soared: he has o. the shadow — 392b
Outstayed: he hath o. his welcome — 102a
Out-vote: tho' we cannot o. them — 209b
Outward: o. be fair, however foul within — 94b
sepulchres..appear beautiful o. — 507b
she is not fair to o. view — 97b
with my o., a Thistle — 29b
Outwatch the Bear — 268a
Oven: put in the o. for Tony and me — 532a
Over: it's o., and can't be helped — 126a
o. the hills and far away — 415a, 533a
o. then, come o. — 231b
o. the water, and o. the sea — 320a
until it doth run o. — 522b
Over-bowed by many benedictions — 48a
Over-canopied with..woodbine — 356b
Overcast: since first our sky was o. — 109a
Overcoat: his o. for ever — 200a
to put on yr. o. — 251a
Overcome: nature is..sometimes o. — 16a
o. evil with good — 513a
o. us like a summer's cloud — 349a
what is else not to be o. — 271a
Overcomes: who o. by force — 272a

Over-driven and under the weather 413b
Overland: the O. Mail 233a
Overmuch: be not righteous o. 499b
Overpaid: high official. .is grossly o. 186a
Overpeer the petty traffickers 352a
Overset: she was o. 111a
Overtaking: neither o. nor meeting 104a
Overthrow: his foes triumph in his o. 176a
    linger out a purposed o. 388b
    of God, ye cannot o. it 512a
    think'st, thou dost o., die not 133a
Overthrown: wrestled well, and o. 325b
Overwhelm myself in poesy 220b
Ovid: O., the soft philosopher of love 140b
    Venus clerk, O. 89b
Owe: much I o. to the Lands 236a
    o. no man anything 513b
    o. no man hate 327a
Owedst: sleep wh. thou o. yesterday 362a
Owes: he o. not any man 249a
Owest: lend less than thou o. 342a
    pay me that thou o. 507a
Owing: grateful mind by o. owes not 273b
Owl: blind as any noon-tide o. 428a
    by a mousing o. hawked at 348b
    clamorous o., that nightly hoots 356b
    curves of the white o. sweeping 263b
    like an o. in an ivy-bush 418b
    like an o. that is in the desert 488a
    moping o. doth. .complain 174a
    nightly sings the staring o. 345b
    O. and the Pussy Cat went to sea 243b
    O., and the Waverley Pen 527b
    o., for all his feathers, was a-cold 221b
    o. that shriek'd, the fatal bellman 347b
    sadder than o.-songs 72a
    white o. in the belfry 438a
    wren. .will fight. .against the o. 350a
Owlet: Ewa-yea! my little o.! 248b
    o. whoops to the wolf below 99b
    the o. Atheism 100b
Owls: a court for o. 502a
    eagle among blinking o. 395b
    his o. was organs 124a
    the answered o. are hooting 73a
    two black o. came and perched 25a
    two O. and a Hen 243a
    when o. do cry 368a
Own: all countries. .his o. 139b
    A Room of One's O. 462b
    beaten men come into their o. 262a
    do what I will with mine o. 507b
    hearer thought it was his o. 443a
    he came unto his o. 510b
    he yet can call his o. 136b
    I have a garden of my o. 261a
    ill-favoured thing, sir, but mine o. 328a
    King enjoys his o. again 292b
    love. .land because it is their o. 178a
    moments wh. he calls his o. 310a
    never mused on sorrow but its o. 77a
    never to set up any of their o. 57b
    she is coming, my o., my sweet 434a
    she knew not 'twas her o. 392a
    so well to know her o. 276a
Own-alone: all by my o. self 181b
Owned: treason is not o. 141a
Owner: bearing the o.'s name 458a
    o. of the axe 444a
Owners: down went the o. 163a
Owse and bottom of the sea 381b
Ox: as an o. goeth to the slaughter 498a
    he eateth grass as an o. 407b
    lion shall eat straw like the o. 501b
    nor his o., nor his ass 480a
    roasted Manningtree o. 377b
    stalled o. and hatred therewith 498a
    stands like an o. in the furrow 233a
    the o. knoweth his owner 501a
    the o. to wrath has moved 29a
    thou shalt not muzzle the o. 494b
Oxen: many o. are come about me 483a
    our o. may be strong to labour 490b
    the years like great black o. 474a
    who drives fat o. 211a
Oxenford: Clerk ther was of O. 88b
Oxford: Half-Way   House   to
    Rome, O. 535a
    I have never seen O. since 288b
    Ipswich and O. 386b
    King. .to O. sent a troop 42b, 445a

Oxford (cont.)
    Koran. .in the schools of O. 162a
    noon on O. town 154b
    O. that has made me insufferable 24b
    O. to him a dearer name 141b
    poetry wh. is in O. made an art 141b
    troops he to O. sent 445b
    what a whole O. is 97b
Oxlips: bold o. 373b
    where o. . .grow 356b
Oxonian: impertinent, being an O. 150b
Oxus: O., forgetting the bright speed 8a
    shorn and parcelled O. 8a
Oyster: as yr. pearl in yr. foul o. 328a
    an o. may be crossed in love 400a
    the world's mine o. 355b
Oysters: all the little O. stood 84b
    by no means unlike o. 123b
    four young O. hurried up 84a
    he had often eaten o. 163a
    if you're ready, O. dear 84b
    o. . .more beautiful than. .religion 315b
    poverty and o. . .go together 126a
Ozymandias, king of kings 396b

P

Pa: my p. requests me to write 124b
Pace: bloody thoughts, with violent p. 362b
    by the first p. that is sick 368b
    creeps in this petty p. 350b
    don't like the p. you are driving 405a
    long-resounding p. 175a
    no p. perceived 388b
    not afraid of 'the p.' 417a
    the moon's soft p. 469b
    the p. is too good to inquire 289a
    unperturb'd p. 441b
Paces: ordered motions, and regu-
    lar p. 42a
    p. about her room again, alone 144b
    she made three p. thro' the room 431b
    two p. of the vilest earth 379a
Pachyderm: he was a Tidy P. 237a
Pacific: he stared at the P. 220b
Pacing: walking up and p. down 432b
Pacings: long mechanic p. 433a
Pack: I will p., and take a train 39b
    p. up your troubles 10b
    p. when it begins to rain 342a
    pour out the p. of matter 323b
    somebody's p. has slid 233a
    some. .that can p. the cards 15a
Package: Ankworks p. 124a
Pack-drill: it 's p. for me 227b
Packed: boxes, all carefully p. 85b
Pack-horse: posterity is a p. 128a
    think rather of the p. 284a
Packs and sets of great ones 344a
Padded man that wears the stays 434b
Paddington: ever-weeping P. 30b
Paddle his own canoe 260a
Paddles: 'ear their p. chunkin' 232a
Paddock calls 345b
Paddocks: cold as p. 190b
Paddy dear, an' did ye hear 525b
Padlock on her mind 305b
Paedobaptist: she's a P. 172a
Pagan: Christian, p., nor man 333b
    on that hard P. world 7a
    p., I regret to say 123b
    P. suckled in a creed outworn 473a
    you find the p.—spoiled 477b
Page: beautiful quarto p. 400b
    elvish p. fell to the ground 317b
    every p. having an ample marge 429a
    hither, p., and stand by me 286b
    I were p. to joy 423a
    p. and monarch, forth they went 286b
    pictures for the p. atone 298b
    pretty p., with the dimpled chin 440b
    to their eyes her ample p. 174a
    trails all about the written p. 476b
    what one sweet p. can teach 293a
Pageant: insubstantial p. faded 367b
    p. of his bleeding heart 6a
    the dreary p. laboured 12b
Pageantry: masks, and antique p. 269a
Pageants: black vesper's p. 324a
    p. of the sea 352a

Pages: untouched the p. lie 113b
Pagett, M.P., was a liar 233a
Pagoda: Moulmein P. 232a
Paian, Apollo 423a
Paid: as if not p. before 387b
    he is well p. that is well satisfied 355a
    I p. them the things 486b
    nothing a-year, p. quarterly 417a
    p. with sighs a plenty 198b
    truth is well p. 106a
    two I am sure I have p. 377b
    we ha' p. in full 234b
    ye are not p. to think 232a
Pain: after long grief and p. 434a
    a piercing p., a killing sin 415a
    arrears of p., darkness 50b
    auntie, did you feel no p. 172b
    born in other's p. 441a
    but relieved their p. 168b
    costs worlds of p. 261b
    creation. .travaileth in p. 513b
    death who puts an end to p. 428b
    die of a rose in aromatic p.? 300b
    equal ease unto my p. 79b
    Eternal Passion! Eternal P. 7b
    give yourself no unnecessary p. 393a
    gods sigh for the cost and p. 43b
    grievous pleasure and p. 48a
    he hath no p. 239b
    herbs to ease their p. 233a
    I am quite sure she felt no p. 50a
    I feel no p. dear mother 523b
    I love to give p. 105a
    inflict p. upon oneself 265a
    in pleasure, but in rest from p. 140b
    I were king of p. 423a
    labour we delight in physics p. 348a
    laughter with some p. is fraught 393b
    love, that is not p. 470a
    my heart puts forth its p. 39a
    narcotics, numbing p. 429b
    new grown with pleasant p. 220b
    no living thing to suffer p. 397a
    no p. felt she 50a
    no pleasure, nor no p. 320b
    now comes the p. of truth 218b
    our joys three parts p. 50b
    Our Lady of P. 421a
    owes. .pleasures to another's p. 112a
    O what p. it is to part! 159b
    p. and anguish wring the brow 318b
    p. and grief to me 484a
    p. and ruin to despise 174b
    p. of finite hearts that yearn 52b
    p. shall not be inflicted 407b
    p. that is all but a pleasure 165b
    p. without the peace of death 76b
    passion, p., or pride 438b
    peril, toil, and p. 184a
    pleasure that's all but p. 165b
    pleasure. .the intermission of p. 321a
    pleasure turns to pleasing p. 409a
    pleasure with p. for leaven 420b
    pleasures banish p. 453b
    riches left, not got with p. 416a
    shall lightly pass the p. 177a
    sorrow, loss or p. 471a
    sudden cry of p. 410b
    superflux of p. 420a
    sweet is pleasure after p. 139a
    tender for another's p. 175a
    that is not akin to p. 247a
    there be any more p. 519b
    thou certain p. 173a
    to go in company with P. 465a
    tongueless vigil and all the p. 420a
    unnumbered hours of p. 77b
    upon the midnight with no p. 220a
    what ignorance of p.? 398b
    what p. it was to drown 384b
    what triumph! hark, what p. 7a
    wicked to deserve such p. 45b
    with no throbs of fiery p. 210b
    without one p. 433a
    with p. purchased, doth inherit p. 344a
Painch, tripe, or thairm 60b
Painful: no p. inch to gain 96b
    one is as p. as the other 14a
    p. pre-eminence 1b
    too p. an endeavour 302a
Pains: all p. the immortal spirit 7b

Pains (cont.)

by p. men come to greater p.	14b
everlasting p.	452b
for my p. a world of sighs	360a
his p. were o'er	167a
his present and yr. p.	381b
labour for his p.	461a
made my p. his prey	408a
p. of death gat hold upon me	489a
p. of love be sweeter far	142a
repays a thousand p.	50a
so double was his p.	408b
taken no p. with its sums	86a
take the p. to set me right	241a
uneasy pleasures and fine p.	147b

Paint: as fresh as p. 403a

does he p.?	49a
flinging a pot of p.	313b
he fain wd. p. a picture	49a
I cannot p. what then I was	472a
let her p. an inch thick	336b
p. the sable skies	138a
putty, brass, an' p.	233b
showed the p., but hid the face	140a
take off yr. coat, grind p.	147a
those who P. 'em truest	1a
to p. the lily	374a
to p. Thy Presence	280a

Painted: as idle as a p. ship 98b

mirror. .is not to be p. upon	254b
p. to the eyes	131a
paltry, foolish, p. things	137a
she p. her face	496b
upon a p. ocean	98b

Painter: he is but a landscape-p. 432b

nature's sternest p.	72b
not a great. .p. can be an architect	314a
once more that landscape p.	432b
some great p. dips his pencil	398a
the sinful p. drapes his goddess	147a

Painters: I hate all Boets and P. 161a

poets, like p., thus unskilled	300a

Painting: amateur p. in water-colour 413a

p. thy outward walls so costly	389b
whose mother was her p.	328b

Paintings: all the allegorical p. 212a

I have heard of your p.	333b

Paints: He p. the wayside flower 76a

Ingres's the modern man who p.	46b
to know a butcher p.	52a

Pair: all in a chaise and p. 108a

aware of a princely p.	254a
blest p. of Sirens	278a
happy, happy, p.	138b
nor p., nor build, nor sing	102a
such a mutual p.	322a

Palace: a p. and a prison on each hand 69a

a p. fit for you and me	414b
cypress in the p. walk	436b
hollow oak our p. is	116a
in his p. of the West	282b
in the lighted p. near	432a
love in a p.	219a
my gorgeous p. for a hermitage	375b
opes the p. of Eternity	266b
p. . .name of wh. was Beautiful	54a
p. of dim night	366b
purple-lined p. of sweet sin	219a

Palaces: builds p. in Kingdom come 261b

dragons in their pleasant p.	501b
fair, frail, p.	3a
hark! at the Golden P.	406b
mid pleasures and p.	294b
plenteousness within thy p.	480b
poor men's cottages princes' p.	352b
saw in sleep old p.	396b
the gorgeous p.	367b
'two-and-thirty p.'	222b
walls, p., half-cities	69a
watch the sunshot p. high	38a

Paladin: Sidney's self, the starry p. 52a

Palæozoic: in the P. time 404a

Palate: against his p. fine 219b

his ample p. took savour	218a
no motion of the liver, but the p.	371a
p., the hutch of tasty lust	197b

Palatinus: but he saw on P. 253b

Pale: art thou p. for weariness 396a

behold a p. horse	518b
by park and p.	438a

Pale (cont.)

great bond wh. keeps me p.!	349a
moon. .p. in her anger	356b
one p. as yonder wan. .moon	393b
over park, over p.	356b
p., and leaden-ey'd	196a
p. as thy smock	364a
p., beyond porch and portal	422a
p. contented sort of discontent	219a
p. grew thy cheek	74b
p. hands I loved	197a
p. wh. held that lovely deer	448b
prithee, why so p.	416a
walk the studious cloisters p.	268b
why so p. and wan	416a

Pale-mouth'd prophet 220a

Palestine: in sunny P. 261b

Paling: piece-bright p. 198a

Pall: in purple nor in p. 522a

Tragedy in sceptred p.	268a
when that began to p.	27b

Palladium of all the. .rights 217a

Pallas: Apollo, P., Jove 131b

Pallets: upon uneasy p. stretching 380a

Palliate what we cannot cure 212b

Pallid: angels, all p. and wan 298a

Pall Mall: shady side of P. 283b

Pall Mall Gazette 440a

Palm: bear the p. alone 337b

dominion over p. and pine	233b
dull thy p. with entertainment	330b
lands of p. and southern pine	426a
lands of p., of orange	426a
quietly sweating p. to p.	202b
to have an itching p.	340b
virginalling upon his p.	373a
win the p., the oak, or bays	260b

Palmer: exerted herself to ask Mr. P. 11b

sad votarist in p.'s weed	267a
sceptre for a p.'s walking staff	375b

Palmerston: pugilist [Lord P.] 17a

Palmerworm: that wh. the p. hath left 504a

Palms: in his p. wh. were hollow 191b

paddling p.	373a
p. before my feet	92a
their fronded p. in air	458b
the p. of her hands	496b
what are frequent in p. . .dates	191b

Palm-trees: City of p. 448a

Palmyra: Balbec and P. 449b

Palomides: by my knighthood, said P. 257a

Palpable: as a mountain, open, p. 377b

thro' the p. obscure	272b

Palsied eld 352a

Palsy: strucken wid de p. 181b

Palter with us with a double sense 351a

Paltry to be Cæsar 325a

Pamere: mountain cradle in P. 8a

Pamphylia: Phrygia, and P. 512a

Pamphleteer on guano 437a

Pan: buy me a new p. 63a

half a beast is the great god P	43b
P. by noon	420b
P. did after Syrinx speed	260b
the great god P.	43b
turned the cat in p. again	524a

Pancras and Kentish Town 30b

Pander of posterity 407b

Pandion: King P. 20b

Pane: a tap at the p. 48b

Panes of quaint device 221b

Pang: e'en the p. preceeding death 168a

ev'ry p. that rends the heart	53a
learn, nor account the p.	50b
p. as great as when a giant dies	352a
p. of all the partings	441a
she feels no biting p.	162b
turned his face with a ghastly p.	99a

Pangs: cost her mother Tellus keener p. 218b

in the sweet p. of it remember	370b
keen were his p.	72a
more p. and fears than wars	386a
p. of dispriz'd love	333a
the p., the internal p. are ready	464b

Panic's in thy breastie 62a

Panjandrum: grand P. himself 155b

Pansie: meet we no angels, P.? 10b

Pansies, that's for thoughts 335b

Pansy: the p. at my feet 466a

the p. freakt with jet	270a

Pant: I p., I sink, I tremble 393b

Pantaloon: lean and slippered p. 326b

Pants: as p. the hart 424b

earth in fast thick p.	101a
ride on the p. triumphing	324a

Papa: else his dear p. is poor 414a

P., potatoes, poultry	123a
the word P.	123a

Papacy. .the ghost of. .Roman Empire 191b

Paper: any news in the p. 11b

golly, what a p.!	413b
grey p. with blunt type!	52a
he hath not eat p.	344b
if all the earth were p.	251b
just for a scrap of p.	567b
make dust our p.	375b
that ever blotted p.	354b
the virtue of p. government	55a
this p. appears dull	410b

Paper-mill: thou hast built a p. 384a

Papist, saint or sinner 305a

Paps with a golden girdle 518a

Paradisaical pleasures of the Mahometans 175b

Paradisal imagineless metal 443a

Paradise: Athens but the rudiments of P. 406a

beautiful as a wreck of P.	393b
but at the gates o' P.	529a
by some supposed true P.	274a
dreams of P. and light	447b
drunk the milk of P.	101b
England is a p. for women	64b
enjoy p. in the next (world)	23b
even with P. devise the snake	154a
gather at the gate of P.	154b
heav'nly p. is that place	78b
how has she cheapen'd p.	293a
in P., if we meet	53a
Italy. .a p. for horses	64b
I was taught in P.	218a
Jane went to P.	230a
Limbo. .the P. of Fools	273b
lost angel of a ruined P.	392a
loth to leave this P.	276b
O P.! O P.	150a
P. by way of Kensal Green	93a
P., so late their happy seat	277a
P. . .subtle, and mighty opium!	120a
p. to what we fear of death	352a
P. within thee, happier far	276b
skip upon the trees of P.	415a
sole propriety, in P.	274b
such are the Gates of P.	30a
the desert were a p.	62b
thought wd. destroy their p.	175a
thou shalt be with me in P.	510a
threats of Hell and Hopes of P.	153a
this other Eden, demi-P.	375a
to him are opening p.	175a
to live in P. alone	261a
weave a p. for a sect	218a
Wilderness is P. enow!	152b

[Paradise Lost] most sublime poem 142a

Paradises: two P. 'twere 261a

Paradox: man is an embodied p. 103b

p. wh. comforts while it mocks	50b

Paradoxes: old fond p. 360b

Paradoxical: that sounds a little p. 135a

Paragon of animals! 332b

Parallel: but ours so truly p. 260a

Parallels: delves the p. in beauty's 388a

Paramount of truths 464b

Paramour: dark to be his p. 366b

thou shalt be my p.	258b

Paramours: worn of p. 409b

Parasol: Mama's p. between them 123a

Parcae thought him one 215a

Parcel: a p. of their fortunes 324a

p. of boilers and vats	210b

Parchment: bound in stale p. 264b

lamb shd. be made into p.	384a
p., being scribbled o'er	384a
virtue of wax and p.	55b

Pard: freckled like a p. 219a

p.-like spirit, beautiful	392a

Pardon: bret-ful of p. 89a

if life was bitter to thee, p.	421a

Pardon (cont.)
I p. something to..liberty 55b
kiss of the sun for p. 177b
p. for too much loving you 361b
p.'s the word to all 329a
the injur'd..they ne'er p. 139b
to p. or to bear it 108a
weep for my p. 324b
Pardon'd and retain the offence? 334b
Parent: bedside of a sick p. 255b
don't object to an aged p. 123b
on p. knees, a naked..child 214a
our first p. knew thee 456b
P. of Good, Almighty 275a
perhaps that p. mourned 242a
that wd. put any p. mad 155a
to lose one p...misfortune 460a
Parentage: p. unguessed 235a
what is yr. p.? 370a
Parents: begin by loving their p. 460b
besmear'd with..p.' tears 271b
education..given..by most p. 410b
joys of p. are secret 14b
learned to bottle our p. twain 228a
lords whose p. were the Lord
knows who 118b
p. first season us 187a
stranger to one of yr. p. 11b
Parfit gentil knight 88a
Paris: fur away ez P. is 250a
Frensh of P. was to hir unknowe 88b
good Americans die they go to P. 460b
good Americans..they die, go to P. 4b
Helen..with wanton P. sleeps 368b
no good girl's lip out of P. 424a
no lord of P., Venyce or Floraunce 143a
P. is well worth a mass 563b
the judgment of P. 554b
Parish: all the world as my p. 456a
bason to be provided by the P. 480a
his pension from his p. 314b
Parish Church: plain as way to p. 326b
Park: over p., over pale 356b
p. where the peach-blossoms blew 242a
stands as Neptune's p. 328b
with a cot in a p. 242a
P. Lane for choice 571b
Parks were the lungs of London 297a
Parliament: crop-headed P. 45b
honest by an act of p. 214b
in the P. of man 432b
Mob, P., rabble 97a
P. has no right to tax..Americans 305a
P. speaking..to Buncombe 81a
Three Estates in P. 81a
Parliamentary: as an old P. hand 167b
Bag of P. Eloquence 81a
Rupert of P. discussion 128a
without party P. government 128b
Parliaments: England..mother of P. 38a
we shall have no more P. 216a
Parlour: is it a party in a p.? 468b
prisoned in a p. snug 110b
'tis the prettiest little p. 201a
will you walk into my p.? 201a
Parlour boarder of a pig 196a
Parlous: in a p. state 327a
Parma: foul scorn that P. or Spain 145a
Parmaceti for an inward bruise 377a
Parnassus: you my chief P. be 402a
Parochial: art must be p. 281a
scorning p. ways 180a
[Thoreau] he was p. 204a
Parrots: like p. at a bagpiper 352b
rabbits is 'dogs' and so's p. 535a
Parsee from whose hat the rays 237a
Parody: devil's walking p. 92a
Parole of literary men 210b
Paronomasia: catch the p. 75a
Parson: a Church of England p. 235a
brandy for the P. 234b
coughing drowns the p.'s saw 345b
his creed no p. ever knew 136b
like a p.'s damn 180b
Monday is p.'s holiday 418a
p. knows enough .. knows a
duke 113a
P. lost his senses 192a
p., much bemused in beer 303a
then the P. might preach 32a
the p. and the p.'s wife 96a

Parson (cont.)
the p., oh! illustrious spark 109b
the p. owned his skill 168b
tickling a p.'s nose 364b
Whig in a p.'s gown 212b
Parsons: p. are very like other men 90b
p. do not care for truth 415b
this merriment of p. 210b
Parsnips: fine words butter no p. 319b
Part: a p. to tear a cat in 356a
being p. in all I have 386b
come in between and bid us p. 443a
come let us kiss and p. 137b
each man has some p. to play 306b
fear God, and take yr. own p. 34a
few, few shall p. 77a
for mine own poor p. 331b
for we know in p. 514b
from yours you will not p. 416a
hast command of every p. 190a
heart must bear the longest p. 187a
his fear is put beside his p. 387a
I am a p. of all 438b
I have forgot my p. 328b
list to the heavy p. 214b
man must play a p. 352b
Man of sorrows had a p. 53a
Mary hath chosen that good p. 509a
neither p. nor lot in this matter 512a
only p. to meet again 161a
ought but death p. thee and me 495a
p. in friendship 74a
precise in every p. 189a
shall we never, never p. 169a
the heart aye's the p. aye 60a
the more p. knew not wherefore 512b
thou and nature can so gently p. 325a
to p. at last without a kiss? 284a
we lose a p. of ourselves 304a
we prophecy in p. 514b
we two now p. 294a
what pain it is to p. 159b
Partaker with the adulterers 485a
Partakers of thy sad decline 109a
Parted: a' p...between twelve and
one 381b
double cherry, seeming p. 357a
I p. from my dear 199a
like friends once p. 392b
mine never shall be p. 276b
never met—or never p. 59a
p. are those who are singing 34b
p. for ever? 318a
the way we p. 422b
when we two p 74b
Parthenia's pride 160a
Parthians, and Medes..Elamites 512a
Partial: acts not by p. but by gen'ral
laws 300b
Particle: a pushing young p. 165b
every air-borne p. 204b
Particular: a London p. 121a
doctrine of p. Election 135a
so singular in each p. 373b
Particulars: do it in Minute P. 30b
minutely organized P. 30b
Parties: p. nobly are subdued 380b
political p. die..own lies 4b
Parting: at the p. of the way 504a
do not let this p. grieve thee 527a
ere the p. hour go by 7a
every p. was to die 431a
in every p...an image of death 144b
p. is all we know of heaven 127b
p. is such sweet sorrow 365b
p.'s well paid with soon again 294a
rive not more in p. 324a
shakes his p. guest by the hand 369a
this p. was well made 341a
Partings: pang of all the p. gone 441a
p. yet to be 441a
Partington: Mrs. P. 405a
Partition: middle wall of p. 515b
yet a union in p. 357a
Partner: a p. Mr. Jorkins 122a
my p. and my guide 463b
p. in the Glory of the Garden 229b
while his loved p. 170a
Partners: by p., in each other kind 450a
Partridge: as the p. sitteth on eggs 503b
'he the best player!' cries P. 151b

Parts: all his gracious p. **374a**
his p...pretty well for a Lord 209a
if p. allure thee 301b
inwards to the p. extreme 380b
my p., my title 359b
nothing else but his p. 209a
one man in his time plays many
p. 326b
p. of it are excellent! 536a
with her enticing p. 524a
Party: ancient forms of p. strife 431a
as a curse to p. strife 464a
at my p.'s call 166a
Breitmann gif a p. 244b
I had..to educate our p. 128b
is it a p. in a parlour? 468b
neither p. loser 380b
none was for a p. 253a
not a select p. 223b
p. is organized opinion 128b
p. is the madness of many 419a
p. of two is like..Scotch terrier 38a
p.-spirit..the madness of many 304a
stick to try p. 128b
that p. conquers in the strife! 316b
to p. gave up what was meant 169b
watchword of the great Liberal p. 38a
vhere ish dat p. now 244b
without p. Parliamentary government is impossible 128b
Pass: all ye that p. by 503b
bounds wh. they shall not p. 488a
bringeth mighty things to p. 489a
but it cannot p. away 396a
for God's sake, let us p. on! 55a
I expect to p. thro' this world 176b, 523b
I shall not p. this way again 176b, 523b
it may not p. away 229b
I will p. nor turn my face 53a
I will p. thro' the land 494a
let him p. for a man 353a
O! let him p. 344a
O Saki, you shall p. 154a
p. by me as the idle wind 340b
p. it along the line 340b
p. it on! 63b
p., like night, from land to land 100a
p. our long love's day 260a
p. the hat for yr. credit's sake 227a
power to shake me as they p. 463a
ships that p. in the night 249a
sideways did she p. 231b
so p. I hostel, hall 438a
the p. was steep and rugged 254a
the same tho' Dynasties p. 179b
thou shalt strangely p. 387b
'try not the P.!' 247a
very well p. for forty-three 167a
we p. and speak to one another 249a
went roaring thro' the p. 254a
Passage: access and p. to remorse 346b
all unseen 'gan to find 344b
any one grand and spiritual p. 222b
a p. wh. you think is..fine 208a
black p. up to bed 414a
carv'd out his p. 346a
commentators each dark p. shun 477a
fret a p. through it 158a
North-West p. to the intellectual 411b
painful p., o'er a restless flood 109a
p. in the game act 410a
sweetest p. of a song 265a
Passages: bright p...strike yr. mind 67a
cheated into some fine p. 223a
p., that lead to nothing 175a
Passed: it remembren, whan it p. is 90a
p. by on the other side 509a
so he p. over 54b
there hath p. away a glory 466a
when she had p., it seemed 247a
Passenger: punch in the presence
of the p. 38b
Passengers: romance! those first-
class p. 232a
we the p. 200b
Passer-by: touch you, a p.! 307b
Passes: sword in hand upon Afric's p. 93b
to know what p. there 275b
who p. by this road so late? 528a
Passeth: not the lie that p. 14a
so soon p. it away 487b

Passing: he cd. not wait their p. 8b
I did but see her p. by 156a, 526b
'p. away' 185a
p. of the sweetest soul 430b
p. thro' nature to eternity 329b
power is p. from the earth 405a
so be my p. 185a
the labouring world are p. by 475b
Passion: all made of p. 327b
all p. spent 278a
bards of P. and of Mirth 219a
beating of so strong a p. 371a
breathing human p. far above 219b
by p. driven 63a
by such poor p. as the maid 324b
chaos of thought and p. 301a
cows are my p. 122b
eternal P.! eternal Pain! 7b
fat gentleman in such a p. 149a
felt the tender p. 160a
held in holy p. still 268a
his pulse failing, P. speechless 137b
I discern infinite p. 52b
I have a p. for the name of 'Mary' 71a
I have no p. for it 207a
in her first p. woman loves 70b
in love and holy p. 464a
interval betwixt one p. and another 411a
it did relieve my p. much 370b
maiden p. for a maid 428a
man that is not p.'s slave 334a
may I govern my p. 304a
no good if a p. is in you 29b
no p. in the mind of man so weak 14a
no p. so..robs..as fear 57b
O well-painted p. 362b
one master p. in the breast 301a
one p. doth expel another 87b
our loyal p. for our..kings 435a
p. ending, doth the purpose lose 334a
p. for fame..instinct of all..souls 55a
p. for hunting something 125a
p. hidden in my veins 565a
p., I see, is catching 339b
p. of a vegetable fashion 165b
p. put to use in my old griefs 44a
p.-winged Ministers of thought 392a
places wh. pale p. loves 23a
ruling p. strong in death 302a
sick of an old p. 135a
some bloody p. shakes yr...frame 363b
strange fits of p. have I known 471a
sure no p. in the human soul 245a
their fury and my p. 367a
the p. such it was to prove 114a
the p. that left the ground 44b
the Queen was in a furious p. 83a
the ruling p.! 121a
the ruling p. conquers reason 302a
this p., and the death of a..friend 357b
to be in a p. you good may do 29b
to inspire hopeless p...my destiny 440a
torture of a lingering..p. 149a
two extremes of p. 344a
was not this thy P. 423b
what is p. but pining? 265a
what..in p. we propose 334a
what P. cannot music raise 139b
when his p. shall have spent 432a
whose every p. fully strives 322b
wilt thou find p., pain 438b
Passionate: beautiful p. body 421a
deep affections make him p. 259a
make p. my sense of hearing 344b
simple, sensuous and p. 279b
Passionately and irretrievably 312b
Passion-flower at the gate 434a
Passionless: hopeless grief is p. 43b
Passions: all thoughts, all p. 101b
all thy p., matched with mine 432b
desolate p., aching hours 206a
great when he acts from the p. 129b
in men, we various ruling p. find 302a
is the devil to have all the p. 390b
men of like p. with you 512b
p. as it is with fire and water 244b
p...got the better of his creed 411b
p. spin the plot! 264a
such angry p. rise 452b
their human p. now no more 175a
when p. are no more 449a

Passions (cont.)
with life all other p. fly 406b
woman's mind oft shifts her p. 160a
women..have..but two p. 91a
Passive: benevolence of the p. order 265a
Passiveness: in a wise p. 464b
Passives: love's p. are his activ'st 114b
Passover: Christ our p. 514a
it is the Lord's p. 494a
Passport: his p. shall be made 383a
Past: audible voice of the P. 81a
books..soul of the P. Time 81a
leave thy low-vaulted p.! 194a
let the dead P. bury its dead 248a
many a woman has a p. 460a
never plan the future by the p. 57b
nostalgia of the heathen p. 243a
o'er the p. its undivided reign 194a
over the trackless p. 182a
parcels of the dreadful P. 433a
P. and the Future are nothing 306b
p. and to come seem best 380a
praise they that will times p. 190a
remembrance of things p. 387b
something..absurd about the p. 24b
that's p. praying for 377b
the Bard! who present, p...sees 31b
they say miracles are p. 322a
they shall not get p. 565a
to lament the p. 56b
upon the p. has power 142b
what's p., and what's to come 369b
what's p. is prologue 367b
world is weary of the p. 394a
'Pastern' as the 'knee' of a horse 207a
Pastime: and think it p. 336a
forgotten of high jinks 319b
p. and our happiness will grow 468b
take his p. therein 488b
Pastoral: eternity: Cold P.! 219b
Pastors: as some ungracious p. do 330b
spiritual p. and masters 481a
Pasture: feed me in a green p. 483a
the Lord my P. shall prepare 2a
the mettle of yr. p. 382a
they sell the p. now 381b
Pastures: England's pleasant p. 31a
fresh woods, and p. new 270a
p. of the blessed 286a
pipe me to p. still 197b
Pat: now might I do it p. 334b
p.-a-cake 532a
p. he comes, like the catastrophe 342a
p. it, and prick it 532a
with a dexterous p. 113a
Patch: cross p., pull the latch 533a
p. up thine old body 380a
while the p. was worn 438a
Patched: is but p. with sin 370a
Patches: thing of shreds and p. 164a
Pate: feather p. of folly 199b
made by an aged old p. 522a
the p. of a politician 336a
you beat yr. p. 299b
young girl to rub my bald p. 304a
Pâtés de foie gras: idea of heaven is
eating p. 404b
Patent: p. for his honours..from
God 60a
so my p. back again is swerving 388b
Path: around his p...taught to swell 223b
broad vine-sheltered p. 312b
Christ is the p. 279b
for if thou p. 338b
if p. there be or none 468a
in the p. of thy commandments 489a
long brown p. before me 458a
make a beaten p. to his door 148b
makes the p. before him..bright 465a
midst the twilight p. 103a
p. of the just is as the..light 497b
p. on the sea's azure floor 393b
ploughed that p. before 393b
primrose p. of dalliance 330b
shew me the p. of life 482b
straight was a p. of gold for him 49b
take the gentle p. 188a
tho' thy p. is dark as night 256b
Paths: a light unto my p. 489a
all her p. are peace 497b
bitter p. wherein I stray 232b

Paths (cont.)
in our opposed p. to persevere 294a
make his p. straight 504b
so many p. that wind 459a
thro' the p. of the seas 482a
trodden the p. of men 392a
yr. weary p., beguiling 43a
Pathless: pleasure in p. woods 69b
Pathos: true p. and sublime 59a
Pathway: beating pulse a p. spy? 263b
don't strew yr. p. with..urs 193b
smote for us a p. 234b
Patience: a drop of p. 363a
close-lipped P. for our..friend 8a
flour of wyfly p. 89b
genius..aptitude for p. 561b
heard of the p. of Job 517b
I laughed him out of p. 323b
in yr. p. possess ye yr. souls 510a
kingdom and p. of Jesus Christ 518a
languid p. of thy face 102a
let p. have her perfect work 517a
Lord, have p. with me 507a
p., and shuffle the cards 575b
p. on a monument 371a
p., the beggar's virtue 262b
p., thou young..cherubim 363a
P. will achieve more than..force 57b
preached up p. 306a
takes a text, and preacheth p. 187a
talk him out of p. 361b
they that have not p. 361b
time and p. will not dry 182a
year by year, in pious p. 233b
Patient: as p. and as still 402a
cure the disease and kill the p. 15b
fortitude, and p. cheer 468b
fury of a p. man 138b
his Mother, who was p., being dead 294a
like a p. etherized 144b
O soul, be p. 35b
p. as the female dove 336b
poor as Job..but not so p. 379b
the p. must minister to himself 350b
with p. inattention 263a
yet be p. 435b
Patiently adjust, amend 180a
Patines of bright gold 355a
Patmos: isle that is called P. 518a
Patriarch: venerable P. guileless held 304b
Patriarchs: the wives in the p.'days 180a
Patrician: a regular p. 166a
Patrick: before they see Sir P. Spens 530a
first word that Sir P. read 529b
lies gude Sir P. Spens 530a
St. P. was a gentleman 27b
Patriot: never was p. yet, but was a
fool 138b
such is the p.'s boast 170a
the Idea of a P. King 33b
Patriotism: duty and p. clad 246a
p., grown Godlike 179a
p. is not enough 86b
p...last refuge of a scoundrel 208b
where they had p., we have cant 295a
Patriots: all these country p. 67b
brave men, and worthy p. 279b
our p. virtue's cause support 160a
Patron: is not a P., my Lord 206b
P. Commonly a wretch 212b
want, the p. and the jail 213b
Patronage: and p. sway 40b
Patroness: my celestial P. 276a
Patter: unintelligible p. 167a
Pattern: as a p. to encourage purchasers 417b
He is our childhood's p. 3b
our p. to live and to die! 48a
thou cunning'st p. 363b
Pattern-man: the State's p. 288b
Paul: by the apostle P., 385a
down by smoky P.'s they bore 439b
P. the aged 516b
P., thou art beside thyself 513a
the Stout Apostle P. 231a
we and P. must take him 227a
with the charity of P. 94b
Pauliad: Christiad than a P. 181a
Pauper: he's only a p. 289b
Pause: how dull it is to p. 438b
in p. when I shall first begin 334b

Pause (cont.)

must give us p.	333a
nor made a p., nor left a void	210b
p., and puff..and p. again	108a
p. in the day's occupations	246b
p. there, Morocco	353b
Pauses: intervals and happy p.	16b
Pavement: a p. of pearl	6a
archways and the p.	12a
thy cold p. were a sod	69b
the p. of her Heaven	116b
Pavements: on the p. gray	475b
p. fanged with..stones	100a
riches of heaven's p.	272a
Pavilion: p. of Heaven is bare	393a
red p. of my heart?	441a
she did lie in her p.	323a
Pavilioned in splendour	172b
Paving-stones: on these gritty p.	232a
Paviours: the p. cry	149a
Paw: in his p., dandled the kid	274a
save free conscience from the p.	278b
the grim wolf with privy p.	269b
Paweth: he p. in the valley	497b
Pawing to get free	275b
Pawnce: the pretty P.	409a
Paws: massive p. of elder persons	25b
'Pax vobiscum' will answer all	319b
Pay: bloomin' good p.	234a
clean work, and for what p.	314a
credit's sake, and p., p., p.!	227a
cut each others' throats for p.	169a
dirty work..and for what p.	314a
envy's a sharper spur than p.	160b
forebore to p.	233b
in heavenly p. a glorious angel	375a
I p. thy poverty, and not thy will	366a
I was to p. the piper	104a
I will p. thee all	507a
make me able to p. for it	296a
more tears..than you shall see me p.	341b
now I must p. for my fun	230b
p. for one by one	235b
p. me that thou owest	507a
p. too much for yr. whistle	157a
saved the sum of things for p.	200a
thou shdst. vow and not p.	499a
wh. I new p. as if not paid	387b
when will you p. me?	533b
wonders what's to p.	200a
Paying: called p. the Dane-Geld	228b
Paynim: each P. voice to prayer	77b
Paynims: three p., three Jews	257a
Pays: base is the slave that p.	381b
his ready visit p.	477a
owes not but still p.	273b
p. him in his own coin	418b
scent wh. p. the best	250a
Pea: but one split p.	440b
Peace: alas! my everlasting p. is broken	195a
all her paths are p.	409b
a moth of p.	360b
angling..begat habits of p.	450b
a p. I hope with honour	128b
arts of war and p.	70b
author of p.	478a
beyond these voices there is p.	428a
but they are in p.	520a
by the p. among our peoples	234b
calm P. and Quiet	268a
cankers of..a long p.	378b
certain knot of p.	401b
chastisement of our p.	503a
come ye in p. here	318a
deep dream of p.	201b
even lovers find their p.	154b
exceeding p. had made Ben Adhem	201b
far our foes, give p. at home	491a
fear, and p. and strife	319b
for ever hold his p.	481b
for the p. of Jerusalem	489b
friendly to p., but not to me	111a
gentleness, in hearts at p.	40a
give p. in our time	478a
God gave her p.	437a
grant us thy p.	479b
grows the flower of P.	448a
had thy p. been as a river	502b
had Zimri p.	496b
haunt of ancient P.	435b

Peace (cont.)

I came not to send p.	506a
if these shd. hold their p.	510a
if thou return at all in p.	496b
I labour for p.	489b
increase of his government and p.	501b
ingeminate the word P.	203a
in His will is our p.	567a
in p., Love tunes the shepherd's	317a
in p. there's nothing so becomes	382a
in..p. thinks of war	64a
I shall have some p. there	475a
is it p.? And Jehu said	496b
I speak of p.	379a
it's interest that keeps p.	116a
kiss our lady P. at home	379b
laughing heart's long p.	40a
less oft is p. in Shelley's mind	395a
let us have p.	173a
love, joy, p., long-suffering	515b
lovers in p., lead on our days	341a
make a wilderness..call it p.	553b
makes a solitude.., calls it p.!	67b
mangled P., dear nurse of arts	383b
men so old as we to keep the p.	364a
merry songs of p.	386b
mountains also shall bring p.	486b
my p. is gone	568a
never was a good war, or a bad p.	157a
nor keep p. between the effect	346b
nor p. within nor calm around	399a
not p. at any price	205b
nymphs..P. and Plenty	116a
O Eastern star! p.! p.!	325b
of p. for evermore	415b
O heart, be at p.	474a
on earth p., good will	508b
our feet into the way of p.	508b
our p., our fearful innocence	467b
over all the human tops is p.	568a
p. above all earthly dignities	386a
p., and the butt	141b
p. be to my sable shroud	269a
p. be to this house	481b, 509a
p. be within thy walls	489b
p. brooded o'er the hush'd domain	131b
p.; come away	430b
p. comes dropping slow	475a
p. divine like quiet night	306b
p. does nothing to relieve	108a
peaceful sloth, not p.	272b
p., good pint-pot!	377b
p. hath her victories	278b
p. in her chamber	311b
p. instead of death let us bring	76b
p. in thy breast!	365b
p. is come and wars are over	199b
p. is in the grave	397a
p. is of..nature of a conquest	386b
P. is poor reading	179b
p. is put in impossible things	92b
p. is what I seek	6b
p...maintained with honour	315a
p. of God, wh. passeth..understanding	480b, 516a
p. on earth, and mercy mild	455b
p., p.; when there is no p.	503b
p., perfect p.	28a
P., retrenchment, and reform	38a
p. shall go sleep with Turks	376a
p. (slays) its ten thousands	304b
P., the human dress	33a
p. to corrupt no less than war	276b
p. to him that is far off	503a
p. to the soul of the man	6a
p. wh. springs from..little things	283a
p. wh. the world cannot give	478b
preached p. to you wh. were afar	515b
preparation of the gospel of p.	516a
quath P.	242b
rest, and p. at the last	288b
righteousness and p. have kissed	487a
ring in the thousand years of p.	431a
rust in p., or rot in hospital	406a
seek p., and ensue it	484a
sez to 'em, 'P., be still!'	227a
shades, where p...can never dwell	271a
shall bring a man p. at the last	484a
soft phrase of p.	360a
sweet P. is crownid with smiles	448a
that publisheth p.	502b

Peace (cont.)

their bodies are buried in p.	521b
The Prince of P.	501b
there abides a p. of thine	6b
there is no p...unto the wicked	502b
there shd. be p. at home	452b
the star of p. return	78a
the wound of p. is surety	369a
this p. sleep with her	386b
thro' P. to Light	306b
thy banished p., thy laurels torn!	405b
thy right hand carry gentle p.	386a
thy servant depart in p.	508b
to a woman trusts his p. of mind	173a
to gain our p., have sent to p.	348b
told me words of p.	434b
to Mercy, Pity, P.	32b
trouble is ended in a little p.	441a
unity, and concord	479a
universal P. lie like a shaft	427a
until I come in p.	496b
wait Thy word of p.	145b
Warwick, p.	384b
weak piping time of p.	384b
what hast thou to do with p.	496b
What is p.? is it war? No.	121a
where they shd. kneel for p.	367a
while he taught you p.	43a
whispers p. within	28a
who desires p., prepare for war	554a
who studying p.	140a
with p. and consolation	278a
work us a perpetual p.	270a
wd. I were sleep and p.	365b
Peaceable: most p. way for you	359a
Peaceably if we can	95b
Peaceful hours I once enjoy'd!	109b
Peacemaker: 'if' is the only p.	328a
Peacemakers: blessed are the p.	505a
Peach: a little p. in an orchard	151a
nectarine and curious p.	260b
that Jemmy Twitcher shd. p. me	160a
Peacock: droops the milk-white p.	436b
eyed like a p.	219a
he is a monstrous p.	475a
Mor the P.	234b
the pride of the p.	31a
Peacocks: ivory, and apes, and p.	496a
p. and lilies	314b
p. strutting by	229b
proud as p.	321b
Peak: blooms below the barren p.	346b
dwindel, p., and pine	346a
Peaks: p. but to the stars are known	6b
p. of honour we had forgotten	246a
Peal: upon our wedding	199a
the wildest p. for years	192a
Pear: a golden p.	532a
cherry and hoary p.	37b
such as are on a Catherine p.	416a
Pearl: a pavement of p.	6a
a p. of great price	507a
a prince, he rises with his pearl	49b
barbaric p. and gold	272a
base Indian, threw a p. away	364a
heaps of p., inestimable stones	384b
no such p. in any gulf	423a
orient p. a double row	78b
p. in every cowslip's ear	356b
p. in yr. foul oyster	328a
the quarelets of p.	190a
Pearls: as a string of p. to me	309b
gates were twelve p.	520a
gospel's p. upon our coast	260a
neither cast..p. before swine	505b
some ask'd how p. did grow	190a
these p. of thought	250b
those are p. that were his eyes	367a
who wd. search for p.	141a
Pears: have you used P.' soap?	523a
rich mellow p.	19b
Peas: the first green p.	247b
Peasant: rends the p. tooth	229a
some belated p. sees	272a
the toe of the p.	336b
we greet the monarch p.	193b
when the Hymalayan p.	228b
yonder p., who is he	286b
Peasantry: but a bold p.	168a
Peasants: hard hands of p.	341a
Peascod: squash is before 'tis a p.	370a

Pease porridge hot — 533b
Pebble: chose a p. from the brook — 109b
  finding a smoother p. — 289a
  labour a p. without cease — 452a
  only p. on the beach — 34b
  you see this p.-stone — 75a
Pebbles: boys that throw p. and mire! — 453a
  on the unnumbered idle p. chafes — 343b
Peccavi—I've Scinde — 535a
Peccavimus; but rave not thus! — 298a
Pecks: p. and starts — 443b
  p. of poison are not p. of salt — 30a
Pecksniff: Mr. P. — 123b
Peculiar: extensive and p. — 126a
Pecuniary: immense p. Mangle — 127b
  its p. affairs — 167b
Pedants: learned p. much affect — 65a
Pedestaled in triumph — 51b
Pedigree: languages..p. of nations — 212b
  lass wi' a lang p. — 285b
Peel: Disraeli called..P.'s Ministry — 17b
  [P.] caught the Whigs bathing — 128a
  P. has no manners — 455a
  P .. Graham, Shiel, Russell — 177b
Peep: from her cabin'd loop-hole p. — 266b
  one that wd. p. and botanize — 468b
  p. about to find ourselves — 337b
  p. thro' their eyes and laugh — 352b
  to p. at such a world — 112a
  treason can but p. to what it wd. — 335b
Peeping in at noon — 195a
Peer: a rhyming p. — 303a
  daffodils begin to p. — 373a
  Stephen was a worthy p. — 361a
Peerage: p., or Westminster Abbey — 287a
  you shd. study the P. — 460b
Peering: into that darkness p. — 298a
Peers: delight of battle with my peers — 438b
  fare like my p. the heroes — 50b
  House of P., throughout the war — 164a
  judgement of his p. — 550b
  most important p...important — 17b
  My Lord in the P. — 40b
  'tis some praise in p. to write — 72a
  valiant p. were plac'd around — 138b
  we love our House of P. — 166b
  yet want her P.' — 409a
Peewees: martyrs the p. crying — 414b
Pegasus: P.'s neck — 299a
  thought it P. — 220b
  turn and wind a fiery P. — 378b
Peggotty: Mr. P. — 122b
Peggy: noble, lovely, little P. — 306a
Pehlevi: divine high piping P. — 152a
Pelagians do vainly talk — 491a
Peleus: wrath of P.' son — 559b
Pelf: I crave no p. — 368a
Pelican: p. in the wilderness — 488a
  wdst. thou have me turn p. — 104b
Pelion: pile Ossa on P. — 557b
Pelleas: Lancelot or P. — 277a
Pellenore: Pelleas or P. — 277a
Pelop: Thebes, or P.'s line — 268a
Pelting each other..public good — 107b
Pembroke's mother — 42b
Pen: before my p. has glean'd — 221a
  draw my p. in defence..bad cause — 142a
  Falernian winged the p. — 75a
  foolish when he had not a p. — 210b
  he held his p. in trust to Art — 131a
  his fingers held the p. — 111a
  I made a rural p. — 32b
  less brilliant p. than mine — 24b
  make thee glorious by my p. — 280b
  my tongue is the p. — 484b
  Nature..take the p. out of his hand — 9b
  nose was as sharp as a p. — 382a
  p...becomes a torpedo to him — 206a
  p. is worse than the sword — 64a
  prevents his holding a p. — 124b
  scarce forbear to bite his p. — 419a
  scratching of a p. — 250a
  thy p. from lenders' books — 343a
  with such acts fill a p. — 137a
  write, p.! — 344b
Penalty: the p. of Adam — 325b
  to abolish the death p. — 563b
Penance: and p. more will do — 99b
  the man hath p. done — 99b
  torturing hour calls us to p. — 272a
Pence: eternal want of p. — 439b

Pence (cont.)
  he took out two p. — 509a
  sold for three hundred p. — 511a
  yet loss of p., full well he knew — 108b
Pencil: dinted with the silver-
    pointed p. — 49a
  his p. our faces — 169b
  his p. was striking — 169b
  p. in the gloom of earthquake — 398a
  p. of the Holy Ghost — 14a
Pendent: round about the p. world — 352a
Pendulum: vibration of a p. — 217a
Penetralium of mystery — 222a
Penetrating: base, sheer, p. power — 9b
Peneus rolls his fountains — 394a
Penknife: saw me take out my p. — 417b
Penman's latest piece of graphic — 52b
Penned: excellently well p. — 370a
Penning: now wd. mock my p. — 36a
Penny: dukes were three a p. — 163b
  if you haven't got a p. — 522b
  in for a p., in for a pound — 164a
  it was a p.-postage-stamp — 85b
  measure of wheat for a p. — 518b
  measures of barley for a p. — 518b
  one a p., two a p. — 535b
  please to put a p. — 522b
  p. plain and twopence coloured — 412b
  p. to Twickenham Town — 261b
  sir, give me one p. — 531b
  to turn a p. in the way of trade — 111a
Penny-fights an' Aldershot — 229b
Pennyworths: buying good P. — 157a
Pens: dip their p...milk of..kindness — 58a
  if all the p...ever poets held — 259b
  let other p. dwell on guilt — 11a
Pension: his p. from his parish — 314b
  P ..An allowance made — 213a
  p. list of the republic — 95b
  think of 'is p. — 234a
Pensioner: a Miser's p. — 463b
Pensioners: cowslips tall her p. — 356b
Pensions and Grenadiers — 411b
Pent: here in the body p. — 280a
  long in city p. — 221a
Pentameter: in the p. aye falling — 101b
Pentecost: like the P. wind — 180a
Pentecostal crew — 228b
Pent-house: hang upon his p. lid — 346a
Pentridge by the river — 21a
Penury: ache, p. and imprisonment — 352a
  p. repress'd their noble rage — 174a
People: a beggarly p.! — 420a
  a glorious p. vibrated again — 396a
  all p. that on earth do dwell — 224b
  all the Lord's p. were prophets — 494a
  an acceptable p. — 479a
  anywhere a p., more unsteady — 103b
  a p...but in the gristle — 55b
  a p. generally corrupt — 58a
  a p. overlaid with taxes — 15b
  a p. whom I have not known — 482b
  a stiff-necked p. — 494a
  based upon her p.'s will — 437a
  bear the miseries of a p.! — 283a
  benefit of a p...never seen — 56a
  be the p. never so impatient — 488a
  bludgeoning of the p. by the p. — 460b
  by..p. you understand..hoi polloi — 142a
  came of decent p. — 27b
  chief glory of every p. — 212b
  chosen P. never conquer'd quite — 294b
  common p. of the skies — 473b
  company of all faithful p. — 480b
  fire and p. do in this agree — 176b
  fool all the p. — 245b
  forget also thine own p. — 484b
  from the p...all springs — 130a
  good of the p. is the chief law — 540b
  government of all the p. — 292b
  government of the p., by the p. — 245b
  happy the p. whose annals..blank — 80b
  he looked upon his p. — 252b
  his p. are free — 282b
  indictment against an whole p. — 55b
  in the P. was my trust — 469b
  it is what the p. think so — 58a
  makes the p.'s wrongs his own — 138b
  maketh the devices of the p. — 483b
  my p. love to have it so — 503b
  new p. takes the land — 93a

People (cont.)
  no doubt but ye are the P. — 230a, 497d
  none of yr. p. stir me — 357a
  nor is the p.'s judgement..true — 138b
  nor tell to various p. — 113b
  no vision, the p. perish — 499a
  one man shd. die for the p. — 511a
  only two sorts of p. — 390b
  O stormy p.! — 89b
  p. arose as one man — 495a
  p. came to theirs — 192a
  p. crushed by law have no hopes — 58a
  p. don't do such things — 567a
  p. hath some divineness in it — 13b
  p. keep even kings in awe — 117b
  p. loved her much — 432b
  p. never give up their liberties — 56a
  p. not too good-natured..conceive — 410a
  p. shouted with a great shout — 494b
  p. suppose me clever — 53a
  p. that delight in war — 486b
  p. that walked in darkness — 501b
  p. the most unfit to be alone — 103b
  person and the p. his apes — 80a
  pink pills for pale p. — 523a
  plenty of p. whose loss..gain — 164a
  singular use for the common p. — 417b
  sits high in all the p.'s heart — 338a
  some p. are more nice than wise — 109b
  speak not when the p. listens — 319a
  spent and sacrificed p. — 421a
  subdue the p. under us — 484b
  such a lot of p.'s Wills — 91b
  surely the p. is grass — 502b
  that has such p. in 't — 368a
  that loves the p. well — 253b
  the city cast her p. out — 323a
  the Lord round about his p. — 489b
  the madness of the p. — 486a
  the p. are the masters — 56a
  the p. cried, 'O No' — 19b
  the p. imagine a vain thing — 481b
  the p. is the true legislator — 57b
  the p., Lord, the p. — 146a
  the p.'s voice is odd — 303b
  the Privileged and the P. — 130a
  therefore fall the p. unto them — 486b
  the voice of the p. — 309a
  this p. hath a revolting..heart — 503b
  Thy mercy on Thy P. — 233b
  thy p. shall be my p. — 495a
  thy p. still are fed — 131b
  understanded of the p. — 491b
  upon the education of the p. — 128b
  voice of the p...the voice of God — 537a
  we are the p. of England — 93a
  when p. walk hand in hand — 104a
  when wilt thou save the p.? — 146a
  wills of thy faithful p. — 479b
  wronged p. yearning to be free — 452b
  ye are..a peculiar p. — 517b
Peopled: the world must be p. — 358b
  this p. earth a solitude — 397a
Peoples: all the p., great and small — 426a
  by the peace among our p. — 234b
  cry of the Little P. — 244a
  new-caught, sullen p. — 236b
  p., distressed by events — 179b
  silent, sullen p. — 236b
Peopling the lone universe — 395b
Peor and Baalim — 270b
Pepper: enjoy the p. when he pleases — 83a
  peck of pickled p. — 533b
  p. and vinegar besides — 84b
Peppered: I am p., I warrant — 365b
  I have p. two of them — 377b
  where they are p. — 379a
Peradventure: know beyond a p. — 462a
  p. the darkness shall cover me — 490a
Perceive: both p. and know what
    things — 479b
  half create, and what p. — 472a
Perceivest: this thou p., wh. makes
    thy love — 388a
Perch and not their terror — 351a
Percy: Esperance! P.! — 379a
  I am not yet of P.'s mind — 377b
  old song of P. and Douglas — 402a
  P., an I brook my life — 531a
  P. out of Northumberland — 530b
Perdition: down to bottomless p. — 271a

Perdition (*cont.*)
p. catch my soul — 361*b*
the son of p. — 511*b*
Perfect: be ye therefore p. — 505*a*
clear springs..ever p. — 78*a*
if thou wilt be p., go and sell — 507*b*
p. democracy..shameless thing — 57*a*
p. the cup as planned! — 51*a*
p. till the nightingales applauded — 49*a*
spirits of just men made p. — 517*a*
the most p. humour..unconscious — 66*b*
Perfectibility: speak of p. as a dream — 266*a*
Perfection: attain to the divine p. — 247*b*
culture..ascertain what p. is — 9*b*
he writes indexes to p. — 170*a*
p. wrongfully disgrac'd — 388*a*
pursuit of p...sweetness — 9*b*
right praise and true p. — 355*b*
the very pink of p. — 171*a*
top of P. not to know them — 104*a*
what's come to p. perishes — 49*a*
Perfections: eyes where all p. keep — 524*a*
know everything..but yr. p. — 104*a*
p. of a fool — 29*a*
with his sweet p. caught — 313*b*
Perfidious bark — 269*b*
Perform: his wonders to p. — 110*a*
they are not able to p. — 483*a*
Performance: all words, and no p. — 262*b*
her p. keeps no day — 78*b*
his p., as he is now, nothing — 386*a*
Perfume: p. and the suppliance of a
minute — 330*b*
scent of odorous p. — 277*b*
strange invisible p. — 323*a*
Perfumed: gently, o'er a p. sea — 298*a*
p. like a milliner — 376*b*
powder'd, still p. — 215*a*
Perfumes: all the p. of Arabia — 350*a*
in the vale p. his wings — 143*a*
rich distill'd p. — 267*b*
Perhaps: I go to seek a great p. — 565*a*
the grand P. — 45*a*
Peri at the gate — 282*a*
Peril: p., toil and pain — 184*a*
those in p. on the sea — 457*a*
Perilous in steep places — 36*a*
Perils: if man cd. see the p. — 24*a*
in p. in the city — 515*a*
p. and dangers of this night — 478*b*
p. both of wind and limb — 65*a*
what p. do environ the man — 65*a*
Period: belong to the Beardsley p. — 24*b*
give an..account of that p. — 24*b*
made one poem's p. — 259*b*
p...human race..most happy — 162*a*
p., power, and enterprize — 403*a*
Peripatetic: magnetic, p. lover — 165*b*
Perish: all his thoughts will p. — 18*a*
he shall p. everlastingly — 478*b*
I shall p. on the shore — 132*a*
it were better to p. — 82*a*
name..that will not p. in the dust — 407*a*
not p., but have everlasting life — 510*b*
our days that p. — 551*a*
p. in our own — 441*a*
p. the thought! — 95*b*
p. thro' their own imaginations — 482*a*
p. with the sword — 508*a*
Rome shall p...write that word — 107*b*
shall not p. from the earth — 245*b*
they shall p., but thou shalt endure — 488*a*
they too shall p. unconsoled — 242*a*
thy money p. with thee — 512*a*
to p. rather, swallowed up — 272*b*
Perished: memorial is p. with them — 482*a*
noblest thing wh. p. there — 184*b*
poor souls, they p. — 367*a*
we p., each alone — 107*b*
Perishes: cause that p. with them — 96*a*
nothing really p. — 14*a*
what's come to perfection p. — 49*a*
Perishing: the remembered p. be? — 119*a*
Periwig: p. and hatband — 290*b*
p.-pated fellow — 333*b*
Perizzites, and the Hivites — 493*b*
Perjured: P. Clarence — 384*b*
p., murderous, bloody — 389*a*
Perjuries: at lovers' p...Jove laughs — 365*a*
Perjury: Jove but laughs at lover's p. — 141*a*
lay p. upon my soul — 354*b*

Perjury (*cont.*)
p. of lovers — 551*b*
Perk'd up, in a glist'ring grief — 385*b*
Permanence wh. the sea cannot claim — 181*a*
Permanent: nought's p...human race — 71*b*
suffering is p. — 463*a*
Permission of all-ruling Heaven — 271*a*
Pernicious weed! — 108*a*
Perpetuity: to merit of p. — 42*b*
Perplexed: p. her, night and morn — 432*b*
p. in the extreme — 364*a*
Perplexity: that stad is in p. — 474*a*
Persecuted: I p. the church — 514*b*
princes have p. me — 489*b*
Persecutest: Saul, why p. thou me? — 512*a*
Persecution: p...bad..way to plant
religion — 41*b*
p. produced its natural effect — 255*b*
popular but some degree of p. — 418*b*
religious p. may shield itself — 56*a*
Persephone: O Singer of P. — 460*a*
Persepolis: in triumph thro' P. — 259*a*
Persever in obstinate condolement — 330*a*
Perseverance: p. in a good cause — 411*b*
p...keeps honour bright — 369*a*
Persevere: our opposed paths to p. — 294*a*
Persia: past their first sleep in P. — 41*a*
Persian: entertaining as a P. Tale — 208*b*
in P. gulfs were bred — 250*b*
the P. on his throne — 74*a*
they are P. attire — 343*a*
Persians: P. taught three useful things — 72*a*
given to the Medes and P. — 504*a*
Persist: if the fool wd. p. in his folly — 31*a*
thus to p. in doing wrong — 369*a*
Persistence: dominant's p. — 52*b*
Person: blush to the cheek of the
young p. — 125*b*
express image of his p. — 517*a*
goodliest p. that ever came — 257*b*
her own p...beggar'd..description — 323*a*
I am a most superior p. — 528*b*
idea of an agreeable p. — 129*b*
licker koncealed about my p. — 451*a*
like a well-conducted p. — 440*b*
my purse, my p...lie all unlock'd — 352*b*
Old P. of Basing — 243*a*
p. and the people — 89*a*
p. gat in monthes tweye — 89*a*
p. who agrees with me — 129*b*
poure p. dwelling up-on land — 89*a*
povre P. of a toun — 88*b*
square p...into the round hole — 405*a*
there's no sich a p. — 124*a*
Personal: no p. considerations — 173*a*
Personated: most feelingly p. — 370*b*
Persons: as unvalued p. do — 330*b*
God is no respecter of p. — 512*a*
neither confounding the P. — 478*b*
no respect of p. with God — 513*a*
paws of elder p. — 25*b*
p. shd. not be joined together — 481*a*
place, p. nor time — 370*b*
Perspiration: genius is ninety-nine
per cent. p. — 143*a*
Perspire: dig till you gently p. — 230*b*
Persuade: beauty..doth of itself p. — 386*b*
pity whom ye can't p. — 420*a*
Persuaded: Death..thou hast p. — 308*a*
for I am p...neither death — 513*b*
fully p. in his own mind — 514*a*
quite p. that all the Apostles — 70*a*
shadow to shadow, well p. — 228*a*
Persuadest: almost thou p. me — 513*a*
Persuading: by p. me to it — 368*a*
by p. others, we convince ourselves — 217*a*
Persuasion: firm removed
mountains — 31*a*
firm p. that a thing is so — 31*a*
not capable of a firm p. — 31*a*
not truth, but p. — 255*b*
p. hung upon his lips — 411*b*
p. tips his tongue — 95*b*
Persuasions: winged P. — 392*a*
Pert as a schoolgirl — 164*b*
Perturbation: polished p. — 381*a*
Peru: from China to P. — 213*b*
Newton at P. — 449*b*
Perverse: all women born are so p. — 35*b*
I'll frown and be p. — 365*a*
Peschiera, when thy bridge cross — 96*b*

Pessimist fears this is true — 75*a*
Pestered with a popingay — 376*b*
Pestilence: desires but acts not,
breeds p. — 31*a*
from the noisome p. — 487*b*
p. that walketh in darkness — 487*b*
purged the air of p. — 369*b*
shakes p. and war — 273*a*
Pestle: among wheat with a p. — 498*b*
Pests of society — 33*b*
Petal: like the p. of a flower — 427*b*
now sleeps the crimson p. — 436*b*
O filigree p.! — 443*a*
Petals: between His p. wide — 475*a*
garden's last p. were shed — 421*b*
pursed its p. up — 46*b*
scriptured p. — 312*b*
Petar: hoist with his own p. — 335*a*
Peter: disciple did outrun P. — 511*b*
in his last binn Sir P. lies — 295*a*
Lord..looked upon P. — 510*a*
office opposite to St. P. — 363*a*
old priest P. Gilligan — 474*a*
once that P. was respected — 468*b*
P. Piper picked — 533*b*
P. saith..I go a fishing — 511*b*
P. was his name — 163*a*
raree-show of P.'s successor — 45*b*
St. P. sat by the celestial gate — 74*b*
Shock-headed P. — 192*b*
thou art P. — 507*a*
'twas P.'s drift to be — 397*a*
twenty times was P. feared — 468*b*
Peterkin: quote little P. — 406*a*
Peter Turf — 366*b*
Petrarch: if Laura had been P.'s wife — 70*b*
Petrarchal coronation — 222*b*
Petrifications of a plodding brain — 72*a*
Petrifies the feeling — 60*a*
Petticoat: draiglet a' her p. — 59*b*
feet beneath her p. — 416*a*
her p. was satin — 231*b*
I for one venerate a p. — 71*b*
in a yellow p. — 534*b*
in the tempestuous p. — 189*a*
out of the Realm in my p. — 145*a*
Petticoats up to the knees — 96*a*
Pews: talk about the p. and steeples — 91*b*
Pewter: long for simple p. — 163*b*
Phalanx: they move in perfect p. — 271*b*
where is the Pyrrhic p. gone? — 71*a*
Phantasies: twilight P. — 392*a*
Phantasma, or a hideous dream — 338*b*
Phantasy: he..had an excellent p. — 214*b*
Phantom: p., Beauty in a mist of
tears — 474*a*
p. of False morning died — 152*a*
quite the p. of ourselves — 6*b*
she was a p. of delight — 470*b*
transient and embarrassed p. — 129*b*
Phantoms an unprofitable strife — 392*b*
Pharaoh: he hardened P.'s heart — 493*b*
P. is sold for balsams — 42*b*
P.'s bitter yoke — 286*b*
P. surnamed the Great — 236*a*
Pharisee: I am a P., the son of a P. — 512*b*
I lived a P. — 513*a*
touching the law, a P. — 516*a*
Pharisees: righteousness of the
scribes and P. — 505*a*
them infernal P. — 250*a*
Pharpar: Abana and P. — 496*b*
Phenomenon: the infant p. — 124*b*
Phials: turning of the p. of wrath — 312*b*
Phidias: awful Jove young P. brought — 147*a*
Phil: fidgety P. — 193*a*
Philip: hast thou not known me, P.? — 511*a*
heard of P. Slingsby — 12*b*
let me see if P. can — 193*a*
P. and Mary on a shilling — 66*a*
P., foozling with his cleek — 172*b*
P. fought men — 244*a*
P. of Macedon..horse-race won — 402*a*
P.'s peerless son — 9*a*
P. Sparrow — 402*b*
Philippi: see thee at P. — 341*a*
Philistia, be thou glad — 485*b*
Philistine: P. must have originally
meant — 9*a*
P. of..literature, Bunyan — 10*b*
P. of..politics, Cromwell — 10*b*

Philistine: (cont.)
P. of..religion, Luther 10b
Philistines: Apostle of the P...
Macaulay 9b
Barbarians, P., Populace 9b
daughters of the P. 495b
[Middle] Class..designations of P. 9b
P. be upon thee 495a
tho' the P. may jostle 165b
Philistinism! we have not the expres-
sion 9a
Phillida: P. and Corydon 35a
P. flouts me 525b
Philologists who chase a..syllable 110b
Philosopher: al be that he was an p. 88b
an ancient sage p. 65a
guide, p., and friend 301b
he was a shrewd p. 65a
I have tried too..to be a p. 144a
poet..at the same time a..p. 102a
the old p. is still among us 255b
there was never yet p. 359a
to a p. no circumstance..minute 170a
Philosophers: and sayings of p. 65b
English..least..pure p. 17b
Philosophic: defence of p. doubt 18a
P. diner-out 48b
p. mind can take 37b
Philosophical: state of p. doubt 102b
Philosophy: adversity's sweet milk p. 366a
Aristotle and his p. 88b
axioms in p. are not axioms 222b
bullied into a certain p. 222a
charming is divine 267b
for fear Divine P. shd. push 430a
hang up p.! 366a
hast any p. in thee, shepherd? 327a
History is P...by examples 33b
if p. cd. find it out 332b
lecture, Love, in love's p. 133b
little p. inclineth..to atheism 15a
luxurious and a love for p. 222b
[natural p.] mother of..science 17a
not faith, but mere P. 41b
obscure regions, of p. 201b
p., in its more rigid sense 413b
p. is nothing but discretion 321a
p. the lumber of the schools 419b
p., that leaned on Heaven 299a
p. will clip an Angel's wings 219a
than are dreamt of in yr. p. 331b
that untaught innate p. 68b
this same p. is a good horse 170b
touch of cold p. 219a
unfit to hear moral p. 369a
unless p. can make a Juliet 366a
vain wisdom all, and fake p. 272b
Phineus: Tiresias, and P. 273a
Phlegm: spit out thy p. 186b
Phœbus: before the wheels of P. 359a
bright P. in his strength 373b
Delos rose, and P. sprung 70b
P.' amorous pinches black 323a
P. Apollo turned fasting friar 264b
P., arise 138a
P. 'gins arise 328b
P., he 'that wandering knight' 376b
P.! what a name 72a
sweats in the eye of P. 383a
towards P.' lodging 366a
wheels of P.' wain 267a
Phoenix: I knew a p. 474b
like the p. midst her fires 72b
P. builds her spicy nest 79b
the maiden p. 386b
the p. builds the p. nest 115a
Phrase: a fico for the p. 355b
choice words, and measured p. 470b
doctor full of p. and fame 9a
p. by wh. such things are settled 71a
p. of wh. bad historians are..fond 255a
portentous p., 'I told you so' 72a
proverbed with a grand-sire p. 364b
soft p. of peace 360a
sudden, unintelligible p. 294a
that's an ill p. 332a
the p. 'unconscious humour' 66b
the p. wd. be more german 337a
Phrases: discourse in novel p. 165a
high-sounding p. 73b
taffeta p., silken terms 345a

Phrygia and Pamphylia 512a
Phylacteries: make broad their p. 507b
Phyllida: but P., my P. 131a
Phyllis: P. is my only joy 321a
P., without frown or smile 321a
wh. the neat-handed P. dresses 269a
Physic: P. of Metaphysic begs
defence 299a
sceptre, learning, p., must 329a
take p., pomp 343a
throw p. to the dogs 350b
Physician: death is our p. 360b
died last night of my p. 306a
Luke, the beloved p. 516b
more needs..divine than the p. 350a
p...hath his favourite disease 151b
p., heal thyself 509a
time is the great p. 129b
whole need not a p. 506a
Physicians: P...are most happy 307a
p. of the utmost fame 26a
things of many p. 508b
what the fever is to the p. 279a
Pia mater: in the womb of p. 344b
Piano-forte is a fine resource 45a
Pibble-pabble: tiddle-taddle nor p. 382b
Pibroch: let the p. shake the air 12a
p. of Donuil Dhu 318b
Piccadilly: good-bye P. 461a
walk down P. with a..lily 165b
Pick: holding his p. more splendid 415b
Picked: you p. from passing men 414a
Picket's off duty for ever 25a
Picking and stealing 481a
Pickle: plague o' these p. herring! 370a
Pick-lock to a place 108a
Pick-purse: 'at hand, quoth p.' 377a
Pickwick: Mr. P. 126a
old unbroken P. walked 93b
P., the Owl and the Waverley 527b
Pickwickian: in its P. sense 126a
P. point of view 126a
Picinnies, and the Joblillies 155b
Picture: beauty, wh. a p. cannot
express 16a
Earth's last p. 236b
it is some p. on the margin 137b
like Mistress Mall's p. 369b
like the p. of somebody reading 223a
lively p. of his father's face 155b
look here, upon this p. 335a
not on his p., but his book 215b
paint my p. truly like me 116a
p. it—think of it 196a
p. placed the busts between 35a, 91b
reluctance to sit for a p. 210a
Turkey carpet bears to a p. 254a
Pictured: her p. urn 175a
Pictures: all his p. faded 29a
apples of gold in p. of silver 498b
beads, p., rosaries 66a
come to the p...have a good cry 186a
cutting all the p. out 25b
faces are but a gallery of p. 15b
my eyes make p. 100b
p. in our eyes to get 132b
the dead are but as p. 348a
the p. for the page atone 298b
use of a book..without p. 82b
with savage p. fill their gaps 419b
you are p. out of doors 360b
Picturesque: quite p. liar 447a
Pie: blackbirds baked in a p. 533a
eating a Christmas p. 532a
to make the gooseberry p. 171a
when the p. was opened 533a
Piece: a p. of him 329b
Pieces: dash'd all to p. 367a
Destiny with Men for P. 153b
helpless P. of the game 153b
peace is broken into p. 195a
p. of eight 413a
the p. are the phenomena 202b
thirty p. of silver 508a
Piecrust: promises and p. 418a
Pieman: Simple Simon met a p. 532b
Pier: from this here p. 19b
I walked upon the p. 19b
Pierce: into his hand, and p. it 496b
the meeting soul may p. 269a
Pierced: hath p. to the rote 88a

Pierced (cont.)
p. and nail'd Him to the Tree 456a
they also wh. p. him 518a
they p. my hands 483a
Piercing even to the dividing asunder 517a
Pierian: drunk deep of the P. spring 137a
taste not the P. spring 300a
Pies: eats the p. and puddings up 192b
one of Bellamy's veal p. 297b
Piety: all thy P. nor Wit shall lure 153b
each to each by natural p. 468a
mistaken and overzealous p. 56a
renowned for larnin' and p. 173a
to p. more prone 3b
Pig: a parlour boarder of a p. 196a
did you say p., or fig? 83a
like a stuck p. 160b
selling of p. in a poke 446a
stole a p., and away he run! 532b
the p. was eat 532b
this p. went to market 533b
Pigeon-livered: I am p. 333a
Pigging..in the same truckle-bed 55a
Pigmy: darling of a p. size 466b
fretted the p. body 138a
Pigs: as naturally as p. squeak 64b
as p. do in a poke 283b
as p. have to fly 83a
in a glas he hadde p.' bones 89a
whether p. have wings 84b
Pike: holy text of p. and gun 65a
I'll p. out his bonny blue e'en 529b
trail'st thou the puissant p. 382b
Pilate: P. saith..what is truth? 511b
what is truth? said jesting P. 14a
Pilchards: thicker than p. at Looe 227b
Pile: earn a monumental p. 111b
face of this tall p. 104b
God hath made the p. complete 430b
o'er many a mouldering p. 185a
Pilgrim: Honour comes, a p. grey 103a
labour night and day to be a p. 54b
life's a single p. 24a
Man! the p. of a day 77b
never tired p.'s links 78b
onward goes the p. band 20b
P. of Eternity 392a
p. of the sky! 471a
p. steps in amice grey 277a
p. steps of spring 36a
Pilgrimage: he overtaketh in his p. 372b
in the house of my p. 489a
thus I'll take my p. 307b
succeed me in my p. 54b
Pilgrimages: folk to goon on p. 88a
Pilgrims: happy band of p. 287a
like p. to th' appointed place 141a
like tombs of p. 313a
p. of the year waxed very loud 264a
Pilgrim's Progress: wished longer..
excepting..P. 212a
Pill: his potion and his p. 191a
Morrison's P. for curing..maladies 81a
outliv'd the doctor's p. 159b
Pillage they with merry march 381b
Pillar: p. of a cloud...p. of fire 494a
rising seem'd a p. of state 272b
sat by a p. alone 433b
she became a p. of salt 493a
the triple p. of the world 322a
you are a well-deserving p. 355a
Pillared shade 276b
Pillars: among her golden p. high 30b
ancient p. rear their..heads 104b
antique p. massy proof 268b
builded over with p. of gold 30b
four p. of government 15a
his legs are as p. of marble 500b
I bear up the p. of it 487a
there Jerusalem's p. stood 30b
Pillicock set on Pillicock-hill 343a
Pillow: finds the down p. hard 329a
his little hammer under the p. 121a
like a p. on a bed 132b
sigh'd upon a midnight p. 326a
stones Thy p., earth Thy bed 405b
'tis my p. white 393a
Pillows: smooth p. sweetest bed 401b
Pills: I swallow countless p. 163a
p...against an earthquake 2b
Pilot: a daring p. in extremity 138a

Pilot (cont.)

I took the oars: the P.'s boy 99b
oh, P.! 'tis a fearful night 22a
P. of the Galilean lake 269b
see my P. face to face 426a
the P. shrieked 99b
Pilotage: in learning p. 264b
Pilots: best p. have needs of mariners 215a
p. are thicker than pilchards 227b
Piminy: miminy, p. 165b
Pimpernel: demmed, elusive P. 290b
p. dozed on the lea 434a
Pimples: roughnesses, p., warts 116a
Pin: heard a p. drop 310a
his friend in merry p. 108b
life at a p.'s fee 331a
pinn'd it wi' a siller p. 530a
see a p. and pick it up 532b
stay not for th' other p.! 186b
with a little p. bores thro' 375b
Pinafore: Captain of the P. 165b
Pinch: death is as a lover's p. 325a
they brought one P. 328a
Pinches: Phœbus' amorous p. black 323a
Pindaric: epic, nay P. art 303b
Pindarus: the house of P. 278b
Pine: beech and odorous p. 37b
dwindel, peak, and p. 346a
most I p. for thee 252a
p. for what is not 398b
p. with fear and sorrow 409a
palm and southern p. 426a
shall I ever sigh and p.? 188a
tallest p. hewn on Norwegian hills 271b
they p., I live 143a
why dost thou p. within 389b
Pine-apple of politeness 400b
Pined: p. and wanted food 465a
p. away seven of my..years 239a
she p. in thought 371a
Pine-logs: bring me p. 286b
Pines: arrowy white p. 444a
eat the cones under his p. 157b
great p. groan aghast 393a
his thunder-harp of p. 403b
instead of p. shall murmur 220b
never get between the p. 27a
old acquaintance among the p. 444a
p. are gossip to the wide world 154b
she stay'd among these p. 138a
Pine-tree: O p., O p. 569b
p.'s withered branch 247a
Pine-trees: black and gloomy p. 248b
Pinion: he nursed the p. 72a
Imagination droops her p. 71a
Pinions: stayed..his p. from flight 423a
the drift of p. 442a
with p. skim the air 157b
Pink: bring hither the P. 409b
lavender water tinged with p. 243b
p. pills for pale people 523a
rose p. and dirty drab 264b
the p. of courtesy 410b
the p. o' womankind 62b
the p., the emblem o' my dear 62b
the very p. of courtesy 365b
the very p. of perfection 171a
the white p., and the pansy 270a
Pin-money: what they call p. 160b
Pinnace, like a fluttered bird 437a
Pinned it wi' a siller pin 530a
Pins: here files of p. extend 302b
Pinto: Ferdinand Mendez P. 104b
Pint-pot: peace, good p.! 377b
Pioneers: p. and all 362a
p.! O p.! 457b
Pious: stored with p. frauds 56b
this just, this p. fraud 160a
Pipe: a p. for my capacious mouth 159a
as my small p. best fits 188b
draw his last breath thro' a p. 239b
drop thy p., thy happy p. 32b
easier to be played on than a p. 334b
he called for his p. 532a
p. and woo her 436b
p. a song about a lamb 32b
p. but as the linnets sing 430a
p. for fortune's finger 334a
p. me to pastures still 197b
p. of half-awakened birds 436a
p. that song again 32b

Pipe (cont.)

p. to the spirit ditties 219b
p., with solemn..puff 108a
piped a silly p., and took tea 222b
put that in yr. p...and smoke it 19b
quite a three-p. problem 135a
rumour is a p. 379b
she loved the Dorian p. 8b
thy small p...shrill and sound 370a
to mine oaten p. inclined 408a
Piped: p. with merry cheer 32b
we have p. unto you 506b
Piper: Hyperion of calves the P. 96a
I was to pay the p. 104a
Peter P. picked a peck 533b
p., pipe that song again 32b
p. sit thee down and write 32b
Tom, Tom the p.'s son 532b
Pipers: all men, especially p.! 50a
five-and-thirty p. 12b
wi' a hundred p. an' a' 285b
Pipes: grate on their scrannel p. 269b
it's knock out yr. p. 229a
soft p., play on 219b
the p. o' Havelock sound! 459a
what p. and timbrels? 219b
Piping: helpless, naked, p. 32a
his p. took a troubled sound 8b
p. down the valleys wild 32a
p. songs of pleasant glee 32a
weak p. time of peace 384b
Pipkin: little p...fits this little jelly 188b
Pippa passes 25a
Pippins: old p. toothsomest 454b
there's p. and seese to come 355b
Piracies shd. not again be sullied 447a
Pirate: sanctimonious p. 351a
to be a P. King 166a
Pistol: when his p. misses fire 171a
Pistols: have you yr. p.? 457b
Piston: steam and p. stroke 284a
Pit: after them to the bottomless p. 275a
black as the P. from pole 185a
Eagle know what is in the p. 29b
enemies have beat us to the p. 341b
he that diggeth a p. 499b
key of the bottomless p. 519b
law is a bottomless p. 4b
man will go down into the p. 18a
many-headed monster of the p. 303b
out of the horrible p. 484a
Stygian smoke of the p. 204a
they have digged a p. before me 485b
they'll fill a p. 378b
when I go down to the p. 483b
Pitch: a bumping p. 287b
he that toucheth p...defiled 520b
nightly my moving tent 280a
of what validity and p. soe'er 369b
roller, p., and stumps 242a
two p. balls..for eyes 344b
when you make p. hot 121a
Pitch-and-toss: one turn of p. 230a
Pitcher: p. be broken at the fountain 500a
Pitchfork: drive out nature with a p. 543a
thrown on her with a p. 418a
Pitfall: with P. and with Gin 154a
Pith: arms..had seven years' p. 360a
enterprises of..p. and moment 333a
Pities: he p. the plumage 292a
taught by the Power that p. me 169a
Pitiful: ah! were she p. 176a
lips say, 'God be p.' 43a
Oh! it was p.! 195b
p., 'twas wondrous p. 360a
Pitiless: ruffians, p. as proud 107b
Pitt: as P. is to Addington 570b
o'er P.'s the mournful requiem 317b
Pity: a p. beyond all telling 475b
arousing p. and fear 559a
cherish p., lest you drive an Angel 32b
crave p. from blustering wind 249b
gently p. whom ye can't persuade 420a
had p. on the least of things 474a
he best can p...felt the woe 160a
hern went p.-zekle 250b
his heart kep' goin' p.-pat 250b
His P. allows them to leave 234b
his p. gave ere charity began 168b
I learn to p. them 169a
in p. and mournful awe 6a

Pity (cont.)

I p. his ignorance 124b
it was great p., so it was 377a
it was the more p. 530b
knows some touch of p. 384b
looked for some to have p. on me 486b
lov'd her that she did p. them 360a
never any p. for conceited people 144b
no p. to myself 385a
no soul shall p. me 385a
P. a human face 33a
p. him afterwards 209a
p. is sworn servant unto love 117a
p., like a naked new-born babe 347a
p. me, then, and wish 389a
p. my simplicity 455b
p. never ceases to be shown 138b
p. renneth sone in gentil herte 89a
p. sitting in the clouds 366a
p. Sultan Mahmud 152b
p. them that weep 78b
p. the sorrows of a poor old man 284b
p. those they torture not 397a
shew thy p. upon all prisoners 479a
the p. of it, Iago 362b
till P.'s self be dead 103a
'Tis P. She's a Whore 155b
'tis true, 'tis p...p. 'tis 'tis true 332a
to Mercy, P., Peace 32b
virtuous poor, one can p. them 460b
what 'tis to p., and be pitied 326b
you feel the dint of p. 340a
Pixes: pictures, rosaries and p. 66a
Place: across a crowded public p. 292b
adorn'd the venerable p. 168b
a dozen dozen in her p. 416a
all move one p. on 83a
all rising to great p. 14b
a pick-lock to a p. 108a
a p. for everything 403a
a savage p.! 101a
at the p. where 'e is gone 230a
before I understood this p. 448a
bounds of p. and time 175a
bourne of Time and P. 426a
cares no more for one p. 407a
earns a p. i' the story 324a
every Christian kind of p. 413b
face one wd. meet in every p. 218a
find they a p. or part 453b
found no p. of repentance 517a
get p. and wealth 303b
grave's a fine and private p. 260a
his p. cd. nowhere be found 484a
his p. know him any more 497a
home..better p. 326a
hovering o'er the p.'s head 115a
I go to prepare a p. for you 511a
in many a secret p. 471b
is there no respect of p...in you? 370b
men in great p. are..servants 14b
night embrac'd the p. 114b
never the time and the p. 49a
no p.,..shd. murder sanctuarize 336a
no p. to go 63b
nor wished to change his p. 168b
not to be changed by p. or time 271a
of p. 'tween high and low 329a
one in all doth hold his p. 339a
one-eyed, blinking sort o' p. 181a
p...not good manners to mention 40b
p. of the slaying of Itylus 422b
p. thereof shall know it no more 488a
p. to stand and love in 44a
p. where men can pray 93b
p. where the tree falleth 499b
p. where thine honour dwelleth 483b
p. wh. thou hast appointed for them 488a
receive yr. reward in a certain p. 40b
reign in this horrible p. 113a
right man to fill the right p. 243a
rising unto p. is laborious 14b
sat him down in a lonely p. 435b
seldom go to..p. I set out for 411a
smallest people..in a great p. 17b
surely the Lord is in this p. 493a
the mind is its own p. 71a
there's p. and means 322a
till there be no p. 501a
time and p. are lost 273a

Place (cont.)
to keep in the same p. 84a
upon the p. beneath 354b
we are grown and take our p. 227b
when she a p. has 189a
where to choose their p. of rest 277a
Whigs not getting into p. 71b
wryte in p. lyte 90b
Placed: securely p. between 113a
Places: all p., all airs make unto me 42a
all p. are distant from Heaven 64a
all p. that the eye of heaven 374b
all p. thou 276b
all p. were alike to him 237a
angels keep their ancient p. 442a
hark, in thine ear; change p. 343b
love all waste and solitary p. 395a
perilous in steep p. 36a
p. of nestling green 202a
plucking bon-mots from their p. 283a
proper words in proper p. 418a
Quires and P. where they sing 478b
Scripture moveth us in sundry p. 478b
slain in thy high p. 495b
strange p. cramm'd 326b
they were in their proper p. 445a
wickedness in high p. 516a
Placid and self-contained 458a
Plagiary: borrowing..is accounted p. 279b
Plague: and that's his p. 64a
any p. come nigh thy dwelling 487b
fiends that p. thee thus 98b
instruments to p. us 344a
oh! p. of his sentiments! 400b
pleasing p. stole on me 457a
p. o' both yr. houses 365b
p. of all cowards 377b
p. of sighing and grief 377b
the red p. rid you 367a
thro' any p., or trouble 488b
Plagued: monster that has p. the nations 111a
Plagues: add unto him the p. 520b
of all the p. a lover bears 450a
two main p., and common dotages 64a
Plaguing: charges of p...in a handsome way 159a
Plaid: beneath the tartan p. 12a
my p. to the angry airt 62a
Plain: as on a darkling p. 5a
base as is the lowly p. 527b
delicate p., called Ease 54a
gleamed upon the glassy p. 466a
great Gromboolian p. 243b
he will make it p. 110a
Homer..is eminently p. and direct 10a
I'm not so old, and not so p. 163b
instead of p. and sere 36a
it's flat and p. 526a
knight was pricking on the p. 408b
nodding o'er the yellow p. 443b
once more reach that p. 448a
p. man in his p. meaning 354b
penny p. and twopence coloured 412b
stretched upon the p. 72a
that p. was but narrow 54a
the way is all so very p. 93b
virtue is..best p. set 16a
Waterloo's ensanguined p. 525b
waveless p. of Lombardy 395a
Plainly and more plainly 253a
Plainness: perfect p. of speech 10a
Plains: by thousands on her p. 185a
her silver-mantled p. 320b
p. of pleasant Hertfordshire 240b
ringing p. of windy Troy 438b
whiten the green p. under 393a
Plain-speaking with Mr. Snagsby 121a
Plaint: tease her with our p. 8b
Plaisters: for wh. there are no p. 158b
Plan: fulfils great Nature's p. 60a
joined in the p. 110b
mighty maze! but not without a p. 300b
nothing..rest on its original p. 58a
p...pleased his childish thought 465a
some usefu' p. or beuk 60b
the simple p., that they shd. take 470b
this was still his simple p. 136b
Plancus: when P. was consul 546b
Planet: born under a riming p. 359a
new p. swims into his ken 220b

Planet (cont.)
p. of Love is on high 434a
p.'s tyrant, dotard Death 24a
p. Venus..gone on business 125a
every wand'ring p.'s course 259a
while Jove's p. rises 47b
Planetary: stops of p. music 393b
Planets: other p. circle other suns 300b
p., filled with Stagyrites 282b
p. in their radiant courses 305a
P...list'ning stood 275b
then no p. strike 329b
the p., and this centre 368b
the p., in their turn 2a
with p. in His care 474a
Plank: have to swab a p. 121a
Planned: perfect woman, nobly p. 470b
Plans: hopeful p. to emptiness 199b
p., credit, and the Muse 146b
Plant: an orange-tree, that busy p. 187b
fixed like a p. 301a
green p. groweth, menacing 92a
love is..a p. 117a
O wicked, wicked p. 238b
Sensitive P. in a garden grew 398a
Plantagenet: thy rose a thorn, P.? 383b
Plantation: longing for de old p. 156a
Planted: I have p., Apollo's watered 514a
Plants: grow up as the young p. 490b
like p. in mines 49b
p. did spring 20b
p. suck in the earth 106b
to his music p. and flowers 385b
under his own vine what he p. 386b
Plastic: dance of p. circumstance 51a
Plat of rising ground 268a
Plate of turtle green 50a
Plates dropp'd from his pocket 325a
Platform: half the p. just reflects 302b
the p., 'twixt eleven and twelve 330b
Platinum: bullets made of p. 25b
Plato: attachment à la P. 165b
Cæsar's hand, and P.'s brain 146a
dozen persons who read..P. 147b
lend an ear to P. 433a
P. is never sullen 255a
P.'s retirement 277a
P. the wise 435b
P. thou reasonest well 1b
taught out of the rule of P. 279b
unsphere the spirit of P. 268a
Plats the manes of horses 365a
Platter: cleanly p. on the board 170a
licked the p. clean 534a
no account of the p. after it 239a
Plautus too light 332b
Play: actions that a man might p. 330a
a little work, a little p. 263a
an hour to p. 287b
as children with their p. 199a
better than a p. 87b
but better at a p. 282b
by a good author, it's a good p. 390a
come ye here to p.? 530b
delicate and refined p. 57b
every day, for food or p. 98b
everything that heard him p. 385b
fair p. of the British..law 135b
for once had p. unstifled 46a
full craftier to p. 89b
girls and boys come out to p. 534b
good p. needs no epilogue 328a
guilty creatures sitting at a p. 333a
hear thy discourse than see a p. 64b
his p. is always fair 202b
I cannot p. alone 184b
I doubt some foul p. 330b
I shd. like so much to p. 413b
is there no p., to ease the anguish 357a
judge not the p. before..p. be done 117b, 307a
learned to p. when he was young 533a
little Arthur wants to p. 534b
may be p. to you, 'tis death to us 244b
multitude can p. upon it 379b
or a' the p. was played 530a
our p. is done 372b
our p. is played out 440a
p. by me, bathe in me 226a
p. out the p. 378a
p. up! and p. the game! 287b

Play (cont.)
p. with him as with a bird 497b
rose up to p. 494a
sees all her sons at p. 5b
seven up and six to p. 172b
sick men p. so nicely 375a
the p. is done 440b
the p...pleased not the million 332b
the p.'s the thing 333a
turn us out to p. 226a
what to say about a p. 390a
witty prologue to a..dull P. 105a
yet cannot p. well 15a
you cannot p. upon me 334b
young barbarians all at p. 69a
you wd. p. upon me 334b
Playbill..tragedy of Hamlet 320a
Playbills: no time to read p. 58b
Played: he p. at the glove 530b
he p. so truly 215a
if this were p. upon a stage now 371b
I have p. the fool 495b
p. by somebody I do not know 223a
p. by everybody I do not know 223a
p. by somebody I do not know 223a
p. by every p. bill 332b
Played-Out: I am also called P. 445a
Playedst: thou p. most foully 348b
Player: he the best p.! 151b
like a strutting p. 368b
p. on the other side is hidden 202b
poor p., that struts and frets 350b
Players: as many of your p. do 333b
lenten entertainment the p...receive 332b
men and women merely p. 326b
one of these harlotry p. 377b
p. in yr. housewifery 360b
the p. have often mentioned it 214b
will you see the p. well bestowed? 332b
Playfellow: my p., yr. hand 324a
Play-house: you and every p. bill 303b
Playing: ever amid our p. I hear 82b
p. of the merry organ 526b
the purpose of p. 333b
Playing fields of Eton 454b
Playmates: I have had p. 240b
Play-place of our early days 113a
Plays: few of our p. can boast..wit 149a
he loves no p., as thou dost 338a
old p. began to disgust 149b
p., in the many games of life 465b
Plaything: a little p.-house 449a
child's a p. for an hour 240b
some livelier p. gives 301a
Playthings: p. come alive 413b
princes have great p. 112b
to love p. well as a child 413a
Playwright: our P. may show 435b
Plea: as I am, without one p. 146a
in law, what p. so tainted 354a
tho' justice be thy p. 354b
Plead: so what I p. is just 198a
Pleasance: p., revel and applause 361b
youth is full of p. 389b
Pleasant: from p. to severe 141a
how p. it is to have money 96b
lies down to p. dreams 53b
of all that was p. in man 169b
p. if one considers it 398a
p. it is, at the end of the day 425a
think him p. enough 243b
very p. hast thou been 495b
Pleasanter the colder 66a
Pleasantness: her ways are ways of p. 497b
p. of an employment 11b
Please: blow on whom I p. 326b
difficult to p. about..victuals 75b
not to p. ourselves 514a
p. her the best you may 525b
she never fails to p. 321a
some circumstance to p. us 419a
studious to p. 213a
to tax and to p. 55a
towered cities p. us 269a
'twas natural to p. 138a
we'll strive to p. you 372b
we that live to p. 213b
whom to p.? you whisper 49a
Pleased: all seemed well p. 275a
had he p. us less 1b
he was well-p...gave him a hint 406b
in whom I am well p. 504b
p. me long choosing 276a

Pleased (*cont.*)
p. with less than Cleopatra 139a
p. with the danger 138a
p. with what he gets 326a
they please, are p. 170a
Pleases: every prospect p. 184a
if one p. one makes more 105b
the pepper when he p. 83a
Pleasing: every p... prudent part 302a
p. consists in being pleased 183b
p. without skill to please 296b
surest method..of p. 90b
this p. anxious being 174b
Pleasure: aching P. nigh 219b
all knowledge..is..p. in itself 13a
body..is capable of much..p. 75a
budge for no man's p. 365b
business first; p. afterwards 440a
but fading p. brings 402a
but the privilege and p. 163b
cabinet of p. 187b
doubtless the p. is as great 65b
egg by p. laid 110b
for thy p. they are..created 518b
for yr. p. you came here 109a
gave p. to the spectators 255b
happiness..is not in p. 140b
hatred is by far the longest p. 71b
I go to my p., business 473b
I have no p. in them 499b
I'm not to be stinted in p. 461a
in trim gardens takes his p. 268a
it becomes a p. 460a
let fall yr. horrible p. 342b
little p. out of the way 87b
love ceases to be a p. 25a
love of p., and the love of sway 302a
Love!..thou doubtful p. 173a
make a bait of p. 186b
man's chief p. is society 117b
mind, from p. less, withdraws 260b
mingled profit with p. 542b
mixture of a lie..add p. 14a
music..only..p. without vice 212a
my p. had I seen 428a
never had I p. with her 257a
never to blend our p. 465b
no p., nor no pain! 320b
not *P.* but *power* 120a
on p. she was bent 108b
painful p. turns to..pain 409a
pain that is all but a p. 165b
P. at the helm 173b
P., blind with tears 392a
p. eternally new 242a
p. in the pathless woods 69b
p. in poetic pains 111b
p. in the strength of an horse 490b
p. is..intermission of pain 321a
p. is labour too 110b
p. never is at home 218a
p. of believing what we see 395a
p. of the fleeting year 388b
p.'s a sin 70a
p. soon shall fade 177a
p., sure in being mad 141b, 150b
p. that boys..head of a school 449a
p. that's all but pain 165b
p. was his business 143b
p. with pain for leaven 420b
receiv'st with p. thine annoy? 387a
refrain from the unholy p. 25b
source of p. is variety 213a
stock of harmless p. 213a
story, feigned for p. 139a
suburbs of yr. good p. 338b
such as have no p. 231a
sweet is p. after pain 139a
the greatest p. I know 240a
the p. of having it over 195a
there is p. for evermore 482b
the shadow of the dome of p. 101b
thy most pointed p. take 415a
turn to p. all they find 175b
type of a perfect p. 460b
ugliest of trades..moments of p. 205b
variety is the soul of p. 25b
was yr. vision of p. wasteful? 48b
wild, and effable p. 244b
what p. lives in height 437a
when Youth and P. meet 68b

Pleasure (*cont.*)
where is no p. ta'en 366b
without one p. and without
  one pain 433a
working wrong, if p. you attain 177a
yet all hope p. 139b
you were queen of p. 423a
Pleasure-dome: stately p. 101a
Pleasure-house: lordly p. 435b
Pleasures: breed that take their p. 228b
coarser p. of my boyish days 472a
hypocrite in his p. 211b
look not on p. as they come 187a
mid p. and palaces 294b
one of the p. of having a rout 195a
other p. all abjure 275b
owes its p. to another's pain 112a
paucity of human p. 212a
purest of human p. 16a
p. are like poppies spread 63a
p. banish pain 453b
p. in a long immortal dream 219a
p. newly found are sweet 463b
p. of life..conversation 404b
p. that to verse belong 217b
p. with youth pass away 407a
seize the p. of the present day 131a
some new p. prove 132a
soothed his soul to p. 139a
sucked on country p. 133a
than all other p. are 142a
these pretty p. might me move 307b
these uneasy p...for curiosity 147b
understand the p. of the other 11a
unreproved p. free 268b
we will all the p. prove 259a
with p. too refined to please 302a
Pledge: I will p. with mine 216a
ne'er refused to p. my toast 306a
O Motherland, we p. to thee 228a
Pledges: p. of a fruitful tree 188b
p. of Heaven's joy 278a
Pledging with contented smack 219a
Pleiades: flocks of shiny p. 192a
sweet influences of P. 497b
Plenteously bringing forth the
  fruit 479b
Plenteousness within thy palaces 489b
Plentiful: more p. than hope 187a
Plenty: here is God's p. 142a
in delay there lies no p. 370b
on the expectation of p. 348a
representing Peace and P. 116a
scatter p. o'er a smiling land 174b
wasna fou, but just had p. 60a
with P. in the maize 437a
Pliable: name of the other P. 54a
Plighter of high hearts 324a
Plodders: small have continual p. 344b
Plods his weary way 174a
Plot: good p., good friends 377a
green p. shall be our stage 357a
gunpowder treason and p. 532a
her p. hath many changes 307a
some melodious p. 219b
the p. thickens 53b
this blessed p., this earth 375a
what the devil does the p. signify 53b
women guide the p. 400b
Plots, true or false 138a
Plotting some new reformation 141b
Plough: following his p. 470a
land you used to p. 199a
men of England, wherefore p. 399a
O Christ, the p. 261b
p. deep and straight 198a
p.—loom—anvil—spade 240a
p. my furrow alone 310b
speed his p. 87a
tested his first p. 45a
we p. the fields, and scatter 76a
Ploughing: is my team p. 199a
Ploughman: hard as the palm
  of p. 368b
heavy steps of the p. 475b
the p. homeward plods 174a
the p. near at hand 268b
whilst the heavy p. snores 357b
Ploughmen: ye rigid P.! 108a
Ploughshare: soldiers of the p. 314b
stern Ruin's p. drives 62a

Ploughshares: beat their swords
  into p. 501a
Plowed with my heifer 495a
Plowers plowed upon my back 490a
Pluck: p. till time and times are done 476a
to p. me by the beard 343a
Plucked: p. by his hand 452a
p. them as we passed 194b
the fruit, she p., she eat 276a
Pluckers: wh. the p. forgot 311b
Plucking at their harps 231a
Plucks: silk thread p. it back again 365b
Plum: biscuit, or confectionary p. 109b
he took out a p. 532a
Plumage: gives out his snowy p. 443b
pities the p. 292a
p. that had warm'd his nest 72b
warmer climes give brighter p. 241a
Plumbing: yr. p.'s strange 236a
Plumbline: and I said, A p. 504b
with p. in his hand 504b
Plume: blast-beruffled p. 179a
ruffles her pure cold p. 429b
Sir P., of amber snuff-box 302b
saw the helmet and the p. 431b
where ye see my white p. shine 252b
Plumed: all p. like estridges 378b
Plumelets: rosy p. 430b
Plumes: in its p. the various light 261a
jets under his advanced p. 371a
Plummet: did ever p. sound 368a
Plump: he hath a cushion p. 99b
rosy Man, right p. to see 468b
Plums: berries and p. to eat 192a
p. and apple trees 192a
Plunder: he shared in the p. 110b
me that p. forbear 399b
no man stop to p. 254a
take your ill-got p. 287b
Plunge: a beggar, he prepares to p. 49b
Festus, I p.! 49b
p. (after shocking lives) 76a
Plunged: as I was, I p. in 337b
p. himself into the..wave 165a
p. in thought again 7a
Pluto: iron tears down P.'s cheek 268b
won the ear of P. 269a
Ply thee home, lady-cow 534a
Plying: a-p. up an' down! 231b
p. her needle and thread 196a
Plymouth Hoe: arl the time o' P. 287b
lazy Scheldt, or wandering P. 169b
Poacher a keeper turned inside 226b
Pobble's toes 243b
Pocket: carry the moon in my p. 48b
crept in at Myra's p.-hole 31b
diadem stole..put it in his p. 335a
scruple to pick a p. 120a
wid a p. full of tin 156a
Pocket-handkerchief: holding his p. 84b
Pocket-handkerchiefs: moral p. 126b
Pockets: plates dropp'd from his p. 325a
young man feels his p. 200a
Pods: when the p. went pop 117b
Podsnap: Mr. P. 125b
Poem: adjunct or true ornament of p. 270b
a tiny poem all composed 427a
frowzy p., call'd the 'Excursion' 71a
he fain wd. write a p. 49a
life of a man..heroic p. 80a
like to be married to a p. 223a
long p. is a test of invention 222a
made one p.'s period 259b
not metres..that makes a p. 148a
ought himself to be a true p. 279a
p. lovely as a tree 225a
p., whose subject is not truth 87b
sake of writing or making a p. 223a
shorter a prize p. is, the better 255a
Poems: I can explain all the p. 85a
I will put in my p. 458b
one of the most sublime p. 142a
p. are made by fools like me 225a
ye are living p. 246b
Poesy: flowers of P. 259b
force of heaven-bred p. 372b
God of life, and p., and light 69a
golden cadence of p. 344b
Nature, Hope, and P. 102a
on the viewless wings of P. 220a

Poesy (cont.)

overwhelm myself in p.	220b
p. *vinum dæmonum*	13a
shower of light is p.	220b
the great end of p.	220b
wit with p. allied	72a

Poet: and the p.'s dream 468b
a p. cd. not but be gay	467a
a P.!..put his heart to school	463a
a p. soaring in the high region	279a
be accounted p. kings	220b
business of a comic p.	104a
business of a p., said Imlac	213b
dreams of a p. doomed at last	212b
every p., in his kind, is bit	419b
flattery lost on p.'s ear	317a
form'd the P. for the King	206a
God is the perfect p.	49b
good p.'s made, as well as born	216a
grete p. of Itaille..Dant	89a
here the p. meets his..muse	113b
honour to the greatest p.	566b
if any p. knew her	43b
if a P. now and then	472b
I for an unhappy p	305b
is this the great p.	158b
like a P. hidden	398a
living the same p. wh. thou'rt now	106b
lunatic, the lover, and the p.	357b
making a p. out of a man	43b
many a wd.-be p. at this hour	36a
Milton..was a true P.	31a
muse on Nature with a p.'s eye	77a
never durst p. touch a pen	345a
'next P.'—(Manners, Ben!)	48b
no..p...without..unsoundness	254b
not deep the P. sung	8a
notes, thy once-loved P. sung	302b
on a p.'s lips I slept	397a
painter's work, so with the p.'s	542b
passionate heart of the p.	433b
P. and Saint!	106b
p. and the dreamer are distinct	218a
p. did feign that Orpheus drew	355a
p. knows..he speaks adequately	148a
p...same time a..philosopher	102a
p.'s eye, in a fine frenzy	357b
p.'s pen turns them to shapes	357b
rightly shd. possess a p.'s brain	137a
sage and serious p., Spenser	279a
say, that when the P. dies	317a
say "This p. lies"	387a
Shakespeare is not our p.	241a
so is a p.'s mind kindled	224a
spare..p. for his subject sake	107b
story-teller..born, as well as a p.	410a
Swift, you will never be a p.	142a
the Hero can be P., Prophet	80b
the limbs of a p.	547b
the Muse, nae p. ever fand her	62b
the p. does not work by square	108a
the p. sing it with such airs	474a
they had no p., and they died	303b
this is truth the p. sings	432a
thy skill to p. were	398b
true p. that you are	50a
vex not thou the p.'s mind	435b
wd. not..be called a p.	33a
whom no p. sings	137a
Poetaster: hunt a p. down	72b
Poetess: a maudlin p.	303a
Poetic: guide into p. ground	111b
more strong than all p. thought	430a
pleasure in p. pains	111b
p. justice, with her lifted scale	298b
Poetical: claim to p. honours	213a
gods had made thee p.	327a
Poet-race shot such..arches	92b
Poetry: all metaphor is p.	94a
angling is somewhat like p.	450b
art of sinking in P.	303b
as a friend he drops into p.	125b
civilization advances, p...declines	254b
cradled into p. by wrong	395a
fair Nine, forsaking P.	31b
Fleshly School of P.	53b
genuine p. and..p. of Dryden, Pope	9b
genuine p...in the soul	9b
grand style arises in p.	10a
I can repeat p. as well	85a

Poetry (cont.)

if p. comes not as naturally	222b
language is fossil p.	148a
made p. a mere mechanic art	111b
mincing p.	378a
Music and sweet P.	21a
not p., but prose run mad	303a
or even enjoy p.	254b
p...best words in the best order	102b
p...in Oxford made an art	141b
p. is conceived..in their wits	9b
p. is the spontaneous overflow	467b
p. of earth is never dead	221a
P...of the smaller intestines	80a
p.'s a mere drug	150b
p. shd. be great and unobtrusive	222a
p. shd. surprise by..excess	222b
p. sinks and swoons	241b
p.'s unnat'ral	126b
Polar star of p.	222a
read a little p. sometimes	197a
saying so in whining P.	134a
scrap of dramatic p.	445b
Shelley's genius..music, not of p.	9a
she that with p. is won	65b
Sir, what is p.?	209a
to the petty, in his p.	183a
to wh. p. wd. be made subsequent	279b
used p. as a medium	460a
we hate p. that has a..design	222a
we shd. drop into p.	125b
what is p.?..noble emotions	314a
where they had p., we have cant	295a
Poets: all p. are mad	64a
all the pens that ever p. held	259b
as we to the brutes, p. are to us	264b
certain also of yr. own p.	512b
I hate all P. and Painters	161a
in the hearts of mighty P.	464b
I shall be among the English P.	223a
many..P...sown by Nature	464a
mighty p. in their misery dead	470b
Milton 's the prince of p.	71a
old p. outsing and outlove us	421b
O p., from a maniac's tongue	43a
our p. steal from Homer	64a
places of..green, for p. made	202a
pleasure..which only p. know	111b
p. are needed to sing the dawn	264b
p. better prove	387b
p.' food is love and fame	393b
p., like painters, thus unskilled	300a
p. (make men) witty	16a
p. that wrapt Truth in tales	79a
p...the unacknowledged legislators	399b
Savill..his opinion touching p.	13b
sensitive race of p.	543b
sights as youthful p. dream	269a
souls of p. dead and gone	219a
theft in other p...victory in him	142a
the P. Militant below!	106b
things, that the first p. had	137a
three p. in an age at most	419b
three p., in three distant ages	141a
to p. to be second-rate	542b
very Janus of p.	142a
we p. in our youth	470a
what the sage p. taught	267b
when amatory p. sing their loves	71a
whose arrows learned p. hold	66a
why don't p. tell?	232a
Pogrom: presented to a P.	124a
Point: aloof from the entire p.	341b
fine p. of his soul	222a
fixed p. in a changing age	136a
not to put too fine a p. upon it	121a
p. against p.	346a
p. me out the way	218b
p. me to the skies	251b
press yr. p. with modesty	108a
swim to yonder p.	337b
the p. envenom'd too!	337a
they do not p. on me	363b
thus I bore my p.	377b
why, 'tis a p. of faith	115a
Points: kindred p. of heaven	471a
Poising every weight	260b
Poison: Adonais has drunk p.	392a
coward's weapon, p.	155b
he swallowed the p. like	526b
if you p. us, do we not die?	354a

Poison (cont.)

I go about and p. wells	259a
ounce of p. in one pocket	254b
pecks of p. are not pecks of salt	30a
p. for the age's tooth	373b
P. while the bee-mouth sips	219b
strongest p. ever known	29b
the potent p. quite o'ercrows	337a
Poisoned: cans of p. meat	93b
some p. by their wives	375b
Poisons all the rest	453a
Poke: as pigges do in a p.	283b
drew a dial from his p.	326a
Pokers: wreathe iron p.	100b
Polar-star of poetry	222a
Pole: all sights from p. to p.	8b
as the needle to the p.	33b
centre thrice to th' utmost p.	271a
needle trembles to the p.	304a
not rapt above the P.	275a
soldier's p. is fallen	324b
spread the truth from p. to p.	2a
were I so tall to reach the P.	453a
wid a ten foot p.	156a
Poles: upon the p. of truth	14a
wheel between the p.	426a
Police: friendship recognized by..p.	413a
I'll send for the P.!	85b
Policeman: go back with P. Day	228a
p.'s lot is not a happy one	166b
want to know the time, ask a P.!	309b
Policy: based either on religion or p.	314b
brow of careful P.	409b
kings will be tyrants from p.	57a
p. to stear clear of..alliance	451b
some love but little p.	376a
Polish it at leisure	142a
Polished idleness	256a
Polite: p. to every country	196b
till the English grew p.	228b
you're exceedingly p.	166a
Politeness: glance of great p.	74b
Pine-apple of p.	400b
when suave p., tempering..zeal	238a
Political: man is..a p. animal	559a
my remembrance of p. affairs	255b
schemes of p. improvement	208a
Politician: a Brownist as a p.	371b
like a scurvy p.	343b
the pate of a p.	336a
Politicians: whole race of p. put together	418a
Politics: confound their p.	79b
Conservatism..mule of p.	129a
finality..not the language of p.	128a
I taste no p. in boil'd	405a
magnanimity in p...wisdom	56a
mistaken zeal in p.	217a
my p...exceedin accommodatin	451a
Philistine of..p., Cromwell	10b
points of practical p.	130a
p. and the pulpit are terms	56b
p. are not an exact science	567b
p. go by the weather	175b
p. in the East..dissimulation	129b
p. is perhaps the only profession	412b
p. we bar	166b
range of practical p.	167b
shoved him into p.	26a
slipped from p. to puns	305a
talking p. after dinner	128b
these are my p.	412b
they p. like ours profess	175b
Poll: but talk'd like poor P.	158b
his heart *was* true to P.	58b
Polly: depends poor P.'s life	159b
little P. Flinders	535a
our P. is a sad slut	159a
P. put the kettle on	121a
P., you might have toy'd	159a
Pretty P., say	159b
Pollywog: like a p.'s tail	451a
Polonies: fine p.	19b
Poltigrue: My Lady P.	26b
Polygamy: before p. was made a sin	138a
justified a chaste p.	79b
Pomander: sweet p.	402b
Pomegranate: from Browning some P.	43b
p. within thy locks	500a
sings on yon p. tree	366a
Pomeranian grenadier	567b

Pomp: all our p. of yesterday — 233b
bright P. ascended jubilant — 275b
grinning at his p. — 375b
Heaven's p. is spread — 464a
his p., without his force — 58b
in lowly p. ride on to die — 266b
p., and feast, and revelry — 269a
praise his humble p. — 407b
pride, p. and circumstance — 362a
puts all the p. to flight — 299b
Sultan after Sultan with his P. — 152b, 153a
sweet than that of painted p. — 325b
take physic, p. — 343a
the p. of power — 174a
the slave of p. — 316a
the tide of p. — 382b
vain p. and glory of the world — 386a
Pompadour: the P.'s Fan — 130b
Pompey: at the base of P.'s statua — 340a
great P. wd. stand — 323a
knew you not P.? — 337b
pibble-pabble in P.'s camp — 382b
Pomps: high Midsummer p. — 8b
p. and vanity of this..world — 481a
Pond: beyond the depths of a p. — 292b
four ducks on a p. — 4a
mantle like a standing p. — 352b
neighbours o'er the Herring P. — 143a
p. edged with grayish leaves — 180a
Sir Thomas again in the p. — 20a
they have their stream and p. — 39a
Ponder: oh, p. well! — 159b
wise will p. these things — 488b
Pondered: I p., weak and weary — 298a
p. sadly, wearied and forlorn — 284b
Poniards: she speaks p. — 358a
Ponies: blind pit p. — 192a
five-and-twenty p. — 234b
Pontgibaud they mended it — 25b
Pontick sea — 362a
'Ponto!' he cried — 26a
Pony: riding on a p. — 18b
Pontus: in P., and Asia — 512a
Pool: it must first fill a p. — 14b
mantle of the standing p. — 343a
p. of private charity — 293a
wood..p. and the elder tree — 119b
Pools: p. are filled with water — 487a
p. I used to know — 199b
Poop was beaten gold — 323a
Poor: all my goods to feed the p. — 514b
all things..in common, being so p. — 33a
and given to the p. — 489a
anger..keeps (dull men) p. — 13b
angry and p. and happy — 93b
annals of the p. — 174a
art thou p. — 118b
as for the virtuous p. — 460b
blessed are the p. in spirit — 505a
but let the p., and Thou within — 187b
come, Thou Father of the p. — 86b
Death, the p. man's..friend — 61b
faith of the p. is faint — 93b
found'st me p. at first — 169a
give to the p. — 507b
good to the p. — 79b
great man helped the p. — 253a
great men have their p. relations — 121b
grind the faces of the p. — 501a
heaven make me p. — 214b
his dear papa is p. — 414a
how apt the p. are to be proud — 371b
how many p. I see — 452b
how p. a thing is man — 464b
I, being p., have only my dreams — 474b
I can dare to be p. — 160b
if thou art rich, thou'rt p. — 351b
inconvenient to be p. — 107b
laws grind the p. — 170a
low estate of the p. — 483a
makes me p. indeed — 361b
marry a rich woman as a p. — 440a
most rich, being p. — 341b
my Friends were p. but honest — 322a
none so p. to do him reverence — 340a
ointment..given to the p. — 511a
p. always ye have — 511a
p. and content is rich — 361b
p., and mean, and lowly — 3b
p., and the maimed, and the halt — 509b

Poor (cont.)
p. are they..have not patience — 361b
p. have cried, Cæsar hath wept — 340a
p., infirm, weak — 342b
p. make no new friends — 29a
p. man at his gate — 3a
p. man is Christ's stamp — 186b
p. man loved the great — 253a
p. Persoun of a toun — 88b
p., reckless, rude — 136b
p. wandering one — 166a
property of the p. — 315a
save the p., feel for the p. — 240b
solitary, p., nasty, brutish — 191b
so lonely and p. of old — 39a
the murmuring p. — 113b
the p. advanced makes friends — 334a
the p. in a loomp is bad — 434b
the p. man had nothing — 495b
they are but p. — 143a
they p., I rich — 143a
tho' I be p., I'm honest — 265b
tho' p. in gear — 62b
too p. for a bribe — 175b
warms the neighbouring p. — 114a
who now do bless the p. — 286b
without thee we are p. — 112b
Poorest he that is in England — 307b
Poorly (poor man) he lived — 155b
Poorness: when I mock p. — 214b
Pop goes the weasel — 257b
Pope: better to err with P. — 72a
galley-bench creaks with a P. — 424a
poor P. will grieve a month — 419a
P...with eye on his style — 10a
wine from the royal P. — 258a
Popery: antiquity inclines..to P. — 158a
Popinjay: pestered with a p. — 376b
Popish Apennines — 226a
Poplar: edg'd with p. pale — 270b
Poplars: p. stand and tremble — 199b
the p. are felled — 110b
Poppies: fume of p. — 221b
pleasures and p. spread — 63a
p. grow in Flanders fields — 256a
p. was nothing to it — 127a
there p., nodding — 114a
Poppy: blindly scattereth her p. — 42b
flushed print in a p. — 442b
not p., nor mandragora — 362a
not the nectarous p. — 6a
Pops: classical Monday P. — 164b
Populace: Barbarians, Philistines, P. — 9b
P. nearly (left out) — 9b
residuum..give the name of p. — 9b
where the p. rise at once — 457b
Popular: base, common and p. — 382b
it will cease to be p. — 460a
render them p. but..persecution — 418b
Popularity: even his darling p. — 56a
Population: only talked of p. — 171a
Populous city pent — 276a
Porcelain: p. of human kind — 141b
rogue in p. — 264b
Porch: p. and inlet of each sense — 267b
white p. of his home — 253b
Porches of mine ears — 331b
Pore: he wd. p. by the hour — 20a
p. upon the brook — 174b
Pores of the ocean — 393a
Pork: dreamed of tasting p. — 305a
pickled p. they loaded she — 440b
Porpentine: the fretful p. — 331a
Porpoise close behind us — 83a
Porridge: pease p. hot — 533b
the halesome p. — 59b
what p. had John Keats? — 50a
Porringer: take my little p. — 472b
Port: by p. and vest — 253a
claret..wd. be p. if it cd. — 570a
come into p. greatly — 148a
in every p. a mistress — 161a
in every p. a wife — 120b
of regal p., but faded — 274b
p. after stormy seas — 408b
p. for men — 210a
p...seen a costlier funeral — 426b
still bent to make some p. — 8b
the p. is near — 457b
there lies the p. — 439a
tho' p. shd. have age — 20a

Port (cont.)
with our sprightly p. — 324b
Portable: get hold of p. property — 123b
Portal: beyond porch and p. — 422a
fiery p. of the east — 375b
Portals: its p. are inhabited — 396a
P. are alternate Night and Day — 153a
Portance in my travel's history — 360a
Portcullis: let the p. fall — 318b
Portents: these are p. — 363b
Porter: all p. and skittles — 127a
moon shines bright on Mrs. P. — 144b
Porters: poor mechanic p. — 381b
Portia is Brutus' harlot — 338b
Portion: he wales a p. — 59b
no p. in us after — 135a
p. of a good man's life — 472a
p. of that around me — 68b
p. of the loveliness — 392b
Portioned: lands were fairly p. — 253a
Portions and parcels of the..Past — 433a
Portmanteau: it's like a p. — 85a
Portrait: p. of a dog that I know — 212a
P. of the Artist as a Young Man — 217b
Portrait-painting: two styles of p. — 124b
Ports: five p. of knowledge — 41a
p. and happy havens — 374b
p. of slumber open — 381a
Posies: thousand fragrant p. — 259a
Position: every p. must be held — 177b
Positive men..most credulous — 410a
Possess: but for you, p. the field — 96b
never once p. our soul — 8b
p. these shores with me — 117a
p. thy heart, my own — 37b
things rank..p. it merely — 330a
thou dost p. the things I seek — 398b
we may p. man's strength — 228a
Possessed: regain love once p. — 278a
Possesses: man p. nothing certainly — 75a
Possessing: too dear for my p. — 388b
wealth or rank p. — 286b
yet p. all things — 515a
Possession: a p. for the bittern — 502a
have p. of them both — 223a
lose p. of that fair — 387a
mad in pursuit, and in p. so — 389a
p. of it is intolerable — 447a
p. of this heavenly sight! — 364a
p. without obligation — 264b
virtue that p. wd. not show us — 359a
Possessions: for he had great p. — 507b
Possessor: receive thy new p. — 271a
Possessors: present p. of power — 56b
Possest: cuts off what we p. — 139b
Possibilities: to believe only p. — 41b
Possible: Christ, that it were p. — 434a
make p. things not held so — 373a
O that 'twere p. — 434a
p. you may be mistaken — 115b
probable, p. shadow of doubt — 163a
with God all things are p. — 507b
Post: against a p. when he was drunk — 382a
only at his p. when under fire — 179b
only one p. a day — 404b
p. allotted by the Gods — 433a
rode inland many a p. — 252a
Postboy: never see a dead p. — 127a
Posteriors of this day — 345a
Posterity: doing something for P. — 2b
I had not told p. this — 214b
look forward to p. — 57a
overheard the judgment of p. — 255b
pander of p. — 407b
P. do something for us — 2b
p. is a pack-horse — 128a
shd. not stand in thy p. — 348b
think of your p. — 1a
thy p. shall sway — 107b
trustees of P. — 130a
Post-chaise: driving briskly in a p. — 209b
Post-haste and romage in the land — 329b
Post-prandial cigar — 53b
Posts of the door moved — 501b
Postscript: here is yet a p. — 371b
most material in the p. — 15b
pith is in the p. — 183a
Postures: the same our p. were — 132b
Posy: home with her maiden p. — 433b
I made a p. — 187b
I pluck a p. — 48b

Pot: deep to boil like a p. 497b
flinging a p. of paint 313b
Joan doth keel the p. 345b
kettle and the earthen p. together? 520b
p. with a cot in a park 242a
put on the p., says Greedy-gut 534b
strawberries..mouth of their p. 13b
there is death in the p. 496b
the three-hooped p. 384a
who the P.? 154a
Potage: mess of p. 522b, 523a
Potash: birthrite for a mess of p.? 451a
Potations: dull and deep p. 161b
forswear thin p. 380b
Potato: bashful young p. 165b
every Irishman..p. in his head 181a
Potatoes: man..is small p. 237a
papa, p., poultry 123a
Potency: books..contain a p. 279a
their changeful p. 369a
Potent: most p. in potting 361a
p., grave, and reverend 359b
Pother o'er our heads 342b
Potion and his pill 191a
Potions: what p. have I drunk 389a
Potomac: all quiet along the P. 25a, 522a
Pots: lien among the p. 486a
p. he made hot with thorns 485b
Potsherd: joke, poor p., patch 197a
p. to scrape himself 497a
Potter: like a p.'s vessel 481b
p. and clay endure 51a
p. power over the clay 513b
who is the P. 154a
Pouch on side 326b
Pouches: coin his p. wad na bide 62a
Poultice: silence, like a p. 194a
Poultry: papa, potatoes, p. 123a
Pouncet-box..he gave his nose 376b
Pound: give thee a silver p. 77a
I owe you a thousand p. 381a
'tis for a thousand p. 108b
Pounding: hard p. this, gentlemen 573a
Pounds: about two hundred p. a year 66a
draw for a thousand p. 2b
for life, six hundred p. a year 419b
give crowns and p. 108b
handsome in three hundred p. 356a
rich with forty p. a year 168b
young Scotsman..with £300 21b
Pour: I will p. out my spirit 504a
Poureth out of the same 487a
Poverty: an age of p. 355a
any crime so shameful as p. 150a
destruction of the poor..their p. 498a
give me..neither p. nor riches 97a
in honoured p. thy voice 399b
I pay thy p., and not thy will 366a
my p., but not my will, consents 366a
p. and oysters..go together 126a
p. come as one that travelleth 498a
p. has strange bedfellows 252a
p. hunger, and dirt 196a
p. is no disgrace 404b
p.'s catching 25b
quiet mind is worse than p. 445a
she scorns our p. 384a
so much p. and excess 295b
steeped me in p. 362b
worst of crimes is p. 390b
worth by p. depressed 213b
Powder: food for p. 378b
keep yr. p. dry 570a
yr. p.'s runnin' low 287b
Powdered: still to be p. 215a
Power: all p. is a trust 130a
all things by immortal p. 442b
almighty be proved Thy p. 51b
a p. I cannot resist 223b
a p. is passing from the earth 465a
balance of p. 450a
bare, sheer, penetrating p. 9b
beauty..hath strange p. 278a
between his p. and thine 215b
breathless, p. breathe forth 323a
call our p. to account 350a
deep p. of joy 472a
depositary of p. is..unpopular 129a
doth exercise a p. 465a
drink the visionary p. 469b

Power (cont.)
drunk with sight of p. 233b
earthly p...show likest God's 354b
empire is..p. in trust 138a
endless wisdom, boundless p. 149b
enduring p., not ourselves 10a
Eternal P., not ourselves 10b
force of temporal p. 354b
gave to the man despotic p. 278a
girded about with p. 486a
greater..p...dangerous the abuse 56b
Horses and P. and War 227a
I feel all the pride of p. sink 55b
if some great P. wd. agree 202b
if there's a p. above us 1b
intoxicated with p. 57b
in p. unpleased 138a
kingdom, and the p., and the glory 505b
knowledge itself is p. 17a
lead life to sovereign p. 435b
literature seeks to communicate p. 120a
love of p...love of ourselves 183b
money has a p. above the stars 66a
mortality o'ersways their p. 388a
never lacks p. to dismiss itself 338a
never willingly abandon p. 57b
new nobility..the act of p. 15a
no hopes but from p. 58a
notions about a superior p. 417b
not pleasure, but p. 120a
of p. and of love 516b
once more the Heavenly P. 426b
one's cruelty is one's p. 105a
palter'd with Eternal God for p. 435a
period,' p., and enterprize 403a
p. belongeth unto God 485b
P. girt round with weakness 392a
p. of Armies is a visible thing 471b
p. of beauty I remember yet 140a
p. of saying things 293a
p. of the crown, almost dead 56b
p. shd. always be distrusted 214a
p. to cancel his captivity 338a
p. to do me harm 363b
p. to love or hate 259a
p. wh. erring men call Chance 267b
p. wh. stands on Privilege 26b
proud Edward's p. 62b
second death hath no p. 519b
seeds of godlike p. 5a
seek p. and to lose liberty 14b
shadow of some unseen P. 394b
something from our hands have p. 463b
some unknown P.'s employ 7a
take, who have the p. 470b
the good want p. 397a
the intellectual p. thro' words 464a
the literature of p. 120a
they that have p. to hurt 388b
tho' of ample p. to chasten 472a
tho' stripped of p. 317b
Thy P. brings all skill to naught 231b
'tis the supreme of p. 220b
titles, p. and pelf 317a
to defy P., wh. seems omnipotent 397b
to every p. a double p. 345a
unlimited p. is apt to corrupt 297a
upon the past has p. 142b
visionary p. attends the..winds 469b
wad some P. the giftie gie us 61b
Wordsworth's healing p. 6b
Powers: deem that there are p. 464b
dreams and p. 422a
fear of some divine..p. 64b
his active p. are still 430b
lay waste our p. 473a
p., that be are ordained of God 513b
p. that will work for thee 472a
principalities, nor p. 516a
rebel p. that thee array 389b
soul..subject unto the higher p. 513b
strange p. of speech 100a
tempt the frailty of our p. 369a
whose p. shed round him 465a
wise p. deny us 323a
ye gloomy P. 82a
Powerful: the p. goodness want 397a
Poyser: Mrs. P. 'has her say' 144a
Practical politics 130a
Practice: in p., tho' not in principle 11b
my p. could get along 135b

Practice (cont.)
my p. is never very absorbing 135a
P. drives me mad 533a
that in p. is sincere 306a
the p. is quiet 135b
without having good p. 212b
Practise: go p. if you please 51a
we p. to deceive 318b
we shall p. in heaven 49a
Practised what he preached 4b
Prado: walked on the P. 226b
Præmissi: not amissi, but p. 186a
Prætorian: God's pale P. 413b
P. here, P. there 319a
Prague: beautiful city of P. 306b
Prairies: from the forests and the p. 248b
Praise: all song of p. is due 401b
all things thou wdst. p. 119b
alms of thy superfluous p. 137b
ambition and the thirst of p. 111b
at the shout of p. 20a
censure of..self is oblique p. 210a
censure, scarce cd. p. 213b
chronicle as rich with p. 381b
damn with faint p. 303a
dispraised, is the most perfect p. 214b
dispraised were no small p. 277a
envy is a kind of p. 160b
expressive Silence, muse, His p. 443a
foolish face of p. 303a
for love—but P., P., P. 458b
game of interchanging p. 193b
garment of p. for the spirit 503b
girded with p. 172b
God hath no better p. 36b
guests..p. it, not the cooks 181a
His p. forth tell 224b
His p. may thither fly 187a
however we do p. ourselves 370b
I can stand a wast of p. 416b
if there be any p. 516a
in the depth be p. 288b
I p. my days for all they bring 35b
I will p. any man..will p. me 323b
I will p. Thee 188a
let us now p. famous men 234b, 521a
little dust of p. 430b
man, nor muse, can p. too much 215b
men wd. therefore p. the Lord 488b
morning and evening to p. thee 486a
named thee but to p. 178a
not be dieted with p. 219b
not unto us the p., or man 232a
of p. a mere glutton 169b
once beat high for p. 281a
only the Master shall p. us 236b
p. above heaven and earth 490b
p., and proof of manly might 408b
p., blame, love 470b
p. enough to fill th' ambition 111b
p. Father, Son, and Holy Ghost 224b
p. for skill not spent amiss 35b
p. God, from whom all blessings 224b
p. Him above, ye heavenly host 224b
p. Him, all creatures here below 224b
p. Him, all ye stars and light 224a
p. him, and magnify him 478a
p. Him, Angels in the height 224a
p. him in his Name JAH 486a
p. him upon the loud cymbals 490b
p. his humble pomp 407b
p. in its own right belong 392b
p. is satire in these sinful days 457a
p. is the best diet 404b
p. it, or blame it too much 169b
p. of it endureth for ever 489a
p. of wh. I nothing know 463b
praises from..whom all men p. 107a
p. the bridge that carried you 103b
p. the Duke of Marlboro' won 406a
p. the Lord by measure 231a
p. the Lord, O my soul 488a
p. the Lord upon earth 490b
p. the Lord with harp 483b
P. the Lord! ye heavens adore Him 224b
p. they that will times past 190a
p. to the Holiest in the height 288b
right p. and true perfection 355b
sea of the world's p. 467a
sickens at another's p. 94b
solid pudding against empty p. 298b

Praise (cont.)
some p. at morning — 300b
song of p. be sung — 304b
song of thanks and p. — 466b
succeed their fathers' p. — 178a
surely added to. to p. — 430a
swells the note of p. — 174a
that hath breath: p. the Lord — 490b
there were none to p. — 470b
they turn from P. — 44a
this is a King's best p. — 313b
'tis some p. in peers — 72a
to bury Cæsar, not to p. him — 339b
to utter all thy P. — 2a
we p. thee, O God — 558b
who Paint 'em truest P. 'em most — 1a
wits to read, and p. to give — 215b
Wonder, Love and P. — 2a
world conspires to. her — 299b
Praised: everybody p. the Duke — 406a
I p. the dead — 499a
more in him to be p. — 214b
p. him to his face — 437b
p., wept and honoured — 299b
who ne'er said, 'God be p.' — 43a
Praises: delight in thy p. — 73b
His p. there may grow — 187a
let the p. of God be — 490b
loud p. sound at heaven's — 36b
sing p. lustily unto him — 483b
sing p. unto his Name — 486a
sing ye p. with understanding — 485a
who p. everybody p. nobody — 209b
Praising: p. all alike, is p. none — 160a
p. what is lost — 322a
too near the p. of myself — 354b
Prank: daisies p. the ground — 37b
Pranks: his p. have been too broad — 334b
let heaven see the p. — 361b
Prattle: thinking his p...tedious — 376a
Pray: all together — 100a
came to scoff, remain'd to p. — 168b
first taught Art to..p. — 312b
I did not p. him to lay bare — 192a
I p. for no man — 368a
I p. you, kind sir — 531b
late and early p. — 473b
live more nearly as we p. — 224a
look you, I'll go p. — 331b
men ought always to p. — 510a
never p. more — 362a
no angels left now..to p. to — 441a
nor p. with you — 353a
one to watch, and one to p. — 2b
O p. for the peace of Jerusalem — 489b
place where men can p. — 93b
p., and sing, and tell old tales — 344a
p. for my soul — 429a
p. for you at S. Paul's — 404b
p., Sweet, for me — 191a
p. with Kit Smart — 207a
p. without ceasing — 516b
so give alms; p. so — 373b
this manner therefore p. ye — 505a
too much sense to p. — 302a
to whom the Dorians p. — 254a
two went to p.? — 115a
wash yr. hands and p. — 229b
watch and p.! — 146a
when I wd. p. and think — 351b
whene'er he went to p. — 169a
Prayed: caught at God's skirts, and p. — 47b
having p. together, we will go — 189a
p. where he did sit — 99b
Prayer: biddeth me to p. — 100a
breathe our evening p. — 451b
call'd the folk to evening p. — 221b
called the house of p. — 507b
each Paynim voice to p. — 77b
four spend in p. — 97b
godly make his p. unto thee — 483b
hear our anxious p. — 411a
he made his p...to a rag — 236a
homes of silent p. — 430a
ill-tasted, home-brewed p. — 175b
in p. the lips ne'er act — 191a
more things are wrought by p. — 429a
offices of p. and praise — 464a
oh, let the p. re-echo — 245b
p. for all who lie beneath — 227b
p. is the soul's sincere desire — 280a

Prayer (cont.)
rises from p. a better man — 264b
that same p. doth teach — 354b
the people's p. — 138a
this p. I make — 472a
thou that hearest the p. — 485b
'tis the hour of p. — 71a
when p. is of no avail — 465a
with storms of p. — 438a
Prayers: are the p. of the saints — 518b
fall to thy p. — 381a
feed on p., wh. are age his alms — 295b
for a pretence make long p. — 508b
God answers sharp..some p. — 43a
have the p. of the church — 418b
I know whose p. — 232b
knelt down with angry p. — 192a
'long p.' I said..'they say' — 6a
mention of you always in my p. — 513a
not trust it without my p. — 42a
of yr. p. one sweet sacrifice — 385b
p. are a disease of the will — 147b
p. would move me — 339a
profit by losing of our p. — 323a
short were the p. we said — 462b
their three-mile p. — 61b
where p. cross — 351b
wd. not say his p. — 534b
Prayer-time: His p. — 447b
Prayeth: p. best, who loveth best — 100a
p. well, who loveth well — 100a
Praying: insisted on people p. with him — 207a
no p., it spoils business — 291b
now might I do it..he is p. — 334b
Prays: he p. but faintly — 376a
leave..thy sister when she p. — 430a
to deny that faintly p. — 307a
wears a coronet, and p. — 113a
Preach: could na p. for thinkin' o't — 62a
I p. for ever — 113b
p. from ten till four — 164b
p. not because..say something — 456a
p. the gospel to every creature — 508b
shd. I p. a whole year — 249a
sure to p. again — 22a
Preached: flock I daily p. — 524a
he practised what he p. — 4b
I have p. to others — 514a
I p. as never sure to preach — 22a
p. peace to you — 515b
p. to death by wild curates — 404b
Preacher: a caulder p. — 61b
he, too, is no mean p. — 471b
judge not the p. — 187a
like the P. found it not — 399a
powerfulest p. — 173a
p. every Sunday put God — 457a
p.'s merit or demerit — 46a
private advantage of the p. — 56b
vanity of vanities, saith the P. — 499a
Preachers: company of the p. — 486a
p. say, Do as I say — 321a
Preaches: wife who p. — 196b
Preaching: a woman's p. — 207b
church..better than any p. — 147b
God calleth p. folly — 187a
p. down a daughter's heart — 432a
the foolishness of p. — 514a
Preamble: long p. of a tale — 89b
Precedence in the grave — 225a
Precedency between a louse..flea — 211a
Precedent: from p. to p. — 439b
p. embalm a principle — 128a, 522a
recorded for a p. — 354b
Precedents: create good p. — 14b
Precept: ending with some p. deep — 305a
example..more..than p. — 213b
impossible p., 'know thyself' — 81b
p. must be upon p. — 502a
Precepts: p. for the teacher's sake — 150b, 193b
these few p. in thy memory — 330b
Precincts of the cheerful day — 174b
Precious: deserve the p. bane — 272a
make vile things p. — 343a
p. stone set in the silver sea — 375a
so p. as the Goods they sell — 154a
so p. as the stuff they sell — 154a
that were most p. to me — 350a
'tis p. of itself — 369a

Precipice: a castle p.-encurled — 46a
Precipices rang aloud — 466a
Precise: too p. in every part — 189a
Precisely: thinking too p. — 335b
Precisian: devil turned p. — 74b, 262b
Predecessors: illustrious p. — 151a
Predestination in the stride — 231b
Predestined Evil round enmesh — 154a
Predicate: as we all p. — 25a
Predominant member — 572b
Pre-eminence: Lord hath the p. — 489a
painful p.! — 1b
Prefaces: all the p. of Dryden — 419b
Preferment: knocking at P.'s door — 8a
p. goes by letter — 359b
so I gain'd p. — 524a
Preferreth all countries before his — 291b
Preferring: in honour p. one another — 513b
Pregnant: a p. bank — 132b
Prejudice: to everybody's p. — 166b
Prejudices: bundle of p. — 238b
it p. a man so — 404b
uncorrupted with literary p. — 213a
Prelate: a religion without a p. — 18b
Prelatical: to be Presbyterial or P. — 279a
Premises: from insufficient p. — 66b
Prentice: her p. han' she tried — 60b
Preparation: dreadful note of p. — 382b
p. of the gospel of peace — 516a
profession for wh. no p. — 412b
Prepare: I go to p. a place — 511a
my shroud..O! p. it — 371a
p. ye the way of the Lord — 502b, 504b
to p. the mind of the country — 128b
Prepared to marry again — 163b
Preposterousest ends — 66a
Prerogative: dead and rotten as P. — 56b
English subject's sole p. — 141b
the first is law, the last p. — 140b
Presage: augurs mock their own p. — 388b
credit things that do p. — 341a
Presagers of my speaking breast — 387a
Presbyter: new P. is but old Priest — 278b
Presbyterial or Prelatical — 279a
Presbyterian true blue — 65a
Presbytry..not a religion for gentlemen — 87b
Prescription: conservatism discards P. — 129a
have we a p. to die — 360b
Presence: better by their p. — 144b
from whose unseen p. the leaves — 396a
His P. shall my wants supply — 2a
knowledge..wh. is the p. of it — 14a
[Napoleon's] p. on the field — 455a
not thro' his p. — 48a
p. of mind in a railway accident? — 535a
p. that disturbs me — 472a
p. that thus rose so strangely — 292b
scanter of yr. maiden p. — 331a
thy p. is the fulness of joy — 482b
to paint Thy P. — 280a
to the p. in the room — 201b
whose p. of mind was amazing — 243a
Present: act in the living P. — 248a
all p. and correct — 522a
an un-birthday p. — 85a
except the p. company — 290b
his p. and yr. pains — 381b
his p. is futurity — 180b
if this p. were the..last night? — 133a
importance only to be p. at it — 444a
no redress for the p. — 129a
nor powers, nor things p. — 513b
no time like the p. — 258a
predominate over the p. — 213a
p. in spirit — 514a
p. joys are more to flesh — 140b
take the p. time — 327b
the Bard! who p...sees — 31b
things just in the p. — 13a
things p., worst — 380a
Presents: con-found all p. wot eat! — 417a
know all men by these p. — 574a
P...endear Absents — 238b
p. the god unshorn — 189a
Preservation, and all the blessings — 479a
Preserve it as yr. chiefest treasure — 25b
Preserver: destroyer and p.; hear — 396a
President: as P. I have no eyes — 245b
P. of the Immortals — 181a

President (cont.)
rather be right than be P. 95b
Presider: fancy Shakespeare this P. 222a
Press: *dead-born from the p.* 201b
god of our idolatry, the p. 110b
I p. toward the mark 516a
liberty of the p. 217a
misused the king's p. 378b
p. it to thine own again 394b
put thy-self in p. 89b
Pressed: good measure, p. down 509a
Presses them and learns them 305a
Pressing: thou p. me to thee 457b
Press-men: Slaves of the Lamp 5a
Presst: yet, gently p. 109a
Pressures: all p. past 331b
Presume: do not p. too much 340b
let none p. to wear 353b
p. not that I am the thing 381a
p. to lay their hand upon the ark 111b
Presumed: lady, if it is to be p. 215a
Presumption in..human con-
trivances 55b
Pretence: against the undivulged p. 348a
faint meaning make p. 140b
Pretences to break known rules 116a
Pretend they ne'er so wise 277b
Pretender: but who P. is 67b
God bless..the P. 67b
Pretexts: tyrants seldom want p. 57b
Pretty: all my p. ones 350a
all the maidens p. 103b
p.! in amber to observe 303a
p. i' the Mantuan! 75b
p. witty Nell 296a
wh. is p., but I don't know 163a
Prevail: culture..perfection..p. 9b
great is truth, and shall p. 40a
shd. strive and shd. p. 289a
truth is great and shall p. 294a
whether it p. or not 294a
Prevaricate: Ralpho, thou dost p. 65a
Prevarication: die in the last dyke
of p. 56a
Prevent: p. girls from being girls 197a
p. us, O Lord 480b
so to p. the time of life 341a
Preventing: Thy special grace p. us 479b
Prevention: hide thee from p. 338b
Prey: expects his evening p. 173b
fear the birds of p. 351a
greater p. upon the less 175b
have they not divided the p. 495a
in England to take a p. 530b
roaring after their p. 488b
thou soon must be his p. 395b
to dumb Forgetfulness a p. 174b
to p. at fortune 362a
with his foot on the p. 435b
yet as p. to all 301a
you who are..the destined p. 390b
Priam: drew P.'s curtain 379b
proud as P. 476a
Priapus: Death and P. 421b
Price: abatement and low p. 369b
all those men have their p. 450a
if blood be the p. of admiralty 234b
knows the p. of everything 460a
[Nabobs] raised the p. of everything 254b
pearl of great p. 507a
raise the p. of corn 67b
raise the volume's p., a shilling 419b
set her own p. 293a
treasures still, of countless p. 223b
What P. Glory? 4a
without money and without p. 503a
wot p. Selvytion nah? 390b
Prick: if you p. us 354a
love..is a p., it is a sting 295b
to p. and sting her 331b
Pricking: p. of my thumbs 349b
p. on the plain 408b
Prickly arms afar 114a
Pricks: indexes..p. to..volumes 368b
kick against the p. 512a
Pride: all their mournful p. 475b
and spite of p. 301a
blend our pleasure or our p. 465b
burning p. and high disdain 317a
considerate p. waiting revenge 272a

Pride (cont.)
fient a p. na p. had he 63a
four not exempt from p. 241b
ha! ha! Family P. 164b
her p. of place 348b
he that is low no p. 54b
I feel all the p. of power sink 55b
I know thy p. 495b
maiden p., adieu! 385b
my high-blown p. 386a
my p. fell with my fortunes 325b
O by aspiring p. and insolence 258b
our faith, our p. 228a
passion, pain, or p. 438b
perished in his p. 470a
p. goeth before destruction 498a
p., in reasoning p., our error lies 300b
p. in their port 170a
p. of the peacock 31a
p. of the rich is all for sale 93b
p., pomp and circumstance 362a
p. ruled my will 288b
p. still is aiming at the bless'd 300b
p. that apes humility 100b, 406b
p. that licks the dust 303a
p. that pulls the country down 361a
p. that puts this country down 524b
relieve the wretched was his p. 168b
ring out false p. 431a
so sleeps the p. of former days 281a
till they decayed thro' p. 409b
'tis p., rank p., and haughtiness 1b
vain was..the sage's p.! 303b
victim of Parthenia's p.! 160a
Pridie: a Day that hath no *p.* 134a
Priest: a fiddling p. 110b
am I both p. and clerk? 376a
answerest thou the high p. so? 511b
churches built to please the p. 61a
day, a dedicated p. 442b
delicate-handed p. 433b
free me from this turbulent p. 571b
guts of the last p. 563b
hearing the holy p. 408b
Hero can be..P. 80b
inspires the pale-eyed p. 270b
I tell thee, churlish p. 336b
I will be thy p. 220b
loud prays the p. 6a
no Italian p. shall tithe 374a
old p. Peter Gilligan 474a
old P. writ large 278b
p. all shaven and shorn 534a
p. continues what..nurse began 140b
p...mere church furniture 113a
p...slave, and the liberticide 391b
p. who slew the slayer 253b
rather go with sir p. 372a
revilest thou God's high p.? 512b
still is Nature's p. 466b
than he listened to the p. 530a
the ghastly p. doth reign 253b
thou art a p. for ever 489a
the true God's p. 79a
what green altar, O mysterious p. 219b
Priestcraft: ere p. did begin 138a
Priesthood: all his p. moans 217b
a royal p. 517b
Priestley's appointment 403a
Priest-like task of pure ablution 220b
Priests: Bishops, P., and Deacons 478b
feet of thine high p. 423b
of p. we can offer a..variety 173a
p. are only men 51a
p. bear rule by their means 503b
p. bless her when she is riggish 323b
p. by the imposition 254b
p. in gold and black 243a
p., tapers, temples 299b
treen p. and golden chalices 205b
war with women nor with p. 406b
yr. neighbour are their..shamming 282b
Prig: Betsy P. 124a
called the latter 'Little P.' 146b
p., for my life, p. 373a
Primate: served the Lord P. 19a
Prime: April of her p. 387a
buried him before the p. 529b
dragons of the p. 430b
in the golden p. of..Alraschid 437a
laurel for the perfect p. 311a

Prime (cont.)
lost but once yr. p. 190b
love is crowned with the p. 327b
return the glory of yr. p.? 395a
splendour of its p. 394a
while we are in our p. 189a
Prime Minister: grand old man the P. 289b
Primeval: this is the forest p. 247a
Primrose: like thy face, pale p. 329a
p. by a river's brim 468b
p. firstborn child of Ver 23b
p. path of dalliance 330b
p. peeps beneath the thorn 169a
p. way to the everlasting bonfire 348a
rathe p. 270a
soft silken p. fading 268a
yellow p. was to him 468b
Primrose Hill and St. John's Wood 30b
Primroses: eggs..like tufts of p. 129a
pale p. 373b
p. make a capital salad 129b
their smiles, wan as p. 217b
Prince: ambition..in a p., the virtue 262b
greatest p. o' the world 324b
great P. in prison lies 132b
Hamlet is a p., out of thy star 332a
Milton's the p. of poets 71a
p. can mak a belted knight 60b
p., he rises with the pearl? 49b
P. of all the land led them on 76b
p. of darkness is a gentleman 343a, 416a
P. of the Latian name 253a
P., P.-Elective on the modern
plan 91b
send the p. a better companion! 379b
social system..of P.'s nails 122a
Spain, or any p. of Europe 145a
the news and P. of Peace 155b
The P. of Peace 501b
thro' the p. of the devils 506a
to have thy P.'s grace 409a
to my P. faithfully 247b
who made thee a p. 493b
Princedoms, Virtues, Powers 275a
Princes: blaze forth the death of p. 339a
counsels of p. 483b
else to foreign p. 385b
hangs on p.' favours 386a
p. and lords may flourish 168a
p...but the breath of kings 59b
p. have great playthings 112b
p. have persecuted me 489b
p. in all lands 484b
p. in this case..hate the traitor 116b
put not yr. trust in p. 490b
sweet aspect of p. 386a
when p. die with us! 379a
where the P. ride at noon 119a
whose merchants are p. 502a
Princess: a p. wrought it me 374a
fitting for a p. 325b
in love with one p. or another 411a
locks of six p. 225b
Principalities: against p., against
powers 516a
nor angels, nor p. 513b
Principle: an *active* P. 464b
Conservatism..shrinks from P. 129a
Englishman..does everything
on p. 391a
first human p. I wd. teach 380b
I *don't* believe in p. 250a
in practice tho' not in p. 11b
killed hisself on p. 127a
loved the p. of beauty 223b
no greatest happiness p. 80b
precedent embalms a p. 128a, 522a
p...of Natural Selection 117b
p. of the English constitution 28b
protection is not a p. 128a
subjects are rebels from p. 57a
that's a p. in life with me 391b
that sensibility of p. 57a
this p. is old, but true 118b
Principles: damn yr. p.! stick to yr.
party 128b
fights you on patriotic p. 391a
first, religious..p. 10b
he has good p. 207a
it ain't by p. nor men 250a

Principles (cont.)
not wear out [p.] in practice 22b
on the most scientific p. 295a
p. of a free constitution 162a
sincere in good p. 212b
we might our p. swaller 250a
Print: all the wickedness..is p. to
him 124a
delight me for to p. my book 191a
faith, he'll p. it 62a
I love a ballad in p. 373b
p. it as it stands 204b
p. of a man's naked foot 118b
p. wd. then surpass all 215b
's death I'll p. it 303a
seeing our names in p. 93b
see one's name in p. 72a
so many Scarers in P. 125b
'tis *devils* must p. 281a
Printed: what p. thing soever 81b
wh. the Saint had p. 286b
Printers: books by wh...p. have lost 158a
Printing: caused p. to be used 384a
Gunpowder, P...Religion 80a
invented the art of p. 81b
Prior: once was Matthew P. 305b
Priority: observe degree, p. 368b
Priscian: *breaking P.'s head* 66a, 299a
P. a little scratched 345a
Prism: especially prunes and p. 123a
Newton, with his p. 469b
Prison: a great Prince in p. lies 132b
a pretty sort of p. 25a
a p. in a p. 127a
came the hero from his p. 12b
Chillon! thy p. is a holy place 69b
chinks and breaches of our p. 57b
home in the girl's p. 391a
I was in p., and ye came unto me 508a
let's away to p. 344a
opening of the p. to them 503a
palace and a p. on each hand 69a
p. of afflicted breath 374a
stone walls do not a p. make 249b
This Lime-tree Bower my P. 101b
this p. where I live 376a
wear out, in a walled p. 344a
what is a ship but a p.? 64a
Prisoner: a p. of Jesus Christ 516b
passing on the p.'s life 351a
p. comes to meet his doom 167a
p. in his twisted gyves 365b
p. is happy, why lock him in? 391a
Prisoners: all p. and captives 479a
bringeth the p. out 486a
keeping them p. underneath 383b
p. left free to choose 391a
set my p. free 45b
wh. he p. call the sky 459b
ye p. of hope 504b
Prison-house: did grind in the p. 495a
secrets of my p. 331a
shades of the p. begin to close 466a
Prisons: improving his p. in Hell 100b
improving the p. of Hell 406b
p. are built with stones of Law 31a
to..Mahomet were p. of flesh 133b
Prithee, pretty maiden 165b
Privacy, an obscure nook for me 49b
Private: consult our p. ends 419a
dog, to gain some p. ends 169a
greatness, with p. men..a blessing 262b
heart's ease..p. men enjoy! 382b
post of honour is a p. station 1b
public good p. respects..yield 277b
public trusts to very p. uses 250a
religion..sphere of p. life 263a
secure of p. right 138b
served no p. end 302b
to serve our p. ends 94b
Privates: her p. we 332a
kings that p. have not too 382b
Privilege: all the p. I claim 11b
but the p. and pleasure 163b
death is the p. 313b
Englishman's heaven-born p. 9b
power wh. stands on P. 26b
p. o' sitting down 144b
Privileged and the People 130a
Prize: all is a p. 198a
fraught with a later p. 394a

Prize (cont.)
love the game beyond the p. 287b
many people p. it 165b
never will the p...be my award! 217b
not all that tempts..is lawful p. 173b
one receiveth the p. 514a
p. of all too precious you 388a
p. the thing ungained 368b
p. we sought is won 457b
shall win you such a p. 287a
the p., the p. secure! 287a
Timotheus yield the p. 139a
we do not run for p. 406a
what we have we p. not 359a
Prizer: precious..as in the p. 369a
Prizes: other won several p. 527a
p. not quantity of dirty lands 371a
to offer glittering p. 28b
wh. in herself she p. 104a
Prizest things that are curious 189b
Probable, possible shadow of doubt 163a
Probably Arboreal 412b
Probationer..of heaven 140b
Problem: a three-pipe p. 135a
p. must puzzle the devil 62b
solve the p. of the age 147b
Proboscis: wreathed his lithe p. 274a
Proceed *ad infinitum* 419b
Proceeding I am charged withal 360a
Proceedings interested him no more 182b
Process: such was the p. 360a
Procession: torchlight p...down yr.
throat 291a
years in long p. 138b
Proconsul: the great P. 254b
Procrastination is the thief of time 477a
Procreation: for the p. of children 481b
Proctors: prudes for p. 435b
Procuress to the Lords of Hell 430a
Prodigal: a P.'s favourite 463b
Heav'n..once was p. before 140a
yet p. of ease 138a
Prodigality: corrupt influence..p. 56a
p. of Nature 384b
Prodigies: Africa, and her p. 4b
'Prodigious!' exclaimed Dominie 319b
Produce: p. it in God's name 81b
p. of the common day 464a
P.! P.! 81b
Product: fraction of a p. 81b
Production: Tragedy is the noblest P. 2a
Profanation: in the less foul p. 351b
sin, nay, p. to keep in 189a
'twere p. of our joys 134a
Profane: coldly p. 113b
for me to p. it 399b
hence, ye p.; I hate ye 107a
p., erroneous, and vain 65b
so surpassingly p...never..before 75a
to Banbury came I, O p. one! 35a
we shd. p. the service of the dead 336b
Profaned: one word is too often p. 399b
p. the God-given strength 318a
Profess and call themselves Christians 479a
Profession: an ornament to her p. 54b
charmed me from my p. 368a
contrary to their p. 479b
debtor to his p. 14a
most ancient p. in the world 237b
only p. for wh. no preparation 412b
panted for a liberal p. 103b
Professionally he declines and falls 125b
Professions wh. are full 444a
Professors of the Dismal Science 81a
Profit: in all labour there is p. 498a
it surely was my p. 428a
mingled p. with pleasure 542b
no p. but the name 335b
no p. grows where is no pleasure 366b
p. by losing of our prayers 323a
taught me language; and my p. 367a
to whose p. 540a
what p. hath a man 499a
what p. is there in my blood 483b
what shall it p. a man 508b
Profited: what is a man p. 507a
Profitless: deem not p. 469b
Profits: little p. that an idle king 438b
oft-times nothing p. more 276a
Profligate, and thin 477b
Profound: thro' the turbulent p. 403a

Prognostics do not always prove 449b
Programme for a British Ministry 128b
Progress: all p. is based 66a
a party of p. or reform 266b
Conservatism..disavows P. 129a
history of England..p. 254a
our p. thro' the world 249a
p. depends on the unreasonable 391a
p...is..a necessity 408a
p. is not real 161b
p...is part of nature 408a
p. is the law of life 49b
p., man's distinctive mark 46a
p. of a deathless soul 133b
p...of wages to work 81a
rake's p. 440a
spoke of p. spiring round 91b
Progression: nothing in p. can rest 58a
Project gather to a head 367b
Projectile: Army shd. be a p. 177a
Projects: fitter for new p. 16a
Proletarians of the world, unite! 528b
Prologue: make a long p. 521b
what 's past is p. 367b
witty p. to a very dull Play 105a
Prologues: p. precede the piece 158b
p. to the swelling act 346a
Promethean: the right P. fire 345a
where is that P. heat 363b
Promise: boldness ill keeper ..of p. 14b
eat the p.-crammed 334a
first commandment with p. 515b
how truly the P. runs 234b
knowing yr. p. to me 434a
p. of strength and manhood 37a
p...soul of an advertisement 213a
p. such a beauteous day 387b
we have Christ's own p. 20a
who broke no p. 302b
word of p. to our ear 351a
you p. heavens free from strife 106b
Promised: I was p. on a time 409b
p. to Harry and his followers 381b
shalt be what thou art p. 346b
Promised Land: marching to the P. 20b
Promises: all God's p. cd. do 294b
his p. were, as he then was 386a
p. and piecrust 418a
p. as sweet 470b
Promontory: a sterile p. 332b
blue p. with trees 324a
I sat upon a p. 356b
stretched like a p. 275b
Promoted everybody 163b
Promotion: none..sweat but for p. 326a
p. cometh neither from the east 487a
Prompt: the foot less p. 9a
Promptings: waited for the heart's p. 144a
Pronounce: p. it faithfully 365a
spell better than they p. 446b
Pronounces lastly on each deed 269b
Proof: assume..wh. is incapable of p. 245a
give me the ocular p. 362a
lapp'd in p. 346a
no sadder p...of his own littleness 80b
sapping the p. from miracles 10a
'tis a common p. 338a
Proofs: not..by p. but signs 293b
p. of holy writ 362a
Prop: my very p. 353b
p. to our infirmity 469b
you do take the p. 355a
Propagate: learn and p. the best 9a
Propagation: was all our p. 132b
Propensities: excite my amorous p. 206b
ruined..their natural p. 58a
Propensity: usual p. of mankind 201b
Property: get hold of portable p. 123b
I'm a man of p. 165b
little snug p. 143b
love, I see, changing his p. 375a
no right to the p. of the poor 315a
p. has its duties 137b
p. is theft 565a
p., p., p. 434b
Prophecies: prognostics..not always
..p. 449b
p., they shall fail 514b
Prophecy: all p., all medicine 392b
the trumpet of a p.! 396b
the wh. observed, a man may p. 380b

Prophecy (cont.)
urn of bitter p. 394a
Prophesy: eat exceedingly, and p. 214b
we p. in part 514b
Prophesyings with accents terrible 348a
Prophet: confound the p. with the
whale 124a
Hero can be. .P. 80b
I am a p. new inspired 374b
I love a p. of the soul 147a
in the name of the P.—figs! 404a
Juxtaposition his p. 96a
man put off the p. 49a
pale-mouth'd p. 220a
p.?. .and more than a p. 506b
p. is not without honour 507a
P. of the Utterly Absurd 234a
'P.!' said I, 'thing of evil' 298b
there is a p. in Israel 496b
What-you-may-call-it is his p.! 123a
wonderful good for the P.! 230a
Prophetess?. .pretty young woman 144a
Prophetic: O my p. soul! 331b
something like p. strain 268b
Prophets: beware of false p. 505b
is Saul also among the p.? 495a
Lord's people were p. 494a
perverts the P. 72a
p. and kings have desired to see 509a
p. of Nature 470a
p. prophesy falsely 503b
the p., do they live for ever? 504b
this is the law and the p. 505b
thou that killest the p. 507b
who spake by the P. 480a
wisest p. make sure. .first 449b
Propinquity does it 451b
Propontic and the Hellespont 362b
Propontis with spray 420b
Proportion: no p. kept! 376a
some strangeness in the p. 16a
state by p. true 260b
Propose: if he do not p. ..true end of
love 132b
in passion we p. 334a
why don't the men p.? 22b
Proposed: he p. seven times 123a
Propositions of a lover 327a
Propriety: a dozen features of p. 222a
does not always evince its p. 11b
frights the isle from her p. 361a
inseparable p. of time 13b
sole p. in Paradise 274b
study first p. 75b
Prose: all that is not p. is verse 564a
I have been speaking p. 564a
I love thee in p. 305b
makes many more in p. 300a
medium for writing p. 460a
moderate weight of p. 241b
never pin up my hair with p. 105a
not verse now, only p. 45a
poets. .best writers next to. .p. 13b
p.. .bear a great deal of poetry 241b
P. can never be too truthful 451a
p. can paint evening 264b
p. run mad 303a
p., words in their best order 102b
shows that p. is verse 72a
the other harmony of p. 142a
whale's back in the sea of p. 222a
Proselytes: new French p. 140b
of Rome, Jews and p. 512a
p. of one another's trade 66a
Proserpin gathering flowers 274a
Proserpina: P. bids you awake 78b
P. for the flowers now 373a
Prospect: dull p. of a distant good 140b
every p. pleases 184a
noblest p. wh. a Scotchman. .sees 207a
so full of goodly p. 279b
T.C. in a P. of Flowers 261a
what a p. this opens 125b
within the p. of belief 346a
Prospects: all his p. brightening 168a
my p. all look blue 163a
Norway, too, has noble wild p. 207a
shining p. rise 1b
Prosper: p. thou our handy-work 487b
p. thou the work of our hands 487b

Prosper (cont.)
they shall p. that love thee 489b
Treason doth never p. 181b
Prospering: we shall march p. 48a
Prosperity: day of p. be joyful 499b
I will wish thee p. 489b
jest's p. lies in the ear 345b
man to have been in p. 90a
man who can stand p. 81a
p. doth best discover vice 14b
p. doth bewitch men 454b
p. is not without many fears 14b
p. is the blessing of the O.T. 14a
p.'s the very bond of love 373b
things wh. belong to p. 14a
Prosperous: 'tis p. to be just 251a
untoward lot, p. or adverse 465b
Prospers: turns Ashes—or it p. 152b
Prostitute: I puff the p. away 142b
Protect: I'll p. it now 284a
Protection: p. is not a principle 128a
P. is not only dead 570b
Protective of his young 443b
Protest: lady doth p. too much 334a
Protestant: a P. Flail 193a
Printing and. .P. Religion 80a
protestantism of the P. religion 55b
P.. .only go to his solicitor 129b
thy P. to be 190a
Protestantism. .is a sort of dissent 55b
Protestants: Bible. .religion of P. 94a
Protestation: absence, hear thou my p. 198a
Proteus rising from the sea 473a
Protracted: I have p. my work 207a
life p. is p. woe 214a
Proud: all the p. and mighty have 143a
all the p. shall be 299b
be not p. of those two eyes 190a
Celia, since thou art so p. 79a
death be not p. 133a
ever fair and never p. 360b
he hath scattered the p. 508b
he was very stiff and p. 85a
how apt the poor are to be p. 371b
how little are the p. 175b
if she be p., is she not sweet? 315a
I might grow p. the while 190a
I shall be very p. and great 414a
knowledge is p. 112b
know not whether I am p. 241b
mighty p.. .to have a spare bed 296b
of wh. I'm suffishuntly p. 451a
p. as peacocks 321b
p. as Priam 476a
p. in heart and mind 343a
P. Maisie is in the wood 319b
p. me no prouds 366a
p., revengeful, ambitious 333b
p. word you never spoke 241b
ridiculous than. .a p. clergyman 151a
save a p. rider on so p. a back 386b
so p., so witty, and so wise 309b
Sorrow p. to be exalted so 524a
the selfish, and the p. 113b
too p. to fight 462a
too p. to importune 175b
to war down the p. 556a
we ain't p.. .ma says it's sinful 124b
why were they p.? 218b
yes, I am p. 303b
you've done yourselves p. 446b
Prouder: never, I ween, was p. seen 19a
Proudie: 'sir!' said Mrs. P. 445b
Proud-pied April 388b
Prove: believing where we cannot p. 429b
Celia, let us p. 216a
examine me, O Lord, and p. me 483b
if thou wouldst p. me 105b
p. all things 516b
p. anything by figures 80b
Proved: error, and upon me p. 389a
I p. thee also 487a
son who p. they weren't 230a
thou, O God, hast p. us 486a
'tis too much p. 333a
to have p. most royally 337a
wh. was to be p. 541a
Proven: worthy proving can be p. 425b
Provence: home, P. and La Palie 96a
in P. called, 'La belle dame' 221b
Provender: appoint him store of p. 340b

Provender (cont.)
for nought but p. 359b
Proverb: even a p. is no p. 223a
p. and a by-word 496a
p. is much matter decocted 157b
p. is something musty 334b
this p. flashes thro' his head 426b
Proverbed with a grandsire phrase 364b
Proverbs: patch grief with p. 359a
Solomon wrote the P. 286a
Proves by thumps upon yr. back 108a
Provided: expression 'P. for' 122b
Providence: assert eternal P. 270b
behind a frowning p. 110a
even God's p. seeming estranged 196a
experience. .to mortals is a p. 175b
fear not, but trust in P. 22a
happy P. kept it 180b
leave the future to. .P. 13a
P. fashioned us holler 250a
P., foreknowledge, will 272b
'P. in it all,' said Sam 127a
p. in the fall of a sparrow 337a
P. sits up aloft 120b
P. their guide 277a
Province: all knowledge to be my p. 16b
Provinces: kissed away kingdoms
and p. 323b
obedience of distant p. 254a
Provincial: he was worse than p. 204a
Proving: nothing worthy p. can be
proven 425b
Provision: make not p. for the flesh 514a
one p. was conspicuous 315a
Provisos: O horrid p.! 105b
Provocation: what p. I have had? 303b
Provoke: do they p. me to anger? 503b
do they not p. themselves 503b
p. the years to bring the. .yoke 466b
Provoked: charity. .is not easily p. 514b
God is p. every day 482a
Provoking: it's very p. 84b
Prow: an emerging p. 8a
gain the cove with pushing p. 48b
their head the p. 139b
Prowl and prowl around 286a
Prudence is a rich, ugly, old maid 31a
Prudent: every p. part 302a
Prudes: p. for proctors 435b
strictest p. shd. know it 305b
Prune thou thy words 288b
Prunella: leather or p. 301b
Prunes: especially p. and prism 123a
Pruning-hooks: spears into p. 501a
Prussia: military domination of P. 10b
war. .national industry of P. 562b
when P. hurried to the field 318a
Prussian: French, or Turk, or P. 166a
Prussians: others may be P. 124a
Prussic acid without any water 19b
Pry: apple reddens, never p. 52b
Psalm: at my door the Hundredth P. 75b
like a p. of green days 307b
practising the hundredth p. 74b
Psalmanazar: George P. 211a
Psalmist: along the P.'s music deep 44a
death, as the P. saith, is certain 380b
sweet p. of Israel 496a
Psalms: David wrote the P. 286a
glad in him with p. 487b
p. and hymns and spiritual songs 515b
purloins the P. 72a
sonnets turned to holy p. 295b
Psaltery, dulcimer 504a
Psyche: be yr. mournful P. 219b
Ptarmigan that whitens 428b
Pub: some one take me to a p. 91b
Public: British p. in one of its. .fits 255a
British P., you who like me not 51a
consider himself as p. property 205a
convartin' p. trusts 250a
echoes back the p. voice 213b
injustice. .of service to the p. 217a
loudest complainers for the p. 56b
man assumes a p. trust 205a
noblest motive is the p. good 410a
pot of paint in the p.'s face 313b
p. be damned 447b
p. schools 'tis p. folly breeds 113a
p. will always clamour for 196b
speak in p. on the stage 149b

Public (*cont.*)
the p. business is undone	66a
the p. buys its opinions	67a
things on wh. the p. thinks long	213a
to the p. good private respects	277b
vexes p. men	439b
Publican: a fawning p.	353a
Publicans: do not even the p. the same?	505a
eateth..with p. and sinners?	506a
Publish: I'll p., right or wrong	72a
p. and be damned	455a
p. it not in..Askelon	495b
p. it to all the nation	305b
Puck: just a streak of P.	185b
Pudding: chieftain o' the p.-race	60b
in p. time came o'er	524a
make a p...as translate Epictetus	206a
Poley, p. and pie	534a
p. in his belly	377b
solid p. against empty praise	298b
Puddings: eats the pies and p. up	192b
Puff: I p. the prostitute away	142b
solemn interposing p.	108a
then pause, and p.	108a
the p. direct	400a
Puffing is of various sorts	400a
Puffs: with the sliding p.	227a
Pug: O most charming p.	155a
Pugging tooth on edge	373a
Pugilist: put in the p.	17a
Puking: infant, mewling and p.	326b
Pull: p. for the shore, sailor	315b
p. out on the trail again!	231b
rather a sudden p. up	126b
willing to p. his weight	310a
Pulling: here p. down	260b
Pulls: who p. me down?	258b
Pulp: p. so bitter	442a
savoury p. they chew	274a
Pulpit: politics and the p.	56b
p., drum ecclesiastic	64b
Pulpits: Babylonian p.	57a
p. and Sundays	187a
Pulse: a p. in the eternal mind	40a
a p. like a cannon	147b
beating p. a pathway spy	263b
feeling a woman's p.	411a
feel that p. no more	281a
his p. failing, Passion	137b
my p. like a soft drum	225b
very p. of the machine	470b
when the p. begins to throb	39a
Pulses: proved upon our p.	222b
Pumice isle in Baiae's bay	396b
Pumps: yr. p. are strange	236a
Pun: cd. make so vile a p.	120a
exhale it in a p.	239b
Punch: p. brothers! p. with care!	38b
p. in the presence of the passenjare	38b
Punctilio: dam p.	264b
Pundit or Papist	305a
Punished in the sight of men	520a
Punishment: all p. in itself is evil	27b
all p. is mischief	27b
my p. is greater than I can bear	492b
p. is to silence, not to confute	213b
the object of p. is prevention	258a
the p. fit the crime	164b
thy mind perplexed? Oh, p.	118b
Puns: slipped from politics to p.	305a
Punt: as the slow p. swings round	8a
Pupil: to be a p. now	374b
Puppets: God, whose p...are we	50a
shut up the box and the p.	440a
Puppy: drink, p., drink	459a
Puppy-dogs: snails and p. tails	534b
Purblind race of miserable men	427b
Purchase: it is all a p.	198a
strong faith shall p. me	79b
Pure: as p. as snow	333b
because my heart is p.	438a
be warm, but p.	72a
blessed are the p. in heart	505a
blest are the p. in heart	224a
chooseth the p. in heart	224a
down so warm, will pass for p.?	115a
impure what God declares p.	274b
more p., as tempted more	465a
not quite—so p. as you	67a
particularly p. young man	165b

Pure (*cont.*)
p. as the naked heavens	467b
p. mind..refuses apple dumplings	238b
P., Ornate, and Grotesque Art	17b
the real Simon P.	86b
to the p. all things are p.	239b
unto the p. all things are p.	516b
whatsoever things are p.	516a
world where all are p.	428a
Purely: I love thee p.	44a
Purer: live the p. with the other half	335a
so p. than the purest	45a
Purest: p. of human pleasures	16a
p. soul that ere was sent	79a
Purgation of such emotions	559a
Purgatory: in a sort of P. blind	217b
no other p. but a woman	23a
to P. fire thou com'st	529a
Purge: I'll p., and leave sack	379a
p. me with hyssop	485a
Purified: every creature shall be p.	258b
Puritan: grand old P. anthem	246b
he is a kind of p.	370b
P. hated bear-baiting	255b
when I saw a P.-one	35a
Purity: all p., all trial	327b
amazing brightness, p.	291b
and awful p.	149b
nought of p. display	169a
p. and place and innocence	274b
p. is the feminine..of Honour	181a
'twixt air and Angels' p.	132a
Purlieus of the Law	149a, 430b
Purple: a Man of p. cheer?	468b
a p. patch or two	541b
I never saw a P. Cow	54b
in p. nor in pall	522a
Lydia, a seller of p.	512b
p. all the ground	270a
p., prankt, with white	398a
p. with love's wound	356b
Purples: bursting into glossy p.	435a
daisies, and long p.	336a
Purpose: a p. in liquidity	39a
a time to every p.	499a
better shall my p. work on him	360b
carry p. up	36a
change to p. strong	288b
embrace the p. of God	434b
flighty p. never is o'ertook	350a
for my p. holds to sail	439a
God is working His p. out	2b
infirm of p.! give me the daggers	348a
my p. is, indeed, a horse	370b
one increasing p.	432b
passion ending, doth the p. lose	334a
p. of the things themselves	338a
pushes his prudent p.	477a
shake my fell p.	346b
supplies us with its own p.	390b
to what p. is this waste?	508a
unconquerable p. shall be realized	239b
with p. of its own	469a
Purposed: end is p. by the..gods	339a
sworn, and am stedfastly p.	489b
Purposes: aery p.	271b
p. mistook fall'n on the inventors	337a
Purse: consumption of the p.	380a
law can take a p. in open court	66b
make my fool my p.	360b
my p., my person, my..means	352b
put money in thy p.	360b
silken or in leathern p.	296b
want of friends, and empty p.	35a
who steals my p. steals trash	361b
Purses: light gains make heavy p.	16a
Pursue: bold only to p.	392a
foes p. him still	386b
my desires..e'er since p. me	369b
or knowing it, p.	142b
provokes me always to p.	293b
p. Culture in bands	456a
p. with eagerness..hope	213b
seem to fly it, it will p.	216a
Pursued: habits, well p. betimes	283a
it is you who are the p.	390b
p. conclusions infinite	325b
p. with yell and blow	98a
Pursuers: fliers and p.	254a
Pursueth: flee when no man p.	498b
Pursuing: faint, yet p.	495a

Pursuing (*cont.*)
still achieving, still p.	248a
talking, or he is p.	490a
Pursuit: mad in p.	389a
mental p. for the Building up	30b
now of that long p.	442a
p. of perfection	9b
what mad p.?	279b
Pursy: fitness of these p. times	335a
Push: p. beyond her mark	430a
p. off, and sitting well in order	439a
p. us from our stools	349a
tarry till they p. us	341b
this p. will cheer me	350b
Pusillanimity: badge of p.	385b
Puss-gentleman: a fine p.	108a
Pussy: Owl and the P.-cat	243b
p. cat, where have you been?	534a
p.'s in the well	534a
Put: p. himself..good behaviour	71a
p. on Christ	481a
that thou here seest p.	215b
Putrefaction: preserve it from p.	211b
Putteth: as he that p. it off	496a
Putty, brass, an' paint	233b
Pu-we: jug-jug, p.	286a
Puzzle: let schoolmasters p.	169b
woman..is a p. to me	439b
Pye: than shine with P.	72a
when the P. was opened	410b
Pyramid: build me a P.	236a
chief of the P. and Crocodile!	221a
star-y-pointing p.	278a
Pyramids: summit of these p.	564b
the sounding coast its p.	415a
Pyramus: death of P. and Thisby	356a
Pyrenees have ceased to exist	563b
Pyrrhic: where is the P. phalanx gone?	71a
you have the P. dance as yet	71a
Pyrrhus: P...another such victory	13b
the rugged P.	332b
Pythagoras: ah P. metempsychosis	253b
way of P.	41b
what is the opinion of P.	372a

Q

Quack, long versed in human ills	114a
Quacks..in the cure of souls	195b
Quad: always about in the Q.	522b
no one about in the q.	527b
Quadrangular: with spots q.	112b
Quagmire: lost in the q.	428a
Quails: we long for q.	141a
Quake: aspes leef she gan to q.	90a
Quaker: knaw'd a Q. feller	434b
we turned out the Q.	17a
Qualifications: what are his q.?— ONE	40b
Qualities: I am endued with such q.	145a
only two q. in the world	390b
Quality: ambition of so airy..a q.	332b
composition and fierce q.	341b
draw the inward q. after them	324a
give us a taste of yr. q.	332b
of q. and fabric more divine	470a
q. of mercy is not strain'd	354b
royal banner, and all q.	362a
the very q. of my lord	360b
true-fix'd and resting q.	339a
unbecoming..q. than to laugh	104a
Qualms: with many, many q.	286a
Quantities: such q. of sand	84a
who, for false q., was whipt	142b
Quantity: all in q., careful	427a
Quantum o' the sin	60a
Quarelets of pearl	190a
Quarles is sav'd by beauties	298b
Quarrel: beware of entrance to a q.	330b
find q. in a straw	335b
have therefore a perpetual q.	55b
in a false q...no true valour	359a
our q. with the foe	256a
q. with my bread and butter	418b
q. with the noblest grace	367b
quite forgot their q.	84a
sudden and quick in q.	326b
that hath his q. just	384a

Quarrel (*cont.*)
the justice of my q. 25*b*, 259*b*
Quarries: rough q., rocks and hills 360*a*
Quarrelled: I have q. with my wife 295*a*
Quarrelling: set them a q. 201*b*
Quarrels: head is as full of q. 365*b*
no q., murmurs, no delay 115*a*
who in q. interpose 160*b*
Quarry: yr. face my q. was 33*b*
Quarry-slave at night 53*a*
Quarter: for q. as 'e ran 235*a*
Quartered safe out 'ere 229*b*
Quarterly: 'I,' says the Q. 73*a*
nor foul like the *Q*. 183*b*
Quartos, their well-order'd ranks 113*b*
Quean: flaunting, extravagant q. 400*b*
Queen: a heart the Q. leant on 48*b*
apparent q. unveil'd 274*a*
a q., long dead, was young 49*b*
a q., with swarthy cheeks 426*b*
beggar maid shall be my q. 425*b*
British warrior q. 107*b*
cold q. of England 92*b*
dropped a tear into the Q.'s ear 29*a*
every lady wd. be q. 302*a*
every lass a q. 226*a*
Gawd save the Q. 234*a*
grace a summer q. 319*a*
he was the Q.'s luve 530*b*
home life of our own dear Q. 573*b*
I am England's q. 231*a*
I am yr. anointed Q. 145*a*
I come, my q. 324*b*
I'll q. it no inch further 373*b*
I saw the Q. of France 57*a*
I wd. not be a q. 385*b*
jealous q. of heaven 328*b*
laughing q. that caught the world's 202*a*
like the Idalian Q. 138*a*
most Gracious Q., we thee implore 525*a*
Mother, Wife and Q. 437*a*
ocean's child, and then his q. 395*b*
old soldier of the Q's. 522*a*
pass on, my Q., forgiven 428*b*
Q. and huntress, chaste and fair 214*b*
Q. asked the Dairymaid 266*b*
q. in a summer's bower 378*a*
q. of curds and cream 373*b*
Q. of Hearts, she made some tarts 83*b*, 532*b*
Q. of land and sea! 131*b*
Q. o' the May, Mother 434*b*
Q. of the Sovereign South 237*a*
Q. rose of the rosebud garden 434*a*
Q. was in a furious passion 83*a*
Q. was in her chamber 231*b*
q. was in the parlour 533*b*
regular Royal Q. 163*b*
remembrance of a weeping q. 375*b*
royal makings of a q. 386*a*
sometime sister, now our q. 329*b*
the mobled q. 332*b*
the Q. had four Maries 530*a*
the q. in a vesture of gold 484*b*
the q., my lord, is dead 350*b*
the q. of Sheba 496*a*
to London to look at the q. 534*a*
you were q. of pleasure 423*a*
Queen Anne: Q's dead 103*b*
Q...smallest..in a great place 17*b*
Queen Eleanor in the ballad 449*b*
Queen Elizabeth: no scandal about Q. 400*a*
Q. of most happy memory 492*a*
Q.'s dead 418*b*
Queen Mab hath been with you 364*b*
Queens: all yr. acts are q. 373*b*
no more housewives, but q. 314*a*
q. have died young and fair 285*b*
Q. hereafter shall be glad 137*b*
q. of higher mystery to the world 314*a*
q. you must always be 314*a*
too often idle and careless q. 314*a*
Queensberry: between me and..Q. 449*a*
Queer: ill-tempered and q. 243*b*
Queer Street is full of lodgers 125*b*
Quench: cascade q. my great love 164*a*
I q. thee, thou flaming minister 363*b*
q. all the fiery darts 516*a*
Quenched them hath given me fire 347*b*
Quest: fair rover..what thy q.? 37*a*
q. of the Golden Girl 244*a*
Questing: the q. beast 257*a*
Question: a q. not to be asked 377*b*
harm nor q. much 132*b*
hurried q. of Despair 68*a*
interrupt..with such a silly q. 411*a*
nor dare I q. with 388*a*
others abide our q. 7*b*
q. not, but live and labour 171*b*
smiling, put the q. by 426*b*
that is the q. 333*a*
that q.'s out of my part 370*a*
the q. is, had he not been 166*a*
'the q. is,' said Humpty Dumpty 85*a*
the q. [with Mr. Podsnap]..was 125*b*
the right q. to ask 314*b*
thrilling view of the surplice-q. 45*b*
Turk..struck out of the q. 81*a*
Questioning: q. is not the mode 209*a*
sweetly q. 188*b*
Questionings: obstinate q. 466*b*
Questions: all q. in the earth 46*a*
ask me no q. 171*a*
great and 'burning' q. 128*b*
I have answered three q. 82*b*
q. but the price of votes 213*b*
them that asks no q. 234*a*
Quibbles, angel and archangel join 303*b*
Quick: every maze of q. 431*a*
for some cry 'Q.' 435*b*
less q. to spring again 9*a*
q. and fresh art thou 369*b*
q., tender, virginal 294*b*
q. a growth to meet decay 189*a*
Quicken thou me in thy law 489*a*
Quickened: no man hath q. his own soul 483*a*
q. now with fire 176*b*
you hath he q. 515*b*
Quickly: behold, I come q. 520*b*
that thou doest, do q. 511*a*
'twere well it were done q. 347*a*
Quickness: too much q...to be taught 302*a*
Quicksands: soundings..q. and the rocks 222*b*
Quiddities: quips and thy q. 376*b*
Quiescence: he boasts his q. 48*a*
Quiet: all q. along the Potomac 25*a*, 522*a*
All Q. on the Western Front 569*b*
anythin' for a q. life 127*a*
beg you will let me be q. 23*b*
be q.; and go a-Angling 450*b*
be q.! be on yr. guard! 566*b*
breathless q., after all their ills 5*b*
calm Peace, and Q. 268*a*
eye made q. by the power 472*a*
fair q., have I found thee 260*b*
in q. she reposes 7*b*
Lethe's gloom, but not its q. 76*b*
men, some to q. 302*a*
my scallop-shell of q. 307*b*
q. and rest and desire 284*b*
q. to quick bosoms is a hell 68*b*
rich, q., and infamous 254*b*
study to be q. 516*b*
what may q. us 278*a*
where the world is q. 422*a*
Quietness: q. and beauty 472*a*
q. and in confidence 502*a*
q., grown sick of rest 322*b*
unravished bride of q. 219*b*
Quietus: his q. make 333*a*
Quill: his substance..thro' a q. 239*a*
the wren with little q. 357*a*
Quillets of the law 383*b*
Quills: q. upon the fretful porpentine 331*a*
tender stops of various q. 270*a*
Quinapulus: what says Q.? 370*a*
Quince: mince, and slices of q. 243*b*
Quincunx of heaven runs low 41*a*
[Quincy] cannot have forgotten 95*b*
Quinquireme of Nineveh 261*b*
Quintessence: heavenly q. they still 259*b*
what is this q. of dust? 332*b*
Quintilian: made Q. stare 278*b*
Quip modest 328*a*
Quips: q. and cranks 268*b*
q. and thy quiddities 376*b*
Quire: full-voiced q. below 268*b*
with thy q. of Saints 133*a*
Quiring to the young-eyed cherubim 355*a*
Quit: is q. for the next 380*b*
John and I are more than q. 305*b*
q. in a single kiss 36*b*
q. oh q. this mortal frame 299*a*
q., q. for shame 416*a*
q. you like men 515*a*
q. yourselves like men 495*a*
thy death well q. shall be 531*a*
Quiver: he stakes his q. 251*a*
his q. full of them 489*b*
q. and beat of the sea! 424*a*
Quivers: with emptying of q. 420*a*
Quotation: classical q. is the *parole* 210*b*
every q. contributes something 212*b*
Quotations: back'd his opinion with q. 306*a*
Quote: kill you if you q. it 54*b*
we all q. 148*b*
Quoter: first q. of it 148*b*

R

Rabbit: a r. in a snare 410*b*
r. fondles his own..face 425*b*
Rabbits is 'dogs' 535*a*
Rabble: army wd. be a base r. 56*a*
Rabboni: saith unto him, R. 511*b*
Rabelais: shake in R.' easy chair 299*b*
Race: all is r. 130*a*
a lull in the hot r. 5*a*
an idiot r. to honour lost 62*a*
another r. hath been 467*a*
appointed for my second r. 448*a*
a simple r.! 317*a*
challenge all the human r. 309*a*
Foal of an oppressed r. 102*a*
giant r. before the flood 140*a*
godly r. he ran 169*a*
God of their succeeding r. 131*b*
held the human r. in scorn 26*a*
he ran his godly r. 168*b*
he rides a r. 108*b*
hindered in running the r. 479*a*
if I have moved among my r. 415*a*
I joined the human r. 167*a*
I wish I loved the Human R. 308*a*
joy whose r. is just begun 398*a*
last of a r. in ruin 92*a*
life's r. well run 292*a*
more lovely ere his r. be run 70*a*
my r. of glory run 277*b*
no longer tolerate the r. 18*a*
oft wd. challenge me the r. 261*a*
our r. shd. not cease to labour 412*a*
place has with the r. of Saints 189*a*
r. is not to the swift 499*b*
r. is run by one and one 235*a*
r. of little odious vermin 417*b*
r. wh. is set before us 517*a*
rear my dusky r. 432*b*
run the straight r. 279*b*
sane and simple r. 429*a*
sooner will his r. be run 190*b*
still in a tree did end their r. 260*b*
they wh. run in a r. run all 514*a*
things shall be! a loftier r. 424*a*
till thou run out thy r. 278*b*
to convince the whole r. 525*a*
type of all her r. 136*b*
unequal laws unto a savage r. 438*b*
waters in their wintry r. 475*b*
who can run the r. with Death? 211*b*
yr. fainting, dispirited r. 7*b*
Races: soft in the level r. 36*a*
Rachel: R.-and-Leah is marriage 96*a*
R. weeping for her children 504*b*
seven years for R. 493*a*
Rack: not a r. behind 367*b*
one r. the name of God 258*b*
r. of a too easy chair 299*a*
r. of this tough world 344*a*
set me on the r. 362*a*
then we r. the value 359*a*
with a thought the r. dislimns 324*b*
Rackets: our r. to these balls 381*b*
Rackrent: like Sir Condy R. 255*b*
Racks, gibbets, halters 290*b*
Radcliffe also condemned bishops' boots 416*b*

Radiance: white r. of Eternity 392b
Radiancy: what r. of glory 286a
Radiant with ardour divine 7b
Radicals: few r. have good digestions 66b
Radish: like a forked r. 380b
r. and an egg 112a
Rafael: R. made a century of sonnets 49a
R. of the dear Madonnas 49b
Rafters: sheds with smoky r. 267a
Rag: bloomin' old r. over 'ead 236b
to a r. and a bone 236a
Ragamuffins: I have led my r. 379a
Rage: all Heaven in a R. 29a
ape an ancient r. 93a
hard, and full of r. 355a
heathen so furiously r. together 481b
I r., I melt 159a
repress'd their noble r. 174a
shunning civil r. 140a
swell the soul to r. 139a
void of noble r. 430a
waves of the sea . . r. horribly 487b
where the r. of the vulture 67b
with hard-favoured r. 382a
with this r. shall beauty hold 388a
Rages: battle r. loud and long 77b
r. of the ages 179b
sudden she r. 160a
Raggedness: window'd r. 343a
Rags: no scandal like r. 150a
r., and hags, and hideous wenches 100a
righteousness are as filthy r. 503b
sat in unwomanly r. 196a
wh. are the r. of time 134a
Ragtime Band 28a
Rahab and Babylon 487a
Rail: anybody else to r. at me 104b
her six young on the r. 47b
I'll r. against all the firstborn 326a
I'll r. and brawl 366b
r. on the Lord's anointed 385a
say that she r. 366b
some folks r. against other folks 151b
Rail'd on Lady Fortune 326a
Railing for railing 517b
Rails: he r., even there 353a
Railway: presence of mind in a r. accident 535a
threatened . . life with a r.-share 86a
Raiment: as r., as songs of the harp 420a
man clothed in soft r. 506b
purchased r. and forbore to pay 233b
r. of camel's hair 504b
sparkling r. bright 3b
yr. r. all red 252b
Rain: able to command the r. 296a
after the r. . . with never a stain 393a
angels of r. and lightning 396a
borne the dirt and r. 284a
but a sliding drop of r. 475a
come with the volleying r. 8b
conflicting wind and r. 342b
droppeth as the gentle r. 354b
earth soaks up the r. 106b
few small drops of r. 529a
flung it to the winds like R. 152b
former and the latter r. 479a
hath the r. a father? 497b
I dissolve it in r. 393a
in arrowy r. 263b
mist and a weeping r. 256a
mist resembles the r. 247a
my food, and summer r. 415a
neither let there be r. 495b
nor the clouds return after the r. 499b
not hail, or r., or any snow 429b
ombrifuge . . case o' r. 75a
or rivers, in the greatest r. 292b
out of the caverns of r. 393b
pack when it begins to r. 342a
r. and wind beat dark December 328b
r. cats and dogs 418b
r. into a fleece of wool 486b
r. into the little valleys 486a
r. is on our lips 406b
r. it raineth every day 372a
r. it raineth on the just 34b
r., r. and sun! 427b
r., r. go away 534b
r. set early in to-night 50a
right as r. 308b

Rain (cont.)
ripple of r. 420a
sendeth r. on the just 505a
send my roots r. 198a
sentest a gracious r. 486a
small r. down can r. 527b
soft with the drops of r. 486a
sound of abundance of r. 496a
the r. a deluge show'rs 90b
the r. is over and gone 500a
the r. is past and over 262a
the soft refreshing r. 76a
the wind and the r. 372a
thresh of the deep sea r. 231b
to cheer it after r. 110b
useful trouble of the r. 427b
wet's the r. 119a
when the dismal r. came down 403b
wh. had outwept its r. 392a
Rainbow: a r. at night 522a
a r. in the morning 522a
another hue unto the r. 374a
awful r. once in heaven 219a
behold a r. in the sky 468a
blend like the r. 281a
God loves an idle r. 192a
paint the r.'s varying hues 318b
rain and sun! a r. in the sky 427b
r. and a cuckoo's song 118a
r. comes and goes 466a
r. round about the throne 518b
r.'s glory is shed 395a
Rainbows: varying r. die away 299a
Rained: when I awoke, it r. 99a
with . . [Burke] while it r. 212a
Rainfall at morning 414b
Rains: he is dissolving in r. 393a
r. and ruins are over 420a
r. are from His dripping wings 475a
straight r. and tiger sky 263b
Rainy: a r. evening to read this 450a
dropping in a very r. day 498b
Raise: I can r. Thee 188a
more skill'd to r. the wretched 168b
not for these I r. 466b
r. me with the just 280b
r. the stone . . thou shalt find me 526a
r. up them that fall 479a
r. yr. joys and triumphs 455b
Raised: r. a mortal to the skies 139a
r. thee up under the apple tree 501a
Raiseth: cross that r. me 1a
Raising: stop r. corn . . begin r. hell 243b
Rake: a r. among scholars 255b
for thus playing the r. 282a
r.'s progress 440a
woman is at heart a r. 302a
Raleigh: Grenville, R., Drake 287b
Rally behind the Virginians 24b
Ralph: Quoth Hudibras, Friend R. 65b
Sir R. the Rover tore his hair 406b
Ralpho, thou dost prevaricate 65a
Ram: a r. caught in a thicket 493a
black r. is tupping yr. white ewe 359b
Rammers: lay their r. by 149a
Ramp up my genius 215b
Rampage: on the R., Pip 123b
Rampallion: you r.! 380a
Rampart: to the r. we hurried 462a
Ramparts: to force my r. 228b
Rams: my r. speed not 21a
to hearken than the fat of r. 495a
you with shelly horns, r.! 264a
Ran: and we r.; and they r. 256b
herd r. violently down a steep 506a
I r. it through 360a
r. about the room and roared 91b
r. a hundred years to a day 194a
r. before Ahab 496a
r. dismay'd away 355a
they r. together 511b
who r. to help me when I fell 425a
Randal: Lord R., my Son 529b
Random: shaft at r. sent 317b
things wh. I do half at r. 222a
Range with humble livers 385b
Ranger: heart of a r. 26a
Ranges: leave then thy foolish r. 448a
lost behind the R. 228b
Ranging: keep the bee from r. 77b
r. in the rain 176a

Rangoon: but he can take R. 455a
R. to Mandalay 232a
Rank: man of r. appeared 210b
man, starts from his r. 79a
marched, r. on r. 263b
nine 'undred r. an' file 234a
r. is but the guinea's stamp 60b
thirteen r. an' follow me! 229a
to r. and wealth are given 150a
unassailable holds on his r. 339a
Rankers: gentlemen-r. 229b
Ranks: even the r. of Tuscany 253b
forming in the r. of war 68b
place in the r. awaits you 306b
r. are breaking like thin clouds 252b
schoolboy rallies the r. 287b
seen in glittering r. 270b
those craven r. to see 253b
Rann and song 476b
Ransom: r. captive Israel 286b
world's r., blessed Mary's Son 375a
worth r. of gold 446a
Raphael, this Babe must eat 407b
Raphaels, Correggios 169b
Rapid: Homer . . is eminently r. 10a
Rapidly: Iser, rolling r. 76b
works done least r. 49a
Rapids are near 282b
Rapier: with unhatched r. 372a
Rapine: march through r. 571a
Rapping: some one gently r. 298a
Rapscallions: kings is mostly r. 446b
Rapt: r. one, of the godlike forehead 465b
r., twirling in thy hand 8a
Rapture: each gay turn thy r. move 300b
first fine careless r. 47a
in regenerate r. turns my face 312b
modified r.! 164b
r. of the forward view 264a
r. on the lonely shore 69b
with r.-smitten frame 77a
Raptures: high r. do infuse 449a
r. and roses of vice 421a
Rare: however r.—r. it be 119a
I think my love as r. 389a
neither rich nor r. 303a
O r. Ben Jonson 217a
rich and r. were the gems 281a
she was indeed a r. one 462a
Raree-show of Peter's successor 45b
Rarely, rarely, comest thou 398b
Rarity: alas! for the r. 195b
Rascal: muddy-mettled r. 333a
rather be called a r. 209a
you see a Whig you see a r. 212a
Rascals: lash the r. naked 363a
law's made to take care o' r. 144a
r. in all countries 210a
Rash: for my sake do not be r. 571b
I am not splenetive and r. 336b
is too r., too unadvis'd 365a
I tell thee, be not r. 70a
Rashes: green grow the r. 6ob
Raspberry: mid the gorse the r. red 441a
Rasselas, Prince of Abyssinia 213b
Rat: cat that killed the r. 534b
how now! a r.? 335a
I smell a r. 65a, 309b
like a r. without a tail 346a
like the sound of a r. 50a
poisoned r. in a hole 418a
r. of Sumatra 136a
Rate of usance 353a
Rated: in the Rialto you have r. me 353a
Rather: I had much r. 523b
Ratify and confirm the same 481a
Ratiocination: pay with r. 64b
Rations: live upon our daily r. 121b
Ratisbon: we French stormed R. 47b
Rats: land-r. and water-r. 353a
let's sing of r. 172b
mice and r. and such small deer 343a
Rattle: hearing 'em r. a little 150a
not care for the child's r. 207b
pleased with a r. 301a
r. his bones over the stones 289b
r. of a globe to play 130a
r. of new-drawn steel 228b
spoiled his new r. 84a
Rattle-note unvaried 263b
Ravage: any nose may r. 52a

Rave: not r., as do many bridegrooms 237b
Peccavimus, but r. not thus! 298a
Raved: but as I r. 188a
Ravelston: Keith of R. 131a
Raven: grim and ancient r. 298b
quoth the r., 'Nevermore' 298b
r. o'er the infected house 362b
smoothing the r. down 267a
snow on a r.'s back 366a
the r. himself is hoarse 346b
yr. locks were like the r. 61a
Ravens: r., clamorous o'er the dead 392a
r. brought him bread 496a
there were three r. 529b
you have seen the r. flock 529b
Ravenswood: laird of R. to R. shall ride 319a
Ravin: ambition, that wilt r. up 348b
Ravish: except you r. me 133a
to murder and to r. 12b
Ravished: at least wd. have r. her 151a
she did not seduce, she r. 264b
you have r. me away 223b
Ravisher: tell the r. of my soul 78a
Ravishment: divine enchanting r. 267a
tones r., or r. its sweet 217b
Raw: eat not of it r. 493b
even as a thing that is r. 485b
Ray: Eden-sweet the r. 264b
emits a brighter r. 168a
fancy's meteor r. 63a
from her towers a r. shall hover 307b
of purest r. serene 174a
r. of light Divine 86b
r. on r. split the shroud 52b
the vale with hospitable r. 169a
this busy r. Thou hast assign'd 447b
wh. dances in thy r. 294b
touch'd with an interior r. 114b
Raymond: it is Richard, it is R. 92b
Raze: desire to r. the sanctuary 351b
Razor: hew blocks with a r. 304a
Razors and carving knives 76a
Razor-strops and the lottery 295a
Razure of oblivion 352a
Reach: height my soul can r. 44a
I cannot r. it 447b
into my hands themselves do r. 260b
man's r. shd. exceed his grasp 44b
rumour..might never r. me more 111b
Reaches: beyond the r. of our souls 331a
r. of a human wit 259b
Read: a little I can read 322b
and more, he r. it 130b
authors whom they never r. 94a
do *you* r. books *through*? 208a
dozen persons who r...Plato 147b
fashion..to read in secret 34a
for aught that ever I cd. r. 356a
I can r. anything 239a
I'd sit and r. all day 223a
I, I cannot r. it 93b
I may r. at my ease 461b
I r., and sigh 187a
I r., before my eyelids dropt 426b
King George will be able to r. that 178b
let me so r. thy life 114b
Madoc will be r. 304b
man ought to r...as inclination 207a
much had he r. 4b
'none at all,' he replied, and r. on 11b
none can r. the comment 429a
none can r. the text 429a
Oh, this I have r. 235a
on bokes for to r., I me delyte 89b
r. and..understand Shakespeare 222b
r. as much as other men 191b
r. hem as they wryte 90a
r., mark, learn,..inwardly digest 479a
r. my little fable 427a
r. not to contradict 16a
r. somewhat seldomer 45a
r. Thee everywhere 224a
r. the perfect ways 386b
r. to thyself alone the songs 37b
slowly r., and dream 476b
testament..I do not mean to r. 340a
that day we r. no more 566b
they never r. 129b
they r. with joy 293a
we r. fine things 222b

Read (*cont.*)
we r. in their smiles 393b
what do you r., my lord? 332a
what..soever I cd. meet with I r. 81b
who runs may r. 224a
write and r. comes by nature 358b
ye have r., ye have heard 235b
Reader: gentle r.! you wd. find a tale 471a
last r. reads no more 194a
O r.! had you in yr. mind 471a
r. breathless, instead of content 222b
R., I married him 38b
r., look not on his picture 215b
r. that makes the good book 148b
sagacious r. of the works of God 112a
the r.'s threatened, not in vain 300a
under this stone, R., survey 149a
Readers: r. to become more indolent 170a
sense of r. uncorrupted 213a
Readest: understand thou what thou r.? 512a
Readeth: he may run that r. 504b
Readiness: r. is all 337a
the r. of doing 189b
Reading: an art of r. 130b
art of r. is to skip 178b
digressions..the soul of r. 411b
easy writing's vile hard r. 401a
for yr. writing and r. 358b
invincible love of r. 161b
I prefer r. 404a
Peace is poor r. 179b
r...device for avoiding thought 184b
r. is to the mind what exercise 410b
r. maketh a full man 16a
when I am not walking, I am r. 239a
Reads: he r. much 338a
who now r. Bolingbroke? 57a
who now r. Cowley? 303b
who often r...wish to write 114a
Ready: Abra was r. 306a
conference (maketh) a r. man 16a
my Lord, we are quite r. 393a
r. to be anything 42b
r. to be thy bride 531b
we always are r. 158b
Real: any less r. and true 390a
becomes r. till it is experienced 223a
forms more r. than living man 397a
many r. ones to encounter 170b
the r. Simon Pure 86b
Reality: in their smiles, and call r. 393b
Realize: 'at length I r.,' he said 85b
Realized: no pleasure if it were r. 266a
Realm: moves to that mysterious r. 53a
out of the R. in my petticoat 145a
this r., this England 375a
whole r. of nature mine 453b
Realms: calls up the r. of fairy 71a
happy r. of light 271a
r. and islands were as plates 325a
whatever r. to see 169b
whom there r. obey 302b
Reap: as you sow, you are like to r. 65b
in due season we shall r. 515b
neither do they r. 505b
r. where he hath sown 234b
regardeth the clouds shall not r. 499b
sow in tears: shall r. in joy 489b
sows, and he shall not r. 420b
that shall he also r. 515b
where I r. thou shdst. but glean 195b
Reaped: corn.. never shd. be r. 445a
Reaper: but after the r. the world 442b
R. whose name is Death 248a
the R. came that day 248a
Time the r. 442b
Reapers, reaping early 431b
Reaping: ever r. something new 432a
grew the more by r. 325a
reapers, r. early 431b
r. where thou hast not sown 508a
Rear: bring up the r. in heaven 41b
r. of darkness thin 268b
r. of yr. affection 330b
Rearward of a conquered woe 388b
Reason: accepted by thy r., solves for thee 46a
alike in ignorance, his r. such 301a
and that's the r. why 463a
but a woman's r. 372b

Reason (*cont.*)
but show no r. can 452a
capability and god-like r. 335b
common law..is..r. 97b
consider the r. of the case 304b
feast of r. and the flow of soul 303b
free from rhyme or r. 299a
give aught other r. why 178a
give you a r. on compulsion! 377b
have I not r. to lament 471a
have r. to think on 67b
high r., and the love of good 217b
his gentle r. so persuasive 443a
how noble in r. 332b
if it be against r. 97b
I'll tell the r. 59a
in erring r.'s spite 301a
in R.'s ear they all rejoice 2a
it's a woman's r. to say 63b
it was a theme for r. 132a
I will not R. and Compare 30b
know the r. why 182b
law, wh. is perfection of r. 97b
longer than he sees r. 376b
love repine, and r. chafe 147a
men have lost their r. 340a
mere r. is insufficient 201b
mix'd r. with pleasure 169b
neither rhyme or r. 283b
noble and most sovereign r. 333b
nothing is law that is not r. 304b
not his r., but his passions 411b
oh, the very r. why 106b
or any other r. why 3a
our r. is our law 276a
passion conquers r. still 302a
pranked in r.'s garb 267b
r. against..the r. of my love 223b
r. and the will of God 9b
r., an *ignis fatuus* of the mind 309b
R. enslaves all whose minds 391a
r. firm, the temperate will 470b
r. has moons 192a
R. in her most exalted mood 470a
r. is the life of the law 97b
R...nods a little 150b
R. still keeps its throne 150b
r. themselves out again 383b
r. thus with life 351b
r. to rule, mercy to forgive 140b
received nor rhyme nor r. 409b
rest may r. and welcome 44b
rules of r., holy messengers 187a
sanctified by r., blest by faith 470a
seven men that can render a r. 408b
so long as..human r. weak 17b
still may r. war with rhyme 216b
tell me the r., I pray 407a
that takes the r. prisoner 346a
the confidence of r. give 404a
their's not to to r. why 426a
the man who listens to R. is lost 391a
the r. no man knows 259a
to have r. for my rhyme 409b
voice of r. is stifled 58a
wants discourse of r. 330a
we r. but from what we know 300b
what..r...tells me I ought to do 55b
whimsey, not r...the female guide 173a
whom r. hath equalled 271a
words cloth'd in r.'s garb 272b
worse appear the better r. 272a
Reasonable man adapts himself 391a
Reasonableness of Jesus 10b
Reasonably be expected to do 456a
Reasoned: r. high of providence 272b
r. or acted consequentially 91a
r. out of..humanity 28b
Reasoners: most plausible r. 183b
Reasoning: fitly shall conceive thy r. 393b
r. and belief 80a
r. but to err 301a
r., self-sufficing thing 468b
the r. is the same 558b
truth by consecutive r. 222a
Reasons: five r. we shd. drink 3a
good r. must..give place to better 341a
never give yr. r. 258a
r. are as two grains 352b
r. are not like garments 120b
r. find of settled gravity 387b

Reasons (*cont.*)
r. made his mouth to water 65a
the heart has its r. 564b
with r. answer you 340a
yr. r. will certainly be wrong 258a
Rebel: R. and Atheist too 133b
up the street came the r. tread 459a
use 'em kindly, they r. 191b
Rebelled against the words of the
    Lord 488b
Rebellion: a little r. now and then 204b
bringing r. broached 383b
r. is as the sin of witchcraft 495a
r. lay in his way 378b
r. to tyrants..obedience to God 34b
rude eye of r. 374b
rum, Romanism, and r. 54b
Rebels: all that they leave of r. 93b
devil here that commonly r. 362b
hear now, ye r. 494a
r. from principle 57a
tho' r. wound thee 375a
Rebounds: hit hard, unless it r. 208b
Rebuff: welcome each r. 50b
Rebuild it on the old plan 265b
Rebuilt: Society requires to be r. 265b
Rebuke: at thy r. they flee 488a
flee at the r. of one 502a
gave me the greatest r. 257a
open r...better than secret love 498b
Rebuked: my genius is r. 348b
Recall a time of happiness 566b
Recalled: only r. by prayer 182a
r. to life 127a
words once spoke can never be r. 127b
Recalling to life..come into fashion 127a
Recapture..fine careless rapture 47a
Receipt: at the r. of custom 506a
special r. of his own 263a
we have the r. of fern-seed 377a
Receive: blessed to give than to r. 512b
r. my soul at last 455b
we r. but what we give 100b
Received: by him best r. 274a
freely ye have r. 506a
good r., the giver is forgot 104a
his own r. him not 510b
Receiver..as bad as the thief 90b
Receives: heart that watches and r. 471b
their good r. 465a
Receiv'st: r. with pleasure thine
    annoy 387a
wh. thou r. not gladly .. 387a
Receiveth: every one that asketh r. 505b
Rechabite poor Will must live 306a
Recipe: rare r. for melancholy 239b
Recked not of the life he lost 69a
Reckless: I am r. what I do 348b
poor, r., rude 136b
Reckoning: Air. A trim r.! 379a
O, weary r.! 362b
the sense of r. 383a
they little r. make 269b
unanel'd, no r. made 331b
Recognizance and pledge of love 364a
Recognize me by my face 445b
Recoil: with impetuous r. 273a
Recollect half the dishes 11a
Recollecting with tears 86a
Recollection: deep affection, and r. 306b
Recollections: those shadowy r. 466b
Recommence: winter..to r. in August 71b
Recommends: air..sweetly r. itself 347a
Recompense: Heav'n did a r...send 174b
Recompose: decomposes but to r. 44b
Reconciles: custom r. us to every-
    thing 57b
feasting r. everybody 296a
Record: no r. of reply 430a
puts a r. on the gramophone 144b
r. the mischiefs he has done 111b
weep to r., and blush 77b
Recorders: flutes and soft r. 271b
Recording: domesticate the R. Angel 413a
Records: all trivial fond r. 331b
sweet r., promises as sweet 470b
Recover: seldom or never r. 325a
thou might'st him yet r. 137b
Recreant: soldier a mere r. prove 368b
Recruity: 'arf-made r. 236b
Red: a still and awful r. 99a

Red (*cont.*)
black to r. began to turn 65b
blossom in purple and r. 434a
curtain'd with cloudy r. 270b
far flashed the r. artillery 77a
flowers whyte and r. 90a
give this cheek a little r. 302a
glowed celestial rosy r. 276a
his r. right hand 272b
in one r. burial blent 68b
making the green one r. 348a
Nature, r. in tooth and claw 430b
never blows so r. the Rose 153a
nor dim nor r. 98b
one cut short and r. 284a
pale, and hectic r. 396a
poor beggars in r. 236b
raspberry r. for the gatherer 441a
r. as a rose is she 98a
r. men scalped each other 254b
r. o'er the forest peers 224a
r. spirits and grey 349b
streaks of r. were mingled 416a
their r. it never dies 131a
thin r. line tipped with steel 315a
Tray grew very r. 192b
upon the wine when it is r. 498b
yr. own geranium's r. 46b
yr. raiment all r. 252b
Red-breast: r., sacred to the house-
    hold 443b
r. sit and sing 101a
r. whistles from a garden 222a
Reddens: where the apple r. 52b
Rede: better reck the r. 60a
recks not his own r. 330b
Redeem: he that doth r. her 377a
r. us from virtue 421b
tho' late, r. thy name 316a
Redeemed from the earth 519a
Redeemer: as our dear R. said 31b
know that my r. liveth 497a
my strength, and my r. 482b
Thou art my helper and r. 484b
to Thee, R., King 286a
Redeeming the time..days are evil 515b
Redemption: married past r. 141a
our great r. from above 270a
slavery, of my r. thence 360a
Red-legged scissor-man 192b
Red Queen sharply interrupted 85b
Red-ripe of the heart 51a
Red Sea: thro' the R. waters 286b
Redskin: Jack R. on the Quest 91b
Red-tape Talking-machine 81a
Reed: a thinking r. 564b
bruised r. shall he not break 502b
clasped a r. 394a
not as a nymph, but for a r. 260b
plucked a hollow r. 32b
r. is as the oak 329a
r. shaken with the wind? 506b
r. wh. grows nevermore again 43b
r. with the reeds in the river 43b
spring into beauty like a r. 244b
staff of this bruised r. 496b
Reeds: bring me an hundred r. 159a
down in the r. by the river 43b
feeds among the r. and rushes 248b
my worn r. broken 119b
Reef of Norman's Woe 249a
Reek o' the rotten fens 328a
Reel: r. in a drunkard..r. out a saint 94b
r. o' Tullochgorum 402b
they r. to and fro 488b
References: verify yr. r. 313a
Refined: come r. with th' accents 117a
love so much r. 134a
Refining: still went on r. 169b
Reflect on the past 425a
Reflection: r. solves the mystery 415b
r., you may come to-morrow 394b
years of r. may..give me 223a
Reflections: monkey..mortifying r. 104a
Reflex of a star 466a
Reform: every r. was once..opinion 147b
r. it altogether 334a
to innovate is not to r. 57b
Reformation: never came r. in a
    flood 381b

Reformation (*cont.*)
plotting some new r. 141b
what then did happen at the R.? 28b
Reformed that indifferently 334a
Reformers: all r. are bachelors 281a
consolations of middle-aged r. 315b
Refrain from the unholy pleasure 25b
Refrains: sends a cheerful hour, r. 278b
Refreshedst it when it was weary 486a
Refreshes in the breeze 301a
Refreshment: fill them full of r. 247a
I accept r. 164a
only place of r...cheated at 149b
Refuge: other r. have I none 455b
thou hast been our r. 487b
thy wings shall be my r. 485b
Refusal: r., thro' her skill..favour 105a
the great r. 566b
Refuse: creeds that r. 421b
nothing r. 146b
r. till the conversion of the Jews 260a
Refused: nothing to be r. 516b
r. about the age of three 93a
Refuses: whom she r., she treats still 105a
Refute: I r. it *thus* 207b
who can r. a sneer? 292a
Regained: only r. by faith 182a
yet but half-r. 396a
Regard: preferring his r. for me 419b
shd. be without r. 348b
we r. not how it goes 61b
Regarded: heard, not r. 378b
lightly r. the counsel 488b
Regardful of the embroiling sky 443b
Regardless of their doom 174b
Regards: love..mingled with r. 341b
Regenerate rapture turns my face 312b
Regent: fair r. of the Night 161a
God bless the R. 403b
moon, sweet r. 265b
r. of love rhymes 344b
Regiment: comes up the R. 228b
led his r. from behind 163a
Monstrous R. of Women 238a
our breasts for r. 259a
R. o' British Infantree 229a
the R.'s in 'ollow square 228b
Regimental in her fittings 237a
Region: in the sleepy r. stay 284a
is this the r., this the soil 271a
main r. of my song 464a
r. cloud hath mask'd him 387b
r. of thick-ribbèd ice 352a
untrodden r. of my mind 220b
where the r. Elenore? 442b
while a fair r. 468a
Regions Cæsar never knew 107b
Register: history..r. of the crimes 162a
Regress is..a downfall, or..eclipse 14b
Regret: O last r., r. can die 430b
wild with all r. 436a
Regrets: congratulatory r. 128b
wild r., and the bloody sweats 128b
Regular: brought r. and draw'd mild 124a
icily r. 433b
Regulated: moral, r. liberty 56b
Regulations Act 459b
Rehearse: better to r..he moot r. 89a
r. the Articles of thy Belief 481a
Reign: better to r. in hell 271b
long to r. over us 193a
o'er the past its undivided r. 194a
omnipotent but friendless is to r. 397a
r. in this horrible place 113a
r. of some luxurious mire 161a
r. whoever may 111a
spurn her bounded r. 213b
this is the second of our r. 132a
to r. is worth ambition 271b
undisturbed their ancient r. 131b
we may r. secure 271b
Reigned with yr. loves 145b
Reigns: Tom the Second r. 140a
Rein: moon plucked at my r. 475a
spite of curb and r. 108b
with loose r. and bloody spur 252a
Reinforcement..gain from hope 271a
Reins: try out my r. 483b
Rejected: despised and r. of men 503a
tho' his suit was r. 320a
Rejoice: again I say, R. 455b, 516a

Rejoice (*cont.*)
bones wh. thou hast broken may r. 485a
come ye before Him, and r. 224b
each to his choice, and I r. 235a
eke r. with me 307a
from age to age thou didst r. 471b
good Christian men, r. 286b
I hear thee and r. 463b
make this heart r., or ache 109b
men r. when they divide the spoil 501b
r. in the Lord always 516a
r. in the Lord, O ye righteous 483b
r., O young man, in thy youth 499b
r. with me..found my sheep 509b
r. with them that do r. 513b
r. ye dead, where'er yr. spirits 37a
we in ourselves r. 100b
wherefore r.? what conquests
    brings he 337b
Rejoiceth not in iniquity 514b
Rejoicing: toiling—r.—sorrowing 249a
Related: to whom r., or by whom
    begot 299b
Relation: a poor r...irrelevant 239a
Relations: augurs and understood r. 349a
even great men have their poor r. 121b
find for them the right r. 204b
maintain the most friendly r. 238a
squire and his r. 121b
to his friends and his r. 167a
Relative: in the r. way 527a
Relaxes: bless r. 31a
Relearn the Law 230b
Release: before I find r. 434b
our deadly forfeit shd. r. 270a
the prisoner's r. 401b
Releasing: thy worth gives thee r. 388b
Relent: echoes wh. he made r. 137b
r. his first avow'd intent 54b
Relentment: in a moist r. 42a
Relic: fair Greece! sad r. 68a
Relics: crosses, r., crucifixes 66a
other's hands these r. came 133a
r., beads, indulgences 273b
that his hallow'd r. shd. be hid 278a
unhonour'd his r. are laid 281a
with thine r. 89a
Relief: certain r. in change 203b
for this r. much thanks 329a
gave that thought r. 466a
not seek for kind r. 33a
oh! give r. 284b
the r. of man's estate 13a
Relieve the wretched was his pride 168b
Religion: against her foes R. 113b
ambition..suspended..r. 57b
amusements in England..vice..r. 404b
as if R. were intended 65a
Bible..is the r. of Protestants 94a
bringeth men's minds about to r. 15a
brings him about again to our r. 158a
brothels with bricks of R. 31a
dogma..principle of my r. 288a
England..bashfulness in..r. 2a
enough r. to make us hate 418b
great in love as in r. 107a
good man was ther of r. 88b
her r. so well with her learning 306a
honesty..either on r. or policy 314b
humanities of old r. 101b
I know of no other r. 288a
in matters of r. and matrimony 91a
in r., what damned error 354a
man's r. is the chief fact 80b
man without r. 181a
men..lost their reason in..r. 42a
men of sense..of one r. 322a
more beautiful than any r. 315b
more fierce in its r. 288a
much r. as my William likes 168a
my pollertics, like my r. 451a
my r. is to do good 292a
mystery begins, r. ends 57b
nothing is so fatal to r. 41b
not impossibilities enough in R. 41b
one r. is as true as another 64b
persecution..bad..to plant r. 41b
Philistine of..r., Luther 10b
philosophy..handmaid to r. 13a
pity r. has so seldom found 111b
(Presbytery)..not a r...gentlemen 87b

Religion (*cont.*)
Printing and the Protestant R. 80a
pure r. and undefiled 517b
pure r. breathing..laws 467b
r., as a mere sentiment 288a
r. blushing veils her..fires 299a
r. but a childish toy 259a
r., if in heavenly truths attir'd 108a
r...in a mixed company 91a
r...invade..private life 263a
r. is powerless to bestow 148b
r. is the opium of the people 526a
r. is thus not simply morality 10a
r., justice, counsel, and treasure 15a
r., knavery, and change 25b
R...of the smaller intestines 80a
r...prevalent..northern colonies 55b
r...remedy for superstition 55b
r.'s in the heart, not in..knees 205b
r. without a prelate 18b
rogues..pretend to be of a r. 291a
rum and true r. 70b
sensible men..of the same r. 129b
slovenliness is no part of r. 456a
some people talk..of r. 143b
straitest sect of pure r. 513a
such evil deeds cd. r. prompt 550a
superstition..r. of feeble minds 57b
take my r. from the priest 171a
talks loudly against r. 411b
their r. they are so uneven 118b
there is only one r. 391a
this man's r. is vain 517b
writers against r. 57b
Religious: dim r. light 268b
first, r. principles 1b
good, but not r...good 181a
hope I will be r. again 155a
if any..seem to be r. 517b
intellect in r. enquiries 288b
man is..a r. animal 57a
O ye R., discountenance 30b
r. factions are volcanoes 56b
r. persecution may shield itself 56a
suspended my r. enquiries 161b
troubled with r. doubt 93a
Relinquished one delight 467a
Relish: imaginary r. is so sweet 369a
Remain: r. with you always 480b
still wd. r. my wit 119b
things have been they r. 96b
Remained: buckets..had so long r. 99a
Remains: all that r. of her 195b
look..on love's r. 50a
what then r...we still shd. cry 17a
whatever r., *however improbable* 136a
Remark: his r. was shrewd 111a
which I wish to r. 182a
Remarkable: nothing left r. 324b
Remedies: all r. refusing 117a
will not apply new r. 15b
Remedy: a r. against sin 481b
force is not a r. 38a
found out the r. 351b
how to r. our own 238b
r. in..nature against tyranny 208a
r. is worse than the disease 15a
sharp r., but a sure one 308a
they sought the r. 327b
things without all r. 348b
Remember: can I r. if thou forget? 422b
dost thou r. Sicily? 460a
for calmness to r. 2b
haply I may r. 311a
he'll r. with advantages 383a
I can't r. how they go 75a
I do now r...small beer 380a
if I do not r. thee 490a
if thou wilt, r. 311a
I'll r. thee, Glencairn 61b
in the morning we will r. them 28b
I r. how you smiled 241b
I r., I r. 195a
I r. the way we parted 422b
I r., when I was in France 374a
I wd. r. Him 24b
Lord, r. me when thou comest 510a
names that men r. 421b
oh! still r. me 281a
O r. not the sins and offences 483a
please to r. the Fifth..November 532a

Remember (*cont.*)
plight shall be sweet to r. 554b
r. 87b
r. and be sad 311a
r., he's yr. brother 420a
r. Lot's Wife 54a, 510a
r. March, the ides of March r. 340b
r. me when I am gone 311a
r. not past years 288b
r. now thy Creator 499b
r. of this unstable world 257b
r. one man saw you, knew you 50a
r. such things were 350a
r. that thou keep holy the Sabbath 480a
r...the best of friends must part 527a
r. the Maine! 526a
r. what I must be now 375b
r. while the light lives yet 421b
still r., if you mean to please 108a
sweet pangs of it r. me 370b
that no man r. me 180b
thy branches ne'er r. 221a
till thou r. and I forget 422b
to r. for years, to r. with tears! 4a
we will r. the name of the Lord 482b
yet will I r. thee 110a
you will wake and r. 46b
Remembered: dream r. on waking 36b
in their flowing cups freshly r. 383a
I wd. have made myself r. 223b
must the r. perishing be? 119a
r. thee in my bed 485b
still r. that he once was young 4b
we in it shall be r. 383a
when we r. thee, O Sion 490a
Remembering: r. happier things 432a
r. him like anything 93a
soul, r. how she felt 469b
what she felt r. not 469b
Remembren, when it passed is 90a
Remembers: and the maid r. 414b
r. its august abodes 241a
r. me of all his gracious parts 374a
Remembrance: appear almost a r. 222b
as the r. of a guest 520a
dear r. of his dying Lord 408b
fits a king's r. 332a
praising..makes the r. dear 322a
r. fallen from heaven 420b
r. of a weeping queen 375b
r. of his holiness 483b
r. of my former love 372b
r. of things past 387b
rosemary, that's for r. 335b
seem to drown her r. 370a
Remembrancer designedly dropt 458a
Reminiscence sing 457b
Reminiscences make one feel so..sad 390b
Remission: without..blood is no r. 517a
Remnant: r. of our Spartan dead! 70b
smell my r. out 187b
Remnants: antiquities..r. of history 13a
Remorse: abandon all r. 362a
farewell r...good to me is lost 273b
r., the fatal egg by pleasure laid 110b
stop up the..passage to r. 346b
Remote: r. from towns he ran 168b
r., unfriended, melancholy 169b
where the r. Bermudas ride 260a
Re-mould it nearer..Heart's Desire 154a
Remove: digs my grave at each r. 187a
drags at each r. a..chain 169b
Removed: as far r. from God 271a
therefore shall she not be r. 484b
Remover to remove 389a
Removes: three r...as bad as a fire 157a
Remus: traffic with proud R.' sons 539a
Render: earth! r. back 70b
r. therefore to all their dues 513b
r. therefore unto Cæsar 507b
to r. with thy precepts less 73b
Rendezvous: I have a r. with Death 321a
my r. is appointed 458a
Rending: soon the r. of the tomb 20b
Renewed: wish I were r. 389a
Renewing is of love 143b
Renounce: r. the devil 481a
r. when that shall be necessary 412a
Renown: citizen of credit and r. 108a
equall'd with them in r. 273a
honour and r. ye 526a

Renown (cont.)
inheritors of unfulfilled r. 392b
land of just and old r. 439b
living, shall forfeit fair r. 317b
mighty men. . of old, men of r. 492b
no banquet, or r. 187a
r., and grace is dead 348a
set the Cause above r. 287b
sing the glorious day's r. 76b
speak no more of his r. 435a
thy worship and r. 484b
'twas I that gave thee thy r. 79a
wight of high r. 524b
Renowned: no less r. than war 278b
Rent: I widen the r. 393a
r. for Mrs. Rip Van Winkle 53a
r. the envious Casca made 340a
why? for r.! 67b
Repair: friendship in constant r. 207a
r. unto the Bell at Edmonton 108a
Repairs of the table 212a
Reparations upon mighty ruins 56b
Repartee: majority is. . best r. 130a
Repay: come again I will r. thee 509a
I will r. 513b
Repeal of. . obnoxious laws 173a
Repeat: I say to thee, do thou r. 445b
r. what he has. . often repeated 308b
Repeateth: he that r. a matter 498a
Repent: do I r. or change 271a
do truly and earnestly r. 480b
from their marble caves, r., r. 137b
I do r. it from my very soul 368a
it doth r. me 397a
leisure marry'd, they r. in haste 105a
marry'd in haste. . r. at leisure 105a
never, my love, r. 294a
nor falter, nor r. 397b
no strength to r. 378b
r. what's past 335a
r. ye; for the kingdom of heaven 504b
shd. I r. me 363b
sware, and will not r. 489a
the weak alone r. 70a
well, I'll r., and that suddenly 378b
Repentance: but sinners to r. 506a
found no place of r. 517a
give r. to her lover 170a
just persons, wh. need no r. 509b
no r. in the grave 452b
r. is the virtue of weak minds 140b
r.. . want of power to sin 141a
Winter Garment of R. fling 152b
with the morning cool r. came 320a
Repented: of her scorn the maid r. 18b
strove, and much r. 70a
Repenting: mirth, that after no r. draws 278b
wooing, wedding and r. 358a
Repents: not believe a man r. 427b
Repetitions, as the heathens do 505a
Repine: do not r., my friends 123b
Replication of yr. sounds 337b
Replied: I r., 'My Lord' 188a
Replies: something that r. 441b
Reply: how nourished? R., r. 354a
I pause for a r. 339b
loving and a fair r. 330a
no record of r. 430a
their's not to make r. 426a
the r. churlish 328a
Report: by evil r. and good r. 515a
ill r. while you live 332b
knew thee from r. divine 456b
my gossip R. 354a
r. me and my cause aright 337a
whatsoever things are of good r. 516a
who hath believed our r.? 502b
who knows how he may r. 278a
Reporters: gallery in wh. the r. sit 254a
in the R.' Gallery yonder 81a
Reports: bring me no more r. 350b
r. of my death. . exaggerated 573a
Repose: between truth and r. 148a
Christian! seek not yet r. 146a
earned a night's r. 249a
her manners had not that r. 431b
hush'd in grim r. 173b
I long for a r. 464a
leave me to r.! 173b
Love their long r. 394a

Repose (cont.)
nature gives way to in r. 347b
rolled around in dark r. 136a
shd. be his last r. 528a
weave the garlands of r. 260b
Reposes: in quiet she r. 7b
Reprehend: if I r. anything 400b
Representative: drollery called a r. government 130a
Representation: taxation and r... united 305a
Reproach: all guiltless, meet r. 362b
eternal r. of the divines 279a
receives r. of being 389a
r. of Christ greater riches 517a
r. to religion and government 295b
writing their own r. 368b
Reprobation: fall to r. 363b
Reproof valiant 328a
Reproofs from authority. . grave 14b
Reprove: r. her when she's right 419a
tho' the sager sort our deeds r. 78a
Reptile: turn myself into a r. 207a
Republic: last r. cried to God 93b
monarchy of what shd. be a r. 171b
pension list of the r. 95b
R. is a government 17b
r. of letters 1a, 170a
R.'s crowning common-sense 437a
Republican: R. form of Government 407b
surly r. 213a
Republics. . appeal to. . understanding 17b
Repudiate the repudiators 150b
Repugnances: national r. do not touch me 42a
Repulsed: love r., but it returneth! 394a
Reputation: bubble r. 326b
made himself of no r. 516a
my r., Iago, my r. 361b
purest treasure. . is spotless r. 374b
r. of five-and-twenty 141a
r., r., r. 361b
wink a r. down 419b
Reputations: fuller's earth for r. 159b
Request: ruined at our own r. 283a
the r. of his lips 482b
Requests: thou wilt grant their r. 478b
Requiem: chants the master's r. 146b
Pitt's mournful r. 317b
to sing a r., and such rest 336b
to thy high r. become a sod 220a
Require: services to do, till you r. 388a
what 'e thought 'e might r. 236b
Required with gentle sway 274a
Requisite and necessary 478a
Requite: I shd. ill r. thee 109b
Requited: both are alike r. 217a
Rere-mice: war with r. 356b
Rescue: to the r. came 288b
Resemble her to thee 449a
Resembled: had he not r. my father 347b
Resentment: get up r. towards persons 288a
Reserved: I am r. for some end 96a
r., carried about 491b
Residence: a forted r. 352a
thro' love's long r. 36a
Resign: few die and none r. 205a
I'd crowns r. to call thee mine 447a
I r. myself to thee 133a
nor, when we will, r. 7a
Resignation gently slopes 168a
Resist: damned are those who dare r. 524a
I cd. r. till I saw you 223b
r. the devil, and he will flee 517b
Resistance: passive r. of the Tol-booth 319b
refinement. . principle of r. 55b
the wrong that needs r. 18b
Resisted: know not what's r. 59a
rejoice that America has r. 297a
Resistless: r., and grand 169b
short, bright, r. course 317b
Resolute: bloody, bold, and r. 349b
Resolution: I pull in r. 351a
my r. is to die 276b
native hue of r. 333a
reach that great r. 41b
r. thus fobbed 376b
road to r. lies by doubt 307a
what r. from despair 271a
Resolutions: great and mighty r. 65a

Resolve: come, Firm R. 59a
prudent purpose to r. 477a
that we here highly r. 245b
Resolved: in doubt is once to be r. 361b
I r. to honour 526a
think I'm best r. 416a
Resolves: dror r. an' triggers 250a
r.; and re-r. 477a
Resort: all r. of mirth 268a
to wh. I most r. 439b
various bustle of r. 267a
Resource: infinite-r.-and-sagacity 237a
piano-forte is a fine r. 45a
Resources of civilization 167b
Respect: idle wind, wh. I r. not 340b
is there no r. of place 370b
means of procuring r. 209a
no r. of persons 513a
r. was mingled with surprise 316b
the r. that makes calamity 333a
Respectable: a r. Hottentot 91a
devil's most devilish when r. 43a
not one is r. or unhappy 458a
the more r. he is 390b
when was genius found r.? 43a
Respected: Peter was r. 468b
Respecter of persons 512a
Respects: my best r. to you 235a
private r. must yield 277b
Responsibility: liberty means r. 391a
Rest: and take thy r. 73b
angels sing thee to thy r. 337a
a r. for the people of God 49a
away the r. have trifled 46a
birdie, r. a little longer 438a
come, r. in this bosom 282a
find r. unto yr. souls 506b
glad, because they are at r. 488b
good r. to all 232b
he robs me of my r. 176a
ill a-brewing towards my r. 353b
in. . labour r. most sweet 86b
I will give you r. 506b
keep her from her r. 350b
might it die or r. at last! 394a
now cometh r. 292a
now she's at r. 140a
one by one crept silently to R. 153a
quietness, grown sick of r. 322b
r. a little from praise 423b
r. comes at length 150a
r. I well know where 35b
r., r. perturbed spirit 331b
r. thy weary head 247a
r. will give a shrug, and cry 419a
r. ye, brother mariners 433a
Sabbath of his r. 141b
safe lodging, and a holy r. 288b
seals up all in r. 388a
set up my everlasting r. 366b
shortly be with them that r. 277b
sky. . is their appointed r. 99a
so late take r. 489b
so may he r. 386a
so sweet to r. 365b
take r. while you may 317b
the r. be all men's 49a
the r. is silence 337a
the r., tho' fair and wise, commend 393b
there the weary be at r. 497a
they have no r. 519b
they r. not day and night 518b
to quiet r. are gone 20b
we are taking r., master 93b
were not my heart at r. 321a
we shall be with those that r. 33b
we shall r., and. . we shall need it 236b
who doth not crave for r.? 150a
will not let them r. 218a
yiue his soule good r 251a
young spirit! r. thee now! 184b
Rested the seventh day 480a
Resting: war with rhyme, r. never! 216b
Restless: for my sake r. heretofore 109a
r., unfixed in principles 138a
sea-wind's, r. night and day 421b
too r., too untamed 5b
Restlessness: round our r., His rest 43b
with repining r. 188a
Restore: I will r. to you the years 504b
let me blood, and not r. 188b

Restore (*cont.*)
time may r. us — 6b
Restraint: I were free from this r. — 105a
Rests, without a stone — 299b
Result: full r. of all — 300a
r. happiness — 122a
Resume: resumption is to r. — 88a
Resumption is to resume — 88a
Resurgam: hatchments, R. — 440a
Resurrection: attain unto the r. — 516a
came also the r. — 515a
certain hope of the R. — 481b
I am the r., and the life — 511a
in the r. they neither marry — 507b
looking for the r. of the body — 491a
Retain: jot of former love r. — 137b
Retard what we cannot repel — 212b
Retention: they lack r. — 371a
Retentive to the strength of spirit — 338a
Retinue: puffed up with this r. — 380b
Retire: r. me to my Milan — 368a
skilled to r., and in retiring — 277a
with a blush r. — 123b
Retired: add to these r. Leisure — 268a
he is r. as noontide — 469a
Retirement: r. urges sweet return — 276a
there must be no r. — 177b
Retort courteous — 328a
Retreat: a friend in my r. — 111a
I will not r. — 158b
loopholes of r. — 112a
make an honourable r. — 327a
woman's noblest station is r. — 251b
Retreats: I tell thee it never r. — 127b
Retrenchment: Peace, r., and reform — 38a
Retrograde if it does not advance — 162a
Return: departed never to r. — 63b
dust r. to the earth — 500a
gone, and never must r. — 269b
if thou r. at all in peace — 496b
let us r. to our sheep — 566b
retirement urges sweet r. — 276a
r. again, come! — 119a
r. no more to his house — 497a
r., r., O Shulamite — 500b
r., that we may look upon thee — 500b
terrible will be..day of their r. — 255b
Returned: Creator from his work r. — 275b
mother's house private r. — 277b
Returning: r. were as tedious — 349b
with vows of r. — 424b
Returns: but unexpectedly r. — 278a
Reuben: Tranter R. — 179b
Revealed: all flesh shall be r. — 502b
last look by death r. — 72b
r. them unto babes — 509a
the glory that shall be r. — 479b
Revel: go r., ye Cupids — 424b
Revelation: inspired by divine — 13a
Revelations: divine Book of R. — 81b
it ends with R. — 460b
Revellers: Bacchus and his r. — 275b
you moonshine r. — 356a
Revelry: pomp, and feast, and r. — 269a
sound of r. by night — 68a
Revels: Antony, that r. long — 339a
elves, whose midnight r. — 272a
our r. now are ended — 367b
what r. are in hand — 357b
Revenge: Cæsar's spirit,ranging for r. — 339b
capable and wide r. — 362b
her r. being nigh — 360b
I'll ne'er pursue r. — 105a
I will most horribly r. — 383b
little R. herself went down — 438a
man that studieth r. — 14a
my great r. had stomach for them — 363b
pride waiting r. — 272a
r. his foul and..unnatural murder — 331b
R. is a kind of wild justice — 14a
r. triumphs over death — 14a
spur my dull r. — 335b
stirr'd up with envy and r. — 270b
study of r., immortal hate — 271a
sweet as my r.! — 328b
sweet is r., especially to women — 70a
sweet r. grows harsh — 363b
Revenges: I will have such r. — 342b
time brings in his r. — 372a
Revenue: instead of a standing r. — 55b
no r. hast, but thy good spirits? — 334a

Revenue (*cont.*)
streams of r. gushed forth — 454a
Revenues: she bears a duke's r. — 384a
Revered: loved at home, r. abroad — 59b
Reverence: have hem in r. — 89b
more of r. in us — 429b
none so poor to do him r. — 340a
mystic r...to a true monarchy — 17a
r. is due to a child — 549b
thousand claims to r. — 437a
yet r., that angel of the world — 329a
Reverend: ah, r. sir., not I! — 46a
it is a r. thing to see — 15a
Reverent: r. eye must see a purpose — 39a
shall I..dare to be r.? — 294b
Reveries: from r. so airy — 112a
Reversion: no bright r. in the sky? — 299a
Reviewers: chorus of indolent r. — 427a
r...wd. have been poets — 102a
Reviewing: read a book before it. it — 404b
Revilest thou God's high priest? — 512b
Revivals: art is the history of r. — 78a
Revive: straight again r. — 78a
Revolt: is it a r.? — 562a
Revolts: it r. me, but I do it — 164a
leaders of r. — 52a
Revolution: No..it is a r. — 562a
r. in the hopes..of men — 470a
R., like Saturn — 565b
Revolutionists: age fatal to R. — 562b
Revolutions: nursery of future r. — 57a
r. are not made with rose-water — 252a
r. are not to be evaded — 129a
r. never go backward — 297a, 321b
Revolving: one r. moon — 138b
r. in his alter'd soul — 139a
r. labours of the year — 161a
Reward: and nothing for r. — 408b
for their r...be brought to shame — 486b
full r. and glorious fate — 79b
Lord r. him according — 516b
no r. is offered — 258a
reap his own old r. — 236b
r. of a thing well done — 148a
what r. shall be given or done — 489b
Rewarded: of thee be plenteously r. — 479b
they shall be greatly r. — 520a
Rewardest..man according to his work — 485b
Rewardeth: happy..he be that r. thee — 490a
Rewards: crimes..are their own r. — 150b
farewell, r. and fairies — 106a
neither r. nor punishments — 203b
Reynolds: prefer a gipsy by R. — 255a
[Sir Joshua R.'] own geese — 449b
when Sir Joshua R. died — 29a
Reynynge: lycke a r. ryver bee — 88a
Rhapsody of words — 335a
Rheims: Lord Archbishop of R. — 19a
Rhetoric(k): for r. he cd. not ope — 64b
ornate r. taught — 279b
r., able to contend — 16a
r. of thine eye — 344b
Rhetorician: all a r.'s rules — 64b
Rheumatic diseases do abound — 356b
Rhine: dwelleth by the castled R. — 247a
henceforth wash the river R. — 100b
king-like rolls the R. — 75b
lordly, lovely R. — 76b
river R., it is well known — 100b
Rupert of the R. — 252b
the watch on the R. — 569b
wide and winding R. — 68b
Rhinoceros, you are an ugly beast — 26a
Rhodope: brighter than..silver R. — 259a
there are no voices, O R.! — 241b
Rhodora! if the sages ask thee — 147a
Rhyme: a ruined r. — 424a
build the lofty r. — 269a
can r. themselves into..favours — 383b
cd. not get a r. for roman — 155a
free from r.'s infection — 216b
free from r.'s wrongs — 216b
have reason for my r. — 409b
in a sort of Runic r. — 298a
I r. for fun — 60b
it was neither r. nor reason — 283b
love.. hath taught me to r. — 344b
making beautiful old r. — 388b
many a mused r. — 220a

Rhyme (*cont.*)
master of unmeaning r. — 72b
Napoleon of the realms of r. — 71b
now it is r. — 283b
outlive this powerful r. — 387b
reason war with r. — 216b
received nor r. nor reason — 409b
r...invention of a barbarous age — 270b
r. is the rock — 138b
r. the rudder is of verses — 65a
shalt set love to r. — 37b
some careless r. — 244a
some free from r. — 299a
some r. a neebor's name — 60b
some r...for needfu' cash — 60b
some r. to court the clash — 60b
suffice me that my murmuring r. — 284a
tyrant r. hath so abused — 216b
was never said in r. — 221b
wove the thing to a random r. — 130b
Rhymed to death as..in Ireland — 402a
Rhymes: baker r. for his pursuit — 52a
pair their r. as Venus..her doves — 71a
r. are so scarce — 75b
ring out my mournful r. — 431a
with uncouth r...deck'd — 174b
Rhyming: Bacon of our r. crew — 241b
bondage of R. — 270b
born under a riming planet — 359a
Rhythm: whole of a new r. — 43b
Rialto: in the R. you have rated me — 353a
what news on the R.? — 353a
Rib: I another r. afford — 276b
smote him under the fifth r. — 495b
the r...made he a woman — 492a
Riband: lord in the blue r. — 55b
r. in the cap of youth — 336a
r. to stick in his coat — 48a
what this r. bound — 449a
Ribbed: r. like a drum — 171b
r. sea sand — 99a
Ribbon: blue r. of the turf — 129b
Ribbons: sleeves with r. rare — 202a
wi' r. on her breast — 530a
Ribs: God..took one of his r. — 492a
seated heart knock at my r. — 346b
under the r. of Death — 267b
Ribstone Pippin: right as a R. — 26b
Rice: beside the ungather'd r. — 248a
mist was on the r.-fields — 232a
Rich: and with thee r. — 112b
art thou r. — 118b
as easy to marry a r. woman — 440a
being r., my virtue then — 374a
call ourselves a r. nation — 314a
camel..than for a r. man — 507b
feed with the r. — 207b
grow r. in that wh. never..rust — 402a
he was r. as r. cd. be — 163b
if I were become a r. man — 27a
if thou art r., thou'rt poor — 351b
let him be r. and weary — 188a
maketh haste to be r. — 498b
making it r., and like a lily — 201b
most r., being poor — 341b
neither r. nor rare — 393a
no sin, but to be r. — 374a
poor and content is r. — 361b
poorly r., and meanly great — 316a
pride of the r. is all for sale — 93b
r. beyond the dreams of avarice — 210b, 280b
r. have no right to the..poor — 315a
r. he hath sent empty away — 508b
r. in good works — 516b
r. in saving common sense — 435a
r. in the simple worship — 219b
r. man in his castle — 3a
r. man's joke is allis funny! — 41a
r. men furnished with ability — 521a
r. men rule the law — 170a
r., not gaudy — 330b
r., quiet, and infamous — 254b
r. with forty pounds a year — 168b
r. with little store — 143a
r. with the spoils of time — 174a
seems it r. to die — 220a
something r. and strange — 367a
there was a certain r. man — 510a
they poor, I r. — 143a
we're r. in love — 62b

Rich (cont.)
wher. I grow r. 533b
wished all men as r. as he 163b
Richard: God for his R. hath 375a
good Sir R., tell us now 437b
it is R., it is Raymond 92b
more terror to the soul of R. 385a
R. doth himself appear 375b
R.'s himself again 95b
R., that sweet lovely rose 377a
Sir R. bore in hand 437b
Sir R., longing to be at 'em 523a
we came in with R. Conqueror 366b
Richardson: in one letter of R. 208a
read R. for the story 208a
works of R...pictures of high life 449b
Richer: for r. for poorer 481b
r. than all his tribe 364a
the r. still the older 66a
Riches: deceitfulness of r. 506b
for that r. where is my deserving 388b
hardly shall they that have r. 510a
Heaven had looked upon r. 418a
he heapeth up r. 484a
his best r., ignorance 168a
if r. increase, set not yr. heart 485b
infinite in a little room 259a
in her left hand r. and honour 497b
Lord, neither poverty nor r. 97a
love is mor than..gret r. 251a
rather to be chosen than great r. 498b
r. are a good handmaid 13b
r. are for spending 15b
r. have wings 112a
r. left, not got with pain 416a
r...make themselves wings 498b
since all the r. of this world 30b
that r. grow in hell 272a
thy heavy r. but a journey 351b
unsearchable r. of Christ 515b
Richest: than the r. (work) without meaning 314b
Richmond: lass of R. Hill 256b, 447a
Richmonds: six R. in the field 385b
Ricks stand grey to the sun 231b
Rid: get r. of the Dane 228b
marry thee..to be r. of thee 105a
mend it or be r. on't 348b
you are r. of a knave 358b
Riddance: die and be a r. 121b
Ridden that wan water 531a
Riddle: devil's r. is mastered 424a
dishcover the r. 85b
glory, jest, and r. of the world 301a
monster that proposed her r. 277b
r. of destiny, who can show 240a
ye had not found out my r. 495a
Riddles of death Thebes never knew 394a
Ride: all-arm'd I r. 438a
as I r., as I r. 52b
for you alone I r. the ring 172b
Haggards r. no more 410b
r. a bit of blood 196a
r. a cock-horse 533b
r. on because of the word 484b
r. on! r. on in majesty! 266b
r. on the pants triumphing 324a
r., r. together, for ever r.? 48a
r. your ways, Ellangowan 319b
riding a joy! For me, I r. 48a
squires r. slowly towards the sea 93a
they returned from the r. 527a
to r., and speak the truth 72a
up he got, in haste to r. 108b
went for a r. on a tiger 527a
when he next doth r. abroad 109a
Rider: as a steed that knows his r. 68a
r. and horse, friend, foe 68b
save a proud r. 386b
secret..between a r. and..horse 417a
the r. was lost 157a
Rides upon the storm 110a
Rideth upon the heavens 486a
Ridge of a noble down 438b
Ridicule: good action into r. 151b
r. is the best test of truth 91a
Ridiculous: made arms r. 277b
sublime and..r...related 291b
sublime to the r. 172a, 564a
Riding: my r. is better 48a
r. o'er the azure realm 173b

Riding (cont.)
r. o'er land 69b
sing, r.'s a joy 48a
Stonewall Jackson r. ahead 459a
wanton troopers r. by 261a
Ridley: be of good Comfort Master R. 242b
Rife and celebrated in the mouths 277b
Riff-raff: epithet wh. the r. apply 197a
Rifle: jest roll to yr. r. 237a
mind you keep yr. r...jus' so! 228b
r. all the breathing Spring 102b
Riflemen: form, R. form 438a
Rift: load every r. of yr. subject 223b
r. within the lute 428b
Riga: a young lady of R. 527a
Rigdum-Funnidos 79b
Rigged with curses dark 269b
Riggish: bless her when she is r. 323a
Right: all is r. as r. can be 164a
allow this aged man his r. 295b
all's right with the world 50a
as men strive for r. 44a
as much r...as pigs have to fly 83a
at yr. age, it is r. 82b
aye upheld the r. 253b
because not all was r. 114a
because r. is r., to follow r. 435b
be r. by chance 107b
Bertram's r. and Bertram's might 319b
born to set it r. 331b
but what's r. and fair 201a
doeth that wh. is lawful and r. 503b
double error sometimes sets us r. 18a
down the r. it maps a..coast 36a
every-single-one-of-them-is-r. 230a
faith that r. makes might 245a
fashion, the..rule of r. 410b
heaven still guards the r. 375a
his r. hand doth embrace me 500a
I am r. and you are r. 164a
in the r. with two or three 250b
I think it only r. 166a
Judge of all the earth do r. 493a
just and r. well managed 276a
know not whether Laws be r. 459b
make me always..do what is r. 202b
makes us r. or wrang 60a
my right there is none to dispute 113a
Nature stood recover'd of her r. 141b
no man has a r. to fix..boundary 292b
on the r. went down into the sea 98a
our country, r. or wrong 118a
public..attains to think r. 213a
rage to set things r. 44b
rather be r. than be President 95b
reprove her when she's r. 419a
r. and wrong he taught 4b
r. as a Ribstone-Pippin 26b
r. as a trivet 126a
r. as rain 308b
R. Divine of Kings..govern wrong 299a
r. man in the r. place 205a, 243a
r. of an excessive wrong 51a
r. of the ignorant man 80b
so circumspect and r. 265a
sword was servant unto r. 408b
take the pains to set me r. 241a
talks about justice and r. 233a
that r. was r...there he wd. abide 114a
that's r. 177a
tho' r. were worsted 52a
to do..great r., do..little wrong 354b
too fond of the r. 169b
whatever is, is r. 301a
when all goes r. 166b
who'll do him r. now 45b
whose life is in the r. 301b
with firmness in the r. 245b
Righteous: be not r. overmuch 499b
dwellings of the r. 489a
let me die the death of the r. 494a
never saw I the r. forsaken 484a
not come to call the r. 506a
rejoice in the Lord, O ye r. 483b
r. are bold as a lion 498b
r., let him be r. still 520b
r. man regardeth the life of his beast 498a
r. put their hand unto wickedness 489b
r. rather smite me friendly 490b

Righteous (cont.)
the r. are in the hand of God 520a
what hath the r. done 482a
Righteousness: becometh us to fulfil all r. 504b
bring me forth in the paths of r. 483a
except yr. r. exceed r. of..scribes 505a
far gone from original r. 491b
hunger and thirst after r. 505a
little hills r. unto the people 486b
living unto r. 481a
looked..for r., but behold a cry 501a
power..wh. makes for r. 10a
r. and peace have kissed 487a
r. exalteth a nation 498a
r. hath looked down from heaven 487a
r. shall go before him 487a
r. unto the King's son 486b
seek..God, and his r. 505b
shall the Sun of r. arise 504b
thy r. as clear as the light 484a
thy r. as the waves of the sea 502b
turneth away from his r. 66b
what r. really is 10b
word..of meekness, and r. 484b
worketh not the r. of God 517a
Righteousnesses are as filthy rags 503b
Righting: good for r. wrongs 246a
Rightly: when this we r. know 29b
Rights: lies in his r. of a man! 44b
Palladium of all the..r. 217a
property has..duties..well as r. 137b
Rigol: this golden r. 381a
Rigorous: move on a r. line 7a
Rigour: my r. relents 55b
r. of the game 239a
Riled: no sense in gittin' r.! 182a
Rill: cool Siloam's shady r. 184a
Rills: gardens bright with sinuous r. 101a
Rim: utmost purple r. 426b
Rimmon: in the house of R. 496b
Rind: burnished with golden r. 274a
how shall taste the r.? 442a
pulp they chew, and in the r. 274a
sweet as the r. was the core is 421a
Ring: bright gold r. on her hand 281a
bright is the r. of words 414b
curfew must not r. to-night 444b
for you alone I ride the r. 172b
he rid at the r. 530b
kneel and draw the chalky r. 113a
like that feat in the r. 195a
only pretty r. time 327b
rare gold r. of verse 5b
r., happy bells, across the snow 431a
r. in the Christ that is to be 431a
r. of pure and endless light 448b
r. out, wild bells, to the wild sky 431a
r. that he had of yr. daughter 354a
round both..shires they r. them 199a
sleeps on his luminous r. 435b
the r. so worn, as you behold 114a
they now r. the bells 450a
this R. given and received 481b
with this R. I thee wed 481b
Ringdove's neck from changing 77b
Ringed round with a flame 421a
Ringlets: green sour r. make 367b
male r. or feminine gold 421b
Ringlet-snake: Fury's r. 433a
Rings: chain of countless r. 146b
his hands are as gold r. 500b
oft, as in airy r. they skim 304a
r. on her fingers 533b
wearers of r. and chains 241a
when the right man r. them 414b
Rio: rolling down to R. 230b
Riot: fierce blaze of r. 374b
spent waves' r. 422a
Riou: gallant good R. 76b
Rip Van Winkle: rent for Mrs. R. 53a
Ripe: a r. and good one 386b
cherry r. 188b
from hour to hour, we r. and r. 326a
what shelter to grow r. 7a
Riper: amuse his r. stage 301a
Such as are of R. Years 481a
Ripeness: certain r. in intellect 222b
r. is all 344a
Ripes: ventiferous r. 194b
Ripped: mother's womb untimely r. 351a

Ripples down a sunny river 241a
Rise: arts that caused himself to r. 303a
but now they r. again 349a
catch the manners..as they r. 300b
created half to r. 301a
dead men r. up never 422a
half of her shd. r. herself 180a
held we fall to r. 52a
i' the dark to r. by. And I r. 51b
off dull sloth, and joyful r. 224b
of hope to r., or fear to fall 473b
raise the wretched than to r. 168b
r. and trip away 241b
R.! for the day is passing 306b
r., honest Muse! 302a
r...like feathered Mercury 378b
r., take up thy bed, and walk 510b
r. up at the voice of the bird 499b
r. up, My love 262a, 500a
run, r., rest with thee 187a
seen those dead men r. 99a
stoop to r. 262b
that we love we r. betimes 324a
twilight that doth not r. nor set 311a
when afar you r. 50a
woe unto them that r. up 501a
wd. thrive must r. at five 532b
ye haste to r. up early 489b
Risen: Christ, the Lord, is r. to-day 455b
we are r., and stand upright 482b
Risen: hoo-ray and up she r. 527b
Rising: all r. to great place 14b
assisted the sun..in his r. 444a
how oft hereafter r. 154a
in his r. seem'd a pillar 272b
r. and cawing at the gun's 357a
r. with Aurora's light 419b
Risk it on one turn 230a
Rite: no noble r. 336a
r. of lust and blood 391b
Rites: for sacred r. unfit 401b
hour when r. unholy 77b
Rival in the light of day 473a
Rivalry: with the dead there is no r. 255a
Rivals: and r. rail 213a
dear to maidens..their r. dead 293a
r. are the worst! 450a
River: above the r. Wey it is 232b
a living r. by the door 414b
Alph, the sacred r. 101a
among the r. sallows 221b
away, you rolling r. 525a
beside the r. make for you 39b
breast of the R. of Time 6a
down in the reeds by the r. 43b
down upon de Swannee R. 156a
dragon-fly on the r. 43b
fame is like a r. 16b
flowing like a crystal r. 435b
ford o' Kabul r. 229a
fountains mingle with the r. 395b
from the r. winding clearly 431b
fruitful r. in the eye 330a
grassy harvest of the r.-fields 8b
grey-green, greasy Limpopo R. 237a
laugh as he sits by the r. 43b
let the great r. take me 436b
like the snow falls in the r. 63a
Love for ever run like a r. 74a
lycke a reynynge r. bee 88a
majestic R. floated on 8a
on a tree by a r. 165a
on either side the r. lie 431b
one more r. to cross 526a
Pentridge by the r. 21a
primrose by a r.'s brim 468b
reed with the reeds in the r. 43b
ripples down a sunny r. 241a
r. at my garden's end 419b
r. comes me cranking in 378a
r. glideth at his own sweet will 472b
r. Weser, deep and wide 50a
runs not a r. by my palace? 440a
sailed on a r. of crystal light 151a
she's fading down the r. 287b
shewed me a pure r. of water 520a
shines over city and r. 435a
spake to the noble r. 253b
there is a r. in Macedon 383b
there's the r. up an' brimmin' 229a
the rush of the r. 25a

River (cont.)
thy peace been as a r. 502b
'tirra-lirra', by the r. 431b
to the r.'s trembling edge 398a
weariest r. winds..safe to sea 422a
we gather at the r. 315b
white flows the r. 414b
Rivers: any discourse of r. 450b
as the r. in the south 489b
being suffered, r. cannot quench 384b
brooks and r. wide 269a
by shallow r. to whose falls 259a
noise of winds and of many r. 420a
r., in the greatest rain 292b
sendeth the springs into the r. 488a
the r. run into the sea 499a
washed by the r. 40a
Rivets: busy hammers closing r. up 382b
Rivulets: place where r. dance 471b
r. hurrying thro' the lawn 437a
Road: 'ammer along the 'ard 'igh r. 535a
and the r. before me 414a
and the r. below me 414a
at the other end of the r. 262a
beset the R. I was to wander in 154a
does the r. wind uphill 311a
drive the r. and bridge the ford 234b
endless r. you tread 199b
force and r. of casualty 353b
free as the r. 188a
golden R. to Samarkand 154b
horse misus'd upon the r. 29a
I like..the r. you are travelling 405a
I'll tak' the high r. 525b
in the moon the long r. lies 199a
I take to the open r. 458a
life may be a pleasant r. 306a
life's r., so dim and dirty 70a
load has tipped off in the r. 233a
long time on the r. 127b
my mistress still the open r. 414a
my r. leads me forth 262a
no expeditious r. to pack 442a
no r. or ready way to virtue 41b
no 'royal r.' to geometry 573b
on a lonesome r. doth walk 99b
one r. leads to London 262a
on the r., the lonely r. 181b
on the r. to Mandalay 232a
r. lies long and straight 413a
r. that leads him to England 207a
r. to bring us, daily, nearer God 224a
R. to fair Elf-land 528a
r. was a ribbon of moonlight 290a
r. went up, the r. went down 25b
rolling English r. 93a
rough is the r. 78b
rough r. easy walking 199b
sad r. lies so clear 294a
shut the r. thro' the woods 236a
the r. is rough and long 38b
the world to be a grassy r. 476a
they are upon the r. 108b
to be out on the r. 262a
use the ocean as their r. 449a
who passes by this r. so late? 528a
Road-rail, pig-lead 261b
Roads: most r. lead men homewards 262a
Roadway: stand on the r. 475b
Roam: dunce that has been sent to r. 110b
ever let the fancy r. 218a
r., whatever realm to see 169b
the other far doth r. 134a
who soar, but never r. 471a
Roaming: R. in the Gloamin' 242b
r. with a hungry heart 438b
where are you r.? 370b
Roar: bark, bellow, and r. 29b
hear the waves r. 6a
I hear the lion r. 110a
I will r., that I will do 356b
lion give a grievous r. 309a
long, withdrawing r. 5a
r...as any sucking-dove 356b
r., as if of earthly fire 218a
r. of the Milky Way 235a
r. their ribs out 167a
swinging slow with sullen r. 268a
Roared: ran about the room and r. 91b
well r., Lion 357b

Roarers: what care these r. 367a
Roaring: r...lions of the Daily Telegraph 9a
r. in the wind 470a
Roast: but to r. their eggs 15b
no politics in boiled and r. 405a
r. me in sulphur 364a
r. with fire, and unleavened bread 493b
strove to rule the r. 306a
Rob: r. a lady..by way of marriage 151b
r. me, but bind me not 133b
Robbed: he's not r. at all 362a
he that is r. not wanting 362a
r. that smiles steals something 360a
'ye have r.', said he 287b
Robber: Barabbas was a r. 511b
Robbery: in scandal as in r. 90b
Robbing: forbids the r. of a foe 94b
Robe: in a r. of clouds 73a
intertissued r. of gold 382b
nor the judge's r. 351b
robb'd me of my R. of Honour 154a
r. of mine..change my disposition 373b
Robert Browning, you writer of plays 48a
Robert Emmet and Wolfe Tone 474b
Robes: arrayed in white r. 519a
garland and singing r. about him 279a
have washed their r...in the blood 519a
his flaming r. streamed out 218a
in all his r. pontifical exprest 442b
in r. of light arrayed 184a
r. loosely flowing 215a
than r. riche, or fithele 88b
when all her r. are on 525a
[Robespierre] sea-green Incorruptible 80b
Robin: Auld R. Gray 20b
bonny sweet R. 336a
call for the r. redbreast 454b
gay R. is seen no more 26a
lilacs where the r. built 195a
little English r. 470a
no r. ever on the deep 119b
R. Redbreast in a Cage 29a
R.'s not near 224b
sweet R. sits in the bush 319b
what will poor r. do then 533a
where the gardener R., day by day 109b
Robin Adair 224b
Robin Hood: here lies bold R. 530b
is R. asleep? 290a
Robinson: John P. R. he 250a
Robinson Crusoe: except..R. 212a
Robin Crusoe 118b
Robs me of that wh. not enriches him 361a
Robustious periwig-pated fellow 333b
Rochefoucauld: good-bye to R. 145a
Rochets shall go down 307a
Rock: all on a r. reclin'd 161a
a pendant r. 324a
for a r. of offence 501b
impregnable r. of Scripture 167b
it is the Inchcape R.! 406b
R. of ages, cleft for me 445a
r. of immortality 38b
r. of the national resources 454a
rhyme is the r. 138b
set my feet upon the r. 484a
shadow of a great r. 502a
she ran upon no r. 111a
then they rested on a r. 84b
the tall r., the mountain 472a
think that you are upon a r. 329a
this r. shall fly 316b
they knew the perilous r. 406b
tree striking r. at the root 263a
upon this r. I will build 507a
water out of this r. 494a
Rocked: he neither shall be r. 522a
r. in the cradle of the deep 461a
she r. it, and rated it 143b
Rocket: he rose like a r. 291b
Rocking: cradle endlessly r. 457b
r. a grown man 58a
Rocking-horse..thought it Pegasus 220b
Rocks: between the ascetic r. 264b
change from r. to roses 305a
lights..twinkle from the r. 439a
mid these dancing r. 101a
mountains and r., fall on us 519a
on crystal r. ye rove 31b

Rocks (cont.)
paled in with r. unscaleable | 328b
rifted r...leads to Hell | 267b
r., and stones, and trees | 463a
r., caves, lakes, fens | 272b
r. for the conies | 488b
r. on the mould | 522a
seas, .white, when r. are near | 454b
she is older than the r. | 293a
valleys and r. never heard | 113a
walled round with r. | 421b
Rod: Aaron's r. | 493b
a creed is r. | 422a
all humbled kiss the r. | 372b
a r. out of the stem of Jesse | 501b
a r. to check the erring | 463b
bruise them with a r. of iron | 481b
every r...of empire. .crooked | 17a
eyeball owns the mystic r. | 52a
honey with the end of the r. | 495a
r. and thy staff comfort me | 483a
r. of the ungodly cometh not | 489b
r. produces. .effect wh. terminates | 206a
spareth his r. hateth his son | 498a
throw away Thy r. | 188a
thy r. of incantation | 161a
Rode: full royally he r. | 412a
I r. upon the Down | 33b
nor second he, that r. sublime | 175a
r. all that day and all night | 257b
r. between the barley-sheaves | 431b
r. the six hundred | 426a
she r. forth, clothed. .with chastity | 427a
steed, wh. he r. at full speed | 243a
Roderick Dhu | 316b
Rods: bleeding from the Roman r. | 107b
Roe: and following the r. | 62a
be thou like to a r. | 501a
Roebuck: he is a gentle r. | 475a
Roes: breasts are like two young r. | 500b
Roger's false flattering tongue | 239b
Rogue: a dainty r. in porcelain | 264b
bewitched with the r.'s company | 377a
busy and insinuating r. | 363a
fiddler, and consequently a r. | 418a
has he not a r.'s face? | 104b
r. and peasant slave | 332b
r. is married to a whore | 234a
Rogues: hear poor r. talk of court | 344a
r. in buckram suits | 377b
r. obey you well | 191b
r. that pretend to. .religion | 291a
you dissentious r. | 328a
Roland to the dark tower came | 343a
Roll: all away began to r. | 30a
few more years shall r. | 33b
never you mind! r. on! | 163a
not in the r. of common men | 378a
r. dem bones | 191a
r. forth, my song | 258a
r. of the world eastward. .palpable | 180b
r. on, thou ball | 163a
r. on, thou deep. .blue ocean | 69b
r. up and down our ships | 134b
r. up that map | 297b
r. upon yr. bed | 284a
Roller, pitch, and stumps | 242a
Rolling: came r. up ragged and brown | 226b
r. down the Ratcliffe Road | 227a
r. down to Rio | 230b
Rolls: dig for buttered r. | 85b
r. impotently on as Thou or I | 153b
r. it under his tongue | 185b
Romage in the land | 329b
Roman: a dog. .than such a R. | 340b
after the high R. fashion | 324b
a R. meal | 112a
a R.'s life, a R.'s arms | 253b
a R. thought hath struck him | 322b
before the R. came to Rye | 93a
bleeding from the R. rods | 107b
butcher'd to make a R. holiday | 69a
cd. not get a rhyme for r. | 155a
heard the snobbish R. say | 24b
his noses cast is of the r. | 155a
I am a R. citizen | 540b
I'm a R. for that | 150a
know the sweet R. hand | 371b
more an antique R. than a Dane | 337a
noblest R. of them all | 341b
not. .holy, nor R., nor an empire | 566a

Roman (cont.)
play the R. fool | 351a
R., be this thy care | 556a
R. by a R. valiantly vanquished | 324b
R.-Saxon-Danish | 118b
Rooshan: ain't it. .no, sir R., R. | 125b
so rude that wd. not be a R. | 339b
the R. and his trouble | 199a
think not, thou noble R. | 341a
virtue with the R. clergy | 226b
writ in a R. chamber | 96a
Romance: a little given to r. | 149b
'Confound R.!' | 230b
resounds in fable or r. | 271b
R. brought up the nine-fifteen | 230b
R.! those first-class passengers | 232a
sitting by the shores of old r. | 463a
symbols of a high r. | 221a
think steam spoils r. at sea | 232a
Romances: r. as they wd. be spiritualized | 449b
r. paint at full length | 70b
to read eternal new r. of Marivaux | 175b
vulgar authors in r. | 65b
with high r. blent | 221a
Roman Empire: calls itself the Holy R. | 566a
fall of the R. | 412a
ghost of the deceased R. | 191b
historian of the R. | 161b
Romanism: rum, R., and rebellion | 54b
Romans: are yet two R. living | 341b
as when the R. came | 235a
called Cassius the last of the R. | 553b
friends, R., countrymen | 339b
last of all the R. | 341b
pristine wars of the R. | 382a
R. call it stoicism | 1b
R. were like brothers | 253a
to whom the R. pray | 253b
wh. came first. .Greeks or the R. | 129a
Romantic: deep r. chasm | 101a
r. Ireland's dead and gone | 474b
Romanticism: tinge it with r. | 136a
Rome: aisles of Christian R. | 147a
at R. live in the Roman style | 537b
at R. she hadde been | 88b
Bishop of R. hath no jurisdiction | 491b
but that I loved R. more | 339b
Church of R. I found wd. suit | 524a
come from R. al hoot | 89a
everyone. .comes round by R. | 51a
falls the Coliseum, R. shall fall | 69a
fate of Cato and of R. | 1a
first in a village. .second at R. | 13a
grandeur that was R. | 298a
Half-way House to R., Oxford | 535a
hook-nosed fellow of R. | 380b
impossible. .R...breed thy fellow | 341b
in all you writ to R. | 385b
insolent Greece, or haughty R. | 216a
it was at R., on the 15 of October | 161b
I've lost R. | 234a
lay thou on for R.! | 253b
let R. in Tiber melt | 322a
London is. .the R. of to-day | 147a
now is it R. indeed | 338a
Oh R.! my country! | 69a
palmy state of R. | 329b
rolls by the towers of R. | 253b
R. been growing up | 131b
R. has spoken | 538a
R., in the height of her glory | 454a
R. is above the Nations | 234b
R. shall perish—write that word | 107b
R., tho' her eagle. .had flown | 449a
R. thy Virgil's name | 109a
sires have marched to R. | 253a
stands the Coliseum, R. shall stand | 69a
stones of R. to rise and mutiny | 340b
strangers of R., Jews | 512a
time will doubt of R. | 71a
varletry of censuring R. | 325a
Voice of Cato is the voice of R. | 214b
when R. falls—the World | 69a
you cruel men of R. | 337b
Romeo: give me my R. | 366a
O gentle R.! | 365a
R., come forth | 366a
R.'s a dishclout to him | 366a
R.! wherefore art thou R.? | 365a

Ronald: Lord R...flung himself | 243a
Ronsard sang of me | 565b
Ronyon: rump-fed r. | 346a
Roof: even upon the topmost r. | 426b
look right thro' its gorgeous r. | 47b
majestical r. fretted | 332b
runs through the arched r. | 270b
whose humble r. is weather-proof | 190b
worthy. .shdst. come under my r. | 506a
Roofs: building r. of gold | 381b
Roof-tree: heavens my wide r. | 12b
Rookery: leads the clanging r. | 432a
Rooks: choughs and r. brought forth | 349a
r. are blown about | 429b
r. came home in scramble | 192a
r. in families homeward go | 180a
Room: altho' the r. grows chilly | 172b
A R. of One's Own | 462b
brings a taper to the outward r. | 133b
coming to that holy r. | 133a
from my lonely r. this night | 12a
from r. to r. I stray | 452b
how little r. do we take up | 401a
infinite riches in a little r. | 259a
is there r. for Mary there? | 315b
large upper r. furnished | 510a
left the r. with silent dignity | 177a
like a bridegroom from his r. | 12b
nae r. at my head | 529a
Rome indeed and r. enough | 338a
r., and verge enough | 173b
set my feet in a large r. | 483b
take the lower r. | 509b
there is not r. for Death | 38b
there was no r. for them | 508b
to make thee a r. | 215b
who sweeps a r. as for Thy laws | 188b
yes, there's r. | 315b
you shall keep yr. r. | 414b
Rooms: know..r. of thy native country | 157b
love the uppermost r. at feasts | 507b
yr. r. at college was beastly | 232b
Rooshan, ain't it, Wegg | 125b
Rooshans: people. .may be R. | 124a
Roost: curses. .come home to r. | 406b
Rooster: hongry r. don't cackle | 182a
Root: axe is laid unto the r. | 504b
have we eaten on the insane r. | 346a
here, r. and all, in my hand | 427a
I am the r. and the offspring | 520b
nips his r. | 385b
r. and father of many kings | 348b
r. of the matter is found in me | 497a
self-control is wisdom's r. | 59a
they had no r., they withered | 506b
thy r. is ever in its grave | 187b
Roots: are r., and ever green | 295b
as if. .r. of the earth. .rotten | 222b
broad on the r. of things | 44b
poison England at her r. | 34a
r. that can be pulled up | 144a
send my r. rain | 198a
Rope: his throat in a r. | 424a
pulled at one r. | 99a
r. that hangs my dear | 159b
sin as it were with a cart r. | 501a
Roper: Son R.,. .the field is won | 283a
Rorum, corum | 290b
Rosaleen: my Dark R. | 258a
Rosalind: no jewel is like R. | 327a
Rosalys: Margaret and R. | 311b
Rosaries: pictures, r., and pixes | 66a
Rosary: my r. | 309b
Rose: against the blown r. | 324a
all June I bound the r. | 49a
any nose may ravage. .a r. | 52a
a r. her mouth | 433b
a r. in the deeps of my heart | 475b
as red as any r. | 531b
blossom as the r. | 502a
breast that gives the r. | 264a
bud, and yet a r. full blown | 191a
budding r. above the r. full blown | 465a
Christmas I no more desire a r. | 344b
die of a r. in aromatic pain? | 300b
disclose unceremoniously the r. | 452a
English unofficial r. | 39b
enough the r. was heaven to smell | 192a
fair as is the r. in May | 90a
go, lovely R.! | 449a

Rose (cont.)

happy is the r. distilled 356a
hath not thy r. a canker 383b
hath not thy r. a thorn 383b
he r. the morrow morn 100a
he wears the r. of youth 323b
him that loved the r. 441a
His blood upon the r. 297b
home, R., and home Provence 96b
I am the r. of Sharon 500a
if love were what the r. is 423a
if this pale r. offend 405b
I have plucked the r. 363b
Iram..is gone with all its R. 152a
I r. the wrong way to-day 25b
it is written on the r. 185a
it wavers to a r. 131a
Jove bestows..the fading r. 79b
lap of the crimson r. 356b
last r. of summer 281b
leaves the R. of Yesterday 152a
look wh. she turn'd when he r. 281b
lost here but it r. afar! 52b
lovely is the r. 466a
mast burst open with a r. 155a
mighty lak' a r. 410a
more labyrinthine buds the r. 52a
most sweet, and inviolate R. 476a
musk of the r. is blown 434a
my fause lover stole my r. 63b
my Luve's like a red red r. 62a
ne'er the r. without the thorn 191a
Nightingale cries to the R. 152a
no thorns go as deep as a r.'s 421a
on thy cheek a fading r. 218b
pluck a red r. from off this thorn 383b
pluck a white r. with me 383b
queen r. of the rosebud 434a
reddens to a r. 452a
red r. cries, 'She is near' 434a
Red R., Proud R., sad R. 476b
Richard, that sweet lovely r. 377a
R. as where some buried Cæsar 153a
r. both at an instant 379a
R. crossed the road 131a
r. just newly born 205a
R. kissed me to-day 131a
r. leaves, when the r. is dead 399b
R. of all Roses, R. of all..World 475b
r. of the fair state 333b
r. or rue or laurel 420b
r. politely in the club 91b
r.-red city 55a
R. that cannot wither 448a
r. up to play 494a
r. was awake all night 434a
r. with all its sweetest leaves 72a
shd. vanish with the R. 154a
slowly, slowly r. she up 531a
sweet r., whose hue angry 187b
that wh. we call a r. 365a
their only thornless r. 424a
thereby beauty's r...never die 387a
the r. growing on's cheek 251b
the r. like a nymph 398a
the r.'s scent is bitterness 441a
tho' a r. shd. shut 221b
under the r. 28a, 239a
up he r., and donn'd his clothes 335b
up r. the son..up r. Emelye 89a, 141a
vernal bloom, or summer's r. 273a
when the r.-blossoms wither 421b
white r. weeps, 'She is late' 434a
wild centuries roves back the r. 119a
within the bosom of the r. 426b
with lily and red r. 284a
without thorn the r. 274a
you r. o' the wrong side to-day 38a
Rose Aylmer 240b
Roseate hues of early dawn 3b
Rosebery and Comyns Carr 93a
Rosebud: r. set with..wilful thorns 435b
rose of the r. garden of girls 434a
without the fragrant r. 191a
Rosebuds: gather ye r. 190a
r. filled with snow 78b
Rose-cheeked Laura 78a
Roseleaf: only a r. down 24a
Rosemary: for you there's r. 373a
there's r...for remembrance 335b
Roses: change from rocks to r. 305a

Roses (cont.)

have the r. heard 434a
it was the time of r. 194b
lilies without, r. within 261a
make thee beds of r. 259a
Morn a thousand R. brings 152b
morning r. newly washed 366b
Oh r. for the flush of youth 311a
on thy turf shall r. rear 73b
plant thou no r. at my head 311a
raptures and roses of vice 421a
rod of criticism with r. 130b
r. across the moon 284b
r. and white lilies grow 78b
r. are her cheeks 433b
r. at first were white 189b
r. have thorns, ..fountains mud 387b
r., red and white 195a
r., r., all the way 50a
r. stick like burrs 52b
r. were all awake 434a
scent of the r. will hang round 281b
seek r. in December 72a
she wore a wreath of r. 22b
so with r. overgrown 261a
strew no more red r. 7a
strew on her r. 7b
sweet musk-r., and with eglantine 356b
tho' my own red r...blow 442b
virgins are soft as the r. 67b
voluptuous garden-r. 435a
where r. and..violets meet 22a
wild, r., and ivy serpentine 398a
Rose-water: revolutions..not made
with r. 252a
r. over a toad 205b
Ross: read Alexander R. over 65a
sing the Man of R. 302a
Rosy: earth not grey but r. 48b
he that loves a r. cheek 79a
left the daisies r. 433b
pass the r. wine 125a
r. is the west 433b
Rot: cold obstruction and to r. 352a
hour to hour, we r. and r. 326a
propagate, and r. 301a
r. high on Temple Bar 93b
r. inwardly and foul contagion 269b
r. itself with motion 322b
the very deep did r. 98b
Rote: learned and conned by r. 341a
Rotten: goodly apple r. 353a
Lord Lilac thought it rather r. 93a
something is r. in..Denmark 331a
Rottenness: firmament is r. 267b
r. begins in his conduct 204b
Rotting: Dungeon, that I'm r. in 79a
mean and mighty, r. 329a
Rotunda: Opulent R. Strike 412b
Rotundity o' the world 342b
Rough: earth's smoothness r. 50b
r. as nutmeg-graters 191b
r. he may be 124a
the r. places plain 502b
Rougher: I beneath a r. sea 107b
Rough-hew them how we will 336b
Roughness breedeth hate 14b
Roughs: among his fellow r. 136b
Round: attains the upmost r. 338b
dance their wayward r. 471a
drunk their Cup a R. or two 153a
everyone..comes r. by Rome 51a
her diurnal r.! 466a
in the heaven, a perfect r. 44b
knew the merry world was r. 439a
large, and smooth, and r. 406a
light fantastic r. 267a
or else goes r. and r. 86b
r. about the cauldron 349b
r. and r. it flew 98a
r. and top of sovereignty 349b
r. me once again! 434a
r. she turned for my noble sake 48a
r. turned he, as not deigning 253b
the golden r. 346b
Roundabouts: what's lost upon the r. 86b
Rounded with a sleep 367b
Roundelay: synge untoe mie r. 88a
Rounder 'twixt the cypresses 49a
Round-faced man in black 183a
Roundhead: below the R. rode 438a

Round-heads and Wooden-shoes 1b
Round-hoofed, short-jointed 386b
Rounds: it's 'Three r. blank' 229a
it was 'R.! What R.?' 234a
unto their r. their music's aid 249b
Roupell: Mr. Charles R. 408a
Rouse: r. and bestir themselves 271b
r. him at the name of Crispian 383a
Rousseau: mock on, Voltaire, R. 31b
not ask Jean Jacques R. 110b
sophist, wild R. 68b
Rout: difference, after all their r. 94b
pleasures of having a r. 195a
ruin upon ruin, r. on r. 273a
wherefore doth yr. r. 252b
Routed: thrice he r. all his foes 139a
Rove: that, where'er we r. 281b
Rover: whither away, fair r. 37a
Roving: Lady Moon, where are you r. 198a
we'll go no more a-r. 74a
Roves back the rose 119a
Row: darned long r. to hoe 250a
Devil knows how to r. 99b
I'll r. ye so quick 261b
mussels all in a r. 533a
of orient pearl a double r. 78b
Oysters..waited in a r. 84b
r., brothers, r. 282b
r., my knights, near the land 79a
saints, who r. on r., burn upward 592a
watermen, that r. one way 64a
weel may the boatie r. 149b
Rowed: all r. fast 570b
r. along, thinking of nothing 120b
Rowing: find me r. against the stream 319a
looking one way, and r. another 54a
r. home to haven 261b
Rowland's oil 126b
Rowley Poley, pudding and pie 534a
Royal: a crowned man r. 422a
a more than r. tomb 16b
high on a throne of r. state 272a
men of r. siege 359b
no 'r. road' to geometry 573b
to be a regular R. Queen! 163b
Royal Exchange: love to frequent..
the R. 2a
Royal George: down went the R. 111a
Royalist: more r. than the king 566b
Royally: to have prov'd most r. 337a
Royalty: flattery..to R...with a
trowel 129a
r...appeals to diffused feelings 17b
r. is a government..one person 17b
Rub: ay, there's the r. 333a
Rubbish: cast as r. to the void 430b
hopeless r. as thy worst 410b
Rubies: price is above r. 499a
r., fairy favours 356b
wisdom is above r. 497a
wisdom is better than r. 498a
Rubious: more smooth and r. 370a
Rubs nor botches in the work 348b
Ruby: a R. kindles in the Vine 152a
Vine her ancient R. yields 152a
Rudder: mixed with the r. 86a
rhyme the r. is of verses 65a
snatched his r. 8b
their tail the r. 139b
Ruddy: now he was r. 495b
Rude: but only rather r. and wild 26a
'it's very r. of him,' she said 84a
r. am I in my speech 360a
society is all but r. 260b
who is here so r. 339b
Rudeliche and large 89a
Rudest work that tells a story 314b
Rudyards cease from kipling 410b
Rue: I'll set a bank of r. 375b
nought shall make us r. 374b
press the r. for wine 319a
rose or r. or laurel 420b
r., even for ruth 375b
sold for endless r. 198b
there's rosemary and r. 373a
wear yr. r. with a difference 335b
Ruffian: menaces of a r. 208b
that father.. 377b
Ruffians, pitiless as proud 107b
Ruffled, and sometimes impaired 267a
Rug: snug, as a bug in a r. 156b

Rugged: antiquarian is a r. being   209b
  those r. names to our mouths   278b
Ruhnken: learn'd professor, R.   304b
Ruin: around the dear r.   281b
  aspect of princes, and their r.   386a
  at the brink of r.   217a
  back, ere the r. fall!   253b
  formed for the r. of our sex   405b
  formless r. of oblivion   369b
  hideous r. and combustion   271a
  hides the r. that it feeds upon   110b
  in a r. that's romantic   165a
  last of a race in r.   92a
  majestic tho' in r.   272b
  man marks the earth with r.   69b
  pain and r. to despise   174a
  predicts the r. of the State   29a
  print no r.-trace   280a
  red r., and. . breaking up of laws   427b
  r. and confusion hurled   2b
  r., and desperation, and dismay   277b
  r. half an author's graces   283a
  r. seize thee, ruthless King!   173b
  r. upon r., rout on rout   273a
  r.—yet what r.!   69a
  seed of r. in himself   7a
  shame and r. wait for you   107b
  spreading r. and scattering ban   43b
  stern R.'s ploughshare   62a
  thou its r. didst not share   131b
  to r. or to rule the state   138a
  whom God to r. has design'd   140b
  you will r. no more lives   135b
Ruined: r. at our own request   283a
  r. by buying. . pennyworths   157a
  r.. . of their natural propensities   58a
Ru͏ning along the illimitable inane   433a
Ruins: flout, the r. grey   317a
  human mind in r.   118a
  mean reparations upon mighty r.   56b
  rains and r. are over   420a
  the r. of the noblest man   339b
Rule: all be done by the r.   323b
  declared absolute r.   274a
  errors of a wise man make yr. r.   29a
  golden r. is. . no golden rules   391a
  good be each man's r.   427a
  good old r. sufficeth   470b
  levell'd r. of streaming light   267a
  little r., a little sway   143a
  no charge of r., nor governance   416a
  no r. is so general. . exception   64a
  not a regular r.   83b
  observed the golden r.   31b
  oldest r. in the book   83b
  only take this r. along   419a
  r. applies to everyone   166b
  R., Britannia   443a
  R. of Three doth puzzle me   533a
  r.. . to do the business of the day   455a
  singing, R. Britannia   525a
  such as did bear r.   521a
  sure the monarch's r. must prove   306a
  they that r. in England   92a
  too fond to r. alone   303a
  to ruin or to r. the state   138a
  to r. the roast   306a
  wd. the r. of it had been so too   214b
  when you've shouted 'R. Britannia'   227a
  who can r. and dare not lie   433b
Ruler: little Benjamin their r.   486b
Rulers: against the r. of the darkness   516a
  r. are not a terror to good works   513b
  R. of the Queen's Navee   166a
Rules: all a rhetorician's r.   64b
  as if r. were not in the schools   65b
  but truth from r.   65b
  he that only r. by terror   426a
  little r. and few   26b
  never shows she r.   302a
  obtruding false r.   267b
  pretences to break known r. by   116a
  r. and models destroy genius   183b
  r.. . are. . the laws of Nature   202b
  r. e'en the wisest. . in learning r.   113b
  twelve good r.   168b
  with old r. jump right   65b
  woman, r. us still   282a
Ruling: r. himself after thy word   489a
  the r. passion conquers reason   302a
Rum: and a bottle of r.   413a

Rum (cont.)
  r. and true religion   70b
  R. on the port   414b
  r., Romanism, and rebellion   54b
  what a R. Go everything is   455b
Rumbled: under the water it r. on   99b
Rumination: by often r.   327a
Rumour: distillation of r.   80b
  have r. of thee there?   442a
  r. is a pipe   379b
  r. of oppression and deceit   111b
Rumours of wars   507b
Rum-ti-Foo: isle of R.   163a
Run: altho' I r. and r.   93b
  cry it up, or r. it down   419b
  day has r. but to the even-song   189a
  good r. I have in my sleep   416b
  gwine to r. all night   156a
  he may r. that readeth   504b
  if they r., why, we follow   158b
  I r., I r., I am gathered   265a
  I therefore so r.   514a
  let us r. with patience   517a
  many shall r. to and fro   504a
  r. about thro' the city   485b
  r., and not be weary   502b
  r. at least twice as fast   84a
  r. into any kind of danger   478a
  r., rise, rest with Thee   187a
  r., tailors, r., or she'll kill you all   534a
  r. the straight race   279b
  r. to and fro like sparks   520a
  see how they r.   533a
  stay, and r. again, and stay   261a
  still as they r. they look behind   174b
  they wh. r. in a race r. all   514a
  those sins thro' wh. I r.   132a
  thoughts. . half r. before   423a
  to my dead heart r. them in!   415a
  to r. for President in 1928   106a
  to r., tho' not to soar   255b
  to wait, to ride, to r.   409b
  up I go till I end my r.   234a
  we do not r. for prize   406a
  we r. because we like it   406a
Runagates contine in scarceness   486a
Runcible spoon   243b
Rune: she. . read her r. to all   313a
Runic: R. rhyme   298a
  some fallen R. stone   6a
Runnable stag   117b
Runnels pebble-stones   217b
Runneth about unto the end of it   482b
Running: call 'r. a man down'   418a
  first sprightly r.   139b
  it takes all the r. you can do   84a
  r. it never runs from us   132a
  r. the way of thy commandments   479b
Runs: fights and r. away   523b
  it never r. from us away   132a
  sprinkles. . with nectar, and. r. on   241a
Run-stealers flicker to and fro   442b
Rupee: chapter on the Fall of the R.   460a
Rupert: R. of debate   252a
  R. of Parliamentary discussion   128a
  R. of the Rhine   252b
Rural: lovely woman in a r. spot   202a
  made a r. pen   32b
  nor r. sights alone, but r. sounds   111b
Rush: as we r., as we r.   443b
Rushing mighty wind   512a
Rushingly, like the Pentecost Wind   180a
Rushy: down the r. glen   4a
Ruskin: leave to squeamish R.   226a
Russel: Daun R. the fox   89a
Russell: R., let me. . call you Edwin   150b
  hack me as you did. . Lord R.   279b
  R. acted. . highest principles   150b
Russia: last out a night in R.   351b
Russian: might have been a R.   166a
Russians: [R.] dash on the thin red
  line   315a
  R. shall not have Constantinople   201b
Rust: eaten to death with r.   380a
  golden hair tarnished with r.   460a
  his good sword r.   101a
  less than the r.   197a
  needles. . now r. disus'd   109a
  that wh. never taketh r.   402a
  the true r. of the Barons' Wars   449b
  to r. unburnished, not to shine   438b

Rust (cont.)
  toy soldier is red with r.   151a
  wear out than to r. out   116a
  where moth and r. doth corrupt   505b
Rustic moralist   174b
Rusticity: refined r.   468b
Rustics: amazed the gazing r.   168b
Rustum: let R. lay about   152b
  Zal and R.   152b
Rusty: want of fighting was grown r.   65a
Ruth: rue, even for r.   375b
  the sad heart of R.   220a
Rutted this morning by the. . guns   261b
Rye: a bag full of r.   533a
  before the Roman came to R.   93a
  between the acres of the r.   327b
  coming through the r.   59b
  fields of barley and of r.   431b
  rob the blighted r.   114a

S

Saba: Arabia and S.   486b
Sabachthani: Eli, Eli, lama s.   508a
Sabæan: blow S. odours   273b
Sabaoth: Lord God of S.   478a
Sabbath: born on the S. day   525a
  eternal S. of his rest   141b
  hail, S.!. . poor man's day   172b
  hallow thus the S. day   101a
  holy was the S.-bell   221b
  keep holy the S. day   480a
  let a S. song   298a
  one s. deep and wide   438a
  S. of the Lord thy God   480a
  S. of the year!   246a
  s. was made for man   508a
  smiled when a s. appear'd   113a
  thou art no s.-drawler   438a
  upon a S. day it fell   221b
Sabbaths: new moons and s.   501a
  s. of Eternity   438a
  those endless s.   287a, 537a
Sable: and of s. hue   534a
  s. silvered   330b
Sabre: with his s. drawn   523a
Sabrina fair   268a
Sack: I'll purge, and leave it   379a
  intolerable deal of s.   378a
  nothing without s.   380b
  s. and sugar be a fault   377b
  s. the lot!   152a
Sackbut, psaltery, dulcimer   504a
Sacks to sew up wives   440a
Sacrament: orbed s.   442b
Sacred: Alph, the s. river   101a
  feed his s. flame   101b
Sacrifice: bodies a living s.   513b
  coming to the s.   219b
  God will provide for s.   223b
  my hands be an evening s.   490b
  pay thy morning s.   224b
  pinnacle of s. pointing   246a
  prayers one sweet s.   385b
  s. for sin, hast thou not required   484a
  s., oblation, and satisfaction   480b
  s. of God is a troubled spirit   485a
  s. to God. . devil's leavings   419a
  s. to the Graces   90b
  stands Thine ancient s.   233b
  thou desirest no s.   485a
  to obey is better than s.   495a
  turn delight into a s.   186b
  unpitied s. in a. . struggle   56b
Sacrificed: passover is s. for us   514a
Sacrificers, but not butchers   338b
Sacrifices: upon such s., my Cordelia   344a
Sacrilege: we have. . consecrated s.   128b
Sad: ah, s. and strange   436a
  gentlemen wd. be as s. as night   374a
  if you find him s.   322b
  know not why I am so s.   352b, 568b
  make a man look s.   357b
  mine a s. one   352b
  more s. are these we daily see   182a
  nobody shd. be s. but I   374a
  s. and bad and mad it was   46a
  s. as angels for. . man's sin   77b
  s. or singing weather   423a
  s. stuff (Shakespeare)   571a

Sad (*cont.*)
s. that she was glad 441a
s. tires in a mile-a 373a
say I'm s. 202a
so s., so fresh, the days 436a
so s., so strange, the days 436a
seem too solemn s. 408b
their songs are s. 92a
the s. moonbeam 35b
thou art absent I am s. 290a
when so s. thou canst not sadder 442a
wind! thou art s. 284b
Winter..sullen and s. 443b
wrought in a s. sincerity 147a
Sad-coloured sect [Quakers] 196b
Sadder: canst not s. 442a
s. and wiser man 100a
s. even than I am 451a
Saddest: I'm s. when I sing 22a, 451a
s. are, 'It might have been' 182a
s. of all Kings crown'd 206a
Saddle: boot, s., to horse 45b
my s. and my bow 531b
Sadly descends the autumn evening 7b
Sadness: a most humorous s. 327a
feeling of s. and longing 247a
He feeleth for our s. 3b
no s. of farewell 426a
s. in the sweet 441a
s. of her might 219b
s. of her s. 21b
Safe: I wish him s. at home 217a
man's perdition to be s. 147a
s. bind, s. find 446b
s. for democracy 462a
s. home, s. home 287a
s. shall be my going 40a
s. though all safety's lost 40a
s. where men fall 40a
to be..honest is not s. 362a
you're perfectly s. 456b
Safely: but to be s. thus 348b
s., s. gather'd in 130b
thro' the World we s. go 29b
Safer: s. being meek 44b
s. to be that wh. we destroy 348b
Safest: die, s. of all 40a
just when we're s. 45a
Safety: counsellors there is s. 498a
man shall eat in s. 386b
pluck this flower, s. 377a
pot of ale, and s. 382a
safe though all s.'s lost 40a
s. and the health of the..state 330b
s., honour, and welfare 479a
s. is in our speed 147b
under the smile of s. 379b
Sagacious, bold, and turbulent 138a
Sagacity: infinite-resource-and-s. 237a
Sage: be neither saint nor s. 236a
calmly spoke the venerable S. 464b
hoary S. reply'd 211b
Newton, childlike s.! 112a
s. beneath a spreading oak 107b
s. in meditation found 399a
there sit the sainted s. 175a
without hardness will be s. 6a
Sager sort our deeds reprove 78a
Sages: holy s. once did sing 270a
Rhodora! if the s. 147a
s. have seen in thy face 113a
than all the s. can 471b
the dozing s. 108a
Said: a thing well s. 142a
by and by is easily s. 334b
finer..than anything wh. he s. 148a
great deal to be s. 27b
he himself has s. it 166a
he s. nought to me 99a
if I s. so, it was so 170a
I s. the thing wh. was not 418a
never s. a foolish thing 309b
never to himself hath s. 317a
s. anything that was remembered 130a
s. I to myself, s. I 164a
s. it that knew it best 14b
s. on both sides 2a
s. or done in earth 189a
s. whot a owt to's a s. 435a
she s., 'I am aweary' 433a
so very little s. 94b

Said (*cont.*)
there's no more to be s. 523b
there's nothing to be s. 207a
'tis well s. again 385b
well s., as if I had s. it 418b
we s. nothing, all the day 132b
Sail: a s.! a s.! 98b
farther, farther s. 457b
fast for fear did he s. 407a
free the white s. spread! 184b
never weather-beaten s. 78b
proud full s. of his..verse 388a
s. and s., with unshut eye 5b
s. the wet seas roun' 231b
sea-mark of my utmost s. 364a
shook out more s. 8b
silver s. of dawn 200a
time..to take in s. 147a
two towers of s. at dawn 96b
we might s. for evermore 439a
white and rustling s. 116a
white s.'s shaking 262a
Sailed: never s. with *me* before 203b
s. by the Lowlands low 531a
s. in to Bethlehem! 524a
s. off in a wooden shoe 151a
s. the wintry sea 249a
she hadna s. a league 529a
they's away for a year 243b
Sailing: come s. to the strand 530a
comes this way s. 277b
failing occurred in the s. 86a
s. o'er life's solemn main 248a
s. o'er sea 69b
three fishers went s. 226b
three ships a-s. there 524a
three ships come s. by 522a
Sailor: before Noah was a s. 371b
do with the drunken s.? 527b
give ear unto the s. 292a
happiest hour a s. sees 164a
home is the s. 415a
ho, s. of the sea! 130b
lass that loves a s. 120b
light in the darkness, s. 315b
never more, S. 119b
no man will be a s. 207a
s. free to choose 236a
s.'s wife had chestnuts 346a
shrine of the s.'s devotion 389b
soldier an' s. too 234a
well for the s. lad 425b
Sailor-boys were all up aloft 525b
Sailor-folk: silly s. 231a
Sailor-men shd. wear these things 19b
Sailors: guard the s. tossing 20a
joys and sorrows s. find 68a
s. but men 353a
s...in every port a mistress 161a
s. of Bristol City 440b
Sails: loves t' have his s. fill'd 87a
not full s. hasting 260b
purple the s. 323a
s. by the Lowlands low 531a
s. fill'd, and streamers waving 277b
s. o' cramoisie 529a
s. ripped, seams opening 109b
still the s. made on 99b
thy white s. crowding 37a
torn s., provisions short 287a
we our s. advance 137a
white dipping s. 262a
Sail-yards tremble 87a
Saint: able to corrupt a s. 376b
accents of an expiring s. 412a
a s. in crape 301b
be neither s. nor sage 236a
by s., by savage, and by sage 304a
each lost day has its patron s. 182a
follow yr. S. 78a
frequent Doctor and S. 153a
his s. is sure of his..heart 295b
in vain the s. adore 137a
little s. best fits 188b
Miracles of S. Somebody 51a
my late espousèd S. 278b
neither S. nor Sophist led 5a
never a s. took pity 99a
Poet and S.! to thee alone 106b
reel out a s. 94b
s. run mad 303b

Saint (*cont.*)
s. sustained it, but the woman died 299b
seem a s. when most..the devil 384b
she cd. make of me a s. 105a
shrine of my dead S. 225a
to catch a s. 351b
weakest s. upon his knees 110a
wh. the S. had printed 286b
worship oft the idol for the s. 457a
St. Aldegonde had a taste 130a
St. Andrews by the Northern Sea 242a
St. Anne: S. was the mother 293a
we'll sing at S. 282b
St. Augustine! well hast thou said 247b
St. Bride: no, by S. of Bothwell 318b
St. Clement's: bells of S. 533b
St. Denis: between S. and St. George 383b
Sainted: ensky'd and s. 351a
St. Gallowglass's Eve 92b
St. George: England and S. 382a
S. that swinged the dragon 373b
Saint Hubert's breed 316a
St. Ives: going to S. 533b
St. James: galice at S. 88b
ladies of S. 131a
St. John: awake, my S. 300b
his last chapter of S. 45a
Primrose Hill and S.'s Wood 30b
S. himself will scarce forbear 419a
S. sate in the horn 524a
there S. mingles 303b
St. Lawrence took his grid 228b
Saint-like: yet not too s. 247b
St. Loy: by S. 88a
Saint Martin's summer 383b
St. Mary's Lake 473a
Saint Michael was the steresman 524a
St. Nicholas soon wd. be there 280b
St. Patrick's day we'll keep 525b
St. Paul: description of the ruins of S.'s 449b
I am designing S.'s 27b
sketch the ruins of S.'s 254b
wh. with S. are literary terms 10a
Saint Praxed's ever was the church 45a
Saints: all s. else be defaced 176b
all the S. adore Thee 184a
avenge..thy slaughtered s. 278b
calls His s. around 36b
drunken with the blood of the s. 519b
fear Him, ye s. 424b
for all the S. 200a
frets the s. in heaven 43a
ghastly glories of s. 423b
greatest s. and sinners 66a
grow into plaster s. 235b
his soul is with S. 101a
lose with my lost s. 44a
men may jest with s. 351b
never be S. in heaven 41b
pair of carved s. 375b
place..with the race of S. 189a
s. engage in fierce contests 66a
s. have dwelt secure 453a
S., Heroes, if we will 5a
s. immortal reign 453b
s. in yr. injuries 360b
s. may do the same things 65b
s. on earth in concert sing 456a
s. will aid if men will call 100a
self-constituted s. 195b
twilight s. 221b
where S. in glory stand 476b
wh. are the prayers of s. 518b
with s. doth bait thy hook 351b
with thy quire of S. 133a
ye fearful s. 110a
ye that are his s. 484a
yet S. their watch are keeping 415b
St. Satan's fold 429a
Saint Valentine is past 357b
Sake: for my noble s. 48a
for old sakes' s. 226a
for whose dear s. 228a
s. of a ribboned coat 287b
Saki, you shall pass 154a
Sairey, Sairey, little do we know 124a
Salad: Garrick's a s. 169a
my s. days 323a
primroses make a capital s. 129b

Salad (cont.)
s. from the brook 112b
s...special receipt of his own 263a
Salade: a round s. 284b
Salamis: sea-born S. 70b
Salary: had a s. to receive 161b
Sale of chapmen's tongues 344b
Sale-room: babble of the s. 80b
Salisbury: blank cheque to Lord S. 172a
likened Lord S. to a lath 568a
S. and Gloucester 383a
when Lord S. makes a..speech 283b
Sallow, virgin-minded 45b
Sallows: among the river s. 221b
mealed-with-yellow s. 198a
Salley gardens 474a
Sally: none like pretty S. 79b
S. is gone 26b
Sally Lunn! 167a
Salmon: for the s.'s tail 360b
it was the s. 126a
the first s. 247b
white as snow in S. 486a
Salmons: there is s. in both 383b
Saloons: Solomon of S. 48b
Salt: fire and s. 529a
kissed..moustache..egg..s. 237b
pecks of poison are not pecks of s. 30a
pillar of s. 493a
s. have lost his savour 505a
s. of the earth 505a
s. on a woman's tail 65b
speech be..seasoned with s. 516a
yr. bread and salt 230a
Salted: wherewith shall it be s.? 505a
Saltness of time 379b
Saltpetre: villainous s. 377a
Salutary: wise and s. neglect 55b
Salutations: eye full of gentle s. 412a
Salute: earth, I do s. thee 375a
I s. thee, Mantovano 439a
s. one another with an holy kiss 514a
s. the happy morn 67b
those about to die s. you 553b
Saluted: inveterate foes s. 141b
Salvation: generally necessary to s. 481a
Him that brought s. down 402b
my bottle of s. 307b
none of us shd. see s. 354b
no s. exists outside the church 537b
now is our s. nearer 514a
s. joins issue with death 51b
seeks her own s. 336a
that publisheth s. 502b
things necessary to s. 491a
tools of working out s. 66a
work out yr. own s. 516a
wot prawce S. 390b
Samaritan: ready..to do the S. 404b
Samarkand: Golden Road to S. 154b
silken S. 221b
Same: another, yet the s. 299a
Christ the s. yesterday 517a
endless years the s. 453a
go onward the s. 179b
go the s. way home 285a
he is much the s. 12a
I sang the s. again 32b
just the s. as that! 310a
matter remains the s. 14a
s. a hundred years hence 124b
s. as you an' me 231b
that ever is the s. 464a
the s. as if he had not been 433a
the s. as me 236b
thou art the s., and thy years 488a
what reason I shd. be the s.? 12a
Samela: fair S. 176a
Samian wine 71a
Samite: white s. 427b
Samminiato: lamping S. 49a
Sammy, vy worn't there a alleybi 126b
Samphire, dreadful trade! 343b
Sampler: ply the s. 267b
Sampson: Dominie S. 319b
Samson: carry the buckler unto S. 41b
Philistines be upon thee, S. 495a
S. hath quit himself like S. 278a
Samuel: Lord called S. 495a
Sanctities: day's dead s. 441b
Sanctuary: desire to raze the s. 351b

Sanctuary (cont.)
help from the s. 482b
s. within the holier blue 51a
until I went into the s. 486b
Sand: abstinence sows s. 30a
always play with s. 26a
beds of s...and rushy isles 8a
foot..plain to be seen in the s. 118b
I on the s. 319b
land of s. and ruin 424a
land of s. and thorns 428a
length of burning s. appears 114a
little grains of s. 82a
name upon the soft sea-s. 241b
o'er and o'er the s. 226b
on the edge of the s. 243b
ribbed sea-s. 99a
roll down the golden s. 184a
s.-strewn caverns cool 5b
speed in' the slushy s. 48b
such quantities of s. 84a
throw the s. against the wind 31b
World in a Grain of S. 29a
Sandal: battering s. 197a
heap cassia, s.-buds 49b
his s. shoon 335b
Sandals: bind on thy s. 420a
S. were for Clementine 280b
Sanded: fell upon the s. floor 294b
so flewed, so s. 357a
Sandford: down by S. 8b
Sands: circled by the s. 263a
come unto these yellow s. 367a
golden s., and crystal brooks 132a
here are s., ignoble things 22b
lone and level s. 396b
ran itself in golden s. 432a
s. begin to hem 8a
s. of Dee 226b
steer too nigh the s. 138a
Sandwich-men of the *Daily Mail* 93b
Sandwiches: tall lady, eating s. 126a
Sane: fitter being s. 44b
Sang: he worked and s. 28a
I s. long years ago 20b
s. it all day long 36b
s. themselves to sleep 192a
s. the uncouth swain 270a
s. within the bloody wood 145a
Sangreal: story of the S. 257b
Sanguelac, the lake of Blood! 427a
Sank: s. by the Lowlands low 531a
s. her in the sea 529a
Sans: s. teeth, s. eyes 326b
s. Wine, s. Song 153a
Sap: from her material s. 343b
s. and sawdust 84a
trees..also are full of s. 488b
world's whole s. is sunk 133b
Sapphire: a purer s. 434a
second s. 43a, 520a
Sapphires: ivory overlaid with s. 500b
living s. 274a
Sappho: burning S. loved 70b
call me S. 101b
S. lay her burning brows 442b
whether my S.'s breast 189b
Saracens to the confines of Poland 162a
Sarah: S. Battle 239a
wherefore did S. laugh? 493a
Sarcasticul: this is rote S. 451a
Sardine: jasper and a s. stone 518b
Sardius: sixth, s. 520a
Sardonyx: fifth, s. 520a
Sashes: his nice new s. 172b
Sassy: sickly but s. 181b
Sat: as he s. facing it 237b
came and s. down here 284b
he s. him down in a lonely place 435b
he that s. was..like a jasper 518b
people s. down to eat 494a
we s., side by side 28b
Satan: auld Hornie, S. 58b
finally to beat down S. 479a
get thee behind me, S. 507a
I beheld S. as lightning 509a
Lord said unto S. 496b
my S., thou art but a dunce 30a
S., bowing low 277a
S. came also among them 496b
S. exalted sat 272a

Satan (cont.)
S. finds some mischief still 453a
S. met his ancient friend 74b
S., so call him 275a
S. stood unterrifi'd 273a
S. trembles, when he sees 110a
the messenger of S. 515b
wh. is the Devil, and S. 519b
Satanic: dark S. mills 31a
S. School 407b
Satchel: schoolboy, with his s. 326b
Satiety: love's sad s. 398b
occasion of s. 16b
Satin: heroine..mad..into white s. 400a
Satire: after all this s. 210b
let s. be my song 72a
praise is s. 457a
s. is a sort of glass 417b
s. or sense..can Sporus feel? 303a
Satisfaction: oblation, and s. 480b
s., if..any in marriage 160a
Satisfied: or, having it, is s.? 440a
things that are never s. 499a
well paid that is well s. 355a
Satisfies: where most she s. 323a
Satisfieth: s. the empty soul 488b
that wh. s. not 503a
who s. thy mouth 488a
Saturday: betwixt a S. and Monday 79b
died on S. 532b
it's jolly old S. 186a
S. night! 186a
S.'s child works hard 525a
that wash on S. 532b
Saturn: hail, S.'s land 557b
now S. is king again 557a
Revolution, like S. 565b
S. and Love their long repose 394a
while S. whirls 435b
Satyr: heel of a s. 420b
Hyperion to a s. 330a
Satyrs: my men, like s. 258b
Saucy airs we meet 160b
Saul: believe me, S., costs worlds 261b
daughters of Israel, weep over S. 495b
O S., it shall be a Face 51b
S. and Jonathan were lovely 495b
S. also among the prophets? 495a
S. hath slain his thousands 495b
S. was consenting unto his death 512a
S., why persecutest thou me? 512a
whose name was S. 512a
Saunders: Clerk S. 529a
Sautrye: fithele or gay s. 88b
Savage: by saint, by s. 304a
s., extreme, rude 389a
s. in his blindness 184a
the noble s. ran 139b
Savageness out of a bear 362b
Savages: cant in defence of s. 211a
Save: can, but will not, s. me 137a
choose whom it s. time 15b
conquer but to s. 76b
died to s. us all 3b
die to s. charges 64a
dust thou wdst. not s. 426a
enough to s. one's own 48a
God s. the king! 79b
life: wh. if I can s., so 379a
many to s. with thyself 7b
s. me from the candid friend 79a
wilt thou s. the people? 146a
you wd. s. none of me 133a
Saved: He that endureth to the end
shall be s. 506a
England has s. herself 297b
he s. others 508a
s. and hold complete 48b
s. the sum of things for pay 200a
there be souls must be s. 361a
we are not s. 503b
whosoever will be s. 478b
Savill was asked by Essex 13b
Saving a little child 183a
Saviour: around the S.'s throne 184a
call'd 'S. of the Nations' 71b
her sins to her S. 196a
hide me, O my S., hide 455b
lived on earth our S. Holy 3b
our S.'s birth is celebrated 329b
S. of 'is country 235b

Saviour (cont.)
speak low to me, my S.   43a
the S. comes, the S. promised long   131b
'tis thy S., hear his word   110a
whereon the S...was born   67b
Savonarola: had S. spoken less   25a
S. love-sick!   25a
Savoury: mints, s., marjoram   373a
Saviour: filths s. but themselves   343b
keep seeming and s.   373a
salt have lost his s.   505a
send forth a stinking s.   499b
Savours: freckles live their s.   356a
Saw: all I can say is—I s. it   49a
coughing drowns the parson's s.   345b
do not s. the air   333b
he thought he s.   85b
I came, I s., I overcame   548a
I s. and loved   161b
I s. him die   528a
I s. no one   136a
nor no man ever s.   366b
no sound of..s. was there   112b
nothing else s. all day long   218b
thy s. of might   327a
we s. thee in thy balmy nest   115a
when I s. him, I fell..as dead   518b
Sawdust: sap and s.   84a
Saws: all s. of books   331b
drawler of old s.   438a
full of wise s.   326b
Saxon: ancient S. phrase   247a
leave the S. alone   233a
S. and Norman and Dane   439a
S.,—I am Roderick Dhu!   316b
S. is not like us Normans   233a
Say: can't s. no fairer   122b
content to s. nothing   210a
did I s. so?   170a
heard him s. again   198b
he knew not what to s.   73a
I can s. little more   370a
if I cd. s. how much   358a
I have somewhat to s.   496a
I mean what I s.   83a
I s. it, that shd. not s. it   23b
I s. to thee, do thou repeat   445b
kind of good deed to s. well   385b
let me s. that thou wert fair   6b
let us not always s.   50b
Master, s. on   509a
Mrs. Poyser 'has her s. out'   144a
must not s. that thou wert true   6b
nothing to s., s. nothing   103b
nothing to what I cd. s.   83a
s. I'm weary, s. I'm sad   202a
s. I sent thee thither   384b
s. nay, s. nay, for shame   473b
s. that she rail   366b
s. that we have no sin   518a
she said, S. on   496a
somewhat to say unto thee   509a
still we s. as we go   311b
we men may s. more   371a
what o'clock I s. it is   366b
what will this babbler s.?   512b
what you s., or what you do   528b
while you're thinking what to s.   84a
yet many things to s.   511b
you have to s. something   456a
you shdn't. s. it is not good   456b
you shd. s. what you mean   83a
Sayest farewell, and lo!   36b
Saying: ancient s. is no heresy   353b
power of s. things   293a
rage of s. something   207a
Tar-baby ain't s. nuthin'   181b
tremble lest a s. learnt   438b
what are the wild waves s.   82b
Sayings..like women's letters   183a
Says little, thinks less   150a
Scabbard: sword, glued to my s.   262b
threw away the s.   203a
Scabs: make yourselves s.   328a
Scaffold: brothel or on the s.   412a
to the s. and the doom   12b
Scaffoldage: footing and the s.   368b
Scaith: Deil he could na s. thee   59b
Scale: he, by geometric s.   65a
hurl'd himself into the s.   282a
I have made a little s.   239b

Seale (cont.)
Justice, with her lifted s.   298b
on every golden s.!   82b
s. weighing delight and dole   329b
Scallop-shell of quiet   307b
Scalp: hairy s. of such a one   486b
Scan: gently s. yr. brother man   59a
s. his work in vain   110a
Scandal: in s., as in robbery   90b
love and s...best sweeteners   151b
no s. about Queen Elizabeth   400a
no s. like rags   150a
retired to their tea and s.   104a
s. while you dine   438b
the s., the incredible come-down   25a
Scandalous: monarch, s. and poor   309b
Scanter of yr. maiden presence   331a
Scapegoat into the wilderness   494a
Scar: from cliff and s.   436a
there is oft a s.   45b
Scarce: rhymes are so s.   75b
Scarceness: continue in s.   486a
Scare me with thy tears   438b
Scarecrow: s. of the law   351a
theatrical s.   120a
Scarers in print   125b
Scarf veiling an Indian beauty   354a
Scarfs, garters, gold   301a
Scarlet: apes, tho' clothed in s.   215b
cowards in s.   173a
in S. town   531a
line of s. thread   494b
lips are like a thread of s.   500a
s. line was slender   225b
tho' yr. sins be as s.   501a
who clothed you in s.   495b
Scars: he jests at s.   365a
strip his sleeve and show his s.   383a
the s. remaining   100a
Scatter: plough the fields, and s.   76a
s., as from an..hearth   396b
s. my ashes   280b
s. their snow around   37b
Scattered: Israel s. upon the hills   496a
land is s. with light   35b
s. his Maker's image   138a
s. the people that delight in war   486b
writes her s. dream   35b
Scatterest: soon as thou s. them   487b
Scatteringly doth shine   260b
Scene: a breath, a little s.   375b
all this s. of man   300b
gay and festive s.   125b
girdid up my Lions and fled the s.   451a
highly impossible s.   163a
last s. of all   326b
live o'er each s.   298b
lonely s. shall thee restore   103a
made a s. of it with my Papa   123a
of what s. the actors?   392a
our lofty s. be acted o'er   339b
proud s. was o'er   298b
see the distant s.   288b
speaks a new s.   307a
sweet is the s. where..friendship   193b
there I laid the s.   112b
upon that memorable s.   261a
very cunning of the s.   333a
Scenery: mountains..end of all..s.   314a
s. is fine..human nature is finer   222b
the s.'s divine   75b
Scenes: changing s. of life   424b
gay gilded s.   1b
no more behind yr. s., David   206b
s. of crowded life   213b
sicken at the shifting s.   435b
s. sung by him   317b
Scent: an amber s.   277b
join not s. to hue   394b
rose's s. is bitterness   441a
s. of the roses   281b
s. survives their close   441a
sweetest flower for s.   398a
whose s. the fair annoys   108a
Scents: murmurs..s. of the infinite Sea   6a
sweet unmemoried s.   36b
their s. the air perfuming   97a
Sceptic: s. could inquire for   65a
knowledge for the s.'s side   301a
Scepticism: s. of the intellect   288b
wise s...of a good critic   251a

Sceptre: her leaden s.   477a
my s. for a palmer's..staff   375b
s. and crown must tumble down   401a
s., learning, physic   329a
s. shows the force   354b
'tis not the balm, the s.   382b
Sceptred: avails the s. race   240b
dead but s. sovereigns   73a
Sceptreless, free, uncircumscribed   397b
Scheldt: by the lazy S.   169b
Scheme: she'll project a s.   476b
sorry S. of Things   154a
Schemes: many s. thou breedest   7b
s. of political improvement   208a
s. o' mice an' men   62a
Scherzando! ma non troppo ppp   163a
Schiller has the material sublime   102b
Scholar: he was a s.   386b
our S. travels yet   9a
s. all Earth's volumes carry   87b
s. among rakes   255b
shewed him the gentleman and s.   63a
what ills the s.'s life assail   213b
Scholars: lore its s. need   224a
nor its great s. great men   194b
s. and gentlemen   469b
the land of s.   170a
School: at the head of a s.   449a
drink..gi'es us mair than..s.   61a
drew me to s. along the..way   109b
example is the s. of mankind   58a
experience keeps a dear s.   157a
goeth to s., and not to travel   15a
he's been to a good s.   315a
microcosm of a public s.   130a
reason for hating s.   24b
Satanic S.   407b
s. of Stratford atte Bowe   88b
such doctrine never was there s.   277b
three little maids from s.   164b
toward s. with heavy looks   365b
unwillingly to s.   326b
Schoolboy: every s. knows it   425a
every s. knows who imprisoned   254b
not the s. heat   431a
s.'s tale..wonder of an hour   68a
s.'s tip   440a
s. whips his taxed top   405a
voice of the s.   287b
what every s. knows   419a
what s. of fourteen is ignorant   255a
whining s.   326b
Schoolboys from their books   365b
School-bred, though s., the boy be virtuous   113a
Schooldays: in my joyful s.   240b
School-divine: Father turns a s.   303b
Schoolgirl: pert as a s.   164b
s. complexion   526a
Schoolman's subtle art   303a
Schoolmaster is abroad   40b
Schoolmastering: continue s.   82a
Schoolmasters: injuries..must be their s.   342b
let s. puzzle   169b
then s. deliver us   187a
Schoolrooms: build s. for the boy   106a
Schools: and in learned s.   3b
bewildered in the maze of s.   300a
cobwebs of the s.   112b
for a' their college and s.   63a
jargon of the s.   305b
jargon o' your s.   60a
public s...nurseries of all vice   151b
public s...public folly breeds   113a
Schooner Hesperus   249a
Schumann's our music-maker   46b
Science: Art and S. cannot exist   30b
cometh at this newe s.   90a
cookery is..a noble s.   64a
detection is..an exact s.   136a
enough of s. and of art   471b
everything that relates to s.   239a
fair S. frown'd not   174b
fairy tales of s.   432a
Geometry..the only s.   191b
his soul proud s. never taught   300b
pretend to despise Art and S.   30b
Professors of the Dismal S.   81a
s. and logic he chatters   305a
s. falsely so called   516b

Science (cont.)
s. is organized knowledge 407*b*
s. moves, but slowly 432*b*
Sciences: books must follow s. 13*b*
mother of the s. 17*a*
Scientific: absence..of..s...opinion 9*b*
a s. faith's absurd 46*b*
theologians..s. terms 10*a*
Scinde: *peccavi*—I've S. 535*a*
Scissor-man 192*b*
Scoff: some that came to s. at him 12*b*
Scope: art, and that man's s. 387*a*
Score: s. and the tally 384*a*
to that kiss a s. 190*a*
Scorer: One Great S. comes 309*a*
Scores out with all men 50*a*
Scorn: disdain and s. ride sparkling 358*b*
dull eye of s. 37*b*
figure for the time of s. 363*a*
fools may our s...raise 160*b*
Fortune knows we s. her 323*b*
foul s. that Parma or Spain 145*a*
haughty s. wh. mocked the smart 6*a*
held the human race in s. 26*a*
I have had many a s. 531*b*
I s. to change my state 387*b*
not a thing to laugh to s. 327*b*
of her s. the maid repented 18*b*
s. not the Sonnet 470*b*
s. of s. 435*b*
s. the spear 392*a*
sound of public s. 276*b*
to wail their s. 117*a*
treat with virtuous s. 163*b*
what a deal of s. looks beautiful 371*b*
Scorned: lov'd, was s. and died 160*a*
not s. in heaven 109*b*
Scorner of the ground 398*b*
Scornful: seat of the s. 481*b*
s., yet with jealous eyes 303*a*
Scorns: he that s. and struggles 93*b*
Scorpion and asp 276*b*
Scorpions: chastise you with s. 496*a*
Scot: some be S. 233*b*
Scotch: English..little inferior to ..S. 289*b*
joke well into a S. understanding 404*a*
party..like the S. terrier 38*a*
S. have found it 209*a*
Scotched the snake, not killed it 348*b*
Scotchman: makes a S. happy 212*b*
much may be made of a S. 208*a*
noblest prospect..S. ever sees 207*a*
S. but what was a man of sense 246*a*
Scotchmen: trying..to like S. 238*b*
Scotia: chief of S.'s food 59*b*
old S.'s grandeur springs 59*b*
Scotland: be in S. afore ye 525*b*
grave livers do in S. use 470*b*
I do indeed come from S. 207*a*
in S., at the Orcades 301*a*
left fair S.'s strand 61*a*
Oats..in S. supports the people 212*b*
poor auld S.'s sake 60*b*
S., Madam..a worse England 209*b*
shivered was fair S.'s spear 318*b*
stands S. where it did 350*a*
succour S., and remede 474*a*
Switzerland..inferior sort of S. 405*a*
that S. led in luve 474*a*
Scots: kills..S. at a breakfast 377*a*
Land o' Cakes, and brither S. 62*a*
our gude S. lords 530*a*
S. lords at his feet 530*a*
S., wha hae wi' Wallace 62*b*
S., whom Bruce..led 62*b*
Scotsman: moral attribute of a S. 21*b*
S. on the make 21*b*
young S...with £300 21*b*
Scott: flat as Walter S. 525*b*
Italy..indifferent to..sick heart of S. 81*b*
not even Sir Walter S. 390*a*
[S.] Ariosto of the North 69*a*
Sir Walter S...little Bartley 416*b*
Scottish: brave old S. Cavalier 12*b*
informs the S. youth 415*b*
Scoundrel: General Good..plea of the s. 30*b*
given them to such a s. 418*a*
he was a s., and a coward 206*b*

Scoundrel (cont.)
man over forty is a s. 391*a*
patriotism..refuge of a s. 208*b*
Scoundrels: healthy hatred of s. 81*a*
Scoured to nothing 380*a*
Scourge: s. inexorably 272*a*
s. of small cords 510*b*
whose iron s. and torturing hour 173*b*
Scourged to his dungeon 53*a*
Scout: blabbing eastern s. 266*b*
flout 'em and s. 'em 367*b*
Scowl: with anxious s. draw near 12*b*
Scowls the far-famed hold 253*a*
Scramble: home in s. sort 192*a*
Scrap of paper 567*b*
Scrape: potsherd to s. himself 497*a*
Scraper: never was s. brave man 186*b*
Scrappy: when work was s. 93*b*
Scraps: s. are good deeds past 369*a*
stolen the s. 345*a*
Scratch: quick sharp s. 48*b*
s. his name on the Abbey-stones 48*a*
s. the Christian 477*b*
Scratched: of purpose to be s. 65*a*
Priscian a little s. 345*a*
s. with a stick 228*a*
Scratching of a pen 250*a*
Screaming out loud all the time 124*b*
Screams: strange s. of death 348*a*
Screen: s. from seeing 420*b*
s. them in those looks 397*b*
Screw yr. courage 347*b*
Scribblative: babblative and s. 407*a*
Scribble, scribble, scribble! 167*b*
Scribbling: insatiate itch of s. 162*b*
Scribes: authority..not as the s. 506*a*
righteousness of the s. 505*a*
Scrip and scrippage 327*a*
Scripture: devil can cite S. 353*a*
impregnable rock of S. 167*b*
I will better it in S. 291*b*
nail't wi' S. 59*b*
S. moveth us in sundry places 478*a*
Scriptures: abjure the S. 258*b*
book of books..holy S. 186*b*
hast known the holy s. 516*b*
mighty in the S. 512*b*
search the s. 510*b*
Scrivener: cropt s. 239*a*
Scroll: long-cramped s. 48*a*
s. of crystal, blazoning 393*b*
with punishments the s. 185*a*
Scruple: some craven s. 335*b*
Scruples dark and nice 65*a*
Scullion: away, you s.! 380*a*
Sculptor: great s...be an architect 314*a*
the godlike s. 147*a*
Sculpture: ancient s...modesty 295*a*
shapeless s. decked 174*b*
Scum: [our army]..is the mere s. 455*a*
Scurvy: some, right s. 263*b*
Scutcheon: a shielded s. 221*b*
honour is a mere s. 379*a*
my s. plain declares 345*b*
Scuttled: that ever s. ship 70*b*
Scylla..Charybdis of Aye and No 288*a*
Scythe: crooked s. and spade 401*a*
mower whets his s. 268*b*
Scythian: Barbarian, S. 516*a*
Snow on S. hills 259*a*
Sea: against a s. of troubles 333*a*
all as hungry as the s. 371*a*
all the s. were ink 251*b*
alone dwell for ever..kings of s. 6*a*
alone on a wide wide s. 99*a*
and a flowing s. 116*a*
and the s. rises higher 92*a*
around the glassy s. 184*a*
as stars look on the s. 252*a*
beneath a rougher s. 107*b*
beneath the bosom of the s. 31*b*
bind the s. to slumber stilly 77*b*
birds on the foam of the s.! 476*a*
blow the earth into the s. 342*b*
blue days at s. 414*b*
boat and went to s. 440*b*
Bohemia..Country near the S. 373*a*
bottom of the deep blue s. 525*a*
bound in with the triumphant s. 375*b*
by life's unresting s. 194*a*
by the deep s. 69*b*

Sea (cont.)
by the sounding s. 297*b*
called the good s. up to Him 231*a*
can see nothing but s. 13*a*
centre all round to the s. 113*a*
cold grey stones, O S.! 425*b*
cross the narrow s. 453*b*
crowned with summer s. 429*b*
dance like a wave of the s. 475*a*
death, like a narrow s., divides 453*b*
desert of the s. 502*a*
dolorous midland s. 424*a*
down to a sunless s. 101*a*
dreary s. now flows 100*a*
earth, nor boundless s. 388*a*
English..(empire) of the s. 80*a*
espouse the everlasting S. 472*b*
even the billows of the s. 385*b*
far over the summer s. 437*b*
fearest nor s. rising 37*a*
feeds her chicks at s.! 227*a*
for his fame the ocean s. 21*a*
for the s.'s worth 359*b*
France and England is..the s. 205*b*
from s. to shining s. 22*a*
from the flowers to the s. 421*b*
garden fronts the s. 421*b*
gave them back their s. 231*a*
go down to the s. in ships 488*b*
grave, under the deep deep s. 195*b*
great and wide s. also 488*b*
great by land as thou by s. 435*a*
great fishpond (the s.) 118*b*
great markets by the s. 154*b*
gurly grew the s. 529*a*
hail to the kings of the s.! 287*b*
heaven broods o'er the S. 467*a*
Helicon..in cliff to the s. 5*b*
he's drown'd in the s. 531*b*
he that commands the s. 15*b*
ho, sailor of the s.! 130*b*
if we gang to s., master 530*a*
I leaped headlong into the s. 222*b*
in a bowl to s. went wise men 295*b*
in peril on the s. 457*a*
in perils in the s. 515*a*
in the flat s. sunk 267*a*
into a s. of dew 151*a*
into that silent s. 98*b*
inviolate s. 437*a*
iron-bosomed s. 313*a*
isles..that o'erlace the s. 46*a*
I've a Friend, over the s. 52*b*
kingdom by the s. 297*b*
lands beyond the s. 467*a*
leagues beyond..there is more s. 312*b*
learn the secret of the s. 248*a*
let nae the s. come in 530*a*
lie mirrored on her s. 192*a*
life's wild restless s. 3*b*
light..upon the shining s. 438*a*
like a bursting s. 442*a*
like to the Pontic s. 362*a*
little fishes of the s. 85*a*
London, that great s. 395*b*
lonely s. and the sky 262*a*
lookin' eastward to the s. 232*a*
looking lazy at the s. 232*a*
Love..has something of the s. 320*b*
lover of men, the s. 424*a*
melts into the s. 434*a*
moon may draw the s. 436*b*
mountains by the winter s. 429*a*
my bark is on the s. 73*a*
nearer the crystal s. 86*a*
never go to s. 166*a*
never sick at s.! 166*a*
never was, on s. or land 468*b*
never was s. so lone 228*b*
not having been at s. 209*b*
nothing in s.-description 314*a*
o'er a perfumed s. 298*a*
one foot in s. 358*a*
one is of the s. 471*b*
on such a full s. are we..afloat 341*a*
ought to ha' sent you to s. 232*b*
our heritage the s. 116*a*
out of the s. came he! 98*a*
out of the swing of the s. 197*b*
over the s. she flies 27*a*
over the s. our galleys went 49*b*

Sea (cont.)

over the s. to Skye	414b
owse and bottom of the s.	381b
paddles in the halcyon s.	310b
plants his footsteps in the s.	110a
Proteus rising from the s.	473a
quiver and beat of the s.	424a
raging waves of the s.	518a
ran purple to the s.	271b
receiveth as the s.	369b
remain in the broad s.	486a
righteousness as the waves of the s.	502b
rude s. grew civil	356b
sailed the wintry s.	249a
sail on the salt s.	529a
sailors . . on the deep blue s.	20a
say of a . .s. that it is old?	181a
scatter'd in the bottom of . .s.	384b
s., and all that in them is	480a
s. being smooth how many . . boats	368b
s.-blooms and the oozy woods	396b
s.-flower moulded by the s.	420b
s. gave up the dead	519b
s. grows stormy	6a
s. hath no king	313a
s. is his, and he made it	487b
s. itself floweth in yr. veins	445a
s. of faith was once . . at the full	5a
s. of glass like unto crystal	518b
s. of glass mingled with fire	519b
s. of Life and Agony	395b
s. of the world's praise	467a
S. shall give up her dead	491a
s., the open s.!	106a
S. that bares her bosom	473a
s. was made his tomb	21a
s., with such a storm	343a
scents of the infinite S.	6a
sepulchre there by the s.	297b
serpent-haunted s.	154b
serve Him on the S.	231a
set in the silver s.	375a
settle somewhere near the s.	236a
she looked across the s.	225b
shine along the s.	423a
shine upon the Aral S.	8a
sight of that immortal s.	466b
somewhere safe to s.	422a
Southward dreams the s.	441a
splash! splash! along the s.	319a
spread like a green s.	395a
springs of the s.	497b
steep place into the s.	506a
stilleth the raging of the s.	486a
stillness of the central s.	431a
strawberries grow in the s.	534a
such pearl in any gulf the s.	423a
sudden came the s.	49b
sun was shining on the s.	84a
sweet it is, when on the great s.	550b
Sword went out to s.	284b
there was no more s.	519b
the s. beneath my feet	35b
the s.! the s.!	560b
the S. where it goes	5a
the Thracian s.	422b
the waters cover the s.	501b
thousand furlongs of s.	367a
tigers or the roaring s.	366a
to a most dangerous s.	354a
to fill the s. and air	99b
to s. . . . but to make him sick	132b
tremendous s. of cloud	40b
trunk spouts out a s.	275b
under Malta by the s.	231a
union with his native s.	464b
unplumb'd, salt, estranging s.	6b
upon the slimy s.	98b
uttermost parts of the s.	490a
vengeance on the s.	231a
Voices roll in from S.	445b
water in the rough rude s.	375a
waters cover the s.	2b
waters of the dark blue s.	69b
we'll beat to open s.	231a
we'll o'er the s.	193a
we men, at s., indite	134b
went down into the s.	98a
went to s. in a bowl	532b
went to s. in a Sieve	243b
we were masters of the s.!	231a

Sea (cont.)

when I put out to s.	426a
whether in s. or fire	329b
whisper, o'er the s.	99a
who hath desired the S.	234a
whose sound was like the s.	467b
why the s. is boiling hot	84b
wide s. of misery	395a
willing foe and s. room	522b
wind of the western s.	436a
wind-ridden restless s.	119b
with Ships the s. was sprinkled	472b
within a walk of the s.	27a
world-embracing s.	293a
world's tempestuous s.	143b
wrinkled s. beneath him crawls	426b
yea, Sussex by the s.!	235a
ye take away the s.!	231a
yet the s. is not full	499a
yonder is the s.	47a
Sea-banks: upon the wild s.	355a
Sea-beast crawled forth	470a
Sea-breakers: by lonely s.	291a
Sea-breeze hand in hand	441a
Sea-change: suffer a s.	367a
Sea-faring: land-travel or s.?	52b
Sea-fight: last s. is fought	111a
Sea-flower moulded by the sea	420b
Sea-fogs lap and cling	235a
Sea-girt: winged s. citadel	68a
Seagreen Incorruptible	80b
Sea-gulfs: among s. hollow	422b
Sea-hall: his long s.	428b
Sea-King's daughter	439a
Seal: as a s. upon thine heart	501a
have not the s. of God	519a
his s. was on thy brow	184b
S. and Maces danced	175a
s. then, and all is done	324b
s. then this bill	133a
yr. hand; this kingly s.	324a
Sealed: but s. in vain	352a
s. it with his hand	529b
s. thee for herself	334a
seiz'd thy . . soul, and s. thee His	114b
something s. the lips	430a
so softly s.	72b
Sea-life: come to like a s.	208b
Sea-line meets the sky	290a
Sealing-wax: gunpowder and s.	85a
ships and s.	84b
s. of love	352a
Seals: to lose the s. thereof	518b
Seaman: mighty S., this is he	435a
Sea-mark of my utmost sail	364a
Seamen: ahead, is all her s. know	97a
s. made reply	437b
s. were not gentlemen	255b
such as s. use at sea	231a
Sea-monster: more hideous . . than the s.	342a
Sea-nymphs hourly ring his knell	367a
Sear: fallen into the s.	350b
Search: after a s. so painful	309b
but s. will find it out	189b
in the s. of the depths	497b
not worth the s.	352b
s. the land of living men	318a
s. the scriptures	510b
Searched: lord, thou hast s. me	490a
Searching: by s. find out God	497a
I am s. everywhere	410b
Seas: all the s. of God	457b
and the waste of s.	320b
breaking the silence of the s.	471a
but s. do laugh	454b
dangers of the s.	292a
dark broad s.	439a
dear hearts across the s.	230a
down to the s. again	262a
floors of silent s.	145a
foam of perilous s.	220a
gemlike plains and s.	452b
guard our native s.	77b
half s. over	418b
his Briton in blown s.	435a
incident o' th' s.	292a
lapidary s.	452a
launch out on trackless s.	457b
makes the hollow s.	260a
multitudinous s. incarnadine	348a

Seas (cont.)

newly come from the s.	308b
no less than labouring s.	192a
on desperate s. long wont	298a
on what s. shall be thy fate	200a
O rushing s.!	96b
raging s. did roar	525b
s. are quiet . . winds give o'er	449a
s. colder than the Hebrides	154b
strange s. of thought	469b
such as pass on the s.	490b
the s. are too long	16b
thro' the paths of the s.	482a
'twixt two boundless s.	282a
up and down the salt s.	227b
vext the dim s.	438b
when the s. were roaring	161a
Seasickness: as universal as s.	390b
Season: comet of a s.	69b
done at the same s.	378a
each thing that in s. grows	344b
'gainst that s. comes	329b
in s., out of s.	516b
in the s. of the year	525a
little s. of love	171b
meat in due s.	488b
s. of all natures, sleep	349b
s. of calm weather	466b
s. of snows and sins	420a
s. she hath dressings fit	525a
s. yr. admiration	330a
the soote s.	416b
things by s. seasoned	355b
think on at another s.	67b
to every thing there is a s.	499a
word spoken in due s.	498a
Seasoned timber, never gives	187b
Seasons: Age . . with . . his s. done	137b
all s. shall be sweet	101a
anew, returning s. bring	296b
as the swift s. roll!	194a
envious s. roll	194a
few more s. come	33b
four s. fill the measure	221a
from s. such as these	343a
in process of the s. have I seen	388b
I play for S.; not Eternities!	264a
knew the s. when to take	437a
lovers' s. run	134a
of all the S., most love Winter	293b
seen the s. through	231b
see the s. alter	356b
the s.' difference	325b
thou hast all s.	185a
with their s. return	273a
Seat: castle hath a pleasant s.	347a
echo to the s. where love	370b
he fell from off the s.	495a
he grew into his s.	336a
late their happy s.	277a
panting for a happier s.	214a
s. of the scornful	481b
this s. of Mars	375a
while memory holds a s.	331b
wild sequester'd s.	103a
with such ease into his s.	378b
you'll look sweet on the s.	116b
Seated: all s. on the ground	424b
s. one day at the organ	306b
s. upon the convex mound	202b
Seaton: Marie S . . . Marie Beaton	530a
Seats: blissful s.	453b
Seaward: on the rail, and looks s.	47b
Seawards: my road leads me s.	262a
salt tides s. flow	5b
Sea-water: salt s. passes by	430a
Sea-wind: no life but the s.'s	421b
Secesher: agin the S.'s fist	445l
Second: allows the s. place	418b
nor s. he, that rode sublime	175a
no s. knows nor third	278a
s. and sober thoughts	185b
s. at Rome	13a
S. Class in the School of Life	198b
s. eleven sort of chap	21b
where each s. stood heir	359b
Seconds: With sixty s.' worth of distance	230a
smile on you—for s.	131a
Secrecy: for s., no lady closer	377a
Nature's infinite book of s.	322b

Secrecy (cont.)
S. the human dress 33a
Secret: bread eaten in s. 498a
ceases to be a s. 25a
know you her s. 307a
learn the s. of the sea 248a
no s. so close 417a
s., black, and midnight hags 349b
s. of the bull and lamb 264a
s. of the shrouded death 263b
s. things belong unto the Lord 494b
s. was the garden 442b
then in s. sin 94b
three may keep a s. 157a
told my s. out 36b
with every s. thing 500a
Secretary of Nature..Bacon 450b
Secrets: from whom no s. are hid 480a
learned the s. of the grave 293a
s. are edged tools 141a
s. in all families 150a
s. of my prison-house 331a
s. of th' abyss to spy 175a
s. with girls, like loaded guns 114a
Sect: attached to that great s. 393b
it found them a s. 255b
most straitest s. of our religion 513a
paradise for a s. 218a
sad-coloured s. [Quakers] 196b
slave to no s. 301b
Sectaries: jarring s. may learn 109b
nation of s. 129a
Sects: diversity of s. 409a
jarring S. confute 153b
Secure: love is not s. 92a
none can thee s. 448a
s. of private right 138b
s., whate'er he gives 214a
stand s. amidst a falling world 2b
Security: hazard his ease, his s. 56a
our watchword is s. 297a
s. is mortals' chiefest enemy 349b
s. of a God 14a
Sed: groweth s. 526a
Sedately: try to walk s. 414a
Sedge: gentle kiss to every s. 372b
s. is withered from the lake 218b
Seditions: way to prevent s. 15a
Seduce: did not s., she ravished 264b
Seduced: that cannot be s. 338a
Seducer: strong s., opportunity 140a
Seduction of martial music 58b
See: all that we s. or seem 298a
all they that s. me 483a
and thou shalt s. 279b
an' for to s. 229a
before they s. Sir Patrick Spens 530a
blind as they that won't s. 418b
Christian, dost thou s. them 286a
dagger wh. I s. before me 347b
damned if I s. it 287b
did you ever s. such fools 533a
I do not s. them here 312b
I do not ask to s. the..scene 288b
'I don't s.,' said the Caterpillar 82b
if I no more shd. s. thyself 312a
if thou shdst. never s. my face 429a
in all things Thee to s. 188a
I now can s. no more 466a
I now do plainly s. 107a
I s., not feel, how beautiful 100b
I s. them all so excellently 100b
I s. what I eat 83a
I s. what was, and is 463b
I shall s. thee again 341a
I want you to s. Peel, Stanley 177b
I was blind, now I s. 511a
know the faces I shall s. 312b
little while, and ye shall s. me 511b
made the eye, shall he not s.? 487b
may I be there to s. 109a
more people s. than weigh 91a
my friend here didn't s. 172b
my Holy S. of love 219a
never hope to s. one 54b
never s. us but..wish us away 158b

See (cont.)
no man s. me, and live 494a
noo mwore do s. yr. feäce 21a
one short hour to s. 434a
O! s. my women 324b
O taste, and s. 484a
play 'Can you s. me?' 441b
rather s. than be one 54b
s. a disenchanted nation 397a
s. all, nor be afraid 50b
s., and eek for to be seye 89b
s. an innumerable company 29b
s. a pin 532b
s. a round disc of fire 29b
s. ere thou go 446a
s. here it is 219a
s. her passing by 156a, 526b
s. me on Sunday 528b
seem to s. the things..dost not 343b
s. ourseis as others s. us! 61b
s., s., King Richard doth himself 375b
s., s. where Christ's blood 258b
s., the conquering hero comes! 283b
s. thee at Philippi 341a
s. those things wh. you s. 509a
s. thou do it not 519b
s. thro' a flight o' stairs 126b
s. to 'Ackney Marshes 22a
s. too much at once 51a
s. what was forbidden 285a
s., where 'mid work of his..hand 466b
s., where she comes 364a
s. ye to it 508a
shall never s. so much 344a
shall s. eye to eye 502b
Spanish fleet thou canst not s. 400a
them they'll s. nae mair 530a
they shall s. our God 224a
thy joys when shall I s.? 523b
to s. and to be seen 142b
to s. God only 133a
to s. her is to love her 59b
to s. her was to love her 59a
to s. what I have seen 333b
until we hardly s. 398a
Venus, let me never s. 306a
virtue cd. s. to do 267a
wait and s. 10b
we s. thro' a glass darkly 514b
what do I s. and hear? 523a
what went ye out for to s. 506b
what you may expect to s. 136a
when do I s. thee most 311b
when I s. you in the light 237a
while I have eyes to s. 190a
yet I s. thee still 347b
you cd. not s. a cloud 84a
you s. me here, you gods 342b
Seed: all have got the s. 427a
beareth forth good s. 489b
garden that grows to s. 330a
good s. on the land 76a
in the morning sow thy s. 499b
robs not one light s. 218a
s. begging their bread 484a
s. in secret slept 34b
s. its harvest 217b
s. of ruin in himself 7a
what sunny s. 447b
Seeds: look into the s. of time 346a
s. and weak beginnings 380b
s. of godlike power 5a
some s. fell by the wayside 506b
the winged s. 396a
Seed-time: fair s. had my soul 469a
s. and harvest, and cold 492b
Seeing: light of all our s. 466b
precious s. to the eye 345a
way of s. (things rightly) 314b
worth s.? yes 210a
Seek: and s. no more 143a
Frenchies s. him everywhere 290b
I s. and adore them 36b
I s. thee in vain 245b
possess the things I s. 398b
s., and ye shall find 505b
s. it in My arms 442a
s. no happier state 274b
s. out—less often sought 73b
s. to do thee good 489b
s. ye first the kingdom of God 505b

Seek (cont.)
s. ye the Lord while he may 503a
shall we not s. it 184b
shd. I s. farther store 321a
sometime did me s. 473b
they who s. the Lord 484a
we s. one to come 517a
what I s., I know 6b
where s. is find 403a
wh., s. thro' the world 294b
you shall s. all day 352b
you wd. not s. me 564b
Seekest: He whom thou s. 442a
s. thou great things 503b
whom thou s. to find him 422a
Seeketh: charity..s. not her own 514b
he that s. findeth 505b
Seeking: s. shall find Him 47a
s. the food he eats 326a
s. whom he may devour 518a
we must still be s. 464b
Seeks: neither s., nor shows his foe 139b
whoever s. abroad 221b
Seel: s. up the ship-boy's eyes 380a
wise gods s. our eyes 324a
Seeling: come, s. night 349a
Seem: all that we see or s. 298a
men shd. be what they s. 361b
show of things, that only s. 409a
wd. they might s. none 361b
Seemed: all s. well pleased 275a
Seeming: by s. otherwise 360b
keep s. and savour 373a
of s. arms..a short assay 140a
Seemly: it is s. so to do 224b
Seems, madam!..I know not seems 330a
Seen: and be no more s. 484a
benefit..people..never s. 56a
blessed are they that have not s. 511b
brother whom he hath s. 518a
had not the great sun s. 36t
he was s. of me also 514b
I have s. nobody since I saw you 405b
lark so far cannot be s. 343b
love God whom he hath not s. 518a
much have I s. 438b
much more had s. 4b
needs but to be s. 301a
needs only to be s. 108a, 140b
resentment..persons..never s. 288a
s. her wave her hand 431b
s. of none save him 219b
s. what she cd. not declare 193a
that you and I have s. 531a
things a' didn't wish s. 180b
to see and to be s. 142b
True Thomas on earth was never s. 528b
we have s. thee, O love 420b
who hath not s. thee 221b
whom having not s., ye love 517b
wd. you had never s. him 363a
yet s. too oft 301a
Seer: bold s. in a trance 432a
sight of Judah's s. 258a
Sees: doubts from what he s. 29b
eye s...what the eye brings 80b
loved so long and s. no more 310a
s. what he foresaw 465b
she neither hears nor s. 463a
think the king s. thee 186b
See, saw, Margery Daw 533b
Seese: pippins and to s. come 355b
Seest: say what thou s. yond 367b
what thou s., write 518a
Seeth: Lord s. not as man s. 495b
Seine: latitude for a s. 446b
red fool-fury of the S. 431a
Seizure: to whose soft s. 368b
Select: most s. and generous 330b
Selection: principle..of Natural S. 117b
Self: arch-flatterer..is a man's s. 14b
by my own-alone s. 181b
chord of S. 432a
concentred all in s. 317a
dearer than s. 68a
each one a murdered s. 312b
for my single s. 337b
from thee to my sole s. 220a
greater to one than one's s. is 458a
infusing him with s. 375b
joy to see my s. now live 190a

Self (cont.)
love seeketh only S. — 32a
poetical character..has no s. — 223a
resign my s. to thee, O God — 133a
swear by thy gracious s. — 365a
sweet s. set her own price — 293a
to thine own s. be true — 330b
Self-begotten bird — 278a
Self-constituted saints — 195b
Self-control: prudent, cautious s. — 59a
self-knowledge, s. — 435b
Self-esteem, grounded on just — 276a
Self-honoured, self-secure — 7b
Selfish: s. being all my life — 11b
unlike the hard, the s. — 113b
Self-knowledge: self-reverence, s. — 435b
skilful in s. — 465a
Self-love: golden calf of S. — 80a
mirror of s. — 262b
sick of s., Malvolio — 370a
sin of s. possesseth — 388a
true s. and social are the same — 301b
Self-lovers: nature of extreme s. — 15b
Self-protection: liberty of action..s. — 266a
Self-revelation: *fluidity* of s. — 204a
Self-reverence, self-knowledge — 435b
Self-sacrifice: spirit of s. — 464a
Self-scanned: self-schooled, s. — 7b
Self-secure: self-honoured, s. — 7b
Self-seeking: free from s. — 240b
Self-sufficing power of Solitude — 469b
Sell: go and s. that thou hast — 507b
I s. my goodly steed — 531b
Selling: lives by s. something — 412a
Selves: dead s. to higher things — 429b
Selwyn: if Mr. S. calls — 156b
Semblance: outward s. of a man — 126b
s. in another's case — 107b
thou, whose exterior s. doth belie — 466b
thy native s. on — 338b
Semblative a woman's part — 370a
Semele: hapless S. — 258b
Seminary: from a ladies' s. — 164b
Sempronius: we'll do more, S. — 1b
Senate: gives his little s. laws — 298b, 303a
shake alike the s. — 303b
with a s. at his heels — 301b
Senates: applause of listening s. — 174b
gauntlet down to s. — 77b
listening s. hang upon thy tongue — 443b
Senators: green-robed s. — 218a
Send: here am I; s. me — 501b
s. the mild Hindoo — 527b
s. them in, for I am..at leisure — 11b
whom shall I s. — 501b
Seneca: high speech of S. — 14a
S. cannot be too heavy — 332b
Senior-junior..Dan Cupid — 344b
Seniors: advice from my s. — 444a
Senlac! Sanguelac — 427b
Se'nnights nine times nine — 346a
Sensation: but s. is s. — 212b
devote myself to another s. — 223b
Permanent Possibility of S. — 413b
of a short, sharp shock — 164b
Sensational: somewhat too s. — 460a
Sensations: for a life of s. — 222a
s. sweet, felt in the blood — 472a
Sense: accounting for the moral s. — 80b
after yr. own s. — 359b
as keen a s. of duty — 166a
batteries of alluring s. — 260b
bind the wandering s. — 104a
bottom of good s. — 210b
but their s. is shut — 350a
can't be Nature, for it is not s. — 94b
claim to common s. — 25b
common s. and good taste — 389b
gather beauty from their s. — 36a
is of s. forlorn — 100a
it enchants my s. — 369a
judge not the Lord by feeble s. — 110a
left an echo in the s. — 216b
live within the s. they quicken — 399b
lovers'..whose soul is s. — 134a
men of s...of one religion — 322a
Metaphysic calls for aid on S.! — 299a
mocks my waking s. — 403b
nor numb'd s. to steel it — 221b
no s. in gittin' riled! — 182a
nothing goes for s., or light — 65b

Sense (cont.)
not when the s. is dim — 24b
palter with us with a double s. — 351a
porch and inlet of each s. — 267b
retains an obscure s. — 469b
satire or s.,..can Sporus feel? — 303a
Scotchman..a man of s. — 246a
seal thy s. in deathly slumber — 119a
s. aches at thee — 363a
s. and outward things — 466b
s. and wit with poesy allied — 72a
s. faints picturing them — 396b
s. is with their senses..mixed — 264a
s. sublime of something far more — 472a
s., wh. when the winds of Spring — 397a
Shadwell never deviates into s. — 140b
shall my s. pierce love — 312a
solid, reasoning good-s. — 91a
some nonsense about s. — 412b
sound..an echo to the s. — 300a
stings and motions of the s. — 351a
take care of the s. — 83a
thro' s. and nonsense — 138b
too quick a s. — 425a
want of decency is want of s. — 128a
wh. s. may reach and apprehend — 132b
who all my s. confined — 304a
wit and s., virtue — 395b
without one grain of s. — 141a
Senseless: else s. and shapeless — 397b
s. and fit man for the constable — 358b
s., tranced thing — 219a
Senses: my s. in forgetfulness — 192a
Parson lost his s. — 350b
my s. wd. have cooled — 350b
power of our s. — 213a
s., for ever in joy! — 51b
unto our gentle s. — 347a
Sensibility: dear s.! — 411a
experience..is an immense s. — 204b
s. of principle — 57a
yet wanting s. — 112b
Sensible: s. men..never tell — 129b
s. men..of the same religion — 129b
s. to feeling as to sight — 347b
woman was *fundamentally* s. — 210b
Sensibly: things they behave s. about — 390a
Sensitive: Frog is justly s. — 26a
S. Plant in a garden grew — 398a
s., yet..heroically fashioned — 465b
Sensual: earthly, s., devilish — 517b
thro'out the s. world proclaim — 283a
Sensualism: strings of s. — 264b
Sent with broom before — 357b
Sentence: he mouths a s. — 94b
makes half a s. at a time — 108a
my s. is for open war — 272a
originator of a good s. — 148b
speak after s.? Yea — 206a
Sentences: in all pointed s. — 212b
Sentiment: nurse of manly s. — 57a
religion as a mere s. — 288a
s. he has such faith in — 400b
s. is what I am not acquainted — 155a
Sentimental: are you in s. mood? — 164a
s. people..fiddle harmonics — 264b
S. Traveller — 411a
the s. reads — 196a
Sentiments: plague of his s. — 400b
s. that no legislature — 17a
them's my s. — 573a
Sentinel: scarcely worth the s. — 171a
s. on Whitehall gate — 252b
the s. stars set their watch — 77b
Sentinels: fixed s. almost receive — 382b
s. to warn th' immortal souls — 259b
Sentries: like s., are obliged to stand — 141b
untroubled s. of the..night — 280a
Sentry: s., shut yr. eye — 234a
wingèd S. — 448a
Sent'st it back to me — 216b
Separate us from the love of God — 513b
Separation: that eternal s. — 412a
September: April, June, and S. — 172a
cool S. morn — 458b
thirty days hath S. — 533a
Sepulchral statues lay — 132b
Sepulchre: a new s. — 511b
be a soldier's s. — 77a
died about the Holy S. — 313a
dome of a vast s. — 396b

Sepulchre (cont.)
first to the s. — 511b
no man knoweth of his s. — 494b
s. in stubborn Jewry — 375a
s. there by the sea — 297b
throat is an open s. — 482a
when it was yet dark, unto the s. — 511b
whole earth is the s. — 560b
why the s., wherein we saw thee — 331a
Sepulchres: whited s. — 507b
Sequel: what s.? streaming eyes — 433a
Sequester'd vale of life — 174b
Sequitur: no more a s. than yourself — 151b
Seraglio Point — 264b
Seraph: a s.-man — 99b
rapt S. that adores — 301a
S. Abdiel, faithful found — 275a
s.-band, each waved his hand — 99b
Seraphim: bright S. in burning row — 278a
sister of the S.! — 114b
sworded S. — 270b
Seraphims: above it stood the s. — 501b
saw the obsequious S. — 115a
Seraphs: wingèd s. of heaven — 297b
Seraph-wings of ecstasy — 175a
Serbonian bog — 272b
Sere: instead of plain and s. — 36a
leaves they were crisped and s. — 298b
tickle o' the s. — 332b
Serene: breathe its pure s. — 220b
s. yet strong — 305b
that unhoped s. — 39a
Serener: far s. clime — 33b
Serfs at my side — 53b
Sergeant: a-layin' on to the S. — 227a
cheer for the S.'s weddin' — 234a
might have been a s. — 170b
'olding on by the S.'s sash — 234a
S. Whatsisname — 233a
this fell s., death — 337a
Sergeants: two-an-thirty S. — 234a
Sericana, where Chineses drive — 273b
Series of new time began — 138b
Serious: dark and s. angel — 36a
in a s. humour — 1b
joke's a very s. thing — 94b
never means anything s. — 233a
nor trusts them with, s. matters — 91a
nothing s. in mortality — 348a
s. and the smirk — 124b
s. things..in a battle — 84b
treats..a s. subject — 10a
Sermon: her funeral s. — 26a
him who a s. flies — 186b
honest and painful s. — 296a
liked the 'S. on the Mount' — 130b
preach a better s. — 148b
s.'s dull defile — 264a
turn out a s. — 60a
Sermons: s. and soda-water — 70b
s. from mystical Germans — 164b
s. in stones — 325b
Serpent: be the s. under 't — 347a
dragon, that old s. — 519b
gold and flowing s. — 243a
it biteth like a s. — 498b
like Aaron's s. — 301a
my s. of old Nile — 323a
s. beguiled me — 492b
s. subtlest beast — 276a
s. was more subtil — 492a
sharper than a s.'s tooth — 342a
the infernal s. — 270b
think him as a s.'s egg — 338b
'tis a strange s. — 323b
trail of the S. — 282a
way of a s. upon a rock — 499a
Serpentine: to dignify the S. — 131a
Serpents: obscene small s. — 421b
wise as s. — 506a
Servant: bid yr. s. once adieu — 388a
form of a s. — 516a
for thy s. heareth — 495a
good and faithful s. — 508a
good s. does not all commands — 329a
hard a life her s. lives — 476a
his s., nor his maid — 480a
is thy s. a dog — 496b
ken when you have a good s. — 319b
lo! that s. stands you picked — 414a
not a brewer's s. — 29a

Servant (*cont.*)
now Thy s. sleeping — 145b
said the small s. — 125a
s. above his lord — 506a
S. of God, well done — 275a
s. of the high God, Galahad! — 284b
s.'s too often a negligent elf — 19b
s. with this clause — 188b
thy s. depart in peace — 508b
ye hae a gude s. — 320a
yr. s.'s cut in half — 172b
Servants: as one of thy hired s. — 509b
equality in the s.' hall — 21b
fire and people..both good s. — 176b
good s., but bad masters — 244b
hired s. of my father's — 509b
his s. with new acquist — 278a
man has a good many s. — 416b
men in great place are thrice s. — 14b
Press-men..S. of Light — 5a
s. of the most high God — 504a
to s. kind — 79b
we are unprofitable s. — 510a
ye s. of the Lord — 131b
Serve: cared greatly to s. God — 287b
freely we s. — 275a
have not known: shall s. me — 482a
Him s. with fear — 224b
I now will s. more strictly — 463b
no man can s. two masters — 505b
s. it right for being so dear — 124b
s. my turn upon him — 359b
s. thee with a quiet mind — 479b
they also s. who only stand — 278b
time to s. and to sin — 420b
Served: as thou hast s. us — 490a
despised as well as s. it — 67a
had I but s. God — 462b
Jacob's seven years — 493a
Serves: s. and seeks for gain — 342a
take the current while it s. — 341a
Serveth: among you as he that s. — 510a
Service: all s. ranks..same with God — 50a
bounden duty and s. — 480b
choke their s. up — 326a
desert in s. — 369a
did me yeoman's s. — 336b
done the state some s. — 364a
essential s. to his country — 418a
he's out on active s. — 227a
hewn with constant s. — 406a
in s. high, and anthems clear — 268b
in thee 't had been good s. — 323b
s. greater than the god — 369a
s. is perfect freedom — 478a
s. of a mind and heart — 465b
s. of the antique world — 326a
s. sweat for duty — 326a
small s. is true s. — 463b
sometimes to do me s. — 359b
song the s. divyne — 88b
'tis the curse of s. — 359b
weary and old with s. — 386a
Services: nor s. to do — 388a
s. of Angels and men — 480a
Servile: freed from s. bands — 473b
s. to all the skyey influences — 351b
Serving: cumbered about much s. — 509a
Serving-man: iron-bound s. — 132a
s., proud in heart — 343a
Servisable: lowly and s. — 88a
Servitors: words..airy s. — 279a
Servitude: bare laws of s. — 139b
impatient of s. — 55b
s. is at once the consequence — 116b
s. that hugs her chain — 175a
Sesame: Open S.! — 567b
Sesquipedalian blackguard — 96a
Sessions of sweet silent thought — 387b
Sestos and Abydos of her breasts — 132b
Set: here is the whole s. — 400b
I s. her on my pacing steed — 218b
meet it is I s. it down — 331b
neck..broken..can never be s. — 320a
play a s. shall strike..hazard — 381b
s. a candle in the sun — 64b
s. himself doggedly to it — 206b
s. thou in my breast — 176a
s. thine house in order — 502b
s. up thyself, O God — 485b
to have it thus s. down — 332a

Set (*cont.*)
virtue..best plain s. — 16a
Setebos, Setebos, and Setebos — 45b
Setter up and puller down of kings — 384b
Setteth not by himself — 482a
Setting: elsewhere its s. — 466a
nearer he's to s. — 190b
Settle: less will you s. to one — 230b
S.'s numbers — 298b
s. somewhere near the sea — 236a
Settled: people wisn to be s. — 148a
such things are s. nowadays — 71a
'tis s. on the lee — 66a
Settlement: parent of s. — 57a
Settleth: lie that..s. in..the mind — 14a
Settling: perpetually s. — 37a
Seven: may lie till s. — 532b
nay, we are s. — 472b
s. maids with s. mops — 84a
s. times s...nature..cant endure — 155a
seventy times s. — 507a
s. whole days, not one in s. — 188a
world on Sixe and S. — 90a
Seven Dials: air of S. — 163b
Seven-fold gifts impart — 491a
Seventeen: grace of Sweet S. — 425b
Maud is not s. — 433a
Seventh day is the Sabbath — 480a
Seventies: gets well into the s. — 413b
Seventy times seven — 507a
Seventy-seven: at s. it is time — 213a
Sever: kiss, and then we s. — 59a
s. themselves, and madly sweep — 357a
to s. for years — 74b
Severe: from lively to s. — 301b
from pleasant to s. — 141a
if s. in aught — 168b
to nothing but herself s. — 79b
wise he was, but not s. — 4b
Severed: their graves are s. — 184b
Severely: s. breedeth fear — 79b
Severity: s. breedeth fear — 14b
s. of perfect light — 428a
summer..with its usual S. — 102a
treats with..s...serious subject — 10a
Severn: clanging from the S. — 227a
or out to S. strode — 93a
S. into the narrow seas — 157b
twice a day the S. fills — 430a
Severs those it shd. unite — 394a
Seville: dogs of S. — 437b
Sewed: prophetic fury s. the work — 362b
Sewell and Cross young man — 165b
Sewers: houses thick and s. — 276a
reign o'er s. and sinks — 100b
Sewing: s. as long as her eyes — 198b
s. at once, with a double thread — 196a
Sex: fair s. is yr. department — 135b
for the ruin of our s. — 405b
here's the S.! — 61a
no stronger than my s. — 338b
s. to the last — 140a
soft, unhappy s. — 25b
spirits..can either s. assume — 271b
the s. whose presence civilizes — 108a
tyrants of thy s. — 104b
weaker s., to piety more prone — 3b
what is yr. s.'s..care — 251b
women are a s. by themselves — 25a
Sexes: cleanliness of the s. — 457b
old ladies of both s. — 123a
old women (of both s.) — 411b
there are three s. — 404b
Sexton: our honest s. tells — 113b
s. tolled the bell — 195a
went and told the s. — 195a
Sextus: false S. — 253a
Herminius glared on S. — 253b
to S. nought spake he — 253b
Seye: eek for to be s. — 89b
Shackles: s. of an old love — 428b
their s. fall — 111b
Shade: after the night's s. — 357a
alone in summer s. — 465b
Amaryllis in the s. — 269b
betwixt the shine and s. — 425a
boundless contiguity of s. — 111b
by the s. it casts — 49b
clutching the inviolable s. — 8a
crowd into a s. — 302b
dancing in the chequered s. — 269a

Shade (*cont.*)
Glenartney's hazel s. — 316a
green thought in a green s. — 260b
hawthorn bush a sweeter s. — 384a
he is old and she a s. — 241a
his stedfast s. sleeps — 435b
I bear light s. — 393a
in s. of Tempe sit — 401b
narrow verged s. — 260b
no s., no shine..November! — 195a
old sit under the s. of it — 122b
pillared s. high overarched — 276b
present hour..marked with s. — 241a
s. and loveliness and mire — 39b
s. of His hand — 442a
s. of melancholy boughs — 326b
s. of that wh. once was great — 472b
s. of the old apple-tree — 461b
s. that follows wealth or fame — 169a
sitting in a pleasant s. — 20b
sitting in the s. — 229b
sly s. of a Rural Dean — 39b
song, or fleeting s. — 189a
vois memorial in the s. — 88a
wander'st in his s. — 387a
Shades: chase the trembling s. away — 115a
doleful s. — 271a
far are the s. of Arabia — 119a
field is full of s. — 442b
fled the s. of night — 274b
home to s. of under ground — 78b
I have lived with S. so long — 180a
mingle s. of joy and woe — 319b
Oh, happy s.—to me unblest — 111a
s. did hide her — 285a
s. of night were falling fast — 247a
s. of the prison-house — 466a
till the s. lengthen — 288b
where s. of darkness — 119a
Shadow: but a s.'s bliss — 353b
cattle..s. of the British oak — 57a
daisy, by the s. that it casts — 463b
double, swan and s.! — 473a
dream itself is but a s. — 332b
earth be but the s. of Heaven — 275a
follow a s. — 216a
hence, horrible s.! — 349a
hide me under the s. of thy wings — 482b
in the s. of the hill — 73a
it is but a s.'s s. — 332b
life..is but the s. of death — 41a
life's but a walking s. — 350b
light but the s. of God — 41a
like a vast s. moved — 448b
man walketh in a vain s. — 484a
neither s. of turning — 517a
on the earth the s. of thee — 312a
or s. of felicity — 449a
out-soared the s. of our night — 392b
saw the lion's s. e'er himself — 355a
S. cloaked from head to foot — 430a
s. of a glorious name — 550a
s. of a great rock — 502a
S. of Shadows on the deed — 474a
s. of some unseen Power — 394b
s. of the dome of pleasure — 101b
s. of the steeple — 96a
s. of the Valois — 92b
s. of Thy wing — 455b
s. to s., well persuaded — 228a
ship's huge s. lay — 99a
substance..that s. seem'd — 272b
treads the s. of his foe — 98a
unhappy s. — 78a
vague s. of surmise — 146b
with colour and with s. — 441b
yr. s. at evening — 144b
Shadowless like Silence — 195b
Shadows: are s., not substantial — 401a
beckoning s. dire — 267a
best in this kind are but s. — 357b
but the s. of us men — 216a
come like s., so depart! — 349b
events cast their s. before — 77a
half sick of s. — 431b
individuals pass like s. — 56a
millions of strange s. — 387b
no s. great appear — 190a
of their s. deep — 476b
our fatal s. — 23a
scattering of all s. — 20b

Shadows (cont.)
s. and windy places 420a
s. come about her eyes 475a
s. flee away 500a
s. numberless 219b
s. of hates 5a
s. of the evening 20a
s., that showed at noon 244a
s. to-night have struck..terror 385a
there be that s. kiss 353b
very s. of the clouds 463a
what s. we are..s. we pursue 55a
Shadrach, Meshach, and Abed-nego 504a
Shadwell: S. never deviates into sense 140b
S.'s genuine night 140b
Shady: s. side of Pall Mall 283b
s. with birch and beech 37b
sunshine in the s. place 408b
Shaft: and winged the s. 72a
O! many a s., at random sent 317b
s. of slander 294a
Shaftesbury: particularly by Lord S. 91a
Shake: acacia wd. not s. 434a
dreams that s. us nightly 348b
here I s. off the bur 441a
never s. thy gory locks 349a
s. me as they pass 463a
s. hands for ever 137b
s. off the dust 506a
s. of his poor little head 165a
s. the massive paws 25b
s. thou to look on 't 324a
Shaken: and is never s. 389a
so s. as we are 376a
taken, To be well s. 103a
Shakers: movers and s. 291a
Shake-scene in the country 176b
Shakespeare: as I despise S. 390a
better done in S. 142a
but S. also says 70b
Christ's heart, and S.'s strain 146a
Dan Chaucer, mighty S. 36a
did S. ?..the less S. he! 47b
fancy S. this Presider 222a
for gentle S. cut 215b
grace before S. 238b
if S.'s genius had been cultivated 90b
immortal S. rose 213b
I was S.'s countryman 452b
Jew that S. drew 304a
like one of S.'s women 395a
Lo, S., since thy time 36a
make room for S. 22a
myriad-minded S. 102a
my S., rise 215b
one wild S., following Nature's 282b
perhaps understand S. 222b
reading S. by flashes 102b
S., and the musical glasses 171a
S., Falstaff..of East-cheap 170b
S., Fancy's child 269a
[S.]..had the largest..soul 142a
S. is not more decidedly the first 255a
S. is not our poet 241a
[S.] is the very Janus 142a
S. led a life of allegory 223a
S. made use of it first 400a
[S.]..naturally learned 142a
S., on whose forehead climb 44a
S...sad stuff 571a
S. shd. be quite forgotten 93a
S., undoubtedly wanted taste 449b
S. unlocked his heart 47b, 470b
S. was of us 48a
S. (whom you and every play-
house) 303b
souls most fed with S.'s flame 93a
stood with S. at the top 230a
sum of S.'s wit 147a
Taylor, the S. of divines 147a
tongue that S. spake 467a
to S. gave as much 140a
what needs my S. 278a
Shaking: fall without s. 280a
Shalimar: beside the S. 197a
Shall: his absolute 's.' 328a
you s. and you shan't 135a
Shallow: Master S., I owe you 381a
s. brookes murmur 401b
s. in himself 277a
vain or s. thought 147a

Shallows: bound in s. 341a
s...in wh. a lamb may wade 185b
with his depths and his s. 62b
Shalott: beside remote S. 431b
the Lady of S. 431a, 432a
Shame: and race of s. 277b
ashamed with the noble s. 226b
certain death by certain s. 233b
deed throughout the life the s. 177a
each deed of s. 247b
erring sister's s. 72b
foaming out their own s. 518a
he was not born to s. 366a
I see the s. they cannot see 294a
let s. say what it will 336a
not serving s. or lust 131a
put him to an open s. 517a
put them to a perpetual s. 487a
secret House of S. 459b
s. and ruin wait for you 107b
s. come when it will 342b
s. distain his name 61b
s. is ashamed to sit 366a
s. it is to see 226a
s. on us, Christian brethren 200b
so much glory and so much s. 255a
the deed of s. 253a
thy father's s. 35b
waste of s. 389a
without great s...never go back 283a
with s. and grief I yield 225a
whose glory is in their s. 516a
Shamed: s. life is hateful 352a
s. thro' all my nature 432b
Shameless: perfect democracy..s. 57a
Shames: candle to my s. 353b
s., on my bare head 362b
Shamming: priests..gentle s. 282b
s. when he's dead 229a
Shamrock is by law forbid 525b
Shandon: bells of S. 306b
Shank: his shrunk s. 326b
his spindle s. 61a
Shannon: on the green banks of S. 76b
Shape: a dancing s. 273a
execrable s. 273a
gave them s. and speech 423a
grim s. towered up 469a
harmony of s. express 305b
in s. and gesture..eminent 272a
let it keep one s. 351a
mystic s. did move behind me 43b
s. from that thy work 247a
s. no bigger than..agate-stone 364b
s. of things to come 455b
stoop from heaven and take the s. 436b
such a questionable s. 331a
take any s. but that 349a
the other s., if s. it might be 272b
to s. it as he wd. 429a
two of far nobler s. 274a
virtue in her s. 274b
when that strange s. 98b
you might be any s. 85a
Shaped: it is s...like itself 323b
Shapen in wickedness 485a
Shapes: fiery and delectable s. 380b
full of fiery s. 378a
full of s. is fancy 369b
its s...thoughts outnumber 396a
'mongst horrid s. 268b
s. and beckoning shadows 267a
s. that haunt thought's 397a
sublime and beauteous s. 397a
turns them to s. 357b
what s. of sky or plain? 398b
Shard: iron s. 233b
shattered in s. on s. 442a
Share: Adam shall s. with me 276a
beyond a mortal's s. 261a
its ruin didst not s. 131b
no one so true did s. it 371a
no, the utmost s. of my desire 190a
s. the good man's smile 168b
to s. it a' 62b
Shareth in our gladness 3b
Sharks: among the s. and whales 525a
Sharon: rose of S. 160b
Sharp: s. as a needle 308a
s. remedy, but a sure one 121b
somebody's s.

Sharp (cont.)
the billiard s. 164b
Sharpeneth the countenance of his
friend 498b
Sharper: I returned it s. 444a
s. than any two-edged sword 517a
s. than a serpent's tooth 126a, 342a
Sharpest you still have survived 147a
Sharpness of death 478a
Sharps: different s. and flats 50a
Shatter: wd. we not s. it 154a
Shattered: many were s. 437b
Shattering all evil customs 428a
Shave: good lather is half the s. 194b
Shaved with a shell when he chose 242a
Shaw: Oh, Captain S.! 164a
Shawms: trumpets also and s. 488a
Shay: one-hoss s. 194a
She: and you are s. 108b
any been but s. 416a
as any s. belied 389a
but alas! it was s. 67b
came innocence and s. 441a
cruellest s. alive 370a
got him a s. 522b
never home came s. 226b
never none but s.! 524b
one woman, and none but s. 424a
part to blame is s. 291b
s., and comparisons are odious 132a
s. beloved knows naught 368b
s. for God in him 274a
s. is the Broad 528b
s., s. is dead 132b
s., supposing him..the gardener 511b
s., while Apostles shrank 21a
that not impossible s. 115a
the chaste, and unexpressive s. 327a
'tis s., and here..lo I 115b
when s. is by I leave my work 79b
who is this only happy S. 294b
Sheaf: above the slender s. 114a
lay thy s. adown 195b
Shearers: at the s.' feast 269b
sheep before her s. 503a
Shears: Fury with th' abhorred s. 269b
wi' her needle an' her s. 59b
Sheath: sword outwears its s. 74a
sword was in the s. 111a
thy sword into the s. 511b
we shall never s. the sword 10b
Sheaves: bring his s. with him 489b
girded up in s. 387a
yr. s. stood round 493a
Sheba: another S. queen 402a
queen of S. 496a
She-bear, coming up the street 155b
Shed: from the straw-built s. 174a
lowly cattle s. 3b
monarch of a s. 170a
prepare to s. them now 340a
with [Burke] beneath a s. 212a
Sheds: found in lowly s. 267a
Sheelah: when S. was nigh 76b
Sheen: deck'd in glorious s. 286a
Sheep: all we like s. 503a
as s. that have not a shepherd 496a
bah, bah, black s. 534b
beat their love o' s. 250b
bleating of the s. in my ears 495a
Bo-Peep has lost her s. 533a
bringing thy s. in thy hand 7b
careth not for his s. 511a
ensample to his s. 88b
feed my s. 511b
fold shall be full of s. 486a
from thy ways like lost s. 478a
giveth his life for his s. 511a
hungry s. look up 269b
I have found my s. 509b
looking on their silly s. 384a
lost s. of the house of Israel 506a
loves, or else their s. 270b
mountain s. are sweeter 295a
of an old half-witted s. 410b
one sickly s. infects the flock 453a
other s. I have 511a
plunge the struggling s. 253a
return to our s. 566b
s. are in the fauld 20b
s. before her shearers 503a

Sheep (cont.)
s.'s in the meadow 535a
s., that were wont to be so meek 283b
s., what wonder if they stray 110b
shepherdess of s. 265a
teeth are like a flock of s. 500a
that looks after the s. 535a
wh. come to you in s.'s clothing 505b
white over with s. 399b
Sheep-bells and the ship-bells 235a
Sheep-hook: how to hold a s. 269b
Sheeps' guts shd. hale souls 358a
Sheep-worry of Europe [Napoleon] 38a
Sheet: a wet s. 116a
float that standard s. 178a
great s. knit at the four corners 512a
old England's winding s. 29b
s. were big enough..bed of Ware 371b
white s. bleaching 373a
wrapped in their winding s. 137a
Sheets: fumble with the s. 382a
kindliness of s. 39a
whitest s. of snow 115a
Sheffield: Brooks of S. 121b
[Shelburne's] parts, Sir 209a
Shelf: from the s...diadem stole 335a
s. of rock or sand 470a
silence of the upper s. 254b
Shell: heart is like a rainbow s. 310b
he shaved with a s. 242a
kill him in the s. 338b
leaving thine outgrown s. 194a
within thy airy s. 267a
smooth-lipped s. 464b
Shelley: Burns, S., were with us 48a
did you once see S. plain 48b
Mrs. S. answered 391b
peace in S.'s mind 395a
[S.] is a..ineffectual angel 9b
S., whom envy never touched 241b
S. with liquid music in the word 36a
sphere for S.'s genius 9a
there S. dreamed 206a
Shells: cockle s., and silver bells 533a
s., of pearly hue 241a
Shelter: I'd s. thee 62a
s. from the stormy blast 453a
what s. to grow ripe 7a
Shelters: naught s. thee 441b
Shem: done with the Tents of S. 231b
it might be S. 236a
S., Ham, and Japheth 492b
Shenandoah, I long to hear you 525a
Shepherd: as sweet unto a s. 176a
call you, S., from the hill 8a
dead s., now I find thy saw 327a
fairest s. on our green 295b
feed his flock like a s. 502b
feed me with a S.'s Care 2a
gentle S., tell me where 200b
God of love my S. is 188a
good s. giveth his life 511a
hast any philosophy in thee, s.? 327a
is the S.'s delight 522a
is the S.'s warning 522a
King of Love my S. is 18a
lark to s.'s ear 356a
Lord is my s. 483a
O faithful s.! to come 7b
sheep that have not a s. 496a
S. and Bishop of yr. souls 517b
s., blowing of his nails 384a
s., blows his nail 345b
s. in Virgil 206b
s., I take thy word 267a
s. of the Hebrid Isles 443a
S. of the Ocean 408a
s. (repented) of his love 18b
s. tells his tale 268b
slighted, s.'s trade 269b
star calls up the s. 352a
the S.'s sweet lot 32b
thou happy S.-boy 466a
truth in every s.'s tongue 307b
weather the s. shuns 180a
wd. not love a s. swain? 176b
Shepherdess of sheep 265a
Shepherding her bright fountains 392b
Shepherds: ground wh. British s. tread 464a
s., looking on their silly sheep 384a

Shepherds (cont.)
that liberal s. give 336a
while s. watched their flocks 424b
Sheridan: [S.] is dull 207b
S. twenty miles away 308b
S. was listened to 310a
Sheriff: stout old s. comes 252a
Sheriffmuir a battle there was 256b
Sherris: valour comes of s. 380b
Sherris-sack hath a two-fold 380b
Sherry is dull 207b
Sherwood in the red dawn 290a
Sheugh: yet in any s. 529a
Shew ourselves glad in him 487b
Shewed unto him all the kingdoms 509a
She-wolf: eats the s.'s young 99b
Shews: admire fair seeming s. 409a
Shield: be thy s. and buckler 487b
broken was her s. 318b
coffin-'eaded s. 229a
idle spear and s. 270a
lady in his s. 431b
s. of faith, wherewith ye shall 516a
s. of the mighty is..cast away 495b
s. was hung on the breast 92a
snatch'd..spear but left the s. 318a
trusty s. and weapon 569a
wisdom the mirrored s. 392a
Shielding men from..folly 407b
Shields: all s. of mighty men 500b
s. in Branksome Hall 316b
Shieling: lone s. 320b
Shift: let me s. for myself 283a
we'll s. our ground 331b
we s. and bedeck and bedrape 421a
Shifting his side (as a lawyer) 110b
Shilling: a Splendid S. 296b
Philip and Mary on a s. 66a
s. a day, bloomin' good pay 234a
volume's price, a s. 419b
Shillings: rather than forty s. 355b
Shimmered: Jeeves s. out 573b
Shine: anxious for to s. 165a
betwixt the s. and shade 425a
come, within our bosoms s. 86b
deceitful s., deceitful flow 282b
every one doth s. 339a
I'll s. on ye yet 116b
let yr. light so s. before men 505b
no shade, no s...November! 195a
nothing does but s. 443a
not to s. in use 438b
qualified to s. in company 419a
see him s. so brisk 376b
s. as it shines now 132a
s. in my arms 176a
s. thro' the gloom 251b
their visitation they shall s. 520a
they s. on all alike 302b
warms you here shall s. on me 374b
wh. scatteringly doth s. 260b
Shined: in her person s. 278b
s. at Lugwardin 445a
Shines: more it's shook, it s. 178b
Shinest: wheresoe'er thou s. 397b
Shingles: naked s. of the world 5a
Shining: I see it s. plain 199b
needles, once a s. store 109a
quietly s. to the quiet moon 101a
season of clear s. 110b
s. nowhere but in the dark 448a
s. with all his might 84a
somewhere the sun is s. 181b
Shins: break my s. against it 326a
Ship: all I ask, is a tall s. 262a
a s., an isle 155a
a s. is floating in the harbour 393b
being in a s. is being in jail 207a
betwixt the costs of a s. 216a
born in a s...River of Time 6a
from fearful trip the victor s. 457b
gart build a bonny s. 529a
he brake that gallant s. 529a
his rapt s. run on her side 87a
idle as a painted s. 98b
it reached the s. 99b
it was so old a s. 155a
land to wh. she wd. (must) go 97a, 472b
like a stately s. 277b
many a tall s. he buried 354a
one leak will sink a s. 54b

Ship (cont.)
O S. of State! 246b
our s. hath touched upon the desarts 373a
s. after s., the whole night long 437b
s. has weathered every rack 457b
s. not far from land 525b
s.'s huge shadow lay 99a
s. I have got in the North Country 531a
s. is anchored safe 457b
s. is clear at last 457a
s. was as still as she cd. be 406b
s. went down like lead 99b
s. wd. not travel due West! 86a
stately s. is seen no more 244a
'there was a s.,' quoth he 98a
the s. that goes 120b
the s. was cheered 98a
undergirding the s. 513a
wap them into our s.'s side 530a
way of a s. 499a
we too take s. O soul 457b
what care I for the s. 130b
what good s. sailed he 130b
what is a s. but a prison? 64a
whither, O splendid s. 37a
Ship-bells ring along the..beach 235a
Ship-boy: seel up the s.'s eyes 380a
Shipman was ther 88b
Shipmate, joy! 457a
Shipping: fishes first to s...impart 139b
sink all the s. there 216a
Ships: as s., becalmed at eve 96b
drew a thousand s. to Tenedos 259b
face that launched a thousand s. 258b
far distant, storm-beaten s. 256b
go down to the sea in s. 488b
howl, ye s. of Tarshish 502a
I spied three s. 522a
like two doomed s. 459b
mighty s. ten thousand ton 192a
move with the moving s. 424a
of shoes and s. 84b
our s. were British oak 10b
past away with five s. of war 437b
roll up and down our s. at sea 134b
s. are but boards 353a
s. are out of gear 437a
she 'as s. on the foam 236b
s., by thousands, lay 70b
s. shall go abroad 231a
s. that pass in the night 249a
s., towers, domes 472b
six s. of the line 437b
something wrong with our bloody s. 22b
stately s. are twirled 192a
stately s. go on 425b
there go the s. 488b
thou shalt break the s. 485a
Thracian s. and the foreign faces 420a
three s. a-sailing there 524a
watch the s. of England go! 228a
weak s. and spirits steer 422a
we've got the s. 201b
with S. the sea was sprinkled 472b
Shipwreck: escaped the s. of time 13a
s. of my..youth 117a
Shire: s...heart of England 137a
thro' all the s. 198b
Shires: round both the s. 199a
s. and towns from Airly 225b
Shirt: merits of a spotless s. 434b
s. wh. ought to be at wash 255b
shroud as well as s. 196a
Shirts: no s. to wear 163a
Shive: cut loaf to steal a s. 368a
Shoal of time 347a
Shoals of honour 386a
Shock: s. them and keep them up 390a
short, sharp s. 164b
we shall s. them 374b
Shock-headed Peter 192b
Shocks: s. of young love-liking 469b
thousand natural s. 333a
withindoors house the s. 198a
Shod: all s. with steel 465b
Shoddy: up goes the price of s. 163b
Shoe: a s. be Spanish 65b
dame has lost her s. 534a
for want of a s. 157a
in a s. she drops a tester 215b

Shoe (cont.)
into a left-hand s. 85b
one, two, buckle my s. 532a
sailed off in a wooden s. 151a
sixpence in her s. 106a
who lived in a s. 533b
Shoes: beautiful are thy feet with s. 500b
ere those s. were old 330a
French..wear wooden s. 170a
he who sees, takes off his s. 43a
him that makes s. 64a
King James..call for his old s. 321a
my s. from the shoemaker 171a
of s. and ships 84b
over s. in love 372b
put off thy s. 493b
s. were clean and neat 84a
s. were number nine 280b
s. were on their feet 403b
surgeon to old s. 337b
Wellington..s. of his soldiers 17b
yr. s. on yr. feet 494a
Shoe-string: careless s. 189a
Shoe-tie: or glist'ring s. 115b
Shone: along the deep proudly s. 76b
s. like a meteor streaming 271b
s. round him o'er the dead 184b
Shook: monk who s. the world 280a
Shoomp: she gife a s. 244b
Shoon: cork-heeled s. 530a
his clouted s. 267b
his sandal s. 335b
takes her buckled s. 131a
walks the night in her silver s. 119b
Shoot: I s. the hippopotamus 25b
I will s. you! 531a
man of war, and can s. 188a
privily s. at them 482a
s. folly as it flies 300b
s. higher than..aims..at a bush 401b
s., if you must 459a
s. out their lips 483a
s. the sleepy, green-coat man 192b
up and s. themselves 39b
nest is in a watered s. 310b
wilt s. into the dark 438a
young idea how to s. 443b
Shooting-stars attend thee 189b
Shoots: aimeth at the sky s. higher 186b
s. at the midday sun 401b
s. higher that threatens..moon 186b
s. of everlastingness 448a
Shop: a man has s. to mind 51b
he talked s. like a tenth muse 523b
shun the awful s. 93a
Shopkeepers: a nation of s. 1a, 403a, 564a
Shopocracy: abuse the s. 289b
Shore: adieu! my native s. 68a
all waters as the s. 421a
ambergris on s. 260a
apples on the Dead Sea's s. 68b
bring him safe to s. 253b
Chorasmian s. 392b
courses from the s. 457a
dies a wave along the s. 18b
fast by their native s. 111a
fright us from the s. 453b
high s. of this world 382b
his control stops with the s. 69b
kingdom of the s. 388a
lash the sounding s. 300a
lights around the s. 313a
low sounds by the s. 475b
more willing bent to s. 78b
my boat is on the s. 73a
naked foot on the s. 118b
Night's Plutonian s. 298b
now upon the farther s. 145b
nymphs on the s. 424b
ornament is but the guiled s. 354a
pull for the s., sailor 315b
rapture on the lonely s. 69b
s. of Araby the blest 273b
s. of the wide world 221a
some false impossible s. 8b
some wide-watered s. 268a
sport upon the s. 466b
stayed upon the green s. 222b
to his own native s. 298a
towards the pebbled s. 388a
unknown and silent s. 240a

Shore (cont.)
wandering from the nightly s. 298b
waves that beat on Heaven's s. 29b
where is that radiant s.? 184b
wild on this world's s. 290a
Shoreditch: bells at S. 533b
Shores: around desolate s. 221a
earth's human s. 220b
exult O s. 457b
made in her concave s. 337b
possess these s. with me 117a
s. of old romance 463a
Shorewards: great winds s. blow 5b
Shorn: came for wool..went home s. 48b
s. and parcelled Oxus 8a
Short: Codlin's the friend, not S. 125a
come s. of the glory 513a
Eternity's too s. 2a
find it wond'rous s. 169a
long while to make it s. 444a
nasty, brutish, and s. 191b
s., and far between 29a
s. and the long of it 355b
s. as any dream 356a
s., bright, resistless course 317b
the lyf so s. 90a
we have as s. a Spring 189a
Shorter: Clement S. 93a
make you s. by the head 145b
s. a prize poem is, the better 255a
Shorter-Catechist [Stevenson] 185b
Shortest: s. of men 19b
s. way..the foulest 13a
Shortness: spend that s. basely 379a
Shot: a long s., Watson 135b
by bullet or by s. 525b
Sahib s. divinely 527b
s. at for sixpence a day 120b
s. heard round the world 146b
s. with the self-same artillery 249b
Shoulder: hand on his s. smote 287b
on any s. that I see 342a
on my leaning s. 474a
s. the sky, my lad 200a
sparrow alight on my s. 444a
what s., and what art 32a
Shoulders: about the s. thrown 189a
bearing on s. immense 6b
borne on our s. 47a
heads do grow beneath their s. 360a
their s. held the sky 200a
turns sides and his s. 453a
Shout: ceased the inhuman s. 69a
made a universal s. 337b
needn't s. so loud 85a
rout send forth a joyous s. 252b
rung the battle s. 194a
s. about my ears 92a
s. of them that triumph 286a
s. round me, let me hear thy shouts 466a
s. that tore hell's concave 271b
s. with the largest 126a
shouted with a great s. 494b
with psalms must s. 187a
Shouted: s. in his ear 85a
sons of God s. for joy 497b
Shouting: captains, and the s. 497b
every man s. in proportion 417a
tumult and the s. 233b
Shouts with his sister at play! 425b
Shove: s. away the worthy..guest 269b
that's all s. be'ind me 232a
Shoved him into politics 26a
Shovel also 230b
Show: all a fleeting s. 282b
I will s. you something 144b
merely to s. that you have one 90b
multitude, that choose by s. 353b
offer it the s. of violence 329b
outward s. of things 409a
Savon? s. him up 25a
s. and gaze o' time 351a
s. it a fair pair of heels 377a
s. me so divine a thing 260a
s., to the apt thoughts of men 341b
s. us how divine..a woman 473a
s. us the Father 511a
s. vilely in me 380a
that we can s. to-day 127b
that within wh. passeth s. 330a
thing they most do s. 388b

Show (cont.)
time with fairest s. 347b
to s. the form it seemed to hide 317b
wealth to me the s. had brought 467a
Shower: a very s. of beauty 465b
crawling out after a s. 20a
dying lamp, a falling s. 392a
s. of light is poesy 220b
s. yr. shooting corns presage 419b
will not s. on me 199b
Showers: after sharpest s. 242b
Aprille with his s. sote 88a
as sun and s. there 385b
blown seas and storming s. 435a
I bring fresh s. 393a
see, what s. arise 384b
s. and dewdrops wet 311a
small s. last long 374b
suck the honied s. 270a
Sydnaean s. 115b
with true-love s. 335b
Showery, Flowery 158a
Showest: have more than thou s. 342a
Showing: men of little s. 234b
Shown: God wd. have her s. 191a
Shows: our s. are more than will 371a
s. of love to other men 337b
so may the outward s. 354a
Shrank: oblivion..s...reproved 392b
Shreds: king of s. and patch 335a
thing of s. and patches 164a
Shrewsbury: bower of wanton S. 302b
long hour by S. clock 379a
Shriek: a solitary s. 70b
short shrill s. 103a
s. from some captured town 136a
to hear a night-s. 350b
with hollow s. 270b
Shrieking: hooting and s. 338a
s. and squeaking 50a
Shrieks to pitying Heav'n are cast 302b
Shrine: Apollo from his s. 270b
best fits a little s. 188b
Melancholy has her sovran s. 219b
pure virgin s. 447b
s., where you alone are placed 176b
this peaceful s. 206a
this Temple keeps its s. 293b
thy s., thy grove 220a
Shrines: a vapour over s.! 44a
Shrink: mortals start and s. 453b
never make thee s. 529a
Shroud: comes to s. me 132b
in a s. of thoughts 68b
my s. of white 371a
peace be to my sable s. 269a
ray on ray split the s. 52b
s. as well as a shirt 196a
white his s. 335b
Shrouds: land-breeze shook the s. 111a
s. thee wheresoe'er thou shinest 397b
Shrunk: how much art thou s.! 379a
swiftly s. away 407b
Shudder: I s. at the word 555a
Shuddering: of s., also, and tears 452a
shall I with s. fall? 264a
Shuffle: patience, and s. the cards 575b
Shuffled off this mortal coil 333a
Shuffling: not so above; there is no s. 334b
Shuh-shuh-gah 248b
Shulamite: return, O S. 500b
Shun: I did s. a year 132a
s. the fault I fell in 531b
s. what I follow 50b
thought she wd. s. me 22b
Shut: but their sense is s. 350a
O s. not up my soul 483b
s. the door after you 143b
s. the door, good John 302b
s. up in measureless content 347b
wisdom..quite s. out 273b
Shutter: before her on a s. 440b
Shutters: close the s. fast 112a
my back-parlour s. 295a
Shuttle: musical s. 457b
swifter than a weaver's s. 497a
Shy: Jesus, wast Thou s. 441b
we are not s. 164a
Shyness: diffidence or s. 164b
Siam: King of S. sent ambassadors 210a
Sibyl: saw the S. at Cumae 313a

Sibyl (cont.)
s., that had numbered in the world 362b
what wdst. thou, S.? 313a
Sichem: divide S. 485b
Sicily: dost thou remember S.? 460a
Syrtes and soft S. 8b
Sick: all his s. men from the land 437b
are you s. or are you sullen? 211b
as s. that surfeit with too much 352b
but they that are s. 506a
can s. men play so nicely 375a
half my men are s. 437b
half s. of shadows 431b
I am s. at heart 329a
I am s. of many griefs 341a
I am sudden s. 322b
kill s. people groaning 259a
lying s. ashore 437b
make any man s. to hear her 296a
more than a little s. 227b
never s. at sea! 166a
not so s., my lord 350b
perhaps was s., in love 301b
say I'm s., I'm dead 302b
see me and be s. 199a
s. almost to doomsday with eclipse 329b
s., and ye visited me 508a
s., as a dog 182b
s. in soul and body both 192a
s. man of Europe, the Turk 564b
s. persons, and young children 479a
tell him, that I am s. of love 500b
the s., O Lord, around thee lay 447a
to sea..but to make him s. 132b
where the s. one roams 196a
yourself and me, I am s. of both 209a
Sicken: appetite may s. 369b
Vanity will s. soon and die 270b
when love begins to s. 340b
Sickened at all triumphs 94b
Sickens at another's praise 94b
Sickle: cd. not make the s. yield 30a
his s. in his hand 248a
s. in the fruitful field 30a
with his s. keen 248a
within his bending s.'s compass 389a
Sicklemen: sunburnt s. 367b
Sickly but sassy 181b
Sickness: by His health, s. 33a
falling s. 338a
in s. and in health 481b
love is a s. 117a
medicine to heal their s. 490b
my long s. of health 368a
s. that destroyeth 487b
thy s. shall depart 227b
very s. in my heart 336a
when yr. s. is yr. soul 199b
Side: be near us at our s. 430a
friends who set forth at our s. 7b
Gods..are on our s. to-day 254a
my hand into his s. 511b
on one s. lay the Ocean 429a
on this s. my hand 376a
passed by on the other s. 509a
rose o' the wrong s. to-day 38a
she standeth by thy s. 531b
s. by s. those chiefs of pride 254a
s. by s. were laid 274b
trumpets sounded..on the other s. 54b
who is on my s.? who? 496b
Side-arms: keeps 'is s. awful 228b
Sides: between the piney s. 435a
holding both his s. 268b
houseless heads and unfed s. 343a
no woman's s. can bide 371a
ruined s. of kings 22b
said on both s. 2a
s. of nature will not sustain it 322b
turns his s. and his shoulders 453a
two separate s. to my head 236a
wear it on both s. 369a
Sideways: looked s. up 99a
s. wd. she lean 218b
Sidney: Friend to Sir Philip S. 177a
miracle of our age..S. 79a
S.'s self, the starry paladin 52a
S.'s sister 42b
S., warbler of poetic prose 112b
Siege: laugh a s. to scorn 350b
men of royal s. 359b

Siege (cont.)
s. of the city of Gaunt 531b
Sieges: battles, s., fortunes 360a
Sieve: in a s. I'll thither sail 346a
to sea in a S. 243b
water through a s. 85b
Sifted: God had s. three kingdoms 247a
Sigh: a s. too much 256a
beadle to a humorous s. 344b
cheat thee of a s. 461b
he gave a deep s. 411a
I'll s. with you 164a
kiss, a s., and so away 115a
passing tribute of a s. 174b
prompts th' eternal s. 301b
regain'd my freedom with a s. 69b
shall I ever s. and pine? 188a
s. for the toothache 358b
s., heart, again in the dew 474b
s. is the sword of an Angel King 30b
s. like Tom o' Bedlam 342a
s. no more, ladies 358a
s. of such as bring cowslips 189a
s. that only one thing 9a
s. that rends thy constant heart 169a
s. that silence heaves 218b
s. to those who love me 73a
some a light s. 24a
then s. not so 358a
took her with a s. 31b
you can hear them s. 162b
Sighed: he s. no more 167a
I s., and said amang them 61b
no sooner loved but they s. 327b
she s. sore, and sang full sweet 143b
s. and look'd, and s. again 139a
s. and looked unutterable 443b
s. at the sound of a knell 113a
s. for the love of a ladye! 167a
we have not s. deep 53a
wept not greatly, but s. 257b
Sighing: genius is with s. sent 270b
it s. cries, Hey ho 117a
plague of s. and grief 377b
poor soul sat s. 363a
s. of a contrite heart 479a
s. thro' all her works 276a
sorrow and s. shall flee 502a
we s. saw 249b
Sighs: add sobs, fiery s. 64b
before my s. did dry it 188a
breast shortening into s. 420b
for my pains a world of s. 360a
her s. the strings do break 78a
made of s. and tears 327b
night of memories and of s. 241a
on the Bridge of S. 69a
paid with s. a plenty 198b
s. are the natural language 321b
Sorrow, with her family of S. 392a
thousand s. to save 371a
winds and waters s. and tears 322b
Sight: alas, a piteous s. 407b
at s. of thee was glad 463b
bury sorrow out of s. 53a
by faith, not by s. 515a
cannot shew so brave a s. 260b
creation downward bend their s. 142b
dislike..at first s. 410a
dulness of our blinded s. 491a
earth, and every common s. 466a
first s. they have changed eyes 367b
gleamed upon my s. 470b
hide them for my aching s. 12a
in the s. of the unwise 520a
it is not yet in s. 400a
it was a heavenly s. 99b
keen discriminating s. 78b
loved not at first s. 259a, 327a
love this s. so fair 224a
many a vanished s. 387b
nor any sound or s. 422a
oft the s. of means to do ill 374b
Oh the pleasant s. to see 225b
out of s. is out of mind 97a
possession of this heavenly s. 364a
sensible to feeling as to s. 347b
s. of any bird 497b
s. of vernal bloom 273a
s. of you is good for sore eyes 418b
s. so touching in its majesty 472b

Sight (cont.)
s. to dream of 100a
s. to make an old man young 427a
so he vanished from my s. 32b
terror on my aching s. 104b
tho' lost to s. 245b
to s. or thought be formed 276a
we were a comely s. 530a
Sighted fifty-three 437a
Sigh-tempests: nor s. move 134a
Sights: all s. from pole to pole 8b
discover s. of woe 271a
frequent s. of what is to be borne 468b
her s. and sounds 40a
see the s. that dazzle 33b
s. as youthful poets dream 269a
so full of ugly s. 384b
such s., or worse 468b
Sign: creaking of a country s. 107b
he dies, and makes no s. 384a
in this s. shalt thou conquer 540b
nay, but I have a s. 41a
outward and visible s. 481a
seeketh after a s. 506b
s. you must not touch 132b
we made no s. 459b
wh. is indeed but s. 359b
Signal: I..do not see the s.! 287a
only a s. shown 249a
s. to a maid 265a
Signals: stood as s. to the land 99b
Signifying nothing 350b
Signiors: grave, and reverend s. 359b
Sign-post: Majesty's head on a s. 255a
Signs: by proofs but s. 293b
my s. and wonders 493b
s. of the times 507a
Sikes, housebreaker 75a
Silence: after-s. on the shore 73b
all s. an' all glisten 250b
a s. in the hills 430a
being of the eternal S. 466b
bless myself with s. 49b
breaking the s. of the seas 471a
calumnies..answered best with s. 216a
come then, expressive S. 443a
elected S., sing to me 197b
eternal s. of these..spaces 564b
ever widening slowly s. all 428b
fish monastic s. keep 132b
foster-child of s. 219b
friendly s. of the mute moon 555a
God strikes a s. 44a
Gospel of S. 572b
his s. will sit drooping 336b
icy s. of the tomb 219a
I kept s...even from good words 484a
in s. and in gloom 12b
in s. sad, trip we 357a
kindly s. when they brawl 425b
let yr. women keep s. 514b
lies are often told in s. 413a
like S., listening to s. 195b
[Macaulay] has..flashes of s. 404b
my gracious s. 328a
parted in s. and tears 74b
power of punishment is to s. 213b
rest is s. 337a
sigh that s. heaves 218b
s. accompanied 274a
S.! and Desolation! 298a
S. and Foresight 473a
s. and sleep like fields 119a
s. augmenteth grief 176b
s. deep as death 76b
s. fell with the waking birds 434a
s. in heaven 519a
S. is deep as Eternity 80a
s. is divine, yet also brutish 81a
S. is golden 81b
s. is..his mother tongue 170b
s. is most noble 420b
S. is of Eternity 81b
s. is only commendable 352b
s. is the perfectest herald 358a
s. is the virtue of fools 13b
s., like a poultice 194a
s. more musical than any song 311a
s. of the many villagers 243a
s. of the sleep-time 52a
s. of the upper shelf 254b

Silence (cont.)
s. sank like music 99b
s. surged softly backward 119b
s. that dreadful bell 361a
s. that is in the starry sky 463a
s. their mourning 424b
s. was pleased 274a
s. we the tempest fear 139b
speech is the small change of s. 265a
still-born S.! 155a
study a long s. 454b
that eternal s. 438b
that man's s. is wonderful 181a
there is a s. where no sound 195b
thunders of white s. 43b
'tis visible s. 312a
towers of s. 119a
to which, in s. hushed, his very soul 464b
two-fold s. was the song 312a
under all speech . . lies a s. 80a
with s. and tears 74b
Silencing: justified in s. mankind 266a
Silent: all s. and all damned 468b
away into the s. land 311a
great joys, like griefs, are s. 259b
impossible to be s. 56a
into that s. sea 98b
s. ? ah, he is s.! 181a
s. as the moon 277b
s. in seven languages 17b
s., let thy morals tell thy mind 299b
s. on his horse 27a
s. stars go by 40a
s., upon a peak in Darien 220b
tongue lies s. in the grave 110a
why art thou s., thou voice 115b
Silently: gentle wind . . s., invisibly 31b
s., and with how wan a face! 401b
s. as a dream the fabric rose 112b
s. steal away 247a
Silk: make his couche of s. 89b
soft as s. 160b
that thing of s. 303a
walk in s. attire 33a
worms . . that did breed the s. 362b
Silken: s. dalliance 381b
s., shy, insinuating 384b
Silks: in s. my Julia goes 190b
Silliness: bay mare shames s. 458a
s. to live when . . is torment 360b
Silly: babe, come s. soul 35b
heard a lot of s. things 186a
s. to gild refined gold 70b
Siloa's brook that flow'd 270b
Siloam's shady rill 184a
Silver: breathe thro' s. 49a
gold and s. becks me 374a
I'll give thee a s. pound 77a
just for a handful of s. 48a
like as s. is tried 486a
little s. crucifix 227a
little s. feet 261a
rocked in s. nor in gold 522a
s. and gold have I none 512a
s. cord be loosed 500a
s. for the maid 228a
s. hae to spare 33a
s., snarling trumpets 221b
s. tassie 60b
s. threads among the gold 308b
thirty pieces of s. 508a
turn forth her s. lining 267a
white-robed, with s. hair 35b
Silvered: head not . . completely s. 112a
Silversmith: Demetrius, a s. 512b
Silvery: coin of s. shine 85b
so s. is thy voice 190b
Silvia: except I be by S. 372b
then to S. let us sing 372b
who is S.? 372b
Similes: most unsavoury s. 376b
play with s. 463b
Similitude: more from the first s. 43a
worst s. in the world 255a
Similitudes: visions, and used s. 504a
Simmery Axe: number seventy, S.! 167a
Simon: one S. a tanner 512a
real S. 86b
S., I have somewhat to say 509a
S. . . lovest thou me 511b

Simon (cont.)
S. Peter saith unto them 511b
S.'s wife's mother 508a
S. the Cellarer 25b
Simple S. met a pieman 532b
Simple: delight in s. things 228a
for as s. he looks 62b
I sought the s. life 114a
mind that is grandly s. 148a
s. great ones gone for ever 433b
s., sensuous and passionate 279b
too s. and too sweet 293a
Simpleness: God . . knowest my s. 486b
s. and gentleness 227b
when s. and duty tender it 357b
Simples: compounded of many s. 327a
Simplicity: cultivate s. Coleridge 239b
in his s. sublime 435a
in low s. 353a
love thee, meek S.! 101b
makes a grace 215a
noble nature . . treats with s. 10a
pity my s. 455b
s. a child 299b
s. of the three per cents. 129b, 320b
truth miscalled s. 388a
Simplify, simplify 444a
Simulacrum: sun . . the dark s. 41a
Sin: before polygamy was . . a s. 138a
be ye angry, and s. not 515b
blossoms of my s. 331b
by that s. fell the angels 386a
convinceth me of s. 511a
dead unto s., and living 481a
died unto s. once 513a
does not win who plays with S. 459b
dreadful record of s. 135b
earth hath no s. but thine 37b
ere s. cd. blight 100b
excepting Original S. 78a
for she knew no s. 140a
for the good man's s. 77b
go, and s. no more 511a
go away and s. no more 525a
guilty of dust and s. 188b
have ye sinned one s. for the pride 235b
he that is without s. 511a
his darling s. is pride 100b
his favourite s. is pride 406b
ignorance . . not innocence but s. 47b
I have a s. of fear 132a
impute my Fall to S. 154a
in s. hath my mother conceived 485a
is the law s.? God forbid 513a
laden with my s. 415b
lukewarmness I account a s. 107a
Milton, Death, and S. 477b
mother I'm living in s. 186a
my s. is ever before me 485a
my s. their door 132a
night that shd. banish all s. 168a
noise and s.! 48b
no s. but ignorance 259a
no s., but to be rich 374a
no s. except stupidity 460a
nothing emboldens s . . as mercy 368a
not known s., but by the law 513a
not let His eye see s. 155b
one cunning bosom s. 187a
one single venial s. 288b
one s. will destroy a sinner 54b
palace of sweet s. 219a
piercing pain, a killing s. 415a
quantum o' the s. 60a
read of that s. in a book 235b
remedy against s. 481b
roots of s. are there 235b
sacrifice for s., . . not required 484a
say that we have no s. 518a
shall we continue in s. 513a
s. as it were with a cart rope 501a
s. if thou wilt . . in secret 94b
s. I impute to each . . ghost 52a
s. of abstinence 130b
s. of self-love possesseth all 388a
s.'s a pleasure 70a
s. shall be no more 149b
s. strongly 550b
s. that amends is but patched 370a
s. that dwelleth in me 513a
s. to covet honour 383a

Sin (cont.)
S. wherewith the Face of Man 154a
s. wh. doth so easily beset us 517a
s. wh. I did shun 132a
s. ye do by two and two 235b
stand in awe, and s. not 481b
taught Original S. 46b
they s. who tell us love can die 406b
this dark world of s. 28a
thy s.'s not accidental 352a
till disproportioned s. jarr'd 278a
time to serve and to s. 420b
'tis s., nay profanation 189a
to s. in loving virtue 351b
wages of s. is death 513a
want of power to s. 141a
weeps incessantly for my s. 31b
where s. abounded, grace . . abound 513a
wilt thou forgive that s. 132a
won others to s. 132a
world's as ugly, ay, as s. 246a
worst s. . . to be indifferent 390a
yr. s. will find you out 494b
Since: s. first I saw 526a
s. nothing all my love avails 47b
Sincere: officious, innocent, s. 210b
Sincerity: in a sad s. 147a
s. is a dangerous thing 460a
unleavened bread of s. 514a
Sinew: bracing brain and s. 226a
Sinewed: she was iron-s. 171b
Sinews: money is the s. of love 150b
neither is money the s. of war 15b
stiffen the s. 382a
twist the s. of thy heart 32a
Sinful: affections of s. men 479b
do no s. action 3a
ma says it's s. 124b
Sing: biginneth s. 90a
byrdes swetely did s. 182b
cannot s. the old songs 20b, 75a
cherubim does cease to s. 29a
come, s. now, s. 23b
die before they s. 100b
'e'd 'eard men s. 236b
elected Silence, s. to me 197b
flowery work doth s. 268b
found in thine heart to s. 422b
hearts unwounded s. 232b
how shall we s. to her 420a
I can't s. . . saddest when I s. 451a
if she shd. s. by day 355b
I'll s., that I may seem valiant 139b
I s. of a maiden 524a
I s. of brooks 188b
let me s. and die 71a
Mary did s. 524a
might not s. so wildly well 298a
more safe I s. 275a
must we s. for evermore 231a
of thee I s. 404a
O s. unto God, and s. praises 486a
nor build, nor s. 102a
nor stayed to hear him s. 36b
now let us s. 109a
Places where they s. 478b
pray, and s., and tell old tales 344a
saddest when I s. 22a, 451a
saints on earth in concert s. 456a
second best to s. them 27a
s. alang wi' me 402b
s. all a green willow 363a
s. a merry madrigal 164b
s. among the branches 488a
s., and build the lofty rhyme 269a
s. a sang at least 60b
s. 'Bah to you' 165b
s. because I must 430a
s. both high and low 370b
s., boys, in joyful chorus 117a
s. cuccu, nu! 522b
S. 'Hey to you' 165b
s. in a hempen string 23a
s. in the summer day 192a
s. in the valley below 523a
s. it as we used to s. it 473a
s. it with a spirit 473a
s. me a song of a lad 414b
s. me yr. song, O! 167a
s. no more ditties 358b

Sing (cont.)
s. no sad songs for me 311a
s. of her with falls 43b
s. 'Kulla-lo-lo!' 232a
s.—s.—Music was given 282a
s. them loud even 370a
s. the savageness out of a bear 362b
s. thou smoothly 78a
s. together, ye waste places 502b
s. to the Lord with cheerful voice 224b
s. unto the Lord a new song 483b
s. us one of the songs 490a
s., while the hours..follow 422b
s., ye gentle maidens 117a
s., ye heavens, and earth reply 455b
so did she s. 249b
still wdst. thou s. 220a
swans s. before they die 100b
then they began to s. 163a
to Silvia let us s. 372b
to s. them too 373b
used to s. in the water 123b
we two alone will s. 344a
we will s. one song 156a
when he did s. 385b
when you s., I'd have you buy 373b
whilst thus I s., I am a King 95b
wrong to s. so wildly 430b
Singe: it do s. yourself 385b
Singed the beard of the Bishop 407a
Singeing..King of Spain's Beard 136b
Singer: after the s. is dead 414b
he, the s., passes 264a
idle s. of an empty day 284a
low as the s. lies 414b
none hear beside the s. 241a
O S. of Persephone! 461a
s. in France of old 424a
s. of sweet Colonus 6a
the music-hall s. 164b
thine ear against the s. 319a
thou the s.; I the song! 163b
when the s. sings them 414b
youngest to the oldest s. 423a
Singers: s. also and trumpeters 487a
s. go before 486b
sweetest of all s. 248b
Singeth with her breast 196a
Singing: angels..s. out of tune 74b
carry up this corpse, s. together 47a
I am sick of s. 423b
love a woman for s. 342a
Master of all s.! 248b
now the time of s. 262b
parted..those who are s. to-day 34b
poured the deathless s. 43a
s. as they shine 2a
s. in the Wilderness 152b
s. of birds is come 500a
s. of Mount Abora 101b
s. so rarely 319b
s. startle the dull night 268b
s. still dost soar 398a
s. to Father, Son 200b
s. will never be done 316a
stinte of s. 89a
suddenly burst out s. 316a
sweet s. in the choir 526b
there is delight in s. 241a
waves of thy sweet s. 394a, 397b
ye have a s. face 23b
Singing-boys: six little S. 19a
Singist: as a s. I am not a success 451a
Single: careless of the s. life 430b
deepest still is s. 120a
forever! 'tis a s. word! 75b
in s. blessedness 356a
married to a s. life 114b
nothing in the world is s. 395b
s. life doth well with churchmen 14b
s. thraldom 17a
wish I were s. again 524b
Single-hearted: grown s. 392b
Singly: who s. hast maintained 275a
Sings: another Orpheus s. 394a
Christian while he s. 110b
grove he s. in now 448a
he s., and he 100a
in his motion like an angel s. 355a
no..pang the while she s. 162b
s. for his supper 534b
Sire: by bleeding S. to Son 72b

Sings (cont.)
s. in his boat on the bay! 425b
s. on yon pomegranate tree 366a
small fowlys s. on the spray 134b
tell me what she s. 471a
wakeful bird s. darkling 273a
waking til she s. 251b
well s. thu, cuccu 522b
Singular in each particular 373b
Singularity: excess, and not by s. 222b
s. is almost invariably a clue 135a
trick of s. 371b
Sinister embroidered on..normal 204a
Sink: not gross to s., but light 386b
not s. i' the scale 50b
or s. or swim 377a
s. by the Lowlands low 531a
s. me the ship 437b
to s. with Lamplough 412b
Sinketh: lie that s. in 14a
Sinking: alacrity in s. 356a
s. as the light wind 221b
that s. feeling 522b
Sinks: it s., and I am ready 241a
reign o'er sewers and s. 100b
slow s., more lovely ere his race 70a
Sinned: against thee only have I s. 485a
Father, I have s. against heaven 509b
for all have s. 513a
have ye s. one sin 235b
more s. against than sinning 342b
Sinner: I of her a s. 105a
joy..over one s. that repenteth 509b
merciful to me a s. 510a
one sin will destroy a s. 54b
Papist, saint or s. 305a
say, poor s., lov'st thou me? 110a
Sinners: but s. to repentance 506a
eateth with publicans and s.? 506a
for we are s. all 384a
God and s. reconciled 455b
greatest saints and s. 66a
if s. entice thee 497b
many po' s. 'll be kotched 182a
mercy upon us miserable s. 478b
s. must with devils dwell 452b
s.; of whom I am chief 516b
s. shall be converted 485a
s.' ways prosper 198a
Sinning: else s. greatly 469b
sinned against than s. 342b
Sins: bare the s. of many 503a
be all my s. remembered 333b
chain of our s. 479a
commit the oldest s. 381a
compound for s...inclin'd to 65a
cover the multitude of s. 517b
dead in trespasses and s. 515b
drunkenness..root of all s. 204a
for the s. of yr. sire..suffer 546a
her s. to her Saviour 196a
her s. were on her head 231b
madness..come on us for our s. 428a
manifold s. and wickedness 478a
our s. lay on the king! 382b
presumptuous s. 482b
repent you of yr. s. 480b
season of snows and s. 420a
set our s. from us 488a
s...scarlet..books were read 26b
s. they love to act 364a
s. thro' wh. I run 132a
thinkin' on their s. 61a
tho' yr. s. be as scarlet 501a
vengeance of our s. 478b
visit the s. of the fathers 480a
weep for their s. 458a
Sion: if S. hill delight thee 270b
loveth the gates of S. 487a
O be..gracious unto S. 485a
sing us one of the songs of S. 490a
strengthen thee out of S. 482b
walk about S. 485a
when we remembered thee, O S. 490a
Sip: be tasted in a s. 125a
Sipping: some s. punch 468b
Sips: three s. the Aryan 52a
Sir: s. priest than s. knight 372a
S., we wd. see Jesus 511a
Sir-come-spy-see 19a

Sire (cont.)
left by his s. 73a
lisp their s.'s return 174a
make their s. stoop 375b
S. of an immortal strain 391b
still from the s. the son shall hear 318b
Sybil Kindred's s. 114a
thy s. was a knight 317b
Siren: drunk of S. tears 389a
the S. waits thee 241a
Sirens: Blest pair of S. 278a
dear me! s., of course 123b
Sires: land of my s. 317b
s. have marched to Rome 253a
Sirius: kingly brilliance of S. 180a
stars..fought against S. 494b
Sisera: mother of S. looked out 495a
Sis Tempy 181b
Sister: erring s.'s shame 72b
garden inclosed is my s. 500b
had it been his s. 523b
Innocence thy S. 260b
kissed her little s. 280b
leave thou thy s. 430a
ministering angel shall my s. be 336b
moon is my s. 26b
my dear, dear S.! 472a
my s. and my s.'s child 108b
my s., good night 26b
my s., my love, my dove 500b
my s.! my sweet s.! 72b
no friend like a s. 311a
our S. the Spring 27a
our sometime s., now our queen 329b
shouts with his s. 425b
S. and Auntie say 236a
s. of the Seraphim! 114b
s. of the spring 396a
s., my s., O..swallow 422b
s.'s husband's niece 85b
s., the whole day long 82b
swallow, my s., O..swallow 422b
we have a little s. 501a
yr. s. is given to government 123b
Sisterly animosity 417a
Sisters: all the S. virtuous 288a
men with s. dear 196a
s. and his cousins 166a
s. under their skins 230b
sphere-born harmonious s. 278a
they were s., we were brothers 172a
twa s. sat in a bour 528b
weird s. 350a
Sit: at last s. down by thee 225b
cure..is not to s. still 230b
here we will s. 355a
I shall s. here..on and off 82b
I s. on a man's back 567a
let us s. upon the ground 375b
rest s. round it 43a
s. by the fire and spin 533a
s. down quickly, and write fifty 509b
s. every man under his vine 504b
s. thou on my right hand 489a
s. thou still when kings..arming 319a
so I did s. and eat 188b
to s. for a picture 210a
to s. upon a hill, as I do 384a
though I s. down now 128a
we wd. s. down 260a
Site: to change their s. 65b
Sits: O! he s. high 338a
Sitting: cheap s. as standing 418b
end of it's s. an' thinkin' 230b
listen where thou art s. 268a
privilege o' s. down 144b
s. careless on a granary 221b
s. well in order 439a
Sitivation at the lighthouse 127a
Six: five, s., pick up sticks 532a
in law's grave study s. 97b
Jonas Kindred..was s. feet high 114a
let's fight till s. 84b
rode the s. hundred 426a
s. hours in sleep 97b
s. of one 259b
to my s. lustres 133b
world on S. and Sevene 90a

xpence: *bang*—went s.!!! 535a
found a crooked s. 532a
I give thee s.! 78b
I only got s. 535b
precious little for s. 535b
shot at for s. a day 120b
s. all too dear 361a
s. at a bookstall 144a
s. in her shoe 106a
song of s. 533a
xpences: pockets were full of s. 129b
two-and-forty s...guinea 211b
ixteen-string Jack 209a
ixty: men above s. years 291a
ixty: s. of pots of ale 65a
ixtyfold: some s., some thirtyfold 506b
ize: s. of pots of ale 65a
those of the largest s. 84b
kater: like the s. on ice 427a
kating over thin ice 147b
keigh: asklent and unco' s. 60a
keleton: hiding the s. 264a
keletons: brown s. of leaves 99b
ketch: first rude s. 228a
kiddaw: red glare on S. 252b
till S. saw the fire 252b
kies: as long as s. are blue 392a
baby small, dropt from the s. 21a
clear as are the frosty s. 438a
cloudless climes and starry s. 74a
distant deeps or s. 32a
exchange thy sullen s. 111b
heifer lowing at the s. 219b
hereditary s. 142b
if morning s., books, and my food 415a
I'll meet the raging of the s. 77a
kindled in the upper s. 146b
looks commercing with the s. 268a
look up at the s. 197b
look upward to the s. 287a
mansions in the s. 453b
only matched in the s. 36a
paint the sable s. 138a
people of the s. 473b
points her to the s. 143a
rush into the s.! 300b
s. are painted with..sparks 339a
s. so dull and grey 225b
s. they were ashen and sober 298b
soaring claim the s. 157b
sparkle in their s. 190a
Stamper of the S. 475a
stars are in the quiet s. 252a
twitter in the s. 222a
watcher of the s. 220b
watch-tower in the s. 268b
Skiff attains the shore 244a
Skill: all s. to naught 231b
doctor-like—controlling s. 388a
foresight, strength, and s. 470b
my s. goes beyond the depths 292b
never-failing s. 110a
or none, or little s. 191a
praise for s. not spent amiss 35b
sharpens our s. 57b
simple truth his utmost s.! 473a
s. comes so slow 117b
s...is nothing without sack 380b
s. runs on the lees 190b
thy s. to poet were 144b
'tis God gives s. 64b
Skilled: s. in analytic 277a
s. to retire, and in retiring 378a
Skimble-skamble stuff 121a
Skimpole: Harold S. 356b
Skin: enamelled s. 503b
Ethiopian change his s. 534a
get a little hare's s. 236a
his s. was dark 415a
I stuff my s., so full within 161a
s. is ivory so white 497a
s. of my teeth 98b
s. was white as leprosy 363b
that whiter s. of hers 497a
tho' after my s. worms destroy 185b
Skin-deep: colours, that are but s. 18a
joys like beauty, but s. 230b
Skins: sisters under their s. 178b
Skip: art of reading is to s. 415a
blue-behinded ape, I s. 344a
I wd. have made them s. 249a
Skipper..taken his little daughter

Skipping: pretty s. grace 261a
Skirts: caught at God's s. 47b
my s. up in the air 35b
s. of happy chance 430b
tents, whose cloudy s. 103a
s. of his clothing 490a
Skittles: all beer and s. 75b, 201a
all porter and s. 127a
loore him on to s. 74b
Skittish in all motions 370b
Skugg lies snug 156b
Skull: found..s. and the feet 496b
Skulls: lay in dead men's s. 384b
Skuttlefish: disputants..mind of the S. 2b
Sky: about us in the s. 199a
above the bright blue s. 265b
all the milky s. 476a
almost touched the s. 192b
banner in the s. 194a
bears the falling s. 199b
bed of daffodil s. 434a
blue ethereal s. 2a
blue s. bends over all 100a
blue s. of spring 4a
Bowl we call the S. 153b
bright reversion in the s. 299a
broad as the blue s. 445b
build in the breezy s. 38a
close against the s. 195a
crimson of the sunset s. 3b
die in yon rich s. 436a
do not know beneath what s. 200a
dusky night ride down the s. 151b
evening s. pavilions it 396a
fearest..nor s. clouding 37a
first our s. was overcast 109a
foam of the s. 475b
forehead of the morning s. 270a
for the s. is red 507a
freeze, thou bitter s. 326b
from the four corners of the s. 140b
give me the clear blue s. 183b
held the s. suspended 200a
hot and copper s. 98b
I stared into the s. 192b
like a diamond in the s. 425a
like a teatray in the s. 83a
like strips of the s. 393a
lonely sea and the s. 262a
lustre in its s. 394b
monarch of the s. 258b
moon upon an empty s. 476a
Music shall untune the s. 139b
my lyre within the s. 298a
nether s. opens 179b
nursling of the s. 393a
obscurest night involved the s. 107b
only one is shining in the s. 470b
Ophiucus huge in th' arctic s. 273a
out of the s. as I came through 256a
pealing up to the sunny s. 433b
pilgrim of the s. 471a
sea-line meets the s. 290a
set their watch in the s. 77b
shine upon the starry s. 30b
shoulder the s. 200a
sinful man beneath the s. 224a
s. belongs to them 99a
s. bounds the ocean 35b
s. grows darker yet 92a
s. imbrued with colour 49a
s. is clear and blue 413b
s. resum'd her light 141b
s. seemed not a s. of earth 469a
s.—what a scowl of cloud 52b
somewhere sings about the s. 71a
spread out against the s. 144b
stars be blown about the s. 476a
that equal s. 300b
that is in the starry s. 463a
th' embroiling s. 443b
they change their s. 543a
thy s. is ever clear 53a, 246b
tiger s. 263b
till Earth and S. stand presently 227a
under that benign s. 39a
whatever s.'s above me 73a
wheeling out on a windy s. 459a
wh. prisoners call the s. 459b
who aimeth at the s. 186b

Sky (*cont.*)
wide and starry s. 415a
wild bells, to the wild s. 431a
Skye: beyond the Isle of S. 530b
over the sea to S. 414b
Skylark: despise the s.'s song 38b
s. wounded in the wing 29a
Slab: gruel thick and s. 349b
Slack: observing me grow s. 188b
the havoc did not s. 76b
Slain: above the noble s. 184b
can never do that's s. 66a
ere thou hast s. another 42b
ever he s. shd. be 530b
fight and no be s. 63a
fight and no be s. 320b
I am s. by a fair cruel maid 371a
many a gallant man was s. 525b
O s. and spent 421a
Saul hath s. his thousands 495b
shall himself be s. 253b
s. the Jabberwock 84a
s. think he is s. 146a
thrice he slew the s. 139a
trade of war I have s. men 359b
vengeance..brooding o'er the s. 317a
when they have s. her lover 77a
who is in battle s. 170a
whom..law, chance, hath s. 133a
Slander: devised this s. 363a
fear not s., censure rash 329a
ring out the..civic s. 431a
shaft of s. 294a
s. any moment's leisure 331a
s., meanest spawn of Hell 432a
to speak no s. 427b
who's angry at a s. 214b
Slanderers: persecutors, and s. 479a
Slang: all s. is metaphor 94a
Slate: have to clean yr. s. 310b
something off a s. 227a
Slates: jury..wrote down..on..s. 83b
Slaughter: arrayed for mutual s. 468a
as a lamb to the s. 503a
as an ox goeth to the s. 498a
breathing..threatenings and s. 512a
canon 'gainst self-s. 330a
great s. of his own side 13b
wade thro' s. to a throne 174b
when it comes to s. 229b
Slaughter'd and made an end 287b
Slav, Teuton, Kelt 426a
Slave: a fingering s. 468b
base is the s. that pays 381b
been s. to thousands 361b
Being yr. s., what shd. I do 388a
but like a sad s. 388a
cogging, cozening s. 363a
here I stand, yr. s. 342b
I am the very s. of circumstance 73b
in giving freedom to the s. 245a
master o'er a s. 466b
meant them for a s. 71a
no more s. States..s. Territories 88a
O! cursed, cursed s. 364a
rogue and peasant s. am I! 332b
s.! I have set my life 385b
s.'s offal 333a
s. to no sect 301b
sleep..soundly as..wretched s. 382b
were a Christian S. 185a
what a s. art thou 377b
wd. have made him a s. 55a
Slavery: chains and s. 62b
s. of the tea and coffee 97a
s. they can have anywhere 56a
s...weed..grows in every soil 56a
taken by the..foe and sold to s. 360a
Slaves: an army of s. 73a
be wholly s. or wholly free 140b
Britons never will be s. 443a
by s. that take their humours 374a
freemen, are the only s. 262b
French..are all s. 170b
land of s. shall ne'er be mine 71a
make s. of the rest 297a
morality of s. 569a
necessity..is the creed of s. 297b
not press you like s. 158b
s. cannot breathe in England 111b
s., howe'er contented, never know 111b

Slaves (*cont.*)

s. who dare not be in the right	250b
s. who fear to speak	250a
tho' ruling them like s.	397b
Slay: but s., and s., and s.	254a
Slayer: red s. think he slays	146a
Slays: moves, and mates, and s.	153b
red slayer think he s.	146a
Sleary babies..Sleary's fits	233b
Sleave of care	348a
Sleep: abuse the curtained s.	347b
after battle s. is best	289a
after-dinner's s.	351b
among the hungry worms I s.	529a
and we must s.	324b
angel spirits of s.	35b
as before, Love,—only s.!	52b
back from the City of S.	228a
be but to sleep and feed?	335b
between a s. and a s.	420b
but as a drunken s.	352a
but cannot break his S.	153a
can s. so soundly as the..slave	382b
care-charmer S.	117a
care is heavy, therefore s. you	119a
charm that lulls to s.	169a
day dies with s.	197b
Death and his brother S.!	393b, 397b
deep and dreamless s.	40a
dewy-feather'd s.	268b
dovecote doors of s.	265a
drowsy approaches of s.	41a
everything but s.	422a
exposition of s.	357a
first s...his last repose	528a
first s. in Persia	41a
first sweet s. of night	394b
flowers, as in their causes, s.	79b
folding of the hands to s.	498a
freed us from everlasting s.	41a
from the fields of s.	466a
gentle s. from Heaven	99a
giveth his beloved s.	44a, 489b
Glamis hath murdered s.	348a
gray and full of s.	476b
great gift of s.	185a
held we..s. to wake	52a
how s. the brave	103a
I am fayn to s.	530b
illumined the land of S.	248a
incommunicable s.	463a
in guileless s.	444b
in s. a king	388b
in thy last long s.	214a
invites one to s.	399b
I shall s., and move with the.. ships	424a
I s., but my heart waketh	500b
I s. out the thought	373a
I s. well, but that's all	284b
keepeth thee will not s.	489b
Macbeth does murder s.	348a
Macbeth shall s. no more	348a
make any one..s. that bedstead	127a
medicine to that sweet s.	362a
mortality..like unwilling s.	221a
no s. till morn	68b
one short s. past	133a
only the s. eternal	422a
or let me s. alway	99b
O s.! O gentle s.	380a
O S.! the friend of woe	406b
O S.! thou flatterer	104a
quiet s. and a sweet dream	262a
rounded with a s.	367b
saw in s. old palaces	396b
season of all natures, s.	349b
shall not s., tho' poppies grow	256a
silence and s. like fields	119a
silence of the s.-time	52a
Sir Roger..s. in..[church]	2a
s. after toil	408b
S. again deceive me	105a
s. al the night with open yĕ	88a
s. an act or two	386b
s. and a forgetting	466a
s.; and if life was bitter	421a
s., death's counterfeit	348a
s. deeply above	30b
s. dwell upon thine eyes	365b
s. full of sweet dreams	217b

Sleep (*cont.*)

s. I can get nane	59a
s. in dull cold marble	386a
s. in one another's arms	393b
s. in spite of thunder	349b
s. in the affliction	348b
s. in the night	420b
s. is a death	42a
[s. is] in fine, so like death	42a
s. is sweet to the labouring man	54a
S.! it is a gentle thing	99a
s., liest thou in smoky cribs	380a
s. like a top	117b
s. not so sound, as sweet	188b
s. of a labouring man	499a
s. on, blest sleep	274b
s. one ever-during night	78a
s. on my Love in thy cold bed	225a
S., O S., with thy rod	161a
s. out this great gap of time	323a
s., pretty wantons, do not cry	119a
s. rock thy brain	334a
s. shall neither night nor day	346a
S. shall obey me	406b
s.'s no softer	49b
s. that is among the lonely hills	463a
s. that knits up..care	348a
S., the certain knot of peace	401b
s. thegither at the foot	61a
s., the innocent s.	348a
s. the s. of death	30b
s. the s. that knows not breaking	316b
s. to fall upon Adam	492a
s., undisturb'd, within this..shrine	206a
s. was aery light	274b
S., why dost thou leave me?	105a
s. will come when thou art fled	399a
s. with it now!	381a
such as s. o' nights	338a
sweet restorer, balmy s.	477a
that s. of death	333a
then s., dear, s.	23b
they are even as a s.	487b
they s., and it is lifted	397b
think of them that s.	76b
this s. is sound indeed	381a
thy sweet child S.	399a
till death like s...steal on	399a
time to awake out of s.	514a
to die; to s.	333a
to haunt thy s.	119b
turns in her s.	307b
uncanopied s. is flying	35b
visit the soul in s.	396a
voice cry, 'S. no more!'	348a
we shall not all s.	515a
what hath night to do with s.?	266b
what's to s.?	161a
when man doth s.	448b
when s. itself must end	41a
whom they s. beside	198b
with the first s.	265a
wd. I were s. and peace	365b
Sleeper: glean of me the s.	442b
never a quiet s.	434b
sun-flushed s.	442b
sun-hazed s.	442b
Sleepers in that quiet earth	39a
Sleepeth: not dead, but s.	506a
peradventure he s.	496a
Sleep-flower sways in the wheat	442b
Sleeping: cursed him in s.	19a
Jock, when ye're s.	319b
kind of s. in the blood	379b
lies my young love s.	263b
s. and the dead are..pictures	348a
s. found by whom they dread	271b
s. hound to wake	90a
s. three on a grid	235b
s., waking, still at ease	296b
s. when she died!	196a
s. woods all night singeth	99b
some s. killed	375b
tha' s. there below	287b
try, by s., what it is to die	42a
wakened us from s.	40a
Sleeps: fitful fever he s. well	348b
he that s. feels not..toothache	329a
in slumbers light she s.	248b
in their s. will mutter	362a
now s. the crimson petal	436b

Sleeps (*cont.*)

one s. where Southern vines	184a
s., and never palates more the dug	325a
s. as may beguile the night	416b
s. on his own heart	469a
s. with the primeval giants	80a
so s. the pride	281a
where the M.F.H. s. he breakfasts	416a
while my pretty one, s.	436a
Sleepy: contentment is a s. thing	445a
in the s. region stay	284a
to bed, says S.-head	534a
Sleet: fire and s.	529a
whistling s. and snow	249a
Sleeve: ace of trumps up his s.	238a
my heart upon my s.	359a
will he strip his s.	383a
Sleeves: lawn s. and rochets	307a
s. with ribbons rare	202a
Sleight: admire his s. of hand	65a
perceive a juggler's s.	65a
Slender: cedar tall and s.	290a
Slept: dying when she s.	196a
first-fruits of them that s.	515a
hath it s. since	347a
he thought I s.	293a
I have not s. one wink	328a
one that wd. have s.	143a
resembled my father as he s.	347a
s. among his ashes cold	221a
s. an hour less	211a
s. in the contriving of lust	343a
s. under the dresser	27b
s. with his fathers	496a
while their companions s.	247b
Slew: he was ambitious, I s. him	339b
Slid into my soul	99a
Slide: let the world s.	23b
Slight: loved so s. a thing	432b
s. all that do	150a
s. not the songsmith	452a
s. what I receive	50b
Slighter: Lilac was of s. stuff	93a
Slime: slimier s.	39a
sprawled thro' the ooze and s.	404a
tare each other in their s.	430b
Slimy: s. things did crawl	98b
thousand s. things	99a
Slings and arrows	333a
Slingsby of the manly chest	12b
Slinks out of the race	279a
Slip: enemies the s. for ever	411b
gave us all the s.	52b
Slipped: he s. up somehow	182a
Slipper and subtle knave	361a
Slippered Hesper	39b
Slips: all s. of hers	195b
greyhounds in the s.	382a
Slits the thin-spun life	269b
Sliver: an envious s. broke	336a
s. and disbranch	343b
Slog—slog—slog—sloggin'	227b
Slogan: cry the s.	12a
rose the s. of Macdonald	12a
Slope: s. of mighty limbs	421a
s. thro' darkness up to God	430b
the s. of faces	112a
upon life's darkening s.	312a
Slopes: orchard s., and the Anio	96a
resignation gently s. the way	168a
Slop-kettle: coffee and other s.	97a
Sloth: but most of s.	186b
love, wh. s. maligns	293b
peaceful s., not peace	272b
resty s.	329a
shake off dull s.	224b
too much time in studies is s.	16a
Slothful: not s. in business	513b
s. man saith, there is a lion	498b
Slough: name of the s. was Despond	54a
Slovenliness is no part of religion	456a
Slovenly will spit on all things	87b
Slow: as tardy as too s.	365b
but so s.!	48b
celerity even itself is s.	190b
come he s., or come he fast	318a
I am s. of speech	493b
I am s. of study	356a
may be life, but ain't it s.?	186a
or were he reckoned s.	36b
s. and steady wins the race	246a

Slow (cont.)
s. howe'er my marches be 225b
s. in pursuit 357a
s., s., fresh fount 214b
s. to speak, s. to wrath 517a
some cry 'S.' 435b
steps solemn, mournful, and s. 459a
sun climbs s. 96b
tarry a while, says S. 534b
unfriended, melancholy, s. 169b
vaster than empires, and more s. 260a
Slowly: s. rose she up 531a
s. she came nigh him 531a
Spring comes s. up this way 100a
Slow-worm: snake, or s. bite thee 189b
Slug-a-bed: get up, sweet S. 189a
Sluggard: foul s.'s comfort 80a
go to the ant, thou s. 498a
s. is wiser in his own conceit 498b
the s.'s cradle 87b
voice of the s. 453a
Slug-horn to my lips 45b
Slugs: killing s. on borders 229b
s. leave their lair 102a
s. that come crawling out 20a
Sluicing: browsing and s. 573b
Slumber: buzzing night-flies to thy s. 380a
ere S.'s chain has bound 282b
honey-heavy dew of s. 338b
I must s. again 453a
lie still and s. 453a
limbs affected s. more 78b
ports of s. open wide 381a
sense in deathly s. 119a
sleep, a little s. 498a
s. did my spirit seal 463a
s. is more sweet than toil 433a
s. out their immortality 113b
to soothing s. seven 214b
will start from her s. 6a
Slumbering: dictates to me s. 276a
might half s. 220b
Slumbers: golden s. kiss yr. eyes 119a
hast thou golden s. 118b
imagine unquiet s. 39a
like infants' s. 224a
pleasing dreams, and s. light! 318b
soul is dead that s. 247b
visit'st my s. nightly 275b
while in s. light she sleeps! 248b
Slung atween the round shot 287b
Slut: I am not a s. 327a
Polly is a sad s. 159a
was not she a dirty s. 533b
Sly: Tough, and de-vilish s.! 122b
Smack: father did something s. 353b
pledging with contented s. 219a
Small: almost too s. for sight 343b
between the s. and great 113a
compare great things with s. 273a
day of s. nations 87a
day of s. things 504b
dull unlettered s. 113a
how s., of all that..hearts endure 213a
how s. the world is 177a
in life's s. things be resolute 250b
just so s. as I 441b
no great and no s. 146a
of s. houndes had she 88b
one that was s. 527a
said 'is it s.?' 243b
showed at noon but s. 244a
s., but how dear to us 21a
s...continual plodders ever won 344b
s. is the worth of beauty 449a
s. matters win..commendation 16b
s. one a strong nation 503a
s. rain down can rain 527b
s. states, Israel, Athens..England 203a
s. things are best 150a
souls of women are so s. 66a
very s. the very great are! 440b
Smaller fleas to bite 'em 419b
Smallest: Queen Anne..s...in great place 17b
Smart: girls that are so s. 79b
joys to feel all s. 187b
scorn wh. mocked the s. 6a
Smatch: some s. of honour 341b
Smattering of everything 121b
Smauker: Mr. S. 127a

Smell: ancient and fish-like s. 367b
cheered with the grateful s. 273b
chill the wintry s. 421a
flower of sweetest s. 468a
Hudibras, I s. a rat 65a
rose was heaven to s. 192a
rose..wd. s. as sweet 365a
shine so brisk, and s. so sweet 376b
s. it on the tree 363b
s. my remnant out 187b
s. of bread and butter 67b
s. sweet, and blossom in their dust 401a
s. the dew and rain 188a
s. too strong of the lamp 411b
sweet keen s. 313a
Smelling out a suit 364b
Smells: grows and s., I swear 216b
it s. to heaven 334b
s. wooingly here 347a
Smell'st: fair and s. so sweet 363a
Smile: and s., s., s. 10b
blush and gently s. 188b
calm thou may'st s. 214a
Cambridge people rarely s. 39b
followed perhaps by a s. 111a
gleam of her own dying s. 392a
good gigantic s. 47b
Heaven's blue s. 393a
her s., it seems half holy 43b
I dare not beg a s. 190a
I hear a s. 116a
jest without the s. 102a
last s. ere he slept 282b
meet again, why, we shall s. 341a
moved to s. at anything 338a
one may s. and s., and be a villain 331b
peculiar sweet s. shone 440a
remember how you s. 241b
share the good man's s. 168b
show their teeth in way of s. 352b
s. at us, pay us 93a
s. dwells a little longer 87a
s., for yr. lover comes 458b
s. his work to see 32a
s. in thine eyes 281a
s. it was pensive and childlike 182a
s. on the face of the tiger 527a
s. on you—for seconds 131a
s. that glowed celestial 276a
s. that was childlike and bland 182a
s. to those who hate 73a
s. upon his fingers' ends 382a
s. we wd. aspire to 386a
s. with the wise 207b
some that s. have in their hearts 340b
the immeasurable s. 293b
the social s. 174a
thrifty wifie's s. 59b
tribute of a s. 317a
twinkling s. of ocean 224a
vast substantial s. 121b
when you gave her a s. 148b
with a s. on her lips 318a
with his watery s. 426b
without frown or s. 321a
with s. so sweet 447a
you shd. forget and s. 311a
you s., Madonna 242a
Smiled: all around thee s. 214a
has s. and said 'Good Night' 26b
He Never S. Again 184b
his little arms, and s. 175a
s. a kind of sickly smile 182b
s. well content 415a
s. when a sabbath appear'd 113a
till that on her it s. 143b
until she s. on me 97b
Smiles: becks, and wreathed s. 268b
breath, s., tears, of all my life 44a
daggers in men's s. 348a
eternal s. his emptiness betray 303a
every time a man s. 411a
flower that s. to-day 190a
kissed into s. again 182a
life is..sobs, sniffles, and s. 185b
neat, with s. so sweet 256b
own sweet s. I see 109a
robbed that s. steals something 360a
seldom he s. 338a
s. awake you 119a
s. before they dwindle 397b

Smiles (cont.)
s., but not as Sultans smile 92b
s. by his cheerful fire 170a
s. sae sweetly on her knee 61b
s., wan as primroses 217b
than s. of other maidens are 97b
their nurslings with their s. 241b
the s. of joy, the tears of woe 282b
the s. that win 74a
tears and s. like us He knew 3b
we read in their s. 393b
when Molly s. beneath her cow 528a
wife s., and lets it go at that 21b
with s. and soap 86a
Smilest: thou s. and art still 7b
Smiling: he hides a s. face 110a
it was s. in my face 347a
I've seen the s. 97a
s., put the question by 426b
s. the boy fell dead 47b
tho', by yr. s., you seem to say so 332b
villain, s., damned villain! 331b
virtue! com'st thou s. 324a
Smirk: serious and the s. 124b
Smite: Christian, up and s. them 286b
rather s. me friendly 490b
rude caitiff s. the other too! 193b
s. all the firstborn 494a
s. once, and s. no more 269b
s. thee on thy right cheek 505a
Smiteth: smite him that s. him 503b
Smith: by naming him S. 194b
Chuck it, S.! 91b
clinging to their crosses..F.E.S.? 91b
combined in Horace S. 395b
first s...first murderer's son 112b
s., a mighty man is he 249a
S., take a fresh cigar! 76a
Smithy: sparks blown out of a s. 476a
village s. stands 249a
Smitten me to my knee 441b
Smock: embroidery of a s.-frock 180b
pale as thy s. 364a
Smoke: above the s. and stir 266b
a man who does not s. 413a
bottle in the s. 489a
counties overhung with s. 284a
dunnest s. of hell 346b
emit so much s. 239b
from the s. into the smother 325b
good cigar is a S. 227b
guide in s. and flame 319b
house was filled with s. 501b
in yon s. concealed 96b
like as the s. vanisheth 486a
only thin s. without flame 179b
put that in yr. pipe..and s. it 19b
s. of their torment 519b
stupefying incense-s. 45a
this stinking s. 204a
w'at you gwine do wid de s.? 182a
Smoked like a chimney 19a
Smoking: blessing this s. is 184b
s...blessing..we owe to America 184b
s. flax 502b
s. of a whackin' white cheroot 232a
Smooth: I am a s. man 493a
large, and s., and round 406a
s. as monumental alabaster 363b
supple and s. to her 192a
true love never did run s. 356a
Smoother: words were s. than oil 485b
Smoothes her charming tones 275a
Smooth-faced snubnosed rogue 433b
Smoothness: temperance..give it s. 333b
turns earth's s. rough 50b
Smote: s. for us a pathway 234b
s. him thus 364a
s. him with the edge of the sword 494a
s. itself into the bread 428a
s. them hip and thigh 495a
they s. me, they wounded me 500b
Smother: from the smoke into the s. 325b
Smutched: soil hath s. it 216b
Smyler with the knyf 570b
Snagsby: Mr. S. 121a
Snail: a whiting to a s. 83a
consume away like a s. 485b
creeping like s. 326b
slug-abed s. 441b
s.'s on the thorn 50a

Snail (cont.)
turn not pale, beloved s.   83b
went to kill a s.   534a
worm nor s., do no offence   356b
Snails: horns of cockled s.   345a
pretty feet like s.   190b
s., and puppy-dogs' tails   534b
Snake: didst devise the S.   154a
like a wounded s.   300a
nor s. or slow-worm   189b
scotched the s., not killed it   348b
S. is living yet   26b
s. lurks in the grass   557b
s. slipt under a spray   435b
s. throws her enamelled skin   356b
with Paradise devise the S.   154a
Snakes: cloud of winged s.   397a
there are no s.   209b
two bright and aged s.   5b
you spotted s.   356b
Snapdragon: gold-dusted s.   8b
s. growing on the walls   288b
Snapped 'em off short   121b
Snapper-up of unconsidered trifles   373a
Snapping: slew the S. Turtle   12b
Snaps and snails   534b
Snare: rabbit in a s.   410b
s. is broken, and we are destroyed   489b
s. of the hunter   487b
world's great s.   324a
Snares of death compassed me   489a
Snarls: they rises, and we s.   124a
Snatch: s. a fearful joy   174b
s. them straight away   364a
Snatched away in beauty's bloom   73b
Snatches: ballads, songs and s.   164a
chanted s. of old tunes   336a
Sneer: devil in his s.   70a
solemn creed with solemn s.   68b
teach the rest to s.   303a
who can refute a s.?   292a
Sneering: without s., teach the rest   303a
Sneers of selfish men   472a
Sneezes: beat him when he s.   82b
Sneezy: Breezy, S.   158a
Snewed in his hous of mete   88b
Snicker: hold my coat and s.   145a
Snicker-snack: blade went s.   84a
Snickersnee: I drew my s.   165a
Sniffles predominating   185b
Snob: admires mean things is a S.   439b
not to be sometimes a S.   439b
Snodgrass: Mr. S.   126a
Snore: can't hear himself s.   447a
fit to s. his head off   84b
Snored: simply sat and s.   91b
Snorer can't hear himself   447a
Snores out the watch   381a
Snow: architecture of the s.   147a
as s. in harvest   385a
blood is very s.-broth   351a
bloodless lay the untrodden s.   76b
chaste as unsunned s.   328b
cherry hung with s.   198b
frost from purest s.   328b
garment of unsullied s.   407a
gone with the s.   36a
half-buried in the s. was found   247a
he giveth s. like wool   490b
if s. be white   389a
I shall be whiter than s.   485a
I sift the s.   393a
ivy-tod is heavy with s.   99b
land of mist and s.   98b
last long streak of s.   431a
lawn as white as driven s.   373b
like S. upon the Desert's..Face   152b
mark'd but the fall o' the s.   216b
mockery king of s.   376b
naked in December s.   374b
never shall love the s. again   36b
rose-buds filled with s.   78b
scatter their s. around   37b
sends the s. in winter   76a
shroud as the mountain s.   335b
s. and vapours   490b
s. falls in the river   63a
s. had fallen, s. on s.   311a
s. hath retreated   467b
s. in Salmon   486a

Snow (cont.)
s. in the glance of the Lord   74a
s. lay round about   286b
s. of ferne yere   90a
s. on a raven's back   366a
s. on field an' hill   250b
s. on Scythian hills   259a
s. shall be their winding-sheet   77a
the s. came flying   37a
they shall be white as s.   501a
tufts of s. on the bare branch   101a
Virgin shrouded in s.   32a
we shall have s.   533a
where the s. lay dinted   286b
whitest sheets of s.   115a
wish a s. in May's..mirth   344b
with a diadem of s.   73a
Snowdon: we've the stones of S.   226a
Snowdonian antelope   395b
Snowdrifts: lie long, high s.   199a
Snowdrop: first s. of the year   438a
Snows: buds that s. have shaken   422a
Cecilia's lap of s.   442b
her couch of s.   392b
Lady of the S.   233a
season of s. and sins   420a
s. of yesteryear   565b
thro' a waste of s.   299a
Snowy, Flowy   158a
Snubnosed rogue   433b
Snuff: only took s.   169b
s., tobacker, and sleep   122a
you abuse s.   102b
Snuff-box: of amber s. justly vain   302b
Snuffed: s. out by an article   71b
s. the tainted gale   316a
Snuffle and sniff and handkerchief   39b
Snug: little s. property   143b
s., as a bug   156b
So: if it was s., it might be   84a
if it were s., it wd. be   84a
well, I told you s.   249a
Soap: have you used Pears' S.?   523a
I used yr. s. two years ago   535b
s. and education..more deadly   446b
What! no s.   155b
washing..with invisible s.   195a
with smiles and s.   86a
Soap-boiler costive   454b
Soar: run, tho' not to s.   255b
shd. spur you to s.   423a
singing still dost s.   398a
s. not too high to fall   262b
thou canst not s.   392a
type of the wise who s.   471a
Soaring: tired with s.   139a
Sob: throb and mutual s.   77b
Sobbed and he sighed   165a
Sobbing: a-sighing and a-s.   528a
Sober: be s., be vigilant   518a
men at whiles are s.   200a
righteous, and s. life   478a
s. as a judge   151a, 240a
to bed go s.   23a
to-morrow we'll be s.   522b
Soberness: words of truth and s.   513a
Sobers: drinking largely s. us   300a
Sobs: add s., fiery sighs   64b
s., sniffles, and smiles   185b
Social: s. intercourse with him   208a
s. system..Prince's nails   122a
true self-love and s...the same   301b
Societies: troops, and sweet s.   270a
Society: chief pleasure is s.   117b
cling together in one s.   469a
Corinthian capital of..s.   57b
desperate odd-fellow s.   444a
equal s. with them to hold   106b
gain to s. at large   164a
hung loose upon s.   206b
man seeketh in s. comfort   13a
man was formed for s.   28b
one great s. alone   469b
ourself will mingle with s.   349a
pests of s.   33b
Pill for..the maladies of S.   81a
s. became my glittering bride   464a
s...conspiracy against..manhood   147b
s. distributes itself   9b
s., friendship, and love   113a

Society (cont.)
s. is all but rude   260b
s. is now one polished horde   71b
s. is wonderfully delightful   460b
s. than solitude is worse   19a
s., where none intrudes   69b
solitude sometimes is best s.   276a
such s. as is quiet   398b
three great classes..s.   9b
unfriendly to s.'s . . joys   108a
when s. requires to be rebuilt   265b
Sock: Jonson's learned s.   269a
Socked: I s. it them hard   227b
Socket: burn to the s.   464a
Sockets: candles burn their s.   200a
s. of fine gold   500b
Socks: when thy s. were on   216a
Socratic manner is not a game   25a
Sod: become a s.   220a
hard and trampled s.   12a
heat was in the very s.   286b
under my head a s.   530b
Soda-water: sermons and s.   70b
Sodden and unkind   26b
Sods: s. with our bayonets turning   462a
under green s. lay   474a
Sofa: accomplished S. last   111b
I sing the S.   111b
wheel the s. round   112a
Soft: all this fair, and s.   260b
cast me in so s. a mould   139a
her voice was ever s.   344a
it s. as silk remains   191b
O so s.! O so sweet is she!   216b
s. as lips that laugh   420b
s. as silk   160b
s. as the breath of even   11a
s. in the level races   36a
Softly: fair and s...he cried   108b
I shall go s. all my years   502b
s., gently, kindly treat   159a
s. she was going up   99a
Softness she and sweet..grace   274a
Soil: fame..grows on mortal s.   269b
fattest s. to weeds   380b
paints the sterile s.   114a
(slavery) grows in every s.   56a
s. hath smutched it   216b
this the s., the clime   271a
Soiled: s. by rude hands   114a
s. with all ignoble use   431a
Sojourner, as all my fathers were   484a
Solace: our s. is, the sad road   294a
s. in the midst of woe   86b
with s. and gladness   402b
Solar: hub of the s. system   194a
s. walk or milky way   300b
Sold: eleventh hour..sees us s.   236a
not have s. her for it   363b
set at naught and s. Him   456a
s. cheap what is most dear   389a
s. for endless rue   198b
s. his birthright unto Jacob   493a
s. my steed, thou'rt s.   289b
Soldan of Byzantium is smiling   92b
Soldier: always tell an old s.   389b
ambition, the s.'s virtue   323a
as an old s. I admit..cowardice   390b
a s.'s grave, for thee the best   73b
Battle was a s. bold   194b
be a s.'s sepulchre   77a
British s. can stand up   390a
come you back, you British s.   232a
drinking is the s.'s pleasure   139a
driveth o'er a s.'s neck   364b
every French s. carries   564b
expect a s. to think   390a
farewell, honest s.   329a
for a s. I listed   120b
for her..the s. fights   21a
for to serve as a s.   236b
God and s. we alike adore   217a
God's s. be he   351a
go to yr. Gawd like a s.   237a
himself have been a s.   377a
in the s. is flat blasphemy   351b
I said an elder s.   340b
let a s. drink   361a
little toy s.   151a
majesty the British s. fights   285b
mourn'd her s. slain   242a

Soldier (cont.)
'Nay,' the s.'s pride touched 47b
not having been a s. 209b
old S. of the Queen's 522a
our s. slighted 217a
s. a mere recreant prove 368b
s., and afeard? 350a
s. an' sailor too 234a
s. fit to stand by Cæsar 361a
s., full of strange oaths 326b
s...is..a quiet grave man 17b
s. is better accommodated 380b
s...not a romantic animal 17b
s. of the Legion lay dying 290a
s., rest! thy warfare o'er 316b
s.'s a man 361a
s.'s pole is fallen 324b
tried and valiant s. 340b
wot the ten-year's. tells 232a
Soldiers: amongst a thousand s. 24a
but we are s. 368b
Ireland gives England her s. 264b
Lord gets His best s. 410a
men like s. may not quit 433a
mustered their s. by two 531b
old s. never die 525b
old s., sweetheart, are surest 454b
onward, Christian s. 20a
others, like s., armed 381b
s. bore dead bodies by 376b
S. of Christ, arise 455b
S. of the ploughshare 314b
steel my s.' hearts 383a
substance of ten thousand s. 385a
Wellington..shoes of his s. 17b
Soldier-saint: O s. 51b
Soldier-saints, who row on row 52a
Soldiery: licentious s. 56a
Sole: dove..s. of her foot 492b
Solecism: eternity without a s. 41b
Solemn: more s. and serene 394b
s. creed with s. sneer 68b
Solemnized their obsequies 42a
Solicit for it straight 363b
Soliciting: still-s. eye 341b
this supernatural s. 346b
Solicitor: Protestant..only go to his s. 129b
wound in the s...very serious 66b
Solid: s. man of Boston 247b
too too s. flesh 330a
Solitary: if you are idle, be not s. 210a
life of man, s...brutish 191b
saw a s. cell 100b
s., and cannot impart it 206b
s. place shall be glad 502a
s. sorrow best befits 218b
took their s. way 277a
to wander s. there 261a
Solitude: a s. almost 107a
bird in the s. singing 74a
bliss of s. 467b
City's voice..soft like S.'s 399a
come to him in s. 469a
he makes a s., and calls it peace! 67b
I love tranquil s. 398b
in s. what happiness? 275b
lamp-lit desk in s. 36a
midst of a vast s. 254b
my faithful s. 105b
O still s. 36a
passing sweet, is s. 111a
race wh...disturbed its s. 18a
self-sufficing power of S. 469b
society than s. is worse 19a
s. sometimes is best society 276a
s.! where are the charms 113a
s.; yet not alone, while thou 275b
Soul to S. retires 152a
sweet retired s. 267a
this delicious s. 260b
this peopled earth a s. 397a
worst s...destitute..friendship 14a
whisper, s. is sweet 111a
whosoever is delighted in s. 15b
Solitudes: misty s. 236a
Solomon: all S.'s wisdom 496a
felicities of S. 14a
greater than S. is here 506b
one man in a thousand, S. says 235a
S. Grundy 532b
S. in all his glory 505b

Solomon (cont.)
S. loved many strange women 496b
S. of saloons 48b
S. wrote the Proverbs 286a
song of songs, wh. is S.'s 500a
Solve 'em in a trice 65a
Some: s. have too much 143a
s. talk of Alexander 526a
s. there be, wh. have no memorial 521b
Somebody: brisk little s. 44b
heart is sair for S. 60b
let's stop s...doing something 186a
mine ain dear s. 424b
must be s.'s son 523a
Saint S. 51a
s.'s catching it now 233a
s. to hew and hack 65a
when everyone is s. 163b
Someone: s. had blundered 426a
s. somewhere sings about the sky 71a
Somerset: rose a canker, S. 383a
Something: driving rapidly from s. 209a
have to say s. 456a
I too will s. make 36b
know s. of everything 524a
s. attempted, s. done 249a
s. evermore about to be 469b
s. in a flying horse 468b
s. in its depths doth glow 5b
s. in it, tricks and all 48b
s. in this more than natural 332b
s. rich and strange 367a
s., s. that replies 441b
s. there is moves me to love 38a
s. there is..doesn't love a wall 157b
s. too much of this 334a
s. very like Him 96b
s. wicked this way comes 349b
s. will come of this 121a
that s. still wh. prompts th'..sigh 301b
time for a little s. 266b
'tis s., nothing 361b
when there's s. doing 238a
Sometimes: s. coming, s. coy 321a
s. this, and s. that 189b
Somewhat to say unto thee 496a
Somewhere: s. I came by 197b
s. the sun is shining 181b
that truth lies s. 109a
Somnus in Homer 41a
Son: an only s., sir 170b
beggarly s. of a gun 75a
body of my brother's s. 99a
by bleeding Sire to S. 72b
coarse-bred s. of a livery..keeper 474b
conceive, and bear a s. 501b
crucify..S. of God afresh 517a
did bear our s. 238b
Duke's.—cook's s. 227a
England's greatest s. 435a
Epicurus owne s. 88b
Fhairshon had a s. 12b
foolish s. is the heaviness 498a
from the sire the s. shall hear 318b
gave his only-begotten S. 510b
good man teach his s. 383a
he was an esquire's s. 531b
his little s. into his bosom 155b
honest man's s. 353b
I obeyed as a s. 161b
kiss the S., lest he be angry 481b
left a s. who—proved they weren't 230a
Lord Randal, my s. 529b
manhood taken by the S. 288b
Monk my s. 407a
must be somebody's s. 523a
my little S., who look'd 294a
my s.—and what's a s.? 238b
my s., if sinners entice thee 497b
my s. in tears 164a
my s.'s wife, Elizabeth 203b
mystical body of thy S. 48oa, 480b
O Absalom, my s., my s. 495b
only s. of his mother 509a
O wonderful s. 334b
s. has done nearly as well 66b
S. of God goes forth to war 184a
S. of Heav'n and Earth 275a
S. of Heaven's eternal King 270a
s. of his old age 493a
S. of man hath not where to lay 506a

Son (cont.)
S. of Morn in weary Night's 30a
s. of man, that thou visitest him 482a
s. of perdition 511b
S. of the old moon-mountains 221a
spareth his rod hateth his s. 498a
struck the father when..s. swore 64b
this is my beloved S. 504b
this is my s...Telemachus 438b
this my s. was dead 509b
this the carpenter's s. 507a
thy s., thine only s. Isaac 493a
to her s. she ches 524a
two-legged thing, a s. 138a
unto us a s. is given 501b
wise s. maketh a glad father 498a
woman, behold thy s.! 511b
worthy to be called thy s. 509b
your tardy s. to chide 335a
Song: acquaints his soul with s. 52a
after all an earthly s. 430b
a goodly manor for a s. 322a
Alexandrine ends the s. 300a
all this for a s. 58b
an old s. made by an aged 522a
as it were a new s. 519a
be the morn of s. 415b
breeze of s. 430b
bright names will hallow s. 68b
brotherhood in s. 217b
but their low, lone s. 82b
but weigh this s. with the great 474b
civil at her s. 356b
conspiracy of our spacious s. 114b
end of ane old s. 572b
fable, s. or fleeting shade 189a
followed by a sacred s. 26a
ful wel she s. the service 88b
glorious the s. 403a
God who best taught s. 51a
greet her with his s. 277a
heard in tale or s. 266b
hear we these monkes' s. 79a
her symphony and s. 101b
his s. of love 36b
hopped with his s. 119b
I have a s. to sing O! 167a
I have no s. to give you 225b
I made another s. 36b
in England's s. for ever 287b
is it accepted of S.? 263a
I the s.! 163b
lark becomes a sightless s. 431a
lasting is the s. 264a
lightnings of his s. 392a
melancholy out of a s. 326a
metre of an antique s. 387a
middle of my s. 108b
morning star of s. 426b
most topical s. 527a
my S., I fear..thou wilt find 393b
my vision with the s. 263b
never go beyond a s. 149a
never may I commence my s. 51a
new s.'s measure 291a
no man cd. learn that s. 519a
no sorrow in thy s. 53a, 246b
oaten stop, or pastoral s. 103a
old and antique s. 370b
one grand sweet s. 225b
one s., and in my brain I sing it 49b
only in you my s. begins 401b
on the wings of s. 568b
orb of s...Milton 464b
our s. is the voice of desire 37a
our s. shall rise to Thee 184a
passage of a s. 265a
penny for a s. 474a
pipe a simple s. 465b
pipe that s. again 32b
rainbow and a cuckoo's s. 118a
rapid plumes of s. 396a
required of us then a s. 490a
roll forth, my s. 258a
self-same s. that found a path 220a
shedding my s. upon height 422b
sing a faery's s. 218b
singing our s. of God 457b
singing s. for s. 241a
sing me a bawdy s. 378b
sing me a s. of a lad 414b

Song (cont.)

sings a solitary s.	467b
sings each s. twice over	47a
sing the Lord's s.	490a
sing unto the Lord a new s.	483b
s. about a lamb	32b
s. and blood are pure	264a
s. charms the sense	272b
s., from beginning to end	246b
s. in thy praise	60b
s. is considered a perfect gem	75a
s. is not truth	452a
s. is sung and past	473b
s. made in lieu of..ornaments	408b
s. of a merry man	167a
s. of Harvest home	3b
s. of sixpence	533a
s. of them that feast	286a
S. on yr. bugles blown	185a
s. that echoes cheerly	431b
s. that nerves a nation's heart	426a
s. that shd. spur you	423a
s. the Syrens sang	42b
s. too daring	305b
s. was wordless	316a
s. wd. have been longer	532b
sound my echoing s.	260a
still govern thou my s.	275b
subject for heroic s.	276a
swallow-flights of s.	430a
swear to the truth of a s.	305b
swift stream of s.	395b
take up thy S.	294a
that glorious s. of old	320b
that piece of s.	370b
the burthen of his s.	28a
the Fair commands the s.	111b
the s. for me!	468a
they teach in s.	395a
thinks two notes a s.	118a
thro' all spheres one s. increase	311b
till I end my s.	409b
time..our tedious s...have ending	270b
turn out a s.	60a
wanted one immortal s.	138a
we'll sing another s.	473a
wherefrom thou my s.	37a
will I frame my s.	91a
wine, woman, and s.	440b
woman, wine and s.	569a
yet my s. comes native	221a
you have heard the s.	231b

Songs: angelic s. are swelling

	149b
best of all trades, to make s.	27a
cannot sing the old s.	20b, 75a
coude s. make and wel endyte	88a
dirty s. and dreary	40a
ever piping s.	219b
fall of s.	414b
fruit for their s.	2b
go, s., for ended	441a
Heine for s.	46b
her matchless s. does meditate	261a
hymns and spiritual s.	515b
lean and flashy s.	269b
let us go hence, my s.	423a
merry s. of peace	386b
my uncared-for s.	36a
our sweetest s. are..saddest	398b
sing no sad s. for me	311a
sombre s. and sweet	421a
song of s., wh. is Solomon's	500a
s. consecrate to truth	399b
s. for me and my aunts	373a
s. may inspirit us	48a
s. of Araby	461b
s. of expectation	20b
s. of happy cheer	32b
s. of his fashion bring	414b
s. of pleasant glee	32a
s. of the harp-player	420a
s. that I made for thee	37b
their s. are sad	92a
the Sussex s. be sung	27a
thou need'st not make new s.	106b
with s. of deliverance	483b
wrote my happy s.	32b

Songsmith: slight not the s. — 452a
Songstress: sober-suited s. — 443b
Sonnet: it turned to a S. — 131a

ode, and elegy, and s.	211b

Sonnet (cont.)

scorn not the S.	470b
s. is a moment's monument	311b
Sonnets: book of Songs and S.	355b
lovers' s. turned to..psalms	295b
Rafael made a century of s.	49a
written s. all his life	70b
Sonneteer: hackney s.	300b
Sons: actions..not always true s.	65a
all *lapis*, all s.	45a
Arcturus with his s.	497b
as many s. as I have hairs	351a
bears all its s. away	453b
best of the s. of the morning!	184a
bind yr. s. to exile	236b
fallen s. of Eve	93b
give them to yr. s.	535b
God's s. are things	256b
if I had a thousand s.	380b
keener pangs..than..her s.	218b
methinks her patient s.	170a
Mothers that lack s.	328a
Muses chose their s. by name	36a
seldom see we s. succeed	178a
s. may grow up as..plants	490b
s. of ale and brede	474a
s. of Belial, flown with insolence	271b
s. of God came to present	496b
s. of God shouted for joy	497b
S. of Martha	234b
S. of Mary	234b
s. of men and angels	455b
s. of the waves	158b
strong heart of her s.	136b
their s., they gave	39a
things are the s. of heaven	212b
third among the s. of light	391b
we arraign her, her s.	6b
yr. s. and..daughters..prophesy	504a
Soon: day returns too s.	74a
death cometh s. or late	253a
Death will come..s., too s.	399a
Night, come s., s.!	399a
s. in yr. arms to feel so small	294a
think it s. when others cry	44a
world..with us; late and s.	473a
you haste away so s.	189a
Sooner: make an end the s.	15b
s. will his race be run	190b
s. it's over, the s. to sleep	226b
Soonest take their flight	289b
Soot: in s. I sleep	32b
Sooth: it is silly s.	371a
Soothe: friend to s. the cares	220b
Soothes: saddens while it s.!	50a
Sop: body gets its s.	45a
Cerberus a s.	104a
Sophia..followed me to India	319b
Sophist: dark-browed s.	435b
Saint never S. led	5a
self-torturing s., wild Rousseau	68b
Sophisters, economists..calculators	57a
Sophistry: his fib or s.	303a
universities incline wits to s.	17a
Sophonisba! Sophonisba! Oh!	443b
Sops in wine	409b
Sordello's story told	52a
Sore: critics, who themselves are s.	72a
s. with loving her	123a
Sores: all kinds of s., and shames	362b
Sorrel: meadow-sweet or s.	420b
Sorrento and Amalfi	241a
Sorrow: brief s., short-lived care	286a
certain of s. in store	233b
doeth it to his s.	498a
down, thou climbing s.	342a
ere the s. comes with years	43a
far from s.	130b
father's s.	176a
from the memory a rooted s.	350b
from the sphere of our s.	399b
give s. words	350a
gray hairs with s. to the grave	493b
has s. thy young days shaded?	281b
heart hath 'scap'd this s.	388b
he died out of s.	531a
I must bury s.	53a
in s. thou shalt bring forth	492b
knowledge increaseth s.	499a
labour without s. is base	314b

Sorrow (cont.)

last his s., first his joy	176a
lightnings of his song in s.	392a
like this s. 'twill come	37b
little fun, to match the s.	263a
Lycidas yr. s. is not dead	270a
moan her s. to the roof	234b
more in s. than in anger	330b
mused on s. but its own	77a
my old s. wakes	203a
nae s. there, John	285b
nature cd. not s. hide	176a
neither s., nor crying	519b
never ate his bread in s.	82a
night of doubt and s.	20b
no greater s. than to recall	566b
no s. in thy song	53a, 246b
not a word of s.	462b
not be in s. too?	33a
not sure of s.	422a
now melt into s.	67b
parting is such sweet s.	365b
pure and complete s.	567a
regions of s., doleful shades	271a
resembles s. only	247a
shd. water this s.	322b
shun the man of s.	113b
sin cd. blight or s. fade	100b
sit by the fireside with S.	394b
so beguile thy s.	368a
solitary s. best befits	218b
some natural s.	471a
s. and sighing shall flee	502a
s. and silence are strong	247a
s. breeds s.	137a
s. dogging sin	187a
s. enough in the natural way	233b
s. for the lost Lenore	298a
s. like unto my s.	503b
s. makes us wise	431a
s. more beauiful than Beauty's	218a
s. never comes too late	175a
s. of the meanest thing	465b
S. proud to be exalted	524a
s.'s crown of s.	432a
s. so royally in you appears	381a
s., that is not s.	470a
S., why dost borrow	217b
S., wilt thou live with me	430b
S., with her family of Sighs	392a
swift joy and tardy s.	441a
tales of s. done	168b
think is to be full of s.	220a
this s.'s heavenly	363b
to come in spite of s.	268b
to S., I bade good-morrow	217b
travail and heavy s.	420b
trouble, s., need	480b
useless or hopeless s.	214a
wear a golden s.	385b
what s. was, thou had'st her know	173b
when in s., when in danger	411a
write s. on the bosom of the earth	375b
you were thrall to s.	423a
Sorrowful: he went away s.	507b
Sorrowing: borrowing goeth a s.	446a
toiling—rejoicing—s.	249a
Sorrows: and carried our s.	503a
as thy s. flow	281a
costly in our s.	411a
desire can make, or s. breed	225a
engluts and swallows other s.	359b
few s., however poignant	404a
for transient s.	470b
here I and s. sit	374a
it soothes his s.	289a
losses are restored and s. end	387b
man of s.	503a
Man of s. had a part	53a
my s. are at an end	159b
my s. have an end	523b
pity the s. of a poor old man	284b
s. of my heart are enlarged	483a
s. of yr. changing face	476b
when s. come, they come not single	335b
Sorry: death's self is s.	215a
do that I shall be s. for	340b
I am very s. for him	567a
I'm s., but we all must die	410a
s. for their childishness	294a
Sort: fellows of the baser s.	512b

ort (*cont.*)
like this s. of thing 245b
orted: with sobs..he s. out 84b
orts: all s. and conditions 479a
s. of things and weather 146b
ot: you drunken s.! 534b
ots: what can ennoble s. 301b
oudan: into the S.'s realm 9a
yr. 'ome in the S. 229a
ought: come, long-s.! 399a
far may be s. 402b
I have never s. the world 211a
I s. him, but his place 484a
I s. no more 441b
less often s. than found 73b
love s. is good 371b
on my bed I s. him 500a
s., for his lost heart was tender 399a
s. it with thimbles 86a
s. thee wandering, set thee right 110a
s. the Lord aright 59b
s. with an indignant mien 107b
they never s. in vain 59b
tho' he sought it carefully 517a
those men that s. him 386b
oul: acquaints his s. with song 52a
a *creative* s. 470a
adieu 'twixt s. and body 313b
affirmations of the s. 148b
a fiery s. 138a
aged s. to damn 93a
a grave unto a s. 374a
agrees..devil and thee about..s. 376b
all that a s. can do 133a
and his s. sincere 174b
angels..call to the s. 448b
as if that s. were fled 281a
a s. of fire 213b
assault and hurt the s. 479b
awake my s. 224b
became a living s. 492a
because his s. was great 136b
become a living s. 472a
be still, my s. 199b
bid the s. of Orpheus 268b
bitterness of my s. 502b
blind his s. with clay 437a
boasts two s.-sides 49b
body and in s. can bind 317a
body nature is, and God the s. 301a
books on the s. 46a
books..s. of the..Past Time 81a
but the s. stands fast 423a
call upon my s. 370a
calm s. of all things 6b
can thy s. know change? 51a
captain of my s. 185a
casket of my s. 221a
catch my flying s. 299b
Chatterton..the sleepless s. 470a
Christe receive thy s. 529a
city of the s. 69a
clothing for the s. divine 29b
conceal the S. within 429b
condense within thy s. 288b
consistency..a great s...nothing 147b
Country's gut her s. 250b
crowd not on my s.! 173b
delivered my s. from death 485b, 489a
deliver my s. from the sword 483a
demands my s., my life 453b
desire..is sweet to the s. 498a
dim s. of a star 423b
dividing asunder of s. and spirit 517a
dull wd. he be of s. 472b
ensnared my s. and body 364a
equal to the s.'s desires 464b
eternal summer in his s. 194a
every s., it passed me by 99a
eye and prospect of his s. 359a
fair seed-time had my s. 469a
fetter, that the s...thrown away! 248a
Fiat in my s. 24a
fine point of his s. 222a
five windows of the s. 30a
flesh helps s. 50b
footsteps of thy s. 43b
for my s., what can it do 331a
for s. is form 409a
found in some part of my s. 363a
freed his s. the nearest way 210b

Soul (*cont.*)
full of heaviness, O my s. 484b
give me my s. again 258b
given my s. for this 423a
give not thy s. unto a woman 520b
good book..essence of a human s. 82a
go, S., the body's guest 307b
half the little s. is dirt 434b
hangs my helpless s. on Thee 455b
hang there like fruit, my s. 329a
happy s. she shall discover 115a
have neither a s. to lose 404b
heard them call my s. 434b
heart and s. do sing 402a
heart and the s. and the senses 51b
heaven of his high s. 441b
he grants the s. again 110b
he had a little S. 282b
height my s. can reach 44a
her love-laden s. 398a
her s. to keep 265a
he shall convert my s. 483a
hidden s. of harmony 269a
hides a dark s. 267a
him whom my s. loveth 500a
his angry s. ascended 12b
his own s. was like that 292b
his heart and s. away 198b
his s. proud science never taught 300b
his s. shall taste the sadness 219b
his s. well-knit 6b
holdeth our s. in life 486a
how prodigal the s. 331a
humanized my s. 468b
hungry s. with goodness 488b
hurl my s. from heaven 364a
I am the s. 422a
I built my s. a..pleasure-house 435b
if his eager s., biting for anger 158a
I gave your yr. own s. 390a
I loafe and invite my s. 457b
in my s. am free 249b
in mystery our s. abides 7a
I refrain my s. 490a
I roamed with my S. 298b
iron entered into his s. 488b
I saw the iron enter into his s. 411a
I thee to me, O s. 457b
it is my s. that calls 365b
John's s. flared into the dark 47a
King Cole was a merry old s. 532a
lay perjury upon my s. 354b
lay thou thy s. full in her hands 315a
leave my s. in hell 482b
leaves s. free a little 45a
let every s. be subject 153b
lie in the S. 571b
lift my s. to heaven 385b
lips suck forth my s. 258b
little s. for a little bears up 423b
little S., let us try 282b
little s., wandering, pleasant 541b
long kiss my whole s. thro' my lips 427a
Love her body from her s. 313a
lose his own s. 507a, 508b
man..in whose rich s. the virtues 136b
man to afflict his s. 503a
man, with s. so dead 317a
marvelling why my s. was sad 441a
may my s. be blasted 391b
measured by my s. 453a
meeting s. may pierce in notes 269a
memorial from the S.'s eternity 311b
men so loose of s. 362a
mercy o' my s., Lord God 256a
merry if he sailed 414b
midmost s. in three 231a
mind and s., according well 429b
mine eyes into my very s. 335a
mood..that wings the s. 143a
most offending s. alive 383a
mount, mount, my s. 376a
my own s. has to itself decreed 220b
my rising S. surveys 2a
my s. doth magnify the Lord 508b
my s. drew back 188b
my s. for Goddës grace 37a
my s. hath a desire and longing 487a
my s. hath her content 361a
my s., if I have a s.! 525a
my s. in agony 99a

Soul (*cont.*)
my s. in a kiss 423a
my s. into the boughs does glide 261a
my s. is among lions 485b
my s. is an enchanted boat 397b
my S., my daughter 442b
my s. once more made trial 469a
my s.'s birth-partner 312a
my s.'s calm retreat 447b
my s.'s in arms 95b
my s. sit thou a..looker-on 307a
my s. smoothed itself 48a
my s. spurned the chains 396a
my s. that lingers sighing 199b
my s., there is a country 448a
my s. thirsteth for thee 485b
my s. with the sinners 483b
my title, and my perfect s. 359b
my unconquerable s. 185a
never once possess our s. 8b
no coward s. is mine 38b
nor s. helps flesh 50b
nor the prophetic s. 388b
no s. shall pity me 385a
no s. that lived, loved, wrought 421a
no s. to be damned 444b
not a smaller s., nor Lancelot 428a
of a reasonable s...subsisting 478b
old man with an old s. 74b
O my brave s.! 457b
O my prophetic s.! 331b
one drop wd. save my s. 258b
one impulse of yr. s. 390a
one s...commit..single venial sin 288b
opened its s. to me 49a
O s., be patient 35b
O thou s. of my s.! 50b
our s. had felt him 6b
our s. is escaped even as a bird 489b
our s. with battle-din 406a
parting s. relies 174b
passing of the sweetest s. 430b
perdition catch my s. 361b
pilgrim s. in you 476b
poetry is conceived..in the s. 9b
poor s. sat sighing 363a
poor s., the centre of my..earth 389b
poor s...thinks no..harm 35b
pour'd..her pensive s. 103a
prayer is the s.'s sincere desire 280a
pressed down my s. 485b
progress of a deathless s. 133b
prophet of the s. 147a
pure s. unto his captain Christ 375b
purest s. that ere was sent 79a
quickened his own s. 483a
receive my s. at last 455b
repent it from my very s. 368a
revolving in his altered s. 139a
roll from s. to s. 436a
sang a kindred s. out 51a
satisfieth the empty s. 488b
save his s. alive 503b
scarce the s. of a louse 235b
seized thy parting s. 114b
[Shakespeare] had the largest..s. 142a
shrinks his s. back on herself 1b
sickness is yr. s. 199b
sighed his s. toward the Grecian 355a
silent s., my brother 421a
since my dear s. was mistress 334a
single s. does fence 260b
so longeth my s. after thee 484b
some s. of goodness 382b
soothed his s. to pleasures 139a
s. abhorred all manner of meat 488b
s. above buttons 103b
s. and body part like friends 115a
s. and body rive not 324a
s. aspiring pants its source 280a
s. fainted in them 488b
s. fleeth unto the Lord 490a
s. from out immortal hell 433a
s. hath not her generous aspirings 239b
s. is competent to gain 464b
s. is dead that slumbers 247b
s. is even like a weaned child 490a
s. is in a ferment 217a
s. is marching on 178a
s. is not more than the body 458a
s. is with the saints 101a

Soul (*cont.*)

s. may not profit by	264b
s. of Adonais, like a star	392b
S. of all the worlds	464b
s. of her beauty and love	398a
s. of man is fed	262a
s. of music shed	281a
s. of our grandam	372a
s. of Sir John Cheek	278b
S. of the Age!	215b
s. of thy turtle-dove	486b
s., remembering how she felt	469b
s. remembering my good friends	375a
s., revolving hopeless strife	35b
s.'s dark cottage	449a
S. that art the Eternity of thought	465b
S. that maketh all	146a
S. that rises with us	466a
s., that she should flee as a bird	482a
s. the body form doth take	409a
s., thou hast much goods	509b
s. to feel the flesh	39a
s. to whom Luther	133b
s., uneasy, and confined from home	300b
s. wears out the breast	74a
s. with all its maladies	292b
stately mansions, O my s.	194a
stature of my s.	264a
still to the lowly s.	224a
stop-sensation in my S.	127b
strains that might create a s.	267b
strong is the S.	5a
subject's s. is his own	382b
sun of my s.	224a
sweet and virtuous s.	187b
taught my s. to fancy aught	448a
tell me, my s., can this be death?	299a
the palace of the S.	68a
the s. to dare	316b
think nobly of the s.	372a
thirst that from the s. doth rise	216a
this night thy s...be required	509b
this s. hath been alone	100a
thou art a s. in bliss	344a
thou free my s.	133a
tho' thy s. sail leagues	312b
thoughtful S. to Solitude retires	152a
thy rapt s. sitting	268a
thy s. and God stand sure	51a
thy s. I know not from thy body	312a
thy s.'s flight, if it find heaven	348b
thy s.'s immensity	466b
thy s. the fixt foot	134a
thy s. was like a star	467b
'tis my outward s.	132b
to bear my s. away	2b
tocsin of the s.	71a
to fret thy s.	409a
to get his glorious s.	258b
to my s. at death I cry	457a
try the s.'s strength on	45a
tumult, of the s.	467b
unmakes but to remake the s.	51b
vainly strives the s. to mingle	120a
veil of the s. therein	420b
very s. listened intensely	464b
wake the s. by tender strokes	298b
wan s. in that golden air	312b
was not spoken of the s.	247b
waters to a thirsty s.	498b
well for the body as the s.	478a
we too take ship, O s.	457b
what of s. was left	52b
what s. was his	464a
wh. enters into one's s.	222a
wh. war against the s.	517b
white bird..his own s.	292b
whiter s. than thine	240b
whom shall my s. believe	50b
whose s. is sense	134a
whose s. was sad	167a
winders to my S.	451a
winged chalice of the s.	313a
with Psyche, my S.	298b
with so full s. but some defect	367b
wit its s.	100b, 527b
wd. harrow up thy s.	331a
wronged great s.	49a
Soul-making: vale of S.	223a
Souls: all the s. that were forfeit	351b
amid men's s., that waver	475b

Souls (*cont.*)

as we wish our s. to be	395a
bear little s. to Heaven	150a
Bishop of yr. s.	517b
borne inward unto s. afar	44a
[corporations]..have no s.	97b
corrupt the s. of those they rule	7a
damp s. of housemaids	145a
division 'tween our s.	341a
drink to poor damned s.	230a
find rest unto yr. s.	506b
for all sparrows' s.	402b
freedom in their s.	424a
good morrow to our waking s.	133a
harmony is in immortal s.	355a
have ye s. in heaven too?	219a
Holy Ghost, our s. inspire	491a
if human s. did never kiss	217b
if s. can weep in bliss	109b
instinct of all great s.	55a
jewel of their s.	361b
kind s., you wonder	293a
knead two virtuous s.	71a
land of such dear s.	375a
left yr. s. on earth	219a
Lord, thou lover of s.	520a
men's defiled s.	407b
mercy upon one of our s.	372a
might discharge their s.	141b
must pure lovers' s. descend	132b
our s. as free	69b
our s. have sight of that..sea	466b
our s., whose faculties	259a
our two s., therefore, wh. are one	134a
peace-parted s.	336b
poor jewel of their s.	412a
possess ye yr. s.	510a
quacks..in the cure of s.	195b
see the s. we loved	434a
s...are but sunbeams	247b
s. at home with God	226b
s. do couch on flowers	324b
s. exult, and London's towers	30b
s...fed with Shakespeare's flame	93a
s. in new French books	45a
S. in their degree	230b
s. lost in the dark	47a
s. mounting up to God	311b
s. negotiate there	132b
s. not lent in usury	264a
s. of Christian peoples	91b
s. of poets dead and gone	219a
s. of the righteous..hand of God	520a
s. of women are so small	66a
s. out of men's bodies	358a
s. stand up erect	44a
s...that die in the battle	96a
s. that have toiled	439a
s. were in our names	263b
s. who dwell in Night	29b
tears for all s. in trouble	258a
there be s. must be saved	361a
they've s. that grovel	75b
thro' such s. alone	51b
times that try men's s.	291b
to play with s.	48a
two s. dwell, alas! in my breast	568a
two s. with but a single thought	568b
vigorous s., high-cultured	77b
we that have free s.	334a
wh. sucks two s.	132b
wh. virtuous s. abhor	280b
Sound: a deep s. strikes	68a
all is not s.	215a
all the s. I heard	198b
as to the tabor's s.	466a
born of murmuring s.	471b
call him up the S.	287b
carolings of such ecstatic s.	179a
except the mill-wheel's s.	393a
full of s. and fury	350b
give an uncertain s.	514b
great shocks of s.	427a
heal the blows of s.	194a
hearest the s. thereof	510b
heart as s. and free	190a
however rude the s.	162b
like the s. of a rat	50a
measures of delightful s.	398b
momentary as a s.	356a
nor any s. or sight	422a

Sound (*cont.*)

no s. is dissonant	102
no s. was heard of..clashing wars	131
o'er my ear like the sweet s.	366
once, it was a magic s.	7?
piping took a troubled s.	8
recoil and jarring s.	273
same s. is in my ears	405
sleep not so s., as sweet	188
s. as a top	160
s. is forc'd, the notes are few	31
s. is gone out into all lands	482
s. must seem an echo	300
s. of abundance of rain	496
s. of public scorn	276
s. of revelry by night	68
s. of royal cheer	432
s. of the cool colonnade	110
s. of the grinding is low	499
s. of those he wrought for	435
s. of water's murmuring	397
s., s. the clarion	283
s. were parted thence	216
sweet is every s.	437
the other not very s.	405
trumpet's wondrous s.	127
tumult sent an alien s.	466
where hath been no s.	195
wooden dialogue and s.	368
you wd. s. me from my lowest	334
Sounding: s. generalities	94
s. labour house	7
s. thro' the town	530
went s. on, a dim..way	464
Soundings: acquainted with the s.	222
Sounds: blowing martial s.	271
concord of sweet s.	355
concord of well-tuned s.	387
in souls a sympathy with s.	112
musician scatters s.	464
replication of yr. s.	337
rural s. exhilarate	111
s. and sweet airs	367
s. will gather beauty	36
s. will take care of themselves	83
strange s. along the chancel	317
tempting s. I hear	33
Soup: let his s. get cold	192
s. he swallows, sup by sup	192
S. of the evening, beautiful S.!	83
take the nasty s. away	192
won't have any s. to-day	192
Soup-and-fish: donning the s.	573
Sour: lofty and s. to them	386
Source: God, the mighty s. of all	403
its s., 'tis beer	264
its s. to mount	280
life's first native s.	409
or ope the sacred s.	175
s. of all my bliss	169
s. of human offspring	274
s. that keeps it filled	263
Thou s. of all our store	86
South: beauty in the S.	436
clanking their chains in the S.	451
come, thou s.	500
compact..between..North..S.	159
fickle is the S.	436
full of the warm S.	219
good s. wind	98
hair twixt s. and s.-west side	64
hills look over on the S.	441
hills of the S. Country	26
Queen of the Sovereign S.	237
rivers in the s.	489
rosy is the S.	433
S., East, and on	47
S. to the blind Horn's hate	231
wanton in the S.	436
Southampton: weekly from S.	230
Southern: boon s. country	9
bore me in the s. wild	32
Southron: matches of the S. folk	442
Southward dreams the sea	441
South-west wind and west wind	420
Sovereign: Civilities with my s.	207
from his s. hand	191
if s. sway may be dissolv'd	138
Magna Charta..will have no s.	97
servants of the s. or state	14
S., and his Dominions	479

Sovereign (cont.)
s. of sighs and groans 344b
trample on their s.'s head 375b
what to be a s. 145a
whilst I, my s., watch the clock 388a
Sovereign'st thing on earth 377a
Sovereigns: dead but sceptred s. 73a
Sovereignty: round and top of s. 349b
to one cd. s. impute 136b
top of s. 218b
wommen desyren..s. 89b
Sow: build for him, s. for him 470b
for, as you s...like to reap 65a
fowls of the air: for they s. not 505b
observeth the wind shall not s. 499b
s. eats up all the draff 216a
s. in tears: shall reap in joy 489b
s. that hath overwhelmed 379b
Sowen som difficultee 89a
Sower went forth sowing 34b
Soweth: whatsoever a man s. 515b
Sowing: we reap our s. 263a
Sown: nor was ever s. 445a
on earth was never s. 471b
Poets that are s. by Nature 464a
where thou hast not s. 508a
Sows, and he shall not reap 420b
Space: annihilate but s. and time 298b
here is my s. 322a
king of infinite s. 332b
nought the lettres s. 90a
sinks downwards thro' s. 179b
somewhere, beyond s. and time 39a
Spaces: silence of these infinite s. 564b
s. where cats are cats 259b
Spade: crooked scythe and s. 401a
cultivated entirely by the s. 266a
fiddle, sir, and s. 319a
if you don't call me s. 418b
must call a s. a s. 162b
nominate a s. a s. 215b
s.! with wh. Wilkinson hath tilled 471a
Spades: let s. be trumps 302b
s..emblem of..untimely graves 112b
Spain: blood-red field of S. 184b
castels than in S. 90a
Cervantes smiled S.'s chivalry 71b
devildoms of S. 437b
into the hands of S. 150b
King of S. is dead 150b
King of S.'s Beard 136b
king of S.'s daughter 532a
Miguel of S. 230a
not left to S. 437b
plateau of S. forming a head 179b
slow old tunes of S. 261b
where are the gallows of S.? 130b
Spake: carl s. oo thing 89b
never man s. like this man 511a
s. by the Prophets 480a
s. full well, in language quaint 247a
s. he; and was buckling tighter 254a
s. on that ancient man 98a
Span: Eve's 178b
life of man less than a s. 17a
spick and s.,-new 65a
Spaniard: French, Italian, S., or
   Dutch 42a
Spaniards: S. seem wiser than they are 15b
to thrash the S. too 136b
Spaniel'd: hearts that s. me 324a
Spaniels civilly delight 303a
Spanish: ambuscadoes, S. blades 364b
fond of S. wine 261b
hear a S. lady 528a
I must learn S. 46b
S. ale shall give you hope 258a
S. fleet thou canst not see 400a
S. Gal-la-lee 531a
S. or neat's leather 65b
S. ships of war 437a
tell her in S. 46b
there is a S. proverb 90b
Spare: advance! S. not 198a
how much he can s. 210a
O s. me a little 484a
s. all I have 150a
s. the beechen tree 76b
s. the humbled 556a
s. the poet for..subject's sake 107b
s. the rod, and spoil the child 65b

Spare (cont.)
s. yr. country's flag 459a
Spared: better s. a better man 379a
Sparely: I fear ye dine but s. 61b
Spares: never s. the child 196a
Spark: nor human s. is left 299a
parson, oh! illustrious s. 109b
shows a hasty s. 341a
s. from Heaven to fall 8a
s. of celestial fire 451b
vital s. of heav'nly flame! 299a
Sparkle for ever 436a
Sparkling: pair of s. eyes 163b
Sparks: as the s. fly upward 497a
s. among the stubble 520a
s. blown out of a smithy 476a
with unnumber'd s. 339a
Sparrow: brawling of a s. 476a
even as it were a s. 488a
hedge-s. fed the cuckoo 342a
hero perish, or a s. fall 300b
in the fall of a s. 337a
'I,' said the S. 528a
life of man..like..s. 24a
my lady's s., O, he's sped 538b
soul of Philip S. 402b
s. alight on my shoulder 444a
s. hath found her a nest 487a
Sparrow-grass: hit look lak s. 181b
Sparrows: for all s.' souls 402b
are not five s. sold 509b
are not two s. sold 506a
more value than many s. 506a
team of s. 251a
when s. build 203a
Spars: under the s. of wh. I lie 190b
Sparta: firm as S.'s king 136b
S. is yr. inheritance 540a
with hounds of S. 357a
Spartan: out of the S. kind 357a
remnant of our S. dead! 70b
Spartans: go tell the S. 560a
Spat on me on Wednesday 353a
Speak: been supposed to s. 71b
both of them s. of something 466a
did he stop and s. to you 48b
heard Chapman s. out loud 220b
hear them s. in our tongues 512a
he can s. and flee! 529a
he shall s. for himself 511a
if I s. to thee in Friendship's 282b
if they s. first 104a
I never will s. word 364a
I only s. right on 340a
I s. too boldly 282b
I s. too coldly 282b
I s. unto them thereof 489b
it was my hint to s. 360a
let him now s. 481b
let not God s. with us 494a
live pure, s. true 427b
losers must have leave to s. 95b
men shall s. well of you 509a
not permitted unto them to s. 514b
of comfort no man s. 375b
one that can s. so well 262b
one to s., and another to hear 444a
province of knowledge to s. 194b
shame for women to s. 514b
slaves who fear to s. 250b
slow to s. 517a
s. after sentence? 206a
s. but one word to me 284b
s. by the card 336b
s.; Cæsar is turned to hear 337b
s. daggers to her, but use none 334b
s. disrespectfully of the Equator 404a
s. for yourself, John 246b
s.; I'll go no further 331a
s. in French when you can't think 84a
s. less than thou knowest 342a
s., Lord; for thy servant heareth 495a
s. low, if you s. love 358a
s. low to me, my Saviour 43a
s. more in a minute 365b
s. no more of his renown 435a
s. no more; thou turn'st mine eyes 335a
s. not when the people listens 319a
s. of me as I am 364a
s. of the better land 184b

Speak (cont.)
s. roughly to yr. little boy 82b
s. softly and carry a big stick 310a
s. the speech, I pray you 333b
s. the thing that's true 452b
s. to Him thou for He hears 427b
s. unto us smooth things 502a
s. very well in the..Commons 130a
s. what to-morrow thinks 147b
s. what you think to-day 147b
s. when he is spoken to 413b
s. when you're spoken to 85b
s. ye comfortably to Jerusalem 502b
therof redeth nat to s. 88b
those that are asleep to s. 500b
'tis mine to s. 403b
upon wh. it is difficult to s. 56a
well didst thou s. 68a
we shal s. of thee 90a
what I think, I must s. 327a
what shd. we s. of 328b
when you s., sweet 373b
who s. the tongue that Shakespeare 467a
wd. not cease to s. 114a
you s. to him again 48b
Speaker: no other s. of my..actions 386b
Speakers: stay, you imperfect s. 346a
Speakest wiser than thou art ware 326a
Speaking: adepts in the s. trade 94b
for their much s. 505a
God be..in my s. 523a
in s. for myself 360a
s. in a perpetual hyperbole 14b
s. things wh. they ought not 516b
sum of things for ever s. 464b
thought him still s. 275b
Speaks: he speaks very shrewishly 370a
Jesus s., and s. to thee 110a
never s. well of me 104b
she s. poniards 358a
s. an infinite deal of nothing 352b
s. the kindest words 244a
s. to Me..public meeting 448b
when he s., the air..is still 381a
Spear: bring me my s. 31a
ever put s. in the rest 257b
footing of a s. 377a
his s., to equal wh. the tallest 271b
idle s. and shield 270a
Ithuriel with his s. 274b
knappeth the s. in sunder 484b
shield an' shovel-s. 229a
shivered was Scotland's s. 318b
snatched the s., but left the shield 318a
will like a dividing s. 5b
Spearmen still made good 318b
Spears: brought him slain with s. 436b
sheen of their s. 74a
s. into pruning-hooks 501a
stars threw down their s. 32a
teeth are s. and arrows 485b
Special: he was..a s. attorney 169b
Specialism: his s. is omniscience 136a
Species: female of the s. 229a
not an individual, but a s. 151a
not the individual, but the s. 213b
than as one of the s. 1b
Specimen: only s. of Burke is, all 183a
Speckled Vanity 270b
Spectacle: s. of human happiness 404b
s. of so much glory 255a
s. unto the world 514a
Spectacles: s. of books to read 142a
s., to shoot the hare 192b
with s. on nose 326b
Spectator of mankind 1b
Spectators: actors or s.? 392a
Spectatress of the mischief 313b
Spectre: dancing s. seems the moon 264a
my S. around me 31b
s.-thin, and dies 220a
Spectre-bark: off shot the s. 99a
Speculation: no s. in those eyes 349a
Speculations: throw out my s. 201b
Speech: a stately s. 470b
better to deal by s. 16a
Consul's s. was low 253a
cd. wed itself with S. 430a
eyesight and s. they wrought 420b
fear my s. distorting 36b
general ear with horrid s. 333a

Speech (cont.)
his ready s. flowed 316b
his s. was coarse 233b
I am slow of s. 493b
in high style, and make a s. 11a
in the seventh s., an interpreter 520b
knavish s. sleeps 335a
let thy s. be short 520b
makes mouths at our s. 421b
manner of his s. 323a
mighty likely s. 159b
neither s. nor language 482b
nor utterance, nor power of s. 340a
on him no s. 241a
smaller parts-o'-s. 75a
speak the s., I pray you 333b
s. be alway with grace 516a
s. created thought 397a
s. is a burning fire 420b
s. is human 81a
S. is of Time 81b
S. is shallow as Time 80a
S. is silvern 81b
s. only to conceal..thoughts 566a
s...small change of silence 265a
spoke the s. of the Gaels 92a
strange powers of s. 100a
sweet music of s. 113a
they thought a malevolent s. 214b
thy s. bewrayeth thee 508a
thy s. is comely 500a
to cast away my s. 370a
tongue blossom into s. 45b
true use of s. 170b
under all s...lies a silence 80a
upon my parts of s. 400b
whose s. Truth knows not 313a
Speeches: all the easy s. 93a
gets his s. by it 310a
I leave it to men's charitable s. 17a
Speed: better may she s. 149b
courage, breath, and s. 316a
deliberate s. 441b
follow thee with all the s. 225a
outstrip thy skiey s. 396b
Oxus, forgetting the bright s. 8a
safety is in our s. 147b
shall teach me s. 374a
s. his plough 87a
s. i' the slushy sand 48b
s., Malise, s.! 316b
Speeds too fast, 'twill tire 344b
Spell: foreigners always s. better 446b
s. it with a 'V' or a 'W'? 126b
went thy s. thro' him 312b
who lies beneath yr. s.? 197a
Speller: Chawcer..wuss s. I know 451a
taste and fancy of the s. 126b
Spells: dealer in magic and s. 167a
Spence: grand old ballad..S. 100b
Spencer: renowned S., lie 22a
Spend: good world..to s...in 38a
much money as I cd. s. 533a
so wol we s. 89b
s. that shortness basely 379a
to s., to give, to want 409b
what we yet may s. 153a
Spendest: whatsoever thou s. more 509a
Spending: riches are for s. 15b
Spenlow: Mr. S. 122b
Spens: Sir Patrick S. 529b
Spenser: a little nearer S. 22a
lodge thee by Chaucer, or S. 215b
serious poet S. 279a
sweet S. moving 469b
thee gentle S. fondly led 241b
Spent: being s., the worse 190b
feels himself s. 111a
s. and maimed among 226a
that we s., we had 526a
time has been properly s. 425a
Sphere: all quit their s. 30b
arrows of that silver s. 398a
cheering the elevated s. 57a
gird the s. with centric 275b
make up a year and a s. 146b
s. for Shelley's genius 9a
their motion in one s. 379a
they the s. 132b
world's storm-troubled s. 38b
Sphere-descended: Music, s. maid 103a

Spheres: abject from the s. 452a
driven by the s. 448b
like the harmonious s. 249b
maintain the music of the s. 42a
moving as the restless S. 259a
propertied as all the tuned s. 325a
rose to touch the s. 44a
seems to shake the s. 138b
shot madly from their s. 356b
s. of action 244b
s. of influence 526a
start from their s. 331a
you ever-moving s. 258b
Sphinx: Minx, or a S. 125b
subtle as S. 345a
Spice, and all that's nice 534b
Spiced: dish more sharply s. 293b
Spices: s. thereof may flow out 500b
upon the mountain of s. 501a
woodbine s. 434a
Spick and span new 65a
Spicy: India's s. shores 107b
s. breezes blow soft 184a
Spider: said a s. to a fly 201a
smallest s.'s web 364b
s.'s touch how exquisitely fine 300b
Spiders: s., flies..ants..in amber 16b
weaving s. come not here 356b
Spider-web: kind of huge s. 204b
Spied: ferlie he s. wi' his e'e 528a
Spier: married, s. nae mair 63a
Spies: if we were God's s. 344a
they come not single s. 335b
ye are s.; to see the nakedness 493b
Spill: spare..rod..s. the child 65b
Spills: guilt..s. itself in fearing 335b
wh. s. the foremost foeman's 316b
Spin: neither do they s. 505b
sit by the fire and s. 533a
Spindle-guide: coupler-flange to s. 231b
Spinnage: world of gammon and s. 122a
Spinners: long-legged s. 356b
made of long s.' legs 364b
Spins like a fretful midge 311b
Spinsters and the knitters 371a
Spire of English grass 178a
Spires: City with her dreaming s. 8b
dim-discovered s. 103a
from all her reeling s. 252b
mount of marble, a hundred s. 426b
s. of Frederick stand 458b
s. whose 'silent fingers' 464b
the s. of form 146b
what s., what farms 199b
ye distant s., ye antique towns 174b
Spirit: progress s. round 91b
Spirit: a dedicated s. 469b
all pains the immortal s. 7b
a s. when her s. looked 312a
before that s. die 415a
body did contain a s. 379a
bold s. in a loyal breast 374b
bound in the s. 512b
bring forth the fruits of the S. 479a
'Brutus' will start a s. 337b
by the S., in sincerity 65b
clear s. doth raise 269b
come, O Creator S. 549b
come, Thou Holy S., come 86b
culture..history of the human s. 10a
curbing his lavish s. 346a
delighted s. to bathe in..floods 352a
diversities..gifts, but the same S. 514a
dividing asunder of soul and s. 517a
dumb s. within 406a
eviller s. than you 406a
expense of s. 380a
extravagant and erring s. hies 329b
fervent in s. 513b
fiercest S. that fought in Heav'n 272a
flesh lusteth against the S. 515b
follow yr. s. 382a
fruit of the S. is love, joy 515b
gentlier on the s. lies 433a
genuine s. of localism 34a
God is a S. 510b
hail to thee, blithe s.! 398a
haughty s. before a fall 498a
healthful S. of thy grace 478b
her cabin'd ample S. 7b
her s.'s vestal grace 293b

Spirit (cont.)
he that ruleth his s. 498a
holding the eternal s. 374a
holy-day rejoicing s. 240a
holy s. of discipline 520a
holy s. of man 420b
humble, tranquil s. 118b
I am thy father's s. 331a
I commend my s. 483b, 510a
if the ill s. have so fair 367b
immortal s. grows 469a
informs my s., ne'er can I believe 464a
invisible s. of wine 361b
it is the generous s. 465a
I was in the s. 518a
lodging for his S. fair 294b
Mammon, the least erected S. 272a
man..kin to God by his s. 15a
meek and quiet s. 517b
merry, nimble, stirring s. 345a
motions of his s. 355b
my s. hath rejoiced in God 508b
my s. is too deeply laden 399b
my s. like a charmed bark 394a
my s. pure and clear 438a
my s. wh. so long darkened 395b
needs s. lack all life behind 51b
no more s. in her 496a
no s. can walk aboard 329b
nought..the s. calms as rum 70b
one fair s. for my minister 69b
pard-like s. 392a
pardon..the s. of liberty 55b
pour out my s. upon all flesh 504a
pure s. shall flow 392b
put a s. of youth 388b
quite o'ercrows my s. 337a
rarer s. never did steer 324b
renew a right s. within me 485a
rest, perturbed s. 331b
retentive to the strength of s. 338a
rural sounds, exhilarate the s. 111b
sacrifice of God is a troubled s. 485a
scorned his s. 338a
shy s. in my heart 472b
sing it with a s. 473a
slumber did my s. seal 463a
speaks to my s. of *thee* 74a
S. and the bride say, Come 520b
s., antithetically mixt 68b
s. bloweth and is still 7a
S. fierce, My s.! 396b
s. giveth life 515a
S., I love thee 398b
s. indeed is willing 508a
s. in my feet 394b
s. in the woods 468a
S. of adoption 513b
S. of Beauty, that dost consecrate 394b
S. of Delight! 398b
s. of divinest Liberty 101a
s. of fear 516b
S. of God moved upon..the waters 492a
s. of health or goblin 331a
s. of my dream 72a
S. of Night! 399a
s. of self-sacrifice 464a
s. of sense hard as the palm 368b
s. of the chainless mind! 69b
s. of the Lord bloweth upon it 502b
s. of the Lord is upon me 503a
s. of the Lord shall rest upon him 501b
S. of the Universe! 465b
s. of the worm beneath the sod 393b
s. of truth, unity, and concord 480b
s. passed before my face 497a
s. shall return unto God 500a
s. so still and quiet 360a
s. that ever took flesh 147b
s. that is in Antony 337b
s. that knows no insulated spot 464b
s. that on this life's..sea 87a
s. that quickeneth 511a
S. that strove for truth 399a
S., wh. art moving everywhere 396a
s. within me constraineth me 497a
S. without spot. (Sidney) 392b
S. with S. can meet 427b
s., yet a woman too! 470b
stablish me with thy free s. 485a

Spirit (*cont.*)

stab my s. broad awake	415a
stirs her s. up	407a
strengthened with might by his S.	515b
strength of thy s.	422b
strike with our s.'s knife	392b
sweet S. comfort me!	190b
take not thy holy s. from me	485a
the anointing S. art	491a
th' enlightened s. sees	448a
there's a wicked s.	3a
they that are after the S.	513b
things of the S.	513b
this gray s. yearning	438b
tho' at times her s. sank	432b
thy s. walks abroad	341b
to break a man's s.	390a
to the s. ditties of no tone	219b
unsphere the s. of Plato	268a
voice did on my s. fall	96b
voice my s. can cheer	245b
with a joyful s. I..die	437b
with too much s. to be..at ease	302a
worser s. a woman	389b
wounded s. who can bear?	498b
yea, saith the S.	519b
yet a s. still	470b
young s.! rest thee now!	184b
Spiriting: do my s. gently	367a
Spiritless: degraded, s. outcast!	78b
Spirit-like, eludes embrace	293b
Spirits: actors..were all s.	367b
all s. are enslaved	397a
angel s. of sleep	35b
beauteous s. do ingirt	78b
black s. and white	265b, 349b
by our own s. are we deified	470a
choice and master s.	339b
come, you s. that tend	346b
drooping s. can raise	107a
flat unraised s.	381a
glorious s. shine!	453b
Heaven with S. masculine	276b
her wanton s. look out	369a
inland petty s. muster me	380b
isolate pure s.	44a
jump with common s.	353b
maketh his angels s.	488a
no revenue..but thy good s.	334a
other s. there are	221a
our s. rushed together	432a
pluck up thy s., man	283a
ruffle our yr. s.	340b
rule our s. from their urns	73a
seven other s. more wicked	506b
she looked the s. up and down	231b
s. are not finely touched	351a
s...can either sex assume	271b
s. from the vasty deep	378a
s. of just men made perfect	517a
s. of those who were homing	180a
s. passing thro' the streets	396a
s. that know all..consequences	350b
stories from the land of s.	101a
their s. are in Heaven!	472b
unhappy s. that fell	258b
weak ships and s. steer	422a
we have the evil s. too	406a
wh. like two s. do suggest me	389b
wonders at our quaint s.	356b
Spiritual: Germany was my s. home	571b
s. is stronger than..material	148b
Spirituality about the face	135b
Spit: my friend may s.	187b
s. on all things fair	87b
s. upon him, whilst I say he lies	375b
Spite: I do to s. the world	348b
it were only to s. them	170a
slander and the s.	431a
Splash! splash! along the sea	319a
Splashing and paddling	43b
Spleen: excite yr. languid s.	165b
in a s., unfolds both heaven	356a
so much..Mirth and S.	2a
Spleeny Lutheran	385b
Splendid: a S. Shilling	296b
load of s. care	283a
s. and a happy land	168b
s. isolation	172a
s. with swords	421a

Splendid (*cont.*)

sundown s. and serene	185a
Splendour: faded s. wan	274b
guilty s.	112a
its s., soon or late, will pierce	49b
more-than-oriental-s.	237a
not in lone s.	220b
over the s. and speed	420a
pavilioned in s.	172b
silvery s. pant with bliss	218b
s. among shadows	399a
s. falls on castle walls	436a
s. in the grass	466b
s. of its prime	394a
stung by the s.	46a
sun..in his first s.	472b
we are children of s.	452a
Splendours, and Glooms	392a
Splenetive: tho' I am not s.	336b
Spliced in the humdrum way	38b
Split: Gawd..won't s. on a pal	237b
ice did s.	98b
s. her in twain	437b
to make all s.	356a
tongue shall be s.	533a
Split'st the unwedgeable	351b
Spohr and Beethoven	164b
Spoil: come and s. the fun	84a
company, hath been the s. of me	378b
household divided the s.	486a
sign'd in thy s.	339b
when they divide the s.	501b
Spoiled the Egyptians	494a
Spoilers: hands of the s.	494b
s. of the symmetry	239a
Spoils: s. that his own hand spread	421b
s. the rod	196a
s. the singing of the nightingale	217b
s. were fairly sold	253a
stratagems and s.	355b
Spoke: all that's s. is marred	364a
checked him while he s.	241a
deny what I have s.	365a
he s., and loos'd our hearts	6b
proud word you never s.	241b
put a s. among yr. wheels	23a
she s., and panted	323a
s. in her cheeks	133b
s. what she shd. not	350a
while he pleading s.	443a
Spoken: glorious things of thee are s.	289a
Lord hath not s. by me	496b
not have s. on't	323b
speak when you're s. to	85b
that never have s. yet	93a
Sponge: married to a s.	353a
Spongy April	367b
Sponsors: mountains are our s.	241b
Spoon: dish ran after the s.	534a
runcible s.	243b
worth a silver s.	522a
Spoons: let us count our s.	207b
we counted our s.	147a
we guard our s.	254a
with my silver s.	295a
world locks up its s.	390b
Sport: all the s. is stale	226a
animals never kill for s.	157b
Cæsar bleed in s.	339a
detested s.	112a
she is s. for Jove	361a
s. for our neighbours	11b
S. that wrinkled Care derides	268b
s., to the wild ocean	372b
s. with Amaryllis in the shade	269b
to s. wd. be as tedious	376b
'unting is..the s. of kings	416b
Sported on the green	406a
Sporting: mates were idly s.	36b
Sports: Christmas brought his s.	318a
excel in athletic s.	129b
joy of youthful s.	69b
play her cruel s.	409a
s. of love	216a
Sportsman wot doesn't kick his wife	416b
Sporus: let S. tremble	303a
Spot: angry s. doth glow	338a
for each one s. shall prove	235a
out, damned s.! out, I say!	350a
reach the S. where I made one	154a
s. that's always barred	164b

Spot (*cont.*)

stir of this dim s.	266b
there is no s. in thee	500b
tip me the black s.	413a
with a s. I damn him	340b
Spots: gold coats s. you see	356b
leopard his s.	503b
s. and clouds in the sun	64a
s. in yr. feasts of charity	518a
s. quadrangular	112b
Spousal: bird of night sung s.	275b
Spouse: dear Christ, thy s.	133a
John Gilpin's s. said	108a
my sister, my s.	500b
S. and Brother	441a
s. of the worm	77b
Sprat: Jack S.	534a
Sprawled thro' the ooze	404a
Spray: champ..chafe..toss in the s.	
cowrin' on the s.	424b
never a s. of yew	7b
snake slipt under a s.	435b
s. the bird clung to	48b
that on yon bloomy s.	278a
twirling..a withered s.	8a
Spread: butter's s. too thick	84b
masters, s. yourselves	356a
money..not good..except..s.	15a
Spreading: s. chestnut-tree	249a
s. of the hideous town	284a
Sprig of bays in fifty years	419b
Sprightly: first s. running	139b
Sprig-muslin drest	180a
Spring: and cd. s. to her	420a
apparelled like the s.	364a
a s. of light	97b
been absent in the s.	388b
blossom the s. begins	420b
blue sky of s.	4a
can S. be far behind?	396b
chilly finger'd s.	217b
clear s., or shady grove	273a
come, gentle S.!	443b
cuckoo, messenger of S.	408a
drunk deep of the Pierian s.	137a
ever-returning s.	458b
falsehood has a perennial s.	55a
farewell! thou latter s.!	376b
flowers that bloom in the s., tra la	165a
floures ginnen for to s.	89b
found in the s. to follow	422b
fresh s., and summer	395a
fresh s. the herald of love's	408a
gay s. leaping cometh	35b
has no second s.	296b
haunted s. and dale	270b
have as short a S.	189a
heart be full of the s.	422b
hounds of s.	420a
how this s. of love resembleth	372b
image of thine eyes in any s.	312a
in the Fire of S.	152b
in the S. a young man's fancy	432a
I thought 'twas the s.	67b
lap of the new come s.	376a
lead the Surrey s. again	232b
linnet courting his lady in the s.	36b
lived light in the s.	5b
made a lasting s.	385b
meadow-gale of s.	99b
melted into s.	39a
middle summer's s.	356b
murmurs of the S.	307b
nae second s.	525b
nightingale all s. thro'	422b
no S., nor Summer beauty	132a
now S. restores the balmy days	539a
O, Baby S.	293b
one master-s. controll'd them all	112a
our Sister the S.	27a
pilgrim steps of s.	36a
rifle all the breathing S.	102b
sister of the s. shall blow	396a
smiling face a dream of S.!	102a
S. a livelier iris changes	432a
s. and foison of the year	387b
S. comes slowly up this way	100a
s., full of sweet days and roses	187b
s. goeth all in white	37b
S. in rarest visitation	397a
s. is come home	441b

Spring (cont.)
s. of love gushed 99a
s. shut up, a fountain sealed 500b
s., the sweet s. 286a
S., time's Harbinger 23b
sweet lovers love the s. 327b
taste not the Pierian s. 300a
that S. shd. vanish 154a
thought 'twas the s...it was she 67b
thou wilt s. to me 428a
thy lover the s. 422b
waters of the crisped s. 119a
white foam of the S. 452a
winter, commonly called the s. 113a
Winter..was changed to S. 397b
year's at the s. 50a
you do bring in the S. 190b
Springe: woodcock to mine own s. 337a
Springen cokkel 89a
Springes to catch woodcocks 331a
Springs: all my fresh s. 487a
fifty s. are little room 198b
four wanton s. 374b
mirth that has no bitter s. 228a
O faintly, gentle s. 214b
red strays of ruined s. 422a
s. into the rivers 488a
s. of the sea 497b
s. o' that countrie 528a
s. renewed by flowing 78a
streams o'erflow yr. s. 260b
three beauteous s. to..autumn 388b
water at those s. 328b
where s. not fail 197b
Springtide: her old s. 206a
Spring-time..pretty ringtime 327b
Sprinkles another's laughing face 241a
Sprinkling: wd. I be s. it 238b
Sprite: an angelic s. 133a
his clear S. yet reigns 391b
picture that orchard s. 192a
Sprites: one of s. and goblins 373a
sweet s., the burden bear 367a
Sprouting despondently 145a
Sprush: cock it fu' s. 193b
Spue thee out of my mouth 518b
Spun my last thread 132a
Spur: danger..s. of all great minds 87b
fame is the s. 269b
I have no s. to prick 347a
Spurgeon: haberdasher to Mr. S. 67a
Spurn not the nobly born 163b
Spurned me such a day 353a
Spurred: Doeg...s. boldly on 138b
Spurs: boy win his s. 143b
s. the lated traveller 349a
s. too fast betimes 374b
Spurt of a lighted match 48b
Spy: all will s. in thy face 132b
to s. out the land 494a
Squad: let the awkward s. 63b
Squadron: 'arf a s. swimmin' 229a
Squamous, omnipotent, and kind 39b
Square: broke a British s. 229a
circles can never make a s. 171a
given a s. deal 310a
grows a glimmering s. 436a
I have not kept the s. 323b
meet you on the s. 239a
s., and above the board 178a
s. with Genesis again 45a
Squares: about the flowering s. 431a
Squash: s. is before 'tis a peascod 370a
this s., this gentleman 373a
Squat like a toad 274b
Squeak: naturally as pigs s. 64b
s. and gibber 329b
Squeaking of the wry-necked fife 353b
[**Squeers**] had but one eye 124b
Squeeze a right-hand foot 85b
Squeezing: with you in the s. of a
lemon 171a
Squinch-owl: say ter der s. 181b
Squire: s. and his relations 121b
s. seemed struck in the saddle 93a
Squires: gallant s. of Kent 252b
last sad s. 93a
nine and twenty s. of name 316b
Squirrel: joiner is 364b
mountain and the s. 146b
Stab my spirit broad awake 415a

Stability: a party of..s. 266a
Stable: commonwealth is fixed and s. 56a
courtly s. 270b
dunghill hard by his own s. 100b
nothing s. in the world 222a
son of a livery s. keeper 474b
s. for his steed 305a
s.-place sufficed 311a
Stables are the real centre 390a
Stablish: s., continue our march 7b
s. me according to thy word 489b
s. me with thy free spirit 485a
Stacher through to meet their Dad 59b
Stack, or the barn door 268b
Stacks: all ready in s. 167a
Staff: every rod or s. of empire 17a
rod and thy s. comfort me 483a
s. of this bruised reed 496b
stay and the s. 501a
yr. s. in yr. hand 494a
Stafford: Lord S. mines 178a
Stag: a runnable s. 117a
s. at eve 316a
Stage: agree on the s. 400a
all the world's a s. 326b
daily s. of duty 224b
dies for love, but on the s. 141a
drown the s. with tears 333a
first reared the S. 213b
green plot shall be our s. 357a
he flits across the s. 129b
hour upon the s. 350b
little man there upon the s. 151b
Muse first trod the s. 298b
old woe step on the s. again 51a
on the s. he was natural 169b
played upon a s. now 371b
shake a s. 216a
speak in public on the s. 149b
s. but echoes back 213b
s. so gloomed with woe 435b
s. where every man must play 352b
the s.'s jewel 215a
this great s. of fools 343b
unperfect actor on the s. 387a
we've still our s. 44b
wonder of our s.! 215b
Stage-coach: follies..faster than a s. 170b
Stagers: heard old cunning s. 65b
Stages: his s. may have been 399b
Stagger like a drunken man 488b
Stagirite: staggered that stout S. 240b
Stagnated: seem well-nigh s. 311b
Stagyrites: planets, filled with S. 282b
Stain: felt a s. like a wound 57a
offered free from s. 252b
saw, with many a s. 114a
s. in thine honour 521a
suns of the world may s. 387b
without fault or s. on thee 37a
world's slow s. 392b
Stained the water clear 32b
Stains: s. and splendid dyes 221b
such s. there are 241a
Stair: build a gorgeous s. 202b
going up another's s. 567a
led her up the s. 230a
rising..by a winding s. 14b
Staircase wit 562b
Stairs: up s., down s. 534b
Stake: deep s. they have 56a
have tied me to a s. 351a
head upon a s. 280b
I am tied to the s. 343a
s. in the country 573b
still hae a s. 59a
thumbscrew and the s. 437b
we are at the s. 340b
Stale: how weary, s., flat 330a
poor I am s. 328b
Stalk: half asleep as they s. 179b
He hangeth on a s. 475a
Stalked off reluctant 29a
Stalking-horse: folly like a s. 328a
Stalky: yr. Uncle S. 237b
Stamford: bullocks at S. fair 380b
by S. town 432b
Stamp: Christ's s. to boot 186b
penny-postage-s. 85b
s. of his lowly origin 117b

Stamper of the Skies 473a
Stamping: Queen..went s. about 83a
Stand: at the casement seen her s. 431b
cannot always s. upright 479b
cd. s. on any ground 137a
do I s. and stare? 48b
farewell, and s. fast 377a
glorious Angels always s. 286a
having done all, to s. 516a
his fav'rite s. between 113a
how does she s.? 525b
how, if a' will not s. 358b
incessantly s. on yr. head 82b
in this we s. or fall 275a
I s. alone, and think 221a
little child I s. 190b
nowhere to s. but on 225a
now who will s. on either hand 253a
one firm spot on wh. to s. 559a
on what he intended to s. 129a
risen and s. upright 482b
she seemed to s. 316a
souls to s. up erect 44a
s. a man a cheese 93b
s. close around 241a
s. not upon the order 349a
s. still, true poet 50a
s. still, you ever-moving spheres 258b
s. to in a month 365b
s. up for Jesus 142b
s. up now, Tomlinson 235a
s. upon my kingdom 375a
strengthen such as do s. 479a
time to s. and stare 118a
we s. to bless Thee 145b
why s. ye here all the day idle? 507b
will s. a-tiptoe when this day 383a
Standard: yr. glorious s. launch 77b
Standest meekly by 289b
Standeth: she s. by thy side 531b
that thinketh he s. 514b
Standfast: Mr. S. 54b
Standing: keep you s. at that door 311a
s. for some false..shore 8b
s. is slippery 14b
Stands: s. Scotland where it did? 350a
sturdy and staunch he s. 151a
what s. if Freedom fall? 229a
Stanhope's pencil writ 477b
Stanley: approbation from Sir
Hubert S. 284b
here S. meets, how S. scorns 252a
on, S., on! 318b
[S.]..Rupert of..discussion 128a
Stanza: who pens a s. 303a
Staple of his argument 304b, 345a
Star: a bright particular s. 322a
against the morning s. 394a
an incredible s. 92b
bid haste the evening s. 275b
bright and morning s. 520b
bright morning s. 270a
bright *Occidental S.* 492a
bright s., wd. I were stedfast 220b
came forth to rebehold each s. 566b
catch a falling s. 134a
constant as the northern s. 339a
curb a runaway young s. 74b
day-s. arise in yr. hearts 518a
desire of the moth for the s. 399b
dim soul of a s. 423b
evening s., love's harbinger 276b
every wandering s. 206a
eve's one s. 218a
fair as a s., when only one 470b
first s. shivers 154a
flowed right for the Polar S. 8a
found the new Messiah by the s. 140b
glittering like the morning's 57a
grapples with his evil s. 430b
great s. early drooped 458b
hitch yr. wagon to a s. 148b
infect to the north s. 358a
inquisition of each s. 443a
knock at a s. 189b
light of the morning s. 31a
lights the evening s. 76a
like a sinking s. 438b
lit by one large s. 263b
loftiest s. of unascended heaven 397b
moist s. under whose influence 329b

Star (cont.)

Moon, with one bright s.   99a
morning s. of song   426b
named a s.   50a
never s. was lost here   52b
O eastern s.!   325b
one s. differeth from another s.   515a
our life's S.   466a
particular beauteous s.   218b
ran against a shooting s.   407a
reflex of a s.   466a
running stream, O morning s.   476a
seen his s. in the east   504b
some fostering s.   452a
splendid, a s.!   52b
S. for every State   462a
s.-inwrought!   399a
s. is called Wormwood   519a
s.-like sparkle in their skies   190a
s. nor sun shall waken   422a
s. of my fate hath declined   74a
s. of peace return   78a
s. or two beside   99a
s., that once had shone   154b
s. to every wandering bark   389a
s. to guide the humble   256b
s to steer her by   262a
s., with lessening ray   6:b
s.-y-pointing pyramid   278a
sunset and evening s.   426a
take away that s. and garter   12a
takes the s.'s height   423b
their s. is a world   49a
there was a s. danced   358a
thy soul was like a s.   467b
to the charge of a s.!   342a
troubling of a s.   442b
twinkle, twinkle, little s.   425a
unfolding s. calls up..shepherd   352a
vague unpunctual s.   39b
youngest-teemed s.   270b
zenith like a falling s.   272a
Star-captains glow   154b
Star-Chamber matter of it   355b
Stare: made Quintilian s.   278b
on the ground I see thee s.   89a
stony British s.   433b
time to stand and s.   118a
Stared: I..s. into the sky   192b
s., with his foot on the prey   435b
Staring and looking upon me   483a
Stark: Molly S. 's a widow   410a
Star-led wizards   270a
Starlight: by the s., naming   47a
River floated..into the frosty s.   8a
s. and by candlelight   445b
there was nae s.   528a
Star-like: from s. eyes doth seek   79a
Starry: this s. stranger   114b
where are those s. woods?   37a
Stars: all the s. looked down   92a
amid a crowd of s.   476b
and calculate the s.   275b
and one the s.   242a
and she forgot the s.   218b
ask of the s. in motion   442a
asks of God, but of her s.   302a
as s. look on the sea   252a
baths of all the western s.   439a
beauty of a thousand s.   258b
between me and the s.   469a
blesses his s...thinks it luxury   1b
blue sky belongs to [s.]   99a
bright, patient s.   218b
by the earnest s.   218a
certain s. shot madly   356b
close up the s.   267a
continuous as the s.   467a
crowned with the s.   445a
crown of twelve s.   519a
cut him out in little s.   366a
Danaë to the s.   436b
doubt thou the s. are fire   332a
eyes were blind with s.   192b
falling s. are shooting   73a
far beyond the s.   448a
fault..is not in our s.   337b
fleet of s. is anchored   154b
for mounting to the s.   566b
glows in the s.   501a
he made the s. also   492a

Stars (cont.)

in his right hand seven s.   518b
in the shining of the s.   429a
kinship with the s.   263b
look at the s.!   197b
morning s. sang together   497b
moves the sun and the other s.   567a
new-bathed s.   8a
night with her train of s.   185a
opposition of the s.   260b
peaks but to the s. are known   6b
praise Him, all ye s. and light   224a
preserve the s. from wrong   464a
risen s. and the fallen   420a
sentinel s. set their watch   77b
shalt thou scale the s.   556b
shine aloft like s.   464b
silent s. go by   40a
some of us are looking at the s.   573a
s. and sunbeams know   7b
s. and the winds are unto her   420a
S. are setting and the Caravan   153b
s. be blown about the sky   476a
S. before him from the Field   152a
s. began to blink   468b
s. came out far over   437b
s. come out, and the night-wind   6a
s. hide their diminished heads   273b
s. in her hair were seven   311b
s. in their calm   5b
s. in their courses   494b
s. in their stations set   206a
s. move still, time runs   258b
s. of heaven fell   518b
s. of midnight shall be dear   471b
s. of the summer night   248b
s. of twilight fair   470b
s. on Campden Hill   92b
s. peep behind her   393a
s. rush out   99a
s.' tennis-balls   454a
s. that have a different birth   396a
s., that in earth's firmament   247a
s. that round her burn   2a
s. the glory of His eyes   297b
s. threw down their spears   32a
s. to set   185a
s., wh. thou hast ordained   482a
s. without a name   220b
Stone that puts the S.   152a
streams full of s.   118a
strives to touch the s.   409b
sun, moon, and s., brother   34a
Syrian s. look down   7a
telleth the number of the s.   490b
the s. came otherwise   45b
two s. keep not their motion   379a
under the passing s.   475b
wandering s., to whom is reserved   518a
when s. are in the quiet skies   252a
with her splendid s.   155a
with s. to see   414a
ye quenchless s.!   280a
yoke of inauspicious s.   366b
Star-scattered: Guests S.   154a
Star-shine at night   414a
Star-showers: dissolved in s.   399a
Star-spangled banner   224b
Start: cannot once s. me   350b
s. it at home   110b
s. not so wildly   334b
s. of the majestic world   337b
straining upon the s.   382a
will s. from her slumber   6a
wd. s. and tremble   434a
Started: she s. one day   527a
s. like a guilty thing   329b
Starting aside like a broken bow   487a
Startle: s. or amaze it with itself   222a
these thoughts may s.   267a
wh. makes thee s. at me   62a
Startles at destruction   1b
Starts: up he s. discovered   274b
Starve: hinders our coming you'll s.   227b
let not poor Nelly s.   87b
s. at door   187b
swear, fool, or s.   142b
that s. with nothing   352b
to s. abroad   140b
Starved: saw their s. lips   219a
s., feasted, despaired   53a

State: all were for the s.   253a
Argyll, the s.'s whole thunder   303b
Atlas of the s.   110b
beweep my outcast s.   387a
burden on the reeling s.   108a
confession of his true s.   333a
done the s. some service   364a
eruption to our s.   329b
falling, with a falling S.   298b
first duty of a S.   314b
founding a firm s.   260b
free church in a free s.   567a
from thy s. mine never..parted   276b
gambler by the s. licensed   29b
glories of our blood and s.   401a
grant me, Heaven, a middle s.   257a
great men..landmarks in the s.   55a
health of the whole s.   330b
healthy s. of political life   266a
his s. empties itself   355b
I am the S.   563b
in a s. of wild alarm   164b
in that s. I came, return   448a
in the youth of a s.   16b
labours of a servile s.   72a
last s. of that man   506b
mock the air with idle s.   173b
my single s. of man   346b
my s. depose   376a
my s., like to the lark   387b
no assistant for a s.   332a
nothing doth more hurt in a s.   5b
obscure sequestered s.   51b
O Ship of S.!   246b
our s. cannot be sever'd   276b
palmy s. of Rome   329b
predicts the ruin of the S.   29a
quit thy s.   186b
rush into the s.   354b
scoffing his s.   375b
seek no happier s.   274b
S. for every Star   462a
s. in wonted manner keep   214b
S.'s mellow forms prefer   175b
S.'s pattern man   288b
S. wh. dwarfs its men   266a
s. without..means of..change   56b
Sun begins his s.   268b
the s. of man   338b
this is the s. of man   385b
thy s. is the more gracious   337a
to ruin or to rule the s.   138a
traduced the s.   364a
whole s. of Christ's Church   480b
with the storms of s.   386a
world of pomp and s.   22b
yet my s. is well   370a
Stately: grow great and s.   414a
rather tall and s.   528b
she is tall and s.   433b
s. homes of England   184b
Statements was interesting   446b
States: indestructible s.   88a
in s. unborn   339b
many goodly s.   220b
no more slave S.   88a
small s., Israel, Athens   203a
s. can be saved without it!   252a
s., like men, have their growth   242a
Union of these S.   458b
Statesman: chemist, fiddler, s.   138b
one s. of the present day   184b
s...if..ridden in omnibuses   184b
s., yet friend to truth!   302b
too nice for a s.   169b
Statesmen: s. at her council   437a
S...betray their friends   160a
Station: give me..a private s.   160b
Stations: know our proper s.   121b
Statistical Christ   291a
Statua: base of Pompey's s.   340a
Statue: hang him up and erect a s.   404b
lips met with under the s.   421b
s. stood of Newton   469b
Statues: sepulchral s. lay   132b
s. on the terraces   229b
towers and tombs and s.   154b
Stature: add one cubit unto his s.   505b
of a tall s.   261a
s. of my soul   264a
to s. of the gods   263b

Status quo: restored the s. 26b
Staunch and strong, a goodly vessel 246b
Stave: Death will listen to yr. s. 394b
Staves: comest to me with s. 495b
Stay: but none can s. 205a
but we wish 'em to s. 158b
can't you s.? 447b
I still will s. with thee 366b
neither have the hearts to s. 66a
no longer s. with you 527a
not making a s. 189b
O! s. and hear 370b
'O s.,' the maiden said 247a
O s.,' thou goodly youth 531b
short time to s. as you 189a
s. a little..end the sooner 15b
s., and run again, and s. 261a
s. for me there 225a
s. me with flagons 500a
s. rather on earth 44a
s., s. at home, my heart 248b
s., s., the king hath thrown 374b
s., s., until the hasting day 189a
s. the morning star 101a
s. then! Thou art so fair! 568a
s. yet here awhile 188b
s., you imperfect speakers 346a
whole s. of bread 501a
without thee here to s. 276b
with thee to go, is to s. here 276b
Stay-at-Home: sweet S. 118a
Stayed: s. in mid passage 423a
while he s. with us 423a
Stays: man that wears the s. 434b
Steadfastness and careful truth 228a
Steadily: saw life s. 6a
Steady: slow and s. wins 246a
s., boys, s. 158b
s. of heart, and stout of hand 317a
s. the Buffs 237b
Steal: cunningly did s. away 187b
maiden herself will s. 281b
silently s. away 247a
s. across the sky 20a
s. a goose from off a common 527b
's.!' foh! 355b
s. from all I may be 69b
s. from his figure 388b
s. my thunder 120a
s. out of yr. company 359a
s. us from ourselves 139b
then s. away, give little warning 19a
thou shalt not s. 480a
to s. away yr. hearts 340a
Stealing: hanged for s. horses 178a
picking and s. 481a
piracies..crime of s. 447a
s. and giving odour 369b
Steals: s. on the ear 200a
s. yr. whole estate 159b
Stealth: do a good action by s. 240a
do good by s. 303b
lusty s. of nature 341b
Steam: exceptin' always S. 231b
forget the snorting s. 284a
s. of rich distill'd perfumes 267b
s. spoils romance 232a
Steam-engine: s...back to the tea-
kettle 128a
Webster..s. in trousers 404b
Steamers: all you Big S. 227b
coffee on board s. 439b
s., white and gold 230b
Stedfast as thou art 220b
Steed: Auster was the fleetest s. 253b
farewell the neighing s. 362a
he purchased a s. 243a
his s. was the best 318a
mounts the warrior's s. 317a
on her milk-white s. 528a
on my pacing s. 218b
sell my goodly s. 531b
sold, my Arab s. 289b
soon I'll mount my s. 172b
stable for his s. 305a
s. in the Kelpie's Flow 319a
s., that knows his rider 68a
s. threatens s. 382b
s. to battle driven 77a
Steeds: brought them their s. 316b
fiery-footed s. 366a

Steeds (cont.)
his s. to water 328b
hurled abroad by reinless s. 312b
s. were white as snow 254a
they'll have fleet s. 318a
Steel: again in complete s. 331a
armed with..complete s. 25b, 259b
clad in complete s. 267b
cold s., boys! 4b
foeman bares his s. 166b
foemen worthy of their s. 316b
girdle me with s. 258a
lift shrewd s. 375a
locked up in s. 384a
long divorce of s. 385b
nor s., nor poison 348b
pinion wh. impelled the s. 72a
rattle of new-drawn s. 228b
shot and s., and scorching flame 12a
s. my soldiers' hearts 383a
s.-true and blade-straight 414b
the hurricane of s. 12a
with his brandished s. 346a
with hoops of s. 330b
Steep: Ismenian s. 277b
monstrous s. of Montmorenci 220b
more beautifully s. 472b
no towers along the s. 78a
s. place into the sea 506a
Sunium's marbled s. 71a
wild and stormy s. 76b
Steeped me in poverty 362b
Steeple: church and no s.! 420a
on it put a s. 27b
shadow of the s. 96a
Steeples: drenched our s. 342b
in s. far and near 199a
still the s. hum 199a
talk about the pews and s. 91b
Steer: converse, happily to s. 301b
s. too nigh the sands 138a
verse can gently s. 141a
with which..s. their courses 65a
Steered: helmsman s. us through 98b
Steersmen: grow good s. 264b
Stella: you S.'s feet may kiss 402a
Stellenbosch: fear o' S. 234b
Stem: moulded on one s. 357a
s. of Jesse 501b
Stenches: two and seventy s. 100a
Step: by him one s. below 368b
first s. wh. counts 562b
if a s. shd. sound 421b
mind the music and the s. 18b
my s. in bliss 36b
one s. enough for me 288b
s. softly, under snow 93b
with s. so active 241a
Stephen: Feast of S. 286b
S. Sly 366b
Stepped in so far 349b
Stepping where his comrade stood 318b
Stepping-stones: rise on s. 429b
Steps: Age, with stealing s. 448b
ask the number of the s. 205b
by backward s. wd. move 448a
by due s. aspire 266b
countest the s. of the Sun 32a
fearful s. pursuing hopes 394b
hear not my s. 347b
invites my s., and points 299a
last s. I climb 395a
master's s. he trod 286b
pilgrim s. of spring 36a
s. almost as silent 469a
s. of virgin liberty 470b
s. solemn, mournful and slow 459a
support uneasy s. 271b
the s. were higher 141b
thy s. retrace 166a
to these dark s. 277b
very s. have left a trace 69b
wandering s. and slow 277a
with how sad s. 401b
Stept: she s. to him, as red 531b
Sterility: into her womb convey s. 342a
Sterling: if my word be s. 376a
Stern: anchors out of the s. 513a
Mull was a-s. 414b
s. and unbending Tories 254b
s. to view 168b

Stern-faced men set out from Lynn 196a
Sternhold: hail S., then 111b
Steward: unjust s. 509b
Stewards: s. of their excellence 388b
s. of the mysteries 514a
Stewer: Jan S. 531b
Stick: carry a big s. 310a
he fell like the s. 291b
kind of burr; I shall s. 352a
s. and a string 214a
s. close to yr. desks 166a
Sticking-place: courage to the s. 347b
'Stickit minister' 319b
Sticks: brittle s. of thorn 190b
five, six, pick up s. 532a
Stiff: he was very proud and s. 85a
s. in opinions 138b
s. upper lip 86a
Stiff-necked people 494a
Stiffness in refusing 478a
Stifling it wd. be an evil 266a
Stiggins: Mr. S. 126b
Stile: against a crooked s. 532a
merrily hent the s.-a 373a
sitting on the s., Mary 28b
Stiles: lame dogs over s. 226a
Still: as patient and as s. 402a
as s. as mouse 155a
be s. and be content 531b
be s., be s., my soul 199b
be s. then, and know 484b
but s. moves delight 78a
Caesar, now be s. 341b
calm and s. 444b
he came all so s. 524b
he won't sit s. 193a
how s. we see thee lie 40a
in yr. own chamber, and be s. 481b
methinks s. doth stand 388b
move s., s. so 373b
ship was as s. as she cd. be 406b
sit s. for once at table 193a
s. as, while Saturn whirls 435b
strength is to sit s. 502a
thou smilest and art s. 7b
Stilleth the raging of the sea 486a
Stillicide: cave's s. 179b
S. a crime 413b
Stillness: a horrid s. 139b
air a solemn s. holds 174a
modest s. and humility 382a
soft s. and the night 355a
s. of the central sea 431a
Still-vext Bermoothes 367a
Sting: death, where is thy s.? 515a
each s. that bids 50b
it is a prick, it is a s. 295b
thy s. is not so sharp 326b
where is death's s.? 251b
Stings: armed in their s. 381b
nasty long s. 20a
s. you for yr. pains 191b
wanton s. and motions 351a
were s. in their tails 519a
Stink: stand by the fire and s. 342a
Stinks: and several s. 100a
s. and stings 303a
Stinte of singing 89a
Stinted: be s. in pleasure 461a
pretty fool, it s. 364b
Stinteth first when she..singe 90a
Stir: above the smoke and s. 266b
let me not s. you 340a
never..s. made the listeners 119b
none of yr. people s. me 357a
no s. in the air 406b
no s. of air was there 218a
s. it and stump it 166b
s. up, we beseech thee, O Lord 479b
things that make the greatest s. 156a
Stirred: in the forest something s. 402a
we have not s. 50b
Stirring: s. thrills the air 179b
s. times we live in 180b
Stirrup: his foot upon the s. 119b
I sprang to the s. 47b
s. and the ground 76a, 522b
s. about her, when she stirs 475a
Stitch! stitch! stitch! 196a
Stitching: our s. and unstitching 474a
Stock: his mind into the common s. 167b

Stock (cont.)
how his s. goes on — 100b
how his s. went on — 406b
Stock-dove: I heard a S. — 468a
Stocking: a s. all the day! — 168a
kneeling ne'er spoiled silk s. — 186b
Stockings: black worsted s. — 255b
come to her in yellow s. — 371b
commended thy yellow s. — 371b
he stood in his s. — 19b
silk s. and white bosoms — 206b
the s. were hung — 280b
Stockish: nought so s., hard — 355a
Stock-jobbers: ears of s. and Jews — 111a
Stocks: ascribe unto stones and s. — 520a
s. in fragrant blow — 8b
they hurt in the s. — 488b
worshipped s. and stones — 278b
Stoic: every S. was a S. — 147b
S. fur — 267b
weakness for the s.'s pride — 301a
Stoicism: Romans call it s. — 1b
Stoics: after the manner of the S. — 14a
Stole: from a better man I s. — 414b
mice, s. in and out — 416a
reason so persuasive s. — 443a
s. a pig, and away he run — 532b
they knew 'e s. — 236b
wonder where you s. 'em — 419b
Stolen: better, had I s. the whole — 414b
s. his wits away — 119a
s. my soul away — 446a
s. waters are sweet — 498a
s. sweets are best — 95b
Stoles: nice white s. — 19a
Stomach: army marches on its s. — 575a
healthy s...conservative — 66b
my great revenge had s. — 363b
my s. is not good — 415a
no s. to this fight — 383a
of an unbounded s. — 386a
proud look and high s. — 488a
s. of a king — 145a
wine for thy s.'s sake — 516b
Stomach-aches: tuned like fifty s. — 121b
Stomacher: her s. was gold — 231b
with the red s. — 132b
Stone: angel took up a s. — 519b
are themselves as s. — 388b
as a huge s. is — 470a
as cold as any s. — 382a
at his heels a s. — 335b
be s. no more — 373b
bows down to wood and s. — 184a
dig and heap, lay s. on s. — 7a
fling but a s. — 175b
for a s. of stumbling — 501b
give him a white s. — 518b
grey s. and grassy clay — 295a
hurt not thy foot against a s. — 487b
let him first cast a s. — 511a
lifted up a single s. — 468a
nor s., nor earth — 388a
one s. the more swings — 232b
precious s. set in the silver sea — 375a
raise the s. — 526a
seeth the s. taken away — 511b
sound of iron on s. — 119b
s. that is rolling — 446b
S. that puts the Stars to flight — 152a
s. that the devil can throw — 183b
s. the twenty-first — 45b
s. where Alexander's ashes lay — 18b
s. wh. the builders refused — 489a
that ligs under a s. — 534a
the conscious s. — 147a
trunkless legs of s. — 396b
turn but a s. — 442a
underneath this s. doth lie — 215b
under this s., Reader — 149a
untroubled heart of s. — 77a
violet by a mossy s. — 470b
virtue is like a rich s. — 16a
we raised not a s. — 462b
will he give him a s.? — 505b
with a s. at my gate — 304a
without a s., a name — 299b
without gout or s. — 304a
you're writing upon s. — 241b
Stones: age in piled s. — 278a
bones over the s. — 289b

Stones (cont.)
five smooth s. out of the brook — 495b
gray s., O Sea! — 425b
inestimable s. — 384b
like s. of worth — 387b
man that spares these s. — 389b
music with th' enamelled s. — 372b
no s. in heaven — 364a
pavements fanged with..s. — 100a
sermons in s. — 325b
softened the s. — 363a
s. and clouts make martyrs — 42a
s. have been known to move — 349a
s. Thy pillow — 405b
s. wd. immediately cry out — 510a
throweth them against the s. — 490a
throw s. at him — 390a
very s. of Rome — 340a
very s. prate — 347b
we've the s. of Snowdon — 226a
worshipped stocks and s. — 278b
you are not s. — 340a
you blocks, you s. — 337b
Stonest them wh. are sent — 507b
Stonewall Jackson riding ahead — 459a
Stony: car rattling o'er the s. street — 68b
Stood: freely they s. who s. — 273b
he s. in his stockings — 19b
long I s. there wondering — 298a
s. between it and the dominion — 256b
s. by me, knee to knee — 99a
they s. aloof — 100a
we have s. apart — 462a
Stooks: stood amid the s. — 195b
Stools: Latin names for horns and s. — 60a
necessity invented s. — 111b
push us from our s. — 349a
Stoop: do I s.? I pluck a posy — 48b
s. into a..sea of cloud — 49b
s. to rise — 262b
therefore does not s. — 465a
Stooping: s. down, as needs he must — 108b
s. thro' a fleecy cloud — 268a
Stoops: she s. to conquer — 170b
to rise, it s. — 46a
Stop: did he s. and speak to you — 48b
let's s. somebody from doing — 186a
made him turn and s. — 137a
so plain a s. — 379b
sound what s. she please — 334a
s. and consider! — 220b
s., Christian passer-by! — 100b
s. everyone from doing it — 186a
s.! for thy tread — 68a
s. to busy fools — 447b
that honourable s. — 361a
the end: then s. — 83b
time..must have a s. — 379a
Stopped: cellar s. him down — 295a
nor s. till where he had got up — 109a
Stopp'st: wherefore s. thou me — 98a
Stoppeth one of three — 98a
Stops: seem to know my s. — 334b
s. his mouth with a kiss — 358a
s. of planetary music — 393b
tender s. of various quills — 270a
Stop-sensation in my Soul — 127b
Store: as large as s. — 188a
cares were to increase his s. — 194b
come, Thou source of all our s. — 86b
Heaven will bless yr. s. — 284b
oft amid thy s. — 221b
spread her wholesome s. — 168a
s. of the first author — 261b
Storehouse: s. for the glory of the
Creator — 13a
s...of life and comfort — 186b
Stores: such s. as silent thought — 471a
Storied: s. of old in high — 267b
s. windows richly dight — 268b
Stories: believe of my own s. — 203b
manifold s., I know — 75b
sad s. of the death of kings — 375b
s. from the land of spirits — 101a
s. of savage men — 55b
s. of thy finisht love — 78b
s. to rede — 19a
whence these s.? — 248b
yon with dismal s. — 54b
Stork: dwelling for the s. — 488b
Storm: and directs the S. — 1a

Storm (cont.)
brows like gathering s. — 62b
falter, are lost in the s.! — 7b
fled away into the s. — 221b
in darkness and in s. — 22b
it is not in the s. — 73b
leave thee in the s. — 342a
pelting of this pitiless s. — 343a
rides upon the s. — 110a
sea, with such a s. — 343a
stemm'd the rude s. — 72a
s...coming on the Chiltern Hills — 91b
S. in a Teacup — 22a
s...in 'David Copperfield' — 314a
Stormcock, and Golden Gain — 232b
Storms: all thy waves and s. — 484b
ere the winter s. begin — 3b
gale when s. are o'er — 18b
greater s. and tempests — 322b
he sought the s. — 138a
s. that rage outside — 8b
sudden s. are short — 374b
where no s. come — 197b
wh. no loud s. annoy — 213a
with the s. of state — 386a
Stormy: beyond the s. Hebrides — 270a
to 'scape s. days — 133a
wild and s. steep — 76b
Story: earns a place i' the s. — 324a
ere their s. die — 179b
honour is the subject of my s. — 337b
how strange a s.! — 403b
how to tell my s. — 360a
I love to hear the s. — 266a
light of thy s. — 218a
my s. being done — 360a
name great in s. — 73b
pretty s. tell — 425a
quite a different s. — 414a
read this little s. — 215a
short in the s. itself — 521b
shuts up the s. of our days — 308a
Sordello's s. told — 52a
still is the s. told — 253b
s. always old and always new — 51a
s. chronicled for one of the truest — 257b
s., feigned for pleasure — 139a
s. for wh. the world — 136a
s.! God bless you — 78b
s. is extant — 334b
s. need be long — 444a
s. of Cambuscan bold — 268b
s. of her birth — 2a
s. of my life — 360a
s. shall the good man teach — 383a
tell me the old, old s. — 179a
that is another s. — 237b
this is the sorrowful s. — 231a
to tell my s. — 337a
Story-dressers: our s. do as much — 64a
Story-teller is born — 410a
Stout: Grubby, who was short and s. — 93a
Stoutness, in moderation — 163b
Strachan: Sir Richard S. — 523a
Strack: he s. the top-mast — 529a
Straddled: then Apollyon s. — 54a
Stradivari: Antonio S.'s violins — 144b
Straggler into loving arms — 240b
Straight: grow s. in the strength — 422b
make s. in the desert — 502b
seven, eight, lay them s. — 532a
shall be absolutely s. — 456b
s. to the self-same mark — 48a
street wh. is called S. — 512a
Straightway I was 'ware — 43b
Strain: drop the drowsy s. — 108a
hold cheap the s. — 50b
like prophetic s. — 268b
of thy happy s. — 398b
she loved..the Dorian s. — 8b
Sire of an immortal s. — 391b
soft is the s. — 300a
s. of man's bred out — 368a
s. of strutting chanticleer — 367a
that s. again — 369b
that s. I heard — 269b
unpremeditated s. — 443a
yon's s., hard s. — 231b
Strained: mercy is not s. — 354b
Straining upon the start — 382a

Strains: blessed s. are telling 149b
mute his tuneful s. 317b
soul-animating s. 470b
such s. as wd. have won the ear 269a
took in s. 267b
Strait: how s. the gate 185a
in a s. so narrow 369a
into a desperate s. 262b
thro' s., rough, dense 273a
Strait-jacket: creed..s. for humanity 264b
Straits: outside the Western S. 8b
Strand: Chelsea to the S. 232a
come sailing to the s. 530a
destined to a barren s. 213b
her name upon the s. 408a
in Craven-street, S. 404a
India's coral s. 184a
I walked along the S. 212a
knits the ivy rugged s. 317b
left fair Scotland's s. 61a
let's all go down the S. 86a
some far northern s. 6a
was walking on the s. 529b
where's the Maypole in the S. 35a
Strands: last s. of man 197a
Strange: how s. it seems, and new! 48b
in language s. she said 218b
more cunning to be s. 365a
nor s. thy doom 37b
passed many a s. streem 88b
something rich and s. 367a
s. and terrible events 324b
s., even in a dream 99a
s. to think by the way 311b
this is more s. 349a
this is wondrous s. 331b
'tis s., but true 72a
'tis s. the mind..snuff'd out 71b
too s., too restless 5b
truth is always s. 72a
'twas s., 'twas passing s. 360a
very s. and well bred 105b
Strangeness in the proportion 16a
Stranger: a wilful s. 414a
I am a s. with thee 484a
I, a s. and afraid 200a
I was a s. 508a
on earth I am a s. 61b
s. doth not intermeddle 498a
s.! 'eave 'arf a brick 535a
s. filled the Stuarts' throne 316b
s. hath thy bridle-rein 289b
s. here in Gloucestershire 375a
s. in a strange land 493b
s., pause and ask thyself 123b
s.'s caste or creed 305a
s. that is within thy gates 480a
s. to one of yr. parents 11b
surety for a s. 498a
this starry s. 114b
to-morrow a s. will say 147b
wheeling s. 359b
Strangers: all the Athenians and s. 512b
by s. honoured 299a
careth for the s. 490b
forgetful to entertain s. 517a
if a man be..courteous to s. 15a
we may be better s. 327a
Strangest: in did come the s. figure 50a
Strangled: throat around, and s. her 50a
Strangling: than s. in a string 198b
Stratagem: tea without a s. 476b
Stratagems: nets and s. 187a
s., and spoils 355b
Stratford atte Bowe: scole of S. 88b
Straw: find quarrel in a s. 335b
lion shall eat s. 501b
oft stumbles at a s. 409b
pipes of wretched s. 269b
s...wh. way the wind is 321a
tickled with a s. 301a
Strawberries: Dr. Boteler said of s. 385a
I saw good s. 385a
only netting s. 229b
s. at the mouth 13b
s. grow in the sea 534a
Strawberry: [Butler] said of the [S.] 67a
like s. wives 13b
Strawberry Hill 449a
Straws: errors, like s. 141a
of hairs, or s., or dirt 303a

Stray: from their own Music..s. 78b
paths wherein I s. 232b
what wonder if they s. 110b
with me you'd fondly s. 159b
Strayed: after wh. I s. 441b
s. from thy ways 478a
tho' thou hast surely s. 166a
Strays: by many winding nooks he s. 372b
s. of ruined springs 422a
Streaks: s. of red were mingled 416a
s. of the tulip 213b
Stream: by mount, and s., and sea 184b
clear and gentle s. 35b
eves by haunted s. 269a
feed, by the s. 32b
freezing s. below 393a
have their s. and pond 39a
in such a crystal s. 398b
I strove against the s. 436b
leaves in the glassy s. 336a
like an ever-rolling s. 453b
little s. best fits 188b
make thy s. my great example 119b
meadow, grove, and s. 466a
mercy of a rude s. 386a
me rowing against the s. 319a
mighty s. of tendency 464b
no s. meanders..level 255a
on the gliding s. 35b
over the still s. 220a
painted meadow, or a purling s. 1b
passed many a straunge s. 88b
round the bosom of the s. 398a
salt weed sways in the s. 5b
scooped the brimming s. 274a
smooth s. in smoother numbers 300a
steep Atlantic s. 266b
still glides the S. 463b
s. that flashest white 431b
s. will not run long 57a
sweetness in the s. 430b
swift s. of song 395b
talk was like a s. 305a
the dark, the silent s. 394b
the s. runs fast 282b
trailing in the cool s. 8a
vagabond flag upon the s. 322b
Streamers: and s. waving 277b
fan spread and s. out 105a
s. waving in the wind 161a
Streams: alone spring the great s. 6b
as shallow s. run dimpling 303a
as s. meander 280a
by those mysterious s. 44b
civil laws..but as s. 13a
fresh s. ran by her 363a
gilding pale s. 387b
his crystalline s. 396b
large s. from little fountains 149b
liquid lapse of murmuring s. 275b
more pellucid s. 467b
sands..dam his s. 8a
sitting by desolate s. 291a
spent the s. 37a
stillest s. oft water fairest 113a
s. full of stars 118a
s. in the desert 502a
s. o'erflow yr. springs 260b
s. their channels deeper wear 61b
s., whereupon ye learn 37a
strength of the s. 420a
what eternal s. 298a
Street: brawls disturb the s. 452b
by jostling in the s. 30a
car rattling o'er the stony s. 68b
clamour of the crowded s. 247b
foot-path of a s. 59b
going past me in the s. 413b
harlot's cry from s. to s. 29b
he at the end of the s. 145a
if the s. were time 145a
key of the s. 127a
lane, highway, or open s. 445b
long unlovely s. 429b
man in the s. 176b
mockers in the roaring s. 244a
ringing down the s. 12a
sell them in the s. 85b
s. of the city was pure gold 520a
s. wh. is called Straight 512a
trouble every s. 137a

Street (cont.)
up the s. came the rebel tread 459a
where the long s. roars 431a
where the s. grows straiter 439b
Streets: children cried in the s. 285a
doors shall be shut in the s. 499b
gibber in the Roman s. 329b
her voice in the s. 497b
in the dark s. shineth 40a
no complaining in our s. 490b
s. are paved with gold 103b
s. broad and narrow 524a
s. were filled with joyful sounds 430a
s. where the great men go 154b
Strength: are not now that s. 439a
as my s. wears away 304a
Christ is thy s. 279b
confidence shall be yr. s. 502a
conscience..s. enough to prevent 171a
delivered by much s. 484a
entangles itself with s. 324b
girded himself with s. 487b
God wd. give him s. 215a
go from s. to s. 487a
grows the s. of all 301a
hast thou ordained s. 482a
have a giant's s. 351b
he hath shewed s. 508b
his s. make stronger 37a
his s. the more is 54b
I may recover my s. 484a
impulse of thy s. 396b
in the s. of this I rode 428a
is practised that s. 7b
king's name is a tower of s. 385a
Lord is the s. of my life 483b
Lord shall renew their s. 502b
man by his great s. 484a
man's s. to comfort 228a
my s., and my redeemer 482b
my s. is as the s. of ten 438a
my s. is made perfect 515b
navy of England..natural s. 28b
O man, thy s. endue 36b
on wh. all s. depends 403a
profaned the God-given s. 318a
promise of s. and manhood 37a
rejoiceth in his s. 497b
somehow tell of yr. own s. 284a
so shall thy s. be 494b
s. and nature made amends 313b
s. by limping sway disabled 388a
s., distance and length 198a
s. in what remains 466b
s. is to sit still 502a
s. might endure for a span 420b
s. setteth fast the mountains 486a
s. then but labour and sorrow 487b
s. without hands 420b
trial of her s. 469a
true s. of guilty kings 7a
try the soul's s. on 45a
unbend yr. noble s. 348a
vexed his immortal s. 36a
Strengthen: s. such as do stand 479a
s. thee out of Sion 482b
s. the wavering line 7b
s. ye the weak hands 502a
to s. whilst one stands 311a
Strengthened: to be s. with might 515b
Strengtheneth: Christ wh. s. me 516a
Strengthens with his strength 301a
Strenuous: doctrine of the s. life 310a
Stretch: s. forth thy mighty hand 200b
s. him out longer 344a
Stretched: s. like a promontory 275b
s. out on the spoils 421b
there was things wh. he s. 446b
Strew: flowers to s. thy way 187a
s. on her roses 7b
s. them in the air 280b
Stricken: I was a s. deer 112a
s. at Waterloo 93a
Strict: death, is s. in his arrest 337a
Strictly: I now will serve more s. 463b
Stride: one s. comes the dark 99a
Strife: a double s. 17a
and void of s. 140a
but I am worn with s. 425a
dull and endless s. 471b
forms of party s. 431a

Strife (cont.)
for the sake of s.   95a
graver had a s.   215b
in the common s.   465a
let there be no s.   492b
life, in ceaseless s.   290a
man of s.   503b
none was worth my s.   241a
nor in the s. we feel benumbed   73b
or a double s.   17a
O s., O curse   44a
party conquers in the s.   316b
phantoms an unprofitable s.   392b
serv'd for that Titanic s.   6b
soul, revolving hopeless s.   35b
stern s., and carnage drear   318b
s. comes with manhood   317b
s. too humble   469b
s. with the palm   5b
the s. is o'er   304b
waters of s.   487a
what is peace?..is it s.?   121a
when the s. is fierce   200a
Strike: Britons, s. home   447b
honour, while you s.   287b
if you s. a child   391a
I s. it, and it hurts   362b
she will s. and sink   390a
s. et when yr. powder's..low   287b
s. it out   208a
s. thy bosom, sage   211b
themselves must s. the blow   68a
thou s. not awry   283a
yet afraid to s.   303a
Strikes: how it s. a Contemporary   47b
s. him dead for thine and thee   436b
s. where it doth love   363b
String: end of a golden s.   30b
harp not on that s.   385a
little bits of s.   26a
one long yellow s.   50a
sing in a hempen s.   23a
strangling in a s.   198b
untune that s.   368b
Strings: her sighs the s. do break   78a
I had two s. to my bow   151b
instrument of ten s.   483b
languid s. do scarcely move!   31b
revives the leaden s.   78a
there are s...in the human heart   121a
Stripe for stripe   494a
Stripes: beaten with few s.   509b
cut 'is s. away   228b
forty s. save one   515a
things worthy of s.   509b
with his s. we are healed   503a
Stripling: crossing the s. Thames   8a
nor spear the s. took   109b
Stripped: when two are s.   259a
Strive: shd. s. afresh against the foe   289a
s., and hold cheap the strain   50b
s. nor weep   52b
s. officiously to keep alive   96b
to s., to seek   439a
we'll s. to please you   372b
Striving to better, oft we mar   342a
Strode after me   469a
Stroke: none so fast as s.   570b
no second s. intend   273a
past the tyrant's s.   329a
some distressful s.   360a
s. most dolorous   257a
tune of flutes kept s.   323a
Strokes: amorous of their s.   323a
little s. fell great oaks   323a
Stroking me gently with the other   417b
Stroll alone through fields   101a
Strong: be s. and of a good courage   494b
but s. in will   439a
cruel he looks, but calm and s.   397a
faithful, s. as death   110a
fifty-score s.   45b
heavens..are fresh and s.   464a
I again am s.   466a
most exquisite and s.   289b
O constancy! be s.   339a
quit you like men, be s.   515a
still going s.   522b
s. against tide, th'..whale   403a
s. came forth sweetness   495a
s. for service still   112a

Strong (cont.)
s. in pursuit the rapid glede   403a
s. is the horse upon his speed   403a
s. is the Soul   5a
s. men shall bow themselves   499b
s. the gier-eagle   403a
s. the tall ostrich   403a
s. thro' the turbulent profound   403a
s. without rage   119b
to keep the s. in awe   385a
to suffer and be s.   247b
victory is not a name s. enough   287a
wants that little s.   193b
we then that are s.   514a
Stronger: s. by weakness   449a
no s. than my sex   338b
s. than the hosts of error   53a
Strongest: Cob was the s.   20a
wine is the s.   520a
Stronghold: safe s. our God is still   569a
turn ye to the s.   504b
Strook: so s. with dread   277b
Strove: a little still she s.   70a
I s., made head   50b
I s. with none   241a
Struck: he s. the top-mast   529a
I s. the board   188a
s. him, and dismiss'd   294a
s. so to the soul   333a
Struggle: alarms of s. and flight   5a
sacrifice in a contemptible s.   56b
say not, the s. naught availeth   96b
s. for existence   117b
what s. to escape?   219b
Struggles and howls at fits   393a
Struggling in vain with ruthless
    destiny   464b
Strumpet: half some sturdy s.   180a
into a s.'s fool   322a
most true; she is a s.   332a
Strumpeted: virtue rudely s.   388a
Strung with subtle-coloured hair   421a
Strunt: but ye s. rarely   61b
Struts: s. and frets his hour   350b
s. his dames before   268b
Stuarts: stranger filled the S.' throne   316b
went out..with the S.   129b
Stubble: base built on s.   267b
showed like a s.-land   376b
sparks among the s.   520a
Stubborn: matters of fact..s. things   444b
s. spearmen still made good   318b
the s. they chastise   113b
too s. and too strange   337b
Stubbornness: impious s.   330a
Stubbs: footman to Justinian S.   572b
S. butters Freeman   528a
Stuck: like a s. pig   160b
Stud: outroot the S.   171b
Studied: more than I have s.   370a
rather s. books than men   17a
s. men from my..close   263b
s. with me at the U—   79a
Studies: air of delightful s.   279a
he s. it in town   110b
s. serve for delight   16a
too much time in s.   16a
Studious: s. let me sit   443b
s. of laborious ease   112a
Study: his s. of imagination   359a
I am slow of s.   356a
labour and intent s.   279a
live to s., and not s. to live   16b
much s. is a weariness   500a
my only s., is man   34a
proper s. of mankind   301a
s. a long silence   454b
s. evermore is overshot   344b
s. first propriety   75b
s. is like the heaven's..sun   344b
s...made him very lean   196a
s. to be quiet   516b
s. was but litel on the bible   88b
s. what you most affect   366b
that did nothing s.   225a
the Fields his s.   33a
thy testimonies are my s.   489a
Studying: s. all the summer night   261a
s. how I may compare   376a
Stuff: bosom of that perilous s.   350b
listen all day to such s.   82b

Stuff (cont.)
made of sterner s.   340a
of s. so fat and dull   336a
see the s. again   186a
skimble-skamble s.   378a
so precious as the s. they sell   154a
s. o' the conscience   359b
such s. in my thoughts   332b
such volumes of s.   243b
we are such s.   367b
what s. 'tis made of   352b
Stuffed: s. with epithets of war   359b
we are the s. men   145a
Stuffs out his vacant garments   374a
Stumble: brother! do not s.   256b
s. that runs fast   365b
Stump: stir it and s. it   166b
Stumps: fought upon his s.   391b
Stung: some bee had s. it   416a
Stunned: one that hath been s.   100a
Stupid: when a s. man is..ashamed   390a
Stupidity: man's immense s.   45b
no sin except s.   460a
such an excess of s.   207b
with s. the gods   569b
Sty: no better than a s.   324b
Stygian: S. cave forlorn   268b
S. smoke of the pit   204a
ye S. set   241a
Style: do it in a high s.   11a
grand s...arises in poetry   10a
his own towering s.   94a
how the s. refines   300b
in so strange a s.   300a
Johnson's s. was grand   103b
just the proper s.   310a
nothing to assert has no s.   390b
Pope..eye on his s.   10a
s. is the man   561b
theirs for their s. I'll read   387b
true definition of a s.   418a
Styles: two distinct s. requisite   130a
Subdue: chasten and s.   472a
he shall s. the people   484b
that must s. at length   301a
Subdued: my nature is s.   389a
parties nobly are s.   380b
Subject: duty..s. owes the prince   367a
every s.'s duty is the king's   382b
grant the artist his s.   204b
puny s. strikes   375a
spare the poet for his s.'s sake   107b
s. for heroic song   276a
s. made to yr. hand   48a
s. of all verse   42b
s. to his birth   330b
s. we old men..of lying!   380b
unlike my s., will I frame   91a
what it is to be a s.   145a
with itself, but with its s.   222a
Subjection: wh. implied s.   274a
Subjects: but show to s.   113b
greatness on her s.' love   306a
good of s. is the end of kings   118b
kings seek their s.' good   189b
my s. for a pair of..saints   375b
paid his s. with a royal wage   39a
s. are rebels from principle   57a
s. still loathe..Government   189b
were their s. wise   112b
Sublime: boundless, endless and s.   69b
egotistical s.   223a
howls the s.   124a
know how s. a thing   247b
my object all s.   164b
never tender nor s.   241b
step is short from the S.   172a
s. and the ridiculous   291b
s. dashed to pieces   102b
s. to the ridiculous   564a
Sublimity: possible s.   469b
Sublunary: dull s. lovers'   134a
Submission: make s...to our King   76b
yielded with coy s.   274a
Submit: must he s.?   375b
never to s. or yield   271a
we s. to women so   78b
wives, s. yourselves   515b
Submits his neck..second yoke   190a
Subscribe: collects, tho' it does not s.   86a
Subscribers: any list of s.   210b

Subscribers (*cont.*)
for s. baits his hook   94*b*
Subscription: shouting..amount of
his s.   417*a*
you owe me no s.   342*b*
Subsist: mine shall s. by me   176*b*
Subsisting: human flesh s.   478*b*
Substance: all the s. of his house   501*a*
dividing the S.   478*b*
or s. might be called   272*a*
s. of a book   238*a*
s. of ten thousand soldiers   385*a*
s. of the ambitious   332*b*
s. of things hoped for   517*a*
wasted his s.   509*b*
what is yr. s.   387*b*
Substances: in yr. sightless s.   346*b*
Substitute shines brightly   355*b*
Substratum: basis or s.   75*a*
Subterranean: the s. dark   200*a*
Subtle: know not well the s. ways   146*a*
serpent was more s.   492*a*
Subtlest: serpent s. beast   276*a*
Subtleties: destroyed by s.   264*a*
Subtilty: brother came with s.   493*a*
s. of the devil   479*a*
Suburb of the life elysian   248*a*
Suburbs: s. at the Elephant   371*b*
s. of yr. good pleasure   338*b*
Succeed: first you don't s.   191*a*
see we sons s.   178*a*
Succeeded: matter she drove at s.   306*a*
Succeeds: an Amurath s.   381*a*
he s., the merit's all his own   95*a*
s. in unknown fate   361*a*
Success: ecstasy, is s. in life   293*a*
from wh. s. is banished   412*a*
given me earnest of s.   346*b*
his surcease s.   347*a*
infallible criterion..s.   57*b*
minute's s. pays   44*b*
mortals to command s.   1*b*
no very lively hope of s.   404*b*
s. in our art   147*i*
s...in political life   128*b*
s...miscarriage..empty sounds   207*a*
s. perhaps may crown us   112*a*
s. was found on Israel's side   110*a*
triumphals of his hop't s.   277*b*
true s. is to labour   413*b*
what good s. soever they have   307*a*
Successful: s. crimes alone..justified   141*a*
tide of s. experiment   204*b*
Succoth: valley of S.   485*b*
Such: altogether s. as I am   513*a*
of s. is the kingdom of God   508*b*
s. wilt thou be to me   134*a*
Suck: I have given s.   347*a*
love..doth s. his sweet   246*a*
s. they no small advantage   486*b*
Suck-a-Thumb   192*b*
Sucklings: babes and s.   482*a*
Sucks: where the bee s.   368*a*
Sudden: s. as sweet   265*a*
too unadvised, too s.   365*a*
Sue: charm of lovely S.   161*a*
less used to s.   316*b*
we were not born to s.   374*b*
Suez: east of S.   232*a*
Suffer: better one s.   138*a*
cannot s. wrong   439*b*
do well, and s. for it   517*b*
I will not s. him   488*a*
not without hope we s.   468*b*
s. a sea-change   367*a*
s. for the truth's sake   480*a*
s. it to be so now   504*b*
s. me to come to thee   455*b*
s. the little children   508*b*
s. to redeem our loss   524*b*
s. us not, at our last hour   481*b*
those that I saw s.   367*a*
to s. all alike   324*a*
to s. and be strong   247*b*
will not s. long   439*b*
ye s. fools gladly   515*a*
Sufferance: corporal s.   352*a*
s. is the badge of our tribe   353*a*
Suffered: being s., rivers cannot
quench   384*b*
had s. many things   508*b*

Suffered (*cont.*)
have s. greatly   438*b*
O! I have s. with those   367*a*
Sufferer: best of men..was a s.   118*b*
Suffereth: charity s. long   514*b*
Suffering: knowledge by s. entereth   44*a*
learn in s...teach in song   395*a*
lounjun 'roun' en s.   181*b*
more exposed to s.   465*a*
out of human s.   467*a*
s. is permanent   463*a*
s. is the lover's part   159*a*
Sufferings: saith my s. then   259*b*
to each his s.   175*a*
Suffers: he s., but..not suffer long   439*b*
Suffice for those who belong to them   458*a*
Sufficiency: elegant s.   443*b*
Sufficient unto the day   505*b*
Suffolk his axe did ply   137*a*
Suffusion: all colours a s.   100*b*
dim s. veiled   273*a*
Sugar: action, we do s. o'er   333*a*
give a s. plum than my time   223*a*
I must s. my hair   83*a*
sack and s. be a fault   377*b*
s. and spice, and all that's nice   534*b*
Sugared: 'ow we're s. about   234*b*
Suggest: spirits do s. me still   389*b*
Suggestion: I yield to that s.   346*b*
they'll take s. as a cat   367*b*
Suicide: echo..from the s.'s grave   165*a*
nothing left for you, not even s.   413*a*
Suing: in s. long to bide   409*a*
Suit: Hearts was her favourite s.   239*a*
honour, or gay s.   187*a*
I be still in s.   188*a*
seem to s. her notion   164*b*
silk s., wh. cost me much money   296*a*
smelling out s.   364*b*
tho' his s. was rejected   320*a*
Suitor: think that you are Ann's s.   390*b*
Suitors: see s. following   361*a*
Suits: out of s. with fortune   325*b*
s. of solemn black   330*a*
wh. now s. with it   347*b*
Sulky sullen dame   62*b*
Sullen: sick or are you s.?   211*b*
Winter..s. and sad   443*b*
Sullenness against Nature   279*b*
Sulphur: quick s. fraught   408*b*
Sultan: pity S. Mahmud   152*b*
S. after S. with his Pomp   152*b*, 153*a*
S.'s Turret with a Shaft   152*a*
Sum: all this mighty s.   464*b*
giving thy s. of more   325*b*
great s. obtained I this freedom   512*b*
make up my s.   336*b*
s. of earthly bliss   275*b*
s. of human wretchedness   73*b*
Sumatra: rat of S.   136*a*
Sumer is icumen in   526*a*
Summed: can it be s. up so   36*b*
Summer: after s. merrily   368*a*
all-hallown S.   376*b*
all on a s. day   83*b*
all on a s.'s day   532*b*
all the wild s.   475*a*
bathing of a s.'s day   469*a*
bears eternal s. in his soul   194*a*
branding s. suns avail   429*b*
chestnuts, s. through   39*b*
compare thee to a s.'s day   387*a*
dews of s. night   265*b*
Diana in her s. weed   176*a*
ditties all a s.'s day   271*b*
English s.'s done   231*b*
eternal s. gilds them   70*b*
expect Saint Martin's s.   383*b*
fades a s. cloud away   18*b*
fantastic s.'s heat   374*b*
flies on s. eves   220*a*
fresh spring and s.   395*a*
goodbye, S., goodbye   459*a*
in a s. seson   242*b*
in s., quite the other way   413*b*
it was a s.'s evening   406*a*
last rose of s.   281*b*
life as on a s.'s day   218*a*
love in s.'s wonderland   290*a*
mery s.'s day   90*a*
middle s.'s spring   356*b*

Summer (*cont.*)
on a s.'s evening   340*c*
see in a s.'s day   356*b*
singest of s.   219*b*
s. and winter, and day and night   492*b*
s. by this sun of York   384*b*
s. clothe the general earth   101*a*
s. comes with flower   184*b*
s. dies the swan   438*a*
s. first was leavy   358*b*
s. is ended, and we are not saved   503*b*
s. is icumen in   526*a*
s. redundant   52*b*
s. set lip   442*b*
s.'s flower is to the s. sweet   388*b*
s.'s green all girded up   387*a*
s.'s joys are spoilt   218*a*
s. skies to mourn   217*b*
s.'s lease hath all too short   387*a*
s.'s ripening breath   365*b*
s.'s velvet buds   381*b*
s. with flowers that fell   420*b*
S...with its usual Severity   102*a*
thick-warbled notes the s. long   277*a*
this guest of s.   347*a*
thou art a s. bird   381*a*
thro' the s. is not heard   394*b*
thy eternal s.   387*a*
thy lord the s.   422*b*
to ensure s. in England   449*b*
was beauty's s. dead   388*b*
when the s. is shed   422*b*
winter, spring, and s.   525*a*
Summer-friends: like s.   188*a*
Summer-house in Christendom   378*a*
Summer-night: tranced s.   218*a*
Summers: a thousand s. are over   422*b*
raw inclement s.   418*a*
shook three s.' pride   388*b*
this many s. in a sea of glory   386*a*
Summerset several times   417*b*
Summertime on Bredon   199*a*
Summits: nations touch at their s.   17*b*
snowy s. old   436*a*
Summon: to s. his array   253*a*
Summoners: these dreadful s. grace   342*b*
Summons: hark to the s.!   318*b*
s. comes to join the..caravan   53*a*
upon a fearful s.   329*b*
Sums: no pains with its s.   86*a*
Sun: against a setting s.   368*a*
all, except their s., is set   70*b*
alone the s. arises   6*b*
apples of the s.   476*a*
as the s. and showers there   385*b*
as the dial to the s.   33*b*
as the s. breaks thro'   366*b*
as the s. in his strength   492*a*
a s. will pierce   44*b*
at the going down of the s.   28*b*
aweary of the s.   351*a*
be ere the set of s.   345*b*
before the rising s.   453*a*
beneath the making s.   36*b*
benedictions—s.'s and moon's   48*a*
best s. we have..Newcastle coal   449*b*
betwixt us and the s.   98*b*
blushing discontented s.   375*b*
bride, on whom the s. doth shine   188*b*
brief the s. of summer   436*b*
bright-haired s.   103*a*
broad s. is sinking   467*a*
busy old fool, unruly S.   134*a*
catch the dying s.   415*a*
chambers of the s.   31*b*
clear as the s.   500*b*
close to the s.   426*b*
common s., the air, and skies   175*a*
countenance was as the s.   518*b*
countest the steps of the S.   32*a*
crimson s. went down   136*a*
dewdrop from the s.   463*b*
doubt thou the sun doth move   332*a*
drum-beat, following the s.   454*a*
dry s., dry wind   446*b*
ere the s. was set   447*a*
ever braved the s.   51*a*
every morning the red s.   3*a*
eyes to behold the s.   499*b*
faint with the hot s.   221*a*
farthing candle to the s.   477*a*

Sun (cont.)

follow and find the s.	422b
follow thy fair s.	78a
gallant will command the s.	366b
glorious S. be born	223b
glorious S. uprist	98b
glorious the s. in mid-career	403a
goblin of the s.	312b
God-curst s.	180a
God Himself is moon and s.	435a
great S. begins his state	268b
guilty of our disasters the s.	342a
had not the great s. seen	36b
hath Britain all the s.	328b
headland, he beheld the s.	464a
heat o' the s.	329a
he maketh his s. to rise	505a
hills, the s. shines sweetly on	529a
hold..to the s. my little taper	71b
hooting at the glorious s.	100b
I am too much i' the s.	329b
insultin' the s.	289b
Juliet is the s.	365a
just as his s. was rising	523a
kings crept out..to feel the s.	43a
kiss of the s. for pardon	177b
labour..he taketh under the s.	499a
lake-reflected s.	397a
lamp of Heaven, the s.	190b
lands beneath another s.	443b
largess universal like the s.	382b
leave the blessed s.	434b
let not the s. go down	515b
let them not see the s.	485b
light a candle to the s.	401a
Linden, when the s. was low	76b
livery of the burnished s.	353a
loss of the s.	91a
loves to live i' the s.	326a
marigold..bed wi' the s.	373a
midnight speak with the S.	447b
Morea's hills the setting s.	70a
most sheene is the s.	242b
my s. sets to rise again	48b
never assisted the s.	444a
never did s. more beautifully	472b
new thing under the s.	499a
no need of the s.	520a
nor s. shall waken	422a
no s.—no moon!	195a
nothing like the s.	389a
not quickened by the s.	464a
o'er thee the s. doth pine	37b
on wh. the s. never sets	289b
owes no homage to the s.	42a
peers the setting s.	224a
plants..wh. never saw the s.	49b
quiet as the s.	421a
rest the s. goes round	449a
rime-ringed s.	231b
round the setting s.	467a
saves a description of the..s.	400a
scarce cd. see the s.	311b
sea-daisies feast on the s.	424a
self-same s. that shines	373b
set a candle in the s.	64b
shall the s. light on them	519a
shall the S. of righteousness arise	504b
shoots at the midday s.	401b
side that's next the s.	416a
smitten with the morning S.	436a
somewhere the s. is shining	181b
splendid silent s.	457a
spots and clouds in the s.	64a
study is like the heaven's..s.	344b
s. and moon of the heart's desire	313a
s. and moon, rejoice	224a
S. and Moon shd. doubt	29b
s. and stars to play with	390a
s. and the rain are flying	414b
s. and the south	422b
s. ariseth, and they get them away	488b
S. came up upon the left	98a
s. climbs slow	96b
s. feels like May	48b
s. had risen to hear him	144a
s. has left the lea	320a
s. has not attain'd his noon	189a
S. himself a fair hot wench	376a
S. himself cannot forget	527b

Sun (cont.)

s. himself must die	77a
s., imagine me the west!	176a
s...in dim eclipse	272a
s...in the lap of Thetis	65b
s. is laid to sleep	214b
s. is mounted	200a
s. itself is but the dark *simulacrum*	41a
s. knoweth his going down	488b
s. looked over the mountain's rim	49b
s., moon, and stars, brother	34a
s. of Austerlitz	564b
s. of heaven prove a micher	377b
s. of my soul!	224a
s. of York	384b
s. shall not burn thee	489b
s. shines always there	29a
S.'s rim dips	99a
s., stand thou still	494b
s. that warms you here	374b
s. thro' the mirk	116b
s. to me is dark	277b
s. upon the upland lawn	174b
S. was flecked with bars	98b
s. was laughing sweetly	475a
s. was shining on the sea	84a
s. went down..stars came out	437b
S., who scattered into flight	152a
s. will be dimmed	18a
s., with ardent frown	316a
swear to a touch o' s.	234a
sweetheart of the s.	195b
sweet tale of the s.	377b
tabernacle for the s.	482b
tapers to the s.	113b
that s., thine eye	387b
the bloody S., at noon	98b
the maturing s.	221b
there to s. itself	470a
the rising of the s.	526b
the s., or the light..not darkened	499b
the unregulated s.	39b
till the s. grows cold	425a
time this s. is set	437b
tired the s. with talking	106b
to have enjoyed the s.	5b
to-morrow let my s...display	107a
to s. myself in Huncamunca's	151b
to the garish s.	366a
under the midday s.	267a
up roos the s.	89a
up rose the s.	141a
was sitting in the s.	406a
west as the s. went down	226b
whan soft was the s.	242b
when the s. in bed	270b
when the s. rises, do you not see	29b
when the s. sets, shadows	244a
when the s. set where were they?	70b
window where the s. came	195a
wind up the s. and moon	74b
with the dying s.	34a
with the s. to match	45b
woman clothed with the s.	519a
yet the early rising s.	189a
Sunbeam: bathe in the fresh s.	397b
motes in the s.	89b
s. in a winter's day	143a
s. quickened thee, O man	241a
Sunbeams: stars and s. know	7b
s. lifted higher	247b
s. out of cucumbers	418a
winds and s.	393b
Sunburn'd sicklemen	367b
Sunday: buried on S.	532b
Christ's S. at morn	524a
killing of a mouse on S.	35a
of a S. morning	199a
on S. heaven's gate	187a
see me on S.	528b
that calm S. that goes on	154b
Sundays: begin a journey on S.	418b
Pulpits and S.	187a
S. of man's life	187a
Sundered in the night	431a
Sundown splendid and serene	185a
Sunflower: as the s. turns	281b
S.! weary of time	32a
where my S. wishes to go	32a
Sung: I've only s. it once	424a
some are s.	441a

Sung (cont.)

s. from noon to noon	284b
Sun-girt city	395b
Sunium: on S.'s height	241a
S.'s marbled steep	71a
Sunk: all s. beneath the wave	111a
in the flat sea s.	267a
some were s.	437b
s. tho' he be	270a
that s. so low	269b
Sunless: down to a s. sea	101a
Sunlight: as moonlight unto s.	432b
s. and the sward	235a
s. clasps the earth	395b
s. drinketh dew	427a
Sunnier side of doubt	425b
Sunny: S. Jim	179a
sat on a s. bank	522a
that s. dome	101b
Sunrise: descried at s...prow	8a
like s. from the sea	394a
lives in Eternity's s.	30b
seen their s. pass	91b
s. blooms and withers	312a
s. in town and country	413a
that august s.	435b
Suns: be where s. are not	33b
blest by s. of home	40a
branding summer s. avail	429b
few more s. shall set	33b
light of setting s.	472a
million million of s.	439a
other planets circle other s.	300b
process of the s.	432b
s. and universes ceased	38b
s. may set and rise	538b
s. of the world may stain	387b
s., that set, may rise	216a
we are what s...make us	241b
Sunset: as after s. fadeth	388a
sail beyond the s.	439a
s. and evening star	426a
s. divides the sky	69a
s. embers	414b
s. ran, one glorious blood-red	47b
there's a s.-touch	45a
'tis the s. of life	77a
turns toward s.	423a
Sunsets exquisitely dying	202b
Sunset-seas: continents of s.	3a
Sunshine: breezes and the s.	76a
by intercepting the s.	559b
from s. to the sunless land	465b
lived more in the broad s. of life	210a
made a s. in the shady place	408b
on a s. holiday	269a
s. is a glorious birth	466a
thunder and the s.	439a
Sunshot palaces high	38a
Sun-thaw: smokes in the s.	101a
Sun-treader, life	50a
Sup: he swallows, s. by s.	192b
let's s. before we go	534b
who sipped no s.	167a
Superb against the dawn	27a
Supererogation: Works of S.	491b
Superfluities: s. of mankind	159b
we must have s.	160b
Superfluity: barren s. of words	159a
s. comes sooner	352b
s. of naughtiness	517b
Superfluous: in the poorest things s.	342b
so s. to demand the time	376a
s. lags the veteran	214a
s...to point out..this is war	1a
Superflux of pain	420a
Superior: most s. person	528b
sick of his s.	368b
Superscription: image and s.	507b
Supersede the last fashionable novel	255b
Superstition: a s. in avoiding s.	15a
religion..remedy for s.	55b
species of s. to another	201b
s...religion of feeble minds	57b
the fabric of s.	57b
Superstitions: end as s.	203a
Superstitious: he is s. grown	338b
more s., more bigoted	288a
ye are too s.	512b
Supped full with horrors	350b
Supper: ate a good s. at night	4a

Supper (*cont.*)
Baptism, and the S. — 481*a*
consider s. as a turnpike — 144*a*
eat my s. there — 472*b*
Hatim call to S. — 152*b*
Hatim Tai cry S. — 152*b*
heard him speak at a s. — 149*a*
hope..is a bad s. — 13*b*
if the s. was to my taste — 411*a*
last sad s. — 428*a*
marriage s. of the Lamb — 519*b*
sings for his s. — 534*b*
s., dinner, luncheon — 50*a*
Supple and smooth to her — 192*a*
Suppliant: S. for his own! — 73*b*
thus the s. prays — 214*a*
Supplications: our common s. — 478*b*
Support: but to s. him after — 368*a*
s. uneasy steps — 271*b*
s. us all the day long — 288*b*
Suppose: 'do you s.,' the Walrus said — 84*a*
Suppressed: guinea-pigs..was..s. — 83*b*
Supreme: disposer S. — 461*b*
France..in none s. — 8*a*
Surcease: with his s. success — 347*a*
Sure: as s. as death — 215*b*
make assurance double s. — 349*b*
not s. of sorrow — 422*a*
one s., if another fails — 52*a*
s. and safe one — 386*a*
s. in all His ways — 288*b*
s. there was wine — 188*a*
s. to each his own — 234*b*
too s. of the amour — 441*a*
Surety: s. for a stranger — 498*a*
wound of peace is s. — 369*a*
Surface of Time's fleeting river — 396*a*
Surfeit: no crude s. reigns — 267*b*
sick that s. with too much — 352*b*
that suffer s., cloyment — 371*a*
Surfeited: they s. with honey — 378*a*
Surfeiting: excess of it, that, s. — 369*b*
Surfeit-swelled: so s. — 381*a*
Surge: rude imperious s. — 380*a*
the murmuring s. — 343*b*
turbulent s. shall cover — 368*a*
Surgeon to old shoes — 337*b*
Surgery: honour hath no skill in s. — 379*a*
Surges: labouring s. of the world — 443*a*
when loud s. lash — 300*a*
Surly: lion..went s. by — 338*a*
Surmise: function is smother'd in s. — 346*b*
vague shadow of s. — 146*b*
we all s., they, this thing — 50*b*
with a wild s. — 220*b*
Surmises: blown by s. — 379*b*
Surname: his s., Leisure — 130*a*
out of his s...coined — 254*b*
Surplice: view of the s.-question — 45*b*
Surplice-peg: shape of a s. — 228*a*
Surplices: flame beside the s. — 243*a*
scarlet cloaks and s. — 243*a*
Surprise: blesses us with s. — 27*a*
Oh! what a s. — 97*a*
poetry shd. s. by..excess — 222*b*
respect was mingled with s. — 316*b*
rise to no little s. — 19*a*
Surprised: discovered and s. — 274*b*
Surprises: millions of s. — 187*a*
politics s. by himself — 126*a*
sometimes a light s. — 110*b*
Surrender: Guards die..not s. — 562*a*
unconditional..s. — 173*a*
yet be forced to s. — 41*b*
Surrey: I dare meet S. — 375*b*
Kent and S. may — 229*a*
S. spring again — 232*b*
Survey: monarch of all I s. — 113*a*
time, that takes s. — 379*a*
when I s. the wondrous Cross — 453*b*
Survival of the Fittest — 117*b*, 408*a*
Survived: you still have s. — 147*a*
Susan: black-eyed S. — 161*a*
Susceptible: rather s. Chancellor — 163*b*
Suspect: always s. everybody — 125*a*
nothing makes a man s. much — 15*b*
s. the thoughts of others — 353*a*
Suspects, yet soundly loves! — 361*b*
Suspected: new opinions..always s. — 246*a*
Suspend: best..cannot s. their fate — 118*a*

Suspended: almost s., we are laid asleep — 472*a*
s. in favour of England — 390*a*
s. my religious enquiries — 161*b*
Suspenders: *not* forget the S. — 237*a*
Suspense: inconvenience of s. — 148*a*
Suspension of disbelief — 102*a*
Suspicion: Caesar's wife..above s. — 574*a*
s. all our lives — 379*a*
s. always haunts the guilty — 384*b*
Suspicions: s. amongst thoughts — 15*b*
with fresh s. — 361*b*
Suspicious: men are s. — 189*b*
Suspiration: windy s. — 330*a*
Sussex: moon from S. downs — 92*b*
smell the S. air — 27*a*
story of S. told — 27*a*
S. moon, untravelled — 92*b*
S. songs be sung — 27*a*
S. weed — 235*a*
yea, S. by the sea — 235*a*
Sustain: nature will not s. it — 322*b*
Sutlers of the Lord — 145*a*
Swab: have to s. a plank — 121*a*
Swaddling: out of his s.-clouts — 332*b*
Swaggering: by s. cd. I never thrive — 372*a*
what..have we s. here — 357*a*
Swain: a frugal s. — 194*b*
dull s. treads — 267*b*
I the happy country swain — 61*b*
no better than a homely s. — 384*a*
sang the uncouth s. — 270*a*
s. did woo, she was nice — 176*a*
Swains: bring the s. together — 414*b*
our s. commend her — 372*b*
Swallow: as the s. by flying — 498*b*
before the swallow dares — 373*a*
flies with s.'s wings — 385*a*
O fleet sweet s. — 422*b*
O summer s. — 422*b*
O S., flying from the..woods — 436*b*
O s. sister, O changing s. — 422*b*
O S., S., flying..South — 436*a*
O tell her, S. — 436*a, b*
s. a nest where she may lay — 487*a*
s.-flights of song — 430*a*
s. has set her six young — 47*b*
s., my sister, O sister s. — 422*b*
s. stopt as he hunted — 435*b*
s. twittering from the..shed — 174*a*
the chaffering s. — 43*a*
to lap and to s. — 459*a*
we might our principles s. — 250*a*
Swallowed: first mouthed..last s. — 335*a*
s. by men's eyes — 378*a*
Swalloweth: he s. the ground — 497*b*
Swallows: engluts and s. other sorrows — 359*b*
gathering s. twitter — 222*a*
s. are making them ready — 459*a*
s. have built in Cleopatra's sails — 324*a*
we saw the s. gathering — 264*a*
Swan: double, s. and shadow! — 473*a*
doth the s. her downy cygnets — 383*b*
every goose a s., lad — 226*a*
I will play the s. — 364*a*
like a sleeping s. — 397*b*
makes a s.-like end — 354*a*
some full-breasted s. — 429*b*
stately-sailing s. — 443*b*
summer dies the s. — 438*a*
S. of Avon — 216*a*
s. on still St. Mary's Lake — 473*a*
the s.'s down-feather — 323*b*
wild-s. pause in their cloud — 435*b*
Swannee: my dear old S. — 75*a*
S. Ribber — 156*b*
Swans: geese are s. — 6*b*
his own geese are s. — 440*b*
s. sing before they die — 100*b*
very like s. — 123*b*
Swap: not best to s. horses — 245*b*
Sward: sunlight and the s. — 235*a*
Swarm of bees in May — 522*a*
Swarry: a friendly s. — 127*a*
Swashing: remember thy s. blow — 364*b*
s. and a martial outside — 325*b*
Swat: Akond of S. — 243*b*
Swath: spares the next s. — 221*b*
Sway: above this sceptred s. — 354*b*
governed by no other s. — 280*b*

Sway (*cont.*)
limping s. — 388*a*
little rule, a little s. — 143*a*
love of s. — 302*a*
more habitual s. — 467*a*
prevail'd with double s. — 168*b*
Swayed: s...upon a rocking horse — 220*b*
wd. she be s. by quite as keen — 166*a*
Sways: by submitting, s. — 302*a*
so s. she level — 370*b*
Swear: and s. nowhere — 134*a*
blessed moon I s. — 365*a*
do not s. at all — 365*a*
s. by thy gracious self — 365*a*
s. by thyself — 132*a*
s., fool, or starve — 142*b*
s. like a comfit-maker's wife — 378*a*
s. me, Kate — 378*a*
s. not at all — 505*a*
s. not by the moon — 365*a*
s...on a parcel-gilt goblet — 380*a*
s. to never kiss the girls — 46*b*
Sweareth unto his neighbour — 482*b*
Swearing: let me alone for s. — 372*a*
Swears with so much grace — 244*a*
Sweat: agony and bloody S. — 478*b*
a muck of s. — 171*a*
Falstaff shall die of a s. — 381*a*
in the s. of thy face — 492*b*
spend our mid-day s. — 307*a*
they do not s. and whine — 458*a*
Sweating: s. devil here — 362*b*
s. palm to palm — 202*b*
Sweats: Falstaff s. to death — 377*a*
regrets, and the bloody s. — 459*b*
s. in the eye of Phoebus — 383*a*
Sweep: madly is the sky — 357*a*
s. on, you fat and greasy citizens — 325*b*
s. the clouds no more — 194*a*
s. thro' her marble halls! — 247*b*
s. through the deep — 77*b*
Sweeps a room as for Thy laws — 188*b*
Sweet: all her task to be s. — 452*a*
all is not s. — 215*a*
as s. unto a shepherd — 176*a*
doth suck his s. — 176*a*
half so s. in life — 281*b*
how it was s. — 46*a*
how s.! did any heart — 399*a*
how s. is the Shepherd's s. lot — 32*b*
if s., give thanks — 421*a*
in the s. o' the year — 373*a*
little s. doth kill — 218*b*
love so young cd. be so s. — 37*b*
O fair! O s. — 402*a*
O so s. is she! — 216*b*
O s. and far from cliff — 436*a*
pleasures newly found are s. — 463*b*
sleep not so sound, as s. — 188*b*
some have found so s. — 433*b*
so..s., as lovely melancholy — 23*a*
so s., the sense faints — 396*b*
so s. was ne'er so fatal — 363*b*
s. and fair she seems — 449*a*
s. and low — 436*a*
s. and virtuous soul — 187*b*
s. as summer — 386*b*
s. as those by hopeless fancy — 436*a*
s. by-and-by — 315*b*
s. is every sound — 437*a*
s. is the breath of morn — 274*b*
s. it is, when on the..sea — 550*b*
s., not lasting — 336*b*
s. reasonableness — 10*b*
s. the coming on — 274*b*
s. their memory still — 109*b*
s. tho' in sadness — 396*b*
s. to myself that am so s. — 294*a*
s. voice, s. lips — 221*a*
s., when the morn is grey — 75*b*
s., when they've cleared away — 75*b*
s. will be the flower — 110*a*
swore my lips were s. — 241*b*
thy chamber window, S.! — 394*b*
'tis s. to him — 101*a*
'tis very s. to look — 221*a*
too simple and too s. — 293*a*
wit enough to keep it s. — 211*b*
with ecstasies so s. — 37*b*
with swift, slow; s., sour — 197*b*
you'll look s. on the seat — 116*b*

Sweet-and-twenty: kiss me, s. 370b
Sweeten this little hand 350a
Sweeteners: best s. of tea 151b
Sweeter: music s. than their own 469a
  s. also than honey 482b
  s. no girl ever gave 461a
  s. than the marriage feast 100a
  s. thy voice 437a
  thereby be the s. 351b
Sweetest: possibly s. 75b
Sweetheart: dead man's s. 199a
  I prithee, s., canst thou tell 531b
  past and gone, s. 531a
  s. of the sun 195b
  Tray, Blanche and S. 343a
Sweeting: pretty s. 370b
Sweetly flows that liquefaction 190b
Sweetmeats: breaths with s. 364b
Sweetness: as may, with s. 268b
  every s. that inspired 259b
  folds the lily all her s. up 437a
  linked s. long drawn out 269a
  loathe the taste of s. 378b
  out of the strong came forth s. 495a
  pursuit of s. and light 441a
  s. in the sad 430b
  s., mercy, majesty 249b
  very s. yieldeth proof 467b
  want words, and s. 216b
  waste its s. on the desert 174a
  wh. are s. and light 417b
  with s. fills the breast 86b
Sweet peas on tiptoe 218b
Sweets: all its s. are gone 221a
  box where s. compacted 187b
  discandy, melt their s. 324a
  instead of s., his ample palate 218a
  nectared s. 267b
  stolen s. are best 95b
  s. and the bitters of love 72b
  s. into your list 202a
  s. that you suck 227b
  s. to the sweet 336b
  s. with s. war not 387a
  Thy s. along with Thee 187a
  wilderness of s. 275a
Sweet-William with its..cottage swell 8b
Swell: are taught to s. 223b
  green s. is in the havens 197b
  s. at full of tide 323b
  s., bosom, with thy fraught 362a
  s. gluts twice ten thousand 221a
Swelling: green buds they were s. 531a
  she's a s. wisibly 126b
Swept: empty, s., and garnished 506b
  s. it for half a year 84a
Swerving: patent back again is s. 388b
Swift: be s. to hear 517a
  dividing his mind 573a
  love is s. of foot 188a
  oh, be s., my soul 200b
  s. Anapæsts throng 101b
  s. as a shadow 356a
  S. expires a driv'ler 214a
  s. in all obedience 234b
  s. things for swiftness 441b
  s. to be hurled 196a
  s. without violence 305b
  S., you will never be a poet 142a
  too s. arrives as tardy 365b
  with s., slow 197b
Swiftness: O s. never ceasing! 295b
  s. did I sue 441b
Swike: ne s. thu 522b
Swimmer: in the..ocean a s. 554b
Swine: cast ye yr. pearls before s. 505b
  gold in a s.'s snout 498a
  husks that the s. did eat 509b
Swing: fellow's got to s. 459b
  I don't want to s. a cat 122b
  out of the s. of the sea 197b
  s. me suddenly into the shade 39b
  v'ice hed sech a s. 250b
Swinged the dragon 373b
Swinges the scaly horror 270b
Swinging: s. round the circle 205b
  s. slow with sullen roar 268a
Swings: one..the more s. into place 232b
  his and that way s. 9a

Swings (cont.)
  we pulls up on the s. 86b
Swinish: hoofs of a s. multitude 57a
Swipes: finish up yr. s. 229a
  s. they take in 27a
Swiss: no money, no S. 565a
Switched his long tail 100b
Switzerland..inferior..Scotland 405a
Swiveller: Dick S. 125a
Swim: but said I cd. not s. 83b
  naughty night to s. in 343a
  s. to Thee, my Maker 280b
Swimmer: never a s. shall cross 424a
  never, I ween, did s. 253b
  some strong s. 70b
  to be crossed by any s. 413b
Swims: new planet s. into his ken 220b
  s., or sinks, or wades 273a
  who s. in sight 424a
Swoop: one fell s. 350a
Swop for my dear old Dutch 94a
Sword: born of thee are s. and fire 427b
  brave man with a s. 459b
  broached on his s. 383b
  die on mine own s. 351a
  employment with the naked s. 186b
  famous by my s. 280b
  fleshed thy maiden s. 379a
  flourishing with his s. 308b
  gird on thy s., O man 36b
  hack thy s. as thou hast done 377b
  [Hampden] first drew the s. 203a
  he had a s. upstairs 474a
  hides a s. from hilts 381b
  his father's s. 281b
  his good s. rest 101a
  I bear my trusty s. 108b
  is the s. unswayed? 385a
  Justice to break her s. 363b
  lift up s. against nation 501a
  lightnings Thy s. 94a
  many have fallen by the..s. 520b
  more splendid than the s. 415b
  mouth went a sharp two-edged s. 518b
  my soul from the s. 483a
  my s. I give 54b
  nor the deputed s. 351b
  not to send peace, but a s. 506a
  oyster..I with s. will open 355b
  pen is worse than the s. 64a
  put up thy s. 511b
  sharp as a two-edged s. 497b
  sharper than any two-edged s. 517a
  since put up my s. 338a
  s., a horse, a shield 250a
  s., glued to my scabbard 262b
  s. he sung a song of death 30a
  s., nor yet a lute 187a
  s. of an Angel King 30b
  s. of Common Sense 263a
  s. of Hazael 496a
  s. outwears its sheath 74a
  s. sleep in my hand 31b
  s. sung on the barren hearth 30a
  s. that severs all 263b
  s. upon thy thigh 484b
  s. was in the sheath 111a
  s. was servant unto right 408b
  S. went out to sea 284b
  take away the s. 252a
  the s., the mace 382b
  they that take the s. 508a
  tongue a sharp s. 485b
  took his vorpal s. 83b
  two-edged s. in their hands 490b
  unsmote by the s. 74a
  we shall never sheathe the s. 10b
  whipster gets my s. 364a
  with s. of justice thee ruleth 143a
  with s.-sway, and with lance's 318b
  with the edge of the s. 494a
Swords: keep up yr. bright s. 359b
  lifting up their s. 154b
  sheathed their s. for lack 382a
  splendid with s. 421a
  stout hearts and sharp s. 28b
  s. into ploughshares 501a
  s. must have leaped 57a
  s. shall play the orators 259a
  turns our s. in our own..entrails 341b
  yet be they very s. 485b

Swords (cont.)
  your s., made rich 339b
Swore: jested, quaffed, and s. 136b
  our armies s. terribly 411b
  Sikes..habitually s. 75a
  s. not at all 27b
  tongue..not my soul that s. 559b
  what to say, he s. 73a
Sworn: had I so s. as you 347a
  I have s., and am..purposed 489b
  I have s. thee fair 389b
Swosser: Captain S. 121a
Swound: noises in a s. 98a
Sybil: contortions of the s. 58b
Sycamore: nightingale in the s. 414b
  sighing by a s. tree 363a
Sydnaean Showers 115b
Sydney, whom we yet admire 97b
Syllable: chase a panting s. 110b
  s. of recorded time 350b
Syllables: heroic s. both ways 71b
  s. jar with time 216b
  these equal s. alone 300a
Syllogisms hang not 107b
Sylph: only s. I ever saw 125a
Symbols: huge cloudy s. 221a
  s. of Eternity 471a
  we are s., and inhabit s. 148a
Symmetry: its s. be as of thunder 314a
  thy fearful s. 31b
Sympathetic gunpowder 66a
Sympathies: vain s.! 463b
Sympathize: I deeply s. 84b
Sympathy: by admiration, by s. 148a
  in the primal s. 466b
  souls a s. with sounds 112b
  s. in choice 356a
  the secret s. 317a
  with our heartfelt s. 165b
  wrought to s. with hopes 398b
Symphonies: five sweet s. 311b
Symphony and song 101b
Symplegades: narrowing S. 420b
Synagogues: chief seats in the s. 507b
Syne: for auld lang s. 59a
Synod: hold a s. in thy heart 280b
  S. of Cooks 207b
Syrens: song the S. sang 42b
Syrian: in the lorn S. town 7a
  S. damsels to lament 271b
  the S. stars look down 7a
Syrinx: Pan did after S. speed 260b
Syrops: lucent s. 221b
Syrups: drowsy s. of Arabia 362a
Syrtes and soft Sicily 8b
System: educated by a s. 265a
  energies of our s. will decay 18a
  I must Create a S. 30b
  social s...Prince's nails 122a
  s. into s. runs 300b
  while they oppose every s. 57b
Systems: atoms or s. into ruin 300b
  our little s. 429b
  wheeling s. darken 442a

T

T: mark it with T 532a
  to a T, sir 150b
Tabbies: we're not as t. are 76a
Tabernacle: dwell in thy t. 482a
  Orient t. 442b
  set a t. for the sun 482b
Table: about my t. to and fro 476b
  Alice looked all round the t. 83a
  carpenter..made you a bad t. 207a
  crumbs..from the rich man's t. 510a
  crumbs wh. fall from..masters' t. 507a
  general joy of the whole t. 349a
  requires the repairs of the t. 212a
  scraped one out of the t. 351a
  set the t. on a roar 336b
  shalt prepare a t. before me 483a
  sit still for once at t. 193a
  t. of the Moveable Feasts 478a
  write it before them in a t. 502a
Table Bay: horse and foot going to T.! 227a
Table-crumbs attract his..feet 443b
Table-lands: the shining t. 435a

Table Mountain: reside at T.   182*b*
Tables: fleshy t. of the heart   515*a*
   leave . . God, and serve t.   512*a*
   make it plain upon t.   504*b*
   my t.—meet it is I set it down   331*b*
   near a thousand t. pined   465*a*
   not yr. trade to make it.   207*a*
Tablets: quick, thy t., Memory!   7*a*
Tabor: as to the t.'s sound   466*a*
Tace . . Latin for a candle   151*a*
Tackle swell with the touches   323*a*
Tadlow walks the streets   149*a*
Tadpole: T. and Taper   129*a*
   when you were a t.   404*a*
Taffeta: doublet of changeable t.   371*a*
   wench in flame-coloured t.   376*a*
Taffy: comes T. dancing   232*b*
   T. was a Welshman   532*a*
   T. was not at home   532*a*
Tag rag, merry derry   290*b*
Tail: brother, thy t. hangs down   234*a*
   cast salt on a woman's t.   65*b*
   Chittabob's t. was the finest   20*a*
   comes she with a tithe-pig's t.   364*b*
   corking-pin stuck through his t.   19*b*
   counsel to the t.   250*b*
   cow with the iron t.   535*a*
   durst not touch her t.   534*a*
   has a nimble t.   216*a*
   her t. came out   19*b*
   he wagged his t., and wet his lip   192*b*
   he with his t. awey   90*a*
   his languid t. above us   475*a*
   hole where . . t. came thro'   100*b*, 406*b*
   improve his shining t.   82*b*
   scaly horror of his folded t.   270*b*
   sensations of its 't.'   17*b*
   such a little t. behind   25*b*
   switched his long t.   100*b*
   t. must wag the dog   228*a*
   their t. the rudder   139*b*
   thereby hangs a t.   361*b*
   thin mane, thick t.   386*b*
   treading on my t.   83*a*
   waving his wild t.   237*a*
   wh. t. she wriggles   216*a*
   wh. was the head . . wh. was the t.   38*a*
Tailor: he called the t. lown   361*a*
   ninth part even of a t.   80*b*
   t. make thy doublet   371*a*
Tailors: four-and-twenty t.   534*a*
   run, t., run or she'll kill you   534*a*
Tails: bring their t. behind them   533*a*
   holding their neighbours' t.   231*a*
   nasty long t.   20*a*
   t. of both hung down   403*b*
   t. you lose   115*b*
   were stings in their t.   519*a*
Taint: but never t. my love   363*a*
Take: easy to t. *more* than nothing   83*a*
   from thee I did but t.   442*a*
   I believe, and t. it   145*b*
   I can't t. more   83*a*
   I saw you t. his kiss!   293*b*
   prays der Lord, T. anyding   1*a*
   shalt not t. the Name of the Lord   480*a*
   these thou shalt not t.   423*b*
   this cannot t. her   416*a*
   t. and break us; we are yours   185*a*
   t. any heart, t. mine   166*b*
   t. any shape but that   349*a*
   t. anything for granted   128*a*
   t. a suck at the lemon   19*b*
   t. heed therefore that the light   509*a*
   t. him for all in all   330*a*
   t. me to a brewery   523*b*
   t. me to you, imprison me   133*a*
   t. my counsel, happy man   163*b*
   t. my Muse and me   215*a*
   t., O t. those lips away   352*a*
   t. some more tea   83*a*
   t. that, you hound, and that!   135*b*
   t. thee with her eyelids   498*a*
   t. what this sweet hour yields   394*b*
   t. what thou wilt away   112*b*
   they shd. t., who have the power   470*b*
   well, let it t. them!   152*b*
   ye shall t. it patiently   517*b*
   you mean you can't t. *less*   83*a*
Taken: deny its use thoughtfully t.   76*a*
   I fear she will be t.   531*a*

Taken (*cont.*)
   Lord hath t. away   496*b*
   not be t. away from her   509*a*
   one shall be t.   508*a*
   tho' much is t., much remains   439*a*
   when t., to be well shaken   103*a*
Takes: blesseth . . him that t.   354*b*
   like that it t. away   73*b*
Taking: a's doing a-t. o' meä?   435*a*
   damnation of his t.-off   347*a*
   folks got t. me for him   244*b*
   in the t. of it breathe   227*b*
   t. in one another's washing   573*b*
   think, boy, of t. a wife   282*a*
Talbot: Warwick and T.   383*a*
Tale: and thereby hangs a t.   326*a*
   an ower true t.   319*a*
   as it were a t. that is told   487*b*
   a t. shd. be judicious   108*a*
   dark words begins my t.   465*a*
   debonair and gentle t.   221*a*
   doth the same t. repeat   466*a*
   every t. condemns me   385*a*
   fair t. of a tub   283*b*
   find a t. in every thing   471*a*
   her terrible t. you can't assail   165*a*
   I cd. a t. unfold   331*a*
   interest to a twice-told t.   72*b*
   I say the t. as 'twas said   317*a*
   long preamble of a t.   89*b*
   many a t. their music tells   282*a*
   mere t. of a tub   454*b*
   my t. of woe   151*a*
   point a moral, or adorn a t.   213*b*
   round unvarnished t. deliver   360*a*
   sad t.'s best for winter   373*a*
   schoolboy's t. . . . wonder of an hour   68*a*
   shepherd tells his t.   268*b*
   sing or say his homely t.   468*a*
   sweet t. of the sun   377*b*
   t. not too importunate   284*a*
   t. shall put you down   377*b*
   t. told by an idiot   350*b*
   t. was undoubtedly true   242*a*
   t. wh. holdeth children from play   402*a*
   t., wh. is strictly true   236*a*
   tattling many a broken t.   296*b*
   tedious as a twice-told t.   374*a*
   telle a t. after a man   89*a*
   telle his t. untrewe   89*a*
   thereby hangs a t.   366*b*
   to him my t. I teach   100*a*
   tongue brings in a several t.   385*a*
Talent: blest with each t.   303*a*
   his single t. well employ'd   210*b*
   T. does what it can   265*a*
   t. instantly recognizes genius   136*a*
   t. of the English nation   141*b*
   that one t. wh. is death to hide   278*b*
Talented: I'm sure he's a t. man   305*a*
Talents: if you have great t.   308*b*
Tales: fear . . increased with t.   14*a*
   our dreams are t.   119*a*
   poets that wrapt Truth in t.   79*a*
   seemed to them as idle t.   510*a*
   t. of love shall tell   53*b*
   tell old t., and laugh   344*a*
   tell t. of thee to . . Jove   342*b*
   wild t. to cheat thee   461*b*
Talismans: books are . . t. and spells   112*b*
Talk: after-dinner t.   434*b*
   an hour's t. withal   344*b*
   but t. of his horse   353*a*
   by beginning to t.   183*a*
   Cabots t. only to God   34*a*
   difference of men's t.   296*a*
   fit time . . to t. of Pensions   411*b*
   have him t. to me   378*a*
   have out his t.   209*b*
   honest talk and wholesome wine   438*b*
   hopes of high t.   394*b*
   I have no small t.   455*a*
   it would t.: Lord how it talk't!   23*b*
   leading one to t. of a book   207*a*
   leave the Wise to t.   153*a*
   let's t. of graves   375*b*
   loves to hear himself t.   365*b*
   made ignoble t.   428*b*
   my fireside with personal t.   468*b*
   night is crept upon our t.   341*a*
   no use to t. to me   198*b*

Talk (*cont.*)
   Pelagians do vainly t.   491*a*
   read not . . to find t.   16*a*
   Sailor-men shd. t. so very queer   19*b*
   some little t. awhile   153*b*
   t. about the rest of us   192*a*
   t. a little wild   385*b*
   t., and not the intrigue . . crime   173*a*
   t. but a tinkling cymbal   15*b*
   t. him out of patience   361*b*
   t. six times with the same . . lady   71*b*
   t. so like a waiting-gentlewoman   376*b*
   t. was like a stream   305*a*
   t. with some old lover's ghost   133*b*
   t. with you, walk with you   353*a*
   the mair they t.   62*b*
   the t. slid north   227*a*
   they always t., who never think   306*a*
   those who t. most about . . marriage   391*a*
   to t. of many things   84*b*
   we'll t. with them too   344*a*
   who t. too much   138*a*
   wished him to t. on for ever   183*b*
   winter t. by the fireside   16*a*
Talked: believe they t. of me   150*a*
   [Coleridge] t. on   183*b*
   Lord, how it t.   23*b*
   so much they t.   94*b*
   t. with us by the way   510*a*
   thin t. to him sevairely   231*a*
   worse than being t. about   460*b*
Talkers: most fluent t.   183*b*
Talking: foolish t. nor jesting   515*b*
   Frenchman must be always t.   210*a*
   he is t., or he is pursuing   496*a*
   he will be t.   359*a*
   never mind her; go on t.   390*b*
   t. about being a gentleman   416*b*
   t. and eloquence . . not the same   215*a*
   t. of Michelangelo   144*b*
   t. politics after dinner   128*b*
   tired the sun with t.   106*b*
   you will still be t.   358*a*
Talking-machine: red-tape T.   81*a*
Talks: he t. it so very fast   150*a*
   liked the way it t.   308*a*
   t. about her hair   443*a*
Tall: divinely t.   426*b*
   gallows . . neat and adequately t.   91*b*
   her stature t.   70*a*
   he's as t. a man as any   369*b*
   rather t. and stately   528*b*
   she is t. and stately   433*b*
   so t., he almost touched the sky   192*b*
   t. as Amazon   219*a*
   t. men had ever very empty heads   13*b*
   were I so t. to reach the Pole   453*a*
Taller by . . the breadth of my nail   417*b*
Tallest of boys   19*b*
Tally: score and the t.   384*a*
Talmud: all the fables in . . the T.   15*a*
Tam: but T. was glorious   62*b*
   T. kent what was what   63*a*
   T. lo'ed him like a . . brither   62*b*
   T.! thou'll get thy fairin'   63*a*
Tamarisks: noon behind the t.   228*a*
Tambourine on her other knee   125*a*
Tame: be not too t.   333*b*
   glass, wh. thou canst not t.   186*b*
   half-wild and wholly t.   235*a*
   who, ne'er so t., so cherish'd   379*a*
Tamed: in one year t.   261*a*
Tamer of the human breast   173*b*
Tamtallan: Time may gnaw T.   62*b*
Tanais: flows the freezing T. thro'   299*a*
Tane unto the tither did say   529*b*
Tang: a tongue with a t.   367*b*
Tanner: one Simon a t.   512*a*
Taper: a t. to the outward room   133*b*
   hold up to the sun my . . t.   71*b*
   hope . . the gleaming t.'s light   168*a*
   Tadpole and T.   129*a*
   t. of conwiviality   125*a*
   yon t. cheers the vale   169*a*
   you saw the t. burning   317*b*
Tapers: hold their glimmering t.   113*b*
   lit her glimmering t.   441*b*
   priests, t. temples   299*b*
   what is frequent in t. . . . wax   182*a*
Tapestry: of a Turkey t.   200*b*

'appertit: Mr. T.   121a
apping: suddenly there came a t.   298a
apsalteerie: may a' gae t. O!   60b
'ar: maiden and the t.   166a
'ara: hangs as mute on T.'s walls   281a
  harp that once thro' T.'s halls   281a
'aradiddles: telling t.   244b
'a-ra-ra-boom-de-ay   316a
'arantara, tarantara   166b
'ar-Baby: he call a T.   181b
  T. ain't saying nuthin'   181b
'ar-barrel: black as a t.   84a
are each other in their slime   430b
ares: clasping t. cling round   114a
  enemy came and sowed t.   506b
  weeds and t. of mine own brain   41b
'arn: the dark t. dry   119b
'arnish late on Wenlock Edge   199b
'arnishing: by nature a t. eye   264b
'arpaulin jacket   459a
'arquin: great house of T.   253a
  T.'s ravishing strides   347b
'arried: have I not t.?   368b
'arry: boatman, do not t.!   77a
  longer will t.   137a
  t. a while, says Slow   534b
  t. the grinding   368b
  t. till I come   512a
  t. till they push us   341b
  why t. the wheels of his chariot?   495a
  you may for ever t.   190b
'arrying: make no long t.   484b
'arshish: howl, ye ships of T.   502a
'arsus: stately ship of T.   277b
'artan: beneath the t. plaid   12a
'artarly: so savage and T.   73a
'arts: she made some t.   83b, 532b
  he stole the t.   532b
  he stole those t.   83b
'ar water]..cheer but not inebriate   28a
'ask: all her t. to be sweet   452a
  but one t. for all   229a
  delightful t.!   443b
  good never will be our t.   271a
  great t. of happiness   415a
  labourer's t. is o'er   145b
  long day's t. is done   324b
  morning sees some t. begin   249a
  my t. accomplished   185a
  sets love a t. like that   202a
  t. for all that a man has   412a
  thy worldly t. hast done   329a
  to this childish t.   415a
  trivial round, the common t.   224a
  weary t. foredone   357b
  what he reads as a t.   207a
'ask-Master: great T.'s eye   278b
'asks: among the t. of real life   465a
  command him t.   362b
  t. in hours of insight willed   7a
'assel-gentle: lure this t. back   365b
'assie: in a silver t.   60b
'aste: all ashes to the t.   68b
  always had a t. for damning   282b
  bud may have a bitter t.   110a
  but t. a little honey   495a
  common sense and good t.   380b
  he had a kind of t.   353b
  her t. exact   165a
  judge of t.   553b
  let me t. the whole of it   50b
  let me t. yr. ware   532b
  mortal t. brought death   270b
  O t., and see, how gracious   484a
  Shakespeare,..wanted t.   449b
  t. my *Anno Domini*   150a
  t. not; handle not   516a
  t. not when..wine cup glistens   319a
  t. of yr. quality   332b
  t. yr. legs, sir   371b
  terrible t. for tippling   163b
  they never t. who always drink   306a
  things sweet to t.   374b
  tho' t., tho' genius bless   103a
  to t. the barrel   62b
  vicissitudes of t.   213b
  wh. th' offended t...rejected   276b
'asted: can't be t. in a sip!   125a
  some books are to be t.   16a
  t. the eternal joys of heaven   258b
'astes: t. greatly alter   207b

Tastes (*cont.*)
  t. may not be the same   391a
  various are the t. of men   3a
Tattle: women..have an entertaining t.   91a
Tattlers also and busybodies   516b
Tattling many a broken tale   296b
Tattycoram   123a
Taught: afterward he t.   88b
  all they've t. me   282a
  he t., but first he folwed   88b
  he t. us little   6b
  in them is plainest t.   277a
  mind what I am t.   425a
  quickness ever to be t.   302a
  say, I t. thee   386a
  t. by the Power that pities   169a
  t. them as one having authority   506a
Taunting: reproofs..grave, and
  not t.   14b
Tavern: as by a good t.   208b
  a t. in the town   527a
  choicer than the Mermaid T.   219a
  creaking couplets in a t. hall   72a
  Voice within the T. cried   152a
  vulgar and t. music   42a
  within the T. caught   153b, 154a
Tavern-chair..throne of..felicity   212a
Taverns: he knew the t. wel   88b
  t. while the tempest hurled   199b
Taw: knuckle down at t.   113a
Tawny: Nightingale! the t.-throated!   7a
Tax: *Excise*: a hateful t.   212b
  to t. and to please   55a
Taxation and representation   305a
Taxed: all the world shd. be t.   508b
  schoolboy whips his t. top   405a
  t. horse, with a t. bridle   405a
Taxes: all t...fall upon agriculture   162a
  as true..as t. is   122a
  except death and t.   156b
  people overlaid with t.   15b
  t. on everything on earth   405a
  whoever pays the t.   230b
Tay: some'll swallow t.   261b
  t. is not my diversion   237a
Taylor..Shakespeare of divines   147a
T.C. in a Prospect of Flowers   261a
Tea: coffee, t., chocolate   4b
  counsel take—and sometimes t.   302b
  dinner, lunch, and t.   26a
  honey still for t.   40a
  if this is coffee, I want t.   536b
  now for the t. of our host   167a
  some sipping t.   468b
  swallowing his t. in oceans   255b
  take some more t.   83a
  t., altho' an Oriental   93b
  t. and comfortable advice   222b
  t. taste of boiled boots   439b
  t. without a stratagem   476b
  to their t. and scandal   104a
  we'll all have t.   121a
Teach: and gladly t.   88b
  go, t. eternal wisdom how to rule   301a
  I can easier t. twenty   353a
  let such t. others who..excel   300a
  mine to t. me   63b
  oh t. me yet somewhat   438a
  she doth t. the torches   365a
  still pleased to t.   300b
  t. him how to tell my story   360a
  t. me at once, and learn   299b
  t. me how a beggar..be answer'd   355a
  t. me, my God and King   188a
  t. me to feel   304a
  t. me to live, that I may dread   224b
  t. ourselves that honourable stop   361a
  t. them how..the mind of man   470a
  t. the orphan-boy   431b
  t. thy necessity to reason   374b
  t. us to bear the yoke   228a
  t. you more of man   471b
  t. you to drink deep   330a
  what you t. them first   207b
Teacher: doctrine for the t.'s sake   118a
  let Nature be yr. t.   471b
  precepts for the t.'s sake   150b, 193b
  tinderest t.   173a
Teachers: daily t. had been woods   463a
  more understanding than my t.   489a

Teaching: follow mine own t.   353a
  t. nations how to live   279b
Teacup: Storm in a T.   22a
  t. times of hood and hoop   438a
Tea-kettle: always back to the t.   128a
Team: is my t. ploughing   199a
  t. of little atomies   364b
Tear: all he had, a t.   174b
  and a t. in her eye   318a
  aye the t. comes in my ee   59a
  claims the homage of a t.   68a
  charm thee to a t.   461b
  dropped a t. into the Queen's ear   29a
  droppe the brynie t.   88a
  drop upon Fox's grave the t.   317b
  Erin, the t. and the smile   281a
  every t. from every eye   29b
  every woe a t. can claim   72b
  fallen a splendid t.   434a
  forbade the rising t.   317a
  for whom a t. you shed   215a
  from yr. eyelids wip'd a t.   326b
  grave rain'd many a t.   335b
  Guy de Vere, hast *thou* no t.   298a
  here did she fall a t.   375b
  meed of some melodious t.   269a
  never a t. bedims   182a
  not a t. must o'er her fall   44a
  persuasive language of a t.   95a
  Recording Angel..dropped a t.   412a
  repressed the starting t.   211b
  shed a bitter t.   84a
  t. be duly shed   103a
  t. blinded his e'e   529b
  t. her tattered ensign down!   194a
  t. him for his bad verses   340b
  t. is an intellectual thing   30b
  t. it from thy Throne   109b
  t. was in his eye   252b
  t...wiped with a little address   111a
  the sympathetic t.   174a
  the unanswerable t.   70a
  think to shed a t.   386a
  toning of a t.   189a
  weep with thee, t. for t.   281b
Tear-floods: no t.   134a
Tears: and the t. of it are wet   323b
  baptized in t.   242a
  beguile her of her t.   360a
  big round t. run down   443b
  bitter t. to shed   106a
  breath, smiles, t., of all my life!   44a
  broomsticks and their t.   474b
  but they are cruel t.   363b
  corn, before my t. did drown   188a
  daffadillies fill their cups with t.   270a
  dashed with light quick t.!   421a
  dearth of woman's t.   290a
  dim with childish t.   405a
  dip their wings in t.   430a
  drew iron t. down Pluto's cheek   268b
  drop, drop, slow t.   155b
  droppings of warm t.   44a
  drop t. as fast as the Arabian   364a
  drop thy foolish t.   426a
  drown the stage with t.   333a
  eyes and t. be the same things   260b
  far too freely moved to t.   26a
  fills the eyes with falling t.   397a
  flow with t. of gold   33a
  fountain of sweet t.   471a
  full of t. am I   376a
  gave me up to t.   383a
  greatness of the world in t.   476a
  had t. for all souls in trouble   258a
  her salt t. fell from her   363a
  her t. fell with the dews   433b
  if you have t.   340a
  I heard her t.   311b
  in t. amid the alien corn   220a
  in the mist of t. I hid from Him   441b
  keep time with my salt t.   214b
  kiss again with t.   436a
  let it wipe another's t.   63b
  like Niobe, all t.   330a
  like summer tempest came her t.   436b
  long drip of human t.   180a
  melted into t. for thee   225a
  mine own t. do scald like..lead   344a
  mine own t. I wash away my balm   376a
  move the muse to t.   108a

Tears (cont.)

my son in t.	164a
my t. must stop	196b
no arithmetic but t.	225a
nothing is here for t.	278a
now am full of t.	474a
of shuddering, also, and t.	452a
our bitter t. o'erflow	266b
owe more t. to this dead man	341b
parted in silence and t.	74b
Pleasure, blind with t.	392a
put my t. into this bottle	485b
rich flames, and hired t.	42a
scare me with thy t.	438b
see sin, but through my t.	155b
sheddeth tender t.	408b
shed t. when they wd. devour	15b
sink'st in thine own t.	119a
some natural t. they dropped	277a
sought it carefully with t.	517a
source of sympathetic t.	175a
t. and laughters for all time!	44a
t. and smiles like us He knew	3b
t. from the depth	436a
t., idle t.	436a
t. live in an onion	322b
t. no bitterness	251b
t. of the sky	91a
t. shall drown the wind	347a
t. that overflow thy urn	241a
t., their little triumphs o'er	175a
T. wash out a Word of it	153b
that sow in t.: shall reap in joy	489b
the big round t. cours'd	325b
therefore I forbid my t.	336a
the smiles of joy, the t. of woe	282b
those seeing t.	260b
tho' t. no longer flow	38b
time with a gift of t.	420b
tired of t. and laughter	422a
too deep for t.	467a
to remember with t.!	4a
to these crocodile's t...add sobs	64b
votive t. and symbol flowers	394a
watered Heaven with their t.	32a
weep thy girlish t.	452a
wipe..all t. from their eyes	519b
wipe away all t.	519a
with the bread of t.	487a
Teas: treat housemaids to his t.	93b
Tease: t. us out of thought	219b
thus t. me together	160a
Teases: because he knows it t.	82b
Tea-shops: low-class t.	35a
Tea-time: creation..expire before t.	404b
Teatray in the sky	83a
Teddington: which is T.	234a
Tedious: cheer one on the t. way	311a
more t. than the dial	362b
t. as a king	359a
t. as a tired horse	378a
thinking his prattle to be t.	376a
Teeming: nor Cynthia t. shows	260b
Tees: my lovelier T.	252b
Teeth: cast me in the t.	484b
children's t. are set on edge	503b
makes my t. watter	155a
show their t. in way of smile	352b
skin of my t.	497a
taking out his false t.	135a
t. and forehead of our faults	334b
tell him to his t.	336a
thy t. are like a flock of sheep	500a
to cast into my t.	341a
weeping and gnashing of t.	506a
whose t. are spears and arrows	485b
with thy sharp t. this knot	325a
Teeth-chattering Month	102b
Teetotaller: beer t., not a cham-	
pagne t.	390a
no woman shd. marry a t.	413a
Tekel, Upharsin	504a
Telegraph: lions of the *Daily T.*	9a
Telemachus: mine own T.	438b
Tell: almost makes me cry to t.	192b
but why I cannot t.	41a
from the grave, to t. us this	331b
I cannot t. what you..think	337b
I can t. you anyhow	54b
I cd. never t. why	165b
if it be love..t. me how much	322a

Tell (cont.)

I have none to t., Sir	78b
I'll swear I can't t. how	457a
in the body, I cannot t.	515a
I shd. answer, I shd. t. you	248b
I t. you that wh. you..do know	340a
Lady, I fain wd. t. how	312a
men of sense never t.	322a
never seek to t. thy love	31b
no method to t. her in Spanish?	46b
sight to dream of, not to t.	100a
sweetheart, canst thou t. me	531b
t. her, that I follow thee	436b
t. her, what I t. to thee	436a
t. it not in Gath	495b
t. me, my heart	251b
t. me not, in mournful numbers	247b
t. me not, Sweet, I am unkind	250a
t. me, O thou..my soul loveth	500a
t. me the old, old story	179a
t. me whom you live with	90b
t. not as new..ev'rybody knows	108a
t. proud Jove	215b
t. tale, tit	533a
t. them I am, Jehova said	403a
t. them that come after	485a
t. the other girls and boys	414a
t. you who you are	90b
'that I cannot t.,' said he	406a
they didn't t., nor make a fuss	236b
what I t. you three times	85b
whereby I can t.	292b
woman who wd. t. one that	460b
ye scarcely t. to ony	60a
you must somehow t. of yr. own	284a
you must not kiss and t.	104b
you never can t.	391b
Teller: bad news infects the t.	322b
truth never hurts the t.	46b
Telling: I am t. you	456b
if thou know'st it, t.	286b
only for t. a man he was wrong	97a
pity beyond all t.	475b
wh. t. what it is to die	430a
Tellus: cost her mother T...pangs	218b
Tempe: divine as the vale of T.	314a
in shade of T. sit	401b
Temper: a tart t. never mellows	203b
because she lost her t. once	234b
do anything, only keep yr. t.	411b
he of a t. was so absolute	136b
of such a feeble t.	337b
one equal t. of heroic hearts	439a
t. is nine-tenths of Christianity	184a
touch of celestial t.	274b
Temperance: as t. wd. be difficult	212a
faith, meekness, t.	515b
healthy by t.	303a
ye must acquire and beget a t.	333b
Temperate: more lovely and more t.	387a
the t. affords me none	79b
Tempes: where fairer T. bloom	394a
Tempest: drive devious, t. toss'd	109b
fierce raged the t.	444b
in taverns while the t. hurled	199b
lowers the t. overhead	247a
no t. gave the shock	111a
silence we the t. fear	139b
t. still is high	455b
windy t. of my heart	384b
Tempests: glasses itself in t.	69b
he on whom Thy t. fell	188a
looks on t. and is never shaken	389a
Tempest-tost: it shall be t.	346a
Templar Knights to bide	409b
Templars: wits and T.	303a
Temple: all the T. is prepared	
within	152a
at the t.'s inner shrine	467a
broke ope the Lord's anointed t.	348a
build the T. in their days	260b
dread T. of Thy worth	232b
drove them all out of the t.	510b
dwell in such a t.	367b
Herostratus..burnt..T. of Diana	42b
his train filled the t.	501b
in the very t. of delight	219b
I saw no t. therein	520a
let each new t.	194a
metropolitan t. in the hearts	464a
polished corners of the t.	490b

Temple (cont.)

second t. was not like the first	140a
some old t., nodding to its fall	301a
t. half as old as Time	310a
T. lost outright	153a
this T. keeps its shrine	293
when t. and tower	278
yr. body is the t.	514
Temple Bar: high over roaring T.	439a
rot high on T.	93
T. to Aldgate Street	160a
Temple-bells: t. are callin'	232a
t. they say: Come you back	232a
Temples: forsake their t. dim	270a
mortal t. of a king	375a
my joyful t. bind	448a
smote the nail into his t.	494b
solemn t.	367a
t. of his Gods	253a
thy t. are like a..pomegranate	500a
Temporal: pass through things t.	479a
Tempt: he tries to t. you	3a
king nor prince shall t. me	12a
shall not t. the Lord thy God	505a
so proudly t. the Son of God	277b
t. my Lady Poltigrue	26b
t. not a desperate man	366b
t. the frailty of our powers	369a
Temptation: cold, and to t. slow	388b
fond of resisting t.	23b
lead us not into t.	505b
man that endureth t.	517a
maximum of t. with..opportunity	391a
most dangerous is that t.	351b
oughtn't to yield to t.	197a
resist everything except t.	573a
t. comes to us in gay..colours	185b
that way going to t.	351b
there hath not t. taken you	514b
to get rid of a t...yield to it	460b
why comes t. but for man to meet	51b
with..t. also make..way to escape	514b
ye're aiblins nae t.	59a
Temptations to belong..other nations	166a
Tempted: extreme annoyance, t. him	26b
more pure, as t. more	465a
one thing to be t.	351a
other men are t. to	65b
suffer you to be t.	514b
t., and yet undefiled	405b
t. by a private whim	26b
they t. me, my beautiful!	290a
Tempting sounds I hear	33b
Tempts yr. wandering eyes	173b
Ten: it's now t. o'clock	266a
nine, t., a good fat hen	532a
t., who in ears and eyes	50b
upper t. thousand of the city	461b
were there not t. cleansed?	510a
Tenant: house and t. go to ground	147b
Tenants: nobler t. of the flood	110b
outlives a thousand t.	336a
t. of life's middle state	113a
Ten Comandments: aren't no T.	232a
went to sea with the T.	351a
Tend upon the hours and times	388a
Tendance: in so long t. spend	409b
Tended her i' the eyes	323a
Tendency: mighty stream of t.	464b
Tender: Bill as is young and t.	440b
distorting his t. love	36b
Dowglas, t. and trewe!	193b
felt the t. passion	160a
quick, t., virginal	294b
t. for another's pain	175a
things that are t. and unpleasing	15b
tho' never t. nor sublime	241b
Tender-handed stroke a nettle	191b
Tenderly: take her up t.	195b
Tenderness: more alive to t.	465a
thanks to its t., its joys	467a
Tenders: shoal of fools for t.	105a
Tendrils strong as flesh and blood	468b
Tenedos: a thousand ships to T.	250b
Tenement: informed the t. of clay	138a
into a clayey t.	79a
threshold of the ruined t.!	297a
Teneriff or Atlas	274b
Tennis-balls: stuffed t.	358b
the stars' t.	454b
Tennyson: hoped T. was writing his	66b

Tennyson (*cont.*)
[T.] cd. not think up to   94*a*
T. was not Tennysonian   204*b*
[T.] ..write verses without. .under-
  standing   102*b*
Wordsworth, T., and Browning   17*b*
Tenor: held the t. of his way   304*b*
  noiseless t. of their way   174*b*
066 and all that   321*b*
Tent: I rede ye t. it   62*a*
  little t. of blue   459*b*
  my t.'s thin roof   393*a*
  my wind-built t.   393*a*
  pitch my moving t.   280*a*
  sits in yon western t.   103*a*
  summer's evening, in his t.   340*a*
Tent-royal of their emperor   381*b*
Tents: fold their t., like the Arabs   247*a*
  ha' done with the T. of Shem   231*b*
  plain man, dwelling in t.   493*a*
  such as dwell in t.   492*b*
  t. of ungodliness   487*a*
  thy tribe's black t.   441*a*
  to yr. t., O Israel   496*a*
  within whose magic t.   36*b*
Tereu, Tereu, by and by   20*b*
Term: I served a t.   166*a*
Termagant: for o'erdoing T.   333*b*
Terminations: terrible as her t.   358*a*
Terminological inexactitude   95*a*
Terms: airs and recollected t.   370*b*
  I come on perfect t.   458*a*
  I like not fair t.   353*a*
  in good set t.   326*a*
  no t. except. .surrender   173*a*
  silken t. precise   345*a*
  t. like grace, new birth   10*a*
  t. too deep for *me*   165*a*
  the happiest t. I have   379*a*
Terrace: a t. walk   419*b*
  blank to Zoroaster on his t.   49*b*
Terrible: I the elder and more t.   339*a*
  make thee t. and dear   399*a*
  t. as hell   272*b*
Terrier: party. .like the Scotch t.   38*a*
Terror: only rules by t.   426*a*
  so full of dismal t.   384*b*
  struck more t. to. .Richard   385*a*
  t. by night   487*b*
  t. haunts the guilty mind   244*a*
  t. of darkness!   87*a*
  T. the human form divine   33*a*
  t. to good works   513*b*
  their perch and not their t.   351*a*
  there is no t., Cassius   340*b*
  without t. great   305*b*
Terrors: its deadly t. clasp   32*a*
  king of t.   497*a*
  new t. of death   4*b*
  scarecrow for superstitious t.   120*a*
  shall be the t. of the earth   342*b*
Tertium Quid: Wife and a T.   237*b*
  T. his sport with T.   181*a*
Tess: his sport with T.   181*a*
Test: best is bad, nor bears Thy t.   45*b*
  bring me to the t.   335*a*
  there lies the t.   94*b*
Testament: Commons hear this t.   340*a*
  thou mak'st a t.   325*b*
Tested his first plough   45*a*
Tester: she drops a t.   215*b*
Testimonies: thy t. are my study   489*a*
Testimony: no t. is sufficient   201*a*
Tetchy and wayward   385*a*
Tether: nae man can t. time or tide   63*a*
  tied the world in a t.   424*a*
Teuton: Slav, T., Kelt   426*a*
Teviotdale: march, Ettrick **and** T.   320*a*
Text: approve it with a t.   354*a*
  a square of t.   429*a*
  God takes a t.   187*a*
  great t. in Galatians   52*a*
  many a holy t. around she strews   174*b*
  neat rivulet of t.   400*b*
  none can read the t.   429*a*
  of that t. a pulled hen   88*b*
  read ev'ry t. and gloss over   65*a*
  to yr. t., Mr. Dean!   145*a*
Texts: difference of t.   409*a*
Texture: we know her woof, her t.   219*a*
Thackeray settled like a meat-fly   313*b*
Thairm: painch, tripe, or t.   60*b*

Thais: lovely T. by his side   138*b*
  lovely T. sits beside thee   139*a*
Thames: crossing the stripling T. at
  Bablock-hithe   8*a*
  flights upon the banks of T.   216*a*
  hill beside the silver T.   37*b*
  not of Gennesareth, but T.!   442*b*
  of our poor T. she never heard!   8*b*
  on T.' broad aged back   409*b*
  sweet T., run softly   409*b*
  T., attended by two nymphs   116*a*
  T. bordered by its gardens   284*a*
  T. is between me and the Duchess   449*a*
  the youthful T.   8*b*
  with no allaying T.   249*b*
Thammuz came next   271*b*
Thamyris and blind Mæonides   273*a*
Thane of Cawdor lives   346*a*
Thank: I t. thee, Jew   355*a*
  I t. the goodness and the grace   424*b*
  make the Moor t. me   361*a*
  t. me no thankings   366*a*
  t. whatever gods may be   185*a*
  t. with brief thanksgiving   422*a*
  t. you. .the agony is abated   255*b*
  then t. the Lord, O t. the Lord   76*a*
Thanked: nobody t. him for it   209*b*
  when I'm not t. at all   151*b*
Thankful: come, ye t. people   3*b*
  pleasant thing it is to be t.   490*b*
  so t. for illusion   96*a*
  the just to be t.   483*b*
Thankfulness: bless yr. name in
  pride and t.   47*b*
Thanks: for this relief much t.   329*a*
  I am poor even in t.   332*b*
  shall the dust give t.   483*b*
  some give t.   293*a*
  such t. as fits a king's   332*a*
  ta'en with equal t.   334*a*
  take the t. of a boy   24*b*
  t. be to the Lord   483*b*
  t. God for anything   206*b*
  t. to the human heart   467*a*
  to give t. is good   421*a*
Thanksgiving: be received with t.   516*b*
  thank with brief t.   422*a*
  with proud t.   28*b*
Tharsis: kings of T.   486*b*
That: take t. you hound, and t.!   135*b*
  1066 and all t.   321*b*
  t. thou doest, do quickly   511*a*
Thatch: house with deep t.   27*a*
  while the nigh t. smokes   101*a*
Thatch-eves: round the t. run   221*b*
Thaw, and resolve itself   330*a*
Theatre: as in a t., the eyes of men   376*a*
  everybody has his own t.   181*a*
  Idols of the T.   16*b*
  this t. of man's life   13*a*
  wait all day long in the t.   413*a*
Theatres: t., and temples lie open   472*b*
  t. of crowded men   218*a*
Theatrical scarecrow   120*a*
Theban: that T. monster   277*b*
  this same learned T.   343*a*
Thebes: riddle of death T. never
  knew   394*a*
  T. did his green. .youth   141*b*
  T., or Pelops' line   268*a*
  walked about. .in T.'s streets   403*b*
Thee: at last sit down by t.   225*b*
  but broken lights of t.   429*b*
  do it as for T.   188*a*
  have not T. in awe   233*b*
  love be great, 'twixt t. and me   21*a*
  minister of t. to me   36*a*
  nearer, my God, to T.   1*a*
  sigh'd for the dawn and t.   434*a*
  Talk awhile of ME and T.   153*b*
  therefore to t. it was given   7*b*
  what have I to do with t.?   510*b*
  who T. by faith. .confessed   200*a*
  without T. I cannot live   224*a*
  without T. I dare not die   224*a*
Theek: we'll t. our nest   529*b*
Theft: Christ. .forgave the t.   51*a*
  suspicious head of t.   345*a*
  wd. be t. in other poets   142*a*
Theirs: t. but to do and die   426*a*
  t. not to make reply   426*a*

Them 's my sentiments   573*a*
Theme: act of the imperial t.   346*a*
  as it is my t.!   119*b*
  it was a t. for reason   132*a*
  the t. too great!   305*b*
Themes: muses on admired t.   259*b*
Themselves: are a law unto t.   513*a*
  behold a greater than t.   338*a*
  outward shows be least t.   354*a*
  vilest things become t. in her   323*a*
Thentente in all   90*b*
Theocrite: 'Praise God!' sang T.   45*a*
Theologians. .employed. .terms   10*a*
Theology: better than this t.   147*b*
  objected to his t.   403*a*
Theophilus: most excellent T.   508*b*
  treatise have I made, O T.   512*a*
Theoric: bookish t.   359*b*
Theorize before one has data   135*a*
There: condemn itself for being t.   350*b*
  cry over me, T., t.   486*b*
  he had been t. before   237*b*
  he was t. ...He himself   45*b*
  if thou wert t.   62*b*
  I have been t.   453*a*
  I shall not be t.   424*a*
  is t. anybody t.   119*b*
  it's t. that I wd. be   232*a*
  not t., not t., my child!   184*b*
  t. am I in the midst of them   507*a*
  t. goes John Bradford   34*b*
  t., t., I wd. go, O my beloved   568*a*
Thereby hangs a tail   361*b*
Thermopylæ: to make a new T.   70*b*
Thersites' body is as good as Ajax   329*a*
These: from t. I wd. be gone   388*a*
  long way with t. thou seest   429*b*
  t. are they wh. came out   519*a*
  t., in the day when heaven   200*a*
Thetis: sun. .in the lap of T.   65*b*
They: every one else is T.   236*a*
  t. at least are for me   441*b*
  t., this thing, and I   50*b*
Thick: as t. as motes   89*b*
  his colours laid so t.   140*a*
  t. and fast they came at last   84*b*
  t. as autumnal leaves   271*b*
  through t. and thin   65*a*, 108*b*, 138*b*
Thicker than my father's loins   496*a*
Thicket: ram caught in a t.   493*a*
  t. closed behind her   429*a*
Thickets: fields and thorny t.   443*b*
  t. to his floods decline   37*b*
Thicksides and *hairy* Aldrich   96*a*
Thief: apparel fits yr. t.   352*a*
  behold, I come as a t.   519*b*
  embrace the impenitent t.   412*b*
  Eugene Aram, tho' a t.   75*b*
  first cries out stop t.   104*b*
  first grand t. into God's fold   273*b*
  giant's robes upon a dwarfish t.   350*a*
  have a t. or two guiltier   351*a*
  if you do take a t.   359*a*
  opportunity makes a t.   16*b*
  rails upon yond simple t.   343*b*
  receiver. .as bad as the t.   90*b*
  steals something from the t.   360*a*
  Taffy was a t.   532*a*
  t. doth fear each bush   384*b*
  t. said the last kind word   51*a*
  Translation's t. that addeth more   261*b*
  when thou sawest a t.   485*a*
  wh. is the justice, wh. is the t.?   343*b*
Thieves: fell among t.   509*a*
  'gainst knaves and t.   372*a*
  land-t. and water-t.   353*a*
  made it a den of t.   507*b*
  shot out sharp after t.   421*b*
  thou best of t.   139*b*
  where t. break through   505*b*
Thigh: bee with honied t.   268*b*
  hollow of Jacob's t.   493*a*
  on his t. a name   519*b*
Thighs: cuisses on his t.   378*b*
Thimbles: sought it with t.   86*a*
Thin: gruel, t., but not too t.   11*a*
  jewels make women. .t.   21*b*
  lips were red, and one was t.   416*a*
  O hear! how t. and clear   436*a*
  profligate, and t.   477*b*
  so t., so pale, is yet of gold   114*a*

Thin (*cont.*)
through thick and t.   65a, 108b, 138b
Thine: as I must on t.   394b
not my will, but t.   510a
only call me t.   101b
Rose Aylmer, all were t.   240b
she be only t.   260b
since I cannot have t.   416a
why not I with or t.?   395b
Wordsworth, both are t.   410b
Thinner, clearer, farther going!   436a
Thing: acting of a dreadful t.   338b
a *Good T.*   321b
a t. well said   142a
beguile the t. I am   360b
blame the t. that's not   294b
bonnie wee t.   59b
but one t. is needful   509a
but that is not the t.   223a
conceive a t. so sad   475a
dejected t. of fortune   343b
doeth the t. wh. is right   482a
draw the T. as he sees It   236b
each t. that in season grows   344b
every blessed t. you hold   163b
excels each mortal t.   372b
fond t. vainly invented   491b
gentle t. like me   475a
good and joyful a t. it is   490a
good t. come out of Nazareth?   510b
handsome wee t.   62a
has this t. appeared again   329b
I am the t. I was   381a
I know a t. or two   166b
ill-favoured t., sir   328a
in his hand..T. became a trumpet   470b
I said the t. wh. was not   418a
I wove the t. to a random rhyme   130b
joyful and pleasant t.   490b
laugh at any mortal t.   71a
learning, what a t. it is   366b
lo'esome wee t.   62a
lose a t...none but fools wd. keep   351b
lovely and a fearful t.   70b
many a t. I sought   387b
miss the many-splendoured t.   442a
most unattractive old t.   165a
motion like a living t.   469a
no new t. under the sun   499a
palsy-stricken, churchyard t.   221b
play's the t.   333a
prize the t. ungained   368b
same t. at the end   44b
seeks a little t. to do   47a
she seemed a t. that cd. not feel   463a
sole unquiet t.   101a
such a t. as I myself   337b
such a t. as thou   359b
sweetest t. that ever grew   467b
that extremely lovely t.   163a
that t. that ends all   325a
the t. that hath been..shall be   499a
t. begot within a pair of minutes   238b
t. devised by the enemy   385a
t. imagination boggles at   75b
t. immortal as itself   331a
t. that she despises   104a
this t. is of God   422a
this t. was not done in a corner   513a
thou art the t. itself   343a
throw away the dearest t. he owed   346b
very t. he'll set you to   30a
we have so much of the t.   9a
what a little t. to remember   4a
what is that t. called Light   95a
what t. dost thou now   422a
what t. of sea or land?   277b
what t. upon his back had got   108b
winsome wee t.   62a
with a great t. to pursue   47a
Things: aggregate of little t.   283a
all good t. are ours   50b
all other t. give place   160b
all other t., to their destruction   132a
all t. are full of labour   499a
all t. are taken from us   433a
all t. change them to the contrary   366a
all t. come to an end   489a
all t. else about   470b
all t. necessary to salvation   491a
all t. show it   160a

Things (*cont.*)
all t. that we ordained   366a
all t. thou wdst. praise   119b
all t. to all men   514a, 524b
all t. uncomely and broken   475b
all t. visible and invisible   480a
all t. were made by him   510b
all t. work together for good   513b
art all t. under Heaven   276b
as rare t. will, it vanished   49a
as t. have been they remain   96b
beauteous forms of t.   471b
brave translunary t.   137a
but for the virtuous t.   91b
cannot but remember such t. were   350a
cannot do the t. that ye wd.   515b
can such t. be   349a
cared for none of those t.   512b
cognisance of men and t.   47b
contemneth small t.   520b
credit t. that do presage   341a
dead selves to higher t.   429b
did the t. play..thro' their wings?   441b
do the t. I ought   425a
dreaming on t. to come   388b
end of all t. is at hand   517b
fair and flagrant t.   114b
feud 'twixt t. and me   36a
fine t. to be seen   93a
foolish t. of the world   514a
forgetting those t. wh. are behind   516a
former t. are passed away   519b
forms of t. unknown   357b
fulfilled of unspeakable t.   423b
full of a number of t.   414a
giver of all good t.   479b
God's sons are t.   256b
good t. will strive to dwell   367b
great ugly t.   20a
how can these t. be   510b
I find..t. very much as 'ow   86b
I look at all t. as they are   439b
I make all t. new   519b
into the life of t.   472a
I speak of the t. wh. I have made   484b
I will do such t.   342b
left undone those t.   478a
let all t. be done decently   514b
let determined t. to destiny hold   323b
lose not the t. eternal   479b
main chance of t.   380b
make possible t. not so held   373a
mass of t. to come at large   368b
mind not high t.   513b
more t. are shewed unto thee   520a
more t. are wrought by prayer   429a
more t. in heaven and earth   331b
my friend, the t. that do attain   416a
mystical better t.   171b
nor t. diurnal   422a
nor t. present, nor t. to come   513b
nothing brings me all t.   368a
O all ye Green T.   478a
on all t. all day long   429a
on t. above, not on t. on the earth   516a
paid them the t. I never took   486b
paltry, foolish, painted t.   137a
people don't do such t.   567a
purpose of the t. themselves   338a
put away childish t.   514b
right judgment in all t.   479b
sad vicissitudes of t.   162b
secret t. belong unto the Lord   494b
see the good t. there   192b
seekest thou great t.   503b
sense and outward t.   466b
shape of t. to come   455b
show..the t. that are not   341b
substance of t. hoped for   517a
such good t. as pass man's   479b
take upon's the mystery of t.   344a
teach thee terrible t.   484b
these t. shall be!   424a
these t. shall be added   505b
t...altered in the building trade   236a
t. and actions are what they are   64b
t. are beyond all use   339a
t. are in the saddle   146b
t. are not what they seem   247b
t. are seldom what they seem   166a
t. are the sons of heaven   212b

Things (*cont.*)
t. at home are crossways   80a
t. bad begun   349a
t. beyond our care   141a
t. forever speaking   464a
t. like that, you know, must be   406a
t. more true and deep   398a
t. noted in thy book   485b
t. outward do draw the inward   324a
t. past redress   375a
t. people make fools of themselves   390a
t. rank and gross in nature   330a
t. standing thus unknown   337a
t. that are more excellent   452b
t. that didn't occur   156a
t. that love night   342b
t. that make the greatest stir   156a
t. that they shall do   432a
t. they ought to do   479b
t. unattempted yet in prose   270b
t. whereof our conscience..afraid   478a
t. wh. are requisite and necessary   478a
t. wh. are written in this book   520b
t., wh. for our unworthiness   480b
t. wh. I have seen   466a
t. without all remedy   348b
t. won are done   368b
t. worthy of stripes   509b
those t. wh. elemented it   134a
thousand slimy t.   99a
through t. temporal   479b
to bring in fine t.   53b
unhappy, far-off t.   471a
unto the pure all t. are pure   516b
very excellent t. are spoken   487a
weak t. of the world   514a
were such t. here as we do speak   346a
whatsoever t. are true   516a
what t...at the Mermaid   22b
what t. were gain to me   516a
when t. were as fine   67b
whoso doeth these t.   482b
wh. t. are an allegory   515b
with enduring t.   469a
worse than senseless t.   337b
yet possessing all t.   515a
you are idle shallow t.   371b
Think: all that we ask or t.   515b
always talk, who never t.   306a
an' no t. lang   62b
as my poor heart doth t.   251b
because I t. him so   372b
books t. for me   239a
but to t. is to be full of sorrow   220a
comedy to those that t.   449b
cd. t. for two minutes together   405a
do then, t. here before   133b
expect a soldier to t.   390a
haply I t. on thee   387b
'I am inclined to t.,' said I   136a
I cannot sit and t.   239a
I do not t. so differently   201b
I don't t.   127a
if they t., they fasten their hands   200a
if you can t...not make thoughts   230a
I sometimes t. that never blows   153a
I t. and t. on things impossible   141b
I t. that thou art just   362a
I t., therefore I am   540b
it is very nice to t.   413b
knew not what to t.   109b
learn to t. Imperially   87a
let me not t. on't   330a
man must t. o' things   231b
must not t. of thee   265a
now I t. it   410b
or t. on 't now   189a
pause and sadly t.   290a
she cd. not t.   114a
she that cd. t.   361a
stay and t. of nought   388a
teach him to t. for himself!   391b
[Tennyson] cd. not t. up to the
    height   94a
t. by fits and starts   200a
t. he never cd. recapture   47a
t., in this battered Caravanserai   152a
t. like other people   391b
t. no more, lad   199b
t. not God at all   277b
t. not, thou noble Roman   341a

Think (cont.)

t. of them that sleep	76b
t. on him that's far awa	59a
t. only this of me	40a
t. only what concerns thee	275b
t. on these things	516a
t. perhaps even less	45a
t. they of their brethren more	287a
t. thou and act	312b
t. what 'e 's been	234a
t. what I have done	348a
t. you mid all this mighty sum	464b
those who greatly t.	299a
'tis sweet to t...where'er we rove	281b
whate'er you t., good words..best	374b
when I wd. pray and t.	351b
who t. too little	138a
Thinker on this planet	148a
Thinkers: not always the justest t.	183b
Thinketh He made it	45b
Thinking: and then to t.!	183b
dignity of t. beings	213a
hardly seem worth t. of	474b
I'm a fool for t.	305a
it ain't t. about it	445b
much drinking, little t.	418a
plain living and high t.	467b
t., feeling, loving	463b
t. for myself at all	166a
t. makes it so	332a
t. of nothing at all	120b
t. of the days that are no more	436a
t. of the old 'un	122a
t. on fantastic summer's heat	374b
t. on my dearie	59a
t. on the frosty Caucasus	374b
t. on their sins	61a
t. too precisely on the event	335b
t...what a Rum Go everything is	455b
with too much t.	302a
Thinkings: solitary t.	217b
Thinks: he most lives who t. most	18a
he t. too much	338a
I know she t. o' me	232a
man t. meanly of himself	209b
never t. of me	527a
says little, t. less	150a
she t. not on what's said	189a
things on wh. the public t. long	213a
t. men honest that but seem	360b
whene'er she t. at all	94b
when he t., good easy man	385b
whether he t. too little	301a
Thinner on bottled beer	165b
Thinness: gold to airy t. beat	134a
Third: then he gave a t.	468b
the t. in yr. bosom	365b
with a shadowy t.	45b
with never a t.	45b
Thirst: I t.	511b
man can raise a t.	232a
neither t. any more	519a
t. after righteousness	505a
t. that from the soul doth rise	216a
t. to know and understand	452b
without provocation of t.	418a
Thirsted scooped..brimming stream	274a
Thirsteth: ho, every one that t.	503a
Thirty: at t. man suspects himself	477a
at t., the wit (reigns)	157a
t. days hath November	172a
t. days hath September	533a
wrong side of t.	418b
Thirty-three: nothing—except t.	70a
Thirty-five: to die at	9a
This: that it shd. come to t.!	330a
t. royal throne of kings	375a
t. was a man	341b
Thisbe: death of Pyramus and T.	356a
T. fearfully o'ertrip the dew	355a
Thistle: a T. across my way	29b
find the stubborn t. bursting	435a
Thistles: docks, rough t.	383b
gather..figs of t.?	505b
t. stretch their prickly arms	114a
Thither: if thou canst get but t.	448a
Thomas: John's ideal T.	194a
pop Sir T. again in the pond	20a
ta'en true T. up behind	528a
the real T.	194a
T., because thou hast seen me	511b

Thomas (cont.)

T., here's my best respects	235a
T.' ideal T.	194a
true T. he pu'd off his cap	528a
true T. lay on Huntlie	528a
true T. on earth was never seen	528b
Thoreau: quote T.'s example	135b
Thorn: breast against a t.	20b, 196a
Elder, Elm, and T.	119b
figs grew upon t.	92a
from off this t. with me	383b
given to me a t. in the flesh	515b
gnarled and writhen t.	235a
instead of the t...the fir tree	503a
kissed beside the t.	37b
left the t. wi' me	63b
ne'er the rose without the t.	191a
no harvest but a t.	188a
Oak, and Ash, and T.	236a
peeps beneath the t.	169a
plant this t., this canker	377a
slug-abed snail upon the t.	441b
then was the t., without..rose-bud	191a
t. thy brow to braid	319a
withering on the virgin t.	356a
Thornburgh: Mrs. T.	451b
Thorn-crowned Man	7a
Thorns: brow of labour..crown of t.	53a
crackling of t. under a pot	499a
fall upon the t. of life!	396b
gather grapes of t.	505b
land of sand and t.	428a
no t. go as deep	421a
once was crowned with t.	224a
pots be made hot with t.	485b
set with little wilful t.	435b
t. that in her bosom lodge	331b
Thoroughfare for all thoughts	223b
Thou: for t. art with me	483a
I am t.	422a
not only t., but also all that hear	513a
t. also	552a
t. art t.	422a
T. beside me singing	152b
t. for whom e'en Jove wd. swear	345a
T.! if t. wast He	47a
t., Lord, and I	119b
t.'s for ever!	62b
t. that hearest the prayer	485b
t. to me art all things	276b
T. wast up by break of day	187a
'tis t. must bring her hame	529b
Thought: any unproportioned t.	330b
armour is his honest t.	473a
a Roman t. hath struck him	322b
as in uffish t. he stood	83b
as silent t. can bring	471a
as swift as t.	345a
best that is known and t.	9a
better than I t.	458a
bound of human t.	438b
built beyond mortal t.	392b
but he t. another	89b
change..in the..modes of t.	265b
chaos of t. and passion	301a
charm, by t. supplied	472a
does not seem a moment's t.	474a
eager t. warbling his Doric lay	270a
elevation of our t.	464b
end of man..action and not a t.	81b
ere T. cd. wed itself	430a
eternity..dreadful t.!	1b
Eternity of t.	465b
even with a t. the rack dislimns	324b
every third t. shall be my grave	368a
evil is wrought by want of t.	196a
exhausting t., and hiving wisdom	68b
Experience is the child of T.	130a
flowers of thy t.	422b
green t. in a green shade	260b
haunt t.'s wildernesses	397a
her body t.	133b
he t. he saw	85b
he t. I t. he t. I slept	293b
hit on the same t.	400a
holy and good t.	521b
human t. or form	394b
in a general honest t.	341b
indolent vacuity of t.	112b
in loftiness of t.	141a
in the light of t.	398a

Thought (cont.)

I shun the t.	265a
I sleep out the t.	373a
I t. so once	160a
Jesu, the very t. of Thee	86b
keep ye t. of us	36a
knows not from her t.	313a
language is..the body, of t.	81b
language is the dress of t.	213a
lean upon the t.	5b
lived with no other t.	297b
love, and t., and joy	471a
magnanimity of t.	477a
man of yearning t. and aspiration	313a
man's t...keeps the roadway	380a
more strong than all poetic t.	430a
my t. whose murder yet is but fantastical	346b
never cd. divine his real t.	70b
nought is worth a t.	305a
oft was t. but ne'er..expressed	300a
O, if I t. that, I'd beat him	370b
one t. of thee puts all the pomp	299b
one t., one grace, one wonder	259b
perish the t.	95b
pleased his childish t.	465a
plunged in t. again	7a
possesses or possessed a t.	68a
question with my jealous t.	388a
reach on with thy t.	312b
rear the tender t.	443b
sessions of sweet silent t.	387b
sight or t. be formed	276a
some hollow t.	469a
some monster in his t.	361b
some sudden t.	244a
speech created t.	397a
splendour of a sudden t.	46a
steadfast of t.	402b
stood awhile in t.	83b
strange seas of t.	469b
sudden t. strikes me	79a
swift as t. in every power	345a
take no t. for the morrow	505b
teach high t.	428a
tease us out of t.	219b
tell of saddest t.	398b
the dome of T.	68a
the pale cast of t.	333a
thing they call a t.	300a
thinking to have common t.	302a
this I have t. that another man t.	235a
t. again, but knew not what	109b
t.-executing fires	342b
t. is free	367b
T. is the child of Action	130a
T. leapt out to wed with T.	430a
t. of grief refuse	37a
t. of our past years	466b
t...secreted by the brain	80a
t.'s the slave of life	379a
t. upon thee when I was waking?	485b
t. wh. saddens while it scothes	50a
t. wd. destroy their paradise	175a
thou wert a beautiful t.	69a
to believe yr. own t.	147b
to have loved..t...done	5b
to let one's t. wander	476a
two souls with but a single t.	568b
untouched by solemn t.	467a
vain or shallow t.	147a
wad ye tak a t.	59a
wh. of you by taking t.	505b
whistled..for want of t.	140a
white celestial t.	448a
wish was father..to that t.	381a
working-house of t.	383b
ye t.? ye are not paid to think	232a
Thoughts: absent t. o' ither	63a
adieu—my morning t.	105b
all his t. perish	490b
all his t. will perish	18a
all stray t., fancies fugitive	51b
all t., all passions	101b
apt t. of men	341b
as thy t. in me	437a
busy t. outnumber	396a
cursed t...nature gives way to	347b
dark soul and foul t.	267a
did their silly t. so busy keep	270b
drawn from t. more far	43b

Thoughts (*cont.*)

drive my dead t.	396b
even so my bloody t.	362b
familiar to my slaughterous t.	350b
feed on t., that voluntary move	273a
feed with lofty t.	472a
feeling of their masters' t.	259b
give thy t. no tongue	330b
gor'd mine own t.	389a
high-erected t.	401b
holds her little t. in sight	265a
how many t. there be	24a
I do begin to have bloody t.	367b
in t. more elevate	272b
in t., not breaths	18a
joy of elevated t.	472a
lift the t. of man	220b
mood when pleasant t. bring sad t.	471a
my sad t. doth cheer	448a
my t. are not yr.	503a
my wanton t. enticed	285a
not make t. yr. aim	230a
of all the t. of God	44a
on hospitable t. intent	275a
only to conceal their t.	566a
our t. as boundless	69b
pansies, that's for t.	335b
please yr. t. in feeding them	324b
ripe t. in my brain	388b
second and sober t.	185b
sensations rather than of t.!	222a
some strange t. transcend	448b
soothing t. that spring	467a
so thy t., when thou art gone	399b
spirits that tend on mortal t.!	346b
stal'd are my t.	176b
such stuff in my t.	332b
suspect the t. of others	353a
suspicions amongst t.	15b
sweet t. in a dream	394b
than I have t. to put them in	333b
these t. may startle well	267a
thou understandest my t.	490a
t. beyond . . reaches of our souls	331a
t. by England given	40a
t. . . come crowding in so fast	142a
t. control that o'er thee swell	288b
t. go blowing through them	40a
t. half linger, half run before	423a
t. of men accurst	380a
t. of men are widened	432b
t. of youth are long, long t.	247b
t. rule the world	148b
t. that arise in me	425b
t., that breathe	175a
t. that do lie too deep for tears	467a
t. that wander thro' eternity	272b
t. to memory dear	319a
t. wh. may assault . . the soul	479b
t. which were not their t.	68b
t. whose very sweetness yieldeth	467b
throng of t. and forms	397b
trouble . . with any such t. yet	382a
undying t. I bear	265a
wayward t. will slide	471a
where branched t., new grown	220b
whose t. are legible in the eye	313b
with wh. t. the day rose	225a
yet in these t. myself . . despising	387b

Thousand: draw for a t. pounds

	2b
little one shall become a t.	503a
make that t. up a million	190a
mind has a t. eyes	34a
night has a t. eyes	34a
one among a t.	497a
one man among a t.	499b
one man in a t.	235a
one man picked out of ten t.	332a
one ten t. of those men	383a
one t. shall flee at the rebuke	502a
ten t. at thy right hand	487b
ten t. times ten t.	3b
t. fragrant posies	259a
t. scattered into Clay	152b
t. shall fall beside thee	487b
who has a t. friends	148b

Thousands: from the t. He hath freed

	87a
makes countless t. mourn!	61b
Saul hath slain his t.	495b
t. counted every groan	6a

Thousands (*cont.*)

t. equally were meant	419a
t. of gold and silver	489a
t. of years, if all were told	474b
to murder t. . . a specious name	477a
Thousandth Man will stand by	235a
Thracian: for the T. ships	420a
the T. sea	422b
Thraldom: single t., or a double strife	17a
Thrall: hath thee in t.	219a
t. to the fair hair	239a
you were t. to sorrow	423a
Thrasonical: Cæsar's t. brag	327b
Thread: at once, with a double t.	196a
feels at each t.	300b
hangs like a blue t.	312a
hinders needle and t.	196b
plying her needle and t.	196a
silk t. plucks it back again	365b
spun my last t.	132a
this line of scarlet t.	494b
t. of his verbosity	304b, 345a
t. of human life	319b
weave their t. with bones	371a
Threaded together on Time's string	187a
Threadneedle Street: Old Lady of T.	167a
Threat: whiles I t. he lives	347b
Threats: no terrors, Cassius, in yr. t.	340b
Threatened: Englishman, being . . t., a lion	87a
t. its life with a railway-share	86a
Three: Church clock at ten to t.	40a
forth went the dauntless T.	253a
God is T., and God is One	288b
kingdoms are less by t.	424a
not t. of my hundred . . left alive	379a
Rule of T. doth puzzle me	533a
the T. in One, the One in T.	233b
this night she'll hae but t.	530a
tho' he was only t.	266b
t. blind mice	533a
t. gentlemen at once	400b
t. hundred grant but t.	70b
t. is company	460a
t. may keep a secret	157a
t. merry boys	23a
t. o'clock in the morning courage	444a
when shall we t. meet again	345b
woodspurge has a cup of t.	313a
Three-and-thirty: dragged to t.	70a
Threefold cord	499a
Threescore: attain to write t.	132a
Thresh of the deep-sea rain	231b
Threshold: across my t.	293a
by the happy t.	437a
goest over the t. thereof	157b
starry t. of Jove's Court	266b
Threw them back again	526a
Thrice: t. came on in fury	253b
t. hadde she been at Jerusalem	88b
t. he routed all his foes	139a
Thrift: due, respective to	293a
large example of wise t.	249b
my well-won t.	353a
t., t. Horatio!	330a
Thrifty: housewife that's t.	400b
Thrill: glory's t. is o'er	281a
Thrive: he that wd. t. swaggering cd. I never t.	532b 372a
Thriven: he that hath t.	532b
Throat: 'Amen' stuck in my t.	347b
and an undulating t.	26b
brazen t. of war	276a
down the t. of Old Time	123b
each t. was parched	98b
feel the fog in my t.	50b
felt you round my t.	197a
his t. they cut from ear to ear	454a
I took by the t.	364a
scuttled ship or cut a t.	70b
speak they thro' their t.	489a
three times her little t. around	50a
t. is an open sepulchre	482a
t. is shut and dried	234b
winding-sheet . . high as her t.	319a
with shriller t. shall sing	249b
yet straining his t.	169b
Throats: cut each other's t., for pay	169a

Throats (*cont.*)

cutting foreign t.	364b
mortal engines, whose rude t.	362a
serpents with soft stretching t.	421b
their patriot t.	213b
Throb and mutual sob	77b
Throbbings: restless t. and burnings	171b
t. of noontide	179b
Throe: a t. of the heart	37a
dare, never grudge the t.!	50b
Throne: a doubtful t. is ice	427b
angels . . fell before . . t.	519a
around the Saviour's t. rejoice	184a
around the t. of God a band	286a
barge . . like a burnish'd t.	323a
before the t. . . a sea of glass	518b
beneath the shadow of Thy T.	453a
cradle and His t.	224a
fierce light wh. beats upon a t.	427b
Gehenna or up to the T.	236b
guiding the fiery-wheeled t.	268a
here is my t., bid kings come	374a
high on a t. of royal state	272a
honour'd for his burning t.	352b
in mercy . . the t. be established	502a
in the midst of the t.	518b
loafing around The T.	183a
love's t. was not with these	311b
Mahmud on his golden T.	152b
nearer the great white t.	86a
on a t. of rocks	73a
Persian on his t.	74a
rainbow round about the t.	518b
river . . proceeding out of the t.	520a
royal t. of kings	375a
sable T. behold of Night	299a
saw a great white t.	519b
seek such t. as this	314a
sits lightly in his t.	366a
something behind the t. greater	297a
the living t., the sapphire-blaze	175a
thou from a t. mounted	438a
t. he sits on	382b
t. of bayonets	203a
T. sent word to a T.	233a
upon a t., high and lifted up	501b
wade thro' slaughter to a t.	174b
when we owed the T.	47a
without fault before the t.	519a
Throned on ocean's wave	393b
Thrones: rose from their t.	392b
T., Dominations, Princedoms	275a
Throng: all the martyr t.	286a
leaving the tumultuous t.	466a
plaudits of the t.	247b
Throstle: blithe the t. sings	471b
t. with his note so true	357a
Throstlecock: ousel and the t.	137a
Throstles: the t. too	426b
Through: after his getting t. it!	195a
do *you* read books t.?	208a
Throve: that on wh. it t. falls off	431b
Throw: he said, T. her down	496b
now t. me again	329a
t. away Thy rod	188a
t. away Thy wrath	188a
t. yr. wedded lady from you?	329a
Thrush: an aged t., frail	179a
heigh! the t. and the jay	373a
rarely pipes the mounted t.	430b
that's the wise t.	47a
Thrust-block: sweatin' t.	232a
Thrusts the thing . . prayed for	43a
Thucydides: T. at Boston	449b
[T. or Xenophon] maintained	33b
Times . . more useful . . than . . T.	97a
Times . . works of T.	97a
Thug and the Druse	92b
Thule: farthest T.	557b
Thumb: bite yr. t. at us	364b
he put in his t.	532a
'twixt his finger and his t.	376b
Thumbs: pricking of my t.	349b
t. are rough and tarred	231a
Thumbscrew and the stake	437b
Thummim: Urim and the T.	494a
Thumped him on the head	85b
Thumps: proves by t. upon yr. back	108a
Thunder: all-dreaded t.-stone	329a
as I pass in t.	393a
at the voice of thy t.	488a

hunder (cont.)
bid the t.-bearer shoot 342b
came a burst of t. sound 184b
cavern under is fettered the t. 393a
dawn comes up like t. 232a
deep t. peal on peal 68b
felt like the t.'s roll 6b
from the moan of t. 392b
glorious the t.'s roar 403a
God made the t...lightning made
  itself 255a
he was as rattling t. 325a
hills with t. riven 77a
hinges grate harsh t. 273a
let the legions t. past 7a
loud roared the dreadful t. 90b
sleep in spite of t. 349b
sound like t.—everlastingly 467a
steal my t. 120a
such sweet t. 357a
symmetry be as of t. 314a
thou, all-shaking t. 342b
t. and the sunshine 439a
t. in the room 127b
t., lightning or in rain 345b
t. of the captains 497b
t. of the Odyssey 242a
t. to t. 137a
to sleep with the t. 446b
what serve for the t.? 364a
thunderbolt: a harmless t. 552b
like a t. he fall 426b
thunderbolts: gods, with all yr. t. 341a
oak-cleaving t. 342b
hundered: volleyed and t. 426a
hunderer's scowl 202b
hunders: Jehovah of the T. 230a
t. in the index 335a
t. of white silence 43b
hunderstorm: streams like the t. 69a
hunderstruck: I stood like one t. 118b
hurlow: remember T.'s answer 404b
T. is a fine fellow 211a
wise as T. looked 156b
hursday: they that wash on T. 532b
T.'s child has far to go 525a
took ill on T. 532b
'twas on a Holy T. 32b
hus: I refute it t. 207b
that we are t., or t. 360b
t. from childhood's hour! 75b
t. have I had thee 388b
t. thou must do 346b
to be t. is nothing 348b
why is this t.? 451b
husness: reason for this t. 451b
hwackum was for doing justice 151b
hyatira: in the city of T. 512b
hy-doxy: Heterodoxy or T. 80b
hyme: among the springing t. 199a
sweet t. true 23b
wild t. blows 356b
hyrsis: T. of his own will went
  away 8b
T., still our Tree is there 9a
hyself: and I—and I—t. 312b
be so true to t. 15b
I am t.—what hast thou done 312b
I no more shd. see t. 312a
many to save with t. 7b
nor thee from t. 312a
read to t. alone 37b
resolve to t. 8b
seekest thou great things for t. 503b
thou continuest such, owe to t. 275a
thou t. to all eternity 312b
t. how wondrous then! 275a
t. thou gav'st, thine own worth 388b
T. with shining Foot shall pass 154a
Tiber: O, T.! father T.! 253b
Rome in T. melt 322a
T. trembled underneath 337b
Tiberius: had T. been a cat 7b
so T. might have sat 7b
the Coin, T. 130b
Tibur is beautiful too 96a
Tickle: if you t. us 354a
I'll t. yr. catastrophe 380a
Tickled: trouts are t. best 66b
Tickling: t. a parson's nose 364b
trout that must be caught with t. 371a

Tiddle-taddle nor pibble-pabble 382b
Tide: all this tinkling t. 475a
at the turning o' the t. 381b
but came the t. 408a
but such a t. as moving 426a
call of the running t. 262a
face upwards on the oily t. 202b
going out with the t. 122b
grey wing upon every t. 474b
I am drifting with the t. 531a
lackeying the varying t. 322b
lived in the t. of times 339b
not this t. 232b
people..born..t.'s..in 122b
people..die..t.'s..out 122b
side by side in the ebbing t. 404a
tether time nor t. 63a
t. in the affairs of men 341a
t. in the affairs of women 71a
t. of human existence 208b
under the whelming t. 270a
upon the swell at full of t. 323a
western t. crept up 226b
written what no t...wash away 241b
Tidings: dismal t. when he frown'd 168b
glad t. of great joy 424b
good t. of good 502b
let ill t. tell themselves 323b
O t. of comfort 523a
Tideless: earth, t. and inert 18a
t. dolorous midland sea 424a
Tides: impelled of invisible t. 423b
salt t. seawards flow 5b
Tidy Pachyderm 237a
Tie: the silken t. 317a
Tied and bound with..our sins 479a
Tiger: a ride on a t. 527a
find a T. well repay 25b
imitate the action of the t. 382a
on the face of the t. 527a
t.'s heart wrapped in a player's 176b
t. that hadn't got a Christian 535b
T., T., burning bright 31b, 32a
T. Tim, come tell me true 19b
Tiger-moth's deep..wings 221b
Tigers: inexorable..than empty t. 366a
tamed and shabby t. 192a
t. of wrath are wiser 31a
Tights: she played it in t. 24b
Tile: where did you get that t.? 310a
Tiles: as many devils..as there are t. 569a
Tills: knows he who t. 146b
Tillyvally, lady 370b
Tim: Tiny T. 121b
Timber: navy nothing but rotten t. 56a
Timbrel: sound the loud t. 282b
Timbrels: playing on the t. 486b
Time: above the wrecks of T. 244a
against that t. when 387b
a good t. coming 256a
a gude t. coming 320a
all of the olden t. 524b
ancient nobility..act of t. 15a
and T. is fleeting 248a
and to the end of t. 206a
a t., and times, and half a t. 519a
a weary t.! a weary t.! 98b
backward and abysm of t. 367a
balance of proud t. 176a
bald cheater, T. 215b
bald sexton, T. 374a
bank and shoal of t. 347a
been so long t. with you 511a
before her t. she died 432b
be not coy, but use yr. t. 190b
bid t. return 375a
books of all t. 314a
bounds of place and t. 175a
bourne of T. and Place 426a
breaks t., as dancers 78b
breast of the River of T. 6a
by T.'s devouring hand 35a
by T.'s slow finger 18b
child of silence and slow t. 219b
chinks that t. has made 449a
choose thine own t. 19a
conspiracy his t. doth take 367b
cormorant devouring T. 344a
corridors of T. 247a
count t. by heart-throbs 18a
creeping hours of t. 326b

Time (cont.)
curtsey..it saves t. 84a
dark hills of t. 33b
dear t.'s waste 387b
demand the t. of the day 376a
did those feet in ancient t. 31a
dismal terror was the t.! 384b
do not squander t. 157a
down the throat of Old T. 123b
dust on antique t. wd. lie 328a
'eard 'em markin' 234a
eighteenth century of T. 80b
envious and calumniating t. 369a
eternity is in love with..t. 31a
even such is t. 307b
events in the womb of t. 360b
figure for the t. of scorn 363a
fly, envious T. 278b
fool all the people all of the t. 245b
foremost captain of his t. 435a
foremost files of t. 432b
for loss of t. 108b
for t. y-lost 90a
foulest birth of t. 393b
friendship as had mastered T. 430b
from this t. forth for evermore 489b
'gainst the tooth of t. 352a
give peace in our t. 478a
grand Instructor, T. 58a
great gap of t. 323a
half as old as T. 55a, 310a
hardest t. of all 134b
harmless folly of the t. 189a
hatched to the woeful t. 348a
he said, 'What's t.?' 47a
he hath but a short t. 519a
his golden locks t. hath to silver 295b
his prison'd t. made me 36a
his youth 'gainst t. and age 295b
holy t. is quiet as a nun 467a
how long a t. lies in one..word 374b
how T. is slipping 153b
if the street were t. 145a
if you want to know the t. 309b
I have no precious t. 388a
in a t. out-worn 474b
in continuance of t. 478a
in His good t.! 49b
innovations..the births of t. 15b
in our t., Thy Grace may give us 228a
inseparable propriety of t. 13b
in such a t. as this 340b
in the afternoon of t. 415a
in the old t. before them 479a
in t. all haggard hawks 238a
in t. small wedges cleave 238a
in t. the flint is pierced 238a
in t. the savage bull 238a
I shall find t., Cassius 341b
it is some t. to go 534b
it is t. to be old 147a
it was the t. of roses 194b
it will last my t. 80a
keeping t., t., t. 298a
kingdoms..in a moment of t. 509a
last syllable of recorded t. 350b
leaves have their t. to fall 185a
[letter-writing] way of wasting t. 283b
little is t. while it is new! 530a
long result of T. 432a
long t. between drinks 524b
look into the seeds of t. 346a
love's not T.'s fool 389a
Love took up the glass of T. 432a
meanwhile, T. is flying 558a
mild and almost mythic t. 294a
mild Heaven t. ordains 278b
Miss Jenkyns beat t. 159a
mock the t. with fairest show 347b
my t. has been properly spent 425a
never the t. and the place 49a
night of t...surpasseth the day 42b
no proper t. of day 195a
nor this the only t. 37b
no t. to see, in broad daylight 118a
not of an age, but for all t.! 216a
now is the accepted t. 515a
now it is high t. to awake 514a
O aching t.! 218a
old T. is still a-flying 190a
old T. makes these decay 79a

Time (cont.)

old T. the clock-setter 374b
only fault's with t. 48b
only t. for grief! 196b
on the sands of t. 248a
O t. too swift 295b
panting T. toiled after him 213b
pluck till t. and times are done 476a
present horror from the t. 347b
procrastination is the thief of t. 477a
quaffing, and unthinking t. 141b
redeeming the t., because the days 515b
rich with the spoils of t. 174a
saltness of t. 379b
seen better faces in my t. 342a
seen the best of our t. 341b
series of new t. began 138b
shipwreck of t. 13a
short t. to stay, as you 189a
silent touches of t. 58a
sing of T. or Eternity 427a
so gracious is the t. 329b
some t., his good t. 49b
somewhere, beyond space and t. 39a
so shall T. be 312b
spared and blest by T. 69a
Speech is of T. 81b
speech is shallow as T. 80a
spirit of the t. 374a
stretch'd forefinger of all T. 436a
struggles with and conquers T. 241b
Sun-flower! weary of t. 32a
syllables jar with t. 216b
take a little t...Tattycoram 123a
take the present t. 327b
temple half as old as T. 310a
tether t. nor tide 63a
that old common arbitrator, T. 369b
that t. may cease 258b
that t. of year thou mayst in me 388a
the Bird of T. 152b
thee conversing I forget all t. 274a
the Gardener, T. 130b
then while t. serves 189a
the rags of t. 134a
there is a t. of life, Sir 212a
the T.-Machine 455b
the t. returns again 30b
the t. will come 129a
threaded together on T.'s string 187a
thro' that long t. 464b
T., a maniac scattering dust 430a
T. ambles withal 327a
t. and my intents are savage 366a
t. and nonsense scorning 53b
t. and order of yr. birth 36a
t. and patience will not dry 182a
t. and place are lost 273a
t. and the hour runs thro' 346b
t., and the ocean 452a
T. an endless song 475b
t...but five days elder 41b
T. but the impression deeper 61b
T. can but make her beauty 475a
t. did beckon to the flow'rs 187b
t. doth settle 198a
t. doth transfix the flourish 388a
t. draws near the birth of Christ 430a
T. driveth onward fast 433a
T...Fate..their Vintage prest 153a
t. for a little something 266b
t. for labour and thought 420b
t. for such a word 350b
t. goes, you say 131a
't. has come,' the Walrus said 84b
t. hath, my lord, a wallet 369a
t. hovers o'er, impatient 214a
t. I might have trod 459b
T. in hours, days, years 448b
t. is come round 341b
t. is like a fashionable host 369a
t. is lost wot is not..hunting 416b
t. is money 156b
t. is our tedious song 270b
t. is out of joint 331b
t. is the greatest innovator 15b
t. is the great physician 129b
T., like an ever-rolling stream 453b
T. makes ancient good uncouth 251a
T. may gnaw Tamtallan 62b
t. may restore us 6b

Time (cont.)

T., not Corydon hath conquer'd 8b
T., Occasion, Chance 397a
t. of life is short 379a
t. of the singing of birds 500a
t. of this mortal life 479a
T. plays the fiddle 131a
t. remembered is grief 420a
t. runs, the clock will strike 258b
T.'s eunuch 198a
T.'s fell hand defaced 388a
T.'s fleeting river 396a
t.'s flies 368a
t.'s furrows I behold 387a
t.'s glory is to calm 386b
t.'s great wilderness 282a
t. shall moult away 416a
T. shall reap 442b
T. shall throw a dart 42b
t.'s iron feet 280a
T.'s noblest offspring 28a
T.'s printless torrent 393b
t.'s wheel runs back 51a
T.'s wingèd chariot 260a
T.'s wrecks and scars 92b
T., that is o'er-kind 228a
t. that shall surely be 2b
t. that takes survey 379a
T., the avenger! 69a
t. the devourer of all things 551b
T. the reaper 442b
T. the Shadow 473a
t. to act them in 333b
t. to be born 499a
t. to win this game 136b
T. travels in divers places 327a
t. turns the old days 421a
T. was when Love and I 167a
t. we may comprehend 41b
t., when all the lights wax dim 190a
t. when meadow, grove and stream 466a
t. when thou mayest be found 483b
t. whereof the memory of man 28b, 245b
t., wh. antiquates antiquities 42b
t., wh. is the author of authors 13a
t. will doubt of Rome 71a
T. will run back 270b
t. with a gift of tears 420b
T. writes no wrinkle 69b
T., you old gypsy man 192b
t., you thief, who love to get 202a
'tis almost fairy t. 357b
'tis but the t. 339a
'tis t.; descend 373b
'tis t. to do 't 350a
to beguile the t., look like the t. 347a
to choose t. is to save t. 15b
too much t. in studies is sloth 16a
to remoter t. bequeath 394a
to t. thou growest 387a
turn backward, O T. 4a
unimaginable touch of t. 468a
very age and body of the t. 333b
Vintage rolling T. hath prest 153a
waiting t., my brothers 134b
wastes her t. and me 449a
what t., what circuit 49b
when T...amber locks to grey 137a
when t. is broke 376a
whips and scorns of t. 333a
whirligig of t. 372a
who, in t., knows whither 117a
with leaden foot t. creeps 204a
world enough, and t. 260a
wrinkled deep in t. 323a

Timely happy, timely wise 223b
Times: all t. when old are good 67b
coldness of the t. 431a
ever lived in the tide of t. 339b
former t. shake hands 65b
giddy-paced t. 370b
how many t. do I love thee 24a
if the t. do bear it 15a
my t. be in Thy hand 51a
nature of the t. deceased 380a
old t. were changed 316b
our t. are in his hand 50b
signs of the t. 507a
spacious t. of great Elizabeth 426b
stirring t. we live in 180a
sundry t. and in divers manners 517a

Times (cont.)

tea-cup t. 438
the good old t. 67
t. are changed with him 413
t. go by turns 407
T. has made many ministries 17
t. have been, that, when the brains 349
t. that try men's souls 291
T...useful..than..Thucydides 97
t. will not mend till the king 292
usage of those antique t. 408
wh. cunning t. put on 354
worst T...succeed the former 190
Time-Spirit..proof from miracles 10
Timon hath made his..mansion 368
Timotheus yield the prize 139
Tin: pocket full of t. 156
Tincture in the blood 118
Tine: my jewel it shd. t. 59
Tingle: ears..heareth it shall t. 495
Tingling: whoreson t. 379
Tinka-tinka-tink 234
Tinkle: grasped it for a t. 24
Tinkling with their feet 501
Tinklings lull the distant folds 174
Tinsel: flapt its t. wing 266
Tintinabulation that so musically 298
Tints that glow 74
Tip: schoolboy's t. 440
star within its nether t. 99
t. me the black spot 413
t. them Long Melford 34
Tippenny: wi' t., we fear nae evil 63a
Tipperary: long way to T. 461a
Tipple: fishes, that t. 249b
Tippled drink, more fine 219a
Tippling: taste for t. 163b
Tips with silver all these..tree tops 365a
Tip-tilted like the petal 427b
Tip-toe upon a little hill 218b
Tire: his duty to gaudy t. 115b
long before I t. 39b
t. of all creation 194a
Tired: dinner waits and we are t. 108b
hunt down a t. metaphor 71b
I am t. of tears and laughter 422a
life..process of getting t. 66b
man is t. of London..t. of life 209b
till t. he sleeps 301a
t. waves, vainly breaking 96b
t. with all these 388a
t. yet strong 265a
Tires: t. betimes that spurs too fast 374b
you in Grecian t. are painted 387b
Tiresias and Phineus 273a
Tiring-house: hawthorn-brake our t. 357a
Tirling at the window 266a
Tirra-lirra: lark, that t. chants 373a
't.' by the river 431b
'Tis done, but yesterday 73b
Tit: tell tale, t. 533a
Titan: thy glory, T. 397b
pale T.-woman 421a
pitiful-hearted T. 377b
the weary T. 6b
T. kiss a dish of butter 377b
Titania: there sleeps T. 356b
Titanic: alley T. 298b
served for that T. strife 6b
Tithe or toll in our dominions 374a
Tithe-pig's tail 364b
Tither: tane unto the t. did say 529b
Titian: nobody cares..about T. 314b
Title: courage prove my t. 325a
does he feel his t. 350a
farced t. running 'fore 382b
honery t. of T. K. 451a
like my t., for it is not mine 414b
read my t. clear 453b
t. from a better man 414b
whatever t. suit thee 58b
who gained no t. 302b
Titled: to feed the t. knave 63a
Titles: as due by many t. 133a
despite those t., power, and pelf 317a
have t. manifold 467a
high though his t. 317a
thy other t. thou hast given away 342a
t. are shadows 118b
what once had beauty, t. 299b
Titwillow: oh willow, t. 165a

Toad: contentment to that t. 233a
  I had rather be a t. 362a
  rose-water over a t. 205b
  t. beneath the harrow 233a
  t., ugly and venomous 325b
Toads: cistern for foul t. 363a
Toast: bring me some t. 535a
  chocolate, butter, and t. 4b
  let the t. pass 400b
  never had a piece of t. 294b
  now for the muffin and t. 167a
  refused to pledge my t. 306a
  t. of the parish 310b
  t. that pleased me most 120b
  to t. our wants 302a
Tobacco: devilish and damned t. 64b
  divine t. 409a
  for thy sake, T. 240a
  going to leave off t. 239b
  goose cooked by t.-juice 76a
  Jones, the t. jar! 76a
  no sweeter t...than the Three
    Castles 440a
  snuff, t., and sleep 122a
  that tawny weed t. 214b
  T., divine, rare 64a
Tobias: Henry and T. 230a
Toby: provide our little T. meat 407b
Tocher: lass wi' a t. 61a
Tocsin of the soul 71a
To-day: call t. his own 142a
  face the stern T. 306b
  if T. be sweet 153b
  I have lived t. 107a, 142a
  I'm to be married t. 163b
  lose..ground won t. 8a
  never do t. what you can put off 535a
  never jam t. 84b
  Rose kissed me t. 131a
  such a day to-morrow as t. 372b
  the day will be t. 37b
  t., all day, I rode 33b
  t., beneath the foeman's frown 136b
  t. he puts forth..leaves 385b
  t. thou shalt be with me 510a
  will not hang myself t. 91b
  wiser t. than he was yesterday 419a
Todger's cd. do it 123b
Toe: clerical, printless t. 39b
  gentleman from top to t. 71b
  light fantastic t. 268b
  taken him in t.! 195a
  with forward t. 263b
Toes: a Pobble's t. 243b
  t. are turned up to the daisies 19b
  warming her pretty little t. 535b
Together: all t. pray 100a
  been t. now for forty years 94a
  forth they went t. 286b
  let us remain t. still 394a
  Life! we've been long t. 18b
  never come t. again 118a
  rise or sink t. 437a
  three men hold t. 424a
  walk t. to the kirk 100a
  wherefore they were come t. 512b
Toil: double t. and trouble 349b
  forget his labour an' his t. 59b
  her men robust for t. 77b
  her strong t. of grace 325b
  his honour and his t. 439a
  horny-handed sons of t. 217a
  horny hands of t. 250a
  'mid t. and tribulation 415b
  mock the hope of t. 114a
  mock their useful t. 174a
  more sweet than t. 433a
  our love and t. 227b
  remark each anxious t. 213b
  sit, and view their t. 117a
  they t. not, neither..spin 505b
  they waste their t. 317a
  t., envy, want 213b
  t. in other men's extremes 238b
  who climbs with t. 24b
  why all this t. and trouble? 471b
  with much t. attain 96b
  yet with great t. 3b
Toiled: he had t. after it 239b
  rest forgot for wh. he t. 387a
  we have t. all the night 509a

Toiling: t.—rejoicing—sorrowing 249a
  t. upward in the night 247b
Toils: distinguished..but by t. 1b
  superior t. 1b
  their t. upbraid 260b
  t. much to earn 111b
Token: show some t. upon me 487a
Tokens: words..t...for conceits 13a
Tolbooth: resistance of the T.-gate 319b
Told: bade me fight had t. me so 149b
  best being plainly t. 385a
  drank as he was t. 192b
  half was not t. me 496a
  hath it not been t. you 502b
  he t. it not 430a
  if all were t. 474b
  I t. you so 72a
  love that never t. căn be 31b
  that was t. to me 235a
  t. me you had been to her 83b
  well, I t. you so 249a
  went and t. the sexton 195a
Toledo: blade, T. trusty 65a
Tolerable and not to be endured 358b
Tolerate: no longer t. the race 18a
Toll: bell to t. me back 220a
  birds sang..t. slowly 43b
  tithe or t. in our dominions 374a
  t. for the brave 111a
Tolled the one bell 199a
Tolls the evening chime 282b
Tom: have been T.'s food 343a
  little T. Tucker 534b
  said T.'s father 282a
  T. he was a piper's son 533a
  T.'s a-cold 343a
  T.'s no more..so no more of T. 71b
  T. the Second..like T. the first 140a
  T., T., the piper's son 532b
  T. was beat 532b
Tomata: Chops and T. Sauce 126b
Tomb: a more than royal t. 16b
  as toward the silent t. 463b
  come this side the t. 118a
  Fidele's grassy t. 102b
  fourfold t. 22a
  from the t. the voice of Nature 174b
  graces..blossom on the t. 113b
  icy silence of the t. 219a
  keeps empty in thy t. 225a
  longing for the t. 476a
  making their t. the womb 388b
  moniment, without a t. 215b
  of her breasts a t. 421a
  press no ponderous t. 73b
  sea was made his t. 21a
  soon the rending of the t. 20b
  stood upon Achilles' t. 71a
  t. by the sounding sea 297b
  world wd. smell like..a t. 395b
Tombs: hark! from the t. 453b
  like t. of pilgrims 313a
  rending t. rebound 127b
  t. of brass are spent 389a
  towers and t. and statues 154b
  upon our brazen t. 344a
Tombstone: fight is a t. white 233a
Tom Jones: than in all T. 208a
Tomlinson: stand up now, T. 235a
Tommy: an 'ealthy T. for a year 229a
  little T. Lin 534a
  T., 'ow's yer soul? 235b
  T. this, an' T. that 235b
Tomnoddy: my Lord T. 19b, 40b
Tom o' Bedlam 342a
To-morrow: altho' t. it seem..dream 36b
  boast not thyself of t. 498b
  eat and drink, for t. we die 515a
  I'll die for him t. 531b
  jam t. 84b
  lose t. the ground won to-day 8a
  not too late t. to be brave 4b
  pine at them beyond t. 220a
  reflection, you may come t. 394b
  so, till t. eve, my Own, adieu! 294a
  such a day t. as to-day 372b
  that may be t. 441a
  that shall be t. 53a
  think t. will repay 139b
  this, no t. hath 132a
  to be put back t. 409a

To-morrow (cont.)
  t., and t., creeps in 350b
  t. blossoms 385b
  t. do thy worst 142a
  t. is our wedding-day 108a
  t. is Saint Crispian 383a
  t. let my sun his beams 107a
  t. let us do or die 76b
  t.'ll be the happiest 434b
  t.'s falser than the former 139b
  t. speak what t. thinks 147b
  t.'s uprising to deeds 284b
  t. the last of many battles 324a
  t. to fresh woods 270a
  t. we'll be sober 522b
  T.!—Why, T. I may be 153a
  t. will be dying 190a
  unborn T. 153b
  will she kiss me t.? 131a
  you can put off till t. 535a
To-morrows: confident t. 464b
Tom Pearse, Tom Pearse 531b
Tom Thumb: thought about T. 211b
Tomtit: a little t. sang 165a
Tone: deep, autumnal t. 396b
  dwells in that mighty t.! 82b
  praises, with enthusiastic t. 164b
  t., and gesture bland 316b
  t. of languid Nature 111b
  t. of the company 90b
  with mellower t. 433a
Tones: smoothes her charming t. 275a
  t. are remembered not 395a
  t. ravishment 217b
Toning of a tear 189a
Tongs and the bones 357a
Tongue: all obliterated T. 153b
  bear welcome in..your t. 347a
  bridleth not his t. 517b
  Death..stopped his tuneful t. 302b
  done unto thee, thou false t. 489b
  every t. brings in a..tale 385a
  fellows of infinite t. 383b
  give thy thoughts no t. 330b
  had t. at will 360b
  hang upon thy t. 443b
  haud yr. t., my daughter 531b
  have fallen by the t. 520b
  heart thinks his t. speaks 358b
  her t. unbound 104a
  his t. dropt manna 272a
  his t. is the clapper 358b
  his t. to conceive 357b
  hold yr. t., and let me love 132a
  I held my t. 484a
  I must hold my t. 330a
  in their Mother T. 481a
  in the vulgar t. 480b
  iron t. of midnight 357b
  I spake with my t. 484a
  it have no t., will speak 333a
  lends the t. vows 331a
  let my t. cleave to..my mouth 490a
  let thy t. tang arguments 371b
  lisping, stammering t. 110a
  love's t. proves dainty Bacchus 345a
  my oracular t. 400b
  my t. is the pen 484b
  my t.'s use is to me 374b
  never ear, did heare that t. 313b
  nor t. to speak 244b
  our t. is known 201a
  rank t. blossom into speech 45b
  Roger's false flattering t. 239b
  rolls it under his t. 185b
  she had a t. with a tang 367b
  she has found her t. 215a
  silence is become his mother t. 170b
  smooth t. whose music 78b
  snakes with double t. 356b
  swete up-on his t. 88b
  that his t. must vent 328a
  their t. a sharp sword 485b
  the t. our trumpeter 328a
  tongue breaketh the bones 520b
  t. can no man tame 517b
  t. from evil speaking 481a
  t. in every wound 340b
  t. is the only edged tool 203b
  t. like a button-stick 227b
  t. shall be split 533a

Tongue (cont.)
t. of the dogs may be red | 486b
t. of him that makes it | 345b
t. sounds ever after as a..bell | 379b
t. so varied | 241a
t. to persuade | 203a
t., well that's a wery good thing | 126a
t., wh. is the birth, becomes..wit | 380b
treasure of our t. | 117a
understanding, but no t. | 330b
while I held my t. | 483b
whose strenuous t. can burst | 219b
wd. that my t. cd. utter | 425b
yr. t.'s sweet air | 356a
Tongues: airy t. that syllable | 267a
bestowed that time in the t. | 369b
conscience..a thousand several t. | 385a
done to death by slanderous t. | 359a
finds t. in trees | 325b
gracious message a host of t. | 323b
heads and t. a-talking | 199b
kindreds, and people, and t. | 519a
lovers' t. by night | 365b
neither evil t., rash judgments | 472a
'tis of aspics' t. | 362a
t. can poison truth | 100a
t. like as of fire | 512a
t. of men and of angels | 514b
t., they shall cease | 514b
to silence envious t. | 386a
walls have t. | 419b
wild t. that have not Thee | 233b
To-night: child again, just for t. | 4a
met in thee t. | 40a
to-morrow not t. | 53a
t. it doth inherit | 7b
t. so full of care | 35b
t. we'll merry be | 522b
Tony: in the oven for T. and me | 532a
Took: all wh. I t. from thee | 442a
'e went an' t. the same as me | 236b
t. her with a sigh | 31b
t. to free-thinking | 527a
ye t. me in | 508a
Tool: Man is a t.-making animal | 157a
Man is a t.-using animal | 81b
Tools: but to name his t. | 64b
few lend..their working t. | 446a
secrets are edged t. | 141a
t. of working out salvation | 66a
t. to him that can handle them | 80a
t. to work withal | 250a
without t. he is nothing | 81b
'Too-quick,' the chain | 435b
'Too-slow' will need the whip | 435b
Tooth: danger of her former t. | 348b
had alwey a coltes t. | 89b
keen and angry t. | 36a
Nature, red in t. and claw | 430b
pugging t. | 373a
sharper than a serpent's t. | 342a
t. for t. | 494a
Toothache: endure the t. patiently | 359a
I have the t. | 358b
I suffer t.'s ills | 163a
sigh for the t. | 358b
sleeps feels not the t. | 329a
Tooth-picks: supply of t. | 205b
Tooth-point: where each t. goes | 233a
Toots: Mr. T. | 122b
Top: couched on the bald t. | 470a
die at the t. | 419a
from the naked t. | 464a
gentleman from t. to toe | 71b
He, wh. is the t. of judgment | 351b
little bit off the t. | 285b
ruffian billows by the t. | 380a
sleep like a t. | 117b
sound as a t. | 160b
t. of every tree | 163b
t. of sovereignty | 218b, 349b
whips his taxed t. | 405a
Topaz: ninth, a t. | 520a
Toper: Lo! the poor t. | 113b
Tophet-flare | 227b
Topics: have but two t. | 209a
Top-mast: he strack the t. | 529a
Tops: spun like whipping t. | 192a
think their slender t. | 195a
t. cleaned with champagne | 416b
Topsawyer | 122a

Topses: boxes without t. | 280b
Topsy: 'never was born!' persisted T. | 415b
Topsy-turvey: studied men from my t. | 263b
Torch: a bright t. | 220b
hand on the t. of life | 550b
since the t. is out | 324b
t. is at thy temple door | 308a
t. that lighted mine | 146b
truth, like a t. | 178b
we throw the t. | 256a
Torchlight procession..throat | 291a
Torches: lighting our little t. | 97b
she doth teach the t. | 365a
Tories: stern and unbending T. | 254b
T. own no argument | 42b
Torment: measure of our t. | 229b
more..t. than a hermit's fast | 219a
no t. touch them | 520a
smoke of their t. | 519b
t. of the night's untruth | 117a
when to live is t. | 360b
Tormented with ten thousand hells | 258b
Torments: of all the t. | 450a
t...become our elements | 272b
t...laid to my charge | 91a
t. lie in..a wedding-ring | 95b
what t. of grief | 147a
Torn: Mary from my soul was t. | 61b
Torpedo: pen..becomes a t. to him | 206a
Torrent: amber t. descended | 96a
t. of a woman's will | 528a
Torrid: animated t.-zone | 146b
t. or the frozen zone | 79b
'Tortoise' is an insect | 535a
Torture: all length is t. | 324b
hum of human cities t. | 68b
pity those they t. not | 397a
t...amusing in itself | 157b
t. not again | 392b
t. of a lingering..passion | 149a
t. of the mind | 348b
t. one poor word | 141a
Tortures: gold, by t. tried | 299b
Tory: T. and Whig in turns | 405a
T. men and Whig measures | 129a
whether I were a Whig or a T. | 417b
what is called the T....party | 115b
Whig and T. a' agree | 402b
wise T...wise Whig..will agree | 210b
Toss: good enough to t. | 378b
I t. i' the air | 51a
may t. him to My breast | 188a
t. of the parish | 310b
Tossed: t. and gored several persons | 207b
t. on the wind ridden..sea | 119b
Toss-pots still had drunken heads | 372a
Total gules | 332b
Totter: t. into vogue | 449b
we maun t. down, John | 61a
Totters forth, wrapped in a..veil | 399b
Touch: by one satiric t. | 419a
far-off t. of greatness | 428b
fear not to t. the best | 307b
her t., might give th' alarm | 457a
I might t. that cheek | 365a
little t. of Harry | 382b
nations t. at their summits | 17b
Nelson t. | 287b
nothing, can t. him further | 348b
of Nelson only a t. | 49a
one t. of nature | 369a
puts it not unto the t. | 280b
soft t. invisible | 223b
t. divine, and the scaled eyeball | 52a
t. me not | 511b
t. not a single bough | 284a
t. not, taste not | 516a
t. of a vanish'd hand | 425b
t. of celestial temper | 274b
t. of cold philosophy | 219a
t. of earthly years | 463a
t., wh. renders..interesting | 320b
t. you, a passer-by | 307b
unimaginable t. of time | 468a
wants the natural t. | 350a
Touched: chord..is t. within us | 112b
t. nothing that he did not adorn | 209b
t. with an interior ray | 114b
Touches: Homocea t. the spot | 523b
such heavenly t. ne'er touch'd | 387a
t. of things common | 44a

Touches (cont.)
who t. this t. a man | 458b
Tough: interesting, but t. | 446b
rather a t. customer | 121a
t., ma'am, t., is J. B. T. | 122b
Toves: the slithy t. | 83b
Tow, row, row | 526a
Toward or untoward lot | 465b
Tower: Cæsar's ill-erected t. | 376a
Giotto's t. | 247a
ivy-mantled t. | 174a
maiden in a palace-t. | 398a
nail my head on yonder t. | 12b
neck is like the t. of David | 500b
nor stony t., nor walls | 338a
Roland to the dark t. came | 45b, 343a
stood like a t. | 272a
that t. of strength | 435a
[T. of London] as nigh heaven | 283a
watchman on the lonely t. [Pitt] | 317b
with a t. and bells | 113b
Towers: cloud-capped t. | 367b
elephants endorsed with t. | 277a
from her t. a ray | 307b
hammer'd from a hundred t. | 427a
no t. along the steep | 78a
sublime on the t. | 393a
tell the t. thereof | 485a
those bricky t. | 409b
topless t. of Ilium | 258b
t., and battlements it sees | 269a
t. and tombs and statues | 154b
t. of silence [clouds] | 119a
two t. of sail | 96b
whispering from her t. | 9a
with walls and t. | 101a
ye antique t. | 174b
ye t. of Julius | 173b
To-witta-woo: pu-we, t.! | 286a
Town: a tavern in the t. | 527a
Ayr, wham ne'er a t. surpasses | 62b
come after me to t. | 445a
down to the end of the t. | 266b
enormous thro' the Sacred T. | 26b
give every t. a limb | 12b
haunted t. to me! | 242a
in Scarlet t. | 531a
little t. of Bethlehem | 40a
man made the t. | 111b
my fate in a country t. | 304a
one-horse t. | 447a
pore Persoun of a t. | 88b
seaward from the t. | 202a
sent them out of t. | 532b
shriek from some captured t. | 136a
sounding thro' the t. | 530b
spreading of the hideous t. | 284a
tavernes wel in every t. | 88b
the country in t. | 551a
the lorn Syrian t. | 7a
they are for the t.'s end | 379a
t...lighter than vanity | 54a
t. of monks and bones | 100a
watching them out of the t. | 226b
what little t. by river or sea | 219b
what's this dull t. to me | 224b
Winkie runs thro' the t. | 266a
Town-crier spoke my lines | 333b
Townland: riding to the t. | 475a
Towns: elephants for want of t. | 419b
London, thou art of t. | 142b
seven wealthy t. contend | 321b
shires and t. from Airly | 225b
t...civic independence flings | 77b
Townshend: persuade Tommy T. | 169b
Toy: eternity to get a t. | 386b
foolish thing was but a t. | 372a
Toyed: might have t. and kist | 159a
Toys: all is but t. | 348a
meddle with my t. | 414a
then cast their t. away | 109a
t. and things to eat | 414a
Trace: misery still delights to t. | 107b
t. upon her face | 164b
Traces, of the smallest spider's web | 364b
Track: around the ancient t. | 263b
come flying on our t. | 443b
grassy t. to-day it is | 232b
t. the deep | 184b
tread again that ancient t. | 448a
Tract: left a little t. | 459b

Tract (cont.)
t. of inland ground 464b
Trade: accident is not my t. 465b
a losing t., I assure you 34a
every t. save censure 72a
except what t. can give 51b
half a t. and half an art 203a
his art, but not the t. 419b
in the t. of war..slain men 359b
in the way of t. 111a
no nation was ever ruined by t. 156b
not accidental, but a t. 352a
now there isn't any t. 186a
others..venture t. abroad 381b
poetry..in London..is a t. 141b
proselytes of one another's t. 66a
samphire, dreadful t. 343b
slighted shepherd's t. 269b
some way of common t. 375b
that t. in love 323b
the old t.'s plyin' 287b
this t. of mine 48b
t...with the living and the dead 142a
two of a t. 160b
war is the t. of kings 140b
what t., thou knave? 337a
Trader: some grave Tyrian t. 8a
Trades: best..t., to make songs 27a
ugliest of t...moments of pleasure 205b
Tradesman thou!..hope..to heaven 142b
Tradesmen: bow, ye t. 163b
Tradition: youth of America..is their
oldest t. 460b
Traditions: these legends and t. 248a
t. of civility 203a
Traffic: warn all t. and detain 232b
Traffickers: overpeer the petty t. 352b
t., the dark Iberians 8b
Tragedies: two t. in life 391a
Tragedy: Fate wrote her a..t. 24b
go litel myn t. 90b
gorgeous T. in sceptred pall 268a
greatest t...except a defeat 455a
out of it simply a t. 460b
play is the t., 'Man' 298a
that is their t. 460a
t. is the imitation of an action 559b
T. is the noblest Production 2a
t. to those that feel 449b
Tragical: very t. mirth 357b
Trail: long, long t. a-winding 225b
old t., our own t. 231b
pull out on the t. again! 231b
still on their t. 444a
t. of the Serpent 282a
t. that is always new 231b
Trails all about the written page 476b
Trail'st thou the puissant pike? 382b
Train: as we rush in the t. 443b
gems of Heav'n, her starry t. 274b
great Mother's t. divine 9a
his t. filled the temple 501b
left my glorious t. 448a
next t. has gone ten minutes 535b
pack and take a t. 39b
t. up a child 498b
t. up a fig-tree 122b
who follows in His t.? 184a
world and all her t. were hurl'd 448b
Train-band captain eke was he 108a
Traitor: but the t. hate 118b
of 'ifs'? Thou art a t. 385a
princes..hate the t. 116b
Traitors: he looked upon the t. 252b
is to hate t. and the treason love 140b
more strong than t.' arms 340a
our doubts are t. 351a
Tram: not a bus but a t. 527a
Trambeams: tender t. 197b
Trammel up the consequence 347a
Tramp: poor old t. explains 185b
t. of twenty-two men 34b
t.! t.! along the land they rode 319a
Trample: t. down abuses 566a
t. on their sovereign's head 375b
weed ye t. underfoot 229a
Trampled and mocked with many 391b
Tramplings of three conquests 42a
Trance: bold seër in a t. 432a
in mad t. strike 392b
no nightly t. 270b

Tranced: senseless, t. thing 219a
Trances: all my days are t. 298a
Tranquil: thine is the t. hour 464a
Tranquillity: after noise, t. 289a
despair and cold t. 392b
divine T. 433a
emotion recollected in t. 467b
feeling of inward t. 148b
I am restoring t. 55b
looking t. 69a
sinking down in its t. 467a
Transatlantic Liberty arose 76b
Transcend our wonted themes 448b
Transcendental: chatter of a t. kind 165a
t. moonshine 81a
Transfigured: her face, the thrice-t. 49a
Transfigures you and me 200b
Transgression: there is no t. 513a
t. of a law of nature 201a
Transgressions: wounded for our t. 503a
Transgressors: intercession for the t. 503a
numbered with the t. 503a
way of t. 498a
Transition: what seems so is t. 248a
Transitory: action is t. 463a
Translated: Bottom!..thou art t. 357a
Translation: he is T.'s thief 261b
may be a mistake in the t. 447b
not a t.—only taken 400a
Translations not unlike to be 200b
Translucent wave 268a
Translunary: brave t. things 137a
Transmigrates: elements once out..
it t. 323b
Transmitter of a foolish face 316a
Transmutes, bereaves 465a
Transported with the View, I'm lost 2a
Trap: mous caught in a t. 88b
Trappings and the suits of woe 330a
Trash: peasants their vile t. 341a
poor t. of Venice 361a
steals my purse steals t. 361b
Travail: if t. you sustain 177a
my great t. so gladly spent 473b
my labour for my t. 368b
that t. on the deep 117a
t. and heavy sorrow 420b
Travaileth: with his lips he t. 420b
Travel: all that t. by land 479a
discredited your t. 322b
ever thought the t. long 313b
goeth to school, and not to t. 15a
how I long to t. back 448a
in a moment t. hither 466b
I t. for t.'s sake 412b
lands I was to t. in 530a
not t. to see English men 411a
our deeds still t. with us 144a
portance in my t.'s history 360a
tho' we t. the world over 148a
to t. hopefully is..better 413b
t. down the years 63b
t. much faster than light 527a
t. forth without my cloak 387b
t., in the younger sort 15a
t. on life's common way 467b
wherever I t. I find it so 26b
Travelled: much have I t. 220b
t. among unknown men 467a
Traveller: 'anybody there?' said
the t. 119b
curious t. from Lima 449b
Farewell, Monsieur T. 327a
forget his fellow t. 527b
from whose bourn no t. returns 333a
I met a t. 396b
lost t.'s dream 30a
misled and lonely t. 267a
region round the t. lies 468a
some t. from New Zealand 254b
spurs the lated t. apace 349a
the Sentimental T. 411a
t. betwixt life and death 470b
t., by the faithful hound 247a
t. came by, silently 31b
t. from the cradle to the grave 397b
t.'s journey is done 32a
t. was to blame 305a
t. with empty pockets 549a
Travellers: inn where t. bait 205a
t. must be content 326a

Travelleth: come as one that t. 498a
Travelling: Captain is a good t. name 150a
t. abroad..t. at home 208a
t. is the ruin of all happiness! 58b
t. towards the grave 469a
worth the t. to 415a
Travels: contemplation of my t. 327a
hedgehog t. furtively 179a
he t. the fastest who t. alone 236b
too old to go again to my t. 87b
'T.'..excursions..in my own
mind 102b
Tray: good dog T. 192b
my poor dog T. 76b
T., Blanche and Sweetheart 343a
Trays: cheap tin t. 261b
Treachery: fear their subjects' t. 384b
killed with my own t. 337a
t.! seek it out 337a
Treacle: fly that sips t. 159b
Tread: beetle, that we t. upon 352a
close behind him t. 99b
Freedom hallows with her t. 74a
if onward ye will t. 287a
on my heart they t. now 375b
so airy a t. 434a
to t. on classic ground 1b
t. softly..you t. on my dreams 474b
t. thou in them boldly 286b
with an undaunted t. 414a
ye who t. the Narrow Way 227b
Treads on it daily..clouted shoon 267b
Treason: and the t. love 140b
bloody t. flourish'd 340a
condoned high t. 128b
[corporations] cannot commit t. 97b
gunpowder t. and plot 532a
in trust I have found t. 145a
kings may love t. 118b
moderation..is a sort of t. 58a
none dare call it t. 181b
Pension..state hireling for t. 213a
popular humanity is t. 1b
there was t. done 26a
they love the t. 116b
t. can but peep 335b
'T.' cried the Speaker 185b
T. doth never prosper 181b
t. has done his worst 348b
t. is but trusted like the fox 379a
t. is not own'd 141a
t. was no crime 138b
Treasons: fit for T., stratagems 355b
Treasure: as yr. chiefest t. 25b
delight or as our t. 187b
earthern vessel, holding t. 46a
he that has stoln the t. 104b
justice, counsel, and t. 15a
of his t. things new and old 507a
precious t., thou art mine 63b
purest t. mortal times afford 374b
rich the t.; sweet the pleasure 139a
she is yr. t. 366b
thou shalt have t. in heaven 507b
t. in earthen vessels 515a
t. of our tongue 117a
we t. beyond measure 163b
what trusty t. in the world 177a
where yr. t. is 505b
Treasurer: Flimnap, the T. 417b
Treasures: better than all t. 398b
lay not up..t. upon earth 505b
lay up..yourselves t. in heaven 505b
new t. still, of countless price 223b
than the t. in Egypt 517a
t. from an earthen pot 187a
t. up his bright designs 110a
Treasuries: sumless t. 381b
Treasury: T. is the spring of
business 17a
treble of the T. Bench 128a
Treat: all eager for the t. 84a
something..to t. my friends 257a
t. unmoneyed men 93b
who gives a child a t. 261b
you shd. t. me thus 150a
Treatise: at a dismal t. rouse 350b
former t. have I made 512a
Treaty: and a t. broken 26a
Trebisond: Marocco or T. 271b
Treble: towards childish t. 326b

Treble (cont.)
t. of the Treasury Bench 128a
Tree: Adam sat under the T. 228a
and on the t. of life..sat 273b
baby on the t. top 29a
bespangling herb and t. 189a
birds still hopping on the t. 413b
break the infant t. 48b
by the Eildon T. 528a
choose our t. 264a
dark t., still sad 72b
drop like the fruits of the t. 263a
fool sees not the same t. 31a
garden of Liberty's t. 77b
God can make a t. 225a
got me boughs off many a t. 187a
he that aims at a t. 186b
highly impossible t. 163a
if he finds that this t. 527b
incense-bearing t. 101a
in the wide waste there still is a t. 74a
I shall be like that t. 419a
it was a trustie t. 530a
laughing leaves of the t. divide 420b
little girl sat under a t. 198b
lone, sky-pointing t. 9a
Mahogany T. 440b
may be ay sticking in a t. 319b
middle t. and highest there 273b
more to my taste than a t. 283b
not growing like a t. 216b
Old Man in a t. 243a
on a t. by a river 165a
our T. yet crowns 9a
pledges of a fruitful t. 188b
poem lovely as a t. 225a
root of my t. 243a
she gave me of the t. 492b
sighing by a sycamore t. 363a
smell it on the t. 363b
some single herb or t. 260b
spare the beechen t. 76b
than he that means a t. 186b
that's why the t. 522b
there's a t., of many, one 466a
these things in a green t. 510a
three ravens sat on a t. 529b
till the t. die 329a
too happy, happy t. 221a
top of every t. 163b
t. did end their race 260b
t. is known by his fruit 506b
t. is living yet 195a
t. of life also 492a
t. of the knowledge of good 492a
t. planted by the water-side 481b
t. striking rock at the root 263a
t...wh. did not know the love 107a
t., whose..taste brought death 270b
t. will wither..before it fall 68b
Tumtum t. 83b
under the greenwood t. 326a
where the t. falleth 499b
wish I were a t. 187a
woodman, spare that t.! 284a
Treen chalices 205b
Trees: all the t. are brown 226a
all the t. are green 226a
all t. do close 260b
among the gusty t. 290a
axe laid..root of the t. 504b
beside the lake, beneath the t. 467a
birch, most shy..of t. 250b
brotherhood of venerable t. 463b
buried among t. 468a
Dryad of the t. 219b
fast as the Arabian t. 364a
filled the t. and flapped 192a
finds tongues in t. 325b
from a t.'s summit 220b
gloomy, friendly T. 445b
grottoes are shaded with t. 399b
hide in cooling t. 221a
high in tufted t. 269a
I see men as t. 508b
it 'whispers thro' the t.' 300a
lady by the t. 474b
leafless t. and every icy crag 466a
loveliest of t., the cherry 198b
music of its t. at dawn 7a
of all the t. in England 119b

Trees (cont.)
O look at the t. 37a
Orpheus drew t., stones 355a
rocks, and stones, and t. 463a
still climbing t. in the Hesperides 345a
tall ancestral t. 184b
t. and houses go wheeling 443b
t...are full of sap 488b
t. at spring do yield 446a
t. began to whisper 434b
t. did grow 20b
t. in whose dim shadow 253b
t. that are in the wood 526b
t. that are therein 490a
t. that grow so fair 236a
t. they are so high 531a
t. to speak 349a
t. upon 't, that nod 324a
t. wept odorous gums 274a
t., where you sit 302b
under the rugged t. 181b
vext garden-t. 8b
when lofty t. I see 387a
with his lute made t. 385b
you lover of t. 46a
Trelawny: shall T. die? 182b
Tremble: t. and despoil themselves 396b
t. lest a saying learnt 438b
t. like a guilty thing 466b
t., thou wretch 342b
Trembled: all who saw them t. 254a
all you t. at before 110b
Hell t. at the hideous name 273a
there is through his..air 179a
Tremblers: boding t. learn'd to trace 168b
Trembles: it t. to a lily 131a
Satan t., when he sees 110a
t., but it cannot pass away 396a
t. in the breast 280a
Trembling: t., hoping, lingering 299a
t...where I had stood 395a
with fear and t. 516a
Trembulation: I feels all over t. 417a
Trencher: dead Cæsar's t. 324a
valiant t.-man 358a
Trenches in thy beauty's field 387a
Trent: o'er the wide vale of T. 252b
why was Burton built on T.? 199b
Trespass: that t. against us 478a
Trespasses: forgive us our t. 478a
who were dead in t. 515b
Tress: threshed..at midnight by a t. 476a
Tresses: breathing t., meekest Eve 103a
fair t. man's imperial race 302b
knees and t. folded 263b
t. like the morn 267b
withered cheek and t. grey 316b
Trial: democracy is on t. 131b
t. by jury..a delusion 120a
t. of her strength 469a
Tribe: badge of all our t. 353a
his t. were..gentlemen 138b
Idols of the T. 16b
may his t. increase 201b
richer than all his t. 364a
thy t.'s black tents 441a
whole t. of fops 341b
Tribes: our supple t. 213b
t., the *Bores* and *Bored* 71b
Tribulation: came out of great t. 519a
companion in t. 518a
'mid toil and t. 415b
necessity, and t. 479a
ye shall have t. 511b
Tribunal: new t. now 51b
Tributaries: brooks are Thames's t. 8b
Tribute: not a cent for t. 181b
passing t. of a sigh 174b
t. to whom t. is due 513b
Trick: into the t. of singularity 371b
long t.'s over 262a
served such another t. 356a
t. of our English nation 379b
t. worth two of that 377a
when in doubt, win the t. 201a
wild t. of his ancestors 379a
yet it is our t. 336a
Trick'd in antique ruff 211b
Tricks: frustrate their knavish t. 79b
plays such fantastic t. 351b
something in it, t. and all 48b

Tricks (cont.)
such t. hath strong imagination 357a
their t. an' craft 61a
their t. and their manners 125b
there are no t. in plain..faith 340b
t. are either knavish or childish 210a
t. that are vain 182a
women are like t. 104b
Tried: can't drop it if I t. 229a
fire seven times t. this 353b
she for a little t. 473b
thou also hast t. us 486a
thou that hast not t. 409a
too much are t. 7a
t. a little, failed much 412b
when he is t., he shall receive 517a
without consent been only t. 291b
Trifle: as 'twere a careless t. 346b
Trifled: away the rest have t. 46a
Trifler: busy t. 108a
Trifles: but t. with one 160a
man of sense..t. with [women] 91a
she who t. with all 160a
t. light as air 362a
unconsidered t. 373a
win us with honest t. 346a
Trigger after his death 206b
Triggers: resolves an' t. 250a
Trimmer: innocent word 'T.' 178a
Trimmings: with the usual t. 127a
Trinities: tangled T. 233b
Trinity: Harrer an' T. College 232b
I the T. illustrate 52a
old fellow of T. 527a
T. Church I met my doom 162b
T. had never been unkind 288b
Trinket at my wrist 442a
Trip: come, and t. it 268b
his words..t. about him 279a
once you t. on it, entails 52a
our fearful t. is done 457a
t. it up and down 522b
t. no further, pretty sweeting 370b
Tripe: painch, t., or thairm 60b
Triple: casement..t. arched 221b
t. cord, wh. no man can break 58a
Trippingly on the tongue 333b
Trips: trochee t. 101b
Trisagion: raise the 'T.' 287a
Trissotin: half T. 254b
Tristram Shandy: novel called.. T.S. 449b
Triton: hear old T. 473a
T. blowing loud 408a
T. of the minnows 328a
Triumph: be pedestaled in t. 51b
in ourselves, are t. 247b
in their t. die 365b
in t. from the north 252b
in t. thro' Persepolis 259a
I t. still, if Thou abide 251b
now is the Victor's t. won 304b
poor..t. o'er the timid hare! 443b
pursue the t. 301b
shout of them that t. 286a
t. over death and sin 408a
we shall not see the t. 127b
what t.! hark 7a
when learning's t. o'er her..foes 213b
who in t. advances 316b
with T. and Disaster 230a
Triumphals: joyless t. 277b
Triumphant: joyful and t. 290a
Triumphs: glories, t., spoils 339b
let the t. of Love 424b
sickened at all t. 94b
their little t. o'er 175a
Triumph-song: distant t. 200a
Trivet: right as a t. 126a
Trivial: rise from t. things 302b
the t. round 224a
Trochee trips 101b
Trod: a time I might have t. 459b
t. that day to God 227b
Trodden: little fire is quickly t. out 384b
t. the winepress alone 503b
Troilus methinks mounted..walls 355a
Trojans we are no more 555b
Troop: farewell the plumed t. 362a
sent a t. of horse 445a
t. cometh..name Gad 493a

Troop (cont.)
t. home to churchyards 357a
while a foreign t. was landed 297a
Troopers: Noll's damned t. 45b
wanton t. riding by 261a
Troops: Æneas shall want t. 324b
in solemn t., and sweet societies 270a
rashly charged the t. of error 41b
t. he to Oxford sent 445b
t. of Midian 286a
Troop-Sergeant-Major 234a
Trope: out there flew a t. 64b
Tropes: he ranged his t. 306a
Trophies: all their t. pass away 244a
cloudy t. hung 219b
down her weedy t...fell 336a
t. unto the enemies of truth 41b
Trophy, sword, nor hatchment 336a
Tropic: under the t. is our language 449a
Trot: to t. the round 137a
Troth: I plight thee my t. 481b
noblest t. dies here 312a
tell t. and shame the devil 216a
Trotting thro' the dark 234a
Troubadour: gaily the T. 22b
Trouble: against them that t. me 483a
all this toil and t. 471b
but a t. of ants 439a
cried unto the Lord in their t. 488b
double, toil and t. 349b
few days, and full of t. 497a
forge a lifelong t. 427b
genius..capacity of taking t. 80b
genius..possessors into t. 66b
have your t. doubl'd 118b
here, where all t. seems dead 422a
in the day of t. 482b
in t. to be troubled 118b
kindness in another's t. 171b
man is born unto t. 497a
man wa'at kin show you t. 181b
mine enemies that t. me 484b
my little t. is ended 441a
one who had seen t. 455b
present help in t. 484b
progress..t. and care 249a
Roman and his t. are ashes 199a
soon smooth away t. 39a
transient, shining t. 172b
t. enough of its own 459a
t., sorrow, need 480b
t. to my dreams 469a
t. weighed upon her 432b
useful t. of the rain 427b
war, he sung, is toil and t. 139a
when there 's t. brewing 238a
women and care and t. 451b
wd. t. him much more 108b
you ain't see no t. yit 181b
Troubled: let not yr. heart be t. 511a
t. with thick-coming fancies 350b
world's storm-t. sphere 38b
Troubles: a sea of t. 333a
Ianthe, little t. pass 241a
I have had t. enough 49a
O God: out of all his t. 483a
pack up your t. 10b
t. of our proud and angry dust 200a
t. of the brain 350b
Troubling: t. of a star 442b
wicked cease from t. 497a
Troublous: not any t. thing before 421a
Trough was full, and faithful Tray 192b
Troul: they t. so merrily 3a
Trousers: bottoms of my t. rolled 145a
Trousers: hitched his t. up 10b
never put on one's best t. 567a
Webster..steam-engine in t. 404b
Trout: a lusty t. 425b
here comes the t. 371a
t. in the milk 135b, 444a
Trouts are tickled best 66b
Trowel: flattery..with a t. 129a
lays it on with a t. 104a
Trowl the brown bowl 319b
Troy: fir'd another T. 139a
half his T. was burned 379b
night when T. was sacked 313b
tale of T. divine 268a
(O T. Town!) 313a
ringing plains of windy T. 438b

Troy (cont.)
T. passed away in one..gleam 475b
was there another T. 474b
where's T.? 35a
Troyan: mounted the T. walls 355a
the T. gestes 90a
Troynovaunt: lusty T. 142b
Truant: every t. knew 168b
t. been to chivalry 378b
t. disposition 330a
Truce: formal t. and as of right 294b
place where one day's t. 56b
quashed in our new t. 36a
Truck of the last mainmast 181a
Truckle-bed: pigging together..
same t. 55a
Trudg'd along unknowing 140a
True: always say what's t. 413b
always think what is t. 202b
an ower t. tale 319a
Arabian Tales were t. 288a
be so t. to thyself 15b
called Faithful and T. 519b
can the devil speak t. 346a
cd. I doubt him t. 241b
England to itself do rest but t. 374b
good to be honest and t. 61a, 524b
heart was t. to Poll 58b
he said t. things 45a
I am the t. Amphitryon 139b
if this be t., indeed 70b
if t., here only 274a
if yr. heart be only t. 58b
I'll prove more t. 365a
I love thee t. 263b
I reckon rather t. 218b
is t. of most we leave behind 97a
kept him falsely t. 428b
like to coins, some t., some light 428a
long enough it will be t. 27b
man had rather were t...believes 16b
most t. it is that I have look'd 389a
nay, had she been t. 363b
never man was t. 35b
nothing t., but Heaven 282b
one religion is as t. as another 64b
part of death no one so t. 371a
possibly quite as t. 47b
prithee, tell me t. 165b
say that thou wert t. 214b
slander makes it t. 6b
so young, my lord, and t. 341b
speak the thing that 's t. 452b
taking t. for false 427b
tale was undoubtedly t. 242a
tell you three times is t. 85b
that he is mad, 'tis t. 332a
thing is not necessarily t. 460b
things more t. and deep 398b
thing they know isn't t. 27b
tho' she were t., when you met her 134a
'tis easy to be t. 321a
'tis t., 'tis pity 332a
'tis t., 'tis t. 198b
to thine own self be t. 330b
t...as taxes is 122a
T. Thomas lay on Huntlie 528a
t. to thee till death 150a
we are sure they are t. 373b
well to be honest and t. 262b
what is t. for you 147b
whatsoever things are t. 516a
wh. are t. of heart 482a
wh. was prov'd t. before 66a
woman t. and fair 134a
worship..considered..equally t. 162a
yet t. it is, as cow chaws 446a
True-fix'd and resting quality 339a
Truepenny: art thou there, t.? 331b
Truest: those who Paint 'em t. 1a
t. and the holiest (story) 257b
Trump: at the last t. 515a
Lord with the sound of the t. 484b
neighing steed, and the shrill t. 362a
Trumpery: with all their t. 273b
Trumpet: anon a t. sounds 442a
blow t., for the world is white 427b
blow yr. own t. 166b
dreads the final T. 180a
glorious the t. 403a
great voice, as of a t. 518a

Trumpet (cont.)
hark! the shrill t. sounds 95b
heard the sound of the t. 494b
he shifted his t. 169b
his t. shrill 408a
it is the sound of the t. 497b
last loud t.'s wondrous sound 127b
let the t. snare the foeman 234b
moved more than with a t. 402a
the Thing became a t. 470b
t. give an uncertain sound 514b
t. of a prophecy! 396b
t. of Germinal 91b
t. of his own virtues 359a
t. shall be heard on high 139b
t.'s loud clangour 139b
t.'s silver sound is still 317b
t. to t. spake 137a
Trumpeters: singers also and t. 487a
Trumpets: blowin' er de t. 182a
blow yr., Angels 133a
he saith among the t., Ha, ha 497b
moment, while the t. blow 436b
pâtés de foie gras to..t. 404b
silver, snarling t. 221b
sound the t. 139a, 244a, 283b
the t. bray 164a
t. also, and shawms 488a
t. of the night 423a
t. sounded for him 54b
up-lifted Angel t. blow 278a
Trumps: if dirt were t. 240b
let spades be t. 302b
Truncheon: marshal's t. 351b
Trundle-tail 343a
Trunk: so large a t. before 25b
t. spouts out a sea 275b
Trunkless, yet it couldn't forget 165a
Trust: all power is a t. 130a
empire is..power in t. 138a
fear not, but t. in Providence 22a
if you can t. yourself 230a
in the People was my t. 469b
in t. I have found treason 145a
liars we can never t. 452b
little t. that when we die 263a
men dare t. themselves with men 368a
on whom I built an absolute t. 346b
O t. not in wrong 485b
put not yr. t. in princes 490b
put their t. in chariots 482b
right of governing..a t. 156b
rude, cruel, not to t. 389a
slew the T. they stood..pledged 294a
soothed by an unfaltering t. 53a
to frail mortality shall t. 17a
T. his sworn brother 373b
t. in all things high 437a
t. in God, and do the Right 256b
t. me not at all 428b
t. no Future, howe'er pleasant 248a
t. none; for oaths are straw 382a
t. on, and think to-morrow 139b
t. that somehow good 430a
t. thou thy Love 315a
t. thy honest offer'd courtesy 267a
t. was with th' Eternal 272a
Trusted: armour wherein he t. 509a
let no such man be t. 355b
Lord in thee have I t. 478a
t. to thy billows 69b
Trustees of Posterity 130a
Trusts: convartin' public t. 250a
nor t. them with, serious matters 91a
t. a frail bark 173a
Trusty, dusky, vivid 414a
Truth: against..multitudes the cause
of t. 275a
as beauty must be t. 222a
ask if t. be there 6b
beauty is t., t. beauty 219b
Beauty, T., and Love 36b
belief of t., wh. is the enjoying 14a
between t. and repose 148a
bread of sincerity and t. 514a
bright countenance of t. 279a
bring t. to light 386b
but t. from rules 65b
candidate for t. 148a
cannot tell how the t. may be 317a
Christianity better than T. 102a

Truth (cont.)

Christ with His lamp of t.	36b
commencing in a t.	346b
constantly speak the t.	480a
desire of fame, and love of t.	428a
divine melodious t.	219a
does t. sound bitter	48a
dost to T. aspire	37a
doubt t. to be a liar	332a
few enthusiasts speak t.	18a
fiction lags after t.	55b
fiend that lies like t.	351a
find where t. is hid	332a
forc'd me, out of thy honest t.	386a
for the t. he ought to die	147a
freeman whom the t. makes free	112b
full round of t.	426a
good that came of telling t.	139b
great is t., and shall prevail	40a
great is T., and mighty	520a
great ocean of t.	289a
habit. .all the test of t.	113b
heavenly it. imparts	224a
how sweet the t.	149b
I am the way, the t.	511a
I held it t.	429b
image of t. new-born	32a
inquiry of t., wh. is the love- making	14a
justice is t. in action	128a
keep abreast of T.	251a
kept thy t. so pure	278b
knowledge of t., wh. is the presence	14a
know then this t.	301b
let t. be told	37b
lie wh. is part a t.	427a
light of t.	121b
looked on t. askance	389a
loved chivalrye, t. and honour	88a
love of t. predominates	148a
mainly he loves the t.	446b
mercy and t. are met together	487a
more and more to disclose t.	13b
never. .feel certain of any t.	223a
no mask like open t.	104a
not t., but things like t.	87b
one t. is clear	301a
oratory. .not t., but persuasion	255b
parsons do not care for t.	415b
Pilate saith. .what is t.?	511b
poets that wrapt T. in tales	79a
possession of t. as of a city	41b
put him in possession of t.	246a
relationship with beauty and t.	222a
ridicule is the best test of t.	91a
ring in the love of t.	431a
rose upon T.'s lips	452a
seeming t. wh. cunning times	354a
see skulking T. . .fled	209a
shall it declare thy t.?	483b
she is made of t.	389a
simple t. miscalled simplicity	388a
sole judge of t.	301a
song is not t.	452a
songs consecrate to t. and liberty	399b
so T. be in the field	279a
speaketh the t. from his heart	482a
Spirit that strove for t.	399a
spread the t. from pole to pole	2a
steadfastness and careful t.	228a
stooped to t.	303a
strife of T. with Falsehood	250b
stupendous t. believed	402b
such a t. as I have meant	473b
suffer for the t.'s sake	480a
swear to the t. of a song	305b
sweet ornament wh. t. doth give!	387b
takes this carp of t.	331b
that t. lies somewhere	251a
then to side with T. is noble	109a
there is no t. in him	511a
they worship T.	39b
this mournful t. . .confess'd	213b
this t. to prove	6b
thy God's, and t.'s	386a
tongues can poison t.	100a
to T. its state is dedicate	397a
trophies unto the enemies of t.	41b
t. and untruth together	15b
T. beareth away the victory	520a

Truth (cont.)

t. be veiled, but still it burneth	394a
t. breathed by cheerfulness	471b
t. by consecutive reasoning	222a
t. can never be told	31a
t. comes out in wine	552b
t., ever lovely. .foe of tyrants	77b
T. forever on the scaffold	250b
t., for its own sake	226b
t. from his lips prevail'd	168b
t. . .golden girdle of the globe	107b
t. has such a face	140b
t. his utmost skill!	473a
t. in every shepherd's tongue	307b
t. in masquerade	71b
t. in the inward parts	485a
t. is always strange	72a
t. is great, and shall prevail	294a
t. is marching on	200b
t. is not in us	518a
t. is. .stranger than fiction	72a
t. is the hyeste thing	89b
t. is well paid when she is sung	106a
t. is within ourselves	49b
t. lies within a little. .compass	33b
t., like a torch	178b
t. never hurts the teller	46b
t. of imagination	222a
t. . .peeps over the glass's edge	45a
T. severe, by fairy Fiction dressed	173b
t. shall be thy warrant	307b
t. shall flourish out of the earth	487a
t. shall make you free	511a
t., Sir, is a cow	207b
T. sometimes will lend her. .fires	72b
t.'s sacred Fort	40b
t. that's told with bad intent	29b
t. the brilliant Frenchman	113a
T. the masculine, of Honour	181a
t. the poet sings	432a
t. thy Bondman let me live!	464a
t. to o'erpeer	328a
t., unity, and concord	480b
t. universally acknowledged	11b
t. . .upon the lips of dying men	8a
t. whereby the nations live	228a
t. will come to light	353b
t. with gold she weighs	298b
t. within thy mind rehearse	438b
two to speak the t.	444a
upon the poles of t.	14a
whatever remains. .must be the t.	136a
what is t.? said jesting Pilate	14a
where t. calls spade a spade	44b
while you live, tell t.	378a
who ever knew T. put to the worse	279a
who never sold the t.	435a
whose speech T. knows not	313a
with t. it quite agrees	165a
word of t., of meekness	484b
words of t. and soberness	513a
worship him in spirit and in t.	510b
yet friend to t.	302b
you saw Waring? T. or joke?	52b
Truthful: name is T. James	182b
too t. or too wise	452a
Truths: bear all naked t.	218b
darkness tell us t.	346a
fate of new t.	203a
irrationally held t.	203a
one way possible of speaking t.	51b
paramount of t.	464b
religion, if in heavenly t. attir'd	108a
some random t. he can impart	469a
tell him disagreeable t.	252a
t. as refin'd as ever Athens	4b
t. begin as blasphemies	389b
t. that wake, to perish never	466b
t. wd. you teach	301b
two t. are told	346a
Truth-teller was our. .Alfred	435a
Try: guiltier than him they t.	351a
little Soul, let us t., t., t.	282b
then let me t. with all my might	425a
t. . .can be such men as he!	5a
t. him afterward	446b
't. not the Pass!'	247a
t., t. again	191a
t.-t.-t.-t.-to think o' something	227b
Trying: she's t. all she can	192b

Trying (cont.)

t. . .to like Scotchmen	238b
Tu quoque	552a
Tub: fair tale of a t.	283b
mere tale of a t.	454b
Tubal Cain was a man of might	256a
Tube: reeking t. and iron shard	233b
Tube-rose: sweet t.	398a
Tubes are twisted	236b
Tubs: from their separate t.	528a
Tucker: little Tom T.	534b
Tuesday: christened on a T.	532b
that wash on T.	532b
T.'s child is full of grace	525a
Tug: then was the t. of war	244a
Tugela side	27a
Tugs: each t. it a different way	72b
Tulgey: the t. wood	83b
Tulip: streaks of the t.	213b
Tulips bloom as they are told	39b
Tullochgorum: Reel o' T.	402b
Tum, tum; then the band played	45a
Tumble: twa wheel-barrows t.	177b
Tumbling: boys. .t. in the street	59b
fortunes. .t. into some. .laps	445a
Tumbrils toiling up the. .way	13a
Tumtum tree	91b
Tumult: depth, and not the t.	83b
Jesus calls us; o'er the t.	467b
'mid this t. Kubla heard	3b
t. and the shouting dies	101b
t. dwindled to a calm	233b
t. of her war	74b
Tumultuous: this t. body	415b
Tun of man	39b
Tune: dost thou like this t.?	377b
get away from the t.	370b
has his t. by heart	236b
Heaven tries earth if it be in t.	251a
incapable of a t.	238b
out of t. and harsh	333b
singeth a quiet t.	99b
sweetly played in t.	62a
t. is something hard	231a
t. the instrument here at the door	133b
we are out of t.	473a
whistled a foolish t.	181b
Tunes: devil. .have all the good t.	191b
found out musical t.	521a
little list of t.	122b
slow old t. of Spain	261b
snatches of old t.	336a
t. that he cd. play	533a
Tunic: all-concealing t.	397a
Tunnel of green gloom	39b
Tunnies steeped in brine	8b
Tupman: Mr. T.	126a
Tupping yr. white ewe	359b
Turbans: silken t. wreath'd	277a
Turbot: price of a large t. for it	314a
(way of t.) an archdeacon	405b
Turbulent: free me from this t. priest	571b
t. of wit	138a
Turf: a grass-green t.	335b
as the t. they trod	469a
blue ribbon of the t.	129b
every t. beneath their feet	77a
green be the t. above	178a
green t. lie lightly on thy breast	299b
lends the light t.	114a
on the dappled t. at ease	463b
shelving bank of t.	398a
thy t. shall roses rear	73b
to bless the t.	103a
t. suck the honied showers	270a
wise t. cloaks the. .cliff-edge	235a
Turgenieff: lips of Ivan T.	204a
Turk: bear, like the T.	303a
French, or T., or Proosian	166a
master comes like any T.	79b
sick man of Europe, the T.	564b
take the T. by the beard!	383b
the unspeakable T.	81a
turbaned T.	364a
when Man is the T.	92b
Turkey: in T. 'ven they cuts	126a
T. carpet. .to a picture	254b
wrong side of a T. tapestry	200b
Turkey-cock: rare t. of him	371a
Turks: say, like those wicked T.	123a

Turks (cont.)
sleep with T. and infidels 376a
[T.].. bag and baggage 167b
T., Infidels, and Hereticks 479b
Turmoil: ceaseless t. seething 101a
Turmoiled in the court 384a
Turn: he made him t. 137a
it is my t. now 287a
I t. to thee as some..afternoon 423a
I wd. to thee and answer 199a
let not each gay t. 300b
perhaps t. out a sermon 60a
the planets, in their t. 2a
to t. you out, to t. you out 228b
t. again to cover the earth 488a
t. again to his earth 490b
t., Angelina, ever dear 169a
t. from us all those evils 479a
t. our captivity 489b
t. out a song 60a
t. thou behind me 496b
t. thou ghost that way 132b
t. to God to praise and pray 47b
t. to him the other also 505a
t. wheresoe'er I may 466a
who will often t. aside 228b
Turned: been t. out several times 239b
cried, and t. away 39b
having once t. round 99b
how all t. to him 52b
in case anything t. up 122a
I t. me to them very wistfully 441b
t. every one to his own way 503a
t. him right and round about 61a
Turner: Mrs. T.'s daughter play 296a
Turneth: he t. it upside down 490b
Turning: at the t. o' the tide 381b
but there's no t. back 311a
by never t. back 311a
neither shadow of t. 517a
Turnip: blood out of a t. 259b
t. than his father 211b
Turnips: who t. cries 211b
Turnpike: consider supper as a t. 144a
Turns: poor head almost t. 7b
t. no more his head 99b
t. of chance below 139a
whoso t. as I, this evening 47b
Turret: Galileo on his t. 49b
the Sultan's T. 152a
Turrets: half-glimpsed t. 442a
Turtle: the love of the t. 67b
t. green and glutinous 50a
voice of the t. is heard 500a
Turtle-dove: bay horse and a t. 444a
soul of thy t. 486b
t. is heard 262b
Turveydrop: Mr. T. 121a
Tuscany: ranks of T. 253b
Tusculan Mamilius 253a
Tusculum: lay on for T. 253b
T. (beautiful T.) 122b
Tush, they say, how shd. God 486b
Tuum: distinctions of meum and t. 239a
Tu-whit, tu-who, a merry note 345b
Twa: fell thir t. between 529a
we t. hae run about 59a
Twain: mischance between us t. 334a
such a t. can do't 322a
t. he covered his face 501b
t. were casting dice 98b
Twal: wee short hour ayont the t. 60a
Tweedledee: Tweedledum and T. 84a
'twixt Tweedledum and T. 67a
Tweedledum: T. and Tweedledee 84a
'twixt T. and Tweedledee 67a
Twelve: Christmas Eve, and t. 180a
jury..may in a sworn t. 351a
parted..between t. and one 381b
platform, 'twixt eleven and t. 330b
since t. honest men..decided 306b
t. good men into a box 40b
T.-Pound Look 21b
Twentieth year is well-nigh past 109a
Twenty: at t. years..will reigns 157a
first t. years are the longest 407a
ivy of sweet two-and-t. 73b
let t. pass 45b
to that t., add a hundred 190a
t. will not come again 198b
Twenty-four: we shall be t. 199b

Twenty-nine distinct damnations 52a
Twenty-six: towards the age of t. 26a
Twice: no man under the sky lives t. 423b
t. pierced His gospel..feet 244a
Twickenham: penny to T. Town 261b
Twig: a-top on the the topmost t. 311b
Twiggy-voo, my boys 284b
Twigs: limed t. for crabs 85b
Twilight: bats..ever fly by t. 15b
disastrous t. sheds 272a
dreaming thro' the t. 311a
in me thou seest the t. 388a
less kind than the grey t. 474b
like t.'s, too, her dusky hair 470b
over Fiesole by t. 49a
told as the t. fails 231a
t. and evening bell 426a
t., and the sunless day 70b
t. gray..in her sober livery 274a
Twilights: gracious t. where his chosen lie 52a
t. were more clear 133b
Twin: don't tell my t. 186a
great T. Brethren 254a
one of us was born a t. 244b
t. halves of one august event 179a
Twine: another o' the t. 530a
twist ye, t. ye 319b
Twin'd my love and me 531b
Twinkle: t., t., little bat 83a
t., t. little star 425a
Twinkled: yr. benefices t. 140b
Twinkling: endureth but the t. 483b
t. of a bedstaff 322a
t. of an eye 515a
Twins: Clara threw the t. 172b
every one bear t. 500a
roes that are t. 500b
those t. of learning 386b
Twirl down the middle 131a
Twist: blossomy t. 442a
t. ye, twine ye 319b
Twitched his mantle blue 270a
Twitcher: Jeremy T. 160a
Twitters: a late lark t. 185a
Two: at the expense of t. 96b
bicycle built for t. 116b
can t. walk together 504a
forefathers deemed it t. 75b
grows t. thereby 186b
if they be t., they are t. so 134a
in favour of t. [eyes] 124b
lies to hide it, makes it t. 452b
nay, not so much, not t. 330a
never by t. and t. 235a
one, t., buckle my shoe 532a
takes t. to speak the truth 444a
those other t. equalled with me 273a
t. and t. only supreme..beings 288a
t. are walking apart 203a
t. at a time no mortal..bear 160a
t. lovely black eyes 97a
t. may keep counsel 365b
t. men I honour 81b
t. o'clock in the morning courage 575a
t. of a trade 160b
t. only, as generally necessary 481a
t. or three are gathered together 478b, 507a
t. things stand like stone 171b
t. to bear my soul away 2b
t. went to pray 115a
we t. stood there 45b
when we t. parted 74b
Two-and-twenty: I am t. 198b
Two-handed engine at the door 269b
Two-legged: unfeather'd t. thing 138a
Twopence: go the length of t. 412b
I care not t. 23a
t. a week, and jam 84b
t. coloured 412b
without the oil and t. 404b
Tyke: bobtail t. 343a
Tyne: Severn to the T. 227a
Type: careful of the t. 430b
funny t...at Leipsig 45a
grey paper with blunt t.! 52a
highest t. of human nature 407b
loose t. of things 463b
noble t. of good 248a

Type (cont.)
t. of all her race 136b
Types: device of Movable T. 81b
Typewriter does not generate 135b
Tyrannies: age, agues, t. 133a
Tyrannous to use it like a giant 351b
Tyranny: appeal from t. to God 69b
bad laws..worst sort of t. 55a
ecclesiastic t.'s the worst 118b
remedy..against t. 208a
serving either calamity or t. 520a
snuff the approach of t. 55b
this t. be overpast 485b
Tyrant: Jealousy, thou t. of the mind! 140b
little t. of his fields 174a
love..that t. of the soul 244a
necessity, the t.'s plea 274a
past the t.'s stroke 329a
planet's t., dotard Death 24a
t. custom 360b
t. duke unto a t. brother 325b
t. rhyme hath so abused 216b
Tyrants: all men wd. be t. 118a
hearts bid the t. defiance 77b
kings will be t. from policy 57a
love..between t. and slaves 170b
necessity..argument of t. 297b
truth..foe of t. 77b
'twixt kings and t...difference 189b
t. of thy sex 104b
t. seldom want pretexts 57b
when t.' crests and tombs 389a
Tyranwel and I have been dead 91a
Tyre: daughter of T. shall be there 484b
one with Nineveh and T. 233b
Tyrian: budded T. 220a
some grave T. trader 8a

U

Ubiquities: blazing u. 148b
Ucalegon: neighbour U. burned 555b
Uffish: in u. thought he stood 83b
Uglier yet is the Hump 230b
Ugliness: who can have made its u? 202b
Ugly: fancy one's old and u. 105a
good than to be u. 460b
I say, you u. beast! 416b
that makes me u. 363a
why wasn't I born old and u? 121a
Ulcers: his poor old u. 185b
Ullin: Lord U.'s daughter 77a
Ulpian at the best 45a
Ulster will fight 95a
Ulva: chief of U.'s isle 77a
Ulysses: a new U. leaves 394a
profitable example in U. 543a
U. come possess these shores 117a
Umbrage: Americans have taken u. 535b
Umbrella: steals the just's u. 34b
Umbro: young boys in U. 253a
Umpire: chaos u. sits 273a
u., the pavilion cat 242a
'Umps,' said Mr. Grewgious 123b
Una for her milk-white lamb 468b
Unaccustomed to the yoke 110a
Unacquainted with the ABC 410b
Unadorned: beauty u. 25b
when u. adorned the most 443b
Unadvised: too u., too sudden 365a
Unaffected: affecting to seem u. 103b
Unafraid: Gentlemen u. 227b
Unalterably, never yours 124b
Unaneled: disappointed, u. 331b
Unanimity is wonderful! 400a
Unapparent: far in the U. 392b
Unapt to perceive 9b
Unarm, Eros 324a
Unashamed: brawling judgments, u. 429a
Unassailable holds on his rank 339a
Unattempted: things u. yet 270b
Unaware: blessed them u. 99a
he knew and I was u. 179a
some morning, u. 47a
Unawares: angels u. 517a
Unbecoming: more u...than to laugh 104a
u. to a woman 460a
Unbelief: blind u. is sure 110a

Unbelief (cont.)
did it ignorantly in u. 516b
gained them by our u. 45a
land of u. and fear 31a
one is u...other is contumely 15a
U. in denying them 148b
u. is blind 267b
Unbend yr. noble strength 348a
Unbends the mind like (women) 159b
Unbent: she u. her mind 239a
Unbewail'd: hold u. their way 323b
Unbidden guests are often welcomest 383b
Un-birthday: an u. present 85a
Unblamed: may I express thee u.? 273a
Unborn: child may rue that is u. 530b
ye u. ages, crowd not 173b
Unbought grace of life 57a
Unbowed: bloody, but u. 185a
Unbroke: keep all vows u. 376a
Unbroken Pickwick 93b
Unburied: bodies of u. men 454b
Unbusy: sole u. thing 102a
Unbuttoned: little ones, u. 113a
Uncanopied sleep is flying 35b
Uncared: O my u.-for songs 36a
Unceremoniously the rose 452a
Uncertain: trumpet give an u. sound 514b
u., coy, and hard to please 318b
Uncertainty: certainty for an u. 213a
Unchanged: doth still remain u. 470a
Uncharitableness: and all u. 478b
Unchipt, unflead 190b
Uncircumcised: daughters of the u. 495b
Uncircumcision: circumcision nor u. 516a
Uncle: married with mine u. 330a
O my prophetic soul! my u.! 331b
u. me no u. 375a
Unclean: man of u. lips 501b
Uncle George: when yr. U. was living 123a
Uncle Stalky: yr. U. 237b
Uncle Toby: U.'s business 412a
U...whistling..Lillaburlero 411b
U...with the fly in his hand 411b
Uncle Tom Cobbleigh 531b
Unclothe: lo I u. and clear 115b
Unclubbable man 207b
Uncoffined: unknelled, u. 69b
Uncomely: all things u. and broken 475b
Uncomfortable: moral when he is only u. 390b
we u. feel 166b
Uncomfortableness of it all 51b
Uncommon: very u. cook 315b
Unconcerned as when yr. infant beauty 320b
Unconfined: let joy be u. 68b
Unconning: thou art so u. 89b
Unconquered: sat u. in a ring 93a
Unconscionable time dying 88a
Unconscious: humour and irony..u. 66b
Unconsciously as heretofore 179a
Uncontrollable: than thou, O u.! 396b
Unconvincing: bald and u. narrative 165a
Uncouth: not unkind because u. 36a
Uncouther: better the u. 52b
Uncover, dogs, and lap 368a
Uncreated: nor three u. 478b
Unction: flattering to yr. soul 335a
Undefiled: my dove, my u. 500b
so shall I be u. 482b
tempted, and yet u. 405b
u. for the u. 226a
Undercliff: violets of the U. 229a
Undercurrent..about his name 314b
Undergirding the ship 513a
Underground: dwell the nations u. 442b
lays lads u. 199b
Underlings: we are u. 199b
Underneath are the everlasting arms 494b
Undersized: he's a bit u. 164a
Understand: fool doth not u. 487b
honour wh. they do not u. 468a
I may not u. 197a
I u. thy kisses 378a
mankind u. (Monarchy) 17a
more things..than men u. 520a
none aid you, and few u. 301b
shire for men who u. 39b

Understand (cont.)
some who did not u. them 305a
still the less they u. 65b
things wh. others u. 469a
thirst to know and u. 452b
thought I to u. this 486b
to admire, we shd. not u. 104b
u. a writer's ignorance 102a
what profits now to u. 434b
when his friends did u. 531b
wot do they u.? 232a
Understanded of the people 491b
Understandest: thou u. my thoughts 490a
u. thou what thou readest 512a
Understandeth: who u. thee not, loves thee not 344b
Understanding: beasts that have no u. 481b
find you an u. 211b
for thy more sweet u., a woman 344b
give it an u. 330b
God be in..my u. 523a
good things as pass man's u. 479b
good u. have all they 489a
he imparted them u. 520b
horse and mule, wh. have no u. 483b
if thou hast u. 497b
ignorant of his u. 102a
in honour hath no u. 485a
in length of days u. 497a
light a candle of u. 520a
more u. than my teachers 489a
passeth all u. 516a
sing ye praises with u. 485a
spirit of wisdom and u. 501b
to the u. they strike a note 42a
u. to direct 217a
wh. passeth all u. 480b
with all thy getting get u. 497b
Understandings: muddy u. 57a
Understands: think she u. 46b
Understood: all who u. admired 305a
by her that bore her u. 428b
Great First Cause, least u. 304a
interpreter..hardest to be u. 400a
then u. I the end 486b
u., and not be believed 31a
Undertakers: as u. walk before 158b
wot 'ud become of the u. 127a
Underwood: green u. and cover 420b
Undescribable: describe the u. 69a
Undid: what they u. did 323a
Un-dish-cover the fish 85b
Undo: I will u. myself 376a
some to u. 119b, 142b
Undoing: my heart's u. 281b
Undone: another victory, we are u. 13b
Caelia has u. me 457a
estate o' the world were now u. 351a
not to leave 't u. 361b
petty done, the u. vast 48a
some to be u. 119b, 142b
to give, to want, to be u. 409b
we have left u. those things 478a
wishest shd. be u. 346b
woe is me! for I am u. 501b
Undress: when I u. me 150b
Undrest: if u. at church 150b
Undulate round the world 458b
Undying thoughts I bear 265a
Unearned increment 265b
Uneasy: coaxin' u. ones 173a
short u. motion 99b
you are u. 203b
Uneducated: Chawcer..was so u. 451a
Unequal: men are made by nature u. 157b
Unextinguishable laugh 41a
Uneven: in..religion they are so u. 118b
Unexpectedness: wh. I call u. 295a
Unexpert: wiles more u. 272a
Unexpressed: uttered or u. 280a
Unexpressive she 327a
Unfaith in ought 428b
Unfamiliar: curious, and u. 189b
Unfeather'd two-legg'd thing 138a
Unfeeling: th' u. for his own 175a
Unfit: for all things u. 169b
u. contrarious moods of men 44a
Unfixed in principles 138a
Unfolding star calls up the shepherd 352a
Unfolds both heaven and earth 356a
Unforgetful: teach the u. to forget 312b

Unfortunate: one more U. 195b
u. Miss Bailey! 103b
Unfriendly: u. to society's..joys 108a
u. to the nose 415a
Unfrowning caryatides 415a
Unfurnished: head..to be let u. 65a
Ungartered, and down-gyved 332a
Ungather'd: beside the u. rice 248a
Ungentlemanly: how u. he can look 417a
Ungodliness: tents of u. 487a
Ungodly: as for the way of the u. 490b
because of the u. 484a
rod of the u. cometh not 489b
seen the u. in great power 484a
u. fall into their own nets 490b
u. perish at..presence of God 486a
Ungratefulness: Do they call virtue there u.? 401b
Unguessed: walk on earth u. at 7b
Unhand: 'u. it, sir!' 445b
u. me, gentlemen 331a
u. me, grey-beard 98a
Unhanged: three good men u. 377b
Unhappiness..comes of his greatness 81b
Unhappy: dare to be u. 313b
inconstant..never to be very u. 160b
instinct for being u. 315a
not one is respectable or u. 458a
to thyself u. chief 35b
Unheard: those u. are sweeter 219b
u. of as thou art 463b
Unholy: hour when rites u. 77b
shrieks and sights u. 268b
Unhonoured: u. his relics are laid 281a
u., and unsung 317b
Unhoped: that u. serene 39a
Unhoused free condition 359b
Unhousel'd, disappointed 331b
Unicorn: lion and the u. 532a
Unicorns: horns of the u. 483a
Un-idea'd girls 206b
Uniform: first I put this u. on 165a
shd. be more u. 195a
u. 'e wore..nothin' much before 229b
u. must work its way 127a
Uniformity: use..before u. 16a
Uniforms: fellows in foolscap u. 67b
Unimpaired: strong for service..u. 112a
Unimportant—important 83b
Unintelligent: as..upper class 9b
Union: an indestructible U. 88a
broken Nature's social u. 62a
our Federal U. 203b
our u. is perfect 127b
sail on, O U. 246b
saved the U. of these States 458b
u. of hands and hearts 425a
u. of total dissent 250b
u. with his native sea 464b
yet an u. in partition 357a
Unit: misses an u. 47a
Unitarian: he became a U. 148a
Unitarianism: convert me to U. 240a
Unite: at last, u. them there 96b
severs those it shd. u. 394a
workers of the world, u.! 528b
United: ev'ry flower is u. 159b
U. Metropolitan Improved 124b
u. thoughts and counsels 271a
United States: rise of the U. 412a
these U. 458b
Unities: preserved the u., sir 125a
Uniting: by u. we stand 127b
Unity: live in u. and godly love 480b
send up U. 232b
to dwell together in u. 490a
u., peace, and concord 479a
Universal: relaxed into a u. grin 112a
this u. frame began 139b
u. dovetailedness 125a
u. frame..without a mind 15a
with a u. blank 273b
Universe: born for the U. 169b
eye with wh. the U. beholds 392b
I accept the u. 82a
in a boundless u. 438b
in God's great u. 134b
into this U., and *Why* 153a
measure of the u. 397a
my u. that feels 44b

Universe (cont.)
  peopling the lone u. 395b
  praised be the fathomless u. 458b
  pretend to understand the U. 81b
  Spirit of the U.! 465b
  to mingle with the U. 69b
  wedded to this goodly u. 464a
  we possessed all the u. 390a
  wide vessel of the U. 382a
Universes: suns and u. ceased 38b
Universities: state of both his u. 445a
  u. incline wits to sophistry 17a
  wants of his two u. 445b
University: than his own mother U. 141b
  true U...collection of books 81a
  U. of Gottingen 79a
  U...place of light 128b
  we are the U. 528b
Unjust: on the u. fella 34b
  u., let him be u. still 520b
  u. steals the just's umbrella 34b
Unkempt about those hedges 39b
Unkind: deformed but the u. 372a
  sodden and u. 26b
  Sweet, I am u. 250a
  Trinity had never been u. 288b
  u. and the unruly 414a
  winter was not u. 36a
Unkindness: drink down all u. 355b
  his u. may defeat my life 363a
  u. may do much 363a
  you elements, with u. 342b
Unknelled, uncoffined 69b
Unknowable: O world u. 442a
Unknowing: u. and unknown 61b
  u. what he sought 140a
Unknown: and to fame u. 174b
  argues yourselves u. 274b
  behind the dim u. 250b
  but keep 't u. 361b
  in some u. power's employ 7a
  she lived u. 470b
  that is to him u. 448b
  things standing thus u. 337a
  to few u. 273b
  to the U. God 512b
  unknelled, uncoffined..u. 69b
Unlearned: amaze the u. 300a
  u., he knew no schoolmen's..art 303a
Unlessoned girl 354a
Unloads: death u. thee 351b
Unlock: cannot u. yr. heart 146b
  only cd. u. the gate 3b
Unloose: I am not worthy to u. 510b
Unloved: unshown, is often left u. 323b
Unlovely as thou seem'st 112a
Unmakes: God u. but to remake 51b
Unmeritable man 340b
Unmindfulness: play in skilled u. 179a
Unmissed but by his dogs 110b
Unmoneyed: treat u. men 388b
Unmoved, cold 101a
Unmuzzled: come among you u. 167b
Unnatural: foul, strange and u. 331b
  let me be cruel, not u. 334b
  poetry's u. 126b
Unnecessary: give yourself no u. pain 393a
Unobserved: am I alone, and u.? 165a
  u. home to his mother's house 277b
Unofficial: English u. rose 39b
Unparticular: nice u. man 180b
Unpitied: unrespited, u. 272b
Unplumbed, salt, estranging sea 6b
Unpopular: I was not u. there 24b
  power is always u. 129a
Unpremeditated: his u. strain 443a
  my u. verse 276a
  u. lay 316b
Unprofitable: stale, flat and u. 330a
  u. of my whole life 161b
Unpunctual: vague u. star 39b
Unqueen: old times u. thee 97b
Unquiet: immovably u. 396a
  sole u. thing 101a
Unreasonable: depends on the u. man 391a
Unreconciled as yet to heaven 363b
Unregulated: there the u. sun 39b
Unremembered: nameless, u. acts 472a
Unremembering way 441a
Unreproved pleasures free 268b
Unrequited: what u. affection is 123a

Unrespited, unpitied 272b
Unrest wh. men miscall delight 392b
Unreturning: over the u. brave 68b
Unrevealed: rest remaineth u. 430a
Unrewarded: nothing went u. 138b
Unrighteousness: mammon of u. 509b
Unripened beauties of the north 1b
Unruly: unkind and the u. 414a
Unsad and ever untrewe 89b
Unsatisfied: cigarette..leaves one u. 460b
Unscathed: thence u. to go 318b
Unseatest: care..perching, u. 75b
Unseduced: unshaken, u. 275a
Unseemly: behave itself u. 514b
Unseen: floats tho' u. among us 394b
  greet the u. with a cheer 52a
  left u. a wonderful piece 322b
  minute and u. 246b
  thou art u., but yet I hear 398a
  u. before by Gods 218a
  u. things above 179a
  walk the earth u. 274b
Unselfishness of an oyster 315b
Unsettle: don't let that u. you 163a
Unsettled: as far as they are u. 148a
Unsex me here 346b
Unshaken, unseduced 275a
Unsham'd, tho' foil'd 141a
Unshapely: wrong of u. things 475b
Unsifted in such perilous circum-
  stances 331a
Unskilled to sunder 96b
Unsought: not u. be won 275b
Unsoundness: certain u. of mind 254b
Unspeakable: the u. Turk 81a
Unspotted from the world 517b
Unstable: remember of this u. world 257b
  u. as water, thou shalt not excel 493b
Unstaid and skittish 370b
Unsubdued: than many u. 394a
Unsuccessful literary man 26b
Unsung: some u. 441a
  unhonoured and u. 317a
Unsunned heaps of miser's 267b
Unsure: to come is still u. 370b
Unsuspected: some u. isle 50a
Unsweet: ears not u. 402a
Untainted: than a heart u. 384a
Untamed: too restless, too u. 5b
Untangled much misfortune bodes 365a
Untender: so young, and so u.? 341b
Unterrified: Satan stood u. 273a
  unseduced, u. 275a
Unthinkable: thundered u. wings 92b
Unthinking: quaffing and u. time 141b
Unthread the rude eye 374b
Untimely: an u. grave 79a
  came I so u. forth 449a
Untouched: u. by solemn thought 467a
  u. the pages lie 113b
Untrue: telle his tale u. 89a
  unsad and ever u. 89b
Untruth: one wilful u. 288b
  torments of the night's u. 117a
  truth and u. together 15b
Untying: knot there's no u. 77b
Unused: fust in us u. 335b
Unvarnished tale 360a
Unvexed with anxious cares 140a
Unwashed artificer 111a
Unweighing fellow 352a
Unwept, unhonoured and unsung 317b
Unwholesome: egg boiled..is not u. 11a
Unwise: in the sight of the u. 520a
Unwithstood: with pomp of
  waters, u. 467a
Unworthiness: for our u. we dare
  not 480b
Unworthy: family was not u. of him 129b
  I was not u. to love her 73b
  merit of the u. takes 333a
Up: Antony..is notwithstanding u. 339a
  be u. and doing 248a
  cannot bear levelling u. 207b
  come U.!..you hugly beast 416b
  gay go u. 533b
  hey! then u. go we! 193a, 307a
  neither u. nor down 526b
  only half way u. 526b
  see me safe u. 283a
  seven u. and six to play 172b

Up (cont.)
  their utmost u. and on 51a
  u. Guards and at them 455a
  u. he got, in haste 108b
  u. in the morning's no' for me 63a
  u., Lord, and let not man 482a
  u. stairs, down stairs 534b
  u.! u.! my friend 471b
  when they were u. 526b
  where he had got u. 109a
Upbeareth me, Ischyros 441a
Upbraideth: giveth..and u. not 517a
Up-gathered now like..flowers 473a
Upharsin: mene, mene, tekel, u. 504a
Uphill: road wind u. all the way 311a
  we shall escape the u. 311a
Uphold the unyok'd humour 376b
Upland: ah, vain!..this u. dim 9a
Uplift: never dared u. the..tunic 397a
Uplifted beyond hope 272a
Upper: all u. crust here 177b
  Englishman of..u. classes 9b
  large u. room furnished 510a
  stiff u. lip 86a
  u. ten thousand of the city 461b
Upraised me where my mother 441a
Upright: who cannot sit u. 108b
Uprising: downsitting, and mine u. 490a
  our wakening and u. 223b
  to-morrow's u...shall be sweet 284b
Uproar: this day's u. 512b
  u.'s your only music 222a
Uprouse ye, then, my merry men! 18a
Upside: turned the world u. down 512b
Upstairs: compel us to be equal u. 21b
  came u. into the world 104b
Up-tails all 215b
Upward: they must u. still 251a
Urania: govern thou my song, U. 275b
  lament anew, U.! 391b
Uranus: perturbed moon of U. 294b
Urban, squat, and packed with guile 39b
Urge: procreant u. of the world 457b
  u. and u. and u. 457b
Uriah in the forefront..battle 495b
Uricon: ashes under U. 199a
Urim and the Thummim 494a
Urn: bubbling and loud-hissing u. 112a
  end by Nelson's u. 92b
  favour thy destin'd u. 269a
  her pictured u. 175a
  storied u. or animated bust 174a
  tears that overflow thy u. 241a
Urns: rule..spirits from their u. 73a
  cold sepulchral u. 108a
Urs: those dreadful u. 193b
Ursa Major: my nativity..under U. 342a
Us: they are not like u. 525a
Usage of those antique times 408b
Usance: rate of u. 353a
Use: come to deadly u. 343b
  have no u. for them 197a
  joys are spoilt by u. 218a
  let diaries..be brought in u. 15a
  let u. be preferred 16a
  rather u. than fame 429a
  still why deny its u. 76a
  such as cannot u. them 215b
  takes away the u. of 't 262b
  things are beyond all u. 339a
  u. a poor maiden so 523a
  u. doth breed a habit 372b
  u. every man after his desert 332b
  u. in measured language 429b
Used: as he hath u. of old 340b
  I am cruelly u. 11b
  I have u. no other 535b
  it will be u. against you 135b
  nothing like being u. to a thing 400b
Used-to-was 445a
Useful: magistrate, as equally u. 162a
Useless: most beautiful things..u. 314b
  u. as a general maxim 254b
  u. each without the other 248b
Uselessness of men above sixty 291a
Uses: thing I love for others' u. 362a
  to u. of a cup 51a
  u. of this world 330a
  very privit u. 250a
Using: love..barren with best u. 117a
Usna's children died 475b

Usquebae: wi u...face the devil   63a
Usurp: none can u. this height   218a
Usurpation: I dare without u.   41a
Usury: his money upon u.   482b
  lent out my heart with u.   239b
  souls not lent in u.   264a
Uther: romance of U.'s son   271b
Utmost: wha does the u.   59a
Utopia: not in U.   469b
  principality in U.   255a
Utter: man cannot u. it   499a
  not u. what thou dost not know   377a
  to u. all thy Praise   2a
Utterance: how divine is u.   264b
  that large u.   218a
  timely u. gave   466a
  with what strange u.   469a
Uttered: u. nothing base   437a
  u. or unexpressed   280a
Uzziah: year that King U. died   501a

V

Vacant: a mind quite v.   110b
Vacuity: indolent v. of thought   112b
Vagrom: comprehend all v. men   358b
Vague, a dizzy, a tumultuous joy   407a
Vain: a' is done in v.   61a
  and full as v.   139a
  because I weep in v.   174a
  call it not v.; they do not err   317a
  in v. with lavish kindness   184a
  let not only mine be v.   198b
  most v., most generous   185b
  Name of the Lord thy God in v.   480a
  Patently Impossible and V.   234a
  profane, erroneous, and v.   65b
  same Garden after me—in v.!   154a
  sweet is..love tho' given in v.   428b
  v. are the thousand creeds   38b
  v. man, said she   408a
  v., mightiest fleets of iron   136b
  v., those all-shattering guns   136b
  why, all delights are v.   344a
Vainly strives the soul   120a
Vale: as a v. of tears   46a
  as that v. in whose bosom   281b
  declin'd into the v. of years   362a
  longest hill must end in a v.   24b
  meet thee in that hollow v.   225a
  sequester'd v. of rural life   304b
  there lies a v. in Ida   435a
  the v. of Soul-making   223a
  the V., the three lone weirs   8b
  v. of misery use it for a well   487a
  violet-embroidered v.   267a
  yon taper cheers the v.   169a
Valentine: Hail, Bishop V.   132b
Valerius loathed the wrong   253b
Vales: and from our lovely v.   245b
  to the hills and the v.   424b
  voice, making all the v. rejoice   32b
Valet: no man is a hero to his v.   561a
  to his very v. seem'd a hero   67b
Valiant: as he was v. I honour him   339b
  be v., but not too venturous   251b
  he who would v. be   54b
  ring in the v. man   431a
  the v. never taste of death   339a
  v. in velvet   185b
Valiant-for-Truth   54b
Valiant-young: more v.   378b
Validity: of what v. and pitch   369b
Valley: all along the v.   431b
  darker grows the v.   263b
  every v. shall be exalted   502b
  he lies now in the little v.   44b
  he paweth in the v.   497b
  Love is of the v.   437a
  sing in the v. below   523a
  there is not..a v. so sweet   281b
  the v. sheep are fatter   295a
  v. between Buxton and Bakewell   314a
  v. of Humiliation   54a
  v. of the shadow of death   483a
  v. wh. was full of bones   504a
Valley-glades: deep in the next v.   220a
Valleys: bright in the fruitful v.   37a
  down to the v. beneath   488a
  far below them in the v.   433a

Valleys (cont.)
  piping down the v. wild   32a
  sendest rain into the little v.   486a
  v. also shall stand so thick   486a
  v. and rocks never heard   113a
  v. of Ionian hills   435a
Vallombrosa: brooks in V.   271b
Valois: shadow of the V.   92b
Valoroso is a man again!   440a
Valour: better part of v.   379a
  false quarrel there is no true v.   359a
  for contemplation he and v.   274a
  for v., is not love a Hercules   345a
  in thine own act and v.   347a
  like v.'s minion carv'd   346a
  much..v. in this Welshman   382b
  my v. is certainly going!   400b
  V. and Innocence   233b
  v. comes of sherris   380b
  who wd. true v. see   54b
Valorous: more childish v.   259b
Value: knows..the v. of nothing   460a
  more v. than many sparrows   506a
  then we rack the v.   359a
  v. dwells not in particular will   369a
  what he most doth v.   465b
Valued: but as 'tis v.   369a
Values: as moneys are for v.   13a
Vampire: like the v., she has been dead   293a
Van first took'st the field   225a
Vanbrugh's house of clay   149a
Vandyke is of the company   158a
Vanish: far from v., rather grows   44b
  hope may v., but can die not   394a
  suddenly v. away   86a
Vanished: as rare things will, it v.   49a
  he v. out of sight   407b
  it v. quite slowly   83a
  v. from his lonely hearth   465b
Vanishest: if thus thou v.   325a
Vanisheth: then v. away   517b
Vanishings: fallings from us, v.   466b
Vanity: all others are but v.   406b
  children of men, they are but v.   485b
  draw iniquity with cords of v.   501a
  every man living is altogether v.   484a
  every man therefore is but v.   484a
  give not yourselves unto v.   485b
  herein is not only a great v.   204a
  lest they behold v.   480a
  lighter than v. itself   485b
  no love, quoth he, but v.   202a
  no need of such v.   358b
  oh, V. of vanities!   440b
  out o' touch o' v.   232a
  speckled V. will sicken soon   270b
  that v. in years   377b
  town..is lighter than v.   54a
  v. and vexation of spirit   499a
  v., like murder, will out   107b
  v. of vanities, saith the Preacher   499a
  wh. is yr. partickler v.   127a
  women..two passions, v. and love   91a
Vanity-Fair: beareth the name of V.   54a
Vanquished: by a Roman valiantly v.   324b
  ingratitude..quite v. him   340a
  the v. had no despite   408b
  v., he cd. argue still   168b
  woe to the v.   550a
Vantage: forehand and v. of a king   383a
  might the v. best have took   351b
Vapour: like a v. over shrines!   44a
  live upon the v. of a dungeon   362a
  v. sometime like a bear   324a
  what is yr. life? it is even a v.   517b
Vapours: congregation of v.   332b
  crudy v. wh. environ it   380b
  the v. weep their burthen   438a
  v. both away   132b
Variable: love prove likewise v.   365a
  v. as the shade   318b
Variableness: in whom is no v.   517a
Variation: admitting any v.   478a
Varieties: different v. of pipe   135b
Variety: fortune is full of fresh v.   21a
  her infinite v.   323a
  Love's sweetest part, V.   133b
  offer a charmin' v.   173a
  sad v. of woe   162b, 299b

Variety (cont.)
  source of pleasure is v.   213a
  v. about the New England weather   446b
  v. is the soul of pleasure   25b
  v.'s the source of joy below   160a
  v.'s the spice of life   111b
Variorum: life is all a v.   61b
Various: a man so v.   138b
  nor tell to v. people v. things   113b
  v. are the tastes of men   3a
  v. hindrances we meet   110a
Varletry: shouting v.   325a
Varus, give me back my legions   538a
Vase: shatter the v., if you will   281b
Vassals and serfs at my side   53b
Vast and middle of the night   330a
Vastness! and Age!   298a
Vasty Hall of Death   7b
Vats of Luna   253a
Vault: fretted v.   174a
  in the v. above the Cherubim   230b
  leave it buried in this v.   215b
  lees is left this v. to brag of   348a
  making the hollow v. resound   202b
  nor, in thy marble v.   260a
Vaulted with such ease   378b
Vaulter: green little v.   202a
Vaulting ambition   347a
Vaunt: all but an empty v.   398b
Vaunt-couriers to..thunderbolts   342b
Vaunting aloud, but racked   271a
Vaward: take thou the v. of me   530b
Veer in the tide   424a
Vegetable: content with a v. love   165b
  my v. love shd. grow   260a
  passion of a v. fashion   165b
Vegetate: one does but v.   58b
  v. in a village   103b
  wish to v. like the country   183b
Veil: death is the v.   397b
  lift not the painted v.   399a
  sacred v. drawn o'er Thy..noon   447b
  this that was the v. of thee?   420b
  took away my v. from me   500b
  v. after v. will lift   5a
  V. thro' wh. I might not see   153b
  wrapped in a gauzy v.   399b
Veils: knew her..thro' all her v.   79a
  v. of the soul therein   420b
Vein: King Cambyses' v.   377b
  not in the giving v. to-day   385a
  this is Ercles'   356a
Veins: azur'd harebell, like thy v.   329a
  my bluest v. to kiss   323b
  open all my v.   280b
  so in my v. red life might stream   219a
Velasquez: why drag in V.?   456b
Velvet: gude lord in the black v.   530a
  mantle warm, and v. capt   109b
  valiant in v.   185b
Venerate: I for one v. a petticoat   71b
  v. art as art   184a
Venetian: turban'd Turk beat a V.   364a
Vengeance: clamour for a v. on the sea   231a
  day of v. of our God   503a
  heav'n awards the v. due   107b
  just my v. complete   47b
  neither take..v. of our sins   478b
  no sense..can rouse to v.   78b
  v., deep-brooding o'er the slain   317a
  v. is mine, I will repay   513b
  v. of Jenny's case   356a
Venice: dirty stones of V.   226a
  here with us in V.   353a
  in V. they do let heaven see   361b
  I stood in V.   69a
  no Lord of Parys, V. or Floraunce   143a
  no, not for V.   354b
  Ocean's nursling, V.   395a
  that cunning whore of V.   363a
  there at V. gave his body   375b
  this poor trash of V.   361a
  V. in their armoury have this inscription   64a
  V., the eldest child of Liberty   472b
  where V. sat in state   60a
Venite: God's great V.   133b
Venom, to thy work   337a
Venture: a bow at a v.   496b
  damn her at a v.   240b

nture (cont.)
naught v., naught have ... 446a
O Luve will v. in ... 62b
ntured: I have v., like little..boys 385b
you have deeply v. ... 73a
ntures: or lose our v. ... 341a
nus: as V. yokes her doves ... 71a
a V. or a angel ... 126b
Cotytto or V. ... 421b
o'er-picturing that V. ... 323a
planet V...gone on business ... 125a
thy V. that must die ... 176a
V. clerk, Ovyde ... 89b
V. herself fastened on her prey 565a
V., let me never see ... 306a
V., take my votive glass ... 306a
V. when she smiles ... 216b
r: first born child of V. ... 23b
racity: heard and saw with v. 175b
rbosity: exuberance of his own v. 128b
thread of his v. ... 304b, 345a
rbs and nouns do more agree 182a
rdict of the world is conclusive 537b
rdure: see no other v. ... 221a
re de Vere: caste of V. de V. 431b
reker's secret ... 204b
rge: room, and v. enough ... 173b
upon the beached v. ... 368a
very v. of her confine ... 342b
rger: an erudite V. ... 19a
rgil at Mexico ... 449b
rify yr. references ... 313a
risimilitude: fine isolated v. 222a
give artistic v. ... 165a
rmillion-spotted, golden ... 219a
rmin: race of little odious v. 417b
swarming with all sorts of v. 20a
rnal seasons of the year ... 279b
rsailles: the Dauphiness, at V. 57a
rse: all that is not prose is v. 564a
a v. may find him ... 186b
bumbast out a blank v. ... 176b
cheered..himself with ends of v. 65b
come, but one v. ... 370b
court others in v. ... 305b
decorate the v. herself ... 72b
facility of the octosyllabic v. 69b
Flask of Wine, a Book of V. 152b
had not my v. extolled thy name 79a
harmonious sisters, Voice and V. 278a
incantation of this v. ... 396b
in high immortal v. ... 267b
leaving great v. unto a..clan 219b
lies the subject of all v. ... 42b
married to immortal v. ... 269a
my unpremeditated v. ... 276a
my v. again shall gild ... 137a
my v. is not a convex ... 187a
my v. yr. virtues rare..eternize 408a
ne'er a v. to thee ... 226a
not v. now, only prose! ... 45a
now one in v. makes many more 300a
of..my v., like not a single line 414b
pleasures that to v. belong 217b
reads v...thinks she understands 46b
receive a strew of weeping v. 225a
rough, hoarse v. ... 300a
run them into v. ... 142a
sail of his great v. ... 388a
still thy v. has charms ... 318a
this be the v. you grave for me 415a
tiresome v.-reciter, Care ... 394b
to join the varying v. ... 303b
too humble to be named in v. 469b
v., a breeze ... 102a
v. can gently steer ... 141a
v...immortalizes whom it sings! 113a
v. is merely prose ... 72a
v. softens toil ... 162b
wanting the accomplishment of v. 464a
Verser: hearken unto a V. ... 186b
Verses: Book of V. underneath the
Bough ... 152b
false gallop of v. ... 327a
quire of bad v. in the other 254b
recited v. in writing ... 521a
rhyme the rudder is of v. 65a
some for writing v. ... 246a
tear him for his bad v. ... 340b
Tennyson write v. without..metre 102b
write halting v., run a mile 413a

Versing: relish v. ... 188a
Versions: hundred v. of (one religion) ... 391a
Verulam: large-browed V. ... 435b
Vesper: black v.'s pageants 324a
Vesper-bell: hark the little v. 100a
Vespers: 'st, there's V. ... 52a
Vessel: a brave v. ... 367a
break them..like a potter's v. 481b
earthern v., holding treasure 46a
gallant trim the gilded v. goes 173b
like a..ghost, the v. swept 249a
make one v. unto honour 513b
steersmen when the v.'s crank! 264b
the v. puffs her sail ... 439a
weigh the v. up ... 111a
wide v. of the universe ... 382a
wife, as..the weaker v. ... 517b
Vessels: treasure in earthen v. 515a
Vest: blood over the purple v. 254a
casting the body's v. aside 261a
thro' the v. wh. seems to hide 397b
Vestal: blameless v.'s lot ... 299b
in v. February ... 293b
Vestals: acidulous v. ... 413a
Vestry: I will see you in the v. 404b
Vesture: as a v. shalt thou change 488a
cast lots upon my v. ... 483a
he hath on his v...a name 519b
muddy v. of decay ... 355a
queen in a v. of gold ... 484b
Veteran on the stage ... 214a
Veterans: world its v. rewards! 302a
Vex: he hoped it wd. v. somebody 210a
mak enow' themselves to v. them 63a
v. not thou the poet's mind 435b
Vexation: multiplication is v. 533a
vanity and v. of spirit ... 499a
v. of a dream ... 357a
Vexed: but I was not v. ... 211a
v. his immortal strength ... 36a
Vexes: the other v. it ... 218a
Vials full of odours ... 518b
Viands: what v. he preferred 150b
Vibrated: better not be v. ... 121a
Vibration each way free ... 190b
Vicar: not the Vicarage, nor the V. 305a
the V. of Bray, sir ... 524a
Vicarage: not the V., nor the Vicar 305a
Vice: ambition, in a private man a v. 262b
boldly rebuke v. ... 480a
end in sight was a v. ... 52a
he lashed the v. ... 419a
music..pleasure without v. 212a
mutual Forgiveness of each v. 30a
no amusements but v. and religion 404b
no v., but beggary ... 374a
old-gentlemanly v...avarice 70b
or any taint of v. ... 372a
prosperity doth best discover v. 14b
raptures and roses of v. ... 421a
spreading v.'s snares ... 94b
than bullied out of v. ... 416b
that reverend v. ... 377b
thine honesty a v. ... 362a
this v. of lying ... 380b
thy body is all v. ... 206b
'tis a v. to know him ... 337a
to sanction V., and hunt Decorum 72a
'twixt a v. and folly, turned 233b
v. is a monster ... 301a
v. itself lost half its evil 57a
virtue itself of v...pardon beg 335a
when v. prevails ... 1b
where th' extreme of v. ... 301a
will no other v. content you? 133b
Viceroy to that..to heaven..gone 132b
Vices: dwelt upon her v. too 26a
of our pleasant v...plague us 344a
of our v. we can frame ... 247b
redeemed thy v. with his virtues 214b
v. may be committed very genteelly ... 208b
Vicinity: so had to leave the v. 527a
Viciousness: in our v. grow hard 324a
Vicissitude: sad v. of things 162b, 412a
Vicissitudes: v. of fortune ... 162a
wild v. of taste ... 213b
Victim: a v. must be found 164b
first insults the v. ... 114a
v. o' connubiality ... 126a

Victims: the little v. play ... 174b
Victor: now is the V.'s triumph won 304b
out spoke the v. then ... 76b
potent v. in his rage ... 271a
to the v...the spoils of the enemy 258a
Victories: after a thousand v. once
foiled ... 387a
peace hath her v. ... 278b
victors are by v. undone 140a
Victorious: make him v. ... 193a
o'er all the ills of life v. 62b
Victors: let the v., when they come 6b
v. are by victories undone 140a
Victory: at every famous v. 406a
courses of the V. were absorbed 181a
glorious thing must be a v., Sir 455a
gotten hast the v. ... 225a
honour was the meed of v. 408b
Joy, Empire, and V. ... 397b
life's v. won ... 292a
O grave, where is thy v.? 515a
such another v., we are undone 13b
that dishonest v. at Chæronea 278b
theft..is only v. in him ... 142a
the V. was gone ... 181a
to gain such a v. as this ... 455a
Truth beareth away the v. 520a
'twas a famous v. ... 406a
v. and praise in its own right 392b
v. is not a name strong enough 287a
v. is twice itself ... 357b
welcome to yr. gory bed, or to v. 62b
Westminster Abbey or v. 287a
Victuals: difficult to please about
their v. ... 75b
v. and the wine rather good 75b
we have no v. ... 440b
View: behold her face at ample v. 369b
Creation widened in man's v. 457a
do you admire the v. ... 84b
Goethe's wide and luminous v. 7a
lends enchantment to the v. 77a
made myself a motley to the v. 389a
observation with extensive v. 213b
point of v., then sinks downwards 179b
rapture of the forward v. 264a
transported with the V. 2a
v. fair Melrose aright ... 317a
v. the landscape o'er ... 453b
View-hollo: Peel's v. ... 173b
Viewing him since, alas, too late! 215a
Views: her happy v. ... 430a
they gave new v. to life 113b
Vigil: tongueless v. ... 420a
will yearly on the v. feast 383a
Vigilance: liberty..is eternal v. 116b
Vigilant: be sober, be v. ... 518a
I am as v. as a cat ... 378b
Vigils: mine eyes their v. keep 286b
Vigour: England..has a secret v. 147b
takes away v. from our arms 56a
the v. of the Lord ... 415b
years steal..v. from the limb 68a
Vigorous: conservatives when they
are least v. ... 148a
Vikings: stir the V.' blood ... 226a
Vile: be he ne'er so v. ... 383a
better to be v. than v. esteemed 389a
find it cowardly and v. 341a
goodness to the v. seem v. 343b
make v. things precious 343a
only man is v. ... 184a
O v., intolerable ... 366b
who is here so v. ... 339b
Vileness: no inner v. that we dread? 430a
Vilest things become themselves 323a
Vilikins and his Dinah ... 526b
Villa: if one must have a v. 283b
Village: a v. less than Islington 107a
loveliest v. of the plain 168a
rather be first in a v. ... 13a
some v. Hampden ... 174a
the v. smithy stands ... 249a
thro' an Alpine v. passed 247a
vegetate in a v. ... 103b
v. maiden she ... 432b
Villagers: in gold and black, the v. 243a
Villages: pleasant v. and farms 276a
Villain: condemns me for a v. 385a
determined to prove a v. 384b
hungry, lean-faced v. 328a

Villain (*cont.*)
I am alone the v. 324*a*
if some eternal v. 363*a*
in tragic life..no v. need be 264*a*
one murder made a v. 304*b*
smile, and be a v. 331*b*
smiling, damned v. 331*b*
v. and he be many miles asunder 366*a*
v. dwelling in all Denmark 331*b*
v. to bereave my life 30*a*
Villains: as if we were v. by necessity 342*a*
God shd. go before such v. 359*a*
Villanous: foreheads v. low 367*b*
that's v., and shows..ambition 334*a*
Villany: clothe my naked v. 384*b*
in me 'tis v. ·
O v.! Ho! let the door be lock'd 337*a*
v. you teach me, I will execute 354*a*
Villatic: tame v. fowl 278*a*
Villiers: great V. lies—alas! 302*b*
Villon, our sad..brother's name 421*a*
Vinci: they spell it V. 446*b*
Vindicate the ways of God to man 300*b*
Vine: best fits a little v. 188*b*
eat in safety under his own v. 386*b*
every man under his v. 504*b*
foxlike in the v. 437*a*
lands of..maize and v. 426*a*
luscious clusters of the v. 260*b*
monarch of the v. 323*b*
Ruby kindles in the V. 152*a*
the gadding v. 269*b*
the mantling v. 274*a*
V. her ancient Ruby yields 152*a*
wife shall be as the fruitful v. 490*a*
wild v. slipping down 420*b*
Vinegar: gave me v. to drink 486*b*
other of such v. aspect 352*b*
pepper and v. besides 84*b*
Vine-leaves in his hair 567*a*
Vines: beggars, fleas and v. 226*a*
bless with fruit the v. 221*b*
foxes, that spoil the v. 500*a*
where Southern v. are drest 184*b*
Vine-sheltered: broad v. path 312*b*
Vineyard: my wellbeloved hath a v. 501*a*
who planteth a v. 514*a*
Vintage: a draught of v.! 219*b*
his V. rolling Time 153*a*
v. of Abi-ezer 495*a*
v. where the grapes of wrath 200*b*
Vintager: Ariadne was a v. 217*b*
Vintners: what the V. buy 154*a*
Vinum dæmonum: call poesy v. 13*a*
Viol: than an unstringed v. 374*b*
Violence: blown with restless v. 352*a*
by v. constrained to do anything 145*a*
essence of war is v. 254*a*
kingdom of heaven suffereth v. 506*b*
offer it the show of v. 329*b*
with v. shall that great city 519*b*
Violent: danger of v. death 191*b*
laid v. hands upon themselves 481*b*
so over v., or over civil 138*b*
virtue in ambition is v. 14*b*
Violently: move v. to their place 14*b*
v. if they must 307*b*
Violet: a grave's one v. 50*a*
dew that on the v. lies 317*b*
fashioned an April v. 452*a*
she is the v. 402*b*
the glowing v. 270*a*
the nodding v. grows 356*b*
throw a perfume on the v. 374*a*
v., amaracus 435*a*
v. by a mossy stone 470*b*
v. in the youth of..nature 330*b*
v. of his native land 430*a*
v. smells to him as it doth to me 382*b*
Violets: by ashen roots the v. blow 431*a*
daisies pied and v. blue 345*b*
fast fading v. 220*a*
from her..flesh may v. spring 336*b*
I wd. give you some v. 335*b*
lilies and v. meet 22*a*
mix v. with anything 129*b*
upon a bank of v. 369*b*
v., and the lily cups 195*a*
v. blue as yr. eyes 434*a*
v. dim, but sweeter than..Juno's eyes 373*a*

Violets (*cont.*)
v. of the Undercliff 229*a*
v.' reclining head 132*b*
v. suddenly bloom at her feet 27*a*
when sweet v. sicken 399*b*
where early v. die 318*a*
who are the v. now 376*a*
wind-flowers and v. 394*b*, 398*a*
Violin: flute, v., bassoon 434*a*
Violins: Antonio Stradivari's v. 144*b*
Viper: Lawyer killing a v. 100*b*
Vipers: O generation of v. 504*b*
to extirpate the v. 12*b*
Virgil: art thou then that V.? 566*b*
Homer and V. are forgotten 304*b*
Rome (sound) thy V.'s name 109*a*
the English V. [Spenser] 224*a*
the Shepherd in V. 206*b*
V. at Mexico 449*b*
Virgilian: worthy of the V. muse 37*a*
Virgin: a v. shall conceive 501*b*
a v.-widow and a *Mourning Bride* 141*a*
bashful v.'s side-long looks 168*a*
every harlot was a v. once 30*a*
now the V. returns 557*a*
pale V. shrouded in snow 32*a*
pre-elect God's V. 313*a*
see the V. blest 270*b*
so tho' a v., yet a bride 79*b*
withering on the v. thorn 356*a*
Virginal: quick, tender, v. 294*b*
Virginalling upon his palm 373*a*
Virgined: lip hath v. it e'er since 328*b*
Virginia: tobacco comes from V. 440*a*
Virginian: I am not a V. 185*b*
Virginians: rally behind the V. 24*b*
Virginity: that long-preserved v. 260*a*
the rash oath of v. 293*b*
Virgins: 'farewell,' she said, 'ye v. all' 531*b*
Martyrs, Prophets, V. 286*a*
of pure V. none is fairer 294*b*
therefore do the v. love thee 500*a*
v. are soft as the roses 67*b*
v. in their ecstasies 428*a*
v. that be her fellows 484*b*
Virgo! gr-r-r 52*a*
Virtue: adversity doth best discover v. 14*b*
ambition..in a prince, the v. 262*b*
as other men after v. 239*b*
assume a v., if you have it not 335*a*
being rich, my v. then shall be 374*a*
blunder'd on some v. unawares 94*b*
call v. there ungratefulness 401*b*
every v., every grace 240*b*
faith..let that arm thy v. 313*b*
fighting the lost fight of v. 412*a*
first upgrowth of all v. 226*b*
fix thy firm gaze on v. and on me 254*a*
flattered into v. 416*b*
forbearance ceases to be a v. 56*b*
from mere natural v. 288*b*
fugitive and cloistered v. 279*a*
goad us on to sin in loving v. 351*b*
greatest offence against v. 183*b*
he must delight in v. 1*b*
if there be any v. 516*a*
if v. feeble were 268*a*
if you can..keep yr. v. 230*a*
in conscious v. bold 298*b*
ladies..who make v. unamiable 410*b*
laments that v. cannot live 339*a*
lean'd to V.'s side 168*b*
let them look upon v. 552*a*
liberty..with order and v. 55*a*
lilies and languors of v. 421*a*
linked with one v. 70*a*
love v., she alone is free 268*a*
more v. than doth live 215*b*
my mouse of v. 370*a*
no distinction between v. and vice 207*b*
no road or ready way to v. 41*b*
no v. like necessity 374*b*
O infinite v.! 324*a*
only amaranthine flower..is v. 112*a*
patriots v.'s cause support 160*a*
redeem us from v. 421*b*
some by v. fall 351*b*
tart, cathartic v. 148*a*
thy mind all v. 206*b*
'tis some v., v. to commend 104*a*

Virtue (*cont.*)
'tis v...not birth..makes us noble
very sinews of v. 4
v.! a fig! 3
v. alone is happiness 3
v. alone is true nobility 1
v. and human knowledge 3
v. cd. see to do what v. wd. 2
v. had gone out of him 5
v. in ambition is violent
v. in her shape how lovely 2
v. is bold 3.
v. is its own reward 1
v. is like a rich stone
v. is the fount whence honour 2
v. itself of vice must pardon beg 3.
v. may be assailed 2
v. of paper government
v. of wax and parchment
v. rudely strumpeted 38
v. she finds too painful 30
v. that possession wd. not show 3:
v. that transgresses..but patch'd 3:
v., wh. cannot know the disgrace 5
v. wh. requires to be..guarded 1:
walls of some high V. 2:
wars that make ambition v. 3:
wh. into words no v. can digest 2:
whose solid v...cd. neither graze 3:
will change to v. and..worthiness 3:
without eradicating the v. 17
Virtues: be to her v. very kind 30
crimes, like v...own rewards 15
curse on his v.
force and fraud..cardinal v. 19
for several v...lik'd several women 36
his v. walk'd their..round 2:
his v. were his arts 5
his v. will plead like angels 34
if..v. did not go forth of us 35
in v. nothing earthly cd. surpass 7
mentioned her v., it is true 2
our v. barren 41
our v. would be proud 32
the trumpet of his own v. 35
my verse yr. v...shall eternize 40
v. neglected then, adored become 11
v. we write in water 38
v. wh. mine eyes had seen 46
whose..soul the v. well did suit 13
world to hide v. in 36
Virtuous: because thou art v. 37
be in general v. 15
but for the v. things you do 9
grow v. in their old age 304*a*, 41
ladies outrageously v. 41
most seeming-v. eye 7:
retired to his v. couch 45
the boy be v. still 11:
who can find a v. woman? 49
Virtuousest: seems wisest, v. 27
Visage: dejected 'haviour of the v. 33
hides not his v. from our cottage 37:
never see me more in the v. 25
Othello's v. in his mind 36
Visages: men whose v. do cream 35:
Vishnu-land what Avatar? 5:
Visible: all things v. 48
Vision: a more delightful v. 57
as thy v. here solicited 421
bright thy v. that delighted 258
by the v. splendid 36
city such as v. builds 396
double the v. my eyes do see 29
double v. is always with me 29
enjoy'd in v. beatific 272
fabric of this v. 367
fatal v., sensible to feeling 347
his life is a watch or a v. 42
in a v. once I saw 10:
my v.'s greatest enemy 29
my v. with the song 263
saw the V. of the world 432
scarce seemed a v. 396
the v. raised its head 20:
the young men's v. 138
v. and the faculty divine ·64
V. of Christ wh. those dost see 29
v. of some person or persons 204
V. of the guarded mount 270
was it a v., or a waking dream? 220

ion (cont.)
hat stately v. mocks my..sense? 403b
where there is no v., the people
  perish 499a
with the v. glorious 415b
ou see my v.'s limited 126b
onary: fled the v. gleam 466a
. joys remove 105a
ions: I have multiplied v. 504a
ost in stormy v. 392b
ay Oberon! what v. have I seen? 357a
. of glory, spare my..sight 173b
oung men shall see v. 504a
it: intending to v. them more 424b
. it by the pale moonlight 317a
. the fatherless and widows 517b
o trusted man his annual v. 443b
what thy short v. meant 240a
itation: in the time of their v. 520a
nightly v. unimplored 276a
winds of Spring in rarest v. 397a
itations: aeolian v. 469a
itings: compunctious v. of nature 346b
its: like angels' v., short 289b
y. like those of angels 29a
ality: not v. enough to preserve it 211b
. in a woman..fury of creation 390b
tals: feed thee out of my own v.? 104b
truvius: you, the best V. 140a
vified: filled and v. by Thee 280a
zards to our hearts 349a
-notes are something 48b
ocabulary of Bradshaw 136a
ocation: as if his whole v. 466b
labour in his v. 376b
'tis my v., Hal 376b
worthy of the v. 515b
gue: totter into v. 449b
ice: after the fire a still small v. 496a
aggravate my v. so 356b
a great v., as of a trumpet 518a
and that a mighty v. 486b
a thrilling v. is sounding 86b
a V. above their beat 441b
a v. less loud 48b
a v. whose sound was like the sea 467b
a v. will run from hedge 221a
because of the bridegroom's v. 510b
bird of the air..carry the v. 499b
bird, or but a wandering v. 463b
but few thy v. 330b
clear sonorous v. 464b
distant v., in the darkness 249a
each a mighty V. 471b
find their sole v. in that..brow 7b
gave thee such a tender v. 32b
harmonious sisters, V. and Verse 278a
hear a v. in every wind 174b
heard a v. cry 'Sleep no more!' 348a
heart and soul and v. 286b
heart and v. opprest 286a
hear the v. of the Bard 31b
her v., and her hair, and eyes 261b
her v...might give th' alarm 457a
her v. in the street 497b
her v. revives the leaden strings 78a
her v. was ever soft 344a
his lip manly v. 326b
his sweet v. he rears 99b
his v. in all her music 392b
his v. was buried among trees 468a
his v. was propertied 325a
I heard a v.; it said 468b
in..poverty thy v. did weave 399b
I sing with mortal v. 275a
is, and is not the v. of God 303b
I thought I knew the v. 235a
it is the v. of a god 512a
joy is the sweet v. 100b
let thy v. rise like a fountain 429a
lift up yr. v.; rejoice 455b
look at me..in that tone of v. 535b
Lord, hear my v. 490a
Mountain's slumbrous v. 396a
my v. ascending high 453a
no magic of her v. 293b
no v.; but oh! the silence 99b
no v. hed sech a swing 250b
no v. or hideous hum 270b
O! for a falconer's v. 365b
or the v. of one beloved 397a

Voice (cont.)
our song is the v. of desire 37a
people's v. is odd 303b
raise for good..supplicating v. 214a
refuseth..the v. of the charmer 485b
reserve the more weighty v. 15b
seasoned with a gracious v. 354a
singest with v. memorial 88a
sing to the Lord with cheerful v. 224b
small v. spake unto me 438b
so charming left his v. 275b
so in a v. 131b
sole daughter of his v. 276a
so silvery is thy v. 190b
sound of a voice that is still 425b
speak in a monstrous little v. 356a
sweeter thy v. 437a
that gentle v. we hear 11a
that V. is round me 442a
there came a v. without reply 147a
the v. of my complaint 483a
the v. of the great Creator 82b
the v. said, Cry 502b
the v. so sweet 216b
this is the same v. 51a
thy gentle v. my spirit can cheer 245b
thy v. and hand shake still 312b
thy v., thy lute 220a
'tis the v. of the lobster 83b
'tis the v. of the sluggard 453a
utter forth a glorious V. 2a
v. and the shape of a woman 222b
v. as the sound of many waters 518b
v. behind me whispered low 459b
v., I have lost it with hollaing 379b
v. I heard this passing night 220a
v. is heard thro' rolling drums 436b
v. is Jacob's v. 493a
v. of Cato is the v. of Rome 214b
v. of him..in the wilderness 502b
v. of joy and health 489a
v. of one crying in the wilderness 504b
v. of the dead was a living v. 431b
v. of the Lord God walking 492b
v. of the Lord maketh the hinds 483b
v. of the people hath..divineness 13b
v. of the people is the v. of God 537a
v. of the people, the v. of God 309a
v. of the schoolboy rallies 287b
v. of the turtle is heard 500a
v. of thy brother's blood 492b
v. said in mastery while I strove 43b
v. so thrilling ne'er was heard 471a
v. that breath'd o'er Eden 224a
v. thro' mazes running 269a
V. within the Tavern 152a
wake thy wild v. anew 318b
what v. did on my spirit fall 96b
when I shall v. aloud 249b
wild v. pealing up 433b
Voiced like a great bell 154b
Voices: ancestral v. prophesying war 101b
brothers, lift yr. v. 20a
great V. roll in from Sea 445b
I hear their gentle v. calling 156b
men, with wailing in yr. v.! 44a
moans round with many v. 439a
music, when soft v. die 399b
our v. keep tune 282b
their v. are heard among them 482b
there are no v., O Rhodopé! 241b
two v. are there 410b, 471b
v. of children..on the green 32b
where beyond these v...is peace 428a
wh. angel v. tell 266a
yr. v...yr. most sweet v. 328a
Void: left an aching v. 100b
nor made a pause, nor left a v. 210b
that his might cd. render v. 38b
Volaterræ: from lordly V. 253a
Volcanoes: range of exhausted v. 128b
religious factions..v. burnt out 56b
Volleyed and thundered 426a
Volscians: flutter'd yr. V. in Corioli 328b
Voltaire: mock on, V., Rousseau 31b
read that moderate man V. 180a
[V.] built God a church 110b
Volubility: I'll commend her v. 366b
Volume: lo here a little v. 115a
lose a v. to [Coleridge] 239a
this fair v. wh. the World..name 137b

Volume (cont.)
v. of forgotten lore 298a
v. of the book it is written 484a
wrote them in a certain v. 49a
Volumes: all Earth's v. carry 87b
from mine own library with v. 367a
I am for whole v. 344b
pricks to their subsequent v. 368b
Voluptuous: music arose with its v.
  swell 68a
Voluptuousness: misanthropy and v. 255a
Vomit: dog is turned to his own v. 518a
dog returneth to his v. 498b
Vorpal: the v. blade 84a
took his v. sword 83b
Vortex of immensity 124a
Votaress: imperial v. passed on 356b
Votarist: like a sad v. 207a
Votary of the desk 239a
Vote: to hunt, and v. 67b
to lend him a v. 169b
Votes: questions but the price of v. 213b
Vovi—I've Oude 535a
Vow: better..that thou shdst. not v. 499a
do not v. 149a
hand in hand even with the v. 331b
I v. to thee, my country 409b
that great v. wh. did..make us one 338b
Vowels: the open v. tire 300a
Vows: cancel all our v. 137b
God keep all v. 376a
hour when lovers' v. seem sweet 73b
I take the tongueless v. 441a
lends the tongue v. 331a
our moist v. denied 270a
prove much in our v. 371a
suck'd the honey of his music v. 333b
v. can't change nature 51a
v., to the blackest devil 335b
v. with so much passion 244a
whose rival amorous v. 37b
Voyage: all the v. of their life 341a
drear was the v., sailor 315b
dry as the..biscuit after a v. 326b
its v. closed and done 457b
never thus cd. v. on 395a
take my last v. 191b
Voyager: lands the v. at last 145b
Vulcan: V. and his whole forge 41a
V.'s stithy 334a
Vulgar: all is v., all clumsy 97a
both the great v., and the small 107a
ca' them v. farin' 285b
familiar, but by no means v. 330b
I saw a little v. Boy 19b
laugh!..such a v. expression 104a
takes place with the v. 13b
when it is looked upon as v. 460a
wicked, my dear, it's v. 535b
work upon the v. with fine sense 304a
Vulgarize the day of judgment 205b
Vulture: where the rage of the v. 67b

W

Wabe: gimble in the w. 83b
Waddy is an infectious disease 237b
Wade: shd. I w. no more 349b
Wae to think upo' yon den 59a
Wafted: spices are w. abroad 434a
Wafture of yr. hand 338b
Wag: Mother's w. 176a
Wage: for wh. they drew the w. 236a
paid his subjects..a royal w. 39a
Wagers: Fools for argument use w. 65b
Wages: be content with yr. w. 509a
give her the w. of going on 439a
I know what w. beauty gives 476a
my scanty w. as well 390a
my w. taken 185a
progress..apportioning..w. to
  work 81a
ta'en thy w. 329a
took their w. and are dead 200a
w. of sin is death 513a
Wagging: better a finger off, as
  ay w. 320a
Waggoner, a small grey-coated gnat 364b
Waggons: cany w. light 273b

ENGLISH INDEX

Waggon-spokes made of..spinners' 364b
Wagon to a star 148b
Wags: how the world w. 326a
  I must confess, are w. too 379b
  you w. that judge by rote 291b
Wail: earth shall w. because of him 518a
  old woes new w. 387b
  yet so does w.? 251b
Wailers: delv'd gold, the w. heap! 44a
Wailing: deeply w. 456a
Wain upon the northern steep 200a
Waist: arms went round her w. 261b
  full bosom to thy slender w. 305b
  her slender w. confined 448b
  round her w. she felt it fold 426b
  strapp'd w., and frozen locks 112a
  then you live about her w. 332a
Waistcoat: get her a flannel w. 159a
  yolk runs down the w. 124b
Waistcoat-buttons: work them into
  w. 85b
Waistcoats: negroes..with flannel w. 126b
Wait: and w. upon her 190b
  each in his office w. 131b
  if you can w. and not be tired 230a
  is this a time to w.? 12a
  learn to labour and to w. 248a
  she'll w. a wee 63b
  that w. upon the Lord 502b
  the lily whispers, 'I w.' 434a
  these w. all upon thee 488b
  w. and see 10b
  w. the 'pointed hour 141b
  w. till the clouds roll by 462b
  w. upon Mary's sons 234b
  we can w. no longer 457b
  who only stand and w. 278b
  wd. not w. for me 199a
Waited: Oysters..w. in a row 84b
  w., duteous on them all 316a
  w. patiently for the Lord 484a
Waiter: if you look at the w. 126a
  one became head-w. 439b
  plump head-w. at the Cock 439b
Waiting: a-w. for their ain dear 530a
  find wings w. there 24b
  not be tired by w. 230a
  the w. time, my brothers 134b
  w. for Sir Richard Strachan 523a
Waiting-gentlewoman: talk so like
  a w. 376b
Waive: take the Cash..w. the Rest 152b
Wake: do I w. or sleep? 220a
  held we..sleep to w. 52a
  I'd go and w. them, if—— 85a
  sleping hound to w. 90a
  survived her own w. 255b
  those who w. and live 396a
  thou wilt not w. till I 225a
  w. and call me early 434b
  w.! for the Sun, who scatter'd 152a
  w. up America 158a
  we w. and whisper awhile 119a
  we w. eternally 133a
  will you w. him? No, not I 535a
  you will w., and remember 46b
Waked: I w., she fled 278b
  I w. to find her 275b
  you have w. me too soon 453a
Waked'st: thou w. me wisely 132a
Waken thou with me 436b
Wakening and uprising prove 223b
Wakes: at wh. he starts and w. 364b
  he haunts w., fairs 373a
  he w. or sleeps with the..dead 392a
  Hock-carts, wassails, w. 188b
  w. it now, to look so green 347a
Waketh: but my heart w. 500b
Waking: dream remembered on w. 36b
  thought upon these when I was w. 485b
  w., no such matter 388b
  w. or asleep, thou of death 398b
  w. with day 317b
Wakings: adieu..agreeable w. 105b
Waldo is one of those people 315b
Wales: God bless the Prince of W. 245b
  golden sea of W. 154a
  one road runs to W. 262a
Walet: his w. lay biforn 89a
Walk: a closer w. with God 109b
  ah, the w. that afternoon 293b

Walk (cont.)
  cloistress, she will veiled w. 369b
  his morning w...in the church-
    yard 319b
  I do here w. before thee 379b
  I w. abroad a nights 259a
  I w. unseen on the dry..green 268a
  men must w...before they dance 303b
  my very w. shd. be a jig 369b
  people w. hand in hand 104a
  shadows that w. by us still 23a
  swiftly w. over the western wave 399a
  take up thy bed, and w. 510b
  they shall w., and not faint 502b
  this is the way, w. ye in it 502a
  try to w. sedately 414a
  w. about Sion 485a
  w. along the Bois Bou-long 162b
  w. by myself in Westminster
    Abbey 1b
  w. in fear and dread 99b
  w. in newness of life 513a
  w. together to the kirk 100a
  w. while ye have the light 511a
  w. with stretched forth necks 501a
  w. with you, and talk with you 155a
  where'er you w. 302b
  will you w. a little faster? 83a
  with Thee, may w. uncowed 228a
Walked: Cat. He w. by himself 237a
  each..w. very crookedly 417a
  Him that w. the waves 270a
  him who w. in glory 470a
  I had not w. above a mile 448a
  w. about..in Thebes' streets 403b
  w. along our roads 241a
  w. he from his birth 227b
  w. on a mile or so 199a
Walkedst whither thou wouldest 511b
Walking: as I was w. all alone 529b
  be but a w. dictionary 87b
  craves wary w. 338a
  I nauseate w. 105a
  Jesus..w. on the sea 507a
  Johnnie Cope, are ye w. yet? 193b
  Joseph was a-w. 522a
  make the rough road easy w. 199b
  Proud Maisie..w. so early 319b
  seen us w. every day? 107a
  w. in an air of glory 448a
  w., like two angels white 37a
  w. up and down in it 496b
  w. up and pacing down 432b
  was w. on the strand 529a
  were w. close at hand 84a
Walks: echoing w. between 276b
  he that w. with the..night 458b
  in my w. it seems to me 26a
  liked the way it w. 308a
  nobody w. much faster 85a
  nothing w. with aimless feet 430b
  now the moon w. the night 119b
  once turned round w. on 99b
  she w.—the lady of my delight 265a
  silent w. I tread 113b
  studious w. and shades 277a
  such quiet w. as these 384a
  take my w. abroad 452b
  w. up and down with me 374a
Wall: built in Jerusalem's w. 30b
  darkly looked he at the w. 253a
  find thy body by the w. 6b
  flower in the crannied w. 427a
  Humpty Dumpty sat on a w. 85a
  I shall leap over the w. 482b
  Jackson standing like a stone w. 24b
  middle w. of partition 515b
  or close the w. up 382a
  our trumpets waken the W.! 234b
  reserve the hanging w. 301b
  seen a mous go by the w. 89b
  serves it in the office of a w. 375a
  shone on the old oak w. 22a
  smite thee, thou whited w. 512b
  something..that doesn't love a w. 157b
  stood against the w. 435b
  that the w. is strong 459b
  the Lord stood upon a w. 504b
  the w. fell down flat 494b
  the whitewash'd w. 168b
  weather on the outward w. 353b

Wall (cont.)
  with our backs to the w. 1
  without a city w.
  Wallace: wi' W. bled 319b
  Waller was smooth 3
  Wallet at his back 3
  Wallow naked in December's snow 3
  Wallowed in a score 1
  Walls: banners on the outward w. 3
  build thou the w. of Jerusalem 4
  close her from thy ancient w.
  deep and wide washes its w.
  Devil-defended 2
  grey bare w. lain guestless 4
  painting thy outward w. 3
  sick people groaning under w. 2
  snap-dragon growing on the w. 2
  stone w. do not a prison make 2
  w. have tongues 4
  w. in the New Jerusalem
  w., palaces, half-cities 6
  watches from his mountain w. 4
  within the spacious w. 1
  with w. and towers were girdled 1
  wooden w. are the best 1
  Walnuts and the wine 4
  Walrus and the Carpenter 84a
  Walsingham: holy land of W. 3
  Walter: good Sir W. met her 2
  Waltz: seductive W.! 7
  swoons to a w. 2
  voluptuous W.! 7
  Waly: w., w. up the bank 53
  w., w. gin love be bonnie 53
  Wand: ammiral, were but a w. 27
  with thine opiate w. 39
  Wander: himself he learned to w. 6
  I w. in the ways of men 6
  I wd. w. if I might 28
  let one's thought w. 47
  may w. ere he die 42
  then w. o'er city, and sea 39
  to w. unchecked thro' a garden 3
  w. in that golden maze 14
  w. where the Muses haunt 27
  we will not w. more 43
  whither shall I w.? 53
  wit! whither w. you? 32
  Wandered: as I w. by the way 39
  I w. by the brook-side 198
  I w. lonely as a cloud 467
  I w. till I died 8
  Wanderer: foiled circuitous w.
  himself w. from the narrow 110
  the w. halts and hears 190
  w. is man from his birth
  weary, wayworn w. bore 298
  Wandering: a w. minstrel I 164
  forget the w. and the pain 154
  have one with me w. 284
  I've been w. away 282
  poor w. one! 166
  restore thy w. Love 105
  sought thee w., set thee right 110
  w. companionless among the stars 396
  w. on as loth to die 467
  Wanderings: comrade of thy w. 396
  he chid their w. 168
  Want: eternal w. of pence 439
  feel there is some hidden w. 398
  first to get what you w. 404
  gift..will never let you w. 216
  I w. what I w. when I w. it 33
  making things wh. he doesn't w. 197
  not what they w. 116
  ring out the w. 431
  saying you w. to know 123
  the House of W. 161
  tho' much I w. 143
  thy w. as an armed man 498
  w. no manner of thing that is good 484
  w. of a thing is perplexing 447
  what can I w. or need? 188
  what does he w.? A pot of beer 125
  what do you w.? A pot of beer 534
  what more can one w.? 460
  Wanted: go where you are w.? 199a
  no nation w. it so much 419a
  not be w. these ten years 297b
  w. one thing..have w. everything 184a
  you w. it, George Dandin 564a

...ting: and art found w. 504a
...ot w. what is stolen 362a
. is—what? 52b
...nton: ah, w. will ye? 176a
w. and a merye 88b
...o further than a w.'s bird 365b
...ie w. smiled 176a
. in the South 436b
., with long delay 35b
., Zephyr sings 143a
...eep not, my w. 176a
...ntoned with thy breakers 69b
...ntonness: in clothes a w. 189a
...ad..only for w. 374a
...nts: it's everything he w. 201a
or w. that little long 169a
...resence shall my w. supply 2a
...rovide for human w. 57a
...o toast our w. 302a
., shd. be provided for 57a
...o them into our ship's side 530a
...r: accurst..that first invented w. 259a
...ll the business of w. 454b
...ll whom w., dearth, age 133a
...midst the ranks of w. 252b
...ncestral voices prophesying w. 101b
...s long as w. is regarded as wicked 460a
...s much and as little of the w. 15b
...t w. 'twixt will and will not 351b
...eautiful that w. and all its deeds 457b
...lood-red blossom of w. 434b
...razen threat of w. 276b
...Brutus, with himself at w. 337b
...arried the great w. from Macedon 9a
...ircumstance of glorious w.! 362a
...ome in yr. w. array 318b
...Dalhoussy, the great God of W. 298b
...elays are dangerous in w. 141b
...lo in the Great W., daddy? 527b
...ssence of w. is violence 254a
...linty and steel couch of w. 360b
...Force and fraud..in w...virtues 191b
...orming in the ranks of w. 68b
...hath all this w. been wrought 257b
...Horses and Power and W. 227a
...House of Peers, throughout the w. 164a
...I did not believe in inevitable w. 242b
...f, therefore, w. shd. ever come 242b
...mage of w., without its guilt 406a, 416b
...nfection and the hand of w. 375a
...n the trade of w...slain men 359b
...n time of peace thinks of w. 64a
...n w., he mounts the warrior's 317a
...n w. the two cardinal virtues 191b
...n w. moral considerations 564a
...John of Austria is going to the w. 92b
...less renowned than w. 278b
...ives in a state of w. by nature 419b
...love's a man of w. 188a
...magnificent, but it is not W. 561a
...Minstrel Boy to the w. is gone 281b
...moderation in w. is imbecility 254a
...my sentence is for open w. 272a
...neither is money..sinews of w. 15b
...neither..learn w. any more 501a
...no discharge in that w. 499b
...no discharge in the w. 227b
...offer w...shd. kneel for peace 367a
...or come ye in w. 318a
...peace to corrupt..w. to waste 276b
...people that delight in w. 486b
...shakes pestilence and w. 273a
...so dauntless in w. 318a
...some slain in w. 375b
...Son of God goes forth to w. 184a
...stand up and take the w. 229a
...stuff'd with epithets of w. 359b
...tell us all about the w. 406a
...the Lord is a man of w. 494a
...there never was a good w. 157a
...there was w. in heaven 519a
...they'll start another w. 186a
...to point out..that this is w. 1a
...to w. against thee more 421a
...to w. and arms I fly 250a
...tumult of her w. 415b
...unsuccessful or suceesful w. 111b
...'unting is..the image of w. 416b
...used to w.'s alarms 194b
...wage no w. with women 406b
...w...boys..is all hell 401a

War (cont.)
w., death, or sickness 356a
w. even to the knife! 68a
w. has its laws 288a
w., he sung, is toil and trouble 139a
w. is the trade of kings 140b
w. its thousands slays 304b
w. lays a burden on the..state 108a
W. makes rattling good history 179b
w...national industry of Prussia 562b
w., nor battle's sound was heard 270a
w.'s a game..were..subjects wise 112b
w.'s annals will cloud into night 179b
w.'s glorious art 477a
W. that will end W. 455b
w., w. is still the cry 68a
weapons of w. perished 495b
we've a w., an' a debt 250b
what can w. but endless w. still breed? 278b
what is peace? is it w.? 121a
when the blast of w. blows 382a
when was a w. not a w.? 78a
where mingles w.'s rattle 318a
who desires peace, prepare for w. 554a
who is able to make w. with him? 519a
wither'd is the garland of w. 324b
Warble: w., child 344b
w. his native wood-notes 269a
Warbled: notes as, w. to the string 268b
Warbler: Attic w. pours her throat 175b
every w. has his tune 111b
Sidney, w. of poetic prose 112b
Warblest at eve 278a
Warburton..rage for saying something 207a
Ward: American nation in th' Sixth W. 143a
Light and Mrs. Humphry W. 91b
thou knowest my old w. 377b
W. has no heart, they say 310a
Warder: w. silent on the hill! 317b
w.! w.! open quickly 12a
Wardrobe: their gay w. wear 269b
Wards: pretty young w. 163b
turn the key..in the oiled w. 221a
Ware: bed of W. 371b
I shd. dine at W. 109a
let me taste yr. w. 532b
ne'er be w. of mine own wit 326a
Warehouse of my knowledge 416b
Warfare: goeth a w...at his own charges? 514a
her w. is accomplished 502b
rest! thy w. o'er 316b
such a thing as legitimate w. 288a
the w. long 200a
Waring: what's become of W. 52b
when I last saw W. 52b
Warly cares, an' warly men 60b
Warm: aha, I am w. 502b
be w., but pure 72a
it is w. work 287a
nursing her wrath to keep it w. 62b
O! she's w. 373b
rises w. and bright 3a
to keep himself w. 533a
too w. to work, Hardy, to last long 287a
to w. their little loves 173b
to w. without heating 28a
w. him at his fire 186b
yr. down so w. 115a
War-man call'd Billy the Norman 120b
Warmed: I w. both hands 241a
Warmer: ys no weder w. 242b
Warming her pretty little toes 535b
Warming-pans: heroes were as good as w. 264b
Warmint: running into the w. 416b
Warms: it w. the very sickness 336a
w. in the sun 301a
Warmth: he w. himself 502b
Warmth: a little w., a little light 263a
awful w. about my heart 222b
I yearn'd for w. and colour 428a
no w., no cheerfulness 195a
w. to swell the grain 76a
Warn: to w., to comfort 470b
w. all traffic and detain 232b
Warned: be w. by my lot 230b
friends, be w. by me 26a

Warning: come without w. 118a
give little w. 19a
give w. to the world 388a
horrid w. gapèd wide 219a
is the shepherd's w. 522a
take w. by the fall 531b
Warns: conscience..w. me not to do 304a
War Office: except the British W. 390a
Warp: weave the w. 173b
Warrant: here's the w., Claudio 352a
Warren's blackin' 126b
Warring: w. in Heav'n 273b
w. within our breasts 259a
Warrior: home they brought her w. dead 436b
like a w. taking his rest 462a
painful w. famousèd for fight 387a
who is the happy W. 465a
Warriors: Clan Alpine's w. 316b
stern joy wh. w. feel 316b
Wars: amidst the w. of elements 1b
Christian men..serve in the w. 491b
clucked thee to the w. 328b
examine the w. of Pompey 382b
fierce w. and faithful loves 408b
he maketh w. to cease 484b
more..fears that w. or women 386a
no sound was heard of clashing w. 131b
peace is come and w. are over 199b
plumed troop, and the big w. 362a
ring out the thousand w. of old 431a
skilful in the w. 448a
their w. are merry 92a
w. and rumours of w. 507b
Warsaw: order reigns in W. 566b
Warts: roughnesses, pimples, w. 116a
Warwick: W. and Talbot 383a
W., peace 384b
Wary: adder..craves w. walking 338a
Was: I am not what I w. 306a
it w. a Turkey 121b
w.—whatever thou hast been 280a
wh. is and wh. w. 518a
Wash: gulfs will w. us down 439a
henceforth w. the river Rhine? 100b
it never comes out in the w. 234b
Lord, dost thou w. my feet? 511a
no tide shall ever w. away 241b
softly w. again and ever again 457b
they that w. on Monday 532b
thou shalt w. me..I..be whiter 485a
w. me in steep-down gulfs 364a
w. me, Saviour, or I die 445a
w. my hands in innocency 483b
w. yr. city of Cologne 100b
Washed: have w. their robes 519a
took water, and w. his hands 508a
w., and dressed, and warmed 261b
w. by Arethusa's fount 176a
Washes: moon..w. all the air 356b
w. its walls on the southern side 50a
Washing: always w., and never.. finished 181a
came up from the w. 500a
seemed w. his hands 195a
taking in one another's w. 573b
Washington: Government at W. lives! 158b
take in at W. Inn 27a
Washingtonian dignity 304b
Waspish: when you are w. 340b
Wasps: bottled w. upon a wall 110b
Wassailing: here we come a-w. 523b
Waste: across this watery w. 96b
his flames must w. away 79a
hushed Chorasmian w. 8a
I love all w. and solitary places 395a
in..wide w. there still is a tree 74a
pale W. widens around 6a
to the bound of the w. 7b
to what purpose is this w.? 508a
weary w. of waters 406b
were I in the wildest w. 62b
young affections run to w. 69a
Wasted: talk not of w. affection 247a
why this charm is w. 147a
Wasteful: was yr. youth of pleasure w.? 48b
Wastel-breed: milk and w. 88b
Wastes her time and me 449a
Wat: poor W., far off upon a hill 386b

Wat (cont.)

to w. their cork-heeled shoon	530a
they w. their hats abune	530a

Watch: a w. and chain, of course | 309b
before the morning w. | 490a
call the rest of the w. together | 358b
cat wd. w. a mouse | 418b
engine [a w.] to our ears | 417b
for the w. to babble and to talk | 358b
his life is a w. | 420b
keeping w. above his own | 250b
Lord w. between me and thee | 493a
men wont to w. on duty | 271b
one to w., and one to pray | 2b
past as a w. in the night | 487b
Saints their w. are keeping | 415b
set a w., O Lord, before my mouth | 490b
she shall w. all night | 366b
short as the w. | 453a
stars set their w. in the sky | 77b
they w. from their graves! | 48a
w. and pray | 146a
w. did thine anxious servants | 444b
w. o'er man's mortality | 467a
w. the wall, my darling | 234a
w.! while in slumbers..she sleeps! | 248b
w. with me one hour | 508a
wear yr. learning, like yr. w. | 90b
where none can w. her | 198a
wh. w. not one another out of fear | 133a
Watch-dog: w.'s honest bark | 70a
w.'s voice that bayed | 168b
Watch-dogs bark | 367a
Watched: he w. and wept | 168b
I have w…am even as..a sparrow | 488a
Watches: endured thro' w. of the dark | 443a
heart that w. and receives | 471b
he w. from his mountain walls | 426b
our judgments as our w. | 300a
Watchful: guard me with a w. Eye | 2a
w. at His gate | 131b
Watching: before I tire of w. you | 39b
w. round you still | 3a
with w. and with study faint | 94b
Watchman: w. on the lonely tower | 317b
w. said, The morning cometh | 502a
w. waketh but in vain | 489b
w., what of the night? | 502a
Watchmen that went about the city | 500b
Watch-tower in the skies | 268b
Watchword: w. is security | 297a
w. of the Liberal Party | 38a
Water: across the stormy w. | 77a
a cup of cold w. only | 506b
and with w. of affliction | 496b
as w. spilt on the ground | 495b
barge..burn'd on the w. | 323a
benison of hot w. | 39a
better deeds shall be in w. writ | 23a
blood is thick, but w.'s thin | 164a
Blood..than w.'s thicker | 202b
but limns the w. | 17a
by trinking up ta w. | 12b
by w. and the Word | 415b
by w. he sente hem hoom | 88b
cast the w. of thy land | 350b
charmed w. burned alway | 99a
Christ walking on the w. | 442b
clouds they are without w. | 518a
conscious w. saw its God | 114b
dense shadowy w. | 202b
dreadful noise of w. | 384b
drink no longer w. | 516b
drops of w. hollow out a stone | 552a
drunk yr. w. and wine | 230a
earth hath bubbles, as the w. has | 346a
fetch you w. out of this rock? | 494a
fish out of the w. | 321b
for the bittern, and pools of w. | 502a
Garden by the W. blows | 152a
good..come of w. and of mud | 39a
he took w., and washed his hands | 508a
I came like W. | 153a
I don't care where the w. goes | 93b
if I were under w. | 222b
I hear lake w. lapping | 475b
indistinct, as w. is in w. | 324b
in the w. under the earth | 480a
I stained the w. clear | 32b
it is an automa, runs under w. | 216a

Water (cont.)

King over the W.	526b
land where no w. is	485b
lay a great w.	429a
like W. willy-nilly flowing	153a
little drops of w.	82a
made the w. wh. they beat	323a
miller sees not all the w.	64b
Minnehaha, Laughing W.	248b
more w. glideth by the mill	368a
name was writ in w.	223b
nor sodden at all with w.	493b
not all the w. in the..rude sea	375a
o'er the w. to Charlie	193a
over the w., and over the sea	320a
over the w. to Charlie	320a
pools are filled with w.	487a
pour this oil..on the w.	24b
Prussic acid without any w.	19b
ready by w. as by land	146a
reasons made his mouth to w.	65a
ridden that wan w.	531a
river of w. of life	520a
rivers of w. in a dry place	502a
salt w. unbounded	234a
same place sweet w. and bitter?	517b
Skuttle Fish..blackens all the W.	2b
so low that she drinks w.	87a
sound of w.'s murmuring	397b
the w. come down at Lodore?	406b
the whole stay of w.	501a
this business will never hold w.	95b
'tis with him in standing w.	370a
too much of w. hast thou	336a
under the w. it rumbled on	99b
unseen, and full of w.	376a
unstable as water…shalt not excel	493b
virtues we write in w.	386a
washing..in imperceptible w.	195a
wash their feet in soda w.	144b
w. but the desert	69a
w. flowed in it dazzled their eyes	531a
w. is best	560a
w. like a stone	311a
w., like a witch's oils	98b
w. of life freely	519b, 520b
w. once a day her chamber	369b
w. shall hear me	406b
w. springs up..boiled	180b
w.'s wider, thank the Lord	202b
w. through a sieve	85b
w., w., everywhere	98b
w. yr. damned flower-pots	52a
wetter w., slimier slime	39a
whar de b'iling w. hit	181b
what's the w. in French	124b
wilderness a standing w.	488b
you will do yr. work on w.	229b
Water-brooks: hart desireth the w. | 484b
Water-colour: amateur painting in w. | 413a
Watered: but it is fed and w. | 76a
w. the whole face of the land | 492a
Waterfall he named her | 248b
Waterflags in flower | 293b
Water-flies: let the w. blow me | 325a
Water-fly: dost know this w.? | 337a
Water-flood: Lord sitteth above the w. | 483b
Water-floods..not come nigh him | 483b
Watering that last year's crop | 144a
Water-land of Dutchmen | 71b
Water-lilies: floating w., broad and bright | 398a
Water-lily: she saw the w. bloom | 431b
Waterloo: he was stricken at W. | 93a
meets his W. at last | 296b
our W., Watson | 135b
that world-earthquake, W.! | 435a
W. House young man | 165b
W.'s ensanguined plain | 525b
W. was won..playing-fields of Eton | 454b
Waterman: jolly young w. | 120b
w., looking one way | 54a
Watermen, that row one way | 64a
Water-mill: noise like that of a w. | 417b
Water-pipes: noise of the w. | 484b
Waters: all that move in the W. | 478a
all w. as the shore | 421a
and the w. murmuring | 268b
as cold w. to a thirsty soul | 498b

Waters (cont.)

as the w. cover the sea	2b, 5
at the w. of strife	4
beams of his chambers in the w.	4
beside the w. of comfort	4
bosom the bright w. meet	2
brook into the main of w.	3
by the w. of Babylon	449b, 4
calm in w., seen	3
cast thy bread upon the w.	4
come ye to the w.	5
cool w. where we used to dwell	10
crept by me upon the w.	30
drifts away like the w.	4
fades o'er the blue	
fen of stagnant w.	40
flowed 'with pomp of w.'	40
gently by his, ye w., glide!	
give place like the pale w.	42
God moved upon the face of the w.	49
into what great w.	41
its w., returning back	24
knowledge of man is as the w.	
luminous home of w.	
many w. cannot quench love	50
mighty w. rolling evermore	
much deeper w. than I had thought	13
nor sound of w. shaken	42
obscure w. slope into a darkness	5
occupy their business in great w.	
once more upon the w.	6
over the waste of w.	7
rocks, unscaleable, and roaring w.	32
see thee in our w. yet appear	21
stolen w. are sweet	49
swell the curled w.	34
the width of the w., the hush	
tho' Thou the w. warp	32
thro' the Red Sea w.	28
to the w. and the wild	47
turning bitter w. into sweetness	14
w. of the crisped spring	11
w. of wide Agony	39
w. on a starry night	
w. on my cheek bestowed	10
w. stand in the hills	48
w. stilled at even	31
w. were his winding sheet	2
w. wild went o'er his child	7
weary waste of w.	40
while the w. nearer roll	45
whore that sitteth upon many w.	51
with a clamour of w.	42
with earth's w. make accord	44
world of w. wild	44
Waterside: tree planted by the w. | 48
Water-springs of a dry ground | 48
Water-tower: great grey w. | 9
Watery: across this w. waste | 9
Watson: a long shot, W. | 13
good old W.! | 13
I thought I knew my W. | 13
it is my belief, W. | 13
W., the fair sex is yr. department | 13
you know my methods, W. | 13
Watts: Boys, give 'em W.! | 182
Waught: right gude-willie w. | 59
Wave: all sunk beneath the w. | 111
a winning w. (deserving note) | 189
brooding on the charmèd w. | 27
chin upon an orient w. | 27
dies a w. along the shore | 18
glassy, cool, translucent w. | 268
in sight of the great third w. | 424
last w. pales | 154
over the western w. | 399
plunged..into the billowy w. | 165
the blind w., feeling round | 428
w. and whirlwind wrestle | 24
w. may not foam | 184
w. that echoes round the world | 428
w. to pant beneath thy power | 396
weak as is the breaking w. | 469
wish you a w. o' the sea | 373
within the w.'s intenser day | 396
Waved: long has it w. on high | 194
Waverley pen | 527
Wavers to a rose | 131
Waves: all thy w. and storms | 484
Britannia rule(s) the w. | 77a, 443

es (cont.)

at came the w.	408a
me as the w. come	319a
ated midway on the w.	101b
ee as the sons of the w.?	158b
om w. serener far	394a
ear the w. roar	6a
eed not the rolling w.	315b
ere shall thy proud w. be stayed	497b
see the w. upon the shore	399a
ght-hearted Masters of the w.	8b
ke as the w. make..the shore	388a
tle w. of Breffny	172a
nged for dash of w.	8a
ever a wave of all her w.	234b
othing, save the w. and I	71a
er the mountain w.	78a
ough the w. no more	111a
ging w. of the sea	518a
e noise of his w.	486a
e w. whitened	421b
e w. bound beneath me	68a
e wild w. whist	367a
red w., vainly breaking	96b
an w. and wet winds labour	422a
..are mighty, and rage horribly	487b
. be upon you at last	423b
. clasp one another	395b
., flowers, clouds, woods, rocks	393b
. of thy sweet singing	394a, 397b
. that beat on Heaven's shore	29b
. you to a more removed ground	331a
hat are the wild w. saying	82b
hen the w. went high	138a
esty w. confound and swallow	349b
vy in the dusk	263b
x: hereafter will the w. and wane	154a
tapers—that's w.	182a
ke as w. melteth	486a
irtue of w. and parchment	55b
. to receive, and marble to retain	67b
xwork: Mrs. Jarley's w. show	125a
y: adorns and cheers our w.	168a
little pleasure out of the w.	87b
s birds their trackless w.	49b
road is the w...to destruction	505b
are not wh. w. we go	146a
im and perilous w.!	464a
ach thing give him w.	322b
und out his uncouth w.	272b
ound thee a w...to rise in	386a
iad she come all the w. for this	284a
eav'n's wide pathless w.	268a
am already on the w.	225a
am the w., the truth	511a
f w. to the Better there be	179b
know the w. she went	433b
n the w. with him	505a
nto their own country another w.	504b
see my w. as birds	49b
ast this w. a-fishing	450b
ed them forth by the right w.	488b
ife with its w. before us lies	279b
ong is the w. and hard	272b
ong w. to Tipperary	461a
nake thy w. plain before my face	482a
ny w...begin with the beginning	70a
New W. to Pay Old Debts	262b
iarrow is..w...leadeth unto life	505b
iever in the w., nor out of the w.	87b
orepare ye the w. of the Lord	502b
oretty Fanny's w.	292b
orimrose w...everlasting bonfire	348a
ebellion lay in his w.	378b
he went her unremembering w.	441a
ome w. of common trade	375b
uch a winning w. with you	105a
hat's the eftest w.	359a
hat thy w. may be known	486a
hat w. madness lies	343a
hee conversing, I forget the w.	161a
the farthest w. about	307a
the w. was long	316b
there was but one w.	382a
the w. of all flesh	105b, 321b, 454b
this is the w. the world ends	145a
this is the w., walk ye in it	502a
this w. and that w., and wh. w.	160a
this w. or that	463a
thorny w. to heaven	330b
to catch the nearest w.	346b

Way (cont.)

tread the Narrow W.	227b
walk yr. mystic w.	165a
wanderer from the narrow w.	110b
w. is all so very plain	93b
w. is long to the sun	422b
w. of all the earth	494b
w. of an eagle	499a
w. of transgressors is hard	498a
w. to heaven..by water as by land	146a
we may lose the w.	93b
what leads the nearest w.	278b
young man cleanse his w.	489a
Wayfaring men, tho' fools	502a
Waylay: to startle, and w.	470b
Ways: blood is nipp'd and w. be foul	345b
can take no middle w.	37b
cheerful w. of men	273b
dwelt among untrodden w.	470b
for w. that are dark	182a
gave him light in his w.	420b
her w. are w. of gentleness	409b
her w. are w. of pleasantness	497b
her w. be unconfined	305b
her w. to roam	40a
how many w. and days!	312b
I am with them, in some w.	459b
know not well the subtle w.	146a
neither are yr. w. my w.	503a
nine and sixty w...tribal lays	230a
oldest sins the newest kind of w.	381a
one of two bad w.	339b
several w. they run	119b
she had not these w.	475a
sure in all His w.	288b
teach thy w. unto the wicked	485a
their incommunicable w. follow	312a
wild hills and rough uneven w.	375a
winding mossy w.	220a
windy w. of men	439a
world and its w...certain worth	52a
yr. great and gracious w.	294a
Wayside: some seeds fell by the w.	506b
Wayward: strange and w. wight	22b
Wayworn wanderer bore	298a
We: w. authors, Ma'am	129a
people like us are W.	236a
put it down w., my Lord	126b
still it is not w.	93a
time stays, w. go	131a
w. must eat w.	440b
Weak: admiration only of w. minds	277a
alack! too w. the conflict	344a
bear the infirmities of the w.	514a
but he is w.; both Man and Boy	469a
concessions of the w...of fear	55b
God hath chosen the w. things	514a
how very w. the very wise	440b
idleness..refuge of w. minds	91a
made w. by time and fate	439a
mortality's too w. to bear	289b
my love is w. and faint	110a
not a child so small and w.	3b
speak for the fallen and the w.	250b
to be w. is miserable	271a
the w. alone repent	70a
w. and beggarly elements	515a
w. as is a breaking wave	469a
w. brother..the worst of mankind	413a
w. one is singled to endure	395a
Weaker: to the w. side inclined	66a
Weakest: fondest, blindest, w.	442a
w. saint upon his knees	110a
Weak-hearted: help the w.	479a
Weakness: all w. that impairs	7b
amiable w.	151b, 400b
is it w. of intellect, birdie	165a
made perfect in w.	515b
no w., no contempt, disparage	278a
one man's w...the strength of all	301a
owning her w.	196a
she strove against her w.	432b
too much w. for the stoic's	301a
w. is not in yr. word	7b
w. of our mortal nature	479b
Weaknesses: his w. are great	227a
w. with a delicate hand	170b
Weal: come w., come woe	320a
never shall be parted, w. or woe	276b
Wealth: all that w. e'er gave	174a
as their w. increases, so enclose	259a

Wealth (cont.)

best riches, ignorance of w.	168a
boundless his w. as wish	317a
bring home the w. of the Indies	210a
consume w. without producing it	390a
get place and w.	303b
in health and w. long to live	478b
let w. and commerce..die	258a
little w. he had	419a
love remembered such w. brings	387b
nobility..prevents the rule of w.	17b
no w. but life	315a
shade that follows w. or fame	169a
Sleep..the poor man's w.	401b
squandering w...his peculiar art	138b
swim'st thou in w.	119a
to rank and w. are given	150a
wait for w., or honours	465a
w. I seek not	414a
w. or rank possessing	286b
w. to me the show had brought	467a
where w. accumulates	168a
where w. and freedom reign	170a
wretched man outlive his *wealth*	355a
Wealthy: healthy, w., and wise	157a
Weaned: soul is even like a w. child	490a
were we not w. till then	133a
Weans: are the w. in their bed	266a
fire-side clime to w. and wife	59a
Weapon: other hand held a w.	496b
trusty shield and w.	569a
Weaponless himself	277b
Weapon-point: at w. they close	318b
Weapons: Christian men..to wear w.	491b
get yr. w. ready	457b
w. of war perished	495b
Wear: nothing else to w.	163b
w. out than to rust out	116a
w. out the everlasting flint	365b
w. without corrival	377a
will us to w. ourselves	259a
Wearer: Mr. William W.	454a
Wearer: by the merit of the w.!	353b
Wearers of rings and chains!	241a
Wearied and forlorn	284b
Wearies me, you say it w. you	352b
Weariness: art thou pale for w.	396a
deep w. and sated lust	7a
for w. of thee	133b
thro' w. they failed	110a
w. can snore upon the flint	329a
w. not on yr. brow	7b
w., the fever, and the fret	220a
yet w. may toss him	188a
Wearing: for w. a black gown	90b
I'm w. awa' to the land	285b
the worse for w.	120b
w. his wisdom lightly	426b
w. o' the Green	525b
w. the white flower	427b
Wears: so w. she to him	370b
w. out his time	359b
w. the turning globe	200a
Weary: art thou w.	286a
a w. time!	98b
be not w. in well doing	516b
eyelids are a little w.	292b
glazed each w. eye	98b
how w., stale, flat	330a
I am w. of days and hours	422a
I'm w. wi' hunting	529b
I sae w. fu' o' care	63b
let him be rich and w.	188a
let us not be w. in well doing	515b
Oh, I am very w.	38b
run, and not be w.	502b
say I'm w., say I'm sad	202a
she, the w. Titan	6b
she was full w. of her watch	143b
there the w. be at rest	497a
w. and ill at ease	306b
w. and kind one linger'd	476a
w. and old with service	386a
w. of breath	195b
w. of earth and laden with my sin	415b
w. with toil, I haste me	387a
Weasel: as a w. sucks eggs	326a
methinks it is like a w.	334b
pop goes the w.!	257b
Weather: and thro' cloudy w.	18b
but winter and rough w.	326a

Weather (cont.)
constant be, come wind, come w. 54b
first talk is of the w. 213a
for the old June w. 46a
hap to the fresh fierce weather 424a
hard grey w. breeds hard..men 226a
if it prove fair w. 416a
ill is the w...bringeth no gain 119a
in calm or stormy w. 311a
in sad or singing w. 423a
in the blue unclouded w. 431b
little we fear w. without 440b
martlet, builds in the w. 353b
mention again it was gorgeous w. 75b
136 different kinds of w. 447a
plaguy twelve-penny w. 418a
politics go by the w. 175b
respite to husbands..w. may send 446a
roof of blue Italian w. 395b
say it will be fair w. 507a
season of calm w. 466b
'tis very warm w...in bed 418a
under the w. 413b
variety about the New England w. 446b
w. ginneth clere 90a
w. the cuckoo likes 180a
w. the shepherd shuns 180a
woo foul w. all too soon 196a
ys no w. warmer 242b
Weather-beaten sail more willing 78b
Weather-cock: there was no w. 463a
Weatherwise: if the Bard was w. 100b
some are w. 157a
Weave: ever so will w. 179a
so fair a fancy few wd. w. 180a
tangled web we w. 318b
w. a circle round him thrice 101b
w. the warp, and w. the woof 173b
Weaves, and is clothed with derision 420b
Web: go fetch a w. 530a
magic in the w. of it 362b
out flew the w. 431b
she left the w. 431b
tangled we w. weave 318b
w. of human things 392b
w. of our life..of a mingled yarn 322a
with as little a w. as this 361a
Webs: and trafficked for strange w. 293a
takes the flood with swarthy w. 429b
Webster: W. steam-engine in trousers 404b
W. was much possessed by death 145a
Wed: she wore when she was w. 433a
star and think to w. it 322a
young lovers lately w. 431b
Wedded: art w. to calamity 366b
Faith, once w. fast 282a
hail w. love, mysterious law 274b
tho' w. we have been 108a
w. to the Earlie's son! 318b
w. to this goodly universe 464a
Wedding: bought her w. clothes 2b
cheer for the Sergeant's w. 234a
get the w. dresses ready 71b
let's have a w. 123b
our w. cheer to a sad burial 366a
peal upon our w. 199a
wooing, w., and repenting 358a
Wedding-day: barefoot on her w. 366b
brightly dawns our w. 164b
drink good wine upon the w. 530b
in tears—and on his w.! 164a
said John, it is my w. 109a
to-morrow is our w. 108a
Wedding-guest: W. here beat his
breast 98a
W. sat on a stone 98a
W. stood still 98a
W.! this soul hath been 100a
Wedding-ring: circle of a w. 95b
Wede: withered w. all away 97a
Wedges: in time small w. cleave 238a
w. of gold, great anchors 384b
Wedlock: joined together in holy w. 481b
W.'s a very awful thing 195a
yet w.'s the devil 73a
Wednesday: he that died o' W. 379a
married on a W. 532b
W.'s child is full of woe 525a
they that wash on W. 532b
Wee: expectant w. things 59b
handsome w. thing 62a

Wee (cont.)
my w., w. thing 158a
sweet w. wife o' mine 62a
this pig said w., w., w. 533b
w., sleekit, cow'rin', tim'rous 62a
w., w. German lairdie 116b
winsome w. thing 62a
Weed: hold no more than Sussex w. 235a
honey from the w. 382b
less than the w. that grows 197a
lust after that tawney w. tobacco 214b
more ought law to w. it out 14a
O thou w.! 363a
pernicious w.! 108a
salt w. sways in the stream 5b
slavery..is a w. 56a
the basest w. that grows 452a
the fat w. that rots itself 331b
the fragrant w. [Mignonette] 112b
w. wide enough to wrap a fairy 356b
w. ye trample underfoot 229a
Weeds: boughs her coronet w. 336a
buy yourself w. 160a
fumiter and furrow w. 343b
grubbing w. from gravel 229b
idle w. that grow 343b
long live the w. 197b
more than mundane w. 39b
rank w., that every art..defy 114a
smell far worse than w. 388b
the fattest soil to w. 380b
to cast her w. 196a
w. and tares of mine own brain 41b
when we're only burning w. 92b
worthless as withered w. 38b
Week: a w. but only four 20b
be accomplished in a w. 413b
dine at Blenheim once a w. 528b
of all the days that's in the w. 79b
sweet to him who all the w. 101a
till the w. after next 85b
twopence a w., and jam 84b
what! keep a w. away? 362b
Weeks: been fou for w. thegither 62b
brief hours and w. 389a
frown on you—for w. 131a
working about six w. in a year 444a
Weel may the boatie row 149b
Weep: all around thee w. 214a
bid me to w., and I will w. 190a
even butchers w. 150b
fair daffodils, we w. to see 189a
find my grave, to w. there 371a
if souls can w. in bliss 109b
I'll w. with thee, tear for tear 281b
I must w...they are cruel tears 363b
I saw my lady w. 524a
I w. for Adonais 391b
I w. for joy to stand 375a
'I w. for you,' the Walrus said 84b
may w., but never see 241a
milk my ewes and w. 373b
moot w. and pleyhe 89a
O! now you w. 340a
scarcely cry 'w.! w.! w.!' 32b
seek it, and w. no more 184b
she must w. or she will die 436b
sore w. she if oon..were deed 88b
strive nor w. 52b
'tis that I may not w. 71a
to Hecuba, what he shd. w. for
her? 333a
w., and you w. alone 459a
w. away the life of care 399a
w., daughter of a royal line 73a
w. for bones in Africa 200a
w. no more, my lady 156a
w. not, my wanton 176a
w. now or nevermore! 298a
w. on; and, as thy sorrows flow 281a
w. the more because I w. in vain 174a
w. to record..blush to give it in 77b
w. with me, all you that read 215a
w. with them that w. 513b
w. you no more, sad fountains 527b
Who would not w., if Atticus were
he! 303a
wilt thou w. when I am low? 67b
wolde w., if she sawe a mous 88b
Weeping: doth that bode w. 363a
do ye hear the children w. 43a

Weeping (cont.)
ever-w. Paddington [?]
eyes swoln with w. 2[?]
goeth on his way w. 4[?]
my eyes are tired of w. [?]
my head is wild with w. 3[?]
not long, the w. and the laughter 1[?]
soon the night of w. 4[?]
strew of w. verse 2[?]
they are w. bitterly [?]
w. and gnashing of teeth 5[?]
w. and watching for the morrow [?]
w. in the playtime of the others [?]
w. thou sat'st 2[?]
w., w. late and early 4[?]
with w. and with laughter 2[?]
world's more full of w. 4[?]
Weeps: why these w.? 4[?]
Wegg: Rooshan; ain't it, W. 1[?]
Weigh: let us not w. them [?]
more people see than w. [?]
read..to w. and consider [?]
w. it down on one side 1[?]
w. the vessel up 1[?]
w. this song with the great 4[?]
w. yr. Gods and you 2[?]
Weight: beneath the furrow's w. [?]
bowed by the w. of centuries 2[?]
by its own w. made stedfast 1[?]
custom lie upon thee with a w. 4[?]
feel the w. of chance desires 4[?]
heavy and the weary w. 4[?]
he carries w.! he rides a race! 1[?]
lay aside every w. 5[?]
nothing to relieve the w. 1[?]
number, w., and measure [?]
oppression of their prodigal w. 3[?]
there was the w...pull'd me down 3[?]
thrice their w. in gold 1[?]
wearing all that w. of learning 4[?]
w. of the superincumbent hour 3[?]
w. of too much liberty 4[?]
willing to pull his w. 3[?]
Weights: deceitful upon the w. 4[?]
Weighty: fame is like a river..drowns
things w. [?]
Weirs: about the glimmering w. 1[?]
the three lone w. [?]
Welcome: advice is seldom w. [?]
always w., keep it handy 5[?]
aye be w. back again [?]
bay deep-mouthed w. 7[?]
bear w. in your eye 3[?]
be w. back again 3[?]
choir of day w. the dawn 3[?]
frolic w. took the thunder 4[?]
he hath outstayed his w. [?]
poor dog..the first to w. [?]
thrice w., darling of the Spring 4[?]
warmest w., at an inn 3[?]
w., all wonders in one sight! 11[?]
w. each rebuff 5[?]
w. ever smiles 3[?]
w. for himself, and dinner 3[?]
w., kindred glooms 4[?]
w. maids of honour 19[?]
w. one and w. all 19[?]
w. peaceful evening in 11[?]
w. the coming..guest 3[?]
w., thou kind deceiver 13[?]
w. to yr. gory bed [?]
w., wild North-easter [?]
when it comes say 'W. Friend' 11[?]
wind of w. and farewell 31[?]
Welcomes: w. little fishes in 8[?]
w...world and his wife [?]
Welcomest when they are gone 38[?]
Welfare of our Sovereign 47[?]
Welkin: hark, how all the w. rings 45[?]
Well: all is not w. 33[?]
all is w., tho' faith and form 43[?]
all shall be w. 35[?]
all things will be w. 29[?]
are you quite w., Laetitia? 26[?]
as w. said..had said it myself 41[?]
a w. of love, a spring of light 9[?]
bed-time, Hal, and all well 37[?]
do w., and suffer for it 51[?]
down by the green w., I'll pause [?]
fair w. or grove he sings in 44[?]
fare thee w. and if for ever 72[?]

Well (cont.)

foolish thing w. done	208a
golden crown like a deep w.	376a
how w. I did behave	199a
I can do very w.	206b
if we do w. here	249a
is it w. with the child?	496b
kiss the place to make it w.	425a
laugh and be w.	175b
learn to write w.	141b
looking w. won't move her	416a
must come, shall come w.	5a
never speak w. of one another	208b
not feeling very w. myself	536a
not wisely but too w.	364a
pussy's in the w.	534a
they were *in* the w.	83a
they were. .w. in	83a
'twill all be w.	154a
use it for a w.	487a
very w. where they are	458a
w. done, said I	115a
w. done, thou good and faithful	508a
w. for him whose will is strong!	439b
w. for the fisherman's boy	425b
w. for the sailor lad	425b
w. of English undefyled	409a
W. of Life to taste	153b
w. of unconscious cerebration	204a
w., 'tis very w.	393a
w. to be merry and wise	262b
who can do all things w.?	94b
Well-a-way: every youth cry *W.*	531a
Well-beloved: myrrh is my w.	500a
my w. hath a vineyard	501a
Well-bred: very strange and w.	105b
Well-connected: scorn the w.	163b
Well-content: sweet W.	118a
Well-doing: continuance in w.	513a
Weller: Mr. W.	126a, b, 127a
Sam W.	126a, b, 127a
Well-favoured: he is very w.	370a
Wellington: W. or Villainton	71b
W. presents his compliments	454b
W...shoes of his soldiers	17b
Wells: buckets into empty w.	112a
John Wellington W.	167a
Well-spent: rare as a w. (life)	80a
Well-spring: holds the bubbling w.	263b
Welsh: devil understands W.	378a
makes W. as sweet	378a
Welshman: Taffy was a W.	532a
valour in this W.	382b
Weltering in his blood	139a
Wen: great w. (London)	97a
Wenceslas: good King W.	286b
Wench: hostess. .a most sweet w.?	376b
O ill-starr'd w.!	364a
stuff fit only for a w.	261b
sun himself a fair hot w.	376a
Wenches: hags, and hideous w.	100a
pinches country w.	215b
Wenlock Edge	199b
Went: I w. by, and lo	484a
what it meant—but she w.!	527a
what w. ye out for to see?	506b
Wept: he watch'd and w.	168b
he w. not greatly, but sighed	257b
he w. to hear	32b
that long before had w.	143b
thou comest, much w. for	430a
turned aside and w.	12b
w. (I heard her tears)	311b
w. like anything to see	84a
w. o'er his wounds	168b
w. over her, carved in stone	433b
w. with joy to hear	32b
we sat down and w.	490a
Were: we w.? why then. .we *are*	26b
Wernher: fair young W. died	27a
Werther had a love	440b
Weser, deep and wide	50a
Wesley's conversation is good	209b
Wessex: in these W. nooks	180b
West: April's in the w. wind	262a
ask me no more if east or w.	79b
blush from W. to East	434a
bosom of the urgent W.	37a
Cincinnatus of the W.	73b
ever was in the W. Country	119a
fishers. .out into the w.	226b

West (cont.)

gathered to the quiet w.	185a
gigantic daughter of the W.	427a
go W., young man	175b
I dearly like the w.	62a
imagine me the w.!	176a
in his palace of the W.	282b
in the regions of the W.	12b
it comes from the w. lands	262a
lady of the W. Country	119a
little birds sung w.	43b
little grey home in the w.	461b
Lochinvar is come out of the w.	318a
never hear the w. wind	262a
O wild W. Wind	396a
rosy is the W.	433b
safeguard of the W.	472b
sailing away to the w.	226b
ship wd. *not* travel due W.!	86a
sunset fadeth in the w.	388a
that 's where the W. begins	87a
there is neither East nor W.	227a
till the W. is East	434a
wan w. shivers	227a
W. is W.	227a
W. to the Golden Gate	231b
when the w. is red	414b
when the wind is in the w.	532b
without declining W.	133a
woman with the W. in her eyes	98a
Western: All Quiet on the W. Front	569b
cooling w. breeze	300a
outside the W. Straits	8b
W. custom of one wife	315a
w. wind, when wilt thou blow	527b
Westminster Abbey: England's Wal-halla [W.]	453b
peerage, or W.	287a
walk by myself in W.	1b
W. or Victory!	287a
Weston: Mr. W.'s good wine	11a
West Port: open the W.	316a
Westward: but w., look, the land	96b
some eastward, and some w.	109a
w. the course of empire takes	28a
Wet: bereft of w. and of wildness	197b
w. with Channel spray	229a
Wether: black w. of St. Satan's	429a
tainted w. of the flock	354b
Wey: above the river W. it is	232b
Whale: confound the prophet with the w.	124a
th' enormous w. emerges	403a
the w.'s way	262a
very like a w.	334b
w.'s back in the sea of prose	222a
Whale-backed Downs	235a
Whales: among the sharks and w.	525a
drag the Atlantic Ocean for w.	446b
great w. come sailing by	5b
O ye w., and all that move	478a
they wd. talk like w.	171b
Wharf: in ease on Lethe w.	331b
Wharfs: adjacent w.	323a
What: he knew w.'s w.	65a
she knows w.'s w., she does	127a
Tam kent w. was w.	63a
tell us w. and where they be	434a
to be we know not w.	139b
w. are these, so withered	346a
w. are they all	146b
w. are they among so many?	510b
w. from this day I shall be	306a
w.! has this thing appear'd	329b
w. have I done for you, England	185a
w. is here?	432a
w. is home without a mother?	182b
w. is it then to have. .no wife	17a
w. is there I wd. not do	185a
w. is this that thou hast done?	492b
w.? I that loved	526a
w.'s gone and w.'s past help	373a
w. we have been makes. .w. we are	144a
w. we can we will be	226a
w. went ye out for to see?	506b
why, or which, or w.	243b
Whatever thou hast been	72b
What-ho! She bumps!	86a
What's-his-name: Sergeant W.	233a
W. but Thingummy	123a
Whatsoever things are true	516a

Whaups are crying

	414b
Wheat: among w. with a pestle	498b
have a cake out of the w.	368b
measure of w. for a penny	518b
orient and immortal w.	445a
sleep among the w.	85b
sways in the w. its head	442b
two grains of w., hid	352b
w. for this planting	247a
w. set about with lilies	500b
when w. is green	356a
Wheel: and the w.'s kick	262a
butterfly upon a w.	303a
fly sat upon. .axle tree. .chariot-w.	16b
I cannot mind my w.	241a
noisy w. was still	198b
rolling Ixionian w.	433a
turns the giddy w. around	162b
upon a w. of fire	344a
w. broken at the cistern	500a
w. had been in the midst of a w.	503b
w. has come full circle	344a
whirling w. of Change	409a
yr. w. is new	236a
yr. w. is out of order	78b
Wheelbarrow: she wheeled her w.	524a
Wheel-barrows tumble when they meet	59b
Wheeling: w. out on a windy sky	459a
w. stranger	359b
Wheels: all the w. run down	226a
call upon the w., master	93b
for w. of Hansom-cabs	85b
hindmost w. of Phoebus' wain	267a
put a spoke among yr. w.	23a
w. within w.	127a
why tarry the w. of his chariot?	495a
Whelks: bubukles, and w.	382a
Whelmed in deeper gulphs than he	107b
When: w. Adam dalfe	178b
w. or how I cannot tell	313a
w. shall I come to thee?	523b
w. shall we three meet again	345b
w. that Aprille	88a
w. that I was and a little. .boy.	372a
Whence: hither hurried *w.*?	153a
w. and what art thou	273a
w., and whither flown	154a
w. are we, and why are we?	392a
w. comest thou, Gehazi?	496b
Why not knowing nor *W.*	153a
Where: Alice, w. art thou?	53b
be. .we know not w.	139b
cries out, 'W. is it?'	100b
echo answers, w.?	68a
fell to earth, I knew not w.	246b
gentle Shepherd, tell me w.	200b
oh w., and oh! w.	217a
O w. hae ye been?	530b
question. .w. you may be	388a
the boy, oh! w. was he?	184b
think of nought save, w. you are	388a
what and w. they be	434a
w. are they, Cotytto or Venus	421b
w. are you going. .Big Steamers	227b
w. are you going to	525b
w. are you now?	197a
w. art thou, my beloved Son	462b
w. is he who can do all things	94b
w. is my boy to-night?	525b
w. is my child?	68a
w. is she now?	350a
w. is the man who has the power	528a
w. lies the land	97a
w.'s George? Gone to Lyonch	528a
w. shall we gang and dine	529b
w. shall we find her	420a
w. shall we our breakfast take?	529b
w.'s now their victor	318a
w. the bee sucks	368a
w. the place? upon the heath	345b
w. was than the pride of man	178b
w. wast thou when I laid	497b
w. wert thou, brother	430a
w.—w. slept thine ire	218a
w. you will never won	529a
will be nobody knows w.	249a
Whereabout: prate of my w.	347b
Where'er we tread 't is haunted	68a
Wherefore: for every why he had a w.	65a

Wherefore (cont.)
O w. shd. I busk my heid? 530a
w. are these things hid? 369b
w. thou alone? 274b
Wheresoe'er: w. in God's..universe 134b
w. I turn my ravished eyes 1b
Wheresomever: with him, w. he is 381b
Wherewithal shall a young man 489a
Wherry: my trim-built w. 120b
Whets, and combs its silver wings 261a
Whetstone: play the part of a w. 542a
Which: not a soul knew w. 244b
w. of you have done this? 349a
Whid: a rousing w. 59b
Whiddon: Dan'l W. 531b
Whiff of grapeshot 80b
Whiffling thro' the tulgy wood 83b
Whig: a *bottomless* W. 211a
Essene, Erastian W. 92b
first W. was the Devil 210a
not like..to see a W...any dress 212b
Tory and W. in turns 405a
Tory men and W. measures 129a
where you see a W...a rascal 212a
whether I were a W. or a Tory 417b
W. and Tory a' agree 402b
W. Dogs shd. not have the best 212a
W. in a parson's gown 212b
W...The name of a faction 213a
wise Tory and a wise W...agree 210b
you are a vile W. 208a
Whigmigmorum 402b
Whigs: caught the W. bathing 128a
W. admit no force but argument 42b
W. *not* getting into place 71b
While: little w. our lips are dumb 433a
little w...shall see me 511b
oh! yet a little w. 472a
Whim: strangest w. has seized me 91b
Whimper: not with a bang but a w. 145a
Whims of an egotist 222a
Whimsey, not reason 173a
Whimsies: they have my w. 305b
Whining: in w. poetry 134a
Whip: in every honest hand a w. 363a
not feel the driver's w. 248a
'Too-slow' will need the w. 435b
w. me such honest knaves 359b
w. me, ye devils 364a
w., of cricket's bone 364b
Whip-lash: shank a guid w. 61a
Whipmegorum 402b
Whipped: she w. them all well 533b
w. her little daughter 535b
Whippersnapper: critic and w. 44b
Whipping: who shd. 'scape w.? 332b
Whips: chastised you with w. 496a
w. and scorns of time 333a
Whipster: every puny w. 364a
Whipt at school 142b
Whirligig of time 372a
Whirlpools: the sensual w. 264b
Whirlwind: drink of the w.'s stream 397b
like a w. up the pass 254a
rides in the W. 1a
shall reap the w. 504a
the sweeping w.'s sway 173b
wave and w. wrestle 246b
Whisker: educated w. 426b
Whiskers: not by yr. individual w. 65b
Whiskey: Freedom and W. 59a
tell me w.'s name in Greek 59a
Whisper: by all ye cry or w. 236b
far-heard w., o'er the sea 99a
full well the busy w. 168b
his W. came to me 228b
to w. at the grates 249b
we wake and w. 119a
w. down the field 231b
Whispering: above me, w. low 241a
come w. by 179b
so I were out of yr. w. 454b
w., with white lips 68b
Whisperings: eternal w. 221a
foul w. are abroad 350a
Whispers: God..w. in the ear 44b
it w. thro' the trees 300a
secret w. of each other's watch 382b
Whist: a good game at w. 239a
comes my husband from his w. 46b
wild waves w. 367a

Whistle: clear as a w. 67a
he cd. w. them back 169b
her joly w. 89a
I'd w. her off 362a
Joseph did w. 524a
let it w. as it will 318a
pay too much for yr. w. 157a
still he'd w. and sing 120b
to a blackbird 'tis to w. 64b
w., and I'll come to you 63a
w. and she'll come to you 23b
w. owre the lave o 't 63a
Whistled: w. a foolish tune 181b
w. and shifted his heavy load 181b
w. as he went 140a
Whistles: quoth she, and w. thrice 98b
w. in his sound 326b
w. o'er the furrowed land 268b
Whistling: alone, w. to the air 323a
w...bars of Lillabullero 411b
w. to keep..from being afraid 139b
White: arrayed in w. robes 519a
black where I read w. 29b
blush to find itself less w. 405b
burnt green, and blue and w. 98b
crowned with milk-w. may 37b
down in black and w. 67b
'elp you a lot with the W. 230b
fleece was w. as snow 177b
floures w. and rede 90a
grew more clean and w. 44a
hair has become very w. 82b
have it here in black and w. 215b
holy w. birds flying after 261b
kisses shd. impair their w. 43b
my beloved is w. and ruddy 500b
nor grew it w. in a single night 69b
nor w. so very w. 78b
O! my soul is w. 32b
O so w.! O so soft! 216b
roses at first were w. 189b
so clean and so w. 453a
spring goeth all in w. 37b
their w. it stays forever 131a
the snow..a moment w. 63a
the w. clouds stray 37b
the W. Man's burden 236b
they more w. shd. be 189b
w. already unto harvest 510b
w. as snow in Salmon 486a
w. as snow their armour 254a
w. as the sun 105b
w. butterflies in the air 37b
w., clear w., inside 229b
w. daisies prank the ground 37b
w. for Eastertide 198b
w. his shroud as the..snow 335b
w. in the blood of the Lamb 519a
w. in the moon the long road 199a
w...is the English child 32b
w.-robed, with silver hair 35b
w. shall not neutralize the black 51b
wild w. horses play 5b
yr. fleece is w. but 'tis too cold 115a
Whited: thou w. wall 512b
w. sepulchres 507b
Whitefoot: come up W. 203a
Whitehall: grass grows..W. Court 296a
sentinel on W. gate 252b
White Horse of the W. H. Vale 91b
Whitens: Ptarmigan that w. 428b
Whiter: w. soul than thine 240b
w. than be the flocks 176a
Whites: all w. are ink 368b
Whither: I know not W. 153a
whence, and w. flown 154a
w. depart the souls 96a
w. goest thou? 558a
w. hurried hence 153a
Whithersoever thou goest 494b
Whiting: a w. to a snail 83a
'extremes meet', as the w. said 196b
Whizz of my cross-bow 99a
Who: and w. are you? 528b
w. can tell how oft he offendeth 482b
w. comes here? A Grenadier 125b, 534b
w. is like unto the beast? 519a
w. is on my side? w.? 496b
w. is she that looketh forth 500b
w. is Silvia? 372b

Who (cont.)
w. is the King of Glory 483a
w. is this? 432a
w. killed Cock Robin? 528a
w., or why, or which 243b
w. saw him die? 528a
w. shall dwell in thy tabernacle 482a
w. was then the (a) gentleman? 178b, 527b
w. will show us any good? 482a
Whole: w. I planned 50b
half is greater than the w. 559b
I am equal and the w. 422a
parts of one stupendous w. 301a
saw life steadily, and saw it w. 6a
that be w. need not a physician 506a
that is, seeing the w. of them 314b
what a w. Oxford is! 97b
whose prayers wd. make me w. 232b
Whoop: merrily we'll w. 232b
Whooping: out of all w.! 459a
Whore: for the young man's w. 207b
judgment of the great w. 519b
more like a w.'s than a man's 232b
Pity She's a W. 155b
posture of a w. 325a
rogue is married to a w. 234a
teach the morals of a w. 206b
that cunning w. of Venice 363a
the woman's a w. 208b
w. and gambler..licensed 29b
Whoring with their own inventions 488b
Whoremaster: evasion of w. man 342a
Whores: never saw so many w. 455a
Whose: see and remark, and say w. 458a
Whosoever will be saved 478b
Why: and W. not knowing 153a
for every w. he had a wherefore 65a
for w.? the Lord our God is good 224b
for w.? thou shalt not leave 482b
he knows not w. 429b
I can't think w. 166b
I cd. never tell w. 165b
man of morals tell me w. 106b
the 'w.' is plain 326b
w. and wherefore in all things 383b
w., Edward, tell me w.? 463a
'w. not?' said the March Hare 83a
w.? thou hast delivered my soul 489a
will know the reason w.! 182b
Wicked: darts of the w. 516a
God help the w.! 377b
I's w. I is 415b
it's worse than w. 535b
let but thy w. men..go 107a
little better than one of the w. 376b
long as war is regarded as w. 460a
must be w. to deserve such pain 45b
never wonder to see men w. 419a
no peace..unto the w. 502b
spirits more w. than himself 506b
tender mercies of the w. 498a
'there is no God,' the w. saith 96a
there's a w. spirit 3a
thy ways unto the w. 485a
when the w. man turneth 503b
w. cease from troubling 497a
w. flee when no man pursueth 498b
Wickedness: against spiritual w. 516a
all w...little to the w. of..woman 520b
from God, that he shd. do w. 497a
goeth on still in his w. 486b
I was shapen in w. 485a
leaven of malice and w. 514a
loose the bands of w. 503a
manifold sins and w. 478a
put their hand unto w. 489b
turneth away from his w. 503b
w. of the world is print to him 124a
W. proceedeth from the wicked 495b
w. that hinders loving 49a
ye have plowed w. 504a
[Wickliff's] ashes into Avon 157b
Widdicombe Fair 531b
Widdrington: as low as..Squire W. 140a
Wide: alone on a w. w. sea 99a
how w. also the east is 488a
how w. the limits stand 168b
nor so w. as a church door 365b
not deep the poet sees but w. 8a

Wide (cont.)
two feet w. — 471b
w. as his command — 138a
Widening slowly silence all — 428b
Wider: gape for thee thrice w. — 381a
Widow: a virgin-w. — 141a
a w. bird sate mourning — 393a
came a certain poor w. — 508b
defendeth the fatherless and w. — 490b
here's to the w. of fifty — 405b
I am a w., poor — 407a
Molly Stark 's a w. — 410a
my basnet a w.'s curch? — 531a
of his mother, and she was a w. — 509a
some undone w. sits — 262b
the W. at Windsor — 236b
w. comes..to cast her weeds — 196a
Widowhood: comfortable estate of w. — 159b
nursling of thy w. — 391b
Widows: and w. in their affliction — 517b
defendeth the cause of the w. — 486a
devour w.' houses — 508a
do as other w., buy yourself weeds — 160a
fatherless children, and w. — 479a
many w. were in Israel — 509a
when w. exclaim loudly — 151a
w. in Corioli — 328a
W...most perverse Creatures — 2a
Wielder of the stateliest measure — 439a
Wife: account w...but as bills — 14b
a letter from his w. — 85b
appear like man and w. — 95a
artist will let his w. starve — 390b
as the husband is, the w. is — 432a
auld w. sat at her ivied door — 75a
a w. for breed — 161a
better accommodated than with a w. — 380b
borrowed my neighbour's w. — 235b
bracelets to adorn the w. — 187a
Brutus' harlot, not his w. — 338b
but I'd have no w. — 114b
Caesar's w., all things to all men — 524b
carline's w.'s three sons — 529a
cleave unto his w. — 492a
damned in a fair w. — 359b
dwindle into a w. — 105b
faithful w., without debate — 416b
fireside clime to weans and w. — 59a
Giant Despair had a w. — 54a
heard a w. sing to her child — 143b
he cd. not act upon my w. — 30a
here lies my w. — 140a
his w. looked back — 493a
hurling them at his w. — 135a
husband frae the w. despises! — 62b
if ever I marry a w. — 240b
if Laura had been Petrarch's w. — 70b
if w. should dine at Edmonton — 109a
I hadna been his w. a week — 20b
I hae a w. o' my ain — 61a
I have married a w. — 509b
I have quarrelled with my w. — 295a
I have a w. — 120b
in every port a w. — 120b
in the lofty character of W. — 122b
kick his w. out of bed — 416b
kill a w. with kindness — 366b
light w...make heavy husband — 355b
Lord Brutus took to w. — 338b
love yr. neighbour's w. — 255a
man and w...never..power to hang — 150a
marriage with his brother's w. — 385b
married without e'er a w.? — 534b
match'd with an aged w. — 438b
minister kissed the fiddler's w. — 62a
monstrous animal a husband and w. — 151b
Mother, W. and Queen — 437a
must be in want of a w. — 11b
my 'oss, my w., and my name — 417a
my true and honourable w. — 338b
my w...poor wretch, is troubled — 296a
neighed after his neighbour's w. — 503b
neither maid nor w. — 425a
no casual mistress, but a w. — 430b
no man..can be true to his w. — 447b
one w. and hardly any mistresses — 315a
one w. is too much — 160a
parson and the parson's w. — 96a
ran after a farmer's w. — 533a

Wife (cont.)
remember Lot's w. — 54a, 510a
sailor's w. had chestnuts — 346a
same face of his wedded w. — 237b
sanctified by the w. — 514a
shalt not covet thy neighbour's w. — 480a
sic a w. as Willie had — 63b
so save a wretched w. — 159b
sweet wee w. o' mine — 62a
tedious as..railing w. — 378a
Thane of Fife had a w. — 350a
the w. smiles, and lets it go — 21b
the w. was pretty — 114a
think, boy, of taking a w. — 282a
think my w. be honest — 362a
this is my w., pray look at her — 528b
this woman to thy wedded w. — 481b
thy bottle, and thy w. — 301b
to have or have no w. — 17a
to look out for a w. — 417a
t'other w. wd. take ill — 160a
uncumber'd with a w. — 140a
weeping w. and children — 451a
we fell out, my w. and I — 436a
when his w. talks Greek — 212a
whose w. shall I take? — 282a
widowed w., and married maid — 319a
w., as unto the weaker vessel — 517b
w. cd. eat no lean — 534a
w. is May, the husband June — 452a
w. of thy bosom — 494b
w. shall be as the fruitful vine — 490a
w. who preaches in her gown — 196b
world and his w. — 4b, 418b
Wifely: flour of w. pacience — 89b
Wig: hat and w. will soon be here — 108b
thy own hare, or a w.? — 239b
w. with the scorched foretop — 255b
Wight: maid and her w. — 179b
she was a w., if ever such w. were — 361a
strange and wayward w. — 22b
unhappy w., born to disastrous — 409b
w. of high renown — 524b
Wights: with worthy w. to reign — 177a
Wigwam: lights the w. — 248b
w. of Nokomis — 248b
Wild: den of w. things in..her eyes! — 192a
half-w. and wholly tame — 235a
her eyes were w. — 218b
her w., w. eyes — 219a
made us nobly w. — 189b
only rather rude and w. — 26a
pray, Mr. W., why bitch? — 151a
revenge is a kind of w. justice — 14a
talk a little w. — 385b
to the waters and the w. — 476a
walking by his w. lone — 237a
waving his w. tail — 237a
Wet W. Woods — 237a
what are the w. waves saying — 82b
what so w. as words are? — 52b
when w. in woods the noble savage — 139b
w. he may be — 124a
Wild-cats in yr. kitchens — 360b
Wilderness: a w. of sweets — 275a
cometh up from the w. — 501a
crying in the w. — 504b
dwellings of the w. — 486a
for a scapegoat into the w. — 494a
for a w. of monkeys — 354a
guess to be a little w. — 261a
Heaven's constellated w. — 397b
in the waste howling w. — 494b
in the w. shall waters break out — 502a
like a pelican in the w. — 488a
lodge in some vast w. — 111b
man in the w. asked me — 534a
ninety and nine in the w. — 509b
perils in the w. — 515a
singing in the W. — 152b
the w. a standing water — 488b
thou wentest thro' the w. — 486a
thro' the w. of this world — 54a
voice..that crieth in the w. — 502b
weeds and the w. — 197b
w. and the solitary place — 502a
w. into a glorious empire — 56a
W. is Paradise enow — 152b
W. were Paradise enow! — 152b
Wildernesses: desert w. — 267a

Wild-fowl: fetch the w. home — 529b
more fearful w. than yr. lion — 357a
Wildness: bereft of wet and of w. — 197b
Wile: follow'd with endearing w. — 168b
sae bright to w. us hame — 63b
Wiles: cranks, and wanton w. — 268b
man of many w. — 560a
of w. more unexpert — 272a
transient sorrows, simple w. — 470b
Wilful: to w. men the injuries — 342b
Wilhelmine: grandchild W. — 406a
Wilkinson: Mr. W., a clergyman — 154b
spade! with wh. W. hath tilled — 471a
Will: all-urging W. — 179b
as in our w. to love or not — 275a
at war 'twixt w. and w. not — 351b
a w. most incorrect — 330a
boy's w. is the wind's w. — 247b
but, Lord, the w. — 137b
cannot kindle when we w. — 7a
cause is in my w. — 339a
consciousness the W. informing — 179b
dwells not in particular w. — 369a
eternal spirit, against her w. — 374a
foreknowledge, w. and fate — 272a
forge his own w. — 166b
good Lord, if thy w. it be! — 531a
good w. toward men — 508b
he that complies against his w. — 66a
his own sweet w. — 472b
his w. his law — 113a
his w. is not his own — 330b
his w. made or suffered them — 397b
humanity's afflicted w. — 464b
if she w., she w. — 528a
in His w. is our peace — 567a
I shd. fulfil thy w. — 484a
it is my duty and I w. — 162b
I w. do..because I w. do it — 63b
I w. it, I insist on it! — 549a
laid me down with a w. — 415a
leave to..Heaven his stubborn w. — 420a
Michael Henchard's W. — 180b
neither, when we w., enjoy — 7a
not my w., but thine — 510a
our shows are more than w. — 371a
our w. that thus enchains us — 395a
poverty, but not my w., consents — 366a
prayers are a disease of the w. — 147b
pride ruled my w. — 288b
puzzles the w. — 333a
take the w. for the deed — 418b
the Mariner hath his w. — 98a
the temperate w. — 470b
the W. has woven with an absent — 179a
the W. is free — 5a
the w., the w.!..Caesar's w. — 340a
the w. to do — 316a
thou hast thy 'W.' — 389a
thowt 'twur the w. o' the Lord — 439a
th' unconquerable w. — 271a
thy w. be done in earth — 505b
torrent of a woman's w. — 528a
we know our w. is free — 207b
what I w. is fate — 275b
what of the Immanent W. — 179a
whose w. is strong — 439b
w. accipitrine — 441a
W. Honeycomb calls these..ladies — 410a
w. in us is over-ruled — 259a
w. like a dividing spear — 5b
W. to boot, and W. in over-plus — 389a
w. you, won't you — 83a
with all my w. — 294a
with half so good a w. — 341b
won my right good w. — 256b, 447a
works his sovereign W. — 110a
yet His w. be done! — 434b
yr. Majesty's w. is law — 165a
you w., Oscar, you w. — 456b
Willed: all we have w. or hoped — 44b
William: my W.'s wife — 168a
religion as my W. like — 168a
you are old, Father W. — 82b, 407a
Williams' pink pills — 523a
Willie (Willy): O love my W.! — 75b
sic a wife as W. had — 63b
W., let me and you be wipers — 50a
W. shall dance with Jane — 522b
Willing: Barkis is w. — 122a
when a man says he's w. — 122a

Will-o'-th'-Wisp mislight me — 189b
Willoughby: Beaumont and W. — 137a
Willow: all a green w., w. — 191a
  Dido with a w. in her hand — 355a
  sing all a green w. — 363a
  sing w., w., w. — 363a
  there is a w. grows aslant — 336a
  violets die, under the w. — 318a
  w. must be my garland — 363a
  w., titwillow — 165a
  w., w., waly — 165b
Willows: where the w. weep — 35b
  w. whiten — 431b
Willow-tree: al under the w. — 88a
  lance a wand of the w.? — 531a
  my harp on a weeping w. — 527a
Wills: blackbirds have their w. — 426b
  let's..talk of w. — 375b
  mention it within thin w. — 340a
  our w. and fates..contrary run — 334a
  our w. are gardeners — 360b
  so we shall make our w. — 172a
  such a lot of people's W. — 91b
  the w. above be done! — 367a
  unruly w. and affections — 479b
  what she w. to do..seems wisest — 276a
  w. of thy faithful people — 479b
Wimpled, whining, purblind — 344a
Win: but he does not w. — 459b
  one shd. lose, the other w. — 259a
  than you to w. again — 92a
  they laugh that w. — 362b
Virtue he had vow'd to w. — 294a
who w. heaven, blest are they — 49a
who would greatly w. — 73a
w. or lose it all — 280b
w-i-n, w. — 124b
yet wouldst wrongly w. — 346b
Winced nor cried aloud — 185a
Winchester: Jane lies in W. — 230b
  while the stones of W. — 230b
Wind: against the w. — 69a
  airts the w. can blaw — 62a
  all ye as a w. shall go by — 423b
  aloud the w. doth blow — 345b
  and the w. blows stronger — 286b
  and the w.'s song — 262a
  Angel of the Off-shore W. — 230b
  argument with an east w. — 251a
  as cauld a w. as ever blew — 61b
  as it were brought forth w. — 502a
  as W. along the Waste — 153a
  a w. is hovering o'er — 393b
  a w. on the heath — 34a
  bay'd the whisp'ring w. — 168b
  beat of the offshore w. — 231b
  betwixt the w. and his nobility — 376b
  bids the w. blow the earth — 342b
  blow, blow, thou winter w. — 326b
  blows the w. to-day — 414b
  blow, thou w. of God! — 226a
  blow, w.! come, wrack! — 351a
  Boston man is the east w. — 4b
  both with w. and stream — 361a
  boy's will is the w.'s will — 247b
  breathing of the common w. — 472b
  chiding of the winter's w. — 325b
  clear as w. — 435b
  cold's the w. — 119a
  conflicting w. and rain — 342b
  constant be, come w., come weather — 54b
  dust wh. the rude w. blows — 343b
  east w. may never blow — 450a
  e'er the w. doth blow — 292a
  every w. of criticism — 211b
  every w. of doctrine — 515b
  except w. stands as never — 446a
  fair stood the w. for France — 137a
  filled with a lusty w. — 87a
  for the gentle w. does move — 31b
  frosty w. made moan — 311a
  frozen w. crept on above — 393a
  gone with the w. — 571a
  good south w. sprung up — 98b
  he that observeth the w. — 499b
  hey, ho, the w. and the rain — 372a
  hiding place from the w. — 502a
  His hammer of w. — 443a
  ill w. turns none to good — 446a
  into the w...pass the pain — 177a

Wind (cont.)
  is the w. in that door? — 257a
  jovial w. of winter — 226a
  large a charter as the w. — 326b
  let her down the w. — 362a
  light w. lives or dies — 221b
  like W. I go — 153a
  loose as the w. — 188a
  Lord was not in the w. — 496a
  loud dry w. blow thro' my ear — 469a
  never hear the west w. — 262a
  nor ever w. blows loudly — 429b
  north w. doth blow — 533a
  nor wild w. sweep — 184b
  O wild West W. — 396a
  O w., the weder ginneth clere — 90a
  passionate w. of welcome — 311b
  pass me by as the idle w. — 340b
  perils both of w. and limb — 65a
  pity for blustering w. — 249b
  reed shaken with the w.? — 506b
  roaring in the w. all night — 470a
  rushing mighty w. — 512a
  shaken of a mighty w. — 518b
  sits the w. in that corner? — 358b
  soft-lifted by the winnowing w. — 221b
  southwest-w. and..west-w. sing — 420a
  soon as the w. goeth over it — 488a
  stop a hole to keep the w. away — 336b
  straw..way the w. is — 321a
  streamers waving in the w. — 161a
  strive to ourselves — 224a
  swoln with w. and the rank mist — 269b
  tears shall drown the w. — 347a
  tempers the w. to the shorn lamb — 573a
  the same w. sang — 421b
  the w. blows out of the gates — 475b
  the w. breathes low — 433a
  the w. sweep man away — 5b
  they have sown the w. — 504a
  thy great w. blows — 476a
  thro' the east-w. — 485a
  thro' the velvet leaves the w. — 344b
  throw the sand against the w. — 31b
  toast..the w. that blows — 120b
  'twill endure w. and weather — 370a
  unhelped by any w. — 101a
  walketh upon the wings of the w. — 488a
  warm w., the west w. — 262a
  western w., when wilt thou blow — 527b
  whenever a March w. sighs — 434a
  when the w. blows — 29a
  when the w. is in the east — 532b
  when the w. is southerly — 332b
  where the w.'s feet shine — 423a
  whistles in the w. — 467b
  whistling made of every w. — 441b
  w. a fiery Pegasus — 378b
  w. and storm fulfilling — 490b
  w. and wave and oar — 433a
  w. beat dark December — 328b
  w. began to roll — 434b
  w. blew due East — 86a
  w. bloweth where it listeth — 510b
  w. blows it back again — 31b
  w. breathing thro' the grass — 39a
  w. doth blow to-day — 529a
  w. is in the palm trees — 232a
  w. of the western sea — 436a
  w. on the heath, brother — 34a
  w.'s in the east — 121a
  w.'s like a whetted knife — 262a
  W. that blows between — 235b
  w. that follows fast — 116a
  W., that grand old harper — 403b
  w. was a torrent of darkness — 290a
  w., w.! thou art sad — 284b
  with this w. blowing — 232b
Wind-flowers: pied w. — 398a
  w., and violets — 394b
Winding-sheet: snow shall be their w. — 77a
  waters were his w. — 21a
  w. is..as high as her throat — 319a
  w. of Edward's race — 173b
Windmill: garlic in a w. — 378a
Window: chamber where there is now w. — 263b
  dash the w.-glass to shivers — 319b
  first against the w. beats — 443b
  light thro' yonder w. breaks — 365a
  little w. where the sun — 195a

Window (cont.)
  Sisera looked out at a w. — 495a
  takes this w. for the east — 117b
  thy chamber w., Sweet — 394b
  tirling at the w. — 266a
  w. to open onto the Lake — 223a
  w-i-n, win, d-e-r, der, w. — 124b
Windows: blank the w. flare — 232b
  by breaking of w. — 283a
  by eastern w. only — 96b
  five w. of the soul — 30a
  I cleaned the w. — 166a
  I wish thar was w. to my Sole — 451a
  make der w. sound — 244b
  look out of the w. be darkened — 499b
  rich w. that exclude the light — 175a
  thou, thus thro' w...call on us — 134a
  up flew the w. all — 108b
  w. richly dight — 268b
Winds: amid the wafting w. — 457b
  between the w. of heaven — 330a
  Burke, who w. into a subject — 171b
  call her w. and waters sighs — 322b
  carried about of w. — 518a
  change, as ye list, ye w. — 161a
  come as the w. come — 319a
  courted by all the w. — 277b
  dead w.' and spent waves' — 422a
  enlarged w. that curl the flood — 249b
  for us the w. do blow — 187b
  gathering w. will call the darkness — 399a
  great w. shorewards blow — 5b
  great w. Thy clarions — 94a
  hear the w. howling — 6a
  imprisoned in the viewless w. — 352a
  in the visitation of the w. — 380a
  light w. go seaward — 202a
  loud w. when they call — 470a
  me howling w. drive devious — 109b
  melodious w. have birth — 31b
  motions of the viewless w. — 469b
  north-east w. blow Sabæan odours — 273b
  on the wings of mighty w. — 412a
  rough w. do shake the darling buds — 387a
  stormy w. did blow — 525b
  stormy w. do blow — 77b
  summer w. that creep from flower — 394b
  the w. blew calm — 285a
  tho' w. blew great guns — 120b
  tho' you untie the w. — 349b
  thunder-zoned w. — 396a
  to all the w. that blew — 435a
  trod, as on the four w. — 261a
  waves and wet w. labour — 422a
  what..w. and waters make us — 241b
  when the w. give o'er — 449a
  where the w. are all asleep — 5b
  wild leaves that w. have taken — 422a
  w. and seas are troublesome — 117a
  w. and sunbeams — 393b
  w. are breathing low — 394b
  w. are quiet as the sun — 421a
  w. are unto her as raiment — 420a
  w. come to me from the fields — 466a
  w. of heaven mix for ever — 395b
  w. of March with beauty — 373a
  W. of the World, give answer! — 228b
  w. somewhere safe to sea — 422a
  w. that will be howling — 473a
  w. were love-sick with them — 323a
  w. whistle shrill — 440b
Windsor: Widow at W. — 236b
Windward of the law — 94b
Windy: shadows and w. places — 420a
  w. side o' the law — 372a
Wine: a bin of W. — 414b
  a Jug of W. — 152b
  as water unto w. — 432b
  best w., for my beloved — 500b
  blood and w. are red — 459b
  bored with good w. — 130a
  Botticelli isn't a w. — 536a
  bring me w. — 286b
  can with w. dispense — 113b
  Catholic that live upon w. — 26b
  come ye here to drink good w. — 530b
  cruse best fits my little w. — 188b
  Cup of this forbidden W. — 153b
  deep in anything but W. — 153b
  desire not to be rinsed with w. — 197b

Wine (cont.)

do crush their w.	260b
doesn't get into the w.	93b
drank the red w. thro' the helmet	316b
drinking the blude-red w.	529b
drink one cup of w.	318a
drinks his w. 'mid laughter free	527a
drink thy w. with a merry heart	499b
drunken, but not with w.	502a
drunk yr. water and w.	230a
fetch to me a pint o' w.	60b
fond of Spanish w.	261b
for its poisonous w.	219b
for to drinken strong w.	89a
for w. inspires us	159b
freighted Chian w.	8b
french w. and fine weather	223a
full of dewy w.	220a
gave her cocktails and w.	527a
giant refreshed with w.	487a
good w., a friend, or being dry	3a
grief in w. we steep	249b
'have some w.,'..March Hare said	83a
he drinks now.	380b
honest talk and wholesome w.	438b
hurt not the oil and the w.	518b
I don't see any w.	83a
I'll not look for w.	216a
invisible spirit of w.	361b
I rather like bad w.	130a
is not old w. wholesomest	454b
it wasn't the w.	126a
let us have w. and women	70b
lordliest in their w.	278a
love at first, like generous w.	66a
love is better than w.	500a
mine host's Canary w.	219a
Mr. Weston's good w.	11a
new friend is as new w.	520b
new w. into old bottles	506a
old w. to drink	13b
our ballast is old w.	295b
outdid the frolic w.	189b
pass the rosy w.	125a
Pehlevi, with W.! W.! W.!	152a
press the rue for w.	319a
red sweet w. of youth	39a
Red W.! the Nightingale cries	152a
rich Canary w.	215a
Samian w.	71a
sans W., sans Song, sans Singer	153a
spill'd the w.	293a
sure there was w.	188a
sweet white w.	261b
talk of Constitutions o'er yr. w.	77b
there is a cup, and the w. is red	487a
this the W., and this the Bread	31b
truth comes out in w.	552b
two main plagues..w. and women	64a
upon the w. when it is red	498b
use a little w. for thy stomach's	516b
victuals and the w. rather good	75b
walnuts and the w.	434b
when the w.-cup glistens	319a
when the w. is in, the wit is out	23b
who loves not w.	440b
who loves not woman, w.	569a
W., a Book of Verse	152b
w. and wax, of gamyn and gle	474a
w. from the royal Pope	258a
W. has play'd the Infidel	154a
w. in rivers	319b
w. is a good familiar creature	361b
w. is a mocker	498b
W. is the strongest	520a
w. maketh merry	499b
w. of life is drawn	348a
W. of Life keeps oozing	154b
w. that maketh glad the heart	488a
with seas of life, like w.	445a
women and w. shd. life employ	159b
Wine-lees and democracy	44b
Wine-press: trodden the w. alone	503b
w. wh. ye tread	252b
Wines: feast of w. on the lees	502a
Wing: beats with light w.	284a
crept so long on a broken w.	434b
damp my intended w.	276a
Death's imperishable w.	312a
flapt its tinsel w.	260a

Wing (cont.)

flits by on leathern w.	103a
got to take under my w., tra la	165a
grey w. upon every tide	474b
his head under his w.	533a
joy is ever on the w.	277b
skylark wounded in the w.	29a
soars on golden w.	268a
soiled glory, and the trailing w.	6a
start a w.!	442a
their victor vaward w.	318a
white clouds on the w.	4a
w. of friendship never moults	125a
with as inconstant w. as summer	394b
without w. of hippogriff	277a
with the shadow of Thy w.	455b
Winged: said the w. minute	264b
w. hours of bliss	77b
w. sea-girt citadel	68a
Wings: all legs and w.	20a
arise with healing in his w.	504b
as the bird w. and sings	50b
clap her broad w.	157b
combs its silver w.	261a
covered with silver w.	486a
defend thee under his w.	487b
dip their w. in tears	430a
each one had six w.	501b
eagle's w. I bore this wren	139a
ears like errant w.	92a
falls from the w. of Night	247a
find w. waiting there	24b
float upon the w. of silence	267a
for their leathern w.	356b
Friendship..Love without his w.	72b
girt with golden w.	267a
glittering ranks with w. display'd	270b
golden hours on angel w.	61a
head, hands, w., or feet	273a
hear the beating of his w.	38a
if I take the w. of the morning	490a
ill news hath w.	136b
in the vale perfumes his w.	143a
lets grow her w.	267a
lie upon the w. of night	366a
little w. are stronger	438a
long expected healing w.	447b
Love with unconfined w.	249b
now with his w. he plays	176a
O, for a horse with w.!	328b
on the viewless w. of Poesy	220a
on what w. dare he aspire	32a
on w. they are carried	414b
play..thro' their w.	441b
poor splendid w. so frayed	421a
prisoners underneath her w.	383b
riches have w.	112a
riches..make themselves w.	498b
rises with healing in his w.	110b
sailing on obscene w.	100b
shakes his dewy w.	117b
shakes the w., and will not stay	142b
she claps her w.	251b
straight on w. I arise	36a
that wh. hath w. shall tell	499b
they now can spare their w.	115a
those quivering w. composed	471a
thundered unthinkable w.	92b
thy w. shall be my refuge	485b
tiger-moth's deep-damask'd w.	221b
walketh upon the w. of the wind	488a
whether pigs have w.	84b
while the w. aspire	471a
W. o' the Mornin'	236b
w. were wet with ranging	176a
with ah! bright w.	197b
ympt with w. of fame	79a
Wink: never came a w. too soon	195a
w. and hold out mine iron	381b
w. a reputation down	419b
Winked: bubble w. at me, and said	188b
'e w. back—the same as us!	236b
w. at 'Omer down the road	236b
Winkie: Wee Willie W.	266a
Winks and shut his apprehension	260a
Winning: glory of the w. were she won!	263b
such a w. way	105a
world be worth the w.	139a
Winnings: one heap of all yr. w.	230a
Wins: game where nobody w.	158a

Winter: age is as a lusty w.

age is as a lusty w.	326a
amusement in a tedious w.-night	417b
bare W. suddenly was changed	397b
but w. and rough weather	326a
Christmas..in the Middle of W.	2a
crown old W.'s head	115b
dark as w. was the flow	76b
English w.—ending in July	71b
ere the w. storms begin	3b
for, lo! the w. is past	500a
for w., spring and summer	525a
furious w.'s rages	329a
her w. weeds outworn	394a
He sends the snow in w.	76a
hounds of spring..on w.'s traces	420a
how like a w. hath my absence	388b
if W. comes, can Spring be far	396b
in freezing w. night	407b
in hoary w.'s night	407b
in the bleak mid-w.	311a
in the haunch of w. sings	381a
in w. I get up at night	413b
it is cold w.'s night	531a
it was not in the w.	194b
it was the w. wild	270a
jovial wind of w.	226a
most love W.	293b
no w. in thy year	53a, 246b
one cold w.'s day	192b
our severest w...the spring	113a
reigns in the w.'s pale	373a
sad tale's best for w.	373a
savour all the w. long	373a
shalt find the w.'s rage	286b
there was no w. in 't	325a
'tis past, the w.	262a
W. comes to rule the varied year	443b
w. fly-fishing	450a
W.-garment of Repentance fling	152b
w. is come and gone	392a
w. lingering chills the lap	170a
w. of our discontent	384b
W., ruler of th' inverted year	112a
W. slumbering in the open air	102a
w.'s not gone yet	342a
w.'s rains and ruins	420a
w. talk by thy fireside	16a
w. was not unkind	36a
w., when the dismal rain came	403b
wd. seem a w.'s day	309b
Winters: fifty w. o'er him	175a
four lagging w.	374b
praise the w. gone	476a
three w. cold..from the forests	388b
when forty w. besiege	387a
w. and keeps warm her note	79b
Wipe away all tears	519a
Wiped: but w. them soon	277a
Wipers: me and you be w.	50a
Wires: across the w.	12a
black w. grow on her head	389a
Wisdom: be famous then by w.	277a
celestial W. calms the mind	214a
criterion of w. to vulgar judgements	57b
due to the want of human w.	242b
excess leads to the palace of w.	31a
folly..wh. confounds its w.	194b
gold..lies at the root of w.	66b
go, teach eternal w.	301a
government is a contrivance of..w.	57a
hiving w. with each..year	68b
if any of you lack w.	517a
it seems the part of w.	112b
Jesus increased in w. and stature	509a
light in W.'s eyes	452a
lion is the w. of God	31a
little w. the world is governed	567b
more of w. in it	471b
nor knowledge, nor w., in the grave	499b
not diffident of w.	276a
no w. in useless..sorrow	214a
of highest w. brings about	278a
pray for w. yet	2b
privilege of w. to listen	194b
provided for by this w.	57a
self-control is w.'s root	59a
she that in w. never was so frail	360b
spirit of w. and understanding	501b
takes..w. from our councils	56a

Wisdom (cont.)
the beginning of w.   489a
there's w. in women   40a
Thine endless w.   149b
this w. descendeth not   517b
those who love want w.   397a
thy w., less thy certainty   410b
to the w. of the just   508b
understand w. secretly   485a
vain w. all   272b
wearing his w. lightly   426b
what is bettre than w.?   89a
w. and goodness to the vile   343b
W. and Spirit of the Universe   465b
W. and Wit are little seen   35a, 91b
w. at one entrance..shut out   273b
W. be put in a silver rod   29b
w. breathed by health   471b
w. crieth without   497b
w. denotes the pursuing of the best   202b
w. excelleth folly   499a
w. goes by majorities   264b
w. has taught us to be calm   193b
w. in minds attentive   112b
w. in the scorn of consequence   435b
w. is above rubies   497a
w. is better than rubies   498a
w. is humble..he knows no more   112b
w. is justified of her children   506b
w. is the principal thing   497b
w. lays on evil men   112b
w. lingers   432b
w. not to do desperate things   444a
w. of our ancestors   56b
w. of the ancients   17a
w. of the crocodiles   15b
w. or even memory   313a
W. say another   58a
W.'s self oft seeks..solitude   267a
w. shall die with you   497a
w. sleep with thee   431a
w. the mirrored shield   392a
w. with mirth   169b
w. and wit are little seen   35a
with the ancient is w.   497a
Wise: a being darkly w.   301a
all things w. and wonderful   3a
and confirm the w.   113b
angling..worthy..of a w. man   450b
are reputed w...saying nothing   352b
beacons of w. men   203a
be lowly w.   275b
be not worldly w.   307a
be w. to-day   477a
be w. with speed   476b
be ye therefore w. as serpents   506a
care..whether he is a W. man   31a
childish valourous than manly w.   259b
cunning men pass for w.   15b
each in each, immediately w.   39b
errors of a w. man make yr. rule   29a
every w. man's son doth know   370b
exceeding w., fair spoken   386b
first be w. and good   278b
fool wd. persist..become w.   31a
ful w. is he..him selven knowe   89a
give unto me, made lowly w.   464a
good to be merry and w.   61a, 524b
grow w. for spite   419a
guid to be merry and w.   61a
healthy, wealthy, and w.   157a
heard a w. man say   198b
hid..from the w. and prudent   509a
holy, fair and w. is she   372b
how very weak the very w.   440b
in a bowl..went w. men three   295b
men are not always w.   497a
more happy, if less w.   73a
more nice than w.   100b
more of the fool than of the w.   14b
more than woman to be w.   281a
more w. when he had   210b
nor ever did a w. one   309b
nor talk too w.   230a
obscurely w., and coarsely kind   210b
pretend they ne'er so w.   277b
smile with the w.   207b
so proud, so witty and so w.   309b
sorrow makes us w.   431a
so w. as Thurlow looked   156b

Wise (cont.)
so w., so young..never live long   385a
taketh the w...own craftiness   497a
there came w. men   504b
the w. of the world..made dumb   119a
the w. want love   397a
they are w. and honourable   340a
those that think them w., are.. fools   3b
tho' w. in show   278b
timely happy, timely w.   223b
'tis folly to be w.   175a
to a w. man ports and..havens   374b
to be w. and eke to love   409b
to be w., and love   369a
to confound the w.   514a
to love is w.   37b
too truthful or too w.   452a
type of the w. who soar   471a
virtuous and w. he was   471a
vocal to the w.   4b
we were very, very w.   560a
what all the w. men promised   98a
what leisure to grow w.   572a
while the great and w. decay   7a
who are a little w...best fools   244a
who can be w., amazed   134a
whoso is w. will ponder   488b
w. are merry of tongue   475b
w., for cure, on exercise depend   140a
w., idle, childish things   441a
w. in his own conceit   498b
w. in yr. own conceits   513b
w. men eat them (feasts)   157a
w. men of Gotham   532b
w. thro' excess of wisdom   148a
w., upright, valiant   468a
with..Khayyám, and leave the W.   153a
wretched are the w.   306a
ye yourselves are w.   515a
Wisely: loved not w. but too well   364a
w. and slow   365b
Wiseman: wise-manned..by W.   51a
Wiser: are w. than their own   40a
French are w. than they seem   15b
grow w. and better   304a
I am w. than the aged   489a
not left a better or w. behind   169b
sadder and a w. man   100a
Spaniards seem w. than they are   15b
speakest w. than thou art ware   326a
to be guided by the w.   80b
w. being good   44b
w. men become   449a
w. than a daw   383b
w. than the children of light   509b
w. than we know   148a
w. to-day than he was yesterday   419a
young man will be w. by and by   427b
Wisest: first and w. of them all   277a
in the mouths of w. men   277b
more than the w. man can answer   103b
only the w. of mankind achieve   404a
rules e'en the w.   113b
seems w., virtuousest..best   276a
the w. fool in Christendom   204a, 563b
w., brightest, meanest of mankind   301b
w. man the warl' saw   60b
w. men have erred   277b
Wish: all yr. w. is woman to win   440b
each w. of my heart   281b
fled from her w.   360b
happy the man whose w. and care   303b
I never fram'd a w.   112b
I often w. the night   195a
I strongly w. for what I..hope   141b
I w. I were where Helen lies   531a
I w. no living things to suffer   397a
I w. you all the joy   354b
long as god-like w.   464a
man in arms shd. w. to be   465a
no addition nor my w.   362b
our utmost w. possessing   161a
she'll w. there wos more   126b
thy own w. w. I thee   344b
to his w. or not   465b
whoever hath her w.   389a
w. I were single again   524b
w. was father..to that thought   381a
Wished: devoutly to be w.   333a
he whom I w. to see   224b

Wished (cont.)
hyacinth I w. me in her hand   138a
I've often w. that I had clear   419b
nor w., nor car'd, nor laugh'd   305b
w. for to hear   224b
w. she had not heard it   360a
Wishes: her little w. and ways   180b
his nest of w. piping   264b
meet you her my w.   115b
my w. cloudy character   115b
sober w. never learned   174b
so many w. feedest   7b
their country's w. blest   103a
Wishing: each w. for the sword   263b
w. me like to one more rich   387a
Wisp on the morass   73a
Wist: had I w., before I kist   530a
Wit: age is in, the w. is out   359a
all yr. Piety nor W.   153b
a miracle, instead of w.   477b
an accepted w. has but to say   167a
an old blind débauchée of w.   449b
are at their w.s' end   488b
as a w., if not first   169b
as metaphysic w. can fly   65a
a spice of w.   414b
a w.'s a feather   301b
becomes excellent w.   380b
beef..does harm to my w.   369b
brevity is the soul of w.   332a
by the w. of man so well devised   478a
cause that w. is in other men   379b
cd. he but have drawn his w.   215b
craves a kind of w.   371b
devise, w.! write, pen!   344b
fancy w. will come   299b
he shoots his w.   328a
his w. invites you   108a
his w. was in his own power   214b
How now, w.!   325b
how the w. brightens   300b
I had but little w.   534b
in w. a man   299b
jest with saints, 'tis w. in them   351b
let w. bear a stroke   446a
loudest w. I e'er was deafen'd   72a
malice mingled with a little w.   140b
more w. than a Christian   369b
ne'er be ware of my own w.   326a
neither w., nor words, nor worth   340a
not his pointed w.   303b
only idea of w...laughing   404a
plays boast of more w.   149a
pleasant smooth w.   11a
reaches of a human w.   259b
Sleep..the baiting-place of w.   401b
some beams of w.   140b
still remains to mortify a w.   303b
still wd. remain my w. to try   119b
sum of Shakespeare's w.   147a
too proud for a w.   169b
true w. is nature to advantage   300a
universal monarchy of w.   79a
vex not..with thy shallow w.   435b
wears his w. in his belly   369a
whole wealth of thy w.   354b
whole w. in a jest   22b
wine is in, the w. is out   359a
wisdom and w. are little seen   35a, 91b
w. and sense, virtue..knowledge   395b
w. enough to keep it sweet   211b
w. enough to run away   66a
w. in all languages   142a
w. in his own eye   104b
w.'s an unruly engine   186b
w.'s the noblest frailty   321b
w. that can creep   303a
w. to persuade   117b
witty fool than a foolish w.   370a
w. will shine thro' the harsh   141a
w. with jealous eye surveys   94b
women..have..sometimes w.   91a
ye have a nimble w.   327a
your w.'s too hot   344b
Witch: mother a w. maun be   531a
nor w. hath power to charm   329b
shalt not suffer a w. to live   494a
water like a w.'s oils   98b
w. the world with..horsemanship   378b
Witchcraft: no w. charm thee   329a
only..w. I have used   360a

Witchcraft (*cont.*)
rebellion is as the sin of w.   495*a*
w. celebrates pale Hecate's   347*b*
Witches: all the wild w.   474*b*
think we're burning w.   92*b*
Witching time of night   334*b*
With: he that is not w. me   506*b*, 509*a*
too much w. us   473*a*
wd. I were w. him   381*b*
Withal: Time ambles w.   327*a*
Withdraw: Anthea must w. from
him   190*a*
Withdrawing: melancholy long, w.
roar   5*a*
Withdrawn: as night is w.   37*a*
Wither: age cannot w. her   323*a*
it needs must w.   363*b*
tree will. long before it fall   68*b*
w. and come to deadly use   343*b*
Withered: dried up, and w.   487*b*
it cd. not w. be   216*b*
no root, they. w. away   506*b*
so w. and so wild   346*a*
w. and wede all away   97*a*
w. in my hand   187*b*
Withereth: rose fast w. too   218*b*
Witherington: for W. my heart was
woe   530*b*
for W. needs must I wail   391*b*
Withers are unwrung   334*b*
Within: from w. were heard murmurings   464*b*
he never went w.   106*b*
I have that w. wh. passeth show   330*a*
improvement is from w. outwards   157*a*
I've that w. for wh...no plaisters   158*b*
kingdom of God is w. you   510*a*
outward be fair, however foul w.   94*b*
that is. w. him does condemn   350*b*
w. the meaning of the Act   528*a*
w. were fears   515*a*
Without: no living with thee, nor
w. thee   2*a*
when I shd. find thee w.   500*b*
w. were fightings   515*a*
Withstand in the evil day   516*a*
Withstood: we w. Christ then   47*a*
Witlings: tho' w. sneer   213*a*
Witness: bore w. gloriously   278*a*
heaven and earth to w.   494*b*
shalt not bear false w.   480*a*
weak w. of thy name   278*a*
Witnesses: cloud of w.   517*a*
mouth of two or three w.   515*b*
w. laid down their clothes   512*a*
Wits: great w...madness allied   138*a*
he shall recover his w. there   336*b*
home-keeping youths have ever
homely w.   372*b*
lord among w.   206*b*
native to famous w.   277*a*
rash bavin w.   378*a*
stolen his w. away   119*a*
their poetry..conceived..in..w.   9*b*
universities incline w.   17*a*
veins of rhyming mother w.   259*a*
warming his five w.   438*a*
we have w. to read   215*b*
w. and Templars   303*a*
w. are gamecocks   160*b*
Wittles: live on broken w.   122*a*
w. and drink to me   122*a*
Witty: anger makes dull men w.   13*b*
I am not only w.   379*b*
it shall be w...shan't be long   91*a*
w., profligate and thin   477*b*
Wive: when I came, alas! to w.   372*a*
Wives: fair be their w.   143*a*
go mad, and beat their w.   76*a*
happy in three w.   240*b*
husbands, love yr. w.   516*a*
like strawberry w.   13*b*
loves into corpses or w.   421*a*
man with seven w.   533*b*
many, many w.   286*a*
old w.' fables   516*b*
our careful w.   382*b*
sacks to sew up w.   440*a*
sky changes when they are w.   327*b*
some poisoned by their w.   375*b*
we have children, we have w.   437*b*

Wives (*cont.*)
w. and mithers maist despairin'   285*b*
w. are young men's mistresses   14*b*
w. in the patriarchs' days   180*a*
w., submit..unto yr. husbands   515*b*
Wiving: hanging and w.   353*b*
Wizards: star-led w.   270*a*
Woa mare!   162*b*
Woe: all yr. Sounds of w.   358*b*
best can pity who has felt the w.   160*a*
beyond this land of w.   18*a*
can I see another's w.   33*a*
companions of our w.   450*a*
death..and all our w.   270*b*
deep, unutterable w.   12*b*
discover sights of w.   271*a*
Europe made his w. her own   6*a*
every w. a tear can claim   72*b*
face was full of w.   524*a*
from w. to w. tell o'er   387*b*
gave signs of w.   276*a*
heads are bowed with w.   266*b*
in her voiceless w.   69*a*
joy and w. are woven fine   29*b*
king tried in fires of w.   206*a*
lock'd the source of softer w.   317*a*
long since cancelled w.   387*b*
man was made for Joy and W.   29*b*
melt at other's w.   173*b*
my heart is sick of w.   38*b*
never shall be parted, weal or w.   276*b*
of all the..hideous notes of w.   72*a*
old w. step on the stage   51*a*
proved, a very w.   389*a*
rearward of a conquered w.   388*b*
sad variety of w.   162*b*, 299*b*
Sleep..the balm of w.   401*b*
Sleep! the friend of W.   406*b*
solace in the midst of w.   86*b*
such a draught of w.   392*a*
such a w., believe me, as wins   524*a*
taste the luxury of w.   281*a*
the song of w...an earthly song   430*b*
the tears of w., deceitful shine   282*b*
they work our w.   78*b*
to feel another's w.   304*a*
trappings and the suits of w.   330*a*
Wednesday's child is full of w.   525*a*
w. comforts w. again   137*a*
w. is me, that I..with Mesech   489*b*
w. to that man by whom..cometh   507*a*
w. to the vanquished   550*a*
w. unto you for ye pay tithe   507*b*
w. unto you, lawyers!   509*a*
w. unto you, when all men..speak
well   509*a*
w. weeps out her division   214*b*
Woe-begone: dead in look, so w.   379*b*
Woeful may cease frae..greeting   525*b*
Woes: an Iliad of w.   120*a*
in all..w. that curse our race   163*a*
old w. new wail   387*b*
still her w. at midnight rise   251*b*
w. wh. Hope thinks infinite   397*b*
worst of w. that wait on age   68*a*
Wolf: Assyrian came down like a w.   74*a*
his sentinel, the w.   347*b*
lion and the belly-pinched w.   342*b*
owlet whoops to the w.   99*b*
the w. that follows   420*b*
w. behowls the moon   357*b*
w...shall dwell with the lamb   501*b*
w. with privy paw   269*b*
Wolfe's great name compatriot   111*b*
Wolfe Tone   474*b*
Wolf's-bane, tight-rooted   219*b*
Wolsey, that once trod the ways   386*a*
Wolves: herded w., bold only to
pursue   392*a*
howling of Irish w.   327*b*
inwardly they are ravening w.   505*b*
left the w. behind   254*a*
paw of hireling w.   278*b*
the w. have preyed   359*a*
w. they howled and whined   254*a*
Woman: ah, wasteful w.   293*a*
all is semblative a w.'s part   370*a*
an honest w.'s son   353*b*
a sweeter w. ne'er drew breath   203*b*
a w.'s noblest station   251*b*
a w.'s preaching   207*b*

Woman (*cont.*)
a w.'s whole life..affections   203*b*
Aziola was some tedious w.   393*a*
barren w. to keep house   489*a*
being for a w.'s sake   474*a*
believe a w. or an epitaph   72*a*
brawling w. in a wide house   498*b*
brought the trembling w. there   30*a*
but the w. died   299*b*
callin' a young w. a Wenus   126*b*
can a w.'s tender care   110*a*
caparisons don't become a..w.   400*b*
cast salt on a w.'s tail   65*b*
changeful is w. always   555*b*
constant you are, but yet a w.   377*a*
contentious w. are alike   498*b*
damnable, deceitful w.   291*b*
die because a w.'s fair?   462*a*
dispell'd when a w. appears   159*b*
do you not know I am a w.?   327*a*
each thought on the w.   226*b*
e'en a w. and commanded   324*b*
every w. knows that   21*b*
excellent thing in w.   344*a*
fair w. wh. is without discretion   498*a*
farewell dear, deluding W.   60*b*
fat white w. whom nobody loves   106*a*
feeling a w.'s pulse   411*a*
fine parts indeed who cheats a w.   159*b*
frailty, thy name is w.!   330*a*
fury, like a w. scorned   104*b*
give not thy soul unto a w.   520*b*
gives to man or w.   198*b*
God made w. for the man   426*b*
good name in man or w.   361*b*
had a w. ever less   61*b*
he is a very pretty w.   155*a*
here rests a w., good   299*b*
he that tastes w., ruin meets   159*b*
how divine..a w. may be made   473*a*
I can tell a w.'s age   166*b*
if a w. have long hair   514*b*
I grant I am a w.   338*b*
I hate a dumpy w.   70*a*
inconstant w...never..unhappy   160*b*
in that one w. I have lost   386*a*
in w.'s eye the unanswerable tear   70*a*
[Irene Adler] always *the* w.   135*a*
I saw the w. drunken   519*b*
is this the silent w.   215*a*
I will take some savage w.   432*b*
lack of w.'s nursing   290*a*
large-brained w.   43*b*
lays his hand upon a w.   444*b*
let still the w. take an elder   370*b*
light, that lies in w.'s eyes   281*b*
lips of a strange w.   497*b*
love..company..improves a w.!   150*a*
lovely w. in a rural spot!   202*a*
lovely w. stoops to folly   144*b*, 170*a*
man and a w. in a garden   460*b*
man he must go with a w.   232*b*
man's desire for the w.   102*b*
man's mind, but a w.'s might   339*a*
man that is born of..w.
  237*a*, 481*b*, 497*a*
man was...W.'s cully made   104*b*
many a w. has a past   460*a*
more sweet understanding, a w.   344*b*
more than w. to be wise   281*a*
nakedness of w...work of God   31*a*
naked thinking heart..to a w.   132*a*
never be by w. loved   29*a*
never trust a w. who tells..age   460*b*
none of w. born..harm Macbeth   349*a*
no, nor w. either   332*b*
no other but a w.'s reason   372*b*
no other purgatory but a w.   23*a*
nothing lovelier..found in w.   276*a*
no w...beauty without a fortune   150*a*
no w.'s heart so big   371*a*
no w. shd. marry a teetotaller   413*a*
no w.'s sides can bide   371*a*
oblidged to call it w.   155*a*
of every ill, a w. is the worst   173*a*
oh w.! lovely w. Nature made thee   291*b*
old w. clothed in grey   239*b*
O most pernicious w.!   331*b*
one hair of a w. can draw   200*b*
one to show a w...loves her   49*b*
one w. can forgive another   159*b*

Woman (*cont.*)

only books were w.'s looks	282a
O w.-country, wooed not wed	45a
O W.! in our hours of ease	318b
perfect w., nobly planned	470b
pleasant to any sort of w.	237b
poor lone w.	380a
post-chaise with a pretty w.	209b
shallow, changing w.	385a
shape of a w. has haunted me	222b
she is a w., therefore	368a
she was a worthy w.	88b
silliest w...manage a clever man	237b
sort of bloom on a w.	21b
so unbecoming to a w.	460a
so unto the man is w.	248b
speaks small like a w.	355b
still be a w. to you	292b
still gentler sister w.	59a
such a w. oweth to her husband	367a
such beauty as a w.'s eye	345a
take a mere beggar-w.	288b
that made a w. cry	256a
that princely w.	239a
the female w.	451a
there shone one w.	424a
the rib..made he a w.	492a
the wickedness of a w.	520b
the w. died also	507b
the w.'s a whore	208b
the w.'s deaf, and does not hear	299b
they are neither man nor w.	298a
think myself a very bad W.	1b
'tis brief..as w.'s love	334a
'tis w., w., rules us still	282a
to a w. not to show..weakness	560b
tongue..good..when it an't a w.'s	126a
to play the w.	386a
torrent of a w.'s will	528a
uncommon pretty young w.	144a
untimely fruit of a w.	485b
very honest w...given to lie	325a
virtuous w. is a crown	498a
vitality in a w.	390b
was never yet fair w.	342b
weak and feeble w.	145a
what is better than a good w.	89a
what is w.?..agreeable blunders	107b
what w., however old	439b
who can find a virtuous w.?	499a
whose heaven shd. be true W.	312a
who takes a w. must be undone	159b
who to a w. trusts	173a
wicked w. liberty to gad abroad	520b
wilt thou have this w.	481b
wine, w., and song	440b
w. among all those..not found	499b
w. as old as she looks	102b
w., behold thy son!	511b
w. clothed with the sun	519a
w. for the hearth	436b
w...gained by every sort of flattery	91a
w., gentle w. dare	407a
w. had a bottom of good sense	210b
w. hath found him already	361a
w. having an alabaster box	508a
w. in her selfless mood	428b
W., in the lofty character of Wife	122b
w. in this humour wooed	384b
w. is a dish for the gods	325a
w...is a puzzle to me	439b
w. is at heart a rake	302a
w. is his game	436b
w. is only a w.	227b
w. is so hard upon the w.	436b
w. is the lesser man	432b
W...last thing civilized by Man	264b
w. like a dew-drop	45a
w., lovely w., does the same	110b
w. loves her lover	70b
w...may marry whom she likes	440a
w. moved is like a fountain	367a
w. must wear chains	150a
w. of so shining loveliness	476a
w. said when she kissed her cow	418b
w.'s at best a contradiction	302a
w. sat in unwomanly rags	196a
w.'s cause is man's	437a
w.'s desire is rarely other	102b
w. seldom asks advice	2b

Woman (*cont.*)

w.'s faith, and w.'s trust	319a
w.'s friendship ever ends in love	160a
w.'s happiest knowledge	274a
w.'s mind oft shifts	160a
w.'s reason to say	63b
w.'s whole existence	70a
w. that deliberates is lost	1b
w. that Lord Brutus took to wife	338b
w. to obey	436b
w. true and fair	134a
w. wailing for her demon lover	101a
w. wakes to love	428b
w. well-reputed, Cato's daughter	338b
w., what have I to do with thee?	510b
w.! when I behold thee flippant	222a
w. who did not care	236a
w. who lived in a shoe	533b
w. whom thou gavest..with me	492b
w. who wd. tell one that	460b
w., wine and song	569a
w. with the heart	436b
w. with the West in her eyes	98a
w. yet think him an angel	439b
worser spirit a w. colour'd ill	389b
wd. it not grieve a w.	358a
yet a w. too	470b
yr. wish is w. to win	440b
Woman'd: see me w.	362b
Woman-head..more than one a bed	133b
Womanhood: good, heroic w.	248a
w. and childhood fleet	247b
Womankind: admire of w. but one	108b
faith in w.	437a
I do think better of w.	222b
packs off its w.	390b
the pink o' w.	62b
worst he can of w.	194b
Womanly: now is pure w.	195b
so w., her demeaning	402b
Womb: chaste lady's pregnant w.	260b
his mother's w. untimely ripped	351a
immensity..in thy dear w.	133a
into her w. convey sterility	342a
like a child from the w.	393b
making their tomb the w.	388b
sadder than the Niobean w.	421a
teeming w. of royal kings	375a
the grave; and the barren w.	499a
w. of nature..perhaps her grave	273a
w. of uncreated night	272b
Women: Achilles..among w.	42b
alas! the love of w.	70b
all w. become like their mothers	460a
all w. born are so perverse	35b
among thy honourable w.	484b
are not w. truly, then..shadows	216a
as the weird w. promised	348b
beautiful w. of antiquity	292b
because w. have cancers	222b
blessed art thou among w.	508b
by bad w. been deceived	277b
by subtleties these w. are!	264a
cry of w. rose	136a
dear dead w., with such hair	52b
devil wd. have him about w.	382a
England is a paradise for w.	64b
experience of w...many nations	136a
fairest among w.	500a
fears than wars or w. have	386a
framed to make w. false	360b
from w.'s eyes this doctrine	345a
happiest w...have no history	144b
hard..for w. to keep counsel!	339a
her w. fair; her men robust	77b
in the room the w. come and go	144b
if w. cd. be fair	120b
I must have w.	159b
in w., two almost divide	302a
Italy a..hell for w.	64b
jewels make w...fat or..thin	21b
Kent, sir..hops and w.	126a
lamps shone o'er fair w.	68a
learn about w. from me	230b
learned about w. from 'er	230b
Legend of Good W.	426b
let us have wine and w.	70b
let yr. w. keep silence	514b
like w.'s letters..in the postscript	183a
lost and worn, than w.'s are	370b
loved many strange w.	496a

Women (*cont.*)

Mary, pity w.!	232b
men and w. with our race	227b
men in w. do require	30b
men that w. marry	247b
men, w., and clergymen	404b
Monstrous Regiment of W.	238a
my fifty men and w.	49a
not denyin' the w. are foolish	144a
old w. (of both sexes)	411b
one of Shakespeare's w.	395a
opinion..of the generality of w.	223a
other w. cloy the appetites	323a
other w. know so much	44b
passing the love of w.	229a, 495b
practise..with men and w.	51a
proper function of w.	144b
say that I know w.	439b
seven w...take hold of one man	501a
several virtues..liked several w.	367b
shame for w. to speak	514b
sick of the hired w.	232b
some w.'ll stay in a man's memory	237b
souls of w. are so small	66a
sweet is revenge, especially to w.	70a
there be w., fair as she	182a
there's wisdom in w.	40a
these tell-tale w.	385a
though w. are angels	73a
tide in the affairs of w.	71a
to passionate w. if it seem	474b
'twixt w.'s love, and men's	132a
two main plagues..wine and w.	64a
uniform..work its way with the w.	127a
wage no war with w.	406b
were w. never so fair	251a
were w. never so false	251a
we submit to w. so	78b
where w. walk in public	457b
wh. w. don't understand	232b
with w. the heart argues	7a
w. and care and trouble	451b
W., and Champagne, and Bridge	26b
w. and elephants never forget	572b
W. and Horses and Power	227a
w. and music..never be dated	171a
w. and wine shd. life employ	159b
w. are angels, wooing	368b
w. are a sex by themselves	25a
w. are like tricks	104b
w. are mostly troublesome cattle	250a
w. are so simple to offer war	367a
W. are strongest	520a
w. can true converts make	150b
w...care..more for a marriage	17b
w. come out to cut up	237a
w. desyren to have sovereyntee	89b
w. do in men require	30b
w. guide the plot	400b
w...have an entertaining tattle	91a
w...have..but two passions	91a
w. have no characters at all	302a
w. labouring of child	479a
w...more like each other than men	91a
w. must be half-workers	328b
w. must weep	226b
w. never look so well	417a
w. of good carriage	365a
w., then, are only children	91a
w...who love their lords	194b
w., worst and best	429a
you shd. be w.	346a
Won: baffled oft is ever w.	72b
I am too quickly w.	365a
I've w.! I've w.!	98b
I've w. others to sin	132a
nothing lost nor w.	66a
not that you w. or lost	309a
other palms are w.	467a
she is w.! we are gone	318a
she w., and Cupid blind did rise	251b
some say that we w.	256b
spirit in wh. thy are w.	458a
where you will never w.	529a
why, having w. her	293b
woman in this humour w.	384b
woman, therefore may be w.	368a
woman, therefore to be w.	384a
Wonder: all a w. and a wild desire	51a
all the w. that wd. be	432b

Wonder (*cont.*)

around the w. grew	199*a*
common w. of all men	42*a*
did w. more and more	108*b*
great w. in heaven	519*a*
in w. love and praise	2*a*
I w., by my troth	133*a*
I w. what you are	425*a*
I w. what you're at	83*a*
mournful that no new w...betide	475*b*
'no w.,' said the lords	425*b*
one w. at the least	259*b*
seek no w. but the human face	218*a*
still the w. grew	168*b*
to work a w., God wd. have	191*a*
we w. at ourselves	463*a*
what w. if a Poet now and then	472*b*
without our special w.	349*a*
w. how the devil they got there	303*a*
w. of an hour	68*a*
w. of our age	176*b*
w. of our stage!	215*b*
w. of this earth	395*a*
w., wh. is the seed of knowledge	13*a*
worship is transcendent w.	80*b*
Wondered: all the world w.	426*a*
Wonderful: all things wise and w.	3*a*
anything that is w.	104*a*
called W., Counsellor	501*b*
how w. is Death	393*b*
my God, how w. Thou art	149*b*
O w., w., and most w.	327*a*
passing strange and w.	393*b*
to add..to this w. year	158*b*
'w.!' I ejaculated	136*a*
Wondering for his bread	112*a*
Wonders: all w. in one sight	115*a*
carry within us the w.	4*b*
declare the w. that he doeth	488*b*
'e w. because 'e is frequent	236*b*
his w. in the deep	488*b*
his w. to perform	110*a*
my signs and w. in..Egypt	493*b*
w. in the land of Ham	488*b*
w. that I yet have heard	339*a*
w. what's to pay	200*a*
w. where he is	443*b*
w. will never cease	142*b*
Wondrous: more w. still..charming fair	31*b*
more w. still the table	31*b*
thyself how w. then!	275*a*
w. the gods, more w...the men	31*b*
w., w., still the cock and hen'	31*b*
Woning fer by weste	88*b*
Won't: Don't! Shan't! W.!	233*a*
if she w., she w.	528*a*
will you, we you	83*a*
Woo: April when they w.	327*b*
Duncan Gray came here to w.	60*a*
so thou wilt w.	365*a*
tell my story..that wd. w. her	360*a*
why, having won her, do I w.?	293*b*
w. foul weather all too soon	196*a*
Wood: behind the little w.	433*b*
bows down to w. and stone	184*a*
brown heath and shaggy w.	317*b*
char the w. ere..limn with it	442*a*
cleave the w.	526*a*
deep and gloomy w.	472*a*
great Birnam w.	349*b*
heap on more w.	318*a*
Hermit good lives in that w.	99*b*
herrings grew in the w.	534*a*
impulse from a vernal w.	471*b*
I walked by the w. side	35*a*
makes wing to the rooky w.	349*a*
misty border of the w.	476*a*
my house in the high w.	27*a*
old w. best to burn	13*b*
old w. burn brightest	454*b*
set out to plant a w.	419*b*
springth the w. nu	526*a*
starlight w., with fearful steps	394*b*
their dark impenetrable w.	318*b*
three (years) in the w.	20*a*
trees that are in the w.	526*b*
true w., of yew-w.	135*a*
what w. a cudgel's of	65*b*
whiffling thro' the tulgey w.	83*b*
within the bloody w.	145*a*

Wood (*cont.*)

w. and the pool and..elder tree	119*b*
w. of English bows	135*a*
you are not w...but men	340*a*
Woodbine: well-attir'd w.	270*a*
with luscious w.	356*b*
w. spices are wafted	434*a*
Wood-birds but to couple now	357*b*
Woodcock: w. near the gin	371*a*
w. to mine own springe	337*a*
Woodcocks: springes to catch w.	331*a*
Wooden walls are the best	106*b*
Wooden-shoes: Round-heads and W.	1*b*
Woodland: about the w. ride	198*b*
our winter w. looks a flower	426*b*
Woodlands: about the w. I will go	198*b*
Woodman: w., spare that tree!	284*a*
w., spare the beechen tree	76*b*
Wood-notes: native w. wild	269*a*
Wood-pigeons breed	399*b*
Woods: from the golden w.	436*b*
Greta w. are green	319*a*
in these wild w. forlorn	276*b*
into the w. my Master went	242*b*
never knew the summer w.	430*a*
no bosomed w. adorn	235*a*
no road thro' the w.!	236*a*
pleasure in the pathless w.	69*b*
sea-blooms and the oozy w.	396*b*
senators of mighty w.	218*a*
sounding Clouden's w.	59*b*
stroll alone thro' fields and w.	101*a*
teachers had been w. and rills	463*a*
these hoary w. are grand	320*b*
there is a spirit in the w.	468*a*
these w. more free from peril	325*b*
those enchanted w.	264*b*
to the sleeping w. all night	99*b*
we'll to the w. no more	199*b*
Wet Wild W.	237*a*
when all the w. are still	278*a*
where are those starry w.?	37*a*
w. decay and fall	438*a*
w. have no voice but..complaining	284*a*
w. on shore look dim	282*b*
w. or steepy mountain yields	259*a*
w. shall to me answer	408*b*
Woodspurge has a cup	313*a*
Wooed: beautiful, therefore to be w.	384*a*
her worth, that wd. be w.	275*b*
love that he hath never w.	36*a*
pensively he w.	468*a*
she w. an Englishman	528*a*
woman-country, w. not wed	45*a*
woman in this humour w.	384*a*
woman, therefore may be w.	368*a*
w. and married and a'	310*b*, 528*b*
Wooer: knight to be their w.	528*b*
Woof: we know her w.	219*a*
w. of my tent 's thin roof	393*a*
Wooing: ha, ha, the w. o't	60*a*
love-making, or w. of it	14*a*
who comes a w. me	225*b*
women are angels, w.	368*a*
w., wedding, and repenting	358*a*
Wooings: romances paint..w.	70*b*
Wool: have you any w.?	534*b*
he giveth snow like w.	490*b*
he had no w. on de top	156*b*
if such as came for w.	48*b*
rain into a fleece of w.	486*b*
tease the huswife's w.	267*b*
where de w. ought to grow	156*b*
Woollen: odious! in w.!	302*a*
Woolly: clothing, w., bright	32*b*
Word: a dictatorial w.	166*a*
a false w. spoken	26*a*
an irksome w. and task	440*b*
a time for such a w.	350*b*
a w. and a blow	54*a*, 139*b*, 365*b*
be a hearer of the w.	517*b*
before thy uncreating w.	299*a*
Bilbo's the w.	104*b*
birth of..w. *flirtation*	91*a*
but even that w. alone	312*b*
by water and the W.	415*b*
captain 's but a choleric w.	351*b*
contempt of thy W.	478*b*
doers of the w., and not hearers	517*b*
every idle w. that men..speak	506*b*

Word (*cont.*)

every w. be established	515*b*
every w. stabs	358*a*
every w. that proceedeth	494*b*, 505*a*
first w. that Sir Patrick read	529*b*
flowering in a lonely w.	439*a*
fool can play upon the w.!	354*b*
for no w. however sounding..to relax	412*b*
for teaching me that w.	355*a*
frantic boast and foolish w.	233*b*
God has not said a w.	50*b*
God the w. that spake it	145*b*
honour his own w.	427*b*
if my w. be sterling	376*a*
I'll talk a w. with this..Theban	343*a*
ill w. may empoison liking	358*b*
in every whispered w.	73*b*
in the beginning was the W.	510*b*
leff w. and take the dede	251*a*
Lord gave the w.	486*a*
man's w. is God in man	427*b*
mute and will not speak a w.	366*b*
nat o. wol he faille	89*a*
ne'er a w. wad ane o' them	531*b*
not a w. of sorrow	462*b*
not eaten thee for a w.	345*a*
observant of His heav'nly W.	131*b*
one w. is too often profaned	399*b*
or a w. be spoken	421*b*
pardon's the w. to all	329*a*
proud w. you never spoke	241*b*
sincere milk of the w.	517*b*
some with a flattering w.	459*b*
some w...like Basingstoke	166*b*
so the W. had breath	430*a*
speak but one w. to me	284*b*
speak no angry w.	3*a*
suit the w. to the action	333*b*
Tears wash out a W. of it	153*b*
that I kept my w.	119*b*
that once familiar w.	22*a*
the w. of Caesar might have stood	340*a*
they hear the W.	234*b*
thief said the last kind w.	51*a*
this w. shall speak for me	344*b*
thy w. is a lantern	489*a*
time lies in one little w.!	374*b*
to-day I pronounced a w.	155*a*
to neither a w. will I say	160*a*
torture one poor w.	141*a*
true and lively W.	480*b*
two meanings packed..into one w.	85*a*
'twas God the w. that spake it	145*b*
wanton springs end in a w.	374*b*
we had no w. to say	459*b*
we have not the w. (Philistinism)	9*a*
we said no w.	459*b*
what the w. did make it	145*b*
when *I* use a w.	85*a*
w., at random spoken	317*b*
w. fitly spoken	498*b*
w. for w. without book	369*b*
w. is but wynd	251*a*
w. of God is quick, and powerful	517*a*
w. spoken in due season	498*a*
W. was made flesh	510*b*
you've spoken the foremost w.!	531*b*
Words: abideth not in w.	229*b*
all their courteous w.	137*b*
all w. forgotten	119*b*
alms-basket of w.	345*a*
a rhapsody of w.	335*a*
artillery of w.	419*b*
barren superfluity of w.	159*a*
bright is the ring of w.	414*b*
but w. are w.	360*a*
choice w., and measured phrase	470*b*
coiner of sweet w.	8*a*
councils his w. will grace	40*b*
darkeneth..by w. without knowledge	497*b*
deceive you with vain w.	515*b*
deeds, not w. shall speak me	23*a*
determination of w. to the mouth	417*a*
dressing old w. new	388*a*
embodied in the mystery of w.	469*b*
few of the unpleasant'st w.	354*b*
finde w. newe	89*a*
fine w. butter no parsnips	319*b*
fine w.!..where you stole 'em	419*b*

Words (cont.)
for all sad w. of tongue 459a
form of sound w. 516b
for the idiom of w. 306a
give sorrow w. 350a
glotoun of w. 242b
good w., I think, were best 374b
hear what comfortable w. 480b
Heaven hath my empty w. 351b
he w. me, girls 325a
high thought, and amiable w. 428a
his w...trip about him 279a
his w. were smoother than oil 485b
immodest w. admit..no defence 128a
in all His w. most wonderful 288b
in w. deceiving 270b
it wasn't the w. 527a
last w...name of M. Angelo 308b
last w. of Higginbotham 403b
let the w. of my mouth 482b
let thy w. be few 499a
like the empty w. of a dream 36b
melting melodious w. 190b
men of few w. are the best 382a
much in few w. 520b
much matter..into few w. 157b
multiplieth w. without knowledge 497b
my w. among mankind 396b
my w. are my own 87b
my w. were now written 497a
neither by hir w. 89b
oaths are..w., and w. but wind 65b
perfect music unto noble w. 437a
play 'po' w.? 75a
proper w. in proper places 418a
prune thou thy w. 288b
repeats his w. 374a
silence..even from good w. 484a
so well thy w. become thee 346a
such as w. could never utter 440b
sweet w., low-crooked curtsies 339a
ten low w. oft creep 300a
these are very bitter w. 380a
these two w...undone the world 321a
the w. so fair 216b
thro' w. and things 464a
'twas throwing w. away 472b
two narrow w., Hic jacet 308a
two w. to that bargain 418b
vulgar languages that want w. 216b
what so wild as w. are 52b
wh. into w. no virtue can digest 259b
while his acrid w. turn 194a
with hard w. and unkiss'd 294a
with lucky w. favour 269a
with these dark w. begins 465a
wit, nor w., nor worth 340a
w. and deeds are..modes 148a
w., and no performance 262b
w. are also actions 148a
w. are like a cloud of..snakes 397a
w. are men's daughters 256b
w. are no deeds 385b
w. are quick and vain 397a
w. are the daughters of earth 212b
w. as hard as cannon-balls 147b
w. divide and rend 420b
w. in Mr. Montgomery's writing 254b
w. into the ends of the world 482b
w., like Nature, half-reveal 429b
w. may be false 321b
w. move slow 300a
w. of learned length 168b
w. of love then spoken 282b
w. of the wise are as goads 500a
w. of truth and soberness 513a
w. once spoke..never be recall'd 127b
w. seemed to them as idle tales 510a
w., that burn 175a
w. that have been so nimble 22b
w...tokens..for conceits 13a
w. to the heat of deeds 347b
w., w., mere w. 369b
w., w. or I shall burst 150a
w., w., w. 332a
yr. w., they rob the Hybla bees 341a
Wordsworth: carnage, so W. tells 71b
happy in three wives as Mr. W. is 240b
let simple W. chime 72b
Mr. W.'s epic poetry 183b
out-babying W. 252a

Wordsworth (cont.)
sedulous ape to..W. 412b
W., both are thine 410b
W.'s eyes avert their ken 7a
W.'s healing power 6b
W. sometimes wakes 71a
W.'s standard of intoxication 401a
W.'s sweet calm 7a
W., Tennyson, and Browning 17b
W. was not prone enough 183a
Wordsworthian or egotistical sublime 223a
Wore: she wore a wreath of roses 22b
she w. when she was wed 433a
w. enough for modesty 53b
w., I think, a chasuble 182b
Work: a little w. 263a
all out of w., and cold fraction 381b
at his dirty w. again 303a
a wonderful piece of w. 322b
blessed..he who has found his w. 81b
bread and w. for all 29a
canst w. i' the earth 331b
clean w., and for what pay? 314a
desireth a good w. 516b
dirty w...and for what pay 314a
do the w. that's nearest 226a
every man's w. shall be..manifest 514a
faints the cold w. 103a
for their w. continueth 234b
his little w. of love 3b
his six days' w. 275b
his w. of glory done 111a
if any wd. not w. 516b
I have protracted my w. 207a
I like w.: it fascinates me 205a
it is warm w. 287a
I want w. 377a
Kaspar's w. was done 406a
left no immortal w. behind me 223b
life's w. well done 292a
man goeth forth to his w. 488b
man stopped w. at this age 291a
'mid w. of his own hand 466b
no one shall w. for money 236b
not breed one w. that wakes 198a
nothing to do but w. 225a
now let it w. 340b
only men who did the w. 236a
patience have her perfect w. 517a
plenty of w. to do 205a
poet..not w. by square or line 108a
progress..of wages to w. 81a
put us to w. anew 236b
rewardest..man according to his w. 485b
said, 'Dear w.! Good night!' 198b
scan his w. in vain 110a
sole w. of a life-time 46a
sport..as tedious as to w. 376b
then smoothed her w. 198b
there is always w. 250a
there is no w. nor device 499b
the righteous w., the public care 91b
those men..that do no w. to-day 383a
to make dictionaries is dull w. 212b
too warm w., Hardy, to last long 287a
to w., and back to bed 261b
to w. a wonder, God wd. have 191a
when all its w. is done 294a
when Nature has w. to be done 148b
when no man can w. 511a
when she is by I leave my w. 79b
when w. was scrappy 93b
when yr. w. is finished 229b
who first invented W. 240b
whose w. is not born with him 250a
woman is the w. of God 31a
w. apace, apace, apace 118a
w. for poor old Ned 156b
w. like a digger on the railroad 147a
w. of noble note 439a
w. of our hands upon us 487b
w. the Ides of March began 341a
w. them to their good 407b
w. till further orders 229b
w. without hope 102a
wrought in the w. 496b
years to be of w. and joy 39a
Worked: he w. and sang 28a
men that w. for England 92a
Workers: w. of the world unite 528b
w. start amid their work 43a

Workest great marvels 478b
Workhouse: home is..the woman's w. 391a
Working: for the joy of the w. 236b
in w., if travail you sustain 177a
w...six weeks in a year 444a
Working-class: vast portion..of the w. 9b
Working-house of thought 383b
Workmanship: dark inscrutable w. 469a
wonder at the w. 267b
Workmen: Master of all Good W. 236b
Works: cast off the w. of darkness 514a
counsels, and all just w. 478b
faith without w. is dead 517b
full of good w. 512a
God now accepteth thy w. 499b
good w. in her husband 276a
his ordinary w. convince it 15a
his w. are the comments on it 223a
how our w. endure 228a
I know thy w. 518b
in w. of labour, or of skill 453a
may see yr. good w. 505a
move immediately upon yr. w. 173a
noblest w...from childless men 14b
noble w. that thou didst 479a
O all ye W. of the Lord 478a
our w. begun, continued 480b
rich in good w. 516b
rulers..not a terror to good w. 513b
still, the more he w. 471a
Saturday's..w. hard for its living 525a
their w. do follow them 519b
vulgar w. of man 469a
w. done least rapidly 49a
w. his sovereign Will 110a
W. of Supererogation 491b
Workshop: England..w. of the world 128a
Worky-day fortune 322b
World: a balm upon the w. 218a
abide in this dull w. 324b
above the w. you fly 83a
a bubble burst, and now a w. 300b
ae half of the w. 320a
a foutra for the w. 381a
against a w. in arms 254b
Alexander at the head of the w. 449a
a little w. made cunningly 133a
all's right with the w. 50a
all the sad w. needs 459a
all the uses of this w. 330a
all the w. and his wife 4b
all the w.'s a stage 326b
all the w. wondered 426a
all the w. wd. stare 109a
all th' inamoured w. will say 249b
America..half-brother of the w. 18a
and saved a w. 282a
anywhere out of the w.! 196a
as good be out of the w. 95b
a' the weary w. to quiet 20b
at wh. the w. grew pale 213b
banish all the w. 378a
become fit for this w. 222a
be'old this w. so wide 229a
bend doth awe the w. 337b
Berkeley destroyed this w. 405a
blackguard made the w. 199b
books..are a substantial w. 468b
bottom of the monstrous w. 270a
brave new w. 368a
brave w., Sir, full of religion 25b
briars, is this working-day w.! 325b
Britain is a w. by itself 328b
broad highway of the w. 393b
burden of the w. 258b
busy w. is hushed 288b
but else, not for the w. 365a
called the New W. into existence 79a
caught the w.'s great hands 202a
chide no breather in the w. 327a
compare this prison..unto the w. 376a
compass of the w. 483a
courts..places to learn the w. in 90b
cup us, till the w. go round 323b
daffed the w. aside 378b
deceits of the w. 478b
deign on the passing w. 213b

World (cont.)
devil..kingdoms of the w. 505a
dry a cinder this w. is 132b
dull w. a business of delight 395b
earth and the w. were made 487b
enjoys the w. aright 436b
enthusiasm moves the w. 18a
ere the w. be passed 168a
estate o' the w. were now undone 351a
even so the w. 312b
excellent foppery of the w. 341b
experience of the w. 145a
extend thy mind o'er all the w. 277a
eyes..nourish all the w. 345a
fair volume wh. we W. do name 137b
fashion of this w. passeth away 514a
fled from this vile w. 388a
folly of the w...confounds 194b
free, the w. before me 458a
furloughs for another w. 141b
gave his honours to the w. 386a
get the whole w. out of bed 261b
girdled with the gleaming w. 433a
give warning to the w. 388a
gleams of a remoter w. 396a
gleams that untravelled w. 438b
God so loved the w. 510b
good and increase of the w. 426b
good-bye, proud w. 146b
good deed in a naughty w. 355b
good w....to spend..in 38a
great morning of the w. 392a
great while ago the w. begun 372a
great w.'s altar-stairs 430b
great w. spin for ever 432b
had we but w. enough 260a
hand that rules the w. 448b
he doth bestride the narrow w. 337b
herald of a noisy w. 112a
hereafter, in a better w. than this 325b
high shore of this w. 382b
his little w. of man 342b
his six days' work, a w. 275b
holds the w. between His bill 475a
hold the w. but as the w. 352b
Holy Ghost over the bent w. 197b
hooker the wide w. round! 236a
how small the w. is 177a
if he shall gain the whole w. 507a
if there's another w. 62a
I have never sought the w. 211a
I have not loved the w. 68b
I have overcome the w. 511b
in a w. I never made 200a
in the morning of the w. 50a
in the very w., wh. is..w. of us all 469b
in the whole wide w. again 416a
in this harsh w. draw thy breath 337a
into a w. wh., wanting there 449a
into the dangerous w. I leapt 32a
is the voice of the w. 42a
joy the w. can give 73b
kind that is not in the w. 476a
knew the merry w. was round 439a
knowledge of the w...in the w. 90b
leaves the w. to darkness 174a
leave the w. unseen 219b
lesser god had made the w. 429a
let the w. mind him 47a
let the w. slide 23b
light of the bright w. dies 34a
little body is aweary of this..w. 352b
little of this great w. 360a
little wisdom the w. is governed 567b
long prayers..in the w. they say 6a
look round the habitable w.! 142b
lords of the w. besides 270b
loved this present w. 516b
love that makes the w. go round 83a, 524b
made the bright w. dim 399b
made the round w. so sure 487b
made the w. to be a grassy road 476a
mad w.! Mad kings! 374a
Mad W., my Masters 354, 425a
make me such another w. 363b
manifold changes of the w. 479b
man is one w. 187b
may the w. go well with thee 527a
mighty w. of eye, and ear 472a
month in wh. the w. bigan 89a

World (cont.)
music is the gladness of the w. 144b
my blemishes in the w.'s report 323b
my country is the w. 292a
myself create my little w. 24a
naked shingles of the w. 5a
naked sword throughout the w. 186b
noble blood of all this w. 339b
nor the w. me 68b
now attracts the envy of the w. 55b
o'er a slumbering w. 477a
of all the w.'s brave heroes 526a
of this bad w. the loveliest 26b
of whom the w. was not worthy 517a
oh w., no w., but..public wrongs 238b
O monstrous w.! 362a
one half of the w. cannot understand 11a
one to face the w. with 49b
on the lunar w. securely pry 139b
on the shore of the wide w. 221a
O w. invisible, we view thee 442a
O w.! O life! O time! 395a
O w.! thou wast the forest 339b
pass thro' this w. but once 523b
peace wh. the w. cannot give 478b
poor W. (said I) 114b
procreant urge of the w. 457b
proud w., said I 115a
quiet limit of the w. 438b
rack of this tough w. 344a
reaching to some great w. 294b
reckless what I do..spite the w. 348b
ring'd with the azure w. 426b
roll of the w. eastward 180b
Rose of all the W. 475b
rotundity o' the w. 342b
round about the pendent w.! 352a
round the w. away 226a
round the w. for ever and aye 5b
rulers of the darkness of this w. 516a
say to all the w.'..a man!' 341b
secure amidst a falling w. 2b
see a W. in a Grain of Sand 29a
see how this w. goes 343b
seek a newer w. 439a
sensual w. proclaim 283a
service of the antique w. 326a
set the w. on Sixe and Sevene 90a
shakers of the w. for ever 291a
shot heard round the w. 146b
shows he is a citizen of the w. 15a
since all the riches of this w. 30b
smile of safety wounds the w. 379b
snug farm of the W. 406b
so, in the w. 339a
so runs the w. away 334b
spectacle unto the w. 514a
spins the heavy w. 199b
start of the majestic w. 337b
stood against the w. 340a
strange to the w. 33a
take note, O w.! 362a
ten to the world allot 214b
than this w. dreams of 429a
that, has the w. here 47a
the care of this w. 506b
their star is a w. 49a
these laid the w. away 39a
the whole w. woke 93a
the w.'s an inn 141a
the w. was young then 307a
the W. went very well then 570a
the w. ye shall have tribulation 511b
this busie w. and I 107a
this dark w. of sin 28a
this gewgaw w. 139a
this is a puzzling w. 144a
this little w., this precious stone 375a
this noble w. of thee 280b
this the w. well knows 389a
this unintelligible w. 472a
this warm kind w. is all I know 106b
this wise w. of ours 386a
this w., I hate ye 46b
this w.'s no blot 202b
this w. so vast
tho' the w. be a-waning 284a
thoughts rule the w. 148b
thou seest the w., Volumnius 341b
thou tell'st the w. it is not worth 325a

World (cont.)
thou vain w., adieu 79a
thro' the W. we safely go 29b
thus I live in the w. 1b
tied the w. in a tether 424a
till the w. is wrought to sympathy 398a
to know the w., not love her 477b
to the ending of the w. 383a
trying to adapt the w. 391a
turned the w. upside down 512b
'twas never merry w. 371b
two words have undone the w. 321a
unspotted from the w. 517b
vanity of this wicked w. 481a
verdict of the w. is conclusive 537b
view the w. as a vale of tears 46a
visiting this various w. 394b
void, the w. can never fill 109b
wash..again this soiled w. 457b
wave that echoes round the w. 428b
way the w. ends 145a
we and the labouring w. 475b
what of the w.'s bane 475a
what wd. the w. be, once bereft 197b
when all the w. dissolves 258b
when all the world is old 226a
when all the w. is young 226a
when in the w. I lived 345b
when Rome falls—the W. 69a
whereon the Saviour of the w. 67b
wh. is the w. of all of us 469b
whole w. cannot shew..another 261a
whoso hath this w.'s good 518a
wide w. dreaming on things 388b
wilderness of this w. 54a
will gaze upon this w. 476b
winds of the W., give answer! 228b
wondrous Architecture of the w. 259a
w. affords or grows by kind 143a
w. and all her train 448b
w. and his wife 418b
w. and its ways have a..worth 52a
w. and love were young 307b
w., as God has made it! 47a
w. as my parish 456a
w...be made safe for democracy 462a
w. be worth the winning 139a
w. below the shadow 231b
w...but an hospital 42a
w. consists of men, women, and
Hervey's 280a
w. contains, the wh. he cd.
approve 399a
w. continues to offer..prizes 28b
w. forgetting, by the w. forgot 299b
w...full of a number of things 414a
W...give thee credit for the
rest 94b
w. has grown grey from Thy
breath 423b
w. has little to bestow 18b
w. has no such flowers 423a
w. in every corner sing 187a
w. is a bundle of hay 72b
w. is all a fleeting show 282b
w. is charged with the grandeur 197b
w. is full of care 451b
w. is full of meat and drink 413b
w. is in a state of chassis 290b
w. is made up..fools and knaves 53b
w. is not for aye 334a
w. is not thy friend 366a
w. is too much with us 473a
w. is weary of the past 394a
w. its veterans rewards 302a
w. laughs with you 459a
w. may end to-night 47b
w. must be peopled 358b
w. now is but the minister 36a
w. of gammon and spinach 122a
w. of happy days 384b
w. of men for me 49b
w. of pomp and state 22b
w. of vile ill-favour'd faults 356a
w. of waters wild 443a
w., or even worldkin 81b
w.'s a bubble 17a
w.'s a jest, and joy's a trinket 410b
w.'s a scene of changes 107a
w.'s as ugly, ay, as sin 246a
w.'s course will not fail 294a

World (*cont.*)
w.'s great age begins anew — 394a
w.'s great men..not..scholars — 194b
w.'s great snare uncaught — 324a
w. shall end when I forget — 422b
w. shd. listen then — 398b
w.'s mine oyster — 355b
w.'s more full of weeping — 476a
w.'s storm-troubled sphere — 38b
w.'s tempestuous sea — 143b
w...still deceived with ornament — 354a
w. surely is wide enough — 411b
w.'s whole sap is sunk — 133b
w. to hide virtues in — 369b
w. was all before them — 277a
w. was very guilty — 344b
W. Well Lost — 139a
w. where all are pure — 428a
w. will..follow only those — 67a
w. will give thee credit — 94b
w. will not believe..man repents — 427b
w. without end. Amen — 478a
w. wd. go round a deal faster — 82b
w. wd. smell like..a tomb — 395b
worst w. that ever was known — 38a
ye are the light of the w. — 505a
yr. back upon the w. — 247b
World-forsakers: world-losers and w. — 291a
Worldlings: mak'st a testament as w. — 325b
world, and w. base — 381a
World-losers and world-forsakers — 291a
Worldly: all my w. goods — 481b
all w. shapes shall melt — 77a
be wisely w. — 307a
breath of w. men — 375a
honours, or for w. state — 465a
thanked my God for w. things — 30b
W. Hope men set their Hearts — 152b
Worldly-Wise-Man — 54a
Worlds: allur'd to brighter w. — 168b
both the w. suffer — 348b
both w. at once they view — 449a
from w. not quickened by the sun — 464a
in never-fading w. — 464b
in w. not realized — 466b
joy for it worth w. — 186b
new w. to buy — 260b
so many w., so much to do — 430b
Soul of all the w. — 464b
the crush of w. — 1b
Wind that blows between the W. — 235b
w. in th' yet unformed Occident — 117a
worth purchasing with w. — 151a
World-terror's wing — 92a
World-without-end: w. bargain — 345b
w.hour — 388a
Worm: big as a round little w. — 364b
Conqueror W. — 298a
don't cackle w'en he fine a w. — 182a
I am a w., and no man — 483a
I am but as a crushed w. — 535b
I want to be a w. — 167b
like a w. i' the bud — 371a
or was I a w.—too low-crawling — 218a
rather tough w. — 165a
sets foot upon a w. — 112b
sharp-headed w. — 438a
spirit of the w. beneath the sod — 393b
spouse of the w. — 77b
the crested w. — 112b
their w. dieth not — 508b
w. at one end..fool at the other — 214a
w. is cloven in vain — 430b
w. is yr. only emperor — 335a
w. mounts thro' all the spires — 146b
w. nor snail, do no offence — 356b
w. that hath eat of a king — 335b
w. that never dies — 39b
w., the canker, and the grief — 73b
Worms: among the hungry w. I sleep — 529a
convocation of politic w. — 335a
devils wd. set on me in W. — 569a
flies, w., and flowers — 453a
he was eaten of w. — 512b
I was one of the w. — 105b
I went to W.; and got more drunken — 304b
made w.' meat of me — 365b
mercy on us w. of earth — 149b
nor w. forget — 124b

Worms (*cont.*)
of w., and epitaphs — 375b
then w. shall try — 260a
with vilest w. to dwell — 388a
w. destroy this body — 497a
w. have eaten them — 327b
w...thy chambermaids — 366b
w. were hallowed that did breed — 362b
Wormwood: end is bitter as w. — 497b
star is called W. — 519a
the w. and the gall — 503b
Worn: when we're w., hacked, hewn — 406a
Worry and devour each other — 109b
Worrying: what's the use of w. — 10b
Worse: as her mind grew w. — 465b
boundless better, boundless w. — 438b
but rather grew w. — 508b
cd. make the w. appear the better — 272a
greater feeling to the w. — 374b
if they spake w., 'twere better — 214b
kept it from being any w. — 180b
leave the w. ones — 25b
nobody seem'd one penny the w. — 19a
other things wh. were w. — 237a
see..better things..follow w. — 551b
the better, the w. — 13b
w., and worst times, still succeed — 190b
w. than an infidel — 516b
w. than fables yet have feigned — 272a
w. to me than dead — 462b
w. when it comes late — 205b
Worship: are come to w. him — 504b
bow down to them, nor w. them — 480a
fell at his feet to w. him — 519b
must w. him in spirit — 510b
simple w. of a day — 219b
thy w. and renown — 484b
with what deep w. — 101a
with wh. I w. thine — 399b
w. her by years — 428a
w. is transcendent wonder — 80b
w. of the great of old — 73a
w. only thee — 109b
w. to the garish sun — 366a
w., wh. prevailed in..Roman world — 162a
ye ignorantly w. — 512b
Worshipped: angels..w. be — 131b
lifted up, or w. — 491b
suspect that I w. the Devil — 30b
w. by the names divine — 30a
Worshipper: drowsy W. outside Nature mourns her w. — 152a, 317a
Worshipp'st at the temple's..shrine — 467a
Worser: throw away the w. part — 335a
Worst: a full look at the w. — 179b
began best can't end w. — 44b
best and the w. of this is — 422b
best is like the w. — 232a
change for the w. — 87a
good in the w. of us — 192a
greatest, nor the w. of men — 68b
his w. is better — 183a
hopeless rubbish as thy w. — 410b
I love to be the w. — 418a
knew the w. too young — 229b
the w. is not, so long — 343b
things present, w. — 380a
thinks the w. he can — 194b
this is the w. — 343b
w. are no worse — 357b
w. inn's w. room — 302b
w. is death — 375a
w. is yet to come — 206a
w. kinde of infortune — 90a
w. returns to laughter — 343b
w. speaks something good — 187a
Worth: all his worldly w. for this — 438a
aught be w. the doing — 33a
comfort of thy w. — 387b
early known thy wondrous w. — 313b
entertain us with no w. — 449a
I am w. more than ever — 296b
in the w. and choice — 214b
much is she w. — 185b
own w. then not knowing — 388b
relic of departed w. — 68a
slow rises w. by poverty — 213b
Temple of thy W. — 232b
the conscience of her w. — 275b
what is the w. of anything — 76a

Worth (*cont.*)
wit, nor words, nor w. — 340a
whose w.'s unknown — 389a
w. a guinea a box — 528b
w. makes the man — 301b
w. of a State..w. of..individuals — 266a
w. the travelling to — 415a
Worthies: than all the W. did — 134a
Worthiness: change to virtue and to w. — 338a
combin'd in beauty's w. — 259b
Worthy: found them w. for himself — 520a
I find thee w. — 250b
Lord, I am not w. — 506a
more w. to leap in ourselves — 341b
nine w. and the best that..were — 257a
no more w. to be called thy son — 509b
of whom the world was not w. — 517a
seem w. of yr. love — 469a
she was a W. womman — 88b
who is w. to open the book — 518b
w. of the vocation — 515b
Wotton: Sir Henry W...lover of angling — 450b
Sir Henry W. used to say — 13b
Would: as I w. they shd. do — 481a
'dare not' wait upon 'I w.' — 347a
under her wings, and ye w. not! — 507b
Wouldst highly that w. thou holily — 346b
Wound: did help to w. itself — 374b
earth felt the w. — 276a
felt a stain like a w. — 57a
gall a new-healed w. — 379b
heal me of my grievous w. — 429b
jests at scars..never felt a w. — 365a
knife see not the w. it makes — 346b
my w. is deep — 530b
tho' rebels w. thee — 375a
tongue in every w. of Caesar — 340b
what w. did ever heal — 361b
whose annual w. in Lebanon — 271b
willing to w...afraid to strike — 303a
w. for w. — 494a
w. in the solicitor..very serious — 66b
w. of peace is surety — 369a
w. that laid thee low — 72a
Wounded: tend the w. under fire — 229b
when w., heal'd thy wound — 110a
w. and left on Afghanistan's — 237a
w. for our transgressions — 503a
w. in the house of my friends — 504b
w. is the wounding heart — 114b
w. spirit who can bear? — 498b
'you're w.! 'Nay' — 47b
Wounds: bind up my w. — 385a
dead Caesar's w. — 340a
faithful are the w. of a friend — 498b
guns, and drums, and w. — 376b
heals his w. — 289a
keeps his own w. green — 14a
kist his w. that were so red — 529b
labour and the w. are vain — 96b
words become thee as thy w. — 346a
w. I had on Crispin's day — 383a
Woundy: they sound so w. great — 3a
Wrack: a way, out of his w. — 386a
blow, wind! come, w.! — 351a
Wracks: thousand fearful w. — 384b
Wragg is in custody — 9a
Wrangle: shall we begin to w. — 526a
Wrap me up in my tarpaulin — 459a
Wrapped: w. in purple robes — 474a
w. up my buth in a mistry — 440b
Wrath: day of w. — 540a
devil..having great w. — 519a
envy and w. shorten the life — 520b
eternal w. burnt after them — 275a
flee from the w. to come — 504b
from the w. of the Lamb — 519a
grapes of w. are stored — 200b
he enter'd full of w. — 218a
his w. endureth but the twinkling — 483b
I told my w. — 32a
my w. did grow — 32a
not in cruelty, not in w. — 248a
nursing her w. to keep it warm — 62b
slow to w. — 517a
soft answer turneth away w. — 498a
sun go down upon yr. w. — 515b
that day of w. — 317b
Thou'lt leave Thy w., and say — 294a

Wrath (cont.)
throw away Thy w. 188a
tigers of w. are wiser 31a
turning of the phials of w. 312b
wh. way shall I fly infinite w. 273b
who the ox to w. has moved 29a
W., by His meekness 33a
w. of men worketh not 517a
w. of Peleus' son 559b
w. of the lion 31a
Wreath: I put on thy w. 218a
subtle w. of hair 132b
sent thee late a rosy w. 216b
Wreathed his lithe proboscis 274a
Wreck: decay of that colossal w. 396b
from its own w. the thing 397b
only not a w. 287a
with sunken w. 381b
Wrecks: above the w. of Time 244a
on the shore vomits its w. 395b
w. of a dissolving dream 394a
Wreke him on a flye 90a
Wren: considered Sir Christopher
    W. 19a
eagle's wings I bore this w. 139a
four Larks and a W. 243a
miracle of a youth Mr. Christopher
    W. 149b
no better a musician than the w. 355b
robin redbreast and the w. 454b
Sir Christopher W. said 27b
who shall hurt the little w. 29a
w. goes to 't 343b
w. with little quill 357a
youngest w. of nine 371b
w., the most diminutive of birds 350a
Wrestle: we w. not against flesh 516a
Wrestled: as he w. with him 493a
God..w. with him 450b
Sir, you have w. well 325b
there w. a man with him 493a
Wrestles: he that w. with us 57b
Wrestling: I wretch lay w. 197a
Wretch: ceremony, such a w. 383a
excellent w.! 361b
hailed the w. who won 69a
haply yon w., so famous 294a
leaves the w. to weep 169a
my wife, who, poor w. 296a
nor the w. undone 113b
on hope the w. relies 168a
Patron. Commonly a w. 364b
pretty w. left crying 328a
sharp-looking w. 107b
such a destined w. as I 342b
tremble, thou w. 59b
w., a villain, lost to love 317a
w., concentred all in self 109b
w. even then 61b
w. that dares not die 78b
w.! whom no sense of wrongs 444b
w. whom 'twere gross flattery 386a
Wretched: how w. is that poor man 477a
the w. he forsakes 130a
w. have no friends 342b
w. in both! 395a
w. men are cradled into poetry 73b
Wretchedness: sum of human w. 368a
w. that glory brings us! 343a
Wretches: feel what w. feel 343a
poor naked w. 193a
Wriggles and giggles 450a
Wring: soon w. their hands 170a
w. his bosom—is to die 135b
you will w. no more hearts 141a
Wrinkle: slip out ..with the first w. 69b
Time writes no w. 68a
w. deeper on the brow 323a
Wrinkled deep in time 196a
Wrist: gyves upon his w. 36a
Writ: heard or w. so oft 389a
I never w., nor no man..loved 384b
stolen forth of holy w. 96a
w. in a Roman chamber 303a
Write: born to w., converse 65b
but a desk to w. upon 413b
cannot w. like Hazlitt 11b
can you contrive to w. so even? 49a
does he w.? he fain wd. paint 183a
does not w. himself down

Write (cont.)
enraged I w. 176b
fingers of..hand wherewith I w. 44a
he said unto me, W. 519b
hope to w. well hereafter 279a
I am resolved to w. on 170a
I live and w. 188a
I sit down to w. 223b
I will w. for Antiquity! 240a
I will w. upon him my new name 518b
I w. as others wrote 241a
I w. for the general amusement 319a
last, till you w. yr. letter 134a
learn to w. well 141b
let others w. for glory 106a
little more I have to w. 189b
look in thy heart, and w. 401b
make me w. too much 117a
man may w. at any time 206b
Muse invoked, sit down to w. 419b
never read books—I w. them 535b
never to w. for the sake of writing 223a
nobody can w. the life of a man 208a
not enough for me to w. 251b
piper, sit thee down and w. 32b
ready man that w. apace 45a
rede hem as they w. 90a
screaming..all the time I w. 124b
sit down quickly, and w. fifty 509b
sometimes wish to w. 114a
tho' an angel shd. w. 281a
were angels to w. 289b
what thou seest, w. in a book 518a
w. and read comes by nature 358b
w. God first 359a
w. it before them in a table 502a
w. me as one that loves 202a
w. me down an ass 359a
w. my name in the dust 536b
w. such stuff for ever 211a
'w. that down,' the King said 83b
w. the vision, and make it plain 504b
you w. with ease 401a
Writer: a late facetious w. 151b
loose, plain, rude w. 64a
tongue is the pen: of a ready w. 484b
understand a w.'s ignorance 102a
you w. of plays 48a
Writers: as w. become more
    numerous 170a
poets..best w., next to..prose 13b
w. against religion 57b
Writes: one who w. amiss 300a
Writest: 'what w. thou?' 201b
Writhed not at passing 221b
Writing: easy w.'s..hard reading 401a
fairy kind of w. 140b
fairy way of w. 2a
fine w. is next to fine doing 223a
for yr. w. and reading 358b
recited verses in w. 521a
some for w. verses 246a
this manner of w. 279a
true ease in w. 300a
w...a mechanic part of wit! 149a
w. increaseth rage 176b
w. (maketh) an exact man 16a
Writing-book: you have lost yr. w.! 193a
Writings: confess thy w. to be such 215b
Written: a well-w. Life 80a
censure freely who have w. well 300a
fails, since this was w. 47b
I have since w. what no tide 241b
my words were now w. 497a
so many people have w. 212b
something so w. to after-times 279a
what I have w. I have w. 511b
w. by mere man..wished longer 212a
w. on terrestrial things 179a
w. such volumes of stuff! 243b
Wrong: all was w. because 114a
bade her w. stay 360b
better hang w. fler than no fler 121b
career of high-handed w. 87a
cradled into poetry by w. 395a
divinely in the w. 476b
do a little w. 354b
doeth grievous w. 426a
easily things go w. 256a
feel I must be w. 460a
Frenchmen can't be w. 177b

Wrong (cont.)
gang a kennin w. 59a
general notions are generally w. 280a
great a w. it is to let 476a
he can't be w. whose life 301b
he has been in the w. 309b
I canna w. thee 59b
I dread, doing no w. 354b
if you w. us..not revenge? 354a
in working w., if pleasures 177a
king can do no w. 28b
love shd. have no w. 35b
makes us right or w. 60a
multitude is always in the w. 128a
nature is usually w. 456b
nets of w. and right 474b
never dreamed..w. wd. triumph 52a
not surely always in the w. 107b
one idea, and that is a w. one 208a
one idea, and that was w. 130a
one w. more to man 48a
O trust not in w. 485b
our country, right or w. 118a
own he has been in the w. 419a
pardon, who have done the w. 139b
pledged to keep from w. 294a
preserve the stars from w. 464a
right and w. he taught 4b
right of an excessive w. 51a
suffer w. no more 253a
telling a man he was w. 97a
to advise her w. 419a
Valerius loathed the w. 253b
we do him w. 430b
we do it w., being so majestical 329b
when everyone is w. 562a
when..nothing goes w. 166b
where is the w. I did them? 48b
who does, not suffers w. 397a
w. extenuates not w. 369a
W. for ever on the throne 250b
w. left unredressed on earth 226b
w. of unshapely things 475b
w. side of a Turkey tapestry 200b
w. side of the door 92a
w. side of thirty 418b
w. that needs resistance 18b
you w. me every way 340b
Wrongs: good for righting w. 246a
mass of public w. 238b
people's w. his own 138b
redressing human w. 427b
w. darker than death 397b
Wrote: gentlemen who w. with
    ease 303b
sorry now, I w. it 54b
this they w. that another man w. 235b
whatever he w., did it better 209b
w. my happy songs 32b
Wroth with one we love 100a
Wrought: but being w., perplexed 364a
first he w. 88b
sound of those he w. for 435a
w. the end unthought 236a
Wye: half the babbling W. 430a
Wynken, Blynken, and Nod 151a

X

Xanadu: in X. did Kubla Khan 101a
Xenophon: X. at New York 449b
[X.] maintained the dignity of his-
    tory 33b
Xiphias to his aim 403a

Y

Yammerton: Major Y. 416b
Yank: boldest thieves, be Y.! 233b
Yankee Doodle came to town 18b
Yarn: I ask is a merry y. 262a
mingled y., good and ill together 322a
Yarrow: my love, the flower of Y. 246b
Yasmin: flowers are dead, Y. 154b
I toward thy bed, Y. 154b
Yawcob Strauss: leaf dot Y. S. 1a
Yawp: my barbaric y. 458a
Y-beten: maker is him-self y. 90a
Ydrad: but ever was y. 408b
gods and men y. 409a

Yea: Chapman's y. was y.   27b
let yr. communication be Y, y.   505a
let yr. y. be y.   517b
the everlasting y.   81b
Yea-forsooth knave   379b
Year: acceptable y. of the Lord   503a
all this y. to thee   446b
another y.! another deadly blow!   468a
atmosphere of a new-fal'n y.   24a
before the mellowing y.   269a
bloom the y. long!   37a
breath and the bloom of the y.   52a
circle of the golden y.   427a
crownest the y. with..goodness   486a
dirge of the dying y.   396b
doctor does not give you a y.   413b
each day is like a y.   459b
fill the measure of the y.   221a
follows so the ever-running y.   383a
grief returns with the revolving y.   392a
heav'n's eternal y. is thine   140b
if all the year were..holidays   376b
in over a y. and a half   424a
in the sweet o' the y.   373a
leading up the golden y.   427a
longest night in all the y.   284b
my most immemorial y.   298b
no winter in thy y.!   53a, 246b
pilgrims of the year   264a
pleasure of the fleeting y.!   388b
read any book..not a y. old   148b
shd. I preach a whole y.!   249a
that time of y. thou mayst..behold   388a
the y. is going   431a
the y. of the great crime   294a
the y.'s at the spring   50a
this many and many a y.   38a
this newe corn from y. to y.   90a
this wonderful y.   158b
thro' many a weary y.   200b
thus with the y. seasons return   273a
till another y. be gone   228a
till you come to Forty Y.   440b
'tis the y.'s midnight   133b
to make up a y. and a sphere   146b
twentieth y. is well-nigh past   109a
will finish up the y.   384a
Winter comes..rule the varied y.   443b
Winter, ruler of th' inverted y.   112a
wisdom with each studious y.   68b
y. after y...voted cent. per cent.   67b
y. only lost to me   188a
y. wake y. to sorrow   392a
y. whose days are long   459b
Yearn: finite hearts that y.   52b
Yearning: unto the man of y. thought   313a
Yearnings: weary longings and y.   171b
Years: add again y. and y. unto y.   132a
ah! happy y.!   68a
all the same a hundred y. hence   124b
and the y. that are past   487a
as the faithful y. return   232b
before the beginning of y.   420b
bring our y. to an end   487b
but y. hath done this wrong   117a
come to the y. of discretion   481a
cuts off twenty y. of life   339a
down the arches of the y.   441b
ere the sorrow comes with y.   43a
few more y. shall roll   33b
for certain y., for certain months   312b
forty y. on   34b
gave up the y. to be   39a
going on now for three hundred y.   460b
go softly all my y.   502b
hair is grey, but not with y.   69b
have him nine y. a-killing   362b
hopes and fears of all the y.   40a
how many y. a mortal man may live   384a
into the vale of y.   362a
it may be for y.   115b
language..learned these forty y.   374b
live a thousand y.   339b
love you ten y. before the Flood   260a
Lundy from his earliest y.   26a
meet thee after long y.   74b
moments big as y.   218a
more y. might crave..precedence   225a
new y. ruin and rend   423b

Years (cont.)
nor the y. condemn   28b
nor the y. draw nigh   499b
of my three score y. and ten   198b
O for ten y.   220b
our age are threescore y. and ten   487b
our noisy y. seem moments   466b
out of me the y. roll   422a
provoke the y. to bring the..yoke   466b
recollecting..how, in earlier y.   86a
sae mony changefu' y.   61b
seemed unto him but a few y.   493a
some lost lady of old y.   52b
Such as are of Riper Y.   481a
sum of six thousand y.   293a
take from seventy y. a score   198b
the golden y. return   394a
the long y. I've been wandering   282a
they come to fourscore y.   487b
thought of our past y.   466b
thousands of y., if all were told   474b
thousand y. in thy sight   487b
thy thousand y. of gloom   429b
thy y. shall not fail   488a
till seven y.' heat   369b
till seven y. were gone   528b
to remember for y.   4a
touch of earthly y.   463a
twelve y. complete..in exile   261a
twice ten tedious y.   108a
what have these y. left to me?   70a
where all past y. are   134a
y. damp my intended wing   276a
y. glide away   20a
y. he number'd scarce thirteen   215a
y. in long procession   138b
y. like great black oxen   474a
y. steal fire from the mind   68a
y. teach much wh...days never know   148a
y. that bring..philosophic mind   467a
y. that the locust hath eaten   504a
Yesterday's Sev'n Thousand Y.   153a
yet wait many y.   409a
Yeas: in russet y.   345a
Yell: Gélert's dying y.   408a
such a y. was there   318b
Yellow: come unto these y. sands   367a
deeper y. on the corn   191a
hair..y. like ripe corn   311b
learn from the Y. an' Brown   230b
the sear, the y. leaf   350b
y., and black, and pale   396a
Yellow-Dog-Dingo behind   230b
Yeoman: did me y.'s service   336b
Yeomen: nine and twenty y. tall   316b
y., whose limbs..made in England   382a
Yerde: man maketh ofte a y.   90a
Yes: Crier cried, 'O Y.!'   19b
Prophets, Virgins, answer, Y.!   286a
'Y.,' I answered you last night   43b
y., there's room   315b
y. verily; and by God's help   481a
Yesterday: all our pomp of y.   233b
and dead Y.   153b
but y. the word of Caesar   340a
call back y., bid time return   375a
children dear, was it y.   6a
Christ the same y., and to-day   517a
great families of y.   118b
leaves the Rose of Y.   152b
no to-morrow hath, nor y.   132a
sweet sleep wh. thou ow'dst y.   362a
that was y.   441a
thousand years..are but as y.   487b
'tis done, but y. a King!   73b
we were saying y.   550a
Y.'s Sev'n Thousand Years   153a
Yesterdays: cheerful y.   464b
y. have lighted fools   350b
Yestreen: new moon late y.   530a
Yew: dusk the hall with y.   7a
never a spray of y.   7b
slips of y. sliver'd in the moon's   349b
solemnly to yonder y.   216b
stuck all with y.   371a
Y. alone burns lamps of peace   119b
Yield: at a touch I y.   436b
find, and not to y.   439a
never to submit or y.   271a
oughtn't to y. to temptations   197a

Yield (cont.)
with shame and grief I y.   225a
y., proud foe, thy fleet   76b
y. them for a day   430b
Yielded: by her y., by him..received   274a
y. with coy submission   274a
Y.-lost: for tyme y.   90a
Yo-ho-ho, and a bottle of rum   413a
Yoke: bring the inevitable y.   466b
bull doth bear the y.   358a
Flanders hath received our y.   449a
he bear y. in his youth   503b
my y. is easy   506b
neck unto a second y.   190a
Pharaoh's bitter y.   286b
take my y. upon you   506b
to bear the y. in youth   228a
ye break every y.   503a
y. of inauspicious stars   366b
Yolk runs down the waistcoat   124b
Yonder all before us lie   260a
Yonghy-Bonghy-Bo   243b
Yore: as it hath been of y.   466a
Yorick: alas! poor Y.   336b
'Cock and a Bull,' said Y.   412a
York: at Y., 'tis on the Tweed   301a
born in..1632, in the city of Y.   118a
noble Duke of Y.   526b
this sun of Y.   384b
You: all too precious y.   388a
and y., and all of us fell down   340a
even as y. and I!   236a
is it really y. again?   46b
to y., to y., all song of praise   401b
unto y. at last she flies   79b
Young: always find us y.   147a
America is a country of y. men   148b
as great with y. as she might goe   529b
a y. man's fancy   432a
both were y.   72a
[Brigham Y.] is dreadfully married   451b
capacities of us that are y.   379b
crime of being a y. man   297a
God guide them—y.   428b
head bit off by it y.   342a
I, being y. and foolish   474a
if y. hearts were not so clever   199b
I have been y.   484a
in Heaven is to grow y.   312a
I was y. and foolish   474a
knew the worst too y.!   229b
learned to play when he was y.   533a
loved when all was y.   226a
love so y. cd. be so sweet   37b
made y. with y. desires   441b
marry? a y. man not yet   14b
my pretty lad is y.   531a
myself when y. did eagerly   153a
nest where she may lay her y.   487a
not so y., sir, to love a woman   342a
or as y. as what she was   231b
rejoice, O y. man, in thy youth   499b
remembered that he once was y.   4b
she died y.   454b
she that was y. and fair   460a
sight to make an old man y.   427a
so wise, so y.   385a
so y., and so untender?   341b
so y. a body with so old a head   354b
so y., so fair   69a
swallow..six y. on the rail   47b
tall y. men in turn   92b
the y. can do for the old   390a
the y., y. children   43a
they were so y., so beautiful   70b
they wd. be y. for ever   199b
those that are with y.   502b
thou wast y., thou girdedst thyself   511b
to be seventy years y.   194a
to be y. was very heaven   465a
went to the Bar as a very y. man   164a
we that are y.   344a
we were y., we were merry   98a
when all the world is y.   226a
whether we be y. or old   469b
y. and old come forth to play   269a
y. and so fair!   195b
y. enough for a boy   370a
y. generations in hail   263a
y. man, I think you're dying   531a

Young (cont.)
y. man will be wiser by and by 427b
y. men are fitter to invent 16a
y. men glittering and sparkling 445a
y. men taken in and done for 225a
y. men..Aristotle thought unfit 369a
y. ones carry pistols 389b
yr. y. men shall see visions 504a
Younger: let thy love be y. 370b
travel, in the y. sort 15a
y. than she are happy mothers 364b
Youngest: but now, thy y., dearest 391b
infallible, not even the y. 443a
y. to the oldest singer 423a
y. was, and highte Canacee 89b
Your: who's y. fat friend 53a
Yours: all I have, devoted y. 386b
what I have done is y. 386b
y. I see is coming down 393a
Yourself: an' y. jus' so 228b
do it y. 19b
go into it y. 30a
keep something to y. 60a
keep y. to y. 126b
speak for y., John 246b
two topics, y. and me 209a
Youth: adventurous and honourable
y. 413a
age approve of y. 51a
age must..be taught by y. 58a
a man loves the meat in his y. 358b
April of yr. y. adorns 186b
a spirit of y. in everything 388b
as y. and thou are of one date 387a
a y., and a well-beloved y. 531b
a y. of frolics 302a
a y. of labour 168a
bear the yoke in his y. 503b
billiards..sign of an ill-spent y. 408a
blest. . with y. for evermore 312a
brisk intemperance of y. 161b
caught our y. 40a
child do deeds of y. 387b
crabbed age and y. 389b
Creator in the days of thy y. 499b
days of our tropic y. 182a
days of our y. are..glory 73b
done it from my y. 113b
dropped from their y. and love 52a
enjoy'd his y. 140a
everything..great..done by y. 129a
every y. cry Well-a-way 531a
face to lose y. for 48a
figure of blown y. 333b
flourish in immortal y. 1b
flourish set on y. 388a
gave my heart another y. 389a
gives his y. delight 301a
glory of y. glowed in his soul 414b
green unknowing y. engage 141b
he wears the rose of y. 323b
hill of everlasting y. 36b
his y. 'gainst time and age 295b
home-keeping y...homely wits 372b

Youth (cont.)
hour of thoughtless y. 472a
if y. knew 563a
I knew a phœnix in my y. 474b
'in my y,' Father William replied 82b
in my y. I never did apply 325b
in. .my y. I remembered my God! 407a
in the lexicon of y. 252a
in the vaward of our y. 379b
in y. it sheltered me 284a
laugh uproariously in y. 39b
lo! as that y.'s eyes burned 312b
mewing her mighty y. 279a
music tells, of y., and home 282a
noble y. did dress themselves 380a
not clean past yr. y. 379b
Nurseries of blooming Y. 468b
offences of my y. 483a
one beloved heard in y. alone 397a
O stay, thou goodly y.! 531b
other companye in y. 88b
our y., our joys, and all 307b
past the bounds of freakish y. 112a
pleasures with y. pass away 407a
red sweet wine of y. 39a
rejoice, O young man, in thy y. 499b
riband in the cap of y. 336a
roses for the flush of y. 311a
shake their wicked sides at y. 474a
ship-wreck of my. .y. 117a
stretch the folly of our y. 93a
stroke that my y. suffered 360a
they had been friends in y. 100a
things Y. needed not 463b
this Y. and Age..strangers still 137b
thoughts of y. are long 247b
thou hast nor y. nor age 351b
thy fair and shining y. 463b
to many a y., and many a maid 269a
what our y. desires 9a
when Y. and Pleasure meet 68b
where y. grows pale 220a
with wh. our y. is fed 394b
y. and age in common 9a
y. and blood are warmer 190b
y. and observation copied 331b
y., beauty, graceful action 138b
y...face towards the upland hill 137b
y., I do adore thee 389b
Y. is a blunder 129a
y. is full of pleasance 389b
y. is the season of credulity 297a
y. is the time to go flashing 413a
y. is vain 100a
y. means love 51a
y. of America..their..tradition 460b
Y. of a Nation..trustees 130a
y. of delight, come hither 32a
y. of England is on fire 381b
y. of pleasure wasteful 48b
Y. on the prow 173b
Y. pined away with desire 32a
y.'s a stuff will not endure 370b

Youth (cont.)
y. shows but half 50b
Y.'s sweet-scented manuscript 154a
y.'s the season made for joys 159b
y. to fortune and. .fame unknown 174b
y. waneth by increasing 295b
y., was full of foolish noise 430a
y., what man's age is like to be 119b
y., who bore, mid snow and ice 247a
y., who daily farther 466b
y. whose hope is high 37a
y. will be served 34a
Youths: feeble and restless y. 96a
y. and maidens gay 100a
y. green and happy 96a
Y-reke: is fyr y. 89a
Y-sowen wonder wyde 89b
Yule-nicht when we were fou' 60a
Yum-Yum: going to marry Y. 164b
Yvetot: there was a King of Y. 561b
Y-wet: whistle wel y. 89a

Zal and Rustum bluster 152b
Zeal: all z...all z. Mr. Easy 259b
a z. of God, but not. .knowledge 513b
furious ardour of my z. 94b
mistaken z. in politics 217a
not too much z. 565b
serv'd my God with half the z. 386a
tempering bigot z. 238a
the z. of thine house 486b
we think it to be z. 537a
z. of the Lord of Hosts 501b
Zealots: let graceless z. fight 301b
Zealous, beneficent, firm 7b
Zebra: striped like a z. 219a
Zed! thou unnecessary letter! 342a
Zembla: at Greenland, Z. 301a
Zenith: dropt from the z. 272a
Zenocrate: ah fair Z., divine Z. 259b
entertain divine Z. 259b
Z., lovelier than the Love 259a
Zephyr: odes to every z. 226a
soft the z. blows 173b
when z. gently blows 300a
while the wanton z. sings 143a
Zest: thy graciousness a warmer z. 36a
Zeus: dear City of Z. 574a
Zimri: had Z. peace 496b
Zion: at ease in Z. 504a
the Lord shall bring again Z. 502b
unto Z., Thy God reigneth 502b
Z., city of our God 289a
Zodiac: Mermaid in the Z. 219a
Zodiacs: three fill'd Z. 215a
Zone: torrid or the frozen z. 79b
Zoo: you may see at the Z. 230b
Zoroaster: blank to Z. on his terrace 49b
the Magus Z., my dead child 397a

LATIN

A

Abibis: tu missus a. 547b
Abiit, excessit 540b
Abire: tempus a. tibi est 544a
Abutere: quousque tandem a. 540b
Academi: inter silvas A. 543b
Achates: fidus. .A. 554b
Acheronta movebo 556b
Acherontis: strepitumque A. avari 557b
Achilli: exuvias indutus A. 555b
impar congressus A. 555a
Achivi: plectuntur A. 543a
Acu: tetigisti a. 552b
Addictus: nullius a. iurare 542b
Adeste, fideles 558a
Admirari: nil a. prope res est una 543a
Adulescentiam: studia a. acuunt 540b
Aenea: nunc animis opus, A. 556a
Aeneae: domus A. Capitoli. .saxum
accolet 556b

Aeneas: quo pater A., quo Tullus
dives 547a
Aeneus: hic murus a. esto 542b
Aequam memento. .servare mentem 545a
Aequora: multa per a. vectus 539b
Aes: robur et a. triplex 544a
Aetas: a. parentum peior 546a
fugerit invida a. 544b
Aevi: quod superest a. 543b
Africa: ex A. semper aliquid novi 552b
Agamemnona: vixere fortes ante A. 547a
Agendum: dum quid superesset a. 550a
Agri: modus a. non ita magnus 548a
Agricolas: O fortunatos nimium. .a. 557b
Alexim: Corydon ardebat A. 556b
Alieni appetens 553a
Alpes: saevas curre per A. 549b
Ama et fac quod vis 538a
Amantem. .quis fallere possit a. ? 555b
Amantium irae 554a
Amantum: Iuppiter. .periuria ridet a. 551b

Amari: surgit a. aliquid 550b
Amaryllida: resonare doces A. silvas 556b
Amavi: sero te a. 537b
Amet: cras a. qui nunquam amavit 558b
Amici, diem perdidi 554a
Amicitia: demum firma a. est 553a
Amo: non a. te, Sabidi 551a
odi et a. 539b
Amor: cedet a. rebus 552a
nunc scio quid sit A. 557b
omnia vincit A. 557b
suprema citius solvet a. die 544b
Amorem: subito deponere a. 539b
Amori dare ludum 546a
Amoris: qui finem quaeris a. 552a
Amphora coepit institui 541b
Ampullas: proicit a. 542a
Angelicam habent faciem 541a
Angelorum: cantabunt laetius a. chori 558b
Angli: quod A. vocarentur 541a
Anguis: latet a. in herba 557a

Angulus: ille terrarum..a. ridet 545a
Angusta: res a. domi 548b
Animae: a. dimidium meae 544a
  a. naturaliter Christianae 554a
Animam: a. praeferre pudori 549a
  liberavi a. meam 538a
Animis: nunc a. opus, Aenea 556a
  tantaene a. caelestibus irae? 554b
Animula vagula blandula 541b
Animum: aequum mi a. ipse parabo 543b
Animus si te non deficit aequus 543a
Anni: singula..a. praedantur 543b
Annos: multos da, Iuppiter, a. 549b
Annus: monet a. et..hora 547a
  nunc formosissimus a. 557a
Anser: inter strepere a. olores 557b
Antecedentem: raro a. scelestum 545a
Apollo: A. pocula..plena ministret 551b
  semper arcum tendit A. 545a
  sic me servavit A. 547b
Apparentibus: de non a. 558b
Appetens: alieni a. 553a
Aqua: scribere oportet a. 539b
Aquae: vicinus iugis a. fons 548a
  scribuntur a. potoribus 543b
Araneam: quare videmus a. 16b
Arator: de tauris narrat a. 552b
Aratro: nullo contusus a. 539b
  postquam tactus a. est 538b
Arbiter: elegantiae a. 553b
Arbitrio popularis aurae 545b
Arbitrium: quem penes a. est 541b
Arbusta: non omnis a. iuvant 557a
Arcades ambo 557a
Arcadia: et in A. ego 574b
Arcum: neque semper a. tendit
  Apollo 545a
Ardet: iam proximus a. Ucalegon 555b
  paries cum proximus a. 543a
Ardui: nil mortalibus a. est 544a
Arduis: rebus in a. 545a
Argutos inter..anser olores 557b
Aris: pro a. atque focis suis 553a
Arma: a. virumque cano 554b
  cedant a. togae 540a
Artes: didicisse fideliter a. 552a
  hae tibi erunt a. 556a
  omnes a. quae ad humanitatem
  pertinent 540b
Artifex: qualis a. pereo 551a
Aspiciam: quando ego te a. 548a
Assis: omnes unius aestimemus a. 538b
Astra: sic itur ad a. 556b
Atticum: sal A. 552b
Audacia certe laus erit 552b
Audax: a. omnia perpeti 544a
  verbis felicissime a. 553a
Aude: sapere a. 543a
Audi alteram partem 537b
Auditis an..ludit..insania 546a
Auditorem: non secus ac notas a. rapit 542a
Augescunt aliae gentes 550b
Auras: evadere ad a. 556a
Auream..mediocritatem 545a
Aureus: non deficit alter a. 556a
Auri sacra fames 555b
Auroram: usque A. et Gangen 546a
Aurum irreperptum 546a
Auxilio: non tali a...tempus eget 555b
Ave: frater, a. atque vale 540a
Avena: musam meditaris a. 405a, 556b
Averno: facilis descensus A. 556a
Avi numerantur avorum 558a
Avis: rara a. in terris 549a
Avite: aliter non fit, A., liber 551a

B

Bandusiae: O fons B. 546a
Barbiton hic paries habebit 546b
Basia: da mi b. mille 538b
Beatum: facere et servare b. 543a
  nihil est ab omni parte b. 545b
Beatus ille, qui procul negotiis 544a
Belli certamina magna tueri 550b
Bellum: praeparet b. 554b
Benefacta: recordanti b. 539b
Beneficium inopi bis dat 553b
Bibendum: nunc est b. 545a
Blandula: animula vagula b. 541b

Bona: sunt b., sunt quaedam medio-
  cria 551a
Bono: cui b. 540b
Bonum: summum b. 540a
Brevis esse laboro 541b
Britanniae: terminus B. patet 553b
Britannos: divisos orbe B. 556b
Brute: et tu, B.? 548b
Brutum fulmen 552b

C

Caelestis origo seminibus 556a
Caelum non animum mutant 543a
Cacoethes: scribendi c. 549a
Calamus saevior ense patet 64a
Callet: duramque c. pauperiem 547a
Campum: quatit ungula c. 556b
Canamus: paulo maiora c. 557a
Canities: donec..c. abest morosa 544b
Cantabit vacuus..viator 549a
Cantare pares 557a
Capax imperii nisi imperasset 553b
Capitoli immobile saxum 556b
Capitis: tam cari c. 545a
Capreis: grandis epistula venit a C. 549a
Carpe diem 544b
Carthago: delenda est C. 538a
  O magna C. 546a
Cassium Romanorum ultimum 553b
Castalia: Apollo pocula C...ministret 551b
Castitatem: da mihi c. 537b
Catilina: quousque..abutere, C. 540b
Catoni: causa..placuit..victa C. 550a
Catonibus: priscis memorata C. 544a
Catulle: C., destinatus obdura 538b
  miser C., desinas ineptire 538b
Catullus: gratias tibi maximas C. 539a
Causa: c. finita est 538a
  victrix c. deis placuit 550a
Causas: rerum cognoscere c. 557b
Cave canem 552a
Cedite Romani scriptores 553a
Cenae: O noctes c. que deum 548a
Censoris: animum c. sumet honesti 543b
Censura: vexat c. columbas 548b
Certamina: c. magna tueri 550b
  haec c. tanta..quiescent 558a
Certum est quia impossibile est 554a
Cervicem: utinam populus Romanus
  unam c. haberet 538a
Cetera quis nescit? 551b
Cethegis: Catonibus atque C. 544a
Chommoda dicebat 539b
Christianae: animae naturaliter C. 554a
Christus: surrexit C. hodie 558b
Chrysippo et Crantore 542b
Cinarae: sub regno C. 546b
Circenses: panem et c. 549b
Circumspice: c., si monumentum
  requiris 19a
  si monumentum requiris, c. 473b, 558b
Civis Romanus sum 540b
Civium: non c. ardor prava iuben-
  tium 545b
Clamorem: compesce c. 545b
Clarum et venerabile nomen 550a
Claudite iam rivos, pueri 557a
Cogimur: omnes eodem c. 545a
Cogito, ergo sum 540b
Cognatione quadam..continentur
  (artes) 540b
Colori: nimium ne crede c. 557a
Columnae: non concessere c. 542b
Communia: proprie c. dicere 542a
Compesce clamorem 545b
Compunctionem: opto..sentire c. 537a
Concordia discors 543a
Confitentem: habes c. reum 552b
Conscire: nil c. sibi 542b
Consule: c. Planco 546b
  fortunatam natam me c.
  Romam 540a
  nata mecum c. Manlio 546b
Consumere: solebamus c. longa..
  tempora 552a
Conticuere omnes intentique 555a
Continentiam: imperas nobis c. 537b
Copula: irrupta tenet c. 544b
Cor: inquietum est c. nostrum 537b
  ulterius c. lacerare nequit 420a
Corde: aegro in c. senescit 549a

Corinthum: contingit adire C. 543a
Cornea: quarum (portae) altera fertur
  c. 556a
Cornu: faenum habet in c. 556a
Corpore: latet hoc sub c. 547b
Corpuscula: quantula..hominum c. 549b
Corrigere: quidquid c. est nefas 545a
Corydon: formosum pastor C. arde-
  bat Alexim 556b
Cotis: fungar vice c. 542a
Crambe repetita 549a
Crantore: Chrysippo et C. 542b
Cras: c. amet qui nunquam amavit 558b
  c. ingens iterabimus aequor 544b
Creantur: fortes c. 546b
Creari: nil posse c. de nilo 550a
Credat Iudaeus Apella 547b
Credens: nil actum c. 550a
Credite posteri 545b
Credula: quam minimum c. postero 544b
Credulus: non ego c. illis 557b
Credunt: quod volunt c. 548b
Crepidam: ne supra c. sutor iudi-
  caret 552b
Crimine ab uno disce omnes 555a
Crucem: si libenter c. portas 537a
Crustula: dant c. blandi doctores 547b
Cubili: dea nec dignata c. est 557a
Culpa: O felix c. 551a
Cumaei: ultima C. venit..aetas 557a
Cunctando restituit rem 541a
Cupidines: O Veneres C. que 538a
Cupidinum: dulcium mater saeva C. 546b
  mater saeva C. 544b
Cupressi: inter viburna c. 556b
Cura: post equitem sedet atra C. 545b
Curiosa: Horatii c. felicitas 552b
Curis: quid solutis est beatius c. 538b
Cursores vitai lampada tradunt 550b
Custodiet: quis c. ipsos custodes 549a
Cycno: nigro simillima c. 549a

D

Damna: per d., per caedis 547a
Damnatur: iudex d. ubi nocens
  absolvitur 553b
Damnosa hereditas 541a
Danaos: timeo D. et dona ferentis 555a
Dat: beneficium inopi bis d. 553b
  bis d. qui cito d. 553b
Davos sum, non Oedipus 554a
Dea: vera incessu patuit d. 555a
Debellare superbos 556a
Decede peritis 544a
Declamatio fias 549b
Decorum: d. est desipere in loco 67a
  dulce et d...mori 545a
Decus: dulce d. meum 544a
Defensoribus: non tali auxilio nec
  d. istis 555b
Definitionis: quam scire eius d. 537a
Dei: estne D. sedes nisi terra? 550a
Delenda est Carthago 538a
Delicta maiorum 546a
Dementat: deus quos vult perdere,
  d. prius 538a
Democritus: rideret D. 543b
Demonstrandum: quod erat d. 541a
Deo: par esse d. videtur 539a
Deorum: parcus d. cultor 545a
Desideratoque: d...lecto 538b
Desiderio: quis d. sit pudor 545a
Desinas: Catulle d. ineptire 538b
Desine..bene velle mereri 539b
Desipere: decorum est d. in loco 67a
  dulce est d. in loco 547b
Desperandum: nil d. 544b
Destinatus obdura 538b
Deteriora sequor 551b
Detrimenti: ne quid res publica d.
  caperet 540b
Deus: d. quos vult perdere 538a
  nec d. intersit 542a
  sit D. propitius huic potatori 558b
Di: d. me terrent 556b
  d. omen avertant 540b
  O d., reddite mi hoc 539b
Dic mihi, Musa, virum 542a
Dicebamus hesterna die 550a

LATIN INDEX

Dicere: quae sentias d. licet 553b
Die: sermonem deficiente d. 552a
Diem: amici, d. perdidi 554a
  carpe d. 544b
  qui ante d. periit 287b
  utinam per unam d...conversati 537a
Dies: d. irae 540a
  nulla d. sine linea 552b
Diffugere nives 547a
Digito: pulchrum est d. monstrari 552a
Dignitate: cum d. otium 540a
Dignum laude virum 547a
Dimidium: animae d. meae 544a
  d. facti qui coepit habet 543a
Dis: d. aliter visum 555b
  non sine d. animosus infans 546a
Discors: concordia d. 543a
Ditis: atri ianua D. 556a
Divis: permitte d. cetera 544b
Divisa in partes tres 548b
Divitias operosiores 545b
Divos: si fas est, superare d. 539a
Dixeris egregie notum 541b
Dixerunt: qui ante nos nostra d. 541a
Dixit: ipse d. 574a
Doceri: fas est ab hoste d. 551b
Docet: ipse d. quid agam 551b
Docte sermones 546a
Dolendum est primum ipsi tibi 542a
Dolorem: iubes renovare d. 555a
Dolorosa: stabat mater d. 554a
Dolos: seu versare d. 555a
Dolosa: cineri d. 555a
Domina: beata mea D. 284b
Dominus: D. illuminatio mea 558a
Domus: d. et placens uxor 545b
  stat fortuna d. 558a
Dona: timeo Danaos et d. ferentis 555a
Dono: cui d...novum libellum 538a
Dormienda: nox est perpetua una d. 538b
Dulce: d. est desipere in loco 547b
  d. et decorum est 545b
  d. ridentem Lalagen 545a
Dulci: miscuit utile d. 542b
Durate, et vosmet..servate 554a
Durum: sed levius fit 545a
Dux femina facti 554b

E

Eadem: semper e. 145b
Ecce homo 558a
Ecclesiam: e. non habet matrem 537b
  salus extra e. non est 537b
Edax: tempus e. rerum 551b
Effugies: non e. meos iambos 540a
Egelidos: ver e. refert tepores 539a
Egestas: turpis E. 556a
  urgens in rebus e. 557b
Ego et Rex meus 385b
Eheu fugaces, Postume 545b
Electro: formicam in e. 16b
Elephanto: altera (porta)..perfecta
  nitens e. 556a
Elissae: meminisse pigebit E. 555b
Emollit mores 552a
Emori: quid moraris e.? 539a
Ense: calamus saevior e. patet 64a
Entia non sunt multiplicanda 574a
Epicuri de grege porcum 543a
Epistula: verbosa et grandis e. 549a
Equo ne credite, Teucri 555a
Equis: currite noctis e. 258b
Equitem: post e. sedet atra Cura 545b
Equum: solve..mature sanus e. 542b
Erupit: excessit, evasit, e. 540b
Eripuit caelo fulmen 551a
Error: me malus abstulit e. 557a
Esuriens: Graeculus e. 548b
Esurienti: mihi e. te 537b
Evasit, erupit 540b
Eventum: semper ad e. festinat 542a
Excessit, evasit, erupit 540b
Excoluere: qui vitam e. per artis 556a
Excrucior: sentio et e. 539b
Exemplaria: vos e. Graeca..versate 542a
Existentibus: de non e. eadem..ratio 558b
Ex(orna): hanc e. 540a
Exoriare aliquis..ultor 555b
Experto credite 556b

F

Fabrum esse suae quemque fortunae 553a
Fabula: de te f. narratur 547b
Facilis descensus Averno 556a
Faece: in Romuli f. 540a
Faenore: solutus omni f. 544a
Faenum habet in cornu 547b
Fagi: Tityre, tu patulae..f. 556b
Fallentis semita vitae 543b
Fallere: quis f. possit amantem? 555b
Fames: auri sacra f. 555b
  malesuada F. 556a
Fanda: omnia f. nefanda 539b
Fandi: mollissima f. tempora 555b
Farrago libelli est 548b
Faucibus: primis in f. Orci 556a
Favete linguis 545b
Favilla: solvet saeclum in f. 540a
Fecisti nos ad te 537b
Felices ter et amplius 544b
Felicitas: Horatii curiosa f. 552b
Felix: f...opportunitate mortis 553b
  f. qui potuit rerum cognoscere
  causas 557b
  O f. culpa 551a
Femina: nemo magis gaudet quam f. 549b
Feros: nec sinit esse f. 552a
Ferrum: in me convertite f. 556b
Festina: f. lente 553a
Festinat: ad eventum f. 542a
Fiat lux 558a
Fide: Punica f. 553a
Fideles: adeste, f. 558a
Fides: nulli cessura f. 551b
Fidus..Achates 554b
Filius istarum lacrimarum 537b
Finem: dabit deus his quoque f. 554b
  respice f. 574b
Fines: sunt certi denique f. 547b
Flagitium: peius leto f. timet 547a
Flammae: veteris vestigia f. 555b
Flammantia moenia mundi 550a
Flebilis: multis..bonis f. occidit 545a
Flectere si nequeo superos 556b
Flere: si vis me f. 542a
Flos: prati ultimi f. 538b
  ut f. in saeptis 539b
Focis: pro aris atque f. 553a
Fons: O f. Bandusiae 546a
Fonte: medio de f. leporum 550b
Formosa: mulier f. superne 541b
Formosam resonare .. Amaryllida
  doces 556b
Fors: quem F. dierum cumque dabit
  lucro appone 544b
Forsan..meminisse iuvabit 554b
Forsitan et nostrum nomen 551b
Fortes: f. creantur fortibus 546b
  vixere f. ante Agamemnona 547a
Fortiter: pecca f. 550b
Fortuna: audentis F. iuvat 556b
  fortis f. adiuvat 554a
  stat f. domus 558a
  te, nos facimus, F., deam 549b
Fortunae: fabrum esse suae..f. 553a
Fortunatam: O f. natam..Romam 540a
Fortunatos: O f. nimium 557b
Fortunatus..deos qui novit 557b
Frater, ave atque vale 540a
Fratrum: par nobile f. 548a
Fruges consumere nati 543a
Frugis: provisae f...copia 543b
Fucos: ignavum f. pecus 558a
Fuere: sed haec prius f. 538b
Fugaces: eheu f., Postume 545b
Fugis: quem f., a, demens? 557a
Fuit Ilium 555b
Fulgore: non fumum ex f. 542a
Fulmen: brutum f. 552b
  eripuit caelo f. 551a
Fumum: f. et opes..Romae 546b
  non f. ex fulgore 542a
Fungar vice cotis 542a
Furor: f. arma ministrat 554b
  ira f. brevis est 543a
Futurum: quid sit f. 544b

G

Gadibus: a G. usque auroram 549a
Galatea: malo me G. petit 557a
Gallia est omnis divisa 548b
Gangen: usque Auroram et G. 549a
Genium loci..precatur 556b
Gens humana ruit 544a
Gentes: multas per g. 539b
Genus: at g. immortale manet 558a
  g. irritabile vatum 543b
  hoc g. omne 547b
Germania: rebellatrix..G. 552a
Gloria: sic transit g. mundi 537a
Gloriae: cupido g. novissima exuitur 553b
Gloriam: ad majorem Dei g. 558b
Gloriosus: miles g. 552b
Graeca: vos exemplaria G...versate 542a
Graecia capta ferum victorem cepit 543b
Graeculus esuriens 548b
Gracilis: quis multa g. 544b
Grais ingenium..dedit..musa loqui 542b
Grammatici certant 541b
Gratias tibi maximas 539a
Gratus: donec g. eram tibi 546a
Graviora: O passi d. 554b
Grege: Epicuri de g. porcum 543a
Gurgite: in g. vasto 554b
Gutta cavat lapidem 552a

H

Habent sua fata libelli 551a
Habita: tecum h. 552a
Hasdrubale interempto 547a
Herbas: miscueruntque h. 557b
Hereditas: damnosa h. 541a
Hesperus: venit H., ite capellae 557b
Hilarem: oderunt h. tristes 543b
Homerus: bonus dormitat H. 542b
Homines: quot h. tot sententiae 554a
  ridiculos h. facit 548b
Homo: ecce h. 558a
  h. sum 554a
Honores: mitte supervacuos h. 545b
Honoribus: intaminatis fulget h. 545b
Honos: semper h. nomenque..mane-
  bunt 555a
Hora: felici optatius h. 539b
  quae rapit h. diem 547a
  suprema mihi cum venerit h. 554a
Horatius: insurgit aliquando [H.] 553a
Horis: inertibus h. 548a
Horrendum, informe, ingens 555b
Horresco referens 555a
Hortis: flos..secretus nascitur h. 539b
Hospes: deferor hospes 542b
  h. comesque corporis 541b
Humani nil a me alienum puto 554a
Hydrops: crescit..dirus h. 545a

I

Iacta alea est 548b
Iam ver..refert tepores 539a
Iambos: non effugies meos i. 540a
Idem velle atque idem nolle 553a
Idola Tribus 16b
Idolorum: quatuor sunt genera I. 16b
Idoneus: vixi puellis nuper i. 546b
Ignara: non i. mali 555a
Igneus est ollis vigor 556a
Ignis: incedis per i. 545a
  velut inter i. luna minores 544b
Ignotum: omne i. pro magnifico 553b
Ignotus moritur sibi 553a
Ilex tonsa bipennibus 547a
Iliade: quid maius nascitur I. 553a
Ilium: fuit I. 555b
Illacrimabiles: sed omnes i. 547a
Imber: firmat sol, educat i. 539b
Imitatores: O i., servum pecus 543b
Immortalia ne speres 547a
Impavidum ferient ruinae 546a
Imperator, morituri te salutant 553b
Imperii: capax i. nisi imperasset 553b
Imperio: tu regere i. populos 556a
Imperium et Libertas 128b
Impossibile: certum est quia i. est 554a
Incedis per ignis 545a
Inceptis gravibus plerumque 541b
Incepto: qualis ab i. processerit 542a
Incipe, parve puer 557a
Inculto latet hoc sub corpore 547b
Indignatio: facit i. versum 548b

Indignatio (cont.)
i. principis mors est 283a
ubi saeva i. 420a
Indocilis pauperiem pati 544a
Infandum, regina 555a
Infans: non sine dis animosus i. 546a
Iniuria: spretae i. formae 554b
Iniquitatem: odi i. 541a
Inmemores non sinit esse sui 552a
Inopem me copia fecit 551b
Inops: magnas inter opes i. 546b
Insania: amabilis i. 546a
Intabescant: virtutem. .i.que relicta 552a
Integer vitae scelerisque purus 545a
Interire: nil vere i. 14a
Intus: ecce i. eras 537b
Invideo: non equidem i. 556b
Iocosae: non hoc i. conveniet lyrae 546a
Iocosi: oderunt. .tristem i. 543b
Iove: ab I. principium musae 557a
Iovem: satis est orare I. 543b
Iovis: quod nec I. ira. .abolere 551b
Ipse dixit 574a
Ira furor brevis est 543a
Irae: amantium i. 544a
dies i. 540a
tantaene animis caelestibus i.? 554b
Irrevocabile: volat i. verbum 543a
Italiae: probrosis altior I. ruinis 546a
Italiam fato profugus. .venit 554b
Ite domum saturae. .capellae 557b
Iter: per i. tenebricosum 538b
Iterabimus: cras ingens i. aequor 544b
Iucundi acti labores 540a
Iudaeus: credat I. Apella 547b
Iudex: i. damnatur 553b
i. honestum praetulit utili 547a
Iudicat: securus i. orbis terrarum 537b
Iudice: sub i. lis est 541b
Iudicium: i. Paridis 554b
i. parium suorum 550b
Iunctura: si. .verbum reddiderit i. 541b
Iunonis: memorem I. ob iram 554b
Iuppiter: et I. hostis 556b
I. est quodcumque vides 550a
I. ex alto. .ridet 551a
I. pluvius 554a
Iura: per populos dat i. 558a
Iustitiam: dilexi i. et odi iniquitatem 541a
Iustum et tenacem. .virum 545b
Iuvenes: vesper adest, i. 539b
Iuventa: calidus i. 546b
Iuventus: rara i. 544a

L

Labor: hic l. est 556a
l. omnia vicit 557b
Labores: iucundi acti l. 540a
Lacrimae: sunt l. rerum 555a
Lacrimarum: filius istarum l. 537b
Lacrimosa: iuxta crucem l. 554a
Laeti triumphantes 558a
Lalagen: dulce ridentem L. 545a
Lampada: cursores vitai l. tradunt 550b
Lapidem: gutta cavat l. 552a
Latericiam: quam l. accepisset 543b
Latio: Graecia. .artes intulit. .L. 543b
Latrone: cantabit. .coram l. viator 549a
Laudamus: Te Deum l. 558b
Laudant illa sed ista legunt 551a
Laudator temporis acti 542a
Laudet diversa sequentes 547b
Lege: tolle l. 537b
Leges: quid l. . .proficiunt 546b
silent enim l. inter arma 540b
Legiones: Quintili Vare, l. redde 538a
Legunt: laudant illa sed ista l. 551a
Lente: O l., l. currite 258b
Lesbia: L. nostra, L. illa 539a
vivamus, mea L. 538b
Lex: salus populi suprema est l. 540b
Libelli: farrago l. est 548b
habent sua fata l. 551a
Libellum: lepidum novum l. 538a
Libenter: fere l. homines. .credunt 548b
Liber: aliter non fit, Avite, l. 551a
Liberavi animam meam 538a
Libertas: Imperium et L. 128b
l. et natale solum 419b
Librorum: sit bona l. . .copia 543b

Lignum: praecipue autem l., sive
virga 17a
Linea: nulla dies sine l. 552b
Lis: sub iudice l. est 541b
Lites: tantas componere l. 557a
Locuta: Roma l. est 538a
Loquendi: ius et norma l. 541b
Lucem: ex fumo dare l. 542a
Lucis tuae radium 549b
Luctus et. .Curae 556a
Lues: immeritus l. 546a
Lugete, O Veneres 538b
Luna: velut inter ignis l. minores 544b
Lunae: amica silentia l. 555a
Lusisti satis 544a
Lux: cum semel occidit brevis l. 538b
fiat l. 558a
Luxuria incubuit 549a
Lydiae: O L. lacus undae 538b

M

Maecenas: M. . .edite regibus 544a
qui fit, M. 547b
Macte nova virtute, puer 556b
Magna est veritas 40a
Magnifico: omne ignotum pro m. 553b
Mala: sunt m. plura 551a
Malo me Galatea petit 557a
Malorum: religio potuit suadere m. 550a
Manlio: consule M. 546b
suo similis patri M. 539a
Manus: tendebantque m. 556a
Mare: oleum. .mittas in m. 24b
qui trans m. currunt 543a
Mari: suave, m. magno 550b
Marmoream se relinquere 538a
Mater: m. saeva Cupidinum 544b
scientiarum m. 17a
stabat m. dolorosa 554a
Materiae: summam m. prorsus
eandem 14a
Matre pulchra filia pulchrior 544b
Matrem: risu cognoscere m. 557a
Mavult homo verum 16b
Maxima debetur puero reverentia 549b
Me, me, adsum qui feci 556b
Medea: ne. .coram populo M.
trucidet 542a
Medias: in m. res 542a
Medicina: sero m. paratur 551b
Medio tutissimus ibis 551b
Mediocria: sunt quaedam m. 551a
Mediocribus esse poetis 542b
Mediocritatem: auream. .m. 545a
Meliboee: O M., deus. .otia fecit 556b
Meliora: video m., proboque 551b
Membra: disiecti m. poetae 547b
Meminisse: haec olim m. iuvabit 554b
Memor: dum m. ipse mei 555b
Memores: quiqui sui m. . .fecere 556a
Mendax: splendide m. 546a
Mens: m. agitat molem 556a
m. cuiusque is est quisque 540a
m. sana in corpore sano 549b
m. sibi conscia recti 555a
Merses profundo 547a
Metuant: oderint, dum m. 540b
Metuit secundis. .sortem. .pectus 545a
Miles: m. gloriosus 552b
numerat m. vulnera 552b
sed m., sed pro patria 287b
Militavi non sine gloria 546b
Minerva: crassa M. 548a
invita. .M. 542b
Miscuerunt herbas 557b
Miseris succurrere disco 555a
Miserrima: quaeque ipse m. vidi 555a
Modus: est m. in rebus 547b
Moles: rudis indigestaque m. 551b
tantae m. erat. .condere gentem 554b
Monstrum horrendum 555b
Monumentum: circumspice, si m.
requiris 19a
exegi m. aere perennius 546b
si m. requiris 473b
Morbi: pallentesque habitant M. 556a
subeunt m. tristisque senectus 558a
Morbo: venienti occurrite m. 552a
Morbum: hunc habet m. 539a
Morem: contra bonum m. 553a

Mores: O tempora, O m. 540b
qui m. hominum. .vidit 542a
sine crimine m. 551b
Moriar: non omnis m. 546b
Moribus: m. antiquis res stat 541a
quid leges sine m. . .proficiunt 546b
Moriens: te teneam m. 554a
Morior in exilio 541a
Morituri: Imperator, m. te salutant 553b
Mortalia: mentem m. tangunt 555a
Mortalibus: nil m. ardui est 544a
Mors: illi m. gravis incubat 553a
indignatio principis m. est 283a
m. sola fatetur 549b
pallida M. aequo pulsat 544b
Mortis: felix. .opportunitate m. 553b
posce animam m. terrore carentem 549b
rapit inclementia m. 558a
timor m. conturbat me 142b
Mulier: m. cupido quod dicit amanti 539b
m. formosa superne 541b
Mundi: flammantia moenia m. 550a
sic transit gloria m. 537b
Munditiis: simplex m. 544b
Murus aeneus esto 542b
Mus: nascetur ridiculus m. 542a
Musa: M. vetat mori 547a
quo, M., tendis 546a
Mutabile semper femina 555b
Mutato nomine de te 547b
Mutatus: quantum. . ab illo
Hectore 555b

N

Naso suspendis adunco 547b
Nasum: totum ut te faciant. .n. 538b
Natale solum dulcedine. .ducit 552a
Natura: si n. negat 548b
Naturae enim non imperatur 17a
Naturam expelles furca 543a
Navita de ventis. .narrat 552b
Nebula: remota erroris n. 549a
Necessitas: n. dat legem 553b
n. non habet legem 553b
Negotiis: qui procul n. 544a
Nequid: ut n. nimis 554a
Nequiores: aetas. .tulit nos n. 546a
Niger: hic n. est 547b
Nihil est ab omni parte beatum 545b
Nihilum: de nihilo n. 552a
Nil: n. admirari 543a
n. posse creari de nilo 550a
Nimis: ut nequid n. 554a
Nives: diffugere n. 547a
Nobilitate: contendere n. 550b
Nocens: nemo n. absolvitur 549b
Nocitura toga, n. petuntur militia 549a
Noctes: n. atque dies niti 550b
O n. cenaeque deum 548a
Nodus: dignus vindice n. inciderit 542a
Nomen: clarum et venerabile n. 550a
nostrum n. miscebitur istis 551b
omne capax movet urna n. 545b
Nominis: stat magni n. umbra 550a
Non sum qualis eram 546b
Nonum prematur in annum 542b
Notus nimis omnibus 553a
Novi: ex Africa semper aliquid n. 552b
Nox: n. est perpetua una dormienda 538b
n. umida coelo praecipitat 555a
Nugas: solebas. .aliquid putare n. 538a
Nulla retrorsum (vestigia) 542b
Nullius addictus iurare in verba 542b
Nullum quod tetigit non ornavit 209b
Numen: nullum n. habes 549b
Numerisque fertur lege solutis 546b
Numerus: nos n. sumus 543a
Numine: quo n. laeso 554b
Nunc est bibendum 545a
Nympha pudica Deum vidit 114b

O

Oblitus meorum obliviscendus 543b
Oblivia: ducere. .iucunda o. vitae 548a
Obliviscendus: meorum o. et illis 543a
Obscurus fio 541b
Occidere: soles o. et redire possunt 538b
Occidit: cum semel o. brevis lux 538b
o., o.. .fortuna nostri 547a

Occumbere: seu certae o. morti 555a
Occupato: nube polum Pater o. 546b
Occurrite: venienti o. morbo 552a
Oderint, dum metuant 540b
Odi: incredulus o. 542a
o. et amo 539b
o. profanum vulgus et arceo 545b
Persicos o., puer, apparatus 545a
Odisse quem laeseris 553b
Oedipus: Davos sum, non O. 554a
Ofellus: quae praecepit O. rusticus 548a
Oleum..mittas in mare 24a
Olores: inter strepere anser o. 557b
Olympo: viamque adfectat O. 558a
Pelion imposuisse O. 546a
Olympum: Ossae frondosum in-
volvere O. 557b
Omen: di o. avertant 540b
procul o. abesto 551b
Omne capax movet urna nomen 545b
Omnes eodem cogimur 545a
Omnia: non o. possumus omnes 557b
o. mutari 14a
Omnium consensu capax imperii 553b
Operosiores: divitias o. 545b
Opes: magnas inter o. inops 546b
Opus: hoc o., hic labor est 556a
iamque o. exegi 551b
Optima quaeque dies..fugit 558a
Orbis: fractus illabatur o. 546a
Orci: in faucibus O. 556a
Ore rotunda 542b
Orna: hanc ex (o.) 540a
Ornavit: nullum quod tetigit non
o. 209b
Ossam: imponere Pelio O. 557b
Ossibus: ex o. ultor 555b
Ostendis: quodcumque o. mihi 542a
Otia: deus nobis haec o. fecit 556b
Otiosum: nunquam se minus o. 540a
Otiosus: nunquam sis ex toto o. 537a
Otium: cum dignitate o. 540a

P

Pacem: p. appellant 553b
qui desiderat p. 554b
Pacis: longae p. mala 549a
p. imponere morem 556a
Pallescere: nulla p. culpa 542b
Pallida Mors 544b
Pallidula rigida nudula 541b
Panem et circenses 549b
Pannus: purpureus..p. 541b
Paratus: in utrumque p. 555a
Parcere subiectis 556a
Parcus deorum cultor 545a
Parentum: aetas p. peior 546a
audiet pugnas vitio p. 544a
Pars: quorum p. magna fui 555a
Partem: audi alteram p. 537b
Parturient montes 542a
Passer mortuus est 538b
Passibus: non p. aequis 555b
Passione interdum movemur 537a
Pater: nube polum P. occupato 546b
Patientia: levius fit p.
Patimur: nunc p. longae pacis mala 549a
Patrem: habere non potest Deum p. 537b
Patria: pro p. mori 545b
pro p., pro liberis 553a
Patronum: optimus omnium's p. 539a
Pauperiem: duram callet p. pati 547a
indocilis p. pati 544a
Paupertas: nil habet infelix p. 548b
Pauperum tabernas 544b
Pecca fortiter 550b
Pecus: imitatores, servum p. 543b
Pede: stans p. in uno 547b
Pelio: imponere P. Ossam 557b
Pelion imposuisse Olympo 546a
Pendulus: dubiae spe p. hora 543b
Pereant..qui ante nos..dixerunt 541a
Perenne: plus uno maneat p. saeclo 538b
Perennius: aere p. 546b
Pereunt et imputantur 551a
Perii: ut vidi, ut p. 557a
Periit: qui ante diem p. 287b
Perituram: venalem et mature p. 553a
Permitte divis cetera 544b
Pernoctant (studia) nobiscum 540b

Perpetua: nox est p.una dormienda 538b
Perpetuum: atque in p., frater, ave 540a
Persicos odi, puer, apparatus 545a
Petis: quod p. hic est 543a
Pictura: p. pascit inani 555a
ut p. poesis 542b
Pictoribus atque poetis 541b
Pierides: me facere poetam P. 557b
Pietate: hoc pro p. mea 539b
Piscem: desinat in p. mulier 541b
Placeo: quod spiro et p. 546b
Planco: consule P. 546b
Pluvius: Iupiter p. 554a
Poema: cupiet fecisse p. 543b
Poena: deseruit pede P. claudo 545b
Poesis: ut pictura p. 542b
Poeta: pessimus omnium p. 539a
Poetae: disiecti membra p. 547b
Poetis: mediocribus esse p. 542b
pictoribus atque p. 541b
Populi: salus p. suprema est lex 540b
vox p., vox dei 537a
Populus: utinam p. Romanus unam
cervicem haberet 538a
Porcum: Epicuri de grege p. 543a
Portae: geminae Somni p. 556a
Portas: si libenter crucem p. 537a
Possidentem: non p. multa..beatum 547a
Possunt, quia posse videntur 556a
Posteri: credite p. 545b
Postume: eheu fugaces, P. 545b
Potoribus: scribuntur aquae p. 543b
Praedantur: singula de nobis anni
p. euntes 543b
Praelatura: subiectione quam in p. 537a
Praesidium et dulce decus meum 544a
Praeteritos referat si Iuppiter annos 556b
Praevalebit: magna est veritas et
p. 40a
Prata: sat p. biberunt 557a
Prematur: nonumque p. in annum 542b
Pretio: omnia Romae cum p. 549a
Priamus: en P. 556a
Primo avulso non deficit 543a
Principibus: p. placuisse viris 543a
Principiis: p. obsta 551b
Principium: ab Iove p. musae 557a
Prius: sed haec p. fuere 538b
Probitas: p. laudatur 548b
Procul: p. hinc, p. este, severae 551b
p. omen abesto 551b
p., o p. este, profani 556a
qui p. hinc 287b
Progeniem vitiosiorem 546a
Progenies: iam nova p. caelo 557a
Propositi: tenacem p. virum 545b
Propositum: meum est p. 558b
Proprie communia dicere 542a
Proximus: iam p. ardet Ucalegon 555b
paries cum p. ardet 543a
Pudor: purpureusque p. 551b
quis desiderio sit p. 545a
Puellae: passer, deliciae meae p. 538b
Puellis: vixi p. nuper idoneus 546b
Puer: O formose p. 557a
te p. in rosa..urget 544b
Pueros: ne p. coram populo Medea
trucidet 542a
Pulchra: O matre p. 544b
Pulchritudo tam antiqua 537b
Pulchrum: qui quid sit p. decit 542b
Pulsanda tellus 545a
Pulveris exigui iactu 558a
Pulvis et umbra sumus 547a
Pumice: libellum..p. expolitum 538a
Punica fide 553a
Puriter: si vitam p. egi 539b
Purpureus..pannus 541b
Pyrrha: grato, P., sub antro 544b

Q

Quadrigis petimus bene vivere 543a
Quadripedante putrem 556b
Quadruviis et angiportis 539a
Quaesieris: tu ne q. 544b
Quaesiveris: nec te q. extra 552a
Qualis ab incepto 542a
Quanta qualia..sabbata 537a
Querimoniis: divulsus q. 544b
Quid est, Catulle? 539a

Quidquid agunt homines 548b
Quies: prima q. mortalibus aegris 555a
Quo, Musa, tendis? 546a
Quorum pars magna fui 555a
Quousque tandem abutere..
patientia 540b

R

Rapit: quae r. hora diem 547a
Rari nantes in gurgite vasto 554b
Rebellatrix. . Germania 552a
Rebus in arduis 545a
Recte: si possis r. 542b
Rectum: nequit consistere r. 547b
Redire: negant r. quenquam
soles occidere et r. possunt 538b
Regere imperio populos..
memento 556a
Reges: quidquid delirant r. 543a
Regis: vexilla r. prodeunt 541a
Religio potuit suadere malorum 550a
Rem: quocumque modo r. 542b
Remi: magnanimis R. nepotes 539a
Renascentur: multa r. quae iam ceci-
dere 541b
Renidet: quodcumque agit, r. 539a
Res: r. angusta domi 548b
r. publica detrimenti caperet 540b
Respice finem 574b
Responsare cupidinibus 548a
Rescribas: nil mihi r. 551b
Retrorsum: vestigia..nulla r. 542b
Reverentia: maxima debetur puero r. 549b
Revocare gradum 556a
Rex: ego et r. meus 385b
Ridentem: audit dulce r. 539a
r. dicere verum quid vetat 547b
Ridete quidquid est domi cachin-
norum 538b
Ripae ulterioris amore 556a
Risu: nam r. inepto res ineptior
nulla est 539a
Robur et aes triplex 544a
Roma locuta est 538a
Romae: omnia R. cum pretio 549a
si fueris R. 537b
strepitumque R. 546b
Romam: fortunatam natam me con-
sule R. 540a
Romana: res stat R. viresque 541a
Romanam condere gentem 554b
Romane: hunc tu, R., caveto 547b
regere..populos, R., memento 556a
Romani: cedite R. scriptores 553a
Romano vivito more 537b
Romanorum: Cassium R. ultimum 553b
Romanus: civis R. sum 540b
imperiumque pater R. habebit 556b
Romuli: in R. faece 540a
Rosa quo locorum sera moretur 545a
Rota: currente r. cur urceus exit? 541b
Ruit: mole r. sua 516a
Rumores: r.que senum severiorum 538b
Rus: O r., quando ego te aspiciam? 548a
r. in urbe 551a

S

Sabbata: qualia sunt illa s. 537a
Sabidi: non amo te, S. 551a
Saeclo: plus uno maneat perenne s. 538b
Saeclorum nascitur ordo 557a
Saepibus in nostris 557a
Sal Atticum 552b
Salaputium disertum 539a
Salus: s. extra ecclesiam non est 537b
s. populi suprema est lex 321a, 540b
una s. victis 555b
Salutem: nullam sperare s. 555b
Salve, magna parens 557b
Sana: mens s. in corpore sano 549b
Sanguinis: semen est s. Christia-
norum 574a
Sapiens: abnormis s. 548a
Sapientia: de S. Veterum 17a
Sapientibus: etiam s. cupido gloriae 553b
Satura quidem tota nostra est 553a
Saturnia: redeunt S. regna 557a
S. tellus 557b
Saturno rege 549a
Scalam: de vitiis nostris s. 538a

Scelestum: raro antecedentem s. 545b
Sceptra: eripuit..mox s. tyrannis 551a
Scientiarum mater 17a
Scientia potestas est 17a
Scire nefas 544b
Scribere oportet aqua 539b
Scripturas: scrutamini s. 321a
Sectari: mitte s. 545a
Securis: nec sumit aut ponit s. 545b
Securus iudicat orbis terrarum 537b
Seges: nunc s. est ubi Troia fuit 551b
Semen est sanguinis Christianorum 574a
Semihiante labello 539a
Semper: quod s., quod ubique 554b
  s. eadem 145b
Senectutem (studia) oblectant 540b
Senectus: tristis s. 558a
Sententiae: quot homines tot s. 554a
Sentire quae velis 553b
Sepulcris: si quicquam mutis gratum
  ..s. accidere..potest 539b
Sera nimis vita est crastina 551a
Serena: sapientum templa s. 550b
Sermo: nec meus hic s. est 548a
Sermones utriusque linguae 546a
Sero te amavi 537b
Servate: vosmet rebus s. secundis 554b
Servetur ad imum 542a
Sesquipedalia verba 542a
Severae: procul este, s. 551b
Severiorum: rumoresque senum s. 538b
Sic vos non vobis 558b
Sicelides Musae 557a
Sidera: suadent..s. somnos 555a
  sublima feriam s. vertice 544a
Signo: in hoc s. vinces 540b
Silent enim leges inter arma 540b
Silvae: nunc frondent s. 557a
Silvas: habitarunt di quoque s. 557a
Simplex munditiis 544b
Simplicitas: nudaque s. 551b
  O sancta s. 548a
Sirmio: salve O venusta S. 538b
Situm: sic melius s. 546a
Sol: inferebatur s. et luna 537b
Solamine: humano pro s. 558b
Soles: s. effugere atque abire sentit 551a
  s. occidere et redire possunt 538b
Solitudinem: ubi s. faciunt 553b
Solum: natale s. dulcedine
  nec minus s. 552a
Solutis: lege s. 540a
Solve: s. metus 546b
  s. senescentem..equum 555a
Solventur risu tabulae 542b
Somni: geminae S. portae 547b
Spartam nactus es 556a
Spatium: da s. vitae 540a
Sperat infestis 549b
Sperabitur: grata..quae non s. 545a
Spinis: exempta..s. de pluribus una 543a
Spiritus: dum s. hos regit artus 544a
  s. intus alit 555b
  veni Sancte S. 556a
Spiro: quod s. et placeo 549b
Splendide mendax 546b
Splendidior vitro 546a
Spretaeque iniuria formae 546a
Stat: stat fortuna domus 554b
  s. magni nominis umbra 558a
Strenua nos exercet inertia 550a
Strepitumque Acherontis avari 543a
Studia adulescentiam acuunt 557b
Stultitia: sapientia..s. caruisse 540b
Suave, mari magno 542b
Subiectione: stare in s. 550b
Successus: hos s. alit 537a
Sufflaminandus: s. erat 556a
Sum: cogito, ergo s. 214b
Summum bonum 540b
Supellex: curta s. 540a
                            552a

Superos: flectere si nequeo s. 556b
  s. quid quaerimus ultra 550a
Suppositos: per ignis s. cineri 545a
Supremum: omnem crede diem..s. 543a
Surrexit Christus hodie 558b

T

Taberna: in t. mori 558b
Tacitae per amica silentia lunae 555a
Tantas componere lites 557a
Tecum vivere amem 546a
Te Deum laudamus 558b
Tellus: pulsanda t. 545a
Tempestas: quo me cumque rapit t. 542b
Temptanda via est 558a
Tempora: O t., O mores 540b
Temporis: laudator t. acti 542a
Temporum: rara t. felicitate 553b
Tempus: fugit irrevocabile t. 558a
  t. abire tibi est 544a
  t. edax rerum 551b
  t...quo..quies..serpit 555a
Tenacem: iustum et t. 545b
Tendebant manus 556a
Tenebricosum: it per iter t. 538b
Tenui musam meditamur 405a, 556b
Testa: pia t. 546b
Tetigisti acu 552b
Teucro: et auspice T. 544b
Thule: ultima T. 557b
Timeo Danaos 555a
Timor: t. mortis conturbit me 142b
  votum t. ira voluptas 548b
Tityre, tu patulae 556b
Tolle lege 537b
Torquatus volo parvulus 539a
Tristes: oderunt hilarem t. 543b
Troia: ubi T. fuit 551b
Troiae: captae post tempora T. 542a
Tu: et t., Brute 548b
  t. quoque 552a
Tullus dives et Ancus 547a
Turpissimus: nemo repente fuit t. 548b
Tutissimus: medio t. ibis 551b
Tyranni: non vultus instantis t. 545b
Tyrannis: eripuit..mox sceptra t. 551a

U

Ubique: quod semper, quod u. 554b
Ulixen: proposuit..exemplar U. 543a
Ultio: in firmi est animi..voluptas u. 549b
  prima est haec u. 549b
Ultor: ex ossibus u. 555b
Ulubris: quod petis hic est, est U. 543a
Umbra: pulvis et u. sumus 547a
Unguem: ad u. factus homo 547b
Unus homo..cunctando restituit
  rem 541a
Urbem: u. excoluit adeo 538a
  u. venalem 553a
Urbis: mores..vidit et u. 542a
Urceus: currente rota cur u. exit 541b
Urna: omne capax movet u. nomen 545b
Utile: qui miscuit u. dulci 542b
Uxor: ab illis incipit u. 549a
  domus et placens u. 545b

V

Vadis: quo v.? 558a
Vae victis 550a
Vagula: animula v. blandula 541b
Vale: frater, ave atque v. 540a
Valere: sed v. vita est 551a
Vanae: quid leges..v. proficiunt 546b
Vare: Quintili V., legiones redde 538a
Varium et mutabile 555b
Vate: carent quia v. sacro 547a
Vatum: genus irritabile v. 543b
Velle: idem v. atque idem nolle 553a
Veneres: lugete, O V. 538b

Veni: v. Sancte Spiritus 549b
  v., vidi, vici 548a
Veniam: dat v. corvis 548b
  v. petimusque damusque 541b
Venienti occurrite morbo 552a
Venite, venite in Bethlehem 558a
Ver egelidos refert tepores 539a
Vera: dinoscere possunt v. bona 549a
Verbum: volat irrevocabile v. 543a
Veritas: in vino v. 552b
  magna est v. 40a
Versate: nocturna v. manu 542a
Verum: mavult homo v. esse 16b
Vesper adest, iuvenes 539b
Vestibulum ante ipsum 556a
Vestigia..nulla retrorsum 542a
Vetustas: deserta v. 544a
  nec edax abolere v. 551b
Vexilla regis prodeunt 541a
Viator: cantabit vacuus...v. 549a
Viburna: inter v. cupressi 556b
Vicisti, Galilæe 548a
Victis: vae v. 550a
Victor..per populos dat iura 558a
Victrix causa deis placuit 550a
Video meliora, proboque 551b
Vidi: ut v., ut perii 557a
Vigor et caelestis origo 556a
Vilia miretur vulgus 551b
Vina proxima morientis ori 558b
Vinces: in hoc signo v. 540b
Vinclum: quoddam commune v. 540b
Vino: in v. veritas 552b
Virenti canities abest morosa 544b
Vires: quodsi deficiant v. 552b
Virginibus puerisque 545b
Virgo: iam redet et v. 557a
Virisque adquirit eundo 555b
Vitae: integer v. scelerisque purus 545a
  iucunda oblivia v. 548a
Virtus: quid v. et..sapientia possit 543a
  v. est vitium fugere 542b
  v. repulsae nescia sordidae 545b
Virtutem videant 552a
Virum: arma v.que cano 554b
Vis: ama et fac quod v. 538a
  iube quod v. 537b
  v. consili expers 546a
  vivida v. animi pervicit 550a
Vitae: fallentis semita v. 543b
  v. summa brevis 544b
Vitam: det v., det opes 543b
  propter v...perdere causas 549a
  si v. puriter egi 539b
Vitiis: de v. nostris scalam..facimus 538a
Vitium: virtus est v. fugere 542b
Vivamus, mea Lesbia 538b
Vive hodie 551a
Vivere: non est v., sed valere vita est 551a
  tecum v. amem 546a
Vivida vis animi pervicit 550a
Vixi: dixisse 'v.' 546b
  v. puellis nuper idoneus 546b
Vocabula: quæ..sunt in honore v. 541b
  specioso v. rerum 544a
Volitare: virum v. per ora 558a
Volo: hoc v., sic iubeo 549a
Volucris dispersit in auras 556b
Voluisse sat est 552b
Voluntas: sit pro ratione v. 549a
Voluptas: trahit sua quemque v. 557a
  votum timor ira v. 548b
Vos: sic v. non vobis 558b
Votis: hoc erat in v. 548a
Votum timor ira voluptas 548b
Vox populi, vox dei 309a, 537a
Vulgus: odi profanum v. 545b
Vulpes aegroto cauta leoni 542b
Vultus: non v. instantis tyranni 545b

Z

Zelum putamus 537c

GREEK

A

Ἄγαν: μηδὲν ἄ. 560b
Ἀλεκτρυόνα: τῷ Ἀσκληπιῷ ὀφείλομεν ἄ. 560a
Ἀλέξανδρος: εἰ μὴ Ἀ. ἤμην 559a
Ἀμύνεσθαι περὶ πάτρης 560a
Ἀνήριθμον γέλασμα 559a
Ἀνθρώπου: οὐδὲν ἄ. δεινότερον 560b
Ἀνθρώπων: πολλῶν δ' ἄ. ἴδεν ἄστεα 560a
Ἀπομειβόμενος: τὸν δ' ἄ. 560a
Ἀρετῆς πέρι ἢ ψόγου 560b
Ἀριστεύειν: αἰὲν ἀ. 560a
Ἀσκληπιῷ: τῷ Ἀ. ὀφείλομεν ἀλεκτρυόνα 560a
Ἄστεα: ἴδεν ἄ. 560a

B

Βιβλίον: μέγα β. μέγα κακόν 559b
Βίος: ὁ β. βραχύς 559b

Γ

Γελάσασα: δακρύοεν γ. 560a
Γέλασμα: ἀνήριθμον γ. 559a
Γηράσκω δ' ἀεὶ πολλὰ διδασκόμενος 560a
Γλῶσσ': ἢ γ. ὀμώμοχ' 559b
Γνῶθι σεαυτόν 560b

Δ

Δακρυόεν γελάσασα 560a
Δεινά: πολλὰ τὰ δ. 560b
Διδασκόμενος: γηράσκω δ' ἀεὶ πολλὰ δ. 560b
Διογένης ἂν ἤμην 559a

E

Ἐπιφανῶν: ἀνδρῶν ἐ. γῆ τάφος 560b
Εὔκολος: ὁ δ' ε. μὲν ἐνθάδ' 559a
Εὕρηκα 559a
Εὐτελείας: φιλοκαλοῦμεν μετ' ε. 560b
Εὐτυχέα: μηδὲ καλέειν ἀλλ' ε. 560b
Εὐτυχέστερος: πατρὸς ε. 560b

H

Ἡλίου: ἀπὸ τοῦ ἡ. μετάστηθι 559b
Ἥμισυ: πλέον ἥ. παντός 559b

Θ

Θάλαττα, θάλαττα 560b
Θεός: ἢ θηρίον ἢ θ. 559a
Θηρίον: ἢ θ. ἢ θεός 559a

I

Ἱπποκλείδῃ: οὐ φροντὶς Ἱ. 559b

K

Κάθαρσιν: παθημάτων κ. 559a
Κτῆμα ἐς ἀεί 560b
Κυμάτων: ποντίων τε κ. 559a

Λ

Λακεδαιμονίοις: ἄγγειλον Λ. 560a

M

Μαλακίας: φιλοσοφοῦμεν ἄνευ μ. 560b
Μέτρον: πάντων χρημάτων μ. 560a
Μῆνιν ἄειδε, θεά 559b

N

Νόον: καὶ ν. ἔγνω 560a

O

Οἰωνός: εἷς ο. ἄριστος 560a
Ὄλβιον: μηδὲ καλέειν κω ὄ. 560b

Π

Πειθόμενοι: τοῖς κείνων ῥήμασι π. 560a
Πολιτικόν: ἄνθρωπος φύσει π. ζῷον 559a
Πολύτροπον: ἄνδρα μοι ἔννεπε, Μοῦσα, π. 560a

P

Ῥεῖ: πάντα ῥ., οὐδὲν μένει 559b

Σ

Σεαυτόν: γνῶθι σ. 560b
Στῶ: ποῦ σ. 559a
Συνετοῖσιν: φωνᾶντα σ. 560a

T

Τάφος: πᾶσα γῆ τ. 560b
Τέχνη: ἡ δὲ τ. μακρή 559b
Τραγῳδία μίμησις 559a

Υ

Ὕδωρ: ἄριστον μὲν ὕ. 560a
Ὑπαρχούσης φύσεως μὴ χείροσι γενέσθαι 560b

Φ

Φιλοκαλοῦμεν μετ' εὐτελείας 560b
Φιλοσοφοῦμεν ἄνευ μαλακίας 560b
Φρήν: ἡ δὲ φ. ἀνώμοτος 559b
Φύλλων: οἵη περ φ. γενεή 560a
Φωνᾶντα συνετοῖσιν 560a

Ψ

Ψόγου: ἀρετῆς πέρι ἢ ψ. 560b

FRENCH

A

Absence est à l'amour 561b
Absents ont toujours tort 562b
Accuse: J'a. 566a
Acte: le dernier a. est sanglant 554b
Adversité de nos meilleurs amis 562a
Aimez qui vous aime 566a
Allons, enfants de la patrie 565b
Âme: aventures de son â. 563a
Ami: n'oserez-vous, mon bel a. 170a
Amiral: tuer..un a. pour encourager 566a
Amour: l'absence est à l'a. 561b
Angleterre..nation de boutiquiers 564a
Animal: cet a. est très méchant 566a
Anne: sœur A., ne vois-tu rien venir 564b
Antan: neiges d'a. 565b
Appétit vient en mangeant 565a
Appris: ils n'ont rien a. 565b
rien oublié et..rien a. 563a
Ardeur dans mes veines cachée 565a
Argent: point d'a. 565a
Arques: nous avons combattu à A. 563b
Assassins: Mm. les a. commencent 563b
Attaque: on l'a. il se défend situation excellente. J'a. 563a
Audace, et encore de l'audace 561a
Austerlitz: soleil d'A. 564b
Autrui: les maux d'a. 562a

B

Bataillons: Dieu est..pour les gros b. 566a
Bâton de maréchal de France 80a, 564b
Belle: temps que j'étais b. 565b
Bien: mieux est l'ennemi du bien 575a
mon b. où je le trouve 574b
Bienfaits: recevoir de plus grand b. 574b
Bois: nous n'irons plus aux b. 561b
Boue: nostalgie de la b. 561a
Boutiquiers: nation de b. 564a
Brioche: mangent de la b. 563b

C

Ça ira 566a
Carrière ouverte aux talents 80a, 564a
Casse: tout passe, tout c. 575a
Centre: mon c. cède 563a
Chandelle: au soir, à la c. 565b
Change: plus ça c., plus..même chose 563b
Changé: nous avons c. tout cela 575a
Chefs-d'œuvre: âme au milieu des c. 563a
Chercher un grand peut-être 565a
Chercherais: tu ne me c. pas 564b
Chevalier sans peur 566a
Cléopâtre: le nez de C. 564b
Clercs: la trahison des c. 574b
Cœur a ses raisons 564b

Comédie: belle que soit la c. 564b
Compagnon de la Majolaine 528a
Congrès ne marche pas 562a
Courage..deux heures après minuit 575a
Crillon: pends-toi, brave C. 563b
Crimes: O liberté! que de c. 565a
Critique: le bon c. est celui 563a
Cultiver notre jardin 566a

D

Danse: congrès ne marche pas, il d. 562a
Défend: on l'attaque il se d. 566a
Déluge: après nous le d. 565a
Déplaît: quelque chose qui ne nous d. pas 562a
Dévorât successivement tous ses enfants 565b
Dieu est..pour les gros bataillons 566a
si D. n'existait pas 566a
Direz, chantant mes vers 565b
Distance n'y fait rien 562b

E

Écrasez l'infâme 566a
Égalité: Liberté É.l 566b

FRENCH INDEX

Embarras des richesses 561a
Empire: ni romain, ni e. 566a
Encourager: pour e. les autres 566a
Enfants terribles 563a
Escalier: esprit de l'e. 562b
Espaces infinis m'effraie 564b
Esprit de l'escalier 562b
État c'est moi 563b

F

Farce est jouée 565a
Fers: il est dans les f. 565b
Fils de Saint Louis 563a
Forces: balance des f. réelles 564a
Fraternité: Egalité! F.! 566b

G

Galère: faire dans cette g.
  vogue la g. 564b
Garde: la G. meurt 565a
Génie..aptitude à la patience 562a
Georges Dandin: vous l'avez voulu, 561b
  G. D. 564a
Giberne: soldat..porte dans sa g. 564b
Gloire: le jour de g. est arrivé 565b
Gouvernement qu'elle mérite 562b
Guerre: à la g., les trois quarts 564a
  ce n'est pas la g. 561a
  g. est l'industrie..de la Prusse 562b

H

Habileté que de savoir cacher 562a
Héros: point de h. pour son valet 561a
Heureux: si h. ni si malheureux 562a
Homme gravement malade 564b
  le style est l'h. 561b
  l'h. n'est qu'un roseau 564b
Honneur: tout est perdu fors l'h. 563a
Hypocrisie est un hommage 562a

I

Infâme: écrasez l'i. 566a
Infini me tourmente 562b
Inventer: il faudrait l'i. 566a
Ira: ça i. 566a

J

Jardin: cultiver notre j. 566a
Jésus: bon Sansculotte J. 562b
Jeunesse: si j. savoit 563a
Jour de gloire est arrivé 565b
Jours: tous les j., à tous points 561a

L

Lasse: tout casse, tout l. 575a
Lauriers sont coupés 561b
Liberté: L.! Egalité! 566b
  O l.! que de crimes 565a
Libre: l'homme est né l. 565b
Louis: fils de Saint L. 563a

M

Magnifique, mais ce n'est pas la
  guerre 561a
Maîtresses: j'aurai des m. 161a
Malade: homme gravement m. 564b

Malherbe: en fin M. vint 574b
Malheureux: si heureux ni si m. 562a
Maux: supporter les m. d'autrui 562a
Méfiez-vous! Les oreilles ennemies 566b
Messe: Paris vaut bien une m. 563b
Meurt: la Garde m. 562a
Mieux: je vais de m. en m. 561a
  m. est l'ennemi du bien 575a
Monde: quand tout le m. a tort 562a
Morales: trois quarts sont des affaires
  m. 564a
Morts: il n'y a pas de m. 562b
Mourra: on m. seul 564b
Moutons: retournons à nos m. 566b

N

Nation: toute n. a le gouvernement 562b
Nécessité: je n'en vois pas la n. 561a
Neiges d'antan 565b
Nez de Cléopâtre 564b
Nostalgie de la boue 561a

O

Ordre règne à Varsovie 566b
Oserez: n'o. vous, mon bel ami 176a
Oublié: rien appris, ni rien o. 565b
  rien o. et n'ont rien appris 563a
Oreilles ennemies vous écoutent 566b

P

Pantoufles: apportez-moi mes p. 564a
Paris vaut bien une messe 563b
Paroles: n'emploient les p. que 566a
Pas: premier p. qui coûte 562b
Passe: tout p., tout casse 575a
Passeront: ils ne p. pas 565a
Patience: aptitude à la p. 561b
Patrie: enfants de la p. 565b
Pends-toi, brave Crillon 563b
Pensée: se servent de la p. 566a
Pensées: pour déguiser leurs p. 566a
Perdu fors l'honneur 564a
Peur: sans p. et sans reproche 563a
Peut-être: chercher un grand p. 566a
Pleurer: peur d'être obligé d'en p. 565a
Plus ça change, p. c'est la même 561b
Premier pas qui coûte 563b
Prêtre: boyaux du dernier p. 562b
Proie: Vénus..à sa p. attachée 563b
Propriété c'est le vol 565a
Prose: ce qui n'est point p. est vers: 565a
  je dis de la p. 564a
Prusse: industrie nationale de la P. 562b
Pyramides: haut de ces p. 564a
Pyrénées: il n'y a plus de P. 563b

R

Raisons: le cœur a ses r. 564b
Reconnaissance..secrète envie 574b
Reprendre mon bien 574b
Reproche: sans peur et sans r. 566a
Reste: j'y suis, j'y r. 574b
Retournons à nos moutons 566b
Révolte: c'est une r.? 562a
Révolution: c'est une r. 562a
  R., comme Saturne 565b
Richesses: embarras des r. 561a
Rideau: tirez le r. 565a
Ridicule: du sublime au r. 564a

Rire: je me presse de r. de tout 561b
Roi: plus royaliste que le r. 566b
  r. d'Yvetot 561b
Rois: dernier des r. fût étranglé 563b
Romain: ni saint, ni r. 566a
Ronsard me célébrait 565b
Roseau: un r. pensant 564b
Royaliste: plus r. que le roi 566b

S

Saint: ni s., ni romain 566a
Sanglant: dernier acte est s. 564b
Saturne: Révolution, comme S. 565b
Seul: on mourra s. 564b
Siècles: quarante s. vous contem-
  plent 564a
Silence: grand talent pour le s. 81a
  s. éternel de ces espaces 564b
Situation excellente. J'attaque 563a
Soldat: tout s. français porte 564b
Soldats, songez que, du haut 564a
Soleil d'Austerlitz 564b
Style est l'homme 561b
Sublime au ridicule 564a
Suis: j'y s., j'y reste 574b
Suisse: point de S. 565a

T

Taisez-vous! Méfiez-vous! 566b
Talent pour le silence 81a
Talents: carrière ouverte aux t. 80a, 564a
Temps que j'étais belle 565b
Tête d'armée 564b
Tort: absents ont toujours t. 562b
  tout le monde a t. 562a
Trahison des clercs 574b
Trouve: mon bien où je le t. 564b
Trouvé: si tu ne m'avais t. 574b
Tuer de temps en temps un amiral 566a

V

Valet: point de héros pour son v. 561a
Varsovie: l'ordre règne à V. 566b
Veines: ardeur dans mes v. cachée 565a
Vent: qu'est au feu le v. 561b
Vénus: c'est V. toute entière 565a
Vers: n'est point prose est v. 564a
Vice: le v. rend à la vertu 562a
Vieille: quand vous serez bien v. 565b
Vieillesse: si. v. pouvoit 563a
Vive: il faut que je v. 561a
Vogue la galère 565a
Vol: la propriété c'est le v. 565a
Vouldras: fay ce que v. 565a
Voulu: vous l'avez v., Georges
  Dandin 564a

Y

Yvetot: un roi d'Y. 561b

Z

Zèle: pas trop de z. 565b

ITALIAN

A

Altrui: lo pane a.   567a
Amor che move il sole   567a

B

Ben trovato   575a

C

Cammin di nostra vita   566b
Chiesa: libera C. in libero Stato   567a

D

Dolore: nessun maggior d.   566b

F

Felice: ricordarsi del tempo f.   566b

G

Galeotto fu il libro   566b

L

Lasciate ogni speranza   566b
Leggemmo: non vi l. avante   566b
Libera Chiesa   567a
Libro: Galeotto fu il l.   566b

M

Maestro di color che sanno   566b
Mezzo: nel m. del cammin   566b
Miseria: felice nella m.   566b
Muove: e pur si m.   567a

O

Onorate l'altissimo poeta   566b

P

Pace: è nostra p.   567a
Pane: lo p. altrui   567a
Piensieri stretti ed il viso sciolto   573b
Poeta: l'altissimo p.   566b
Proverai sì come sa di sale   567a
Puro e disposto   566b

R

Ricordarsi del tempo felice   566b
Rifiuto: il gran r.   566b
Riveder le stelle   566b

S

Sanno: Maestro di color che s.   566b
Scale: per l'altrui s.   567a
Scendere e il salir   566b
Speranza: lasciate ogni s.   566b
Stato: libera Chiesa in libero S.   567a
Stelle: riveder le s.   566b
   salire alle s.   566b
   sole e l'altre s.   567a

T

Trovato: è molto ben t.   575a

V

Virgilio: or se' tu quel V.   566b
Viso sciolto.   573b
Volontate: e la sua v.   567a

SPANISH

C

Caballero de la Triste Figura   567b

F

Figura: Caballero de la Triste F.   567b

L

Linajes: dos l. solos hay   567b

T

Tenir: el t. y el no t.   567b

GERMAN

A

Anders: ich kann nicht a.   569a

B

Bedeuten: was soll es b.   568b
Bestie: blonde B.   569b
Blätter: grün sind deine B.   569b
Blonde Bestie   569b
Blut und Eisen   567b
Böse: jenseits von Gut und B.   569a
Burg: feste B. ist unser Gott   569a

C

Canossa: nach C. gehen wir nicht   567b

D

Dächern: Ziegel auf den D.   569a
Deutschland über alles   568a
Dinge: zwei D. erfüllen das Gemüth   568b
Drang: Sturm und D.   568b
Dummheit: mit der D. kämpfen Götter   569b

E

Ehrlicher Makler   567b
Eisen: Blut und E.   567b

F

Flügeln des Gesanges   568b
Fragen: ich will dich f.   568b

G

Gedanke: zwei Seelen und ein G.   568b
Geliebter: O mein G.   568a
Geographischer Begriff   569a
Gesang: Weib und G.   569a
Gesanges: aus Flügeln des G.   568b
Gesetz: moralische G. in mir   568b
Gipfeln: über allen G. ist Ruh'   568a
Gold-Orangen glühn   568a
Gott: feste Burg ist unser G.   569a
Götter: Dummheit kämpfen G.   569b
Gott-trunkener Mensch   569b
Grolle: ich g. nicht   568b
Gut: jenseits von G. und Böse   569a

H

Hast: ohne H., aber ohne Rast   568b
Herren-Moral   569a
Herz: mein H. ich will dich fragen   568b
   mein H. ist schwer   568a
   wenn das H. auch bricht   568b
Herzen: zwei H. und ein Schlag   568b
Himmel: bestirnte H. über mir   568b
Hunde, wollt ihr ewig leben?   568a

I

Italien ist ein geographischer Begriff   569a

K

Kann: ich k. nicht anders   569a
Kennst du das Land   568a
Knochen: die gesunden K.   567b

L

Land: kennst du das L.   568a
Laub: im dunkeln L.   568a
Leben: Narr sein L. lang   569a
   wollt ihr ewig l.?   568a
Licht: mehr L.!   568b
Liebe: was ist denn L.?   568b
Lorbeer: hoch der L. steht   568a

M

Makler: Ehrlicher M.   567b
Märchen aus alten Zeiten   568b
Mensch: Gott-trunkener M.   569b
Moral: Herren-M. und Sklaven-M.   569a
Musketiers: pommerschen M.   567b
Myrte: die M. still   568a

N

Narr: der bleibt ein N.   569a
Neues: im Westen nichts N.   569b

P

Politik..keine exakte Wissenschaft   567b
Pommerschen: einzigen p. Musketiers   567b

R

Rast: ohne Hast, aber ohne R.   568b
Rhein: die Wacht am R.   569b
Ruh': meine R.' ist hin   568a
   über allen Gipfeln ist R.'   568a

S

Schlag: zwei Herzen und ein S.   568b
Schön: du bist so s.   568a
Seelen: zwei S. und ein Gedanke   568b
   zwei S. wohnen..in meiner Brust   568a
Sinn: nicht aus dem S.   568b
Sklaven-Moral   569a
Sturm und Drang   568b

T

Tannenbaum, O Tannenbaum   569b
Teufel: so viel T.   569a
Traurig: ich so t. bin   568b

V

Verweile doch! du bist   568a

W

Wacht: die W. am Rhein   569b
Waffen: gute Wehr und W.   569a
Weib: Wein, W. und Gesang   569a
Weiss nicht, was soll es bedeuten   568b
Westen: im W. nichts Neues   569b
Wind: sanfter W. vom blauen Himmel   568a
Worms: Dächern waren zu W.   569a

Z

Ziegel auf den Dächern   569a
Zeiten: Märchen aus alten Z.   568b
Zitronen: wo die Z. blühn   568a

20 50

SET IN
GREAT BRITAIN
AT THE
UNIVERSITY PRESS
OXFORD
AND
PRINTED BY
R. & R. CLARK LTD
EDINBURGH